Encyclopedia of Ukraine

Encyclopedia of

UKRAINE

VOLUME III
L-Pf

Edited by
DANYLO HUSAR STRUK

under the auspices of

the Canadian Institute of Ukrainian Studies (University of Alberta),

the Shevchenko Scientific Society (Sarcelles, France), and

the Canadian Foundation for Ukrainian Studies

UNIVERSITY OF TORONTO PRESS INCORPORATED

Toronto Buffalo London

© University of Toronto Press Incorporated 1993
Toronto Buffalo London
Printed in Canada

ISBN 0-8020-3993-6
Collector's Edition: ISBN 0-8020-3008-4

Canadian Cataloguing in Publication Data
Main entry under title:
Encyclopedia of Ukraine

Revision of: Entsyklopediia ukraïnoznavstva.
Vols. 1–2 edited by Volodymyr Kubijovyč;
vols. 3–5 edited by Danylo Husar Struk.
Includes bibliographical references.
Contents: Map and gazetteer volume. –
V. 1. A–F – V. 2. G–K – V. 3. L–PF – V. 4. PH–SR – V. 5. ST–Z.
ISBN 0-8020-3993-6 (v. 3)

1. Ukraine – Dictionaries and encyclopedias.
2. Ukraine – Gazetteers.
I. Kubijovyč, V. (Volodymyr), 1900–85.
II. Struk, Danylo Husar, 1940–.
III. Canadian Institute of Ukrainian Studies.
IV. Naukove tovarystvo imeny Shevchenka.
V. Canadian Foundation for Ukrainian Studies.
VI. Title: Entsyklopediia ukraïnoznavstva.

DK508.E52213 1984 fol   947'.71'003   C84-099336-6

Volodymyr Kubijovyč, *Editor-in-Chief, volumes 1, 2*

Danylo Husar Struk, *Editor-in-Chief, volumes 3, 4, 5*

The publication of this volume

has been made possible in part

through a grant from the Province of Manitoba

in recognition of the contribution of Ukrainian pioneers

to the development of the province.

EDITORIAL STAFF

CONTRIBUTORS

Preface to Volumes 3 to 5

These last three volumes of *Encyclopedia of Ukraine* are the culmination of a process that began in 1948 in Munich when the Shevchenko Scientific Society, the oldest Ukrainian learned association, directed its 'human and material resource ... toward preparing and publishing *Entsyklopediia ukraïnoznavstva*.' In the preface to volume 1 of *Encyclopedia of Ukraine*, the late Volodymyr Kubijovyč outlined the historical process that began the transformation of the 10-volume *Entsyklopediia ukraïnoznavstva* into a major English-language reference work on Ukraine. As editor in chief of volumes 1 and 2, Professor Kubijovyč anticipated that the completed *Encyclopedia of Ukraine* would be published in four consecutive volumes, appearing at intervals of two to three years. As is evident, that schedule proved unrealistic. Furthermore, a fifth volume was necessary to accommodate what was an almost overwhelming amount of information. It was deemed technically effective, moreover, to publish volumes 3–5 simultaneously. Simultaneous publication would have the additional advantage that a more thoroughly integrated reference work would be produced within a shorter time frame. In retrospect the decision was a prudent one because it allowed for at least some information about the rapid changes taking place in Ukraine after the collapse of the Soviet Union to be incorporated into all three remaining volumes.

Scholarly excellence, which guided the editors and staff of volumes 1 and 2, has remained a goal in the writing of the last three volumes. We feel confident that *Encyclopedia of Ukraine* fulfills the basic requirements of an encyclopedia in that it preserves the facts and presents information accurately and objectively. These requirements are particularly acute in the light of the inaccuracies, distortions, and gaps that have plagued scholarship concerning Ukraine both in Soviet-ruled Ukraine and throughout the world. The critical response to volumes 1 and 2 was encouraging, and it confirmed the need for such a reference work. Numerous positive, some even glowing, reviews appeared in both academic journals and local press. The first printing of 5,000 copies of volume 1 was sold out within three months, and orders came from around the world, including China, Japan, Europe, and Australia.

As might be expected, changes are inevitable over the course of a project with as long a history as that of the encyclopedia. The succession of a new editor in chief for volumes 3–5, following the death of Professor Kubijovyč in 1985, has resulted in the introduction of a new perspective to the encyclopedia. A number of things, however, have remained unchanged. Three styles of transliteration continue to be used; a bibliography continues to be included at the end of longer articles, with the simple aim of directing the reader looking for more in-depth analysis and greater detail to other sources; and articles continue to be written in a manner that addresses the needs of an English-speaking Western audience. In addition, every attempt has been made to maintain, if not improve upon, the features, scope, and quality of the first two volumes.

Since the publication of volume 2 in 1988, monumental changes have taken place in Ukraine. In its transition from a republic within the USSR to an independent sovereign state, Ukraine has undergone many economic, political, social, and cultural transformations. For the editorial staff of the encyclopedia it became of prime importance to keep abreast of the rapidly changing situation and to provide the most up-to-date and accurate information possible. Given that almost 90 percent of volumes 3–5 had been written and given final approval by the editorial board by early 1992, not all additions and revisions received after that date could be incorporated if the publication date was to be met. In some instances, even the revision may now appear to be outdated. Notable changes have been made in terminology and geographical names. For example, the Ukrainian-language acronym AN URSR used throughout volumes 1 and 2 for the

Academy of Sciences of the Ukrainian SSR has been changed whenever possible to ANU to reflect the renaming of that institution as the Academy of Sciences of Ukraine (Akademiia nauk Ukrainy). After the first appearance of AN URSR in an entry, 'now ANU' has been inserted in parentheses, and ANU has been used thereafter regardless of the date to which reference is being made. 'The Ukrainian SSR' has been replaced by 'Ukraine,' except in specific cases where a distinction between Soviet-occupied Ukraine and Western Ukraine prior to and during the Second World War is intended. 'Belorussia' or 'the Belorussian SSR' has been changed in almost every instance to 'Belarus.' 'Moldavia' has been changed to 'Moldova,' however, only in post-1991 references. 'Russia' is used instead of 'the RSFSR' to refer to post-Soviet Russia, and the acronym RF is used to refer to the non-ethnic Russian or mixed-ethnic parts of the current Russian Federation. The acronym SSR has been dropped for all other former republics of the dissolved Soviet Union. With independence, the pre-Soviet names of some Ukrainian towns and cities have been restored (notably Luhanske and Mariiupil), and the encyclopedia reflects the changes in toponymy.

From the outset the initiators of *Encyclopedia of Ukraine* realized not only that technically the project would be a major undertaking, but that financially it would require millions of dollars. The Canadian Institute of Ukrainian Studies at the University of Alberta committed one-third of its yearly budget to the encyclopedia through the entire project. Other funding was provided by the Canadian Foundation for Ukrainian Studies, which focused its activities on fund-raising campaigns in support of the encyclopedia throughout the Ukrainian communities in Canada and the United States. There was support for the project outside of the Ukrainian community as well. All of Canada contributed, through a federal grant, toward the publication of volume 4, and the provinces of Saskatchewan, Manitoba, and British Columbia generously subsidized the publication of volumes 2, 3, and 5 respectively.

To say the least, the task was monumental. It never would have been completed without the strong commitment of a very dedicated team. For many, their involvement was a labor of love prompted by a strong belief in the encyclopedia. Special thanks and recognition are due not only to the subject editors, who fulfilled their responsibilities diligently and eagerly in exchange for a token honorarium, but also to the in-house staff, who often worked beyond the call of duty. We greatly appreciate the unremunerated dedication and assistance of Stefania Kucharyshyn in drawing many of the maps and co-ordinating the preparation of all the maps for the last three volumes. The scholarly quality of the encyclopedia is, to a great extent, attributable to the dedication, knowledge, and exactitude of the editorial board, and the appearance of the encyclopedia on schedule is a result of the unwavering support of the Canadian Institute of Ukrainian Studies and the consistent efforts of the successive executives and board members of the Canadian Foundation for Ukrainian Studies, who donated time and money to help us complete the five-volume set.

To ensure the validity, viability, and utility of *Encyclopedia of Ukraine* for many years to come, plans have been made for triennial updates. As a first step in improving the encyclopedia's usefulness, a comprehensive name index will be prepared and published in a separate volume within two years. We genuinely believe that the initial goals established for the encyclopedia by V. Kubijovyč have been upheld, and that *Encyclopedia of Ukraine* will be of value to all those interested in Ukraine, its people, and their descendants.

Danylo Husar Struk

L

Rev Vasyl Laba

Laba, Vasyl (Basil), b 1 September 1887 in Berteshiv, Bibrka county, Galicia, d 10 November 1976 in Edmonton. Priest and theologian; full member of the Shevchenko Scientific Society from 1947. After being educated at the universities of Lviv, Innsbruck, Fribourg, and Vienna (D TH, 1914), Laba was ordained in 1912 and served as field chaplain in the Austrian army (1914–18), chief chaplain in the Ukrainian Galician Army, and acting vicar-general of the Ukrainian Catholic archeparchy of Lviv in Kamianets-Podilskyi (1919–20). In the interwar period he taught at a gymnasium in Lviv and at the Greek Catholic Theological Seminary (from 1926) and the Greek Catholic Theological Academy (from 1930). He wrote a monograph on biblical hermeneutics (1928) and a three-volume survey of patristics (1930–2). During the Second World War he was chief chaplain in the *Division Galizien. As a postwar refugee he was the first rector of the Ukrainian Catholic seminaries in Hischberg, Germany (1945–8), and Kulemborg, Holland (1948–50). In Canada after 1950, Laba served as vicar-general of the Ukrainian Catholic eparchy of Edmonton; he was also prorector and professor at the Ukrainian Catholic University in Rome (1963–76).

Laba River. A left-bank tributary of the Kuban River. It is 214 km in length and drains a basin area of 12,500 sq km. The Laba begins at the confluence of the Velyka Laba (130 km in length) and the Mala Laba rivers, which arise from glaciers in the northern Caucasus. The Laba passes through a deep valley and then flows through Subcaucasia and the Kuban Lowland steppe. Floodplains are found at its mouth. The Laba is a potential source of hydroelectric power.

Labai, Yosafat [Labaj, Josafat], b 3 June 1895 in Yazenytsia, Kaminka-Strumylova county, Galicia, d 11 July 1962 in Argentina. Religious and educational figure. In 1912 he entered the Basilian St Nicholas's Monastery in Krekhiv. He was ordained in 1925 and served as the superior of St Onuphrius's Monastery in Dobromyl, the rector of St Josaphat's Ukrainian Pontifical College in Rome (1935–55), and a missionary in Montevideo (1955–6) and Buenos Aires (from 1956).

Labor Alliance of Ukrainian Students (Obiednannia pratsi ukrainskykh studentiv). An umbrella body of Ukrainian student groups in Lviv which was active from June 1942 until the summer of 1944. The alliance united Ukrainian student groups organized at local faculties and institutions of higher education; the groups included 471 students in medicine, 402 in technical sciences, 212 in agronomy, 119 in veterinary sciences, 104 in pharmacology, 80 in forestry, the Ukrainian students' sports club (450), and the student banduryst choir (46). The alliance was led by B. *Lonchyna, and published the monthly *Students'kyi prapor.

Labor alliances (Obiednannia pratsi; German: Arbeitsgemeinschaften). Professional and special interest organizations which operated in the Generalgouvernement in 1941–4 under the auspices of the *Ukrainian Central Committee (UTsK). These groups had their origins in the various branches (or 'sections') that were created under the umbrella of the UTsK to allow for the continuity of activity by Ukrainian associations that had been closed by the Nazi regime. They functioned largely with a nominal connection to the UTsK until May 1941, when they were linked directly to the appropriate departments of the UTsK (mainly the economics, cultural work, and social welfare sections), and their activities were directed by 'men of trust' appointed by the president of the UTsK.

The first and largest alliance was the *Ukrainian Teachers' Labor Alliance, with a membership of over 8,000. The second-largest association was the Labor Alliance of the Medical-Sanitation Service, headed by R. Osinchuk. It was subdivided into four groups, physicians, veterinarians, pharmacists, and nurses, and oversaw the work of the Abstainers' Alliance, headed by M. Nykyforchyn. Various student societies were represented by the *Labor Alliance of Ukrainian Students. Artists and writers had their own alliances: the Labor Association of Ukrainian Pictorial Artists was headed by I. Ivanets, the Labor Alliance of Writers, by H. Luzhnytsky, the Labor Alliance of Musicians, by S. Liudkevych, the Labor Alliance of Journalists, by O. Bodnarovych, and the Labor Alliance of Theater Artists, by V. Blavatsky. The Labor Alliance of Tradesmen was formed from the *Zoria trade association and headed by N. Kushyk. Labor alliances of scientists, jurists, engineers and technicians, businessmen, industrialists, workers, office workers, clergy, and home owners had a smaller membership.

K. Pankivsky

Labor armies. Units of the Red Army that were used partly in rebuilding industry in Soviet Russia and Ukraine during 1920–1. In January 1920 the Third All-Russian

LABOR CAMPS IN THE FORMER USSR

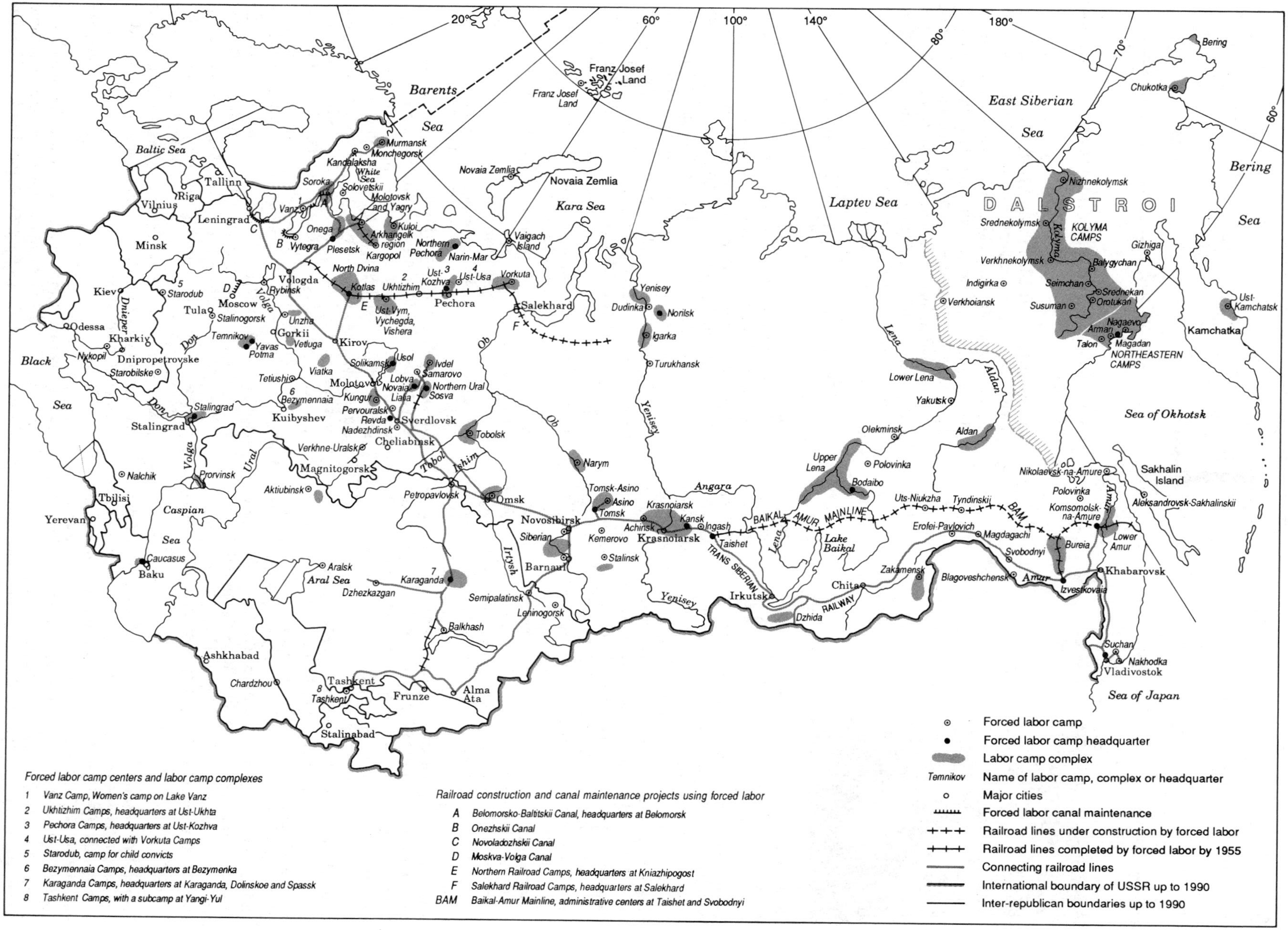
Forced labor camp centers and labor camp complexes
1 Vanz Camp, Women's camp on Lake Vanz
2 Ukhtizhim Camps, headquarters at Ust-Ukhta
3 Pechora Camps, headquarters at Ust-Kozhva
4 Ust-Usa, connected with Vorkuta Camps
5 Starodub, camp for child convicts
6 Bezymennaia Camps, headquarters at Bezymenka
7 Karaganda Camps, headquarters at Karaganda, Dolinskoe and Spassk
8 Tashkent Camps, with a subcamp at Yangi-Yul
Railroad construction and canal maintenance projects using forced labor
A Belomorsko-Baltitskii Canal, headquarters at Belomorsk
B Onezhskii Canal
C Novoladozhskii Canal
D Moskva-Volga Canal
E Northern Railroad Camps, headquarters at Kniazhipogost
F Salekhard Railroad Camps, headquarters at Salekhard
BAM Baikal-Amur Mainline, administrative centers at Taishet and Svobodnyi
Forced labor camp
Forced labor camp headquarter
Labor camp complex
Temnikov Name of labor camp, complex or headquarter
Major cities
Forced labor canal maintenance
Railroad lines under construction by forced labor
Railroad lines completed by forced labor by 1955
Connecting railroad lines
International boundary of USSR up to 1990
Inter-republican boundaries up to 1990
20°
60°
100°
140°
180°
80°
70°
60°
Barents Sea
Baltic Sea
Black Sea
Caspian Sea
Aral Sea
Kara Sea
Laptev Sea
East Siberian Sea
Bering Sea
Sea of Okhotsk
Sea of Japan
White Sea
Franz Josef Land
Novaia Zemlia
Vaigach Island
Sakhalin Island
Kamchatka
D A L S T R O I
KOLYMA CAMPS
NORTHEASTERN CAMPS
Murmansk
Monchegorsk
Kandalaksha
Soroka
Solovetskii
Molotovsk and Yagry
Kuloi
Arkhangelsk region
Northern Pechora
Narin-Mar
Onega
Plesetsk
Kargopol
Vanz
Vytegra
Leningrad
Tallinn
Riga
Vilnius
Minsk
Kiev
Odessa
Kharkiv
Nykopil
Dnipropetrovske
Starobilske
Starodub
Moscow
Tula
Stalinogorsk
Temnikov
Yavas
Potma
Gorkii
Unzha
Vetluga
Vologda
Rybinsk
North Dvina
Kotlas
Ukhtizhim
Ust-Kozhva
Ust-Usa
Vorkuta
Pechora
Salekhard
Ust-Vym, Vychegda, Vishera
Kirov
Viatka
Solikamsk
Usol
Ivdel
Samarovo
Lobva
Novaia Liallia
Northern Ural
Sosva
Molotov
Kungur
Pervouralsk
Revda
Nadezhdinsk
Sverdlovsk
Cheliabinsk
Verkhne-Uralsk
Magnitogorsk
Tetiushi
Bezymennaia
Kuibyshev
Stalingrad
Nalchik
Tbilisi
Yerevan
Baku
Caucasus
Prorvinsk
Aktiubinsk
Ashkhabad
Chardzhou
Tashkent
Stalinabad
Frunze
Alma Ata
Balkhash
Aralsk
Karaganda
Dzhezkazgan
Semipalatinsk
Leninogorsk
Petropavlovsk
Tobolsk
Omsk
Novosibirsk
Siberian
Barnaul
Kemerovo
Stalinsk
Narym
Tomsk-Asino
Asino
Tomsk
Krasnoiarsk
Achinsk
Kansk
Ingash
Taishet
TRANS SIBERIAN RAILWAY
Irkutsk
Dzhida
Chita
Lake Baikal
Zakamensk
BAIKAL AMUR MAINLINE
BAM
Dudinka
Yenisey
Norilsk
Igarka
Turukhansk
Upper Lena
Bodaibo
Polovinka
Olekminsk
Lower Lena
Yakutsk
Aldan
Verkhoiansk
Indigirka
Nizhnekolymsk
Srednekolymsk
Verkhnekolymsk
Balygychan
Seimchan
Srednekan
Orotukan
Susuman
Nagaevo
Arman
Talon
Magadan
Gizhiga
Chukotka
Bering
Ust-Kamchatsk
Uts-Niukzha
Tyndinskii
Erofei-Pavlovich
Magdagachi
Svobodnyi
Blagoveshchensk
Bureia
Izvestkovaia
Komsomolsk-na-Amure
Nikolaevsk-na-Amure
Aleksandrovsk-Sakhalinskii
Lower Amur
Khabarovsk
Suchan
Nakhodka
Vladivostok
Volga
Don
Dnieper
Ural
Tobol
Ishim
Irtysh
Ob
Angara
Lena
Amur

Congress of Soviets of the National Economy called for the militarization of workers through the army recruiting machinery and the transfer of labor. On 15 January 1920 the Soviet Third Army in the Urals was transformed into a labor army and was put to work in the civilian economy. On 21 January 1920 the Supreme Council of People's Commissars of the RSFSR and the All-Ukrainian Revolutionary Committee decided to form the Ukrainian Labor Armies out of troops on the southwestern front. Since fighting continued in Ukraine during the 1920s, the labor army was limited to Kharkiv and the Donbas. In Kharkiv the Communist party objected strongly to the use of army labor and called on the trade unions to provide the labor. Its position received the majority of votes at the Fourth Congress of the CP(B)U on 16 March 1920. Nonetheless, the Donbas coal mines were brought under military control on 14 April 1920. In January 1921 the Ukrainian Labor Army numbered only 31,000 workers, compared to over two million in Russia. It was dissolved in March 1921 at the 10th Congress of the Russian Communist Party (Bolshevik). With the introduction of the NEP the Council of Labor and Defense of the RSFSR dissolved all labor armies, on 30 December 1921.

Labor Association of Ukrainian Pictorial Artists (Spilka pratsi ukrainskykh obrazotvorchykh mysttsiv). An artists' organization established in 1941 in German-occupied Lviv under the aegis of the Ukrainian Central Committee. In 1942 its membership was about 100. Under its presidents, M. Osinchuk and I. Ivanets (1942–4), it organized public discussions and an exhibition of 48 artists (December 1941), a retrospective exhibition of the works of I. Trush, O. Novakivsky, P. Kholodny, Sr, and P. Kovzhun (June 1942), an exhibition of works by 69 artists on the 25th anniversary of the Kiev Academy of Arts (January 1943), a retrospective exhibition of the works of O. Kulchytska (May 1943), and an exhibition of 99 artists (December 1943). The association ceased its activities in 1944.

Labor camps (aka corrective-labor camps). The principal type of punitive institution in the former Soviet Union. There were five classes of labor camps (in order of increasing severity): exile colony, ordinary-regime camp, intensified-regime camp, strict-regime camp, and special-regime camp. Exile colonies were for prisoners who were deemed to be 'solidly on the path to reform.' Ordinary-regime camps held prisoners (male or female) serving sentences of less than three years for other than very serious crimes or serving the initial portion (not more than three years) of longer composite sentences for major offenses. Intensified-regime camps were for men sentenced to more than three years for serious offenses. Women and men convicted of serious state crimes (usually for political dissent) and 'especially dangerous recidivists' were incarcerated in strict-regime camps. The special-regime camps were for men with commuted death sentences and 'especially dangerous recidivists.' Prison officials had the power to change a prisoner's category depending on his or her behavior. A particularly uncooperative prisoner could be moved from a camp to a prison, where conditions were even harsher. Apart from the lack of freedom, the most punitive feature of labor camps was their semistarvation diet. Working men in the strict-regime camps should con-

Strict- and special-regime camps in the former Ukrainian SSR

Type	Location	Date of most recent information
Strict/ special	Kherson	1977
Special	Dobrovody, Ternopil oblast	1984
Special	Iziaslav, Khmelnytskyi oblast	1986
Special	Korosten, Zhytomyr oblast	1982
Special	Lozivske, Voroshylovhrad oblast	1985
Strict	Bila Tserkva, Kiev oblast	1985
Strict	Brianka, Voroshylovhrad oblast	1982
Strict	Chernukhyne, Voroshylovhrad oblast	1983
Strict	Dniprodzerzhynske, Bahlii district	1975
Strict	Katerynivka, Rivne oblast	1984
Strict	Kirovohrad	1976
Strict	Kirovske, Donetske oblast	1986
Strict	Komisarivka, Voroshylovhrad oblast	1986
Strict	Ladyzhyn, Vinnytsia oblast	1985
Strict	Lviv, Shevchenko Street	1986
Strict	Lviv, Stryi Street	1985
Strict	Makorty, Dnipropetrovske oblast	1986
Strict	Manevychi, Volyhnia oblast	1986
Strict	Odessa, Chornomorska Doroha	1979
Strict	Olshanske, Mykolaiv oblast	1985
Strict	Perevalske, Voroshylovhard oblast	1986
Strict	Sukhodolske, Voroshylovhrad oblast	1985
Strict	Volnianske, Zaporizhia oblast	1984
Strict	Zhovti Vody, Dnipropetrovske oblast	1974

sume 3,100 to 3,900 calories per day, and women, 2,400 to 2,700 calories, according to the World Health Organization (WHO). Their actual diet contained 2,100 calories and could be reduced to 1,300 calories on disciplinary grounds. Carbohydrate-to-protein ratios far exceeded maximums set by the WHO, and the quality of food was very poor: there were no fresh fruits or vegetables, fish (the main protein) was sometimes rotten, and food was often infested with maggots and cockroaches.

Honest labor, according to official theory, was an integral part of the prisoner's re-education. But the more evident purpose of camp labor was economic and punitive. The economic output of labor camps was large enough to figure as a separate factor in Soviet planning. But the punitive purpose of prison labor was the chief reason for the presence of police organs. The labor was strenuous, fatiguing, and often dangerous. Workplaces were underventilated and underheated in the winter. Clothing for outdoor workers was inadequate. Machinery was old and in ill repair. Failure to meet high production quotas was punished with lower food rations and the loss of correspondence or visiting rights. Injuries were common, particularly in three uranium-mining camps in Ukraine, where few prisoners survived their sentences. Poor diet and hard work often resulted in illness. Medical treatment in the labor camps was poor and often withheld altogether. Prisoners have also been known to have refused operations, because of the ineptness of the medical staff. Besides material hardships prisoners endured various restrictions of their rights, including censorship and mail limitations (they could send from one to three letters a month, depending on the type of camp). In some camps all prisoners were shaved bald on admission. In some prisons, particularly in the RSFSR, only Russian could be used.

Over a hundred labor camps in the Ukrainian SSR were known in the West (see table). A number of them were designed for amputees and seriously ill prisoners, and 12 of them were for 14-to-18-year-olds. Political prisoners were sent usually to labor camps outside Ukraine. The prison population of the USSR was a state secret. According to Amnesty International estimates based on semiofficial sources, there were at least one million prisoners in the USSR in the 1970s, of whom more than 10,000 were political prisoners. Approx 40 percent of all political prisoners in the USSR were Ukrainians.

The principal legislation governing Ukrainian labor camps was the *Criminal Code of the Ukrainian SSR (1961), the *Corrective-Labor Code of the Ukrainian SSR (1971), which was based on the foundations of the Corrective-Labor Legislation of the USSR and the Union Republics (1969), and the Rules of Internal Order for Corrective-Labor Institutions, which gave prison administrators wide discretionary powers. Because the central procuracy was ineffective in monitoring the camps, the codes afforded the inmates hardly any protection from arbitrary and cruel treatment by the staff. (See also *Concentration camps, *Forced labor, and *Penitentiary system.)

BIBLIOGRAPHY
Amnesty International. *Prisoners of Conscience in the USSR: Their Treatment and Conditions* (London 1975)
Shifrin, A. *The First Guidebook to Prisons and Concentration Camps of the Soviet Union* (Uhldingen 1980)
                                        A. Feldman, C. Freeland

Labor Congress (Trudovyi kongres, aka Kongres trudovoho narodu Ukrainy [Congress of the Working People of Ukraine]). An all-Ukrainian legislative assembly convened by the *Directory of the UNR in Kiev on 22 January 1919. To counteract more effectively the Bolshevik influence in the cities, the Directory and the representatives of Ukrainian political parties decided at their meeting in Vinnytsia at the beginning of 1918 to base their political support on the so-called labor principle. According to that principle political power in the counties and the gubernias was to belong to councils of workers, peasants, and the working intelligentsia, excluding landowners and capitalists, and the central government was to rest on a labor congress. Instructions on the election to the Congress of the Working People of Ukraine, issued on 26 December 1918, provided for 593 deputies, 528 of them from the UNR and 65 from the Western Ukrainian National Republic (ZUNR). Because the Directory did not control all Ukrainian territory, the elections could not be conducted throughout Ukraine. The first and only session of the Labor Congress lasted from 22 January to 28 January 1919; it was held in the Kiev Opera House. Almost 400 delegates, including a 36-member delegation from the Ukrainian National Rada (of the ZUNR) and representatives of the Polish, Russian, and Jewish minorities, attended the session. After failing to agree on a chairman of the presidium the congress elected three vice-chairmen – S. Vityk (a member of the Ukrainian Social Democratic party in Galicia), D. Odryna (a Ukrainian Socialist Revolutionary from the Peasant Association), and T. Starukh (from a block of Galician parties) – and five secretaries – S. Bachynsky (a Ukrainian Socialist Revolutionary from the Peasant Association), V.

Zlotchansky (from the Ukrainian Social Democratic Workers' party), I. Bisk (from the Russian Social Democratic Workers' party), L. Havryliuk (from the Russian Party of Socialist Revolutionaries), and M. Vorony (from the Ukrainian Social Democratic Workers' party [Independentists]). On the evening of 22 January the congress ratified the union of the UNR and ZUNR that had been proclaimed earlier in the day. On the last day of its session it approved the policies of the Directory and transferred its powers to the Directory until the next session. It also set up six parliamentary commissions – defense, agrarian affairs, budget, foreign affairs, food supply, and culture and education – but in the circumstances those could not perform their duties. Finally, the congress adopted the principle of universal suffrage for future parliamentary and local elections. Military setbacks forced the Labor Congress to end its session prematurely.

BIBLIOGRAPHY
Khrystiuk, P. *Zamitky i materiialy do istorii ukrains'koi revoliutsii 1917–1920 rr.* (Vienna 1922; repr, New York 1969)
Siropolko, S. 'Diial'nist' Kul'turno-osvitn'oï komisii Trudovoho kongresu,' *Kalendar Dnipro na 1939 rik* (Lviv 1938)
Stakhiv, M. *Ukraïna v dobi Dyrektorii UNR*, 3 (Scranton 1963)
                                        A. Zhukovsky

Labor law. The body of laws that regulate matters such as terms of employment, wages, vacations and leave, conditions of work, labor organizations, collective bargaining, labor conflicts, and social security.

With the rapid development of industry in the 19th century, labor relations came to be governed by civil law. Labor was viewed as a commodity, sold by the worker to an employer for a certain remuneration. The employer's stronger position allowed him to exploit workers. In Western and Central Europe, including the Austro-Hungarian Empire, trade unions were recognized as legal representatives of workers only at the end of the 19th century. In the Russian Empire the trade-union movement grew very slowly and became a target of political repression after the Revolution of 1905. (For pre-Soviet labor law in the Russian Empire, see *Factory legislation.)

After the First World War, the belief that labor is not a commodity but a social asset, and hence should not be subject to civil law, became widespread. From that time, the slow disengagement of labor law from civil law began. In the 1920s, the 8-hour workday was introduced in Czechoslovakia, Rumania, and Poland. Government institutions such as the Labor Inspectorate under the Ministry of Labor and Social Security in Poland were established to regulate working conditions. Laws were passed in Poland to protect women and minors in the work force (1924), to guarantee vacations and holidays (1922), and to regulate collective labor agreements. In 1928 the Polish government set up labor courts with representatives from industry and workers. Laws on *social security were introduced. None of these measures had much of an effect in the Ukrainian territories under Poland, Czechoslovakia, or Rumania, since industry was poorly developed in those regions and only a few Ukrainians worked in industrial or commercial enterprises. Moreover, the mass of agricultural workers lacked any form of work protection.

In the USSR a different system of labor relations and labor law emerged. The state became the sole owner of the means of production, and relations between workers and a private entrepreneur were replaced by relations between workers and the state, which was represented by the Party bureaucracy. According to Soviet ideology, state ownership was synonymous with national ownership, and every citizen was a co-owner of state property. Work in the socialist economy was the constitutional obligation of every able-bodied citizen. Anyone who refused to work and lived off an illegal income was a 'parasite' and subject to prosecution. The obligation to work was tied to the right to work, ie, to the right to a job commensurate with one's specialization and qualifications, and to an appropriate wage. Labor law was the body of norms that regulated the social relations of workers at their enterprises, organizations, and institutions.

In 1922 the Labor Code of the Ukrainian SSR, almost a literal translation of the RSFSR code, was introduced. This code covered only the general features of labor relations; the details were settled by various instructions of individual ministries. The new labor code, based on the Legislative Foundations of the USSR and Union Republics on Labor (1971), was passed in 1972. The code regulated labor relations of all manual and office workers, first 'to promote the growth of labor productivity, to increase the effectiveness of social production and to improve the material and cultural living standards of the workers, to strengthen labor discipline' (art 1, par 1). To regulate conditions of work and protect the rights of manual and office workers was only its second purpose. Every worker was required to maintain labor discipline, which was defined by the Rules of Internal Labor Order (latest edn, 1983).

The right of individuals to join trade unions was guaranteed in the constitutions of the Ukrainian SSR (art 106) and the USSR (art 126). The Party played the leading role in trade unions. The relationship between the state, which, too, was controlled by the Party, and the trade unions was characterized as 'socialist co-operation.'

Collective agreements in the USSR had little in common with agreements between companies and trade unions in a free-market system. Under Soviet labor law, a collective agreement was established between a trade-union committee that represents the workers and the management of an enterprise (art 11 of the Labor Code). It set forth the responsibilities of the workers and management in fulfilling the production plans, improving the technology, and organizing production, payment of bonuses, and the training of cadres. Since wages, hours of work, holidays, and other basic issues were settled by legislation, not by collective bargaining, they were not an essential part of the agreement. The form and content of collective agreements were regulated by separate instructions.

In principle, workers were free to choose their place of work. In accepting a job, the worker became a member of the enterprise collective; he automatically received the rights and assumed the responsibilities of the collective. The worker had the right to break the contract by providing two weeks' notice. He could be dismissed from work for reasons set forth in the law and with the formal consent of the trade-union committee at the enterprise. Because, officially, there was no unemployment in the USSR, there was no assistance for unemployed workers. A worker who quit or was dismissed received two weeks' severance pay (art 44 of the Labor Code).

The regulation of work was based on various normative documents. These regulations could apply to only some or to all branches of the economy. By jurisdiction they could be all-Union, republican, or local. All these issues were addressed in the Statute on the Method for Developing Normative Documents for Regulating Labor, adopted in 1968 by the USSR State Committee of Labor and the Presidium of the All-Union Soviet of Trade Unions.

Wages depended largely on the fulfillment of production quotas. In the planned economy of the USSR, they were set centrally for the entire Union. Wages were also influenced by locality: in the Asiatic part of the Union or in the north, wages were higher than in Ukraine. Workers had no say in deciding the wage scales. Bonuses, which were awarded for fulfilling and overfulfilling production plans, were regulated by separate decrees. Workers' wages were treated separately from the wages of engineering and technical personnel. The remuneration of higher functionaries, particularly the privileged class (the so-called *nomenklatura* workers), was much higher than that of ordinary workers; their bonuses were also more substantial.

Conflicts between workers and management arising from the implementation of labor law (eg, regarding dismissals) were settled by (1) special commissions set up at enterprises or organizations and consisting of an equal number of trade union and management representatives, (2) trade union committees, and (3) people's courts. Disputes involving higher management were settled in higher-level courts. Disputes over labor quotas and wage rates were ruled out: these questions were the exclusive responsibility of the central organs. Strikes were seen as criminal acts.

Labor legislation for manual and office workers did not apply to collective farmers, who were considered to be co-owners of their farm. Neither the courts nor the procuracy had the right to interfere in internal labor relations on collective farms. Until the mid-1960s collective farmers were paid according to the *workday system.

BIBLIOGRAPHY
Smirnov, O. *Priroda i sushchnost' prava na trud v SSSR* (Moscow 1964)
Conquest, R. (ed). *Industrial Workers in the USSR* (London 1967)
Sovetskoe trudovoe pravo (Kiev 1981)
Kodeks zakoniv pro pratsiu Ukraïns'koï RSR (Kiev 1984)
                                                        A. Bilynsky

Labor productivity. The relation of output to the labor necessary for its production. In the former USSR labor productivity was defined as the national income produced (NIP) at constant prices per average annual worker in material production. In industry labor productivity was the gross output per average industrial worker; in agriculture, the gross output of the socialized sector (collective and state farms and enterprises) per agricultural worker (the output of private plots was ignored); in transportation, the output (in ton-kilometers) per worker. Other production inputs, such as capital and land, were not taken into account. Since Soviet growth rates for national income and industrial production were measured differently than in the West (resulting in rates almost double those arrived at by Western methods), the growth rates of labor productivity were correspondingly higher, except in agriculture and transportation, where they can be compared with Western productivity growth rates virtually without adjustment.

TABLE 1
Growth of labor productivity in Ukraine, 1970–89
(percentage of 1960 rate)

	1960	1970	1975	1980	1985	1989
Social labor productivity	100	184	224	260	317	368
Industry	100	162	209	234	268	322
Agriculture (socialized)	100	155	174	207	250	317
Construction	100	153	197	215	246	275

TABLE 2
Growth of labor productivity in Ukraine by industry in the 1980s
(percentage of 1980 rate)

	1980	1985	1989
Industry as a whole	100	114	136
Heavy industry	100	116	140
Energy	100	101	109
Electric power	100	104	115
Fuel	100	98	103
Metallurgical industry	100	108	126
Machine building	100	127	163
Chemical wood products	100	122	148
Chemicals & petrochemicals	100	121	147
Lumber, woodworking, pulp & paper	100	123	152
Building materials	100	112	132
Light industry	100	113	131
Textiles	100	108	128
Clothing	100	117	131
Leather, shoes, & furs	100	114	131
Food	100	116	135

Until recently labor productivity was greatly emphasized in Soviet statistics, and Party programs called for surpassing the productivity of capitalist countries. In the 1980s Soviet labor productivity fell as NIP and industrial and agricultural output declined. According to official (optimistic) comparisons between the USSR (no such measurements were made for the Ukrainian SSR) and the United States, in the mid-1980s labor productivity in Soviet industry was 55 percent of that in American industry (in 1970 it was 53 percent, and in 1960, 44 percent). Since 1988–9 such comparisons have not been made.

The official growth rates of labor productivity in various branches of Ukraine's economy are given in the tables.

BIBLIOGRAPHY
Savenko, L. Produktyvnist' pratsi: Dynamika i rezervy zrostannia (Kiev 1979)
Ivanov, N. (ed). Proizvoditel'nost' truda i fondootdacha: Problemy rosta (Kiev 1990)

A. Revenko

Labor reserve schools (shkoly trudovykh rezerviv). Vocational training schools below the level of *tekhnikum which were subordinated to a highly centralized institution, the State Labor Reserves of the USSR. The State Labor Reserves was established as an all-Union institution by a decree of the Presidium of the Supreme Soviet on 2 October 1940 and had the task of increasing the number of semiskilled workers for agriculture and industry. Labor reserve schools were filled by means of drafts of young men and women between the ages of 14 and 17. Every collective farm was obliged to send 2 youths per 100 adult members to these schools each year. In urban communities all secondary-school pupils of the appropriate age whose marks were below 'good' were subject to the draft. Training in labor reserve schools lasted from one-half to two years, depending on the type of school. Initially, three types of labor reserve schools were established, trade schools, railway schools, and factory-industrial schools. The student draftees were assigned to schools and state-funded residences scattered throughout the USSR (mainly in the Urals and Siberia). They received a narrow trade education of poor quality. There were 1,500 labor reserve schools established in 1940, with 800,000 drafted youths; 316 schools (with 130,000 draftees) were in Ukraine. During 1945–68, 15,380,000 pupils completed programs at labor reserve schools in the USSR; 27 percent of them were from Ukraine. Upon graduation students were obliged to work in places assigned by the Ministry of Labor Reserves in Moscow. The compulsory aspects of labor reserve schools lasted until 1950. In March 1955 the draft was abolished, and after July 1959 the 624 schools in existence were transformed into urban and rural *vocational-technical schools.

L. Szuch

Labor resources. The part of a country's population possessing the physical and mental ability and knowledge to work. A country's labor resources determine its potential work force.

The labor resources of Ukraine and the USSR as a whole consisted formally of men aged 16 to 59 and women aged 16 to 54, except for the handicapped and for early pensioners, such as officers of the armed forces and the KGB, miners, and chemical workers. Labor resources do not coincide with the actual work force, because (1) most young people are still secondary or postsecondary students, (2) many young and middle-aged women are at home managing households and raising children, (3) in agriculture the working age is much longer, from age 10 to 12 to advanced old age (this was true especially in the first half of the 20th century), and (4) many men and women continue working after having reached the age of retirement (60 and 55 respectively).

Only recently have economists begun to take a special interest in labor resources; therefore, no data exist for the 19th and early 20th centuries. But it is known that approx 60 percent of the rural population in the nine Ukrainian gubernias of the Russian Empire was 12 to 60 years old. That group can be viewed as constituting the labor resources of the period; the number of those over 60 who were still working was compensated for by that of the disabled in the younger age-groups. There were 5.3 million males and females aged 12 to 60 in the Ukrainian gubernias in 1811, 6.9 million in 1851, and 15 million at the beginning of the 20th century. The labor resources of the period in the contemporary sense of the term (men aged 16 to 59 and women aged 16 to 54) consisted of approx 49 percent of the population. Intensive emigration in 1891–1914 from the gubernias to Siberia and Turkestan (approx 1.6 million people, mostly peasants) and the United States (1 million people, mostly Jews) and the large population losses that occurred during the First World War were reflected in a sharp decline in labor resources. By the February Revolution of 1917 the number of males and females aged 12 to 60 was 19 million (four times what it was a century earlier), and the labor resources by contemporary standards amounted to only 15.5 million. Large population losses also occurred during the struggle for Ukrainian independence (1917–20). Consequently, the 1926 Soviet census indicated that there were 15 million men and women aged 16 to 59 and 16 to 54 respectively in Soviet Ukraine, that is, fewer than before the 1917 Revolution. Border changes also played some role in the decline.

The forced *collectivization of agriculture and the ensuing repression of the so-called *kulaks, the man-made *famine of 1932–3, and the *terror resulted in massive population losses in all age-groups. The growth of Soviet Ukraine's labor resources was thus slowed down. It was not halted, however, because a large group born in the 1920s entered the labor force, and because in Ukraine immigration exceeded out-migration in the 1930s. The 1939 Soviet census listed 8.7 million men aged 16 to 59 and 8.9 million women aged 16 to 54; for the first time the number of women exceeded that of men in the labor resources. The women's share of the total population had increased to 57 percent (from 50 percent at the turn of the century).

The Soviet Ukrainian population suffered huge losses during the Second World War, but the annexation of most of Western Ukraine resulted in an increase in Ukraine's labor resources. By 1959 they totaled 24.9 million people (11.3 million men and 13.6 million women), and their share within the total population had increased to 59.5 percent. In the 1960s, however, their growth slowed down. In the 1970 census there were 26.2 million: the number of men had grown to 12.7 million, but the number of women, 13.5 million, was basically unchanged, and their combined share within the total population had fallen to 55.6 percent. In the 1960s and 1970s there was a shortage of labor resources as the relatively small group

born during the Second World War entered the work force, and as the generation born during the 1910s left it. By the 1979 census, however, the situation had begun to improve: the labor resources consisted of 28.8 million people (14.3 million men and 14.5 million women), constituting 58 percent of the total population. By 1986 the labor resources had grown slightly to 29.5 million people, but their share within the population remained unchanged at 58 percent. It has been projected that by 2000 the number of people will increase slightly, to 29.9 million; their share within the population will be 55–56 percent.

The division of the labor resources by gender and age has great significance for a country's economic life. The 1897 imperial census indicated a predominance of males in almost every age category and a rapid decline in the numbers within each succeeding age group. In the years 1926–39, females predominated in all age categories, the population under 40 declined steadily, and that between 40 and 50 fell sharply (see table 1). After the Second World War a great discrepancy occurred in the number of men and women in the older age-groups; this discrepancy is moving with the older age-groups and by the end of the century will not have any impact on the gender structure of the labor resources.

Through the 20th century a gradual aging of the labor resources has occurred. The younger groups have gradually decreased in number, and the older groups increased. Several factors have simultaneously influenced this development: fluctuating birth rates, losses due to wars and mass repression, and an increase in life span. Consequently, the general pattern have been subject to complex fluctuations. The share of actual labor resources within the population has declined gradually, from 35.2 percent in 1897 to 31.5 percent in 1939; has grown, to 39.9 percent in 1959 and 48.9 percent in 1970; and has again declined, to a projected 45.5 percent in 2000 (see table 2).

Actual employment of the labor resources varies by age-group (see table 3). Only about half of those in young-

TABLE 1
Ukraine's population and labor resources, 1897–1990 (in 1,000s)

Year	Population total No.	Male/female	Labor resources by age-group and gender						
			15–19 Male/female	20–29 Male/female	30–39 Male/female	40–49 Male/female	50–54 Male/female	55–59 Male/female	60–65 Male/female
1897	21,246	10,669	1,070	1,658	1,294	958	371	259	415
		10,577	1,141	1,635	1,276	922	390	262	377
1926	29,019	14,095	1,669	2,228	1,685	1,183	428	335	551
		14,924	1,854	2,756	1,827	1,232	486	428	650
1939*	30,947	14,754	1,437	2,924	2,375	1,405	499	430	467
		16,193	1,526	3,076	2,588	1,632	600	550	740
1959	41,869	18,575	1,742	3,624	2,681	1,857	917	682	964
		23,294	1,769	3,835	3,736	3,066	1,435	1,265	1,705
1970	47,126	21,305	1,962	2,972	3,602	2,828	728	979	1,413
		25,821	1,900	3,127	3,844	3,851	1,211	1,777	2,624
1979	49,609	22,616	2,128	3,824	2,941	3,398	1,545	879	1,418
		26,993	2,000	3,870	3,180	3,753	2,082	1,573	2,790
1990	51,800	24,000	1,875	3,883	3,700	2,820	1,765	1,257	1,853
		27,800	1,865	3,865	3,770	3,070	2,045	1,528	3,147

*Soviet Ukraine before the annexation of the western oblasts

TABLE 2
Percentage of Ukraine's population in certain age-groups and in its labor resources, 1897–2000

Year	Age-group							Labor resources	
	15–19	20–29	30–39	40–49	50–54	55–59	60–69	Official[a]	Actual[b]
1897	10.4	15.5	12.1	8.8	3.6	2.6	3.7	49.0	42.6
1926	12.1	17.2	12.1	8.3	3.1	2.6	4.1	51.7	43.3
1939	9.6	19.4	16.0	9.8	3.4	3.1	3.9	57.0	51.7
1959	8.4	17.8	15.3	11.8	5.6	4.6	6.4	59.5	55.1
1970	8.2	12.9	15.8	14.2	4.1	5.8	8.6	55.6	52.8
1979	8.3	15.5	12.3	14.4	7.3	4.9	8.5	58.0	54.4
1990	7.1	14.7	14.2	11.2	7.2	5.3	9.5	55.4	52.6
2000	7.6	13.9	14.0	13.5	6.2	3.5	10.3	55.7	51.1

[a]Men aged 16 to 59 and women aged 16 to 54
[b]Men and women aged 20 to 59

TABLE 3
Employed labor resources in Ukraine and the USSR in 1970 (percentage of age-group)

	Age-group							
	16–19	20–29	30–39	40–49	50–54	55–59	60–69	16–59
Ukraine	48.0[a]	88.1	94.1	90.6	79.2	42.2	14.4[b]	88.8[c]
USSR	47.9[b]	87.3	91.6	91.8	80.0	43.2	15.1[b]	88.1[c]

[a]Including employed people under 16
[b]Including all employed people over 60
[c]Men aged 16 to 59, women aged 16 to 54, and all employed people regardless of age

er and older age-groups are employed, whereas nearly 90 percent of middle-aged people work. On the whole, approx 88 percent of the labor resources are employed. In Ukraine, as was the case in the USSR as a whole, the employment of male and female labor resources differed (see table 4). The share of Ukraine's labor resources within the entire population of the USSR gradually decreased from approx 20–22 percent before the Second World War to 20.8 percent in 1959, 19 percent in 1979, and about 18 percent when the USSR ceased to exist.

TABLE 4
Labor resources in Ukraine by gender and age in the 1979 USSR census (percentage employed in each gender group/age-group)

Age-group	Males	Females	Both genders
14	0.3	0.2	0.2
15	1.6	1.5	1.6
16–17	21.0	20.5	20.7
18–19	69.7	63.7	66.8
20–29	91.5	88.7	90.1
30–39	98.1	91.1	94.5
40–49	97.0	93.5	95.2
50–54	90.0	81.1	84.9
55–59	78.3	28.7	46.2
60–64	29.3	10.5	16.9
65–69	15.4	5.1	8.4
Over 70	5.3	1.4	2.5
Over 14	74.5	60.3	66.7

Ukraine's labor resources have been gradually redistributed. The number of self-employed people (at home or on private plots) and agricultural workers has decreased, and the number of blue- and white-collar workers (especially in education, health care, communal and consumer services, and science) has increased. The redistribution has necessitated an increase in educational levels. Whereas there were 2,607,000 elementary-school children (only 29,000 in senior grades) in Ukraine in 1914–15, there were 6,830,000 (310,000 in senior grades) in 1940–1, 6,722,000 (604,000 in grades 9–11) in 1960–1, 8,414,000 (1,596,000 in senior grades) in 1970–1, and 7,500,000 (nearly 2,000,000 in senior grades) in the 1980s. Among all the employed in Ukraine in 1959, 9.9 percent had higher, incomplete higher, or specialized secondary educations; the figure rose to 17.5 in 1970 and 26 in 1979. With respect to the educational level of the work force, Ukraine lagged behind Armenia, Georgia, Lithuania, Latvia, Estonia, and the Russian SFSR. General and incomplete secondary educations had been attained by 33.9 percent in 1959, 49.3 percent in 1970, and 55.3 percent in 1979. In secondary education Ukraine was ahead of the Russian SFSR, Belorussia, Moldavia, Latvia, Lithuania, and Estonia, but not the Caucasian and Central Asian republics.

BIBLIOGRAPHY
Ptukha, M. (ed). *Demohrafichnyi zbirnyk* (Kiev 1926)
Rashin, A. *Naselenie Rossii za 100 let (1811–1913 gg.): Statisticheskie ocherki*, ed S. Strumilin (Moscow 1956)
Korchak-Chepurkovskii, Iu. *Izbrannye demograficheskie issledovaniia* (Moscow 1970)
Chumachenko, N. (ed). *Naselenie i trudovye resursy Donbassa* (Kiev 1977)
Kostakov, V.; Manevich, L. (eds). *Regional'nye problemy naseleniia i trudovye resursy SSSR* (Moscow 1978)

S. Maksudov

Labor school (*trudova shkola*). A school in which instruction is combined with practical experience and which prepares the student for a technical-scientific occupation. Though the idea of labor schools originated during the Renaissance, it found its fullest expression in the writings of the 19th-century British social reformer Robert Owen. In Ukraine the term labor schools originally referred to all schools which offered a general elementary and *incomplete secondary education for children between the ages of 8 and 15. (See *Seven-year schools.) Work on the curriculum of a *unified labor school was started late in 1917 by a special commission created by the Ministry of Education of the Ukrainian National Republic. (See *Elementary schools.) In 1925–8 some labor schools were transformed into *factory seven-year schools in the cities, and some village labor schools were reorganized into *schools for rural youth. In 1934, general elementary schools with grades one to seven were re-established and named seven-year schools. In 1958 all seven-year schools were reorganized into *eight-year schools. (See also *Education, *Secondary education.)

Laborets River [Laborec]. A right-bank tributary of the Liatorytsia River in eastern Slovakia. It is 135.5 km in length and drains a basin area of 4,523 sq km. Its source is near the Lupkiv Pass in the Lemko region, and it flows through the Low Beskyd and the Tysa Lowland. Its main tributaries (both left-bank) are the Chirokha and the Uzh rivers.

Labosh, Fedir [Laboš] (Fedor), b 24 January 1902 in Djurdjevo, Bačka region, Serbia, d 5 November 1977 in Zagreb. Economist and historian. After obtaining a PH D in Zagreb (1928) he worked as an economist for the city in the postwar period. At the same time he studied the history of Ukrainians in the Bačka region and wrote essays on this topic, as well as *Ystoryia rusynokh Bachkei, Sremu y Slavonyï, 1745–1918* (History of the Ruthenians of Bačka, Srem, and Slavonia, 1745–1918).

Labradorite. A mineral consisting of plagioclase feldspar of the albite-anorthite series that is usually gray to black in color. Its red, blue, or green iridescence makes labradorite a valued gemstone and ornamental and facing material. Anorthosite and igneous rock, composed mainly of coarse-grained labradorite crystals, are found in Ukraine. Deposits of high-grade anorthosite occur in Cherniakhiv raion (Holovyne, Horbuliv, Slipchytsi) and Volodarske-Volynske raion (Novyi Bobryk, Kamianyi Brid, Poronivka, Turchynka), in Zhytomyr oblast; in Horodyshche raion, in Cherkasy oblast; and in Novomyrhorod raion, in Kirovohrad oblast. Labradorite facing can be seen on many of Kiev's buildings and in its subway stations.

Lada. A Slavic and Latvian-Lithuanian deity of fertility and marriage. Her cult was widespread in Ukraine and has left its mark on ritual songs. One of four deities depicted on the *Zbruch idol is a woman with a ring in her right hand. Some scholars, including B. Rybakov, claim that the female figure is Lada. The oldest written references to the Lada cult are found in 15th-century Polish church prohibitions of pagan rituals. In Ukraine the Lada cult is first mentioned in I. Gizel's *Sinopsis* (1674); she is referred to as a goddess from the time of Volodymyr the Great. Lada's feast, which was celebrated with games in her honor, was part of the spring rituals. Some scholars, such as E. Anichkov and A. Brückner, denied Lada's existence in Slavic mythology and explained the frequent use of the word in folk songs as a mere refrain. But the pervasiveness of this refrain in all Slavic and even Baltic folklore casts doubt on that theory. Some colloquial expressions allude to the cult of Lada: in Volhynia *laduvaty* means to conduct a wedding, and in Transcarpathia and the Prešov region *ladkanky* are wedding songs, and *ladkaty* is to sing wedding songs.

Sophia Lada: *Prairie Fantasy III* (gouache, 1986)

Lada, Sophia, b 17 October 1941 in Cracow. Painter. She was a student at the Moore College of Art in Philadephia and the Pennsylvania Academy of Fine Arts (1964) and studied iconography with S. Hordynsky (1976–7). In the early 1980s she was curator of the Oseredok Art Gallery and Museum in Winnipeg. Lada's works are influenced by symbolism, surrealism, and Ukrainian folk art. Her favorite subjects are female figures in the magic world of nature and fairy tales. In a cycle of eight paintings she portrayed the sun's course during the four seasons of the year and related changes in color. Solo exhibitions of her works have been held in Philadephia (1972, 1973, 1979), St Paul (1973), Toronto (1974), Baltimore (1974), Warren, Michigan (1978), and Windham, New York (1980).

Ladan, Pavlo (pseuds: Nedobyty, Netiaha), b 29 February 1892 in Ulashkivtsi, Chortkiv county, Galicia, d 27 April 1933. Communist activist. After emigrating to Canada (1910) and the United States (1915) he worked on the railway and in factories. He was active in immigrant socialist and communist organizations and served as secretary and editor of the Ukrainian-American newspaper *Robitnyk*. To avoid a five-year prison term for political activities, he escaped to Europe, where he worked with the External Bureau for Aiding the Communist Party of Eastern Galicia in Prague, Vienna, and Berlin (1921–3). From 1924 he was a member of the Central Committee of the Communist Party of Western Ukraine (KPZU), a candidate of the Comintern's Executive Committee, and the KPZU representative in the Polish section of the Comintern. In 1926 he returned to the United States and served on the executive committee of the Ukrainian Federation of the Communist Party of America (later the United Ukrainian Toilers Organization). In 1930 he was recalled to the CC KPZU and appointed editor of its journal *Nasha pravda* in Berlin. In the final two years of his life he held an important position at the Secretariat of the Politburo of the CC KPZU. He died in the Stalinist terror.

Ladan (aka Ladyn). III-13. A town smt (1990 pop 7,600) on the Udai River in Pryluka raion, Chernihiv oblast. It is mentioned in documents as early as 1619, when its Monastery of the Holy Protectress was converted into a nunnery. Today the town has a fire-equipment plant, a secondary school, and a technical school.

Ladny, Vadym [Ladnyj], b 27 December 1918 in Kharkiv. Architect. A graduate of the Kharkiv Civil-Engineering Institute (1946), he has worked in Kiev, where together with other architects he designed the building of the AN URSR (now ANU) Section of Social Sciences (1954), the river port (1961), the Rusanivka Island housing complex (1964–71), the apartment buildings on Brest-Litovsk Prospect (1961–72), the Slavuta hotel (1972), the physics complex at Kiev University (1973), and the Obolon housing complex (1974–85).

Ladomyrova Gospel (Ladomyrivske uchytelne yevanheliie). A 17th-century manuscript of 242 folios written in the *pivustav* script that was discovered at the Ladomyrova Monastery in the Prešov region. It consists of didactics and Sunday Gospel readings. Its anti-Reformation teachings indicate that it was written during the spread of Lutheranism. Its language, which has local dialectal elements, was studied by I. *Pańkevych (*Naukovyi zbirnyk Tovarystva Prosvita v Uzhhorodi*, 1923). The gospel was copied from the same original as the didactic gospel found in I. Kapyshovsky's eparchial library in Prešov, which had been composed in the vernacular of the Boiko–Sian dialectal boundary. There are textual parallels between the Ladomyrova and the *Peresopnytsia gospels.

Ladyka, Dmytro, b 14 August 1889 in the Ternopil region, d 1945 in Dresden. Lawyer, civic figure, and politician. He was active in the Prosvita society, the Union of Ukrainian Progressive Youth (Kameniari), and the Ukrainian Socialist Radical party, of which he sat on the executive council. An effective public speaker, he defended Ukrainian activists in political trials and was elected to the Polish Sejm from the Ternopil district in 1928 and 1930. In parliament he served as secretary of the Ukrainian socialists' caucus (1928–30). He died in the bombing of Dresden.

Ladyka, Vasyl (Basil; secular name: Volodymyr), b 2 August 1884 in Drohobych, Galicia, d 1 September 1956 in Winnipeg. Basilian missionary and Ukrainian Catholic

Dmytro Ladyka   Archbishop Vasyl Ladyka

archbishop of Canada. Ladyka entered the Basilian novitiate in 1903 and took monastic vows in 1909, the year he was sent to Canada. He graduated from the Grand Séminaire in Montreal and was ordained in 1912. He worked as a missionary in Manitoba (1912–13) and in Saskatchewan and Alberta (1913–22), and as rector of St Josaphat's Church in Edmonton (1922–9). He was consecrated bishop of Winnipeg and designated head of the Ukrainian Catholic church in Canada in May 1929, and was elevated to the rank of archbishop in 1948. He strengthened the church in Canada by promoting such lay organizations as the *Ukrainian Catholic Brotherhood, the Ukrainian Catholic Women's League, and Ukrainian Catholic Youth, and by establishing *Ukraïns'ki visti* as the church's weekly organ in 1929.

Ladyzhensky, Gennadii [Ladyženskij, Gennadij], b 4 February 1853 in Kologriv, Kostroma gubernia, Russia, d 15 September 1916 in Kologriv. Russian painter. He studied at the St Petersburg Academy of Arts (1870–9) and was elected a member in 1910. From 1882 to 1914 he lived in Odessa. There he taught painting at the Realschule and at the art school (Ye. Bukovetsky and P. Volokidin were his students), painted watercolor genre scenes, portraits, and landscapes, and was a founding member of the *Society of South Russian Artists. His works include *Tiller* (1885), *Flock in the Steppe* (1885), *Road in the Kherson Steppes*, *Evening at a Khutir*, *The Sea* (1885), *Winter in the South* (1889), *Ukraine* (1889), *Banduryst* (1891), *Granite Unloading at the Odessa Port* (1898), and *Khadzhybei* (1899). A book about Ladyzhensky by V. Afanasiev was published in Kiev in 1966.

Ladyzhensky, Mykola [Ladyžens'kyj], b 28 March 1906 in Litynia, Drohobych county, Galicia, d 11 May 1975 in Lviv. Geologist; corresponding member of the AN URSR (now ANU) from 1972. He graduated from the Cracow Mining Academy in 1936 and worked as a geologist in the Pioner Oil Company in Lviv. After the war he was a lecturer at the Lviv Polytechnical Institute (1945–51) and a department head at the Institute of Geology and Geochemistry of Fossil Fuels of the AN URSR (1951–75). He researched the geological structure and the mineral deposits (mainly oil and natural gas) of the Carpathian Mountains and the Crimea. He was also interested in the industrial application of menilite schists found in the Carpathians.

Ladyzhets, Volodymyr [Ladyžec'], b 17 June 1924 in Kharkivtsi, Lityn county, Podilia gubernia. Writer and poet. In 1949 he was appointed culture editor of the oblast newspaper of Transcarpathia, and later, editor in chief of the oblast publishing house. As a poet he published several collections, including *Slavliu trud* (I Glorify Labor, 1950), *Liryka* (Lyrical Poetry, 1959), *Mizh berehamy* (Between the Banks, 1962), and *Vichne kolo* (The Eternal Circle, 1978). Among his prose works are short stories, published in numerous collections including *Iasnovyd* (The Seer, 1974), and the novels *Perekhrestia* (The Crossroads, 1967) and *Za brustverom – svitanok* (Beyond the Rampart It's Dawn, 1976). He has also written fables, stories, and poetry for children.

Ladyzhyn [Ladyžyn]. V-10. A city (1990 pop 20,000) on the Boh River in Trostianets raion, Vinnytsia oblast. In the 13th century it belonged to Galicia principality and had a fortress, which withstood the Tatar invasion of 1240. It is first mentioned in a historical document in 1362, when it was captured by Lithuania. During the Cossack-Polish War of 1648–57 it was a company center of Uman regiment. In 1648 M. Kryvonis defeated a Polish regiment near Ladyzhyn. By 1699 it was the scene of many battles among the Cossacks, Poles, and Turks. The town participated in the Cossack and popular uprising of 1702–4 and the haidamaka uprising of 1768. In October 1919 the Ukrainian Sich Riflemen fought A. Denikin's army near Ladyzhyn, and in August of the following year the UNR Army fought the Red Army in the area. Today the town has a thermoelectric station, a reinforced-concrete plant, a silicate bricks plant, a granite quarry, and an oil-pressing plant. Two settlements from the Neolithic period and two from the 6th to 7th centuries have been excavated near Ladyzhyn. The ruins of the Ladyzhyn fortress are visible today.

Lahoda. A noble family of the Poltava region, descended from Vasyl Lahoda (d 1702), who was captain of Khorol regiment (1685) and osaul of Myrhorod regiment (1691–1701). His son, Oleksander Lahodenko, was flag-bearer (*khorunzhyi*) of Myrhorod regiment (1723–32).

Lahoda, Alla, b 6 February 1937 in Kiev. Ballerina. Upon graduating from the Kiev Choreography School (1955) she joined the Kiev Theater of Opera and Ballet, with which she appeared as Kylyna in M. Skorulsky's *The Forest Song*, Zarema in B. Asafev's *Fountain of Bakhchesarai*, the Mistress of the Copper Mountain in S. Prokofiev's *Stone Flower*, Kitri in L. Minkus's *Don Quixote*, and the Golden Lady in *Symphonic Dances* (music by S. Rachmaninoff).

Lahoda, Valentyn (pseud of Valentyn Lahodzynsky), b 27 May 1913 in Stepantsi, Kaniv county, Kiev gubernia. Poet. Before the Second World War he worked as a correspondent for the Donbas newspaper *Molodyi robitnyk*, and later he became a radiobroadcast editor in Donetske and Dnipropetrovske. After the war he devoted himself to writing. He has published collections of lyric poetry, such as *Kviten'* (April, 1953) and *Natkhnennia* (Inspiration, 1960), and collections of satirical and humorous poetry: *Shcho posiiesh, te i pozhnesh* (What You Sow, You Shall Reap, 1955), *Mokrym riadnom* (With a Wet Sheet, 1956), *Khoch krut', khoch vert'* (Though You Twist or Turn, 1962), *Hariacha zavyvka* (Hot Wrap, 1968), and *Spasybi za uvahu*

(Thanks for Your Attention, 1976). He has also translated some Hungarian poetry into Ukrainian.

Mykola Lahodynsky

Lahodynsky, Mykola [Lahodyns'kyj], b 1866, d 1919. Lawyer and civic and political leader in Galicia. After opening a law office in Deliatyn (near Kolomyia) in 1900, he organized the Ruska Kasa credit union and branches of the Prosvita society, Silskyi Hospodar, and Ruska Besida in the town. An effective regional organizer for the Ukrainian Radical party, he was elected to its chief executive committee and, during the First World War, to its presidency. He was elected twice (1907 and 1911) to the Austrian parliament in Vienna, where he served as deputy leader of the Ukrainian Parliamentary Club. He was also a deputy to the Galician Diet from 1913, as well as a member of the General Ukrainian Council and the Ukrainian National Rada.

Lakes. Natural, nonflowing bodies of water that fill depressions on the earth's surface and lack direct exchange with the sea. In Ukraine lakes are numerous but small. The contiguous ethnographic territory of Ukraine contains some 4,000 lakes. Within the borders of Ukraine there are over 3,000 lakes with a combined surface area of more than 2,000 sq km, which constitutes nearly 3.5 percent of the country's total land area. The mean surface area of the lakes in Ukraine is 0.67 sq km. Only 30 lakes exceed 10 sq km in surface area, and 13 exceed 30 sq km.

The majority of lakes in Ukraine are of fluvial origin, commonly associated with the changing shapes and configurations of the river channels in the floodplains of large rivers. Such lakes tend to be small and shallow, are rich in fish, and contain fresh but sometimes muddy water. The largest number of such lakes are found in the floodplains of the Dnieper, the Kuban, the Prypiat, and the Desna, with smaller numbers along the Dniester, the Donets, the Orel, the Samara, and other rivers. The construction of the Dnieper Cascade resulted in the creation of a system of reservoirs in most of the little lakes of the Dnieper floodplain. Also of fluvial origin are the saline Lake Manych-Gudilo (Manych-Hudylo in Ukrainian; 300 sq km) and other lakes along the Manych River.

There are a large number of lakes in western Polisia. They can be divided into several groups. In northwestern Polisia (Brest oblast), notably in the drainage basin of the Yaselda River, there is a grouping of middle-sized lakes – Vyhonivske (surface area, 26.5 sq km; maximum depth, 2.7 m), Chorne (17.2 sq km; 2.2 m), Sporivske (13.2 sq km; 2.1 m) – and a number of smaller ones. Located in swampy terrain, many of those lakes are joined either by slow-flowing streams or by canals, built mostly for the purpose of drainage. Along the upper reaches of the Prypiat River in western Polisia (mostly Volhynia oblast), there are shallow Lake Tur (13.5 sq km; 2.6 m), Lake Orikhove, Lake Volianske, Lake Bile, Lake Liubiazh, Lake Nobel, and other, smaller lakes. Like the lakes along the Yaselda River they are located in the midst of swamps, are often underlain by peat deposits, and thus belong to the dystrophic class. Some of those lakes are of fluvial origin; others are of glacial or even eolian origin, where the drainage was impeded by sand dunes. Another group of lakes, located between the headwaters of the Prypiat and the Buh rivers, includes Lake Svytiaz (24.2 sq km; 58.4 m), Lake Pulemet (16.3 sq km; 19.2 m), and other, smaller lakes. Those lakes are deeper, obtain their clear water from springs in chalk formations, and are considered to be of karstic origin. In addition there are small, shallow lakes scattered through southwestern Polisia between the Turiia and the Styr rivers and in Volodava Polisia (in southern Podlachia, now part of Poland). All the lakes of western Polisia have a moderate or below-average level of mineralization.

The largest lakes of Ukraine are located along the coast of the Black and Azov seas. The combined surface area of those lakes makes up nearly 59 percent of the lake area in Ukraine. Some of them are former shallow marine bays (lagoon lakes), and others are enclosed flooded river estuaries (limans). Both are separated from the sea by narrow sandbars. Coastal lakes are large but shallow and have considerable (if not high) levels of salinity. Those with very high mineral content are significant for salt mining and the chemical industry and are used for medicinal purposes. In the southwest the largest coastal lakes also include the freshwater, liman-like lakes blocked off by the levees of the Danube: Lake Kahul (90 sq km; 6.0 m), Lake Yalpukh (149 sq km; 2.0 m), Lake Katlabukh (68 sq km; 4.0 m), and Lake Kytai (60 sq km; 5.0 m). There are small, fluvial lakes in the floodplain of the Danube as well. Between the mouths of the Danube and the Dniester are Lake Sasyk (also known as Lake Kunduk; 210 sq km; 3.0 m; in the process of being desalted), Lake Shahany (70 sq km; 2.0 m), Lake Alibei (72 sq km; 2.0 m), Lake Burnas (22.6 sq km; 1.9 m), and the Budatskyi Liman (30.0 sq km; 2.0 m). At the mouth of the Dniester River are the Kuchurhan Liman (20 sq km; 5.0 m) and the Dniester Liman (360 sq km; 2.5 m). Between the Dniester and the Boh limans are the Khadzhybei Liman (70 sq km; 13 m), the Kuialnyk Liman (61 sq km; 3 m), the Tylihul Liman (150–170 sq km; 21.0 m), and the Berezan Liman (60 sq km; 3.2 m). On the northern coast of the Azov Sea are Lake Molochne (170 sq km; 9.0 m) and the Miius Liman. Along the Kuban Lowland coast are Lake Khanske, the Hirkyi Liman, the Solodkyi Liman, and many other lakes in the delta of the Kuban River, including the Kirpili Liman, Lake Skeliuvate, the Boikiv Liman, the Ponura Liman, the Skhidnii Liman, the Kurchanskyi Liman, the Akhtanyzovskyi Liman, the Tsokur Liman, the Kyzyltashskyi Liman, and the Vytiazivskyi Liman. Those numerous shallow (1 to 1.5 m) lakes are rich in fish life and occupy a combined surface area of 1,360 sq km. In the Crimea there are shallow, salty lakes south of the Perekop Isthmus, including Lake Chervone (Krasne; 34 sq km; 1.0 m), Lake Kyiatske (12.5 sq km; 0.4 m), Lake Kyrleutske (20.8 sq km; 0.6 m), and Lake Aihulske (37.5 sq km; 0.3 m), probably outlying remnants of the shallow Lake Syvash. Other coastal lakes in the Crimea include Lake Donuzlav (48 sq km; 27 m), Lake Sasyk (75 sq km; 1.2 m), and Lake Saky (8.1 sq km; 1.5 m) on the west side, and Lake Aktashske (27 sq km; 0.1 m), Lake Chokratske (8.5 sq km; 0.8 m), Lake Tobechytske (19 sq km; 0.5 m), and Lake Uzunlarske (21.1 sq km; 0.1 m) on the Kerch Peninsula.

Besides those in western Polisia and the coastal zone and along the floodplains, there are few lakes of appreciable size in Ukraine. There are karstic lakes in southwestern Polisia (formed as a result of the erosion of chalk), in Podilia and Pokutia (the erosion of gypsum), in the mountains and foothills of the Crimea (the erosion of limestone), and in the Donbas near Slovianske (the erosion of salt). To the karstic lakes may also be added the seasonal lakes, which occupy *pody (depressions formed as a result of the compaction of waterlogged loess) in the spring.

The few lakes in the Carpathian Mountains have a variety of origins, including tectonic, postglacial (notably the tarns of the Chornohora Mountains), and volcanic (such as the Morske Oko in the Vyhorlat Mountains) origins. All those lakes are small (the largest being Lake Synevyr) and contain clear, fresh water. Lakes found in the Caucasus Mountains are of similar origin and have similar characteristics.

In addition to natural lakes there are many artificial ponds (about 18,000) and water reservoirs in Ukraine. The six large reservoirs on the Dnieper River alone occupy a combined surface area of over 7,000 sq km. The combined area for all ponds and reservoirs in Ukraine (January 1986) is 11,730 sq km; they retain 57.8 cu km of water.

BIBLIOGRAPHY
Burkser, Ie. *Soloni ozera ta lymany Ukraïny* (Kiev 1928)
Dunai i pridunaiskie vodoemy v predelakh SSSR. Vol 36, *Trudy Instituta gidrobiologii AN SSSR* (Moscow 1961)
Polivannaia, M. 'Ozera,' in *Priroda Ukrainskoi SSR: Moria i vnutrennie vody* (Kiev 1987)
Spravochnik po vodnym resursam (Kiev 1987)

I. Stebelsky

Bishop Hryhorii Lakota

Lakota, Hryhorii, b 31 January 1883 in Holodivka, Rudky county, Galicia, d 12 November 1950 in Abez, Komi ASSR. Ukrainian Catholic bishop and scholar. He was ordained in 1908, and completed his D TH at Vienna University in 1913. He then taught church history and canon law and served as rector (1918–26) at the Peremyshl Greek Catholic Theological Seminary. In 1924 he became assistant bishop of Peremyshl eparchy, a position he retained until he was arrested in 1946 by the Polish authorities. He was handed over to the Soviet authorities and sentenced to eight years in a Vorkuta labor camp, where he died. While in Peremyshl, Lakota wrote a commentary on marriage law in the church codex of 1921 and *Try Synody Peremys'ki v XVI–XIX st.* (Three Synods of Peremyshl in the 16th–19th Centuries, 1939).

Laktionov-Stezenko, Mykola, b 15 February 1929 in Novovolodymyrivka (now in Kirovohrad oblast). Film director. In 1961 he completed studies at the Faculty of Screenwriters of the State Institute of Cinematography in Moscow; since then he has worked in Kiev at the Studio of Chronicle-Documentary Films. His first film was *Suchasni zaporozhtsi* (Contemporary Zaporozhian Cossacks, 1964).

Lakyza, Ivan, b 24 November 1895 in Starzyska, Radom gubernia, Poland, d 27 July 1938. Soviet literary critic. In the 1920s and 1930s his articles and reviews appeared in *Zhyttia i revoliutsiia, Hart,* and *Prolitfront.* He was also the author of popular critical biographies of M. Kotsiubynsky (1928) and T. Shevchenko (1929) and the collection of critical essays *Pys'mennyk i krytyk* (The Writer and the Critic, 1928). In 1937 he moved to Moscow, where he worked in the People's Commissariat of Education. His critiques of certain writers (eg, B. Antonenko-Davydovych, V. Pidmohylny) contributed to their persecution; subsequently he himself became a victim of the Stalinist terror.

Lam, Jan, b 16 January 1838 in Stanyslaviv, Galicia, d 3 August 1886 in Lviv. Polish writer and publicist. He studied law at Lviv University and worked as a provincial-school teacher. He took part in the Polish Insurrection of 1863–4. From 1866 he was a journalist in Lviv; there he became editor of the liberal daily *Dziennik Polski* (1869–86) and wrote several novels replete with Ukrainianisms and satirical depictions (à la C. Dickens) of Galician society. In his publicism he portrayed the Ukrainian Cossacks (eg, Hetman B. Khmelnytsky), T. Shevchenko, and the Galician Ukrainophiles sympathetically. In the introduction to his historical poem *Zawichost* (1862), about the battle between the forces of Princes Leszek of Cracow and Roman Mstyslavych of Galicia-Volhynia in 1205, Lam argued that medieval Rus' and the Ukrainian language were not Russian but separate and distinct entities. His literary works were republished in four volumes in Warsaw in 1956–7, and a selection of his publicism appeared in 1954.

Lamakh, Valerii [Lamax, Valerij], b 6 March 1925 in Lebedyn, Kharkiv gubernia, d 1978. Graphic artist, painter, and muralist. A graduate of the Kiev State Art Institute (1948), he designed posters, took part in the creation of the mosaic wall panels inside the Kiev River Station (1961) and Boryspil Airport (1965), and created the monumental wall panel inside the Palace of Culture of the Chemical Production Complex in Dniprodzerzhynske (1968–70). In the early 1960s he did paintings (only recently brought to public attention) that could be considered examples of abstract expressive in Ukrainian art.

Laments (*holosinnia*). Folk poetry connected with the traditional funeral rites. Their original function was to propitiate the deity for the soul of the departed and to secure its support for the living kin. With time their magical purpose was forgotten, but their ritual use was preserved.

The laments are usually performed by the deceased's closest female relative – the wife, mother, or sister. But there are also fine examples of children's laments for their parents and husbands' for wives or children. In some regions, if the relatives would not recite them, semiprofessional wailers were hired.

Laments have a traditional form – a recitative style punctuated frequently by exclamations. They have distinctive imagery, emotive epithets, metaphors, similes, and lyrical appeals to the departed. The wailer is free to improvise within certain limits. She expresses grief at the loss of a family member and at the same time recounts in vivid detail the life she shared with the departed. Laments were recited also over natural disasters, such as crop failure, fire, or famine; these songs are related to the wailings over recruits. Formally, laments are related to the dumas and are one of the oldest recorded folk genres. A fine example of the genre from the end of the 12th century is the lament of Anna Yaroslavna in *Slovo o polku Ihorevi.* Folklorists began studying and collecting laments in the 19th century. One of the largest collections (299 items) was gathered by I. *Svientsitsky. Laments in use by Ukrainians in Poland, Czechoslovakia, and Rumania were recorded only after the Second World War.

BIBLIOGRAPHY
Svientsits'kyi, I. 'Pokhoronni holosinnia,' *Etnohrafichnyi zbirnyk,* 31–2 (1912)

M. Mushynka

Lan, Oleksander (pseud of Kyrylo Korshak), b 1897 in Horodyshche, Cherkasy county, Kiev gubernia, d 1943. Poet and archeologist. He graduated from the Kiev Institute of People's Education in 1928. In 1924 his poetry began to appear in journals, such as *Nova hromada, Chervonyi shliakh,* and *Hlobus.* Only three collections of his poetry were published: *Otavy kosiat'* (They Are Cutting the Aftercrops, 1928), *Doloni ploshch* (The Palms of Plazas, 1930), and *Nazustrich sontsiu* (To Meet the Sun, 1930). His articles on archeology appeared in *Khronika arkheolohiï ta mystetstva* (1930–1), *Nauka i zhizn'* (1935), and *Naukovi zapysky Instytutu istoriï material'noï kul'tury* (1934–5).

Lan. A publishing house established in Kiev in 1909 by O. Hrushevsky. Directed by Yu. *Tyshchenko, it published, using the *Zhelekhivka script, books for children and teenagers by Tyshchenko (on the life of plants and the Crimea), M. Shapoval (on the forest), Yu. Budiak (on savage peoples), M. Hrushevsky (his historical story about Hetman B. Khmelnytsky), S. Rudnytsky (on the physical geography of Ukraine), and V. Koroliv-Stary (on healing domestic animals); a collection of L. Hlibov's fables; A. Hrushevska's story *Nad morem* (At the Sea); and collections of stories by R. Kipling (trans Tyshchenko), E.T. Seton (trans Tyshchenko), W. Hauff (trans O. Oles), and others. The books' covers were designed by I. Buriachok. Lan ceased operating in 1913 after Tyshchenko was forced to emigrate.

Lancasterian schools (*liankasterski shkoly*). Inexpensive elementary schools in which older and better students lead the school activities in groups under the teacher's supervision. The Lancasterian school system was brought to Ukraine from France by Gen N. Raevsky and the Decembrist M. Orlov, who reformed the system and in 1818 founded a large military school for orphans in Kiev. Other Lancasterian schools in Ukraine were established in Horodyshche, Cherkasy county, through the initiative of Count M. Vorontsov, in the village of Babai, near Kharkiv (1832), and in many other locations. The Lancasterian school system failed to establish itself in Ukraine and soon disappeared.

Lancer regiments (*pikinerski polky*). Formations of military colonists created in 1764 by the Russian government to settle the newly created *New Russia gubernia and defend it from the Turks and Crimean Tatars. The lancers (*pikinery*), who were named after the pikes they used as one of their weapons, were recruited mostly from among the Cossacks of Poltava and Myrhorod regiments (Donets and Dnieper regiments), but also from among Ukrainian and Russian peasants; Serbian, Montenegrin, and Hungarian colonists (Yelysavethrad and Luhanske regiments); and in 1776 from former Zaporozhian Cossacks (Poltava and Kherson regiments). Lancers lost their Cossack privileges and were forced to remain in military service, pay taxes, and fulfill feudal obligations to the state. In 1767 the lancers in Kremenchuk and Vlasivka, in the Dnieper Regiment, sent a representative, P. Denysenko, to Moscow to protest their oppression, but the petition was in vain. Their condition worsened considerably after the outbreak of the Russo-Turkish War (1768–74). Influenced by the *Koliivshchyna rebellion in Right-Bank Ukraine, the Donets and Dnieper regiments mutinied in 1769. Several hundred lancers joined forces with Zaporozhian Cossack rebels to fight the tsar's punitive detachments. The revolt was suppressed brutally in 1770. Ya. Holovaty and other leaders, as well as many mutineers, were whipped and sentenced for life to hard labor in Siberia; many of them died in transit. The other members of the Donets Regiment were sent to fight the Crimean Tatars. They distinguished themselves in battle at Perekop (1770) and Kaffa and in the 1774 rout of the Tatar-Turkish forces in the Crimea. When Russia annexed the Crimean Khanate in 1783, the regiments lost their defensive importance and were transformed into three light-cavalry regiments.

Lanckoroński, Przecław, ?–1531. Ukrainianized Polish nobleman, starosta of Khmilnyk, and military leader at the beginning of the 16th century. With O. *Dashkevych he organized Cossack forces to defend the population against Tatar incursions. He went on military campaigns with the Cossacks in 1516 to Akkerman, in Moldavia (then a Turkish-held territory), and in 1528 to Ochakiv, on the Black Sea. He figures in many folk legends and sayings.

Land charters (*zemski ustavni hramoty*). Legal documents of the Grand Duchy of Lithuania granted by the grand dukes to particular territories and their inhabitants to confirm their ancient rights and to define their relation to the central government. In contrast to charters of privilege, which sometimes introduced new rights, land charters confirmed traditional rights. Eight land charters deal with Ukrainian lands within the Grand Duchy and two Ukrainian lands within the Polish Commonwealth. The more important charters were Jagiełło's charter to Lutske land (1424 or 1430), Casimir IV Jagiełłonczyk's charter to Galicia (1456), the charter to Dorohychyn land (1516), two charters (1501 and 1509) to Volhynia, and one (1501) to Bielsk county in Podlachia. Many of them were based on earlier charters which have not been preserved. These documents contain material on civil, criminal, private, and procedural law, and some information about the institutions and norms of old Ukrainian customary law. The later charters have a more distinct estate character.

Land community (*zemelna hromada*, aka land society [*zemelne tovarystvo*]). In early Soviet Ukraine an association of peasant households that collectively received from the state the right to use fields, meadows, and pastures. Resembling the Russian *obshchina, the unit was established on 27 May 1922 and was confirmed by the USSR Land Code of 30 July 1930. Membership in a land community was compulsory. A general meeting of members had the right to decide on one of three forms of land use: (1) communal use, whereby cultivated land was redistributed periodically to each family household according to its size; (2) the distribution of land to each household on a permanent basis; or (3) common cultivation by an artel, whereby the artel could take on the function of the land community. Regulations permitted a household or group of households to choose forms of land use different from those prevalent in the land community; such households were allocated land for the purpose. In 1928 the Soviet government began restricting the rights of land communities, and in 1930, as a result of *collectivization policies, it abolished them.

Land courts (*zemski sudy*). Nobility courts which functioned in Poland (Polish: *sąd ziemski*) and the Grand Duchy of Lithuania from the mid-15th century. They were introduced in Right-Bank Ukraine in the 16th century. Each court served a voivodeship or land (*zemlia*) in handling civil litigation cases. The three-member court was elected by the nobles of the region and confirmed for life by the king. Its verdicts could be appealed to the dietine courts in Poland or to the grand prince in Lithuania.

In 1763 Hetman K. Rozumovsky reintroduced the land courts, as defined in the Lithuanian Statute, in Left-Bank Ukraine. Twenty courts were established, two per regiment and three in the Nizhen regiment. Each consisted of three officers, elected for life from among military fellows. They ruled on most civil matters, and their verdicts could be appealed to the general court in Chernihiv. As the gubernial system was extended to Ukraine, these courts were abolished, in 1782. They were restored in 1796 by Paul I as elected courts, one per county, and their authority was enlarged to cover criminal cases. The land courts were finally abolished in 1831.

Land law (*zemelne zakonodavstvo*). Legal norms that regulate land ownership, tenure, and use. In the USSR land law is a wide legal area embracing all land relations and various socialist forms of land use. In non-Soviet countries land ownership and use is regulated mostly by private law (property, contracts, and so on). Only some land legislation belongs to public law, particularly the legislative or administrative acts that limit the freedom of transfer, division, consolidation, and expropriation. (For earlier land acts under the Russian Empire and Austria-Hungary, see *Land tenure system and *Land reforms.)

During the period of Ukrainian statehood in 1917–20, land ownership and distribution was one of the most pressing problems. It was the subject of a series of proclamations and legislative acts. The First Universal of the Central Rada announced the expropriation of the estates of the landowners, the state, the tsar, and the church, and reserved the right of the Ukrainian parliament to make land legislation. The Third Universal abolished the gentry's right to own estates and other lands not worked directly by them, and transferred, without compensation, this 'property of all the toiling people' to the people. The Constituent Assembly of Ukraine was to enact the law that would bring order to land tenure; until then, local land committees would administer expropriated lands. The Fourth Universal proclaimed the abolition of private land ownership and the socialization of land in the UNR.

On 31 January 1918 the Central Rada passed a special land law which restated the main points of the Third Universal and preserved the principle of socialization. Inspired by the land program of the Ukrainian Party of Socialist Revolutionaries, it allowed former owners to retain the use of tracts, whose size was to be determined, according to local conditions, by the land administration consisting of land committees (village, district, and gubernia) and a central government land agency. The law provided for land use by individuals, co-operatives, the state, and other public corporations. It was implemented after the Bolsheviks had been pushed out of Ukraine in March 1918.

By his decree of 29 April 1918, Hetman P. Skoropadsky abolished the Central Rada's land law and dissolved the land committees. This decree and the Hetman's provisional law proclaimed that the right of ownership was inalienable, and that private property could be expropriated only with compensation. A special commission drafted a land reform bill (known as Minister V. Leontovych's bill), which was enacted in November 1918. It required estates over 200 desiatins (218 ha) to be sold to the State Land Bank and to be distributed among peasant farmers in parcels of up to 25 desiatins.

Instead of reinstating the Central Rada's land law, the Directory of the UNR on 9 January 1919 enacted M. Shapoval's modified version of the law of 31 January 1918. It granted in perpetuity a maximum of 15 desiatins to individual farmers and socialized all other land without compensation. Thus, private farms worked by their owners were retained, while voluntary co-operative farming was encouraged. Shifting battlefronts, however, prevented this law from being implemented.

The Ukrainian National Rada of the Western Province of the Ukrainian National Republic on 14 April 1919 adopted a land law which preserved the principle of private ownership. At the same time it expropriated, for the purpose of redistributing land among landless peasants and small farmers, the following categories of land: (1) manorial tracts which had been excluded from village community jurisdiction by the law of 1866; (2) church and monastic lands; (3) estates that were not worked by the owners themselves; (4) lands acquired through speculation; and (5) all other lands in excess of a limit to be defined by a separate law, which would also determine compensation for expropriated land. The Polish occupation of Western Ukraine prevented the National Rada from implementing these reforms. (For Polish land legislation in the interwar period see *Land reforms.)

Soviet Ukraine. The land law of the Ukrainian SSR was inspired by the Russian government's decree of 21 November 1917 and nationalization law of 27 January 1918, and was adopted by the Second All-Ukrainian Congress of Soviets in March 1918. The new law abolished private

ownership of land and proclaimed all land to be the property of 'the entire toiling people.' Subsequently, the Provisional Workers' and Peasants' Government of Ukraine declared, on 28 January 1919, that all cultivated landowners' estates belonged to the state and would be converted by the People's Commissariat of Land Affairs into state farms and communes. On 22 January 1920 the Ukrainian Soviet government published the Basic Principles of Organizing Land Affairs in Ukraine, which took into account some of the peasantry's demands. The land law of 5 February 1920, which was based on these principles, echoed the first law on land nationalization. All land not worked directly was to be distributed without compensation to the peasants and controlled by land communities. The owners of the confiscated lands were to be expelled immediately from their farms. This law was approved by the Fourth All-Ukrainian Congress of Soviets in May 1920.

On 27 May 1922 the All-Ukrainian Central Executive Committee (VUTsVK) issued the Fundamental Law on the Toilers' Land Use and on 16 October 1922 approved the Land Code of the Ukrainian SSR. Modeled on the land law of the Russian SFSR, the new law permitted the limited use of hired labor and land leasing.

In the Union constitution of 1924 the USSR legislature received the power to define the general principles of the land law, while republican governments could determine, in harmony with the Union law, only the rules of land use. The last more or less autonomous land acts of the Ukrainian SSR were the government decrees of 1927, which introduced several changes in the Land Code of the Ukrainian SSR. By 15 December 1928 the Central Executive Committee of the USSR published the General Foundations of Land Use and Land Tenure, which applied to Ukraine as well as to other republics.

Radical changes in Ukraine's land law occurred when the All-Union Communist Party (Bolshevik) approved (5 January 1930) the resolution on speeding up the collectivization of agriculture, and the Union law depriving the kulaks of the right to use or lease land or to hire labor. The Presidium of the VUTsVK repeated this new law in its resolution of 23 August 1930, thus negating a large portion of Ukraine's Land Code of 1922. Land use by collective farms was regulated almost entirely by the Union law, primarily by the Model Statute for the Agricultural Artel of 1 September 1930 (modified on 17 February 1935). A 1930 Union law granted the collective farms 'perpetual use' of their land. Other important acts regulating land use in Ukraine included the decrees of the USSR government in 1939 on the size of private plots held by collective farmers, manual workers, and office workers, and on the abolition of the *khutir* homesteads. In the postwar period the USSR government proclaimed (7 June and 17 July 1950) the voluntary consolidation of collective farms. In practice, however, the process was not voluntary, but imposed by the Party and by the state machine.

The power of the Union republics in land affairs was a contentious issue between the advocates of Moscow centralism and of republican autonomy in the 1920s. It was settled at the time in Moscow's favor by faits accomplis. Thus, the theoretical question of land ownership was settled in 1929–30 in favor of the USSR by the almost complete replacement of Ukraine's land law by the Union law. In 1956–8 the issue of codifying the land laws of the Union republics was raised, and proposals were made to expand the rights of the republics in this area and to let the USSR government decide only basic questions of land use, tenure, and cadastre. The issue was resolved in a manner similar to that of the 1924 arrangements. The Foundations of the Land Law of the USSR and the Union Republics (approved by the Supreme Soviet of the USSR on 13 December 1968) remained within the competency of the Union government, while the specific codes and other acts based on these foundations were determined by the republics. Thus, the Land Code of the Ukrainian SSR (1970) repeated and was built on the Foundations, as were the codes of the other republics. In practice the Union agencies retain the right to take the initiative even in matters that belong to the jurisdiction of the republics.

Other sources of land law are the Model Statute of the Collective Farm (in effect since 27 November 1969); resolutions of the Union and republican councils of ministers; orders and instructions of ministries and departments; and decisions of local soviets. In principle, the norms of civil law do not apply to land affairs.

The general changes which came about with 'perestroika' under M. Gorbachev also affected land use. On 6 March 1990 a new set of Fundamental Principles of Land Legislation was announced. Also being considered is a law establishing the right to private property. The privatization of land and property, however, is still a difficult issue.

BIBLIOGRAPHY
Vytanovych. I. *Agrarna polityka ukraïns'kykh uriadiv 1917–1920* (Munich–Chicago 1968)

Indychenko, P. *Radians'ke zemel'ne pravo* (Kiev 1971)
Zakonodavchi akty pro zemliu (Kiev 1972)

V. Holubnychy, V. Markus, M. Stakhiv

Land melioration. Major improvement of the productivity of the soil by tillage, *crop rotation, irrigation, drainage, use of fertilizers, or chemical reclamation. Tillage changes the soil structure, kills weeds, and lays crop residues by physical means, such as plows, harrows, rollers, and pulverizers. Excessive tillage may result in crusting, impede water storage, and increase runoff. Crop residue, or mulch, prevents rain injury to the soil surface. Crop rotation helps preserve favorable soil structure, reduce erosion, and supply nitrogen to the soil. During N. Khrushchev's regime fallow-land area was greatly reduced in Ukraine, with increased soil erosion as a result. *Irrigation and *drainage transform arid or swampy land into arable land. In 1979, 2,478,000 ha in Ukraine were under irrigation, and 3,065,000 ha were under drainage. The largest area of reclaimed wetland is in Polisia. Excessive irrigation can cause soil salinization. The need for chemical fertilizers to maintain agriculture productivity has increased. The use of chemical fertilizers in Ukraine is lower than in the West, but it has increased rapidly in recent years, from 14.6 kg per ha in 1960 to 157.2 kg per ha in 1987. Chemical reclamation is the indirect use of minerals to improve soil conditions. Liming combats excessive acidity, and gypsum, excessive alkalinity. In Ukraine liming is used in the chernozem zones, such as Polisia.

LAND MELIORATION

Land Mortgage Bank (Zemelnyi bank hipotechnyi). A joint-stock bank established in Lviv in 1910 to provide peasants with loans for land purchases and farm improvement. It was the first Ukrainian bank in Galicia. It was set up with an equity fund of one million kronen, which was raised by selling 2,500 shares at 400 kronen each. By 1914 it had issued 1,850 long-term mortgage loans to peasants for a total sum of 7,356,000 kronen. The general devaluation after the First World War reduced the bank's equity sharply, but by the 1930s it had risen to 5 million zlotys, and assets amounted to 800,000 zlotys. A branch was set up in Stanyslaviv. The bank's directors were O. *Kulchytsky (1910–30) and V. Sinhalevych. When Soviet troops occupied Galicia in 1939, the bank was nationalized.

Land reforms. Legislative and administrative measures aimed at redistributing land among various social groups. They have been known in Ukraine since medieval times. Some, such as the *voloka* land reform of the mid-16th century, radically altered the relation of different social strata to the land. Great socioeconomic changes such as the limiting or abolition of serfdom (1783 and 1848 in Austria, 1861 in Russia) involved significant changes in land tenure and use (see *Serfdom). The modern concept of land reforms, which is tied to a political and economic struggle for a fairer distribution of land among groups of individual landowners or land users, is of recent origin.

The land reforms which followed the abolition of serfdom in the Russian Empire left Ukrainian peasants with less land at their disposal: 30.8 percent of the land formerly used by the peasantry was detached and retained by the landowners. Of a total land fund of 48.1 million ha in the nine Ukrainian gubernias, 21.9 million ha (45.7 percent) were transferred to the peasants, 22.5 million ha (46.6 percent) were retained by the large landowners, and the remaining 3.7 million ha (7.7 percent) belonged to the state or the church. The peasants had to pay the former owners for the land through a system of *redemption payments: the state bought the land from the landowners and sold it to the peasants on credit. This land reform failed to appease the peasant's land hunger. The small size of peasant holdings and, hence, the low productivity of most peasant farms, the land shortage, and rural overpopulation, which became acute in Ukraine by the end of the 19th century, had a marked influence on the Revolution of 1905. The *Stolypin agrarian reforms (1906) were an attempt to alleviate the crisis. These measures, however, benefited only the middle and wealthier peasantry. The poor peasants could not improve their lot and had to sell their remaining holdings, and thereby swelled the ranks of the rural proletariat.

The Revolution of 1917 also included land reforms. Ukraine's national governments worked out the principles of land reforms but were not able to carry them out (see *Land law). The reforms that were put into practice were either local or temporary. Bolshevik land policy amounted to land revolution rather than reform, in that it involved the expropriation and socialization of land (see *War communism, *New Economic Policy, *Collectivization, *Land tenure system, and *Land law).

After the abolition of serfdom on Ukrainian territories controlled by Austria, peasants could own the land they had used. At the time, landowners owned 2,461,000 ha (44.4 percent), and peasants owned 3,069,000 ha (55.6 percent). The landowners were reimbursed by the state, and the peasants were given 40 years to settle their debt to the state. Despite the reduction of large estates by parcelation, the land crisis continued, just as it did in eastern Ukraine. In fact, there were no fundamental land reforms in Ukrainian territories under Austria-Hungary. The Galician Diet, which had the power to pass land laws, was controlled by Polish landowners who rejected reform. Some political parties in Galicia included land reform in their platforms.

In the interwar period the Polish, Czechoslovak, and Rumanian regimes in Western Ukraine introduced land reforms in the modern sense. In Poland a law was passed on 15 July 1920 by which large estates were expropriated at prices set by land administrations. Landowners were allowed to retain up to 180 ha (60 ha near the cities); on Ukrainian territories the maximum size of an estate was 400 ha. Excess land was parceled out among small farmers and landless peasants, primarily soldiers and invalids of the Polish army. In 1919–23 the Polish authorities conducted extensive land reforms: about 450,000 ha in Western Ukraine were parceled out to colonists, particularly veterans, from the Polish heartland. Ukrainian peasants received scarcely 6 percent of the distributed land. The parcelation was conducted, with the approval of the Polish Ministry of Agriculture, either by the owners themselves or by select Polish banks. The Ukrainian parcelation society in Lviv, Zemlia, did not get a concession to parcel land. The Polish law of 28 December 1925 restricted further access of Ukrainian peasants to parceled land. In 1934 state bodies (voivodeship governments) took over the implementation of land reforms from land administrations.

In Bukovyna and Bessarabia, land reform was based on the law of 30 July 1921, which limited the estates of non-Rumanians to 100 ha and of Rumanians to 250 ha, and expropriated all the lands of the Orthodox Religious Land Fund. Of the 144,000 ha designated for distribution, only 63,000 ha were distributed by the end of 1926. One-third of it went to Ukrainians. The state reimbursed the former landowners at a rate set by a special commission, while the peasants paid the state half the rate plus the costs of surveying and registration. A large part of the undistributed land was leased by the government or was reserved for settling Rumanian colonists among the Ukrainian population.

In Transcarpathia, the Czechoslovak government effected a partial land reform in 1922–8. Expropriated parts of estates were distributed among the small farmers and landless peasants, 86 percent of whom were Ukrainian. State lands consisting of forests, pasture, and meadows, however, were not subject to redistribution. Thus, this reform did little to alleviate the plight of the Transcarpathian peasantry.

With the Soviet occupation of Western Ukraine, the land tenure system was altered radically.

BIBLIOGRAPHY
Zalozets'kyi, R. *Zemel'na reforma na Ukraïni* (Vienna–Kiev 1918)
Pavlykovs'kyi, Iu. *Zemel'na sprava u Skhidnii Halychyni* (Lviv 1922)
Mytsiuk, O. *Agrarna polityka*, 2 vols (Poděbrady 1925)
Karpats'ka Ukraïna (Lviv 1939)
Bukovyna, ïï mynule i suchasne (Paris–Philadelphia–Detroit 1956)

Land tenure system. The system of holding and using land that defines the rights and obligations of the owner, occupant, and cultivator of the land. In ancient Rus' clans settled and took possession of virgin lands. As extended families separated from the clan, they established with the clan's consent their own *dvoryshche, which usually consisted of several *dym or farmsteads held by blood-related families. The dvoryshche collectively owned all the fields, forests, meadows, and water sources that had been occupied and worked in some way by the members of the family. Working members of the family (potuzhnyky) were allotted shares of the dvoryshche's land for their use. Land that did not belong to any dvoryshche was used by the clan for its general needs.

The idea of private land ownership first arose in the Princely era. The concept took root when the population began to shift west and north to territories that were safer from the steppe nomads. Officials of the princes began to fence off free and communal lands, at first claiming only exclusive use of them in exchange for services. Eventually they claimed full ownership. In the 12th and 13th centuries the claims to the land of princes, boyars, hromady, and free peasants expanded. The larger estates owned by princes, boyars, or the church were surrounded by service villages or were worked by semifree *zakupy and *izhoi. Apart from the obligatory *tribute to the prince, the peasants had free use of their property. There is no evidence that the princes of Rus', unlike the rulers in Western Europe, ever claimed title to all the land. Like any other individual the prince had a right to the land he used for the needs of his own court. References to princely grants of villages probably concern villages owned by the princes. Transfers of princely land to heirs and purchases of boyar estates are also mentioned in early documents. The reports of land grants in return for services, which appear in the chronicles, indicate that feudal relations were introduced in the Galician-Volhynian principality only when it began to decline.

A feudal system of land tenure similar to that in Western Europe was established in Ukraine in the 15th and 16th centuries under Lithuanian and Polish rule. In that period land tenure was tied to compulsory military service. The ultimate right to all the land belonged to the Lithuanian grand duke, who divided the land among his princes and boyars in exchange for services. They, in turn, gave others use of their land in return for military service or tribute. Even large economic units, such as the dvoryshche, are often referred to as 'services.' Free peasants worked land that was held directly by the grand duke or by princes, boyars, or the church. The peasants could freely dispose of their use of the land (buy, sell, and inherit), provided their obligations to the landholders were met.

The first two editions of the *Lithuanian Statute (1529, 1566) indicate that there were attempts to introduce the kind of social and economic relations found in Poland: to set off the privileged and unprivileged estates, to separate military service from land tenure, and to limit the right to own land to the grand duke, the gentry, and the church. At the end of the 15th century the old dvoryshcha were broken up and divided into voloky (see *voloka land reform).

During the 15th century Polish law was introduced in Galicia, the Kholm region, and Podlachia. Previous distinctions among free, semifree, and bonded peasants were gradually erased: all peasants became serfs bound to the land without the right of movement and, besides making payments in kind, increasingly forced to do corvée. The nobles became not merely the ruler's stewards but outright owners of the land.

These changes were hastened by the growth of the Polish grain trade. In 1466 Poland gained a Baltic port, which gave it access to western and northern European markets.

The magnates and wealthier gentry set up large grain farms, called *filvarok, on the best land and increased corvée. By the end of the 16th century 78 percent of the land belonged to the nobility, 3 percent to churches and monasteries, and 19 percent to the crown.

After the Union of Lublin (1569) Polish law was extended to other parts of Ukraine. Polish magnates and gentry began to accumulate large landholdings in Ukraine, acquired parts of the crownlands for their services, and gradually enserfed the rural population. These processes met with resistance, however. It was difficult to establish filvarok in the steppes, and settlers rejected the expiry of their short-term leases with the landowners. The social unrest arising from such conditions finally exploded, in B. Khmelnytsky's social and political revolution.

In Transcarpathia the obligations of the peasants and the privileges of the gentry were codified in the Tripantitum of 1546. In Bukovyna at that time, the Moldavian voivodes distributed latifundia among their gentry and boyars. The vulnerability of those regions to Turkish and Tatar raids made it impossible for the landowners to exploit the peasants as severely as in Galicia.

Under the Hetman state there were several forms of land tenure. The few members of the gentry who had supported B. Khmelnytsky retained their ownership rights. The emerging Cossack starshyna gained access to large landholdings, which were tied to certain offices in the state. The starshyna did not acquire the same rights as the gentry until the reign of D. Apostol, when its inheritance right was recognized. The Cossack estate secured the right of perpetual ownership and unrestricted enjoyment of its lands.

According to unwritten customary law, peasants could take possession (zaimka) of unoccupied lands. They also had the right to choose their master or to become *landless peasants (pidsusidky). Thus, peasants had full disposal of the land they used. Also, peasants on gentry or monastery estates initially had the right to dispose of the land they cultivated, although they were indentured. The peasants who lived on the free military estates, which belonged to the state, retained the right to dispose of the land they used longest. When at the end of the 17th century the Russian tsar began to interfere in land affairs in Ukraine by granting estates to officers and monasteries without the hetman's approval, the land rights of the peasantry began to diminish as well.

From the mid-18th century more and more of the land and peasants in Ukraine fell into the hands of Russian nobles and officials. As Russian power in the hetmanate increased, the number of free peasants decreased: according to the *General Survey of Landholdings conducted by Hetman D. Apostol in 1729–31, only a third of the peasants were free commoners. Under pressure from Russian authorities Hetman I. Skoropadsky enserfed even some Cossacks. Serfdom was established officially in Left-Bank Ukraine in 1783 by an edict of Catherine II, and in Southern Ukraine in 1796.

In the Russian Empire most land was owned by landowners, the state, and the church. Of the other estates only Cossacks retained the full right to own land. The peasants were serfs either of the landlords (2,493,000 in 1858) or of the state (1,682,000). Their legal tie with a certain plot was dissolved: the 1808 law prohibiting the sale of peasants without land was repealed in 1841. Henceforth, peasants and land could be sold separately. The development of

TABLE 1
Distribution of farms in Russian-ruled Ukraine in 1917 according to seeded area (percentages)

Type of farm (in desiatins [des])	Polisia	Right Bank	Left Bank	Steppe	Ukraine as a whole
No seeded land	9.7	13.5	18.6	19.1	16.0
Under 1 des	17.7	24.8	3.6	7.1	16.2
1–4 des	42.6	51.1	34.9	22.3	37.8
4–9 des	24.4	9.5	23.4	24.0	18.5
9–15 des	4.6	0.9	6.5	13.6	6.4
Over 15 des	1.0	0.2	3.0	13.9	5.1

TABLE 2
Distribution of land in Ukraine among different users, 1955–87 (in 1,000 ha)

Type of use	1955	1966	1974	1987
Collective farms	44,981	38,678	37,385	35,821
including private plots	(2,388)	(2,129)	(2,001)	(1,663)
State enterprises	4,949	9,938	10,932	11,917
including state farms	(3,991)	(8,675)	(9,521)	–
Wage and salary workers' (private) plots	287	483	597	753
State lands and forests	6,229	–	8,536	8,702
Other land users	3,193	–	2,921	3,069
Total land area	59,639	49,099	60,371	60,262

Figures in parentheses are not included in total land area.

commercial farming and of agricultural processing industries accelerated the separation of peasants from the land. A monthly payment for labor in foodstuffs became more common. In Ukraine serfs almost universally provided corvée rather than quitrent (see *Serfdom).

The emancipation of serfs in the Russian Empire in 1861 entailed basic changes in land tenure. Of 48.1 million ha of land in the nine Ukrainian gubernias the peasants received 21.9 million ha, the landowners retained 22.5 million ha, and the church and state held on to 3.7 million ha. The state compensated the landowners for the land transferred to the peasants and then collected redemption payments spread over 40 years from the peasants. *Servitudes, such as meadows and forests, were left intact until 1886 for use by the village and the landlord.

The amount of land allotted to each peasant household varied with the region, the size of the plot previously used by the peasant, and the type of farmer-owner. State serfs received on average 7.5 desiatins per household, landlords' serfs only 5 desiatins. Of the households that got land, 3 percent received less than 1 desiatin, 16 percent from 1 to 3 desiatins, 67 percent from 3 to 10 desiatins, and 14 percent over 10 desiatins. Only some of the transferred land went to individual households: in the steppe region of Ukraine the Russian *obshchina system of land tenure prevailed. By the end of the 1870s, 45 percent of all farms in Ukraine had come under the *obshchina* system: 95 percent of the allotted land in Katerynoslav gubernia, 95.3 percent in Kharkiv gubernia, and 88.8 percent in Kherson gubernia, but only 5.4 percent in Podilia, 5.9 percent in Poltava gubernia, and 6.7 percent in Kiev gubernia. The inadequate parcels of land received by the peasants were reduced even further by division among heirs. As a result,

although the total land owned or rented by peasants grew somewhat, the average peasant holding declined from 12.3 ha in 1877 to 9.4 ha in 1905. The land shortage increased social tension in the countryside. In response to peasant unrest the *Stolypin agrarian reforms allowed peasants to leave the *obshchina* system with an allotment of their own land. They could also consolidate their parcels of land into one holding contiguous to (*khutir) or at a distance from (*vidrub*) the farm buildings. Land banks and other credit institutions encouraged the spread of individual farmsteads of either type. Peasant unrest in 1902–6 aroused insecurity among landowners and accelerated the transfer of land to the peasants. At the outbreak of the First World War, peasant landholdings in the Ukrainian gubernias increased to 32 million ha, or 65 percent of the total land fund. More than half of all peasant households, however, lacked enough land to support themselves (see table 1).

The 1917 Revolution opened a new period in agrarian relations. The social and political demands of the Ukrainian people were rejected by the Provisional Government; hence, Ukraine began to develop its own agrarian legislation only after its proclamation of independence. The war with Russia and the rapidly changing political situation made it impossible for the government to implement *land laws.

In Soviet Ukraine a new land law was passed only in October 1922. Maintaining the principle of the nationalization of all land, it recognized the peasants' right to use the land in perpetuity. The land was not distributed directly to the peasants but was handed over to *land communities for distribution. The communities could decide the terms of tenure; they usually chose the traditional form of farming for Ukraine, the individual farmstead. The state retained use of the forests (3.7 million ha) and a small portion of arable land (1.4 million ha), on which it set up state farms and communes. In 1927, peasant farms had 36.8 million ha at their disposal. The number of peasant households increased, from 3.5 million in 1916 to 5.2 million in 1928. The *collectivization in 1930–1 made fundamental changes in the land tenure system of Soviet Ukraine. Individual farms were abolished, and use of the land was given to collective farms, state farms, and state enterprises (see table 2).

Western Ukraine. After Austria's annexation of Galicia and Bukovyna, some changes in the land tenure system were made by Maria Theresa and Joseph II in the spirit of enlightened absolutism and physiocratic doctrine. Cadastres were conducted, and corvée was regularized. In 1787 a legal distinction between the demesne or tabular land belonging to the landlord and rustical land belonging to the peasantry was introduced, and the latter category of land could no longer be appropriated by landowners and added to their *filvarky*. Under Joseph II a cadastre was prepared to serve as the basis of tax reform and urbarium standardization, which was to replace corvée with monetary rents. According to the preliminary cadastre of 1819, 61 percent of peasant farms could not be self-sufficient in the prevailing economic system. The Napoleonic Wars and the chaos in their wake put an end to reforms and strengthened the position of the *filvarok* owners, who provided the army with supplies. Ignoring the law of 1787, they managed to annex 1 million morgen (580,000 ha) of rustical land by 1848.

Although the land reform of 1848 gave peasants ownership of the land which previously they had had the use of, it did not provide for the economic development of the peasant farms. Restrictions on the division of peasant holdings, their mortgaging, and their sale to nonpeasants were rarely observed. Consequently, in 1819–59 the number of peasant farms grew by 55 percent, and the number of small holdings under 5 morgen almost doubled. When the restrictions were removed in 1868, and new laws, such as the law on unrestricted credit, which legalized usury, were introduced, peasant land became subject to speculation. From 1875 to 1884 some 23,650 peasant farms were auctioned off. Some farmland was withdrawn from production, and many peasant holdings were subdivided to the point at which they could not support their owners. In 1902, 42.3 percent of farms consisted of less than 2 ha, 37.3 percent of 2–5 ha, 14.9 percent of 5–10 ha, and barely 5.5 percent of over 10 ha.

In 1852–60, large landholdings accounted for 44.8 percent of the land fund. By 1912 they accounted for 37.8 percent of the land, 16.3 percent of which belonged to latifundia of over 10,000 morgs. Thus, within 50 years 275,700 ha of the large estates were divided and sold to small holders, most of whom were Polish. Only 38,000 ha of that land was bought by Ukrainian peasants. The proletarianization of the Ukrainian peasantry grew rapidly, restrained only to some extent by immigration, spreading education, and rising national consciousness.

In Ukrainian territories under Polish control, the land reforms of 1920 and 1925 brought some changes in the land tenure system. Some large estates were broken up, and certain limitations were imposed on the sale of land. Ukrainian peasants gained hardly anything from the distribution of the parceled lands. Almost half of the farms (42 percent) in Western Ukraine were under 2 ha, 39 percent were 2–5 ha, 14 percent were 5–10 ha, and 5 percent were over 10 ha. Landholders of the last category owned 44 percent of the land. Ukrainian peasants were hit hardest by the land shortage.

Changes in the land tenure systems of Bukovyna and Transcarpathia paralleled those in Galicia. Most farms were very small: at the turn of the century in Bukovyna 56 percent of farms consisted of less than 2 ha, 29 percent of 2–5 ha, 10 percent of 5–10 ha, and only 5 percent of farms, occupying 61 percent of all the land, of over 10 ha. Rumanian agrarian reforms did little to alter the picture. In Transcarpathia under Czechoslovak rule, peasants owned only 36 percent of the land (but 88 percent of the arable land). Forty-five percent of the farms were under 2 ha, 30 percent were 2–5 ha, and 17 percent were 5–10 ha. The 8 percent of farms over 10 ha accounted for 77 percent of the land area.

During the first Soviet occupation of Western Ukraine in 1939–41, the property of the church and large landowners was nationalized. According to Soviet data 45 percent of the confiscated lands in Galicia and Volhynia was distributed among landless peasants and small landholders. Private ownership of up to 40 ha was permitted. In the summer of 1940 collectivization commenced in Western Ukraine, and by the outbreak of the German-Soviet War 14 percent of the farms had been collectivized. During the occupation in 1941–4 the Germans nationalized all Soviet government property and converted state farms and some of the collective farms into state farming enterprises. In 1944–5 the Soviets again distributed some of the confiscated land among peasants. In the summer of 1948 they launched a massive collectivization drive, which was completed in 1951. From that time one tenure system prevailed throughout Soviet Ukraine.

BIBLIOGRAPHY
Budzynovs'kyi, V. Khlops'ka posilist' (Lviv 1901)
Voinarovs'kyi, T. Vplyv Pol'shchi na ekonomichnyi rozvii Ukraïny-Rusy (Lviv 1910)
Hrushevs'kyi, M. Studiï z ekonomichnoï istoriï Ukraïny (Kiev 1918)
Pavlykovs'kyi, Iu. Zemel'na sprava u Skhidnii Halychyni (Lviv 1922)
Slabchenko, M. Materiialy do ekonomichno-sotsiial'noï istoriï Ukraïny XIX st., 2 vols (Odessa 1925, 1927)
– Borot'ba za systemy zemlevolodinnia i formy hospodarstva v Ukraïni 19–20 st. (Odessa 1927)
Olezhko, N. Agrarna polityka bol'shevykiv (Munich 1947)
Hurzhii, I. Rozklad feodal'no-kriposnyts'koï systemy v sil's'komu hospodarstvi Ukraïny pershoï polovyny XIX st. (Kiev 1954)
Kononenko, K. Ukraine and Russia: A History of the Economic Relations between Ukraine and Russia (1654–1917) (Milwaukee 1958)
Macey, D. Government and Peasant in Russia, 1861–1906 (DeKalb, Ill 1987)

K. Kononenko, I. Vytanovych

Land use. Farmland is the most important category of land in Ukraine (see table 1). The high percentage of cultivated land in Ukraine at the beginning of the 20th century can be attributed only in part to geographical conditions. With little industrial development to alleviate the problems caused by high taxation and high population density, Ukrainian peasants were compelled to cultivate every patch of arable land. Even in hilly Western Ukraine, not to mention the fertile steppe and forest-steppe regions, the proportion of tilled land (49.1 percent) was higher than in either contemporary England (at 12.9 percent) or contemporary Italy (at 42.6 percent).

Intensive cultivation has led to the deterioration of the best agricultural areas in Ukraine. From 1933 to 1975 the amount of tilled land in the steppe region decreased from 80 percent to 72 percent, and in the forest-steppe region, from 77 percent to 70 percent. In spite of *land melioration in recent years, the earlier proportion of arable land has not been regained. Oddly enough, poorer soil types have fared better. Protected by bogs and mountains from too much cultivation in earlier centuries, Polisia and Transcarpathia have been subjected to extensive melioration in recent times. Between 1933 and 1975 the proportion of tilled land in Polisia increased from 30 percent to 36 percent, as a result of the draining of over 1.5 million ha of bog. In Transcarpathia the proportion of tilled land increased from 14 percent to 21 percent, at the expense of native forests. (See *Arable land.)

Technology has changed the character of hayfields and pastures. In the past, progress was measured by the conversion of hayfields and pastures into tilled land. Now hayfields and pastures themselves are being improved. Traditionally, hayfields and pastures were all either natural meadows or land left fallow in the crop rotation process. By 1979, however, one in six hayfields was cultivated; the figure for natural hayfields improved by surface and root cultivation methods would be much higher. In general the proportion of other fields varies inversely with the proportion of tilled land. Hence, in Polisia and Transcarpathia hayfields and pastures account for 25–30 percent of the territory, in the forest-steppe, for approximately 15 percent, and in the steppe, for less than 5 percent. (See *Hayfields and *Pasture.)

TABLE 1
Land use in relation to total land fund, 1913–87 (percentages)

Use	Galicia 1913	Ukr under Russia 1913	Ukr SSR 1926–7	W Ukr ca 1933	Ukr SSR ca 1935	Ukrainian SSR 1935	1950	1955	1966	1975	1987
Tilled land	49.1	70.3	72.3	45.0	76.0	68.0	68.0	60.0	57.6	56.5	56.8
Hayfields and	12.6	12.3	4.3	12.7	4.8	4.1	13.0	5.1	4.2	3.8	3.5
Pasture	9.1		–	7.9		4.2	–	8.3	7.7	7.8	8.0
Orchards & vineyards	–	–	–	–	–	1.0	1.0	1.3	2.2	2.5	1.5
Forests	25.7	10.6	8.8	23.7	8.3	7.5	12.0	–	15.0	–	14.4
Wetlands	0.4	–	–	–	–	–	–	–	6.3	–	–
Other	–	6.8	–	10.6	–	15.1	6.0	25.9	7.0	29.3	15.7
Used	0.0	–	6.7	–	5.5	–	–	–	–	–	–
Unused	3.1	–	7.9	–	5.4	–	–	–	–	–	–
Total area (in million ha)	9.4	51.6	43.4	13.2	43.4	44.6	60.1	60.1	60.4	60.4	60.4

TABLE 2
Percentage of sown area devoted to different crops, 1913–83

	Galicia 1913	1991 Terr Ukr SSR 1913	Galicia 1920s	Ukr SSR 1920s	Ukrainian SSR 1930	1935	1940	1950	1960	1970	1980	1983
Grain	68*	90	75	85	79	7	68	6	41	47	49	48
Industrial crops		4	1	6	9	9	9	9	11	12	12	12
Potatoes and other vegetables	16	4	19	8	7	8	9	8	8	8	7	7
Forage		2	6	2	6	8	14	17	40	33	32	34
Not subdivided	16	0	1	0	0	0	0	0	0	0	0	0
Sown area (in million ha)	2.5	22.9	2.3	24.1	28.4	25.7	31.1	30.7	33.6	32.8	33.6	33.1

*Including only wheat, rye, barley, and oats
 Including some legumes

In comparison with those in other European countries Ukraine's forests cover a relatively small proportion of the country's area. They are concentrated mostly in Polisia and the Carpathian Mountains. Some attempts have been made to maintain forests: 159,000 ha of forest land were either regenerated or developed each year in the 1950s. But the pace of forestation declined steadily through the next two decades, so that only 73,300 ha were forested in 1980 (see *Forest management). Because they demand intensive farming techniques orchards and vineyards account for very little of the land use in the Ukrainian SSR. Nonetheless, their output figures prominently in the production of private plots and in the economy of the southern oblasts (see *Orcharding and fruit farming and *Viticulture).

Arable land use in Ukraine has been evolving in two main directions. First, the amount of land left fallow has declined to almost 5 percent. In the past the *long-fallow system, and various *short-fallow systems, served to avert soil erosion and exhaustion. Today those methods of conservation are uneconomical, but other methods of land conservation are often poorly applied in Ukraine. Fertilizer is usually in short supply. Ambitious irrigation and drainage schemes have resulted in the salinization of some regions, such as the Budzhak steppe, and have exacerbated water shortages in other regions.

The second trend in Ukrainian agriculture, increasing crop specialization, has also been poorly administered. Specialization was first officially encouraged during the collectivization period, but the ravages of the famine and insufficient funds doomed the policy to failure. It was replaced in 1933 by a policy of regional self-sufficiency, which led to wasteful practices, such as the cultivation of sugar beets in the hot steppes of Central Asia and of cotton in the cool Ukrainian steppes. When revived under N. Khrushchev, specialization was taken to extremes and resulted in economic and ecological imbalances.

C. Freeland, V. Kubijovyč

Landau, Lev, b 22 January 1908 in Baku, Azerbaidzhan, d 1 April 1968 in Moscow. One of the leading theoretical physicists of the 20th century; full member of the USSR Academy of Sciences from 1946. A graduate of Leningrad University (1927), he studied at N. Bohr's Institute for Theoretical Physics in Copenhagen, headed the theoretical physics department at the Ukrainian Physical-Technical Institute in Kharkiv (1932–7), and held the chair of general physics at Kharkiv University (1935–7). In its time, Landau's school of theoretical physics in Kharkiv was the center of Soviet physics research. In 1937 Landau moved to Moscow to head the theoretical physics department at the USSR Institute for Physics Problems. Notwithstanding his prominence, in 1938–9, during the Yezhov terror, Landau was imprisoned. Subsequently he taught at Moscow University (1943–7, 1955–68). Landau made important contributions to almost every area of physics. While in Kharkiv, he developed the theories of diamagnetism and antiferromagnetism; provided theoretical explanations of the domain structure of ferromagnets, ferromagnetic resonance, and photoelectric effects in semiconductors (with E. Lifshits); and did pioneering work on the kinetics of electron plasma. Among his later contributions, his theory of superfluidity, for which he received the Nobel Prize in 1962, and his theory of superconductivity deserve to be singled out.

Landforms (*heomorfolohiia*). Discrete features of the earth's land surface, the shape, form, and nature of which were studied in the past as part of the discipline of physiography. That discipline's modern derivative, which emphasizes the study of the origin of landforms, is known as geomorphology.

The origins of landforms. The present landforms of Ukraine, like those in other parts of the world, exist in a particular stage of their formation by the interaction of internal forces of the earth and external agents. The movement of the earth's crust and the resulting geological structure have had a profound influence on the shapes and sizes of landforms. Among the land-sculpting agents, running water and glaciers have had the greatest effect on the landforms of Ukraine; wave action and wind have had less impact.

Variation in the geological structure has resulted in a great range of types of bedrock in Ukraine that offers varying resistance to all agents of weathering and erosion. The same erosive forces affect hard crystalline rocks, soluble limestones, soft clays, and friable loess. The different types of bedrock and, in turn, of parent material were formed in different ways in different geological periods.

Tectonic processes have had a direct effect on the formation of major landforms. Mountains were formed in a southern belt of recent orogenic movement – the Carpathians, the Crimean Mountains, and the Caucasus (see map 1). In a middle belt some upland areas, such as the Ukrainian Crystalline Shield and, to a lesser degree, the Donets Ridge, have experienced prolonged periods of uplift. Other regions to the north and south include lowlands or basins that have experienced subsidence.

Areas of most intense uplift have been subjected to intensive erosion, mostly by running water, which has cut deep valleys into the landmasses. In the mountains the resulting local relief exceeds 500 m (see map 2). Uplands with local relief of 80–300 m are common. Areas of downsinking, by contrast, have been characterized by aggradation by marine, lacustrine, fluvial, and even eolian deposition. The relief in such areas has been on the decline and seldom exceeds 40 m. Boundaries between areas of uplift and subsidence are expressed in elevational differences, as along the northern edge of Podilia and the high right bank of the Dnieper. Rivers often follow such boundaries – the Boh River along the southwestern edge of the Crystalline Shield, for example, or the Don along the northeastern edge of the Voronezh Massif.

Glaciation played an important part in the formation of the landforms of Ukraine. Except for a belt of folded mountains, most of the uplands and lowlands were covered by thick layers of Quaternary deposits that derived, in one way or another, from glaciation. Northern Ukraine either underwent glaciation or was located near the edge of the Pleistocene continental ice sheet and thereby gained either glacial or glacio-fluvial accumulations. Areas to the south, by contrast, were free of ice and ponding but accumulated thick loess deposits, possibly originating from periglacial dust carried by the wind. Running water

Limit of zones

Limit of regions

0   100   200 km

1 LANDFORM REGIONS

2 LOCAL VARIATIONS OF ELEVATION

carved gullies in the easily erodible loess, thereby creating a landscape of fluvial erosion.

After the ice sheets had receded, the entire territory of Ukraine was subjected to the external forces responsible for the shaping of the present landforms. They are essentially minor topographic changes associated with surface water erosion, riverbank erosion and fluvial deposition, wind erosion and deposition, shoreline and coastal erosion and deposition, and other processes.

Landform assemblages. There are four distinctive landform assemblages in Ukraine (see map 3), each associated with a different prevailing process: (1) mountain landforms, (2) landforms associated with glacial topography, (3) landforms associated with the fluvial erosion of loess, and (4) coastal landforms along the Black Sea and the Sea of Azov. Within each assemblage there are recognizable morphological variations.

Mountain landforms are associated with powerful endogenous mountain-building forces (orogeny) and intensive subsequent erosion. Young, folded mountains belonging to the Alpine mountain system are found in the southern fringes of Ukraine – the Carpathians, the Crimean Mountains, and the Caucasus.

The Carpathians, at present of medium elevation, underwent a number of orogenic movements. The main phase of folding occurred in the Tertiary period, when the Carpathians rose out of the Paratethys Sea. Subjected to great lateral compression from the south, the upwarped flysch strata, consisting of interbedded coarse clastic materials, sandstones, and shales, buckled into large nappes and overthrust blocks that moved northeastward toward the foreland and covered the younger strata of Subcarpathia. Although the softer materials of the folded and faulted structures were subsequently eroded, those associated with the harder compressed rock remained as two

parallel flysch ridges: the outer (or overthrust) fold zone and the inner (or Magura-Chornohora) anticlinal zone. Between them the central synclinal zone (also known as the Middle Carpathian Depression) was further accentuated by the erosion of the soft underlying shales and sandstones. The extreme southern belt of the Ukrainian Carpathians (the Volcanic Carpathians, or the Vyhorlat-Tupyi group) was formed by effusives associated with Neogene faulting. That chain of mountains and conic peaks is separated from the inner anticlinal zone of the flysch belt by a long valley developed on soft shales.

Landforms of the flysch Carpathians are typical of folded mountains of medium elevation. Gently sloping, broad, and little-dissected parallel ridges and valleys contrast with the deeply incised (up to 1,000 m) transverse valleys that cut through the ridges. The transverse valleys, containing the main tributaries of the Dniester River in the north and those of the Tysa River in the south, are characterized by steep slopes, rocky bottoms, rapids, and even waterfalls. In turn the affluents of the aforementioned tributaries have carved out side valleys in soft shales parallel to the mountain ridges, thereby creating a trellised drainage pattern controlled by the folded strata. Only the highest parts of the Carpathians, mainly the Hutsul Alps and the Chornohora, possess traces of mountain glaciation, such as cirques, hanging troughs, moraines, several small moraine-dammed lakes, and talus cones below very steep slopes resulting from rock slides.

The Volcanic Carpathians are fragmented by the Tysa and its tributaries into a chain of discrete mountains: the Vyhorlat, Makovytsia, Syniak, Velykyi Dil, Tupyi, and Hutyn. They are characterized by massive, broad ridges and dormant volcanic cones topped with craters or calderas (in places filled with water).

Subcarpathia, abutting to the northeast of the Car-

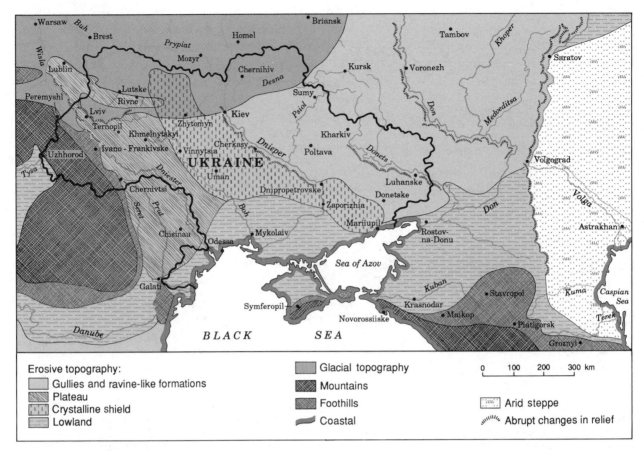

Erosive topography:
⬜ Gullies and ravine-like formations
▨ Plateau
▦ Crystalline shield
▥ Lowland

▥ Glacial topography
▦ Mountains
▦ Foothills
〜 Coastal

⬚ Arid steppe
ᶯᶯᶯ Abrupt changes in relief

0   100   200   300 km

3 LANDSCAPES

pathians, is an area of transition from mountains to lowlands. It consists of foothills interspersed with some basins and lowlands along the Dniester and the Prut rivers. Structurally the uplands are usually broad anticlines, and the basins depressions. The uplands (300–500 m above sea level, or asl) rise above the valleys of the Dniester tributaries that dissect them. Valleys often contain up to six or seven terraces and occasional stone pavements. The basins (the Stanyslaviv Depression and the Kolomyia-Chernivtsi Lowland) contain alluvial deposits which have been eroded by the present rivers to form two or three terraces. The Upper Dniester Lowland is an alluvial-outwash plain, containing deposits brought by streams from the Carpathians and glacial meltwaters from the northwest. The Sian Lowland contains moraine, glacio-fluvial, and alluvial deposits. There continental glaciation contributed to the washboardlike relief and the presence of surface boulders (erratics) and kame terraces.

The Crimean Mountains are remnants of a large folded system, part of which downfaulted below sea level. Repeated uplifting and subsiding during the Tertiary and the Quaternary periods caused active erosion to alternate with peneplanation.

The Crimean Mountains consist of three parallel ranges in the west and two in the east. The low northern ranges (300–500 m asl) are longitudinal monoclines of the northern wing of the Crimean anticline. Hence they have gentle northern slopes and steep southward-facing escarpments

(cuestas) which appear wherever their Tertiary limestone is exposed. The cuestas face insular, tablelike mountains that rise gradually to form the highest coastal range, the Yaila. It is the axis of the anticline and consists of hard, Jurassic limestone. The top of the range forms a high (1,000–1,500 m asl) plateau, which drops suddenly (300–800 m) to the southern coast. Toward the east the mountains break up into numerous ridges and peaks and decline to below 1,000 m asl.

The Yaila, notably its western part, is known for karst features of the Mediterranean type. Karoo fields prevail in areas devoid of topsoil. Funnel-like sinkholes, gullies, and precipitous ravines with year-round snow are some of the surface manifestations of rapid water seepage and its dissolving action on the limestone. Caves with stalactites and stalagmites (notably the Byndash-Koba and the Suuk-Koba, near Chatyr-Dag), together with underground lakes and rivers, constitute the subterranean karst manifestations. The southern slopes of the Yaila are dissected by deep canyons.

The northwestern section of the Caucasus Mountains lies in Ukrainian ethnographic territory. It consists of the western terminus of the Great Caucasus Range, which corresponds to a narrow, western end of the Caucasus anticline, and is bounded by the Kuban Lowland to the north and the Novorosiiske syncline (along the coast) to the south.

The extreme western end of the Great Caucasus, also

known as the Black Sea Caucasus, is composed of Eocene flysch as well as Cretaceous and Jurassic limestones. The main ridge (600–900 m asl), along with occasional lower parallel ridges, forms a gentle landscape characteristic of mountains of medium elevation. From the coast north of Anapa the ridge rises gradually eastward, to reach a peak of 2,867 m asl at Mt Fisht. East of Mt Fisht the Great Caucasus continues as the Western Caucasus and then joins the Central Caucasus.

North of the main ridge of the Western Caucasus, but south of the Eastern Kuban Lowland, is an uplifted and fragmented fringe of the Scythian Platform. From the north it forms a rising monocline. Capped with hard Jurassic and Cretaceous limestones, it reveals two parallel southward-facing high cuestas, the Chorni (Russian: Chernye) Mountains (1,000–1,500 m asl) and the Skeliastyi (Russian: Skalistyi) Ridge (1,500–2,000 m asl). Between the latter and the main ridge of the Western Caucasus is a long and narrow depression, which makes up the southernmost fringe of the Scythian Platform. The Kuban and its tributaries, originating from the Western Caucasus, carved parallel valleys across the depression and deep, narrow gaps through the cuestas, thereby fragmenting them into a number of separate ridges. The rivers and streams there form a typically trellised drainage pattern.

North of the Caucasus and east of the Kuban Lowland, landforms of pronounced relief associated with the foothills extend to the Stavropol Upland. That plateau (500–800 m asl in the west, but only 200–400 m asl in the east) is an uplifted, slightly tilted and eroded fragment of the Scythian Platform. Rivers and seasonal streams have cut deep (100–200 m) valleys into the Tertiary sandstones and limestones. In the south, between the Stavropol Upland and the Central Caucasus, stands a cluster of laccoliths – irregular formations of igneous rocks that were intruded between layers of sedimentary rocks. Now they remain exposed as high, individual hills or small mountains (1,000–1,400 m asl) in the vicinity of Piatigorsk.

Glacial landforms were shaped by the processes associated with continental ice sheets. Glacial landforms occur throughout the northern Ukrainian lowland, north of the line   Lublin–Kholm–Volodymyr-Volynskyi–Zhytomyr–Kiev–Nizhen–Putyvl. They are also found in the Sian and upper Dniester lowlands.

Three types of glacial landform associations exist: (1) those associated with the ground moraine formed under an ice sheet, (2) those associated with the terminal moraine formed along an ice front, and (3) those associated with the outwash plains formed by braided streams of meltwater flowing out of the glacier. Glacial landforms do not coincide precisely with the area once covered by the ice sheet. Some formerly glaciated areas (such as the Dnieper ice lobe in the Dnieper Lowland) were subsequently covered with thick layers of loess. Meanwhile, outwash plains often reached southward beyond the greatest extent of the ice sheet.

Ground moraine landforms prevail in the basins of the upper Dnieper, the Desna, and the middle Buh, as well as in the margins of Polisia. In general they appear as occasional low hills rising gently over a predominantly flat to gently undulating plain. Fields of such hills, facing mostly in the same (northeast to southwest) direction, have been identified as eskers and kames or kamelike hills in an area 25–100 km to the north of Zhytomyr, near what was once

the western edge of the Dnieper ice lobe. Whereas the ground moraine consists of till composed mostly of clay and some interspersed boulders, the eskers and kames, as former beds of glacial and periglacial streams, consist of water-worked sands and gravels. After the ice sheet melted, the surface was exposed to the accumulation of outwash deposits, sedimentation in ponds, and wind and water erosion.

Terminal moraine landforms are found in the Volodava area, near Lake Svytiaz, Liuboml, and Kovel. They become more pronounced east of Kovel near Poverske (see see map 4), on the western side of the Stokhid River, and then form a broad, crescent-shaped belt that extends eastward north of Manevychi through Volodymyrets and Dubrovytsia, on the west side of the Horyn River. Hills of varied composition (boulder, sandy and clayey till) rise 20–40 m above the flat, swampy lowland in successive curving rows, usually forming local watersheds. Between the morainic hills are broad river valleys and swampy lowlands or local depressions with occasional kettle lakes. Here and there, crossing the lowlands, are long, narrow eskers (map 4), which originated as bottom deposits of sediment-laden glacial streams.

Outwash plains mostly lie in front of the terminal moraine, though there are lowland areas behind the terminal moraine that may also possess an outwash surface. Major outwash plains, located in front of the Dnieper (maximum) glaciation, are found in southcentral Polisia (a broad area from Lutske and Sarny in the west to just west of Korosten and Zhytomyr in the east) and in Little Polisia (from Nesterov, north of Lviv, toward Slavuta in the east). Outwash plains interspersed among terminal moraines and ground moraines are found in western Polisia (northwest of Lutske), Kievan Polisia (northwest of Kiev), and Chernihiv Polisia (mostly northeast of Chernihiv). The outwash plains consist of flat, glacio-fluvial and glaciolacustrine deposits. Wind action sifted the sandy surfaces into dunes, and poor subsurface drainage resulted in much of the lower areas' remaining in small bodies of water and swamps. Occasional low, flat-topped hills, or denudational remnants, add another form of topographic relief to the generally flat landscape.

Water erosion landforms prevail in areas that were not subjected to glaciation. Common landforms include gullies, ravines, landslides, and loess karst. Conditions for gullying and the formation of ravines are particularly favorable in the uplands, where loess and other friable strata can be easily washed away by surface running water. Although the nonglaciated areas are mostly lightly forested and hence not well protected from the elements, the trampling of vegetation by herd animals and especially the removal of natural vegetation by human activity have intensified both water and wind erosion.

Despite the presence of loess cover throughout the areas dominated by water erosion landforms, there are distinct regional variations associated with elevation and geology. Thus, after tectonic movements raised the Western Ukrainian uplands, a new erosion cycle initiated the sculpting of the Cretaceous-Tertiary limestones into a plateau landscape of scarps, gorges, ravines, and gullies. In central Ukraine, where the Ukrainian Crystalline Shield is close to the surface, a landscape of less deeply incised, rocky-bottomed river valleys developed. Farther east, in the Dnieper Lowland and the Central Upland, a landscape

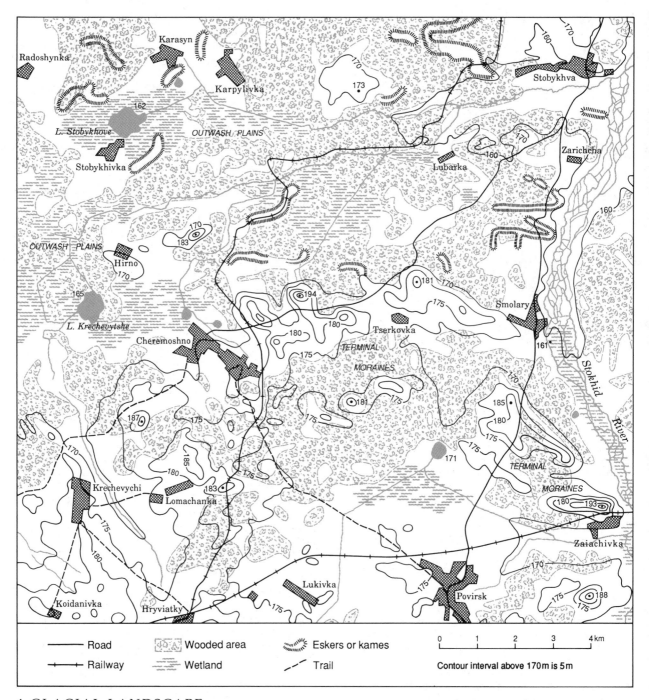

——— Road	🔲 Wooded area	⋙ Eskers or kames
┼┼┼ Railway	≈≈ Wetland	⋯ Trail

0   1   2   3   4 km

Contour interval above 170 m is 5 m

4 GLACIAL LANDSCAPE

of gullies and ravinelike formations evolved. In the Black Sea Lowland the plains above the river valleys developed many small surface depressions known as *pody*.

Plateau landforms are found in the Roztochia Upland, Podolian Upland, Volhynia-Kholm Upland, and Pokutian-Bessarabian Upland. They all consist of plains dissected by deep valleys or gullies, although local variations occur in which a complex of specific landforms are prevalent. The most spectacular canyons are found along the southern side of the Podolian Upland. The Dniester River, which bounds the Podolian Upland in the south, occupies

the largest gorge. Both the Dniester River and its tributaries have deeply incised meanders (see map 5). Upriver, along the northern side of the Pokutian Upland, surface karst features, such as sinkholes and caves, become prominent. Still farther to the northwest, on the northern side of the Dniester River, the chalk deposits of the Opilia Upland (in the western end of Podilia) are carved into wider, more gently sloping tributary river valleys, and form rolling terrain. Northwest of Lviv a chalk ridge forms the Roztochia water divide, which was subjected to deep gullying. Southeast of Lviv and then extending eastward, the north-

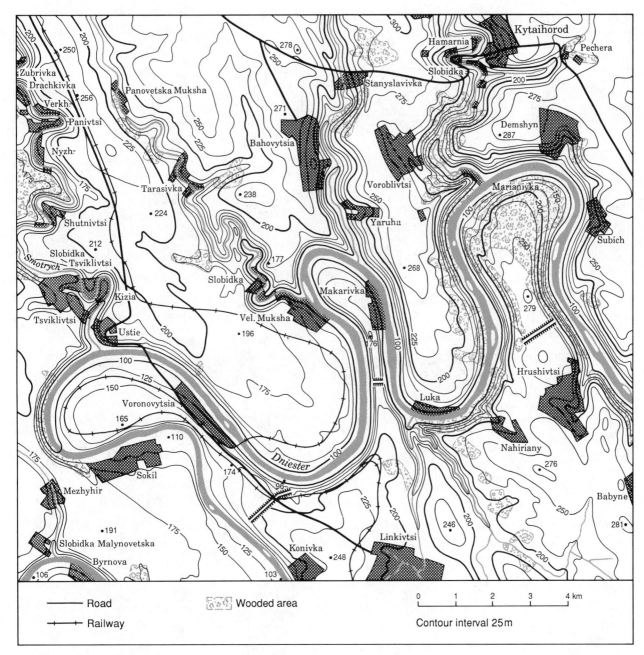

5 PLATEAU AND CANYON LANDSCAPE

ern side of the Podolian Upland is characterized by a severely gullied or ravined escarpment along which are a
number of isolated plateau remnants, or mesas (see map
6). To the north the Volhynia-Kholm Upland, underlain
by chalk, forms a gully-eroded landscape similar to that of
the Roztochia.

The Crystalline Shield landforms represent another
variation of the plains dissected by rivers, ravines, and
gullies. Once river valleys cut through the surface loess
and the thin, underlying Tertiary sediments, their characteristics change as they reach and begin to erode the Crystalline Shield. The river valleys narrow, their longitudinal
profiles become irregular, and their stream channels become rocky and replete with rapids. Crystalline rocks
form steep walls of gorges, as along the Dnieper River be-

tween the cities of Dnipropetrovske and Zaporizhia,
along the Dniester River near Yampil, and along the middle segment of the Boh River and its tributaries. Fault lines
in the Ukrainian Crystalline Shield have controlled the
alignment of many rivers. Almost the entire Boh River follows the tectonic rim of the Ukrainian Crystalline Shield,
as does the Dnieper River from Kiev to Dnipropetrovske.
The high right bank of the Dnieper, which is underlain by
the Ukrainian Crystalline Shield, rises 50–160 m above the
Dnieper Lowland on the other side of the river. The loess-
covered high right bank, notably at Kiev, is dissected by a
number of gullies and ravines (see map 7). The sandy left
bank, by contrast, is nearly flat and is poorly drained. It
possesses characteristics of Pleistocene glacio-fluvial deposits associated with the Dnieper ice lobe that pushed

Road

Railway

Wooded area

Wetland

| 0 | 1 | 2 | 3 | 4 km |

Contour interval 25 m

6 LVIV AND VICINITY

down the Dnieper Lowland and then melted. As the rising Crystalline Shield dammed the southward flow of the lobe's outwash water, the lowland accumulated large quantities of sand, which was subsequently wind-worked on the Dnieper terraces into dunes.

Gullies and ravinelike formations not only dominate the southern reaches of the Central Upland and the Do-

nets Ridge but are an important component of the landscape in the higher elevations of the Dnieper Lowland. Contributing to their evolution are the presence of a thick loess cover underlain by unconsolidated sedimentary deposits, summer downpours typical of a continental climate, and the absence of forest cover. A distinct feature of the landscape is the partially trellised drainage pattern in-

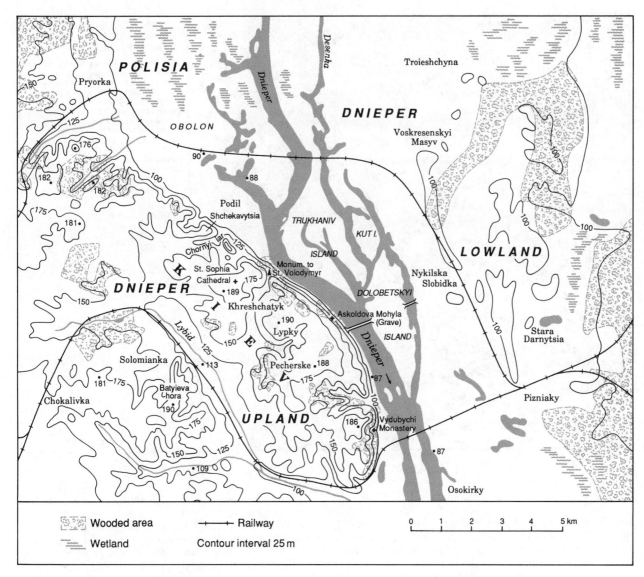

7 KIEV AREA

Map labels: POLISIA · Pryorka · ⊙176 · 182 · 182 · 181 · 150 · OBOLON · 90 · 88 · Podil · Shchekavytsia · Chornyi Iar · K I E V · St. Sophia Cathedral ✝ · 189 · Khreshchatyk · 190 · Lypky · DNIEPER · 150 · 175 · 181 · Solomianka · 113 · Batyieva Chora · 190 · Chokalivka · 175 · 190 · Pecherske · 188 · UPLAND · 175 · 125 · 150 · 109 · 186 · 100 · 100 · 125 · 150 · Dnieper · Desenka · Troieshchyna · DNIEPER · Voskresenskyi Masyv · TRUKHANIV · ISLAND · KUT I. · Monum. to St. Volodymyr · DOLOBETSKYI · Askoldova Mohyla (Grave) · ISLAND · 87 · Vydubychi Monastery · 87 · LOWLAND · 100 · Nykilska Slobidka · 100 · Stara Darnytsia · Pizniaky · Osokirky · Lybid · 100 · 100 · 150

Legend: ⬚ Wooded area — ┼┼┼ Railway — ∿ Wetland — Contour interval 25 m

0 1 2 3 4 5 km

volving repeated asymmetrical valleys of the parallel-flowing rivers. Each river valley possesses a high right (western) bank, dissected by ravines and gullies, and a low left (eastern) bank with a wide floodplain containing marshes and oxbow lakes (see map 8). Above the floodplain the lower terraces of the left bank often possess sand dunes. Eastward the higher terraces merge with the gently rising, slightly undulating plain, toward the watershed with the next river. The surface, covered with thick layers of loess, is dissected by ravines and gullies.

The loess and alluvial landforms of the Black Sea and Sea of Azov regions as well as the Kuban Lowlands generally lack ravine and gully features, except where there is a marked variation in local relief. The flat plains above the river valleys, notably the Black Sea Lowland between the Boh and the Molochna rivers, contain many small, saucer-like depressions (*pody*). Ranging in length from several meters to several kilometers and in depth from several centimeters to five or six meters, they are filled with water in the spring and support succulent grass in the summer. Higher water tables in the Kuban Lowland support many small lakes that fill the depressions throughout the year and a denser, year-round river network that connects them.

Proximity to the sea affected the geomorphology of the lower portions of the lowlands. In the early Tertiary period the Pontic Sea transgression left its mark in the form of relict low coastal bluffs and beaches between the Inhul and the Molochna rivers (approx 75–100 km inland from the present Black Sea coast). Also apparent are remnants of the old deltaic deposits of the Tertiary period in those places where the pre-Dnieper, the pre-Danube, and the pre-Kuban flowed into the sea. A decline of the sea level in the Pleistocene accelerated river erosion, but its subsequent rise to the present level and a gentle subsidence along the present coast contributed to river aggradation. The result was the formation of broad floodplains with braided streams and little lakes or floodplains containing

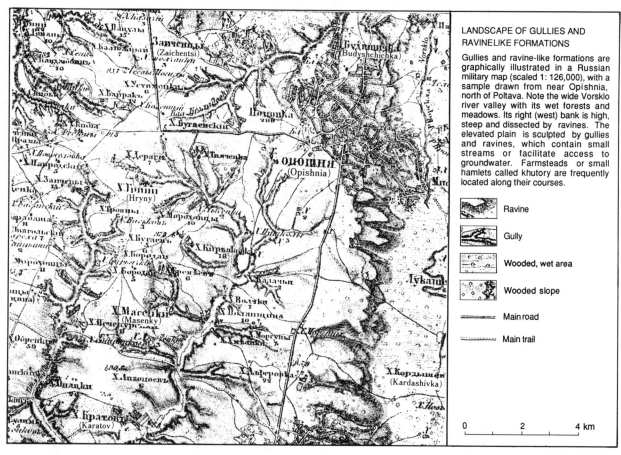

LANDSCAPE OF GULLIES AND RAVINELIKE FORMATIONS

Gullies and ravine-like formations are graphically illustrated in a Russian military map (scaled 1: 126,000), with a sample drawn from near Opishnia, north of Poltava. Note the wide Vorsklo river valley with its wet forests and meadows. Its right (west) bank is high, steep and dissected by ravines. The elevated plain is sculpted by gullies and ravines, which contain small streams or facilitate access to groundwater. Farmsteads or small hamlets called khutory are frequently located along their courses.

Ravine

Gully

Wooded, wet area

Wooded slope

Main road

Main trail

0   2   4 km

8 LANDSCAPE OF GULLIES AND RAVINELIKE FORMATIONS

streams with broad meanders and many oxbow lakes.

Coastal landforms are in an active state of development along the Black Sea and the Sea of Azov. They are shaped by water movement – wave action, longshore currents, and tides. Fluvial action – the sculpting of the land surface or the infusion of silt-laden water by rivers – also affects the formation of coastal landforms. Such interaction is particularly evident in the formation of deltas.

The Danube Delta is a flat and swampy alluvial plain with many lakes. Three principal estuaries of the Danube, the Kiliia, the Sulina, and the Sfântu Gheorghe, flow into the sea, but there are more interconnected distributaries and small lakes. Offshore bars separate the delta from the sea and threaten navigation at low tide. Spring floods inundate the delta. Levees form the banks along the major channels and block off local tributaries, which usually form terminal lakes.

Liman-type estuaries and coastal bluffs extend from the Danube to the Dnieper River. Those features were formed in conjunction with coastal submergence. The headlands, made up of Tertiary limestone underlain by soft clays, were eroded back to produce a straightened, clifflike coast with a narrow beach at the bottom of the bluff. Coastal submergence and the resulting marine transgression into river valleys formed broad, flooded estuaries. The latter became either partly separated or completely cut off from the sea by barrier islands or barrier beaches (respectively) built up by longshore currents with material eroded from the headlands, and thus assumed the shape of the classical limans. The larger rivers, such as the Dniester, the Boh, and the Dnieper, maintained a large enough discharge to clear the marine littoral deposits. The small rivers, however, did not generate enough power to break through the barrier beaches that sealed off their limans from the sea.

The limans and coastal bluffs were also formed at higher elevations, when a relatively brief but recent marine transgression occurred on the coast in earlier periods. The Dnieper Liman, for example, shows evidence of a relict coastal bluff of the Pleistocene epoch (Dnieper age), now found somewhat inland, which runs from the present coast at Shyroka Balka eastward to Kherson (note the respective 10- to 25-m contours in map 9).

Shallow bays and long, narrow spits dominate the coast south and east of the Dnieper-Boh Estuary. The configuration is related to the unconsolidated and easily erodible materials of the low, flat coastal plain that was formed as the pre-Dnieper delta of the Middle and Upper Pliocene and renewed in the Polisia age of the Pleistocene. Subsequently the longshore currents straightened out the old deltaic headland and carried the material both west and east to form, respectively, the Tendriv Spit and Dzharylhach Island.

Another variation of coastal bluffs with limans and spits is found along the northern coast of the Sea of Azov. There spits occur alongside the mouths of rivers that discharge sediment-laden water into the sea. They consist of river-fed sediment which has been shaped by longshore currents into a series of southwestward-pointing hooks.

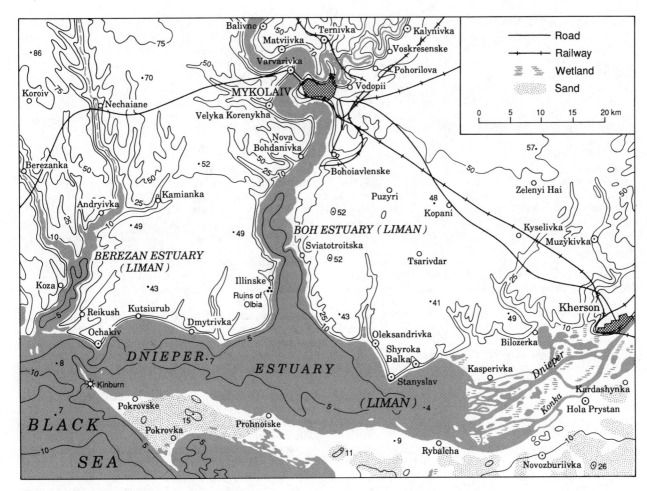

9 DNIEPER ESTUARY

The Arabat Spit, located on the western side of the Sea of Azov and enclosing the salty Syvash Lake of the Crimea, is the longest in Ukraine, at 113 km. On the eastern side of the Sea of Azov the coastal bluffs along Tahanrih Bay change in the south to low, accumulative sandy shorelines enclosing the lakes and bays of the Kuban Delta and the Taman Peninsula.

The western coast of the Crimea is a combination of rock platforms along the Tarkhankut Upland, an accumulative sandy plain along Kalamitska Bay, an abrasive bluff coastline just south of it, and another rock platform coast along the western terminus of the Crimean Mountains. Since the southwestern coast is perpendicular to the Crimean Mountains, the valleys in the mountains form deep bays which favor the building of ports. The southern coast of the Crimea, which parallels the Yaila Range, is an abrasive mountainous coast, with narrow, pebbly beaches in small local embayments. Landforms along the promontories include wave-cut cliffs, sea caves, stacks, and arches. A similar mountainous coast is found along the Black Sea Caucasus. The Kerch Peninsula, by contrast, is bounded by a combination of rock platforms, abrasive-accumulative coasts in open bays, and accumulative sandy plains in sheltered embayments.

BIBLIOGRAPHY
Levakovskii, I. *Ocherki rel'efa Khar'kovskoi gubernii* (Kharkiv 1863)

Tutkovskii, P. *Orograficheskii ocherk Tsentral'nogo i Iuzhnogo Poles'ia* (Moscow 1913)
Tutkovs'kyi, P. *Pryrodnia raionyzatsiia Ukraïny* (Kiev 1922)
Polians'kyi, Iu. *Terasy, lesy i morfolohiia Halyts'koho Podillia nad Dnistrom* (Lviv 1929)
Sobolev, D. *Eskizy geomorfologii Ukrainy.* Vol 7, *Biulleten' Moskovskogo obshchestva ispytatelei prirody* (Moscow 1929)
Lichkov, B. *O stroenii rechnykh dolin Ukrainy* (Leningrad 1931)
Dmytriiev, M. (Dmitriev, N.) *Rel'ief URSR: Heomorfolohichnyi narys* (Kharkiv 1936)
Gladtsin, I. *Geomorfologiia SSSR: Geomorfologiia evropeiskoi chasti SSSR i Kavkaza* (Leningrad 1939)
Pashkevych, S. 'Morfolohichni kraievydy ukraïns'kykh zemel',' in *Heohrafiia ukraïns'kykh i sumezhnykh zemel'*, ed V. Kubijovyč (Cracow–Lviv 1943)
Anuchin, D.; Borzov, A. *Rel'ef evropeiskoi chasti SSSR* (Moscow 1948)
Bondarchuk, V. *Heomorfolohiia URSR* (Kiev 1949)
Karandeeva, M. *Geomorfologiia evropeiskoi chasti SSSR* (Moscow 1957)
Tsys', P. *Heomorfolohiia URSR* (Lviv 1962)
Zamorii, P. *Chetvertynni vidklady Ukraïns'koï RSR* (Kiev 1962)
Fiziko-geograficheskoe raionirovanie Ukrainskoi SSR (Kiev 1968)
Sokolovs'kyi, I. *Zakonomirnosti rozvytku rel'iefu Ukrainy* (Kiev 1973)
Marynych, O.; Lan'ko, A.; Shcherban', M.; Shyshchenko, P. *Fizychna heohrafiia Ukraïns'koï RSR* (Kiev 1982)

M. Dolnytsky, I. Stebelsky

Landless peasants (*pidsusidky* 'those under neighbors'). The collective name for various categories of impoverished peasants in 16th- to 18th-century Ukraine who did not have their own land but worked for neighbors who did – primarily Cossack captains, common Cossacks, and monasteries – in exchange for shelter and garden plots. Some *pidsusidky* had their own homes and even oxen and farm tools, but not arable land. Others were peasants and Cossacks who sold their land to neighbors to avoid taxation, military service, and other feudal obligations. Because many peasants chose to sell, in the 1690s the government of the Hetman state in Left-Bank Ukraine began restricting the possibilities and forcing *pidsusidky* to perform corvée. In the Hetman state in 1732, 7 percent of the peasant and Cossack households included *pidsusidky*. Most of the *pidsusidky* in Left-Bank and Slobidska Ukraine became serfs after Catherine II introduced serfdom there in 1783.

Landowners (*zemlevlasnyky, pomishchyky*). The owners of large and medium-sized estates, who constituted the leading social group in Ukraine before 1917 as a result of their economic strength, political influence, and (in the case of the nobility) estate privileges. Their Ukrainian designation was derived from the practice of *pomistia* or service tenure in the Russian Empire, which existed in the 15th to 18th centuries concurrently with the older *votchyny*, or patrimonial estates. By the 18th century *pomistia* holdings had virtually become hereditary. Consequently, in 1714 Peter I instituted a single system of land ownership that abolished the legal distinction between the two types of holding. From then the term *pomishchyk* was increasingly used in Ukraine, where landowners had previously been known as *didychi* (full and hereditary landowners) or *derzhavtsi* (service-tenure holders). Until the mid-19th century the right to own land and the peasants (serfs) bound to it (or to the person of the landowner) was exclusively in the hands of the *nobility. After the reforms in 1861 changed the *land tenure system, a substantial number of merchants became landowners, albeit without the estate privileges or political influence of the aristocracy.

The national composition of landowners in Ukraine was not homogeneous. In the central and eastern parts of the country the *didychi* and *derzhavtsi* were almost exclusively Ukrainian until the 16th century. In Western Ukraine the landowning class included Ukrainians, Poles, and (in Transcarpathia) Hungarians; on the borders of Ukraine and Belarus, Belarusian-Lithuanian landowners made their presence felt. After the Union of Lublin Polish magnates and nobility began settling in central Ukraine. Beginning with the 16th century, Russian *pomishchyky* began arriving on the northern reaches of Left-Bank Ukraine. During the tenure of Hetman B. Khmelnytsky and the subsequent Ruin Polish landowners disappeared completely from Left-Bank Ukraine and were largely absent from the Right Bank until the 18th century. Subsequently, they continued to be an influential force, right up to 1917, notwithstanding certain confiscations of property by the Russian government in the wake of the partitions of Poland and the Polish insurrections of 1830–1 and 1863–4. Among the owners of massive latifundia during that period were the *Potocki, Branicki, *Sanguszko, and Lubomirski families.

Starting in the late 18th century many lands formerly controlled by Polish magnates fell into the hands of Russian landowners (such as G. Potemkin and the Samoilov, Bobrinsky, Engelhardt, Stroganov, Shuvalov, Vorontsov, Vorontsov-Dashkov, Lopukhin, Demidov, San-Donato, Naryshkin, Balashov, and Uvarov families) through government redistribution, sale (occasionally forced), or inheritance. Some Ukrainian families, including the *Hudovych and *Troshchynsky, also benefited from such shifts in ownership.

The Ukrainian landowners of Left-Bank and Slobidska Ukraine, largely the descendants of Cossack officers, constituted a majority of the large property owners in those areas until the Revolution of 1917. There emerged a number of Russian or other foreign holdings in the early 18th century, however, alongside the older estates of the Galagan, Hudovych, Kapnist, Khanenko, Kochubei, Lashkevych, Myloradovych, Sudiienko, Skoropadsky, Tarnovsky, and other families. They included, among others, the Rumiantsev, Golitsyn, Dolgorukov, Yusypov, and Meklenburg-Strelitzi lines. A number of Ukrainian estates passed in the 19th century from Ukrainian to Russian control by way of marriage, such as those acquired by the Lamsdorf-Galagan, Musin-Pushkin, Repnin, and Zhemchuzhnikov families.

In Southern Ukraine the Ukrainian landowners were mostly descendants of Zaporozhian Cossacks. The region's numerous Russian and other foreign landowners had acquired estates by tsarist edict (mostly during the reign of Catherine II) or through purchase. The more important foreign landowners included the Potemkin, Viazemsky, Prozorovsky, Mordvinov, Vorontsov, Kankrin, Popov, and Romanov families.

Merchant landowners appeared in Ukraine in the mid-19th century, notably the Tereshchenko (from the Chernihiv region) and Kharytonenko (from the Kharkiv region) families. In the late 19th century a few wealthy Ukrainian landowners (Ye. *Chykalenko, V. *Leontovych, and others) became active in the Ukrainian national movement.

Western Ukraine. There were a substantial number of Ukrainian boyars in the Principality of Galicia-Volhynia until the mid-14th century. After the Polish annexation of Galicia most of them lost their estates. Many of them traveled eastward to Volhynia, where a number of Ukrainian princely and magnate families (Chetvertynsky, Czartoryski, Ostrozky, Sanguszko, Wiśniowiecki, Zbaraski, and others) consolidated themselves under Lithuanian rule. In addition new Ukrainian-Belarusian-Lithuanian landowning families (Koretsky, Zahorovsky, Zasławski, and others) emerged. In Galicia, the Kholm region, and Podlachia wealthy Polish families, such as the Branicki, Dzieduszycski, Poniatowski, Potocki, Rzewuski, and Tarnowski, established huge latifundia. Only a few of the old Rus' boyar families continued to hold their estates, among them the Bybelsky, Danylovych, Melshtynsky, Shumliansky, and Tustanovsky lines.

In Bukovyna, which was part of the Galicia-Volhynia state in the 12th to 14th centuries and then under Moldavia, estates were granted to boyars for state and military service as well as to certain established families that later became assimilated.

In Transcarpathia, through the 13th to 17th centuries (particularly after the seizure of the crown by the Anjou dynasty in the early 14th century) the largest estates were given to Hungarian or Hungarianized Italian, French,

Wallachian, and German magnates. Among them were the Aba, Bokshai, Dovhai (a Ukrainian feudal line), Draha, Drugeth, Ilosvaj, Paloczi, Perényi, Petenko, and Ragali families.

Initially the estates were granted to foreigners in Western Ukraine as service tenure, but the lands soon became hereditary. Under the influence of a foreign elite the old Rus' families assimilated with foreign (especially Polish) landowners, often through conversion to the Latin rite upon marriage. Only a few families held to the traditional Rus' religion and nationality; most of them were petty gentry.

In 1785, not long after the annexation of Galicia by Austria, a register was made of 1,500 local *didychi* who controlled 5,300 *filvarky*, or manors. Among them were 40 magnates who controlled 2,800 manors. Some of that group (including the Jabłonowski, Lubomirski, Potocki, Rzewuski, Sanguszko, and Zamoyski families) owned estates in Russian-controlled Ukraine. Owing to a curial electoral system Galician and Bukovynian *didychi* exercised a decisive influence in local affairs even after the adoption of the Austrian constitutions of 1860 and 1867 (in 1883, they constituted 70 percent of the parliamentary representatives in the Galician Diet). They also carried weight in the central Viennese government and parliament.

The owners of large estates in Galicia and Bukovyna usually did not administer them themselves; they preferred to hire managers or to rent them out. As a result, by the late 19th century many estates had gone into decline, and were changing hands frequently or being auctioned following bankruptcy. Ownership often passed to various repossessors and creditors. The estates could also be parceled out to the local peasantry. Many estates in Galicia were taken over by Jews and Austrian Germans. In the 1870s, Viennese and other financial institutions began buying up large tracts of the region's forest. Among the notable Ukrainian *didychi* of Western Ukraine were T. *Dembytsky, I. *Fedorovych, and the Sheptytsky and Tyshkevych families. In Bukovyna Rumanian boyar landowners gradually were joined by Armenians, Germans, and Jews.

Despite the introduction of *land reforms and other political changes during the interwar period, Polish landowners in Galicia and northwestern Ukraine managed to maintain their grasp on their holdings to a greater extent than in Poland proper. Similarly, Rumanian landowners maintained their positions in Bukovyna. In Transcarpathia Ukrainians benefited only marginally from land reform. In all those areas the landowners remained influential, although they lost their estate privileges and entrenched political positions.

BIBLIOGRAPHY
Romanovich-Slavatinskii, A. *Dvorianstvo v Rossii ot nachala XVIII veka do otmeny krepostnogo prava* (St Petersburg 1870; 2nd edn, Kiev 1912)
Lazarevskii, A. *Opisanie staroi Malorossii*, 3 vols (Kiev 1888–1902)
Linnichenko, I. *Cherty iz istorii soslovii Iugo-Zapadnoi (Galitskoi) Rusi XIV–XVI vv.* (Moscow 1894)
Voinarovs'kyi, T. *Vplyv Pol'shchi na ekonomichnyi rozvii Ukraïny-Rusy* (Lviv 1910)
Baranovych, O. 'Narysy magnats'koho hospodarstva na pivdni Volyni u XVII st.,' *Studiï z istoriï Ukraïny* (Kiev 1926–8, 1930)
Mytsiuk, O. *Narysy z sotsiial'no-hospodars'koï istoriï Pidkarpats'koï Rusy*, 2 vols (Uzhhorod 1936, 1938)
Ivanov, L. 'Raspredelenie zemlevladeniia na Ukraine nakanune revoliutsii 1905–1907 gg.,' *Istoricheskie zapiski*, 60 (Moscow 1958)
Serczyk, W.A. *Gospodarstwo magnackie w województwie podolskim w drugiej połowie XVIII wieku* (Wrocław 1965)
Anfimov, A. *Krupnoe pomeshchich'e khoziaistvo Evropeiskoi Rossii (kontsa XIX–nachala XX veka* (Moscow 1969)
Franko, I. 'Zemel'na vlasnist' v Halychyni,' in *Ivan Franko: Zibrannia tvoriv*, 44, bk 1 (Kiev 1984)
Rosman, M. *The Lord's Jews: Magnate-Jewish Relations in the Polish-Lithuanian Commonwealth* (Cambridge, Mass 1990)

O. Ohloblyn, I. Vytanovych

Landscape art. The depiction of natural scenery. In Ukrainian art highly conventionalized landscape elements were used in icons (eg, *The Transfiguration* [14th century] in the Church of the Mother of God in Busovysko, near Turka, Galicia). Architectural settings became part of the separately enclosed scenes in icons illustrating the lives of the saints (eg, in the icon of SS *Cosmas and Damian* [15th century] from Tylych in the Lemko region). During the Renaissance landscapes in icons became less schematized and began looking more like the surrounding Ukrainian countryside (eg, in *The Dream of Jacob* [1650] in the iconostasis of the Church of the Holy Ghost in Drohobych). Architecture and local scenery were important elements in the icons of I. Rutkovych (*Christ by the Well* [1697–9] in the iconostasis of the church in Skvariava Nova, near Zhovkva, Galicia) and Y. Kondzelevych (*The Dormition* in the Białystok Monastery [17th century]). Landscapes also appeared as backgrounds to portraits (portrait of Yevdokiia Zhuravko [18th century]).

Some of the earliest landscapes were settings for religious engravings. At first they were variations on landscapes borrowed from Western European models, but later, local elements emerged. In 1669 Master Illia depicted the Dnieper River in his engraving *The Coming of Iconographers from Constantinople*. Similar engravings by L. Tarasevych showed an even greater preoccupation with local scenery. In 1674 N. Zubrytsky engraved the siege of the Pochaiv Lavra, and in 1699 D. Sinkevych engraved the architectural ensemble of the Krekhiv Monastery; both were from a bird's-eye view. Depictions of churches and secular buildings appeared in the engraved theses produced in the 17th and 18th centuries by the Kievan Cave Monastery Press. H. Levytsky engraved a realistic panorama of the land and architecture for the thesis dedicated to Metropolitan R. Zaborovsky (1739). *Ifika iieropolitika* (1712) contained N. Zubrytsky's engraving of a windmill on a river bank.

In the 18th century, landscapes gained greater prominence in religious pictures (eg, the depiction of Mt Sinai in the mural in the west wall of St George's Church in Drohobych). One of the earliest attempts to convey the local scenery was made by M. Terensky (the town of Dubets as seen through a window in his *Krasytsky Family Portrait* [1753]). V. Hryhorovych-Barsky popularized landscape art through his drawings of his travels (1723–47) in Europe and the Near East.

At the beginning of the 19th century landscapes became an integral part of icon compositions. In *Mary and Elizabeth* in the iconostasis of the church in Sulymivka, Poltava gubernia (ca 1830), the foliage and trees dominate the composition.

Landscape painting did not, however, become an independent genre in Ukrainian art until the 19th century. Romanticism inspired artists to record faithfully the pastoral scenery of thatched-roof cottages and the surrounding countryside. Among them were I. *Soshenko (*The Ros River near Bila Tserkva*), T. *Shevchenko, and B. *Shternberg (*View of [the] Podil [District] in Kiev*, 1837). Shevchenko painted watercolor landscapes of interesting architecture when he worked for the Archeographic Commission of Kiev University. He did two landscapes (*Kiev* and *Vydubychi Monastery*) for his series of etchings on Ukrainian topics called *'Zhivopisnaia Ukraïna' (1844). In exile he depicted the surrounding countryside in numerous drawings and watercolors; they included landscapes of the Aral Sea coast (1848–9), the Mangishlak Peninsula (1851), and the area around the Novopetrovsk Fortress (1853–7).

With time two types of landscape art developed, the poetic and the epic. Among the 19th-century artists who devoted much of their work to Ukrainian landscapes were two artists of non-Ukrainian origin, I. *Aivazovsky, who is famous for his marine paintings, and A. *Kuindzhi, who painted Romantic moonlit scenes. Other Ukrainian artists who devoted their efforts to landscape painting were S. *Vasylkivsky, I. *Pokhytonov, and S. *Svitoslavsky. In the early 20th century P. *Levchenko painted intimate lyrical views in impressionist colors capturing the fleeting effects of light in both urban and rural scenes (*Fountain near the Golden Gate* and *Cottage, Zmiiv*, 1915). V. *Krychevsky and A. *Manevich also worked in the impressionist manner. Symbolism was dominant in the fantasy landscapes of Yu. *Mykhailiv (*Music of the Stars*, 1920s).

Summer Day in Ukraine (late 19th century) by P. Levchenko

In Western Ukraine I. *Trush painted idyllic sunsets, ordinary fields, and panoramic views (*The Dnieper*, 1910) only slightly influenced by impressionist colors, and O. *Kulchytska depicted informal scenes using an impressionist palette (*Willows*, 1907). O. *Novakivsky became known for his expressionist views of the countryside (*Mount Grehit*, 1931) and urban scenes (numerous views of St George's Cathedral in Lviv). Landscape painting was also prominent in the work of the Transcarpathian artists Y. *Bokshai (*First Frost*, 1927), E. *Hrabovsky (*Thaw*, 1921), and Z. *Sholtes (*Wooden Church*, 1939).

In the 1930s, after *socialist realism was imposed as the only sanctioned artistic method in the USSR, landscape painting in Soviet Ukraine was limited to views of collective farms (eg, H. Svitlytsky's *Collective Farm in Blossom* [1935] and M. Burachek's *Collective-Farm Road* [1937]) and industrial sites. Pure landscape painting was revived in Ukraine after the Second World War through the influ-

ence of Western Ukrainian artists, such as Y. Bokshai, R. *Selsky, and V. *Manastyrsky. But landscapes were painted in a naturalistic manner in keeping with socialist realism. During the Khrushchev 'thaw' landscape painting regained some of its lost prominence largely as a result of efforts by O. *Shovkunenko (*Evening Rays*, 1955), M. *Hlushchenko (*Spring*, 1959), S. *Shyshko (*Mountain Pasture*, 1951), and D. *Shavykin (*Evening on the Dnieper River*, 1957) in Kiev; R. Selsky and his wife, M. *Selska, in Lviv; and Y. Bokshai, A. Kashai, and F. *Manailo in Uzhhorod.

In Lviv R. Selsky popularized Carpathian landscapes (eg, *Chornohora*, 1968), seascapes, and views of Crimea, often using natural scenery to create constructs of color and form (*Thicket*, 1968). V. Manastyrsky painted landscapes characterized by rhythmic patterns of flat pigment (eg, *Under the Mountain Sokil*, 1962). H. *Smolsky, O. *Shatkivsky, S. Koropchak, and D. Dovboshynsky have painted landscapes in a variety of figurative styles. Landscapes have been particularly prominent in the work of V. *Patyk, who paints with great spontaneity and expressive hues (*Summer*, 1972), and L. *Medvid, whose monochromatic, highly realistic views, with forms reduced to their essentials, are a departure from socialist realism (*Heat Wave*, 1969).

Chornohora (1968) by R. Selsky

In Kiev T. *Yablonska painted panoramic views of the land in the 1960s (*Nameless Heights*, 1969) and eventually turned to landscape studies in contrasts of light in the manner of the French impressionists (*Our Beautiful Kiev*, 1986). Realistic landscapes depicting the beauty of the Ukrainian countryside have dominated in the work of V. *Nepyipyvo. The Kiev artists H. Havrylenko, Ya. Levych, A. Lymariev, and M. *Vainshtein devoted considerable time to landscapes that did not conform to socialist realism, as did Y. *Yehorov, O. Voloshynov, V. Basanets, V. *Strelnikov, and V. *Tsiupko in Odessa. Both Strelnikov (*By the White House*, 1979) and Tsiupko (*Boats*, 1978) have painted landscapes bordering on abstraction and abstractions inspired by landscapes. There are folk-art elements in V. *Padun's landscapes of rural Ukraine around Dnipropetrovske (*Old Village*, 1979). Unusual but realistic landscapes, as well as nightmarish, surrealistic scenes of desolate places, have been created by I. *Marchuk, who works with a weblike technique (*Night in the Steppe*, 1984). Ye. Hordiiets (*Pink Rocks*, 1986) paints meticulous photorealist landscapes that often contain elements of the fantastic, as do the works of V. Pasyvenko and D. *Stetsko. Expressionism prevails in the landscapes of M. *Popov and Yu. *Lutskevych.

Of the Ukrainian landscape artists who worked outside their homeland, the most prominent was O. *Hryshchenko (A. Gritchenko), who achieved recognition in France for his landscapes and seascapes (*Morning in Provence*), painted mostly in an expressionist manner. M. *Krychevsky, who worked in Paris from 1929, specialized in sensitive watercolor views of the city. A. *Solohub has concentrated on watercolor landscapes of Paris and Istanbul, and Z. *Lisovska has specialized in gouaches of landscapes of the Swiss Alps. Expressionistic glimpses of France alongside those of his native Carpathian scenery constitute the major portion of the work of O. *Mazuryk, who has worked in Paris since 1968 (*Villaret*, 1971; *Carpathian Church*, 1985).

In the United States vibrant colors and expressive brush strokes have been typical of the work of M. *Moroz (*Bar Harbor, Maine*), M. *Nedilko (*Seascape*), and L. *Hutsaliuk (*Architectural Landscape*). Other artists who have painted landscapes there include V. *Krychevsky, Jr, M. *Radysh, K. Krychevska-Rosandych, and M. Harasovska-Dachyshyn. Of the artists who emigrated to Canada M. *Levytsky has painted numerous semiabstract landscapes (*Spanish Town*, 1965), H. *Novakivska has experimented with textural effects (*Along the Road*), and M. *Styranka has concentrated on delicate watercolor views (*Winter*, 1988). W. *Kurelek, the most famous Canadian artist of Ukrainian origin, depicted the Canadian landscape from coast to coast in a highly personal, realistic manner often bordering on the primitive (*Fields*, 1976). W. *Lobchuk, D. *Proch, P. *Shostak, and D. *Stryjek have also painted Canadian landscapes.

D. Zelska-Darewych

Landscaping. The conscious modification and shaping of outdoor environments for human use. In the past, landscaping was carried out by traditional farmers and builders and, later, by those trained in gardening, agriculture, horticulture, silviculture, hydraulics, and architecture. The field was generally regarded as horticultural, but by the mid-19th century the term landscape architecture was being used to suggest professionalism in landscape design. Today, landscape architects are involved in projects that are considered more part of *urban planning or urban design.

From the late Neolithic to the Copper Age the *Trypilian culture is represented by the remains of rectangular clay houses grouped into settlements laid out on terraces or hills in circular fashion. From the Bronze and Iron ages major landscape features include Cimmerian and Scythian burial mounds, walled settlements and long earthen defense walls, and megalithic structures (temples and stone idols). The ancient Greek colonization of the Black Sea coast (7th–6th centuries BC) brought with it the construction of cities (Chersonesus, Olbia, Tyras, and others) with a regular-grid street pattern, quarried stone buildings, and stone defense walls. In the Princely era (9th–14th centuries AD) cities in the forest-steppe and forest zones contained defense walls, tower gates (such as the Golden Gate of Kiev), palaces, and, above all, brick and stone churches in the Byzantine style (such as the *St Sophia Cathedral in Kiev). In time, church construction assumed local architectural styles (the Kiev, Chernihiv, and Volhynia schools of the 12th–13th centuries), which developed into the Ukrainian architectural style (14th–16th centuries).

Meanwhile a traditional folk architecture prevailed, as evidenced in the layout of villages as well as the construction of houses and the fencing and plantings around them. Even small, wooden churches, built using folk techniques, developed their own regional styles and were given pride of place on the highest points of land.

The Renaissance brought with it the baroque style, with its complex design and ornate decorations. That style, which was modified into the Ukrainian baroque, was applied (in the 18th century) to the hetman palaces, large urban structures, and churches. Even village churches were built in the style and were prominently sited on the highest elevations. Urban and palace gardens of the period were laid out by professional landscapers, who used the ornate geometric and highly structured French palace garden as a model. By the late 18th century, however, the baroque style was being replaced by imperial neoclassicism. With the accelerating growth of cities, elements of classical architecture were applied to municipal and large residential complexes in Kiev, Poltava, Odessa, and other cities. New settlements were laid out in regular-grid patterns in contrast to the irregular and somewhat concentric street patterns of old towns. At the same time the romanticism of the period was reflected in the establishment of English or landscape parks. Such professionally landscaped parks were usually established at locations with picturesque relief. The designers supplemented existing natural shrubs and trees with newly introduced exotics, natural bodies of water with ponds and fountains or waterfalls, and natural slopes with cliffs and incorporated other architectural elements or decorative objects. Parks of that type included Oleksandriia in Bila Tserkva (1793) and Trostianets in the Chernihiv region (1834).

From the late 19th century, industrialization propelled the growth of cities. Along the newly built railroad lines mushroomed industrial structures and, nearby, cramped residential apartments for workers. In the most attractive locations were erected elaborate homes for the elite, professionally landscaped in parklike settings. Commercial and civic buildings were designed in an eclectic style, which by the end of the 19th century turned to modern and Ukrainian moderne style (as exemplified by the Lviv Polytechnical Institute, 1873–7, and the gubernia zemstvo building in Poltava, 1905–9). Structures were built with new materials (glass, metal frame, reinforced concrete) and techniques (cantilevers).

In the countryside farmland was expanded to new limits by means of technology. The forest-steppe and the steppe were transformed into fields of crops, mostly grain. Forested swamplands were drained, and mountain forests were subjected to lumbering and drilling for oil. The transformation of the natural landscape was purely utilitarian. Professional landscaping was restricted to parks and the immediate surroundings of buildings, and the peasantry landscaped the small holdings around their houses in traditional ways, with fences, flower beds, orchards, and vegetable gardens.

In the Soviet period urban growth was guided by the principles of socialist state planning. In Ukraine most cities were already well established, and Zaporizhia was the only major city that developed on the basis of socialist urban planning. Elsewhere various new elements were simply added to existing patterns. A high priority was placed on the building of giant industrial objects and large institutional buildings for the promotion of socialist culture, including clubs, palaces of culture, and parks of culture and relaxation. Most churches were closed and then stripped and converted to other uses or destroyed. Only in the late 1980s and early 1990s, following a legal guarantee of religious freedom, were churches reopened.

During the reconstruction that followed the Second World War new residential areas were laid out, with apartment blocks forming integrated groupings or microraions, where residents theoretically would be able to obtain all the necessary basic services. They were characterized architecturally by large (if not daunting) scale, simplicity of form, and prefabricated mass production. Trees were planted to set off the buildings from the roads, but special professional landscaping was generally restricted to highly visible central districts and public buildings. The construction of gigantic war memorials was accompanied by matching bold, rampart-inspired landscaping. In the countryside priority was given to the construction of very large state- and collective-farm production buildings (livestock housing, concrete silos) and institutional buildings (administration offices, meeting halls, schools). Although a few villages were developed as socialist showcases with two-storied residential housing and sometimes even multistoried apartment buildings, the onus was on the peasantry to rebuild their homes using wood-frame or brick construction according to established designs. Housing was to be consolidated into larger settlements around the institutional buildings on the basis of a new grid street pattern. In that planned restructuring, devised by the Ukrainian Scientific Research and Planning Institute of Civil Rural Construction, the rich diversity of traditional house styles, fences, and garden-orchard landscaping was often abandoned for an orderly, suburban appearance.

Throughout Ukraine monuments to V. Lenin or the memory of the Second World War were erected in prominent places and landscaped with pavement and geometric flower beds. Other figures compatible with official Soviet ideology were also honored with monuments; T. Shevchenko was the Ukrainian figure most often honored in that way. The monuments to Lenin began being disassembled in 1990 and replaced by monuments to prominent Ukrainian persons or events, landscaped with appropriate flower beds and trees, such as *viburnum.

BIBLIOGRAPHY
Vologodtsev, I. Osobennosti razvitiia gorodov Ukrainy (Kharkiv 1930)
Iurchenko, P. Ukraïns'ka narodna arkhitektura (Kiev 1947)
Sichyns'kyi, V. Pam'iatky ukraïns'koï arkhitektury (Philadelphia 1952)
Rubtsov, L. Sadovo-parkovyi landshaft (Kiev 1956)
Lypa, O. Vyznachni sady i parky Ukraïny ta ïkh okhorona (Kiev 1960)
Gradostroitel'stvo: Landshaftnaia arkhitektura (Kiev 1961)
Deleur, G.; Khokhol, Iu. Arkhitektura sela: Planirovka i zastroika (Kiev 1979)
Pereustroistvo sel Ukrainskoi SSR (Kiev 1981)

I. Stebelsky

Lange, Nikolai, b 24 March 1858 in St Petersburg, d 15 February 1921 in Odessa. Russian psychologist; one of the founders of experimental psychology in the Russian Empire. He graduated from St Petersburg University (1882) and worked in W. Wundt's laboratory in Leipzig. As a professor at Odessa University (1888–1921) he founded a psychology laboratory (1895) and organized the Higher Courses for Women in Odessa (1903). In his work Psikhologiia (Psychology, 1922), influenced by Wundt, he proposed a philosophical basis for psychology and defended the dualistic theory of 'psychophysical reciprocal actions' while refuting social Darwinism. He also wrote Dusha rebenka v pervye gody zhizni (The Soul of a Child in the First Years of Life, 1891), Psikhologicheskie issledovaniia (Psychological Research, 1893), and Teoriia Vundta o nachale mifa (Wundt's Theory on the Origin of Myth, 1912).

Langeron, Louis-Alexandre Andrault, b 13 January 1763 in Paris, d 16 July 1831 in St Petersburg. A French nobleman, Russian general, count (from 1799), and political figure. In 1790, during the French Revolution, he emigrated to Russia and served as an officer in the Russian infantry. During the Russo-Turkish War of 1806–12 his adjutant was I. *Kotliarevsky. From November 1815 to May 1823 he was governor-general of *New Russia in Southern Ukraine and commander in chief of the Boh and Black Sea Cossack armies. While governor-general, until 1820 he was also chief of the Odessa autonomous administrative territory (gradonachalstvo). He promoted the growth of Odessa's port, established the first public utilities in Odessa, and was a major benefactor of the *Richelieu Lyceum, the girls' school, and the Greek commercial school there. He was also one of the founders of *Freemasonry in Ukraine.

Language, Ukrainian. The second most widely spoken language of the 12 surviving members of the Slavic group of the large Indo-European language family. Geographically, it is classified with Russian and Belarusian as an East Slavic language. Actually, like Slovak, it occupies a central position: it borders on some West Slavic languages, and it once bordered on Bulgarian, a South Slavic language, before being separated from it by Rumanian and Hungarian. Accordingly, Ukrainian shared in the historical development of all three branches of the *Slavic languages. Today Ukrainian borders on Russian in the east and northeast, on Belarusian in the north, and on Polish, Slovak, and two non-Slavic languages – Hungarian and Rumanian – in the west. Before the steppes of southern Ukraine were resettled by the Ukrainians, this was an area of contact with various Turkic languages, such as Crimean Tatar.

Within its geographic boundaries Ukrainian is represented basically by a set of *dialects, some of which differ significantly from the others. Generally, however, dialectal divisions in Ukrainian are not as strong as they are, for example, in British English or in German. Traditionally, scholars have divided Ukrainian dialects into three main groups, *northern, *southwestern, and *southeastern, and these have been subdivided further. Standard Ukrainian, which is accepted as such by the speakers of all the dialects and represents Ukrainian to outsiders, is a superstructure built on this dialectal foundation. It is the only form of Ukrainian taught in school and, except for clearly regional manifestations, used in literature. The standard language is based mainly on the Poltava-Kiev dialects of the southeastern group, but it also contains many features from other dialects, particularly the southwestern ones.

(For an account of its historical development, see *Standard Ukrainian.)

Phonetics and phonemics. Six vocalic phonemes – Four unrounded (low back /a/, mid-front /e/, high-front /i/, and central-high, mid-front /y/) and two rounded (mid-back /o/ and high-back /u/) – characterize the phonetics and phonemics of Modern Standard Ukrainian. All vowels may appear in the stressed or unstressed position, but in unstressed syllables the distinction between /e/ and /y/ is neutralized, and the phonetic environment determines whether the phonetic realization is closer to /e/ or to /y/; eg, in *nésenyj* 'carried' the /e/ in the first syllable is stressed, but in *nesé* (3rd pers sing) it is unstressed and is slightly shifted towards an *y*, while in *nesý* 2nd pers sing imp it is closer to *y*. No other vowels are subject to qualitative changes in the unstressed position. Stress in Ukrainian is weak in terms of expiratory energy and is marked primarily by lengthening. On the other hand there is no phonemic length outside of stress; ie, the length is a concomitant of the stress. In normal speech, vowels undergo no reduction. This combination of features does not occur in any adjacent Slavic language.

The inventory of consonants in Modern Standard Ukrainian consists of labials, dentals, postdentals, velars, and one pharyngeal. (1) The labials are represented by /b/, /v/, and /m/; /v/ is realized only as /w/ in word- and syllable-final position, while in the prevocalic position the choice of bilabial or labiodental articulation is optional. There is also a labial /f/, but only in foreign words; it is alien to most dialects, where, more often than not, it is replaced by the affricate /xv/. (2) The dentals are /t/, /d/, /s/, /z/, the lateral sonorant /l/, the trill /r/, and the affricates /c/ and /3/ (spelled *dz*). All dentals (/r/ only in the word-final position) appear also in palatalized versions as /t'/, /d'/, /s'/, /z'/, /l'/, /r'/, /c'/, and /3'/, so the number of dental phonemes is doubled. (3) The postdentals are /š/, /ž/, and the affricates /č/ and /ǯ/ (spelled *dž*). Except for the extraphonemic (automatic) palatalization before *i*, they are not subject to palatalization. (4) The velars are /k/, /g/ (mostly in foreign words), and /x/. (5) Finally, there is the pharyngeal /h/. The velars and the pharyngeal are subject to nonphonemic palatalization before *i*.

Thus, the total number of consonantal phonemes is 31 or, if the glide /j/ (alternating in some positions with /i/) is counted as a consonant, 32. Furthermore, 18 consonants may also appear in a lengthened version, 8 of them – /b/, /v/, /m/, /d/, /z/, /s/, /n/, and /j/ – only on morphemic boundaries (ie, where two identical consonants occur, one at the end of one morpheme and the second at the beginning of the next morpheme), eg, *viddaty* = *vid + daty* 'to give away'; 10 others – /t'/, /d'/, /s'/, /z'/, /c'/, /n'/, /l'/, /š/, /ž/, and /č/ (if lengthened, the last also undergo palatalization, which is otherwise alien to them) – also appear on morphemic boundaries, but not as a result of the occurrence of two identical consonants, eg, *volossja* 'hair'. If the latter 10 are considered as having phonemic value, the number of consonant phonemes rises to 42. This excess of consonants (42) over vowels (6) does not mean, however, that Ukrainian is a 'consonantal' language, because it has a large number of open syllables and relatively few consonant clusters.

While oppositions in palatalization and length are limited to certain groups of consonants, the opposition in voicing is much more pervasive and encompasses all consonants except the resonants (/l/, /n/, /r/, /m/, and /j/). In a few cases it applies even to consonant pairs whose members differ in articulation: /x/ and /h/, and, inasmuch as /f/ belongs to the phonemic system of the language, /v/ and /f/.

Both vowels and consonants undergo alternations, most of which are unproductive and are applied traditionally. The only productive ones are the alternations (1) of distinctive /e/ and /y/ with their nondistinctive alternant, depending on stress; (2) of voiceless consonants with corresponding voiced ones before another voiced consonant – eg, *borótysja* 'to fight': *borot'bá* 'fight', pronounced [*borod'bá*] – but not vice versa; and (3) of dental spirants and affricates with corresponding postdentals before postdentals and vice versa; eg, *brjázkaty* 'to clang': *brjažčáty*, *neséš* 'carry' 2nd pers sing: *neséšsja* 'being carried' 2nd pers sing, pronounced [*nesés's'a*].

All other alternations, although they may be frequent, are unproductive and purely traditional or morphologized; for example, the alternation of nonpalatalized consonants susceptible to palatalization with their palatalized counterparts occurs before the ending *-i* in substantives, but not in adjectives; eg, *krajina* 'country': *kraji[n']i* dat-loc sing, but *zelenyj* 'green' nom sing and *zeleni* nom pl with no palatalization of *n*. The most frequent nonproductive alternations of vowels are *i : o* or *e* and *o, e* (nonalternating with *i* as a rule) : # (zero). The former is an earmark of Ukrainian; the latter is shared by most Slavic languages (with variation in the phonetic character of the vowels involved). Both are partially morphologized; eg, *i* typically replaces *o* or *e* in the final syllables ending in a consonant in the nominative singular form vs other cases (*pit* 'sweat', *pič* 'stove': *potu*, *peči* gen sing), in the genitive plural with the zero ending in feminine and neuter substantives (eg, *noha* 'foot': *nih* gen pl), before the suffix *-n-* in adjectives (eg, *ničnyj* 'nightly': *noči* gen sing), and in other instances. The same set of morphological conditions determines the alternation of *o* and *e* with #. But in both cases there is no absolute predictability as to the choice of the alternants.

In consonants the most frequent alternations are those of velars and the pharyngeal with postdentals and with palatalized dentals: *k : č : c', x : š : s', h : ž : z'*. Postdentals typically occur before *-e* in the vocative, before the endings in verb forms of the present tense (all or in the 1st pers sing), in the imperative (eg, *pekty* 'to bake': *peču* 1st pers sing, *pečy* 2nd pers sing imp), and before certain suffixes (eg, *ruka* 'hand': *ručka* 'little hand'), while dentals are found in the dative and locative cases ending in *-i* of nouns (eg, *rux* 'motion': *u rusi* 'in motion') as well as before some suffixes (eg, *kozak* 'Cossack': *kozac'kyj* attrib), but not in words that were introduced relatively recently (eg, *N'ju-Jork* 'New York': *n'ju-jorks'kyj* attrib).

Word structure. All words consist of morphemes. Uninflected words consist of one or more morphemes (eg, *na* 'on', *na-v-kol-o* 'around'). Inflected words contain two or more morphemes, although the last morpheme may be a phonetic zero (eg, *kit-#* 'cat', *vesn-a* 'spring', *vy-kon-av-ec'-#* 'executor'). Morphemes are subject to morphemic alternations and, consequently, may appear in several manifestations (eg, *kit-#* vs *kot-a* gen sing, *vykonav-ec'* vs *vykonav-[c'-a]* gen sing).

All morphemes are meaningful in principle. Roots, suffixes, and prefixes carry referential meanings, endings carry grammatical meanings. In individual cases, however, the referential meaning may be blurred, and the separateness of a morpheme is conveyed only by its not belonging to the adjacent morphemes (eg, *pys'-m-o* 'writing', with a referentially desemanticized suffix, *krematorij-#* 'crematorium', with only the suffix carrying a referential meaning).

The root can be monosyllabic or polysyllabic (eg, *sel-o* 'village', *molok-o* 'milk', *skovorod-a* 'frying pan'). As a rule, in nouns it ends in a consonant. The verb also admits roots ending in a vowel. Prefixes can consist of a single consonant or one or two syllables (eg, *s-kazaty* 'to say', *do-vesty* 'to prove', *pere-nesty* 'to transfer'). Suffixes are consonantal, monosyllabic, or disyllabic (eg, *kin-s'k-yj* 'horse' adj, *robit-nyk* 'worker', *nacional-izacij-a* 'nationalization'). Endings can consist of a vowel, a vowel plus a consonant, or two vowels separated by a consonant (eg, *holov-a* 'head', *holov-oju* instr sing, *holov-am* dat pl). Prefixes precede and suffixes follow roots, and endings follow all the other morphemes listed so far (eg, *za-mov-l-ennj-a* 'order').

As in other Slavic languages, endings typically carry several grammatical meanings simultaneously (-*a* in *za-movlennj-a* conveys at the same time gender, number, and case). In the derivation process a limited number of what could be suffixes follow endings. These so-called postfixes characterize some verbs and pronouns (eg, *smij-a-ty-sja* 'to laugh' cf *smij-u-sja* 1st pers sing, *jak-yj-nebud'* 'any one' cf *jak-oho-nebud'* gen sing).

The part played by suffixes is not limited to derivation: more often than not, the suffix determines where the stress occurs and its movement; in the case of the last suffix, it also determines the choice of ending in the basic word form and, by the same token, the paradigmatic type of the word. The suffix -*ar*, for example, identifies the word as a masculine noun with a zero ending in the nominative singular having the so-called soft type of declension (eg, *lik-ar* [gen *likar'a*] 'physician'). Typically, only affective suffixes may be used in various parts of speech and, within this framework, in various paradigmatic types; eg, *kozak: kozač-en'k-o* 'Cossack', *molodyj: molod-en'k-yj* 'young', *pizno: pizn-en'k-o* 'late', *jisty: jist-on'k-y* 'to eat'.

Quite a few suffixes require certain phonetic changes in the preceding phoneme, most often in the root. Particularly affected is the final velar/pharyngeal of the preceding morpheme, most often with the suffix -*n*- in the derivation of adjectives from other parts of speech (eg, *muzyk-a* 'music': *muzyč-n-yj* 'musical'). There are also cases of fusion of consonants on the boundary of a morpheme with the succeeding suffix (eg, *rob-it-nyk* 'worker' + the collective suffix -*stv-(o)* – *robitny-ctv-o*, where *c* cannot be assigned entirely to either the preceding or succeeding morpheme). As a result of these peculiarities, morphemes in Ukrainian appear not only in their 'regular' form, but also as a set of relationships based on that form.

The primary function of prefixes is to point to spatial relations, while other modifications in the meaning of a word are conveyed mostly by suffixes. Hence, prefixes are especially typical of verbs, and suffixes appear mostly in nouns. But since words are derived as a rule not from roots alone, but from entire stems, prefixes occur widely in nouns, and nominal suffixes enter some verbs. But in such cases they usually occur together with other affixes characterizing the derived part of speech. The prefix *po-*, for example, is basically verbal (eg, *xodyty* 'to walk':

poxodyty 'to walk for a while'), but it is transferred to substantives (eg, *poxodžennja* 'origin' along with the suffix -*en'*-) and adjectives (eg, *poxidnyj* 'derivative' along with the suffix -*n*-); the suffix [-*eñ*'] belongs basically to substantives (eg, *značennja* 'meaning'), although it is transferred to adjectives (*značennevyj*, along with the suffix -*ev*-).

As a rule, neither suffixes nor prefixes have completely definite meanings; they have a variety of connotations. Thus, the same affix in different words may have different meanings (eg, *kerivnyk* 'leader' [a person], *ličyl'nyk* 'meter' [an instrument]) and sometimes even contrary meanings (eg, *zlizty na derevo* 'to climb up a tree', *zlizty z dereva* 'to climb down [off] a tree'). There are only a few suffixes with narrow and precisely defined meanings, but these are usually not very productive (eg, the suffix -*yzn(a)* meaning an inheritance: *didyzna* 'ancestral inheritance', *materyzna* 'maternal inheritance').

Word compounds are fairly frequent in Ukrainian, but they play a subordinate part in word formation. In substantives, adjectives, adverbs, and verbs, compounds are usually formed by connecting two stems with so-called linking vowels: -*o*-, -*e*- (in substantives), and -*y*- (in cases where the first part is a numeral); eg, *syn'-o-zelenyj* 'blue-green', *zeml-e-trus* 'earthquake', *šest-y-kutnyk* 'hexagon'. Word juxtaposition, in which the first component becomes part of the compound without undergoing any change (if there is an ending, it also becomes part of the compound; eg, *žalju-hidnyj* 'pitiful', *kil'ka-poverxovyj* 'several-storied'), is not very productive in the inflectional parts of speech, except in the derivation of compound numerals (eg, *dvisti sorok p'jat* '245', *dvisti sorok p'jat'ox* '245' gen), but it is normal in the derivation of prepositions (eg, *ponad* 'above', *z-pid* 'from under'), particles (*xiba ž bo* 'unless'), and interjections (*tap-talap* 'plop'). The derivation of substantives, especially of the names of states, institutions, organizations, and positions, allows for several types of abbreviation.

Parts of speech and inflection. Each word belongs to a certain part of speech, which is characterized by its function and its inflection or lack thereof. The substantive, adjective, numeral, pronoun, and verb can be inflected. There are three chief types of inflection: (1) nominal, (2) adjectival and pronominal, and (3) verbal. Some numerals have a special type of inflection.

Substantives are inflected (declined) by number and case. (For gender in substantives, see *Gender.) Number (singular vs plural) is basically a semantic category, but it is also used for the grammatical agreement of adjectives in the broad sense, and of verbs with substantives. The cases reflect the syntactic role of the substantive in the utterance. The nominative case usually indicates the syntactic independence of the substantive and is the form in which it functions as the subject of a sentence. The other cases indicate syntactic dependence on a verb or other part of speech. The accusative and dative cases mostly show objective relations. The genitive and instrumental cases express temporal, spatial, and causative relations, although in special instances they indicate the substantive as an object. All of the dependent cases are used with and without prepositions. The last dependent case, the locative, is used only with prepositions and shows almost exclusively temporal and spatial relations. In addition, masculine and feminine substantives in the singular have a special vocative case, which is occasionally replaced by the nominative case in informal speech.

Each case is characterized by its ending or endings. Often the same endings occur in the dative and the locative sing (eg, *knyzi* from *knyha* 'book'), in the nominative and accusative (*lyst, lysty* 'letter' sing and pl), and in the genitive and accusative (*xlopcja*, from *xlopec'* 'boy', *duba* from *dub* 'oak'). In certain declensions the endings are the same in the genitive, dative, and locative singular, in the nominative and accusative plural (eg, *jabluni* from *jablunja* 'apple tree', *tini* from *tin'* 'shade'), and in the genitive singular and nominative and accusative plural (*xaty* from *xata* 'cottage'). Cases with the same ending are sometimes distinguished by the accent (gen sing *xáty*, nom and acc pl *xatý*), but more often by the type of inflection that the substantive belongs to and by the place and role of the given form in the sentence.

The inflectional type of each substantive has no direct semantic or syntactic connotations. It is assigned to each substantive on the basis of the latter's gender and ending. Substantives with -*a* endings are usually feminine; those with zero endings are either masculine or feminine; those with -*o* endings are either neuter or masculine; and those with -*e*, and -*a* endings are neuter (a residual type of neuter ending in -*a* uses the insertions -*at*- and -*en*- in the oblique cases).

Some cases have two endings for the same inflectional type. Sometimes the second endings are relics of old usage and are employed in certain particular words (especially in the nom pl: eg, *vuxa* from *vuxo* 'ear', but *oči* from *oko* 'eye'), or are determined by certain suffixes (eg, the vocative *konju* from *kin'* 'horse', but *xlopče* from *xlopec'* 'boy'; the loc sing *na jazyci* from *jazyk* 'tongue', but *na dubku* from *dubok* 'oaklet'), or by accent (the gen sing *do stolá* and *do stólu* from *stil* 'table'). Sometimes their use depends on semantic categories. The chief of these, although they do not affect the endings consistently, are the personal category (eg, acc sing *baču komyn* 'I see a chimney' vs *baču xlopcja* 'I see a boy', but also *baču duba* 'I see an oak'; the loc sing *na xlopcevi* from *xlopec'* 'boy' vs *na kinci* from *kinec'* 'end'), and the category of 'having form' (wholeness) as opposed to 'lack of form' (eg, gen sing *učnja, metra, cvjaxa* from *učen'* 'pupil', *metr* 'meter', *cvjax* 'nail', but *nastupu, jačmenju* from *nastup* 'advance', *jačmin'* 'barley').

In the adjectival-pronominal declension the number and gender, as well as the case, have a purely formal function, as a means of agreement. This declension has only one type for all words, except for a few variations in certain forms of the pronoun (eg, fem gen sing *čornoji, syn'oji, jakoji* from *čornyj* 'black', *synij* 'blue', *jakyj* 'which', but *cijeji, tijeji, čyjeji* from *cej* 'this', *toj* 'that', *čyj* 'whose'), and always keeps the accent in the same place throughout the entire paradigm (with a few exceptions in some pronouns). The pronouns *ja* 'I', *ty* 'thou', *my* 'we', *vy* 'you', and *sebe* 'oneself' do not belong to this type; they have a suppletive declension (eg, *ja* 'I', gen *mene*, instr *mnoju*). The pronouns *vin* 'he', *xto* 'who', and *ščo* 'what' belong to the adjective declension in indirect cases but have another root in the nominative (*vin – joho, xto – koho, ščo – čoho*).

In Ukrainian the moods of the verb are relatively underdeveloped and undifferentiated. They include the indicative, which expresses real and often unreal actions; the conditional, which expresses both potential and unreal actions; and the imperative. The tenses are even less

developed and distinct. Neither the conditional, the infinitive, nor the participle has tense forms, and in the indicative the present is often used to denote also the future and the past. Conjugation is limited practically to the present tense, and persons are indicated chiefly by endings containing consonants: -*š* in the second person singular, -*t'* (or the simple stem) in the third person singular, -*mo* in the first person plural, and -*te* in the second person plural; these consonants are usually preceded by the vowels -*e*- or -*y*-, which are distinguished only if stressed. The third person plural is marked by -*t'* preceded by -*u*- or -*a*- (eg, *berut', kryčat'* from *braty* 'to take', *kryčaty* 'to shout'). The first person singular has the ending -*u*. Only three verbs have a different conjugation: *jisty* 'to eat', *daty* 'to give', and *(rozpo)visty* 'to tell' (*jim, jisy, jist', jimo, jiste, jidjat'*). The verb *buty* 'to be' has no personal forms in the present: *je(st')* is used for all persons.

The personal form is used chiefly in agreement with the subject. The past tense and the more rarely used pluperfect (which actually shows an impeded action), however, lack personal forms and agree (in the singular) with the gender of the subject (eg, *vin upav* 'he fell', *vona upala* 'she fell', *vono upalo* 'it fell'). The future tense of imperfective verbs is formed from the infinitive + the future tense of the verb *buty* 'to be' or by the consonant -*m*- with the usual personal endings added to the infinitive (eg, *budu braty* or *bratymu* 'I shall take', *budeš braty* or *bratymeš* 'thou shall take'). The conditional mood is formed from the past indicative + the particle *b(y)*. The second person singular and first and second person plural of the imperative are used as a rule without a subject. In the singular the imperative has the ending -*y* when the ending is accented, and a zero ending when the accent is on the root; similarly, in the plural the endings are -*im(o)* and -*it'* or -*mo* and -*te* (eg, *berý, berím, berít'* from *braty* 'to take', *stan', stán'mo, stán'te* from *staty* 'to stand').

The typical system of the Slavic verb with its two stems – the infinitive stem (the infinitive, the past, and the conditional mood, originally aorist-stem) and the present-tense stem (the present tense, the future of perfective verbs, the imperative) – has been retained in Ukrainian but is greatly simplified in many verbs. The infinitive ends in -*ty* (eg, *braty* 'to take', *mohty* 'to be able to', *pekty* 'to bake'). The only widely used participles are passive ones in -*nyj, -tyj*, and non-passive -*lyj* (eg, *vzjatyj* from *vzjaty* 'to take', *davanyj* from *davaty* 'to give', *rozkvitlyj* from *rozkvitnuty* 'to bloom'). There are also indeclinable gerunds in -*čy* and -*šy* (eg, *beručy, bravšy* from *braty* 'to take') and an indeclinable impersonal form in -*no* or -*to* (eg, *prošeno*, from *prosyty* 'to ask', *vzjato*, from *vzjaty* 'to take').

The only really productive category running through all forms of the verb is the aspect – perfective and imperfective. In principle every verb is found in these two aspects, which are formed by the use of different suffixes and prefixes or, less frequently, by accent changes. The iterative meaning is usually not expressed independently and is not distinguished from the usual durative form.

Structure of utterance. All utterances are characterized by an intonation appropriate to the character of the message. The organization of utterances consisting of more than one word relies on grammatical ties and word order. The more obvious these principles of organization, the weaker the intonation, whose role is essentially facultative. There are two kinds of grammatical ties, agreement and government. Agreement takes place between adjectives, including adjectival pronouns and some numerals, and substantives, and between verbs and the nouns that serve as sentence subjects. It is manifested in the categories of case, number, gender (where applicable), and person (when the verb applies to a personal pronoun); eg, *mala rička* 'small river', *maloji ričky* gen sing, *male misto* 'small city', *mali mista* nom pl, *dytyna plače* 'the child cries', *dity plačut'* 'the children cry', *ty plačeš* 'thou art crying'. Government is based on the fact that to convey a certain meaning words may have an inherent requirement for a certain case, or for a certain preposition and the case form, of the dependent noun; eg, *braty* + acc, *xotity* + gen; ie, *beru čaj* 'I take (some) tea', *xoču čaju* 'I want (some) tea'. Government can also require the infinitive, but since the infinitive is not declined, one can speak here of zero-government; eg, *xoču pyty* 'I am thirsty', literally 'I want to drink'. Likewise, if adjectives are replaced with adverbs, which cannot be inflected, one can speak of zero-agreement; eg, *micne koxannja* 'strong love' – *micno koxaje* 'he/she loves strongly'. Agreement and government run through all constituent words in an utterance and make it a syntactic unity, often to a redundant degree.

As a rule, endings bear the grammatical ties between words. Except in formal expressions, therefore, a fixed word order in utterances did not develop in Ukrainian. It is mandatory only for prepositions to precede nominal phrases (eg, *na stoli* 'on the table'); for conjunctions to stand between the phrases they connect (*bat'ko j syn* 'father and son'); and for some particles to stand initially (*xaj skaže* 'let him say'), others to succeed the first word in an utterance (*Otake to stalosja* 'That is what happened'), and still others to precede the word to which they refer (*til'ky ty* 'only thou'). Otherwise one can order words in an utterance with relative freedom. In the neutral word order the subject precedes the predicate (eg, *vin ide* 'he goes'), governing words precede governed words (*beru kartu* 'I take the map'), and adjectives precede their substantives (*bilyj budynok* 'white building'). Statistically, however, this is not the prevalent order, particularly in the case of the subject-predicate order. Often it is replaced by the emphatic word order, in which the most important word appears at the end of the utterance (eg, *Ne znaju, jak dovho tam lyšatymet'sja nadija*, literally 'I do not know how long there will remain hope'). In narrations of parallel events it is replaced by the narrative word order, in which the predicate is at the beginning of the sentence (eg, *Svitylo sonce, kryčaly ptaxy, vijav viterec'*, literally 'Shone the sun, called the birds, blew the wind').

The use of passive and possessive types of sentences is limited in Ukrainian. Impersonal sentences of various types, however, are extensively used. While as a rule the subject is in the nominative case, in impersonal sentences it is in the dative (eg, *Meni sumno* 'I am sad') or the instrumental; the latter occurs in such subjectless sentences as *Napysano stattju* 'The article is written', which may be, but is usually not, supplemented by the agent in the instr: *Petrom* 'by Peter'). Certain unproductive impersonal sentences do not admit any mention of an agent (eg, *Smerkaje* 'Dusk is falling').

Vocabulary. The circumstances in which Standard Ukrainian evolved have largely determined the peculiarities of its vocabulary. It did not develop in an urban environment; hence, it is based mostly on the peasant vernacular. In the second half of the 19th century many writers modeled their language as a matter of principle on rural folk speech. This 'populist' trend accounts for the highly developed vocabulary in Standard Ukrainian of rural life and labor, in which synonyms abound. A great number of locutions are obviously of peasant origin: eg, *u kopy vklasty* 'to make up into sheaves = to beat [mercilessly]', *mov korova zlyzala jazykom* 'as if a cow had licked it up with her tongue = disappeared without a trace'.

In the absence of a single urban center whose spoken Ukrainian could serve as a model for the literary language, the intelligentsia relatively frequently absorbed expressions of local and foreign origin into their vernacular. As a result many words with the same meaning as already accepted words passed into the literary language (eg, *čoven* and *lodka* 'boat', *misto* and *hórod* 'city', *pojizd* and *potjah* 'train'). Many such words are considered localisms and are used only to provide local color (eg, western Ukrainian *gazda* for the standard *hospodar* 'master of the house', and *kryminal* for *vjaznycja* 'prison'); many others are accepted as having equal stylistic status (eg, southeastern Ukrainian *leleka*, northeastern *čornohuz*, and western *busol* and *buz'ko* 'stork').

Many words, including synonyms connected with concepts of urban life, entered Ukrainian standard vocabulary not via peasant dialects but from the languages of nations bordering on or ruling various Ukrainian territories. Thus Ukrainian, which originally showed little social differentiation, has gradually evolved into a language based on the speech of (1) the peasantry, (2) the intelligentsia and professionals, (3) neighboring colonizing nations, and (4) various urban social groups (*jargon and *slang).

After the 1917 Revolution, concerted efforts to develop a scientific and technical *terminology based on the popular language were made, particularly by special terminological institutes affiliated with the All-Ukrainian Academy of Sciences. Since the onset of Stalinism, however, the application of this terminology has been hampered and even paralyzed by the Soviet policy of linguistic *Russification. Nonetheless, the vocabulary and phraseology of modern literary Ukrainian have developed far beyond their rural origins and constitute a rich and complex system derived from various linguistic sources.

Today the vocabulary of Standard Ukrainian has two characteristic features. (1) It is relatively close to the speech of the people without being confined to the language spoken in any one locality. At first Standard Ukrainian developed mainly from the dialects of the Poltava and southern Kiev regions. Soon, however, quite a few words from other dialects, particularly those of Galicia via the Galician intelligentsia, were absorbed into it. Hence, its vocabulary ceased to be connected with any one dialect or dialectal group, although Kiev-Poltava elements still undoubtedly predominate. The Galician dialects have contributed a particularly large number of abstract terms, names of objects, and words associated with urban life (eg, *zasada* 'principle', *vlastyvist'* 'peculiarity', *zarozumilist'* 'arrogance', *vidčuvaty* 'to feel', *rozpuka* 'despair'). As a result, certain homonyms arose (eg, *aby* 'if only' and 'in order'; *vidčyt* 'account' and 'lecture'). (2) Ukrainian includes many loan words, particularly from German, Turkish, Tatar, and Polish, and in more recent times many Europeanisms, especially with Latin or Greek components (eg, *konto* 'account', *kolit* 'colitis', *akcija* 'action', *demokratija* 'democracy', *pilot* 'pilot', and *generator* 'generator'). (In general, the number of borrowings has far exceeded the number of loan translations and neologisms replacing foreign words, a point on which Ukrainian differs significantly from Czech, for example.) These words have usually had a nominative function and have gradually undergone the normal course of phonetic, morphological, and other forms of naturalization; hence they, do not have a special stylistic function that would cause them to stand out, even when they have autochthonous synonyms (eg, *evoljucija – rozvytok* 'evolution', *avijacija – litunstvo* 'aviation'). In this respect Ukrainian is fundamentally different from such double-layered languages as Russian, with its Church Slavonic elements, and English, with its Latin and French elements. For stylistic expression, it has drawn more on its own resources than on a blend with another literary language. Certain 20th-century poets have introduced Church Slavonicisms into their poetic language (eg, M. Bazhan: *brennyj* 'perishable', *suščyj* 'real', *lža* 'lie', *lanyta* 'cheek', and M. Orest: *rekty* 'to speak', *diva* 'virgin', and *stokrat* 'a hundred times'), but few of these have been incorporated into the vernacular. Church Slavonicisms, like other foreign elements, in Ukrainian have had for the most part specifically nominative functions and have been used mainly to express church or religious concepts (eg, *vladyka* 'bishop', *xram* 'temple', *svjaščennyj* 'sacred'). By and large the poetic genres in Modern Standard Ukrainian are distinguished by semantics and imagery rather than by peculiarities of vocabulary. The total number of words in contemporary Ukrainian is about 150,000.

Historical development

Proto-Ukrainian (6th to mid-11th century AD). The formative period of Proto-Ukrainian began with the appearance of distinctive features in the dialects of *Common Slavic spoken in and west of the middle Dnieper Basin that were not shared entirely with adjacent Slavic dialects. Ukrainian arose as a separate language through the accumulation of such features. Phonological changes during the disintegration of Common Slavic resulted in a reduction of the number of vowels from 20 in late Common Slavic to 9 in Proto-Ukrainian and an increase of consonants from 15 to 30 or 31. Most of these changes also occurred in other Slavic dialects, but they differed in essential details, which delimited the Proto-Ukrainian dialects from all adjacent ones; for example, the labialized character of *b* distinguished the Proto-Ukrainian dialects from Proto-Polish ones; the preservation of *i* and the rise of *y* (from *ĭ, ŭ*) before *j* distinguished them from Proto-Russian dialects; the differentiation of *o* and *a* in unstressed syllables distinguished them from Proto-Belarusian dialects; and the reflexation of *ě* as *ie* (later *ė*) in the southwest Proto-Ukrainian dialects distinguished them from all adjacent dialects, as well as from the northern Proto-Ukrainian dialects.

The most important phonetic changes in the Proto-Ukrainian dialects (many of which, but not all, were shared with some adjacent Slavic dialects) were (1) the rise of *y* from *ū*, (2) the rise of *jers (ъ* and *ь*) from *u* and *i* respectively, (3) the rise of an only short *o* and only long *a* and the subsequent loss of phonemic length and pitch, (4) the palatalization of consonants before *ь* and *ě*, and (5) the rise of so-called pleophony.

The roots of the oldest dialectal features can be traced back to the Proto-Ukrainian period. The Rus' Primary Chronicle mentions seven Slavic tribes that inhabited Ukraine's territory: the Siverianians, Polianians, Dulibians, Derevlianians, Ulychians, Tivertsians, and White Croatians. It is not known whether or not each tribe had its own dialectal peculiarities; there is, however, a clear difference between the dialects of Polisia as far south as Kiev on the one hand, and those of Galicia and Podilia on the other. The northern dialects preserved *kv* before *ě* (from Indo-European *oi*; eg, *kvit* vs the southern dialectal *cvit* 'flower'), preserved or restored *sk* before *ě* (eg, *po dъskě* vs the southern *dъscě* 'on board'), and went farther than the southern dialects in replacing *ǯ* by *ž* (*meža* vs the southern *meǯa* 'boundary'). The northern dialects depalatalized soft *r*; conditioned several changes in vowels by stress (eg, *ę* > 'a* if stressed but *e* if unstressed: *p'atь* 'five', but *petý* gen); and modified *e* before a weak *ъ*, which change later resulted in a diphthong under stress (eg, *neslъ* > *néslъ* > *n'ᵤos* 'he carried', but *metъlà* 'broom', Standard Ukrainian = *nis, mitla*). Presumably, the opposition between the northern and southern dialects arose before they were united in what is now Ukrainian. A process of integration (not of differentiation, as with later Ukrainian dialects) occurred, probably for historical reasons – the political dominance of Kiev and, later, mass migrations caused by the invasions of various Turkic tribes.

In morphology, the Proto-Ukrainian dialects inherited fairly complicated systems of declension and conjugation from Common Slavic. In declension, substantives had several types of inflection with seven cases (nominative, genitive, dative, accusative, instrumental, locative, and vocative) and three numbers (singular, dual, plural). Each substantive was assigned to a gender (masculine, feminine, and neuter), but the choice of ending was based not on gender but, as inherited from Indo-European, on stems, originally shown by the component that stood between the ending proper and the preceding part of the word, be it the root or a suffix. There were several basic types of stems: *o, jo, u, i, a, ja,* and consonantal *r, s, n, nt,* and *ū*. Because of morphological levelings and, especially, phonetic changes, however, the distinction between stems had already become obscure in Common Slavic and was later obliterated, so it was only by tradition that the distinction was maintained. Thus, the shift of nouns from one group of stems to another and of specific case endings from one stem-type to another began. Since confusions in stem are quite frequent in the oldest extant manuscripts, it can be assumed that the shifts began well into the Proto-Ukrainian period; eg, the original *u*-stem *synъ* 'son' (cf Lithuanian and Old Indian *sūn-u-s*), which in the genitive singular should have the ending *-u*, appears in the *Izbornik* of Sviatoslav (1073) in two forms, the old *synu* and the new *syna*, transferred from the *o*-stems. Such switches were particularly frequent in nouns of the same gender, and the result was an extensive rearrangement of the declensional types on the basis of gender, a process that even now is not quite complete. The fastest reshuffling occurred in consonantal stems.

The adjective had two types of declension: (1) the nominal, that is, the same as in the substantive, most often of masculine and neuter *o*-stems and of feminine *a*-stems; and (2) the pronominal, in which the demonstrative pronoun *i (jь)* was added to the nominal form in the same case as the latter, with subsequent simplifications. For example, the nominal *malъ* 'small' became the pronominal *malъ*

+ *jъ* 'that small [child, etc]', in the genitive singular masculine *mala* + *jego*, hence *malajego, malaago*, and, under the influence of the 'hard' pronominal declension (*togo*), later *malogo/maloho*.

The verb had five tenses – present, perfect, imperfect, aorist, and pluperfect – but no single form for the future tense, which was conveyed periphrastically by means of such auxiliary verbs as *imu* 'take', *xoču* 'wish', and *načьnu* 'begin' + the infinitive. There was also a well-developed system of participles: present active (eg, *moga* masc, *moguči* fem), past active (*nesъ* masc, *nesъši* fem), and passive in -*mъ*, -*tъ*, and -*nъ*. The moods were the indicative, conditional (*byxъ neslъ* 'I would carry'), and imperative. Besides the infinitive (*nesti* 'to carry') there was the supine, which was used after verbs of motion in space (*nestъ*). This rather complicated system, which had arisen in Common Slavic and differed essentially from Indo-European, was fairly well preserved in the Proto-Ukrainian dialects and carried over into the 12th century.

Old Ukrainian (mid-11th to late 14th century). The period of Old Ukrainian dates from the same time as the oldest extant Rus' texts and coincides with the rise and fall of Kievan Rus'. The year 1387, when Polish supremacy over Galicia and Lithuanian supremacy over most of Ukraine were firmly established, can be considered a conventional cutoff date.

The phonetic changes during this period were (1) the transformation (ca 1125) of *y* into *i* after the velars *g, k*, and *x* (eg, *ruky > ruki* 'hands'), a change limited at the time to northern Ukraine; (2) the spirantization (ca 1200) of *g* (*g* > *h*), which occurred on all of Ukrainian territory (eg, *noga* > *noha* 'foot'); (3) the dispalatalization in the 13th century of labials in the syllable- and word-final position (eg, *holub'* > *holub* 'pigeon'); and (4) the change (ca 1260 in the territory stretching from Bukovyna to western Volhynia) of *i* into a vowel intermediate between *i* and *y* (denoted in the modern Ukrainian alphabet by the letter *и*).

The most consequential sound change in the Old Ukrainian period was the loss of the jers. This loss had occurred in some positions earlier, but it reached its culmination between 1144 (the year of the *Halych Gospel, which reflects the old situation) and 1161 (the year of the inscriptions on the Cross of Princess Eufrosiniia of Polatsk, which reflects the new situation). The jers were treated in two ways and accordingly are labeled weak or strong: the former were lost without replacement, and the latter coalesced with either *e* (*ь*) or *o* (*ъ*). The jers were strong before *r* and *l* between consonants (eg, *vьrxa* 'top' gen sing, *tъrga* 'market' gen sing > *verxa, torga*) and before a syllable containing a weak jer (eg, *sъnъ* 'sleep', *dьnь* 'day' > *son, den'*). All other jers were weak.

Among the many consequences of the loss of the jers, the most important were (1) the introduction of closed syllables and zero morphemes; (2) the alternation of *e* and *o* with ø; (3) the appearance of numerous consonant clusters, many of which were gradually simplified in the course of development; (4) a growth in the functional load of the opposition of nonpalatalized and palatalized consonants; (5) the alternation of *v*- with *u*- (eg, *vnuk : unuk* 'grandson'); (6) the change -*e* > -*a* in the sequence -*ьje* (eg, *zelьje* 'grass' > *zilja*, Standard Ukrainian *zillja*); and (7) the change of *o* and *e* before a syllable in which a jer was lost (eg, *stolъ* 'table' and *pečь* 'stove'). The last change proceeded differently in southern and northern Ukrainian. In the

south, *e* and *o* in the given position were narrowed (marked sometimes in linguistic studies as *ė* and *ȯ*), and so began an evolution that resulted in *i* in modern Ukrainian and gave rise to the alternation of *i* with *e* and *o* (eg, *stil : stola* gen sing, *pič : peči*). In the north, *e* and *o* in the given position, but only under stress, diphthongized into ᵢe and ᵤo respectively and later were further modified; *e* changed before *ъ* only if *ъ* was originally stressed (eg, *neslȯ* 'carried' vs *médъ* 'honey', modern northern Ukrainian *n'ᵤos, med*).

In Old Ukrainian manuscripts the changes in *e* and *o* are reflected differently. The new reflexes of *e* coalesced with the pronounciation of *ě* (*jat'*), and from 1161 they were often spelled as *ě* (*ѣ*). This so-called new *jat'* was henceforth the most typical earmark of Ukrainian manuscripts. There was no way of marking directly the new reflexes of *o* in the traditional alphabet, and this change remained unmarked until the 14th century, when some scribes began using the letter omega (*ω*) for that purpose (it first appeared in the Hankenstein Codex).

No changes as sweeping as this occurred in Old Ukrainian morphology. In the nominal declension the adaptation of the excess of inherited endings to genders continued. The zero ending in the genitive plural was preserved in feminines in -*a*, but tended to be eliminated in masculines (eg, *zimъ* 'winters' vs *běsovъ* 'devils'). In the genitive singular differentiation on the basis of semantic categories took place: the *o*-stem ending -*a* gradually became reserved for substantives denoting concrete and shaped objects, while the *u*-stem -*u* was applied to abstract and shapeless objects. The category of person became clear in the accusative singular (but not plural) where the genitive was introduced in names of human beings (eg, *jesi slěpilъ brata* 'you blinded your brother', the older form being *bratъ* as in the nom). Use of the dual remained strong in substantives, but by the end of the Old Ukrainian period its use had declined in verbs and virtually disappeared in pronouns.

In conjugation two uniquely Ukrainian features emerged. (1) In the 12th century the generalization of *ě* in plural endings of the imperative began (eg, *xvalěte* 'praise'; originally *ě* characterized only class 1 and 2 verbs, while class 3 and 4 verbs had *i*). (2) The verb 'to be' took the ending -*mo* in the first person plural (*jesmo*), and this ending later spread to all verbs. In the 13th century use of the imperfect and aorist began declining, and probably by or in the 14th century they were no longer used in the spoken language. In the 14th century the supine was lost; the ending -*š* in the second person singular of the present tense spread at the expense of the older ending -*ši* (eg, *meteš* instead of *meteši* 'you sweep'); and in the future tense the forms using the auxiliary first person *budu* ('will be' + *l*-participle) and *imu* ('take' + infinitive) crowded out the constructions using *xoču* ('want') and *počьnu* ('will begin'). These developments reflected the tendency of speakers to simplify the morphological system while preserving its essentially conservative character.

Syntax also remained rather conservative, although the use of prepositional phrases, hypotactic constructions, and the instrumental of predication instead of cases in agreement increased. Judging by the extant texts, however, older constructions prevailed.

Owing to extensive contacts with Central Europe and the Turkic peoples of the steppe, many loanwords were added to the vocabulary of Old Ukrainian. The political and religious influence of the Byzantine Empire in Rus', in particular, resulted in the mass borrowing of Greek words and phrases through direct absorption, loan translations (eg, *blahoslovyty* 'to bless' based on the Greek *eulogeō*), and semantic adaptation. Most of these borrowings, however, did not penetrate into the spoken language of the uneducated masses; others were lost later, after the fall of Constantinople and the reorientation of Ukrainian culture toward Western Europe. Yet their general impact on the flexibility of Ukrainian cannot be denied.

Internecine strife among the princes of Rus' and the Mongol invasions of the 13th and 14th centuries gave rise to the westward migration of much of the population of central and northern Ukraine, a general decentralization of national life, and, consequently, the formation of western and northwestern Ukrainian dialects, for example, the *Dniester, *Sian, *Boiko, and *Lemko dialects in the 13th century, and the western *Polisian, *Bukovyna-Pokutia, and *Hutsul dialects in the 14th century.

Early Middle Ukrainian. The period from the late 14th to the third quarter of the 16th century (conventional cutoff dates, 1387 and 1575) coincided with the consolidation of the Lithuanian-Ruthenian state in most of Ukraine, except in Polish-ruled Galicia and Hungarian-ruled Transcarpathia, and with the rise of the Cossacks. Regular incursions by the Crimean Tatars again forced the Ukrainian population to migrate west and northwest, and by the beginning of the 16th century Zhytomyr, Kiev, and Oster marked the eastern and southern boundary of Ukraine. The influx of most of the Ukrainian-speaking population into a relatively small territory and their subsequent return as Cossack settlers to central Ukraine and expansion into the formerly uncolonized southern and eastern regions left a lasting imprint on the Ukrainian language and assured the relative uniformity of Ukrainian throughout a vast territory, except in the most western and northern parts of Ukraine. The *South Volhynian, *Podilian, and central *Transcarpathian dialects can be traced back to this period, as can the split of most of the Polisian dialects into eastern and central variants (in the 16th century).

Most of the sound changes in this period arose in and were limited to the southern part of the reduced Ukrainian populated territory; they did not spread to the north or the Carpathian region. The most important consonant changes were (1) the alteration *l* > *w* before a consonant after an *o* that originated from *ъ* (eg, *vьlkъ* > *vo[w]k*, now spelled *vovk* 'wolf'); (2) the absorption of *j* by the preceding dental or postdental, resulting in long palatalized dentals and postdentals (eg, *[zil'ja]* > *[zill'a]* 'herb', *[zbižž'a]* 'grain'); and (3) the beginning of dispalatalization of (short) postdentals, which had been soft since their appearance in Common Slavic. The first of these changes arose in northern Ukraine and spread south and west only in the 17th century. The second originated in Bukovyna and gradually spread north. The third spread independently out from many centers.

The important vowel changes were (1) the complete merging of the older *i* and *y* in a middle sound, a change that did not affect the westernmost dialects apart from the Hutsul dialect; (2) the change of the reflex of *ě* into *i*, which stopped short of the borders of the eastern and central Polisian dialects; and (3) the change of *ȯ* (the reflex of *o* before a syllable with a weak jer) into *u* and further into *ü*

(eg, *kotъ* > *kȯt* > *kut* > *küt*, now *kit* 'cat'). (Since this *u* never coalesced with the original *u*, it may be denoted as u_2; it is a phenomenon of the southern dialects.) For the first time in the history of the southern dialects changes arose that were motivated by the stress or lack of it on a given syllable: (1) the assimilative change *o* > *a* before a syllable with a stressed *a* (eg, *bohátyj* > *bahátyj* 'rich'), which originated in the north and stopped short at the then Lithuanian-Polish border; (2) the change of unstressed *o* into *u* before a stressed *u* or (depending on the dialect) in all unstressed syllables (eg, *zozúlja* 'cuckoo', pronounced *[zuzúl'a]*); and (3) the merging of unstressed *e* and *y*, which today characterizes the standard language and all dialects except the eastern and central Polisian.

The most important morphological changes took place in declension. Because of the coalescence of *y* and *i*, masculine substantives, originally of *o*-stems, lost the distinction between the nominative and the accusative plural, except those with stems ending in *k*, *x*, and *h*: for example, previously the nominative plural of *sad* 'garden' and *dux* 'spirit' was *sadi* and *dusi*, and the accusative plural was *sady* and *duxy*; now the distinction was lost entirely between *sadi* and *sady*, and limited to the consonant alternation in *dusi* ~ *duxy*: *sady*, *dusy*, *duxy*. Subsequently, the alternation of consonants in the nominative plural was eliminated, and the two case forms merged. Since feminines in -*a* also had the ending -*y* in both cases, this change in the masculines was tantamount to the obliteration of masculine-feminine gender distinctions in the plural. Accordingly, a trend toward uniform endings, mostly in *o*- and *a*-stems and occasionally in *i*-stems, in the dative, instrumental, and locative plural arose; for example, instead of *sadom*, *sady*, and *saděx* use of the forms *sadam*, *sadamy*, and *sadax* started expanding. Gender unification among plurals extended also to adjectives.

These processes did not reach completion in the Early Middle Ukrainian period, but the trends were clearly discernible. Other significant developments included the spread, except in the northern dialects, of the ending -*ovy* in the dative singular of masculines (eg, *sadovy* 'orchard'); the replacement of the accusative plural by genitive plural forms in nouns denoting persons (eg, *znaju bratenyky* by *znaju bratenykuv* 'I know the brothers'); and the elimination of -*y* in monovocalic endings of soft substantives (eg, *na zemly* was replaced by *na zemli* 'on the ground').

In syntax the notable changes were (1) the transformation of active participles into indeclinable gerunds, (2) the expansion of the instrumental predicative, and (3) the rise of the impersonal sentence with the predicate ending in -*no* or -*to* based on the passive participle but capable of taking a direct object in the accusative case (eg, *prystavnyka oskarženo* 'the doorman was accused', 1556).

In the vocabulary of this period, the influences of Lithuanian (mostly via Belarusian) were insignificant, and Belarusian influences themselves were not strong, even though most of Ukraine and Belarus were part of the Grand Duchy of Lithuania. Military and peaceful encounters with the Crimean Tatars, however, particularly after an organized Cossack military had been established, resulted in the absorption of quite a few Turkic words, especially military and commercial terms, into the common language. The most significant development was the expansion of borrowing from Polish, and from Latin, German, and Czech, often via Polish. Loanwords from these languages influenced much more than just Ukrainian administrative, commercial, and cultural terminology: they often replaced established words in the basic vocabulary. As a result of this trend, which continued with undiminished strength for a century and a half, the vocabulary of Ukrainian became closer to that of West Slavic than to that of Russian or Church Slavonic.

Middle Ukrainian. This period began with the consolidation of Polish rule throughout Ukraine after the Union of Lublin (1569), except in Transcarpathia and a small Muscovite-ruled northeastern region, and included the Cossack rebellions, the Cossack-Polish War of 1648–57, the rise and decline of the Cossack Hetman state, and the curtailment of Ukrainian autonomy under Russian rule (conventional cutoff dates, 1575 and 1720). The most significant linguistic development in this period was the formation, on a vast territory, of the southeastern dialect, which later served as the foundation of Modern Standard Ukrainian. This dialect arose in the middle Dnieper Basin and gradually spread southward to the Azov and Black seas as the steppes were settled by speakers of the southwestern and northern dialects. Political turmoil and population mobility created conditions that were conducive to the intermingling of new settlers and to the creation of a relatively uniform new 'synthetic' dialect.

In phonology the major development was the change of *ü* into *i*, which introduced the alternation *o : i* (eg, Old Ukrainian *kotъ* > *ku₂t* > *küt* > *kit : kota* gen sing 'cat'), one of the most striking features of modern Ukrainian (the earliest documentation of it dates from 1653). The consonants /g/, /ʒ/, and /ǯ/ were introduced and/or stabilized to a certain degree during this period. With these two developments the formation of the phonemic and morphophonemic systems of modern Ukrainian was basically completed, and thereafter only minor changes and adjustments took place: (1) the partial dispalatalization of *c'*; (2) the change *e > o* after palatalized dentals before a non-palatalized consonant (eg, *len > l'on* 'flax', *semyj > s'omyj* 'seventh') typical of the southeastern dialects; (3) the dispalatalization of *r'* in the southwestern dialects (except for some Carpathian dialects); (4) the reintroduction ca 1640 of *k* and *h* in the infinitives of verbs of the modern type (eg, *stryhty* from the older *stryčy* 'to cut hair'; and (5) the generalization ca 1720 of *č* and *ž* in the present tense of these verbs (*stryžu* 1st pers sing from the older *stryhu* 1st pers sing, *stryžeš* 2nd pers sing).

In morphology several earlier developments became stabilized, and in some cases of competition one competing variant was eliminated. Although they were not limited to the southeastern dialects, these processes were typical of them: (1) the consistent elimination of the ending *y* in the dative-locative of substantives of the soft declension (eg, *na zemli* instead of *na zemly* 'on the ground') and the expansion of this *-i* to the *-ovy* ending of masculine substantives (eg, *bratovy > bratovi* 'brother'); (2) the acceptance of the form *ščo* 'what' in place of the older *što*; (3) the stabilization of the verbal ending *-mo* in the first person plural of the present tense (eg, *nesemo* 'we carry'); (4) the replacement of *-te* after a vowel in the second plural imperative by *-t'* (eg, *nesit'* 'carry'); (5) the stabilization of past tense forms (original perfect) without an auxiliary verb (eg, *ja brav* instead of the older *bral jesmъ* 'I took'); and (6) in the interaction of the adjectival and pronominal declensions, the replacement of disyllabic by monosyllabic

and trisyllabic by disyllabic endings (eg, *malaja > mala* 'small' nom sing fem, *malajeho > maloho* gen sing masc), which except for a few relics led to the decline of nominal forms of adjectives of the type *mal* (nom sing masc).

By the end of the Middle Ukrainian period the morphological system of the southeastern dialects was almost identical to that of Modern Standard Ukrainian, while the peripheral northern and southwestern dialects to a large extent still preserved the old forms. The syntactic norms of the spoken language did not differ any more substantially from modern Ukrainian either. In vocabulary the language of the Middle Ukrainian period continued to be open to Western, particularly Polish and Latin, influences, even at the height of Ukrainian-Polish political conflicts. In fact, Polish lexical and phraseological influences persisted, although in attenuated form, until the first quarter of the 20th century.

(For developments in the Ukrainian language after 1720, see *Standard Ukrainian.)

BIBLIOGRAPHY

Smal-Stockyj, S.; Gartner, T. *Grammatik der ruthenischen (ukrainischen) Sprache* (Vienna 1913)

Buzuk, P. *Narys istoriï ukraïns'koï movy* (Kiev 1927; photoreprint, Munich 1985)

Tymchenko, Ie. *Kurs istoriï ukraïns'koho iazyka* (Kiev 1927; 2nd edn [censored], Kiev–Kharkiv 1930)

Smal'-Stots'kyi, S. *Ukraïns'ka mova, ïï pochatky, rozvytok i kharakter, ïï prykmety* (Lviv 1933)

Zhytets'kyi, P. *Narys literaturnoï istoriï ukraïns'koï movy v XVII vitsi* (Lviv 1941)

De Bray, R.G.A. *Guide to the Slavonic Languages* (London 1951)

Bulakhovs'kyi, L. *Pytannia pokhodzhennia ukraïns'koï movy* (Kiev 1956)

Kovaliv, P. *Leksychnyi fond literaturnoï movy kyïvs'koho periodu X–XIV st.* (New York 1962)

Hol'denberh, L.; Korolevych, N. *Ukraïns'ka mova: Bibliohrafichnyi pokazhchyk (1918–1961 rr.)* (Kiev 1963)

Bulakhovs'kyi, L. *Vybrani pratsi v piaty tomakh*, vol 2, *Ukraïns'ka mova* (Kiev 1977)

AN URSR Instytut movoznavstva im. O.O. Potebni. *Istoriia ukraïns'koï movy*, 4 vols (Kiev 1978–83)

Shevelov, G.Y. *A Historical Phonology of the Ukrainian Language* (Heidelberg 1979)

Zilyns'kyj, I. *A Phonetic Description of the Ukrainian Language* (Cambridge, Mass 1979)

G.Y. Shevelov

Language legislation. The body of laws, decrees, instructions, and other administrative acts that define the status of the official language and the minority languages within a society, and particularly in the administration, the courts, and education. Language legislation in the modern sense has developed since the 19th century, mostly in multinational states, and has been involved in the cultural and political rebirth of stateless nations.

The status of the Ukrainian language on Ukrainian territories was defined, except during Ukraine's brief period of independence, by foreign powers. In the Russian Empire there was no special legislation on language; Russian was the only language of government. The languages of the so-called *inorodtsi* (Poles, Finns, and Transcaucasian peoples) were admitted to some extent in the church, the courts, and the schools. Ukrainian did not have even these limited rights: it was prohibited by P. *Valuev's circular (1863) and by the *Ems Ukase (1876). When censorship was abolished in 1905, the ban on Ukrainian publications was lifted for a brief period. Subsequently, administrative measures were used to restrict the role of the Ukrainian language in the press and at public meetings. Russian continued to be the language of instruction in schools for the Ukrainian population. Representations to the State Duma and the administration in defense of Ukrainian proved fruitless (see *Language policy.)

Under Austrian rule the legal status of Ukrainian remained undefined for a long time. Although Ukrainian was recognized as a regional language in 1786, German and Polish predominated in government and in the school system in Galicia, and German and Rumanian in Bukovyna. After the 1848 Revolution laws and decrees were published in Ukrainian in the two provinces. The 1867 Constitution recognized the equality of all the peoples of Austria and their 'right to preserve and cultivate their national traditions and language,' but this recognition was not followed up with practical legislation. In practice, Polish was recognized as the official language of government and the courts in Galicia, and German remained the official language in Bukovyna. Ukrainian was admitted as a second regional language in the administration and the courts. On the local level, communities could choose the language in which they conducted their affairs, and Ukrainian communities usually chose Ukrainian. But the county administration in Galicia was conducted in Polish, and in Bukovyna in German. Ukrainian deputies to the Galician and Bukovynian diets had the right to address the assemblies and to make submissions in Ukrainian. The Galician Diet had the power to legislate the language of instruction in secondary schools, while local communities chose the language to be used in elementary schools.

In Transcarpathia under Hungarian rule, Hungarian was the official language of government, and local languages were tolerated, grudgingly, only in the lower courts. In 1848–9 Ukrainian was accepted to some extent as the official language in the so-called Ruthenian district. The school system, too, was subjected to Magyarization, which was officially approved in A. *Apponyi's law (1907).

In January 1919, Ukrainian was recognized by the Directory as the official language of the UNR, but the national minorities were guaranteed, by the law on *national-personal autonomy, broad linguistic rights (25 January 1918). The laws were published usually in Ukrainian and Russian, but the languages of other nationalities were acceptable in communications with government institutions. During the Hetman regime the government, in principle, was to have been run in Ukrainian, but many departments operated in Russian or in both Ukrainian and Russian. In the Western Province of the Ukrainian National Republic (ZO UNR), the official language law of 15 February 1919 recognized the right of national minorities (Poles, Jews, and Germans) to communicate with the government in their own languages. The education law of the ZO UNR (13 February 1919) granted minorities the right to conduct schools in their own languages.

In the interwar period different laws governed minority languages in the three parts of Western Ukraine – under Poland, Rumania, and Czechoslovakia. All three states were bound by international agreements to respect the rights of the Ukrainian language: Poland was bound by a treaty with the Entente (28 June 1919), the Peace Treaty of Riga (18 March 1921), and the decision of the Conference of Ambassadors (14 March 1923) approving Poland's annexation of eastern Galicia; Rumania, by the Treaty of Sèvres (10 August 1920); and Czechoslovakia, by the Treaty of Saint-Germain (10 September 1919).

In Poland the use of Ukrainian by administrative bodies was regulated by three special laws passed on 31 July 1924. Polish was to be used internally in government agencies, and Ukrainian was permitted only in oral or written representations to the county or voivodeship authorities in Lviv, Volhynia, Ternopil, Stanyslaviv, and Polisia voivodeships. The authorities had to answer such petitions in Polish and Ukrainian. Municipal councils were allowed to make their own decisions on the use of Ukrainian, and rural communities were to use the language of the petitioner and could keep records in two languages. Proclamations of local and higher government bodies were published in Ukrainian as well as in Polish. The law permitted the use of Ukrainian in the courts, the prosecutor's office, and notary offices for positions, testimonies, and lawyers' speeches. Judgments and other court documents could be prepared in Ukrainian as well as Polish, at the demand of the parties. The language of instruction in the schools was governed by a separate law (*Lex Grabski*): instruction could be in Ukrainian if the Ukrainian population of the community was at least 25 percent, or if the parents of 40 elementary-school or 150 secondary-school students demanded it. Ukrainian private schools were permitted. The details of language use were settled by executive order from the government or particular ministries. The actual use of Ukrainian in government was very different from what the law might lead one to expect. Only Polish was admitted in municipal and county government: positions were accessible only to Polish-speaking individuals. In Polisia, the Kholm region, and Podlachia, Ukrainian had, in fact, no rights. The Polish authorities did not respect the school legislation; hence, almost all Ukrainian schools became Polish or bilingual.

In Czechoslovakia the legislation with respect to Ukrainian was more liberal than anywhere else. In eastern Slovakia the law of 29 February 1920 granted Ukrainian the same rights as the languages of other national minorities, and in Subcarpathian Ruthenia (Transcarpathia), Ukrainian was the second official language. It was used consistently along with Czech in government communications with the public. Within the government it was used only at the lower, local, levels. Transcarpathia's autonomous diet was to define the official status of the Ukrainian language and decide which version of 'Ruthenian' – Ukrainian, Russian, or the artificial local language (*yazychiie) – was to be the official language. All three versions were tolerated in practice. In 1938–9 the autonomous government of Carpatho-Ukraine adopted literary Ukrainian as the official language. During the Hungarian occupation (1939–44) the rights of the local 'Ruthenian language' were restricted: it was used by officials only to communicate with the public (law of June 1939).

In territories under Rumania, Ukrainian was banned from government, the courts, and even the Orthodox church. The law of 26 July 1924, in particular, denied Ukrainians the status of a national minority and defined them as Rumanians who had forgotten their native tongue. In 1925 compulsory Rumanianization was introduced in the schools.

Until 1989 the Ukrainian SSR did not have a special law on language, only some general declarations about the equality of the different languages in the USSR, and the right of all citizens of Soviet Ukraine to use their native tongue (art 20 of the 1925 Constitution). Ukraine's Constitution of 1937 (art 101) guaranteed the use of Ukrainian in the schools. In fact, the use of Ukrainian, Russian, and other languages in Ukraine was governed by internal Party resolutions and instructions. Although Ukrainian was formally considered the official language, from the very beginning the laws have been published in both Ukrainian and Russian. Government business is conducted in either language, depending on what ministry a given agency comes under – a republican or a Union ministry. But even this criterion is not applied consistently. At the beginning of the Soviet period Russian was dominant. Starting in 1924, the government, the higher schools, and to some extent even the military were Ukrainized (see *Ukrainization). After 1933 Russian was reintroduced widely into the schools, the courts, local and oblast government, and republican ministries. Minority languages were widely used in local government and in the cultural life of national regions and rural soviets only until 1933 (see *Russification and *Language policy).

On 28 October 1989 the Supreme Soviet of the Ukrainian SSR passed the law 'On Languages in the Ukrainian SSR,' which gives official status to Ukrainian and provides for the gradual introduction of Ukrainian in legislation (along with Russian); in ministry and local-government decrees (in 3 to 5 years); in the internal work of government agencies, Party organs, and civic organizations and enterprises (in 3 to 5 years); in the court system along with minority languages (in 3 to 5 years); in international treaties and agreements, in the school system from kindergarten to higher educational institutions (according to parental choice, in 5 to 10 years); in scientific publications (alongside Russian); and in the mass media (alongside other languages). The bill guarantees the use of minority languages in the schools and local government of regions settled by national minorities. Russian is recognized as the language of international communication within and beyond Ukraine. The law is probably too weak to reverse the results of half a century of official Russification and discrimination against the Ukrainian language.

V. Markus

Language policy. Historically, rulers of multinational states have pursued policies aimed either at preserving the languages of all their constituent nations or, as in most cases, at raising the language of the dominant national group to a privileged and even exclusive status by restricting and sometimes forbidding the use of the other languages. In the latter case the stateless nations have tended to defend their languages as necessary factors in their collective survival.

Under Lithuanian and Polish rule. The language of government in the Grand Duchy of Lithuania, which after the disintegration of Kievan Rus' absorbed most of its lands, was Belarusian with a substantial infusion of Ukrainian. In Galicia and the Kholm region, which after the demise of the Principality of Galicia-Volhynia came under the rule of Poland, the language of government was Latin and, later, Polish. Thus in the 15th century Ukrainian was excluded almost entirely from the courts and government in these regions. Despite Polish guarantees set forth as preconditions to the Union of Lublin (1569) and reaffirmed several times (eg, in 1591 and, finally, in 1681), Polish authorities flouted the rights of Ukrainian and imposed Polish in the lands ceded by Lithuania to Poland under the union, in Volhynia, Podlachia, and the Kiev, Bratslav, and Chernihiv regions. For over a century Ukrainians actively defended their language. In 1569 and 1577, for example, the Ukrainian nobility of Volhynia and the Bratslav land sent protests to the Polish king. The so-called Constitutional Sejm finally passed a law in 1696 abolishing the use of Ukrainian in government administration. The language continued to be used only in the church.

Under Russian rule. Russian authorities adopted a restrictive policy toward Ukrainian even before the Pereiaslav Treaty of 1654: the ukases of 1627 and 1628 ordered books printed in Lithuania in the Ukrainian variant of Church Slavonic to be confiscated and burned. When the Kiev metropoly lost its autonomy in 1684, Ukrainian publications became subject to Russian censorship. In 1721 the Kievan Cave Monastery and the Chernihiv printing press were forbidden to print anything but church books, and these had to conform to Russian standards. Similar ukases were issued in 1727 and 1728. In 1735 books printed in Ukraine were banned from the churches, and the Russian pronunciation of Church Slavonic was imposed in the services. In the latter half of the 18th century Russian was introduced as the language of instruction at the Mohyla Academy and then other schools in Ukraine.

Starting with P. *Valuev's secret circular (1863), the Russian government tried to suppress the new Ukrainian literary language based on the vernacular. Declaring that 'there was not, is not, and can be no distinctive Little Russian language,' the minister forbade the printing of religious, scientific, and educational works in Ukrainian. The *Ems Ukase (1876) prohibited Ukrainian publications from being imported, held in school libraries, and printed, and Ukrainian plays and readings from being staged. Only belles lettres (but not translations of foreign literature) and historical documents could be published in Ukrainian, and then only in a modified Russian alphabet known as *yaryzhka. Although toward the end of the century censorship became less strict, Ukrainian was regarded as a dialect of Russian and was excluded from education and civic life. The church, the schools, and the army were the chief instruments of Russification. Also, the tsarist government encouraged Ukrainians to emigrate to other parts of the empire for seasonal or permanent jobs, and Russians to work in Ukraine. The laws of 1869 and 1886, which were in effect to 1917, introduced premiums for all civil servants of non-local origin in Right-Bank Ukraine. Officially, the purpose was to de-Polonize the region. A similar policy was conducted by the Russian Orthodox church. The measures attracted many Russians.

During the brief period of liberalization after the Revolution of 1905, Ukrainian periodicals, books, grammars, and dictionaries and P. Morachevsky's translation of the Bible (submitted to the censors back in 1863) were permitted to appear. Yet various administrative obstacles and censorship restrictions made it difficult to publish Ukrainian periodicals and books. Russian remained the only official language, and in spite of liberals in the Third and

Fourth State dumas, Ukrainian continued to be banned from education, the courts, the church, and public life. With the outbreak of the First World War, the Ukrainian press and publishing houses, including those in Russian-occupied Galicia and Bukovyna, were shut down by the authorities.

Under Austrian and Hungarian rule. The status of the Ukrainian language in Galicia and Bukovyna improved considerably when they became part of the Austrian Empire in the 1770s. The government allowed Ukrainian to be used in the schools and civil service in the crownlands. In 1787 Ukrainian was introduced as the language of instruction at the *Studium Ruthenum of Lviv University, and in 1818 in the elementary schools. In Galicia opposition to Ukrainian came not so much from the Austrian authorities as from the Polish community. At the demand of the Supreme Ruthenian Council, Ukrainian was introduced during the Revolution of 1848–9 in the school and administrative system of Galicia, but in a short while German was reinstated as the official language and the language of instruction in secondary schools and Lviv University. The government's attempt to impose the Latin alphabet on Ukrainians provoked the so-called *Alphabet war, in which the government eventually conceded defeat.

The Austrian constitution of 1867 declared the equality of the empire's nations and their languages, but owing to Polish political influence Polish became in effect the official language in Galicia, and Ukrainian was relegated to a secondary and regional status. Although elementary schools for Ukrainian children were usually run in Ukrainian, secondary and higher education in Ukrainian received little public funding and depended mostly on individual patrons or community organizations such as Prosvita.

In Bukovyna the official language was German; Ukrainian had an auxiliary role. But in the second half of the 19th century, Ukrainian elementary and secondary education enjoyed more favorable conditions there than in any other region of Ukraine. In Transcarpathia, from 1844 Hungarian was the only official language, and after the Compromise of 1867 Magyarization pressures increased. The number of Ukrainian elementary public schools fell from 353 in 1881 to 88 in 1899 and 23 in 1906. A. *Apponyi's law (1907) led to the elimination of the remaining Ukrainian schools.

The period of Ukrainian statehood. After the February Revolution of 1917, the status of the Ukrainian language changed dramatically. For the first time in recent history it acquired an official function in government, the courts, the military, and public life. Some progress in Ukrainianizing educational and academic institutions, the press and book publishing, and civic and cultural organizations was made. The language issue, however, was not mentioned in any of the Central Rada's four universals, and it was only in January 1919 that the UNR Directory proclaimed Ukrainian as the official language. The Ukrainian governments were too weak and short-lived to overcome the social and cultural effects of centuries of Russification, particularly in the cities and towns. In the Western Ukrainian National Republic (1918–19) Ukrainian was given official status, but linguistic rights were granted also to national minorities.

Interwar Western Ukraine. Although Poland was bound by international agreements to respect the linguistic and cultural rights of Ukrainians, the Polish authorities tried to remove Ukrainian from government and education. In 1923 it was excluded from the Sejm and Senate, and in 1924 Polish was recognized as the only official language of the republic. In the predominantly Ukrainian voivodeships of Lviv, Stanyslaviv, Ternopil, Polisia, and Volhynia, Polish was to be used internally, in government institutions, but Ukrainian could be used externally, in dealing with the public. In education the authorities discriminated against Ukrainian-language schools and promoted bilingual or Polish-language schools. This policy was more successful in Volhynia, Podlachia, Polisia, and in the Kholm and Lemko regions than in Galicia, where Ukrainians were better organized politically and economically.

In Transcarpathia the Czechoslovak government allowed Ukrainian and the local Transcarpathian dialect to be used in schools, the press, the courts, and the civil service. In the 1930s, however, the government became more sympathetic to the Russophile tendency. The Hungarian occupational regime of 1939–44 prohibited the use of Standard Ukrainian, but allowed the Transcarpathian dialect to be used by the government in communicating with the public and as a language of instruction in primary and secondary schools.

In Bukovyna and Bessarabia, the chauvinist Rumanian regime pursued a policy of total Rumanianization. The 1923 Constitution proclaimed Rumanian as the only official language and did not mention the linguistic rights of national minorities. Ukrainian was banned from the civil service, education, and even the church. Briefly, in 1929–33, elementary schools with a majority of Ukrainian pupils were allowed to teach six to eight hours per week in Ukrainian.

Soviet Ukraine. Soviet language policy, based on the Communist party's *nationality policy, was inconsistent. Although V. Lenin declared his support for the free development of the national languages of the Russian Empire, the Party's behavior in the first few years of the Bolshevik regime in Ukraine contradicted this principle. Russian was the dominant language in the government, the Party, and postelementary education. Demands for the equality of Ukrainian met with opposition from Russian Bolsheviks. In 1921, for example, Kh. Rakovsky wrote that recognition of Ukrainian as the official language could lead to rule by Ukrainian bourgeoisie and kulaks. Yet pressure from the people, the Ukrainian intelligentsia, and influential Ukrainian Bolsheviks such as M. Skrypnyk, O. Shumsky, V. Blakytny, and H. Hrynko persuaded the 12th Party Congress in 1923 to launch the indigenization policy, which in Ukraine became the *Ukrainization policy. As a result, Ukrainian became widely used in government, public life, education, the arts, and scholarship. Much was done to develop and standardize the language. By 1933, however, the policy was abandoned, though not officially revoked, and a full-scale attack on Ukrainian culture was begun. The gains Ukrainian had made were quickly reversed: as a medium of communication it was virtually eliminated from all spheres except village life and elementary education. Russification in the urban and industrial centers was intensified. Ukrainian linguists were accused of separating Ukrainian from Russian and were prosecuted as 'nationalist saboteurs.' The publication of Ukrainian dictionaries and linguistic studies was halted, and the old language textbooks were removed from the schools. A commission was set up at the People's Commissariat of Education to review Ukrainian terminology and orthography. With the official adoption of the theory of the convergence of Russian, Ukrainian, and Belarusian, Ukrainian orthography, terminology, and syntax were revised to bring them closer to Russian. The 14th Congress of the CPBU in 1938 resolved 'to liquidate the effects of enemy wrecking in the teaching of Russian in schools.' Lacking any legal guarantees, Ukrainian quickly lost ground in regions of Ukrainian settlement outside Ukraine. During the Soviet occupation of Western Ukraine (1939–41) some local concessions to Ukrainian were made in order to gain popular support for Soviet rule.

After the Second World War the Stalinist language policy remained virtually intact. The Russian language was deemed superior to the other national languages, as 'the language of a higher culture, of the October Revolution, of Lenin and Stalin.' It was propagated as the 'second native language' of all non-Russians in the USSR. The education law adopted by Ukraine's Supreme Soviet in 1959 gave parents the 'democratic' right to choose their child's language of instruction – Ukrainian or Russian. The CPSU Program (1961) even spoke of the creation of a homogeneous *Soviet people and the gradual disappearance of national distinctions, particularly in language. Translated into practice, this meant the official promotion of Russian in all spheres of life and the discouragement of the use of other languages. In the cities and industrial centers Ukrainian regressed to its position in tsarist times.

The courageous struggle of a handful of intellectuals against Russification was brutally suppressed in the 1960s and 1970s. The discriminatory resolution 'On the Further Improvement [ie, intensification] of the Learning and Teaching of the Russian Language in the Union Republics' adopted by the USSR Council of Ministers in 1978 further increased the incentives for studying Russian at all levels of the educational system. As M. Gorbachev's political reforms took hold in the late 1980s, Soviet language policy came under increasing criticism. In October 1989 the Supreme Soviet of the Ukrainian SSR recognized Ukrainian as the official language of the republic and set forth a schedule for the gradual Ukrainianization of all public institutions in Ukraine. Yet on 24 April 1990 Russian was decreed the official language of the Soviet Union by the Supreme Soviet of the USSR.

Postwar Eastern Europe. In the Polish People's Republic, the indigenous Ukrainians were subjected to a policy of linguistic assimilation, although from 1956 Ukrainian periodicals were published and a modicum of Ukrainian-language education was allowed. The Ukrainians in the Prešov region of eastern Slovakia have enjoyed relatively broader linguistic rights since 1945, while those in Rumania have had relatively fewer rights. In Yugoslavia, Ukrainians in the Bačka region of Serbia and in Banja Luka in Bosnia have published periodicals in Ukrainian and the Bačka dialect and have run elementary and secondary schools in the Bačka dialect.

(See also *Education, *Language legislation, *Nationality policy, and *Russification.)

BIBLIOGRAPHY
Smal'-Stots'kyi, R. Ukraïns'ka mova v Soviets'kii Ukraïni (Vienna 1936; repr, New York 1969)

Smal-Stocki, R. The Nationality Problem of the Soviet Union and Russian Communist Imperialism (Milwaukee 1952)
Chaplenko, V. Bil'shovyts'ka movna polityka (Munich 1956)
Kolasky, J. Education in Soviet Ukraine: A Study in Discrimination and Russification (Toronto 1968)
Chaplenko, V. Istoriia novoï ukraïns'koï literaturnoï movy (XVII st.– 1933 r.) (New York 1970)
Strumins'kyj, B. 'The Language Question in the Ukrainian Lands before the Nineteenth Century,' in Aspects of the Slavic Language Question, 2, East Slavic, ed R. Picchio and H. Goldblatt (New Haven, Conn 1984)
Solchanyk, R. 'Language Politics in the Ukraine,' in Sociolinguistic Perspectives on Soviet National Languages: Their Past, Present and Future, ed I. Kreindler (Berlin–New York–Amsterdam 1985)
Bruchis, M. One Step Backward, Two Steps Forward: On the Language Policy of the Communist Party of the Soviet Union in the National Republics (New York 1988)
Shevelov, G. The Ukrainian Language in the First Half of the Twentieth Century (1900–1941): Its State and Status (Cambridge, Mass 1989)
Kirkwood, M. (ed). Language Planning in the Soviet Union (New York 1990)

V. Markus, R. Senkus

Laniuk, Yurii [Lanjuk, Jurij], b 7 June 1957 in Lviv. Composer and cellist. Laniuk studied under the Polish composer A. Nikodemowicz and completed the Lviv Conservatory course in 1980. In 1975 he received first prize in the Lysenko Competition in Kiev and in 1990 he was the recipient of the L. Revutsky Prize for his chamber quartet 'Dva ruchaï' (Two Brooks). His compositions include works for cello ('Diptych,' 1988) as well as Chant pour un Equinoxe for baritone, soprano, and chamber orchestra (1991). While active as a composer, Laniuk also teaches cello and composition at the conservatory.

Lanivtsi [Lanivci]. IV-7. A town smt (1990 pop 9,100) and raion center in Ternopil oblast, situated on the Zherdia River. It was first mentioned in documents as early as 1444. It has a reinforced-concrete structures plant, a sugar refinery, a dairy, and a regional museum.

Lanka. See MARS.

Yurii Lapchynsky

Lapchynsky, Yurii [Lapčyns'kyi, Jurij], b 1887, d 1938. Bolshevik party leader and government official. As a leading Bolshevik in Kremenchuk, he chaired the local soviet of workers' and soldiers' deputies in 1917. By December

1917 he was head of the People's Secretariat and a member of the Central Executive Committee of the Soviets of Ukraine. During the Hetman regime he was plenipotentiary of the Provisional Workers' and Peasants' Government of Ukraine in Chernihiv, and in 1919, chairman of the Chernihiv Gubernia Revolutionary Committee and a member of the All-Ukrainian Central Executive Committee and the Kiev Gubernia Revolutionary Committee. An early advocate of Ukrainian autonomy within a federated party and state, he headed the so-called Federalist Opposition within the CP(B)U in 1919. Along with P. Popov and P. Slynko he demanded at the Homel Party Conference in November 1919 an independent Communist party for Ukraine and a Soviet Ukrainian state equal to and federated with the RSFSR. He accused the Russian Communist Party (Bolshevik) of subjugating Ukraine and treating it as a colony. In 1920 Lapchynsky resigned in protest from the CPBU and joined the Ukrainian Communist party, which, however, merged in 1925 with the CP(B)U. In 1928–30 he served as Soviet consul in Lviv. In the early 1930s he was attacked for Ukrainian nationalism and purged from the party. Eventually he perished in the Stalinist terror.

I. Myhul

Laponohov, Oleh, b 15 September 1930 in Kiev. Neurosurgeon. A graduate of the Kiev Medical Institute (1954), he worked in the Kiev Scientific Research Institute of Neurosurgery, from 1969 as director of the functional neurosurgery division. His work concerned the application of operational intervention to functional disorders of the brain and spinal medulla, and cryosurgery for diseases of the central nervous system.

Lappo, Ivan, b 29 August 1869 in Tsarskoe Selo, Russia, d 23 December 1944 in Dresden. Russian historian and specialist in Lithuanian-Ruthenian law. A graduate of St Petersburg University (1892), he lectured at Tartu University (1905–19), the Russian University in Prague (1921–33), and Kaunas University (1933–40). His major publications were *Velikoe kniazhestvo litovskoe za vremia ot zakliucheniia Liublinskoi unii do smerti Stefana Batoriia* (The Grand Duchy of Lithuania in the Period from the Union of Lublin to the Death of Stephen Báthory, 1901), *Velikoe kniazhestvo litovskoe vo vtoroi polovine XVI stoletiia* (The Grand Duchy of Lithuania in the Second Half of the 16th Century, 1911), *Litovskaia metrika* (The Lithuanian Register, 3 vols, 1910–14), and *Litovskii statut 1588 goda* (The Lithuanian Statute of 1588, 2 vols, 1934, 1938).

Lappo-Danilevsky, Aleksandr [Lappo-Danilevskij], b 27 January 1863 in Udachne, Katerynoslav county, d 7 February 1919 in Petrograd. Russian historian, archeologist, and professor in St Petersburg. Most relevant for Ukrainian studies are his publication *Skifskie drevnosti* (Scythian Antiquity, 1887; 2nd edn 1897) and his study of 14th-century wax seals from the Principality of Galicia-Volhynia.

Lapsky, Ostap [Laps'kyj], b 7 July 1926 in Hutsky, near Kobryn, in Polisia voivodeship (now in Belarus). Ukrainian philologist, poet, newspaper and radio journalist, translator, and community figure in postwar Poland. A graduate of Warsaw University (1955), since 1957 he has taught Ukrainian literature and held the university's chair

of Ukrainian philology. He helped prepare the Warsaw edition of the Ukrainian-Polish dictionary (1957), has contributed articles on Ukrainian writers to *Mały słownik pisarzy europejskich narodów ZSRR* (A Concise Dictionary of Writers of the European Nations of the USSR, 1966) and the journal *Slavia Orientalis*, and has written textbooks and edited anthologies for Ukrainian-language elementary schools. He has been an active member of the Ukrainian Social and Cultural Society and a contributor to its paper, *Nashe slovo*, and its yearbook, and has served as an adviser to Ukrainian-language teachers in Poland. His poems have appeared in Ukrainian-language periodicals in Poland and Ukraine. He has translated some of the poetry of T. Shevchenko, P. Tychyna, and V. Korotych into Polish, and some of the poetry of J. Słowacki, J. Tuwim, and J. Harasymowicz into Ukrainian.

Toma Lapychak

Lapychak, Toma [Lapyčak], b 17 October 1914 in Nyzhankovychi, Peremyshl county, Galicia, d 2 April 1975 in Houston, Texas. Physician, political activist, and publicist. He studied medicine in Cracow and took part in the work of the OUN (Melnyk faction). In 1941–2 he became a member and then chairman of the Regional Executive of the OUN before being imprisoned by the Nazis in a concentration camp. After the war, in 1945, in Germany, he joined the Leadership of the Ukrainian Nationalists (PUN) and edited the monthly *Orlyk* (1945–9) in Berchtesgaden. Later he edited *Samostiina Ukraïna* in Chicago (1950–5) and *Likars'kyi visnyk* (1962–6) and **Ukraïns'ke zhyttia*. Together with M. Shlemkevych he founded the Ukrainian Research and Information Institute in Chicago. He is the author of *Ukraïns'kyi natsionalizm* (Ukrainian Nationalism, 1962), in which he criticizes all the factions of the OUN. A book on his life's work was published by A. Bilynsky in 1986.

Larin, Borys, b 17 January 1893 in Poltava, d 26 March 1964 in Leningrad. Linguist; corresponding member of the AN URSR from 1945; member of the Lithuanian Academy of Sciences from 1949. A graduate of Kiev University (1914) and from 1931 a professor at Leningrad University, Larin authored several major works on the history of the Russian and Lithuanian languages and on comparative linguistics. As a lexicographer he published a number of 16th- and 17th-century Western European dictionaries and grammars of Russian, which contain materials showing Ukrainian influences on Russian. He wrote critical articles on literature, including the poetry of P. Tychyna (1920), and designed a program for collecting information for a dialectal atlas of the Ukrainian language (1948, 1949).

Rostyslav Lashchenko

Lashchenko, Rostyslav [Laščenko], b 1 September 1878 in Yelysavethrad, Kherson gubernia, d 30 October 1929 in Prague. Historian of law. After graduating in law from Kiev University (1905) he worked as a court official and judge (1909–17). He was elected president of the Kiev county justices of the peace (1917), chairman of the first department of the Kiev Court of Appeal (1918), and president of the appeals court (1919). At the same time he was a member of the Ukrainian Scientific Society in Kiev, the Commission for the Study of Ukraine's Customary Law at the Ukrainian Academy of Sciences, and the faculty of the Ukrainian State University. In 1920 he emigrated, first to Lviv and then to Prague, where he founded and presided over the Ukrainian Law Society and lectured on the history of Ukrainian law at the Ukrainian Free University and the Ukrainian Husbandry Academy in Poděbrady. Besides important articles on the Lithuanian Statute and the Pereiaslav Treaty, he wrote several monographs: *Lektsiï po istoriï ukraïns'koho prava* (Lectures on the History of Ukrainian Law, 2 pts, 1923–4), *Tsyvil'ne pravo* (Civil Law, 1925), and *Kopni sudy na Ukraïni* (Community Courts in Ukraine, 1926–7).

Lashchevsky, Varlaam [Laščevs'kyj], b ca 1710, d 28 July 1774 in Moscow. Classical philologist, churchman, and dramatist. After completing his studies at the Kiev Academy (1726–37), he took monastic vows and was appointed a lecturer at the academy (1739–47). He taught courses in Greek, for which he wrote a grammar in Latin (1746) that was later revised by H. *Shcherbatsky and republished several times in Leipzig and Moscow. It was used for most of the 19th century in Orthodox seminaries. In 1747 Lashchevsky revised and wrote the preface to a translation of the Old Testament (1751). In 1752 he was appointed rector of the Slavic-Greek-Latin Academy and archimandrite of the Don Monastery in Moscow. His morality play *Tragedokomediia* ... (Tragicomedy ...) was published by N. Tikhonravov in his *Letopisi russkoi literatury i drevnostei* (Chronicles of Russian Literature and Antiquities, vol 1, 1859) and by V. Riezanov in his anthology of Ukrainian drama. H. Skovoroda, who was Lashchevsky's student at the Kiev Academy, quoted from Lashchevsky's tragicomedy *Peresliduvana tserkva* (Persecuted Church).

Lashchuk, Yurii [Laščuk, Jurij], b 2 March 1922 in Lypky, Rivne county, Volhynia. Art scholar. A graduate of the Lviv Institute of Applied and Decorative Arts (1953), he lectured there (1962–75) and obtained a doctorate in 1974. A specialist in folk pottery, he has written books on Hutsul (1950), Transcarpathian (1960), and Kosiv (1966) ceramics and on Ukrainian potters (1968) and is a co-author of a history of Ukrainian decorative art (1969) and vols 2 and 4 of the ANU history of Ukrainian art (1967, 1969–70).

Lashkarev, Petr [Laškarev, Pjotr], b 1833 in Kursk gubernia, d 28 August 1899 in Kiev. Church historian. He graduated from the Kiev Theological Academy and then taught canon law and church history there (from 1866) and at Kiev University (from 1885). He published articles on canon law and other topics in *Trudy Kievskoi dukhovnoi akademii* and other journals, and six of his articles on early churches and church architecture in Kiev were collected in *Tserkovno-arkheologicheskie ocherki, issledovaniia i referaty* (Church Archeology Outlines, Research, and Essays, 1898).

Lashkarov, Vadym [Laškar'ov] (Lashkarev, Vadim), b 7 October 1903 in Kiev, d 1 December 1974 in Kiev. Physicist; AN URSR (now ANU) full member from 1945. A graduate of the Kiev Institute of People's Education (1924), he conducted research at the Kiev Polytechnical Institute (1925–30). From 1939 he headed the semiconductor department at the ANU Institute of Physics in Kiev and taught physics at Kiev University. In 1951–6 Lashkarov contributed significantly to the development and theory of germanium semiconductor devices. In 1960 the semiconductor department at the Institute of Physics became the core of the newly formed ANU *Institute of Semiconductors, which Lashkarov directed until 1970. In 1956 Lashkarov initiated *Ukraïns'kyi fizychnyi zhurnal*. As its chief editor until his death, he was primarily responsible for its high professional level. After his death the journal succumbed to Russification pressures, and during 1978–89 it was published exclusively in Russian.

Oleksander Lashkevych

Lashkevych, Oleksander [Laškevyč], b 1842 in Starodub, Chernihiv gubernia, d 1889. Historian and civic leader. He studied at Kiev University and became involved in peasant reforms in the Kiev and Podilia regions (1860s) and in zemstvo and legal reforms in the Chernihiv region (1870s and 1880s). He was a member of the Old Hromada in Kiev and an editor and publisher of *Kievskaia *starina* (1888–9). His works on the history of 18th-century Left-Bank Ukraine were published in journals such as *Kievskaia starina* (where his recollections were also published, posthumously, in 1899, no. 67) and *Russkii arkhiv*.

Laskarev, Vladimir, b 9 July 1868 in Biriuchi, Voronezh gubernia, Russia, d 10 April 1954 in Belgrade, Yugoslavia. Russian geologist. After graduating from Odessa University in 1892, he taught there until 1920. He subsequently emigrated and was appointed a professor at Belgrade University. In 1901–7 he conducted geological research in Podilia and Volhynia, and in 1915 he published his major work, on the structure of river valleys in Ukraine. He also wrote many geological studies of the Balkan countries.

Laskarzhevsky, Valerii [Laskarževs'kyj, Valerij], b 24 March 1947 in Kiev. Painter. He studied at the Kiev State Art Institute and the Moscow Higher Applied Art School. His work is figurative and realistic but with elements of the unusual. Laskarzhevsky was one of eight Kiev artists chosen for the Exhibition of Young Ukrainian Artists in Moscow in 1985.

Laskavy, Mykhailo [Laskavyj, Myxajlo], b 1862, d 1954 in Shanghai. Actor and stage director. In 1890 he began his theatrical career in Saksahansky's troupe; then he worked in P. Prokhorovych's and T. Kolesnychenko's troupes in Ukraine. In 1912–16 he toured with K. Kameliuk-Kamensky's troupe in Siberia, Japan, and China. From 1926 he was a theatrical director at the Ukrainian National Home in Harbin, Manchuria.

Laslo-Kutsiuk, Mahdalyna [Laslo-Kucjuk] (Laszlo-Kuţiuk, Magdalena), b 30 August 1928 in Timişoara, Rumania. Literary scholar. She studied at Cluj, Bucharest, and Kharkiv universities and taught Ukrainian language and literature at Bucharest University (1954–83). Her perceptive comparative and structuralist studies of modern Ukrainian literature have been published in Soviet Ukrainian and Rumanian journals and as the collections *Velyka tradytsiia* (The Great Tradition, 1979) and *Shukannia formy* (The Search for a Form, 1980). She has also produced a doctoral monograph on Rumanian-Ukrainian literary relations (1974, in Rumanian) and textbooks on Ukrainian poetics (1974) and Soviet Ukrainian literature (2nd edn 1976). She has compiled anthologies of 19th-century Ukrainian stories (1973) and 20th-century Ukrainian poetry (1976) and edited the complete works of S. Yarychevsky (2 vols, 1977, 1979).

Lasovska-Kruk, Myroslava [Lasovs'ka-Kruk], b 11 March 1919 in Galicia. Painter, graphic artist, and writer; wife of V. Lasovsky. She studied graphic art with S. Zhuravsky in Sokal, sculpting with O. Stovbuniak in Landeck, and painting with V. Lasovsky. Having left Ukraine at the end of the war, she settled in Argentina and, in 1959, the United States. She exhibited her work with the Ukrainian Artists' Association in the USA. She has written several novels, such as *Pid chornym nebom* (Under a Black Sky, 1966) and *Dzvinka molodist'* (Reverberating Youth, 1982–3), and plays, such as *L'odolom* (Icebreaker, 1974) and *Volodymyr Velykyi* (Volodymyr the Great, 1988). She has been a leading member of the Association for the Advancement of Ukrainian Culture, the Women's Alliance of the *Organization for the Defense of Four Freedoms for Ukraine,

and the World Federation of Ukrainian Women's Organizations.

Volodymyr Lasovsky: *Self-Portrait* (oil, 1961)

Lasovsky, Volodymyr [Lasovs'kyj], b 3 July 1907 in Soroky, Buchach county, Galicia, d 11 November 1975 in New York. Painter and art essayist and theoretician. He studied at the Novakivsky Art School in Lviv (1928–33) and F. Léger's Académie Grand Chaumier in Paris (1934) and was a key member of *RUB and the *Association of Independent Ukrainian Artists in Lviv. A postwar émigré in Austria and Paris, he lived in Argentina from 1948 and moved to New York in 1959. Lasovsky painted portraits in a classical manner and Légeresque semiabstract compositions with geometric figures. In Buenos Aires he taught art history at a Ukrainian theater studio, and in New York he headed the branch of the Ukrainian Artists' Association in the USA, directed Ukrainian plays, and was chairman of the Council on Cultural Affairs of the World Congress of Free Ukrainians. A book about him was published in 1980 in Toronto.

Lassota von Steblau, Erich, b 1550, probably in Bleischwitz (Błażejowice), Silesia, d 1616 in Košice, Slovakia. Silesian nobleman, soldier of fortune (in Spain and Portugal), and Austrian diplomat. He studied at Leipzig and Padua universities. From 1585 he was a courier of Emperor Rudolph II and an adviser (from 1589, lord high steward) to Archduke Maximilian. In 1594, as Rudolph's envoy, Lassota traveled to the Zaporozhian Sich to enlist the Zaporozhian Host as allies in Austria's war with Turkey. The diary of his mission is a valuable source for the history and geography of late 16th-century Ukraine, particularly of the Zaporizhia. It describes in detail his stay at the Sich, the life of the Cossacks, and his stay in Kiev, Lviv, and other towns in Galicia and Right-Bank Ukraine. Lassota's diary of 1573–94 was published in German in Halle in 1866. His diary of the year 1594 has been translated into Russian (1873, 1890 [trans K. Antonovych-Melnyk, ed V. Antonovych]), Polish (1972), and English (1975). Excerpts from it have been translated into Ukrainian by D. Yavornytsky, V. Domanytsky, M. Hrushevsky, and V. Sichynsky.

BIBLIOGRAPHY
Wójcik, Z. (ed.) *Eryka Lassoty i Wilhelma Beauplana opisy Ukrainy*, trans Z. Stasiewska and S. Meller (Warsaw 1972)
Wynar, L. (ed). *Habsburgs and Zaporozhian Cossacks: The Diary of Erich Lassota von Steblau, 1594*, trans O. Subtelny (Littleton, Colo 1975)

Lassowsky, Jaropolk [Lasovs'kyj], b 17 October 1941 in Lviv. Composer, conductor, violinist, and pedagogue. Educated in music education at New York University (MA, 1969) and music theory at Ohio State University (1981), he is professor of music and conductor of the University Symphony at Clarion University of Pennsylvania as well as concertmaster of the Montreux Festival Symphony and the OPUSI Chamber Orchestra of Cleveland. He is also a member of the New Jersey Symphony, the New Hampshire Music Festival Orchestra, and the Columbus Symphony. His compositions include 'Symphonic Etude,' 'Toccata for Piano,' 'Rhapsody for Flute Solo,' 'Triptych for Violin and Piano,' 'Trio Brevis,' *Daisy* (a musical comedy), and numerous vocal settings of Ukrainian poets. Lassowsky also translated and annotated *Selected Works* by V. *Stus (1987).

Lastivka, Petro, b 5 July 1922 in Savyntsi, Vasylkiv county, Kiev region. Stage and film actor. In 1949 he completed study in the cinema school at the Kiev Artistic Film Studio. He worked as an actor in Ukrainian theaters in Uzhhorod and Chernihiv in 1945–60, joined the Ternopil Ukrainian Music and Drama Theater in 1960, and has been its artistic director since 1988. He acted in the film *Duma pro Kovpaka* (The Ballad about Kovpak, 1976) and wrote the plays *Divchyna z Desny* (The Girl from the Desna River, 1959) and *Oblychchiam do sontsia* (Facing the Sun, 1968).

Lastivka. A Russophile magazine for children, published in Lviv from 1869 to 1881. A supplement to *Uchytel'* until 1875, it appeared weekly until 1874, and then twice a week. The editor and publisher was M. Klemertovych. *Lastivka* published articles on religion and history by I. Halka, A. Dobriansky, D. Vintskovsky, and Y. Markov, and on economic and agricultural subjects by H. Vretsona, I. Naumovych, and others.

Lastôvka. An almanac compiled and published by Ye. Hrebinka in St Petersburg in 1841. It had 382 pages and contained works by L. Borovykovsky, Ye. Hrebinka, H. Kvitka-Osnovianenko, V. Zabila, I. Kotliarevsky, P. Korenytsky, P. Kulish, P. Pysarevsky, O. Chuzhbynsky, and

Lastôvka (title page)

T. Shevchenko. It also included folk songs, popular proverbs, and folktales.

Latin alphabet. The oldest extant literary monuments in Ukraine written in the Latin alphabet (LA) date from the 16th ('The Song of Shtefan the Voivode' in a Czech version of the alphabet) and 17th centuries ('The Song about the Massacre of the Jews of Berestechko,' J. Gawatowicz's *intermedii*, and Kondracki's song collection in a Polish version). In the 19th century conscious efforts at popularizing the use of the LA in Ukraine were made by Y. *Lozynsky and the writers of the Ukrainian school in Polish literature. The first system for a LA for Ukrainian was proposed by F. Miklosich in vol 1 of his *Vergleichende Grammatik der slavischen Sprachen* (1852). Based on the Czech (č, š, ž, dž) and Croatian and Polish (t', d', ś, ź, ć, dź, l', ń) versions of the LA, it was widely used for some time in transcribing Ukrainian words in scholarly bibliographies; in 1859 J. Jíreček relied on it in his proposal for an official LA for Galicia's Ukrainians, which provoked the so-called *Alphabet war. Later attempts at popularizing a combined Latin-*hrazhdanka alphabet (eg, by M. Drahomanov) and a mixture of the versions of the LA used in various Slavic, Germanic, and Romance languages did not take root in Ukraine; and in 1927 a proposal for Latinizing the Ukrainian script by M. Yohansen, B. Tkachenko, M. Nakonechny, and others was rejected by Ukraine's linguistic authorities, though V. Simovych supported it in principle.

Latinisms. Words and expressions borrowed from the Latin. Proto-Slavic was practically devoid of Latinisms, because of the relative lateness of Slavic-Roman contacts. A few Latin words entered it, partly via the Germanic languages, only in the period of its disintegration. These words referred to cultivated plants, eg, *čerešnja* 'cherry' from *cerasus, red'ka* 'radish' from *rādīcem, ljača* 'lentil' from *lens*; items of trade, eg, *ocet* 'vinegar' from *acētum, vyno* 'wine' from *vīnum*; and rites and beliefs, eg, *koljada* 'carol' from *calendae, rusalka < rusalija*, an ancient spring ritual, from *rosālia*, and *pohanyn* 'pagan' from *pāgānus*. After the Christianization of Rus', Latinisms entered Old Ukrainian through Church Slavonic and Greek: eg, *oltar* 'altar' from *altare; ruha* 'church land' from *rogāre; tjablo*, a row of icons above the 'royal doors' of the iconostasis, from *templum* or *tabula*. Latin was the official language of government and law in the Polish Commonwealth; hence, the number of Latinisms entering Ukrainian increased sharply from the mid-16th century on. At the beginning of the 17th century, the teaching and use of Latin became widespread in Ukraine's schools, and many new Latinisms, referring mostly to cultural concepts, entered Ukrainian: eg, *avtor* 'author' from *auctor*, *apeljacija* 'appeal' from *appellātio*, *lekcija* 'lesson' from *lēctiō*, *instrument* 'instrument' from *instrūmentum*, *minuta* 'minute' from *minuta*, *posesija* 'leased land' from *possessus*, *sēkrēt* 'secret' from *secretus*. Most Latinisms that entered Ukrainian during the period of Polish rule existed in and were introduced via Polish.

Since the 18th century, Latinisms already existing in various Western European lexicons, particularly scientific terms, have entered Ukrainian in increasing numbers, mostly via German, Polish, or Russian. In addition, the use of several, often modified, Latin suffixes (*-al'nyj* from *-al*, *-abel'nyj* from *-abelis*, *-izm* from *-ismus*, *-acija* from *-atio*, *-ura* from *-ura*) and a few borrowings from Latin syntax (the predicate verb at the end of a sentence, used in the literary language of the 17th and 18th centuries) have become common in Ukrainian.

O. Horbach

Latorytsia River. See Liatorytsia River.

Latsis, Martin (real name: Sudrabs, Jan), b 28 December 1888 in Latvia, d 20 March 1938. He was active in Riga in the 1905 Revolution and in Petrograd in the 1917 Revolution. After the Bolshevik coup he served on the colleges of the People's Commissariat of Internal Affairs and of the All-Russian *Cheka. As chairman of the All-Russian (July–November 1918) and the All-Ukrainian (1919–21) Cheka, he waged a campaign of terror against the Party's political opponents, Ukrainian insurgents, peasants, and the intelligentsia. After 1921 he held high posts in the administration of the economy and in the Party. He perished in the Stalinist terror and was rehabilitated in the 1950s.

Latsky, Volf [Lac'kyj, Vol'f] (pseud: Bertoldi), b 1881 in Kiev, d 1940 in Tel Aviv. Jewish-Ukrainian political figure and journalist in Kiev. The founder and leader of the Jewish People's party in Ukraine, in April 1919 he served as minister for Jewish affairs in the UNR government. Some of his works deal with the Denikin army's Jewish pogroms in Ukraine.

Latta, Vasyl, b 29 December 1921 in Pčoliné, Humenné district, Czechoslovakia, d 27 June 1965 in Bratislava. Linguist. A graduate of Bratislava (1947) and Leningrad (1949) universities, Latta taught at Bratislava University beginning in 1954 and became a professor there in 1962. He prepared a three-volume atlas of Ukrainian dialects in Slovakia (1991) based on his extensive field research on the Ukrainian dialects of Eastern Slovakia, and published several articles on the phonology of these dialects and an important article on the Slovak-Ukrainian linguistic border (1962).

Latvia. A Baltic state (1991 pop 2,694,000) with an area of 64,500 sq km. Its capital is *Riga. In 1989 the population of Latvia stood at 2,666,600, including 1,387,800 Latvians, 906,000 Russians, 120,000 Belarusians, and 92,100 (3.45 percent) Ukrainians. There were some 71,000 Latvians living elsewhere in the former USSR (7,200 in the Ukrainian SSR, and 46,800 in the RSFSR). Latvians have settled in other European countries, Australia, the United States, Canada, and Argentina.

In the 10th to 12th centuries the southeastern part of Latvia formed part of Kievan Rus' (the Polatsk and Pskov lands). In the 13th century Latvia was ruled by the Teutonic knights, and from the mid-16th century it was part of the Polish-Lithuanian Commonwealth. Northern Latvia was annexed by Sweden in 1629 and then by Russia in 1721. The entire country came under Russian control in 1772 and remained so until 1918. A Latvian national renaissance began in the latter half of the 19th century, and paved the way for the establishment of an independent Latvian republic at the end of 1918. In June 1940 Latvia was occupied by the Bolsheviks, who transformed it into the Latvian SSR. After a reoccupation by the Germans in 1941–5, Latvia again came under Soviet control.

Ukrainian-Latvian relations began toward the end of the 19th century. In Riga there was a small Ukrainian community of civil servants, workers, and students of the local polytechnical institute. In the early 1900s the Ukrainians established the cultural association Hromada, which organized the commemoration of the centenary of the birth of T. Shevchenko in 1914. In the state Duma, Ukrainians and Latvians collaborated within the Union of Autonomists. The Ukrainian activists I. Shrah and P. Chyzhevsky in particular had close connections with Y. Chakste, a Duma member who later became the first president of the Latvian republic. During the time of the Directory there was a Ukrainian diplomatic mission in Riga headed by V. Kedrovsky. On 18 March 1921 the peace treaty between Poland, the USSR, and the Ukrainian SSR was signed in Riga. In the interwar period there was a small Ukrainian colony in Riga, which in 1933 founded the Latvian-Ukrainian Association.

After the Second World War a major influx of non-Balts including many Ukrainians moved into Latvia from other parts of the Soviet Union. According to the 1959 census, 1.4 percent (29,000) of the population consisted of Ukrainians and 26.6 percent of Russians. Twenty years later the percentage of Ukrainians had more than doubled.

Ukrainian-Latvian cultural ties began in the 1890s with the translations into Latvian of Ye. Hrebinka, T. Shevchenko, M. Vovchok, I. Franko, M. Kotsiubynsky, V. Stefanyk, and O. Kobylianska. The translations of Shevchenko's works were especially publicized on the occasion of the 50th anniversary of his death and the centenary of his birth (1911 and 1914). After the Soviet occupation of Latvia in 1940, these ties were promoted not in their own right but as part of the USSR's 'friendship of nations' propaganda. Ukrainian classics by authors such as Shevchenko were translated into Latvian, as were works of contemporary authors, such as P. Tychyna, M. Rylsky, M. Bazhan, O. Korniichuk, Yu. Yanovsky, M. Stelmakh, and O. Honchar. Ukrainian plays and movies were staged or screened in Latvia, and Ukrainian Festival Weeks were held annually in June. At the same time many works of Latvian writers, notably Ya. Rainis, L. Laitsens, and A. Upit, were translated into Ukrainian, and Latvian plays were a regular part of the repertoire of theaters in the Ukrainian SSR.

The liberalization policy toward the end of the 1980s led to a renewed effort on the part of Latvians to free themselves from the Soviet Union. Popular support for independence manifested itself in the Popular Front of Latvia (LTF) and the National Independence Movement of Latvia (LNNK). After the LTF and the LNNK won a majority

Title page of *Storozha*, a Ukrainian journal recently published in Latvia

Larysa Latynina

in the elections to the republic's legislature, the restoration of the 'Republic of Lithuania' was declared by the Supreme Council on 4 May 1990. Nearly 74 percent of those who voted supported this declaration of independence.

Since 1988 a Ukrainian youth club has been active in Riga. The newspaper *Trybuna* has appeared there also since 1988; in its early days it published materials which at that time were still forbidden in Ukraine. The printing presses of Riga were often used to print Ukrainian newspapers (eg, *Holos vidrodzhennia*), which were then smuggled into Ukraine. There has existed mutual support and co-operation between the LTF and the Ukrainian movement for democratization, Rukh. Riga was the site of the founding meetings of several democratic organizations from other republics of the Soviet Union and of the Ukrainian National Democratic League (now the Ukrainian National Democratic party). In 1991 V. Strutynsky began to edit in Riga the journal *Storozha*, devoted to politics, culture, and history.

A. Zhukovsky

Latynina, Larysa (née Dyrii), b 27 December 1934 in Kherson. World-class gymnast. A graduate of the Kiev Institute of Physical Culture (1959), she won a record number of Olympic medals (nine gold, five silver, and four bronze) and was the all-round women's gymnastics champion at the 1956, 1960, and 1964 Olympic Games; she was also the women's gymnastics world champion in 1958 and 1962, the European champion in 1957 and 1961, and a USSR champion 11 times (1956–64). In the history of individual and team events in gymnastics and sports in general, she won the largest number of competitions. In 1966 she moved to Moscow, where until 1977 she coached the USSR women's gymnastics team and served as an international-class judge. From 1977 she was a member of the Organizing Committee of the 1980 Olympic Games. Latynina wrote the books *Soniachna molodist'* (Sunny Youth, 1958) and, in Russian, *Ravnovesie* (Equilibrium, 1975) and *Gimnastika skvoz' gody* (Gymnastics through the Years, 1977).

Latynnyky. The name given to Ukrainian-speaking Roman Catholics in Polish-ruled Western Ukraine, who were either Ukrainian converts to Roman Catholicism or the descendants of Polish colonists who had partially assimilated to the Ukrainian culture. They arose in the late 19th to early 20th century, and by 1939 their number was estimated at 700,000 (515,000 in Galicia and the rest in Volhynia and Podilia). Most *latynnyky* were peasants. When the new frontiers between Poland and the Ukrainian SSR were established after the Second World War, some *latynnyky* emigrated to Poland, but the majority remained and mostly became Ukrainianized. (See also *Poles in Ukraine.)

Latyshev, Georgii [Latyšev, Georgij], b 4 February 1907 in Bezhitsa (now part of Briansk), Russia, d 3 April 1973 in Kiev. Nuclear physicist; AN URSR (now ANU) corresponding member from 1945 and full member of the Kazakh SSR Academy of Sciences from 1958. A graduate of the Leningrad Polytechnical Institute (1929), from 1930 to 1941 he worked at the Ukrainian Physical-Technical Institute in Kharkiv. In 1932 Latyshev, K. *Synelnikov, A. *Walter, and A. *Leipunsky became the first in the USSR to induce nuclear disintegration by artificially accelerated particles. In 1958 he organized the Institute of Nuclear Physics of the Kazakh Academy of Sciences in Alma Ata, which he served as director. In 1965 he moved to Kiev. There he worked at the ANU Institute of Physics and, from 1970, at the Institute for Nuclear Research.

Latysheva, Klavdiia [Latyševa, Klavdija], b 14 March 1897 in Kiev, d 11 May 1956 in Kiev. Mathematician. She studied at the Kiev Institute of People's Education (later Kiev University) in 1920–8, where she remained as a faculty member until her death. In the late 1920s and early 1930s, she worked closely with M. Krylov and M. Kravchuk. She was the first woman in Ukraine to attain a doctorate and then a full professorship in the field of mathematics. Her most famous work is a theorem on the necessary and sufficient conditions for the existence of closed-form solutions of differential equations with polynomial coefficients.

Laurentian Chronicle (Lavrentiivskyi litopys). One of the oldest compendiums of Rus' *chronicles. It is named after the monk Lavrentii, who copied it in 1377 for Prince Dmitrii Konstantinovich of Suzdal. The original is preserved at the St Petersburg Public Library. It contains the chronicle *Povist' vremennykh lit* (second redaction, 1116) and the chronicle compiled for Prince Mikhail Yaroslavich of Vladimir, which describes events until 1305. The pages for the years 898–922, 1203–5, 1263–83, and 1288–94 are missing. The text of Prince Volodymyr Monomakh's testament, *Poucheniie ditiam*, appears in the middle of a narrative about people imprisoned by Alexander the Great of Macedonia and Monomakh's epistle to Prince Oleh Sviatoslavych. The chronicle was discovered in 1792 at the Vladimir Monastery of Christ's Nativity by A. Musin-Pushkin and was published in its entirety in 1846 as the first volume of the full collection of the Rus' chronicles. A second edition, edited by E. Karsky, was published in 1926–8 and reprinted in 1962.

Lausitz culture. See Lusatian culture.

Lava **courts** (literally, bench courts). Courts introduced in the 17th century in cities of Poland and Ukraine that enjoyed the rights of Magdeburg law. They consisted usually of three to seven assessors (*lavnyky*) and were headed by the mayor. According to the law, the members were elected by the free residents, but in practice new members were often appointed by sitting members. The courts had jurisdiction over the residents of the city and the suburban villages in civil and criminal matters. In the 18th century their authority was restricted to petty disputes over property. They were abolished in the mid-19th century after the abolition of Magdeburg law. Later, the name was applied to jury courts in Ukrainian territories under Austrian rule.

Lavra (from the Greek word meaning 'walled part of a city'). Originally a term applied to fortified monasteries in Palestine, it was later used to designate any large or important monastery that came under the direct jurisdiction of the highest church body (eg, the metropolitanate or patriarchate) in a country. In Ukraine, the title *lavra* was conferred on only two Orthodox monasteries, the *Kievan Cave Monastery in 1688 and the *Pochaiv Monastery in 1833, although unofficially it had been used for the latter as early as the 18th century. In the 19th and 20th centuries the local bishop bore the title 'priestly archimandrite' of the given *lavra*, and it was directly administered by his appointee, who had the title 'archimandrite.'

Lavrenko, Yevhen, b 23 February 1900 in Chuhuiv, Kharkiv gubernia, d 18 July 1987 in Leningrad. Geobotanist and phytogeographer; full member of the USSR Academy of Sciences from 1968. He graduated from the Kharkiv Institute of People's Education (1922) and worked at the Kharkiv Botanical Gardens (1921–8) and the Kharkiv Institute for the Protection of Nature (1926–9). He taught at the Kharkiv Agricultural Institute in 1929–34 and then moved from Kharkiv to work in the Leningrad Botanical Institute. Lavrenko's scientific research was devoted mainly to steppe vegetation in the USSR, a field in which he introduced new classifications, as well as to the regionalization and mapping of vegetation. He wrote numerous works on the geobotany of Ukraine, particularly its steppes and marshlands. Lavrenko also worked on the history of flora and vegetation and introduced a concept of the phytogeosphere as a part of the biosphere.

Lavrentev, Mikhail, b 19 November 1900 in Kazan, d 15 October 1980 in Moscow. Mathematician; full member of the AN URSR (now ANU) from 1939 and of the USSR Academy of Sciences from 1946. Lavrentev graduated from Moscow University in 1922 and received his doctoral degree there in 1933. From 1939 to 1941 and 1944 to 1949 he was director of the ANU Institute of Mathematics. From 1945 he was vice-president of the ANU. He became director of the Institute of Mechanics and Computational Technology of the USSR Academy of Sciences (1950–3) and in 1957–75 was vice-president of the USSR Academy of Sciences and head of its Siberian division. From 1975 he worked at the Moscow Institute of Physics and Technology. Lavrentev's fundamental works in mathematics are devoted mostly to the theory of sets, the general theory of functions, the theory of conformal and quasi-conformal

mappings, and the theory of differential equations. In each of these areas he developed new directions. He also obtained new results and initiated new areas of research in mechanics and applied physics.

Yurii Lavrinenko

Lavrinenko, Yurii (Lawrynenko, Jurij; pseud: Yu. Dyvnych), b 3 May 1905 in Khyzhyntsi, Zvenyhorod county, Kiev gubernia, d 14 December 1987 in New York. Literary scholar, critic, and publicist. He graduated from the Kharkiv Institute of People's Education in 1930 and then obtained a PH D from the Institute of Literature of the AN URSR (now ANU). He was arrested several times between 1933 and 1935, and from 1935 to 1939 he was imprisoned in the concentration camp in Norilsk. He was exiled after his release, and in 1950 he emigrated to the United States. He began publishing his works while he was still a student. His historical-literary works are devoted mainly to research on the Ukrainian renaissance of the 1920s. The bibliography of his literary-critical and publicistic works contains more than 300 entries. His books include the literary portraits *Blakytnyi-Ellan* (1929), *Vasyl' Chumak* (1930), *Tvorchist' Pavla Tychyny* (The Works of Pavlo Tychyna, 1930), *V maskakh epokhy* (In the Masks of an Era, coauthor, 1948), the anthology *Rozstriliane vidrodzhennia* (The Executed Renaissance, 1959), the collection of his literary-critical articles *Zrub i parosty* (The Stump and Its Offshoots, 1971), and the monograph *Vasyl' Karazyn* (1975). His essays include *Na shliakhakh syntezy kliarnetyzmu* (On the Roads of the Synthesis of [the Poetic Style] Clarinetism, 1977) and *Pavlo Tychyna i ioho poema 'Skovoroda' na tli epokhy* (Pavlo Tychyna and His Poem 'Skovoroda' in the Context of the Era, 1980). His historical-publicistic works include *Sotsiializm i ukraïns'ka revoliutsiia* (Socialism and the Ukrainian Revolution, 1949) and *Na ispyti velykoï revoliutsiï* (At the Test of the Great Revolution, 1949). He also wrote *Ukrainian Communism and Soviet-Russian Policy toward the Ukraine: An Annotated Bibliography, 1917-1953* (1953) and his memoirs, *Chorna purha* (The Black Blizzard, 1985).

I. Koshelivets

Lavriv folios (Lavrivski lystky). Five folios copied in the 12th century from an Old Church Slavonic text of the Gospels and some sermons. The language of the manuscript bears some faint traces of Ukrainian. The fragment was published and analyzed by O. Kolessa in *ZNTSh*, vol 53, 1903.

Lavriv St Onuphrius's Monastery

Lavriv Saint Onuphrius's Monastery (Lavrivskyi

Manastyr sv. Onufriia). A monastery in Lavriv, Lviv
oblast. According to legend, the monastery was built in
1278 over the burial site of Prince Lev Danylovych. It became a notable monastic center in the Peremyshl eparchy
and later an important Basilian educational center. The
(contemporary) Lavriv church, erected in the 15th century
in a Byzantine-Athos style, was rebuilt in the 17th century
and greatly altered in the 19th century. It contains valuable polychromatic 15th- and 16th-century frescoes. The
monastery buildings now standing were built after major
fires in 1767 and 1909. A center for monastic training, the
Lavriv Monastery also housed the main school for the district from 1789 to 1911 (and for many years the only school
in Galicia with Ukrainian-language instruction). After
1911 the school was turned into a gymnasium. A valuable
library and archives were located on the site. The monastery was liquidated by the Soviet authorities in 1945–6 and
replaced by a school and residence for deaf-mutes. The
church soon fell into disrepair, and the iconostasis was destroyed.

Rev Ivan Lavrivsky   Rev Ivan Lavrivsky
(1773–1846)   (1822–73)

Lavrivsky, Ivan [Lavrivs'kyj] (Lavrovsky), b 15 May
1773 in Terka, Lisko county, Galicia, d 1846 in Peremyshl,
Galicia. Greek Catholic priest, educator, and civic figure.
He graduated (D TH, 1801) from and taught at Lviv University before becoming a teacher of religion, pastoral the-

ology, and Greek at the Lviv Lyceum (1805–14). He served
as rector of the Greek Catholic Seminary in Lviv (1814–
20) and then as a professor of biblical studies at the Peremyshl Theological Institute and a priest at the Peremyshl
cathedral. His major writings (all of which remain unpublished) include a Church Slavonic grammar for
seminarians, a translation of the Primary Chronicle into
Polish, and a Ukrainian-Polish-German dictionary. A promoter of the use and study of the Ukrainian language,
Lavrivsky was one of the pioneers of the Ukrainian revival in Galicia. He donated his large library to the Peremyshl
chapter and his estates to a foundation for promoting elementary education in Ukrainian and aiding widows and
orphans of the clergy.

Lavrivsky, Ivan [Lavrivs'kyj], b 1822 in Lopianka, Dolyna county, Galicia, d 25 May 1873 in Kholm. Composer
and priest. Having developed his musical skills while
studying in Peremyshl, he became conductor of the cathedral choir there. His original compositions were comparable in style to those of M. *Verbytsky and constitute part
of the 'Peremyshl school' that stood at the heart of Ukrainian musical development during the mid-19th century.
Lavrivsky later moved to Cracow (1854–63) and Lviv
(1863–6) before being appointed professor and vice-rector
of the theological seminary in Kholm. His choral works include both religous and secular compositions such as 'Autumn,' 'Zaspivai my, soloviiu' (Sing for Me, Nightingale),
'Richen'ka' (The Streamlet), as well as the popular operettas Oman ochei (A Wile of the Eyes), Roksoliana, and Pan
Dovhonos (Mister Long Nose).

Lavrivsky, Markel (Antin) von Plöcken [Lavrivs'kyj],
b 14 April 1887 in Sebechiv, Sokal county, Galicia, d 14
April 1927 in Vienna. Highest-ranking Ukrainian officer
in the Austrian army. He graduated from the Wienerneu-
stadt Academy and by 1914 had served in various infantry
units and commanded the 77th Infantry Regiment. During the First World War, Lavrivsky was promoted to gen-
eral-major and subsequently to field marshal–lieutenant
and decorated with the Order of Leopold.

Lavrivsky, Mykhailo [Lavrivs'kyj, Myxajlo] (Lawriwsky, Michael), b 7 March 1952 in Barmera, South Australia.
Economist and civic figure. A graduate of Adelaide University (PH D, 1982), he became a senior lecturer in finance
at La Trobe University, Melbourne, in 1984 and full professor in 1990. The editor and founder of Australian-Ukrainian Review (1982–), he was instrumental in establishing
Ukrainian studies at Monash University in 1983. He has
held several leading positions in Ukrainian community
organizations, including the Federation of Ukrainian Organizations in Australia. His publications include Ownership and Control of Australian Corporations (1978) and
Corporate Structure and Performance (1984).

Lavrivsky, Yuliian [Lavrivs'kyj, Julijan], b 1821, d 5
May 1873 in Lviv. Lawyer, civic figure, and political leader. A member of the Ruthenian Congress in 1848, he
joined the Halytsko-Ruska Matytsia society and became
the first chairman of its law department. He was a founder
and long-term president of the Ruska Besida society (see
*Ukrainska Besida) and its theater as well as president of
the *Prosvita society (1870–3). In 1861, while serving as a

Yuliian Lavrivsky

state procurator in Sambir, he was elected to the Galician Diet, and in 1870 he was appointed its deputy marshal. In 1869 he offered the Poles co-operation in the administration of Galicia in return for their granting the Ukrainian language the same status as Polish in government and education. The Polish-controlled provincial executive, however, rejected the offer. Lavrivsky founded the populist newspaper *Osnova* in 1870 and translated the Austrian civil code into Ukrainian.

Lavrov, Fedir, b 24 February 1903 in Veremiivka, Zolotonosha county, Poltava gubernia, d 9 December 1980 in Kiev. Folklorist. He served as director of the Mystetstvo publishers (1937) and the Kiev Institute of Foreign Languages. Then he chaired the ethnography (1951–2) and oral folklore (1952–62) departments at the AN URSR (now ANU) Institute of Fine Arts, Folklore, and Ethnography. In 1939 he helped organize the First Ukrainian Republican Congress of Kobzars and Lirnyks in Ukraine. His chief works consist of a handbook on folklore (1940), a guide to collecting folklore (1949, 1951), a guide to recording folk poetry (1957), biographies of the kobzars F. Kushneryk (1940), O. Veresai (1955), and Ye. Movchan (1958), *Ukrains'ka narodna antyrelihiina satyra* (Ukrainian Antireligious Folk Satire, 1965), and *Kobzari* (Kobzars, 1980).

Lavrov, Pavlo, b 12 July 1903 in Radivtsi, Letychiv county, Podilia gubernia, d 1 June 1973 in Kiev. Marxist historian. A graduate of the Kiev Institute of People's Education (1933), he chaired the Department of the History of the Ukrainian SSR at Kiev University (from 1939) and served as dean of the history faculty. He wrote books on the peasant movement in Podilia gubernia in the first third of the 19th century (1946), the workers' movement in Ukraine in 1913–14 (1957, doctoral diss) and 1910–14 (1966), and Soviet Ukrainian historiography on the workers' movement in Ukraine in 1912–14 (1962).

Lavrovsky, Nikolai [Lavrovskij, Nikolaj], b 4 December 1825 in Vydropusk, Torzhok county, Tver gubernia, Russia, d 1 October 1899 in Kochetok, Zmiiv county, Kharkiv gubernia. Russian philologist and educator; full member of the Russian Academy of Sciences from 1890. A graduate of the Main Pedagogical Institute in St Petersburg, he taught at Kharkiv University (1853–74, professor from 1858) and then served as director of the Nizhen Historical-Philological Institute (1875–82) and rector of Warsaw Uni-

versity (1889–90). He wrote books on the language of the treaties between Rus' and the Greeks (MA diss, 1853), on schools in medieval Rus' (PH D diss, 1854), and on M. Lomonosov (1865).

Lavrovsky, Petr [Lavrovskij], b 25 March 1827 in Vydropusk, Torzhok county, Tver gubernia, Russia, d 12 March 1886 in St Petersburg. Russian philologist; corresponding member of the Imperial Academy of Sciences from 1856. After graduating from the Main Pedagogical Institute in St Petersburg (1851) he taught Slavic languages at Kharkiv University. Then he served as rector of Warsaw University (1869–72) and curator of the Orenburg (1875–80) and Odessa (1880–5) school districts. Some of his numerous works on Slavic languages were devoted to the history and distinctive nature of Ukrainian, eg, *Obzor zamechatal'-nykh osobennostei narechiia malorusskogo sravnitel'no s velikorusskim i drugimi slavianskimi narechiiami* (A Survey of the Main Peculiarities of the Little Russian Dialect in Comparison with the Great Russianand Other Slavic Dialects, 1859) and *O iazyke severnykh russkikh letopisei* (On the Language of Northern Rus' Chronicles, 1852). Disagreeing with M. *Maksymovych, Lavrovsky sided with N. Pogodin and claimed that the language used in Kievan Rus' was Russian.

Lavruk, Pavlo, b 1865, d ? Political figure. A peasant of the Kolomyia region active in the Ukrainian Radical party and in the Sich movement, he was elected in 1911 to the Austrian parliament in Vienna and in 1913 to the Galician Diet. In 1921 he was expelled from the Radical party for advocating co-operation with the Polish government in Galicia.

Lavrushyn, Volodymyr [Lavrušyn], b 28 May 1912 in Kharkiv. Chemist. A graduate of Kharkiv University (1935), he worked at postsecondary institutions in Kharkiv (1945–53) and taught from 1953 at Kharkiv University, where he was rector from 1960 to 1966. His main research has been in physical organic chemistry, particularly the structure and reactivity of organic compounds.

Lavryk, Semen, b 2 November 1915 in Velyka Slobidka, near Ustia, Kamianets-Podilskyi county, Podilia gubernia, d 7 July 1990 in Kiev. Physician and hematologist; corresponding member of the AN URSR (now ANU) from 1979. A graduate of the Vinnytsia Medical Institute (1940), he was rector of the Kiev Medical Institute (1970–84) and director of the laboratory of the Kiev Scientific Research Institute of Hematology and Blood Transfusion. He wrote approx 160 works, including 2 monographs.

Lavryshevo Gospel (Lavryshevske yevanheliie). A manuscript of an Aprakos-type gospel transcribed in the 14th century from a Macedonian original. It consists of 183 parchment folios with double columns. In the 15th to 17th centuries the manuscript belonged to the Lavryshevo Monastery of the Mother of God, near Navahrudak, Belarus. It is now preserved at the Czartoryski Library in Cracow. Its language displays Polisian features such as a new ѣ, a hardened r, a confusion of ѣ with y and y with ы, and sporadic *akan'e*. The manuscript and its language were described by T. Friedelówna in *Ewangeliarz Ławryszewski* (The Lavryshevo Gospel, 1974).

Law. The set of compulsory rules governing relations among individuals as well as institutions in a given society. Being part of the national culture, the law is influenced by the beliefs of a society and is inextricably involved in its social, political, and economic development. The term for law, *pravo*, is common to all Slavic languages. Originally, it meant 'judgment' or 'trial.' Other Ukrainian historical terms for law are *pravda, zakon, ustav, obychai, poshlyna, pokon, urok,* and *staryna.*

Before states were formed, communities on Ukrainian territory were governed by *customary law. The history of Ukrainian law is divided into periods according to the distinctive states that arose in Ukraine.

In the Princely era (9th–14th centuries) the main sources of law were customary law, agreements such as international treaties, compacts among princes, contracts between princes and the people, princely decrees, *viche* decisions, and *Byzantine law. The most original legal monument of the period is *Ruskaia Pravda*, which includes the principal norms of substantive and procedural law. The distinctions between public and private law and between civil and criminal law were unknown. The medieval Rus' state declined, but its law continued to function. In the 14th to 15th centuries it was known as *Rus' law in Ukrainian territories under Polish rule. Gradually, it was replaced by public as well as private *Polish law. At the same time (14th–17th centuries) *Lithuanian-Ruthenian law developed in Ukrainian territories within the Grand Duchy of Lithuania. The laws compiled in the *Lithuanian Register and the *Lithuanian Statute remained in force within the Polish-Lithuanian Commonwealth and, to some extent, in the Hetman state.

Under Polish and Lithuanian rule different foreign laws were adopted in Ukrainian regions for restricted local use. Among villages governed by Rus' law were scattered communities founded on *Wallachian law or *Germanic law. Armenian and Jewish colonies enjoyed internal autonomy and governed themselves by their own law. Municipal self-government based on *Magdeburg law dates back to the 13th century and survived as late as the 19th century in Ukraine.

The law of the Cossack period was based on the Hetman's treaties and legislative acts, the Lithuanian Statute, compilations of customary and Germanic law, and court decisions. After many years of work, the law was compiled and systematized in the *Code of Laws of 1743. The autonomous Hetman state had its own law, based mostly on the Lithuanian Statute. With the abolition of Ukrainian autonomy at the end of the 18th century, Russian law, first public and then civil, was introduced in Russian-ruled territories. In Western Ukraine, Austrian law was introduced in 1772–5. In 1919–39 some of the territory was governed by Polish law and some by Rumanian law, while Transcarpathia came under Hungarian and Czechoslovak law. These regimes in Western Ukraine tolerated Ukrainian customary law as a supplementary source of legal norms.

Except for state and political laws, the laws of the former regimes remained in force during the brief period of national independence (1917–20). Ukrainian legislators and jurists did not have time to construct an independent system of law.

A new kind of law, known as 'socialist,' 'revolutionary,' and 'Soviet,' arose in the Ukrainian SSR and the USSR. The Soviet regime abolished the previous laws and legal institutions and introduced its own legal order, which was codified, eventually, as Soviet law. Soviet norms were determined not only by the constitution and the laws or decrees of the government, but also by the Party program, the decisions of the leading organs of the CPSU, and the current Party line. Thus, law was an instrument of politics. The Soviet state was not a law-governed but a police state, in which law played only a subservient role. It lacked constitutional guarantees of individual rights and firm principles of legality that were binding on the authorities. The state was the source of law, but stood beyond the law.

In codifying Soviet law in the 1920s the regime attempted to overcome the revolutionary chaos that arose out of the disintegration of the old legal order and the political experimentation with the idea of the 'withering away of the state.' The introduction of the New Economic Policy also called for a clearly defined system of laws. The new codes remained European to a large degree, in their classification scheme, their institutions and principles of procedural law, and their terminology. The idea of a distinctive Soviet economic law based on Marxism was rejected in favor of a legal system similar to that in bourgeois societies. A uniform system of laws for the whole USSR and separate republican codes slightly different from each other were drawn up. The same principle was followed in the 1950s and 1960s, when new codes were worked out. The accumulation of legislation since the 1920s and the demand for a more liberal system of 'socialist legality' prompted the government to undertake the task of codification.

Soviet legal theory did not recognize the traditional distinction between public and private law. Soviet law was based on the social ownership of the means of production and a centrally planned economy. By regulating production and consumption the state controlled the essentially private sphere of people's lives. Hence, even family, marital, and inheritance relations were not exclusively private. Yet the general division of law into branches accepted in the West was preserved. State law was divided into branches such as *administrative law, financial law (consisting of budgetary law, tax law, credit law, insurance law, and audit law), electoral law, *language legislation, and education law. Some authors also distinguished, within state law, constitutional law, which defined the process of *legislation. Branches that regulated economic relations – water management law, maritime law, and air transport law – fell clearly under public law. Economic law included also *forest legislation, *land law, and collective-farm law. Relations between manual or office workers and the employer (the state or enterprise) were regulated by *labor law, which was public, not private, in nature. The basic part of private law in the USSR was *civil law. The main branches of civil law were property law, *family law, *inheritance law, *housing legislation, and law of *contract. *Copyright and *patent law were special sections of the last branch. The process of civil litigation was governed by the law of *civil procedure.

The latest codification of Ukraine's *criminal law took place in 1960. The code dealt with offenses against the social order and individuals who were punishable by the state. The severest sanctions were applied to *political crime. Another branch of criminal law was criminal military law. The judicial process in criminal cases was governed by the law of *criminal procedure. The norms defining the institutions and operation of the *penitentiary system are contained in the *Corrective-Labor Code (1971).

Besides norms that regulate legal relations and define the legal order within a state, there are norms that regulate relations between sovereign states or between states and international organizations. International law is based on treaties, legal customs, legal principles, and court decisions. The Soviet theory of international law accepted the principle of exclusive sovereignty and refused to recognize the precedence of international legal norms over national laws. Because Ukraine has enjoyed independence for only brief periods, its contribution to the development of international law has been slight, and its *international legal status has been somewhat problematic.

*Canon law, which governs the internal life of the Catholic and Orthodox churches, today lies outside the secular legal system run by the state.

Problems of legal theory and the history of Ukrainian law have been researched by Ukrainian scholars (see *Legal scholarship). Legal education is provided in Ukrainian institutions of higher learning (see *Law studies). To maintain high professional standards Ukrainian jurists and lawyers have established their own *legal press and have organized professional associations, such as the *Society of Ukrainian Lawyers in Lviv, the *Ukrainian Law Society in Kiev, the *Ukrainian Law Society in Prague, and the Association of Ukrainian Lawyers in the United States and Canada.

Law enforcement. See Police and Procurator's office.

Law studies. The system of preparing members of the legal profession for the practice of law. The aims, teaching methods, and requirements of legal education vary with social, political, and legal context.

In Kievan Rus', the Galician-Volhynian Principality, and the Cossack state, there was no formal legal education. Court officials became familiar with the basic codes and customary law through practice. They read the legal literature, which was translated, usually from Byzantine sources. Law was taught in court schools in the 13th and 14th centuries in Volhynia, Kiev, and Lviv. The Ostrih Academy taught law. *Brotherhood schools in the 16th and 17th centuries, the colleges of the 18th century, and the Kievan Mohyla Academy did not teach law as a separate discipline, but their rhetoric and theology courses covered some elements of law. Monastery schools also taught elements of law. In the 16th to 18th centuries, Ukrainian students acquired a basic legal education in academies and universities in Cracow, Prague, and Western Europe. From the mid-18th century Ukrainians from central and eastern Ukraine could study law at the universities of Moscow (est 1755) and St Petersburg (est 1819). The Ukrainian legal specialist and economist M. *Baluhiansky taught law and served as rector at the latter university.

In Russian-ruled Ukraine a system of legal education was introduced in the early 19th century with the founding of the first universities and lyceums. The universities of Kharkiv, Kiev, and Odessa had law faculties. According to the 1863 statute governing universities in the empire, the four-year legal program included the history of legal philosophy, Roman law, civil law and judicial procedure, criminal law and procedure, the history of Russian law, state law, international law, financial and commercial law and procedure, church law, political economy, and statistics. In addition, law students had to take courses in logic, Roman history, Russian history, forensic medicine, and a foreign language. Orthodox students were also required to study theology. Legal education was also offered by lyceums, which prepared young men of the privileged estates for careers in government. The *Nizhen Lyceum, which specialized in legal education from 1840 to 1875, trained officials for legal institutions. In the early 19th century, courses in canon law were introduced at the Kiev Theological Academy and at various seminaries.

In Ukrainian territories under Habsburg rule, legal education was offered from 1784 at Lviv University and from 1875 at Chernivtsi University. In 1862 and 1872 the first law chairs with Ukrainian as the language of instruction were set up in Lviv. Ukrainian students studied law also in Vienna, Cracow, and Graz. Instruction lasted for four years and covered three basic areas: history (including legal history, Roman law, theory), jurisprudence (civil, criminal, and procedural law), and political science (state law, positive and administrative law, and economics). Those who passed state examinations were qualified to work in the legal system. Lawyers had to complete a doctorate of law, eight years of articling, and an examination by the chamber of advocates.

Under the Polish regime in the interwar period, legal education culminated in a master of law degree, which qualified the holder for positions in the courts or government or for private practice. A doctorate of law was an academic degree which required the writing of a dissertation and the passing of rigorous examinations. The *Lviv (Underground) Ukrainian University (1921–5) had a law faculty with 23 lecturers and over 600 students.

Transcarpathian lawyers were trained at the universities of Vienna and Budapest, or the law schools in Košice and Nagyvárad (Oradea), where training lasted two years. In the interwar period residents of Transcarpathia could study law at a school for notaries in Košice, in Czechoslovak universities, or at the Ukrainian Free University (est 1921) in Prague. With its faculty of law and socioeconomic studies, this university became the main center for Ukrainian legal education abroad.

Under the educational reforms of the early 1920s in the Ukrainian SSR, law faculties were transferred to institutes of the national economy. Legal education became completely controlled by the Communist party, and subservient to its aims and directives. The leading specialists and professors were trained mostly at higher Party schools. In 1922 a law department was established at the Institute of Red Professors. In 1931 the Institute of Law and Soviet Construction (est 1929) became part of the All-Ukrainian Association of Marxist-Leninist Scientific Research Institutes. Its role was to train lecturers in law for higher educational institutions and conduct law research. With the revival of universities in Ukraine, law faculties were reopened at the universities of Kiev and Odessa. The Kharkiv Juridical Institute (est 1935) had four faculties: Soviet formation, law, economic law, and international law. In 1934 a system of law schools with a one-year program was set up to train raion-level cadres, such as procurators and people's judges.

Today, legal education is offered at Kiev, Lviv, and Odessa universities and at the Kharkiv Juridical Institute.

These institutions train legal specialists with higher qualifications for the courts, the procuracy, the investigative branch, and the administrative courts, as well as legal advisers to government bodies and community organizations. In addition to the regular five-year programs, they offer six-year correspondence and night courses. Special correspondence courses and seminars are open to employees of legal institutions who wish to upgrade their qualifications. Kiev and Lviv universities provide one-year courses or seminars for lower court judges, notaries, assessors, and court secretaries. All economics and finance students are required to take courses in law.

In the late 1950s a system of community universities of legal sciences was created to propagate knowledge of Soviet law. By 1960 there were 36 such universities in Ukraine, and by April 1966 there were 156. Most of the students were from the militia, or were members of social courts, or were people's assessors, factory directors, or Party, trade-union, or Komsomol functionaries. The program, usually lasting one year, consisted of monthly lectures on civil, administrative, criminal, and international law, and on Soviet construction.

I. Bakalo

Lawriwsky, Michael. See Lavrivsky, Mykhailo.

Lawryshyn, Zenoby [Lavryšyn, Zenovij], b 4 June 1943 in Rudnyky, Galicia. Composer, conductor, and pianist. A graduate of the Royal Conservatory of Music (1961) and the University of Toronto (MUS M, 1969), he studied under L. Kolessa and A. Jolivet (Paris). His concert appearances have included works by J.S. Bach, L. van Beethoven, F. Chopin, G. Fauré, and M. Ravel, as well as the Ukrainian composers M. Lysenko, V. Barvinsky, V. Dovzhenko, and V. Kosenko. Lawryshyn was a founder of the Ukrainian-Canadian Opera Association and served as its chorus master from 1978. His main works include two symphonies; chamber music; incidental music for plays such as *Romantychna vatra* (Romantic Bonfire), *Lisova pisnia* (Forest Song) and *Cassandra*; *Panakhyda* (Requiem) for mixed chorus; and music for the films *Nikoly ne zabudu* (I Shall Never Forget, 1969), *Marichka* (1973), and *Harvest of Despair* (1985). Lawryshyn won the Golden Sheaf Award of Excellence for the last work at the 1985 Yorkton Festival of Short and Video Films.

Lazarchuk, Andronyk [Lazarčuk], b 15 January 1870 in Ukhovets, Kovel county, Volhynia gubernia, d 6 September 1934 in Borzna, Chernihiv oblast. Painter and pedagogue. A graduate of the St Petersburg Academy of Arts (1895) and its pedagogical program (1905), he taught painting in schools in Kovel, Konotip, Kremianets, and elsewhere. From 1915 he taught in Borzna, where he initiated the creation of the town's museum, which he directed until 1925. His genre paintings include *In a Peasant House*, *A Family Group*, *Reading a Letter*, a portrait of T. Shevchenko, and self-portraits. Lazarchuk also illustrated O. Pchilka's newspaper *Ridnyi krai* (1907–14). An exhibition of 67 of his works was held at the Volhynian Regional Museum in Lutske in 1987.

Lazarchuk, Ipolyt [Lazarčuk], b 13 August 1903 in Pochaiv, Kremianets county, Volhynia gubernia, d 23 February 1979 in Kiev. Animator; son of A. *Lazarchuk. After graduating from the Kiev State Art Institute (1929) he

worked at the Kiev Artistic Film Studio. He was assistant director of one of the first animated sound films in Ukraine, Ye. Horbach's *Murzylka in Africa* (1934), and created the first color animated film in Ukraine, *Lisova uhoda* (The Forest Treaty, 1936). Later he worked at the Kiev Studio of Popular Science Films.

Lazarenko, Andrii, b 27 November 1901 in Kiev, d 13 September 1979 in Lviv. Botanist; corresponding member of the AN URSR (now ANU) from 1951. After graduating from the Kiev Institute of People's Education in 1924, he worked at the ANU Institute of Botany (1922–41, 1943–5), chaired a department of the Lviv Division of the Institute of Botany (1945–9, 1954–6, and 1964–79), directed the ANU Institute of Agrobiology (1951–3), and chaired a department at Lviv University (1945–58). His works deal with the classification and geographical distribution of mosses in Ukraine, Belarus, Central Asia, and the Far East. For five years (1959–64) he was barred from teaching and from continuing his research because he had openly criticized I. Michurin's legacy in Soviet agrobiology.

Lazarenko, Yevhen, b 26 December 1912 in Kharkiv, d 1 January 1979 in Kiev. Geologist and mineralogist; full member of the USSR Academy of Sciences from 1969. He graduated from Kharkiv University (1934) and taught at Voronezh University from 1938. He taught at Lviv University from 1944, became a professor there in 1948, and served as rector from 1951 to 1963. He was head of the AN URSR (now ANU) Institute of Geological Sciences (1969–71) and department head at the ANU Institute of the

Andronyk Lazarchuk: *Portrait of a Girl in a Black Hat* (oil)

Yevhen Lazarenko

Geochemistry and Physics of Minerals (from 1972). Lazarenko initiated the Ukrainian Mineralogical Society and served as its first president (1970) and was vice-president of the All-Union Mineralogical Society (1971). Lazarenko's main works were devoted to general mineralogy as well as to the mineral resources of Ukraine. He wrote several textbooks on mineralogy and coauthored a mineralogical dictionary.

Lazarev, Boris, b 6 August 1906 in Myropillia, Okhtyrka county, Kharkiv gubernia. Low-temperature physicist; AN URSR (now ANU) full member from 1951. A graduate of the Leningrad Polytechnical Institute (1930), he worked at the Leningrad Physical-Technical Institute (1930–6) and at the ANU Physical-Technical Institute in Kharkiv (from 1937). He made substantial contributions to low-temperature physics, particularly to the development of powerful superconducting solenoids. He established a relationship between superconducting properties and the topological structure of the Fermi surface in metals, and contributed to cryogenic vacuum technology.

Lazarevska, Kateryna [Lazarevs'ka], b 1879, d 1940? Historian and archeographer; daughter of O. *Lazarevsky. She worked at the VUAN, where she researched the socioeconomic and cultural history of 18th- and 19th-century Ukraine, the history of guilds in the Kiev and Chernihiv regions (pub in ZIFV, vol 5), and the Lazarevsky family genealogy (pub in *Ukraïns'kyi arkheohrafichnyi zbirnyk*, 1927, no. 2). She was the archeographic editor for vols 1–4 of *Ukraïns'kyi arkhiv* (1929, 1931) and vol 1 of the chronicle of S. Velychko (1926). The journal *Ukraïna* published her articles on the letters of O. Bodiansky to her father (1926, no. 1), the general survey of landholdings of Starodub regiment (1928, no. 4), T. Shevchenko and the Lazarevsky brothers (1928, no. 4), noble estates in the Starodub region in the first half of the 18th century (September 1929), M. Kulish and M. Vovchok (July–August 1929), and materials for the biography of S. Nis (September 1929). Lazarevska's later fate is uncertain; it is known only that she was released from prison in 1933.

Lazarevsky [Lazarevs'kyj]. A Cossack family from the Chernihiv region that included a number of noteworthy figures in 19th-century Ukrainian culture. Matvii (1778–1857) left some interesting memoirs about the Chernihiv region in the first quarter of the 19th century. His oldest son, Vasyl (b 27 February 1817, d 18 April 1890), held gov-

ernment positions in Kharkiv, Orenburg (1847–8), and St Petersburg (from 1848). He translated W. Shakespeare's plays and French literature into Russian, published a few sketches in Russian journals, and compiled a Ukrainian dictionary (unpublished). Mykhailo (b 12 July 1818, d 3 May 1867) served as an official in Tobolsk (1841–6) and Orenburg (1846–50), where he became one of T. Shevchenko's best friends. He helped the poet financially and, after getting a position in St Petersburg, worked for Shevchenko's release from exile. He took care of the ailing poet in St Petersburg, arranged his funeral and the transportation of his body back to Ukraine, and acted as the executor of his estate. In 1858 Shevchenko presented his diary and self-portrait to Mykhailo. Other members of the family include Fedir (b 20 April 1820, d 13 August 1890) and Oleksander *Lazarevsky and his children, Borys, a Russian writer, Hlib, and Kateryna *Lazarevska.

Oleksander Lazarevsky

Lazarevsky, Oleksander [Lazarevs'kyj], b 20 June 1834 in Hyrivka, Konotip county, Chernihiv gubernia, d 13 April 1902 in Pidlypne, Konotip county. Historian. He graduated in 1858 from St Petersburg University, where he studied under M. Sukhomlinov. After the abolition of serfdom he helped implement reforms in the Chernihiv region as a representative to the Chernihiv Conference of Justices of the Peace (1861–3) and was secretary of the Chernihiv Statistical Committee. From 1868 he served in a judicial capacity in Chernihiv, Poltava, Kremenchuk, Nizhen, and Kursk. In 1880 he moved to Kiev, where he was a member of the Kiev Judicial Chamber, played an active role in the *Historical Society of Nestor the Chronicler and its publications, and was one of the founders of the journal *Kievskaia starina*.

As a student Lazarevsky contributed articles to *Chernigovskie gubernskie vedomosti* and prepared *Ukazatel' istochnikov dlia izucheniia malorossiiskogo kraia* (A Guide to Sources for the Study of the Little Russian Land, 1858). In the mid-1860s he researched the socioeconomic and cultural history of Left-Bank Ukraine during the 17th and 18th centuries. He wrote a fundamental study of the peasantry titled 'Malorossiiskie pospolitye krest'iane, 1648–1783' (Little Russian Common Peasants, 1648–1783, *Zapiski Chernigovskogo statisticheskogo komiteta*, vol 1 [1866]) and articles about the Cossack *starshyna* and nobility in *Russkii arkhiv* (1875–6) and *Kievskaia starina* (1882–93). He made an outstanding contribution to the history of colonization, administration, and land tenure in *Opisanie Staroi Malorossii* (A Description of Old Little Russia, 3 vols, 1888–1902). He also wrote a commentary on the historical monographs of D. Miller on the Little Russian nobility and the statute courts (1898) and a study of early Ukrainian historiographers in *Kievskaia starina* (1897, nos 1–2), as well as numerous genealogies. His articles published in *Kievskaia starina* were reprinted in a five-volume edition of his works (1891–9). In the field of Ukrainian archeography Lazarevsky edited M. Khanenko's diary (1884), the diary of the general treasurer Ya. Markovych (3 vols, 1893–7), materials from the archives of the Sulyma (1884), Motyzhynsky (1890), Poletyka (1891), and other families, the Liubech archive of Count M. Myloradovych (1898), the correspondence of H. Poletyka (1895), and, in collaboration with M. Konstantynovych, *Obozrenie Rumiantsevskoi opisi Malorossii* (A Survey of the Rumiantsev Census of Little Russia, 3 vols, 1866–73).

Lazarevsky's approach to history was based on his populist ideas. He emphasized the exploitation of peasants by the Cossack *starshyna* and regarded the Hetman state and its leading figures with disapproval. But he treated fairly those Ukrainian nobles who made a contribution to Ukrainian culture. He paid little attention to the disastrous influence of Russian policy in Ukraine, but Ukrainian historians noted the one-sidedness without denying his enormous contribution; in contrast, Soviet historians approved of his partiality.

Lazarevsky left around 450 published works. His valuable collection of manuscripts and books, bequeathed to Kiev University, has been preserved along with his archive at the Central Scientific Library of the Academy of Sciences of Ukraine in Kiev.

BIBLIOGRAPHY
Tkachenko, M. 'Spysok prats' O.M. Lazarevs'koho i prats' pro n'oho,' *Ukraïns'kyi arkheohrafichnyi zbirnyk*, vol 2 (1927)
Kovalenko, L. 'Do pytannia pro istorychni pohliady O.M. Lazarevs'koho,' *UIZh*, 1958, no. 4
Marchenko, M.; Polukhin, L. *Vydatnyi istoryk Ukraïny O.M. Lazarevs'kyi* (Kiev 1958)
Sarbei, V. *Istorychni pohliady O.M. Lazarevs'koho* (Kiev 1961)
O. Ohloblyn

Lazarevych, Ivan [Lazarevyč], b 29 March 1829 in Mahiliou, Belarus, d 23 March 1902 in Kharkiv. Obstetrician and gynecologist. A graduate of Kiev University (1853), he obtained his doctorate of medicine in 1857 and was a professor at Kharkiv University from 1862. He refined and invented obstetrical instruments and suggested the internal examination of pelvic tissues and organs. He was vice-president of the Second International Medical Congress (Florence, 1869), honorary president of the gynecological section of the 1883 International Medical Congress, and honorary member of the London Obstetrical Society, the Boston Gynecological Society, and Russian physicians' societies in St Petersburg, Moscow, and Kiev. He wrote *Kurs akusherstva* (A Course in Obstetrics, 2 vols, 1877, 1879).

Lazarian, Vsevolod [Lazarjan], b 16 October 1909 in Orikhiv, Berdianske county, Tavriia gubernia, d 24 December 1978 in Dnipropetrovske. Mechanical engineer; full member of the AN URSR (now ANU) from 1972. A graduate of the Dnipropetrovske Mining Institute (1931), he was director of the Dnipropetrovske Institute of Railway

Transport Engineers (1941–58) and head of the Dnipropetrovske branch of the ANU Institute of Mechanics (1968–78). He made contributions to the theories of motion stability, elasticity, and oscillations and solved a number of practical problems in general mechanics and railway transport.

Lazariev, Hryhorii [Lazarjev, Hryhorij], b 20 April 1907 in Tahanrih, Don Cossack province, d November 1989 in Poltava. Stage actor. He began his theatrical career in the Makiivka Theater of Working Youth (1931–4). After returning from exile in Barnaul, he worked in theaters in Chernihiv, Mykolaiv (1939–45), and Kherson (1945–57). Since 1957 he has been a leading actor in the Poltava Ukrainian Music and Drama Theater.

Lazechko-Haas, Myra. See Haas, Maara.

Lazorsky, Mykola [Lazors'kyj] (pseud of Mykola Kork), b 27 October 1890 in Poltava, d 13 March 1970 in Melbourne, Australia. Novelist, publicist, and editor. During the 1920s he edited a journal in Poltava, prepared school textbooks in geography, and published fiction in journals, such as *Znannia* and *Nova hromada*. During the terror of the 1930s he was arrested and imprisoned for 10 years. After the Second World War he settled in Australia. As a writer Lazorsky specialized in the historical novel and the short story. He has published three large novels, *Het'man Kyrylo Rozumovs'kyi* (1961), *Stepova kvitka* (The Steppe Flower, 1965), and *Patriot* (The Patriot, 1969). His short stories and essays have been published posthumously in the collection *Svitlotini* (Light and Shadows, 1973).

Fedir Lazoryk   Ivan Le

Lazoryk, Fedir (pseuds: Fed Makovychanyn, Dalnozir), b 1 April 1913 in Becherov, Bardejov county, Slovakia, d 4 July 1969 in Prešov. Ukrainian poet, novelist, and journalist in Czechoslovakia. He published several collections of poetry, including *Slovo hnanykh i holodnykh* (The Word of the Persecuted and the Hungry, 1949), *Velyka syla* (A Great Force, 1955), *Snizhni khryzantemy* (Snowy Chrysanthemums, 1968), and *Karpats'ka zamana* (Carpathian Lure, 1971); two novels, *Svitanok nad selamy* (Dawn over Villages, 1953) and *Vik nash festyval'nyi* (Our Festival Age, 1958); and stories for children. He edited the journals *Priashevshchina*, *Druzhno vpered*, and *Duklia* and the newpaper *Nove zhyttia*. The folk songs he collected were published in *Spivanochky moï* (My Songs, 1956).

Lazurenko, Danylo, b 24 December 1902 in Vilshana, Kupianske county, Kharkiv gubernia. Stage director. After graduating from the Kharkiv Music and Drama Institute (1929) he worked in the Kharkiv Chervonozavodskyi Ukrainian Drama Theater (1930–3), the Donetske Ukrainian Drama Theater (1933–48, from 1938 as artistic director), and the Dnipropetrovske Ukrainian Drama Theater (1949–59) and, as principal stage director, in the Mykolaiv Ukrainian Theater of Drama and Musical Comedy (1959–61).

Le, Ivan (pseud of Ivan Moisia), b 22 March 1895 in Moisyntsi, Zolotonosha county, Poltava gubernia, d 9 October 1978 in Kiev. Writer. One of the founders of Soviet Ukrainian literature, he began to be published in the early 1920s. He wrote collections of stories and novels, such as *Budni* (Weekdays, 1926), *Iukhym Kudria* (1926), and *Tanets' zhyvota* (The Belly Dance, 1928). His most popular work was *Roman mizhhir'ia* (The Intermountain Novel, 1929), which was published many times and later somewhat modified because of the treatment of the problem of national relations between Russians and the peoples of Asia in the original. Later he wrote the novel *Integral* (1931) in the official vein. His historical novels *Nalyvaiko* (1940) and *Khmel'nyts'kyi* (3 vols, 1957–65) were written in accordance with official Soviet historiography.

Le Clerc, Nicolas-Gabriel, 1726–98. French physician, writer, and historian. In 1759–62 Le Clerc was in Ukraine as private physician to Hetman K. Rozumovsky. In 1769–75 he lived in Russia, where he became an honorary member of the Imperial Academy of Sciences. During his stay in Ukraine Le Clerc collected valuable material on the history of the Cossacks and the Zaporozhian Sich (which he visited). He later wrote *Histoire physique, morale, civile, et politique de la Russie ancienne et moderne* (3 vols, 1783–5), which was severely criticized by the imperial government and Russian and Russophile scholarly circles (eg, in I. Boltin's *Primechaniia na istoriiu drevniia i nyneshniia Rossii g. Leklerka* [Comments on the History of Ancient and Modern Russia by Le Clerc, 2 vols, 1788]). He was also the author of *L'histoire des Cosaques de Boristhènes* (1776), which has not survived.

League for the Liberation of the Peoples of the USSR. See Paris Bloc.

League of American Ukrainians (Liga amerykanskykh ukraintsiv). A pro-communist Ukrainian organization in the United States. The league was created in 1924 under the name of the United Ukrainian Toilers Organization (Soiuz ukrainskykh robitnychykh organizatsii, or SURO) as an ideological successor to the pro-Bolshevik wing of the Ukrainian Federation of the Communist Party of America. The league presented itself as a defender of the economic interests of Ukrainian American workers and maintained an affiliation with the Communist Party of America. It also established a Ukrainian section of the International Workers' Order in 1935, known as ORDEN or the Ukrainian American Fraternal Union, as a front organization. It was an ideological supporter of Soviet power and solicited support for the 'liberation' of Western Ukraine through its incorporation into the Ukrainian SSR. The league had a highly antagonistic relationship with the

mainstream Ukrainian organizations in the United States and carried on a polemic with them which was particularly severe in the 1930s and 1940s. The major Ukrainian associations have criticized the league for its unswerving loyalty to the Soviet Union and its uncritical posture on the question of national independence for Ukraine. The league's membership declined precipitously after the Second World War, with the onset of the Cold War and the realization of a period of economic prosperity.

League of Nations. An international organization incorporated in the 1919 Treaty of Versailles with the aim of preserving world peace and collective security and fostering international co-operation. From 1920 the seat of the league was in Geneva, Switzerland. Among the league's members were states that occupied parts of Ukraine – Poland, Rumania, Czechoslovakia, and the USSR (1934–9). In 1920 the UNR government failed to gain admission to the league. In 1920–3 the *governments-in-exile of the UNR and the Western Ukrainian National Republic repeatedly submitted protests to the league regarding the occupation of Ukrainian lands by Poland and the USSR. Only once – on 23 February 1921 – did the league take into consideration the protests of President Ye. Petrushevych and acknowledge that eastern Galicia was militarily occupied by Poland.

Because the league was responsible for ensuring that the rights of national minorities guaranteed in a treaty signed by Poland, Rumania, and Czechoslovakia were observed, Ukrainians (including Magyarophile and Russophile circles in Transcarpathia) submitted memoranda to the league when such rights were violated. The largest number of such memoranda were submitted by the Ukrainian Parliamentary Representation and its individual members in the Polish Sejm. In them they protested Poland's discriminatory educational policies, the officially sanctioned colonization of Western Ukrainian lands by Polish army veterans, the persecution of the Ukrainian co-operative movement, the abuse and torture of Ukrainian political prisoners, and the 1930 *Pacification of Galicia by the Piłsudski regime. Because of the unsympathetic attitudes of members of the league's Secretariat and the league's complex procedural norms, only the memorandum regarding the Pacification was passed on by the Secretariat to the league's Council.

The only occasion on which the league took note of Soviet Ukrainian affairs was at the September 1933 secret Council meeting on the famine in Ukraine. The league had the legal authority to care for refugees from the former territories of the Russian Empire, including Ukraine, but it did not formally grant Ukrainian émigrés separate recognition (see *Emigration). Ukrainian interests were defended in the league's various agencies primarily by Ukrainian parliamentarians in interwar Poland and by O. *Shulhyn, the unofficial representative of the UNR government-in-exile.

An International Federation of League of Nations Societies promoted co-operation with the league and propagated its ideas. The émigré Ukrainian League of Nations Society and the Western Ukrainian League of Nations Society (Vienna, 1921–4) were admitted to federation at its Prague Congress in June 1922. The first was headed by M. *Zalizniak, the latter by R. *Perfetsky. In 1925 the Ukrainian Group of the International University Federation for the League of Nations was founded at the Ukrainian Husbandry Academy in Poděbrady, Bohemia. Although the league was a political instrument of the victorious European powers in the First World War and did not, by and large, recognize Ukrainian national demands, Ukrainian petitions to the league and the participation of Ukrainians in the International Federation facilitated the dissemination of information about Ukrainian affairs in international circles. In 1946 the league was dissolved by its 21st Assembly and was replaced by the Organization of *United Nations.

League of Ukrainian Catholics of America (Liga ukrainskykh katolykiv, or LUC).

A social organization for Eastern rite Catholics of Ukrainian origin. It was established in 1933 as a cultural, social, and religious association of young Catholics and was known initially as the Ukrainian Catholic Youth League in America. The first head of the league was B. *Katamai. In the early 1960s its name was changed to the current one. The league provides scholarships for theology students and aid to needy Ukrainians and organizes three national gatherings each year: a convention, a sports competition, and a religious retreat. From 1933 it published a monthly magazine, *Ukrainian Youth*, initially in Ukrainian and then in English. Since 1966 it has published *Action*.

League of Ukrainian National Homes. See Union of Ukrainian Community Centres of Canada.

Members of the League of Ukrainian Nationalists. Sitting, from left: M. Stsiborsky, M. Tobilevych, T. Pasichnyk-Tarnavsky, L. Kostariv, M. Zahryvny; standing: Yu. Rudenko, Yu. Artiushenko, D. Pasichnyk, R. Myniv, D. Demchuk, O. Chekhivsky, K. Dudariv, Ya. Herasymovych

League of Ukrainian Nationalists (Legiia ukrainskykh natsionalistiv, or LUN).

A nationalist organization formed in Poděbrady on 12 November 1925 out of three closely related societies, the Ukrainian National Alliance, the Union of Ukrainian Fascists, and the Union for the Liberation of Ukraine. Its purpose was to develop a distinctive Ukrainian nationalist ideology and to unify the national struggle. During its four years of existence the LUN counteracted Sovietophile tendencies and the influence of communist doctrine among Ukrainian émigrés and co-operated in the formation of the OUN. Its membership consisted mostly of émigrés from the Dnieper region (veterans of the UNR Army and students) and included people such as Ye. Malaniuk, L. Mosendz, D. Demchuk, Ya. Moralevych, and M. Seleshko. Branches of the league sprang up in Prague, Brno, Berlin, and Luxembourg, but Poděbrady remained its main center. Its president was M. *Stsiborsky. In 1927 the LUN published two issues of *Derzhavna natsiia* under the editorship of Malaniuk.

League of Ukrainian Organizations. See Ukrainian Workers' League.

Leather industry.

A branch of *light industry that manufactures leather from animal hides. Leather is used mainly in the manufacture of footwear, coats, and gloves.

The leather industry has existed in Ukraine since the time of Kievan Rus', but factories were not established until the second half of the 19th century, and they were limited to Kiev (Berdychiv) and Kherson (Odessa) gubernias. In 1865 there were 449 leather enterprises in Russian-ruled Ukraine, with an output valued at 1,364,000 rubles. Most of them were small workshops run by tradesmen. Volhynia gubernia, with the highest number of leather enterprises, for example, had 166 enterprises in 1884, but they employed only 470 workers and produced only 300,000 rubles' worth of goods. At the same time 52 enterprises in Kiev gubernia employed 443 workers and had an output valued at 1,023,000 rubles. In 1912, 36 modern factories in Kiev and Kherson gubernias produced 85 percent of Ukraine's leather output.

The leather industry was an important branch of Ukraine's light industry: it employed 1,700 workers, or 15.2 percent of the work force in light industry, in 1913 and produced 35.7 percent of the industry's gross output. The emphasis was on the production of heavy leather, much of which was exported to Russian manufacturing centers and then reimported as soft leather goods. In 1913 Ukraine manufactured 16 percent of heavy leather but only 10 percent of leather goods. That year Ukraine produced 4,900 t of heavy leather and 130,000 sq m of soft leather.

During the First World War Ukraine's share of leather production rose to 20–24 percent as the imperial government encouraged concentration to meet military needs. During the revolution and foreign occupation the industry's output fell by half. During the 1920s and 1930s the industry became more concentrated, specialized, and modernized. By 1940 its output was five times greater than it had been in 1913. In 1940 Ukraine produced 8,318,000 sq m of soft leather and 15,000 t of heavy leather, or 17.9 percent and 21.5 percent of the USSR output respectively.

After the Second World War the leather and footwear industries had the slowest growth rates of all branches of light industry. In 1950 Ukraine's output of 5,123,000 sq m of soft leather and 8,200 t of heavy leather was still far below the 1940 output. But production grew steadily thereafter, with soft leather becoming increasingly important. The output of heavy leather has declined since 1970. In 1973 Ukraine produced 22,630,000 sq m of soft leather (20.7 percent of the USSR output) and 31,464 t of heavy leather (21.6 percent of the Union output). By 1983 soft leather had overtaken heavy leather in republican importance: heavy leather production declined to 25,041 t (20.2

percent of the USSR ouput), whereas soft leather production rose to 25,313,000 sq m (22.4 percent of the USSR output).

As leather production became increasingly mechanized, employment in the industry fell. In 1954, 4,203 workers were employed in the leather industry in Ukraine (16.8 percent of all Soviet leather workers), whereas in 1970 only 3,775 were employed, in 24 leather works (19.6 percent of all Soviet leather workers). The main leather factories are in Kiev, Kharkiv, Berdychiv, Vasylkiv, Ivano-Frankivske, Odessa, and Lviv.

B. Somchynsky

Mykola Lebed

Lebed, Mykola [Lebed'], b 23 November 1909 in Strilychi Novi, Bibrka county, Galicia. Revolutionary and Ukrainian nationalist leader. In 1930–2 he organized the OUN youth wing in Western Ukraine, and in 1932–4 he served as liaison between the OUN national executive in Galicia and the OUN leadership abroad. He was sentenced to death for helping to organize the 1934 assassination of B. *Pieracki, but the sentence was commuted to life imprisonment. In September 1939 he escaped from prison, after which he sided with S. *Bandera in the power struggle within the OUN and became one of the Bandera faction's top leaders. After Bandera and most members of Ya. Stetsko's provisional administration were arrested by the Gestapo in 1941, Lebed (under the pseudonym Maksym Ruban) assumed control of the OUN underground struggle against the Nazis in Ukraine and played an important role in organizing the *Ukrainian Insurgent Army (UPA). In the summer of 1943 Lebed became the OUN chief of foreign affairs. He was a founder of the *Ukrainian Supreme Liberation Council (UHVR) and its general secretary for foreign affairs. In July 1944 he left Ukraine to establish contacts with the Allies, and in 1949 he settled in the United States, where he headed the *Prolog Research Corporation (1952–73). He has written the documentary memoir *UPA* (1946; 2nd edn 1987) and numerous articles in the Ukrainian press.

M. Prokop

Lebedev, Anatolii, b 1 February 1931 in Sushchevo, Viazma okrug, Zapadnaia oblast, RSFSR. Specialist in mechanics; full member of the AN URSR (now ANU) since 1988. He graduated from the Kiev Polytechnical Institute (1954) and taught there. From 1960 he worked at the AN URSR Institute of Metal Ceramics and Special Alloys (now the Institute for Problems of Materials Science) and since 1966 at the Institute for Problems of the Strength of Materials. He has done research on the criteria of strength and the factors affecting the strength of materials under conditions of stress at high and low temperatures.

Lebedev, Sergei, b 2 November 1902 in Nizhnii Novgorod, Russia, d 3 July 1974 in Moscow. Russian scientist in the fields of electrodynamics and computer sciences; full member of the AN URSR (now ANU) from 1945 and of the USSR Academy of Sciences (AN SSSR) from 1953. A graduate of the Moscow Higher Technical School (1928), he founded and directed the Institute of Electrodynamics of the AN URSR (1946–51). Under his leadership the institute constructed the digital computing machine *MEOM in 1950. From 1953 Lebedev was director of the Institute of Exact Mechanics and Computing Technics of the AN SSSR. His work dealt with the problems of reliability and automation in power systems, computer technology, and digital instruments theory.

Lebedev, Vladimir, b 6 June 1922 in Dankov, Riazan gubernia, Russia. Specialist in electric welding; full member of the AN URSR (now ANU) since 1972. He graduated from the Moscow Energetics Institute (1944). He worked at the AN URSR Institute of Electric Welding in Kiev and was appointed deputy director there in 1970. His publications deal with the design of arc welding devices and butt welding techniques.

Lebediev, Petro [Lebedjev], b 23 August 1885 in Pyriatyn, Poltava gubernia, d 3 May 1948 in Moscow. Geologist and petrographer; corresponding member of the USSR Academy of Sciences from 1939. He graduated from the St Petersburg Polytechnical Institute in 1909 and St Petersburg University in 1912. He taught at Rostov-na-Donu University and the Leningrad Polytechnical and Leningrad Mining institutes. He conducted geological research in Karelia, Caucasia, Transcaucasia, the Far East, and Ukraine, particularly near Mariiupil and in Volhynia. His works, in petrography, mineralogy, and geochemistry, include *Petrohrafiia Ukraïny* (Petrography of Ukraine, 1934), which he coauthored.

Lebedyn. III-15. A city (1990 pop 32,800) and raion center in Sumy oblast. It was founded in 1654, and in 1658 it became a company center of Sumy regiment and was renamed Lebiazhyi Horod. During the war of 1708–9 the command of the Russian army was stationed in Lebedyn, and later Hetman I. *Mazepa's supporters were interrogated and punished there. In the 19th century Lebedyn was a county center in Kharkiv gubernia. Today the city has a machine-tool and a metalworking plant, a furniture factory, a fruit-canning and a meat-packing plant, a mixed-feed factory, a building-materials plant, and a textile factory. Its art museum contains portraits from P. Polubotok's private collection (early 18th century). There is a memorial museum dedicated to the famous singer B. *Hmyria. The most important architectural monument is the wooden Church of the Resurrection, built in 1748. A settlement of the *Cherniakhiv culture (2nd–4th century) has been excavated near Lebedyn.

Lebedynets, Mykhailo [Lebedynec', Myxajlo], b ?, d 1 December 1934. Writer and poet. From 1918 to 1921 his poetry and prose appeared in journals, such as *Mystetstvo*,

Lebedyn: St Nicholas's Church (early 18th century)

Universal'nyi zhurnal, and *Shliakhy mystetstva*. His published works include a collection of poetry, *Chervonyi vinok* (A Red Garland, 1919), and two collections of short stories, *Pasma zhyttia* (Skeins of Life, 1919) and *Vikno rozchynene* (The Window Is Open, 1922). He was executed during the Stalinist terror.

Lebedynsky, Ivan [Lebedyns'kyj], b 12 October 1888 in Breusivka, Kobeliaky county, Poltava gubernia, d 1942. Economist and statistician. In the 1920s he worked in the trade statistics department at the Central Statistical Administration of the Ukrainian SSR and taught at the Kharkiv Institute of People's Education and then at the Kharkiv Institute of Finance and the Economy. His pioneering work on price indexes was published as *Pro chysla-pokazhchyky (indeksy) ta iak ïkh vykorystovuvaty* (On Numerals-Indicators [Indexes] and How to Use Them, 1927) and *Selians'kyi indeks na Ukraïni: Metodolohichni osnovy ioho vyrakhovuvannia* (The Peasant Index in Ukraine: The Methodological Bases of Its Computation, 1928). His demographic study of Kharkiv was broken off in 1932–3 and was taken up later by M. Kurman and published as *Naselenie bol'shogo sotsialisticheskogo goroda* (The Population of a Large Socialist City, 1968).

Lebedynsky, Sylvestr [Lebedyns'kyj, Syl'vestr], b 1750, d 5 November 1808. Orthodox bishop and biblical scholar. He was educated at the Kiev Theological Academy and served as rector of the Kazan Theological Academy (1797–9) before being consecrated bishop of Pereiaslav. He was then bishop of Poltava (1803–7) and archbishop of Astrakhan. He wrote *Compendium theologiae dogmaticae* (1799).

Lebedyntsev, Kostiantyn [Lebedyncev, Kostjantyn], b 25 October 1878 in Radom, Poland, d 25 September 1925 in Kiev. Mathematician and pedagogue; son of T. Lebedyntsev. A graduate of Kiev University (1900), he taught at various secondary schools in Kiev until and after the Revolution of 1917. He became a consultant for the People's Commissariat of Education and an assistant rector of the Kiev Institute of People's Education. A proponent of new educational methodology, he edited the journal *Pedagogicheskaia nedelia* and wrote textbooks on algebra (1911) and general mathematics (1925).

Teofan Lebedyntsev   Kharyton Lebid-Yurchyk

Lebedyntsev, Teofan [Lebedyncev] (Lebedintsev, Feofan), b 24 March 1828 in Zelena Dibrova, Zvenyhorod county, Kiev gubernia, d 24 March 1888 in Kiev. Historian and educator. He studied at the Voronezh and Kiev seminaries and at the Kiev Theological Academy, where in 1861–4 he was a professor, and then directed the Kholm, Lublin, and Radom school districts, in 1864–80. A specialist in the history of the Orthodox church and its brotherhoods in Ukraine, he founded and edited a periodical for village clergy titled *Rukovodstvo dlia sel'skikh pastyrei* (Kiev, 1860–3), in which he published a number of his own articles, and wrote for the journal *Osnova*. Lebedyntsev was one of the founders of the journal **Kievskaia starina* (1882) and the editor of the second and third volumes of the *Arkhiv Iugo-Zapadnoi Rossii*. He wrote four sermons in Ukrainian (1861–3), the study *Bratstva, ikhnia kolyshnia i nynishnia dolia ta znachennia* (Brotherhoods, Their Former and Present-Day Destiny and Significance, 1862), and memoirs of the poet T. Shevchenko (published in *Kievskaia starina*).

Lebid, Ananii [Lebid', Ananij], b 1889 in Keleberda, Zolotonosha county, Poltava gubernia, d 1939. Poet and literary scholar; member of the writers' group **Pluh. He wrote the monograph *M. Kotsiubynskyi: Zhyttia i tvorchist'* (M. Kotsiubynsky: His Life and Work, 1929) and also contributed articles to *Zapysky Istorychno-filolohichnoho viddilu VUAN*, *Ukraïna*, and *Zhyttia i revoliutsiia*. Together with M. Rylsky he compiled the anthology *Za 25 lit* (In 25 Years, 1926). In addition he wrote poems and songs for the contemporary press. He was arrested in 1929 in connection with the show trial of the *Union for the Liberation of Ukraine but was released. He was arrested again in 1935 and sentenced to 10 years' imprisonment in a concentration camp, where he perished.

Lebid, Dmytro [Lebid'], b 21 February 1893 in Lotsmanska Kamianka (now a part of Dnipropetrovske), Katerynoslav county, Katerynoslav gubernia, d 30 October 1937. Party leader and Soviet state official. A member of the Katerynoslav ('right') Bolshevik faction, after the February Revolution in 1917 he headed the Bolshevik organization of the Katerynoslav railway and the gubernia militia. He rose in the CP(B)U to become a member of the Audit Commission (1919) and the Organizational Bureau (1920) and a candidate member (1920–2) and full member (1922–4) of the Politburo. As second secretary of the CC CP(B)U in 1920–4, he opposed the policy of *Ukrainization. According to his theory of the 'struggle of two cultures,' the Russian urban, proletarian culture would triumph over the Ukrainian rural, peasant culture. From 1924 he held high posts in the Russian Communist Party (Bolshevik). After being arrested during the terror in 1937, he was executed by the NKVD. He was rehabilitated in the 1960s.

Lebid-Yurchyk, Kharyton [Lebid'-Jurčyk, Xaryton], b 1877 in eastern Podilia, d 1945 in Germany. Economist. In 1917–21 he was in the UNR civil service, in which he headed a department of the state treasury and served as deputy minister of finance (1919–21). He lectured in economics at Kamianets-Podilskyi Ukrainian State University. After emigrating to Poland and then to Germany he became a fellow of the agriculture department at the Ukrainian Scientific Institute in Berlin. He specialized in the Ukrainian sugar industry and state finances and wrote *Biudzhetove pravo* (Budget Law, 1927) and *Das erste ukrainische Staatsbudget für das Jahr 1918* (1929).

Left Opposition. The name of a faction led by L. *Trotsky within the Bolshevik party. Leaders of the Left Opposition in Ukraine included Kh. Rakovsky, M. Holubenko, Ya. Livshits, and P. Rozengaus. In 1923 the Left Opposition had half the votes in the Kiev Party organization. In its struggle against bureaucratization it obtained the passive support of some Ukrainian national-communist currents (mainly former *Borotbists.). Most Ukrainian Communists were critical of the Left Opposition's neglect of the national question and of its insistence on rapid industrialization. Some members of the *Communist Party of Western Ukraine, however, were sympathetic to it. During the Stalinist terror of the 1930s many former Left Oppositionists were arrested and sent to labor camps in the Arctic Vorkuta region, where they were executed in 1936–8.

In the second half of the 1930s a group of Ukrainians of the Communist Party of Canada emerged as supporters of the Fourth International, founded in 1938 by the Left Opposition, and published the newspaper *Robitnychi visty* in Toronto (1933–8). Under their influence Trotsky wrote articles in support of Ukraine's independence after the Soviet occupation of Western Ukraine in 1939.

Left-Bank Ukraine (Livoberezhia). A territorial-administrative-geographic region consisting of the Ukrainian lands east of the Dnieper River. In the 17th and 18th centuries Left-Bank Ukraine became a major Ukrainian economic, political, and cultural center administered as 10 Cossack regimental districts (Starodub, Chernihiv, Nizhen, Pryluka, Lubni, Hadiach, Kiev, Pereiaslav, Myrhorod, and Poltava) that formed the *Hetman state (Hetmanate). By extension *Slobidska Ukraine, which had a comparable social and economic order, sometimes has been regarded as part of the Left-Bank realm, even though it was never linked administratively with the Hetmanate and had a separate historical development. The Left-Bank lands have commonly been considered the heartland of Ukrainian ethnic territory. The former Left-Bank Ukraine now constitutes the oblasts of Chernihiv and Poltava, the left bank of Kiev and Cherkasy oblasts, the city of Kiev and its right-bank environs, northern Dnipropetrovske oblast, and northwestern Sumy oblast. The Starodub regiment lands are now within Briansk oblast in the Russian Federation.

The Dnieper waterway provided a specific geographic focus for the Left-Bank region as its dividing line with *Right-Bank Ukraine. The formal partitioning of the two regions made the Dnieper a frontier zone and thereby compelled the Left Bank to reorient itself politically and economically toward Moscow. The Dnieper regained importance only after 1795, when Right-Bank Ukraine had been incorporated in toto into the Russian Empire.

The establishment of the Left Bank as a distinctive geographic and political entity came as an offshoot of the *Cossack-Polish War of 1648–57. Following Hetman B. Khmelnytsky's death (1657) the Cossack polity was racked by dissension between officers and rank-and-file Cossacks, and between pro- and anti-Polish political orientations. The dissension produced a split in Cossack ranks that acquired a specific geographical dimension when the Left-Bank regiments refused to follow the acting hetman, Yu. Khmelnytsky, who supported the Poles against Moscow at the Battle of Chudniv (1660), and elected I. Somko as their leader. Khmelnytsky remained hetman of Right-Bank Ukraine, thereby initiating the division of Ukraine into Left and Right banks. The division soon acquired additional significance in international affairs as a result of the Treaty of *Andrusovo (1667), which established the Dnieper as the dividing line between Russian and Polish zones of influence.

In 1668 the Right-Bank hetman, P. *Doroshenko, successfully united the Cossack regiments on both banks of the Dnieper under his leadership. Internal Right-Bank conflicts and external threats from Poland and Turkey, however, forced his return to the Right Bank. In the interim the acting Left-Bank hetman, D. *Mnohohrishny, was forced by circumstance to break with Doroshenko and swear allegiance to Moscow. Thenceforth the Left Bank remained continuously under Russian influence.

In 1676 Hetman I. *Samoilovych invaded Right-Bank Ukraine, defeated Doroshenko, and proclaimed himself hetman of both banks. In 1678, while retreating before a Turkish advance, Samoilovych forcefully attempted to remove the population of Right-Bank Ukraine to the Left Bank and Slobidska Ukraine.

The *Eternal Peace of 1686 between Russia and Poland cemented the previous Treaty of Andrusovo and confirmed Poland's claim to Right-Bank Ukraine. Russia obtained undisputed control over Left-Bank Ukraine, consisting of the *Hetmanate and a portion of *Zaporizhia. In 1703 Hetman I. *Mazepa occupied Right-Bank Ukraine and was briefly hetman of both banks.

In the 18th century the autonomy of Left-Bank Ukraine was steadily eroded until the Hetmanate was abolished in 1782. From 1796 to 1802 the Left Bank was reconstituted as an administrative territory in *Little Russia gubernia.

Although the Left Bank had ceased to function as an administrative unit, certain features continued to distinguish it as unique for the remainder of the imperial period. The Left-Bank gentry, the former Cossack *starshyna* and its descendants, contributed disproportionately to the formation of a conscious Ukrainian intelligentsia from the end of the 18th to the early 20th centuries. The life of the agricultural population was also distinctive in Left-Bank Ukraine. There free and state peasants, the descendants of rank-and-file Cossacks, formed a significant portion of the rural population, and landlords' serfs were fewer than in Galicia or Right-Bank Ukraine. As well, a characteristic form of peasant settlement, the *khutir*, or single farmstead, was found there. (See also *History of Ukraine.)

A.G. Beniuk

Legal defense. In criminal proceedings, a person empowered to defend the legitimate interests of the defendant and to ensure the observance of the defendant's procedural rights. In the USSR lawyers, trade-union representatives, and relatives could be appointed defense counsel. The appointment procedure and the duties and rights of the defense counsel were defined in the Legislative Foundations of Criminal Jurisprudence of the USSR and Union Republics (1958) and the Code of Criminal Procedure of the Ukrainian SSR (1960). The law required representation by a defense counsel in the following cases: when the defendant, because of physical or mental handicaps, cannot defend himself or herself; when the defendant is a minor; when the defendant does not know the language of the court; when capital punishment is a possible verdict; when compulsory medical treatment is at issue; when there is a conflict of interest between codefendants; when one of the codefendants is represented by a defense counsel. Under Soviet law, the defendant could obtain defense counsel only after the pretrial investigation was completed. Thus, the defendant had no legal assistance during a most crucial stage of the legal process, when false confessions and testimony had been forced routinely from the accused.

Legal press. Periodicals devoted to issues of law and of the legal profession, including the official gazettes of legislatures and reports of the courts.

Gazettes. The earliest gazettes of laws valid in Ukrainian territories were published in Vienna by the Austrian government and were entitled *Allgemeines Reichs-, Gesetz- und Regierungsblatt für das Kaiserthum Österreich* (1848–52), *Reichsgesetzblatt für Kaiserthum Österreich* (1853–69), and *Reichsgesetzblatt für die im Reichsrathe vereinten Königreiche und Länder* (1870–1918). These gazettes were translated into all the languages of the empire. In Ukrainian they came out as *Obshchii zakonov derzhavnykh i pravytel'stva Vistnyk dlia tsisarstva Avstrii* (1849–53), then as *Vistnyk zakonov derzhavnykh i pravytel'stva* (1854–8), and finally as *Vistnyk zakonov derzhavnykh dlia korolevstv i kraev v derzhavnoi dumi zastuplenykh* (1872–95) and *Vistnyk zakoniv derzhavnykh dlia korolivstv i kraïv, zastuplenykh v Derzhavnii*

Radi (1896–1916). Austria's provincial governments published their own gazettes: in Galicia *Provinzialgesetzsammlung des Königreichs Galizien und Lodomerien* (1819–48) was followed by *Allgemeines Landes-Gesets- und Regierungs-Blatt für das Kronland Galizien und Lodomerien mit den Herzogthümern Auschwitz und Zator und dem Grossherzogthume Krakau*, which was translated into Ukrainian as *Vseobshchii dnevnyk zemskykh zakonov i pravytel'stva dlia koronnoi oblasty Halytsii i Volodymerii s kniazhestvom Osvitsymskym i Zatorskym i velykym kniazhestvom Krakovskym* (1851–2), and then by *Landes-Regierungsblatt für das Kronland Galizien und Lodomerien mit den Herzogthümern Auschwitz und Zator und dem Grossherzogthume Krakau* (1853–1914), which appeared also in Ukrainian as *Vistnyk kraievoho pravytel'stva dlia koronnoi oblasty Halytsii* ... For a time, the separate vicegerency in eastern (Ukrainian) Galicia issued *Landes Regierungsblatt für das Verwaltungsgebiet der Statthalterei in Lemberg* (1854–9), which came out in Ukrainian under different titles as *Vistnyk kraevoho pravytel'stva dlia upravytel'stvennoi oblasty namistnychestva v L'vovi* (1854–7) and *Vistnyk riadu kraevoho dlia oblasty administratsiinoi Namistnytstva vo L'vovi* (1858–9). For Bukovyna, *Allgemeines Landes-Gesetz- und Regierungsblatt für das Kronland Bukowina* (1850–1914) was published in Chernivtsi and translated under the title *Obshchii zakonov kraevykh i pravytel'stva Vistnyk dlia korunnoho kraiu Bukovyny*. In the 1850s the gazette *Landesgesetz und Regierungsblatt für Kronland Ungarn* was published as *Zemskii pravytelstvennyi Vistnyk dlia korolevstva Uhorshchyny* for the Ukrainian population in the Hungarian crownlands.

In Russian-ruled Ukraine there was no legal gazette before 1917. New laws were published in the official gubernia newspapers (*gubernskie vedomosti*), which were established in the Ukrainian gubernias in the 1860s.

During the struggle for Ukrainian independence (1917–20), every Ukrainian government issued a regular legal gazette. The Central Rada published *Vistnyk Heneral'noho Sekretariiatu Ukraïny* (1917–8) and *Vistnyk Rady Narodnikh Ministriv Ukraïns'koï Narodn'oï Respubliky* (1918). *Derzhavnyi vistnyk* (1918) came out under the Hetman regime. Under the UNR Directory, *Vistnyk Ukraïns'koï Narodn'oï Respubliky* (1918–19) was changed to *Vistnyk derzhavnykh zakoniv* (1919–20). The government of Western Ukraine published *Zbirnyk zakoniv, rozporiadkiv, ta obizhnykiv proholoshenykh Derzhavnym Sekretariiatom Zakhidnoï Ukraïns'koï Narodnoï Respublyky* (1918) and then *Vistnyk derzhavnykh zakoniv i rozporiadkiv Zakhidnoï Oblasty Ukraïns'koï Narodnoï Respublyky* (1919). In addition, many ministries issued their own gazettes, usually entitled *Vistnyk* or *Visty*.

In the interwar period, a Ukrainian-language legal gazette was published only in Transcarpathia. It was called *Uriadova hazeta Zems'koho Uriadu dlia Pidkarpatorus'koï Rusy* (1919–28) and then *Zems'kyi vistnyk* (1928–38). The gazette of autonomous Carpatho-Ukraine was *Uriadovyi vistnyk Pravytel'stva Pidkarpats'koï Rusy* (1938), which was renamed *Uriadovyi vistnyk Pravytel'stva Karpats'koï Ukraïny* (1939). Laws for Polish- and Rumanian-ruled Ukrainian territories appeared only in Polish or Rumanian gazettes.

The first Soviet government in Ukraine issued its gazette in both Ukrainian and Russian, under the same title as the gazette of the more popular UNR government, *Vistnyk Ukraïns'koï Narodn'oï Respubliky* (December 1917–March 1918). Then the regime published the bilingual

Zbirnyk uzakonen' i rozporiadzhen' Robitnycho-selians'koho uriadu Ukraïny (1919–29) and *Zbirnyk zakoniv ...* and the newspaper **Visti VUTsVK* (1921–41). In Moscow the gazette of the all-Union government was also issued in Ukrainian. From 1941 the official publication of the Ukrainian Supreme Soviet was the bilingual **Vidomosti Verkhovnoï Rady URSR*. The gazette of the USSR Supreme Soviet was published in the languages of the republics, including Ukrainian, but from 1960 it has come out only in Russian. In the 1920s and 1930s some laws and official pronouncements were published in journals of the People's Commissariat of Justice and various court bulletins. Most of these publications appeared in both Ukrainian and Russian. Various commissariats and executive committees published their own bulletins and official magazines. Some decrees and instructions of the ministries were published in national newspapers, such as *Radians'ka Ukraïna* (Kiev) and *Izvestiia* (Moscow), and oblast or city newspapers run by the Party or by the Soviets.

Journals. The first professional law journals published in Ukrainian were **Chasopys' pravnycha* (1889–99), *Chasopys' pravnycha i ekonomichna* (1900–12), and **Pravnychyi vistnyk* (1910–13) in Lviv. Within the Russian Empire there were no Ukrainian-language legal periodicals. Ukrainian jurists published in Russian journals, such as *Zhurnal Iuridicheskogo obshchestva*, *Iuridicheskii vestnik*, and *Vestnik prava*. During the period of Ukrainian independence the monthly *Zakon i pravo* (1918) appeared briefly in Kiev.

In the interwar period, **Zhyttia i pravo* (1928–39) appeared quarterly in Lviv, and the popular monthly *Pravni porady* (1933) came out briefly in Kolomyia. In addition, Western Ukrainian newspapers often carried articles on theoretical and practical legal issues. In Soviet Ukraine the journal *Vestnik sovetskoi iustitsii na Ukraine* (1922–9) was published in Russian until it was renamed (1929–30) **Visnyk radians'koï iustytsiï*. At the same time the People's Commissariat of Justice issued **Chervone pravo* (1926–31). The last two journals were replaced in 1931 by **Revoliutsiine pravo*. After the Second World War no Ukrainian legal journal was published in the USSR for many years, and Ukrainian jurists had to publish their works in various Russian periodicals, such as *Sovetskoe gosudarstvo i pravo* and *Sotsialisticheskaia zakonnost'*. It was only in 1958 that **Radians'ke pravo* was established as the organ of the Ministry of Justice, the procuracy and the Supreme Court of the Ukrainian SSR, and the Sector of State and Law of the AN URSR.

Outside Ukraine, the Association of Ukrainian Lawyers in New York published irregularly the professional journal *Pravnychyi visnyk* (4 vols, 1955–79).

A. Bilynsky, V. Markus

Legal scholarship. The study of law in Ukraine began with the emergence of an organized state in Kievan Rus', when **customary law was systematized in collections such as *Zakon Ruskii* and *Ruskaia Pravda*. The treaties negotiated between Kievan Rus' and Byzantium articulated for the first time the principles of international private law and testify to the legal sophistication of the princes' officials. The Church Slavonic translations of the Greek *Nomocanon* known as **Kormchaia kniga* indicated that there were close ties between Byzantine and Rus' legal specialists. The publication of three editions of the **Lithuanian Statute* in the 16th century confirms that Western-trained legal specialists were active at the time in Ukraine.

In the 18th century, the more prominent legal scholars were V. Stefanovych, the chairman of the committee that prepared the Code of Laws of 1743, and F. Chuikevych, the author of *Sud i rozprava* (Court and Trial, 1750).

As the Ukrainian state declined and became integrated into the Russian Empire, the conditions for an independent tradition of legal scholarship disappeared. Law graduates of the Kievan Mohyla Academy who continued their studies in West European universities served usually in St Petersburg or Moscow.

As a modern discipline, legal scholarship in the Russian Empire dates from the second half of the 18th century. Initially, its area of interest was natural law. This branch of philosophy was developed by foreign thinkers, mostly German ones. V. Zolotnytsky, a Ukrainian, wrote the first independent monograph on natural law in the Russian Empire (1764). The first law professor at Moscow University born in the Russian Empire was another Ukrainian, S. Desnytsky, who completed his doctorate of laws at Glasgow University and advocated at independent judiciary. Several Ukrainians from Transcarpathia – P. Lodii, V. Kukolnyk, and M. Baluhiansky – were invited to St Petersburg and became prominent legal scholars.

In the 19th century the newly established universities in Kharkiv, Kiev, and Odessa, as well as Nizhen Lyceum and the Kiev Theological Academy (canon law), emerged as the centers of legal scholarship in Ukraine. By then the philosophy of law was replaced in the Russian Empire by the encyclopedic study of law. A Ukrainian graduate of Kharkiv University, P. Degai, wrote the first Russian textbook on law, *Posobie v pravilakh izucheniia rossiiskikh zakonov ili materialakh entsiklopedii, metodologii, i istorii literatury rossiiskogo prava* (A Textbook on the Rules of the Study of Russian Laws, or Materials for the Encyclopedia, Methodology, and History of the Literature of Russian Law, 1831). M. Pyliankevych (1819–56), a professor of law at Kiev University, defended a Hegelian position in his *Istoriia filosofii prava* (History of the Philosophy of Law, 1870). O. Lokhvytsky (1830–84), who taught law at the Richelieu Lyceum in Odessa and then at St Petersburg University, studied issues of maritime law and the international law of war. Many of the law professors in Ukraine were Russian, Polish, or German. The more prominent Ukrainian legal scholars of the late 19th and early 20th centuries were L. Bilohryts-Kotliarevsky, a specialist in criminal law; O. Huliaiev, in civil law; V. Karpeka, in civil and financial law; S. Ornatsky (1806–84), in civil law; O. Fedotov-Chekhovsky, in civil and Roman law; H. Hordiienko (d 1849), in criminal law; and P. Lashkarev, in church law. The criminologist S. Bogorodsky played a major role in establishing the law faculty of Kiev University. His student, O. Kistiakovsky, was a specialist in criminal and Ukrainian customary law. V. Nezabytovsky (international law), O. Eikhelman (international law), and B. Kistiakovsky (philosophy of law) served as professors at Kiev University. At Kharkiv University the more important law professors were D. Kachenovsky, V. Danylevsky, V. Yastzhembsky (international law), V. Hordon (civil law and procedure), and M. Chubynsky (criminology). At Odessa University P. Kazansky specialized in international and administrative law, O. Borovykovsky in civil law, and Yu. Pryhara in constitutional law. Some law professors of Ukrainian origin taught at other universities in the Russian Empire: O. Yashchenko and V. Grabar at Tartu University, V. Aleksandrenko at Warsaw

University, and M. Kravchenko at Tomsk University.

In the 19th century much research was done on the legal history of Ukraine. Polish historians, such as T. Czacki and I. Daniłowicz, and Russian scholars, such as V. Sergeevich, K. Nevolin, V. Chicherin, M. Diakonov, P. Silvansky, and M. Vladimirsky-Budanov, studied the law of Kievan Rus', the Lithuanian-Ruthenian state, and the Hetman state. The Ukrainian national revival of the 19th century encouraged wide research on the legal institutions and structure of the Hetman state. Many historical studies were published in journals, such as *Chteniia v Istoricheskom obshchestve Nestora-letopistsa* and *Kievskaia starina*, and in the collection *Arkhiv Iugo-Zapadnoi Rossii*. The most important legal monument published separately was the Code of Laws of 1743, with a commentary by O. Kistiakovsky (1879). In the early 20th century major contributions to Ukrainian legal history were made by M. Vasylenko, D. Miller, M. Slabchenko, M. Maksymeiko, Y. Malynovsky, F. Leontovych, M. Liubavsky, O. Balzer, I. Lappo, S. Kutrzeba, and S. Yushkov. Some of these scholars continued to publish in the Soviet period.

In Western Ukraine the major centers of legal scholarship were the universities of Lviv and Chernivtsi. Several professors of Lviv University were Ukrainians: O. Ohonovsky (private law), P. Stebelsky (criminal law), and S. Dnistriansky (civil and state law). The first attempts to standardize Ukrainian legal terminology were made by the editorial board of Austria's official legal gazette, *Allgemeines Reichs-, Gesetz- und Regierungsblatt für das Kaiserthum Österreich* (1848–52). An official commission, which included I. Holovatsky, H. Shashkevych, and Yu. Vyslotsky, compiled a Ukrainian-German legal and political dictionary, *Juridisch-politische Terminologie für die slavischen Sprachen Österreichs: Deutsch-ruthenische Separat-Ausgabe* (1851). Galicia's Ukrainian center for legal scholarship was the Legal Commission of the Shevchenko Scientific Society (NTSh) in Lviv. It published four volumes of the Pravnycha Biblioteka (Legal Library) series, three volumes of *Zbirnyk Pravnychoï komisiï* (1925–9), and the journals *Chasopys' pravnycha* (1889–99) and *Chasopys' pravnycha i ekonomichna* (1900–12). The quarterly *Pravnychyi vistnyk* of the Society of Ukrainian Lawyers in Lviv published articles on legal history and theory. The more prominent law scholars in Western Ukraine included K. Levytsky, M. Lozynsky, V. Okhrymovych, V. Verhanovsky, S. Baran, V. Paneiko, and V. Levynsky.

In the Ukrainian SSR the development of legal scholarship was difficult and uneven. In the early 1920s the All-Ukrainian Academy of Sciences became the center for research on Ukrainian legal history. The *Commission for the Study of the History of Western-Ruthenian and Ukrainian Law and the *Commission for the Study of Ukraine's Customary Law were established in January 1919 within its Socio-Economic Division. Their primary aim was to study the archival material in Kiev and Moscow. Each commission published its *Pratsi*, which addressed a range of topics, including Lithuanian-Ruthenian law by M. Vasylenko and S. Borysenok, the sociolegal structure of the Zaporozhian Sich by M. Slabchenko, the law of Kievan Rus' by M. Maksymeiko, the legal institutions of the Hetman state by I. Cherkasky, L. Okinshevych, V. Hryshko, and V. Novytsky, and customary law by S. Borysenok, A. Kryster, M. Tovstolis, Y. Malynovsky, and O. Dobrov. Among these scholars the prevailing view was that an independent Ukrainian legal tradition developed continu-

ously from Kievan Rus' to the abolition of the Hetman state. At the beginning of the 1930s the two commissions were dissolved, and research on Ukrainian legal history was interrupted for two decades. It was only in the 1950s that K. Sofronenko's monograph on the Little Russian Office (1951) and V. Diadychenko's book on the sociopolitical system of Left-Bank Ukraine in the 17th and 18th centuries (1959) appeared. In the 1960s V. Kalynovych, A. Tkach, and A. Pashuk also contributed to the history of prerevolutionary law.

Research institutions outside the academy were strongly influenced by Marxism-Leninism and primarily served the economic and political interests of the state. Kharkiv, the first capital of Soviet Ukraine, was the center of legal research and discussion. The Ukrainian Law Society and the People's Commissariat of Justice published jointly *Vestnik sovetskoi iustitsii na Ukraine* (1922–8) and then *Visnyk radians'koï iustytsiï*, which was merged with *Chervone pravo* (1926–31) to form *Revoliutsiine pravo* (1931–41). Jurists tried to develop new branches of law such as co-operative and trade law to handle the new situation. In their works the law was presented generally in traditional terms, as a set of abstract and universally binding norms. This concept of law was accepted by the more prominent jurists of the 1920s, O. Malytsky, H. Volkov, Ye. Nemyrovsky, V. Diablo, V. Boshko, and R. Babuk. Legal specialists, such as M. Paliienko, M. Reikhel, V. Kobalevsky, and A. Evtikhiev, concentrated on constitutional and administrative law. M. Mitilino, S. Landkof, and P. Kovanko-Kovankovsky developed economic law, and V. Koretsky, V. Grabar, L. Velychko, Ye. Kelman, and M. Lozynsky worked on international law.

In the late 1920s legal scholarship began to decline quickly. The theory that technical and organizational norms take precedence over legal ones (legal nihilism) gained favor. Juridical institutes and law faculties were closed. This trend did not last long, since the Soviet authorities demanded severe norms, which assumed a voluntaristic nature. The school of so-called socialist law regarded law as the necessary expression of the will of the state. It was represented by A. Vyshinsky, the general procurator of the USSR. In Ukraine the few active legal scholars confined themselves mostly to commentaries on positive Soviet law: S. Vilniansky on civil law, B. Sokolov on state law, A. Pasherstnyk on labor law, V. Serebrovsky on inheritance law, and S. Landkof on civil law.

It was only after Stalin's death that the Party decided to reject voluntarism and legal relativism, and return to 'socialist legality.' To work out new legal codes it raised the level of legal scholarship. In 1949 the Sector (since 1969, Institute) of State and Law became the chief center of legal scholarship in Ukraine. From 1958 it collaborated with several state agencies in publishing *Radians'ke pravo*. There was an increase in the number of legal publications, the number of law schools (see *law studies), and the enrollment of law students. The publication of the two-volume collective work *Istoriia derzhavy i prava Ukraïns'koï RSR (1917–1967)* (The History of the State and Law of the Ukrainian SSR [1917–1967], 1967) was a significant achievement. Associates of the Kharkiv Juridical Institute prepared several collections of papers entitled *Pytannia derzhavy i prava Ukraïns'koï RSR* (Questions of State and Law of the Ukrainian SSR, 1952–8) and *Pytannia istoriï derzhavy i prava Ukraïns'koï RSR* (Questions of the History of State and Law of the Ukrainian SSR, 1953–7). The law faculty of Kiev University began to publish an inter-departmental collection, *Problemy pravoznavstva* (Problems of Jurisprudence) in 1965. V. Koretsky, P. Nedbailo, Ye. Nazarenko, and V. Tsvietkov dealt with theoretical questions of law and the state. B. Babii, P. Mykhailenko, L. Potarykina, A. Taranov, V. Terletsky, and S. Fuks studied the history of the state and law of the Ukrainian SSR. S. Vilniansky, V. Maslov, H. Matvieiev, M. Hordon, V. Koleichykova, and M. Orydoroha have done work on civil and family law. P. Indychenko, V. Muntian, S. Pidopryhora, and V. Yanchuk specialized in land and co-operative farm law. Ya. Brainin, S. Tykhenko, M. Hrodzynsky, P. Zavorotko, and Ya. Shutin have written on criminal law and procedure. International law has been studied by V. Koretsky, K. Zabihailo, M. Korostarenko, I. Lukashchuk, and N. Ulianova, and the law of other countries has been studied by Ye. Tykhonova, S. Makohon, H. Aleksandrenko, and Ya. Pliasun. Besides juridical institutes and universities, legal research is also conducted at the Kiev and Kharkiv scientific research institutes of forensic experts. Some noted Ukrainian jurists, such as S. Bratus, V. Lisovsky, and V. Serebrovsky, worked in the USSR outside Ukraine.

In Western Ukraine in the interwar period, the legal commission of the NTSh continued to be the main center of legal research. It was headed by V. Verhanovsky. The works of its associates were published in *Zhyttia i pravo*. The more productive legal scholars were S. Baran, V. Starosolsky (state law), Yu. Paneiko (professor of state and administrative law at Cracow, then Vilnius, university), and M. Chubaty (history of Ukrainian law).

Outside Ukraine law research was conducted at the law faculty of the Ukrainian Free University (UVU) in Prague by émigré scholars, such as O. Eikhelman (state and international law), S. Dnistriansky (state law), M. Lozynsky (state law), S. Shelukhyn, R. Lashchenko, A. Yakovliv (history of Ukrainian law), K. Losky (Roman law), and O. Odarchenko (financial law). O. Lototsky, V. Bidnov, and V. Zaikin at the Ukrainian Scientific Institute in Warsaw worked on the history of Ukrainian canon law. After the Second World War law research has continued at UVU, the NTSh, the Ukrainian Academy of Arts and Sciences, and the Association of Ukrainian Lawyers in the United States, which had published three collections of *Pravnychyi visnyk* by 1971. Most Ukrainian law scholars have been interested in the history of Ukrainian law or in Soviet law. Contributors to the former field include V. Hryshko, L. Okinshevych, Ya. Padokh, and A. Yakovliv. Ukrainian state law has been studied by S. Ivanytsky, V. Lysy, and M. Stakhiv; and B. Halaichuk, V. Markus, and R. Yakemchuk have written on international law. Critical studies of Soviet law have been written by A. Bilynsky and Yu. Starosolsky, and O. Yurchenko. M. Chubaty, M. Wojnar, and V. Pospishil have specialized in canon law. Other areas of law and jurisprudence have been studied by E. Pyziur, J. Fedynskyj, T. Ciuciura, and W. Tarnopolsky.

BIBLIOGRAPHY
Babii, B. *Pravovye issledovaniia v Akademii nauk Ukrainskoi SSR, 1919–1973* (Kiev 1974)
— *Ocherk razvitiia pravovykh issledovanii v Ukrainskoi SSR, 1919–1984* (Kiev 1984)

A. Bilynsky, V. Markus, Yu. Starosolsky

Legal system. See Civil procedure, Criminal procedure, and Court system.

Legends (from Latin *legenda*, 'that which is to be read'). In the Western tradition a legend was originally a text about the life of a saint that was prescribed reading in churches on that saint's day and during meals in monasteries. Because medieval legends, such as those in *Legenda aurea*, were similar to fairy tales, the term was extended to refer to various kinds of tales (historical, folk, and religious). Now the term is used for tales in which the characters are actual historical personages, including saints. In Ukraine, in addition to religious legends and apocrypha, there were also legends about Rus' princes, Cossacks, hetmans, haidamakas, opryshoks, and other famous people (eg, M. Churai, H. Skovoroda, T. Shevchenko). They were published by P. Kulish in his *Zapiski o Iuzhnoi Rusi*, by O. Afanasiev-Chuzhbynsky in his *Narodnye legendy* (Folk Legends, 1859 and 1921), and, chiefly, by researchers of Ukrainian fairy tales, such as M. Chubynsky, M. Drahomanov, and V. Hnatiuk. Manuscripts of folk legends were collected and edited by I. Franko and published in 1899. The historical legends that appeared in the oldest Ukrainian chronicles were collected by F. Giliarov in his *Predaniia Russkoi Nachal'noi letopisi* (The Legends of the Rus' Primary Chronicle, 1878). Many legends became part of the Cossack chronicles. *Istoriia Rusov* could be considered a historical legend. Legends have reappeared in the historical novel and drama, and folk legends are frequently drawn upon in Ukrainian poetry.

Legend continues to play a role in contemporary Ukrainian literature. Using legends as a base O. *Dovzhenko wrote his scenario *Zvenyhora*, and L. *Kostenko compared her novel-in-verse *Marusia Churai* to a legend. Legends play a prominent role in the works of D. Pavlychko, B. Stelmakh, V. Vovk, E. Andiievska, and other contemporary writers.

D. Chyzhevsky, D.H. Struk

Léger, Louis-Paul-Marie, b 13 January 1843 in Toulouse, d 30 April 1923 in Paris. Pioneering French Slavist; member of the Russian Imperial Academy of Sciences from 1884 and the Académie Française from 1900. Through his research, travels in Ukraine, and correspondence with M. Drahomanov he developed an interest in Ukrainian folklore and literature, particularly in the poems of T. Shevchenko, some of which he translated. He also translated several Ukrainian folktales and the Primary Chronicle (1884). He was the first to teach Ukrainian language and literature in France, in the years 1904–6 at the Collège de France in Paris. He wrote many works in Slavic studies, including articles and encyclopedia entries about Shevchenko and other Ukrainian writers and a study of N. Gogol.

Legion of Ukrainian Nationalists (Legion ukrainskykh natsionalistiv or Druzhyny ukrainskykh natsionalistiv). A Ukrainian military formation in the German army during the Second World War. The term 'Legion' was used as a popular name, in an analogy with the Legion of Ukrainian Sich Riflemen, for an OUN-organized military unit which under Col R. *Sushko's command attempted to participate in September 1939 in the German-Polish War. The unit was formed initially in Austria of former soldiers of the Carpathian Sich, who in June 1939 had been released from Hungarian internment. At the end of August 1939 the legion consisted of two understrength infantry battalions, which arrived on 3 September in the vicinity of Prešov, Slovakia. On 24 September it crossed the former Czech-Polish border and started to advance through the Lemko region, but the Germans quickly intervened and demobilized it. In April 1941 the military department of the OUN (Bandera faction), headed by D. *Hrytsai, recruited two battalions with the approval of German military (Wehrmacht) circles. The northern battalion, Spezialgruppe Nachtigall, consisted of three companies, commanded by Lt A. Herzner, that underwent final military training near Neuhammer, in Upper Silesia. The southern battalion, Spezialgruppe Roland, was commanded by Maj Ye. Pobihushchy and was trained near Wiener-Neustadt in Austria.

With the outbreak of the German-Soviet War, Nachtigall marched alongside the German army through Radymno, Lviv, and Ternopil. Placed under the command of Maj Heinz on 13 July 1941 and renamed the Second Battalion of the Brandenburg Regiment No. 800, it was sent into front-line combat in the vicinity of Proskuriv (Khmelnytskyi) and, later, Vinnytsia. During the latter part of August, Nachtigall was taken out of the combat zone and transported to Cracow, where it was disarmed and returned to Neuhammer for internment. Roland marched through Rumania and Moldavia and entered Ukraine on 25 July. In August, before it could see any action, it too was disarmed and recalled to Austria.

In mid-October 1941 at Frankfurt an der Oder, both units were integrated into Schutzmannschaftbataillon 201, under a one-year contract. The entire chain of command (22 officers) was Ukrainian: Maj Ye. Pobihushchy was battalion commander, and R. *Shukhevych, M. Brygider, V. Sydor, and V. Pavlyk were company commanders. The battalion's initial strength was over 600. On 19 March 1942, after intensive retraining, it was sent to Belorussia to protect communication lines and to combat Soviet partisans. The battalion's commanders protested repeatedly against German policy in Ukraine. In November 1942, when its soldiers refused to renew their contract, they were disarmed in Mahiliou, discharged, and sent home. The officers were brought to Lviv and on 8 January 1943 incarcerated in a Gestapo prison. Several of them, including R. Shukhevych, escaped and joined the UPA.

BIBLIOGRAPHY
Druzhyny ukraïns'kykh natsionalistiv u 1941–1942 rokakh (Munich 1953)
Kal'ba, M. (comp.) *U lavakh Druzhynnykiv* (Denver 1982)
Pobihushchyi, Ie. *Mozaïka moïkh spomyniv* (Munich–London 1982)
Kal'ba, M. (comp.) *'Nakhtigal' (Kurin' DUN) u svitli faktiv i dokumentiv* (Denver 1984)

P. Sodol

Legislation. The action of making laws, ordinances, or edicts that carry authority in a given society by virtue of their promulgation by an individual or body invested with legislative power. The Ukrainian word for law (*zakon*) dates back to the medieval period and also refers to customary norms. Under the influence of Byzantine legal practice, the term became restricted to normative acts issued by the prince, usually in written form. Other terms for law used in the medieval period were *pokon, pravo, ustav,* and *urok*. Initially, legislative power belonged to the monarch, who sometimes shared it with representatives of the higher estates. In modern times it belongs, as a rule, to popular bodies, such as parliaments, representing a wider constituency.

In medieval Rus' legislative power was shared by the prince, *viche, and *Boyar Council, but the distribution of power among them varied with principality and time. Bishops and hegumens made laws governing church affairs and affecting church people. Congresses of princes were voluntary and irregular; hence, they lacked legislative authority. M. Vladimirsky-Budanov has argued that such congresses had the right to issue laws for a given territory; eg, a part of the *Ruskaia Pravda* was adopted at the Vyshhorod congress of Yaroslav the Wise's sons (1072).

During the Lithuanian-Ruthenian period, the grand duke enjoyed legislative authority in the Vilnius principality, and the appanage princes made law in their own realms. From the 15th century the grand duke began to legislate for the entire duchy, sharing his power with the Council of Lords and the Great Diet. The most important laws of this period were set forth in the *land charters, the *sudebniki,* and the *Lithuanian Statute.

In the Hetman state, legislative authority was held by the hetman, who usually consulted the *starshyna* and obtained their approval. Sometimes the General Military Council also issued laws. As Ukraine's autonomy declined in the 18th century, legislative power passed to the Russian tsar, who exercised it partly through the *Little Russian Collegium. At the Zaporozhian Sich the Sich Council and the council of officers made law. As in the previous period, no clear divisions of power existed among various branches of government. Sometimes they co-operated in implementing the law, and sometimes they competed.

In the Russian Empire the tsar was the only legislative authority until 1905, although he consulted with the State Council and the Committee of Ministers. After 1905 he shared this power with the State Duma. In the Austro-Hungarian Empire, law-making was the emperor's exclusive right until 1867. Then, under the constitutional monarchy and Assembly of Deputies (Abgeordnetenhaus), laws were passed by the State Council (Reichsrat). In the interwar period, legislation for Ukrainian territories under Polish, Rumanian, and Czechoslovak rule was passed by the respective national parliaments and state presidents. Only the diet of Subcarpathian Ruthenia within Czechoslovakia was to have enjoyed the power to make law for the autonomous territory.

During the period of Ukrainian statehood in 1917–20, various bodies under different regimes exercised legislative power. On 8 December 1917 the Central Rada passed a law reserving for itself 'the exclusive and indivisible right to make law for the UNR,' and it exercised this power through its executive committee, the Little Rada. The *Constitution of the UNR, adopted on 29 April 1918, endowed the National Assembly with supreme legislative power and gave the right to propose legislation to its presidium, the Council of National Ministers, groups of deputies, local governments, and citizens themselves (submitting petitions with 100,000 signatures). Under the Hetman government, laws were drafted by the various ministries and passed by the Council of Ministers, but acquired force only after being ratified by the hetman. This system of legislation was to function only until parliament was convened. The Directory of the UNR, as a revolutionary organ, claimed all the powers of government, including the legislative power which it exercised with the Council of National Ministers. The Labor Congress (1919) transferred its legislative power to the Directory until the next session, which could not be held because of the Bolshevik victory in Ukraine. According to the Law on the Temporary Supreme Government and the Legislative System of the UNR (12 November 1920), legislative authority in the UNR was to belong to the State People's Council, and the president of the Directory was merely to ratify laws. The *Government-in-exile of the UNR, however, left the legislative power with the Council of National Ministers and the president of the Directory.

In the Western Ukrainian National Republic (ZUNR), legislative authority was held by the Ukrainian National Rada, which transferred it on 9 June 1919 to the Dictatorship of the Western Province of the UNR.

In Soviet Ukraine, legislative power was vested formally in the All-Ukrainian Congress of Soviets and the All-Ukrainian Central Executive Committee (VUTsVK) by the first constitution of the Ukrainian SSR (14 March 1919). In practice, however, it was usually the Presidium of the VUTsVK and the *Council of People's Commissars that exercised this power. The constitution of January 1937 created the *Supreme Soviet of the Ukrainian SSR as Ukraine's highest and only legislative body, and its status was confirmed by the most recent constitution (1978). In practice, the Presidium of the Supreme Soviet took over most of its legislative functions: it issued general normative acts called *ukazy*, which differed from formal laws only in name, and these were later ratified as laws by the Soviet. Fundamental areas of the law in Ukraine came under the power of the Supreme Soviet of the USSR in Moscow. All laws passed by the USSR Supreme Soviet were valid on Ukrainian territory. In the case of conflict between Ukrainian and USSR law, the latter prevailed. The declaration of *sovereignty (16 July 1990) placed Ukrainian law above the law of the USSR in the Ukrainian SSR.

During periods of revolutionary change, new regimes generally abolish old legislation in whole or in part. The Central Rada retained the basic legislation of the Provisional Government and even of the tsarist regime (especially civil, criminal, and trade legislation). Only some of the legislation was explicitly replaced by new laws. The Hetman government retained even more of the old legislation, including much of the administrative law, but discarded the political and social legislation of the Central Rada. The Directory, in turn, overturned the hetman's legislation. In the ZUNR, almost all of the Austrian laws remained in force. The Soviet regime abolished the legislation of all former governments in Ukraine and, through a series of decrees, introduced Soviet Russian laws in Ukraine.

In most modern states, laws come into force when they are published in official gazettes. For gazettes published by Ukrainian governments, see *Legal press.

V. Markus

Legislative foundations of the USSR and Union republics. All-Union laws that define the fundamental general statutes, principles, and tasks of Soviet legislation in a specific branch of law. The Constitution of the USSR empowered the USSR Supreme Soviet to make such laws, which played an important role in maintaining legal cen-

tralization and obedience to central political authority. They were binding principles, on which all republican legislation had to be based. The following legislative foundations were established: criminal (1958), court organization (1958), civil (1962), marriage and family (1968), corrective-labor (1969), health (1970), water (1971), labor (1971), education (1973), mineral resources (1975), forest (1977), administrative (1980), land (1980), and housing (1982) law.

Legumes (Leguminosae or Fabaceae; Ukrainian: *bobovi*). A family of dicotyledonous plants with over 500 species and 13,000 varieties, 300 of which grow in Ukraine. Because of their high protein content and their nitrogen fixation role, legumes are of great economic importance. Some are sources of oil or medicinal substances. Domesticated varieties fall into two main categories: seed legumes, including *peas, beans, *peanuts, lentils, *soybeans, and lupine, and legume forage grasses, including lucerne, clover, esparcet, and *vetch. The land devoted to seed legumes increased in the Ukrainian SSR from 836,000 ha in 1940 to 1,681,000 ha in 1986 despite the concurrent decrease in land devoted to all seed crops from 21,385,000 ha to 16,214,000 ha. No separate figures are available for grass legumes, which are an important part of the *feed base.

Lehotsky, Teodor [Lehoc'kyj] (Hungarian: Tivadar Lehoczky), b 5 October 1830 in Fucine, Italy, d 25 November 1915 in Mukachiv, Transcarpathia. Lawyer and noted archeologist, historian, and ethnographer of Transcarpathia. He founded a museum in Mukachiv that bore his name and to which he donated his archeological collection (now in the Transcarpathian Regional Studies Museum in Uzhhorod). His main works are a three-volume monograph in Hungarian on Bereg *komitat* (1881–2), collections of Hungarian-Ruthenian folk songs (1864) and proverbs (1877), and articles and books on the archeology of Transcarpathia, among them *Adatok hazánk archaeologiájához* (Contributions on the Archeology of Our Homeland, 2 vols, 1892, 1912) and *Beregmegyei régiségek* (Antiquities of Bereg *Komitat*, 1896).

Lehr-Spławiński, Tadeusz, b 20 September 1891 in Cracow, d 17 February 1965 in Cracow. Polish Slavist. A professor of Lviv (1922–9) and Cracow (1929–62) universities, he wrote a number of important works in Slavic and Ukrainian linguistics. Regarding the question of the origin of Ukrainian he defended the theory of a common Old Rus' language. He studied Ukrainian phonetics and certain problems in morphology from the neogrammarian viewpoint, and his ideas on the formation of Ukrainian dialects partly influenced I. *Zilynsky. His most important works on the history of Ukrainian are collected in *Studia i szkice wybrane z językoznawstwa słowiańskiego* (Selected Studies and Essays in Slavic Linguistics, vol 1, 1957).

Leipunsky, Aleksandr [Lejpunskij], b 7 December 1903 in Drahli, Hrodna gubernia (now in Poland), d 14 August 1972 in Moscow. Nuclear physicist; full AN URSR (now ANU) member from 1934. A graduate of the Leningrad Polytechnical Institute (1926), from 1929 to 1941 he worked at the Kharkiv Physical-Technical Institute, and from 1933 to 1937 he served as its director. From 1944 to 1952 he worked at the AN URSR Institute of Physics in Kiev,

Aleksandr Leipunsky

and in 1944 served as its director. An ingenious experimentalist, he contributed significantly to the early development of nuclear instrumentation and nuclear-reaction studies in Ukraine. Together with A. *Walter, K. *Synelnykov, and G. *Latyshev he was the first in the USSR to induce the disintegration of a stable nucleus (lithium) by means of accelerated protons (1932). Leipunsky is internationally known for the first experimental evidence of the existence of the neutrino, obtained in 1934 while he was working as a visiting scientist in E. Rutherford's laboratory in Cambridge, England. The later years of his life were devoted to the development of nuclear-power technology.

Leisure (*dozvillia*). Time spent neither working nor performing necessary tasks. Theories about the nature and role of leisure range from the view that leisure can compensate for uninteresting work to the opposite view, that the quality of leisure is dependent on the quality of work. Theories about leisure were particularly influential in Soviet Ukraine because social planners had the power to control the amount and, to a certain extent, the type of leisure most people enjoyed. Just before the demise of the Soviet Union thinking about leisure was rather ambiguous. Soviet ideologists emphasized, as had K. Marx, the central importance of work in the life of the individual, even though work had not become as challenging or fulfilling as Marx had envisioned it would be in a communist society. Furthermore, the Marxist emphasis on the need to create conditions in which all members of society would be able to reach their full potential was often taken by Soviet technocrats as leave to ensure that all individuals spent a minimum amount of time engaged in 'good' (ie, officially approved and sponsored) leisure activities and to limit access to 'bad' forms of leisure (ie, passive entertainment).

Demographic trends forced planners to modify their position. The postwar generation was better educated than its predecessors and had at most only dim memories of war, revolution, and Stalinist excesses. Many members of that generation came to rely on leisure for the satisfaction that neither work nor political involvement afforded them. A 1973 study of Soviet workers in an electronics factory, for example, showed that 31 percent considered leisure to be their principal life interest, whereas only 17 percent felt that work was of central importance. A 1974 study showed a negative correlation between the quality of work and interest in leisure; nevertheless, improving the quality of leisure could have been an easier solution to dissatisfaction with work than changing the nature of work itself.

Since the time necessary to attend to personal needs is generally invariable, work outside the home and housework are the two factors that have determined the amount of leisure time available. Although the working day for industrial workers had not diminished significantly in the postwar period, the introduction of the five-day workweek decreased the number of hours worked per week. The change had an important bearing on leisure time: surveys indicated that workers were more likely to use an additional day off as leisure time than to use extra time per day for that purpose.

The workweek of the Soviet elite was probably longer than that of factory workers. Much of the additional burden came on weekends: in 1971, for example, administrators and members of the intelligentsia worked an average of five hours per weekend day. Farmers worked longer hours than all but administrators and the highest officials. An attempt to distribute farm work more evenly throughout the year only resulted in increased work in the winter.

Housework has restricted leisure time almost as much as has work outside the home. Many basic domestic tasks have been and still are time-consuming. In a 1966 Kiev study, for example, 38 percent of the households surveyed spent 2 to 2.5 hours, and 40 percent spent 1 to 1.5 hours, per day shopping for food. Women have borne most of the burden of housework, which has been almost a second job for them. Decreasing the time devoted to housework was long an aim of the Soviet regime, at least in theory. The reality, however, was that the large amount of time spent on housework barely changed. Not only were Soviet planners unable or unwilling to provide enough appliances and services to make household tasks easier, but social attitudes diminished the effect of the few improvements that were made. Custom as much as practical need dictated the amount of housework done: as more nonworking time has become available, women have often begun to do more housework. The social pressure on women to spend much of their time in housework has not been challenged by a more equitable involvement of men in household tasks. The share of housework done by men is unaffected by class or education, and increasing that share was overlooked by Party ideologists as a way of decreasing women's share. Instead a theoretical emphasis was placed on the socialization and mechanization of housework.

On the whole, the empirical data on the relationship between the type of work done and the nature of leisure was in accord with the official Soviet view that more challenging jobs ought to predispose workers to more challenging types of leisure. Managers, academics, and skilled workers spent more of their leisure time actively (in sociopolitical participation, study, and amateur creativity), whereas unskilled workers devoted more of their leisure time to entertainment (watching television, reading, going to the theater or cinema). In a 1973 study, however, a significant minority of unskilled workers seemed to compensate for the unchallenging nature of their work by devoting as much leisure time to active pursuits as did managers, researchers, and skilled workers. Women devoted a greater proportion of their total free time to active forms of leisure, but their actual participation was smaller.

Overall, the use of leisure time in Soviet Ukraine was characterized by (1) a large though decreasing amount of time spent reading, from 1.26 hours per day for male workers and 0.32 hour for female workers in 1923–4 to 0.45 and 0.3 hour respectively in 1978, and from 1.28 hours in all forms of study for male collective farmers and 0.67 hour for female collective farmers in 1934 to 0.68 and 0.20 hour respectively in 1964; (2) an increase in radio listening and television viewing, from 1.08 hours for male workers and 0.61 hour for female workers in 1967–8 to 1.76 and 1.3 hours respectively in 1978; (3) a significant amount of time spent on social visits, with an increase from 0.65 hour for male workers and 0.5 hour for female workers in 1923–4 to 0.93 and 0.64 hour respectively in 1978; and (4) a decline in previously high sociopolitical participation and time devoted to adult education. The apparent preference for recreational and cultural leisure activities bore out the findings of a 1967 survey, in which 75 percent of the respondents said they gave priority to recreational and cultural forms of leisure. The decline in adult education and sociopolitical participation can be attributed in part to historical and demographic changes: adults whose education had been inadequate because of the exigencies of revolution or war had all completed remedial adult classes by the time of the study. Sociopolitical work, moreover, was less prominent in postwar Soviet society than it had been in the revolutionary 1920s.

BIBLIOGRAPHY
Gordon, L.; Klopov, E. *Man after Work: Social Problems of Daily Life and Leisure Time Based on the Surveys of Workers' Time Budgets in Major Cities of the European Part of the USSR* (Moscow 1975)
Zuzanek, J. *Work and Leisure in the Soviet Union: A Time-Budget Analysis* (New York 1980)
Moskoff, W. *Labour and Leisure in the Soviet Union: The Conflict between Public and Private Decision-Making in a Planned Economy* (London and Basingstoke 1984)
Mashika, T. *Zaniatost' zhenshchin i materinstvo* (Moscow 1989)
C. Freeland

Aleksandr Leites

Leites, Aleksandr [Lejtes] (Oleksander), b 15 December 1899 in Brest-Litovsk, d ? Literary critic and scholar. In the 1920s he lived in Kharkiv, where he belonged to the writers' groups *Hart, *Vaplite, and *Prolitfront and published theoretical and critical brochures and articles about Soviet Ukrainian, Russian, and Western European literature and writers. He also wrote *Syluety Zakhodu* (Silhouettes of the West, 1928) and compiled, with M. *Yashek,

Desiat' rokiv ukraïns'koï literatury (1917–1927) (Ten Years of Ukrainian Literature [1917–27], 2 vols, 1928), an important biobibliographic and documentary source. During the terror of the 1930s he moved to Moscow; there he continued writing, but, for political reasons, not on Ukrainian literature.

Leksykohrafichnyi biuleten' (Lexicographic Bulletin). An annual compendium of lexicographic studies published in the years 1951–5, 1958, 1960–1, and 1963 (nine issues) by the AN URSR Institute of Linguistics. Its chief editors were I. Kyrychenko (1951–5) and V. Ilin (1958–63). Published in it were articles dealing with the history and prospects of Ukrainian lexicography, and the theoretical, ideological, methodological, terminological, and practical aspects of new dictionaries and the lexicons of certain Ukrainian dialects and writers (M. Kotsiubynsky, T. Shevchenko), as well as reviews of dictionaries by over 40 Soviet Ukrainian linguists and lexicographers.

Leluk, Nicholas [Leljuk], b 23 February 1935 in Hillcrest, Alberta. Pharmacist and politician of Ukrainian descent. Educated at the universities of Toronto and Wisconsin, Leluk was executive assistant to the registrar of the Ontario College of Pharmacy (1961–9) and executive director of the Council on Drug Abuse (1969–71) before his election to the Ontario legislature in 1971 as a Progressive Conservative member for York West. He served as minister of correctional services (1981–5) and minister of citizenship and culture (May–June 1985).

Lemish, Yurii. See Kuk, Vasyl.

Lemkivshchyna (Lemko Land). A quarterly organ of the World Federation of Lemkos, published in New York City since 1979. The successor to *Lemkivs'ki visti*, it contains news, articles on the history and culture of the Lemko region, memoirs, belles lettres, and historical documents; it devotes considerable attention to the plight of the Ukrainian Catholic church in the Lemko region, Polish injustices against the Lemkos, and official efforts to Polonize the Lemkos. It also reports on Lemko activities in North America. *Lemkivshchyna* has been edited by O. Pytliar and then by an editorial board.

Lemkivshchyna Museum (Muzei Lemkivshchyna). A Lemko regional museum established in Sianik in 1930. Housed in the residence of the Ukrainian Catholic priest, the museum contained approx 650 books, 3,000 documents, 450 coins, 300 samples of embroidery, 200 Easter eggs, and 170 icons. In the 1930s members of the museum society surveyed over 100 villages in the Lemko region and published three volumes of materials and articles. The museum's founder and director was L. *Gets. During the German occupation (1939–44) the museum was merged with the Polish Museum of the Sianik Land, and after the war its holdings were transferred to the local Polish museum.

Lemkivs'ki visti (Lemko News). A monthly paper published from 1964 to 1975 in Yonkers, New York, by the Organization for the Defense of Lemkivshchyna, and from 1975 to 1979 in Toronto by the Federation of Lemkos in Canada. It succeeded *Holos Lemkivshchyny*, published from 1958 to 1964 in Yonkers and edited by S. Zhenetsky.

Lemkivs'ki visti

From 1975 it was the organ of the World Federation of Lemkos. The paper was edited by Yu. Tarnovych (1964–70), I. Eliiashevsky (1970–4), and then an editorial board. It devoted considerable attention to the plight of the Lemkos under Polish rule and their persecution and forced resettlement after the Second World War. It published news, memoirs, belles lettres, historical documents, and articles on the culture and history of the Lemkos, some of which were written in the Lemko dialect. *Lemkivs'ki visti* also contained reports on Lemko activities in North America. In early 1979 it was succeeded by **Lemkivshchyna*.

Lemko Apostolic Administration (Lemkivska apostolska administratura). A Greek Catholic church administrative unit in the **Lemko region of Galicia. It was founded by the Vatican's Congregation for Eastern Churches in 1934, under pressure from the Polish government, to prevent the Ukrainianization of the Lemko region. Consisting of 9 chapters and 121 parishes detached from Peremyshl eparchy, the administrature was under the direct authority of the congregation in Rome. Its seat at first was the township of Rymanów, and then Sianik. The administrators, appointed by the Vatican, were Revs V. Mastsiukh (1934–6), Ya. Medvetsky (1936–40), and O. **Malynovsky (1940–6). Until 1940 a pro-Polish, anti-Ukrainian spirit dominated in the administration, which accepted the premise that the **Lemkos were distinct from Ukrainians. Theology students from the region were obliged to study in Polish Roman Catholic seminaries in Cracow and Tarnów. The Lemko Apostolic Administration ceased to exist in 1946, when most Ukrainians were deported from the Lemko region.

Lemko Association (Lemko-Soiuz). A social fraternal society established in Cleveland, Ohio, in 1929 as Lemko-Soiuz which assumed its present name in 1931. The association was formed by Lemkos in the United States (with some Canadians) who were not satisfied with the existing Ukrainian, Galician Russophile, or Carpatho-Rusyn fraternal societies in North America. The association assumed publication of the Lemko-dialect newspaper *Lemko* (1930–8) and brought out its own publication, *Karpats'ka*

Rus' (1938–). Throughout the 1930s the group expanded the number of its branches, and in 1938 it moved its headquarters to Yonkers, New York. In 1959 the association established a summer resort in Monroe, New York, where the organizational headquarters were again relocated. Initially dominated by Russophiles, the group had strong pro-Soviet sympathies. More recently its members have come out in favor of a separate Carpatho-Rusyn identity. The organization has also launched English-language publications in an effort to appeal to an American-born membership.

Lemko Company of the Ukrainian Insurgent Army (Lemkivska sotnia UPA). A military unit organized in October 1945 in Lisko county, Lemko region. Composed mostly of local peasants with no military training, it was assigned to Capt V. Mizerny's (nom de guerre: Ren) battalion and given the code names 95a and Udarnyk 5. Its zone of operations was the 26th Tactical Sector of the UPA. Under Lt S. **Stebelsky's (Khrin's) command, the company expanded quickly, and by the spring of 1946 it had six platoons and approx 260 men. In April 1946 two of the platoons were detached to form the company Udarnyk 8. The Lemko Company became widely known as an active fighting force. In the first 18 months it fought more than 100 engagements with Polish army or police units. The most famous of them was its successful ambush on 28 March 1947 of Gen K. Swierczewski, Poland's deputy defense minister. In April–June 1947 the company suffered severe losses in almost continuous combat with Polish units, which were conducting **Operation Wisła, and on 29 June it was forced to retreat into the USSR. After several weeks of skirmishes with NKVD border guards, it was strengthened with soldiers from the demobilized Udarnyk 8 and reorganized into two platoons. On 15 August 1947 it was placed under Lt Stakh's command and sent into western Drohobych oblast. On 10 September 1948 it was demobilized, and its soldiers were assigned to the armed underground.

P. Sodol

Lemko dialects. Dialects spoken by the **Lemkos. They belong to the group of Ukrainian **southwestern dialects and are related to the **Sian, **Boiko, and Middle-**Transcarpathian dialects. Situated on the western edge of Ukrainian ethnic territory and wedged in between Polish and Slovak dialects, the Lemko dialects (LD) have developed some striking peculiarities not found in other Ukrainian dialects.

As a result of Slovak expansion into the Prešov region, a belt of transitional, mixed Ukrainian-Slovak dialects emerged. Polish expansion to the southeast resulted in a mixed dialect which was transitional to the Sian dialect and became limited to an island of 10 villages south of Rzeszów (see **Zamishantsi). According to Polish Slavists, such as Z. Stieber, the Lemko dialectal wedge in the Carpathian Mountains between the eastern Slovak and Polish dialects was the result of 14th- and 15th-century Ukrainian colonization (from the Sian region, according to I. Pankevych) of the highland that constituted a sparsely settled bridge between the Little Polish and Prešov (originally transitional Polish-Slovak) dialects. Czech and Slovak Slavists, such as F. Tichý and J. Víra, believed that the southwestern Lemko region was originally a sparsely settled Slovak highland that became Ukrainianized. Ukrainian scholars (V. Hnatiuk, S. Tomashivsky, I. Verkhratsky, Y. Shemlei) held that the LD, except the westernmost ones, are autochthonous. The eastern boundary of the LD runs along the watershed of the Liaborets, Oslava, and Sian rivers. Their southeasterly expansion gave rise between the Laborets and Tsirokha rivers to a belt of dialects transitional to the Middle-Transcarpathian dialects.

The LD have many distinguishing features: (1) *i* from *ō* (eg, *nis* 'nose', but in the west *nыs*); relatively frequent *'u, ju* from *ē* (eg, *n'us* 'carried' from *nestý* 'to carry', *pjuk* [Standard Ukrainian (SU) *pik*] 'he baked'); (2) preservation of (a) the distinction between Proto-Slavic *u₁ – i* in the form *ы – y* (eg, *sыn – sýn'yj* [SU *syn – sýnij*] 'son – blue') and (b) the old groups *kы, hы, xы, gы* (eg, *múxы, nóhы, rúkы* [SU *múkhy, nóhy, rúky*] 'flies, legs, hands'); (3) *dž* in place of the Proto-Slavic *d + i̯* (eg, *médža* [SU *mežá*] 'border'); (4) a stable stress on the penultimate syllable of a word (eg, *moйóko, rúka* [SU *molokó, ruká*] 'milk, hand'); (5) the combinations *-ыr-, -ыl-* (*-ый-*) in place of the Proto-Slavic *-rъ-, -rь-, -lъ-, -lь-* between consonants (eg, *hыrmíty, sыйza* [SU *hrymíty, sl'ozá*] 'to thunder, tear'); (6) hardness of final softened dentals (eg, *óhen, hist* [SU *vohón', hist'*] 'fire, guest'); (7) preservation of *-l* in eastern LD in such forms as *bыl* [SU *buv*] 'he was' (in the central and western LD every hard *l* at the end of syllables and before back vowels is pronounced *ŭ* as in Polish [eg, *moйóko* 'milk']); (8) dorsal pronunciation of the softened dentals *s', z', c', dz'*; (9) change of the preposition-prefix *v* + vowel or voiced consonant into *h* (eg, *h zými, hmérty* [SU *v zymí, vmérty*] 'in winter, to die') and of *v* + voiceless consonant into *x* (eg, *xpásty* [SU *vpásty*] 'to fall'); (10) absence of prothetic consonants (eg, *óna, ápko* [SU *voná, jábluko*] 'she, apple'); (11) the ending *-om* in the instrumental singular of feminine nouns (eg, *tom dóbrom rúkom* [SU *tijéju dóbroju rukóju*] 'with that good hand'); *-oj* in the genitive singular of feminine adjectives (eg, *dóbroj* [SU *dóbroi*] 'good'); and *-ы* in the nominative plural of adjectives (eg, *dóbrы l'úde* [SU *dóbri ljúdy*] 'good people'); (12) the influence of hard endings on the soft declension (eg, *koval'óvy, kovál'om, z n'om* [SU *kovalévi, kovalém, z néju*] 'smith' dat sing, instr sing, 'with her'); (13) archaic endings in the plural of masculine nouns: (a) nominative *-y, -e, -ove* (eg, *s'piváсy, vol'áre, voйóve* [SU *spivaký, voljarí, volý*] 'singers, ox herders, oxen'); (b) dative *-im* (eg, *vól'im* [SU *volám*] 'oxen'); (c) locative *'ix, -'ox* (eg, *na vól'ix, na l'úd'ox* [SU *na voláx, na ljúdjax*] 'on oxen, on people'); (14) verbal personal endings in the present of the type *trýmam, -aš, -at, -áme, -áte, -ájut* (*-ãut', -ãvut*) (SU *trymáju, -ješ, -je, -jemo, -jete, -jut'*) 'hold'; the imperative forms *ber, bérme, bérte* (SU *berý, berím, berít'*) 'take'; the conditional forms *xódyй bыm, -bыs, -bы, xodýly bыzme, -bыste, -bы* (SU *xodýv by, xodýly b*) 'would have gone'; past tense endings *xódyй jem, -jes, xodýly (je)zme, -(je)ste* (SU *xodýv, xodýly*) 'went'; (15) adverbial forms in *-i* (eg, *ŭádn'i* [cf Polish *ładnie*] 'nicely'; (16) lexical peculiarities (eg, *štыrdés'at, xыža, vыhl'ad* [SU *sórok, xáta, viknó*] 'forty, cottage, window'), including Polonisms, Slovakisms, and Hungarian loanwords.

Certain peculiarities of the LD can be found in 16th- to 18th-century literary monuments. The most extensive studies of the LD have been done by I. Verkhratsky, I. Pankevych, and Z. Stieber, the author of a linguistic atlas of the ancient Lemko region (8 parts, 1956–64) and *Dialekt Łemków: Fonetyka i fonologia* (The Lemko Dialect: Phonetics and Phonology, 1982). The LD have been studied also by Y. Shemlei, V. Hnatiuk, I. Zilynsky, and Y. Dzendzelivsky.

O. Horbach

Lemko region (Lemkivshchyna). The territory traditionally inhabited by the *Lemkos forms an ethnographic peninsula 140 km long and 25–50 km wide within Polish and Slovak territory. After the deportation of Lemkos from the northern part in 1946, only the southern part, southwest of the Carpathian Mountains, known as the *Prešov region in Czechoslovakia, has remained inhabited by Lemkos.

The Lemko region occupies the lowest part of the Ukrainian Carpathian Mountains – most of the *Low Beskyd, the western part of the *Middle Beskyd, and the eastern fringe of the *Western Beskyd. The landscape is typical of medium-height-mountain terrain, with ridges reaching 1,000 m and sometimes 1,300 m. Only small parts of southern Low Beskyd and the northern Sian region have a low-mountain landscape. A series of mountain passes along the Torysa and Poprad rivers – Tylych (688 m), Duklia (502 m), and Lupkiw (657 m) – facilitate communications between Galician and Transcarpathian Lemkos.

The northern border with the Poles runs along the first mountain ridges, which closed off the Ukrainian ethnic territory from the low foothills populated densely by the Poles (south of the Ptaszkowa–Szymbark–Cieklin–Żmigród–Dukla–Rymanów line). Toward the east the Ukrainian-Polish border descends from the highlands and runs across the foothills and the Sianik Depression, which is an ethnically mixed zone. The southern, Slovak limit of the Lemko region has many ethnic islands and peninsulas: the Slovaks expanded far north along the wide valleys of the Torysa, Toplia, Ondava, and Laborets rivers, whereas the Lemkos generally inhabited the mountains. The eastern border with other Ukrainian ethnic groups consists of a wide Lemko-Boiko transitional belt from the Oslava to the Solynka River.

Until 1946 the Galician Lemko region comprised the southern part of Nowy Sącz, Gorlice, Jasło, Krosno, and Sianik counties, the southwestern part of Lisko county, and four villages of Nowy Targ county. Altogether the area covered nearly 3,500 sq km and had a population of 200,000, of which 160,000 (1939) were Ukrainians inhabiting about 300 villages. North of the homogeneous Lemko region lie one large and a few small islands of *zamishantsi, whose dialect is close to the Lemko dialect. The Transcarpathian Lemko region occupies most of the Prešov region – about 3,000 sq km with a population of 110,000 and a series of ethnic islands. The number of Lemkos in Galicia in 1939 was estimated at (depending on whether or not the transitional groups were included) 140,000 to 200,000, and in the Prešov region, 100,000 to 140,000. The Lemko region is extended sometimes – mistakenly – to the Dynów and the entire Lisko region.

History. The southern Lemko region belonged to Kiev's sphere of influence from the mid-10th century to the 1020s, when it came under the rule of Hungary. The eastern part of the northern Lemko region, extending to the Wisłoka River, belonged to the Kiev, and then the Galician-Volhynian, state. After Casimir III occupied the eastern part of the Lemko region in the 1340s, the entire Lemko region came under the rule of Poland until 1772. The eastern part formed the so-called Sianik land, which was part of Ruthenia voivodeship; the western part was integrated into Cracow voivodeship.

From the mid-14th century three colonization waves penetrated the Lemko region: Slovak-German colonists from the southwest, who settled in Transcarpathia; German-Polish colonists from the northwest; and Ukrainians, with Wallachian herdsmen, who settled in the east. The non-Ukrainian colonists occupied the lower, agricultural zone of the foothills and denationalized most of the Ukrainian inhabitants, particularly those between the Wisłoka and Sian rivers. The Ukrainian settlers occupied the sparsely populated wooded Beskyds. Their villages were usually founded on *Wallachian law, and they engaged in animal husbandry. In the western Lemko region, which never belonged to Galicia-Volhynia, the Ukrainian colonists wedged themselves in between the Poles and the Slovaks, although some scholars claim that they overpowered a scanty Polish population that had lived there for a long time. Colonization ended in the 16th century, although some new settlements sprang up in the 17th century. By the end of the 16th century the contemporary *Lemko dialects had been formed (I. Pankevych), and the dialects' boundaries, which with minor changes lasted until 1946, had been established. In spite of political divisions, Galician and Transcarpathian Lemkos maintained close ties: the farmers steadily migrated south, where corvée was less oppressive. The Galician Lemkos took part in the Austrian-Transylvanian struggle in the 17th century and in the Ferenc II Rákóczi uprising at the beginning of the 18th century. The Lemko region was shaken also by peasant revolts, especially in B. Khmelnytsky's and A. Kostka Napierski's times. The northern Lemko region and, until the 15th century, Transcarpathia belonged to *Peremyshl eparchy. Under Austrian rule (from 1772) the ties between the Lemko region and the rest of Galicia were weak; hence, the Lemko national awakening began only at the end of the 19th century (see *Lemkos).

Population. In 1939 the population density in the Sianik Depression was 110 per sq km, and in the rest of the Galician Lemko region, 55 per sq km. Only 15 percent of the population was urban. The only city was Sianik; the other population centers – Muszyna, Krynytsia, Bukivsko, and Balyhorod – were merely towns. The cities closest to the region – Nowy Sącz, Grełów, Gorlice, Żmigród, Dukla, and Rymanów – were predominantly Polish and Jewish. Excluding the northern Sianik region, Ukrainians accounted for 82 percent of the population, Poles 13 percent, and Jews 5 percent. In the Sianik region apart from the city, Ukrainians accounted for 60 percent, and in the city, for only 8 percent of the population.

Economy. The basic occupation in the region is farming, which meets only local demand. Before the 1880s ox grazing and sheepherding were important. The animals were bought in the spring in the Boiko and Hutsul regions and then sold in the fall in neighboring towns. After the

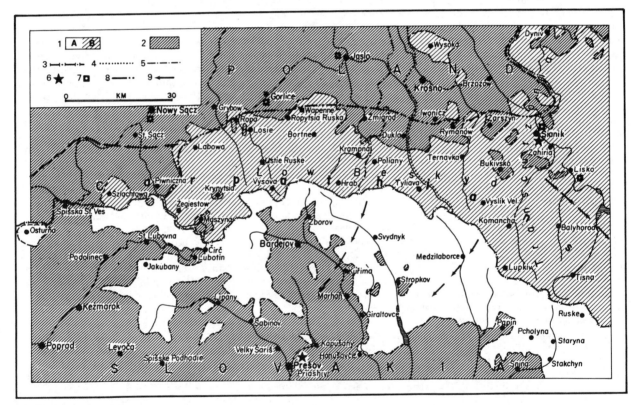

LEMKO REGION

1. The territory of *Lemkivshchyna* (including isolated areas) in 1939, spreading over: A, Slovakia; B, Poland (Ukrainians were deported from this territory in 1945–7)
2. The territory inhabited by Poles and Slovaks
3. Polish-Czechoslovak border
4. Boundary of Halych principality (Galicia)
5. Boundary (western) of Lviv voivodeship
6. Episcopates for the Ukrainian population, liquidated by the Polish (1945) and Czech (1950) governments
7. Centers from which Ukrainian inhabitants were deported to the USSR
8. Northern boundary of UPA operations on Polish territory
9. The direction of the UPA expeditions into Western Europe

*servitudes were abolished and grazing in the forests was restricted, animal husbandry declined, and dairy farming and crop growing (oats, potatoes, flax, and, in the northern Sianik region, rye and wheat) expanded. Secondary occupations included lumbering; handicrafts and cottage industries, such as weaving; woodworking; quarrying; and selling grease. Until 1914 seasonal labor in Hungary during harvesting and temporary work in North America were important sources of revenue. The Lemkos also found work and markets for their dairy products, berries, and mushrooms at spas and health resorts in Shchavnytsia, Krynytsia, Zhegestiv, Vysova, Iwonicz, and Rymanów.

Culture. The Lemko region produced many Ukrainian activists and intellectuals, few of whom could find employment there. Most of them were descendants of old clerical families. Many religious leaders, including Y. Sembratovych, S. Sembratovych, T. Poliansky, Yu. Pelesh, and Y. Kotsylovsky, and some scholars, such as Rev Y. Delkevych and Rev T. Myshkovsky, came from the region. Authors of Lemko origin who wrote about the region include Rev V. Khyliak, B. Antonovych, I. Fylypchak, Yu. Tarnovych, H. Hanuliak, and I. Rusenko. The composer M. Verbytsky and the singers M. Menzinsky and the Baiko sisters are of Lemko descent. Contemporary artists whose Lemko heritage is reflected in their work are M. Chereshnovsky, V. and I. Odrekhivsky, H. Petsukh, and Nykyfor.

Research work on the Lemko region reached a high point in the 1920s and 1930. It focused mostly on the Lemko dialects (I. Verkhratsky, I. Zilynsky, I. Pankevych, Y. Shemlei, and Z. Stieber) and ethnography (V. Hnatiuk, F. Kolessa, I. Falkivsky, and R. Reinfuss). There are only a few works on the history of the Lemko region (M. Korduba, M. Andrusiak) and several works in contemporary history (I. Fylypchak, Yu. Tarnovych, F. Kokovsky, and V. Buchatsky). Current information about the region can be found in the Lemko press – *Lemkivs'ke slovo* (Warsaw) and *Lemkivshchyna* (New York).

BIBLIOGRAPHY
Tarnovych, I. *Iliustrovana istoriia Lemkivshchyny* (Lviv 1936; 2nd edn, New York 1964)
Lemkivshchyna: Materiial'na kul'tura (Cracow 1941)
Stieber, Z. *Topomastyka Łemkowszczyzny*, 2 vols (Łódź 1948–9)
Buchats'kyi, V. *Lemkivshchyna: Istorychno-pobutova rozvidka* (Toronto 1959)
– *Lemkivsbchyna i lemky* (Toronto 1961)
Stavrovs'kyi, O. *Slovats'ko-pol'sko-ukraïns'ke prykordonnia do 18 stolittia* (Bratislava 1967)
Strumins'kyi, B. (ed) *Lemkivshchyna: Zemlia, liudy, istoriia, kul'tura*, 2 vols (New York–Paris–Sydney–Toronto 1988)
                                                          V. Kubijovyč

Lemkos (*lemky*). A Ukrainian ethnic group which until 1946 lived in the most western part of Ukraine on both sides of the Carpathian Mountains and along the Polish-Slovak border (see *Lemko region).

The name seems to be derived from the frequent use of the word *lem* 'only' by the Lemkos. They usually call themselves *rusnak* or *rusyn* (Ruthenian). Scholars and the intelligentsia began to use the name Lemko for the western groups of Ukrainian highlanders in the mid-19th century, and by the end of the century some Lemkos had accepted the name. It is not used widely in the *Prešov region.

The intrinsic conservatism of the Lemkos preserved them from Polonization but at the same time impeded the rise of Ukrainian national consciousness. The Old Ruthenian cultural mainstream, led mostly by local priests, turned in a Russophile direction in the 1900s and received support from the Russian tsarist government. The Russophiles stressed education in the Russian spirit and established boarding schools for young Lemkos in Nowy Sącz, Sianik, and Gorlice. The Ukrainian national movement gained strength among the Lemkos only toward the end of the 19th century and was centered in Nowy Sącz and Sianik. Its leading activists were P. Linynsky, V. Yavorsky, M. Kubiiovych, Rev O. Hadzevych, and Rev M. Dorotsky in Nowy Sącz, and Rev O. Konstantynovych, O. Gudzo, V. Buchatsky, V. Konstantynovych, and Y. Lukashevych in Sianik. A struggle arose between the Ukrainian and the Russophile tendencies. Some indication of their relative strength can be found in the fact that by 1912 there were 22 Prosvita reading rooms and 109 branches of the Russophile Kachkovsky Society in the Lemko region. At the same time there were 185 Ukrainian and 32 Polish schools in the region; 170 villages had no schools.

During the First World War the region was the site of several battles (1914–15) and sustained some damage. The Austrian authorities took repressive measures against the Ukrainians, in particular the Lemko Russophiles. The stuggle for Ukrainian statehood promoted the growth of Ukrainian consciousness among the Lemkos. After the demise of the Austro-Hungarian Empire, the Sianik Commissariat of the Western Ukrainian National Republic (ZUNR), headed by Rev P. Shpylka, remained active until mid-February 1919 and became known as the Komancha Republic. At the same time the Russophile group in the western Lemko region proclaimed the so-called Lemko Republic and used its official paper, *Rus'ka rada*, to agitate for the annexation of the Lemko region by Czechoslovakia.

In the 1920s the Ukrainian movement, supported by young priests and school teachers, began to predominate. Its principal center was Sianik, and its leading figures were Rev I. Kachmar, V. Blavatsky, S. Vanchytsky, and F. Kokovsky. At this time some Lemkos, mostly in the central region, converted to Orthodoxy, which was hostile to the Ukrainian movement. By 1935, of the 145,000 Lemkos in the territory of the Lemko Apostolic Administration, 18,000 were Orthodox. The Polish government attempted to halt the further development of the Ukrainian movement. It supported the Russophiles in order to keep the Lemkos divided and then tried to turn the Lemkos into a Polish ethnic group. The project was carried out under the auspices of the Polish Ministry of War and the Bureau of Nationality Policy under the Presidium of the Council of Ministers. The bureau's Research Commission for the Eastern Lands, reorganized into a special Lemko section in 1934, was to provide a 'scientific' justification for the project. In 1934 the Lemko region was separated from the Peremyshl eparchy and formed into a separate *Lemko Apostolic Administration with a Russophile hierarchy. Ukrainian teachers were replaced by Poles. The Lemko dialects and a special Lemko primer were introduced in the schools, and Polish patriotism was stressed. In 1938 the schools became bilingual. The authorities supported the anti-Ukrainian organization Lemko-Soiuz and the Polonophile weekly *Łemko* (1934–9). In the western Lemko region the links between the Ukrainian co-operatives and their central organization in Lviv, the Audit Union of Ukrainian Co-operatives, were severed, and nearly all the Prosvita reading rooms were closed down. The law on border zones was used as a pretext for deporting nationally conscious Ukrainians from the Lemko region, and Ukrainian organizations were placed under police surveillance. To counteract the Polish policy the Prosvita society in Lviv set up the Lemko Commission. Its task was to promote Ukrainian culture and education in the Lemko region and to disseminate information about the Lemkos among the Ukrainian public. The semimonthly *Nash lemko* (1934–9) and book series Biblioteka Lemkivshchyny (Library of the Lemko Region) served the same purpose. The *Lemkivshchyna Museum was set up in Sianik in 1930. In the United States the *Organization for the Defense of Lemkivshchyna was established to support the Ukrainian movement in the Lemko region.

Under the German occupation (from September 1939) the Ukrainian cultural-educational movement developed rapidly despite difficulties. A number of Ukrainian secondary vocational schools in Sianik and Krynytsia, a teachers' seminary in Krynytsia, the Ukrainian educational societies (UOT), and Ukrainian co-operatives were set up. The activists were local Lemkos and Ukrainian refugees from Soviet-occupied Galicia. With the nomination of Rev O. *Malynovsky to the post of apostolic administra-

Scene from a Lemko wedding

tor and the creation of a separate Lemko Orthodox eparchy under Archbishop P. *Vydybida-Rudenko, the Russophile influence in religious life was overcome. The Ukrainian Central Committee and its branches – the Ukrainian relief committees in Sianik (under P. Bilaniuk), Krynytsia (under O. Navrotsky), and Jasło (under H. Nychka) – oversaw the social and cultural work in the region.

The Soviets occupied the eastern part of the Lemko region in the summer of 1944 and the western part in early 1945. Taking advantage of the war situation the Polish underground assassinated prominent Lemkos and, in the mixed Lemko-Polish areas, even slaughtered Lemkos in mixed villages. Some 4,000 Lemkos had been resettled in the Ukrainian SSR in 1940 under the Soviet-German treaty on voluntary population exchange. The resettlement of Lemkos was resumed under the Polish-Soviet agreement of 16 August 1945, which also determined the Polish-Soviet border and finally surrendered the entire northern Lemko region to Poland. The operation was hindered by the *Ukrainian Insurgent Army, which was active in the eastern Lemko region from 1944. Under Polish pressure most Lemkos (up to 80 percent) had been moved to Ukraine by mid-1946, and the remainder, with few exceptions, were resettled in 1947 among Poles on former German lands which now belonged to Poland (see *Operation Wisła). The depopulated Lemko region was settled partly by Poles, but most of it remained unsettled.

Peasants in the Lemko village of Polonna

Until 1956 the Lemkos as well as all the other Ukrainians in Poland had no national rights (see *Poland). Ukrainian cultural and educational activity centered around the *Ukrainian Social and Cultural Society. In 1957 the supplement *Lemkivs'ke slovo* was added to the society's weekly *Nashe slovo*, and in 1959 a separate section for the development of Lemko culture was established within the society. Only a few Lemkos have been allowed to return to their homeland – by 1957–8 only some 4,000 of the 30,000 to 40,000 Lemkos in Poland. They are dispersed in the Gorlice and Sianik regions and form a majority in only a few villages. The return movement has been halted, although large areas of the Lemko region are uninhabited; in Lísko county, for example, the population density is 25 per sq km, whereas in 1939 it was 70 per sq km. Schools in which Ukrainian is taught are the exception in the Lemko region. Until recently Lemkos did not have their own priests; they often were, and still are, subject to greater discrimination than before the Second World War.

The Lemkos who moved to Ukraine were settled mainly in former Polish villages in the Ternopil, Sambir, and Lviv regions. Some live in the Donbas. In Ukraine, as in Poland, they have tried to preserve their own folklore, especially their songs and dances. But the younger generation is losing its distinctive traits. Some Ukrainian monuments have been preserved in the Polish museums in Sianik, Nowy Sącz, Rzeszów, and Peremyshl as well as in Lviv. Most of them, however, have been destroyed, or, lacking government protection, continue to deteriorate. Representatives of Solidarność have criticized the Polish authorities for resettling the Lemkos, but most Poles consider the Lemkos to be part of the Polish, not the Ukrainian, nation.

The Lemkos are a distinct ethnic group within the Ukrainian nation. Their dialects and spiritual and material culture preserved some unique archaic elements that were lost by other Ukrainian ethnic groups. They also absorbed some Slovak and Polish influences, especially linguistic ones (see *Lemko dialects). More than any other Ukrainian ethnic group the Lemkos are attached to their homeland, traditions, and church and are impervious to external influence. They are more united than other groups, even when they are outside their native land. The Lemkos form several distinct subgroups. The western Lemkos (roughly from the Duklia Pass in the east) have more archaic characteristics than the eastern Lemkos, who have some features in common with other Ukrainian groups, such as the Boikos.

The Lemkos' material culture is considerably poorer than that of the Hutsuls. Their culture is more utilitarian. Their homesteads are built of wood and usually consist of a single building, with the corridor separating the living quarters from the stable. The sloping bilateral roof is covered with shingles in the western and with straw in the eastern Lemko region. Church architecture is similar to that of the Boikos, except that Lemko churches are topped with external baroque domes and high belfries over the vestibules. Lemko dress is similar to that of the Boikos but is more attractive because of a finer selection of cloth, colors, and embroidery. Lemko women wear a fancy necklace (*sylianka*) made of colorful beads. The distinctive men's overcoat (*shuba*) is made of homemade felt. The Lemkos are known for their wood carving, which is highly developed in resort areas and around Sianik. Lemko folklore is particularly rich in songs. Most of them, especially the wedding and humorous songs, were composed by the Lemkos, but some are variants of widely known Ukrainian songs. Slovak folklore had a considerable influence on the Lemkos. Lemko melodies have a remarkable variety of forms, a rich ornamentation, and a wide rhythmic range.

Lemkos in North America. In the 1870s Lemkos from the Prešov region were the first Ukrainian immigrants in the United States. Up to the end of the 19th century the majority of Ukrainian immigrants in the country were Lemkos. They were the founders of the first Ukrainian organizations. Because of the large influx of Lemko immigrants up to the 1930s, some 100,000 to 150,000 Americans and Canadians today are of Lemko origin. Their largest concentrations are in Pennsylvania and around Cleveland. The Lemkos in North America are divided into three large camps: the Ruthenian, Ukrainian, and Russophile. The first consists mostly of Lemkos from the Prešov region. The Greek Catholic Lemkos from Transcarpathia (with a few from Galicia) belong to *Pittsburgh metropoly; those from Galicia belong to Ukrainian Catholic eparchies. Orthodox Lemkos belong mostly to the Orthodox Church of America and the Carpatho-Ruthenian Greek-Catholic Orthodox Church of America as well as the Ukrainian Orthodox church. Most Lemkos belong to Ruthenian or Russophile, and fewer to the Ukrainian, mutual aid insurance societies. The *Lemko Association (est 1929) is a relief organization of conservative Russophile

Young Lemkos in the village of Repid

Lemkos; the Organization for the Defence of Lemkivshchyna (est 1936) is a Ukrainian patriotic association. The Ukrainophile Lemko press has included the monthly *Lemkivs'kyi dzvin* (Philadelphia and Passaic, NJ, 1936–9), edited by M. Dudra; *Lemkivshchyna* (Toronto, 1949–52), edited by Yu. Tarnovych; *Holos Lemkivshchyny* (Yonkers, NY, 1963–), edited by S. Zhenetsky; **Lemkivs'ki visti* (Yonkers, 1958–75 and Toronto, 1975–9), edited by S. Zhenetsky and then Yu. Tarnovych; **Lemkivshchyna* (New York, 1979–), edited by U. Liubovych, O. Pytliar, and then M. Dupliak; and *Lemkovyna* (Yonkers, 1971–81), edited by S. Kychura. The Russophiles founded *Lemko* (1928–36) and *Karpatska Rus'* (1939–), both organs of the Lemko Association.

BIBLIOGRAPHY

Kolessa, F. 'Narodni pisni z halyts'koï Lemkivshchyny,' *Etnohrafichnyi zbirnyk NTSh*, 39–40 (1929)

Smoleński, J. 'Łemkowie i Łemkowszczyzna,' *Wierchy*, 13 (Cracow 1935)

Iadlovs'kyi, S. (ed). *Shematyzm hreko-katolyts'koho dukhovenstva Apostol's'koï administratsiï Lemkivshchyny* (Lviv 1936; repr, Stamford 1970)

Reinfuss, R. 'Łemkowie,' *Wierchy*, 14 (Cracow 1936)

Tarnovych, Iu. *Lemkivshchyna: Materiial'na kul'tura* (Cracow 1941)

Reinfuss, R. 'Łemkowie jako grupa etnograficzna,' *Prace i materiały etnograficzne*, 7 (Wrocław 1948–9)

Shakh, S. *Mizh Sianom i Dunaitsem* (Munich 1960)

Buchats'kyi, V. *Lemky – Ukraïns'ke hirs'ke plemia* (Winnipeg 1962)

Lemkin, I. *Istoriia Lemkoviny* (Yonkers 1969)

Kwilecki, A. *Łemkowie: Zagadnienie migracji i asymilacji* (Warsaw 1974)

Strumins'kyi, B. (ed). *Lemkivshchyna: Zemlia – liudy – istoriia – kul'tura*, 2 vols (New York–Paris–Sydney–Toronto 1988)

V. Kubijovyč

Lemko-Soiuz. See Lemko Association.

Lemkovyna. Ukrainian amateur song and dance ensemble in Poland. It was formed in 1969 by R. Sobolevsky and F. Hoch out of local Lemko choirs and dance groups of the **Lemko region. From the beginning its conductor has been Ya. Trokhanovsky. Its repertoire consists mostly of Lemko folk songs arranged for four voices by R. Sobolevsky and Ya. Trokhanovsky, but it also includes some original works by the conductor and Ya. Poliansky (words by P. Stefanivsky and P. Trokhanovsky), and by noted Ukrainian composers, such as S. Liudkevych and A. Kos-Anatolsky. Its leading soloists are M. Steranka, V. Dudra, P. Karel, O. Haitko, M. Vorobets, and N. Hrbal. The dance group is accompanied by a folk instrument orchestra. The ensemble has performed in Cracow, Warsaw, and Wrocław in Poland and Lviv, Ternopil, Boryslav, and Ivano-Frankivske in Ukraine. It toured Canada and the United States in 1987.

Lemyk, Mykola, b 4 April 1914 in Solova, Peremyshliany county, Galicia, d October 1941 in Myrhorod, Poltava oblast. Revolutionary figure. He studied law at Lviv University and joined the youth branch of the OUN in the early 1930s. In protest against the man-made famine in Ukraine Lemyk assassinated O. Mailov, a representative of the Soviet consulate in Lviv, on 21 October 1933. His death sentence was commuted to life imprisonment, and he escaped from a Polish prison convoy after the fall of Poland in September 1939. In 1941 he was one of the leaders

Mykola Lemyk   Wasyl Lencyk

of the OUN expeditionary groups in Eastern Ukraine. He was hanged by the Gestapo.

Lenartowicz, Teofil, b 27 November 1822 in Warsaw, d 3 February 1893 in Florence. Polish poet. He developed an interest in Ukrainian folklore and translated Ukrainian songs into Polish. In his poem 'O Wernyhorze' (On Vernyhora, 1848) he portrayed the haidamaka movement in Ukraine. He befriended the exiled Cossack Zhurba, to whom he dedicated two poems. In his verses on Ukrainian themes – 'Ukraińska bajda' (Ukrainian Baida), 'Oboz Chmielnickiego' (Khmelnytsky's Camp), 'Złota hramota' (The Golden Charter), and 'Książę na Ostrogu' (Prince of Ostrih) – he called for a united Ukrainian-Polish struggle against the Russian tsarist regime. He wrote one poem ('Krim Geraj,' 1866) in Ukrainian.

Lencyk, Wasyl [Lencyk, Vasyl'], b 17 March 1912 in Mazurivka, Zhydachiv county, Galicia. Historian, pedagogue, and Catholic activist; full member of the Shevchenko Scientific Society since 1961. He studied at the Greek Catholic Theological Academy in Lviv, the Ukrainian Free University in Munich (PHD, 1947), and, after emigrating to the United States in 1949, Fordham University in New York (PH D, 1961). He taught at the Ukrainian Free University (1948–9), St Basil's College in Stamford, Connecticut (1955–88), and Seton Hall University (from 1962), and in 1963 he was appointed a professor of church and world history at the Ukrainian Catholic University in Rome. From 1978 he was general secretary of the Supreme Council of the Shevchenko Scientific Society and a member of its American executive. From 1964 he was director of the **Ukrainian Diocesan Museum in Stamford. He was president of the **Obnova Society of Ukrainian Catholic Students (1954–8) and in 1991 he received the papal medal Pro Ecclesia et Pontifice. He contributed to *Entsyklopedia ukraïnoznavstva* and to *Encyclopedia of Ukraine* (church subject coeditor) and the *New Catholic Encyclopedia* (1979), and he wrote *The Eastern Catholic Church and Czar Nicholas I* (1966).

Lenin, Vladimir (pseud of V. Ulianov), b 22 April 1870 in Simbirsk (now Ulianovsk), Russia, d 21 January 1924 in Gorkii, near Moscow. Russian revolutionary, founder of the Bolshevik party, leader of the Communist revolution, and head of the Soviet state. After being expelled from Kazan University he studied K. Marx and adopted his ideas.

Lenin made important additions to Marxist doctrine in response to the demands of revolutionary practice. These additions form *Leninism, which reveals Lenin's skill as a tactician and his political flexibility. A key contribution was the concept of the revolutionary party, developed first in his *What Is to Be Done?* (1902) and *One Step Forward, Two Steps Back* (1904). Another was the concept of 'democratic centralism.' In *The State and Revolution* (1917) he justified his decision to seize power and to establish the 'dictatorship of the proletariat.' Lenin often reversed himself; he used the State Duma, for example, as a propaganda forum, recognized briefly the Ukrainian National Republic, established the Far Eastern Republic (1920–2) to further Bolshevik foreign policy, and introduced the New Economic Policy (1921) to restore the economy.

Lenin accepted violence and terror as legitimate tools of class war. He created the Soviet security police, the *Cheka. He established the prototype of the totalitarian dictatorship, which tried to remake society and human nature and claimed the right to control all aspects of life. Lenin's ideological teachings and organizational methods paved the way for J. *Stalin's brutal dictatorship.

His initial indifference and even hostility to the nationality issue expressed itself in his rejection of the ethnic criterion in party organization, his opposition to the Jewish Bund, and his commitment to centralism. The class struggle ruled out any national loyalties. He perceived 'national culture' as an instrument of the national bourgeoisie (landowners, priests, and the bourgeoisie). Lenin never visited Ukraine and only slowly acquired some understanding of its peculiar position. By 1912 he had associated Ukraine with Poland and Finland in his criticism of tsarist policies. Although he condemned nationalism, he paid lip service to the right of national self-determination, including independence, assuming all the time that it would not be exercised. He saw ethnic assimilation as 'progressive,' although he acknowledged the right of each people to use its own language and advocated language tolerance. Lenin believed that the right of national self-determination would be transformed dialectically into its opposite, and that 'sometimes greater bonds obtain after free separation.' He denounced Ukrainian socialists, such as D. Dontsov and L. Yurkevych (L. Rybalka), for advocating a separate Ukrainian Social Democratic Workers' party. He replied with abuse when Rybalka pointed out the inconsistency between Lenin's acceptance of national self-determination and his belief in the progressiveness of large states and in their continued existence. Rybalka had argued that the professed internationalism of the Bolsheviks was a veiled form of traditional Russian imperialism: Lenin's talk of the 'fusion of nations' and his desire to prevent the breakup of Russia were incompatible with his promise of national self-determination. Russia's collapse in 1917 compelled Lenin to confront the nationalities question on the practical level. He criticized the Provisional Government for refusing to grant Ukraine autonomy and used Ukrainian grievances to weaken the central government. But upon coming to power he adopted a hostile attitude to Ukrainian independence: he launched an invasion of Ukraine in January 1918. Although he was forced to recognize Ukraine's independence in the Peace Treaty of *Brest-Litovsk, he sent the Red Army into Ukraine again in January 1919 and again in late 1919. To win Ukrainian support for the Bolshevik regime he set up a nominally autonomous Ukrainian Soviet government and promised to promote the Ukrainian language and culture. After consolidating his control over the peoples of the former Russian Empire, Lenin adopted, out of regard for their national feelings, a federated instead of a unitary form of state, in 1922. He pointed to Russian great-power chauvinism as the cause of nationalism in the smaller nations of the USSR. Some of his tactical opinions on the nationality problem provided the basis for the Soviet policy of *Ukrainization that was introduced in 1923. After 72 years of near idolatry, Lenin is finally being seen for the imperialist and dictator that he really was. Since the end of 1990 open criticism of Lenin and what he stood for has spread through Ukraine and resulted in the dismantling of Lenin monuments in most cities.

BIBLIOGRAPHY
Fischer, L. *The Life of Lenin* (New York 1964)
Possony, S. *Lenin: The Compulsive Revolutionary* (Chicago 1964)
Dziuba, I. *Internationalism or Russification?* (London 1968)
Rybalka, L. *Rosiis'ki sotsial-demokraty i natsional'ne pytannia* (Munich 1969)
V.I. Lenin pro Ukraïnu (Kiev 1969)
Bakalo, I. *Natsional'na polityka Lenina* (Munich 1974)

J. Reshetar

Lenin Lake. V-16. An artificial lake near the mouth of the Samara River that connects to the Dnieper water reservoir above the dam of the *Dnieper Hydroelectric Station in Zaporizhia. The lake is 10 km long and up to 3 km wide and has a basin area of 17 sq km.

Lenine. VIII-16. A town smt (1990 pop 8,900) and raion center on the North Crimean Canal in Crimea oblast. It was founded at the end of the 19th century as Sim Kolodiaziv. In 1957 it was reclassified as an smt and renamed Lenine. It has a winery, a mixed-feed factory, and a panels plant.

Leningrad. See Saint Petersburg.

Leningrad Society of Researchers of Ukrainian History, Literature, and Language (Leninhradske Tovarystvo doslidnykiv ukrainskoi istorii, pysmenstva ta movy). The Leningrad branch of the Historical-Philological Society of the All-Ukrainian Academy of Sciences, established in 1922. It published two issues (1928, 1929) of the scholarly publication *Naukovyi zbirnyk*, edited by the director of the society, V. Peretts. Among its 40 members were V. Adriianova-Peretts, I. Abramov, D. Abramovych, O. Barannykov, V. Danyliv, A. Liashchenko, I. Rybakov, and I. Fetisov. The affiliated Ethnographic Commission, also headed by Peretts, studied the socioeconomic and cultural life of Ukrainians outside Ukraine, mainly in the Kuban. Other branches of the Historical-Philological Society existed in Odessa, Vinnytsia, Zhytomyr, and elsewhere. The Leningrad Society was liquidated at the beginning of the 1930s.

Leninism. A strategy of Marxist revolution designed by V. Lenin for the specific needs of tsarist Russia and the political circumstances in Europe in the early 20th century. In view of Russia's backwardness, Leninism can be interpreted more widely as a strategy of building socialism under adverse or 'unripe' conditions. The problem confronting Lenin at the turn of the century was that, several decades after K. Marx's confident predictions about the dissolution of capitalism and nationalism, neither had disappeared. Lenin explained their persistence by pointing out that capitalism had weakened the revolutionary movement by making some concessions to workers and promoting 'trade-union consciousness.' Hence, Lenin proposed, in *What Is to Be Done?* (1902), that Marxists organize themselves around a nucleus of professional revolutionaries who could not be diverted from revolution. Then, in *Imperialism, the Highest Stage of Capitalism* (1917), he argued that because capitalism had avoided collapse by exploiting overseas markets, the strategy of revolution had to be extended to the Third World, which was part of an 'international proletariat.' In the new circumstances, nationalism (or anticolonialism) was a progressive force. Linking 'Great Russian chauvinism' with imperialism, Lenin persuaded the Russian Social Democratic Workers' party to adopt self-determination as official policy. Since he identified oppression with capitalism and class-divided societies, Lenin saw no contradiction in advocating both the 'right of self-determination' and the 'closest unity of the proletariat of all nationalities.' The right of self-determination, he assumed, would be exercised only against the tsarist regime, not against a socialist one. For Lenin, national liberation was an expedient means to socialist revolution, not a goal in itself.

Leninism represented a militant but minority position within the socialist movement. In contrast to the more moderate Mensheviks or Socialist Revolutionaries, Lenin insisted that Russia was on the verge not merely of a bourgeois-democratic revolution but of a proletarian revolution that would usher in socialism. His strategy took into account the widespread unrest in Russia while sidestepping its causes and their relation to Marxist theory. Lenin believed that the Party as the disciplined vanguard of the proletariat could take the place of a mass working-class uprising, and that it would be supported by the rebellious peasantry and nationalities, which had been oppressed under tsarist rule. Once revolution had occurred in Russia, the 'weak link' in the chain of capitalist states, socialism would sweep through the rest of Europe. Although he was wrong about Europe, Lenin succeeded in overthrowing the Provisional Government and consolidating Bolshevik power throughout most of the former Russian Empire.

During the revolutionary period Leninism complicated and radicalized the political choices available to the Ukrainian leaders. Although the political profile of the Central Rada was democratic and moderately socialist, the Rada was temporarily allied with the Bolsheviks, the most militant faction of the Petrograd Soviet, against the Provisional Government, which was hostile to Ukrainian autonomy. Upon taking power Lenin redrew the military and political battle lines. He sent the Red Army to quash the independence movement in Ukraine. Identifying socialism with Bolshevism and branding everyone else 'counterrevolutionary,' he pushed the entire political spectrum leftward and forced the Ukrainian government to adopt a hastily and poorly constructed agrarian reform program, which alienated the wealthier peasants without satisfying the rural majority. The Ukrainian government was faced not only with an armed struggle against the Red Army but also with a political struggle for the support of the Ukrainian peasantry.

With the end of the Civil War Lenin retreated from strictly socialist principles and introduced the *New Economic Policy and a 'cultural revolution' to give the new regime a chance to take root.

In Ukraine Leninism was at first seen as an effort to reconcile Bolshevism and nationalism. To appeal to the Ukrainian intelligentsia and peasantry Lenin granted Ukraine a degree of autonomy within the federal Soviet state and laid the foundations for the policy of *indigenization and *Ukrainization. Basically, Lenin gave legitimacy to the belief, prevalent among leading figures of the CP(B)U during the 1920s, that defending Ukrainian national interests was compatible with the social aims of communism (see *National communism).

BIBLIOGRAPHY
Pipes, R. *The Formation of the Soviet Union: Communism and Nationalism, 1917–1923* (Cambridge, Mass 1954)
Meyer, A. *Leninism* (Cambridge, Mass 1957)
Fedenko, P. *Marksysts'ki i bol'shevyts'ki teorii natsional'noho pytannia* (Munich 1960)
Conquest, R. *V.I. Lenin* (New York 1972)
Mace, J.E. *Communism and the Dilemmas of National Liberation: National Communism in Soviet Ukraine, 1918–1933* (Cambridge, Mass 1983)

Z. Sochor

Lenins'ka pravda (Leninist Truth). An organ of the Sumy oblast CPU Committee and Soviet of People's Deputies until 1991. It first appeared in 1917 in Russian as *Izvestiia Sumskogo soveta rabochikh i soldatskikh deputatov*. In the next few years it was called *Kommuna* (1918–19), *Vlast' sovetam* (1919–20), and *Stiah pratsi* (1921–2). It was renamed *Plug i molot/Pluh i molot* in 1922, and from 1924 it appeared only in Ukrainian. The name *Lenins'ka pravda* was adopted in 1952. In 1980 it had a circulation of 123,000 copies and was published five times per week.

Leninske [Lenins'ke]. V-20. A town smt (1990 pop 5,300) in Sverdlovske raion, Luhanske oblast. It was founded as a workers' settlement of mine no. 9 in 1900 and was renamed Leninske in 1944. There are three coal mines and a railway station in the town.

Stepan Lenkavsky

Lenkavsky, Stepan [Lenkavs'kyj], b 6 July 1904 in Zahvizd, Stanyslaviv county, Galicia, d 30 October 1977 in Munich. Revolutionary leader and nationalist ideologist. He became active in clandestine student groups before graduating from secondary school in Stanyslaviv. While studying philosophy in Lviv he joined the Union of Ukrainian Nationalist Youth and became its leading ideologist and, eventually, a member of its executive council. In 1929 he participated in the founding conference of the OUN and assumed the post of ideology officer for the OUN national executive in Western Ukraine. Besides contributing articles to the legal and underground nationalist press he composed the 'Decalogue of the Ukrainian Nationalist-Revolutionary,' the official membership oath of the OUN. He was a member of the Lystopad group of nationalist writers. His political activity led to his imprisonment by the Poles (1932–6). From the very beginning of the internal dissension in the OUN Lenkavsky sided with S. *Bandera. As one of the authors of the *'Proclamation of Ukrainian Statehood' in 1941, he was imprisoned by the Germans for three and a half years, mostly in Auschwitz. After the war he held top posts in the External Units of the OUN, and at Bandera's death he assumed leadership of the organization (1959–68). After voluntarily stepping down as leader he remained as chief of propaganda and editor of the newspaper *Shliakh peremohy. In the last years of his life he edited a number of books and helped prepare a collection in honor of Ye. Konovalets.

Lenkewich, Ambrose [Lenkevyč, Amvrosija], b 18 January 1876 in Western Ukraine, d 13 May 1953 in Komarno, Manitoba. Pioneer Ukrainian Catholic nun. Lenkewich entered the Order of *Sisters Servants of Mary Immaculate in 1895 and emigrated to Canada (settling initially in Mundare, Alberta) in 1902 with the first group of Ukrainian Catholic missionaries. She was the order's provincial superior (1902–26), and a member of its provincial council until 1939.

Lenkivtsi settlement. An early Trypilian settlement discovered near the village of Lenkivtsi in Kelmentsi raion, Chernivtsi oblast, in 1947 and excavated in 1950–3.

Lentsyk, Vasyl. See Lencyk, Wasyl.

Leo XIII (secular name: Vincenzo Giocchino Pecci), b 2 March 1810 in Carpineto Romano, Italy, d 20 July 1903 in Rome. Pope in 1878–1903. During his papacy a number of initiatives were undertaken in relation to Eastern rite Catholics, including the reformation (1882) of the *Basilian monastic order, the creation (1885) of a new eparchy in Stanyslaviv, and the founding (1897) of a Ukrainian seminary in Rome. Leo XIII also endorsed the resolutions of the Lviv Synod of 1891, and proclaimed (1894) the edict *Orientalium dignitas Ecclesiarum*, confirming the principle of territoriality enunciated in 1890 by the Sacred Congregation for the Propagation of the Faith. The edict limited the jurisdiction of Eastern ecclesiastical authorities to their traditional territories, thereby effectively placing immigrant Ukrainian Catholics under the authority of Latin rite hierarchs in North America. This measure led to considerable dissension and was a major factor behind the conversion of thousands of Catholic Ukrainians to Orthodoxy or other denominations. Leo XIII placed three Halych metropolitans in office and made S. *Sembratovych a cardinal (1895). He also ordered the preparation of a plan for a Lviv-based Ukrainian patriarchate that was opposed by the Hungarian Roman Catholic primate because the new body would incorporate Transcarpathian eparchies.

Leonidze, Georgii, b 27 December 1899 in Patardzeuli, Georgia, d 9 August 1966 in Tbilisi. Georgian writer and national poet, and literary scholar. As a poet he is famous for his lyrical works and his epic *Childhood and Youth* (1939). He visited Ukraine and wrote the cycle *In Myrhorod* and other poems about Ukraine. His admiration of T. Shevchenko is expressed in several essays on the Ukrainian poet and in some poems dedicated to him: 'To Taras Shevchenko,' 'Greetings from Georgia,' and 'The Poet-Prometheus.' Leonidze translated works by Shevchenko, I. Franko, Lesia Ukrainka, and P. Tychyna and sections of *Slovo o polku Ihorevi* into Georgian.

Leontovych, Fedir [Leontovyč], b 1833 in Popivka, Konotip county, Chernihiv gubernia, d 1911 in Kislovodsk, Terek oblast, Russia. Law historian. After graduating in law from Kiev University (1860) he lectured there (1860, 1863–5), at Odessa University (1861–3, 1865–91), and at Warsaw University (1892–1911) on the history of Russian law. He was also rector (1869–77) and prorector of the university in Odessa. Specializing in the law of medieval Rus' and the Caucasian peoples, he wrote a number of important works on Lithuanian-Ruthenian law: *Krest'iane iugo-zapadnoi Rossii po litovsko-russkomu pravu XV–XVI vekov* (The Peasants of Southwestern Russia in Lithuanian-Ruthenian Law of the 15th–16th Centuries, 1863), *Russkaia Pravda i Litovskii statut* (Ruskaia Pravda and the Lithuanian Statute, 1864), *Ocherki istorii litovsko-russkogo prava* (Outlines of the History of Lithuanian-Ruthenian Law, 1894), *Rada velikikh kniazei* (The Council of the Grand Princes, 1907), and *Tsentral'nye sudebnye uchrezhdeniia v Velikom Kniazhestve Litovskom* (The Central Judicial Institutions in the Grand Duchy of Lithuania, 1910). He published over 750 documents, dating from 1413 to 1507, from the Lithuanian Register.

Mykola Leontovych

Leontovych, Mykola [Leontovyč], b 13 December 1877 in Monastyrok, Bratslav county, Podilia gubernia, d 23 January 1921 in Markivka, Haisyn county, Podilia gubernia. Composer, conductor, and teacher. After graduating from the theological seminary in Kamianets-Podilskyi in 1899, he worked as a teacher at various schools in Kiev, Katerynoslav, and Podilia gubernias. He furthered his musical education on an ongoing basis through private study in St Petersburg, where he earned his credentials as a choirmaster of church choruses, and in Kiev, where he studied under B. Yavorsky. In spite of the popularity of his compositions, Leontovych was modest about his work and remained a generally unrecognized figure until he was brought to Kiev in 1918–19 to teach at the Conservatory and the M. Lysenko Institute of Music and Drama. He died in tragic circumstances several years later, being shot by a robber at his parents' home.

Leontovych's musical heritage consists primarily of more than 150 choral compositions inspired by the texts and melodies of Ukrainian folk songs. His earlier works consist mainly of strophic arrangements of folk songs; in later years he developed a strophic-variational form strongly related to the text. A group of his compositions, including 'Shchedryk' (Epiphany Carol), 'Dudaryk' (The *Duda* Player), and 'Hra v Zaichyka' (Playing Rabbit), depart from the simple settings of folk songs and constitute his most original and artistic compositions. Leontovych also wrote several religious works (a liturgy, cantatas), and choral compositions to the texts of various poems (including *L'odolom* [Icebreaker] and *Litni tony* [Summer Tones] by H. Chuprynka). The harmony of his choral compositions is rich and innovative, an important role being played by vocal polyphony, including the use of imitation techniques. His unfinished opera *Na rusalchyn velykden'* (On the Water Nymph's Easter), based on B. Hrinchenko's fairy tale, was the first attempt at a Ukrainian fantastic opera.

Leontovych's creativity played an important role in the development of Ukrainian choral tradition and influenced composers of succeeding generations. His works were popularized by the *Ukrainian Republican Kapelle and became the basis of the repertoire of many choral groups (O. *Koshyts). They obtained high praise from critics as well as widespread popularity in Ukraine and elsewhere. Particularly well known is his 'Shchedryk,' which is commonly called 'The Carol of the Bells' in English.

BIBLIOGRAPHY
Dovzhenko, V. *M.D. Leontovych: Zbirka statei ta materialiv* (Kiev 1947)
Hordiichuk, M. (ed). *M.D. Leontovych: Narys pro zhyttia i tvorchist'* (Kiev 1956)
Diachenko, V. *M.D. Leontovych* (Kiev 1969)
Ivanov, V. *Mykola Leontovych: Spohady, lysty, materialy* (Kiev 1982)
                                                                W. Wytwycky

Leontovych, Oleksander [Leontovyč], b 11 November 1869 in Kiev, d 15 December 1943 in Moscow. Physiologist and neurohistologist; full member of the VUAN and AN URSR (now ANU) from 1929. He graduated from Kiev University in 1893 and wrote his doctoral thesis on the double innervation of human skin in 1900. He was a teacher at the agriculture department of the Kiev Polytechnical Institute (1898–1912), a professor of animal physiology at the Moscow Agricultural Institute (from 1923), and director of the physiology division at the AN URSR Institute of Clinical Physiology (from 1936). He wrote nearly 80 works on the physiology and histology of the peripheral nervous system, proposed a theory of the neuron as an alternating current transmitter (1928–39), researched the physiological regeneration of the nervous system, and perfected a method of staining nervous tissue. A monograph on him was written by N. Bodrova and B. Kraiukhin (1950).

Leontovych, Pavlo [Leontovyč], b 9 March 1825 in Shchutkiv, Galicia, d 19 May 1880 in Ruda Krekhivska,

Zhovkva county, Galicia. Poet and writer; Ukrainian Catholic priest by vocation. He was one of the publishers of the almanac *Lirvak iz nad Siana* (Lira Player from the Banks of the Sian, 1852), in which some of his poems and stories appeared under the pseudonym Pavlo iz Shchutkova. His articles, stories, fables, and poetry were published in journals, such as *Novyny* and *Vechernytsi*, in the newspaper *Slovo*, and in several literary collections.

Volodymyr Leontovych
(1866–1933)

Leontovych, Volodymyr [Leontovyč] (pseud: V. Levenko), b 5 August 1866 in Orikhovshchyna *khutir*, Lubni county, Poltava gubernia, d 10 December 1933 in Prague. Civic leader and writer. After graduating in law from Moscow University (1888) he managed his father's estates and was active in local zemstvo affairs and in the Ukrainian cultural movement. He was a member of the Hromada of Kiev and the Society of Ukrainian Progressives as well as a contributor to *Zoria, Kievskaia starina, Literaturno-naukovyi vistnyk,* and *Hromads'ka dumka.* The daily *Rada* was financed by him. In 1917 Leontovych sat on the Central Rada, and in 1918 he served as minister of agriculture in F. Lyzohub's cabinet of the Hetman government. When the Bolsheviks occupied Ukraine, he emigrated to Berlin and then to Prague. Leontovych wrote novelettes on contemporary life, such as *Khronika rodyny Hrechok* (A Chronicle of the Hrechka Family, 1922), short stories, and memoirs, such as *Spomyny utikacha* (Memoirs of a Refugee, 1922). He collaborated with O. Yefymov on a Russian-Ukrainian legal dictionary (2 edns, 1917, 1919).

Leontovych, Volodymyr [Leontovyč], b 27 July 1881 in Hadiache, Poltava gubernia, d 29 April 1968 in Kiev. Construction engineer and architect. He graduated from the Kiev Polytechnical Institute in 1906, where he studied the architecture of historic buildings in Ukraine, particularly in Volhynia, and conducted the restoration of major architectural monuments in Zhytomyr and the ancient castle in Ostrih. With V. Maksymov and I. Izhakevych he erected the church-monument at the *Kozatski Mohyly Museum and Preserve near Berestechko. Leontovych also taught at engineering schools and wrote papers on the applications of geodesic measurements in civil engineering.

Leontovych Music Society (Muzychne tovarystvo im. M.A. Leontovycha). A national music society named in honor of M. *Leontovych formed in Kiev in 1922 out of the M. Leontovych Memorial Citizens' Committee (est 1921). With branches in Kharkiv, Poltava, Vinnytsia, Chernihiv,

First presidium of the Leontovych Music Society (1922). Sitting, from left: O. Chapkivsky, Yu. Mykhailiv, M. Kocherovsky, D. Koliiukh; standing: P. Kozytsky, T. Melnykiv, Yu. Mezhenko, P. Tychyna, S. Durdukivsky

Tulchyn, Mykolaiv, Izium, and other cities, it consisted of more than 30 music collectives and more than 300 individuals. Dedicated to Ukrainian musical development, the society organized courses of instruction, concerts, and academic research, in addition to publishing the journal *Muzyka. Notable members of the society included M. Verykivsky, M. Hrinchenko, K. Kvitka, P. Kozytsky, and M. Radziievsky. The society was criticized by Soviet authorities for supposedly propagandizing modern Western styles of music, such as expressionism and constructivism, and gradually was forced to give over control of its branches' activities to the Chief Political Education Committee of the People's Commissariat of Education and to direct its composers to create works 'for the masses.' In 1928 the association was restructured as the All-Ukrainian Society of Revolutionary Musicians (VUTORM), which functioned until the creation of the *Union of Composers of Ukraine in 1932.

Leontovych String Quartet (Kvartet im. M. Leontovycha). A group established in 1971 to continue the traditions of the *Leontovych Music Society of the 1920s. Based in Kiev, its members (1988) include S. Kobets and Y. Kharenko (violins), V. Barabanov (viola), and V. Pentaleiev (cello). Since 1978 the quartet members, who also work as instructors at the Kiev Conservatory, have been playing rare instruments made by Italian masters of the 17th and 18th centuries. The quartet won acclaim at both the 16th Leo Weiner International Competition and the 2nd International Festival of String Quartets in Vilnius. In 1988 it visited the United States to perform at the United Nations in New York and at the 'Music Mountain' festival in Connecticut. The quartet's repertoire includes works by F. Haydn, P. Tchaikovsky, and S. Barber, as well as M. Lysenko, M. Skoryk, I. Shamo, A. Filipenko, and M. Leontovych.

Lepkaliuk, Myroslav [Lepkaljuk], b 4 April 1919 in Kosiv Staryi, Kosiv county, Galicia. Engineer, businessman, and community activist. After studying in polytechnical schools in Danzig and Stuttgart, he moved to the United States in 1947 and worked as an engineer. In 1954 he established his own company of bridge designers, whose larger projects included the Fall River Bridge in Massachusetts and the Mississippi River Bridge at Luling, Louisiana. He has headed the Ukrainian Society of Engineers of America (1949–51) and the Ukrainian People's Home in New York (1952–4).

Lepkova-Jastremsky, Olga [Lepkova-Jastrems'ka, Ol'ha] (née Ivanchuk), b 30 March 1906 in Boryslav, Galicia. Opera and concert singer (mezzo-soprano). She studied piano and voice at the Cracow Conservatory and graduated from the Lysenko Higher Music Institute in Lviv. She also studied under A. Didur and in Vienna. She sang and toured with the Lviv State Opera under the stage name Lepkova. Best remembered for her role as Oksana in M. Lysenko's *Zaporozhian Cossack beyond the Danube*, she remained in the United States following a 1938 concert tour in North America.

Bohdan Lepky

Lepky, Bohdan [Lepkyj], b 4 November 1872 in Krehulets, Husiatyn county, Galicia, d 21 July 1941 in Cracow. Galician writer, literary scholar, civic figure, and artist; member of the Shevchenko Scientific Society from 1932; son of S. *Lepky.

Lepky studied at Lviv, Vienna, and Cracow universities and then taught in gymnasiums in Berezhany (1895–9) and at Cracow University (1899–1914). His home in Cracow was a well-known meeting place for Ukrainian writers, artists, and scholars. During the First World War he taught in Vienna; he also worked in the Ukrainian Cultural Council there and for the Union for the Liberation of Ukraine, as a teacher of Ukrainians interned in German prisoner-of-war camps in Wetzlar and Rastatt. From 1921 to 1926 he lived in Berlin; he worked there for the Ukrainske Slovo publishers and the Ukrainian Red Cross and taught courses organized by the Association of Ukrainian Students. From 1926 to 1939 he again taught at Cracow University (from 1932 as the holder of the chair of Ukrainian literature) and was a major promoter of Ukrainian culture in Polish circles. He received an honorary doctorate from the Ukrainian Free University. In 1938–9 he was a member of the Polish Senate. From 1939 he worked for the Ukrainske Vydavnytstvo publishers in Cracow.

Inspired by M. Vorony, V. Shchurat, and I. Franko, Lepky debuted as a writer in 1895. In 1906 he became a founding member of the *Moloda Muza writers' group. Some of his poems were put to music by Ukrainian composers; the requiem song 'Zhuravli' (Cranes), composed by his brother, Lev, is the most famous of them. From 1898 to 1911 over a dozen collections of Lepky's realistic stories (about the peasants' plight, the rural clergy, and generational conflict) and impressionistic prose poems appeared. Between the years 1901 and 1920 he also published over 15 collections of predominantly neoromantic and lyrical (elegiac and introspective) but also social and patriotic poetry. A good half of Lepky's poems and almost all of his stories were republished in two volumes titled *Pysannia* (Writings) in 1922.

After the war Lepky turned to writing historical novels, such as the (unfortunately esthetically uneven) Ukrainian historical prose epic *Mazepa*, which consists of the novels *Motria* (2 vols, 1926), *Ne vbyvai* (Do Not Kill, 1926), *Baturyn* (1927), *Poltava* (vol 1: *Nad Desnoiu* [At the Desna, 1928]; vol 2: *Boï* [Battles, 1929]), and the posthumously published *Z-pid Poltavy do Bender* (From [the Battle of] Poltava to Bendery, 1955). He also wrote the historical novels *Sotnykivna* (The Captain's Daughter, 1927), *Vadym* (1930), and *Krutizh: Istorychni maliunky z chasiv Het'mana Ivana Vyhovs'koho* (The Abyss: Historical Pictures from the Time of Hetman Ivan Vyhovsky, 1941) and the publicistic-philosophical novels *Pid tykhyi vechir* (Toward a Quiet Evening, 1923), *Zirka* (A Star, 1929), and *Veselka nad pustarem* (The Rainbow over the Wasteland, 1930). In the 1930s he also wrote stories and poems for children.

Lepky published articles on Ukrainian literature in Polish and Western Ukrainian periodicals and handbooks. He prepared and wrote critical introductions and notes to Halytska (later Ukrainska) Nakladnia and Ukrainske Slovo editions of works by T. Shevchenko (3 vols, 1918–19 and 5 vols, 1919–20), M. Vovchok (3 vols, 1923), I. Kotliarevsky (2 vols, 1922), P. Kulish (4 vols, 1922–3), O. Storozhenko (2 vols, 1922), and other writers. He also wrote one of the first surveys of old Ukrainian literature (2 vols, 1909, 1912), biographies of Shevchenko (1911, 1918) and M. Shashkevych (1912), the book of literary essays *Nezabutni* (The Unforgettable, 1922), a Polish survey of Ukrainian literature (1930), a book on the problem of translating lyric poetry (1934), and the survey *Nashe pys'menstvo* (Our Literature, 1941). Lepky's memoirs of Franko, V. Stefanyk, and W. Orkan appeared as *Try portrety* (Three Portraits, 1937), and his collected autobiographic prose was republished posthumously as *Kazka moho zhyttia* (The Tale of My Life, 1967). A selection of Lepky's works appeared in a single volume in Ukraine in 1990.

He compiled songbooks, primers, and the poetry anthology *Struny* (Strings, 2 vols, 1922) and translated the medieval epic *Slovo o polku Ihorevi* (The Tale of Ihor's Campaign) into Polish (1905) and modern Ukrainian (1915) and works by M. Kotsiubynsky, Shevchenko, and other Ukrainian writers into Polish. He translated German, Polish, Russian, and English poetry, fairy tales by the Grimm brothers, other children's stories, O. Wilde's *Salome*, and D. Defoe's *Robinson Crusoe* into Ukrainian. He was also an accomplished artist. In 1932 a 60th-birthday exhibition of his landscapes, portraits, and historical paintings was organized in Cracow.

BIBLIOGRAPHY

Vernyvolia, V. [Simovych, V.]. 'Bohdan Lepkyi (narys literaturnoï diial'nosty i sproba kharakterystyky pys'mennyka za dvadsiat' piat' lit ioho pys'mennyts'koï pratsi),' in *Bohdan Lepkyi: Pysannia*, vol 1 (Kiev–Leipzig 1922)

Kuzelia, Z. (ed). *Zolota Lypa: Iuvileina zbirka tvoriv Bohdana Lepkoho z ioho zhyttiepysom, bibliografiieiu tvoriv ta prysviatamy* (Berlin 1924)

Pelens'kyi, Ie. (ed). *Bohdan Lepkyi, 1872–1941: Zbirnyk u poshanu pam'iati poeta* (Cracow–Lviv 1943)

Lev, V. *Bohdan Lepkyi, 1872–1941: Zhyttia i tvorchist'*, vol 193 of *ZNTSh* (1976)

R. Senkus

Lepky, Danylo [Lepkyj] (pseuds: Sava Slyvych, D.L. Khomiv, and Sviashchenyk), b 29 December 1858 in Litynia, Sambir circle, Galicia, d 20 March 1912 in Staryi Sambir, Sambir county, Galicia. Priest, writer, and ethnographer. After graduating from the Peremyshl Theological Seminary (1884) he served as a priest in various villages. In 1900 he was appointed to Staryi Sambir, where he organized a credit and loan association (1901) and headed the local Prosvita society. He was a member of the Ethnographic Commission of the Shevchenko Scientific Society. His short stories began to appear in 1880 in *Zoria*, in which he also published ethnographic and folk art studies. His articles and fiction appeared in *Dilo*, *Bat'kivshchyna*, Prosvita almanacs, and other Galician periodicals. He also wrote children's stories, which appeared in *Dzvinok*, and novels about the common people.

Lev Lepky

Lepky, Lev [Lepkyj] (pseud: Lele), b 7 December 1888 in Poruchyn, Berezhany county, Galicia, d 28 October 1971 in Trenton, New Jersey. Journalist, writer, and songwriter; brother of B. *Lepky. During the First World War he was an organizer and officer of the Ukrainian Sich Riflemen (USS). While serving as a press officer he wrote songs for the USS, several of which became popular, eg, 'Oi vydno selo' (The Village Is Nigh) and the music to 'Zhuravli' (The Cranes; lyrics by B. Lepky). Many of these were later published in *Velykyi spivanyk Chervonoï Kalyny* (The Great Chervona Kalyna Songbook, 1937). In the interwar period he worked as an editor at the *Chervona Kalyna publishing co-operative in Lviv, which he cofounded, and edited its monthly *Litopys Chervonoï kalyny* (1929–39) and its annual almanacs. He also published and edited the humor journal *Zyz* (1924–6), and cofounded and directed the spa at Cherche (1928–39) and the puppet theater Vertep Nashykh Dniv. During the Second World War he was an editor of *Krakivs'ki visti*. A postwar refugee, in 1952 he settled in the United States, where he helped to revive the Chervona Kalyna publishers in New York City and continued organizing USS veterans.

Lepky, Sylvestr [Lepkyj, Syl'vestr] (pseuds: Marko Murava, Borys Boryslav, Borys Lepky, Vasylyshyn, M-o), b 31 December 1845 in Kulykiv, Zhovkva circle, Galicia, d 5

June 1901 in Zhukiv, Berezhany county, Galicia. Priest, writer, and community activist; father of B. *Lepky and L. *Lepky. He graduated from the Greek Catholic Theological Seminary in Lviv in 1871 and then served as a parish priest in various Galician villages. He established a number of Prosvita and Sich reading rooms and assisted in the publication of an edition of T. Shevchenko's works (1867). His verse and fiction, intended to arouse the national consciousness of Ukrainians, appeared in the newspapers *Bukovyna*, *Dilo*, *Pravda*, and *Zoria*. He also published a number of articles and pamphlets on philosophy, literature, sociology, economics, and agronomy. His story *Horyt'* (It Burns, 1901) was given a prize by the Prosvita society and published under separate cover in Lviv. A collection of his verse, *Knyzhka horia* (A Book of Grief, 1903), appeared posthumously.

Lerman, Zoia, b 14 June 1934 in Kiev. Painter. A graduate of the Kiev State Art Institute (1959), from 1974 to 1977 she attended the USSR Academy of Arts Workshop in Kiev. In the 1960s she participated in exhibitions organized by young artists in cafés and various institutions. Lerman works from memory and imagination in a figurative style often depicting women. Her palette is full of light because of her use of white pigment (eg, *Girl from Poltava* [1971] and *Kiev Woman* [1981]).

Lesawyer, Joseph [Lysohir, Josyp], b 25 May 1911 in Northampton, Pennsylvania. Community leader and businessman. A real estate broker by profession, he was active in Ukrainian American organizational life as vice-president (1950–4) and president (1961–78) of the Ukrainian National Association and vice-president (1961–78) of the Ukrainian Congress Committee of America. He also served as president (1971–3) of the World Congress of Free Ukrainians.

Lesawyer, Mary (Lysohir, Mariia), b 8 October 1917 in Shamokin, Pennsylvania. Opera singer (lyric soprano). After studying music at the Juilliard School, she launched her operatic career with the New York City Opera and for nearly two decades performed in major operas. She appeared in numerous Ukrainian musical productions in the United States, Canada, Europe, and South America and sang in Ukrainian operas such as M. Lysenko's *May Night*, S. Hulak-Artemovsky's *Zaporozhian Cossack beyond the Danube*, M. Arkas's *Catherine*, and P. Pecheniha-Uhlytsky's *The Witch*. She also collaborated with Ukrainian-American composers M. Haivoronsky, P. Pecheniha-Uhlytsky, O. Koshyts, and M. Fomenko.

Lesevych [Lesevyč]. A Cossack *starshyna* family from the Poltava region. The line's founder was Kostiantyn, a notable military fellow of Lubni regiment (1724). His son, Danylo, was captain of Kovalivka company in Hadiache regiment (1738–68) and then regimental judge (1768–70). The philosopher V. *Lesevych is descended from the line.

Lesevych, Volodymyr [Lesevyč], b 27 January 1837 in Denysivka, Lubni county, Poltava gubernia, d 26 November 1905 in St Petersburg. Philosopher and community figure; full member of the Shevchenko Scientific Society (NTSh). A graduate of the St Petersburg Military Engneer-

Volodymyr Lesevych

ing School (1855), he served as an officer in Caucasia for three years and then entered the Academy of the General Staff. In 1861 he retired to his estate in Denysivka, where in 1864 he established one of the first elementary schools for peasants with Ukrainian as the language of instruction. A staunch populist and supporter of the Ukrainian national revival, he defended iuse of the Ukrainian language in the Russian press, subsidized M. Drahomanov's émigré activities in Geneva and publications of the Ukrainian Radical party in Galicia, and cofounded the *Philanthropic Society for Publishing Generally Useful and Inexpensive Books in St Petersburg, where he resided. For aiding the revolutionary *Narodnaia Volia, he was exiled to Siberia (1879–81) and then forbidden to live in the capital until 1888. Lesevych was one of the founders of positivism in the Russian Empire. Recognizing the importance of epistemology, he became critical of his earlier Comtean outlook and turned to R. Avenarius's empiriocriticism in formulating his own mature position. The role of philosophy, according to his theory of 'critical realism,' was to synthesize the results of the special sciences into a scientific worldview. He himself did not manage to complete this task. Besides numerous articles in philosophy, Lesevych wrote four books in Russian: a survey of the development of the idea of progress (1868), a critical study of the basic principles of positive philosophy (1877), *Pis'ma o nauchnoi filosofii* (Letters on Scientific Philosophy, 1878), and *Chto takoe nauchnaia filosofiia?* (What is Scientific Philosophy? 1891). He bequeathed his library to the NTSh in Lviv. A three-volume collection of his works (1915–17) was published in Moscow.

T. Zakydalsky

Leshchenko, Leonid [Leščenko], b 2 June 1931 in Horodnytsia (now in Uman raion, Cherkasy oblast). Historian. He graduated from Kiev University (1954) and received a doctorate in 1985. In 1978 he began working at the AN URSR (now ANU) Institute of Social and Economic Problems of Foreign Countries. He has written books on Ukraine in the international arena in 1945–9 (1969), the Soviet-Canadian alliance and co-operation against Nazi Germany in 1941–5 (1973), and the farmers' movement in Canada in 1900–39 (1979) and coedited a handbook on Ukrainians living outside the USSR (1991).

Leshchenko, Mykola [Leščenko], b 19 February 1911 in Burchak, Melitopil county, Katerynoslav gubernia. Soviet historian. He lectured at Kiev University (1945–9) and worked at the AN URSR (now ANU) Institute of History. His works examined Ukrainian historiography and the history of the Ukrainian peasantry; among them is *Klasova borot'ba v ukraïns'komu seli v epokhu domonopolistychnoho kapitalizmu, 60–90-ti roky XIX st.* (The Class Struggle in the Ukrainian Village in the Period of Premonopolistic Capitalism, 1860s–1890s, 1970).

Leshchynsky, Filofei [Leščyns'kyj, Filofej], b 1650 in Galicia, d 31 May 1727. Churchman. He studied at the Kievan Mohyla Academy and was a monk at the Kievan Cave Monastery before becoming metropolitan of Siberia (1702–11). He was forced to retire to a monastery because of ill health and later resumed his post as metropolitan (1715–21). He was one of the most prominent Orthodox missionaries in Siberia. In 1703 he founded a seminary in Tobolsk that existed until 1721. It is estimated that his mission converted over 40,000 people to Christianity.

Lesia Ukrainka. See Ukrainka, Lesia.

Lesia Ukrainka Theater (Ukrainskyi dramatychnyi teatr im. Lesi Ukrainky). The first Soviet theater in Western Ukraine, established in Lviv in September 1939 on the basis of the former casts of the Kotliarevsky and Stadnyk theaters. The artificial union of these theaters, along with the Soviet repertoire, caused disagreement among the directors, Y. Stadnyk, O. Lein, V. Vasylko, V. Blavatsky, and B. Balaban, and produced no great theatrical results. The theater ceased activity in June 1941 and was succeeded by the *Lviv Opera Theater.

Lesia Ukrainka Theater in Kiev. See Kiev Russian Drama Theater.

Lesiv, Mykhailo (Łesiów, Michał), b 3 May 1928 in Stara Huta, Buchach county, Galicia. Slavist and educator. A graduate of the Catholic University in Lublin and Warsaw University (PH D, 1962), since 1956 he has taught at Lublin University. His publications include articles on the language of 17th-century Ukrainian plays and verse, Ukrainian-Polish linguistic relations, and the Ukrainian dialects of the Kholm and Podlachia regions. He has written a monograph on the place-names of the Lublin region (1972) and on pronouns in literary Ukrainian of the 17th and 18th centuries (1977).

Lesiv, Yaroslav, b 3 January 1943 in Luzhky, Dolyna raion, Ivano-Frankivske oblast, d 6 October 1991 near

Yaroslav Lesiv

Bolekhiv, Ivano-Frankivske oblast, in an automobile accident. Teacher, poet, and human rights activist. In 1967, while working as a physical education teacher in Kirovohrad oblast, he was sentenced to six years' imprisonment for his participation in the clandestine *Ukrainian National Front. An inmate of the Vladimir prison from 1970, he was released in March 1973 and allowed to return to Ukraine. In 1979 he joined the *Ukrainian Helsinki Group. Consequently he was arrested in Bolekhiv in November 1979, and sentenced in 1980 to two years in a labor camp near Sarny, Rivne oblast. In November 1981 he was sentenced to five more years of strict-regime labor, from which he was released in 1986. A book of his poetry, *Myt'* (Moment), was published in New York in 1982.

Leskov, Nikolai, b 16 February 1831 in Gorokhov, Orel gubernia, Russia, d 5 March 1895 in St Petersburg. Russian writer. He lived in Kiev from 1849 to 1857; there he learned the Ukrainian language and became acquainted with the life of the Ukrainian people and their culture. Leskov wrote stories on Ukrainian themes, such as 'Nekhreshchenyi pop' (The Unbaptized Priest, 1877), 'Starinnye psikhopaty' (Ancient Psychopaths, 1885), 'Pecherskie antiki' (Pecherske [District] Eccentrics, 1883), and 'Zaiachii remiz' (The Rabbit Warren, 1917). Leskov was personally acquainted with O. Markovych and T. Shevchenko. He wrote articles and memoirs about Shevchenko, such as 'Posledniaia vstrecha i posledniaia razluka s Shevchenko' (The Last Encounter and the Last Farewell with Shevchenko, 1861) and 'Zabyta li Tarasova mogila?' (Is Taras's Grave Forgotten?, 1882).

Lesniak, Omelian [Lesnjak, Omeljan], b 24 April 1882 in Horodenka, Galicia, d near the end of 1953 in Vienna. Senior army officer. As an officer of the Austrian army, in 1916 he commanded the First Battalion of the Legion of Ukrainian Sich Riflemen and was captured by the Russians. After returning to Galicia in 1919, he enlisted in the Ukrainian Galician Army (UHA) and took command of the Zolochiv Military District. In July 1919 he was appointed commander of the Third Brigade of the UHA. Then, as a major, he served in the Supreme Headquarters of the UHA. In the interwar period he lived in Prešov, Czechoslovakia, and after the war in Vienna, where in 1946 he was arrested by the MVD. He was released from Soviet imprisonment in 1953, and returned to Vienna.

Lesnyk, Andrii, b 19 August 1916 in Halzhbiivka, Yampil county, Podilia gubernia. Physicist; corresponding member of the AN URSR (now ANU) since 1976. Since 1947 he has worked at the ANU Institute of Metal Physics. His research deals with the thermodynamics of alloys, the theory of phase transformations in binary alloys, and the physical properties of magnetic films.

Lesur, Charles-Louis, b 24 August 1770 in Guise (Picardie), France, d 1849. French historiographer and publicist. He worked for the Comité du Salut Public (from 1792), where he was Talleyrand's protégé, and for the Ministry of External Relations (from 1812). His *Histoire des Kosaques* (1813; 2nd edn, 2 vols, 1814) was commissioned by Napoleon on the eve of the Russian campaign; the second edition was published with revisions and addenda following the change of the French regime. Based on earlier works about Ukraine by J. *Długosz, G. le Vasseur de *Beauplan, P. *Chevalier, and J.-B. *Scherer, it emphasized Cossack aspirations for independence.

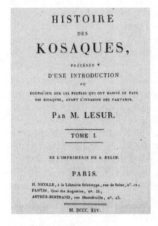

Title page of Charles-Louis Lesur's *Histoire des Kosaques* (1814)

Vadym Lesych

Lesych, Vadym [Lesyč] (pseud of Volodymyr Kirshak; other pseuds: Yaroslav Dryhynych, Yaroslav Yary), b 1909 in Galicia, d 24 August 1982 in New York. Poet and essayist. After studying journalism at Warsaw University, he worked as a journalist and art critic. In 1948 he emigrated to the United States. He began publishing his poetry in 1929 in journals, such as *Literaturno-naukovyi vistnyk* and *Nazustrich* in Lviv and *My* in Warsaw. His early poetry, marked by a predilection for symbolism and dramatic lyricism, is written in strophes that are almost baroque in form. In his later works he stripped the structures of some of their formal elaborateness and incorporated elements of expressionism and narrative lyricism. He is author of nine collections of poetry – *Sontseblysky* (Sun Flares, 1930), *Vidchyniaiu vikno* (I Open a Window, 1932), *Rizbliu viddal'* (I Sculpt the Distance, 1935), *Lirychnyi zoshyt* (A Lyrical Notebook, 1953), *Poeziï* (Poems, 1954), *Rozmova z bat'kom* (Conversation with Father, 1957), *Kreidiane kolo* (The Chalk Circle, 1960), *Kam'iani luny* (Stone Echoes, 1964), and *Vybrani poeziï* (Selected Poems, 1965) – the narrative poem *Naperedodni* (On the Eve, 1960), and numerous essays and articles on literary and artistic themes.

D.H. Struk

Lesyn, Vasyl, b 21 March 1914 in Khotiivka, Sosnytsia county, Chernihiv gubernia, d 1991. Literary scholar. He studied literature at Lviv University. In 1952 he was appointed to the chair of history of Ukrainian literature there. He was a specialist on M. Cheremshyna, L. Martovych, and V. Stefanyk and wrote *Les' Martovych: Literaturnyi portret* (Les Martovych: A Literary Portrait, 1963), *Tvorchist' Vasylia Stefanyka* (The Works of Vasyl Stefanyk, 1965), *Vasyl' Stefanyk: Maister novely* (Vasyl Stefanyk: Master of the Novella, 1970), and *Marko Cheremshyna* (1974). His studies on literary theory include *Kompozytsiia i siuzhet literaturnoho tvoru* (Composition and Plot in a Literary Work, 1960) and *Realistychnyi obraz u khudozhn'omu tvori* (Realistic Portrayal in a Creative Work, 1976). Together

with O. Pulynets he compiled a short dictionary of literary terms (1961).

Leszczyński, Stanisław. See Stanislaus I Leszczyński.

Letopis' Ekaterinoslavskoi gubernskoi uchenoi arkhivnoi komissii. See Archival commissions.

Letychiv: the Potocki family's castle and the Dominican church and monastery. Lithograph of a drawing by N. Orda (1860s)

Letychiv or **Liatychiv** [Letyčiv or Ljatyčiv]. IV-8. A town smt (1990 pop 11,600) and raion center in Khmelnytskyi oblast, located on the Vovk River in the eastern part of the Podolian Upland. It belonged to Galicia principality until 1362 and then came under Lithuanian control. During the period of Lithuanian control a fortress was built there. The town is first mentioned in a historical document in 1411. In 1434 it came under Polish rule, and in 1466 it was granted the rights of *Magdeburg law. In the 15th and 16th centuries it was devastated several times by the Turks and Crimean Tatars. Letychiv played an important role during the Cossack-Polish War of 1648–57. By the end of the century it had witnessed many battles among Cossacks, Poles, and Turks. It took part in the Cossack and popular uprising of 1702–3. After the second partition of Poland in 1793, the town was annexed by Russia and turned into a county center in Podilia gubernia. At the beginning of the 19th century Letychiv played a leading role in the popular uprisings led by U. *Karmaliuk, who was buried there in 1835. Today it has a press assembly plant, a brickyard, a building-materials plant, and a furniture factory. Its architectural monuments include the walls and a tower of the 16th-century castle and two 17th-century Orthodox and Roman Catholic churches. Tools from the Trypilian culture and two early Slav settlements have been discovered near Letychiv.

Leuven (French: Louvain). A Flemish city in Belgium (1985 pop 85,000), and the site of a famous Catholic university (est 1425). Ukrainians (initially from Galicia) have attended the university since 1931, when Metropolitan A. Sheptytsky, with the assistance of the Belgian Jesuit R. Jourdain, sent 50 students for studies there. In 1932–85 approx 100 Ukrainians graduated from Leuven University, three of whom went on to become professors there: V. Gapyshyn, Y. Shukhevych, and R. Yakemchuk. Another

Ukrainian students at Leuven University in 1933

graduate, Zh. Protsyshyn, became a professor at Ghent University. Most of these alumni, among them V. *Mackiw, I. *Ševčenko, M. *Hermaniuk, and O. *Bilaniuk, emigrated to North America, and only about 20 percent stayed on in Belgium. A Ukrainian department was situated at one of the city's libraries. It published books on Ukraine and the monthly *Holos Khrysta Cholovikoliubtsia* (1946–70), which was subsequently taken over by the apostolic visitature.

Vasyl Lev   Prince Lev Danylovych

Lev, Vasyl, b 7 February 1903 in Staryi Yazhiv, Yavoriv county, Galicia, d 23 March 1991 in New York. Linguist and literary historian; member of the Shevchenko Scientific Society from 1947 and of the Ukrainian Academy of Arts and Sciences in the US. After graduating from Lviv University (PH D, 1930) he taught languages in secondary schools in Lviv and then lectured at Lviv University (1937–41). After the war he was a lecturer and professor at the Ukrainian Free University in Munich (1944–9, 1963–88) and then a professor of Ukrainian and Church Slavonic at St Basil's College in Stamford (1952–8), Marywood College (1958–72) in Scranton, and the Ukrainian Catholic University in Rome (1963–88). Lev wrote numerous works, including articles on T. Shevchenko, Lesia Ukrainka, I. Franko, and B. Lepky; linguistic studies of the Krekhiv *Apostol* (1929); articles on the Ukrainian translation of M. Bielski's chronicle (1935); T. Shevchenko's early poetry (1946); and the members of the Ruthenian Triad (1953). With I. Verbiany he compiled a Ukrainian-English and English-Ukrainian dictionary (1947–8). He was a co-editor of the collected works of V. Grendzha-Donsky (1981–8) and of historical collections on the Ternopil (vol 2, 1970), Berezhany (1970), Yavoriv (1984), and Komarno-Rudky (1987) regions.

Lev Danylovych [Lev Danylovyč], b ca 1228, d ca 1301. Prince of Galicia from 1264; son of King *Danylo Romanovych, brother of *Mstyslav and *Shvarno Danylovych, and father of *Yurii Lvovych. He had dynastic ties with Hungary through his marriage to Konstancia, the daughter of Bela IV. Lev inherited the Halych, Peremyshl, and Belz lands from his father in 1264. In 1268 he murdered *Vaišvilkas after Vaišvilkas abdicated and gave the Grand Duchy of Lithuania to his son-in-law, Shvarno, instead of to Lev. Lev inherited the Kholm and Dorohychyn lands after Shvarno's death ca 1269. He made Lviv (which was named after Lev) his capital in 1272. A vassal of the *Tatars from the early 1270s, he had their support during his campaigns against Lithuania (1275, 1277), Poland (1280, 1283, 1286–8), and Hungary (1285). He made a pact with Wenceslas II of Bohemia in 1279 and, as his ally, tried unsuccessfully to seize Cracow in 1280. Lev's long war with Poland brought little gain. He annexed to his realm part of Transcarpathia (including Mukachiv) ca 1280 and part of the Lublin land ca 1292.

Lev Society (Tovarystvo Leva). An independent civic organization in Lviv dedicated to preserving the historical and cultural heritage of Ukraine, formed in 1987. The society has focused its energies on national, cultural, and ecological undertakings. Its most important projects were the restoration of Lviv's Lychakiv Cemetery and undertakings to preserve and reclaim several Ukrainian historical sites. A project attempting to revive folk handicrafts resulted in the establishment of a school in Bilyi Kamin to teach an ancient form of Ukrainian pottery known as black ceramics. In 1988 the society organized an expedition on the Dniester River to call attention to the river's ecological problems (specifically the disruption of the natural flow by man-made dams and the severe pollution). Originally the society had 175 postgraduate members (average age, 25), but by 1991 the membership had dropped to 50 (average age, 18). The presidents of the society have been O. Sheika, I. Hryniv, I. Zakharchyshyn, and Ya. Rybak.

Lev Yuriiovych [Jurijovyč] (Lev II Yuriiovych), b ?, d not later than June 1323. Galician prince; son of *Yurii Lvovych. After his father died (in 1308 or, according to other sources, in 1315), Lev ruled the Principality of Galicia-Volhynia together with his older brother, *Andrii Yuriiovych. Later he ruled Galicia separately. The brothers' policy was to weaken the principality's vassalage to the Golden Horde by maintaining alliances with the *Teutonic Knights and with Poland. The brothers died in battle against the Tatars.

Levada, Oleksander (full surname: Kosiak-Levada), b 26 November 1909 in Kryvchunka, Tarashcha county, Kiev gubernia. Writer. In the postwar years he was appointed to various state positions, among them those of deputy minister of culture of the Ukrainian SSR (responsible for cinema) and vice-president of the Derzhkino. He is the author of books of essays, such as *Bezvirnyky shtur-*

Oleksander Levada

Ivan Levakovsky

muiut' Dnipro (The InfidelsAre Storming the Dnieper, 1931) and *Balkans'kyi shchodennyk* (A Balkan Diary, 1946); the collections of poetry *Poeziï* (Poems, 1941) and *Berezen'-zhovten'* (March–October, 1973); and the novel *Pivdennyi zakhid* (Southwest, with I. Le, 1950). He also wrote numerous plays, published in the collection *Dramy i komediï* (Dramas and Comedies, 1967), of which the most popular was the tragedy *Favst i smert'* (Faust and Death, 1960). His later works include the plays *Zdrastui, Prypiat'* (Greetings, Prypiat, 1973) and *Persten' z diiamantom* (The Diamond Ring, 1977), the collections of screenplays *Bereh nadiï* (The Shore of Hope, 1967) and *Kinopovisti* (Film Narratives, 1977), *Tvory u 4-kh tomakh* (Works in 4 Volumes, 1979–80), and *Dva kol'ory* (Two Colors, 1989).

Levakovsky, Ivan [Levakovs'kyj], b 1828 in St Petersburg, d 27 March 1893 in Kharkiv. Geologist. He graduated from Kharkiv University (in 1852), lectured there (from 1860), and became its first professor of geology (1864). He helped to organize the *Kharkiv Society of Naturalists in 1869 and served as its president until his death. Levakovsky conducted geological research in Ukraine, especially in the Crimea (he outlined the asymmetric structure of the Crimean Mountains) and the southwestern parts of the Donets Basin. He also studied the hydrogeography and soil structure of Ukraine, as well as the geomorphology and tectonics of Right-Bank Ukraine, and wrote the first geology textbook in the Russian Empire (1861–4).

Levanda, Ivan (Ioan; real surname: Sikachka), b March 1734 in Kiev, d 6 July 1814 in Kiev. Churchman and eminent preacher. In 1786 he became pastor of the St Sophia Cathedral in Kiev. Levanda wrote approx 200 sermons and homilies, over 100 of which were collected and published in 1821. Initially influenced by baroque and Polish oration, he eventually developed a unique narrative style, characterized by clarity and realism. He was interested in Ukrainian history and acquired a large collection of historical documents. He also had a large circle of friends among Ukrainian activists, including V. Kapnist, O. Lobysevych, and O. Shafonsky. Levanda is buried in the St Sophia Cathedral.

Levandovsky, Viacheslav [Levandovs'kyj, Vjačeslav], b 23 February 1897 in Kiev, d 18 April 1962 in Moscow. Pioneering animator. While studying at the Kiev Theater

Academy (1918) and the Ukrainian State Academy of Arts (1920–2) he designed sets for a number of theaters and worked as a commercial artist in Kiev. In 1927 he directed a documentary film about the first 10 years of Soviet rule incorporating animation and graphics. In Odessa he made the first Ukrainian animated cartoon, *Kazka pro solom'ianoho bychka* (Tale about the Straw Bullock, 1927). In 1928 he made another in Kiev, *Kazka pro Bilku-hospodyniu ta Myshku-zlodiiku* (Tale about Squirrel the Housewife and Mouse the Thief, 1928). In 1932 he began working in Odessa on one of the first Ukrainian animated sound films, *Tuk-Tuk ta ioho tovarysh Zhuk* (Tuk-Tuk and His Friend Zhuk), which was completed in 1935 by Ye. Horbach and S. Huietsky. From 1933 Levandovsky made animated films at Mosfilm studios in Moscow.

Levanidov, Andrei, b and d ? Russian general. He was commander of the Starodub Carabineer Regiment (1785), corps commander in Kiev (1790–4), and governor-general of Slobidska Ukraine (1796–7). He had ties with Ukrainian autonomist circles and was the protector of A. *Khudorba and A. *Vedel. He took an interest in the history of Ukraine and left a collection of manuscripts called *Andrei Levanidov Malorossiiskii Letopisets* (Andrei Levanidov, a Little Russian Chronicler, ca 1790), which is preserved in the National Museum in Lviv.

Olena Levchanivska

Levchanivska, Olena [Levčanivs'ka] (née Hrodzynska), b 27 January 1881 on the Horodno estate in Volhynia, d 1943 in Kazakhstan. Civic and political leader. After completing her education in St Petersburg and Moscow ca 1907, she became a school organizer and teacher. She returned to the Volhynia region in 1919 and became active in the social welfare and charitable work of the Prosvita society in Kovel and Lutske. In 1922–8 she was a deputy to the Polish Senate and a member of its foreign affairs commission. She was particularly critical of the treatment of Ukrainians under the Poles and spoke out openly on that subject, most notably at the Congress of Minorities called by the League of Nations in Geneva in 1925. She was arrested by the Soviets in 1939 and deported in 1940. She later died in a prison camp in Kazakhstan.

Levchenko, Fedir [Levčenko], b 20 June 1876 in Kononivka, Lubni county, Poltava gubernia, d 24 April 1937 in Zhytomyr. Soil scientist. He graduated from the Kiev Polytechnical Institute in 1904. He then lectured at the Kiev Agricultural Institute (1922–30) and chaired a department at the Kiev Agricultural Engineering Institute of the Sugar Industry and the Zhytomyr Agricultural Institute. In 1908–11 he studied the soil structure of the Turgai steppe and the Karakum desert; subsequently he did soil research in Ukraine. His writings and soil maps were later used in the preparation of soil maps of Ukraine.

Levchenko, Hryhorii [Levčenko, Hryhorij], b 30 November 1901 in Novoselytsia, Skvyra county, Kiev gubernia, d 19 February 1944 in Kiev. Linguist. A graduate of the Kiev Institute of People's Education (1926), he was a docent at Kharkiv and, later, Kiev University. Levchenko wrote a number of pioneering works on 19th-century literary Ukrainian, including an article on T. Shevchenko's role in the history of literary Ukrainian (1939) and *Narysy z istoriï ukraïns'koï literaturnoï movy pershoï polovyny XIX st.* (Essays on the History of Literary Ukrainian in the First Half of the 19th Century, 1946).

Levchenko, Mykhailo [Levčenko, Myxajlo], 1830–1892. Lexicographer. His *Opyt russko-ukrainskogo slovaria* (An Attempt at a Russian-Ukrainian Dictionary, 1874) was one of the first dictionaries of its kind. It contained approx 7,600 Russian and 9,000 Ukrainian words (including synonyms). The Ukrainian vocabulary was derived mostly from the southeastern dialects. In spite of its small range, the dictionary played an important role in normalizing literary Ukrainian. Levchenko also contributed articles on Ukrainian terminology and place-names to *Osnova* (1861).

Mykola Levchenko

Petro Levchenko:
Self-Portrait (oil)

Levchenko, Mykola [Levčenko], b 1900 in the Chernihiv region, d 1934 in Kiev. Folklorist and literary scholar. After graduating from the Kiev Archeological Institute and the Kiev Institute of People's Education he served as A. Krymsky's secretary at the All-Ukrainian Academy of Sciences. In 1927 he was put in charge of publishing at the academy. A specialist in folk prose, he edited the still-unsurpassed collection *Kazky ta opovidannia z Podillia* (Fables and Stories from Podilia, 1928) and *Opovidannia selian za chasy hromadians'koï viiny na Vkraïni* (Peasant Stories from the Civil War in Ukraine, 1926) and wrote a study of the warrior Illia Muromets in medieval Ukrainian folktales (1927). His two-volume collection *Z polia folkl'orystyky ta etnohrafiï* (From the Field of Folklore Studies and Ethnography, 1927–8) was an important contribution to the history of Ukrainian folk culture. Also a literary scholar, he

published V. Antonovych's correspondence in *Zapysky Istorychno-filolohichnoho viddilu UAN* (no 16, 1928) and collaborated with A. Krymsky on the collection *Znadoby do zhyttiepysu Stepana Rudans'koho* (Materials for the Biography of Stepan Rudansky, 1926). He also published some recollections about Rudansky (1929). After being arrested at the end of 1929 in connection with the *Union for the Liberation of Ukraine showtrial, he refused to sign any fabrications and was sent to the GULAG without trial. He was released from labor camp in the fall of 1934, and returned to Kiev. Unable to find work and resume normal life, he committed suicide.

M. Mushynka

Levchenko, Petro [Levčenko], b 11 July 1856 in Kharkiv, d 27 January 1917 in Kharkiv. Painter and pedagogue. He studied art in Kharkiv under D. Bezperchy, at the St Petersburg Academy of Arts (1878–83), and in Paris and Rome. From 1886 he lectured at the Kharkiv Painting School. He was a member of the *Society of South Russian Artists and a participant in almost all of the exhibitions of the *Peredvizhniki (1886–1904), and from 1900 his works displayed the influence of the impressionists. Levchenko did some 800 landscapes and genre paintings. A posthumous retrospective exhibition of 700 of his paintings was held in Kharkiv in 1918. Monographs about him were written by M. Pavlenko (1927), Yu. Diuzhenko (1958), and M. Bezkhutry (1984).

Levchenko, Serhii [Levčenko, Serhij], b 1902 in the Chernihiv region, d 24 June 1969 in Kiev. Linguist and lexicographer. Levchenko studied at the Chernihiv Institute of People's Education and the Kharkiv branch of the AN URSR Institute of Linguistics. After the Second World War he was appointed a lecturer at Kiev University and a senior research associate of the Institute of Linguistics. He wrote a candidate's dissertation on the language of O. Korniichuk (1947) and a course on Ukrainian phonetics (1955), contributed to several dictionaries and reference works, and coedited the last four volumes of the six-volume Ukrainian-Russian dictionary (1953–63).

Levchenko, Yurii [Levčenko, Jurij], b 1956 in Korostyshiv, Zhytomyr oblast. Painter. Although Levchenko graduated from the Kiev State Art Institute in 1980, his work was not accepted for exhibitions until 1987. His paintings *Gold and Purple* and *Reign of Darkness*, dedicated to the millennium of Christianity in Ukraine, were part of the 1988 Dialogue through the Ages Exhibition in Kiev. In them, using Christian symbolism of the Crucifixion and fire, Levchenko suggests parallels with human suffering.

Levchuk, Dmytro [Levčuk], b 28 May 1900 near Kobryn, Hrodna gubernia, Polisia, d 18 July 1977 in Philadelphia. Economist and journalist. After graduating from Kiev University in law (1930) and economics (1931) he worked in state enterprises and taught law in a variety of institutions. He emigrated to the United States after the Second World War. There he became an ideologue for the hetmanite movement, published numerous articles on Soviet affairs in *Ameryka* and *Bat'kivshchyna*, and wrote several books, including the posthumous *Zasnuvannia Moskoviï ta shliakh utvorennia despotychnoï imperiï* (The Establishment of Muscovy and the Path to the Creation of a Despotic Empire, 1979).

Tymofii Levchuk   Ivan Levynsky

Levchuk, Tymofii [Levčuk, Tymofij], b 19 January 1912 in Bystriivka, Skvyra county, Kiev gubernia. Film director. Upon graduating from the Kiev Cinematography Institute (1934) he joined the Kiev Artistic Film Studio as a director. Among his films are *Ivan Franko* (1950); adaptations of two O. Korniichuk plays, *V stepakh Ukraïny* (In the Steppes of Ukraine, 1952) and *Kalynovyi hai* (The Viburnum Grove, 1953); the trilogies *Kyianka* (The Kiev Girl, 1958–60) and *Duma pro Kovpaka* (Duma about Kovpak, 1975–8); the feature films *Zakon Antarktydy* (The Law of Antarctica, 1963) and *Kosmichnyi splav* (The Cosmic Raft, 1964); and *Pomylka Onore de Bal'zaka* (Honoré de Balzac's Mistake, 1968), *Sim'ia Kotsiubyns'kykh* (The Kotsiubynsky Family, 1971), *My zvynuvachuiemo* (We Accuse, 1983), and *Iakshcho voroh ne zdaiet'sia* (If the Enemy Does Not Surrender, 1984). Since 1963 he has served as first secretary of the Union of Cinematographers of Ukraine.

Levenets [Levenec']. A Cossack *starshyna* family in the Poltava region in the 17th and 18th centuries. Prokip (d 1691) served briefly as colonel of Poltava regiment (1674, 1677–8) and distinguished himself in the Chyhyryn campaigns (1677–8). In 1685 he was promoted to the rank of fellow of the standard by Hetman I. Samoilovych. In 1687 he became regimental quartermaster and was even a candidate for the hetman's office. His son, Ivan (d ca 1736), was captain (1687) and then colonel of Poltava regiment (1701–9). In 1708 he turned against Hetman I. Mazepa. He did not aid the Russian side, however, and was dismissed from office. In 1711 he was appointed fellow of the standard, and in 1724 he became one of the three directors of the General Military Chancellery. His son, Ivan (d 1747), was osaul (1726–37) and quartermaster (1737–47) of Poltava regiment.

Levshin, Aleksei [Levšin, Aleksej], b 1799, d 28 September 1879 in Kursk gubernia. Russian civic and political leader. A graduate of Kharkiv University (1818), in 1831–7 he was mayor of Odessa, where he founded a public library and published *Odesskii vestnik*. In 1856–9 he was undersecretary to the imperial minister of internal affairs, and in 1857, as a supporter of the abolition of serfdom, he prepared a project for land reforms. His memoirs, *Dostopamiatnye minuty v moei zhizni* (Unforgettable Minutes in My Life), were published in *Russkii arkhiv* (1885, no. 8).

Levy en masse (*opolchennia*). An armed force of a temporary nature recruited on a voluntary basis from the general population in a national emergency, such as a war. In the Princely era (9th–14th centuries), a levy en masse of burghers and peasants was raised by the prince when the realm was threatened with invasion. The volunteers were organized by territory, each land forming its own *tysiacha* (thousand) commanded by a *tysiatskyi*. They were armed with different weapons and formed a light infantry that played a minor role in battle. In the Grand Duchy of Lithuania (until the mid-16th century) the levy en masse was similiarly organized, but in the Polish Commonwealth it affected mostly the gentry. In the Russian Empire and Austria-Hungary, after the introduction of compulsory *military service, levy en masse was an exceptional measure. It was used to reinforce the active army and provide a rear guard. During the Napoleonic Wars a levy en masse was raised throughout the Russian Empire, in the second half of 1812. The Ukrainian gubernias provided 19 Cossack cavalry regiments and 4 Cossack infantry regiments (totalling 23,000 men), 3 Buh Cossack cavalry regiments (1,700 men), and over 12 cavalry and 16 infantry regiments of the other estates (47,000 men). Another levy en masse was called during the Crimean War. In Austrian-ruled Galicia during the Revolution of 1848–9 the *National Guard and the *People's Militia were formed. In both world wars levies en masse were raised, in the First World War by both Russia and Austria-Hungary, and in the Second by the USSR. There was no levy en masse in Ukrainian armies.

Levynsky, Ivan [Levyns'kyj], b 6 July 1851 in Dolyna, Stanyslaviv county, Galicia, d 4 July 1919 in Lviv. Architect. A graduate of the Lviv Technical Academy (1875), he opened an architectural firm, a building-materials company, and an artistic pottery studio in Lviv. There he designed and built many public buildings in the Moderne style, in which he incorporated motifs from Ukrainian folk architecture and ornamentation. They include the Chamber of Commerce and Industry, the main railway station, the George Hotel, hospitals, clinics, the building of the *Dnister insurance company (1905), the student residence of the Ukrainian Pedagogical Society, the Akademichnyi Dim student residence, the Narodnia Hostynnytsia building, the building of the Lysenko Higher Institute of Music (1916), and the new building of the *Academic Gymnasium. He also designed and built sanatoriums and hospitals in Vorokhta, Zolochiv, Kolomyia, Zalishchyky, Horodenka, and Ternopil. Levynsky was a patron of the Postup society for workers' enlightenment, the Silskyi Hospodar society, the Osnova student society, and other associations; a founding member of the Prosvita society; and a member of the board of the National Museum. In 1903 he became a professor of architecture at the Lviv Polytechnical Institute. During the 1914 Russian retreat from Galicia he was deported to Kiev. There after the February Revolution, he founded the Pratsia agronomic and technical society and built the wooden Ukrainian Catholic church in the Hutsul style. After returning to Lviv in 1918, he founded the Pratsia society there.

S. Hordynsky

Levynsky, Stepan [Levyns'kyj], b 1897 in Lviv, d 8 October 1946 in Gap, France. Civic figure, engineer, and Orientalist; the son of I. *Levynsky. He studied at the Lviv Polytechnic and the Brussels Colonial Institute and received doctoral degrees from the Polytechnical School and National Institute of Oriental Languages and Civilizations in Paris. From 1936 to 1940 he worked in the economics section of the Polish consulate in Harbin, Manchuria, and was active in the Ukrainian community there, by contributing to *Man'dzhurs'kyi vistnyk* and helping compile a Ukrainian-Japanese dictionary. He then studied in Beijing (1940–1) and was an official Japanese translator for the French government of Indochina in Saigon (now Ho Chi Minh City; 1942–5). He translated Japanese literature into Ukrainian and published many accounts of his extensive travels, including *Vid Vezuviia do piskiv Sahary* (From Vesuvius to the Sands of the Sahara), *Z iapons'koho domu* (From a Japanese Home, 1932), and *Skhid i Zakhid* (East and West, 1934).

Volodymyr Levynsky   Anastasiia Levytska

Levynsky, Volodymyr [Levyns'kyj], b 8 August 1880 in Drohobych, Galicia, d 19 December 1953 in Vienna. Editor, journalist, and political leader and theorist. A dissenter who left the Ukrainian Radical party in 1900 and helped establish the *Ukrainian Social Democratic party, Levynsky edited the party's papers *Volia, Zemlia i volia* (1907–12), and *Vpered* (1912–13), as well as the monthly *Dzvin* in Kiev (1913–14). During the First World War he worked in Vienna and Geneva, and later he belonged to the External Group of the Ukrainian Communist party in Vienna, where together with V. Vynnychenko he edited its weekly *Nova doba* (1920–1). In the 1930s he returned to Lviv and contributed articles to *Nova Ukraïna* in Prague, and *Nova kul'tura, Kul'tura, Novi shliakhy*, and *Kooperatyvna respublyka*. His most important publications are *Narys rozvytku ukraïns'koho robitnychoho rukhu v Halychyni* (An Outline of the Development of the Ukrainian Workers' Movement in Galicia, 1914), *Tsarskaia Rossiia i ukrainskii vopros* (Tsarist Russia and the Ukrainian Question [also in Ukrainian], 1917), *Narodnist' i derzhava* (Nationality and the State, 1919, trans into French), *Sotsiialistychna revoliutsiia i Ukraïna* (The Socialist Revolution and Ukraine, 1920), *Relihiia, nauka i sotsiializm* (Religion, Science, and Socialism, 1920), and *Sotsiialistychnyi Internatsional i ponevoleni narody* (The Socialist International and Subjugated Peoples, 1920, also trans into French).

Levytska, Anastasiia [Levyc'ka, Anastasija] (real name: Kashko), b 16 February 1898 in Kulykivka, Chernihiv gu-

bernia, d 6 November 1955 in Kharkiv. Opera singer (mezzo-soprano). After graduating from the Lysenko Music and Drama Institute in Kiev, she worked as a soloist with the Kiev (1927–30) and the Kharkiv (1930–49) theaters of opera and ballet and then served as professor at the Kharkiv Conservatory (1950–5). Her most important roles included Odarka in S. Hulak-Artemovsky's *Zaporozhian Cossack beyond the Danube*, Nastia in M. Lysenko's *Taras Bulba*, Liubasha in N. Rimsky-Korsakov's *The Tsar's Bride*, Liubov in P. Tchaikovsky's *Mazeppa*, Solokha in M. Mussorgsky's *Sorochyntsi Fair*, Carmen in G. Bizet's *Carmen*, and Delilah in C. Saint-Saëns's *Samson and Delilah*.

Levytska, Halyna [Levyc'ka], b 23 January 1901 in Porokhnyk, Jarosław county, Galicia, d 13 July 1949 in Lviv. Pianist, publicist, and pedagogue; spouse of I. *Krushelnytsky. She studied music at the Lysenko Higher Institute of Music in Lviv and at the Vienna Academy of Music (1916–20), lectured at the Lysenko Institute (1921–39), and was professor at its successor, the Lysenko Conservatory (1940–1 and 1944–9). She toured Western Ukraine, Poland, Prague, Vienna, and elsewhere with a repertoire including works by L. von Beethoven, C. Frank, F. Chopin, and F. Liszt. In 1936–7 she gave a series of piano recitals in Lviv devoted to Ukrainian and foreign piano music. She also performed works by contemporary Ukrainian composers, including L. Revutsky, V. Kosenko, P. Kozytsky, B. Liatoshynsky, R. Simovych, M. Kolessa, and A. Rudnytsky.

Levytska, Nataliia. See Nychka, Nataliia.

Olena Levytska

Levytska, Olena [Levyc'ka], b 30 May 1873 in Ozhydiv, Zolochiv county, Galicia, d 24 October 1963 in New York. First Ukrainian woman industrialist in Galicia. After leaving the teaching profession she worked for 15 years at a chemical factory in Warsaw. In 1907 she and her brother set up the Zoria chemical products factory, which she ran by herself after his death in 1914. As a member of the Union of Ukrainian Women she encouraged women to enter professions traditionally closed to them.

Levytska, Olha [Levyc'ka, Ol'ha] (née Buchma; stage name: Szpychlerska), b 15 December 1879 in Pustomyty, Lviv county, Galicia, d 19 March 1925 in Stanyslaviv (now Ivano-Frankivske), Galicia. Actress and singer (soprano); sister of A. *Buchma. She sang in the Polish opera theater in Lviv and then joined the Ruska Besida Theater in 1898. In 1913 Y. Stadnyk left the Ruska Besida Theater, and

Levytska joined his Lviv Ukrainian People's Theater. In 1916–18 she worked in the Theater of the Legion of Ukrainian Sich Riflemen with K. Rubchak.

Popovych appeared in the *Ukrainian Art Digest*, no. 7 (1968).

S. Hordynsky

Vira Levytska   Borys Levytsky (1915–84)

Sofiia Levytska: *Tempest* (woodcut)

Levytska, Sofiia [Levyc'ka, Sofija], b 9 March 1874 in Vykhylivka, Proskuriv county, Podolia gubernia, d 20 September 1937 in Paris. Painter, woodcut artist, and translator; sister of Modest *Levytsky. She studied at L'Ecole des beaux arts in Paris (1905) and exhibited at the Salon des Artistes Indépendants and Salon d'Automne, of which she became a member in 1910. She was close to the cubists, and her painting *White Rhinoceros in the Garden of Eden* (1911) attracted the attention of G. Apollinaire. In 1912 she exhibited with the Section d'Or together with A. Archipenko and held her first individual exhibition in the Galerie Weil. Her translation into French of N. Gogol's *Evenings on a Farm near Dykanka*, illustrated with her own woodcuts, was published in 1921. Her artistic salon in Paris attracted the elite of French artists and writers, among them R. and J. Duffy, D. de Segonzac, P. Valéry, and E. Bernard. Her large-scale compositions with genre scenes – eg, *Harvesting Grapes*, *The Girl on Horseback*, *Clowns*, *Church in Vence* – are painted in a postimpressionist style typical of the L'Ecole de Paris. She did ornamental woodcuts for the collector's edition of P. Valéry's *Le Serpent* (1925) and illustrations for *La Chronique de Joinville*, G. de Louche's *Le Jardinet*, and Paris editions of *La Revue musicale*. Her graphic work was exhibited many times in France and at Ukrainian group exhibitions in Paris, Lviv, Berlin, Prague, Warsaw, and Rome. A posthumous exhibition of her works was held in Paris in 1938. A study of the artist by V.

Levytska, Vira [Levyc'ka] (née Herasymovych-Vyshnevska), b 26 February 1916 in Porytske (now Pavlivka), Volodymyr-Volynskyi county, Volhynia gubernia. Stage actress. She began her theatrical career in the Zahrava Theater in Peremyshl (1933–8) and then worked in the Kotliarevsky Theater (1938–9) and the Lesia Ukrainka Theater (1939–41), in the drama sector of the Lviv Opera Theater (1941–4), and in the Ensemble of Ukrainian Actors in West Germany (1945–9). She performed the title role in J. Anouilh's *Medea*, staged by Teatr u Piatnytsiu in Philadelphia. Levytska retired from the stage in 1970.

Levytsky, Andrii. See Lewicky, Andrew.

Levytsky, Borys [Levyts'kyi], b 9 May 1890 in Uman, Kiev gubernia, d 2 May 1953 in Poltava. Veterinary surgeon and zootechnician. A graduate of the Kharkiv Veterinary Institute (1914), he lectured at the Derhachiv School of Agriculture (1914–19) and was a scientific researcher at the Poltava Epizootic (1922–3) and Zootechnical (1922–30) stations. A professor (from 1950) at the Poltava Agricultural Institute, he wrote numerous works dealing with animal diseases and feed technology and proposed a method of leavening animal feed.

Levytsky, Borys [Levyc'kyi] (Lewytzkyj), b 19 May 1915 in Vienna, d 28 October 1984 in Munich. Journalist, political activist, and Sovietologist. While studying philosophy and psychology at Lviv University (MA, 1938) he edited *Nove selo* (1936–9) and was active in the OUN. With the outbreak of the Soviet-German War he went east with I. *Mitrynga's group and helped found the *Ukrainian People's Democratic party. After the war he left the OUN and helped organize the *Ukrainian Revolutionary Democratic party, in which, together with I. Maistrenko, he headed a leftist faction and edited *Vpered (1949–56). In 1948 he founded his own research bureau for Soviet affairs, which published a monthly bulletin about the higher officials of the Party. In the 1950s he was a contributor to the German liberal daily *Süddeutsche Zeitung* in Munich (under the pen name Paul Sikora) and research associate of the East European Research Service in Düsseldorf. In the 1970s he worked as a specialist on Soviet affairs for the German Social Democratic party. He wrote numerous works on the Soviet Union, including *Vom roten Terror zur sozialistischen Gesellschaft* (1961), *Die Sowjetukraine, 1944–1963* (1964), *Die rote Inquisition* (1967; trans: *The Uses of Terror*, 1971), *The Soviet Political Elite* (1969), *Die sowjetische Nationalitätenpolitik nach Stalins Tod, 1953–1970* (1970), *Die Marschälle und die Politik* (1971), *Sowjetische Entspannungspolitik heute* (1975), and *Politics and Society in Soviet Ukraine, 1953–1980* (1984). He also compiled several biographical dictionaries, such as *The Stalinist Terror in the Thirties* (1974) and *Who's Who in the Socialist Countries* (1978).

B. Osadchuk

Dmytro Levytsky: *Portrait of P. Demidov* (oil, 1773)

Levytsky, Dmytro [Levyc'kyj] (Russian: Levitsky, Dmitrii), b 1735 in Kiev, d 16 April 1822 in St Petersburg. The most prominent portraitist of the classicist era in the Russian Empire. He acquired his basic training from his father, H. *Levytsky, and helped him do engravings for the Kievan Cave Monastery Press. In 1753–6 he helped his father and A. Antropov decorate *St Andrew's Church in Kiev. From 1758 to 1761 he worked in St Petersburg, where he likely studied with Antropov, L.-J.-F. Lagrené, and G. Valeriani. From 1762, while living in Moscow he was a portraitist in great demand among the Russian aristocracy. He moved to St Petersburg in 1769, and he won the highest award at the summer exhibition in 1770 held by the St Petersburg Academy of Arts and was elected a member of the academy. A teacher of portraiture at the academy (1771–88), he retired to Ukraine in 1788, but in 1795 he returned to St Petersburg to become portraitist at the imperial court.

Building on the baroque, classicism, and Western European traditions, Levytsky created a school of portrait painting. His portraits reveal his expert knowledge of drawing, composition, color, and the appropriate gesture. He executed over 100 portraits, including ones of Empress Catherine II, other members of the Russian imperial family, King Stanislaus I Leszczyński, the French encyclopedist D. Diderot (now in the Geneva Museum of Art and History), his own father, brother, and daughter, and six of the first graduates of the Smolny Institute for aristocrats' daughters. Many Ukrainian (eg, L. Myrypolsky, S. Maiatsky, L. Kalynovsky) and Russian portraitists studied with Levytsky at the academy, and his works influenced V. *Borovykovsky.

BIBLIOGRAPHY
Horlenko, V. *Dmytro Levyts'kyi* (Poltava 1919)
Chukin, I. *Dmytro Levyts'kyi* (Kharkiv 1930)
Moleva, N.M. *Dmitrii Grigor'evich Levitskii* (Moscow 1980)
Iablonskaia, T. (comp). *Levitskii* (Moscow 1985)

S. Yaniv

Dmytro Levytsky (1877–1942)   Fedir Levytsky

Levytsky, Dmytro [Levyc'kyj], b 1877 in Dobrachyn, Sokal county, Galicia, d 31 October 1942 in Bukhara, Uzbek SSR. Lawyer and civic and political leader. After graduating from the law faculty of Vienna University he practiced law in Rava Ruska (1912–14) and then briefly in Berezhany. An officer in the Austrian army, he was captured by the Russians in 1915 and deported to Tashkent. During the revolution he organized and headed the Galician-Bukovynian Committee in Kiev. During the Hetman regime he was secretary of the oppositional Ukrainian National Union and then chief of the UNR diplomatic mission to Denmark (1919–21). Upon returning to Galicia he edited the daily *Dilo* (1923–5) and served as the first president (1925–35) and then vice-president (1936–9) of the *Ukrainian National Democratic Alliance (UNDO), which he helped found. After being elected to the Polish Sejm (1928–35) he chaired the *Ukrainian Parliamentary Representation in the assembly. He formed and led the Ukrainian Co-ordinating Committee (1936–9), which represented all the legal Ukrainian parties in Galicia. He was arrested by the Soviets in September 1939 and was imprisoned in Moscow until the outbreak of the German-Soviet War, after which he was permitted to live in Uzbekistan.

Levytsky, Fedir [Levyc'kyj], b 14 May 1858 in Novoukrainka, Yelysavethrad county, Kherson gubernia, d

19 February 1933 in Chernihiv. Actor (mainly comedic) and director. After working as a teacher in Novoukrainka (1877–87) and founding an amateur theater he began his professional career in M. Kropyvnytsky's troupe, joined M. Sadovsky's troupe (1892–7), founded and directed his own troupe in 1905–8, and then entered Sadovsky's Theater in Kiev (1909). Later he was a leading actor in the Ukrainian National Theater (1917-18) and the State Drama Theater (1917–19). After serving in Chernihiv okruha as an instructor of amateur village theaters he returned to Kiev in 1925, to the Shevchenko First Theater of the Ukrainian Soviet Republic. In 1930 he joined the Zhovten Theater in Leningrad. His last year was with the local theater in Lubni. Characteristic of Levytsky's acting was an ability to extend the dramatist's intention and refresh it by strong improvisation. His repertoire consisted mostly of roles of dramas in the ethnographic theater of manners, including the Clerk in I. Karpenko-Kary's *Burlaka* (The Vagabond), Cherevyk in M. Starytsky's *Sorochyns'kyi iarmarok* (The Fair at Sorochyntsi, based on N. Gogol), the Bailiff in M. Kropyvnytsky's *Po revizii* (After the Inspection). He was also successful in roles such as Makar in V. Vynnychenko's *Moloda krov* (Young Blood), Kopystka in M. Kulish's *97*, and, in the non-Ukrainian repertoire, Chris in E. O'Neill's *Anna Christie*, Engstrand in H. Ibsen's *Gengangere*, and Zemlianika in Gogol's *Revizor* (The Inspector General). A biography, by V. Vasylko, was published in Kiev in 1958.

V. Revutsky

Levytsky, Hryhorii [Levyc'kyj, Hryhorij] (né Nis), b ca 1697 in Maiachka, Poltava regiment, d 19 May 1769 in Maiachka. Baroque master engraver and painter. Levytsky studied engraving in Wrocław (until 1735). From ca 1738–41 he was an Orthodox priest in Maiachka and continued to do engravings for the Kievan Cave Monastery Press. Over 40 of his engravings illustrate the press's Gospel (1737), Psalter (1737), and *Apostol* (1737–8, 1752), and the title pages and ornamentation of Kievan students' theses in verse, such as those in honor of R. Kopa (after 1730), I. Nehrebetsky (1738), Metropolitan R. Zaborovsky (1739), and D. Tuptalo (1752). He also prepared four engraved boards for M. Kozachynsky's collection of theses on Aristotle's philosophy (Lviv 1745), containing portraits, coats of arms, cartouches, allegories, symbols, views of Kiev's architectural monuments, genre scenes, and O. Rozumovsky's family tree. In 1753–6, together with his son, D. Levytsky, and A. Antropov, Levytsky painted rococo murals inside St Andrew's Church in Kiev. A book about him by V. Fomenko was published in Kiev in 1976.

Levytsky, Hryhorii [Levyc'kyj, Hryhorij] (Lewitsky), b 19 November 1878 in Bilky, near Popilnia, Skvyra county, Kiev gubernia, d 20 May 1942 in a Soviet prison camp, location unknown. Botanist, cytologist, and cytogeneticist; corresponding member of the USSR Academy of Sciences (1932). A graduate of the biology faculty of Kiev University in 1902, where he studied with the cytologist S. Navashin, he began teaching in 1904 at the Kiev Polytechnical Institute. He was arrested in 1907 for his involvement with the All-Russian Union of Peasants and exiled abroad for four years. While working at the Russian marine biological station at Villefranche and in the laboratory of E. Strasburger at the University of Bonn, Levytsky studied the 'chondriosomes' (mitochondria) of plant cells, devel-

Hryhorii Levytsky: *St John The Evangelist*, engraving in the *Apostol* printed by the Kievan Cave Monastery Press (1738)

oped fixative techniques, worked out the microscopic organization of plant cells, and observed their continuity through cell division. After his return to Kiev in 1911, Levytsky was a professor at the polytechnical institute until 1921, when he was charged with Ukrainian nationalism and dismissed by the Bolsheviks. In 1922–5 he directed the cytology laboratory of the Ukrainian Sugar Trust and organized the trust's Scentific Selection Institute. He wrote one of the first textbooks in the field of cytogenetics, *The Material Basis of Heredity* (1924), and redefined the terms 'karyotype' and 'idiogram' in their modern sense.

BIBLIOGRAPHY
Rubtsova, Z. *Razvitie evoliutsiinnoi tsitogenetiki rastenii v SSSR (1920–1940-e gody)* (Leningrad 1975)

M. Adams

Levytsky, Ivan [Levyc'kyj], b 18 January 1850 in Berlohy, Kalush county, Galicia, d 30 January 1913 in Lviv. Bibliographer and writer; member of the Shevchenko Scientific Society and head of its Bibliographic Commission (from 1909). His more important works include a

Ivan Levytsky (1850–1913)   Kost Levytsky

Galician-Ruthenian bibliography of the 19th century with an overview of Ruthenian publications in Hungary and Bukovyna in 1801–86 (2 vols, 1888, 1895), a Galician-Ruthenian bibliography for 1772–1800 (1903), a bibliography of Ukrainian works published in Austria-Hungary in 1887–93 (3 vols, 1909–11), and a biographical dictionary of 19th-century Transcarpathian Ruthenians (incomplete, 4 issues, 1898). He also published a bibliography of M. Hrushevsky's works, a history of education in Galicia under Austria, and popular historical tales (under the pseudonym Ivan iz Berloh).

Levytsky, Ivan [Levyc'kyj], b 16 November 1875 in Mala Luka, Husiatyn county, Galicia, d 8 April 1938 in Lviv. Composer, choir conductor, and pedagogue. From 1910 he lectured at the Ukrainian Teachers' Seminary and the Lysenko Higher Institute of Music in Lviv. He wrote music for violin (*Nocturne, Romance*), choir, and vocal solo. He set many of T. Shevchenko's verses to music and also wrote music textbooks, most notably *Narys istoriï muzyky* (An Outline of the History of Music, 1921).

Levytsky, Kost [Levyc'kyj, Kost'], b 18 November 1859 in Tysmenytsia, Tovmach county, Galicia, d 12 November 1941 in Lviv. Lawyer, publicist, civic and economic organizer, and prominent political leader in Galicia; full (from 1899) and honorary member of the Shevchenko Scientific Society. A graduate of Lviv University, he opened a law office in Lviv in 1890 and became active in various areas of Ukrainian community life. He edited *Chasopys' pravnycha* (1889–1900), which he helped found. As a member of the executive he transformed the Prosvita society from a purely educational into an educational-economic institution. To build a firm economic foundation for the social and political development of the Ukrainian community in Galicia, he helped found a whole string of important economic organizations, such as Narodna Torhovlia, the Dnister insurance company, Tsentrobank (which he directed in 1898–1939), the *Audit Union of Ukrainian Co-operatives (which he headed in 1904–14), the Land Mortgage Bank, and the Karpatiia mutual insurance company.

A populist by conviction, he helped to organize the People's Council and served as its secretary and vice-president (1885–99). Then, after joining the National Democratic party, he served as secretary and chairman (from 1902) of its executive, the Popular Committee. In 1907 he was elected deputy to the Austrian parliament, and in 1908, to the Galician Diet. As head of the strongest Ukrai-

nian party and chairman of the Ukrainian clubs in the parliament and the Diet, he had become the most influential Ukrainian political leader in Galicia by 1910.

During the First World War Levytsky played a prominent role in the independence movement in Western Ukraine. In 1914 he was elected president of the Supreme Ukrainian Council in Lviv, and in 1915–16, of the *General Ukrainian Council in Vienna. When the Austrian government proposed in 1916 to set up a separate and autonomous Galicia under Polish control, the disillusioned Levytsky resigned as chairman of the Ukrainian Parliamentary Representation. As head of the Lviv delegation of the Ukrainian National Rada, which had decided to establish a Ukrainian state on Austro-Hungarian territories, he ordered the Central Ukrainian Military Council to stage an armed coup in Lviv on 1 November 1918. A week later he became the first head of the State Secretariat of the Western Ukrainian National Republic. A year later, when the Poles occupied Galicia, Levytsky served as secretary of press and propaganda and then of foreign affairs in Ye. Petrushevych's government-in-exile. After returning to Galicia in 1923, he directed his energies to strengthening Ukrainian professional, economic, and cultural institutions. He served as president of the Union of Ukrainian Lawyers, editor of *Zhyttia i pravo*, and director of Tsentrobank. Although he sat on the executive of the Ukrainian National Democratic Alliance, he did not engage in active politics. When the Soviets occupied Galicia in 1939, he chaired the Ukrainian Relief Committee and headed a delegation from the Ukrainian community to the new authorities. He was promptly arrested and was imprisoned in Moscow until the spring of 1941. After the German invasion he helped organize and headed the short-lived Ukrainian National Council in Lviv.

In addition to numerous articles on political, legal, and historical issues Levytsky wrote a number of monographs, including *Istoriia politychnoï dumky halyts'kykh ukraïntsiv 1848–1914* (A History of the Political Thought of Galician Ukrainians, 1848–1914, 2 vols, 1926), *Istoriia vyzvol'nylh zmahan' halyts'kykh ukraïntsiv z chasu svitovoï viiny* (A History of the Liberation Struggle of Galician Ukrainians during the Period of the [First] World War, 3 vols, 1929–30), *Velykyi zryv* (The Great Upheaval, 1931; repr 1968), and *Ukraïns'ki polityky* (Ukrainian Politicians, 1936); he also compiled *Deutsch-ukrainisches juridisches Wörterbuch* (1893; 2nd rev edn 1920).

V. Mudry

Levytsky, Leopold [Levyc'kyj, Leopol'd], b 7 August 1906 in Burdiakivtsi, Borshchiv county, Galicia, d 14 May 1973 in Lviv. Painter and graphic artist. He studied at the Cracow Academy of Fine Arts (1925–32) and its Paris branch (1930–1). For his involvement in the Communist Party of Poland and his political artwork he was expelled from the academy and twice imprisoned (1932, 1935–6). From 1944 Levytsky worked in Lviv, where he became head of the Union of Artists branch in 1949. He created hundreds of linocuts, etchings, monotypes, and lithographs; several linocut series, including the large 'From the Tales of My Father' (1946–7), 'From My Memories' (1946–8), 'Women' (1905–6), and 'Carpathians' (1968–72); over 30 oil paintings (eg, the socialist-realist *Ivan Franko in His Father's Smithy* [1953]); the watercolor series 'Village Vrasiv in Lviv Oblast' (1955–6); and illustrations for editions of works by Western Ukrainian Communist writers,

Leopold Levytsky: *Woman* (monotype, 1960s)

Modest Levytsky

Cardinal Mykhailo Levytsky

such as Ya. Halan, S. Tudor, O. Havryliuk, and P. Kozlaniuk. Many of his early works show the influence of cubism and expressionism. A book about him by G. Ostrovsky was published in Moscow in 1978.

Levytsky, Modest [Levyc'kyj] (pseuds V. Makohonenko, M. Pylypovych), b 25 July 1866 in Vykhylivka, Proskuriv county, Podilia gubernia, d 16 June 1932 in Lutske, Volhynia voivodeship. Physician, civic leader, and writer. After graduating from Kiev University in 1893, he practiced medicine in Kovel, Okny, Boiarka (near Kiev), Radyvyliv, and Bila Tserkva. In 1918–19 he headed the sanitary and cultural-educational departments of the UNR Ministry of Highways. In 1919 he served as adviser, and later, as head, of the UNR diplomatic mission to Greece. As an émigré he directed a tuberculosis hospital for Ukrainian veterans in Zakopane (1922) and then lectured at the Ukrainian Husbandry Academy in Poděbrady. In 1927 he settled in Lutske, where he practiced medicine and taught Ukrainian in secondary school. He wrote short stories, recollections, popular medical pamphlets, and translations. His stories appeared in periodicals, such as *Kievskaia starina*, *Rada*, *Nova hromada*, and *Literaturno-naukovyi vistnyk*, under the pseudonyms M. Pylypovych and Vybornyi-Makohonenko, and in separate collections, including *V sudi* (In Court, 1918), *Gloria vistis* (1925), *Zemlytsia ridna* (Native Land, 1926), and *Tiazhka doroha* (The Hard Road, 1928). He translated several novels into Ukrainian, including H. Sienkiewicz's *Quo vadis*, and Sh. Asch's play *Got fun Nekomeh* (The God of Vengeance).

Levytsky, Mykhailo [Levyc'kyj, Myxajlo], b 1774 in Lanchyn, Stanyslaviv circle, Galicia, d 14 January 1858 at the Univ Monastery, Zolochiv circle, Galicia. Ukrainian Catholic metropolitan and cardinal. After studying theology at the Barbareum in Vienna, he was ordained (1798) and appointed professor of biblical studies at the Greek Catholic Theological Seminary in Lviv. In recognition of his abilities he was made a canon in 1808 and then consecrated bishop of Peremyshl (1813). With the assistance of I. *Mohylnytsky, he launched a major campaign in the field of education: he established 383 new parish schools in the eparchy, petitioned the government for Ukrainian-language instruction in schools, and established a clerical society to print religious and educational materials. He was elevated to the office of metropolitan of Halych and archbishop of Lviv in 1816 and continued his duties in Peremyshl until 1818. As metropolitan, Levytsky continued to press for educational development and the formation of new schools. His conservative attitudes, however, led to conflict with a new generation of intelligentsia (most notably the *Ruthenian Triad) over questions of language (he favored an *etymological orthography, while they advocated a phonetic system) and national identity (he regarded Galician Ukrainians as a separate nation [see *Old Ruthenians], while they accepted a pan-Ukrainian identity). Levytsky enjoyed the complete confidence of the Austrian emperor and obtained concessions from him for his church. In 1848 the emperor named him primate of Galicia, though this position had previously always been held by the Roman Catholic bishop of Lviv. In 1856 Pope Pius IX appointed Levytsky a cardinal, the second Ukrainian in history to receive this honor. By this time he had largely withdrawn from public life because of ill health and was confined to the monastery in Univ.

Levytsky, Mykhailo [Levyc'kyj, Myxajlo], b 9 February 1891 in Yavche, Rohatyn county, Galicia, d 1933. Galician Communist activist. During the First World War he was interned by the Russians as a POW in Central Asia. He joined the Bolshevik party and edited the Ukrainian paper *Tashkents'ka rada* in Tashkent (1918). In 1919 he was sent to Lviv as a member of the Provisional Committee and the underground CC of the Communist Party of Eastern Galicia (KPSH). He was elected to the CP(B)U Galician Organizing Committee (1920) and then to the KPSH Politburo and the *Galician Revolutionary Committee. From late 1921 he served as Soviet plenipotentiary in Austria, Germany, and

Czechoslovakia. Upon returning to Ukraine he was elected a member of the CP(B)U Central Control Committee in 1925 and candidate member of the CC CP(B)U in 1927. Accused of belonging to a 'Ukrainian National Center' headed by M. Hrushevsky, he was arrested and probably executed.

Levytsky, Mykola [Levyc'kyj], b 8 June 1819 in the Chernihiv region, d 14 February 1885 in Kiev. Pedagogue. He graduated from the Kiev Seminary in 1841 and studied at Kiev University. From 1846 he taught in the regions of Kiev and Chernihiv, and from 1858 in secondary schools in the city of Kiev. He proposed a new system of elementary education which would develop a child's mind, fulfill society's physical, moral, and esthetic requirements, and instill and develop in children the desire for useful activity. Levytsky is the author of a number of scholarly articles on methodology and education at the elementary school level. His major work is *Ocherki kursa gramotnosti* (Outline for a Course in Literacy, Kiev 1874).

Mykola Levytsky (1859–1936)

Levytsky, Mykola [Levyts'kyj], b 7 April 1859 in Khmilna, Kaniv county, Kiev gubernia, d 1 December 1936 in Kiev. Pioneer of the artel and co-operation movement in Ukraine. After being expelled from Moscow University he graduated in law from Kharkiv University in 1885 and worked as secretary of the Oleksandriia zemstvo and then as a lawyer in Yelysavethrad. A convinced populist, he devoted his spare time to propagating and organizing artels among farmers, tradesmen, and industrial workers. The first artels were established in 1887 in Oleksandriia county, and spread quickly. Under Levytsky's influence 125 agricultural artels, with a membership of over 3,000 peasants, arose in 1894–8. Many of them were short-lived. Beginning in 1903 Levytsky organized artels in Yelysavethrad, Odessa, Kiev, Balta, Vinnytsia, and other cities. In his articles on the model contract for farmers' artels he proposed various credit and insurance schemes for such artels. In the revolutionary period he was active in the Ukrainian co-operative movement and served in the Central Rada.

Levytsky, Mykola [Levyts'kyj], b 1880, d 1935. Lawyer and political leader. A member of the Ukrainian Social Democratic Workers' party (USDRP), he sat on the Central Rada and represented the UNR at the negotiations with the Central Powers in Brest-Litovsk. He served in the Hetman government as assistant director of the Department of Ex-

ternal Relations at the Ministry of Foreign Affairs and took part in peace negotiations with Soviet Russia. Under the Directory he was a member of the UNR diplomatic mission in Paris. He returned to Ukraine in 1923 and worked in Kharkiv. After being arrested in 1929, he was sent to a prison camp in Krasnoiarsk oblast, where he died several years later.

Myron Levytsky: *Yaroslavna* (oil, 1961)

Levytsky, Myron [Levyc'kyj] (Lev), b 14 October 1913 in Lviv. Painter, graphic artist, journalist, and writer. After studying at the Novakivsky Art School in Lviv (1931–3) and at the Cracow Academy of Arts (1933–4) he worked as a book illustrator and designer in Lviv (from 1935) and published and edited the monthly *My i svit* (1938–9). During the Soviet occupation of Galicia he worked as staff artist at the AN URSR archeology department in Lviv and at the Lviv Historical Museum. During the Nazi occupation he worked for the Ukrainske Vydavnytstvo publishing house and then as a war correspondent of the Division Galizien paper, *Do peremohy* (1943–4). A postwar refugee in Austria, he emigrated to Canada in 1949 and worked in Winnipeg as art editor of I. Tyktor's publishing house and editor of the humor magazine *Komar* (1949–50) before settling in Toronto in 1954. After he had spent two years painting in Paris, his first one-man exhibition was held there, in 1958. Other solo exhibitions were held in Toronto (1961, 1963, 1964, 1973, 1976, 1978), Waterloo (1965), New York (1964, 1974), Detroit (1972), Ottawa (1975), Edmon-

ART 1) V. Patyk: *Autumn in Chornohora* (oil, 1988; private collection). 2) M. Levytsky: *The Day of the Pentecost* (oil, 1968; courtesy of H. Levytska). 3) O. Novakivsky: *Still Life* (pastel, 1916; National Museum, Lviv). 4) O. Mazuryk: *Resurrection* (tempera, 1975; private collection). 5) K. Malevich: *Suprematist Composition* (oil, 1916; State Russian Museum, St Petersburg). 6) A. Petrytsky: Costume design for *William Tell* (cardboard, pencil, appliqué, silver, ink, 1926; Theater Museum, Moscow). 7) Z. Lisovska: *Halyna* (gouache, 1987; private collection).

ton (1977), Chicago (1984), Lviv (1991), and Kiev (1992). Levytsky's canvases are characterized by their rich color harmonies, flowing linearity, and stylized, abstracted forms (eg, *Moroccan Musicians* [1964], *Spanish Town* [1965], and *Portrait of My Wife, Halyna* [1985]). His interests range from portraiture, urban landscapes, classical and Ukrainian mythology, nudes, literature, and history to icons and religious themes (eg, numerous Madonnas and the oil *Day of the Pentecost* [1968]). He has painted the murals and icons in 10 Ukrainian Catholic churches (5 in Canada and 5 in Australia). Levytsky has been instrumental in modernizing Ukrainian sacred art and freeing it from the confines of the traditional Ukrainian-Byzantine style (eg, in the Church of the Holy Eucharist [1974–5] in Toronto and St Andrew's Church [1979–80] in Lidcombe, Australia). He has designed and illustrated over 300 books and magazines and many bookplates, in which he has used a distinctive type of lettering and graphic style. Levytsky has also written a short story collection, *Likhtari* (Lanterns, 1982). A monograph about him by D. Zelska-Darewych was published to coincide with the retrospective exhibition of his works in Toronto and Winnipeg in 1985.

D. Zelska-Darewych

Levytsky, Oleksii [Levyc'kyj, Oleksij], b 10 October 1887 in Kiev, d 18 June 1959 in Dornstadt, near Ulm, Germany. Comic actor. He began his career in O. Suslov's troupe in 1905. In 1910–18 he worked in I. Sahatovsky's troupe, with a hiatus in the Ruska Besida Theater (1913–14). Levytsky joined Sadovsky's Theater in 1919, and in 1920–44 he worked in various Ukrainian troupes in Galicia, and then, until 1949, in the Ensemble of Ukrainian Actors in West Germany.

Orest Levytsky   Osyp Levytsky

Levytsky, Orest [Levyc'kyj] (pseuds O. or L. Orlenko, Orelsky, Levko Maiachynets, Levko Maiachenko, Levko Maiachsky), b 6 January 1849 in Maiachka, Kobeliaky county, Poltava gubernia, d 9 May 1922 in Drabiv, Zolotonosha county, Poltava gubernia. Historian, archeographer, and writer; full member of the Shevchenko Scientific Society from 1910 and the Ukrainian Academy of Sciences from 1918; great-grandson of D. *Levytsky. After completing a program at the Poltava Theological Seminary (1869) he studied at Kiev University (1870–4) under his mentor V. *Antonovych and then taught until 1909 in a Kiev gymnasium. An active member of the *Hromada of Kiev, he researched and published archival materials and studies

pertaining to 16th- to 18th-century Ukrainian history, folkways, marriage, social relations, customary law, and religious social movements. He was secretary (1874–1921) of the *Kiev Archeographic Commission and editor of its publications, a full member (from 1878) of the *Historical Society of Nestor the Chronicler and its vice-president (from 1902), and a frequent contributor to *Kievskaia starina*. After retiring Levytsky was also a member of the editorial board of the journal *Ukraïna* (1914–18) and served as vice-president of the Ukrainian Scientific Society in Kiev. He was elected acting president of the Ukrainian Academy of Sciences in December 1919 and president in March 1922, and he also headed the VUAN Legal Terminology Commission (from 1919), the entire Social-Economic Division (from May 1920), and its Commission for the Study of Customary Law.

Levytsky's works include studies of Ukraine in the second half of the 17th century (1875), the Samovydets Chronicle (1878), Socinianism in Poland and Right-Bank Ukraine (1882), the Ruthenian church in the late 16th-century Polish-Lithuanian state (1884), B. Khmelnytsky (1884), folkways in 16th-century Volhynia and the Poltava region (1888, 1891), social and political life in Kiev and Right-Bank Ukraine in 1811–12 (1891), the first 50 years of the Kiev Archival Commission (1893), life in Little Russia in the second half of the 17th century (1902), the peasantry in Right-Bank Ukraine in 1826–50 (1906), and family life in 16th- and 17th-century Right-Bank Ukraine (1909). His historical stories about life in 16th-century Volhynia and the Hetman state were published in *Literaturno-naukovyi vistnyk* and separately as *Volyns'ki opovidannia* (Volhynian Stories, 1914), *Hanna Montovt* (1926), *Istorychni opovidannia* (Historical Stories, 1930), and *Po sudakh Het'manshchyny* (At the Law Courts of the Hetmanate, 1940). A bibliography of his works was published in *Zapysky Sotsiial'no-ekonomichnoho viddilu VUAN*, vol 1 (1923).

BIBLIOGRAPHY
Vasylenko M. 'Akademyk Orest Ivanovych Levyts'kyi,' *Zapysky Sotsiial'no-ekonomichnoho viddilu VUAN*, 1 (1923)
Moskvych L.; Storchak A. 'Vydatnyi istoryk, arkheohraf-arkhivist (Do 120-richchia vid narodzhennia O.I. Levyts'koho),' *UIZh*, 1968, no. 12
Moskvych, L. 'Tvorchyi shliakh O.I. Levyts'koho,' *Istoriohrafichni doslidzhennia v Ukraïns'kii RSR*, 4 (Kiev 1971)

A. Zhukovsky

Levytsky, Osyp [Levyc'kyj], b 21 December 1886 in Verbizh, Kolomyia county, Galicia, d 11 June 1973 in Fort Wayne, Illinois. Educator. A graduate of Graz University (1913), during the First World War he served in the Austrian army and later in the Ukrainian Galician Army as chief of its press bureau and then as officer for special assignments. After the war he taught at and later became principal of the Ukrainian gymnasium in Stanyslaviv and organized scouting troops for the *Plast Ukrainian Youth Association. At the end of the Second World War he directed gymnasiums in Krynytsia and Vienna. After emigrating to the United States in 1949, he organized and supervised a Ukrainian school in Chicago and served as an inspector of schools for the Ukrainian Congress Committee of America (1954–62). He wrote a book of recollections, *Halyts'ka armiia na Velykii Ukraïni* (The Galician Army in Central Ukraine, 1921), and helped to edit the first two volumes of *Ukraïns'ka halyts'ka armiia* (The Ukrainian Galician Army, 1958–60) and *Al'manakh stany-slavivs'koï zemli* (Almanac of the Stanyslaviv Region, vol 1, 1975).

Levytsky, Parfenii [Levyc'kyj, Parfenij] (secular name: Pamfil), b 10 October 1858 in Plishyvets, Hadiache county, Poltava gubernia, d January 1922 in Poltava. Orthodox bishop. A graduate of the Kiev Theological Academy (1882), he worked as an inspector of religious schools before being consecrated bishop of Mozhaisk (near Moscow) in 1899. As bishop of Kamianets-Podilskyi (1904–9) he supported the Ukrainianization of church life. He supervised the editing and publication of the first Ukrainian translation of the Gospels in the Russian Empire and introduced its use in services, and in 1907 he asked the Holy Synod for permission to introduce Ukrainian into local parish schools. Levytsky also made frequent tours of his eparchy, on which he delivered sermons in Ukrainian and encouraged his priests to do the same. His conduct earned him the enmity of the conservative and chauvinistic Russian hierarchy of the church, and he was transferred to Tula.

Levytsky returned to Plishyvets after the February Revolution of 1917. Although in official retirement, he soon organized a Ukrainian Orthodox brotherhood in Poltava and then consented to be bishop of Poltava after the emigration of the serving bishop. At the request of the *All-Ukrainian Orthodox Church Council, he agreed to assume the leadership of the newly formed *Ukrainian Autocephalous Orthodox church (UAOC) in 1920 and was elected metropolitan of Kiev in May 1921. Under pressure from the hierarchy of the Russian church, however, he withdrew his candidacy and severed ties with the UAOC. He died soon afterward.

Levytsky, Roman [Levyc'kyj], b 18 August 1908 in Rohachyn, Berezhany county, Galicia. Banduryst-singer (bass-baritone), conductor, and teacher. After studying music at the Cracow State Conservatory (solo voice faculty, 1928–30) and graduating from the University of Cracow, he began a career in teaching bandura and voice and conducting choruses in Western Ukraine. Emigrating after the war to Germany and then the United States, in 1954–79 he taught bandura at the Ukrainian Music Institute of America in New York. He toured and appeared as leading soloist with such choruses as Vatra, Dumka, and the Ukrainian Bandurist Chorus. He later became a member and soloist (bandura) of the Kean College Choir in Union, New Jersey. In his appearances he favors works by D. Bortniansky, A. Vedel, M. Verbytsky, M. Lysenko, M. Leontovych, F. Kolessa, and O. Bilash, many of which he has recorded.

Levytsky, Severyn [Levyc'kyj] (pseud: Siryi Lev), b 6 March 1890 in Shchyrovtsi, Radekhiv county, Galicia, d 30 January 1962 in Buffalo, New York. Pedagogue and scout leader. He graduated from Lviv University and taught at the teachers' seminary in Lviv during the interwar period. He headed the Supreme Executive of the *Plast Ukrainian Youth Association in 1924–34. After the outlawing of Plast by the Polish authorities he devoted his efforts to ensuring youth activism according to the movement's principles. In 1941–5 he taught in schools set up by the *Ukrainian Central Committee and headed its *Ukrainian Teachers'

Severyn Levytsky   Volodymyr Levytsky
                          (1854-1939)

Labor Alliance. He emigrated to Germany in 1945. In 1947, at a Plast jamboree in Regensburg, he was elected *Nachalnyi Plastun* (Head Scout). He moved to the United States in 1949. He published many articles on educational matters in the Ukrainian press. His work on the early history of Plast, *Ukraïns'kyi plastovyi ulad, 1911–45* (The Ukrainian Order of Plast, 1911–45, 1967), was published posthumously.

Levytsky, Venedykt Rudolf [Levyc'kyj], b 24 May 1783 in Ivanivtsi, Zhydachiv circle, Galicia, d 14 January 1851 in Lviv. Priest, pedagogue, and censor. A graduate of Lviv University (PH D, 1810), he was a priest at St George's Church in Lviv, vice-rector (1815–19) and rector (1820–4) of the Greek Catholic Theological Seminary, and professor of moral theology at Lviv University (from 1818). From 1828 to 1847 he was dean of the theology faculty of Lviv University. From 1832 Levytsky also served as a censor of Cyrillic books for the Austrian government in Galicia. In this capacity he fought the modernization of Ukrainian (favoring the *etymological spelling based on Church Slavonic) and opposed the publication (and importation, if they were published elsewhere) of works such as *Rusalka Dnistrovaia*, because they were too close to the vernacular. He also criticized *Rusalka Dnistrovaia* for its political liberalism, although it had been approved for publication by the Viennese censor. In 1837 he again became rector of the Lviv seminary. He published two textbooks on biblical studies and several articles on religious topics.

Levytsky, Volodymyr [Levyc'kyj], b 6 June 1854 in Starostyntsi, Vinnytsia county, Podilia gubernia, d 26 October 1939. Economist and statistician; full member of the AN URSR (now ANU) from 1925. A graduate of Odessa University (1878), he taught political economy at the Demidov Lyceum in Yaroslavl, at Kharkiv University (1893–1917), and at the Kharkiv Agricultural Institute (1919–30). He wrote a number of books in economic history and political economy, including *Sel'skokhoziaistvennyi krizis vo Frantsii (1861–1892)* (The Agricultural Crisis in France [1861–1892], 1899), *Istoriia politicheskoi ekonomii v sviazi s istoriei khoziaistvennogo byta* (The History of Political Economy in Relation to the History of Agricultural Life, 1914), and *Ocherki istorii khoziaistvennogo byta narodov drevnego Vostoka: Vaviloniia, Egipet* (Outlines of the History of the

Economic Life of the Peoples of the Ancient East: Babylonia, Egypt, 1926).

Volodymyr Levytsky (1872-1956)

Yevhen Levytsky

Levytsky, Volodymyr [Levyc'kyj], b 31 December 1872 in Ternopil, Galicia, d 13 August 1956 in Lviv. Mathematician and physicist; full member of the Shevchenko Scientific Society (NTSh) from 1899. Levytsky graduated from Lviv University (PH D, 1901) and then taught mathematics and physics in gymnasiums in Lviv and Ternopil as well as at the Lviv (Underground) Ukrainian University. From 1940 to 1956 (with interruptions due to war) he taught at the Lviv Pedagogical Institute. For many years he headed the mathematical–natural sciences–medical section of the NTSh in Lviv and edited its publications; he twice served as NTSh president (1931–5). He wrote numerous scientific papers, mostly devoted to the study of functions of complex variables as well as problems in theoretical physics. He is also known for his work in mathematical, physical, and chemical terminology.

Levytsky, Volodymyr [Levyc'kyj], b 16 August 1888 in Krychka, Nadvirna county, Galicia, d 14 February 1980 in New York. Community leader. He worked for the *Union for the Liberation of Ukraine in German internment camps (1915–18) and then headed the press office of the UNR mission in Berlin (1919–20). After emigrating to the United States in 1924, he became a leading member of *Oborona Ukrainy and editor of its *Orhanizatsiini visti* (1936–41). In 1930 he organized a choir in Scranton, Pennsylvania, and in 1933 he was director of the Ukrainian pavilion at the world's fair in Chicago. He served as vice-president of the *Ukrainian Fraternal Association (1933–41). At the same time he was a secretary of Oborona Ukrainy and chief editor of its *Hromads'kyi holos*. He gradually adopted a Sovietophile outlook that helped cause a split in Oborona Ukrainy at its 1947 convention.

Levytsky, Volodymyr. See Lukych, Vasyl.

Levytsky, Vsevolod [Levyc'kyj], b 2 September 1913 in Radekhiv, Galicia, d 31 December 1976 in Winnipeg. Political activist. He was arrested in 1933 for being a member of the OUN and was forced to leave Ukraine. While studying medicine at Zagreb, he was appointed to the leadership of the OUN and served as contact with the Croat

underground. When civil war erupted in Spain, he was sent there to organize Ukrainian units of the Spanish foreign legion. This idea fell through, but Levytsky himself joined the Falange and was wounded in action. He returned to Galicia with the rank of captain and helped organize the *Division Galizien in 1943. By the end of that year he had been arrested by the Gestapo, and he spent the rest of the war in a concentration camp. In 1948 he emigrated to Canada. He was active in Ukrainian veterans' organizations in Winnipeg. From 1973 he was curator of the Ukrainian military history museum of the Ukrainian Academy of Arts and Sciences.

Levytsky, Yaroslav [Levyc'kyi, Jaroslav], b 3 May 1878 in Pistyn, Kosiv county, Galicia, d 1961. Catholic priest, scholar, and publicist. He was ordained in 1901 after finishing theological studies in Lviv, and then taught at the Academic Gymnasium, the Greek Catholic Theological Academy, and the Ukrainian theological faculty at Lviv University (from 1921). He wrote many works, including *Katolyts'kyi narodnii katekhyzm* (The Catholic Folk [Popular] Catechism, 3 vols, 1913–14), a translation of the New Testament (1921), several surveys of church history, a survey of early Ukrainian homiletics (1930; 2nd edn 1973), and numerous popular and scholarly works. He also edited many journals, including *Nyva* (1904–7 and 1910–18) and *Osnova* (1906–13).

Levytsky, Yevhen [Levyc'kyj, Jevhen], b 17 January 1870 in Sydoriv, Husiatyn county, Galicia, d 21 November 1925 in Vienna. Journalist, civic figure, and political leader. While studying at Lviv University he became critical of the populists and helped found the *Ukrainian Radical party. He later helped establish the *National Democratic party (1899) and was a coauthor of its program. Its unification under the command of the Popular Committee was largely his accomplishment. He also edited the party's newspapers *Buduchnist'* (1899), *Svoboda* (1902), and *Dilo* (1903–6). In 1907 and 1911 he was elected from the Stanyslaviv district as deputy to the Austrian parliament, where he played a leading role in the Ukrainian caucus. As a member of the *Union for the Liberation of Ukraine, he went on lecture tours of Germany and Austria during the First World War and published German-language booklets in an effort to gain public support for Ukrainian independence. In 1919–20 he served as envoy of the Ukrainian National Rada in Berlin and Prague. Afterward he resumed his law practice in Vienna.

Levytsky, Yosyp [Levyc'kyj, Josyp], b 1801 in Tovmachyk, Kolomyia circle, Galicia, d 24 May 1860 in Nahuievychi, Sambir circle, Galicia. Writer, philologist, publicist, and Ukrainian Catholic priest. After completing his theological studies in Vienna he taught Church Slavonic in Peremyshl (1825–53) and served as curator of several parishes. His translations of German literature (J. Schiller and J. Goethe) and his own fables and verses began to appear in *yazychiie in 1822. In 1834 he wrote *Grammatik der ruthenischen oder kleinrussischen Sprache in Galizien*. Levytsky believed that *Church Slavonic should be the basis for literary Ukrainian, although the revised version of this grammar, *Grammatika iazyka russkogo v Galitsii* (Grammar of the Ruthenian Language in Galicia, 1849 and 1850), was closer to the vernacular. In his grammar and in *Priruchnyi slovar slaveno-pol'skii* (Slavonic-Polish Reference Dictionary, 1830) he intermixed elements of the Ukrainian vernacular (*Sian dialects of the Peremyshl region) with elements of Church Slavonic and Russian. In the 1830s he engaged in polemics with Y. *Lozynsky, criticizing particularly his proposals to adopt the Latin alphabet for Ukrainian.

Vasyl Levytsky-Sofroniv

Levytsky-Sofroniv, Vasyl (Sofroniv-Levytsky) [Levyc'kyj, Vasyl'], b 14 December 1899 in Stryhantsi, Stryi county, Galicia, d 1 November 1975 in Toronto. Editor and author. Levytsky graduated from Charles University in Prague and worked as an editor of *Hospodars'ko-kooperatyvnyi chasopys* (1927–43) and *Litopys Chervonoï kalyny* (1929–39) in Lviv. He came to Canada in 1950 and worked on the editorial staff of *Vil'ne slovo* (1954–60) and *Novyi shliakh* (1960–72). He served as president of the Ukrainian Journalists' Association in Canada (1967–9). He is the author of 14 volumes of fiction, plays, and essays. He also translated French and German classics into Ukrainian. An edition of his selected works was published in 1972.

Lewicki, Anatol, b 4 April 1841 in Prysivtsi, Zolochiv district, Galicia, d 25 April 1899 in Cracow. Polish historian. The son of a Ukrainian Greek Catholic priest, he studied at Lviv University (1862–6) and was a gymnasium teacher in Peremyshl (1867–79) and Lviv (1879–83) before becoming a professor of history at Cracow University in 1883. He was elected a member of the Polish Academy of Sciences in 1890. He wrote articles on the history of 14th- to 16th-century Ukraine, coauthored a Polish secondary-school textbook on the history of Poland and adjacent Ruthenian lands (1884; 7th edn 1917), and wrote books on ancient Peremyshl (1881) and Grand Duke Švitrigaila of Lithuania (1892). He also published a list of archival sources for Polish history.

Lewicky, Andrew [Levyc'kyj, Andrij], b 6 June 1945 in Oberaldorf, Bavaria. Ophthalmologist. A graduate of Northwestern University (MD, 1970), he is an assistant professor of ophthalmology at Rush Medical College and codirector of the opthalmology section at the Illinois Masonic Medical Center in Chicago. A specialist in cataract surgery, in 1981 he invented a surgical instrument (the Chamber Maintainer System) that makes cataract extraction and intraocular lens insertion safer and easier.

Lewytzkyj, Borys. See Levytsky, Borys.

Lexicography. The making of dictionaries. Ukrainian lexicography dates back to the 16th century, when the first *alfavyty* and *azbukovnyky*, handwritten glossaries of Hebrew, Greek, and Church Slavonic words in the Holy Scriptures and other religious writings, were prepared. These were followed by the first printed lexicons, compiled by L. *Zyzanii (1596; repr 1964) and P. *Berynda (1627, 1653; repr 1961), reversed as a Church Slavonic (Ukrainian)-Polish lexicon in Suprasl 1722, repr 1751, 1756, and 1804 in Pochaiv. A. Calepino's 1590 Latin-multilingual dictionary served as the basis for a 'Heptaglot' including Ukrainian translation of approx 2,500 Latin words that was prepared somewhere in the Ottoman Empire in the early 17th century (manuscript preserved at the Bodleian Library, Oxford). With the introduction of Latin courses at the Kievan Mohyla College, Ye. *Slavynetsky prepared a Latin-Slavonic (Ukrainian) lexicon (1642; repr 1973) based on the Polish part of A. Calepino's and G. Knapski's 1621 Polish-Latin dictionary. He revised this with A. *Koretsky-Satanovsky's help ca 1650 in Moscow (repr Rome 1968, Kiev 1968, 1973). Later Slavynetsky prepared a Greek-Slavonic-Latin lexicon (before 1675; manuscript preserved at the Moscow Patriarchal Library), which served as the basis for F. Polikarpov-Orlov's printed lexicon (1704). A reverse dictionary of Berynda's, *Synonima slavenorosskaia* (Slavonic-Ruthenian Synonyms), was compiled anonymously in the middle of the 17th century (repr 1889, 1964).

In the early 1700s an anonymous 'Dictionarium Latino-Rutenicum' of approx 20,000 words in the Ukrainian redaction of Church Slavonic was prepared (manuscript preserved at the Franciscan monastery in Dubrovnik). In 1718–24, I. Maksymovych prepared an unpublished Latin-Slavonic dictionary based on G. Knapski's 1626 Latin-Polish dictionary (facsimile edn Rome, 1991).

Ukraine under Russian rule. In the Russian Empire, the earliest lexicographic works containing vernacular Ukrainian words appeared in St Petersburg. The comparative dictionary edited by P. Pallas (2 vols, 1787, 1789) included a glossary of 285 Ukrainian words compiled by H. Bacmeister. Other Ukrainian-Russian dictionaries were prepared in the 1830s; the only extant manuscripts are 19 notebooks containing 4,500 words (ca 1835), which have been ascribed to A. Metlynsky, and P. Biletsky-Nosenko's pioneering dictionary of over 20,000 Ukrainian word nests (1838–43), which was published only in 1966.

The first Ukrainian-Russian dictionaries to be published separately were by O. Afanasiev-Chuzhbynsky (6,000 words from *A* to *Z*, in *Izvestiia Otdela russkago iazyka i slovesnosti Imperatorskoi akademii nauk,* 1855, parts 1–2, 4), K. Sheikovsky (*A–B,* 1862; *T–Ya,* 1883, 1886), M. Zakrevsky (11,127 words, 1861), F. Piskunov (ca 8,000 words, 1873, 1882), and V. Dubrovsky (1909, 1914). The first separately printed Russian-Ukrainian dictionary was by M. Levchenko (7,600 words, 1874). After the imposition of the *Ems Ukase (1876), two decades passed before the next two Russian-Ukrainian dictionaries – by M. Komarov et al (37,000 words, 4 vols, 1893, 1894, 1896, 1898, published under the pseuds M. Umanets and A. Spilka in Austrian-ruled Lviv, repr, Berlin 1924; aka 'Russian-Galician dictionary,' published under the pseud A. Hurt in Vienna 1896–8) and by Ye. Tymchenko (40,000 words, 2 vols, Kiev 1897, 1899) – were published. The most important Ukrainian vernacular–Russian dictionary was initiated by

P. *Kulish in 1861, compiled and edited successively by P. Zhytetsky, V. Naumenko, and Ye. Tymchenko, and completed by B. *Hrinchenko (68,000 words, 4 vols, 1907–9; repr, Berlin 1924, Kiev 1925, 1958–60). It played a decisive role in the later standardization of literary Ukrainian.

A few specialized dictionaries dealing with vernacular botanical, agricultural, and technical terms were published (see *Terminology). Ukrainian vernacular terms were also included in N. Annenkov's Russian botanical dictionary (1859, 2nd edn 1878), the Imperial Academy's Russian dictionary edited by Ya. Grot and A. Shakhmatov (1891–1916), and I. Sreznevsky's dictionary of Old East Slavic (4 vols, 1893, 1895, 1903, 1912; repr, Moscow 1958).

The only lexicons published in the Russian Empire with explanations in Ukrainian were a dictionary of 1,500 foreign terms and little-understood words (1906; repr after 1914 in Winnipeg) by V. Domanytsky and a dictionary of T. Shevchenko's vocabulary (7,000 words, 1916) by Nestor Litopysets (pseud of N. Malecha).

Western Ukraine under Austrian rule. In Galicia, Y. Levytsky's Slavonic-Polish dictionary (1830, based on the Suprasl lexicon 1722, repr 1751, 1756, and 1804 in Pochaiv) contained Ukrainian vernacular words. Ukrainian lexicography did not truly develop in Galicia and Bukovyna, however, until the latter half of the 19th century. Nearly a century of Austrian rule passed before the first German-Ukrainian dictionary, compiled by O. Partytsky (35,000 words, 1867), was published. One by V. Kmitsykevych (34,000 words, 1912) appeared almost a half-century later. The first Ukrainian-German dictionary (over 64,000 words) was compiled by Ye. Zhelekhivsky and S. Nedilsky (2 vols, 1884, 1886; repr 3 vols, 1982). It served as the foundation for the Ukrainian-German dictionary by O. Popovych (1904; repr [ca 25,000 words] 1911). I. Ohonovsky's Greek-Ukrainian dictionary of 13,000 words and names in Homer's *Odyssey* and *Iliad* (1900), Yu. Kobyliansky's Ukrainian-Latin (1907) and Latin-Ukrainian (17,000 words and phrases, 1912) dictionaries, and Y. Tanchakovsky's small Ukrainian-Polish dictionary (1910) were used in Galicia's Ukrainian schools.

Several specialized dictionaries of legal, political, administrative, botanical, mathematical, physical, chemical, and economic terms were compiled (see *Terminology).

In Transcarpathia, where the official language was Hungarian, Ruthenian-Hungarian dictionaries were published by O. Mytrak (ca 70,000 words, 1881) and L. Csopey (ca 20,000 words, 1883). The Ruthenian part was a combination of the Transcarpathian dialects and *yazychiie.

Independent Ukraine, 1917–19. After the February Revolution, Ukrainian became the major language of communication. The acute shortage of dictionaries was remedied to some extent by the publication of a dictionary of grammatical terminology and orthography approved by the Society for School Education (1917); an orthographic dictionary by H. *Holoskevych (3 edns, 1918); over 20 Russian-Ukrainian dictionaries by authors such as V. Buriachenko (1917), S. Ivanytsky and F. Shumliansky (2 vols, 1918), M. Kamenetsky (1918), O. Konysky (3 edns, 1918), M. Kolomyichenko (1918), D. Lebid (1918), the Chas publishing house (1918), B. Stepanenko (2 edns, 1918), P. Terpylo (3 edns, 1918), A. Tomylenko and M. Antonovych (1918), P. Shestopal (1918), and V. Hrebinkovsky (1919); Ukrainian-Russian dictionaries by F. Bezkrovny and S. Pereiaslavets (1917), V. Dubrovsky (edns 3–6, 1917–18),

and two anonymous authors (1917, 1918); a dictionary of foreign terms by Z. Pyptenko (1918); a dictionary of Ukrainian physical terminology by the Ukrainian Scientific Society (1918); a Russian-Ukrainian legal dictionary by V. Leontovych and O. Yefymov (2 edns, 1917, 1919); a dictionary of physics terms by O. Kurylo and H. Kholodny (1918); and 20 small (8–60-page) terminological dictionaries (10 of them Russian-Ukrainian ones) in the fields of medicine, geography, science, mathematics, law, and administration.

Western Ukraine, 1918–41. Ukrainian lexicographic works published in Galicia in this period included a German-Ukrainian dictionary by M.N. (1918); a Ukrainian-Polish dictionary by I. Svientsitsky (1920); a nomenclature of higher plants by M. Melnyk (1922); a Ukrainian stylistic dictionary by I. Ohiienko (1924); an orthographic dictionary by K. Kysilevsky (1927, 1934); a Ukrainian-Polish and Polish-Ukrainian dictionary by Ye. Hrytsak and K. Kysilevsky (1931); a Ukrainian-German dictionary by V. Kalynovych (5,000 words, 1931); a musical dictionary by Z. Lysko (1933); I. Ohiienko's dictionary of words not used in literary Ukrainian (1934); a botanical dictionary by S. Makowiecki, of 3,500 Latin names and 21,253 Ukrainian equivalents transliterated using the Polish alphabet (1936); a pocket dictionary of foreign terms by R. Borys and S. Skorbut (1937); a dictionary of foreign terms by M. Matchak (1938); an orthographic dictionary by O. Paneiko (1941); and a German-Ukrainian dictionary by Ya. Yarema (1941).

In Czechoslovakian-ruled Transcarpathia, Hungarian-Ruthenian (Transcarpathian dialect) dictionaries by N. Beskyd (1919), O. Mytrak (1922), and E. Bokshai, Yu. Revai, and M. Brashchaiko (1928) and a Hungarian-Ruthenian dictionary of legal terms by E. Toronsky (1925–7) were published.

Soviet Ukraine, 1920–32. In the first decade of Soviet rule, lexicographers, most of them in Kiev, concentrated on the preparation of practical Ukrainian-Russian and Russian-Ukrainian dictionaries and the development of a standard *orthography and scientific *terminology. New Ukrainian-Russian dictionaries by D. Yavornytsky (*A–K*, 5,000 words, 1920), L. Savchenko (1923; 2nd edn 1924; 3rd and 4th edns 1925; 5th edn 1926), A. Nikovsky (1927), V. Mankivsky and M. Shcherbak (1929; 2nd edn 1930), and O. Iziumov (1930) were published. The seminal Ukrainian-Russian dictionary edited by B. Hrinchenko was republished in 1925, and S. Yefremov, A. Nikovsky, and others began working on a revised third edition incorporating examples from contemporary literary sources (the first edition had been based on literature written before 1870); only vols 1–3 (*A–N*, 1927–8) were published.

New Russian-Ukrainian dictionaries by the State Publishing House of Ukraine (5 edns, 1923–5), L. Savchenko (1925), O. Iziumov (1926; 2nd and 3rd edns 1927), M. Yohansen, M. Nakonechny, K. Nimchynov, and B. Tkachenko (1926), and H. Sabaldyr (1926) appeared, and the Russian-Ukrainian dictionary edited by M. Komarov et al was reprinted (1925). The VUAN Commission for the Compilation of a Dictionary of Contemporary Ukrainian published a 2,000-page Russian-Ukrainian dictionary (letters *A–P*) edited by S. Yefremov, V. Hantsov, H. Holoskevych, M. Hrinchenko, A. Krymsky, and A. Nikovsky (vol 1, 1924; vol 2 [3 parts]: 1929, 1932–3; vol 3, parts 1–2, 1927–8); it is one of the finest achievements of Ukrainian lexicography.

Also appearing were orthographic dictionaries by H. Holoskevych (4th–7th edns 1922, 1924, 1926, 1930), O. Iziumov (60,000 words, 1931; revised by O. Paneiko, 1941), H. Sabaldyr and O. Kolomatska (25,000 words, 1930), and other authors; dictionaries of foreign terms by the Chas publishing house (1924) and O. Badan-Yavorenko (1932); a dictionary of Ukrainian administrative phraseology (1926, 1927) by V. Pidmohylny and Ye. Pluzhnyk; a German-Ukrainian dictionary by I. Sharovolsky (20,000 words, 1929; rev edn 1948); a Russian-Ukrainian dictionary of proverbs by H. Mlodzynsky (1929); part of a historical dictionary of the Ukrainian language that Ye. Tymchenko (ed) and others had compiled at the turn of the 20th century (*A–Zh*, 1930, 1932; repr, Munich 1985); and a dictionary of foreign terms by I. Boikiv, O. Iziumov, H. Kalyshevsky, and M. Trokhymenko (1932; repr, New York 1955).

Terminological research and compilation was co-ordinated initially in Kiev by a terminological commission (est 1918) at the Ukrainian Scientific Society and the VUAN Orthographic and Terminological Commission (est 1919). In 1921 these commissions were amalgamated to form the VUAN *Institute of the Ukrainian Scientific Language (IUNM). Before it was disbanded in 1930, the IUNM published 20 Ukrainian-Russian dictionaries in the mathematical, technical, natural, and social sciences. In 1931–3 the Institute of Linguistics continued the work of the IUNM. About 70 terminological dictionaries came out in Ukraine by 1933.

Soviet Ukraine since 1933. During the Stalinist terror most Ukrainian lexicographers were repressed as 'bourgeois nationalist saboteurs,' and their works were blacklisted (see *Language policy). Thenceforth a Russified scientific orthography and terminology, expunged of all words deemed archaic, dialectal, or 'contrived' (ie, introduced in the 1920s), was imposed and published in 5 VUAN terminological bulletins (medicine, mathematics, botany, physics, manufacturing, ed P. Mustiatsa, 1934–5), 10 Russian-Ukrainian terminological dictionaries for secondary schools (1933–5), 2 AN URSR Russian-Ukrainian dictionaries (S. Vasylevsky et al, 1937; ed M. Kalynovych, L. Bulakhovsky, and M. Rylsky, 80,000 words, 1948; rev edns 1955–6, 1961–2), an orthographic dictionary (D. Levi, H. Levchenko, and L. Rak, 1936), a dictionary of medical terms (I. Kyrychenko et al, 1936), a Latin-Ukrainian-Russian medical dictionary (M. Knipovych, 1948), and other Russian-Ukrainian and orthographic dictionaries.

Russified orthography, vocabulary, and terminology have remained normative in the many Soviet Ukrainian dictionaries published since Stalin's death. Nonetheless, the post-Stalin era has been the most productive period in Ukrainian lexicography in terms of the number and variety of dictionaries published. Many orthographic dictionaries and handbooks have appeared (I. Kyrychenko, 40,000 words, 1955, rev edn 1960; M. Pohribny, 50,000–52,000 words, 1959, rev edn 1964; I. Vykhovanets et al, 50,000 words, 1973; A. Buriachok, L. Palamarchuk, V. Rusanivsky, and N. Totska, 1973; S. Holovashchuk et al, 114,000 words, 1975, 1977; S. Holovashchuk, 40,000 words, 1979, 1989). The AN URSR (now ANU) has sponsored the preparation and publication of several major multivolume dictionaries: the largest Ukrainian-Russian and Russian-Ukrainian dictionaries (ed I. Kyrychenko et al, 6 vols, 121,700 words, 1953, 1958, 1961–3; ed I. Bilodid et al, 3

vols, 1968, rev edn 1980–1), the largest dictionary of the Ukrainian language (ed I. Bilodid et al, 11 vols, 1970–80), the first dictionary of 14th- to 15th-century Middle Ukrainian (ed L. Humetska et al, 2 vols, 1977–8), and the Ukrainian etymological dictionary in seven projected volumes (ed O. Melnychuk et al; vol 1: *A–H*, 1982; vol 2, *D–Koptsi*, 1985; vol 3, *Kora–M*, 1989). These have served as the foundation of a Russian-Ukrainian dictionary for secondary schools (D. Hanych and I. Oliinyk, 1962; 5th edn 1979), the AN URSR Ukrainian-Russian dictionary (ed V. Ilin, 65,000 words, 1964; 4th edn 1976), and a one-volume school dictionary of the Ukrainian language (ed D. Hrynchyshyn, L. Humetska, et al, 1978).

Over 15 other bilingual dictionaries have appeared: four English-Ukrainian (M. Podvezko, 50,000 words, 1948, 1951; M. Podvezko, 25,000 words, 1955, 1965; M. Podvezko and M. Balla, 65,000 words, 1974, repr Edmonton 1988; Yu. Zhluktenko, N. Bykhovets, and A. Shvants, 20,000 words, 1978, 1982, 1984), a Ukrainian-English (M. Podvezko, 60,000 words, 1952; rev edn 1957, 1962, 1965), four German-Ukrainian (ed I. Sharovolsky, 2nd edn, 25,000 words, 1955; V. Leshchynska, O. Mazny, and K. Sylvestrova, 50,000 words, 1959; V. Bukhbinder, 2,500 words, 1972; ed Ye. Lysenko, 20,000 words, 1978, 1983), a (the first) French-Ukrainian (O. Andriievska and L. Yavorovska, 50,000 words, 1955), a Polish-Ukrainian (ed L. Humetska et al, 2 vols [3 books], 1958–60), (the first) two Ukrainian-French (O. Andriievska and L. Yavorovska, 50,000 words, 1963; M. Lysenko and Y. Donets, 1985; K. Andrashko, O. Kolomyiets, and K. Tyshchenko, 20,000 words, 1986), a (the first) Bulgarian-Ukrainian (I. Stoianov and O. Chmyr, 43,000 words, 1988), and a major Czech-Ukrainian (AN URSR, 2 vols, 1988–9) dictionary. The only two English-Ukrainian phraseological dictionaries (K. Barantsev, 7,000 phrases, 1956; 30,000 phrases, 1969), a dictionary of 2,500 synonyms in the English language (K. Barantsev, 1964), and a Russian-Ukrainian-Hungarian phraseological dictionary (V. Laver and I. Zikan, 1985) have also appeared.

In 1957 a Dictionary Commission headed by Y. Shtokalo was founded at the ANU Institute of Linguistics. It has co-ordinated the compilation of over 20 Russian-Ukrainian specialized terminological dictionaries (see *Terminology).

In the 1950s and 1960s many other specialized dictionaries appeared: a Russian-Ukrainian dictionary of geographic names (A. Kara-Mosko and M. Tokarsky, 1953), a dictionary of linguistic terms (Ye. Krotevych and N. Rodzevych, 1957), two dictionaries of Ukrainian synonyms (A. Bahmet, *Vitchyzna*, 1959, no. 2–1961, no. 12; P. Derkach, ed and rev S. Levchenko, 1960), dictionaries of terms in literary scholarship (V. Lesyn and O. Pulynets, 1961; rev edns 1965, 1971), a Ukrainian-Russian and Russian-Ukrainian dictionary of personal names (ed I. Kyrychenko, 1954; ed S. Levchenko, 1961, 1967; L. Skrypnyk, 1972, 1976, 1986), a brief geological dictionary (V. Vyshniakov, 1962), a Ukrainian-Russian dictionary of geographic names in the Ukrainian SSR (V. Nezhnypapa, 1964; rev edn 1971), a dictionary of T. Shevchenko's language (ed V. Vashchenko et al, 2 vols, 1964), a short dictionary of musical terms (S. Pavliuchenko, 1965), a Ukrainian phraseological dictionary (N. Batiuk, 1966), a political dictionary (1966; 3rd edn 1982), a dictionary of over 2,200 Ukrainian idioms (H. Udovychenko, 1968), a handbook of

Ukrainian surnames (Yu. Redko, 1969), and a brief Russian-Ukrainian dictionary of printing and publishing terms (V. Bova and M. Dolomino, 1969).

Even more specialized dictionaries were published in the 1970s and 1980s: a Ukrainian-Russian and Russian-Ukrainian phraseological dictionary (I. Oliinyk and M. Sydorenko, 1971; rev edn 1978), a dictionary of musical terms (Yu. Yutsevych, 1971; rev edn 1977), a dictionary for fans of cinema (M. Panfilov, 1971), a numismatic dictionary (V. Zvarych, 1972), a toponymic dictionary of the Ukrainian SSR (M. Yanko, 1973), an economic dictionary (ed P. Bahrii and S. Dorohuntsov, 1973), a dictionary of foreign words (ed O. Melnychuk, 1974; 2nd rev edn 1985), a juridical dictionary (eds B. Babii, V. Koretsky, and V. Tsvetkov, 1974), an economic-agricultural dictionary (O. Krysalny, 1975), a dictionary of Shevchenko studies (2 vols, Ye. Kyryliuk et al, 1976–7), a dictionary of the language in H. Kvitka-Osnovianenko's works (3 vols, 1978), a dictionary of Ukrainian rhymes (A. Buriachok and I. Huryn, 1979), a dictionary of Ukraine's hydronyms (ed A. Nepokupny, O. Stryzhak, and K. Tsiluiko, 1979), a dictionary of associative norms in the Ukrainian language (N. Butenko, 1979), a scientific dictionary (I. Bilenko, 1979), a frequency dictionary of words in Soviet Ukrainian prose from 1945 to 1970 (ed V. Perebyinis, 2 vols, 1981), a dictionary reference book of morphemic analysis (I. Yatsenko, 2 vols, 1981), a morphemic dictionary (L. Poliuha, 1983), a major Ukrainian phraseological dictionary (H. Udovychenko, 2 vols, 1984), a Ukrainian morphological dictionary of medical terminology (O. Fedotov, O. Ochkurenko, and K. Fenchyn, 1985), a dictionary of classical mythology (ed A. Biletsky, 1985), a new dictionary of linguistic terms (D. Hanych and I. Oliinyk, 1985), a brief dictionary of Ukrainian periphrases (M. Kolomiiets and Ye. Rehushevsky, 1985), a Ukrainian reverse dictionary (ed S. Bevzenko, 1985), a dictionary of Ukrainian paronyms (D. Hrynchyshyn and O. Serbenska, 1986), a biological dictionary (ed K. Sytnyk and V. Topachevsky, 2nd rev edn, 1986), a philosophical dictionary (V. Shynkaruk, 2nd rev edn, 1986), a dictionary of over 2,000 pairs of Ukrainian antonyms (L. Poliuha, 1987), an encyclopedic dictionary (A. Kudrytsky et al, 3 vols, 1986–7), a dictionary of over 21,000 Ukrainian abbreviations and acronyms (ed M. Feshchenko and V. Zhaivoronok, 1988), a dictionary of Ukrainian phraseological synonyms (M. Kolomiiets and Ye. Rehashevsky, 1989), and a dictionary of difficult language usage in Ukrainian (S. Yermolenko, 1989).

Since the 1950s dialectal dictionaries of Odessa oblast (O. Melnychuk, *Leksykohrafichnyi biuleten'* [*LB*], 2 [1952]), Sumy oblast (I. Pryimak, 1957; A. Moskalenko, Odessa 1958), Transcarpathia (Y. Dzendzelivsky, 1958; H. Hrytsak, typescript, 1962), the lower Dniester region (Y. Dzendzelivsky, *LB*, 6 [1958]; A. Berlizov, 1959), right-bank Cherkasy oblast (P. Lysenko, *LB*, 6 [1958]), Zhytomyr oblast (L. Palamarchuk, *LB*, 6 [1958]), the Poltava region (V. Vashchenko, 1960), Polisia (P. Lysenko, 1961, 1974; M. Nykonchuk, 1979), Bukovyna (V. Prokopenko, in *Karpatskaia dialektologiia i onomastika*, ed G. Klepikov, Moscow 1972), the Boiko region (M. Onyshkevych, 2 vols, 1984), and western Volhynia (M. Korzoniuk, in *Ukraïns'ka dialektna leksyka*, ed I. Matviias et al, 1987) have been published.

Interwar Eastern and Central Europe. Ukrainian émigrés, most of them affiliated with the *Ukrainian Free

University and *Ukrainian Husbandry Academy in Czechoslovakia and the *Ukrainian Scientific Institutes in Berlin and Warsaw, also compiled dictionaries. They published a dictionary of foreign terms (Z. Kuzelia, Leipzig 1919), the first two Czech-Ukrainian dictionaries (N. Kovalevska-Koroleva, 1920; N. Shcherbyna, 1924), some terminological dictionaries, two German-Ukrainian dictionaries (H. Nakonechna, 1939, 1941; the Ukrainske Vydavnytstvo publishing house, 1941), two Ukrainian-German dictionaries (J. Rudnyckyj, over 20,000 words, 1940, 1941; Z. Kuzelia and J. Rudnyckyj, 98,000 words, 1943, repr Wiesbaden 1983), and a Ukrainian-Italian dictionary (Ye. Onatsky, 1941). The Ukrainian-Russian dictionary edited by B. Hrinchenko was reprinted in Berlin in 1924. Also of note were the German-Ukrainian and Ukrainian-German dictionary of military terminology (I. Ilnytskyj-Zankovych, 1938) and German-Ukrainian and Ukrainian-German dictionary of aviation terminology (I. Ilnytskyj-Zankovych, 1939).

The New World. The earliest dictionaries published outside Ukraine appeared in Canada: M. Yasenitsky's *Pocket Dictionary of the Ukrainian-English and English-Ukrainian Languages* (1914) and E. Kozlovsky's *English-Ukrainian Pocket Dictionary* (1917, 1923). Since that time other dictionaries have appeared in Canada, most of them after the Second World War: H. Platsko's (1929) and J. *Krett's (1931) Ukrainian-English and English-Ukrainian dictionaries, F. Dojacek's *New English Interpreter and Ukrainian-English and English-Ukrainian Dictionary* (1930), C. Andrusyshen and J. Krett's *Ukrainian-English Dictionary* (1957; repr 1981, 1985), I. Ohienko's *Grammatical and Stylistic Lexicon of Shevchenko's Poetry* (1961), V. Ninovsky's Ukrainian reverse dictionary (1969), J. Rudnyckyj's *Etymological Dictionary of the Ukrainian Language* (2 vols, 1962–75, 1978–82), F. Bohdan's *Dictionary of Ukrainian Surnames in Canada* (1974), P. Shtepa's dictionary of foreign terms (1977), I. Ohiienko's etymological-semantic dictionary (3 vols, A–O, 1979, 1982, 1988), P. Shtepa's phraseological dictionary (1980), and W. Niniows'kyj's *Ukrainian-English and English-Ukrainian Dictionary* (24,000 words, 1985). M. Podvezko's English-Ukrainian and Ukrainian-English dictionaries (1958) and I. Ohiienko's 1924 Ukrainian stylistic dictionary (1978) have been reprinted.

In the United States the first Ukrainian-English and English-Ukrainian dictionary was M. Surmach's pocket dictionary (1931). Several Ukrainian dictionaries have been published since the Second World War: an English-Ukrainian nautical dictionary (W. Stepankowsky, 1953), an English-Ukrainian dictionary (J. Salastin, 1956), a Ukrainian dictionary of foreign terms (A. Orel, 3 vols, 1963–6), an anatomical dictionary (F. Tsekhivsky and O. Cherniavsky, 1971), two orthographic dictionaries (P. Kovaliv, 1977; ed J. Rudnyckyj and K. Tserkevych, 1979), an English-Ukrainian scientific and technical dictionary (A. Wowk, 1982), and an English-Ukrainian dictionary of color names (A. Wowk, ed B. Struminsky, 1986). Several dictionaries have been reprinted: H. Holoskevych's orthographic dictionary (8th edn 1952, 1962); I. Boikiv, O. Iziumov, H. Kalyshevsky, and M. Trokhymenko's 1932 dictionary of foreign terms (1955); M. Podvezko's *Ukrainian-English Dictionary* (1954, 1963, 1973); M. Halyn's 1926 Latin-Ukrainian medical dictionary (1969); I. Ohiienko's 1934 dictionary of words not used in literary Ukrainian (1973); P. Derkach's 1960 dictionary of Ukrainian synonyms (rev edn, ed V. Volkov, N.

Pazuniak, K. Tserkevych, 1975); A. Bahmet's 1959–61 dictionary of Ukrainian synonyms (*A–P*, ed H. Luzhnytsky and L. Rudnytzky, 1982); the Russian-Ukrainian dictionary of legal terms (ed A. Krymsky, 1984); M. Knipovych's 1948 Latin-Ukrainian-Russian medical dictionary (1985); and P. Oesterle's 1944 German-Ukrainian medical dictionary (1986).

In Argentina, a Ukrainian-Spanish and Spanish-Ukrainian dictionary by T. Petrivsky was published in Buenos Aires as early as 1930. In Australia, a few dictionaries by postwar Ukrainian immigrants have appeared: an orthographic dictionary (D. Nytchenko, 1968, 1985), a *Ukrainian-English Dictionary for Popular Use* (M., W., and A. Dejko, 50,000 words, 1979), and an *English-Ukrainian Dictionary for Popular Use* (M., W., and A. Dejko, 50,000 words, 1979).

Postwar Western Europe. A few dictionaries by and for displaced persons were published in Germany immediately after the Second World War: V. Zakharkiv's (1945–6) and V. Lev and I. Verbiany's (1947) Ukrainian-English and English-Ukrainian dictionaries and A. Orel's orthographic dictionary (1946). Since that time the dictionaries published in Germany have been O. Horbach's dialectal dictionaries of the northern Dniester region (*Naukovi zapysky UTHI* [*NZUTHI*], vol 7 [1965]), northern Dobrudja (*NZUTHI*, vol 15 [1968]; *Zapysky NTSh*, vol 185 [1969]), Terebovlia county (*NZUTHI*, vols 19–20 [1969–70]), western Polisia (*NZUTHI*, vol 25 [1973]), the Prešov region (1973), and southern Volhynia (1973); M. Savchuk's German-Ukrainian electrotechnical dictionary (*UTHI*, 1981); and V. Irklievsky's etymological dictionary of Ukrainian surnames (1987). In Rome, a small Church Slavonic–Ukrainian–English dictionary (D. Popovych and K. Pasichny, 1962) and Ye. Onatsky's Ukrainian-Italian (2nd enlarged edn 1977) and Italian-Ukrainian (1977) dictionaries have been published.

Postwar Eastern Europe. In Poland, a Ukrainian-Polish dictionary (30,000 words, ed S. Hrabiec and P. Zwoliński, 1957) was published. In Czechoslovakia, the indigenous Ukrainians have published a Ukrainian-Slovak dictionary (I. Popel, ed M. Buchynska, 1960), a Ukrainian vernacular–Russian dictionary compiled by Ya. Holovatsky in 19th-century Galicia and Transcarpathia (*Naukovyi zbirnyk Muzeiu ukraïns'koï kul'tury u Svydnyku*, vol 10 [1982]), and the first Slovak-Ukrainian dictionary (P. Bunhanych, 40,000 words, 1985). A Hungarian-Ukrainian dictionary (L. Vladimir, K. Halas, V. Dobosh, et al, 1961) and a Ukrainian-Hungarian dictionary (L. Katona, 1963) have been published by the Hungarian Academy of Sciences. In Bucharest, a Rumanian-Ukrainian (30,000 words, 1963) and a Ukrainian-Rumanian (35,000 words, 1964) dictionary were compiled by native and Soviet lexicographers and edited by G. Cocotailo. In Yugoslavia, the indigenous Ukrainians have prepared a Serbo-Croatian–'Rusinian' (Bačka dialect) and 'Rusinian'–Serbo-Croatian elementary-school dictionary (M. Kochysh, 1970), a Serbo-Croatian–'Rusinian'–Ukrainian school dictionary (M. Kochysh, 1972), and the first Ukrainian–Serbo-Croatian and Serbo-Croatian–Ukrainian dictionary (A. Menac and A. Koval [a Soviet lexicographer], 1979).

BIBLIOGRAPHY
Moskalenko, A. *Narys istoriï ukraïns'koï leksykohrafiï* (Kiev 1961)
Horets'kyi, P. *Istoriia ukraïns'koï leksykohrafiï* (Kiev 1963)
Palamarchuk, L. *Ukraïns'ka radians'ka leksykohrafiia (Pytannia istoriï, teoriï ta praktyky)* (Kiev 1978)

Nimchuk, V. *Staroukraïns'ka leksykohrafiia v ïï zv'iazkakh z rosii-s'koiu ta bilorus'koiu* (Kiev 1980)

O. Horbach, R. Senkus

Lexicology. A branch of linguistics dealing with the study of the meaning, usage, derivation, and history of words and word elements. In Ukraine lexicological problems were usually treated in terms of their practical application, in connection with the establishment of a system of Ukrainian *terminology and of a standard literary Ukrainian lexicon, by scholars such as H. Kholodny (the general principles of terminology), T. Sekunda (the principles of technical terminology), M. Osypiv, Ye. Hrytsak (neologisms), and M. Hladky (author of *Mova suchasnoho ukraïns'koho pys'menstva* [The Language of Contemporary Ukrainian Literature, 1930] and *Nasha hazetna mova* [Our Newspapers' Language, 1928]) and by various authors of articles on *lexicography and the theory and practice of translation. Other linguists, such as O. Syniavsky, M. Sulyma, I. Ohiienko, G.Y. Shevelov, H. Levchenko, I. Bilodid, P. Pliushch, and I. Hrytsiutenko, devoted much attention to lexicological problems in their studies of the language of various writers. Chapters by I. Troian in *Pidvyshchenyi kurs ukraïns'koï movy* (An Advanced Course in the Ukrainian Language, 1930, ed L. Bulakhovsky), by Yu. Sherekh in his *Narys ukraïns'koï literaturnoï movy* (Outline of the Ukrainian Literary Language, 1951), and by P. Horetsky in vol 1 of *Kurs suchasnoï ukraïns'koï literaturnoï movy* (A Course in the Contemporary Ukrainian Literary Language, 1951, ed L. Bulakhovsky) contained systematic but brief surveys of the lexicon of literary Ukrainian.

Since the 1930s the AN URSR (now ANU) Institute of Linguistics has been the co-ordinating center of Ukrainian lexicology. In 1965–9 it published the serial *Leksykolohiia ta leksykohrafiia*. Until recent times Ukrainian theoretical lexicology was underdeveloped and was limited to M. Kalynovych's work on the concept of the word and B. Larin's research on urban speech. In the 1970s several publications on theoretical lexicology appeared: the collection *Pytannia strukturnoï leksykolohiï* (Questions of Structural Lexicology, 1970), L. Lysychenko's *Leksykolohiia suchasnoï ukraïns'koï movy: Semantychna struktura slova* (The Lexicology of the Contemporary Ukrainian Language: Semantic Structure of the Word, 1977), M. Kocherhan's *Slovo i kontekst* (The Word and Context, 1980), and particularly *Z istoriï ukraïns'koï leksykolohiï* (From the History of Ukrainian Lexicology, 1980). Despite their shortcomings, such as political bias and excessive descriptivism, the collectively written *Leksyka i frazeolohiia* (Lexicon and Phraseology, vol 4 of *Suchasna ukraïns'ka literaturna mova* [The Contemporary Ukrainian Literary Language, 1973]) and *Istoriia ukraïns'koï movy: Leksyka i frazeolohiia* (History of the Ukrainian Language: Lexicon and Phraseology, 1983), both edited by M. Zhovtobriukh and V. Rusanivsky, mark a breakthrough in Ukrainian lexicology.

Lezhohubsky, Teodosii [Ležohubs'kyj, Teodosij], b 21 January 1869 in Rybnyky, Berezhany county, Galicia, d 1919. Priest, preacher, educator, and civic leader. A graduate of the Central Seminary in Vienna (1891), from 1913 he was principal of the gymnasium run by the Basilian order of nuns in Lviv. He was vice-president of the Prosvita society and sat on the Popular Committee of the National Democratic party. His sermons were published posthumously in five volumes (1933–6).

Rev Teodosii Lezhohubsky   Antin Liakhotsky

Liadova River [Ljadova]. A left-bank tributary of the Dniester River. It is 93 km long and drains a basin area of 748 sq km. The Liadova flows through the Podolian Upland within the borders of Khmelnytskyi oblast and Vinnytsia oblast and joins the Dniester near Mohyliv-Podilskyi. The river is used for irrigation and pisciculture.

Liakhotsky, Antin [Ljaxoc'kyj] (pseud: Kuzma), b 1853 in Zhytomyr, Volhynia gubernia, d 24 April 1918 in Lausanne, Switzerland. Political activist. After being arrested for his involvement with a revolutionary circle in Kiev, he escaped to Geneva in 1878 and became manager of the Ukrainska Drukarnia press, set up by M. Drahomanov. After Drahomanov's departure (1889) he assumed full control of the printing house, which published about 110 books, pamphlets, and journals. He had close contacts with various Ukrainian and Russian circles opposed to the tsarist regime, and after the Revolution of 1905 he headed the Ukrainian hromada in Geneva, which consisted largely of young revolutionaries.

Liakhovych, Yaryna [Ljaxovyč, Jaryna] (Lachowicz, Yarina), b 2 October 1942 in Ukraine. Artist. After the Second World War, together with her parents she emigrated to Australia. She studied under D. Baker and completed a degree in fine arts at the Royal Institute of Technology in Melbourne. She paints in a modern abstract style and has received numerous awards and prizes at public exhibitions.

Liakhovych, Yevhen [Ljaxovyč, Jevhen], b 4 June 1900 in Ushnia, Zolochiv county, Galicia, d 16 October 1976 in Deerfield Beach, Florida. Journalist and community leader. From 1923 he studied at the Polytechnic Institute of New York in Brooklyn and promoted the Ukrainian Military Organization and then the OUN and their ideology in the United States. In 1933–5 he was the official OUN representative in Great Britain, contributed to *Rozbudova natsiï*, and wrote the brochure *The Ukrainian Question* to inform the British government and public about Ukrainian aspirations. After returning to the United States in 1935, he became a leading member of the pro-OUN Organization for the Rebirth of Ukraine and was an associate editor of the daily *Svoboda* (1936–42). After the Second World War he founded the *Organization for the Defense of Four Free-

doms for Ukraine, served as its first president (1946–8), and contributed to the Ukrainian-American press.

Liakhy [ljaxy]. An old Ukrainian name for the Poles, used for the first time in the 11th century in *Povist' vremennykh lit* (The Tale of Bygone Years) and other chronicles. The word is believed to have evolved from *liada* (uncultivated field). At first it probably designated only a tribe of western Slavs bordering on Rus'; the chronicle mentions the 981 campaign of Volodymyr the Great against the *liakhy*, for example. Later the term was applied to Poles in general. In folk songs not only Poles but enemies in general are called *liakhy*. In the last few centuries the term has been used in a pejorative sense, sometimes to designate Polish gentry.

Lialychi [Ljalyči]. The former estate of Count P. *Zavadovsky, now a town in Surazh raion, Briansk oblast, RF. Lialychi has a monument of 18th-century Ukrainian architecture – a three-story palace built by G. *Quarenghi (1797–1800) in the classical style, with a six-column Corinthian portico, loggias on the side façades, and one-story wings. The so-called Italian Hall in the central part of the palace is covered by a dome. Two orangeries frame the main courtyard, beyond which is an orchard and a landscaped park. In the park stand a summer palace with a four-column Tuscan portico and façade; the Temple of Thanksgiving – a circular pavilion covered by a flattened dome supported by 12 Corinthian columns, in the center of which is a statue of Count P. Rumiantsev; and a church with five cupolas, which is connected by a colonnade to identical belfries at either end, and by an alley to the main palace. The palace's interior was lavishly decorated with sculptures, murals with geometric and floral designs, rare plants, marble, and plaster ornamentation. The palace was damaged during the Second World War and was restored.

Lianytsky, Oleksander [Ljanyc'kyj], b and d ? Painter in late-17th-century Lviv. Works ascribed to him include the iconostasis and fresco icons in the Dormition Church's Chapel of the Three Saints (1698) and the frescoes in the Nestorivtsi residence (discovered in 1910). He probably also painted the portraits of M. and A. Krasovsky (ca 1714).

Liapunov, Aleksandr [Ljapunov], b 6 June 1857 in Yaroslavl, Russia, d 3 November 1918 in Odessa. Russian mathematician and engineer; from 1902 full member of the St Petersburg Academy of Sciences. Liapunov graduated from the University of St Petersburg in 1880, and from 1885 was a docent and then (1892) professor at Kharkiv University. He was active in the *Kharkiv Mathematics Society, as vice-president (1891–8), president (1899–1902), and publications editor. While in Kharkiv Liapunov conducted research in mathematical physics and the theory of probability and obtained important results in both fields. One of his great achievements was the rigorous development of the fundamental concepts of stability theory (now known as the Liapunov-Poincaré theory of stability), which he published in his doctoral dissertation in 1892. In this and succeeding works, he obtained a series of fundamental results on the solution of ordinary linear and nonlinear differential equations. Liapunov's work 'Some Questions Connected with the Dirichlet Problem' (1898) was of great importance to mathematical physics. It investigated the properties of the potential arising from charges and dipoles distributed on a surface, and later led to the study of double-layer potential in the case of dipoles. Liapunov was the first to demonstrate the symmetry of the Green's function for the Dirichlet problem, and to prove that the solution may be represented by a surface integral. His contributions to probability theory included the introduction and the study of the method of characteristic functions and a general proof of the central limit theorem of probability, which covered much wider conditions than proofs of his predecessors. Liapunov's scientific work received wide recognition. In 1902 he moved to St Petersburg as successor to P. Chebyshev as an academician in applied mathematics.

W. Petryshyn

Liapunov, Boris [Ljapunov], b 6 August 1862 in Bolobonovo, Kurmysh county, Simbirsk gubernia, Russia, d 22 February 1943 in Borovoe, Akmolinsk oblast, Kazakhstan. Russian Slavist; full member of the USSR Academy of Sciences from 1923. After graduating from St Petersburg (1881–5) and Kharkiv (1886–91, where he studied under M. Drinov and O. Potebnia) universities, he taught at Kharkiv (1892–1900) and Odessa (1900–23) universities and then worked at various institutions in Leningrad. His publications deal with Proto-Slavic, Old Church Slavonic, the etymology of Slavic words, and a number of old Ukrainian monuments such as the Dobrylo Gospel of 1164 and the Odessa Gospel. In his booklet *Edinstvo russkogo iazyka v ego narechiiakh* (The Unity of the Russian Language in Its Dialects, 1919) he defended the theory of a common Russian language in the Princely era. A bibliography of his works can be found in *Voprosy iazykoznaniia* (1958, no. 2). His article on the earliest relations between Russian and Ukrainian and their separation was published posthumously in 1968.

Liashchenko, Arkadii [Ljaščenko, Arkadij], b 26 January 1871, d 1931. Historian of Ukrainian literature; full member of the Shevchenko Scientific Society; corresponding member of the Academy of Sciences of the USSR; member of the Leningrad Society of Researchers of Ukrainian History, Literature, and Language. His articles on old Ukrainian literature and on 19th-century literature appeared in various scholarly journals and in collections published by the VUAN and the Leningrad Society.

Liashchenko, Petro [Ljaščenko], b 22 October 1876 in Saratov, Russia, d 24 July 1955 in Moscow. Economist specializing in agrarian studies and economic history; corresponding member of the USSR Academy of Sciences from 1943 and full member of the AN URSR (now ANU) from 1945. After graduating from St Petersburg University (1900) he lectured there (1903–12) and at Tomsk University (1913–17). After the revolution he served as a university professor in Rostov-na-Donu and Moscow and as a senior research associate of the Institute of Economics in Kiev. He wrote over 150 works, including *Ocherki agrarnoi evoliutsii Rossii* (Outlines of the Agrarian Evolution of Russia, 2 vols, 1908, 1913), *Krest'ianskoe delo i poreformennaia zemleustroitel'naia politika* (The Peasant Problem and the Postreform Land Tenure Policy, 2 vols, 1913, 1917), and *Istoriia*

Petro Liashchenko

narodnogo khoziaistva SSSR (3 vols, 1947–8; trans as *History of the National Economy of Russia*, 1949).

Liashenko, Luka [Ljašenko], b ca 1894, d ? Film actor, director, and screenwriter. He worked at the Ukrainfilm studio in the 1930s, where he appeared in the films *Zemlia* (The Earth, 1930), *Khlib* (Bread, 1930), *Avangard* (The Avant-Garde, 1932), and *Ostannii port* (The Last Port, 1935), and directed *Shturm zemli* (The Storming of the Earth, 1930), *Vovchi stezhky* (Wolf Paths, 1931), for which he wrote the screenplay, and *Na peredovykh pozytsiiakh* (In Leading Positions, 1932). He was arrested in 1935 during the Stalinist terror.

Liashenko, Vasyl [Ljašenko, Vasyl'], b 12 February 1902 in Nosivka, Nizhen county, Chernihiv gubernia. Solid-state physicist. A graduate of the Kiev Institute of People's Education (1928), he worked at the AN URSR (now ANU) Institute of Physics (1930–60) and Institute of Semiconductors (from 1960) and taught at postsecondary schools in Kiev. He has made substantial contributions to the understanding of carrier-density phenomena in semiconductor surface states and their role in photoconduction and catalysis.

Liashko, Ivan [Ljaško], b 9 September 1922 in Matskivtsi, Lubni county, Poltava gubernia. Mathematician and cyberneticist; full member of the AN URSR (now ANU) since 1973. A graduate of the Kiev Pedagogical Institute (1952), he began to work at Kiev University in 1955, where in 1965 he became a professor and head of the department of mathematical physics. In 1978 he became president of the Znannia Society of the Ukrainian SSR. His principal works deal with the mechanics of solid media, computational mathematics, and cybernetics. He has made important contributions to the theory and application of approximate analytic methods for solving boundary value problems. Also of great importance are his contributions to the development of computer-controlled packet switching automatic system control by means of branching. He has obtained significant results in studying the linear filtering of pink noise and the control problem with bilinear quality criteria.

Liashko, Oleksander, b 30 December 1915 in Rodakove, Slovianoserbske county, Katerynoslav gubernia. A Party functionary and Soviet official. A graduate of the Donetske Industrial Institute (1947), he rose in the Party apparatus to the positions of first secretary of the Donetske Oblast Committee of the CPU (1960–3) and second secretary of the CC (1966–9). In 1969–72 he served as chairman of the Presidium of the Supreme Soviet of the Ukrainian SSR and chairman of Ukraine's Council of Ministers (1972–87). He was a member of the CC CPU (1960–84), the CC CPSU (1961–87), and the Presidium (1963–6) and the Politburo of the CPU (1966–87). Until his retirement in July 1987, Liashko was an obedient executor of Moscow's centralist policies.

Liaskoronsky, Sylvestr [Ljaskorons'kyj, Syl'vestr], b ?, d 19 May 1754 in Kiev. Othodox churchman and writer. He graduated from the Kievan Mohyla Academy and then taught there (1729–41) before becoming hegumen of the Holy Spirit Monastery in Vilnius and archimandrite of the Nizhen Annunciation (1745) and Kiev Epiphany Brotherhood (1746–51) monasteries. He also served as rector and professor of theology at the Kiev academy (1746–51). He wrote the tragicomedy *Obraz strastei mira seho* (A Portrait of the Passion of This World, 1729), which was thematically linked to the Easter cycle.

Vasyl Liaskoronsky   Borys Liatoshynsky

Liaskoronsky, Vasyl [Ljaskorons'kyj, Vasyl'], b 5 January 1860 in Zolotonosha, Poltava gubernia, d 1 January 1928 in Kiev. Historian and archeologist. He graduated from Kiev University in 1885 where he studied under V. Antonovych and I. Luchytsky. He participated in several archeological excavations throughout Ukraine (with V. Khvoika and others), publishing articles about the findings in *Kievskaia starina* and elsewhere. He edited the bulletins of the all-Russian archeological congresses held in Kiev in 1899, Kharkiv in 1902, and Katerynoslav in 1905, and led several expeditions under the auspices of the congresses. A privatdocent at Moscow University (1903–7), eventually he was allowed to assume a similar position at Kiev University (1907–9) before becoming a full professor at the Nizhen Historical-Philosophical Institute (Lyceum) in 1909. After the Revolution he worked in a variety of institutions, but his most important appointment was as the head of the archeological department of the All-Ukrainian Archeological Committee.

A specialist in historical geography, historical topography, numismatics, and other ancillary historical disciplines, Liaskoronsky's major works include *Istoriia Pereia-*

slavskoi zemli s drevneishikh vremen do poloviny XIII st. (The History of the Pereiaslav Land from the Earliest Times to the 13th Century, 1897 [his PH D dissertation]), *Inostrannye karty i atlasy XVI i XVII vv. otnosiashchiesia k Iuzhnoi Rossii* (Foreign Maps and Atlases of the 16th and 17th Centuries Concerning Southern Russia, 1901), *Gil'om Levasser de-Boplan i ego istoriko-geograficheskie trudy otnositel'no Iuzhnoi Rossii* (G. Le Vasseur de Beauplan and His Historico-Geographic Works on Southern Russia, 1901), and dozens of articles on excavations of the Trypilian culture, kurhans throughout Ukraine, and excavations of the Saint Sophia Cathedral, the Golden Gate, and other sites around Kiev. A biography of Liaskoronsky and bibliography of his works by K. Melnyk-Antonovych appeared in *ZIFV*, no. 24 (1929).

Liatorytsia River [Ljatorycja] (aka Latorytsia). A left-bank tributary of the Bodrog River (which it joins in southeastern Czechoslovakia). It is 144 km long and drains a basin area of 2,735 sq km. It flows through the Polonynian Beskyd and Volcanic Ukrainian Carpathians within the borders of Transcarpathia oblast. Its main tributaries are the Stara (right-bank) and the Vicha and Kerepets (left-bank). Its waters are used for industrial and domestic consumption as well as for irrigation. The river flows through the city of Mukachiv.

Liatoshynsky, Borys [Ljatošyns'kyj], b 3 January 1895 in Zhytomyr, d 15 April 1968 in Kiev. Composer and teacher. He graduated in law from Kiev University in 1918, and then in music (studying under R. Glière) from the Kiev Conservatory in 1919. He lectured at the conservatory from 1920 and was appointed professor of composition there in 1935. He also held a professorship at the Moscow Conservatory in 1935–8 and 1941–4.

Liatoshynsky is one of the initiators and main representatives of the modern school in Ukrainian music, using expressionistic style and atonal technique. His mastery of composition and instrumentation is shown throughout his repertoire. He began his work in the style of A. Scriabin, but later came under the influence of the French impressionists, and finally under west European expressionism. His contribution to Ukrainian music lies in a skillful blending of Ukrainian themes with contemporary European style. Together with L. *Revutsky, he exerted a profound influence on Ukrainian composers of the younger generation. His main works include the operas *Zolotyi obruch* (The Golden Ring, 1929, based on the I. Franko novelette *Zakhar Berkut*) and *Shchors* (1937–8), five symphonies, an *Overture on Four Ukrainian Folk Themes* (1926), the suites *Taras Shevchenko* (1952) and *Romeo and Juliet* (1955), the *Slavic* concerto for piano and orchestra (1953), and the completion and orchestration of R. Glière's *Concerto for Violin and Orchestra* (1956). He also composed the cantatas, for chorus and orchestra, *Testament* and *Urochysta* (The Solemn One) in 1939; a piano quintet; five string quartets; two piano trios; and many other works for the piano (two sonatas, ballads, and preludes) and the violin. He wrote nearly 50 solo songs to poems by T. Shevchenko, I. Franko, M. Rylsky, V. Sosiura, H. Heine, A. Pushkin, and others; music for the films *Karmeliuk* (1932), *Ivan* (1932, with Yu. Meitus), *Taras Shevchenko* (1950), *Ivan Franko* (1956, with M. Kolessa), *Hryhoryi Skovoroda* (1959), and others; and arrangements of Ukrainian folk songs.

Liatoshynsky also edited and arranged the score for the comic opera *Eneïda* (1927) and for the new edition of M. Lysenko's opera *Taras Bulba* (1936–7).

BIBLIOGRAPHY
Belza, I. *B.M. Liatoshyns'kyi* (Kiev 1947)
Zaporozhets, N. *B.N. Liatoshinskii* (Moscow 1960)
Samokhvalov, V. *Borys Liatoshyns'kyi* (Kiev 1974)
W. Wytwycky

Oksana Liaturynska   Bishop Ivan Liatyshevsky

Liaturynska, Oksana [Ljaturyns'ka] (pseuds: Roksana Vyshnevetska, Oksana Pechenih, Oksana Cherlenivna), b 1 February 1902 in Katerburg, Kremianets county, Volhynia gubernia, d 13 June 1970 in Minneapolis, Minnesota. Writer and sculptor. In 1924 she emigrated; she lived first in Czechoslovakia, then in Germany, and finally in the United States. She began her literary career in Prague and belonged to the Prague group of Ukrainian writers. Her poetic miniatures are noted for their economy of expression and historical themes. Several collections of her poetry were published, including *Husla* (the title refers to a multistring musical instrument; 1938) and *Kniazha emal'* (Princely Enamel, 1941; 2nd edn 1956). She also wrote a book of novellas, *Materynky* (Wild Thyme, 1946). Two collections of her poems for children were published, *Bedryk* (An Epiphany Carol, 1956) and, posthumously, *Iahilka* (A Spring Song, 1971). In her sculptures a synthetic monumental form is predominant. In 1932 she designed the monument to fallen soldiers in Pardubice; in 1939, Ye. Konovalets's grave monument in Rotterdam; in 1941, I. Bilyk's grave monument in Milvazanky; and in 1949, A. Zhyvotko's grave monument in Aschaffenburg. She sculpted busts of T. Shevchenko, S. Petliura, and Ye. Konovalets, historical portraits, and, using different techniques, compositions in various materials. She also created a series of model dolls and worked with ceramics.

Liatychiv. See Letychiv.

Liatyshevsky, Ivan [Liatyševs'kyj], b 17 October 1879 in Bohorodchany, Stanyslaviv county, Galicia, d 27 November 1957 in Stanyslaviv (Ivano-Frankivske). Catholic bishop and professor. After studying in Vienna and Innsbruck he was ordained in 1907 and then taught in Stanyslaviv at a gymnasium and the theological seminary. In 1918–19 he was director of church and religious affairs for the Western Ukrainian National Republic. He became a canon of Stanyslaviv eparchy in 1928 and was consecrated auxiliary bishop of Stanyslaviv in 1930. He was arrested by the Soviet authorities in 1945 and sentenced to 10 years in a labor camp. He returned to Stanyslaviv in 1955.

Liberalism. A political philosophy and movement that aims to maximize individual freedom by means such as representative democracy, the separation of powers, the protection of individual liberties, and the removal of restrictions on private initiative.

Historically, liberalism has flourished mostly in Western Europe and North America, where the growth of substantial middle classes with access to wealth and social mobility has led to a broad social consensus. In Ukraine, as in Eastern Europe generally, liberalism has been identified with a minority of the intelligentsia. In the late 19th century the zemstvos were the vehicle of liberal opposition to tsarist absolutism in the Russian Empire, which included most of Ukraine. M. Drahomanov's *Volnoe slovo* (Geneva 1881–3) was considered the organ of the Zemstvo Union. After the Revolution of 1905 liberal activity intensified. The *Ukrainian Democratic Radical party (UDRP), whose program resembled that of the Russian Constitutional Democrats, was established in 1905. Drawing support from the intelligentsia, the lower and middle bourgeoisie, and the middle peasantry, the UDRP accounted for more than three-quarters of the Ukrainian representation in the Second State Duma. A moderate element of the URDP, led by M. Hrushevsky, S. Yefremov, and Ye. Chykalenko, formed the *Society of Ukrainian Progressives. In 1917 members of the society founded the *Ukrainian Party of Socialists-Federalists (UPSF). Composed of liberal intellectuals but lacking a mass base, the party played an important role in the early stages of the Ukrainian revolution. It supplied well-qualified functionaries to the Central Rada and subsequent governments. The UPSF supported a democratic federation with Russia, constitutional government, and a moderate form of evolutionary socialism. Given the revolutionary situation, the party did not succeed in implementing its program.

In Western Ukraine the *National Democratic party (est 1899) and its successor, the *Ukrainian National Democratic Alliance (1925–39), supported a liberal program. Both parties were coalitions which claimed to stand above the class struggle and to represent the aspirations of the Ukrainian people to national independence. They sought to achieve this independence by parliamentary means and called for the autonomy of Western Ukraine, first in the Habsburg Empire and then in Poland. The National Democrats dominated Ukrainian political life in Galicia before the First World War. The alliance's influence declined, because its policy of accommodation with the Polish government proved to be counterproductive, and because political life became rapidly radicalized in the 1930s. With the Soviet occupation of Western Ukraine the alliance was dissolved. Its later revival in the emigration was merely symbolic. The *Ukrainian Democratic Alliance, established in New York in 1976, represented an attempt by émigré Ukrainian politicans to co-operate with each other on the basis of a liberal consensus.

M. Yurkevich

Liberec. A city (1975 pop 76,000) in northern Czechoslovakia. In March 1920 an internment camp for soldiers of the Ukrainian Galician Army, mostly from Gen A. *Kravs's army group, was set up in its vicinity. It held over 1,000 internees, including 450 officers, 560 soldiers, and 90 women and children. An intensive cultural-educational program was directed by the Cultural and Educational Circle. It included various courses and the publication of the semimonthly *Ukraïns'kyi skytalets'*. V. *Andriievsky was one of the organizers. In April 1921 the camp was moved to *Josefov. A monument to Ukrainian soldiers has been erected in Liberec.

Liberman, Ovsii, b 2 October 1897 in Slavuta, Khmelnytskyi oblast, d 12 March 1983 in Moscow. Economist and engineer. After graduating from Kiev University (1920) and the Kharkiv Engineering and Economics Institute (1933) he lectured in economics at the latter (1947–63) and in statistics at Kharkiv University (1957–63). His 1962 article in *Pravda* opened a wide discussion on new economic policies. Liberman advocated less control by central planners, and rewards to enterprises based on a profit index, to raise the efficiency of the Soviet economy. Some of his ideas were incorporated in A. Kosygin's reforms in 1965. His major works were *Puti povysheniia rentabel'nosti sotsialisticheskikh predpriiatii* (Ways of Raising the Profitability of Socialist Enterprises, 1956) and *Ekonomicheskie metody povysheniia effektivnosti obshchestvennogo proizvodstva* (1970; trans as *Economic Methods and the Effectiveness of Production*, 1971).

Libovicki, Vladimir, b 10 November 1906 in Cheski Novyny, near Ustyluh, Volhynia gubernia, d 18 December 1984 in Prague. Czech ballet dancer and choreographer. Libovicki studied in the ballet school of V. Avramenko in Rivne, where he was trained in Ukrainian folk dance. In 1937 he was appointed artistic director of the Regional Theater in Uzhhorod, where he favored Ukrainian as the language used during rehearsals. In 1938 Libovicki joined the *Nova Stsena theater, where he worked as a director and choreographer and later became artistic director. He was noted for his production of O. Oles's dramatic poem *Nad Dniprom* (On the Banks of the Dnieper). Libovicki played a leading role in the film about Hutsul life *Polonyns'ke kokhannia* (Love in the Mountain Meadows, 1938), the first Ukrainian-language motion picture made in Transcarpathia (it was destroyed in processing). In 1954 Libovicki was appointed choreographer in the operetta group of the Ukrainian National Theater in Prešov. In 1955 he was coauthor, with the composer P. Spisak, of *Marijka*, the first full-length Ukrainian ballet to originate in Czechoslovakia.

Libraries. Information concerning the earliest libraries in Ukraine can be found in chronicles from the 11th century. The oldest Kievan chronicle, *Povist' vremennykh lit*, contains a special section in the year 1037 devoted to Prince Yaroslav the Wise, describing him as a man well versed in books and identifying him as the founder of the first library in Kiev, housed at the St Sophia Cathedral. On the basis of information gathered from preserved specimens of Kievan literature, it has been established that the cathedral library at St Sophia contained approx 500 volumes, including original Greek manuscripts, translations from the Greek prepared by Bulgarian and native authors, and some original books written by Kievan authors. During Yaroslav's reign another library was established (ca 1050) at the Kievan Cave Monastery; it is considered the first monastery library in medieval Ukraine. Thereafter, church and monastery libraries were established in other cities. Private collections were developed by the Kievan princes, and other, smaller private collections were owned by the aristocracy as well as by some priests and monks.

During the 16th century numerous collections of manuscripts (and, later, books) were established by church brotherhoods. The most famous of the libraries belonged to the Lviv Dormition Brotherhood (est 1585–6). That extensive collection of manuscripts and books apparently employed a rudimentary classification system, a significant advance over the simple inventories of earlier monastery libraries (see *Library science). The Lviv Dormition Brotherhood Library was active for many centuries (it survived as the Stauropegion Institute until 1939). Similar brotherhood libraries were established in Western Ukraine in Ostrih, Lutske, Brest, and Drohobych, and in Kiev and Chernihiv. The prominent Kievan Mohyla Academy housed the largest library in 17th-century Ukraine (10,000 vols).

During the 17th and 18th centuries many private collections were developed, most belonging to clergy. Among them were the libraries of P. Mohyla, D. Tuptalo, T. Prokopovych, I. Galiatovsky, L. Baranovych, and S. Yavorsky. Significant private collections were also owned by members of the Ukrainian Cossack nobility (eg, Ya. Markovych, H. Poletyka, M. Khanenko), scholars (eg, I. Samoilovych, A. Rigelman), members of the Ukrainian gentry (eg, I. Lukashevych), government officials (eg, O. Bezborodko, K. Rozumovsky), and merchants (eg, S. and I. Kuliabka, S. Lashkevych).

19th and early 20th centuries. The Kievan Mohyla Academy and similar but smaller institutions (colleges) that were established in Chernihiv (1700), Kharkiv (1727), and Pereiaslav (1738) all had significant academic libraries which later provided the groundwork for library services at the newly created university libraries. By 1917 the library at Kharkiv University (est 1805) consisted of 250,000 volumes. The Kiev University Library (est 1834) developed from the nucleus of the Kremianets Lyceum Library and had grown to over 500,000 volumes by 1913. The Odessa University Library began with the collection of the Richelieu Lyceum and had grown to 314,000 volumes by 1913.

During the 19th century specialized libraries also began to appear, many connected with archival commissions in gubernia capitals or started by scholarly societies (eg, the Historical Society of Nestor the Chronicler in Kiev, the Odessa Historical Society, the Volhynia Research Society in Zhytomyr). In larger cities *public libraries and reading rooms were established. The Odessa Municipal Library (founded 1829) was the first such library in Ukraine; it also became one of the largest, with 60,000 volumes in 1890 and 162,000 in 1911. The Kiev Municipal Library (founded 1866) housed a significant Ukrainian collection donated by M. Yuzefovych. Additional public and private libraries were organized by zemstvos and civic clubs.

After the Revolution of 1905, during a short period of relative laxity in Russian censorship, several private

Ukrainian libraries came into existence, sponsored by
*Prosvita societies and Ukrainian clubs. Following the dis-
solution of those organizations by the Russian government in 1912, the activities of the libraries were curtailed
or completely abandoned. There were 2,739 small rural libraries in Ukraine by 1913 (or one for approx 180 villages),
with an average of 400 volumes per library or reading
room.

Conditions in Western Ukraine under Austro-Hungarian rule were more favorable for the development of
Ukrainian book collections. The oldest university library
in Ukraine was founded in Lviv in 1784, and consisted of
340,000 volumes before the Second World War. Other important research libraries in Lviv were the Ossolineum Institute (est 1817, with 298,000 vols), the Lviv Polytechnical
Institute Library (est 1844, with 84,000 vols), the Baworowski Foundation Library (est 1856, with 55,000 vols),
the National Museum Library (est 1905), the Prosvita Library (20,000 vols), and the Municipal Library (est 1911,
with 20,000 vols). By the late 19th century the People's
Home Library (est 1849) housed a large collection of
Ucrainica, including 100,000 volumes and many manuscripts and documents. The Ukrainian Catholic church
had an important library in the Greek Catholic Theological Academy in Lviv (est 1783, with 8,500 vols) and in
other cities, such as Peremyshl. Significant book and
manuscript collections were also maintained at the monasteries of the Order of St Basil the Great in Lviv (42,000
vols), Krekhiv (15,000 vols), and Buchach (15,000 vols). In
rural communities and smaller towns a network of small
libraries was developed by the Prosvita (3,000 libraries)
and Kachkovsky societies. They were usually attached to
reading rooms in educational institutions.

The most important Western Ukrainian research library was established in Lviv by the Shevchenko Scientific
Society in 1894; it had 90,000 volumes in 1914 and over
200,000 volumes in 1938, including 1,500 manuscripts.
Under the direction of I. Krevetsky and V. Doroshenko the
library became an internationally recognized center for
depository material and bibliographical research, and it
established interlibrary loans with all leading university
libraries in Europe. In 1939 the library was transformed
into a separate unit of the Soviet Ukrainian Academy of
Sciences.

In Bukovyna the largest library was at Chernivtsi University (420,000 vols in 1936). The Ruska Besida society
maintained a network of 150 smaller libraries for the use
of the local population. In comparison with that in Galicia,
library development in Transcarpathia was modest.
Among its oldest libraries were the monastic libraries established by the Basilian order at Chernecha Hora (est
1720, with 8,000 vols) and the Greek Catholic church in
Hrushiv (est 1775, with 15,000 vols). The library of the
Prosvita society in Uzhhorod (est 1921) also ran a small rural network of libraries (235 in 1935). Following the Soviet
occupation of Galicia and Volhynia (1939), Bukovyna
(1940), and Transcarpathia (1945) all existing libraries
were nationalized and incorporated into the Soviet centralized library system.

Under the Soviet regime. During its independence
(1918–21) Ukraine experienced a growth in libraries and
book production. On 2 August 1918 the National Library
of the Ukrainian State was established with a nucleus of
40,000 volumes. Its collection had grown to 500,000 volumes by 1919 and over one million volumes by 1921.

In November 1922 the Soviet authorities issued a decree
on the 'Establishment of the Unified System of Libraries,'
which authorized the maintenance of academic libraries
by the People's Commissariat of Education and the creation of a network of people's (public and regional) libraries in cities and villages. A number of larger libraries were
established from nationalized book collections, including
the Central Children's Library in Mykolaiv, the Central
Jewish Library in Kiev and a similar Jewish library in
Odessa, the Polish State Central Library in Kiev, and other
specialized larger libraries, such as the October Revolution Library in Katerynoslav.

The largest library in Ukraine during that period was
still the National Library, which was renamed the National (or All-People's) Library of Ukraine in 1919 (from 1965
the *Central Scientific Library of the AN URSR [now ANU]).
Many specialized private collections, and even entire libraries, were transferred to that central library. In 1932 the
National Library housed 2.5 million volumes in Kiev and
125,000 in its Vinnytsia branch. Following the abolish-
ment of the autonomy of the VUAN and its reorganization
by the Soviet authorities into the AN URSR in the 1930s, the
Kiev and Vinnytsia libraries merged, and their holdings
were consolidated into a single library belonging to the
academy, consisting of over 7 million volumes (1936).

During the 1920s all universities were abolished and replaced by 'institutes of public education,' and their library
collections (except textbooks) were transferred either to
the National Library in Kiev or to local central libraries. As
a result of the reorganization the Odessa State Library
became the second-largest library in Ukraine (2.3 million
vols in 1932); smaller collections were found at the
Kharkiv Central Library, the Poltava Central Scientific Library, and elsewhere.

In 1934 the universities were re-established, and by
1935 the Kharkiv University Library had 740,000 volumes,
the Kiev University Library, 700,000 volumes, and the
Odessa University Library, 250,000 volumes. The Soviet
government was also interested in developing the network of public (or 'people's') libraries in the cities and villages, which in 1922 had consisted of 3,067 libraries and
approx two million volumes. The number of such libraries
increased rapidly to 10,000 libraries with 21 million volumes in 1933 and 16,000 libraries with 27 million volumes
in 1938.

Repressions and reforms of the Soviet regime in the
1930s stifled the development of libraries in Ukraine. A
decree 'About Library Work in the Soviet Union' (March
1934) brought to an end the limited autonomy enjoyed by
Ukrainian libraries during the 1920s. Strong censorship
was introduced in academic libraries, and many books
found unfavorable to communist ideology were removed.

Research libraries suffered particularly great losses
during the German-Soviet War of 1941–5. When Ukraine
was occupied by German troops, many collections were
destroyed during the hurried evacuation of the Soviet
authorities, and remaining collections were seriously
depleted by the Germans. Some of the lost collections
were recovered after the end of the war; the National Library (in 1948–65 the State Public Library of the Ukrainian
SSR), for example, recovered its old imprints and manuscripts, which had been evacuated by the Soviet authorities to Ufa in 1941, and also part of the collection taken to
Germany.

Such losses have continued to occur on a smaller scale. During the 1960s and 1970s a number of valuable collections of Ukrainian prerevolutionary materials were destroyed in unexplained circumstances, either by fire or through some kind of negligence. In May 1964 arson in the Central Scientific Library of the ANU resulted in the loss of the singular collection of M. Hrushevsky, as well as of other historical materials. Not long afterward the famous Vydubychi Monastery and its library, containing rare books from the 17th and 18th centuries, were also destroyed by fire. In the early 1970s a significant part of the rare books collection of S. *Maslov was lost from the Kiev University Library, apparently through negligence. In 1974 a fire destroyed a large number of books of V. Kolosova's collection in the library of the ANU Institute of Linguistics. Historic musical documents, housed at the library of the Lysenko Higher Institute of Music in Lviv, perished in 1977.

Postwar library development in the Soviet Union was influenced by such All-Union decrees as 'On the Current Status of Libraries and Their Improvement' (1959) and 'The Increasing Role of Libraries in the Communist Education of Workers and in the Scientific and Technological Process' (1974). A high degree of standardization and uniformity was applied in library organization and services, in spite of the existing diversity of nationalities, cultures, and library traditions. The Soviet press and library professional literature stressed that the principal task of libraries was to propagandize the resolutions of Party congresses and to explain the policy and decisions of the Communist party and the Soviet government. Most of the public libraries and many academic and specialized libraries in Ukraine were under the jurisdiction of the Ukrainian SSR Council of Ministers and the Ministry of Culture.

Political vigilance in regard to book selection was enforced by a network of distributing centers which published lists of recommended book acquisitions and were actively involved in centralized acquisition processing. The largest distributing center for research libraries, supplying over 2,000 such institutions throughout the Soviet Union, was located in Moscow; regional distribution centers in Ukraine existed in Kiev, Kharkiv, Odessa, and Lviv. They were the main source for the bulk of acquisitions by academic, public, and school libraries. In that centralized system each library was supplied with books under an annual contract that specified the particular library's subject of interest, the average number of copies required, and the proposed expenditure on acquisitions during the year.

The rise and fall of leading personalities in the Soviet Union, and especially in Ukraine, accompanied by abrupt shifts and turns in official policies, resulted in a constant process of weeding library collections of 'deteriorated material' and 'obsolete publications.' An estimated 4 percent of public library holdings in the USSR were withdrawn from circulation every year; several factors indicate that the percentage was significantly higher in Ukraine. According to the observations of Western scholars, special collections of confiscated material existed in many of the larger libraries (see *Spetsfondy). Those collections included books by 'enemies of the people,' 'obsolete' histories, foreign works inimical to the Soviet Union, and even pornography.

In a typical Soviet library there were usually at least two types of catalogs. The readers' or public catalog provided a selective coverage of the collection; occasionally it contained annotations guiding the user to the most 'popular' or politically significant material. The official catalog served as an inventory of library holdings, supposedly covering the whole collection (and possibly including some innocuous foreign material). Only researchers and some advanced students with written authorization were allowed to consult the official catalog. It is believed that special inventories or catalogs of removed and politically undesirable materials were maintained in most research libraries and in some larger district libraries. When certain Soviet personalities were rehabilitated, their works might have been reinstated, at least in the official catalog.

New building of the Central Scientific Library of the Academy of Sciences of Ukraine

As of 1985 the Central Scientific Library of the ANU was the largest library in Ukraine. It housed some 12 million volumes, including 291,000 manuscripts, 1.6 million periodicals, 40,000 unpublished dissertations, and a substantial number of nonbook materials. Of special interest were its holdings of incunabula and rare books. That library, along with several others in Ukraine, received depository copies of all books published in the Soviet Union. Its affiliate, the *Lviv Scientific Library of the ANU, had approx six million items, including 75,000 manuscripts and a substantial number of rare books.

University libraries with significant collections can be found at Kiev University (2.7 million vols in 1985), Lviv University (2.5 million vols), Kharkiv University (2.3 million vols), Odessa University (3.5 million vols), Chernivtsi University (1.7 million vols), Uzhhorod University (1.2

million vols), and Dnipropetrovske University (1.2 million vols). Smaller collections are housed at some 140 libraries of pedagogical institutes, such as the Kiev Pedagogical Institute (700,000 vols) and the Drohobych Pedagogical Institute (415,000 vols); ANU institutes, such as the Institute of Linguistics (150,000 vols) and the Institute of History (120,000 vols); and libraries subordinated to various ministries, such as the Library of the Ministry of Culture (130,000 vols) and the Ministry of Education Pedagogical Library (260,000 vols).

By the 1980s there were also over 2,000 specialized libraries in Ukraine, the largest of which were the State Republican Scientific and Technical Library of the Ukrainian Scientific Research Institute of Scientific-Technical Information and Technical-Economic Research in Kiev (est 1935, with 1.7 million vols), the Library of the Kiev Institute of Light Industry (est 1930, with 600,000 vols), and the Central Research Library of the Ministry of Agricultural Industries (est 1944, with 360,000 vols). The Ukrainian SSR had approx 100 large industrial libraries, such as the Kiev Library of Building Industries (est 1944, with 330,000 vols) and the Kiev Library of Automobile Transportation of the Ministry of Special Education (est 1945, with 288,000 vols), and several hundred smaller libraries. Among the 36 sizable agricultural libraries was the Central Scientific Agricultural Library in Kiev (est 1921, with 480,000 vols). There were 73 medical libraries, the largest of which was the Republican Scientific Medical Library in Kiev (est 1930, with 850,000 vols). Many larger regional libraries also served as public district libraries, and usually reflected regional economic and professional interests. The Korolenko State Scientific Library in Kharkiv (est 1886 as a public library), for example, housed 5.8 million volumes, with emphasis on science and technology, and the State Regional Library for Adults in Donetske (est 1926) contained 1.4 million volumes, with emphasis on technology, particularly mining and metallurgy.

Most secondary and eight-year schools had their own libraries of 2,000 to 5,000 volumes. Larger libraries were found in the professional schools, including tekhnikums. The elementary schools, especially in rural districts, had rather small collections, and children used local libraries for supplementary reading. In 1980 there was a total of 59,300 libraries in Ukraine (including school libraries), with combined holdings of 883 million volumes; in 1985 there were 57,900 libraries in Ukraine (compared to 165,000 in the RSFSR), with 1,011 million volumes (compared to 3,019 million vols in the RSFSR). (See the table.)

Public libraries in Ukraine, 1984

Type of library	No. of libraries	Holdings in thousands of vols
Oblast	37	100,766
Raion	521	18,850
Urban	1,852	46,621
Rural	18,242	144,672
Children's	1,242	38,658
Collective-farm	138	467
Trade-union	3,935	55,588
Total	25,995	411,167

Abroad. Through the efforts of Ukrainian émigrés, many educational institutions, churches, civic clubs, and professional organizations have supported libraries of varying size and utility. Some important collections of Ukrainian materials were transferred out of Ukraine to existing university and state libraries. The Austrian State Library, for example, obtained depository copies of all Ukrainian books published in Austria up to 1918. After the First World War the largest émigré Ukrainian libraries were founded in Czechoslovakia, at the Ukrainian Free University in Prague (est 1922, with 10,000 vols in 1938), the Ukrainian Husbandry Academy in Poděbrady (est 1922, with 30,000 vols), the Ukrainian Higher Pedagogical Institute in Prague (est 1923, with 11,000 vols in 1936), the Museum of Ukraine's Struggle for Independence in Prague (est 1925, with 10,000 vols in the main collection and 35 special collections, including more than 1,000 complete sets of Ukrainian periodicals and newspapers), and the Ukrainian Historical Chamber in the Czechoslovakian Foreign Ministry in Prague (est 1931, with 17,000 vols in 1936). With the occupation of Czechoslovakia by the Soviet army in 1945, most of those collections were taken to the Soviet Union, destroyed, or partially integrated into the Slavic collection of the Prague University Library.

The libraries of the Ukrainian scientific institutes in Berlin (est 1926, with 32,000 vols) and Warsaw (est 1930, with 7,000 vols and several special collections, including the archives of M. Drahomanov) were destroyed during the Second World War. The *Petliura Ukrainian Library in Paris (est 1929, with 15,000 vols by 1940) was confiscated and shipped to Germany during the war. It was re-established in Paris after the war (10,000 vols).

Postwar Ukrainian émigrés established new libraries as part of scholarly and educational institutions. Two important libraries were founded in Rome, at the Ukrainian Catholic University (20,000 vols) and St Josaphat's Ukrainian Pontifical College (15,000 vols, including valuable archives pertaining to the history of the Ukrainian Catholic church). In Munich a significant collection of Ucrainica was established by Ukrainian émigrés at the Ukrainian Free University Library (12,000 vols). During the 1950s the Shevchenko Scientific Society Library was transferred from Munich to Sarcelles, France (in 1978 it had 20,000 vols), and in 1950 the Ukrainian Academy of Arts and Sciences Library, originally in Augsburg, Germany, was transferred to New York (in 1978 it contained 20,000 vols and a rich collection of manuscripts).

Other libraries established in the United States during the 1950s were the St Basil's College Library (15,000 vols) and the Ukrainian Diocesan Museum and Library (20,000 vols) in Stamford, Connecticut, the Ukrainian National Museum Research Library in Chicago (12,000 vols), the Ukrainian Orthodox Church of America Library in South Bound Brook, New Jersey (14,000 vols), and the Ukrainian Museum-Archives in Cleveland (6,000 vols).

The largest collections of Ukrainian materials in the United States are found at the Library of Congress (61,500 vols), the University of Illinois (45,000 vols), the New York Public Library (25,000 vols), Harvard University (60,000 vols), the University of Michigan (18,000 vols), Indiana University (18,000 vols), the University of Chicago (16,000 vols), and the University of California at Berkeley (15,000 vols).

In Canada significant Ukrainian collections are housed

in libraries at the Basilian Fathers' Museum in Mundare, Alberta (20,000 vols), the Ukrainian Fraternal Society in Vancouver (8,000 vols), the St Vladimir Institute (22,000 vols) and the Ukrainian National Federation (20,000 vols) in Toronto, and St Andrew's College (40,000 vols) and the Ukrainian Cultural and Educational Centre (20,000 vols) in Winnipeg.

Collections of Ukrainian materials are also housed in the libraries of the University of Toronto (20,000 vols), the University of Alberta (15,000 vols), and the University of Manitoba (30,000 vols). The National Library and the Public Archives of Canada, located in Ottawa, have significant collections of Ukrainian-Canadian folklore and Ucrainica (the latter including the personal archives of V. Kubijovyč).

Large collections of Ukrainian materials and Ucrainica are housed in leading university and research libraries in Europe (Warsaw, Prague, Vienna, Helsinki, Paris, Munich, London), in the Svydnyk Museum of Ukrainian Culture (now the Dukhnovych Museum) in Slovakia, in Rumanian libraries, in Moscow (the Lenin Library and the Saltykov-Shchedrin Library), and in the libraries of the Russian Academy of Sciences in Moscow and St Petersburg.

BIBLIOGRAPHY
Bykovs'kyi, L. *Natsional'na biblioteka Ukraïns'koï derzhavy* (Berlin 1923)
Krevets'kyi, I. *Biblioteka Naukovoho tovarystva im. Shevchenka* (Lviv 1923)
Balyka, D. *Biblioteka v mynulomu* (Kiev 1925)
Zlenko, P. *Pryvatni biblioteky v mynulomu na Ukraïni* (Lviv 1937)
'Library of the Academy of Sciences of the Ukrainian Soviet Socialist Republic,' UNESCO *Bulletin for Libraries*, no. 12 (May 1958)
Horecky, P. *Libraries and Bibliographical Centers in the Soviet Union* (Bloomington, Ind 1959)
Hutians'kyi, S. (ed). *Tsentral'na naukova biblioteka: Bibliohrafichnyi pokazhchyk, 1919–1969* (Kiev 1970)
Francis, S. (ed). *Libraries in the USSR* (Hamden, Conn 1971)
50 rokiv Tsentral'noï naukovoï biblioteky AN URSR (Kiev 1974)
Istoriia Tsentral'noi nauchnoi biblioteki Akademii nauk Ukrainskoi SSR (Kiev 1979)
Gol'denberg, L.; et al (eds). *Kniga i knizhnoe delo v Ukrainskoi SSR: Sbornik dokumentov i materialov*, 2 vols (Kiev 1985–6)
Grimsted, P. *Archives and Manuscript Repositories in the USSR: Ukraine and Moldavia*, vol 1, *General Bibliography and Institutional Directory* (Princeton 1988)

B. Wynar

Library science. Although *libraries are known to have existed in the Kievan Rus' period, the first recorded name of a Ukrainian library scientist is that of P. Yarkovsky. In 1809–32 he was chief librarian of the Kremianets Lyceum, where he taught bibliology and established a bibliographic system. He also served as director of the library of Kiev University.

In the 19th century, library sciences were entirely applied and rarely theoretical. In 1838 S. Bohorodsky and E. Hofman's *Nastavlenie bibliotekariu universiteta sv Vladimira* (Instructions for the Librarians of St Vladimir's [Kiev] University) was published. Innovations in the field appeared in N. Bunge's *Pravila biblioteki* (Rules of the Library, 1880) and other trade publications.

Around that time a number of excellent catalogs and inventories were compiled at the libraries of Kharkiv University (V. Dzhunkovsky, 1824, 1866), Kiev University (A. Krasovsky, 5 vols, 1854–8), Odessa University (O. Ko-

chubynsky, S. Yaroshenko, 3 vols, 1878–1914), and the Kiev Theological Academy (A. Krylovsky, 14 vols, 1890–1915). Collections of manuscripts held by libraries attracted particular attention; descriptions of such collections, however, were more archeographic than bibliographic. Among them were M. Petrov's *Opisanie rukopisnykh sobranii, nakhodiashchikhsia v Kieve* (Description of Manuscript Collections Found in Kiev, 3 vols, 1891–1904), I. Svientsitsky's guide to the collections of the People's Home in Lviv, and S. Maslov's *Obzor rukopisei Biblioteki Imperatorskogo universiteta sv. Vladimira* (Survey of Manuscripts in the Library of the Imperial University of St Vladimir [Kiev], 1910). M. Popruzhenko, S. Ptashytsky, and V. Suboch wrote studies on the collections of individual libraries. In 1910 Z. Kuzelia promoted the establishment of a public library system.

Specialized studies in library science became widespread in the 1920s and 1930s. Yu. Mezhenko studied planning in large and scientific libraries (1923, 1926), D. Balyka studied literacy education (1926, 1927), M. Vasylenko (1919) and O. Ohloblyn (1927) studied the history of the Kremenets Lyceum Library, and L. Bykovsky produced a systematic overview of problems in library science (1923). Catalogs were compiled on Ukrainian materials in the libraries of Kiev (V. Barvinok), Kamianets-Podilskyi (Ye. Sitsinsky), Leningrad and Samara (V. Peretts), and Paris (E. Borschak). Many works were published about the libraries in Kiev (L. Bykovsky, S. Posternak, M. Saharda), Odessa (I. Faas, B. Komarov, Yu. Tiuneeva), and Lviv (B. Barvinsky, V. Doroshenko, I. Krevetsky). B. Bodnarsky promoted the decimal system of classification.

The field of library studies became more intensive and varied after the All-Ukrainian Council of Library Workers in Kharkiv (November 1923) and the Conference of Scientific Libraries of the Ukrainian SSR in Kiev (December 1925). A chair of library science was established in 1925 at the National Library of Ukraine (from 1965 the *Central Scientific Library of the AN URSR [now ANU]). Library science publications included *Bibliotechnyi zbirnyk* (3 issues, 1926–7) and *Zhurnal bibliotekoznavstva ta bibliohrafiï* (4 issues, 1927–30).

The repressive policies of the succeeding years, designed to destroy Ukrainian culture, interrupted the development of Ukrainian library science, and many scholars and workers in the field were persecuted.

After the Second World War Ukrainian library science was, until 1991, completely subordinated to the central authorities in Moscow (although work in Lviv maintained an element of national content). The *Lviv Scientific Library of the ANU has regularly published thematic anthologies (with varying titles) from 1972. Guides to incunabula in Ukrainian libraries have been published by M. Heppener, F. Maksymenko, and V. Mykytas. Other researchers in the field include M. Humeniuk, D. Isaievych, Ye. Kolesnyk, M. Valo, and H. Zlenko.

BIBLIOGRAPHY
Mezhenko, Iu. *Bibliotechna tekhnika* (Kiev 1922)
Bykovs'kyi, L. *Zamitky pro knyhoznavstvo ta knyhovzhyvannia* (Poděbrady 1923)
Siropolko, S. *Korotkyi kurs bibliotekoznavstva* (Lviv 1923)
Levyts'kyi, V. *Poradnyk dlia bibliotekariv* (Lviv 1938)
Chandler, G. *Libraries, Documentation, and Bibliography in the USSR, 1917–1971: Survey and Critical Analysis of Soviet Studies, 1967–1971* (London 1972)

Skrypnyk, T. *Istoriia bibliotechnogo dela na Ukraine, 1917–1932* (Kharkiv 1975)
'Naiholovnisha ukraïns'ka literatura pro bibliotekoznavstvo,' *Ukraïns'ka knyha*, 1976, no. 1
Kasinec, E. *Slavic Books and Bookmen* (New York 1984)

S. Bilokin

Lice (*voshi*). Any of the more than 3,000 species of insect parasites of the order Phthiraptera. Infestation with lice is fostered by inadequate sanitation and crowded living conditions. The human louse (Anoplura, *Pediculus humanus*) carries three dangerous diseases: relapsing fever, trench fever, and *typhus. During the First World War and the ensuing struggle for Ukrainian independence the Ukrainian army and the Ukrainian population were decimated by lice-borne typhus. The fact that typhus is transmitted by lice was first demonstrated by the Ukrainian microbiologist M. *Hamaliia, in 1908. Two years later, Hamaliia proved the value of eradicating lice as a means of eliminating typhus.

Lichkov, Boris [Ličkov], b 30 July 1888 in Irkutsk, Siberia, d ? Geologist. A member of the Ukrainian Scientific Society in Kiev, he taught at the Kiev Institute of People's Education in the 1920s. Together with V. Luchytsky he founded the Ukrainian Geological Committee in 1917 and then established it as an autonomous branch of the St Petersburg Geological Committee in 1922. His main scholarly interests were the geology and geomorphology of the Dnieper region. With Luchytsky he established a scheme of the hydrogeological regions of Ukraine. Lichkov disappeared in 1934 during the Stalinist terror.

Lider, Danylo, b 8 May 1917 in Viktorivka, Donets county, Don Cossack Region. Scenery designer. He graduated from the Repin Institute of Painting, Sculpture, and Architecture in Leningrad in 1956 and then worked in Leningrad, Moscow, and Cheliabinsk before moving to Kiev. In 1964 he designed scenery for the Kiev Operetta Theater and the Kiev Russian Drama Theater, and in 1965 he began working as principal designer for the Kiev Ukrainian Drama Theater (eg, he designed sets for I. Kocherha's *Yaroslav Mudryi* [Yaroslav the Wise, 1970]).

Liège. A city in Belgium (1990 pop 199,000); the center of its Walloon section, and site of the country's largest concentration of Ukrainians. Until 1919 the few Ukrainians who lived there formed the Ruthenian Neutral Circle (Cercle Neutre Ruthène). In the interwar period the Ukrainian community grew to about 200, including many political exiles and 25 students. Main organizations included the Ukrainian Hromada and the Society of Former Ukrainian Combatants in Belgium. In 1945 the number of Ukrainians in the city grew to 2,000, the increase consisting mainly of women from displaced persons' camps in Germany. After a wave of emigration to North America, the community in Liège stabilized at around 1,000. There are two local Ukrainian parishes, one Catholic and one Orthodox. Other organizations include the Union of Ukrainians in Belgium (SUB), branches of the Ukrainian Relief Committee, the Ukrainian Women's Association of Belgium, and the Ukrainian Youth Association (SUM). The St Sophia Community Center was built in Liège in 1978 and is used by local cultural and religious groups.

Liekh, Ivan [Ljex], b 1868 in Zhovkva, Galicia, d 7 December 1950 in Prudentópolis, Brazil. He emigrated to Brazil as a young man and worked from 1899 as a teacher in the first Ukrainian school in Prudentópolis. In 1910 he was put in charge of organizing new immigrant colonies. For his contribution to the development of Paraná he was appointed colonel of the 61st Cavalry Regiment, and he held a number of municipal offices.

Illia Lifshyts   Yevhen Lifshyts

Lifshyts, Illia [Lifšyc', Illja] (Lifshits, Ilia), b 13 January 1917 in Kharkiv, d 23 October 1982 in Moscow. Theoretical physicist; full member of the AN URSR (now ANU) from 1967 and the USSR Academy of Sciences from 1970. A graduate of Kharkiv University (1936) and the Kharkiv Polytechnical Institute (1938), he worked at the ANU Physical-Technical Institute in Kharkiv (1937–68) and was a physics professor at Kharkiv University (1944–64). He moved to Moscow in 1968. He made significant contributions to the electron theory of metals, the dynamic theory of real crystals, the theory of disordered systems, and the kinetics of second-order phase transitions.

Lifshyts, Yevhen [Lifšyc', Jevhen] (Lifshits, Evgenii), b 21 February 1915 in Kharkiv, d 29 October 1985 in Moscow. Theoretical physicist; full member of the USSR Academy of Sciences from 1979. A graduate of the Kharkiv Polytechnical Institute (1933), he worked at the AN URSR (now ANU) Physical-Technical Institute in Kharkiv (1933–8). In 1939 he moved to Moscow. He made significant contributions to ferromagnetism and relativistic cosmology, and with L. *Landau authored the landmark 10-volume textbook series *Course of Theoretical Physics*, which was translated into English and many other languages.

Liga vyzvolennia Ukrainy. See Canadian League for Ukraine's Liberation.

Light industry. A group of industries that produce consumer goods from different raw materials. It includes the primary processing of cotton, wool, silk, leather, hemp, linen, jute, and fur; the production of synthetic textiles; and the manufacture of fabrics, clothing, furs, and shoes.

In Ukraine light industry originated with domestic handicrafts and cottage industry in the early 10th century. By the 12th century some of the trades in the larger cities

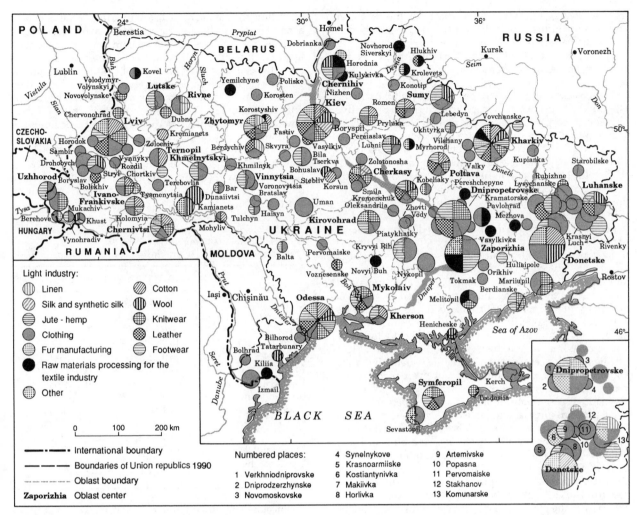

Light industry:
- Linen
- Silk and synthetic silk
- Jute - hemp
- Clothing
- Fur manufacturing
- Raw materials processing for the textile industry
- Other
- Cotton
- Wool
- Knitwear
- Leather
- Footwear

————·— International boundary
———— Boundaries of Union republics 1990
- - - - - Oblast boundary
Zaporizhia Oblast center

Numbered places:
1 Verkhniodniprovske
2 Dniprodzerzhynske
3 Novomoskovske
4 Synelnykove
5 Krasnoarmiiske
6 Kostiantynivka
7 Makiivka
8 Horlivka
9 Artemivske
10 Popasna
11 Pervomaiske
12 Stakhanov
13 Komunarske

had begun to participate in a wider commercial network. In the 14th to 16th centuries the division between the towns and the villages became sharper as a distinct stratum of independent tradesmen arose and organized itself into guilds, first in Western Ukraine and then in the Dnieper region. Some branches of light industry, particularly woolen-cloth and linen manufacturing, were established in the 17th century. The woolen factories were usually owned by landowners and employed serf labor, but leather work manufactures were mostly under the control of merchants and burghers.

In the second half of the 19th century, Russian economic policy discouraged the development of light industry on a larger scale in Ukraine and encouraged it in central Russia and Poland. As a result most branches of light industry in Ukraine continued to operate at the level of the cottage industry and trade shop. A few larger factories were set up only in the leather and jute-hemp industries: leather factories in Berdychiv, Kiev, and Vasylkiv (1855–65), a jute factory in Odessa (1885), and a rope factory in Kharkiv (1896). The success of the policy is evident in the number of workers employed by large and small manufacturing enterprises in Ukraine (see table 1). In 1912 there were only one clothing and two footwear factories in Ukraine. Ukraine's textile industry accounted for only 0.9 percent of the empire's output. In 1913 light industry ac-

counted for only 2.6 percent of the output of large enterprises in Ukraine and for only 2 percent of Ukraine's labor force. Hence, Ukraine exported a large part of its raw materials (wool, leather, etc) to central Russia, Poland, and other regions of the empire and imported manufactured goods. The great disproportion between light and heavy industry in Ukraine underlines the colonial nature of Ukraine's economy at that time.

A similar situation existed in the western Ukrainian territories under Austrian rule. In 1910 there were only 15 light-industry enterprises employing over 20 workers. Among them were several textile factories that employed 100 to 150 workers, such as Heller's weaving factory in Kolomyia, the linen and batting factories in Stanyslaviv, the kilim-weaving factory in Hlyniany, and a few clothes factories in Lviv and Stanyslaviv. Most light-industry en-

TABLE 1
Number of workers in large and small enterprises in Ukraine in 1912 (in 1,000s)

Branch of industry	Large	Small
Fiber processing	8.9	156.8
Leather and footwear manufacturing	1.7	73.7
Clothes manufacturing	0.4	47.0

terprises were small-scale, particularly in the footwear and clothing industries. Light industry in Ukraine did not follow the pattern of development, into large-scale manufacturing, that took place in Western Europe, North America, and some parts of the Russian Empire in the 19th century.

In the 1920s during the NEP period, light industry in the Ukrainian SSR grew somewhat, through private initiative and some reorganization of the manufacturing process. The output of the textile industry grew from 34.6 million rubles' worth in 1913 to 69.2 million in 1927 (at fixed 1926–7 prices). The fur and leather footwear industries expanded sixfold. The clothing industry, which had been hardly visible, produced 119.4 million rubles' worth of goods. Small enterprises of the knitwear industry multiplied rapidly in the 1920s, thanks mainly to private initiatives. In general, Ukrainian light industry attained its prewar level of production in 1923–5. Most of the production continued to be concentrated in small enterprises. In 1926–7, large factories produced 1.32 million pairs of leather footwear, and small enterprises, 7.22 million pairs. Large and small enterprises of the clothing industry produced 24.3 million and 153.8 million rubles' worth of goods respectively. As agriculture was collectivized and supplies of raw materials decreased, and as the development of heavy industry was speeded up, light industry stopped expanding. Most of the smaller enterprises were abolished. By 1932 Ukraine's textile production had not even reached the prewar level. The output of woolen and semiwoolen fabrics had increased only slightly, from 5,285,000 m in 1913 to 6,625,000 m in 1932. The footwear, knitwear, and clothing industries fared somewhat better. During the First Five-Year Plan new leather factories were built in Kiev, Kharkiv, and Poltava, and the Gorky Clothing and Luxemburg Knitwear factories in Kiev were reconstructed. From 1927 to 1932, the output of Ukraine's light industry rose from 404 to 1,369 million rubles' worth. Most growth occurred in the clothing and knitwear industries. The industry's largest enterprises in the interwar period were the knitwear plants in Kiev, Kharkiv, and Odessa; the woolen-cloth complex in Kiev; the cotton-spinning factory in Poltava; the Gorky Clothing Factory in Kiev; and a number of leather factories in the larger cities. In 1940 light industry accounted for 10 percent of the output of large-scale production in Ukraine (2.6 percent in 1913). Its share in the USSR output was highest in the jute-hemp (28.6 percent), knitted underwear (24.6 percent), footwear (19 percent), and socks and hose (16 percent) industries. Light industry was weakest in the Donbas. Ukraine continued to import many textile goods from Russia and other parts of the Soviet Union.

After the Second World War the output of Ukraine's light industry grew significantly, owing to larger harvests of industrial crops and improvements in technology. In 1959–69, 33 new large enterprises were set up, and 79 were expanded and rebuilt. The largest cotton manufacturing complex in the USSR was built in Kherson, as well as a cotton mill in Ternopil, a wool-carding plant in Chernihiv, a silk manufacturing plant in Darnytsia, linen factories in Rivne and Zhytomyr, a shoe factory in Lubni, cotton-spinning factories in Lviv and Kiev, and clothing plants in Artemivske, Drohobych, Mykolaiv, and Pereiaslav-Khmelnytskyi. Today there are about 600 light-industry enterprises in Ukraine. The level of concentration and co-operation among factories has improved. Since the 1960s a number of production associations have been formed, such as the Prohres footwear company, the Svitanok leather company, and the Maiak clothing company, all in Lviv; the Zoria clothing company in Drohobych; and the Ukraïna clothing company in Kiev. The level of capital investment in light industry rose considerably: beginning with the Ninth Five-Year Plan, more than a billion rubles have been invested. The production of synthetic fibers out of residual products of the oil, coal, and gas industries, which in the 1980s accounted for 20 percent of the output, contributed to the growth of light industry. The production process has been highly automated. Table 2 gives an overview of the growth of light industry in Ukraine from 1913 to 1988.

TABLE 2
Output of Ukraine's light industry, 1913–88
(percentage of the Russian Empire or USSR output in parentheses

	1913	1940	1960	1980	1986	1988
Cotton fabrics (millions of m)	4.7 (0.2)	13.8 (0.3)	96.0 (1.5)	–	–	–
Woolen fabrics (millions of m)	5.3 (4.9)	12.0 (10.0)	19.1 (5.6)	–	–	–
Silk fabrics (millions of m)	–	40.0 (4.9)	–	–	–	–
Knitted outerwear (millions of items)	–	12.0 (20.5)	21.7 (19.4)	79.0 (16.5)	81.6	–
Knitted underwear (millions of items)	–	30.3 (24.3)	106.9 (22.6)	214.8 (18.8)	246.0	–
Hose (millions of pairs)	–	79.4 (16.3)	212.9 (22.1)	353.7 (21.2)	398.2 (20.2)	413.7
Leather footwear (millions of pairs)	–	40.8 (19.3)	76.8 (18.3)	177.2 (23.8)	186.9 (23.3)	190.8

Since the mid-1970s statistical data on Ukraine's output of cotton, woolen, and silk textiles have not been published. Figures exist only for the entire USSR. It is reasonable to estimate that Ukraine's share of the USSR output decreased steadily. There are no figures on Ukraine's production of linen. Ukraine's output of semimanufactured goods, such as textile fibers and yarns, is given in table 3.

The distribution of light-industry plants in Ukraine remains uneven. The Donets-Dnieper economic region, where heavy industry is highly concentrated, accounts for only 15 percent of the country's textiles output, up from 6.5 percent in 1970 and 10.5 percent in 1975. The respective percentages for the southwestern region in 1970 and 1975

TABLE 3
Production of textile fibers and yarns, 1940–87
(in 1,000 metric tonnes)

	1940	1970	1980	1987
Linen fiber	1.3	40.7	67.4	106.3
Hemp fiber	24.6	34.6	12.5	15.3
Washed wool	11.2	35.1	35.1	34.8
Raw silk		0.2	0.1	0.1
Cotton yarn	12.2	94.4	135.7	157.6
Linen yarn	1.3	21.1	24.1	27.5
Wool yarn	6.0	34.7	48.0	44.2

were 24.6 and 45.3, and for the southern region, 68.9 and 44.2. The southwestern economic region contains all of Ukraine's linen industry and 75 percent of its silk industry. There is a silk textiles complex in Cherkasy and a technical textiles plant in Lysychanske. The leather industry is also distributed unevenly: 75 percent of it is in the southwestern region, and another 12 percent is in two other regions. Such uneven distribution raises the cost of the industry's products, as does the practice of exporting yarn, washed wool, and other semimanufactured goods to Russia. The cotton industry in Ukraine is dependent on raw materials imported from Central Asia and Transcaucausia. Except for the clothing and knitwear industries, which at least meet some of the demands, there is little evidence to suggest that the situation of Ukraine's light industry will improve in the near future.

BIBLIOGRAPHY
Vynar, B. *Rozvytok ukraïns'koï lehkoï promyslovosty* (Denver 1955)
Lehka promyslovist' Ukraïny 1917–57 (Kiev 1957)
Nesterenko, O. *Rozvytok promyslovosti na Ukraïni*, vol 3 (Kiev 1966)
Lehka promyslovist' Ukraïns'koï RSR za 50 rokiv radians'koï vlady (Kiev 1967)
Derev'iankin, T. *Ekonomichnyi rozvytok Radians'koï Ukraïny, 1917–70* (Kiev 1970)
Rizhkov, I. *Nauchno-tekhnicheskii progress i effektivnost' osnovnykh fondov v legkoi promyshlennosti* (Kiev 1973)

B. Wynar

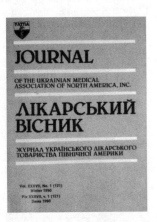

Likars'kyi visnyk (New York)

Likars'kyi visnyk (Physician's Herald). The official journal of the *Ukrainian Medical Association of North America, published since May 1954, at first semiannually and since 1958 quarterly. In 1962 its office moved from New York to Chicago. About one-third of the journal is devoted to scientific articles, including original research, conference papers, and reviews of medical publications. Another third addresses issues from the history of Ukrainian medicine, such as medical terminology, surviving practices of *folk medicine, personal memoirs, and histories of medical institutions. The remaining third deals with current affairs: reports of the association's sections, bulletins from the executive, biographies, and obituaries. The journal has been edited by R. Osinchuk (1954–5, 1958–61), Ya. Voievidka (1956–7), T. Lapychak (1962–6), and P. Dzul (since 1967). Its covers have been designed by J. Hnizdovsky, O. Moshynska, E. Kozak, G. Khudikian, and L. Palii.

Likars'kyi vistnyk (Physician's Herald). A professional and scholarly journal of the *Ukrainian Physicians' Society in Lviv, published monthly in 1920, quarterly in 1921–35, and bimonthly in 1935–9, then also under the auspices of the Medical Commission of the Shevchenko Scientific Society. The first editor was I. Kurovets. The editorial board consisted of T. Burachynsky, Yu. Dobrylovsky, S. Drymalyk, Yu. Kordiuk, Ye. Lukasevych, M. Muzyka, I. Ortynsky, M. Panchyshyn, and S. Parfanovych.

Liknep. See Elimination of illiteracy.

Likowski, Edward, b 26 September 1836 in Września, Poland, d 20 February 1915 in Poznań. Polish church figure and historian. He studied theology in Münster, was ordained in 1861, and was a professor of canon law and church history at the Poznań Theological Seminary from 1865. A member of the Polish Academy of Sciences from 1886, he wrote scholarly monographs in Polish on the history of the union of the Ruthenian and Roman churches (1875), the history of the Uniate church in Lithuania and Ruthenia (ie, Ukraine and Belarus) in the 18th and 19th centuries (1880; 2nd edn 1906), and the 1596 Church Union of Berestia (1896; 2nd edn 1907; Ukrainian trans 1916). In Poznań he served as the vicar-general and vicar of the archdiocesan chapter. He was elevated to the rank of archbishop in 1914.

Liliecrona, Gustaf, b 10 October 1623, d 19 April 1687. Swedish diplomat and statesman. He was an emissary to Ukraine in June–October 1657, sent to negotiate a Swedish-Ukrainian alliance against Poland. Through Liliecrona the Swedish king Charles X Gustav informed Hetman B. *Khmelnytsky that his government had no objections to Khmelnytsky's uniting eastern Ukraine with the western Ukrainian lands then under Polish rule. Khmelnytsky and representatives of the *Cossack *starshyna* agreed to strengthen the Ukrainian-Swedish union in their mutual war against Poland, and they proposed Ukrainian mediation in the matter of restoring peace between Sweden and Russia. The negotiations resulted in the signing of the Korsun Treaty of Alliance on 17 October 1657. The instructions of King Charles to Liliecrona and the diplomat's correspondence with the Swedish government represent a valuable source for the political history of Ukraine during that time. The materials were published in *Arkhiv Iugo-Zapadnoi Rossii* (pt 3, vol 6 [1908]).

Lily of the valley (*Convallaria majalis*; Ukrainian: *konvaliia*). A low perennial herb of the lily family Liliaceae, usually with two large oblong leaves and a raceme of small, fragrant, bell-shaped white flowers. In Ukraine it grows wild in woods and shrubbery and is cultivated as a decorative plant. A valuable *medicinal plant, lily of the valley contains glycosides, and infusions of the flowers are used in the treatment of heart conditions.

Lime industry. A branch of the building-materials industry that produces lime or quicklime by roasting limestone or chalk under controlled conditions. Lime is used as a building material, a flux in steel making, a fertilizer, and a chemical in the manufacture of sugar, paper, and glass and in waste treatment. By the end of the 18th century lime works had been set up in Podilia and the Chernihiv and Novhorod-Siverskyi regions by monasteries and landlords. The industry expanded in the 19th century, but factories remained small, with 18 to 40 workers. In 1875 there were 79 factories in Russian-ruled Ukraine, employing 889 workers and producing 101,000 rubles' worth of lime. By 1895 the number had risen to 232 factories, employing 1,233 workers and producing 273,000 rubles' worth of lime. After 1917 the greatest expansion of the lime industry was in the Donbas. In 1928 Ukraine produced 192,100 t of lime, or 36.9 percent of the total Soviet output. Ukraine's share of the Soviet output declined in the 1950s and rose in the mid-1960s. In 1967 Ukraine produced 6,982,000 t, or 35.5 percent of the Soviet output, and in 1982, 8,727,000 t, or 30.4 percent. Donetske, Dnipropetrovske, Kharkiv, and Vinnytsia oblasts account for 90 percent of the republic's lime output.

Limestone (*vapniak*). A sedimentary rock consisting chiefly of calcium carbonate (over 50 percent), primarily in the form of calcite, but in very young rocks also of aragonite. A third calcium carbonate mineral, vaterite, occurs only in traces, because it quickly alters to calcite. There is a continuous series of transition to dolomite (the calcium-magnesium carbonate), most of the time through secondary dolomitization and consequent recrystallization. *Marble is a metamorphosed equivalent of either limestone or dolomite. The color is mostly white or gray, but it can vary widely, if the rock is stained by traces of impurities. In the commercial manufacture of lime, limestone refers to any rock which contains at least 80 percent carbonate of calcium or magnesium, and which slakes when water is added upon calcination (thermal decomposition).

Limestone of different ages is found in various forms nearly everywhere in Ukraine (except in its central reaches). The oldest are the thick deposits of crinoid Silurian limestones in the Zbruch River valley; they are followed by the Devonian dolomitic limestones of southwestern Podilia, the southern Donets Ridge, and the southwestern part of the Dnieper-Donets Trough. Carboniferous limestones form thick deposits in the Donets Basin. Jurassic limestones are known in the southern part of the Crimean Mountains and the Caucasus and in the southern part of the Opilia Upland and are found at considerable depths in the Dnieper-Donets Trough. Cretaceous limestones are exposed in Podilia, Roztochia, the Volhynia-Kholm Upland, and, less commonly, the Carpathian Mountains. They form large deposits in the northern part of the Crimean Mountains and the Caucasus, lie at considerable depths in the Black Sea Depression, the Dnieper-Donets Trough, and the Prypiat Trough, and rest on the southern slopes of the Voronezh Massif. Paleogene marls occur in the Donets Basin, and Miocene bryozoan and reefy limestones in western Ukraine.

The limestones of the Donets Basin are of the greatest industrial use. Most notable are the large, high-quality deposits of fluxstone mined at Komsomolske, Dokuchaievske, and Novotroitske (respectively southeast, south, and southwest of Donetske), as well as at Balaklava (a suburb of Sevastopil) and (of lesser quality) at Bila Krynytsia and other sites south of Kryvyi Rih. Much limestone is mined for cement in Vynnytsia and Mykolaiv oblasts. Limestone is used as building stone largely in the Crimea, the Donets Basin, Kharkiv oblast, and Podilia.

Chemical and other industrial uses of limestone correspond to the location of the respective industries.

P. Sonnenfeld

Limnychenko, Vasyl. See Melnyk, Vasyl.

Limnytsia River [Limnycja] (aka Lomnytsia). A right-bank tributary of the Dniester River. The Limnytsia is 122 km long and drains a basin area of 1,530 sq km. It has its source in the Gorgany Range of the Ukrainian Carpathians and flows through Ivano-Frankivske oblast. Throughout its course the Limnytsia is a mountain river. Its waters are used for industrial, agricultural, and domestic consumption and irrigation.

Linden (*Tilia*; Ukrainian: *lypa*). A large deciduous tree of the family Tiliaceae, reaching heights of 15–25 m and a trunk diameter of 2 m. Some lindens grow for 500 to 1,000 years. Lindens are widely cultivated as ornamental trees in parks. There are approx 50 known species of linden, 4 of which are found in Ukraine's deciduous and mixed forests. The most common is the little-leaf linden (*T. cordata*; Ukrainian: *lypa sertseva*). The wide-leaf linden (*T. platyphyllas* Scop.) and silver linden (*T. argentea* Desf.) are found in Western Ukraine. The Crimean or green linden (*T. euchlora* Koch.) is found in the Crimean Mountains. Linden wood is soft yet strong. It is widely used in Ukraine for the production of furniture, cabinets, musical instruments, veneer, and millwork. The bark of young trees is used in basketweaving, footwear, and twine. The fragrant, creamy golden flowers are rich in nectar; dried flowers are brewed as a diaphoretic tea and as a gargling solution.

Linear Spiral-Meander Pottery culture: pottery excavated near Nezvyzko, Horodenka raion, Ivano-Frankivske oblast

Linear Spiral-Meander Pottery culture (Liniino-strichkovoi keramiky kultura). An early Neolithic culture that existed throughout western, central, and eastern Europe and in the upper Dniester and western Volhynia regions of Ukraine in the late 5th to mid-4th millennium BC. The settlements of this culture in Ukraine commonly featured semi-pit dwellings with hearths inside and storage pits outside. Both full body burials and cremation were practiced by the people of this culture. Their pottery was known for its globular shape, thin walls, and distinctive linear ornamentation employing frequent spirals. The culture's major occupations included agriculture and animal husbandry.

Linen industry. A branch of the *textile industry that produces linen cloth, sacking, twine, cords, and other goods from *flax fibers. Like other branches of light industry in Ukraine, the linen industry is and has been underdeveloped in relation both to Ukraine's output of flax fiber and to the needs of the population.

The cultivation of flax and the domestic weaving of linen have always played an important role in the Ukrainian economy. Linen was made as early as the Trypilian period. In the 18th century it was said that every household had flax in the fields and a loom at the hearth. The first linen manufactories were established in the 18th century in the flax-growing northern regions. The main centers of linen manufacture in Russian-ruled Ukraine were Pochep, Sheptaky, and Topal, in the Chernihiv region, Rivne, in Volhynia, and Shpola, in the Kiev region. In 1750 the Pochep manufactory was transferred to Russia in accordance with imperial discrimination against Ukrainian manufacturing.

Western Ukraine under Austrian rule grew almost a quarter of the empire's flax (23 percent in the 1840s). The linen industry, valued at 13 million florins, accounted for a quarter of the region's industrial output. Characteristically, only the initial processing of flax fibers was done in Western Ukraine; the finished goods were manufactured in Vienna, Brno, or Pest.

Output of Ukraine's linen industry, 1940–87

Product	1940	1960	1970	1980	1987
Flax fiber (in 1,000 t)	1.3	20.4	40.8	67.4	106.3
Linen yarn (in 1,000 t)	1.3	0.4	21.1	24.1	27.5
Linen cloth (in million m)	2.1	0.35	48.7*	–	–

* Figure for 1968

Linen factories appeared in the Ukrainian gubernias only toward the end of the 19th century, but up to the revolution most of the linen output came from the cottage industry. As new flax varieties were introduced, fiber processing grew rapidly. Its growth rate was not matched by that in linen spinning or weaving (see the table). By 1970 there were 18 linen factories in Ukraine: 8 in Chernihiv oblast, 6 in Zhytomyr oblast, and 1 each in Volhynia, Kiev, Lviv, and Rivne oblasts. The *Zhytomyr and the *Rivne linen manufacturing complexes went into operation in 1962 and 1964 respectively and have raised the republic's output of linen cloth. The linen industry in Ukraine, however, remains underdeveloped in relation to its material base: in 1983 Ukraine grew almost a quarter of the USSR's flax but produced only 11 percent of its linen yarn.

C. Freeland

Linguistic geography. A trend in linguistics begun by J. Gilliéron, who proposed to recover the history of a given language from the present-day territorial distribution of linguistic data. Linguistic geographers study dialects systematically and compile dialectal atlases. In the Slavic countries this scholarly trend had the greatest following in Poland.

Although a pioneering work in linguistic geography, P. *Buzuk's dialectological study of the Poltava region, was written in Ukraine in 1929, the first Ukrainian dialectal atlas did not appear until almost three decades later. Some data on Ukrainian dialects appeared in J. Tarnacki's comparative study of Polish dialects in Mazovia and Polisia (1939) and the dialectological atlas of the Belorussian language (1963). Some works on Ukrainian dialects, such as Pankevych's book on the Transcarpathian dialects (1938), H. Shylo's on the southwestern dialects north of the Dniester River (1957), V. Vashchenko's on the Poltava dialect (1957), and K. Dejna's on the Ternopil region's dialects (1957), contain a number of maps and can be considered embryonic dialectal atlases. Atlases of Ukraine's dialects began to appear only in the 1950s; they include Z. Stieber's atlas of the Lemko region (8 parts, 1956–64), Y. Dzendzelivsky's atlas of Transcarpathia oblast (2 parts, 1958–60), the Carpathian dialectological atlas by S. Bernshtein et al (1967), J. Rieger's atlas of Boiko dialects (6 vols, 1979–86), F. Czyżewski's atlas of Polish and Ukrainian dialects (1986), and Z. Hanudel's south Lemko dialect atlas (2 vols, 1981–9). Work on a dialectal atlas covering all of Ukraine began in 1948–9, using B. Larin's program for collecting data. With Larin's departure to Leningrad, F. *Zhylko, the leading linguistic geographer in Ukraine, became the director of the atlas project. He propagated the principles of linguistic geography in his *Narysy z dialektolohiï ukraïns'koï movy* (Studies in the Dialectology of the Ukrainian Language, 1955; 2nd edn 1966), organized annual conferences on Ukrainian dialectology, and edited several collections of conference papers, including *Ukraïns'ka linhvistychna heohrafiia* (Ukrainian Linguistic Geography, 1966). The project came to a standstill when Zhylko moved to Moscow, but it was eventually revived under the direction of I. Matviias. The first two volumes of *Atlas ukraïns'koï movy* (Atlas of the Ukrainian Language, 1984, 1988) cover Polisia, the central Dnieper region, Volhynia, the Dniester region, and Transcarpathia and adjacent territories. The change of editors and revisions in the project's program, including the reduction of the number of projected volumes from six to three, had a detrimental effect, and the atlas does not measure up to its Polish, Slovak, Bulgarian, and Belorussian counterparts. Of great importance for a description of Ukrainian linguistic geography is also the *Obshcheslavianskii dialektologicheskii atlas* (General Slavic Dialectological Atlas), published in a series from 1988. Besides work on the linguistic atlas, other studies in linguistic geography have been written by V. Vashchenko (the Dnieper region), P. Lyzanets (Transcarpathia), V. Latta (the Prešov region), M. Nykonchuk, and others.

Linguistics. The origins of language study in Ukraine date back to Kievan Rus'. The *Izbornik* of Sviatoslav (1073), which was transcribed from the Bulgarian, contained a chapter 'On Images' by the Byzantine author G. Choiroboschos. We do not know whether the contemporary treatise 'On Letters,' by the Bulgarian monk Khrabr, transcriptions of which are dated not earlier than the 15th century, was known at the time, and have no information about linguistic works of local origin.

A somewhat more independent approach to language studies was adopted in Ukraine only at the end of the 16th and in the first half of the 17th century. This development was conditioned by the polemics over the Church Union of Berestia and by the needs of education. Ideologically, it was grounded in the project of reviving Church Slavonic and Greek; hence, attention was focused on preparing grammars and dictionaries of these languages. Besides primers and elementary school textbooks, some important grammars were published: *Khramatyka slovens'ka iazyka* (Grammar of the Slavic Language, 1586), *Adelphotes* (1591), L. Zyzanii's Slavonic grammar with a small dictionary (1596), M. Smotrytsky's Slavonic grammar (1619), and P. Berynda's Slavonic-Ruthenian lexicon (1627). For some time these works determined the grammatical and lexical tradition not only in Ukraine, but also in Russia and Serbia and to a certain extent even in Rumania. Based on Western European textbooks of Latin and Greek by Donatus, Alvares, Lascaris, Moschopoulos, and others, they mechanically combined medieval scholastic traditions with elements of humanistic grammar. No observations about vernacular usage were made.

In the early 19th century, as universities were founded and romantic-national ideas spread in Ukraine, language studies underwent a renewal and adopted new methods and subjects. Because of Ukraine's colonial status, the development of philology in Ukraine was in some ways distinctive. As state-supported and -controlled institutions, the universities in Ukraine were Russian, Polish, or German-Austrian, not Ukrainian. The study of Ukrainian – called the Little Russian dialect under Russia and Ruthenian under Austria-Hungary and Poland – was not forbidden, but neither was it encouraged. Furthermore, treated as provincial, the universities in Ukraine were constantly drained of their most talented young scholars by universities in the imperial capitals. Thus, I. *Sreznevsky and D. *Ovsianiko-Kulikovsky were drawn away from Kharkiv to St Petersburg, A. *Sobolevsky from Kiev to St Petersburg, and A. Brückner from Lviv to Berlin.

To overcome these obstacles to the development of linguistics in Ukraine, central academy-like institutions were set up. In the 19th century there were only three such schools in Ukraine: the school of philosophical linguistics at Kharkiv University, the F. Miklosich school in Galicia and Bukovyna, and the O. Potebnia school at Kharkiv University. Only the last originated in Ukraine; the first emulated German and Russian examples, and the second was transplanted from Vienna.

Philosophical linguistics, which was inspired by the French encyclopedists and influenced to a slight extent by the German Romantics, was cultivated in the first two decades after the founding of Kharkiv University (1805). Its adherents were interested in universal grammar, the origin and development of languages, the value of language, and the poetic and rhetorical uses of language. Their main works were I. Rizhsky's *Opyt ritoriki* (An Essay on Rhetoric, 1796; 2nd ed 1805; 3rd ed 1822) and *Vvedenie v krug slovesnosti* (Introduction to the Sphere of Language, 1806), I. Tymkovsky's *Opytnyi sposob k filosoficheskomu poznaniiu rossiiskogo iazyka* (The Empirical Method for the Philosophical Study of the Russian Language, 1811), and R. Honorsky's and M. Paki-de-Sovini's writings.

Romanticism in linguistics is associated with I. Sreznevsky at Kharkiv University and M. *Maksymovych at Kiev University. Sreznevsky initiated research on the history of Ukrainian and Russian and on Slovenian dialectology. Maksymovych was interested primarily in the history of Ukrainian and other Slavic languages. Occa-

sionally, he adapted the facts to fit his national-romantic theory. Other representatives of Romanticism were not associated with any university, but were autodidacts and dilettantes. They discovered and introduced into scientific discussion many facts about contemporary Ukrainian, but most of their generalizations and historical speculations were unscientific. Nonetheless, a number of Ukrainian grammars were produced by amateurs, such as O. Pavlovsky (1805, publ 1818), M. Luchkai (1830), I. Mohylnytsky (1823, publ 1910), Y. Lozynsky (before 1833, publ 1846), Y. Levytsky (1834), and I. Vahylevych (1845). *Rozprava o iazytsi iuzhnoruski i ieho narichiiakh* (Treatise on the South Ruthenian Language and Its Dialects, 1849) by Ya. Holovatsky, the first holder of the chair of Ruthenian philology at Lviv University, can also be included among these grammars.

More serious scientific research began with the arrival of P. *Lavrovsky at Kharkiv University in 1851 and of A. Małecki at Lviv University in 1856. The former worked mostly in the history of Russian, the latter in Polish grammar, but both used comparative Slavic materials. Together with A. Kochubinsky at Odessa University (from 1871) they were representatives of positivist, preneogrammarian linguistics.

The first members of F. *Miklosich's pragmatic school in Ukraine were O. Ohonovsky, holder of the chair of Ruthenian philology at Lviv University (from 1874), and his successor to the chair in 1895, O. Kolessa. At Chernivtsi University, S. Smal-Stotsky (1885–1918) and O. Kaluzhniatsky (1875–1914) promoted this linguistic school in Bukovyna. Unlike their teacher, these scholars were not interested in comparative studies but in the history of Ukrainian.

O. *Potebnia, holder of the chair of Russian language and literature at Kharkiv University (1874–91), was the only noted linguist of the period at a university in Russian-ruled Ukraine with a clearly defined Ukrainian identity. Specializing in the field of general linguistics, he embraced the ideas of J. Herbart and R. Lotze's school of psychology and developed an original concept of language bridging linguistics and literary theory. His followers, including D. Ovsianiko-Kulikovsky, V. Khartsiiev, B. Lezin, and O. Vetukhiv, were grouped around the serial *Voprosy teorii i psikhologii tvorchestva* (8 vols, 1907–23). The Russian A. Sobolevsky, who taught at Kiev University (1882–8), regarded Ukrainian as a Russian dialect and proposed the theory of Kiev's 'Great-Russian' origins. Political circumstances prevented two remarkable Kiev linguists from pursuing university careers: K. Mykhalchuk expounded highly original, quasi-structuralist ideas on the history of Ukrainian phonetics, and P. Zhytetsky wrote the first history of Ukrainian phonetics (1876) and historical surveys of literary Ukrainian of the 17th and 18th centuries (1889, 1900).

In Slavic linguistics the chief neogrammarians in Ukraine were A. Brückner at Lviv University (1878–81), S. Kulbakin (1905–19), Ya. Endzelin at Kharkiv University (1911–20), O. Lukianenko at Kiev University (1907–20), and B. Liapunov at Odessa University (1903–23). In general linguistics the school was represented by the phoneticist A. *Tomson at Odessa University (1897–1932) and the Sanskritologists T. Knauer at Kiev and V. Schertzl at Kharkiv (1870–84) and Odessa (1884–96) universities. M. *Hrunsky of Kiev University (1915–41) and V. *Rozov (1903–16), who in 1913–14 read the first course in the history of Ukrainian at Kiev University, were less consistent in their neogrammarian approach. At this time the dilettantes in Ukrainian linguistics, such as V. Naumenko in Kiev, I. Verkhratsky in Lviv, and A. Krymsky, an Orientalist in Moscow, adhered to old philological ideas. In 1906 the first department of Romance and Germanic languages in Ukraine was set up at Kiev University. The first studies in Romance linguistics were S. Savchenko's works on the genesis of the Romance languages (1916) and the history of Provençal (1918).

The Revolution of 1917 marked a turning point in the development of linguistics in Ukraine. The Ukrainian Academy of Sciences (est 1918), along with the universities, became an important center of learning. Ukrainian linguistics became for the first time a distinct discipline in institutions of higher learning. During the period of Ukrainian independence and the subsequent years of *Ukrainization, Ukrainian linguists in Soviet Ukraine had to prepare textbooks of Ukrainian for students and adults, compile high-quality dictionaries (see *Lexicography and *Terminology), and normalize Standard Ukrainian and its orthography.

In the process of normalization two groups with radically different tendencies emerged: the 'ethnographic' group – Ye. Tymchenko, S. Smerechynsky, and O. *Kuryko (until 1925) – which based itself on the principle of *purism; and those who rejected this romantic-nationalist approach – O. *Syniavsky, O. Kurylo (after 1925), M. Sulyma, and K. Nimchynov. The first syntheses of the results of normalization were O. Syniavsky's *Normy ukraïns'koï literaturnoï movy* (The Norms of Literary Ukrainian, 1931) and vols 2 and 3 of the VUAN Russian-Ukrainian dictionary (1927, 1933).

At the same time research was actively conducted in Ukrainian dialectology and the history of the Ukrainian language. Besides descriptions of particular dialects, significant attempts at explaining the genesis of Ukrainian dialects were made by V. *Hantsov, O. Kurylo, and I. *Zilynsky. Descriptive studies of particular literary monuments and analyses of the language used by individual writers were published. P. Buzuk (1927) and Ye. *Tymchenko (1930) wrote the first comprehensive histories of the Ukrainian language, and M. Sulyma (1927) wrote a history of the literary language. Vol 1 of a historical dictionary of Ukrainian (2 parts, 1930, 1932) came out under Ye. Tymchenko's editorship.

Although research on the Ukrainian language prospered in the early Soviet period, other areas of linguistics were neglected. In general linguistics only L. *Bulakhovsky's *Osnovy movoznavstva* (Foundations of Linguistics, 1928–9) was published during this period. Also in the early 1930s O. Kurylo tried to transplant some of the achievements of structuralism to Ukraine. Comparative Indo-European linguistics was almost completely neglected. The little that was published in comparative Slavic linguistics was written by L. Bulakhovsky (on Slavic accentology, particularly frequency in Czech) and M. Hrunsky (on Church Slavonic). In Oriental linguistics only some textbooks appeared, eg, A. *Krymsky's *Tiurky, ikh movy ta literatury* (Turki, Their Languages and Literatures, 1930), T. Kezma's Arabic grammar (1928), and T. Hrunin's Turkish grammar (1930). E. Spivak and M. Shapiro of the VUAN Hebraist Commission conducted research on Yiddish. Romani dialects were studied by O. Barannykov (1931).

The Stalinist terror of the 1930s put an end to the development of Ukrainian linguistics. Almost every noted linguist except L. Bulakhovsky and M. Hrunsky was repressed, or perished. The newly founded Institute of Linguistics became a tool of Russification. Except for H. Levchenko's work on literary Ukrainian of the first half of the 19th century (1939, 1946) and L. Bulakhovsky's university textbooks of Russian, not one serious work on Ukrainian, Russian, Slavic, or general linguistics appeared during the 1930s and 1940s.

In Rumanian-ruled Bukovyna during the interwar period linguistic research at Chernivtsi University died out completely. In Polish-ruled Galicia, Lviv University became an important, though up to 1939 exclusively Polish, linguistic center. Among the noted linguists who worked there were the Polonists K. Nitsch (1917–20), H. Gaertner (1926–35), and W. Taszycki (1929–41, 1944); the Slavists T. Lehr-Spławiński (1922–9) and Z. Stieber (1937–9, 1944–5); the Indo-Europeanists A. Gawroński (1917–27) and J. Kuryłowicz (1929–45); the Germanists W. Dołmajer (1913–32) and O. Kuryłowicz (1932–9); the Romance linguists E. Porębowicz (1899–1931) and Z. Czerny (1924–46); the Anglicist W. Tarnawski (1924–41); the classical philologists S. Witkowski (1902–35), R. Gansiniec (1920–46), and J. Kowalski (1920–45); and the student Polonists S. Bąk, W. Kuraszkiewicz, T. Milewski, S. Hrabec, and K. Dejna. The chair of Ruthenian philology was occupied for the first time by a Pole, J. Janów (1927–45). Linguists associated with the Shevchenko Scientific Society, including O. Kolessa, I. Svientsitsky, V. Lev, K. Kysilevsky, J. Rudnyckyj, and I. Pankevych, conducted research in the spirit of F. Miklosich and V. Vondrák, concentrating mostly on dialects and literary monuments. The society's research program expanded with the arrival from Prague in 1933 of V. *Simovych, the author of pioneering structuralist works in the history of Ukrainian and of interesting works in onomastics. A. Artymovych, a professor at the Ukrainian Free University in Prague, also used the structuralist method. The Ukrainian Scientific Institute in Warsaw was another secondary center for Ukrainian linguistics. It published several works by Galician linguists, such as M. Pshepiurska-Ovcharenko, V. Lev, and M. Pushkar, and supported the work of I. *Ohiienko and R. *Smal-Stotsky. Ohiienko, a representative of the 'ethnographic' tendency, propagated the methods of the Kiev philological school and published *Ridna mova* (1933–9), the first popular Ukrainian linguistic journal. Smal-Stotsky studied specific grammatical categories of contemporary Ukrainian using A. Marty's psychological approach.

Since the Second World War and particularly since Stalin's death, the number of linguists and their publications in Soviet Ukraine has increased. *Movoznavstvo*, the journal of the Institute of Linguistics, was revived in 1941 under L. Bulakhovsky's editorship and has raised its scientific standards. Several new linguistic serials were founded: *Ukraïns'ka mova v shkoli* (1951), renamed in 1963 *Ukraïns'ka mova i literatura v shkoli*; *Diialektolohichnyi biuleten'* (9 issues, 1950–62); *Leksykohrafichnyi biuleten'* (9 issues, 1951–63); and *Doslidzhennia i materialy z ukraïns'koï movy* (6 vols, 1959–64). The Lviv branch of the AN URSR published *Doslidzhennia z movy ta literatury* (2 vols, 1954–7) and *Doslidzhennia i materialy z ukraïns'koï movy* (6 vols, 1959–64). Many collections of articles have been published, including *Slov'ians'ke movoznavstvo* (Slavic Linguistics, 5 vols, 1958–67), *Filolohichnyi zbirnyk* (Philological Collection, 1958), and *Slavistychnyi zbirnyk* (Slavistic Collection, 1963). Collections dealing specifically with dialectology, syntax, the history of Ukrainian grammar, lexicology, onomastics, and stylistics have appeared. The most important synthetic works on Ukrainian that appeared in the decade after Stalin's death were L. Bulakhovsky's book on the origin of the Ukrainian language (1956), L. Humetska's survey of the word-formation system of the Ukrainian language in 14th- and 15th-century official documents (1958), S. Bevzenko's book on the historical morphology of the Ukrainian language (1960), A. Gensorsky's studies of the language of the Galician-Volhynian Chronicle, and F. Zhylko's dialectological research.

Despite a considerable growth in the range of subjects studied and a budding interest in methodological problems (particularly I. Kucherenko's studies in the methodology of morphology), linguistics in Soviet Ukraine in the early 1960s still had many shortcomings. Political bias and propaganda continued to mar many works, particularly I. *Bilodid's (ed) *Kurs istoriï ukraïns'koï literaturnoï movy* (A Course in the History of the Ukrainian Literary Language, 2 vols, 1958, 1961). When the AN URSR was subordinated to the USSR Academy of Sciences in 1963, the publication policy of its institutes, including the Institute of Linguistics, changed drastically. Most periodicals and series were abolished and replaced by occasional collections of articles on specific research questions or individuals such as O. Potebnia, T. Shevchenko, or M. Lomonosov. Only the bimonthly *Movoznavstvo* survived. The publication programs of universities also suffered severe cuts. The only remaining linguistics periodical that serves all the republic's universities is the annual *Ukraïns'ke movoznavstvo* (est 1974). The precarious situation in linguistics is illustrated by the dictionary of the language of H. Kvitka-Osnovianenko's works (3 vols, 1978–9) that was issued by Kharkiv University in only 350 copies, none of which appeared in bookstores. Thus, the Institute of Linguistics and the Institute of Social Sciences in Lviv have become the only serious publishers in Ukrainian linguistics.

During the years 1964–84 the Institute of Linguistics explored some areas that previously had not been systematically studied: the intonation of the contemporary vernacular (four collections of articles), the peculiarities of speech (three collections), and onomastics (six collections). In 1966–70 it published four collections of articles on statistical and structural methods in linguistics. Subsequent collections on topics such as the philosophical questions of linguistics (1972) and language and time (1977) have been marred by propaganda. Most of the studies dealing with Ukrainian have been in dialectology: altogether, seven collections of articles on Ukrainian dialects have appeared. Only three collections have been published on the morphology of modern Ukrainian, one on syntax, four on lexicology, two on the history of linguistic studies, and one on the history of Ukrainian. More monographs than before were published on historical subjects, but generally, the Ukrainian language and its history have been underemphasized. The only exceptions to this rule have been (1) a series of publications of Middle Ukrainian texts, such as 14th- and 15th-century charters; dictionaries by L. Zyzanii, P. Berynda, and Ye. Slavynetsky; grammars by L. Zyzanii, M. Smotrytsky, and I. Uzhevych; and 16th- and 18th-century chancellery documents, but no religious texts; and (2) comprehensive textbook series, such as one on Modern Standard Ukrainian (5 vols, 1969–73) edited by

I. Bilodid et al, and the one on the history of Ukrainian (4 vols, 1978–83) edited by A. Hryshchenko et al. Some valuable reference works have appeared also; eg, a dictionary of 14th- and 15th-century Ukrainian (2 vols, 1977–8) based on the language of old charters, edited by L. Humetska and I. Kernytsky; the first three of seven volumes of a Ukrainian etymological dictionary (1982–), edited by O. Melnychuk et al; the first two volumes of a three-volume atlas of Ukrainian dialects (1984–), edited by I. Matviias et al; a dictionary of Ukrainian hydronyms (1979), edited by K. Tsiluiko et al; and an eleven-volume Ukrainian dictionary (1970–80), edited by I. Bilodid et al. The almost complete restriction of research to the Institute of Linguistics and the emphasis on collections of articles and collectively prepared reference tools made creative individual scholarship in linguistics almost impossible. Soviet linguists became merely executors of a centrally prescribed program, subject to the dogmas of political ideology. Hence, scholarly discussion was virtually nonexistent in Soviet Ukrainian publications.

Another major change in Ukrainian linguistics was brought about by a shift in Soviet nationality and *language policy. At the all-Soviet conferences on teaching Russian held in Tashkent in 1975 and 1979, it was announced that as the universal medium of communication in the USSR, Russian must become through education the 'second native language' of all non-Russians. Accordingly, the Institute of Linguistics in Kiev began feverishly publishing books to promote Russian in Ukraine. As a rule its publications were in Russian and bore titles (in translation) such as *The Russian Language – The Language of International Communication and of the Unification of the Peoples of the USSR* (1976), *A Comparative Study of the Russian and Ukrainian Languages* (1975), *The Culture of Russian Speech in Ukraine* (1976), *The Russian Language as a Source of Enrichment of the Languages of the USSR* (1979), and *The Functioning of the Russian Language in a Close Linguistic Environment* (1981). The institute also began publishing, only in Russian, books on general linguistics.

In the West, linguists have concentrated mostly on problems of Ukrainian grammar and stylistics (eg, J. Barnstead, C. Bethin, V. Yashchun, P. Kovaliv, V. Swoboda), the history of Ukrainian (G.Y. *Shevelov, B. Struminsky, P. Wexler), etymology (J. *Rudnyckyj), dialectology (O. *Horbach, B. Struminsky), Old Ukrainian texts (O. Horbach, V. Swoboda, G. Perfecky, I. Gerus-Tarnawecka), and onomastics (J. Hursky, W. Zyla). (See also *Dialectology, *Grammar, Ukrainian *Language, *Lexicography, *Lexicology, *Morphology, *Orthography, *Standard Ukrainian, *Stylistics, and *Syntax.)

BIBLIOGRAPHY
Bulich, S. *Ocherk istorii iazykoznaniia v Rossii* (St Petersburg 1904)
Ohiienko, I. 'Ohliad ukraïns'koho iazykoznavstva,' *ZNTSh*, 79–80 (1907)
Jagić, V. *Istoriia slavianskoi filologii* (St Petersburg 1910)
Beloded, I.; Borkovskii, V.; Goretskii, P. *Izuchenie ukrainskogo i beloruskogo iazykov* (Moscow 1958)
Horbach, O. 'Pisliavoienni movoznavchi publikatsiï v URSR,' *Suchasnist'*, 1961, no. 12; 1962, no. 1
Shevelov, G. 'Belorussian and Ukrainian,' *Current Trends in Linguistics* (The Hague), 1 (1963)
Bahmut, A. (ed). *Movoznavstvo na Ukraïni za p'iatdesiat' rokiv* (Kiev 1967)
Pavliuk, M. *Osnovni etapy rozvytku ukraïns'koho movoznavstva dozhovtnevoho periodu* (Kiev–Odessa 1978)

Bilodid, I. (ed). *Rozvytok movoznavstva v URSR, 1967–1977* (Kiev 1980)

Hryshchenko, A. 'Dosiahnennia ukraïns'koho radians'koho movoznavstva,' *Movoznavstvo*, 1982, no. 6

Jurkowski, M. 'Ukrainistyka jezykoznawcza w Polsce Ludowej,' *Przegląd humanistyczny* (Warsaw), 1984, no. 2

Semchyns'kyi, S. 'Movoznavstvo u Kyïvs'komu universyteti,' *Movoznavstvo*, 1984, no. 4

Nimchuk, V. *Movoznavstvo na Ukraïni v XIV–XVII st.* (Kiev 1985)
G.Y. Shevelov

Linguistics, Institute of the Academy of Sciences of the Ukrainian SSR. See Institute of Linguistics of the Academy of Sciences of the Ukrainian SSR.

Linnet (*Carduelis cannabina*; Ukrainian: *ziablyk, konoplianka*). A common, small Old World finch of the family Carduelidae, approx 15 cm long, weighing 23 g. The male has a crimson crown and breast, brown-streaked back, and white-edged, forked tail; the female and young are grayish brown. Linnets are valuable for controlling insects.

Linnyk, Volodymyr (Linnik, Vladimir), b 6 July 1889 in Kharkiv, d ? Physicist specializing in applied optics and optical mechanics; full member of the AN URSR (now ANU) from 1939. He graduated from Kiev University (1914) and worked at the Kiev Polytechnical Institute and the State Optical Institute (from 1926). His main contributions were in the fields of X-ray optics (where his formulations are considered classical), applied optics (interferometry, spectroscopy, microscopy), photoelectronics, and astronomical optics. He invented numerous optical instruments, among them the widely used Linnyk microinterferometer, microprofilometers, and double microscopes, as well as various astronomical and measuring-type interferometers, collimators, microscope attachments, and astronomical instruments.

Linova, Yevgeniia [Lin'ova, Jevgenija] (née Paprits), b 9 January 1854 in Brest-Litovsk, d 1919. Russian singer, folklorist, conductor, and educator. In 1890 she came to the United States, organized a choir, and presented concerts of Ukrainian and Russian folk songs in New York, Boston, Philadelphia, and Chicago. In 1896 she returned to Russia, bringing with her a phonograph, which she adapted for collecting folk songs. A year later she made the first phonograph recordings of Ukrainian choral music. On her initiative a musical ethnography commission was set up at the Society of Lovers of Natural Science, Anthropology, and Ethnography. During her expedition to the Poltava region (1904) she recorded about 120 songs, 18 of which appeared in her *Opyt zapisi fonografom ukrainskikh narodnykh pesen* (An Attempt to Record Ukrainian Folk Songs with a Phonograph, 1906). In 1913 she collected folk songs in Galicia and Czechoslovakia. Linova illustrated her lectures at international conferences in Vienna (1909), London (1911), and Paris (1914) with her recordings. Of her large collection, 116 drums have been preserved in Soviet archives.

Lintur, Petro, b 4 May 1909 in Horonda, Bereg komitat, Transcarpathia, d 3 November 1969 in Uzhhorod, Transcarpathia. Folklorist and literary scholar. After graduating from Prague University (1937) he taught at a gymnasium in Khust and lectured at Uzhhorod University (1953–69). He collected almost 1,500 folktales and over 3,000 folk songs and wrote 18 books and 43 scholarly articles. His more important folklore collections are *Zakarpats'ki kazky Andriia Kalyna* (Transcarpathian Tales of Andrii Kalyn, 1955), *Narodni balady Zakarpattia* (Folk Ballads of Transcarpathia, 1959, 1966), *Maister Ivanko* (Master Ivanko, 1960), *Kazky zelenykh hir* (Tales of Green Mountains, 1965), *Dido Vsevido* (Grandfather See-All, 1969), and *Kazky odnoho sela* (A Village's Tales, 1979). His *Ukrainische Volksmärchen* (1972) is an anthology of Ukrainian folktales in German translation. Lintur also studied the works of 19th-century Transcarpathian writers, such as O. Dukhnovych and I. Silvai.

Liubov Linytska

Linytska, Liubov [Linyc'ka, Ljubov], b 27 December 1865 in Preobrazhenske, Oleksandrivske county, Katerynoslav gubernia, d 5 February 1924 in Kiev. Actress and singer (mezzo-soprano). She completed gymnasium in Kharkiv and began her professional career in M. Kropyvnytsky's troupe (1889). She worked in Saksahansky's troupe (1892–1909, with interruptions), Sadovsky's Theater in Kiev (1909–15), the Society of Ukrainian Actors (1915–17), and the Ukrainian National Theater (1917–18) and appeared sporadically in the State People's Theater in 1918 and in the Zhovten Theater (from 1923). During her artistic career she created 120 different characters (young and old) from the ethnographic theater of manners, as well as roles in W. Shakespeare's plays (Gertrude in *Hamlet* and Emilia in *Othello*). Among her best roles were the romantic leading ladies in M. Kropyvnytsky's *Olesia*, M. Starytsky's *Marusia Bohuslavka*, I. Karpenko-Kary's *Handzia* and *Beztalanna* (The Fortuneless Maiden), L. Starytska-Cherniakhivska's *Het'man Doroshenko*, J. Gordin's *Mirele Efros*, and H. Heijermans's *The Good Hope*. A biography of Linytska was published in Kiev in 1957.

Linytsky, Petro [Linyc'kyj], b 5 December 1839 in Okhtyrka, Kharkiv gubernia, d 25 June 1906 in Kiev. Philosopher and theologian. After graduating from the Kiev Theological Academy (M TH, 1865) he was appointed a lecturer there; later he headed its departments of the history of philosophy and, from 1887, logic and metaphysics. Influenced strongly by German idealism, he argued that reason, with its a priori concepts, is capable of attaining necessary truth about reality, and constructed his own philosophical system, which he presented in *Osnovnye voprosy filosofii* (The Fundamental Questions of Philosophy, 1901). Philosophy's conflicts with science and religious faith could be avoided, according to Linytsky, by restricting each to its proper sphere: science to sensible experience, philosophy to formal knowledge, and faith to a few revealed truths necessary for personal salvation. Linytsky also wrote a survey history of philosophical teachings (1874) and monographs on ancient Greek moral and religious concepts (1870), Plato's theology (1876; his PH D diss), speculation (1881), Slavophilism and liberalism (1882), social activity and the origins of social organization (1884), cognition and thought (1895, 1897), metaphysics (1897), and the philosophy of E. von Hartmann.

Lipatov, Yurii, b 10 July 1927 in Ivanovo-Voznesensk, RSFSR. Polymer chemist; corresponding member of the AN URSR (now ANU) since 1969 and full member since 1973. After graduating from the Moscow Petroleum Institute (1949) he worked in Moscow and Minsk. From 1965 to 1985 he directed the ANU Institute of Macromolecular Chemistry. He outlined the theoretical mechanism of interaction between the polymer matrix and various organic and inorganic fillers, and developed a new hypothesis on the mechanism of interphase phenomena in composite materials, taking into account the thermodynamics of compatibility and of colloidal chemical processes. His monographs *Physical Chemistry of Filled Polymers* (1979) and *Colloid Chemistry of Polymers* (1988) have been published in English translation.

Lipatova, Tatiana, b 23 April 1924 in Moscow. Chemist. A graduate of the Moscow Petroleum Institute (1949), she has worked at the AN URSR (now ANU) institutes of Macromolecular Chemistry (1965–76) and Organic Chemistry (since 1976). The main thrust of her research has been in kinetics and mechanism of polymerization reactions. She developed a new area in macromolecular chemistry – the formation of biologically compatible polymeric materials for use in prosthetic implants.

Lipetsky, Yevsevii [Lipec'kyj, Jevsevij], b 5 June 1899 in Verbivtsi, near Zastavna, Bukovyna, d 18 June 1970 in Bayreuth, West Germany. Realist painter. He studied at the Munich (1910–15) and Vienna art academies. From 1918 he lived in Chernivtsi, where he taught art at a Ukrainian gymnasium, ran an art school, and painted sets for Ukrainian stage productions. From 1941 he lived in Germany. Lipetsky painted many portraits of foreign dignitaries (eg, members of the Austrian royal family) and Bukovynian cultural, church, and political leaders (eg, Metropolitan N. Kotliarchuk, O. Kobylianska, I. Nedilsky), landscapes, and genre scenes. He also did many restorations, among them the iconostasis in the church of Khreshchatyk, near Zastavna, and paintings in the Krekhiv Monastery, and designed book covers and diplomas.

Lipiński, Karol, b 30 October 1790 in Radzyń Podlaski, Poland, d 16 December 1861 in Urliv, Zboriv county, Galicia. Polish composer and violinist. A concertmaster (1809), then kapellmeister (1812–14) of the Lviv Municipal Theater, he collaborated with F. Mozart in staging the works of his father (W. Mozart) and other classics, and performed in concert in Lviv, Kiev, Kamianets-Podilskyi, and Kremianets. He later provided the musical notation and accompaniment to W. *Zaleski's collection of *Pieśni polskie i ruskie ludu galicyjskiego* (Polish and Ruthenian Songs of the Galician People, 1833). In his compositions, Lipiński often took advantage of Ukrainian folk melodies.

Yevsevii Lipetsky: *Lukian Kobylytsia*

Lipliave. A Slavic burial ground of the 10th to 12th centuries AD near Lipliave, Kaniv raion, Cherkasy oblast. Seventy-nine kurhans were excavated there in 1906, 1913–14, and 1949. Each kurhan contained a single individual burial, usually in a pit. A variety of grave goods, including iron knives, scissors, and axes, pottery vessels, and ornaments, were recovered.

Lipovany. See Old Believers.

Liquor and spirits distilling. A branch of the *food industry that produces distilled and rectified alcohol from food substances, such as grains, potatoes, fruits, honey, and beets, and yields by-products, such as baking and feed yeasts, feed vitamins, esters, and acids. Distilled spirits are used in the food-processing industry, chemistry, medicine, and technology.

Before 1914. The manufacture of distilled alcohol has been known since ancient times and has been practiced in Europe for millennia. In Ukraine distilling became widespread in the first half of the 16th century. Mead, beer, and whiskey (*horilka*, usually made from rye) were the main alcoholic beverages. Usually the distilleries were owned by the gentry, and their porduction was sold locally in taverns leased to Jews (see *Propination). The exclusive right to make and sell liquor proved one of the main sources of the gentry's income. Distilleries were common in the Hetman state and were owned by the Cossack *starshyna*, burghers, and monasteries.When the Russian and Austro-Hungarian governments established state monopolies on liquor sales in Ukraine, the excise tax (78 per cent in 1913) generated a considerable part of the state revenue.

In the 17th century a distillery was a small enterprise with four to six stills tended by a few local peasants. In the second half of the 18th century, distilling technology improved: the crude alembic producing a single bucket (12.3 L) of whiskey a day was replaced by a superior English fire box still with a capacity of 4 to 25 buckets a day. Larger distilleries and specialized factories were established. According to the Russian cadastre of 1782, 2,666 out of 2,863 (93 percent) manufactories in Left-Bank Ukraine were distilleries. In 1801, 7,839 distilleries in the Dnieper region produced 62 million L of whiskey. In the 1820s the first steam distilleries appeared in Ukraine. Many old manufactories were replaced by fewer but larger modern ones. The number of distilleries decreased, but the production of spirits (40 percent alcohol) increased (see table 1).

The number of distilleries fell sharply after the abolition of serfdom in 1861, because unpaid serf labor was no longer available. But distillery owners in Ukraine had the advantage of locally supplied raw materials and a ready consumer market – hence, the preponderance of small distilleries owned by landowners. As distilling technology improved, the distilling of spirits was gradually separated from the distilling of whiskey and became an independent industry. Polisia and Left-Bank Ukraine, where raw materials (potatoes, rye, molasses) were produced, had the largest number of distilleries; the largest factories were located in Katerynoslav, Kiev, and Kharkiv gubernias. In 1899–1900, 226.3 million L of spirits were produced. In 1897 the distilling industry employed 6,000 full-time workers and a large number of seasonal laborers. Ukraine produced 29 percent of the spirits in the Russian Empire, 90 percent of which were used for whiskey production.

In the Ukrainian territories under Austria-Hungary, liquor distilling was the most developed branch of the food industry. As in Russian-ruled Ukraine, small distilleries belonging to the landed gentry predominated. At the beginning of the 20th century there were about 400 distilleries in Galicia, producing about 30 million L of liquor per year (an average of 75,000 L per factory, compared to 680,000 L in Russian-ruled Ukraine).

1914–41. During the First World War and the struggle for Ukrainian independence (1917–20) the distilleries in central and eastern Ukraine ceased to operate. In 1921 only 21 distilleries were in operation, producing 130 million L of spirits. Production rose during the NEP period. In 1928, 82 factories, employing 4,300 workers, produced 67 million L of raw alcohol. By the mid-1930s production had reached the prewar level. By 1940 the annual output had risen to 264.8 million L of raw alcohol. The increase in spirits production was a result of the utilization of ethanol (over 50 percent) in the production of synthetic rubber and other chemical products.

In Western Ukraine distilling declined significantly in the interwar period. In 1926 there were only 287 small distilleries in Galicia, with an output of 115,000 L. In the northwestern territories there were 452 small distilleries, producing 12,000 L per year. Galicia's production remained low because of a decrease in alcohol consumption and the competition from the more developed distilleries in western Poland.

1945–78. After the disruption of the war period the distilling industry attained its prewar level of production only in 1951. Since then production has grown steadily. The distilleries themselves have been modernized, and production has been concentrated. Most of the small dis-

TABLE 1
Output of spirits in the Ukrainian gubernias, 1801–1913

	1801	1840	1860	1913
Number of distilleries	7,839	3,595	2,407	586
Output (in million L)	61.5	197	228	400

TABLE 2
Output of raw alcohol within the borders of present-day Ukraine, 1913–78 (in million L)

1913	160	1945	66
1928	67	1950	228
1932	107	1960	387
1937	209	1970	564
1940	265	1978	731

tilleries in Western Ukraine were closed down. The number of distilleries in Ukraine fell from 348 in 1940 to 93 in 1965 and then stabilized. In 1970 the average annual output per distillery was 5.9 million L. Table 2 presents the growth in raw-alcohol production in the territories of present-day Ukraine (calculated at 100 percent alcohol – hence the discrepancy with table 1). Ukraine produces 34.5 percent of the raw USSR output of alcohol and 9 percent of the world output. It is the third-largest producer of alcohol in the world (after the United States and Russia).

In 1963 the distilling industry in the Ukrainian SSR employed 10,800 people. In spite of its absolute growth, its share in the food industry has decreased: it now constitutes only about 2 percent of the industry. Major changes have occurred in the type of raw materials predominantly used by the industry. In 1913 sugar-beet molasses yielded 6 percent of the alcohol produced, potatoes, 73 percent, and grains (rye, corn, etc), 21 percent. In 1940 molasses yielded 38 percent, and potatoes and grains, 62 percent. In 1958 the respective percentages were 23 and 77, in 1970, 85 and 15, and in 1978, 92 and 8.

The geographical distribution of the industry is similar to what it was in the past. Most distilleries are located in the forest-steppe belt, and some in the forest belt. The largest enterprises are the Lokhvytsia and Andrushivka spirits distilling complexes; they are followed by the distilleries in Bar and Kalynivka (Vinnytsia oblast), Ivashky (Kharkiv oblast), Kosari (Cherkasy oblast), and Luzhany (Chernivtsi oblast). Ukraine produces over 200 brands of liquor. The largest liquor distilleries are located in Lviv, Artemivske, Donetske, Voroshylovhrad, Dnipropetrovske, and Kharkiv. Today alcohol is exported to former Soviet republics and abroad. Research for the distilling industry has been conducted since 1958 at the Ukrainian Scientific Research Institute of the Spirits and Liqueur-Whiskey Industry in Kiev.

BIBLIOGRAPHY
Nesterenko, O. *Rozvytok promyslovosti na Ukraïni*, vols 1–2 (Kiev 1959, 1962)
Rudnitskii, P. *Ekonomika spirtovogo kombinirovannogo proizvodstva* (Kiev 1969)
Holobuts'kyi, V. *Ekonomichna istoriia Ukraïns'koï RSR: Dozhovt-nevyi period* (Kiev 1970)
Treml, V. *Alcohol in the USSR: A Statistical Study* (Durham, NC 1982)
V. Kubijovyč, B. Wynar

Lira (hurdy-gurdy). A folk string instrument. It was introduced in Ukraine from the West and spread rapidly during the 15th century. The sound is produced by cranking a rosined wheel against strings within the instrument. Most frequently, the *lira* has three strings; the two lower strings are monotonic, and the higher string leads the melody. The instrument was played commonly in Ukraine until the 20th century by itinerant musicians called *lirnyks.

Lirnyk

Lirnyks. Wandering folk minstrels, often blind, who accompanied themselves on a *lira.* They appeared in Ukraine in the 15th century and had formed a guild by the end of the 17th century. There were special schools for them. Their repertoire consisted mainly of religious songs, although humorous and satirical songs were also popular. Some lirnyks specialized in historical songs and dumas.

Lisanevych, Borys [Lisanevyč] (Lisanevich, Boris), b 1904 on Lisanevychivka *khutir*, Odessa county, Kherson gubernia, d 20 November 1985 in Kathmandu, Nepal. Adventurer and big game hunter. After his education at the Cadet Academy of Odessa he was a dancer in S. Diaghilev's Ballet Russe. In 1933 Lisanevych went to India, where he became a guide for big game hunting expeditions, a popular host, and a confidant of maharajas. He was the founder of the famous Club 300 in Calcutta and is regarded as the father of modern tourism in Nepal. In 1954 he opened the Royal Hotel in Kathmandu, which be-

came a meeting place for royalty, international celebrities, and Himalayan mountaineering expeditions. His life is described in M. Peissel's *Tiger for Breakfast: The Story of Boris of Kathmandu – Adventurer, Big Game Hunter, and Host of Nepal's Famous 'Royal Hotel'* (1967).

Lisenkov, Nikolai, b 4 August 1865 in Moscow, d 11 October 1941 in Odessa. Russian anatomist and surgeon. A graduate of the medical faculty of Moscow University (1893), he served as a professor at Odessa University (1902–41, from 1923 the Odessa Medical Institute) and founded the anatomy museum in Odessa. He researched brain disorders and operative methods in heart, brain, and neurosurgery. He wrote textbooks in operative surgery and topographic and normal anatomy and proposed a method of preserving anatomical specimens.

Lishansky, Yukhym [Lišans'kyj, Juxym], b 9 October 1905 in Kiev, d 21 May 1982 in Kiev. Stage director and pedagogue. In 1922 he completed the third studio course at the Moscow Art Theater, and in 1925–6 he apprenticed at Berezil. In 1927–30 he worked in the Kharkiv and Kiev theaters of opera and ballet. In 1931–41 he was stage director at the Kiev Theater of the Red Army, and in 1946–82 stage director and pedagogue in the opera studio at the Kiev Conservatory.

Ivan Lishchynsky

Lishchynsky, Ivan [Liščyns'kyj], b 1883, d 1941. Educator and civic and political leader. A teacher by profession, under the Western Ukrainian National Republic he served as school inspector of the Drohobych district (1918–19). After the war he edited *Uchytel's'ke slovo* (1921–2) and was president of the Organization of the Ukrainians of Lviv (1922–6) and of the Ukrainian Teachers' Mutual Aid Society (1925–9). He was also active in politics, first as a member of the executive and the Central Committee of the Ukrainian Labor party and then as a deputy of the Ukrainian National Democratic Alliance to the Sejm (1928–30). In 1930 he was imprisoned in Brest by the Polish authorities for his political activities.

Lishko, Valerii [Liško, Valerij], b 26 October 1937 in Kiev. Biochemist; AN URSR (now ANU) corresponding member since 1979 and full member since 1982. After graduating from Kiev University (1960) he joined the ANU Institute of Biochemistry and became its deputy director in 1970 and director in 1977. Lishko's research has dealt with the molecular mechanisms of active and passive ion transport through organic membranes. He developed ways of identifying channels of nerve and muscle membranes in noncellular systems.

Liskevych, Taras [Liskevyč], b 14 October 1948 in Munich, Germany. Ukrainian-American sports figure. He graduated from Loyola University in Chicago (1970) and Ohio State University (PH D in physical education, 1976). He was assistant coach of the US women's volleyball team that competed in the 1975 Pan-American Games, and head coach of the men's volleyball team at Ohio State University (1975–6) and the women's volleyball team at the University of the Pacific (Stockton, California, 1976–84). Since 1985 he has been head coach of the US women's volleyball team that competed in the 1988 and 1992 Olympic Games and other international competitions. He cofounded the American (formerly Collegiate) Volleyball Coaches Association and is the coauthor of *A Pictorial Analysis of Power Volleyball* (1972) and author of *Volleyball Is a Hit.*

Lisko [Lis'ko] (Polish: Lesko). IV-3. A town (1968 pop 2,600) on the Sian River in the eastern Lemko region, now a county town in Poland's Krosno voivodeship. In 1932 the Ukrainian peasants of the region revolted against the Polish authorities and landlords. The army was summoned, and 6 peasants were killed, 15 injured, and nearly 100 arrested. Soviet sources present the rebellion as a communist-led action by united Ukrainian and Polish peasants and workers. Until 1939 Lisko county was part of Lviv voivodeship under Poland. Its population was 81,600, of whom 86.2 percent were Ukrainians. In 1947 almost all the Ukrainians were resettled.

Lisnytsky, Hryhorii [Lisnyc'kyj, Hryhorij], b ? in the Kiev region, d 1664. Nobleman and Cossack colonel. He was sent by Hetman B. Khmelnytsky to the Siverske region (1648), and later he served as colonel of Myrhorod regiment (1652–8, with interruptions) and general judge (1657, 1661–2). He was sent as an envoy to Moscow in 1658 and to Poland in 1659. An opponent of Muscovy, he took part in the preparation of the treaties of *Hadiache and *Slobodyshche. A member of the Lviv Brotherhood from 1662, he was killed by the Poles.

Lisovska, Nastia. See Roksoliana.

Lisovska, Zoia [Lisovs'ka, Zoja], b 14 April 1925 in Lviv. Artist; daughter of R. *Lisovsky and S. *Turkevych-Lukiianovych and wife of Oleh *Nyzhankivsky. A postwar refugee, she studied at the Vienna Art Academy (1945–6), received a national diploma in design from the London Polytechnic of Art (1951), and studied painting at the Rome Academy of Fine Arts (1952–5). A resident of Geneva, where she teaches painting and drawing, she has created paintings (gouache landscapes, portraits, and other compositions), frescoes, stained-glass windows, mosaics, enamels, ceramics, sculptures, lithographs, and wood engravings. Solo exhibitions of her works have been held in Munich (1957), Geneva (1960), Rio de Janeiro (1961), New York City (1964, 1970), Toronto (1964, 1984), and Chicago (1974). Joint exhibitions of the works of Lisovska, her father, and her daughter, L. *Nyzhankovska, were held in

Zoia Lisovska: *The Passion* (gouache, 1953)

New York, Philadelphia, and Washington, DC, in 1989, in London in 1990, and in Lviv in 1991.

Lisovsky, Heraklii [Lisovs'kyi, Heraklij] (secular name: Yosyf Odrovuzh-Lisovsky), b 1734 in Usachy, Belarus, d 30 August 1809 in Polatsk. Ukrainian-Belarusian Catholic metropolitan in 1806–9. Although born into a Latinized noble family, Lisovsky found the Eastern rite appealing and entered the Basilian order after studying philosophy and theology in Polatsk. In 1778 he became archimandrite of the St Onuphrius Monastery in Orsha, and in 1784, archbishop of Polatsk. In 1806, after the death of Metropolitan T. *Rostotsky, Tsar Alexander II appointed him de facto metropolitan of Kiev, although under the altered title 'Metropolitan of the Uniate Church in Russia.' During his lifetime Lisovsky faced numerous problems in trying to re-establish the jurisdictional and administrative structure of the Greek Catholic church after the successive partitions of Poland had transferred much of the territory in which the church was based to Russian control.

Lisovsky, Oleksii [Lisovs'kyj, Oleksij], b 24 February 1861 in Machukhy, Poltava county, d 1934 in Krasnodar, Kuban region. Literary scholar and folklorist. After graduating in law from the University of Odessa (1886) he worked at the Odessa and Kharkiv courts. He did research on kobzars and wrote *Opyt izucheniia malo-russkoi dumy* (An Essay on the Study of the Little-Russian Duma, 1890) and *Glavnye motivy v poezii T.G. Shevchenko* (The Main Motifs in the Poetry of T.H. Shevchenko, 1893). Many of his articles appeared in the provincial papers. He was persecuted by the authorities for his liberal ideas.

Lisovsky, Robert [Lisovs'kyj], b 29 December 1893 in Oleksandrivske (now Zaporizhia), d 28 December 1982 in Geneva. Painter and graphic artist; husband of S. *Turkevych-Lukiianovych and father of Z. *Lisovska. He studied in Kiev at O. Murashko's art school, under M. Boichuk and H. Narbut at the Ukrainian Academy of Arts (1917–20), and at the Berlin Academy of Arts (1927). An émigré from 1920, he worked as a graphic artist in Lviv and was a professor of graphic art at the *Ukrainian Studio of Plastic Arts in Prague (1929–45). After the Second

Robert Lisovsky   Vasyl Lisovy

World War he lived in London and, from 1962, Geneva. Lisovsky exhibited in Kiev, Lviv, Warsaw, Berlin, Prague, and Rome. He was a masterful book illustrator and designer, whose expressionism incorporated traits of the Kievan baroque in an original and modern fashion. Lisovsky, P. *Kovzhun, and M. *Butovych were the three most eminent Ukrainian book artists of the 1920s and 1930s. Lisovsky also designed the *trident with a sword, bookplates, and O. Basarab's tombstone (1924) in Lviv and painted in watercolors and oils (flowers, landscapes, still lifes, and portraits).

Lisovy, Oleksander [Lisovyj], b 1 June 1938 in Serov, Sverdlovsk oblast, RSFSR. Cameraman. A graduate of the State Institute of Cinematography in Moscow, he has worked at the Kiev Studio of Chronicle-Documentary Films since 1955. Among his films are *Pisnia* (The Song, 1968), *Uchytel'* (The Teacher, 1970), *Zakharova ridnia* (Zakhar's Family, 1972), *Persha borozna* (The First Furrow, 1974), *Kantata pro Chervonyi orkestr* (Cantata on the Red Orchestra, 1975), and the full-length films *Ukraïna: Zemlia i liudy* (Ukraine: The Land and the People, 1970) and *Rozum, chest', i sovist' epokhy* (The Reason, Honor, and Conscience of the Epoch, 1977).

Lisovy, Petro [Lisovyj] (pseud of Petro Svashenko), b 22 June 1891 in Derhachi, Kharkiv county, Kharkiv gubernia, d 17 January 1943? Writer. From 1920 to the early 1930s his works were published in *Literaturnyi iarmarok*. His sketches and short stories about peasant life appeared in the collection *V revoliutsiiu* (Into the Revolution, 1927). He wrote several novelettes–family chronicles – *Nashi slobozhany* (Our Free Settlers, 1930), *Za Zbruchem* (Beyond the [River] Zbruch, 1932), *Chervona raketa* (The Red Rocket, 1932), and *Harri Smit, abo Ianki v ukraïns'kykh preriiakh* (Harry Smith, or A Yankee on the Ukrainian Prairies, 1933) – and two novels, *Mykola Iarosh* (1928) and *Zapysky Iuriia Dibrovy* (The Notes of Yurii Dibrova, 1930). He was arrested and exiled during the terror of the mid-1930s.

Lisovy, Vasyl [Lisovyj, Vasyl'], b 5 May 1937 in Stari Bezradychi, Obukhiv raion, Kiev oblast. Philosopher and dissident. After graduating from Kiev University (1961), he taught logic and esthetics at the Ternopil Medical Insti-

tute (1962–6) and then returned to Kiev for postgraduate studies. In 1970 he received his candidate's degree and became a research associate of the AN URSR (now ANU) Institute of Philosophy and a lecturer at Kiev University. The articles Lisovy published in 1970–2 – three on ordinary language, one on the history of logic, and one a critique of scientism – reveal a perceptive and original thinker. After sending an open letter to the CC CPSU protesting the wave of arrests of Ukrainian writers and artists in early 1972 and calling for greater openness and democracy, he was arrested on 6 July 1972 and sentenced in November 1973 to seven years in a Mordovian labor camp and three years' exile in the Buriat ASSR for anti-Soviet agitation and propaganda. In 1980 he was sentenced to an additional year of imprisonment for 'parasitism.' He was released in 1983, but he was not permitted to work in philosophy until the beginning of 1990, when he was reinstated in his position at the Institute of Philosophy.

Lisovyk, Oleksander (pseud of Hnyda), b ca 1895 in Poltava gubernia, d ca 1933. Revolutionary figure. A member of the underground Socialist Revolutionary Youth Association (1915–16), after the 1917 Revolution he joined the *Borotbists and became a leading organizer of the partisan struggle in the Poltava region, against the Germans, the Hetman goverment, and the Denikin army. He took part in negotiations with N. *Makhno to form an independent Ukrainian Red Army. In 1919 he headed the Soviet Department of Education in Poltava gubernia, and from December 1919 he edited the Borotbist paper *Ukraïns'kyi proletar* in Katerynoslav. After the Borotbists merged with the CPBU in 1920, he chaired the Artemivske Okruha Executive Committee and sat on the Presidium of the All-Union Central Executive Committee. In the early 1930s he directed the Chief Administration of Automobile Transportation in Soviet Ukraine. He was arrested with other former Borotbists during the Stalinist terror, and executed.

Lisovyk. A figure of Ukrainian folk demonology who controlled the forests and their riches – the trees, animals, and birds. Every forest had its own *lisovyk*, who appeared in the form of a human being, a giant with horns, a tree, or an animal. He could be recognized by the absence of a shadow. He lived in the woods or in inaccessible places and in winter inhabited caves or deserted shepherds' huts, where he whistled and sang. He could lead people astray in the forest or could help hunters by sending animals into their paths. In the Hutsul region the *lisovyk* was represented as a shepherd. After Ukraine's conversion to Christianity St George also became a protector of animals and cattle.

Listok (Sheet). A Transcarpathian Russophile 'religious-literary journal' published semimonthly in Russian in Uzhhorod from September 1885 to December 1903. Its editor was Ye. Fentsyk. Only one issue appeared after Fentsyk's death; it was edited by A. Voloshyn. *Listok* published editorials on religious and political topics; sermons; religious, historical, ethnographic, linguistic, and philosophical articles; poetry; and prose. In 1891–3 it also published an irregular popular education supplement in the Transcarpathian dialect. The journal's contributors were mostly Transcarpathian writers and intellectuals, such as O. Dukhnovych, A. Kralytsky, O. Mytrak, S. Pasichynsky, O. Pavlovych, I. Silvai, Yu. Stavrovsky, and Yu. Zhatkovych. It had few subscribers (150 in 1887; 25 in 1903).

Liszt, Franz, b 22 October 1811 in Raiding, Hungary, d 31 July 1886 in Bayreuth, Germany. Hungarian composer and virtuoso pianist. Ukrainian themes and melodies are evident in a number of Liszt's works. He was familiar with Ukraine, and had his final concert tour there in 1847 (appearing in recitals in Kiev, Zhytomyr, Nemyriv, Berdychev, Kremianets, Lviv, Odessa, Mykolaiv, and Yelysavethrad). He stayed on through late 1847, visiting the estates of Princess Carolyne von Sayn-Wittgenstein at Voronyntsi in Podilia, where he composed two piano pieces ('Ballade d'Ukraine' and 'Complainte') based on Ukrainian folk songs. These were later incorporated into the set *Glanes de Woronince*. In 1840 Liszt finished a transcendental étude, *Mazeppa*, for piano, after the poem by V. Hugo, and in 1851 he composed a symphonic poem of the same title. In 1855 he arranged *Mazeppa* for two pianos, and in 1874 for piano four hands. In 1881 Liszt orchestrated *Danses galiciennes* by his student J. Zarębski (originally for piano four hands), the last movement of which is a **kolomyika*.

Litavry (Kiev)

Litavry (Kettledrums). A literary and art weekly published in Kiev in the autumn of 1941. The editor was O. Teliha. It was banned by the Nazi authorities after the first four issues.

Litavry (Kettledrums). A journal of literature, art, and popular science; the organ of the Association of Ukrainian Scholars, Writers, and Artists in Austria. It was published in Salzburg in 1947 and 1948. The editor in chief was Yu. *Klen, and the editorial board included Yu. Dyvnych, I. Koshelivets, B. Nykolyn, and B. Oleksandriv. The journal contained poetry by V. Skorupsky, H. Cherin, Klen, I. Kovaliv, and M. Orest; prose by I. Kachurovsky (as well as his poetry), O. Satsiuk, M. Tsukanova, and O. Zvychaina; articles on literature by V. Derzhavyn and B. Romanenchuk; and literary reviews by Dyvnych, Klen, Oleksandriv, and Romanenchuk. It published translations from German, English, and Belarusian literatures as well as

Litavry (Salzburg)

obituaries (eg, of M. Matviiev-Melnyk, I. Bryk, M. Trzhepel, and Klen). The 1947 September–December issue was edited by B. Nykolyn, who was later succeeded by Romanenchuk.

Literacy (*pysmennist*). The ability to read and write in a person who has reached a certain age (nine years being the age standard commonly used in Ukrainian lands for statistical purposes); a distinction is made between full and partial literacy, or the ability to read but not write. At the beginning of the 20th century the majority of the population in Ukrainian lands was illiterate, a result of the state neglect of education (in lands ruled by Austria and Hungary), the absence of legal provision for enforcing compulsory education (in lands ruled by Russia), and a weakly developed network of schools. Instruction in foreign (non-Ukrainian) languages and the short length of the school year also hindered full literacy, even among elementary school graduates. Concerted efforts aimed at increasing literacy were made in Russian-ruled Ukraine by *literacy societies and in Western Ukraine by the *Prosvita society.

An 1886 survey showed that 16 percent of Russian army recruits from Right-Bank Ukraine and 26 percent of those from the Left-Bank region were literate (the latter figure reflects a growth in *zemstvo schools). The 1897 Russian census revealed that 26 percent of the total population over nine years of age in the Ukrainian gubernias was literate; the figure for Ukrainians there stood at 23.6 percent (38.6 percent of men, 12.4 percent of women). With the expansion of the school system the figure had grown to approx 42 percent of the total population by 1914.

The transition to using Ukrainian as the language of instruction in schools (from 1917), the further expansion of the school system, the introduction of mandatory education measures, and the work of the Liknep (*elimination of illiteracy) network during the 1920s and 1930s resulted in increased literacy. Table 1 illustrates the success of these undertakings in popular education.

Notwithstanding such progress, the literacy rate of Ukrainians in the Ukrainian SSR in 1926 was below that of the other national groups in the republic (see table 2). According to Soviet census figures the literacy rate in the Ukrainian SSR continued to rise and reached 85.3 percent in 1938.

The literacy rate among Ukrainians in Western Ukraine

TABLE 1
Literacy in the nine Ukrainian gubernias of the Russian Empire, 1897, and the Ukrainian SSR, 1926 (in percentages)

Age	Total population		Urban		Rural	
	1897	1926	1897	1926	1897	1926
Males						
5–8	5.7	12.8	19.4	23.8	4.3	11.7
9–14	43.4	76.0	69.5	86.6	40.3	74.9
15–19	47.9	79.2	71.7	89.7	44.5	77.9
20–24	47.1	88.2	64.2	94.1	41.4	86.8
25–29	44.4	87.2	68.2	93.8	39.9	86.0
30–39	39.0	83.5	65.4	92.1	34.7	81.9
40–49	31.7	72.6	59.1	87.0	27.5	70.0
50–59	23.6	55.4	53.9	79.1	19.5	51.4
60+	17.3	35.3	45.0	65.0	13.8	31.5
All ages	34.2	68.6	59.9	83.6	30.2	66.2
Females						
5–8	3.1	9.9	12.7	22.8	2.1	8.6
9–14	16.3	54.7	49.0	82.4	12.2	51.4
15–19	16.9	54.8	45.6	82.1	12.3	50.8
20–24	15.8	56.8	46.4	84.1	10.8	52.0
25–29	12.6	47.3	40.9	79.4	8.3	41.2
30–39	10.4	37.3	35.4	70.5	6.7	31.2
40–49	8.0	22.4	28.3	56.6	5.1	16.5
50–59	7.0	14.7	23.9	46.8	4.5	9.2
60+	6.2	9.6	19.5	34.2	4.0	5.4
All ages	11.2	37.7	35.3	66.8	7.5	33.2

TABLE 2
Literacy in the Ukrainian SSR by nationality and sex, 1926 (in percentages)

	Males	Females
Total population	68.6	37.7
Ukrainians	66.5	32.5
Russians	76.5	51.2
Jews	84.1	74.2
Poles	60.0	45.7

TABLE 3
Literacy rates in Ukrainian territories under Poland, 1921 and 1931 (in percentages)

	1921	1931
Total population	50.5	64.7
Towns and cities	75.1	85.0
Villages	44.6	59.6
Males	57.2	73.8
Females	44.4	56.0

was significantly higher than in Russian-ruled Ukraine. In 1900, 25 percent of Ukrainians there were literate; in 1910 the figure reached 43 percent (compared to 47 percent of the total population). The literacy rate continued to grow through the 1920s and 1930s (see table 3).

According to Soviet sources illiteracy ceased to exist in the Ukrainian SSR. Census figures from 1970 show that 99.7 percent of 5- to 49-year-olds were literate.

V. Kubijovyč

Literacy societies (*tovarystva hramotnosty*). Community-based societies for popular education that were active in the Russian Empire from the second half of the 19th century until 1917. Their chief purpose was to increase literacy and general knowledge among the population at large. The work of these groups resulted in the establishment of *Sunday schools and library-reading rooms, in the organization of public readings and lectures as well as literary and musical evenings, and in the printing of popular literature for broad distribution. Most of this activity was centered in larger towns and cities, with only occasional forays into villages. The oldest group of this type in Ukraine, the *Kharkiv Literacy Society, was founded in 1869. It focused mainly on publishing popular works, but few of its titles were in Ukrainian. The Kiev Literacy Society, founded in 1882, was more active in Ukrainian-language work. It published Ukrainian literature (including the works of T. Shevchenko) and built the People's Home in 1902, which provided a facility for Ukrainian theater and lectures and later for a Prosvita organization. The *Kiev Literacy Society was also active in Right-Bank Ukraine, where it had affiliates and provided assistance for educational programs in Kiev, Podilia, and Volhynia gubernias. Similar societies formed in the 1890s included the Society for Spreading Popular Literacy in Katerynoslav Gubernia and the Poltava Society for the Development of Popular Education. A Volhynian literacy society was formed in the 1900s. These various societies for popular education tended to limit their work to larger centers and in fact did little to spread literacy in the Ukrainian language. A similar sort of work was taken up in Central and Eastern Ukraine after 1905 by the *Prosvita society. The cause of Ukrainian-language popular education was taken up during the Soviet period by the Het' Nepysmennist (Away with Illiteracy) society (1923–36), which had 1,500 branches and affiliates and a membership of 59,000 in 1925.

Literary criticism. In Ukraine the beginnings of criticism as a separate literary genre coincide with the rebirth of *literature studies in the early decades of the 19th century. Some scholars, however (eg, M. Plevako), suggest a later date because of the virtual absence of Ukrainian-language periodicals until the 1860s.

Early 19th-century Ukrainian literary criticism was linked to the debate on whether or not real literature could be written in Ukrainian. Assertions that it could were first formulated by O. Lobysevych in a letter (1794) to H. Konysky and by Ya. *Markovych in his *Zapiski o Malorossii* ... (Notes on Little Russia ..., 1798). Some early remarks of a critical nature can be found in O. *Pavlovsky's 'Grammar of the Little Russian Dialect' (1818), and the first journals published in Ukraine, *Khar'kovskii Demokrit* (1816), *Ukrainskii vestnik* (1816–19), and *Ukrainskii zhurnal* (1824–5), devoted some passing attention to the question of the viability of a Ukrainian-language literature. The last of the aforementioned journals (1825, no. 5) published a favorable article by I. *Kulzhynsky on the history and nature of 'Little Russian' poetry. Most Russian critics reacted negatively to works published in Ukrainian. Among them were M. *Kachenovsky, the author of an article in *Vestnik Evropy* in 1815 that was hostile to Ukrainian writing in general and I. Kotliarevsky's *Eneïda* (Aeneid) in particular, and V. *Belinsky. Consequently, Ukrainian critics at that time, and even more so later, were forced to limit themselves almost exclusively to defending the right of a Ukrainian literature to exist.

One of the first critical surveys of works in Ukrainian was written by M. *Kostomarov and published in the 1844 literary miscellany *Molodyk*. The first significant contributions to the development of Ukrainian literary criticism, however, were made by P. *Kulish in the late 1850s and early 1860s, particularly in the miscellany *Khata* (1860) and the journal *Osnova* (1861–2). Kulish argued that the Ukrainian language and literature were independent of the Russian, and expressed the hope that writers would produce works that would reflect the Ukrainian identity. He believed that the genres of travesty and burlesque were inimical to Ukrainian literature because they made it appear as fit only for expressing vulgar wit, and he consequently condemned Kotliarevsky and P. Hulak-Artemovsky for the disrespect he felt they had shown in their works for the Ukrainian language. Kulish esteemed the Ukrainian tales of H. Kvitka-Osnovianenko, however, and he was one of the first critics to emphasize the importance of T. Shevchenko's poetry for all the Slavic nations. Although he adhered to the idealized populist notion of the peasantry as the embodiment of the Ukrainian people (*narodnist*) and remained loyal to the ethnographic principle, Kulish had high esthetic standards and considered it the duty of literary critics to struggle against talentless scribblers and epigones. The critical attitudes of Kulish and his supporters in the 1850s and 1860s evolved into *populism, the ideas of which dominated Ukrainian literary criticism until the early 20th century. (The pseudopopulism of Soviet literary criticism from the 1940s to 1960s was of a different origin.)

In Austrian-ruled Galicia literary criticism appeared somewhat later than in Russian-ruled Ukraine. There it was also linked to the movement in support of writing in the vernacular that began with the publication of the miscellany *Rusalka Dnistrovaia* (1837) by the *Ruthenian Triad. In his many articles the triad's Ya. *Holovatsky propagated the idea that literature written in the vernacular could not be limited in scope but should deal with all aspects of life. He also promoted in Galicia the Ukrainian works written in Russian-ruled Ukraine. The question of how a 'Ruthenian' literature could develop, and especially the related issue of language and *orthography, was debated in two miscellanies titled *Vinok rusynam na obzhynky* (1846–7), in the newspaper *Zoria halytska*, in other Galician publications of the mid-19th century, and at the 1848 *Congress of Ruthenian Scholars. In the following decades antipopulist tendencies in Galicia were manifested by advocates of the use of Church Slavonic (eg, M. Malynovsky) and by the *Russophiles (eg, A. Petrushevych). As a result writing in the bookish *yazychiie became widespread, despite the harsh criticism of *Osnova* and particularly M. *Maksymovych. In neighboring Transcarpathia the Ruthenian literary rebirth of the 1860s had a slightly different orientation. Its primary spokesman, O. *Dukhnovych, did not support the use of the vernacular in literature; he thereby made it possible for later Transcarpathian Russophiles to exploit his name for their purposes. Neither the Russophiles nor the supporters of the *yazychiie in Galicia and Transcarpathia produced notable literary critics.

In the 1860s, after the 1863 tsarist ban on printing Ukrai-

nian-language publications, the center of Ukrainian literary activity shifted to Galicia, and the ideas of the *Osnova* writers attracted a substantial following there. Articles from *Osnova*, particularly those by Kulish and Kostomarov, were reprinted in the Lviv journal *Pravda* (1867–98), which became the most important Ukrainian publication of its time. *Pravda* was greatly influenced by Kulish and then, for many years, by O. *Konysky. I. *Nechui-Levytsky, a prominent populist writer and literary critic living in Russian-ruled Ukraine, debuted in *Pravda* and contributed regularly to it. In his now-famous article in *Pravda* on contemporary literary directions (1878) he formulated three principles of literary creativity (verisimilitude, nationality, and *narodnist*) and harshly condemned the widespread orientation of Ukrainian writers to Russian literature.

In the 1870s the key figure in Ukrainian literary criticism was M. *Drahomanov. Drahomanov introduced the idea of progress and emphasized the importance of social questions in literature. In a longer work on Shevchenko, the Ukrainophiles, and socialism (1879) Drahomanov condemned the cult of Shevchenko and the tendentious approaches to his poetry; at the same time he presented a social and cultural framework for the study of Shevchenko's poetry. Although because of his federalist convictions Drahomanov had an artificial, untenable schema of four literatures (the Russian, 'Great Russian,' Ukrainian, and Galician) that virtually no one accepted during or after his lifetime, more than any of his contemporaries he stimulated and enlivened critical thought and provoked a lively polemic in Galician literary circles. In general he hoped that Ukrainian literature would develop in step with the Western and Central European literary movements. Drahomanov pioneered the sociological approach in Ukrainian literary criticism. That approach greatly influenced contributors to *Pravda*, such as I. *Rudchenko in Russian-ruled Ukraine and V. *Navrotsky in Galicia.

Konysky was another prominent advocate of the independence of Ukrainian literature and of the adoption of 'universal liberal ideas ... directly from European sources' rather than through the medium of Russian literature. Other contributors to *Pravda*, such as M. *Buchynsky, O. *Ohonovsky, and V. *Barvinsky, advocated populist perspectives and came into conflict with Drahomanov.

In the mid-1870s Drahomanov's ideas influenced the Lviv student journal *Druh* and its principal contributor, I. *Franko. In his 1876–7 articles in *Druh* Franko was the first Ukrainian literary critic to discuss philosophical and esthetic problems as they related to literature and the relationship between poetry and life. In his article on literature, its tasks, and its most important traits, published in the 1878 literary miscellany *Molot*, Franko reprehended the narrowness of the populist approach, particularly the views expressed by Nechui-Levytsky in his article of that year. Later, however, in his articles in *Zhytie i slovo* and *Literaturno-naukovyi vistnyk* (LNV), Franko transcended Drahomanov's positivist critique and developed a broader understanding of literature as art.

From 1882 to 1907 the principal forum of literary criticism in Russian-ruled Ukraine was the journal *Kievskaia starina* (it appeared as *Ukraïna* in 1907). One of its authors was V. *Horlenko, who had been influenced by the critical method of C.-A. Sainte-Beuve and H. Taine and contributed articles about earlier and contemporary 19th-century

Ukrainian writers and book reviews from a cultural-historical perspective.

At the beginning of the 20th century modernist literary criticism became popular in Ukraine. In 1901 LNV published M. *Vorony's modernist manifesto, in which he exhorted Ukrainian writers to abandon the populist model, to write poetry the quality of which mirrored contemporary world standards, and to embrace the principle of pure art. The modernist esthetic was advanced by the Lviv journal *S'vit (1906–7) and by the Galician modernist writers' group *Moloda Muza, which emulated European contemporaries, such as M. Maeterlinck, H. Ibsen, and F. Nietzsche, and the earlier C.-P. Baudelaire. The leading Ukrainian modernist critic was M. *Yevshan. In his articles in the Kiev journal *Ukraïns'ka khata and his book Pid praporom mystetstva (Under the Flag of Art, 1910) he analyzed the works of Ukrainian modernist writers and tried to formulate the esthetic principles of modernist literary criticism. Those principles remained vague and contradictory, however. Another modernist critic, O. *Lutsky, formulated the fundamental positions of Moloda Muza in his contributions to Dilo and S'vit.

In addition to the modernists a neopopulist criticism based on the earlier, 19th-century, populist perspective flourished in the early 20th century. Its leading exponent was S. *Yefremov, who rejected the esthetic approach as inappropriate for evaluating Ukrainian literature. Instead Yefremov based the value of a literary work on whether or not it promoted the ideal of national liberation, and whether or not its content and form (particularly its language) were suitable for the reading public at large.

From 1902 until the outbreak of the First World War a heated discussion took place among the representatives of various critical methods. It was sparked by Yefremov's antimodernist article 'V poiskakh novoi krasoty' (In Search of a New Beauty, 1902). In the ensuing debate the modernist critics (eg, Lutsky and H. *Khotkevych) published their views in LNV and Ukraïns'ka khata, and the neopopulists published theirs in Kievskaia starina and Nova hromada. Franko was critical of the modernists because he believed firmly that a literary work should enlighten the reader and focus on social issues. At the same time, however, he spoke out against Yefremov because he believed authors had the right to provide a 'psychological analysis of social phenomena' and to try out new forms of artistic expression. Lesia *Ukrainka shared many of Franko's critical views regarding both Ukrainian and foreign literature.

The February Revolution of 1917, the ensuing Ukrainian struggle for independence, and the first decade of Soviet rule in Ukraine stimulated literary activity. During the brief period of Ukrainian independence the journal *Knyhar (1917–20) published many articles and reviews by M. *Zerov, P. *Zaitsev, V. *Koroliv-Stary, and other critics. During that period a variety of literary currents, each with its own critical method, quickly evolved. Criticism was published in ephemeral journals and miscellanies and separately in the essay collections of P. *Tychyna, M. *Semenko, Ya. *Savchenko, M. *Rylsky, and A. *Nikovsky (in his Vita nova [1919], Nikovsky discussed modern poetry in the context of the Ukrainian rebirth). The short-lived rebirth also produced occasional criticism by the symbolists (eg, Ya. Savchenko, D. *Zahul, and Yu. *Mezhenko) and writers of the Proletkult movement (who rejected art in its

traditional sense), more enduring criticism by the *Neoclassicists Zerov and P. *Fylypovych, and many other critical opinions.

By the mid-1920s two main currents of literary criticism had crystallized in Soviet Ukraine. On the one side there was a proregime current consisting more of advocates of official Bolshevik views than orthodox Marxists. On the other there were critics who opposed the proregime line but supported diverse artistic credos (eg, the members of *Vaplite and the essentially apolitical Neoclassicists). This basic bipolarization of critical opinion became most evident during the Soviet Ukrainian *Literary Discussion of 1925–8. The chief spokesmen of the Party line were the vulgar Marxists V. *Koriak, S. *Shchupak, and H. *Ovcharov and the politically more consistent B. *Kovalenko, who advocated the use of 'proletarian realism,' a precursor of the official method of *socialist realism that became obligatory in the 1930s. Key representatives of the oppositional current were the Vaplite leader M. *Khvylovy and the Neoclassicist Zerov. Those critics advocated the view that writers had to develop a high level of literary craft and familiarity with the best literary achievements of the West. The 'opposition' also included unaffiliated critics, such as O. *Biletsky. Biletsky played an important role in the development of Ukrainian literary criticism by pioneering a multidimensional approach that focused on the formal, esthetic aspects of a literary work and on Ukrainian literature in the context of Western literature.

In 1932 the CC of the all-Union Party adopted a resolution that abolished all literary groups, created a single writers' union subordinated to the Party, forbade all literary criticism not sanctioned by the Party, and proclaimed socialist realism to be the only literary method that Soviet writers could use. Consequently all independent literary criticism disappeared, and most critics, including not only many of those in the 'opposition' (eg, Zerov, Fylypovych, M. *Mohyliansky) but also the representatives of Party opinion (including Koriak, Shchupak, and Kovalenko), were arrested during the Stalinist terror. Most of them were shot, or perished in concentration camps; those who survived remained silent until the post-Stalin thaw two decades later.

During the interwar years literary criticism in the non-Soviet territories of Western Ukraine and in the Ukrainian émigré community was linked not to literary trends but to literary-cum-political journals and newspapers. M. *Shapoval, P. *Bohatsky, and other émigré followers of M. Hrushevsky's sociological approach or the neopopulist Yefremov contributed to the Prague-based journal *Nova Ukraïna; V. *Pisniachevsky, M. *Slavinsky, and other émigré and Galician critics contributed to National Democratic or socialist publications. Only a few critics modeled their work on Western European modernist criticism: M. *Rudnytsky, M. *Strutynsky, and several younger contributors to the literary miscellany Terem (1919) and the journals *Mytusa (1922) and LNV (from 1922). The modernist critics came to be viewed as 'liberals.' Liberal views (eg, of Rudnytsky, V. *Simovych, O. *Bodnarovych, and Ya. and S. *Hordynsky) were published in the daily newspaper Dilo, the biweekly Nazustrich (from 1934), and the Warsaw-based bimonthly My (from 1935).

The Western Ukrainian and émigré nationalist movement that emerged in the early 1920s rejected not only the communist, but also the populist and esthetic approaches to literature. The most influential nationalist critic was D. *Dontsov, the editor from 1922 of *LNV* and its successor in 1933, *Vistnyk*. Other critics of the nationalist school were M. *Mukhyn, Ye. *Malaniuk, Yu. *Lypa, Yu. *Klen, V. *Doroshenko, I. *Korovytsky, B. *Kravtsiv, and, especially, L. *Lutsiv. Similar criticism appeared in the journal *Dazhboh* (1932–5), which published articles and reviews by the publisher Ye. *Pelensky and by B.I. *Antonych, Y. Shemlei, and B. *Romanenchuk; and in *Obriï* (1936) and *Naperedodni* (1937–8), where O. *Hrytsai, D. *Vikonska, O. *Olzhych, and V. Rudko published their articles. Mukhyn and Hrytsai also contributed to the principal nationalist organ in Bukovyna, *Samostiina dumka*. Among the Western Ukrainian nationalist critics D. *Nykolyshyn devoted the most attention to Soviet Ukrainian literature.

Interwar Catholic criticism in Galicia was characterized by its anticommunism and antiliberalism. It was published in the journals *Postup* and *Dzvony* and the newspapers *Meta* and *Nova zoria* by M. *Hnatyshak and O. *Mokh. H. *Luzhnytsky (pseud: L. Nyhrytsky), the principal literary critic for the periodicals published by I. Tyktor's publishing house, shared many of the Catholic critics' views. Other critics who contributed to Tyktor's periodicals, particularly the literary-scientific supplement to *Novyi chas* (1937–9), were liberal or nationalist (eg, S. *Siropolko, M. *Holubets, S. Hordynsky, Pelensky, and Romanenchuk).

Communist critics in Western Ukraine were insignificant, both in number and in influence. In the 1920s they contributed to the Lviv journals *Nova Kul'tura*, *Kul'tura*, and *Vikna*. In the late 1920s and early 1930s Galician Sovietophile critics, such as A. and I. *Krushelnytsky, published their views in *Novi shliakhy* and *Krytyka*. After their emigration to Soviet Ukraine and the beginning of the Stalinist terror there, Sovietophile criticism virtually disappeared in Western Ukraine.

During the Second World War the principal organs of Ukrainian literary criticism were the Prague-based nationalist journal *Proboiem* and the Lviv journal *Nashi dni*, to which Simovych, Yu. *Stefanyk (pseud: Yu. Hamorak), and new émigrés from central and eastern Ukraine contributed.

After the war the state of literary criticism in Soviet Ukraine remained fundamentally unchanged. In addition, in the late 1940s, critics with German or Jewish roots (eg, Ye. *Adelheim and I. *Stebun) were persecuted as 'rootless cosmopolitans.' During the first postwar decade Soviet critics applauded the pseudo-*narodnist* of authors who utilized the structures of folk literature. A controlled revival in literary criticism began during the post-Stalin thaw of the mid-1950s, when noteworthy articles by older critics, such as Biletsky, Rylsky, and the labor-camp survivor B. *Antonenko-Davydovych, were allowed to be published.

During the Soviet Ukrainian cultural rebirth of the early 1960s a new criticism arose for the first time since the 1920s. The leading new critics were I. *Dziuba, I. *Svitlychny, Ye. *Sverstiuk, I. Boichak, M. Kotsiubynska, and V. *Stus. Their articles and surveys, in which they applied esthetic criteria rather than the scholastic principles of socialist realism, were interesting attempts at reconceptualizing 'rehabilitated' writers of the 1920s (eg, V. Svidzinsky, Ye. Pluzhnyk, and O. Vlyzko) and sober evaluations, devoid of traditional Soviet biases, of literary developments in Ukraine. The forgotten genre of the literary feuilleton was revived by the critics A. Shevchenko, M. Kosiv, L. Senyk, and M. *Malynovska, who parodied the ideologized writings of the Soviet literary 'generals' and the dubious examples of the class and *narodnist* approach. In various literary debates V. *Donchyk, H. *Syvokin, A. *Makarov, M. Ilnytsky, and V. Ivanysenko challenged orthodox stalwarts such as M. *Shamota, A. *Trypilsky, B. *Buriak, and D. *Shlapak. The latter group continued exhorting critics in a directivelike fashion to adhere to Party-sanctioned sociological schemata, in which the only measure for evaluating a literary work remained whether or not it helped to educate readers in the spirit of communist morality and mobilized them to build a 'radiant future for all of progressive humanity.'

The 1972 CC CPSU resolution 'On Literary-Artistic Criticism' made it clear, however, that the Party was not prepared to relinquish its strict control over literature and criticism, and that critics would have to continue playing the role of censor and policeman in literature. The chill of ideological scholasticism and state intervention again enveloped all publications, and *Komunist Ukraïny* and other Party periodicals resumed publishing articles by Shamota and other literary 'commissars' that denounced many talented writers and their works. Only through the *samvydav network were works such as Sverstiuk's *Cathedral in Scaffolding*, Dziuba's *Internationalism or Russification?*, and Svitlychny's and Stus's articles disseminated in Ukraine.

Those critics were soon subjected to brutal repression, and the 1970s proved in fact a barren decade in terms of literary criticism. The only partial exceptions are L. *Novychenko's books on Tychyna (1979) and Rylsky (1980). In the 1970s the eight-volume multiauthor history of Ukrainian literature (1967–71) prepared by the AN URSR (now ANU) Institute of Literature was censured by Party critics. Its authors were rebuked for devoting excessive attention to the Ukrainian classics and uncritically examining Soviet Ukrainian literature of the 1920s.

Only on the eve of the 1980s did a group of younger critics, born in the 1940s and 1950s – among them M. *Zhulynsky, V. Melnyk, V. Briukhovetsky, O. Nykanorova, M. Strelbytsky, V. Panchenko, S. Hrechaniuk, T. Salyha, L. *Skyrda, M. *Riabchuk, V. Morenets, L. Taran, and N. Bilotserkivets – become influential. Although they had to conform to rules imposed by the Party and occasionally had to exalt socialist realism, they applied esthetic criteria in their criticism and used Aesopian language to discuss the social phenomena depicted in literary works. On the pages of *Literaturna Ukraïna*, where the editor in charge of literary criticism was M. *Slaboshpytsky, lively exchanges of views were published on the state of Ukrainian prose, poetry, and literature for children and adolescents, and on the ethical code of literary criticism.

In the perestroika years Ukraine's journals and newspapers were filled with what would earlier have been 'criminal' references to proscribed writers, and concerted efforts were made to enrich the public's knowledge of how Ukrainian literature had truly developed, about the many writers repressed during the Stalinist terror, and about Ukrainian émigré literature. Nevertheless the first two volumes (1988, 1990) of a projected five-volume Ukrainian encyclopedia of literature prepared at the ANU Institute of Literature still refer to émigré writers, such as I. Bahriany, V. Barka, and T. Osmachka, as Ukrainian bourgeois nationalists, and the newest history of Ukrainian literature prepared at the institute (2 vols, 1987–8) avoids mentioning such writers altogether or treats them as enemies of the people, and presents superficial, simplistic accounts of the tragic fate of most 20th-century Ukrainian writers. But newspapers and journals of the late 1980s and early 1990s have published many previously banned literary works and have provided detailed accounts of their authors. In the process literary criticism and literature studies have overlapped in their discussion of the literature of the past decades, and the distinction between criticism and publicism has become blurred in recent articles (eg, by Dziuba, Sverstiuk, O. Pakhlovska, L. Kostenko, and O. Zabuzhko) addressing the acute problems of national survival.

In the postwar period G.Y. *Shevelov (pseud: Yu. Sherekh) has been the most influential literary critic within the Ukrainian émigré community in the West. In his articles in the journal *Arka* (1947–8) he formulated the principles of a 'national-organic style' and stimulated a lively discussion that continued for some time. Another émigré critic, V. *Derzhavyn, produced articles that combined the Neoclassicist and modernist approaches. In the 1950s and 1960s Yu. *Lavrinenko wrote insightful articles and reviews of Soviet Ukrainian and émigré literature (particularly the poets of the New York Group), and M. *Hlobenko and I. *Koshelivets wrote surveys of Soviet Ukrainian literature and articles about individual Soviet and émigré writers. In the 1960s Kravtsiv contributed systematic surveys of Soviet Ukrainian literature to the monthly journal *Suchasnist'*. The principal intellectual forum within the émigré community since 1960, *Suchasnist'* has also published criticism by B. *Boychuk, Doroshenko, J. *Fizer, Korovytsky, Koshelivets, I. *Kostetsky, H. *Kostiuk, B. *Rubchak, and D.H. *Struk. Some of the other notable émigré critics in the postwar period are Lutsiv, Romanenchuk, Stefanyk, O. Tarnavsky, and A. Yuryniak.

BIBLIOGRAPHY
Hordyns'kyi, Ia. *Literaturna krytyka pidsoviets'koï Ukraïny* (Lviv 1939; repr, Munich 1985)
Bernshtein, M. *Ukraïns'ka literaturna krytyka 50–70-kh rokiv XIX st.* (Kiev 1959)
Ivan'o, I. *Ocherki razvitiia esteticheskoi mysli Ukrainy* (Moscow 1981)
Fedchenko, P. *Literaturna krytyka na Ukraïni pershoï polovyny XIX st.* (Kiev 1982)
Briukhovets'kyi, V.; Kovalenko, L.; Naienko, M. 'Literaturoznavstvo i krytyka,' in *Istoriia ukraïns'koï literatury*, vol 2, *Radians'ka literatura*, ed L. Novychenko (Kiev 1988)
Fedchenko, P. (ed). *Istoriia ukraïns'koï literaturnoï krytyky: Dozhovtnevyi period* (Kiev 1988)
Donchyk, V. (ed). *20-i roky: Literaturni dyskusiï, polemiky: Literaturno-krytychni statti* (Kiev 1991)
I. Koshelivets, B. Kravtsiv, M. Slaboshpytsky

Literary Discussion. A wide-ranging debate during 1925–8 which coincided with the implementation of a policy of Ukrainization and engaged figures active in the political and cultural life of the new Soviet Ukrainian republic. The polemical pamphlets of M. *Khvylovy, which were serialized in *Kultura i pobut* (1925–6), outlined the themes and defined the tone of the debate, which came to be known as the Literary Discussion. Among the issues raised were the right of Ukrainian literature to set its own course, the relationship of current writing to past cultural values, the role of literary organizations, and the function of literature and criticism.

Two fundamental camps emerged. On one side stood Khvylovy, the literary organization Vaplite, and the Neoclassicists, who insisted on the deprovincialization of Ukrainian writing, the assimilation of European literary classics, and the cultivation of high artistic achievements. On the other side stood figures such as M. *Skrypnyk and A. *Khvylia, who acted as spokespeople for the Party, and critics such as V. *Koriak, S. Shchupak, and B. Kovalenko. They supported the *All-Ukrainian Association of Proletarian Writers (VUSSP), an organization sponsored by the Party for the purpose of defeating Vaplite. The VUSSP tended to see intellectual life in Ukraine as a reflection of Russian trends, considered works of the past as potentially pernicious, and applied a crude sociological analysis to and held a utilitarian view of literature. Its members felt that literature must implement the Party's directives and shape the new communist society. Still other figures, such as O. *Biletsky, avoided any organizational involvement and stressed the need for a multifaceted approach to literature and the value of formal analysis.

The Literary Discussion is generally considered to have ended in February 1928, after a formal debate took place in Kharkiv, presided over by Skrypnyk. The issues raised by the Literary Discussion continued, however, to agitate Ukrainian intellectuals and to enliven the pages of literary journals until the early 1930s.

BIBLIOGRAPHY
Leites, A.; Iashek, M. *Desiat' rokiv ukraïns'koï literatury (1917–1927)*, 2 vols (Kharkiv 1928; repr, Munich 1986)
Luckyj, G.S.N. *Literary Politics in the Soviet Ukraine, 1917–1934* (New York 1956 and 1971)
Khvylovy, M. *Cultural Renaissance in Ukraine: Polemical Pamphlets, 1925–1926* (Edmonton 1986)
Donchyk, V. (ed). *20-i roky: Literaturni dyskusiï, polemiky: Literaturno-krytychni statti* (Kiev 1991)
Shkandrij, M. *Modernists, Marxists, and the Nation: The Literary Discussion in Ukraine during the 1920s* (Edmonton 1992)
M. Shkandrij

Literary Fund (Literaturnyi fond). The popular name for a private relief fund for writers in need, established in St Petersburg in 1859 as the Society for Assistance to Needy Writers and Scholars. The only branch in Ukraine existed in Odessa. The society was open to all writers in the Russian Empire as well as to all other interested persons. Its funds came from dues, bequests, donations, and proceeds from readings, concerts, and publications, as well as from the Ministry of Education. Its aim was to give financial assistance to writers or bereaved families of writers, to have their works published, and to help young and talented but needy persons to attain an education toward a literary or teaching career. Subsistence grants were not made public until after the recipient's death. It is believed that among Ukrainian writers T. Shevchenko, M. Vovchok, M. Kotsiubynsky, and P. Hrabovsky all received aid from the fund. The literary fund society ceased to exist in 1918. A fund with similar aims of all-encompassing aid to needy writers was established in the USSR in 1934; it was run by the state and was under the auspices of the Writers' Union of the USSR. Grants, however, were restricted to writers faithful to the Party. In the same year a branch was opened in Kiev with subbranches in Kharkiv, Donetske, Lviv, and Odessa. Under the fund's auspices were also the 'buildings of creativity' in Irpin and Odessa, the writers' building in Kiev, living quarters, clubs, and the like.

Literary journals. Periodical publications, usually appearing monthly, devoted to the publication of literary works and literary criticism. Initially the scope of such periodical publications was broader: they included, in addition to literary works, articles on social, political, and civic themes. The first such general literary magazines to appear in Ukraine were *Khar'kovskii Demokrit (1816), *Ukrainskii vestnik (1816–19), and *Ukrainskii zhurnal (1824–5). Much more than just a literary journal, *Osnova (1861–2) played an important social and organizational role by providing a forum for the fledgling Ukrainian vernacular literature.

In Ukraine under Austro-Hungarian rule periodical literature began with journals, such as *Pchola (1849), *Vechernytsi (1862–3), *Meta (1863–6), *Rusalka (1862–6), and *Pravda (1867–96). The 1870s and 1880s saw the appearance of literary journals with a more radical perspective, such as *Druh (1874–7), *Hromads'kyi druh (1878–9), and *S'vit (1881–2). *Zoria (1880–97) became a general journal representative of Ukrainian literature in the 1890s. Unlike Zoria, which had a conservative orientation, Narod (1890–5) and *Zhytie i slovo (1894–7) were started by writers and scholars with radical and socialist ideas. In 1898 M. Hrushevsky established *Literaturno-naukovyi vistnyk, a single literary-scientific journal uniting all Ukrainian literary trends and the most prominent critics and scholars from all Ukrainian territories. The journal played a leading role in Ukrainian literary development until 1919. Since publication in Ukrainian was forbidden by the *Ems Ukase, the scholarly literary journal *Kievskaia starina (1882–1906) was published in Kiev in Russian. In 1907 it was renamed *Ukraïna, and four issues appeared in Ukrainian. The first literary journal after the liberalization of 1905 was *Nova hromada (1906), but its importance diminished with the transfer of Literaturno-naukovyi vistnyk to Kiev in 1907. Nevertheless, with the emergence of new literary trends, another literary journal was established in Kiev, *Ukraïns'ka khata (1909–14), which became the forum for Ukrainian 'modernism.' It opposed the traditional Ukrainophilism and conservative populism.

In Lviv the new literary and art magazines founded by followers of modernist trends included the monthly *Ruska khata (1905–6), the short-lived *S'vit (1906–7), Bdzhola (1908), and Buduchnist' (1909–10). Emphasizing art and literature was the semimonthly magazine *Iliustrovana Ukraïna (1912–13).

The cultural and national renaissance after the dissolution of the Russian and Austro-Hungarian empires was also marked by an increase of literary journals. Literature, criticism, popular science, and art were represented by *Nashe mynule (1918–19), *Mystetstvo (1919–20), and *Knyhar (1917–20), which also included a section on bibliography. In addition to the revived Literaturno-naukovyi vistnyk in Kiev, there were the *Universal'nyi zhurnal (1928–9) in Kharkiv and the monthly *Shliakh, which appeared in Moscow in 1917 and was transferred to Kiev in 1918, where it continued in the tradition of Ukraïns'ka khata until 1919. The symbolists were represented by the almanac *Muzahet (1919), and the futurists published *Semafor u maibutnie (1922), Katafalk mystetstva (1922), Gong komunkul'ta (1924), and the monthly *Nova generatsiia (1927–30). The leftist writers close to the futurists were organized in the group Avanhard, and published a bulletin, Biuleten' Avanhardu (1928–9, three issues). The all-Ukraini-

an peasant writers' union, Pluh, published its journal *Pluh (1925–33).

The monthly *Zhyttia i revoliutsiia was published in Kiev between 1925 and 1934. It recruited contributors from many groups, including *MARS and the *Neoclassicists. It also devoted some space to the cultivation of Ukrainian traditions and cultural ties with the West. An important literary function was performed by Kul'tura i pobut, a literary supplement to *Visti VUTsVK. M. *Khvylovy's group published the bimonthly *Vaplite beginning in 1926; it was forced to close in 1927. Khvylovy tried to continue the tradition of an engaging literary journal in the monthly *Literaturnyi iarmarok (1928–30, 12 issues) and, when that too failed, in *Prolitfront (1930).

The most prestigious forum of literature, art, criticism, and political opinion was the Kharkiv monthly *Chervonyi shliakh (1923–36), which replaced *Shliakhy mystetstva (1921–3) and united writers of all persuasions. Some other literary journals published in Kharkiv were the semimonthly Selians'kyi zhurnal (1929–31); the literary monthly for agricultural workers, Traktor; and the semimonthly of the All-Ukrainian Association of Proletarian Writers, Literaturnyi pryzov (1931–2). That association also published the most important Russian-language literary journal, Krasnoe slovo (1927–32), which became Litstroi in 1933 and Sovetskaia literatura in 1934.

In addition to Zhyttia i revoliutsiia, *Molodniak (1927–37), the journal of the Central Committee of the Young Communist League of Ukraine, and the literary art magazine Nova hromada (1923–9) were published in Kiev. As a supplement to the Odessa newspaper Chornomors'ka komuna, there was the literary journal *Shkval (1924–33) and the literary, art, and critical publication Metalevi dni (1930–3). The latter two periodicals merged in Literaturnyi zhovten' (1934–5). Literary magazines published in other cities were Chervonyi krai (1927–8) in Vinnytsia; the monthly Zoria (1925–34) in Dnipropetrovske, renamed Shturm (1935–7); the monthly Tempy (1931) in Zaporizhia; the monthly Kryvbas (1931–3) in Kryvyi Rih; the monthly Stapeli (1931–2) in Mykolaiv; and Zaboi (1923–32), renamed Literaturnyi Donbas in 1933.

The bibliographical journals Knyhar (1917–20), Knyha (1923–4), and Nova knyha (1924–5) published some criticism and also recorded current book production. In the late 1920s there were the bimonthly of literary studies *Literaturnyi arkhiv (1930–1), published by the Taras Shevchenko Scientific Research Institute, and the Marxist journal of literary criticism Krytyka (1928–32), renamed Za markso-lenins'ku krytyku in 1932 and *Literaturna krytyka in 1936. Emigré writers from Western Ukraine published in Soviet Ukraine *Zakhidnia Ukraïna (1927–9; and as a monthly, 1930–3). Once *Ukrainization was abandoned as a government policy, and the various literary groups were unified into the *Writers' Union of Ukraine, most literary journals ceased to exist; only Radians'ka literatura (1933–41, later renamed *Vitchyzna), Literaturna krytyka (1936–41), and *Literaturnyi zhurnal (1936–41, replacing Chervonyi shliakh) were permitted.

In Western Ukraine, which found itself under Polish rule after the Treaty of Versailles, the most influential literary journal was D. *Dontsov's Literaturno-naukovyi vistnyk. Other literary journals with a nationalist orientation were *Dazhboh (1932–5), *Obriï (1936–7), and *Naperedodni (1937–8). At the opposite end of the political spectrum

Literary journals

were the communist journals *Vikna (1927–32) and *Novi shliakhy (1929–32). The short-lived *Mytusa (1922) and, later, *Nazustrich (1934–9) were more concerned with literature than politics, whereas *Dzvony (1931–9) reflected a Catholic viewpoint. In Bukovyna under Rumanian occupation the primary literary journal was *Samostiina dumka (1931–7), and in Hungarian-ruled Transcarpathian Ukraine, the journal *Nasha zemlia (1927–9). Literary journals also appeared among the émigrés after the revolution and the First World War, such as Na perelomi (1920) and Vyzvolennia (1923) in Vienna, *Nova Ukraïna (1922–8) and *Proboiem (1933–43) in Prague, and *My (1933–9) in Warsaw.

When the Soviet Union occupied Western Ukraine at the beginning of the Second World War, all literary journals ceased publication. The only permitted literary journal was Literatura i mystetstvo (1940–1) in Lviv. In 1941–5, during the German occupation of Ukraine, the only literary publications permitted were the short-lived biweekly literary newspaper *Litavry (1941) in Kiev and the monthly journal *Nashi dni (1942–4) in Lviv.

The trend in Soviet Ukraine toward a centralized press, which began in the 1930s, continued after the Second World War. All the literary journals were official organs of the various branches of the Writers' Union of Ukraine. Today the literary journals are the monthly Vitchyzna, the Russian-language *Raduga, *Vsesvit (since 1958 a monthly devoted to art and literature abroad), and *Kyïv in Kiev; *Prapor (now Berezil') in Kharkiv; *Zhovten' (now Dzvin) in Lviv; and *Donbas in Donetske. *Slovo i chas (Radians'ke literaturoznavstvo until 1990) is devoted to literature studies. *Ranok and *Dnipro appeared as organs of the Komsomol.

Some literary journals have appeared among Ukrainians outside of Ukraine. *Duklia is the literary journal of the native Ukrainian population of Slovakia and is published every two months in Prešov. Beginning in July 1990 Nash holos began to appear in Rumania. After the Second World War a number of literary-artistic journals were established among the Ukrainian émigrés in DP camps: collections of *MUR (Munich, Regensburg 1946–7), the highly sophisticated journal *Arka (Munich 1947–8), the journal Litavry (Salzburg 1947–8), the scientific-literary journals Ukraïna i

svit (Hannover, 1949–69) and My i svit (Mittenwald, 1950; Paris, 1951–5; Toronto and Niagara Falls, 1955–85). The newspaper Ukraïns'ka literaturna hazeta, established in 1955, combined with Suchasna Ukraïna in 1961 to become the literary-artistic and social monthly *Suchasnist'. Although under the auspices of the *Ukrainian Supreme Liberation Council, Suchasnist' maintained a nonpartisan approach to literature and thus served as the major literary journal in the emigration. In 1992 it began publication in Kiev. Other more local or more political journals exist as well: the nationalist monthly *Vyzvol'nyi shliakh (London, since 1948); the monthly *Novi dni (since 1950) and the irregular Terminus (five issues since 1986), both published in Toronto; and the now-defunct *Kyïv (1950–64) in Philadelphia. The latest literary journal is a joint venture of Ukrainian writers in the West and in Ukraine called *Svito-vyd. (See also *Press, *Humoristic and satiric press, *Children's magazines, and *Almanac.)

D.H. Struk

Literary memorial museums. Collections of documents, manuscripts, printed works, monuments, photographs, and personal effects of noted Ukrainian writers usually established in buildings where those writers lived and worked. There are about 30 such museums in Ukraine, among them the Mykhailo Kotsiubynsky museums in Vinnytsia (est 1927) and Chernihiv (est 1935); the Vladimir Korolenko museums in Poltava (est 1928) and Zhytomyr (est 1973); the Nikolai Gogol Museum in Velyki Sorochyntsi, Poltava oblast (est 1929); the Taras Shevchenko Museum in Shevchenkove, Zvenyhorodka raion, Cherkasy oblast (est 1939); the Panas Myrny Museum in Poltava (est 1939); the Ivan Franko museums in Lviv (est 1940), Ivan Franko (formerly Nahuievychi), Drohobych raion (est 1946), and Kryvorivnia, Verkhovyna raion, Ivano-Frankivske oblast (est 1960); the Vasyl Stefanyk Museum in Rusiv, Sniatyn raion, Ivano-Frankivske oblast (est 1941); the Olha Kobylianska Museum in Chernivtsi (est 1944); the Marko Cheremshyna Museum in Sniatyn, Ivano-Frankivske oblast (est 1949); the Ivan Kotliarevsky Museum in Poltava (est 1952); the Ivan Nechui-Levytsky Museum in Stebliv, Cherkasy oblast (est 1959); the Markiian Shashkevych Museum in Pidlissia, Zolochiv raion, Lviv oblast (est 1959); the Yaroslav Halan Museum in Lviv (est 1961); the Oleksander Dovzhenko Museum in Sosnytsia, Chernihiv oblast (est 1961); the Lesia Ukrainka museums in Kiev (est 1962) and Novohrad-Volynskyi (est 1971); the Mykhailo Pavlyk Museum in Kosiv, Ivano-Frankivske oblast (est 1967); the Leonid Hlibov Museum in Chornyi Ostriv, Khmelnytskyi oblast (est 1968); the Maksym Rylsky Museum in Kiev (est 1968); the Hryhorii Skovoroda Museum in Skovorodynivka, Zolochiv raion, Kharkiv oblast (est 1972); the Oleksander Korniichuk Museum in Kiev (est 1975); and the Pavlo Tychyna Museum in Kiev (est 1980). The *Kiev Shevchenko Museum (est 1949), the Yurii *Fedkovych Museum in Chernivtsi (est 1945; branch in Putyliv), and the Anton Makarenko Museum in Kremenchuk (est 1951) are classified as cultural-educational institutions. A few are also preserves: the Ivan Karpenko-Kary Khutir Nadiia Museum-Preserve near Kirovohrad (est 1956), the Lesia Ukrainka Museum-Homestead in Kolodiazhne, Kovel raion, Volhynia oblast (est 1949), the Shevchenko Building-Museum in Kiev (est 1927), and the Shevchenko *Kaniv Museum-Reserve in Kaniv (est 1925).

Beyond Ukraine there are several literary museums dedicated to Ukrainian writers: the Marko Vovchok Building-Museum in Nalchik, Kabardino-Balkar AR, the Lesia Ukrainka Museum in Surami, Georgia, and the Shevchenko Museum in Fort-Shevchenko, Kazakhstan.

Literatura v shkoli. See *Ukraïns'ka mova i literatura v shkoli*.

Literature. Ukrainian literature did not have a smooth path of development. The language for writing (see *Standard Ukrainian), introduced with Christianity and used for religious ritual, changed at a slower pace than did the spoken word. The rift between the spoken and the written language widened over the years, owing to political events (the numerous invasions of the Mongols and the Tatars; the subjugation of Ukraine by other states, Lithuania, Poland, Russia, and Austria-Hungary; and the outright prohibitions of the Ukrainian language in print). The outcome of the divergence between the written and the spoken language was the adoption in the 19th century of a completely 'new' literary language based on the spoken variant. Although beneficial for the growth of Ukrainian national awareness, it had a detrimental effect on the development of literature. Mostly, noticeably the continuity between pre- and post-19th-century literature seemed lost. Even literature in the vernacular did not develop smoothly. Ukraine at that time was split between two empires, a state of affairs that gave rise to regional vernacular differences and somewhat different tempi of literary growth. Nevertheless, in presenting Ukrainian literature as a whole, the literary process of the last millennium can be viewed as a continuum with several broad periods: the Kievan, the Cossack, the vernacular, the renaissance of the 1920s, and the contemporary. This periodization serves as a historical time frame; it does not divide according to esthetic or philosophical currents, more than one of which may be present in the literature of a given time period. More detailed periodizations have sometimes been used but would be inappropriate in a concise survey.

The Kievan period. Both translated literature and a rich oral tradition played an important role in the development of original literature in Kievan Rus'. The christening of Kievan Rus' in 988 gave impetus to a dissemination of various adaptations (from the Balkan Slav originals) and translations (mainly from Greek) of religious texts. Besides Gospels (*Ostromir Gospel, 1056–7), Acts of the Apostles, and Psalters, of interest for the development of an independent literature were collections of sermons and lives of saints. The translations in such collections were often augmented with local materials, and existed in several redactions. The earliest and most notable such collection was the *Izbornik* of Sviatoslav (1073 and 1076), and the latest, a 14th-century compendium of teachings titled *Izmarahd* (The Emerald). Also popular were such gatherings of aphorisms and sermons as *Pchela* (The Bee) and *Zlataia tsip* (The Golden Chain), which circulated in various editions. The oldest and most noted didactic work is *Slovo o zakoni i blahodati* (A Word on Law and Benevolence, 1050) by Ilarion, the first native metropolitan of Kiev. Somewhat more worldly are the teachings of *Volodymyr Monomakh titled *Poucheniie ditiam* (An Instruction for [My] Children, ca 1117), included in the Primary Chronicle. Noteworthy as a sermonizer in the 12th century was Bish-

op Cyril of Turiv. His art is especially discernible in *Slovo v novu nediliu po Pastsi* (A Word on the First Sunday after Easter, ca 1170).

A more subtle form of didactic literature can be found in the numerous lives. Modeled on translated hagiographies, lives of St Anthony of the Caves, St Volodymyr the Great, St Olha, and others were written and collected in the *Kievan Cave Patericon, the most remarkable collection of lives in the Kievan period. Also noteworthy are the early *chronicles, which are unique for their wealth of information and their blending of fact and fiction, written sources and eyewitness accounts (eg, the tale of Borys and Hlib). The chronicles were compiled by anonymous scribes and copied many times. They can be divided into three parts, the Primary Chronicle (up to the 12th century), the Kievan Chronicle (from 1118 to 1190), and the Galician-Volhynian Chronicle (from the beginning of the 13th century to 1292).

Quite prevalent were apocryphal writings (*Khozhdeniie Bohorodytsi po mukakh* [The Mother of God's Journey through Suffering (Hell), mid-12th century]) as well as translated tales, such as *Varlaam i Ioasaf* or *Aleksandriia (end of the 11th century). Also popular was the first 'travelogue,' *Zhytiie i khozhdeniie Danyla, rus'koï zemli ihumena* (The Life and Pilgrimage of Danylo, Hegumen of Rus', ca 1100). The most unusual and outstanding monument of old Ukrainian literature, however, is the secular epic poem *Slovo o polku Ihorevi (The Tale of Ihor's Campaign, ca 1187). Particularly rich in poetic tropes (epithets, similes, metaphors, metonymy, hyperbole, and personification), the work suggests a sophistication indicative of a rich tradition of folk and martial literature with highly developed poetics. But the plea of the anonymous author for unity among the princes fell on deaf ears. The Kievan state, disunited, was too weak to withstand the onslaughts from the East. Kiev fell to the Mongols in 1240, and the Principality of *Galicia-Volhynia became the focus of political and cultural life in Ukrainian lands. The incorporation of Volhynia into the Grand Duchy of Lithuania (1340) marks the end of the period and of significant literary activity. No major literary monuments remain from the 14th and 15th centuries.

The Cossack period, or the Middle period of Ukrainian literature, began in the 16th century; its vitality was eventually smothered by Russian domination, in the 18th century, together with all vestiges of Cossack independence. It was a period of great unrest and political upheaval which culminated in the *Cossack-Polish War, and of religious strife between the Uniates and the Orthodox, which centered around the Church Union of *Berestia in 1596. Yet the period is also noted for its vibrant and varied cultural activity. When this period began, Ukraine was part of the Polish-Lithuanian state and thus was open to influences from the West, especially to the post-Renaissance, post-Reformation emphasis on learning. It is not surprising that the Orthodox *brotherhoods, experiencing their heyday at that time, established schools (the *Lviv Dormition Brotherhood in the 1580s and the *Kiev Epiphany Brotherhood in 1615). Besides being bastions against Polonization the schools served as centers of literary creativity. The most famous and important school was the Kievan Mohyla College (later Academy), founded by Metropolitan P. *Mohyla in 1632. Of immeasurable importance for the development of literature was the establishment of the first printing press in Lviv by I. *Fedorovych in 1574 and of subsequent printing houses by the brotherhoods. Even prior to the printing of the Lviv *Apostol* (1574) and the Ostrih Bible (1581) several new translations of the Gospels appeared. Under the influence of Protestantism from the West, those publications were intended to make the word of God more understandable to the people (eg, F. *Skoryna's publications [1517–25], the Peresopnytsia Gospel [1555–6], the Krekhiv *Apostol* [1563–72], the Volhynian Gospel [1571]).

One consequence of religious controversy over the Church Union of Berestia was a rich polemical literature. The multitude of works which appeared varied in size and form from short, sharply worded 'epistles' to long scholarly exposés (eg, the *Palinodiia* of Z. Kopystensky [1621]). Typical of many of them is the fiery tract by an anonymous polemicist *Perestoroha* (Warning, 1605–6), which lauds the brotherhoods for spreading education and cautions against Catholicism (the 'Union'), which will destroy that achievement. In another interesting anonymous polemic, *Protestatsiia* (Protestation, 1620), the author draws a direct historical line of development between contemporary Ukraine and Kievan Rus'. Notable for their literary artistry are the writings of Metropolitan I. *Potii (eg, *Uniia* ... [Union, 1595]) defending the Uniates and the plea for Orthodoxy by M. *Smotrytsky, *Trenos , to iest lament* ... (Threnos, or the Lament ... , 1610). But it is the 20–odd extant writings of the maximalist defender of Orthodoxy and Eastern asceticism, I. *Vyshensky, which occupy the most important place in the polemical literature of the period.

Related to polemical writing and equally developed was the art of sermonizing. Some of the most noted practitioners were Smotrytsky, Mohyla, L. *Baranovych, K. *Stavrovetsky-Tranquillon, A. *Radyvylovsky, St Dymytrii *Tuptalo, and S. *Yavorsky. Copious use of allegory and allusion and the inclusion of various tales, translations, anecdotes, and apocryphal writings were the norm, and special emphasis was placed on the form and style of the sermon. I. *Galiatovsky, for example, added to his collection of sermons (*Kliuch razumieniia* [Key of Understanding, 1659]) a large treatise on how to compose a proper sermon.

The popularity of the sermonizer's use of the unusual and the fantastic as illustration, and of tales accepted as 'knowledge,' was reflected in the publication of collections dealing with miracles and the lives of saints. Notable in that respect were the republications of the Kievan Cave Patericon, first by S. Kosiv in Polish as *Paterikon* (1635) and then in Ukrainian (1661); the collections of short stories dealing with the miracles of the Mother of God (eg, Galiatovsky's *Nebo novoie* [New Heaven, 1665] and Tuptalo's *Runo oroshennoie* [The Bedewed Fleece, 1680]); and Tuptalo's famous *menaion of daily readings, *Chet'i minei* (1689–1705).

Fascination with the lives of saints and with the extraordinary also gave rise to a renewed interest in history, which fostered the development of the historiographic genre. T. *Safonovych, a teacher in the Kievan Mohyla College, compiled a history (*Kroinika*) in 1672 composed of previous Rus' as well as Polish chronicles. Even more prominent was the historical compilation *Sinopsis*, published in 1674 in Kiev and attributed to I. *Gizel. The work was republished many times and remained a basic histor-

ical text throughout the period. The momentous upheavals of the B. *Khmelnytsky period were recognized for their historical importance by the contemporary participants. Several Cossack chronicles appeared. Although strictly speaking those chronicles belong more to historiography than to literature, their style and influence on the Ukrainian Romantics played an important role in the later development of literature proper. Three chronicles deserve special mention: the anonymous Samovydets (Eyewitness) Chronicle, which begins with the Khmelnytsky uprising and ends in 1702; the H. Hrabianka Chronicle (1710), which concentrates on the Khmelnytsky period but begins in antiquity and ends at the beginning of the 18th century; and the S. Velychko chronicle, completed after 1720. The last is perhaps the most lively and interesting of the three. In vivid and colorful language Velychko chronicles events and attempts to give the reasons for them, as well as to draw a moral for future generations. Not quite in the same genre but equally lively and interesting is the autobiography of I. *Turchynovsky. His adventures vividly portray the life of the wandering students-preceptors who played an important role in the development of literature, especially poetry and drama.

Although the religious tales, sermons, and secular chronicles are of interest, they nonetheless belong more to the realm of the 'written word' than to literature. Literature in its purer form developed in poetry and drama. Although a large corpus of poems survived (many of them in manuscript), no really major poet emerged. Many of the poems are of unknown authorship. Some have the name of the author encoded into the poem, acrostics being popular at the time; there are also poems in various shapes (cross, half-moon, pyramid, etc) and so-called crabs, which could be read both from left to right and from right to left. Such excess, playfulness, and ornamentation have promted some scholars (eg, D. *Chyzhevsky) to refer to the period as the *baroque. Poetics were taught at the Kievan Mohyla Academy and in the brotherhood schools (a course written by M. *Dovhalevsky [1736] and another by H. *Konysky [in Latin, 1744] are extant), and most of the poems show traces of having been school exercises. Written in syllabic meters, they mix images from the Christian and the ancient worlds. Allegory is a predominant trope (as in the extremely popular 17th-century didactic collection of prose and poetry with allegorical drawings, *Ifika iieropolitika*), and much use is made of certain set images ('emblems' – a scythe for death, dove for purity, etc). Along with poems of religious or moral content, which stress the vanity and brevity of earthly life, there are numerous panegyrics and heraldic poems devoted to verbal description and the glorification of coats of arms. Epigrams are also quite widely represented. Those by the archpriest I. *Velychkovsky are perhaps the most interesting.

Remarkable among the many religious poetasters were Stavrovetsky-Tranquillon (*Perlo mnohotsinnoie* [A Priceless Pearl, 1646]), who used lines of irregular length close to those of folk *dumas; I. *Maksymovych, who presented religious truths in a broad narrative manner (*Bohorodytse Divo* [Virgin Mother of God, 1707] and *Otche nash* [Our Father, 1709]); and *Klymentii, known as Zynovii's son, who is notable for the sheer number (369) of opinionated poems which he composed at the beginning of the 18th century. Arguably the best poet of the period, the peripatetic philosopher H. *Skovoroda wrote religious and morally didactic poetry. The popularity of his live-and-let-live theocentric philosophy as expressed in the collection *Sad bozhestvennykh pesnei* (Garden of Divine Songs, 1753–85) can be seen in the fact that some of the poems (eg, nos 10 and 18) became folk songs. His *Basni Khar'kovskiia* (Kharkiv Fables, 1774) marks the beginning of the fable genre in Ukrainian literature. Quite widely known toward the end of the period was the collection of religious poetry *Bohohlasnyk* (The Praise Book, 1790), from Pochaiv, with many poems based on legends and apocrypha about the Mother of God.

Among the more worldly poems are numerous panegyrics, such as those written in honor of Metropolitan P. Mohyla (eg, *Evkharistirion, albo vdiachnost'* [Eucharisterion, or Gratitude, 1632], *Evfoniia veselobrmiachaia* [Joyful Ringing Euphony, 1633]). One of the earliest such poems was *Vizerunk tsnot* (A Pattern of Virtue, 1618), by O. Mytura in honor of Ye. *Pletenetsky. K. *Sakovych wrote a eulogy to Hetman P. Sahaidachny (*Virshi na zhalosnyi pohreb zatsnoho rytsera Petra Konashevycha Sahaidachnoho ...* [Poems for the Grievous Funeral of the Knight Petro Konashevych Sahaidachny, 1622]) in which he praised the role of the Cossacks as defenders of Ukraine against the Tartars. The *Alfavit sobrannyi rifmami slozhennyi ot sviatykh pisanii ...* (An Alphabet Compiled and Rhymed from the Holy Writings ..., 1705) consists of short narratives about sins and punishments. Remarkable for its separatist aspirations was S. *Divovych's *Razgovor Velikorossii s Malorossiei* (A Conversation of Great Russia with Little Russia, 1762). The few poems attributed to Hetman I. *Mazepa stand out because of their lyricism coupled with concern for the Cossack nation.

Equally important was the development of the dramatic genre. Western European morality, miracle, and mystery plays were part of the Jesuit school curriculum in Poland and from there entered the curriculum of the brotherhood schools. Joined with the study of poetics, *school drama concentrated on the development of poetic dialogue. One early example of a dramatic dialogue is the collection of Christmas poems of P. *Berynda (1616). Soon afterward, full-length dramas were composed, such as the widely known play by an anonymous author *Aleksii, chelovik Bozhyi* (Alexis, Man of God, 1673). To captivate the audience and to provide relief from their often-heavy didacticism, plays were interrupted by entr'actes consisting of humorous dialogues called *intermedes. Those contained rather down-to-earth slapstick humor, but also, at times, social commentary in the form of mocking stereotypes of members of the various social strata of the time – Polish lords, Jews, Cossacks, Gypsies, and peasants – as in an untitled play by M. Dovhalevsky (1737) or in H. Konysky's *Voskreseniie mertvykh* (The Resurrection of the Dead, 1746). Students and seminarians were more than willing to compose intermedes, especially for the plays which were part of the repertoire of the puppet theater, the *vertep. (Texts for *vertep* dramas have survived only from the 1770s.) Since the students and wandering precentors presented the *vertep* at village and city fairs, both the serious mystery plays and the slapstick interludes reached a wide audience. The most famous play of the time, *Vladimir* (1705) by T. *Prokopovych, is unusual in its blurring of the strict division between the serious and the comic. Glorifying Volodymyr the Great for christening

Rus', Prokopovych merges the comic and derisive elements with other elements of the play and so initiates the genre of tragicomedy. A much weaker tragicomedy, dealing with the fall in morals of the day, is V. Lashchevsky's *Tragedokomediia ...* (1742). Of interest also is the drama *Mylost' Bozhiia Ukrainu ... svobodyvshaia* (God's Grace Which Has Liberated Ukraine ..., 1728), by an anonymous author. It moves away from religious themes and deals with events during the Khmelnytsky period. The use of personifications in the play to portray such 'personages' as Ukraine or News (in Ukrainian both are singular and feminine: *Ukraïna, Vistka*) is also quite typical of the time.

Although the Cossack period in Ukrainian literature lasted until the end of the 18th century, it had begun to decline in 1654 with the signing of the *Pereiaslav Treaty, when Ukraine came under ever-increasing Russian domination. In 1667 the *Andrusovo Treaty divided Ukraine between the Russian and the Polish states. In 1709 Hetman Mazepa, in league with Charles XII of Sweden, failed in his attempt to wrest Ukraine from Russian control. In 1720 Peter I of Russia banned all ecclesiastical printing in Ukrainian by decree, and in 1723 the Cossack state lost the right to choose its own hetmans. Catherine II of Russia had the Zaporozhian Sich razed in 1775; in 1783 serfdom was introduced in Ukraine. By 1785 the remaining Cossack *starshyna* had been given the status of nobility so that its absorption into the Russian nobility would be facilitated. All through the Cossack period most of what was written in Ukraine was written in the bookish language, which in the 18th century came under the strong influence of the Russian language and consistently grew farther away from the vernacular.

Also important in ending the Cossack period in Ukrainian literature was the rise of classicism in the literature of the West. The influence of classicism began to be felt in the Russian Empire in the second half of the 18th century. Of the prescriptive tenets of classicism the most important for the further development of Ukrainian literature was that which defined the three styles of literary writing, high, middle, and low. Classicism recognized different registers of language: only odes, tragedies, and scholarly writings were written in the high style (ie, the bookish scholarly language; in Ukraine at the time that meant Russian); drama and prose were relegated to the middle style (a mixture of the bookish and the vernacular spoken by clerks and other literate people); and comedy, burlesque, and travesty were written in the low style (the language of the peasantry; in 'Little Russian,' Ukrainian).

Vernacular literature. It is not surprising then that travesty links the Cossack period with the period of the vernacular. The transposing of high and serious works of antiquity studied in school into the 'low' language of the common people was popular. Many verse-travesties have survived from the 18th century. Some, such as *Iarmarok* (The Fair, 1790) and *Zamysl na popa* (The Plot against the Priest, 1790) by I. *Nekrashevych, tend more toward the burlesque; others, such as *Virgilievi pastukhy ... v malorosii-s'kyi kobeniak pereodiahneni* (Virgil's Shepherds ... Dressed in a Little Russian Vest, ca 1794) by O. Lobysevych, rely more heavily on the humor derived from the use of the common language. It is in that spirit that the 'father' of Ukrainian vernacular literature, I. *Kotliarevsky, wrote his famous epic poem, *Eneïda* (Aeneid, pts 1–3, 1798; pt 4, 1809; pts 5–6, ca 1820; first complete edn 1842).

The work, which appeared in its entirety only after Kotliarevsky's death, was a tremendous success, no doubt because of its skillful travesty of the Roman classic and its able use of the Ukrainian vernacular to reveal that language's wealth of picturesque idioms. Although Kotliarevsky was only following the dictates of classicism and did not set out to 'create a literature in the vernacular,' his highly sensitive ear for the idiomatic language, sharp eye for ethnographic detail, and talent as a writer produced the unexpected. No small part of the success of the travesty lay in the fact that Kotliarevsky abandoned the stilted syllabic versification which had never quite suited the randomly stressed Ukrainian, and wrote the *Eneïda* in a 10-line strophe of four-foot iambs, thereby giving a start to the use of syllabo-tonic metrics in Ukrainian literature. Surprised by his own success, Kotliarevsky nonetheless seemed to realize the importance of his work, for he injected a serious tone in the last three sections of the epic and also went on to write two plays in the newly 'discovered' language, *Natalka Poltavka* (Natalka from Poltava) and *Moskal' charivnyk* (The Soldier Sorcerer), both in 1819.

The most important follower of Kotliarevsky in the genre of travesty was P. *Hulak-Artemovsky, noted for his travestied adaptations of the odes of Horace (*Do Parkhoma*) and the expanded adaptation of a fable by the 18th-century Polish writer I. Krasicki (*Pan ta sobaka* [Master and His Dog, 1818]). Hulak-Artemovsky's attempt to use Ukrainian outside of travesty or burlesque, as in his translation of J.W. von Goethe's *Fisherman*, produced awkward results. His language was still too much in the register of the burlesque. H. *Kvitka-Osnovianenko, the initiator of the Ukrainian short story, was more successful in his attempt to write 'serious' works in the vernacular. Although his play (*Svatannia na Honcharivtsi* [The Betrothal in Honcharivka, 1836]) and early stories still reflect the burlesque tradition (eg, 'Saldats'kyi patret' [A Soldier's Portrait]), his later stories are more somber in tone and are imbued with the sentimentalism that was fashionable at the time. Whereas Kotliarevsky in his comedies showed that Ukrainian peasants could laugh and were funny, Kvitka-Osnovianenko (his collection of stories appeared in 1834) did no more than show that they are capable of tears and sadness.

As classicism gave way to *romanticism its rigid laws were abandoned. Gone were the high and low styles. The Romantics were genuinely interested in folk legends, songs, myths, and the heroic past. Several histories appeared, the most notable being *Istoriia Rusov* (printed in 1847 but written at the beginning of the century and circulated in manuscript form). The authorship is uncertain; but although the language of the work is Russian, its message is that of Ukrainian patriotism. Also important is *Istoriia Maloi Rossii ...* (History of Little Russia ..., 1822) by D. *Bantysh-Kamensky.

Several collections of Ukrainian songs and dumas appeared in quick succession, the most influential of them N. *Tsertelev's first gathering of dumas (1819) and M. *Maksymovych's *Malorossiiskie pesni* (Little Russian Songs, 1827). At Kharkiv University young scholars imbued with the spirit of romanticism formed a group (see *Kharkiv Romantic School) around I. *Sreznevsky, a Ukrainophile Russian scholar and ethnographer. Their interest in and collection of folklore confirmed their belief that the Ukrainian folk tradition was indeed rich in content and language and convinced them of the inaccuracy of the notion that the vernacular language could be used only for humorous literature. They developed new genres, translated and imitated works from other literatures, and wholly embraced J. *Herder's idea that Slavic folk poetry was closer to nature and less soiled by corrupt civilization that that of other peoples. The most prominent of the Kharkiv group were L. *Borovykovsky, whose ballads and whose contribution to the development of poetic vocabulary make him a precursor of T. *Shevchenko; A. *Metlynsky, a poet full of nostalgia for the heroic past of the Cossacks and pessimism for the future; and the lyrical poet M. *Petrenko, known for one extant poem, in which he captures supremely the eternal quest to escape into boundless space. Most of the authors of the period also wrote in Russian; some did so exclusively and thus belong to Russian literature. The famous N. *Gogol is a prime example.

Although by the early 19th century Polonization had progressed in *Galicia as far as Russification had in central Ukraine, if not farther, the national awakening in terms of a turn to the vernacular occurred there at almost the same time as in Russian-ruled Ukraine. The 1837 publication of a collection of poems in the vernacular, *Rusalka Dnistrovaia* (Dniester Water Nymph), published in Buda, Hungary (its printing was not permitted in Galicia), marks the beginning of Ukrainian vernacular literature in Galicia. The collection was the effort of three Lviv seminarians, Ya. *Holovatsky, I. *Vahylevych, and, the most talented author and the leader of the 'trinity,' M. *Shashkevych (see *Ruthenian Triad).

Such authors as M. *Ustyianovych ('Mest' verkhovyntsia' [The Highlander's Vengeance, 1849]) and A. *Mohylnytsky continued to write in the Romantic tradition in Galicia, but Kiev became the center of romanticism in the 1840s. Kiev was the seat of the *Cyril and Methodius Brotherhood, which consisted, among others, of T. Shevchenko, P. *Kulish, and M. *Kostomarov, the last of whom provided a link with the Kharkiv school of the 1830s. Yet unlike the Kharkiv school the brotherhood had a definite, if rather utopian, political and national program: it called for a Slavic federation and believed that Ukraine, where the Cossack traditions of freedom and democracy had flourished, would provide the leadership in the federation. Those ideas were incorporated into *Knyhy bytiia ukraïns'koho narodu* (The Books of Genesis of the Ukrainian People), written by Kostomarov. He also wrote drama on the Shakespearean model, philosophical poetry, and literary criticism. Another prominent member of the brotherhood, Kulish is noted primarily for his novel-chronicle *Chorna rada* (The Black Council, 1857), the first historical novel written in Ukrainian. Kulish was also a poet, a translator (of W. Shakespeare and the Bible), and a publisher (see *Osnova). Although Kulish's prose works far surpassed those of his predecessor Kvitka-Osnovianenko, as a poet he could not surpass Shevchenko.

Unlike Kulish Shevchenko was imbued with the Romantic spirit of revolt, and with him Ukrainian romanticism reached its pinnacle. Shevchenko had the ability to express profound thought in seemingly simple words. With the appearance of his *Kobzar* (The Minstrel, 1840), and his 'Haidamaky' (The Haidamakas, 1841) Shevchenko dispelled all doubt as to whether the Ukrainian vernacular was suitable for a full-range literature. His poems consist of simple lyrics, ballads, Byronic poems, social and political satire, didactic exhortations, and paraphrases of biblical texts. He was popular in his day, and his popularity continued to grow and with it the influence of his poetry. Though Kotliarevsky is the 'father' of literature in the Ukrainian vernacular, Shevchenko is the father of the national revival which culminated in an independent state in 1918.

The death of Shevchenko in 1861 for all practical purposes marks the end of the Romantic movement in Ukraine, although Romantic works continued to be written not only by his epigones but also by some talented writers. The most prominent of the belated Romantics were the poet Ya. *Shchoholev, the prosaist O. *Storozhenko, who in his stories and in an unfinished novel dealt with the fantastic elements of the Cossack past, and Yu. *Fedkovych. Fedkovych is known primarily for his lyrics, imbued with German romanticism and full of Hutsul folklore, with which he brought about a revival of Ukrainian literature in Bukovyna.

Barring those few exceptions, the majority of writers of the time followed the new literary trend of realism and its philosophy of positivism. They stressed the importance of the exact sciences, expressed belief in evolution and progress, preached democracy, and tried to portray reality in an objective, naturalistic manner (naturalism). To be sure, the transition from romanticism to realism was not a sudden one; both elements can be detected in the works of many writers. The best example of the duality is found in the prose of M. *Vovchok, the first major woman writer in Ukrainian literature. In her short stories (1857) she joined elements of the former ethnographic romanticism (descriptions of various folk customs, ceremonies, and dress) with themes of serfdom, and she was one of the first to speak out against the evils of such a social system. Other notable writers on the border of the two movements were S. *Rudansky, whose collection of verse based on folk humor (*Spivomovky*) is unique, and L. *Hlibov, a sensitive lyricist noted mainly, however, for his adaptation of traditional fable plots into Ukrainian by using Ukrainian motifs and folklore to illustrate them.

Realism, however, had its greatest impact on the development of prose, especially of the long short story, the novelette (*povist'*). The genre proved most suitable for conveying the populist message. The first to introduce populist propaganda into his writings was O. *Konysky. The real masters of 19th-century Ukrainian realistic prose were I. *Nechui-Levytsky and P. *Myrny. Nechui-Levytsky formulated the principles of Ukrainian populist realism (a work must be realistic in its portrayal of the world, national in inspiration, and populist in ideology) to which both writers adhered. B. *Hrinchenko was also an important practitioner of the realistic novelette, although he is better known as a poet and lexicographer.

In the second half of the 19th century the tsarist regime severely curtailed literary activity through the Valuev circular of 1863 (see P. *Valuev) and the *Ems Ukase of 1876, which prohibited most publication in the Ukrainian language. Since those decrees were not repealed until 1905, many works remained unpublished or had to be published outside of the Russian Empire, most often in Galicia, where no such restrictions existed. Some works appeared too late to have any influence on the literary process. Such was the case with the family-chronicle novel

Liuboratski by A. *Svydnytsky, written in 1861–2 but not published until 1898. Some scholars and writers even left Russian-ruled Ukraine for Galicia, most notably the historian M. *Hrushevsky. Others went farther west, as did the journalist, scholar, and political ideologist M. *Drahomanov, who in 1876 settled in Geneva, where he published the journal *Hromada*. Through his socialist works he exercised a profound influence on intellectual life in Ukraine.

The most important writer to be influenced by Drahomanov was I. *Franko, the dominant Ukrainian literary figure in the last quarter of the 19th century. Franko's choice of the Ukrainian vernacular over the *yazychiie, the dialect advocated by the *moskvofily* (see *Russophiles), irrevocably confirmed the end of that movement in Galicia. Franko was a universalist. He was equally at ease with the realistic novelette, the lyrical poem, the epic poem, drama, the essay, the political pamphlet, and translation. He was a first-rate philologist and literary critic, as well as an avid collector and cataloger of folk literature. He could not, however, always reconcile his feeling of duty toward his people with the strict artistic demands of a work of literature. As a consequence his literary output is uneven. Nevertheless, owing to his efforts Ukrainian literature made enormous advances in the development of genres and themes.

The desire of the realists to reach as wide an audience as possible with their positivistic message, coupled with the tsarist prohibition of Ukrainian publications, made theater important and spurred the writing of drama. The three most noted dramatists were M. *Starytsky, M. *Kropyvnytsky, and I. *Karpenko-Kary. Starytsky had a predilection for melodrama, and in addition to writing his own plays he adopted and improved works of others. All three mixed ethnographic romanticism with realism, especially in their comedies, but Karpenko-Kary was the first to succeed with historical drama. In his works the line between comedy and tragedy is no longer distinct, and the love intrigue does not necessarily provide the central conflict.

Toward the end of the 19th century realism in Ukrainian literature started to give way to modernism. Some writers no longer aimed for a naturalistic 'copy' of reality, and instead elected an impressionist mode. Along with that change the novelette gave way to the short story. In drama the action passed inward, to explore the psychological conflicts, moods, and experiences of the characters. Poetry abandoned its realistic orientation in favor of the symbolic; emphasis on content gave way to a fascination with form. The work of M. *Kotsiubynsky marks the transition from realism to modernism. His first stories were in the vein of Nechui-Levytsky and Myrny. Later he adopted and perfected the impressionistic manner of narration (eg, *Intermezzo*). O. *Kobylianska, a woman writer contemporary of Kotsiubynsky, was not so much an impressionist in her manner as a neoromantic. She instilled in her heroes (often women) an aloofness and an aristocracy of spirit. The neoromantic tendency in modernism prompted a rekindling of interest in folklore and resulted in the appearance of three remarkable works of literature: H. *Khotkevych's novel *Kaminna dusha* (A Soul of Stone, 1911), which in its treatment of female sexuality anticipates D.H. Lawrence; Lesia *Ukrainka's play *Lisova pisnia* (A Forest Song, 1911); and Kotsiubynsky's novelette *Tini zabutykh predkiv* (Shadows of Forgotten Ancestors, 1913).

The master of the very short impressionistic story was V. *Stefanyk. Condensed, dramatically charged, their subtle orchestration owing much to the local dialect of Stefanyk's heroes, his stories reveal the anguish at the heart of human existence. Two other writers who joined with Stefanyk to form the Pokutia triad were M. *Cheremshyna and L. *Martovych. They used methods similar to those of Stefanyk but rarely achieved the same results. The novelist and dramatist V. *Vynnychenko was deeply interested in the psychological experiences and especially the morality of the intelligentsia. Other modernist prose writers of note were S. *Vasylchenko, A. *Teslenko, and B. *Lepky.

Lepky also wrote poetry, as did most of the other members of the modernist group represented by *Moloda Muza. The most prominent in that group of Galician modernists were P. *Karmansky, with his end-of-the-century pessimism, and V. *Pachovsky, remarkable for his formal diversity. A modernist group in Russian-ruled Ukraine, centered around the journal *Ukraïns'ka khata*, produced no major poets. Outside of that group stood O. *Oles, by far the most popular lyricist of the period, the spirit of whose lyrics waxed and waned with the success and failure of the revolutions of 1905 and 1917; V. *Samiilenko, with his satiric verse; A. *Krymsky, with his exoticism; and H. *Chuprynka, memorable for his experimentation in sound. All of them contributed to the development of modernist poetry. Average poets but important to the modernist movement were M. *Vorony, the author of a modernist manifesto of 1901, and S. *Cherkasenko, who introduced elements of *symbolism into Ukrainian drama.

Although the realist Franko wrote some modernist verse (*Ziv'iale lystia* [Withered Leaves, 1896]), by far the most renowned poet of the modernist era was Lesia Ukrainka. More Romantic than modernist in style, her lyrics reflect wilful determination to conquer the disease that afflicted her body. The fighting spirit of her poems made them timely for the increasing struggle of Ukrainians for self-realization. Yet her greatest achievement was in the realm of the poetic drama. She chose universal themes and gave them her own unique treatment, as in *Kaminnyi hospodar* (The Stone Host, 1912), where she provided an early feminist treatment of the Don Juan motif.

The renaissance of the 1920s. The vernacular period came to an end with the First World War. The downfall of the Russian and Austro-Hungarian empires, the revolution, the establishment of an independent Ukraine (even if for a very short time), and, finally, the relative leniency of the Soviet regime during the period of *Ukrainization in the 1920s all led to a stupendous renaissance of literary activity. New writers appeared by the dozen. They formed literary groups and organizations (Lanka, *MARS, *Hart, *Pluh, *Nova Generatsiia, *Vaplite, *Prolitfront), published almanacs and magazines (such as the highly imaginative *Literaturnyi iarmarok*), and espoused various literary trends (symbolism, expressionism, impressionism, futurism, neoclassicism, neorealism, etc). There was a boom in literary criticism and scholarship. New histories of literature were written. It was the most vital era in Ukrainian literary history.

The most renowned poet of the time was P. *Tychyna. An innovator in form, rhythm, and imagery, he was the embodiment of what has since his day been called a 'romanticism of vitaism' (Yu. *Lavrinenko). A predilection for canonic metrics and classical harmony united a group of five poets commonly referred to as the *Neoclassicists. The group was centered around M. *Zerov and included M. *Rylsky, M. *Drai-Khmara, P. *Fylypovych, and Yu. *Klen. M. *Bazhan was an exponent of expressionism, and M. *Semenko propagated futurism. Other important poets of the time were V. *Blakytny, O. *Vlyzko, Ya. *Savchenko, D. *Falkivsky, D. *Zahul, G. *Shkurupii, V. *Polishchuk, M. *Yohansen, T. *Osmachka, the prolific lyricist V. *Sosiura, and the philosophical poet Ye. *Pluzhnyk.

The 1920s were by no means a renaissance only for poetry. The prose of M. *Khvylovy, with its erratic telegraphic style, and his pamphlets, with their turbulent exhortations and rhetorical questions, were part and symptom of the prevalent spirit of national vitality. Khvylovy's pamphlets, which provoked the *Literary Discussion, and his attempt at grouping writers into organizations – Vaplite and Prolitfront – to create a new proletarian Ukrainian culture make him the most important single author of the period from a literary and cultural but also a political point of view. Ukrainian prose was enriched by the lyrically romantic works of Yu. *Yanovsky and by V. *Pidmohylny, who gave Ukrainian literature its first modern novel in the neorealistic tradition. Ukrainian drama reached its apogee in the works of M. *Kulish especially during his collaboration with L. *Kurbas and the *Berezil theater. Other prose writers of note were M. *Ivchenko, A. *Holovko, I. * Senchenko, H. *Epik, V. *Gzhytsky, A. *Liubchenko, B. *Antonenko-Davydovych, O. *Slisarenko, the lyrical impressionist H. *Kosynka, the humorist O. *Vyshnia, and the essayist and parodist K. *Burevii. All of them were soon to be repressed.

The contemporary period. The renaissance of the 1920s ended abruptly and brutally. By the 1930s the Communist party had taken full control over literature; all independent organizations were abolished, and writers were forced into the *Writers' Union of Ukraine. The great terror began, and by 1938 most of the writers had either accepted Party control or been imprisoned, killed, or driven to suicide. It is estimated that over 250 writers perished during the decade, and the shortest but most intense period of Ukrainian literary development thus ended. *Socialist realism was proclaimed the sole acceptable literary manner. Authors who survived the terror (eg, Tychyna, Rylsky, Bazhan, Yanovsky, Sosiura) were cowed into submission. They renounced their former literary works and wrote panegyrics to J. Stalin and to the Party. Other themes (eg, collectivization, five-year plans, industrialization) were decreed and enforced from above. The 1940s and 1950s in Soviet Ukrainian literature were lean years with respect to literary quality. Representative of the period were the novels of N. *Rybak, I. *Le, L. *Pervomaisky, Yu. *Smolych, P. *Panch, I. *Vilde, and M. *Stelmakh; the dramas of O. *Korniichuk, I. *Mykytenko, and I. *Kocherha; and the poetry of Tychyna, Rylsky, and A. *Malyshko. The exception was the highly individualistic V. *Svidzinsky.

Between the world wars the national struggle continued to be the dominant theme of literature in Western Ukraine and among the political émigrés in Prague. Most representative of the émigré group both in theme and style was the nationalist-romantic poetry of Ye. *Malaniuk. A fighting spirit and historical determinism mark the works of many poets of the nationalist school, such as Yu. Drahan, Yu. *Lypa, L. *Mosendz, O. *Stefanovych, O.

*Liaturynska, S. *Hordynsky, B. *Kravtsiv, and two who fell victim to the Gestapo terror in Ukraine, O. *Olzhych and O. *Teliha. Teliha managed by her extreme sensitivity to soften the often-sharp edges of nationalist poetry. Quite apart from the nationalist group stood the most unusual poet of the period, the imagist B.I. *Antonych, and the pro-communist V. *Bobynsky.

Ukrainian literature outside of Soviet Ukraine experienced an unusually intensive period of development in the displaced persons' camps in West Germany and Austria immediately after the Second World War. Thrown together from various regions of Ukraine, writers managed to replay on a small scale the activity of the 1920s. They convened congresses, organized literary activity (see *MUR), and published almanacs, journals, and books. A key role in the activity was played by the linguist, scholar, and literary critic G.Y. *Shevelov and the novelist U. *Samchuk. Variety and impetus came from a large group of authors, some of whom, such as Osmachka, Klen, I. *Bahriany, M. *Orest, and D. *Humenna, had managed to escape the purges in Soviet Ukraine. Also of note were the dramatist, poet, and publisher I. *Kostetsky; the politically ambivalent Yu. *Kosach; the poets V. *Barka, V. *Lesych, and newcomers to literature, O. *Zuievsky, Ya. *Slavu-tych, L. Poltava, and I. *Kachurovsky (who also wrote prose). The episode came to an end in the early 1950s as the majority of the authors died or emigrated to North America and continued their literary work there.

There had been Ukrainian literary activity in North America since the turn of the century. Many of the early works were poems, written in simple, folklike verse, expressing longing for Ukraine or for acceptance in the strange new land. A few figures stand out, among them the dramatist M. *Irchan (who returned to Soviet Ukraine), the poet M. *Mandryka, and the novelist-chronicler I. *Kiriak. With the advent of the immigrant writers after the Second World War, literary activity increased; it was especially enlivened by the appearance in the late 1950s of a group of younger authors known as the *New York Group. There was little stylistic convergence between the depoetized strophes of G. *Tarnawsky, the sensual earthy images of B. *Boychuk, the surrealism of E. *Andiievska, the erudite allusions of B. *Rubchak, the mythical exoticism of V. *Vovk, and the otherworldliness of P. Kylyna (P. *Warren), but the members of the group were united in their attempt to create modern poetry devoid of immediate links to the tradition of nationalist poetry. Andiievska has also contributed significantly to the development of the modern Ukrainian novel. Some of the other writers who continued their literary activity in North America were the poets Barka, Lesych, Zuievsky, Slavutych, Poltava, V. *Skorupsky, B. *Oleksandriv, Yu. *Kolomyiets, O. *Tarnavsky, and B. Kravtsiv; the satirists O. *Smotrych and B. *Nyzhankivsky (Babai); the humorists I. *Kernytsky and M. *Ponedilok; and the novelists Samchuk and O. *Izarsky. Literary essays and criticism continued to be written by Yu. Sherekh (G.Y. Shevelov), Lavrinenko, and I. *Koshelivets.

After the death of Stalin in 1953 and the 'de-Stalinization' speech by N. Khrushchev at the 20th Party Congress in February 1956, the controls over literature in the Soviet Union began to slacken. A former member of Vaplite, the film director O. *Dovzhenko initiated the 'thaw' in Ukrainian literature with the publication of his autobiographical novelette *Zacharovana Desna* (The Enchanted Desna,

1957). The process of rehabilitation of some of the authors destroyed in the 1930s began slowly. Contemporaries of the purged authors wrote their memoirs of the times (eg, Yu. Smolych and his three volumes about the era of 'restlessness' [*nespokii*], 1968, 1969, and 1972). The rediscovery of the 1920s had a profound influence on the generation that was born just before or during the Second World War and began publishing in the 1960s. The so-called *shestyde-siatnyky* (the Sixties) succeeded in a span of 10 years in revitalizing all genres of Ukrainian literature. Among the most prominent authors were, in poetry, L. *Kostenko, I. *Drach, V. *Korotych, M. *Vinhranovsky, and V. *Symonenko; in prose, Ye. *Hutsalo, H. *Tiutiunnyk, and Valerii *Shevchuk; in literary and cultural criticism, I. *Dziuba, I. *Svitlychny, and Ye. *Sverstiuk; and in drama, O. *Kolomiiets. Some authors, such as the poet D. *Pavlych-ko and the novelists O. *Honchar, L. Pervomaisky, R. *Ivanychuk, Yu. *Mushketyk, and P. *Zahrebelny, entered a newly creative phase. Although almost immediately new repressions occurred, in the 1970s, a second generation of writers managed to appear. Among them the most notable were the poets I. *Kalynets, V. *Stus, and V. *Holoborodko and the prosaist V. *Drozd. With the exception of Kostenko and Shevchuk, who ceased publishing for a decade, most of the authors of the 1960s and 1970s either accepted the strictures of Party control (eg, Korotych, Drach, Dziuba, and Pavlychko) or were repressed (eg, Svitlychny, Sverstiuk, Kalynets, Holoborodko). Symonenko, Tiutiunnyk, and Stus died, Stus in a prison camp of the Gulag.

The changes in the USSR in the six years before its dissolution in 1991 rekindled interest in the 'white spots' – all that which had been removed from the history of Ukrainian literature. Writers who had been absent from Ukrainian literature since the 1930s have now been republished (Khvylovy, Zerov, Pidmohylny, etc), as have poems by poets repressed during L. Brezhnev's regime, such as Kalynets, M. *Vorobiov, and T. *Melnychuk. The literary scholar M. *Zhulynsky has filled in some of the missing literary biographies. A new phenomenon in the development of Ukrainian literature has been the appearance of the urban avant-garde groups Bu-Ba-Bu (V. Neborak, Yu. Andrukhovych, O. Irvanets), LuHoSad (I. Luchuk, N. Honchar, R. Sadlovsky), and Propala Hramota (S. Lybon, Yu. Pozaiak, V. Nedostup). Their poetry is marked by a desire to *épater*, and frequently resorts to parody and satire. New in the development of Ukrainian prose are the urban and demimonde environments and expanded lexical registers in the prose works of Andrukhovych and V. Yavorsky. Among other younger writers of interest are the poets V. Herasymiuk, I. Malkovych, I. Rymaruk, O. Lysheha, and O. Zabuzhko.

Ukrainian literature had a brief flowering in the 1960s in Czechoslovakia, during the Prague Spring. Most noteworthy were the psychological short stories of Ye. *Biss and V. *Datsei, the poetry of S. *Makara and S. *Hostyniak, the criticism of Yu. *Bacha, and the scholarship of O. *Zilynsky, M. *Molnar, and M. *Mushynka. Although no major figures have emerged, some Ukrainian literary activity exists in Yugoslavia, Rumania, Poland, and other countries where Ukrainians have settled (see *Canada, *Great Britain, *Brazil, *Australia, *France, *Germany, and *United States, and also *Literary criticism, *Literature studies, *Drama, *Poetry, and *Prose).

BIBLIOGRAPHY

Petrov, M. *Ocherki istorii ukrainskoi literatury XIX stoletiia* (Kiev 1884)

Ohnovs'kyi, O. *Istoriia literatury rus'koi* (Lviv 1891–3)

Franko, I. *Apokryfy i legendy z ukraïns'kykh rukopysiv: Pam'iatky ukraïns'ko-rus'koï movy i literatury*, 5 vols (Lviv 1896–1910)

Pypin, A. *Istoriia russkoi literatury*, 4 vols (St Petersburg 1911–13)

Iefremov, S. *Istoriia ukraïns'koho pys'menstva*, 4th edn, 2 vols (Kiev–Leipzig 1919, 1924)

Vozniak, M. *Istoriia ukraïns'koï literatury*, 3 vols (Lviv 1920–4)

– *Stare ukraïns'ke pys'menstvo* (Lviv 1922)

Hrushevs'kyi, M. *Istoriia ukraïns'koï literatury*, 5 vols (Kiev–Lviv 1923–7; repr, New York 1959–60)

Zerov, M. *Nove ukraïns'ke pys'menstvo* (Kiev 1924; repr, Munich 1960)

Peretts, V. *Slovo o polku Ihorevim: Pam'iatka feodal'noï Ukraïny-Rusy* (Kiev 1926)

Plevako, M. (ed). *Khrestomatiia novoï ukraïns'koï literatury*, 2 vols (Kharkiv 1928)

Zerov, M. *Vid Kulisha do Vynnychenka* (Kiev 1929)

Rudnyts'kyi, M. *Vid Myrnoho do Khvyl'ovoho* (Lviv 1936)

Chyzhevs'kyi, D. *Ukraïns'kyi literaturnyi barok: Narysy*, 3 vols (Prague 1941–4)

Zerov, M. *Do dzherel* (Cracow 1943; repr, State College 1967)

Gudzii, N.K. *History of Early Russian Literature* (New York 1949)

Vozniak, M. *Pochatky ukraïns'koï komediï*, 2nd edn (New York 1954)

Gudzii, N.K. (ed). *Khrestomatiia po drevnei russkoi literature*, 6th edn (Moscow 1955)

Derzhavyn, V. (ed). *Antolohiia ukraïns'koï poeziï* (London 1957)

Ryl's'kyi, M. (ed). *Antolohiia ukraïns'koï poeziï*, 4 vols (Kiev 1957)

Khudozhnia literatura vydana na Ukraïni za sorok rokiv (Kharkiv 1958)

Lavrinenko, Iu. (ed). *Rozstriliane vidrodzhennia: Antolohiia 1917–1933* (Paris 1959)

Antolohiia ukraïns'koho opovidannia, 4 vols (Kiev 1960)

Bilets'kyi, O.; et al (eds). *Ukraïns'ki pys'mennyky: Biobibliohrafichyi slovnyk*, 5 vols (Kiev 1960–5)

Andrusyshen, C.H.; Kirkconnell, W. (eds). *The Ukrainian Poets, 1189–1962* (Toronto 1963)

Koshelivets', I. *Panorama nainovishoï literatury v URSR* (New York 1963; 2nd rev edn, Munich 1974)

– *Suchasna literatura v URSR* (New York 1964)

Kyryliuk, Ie.; et al (eds). *Istoriia ukraïns'koï literatury*, 8 vols (Kiev 1967–71)

Bilets'kyi, O. *Khrestomatiia davn'oï ukraïns'koï literatury*, 3rd rev edn, (Kiev 1967)

Kravtsiv, B. (ed). *Shistdesiat poetiv shistdesiatykh rokiv: Antolohiia novoï ukraïns'koï poeziï* (New York 1967)

Ryl's'kyi, M; et al (eds). *Ukraïns'kyi dramatychnyi teatr*, 2 vols (Kiev 1967)

Zilyns'kyi, O. (ed). *Literatura chekhoslovats'kykh ukraïntsiv, 1945–1967* (Bratislava 1968)

Boichuk, B.; Rubchak, B. (eds). *Koordynaty: Antolohiia suchasnoï ukraïns'koï poeziï na zakhodi*, 2 vols (Munich 1969)

Čyževs'kyj, D. *A History of Ukrainian Literature: From the 11th to the End of the 19th Century* (Littleton, Colo 1975)

Donchyk, V. (ed). *Dialektyka khudozhn'oho poshuku: Literaturnyi protses 60–80-kh rokiv* (Kiev 1989)

Rymaruk, I. *Visimdesiatnyky: Antolohiia ukraïns'koï poeziï* (Edmonton 1990)

Zhulyns'kyi, M. *Iz zabuttia – v bezsmertia (Storinky pryzabutoï spadshchyny)* (Kiev 1990)

Musiienko, O. (ed). *... Z poroha smerti ... Pys'mennyky Ukraïny – zhertvy stalins'kykh represii* (Kiev 1991)

                                                    D.H. Struk

Literature, Institute of the Academy of Sciences of Ukraine. See Institute of Literature of the Academy of Sciences of the Ukrainian SSR.

Literature for children. See Children's literature.

Literature in translation. Ukrainian belles lettres have been translated into many languages of the world. In addition to major Western European languages (English, French, Spanish, German, Italian), Slavic languages (Russian, Belarusian, Polish, Bulgarian, Czech, Slovak, Serbo-Croatian, Slovenian), and languages of the non-Slavic peoples of the former USSR, translations from Ukrainian literature are available in languages such as Albanian, Arabic, Bengali, Chinese, Danish, Dutch, Esperanto, Finnish, Flemish, Greek, Hebrew, Hungarian, Icelandic, Japanese, Kanarese, Korean, Mongolian, Norwegian, Punjabi, Portuguese, Rumanian, Sinhalese, Swedish, Tamil, Telugu, Turkish, Vietnamese, and Yiddish. A special edition of T. Shevchenko's poem 'Zapovit' (Kiev 1989) is a polyglot anthology in 147 languages. A polyglot edition of I. Franko's 'Kameniari' (Kiev 1983) includes 67 versions of the poem translated into 37 languages. The novelist O. Honchar is the most widely translated contemporary Ukrainian writer. By 1985 his novel *Praporonostsi* (The Standard-bearers) had 40 Russian editions, 21 editions in languages of the peoples of the USSR, and 55 editions outside of the Soviet Union. In many languages, however, Ukrainian literature is represented only by a few samples. The widest coverage is probably in Russian: a Russian edition of Shevchenko's *Kobzar* appeared as early as 1860, during the poet's lifetime. There are hundreds of books translated from Ukrainian literature into Russian, both contemporary and classic, many in multivolume editions. Systematic translations into Western European languages have been undertaken only recently, notably by the Dnipro Publishers of Kiev (translations into English, French, and Spanish of contemporary and classic Ukrainian literature, anthologies of Ukrainian poetry and prose), by the Ukrainian Academic Press of the United States (translations into English mostly of classic authors, an anthology of Ukrainian prose), by Bayda Books of Australia (mostly contemporary authors, translated into English), and, as part of systematic efforts, by individual translators, such as V. Selianska (*Vovk) (translations into Portuguese: anthologies of poetry and prose, works of classic authors) and A.H. *Horbach (translations into German: anthologies of 20th-century Ukrainian prose, popular fiction, and works of dissident poets of Ukraine).

Translations into English. Ukrainian dumas attracted the attention of literary scholars in England and America as early as the middle of the 19th century. Scholarly discussions and/or translations of dumas appeared in *Foreign Quarterly Review* (1840–1), *American Eclectic* (1841), Talvj's *Historical View of the Languages and Literature of the Slavic Nations* (1850), and *Athenaeum* (1873). The first note on Shevchenko, a paraphrase of a few lines from his poem 'The Caucasus,' was, as far as can be determined, in the *Alaska Herald* of 1 March 1868. The earliest-known account of Shevchenko's life and work was J. Austin Stevens's English version of E. Durand's French article published in the *Galaxy* (New York, October 1876). Among the pioneer translators of Shevchenko's poetry were W.R. Morfill, F.P. Marchant, and E.L. Voynich. The first book of Shevchenko's poetry (*Six Lyrics from the Ruthenian of Taras Shevchenko* in E.L. Voynich's translation) and the first separately published essay (*T. Schevchenko, the National Poet of Oukraina* by L.P. Rastorgoueff) were both published in London in 1911. The earliest-known books of Ukrainian prose are M. Vovchok's *Maroussia, a Maid of Ukraine* (New York, 1880s and 1890), which was translated indirectly from the French version coauthored by P.-J. Stahl, and R.N. Bain's collection *Cossack Fairy Tales and Folk Tales* (London 1894), which may well be the first book of translations directly from the Ukrainian language. A collection of Ukrainian folk songs and selected poems by Shevchenko, S. Rudansky, H. Vorobkevych, and Yu. Fedkovych in the English version of F.R. Livesay (New York 1916) was probably the first English anthology of Ukrainian poetry.

Translations from Ukrainian literature and writings about Ukrainian literature had a dramatic quantitative increase in the 1960s, 1970s, and, especially, 1980s. Although many Ukrainian writers remain unrepresented or underrepresented in English, enough Ukrainian belles lettres are available to make university-level courses based exclusively on primary sources in translation possible. The quality of translation is on the rise, and literary criticism occasionally reaches the level of profound analytical study.

Anthologies. There are several anthologies of Ukrainian poetry. The most important are *The Ukrainian Poets, 1189–1962* (Toronto 1963; trans C.H. Andrusyshen and W. Kirkconnell), *Anthology of Soviet Ukrainian Poetry* (Kiev 1982; comp Z. Honcharuk), *Poetry of Soviet Ukraine's New World* (1986), and *Four Ukrainian Poets: Drach, Korotych, Kostenko, Symonenko* (1969; ed G.S.N. Luckyj, trans M. Bohachevsky-Chomiak and D.H. Struk). Ukrainian fiction is represented by the following anthologies: *Their Land* (1964; ed M. Luchkovich), *Stories of the Soviet Ukraine* (1970), *Modern Ukrainian Short Stories* (1973; ed G.S.N. Luckyj), *Valor: Stories by Soviet Ukrainian Writers about the Great Patriotic War of 1941–1945* (1975), *Written in the Book of Life: Works by 19th- and 20th-Century Ukrainian Writers* (1982; trans M. Skrypnyk), *Soviet Ukrainian Short Stories* (1983 and bk 2, 1985), and *Before the Storm: Soviet Ukrainian Fiction of the 1920s* (1986; ed G.S.N. Luckyj, trans Yu. Tkach). Anthologies of Ukrainian folklore include *Ukrainian Folk Tales* (1964; trans M.H. Bloch), *Ukrainian Dumy* (1979; trans G. Tarnawsky and P. Kilina), *Down Singing Centuries* (1981; trans F.R. Livesay), *Ukrainian Folk Tales* (1985; trans I. Zheleznova), and *How Ivan Went to See the Sun* (1989; trans A. Bilenko). A general representative anthology of émigré writers is conspicuous by its absence. There are, however, anthologies by country – of Ukrainian writers of Canada, *Yarmarok* (1987; eds J. Balan and Yu. Klynovy), which includes both poetry and prose; and of Australia, the collection of prose *On the Fence* (1985; ed D. Chub, trans Yu. Tkach) and *Australia's Ukrainian Poets* (1973; trans R.H. Morrison). Literary history and criticism are represented by such important collections (where some of the material has been translated from Ukrainian) as *Taras Ševčenko, 1814–1861* (1962; eds V. Mijakovskyj and G.Y. Shevelov), *Shevchenko and the Critics, 1861–1980* (Toronto 1980; ed G.S.N. Luckyj), and *Studies in Ukrainian Literature* (New York 1986; ed B. Rubchak).

Individual writers. Among translations of Ukrainian classics Shevchenko is most fully represented. *The Poetical Works of Taras Shevchenko* (1964; trans C.H. Andrusyshen and W. Kirkconnell) contains all the poems Shevchenko ever wrote in Ukrainian. Outstanding among other Shevchenko collections are *Taras Shevchenko, the Poet of Ukraine: Selected Poems* (1945; trans C.A. Manning),

Shevchenko's Thoughts and Lyrics (1961), *Song Out of Darkness* (1961; trans V. Rich), *Selected Works: Poetry and Prose with Reproductions of Paintings by T. Shevchenko* (1964 and 1979; ed J. Weir), *Selected Poetry* (1977 and 1989), and *Selections, Poetry, Prose* (1988; trans J. Weir). Among the critical and biographical studies of Shevchenko in addition to the aforementioned mention must be made of *Taras Shevchenko: A Life* by P. Zaitsev (1988; trans and ed G.S.N. Luckyj), and *The Exile*, a biographical novel by Z. Tulub (1988; trans A. Bilenko).

Books of Franko's poetry and prose include *Ivan Franko, the Poet of Western Ukraine: Selected Poems* (1948 and 1968; trans P. Cundy), *Poems and Stories* (1956; trans J. Weir), *Boa Constrictor and Other Stories* (1957; trans F. Solasko), *Stories* (1972), *Moses and Other Poems* (1973; trans V. Rich), *Short Stories* (1977), *Fox Mykyta* (1978; trans B. Melnyk), *Ivan Vyshensky* (1983; trans R.O. Tatchyn), *When the Animals Could Talk* (1984 and 1987; trans M. Skrypnyk), *Selections: Poems and Stories* (1986; trans J. Weir), *Moses and Other Poems* (1987; trans A. Hnidj), and *Zakhar Berkut* (1987; M. Skrypnyk). Lesia Ukrainka is represented by *Spirit of Flame* (1950; trans P. Cundy), *Lesya Ukrainka: Life and Work* (1968; ed C. Bida, trans V. Rich), *In the Catacombs* (1971; trans J. Weir), *Hope: Selected Poetry* (1975; trans G. Evans), and *Forest Song* (1985; trans G. Evans). M. Vovchok, in addition to the pioneering translation of *Maroussia, Maid of Ukraine*, has two recent books in English, *After Finishing School* (1983; trans O. Kovalenko) and *Ukrainian Folk Stories* (1983; trans N. Pedan-Popil). There exists a translation of P. Kulish's novel *The Black Council* (1973; trans G.S.N. and M. Luckyj). H. Kvitka-Osnovianenko's novel *Marusia* (trans F.R. Livesay) was published in New York in 1940. Translations of M. Kotsiubynsky appear as *Chrysalis and Other Stories* (1958; trans J. Guralsky), *The Birthday Present and Other Stories* (1973), *Fata Morgana* (1976; trans A. Bernhard), *Fata Morgana and Other Stories* (1980; var trans), and *Shadows of Forgotten Ancestors* (1981; trans M. Carynnyk). The short stories of V. Stefanyk are available in at least three collections: *The Stone Cross* (1971; trans J. Wiznuk and C.H. Andrusyshen), *A Study of Vasyl Stefanyk: The Pain at the Heart of Existence* (1973; trans and commentary by D.H. Struk), and *Maple Leaves and Other Stories* (1988; trans M. Skrypnyk). I. Nechui-Levytsky's *Mikola Dzerya: A Long Story* was published in Kiev in 1985 (trans O. Kovalenko).

Translations of prose works include S. Vasylchenko's *Stories* (1984; trans O. Kovalenko); A. Teslenko's *Stories* (1981; var trans); M. Khvylovy's *Stories from the Ukraine* (1960; trans G.S.N. Luckyj); V. Pidmohylny's *A Little Touch of Drama* (1972; trans G.S.N. and M. Luckyj); A. Holovko's *The Weeds* (1976; trans A. Bilenko) and *The Red Kerchief* (1979; trans A. Bilenko); B. Antonenko-Davydovych's *Behind the Curtain* (1980; trans Yu. Tkach) and *Duel* (1986; trans Yu. Tkach); V. Gzhytsky's *Night and Day* (1988; trans I. Press); O. Vyshnia's *Hard Times* (1981; trans Yu. Tkach); A. Dovzhenko's *The Enchanted Desna* (1982; trans A. Bilenko); Yu. Yanovsky's *The Horsemen* (1989; trans S. Sinhayivsky); M. Stelmakh's *Let the Blood of Man Not Flow* (1962; trans E. Manning and O. Shartse); O. Honchar's *The Standard-bearers* (1948; trans N. Jochel), *Short Stories* (1950s; trans V. Shneerson), *The Cyclone* (1972; trans A. Ingman), *The Shore of Love* (1980; trans D. Sinclair-Loutit), *Man and Arms* (1985; trans A. Bilenko), and *The Cathedral* (1989; trans Yu. Tkach and L. Rudnytzky); P. Zahrebelny's *From the Point of View of Eternity* (1978; trans C. English); Ye. Hutsalo's *A Prevision of Happiness and Other Stories* (1974; trans E. Manning); O. Berdnyk's *Apostle of Immortality* (1984; trans Yu. Tkach); Valerii Shevchuk's *The Meek Shall Inherit* (1989; trans V. Kholmogorova); Vasyl Shevchuk's *Blood Brothers* (1980; trans Yu. Tkach); A. Dimarov's *Across the Bridge* (1977; trans Yu. Tkach); V. Malyk's *The Cossack Ambassador* (1985; trans S. Sinhaivsky); D. Mishchenko's *The Siverianians* (1986; trans O. Olexiv); Yu. Mushketyk's *Cruel Mercy* (1986; trans O. Panasyev); V. Nestaiko's *Two Toreadors from Vasukovka Village* (1983; trans F. Glagoleva) and *In the Land of the Sunbeam Bunnies* (1986; trans A. Bilenko); M. Pryhara's *The Cossack Holota* (1985; trans M. Skrypnyk); V. Blyznets's *In the Land of the Living Lights* (1987; trans V. Ruzhitsky); R. Sambuk's *The Jeweler from Capuchins Street* (1982; trans A. Bilenko); M. Vinhranovsky's *Summer Evening* (1987; trans A. Bilenko); H. Tiutiunnyk's *Cool Mint* (1986; trans A. Bilenko); V. Zemliak's *The Swan Flock* (1982) and *Green Mills* (1984), both trans by A. Bilenko; V. Vladko's *Descendants of the Scythians* (1986; trans O. Panasyev); B. Kharchuk's *A Measure of Life and a Measure of Death* (1989; trans O. Panasyev). Translations of émigré writers include V. Vynnychenko's *Selected Short Stories* (1991; trans S. Prokopov); I. Kiriak's *Sons of the Soil* (1959 and 1983; trans M. Luchkovich); I. Bahriany's *The Hunters and the Hunted* (1954 and 1956); T. Osmachka's *Red Assassins* (1959); I. Kachurovsky's *Because Deserters Are Immortal* (1979; trans Yu. Tkach); V. Sokil's *And Then There Was Glasnost* (1990; trans K. Windle); M. Ponedilok's *Funny Tears* (1982; trans Yu. Tkach); I. Bodnarchuk's *The Generations Will Get Together* (1986; trans Yu. Tkach); and H. Meriam-Luzhnytsky's *Twelve Letters from F.A. Sheptytsky to His Mother* (1983; trans R.O. Tatchyn).

Among the poetry of individual poets are P. Tychyna's *Selected Poetry* (1987; var trans); M. Rylsky's *Selected Poetry* (1980; trans G. Evans); B.I. Antonych's *Square of Angels* (1977; var trans); I. Drach's *Orchard Lamps* (1978; ed S. Kunitz; 2nd edn 1989); V. Stus's *Selected Poems* (1987; trans J. Lassowsky); I. Kalynets's *Crowning the Scarecrow* (1990; trans M. Carynnyk); L. Kostenko's *Selected Poetry: Wanderings of the Heart* (1990; trans M. Naydan); V. Holoborodko's *Icarus with Butterfly Wings* (1991; trans M. Stefaniuk); O. Teliha's *Boundaries of Flame* (1977; trans O. Prokopiv); V. Symonenko's *Granite Obelisks* (1976; trans A.M. Chirovsky); and, of the émigré poets, Ya. Slavutych's *The Conquerors of the Prairies* (1974 and 1984; var trans) and *Oasis* (1959; trans M. Manly); G. Tarnawsky's *This Is How I Get Well* (1978; trans by author); V. Vovk's *Meanders* (1979; trans M. Lukianowicz) and *Mandala* (1980; trans O. Gomes); and B. Boychuk's *Memories of Love* (1989; trans M. Rudman and D. Ignatow).

Drama is represented in English by O. Korniichuk (*Wings*, 1956; trans J. Gibbons), M. Kulish (*Sonata Pathétique*, 1975; trans G.S.N. and M. Luckyj), and I. Kocherha (*Yaroslav the Wise*, 1982; trans W. May).

Notable among memoirs, diaries, and biographical works are O. Dovzhenko's *The Poet as a Filmmaker* (Cambridge, Mass 1973; trans and commentary by M. Carynnyk), M. Osadchy's *Cataract* (1976; trans M. Carynnyk), V. Drozd's *The Road to Mother* (1987; trans V. Castelli and S. Vladkov), and O. Asher's *Letters from the Gulag: The Life, Letters, and Poetry of Michael Dray-Khmara* (1983).

Outstanding among books of literary history and criticism are D. Chyzhevsky's *A History of Ukrainian Literature*

(1975), Ye. Sverstiuk's *Clandestine Essays* (1976; ed and trans G.S.N. Luckyj), M. Khvylovy's *The Cultural Renaissance in Ukraine* (1986; ed and trans M. Shkandrij), and Ye. Shabliovsky's *Ukrainian Literature through the Ages* (1970).

Translations of Ukrainian belles lettres in the periodical press have appeared most frequently in the pages of such journals as *Ukraine, Ukrainian Canadian, Soviet Literature, Ukrainian Review* (London), *Journal of Ukrainian Studies* (Edmonton), *Forum* (Scranton), and *Smoloskyp* (Ellicott City, Maryland). Articles of literary criticism are published in many English-language journals devoted to Slavic studies, most notably in *Harvard Ukrainian Studies, Slavonic and East European Review, Slavic and East European Journal, Canadian Slavonic Papers, Annals of the Ukrainian Academy of Arts and Sciences in the US,* and *Journal of Ukrainian Studies.*

BIBLIOGRAPHY

'Rosiis'ka literatura i T.H. Shevchenko,' *Shevchenkivs'kyi slovnyk,* vol 2 (Kiev 1977)

Franko, I. *Kameniari movamy narodiv svitu* (Kiev 1983)

Koval', V. 'Praporonostsi v pokhodi,' *Vsesvit*, 1985, no. 5

Denysova, T.; et al (eds). *Ukraïns'ka literatura v zahal'no-slov'ians'komu i svitovomu literaturnomu konteksti,* vol 3, *U vzaiemynakh z literaturamy Zakhodu i Skhodu* (Kiev 1988)

Tarnawsky [Tarnavs'ka], M. *Ukrainian Literature in English: Books and Pamphlets, 1890–1965* (Edmonton 1988)

Piasecky, O. *Bibliography of Ukrainian Literature in English and French: Translations and Critical Works, 1950–1986* (Ottawa 1989)

Shevchenko, T. *Zapovit movamy narodiv svitu* (Kiev 1989)

Tarnawsky [Tarnavs'ka], M. *Ukrainian Literature in English: Articles in Journals and Collections, 1840–1965* (Edmonton 1992)

M. Tarnawsky (Tarnavska)

Literature studies. Literary scholarship in Ukraine originated in the baroque period. M. Smotrytsky was the first to transcend the bounds of grammar proper, in the scholarly treatment of prosody in his Slavonic grammar (1619). At the Kievan Mohyla College (later Academy) students received thorough instruction in the study of styles, as is evident from the theorizing elements in their panegyrics to P. Mohyla that appeared in books published by the Kievan Cave Monastery Press, among them *Imnolohiia ...* (Hymnology ..., 1630), *Eufonia veselobrmiachaia* (Joyful Ringing Euphony, 1633), and, particularly, *Evkharistirion ...* (Eucharisterion, 1632). In 1705 T. Prokopovych taught a course on the theory of literature at the academy; in his lectures (pub 1786) he examined the various literary genres in a comprehensive and professional manner. With the exodus of Ukrainian scholars into the Russian imperial service in Moscow and then St Petersburg, the study of literature in Ukraine declined.

From the 19th century to 1917. Literature studies in Ukraine were revived in entirely different circumstances in the first half of the 19th century. Inspired by the ideas of European romanticism, the scholars M. Maksymovych, I. Sreznevsky, O. Bodiansky, M. Kostomarov, Ya. Holovatsky, and I. Vahylevych published surveys of Ukrainian literature in almanacs and periodicals. In Western Ukraine the first survey of the kind appeared in I. Mohylnytsky's *Vidomost' o russkom iazytsi* (Information about the Ruthenian Language, 1829). Later P. Kulish's survey articles in the journals *Russkii vestnik* (1857, no. 2) and *Osnova* (1861, no. 1) and in his almanac *Khata* (1860) were particularly important for their time.

In the late 1860s the first cultural-historical studies of the development of Ukrainian literature from the perspective of evolutionary historicism were written; notable examples are the surveys of Ukrainian literature by the Russians I. Pryzhov (in his book on Little Russia, 1869) and A. *Pypin and V. Spasovich (in their history of Slavic literatures, 2nd edn, vol 1, 1879). Of particular note are M. Drahomanov's series of articles on Russian and Ukrainian literature (*Pravda* [Lviv], 1873, nos 4–6, 16–21; 1874, nos 1–9) and his study of T. Shevchenko, the Ukrainophiles, and socialism (*Hromada* [Geneva], no. 4 [1879]). Unlike his Romantic precursors, Drahomanov examined Ukrainian literature from the perspective of realism and democracy.

A valuable bibliographic guide to Ukrainian writers was M. (N.) *Petrov's Russian-language history of 19th-century Ukrainian literature (1884). It had a major weakness, however: Petrov claimed that the development of Ukrainian literature was dependent on its Russian counterpart. In his 1888 critique of Petrov, M. *Dashkevych argued that Ukrainian literature evolved independently, and his response, together with Petrov's work, laid the foundation for further literary studies. Around the same time O. *Ohonovsky's history of Ruthenian literature (4 pts, 1887–94) was published in Galicia. Ohonovsky's thesis that the writing of Kievan Rus' was the initial stage of Ukrainian literature elicited bitter criticism from Pypin and other Russian historians. The responses by Ohonovsky and his defenders M. Komarov and I. Nechui-Levytsky (the latter writer's *Ukraïnstvo na literaturnykh pozvakh z Moskovshchynoiu* [The Ukrainian Entity in Literary Challenges with Russia, 1891]) sparked a debate which was reminiscent of an earlier one between Maksymovych and the Russian historian M. Pogodin.

In the 19th century many literary works and chronicles of the medieval and Cossack periods were published by Russian scholarly societies, by the Shevchenko Scientific Society in Lviv, and in the documentary collections *Akty, otnosiashchiesia k istorii Iuzhnoi i Zapadnoi Rossii* (Documents Pertaining to the History of Southern and Western Russia) and *Arkhiv Iugo-Zapadnoi Rossii* (The Archive of Southwestern Russia). Their publication facilitated in-depth studies of medieval and early modern Ukrainian literature by M. Sumtsov, M. *Markovsky, A. Krymsky, M. (N.) Petrov, P. Zhytetsky, and other scholars from the 1880s on. A particularly important role in the furthering of such literary studies was played by I. *Franko in Galicia and by V. *Peretts in Russian-ruled Ukraine; the pre-eminent representative of the so-called philological school, Peretts trained such scholars as L. Biletsky, S. Maslov, I. *Ohiienko, O. Nazarevsky, and V. Adriianova-Peretts. Many studies appeared in the journals *Zapysky NTSh* and *Literaturno-naukovyi vistnyk* in Lviv and *Kievskaia starina* and *Ukraïna* in Kiev.

In the late 19th and early 20th centuries much attention was devoted to modern Ukrainian literature, particularly to Shevchenko studies, by Franko, V. *Shchurat, K. *Studynsky, O. *Kolessa, O. *Konysky, Yu. *Romanchuk, V. *Horlenko, and other scholars. At that time a utilitarian, 'neopopulist' approach to literary studies became dominant. Its primary exponent was S. *Yefremov; B. Hrinchenko, I. Steshenko, and O. *Hrushevsky were other prominent neopopulists. In contradistinction to the neopopulists a small group of scholars (M. *Yevshan, V. *Doroshenko, and others) advocated an esthetic approach to the study of literature.

Soviet Ukraine

The interwar years. Literature studies entered an entirely new phase in the early Soviet period. Until the onset of the Stalinist terror in the early 1930s, the Historical-Philological Division of the All-Ukrainian Academy of Sciences (VUAN) published many articles in the field of literary theory in its periodicals and collections, authoritative annotated texts of old Ukrainian literature, and pioneering monographs by such scholars as Peretts (on the medieval epic *Slovo o polku Ihorevi* [The Tale of Ihor's Campaign, 1926]), D. Abramovych (on the Kievan Cave Patericon, 1931), and V. Riezanov (5 vols on Ukrainian drama, 1926–9). M. Hrushevsky published a major history of old Ukrainian literature (5 vols, 1923, 1925–7) using a cultural-historical approach that was similar to that of the neopopulists. M. *Zerov, P. *Fylypovych, M. *Drai-Khmara, V. *Petrov, M. *Mohyliansky, O. *Doroshkevych, O. *Biletsky, Ya. *Aizenshtok, A. *Shamrai, M. *Novytsky, Markovsky, A. *Muzychka, A. *Leites, M. *Plevako, P. Rulin, T. Slabchenko, and O. *Bahrii made pioneering contributions to the study of modern Ukrainian literature; their work was published separately or in numerous VUAN serials and collections of articles. Shevchenko studies in particular flourished. Scholars edited, provided scholarly introductions to, and annotated the collected or selected works of Shevchenko and most other prominent Ukrainian writers that were published by the State Publishing House of Ukraine and several co-operative publishers (Rukh, Knyhospilka, Slovo, and others). Formalistic research thrived, and new textbooks on the history of Ukrainian literature and theoretical studies (by B. *Yakubsky, D. *Zahul, B. *Navrotsky, H. *Maifet, and others) appeared. Scholars also published their research and criticism in several literary journals, particularly *Chervonyi shliakh*, *Zhyttia i revoliutsiia*, and *Krytyka*.

At the same time, however, literature studies were hampered by political interference in scholarship. Marxist critics representing the Party line (V. *Koriak, A. Richytsky, V. Yurynets, I. *Lakyza, S. *Shchupak, Ye. *Hirchak, A. *Khvylia, B. Kovalenko, H. Ovcharov, and, later, I. Stebun, S. *Shakhovsky, and others) falsified the history of Ukrainian literature, and with the Stalinist assault on bourgeois nationalism and the resulting *terror and physical destruction of almost an entire generation of Ukrainian intellectuals in the early 1930s, literature studies virtually disappeared. Restrictions on what the few surviving scholars could research and write effectively negated the achievements of the 1920s.

The postwar years. There was no noticeable change until the post-Stalin 'thaw' that began in the mid-1950s. At that time the ANURSR (now ANU) *Institute of Literature became the central, co-ordinating institution of literature studies in Ukraine, and a special commission chaired by the institute's director was created to guide and determine the work of literary scholars at all postsecondary institutions in Ukraine.

Since the mid-1950s the development of literature studies in Ukraine has been uneven. Truly scholarly works in literary theory, particularly in esthetics, have been sorely lacking. With the exception of I. Ivano's *Ocherk razvitiia esteticheskoi mysli Ukrainy* (Outline of the Development of Ukraine's Esthetic Thought, 1981), which, significantly, was published in Russian and in Moscow, most of what has been written in the field of literary theory has been dogmatic and propagandistic. Soviet Ukrainian theorists were not allowed to, or did not, deal with Western theories in their research. Only a few works devoted to general or concrete theoretical subjects have been published; among them are P. Volynsky's book on the foundations of literary theory (1962), V. Kovalevsky's book on rhythmic devices in Ukrainian literary verse (1960), and V. Lesyn and O. Pulynets's brief dictionary of literary terms (1961).

Research on 11th- to 13th-century Ukrainian literature has generally been neglected in the postwar period. It has been discussed in Ukrainian in journal articles, in a chrestomathy of old Ukrainian literature (1948; 3rd edn 1967) edited by O. Biletsky, in a few other reference books on Ukrainian literature, and in M. Hrytsai, V. Mykytas, and F. Sholom's university textbook on old Ukrainian literature (1978, the first of its kind). Usually, however, it has been approached within the parameters of Russian literature and written about in Russian. *Slovo o polku Ihorevi* is a case in point. Three editions of various renderings of it into modern Ukrainian were prepared, by Maslov (1953), M. *Gudzii (1955), and L. *Makhnovets (1967), but most scholarly studies of it, even by the Ukrainians Gudzii, L. Bulakhovsky, M. Sharleman, P. Popov, and M. Hetmanets, have been published in Russian in Moscow.

Similarly, most of the postwar research on 14th- to 18th-century Ukrainian literature was, until the late 1950s, conducted in Moscow. Soviet editions of the works of I. Vyshensky (1955) and Prokopovych (1961), for example, were first published in Russian in Moscow. A volume of Peretts's research (1962) also appeared there in Russian, even though it dealt with 16th- and 17th-century Ukrainian literature. In the early 1960s a few important publications concerning the period appeared in Ukraine: a collection of articles about the 17th- and 18th-century Ukrainian translated narrative (1960), edited by B. Derkach, with an appendix of valuable original texts; a collection of articles about Ukrainian intermedes (1960), edited by Makhnovets; H. *Syvokin's book on old Ukrainian poetics (1960); an annotated edition of H. Skovoroda's works (2 vols, 1961); Ya. Dzyra's pioneering article on S. Velychko's Cossack chronicle and its influence on Shevchenko in the journal *Vitchyzna* (1962, no. 5); and Makhnovets's book on satire and humor in 16th- to 18th-century Ukrainian prose (1964).

A resurgence of scholarship on the literature of the period began in the early 1970s, and a few other important works were published: annotated editions of the works of Klymentii, Zynovii's son (1971), I. Velychkovsky (1972), and Skovoroda (2 vols, 1973); a modern Ukrainian edition of M. Dovhalevsky's *Poetyka* (Poetics, 1973), translated and annotated by V. Masliuk; Makhnovets's biography of Skovoroda (1972); and H. Sydorenko's book on Ukrainian versification (1972). After the 1972–3 KGB crackdown on Ukrainian dissidents and 'nationalist' intellectuals in general, nothing of lasting value was published in Ukraine until the late 1970s. Since that time, particularly since the reforms of 1985, there has been a perceptible liberalization in scholarship, and important new books have appeared: an annotated anthology of late 16th- and early 17th-century Ukrainian poetry (1978), edited by V. Kolosova and V. Krekoten; a modern Ukrainian edition of Prokopovych's philosophical works (3 vols, 1979–81); a collection of articles on the literary legacy of Kievan Rus' and 16th- to 18th-century Ukrainian literature (1981), edited by O. *Myshanych; P. Yaremenko's books on Vyshensky (1982)

and Smotrytsky (1986); an annotated anthology of 18th-century Ukrainian literature (1983), edited by Myshanych; a book on A. Radyvylovsky's stories (1983), edited by Krekoten; Masliuk's book on poetics and rhetoric in Latin in the 17th and first half of the 18th century and their role in the development of literary theory in Ukraine (1983); O. Apanovych's book (in Russian) on the handwritten secular book in 18th-century Ukraine (1983); a collection of articles on 16th- to 18th-century Ukrainian literature and other Slavic literatures (1984), edited by Myshanych; M. Sulyma's study of late 16th- and early 17th-century Ukrainian versification (1985); an annotated edition of I. Galiatovsky's *Kliuch razuminiia* (Key of Understanding, 1985); annotated anthologies of 16th- and 17th-century Ukrainian poetry (1987, 1988), edited by V. Yaremenko; and a collection of scholarly articles on Ukrainian literature of the baroque period (1987), edited by Myshanych.

Most postwar Soviet scholars have focused their attention on 19th- and 20th-century literature. Many works (by N. Krutikova and others) have dealt with the subject of Ukrainian-Russian literary ties and have been of a propagandistic nature, emphasizing the salutary influence of Russian literature and writers. There have, however, been works – by M. Bernshtein, Volynsky, O. Babyshkin, N. Kalenychenko, M. Yatsenko, P. Fedchenko, and others – which, despite their political bias, have provided abundant factual material from previously banned sources (by Kulish, Drahomanov, and others) on individual periods and problems and on such topics as journalism and literary criticism. Numerous articles and monographs on individual writers, notably on Shevchenko, Franko, Lesia Ukrainka, M. Kotsiubynsky, V. Stefanyk, and O. Kobylianska, have appeared, as have biographies, analyses of particular aspects of the works, and even collections of primary materials and memoirs of most luminaries of 19th- and early 20th-century Ukrainian literature. Until the late 1980s, analyses were usually politically biased, however, and in certain cases authors even bowdlerized or falsified texts to try to show the love of certain Ukrainian writers for things Russian. Some of the leading postwar specialists on pre-Soviet modern Ukrainian literature have been, besides those already mentioned, I. Bass, O. Biletsky, L. Bolshakov, V. Borodin, D. Chaly, O. Dei, Derkach, V. Herasymenko, O. Honchar, Hrytsai, M. Hrytsiuta, Yu. *Ivakin, Kalenychenko, A. Kaspruk, L. Khinkulov, Yu. Kobyletsky, P. Kolesnyk, Ye. *Kyryliuk, O. Kyselov, Lesyn, M. Levchenko, Z. Moroz, Mykytas, O. Honchar, I. Pilhuk, F. Pohrebennyk, Popov, P. Prykhodko, Ye. *Shabliovsky, S. Shakhovsky, V. Shubravsky, Stebun, L. Stetsenko, Sydorenko, M. Syvachenko, H. Verves, Volynsky, M. *Vozniak, O. Zasenko, and S. Zubkov.

In post-Stalinist scholarship on Soviet literature, in accordance with the Party line, most writers who had been destroyed in the terror of the 1930s were posthumously rehabilitated by way of selective, limited republication of their works (the exception being I. Mykytenko, who has been widely studied and republished). Their biographies, however, have been presented in a distorted manner to emphasize their Soviet patriotism, and any discussion of the reason for their untimely deaths was deliberately avoided until the reforms of 1980s. Until the late 1980s, authors of monographs and articles about the writers of the 1920s generally distorted and even denigrated their pre-socialist-realist writings (eg, L. *Novychenko's 1959 book on P. Tychyna's early poetry and S. *Kryzhanivsky's 1960 book on M. Rylsky) and were not allowed to discuss, except in passing and in a biased manner, the lives and works of various important literary figures (eg, M. Khvylovy, V. Vynnychenko, and Yefremov) who were deemed anti-Soviet. The foremost postwar specialists on Soviet Ukrainian literature have been Ye. Adelheim, Babyshkin, O. Diachenko, V. *Donchyk, I. Duz, I. *Dzeverin, V. Fashchenko, K. Frolova, Z. Holubieva, A. Ishchuk, Kobyletsky, L. Kovalenko, P. Kononenko, B. Korsunska, N. Kostenko, Kryzhanivsky, N. *Kuziakina, O. Kylymnyk, Y. Kyselov, M. Naienko, Novychenko, M. Ostryk, S. Plachynda, V. Radchenko, M. Rodko, I. Semenchuk, Shabliovsky, Shakhovsky, D. Shlapak, Ye. Starynkevych, Sydorenko, M. Syrotiuk, Syvokin, A. Trostianetsky, A. Trypilsky, D. Vakulenko, and M. *Zhulynsky.

Advances in literature studies have nonetheless occurred in the post-Stalinist period. Works of many, though not all, writers banned under Stalin from the scholarly purview have been included in various books, such as Rylsky and M. Nahnybida's anthology of Ukrainian poetry (4 vols, 1957) and an anthology of the Ukrainian short story (1960) edited by O. Biletsky et al. Studies of genres, particularly in pre-Soviet literature, have been freely developed (eg, H. Nudha's books on parody in Ukrainian literature [1961], the Ukrainian ballad [1970], and the Ukrainian poetic epic and dumas [1971]). A few collections of materials for the study of Ukrainian literature (eg, a study edited by O. Biletsky [5 vols, 1959–63]), valuable works in literary bibliography (by L. Holdenberh, M. Moroz, I. Boiko, and others), and Dei's dictionary of Ukrainian pseudonyms and cryptonyms (1969) have appeared. Hundreds of monographs, textbooks, literary biographies and 'portraits,' chrestomathies, and collections of articles, documents, and memoirs have been issued, and scholars have had the opportunity to publish in many periodicals, including *Radians'ke literaturoznavstvo* (now *Slovo i chas*), *Ukraïns'ke literaturoznavstvo*, *Ukraïns'ka mova i literatura v shkoli*, *Inozemna filolohiia*, *Problemy slov'ianoznavstva*, and *Slov'ians'ke literaturoznavstvo i fol'klorystyka*. The study of classical literature has been fostered by such scholars as O. Biletsky, M. Bilyk, Y. Kobiv, M. Kuzma, Masliuk, Yu. Mushak, F. Lutska, E. Kudrytsky, Yu. Sak, and Y. Bahlai; and Shamrai, D. Zatonsky, T. Yakymovych, Verves, M. Sokoliansky, Yu. Pokalchuk, V. Shevchuk, T. Denisova, D. Nalyvaiko, I. Zhuravska, and O. Pakhlovska, and other scholars have written monographs on European, American, and other foreign literature.

Until the late 1980s, however, prominent scholars who survived Stalinism, including O. Biletsky, the 'dean' of postwar Soviet Ukrainian literary scholarship, have not had many of their earlier, superior writings republished in representative editions of their works. Formalist and other 'esthetic' approaches were viewed as being incompatible with the obligatory Marxist-Leninist method. All manuscripts were subject to several levels of scrutiny – by the self-censoring authors themselves, the supervising editor of a publication, and the editorial board – and then still had to be sanctioned by a state censor. Consequently, all histories of Ukrainian literature, such as those published in two vols in 1954–7 and 1987–8 and in eight vols (nine books) in 1967–71, were written by 'collectives' of authors; the orthodox purity of all the individual contributions was thus safeguarded.

Western Ukraine and abroad, 1918–39. Under interwar Polish rule Lviv was the main center of literature studies in Western Ukraine. Ukrainian scholars were barred from Lviv University by the Polish authorities, and survived by teaching in gymnasiums or working for Ukrainian community organizations. They could, however, publish their works in Galicia, without having to endure the political constraints placed on their Soviet colleagues, in the serials of the *Shevchenko Scientific Society (NTSh), in *Literaturno-naukovyi vistnyk*, and in other periodicals. Older scholars, such as I. Bryk, Doroshenko, Ya. *Hordynsky, D. Lukiianovych, Shchurat, Studynsky, I. *Svientsitsky, and Vozniak, remained productive, and important contributions were also made by their younger colleagues in Lviv, notably M. *Hnatyshak, V. *Lev, L. *Lutsiv, H. *Luzhnytsky, Ye. *Pelensky, V. *Radzykevych, M. *Rudnytsky, and M. *Tershakovets.

In the 1920s and 1930s most scholars who fled from Soviet rule found refuge in Czechoslovakia, Poland, Austria, Germany, and France. Together with Galician and Bukovynian expatriates also living there they founded many new scholarly institutions, such as the Ukrainian Free University, the Ukrainian Higher Pedagogical Institute, the Ukrainian Historical-Philological Society in Prague, and the Ukrainian Scientific Institute in both Berlin and Warsaw, all of which maintained close ties with the NTSh in Lviv. Valuable contributions to literature studies were published in the serials and collections of those institutions in Western Ukrainian, Czech, Polish, and German periodicals and in individual books by D. Antonovych, L. *Biletsky, P. *Bohatsky, K. Chekhovych, D. *Chyzhevsky, D. Doroshenko, O. Kolessa, V. *Simovych, and S. *Smal-Stotsky in Prague, V. Birchak in Uzhhorod, Ye. Perfetsky in Bratislava, B. *Lepky in Cracow, I. Ohiienko and P. *Zaitsev in Warsaw, O. *Hrytsai in Vienna, and E. *Borschak in Paris. Several Czech scholars, notably V. Charvát, A. Hartl, J. Horák, J. Máchal, and F. Tichý, also published works about Ukrainian literature.

Postwar scholarship outside Ukraine

Western Europe. After the Second World War many scholars sought refuge from Soviet rule and occupation as displaced persons in the Allied occupation zones in Germany. The Shevchenko Scientific Society and Ukrainian Free University were re-established in Munich, and a new body, the Ukrainian Free Academy of Sciences (UVAN), was created in Augsburg in 1945. By the late 1940s most refugees had resettled overseas. Emigré literary scholars who have lived in postwar West Germany in the period after 1950 and have made important contributions to the study of Ukrainian literature are Yu. *Blokhyn, Chyzhevsky, V. *Derzhavyn, A.H. Horbach, I. *Kachurovsky (since 1969), I. *Koshelivets, and I. *Kostetsky. Another, V. Petrov, returned to Ukraine in 1949, and another, M. *Hlobenko, moved to France in 1951. Only one prominent émigré literary scholar, V. *Swoboda, has lived and published in Great Britain. In France contributions to literature studies have been made more recently by M. Scherrer, E. Kruba, and L. *Pliushch.

Canada. G.S.N. *Luckyj, who became chairman of the Slavic studies department at the University of Toronto in 1954, has played a leading role in the advancement of Ukrainian literature studies at Canadian and American universities through his pioneering English-language books, translations, and articles. Two prominent interwar scholars, L. Biletsky and Ohiienko, continued their literary activity after moving from Germany to Winnipeg. Other Canadian university professors have also contributed articles and books in English: the émigrés C. *Bida and V. Revutsky, and the younger, North American–educated M. Shkandrij and D.H. *Struk. Academics who have written articles and prepared anthologies include the Canadian-born C. Andrusyshen and W. Kirkconnell (an Anglo-Canadian) and the émigré Ya. Slavutych. The émigré academics A. Malycky, N. Pedan-Popil, J. Rozumnyj, W. Smyrniw, W. Shelest, and O. Zuievsky and the younger, North American–educated R. Bahry, O. Ilnytzkyj, R. Karpiak, I. Makaryk, N. Pylypiuk, and M. Tarnawsky have contributed articles. Other postwar émigrés in Canada who have written books or articles on Ukrainian literature are M. Carynnyk, O. Chernenko, A. Horokhovych, O. Kopach, D. Kozii, P. Roienko, Yu. Rusov, Yu. Stefanyk, M. Solovii, and Yu. Voichyshyn. Books on Ukrainian-Canadian literature have been written by the émigrés O. Hai-Holovko and M. Mandryka, by the Canadian-born J. Balan, and by the Ukrainian-Canadian Communist writer P. Krawchuk.

United States. Of the Ukrainian literary scholars who emigrated to the United States after the Second World War H. *Kostiuk, B. *Kravtsiv, and Yu. *Lavrinenko, in particular, have produced important literary studies, anthologies, and editions of the repressed Soviet Ukrainian writers of the 1920s and 1930s. Books in Ukrainian have also been written and/or edited by other émigrés, including V. Barka, V. Bezushko, B. *Boychuk, V. *Chaplenko, O. Drai-Khmara-Asher, P. *Holubenko, S. Hordynsky, Lev, Lutsiv, Luzhnytsky, P. *Odarchenko, S. Pohorily, Radzykevych, B. *Romanenchuk, and A. *Yuryniak. Among American academics Ukrainian literature was first treated systematically in the 1940s and 1950s by C. *Manning of Columbia University. Since the 1950s, émigré scholars have taught at American universities and published English-language studies of Ukrainian literature. Books and articles have been written by the professors S. Chorney, J. *Fizer, G. *Grabowicz, and L. *Rudnytzky, and articles have been contributed by other university scholars, such as L. Onyshkevych, M. Ovcharenko (Pshepiurska), B. *Rubchak, G.Y. *Shevelov, and W. *Zyla. Bibliographic research in Ukrainian literature has been conducted by M. Tarnavska.

Eastern Europe. Until the late 1980s postwar Ukrainian literature studies developed in Poland, Czechoslovakia, and Rumania not without ideological constraints. Nonetheless, important works were produced there, particularly in the area of the literary relations between those countries and Ukraine. Scholars in Poland have written on both old and modern Ukrainian literature. Books and articles have been produced there by the Ukrainian S. *Kozak and the Poles M. Jakóbiec, M. Kuplowski, P. Lewin, R. Łużny, F. *Nieuważny, and E. Wiśniewska. Articles have been written by Ukrainians, such as Ya. Hrytskovian, M. Ivanek, V. *Mokry, V. Nazaruk, A. Serednytsky, and M. Syvitsky, and by the Poles G. Pazdro, F. Sielicki, and P. Zwoliński. Ukrainian literature studies in Czechoslovakia have focused on Ukrainian-Czechoslovak literary relations, the history of Transcarpathian literature, and contemporary Ukrainian writing in the Prešov region. Books and/or articles have been written there by the Ukrainian scholars Yu. *Bacha, Z. Genyk-Berezovska, F. Kovach, M. *Molnar, M. Roman, O. Rudlovchak, Y. Shlepets, and O.

*Zilynsky and by the Czechs M. *Nevrlý and V. Židlický. In Rumania there has been only one prominent scholar of Ukrainian literature, M. *Laslo-Kutsiuk in Bucharest.

Elsewhere. Ukrainian literature studies in other parts of the world have had few contributors. In Brazil V. *Vovk has taught and written in Portuguese on Ukrainian literature. In Argentina I. Kachurovsky wrote in Spanish on Ukrainian literature while living there in 1948–69. In Australia studies of Ukrainian literature have been written by the émigrés Bohatsky, O. Fylypovych, S. Haievsky, and D. *Nytchenko (Chub). Since the early 1980s the first Australian university lecturer in Ukrainian literature, M. *Pavlyshyn of Monash University, has published articles on modern Ukrainian writers and on Ukrainian literature in Australia.

(See also *Bibliography, *Classical studies, *Literary criticism, and *Slavic studies.)

BIBLIOGRAPHY
Peretts, V. *Natsional'naia politika v SSSR i uspekhi ukrainskogo literaturovedeniia v 1917–1932 gg.* (Leningrad 1933)
Bilets'kyi, L. 'Ohliad prats' iz istorii pys'menstva ta literaturoznavstva,' in *2. ukraïns'kyi naukovyi z'ïzd u Prazi* (Prague 1934)
Kostiuk, H. 'Ukraïns'ke naukove literaturoznavstvo v pershe porevoliutsiine p'iatnadtsiatylittia,' in *Zbirnyk na poshanu ukraïns'kykh uchenykh znyshchenykh bol'shevyts'koiu Moskvoiu,* ed M. Ovcharenko, ZNTSh 173 (Paris and Chicago 1962)
Bilets'kyi, O. 'Shliakhy rozvytku dozhovtnevoho ukraïns'koho literaturoznavstva,' in his *Zibrannia prats' v p'iaty tomakh,* vol 2 (Kiev 1965)
Komyshanchenko, M.; et al (eds). *Ukraïns'ke radians'ke literaturoznavstvo za 50 rokiv* (Kiev 1968)
Hol'denberh, L. *Literaturoznavcha knyha v Ukraïns'kii RSR: Pytannia teorii ta istorii* (Kiev 1980)
Hurladi, M. *Na poklyk zhyttia: Rozrobka ideino-estetychnykh problem literaturoznavstva na Ukraïni v pisliavoienni roky* (Kiev 1984)
Briukhovets'kyi, V.; Kovalenko, L.; Naienko, M. 'Literaturoznavstvo i krytyka,' in *Istoriia ukraïns'koï literatury,* vol 2, ed L. Novychenko (Kiev 1988)
                                    I. Koshelivets, R. Senkus

Literaturna hazeta. See *Literaturna Ukraïna.*

Literaturna krytyka (Literary Criticism). A Marxist monthly of literary criticism, scholarship, theory, and bibliography; art, theater, film, and folklore were also discussed. It was first published in Kharkiv in January 1928, and until April 1932 it was the unofficial organ of the *All-Ukrainian Association of Proletarian Writers and was called *Krytyka.* M. Skrypnyk, A. Khvylia, V. Desniak, V. Koriak, T. Taran, I. Kulyk, T. Stepovy, and Ya. Savchenko belonged to its editorial board. Among its contributors were Ya. Aizenshtok, V. Atamaniuk, O. Biletsky, M. Dolengo, I. Kapustiansky, Ye. Kyryliuk, H. Maifet, M. Motuzka, I. Mykytenko, M. Novytsky, O. Poltoratsky, V. Sedliar, I. Vrona, and F. Yakubovsky. From May 1932 the journal was the organ of the newly founded *Writers' Union of Ukraine and was called *Za markso-lenins'ku krytyku.* Thenceforth its content was excessively dogmatic and Stalinist; among its contributors in that period were P. Kolesnyk, B. Kovalenko, I. Kulyk, Ye. Kyryliuk, A. Paniv, L. Pidhainy, S. Shchupak, A. Trostianetsky, and Yu. Yosypchuk. From 1934 the journal was published in Kiev. It was renamed *Literaturna krytyka* in December 1935 and *Radians'ka Ukraïna* in January 1941. The last issue of the journal appeared in February 1941.

Literaturna Odesa. A publicistic almanac of the Odessa branch of the Writers' Union of Ukraine. It was published between 1948 and 1958 in Odessa in both Ukrainian and Russian and contained articles on literature and art.

Literaturna Ukraïna

Literaturna Ukraïna (Literary Ukraine). A literary newspaper founded by a resolution of the CC CPBU as the organ of the *All-Ukrainian Association of Proletarian Writers. It began publication on 21 March 1927 in Kiev under the name *Literaturna hazeta* (1930–4 published in Kharkiv). Between 1941 and 1945, it was published as *Literatura i mystetstvo*, in Luhanske, Ufa, Moscow, Kharkiv, and, in 1944, Kiev. From 1945 to 1962 it was again called *Literaturna hazeta* and published in Kiev. It was renamed *Literaturna Ukraïna* in 1962. It has been first a fortnightly, later a weekly, from 1957 a biweekly, and since 1985 a weekly. *Literaturna Ukraïna* was the first literary newspaper that unwaveringly toed the Party line; it supported the so-called proletarian writers and had already declared war on Ukrainian culture in the 1920s. *Literaturna Ukraïna* played an important part in condemning not only the so-called bourgeois literature, of the members of MARS for example, but also that of the members of Vaplite, Prolitfront, and Nova Generatsiia, who although they called themselves 'proletarian,' were in fact opposed to the Party line in literature. In 1932 it became the organ of the *Writers' Union of Ukraine and was the mouthpiece of J. Stalin's, later N. Khrushchev's, literary policies. In the first years of its existence B. *Kovalenko played a major part in establishing the newspaper's orientation. Its editors in chief have been I. Le, P. Usenko, L. Novychenko, M. Shamota, A. Khyzhniak, and, since 1980, P. Perebyinis, I. Kocherha, D. Tsmokalenko, P. Zahrebelny, and B. Rohoza. In the mid-1980s the newspaper assumed the role of defender of the Ukrainian language, and in the early 1990s it became an organ for national revival and independence.

Literaturnoe zavedenie priashevskoe. See Prešov Literary Society.

Literaturno-naukova biblioteka (Literary-Scientific Library). A series of books and booklets published by I. *Franko in Lviv from 1889 to 1898. It included Franko's narrative poem *Smert' Kaïna* (The Death of Cain); his novel *Dlia domashn'oho vohnyshcha* (For the Home Hearth); his habilitation dissertation on I. Vyshensky; T. Shevchenko's narrative poem 'Perebendia,' with Franko's introduction; M. Drahomanov's *Avstrorus'ki spohady* (Austro-Ruthenian Memoirs) and *Chudats'ki dumky pro ukraïns'ku natsional'nu spravu* (Eccentric Thoughts about the Ukrainian National Problem); a poetry collection by U. Kravchenko; V. Shchurat's translation of G. Flaubert's *La légende de Saint Julien l'Hospitalier*; other translations; and reprints of Franko's writings from the socialist periodicals *Narod* and *Zhytie i slovo*.

Literaturno-naukovyi vistnyk

Literaturno-naukovyi vistnyk (Literary Scientific Herald, or LNV). A monthly journal published in 1898–1906 in Lviv, in 1907–14 and 1917–19 in Kiev, and in 1922–32 again in Lviv. It was founded on the initiative of M. Hrushevsky as the organ of the Shevchenko Scientific Society (NTSh), incorporating the journals *Zoria* (published by the NTSh) and *Zhytie i slovo* (published by I. Franko). From 1905 it was published by the Ukrainian-Ruthenian Publishing Company. *LNV* became the foremost literary-scientific journal of the day. The editorial board consisted of M. *Hrushevsky (editor in chief), I. *Franko, O. Borkovsky, and O. Makovei. The latter two soon resigned and were replaced by V. *Hnatiuk. The de facto editor during the first period of *LNV* in Lviv was Franko, who published a large number of his own poems, stories, and tales therein, as well as literary critiques, history articles, and reviews. He also obtained the collaboration of leading writers from all parts of Ukraine, including established writers, such as H. Barvinok, O. Konysky, and D. Mordovets, and younger writers, such as V. Vynnychenko, M. Vorony, B. Hrinchenko, I. Tobilevych, A. Krymsky, V. Leontovych, V. Samiilenko, L. Starytska-Cherniakhivska, Lesia Ukrainka, K. Hrynevycheva, P. Karmansky, Yu. Kmit, B. Lepky, O. Makovei, L. Martovych, V. Pachovsky, V. Stefanyk, M. Cheremshyna, M. Yatskiv, and O. Kobylianska.

After the Revolution of 1905, when publication in Ukrainian became possible in Russian-ruled Ukraine, Hrushevsky transferred *LNV* to Kiev, where he took over the editorial responsibility and published his own belletristic works, signed 'M.Z.' (Mykhailo Zavoloka), publicistic articles, reports, and reviews. So that the circulation of *LNV* could be extended to Galicia and Bukovyna, the journal was sent in folio to Lviv, where it was then bound at the NTSh shop. Later the Lviv editorial office was created and managed by M. Yevshan. New contributors included S. Cherkasenko, H. Chuprynka, D. Lukiianovych, O. Hrushevsky, M. Zalizniak, V. Lypynsky, A. Nikovsky, M. Porsh, V. Sadovsky, M. Stasiuk, I. Feshchenko-Chopivsky, K. Shyrotsky, V. Doroshenko, I. Dzhydzhora, M. Yevshan, Ye. Levytsky, M. Lozynsky, M. Mochulsky, and L. Tsehelsky. Until the beginning of the First World War *LNV* played an important part in uniting the cultural forces that had been separated in consequence of the division of Ukraine between the Russian and Austro-Hungarian empires.

In 1914, like all Ukrainian press, *LNV* was banned. When the tsarist regime fell in 1917, the journal resumed publication under the editorship of O. Hrushevsky. New contributors included P. Tychyna, M. Rylsky, Ya. Savchenko, and M. Ivchenko. Conditions in Kiev, however, were unfavorable for its progress, and in 1920 *LNV* was again banned, this time by the Soviet authorities.

In 1922 *LNV* was revived in Lviv with the financial support of former Sich Riflemen. The editorial committee consisted of V. Hnatiuk, V. Doroshenko, M. Halushchynsky, Ye. Konovalets, Yu. Pavlykovsky, and I. Rakovsky, and was headed by D. *Dontsov. The idea behind the revival of *LNV* was to unite all the literary forces in Western Ukrainian territories and in the diaspora that defended a Ukrainian national standpoint. Former eminent contributors were followed by younger collaborators, such as B.I. Antonych, N. Livytska-Kholodna, Ye. Malaniuk, Yu. Lypa, B. Kravtsiv, O. Olzhych, and O. Stefanovych. The editorial board, however, progressively ceased to function, and Dontsov, the editor in chief, caused a portion of the collaborators to quit because of his nationalistic ideological attitude. The declining artistic standard of the journal, combined with financial difficulties, caused *LNV* to cease publication at the end of 1932. Dontsov thereupon began publishing his own journal, *Vistnyk. In 1948–9 two more issues of *LNV* appeared in Regensburg, edited by V. Shulha.

The first 20 volumes of *LNV* were cataloged by V. Domanytsky (1903), and M. Svientsitska later compiled an index of the entire edition (nd).

BIBLIOGRAPHY
Doroshenko, V. 'Literaturno-naukovyi Visnyk (1898–1914, 1917–1919, 1922–30),' *LNV*, vol 1 (Regensburg 1948)
                                                              V. Doroshenko

Literaturnyi arkhiv. A bimonthly journal of literature studies which was the organ of the Taras Shevchenko Scientific Research Institute. It was published in Kharkiv in 1930–1 and was edited by D. Bahalii, O. Biletsky, O. Doroshkevych, and S. *Pylypenko (chief editor).

Literaturnyi Donbas (Literary Donbas). A literary and art almanac of the Donetske branch of the Writers' Union of Ukraine. It was originally published under the title *Zaboi and was renamed *Literaturnyi Donbas* in 1932. In 1933 it was moved from Artemivske to Staline (now Donetske). From its 10th issue it was printed in Russian. It was published monthly at first, bimonthly in 1936, five times a year in 1937 and 1938, and bimonthly again in 1939. It ceased publication during the Second World War

and resumed publication in 1946. Since 1958, under the title *Donbass*, it has appeared as a bilingual Ukrainian-Russian quarterly, although in fact it has been almost exclusively in the Russian language. It mostly features works on the subject of life in the mines.

Literaturnyi iarmarok: dust jacket (watercolor by A. Petrytsky) and title page

Literaturnyi iarmarok (Literary Fair). A literary and art almanac in Kharkiv, edited by M. *Khvylovy. Twelve issues appeared between December 1928 and February 1930. Officially nonpartisan, *Literaturnyi iarmarok* was in fact the organ of the group of former members of the dissolved *Vaplite. The literary-historical significance of the almanac lies in its representing one of the last organized attempts to resist the Communist party's efforts to force all writers to adopt socialist realism. *Literaturnyi iarmarok* published works which were later labeled bourgeois-nationalist, including M. Kulish's plays, Khvylovy's satires *Ivan Ivanovych* and *Revizor* (The Inspector General), V. Gzhytsky's novel *Chorne ozero* (The Black Lake), I. Senchenko's *Chervonohrads'ki portrety* (Chervonohrad Portraits), V. Sosiura's poem *Mazepa*, poetry and prose by V. Mysyk, O. Vlyzko, and M. Yohansen, and intermedes by O. Vyshnia and V. Yurynets. Attacks from the official critics even provoked an original arrangement of the almanac, in which modernism (particularly the illustrations) was combined with traditional Ukrainian forms (framing and linking the whole text were intermedes, which were written by different authors in each issue). After the forced liquidation of *Literaturnyi iarmarok* the nucleus of its contributors, together with many other writers, founded the group *Prolitfront, which published a journal of the same name.

                                                              I. Koshelivets

Literaturnyi sbornik (Literary Miscellany). A literary and historical serial published by the *Halytsko-Ruska Matytsia Society in Lviv in 1865–6, 1868–9, 1874, 1885–6, 1889, 1891, and 1897. Until 1869 it was called *Naukovyi sbornik*. The serial contained pioneering articles in Galician history, philology, and ethnography and some belletristic works by Ya. Holovatsky, A. Petrushevych, M. Ustyianovych, V. Stefanovych, I. Sharanevych, O. Lepky, V. Terletsky, M. Kostomarov, I. Hushalevych, I. Ozarkevych, and others. The serial also published information about the society's activities and other scholarly developments in Lviv. The 1874, 1891, and 1897 issues consisted primarily of A. Petrushevych's Galician-Volhynian chronicle for the years 1600–1772. From 1885 B. Didytsky was the serial's editor.

Literaturnyi zhurnal (Literary Journal). A monthly of socialist-realist literary and art criticism and publicism. It was published in Kharkiv from August 1936 as an organ of the Writers' Union of Ukraine and replaced the prominent journal *Chervonyi shliakh*. It ceased publication in 1941 after 58 issues.

Lithography: illustration for H.C. Andersen's *Snow White* by M. Murashko (1873)

Lithography. The method of printing a text or drawing from a smooth limestone surface onto paper, invented in 1796 by A. Senefelder in Germany. It was introduced in Ukraine in the 1820s at the art studio of the Kievan Cave Monastery and private studios in Lviv, Kiev, Odessa, and Mykolaiv. In 1828 the engraving shop at the Mezhyhiria Faience Factory near Kiev began using lithography to decorate unglazed china. The studio Mykolaiv (est 1829) printed navigational charts, manuals, and, later, illustrations. In Odessa the studio of A. Braun (est 1829) ran prints of artistic views of Odessa, Crimea, and other places in southern Ukraine. In Lviv, lithographs were printed at the studio of J., P., and K. Piller (from 1822), the Ossolineum Institute (1830–4), and the Stauropegion Institute (from 1846). From the 1830s on, lithography studios at Kharkiv and Kiev universities printed illustrations for textbooks, document collections, albums, and literary almanacs.

In Ukraine the first master lithographers were from Central Europe – L. Kwaas from Saxony, H. Schöngold from Switzerland, and O. Braun, I. Walner, J. Piller, and A. Lange from various German lands. They produced lithographs of their own drawings and of works by Ukrainian artists. In the first half of the 19th century lithography was mastered by Ukrainian artists (eg, I. Vendzylovych and S. Vozniak in Galicia). In the second half significant achievements in lithography were attained by K. *Trutovsky, O. *Slastion, and M. *Murashko. The notable lithography workshops existed at the Kievan Cave Monastery Press, which printed large runs of landscapes of this ancient site and other churches in Kiev, as well as oleographed icons, and at the printery of S. Kulzhenko, which issued both religious and secular lithographs. In the 20th century, lithography played an important role in book *illustration

and *poster art as well as flourishing in its own right as a graphic art. Notable 20th-century Ukrainian lithographers are O. Slastion, M. *Zhuk, I. *Padalka, V. *Zauze, O. *Dovhal, V. *Kasiian, V. *Myronenko, M. *Derehus, H. *Pustoviit, H. *Bondarenko, V. *Averin, V. Parchevsky, V. *Savin, Ye. *Svitlychny, O. *Liubymsky, and A. Nasedkin. (For a bibliography, see *Graphic art.)

D. Stepovyk

Lithuania (Lithuanian: Lietuva; Ukrainian: Lytva). A country on the eastern shore of the Baltic Sea. Its capital is *Vilnius. The Lithuanians belong to the Baltic group of Indo-European nations. They have had a long history of linguistic, cultural, and political interaction with their Slavic neighbors, including the Ukrainians. In 1940–1 and from January 1945 to March 1991 Lithuania constituted a Soviet republic, with an area of 65,200 sq km. In 1989 it had a population of 3,674,802, of whom 2,924,251 (79.6 percent) were Lithuanians, 344,455 (9.4 percent) were Russians, 257,994 (7 percent) were Poles, 63,169 (1.7 percent) were Belarusians, and 44,789 (1.2 percent) were Ukrainians. Of the Ukrainians living in Lithuania in 1989, 51 percent gave Ukrainian as their native language, 45.3 percent gave Russian, and only 0.3 percent gave Lithuanian; only 16.8 percent could speak Lithuanian.

There are over 3.5 million Lithuanians in the world today. The largest concentrations outside Lithuania are in the United States (over 330,000 in 1970), Russia (70,427 in 1989), Latvia (34,630 in 1989), Canada (14,725 in 1986), Ukraine (11,278 in 1989), and Poland (approx 10,000).

The medieval Lithuanian tribes (including the *Yatvingians) frequently fought over territories with the Rus' princes of Kiev, Galicia-Volhynia, and Polatsk and with the *Teutonic Knights. Not until the early 13th century, however, did they create a common political entity. In 1225 the majority of the Lithuanian tribes were united under the rule of *Mindaugas, and formed the Grand Duchy of Lithuania. Taking advantage of the disintegration of Rus' under the impact of the Mongol invasion, Mindaugas conquered *Chorna Rus' and parts of Polatsk principality and entered into a military alliance and dynastic union with the Principality of *Galicia-Volhynia. In the 1250s King Danylo Romanovych of Galicia-Volhynia routed the Yatvingian tribes inhabiting what is today northern Podlachia, and their territory was divided among the princes of Galicia-Volhynia and Mazovia and the Teutonic Knights. Chorna Rus' came under the rule of Danylo's son Roman Danylovych.

In 1267 Mindaugas's son and successor, *Vaišvilkas, abdicated the Lithuanian throne in favor of his brother-in-law, Danylo's son *Shvarno Danylovych. Thus Lithuania and Galicia-Volhynia were briefly (until Shvarno's death in 1269) ruled by one dynasty. Lithuania's internecine conflicts and wars with its neighbors temporarily halted its southward and eastward expansion. Expansion resumed during the reign of Grand Prince *Gediminas (1316 to ca 1340), who conquered most of Belarus and the Ukrainian lands of Turiv-Pynske and northern Volhynia. With the demise of the Principality of Galicia-Volhynia in 1340, Volhynia came under the rule of Gediminas's son *Liubartas. In the 1360s, during the reign of Gediminas's son *Algirdas, the *Lithuanian-Ruthenian state was consolidated, and extended over all the Belarusian and most of the Ukrainian lands except Galicia, which was annexed by

Poland. During the height of its expansion Lithuania's possessions included nearly half of the former territory of Kievan Rus'. Only 10 percent of the realm was inhabited by Lithuanians, and the official culture, language, and religion of the new state became Ruthenian (ie, Ukrainian-Belarusian). An Orthodox *Lithuanian metropoly was created. Following the Lithuanian-Polish dynastic Union of *Krevo (1385) Lithuania ceased to be completely independent and became officially Catholic. Polish control increased steadily, particularly after the demise of the *Jagiellon dynasty in 1572. After the Union of *Lublin (1569) Lithuania was left with only limited autonomy within the Polish Commonwealth, having ceded most of its Ukrainian lands to *Poland and accepted the Polish crown and a common parliament. With time Polish culture and religious influence displaced Ruthenian influence and resulted in the Polonization of the Lithuanian-Ruthenian nobility. In 1529 the Lithuanian-Ruthenian state adopted a new law code, the *Lithuanian Statute, revised in 1566 and again in 1588, introducing Polish concepts into its criminal and civil sections. Polish domination of Lithuania did not cease after the partitions of Poland and the occupation of nearly all of ethnic Lithuania by the Russian Empire. Although Polish was banned as the official language in 1822, only after the unsuccessful Polish Insurrection of 1830–1 did Russification and the suppression of Lithuanian culture intensify. In the second half of the 19th century a Lithuanian national rebirth occurred, led by the intelligentsia of peasant origin and bolstered by Lithuanian immigrants in the United States and the nearly 150,000 Lithuanians living in the Prussian-ruled Klaipėda (Memel) region. During the First World War Lithuania was occupied by the Germans (1915–18), and after several preliminary efforts Lithuania became an independent republic in November 1918. The Vilnius region, however, which was inhabited by Belarusians, Poles, and Lithuanians, was forcibly annexed by Poland in 1920. After two decades of domestic instability and tensions with Poland and later Nazi Germany (culminating in Germany's annexation of the Klaipėda region in March 1939) Lithuania was occupied by the USSR in June 1940. Soviet oppression was followed by that of the Nazi occupation (June 1941 to January 1945). Thereafter Lithuania remained a Soviet republic until March 1991, when it regained its independence.

Toward the end of the 19th century Lithuanian-Ukrainian relations were renewed. In the Russian State Duma Ukrainian and Lithuanian representatives collaborated within the *Autonomists' Union, and O. Lototsky maintained close ties with the Lithuanian leader V. Matulaitis. Lithuanian students in Kiev co-operated with Ukrainian student organizations. At the peace talks with the Central Powers culminating in the Peace Treaty of Brest-Litovsk in 1918, the future Lithuanian prime minister A. Voldemaras secretly took part in the UNR delegation as an adviser so as to inform the Lithuanians of the progress of the negotiations with the Germans. The newly formed Ukrainian and Lithuanian republics did not have the opportunity to solidify relations, however. After the unsuccessful Ukrainian struggle for independence Lithuania supported the revolutionary struggle of the Ukrainian Military Organization (UVO) and the OUN in Polish-ruled Western Ukraine through semiofficial organizations, such as the Lithuanian Riflemen's Association and the Union for the

Liberation of Vilnius (headed by M. Biržiška). The UVO organ *Surma was printed in Kaunas, and Ukrainian-Lithuanian activists were issued Lithuanian passports and granted asylum. The Ukrainian-Lithuanian Society in Kaunas (1927–35), headed by Biržiška, informed the Lithuanian public about the Ukrainian question through its bulletin *Lietuvių Ukrainiečių Draugijos Zinios* (1933–5). The UVO and, later, OUN representative I. Reviuk-Bartovych resided in Kaunas. In the West émigré Ukrainians collaborated with émigré Lithuanians in the Anti-Bolshevik Bloc of Nations and other organizations.

The Lithuanian-Ukrainian bulletin published in Kaunas in 1933–5

There were also cultural ties between Lithuania and Ukraine. Before the First World War theatrical troupes from Russian-ruled Ukraine toured Lithuanian towns several times, and from 1912 I. Kotliarevsky's play *Natalka Poltavka* (Natalka from Poltava) was part of the repertoire of many Lithuanian amateur theatrical groups. In the 1880s J. Andziulaitis's translations of several of T. Shevchenko's poems were published in Lithuanian journals. In 1891, stories by I. Franko were also translated. From 1909 L. Gira translated and popularized Shevchenko's poetry; his translations were published as a separate volume in 1912. Gira also wrote the first Lithuanian article about Shevchenko. In 1914, despite the tsarist ban, a celebration of Shevchenko's centenary was organized by the writer J. Žemaitė in Lithuania. Throughout the postwar Soviet period many Lithuanian poets translated Shevchenko's works. Separate editions of them were published in 1951, 1955, and 1961, and in 1964 V. Abramavičius's book about Shevchenko in Vilnius was published. Works by Lesia Ukrainka, M. Kotsiubynsky, M. Rylsky, P. Tychyna, O. Vyshnia, O. Honchar, M. Stelmakh, and other Ukrainian writers have also been translated into Lithuanian. Lithuanian-Ukrainian literary relations were surveyed in a book by K. Korsakas (1954). Lithuanian writers whose works have been translated into Ukrainian include S. Nėris, A. Venclova, Žemaitė, P. Cvirka, J. Baltušis, E. Mieželaitis, and M. Sluckis. Plays by Franko, O. Korniichuk, V. Mynko, and other Ukrainian dramatists have been staged in Lithuania, and since 1955 S. Hulak-Artemovksy's opera *Zaporozhets' za Dunaiem* (Zaporozhian Cossack beyond the Danube) has been part of the repertoire of the Vilnius Opera and Ballet Theater. Similarly, Lithuanian plays have been staged in Ukraine. Since 1961, 10-day festivals of Ukrainian literature and art have been held in Lithuania, and in 1968 the 17th Shevchenko scholarly conference was held in Vilnius.

In December 1988 the Hromada of Ukrainians of Lithuania was formed in Vilnius, and in October 1989 the

Constituent Congress of Ukrainians in Lithuania was held there. The Hromada supported the Lithuanian independence movement and has had close ties with the Popular Movement of Ukraine (Rukh). Hromada branches are active in Vilnius, Kaunas, Klaipėda, Mažeikiai, and Jonava. Ukrainian choirs have been formed in Vilnius and Klaipėda, and Ukrainian Sunday schools in Vilnius and Jonava.

BIBLIOGRAPHY
Trots'kyi, M. *Lytovtsi* (Vienna 1917)
Jurgéla, C. *History of the Lithuanian Nation* (New York 1948)
Gerutis, A. (ed). *Lithuania: 700 Years* (New York 1969)
Trembits'kyi, V. 'Vil'na i Kyïv z perspektyvy storich (Do pytannia lytovs'ko-ukraïns'kykh vidnosyn),' *Al'manakh Ukraïns'koho narodnoho soiuzu na rik 1972* (Jersey City and New York)
Ochmański, J. *Historia Litwy*, 2nd rev edn (Wrocław, Warsaw, Cracow, Gdańsk, and Łódź 1982)
Budreckis, A. (ed). *Eastern Lithuania: A Collection of Historical and Ethnographic Studies* (Chicago 1985)
V. Kubijovyč, A. Zhukovsky

Lithuanian metropoly. An Orthodox church province that existed in the 14th and 15th centuries within the Grand Duchy of Lithuania. It was founded following the occupation of much of western Ukraine by Lithuania. When Roman, the Kievan metropolitan, transferred his see to Moscow, the Lithuanian princes Gedimiras and, later, Algirdas demanded a separate metropoly, free of Muscovite control. The Patriarch of Constantinople agreed and consecrated Roman 'metropolitan of Lithuania and Volhynia' in 1355, with his see in Navahrudak (Belarus) and jurisdiction over the eparchies of Polatsk and Turiv, Volodymyr, Lutske, Kholm, Halych, and Peremyshl. After Roman's death in 1361, the metropolitan of Kiev moved to prevent the appointment of a successor. Later the western eparchies of the metropoly were transferred to the renewed *Halych metropoly. In 1376 Grand Duke Vytautas succeeded in having *Cyprian consecrated as metropolitan, who in 1389 assumed control over all eparchies of the Halych and Kiev metropolies. He resided in Moscow, and had the title 'Metropolitan of all Rus'.' Cyprian's successor, however, was not accepted in the Lithuanian-controlled territories of Ukraine, and a synod of the bishops of Polatsk, Smolensk, Lutske, Chernihiv, Volodymyr, Turiv, Peremyshl, and Kholm elected G. *Tsamblak as metropolitan of Lithuania in 1415. After Tsamblak died in 1419, the Lithuanian eparchies once again came under the authority of Moscow. A final attempt to renew the Lithuanian metropoly under Bishop Herasym of Smolensk (1431–5) failed.

Lithuanian Register (Lithuanian: Lietuvos Metrika; Ukrainian: Lytovska metryka). A register listing and describing documents issued and received by the chancellery of the Grand Duchy of Lithuania from the end of the 14th century to 1794. The name is applied also to the chancellery archive, which consisted of 566 volumes of registration lists, and to a variety of original documents or copies – treaties, instructions to ambassadors and their reports, charters granting lands or privileges, permits and licenses, court decisions, appointment lists, and military instructions. The earliest documents were written mostly in the chancellery version of Ruthenian; others were written in Latin, Polish, German, and even Arabic. At the beginning of the 16th century the archive was moved from Trakai castle to the Low Castle in Vilnius. When in 1569 Volhynia, Bratslav, and Kiev palatinates were transferred to Poland by the Treaty of Lublin, the documents pertaining to those territories were deposited in a special Volhynian Register in Warsaw, and documents connected with Galicia were preserved at the Crown Register in Cracow. In 1765 the Crown Register was moved to Warsaw and was supplemented with the rest of the Lithuanian Register from Vilnius. After the partition of Poland the Lithuanian Register was transferred to the Russian imperial archive in St Petersburg, and the Volhynian Register and the Galician documents of the Polish national archive were integrated with it. In 1887 the archive was moved to Moscow. Today it is located at the Central State Archive of Old Documents in Moscow. Some materials from the Lithuanian Register have been published in the collections *Akty, otnosiashchiesia k istorii Iuzhnoi i Zapadnoi Rossii* (Documents on the History of Southern and Western Russia, 1863–92) and *Akty, otnosiashchiesia k istorii Zapadnoi Rossii* (Documents on the History of Western Russia, 1846–53) and in publications of the Kiev Archeographic Commission.

BIBLIOGRAPHY
Grimsted, P.; Sułkowska-Kurasiowa, I. *The 'Lithuanian Metrica' in Moscow and Warsaw: Reconstructing the Archives of the Grand Duchy of Lithuania* (Cambridge, Mass 1984)
A. Zhukovsky

Title page of the third Lithuanian Statute (1588)

Lithuanian Statute. The code of laws of the *Lithuanian-Ruthenian state, published in the 16th century in three basic editions. It was one of the most advanced legal codes of its time. Before its appearance, Lithuanian-Ruthenian law was based on *Ruskaia Pravda and Lithuanian, Ukrainian, and Belarusian customary law. The First or Old Lithuanian Statute, ratified by the diet in Vilnius in 1529, consisted of 243 articles (272 in the Slutsk redaction). Organized under 13 sections, these articles included norms of contract, procedural, criminal, and civil law, as well as state statutes. The overriding concern of this code was to protect the interests of the state and nobility, especially the magnates. The Second Lithuanian Statute (367 articles in 14 sections), often called the Volhynian version because of the influence of the Volhynian nobility in its preparation, was ratified in 1566. It brought about major administrative-political reforms, such as the division of the country into counties, and especially expanded the privileges of the lower gentry by admitting it to the diet. It confirmed in legal terms the leading role of the nobility in the state and further restricted the rights of the peasantry (cities were governed by *Magdeburg law). The Third Lithuanian Statute, consisting of 488 articles in 14 sections, was compiled after the union of the Grand Duchy of Lithuania with Poland in 1569 and was ratified by Sigismund III Vasa in 1588. In this edition many Polish concepts were introduced into the criminal and civil law, which were systematized anew. For the first time, it established a unified code of laws for the entire Lithuanian-Ruthenian state and the entire population; in this respect it differed from the earlier editions, which were collections of local laws. It also entrenched the privileges of the nobility and completed the enserfment of the peasants.

All three editions of the Lithuanian Statute were written in the contemporary Ruthenian chancellery language, which was a mixture of Church Slavonic, Ukrainian, and Belarusian. The first two appeared only in manuscript form; the last was printed in Vilnius. In 1614 the first Polish translation was published, and in 1811 a Russian translation, based on the Polish one, appeared. The Lithuanian Statute was one of the sources used in preparing the first Muscovite code of law (1649).

The Lithuanian Statute remained for several centuries the basic collection of laws in Ukraine, even in the territory annexed by Poland. It was the main source of Ukrainian law for the Hetman state and the basic source of the *Code of Laws of 1743. In Right-Bank Ukraine it remained in force until 1840, when it was annulled by Nicholas I. Some parts of it were incorporated into the collection of Russian laws and remained valid in Chernihiv and Poltava gubernias until the Revolution of 1917.

BIBLIOGRAPHY
Lashchenko, R. 'Lytovs'kyi statut, iako pam'iatnyk ukraïns'koho prava,' in *Naukovyi zbirnyk Ukraïns'koho universytetu v Prazi*, 1 (1923)
Vasylenko, M. 'Iak skasovano Lytovs'koho Statuta,' *Zapysky Sotsiial'no-ekonomichnoho viddilu*, 2–3 (1926)
Lappo, I. *Litovskii statut 1588 goda*, 2 vols (Kaunas 1934, 1938)
Okinshevich, L. *The Law of the Grand Duchy of Lithuania: Background and Bibliography* (New York 1953)
Tkach, A. *Istoriia kodyfikatsiï dorevoliutsiinoho prava Ukraïny* (Kiev 1968)

T. Ciuciura

Lithuanian-Ruthenian law. The system of law of the Lithuanian-Ruthenian state or, more precisely, the Grand Duchy of Lithuania, which from the 14th to the 18th century included Lithuania, Belarus, and most of Ukraine (to the Union of Lublin in 1569). The systematic study of Lithuanian-Ruthenian law began in the first half of the 19th century. Polish historians considered it a local variant of Polish law, and Russian historians usually referred to it as 'western Russian' law and treated it as part of Russian law. Eventually, it was studied by Lithuanian, Belarusian, and Ukrainian historians and legal scholars, who accepted it as part of the legal history of all three nations.

Lithuanian-Ruthenian state. A feudal state of the 13th to 16th centuries that included Lithuanian, Belarusian, and Ukrainian territories. Each of its constituent principalities enjoyed a wide-ranging autonomy. The ruler was the grand duke, who was assisted by a boyars' council.

From 1323 the capital was Vilnius. The state was shaped by its struggles with the *Teutonic Knights, the Principality of Galicia-Volhynia, the Tatars, and then Poland and Muscovy. Lithuania began to encroach on Ukrainian and Belarusian territories during the reign of its founder, *Mindaugas (1236–63). *Gediminas (1316–41) and his son, *Algirdas (1345–77), annexed the Pynske, Berestia, Chernihiv-Siversk, Podilia, Pereiaslav, and Kiev regions. Weakened by Tatar attacks and internal strife, the Ukrainian princes offered little resistance to Lithuanian hegemony and joined its administrative system.

Political and cultural life in the Lithuanian-Ruthenian state was based on the traditions of the Kiev and Galician-Volhynian states. An official Ruthenian language evolved from the language used in Rus'. The legal system was based on the legal traditions of Rus' (see *Lithuanian-Ruthenian law and *Lithuanian Statute). The Lithuanians also benefited from the military expertise of Rus' in organizational and fortification skills. Dynastic ties between the princes of Rus' and Lithuania helped to maintain the Ruthenian influence. The Ruthenian princes belonged to the duke's councils and were part of the ruling class. The Orthodox church was allowed to develop freely, and it played an important role in the country's cultural and educational life. Manufacturing and trade developed rapidly in the towns and cities. The situation changed abruptly after 1385, when *Jagiełło (1377–92) concluded the Union of *Krevo and assumed the Polish crown.

Jagiełło's pro-Polish policies aroused strong Lithuanian-Ruthenian opposition. The ruling classes resisted the Polonization and the Latinization of political and cultural life. Initially the opposition was headed by *Vytautas (1392–1430), who supported the Ukrainian princes and intended to make Lithuania-Ruthenia independent of Poland and to expand it southward and eastward. After being defeated by the Tatars in 1399, however, he had to come to terms with Jagiełło. The Union of *Horodlo (1413) gave the nobles of the Lithuanian-Ruthenian state, who were Catholic, equality with the Polish nobility but restricted the participation of Orthodox (mostly Ruthenian) lords in state affairs. A new opposition was headed by Jagiełło's brother, *Švitrigaila (1430–5). His pro-Ruthenian policy resulted in a split in the Lithuanian-Ruthenian state: the pro-Polish forces installed *Zygimantas (1435–40) as grand duke, and Švitrigaila established his power base in Volhynia, which for a brief period became a separate state. After the death of Zygimantas *Casimir IV Jagiellończyk (1440–92) was proclaimed grand duke. He continued his predecessor's pro-Polish centralist policy. To appease the growing opposition of the Ruthenian princes, *Olelko Volodymyrovych (the grandson of Algirdas) was appointed ruler in Kiev. The measure strengthened Ruthenian influence on state policy for a time. After Švitrigaila's death (1452) the Volhynian principality was abolished, and after *Semen Olelkovych's death (1470) Casimir installed the Polonized M. Gasztod (Gasztołd) as voivode of Kiev. The Ruthenian princes responded to the growing Polish influence by organizing a conspiracy under the leadership of *Mykhailo Olelkovych. The plot was uncovered in 1481, and many of its participants were executed.

The rise of Polish power prompted many Orthodox Ukrainian and Belarusian princes to look for aid to Muscovy, which had defeated the Tatars and was consolidating its centralist state. Ivan III of Muscovy proclaimed himself the defender of Orthodoxy and heir to the Kiev dynasty. His action increased tensions and military conflicts between Lithuania and Moscow. By the early 16th century most of the Chernihiv and Siversk territories had been annexed by Muscovy. In 1508 Prince M. *Hlynsky and his brothers led an anti-Lithuanian revolt aimed at separating Ukraine and Belarus from Lithuania and renewing the state of Rus'. Theirs was the last attempt of the Ukrainian princes to oppose Lithuanian and Polish power.

Poland spared no effort to bring Lithuania under its control and to transform the personal union signed at Krevo into a complete fusion of the two states. To that end it exploited the lesser Lithuanian nobility, which was promised equal status with the Polish nobility. The Lithuanian aristocracy, magnates, and upper nobility continued to oppose the union, which they saw as signaling the demise of the Lithuanian-Ruthenian state. In spite of strong Lithuanian opposition the union of the two states in the Polish Commonwealth was proclaimed in Lublin (1569). Lithuania preserved some of its autonomy, but the Ruthenian lands formerly under its control were divided. Except for parts of Podlachia and Polisia the Ukrainian lands fell under Polish rule, and virtually all the Belarusian lands remained under Lithuania. Lithuania's legal status within the commonwealth remained unchanged until Poland was partitioned in 1772, 1793, and 1795. (See also *Lithuania.)

BIBLIOGRAPHY

Lelewel, J. *Dzieje Litwy i Rusi aż do unji z Polską w Lublinie*, 2nd edn (Poznań 1844)
Antonovich, V. (ed). *Gramoty velikikh kniazei litovskikh (1390–1569)* (Kiev 1868)
– *Ocherk istorii Velikogo Kniazhestva Litovskogo do poloviny XV v.* (Kiev 1885)
Dashkevich, N. *Zametki po istorii Litovsko-russkogo gosudarstva* (Kiev 1885)
Leontovich, F. *Ocherki iz istorii Litovsko-russkogo prava: Obrazovanie territorii Litovskogo gosudarstva* (St Petersburg 1894)
Maksimeiko, N. *Seimy Litovsko-russkogo gosudarstva do Liublinskoi unii 1569* (Kharkiv 1902)
Liubavskii, M. *Ocherk istorii Litovsko-russkogo gosudarstva do Liublinskoi unii vkliuchitel'no* (Moscow 1910)
Picheta, V. *Istoriia Litovskogo gosudarstva do Liublinskoi unii* (Vilnius 1921)
Chubatyi, M. 'Derzhavno-pravne stanovyshche ukraïns'kykh zemel' lytovs'koï derzhavy pid kinets' XVI st.,' *ZNTSh*, 134–5, 144–5 (Lviv 1924–6)
Kolankowski, L. *Dzieje Wielkiego Księstwa Litewskiego za Jagiellonów, 1377–1499*, 1 (Warsaw 1930)
Jablonowski, H. *Westrussland zwischen Wilna und Moskau* (Leiden 1955)
Pashuto, V. *Obrazovanie Litovskogo gosudarstva* (Moscow 1959)
                                                        L. Wynar

Litko, Anatolii, b 23 September 1934 in Horodnie, Bohodukhiv county, Kharkiv oblast. Stage director and actor. In 1963 he graduated from the Kharkiv Institute of Arts, and in 1965 he staged his first production in the Kharkiv Ukrainian Drama Theater. He then worked in the Mykolaiv Ukrainian Theater of Drama and Musical Comedy (1965–74). He has been artistic director in the Dnipropetrovske Ukrainian Music and Drama Theater (1979–85) and, since 1987, in the Mykolaiv Russian Drama Theater.

Litky Gospel (Litkivske yevanheliie). A gospel transcribed at the end of the 16th century in Volhynia from a Church-Slavonic gospel printed in Kiev. The 255-page manuscript was discovered in Litky (now in Brovary raion, Kiev oblast). According to O. Hruzynsky it was written between 1595 and 1600 in the Monastery of the Lutske Brotherhood of the Elevation of the Cross. A Ukrainian translation of a part of St Luke's Gospel was inserted on folios 122 (reverse) to 146. The first part of the insert corresponds to the text of the *Peresopnytsia Gospel (1556–61); the second part is mostly Church Slavonic. The language of the Ukrainian part of the Litky Gospel was studied by O. Hruzynsky, who published this part in *Chteniia v Istoricheskom obshchestve Nestora-letopistsa* (vols 22–23).

Litopys Boikivshchyny   *Litopys Chervonoï kalyny*

Litopys Boikivshchyny (Chronicle of the Boiko Region). A journal dedicated to the study of the ethnography, history, geography, music, dialect, and economy of the Boiko region, published by the Boikivshchyna Society in Sambir, Galicia, in 1931–9 (nos 1–11) and in Philadelphia since 1969. Since 1969 the editors have been O. Berezhnytsky (1969–79) and M. Utrysko (1979–89). By 1989, 60 issues had been published.

Litopys Chervonoï kalyny (Chronicle of Chervona Kalyna). An illustrated monthly of the *Chervona Kalyna publishing house in Lviv. It came out in 1929–39 and was devoted mainly to the struggle for Ukrainian independence in 1914–21. It contained memoirs, bibliographies, reviews of historical books published in the interwar period, photographs, and documents. The editors were L. *Lepky and V. *Levytsky-Sofroniv. Publication of the journal was renewed in 1990 in Lviv under the editorship of O. Khodak.

Litopys druku URSR (Chronicle of Print of the Ukrainian SSR). The bibliographic organ of the Soviet Ukrainian state, published by the Book Chamber of the Ukrainian SSR since 1924. Originally called *Litopys ukraïns'koho druku*, it was published as a monthly in 1924, a semimonthly in 1925–6, a weekly in 1927–8, and a quarterly in 1929–30. During that period it provided bibliographic descriptions of all publications appearing in Soviet Ukraine and all Ukrainian-language publications elsewhere, and published bibliographic surveys and articles. The serial was suspended in October 1930. Revived under its present name in 1935, since that time it has published bibliographic descriptions of all publications in Soviet Ukraine. Its periodicity has varied from 12 to 52 issues per year, with a hiatus in the years 1942–6. Bibliographic descriptions of books, journal and newspaper articles, book reviews, musical scores, and periodicals have been published in the separate serials *Litopys knyh* (since 1935), *Litopys zhurnal'nykh statei* (since 1936), *Litopys retsenzii* (since 1936), *Litopys hazetnykh statei* (since 1937), *Litopys muzychnoï literatury* (since 1954), and *Litopys periodychnykh vydan' URSR* (since 1972).

Litopys hazetnykh statei (Chronicle of Newspaper Articles). A semimonthly bibliographic serial published in Kiev by the Book Chamber of the Ukrainian SSR since 1937. Until 1954 it was called *Litopys druku: Hazetni statti*. The serial indexes the most important articles, literary works, and documentary materials appearing in Ukraine's republican newspapers, and all literary works and articles on local affairs appearing in its oblast newspapers. Each issue also contains a name and place index and a list of newspapers surveyed.

Litopys knyh (Chronicle of Books). A monthly serial published by the Book Chamber of the Ukrainian SSR since 1935. Until 1953 it was called *Litopys druku: Knyhy*. The serial provides bibliographic descriptions of books, brochures, and dissertation abstracts published separately in Soviet Ukraine.

Litopys revoliutsii (Chronicle of the Revolution). A journal on the history of the CP(B)U and the years 1917–21 in Ukraine, published in Kharkiv in 1922–33. Until 1928 it was published in Russian as *Letopis' revoliutsii*, and thereafter, in Ukrainian. It usually came out every two months. Altogether 57 issues appeared. They contained large amounts of material later omitted from the official history of the CP(B)U.

***Litopys ukraïns'koho druku*.** See *Litopys druku URSR*.

Litopys UPA: title page of vol 17

Litopys Ukraïns'koï povstans'koï armiï (Chronicle of the Ukrainian Insurgent Army). A series of volumes containing documents and source materials relating to the history of the UPA. Each volume or group of volumes is devoted to a specific theme and has a separate title. *Litopys* is published jointly by two UPA veterans' organizations, the Former Members of the Ukrainian Insurgent Army and the Society of Former UPA Soldiers, and is edited by Ye. Shtendera and P. Potichnyj. Since 1976, 21 volumes have come out.

Litopys zhurnal'nykh statei (Chronicle of Journal Articles). A semimonthly serial published by the Book Chamber of the Ukrainian USSR since 1936. Until 1960 it was a monthly called *Litopys druku: Zhurnal'ni statti*. It provides bibliographic descriptions of articles, documentary materials, and literary works appearing in all periodicals published in Soviet Ukraine.

Litoshenko, Leonid [Litosěnko], b 2 June 1907 in Kursk, Russia, d 18 May 1972 in Kursk. Ukrainian graphic artist and architect. He designed many bookplates using primarily needle and linoleum engraving, and also engraved in celluloid. Using S. Taranushenko's work as inspiration he created the engraving series 'Windmills' (1944) and 'Ukrainian Folk Furniture' (1944). He also edited three albums of O. Kulchytska's works (1956, 1957, 1960) and amassed a huge collection of bookplates (over 3,500).

Little Entente. A series of alliances among Czechoslovakia, Rumania, and Yugoslavia, made in 1920–1 and consolidated in a single treaty in May 1929. Its purpose was to protect its members against the threat of Hungarian or Austrian aggression and to preserve the territories acquired from Austria after the First World War. Although each member of the Little Entente justified its own claim to independence by the principle of national self-determination, not one of them applied the principle to Ukrainian Transcarpathia; instead they regarded demands for self-determination in that region as an internal problem. The alliance disintegrated after the Munich Agreement (1938) and was formally ended in February 1939.

Little Poland (Polish: Małopolska). The historical territory of Poland in the basin of the upper and middle Vistula River, inhabited by the Vistulans. It became part of the Polish state at the end of the 10th century. The name Little Poland, distinct from the name Great Poland (western Poland), was used to refer to Cracow, Lublin, and Sandomierz voivodeships and, after the Union of Lublin in 1569, to the eight so-called Ruthenian voivodeships, or all the Ukrainian territory under Poland, as well. In the interwar period the Polish government used the name Little Poland for the former Austrian crownlands of Galicia and Lodomeria and the artificial name Eastern Little Poland (Małopolska Wschodnia) for the Ukrainian part of Galicia.

Little Polisia (Male Polissia). A depression in western Ukraine lying between the Volhynia-Kholm Upland in the north and the Podolian Upland in the south and between Roztochia in the west and Podilia (near Shepetivka) in the east. In the south Little Polisia is delineated by a steep, 70–150 m escarpment running along the line Shepetivka–Kuniv–Kremianets–Olesko–Pidiarkiv–Lviv–Nesterov–Rava-Ruska. In the north it is bounded by a 40–60 m rise along the line Krupets–Ostrih–Verba–Berestechko–Chervonohrad–Uhniv. The length of Little Polisia is approx 300 km; its width varies from 20–25 km in the east to 40–70 km in the west, where it encompasses the Upper Buh

River Basin. It is narrowest (5 km) near Ostrih. Its highest elevation is 245 m above sea level.

The foundation of Little Polisia consists of Upper Cretaceous marls, covered with glacial and alluvial deposits. The depression probably originated in the Pliocene. Its glacial landscape has been formed mostly by the action of meltwaters. The latter, dammed by the continental glacier blocking the north side of the Upper Buh River Basin, overflowed eastward, carving the Little Polisia spillway. After the glacier had melted, the Buh, the Styr, the Ikva, the Viliia, and the Horyn rivers began to flow north, and the spillway was transformed into a series of river basins (the Buh, the Styr, the Ikva, and the Horyn), separated by low watersheds. Little Polisia is thus mostly an outwash plain, although in the west, where the ice lobe was present, there are some moraine-outwash deposits, and even lacustrine-loess plains at elevations of 190–270 m, carved gently by slow rivers. Podzols, meadow soils, and bog soils prevail. The eastern part resembles Polisia: it is well forested, swampy, and choked with barchan sand dunes. Forests of pine, birch, oak, aspen, and hornbeam cover about 30 percent of the territory. Hayfields (often waterlogged) and pastures account for over 25 percent, and cultivated land makes up about 40 percent of the area. The population density is approx 50 persons per sq km. Only about 30 percent of the population is urban. Except for Kamianka-Buzka, the towns of Little Polisia are located along the borders with the uplands.

I. Stebelsky

Little Rada. See Central Rada.

Little Russia (Mala Rus', later Malorosiia). The name appeared in Byzantine sources at the beginning of the 14th century and was used for the church administrative unit covering the territory of the Galician-Volhynian state. In Byzantine documents and eparchy registers Halych metropoly (est 1303), consisting of six eparchies (Halych, Peremyshl, Volodymyr, Kholm, Lutske, and Turiv), was known as *Micra Rosia* (Little Rus'). From 1354 the name *Macra Rosia* (Great Rus') was used for the 13 eparchies under the Kiev metropolitan, namely, the Ukrainian eparchies of Kiev, Chernihiv, Pereiaslav, and Bilhorod and 9 Belarusian and Russian eparchies. It was probably under the influence of Byzantine church nomenclature that Prince Yurii II Boleslav called himself *Dux totius Russiae Minoris* in a charter of 1335. Galician kings and princes usually used the title *Rex Russiae, Dux totius terrae Russiae*, or *Dux et Dominus Russiae*.

The name Little Russia does not appear in 15th- or 16th-century documents. Only in the first half of the 17th century did it begin to be used in church correspondence between Kiev and Moscow. Until almost the end of the 17th century the names Rus' (Latin: *Russia*), Ruthenian land (Polish: *Ziemia Ruska*) and Red Rus' (Latin: *Russia Rubra*) were used in chronicles and maps to designate western Ukrainian territory. The term Great Rus', which had been applied originally to the eparchies of Kiev metropoly, was used later to refer to the territories of Novgorod and then Suzdal and Moscow, although until the 18th century those territories were usually called Muscovy in books and on maps. Great Russia was used by foreigners, however, to designate the Ukrainian state of B. Khmelnytsky, whom they titled Master and Hetman of Great Russia (1650). Af-

ter the Pereiaslav Treaty of 1654 Tsar Aleksei Mikhailovich added to the usual title of the Muscovite tsars the phrase 'of all Great and Little Russia.' Later the term Little Russia (*Malaia Rossiia* or *Parva Rossia*), as the designation of the Ukrainian territory united with Muscovy, began to be adopted in Ukrainian official documents, chronicles, and literature. The name does not appear on the geographical maps of Ukraine published by the Russian Academy of Sciences in 1736–8 or in the Russian atlas of 1745.

Malorossiia, which is derived from *Malaia Rossiia*, began to be used in official nomenclature in the 18th century to refer only to Left-Bank Ukraine, that is, to the Hetman state. In 1781 the Hetman state was abolished and replaced by three vicegerencies, Chernihiv, Novhorod-Siverskyi, and Kiev. In 1796 they were merged to form Little Russia gubernia (excluding Kiev), which in 1802 was divided into Poltava and Chernihiv gubernias. The official terms Little Russia (*Malorossiia*), Little Russian (*malorusskii*), and Little Russians (*malorossy*) were used for Russian-ruled Ukraine and its inhabitants only in the 19th and at the beginning of the 20th century. Ukrainians living outside the Russian Empire were also called Little Russians. But the name Ukraine was also quite widely used in Russian scientific and literary publications. The name Little Russia was sometimes restricted only to Left-Bank Ukraine within the limits of Poltava, Kharkiv, and Chernihiv gubernias. After the Revolution of 1917 the terms Little Russia and Little Russian were dropped from general and official usage. Ukrainians did not approve of the term Little Russia, and it does not appear in Ukrainian folklore.

BIBLIOGRAPHY
Hrushevs'kyi, M. 'Velyka, Mala i Bila Rus',' *Ukraïna*, 1917
Solov'ev, A. 'Velikaia, Malaia i Belaia Rossiia,' *Voprosy istorii*, 1947, no.7
Borschak, E. 'Rus', Mala Rosiia, Ukraïna,' *Revue des études Slaves*, 24 (1948)
Gregorovich, A. *Ukraine, Rus', Russia and Muscovy: A Selected Bibliography of the Names* (Toronto 1971)
B. Kravtsiv

Little Russia gubernia. An administrative territory of the Russian Empire set up in 1796. It consisted of the former Kiev (except for the city itself and its region on the right bank of the Dnieper), Novhorod-Siverskyi, and Chernihiv vicegerencies as well as the town of Kremenchuk and the former Poltava and Myrhorod regiments. The capital of the gubernia was Chernihiv. The court system of the Hetman state, including the general court, the estate land courts, and the *pidkomorskyi* courts, was restored in the gubernia. In 1802 Little Russia gubernia was divided into Chernihiv and Poltava gubernias.

Little Russian Collegium (Malorosiiska kolehiia; Russian: Malorossiiskaia kollegiia). Two distinct administrative institutions set up in Ukraine in the 18th century by the imperial Russian government. The first collegium was established by Peter I on 29 April 1722 in Hlukhiv. Its purpose was to oversee and monitor the activities of the hetman and his officers as well as the regimental and company *starshyna* in Ukraine. The collegium consisted of six staff officers from Russian regiments and garrisons stationed in Ukraine and a procurator, all of whom were appointed by the tsar and were to serve only one year. Its chairman was Brigadier S. Veliaminov. At the same time responsibility for Ukrainian affairs in St Petersburg was transferred from the Collegium of Foreign Affairs to the Senate (ie, from external to internal affairs). Taking advantage of the interregnum after Hetman I. Skoropadsky's death, when only an acting hetman, P. Polubotok, was appointed, the collegium usurped the powers of the hetman and acted as the highest administrative, judicial, and financial body in Ukraine. It reviewed the instructions of the hetman's office, served as an appeals court, and made fiscal decisions (increasing taxes fivefold). Its interference in the affairs of the hetman administration and arbitrary behavior aroused the indignation of the *starshyna* and sparked many protests from the hetman's office. Peter II promised to abolish the collegium and finally did so on 29 September 1727.

The second collegium was established by a decree of Catherine II, issued on 10 November 1764. With the abolition of the Hetman state it was to act as the highest governing body in Ukraine. Its task was to eradicate the last vestiges of Ukraine's autonomy, destroy the Cossack *starshyna*, and increase the economic exploitation of Ukraine. It consisted of eight permanent members appointed by the central government – four Ukrainians chosen from the general *starshyna* and four Russians. The president of the collegium was Count P. *Rumiantsev, who was also the governor-general of Ukraine and the commander in chief of all troops on its territory. His jurisdiction extended to the Zaporizhia. In 1782 the administrative system of Russian-ruled Ukraine began to be reorganized. Three vicegerencies were set up, and the second Little Russian Collegium was finally abolished on 20 August 1786.

BIBLIOGRAPHY
Dzhydzhora, I. 'Reformy Malorosiis'koï kolegiï na Ukraïni v 1722–3 rr.,' in *Iuvileinyi zbirnyk prysviachenyi profesorovy Mykhailovy Hrushevs'komu* (Lviv 1906)
Maksimovich, G. *Deiatel'nost' gr. P. Rumiantseva-Zadunaiskogo po upravleniiu Malorossiei* (Nizhen 1913)

O. Ohloblyn

Little Russian mentality (*malorosiistvo*). An inferiority complex in some Ukrainians, particularly among the intelligentsia, with respect to the Russians. Its essential components are admiration and identification with Russian culture and imperial tradition and a denial of Ukrainian distinctiveness, accomplishment, and political aspirations. According to M. *Drahomanov the mentality is typical of Russified Ukrainians, whose national identity was shaped by alien pressures. Their experience led them to absorb mostly the bad qualities of the alien Russian culture and to reject the good qualities of their own culture. For V. *Lypynsky the Little Russian mentality is a sickness arising out of Ukraine's lack of statehood. Ye. *Malaniuk defined the political Little Russian complex as a lack of national spiritual sovereignty, 'the lack of the most elementary national instinct and the paralysis of political will,' and a 'national defeatism' that was manifest in self-hatred in the 18th century and later in surrender to Moscow and servility to its rulers. A similar analysis can be found in M. *Khvylovy. Among the intelligentsia of Western Ukraine there was a somewhat analogous complex with respect to the Poles, expressed in the self-definition '*gente Ruthenus, natione Polonus*' and labeled *khrunivstvo* (piggishness) by Ukrainians. Ukrainians in Transcarpathia who were de-voted to Hungary were called *Magyarones. There is a distinction between the Little Russian mentality and Russophilism (see *Russophiles), although the two were sometimes similar in their expression and their results.

B. Kravtsiv

Little Russian Office (Russian: Prikaz Malyia Rossii, Malorossiiskii prikaz). A Muscovite agency established in 1663 to represent the tsar's interests in the Left-Bank or Hetman state. The office was based in Moscow and had a staff of approx 20. It maintained ties on the tsar's behalf with the hetman's government and representatives in Moscow, kept the tsar informed of developments, gathered intelligence, supervised and supplied the Muscovite garrisons in several of the Hetmanate's towns, mitigated conflicts between them and the people, oversaw the construction of fortresses and bridges, looked after the interests of Russian merchants in Ukraine, issued travel permits, and settled jurisdictional disputes. The office also monitored the administrative institutions of the Hetman state and the hetman's correspondence with foreign rulers, reviewed the hetman's appointments, and interfered in the affairs of the Orthodox church in Ukraine. From 1707 it had a resident general in the hetman's capital. The head of the Little Russian Office also usually headed the Muscovite Office of Foreign Envoys and was responsible directly to the tsar. The office was replaced in 1722 by the *Little Russian Collegium.

BIBLIOGRAPHY
Diadychenko, V. *Narysy suspil'no-politychnoho ustroiu Livoberezhnoï Ukraïny kintsia XVII–pochatku XVIII st.* (Kiev 1959)
Sofronenko, K. *Malorossiiskii prikaz Russkogo gosudarstva vtoroi poloviny XVII i nachala XVIII veka* (Moscow 1960)

A. Zhukovsky

Little Russian Secret Society (Malorosiiske taiemne tovarystvo). A political organization active in the early 1820s in Left-Bank Ukraine. It was organized and headed by V. *Lukashevych, marshal of the nobility of Pereiaslav county. Although precise information about the society is not available, from the testimony of many leading activists of the Decembrist movement it appears that the society's main goal was to gain independence for Ukraine. The society had its 'catechism,' which to the question 'Where did the sun rise?' prescribed the reply 'In Chyhyryn.' A number of landowners from the Poltava region, including S. Kochubei, V. Tarnovsky, and the Oleksiiv brothers, belonged to the society and were arrested in 1826 in consequence. Lukashevych and the society developed contacts with some professors of the Nizhen Lyceum and some residents of Kiev and other towns of Left-Bank Ukraine, as well as with clandestine Polish organizations, but probably avoided closer ties with Russian Decembrists. During the tsarist investigation in St Petersburg in 1826 Lukashevych denied that such a society had ever existed. All its members were released quickly, but Lukashevych was confined to his estate in Boryspil for the rest of his life.

Liturgical books. Books that contain the text and instructions for liturgical services. These books contain basic church services (the Divine *Liturgy, vespers, matins, and so forth) and/or special services (such as baptisms, weddings, and funerals). General liturgical books include the *Liturgicon (*sluzhebnyk*); *chasoslov (Horologion); *Octoechos (*oktoikh*); *Menaion (*mineia*); *Triodion (*triod'*); and *Typikon (*typikon* or *typyk*), which contains the statutes governing services. Special or individual services are contained in the *trebnyk, Acathistus (*akafisnyk*), Breviary (*molytoslov*), and other books. Liturgical books that provide both text and notes (for singing) include the Octoechos; *Hirmologion; and *triod notna*, a type of Triodion. The *bohohlasnyk* includes text and notes for popular religious songs and hymns sung in the Ukrainian Catholic church. A final category of liturgical books includes those with texts of the Scriptures: the Bible, *Apostol, and *Psalter.

The earliest liturgical books used in Ukraine were Church Slavonic translations of Byzantine texts. The subsequent history of Ukrainian liturgical books is linked closely to major changes in the history of the Ukrainian churches, including the devastation suffered during the Mongol invasion, the strife resulting from division into two churches, subordination to the Russian Orthodox church in the 18th to 20th centuries, the brief renaissance of the 20th century, repression under Soviet rule, and existence as a diaspora church outside of Ukraine. Each such major change in the circumstances of the churches has been accompanied by calls to revise extant church texts. During the 16th–century Ukrainian Orthodox revival, for example, discussions begun at sobors in 1591 and 1593 resulted in an extensive review of church texts (which were checked against Greek originals and earlier Church Slavonic versions) and revision of the *Trebnyk* (1606), Liturgicon (1617 and 1620), Triodion (1627 and 1631), Menaion (1638), and other books. With the strengthening of Russian control over Ukrainian church affairs, liturgical books were Russified and purged of Ukrainian elements, and for much of the 18th and 19th centuries the Russian church officially prohibited the printing and distribution of Ukrainian liturgical books. At the same time, Ukrainian Catholic liturgical books and practices were being subjected to strong Latinizing and Polonizing pressures, evident, for example, in the decisions of the Synod of *Zamostia of 1720.

Many of these trends were reversed in the 20th century. The *Ukrainian Autocephalous Orthodox church attempted to Ukrainianize the church rite in the 1920s and commissioned the preparation of several new liturgical books in Kiev. Such work was also undertaken in the interwar period by scholarly institutions located in Lviv, Warsaw (the *Ukrainian Scientific Institute), and Lutske (the *Mohyla Society). Under the leadership of Metropolitan A. *Sheptytsky, the Ukrainian Catholic church also worked to Ukrainianize its liturgical books, beginning in the early 20th century. This effort was reflected in the publication of a new Liturgicon in 1906. It was continued under Cardinal Y. *Slipy, who personally oversaw the preparation of several revised texts after his arrival in Rome in 1963. Since the Second World War most work on the revision of liturgical books has been carried on outside Ukraine, in Rome, South Bound Brook (United States), and Winnipeg (Canada). The Liturgical Commission of the Ukrainian Catholic church was especially active in the 1960s and 1970s, when it published Ukrainian translations of several church texts that had existed only in Church Slavonic. (See also *Church rite.)

I. Korovytsky

Liturgical language. The language used in church services. Although Latin remained the only liturgical language in the Western church for many centuries, from the beginning the Eastern Christian church encouraged the use of the vernacular (eg, Syrian, Armenian, Georgian) in newly established churches. In the 9th century the basic liturgical texts were translated by the Byzantine missionaries Cyril (see *Saint Cyril) and Methodius into a form of Old Bulgarian that later became known as Old *Church Slavonic. This language was to serve as the main church language of Rus'-Ukraine (as well as of other Eastern rite Slavic churches) for many centuries.

The Church Slavonic language used in Ukraine was phonetically Ukrainianized virtually from its adoption to make it more comprehensible for believers. In the 16th century, in part under the influence of the Reformation, some attempts were made to introduce the vernacular for use in churches, and several translations of the Gospels were made.

The widespread use of the Ukrainian variant of Church Slavonic (as well as attempts to introduce the vernacular) ceased following the subjugation of the Ukrainian Orthodox to the Russian Orthodox church in the late 17th century. Church hierarchs launched a full assault on the Ukrainian language by condemning the Ukrainian pronunciation of Church Slavonic in singing, sermons, and the performance of rites and replacing it with a Russian pronunciation. This measure was accompanied by heavy censorship of church books printed in Ukraine. For the next two centuries the traditional form of Ukrainian liturgical articulation was retained only outside the boundaries of the Russian Empire (in Galicia, Bukovyna, and Transcarpathia).

With the renewal of Ukrainian statehood in 1917–20, the Ukrainian Autocephalous Orthodox church (UAOC) revived the traditional Ukrainian articulation of Church Slavonic and introduced the vernacular for use in some parts of the service. Within a relatively short period of time a circle of scholars (including Metropolitan V. *Lypkivsky) had translated many essential church texts, including the *Liturgicon and *trebnyk, into modern Ukrainian. After the Russian Orthodox church re-established its dominance in Ukraine following the liquidation of the UAOC in the 1930s, the Ukrainian vernacular and the Ukrainian form of Church Slavonic were not recognized as liturgical languages. A revival of Ukrainian liturgical language during the Second World War (under the German occupation) was likewise short-lived. Churches of the official Russian Orthodox church in Ukraine (since 1990 called the Ukrainian Orthodox church) today use the Russian form of Church Slavonic except in the Western Ukrainian areas annexed in 1945, where a traditional Ukrainian articulation is tolerated. The UAOC, revived again in the late 1980s, has again introduced Ukrainian into common use. The various *Evangelical Christian denominations in Ukraine are generally either Russian or Ukrainian.

During the interwar period the use of vernacular Ukrainian as a liturgical language made considerable headway in Ukrainian parishes of the *Polish Autocephalous Orthodox church. The texts most commonly used included the Kiev translations of the 1920s and works prepared by I. *Ohiienko; the *Ukrainian Scientific Institute in Warsaw; and the *Mohyla Society in Lutske, which published texts of individual services and monographs about the distinctiveness of the Ukrainian church. A large-format Gospel published by the Orthodox metropoly in this same period provided a much-needed addition to the basic library of Ukrainian liturgical texts. After the Second World War, when Poland became a Soviet satellite, church life was simultaneously Polonized and Russified, and the use of Ukrainian was severely limited.

Ukrainian is used as a liturgical language by Ukrainian Catholic, Orthodox, and Protestant churches in the West. Orthodox churches and Protestant denominations generally started moving toward the use of vernacular Ukrainian in the early 20th century; the Ukrainian Catholic church retained Church Slavonic until the 1960s. The Second Vatican Council decreed that in the Latin rite the use of the vernacular as a liturgical language was permissible. The synod of Ukrainian bishops accepted the decree for the Ukrainian Catholic church and initiated the change (despite opposition from some believers). Since then, English has overtaken Ukrainian as the language of the church in many parishes in North America.

BIBLIOGRAPHY
Korolevsky, C. *Living Languages in Catholic Worship: An Historical Inquiry*, trans D. Attwater (Westminster, Md 1957)
Fedoriv, Iu. *Yaka mova Hospodu Bohu naimylisha?* (Toronto 1977)
I. Korovytsky, A. Velyky

Title page of the Liturgicon printed by the Kievan Cave Monastery Press in 1629

Liturgicon (*sluzhebnyk*). Also called a missal, a church book that contains the text of the prayers of the priest, deacon, and participants – as well as ritual prescriptions – which are required for the performing of a Divine *Liturgy. The complete or *velykyi* (Great) Liturgicon includes the text for the four forms of the Liturgy and the full range of gospel and epistle readings that they might require, as well as other prayers.

The oldest Church Slavonic Liturgicons – those used in Kievan Rus' – were attributed to Anthony the Roman (d 1147) and Barlaam (d 1192). Modern Liturgicons are based upon the Diataxis of Philotheus Coccinus, the Patriarch of Constantinople (1352–76), which was translated into Old Church Slavonic and introduced into the Ukrainian church by the Kievan metropolitan Cyprian (d 1406). The most important Liturgicon for the Ukrainian Orthodox church was compiled and edited by Metropolitan P. Mohyla in Kiev in 1629 (revised in 1639). It was used in all Orthodox churches until the Russian Holy Synod adopted the Synodal text and imposed it on the Ukrainian church in 1721. The first known Ukrainian Catholic text of the Liturgicon appeared in Vilnius in 1617. The Liturgicon in an enlarged format (by Metropolitan K. Zhokhovsky, 1692) included the epistle and gospel readings with all the propers of the movable and immovable feasts and the liturgical hours; it was greatly influenced by Roman Catholic practices. Revised and republished in 1905 (after the Lviv Synod of 1891), this basic text was used until 1941, when, at the request of the Ukrainian Catholic bishops, the Vatican promulgated a new version based on the Liturgicon used prior to 1692. All Ukrainian Catholic Liturgicons used Old Church Slavonic, and it was only in 1968 that a modern Ukrainian version was approved for use in the church. Several translations of Liturgicons have been prepared for the Ukrainian Orthodox church since 1917, including a complete set undertaken by a commission of the *Ukrainian Scientific Institute in Warsaw during the 1930s and another prepared at the Theological Research Institute in New York in 1963. There is, however, no single standard Liturgicon adopted by all Orthodox jurisdictions.

I. Korovytsky, M. Vavryk

Liturgy, Divine (*Bozhestvenna Liturhiia*). A eucharistic church service performed by a priest or bishop, with the assistance of a deacon; known commonly as the Mass in the Latin rite. The most fundamental of Christian church services, the Divine Liturgy symbolically commemorates the earthly life, death, and resurrection of Jesus Christ. The four Divine Liturgies used by Ukrainians date from the 4th century but acquired their present format in the 9th century. The Divine Liturgy of St John Chrysostom is the most commonly used and is celebrated on Sundays and weekdays. The Divine Liturgy of St Basil the Great is observed 10 times a year and is distinguished mainly by the longer silent prayers said by the priest. The Divine Liturgy of the Presanctified Gifts is performed on Wednesdays and Fridays during the Great Lent and on the first days of the week preceding Easter. It is notable for using eucharistic species consecrated during a previous Liturgy. The Divine Liturgy of the Holy Apostle Jacob (James) is celebrated once a year, on his feast day (5 November [23 October OS]).

The Divine Liturgy might be described as a series of connected prayer sequences or as the divine drama (*leitourgia*). It is celebrated in three parts: (1) the prayers of entry, with vesting and Proscomydiia (Prothesis); (2) the Liturgy of the Catechumens or the Word; and (3) the Liturgy of the Faithful or the Eucharist, which includes the Anaphora and Communion. Proscomydiia is an elaborate rite during which the priest prepares the bread and wine to be used in the Communion. The Liturgy of the Catechumens begins with the Great Litany of Peace, includes the processional entrance of the priest with the Gospel, and is centered around the reading of the New Testament letters (*Apostol*) and Gospel and a sermon or a homily. It concludes with the admonition of the catechumens (unbaptized) to leave; they are not permitted to participate in the rest of the service. The Liturgy of the Faithful reaches its climax during the Anaphora, which is centered around transubstantiation or the transformation of the bread and wine into the Body and Blood of Jesus Christ (consecration). It is followed by the Communion or distribution of the consecrated species among the congregation of believers. It includes the recitation of the Creed and the Lord's Prayer. The texts of the Liturgies can be found in a *Liturgicon.

The Ukrainian celebration of the Liturgy involves numerous well-developed practices, including the assistance of deacons in the service (when they are available), a pronounced spatial division between priest and congregation (accented during certain portions of the Liturgy by the opening or closing of the middle or Royal Gates of the *iconostasis), symbolic processions by the bishop or a priest and his retinue around the altar, and the extensive use of candles and incense. Likewise, the choral accompaniment to the Liturgy is well defined and highly regarded (see *Church music). Additional services commemorating feast days or other occasions are commonly performed separately from but in conjunction with the Liturgy (see *Church holidays).

The Ukrainian Orthodox and Catholic churches, like all Eastern Slavic churches, maintain their own specific ritual forms in celebrating the Divine Liturgy. These are particularly evident if compared to the liturgical norms of the Russian Orthodox church. The priest in a Ukrainian church, for example, traditionally reads the Gospel facing the congregation, while in the Russian church he is turned away from them; moreover, the Ukrainian priest keeps the Royal Gates of the iconostasis open considerably longer than does the Russian. After the subjugation of the Ukrainian Orthodox to the Russian Orthodox church in the 18th century, numerous Russian elements were introduced into the Liturgy. The Ukrainian Autocephalous Orthodox church that emerged after 1917 reformed the Liturgy (including abbreviations) and revived many old Ukrainian traditions. These traditions are now observed by most Ukrainian Orthodox jurisdictions in the West, but the official Ukrainian Orthodox church under the Moscow patriarch retains many Russian elements in its Liturgy.

In Galicia, Ukrainian Catholic liturgical practice was subjected to Latinizing influences through Polish Roman Catholicism until the end of the 19th century. The *Lviv Synod of 1891 undertook a number of reforms intended to restore a more traditional form of observance, but with only limited success. In the late 1920s Metropolitan A. *Sheptytsky also favored a return to traditional practices, and a special commission tried to standardize liturgical practices. More recently, the Liturgical Commission under the Congregation for Eastern Churches at the Vatican published authoritative editions of the three major Liturgies used in the Ukrainian Catholic church, which have given rise to greatly increased standardization since the 1960s.

BIBLIOGRAPHY
Fedoriv, Iu. *Obriady Ukraïns'koï Tserkvy: Istorychnyi rozvytok i poiasnennia* (Rome–Toronto 1970)
Solovey, M. *The Byzantine Divine Liturgy: History and Commentary*, trans D. Wysochansky (Washington, DC 1970)
Kucharek, C. *The Byzantine-Slav Liturgy of St John Chrysostom: Its Origin and Evolution* (Allendale, NJ–Combermere, Ont 1971)
Schulz, H. *The Byzantine Liturgy: Symbolic Structure and Faith Expression* (New York 1986)

I. Korovytsky

Litvin, Mikolas. See Michalon Lithuanus.

Lityn. IV-9. A town smt (1990 pop 7,200) on the Zhar River and a raion center in Vinnytsia oblast. Lityn is first mentioned in a historical document in 1431. At that time a fortified castle, situated on an island in the Zhar River, was built there. In 1578 Lityn was granted the rights of *Magdeburg law. The town was heavily damaged in the Cossack-Polish War of 1648–57. It was involved in the popular rebellions of 1687 and 1702–3 and in the haidamaka uprisings of 1750 and 1768. After the second partition of Poland in 1793, Lityn was annexed by Russia, and became a county center in Podilia gubernia. At the beginning of the 19th century it took part in U. *Karmaliuk's rebellion. He was imprisoned there in 1822–3, 1827, and 1830–2, and escaped twice (1827, 1832). In 1919–20 Otaman Ya. Shepel's partisans fought the Red Army and A. Denikin's army in the vicinity of Lityn. The Ukrainian Galician Army and the UNR Army were also active in the region, in 1919 and 1920 respectively. Today Lityn has a fruit- and vegetable-canning factory, a mixed-feed factory, two granite quarries, and a regional museum.

Liubachiv [Ljubačiv] (Polish: Lubaczów). III-4. A town (1989 pop 11,600) on the Liubachivka River and a county center in Poland's Peremyshl voivodeship. It was part of Peremyshl principality in Kievan Rus' at the end of the 11th century. In 1344 it was annexed by Poland, and Casimir III built a castle there. For a period in the 17th century it was held by the Cossacks. In 1717 A. Sieniawski established a famous glass-works there.

Metropolitan Myroslav Liubachivsky

Liubachivsky, Myroslav [Ljubačivs'kyj], b 24 June 1914 in Dolyna, Galicia. Ukrainian Catholic cardinal and metropolitan. Having studied at the Greek Catholic Theological Academy in Lviv, at the Catholic University in Innsbruck, in Sion, Switzerland (D TH, 1941), and at the Gregorian University in Rome, he arrived in the United States in 1947. After a period of teaching and pastoral work at St Basil's Seminary in Stamford and other locations, he was assigned to a parish in Cleveland. In 1968 he became spiritual director of St Josaphat's Seminary in Washington, and in 1977 he assumed the same post at St Basil's Seminary. In 1978 Liubachivsky was named archbishop of Philadelphia and metropolitan of the Ukrainian Catholic church in the United States. In 1979 he was made coadjutor and successor to Cardinal Y. Slipy at an extraordinary synod of Ukrainian Catholic bishops. When Slipy died in 1984, Liubachivsky became archbishop major of Lviv, metropolitan of Halych, and head of the Ukrainian

Catholic church. In 1985 Pope John Paul II appointed him a cardinal. Liubachivsky has traveled extensively to visit his followers, and in 1991 he was finally permitted to travel to his see of Lviv. He has been actively involved in the rebirth of the church in Ukraine in presiding over the re-establishment of a formal church structure and regular eparchies. He has also published collections of sermons and other works.

Liubar [Ljubar]. IV-8. A town smt (1990 pop 2,700) on the Sluch River and a raion center in Zhytomyr oblast. It originated as Liubartov in the mid-14th century when the Lithuanian duke Liubartas extended the old town of Bolokhiv by building a castle on the right bank of the river. Liubartov became the center of one of the principalities of the Lithuanian state. In 1569 it came under Polish rule, and in 1604 it was renamed Liubar. An important trading center, Liubar was destroyed by the Crimean Tatars in 1593 and 1618. It played an important role in the Cossack-Polish War of 1648–57. In the 1760s there was a strong haidamaka movement in the region. In 1793 Liubar came under Russian rule and played a part in the Decembrist movement. In the 19th century it was an important economic center in Volhynia, but it declined under Soviet rule, and it became an smt in 1924. Today Liubar has a food industry. Its architectural monuments include a Dominican Catholic church built in 1752 and a monastery built in 1634 in the Renaissance style. Archeologists have discovered several settlements of the *Trypilian culture, Bronze Age, early Iron Age, and *Cherniakhiv culture near Liubar.

Semen Liubarsky

Liubarsky, Semen [Ljubars'kyj], b 1878, d July 1944 in Skryhichyn, Hrubeshiv county, Kholm region. School teacher and civic and church activist. He was a member of the Central Rada (1917–18) and, in the interwar period, a deputy to the Polish Sejm (1922–8). He published articles on the history and ethnography of the Kholm region.

Liubart, Varvara [Ljubart] (real surname: Kolyshko), b 26 April 1898 in Poltava, d 4 November 1967 in Lviv. Stage actress. She studied in St Petersburg at the conservatory and at the drama school in the Aleksandrian Theater (1916–18). She joined the State People's Theater under P. Saksahansky in 1918 and continued in his People's Theater (1919–22). In 1922 she was one of the founders of the Zankovetska Theater in Kiev, with which she stayed when it moved to Lviv in 1944. Her best roles were Desde-mona in W. Shakespeare's *Othello*, Hilda in I. Kocherha's *Svichchyne vesillia* (Svichka's Wedding), and Anna in I. Franko's *Ukradene shchastia* (Stolen Happiness).

Liubartas [Ljubartas] (Ukrainian: Liubart), b ?, d ca 1385. Lithuanian-Ruthenian duke of Volhynia; son of Grand Duke *Gediminas. Ca 1322 he married a daughter of Prince *Andrii Yuriiovych of Galicia-Volhynia. After Liubartas accepted Orthodoxy and was baptized as Dymytrii, Andrii awarded him the Lutske land. After Andrii's death ca 1323, his successor and Liubartas's cousin, *Yurii II Boleslav, granted Liubartas the Volodymyr-Volynskyi land. In 1340, after Yurii was poisoned, the boyars offered the Galician-Volhynian throne to Liubartas. Liubartas's and Yurii's brother-in-law, *Casimir III of Poland, contested Liubartas's rule, however. War between Poland and Liubartas and his brothers lasted for 40 years. By 1349 Casimir had seized Galicia, and by 1366 he controlled all of Volhynia except the Lutske land. After Casimir's death in 1370, Liubartas and his brother Kęstutis failed to regain Galicia but recaptured all of Volhynia, which thereafter remained under Lithuanian-Ruthenian rule until 1569. Liubartas was succeeded briefly by his son, Fedor, who ca 1387 was forced to surrender his lands to his cousin, *Vytautas.

Liubashivka [Ljubašivka]. VI-11. A town smt (1990 pop 9,900) in the northwestern part of the Black Sea Lowland and a raion center in Odessa oblast. It was founded in the late 18th century, and became an smt in 1957. Liubashivka has a mixed-feed factory, a dairy, an oil-pressing plant, a grain elevator, and a regional museum.

Liubavsky, Matvii [Ljubavs'kyj, Matvij] (Liubauski, Matsvei), b 13 August 1860 in Bolshie Mozhary, Riazan gubernia, d 22 November 1936 in Ufa. Historian of Belarusian origin; full member of the USSR Academy of Sciences from 1929. He was a student of V. Kliuchevsky and later became a professor at Moscow University (1901–17, rector from 1911). A specialist in the history of the Lithuanian-Ruthenian state, he wrote *Oblastnoe delenie i mestnoe upravlenie Litovsko-Rus'kogo gosudarstva ko vremeni izdaniia pervogo Litovskogo statuta* (Regional Division and Local Government in the Lithuanian-Ruthenian State to the Time of the Publication of the First Lithuanian Statute, 1898), *Litovsko-russkii seim* (The Lithuanian-Ruthenian Diet, 1901), and *Ocherk istorii Litovsko-Russkogo gosudarstva* (Survey of the History of the Lithuanian-Ruthenian State, 1910), as well as *Istoriia zapadnykh slavian* (History of the Western Slavs, 1917; 2nd edn 1918) and a study in Belarusian of the Lithuanian-Belarusian state at the beginning of the 16th century (1926). M. Hrushevsky published *O knige M.K. Liubavskogo 'Lektsii po drevnei russkoi istorii do kontsa XVI v.'* (On the Book by M. Liubavsky 'Lectures in Ancient Ruthenian History to the End of the 16th Century,' 1915), and I. Borozdin's bibliography of Liubavsky's works was published in the commemorative *Sbornik stattei v chest' M.K. Liubavskogo* (Collection of Articles in Honor of M. Liubavsky, 1917). After the revolution Liubavsky was exiled to Ufa.

Liubchenko, Arkadii [Ljubčenko, Arkadij], b 7 March 1899 in Staryi Zhyvotiv, Uman county, Kiev gubernia, d 25 February 1945 in Bad Kissingen, Germany. Writer. He

Arkadii Liubchenko   Panas Liubchenko

was active in the literary movement of the 1920s and 1930s, as secretary of the literary association Hart, co-founder and permanent secretary of Vaplite, and co-founder of Prolitfront and the almanac *Literaturnyi iarmarok*. He edited the State Publishing House of Ukraine editions of V. Vynnychenko's selected works (1927) and V. Stefanyk's selected works (1928). He also worked in the editorial office of the newspaper *Vil'na Ukraïna* in Kharkiv (1941–2). He began to publish his work in 1918, including the neoromantic-impressionist collections of stories and novels *Buremna put'* (The Tempestuous Road, 1927), *Vona* (She, 1929), and *Vitryla tryvoh* (The Sails of Anxieties, 1932) as well as articles, essays, and translations of the French authors A. Daudet and F. Mauriac. His *Shchodennyk* (Diary, 1951) was published posthumously.

Liubchenko, Mykola [Ljubčenko] (pseud: Kost Kotko), b 29 February 1896 in Kiev, d 25 November 1937. Writer. During the revolution he was a leading member of the *Borotbists and edited that group's organ, *Borot'ba*. Later, as a member of the CP(B)U, he edited *Komunist* (see *Radians'ka Ukraïna*). He began to publish his works in 1911. During the Soviet period his feuilletons appeared in the press, and several collections of his satirical sketches, particularly aimed at the Ukrainian National Republic, were published: *Petliuriia* (1921), *Proty Symona Petliury* (Against S. Petliura, 1921), and *Istukrev* (1928). He was arrested in 1934, imprisoned in the Soviet Arctic, and executed there by the NKVD.

Liubchenko, Panas [Ljubčenko], b 14 January 1897 in Kaharlyk, Kiev county, Kiev gubernia, d 29 August 1937 in Kiev. Soviet political leader. A member of the Central Committee of the Ukrainian Party of Socialist Revolutionaries, in 1918 he headed its leftist faction, known as the *Borotbists. Eventually, when internationalists within the party, which split off and in 1918–20 reorganized, formed the Ukrainian Communist party (of Borotbists), and merged with the CP(B)U, he became secretary of the Party's Kiev Gubernia Committee, head of the Chernihiv Gubernia Executive Committee (1921–2), and president of the All-Ukrainian Association of Agricultural Co-operatives (1922–5). In 1927 he was promoted to the position of secretary of the CC CP(B)U, and in 1934, to that of full member of the Politburo. At the same time he was deputy

chairman (1933) and chairman (1934–7) of the Council of People's Commissars of the Ukrainian SSR. Liubchenko carried out the Party's centralist policies in Ukraine. In the show trials of the Union for the Liberation of Ukraine he acted as a 'people's prosecutor' from the All-Ukrainian Council of Trade Unions. He also played a political role in the collectivization and the grain requisition, which precipitated the 1932–3 famine in Ukraine. He seems to have committed suicide while facing imminent arrest. At the Moscow show trials he was accused posthumously of creating a nationalist-fascist organization. He was rehabilitated in the early 1960s, and his biography was published in 1970.

V. Markus

Liubech [Ljubeč]. II-11. A town smt (1990 pop 3,800) on the left bank of the Dnieper River in Ripky raion, Chernihiv oblast. One of the oldest towns in Ukraine, Liubech is first mentioned in the chronicles in 882, when it was captured by Prince Oleh. In the 10th and 11th centuries it was an important center of the Chernihiv region. It was the birthplace of St Anthony, the founder of the Kievan Cave Monastery. It was the site of the Battle of *Liubech in 1016 and of the *Liubech congress of princes in 1097 and a similar congress in 1135. Liubech was burned down by Prince Rostyslav in 1147 and by the Cumans in 1157. It was annexed by Lithuania in 1356, and under the Treaty of Lublin it was transferred to Poland and became a starostvo center. The town played an important role in the Cossack-Polish War of 1648–57 and then came under Muscovy's rule. From then Liubech declined and lost political significance. In 1958 it became an smt. Today Liubech has a fruit-drying plant, a cheese workshop of the Ripky dairy, and a fish farm. Archeologists have discovered 16 settlements from the Neolithic Period, 6 settlements from the early Iron and Bronze ages (8th–2nd century BC), and 5 Slav settlements around Liubech. The remnants of the medieval castle have been uncovered, and a stone building from the 17th century has survived.

Liubech, Battle of. A battle between the sons of Volodymyr the Great, Sviatopolk I and Yaroslav the Wise, in 1016 near the town of Liubech. Volodymyr's death in 1015 precipitated a struggle among his sons for the throne of Kiev. Sviatopolk proclaimed himself grand prince and ordered his half-brothers, Borys and Hlib, as well as Sviatoslav, prince of the Derevlianians, killed. Upon learning of his crime, Yaroslav gathered an army of 40,000 Novgorodians and 1,000 mercenary Varangians and marched against Sviatopolk. After being defeated at Liubech Sviatopolk fled to his father-in-law, Bolesław I the Brave, in Poland, and Yaroslav assumed the throne of Kiev (see *Yaroslav the Wise).

Liubech congress of princes. A conference of the princes of Kievan Rus', convened at the initiative of Volodymyr Monomakh in Liubech in 1097. Its purpose was to end the conflicts among the princes and to unite them in the struggle against the Cumans. Besides Volodymyr Monomakh the congress was attended by five princes: Sviatopolk II Iziaslavych, the grand prince of Kiev, Oleh Sviatoslavych of Chernihiv, Davyd Sviatoslavych of Smolensk, Davyd Ihorevych of Volodymyr-Volynskyi, and Vasylko Rostyslavych of Terebovlia-Peremyshl. The congress abolished the seniority principle of succession and adopted the principle of patrimony, whereby each prince would possess the lands ruled by his father. The congress thereby transformed a formally unitary state into a group of independent states joined together in a unique kind of federation, in which issues of common interest were settled at princely congresses. The Liubech congress decided to conduct a joint campaign against the Cumans. The congress did not succeed in ending the strife among princes, which weakened and eventually undermined Rus'.

Liubeshiv [Ljubešiv]. II-6. A town smt (1990 pop 5,100) on the Stokhid River and a raion center in Volhynia oblast. It is first mentioned in a historical document in 1484, when it was under Lithuanian rule. In 1569 it became part of the Polish Commonwealth, and at the end of the century a Piarist monastery was built there. In 1706 the town was destroyed by Charles XII of Sweden. After the partition of Poland in 1795, Liubeshiv was annexed by Russia, and became a *volost* center in Pynske county, Minsk gubernia. Today it is an agricultural town with a silicate brick factory and several food-processing enterprises. Its old monastery and 18th-century park are tourist attractions.

Liubin Velykyi [Ljubin' Velykyj]. IV-4. A resort town smt (1988 pop 5,000) on the Vereshytsia River in Horodok raion, Lviv oblast. It has been known since the 13th century, and received the status of smt in 1964. From March to May 1919 the Ukrainian Galician Army fought several battles against the Polish army around Liubin Velykyi. The resort's hydrogen sulfate and calcium sulfate springs and muds are used for curative baths.

Liuboml [Ljuboml']. II-5. A city (1990 pop 10,200) in the southwestern part of Volhynian Polisia and a raion center in Volhynia oblast. Liuboml is first mentioned in the Hypatian Chronicle under the year 1287. It was Prince *Volodymyr Vasylkovych's favorite town, and his place of death in 1288. In the 14th century a castle was built there, and in 1541 the town was granted the rights of *Magdeburg law. From 1768 it belonged to the Branicki family, who built a palace and park there. In the interwar period Liuboml was a county center in Volhynia voivodeship. The city has the Svitiaz Machine-Building Plant, two lumber mills, and a regional museum. Its architectural monuments include the Church of St Gregory (1264), a Catholic church (1412), castle catacombs (15th–16th century), and a partly preserved 18th-century trading center. A burial site from the 3rd to 4th centuries and two fortified settlements from the time of Kievan Rus' have been excavated near Liuboml.

Liubomyrsky, Hryhorii [Ljubomyrs'kyj, Hryhorij], b 13 February 1865 in Vasylkiv, Kiev gubernia, d 14 February 1937 in Kiev. Music teacher and composer. A cofounder of the *Lysenko Music and Drama School in 1904, he taught there and at its successor institutions, the Lysenko Music and Drama Institute (from 1918) and the Kiev Conservatory (from 1934). His compositions include a Symphony in G-flat, *Elegy*, and eastern dances. He also wrote textbooks on elementary theory of music and harmony and articles in music journals. Liubomyrsky taught many individuals who figured prominently in Ukrainian musical life, including K. Stetsenko, O. Koshyts, and V. Verkhovynets.

Hryhorii Liubomyrsky   Stepan Liubomyrsky

Liubomyrsky, Stepan [Ljubomyrs'kyj] (pseud of Liubomyr Stepan Rykhtytsky; other pseuds: Stepan Elerson, Mykola Khortytsia), b 21 April 1921 in Drohobych, Galicia, d 16 July 1983 in Chicago. Writer. Liubomyrsky's studies at Lviv University were interrupted when the university was shut down by the Germans. He joined the *Division Galizien in 1943. His writing career began in the POW camp in Rimini, Italy, in 1946 with the collection of stories *Son litn'oï nochi* (Dream of a Summer's Night, under the pseud Stepan Elerson). His second work, *Zhorstoki svitanky* (Cruel Dawns, 1947), was the first in a long series of novels devoted to the underground struggle for Ukraine's independence. Some of his novels, which were heavy on intrigue and full of national pathos, were extremely popular (*Plem'ia Vovkiv* [The Clan of Wolves, 1951], *Mizh slavoiu i smertiu* [Between Glory and Death, 1953], and *Pid molotom viiny* [Under the Hammer of War, 4 vols, 1955–6], although of little literary value and marred by two-dimensional characterizations. In his later novels, including the posthumous trilogy *Slidamy zapovitu* (Following the Testament, 1985), plot often gives way to ideological preaching. His first novel, *Zhorstoki svitanky*, was made into a film in 1965, produced by W. Wasik in Canada. Liubomyrsky wrote two more film scenarios for the Canukr film production company in Oshawa, Ontario: *Nikoly ne zabudu* (I Shall Never Forget, 1969) and *Zashumila verkhovyna* (Whispering Highlands, 1975).

D.H. Struk

Liubotyn [Ljubotyn]. IV-16. A city (1990 pop 29,000) in Kharkiv raion, Kharkiv oblast. Founded in the mid-17th century, Liubotyn served as a company center of Kharkiv regiment. In the mid-18th century the region was involved in the haidamaka movement. Since the 1880s Liubotyn has been an important railway junction on the Kharkiv–Mykolaiv line. It was given city status in 1938. It has several railway-related enterprises, a textile plant, a brickyard, a liquor distillery, and a dried yeast–feed factory. A Scythian settlement from the 2nd millennium BC has been discovered near Liubotyn.

Liubotyn fortified settlement. An important archeological site located approx 25 km west of Kharkiv. Utilized extensively from the 7th to the 4th century BC, the site is noted for its defensive walls of earth and wood. Artifacts uncovered in the course of excavation in the early 1960s indicate that Liubotyn was a highly developed bronze and iron manufacturing center.

Liubovsky, Petro [Ljubovs'kyj], b and d ? Philosopher and teacher of the early 19th century. After graduating from Kharkiv University (1808) he taught at the Kharkiv Gymnasium for five years and was a member and secretary of the Kharkiv Scientific Society (est 1812). He recognized the role of both experience and reason in knowledge and claimed that language was necessary to thought. He wrote short textbooks in Russian on experimental psychology (1815) and logic (1817).

Liubovych, Petro [Ljubovyč], b 1826 in Staryi Zbarazh, Zbarazh county, Galicia, d 1869 in Hrymaliv, Skalat county, Galicia. Composer and conductor. After graduating from the Lviv Theological Seminary in 1853, he was ordained and appointed conductor of a church choir in Peremyshl. He wrote a liturgy for mixed choir and a piano potpourri *Ulubione sola ruskie* (Favorite Ruthenian Solos), the first collection of Ukrainian piano music. He also arranged folk songs.

Liubovych, Uliana. See Starosolska, Uliana.

Oleksandra Liubych-Parakhoniak

Liubych-Parakhoniak, Oleksandra [Ljubyč-Paraxonjak] (Parakhoniak), b 14 March 1892 in Stanyslaviv, Galicia, d 23 February 1977 in Vynnyky (a suburb of Lviv). Opera singer (lyric-dramatic soprano). She was a student of O. Myshuha and the first performer of most of S. Liudkevych's solo songs. From 1917 she performed at the Lviv Municipal Theater as well as in the theaters of Cracow, Poznań, and Torun, notably the name-roles in S. Moniuszko's *Halka* and G. Verdi's *Aida*. She also toured Germany and Czechoslovakia. She quit the stage in 1937.

Liubymenko, Volodymyr [Ljubymenko], b 16 January 1873 in Veidelevka, Valuiky county, Voronezh gubernia, d 14 September 1937 in Leningrad. Botanist and plant physiologist; corresponding member of the USSR Academy of Sciences from 1922 and 1929 full member of the VUAN (now ANU) from 1929. A graduate of the Forestry Institute in St Petersburg (1898), he worked in France and at various scientific institutions in Leningrad. In 1928 Liubymenko organized the Institute of Applied Botany in Kharkiv, and in 1929 he became head of the Department of Chemical Plant Physiology at the VUAN Institute of Botany. Most of his research dealt with the chemical aspects of plastids and pigments, photosynthesis, and photoperiodism. Besides publishing over 200 research papers he wrote the influential *Kurs obshchei botaniki* (A Course in General Botany, 1923). Liubymenko was critical of T. *Lysenko's theory of plant development, and died in the 1937 terror perhaps as a result.

Liubymivka fortified settlement and kurhans. Remains of a fortified settlement that existed from the 3rd century BC to the 3rd century AD, and a group of 60 kurhans of various dates, located near the present-day village of Liubymivka, Kakhivka raion, Kherson oblast. The settlement was situated on the left bank of the Konka River (now the left bank of the Kakhivka Reservoir). Excavations of the site were done in the 1920s (by the Kherson Historical Museum), 1951–2, 1968–9, and 1978 (by the AN URSR Institute of Archeology). The fortified settlement covered 3.5 sq ha and was surrounded by ramparts (5–10 m high) and a trench (6–25 m wide). Uncovered in the settlement were domestic stone dwellings, commercial buildings, and a cobblestone square. Pottery of local and foreign manufacture, tools, amphoras, coins, and other items were recovered in the course of excavations. The primary subsistence activity of the inhabitants was agriculture and animal husbandry; crafts and trade with such cities as *Olbia and *Chersonese Taurica were also important.

Liubymsky, Oleksandr [Ljubyms'kyj], b 26 March 1907 in Melitopil, Tavriia gubernia, d 19 April 1981 in Kharkiv. Painter. A graduate of the Kharkiv Art Institute (1932), he later taught there (1947–65). He painted landscapes, such as *Evening in the Steppe* (1937) and *At Dawn* (1957); socialist-realist genre scenes, such as *Descent into the Mine* (1932) and *Competition of Blast-Furnace Workers*; and, with M. Rybalchenko, large decorative panels, such as *Gathering Apples* (1939, for the Ukrainian pavilion at the USSR Exhibition of Economic Achievements in Moscow), *Toward the Star* (1969), and *At Lunch Break* (1977).

Liubynetsky, Roman [Ljubynec'kyi], b 3 December 1885 in Chesnyky, Rohatyn county, Galicia, d 30 June 1945 in Komarov, near Plzeň, Czechoslovakia. Opera singer (lyrical tenor) and teacher. He graduated from the Academy of Music in Vienna (1914) and was a soloist at the opera theaters of Dresden (1914–15), Cracow (1917–18), and Zagreb (1918–29). His main roles included Faust in C. Gounod's *Faust*, Cavaradocci in G. Puccini's *Tosca*, and Don José in G. Bizet's *Carmen*. In 1929–44 he was a professor at the Lviv Conservatory.

Liubynsky, Mykola [Ljubyns'kyj], b 5 October 1891 in Strikhivtsi, Nova Ushytsia county, Podilia gubernia, d 1930s. Political activist. A member of the Ukrainian Party of Socialist Revolutionaries, he sat on the Central Rada and the Little Rada. He represented the UNR at the Brest-Litovsk peace conference and signed an appeal to the German people for military assistance (12 February 1918). In March and April 1918 he served as UNR minister of foreign affairs in V. Holubovych's cabinet. Later, under the Soviet regime, he worked at the VUAN Institute of the Ukrainian Scientific Language in Kiev and was a member of the edi-

Mykola Liubynsky   Stanyslav Liudkevych

torial board of *Visnyk instytutu ukraïns'koï naukovoï movy* (1930). He was arrested in the 1930s, and his fate is unknown.

Liubynsky, Vsevolod [Ljubyns'kyj], b 1840 in Kiev gubernia, d 1920. Pharmacologist and political leader. An active member of the Ukrainian People's Hromada, established by P. Skoropadsky in 1917, he participated in Skoropadsky's coup d'état and served in F. Lyzohub's and S. Gerbel's cabinets as minister of public health. He was a strong advocate of Ukrainianization in the Hetman government and in his own ministry placed Ukrainian officials in key positions.

Liubystok, Hryhorii [Ljubystok, Hryhorij], b and d ? Bandurist. From 1730 he served as musician at the court of Elizabeth I in St Petersburg. He attempted an escape to Ukraine in 1731 but was unsuccessful. In 1749 he was ennobled and granted the rank of colonel. He received an estate near Lubni, where he lived for the rest of his life. Liubystok was also active in the effort to restore the office of the hetman, which was filled by K. Rozumovsky in 1750.

Liudiie. The old term for the common people as distinct from the nobles and boyars of Kievan Rus'. Most of them were free: they paid the prince tribute but were not required to perform personal services. According to **Ruska-ia Pravda* the penalty for killing a *liudin* was a single **vyra*, and for killing a prince's officer, a double *vyra*. In the 11th and 12th centuries various subclasses of *liudiie* were distinguished, including *chorni* (free town workers, mostly tradesmen), *narochyti* (wealthy merchants), and *tserkovni* (charges of the church).

Liudkevych, Stanyslav [Ljudkevyč], b 24 January 1879 in Jarosław, d 12 September 1979 in Lviv. Composer, musicologist, folklorist, and pedagogue; member of the Shevchenko Scientific Society since 1935. He was taught piano as a child by his mother, and continued to study in Lviv under M. Soltys and in Vienna under O. Zemlinsky and P. Gredener (composition and instrumentation) and Guido Adler (musicology), where he obtained a PH D in 1907 with a dissertation on program music. He taught in gymnasiums in Lviv and Peremyshl in 1901–7; in 1908 he

was appointed director of the M. Lysenko Institute of Music in Lviv, and in 1919 he became an inspector of its branches and a lecturer in music theory. From 1939 he taught at the Lviv State Conservatory and then held the Chair of Composition until his retirement in 1972.

Liudkevych began composing choral works while still a gymnasium student. His symphonic cantata *The Caucasus* (1902–13), inspired by T. Shevchenko's poem of the same name, is considered one of the most eminent works in Ukrainian music of that time. Other choral compositions include *The Eternal Revolutionary* (1898), *The Reaper* (1901), *Khor pidzemnykh kovaliv* (The Chorus of Underground Blacksmiths, 1905), *Oi, vyhostriu tovarysha* (Oh, I'll Hone My Knife, 1917), and *The Testament* (1934). His symphonic compositions include *Strilets'ka rapsodiia* (The [Sich] Riflemen's Rhapsody, 1920), *Kameniari* (The Stonecutters, 1926, 2nd edn 1956), and *Vesnianky* (Spring Songs, 1935). He also wrote a piano trio, minor works for the piano and the violin, solo songs, the unfinished opera *Bar Kokhba* (1926), and arrangements of folk and riflemen songs. In his later period, he composed orchestral works, including *Symfonietta* (1943), *Koliadnytsia* (Christman Caroller, 1944), *Iunats'ke rondo* (The Rondo of Youth, 1946), the symphonic poem *The Dnieper* (1948), *Prykarpats'ka symfoniia* (The Subcarpathian Symphony, 1952), concertos for piano and for violin, and the opera *Dovbush*.

Liudkevych edited works by earlier composers, including M. Verbytsky, O. Nyzhankivsky, V. Matiuk, and S. Vorobkevych. He composed and orchestrated the additional act in S. Hulak-Artemovsky's opera *Zaporozhian Cossack beyond the Danube* and orchestrated M. Lysenko's operas *Nocturne* and *Utoplena* (The Drowned Maiden). Liudkevych is the author of various theoretical works on Ukrainian music, including *Zahalni osnovy muzyky* (The Basic Principles of Music, 1921) and *Materiialy do nauky sol'fedzho i khorovoho spivu* (Materials for the Study of Solfège and Choral Singing, 1930). With O. Rozdolsky he compiled *Halyts'ko-rus'ki melodiï* (Galician-Ruthenian Melodies, 2 vols of *Etnohrafichnyi zbirnyk*, 1906–7). He wrote numerous commentaries and reviews, and edited articles on music in the journals *Artystychnyi vistnyk* (1905), *Muzychnyi lystok* (1925), and *Muzychnyi vistnyk* (1929–34).

A major anthology of Liudkevych's writings was published in Kiev in 1973 but immediately withdrawn from circulation. In 1976 a reprint edition of this work was published in the United States, and a considerably shortened anthology appeared in the Ukrainian SSR.

Liudkevych played an important part in developing musical culture in Ukraine through his activity in the *Boian society and in the *Lysenko Higher Institute of Music. His compositions are characterized by highly professional skill and a tendency toward monumentalism and drama.

BIBLIOGRAPHY

Zahaikevych, M. *S.P. Liudkevych: Narys pro zhyttia i tvorchist'* (Kiev 1957)

Shtunder, Z. (ed). *S. Liudkevych: Doslidzhennia, statti, retsenziï* (Kiev 1973)

Pavlyshyn, S. *Stanislav Liudkevych* (Kiev 1974)

Zahaikevych, M. (ed). *Tvorchist' S. Liudkevycha: Zbirnyk stattei* (Kiev 1979)

Vytvyts'kyi, V. 'Stanyslav Liudkevych zblyz'ka,' *Suchasnist'*, 1979, no. 6

Teren-Ius'kiv, T. *Natsional'no-derzhavna motyvatsiia tvorchosty S. Liudkevycha* (London 1984)

A. Rudnytsky, R. Savytsky

Liudyna i svit (Man and World). A monthly published by the Znannia Society of Ukraine in Kiev since October 1960. Until 1964 it was called *Voiovnychyi ateïst*. Until 1990 it included articles on atheism and the methodology of atheistic propaganda and propagated new Soviet feasts and rites to replace traditional church holidays.

Arkhyp Liulka

Liulka, Arkhyp [Ljul'ka, Arxyp], b 23 March 1908 in Savarka, Kaniv county, Kiev gubernia, d 1 April 1984 in Moscow. Airplane engine designer; full member of the USSR Academy of Sciences from 1968. He graduated from the Kiev Polytechnical Institute (1931), worked in Kharkiv, Leningrad, and Moscow, and taught at the Kharkiv Aviation Institute. He headed the Aircraft Design Bureau of the State Committee for Aviation Engineering at the USSR Council of Ministers and from 1965 worked in the USSR Ministry of the Aircraft Industry. He designed the first Soviet turbo-compressor jet engine (1937–9) and other turbo jet engines, such as the AL-3 and AL-5, and worked on new fuels.

Liutkovych-Telytsia, Pavlo [Ljutkovyč-Telycja] (Domzhyv-Liutkevych), b ? in Western Ukraine, d 1634 in Chorna, Volhynia. Churchman and printer. He ran a series of printing presses in Uhortsi, near Sambir (1617–21); in Minsk, Belarus (1622); and in Volhynia at the Chetvertnia (1624–5), Lutske (1625–8), and Chorna monasteries. He was also hegumen of the SS Peter and Paul Monastery in Minsk (from 1611) and the monastery in Chorna (1628–34). Seven of the nine books he is known to have printed have been preserved, including his own panegyric to O. Sheptytsky (1622). He printed panegyrics, theological works, poetry, and textbooks.

Liutsenko, Oleksander [Ljucenko], b 12 August 1806, d 9 February 1884 in St Petersburg. Archeologist. While serving as director of the Kerch Archeological Museum from 1853 to 1878, he conducted excavations of Scythian and Hellenic monuments in Katerynoslav gubernia, the Taman Peninsula, and the Crimea near Kerch. He excavated the well-known *Oleksandropil and *Melek-Chesmen kurhans. The finds that he discovered are preserved at the Kerch Museum and the Hermitage in St Petersburg.

Among his archeological studies is the monograph *Drevnie evreiskie nadgrobnye pamiatniki, otkrytye v nasypakh Fanagoriiskogo gorodishcha* (Ancient Hebrew Grave Monuments Found in the Mounds of the Phanagoria Fortified Settlement, 1881).

Livadiia Palace (now a sanatorium)

Livadiia [Livadija]. IX-15. A town smt (1990 pop 1,900) on the southern coast of the Crimea 3 km southwest of Yalta and under the administration of the Yalta city council. In the 18th century there was a Greek settlement at the site, which in the second half of the 19th century became an estate of the Russian royal family. After the Revolution of 1917 it was transformed into a health resort. Some sessions of the Yalta Conference in 1945 were held in Livadiia. Today the town has a vineyard and a winery, several sanatoriums, and resorts for victims of heart, lung, and nerve diseases. Livadiia's most important architectural monument is the Grand Palace, designed by M. Krasnov in 1910–11 and surrounded by a park designed by I. Peter in 1834. Traces of Copper Age and Taurian settlements and a burial place from the 1st century have been found near the town. The ruins of a 10th- to 12th-century castle are nearby.

Livchak, Osyp [Livčak] (Lyvchak), b 1839 in Tysova, Peremyshl county, Galicia, d 1914 in Petrograd. Inventor and writer. He obtained his education at Lviv and Vienna universities and in Vienna was editor of the journals *Strakhopud (1863), *Zolotaia hramota* (1864–7), and *Slavianskaia zaria* (1867–8). From 1869 he lived in Vilnius and St Petersburg. He designed a prototype of a linotype (1881, years before a similar construction was presented by O. Morgentaller in the United States), a diascope (type of periscope), and an all-purpose sighting mechanism that was awarded a gold medal by the Paris Academy (1886). His automatic meter indicating the speed and distance traveled by a locomotive was awarded a gold medal by the Russian Technical Society (1900). Livchak was the author of several books on technical topics as well as some original literary works.

Livesay, Florence Randal (family name: Randal), b 3 November 1874 in Compton, Quebec, d 28 July 1953 in Toronto. Journalist and author. She translated into English a volume of Ukrainian verse, *Songs of Ukraina* (1916), with the assistance of P. *Krat and others. She also translated H. Kvitka-Osnovianenko's *Marusia* (1940), assisted by Krat and T. *Humeniuk. A collection of her various

Florence Randal Livesay   Natalia Livytska-Kholodna

translations (including dumas) and writings on Ukrainian topics was published in 1981 as *Down Singing Centuries: Folk Literature of the Ukraine.*

Livestock. See Animal husbandry, Cattle raising, Horse breeding, Hog raising, Sheep farming, and Goat farming.

Living church (Zhyva tserkva). A major faction of the *Renovationist church that was active in the Ukrainian SSR during the 1920s and 1930s. The church was formed in 1922 by liberal-minded Russian Orthodox clergymen who took advantage of a standoff between the Patriarchal Russian church headed by Tikhon and the Soviet regime to ascend to a position of religious prominence. Since the church shared a general distrust of the traditional episcopal authority and the conservative monasteries with the newly formed Ukrainian Autocephalous Orthodox church (UAOC), the Living church initially hoped to co-operate with the latter (this would also have provided the fledgling group with a well-developed base of operations). The UAOC, wary of what it viewed as essentially a Russian church and cautious in order to guard its independence, rejected the offer. The Living church then formally structured itself in 1923 into the Ukrainian Orthodox (Synodal) church under the leadership of a Kharkiv-based metropolitan, P. Pegov.

For the next several years the Living church sought to submerge Orthodox groups in Ukraine under its leadership. It hoped to attract adherents of the Patriarchal church by following a relatively conservative (compared with the Russian Renovationist) course of action. In order to undermine the UAOC, the church set off on a much-proclaimed process of Ukrainization and even declared itself autocephalous in 1925. These moves were largely tactical, however, and the church remained essentially Russian in character and tied to its founding body. The Renovationists were assisted by Soviet authorities, who preferred them to the more conservative Patriarchal church and the more nationalistic UAOC. The regime even coerced a number of Patriarchal clergymen and parishes to join the Living church. As well, it was free to publish books and journals (*Golos pravoslavnoi Ukrainy* and later *Ukraïns'kyi pravoslavnyi blahovisnyk*) and to run a theology school in the Kievan Cave Monastery. Nevertheless, it failed to gain many adherents, although some UAOC parishes, especially in Podilia, did join.

The Living church fell victim to a massive antireligion campaign that swept the USSR after 1929. Even before that, the number of its priests had declined from 3,500 in 1925 to 2,200 in 1928. This downturn in its fortunes was hastened by the political reconciliation of the Patriarchal church with Soviet authorities in 1927. By 1941 not a single functioning Living church parish remained in Ukraine.

Living standard. See Standard of living.

Livytska, Mariia [Livyc'ka, Marija] (née Tkachenko), b 9 April 1879 in Berdychiv, Kiev gubernia, d 16 August 1971 in Yonkers, New York. Civic and political figure; wife of A. *Livytsky and mother of M. *Livytsky. As a student in Kiev she was active in the student hromada. After joining the Revolutionary Ukrainian party and its successor, the Ukrainian Social Democratic Workers' party, she was involved in revolutionary activity in Lubni, and in 1909 she was a defendant in the trial of the so-called *Lubni Republic. In 1917 she was active in the political life of the Poltava region. She emigrated in November 1920 to Poland, where she served as president of the Union of Ukrainian Emigrant Women in Poland (1927–39). From 1944 she lived in Germany, and from 1954, in the United States. Her memoirs, *Na hrani dvokh epokh* (Between Two Epochs, 1972), deal with events prior to 1920.

Livytska-Kholodna, Natalia [Livyc'ka-Xolodna, Natalja], b 1902 in the Poltava region. Poet; daughter of A. *Livytsky. She was active in Ukrainian women's organizations and coedited the journal *Zhinka*. A displaced person after the Second World War, she eventually settled in the United States. Her poetry appeared in various journals – *Literaturno-naukovyi vistnyk*, *Vistnyk*, *My*, and others – and was published in several collections, including *Vohon' i popil* (Fire and Ashes, 1934) and *Sim liter* (Seven Letters, 1937). She wrote a biography of T. Shevchenko for young readers, *Shliakh veletnia* (A Giant's Path, 1955). She has also translated from French and Italian into Ukrainian.

Andrii Livytsky   Mykola Livytsky

Livytsky, Andrii [Livyc'kyj, Andrij], b 9 April 1879 in Lypliava, Zolotonosha county, Poltava gubernia, d 17 January 1954 in Karlsruhe, Germany. Jurist and civic and political leader. After graduating from Galagan College in Kiev and the law faculty of Kiev University he worked as a lawyer and civic judge. He was active in the Ukrainian movement as president of the student hromada in Kiev, and in 1901 he joined the *Revolutionary Ukrainian party and became president of its Lubni branch. He was arrested in 1905 for his political activities and tried as the chief instigator of the so-called Lubni Republic and Civil Self-Defense, which opposed Jewish pogroms. From 1905 to 1920 Livytsky was a leading member of the Ukrainian Social Democratic Workers' party. In 1917–18 he sat on the Central Rada and the Central Committee of the Peasant Association, served as the UNR commissioner of Zolotonosha county and then of Poltava gubernia, and belonged to the Ukrainian National Union, which prepared the uprising against the Hetman government (November 1918). Under the UNR Directory he chaired the commission for convening the Labor Congress, which he attended. In April 1919 he was appointed minister of justice and deputy prime minister of the UNR government, and in August he was also appointed director of the Ministry of Foreign Affairs. In October 1919, as head of the diplomatic mission in Poland, he was given the difficult assignment of forging an alliance against Soviet Russia. His negotiations in Warsaw culminated in the Treaty of *Warsaw.

One year later Livytsky became head of the UNR government and went with it into exile in Tarnów, Poland. At the end of 1921, after the tragic outcome of the Second Winter Campaign, he persuaded his colleagues to set up the *Government-in-exile of the UNR. While living in Warsaw he collaborated with S. Petliura, the leader of the Directory, in managing the government's diplomatic, political, and military affairs. After Petliura's death in 1926, Livytsky succeeded him as vice-president of the Directory and chief otaman of the UNR Armed Forces and thenceforth headed the government-in-exile. During the Second World War he was confined to Warsaw by the Germans. On his express instructions V. Prokopovych (and the head of the government, O. Shulhyn) in Paris assumed the temporary presidency of the Directory and declared the UNR government's support of France, Britain, and Poland against Germany. In 1945 Livytsky reactivated the UNR government-in-exile and invited representatives of the new emigration to join it. In 1946 he instructed I. Mazepa to unite all political parties around the state center of the UNR, and that union eventually resulted in the organization of the Ukrainian National Council (1948). At the first session of the council Livytsky was elected president of the UNR government-in-exile for life. In 1965 his remains were transferred to the Ukrainian cemetery in South Bound Brook, New Jersey.

K. Pankivsky

Livytsky, Mykola [Livyc'kyj] (pseud: V. Tkach), b 9 January 1907 in Zhmerynka, Vinnytsia county, Podilia gubernia, d 8 December 1989 in Philadelphia. Political leader and journalist; son of A. *Livytsky. He studied in Prague, Warsaw, and Geneva and in 1925–7 headed the Ukrainian Students' Hromada in Warsaw. In 1932–9 he served as the representative of the *Government-in-exile of the UNR in Geneva, and in 1945–6 he helped establish the *Ukrainian National State Union (which he headed in 1950–67). In 1949 he became a member of the executive of the Ukrainian National Council, and in 1957 became its head as well as director of foreign affairs. He was elected president of the Government-in-exile of the UNR in 1967 at the 6th session of the Ukrainian National Council. In 1984 he moved to Philadelphia. Livytsky published many articles and publicistic works for a wide range of Ukrainian periodicals and publicistic brochures; a number of them are compiled in *Vidnosyny Zakhid-Skhid i problemy ponevolenykh Moskvoiu narodiv* (East-West Relations and the Problems of Nations Enslaved by Moscow, 1975).

Lizards (Lacertidae; Ukrainian: *yashchirky*). A family of the suborder Sauria of the order Squamata, class Reptilia, representing a large group of scaly reptiles found throughout the world in tropical and temperate zones; its genus *Lacerta* includes most of the species of European lizards. Lizards are multicolored and blend with their surroundings. Most feed on insects and small invertebrates, some eat snails and crabs, and others are vegetarians. Lizard eggs, enclosed in a soft, leathery shell, are laid under rocks, in crevices, or in the sand. In Ukraine the green lizard (*L. viridis*) lives in the steppe on the right bank of the Dnieper River. The fast lizard (*L. agilis*) is found all over Ukraine. The viviparous lizard (*L. vivipara*) inhabits areas of Polisia, the northwestern forest-steppe, and the Carpathian Mountains. The Crimean lizard (*L. taurica*) lives along the shores of the Black Sea. The cliff lizard (*L. saxicola*) is also a Crimean native. The blindworm (*Anguis fragilis*; Ukrainian: *veretinnytsia*) has an apodal body and is found throughout Ukraine, with the exception of the Crimea and some steppe regions. The rare scheltopusik (*Ophisaurus apodus*; Ukrainian: *zhovtobriukh*; Russian: *zheltopuzik*), a reddish brown, legless lizard up to 1.5 m long, can be found in the dense vegetation of the Crimea and the Caucasus Mountains. The sand lizard (*Eremias arquata*) inhabits semidesert, arid steppe, and forest-steppe areas. Other species include the Crimean gymnogecko (*Gymnodactylus kotshyi*), the multicolored chameleon (*Chameleon deremensis*), the steppe lizard (*Agama sanguinolenta*), and the short-tail lizard (*Trachysaurus rugosus*).

I. Masnyk

Loanwords. See *Anglicisms, *Gallicisms, *Germanisms, *Hellenisms, *Hungarian loanwords, *Iranianisms, *Latinisms, *Polonisms, *Rumanianisms, *Russian-Ukrainian linguistic relations, *Slovak-Ukrainian linguistic relations, and *Turkisms.

Lobachevsky, Nikolai [Lobačevskij, Nikolaj], b 1 December 1772 in Nizhnii Novgorod (now Gorkii), Russia, d 24 February 1865 in Kazan, Russia. Russian mathematician of Ukrainian ancestry. He studied at the university in Kazan (1807–11), where in 1814 he became adjunct professor, in 1822 full professor, and in 1827–46 rector. He and J. Bolyai independently founded non-Euclidean geometry (published 1829 and 1831, respectively). Lobachevskian geometry was based on the same fundamental premises as Euclidean, except for the parallel postulate. Lobachevsky's parallel postulate is as follows: through a point not on a given line, there pass at least two lines lying in the same plane and not intersecting the line. This replacement of Euclid's parallel postulate heralded a new era in the development of geometry and mathematics in general.

Lobach-Zhuchenko, Boris [Lobač-Žučenko], b 16 November 1899 in St Petersburg. The foremost authority on M. *Vovchok (his grandmother). He is the author of a chronicle of her life and works (1969; 2nd edn 1983), a book about Vovchok in the Caucasus (1976) based on family archives, a biography of Vovchok (1979), and a collection of reminiscences and information about her (1987).

He has also coedited editions of Vovchok's letters (2 vols, 1984) and letters to her (2 vols, 1979) and compiled (with L. Ilnytska) a bibliography pertaining to Vovchok and her contemporaries (1983).

Danylo Lobai

Andrii Loboda

Lobai, Danylo [Lobaj](Lobay), b 30 December 1893 in Ulvivky, Sokal county, Galicia, d 27 December 1966 in Toronto. Journalist and community leader. Lobai was active in Sich and Prosvita societies in his native village. He emigrated to Canada in 1913 and joined the *Federation of Ukrainian Social Democrats in Winnipeg. Coeditor of *Robochyi narod* (1914–18) and its successor, *Ukraïns'ki robitnychi visti* (1919–35), Lobai was a founder and stalwart lieutenant of the *Ukrainian Labour-Farmer Temple Association (ULFTA) as well as a member of the *Communist Party of Canada (CPC). In August 1935, disturbed by the Great Famine and purges in Soviet Ukraine, the growing domination of the ULFTA by the CPC, and the disappearance of two former ULFTA members (M. *Irchan and I. Sembai) who had returned to the USSR, Lobai left the ULFTA with a group of disenchanted followers. He then founded the League of Ukrainian Organizations (renamed *Ukrainian Workers' League [UWL] in 1940) and edited its papers *Pravda* (1936–8) and *Vpered* (1938–40). He became president of the UWL (1940–66), a founding member of the Ukrainian Canadian Committee (now Congress) and a member of its presidium, and an active member of the Ukrainian National Home in Winnipeg. From 1948 until 1965 he was coeditor of *Ukrains'kyi holos* in Winnipeg. Lobai was the author of *Za diisne vyiasnennia polozhennia na Radians'kii Ukraïni* (For a Truthful Clarification of the State of Affairs in Soviet Ukraine, 1935) and *Neperemozhna Ukraïna* (Unconquerable Ukraine, 1950). His account of the relationship between the ULFTA and the CPC as well as of the events leading to his break with the former was published in the 1949 *Propam'iatna knyha* (Memorial Book) of the Winnipeg Ukrainian National Home.

B. Krawchenko

Lobanov-Rostovsky, Yakov [Lobanov-Rostovskij, Jakov], 1760–1831. Russian prince. He was the governor-general of Left-Bank Ukraine in 1808–16. In 1812 he directed the organization of 17 Little Russian regiments for the war against Napoleon. He promised to reward the participants by restoring their former Cossack privileges. His promise was not kept, and the soldiers were again enserfed after the war. His severe policy of Russian cen-

tralism provoked open dissatisfaction among the Ukrainian nobility.

Lobay, Mary [Lobaj, Marija], b 24 June 1920 in Wasel, Alberta. Educator and community leader; sister of W. Hawrelak. A graduate of the University of Alberta (M ED, 1966), she worked as a teacher and administrator in the Edmonton public school system for many years. She sat in the senate of the University of Alberta (1978–84, 1986–) and on its board of governors (1986–). She was the founding president of the Friends of the Ukrainian Heritage Cultural Village and a member of the Canadian Multiculturalism Council (1985–8). In 1988 she was appointed a member of the Order of Canada.

Lobchuk, William (Lobčuk), b 20 December 1942 in Neepawa, Manitoba. Printmaker. After graduating from the University of Manitoba (1966) he opened the first silkscreen printing shop in Winnipeg, which became a meeting place for artists. Lobchuk has been active in the Manitoba Arts Council and the Canadian National Committee of the International Association of Art, and a board member of the Ukrainian Cultural and Educational Centre, which runs the Oseredok Art Gallery in Winnipeg. Most of his serigraphs depict the Canadian prairie and convey the flatness of the land and the majesty of the sky through horizontal composition and intense hues. Lobchuk uses photosensitive block-out film, thereby combining the photographic richness of texture with the flat hard-edge areas of color and line (eg, *Sunflower Sunset* and *Moo One*).

Loboda, Andrii, b 26 June 1871 in Švenčonys, Lithuania, d 1 January 1931 in Kiev. Folklorist, literary scholar, and pedagogue; full member of the Shevchenko Scientific Society, and the VUAN (now ANU) from 1922, corresponding member of the USSR Academy of Sciences from 1924, and honorary member of the Leningrad Ethnographic Society from 1925. After graduating from Kiev University (1894) he taught there and at St Olha's Women's Institute in Kiev. He edited the university's journal and was secretary of the Faculty of History and Philology. He was the first professor to offer a course in 19th-century Ukrainian literature at Kiev University. After 1919 he served as vice-president and administrative head of the VUAN, head of the ethnographic section of the Ukrainian Scientific Society in Kiev (1920–1), director of the VUAN Ethnographic Commission (1921–30) and Regional Studies Commission (from 1923), and editor of *Etnohrafichnyi visnyk* (1925–31), *Biuleten' Etnohrafichnoï komisiï* (1926–30), various collections such as *Materialy do vyvchennia vyrobnychykh ob'iednan'* (Materials for the Study of Manufacturing Associations, 1929–31), and O. Andriievsky's bibliography of Ukrainian folklore (1930). His earliest books dealt with the *bylyny* (1895, 1896, 1904). Then he wrote several reference works on the Russian oral tradition (four editions, 1909–14) and on 18th-century Russian literature.

Altogether he published nearly 100 scholarly works and edited many folklore collections. He was a proponent of the comparative historical method in folklore studies. In the late 1920s he emphasized the need to collect and to study 'contemporary' folklore without corrupting it. In *Etnohrafichnyi visnyk* (1925) he published a programmatic article on the current state and tasks of Ukrainian ethnography.

M. Mushynka

Loboda, Hryhorii, b ? in the Kiev region, d May 1596. Hetman of the registered Cossacks (1593–6, with interruptions). In 1594 and 1595 he and S. *Nalyvaiko took part in the anti-Turkish campaign in Moldavia as allies of Rudolf II. During the Cossack rebellion of 1596 Loboda and Nalyvaiko raided Kiev voivodeship and Belarus. Loboda was assassinated by Nalyvaiko's supporters during the Battle of Solonytsia for attempting to come to terms with the Poles.

Loboda, Liudmyla (née Topolina), b 11 November 1945 in Magnitogorsk, Russia. Painter and graphic artist; wife and student of Volodymyr *Loboda. She moved to Dnipropetrovske in 1958 and graduated from the Dnipropetrovske Institute of Civil Engineering in 1969. Her works include landscapes, figural compositions, nudes, and portraits of Ukrainian writers and artists. She works in a figurative manner combining an expressionistic brush stroke with dark energetic lines and a subdued, clear palette (eg, *Church in Boryslav* and *Land Washed by Rain* [1987]). She has produced many series of linocuts inspired by the writings of T. Shevchenko, N. Gogol, A. Pushkin, E.A. Poe, and other writers; depicted well-known figures, such as L. Kurbas, B.I. Antonych, A. Archipenko, and V. Stus; and illustrated several children's books.

Liudmyla Loboda: *Family* (oil, 1985)

Loboda, Viktor, b 1823, d after 1876. Political activist and writer. After graduating from a civil engineering course in St Petersburg, he worked in the civil service in Ukraine and Russia and was a member of the Poltava Hromada. In 1862 he was arrested for participating in political circles with 'an extreme Little Russian tendency' (in fact, for advocating political independence for Ukraine) and exiled to Perm gubernia. In 1868 he was released without the right to return to Ukraine. He wrote literary works, publicistic articles, and recollections of T. Shevchenko in *Kievskaia starina*.

Volodymyr Loboda: *Prickly Conversation* (oil, 1988)

Loboda, Volodymyr, b 6 July 1943 in Dnipropetrovske. Painter and graphic artist; husband of L. *Loboda. A graduate of the Dnipropetrovske Institute of Civil Engineering (1971), he has worked as a visual artist. His expressionist manner conveys an atmosphere of impulsive energy and turmoil through slashing lines, dark outlines, and bright colors (eg, *Men and Women: Dialogue* [1983] and *Waiting* [1987]), and his emotionally charged linocuts echo the expressive qualities of his paintings. Loboda works in series, some of which commemorate events, such as the 1922–3 famine and the millennium of Christianity in Ukraine, and some of which commemorate people, including his favorite poet, T. Shevchenko, and artists, such as F. de Goya, P. Picasso, D. Velázquez, and Rembrandt (the 360-print series 'Great Wandering in Ukraine' [1986]). Loboda is not a member of the Union of Artists of Ukraine and has been an outspoken critic of the restrictions placed on artists by *socialist realism. He has striven to create an art synthesizing Ukrainian artistic traditions and the achievements of world art. Since moving to Lviv in 1982, he has influenced the work of several younger artists there (eg, P. and A. Humeniuk).

Łobodowski, Józef, b 19 March 1909, d 18 April 1988 in Madrid. Polish poet, literary critic, and translator. Before the Second World War he published a few collections of engagé poetry in Poland. From 1945 he lived in Spain, where he published over a dozen more collections. He continued the tradition of the *Ukrainian school in Polish literature and wrote many poems on Ukrainian themes; they are included in *Rozmova z Ojczyzną* (Conversation with the Fatherland, 1936), *Złota gramota* (The Golden Charter, 1954), *Pieśń o Ukrainie* (Song about Ukraine,

1959), and other collections. From the 1930s on he also translated into Polish works by many Ukrainian writers, among them T. Shevchenko, Lesia Ukrainka, I. Bahriany, L. Mohylianska, and O. Teliha, and he wrote about those authors and Ukrainian literature in general, mostly in the Polish émigré monthly *Kultura*. His poetry has been translated into Ukrainian by S. Hordynsky, B. Kravtsiv, Ya. Slavutych, and L. Poltava.

Lobodych, Roman [Lobodyč], b 8 January 1893 in Soroky, Buchach county, Galicia, d 22 August 1969 in Philadelphia. Priest and church and civic leader. After completing his theological studies at Lviv University, he was ordained (1917) and served as chaplain in the Austrian army on the Italian front. Upon his release from a POW camp, he joined the Ukrainian Galician Army as chaplain. After the war he worked in various parishes before being appointed canon and vicar of the Stanyslaviv cathedral in 1930. A candidate of the Ukrainian Catholic People's party, he was elected to the Polish Senate in 1935. Three years later he was appointed canon of the metropolitan's chapter and vicar of St George's Cathedral. During the Second World War he served as chaplain of the Division Galizien (1943–5), and in 1947, he emigrated to the United States, where he organized a parish in Los Angeles. He also served as the first rector of the Ukrainian seminary in Washington, DC, chaplain of the Basilian orphanage in Philadelphia, and president (1957–9) of the Providence Association of Ukrainian Catholics in America.

Lobysevych, Opanas [Lobysevyč], b 1732 in Pohar, Starodub regiment, d 1805. Writer; pioneer of the Ukrainian national renaissance. He studied at the Kievan Mohyla Academy (1747–52) and then at the university at the St Petersburg Academy of Sciences (1754–60). Later, in Novhorod-Siverskyi, he became county (1783) and gubernial (1785–7) marshal of the nobility and one of the leading members of the Novhorod-Siverskyi group of patriots (1780–90). Lobysevych is the author of *Vergilievikh pastukhov...v malorossiiskii kobeniak pereodetykh* (1794), a Ukrainian adaptation of Virgil's *Bucolics*. The work was lost. His Russian translations from Latin and French were published in the journals *Trudoliubivaia pchela* (1759) and *Baryshek vsiakiia vsiachini* (1770).

Local government. See Municipal government, County, and Gubernia.

Local industry. In the Soviet economy, a group of enterprises producing mostly consumer goods and subordinated to the Ministry of Local Industry and to oblast and raion soviets. Local industry utilizes mainly local raw materials and dicarded materials and, besides regular workers, employs retired, disabled, and seasonally unemployed help. By employing resources that would have remained unused, local industry helps to raise the standard of living. It accounts for a substantial share of the consumer-goods output. Taxes paid by local industry provide most of the revenue for local government; thus, the industry serves as the basis of local autonomy and initiative.

The administrative subordination of local industry changed several times in the Soviet period. In 1927, when raions were introduced, and the powers of local soviets were determined, enterprises using local raw materials and selling their output on local markets were classified as local industry. Some of the enterprises were quite large. In 1927 local industry accounted for 30 percent of producer-goods output. During the First Five-Year Plan investment in local industry was controlled from Moscow, and starting in 1933 the industry's output was included in the central planning. Such a system restricted local initiative. A Ukrainian People's Commissariat of Local Industry (est 1934) assumed supervision over medium and large enterprises, which had been under the jurisdiction of local soviets. This part of industry became known as the narrower local industry. The smaller enterprises, called the broader local industry, continued to be overseen by local soviets. In 1936 the broader local industry produced slightly over one-third of Ukraine's industrial output, including almost all shoes, knitwear, clothes, lignite, peat, china, printed matter, furniture, and paper, 81 percent of metal consumer goods, 76 percent of electric power, and almost 70 percent of canned goods and beer. It employed 47 percent of the work force. The narrower local industry produced 10.9 percent of the industrial output and employed 8.3 percent of the work force. In the late 1930s several larger enterprises were transferred to newly created industrial secretariats, and in 1939 all small enterprises, which had been under raion jurisdiction, were brought under the Secretariat of Local Industry. Centralization hampered the efficient use of local resources and lowered the standard of living.

In 1957 the Ministry of Local Industry, along with most of the industrial ministries, was abolished. Its larger enterprises were placed under *regional economic councils (sovnarkhozy)*, and the rest were returned to the jurisdiction of local soviets. The term 'local industry' was restricted to the latter, which in 1959 produced 12.8 percent of all producer goods and 33 percent of all consumer goods. In 1960 this group of enterprises accounted for 24.8 percent of the output of Ukraine's light industry, 22.6 percent of its food-industry output, 21.5 percent of its woodworking-industry output, 95 percent of the washing machines produced, and 96 percent of the children's bicycles produced. The recentralization of local industry began with the subordination of all its enterprises to the *sovnarkhozy* in 1963 and culminated in the resurrection of the Ministry of Local Industry in 1965.

Since then production has tended to become more and more concentrated: the number of enterprises under ministry supervision decreased from 912 in 1965 to 388 and 4 republican production associations in 1985. The enterprises, including 43 production associations, subordinated to local soviets, increased their total output by a factor of 2.3 from 1970 to 1984. Republican associations subordinated to the Ministry of Local Industry increased their output as follows: the peat industry by a factor of 2.3, the musical instruments industry by a factor of 1.8, the handicrafts industry by a factor of 2, and the mechanical equipment industry by a factor of 1.3. The productive potential of local industry has grown. In the early 1980s a number of new enterprises were set up: a folk-instruments factory in Lviv, a consumer-metal products factory in Rivne, a drafting equipment plant in Odessa, a research and development enterprise in Kirovohrad, and a folk-handicrafts plant in Pryluka. The industry's fixed assets, however, are inadequate and largely obsolete. About 30 percent of its equipment has to be replaced. In the production of musical instruments 50 percent of the equipment must be replaced. Consumer goods, amounting to over 10,000 separate items, account for three-quarters of the industry's total output. Many products that previously came under other industrial ministries are now produced by the local industry. The output of chemical, petrochemical, plastic, and polymer products increased by five times from 1966 to 1984. The local industry makes stainless steel products, steel enameled products, electroplated items, children's bicycles and carriages, sleds, skates, locks, and other metal products. Wood products of the local industry, such as furniture, school and office equipment, wagons, wheels, and barrels, increased by a factor of six in the last two decades. Most important among the industry's products are light-industry goods, such as clothes, textiles, footwear, and leather items. Their output increased by eight times from 1966 to 1984.

The artistic-handicrafts industry consists of 5 production associations and 22 enterprises. Its output includes wood carvings, kilims and decorative weavings, embroidery, and ceramics. In 1985 its annual output was valued at 225 million rubles. The musical instruments industry is organized in an industrial association of 11 enterprises.

BIBLIOGRAPHY
Verba, P. *Mistseva promyslovist' ta dzherela ïi rozvytku* (Kharkiv 1959)
Bohaienko, V. *Rezervy zbil'shennia vyrobnytstva tovariv narodnoho spozhyvannia v mistsevii promyslovosti* (Kiev 1960)
V. Holubnychy, I. Koropeckyj

Locomotive industry. A branch of the machine-building industry specializing in locomotive engines. The first locomotive works in Ukraine were established in Kharkiv in 1895 and Luhanske in 1896. In 1901 those factories became part of a Russian syndicate called the Locomotive Union. By 1912 the Kharkiv factory had built 1,846 engines, and in 11 years (1900–11) the Luhanske factory built about 1,500. In 1913 Ukraine's output was 189 locomotives, or 40 percent of the Russian Empire's output. After the revolution of 1917 the locomotive industry in Ukraine continued to grow, and the traditional centers of Kharkiv and Luhanske expanded greatly. By 1940 Ukraine was producing 672 locomotives per year, or 73.5 percent of USSR's output. During the Second World War the industry was completely ruined, and it did not achieve its prewar level until 1954. By 1957 the conversion from steam to diesel and electric locomotive production was complete. Output of diesel locomotives peaked in 1967, when 1,439 units were produced. In 1983 Ukraine produced 1,306 locomotives. Ukraine has continued to specialize in locomotive production; it increased its share of Soviet production in 1983 to 95 percent. The major locomotive works are the *Luhanske Diesel Locomotive Building Consortium and the Kharkiv Transport Machine-Building Plant.

Lodii, Petro [Lodij], b 15 May 1764 in Zboi, in the Prešov region, d 22 June 1829 in St Petersburg. Philosopher, jurist, and educator. After studying philosophy in Nagyvárad (now Oradea, Rumania) and theology in Uzhhorod and Lviv, he taught philosophy, mathematics, and law at the *Studium Ruthenum in Lviv (1787–1802), served as dean of its philosophy faculty (1797), taught at Cracow University (1803), and held the chair of philosophy and law at the

Petro Lodii

St Petersburg Pedagogical Institute (1804–19) and its offspring, St Petersburg University (1819–29). He also lectured at other higher schools in St Petersburg and was principal of the St Petersburg Commercial School (1819–25) and dean of the university's philosophy and law faculty (1819–25). Lodii's translation of a part of C. Baumeister's *Elementa Philosophiae* dealing with practical philosophy (1790) is important for the development of Ukrainian philosophical terminology. Lodii wrote one of the best Russian logic textbooks of his time (1815); it provides an introduction not only to logic but to philosophy in general and is one of the first attempts in the Russian Empire to refute I. Kant's system. Embracing deism in theology and realism in epistemology, Lodii followed C. Wolff on most philosophical issues. His contribution to practical philosophy consists of *Teoriia obshchikh prav* (A Theory of Universal Laws, 1828).

Lodomeria. The Latin name of Volodymyr-Volynskyi principality, as in *Regnum Galiciae et Lodomeriae*. It appeared in the title of Andrew II of Hungary (*Galiciae Lodomeriaeque rex*) starting in 1206 and in the title of the Austrian emperors after Austria's annexation of Galicia in 1772. In the manifesto of 18 September 1772 Maria Theresa justified the annexation of Galicia on the ground that Lodomeria was a former possession of Hungary.

Loeffler, Charles, b 30 January 1861 in Mulhouse, Alsace, d 19 May 1935 in Medfield, Massachusetts. American composer and violinist of French birth. As a young child he lived in the town of Smila, near Cherkasy, before moving to Hungary, Switzerland, France, and then the United States. An impressionistic cosmopolitan, he drew his inspiration from many sources. His *Les Veilles de l'Ukraine* (1891), based on Gogol's *Evenings on a Farm near Dykanka*, is a suite of four movements for violin and orchestra. It was first performed in Boston on 20 November 1891 with the composer as soloist and the Boston Symphony Orchestra conducted by A. Nikisch. One of his orchestral poems, *Memories of My Childhood* (1923), reflects the modal feelings of Ukrainian songs and dances.

Loess. Deposits of unstratified fine-grained, pale buff yellow mineral particles. The particles in loess consist mostly of silt (up to 60 percent; particles 0.05 to 0.005 mm in diameter), although some clay (10–20 percent; particles less than 0.005 mm) and fine sand (up to 7 percent; particles 0.1 to 0.25 mm) are also present. The minerals that make up the particles are mostly quartz, followed by feldspar, mica, kaolinite, and montmorillonite. The soils that form on loess tend to be neither too wet nor too dry, and the chemical properties of loess provide the soil with high levels of fertility. Loess covers nearly three-quarters of the surface territory of Ukraine. It is found at various elevations, including uplands, slopes, plains, and valley terraces. Only the mountains, the glaciated lacustrine plains of Polisia, and the floodplains of major river valleys are devoid of loess. The thickness of loess in Ukraine ranges from several tens of centimeters to 40 to 50 meters (near Dnipropetrovske); the most common thickness is 5 to 10 meters (as in the Podolian Upland and the Azov Upland).

Loev (Ukrainian: Loiv [Lojiv]). II-11. A town smt (1972 pop 5,000) and raion center in Homel oblast, Belarus. It is situated on the Ukrainian-Belarus border near the confluence of the Sozh and the Dnieper rivers. In 1649 a Lithuanian-Polish army led by Prince J. Radziwiłł defeated Col M. Krychevsky's Cossack forces near the town.

Logic. A branch of *philosophy dealing with the forms of valid reasoning. Formal logic, which was first systematized by Aristotle, deals with the nature of concepts, propositions, and syllogistic arguments. Mathematical or symbolic logic, which is a formal logic more powerful than the traditional Aristotelian logic, was developed in the 19th century. Dialectical logic is the branch of dialectical materialism dealing with the categories and the three laws of thought.

In Ukraine the earliest knowledge about logic was derived from Slavonic translations of Byzantine sources. The *Izbornik* of Sviatoslav (1073) contains St Maximus the Confessor's and Theodore of Rhaithu's discussion of concepts, definitions, and categories based on Aristotle's *Organon* and Porphyry's *Isagoge*. A late 13th- to early 14th-century Slavonic translation of St John of Damascus's *Dialectica* reached Rus' in the first half of the 15th century. Toward the end of the 15th century two important additions were made to the literature on logic: *Lohika Aviasafa* (Aviasaf's Logic, 1483), a compilation based on al-Ghazali's *Aims of the Philosophers*, and *Knyha, hlaholemaia lohika* (The Book Called Logic), a compilation based on M. Maimonides' *Logical Terms*. Both of these works were translated most probably in Kiev and were based on Hebrew, not Byzantine, sources. Their treatment of logic was much fuller than that in the *Izbornik* and *Dialectica*: it covered not only concepts, definitions, and categories, but also propositions, inferences, and syllogisms. Instead of adopting the Church Slavonic technical vocabulary of the earlier works, they introduced a terminology based on the Ukrainian vernacular.

With the introduction of European forms of higher education in the 17th century, logic became an important and permanent part of the curriculum. At the Kievan Mohyla Academy one year of the three-year philosophy program was devoted to logic, which was valued primarily for its usefulness in rhetoric. The short introductory course, called dialectic or minor logic, was taught often at the end of the rhetoric course. The full course, called major logic, discussed the nature of terms, categories, predicables, universals, propositions, inference, and syllogisms, as well as the concept of science and logic. Although the courses differed from each other because each lecturer prepared his own course, they were patterned more or less on Peter of Spain's textbook. The core of Aristotle's

logic was supplemented with new ideas and techniques worked out by scholastic and neoscholastic thinkers. Occasionally the Kievan professors raised objections to Aristotle and offered their own solutions to problems. Over 30 logic manuals prepared in Kiev have survived, including the courses of Y. Kononovych-Horbatsky (1639–40), I. Gizel (1645–6), S. Yavorsky (1691), Y. Turoboisky (1702), T. Prokopovych (1708), Y. Volchansky (1717), S. Kalynovsky (1729), M. Kozachynsky (1743), H. Konysky (1749), and H. Shcherbatsky (1751). Only a few of them have been translated, wholly or partly, from Latin into Ukrainian. Ya. Kozelsky, a graduate of the academy, devoted a section of his *Filosoficheskie predlozheniia ...* (Philosophical Propositions ..., 1768) to logic. In the mid-18th century Wolffian philosophy was adopted by the academy, and C. Baumeister's logic textbook became the basic source for its courses in logic. The Wolffian tradition was continued into the 19th century by P. Lodii, whose *Logicheskie nastavleniia ...* (Logical Principles ..., 1815) was the best textbook in the Russian Empire at the time.

In the 19th century, logic studies were strongly emphasized at Kharkiv University. Its first rector, I. Rizhsky, had taught logic in Moscow and had written a textbook (1790) based on C. Baumeister. T. Mochulsky (1811), L. Jacob (1811, 1815), I. Liubachynsky (1817), and P. Liubovsky prepared logic textbooks in Russian; J. Schad explored the nature of formal logic in contrast to transcendental logic in his *Institutiones philosophiae universae ...* (1812). The mathematics professor T. Osipovsky translated E.B. de Condillac's (1805) *La Logique* into Russian. At Kiev University O. Novytsky published a large textbook on logic and scientific methodology (1841) and a short version of it (1846, 1848). A section of the third volume of S. Hohotsky's philosophical lexicon (1866) was devoted to logic. In Odessa O. Mykhnevych wrote an elementary logic textbook for the students of the Richelieu Lyceum (1848; 2nd edn 1874). Toward the end of the 19th century Odessa University became a leading center of logic studies. There N. Lange wrote a textbook (1891; repr 1894, 1898, 1903, 1910) that was accepted as the standard in the field. His colleagues I. Sleshynsky (1893), Ye. Bunytsky (1896), and S. Shatunovsky (1917) followed the development of mathematical logic in the West and made their own contributions to it. P. Poretsky, a graduate of Kharkiv University and professor of astronomy at Kazan University, made some important discoveries in mathematical logic (1881, 1884, 1902). The leading logicians at Kiev University were F. Kozlovsky, whose logic textbook went through 4 editions (1894–1907), and G. Chelpanov, whose textbook went through 10 editions (1906–18). At Kharkiv University F. Leikfeld worked on the nature of hypothetical judgment (1906), and S. Glagolev pointed out the shortcomings of traditional syllogistic logic (1907, 1910).

In the Soviet period formal logic continued to be taught according to pre-Soviet textbooks written by G. Chelpanov (repr 1918, 1924) and N. Lange (repr 1918). Research in mathematical logic was continued at Odessa and Kharkiv universities, but the attention of philosophers was concentrated increasingly upon dialectical logic. To define the place of the dialectic in the general system of knowledge, Marxist thinkers had to show how it was related to traditional (formal) logic. For over a decade this relation was the main subject of discussion. V. Asmus in his book on dialectical materialism and logic (1924) and O.

Bervytsky in his book on logic and dialectic (1929) conceded that formal logic, being static and discrete, cannot reflect, as dialectical logic does, constantly changing and interconnected reality, and yet they defended the usefulness of formal logic for systematizing knowledge and even for expanding it.

By the early 1930s opinion had turned against this conciliatory position: if formal logic did not correspond to reality, then it was false and could not be useful. This conclusion was stated clearly in a collection of articles published in Kharkiv on dialectical materialism (1932). Mathematical logic was associated with formal logic and denounced as mechanistic (V. Yurynets), abstract, and useless (Ya. Kaufman). As these logics were dismissed from the schools and research institutes, the development of dialectical logic was encouraged. Following V. Lenin's instructions, published in his *Philosophical Notebooks* (1929), to work out a materialist interpretation of G. Hegel's dialectic and give a materialist treatment of the categories, philosophers such as O. Bervytsky, T. Stepovy, O. Vasileva, Ya. Bludov, R. Levik, N. Milhevsky, and S. Semkovsky wrote many articles on Hegel's logic, and P. Demchuk, T. Stepovy, V. Hadzinsky, and V. Boiko analyzed various logical categories.

After the Second World War the discussion of the relationship between formal and dialectical logic was reopened by the 1946 CC CPSU decision to reintroduce formal logic into the educational program. Old Russian textbooks by G. Chelpanov (1945, 1946) and S. Vinogradov and A. Kuzmin (1949, 1952, 1953, 1954) were republished (sometimes in translation), and new ones were prepared by V. Asmus (1947, 1954) and M. Strogovich (1949). Some of them were translated into Ukrainian. J. Stalin's new position on language as a realm outside the economically determined superstructure gave the defenders of formal logic an additional argument in its favor. The theoretical debate over formal logic dragged on for many years, while the subject spread quickly in the schools and institutes. In Kiev one of the chief defenders of mathematical logic was V. Beliaev, a historian of Aristotelian logic. The rapid development of cybernetics and the philosophy of science in Kiev stimulated interest in mathematical logic. P. Kopnin, the director of the AN URSR (now ANU) Institute of Philosophy (1962–8), wrote a number of influential books on dialectics as logic (1961, 1973) and on logic and science (1968, 1973). His colleague M. Popovych discussed the basic methods of modern logic and its cognitive status and relation to the dialectic (1971). F. Moskalenko explored the relationship between inductive and deductive logic and wrote a history of inductive logic in the Russian Empire (1955); V. Melnikov (1959), V. Nichyk (1960), and M. Bulatov (1981) studied the nature of the categories; S. Krymsky speculated on the evolutionary emergence of logical forms and laws (1962); and M. Popovych examined the role of cultural context in the history of logic (1979). The development of logic in Ukraine has been investigated by V. Nichyk, S. Krymsky, and I. Paslavsky.

In interwar Western Ukraine the psychologist S. Balei taught logic at the Lviv (Underground) Ukrainian University and wrote an elementary textbook (1923). As a member of the Polish Lviv Philosophical Association he was acquainted with the new work done by Polish logicians in Lviv. Rev V. Maksymets taught logic at the Greek Catholic Theological Academy in Lviv (1931–9).

Outside Ukraine logic has been taught at Ukrainian postsecondary schools in interwar Prague and postwar Munich. D. Chyzhevsky wrote an outline (1924) of his logic course at the Ukrainian Higher Pedagogical Institute in Prague.

BIBLIOGRAPHY
Nichyk, V. 'Lohika,' in *Rozvytok filosofiï v Ukraïns'kii RSR*, ed V. Ievdokymenko et al (Kiev 1968)
Paslavs'kyi, I. 'Rozvytok lohichnykh idei u vitchyznianii filosofiï druhoï polovyny XV st.,' *Filosofs'ka dumka*, 1986, no. 6
T. Zakydalsky

Ruslan Logush: *Celestial Composition '82* (silk screen)

Logush, Ruslan [Loguš], b 4 June 1950 in Montreal. Canadian silk-screen artist of Ukrainian origin. A graduate of Sir George Williams University in Montreal, he has worked independently in Studio Graphia, a group of 10 Canadian artists. Solo exhibitions of his works have been held in Minneapolis (1973), Winnipeg (1973), Toronto (1974), and Montreal (1976). He has also taken part in various group shows, among them Salon International de l'Art Libre in Paris (1972, honorable mention), the International Print Biennale in Cracow (1974), the Olympic Exhibition in Montreal (1976), and the Ukrainian Artists International Exhibition in Toronto (1982). In works such as *Celestial Composition '82'* or *St. Luke Chapter 27:11* he has tried to express cosmogony through geometric forms suggesting planets in their orbits, subordinated to the divine laws of cosmic motion.

Lohos

Lohos (Logos). A scholarly quarterly concerned with theological and philosophical questions and with Ukrainian church history. It was founded by Rev M. *Hermaniuk in Waterford, Ontario, in 1950 and published by the Redemptorist Fathers in Yorkton, Saskatchewan, until 1983. The quarterly was edited by Revs Hermaniuk (1950–1), V. Malanchuk (1951–61), M. Hrynchyshyn (1961–6), and S. Shawel (1966–83). Circulation fell from 1,000 during the 1950s to 150 in 1983.

Hryhorii Lohvyn   Mykhailo Lomatsky

Lohvyn, Hryhorii, b 22 May 1910 in Kosivka, Oleksandriia county, Kherson gubernia. Ukrainian art scholar. A graduate of the Kharkiv (1934) and Moscow (1941) art institutes, he obtained a doctorate in 1968. Lovhyn has written extensively on the medieval, Renaissance, and baroque architecture, painting, sculpture, book miniatures, and decorative art of Ukraine. He has published, in Russian, books on the architectural monuments of Kiev (1960, 1967, 1982), 10th- to 18th-century Ukrainian art (1963), and the architectural monuments of Chernihiv, Novhorod-Siverskyi, Hlukhiv, and Putyvl (1965, 1980) and a guidebook to the artistic monuments of Ukraine and Moldavia (1982). His best-known Ukrainian work is *Po Ukraïni* (Through Ukraine, 1968), a book on Ukraine's old artistic monuments. Some of his works have been translated into English, namely *Kiev's Hagia Sophia* (1971) and *Into the Deep Past: Miniatures and Ornaments in Old Manuscripts of the 11th–18th Centuries* (1977). More recently he published a monograph in Ukrainian on engravings in 16th- to 18th-century Ukrainian books (1990). Lohvyn also coauthored a book on Ukrainian medieval painting (1976, with L. Miliaieva and V. Svientsitska), contributed chapters to vols 2 and 3 of the AN URSR six-volume history of Ukrainian art (1967–8), and was the editor in charge of vols 3 and 4 of the four-volume guide in Russian to the monuments of urban construction and architecture in Ukraine (1985, 1986).

S. Hordynsky

Lohvyn, Yurii, b 5 February 1939 in Kremenchuk, Poltava oblast. Graphic artist and writer; son of H. Lohvyn. A graduate of the Kiev State Art Institute (1965) and the Higher Literature Courses of the Gorky Institute of Literature in Moscow, he has worked as a book illustrator and created many series of color linocuts and engravings on plastic and wood, among them 'My Forefathers,' 'The Earth and People,' and 'Ukrainian Folk Ballads.' Among

Yurii Lohvyn: *Over the Mountains* (wood engraving)

the books he has illustrated are H. Kosynka's *Sertse* (The Heart, 1967) and P. Tychyna's poem *Skovoroda* (1971). His artistic works show the influence of N. Rerikh and H. Narbut. He is the author of prose collections, such as *Pivnichne siaivo* (The Northern Lights, 1961), *Vohon' na skeli* (The Fire on the Cliff, 1965), *Daleka veselka* (The Distant Rainbow, 1970), *Znaiomyi lev: Pys'mena mynulykh dniv* (The Known Lion: Writings of Past Days, 1972), *Kolir dlia neba* (Color for the Sky, 1978), and *Zakliatyi vershnyk* (The Damned Rider, 1990), and the historical novel *Taiemnytsia odnoho diamanta* (The Secret of One Diamond, 1989).

Lohvynenko, Vitalii, b 28 January 1928 in Dycheskulove, Zinovivske (now Kirovohrad) okruha, d 1990. Writer. He began to publish in 1952. Several collections of his short stories have appeared: *Davni rany* (Old Wounds, 1961), *Suzir'ia* (Constellation, 1963), and *Biostrumy* (Biocurrents, 1970). He also published a number of novels: *Lita molodiï* (Years of Youth, 1957), *Vinchannia* (The Marriage, 1965), *Rubikon* (The Rubicon, 1966), *Vazhka voda* (Heavy Water, 1972), and *Rosava* (1975). Selections of his works were published in two volumes titled *Vybrane* (Selections, 1986). Many of his works were translated into Russian.

Lokachi [Lokači]. III-5. A town smt (1990 pop 3,600) and raion center on the Luha River in southwestern Volhynia oblast. It is first mentioned in historical documents in 1542. After the third partition of Poland in 1795, it came under Russian rule. Among its architectural monuments are an ancient chapel and a church built in 1609.

Lokhvytsia: Monument to H. Skovoroda by I. Kavaleridze (1922)

Lokhvytsia [Loxvycja]. III-14. A town (1990 pop 13,600) on the Lokhvytsia River and a raion center in Poltava oblast. It is first mentioned in historical documents in 1320. In 1628 it was granted town status, and belonged to the Vyshnevetsky family. Lokhvytsia played an important role in the Cossack and popular uprisings of the 1630s. In 1648–9 and 1658–1781 it was a a Cossack company center. In 1802–1923 Lokhvytsia was a county center in Poltava gubernia. Today it has a sewing factory and a food-processing plant. Near Lokhvytsia archeologists have found several burial sites of the *Cherniakhiv culture (2nd–5th century), a settlement of the *Romen-Borshcheve culture (8th–10th century), and a medieval fortress which belonged to Pereiaslav principality.

Lokhvytsia Sugar Refining Complex (Lokhvytskyi tsukrovyi kombinat). A refining enterprise established in 1928 in Chervonozavodske, now in Lokhvytsia raion, Poltava oblast. When the refinery went into operation in 1929, its processing capacity was 20,000 centners of sugar beets per day. In 1930 a local state farm was linked with the refinery, and a complex thereby formed. In 1979 the complex had a capacity of 93,000 centners of beets per day.

Lokhvytsky, Kindrat [Loxvyc'kyj], b 20 March 1774, d late 1830s. Mystic and amateur archeologist in Kiev. In the course of excavations he discovered in 1824 the foundations of the Church of the *Tithes, in 1832 the remains of the *Golden Gate, in 1833 the foundations of St Irene's Church dating back to the times of Yaroslav the Wise, and ruins of unidentified buildings from the Princely era. He amassed a valuable collection of coins and medals from various historical periods.

Lokota, Ivan, b 3 June 1884 in Velykyi Bychkiv, Transcarpathia, d 20 November 1942 in the USSR. Communist organizer and leader in Transcarpathia. A member of the Communist Party of Czechoslovakia from 1921, he belonged to the Party's regional committee for Transcarpathia (1924–9) and its Central Committee (1929–39). In 1929 he was elected to the Senate, but three years later he was arrested by the Czechoslovak authorities, imprisoned for subversive activity, and deprived of his seat. In 1937, before having served his full sentence, he was released because of failing health, and in 1940 he fled to the USSR.

Lomachka, Svyryd. See Oleksandriv, Borys.

Lomatsky, Mykhailo [Lomac'kyj, Myxajlo], b 23 November 1886 in Husiatyn, Galicia, d 1968 in Munich. Writer. From 1906 he worked as a village school teacher and itinerant tutor in Galicia. After being persecuted by the Polish authorities and imprisoned during the 1939–41 Soviet occupation he sought refuge following the Second World War in Germany; there he taught and helped to organize the Ukrainian Youth Association in displaced persons camps and contributed to Ukrainian émigré newspapers. Between 1956 and 1968 he published 13 books of ethnographic sketches and Romantic-historical prose about the colorful inhabitants of the Hutsul region, where he had once lived and taught.

Łomnicki, Marian, b 9 September 1845 in Bavoriv, Ternopil circle, Galicia, d 26 September 1915 in Lviv. Polish natural scientist of Ukrainian origin; full member of the Shevchenko Scientific Society from 1914. He studied at Cracow and Vienna universities (1864–8), worked in Stanyslaviv and Lviv, and became director of the Dzieduszycki Museum in Lviv (from 1905). His work included entomological, malacological, geological, and paleontological studies of Western Ukraine. He was a major contributor to the *Atlas Geologiczny Galicji* (Geological Atlas of Galicia, 1895–1902).

Lomykovsky, Ivan [Lomykovs'kyj], b ? in Volhynia, d 1714 in Iaşi, Moldavia. Cossack officer. He was general chancellor under Hetman M. Khanenko, and in the 1670s he moved to Left-Bank Ukraine, where he became a member of the Ukrainian government, as general standard-bearer (1689–91), acting hetman (1690), general osaul (1692–1707), and general quartermaster (1707–9). He strongly advocated Ukraine's break with Moscow and knew about I. Mazepa's negotiations with the Swedes. After the defeat at Poltava he emigrated with Mazepa to Bendery.

Lomykovsky, Vasyl [Lomykovs'kyj, Vasyl'], b 26 January 1777 in Meliushky, near Khorol, New Serbia gubernia, d ca 1848. Historian and ethnographer, and agronomist by profession. After retiring from military service he experimented with new agricultural methods and collected historical materials. He compiled the first collection of

Ukrainian dumas (16 in all), which was published by P. Zhytetsky in 1893, and a valuable dictionary of contemporary Ukrainian, which was published in *Kievskaia starina* and by O. Lazarevsky as a separate book in 1894. In 1809 he also translated J.-B. *Scherer's *Annales de la Petite-Russie ou Histoire des Cosaques ...* (1788) into Russian.

Lomynsky, Fedir [Lomyns'kyj], b 1 February 1856 in Kiev, d 30 November 1927 in Kiev. Histologist. A graduate of Kiev University (1882), he worked in its histology department from 1891 (from 1905 as chairman; in 1921 the department was transferred to the Kiev Medical Institute). His research centered on microbial parasitism and cytology (intracellular). He was the first to observe (1882) that nerve cells could divide (karyokinesis), and he described the phenomenon of neuronophagy (the engulfment of damaged neurons by leukocytes) in 1884. He also demonstrated the transmission of anthrax to humans and animals through grasses and other cultivars.

Bohdan Lonchyna

Lonchyna, Bohdan [Lončyna, Bohdan], b 2 January 1917 in Lviv, d 27 March 1985 in Detroit. Pedagogue, community figure, and Catholic activist. He studied Western European and Romance languages at the universities of Lviv (1935–9) and Vienna (1940–2) and during extended tours of the Continent. He worked as a student affairs officer for the Ukrainian Central Committee in 1942–4; in this position he drew upon his involvement with the Obnova Society of Ukrainian Catholic Students and the Sich student society as he headed the Labor Alliance of Ukrainian Students and edited the monthly *Students'kyi prapor*. Lonchyna subsequently emigrated to the United States, where he taught at Steubenville College in Ohio (1949–59) and the University of Detroit (1959–72). In addition he served as a dean of the Ukrainian Catholic University in Rome and organized its summer programs in 1972–84, fostered an Obnova society of Ukrainian Catholic intellectuals, and headed the Ukrainian Patriarchal Society of the United States (1979–83) and the Ukrainian Patriarchal World Federation (1982–5). His writings include a textbook on Ukrainian culture (1971) and translations into Ukrainian of *Poema de Mio Cid* (1972) and *Chanson de Roland* (1977).

London. The capital of Great Britain (1988 pop 6,735,400), situated on the Thames River in southeastern England. It has an active port and is one of the world's leading financial, trading, industrial, and cultural centers. Concerted Ukrainian presence in London begins on the eve of the First World War. In 1912–15 G. *Raffalovich (pseud Bedwin Sands), a naturalized Briton of French and Jewish (from Odessa) background, published valuable materials there about Ukrainian affairs and advocated Ukraine's independence. In 1919–23 the diplomatic missions of the Western Ukrainian National Republic (ZUNR) and UNR governments existed in London and were staffed by A. Margolin, Ya. Olesnytsky, M. Stakhovsky, M. Vishnitser, and S. Vytvytsky. In 1931–40 Ya. Makohin sponsored the Ukrainian Press Bureau there; its director was V. *Kaye-Kysilewsky until 1938–9, when it was headed by the Ukrainian Canadian S. Davidovich. In 1932–4 a hetmanite group led by V. Korostovets published a bulletin, the *Investigator*, in London. In 1933–5 Ye. Liakhovych served as the Organization of Ukrainian Nationalists' representative in the city.

During the interwar period there was a growing interest in Ukrainian issues among Britons. The *Slavonic Review*, whose contributors included M. Andrusiak, E. Borschak, D. Doroshenko, I. Mazepa, I. Mirchuk, V. Paneiko, R. Smal-Stotsky, O. Shulhyn, and A. Voloshyn, provided a forum for the discussion of Ukrainian matters.

In 1935 the Anglo-Ukrainian Committee was established, with Lord Dickinson, Lord Noel-Buxton, several MPs, and the noted historians G. Gooch and R. Seton-Watson among its members. Other Londoners who involved themselves with Ukrainian affairs included the intelligence specialist T. *Philipps, the lawyer and politician A. Lincoln, the businessman and politician C. Malone, and the publicist L. Lawton. After the war the publicist A. Herbert and a Catholic activist and editor of the weekly *Tablet*, D. Woodruff, were also sympathetic to Ukrainian concerns.

In August 1943 the Ukrainian Canadian Servicemen's Association moved its headquarters from Manchester to London. In 1945 it initiated the *Central Ukrainian Relief Bureau. In August 1945 the Association of Ukrainian Soldiers in the Polish Armed Forces was established in London, and this organization enabled many Ukrainians, particularly those who had served in the *Polish Second Corps under W. Anders, to begin settling in the city in 1946. In 1947 former members of the *Division Galizien (approx 8,500 men) were relocated from Italy and joined by many immigrants from the displaced persons' camps in Germany.

Today the Ukrainian community in London consists of about 1,500 people. Initially they were predominantly factory and trade workers, but the second generation has managed to establish itself in professions, such as law, medicine, teaching, journalism, and computer science.

The Ukrainian organizations in London include the *Association of Ukrainians in Great Britain (SUB, est 1946), the *Federation of Ukrainians in Great Britain (est 1949), the Anglo-Ukrainian Committee, the Mazepa Society, the Polish-Ukrainian Society, the Academic Society, the Students' Hromada, the Ukrainian Graduates and Professional Association, the Ukrainian Press Agency, the Ukrainian Central Information Service, the Ukrainian

The monument in London to St Volodymyr (sculptor Leonid Molodozhanyn), erected in 1988 in commemoration of the millennium of Christianity in Ukraine

Society, the Society of Ukrainian Litterateurs, the Association of Ukrainian Women, and the Ukrainian Former Combatants in Great Britain. There are also branches of international organizations, such as the Ukrainian National Council, the Anti-Bolshevik Bloc of Nations, the Ukrainian Democratic Alliance (1970–1980s), the Ukrainian Helsinki Union, the Ukrainian Catholic University, the St Sophia Religious Society, the Plast Ukrainian Youth Association, and the Ukrainian Youth Association (SUM). The apostolic exarchate for Ukrainian Catholics in Great Britain and the eparchial administration of the Ukrainian Autocephalous Orthodox church have cathedrals in the city. The headquarters of most British Ukrainian organizations, a number of which have their own buildings, are in London.

Two publishing houses, *Ukrainian Publishers Ltd and Nashe Slovo, were active for some time, but only the former, the larger company, now remains. The weekly *Ukraïns'ka dumka* (the organ of SUB), the monthlies *Vyzvol'-nyi shliakh, Soviet Nationality Survey,* UGPA *Newsletter,* and *Press Releases of the Ukrainian Press Agency,* and the quarterlies *Ukrainian Review, Vidomosti eparkhiial'noho upravlinnia* UAPTs, and *Surmach* (a veterans' publication) are all published in London. The Catholic quarterly *Nasha tserkva* was issued in 1953–75, and irregularly for a few years after that, before being replaced by the irregular *Tserkovni visti.*

The libraries of the British Museum and the London School of Slavonic and East European Studies have large holdings of valuable material concerning Ukraine and Ukrainians.

(See also *Great Britain.)

C. Zelenko

Long-fallow system. A method of land cultivation that alternates short periods (usually about 3 years) of crop raising with long periods (up to 25 years) of idleness. Livestock is often pastured on the fallow land. During the first two or three idle years a weedy fallow of annual and biennial plants appears; it is followed by rhizomatous plants and then by grasses as the soil becomes more compact. Finally the wild vegetation typical of the region comes to predominate. During the fallow period the soil's fertility and moisture are restored. Because of its inefficient use of land, the system is rarely practiced today. It has been replaced by no- or low-tillage systems, crop rotation, and the application of fertilizers and herbicides.

The long-fallow system in Ukraine dates back to the Trypilian culture (4,500–2,000 BC). As population increased and land became scarcer, the system had to be abandoned. In the central regions of Kievan Rus' the fallow period, initially, was reduced to as few as three years, and then the fallow system was replaced altogether by a two- or three-year crop rotation system. In the thinly populated steppe and Transcarpathian regions the long-fallow system survived longer. It was still practiced there in the mid-19th century, although it had disappeared from Western Europe by the 16th century. In 1917, substantial tracts in Ukraine (318,000 ha in Kharkiv gubernia and 187,000 ha in Poltava gubernia) lay fallow, most of them belonging to big landowners. As late as the 1930s 500,000 ha of long-fallow land were being used for sheep pasturing.

C. Freeland

Lopan River [Lopan']. A left-bank tributary of the Udy River (which it joins at Kharkiv). It is 96 km long (78 km in Ukraine) and drains a basin area of 2,000 sq km. The Lopan flows through the Central Upland within the borders of Belgorod oblast (RFR) and Kharkiv oblast. Its waters are used for industrial and domestic consumption. The main cities located along the river are Kharkiv and Derkachi.

Lopatynska, Filomena [Lopatyns'ka] (née Kravchuk), b 1873 in Chernivtsi, d 26 March 1940 in Odessa. Opera singer (soprano); spouse of L. *Lopatynsky and mother of F. *Lopatynsky. A graduate of the Lviv Conservatory (1904), she performed in 1891–7 at the Ruska Besida Theater in Lviv and later at the Lviv Municipal Opera Theater. For some time she was with the Chernivtsi German theater, although she continued to appear on the Ukrainian stage. In 1915–16 she joined L. Kurbas's Ternopilski Teatralni Vechory theater, and in 1917–23 she performed with the Ukrainian Theater in Chernivtsi and other troupes in Galicia. From the mid-1920s she lived in Soviet Ukraine. Her more important roles included Maryna in N. Kybalchych's *Katria Chaikivna,* Tatiana in P. Tchaikovsky's *Eugene Onegin,* and the title roles in D. Sichynsky's *Roksoliana,* S. Moniuszko's *Halka,* and G. Bizet's *Carmen.*

Filomena Lopatynska   Favst Lopatynsky   Lev Lopatynsky   Yaroslav Lopatynsky (1906–81)

Lopatynsky, Demian [Lopatyns'kyj, Demjan], b 12 March 1866 in Lviv, d 8 February 1951 in Newark, New Jersey. Priest and church and civic leader. After serving in several rural parishes he was appointed canon of the Greek Catholic Lviv metropoly and catechist for secondary schools. A populist by conviction, he became one of the leading members of the National Democratic party and, later, the Ukrainian National Democratic Alliance. He served on the Lviv municipal council, chaired the board of directors of the Dilo Publishing Company (1910–39), and served on the board of Narodna Torhovlia. Under his care the Dormition Church in Lviv was restored. After emigrating in 1944, he organized parishes in Germany and England, and in 1950 he joined his family in the United States.

Lopatynsky, Favst [Lopatyns'kyj], b 1899 in Lviv, d 1937. Stage actor and director and film director; son of F. *Lopatynska and L. *Lopatynsky. He began his stage career in the Ternopilski Teatralni Vechory (1915–16) and then worked in Molodyi Teatr (1917–19), the Theater of the Western Ukrainian National Republic (1919), Kyidramte (1920–2), Berezil (1922–7), and the Fairy-Tale Theater in Kharkiv (1926–7). During 1926–33 he was a film director at the Odessa and Kiev Artistic Film studios. He was arrested during the Stalinist terror, and died in a concentration camp. In acting and stage directing Lopatynsky was a follower of L. *Kurbas's system. He played Yarema in *Haidamaky* (The Haidamakas, based on T. Shevchenko) and Leon in F. Grillpartzer's *Weh' dem, der lügt* and directed the Berezil productions of *Novi idut'* (The New Are Coming, based on O. Zozulia, 1923), *Mashynobortsi* (adapted from E. Toller's *Die Maschinenstürmer*, 1924), and *Poshylys' u durni* (They Made Fools of Themselves, adapted from M. Kropyvnytsky, 1924). In 1922 Lopatynsky was in charge of Berezil's second experimental workshop. He filmed *Synii paket* (Blue Package, 1926), *Vasia – reformator* (Vasia the Reformer, with O. Dovzhenko, 1926), and *Karmeliuk* (1931). He was also the author of the drama *Kozak Holota* (1927).

Lopatynsky, Lev [Lopatyns'kyj], b 29 February 1868 in Lviv, d 7 September 1914 near Yaniv, Galicia. Actor, author, and public figure; husband of F. *Lopatynska and father of F. *Lopatynsky. After studying law at Lviv University he graduated in drama from the Vienna Conserva-

tory (1891–92) and then was an actor in the Ruska Besida Theater, of which he became director in 1898. As an actor he played mostly heroic character roles, including Hnat in T. Shevchenko's *Nazar Stodolia* and Robert Heinecke in H. Sudermann's *Die Ehre*. He wrote the plays *Do Braziliï* (To Brazil, 1878), *Svekrukha* (The Mother-in-law, 1899), and *Parazia* (1901) and the book *Zur Psychologie des Schauspielers* (1893). After abandoning his stage career Lopatynsky edited the newspapers *Ruslan* (1898–1907) and *Bukovyna* and practiced law in Sambir and Kopychyntsi.

Lopatynsky, Teofilakt [Lopatyns'kyj], b 1670 in Volhynia, d 6 May 1741. Theologian and churchman. A graduate of the Kievan Mohyla Academy, he taught there and then served as rector of the Moscow Slavonic-Greek-Latin Academy (1706–22). He was a member of the Russian Holy Synod, bishop of Tver (1723–5), and archbishop of Pskov (1725) and then of Tver (1726–36). Lopatynsky was one of a number of Ukrainian hierarchs grouped around Metropolitan S. *Yavorsky who sought to reform the Orthodox church in Russia but opposed the more radical positions, the destruction of the patriarchate, and the complete subservience to the state espoused by T. *Prokopovych. Lopatynsky helped prepare a new edition of the Ostrih Bible and published Yavorsky's *Kamen' very ...* (The Stone of Faith ..., 1718). For his opposition to Prokopovych, Lopatynsky was arrested in 1736 and defrocked in 1738. He was released in 1740. He left several unpublished manuscripts on philosophical and religious topics.

Lopatynsky, Yaroslav [Lopatyns'kyj, Jaroslav], b 19 August 1871 in Dolyna, Galicia, d 14 January 1936 in Holohirky, Zolochiv county, Galicia. Composer. A graduate of the Vienna Medical Institute (1898), he worked as a village physician in Pomoriany (Zboriv county) and then in Holohory. He served as a doctor with the Ukrainian Galician Army from 1918 and was eventually captured and imprisoned in Ukraine. He returned to Holohory in 1923. Lopatynsky's compositions include pieces for piano, approx 100 songs for solo voice and for chorus ('Vstavai, Ukraïno' [Arise, Ukraine, 1905]), and stage works, such as the opera *Oksana*, the comic opera *Enei na mandrivtsi* (Aeneas on a Journey, 1911), the children's opera *Zirka shchastia* (Star of Happiness), the fantastic opera *Kazka skel'* (Tale of the Cliffs), and several operettas.

Lopatynsky, Yaroslav [Lopatyns'kyj, Jaroslav], b 9 November 1906 in Tbilisi, Georgia, d 10 March 1981 in Donetske. Ukrainian mathematician; full member of the AN URSR (now ANU) from 1965. Lopatynsky graduated from Azerbaidzhan University in 1926. He taught at institutions of higher learning in Baku, and in 1945–63 he held a chair in differential equations at Lviv University. After working two years at Moscow's Industrial Institute, in 1966 Lopatynsky became head of the Section of Partial Differential Equations at the ANU Institute of Applied Mathematics and Mechanics in Donetske. Most of his basic research was devoted to the development of the theory of linear and nonlinear partial differential equations. During his Lviv period Lopatynsky obtained important results in the theory of systems of elliptic linear equations, for which he constructed local fundamental solutions. He also developed a method of reducing general boundary value problems to regular integral equations. Lopatynsky was the first person to formulate a condition on the relation between the coefficients of the system and the coefficients of the boundary operators which is necessary and sufficient for the normal solvability of boundary value problems. This is now known as the Lopatynsky Condition. He also obtained some basic results in the solvability of the Cauchy problem for operator equations in Banach spaces. In addition to his scientific articles Lopatynsky wrote *Introduction to the Contemporary Theory of Partial Differential Equations* (1980).

W. Petryshyn

Lopatynsky, Yurii [Lopatyns'kyi, Jurij] (noms de guerre: Kalyna, Sheik), b 12 April 1906 in Ternopil, Galicia, d 16 November 1982 in Hunter, New York. UPA staff officer. Having received officer training in the Polish army (1928–30), he served as an officer in the Carpathian Sich (November 1938–March 1939) and in the Nachtigall Legion of Ukrainian Nationalists (April–September 1941). After spending 18 months in the Sachsenhausen concentration camp he returned to Ukraine in December 1944 and served at UPA headquarters. In May 1945 he conducted negotiations with the Polish Home Army. At the end of the year he arrived in Munich and became deputy chief of the UPA Mission. He was promoted to lieutenant colonel (1950) and awarded the Gold Cross of Merit (1952). After emigrating to the United States (1953) he served as president of the Former Members of the UPA and board member of the *Prolog Research Corporation.

Lopukhov, Oleksandr [Lopuxov], b 12 September 1925 in Horodnia, Chernihiv okruha. Painter. Lopukhov studied at the Kiev State Art Institute (1947–53) and has taught there since 1953 and served as its rector (1973–85). In 1983 he was elected head of the Union of Artists of Ukraine. His paintings, many of which are in the Kiev Museum of Ukrainian Art, portray revolutionary and military themes in the spirit of Soviet patriotism. His best-known works are *To Petrograd (V.I. Lenin)* (1953), *The Arrest of the Provisional Government* (1955–7), *The Arsenal Rebels* (1956–60), *War* (1968–9), *Moonlight Sonata* (1968–70), and *Victory* (1973–5). An album of his works was published in Kiev in 1975.

Los, Fedir [Los'], b 19 June 1908 in Pivnivshchyna, Horodnia county, Chernihiv gubernia, d 21 July 1980 in Kiev. Historian. He lectured at institutions of higher education (1931–5) and at Kiev University (1949–65, as professor from 1954) and worked at the AN URSR (now ANU) Institute of History (1935–79, as assistant director in 1948–58). His works deal with the Stolypin reforms, the Revolution of 1905 (1955), and the history of the working class (1955, 1962) in Ukraine; he also authored secondary-school history textbooks.

Ukrainian Catholic Church of the Nativity of the Blessed Virgin Mary in Los Angeles

Los Angeles. The second-largest city (1990 pop 3,485,400) in the United States and a major financial, manufacturing, research, and entertainment center on the Pacific coast in southern California. Few Ukrainians settled in Los Angeles before the Second World War. The earliest arrival came in the 19th century, and by 1938 the number had grown to about 150. By 1948 there were approx 500 Ukrainian families in the area, and in 1980, 11,300 residents of Ukrainian origin. The community's activities are centered around the Ukrainian Culture Center, which arose out of the Ukrainian Club in 1946. Headed for many years by M. Novak, the center organized concerts, dances, and plays and raised funds for Ukrainian refugees. In 1961 it bought its own building, the Ukrainian National Home. The Ukrainian Orthodox parishes of St Volodymyr and St Andrew date from 1946 and 1951 respectively. The Ukrainian Catholic parish of the Nativity of the Blessed Virgin Mary was founded in 1947, and a Ukrainian Evangelical Baptist church in 1963. As the community grew, new organizations, such as branches of the Ukrainian National Association (1949), the Ukrainian Fraternal Association (1951), the Ukrainian National Aid (1963), the Ukrainian National Women's League (1957), the Plast Ukrainian Youth Association (1965), and the Ukrainian Youth Association (SUM, 1967), were set up. A Ukrainian credit union was organized in 1964.

Losenko, Antin, b 10 August 1737 in Hlukhiv, Nizhen regiment, d 4 December 1773 in St Petersburg. Painter; a leading exponent of historical painting in the classicist style. He was brought to St Petersburg to sing in the imperial court choir in 1744. After his voice changed, he was sent to study art under I. Argunov (1753–8) and at the St Petersburg Academy of Arts (1759–60), which gave him bursaries to study in Paris (1760–5) and Rome (1766–9).

Antin Losenko: *Zeus and Themis* (oil, 1769)

Losenko became a member of and professor at the academy in 1770, served as its director (1772–3), and wrote its textbook on human proportions (1772). His oeuvre includes paintings on biblical and mythological themes, such as *The Miraculous Draught of Fishes* (1762), *Abraham's Sacrifice* (1765), *Cain* (1768), *Abel* (1769), *Zeus and Themis* (1769), and *Hector's Parting with Andromache* (1773); paintings on historical themes, such as *The Holy Apostle Andrew* (1769) and *Grand Prince Volodymyr and Rohnida* (1770); portraits of prominent personalities; a self-portrait; and approx 200 drawings of nude figures and parts of the body, which were held up as models of excellence to students at the academy for many years. Losenko introduced to Russian painting the *pompier* style and influenced the work of several artists, including I. Akimov, P. Sokolov, and G. Ugriumov. Most of his works are preserved at the Russian Museum in St Petersburg and the Tretiakov Gallery in Moscow. Books about him have been written by A. Kaganovich (1963) and E. Gavrilova (1977).

Loshkarev, Mikhail [Loškarjov, Mixail], b 24 January 1913 in Orenburg, Russia, d 13 October 1986 in Dnipropetrovske. Electrochemist; AN URSR (now ANU) corresponding member from 1967. After graduating from the Ural Industrial Institute (1936) he worked there and at the Ivanovo Chemical Technology Institute. From 1948 he chaired a department at the Dnipropetrovske Chemical Technology Institute, where he also served as rector (1951–72). A specialist in the kinetics of electrochemical processes, he developed a theory of the effect of surface-active agents on the kinetics of electrode processes and studied the cathodic separation of metals.

Losky, Ihor [Los'kyj], b 15 December 1900 in Lublin, Poland, d 27 May 1936 in Lviv. Historian; son of K. *Losky. As a student at the Ukrainian gymnasium in Kiev he took part in the Battle of *Kruty. After graduating from the Ukrainian Free University in Prague (PH D, 1927) he worked at the Ukrainian Scientific Institute in Berlin (1927–32) and then taught French and German at the Greek Catholic Seminary in Lviv. He contributed historical articles to *Zhyttia i znannia* and helped edit *Khliborobs'kyi shliakh* and *Ridna shkola*. He specialized in the culture of the Hetman state and 19th-century revolutionary movements in Ukraine.

Kost Losky

Losky, Kost [Los'kyj, Kost'], b 28 January 1874 in St Petersburg, d 14 October 1933 in Prague. Jurist, civic and political figure, writer, and publicist; full member of the Shevchenko Scientific Society. He graduated in history and law from Warsaw and St Petersburg universities and then served as a government official in the Kholm region, where he became a leading figure in the Ukrainian movement. In 1905 he founded a branch of the Prosvita society in Hrubeshiv and a publishing house for popular Ukrainian books. He was a copublisher of the newspaper *Buh*. In 1917 he served as assistant gubernial commissioner for Galicia and then as chairman of the Kholm Gubernia Council. Losky was a member of the Central Rada and director of a department in the Secretariat of Internal Affairs and then in the UNR Ministry of Foreign Affairs. In 1918 the Hetman government sent him as an envoy to Finland, and later, to Sweden and Norway. In 1920 he settled in Prague and turned to academic work: he was appointed a professor of Roman law, dean of the law and social sciences faculty (1927–8), and prorector (1929–30) of the Ukrainian Free University. His main publications were *Ukrainskii vopros: Rossiia i Antanta* (The Ukrainian Question: Russia and the Entente, 1918), *Narys ryms'koï istoriï* (An Outline of Roman History, 1919), *Korotkyi narys hrets'koï istoriï* (A Brief Outline of Greek History, 1921), *Istoriia dzherel ryms'koho prava* (History of the Sources of Roman Law, 1921), and *Istoriia i systema ryms'koho pryvatnoho prava* (The History and System of Roman Private Law, 2 vols, nd). He also published a collection of feuilletons and articles, *Vid velykoho do smishnoho* (From the Sublime to the Ridiculous, 1919), and some translations of A. Chekhov and H. Heine.

Bishop Basil Losten Bishop Innocent Lotocky

Olena Lototska Antin Lototsky

Losten, Basil, b 11 May 1930 in Chesapeake City, Maryland. Ukrainian Catholic bishop in the United States. Ordained shortly after completing his studies at the Catholic University of America in Washington, DC (1957), he became personal secretary to Metropolitan A. *Senyshyn. He was appointed by the Vatican in 1971 as auxiliary bishop of Philadelphia archeparchy, without consultation with the synod of Ukrainian Catholic bishops (headed by Cardinal Y. Slipy). In 1976–7 Losten was administrator of Philadelphia archeparchy, and in 1977 he became bishop of Stamford eparchy. In June 1990 Cardinal M. Liubachivsky appointed him special emissary to assist in the rebirth of the Ukrainian Catholic church in Ukraine.

Losynivka. III-12. A town smt (1990 pop 4,800) in Nizhen raion, Chernihiv oblast. It is first mentioned in historical documents in 1627. Losynivka has a brick factory and a bread-baking complex. Several medieval settlements have been discovered near the town.

Lotocky, Innocent [Lotoc'kyj, Inokentij], b 3 November 1915 in Petlykivtsi, Buchach county, Galicia. Ukrainian Catholic bishop. After studying in Dobromyl and Lavriv he was ordained in 1940 in Czechoslovakia. He completed further studies in Vienna (1945), served in Belgium, and moved to the Pittsburgh area in 1946 to become acting provincial of the Basilian order in the United States. In 1957–81 Lotocky was a pastor at churches in New York City, Glen Cove (New York), Chicago, and Hamtramck (Michigan). In 1981 he was consecrated bishop of Chicago eparchy.

Lototska, Olena [Lotoc'ka] (née Folys), b 23 May 1894 in Liubycha Kniazie, Rava Ruska county, Galicia, d 2 December 1975 in Albany, New York. Activist of the women's movement. She emigrated to the United States with her first husband, Rev V. Dovbushovsky, in 1912, and after his death married V. *Lototsky. She was a founder and longtime president (1931–4, 1943–65) of the *Ukrainian National Women's League of America. She was also the moving force behind the convening of the First Ukrainian Women's Congress in America (1932), the founding of the journal *Nashe zhyttia (1944), and the organizing of the 1948 World Congress of Ukrainian Women in New York, which gave rise to the *World Federation of Ukrainian Women's Organizations. She served as vice-president and then president (1969–72) of the federation and helped organize the Second World Congress of Ukrainian Women

in 1959. She maintained contacts with various international women's associations and attended international women's conferences in Washington (1925), Helsinki (1954), Montreal (1957), and Paris (1958).

Lototska-Tokarzewski, Oksana [Lotoc'ka-Tokarževs'ka], b 1887, d 1950 in London. Community activist; daughter of O. *Lototsky and wife of J. *Tokarzewski-Karaszewicz. She served as a secretary of the Ukrainian diplomatic mission in Turkey (1919–20) before moving to France, where she was active in organizing exhibitions of Ukrainian art and various concerts. She represented Ukrainian women at international women's congresses in Vienna (1921) and Paris (1926). She moved to Italy in 1936 and published articles on Ukrainian affairs in *Osservatore Romano*. Later she settled in England, where she continued her community involvements.

Lototsky, Antin [Lotoc'kyj] (pseud: Ya. Vilshenko), b 1881, d 28 May 1949 in Lviv. Writer and pedagogue. For many years he taught at a gymnasium in Rohatyn. He wrote novelettes, short stories, and tales in verse for children and adolescents: *Tsvity z polia* (Flowers from the Field, 1907), *Vedmedivs'ka popivna* (The Priest's Daughter from Vedmedivka, 1909), *Trylisy* (1910), *Smertne zillia* (Deadly Herbs, 1921), *Naïzd obriv* (The Raid of the Avars, 1923), *Try pobratymy* (The Three Blood Brothers, 1934), *Bulo kolys' na Ukraïni* (Once upon a Time in Ukraine, 1934), *Kozak Baida* (The Cossack Baida, 1936), *Roksoliana* (1936), *Otrok kn. Romana* (Prince Roman's Page, 1937), and *Kniazha slava* (The Princes' Glory, 1939). Most of those works have historical themes and are marked by a fine sensitivity to the psychology of children. Some of them have been reprinted several times. Lototsky coedited several children's magazines, such as *Svit dytyny* and *Nash pryiatel'*.

Lototsky, Oleksander [Lotoc'kyj] (pseuds: O. Bilousenko, O. Liubenky, and Spectator), b 22 March 1870 in Bronnytsia, Mohyliv county, Podilia gubernia, d 22 October 1939 in Warsaw. Civic and political figure, writer, publicist, and scholar; full member of the Shevchenko Scientific Society (from 1900) and the Ukrainian Scientific Society in Kiev. After graduating from the Kiev Theological Academy in 1896, he worked (1900–17) in the Ministry of State for the Control of Finances in Kiev and then in St Petersburg, where he rose to the position of deputy gener-

Oleksander Lototsky   Volodymyr Lototsky

al comptroller. An active member of the *Society of Ukrainian Progressives from 1908, he assisted in establishing the Ukrainian caucus in the Russian State Duma. He became head of the *Ukrainian National Council in Petrograd in 1917 and then gubernial commissioner of Russian-occupied Bukovyna and Pokutia. His positions in the UNR government included that of secretary general (September–November 1917) and state comptroller (1918) in the General Secretariat of the Central Rada, and in the Hetman government he was minister of religious affairs (October–November 1918). As acting minister of religious affairs under the UNR Directory Lototsky was instrumental in the declaration of autocephaly by the Ukrainian Orthodox church (1 January 1919). He also went to Constantinople as minister plenipotentiary to obtain the patriarch's recognition of that church's new status. He emigrated in 1920 to Vienna, then Prague, and finally Warsaw. He served as a docent and eventually professor of canon law at the Ukrainian Free University (1922–8) and professor of Orthodox church history at Warsaw University (1929–39). He was a founder and director (1930–9) of the *Ukrainian Scientific Institute in Warsaw. He was also minister of internal affairs and deputy premier in the *Government-in-exile of the UNR (1927–30).

Lototsky's earliest publications (1889) were children's books. He published readers and the anthology *Vinok* (The Wreath) and helped found the Vik publishing house. In the 1890s his scholarly and popular studies began to appear in *Kievskaia starina*, *Pravda* (Lviv), *Literaturno-naukovyi vistnyk*, and *Zapysky Naukovoho tovarystva im. T. Shevchenka*. He contributed articles on economics to Russian economic journals, *Ukrainskii vestnik*, and *Ukrainskaia zhizn'*. He wrote many articles on the history of schools in Ukraine and Russia. As a publicist he contributed hundreds of articles to leading (usually liberal) Russian journals and newspapers defending Ukrainian causes. As a church activist he collaborated with the Synod in publishing a Ukrainian translation of the Gospel, wrote textbooks on the Old and New Testaments, and belonged to the commission for translating liturgical books at the Ukrainian Scientific Institute in Warsaw. Lototsky was also active in civic affairs. He promoted the printing of Ukrainian books, and in the 1900s he was active in the revival of Ukrainian-language publishing. He defended Ukrainian interests before the St Petersburg bureaucracy. A liberal democrat and a republican, he belonged to the Ukrainian

Democratic Radical party, which later became the *Ukrainian Party of Socialists-Federalists. Lototsky remained active while abroad in writing articles for foreign journals (Turkish, Greek, Finnish, Czechoslovakian, Polish, and French) and participating in various civic and cultural undertakings.

Lotosky's major writings include studies of cathedral chapters in Ukraine in the 15th and 16th centuries (1896) and of the social position of the secular clergy in Ukraine and in Russia in the 18th century (1898), as well as *Ukraïns'ki dzherela tserkovnoho prava* (Ukrainian Sources of Ecclesiastical Law, 1931; repr 1984) and *Avtokefaliia* (Autocephaly, 2 vols, 1935, 1938). His memoirs, *Storinky mynuloho* (Pages of the Past, 4 vols, 1932–4) and *V Tsarhorodi* (In Constantinople, 1939; repr 1966), are valuable sources for the history of Ukrainian cultural and civic life in the late 19th and early 20th centuries.

R. Smal-Stotsky

Lototsky, Volodymyr [Lotoc'kyj], b 15 May 1883 in Shchepaniv, Berezhany county, Galicia, d 17 March 1958 in Philadelphia. Journalist and civic activist; husband of O. *Lototska. As a member of the Ukrainian National Democratic party, he worked as an editor of *Dilo* and chief editor of *Svoboda* (1910–13) in Lviv. After emigrating to the United States in 1913, he worked on the staff of *Svoboda* and eventually became its chief editor (1919–26). He then headed the paper *Ameryka* in Philadelphia (1927–43) and *Narodna volia* in Scranton, Pennsylvania (1943–6). Lototsky was active in many Ukrainian organizations and served as secretary of the Education Commission of the Ukrainian National Association, a member of the General Ukrainian Committee (1915), secretary of the Ukrainian National Committee (1918), and secretary of the League of Four Nations (1919).

Lotykove. V-19, DB II-5. A town smt (1986 pop 4,000) in Slovianoserbske raion, Luhanske oblast. Founded at the beginning of the 20th century as Ivanivskyi Rudnyk, it was renamed Gustav in 1912 and Lotykove in 1919 (in honor of the Bolshevik V. Lotyk). It has a coal mine and a building-materials plant.

Louvain. See Leuven.

Lovchyi. The game warden at a prince's court in Rus'. He was responsible for managing the lands, game, and personnel related to hunting. For his renumeration he was allowed to collect a special tax called *lovche* in cash or kind from the local town or village population. The post was prestigious, for the princes attributed great importance to hunting. The earliest reference to the position is found in Volodymyr Monomakh's *Poucheniie ditiam*.

Low Beskyd (aka Lemko Beskyd). The section of the Beskyd Mountains between the Bila River at Tylych Pass and the Toplia River in the west, and between the Sian River along Oslava and Lupkiv Pass and the Laborets River in the east. The Low Beskyd has the lowest elevation and widest area of the external flysch part of the Carpathians. It includes, from north to south, the Carpathian foothills, the Gorlice-Sianik Basin, and the Low Beskyd itself.

Low Beskyd: eastern part of the Gorlice-Sianik Basin

The foothills, composed of soft sand-hills, slate, clay, and marls, roll gently along a path 30–50 km across. Wide ridges reaching 350–450 m in height rise 150–200 m above wide valleys. A truly mountainous aspect is found only on the Chornorih Ridge (592 m) north of Krosno and in the eastern part along the middle Sian River (Peremyshl foothills). That area was settled by a pocket of Ukrainians (see *Zamishantsi*).

The Gorlice-Sianik Basin is a zone nearly 80 km in length and 8–12 km in width between the foothills and the Low Beskyd itself. Partially forested, it includes several plateaus (270–350 m) and low hills. Owing to advantageous natural conditions and a favorable location, the area is densely populated, with 150 to 200 persons per sq km. Its eastern region (including the town of Sianik) was populated by Ukrainians until 1946.

The Low Beskyd itself, which rises 200–300 m above the Gorlice-Sianik Basin, constitutes a long-standing ethnographic border between Ukraine and Poland. The Low Beskyd is the lowest and (along with the Middle Beskyd) the gentlest part of the Carpathians. Only a few peaks exceed 1,000 m (such as Busiv, at 1,010 m), and a large portion of the region consists of elevations similar in landscape to foothills. The ravines are also low and easily traversed. The most massive ridges reach over 800 m in the middle part of the Low Beskyd, but only on the Galician side. The southwestern region is characterized by insular hills, and the eastern region has a lattice structure (lengthwise ridges and valleys). In the south, between the Toplia and the Laborets rivers, the Low Beskyd becomes the Ondava Highlands, at 400–500 m, which are crossed by relatively deep perpendicular valleys at 200–300 m.

The Low Beskyd is the largest deforested area in the Ukrainian Carpathians (29 percent forested, 40 percent cultivated, 26 percent hayfields and pasture). The forests in the lower regions consist of oak, elm, linden, and other trees; beech and fir are common in the upper reaches.

Until 1946 the entire northern (Galician) part of the Low Beskyd lay in Ukrainian ethnographic territory, and the southern (Transcarpathian) part was mainly Ukrainian and partly Slovak. The Ukrainian population consisted predominantly of *Lemkos. Since the resettlement of Ukrainians from the Lemko region, Ukrainians have been found only in the southern parts of the Low Beskyd.

V. Kubijovyč

Lower-Don Lowland. A large lowland in the lower Don Valley that includes most of the *Don region (territory of the Don Cossacks). It consists of four geographical regions. The first is the Azov Lowland, in the southwest, which joins the Kuban Lowland (and is sometimes known as the Kuban-Azov Lowland). In the east is a second formation, the Sal-Manych Ridge, which has an eroded terrain that drops sharply in the east to the Caspian Lowland. The third region, the Kuma-Manych Depression, is located in the south. The fourth region, the Don Ridge in the northwest, has a broken relief that represents an extension of the Central Upland.

Łoziński, Władysław (pseud: Władysław Lubicz), b 29 May 1843 in Opari, Drohobych county, Galicia, d 20 May 1913 in Lviv. Polish writer, literary critic, and historian. He produced a number of historical novels, including *Czarne godziny* (Black Hours, 1869) and *Hazardy* (Risks, 1870), and numerous stories published in over 10 collections. As a historian he took a special interest in the past of the burghers and nobility of Galicia, in the works *Patrycjat i mieszczaństwo lwowskie w XVI–XVII w.* (The Lviv Patriciate and Burghers in the 16th–17th Centuries, 1890), *Kupiectwo lwowskie* (The Lviv Merchant Class, 1891), *Sztuka lwowska* (Lviv Art, 1898), *Prawem i lewem: Obyczaje na Czerwonej Rusi* (With the Right and Left: Customs in Red Ruthenia, 1903), and *Życie polskie w dawnych wiekach* (Polish Life in Ancient Times, 1907).

Lozivskyi [Lozivs'kyj]. V-17. A town smt (1990 pop 7,000) in Slovianoserbske raion, Luhanske oblast. It was founded in 1949 and has a coal mine and a coal-enrichment plant. A number of kurhans from the 11th to 13th century are located near Lozivskyi.

Lozova. V-17. A city (1990 pop 73,700) and raion center in Kharkiv oblast. It was founded in the late 1860s during the construction of the Kursk–Kharkiv–Azov railway line. In April 1918 the UNR Army fought several battles against the Red Army near Lozova. Today the city is a major railway junction and has several railway-related enterprises, a metallurgical machinery plant, a machine-building factory, and a tractor plant.

Lozovsky, Oleksander [Lozovs'kyj], b 12 September 1900 in Kiev, d 22 March 1922 in Kiev. Graphic artist. He studied at the Ukrainian State Academy of Arts (1918–22).

Oleksander Lozovsky: cover design of a poetry collection by P. Tychyna (1920)

His teachers, of major influence on him, were H. *Narbut and M. *Boichuk. Lozovsky designed the covers of P. Tychyna's early poetry collections *Soniashni klarnety* (Solar Clarinets, 2nd edn, 1920), *Zamists' sonetiv i oktav* (Instead of Sonnets and Octaves, 1920), and *Pluh* (Plow, 1920); an edition of M. Kotsiubynsky's works (1922); S. Vasylchenko's collection *V kholodku* (In the Shade, 1922); and several editions of scores of Ukrainian folk songs (1921). At the academy he exhibited his prints *Malachite, Annunciation, St John the Baptist*, and *Memento mori* in 1920 and portraits of V. Lenin and H. Skovoroda in 1921.

Mykhailo Lozynsky   Roman Lubkivsky

Lozynsky, Mykhailo [Lozyns'kyj, Myxajlo], b 1880, d 23 October 1937. Lawyer, publicist, and political figure. He was a collaborator with the *Union for the Liberation of Ukraine, editor of *Hromads'kyi holos*, a longtime contributor to and coeditor of *Dilo*, and a contributor to *Hromads'ka dumka, Rada*, and *Haslo*, the official organ of the Revolutionary Ukrainian party (RUP). In March 1919 he served as undersecretary of foreign affairs for the Western Province of the Ukrainian National Republic, a member of the delegation for negotiating the Ukrainian-Polish peace treaty, and a participant at the Paris Peace Conference. In 1921–7 he was a professor of international law at the Ukrainian Free University in Prague. Later he emigrated to the USSR and chaired the Department of Law at the Institute of the National Economy and worked at the Ukrainian Institute of Marxism-Leninism in Kharkiv. Lozynsky's works, dealing with the modern history of Western Ukraine, included *Pol'skyi i rus'kyi revoliutsiinyi rukh i Ukraïna* (The Polish and Ruthenian Revolutionary Movement and Ukraine, 1908), *Utvorennia ukraïns'koho koronnoho kraiu v Avstrii* (1915; pub in German as *Die Schaffung einer ukrainischen Provinz in Oesterreich*, 1915), *Halychyna v zhyttiu Ukraïny* (Galicia in the Life of Ukraine, 1916), *Halychyna v rr. 1918–1920: Rozvidky i materiialy* (Galicia in the Years 1918–20: Research and Materials, 1922; repr 1970), *Uvahy pro ukraïns'ku derzhavnist'* (Remarks Concerning Ukrainian Statehood, 1927), and *U desiatyrichchia halyts'koï revolutsiï: Fakty i sproba otsinky* (On the Tenth Anniversary of the Revolution in Galicia: Facts and an Attempted Evaluation, 1928). He was also the author of a textbook on international law (1922) and a collection dedicated to S. Dnistriansky, *Okhorona natsional'nykh menshostei* (Defense of National Minorities, 1923), as well as research articles on M. Drahomanov, M. Pavlyk, and others. In 1930 he was arrested and deported to the Northern Urals, where he was shot.

Lozynsky, Volodymyr [Lozyns'kyj], b 1855, d 1914. Civic figure. A forester by profession, he was active as a young man in Narodnaia Volia and in the Russian Socialist Revolutionary party. Later he supported the Ukrainian Popular Defense and, during its suppression in 1909, saved many of its members. He published and edited the satirical magazine *Shershen'* in Kiev (1906) and provided financial support for *Svitlo* (1910–14) and *Ukraïns'kyi etnohrafichnyi zbirnyk* (1914).

Lozynsky, Yevhen [Lozyns'kyj, Jevhen], b 18 May 1909 in Tysmenytsia, Tovmach county, d 17 December 1977 in New York. Political activist. He joined the Ukrainian Military Organization and the OUN while he was still a gymnasium student, and he was imprisoned several times by the Polish authorities for his political activities. In 1932 he graduated in law from Cracow University. As a leading member of the OUN (Bandera faction) he was arrested in September 1941 and spent a number of years in German concentration camps. After the war he was placed in charge of social affairs in the OUN leadership in Munich. He emigrated to the United States and became a leading figure in pro-Banderite organizations there and served as president of the *Self-Reliance Association of American Ukrainians. He was also a member of the executive of the Ukrainian Congress Committee of America.

Lozynsky, Yosyp [Lozyns'kyj, Josyp], b 20 December 1807 in Virky, near Peremyshl, d 11 August 1889 in Yavoriv, Galicia. Ethnographer, publicist, grammarian, and Greek Catholic priest. Influenced by the Slovenian philologist J. Kopitar and the debates on South Slavic orthography, he proposed to adopt the *Latin alphabet for Ukrainian (1834) and provoked considerable opposition from the Ukrainian intelligentsia, including M. *Shashkevych. He wrote a valuable grammar of the Ukrainian vernacular, *Gramatyka języka ruskiego (małoruskiego)* (Grammar of the Ruthenian [Little Russian] Language, 1846), and published in the Latin alphabet a collection of Western Ukrainian wedding songs, *Ruskoje wesile* (The Ruthenian Wedding, 1835). Lozynsky consistently opposed *yazychiie as literary Ukrainian and polemicized with Y. *Levytsky on the issue. He wrote a study of folk games (1860) and a biography of I. Snihursky (1851).

Lubart. See Liubartas.

Lubchenko, Andrii [Lubčenko, Andrij], b 27 October 1921 at Lomakivskyi *khutir*, Myrhorod county, Poltava gubernia, d 26 November 1977 in Kiev. Solid-state physicist. A graduate of Lviv University (1951), he worked in Kiev at the AN URSR (now ANU) institutes of Physics (1957–66), of Theoretical Physics (1966–71), and for Nuclear Research (1971–7). He made significant contributions to the field of the optical properties of solids.

Lubenets, Tymofii [Lubenec', Tymofij], b 21 February 1855 in Krolevets, Chernihiv gubernia, d 14 April 1936. Pedagogue and education activist. He taught at a gymnasium in Kiev from 1883 to 1889. He became an elementary school inspector for the Kiev school district in 1889 and later the director of elementary schools for Kiev gubernia. He wrote grade-school textbooks and methodological studies, supported *Sunday schools, and advocated teaching in the Ukrainian language. He published a Ukrainian primer in Lviv under the pseudonym of Norets which cost him his position as director of elementary schools.

Lubensky, Stepan [Lubens'kyj] (Lubenchenko), b and d ? Early-18th-century icon painter. A presbyter at St Nicholas's Church in Kiev, he painted the iconostases in the Dormition Cathedral of the Kievan Cave Monastery (from 1720) and St Michael's Golden-Domed Monastery in Kiev.

Lubkivsky, Roman [Lubkivs'kyj], b 10 August 1941 in Ostrivets, Ternopil oblast. Poet, editor, and translator. He graduated from the pedagogical faculty at Lviv University (1963). He was deputy chief editor of the Lviv literary monthly *Zhovten'* (1966–80), and since 1981 he has headed the Lviv branch of the Writers' Union of Ukraine. In 1990 he was elected to the Supreme Soviet from the Yavoriv district. In 1992 he was appointed the first ambassador of newly independent Ukraine to Czechoslovakia. His poetry collections are *Zachudovani oleni* (Mesmerized Deer, 1965), *Hromove derevo* (The Thunderous Tree, 1967), *Ramena* (Shoulders, 1969), *Smoloskypy* (Torches, 1975), and *Zvizdar* (The Stargazer, 1977). He has compiled and translated the poetry anthologies *Slov'ians'ke nebo* (The Slavic Sky, 1972) and *Slov'ians'ka lira* (The Slavic Lyre, 1983), edited other books of translated poetry, and written literary criticism and publicism.

Lublin (Liublin). II-3. A city (1990 est pop 349,600) in eastern Poland and a voivodeship center. In the Middle Ages Lublin was an important Polish city on the border with Kiev and then Galicia-Volhynia principalities. In 1244 it was captured by Danylo Romanovych, and ca 1289, by his son Lev. Until 1302 Lublin was part of the Galician-Volhynian state. In 1474 it became the seat of a Polish voivode, and in 1578, of the crown tribunal, the highest court for southern Poland. In the 16th and early 17th centuries Lublin was an important trade center and the seat of many Polish diets. The Union of *Lublin (1569) was signed at one such session. Ukrainians constituted an important segment of the city's population. Lublin was also at that time an important Ukrainian religious center. In 1593 an Orthodox brotherhood modeled on the Lviv Dormition Brotherhood was established at the Church of the

Lublin: 15th-century Ruthenian frescoes in the Trinity Chapel

Lublin: 15th-century Ruthenian frescoes in the Trinity Chapel

Savior, and in 1607 a school was added. In the mid-17th century the church was acquired by the Basilian monks, who founded a monastery that remained active until 1864. Hetman B. Khmelnytsky occupied Lublin a number of times in 1648–9. In the second half of the 17th century the local Ukrainian population was thoroughly Polonized.

From 1815 Lublin belonged to the Congress Kingdom of Poland and then became a Russian gubernial town under direct rule of St Petersburg. It was the administrative center of Lublin gubernia, which included the Kholm region until 1912. Until 1914 few Ukrainians lived in the city.

In the interwar period Lublin was the center of a voivodeship which included the Kholm region and Podlachia. A Ukrainian colony of 300 to 400 people was established in the city. A few dozen Ukrainians studied at the Polish Catholic university. During the German occupation, mainly in 1939–41, the number of Ukrainians in Lublin grew to 1,000 as Ukrainians fled Soviet-occupied Western Ukraine. Lublin was the home of the Ukrainian Relief Committee, two Ukrainian parishes (one Catholic and one Orthodox), and a district office of the Ukrainian Central Committee (headed by V. Tymtsiurak and then L. Holeiko). From 1960 the local Ukrainian colony belonged to the Ukrainian Social and Cultural Society in Warsaw. A part of the archive and library of the former Greek Catholic Peremyshl·eparchy is housed in the library of Lublin Catholic University. The Trinity Chapel contains frescoes by the Ukrainian painter *Andrii (1415). The Church of the Transfiguration, built in 1607, represents the Ukrainian adaptation of the Renaissance style.

Lublin, Union of. A union agreement between the Grand Duchy of Lithuania and the Kingdom of Poland, signed on 1 July 1569 at a joint assembly of Lithuanian and Polish deputies in Lublin. The treaty gave birth to a single state, the Polish-Lithuanian Commonwealth, with a common elected monarch combining the offices of the Polish king and the Lithuanian grand duke, a common diet and senate, a joint foreign policy, and one monetary system. The Grand Duchy preserved its autonomy with its own laws, government, administration, courts, army, and finances. The treaty was signed by Lithuania at a time when it needed Polish help in its war against Muscovy. For Poland the treaty provided a means of acquiring some

Lithuanian territory. Under the treaty Poland (the Polish crown) obtained the Ukrainian territories of Podlachia, Volhynia, Podilia, and the Bratslav and Kiev regions. The nobility of those territories were given the same rights and privileges as the Polish nobility. The Grand Duchy retained, apart from Lithuanian territory, Belarus and the Berestia and Pynske regions. Thus the union gave Poland control over a large part of Ukrainian territory, where it proceeded to subjugate and exploit the indigenous population.

BIBLIOGRAPHY
Dnevnik Liublinskogo seima 1569 goda: Soedinenie Velikogo Khiazhestva Litovskogo s Korolevstvom Pol'skim (St Petersburg 1869)
Kutrzeba, S.; Semkowicz, W. (eds). *Akta unii Polski z Litwą 1385–1791* (Cracow 1932)

Lubni or **Lubny.** III-13, 14. A city (1990 pop 59,800) and raion center in Poltava oblast. It was founded as a fortified frontier town in 988 by Prince Volodymyr Sviatoslavych of Kiev. In 1107 the Rus' princes defeated the Cumans in battle there. Lubni was destroyed by the Mongols in 1239. Rebuilt in the latter half of the 16th century by the Wiśniowiecki family, Lubni was granted the rights of *Magdeburg law. In May 1596 the Polish army crushed the Cossack-peasant rebellion led by S. Nalyvaiko and H. Loboda in the Battle of Solonytsia near Lubni. In 1637–8 the town was a center of Cossack-peasant unrest. It was a regimental capital in the Hetman state (1648, 1658–1781) and then a county town in Poltava gubernia in the Russian Empire (1802–1917). A botanical garden with medicinal plants and the first field apothecary in Ukraine were established there in the early 18th century.

Today Lubni is an industrial city with machine building and metalworking as its chief industries: the largest plants are the Komunar Machine-Tool Plant, the Komsomolets Machine-Building Plant, and a computing-machine plant. A branch of the All-Union Scientific Research Institute of Medicinal Plants operated in Lubni. The city has an art gallery and a regional museum (est 1897). The *Mhar Transfiguration Monastery is located nearby.

Lubni regiment (Lubenskyi polk). An administrative territory and military formation of the Hetman state. The regiment was formed in 1648 at the outbreak of the Khmelnytsky uprising but in 1649 was divided into Myrhorod and Kropyvna regiments. It was reconstituted in 1658 when Kropyvna regiment was abolished. Until the mid-18th century the regiment had 13 companies, and later, 23. In 1721 its population was approx 22,000, including 10,700 Cossacks. It could field almost 2,700 infantry and 4,000 cavalry troops. According to the 1764 census the regiment encompassed 21 towns and 1,609 villages and estates and had a population of 147,000, including over 68,000 Cossacks. Its Cossacks took part in several Russian military expeditions, the Great Northern War (1700–21), the Russo-Turkish War (1735–9), and the Seven Years' War (1756–63). In 1781 Lubni regiment was dissolved, and its territory was divided between Kiev and Chernihiv vicegerencies.

Lubni Republic (Lubenska respublika). The name of a trial held in 1909 at the Military Circuit Court in Kiev. Of the 57 defendants the principal ones were A. *Livytsky, M. Livytska, V. and M. Shemet, and M. Sakharov. Among the lawyers conducting the defense were M. *Mikhnovsky and A. *Margolin. The charge of conspiracy to overthrow the tsarist government stemmed from the activities of the Revolutionary Coalition Committee, which was formed in Lubni at the outbreak of the Revolution of 1905 by the Ukrainian Social Democratic Workers' party and other socialist parties, such as the Jewish Bund and Poale Zion. Having been frustrated in its plans by the failure of the revolution at the center, the committee set up a combat force known as Lubni Self-Defense or Civil Self-Defense under A. Livytsky's command to counteract Jewish pogroms organized by the Black Hundreds and to stop the arrests of revolutionaries. A court of appeal revoked the military court's harsh sentences and acquitted all the defendants.

Lubok **literature** (from *lub* 'linden plank'; hence, a woodcut print). Inexpensive illustrated books for the mass reader in which certain genres of poetry and prose were commonly published. They first appeared in the second half of the 18th century, after *lubok* pictures began to circulate. In their day the booklets served the function of modern-day comic books. The most popular of them were songbooks of Little Russian folksongs, such as *Molodyi chumak* (The Young Wagoner, 1884), *Banduryst* (The Banduryst, 1887), and *Slipyi kobzar* (The Blind Kobzar, 1899); lives of saints; legends; booklets of religious and moral instruction, such as *Lysty z neba* (Letters from Heaven); calendars; collections of anecdotes, such as *Veselyi opovidach* (The Witty Narrator) and *Pobrekhen'ky* (Tall Tales); collections of folktales; collections of everyday sketches, such as *Byla zhinka muzhyka* (A Wife Beat Her Husband), *V mistechku Dzhulyni trapylas' novyna* (In the Town of Dzhulyna an Amazing Thing Happened), and *Iak kum Bandura chortiaku piimav, ta ne vtrymav* (How Godfather Bandura Caught a Devil but Could Not Hold Him); dream books; ghost stories; declaimers; adventure and pseudo-historical novels, such as *Naimychka, povest' iz malorossiiskoi zhizni* (The Servant Girl, a Novelette about Little Russian Life) and *Ivan Stepanovich Mazepa, malorossiiskoi getman* (Ivan Stepanovych Mazepa, the Little Russian Hetman). Many of the books were translations from Russian, particularly of N. Gogol's *Taras Bul'ba* (which appeared under the sensationalized titles *Rozbiinyk Taras Chornomor* [The Brigand Taras Chornomor] and *Pryhody otamana Urvana* [The Adventures of Otaman Urvan]), *Vii*, and *Nich pid Rizdvo* (The Night before Christmas). Some translations of classic Western writers, such as W. Shakespeare, Dante, and A. Dumas, were also published in *lubok* form. I. Kotliarevsky's *Eneïda* (Aeneid) and *Natalka Poltavka* (Natalka from Poltava) circulated widely in such editions. *Lubok* literature was also widely known among Ukrainian immigrants in the New World.

Lubok **pictures.** A form of graphic art for the common people, combining a printed and colored image with a subscript (often a simple verse). *Lubok* pictures were popular in Ukraine from the end of the 18th century. The name is derived from *lub*, the linden plank in which the picture was engraved or the linden bark from which the baskets for transporting the pictures were woven. In the 19th century, *lubok* pictures were produced by means of li-

Lubok illustration to the Bible by Illia (wood engraving, 17th century)

Lubok sheet by E. Denbrovsky (wood engraving, late 18th century)

thography and chromolithography and offered a cheap way of decorating peasant homes. They depicted scenes illustrating folk songs, tales, legends, the Bible, literary works, and proverbs. Sometimes they carried a critical or satirical comment on the political order. In prerevolutionary Ukraine many *lubok* pictures were printed in Odessa by Yu. Fesenko and at the Kievan Cave and Pochaiv monasteries. The tradition was revived during the Second World War by H. Bondarenko, A. Rieznychenko, V. Fatalchuk, and L. Chernov. The stylistic qualities of the genre are sometimes used in Soviet posters and illustrations of children's books.

Lubok **theater.** A pseudo-ethnographic, popular theatrical genre of a coarse artistic quality, performed by *touring theaters. Approx 70 *lubok* theater troupes existed during the 1880s and 1890s, with the actors and directors creating the repertoire themselves. To a certain degree *lubok* theater developed as an antipode of the ethnographic theater, which strove to portray village life in a realistic way or the Ukrainian heroic past in a colorful poetic form. *Lubok* theater twisted these portrayals into grotesque caricature and farce. It was not interefered with by the tsarist government, and some *lubok* theater troupes in Russian-ruled Ukraine were active until the NEP. Satires based on *lubok* theater performances were produced by the Ukrainian Drama Theater and by Berezil.

Lucaris, Cyril, b 13 November 1572 in Crete, d 27 June 1638 near Constantinople. Greek theologian and patriarch. He was exarch in the Polish-Lithuanian Commonwealth of the Patriarch of Alexandria Meletios Pegas, and rector of the theological academy in Vilnius. He participated in the Orthodox sobor that opposed the Church Union of *Berestia in 1596, and worked to undo the union and restore Orthodox hegemony in Ukraine. He was elected Patriarch of Alexandria in 1602 and Patriarch of Constantinople in 1620. His support for many Protestant reforms earned him the enmity of the conservative clergy, and he was deposed (and reinstalled) as patriarch five times. Lucaris maintained close relations with Ukraine and in 1623 ratified the statutes of the Lutske Brotherhood of the Elevation of the Cross and its school. In 1633 he confirmed the election of P. *Mohyla as Kievan metropolitan and named him exarch of the Patriarch of Constantinople.

Luchakivsky, Kostiantyn [Lučakivs'kyj, Kostjantyn], b 19 April 1846 in Yavche, Berezhany circle, Galicia, d 24 March 1912. Educator and classical philologist. A graduate of the universities of Lviv and Vienna, Luchakivsky taught Greek, Latin, and Ukrainian at the Academic Gymnasium of Lviv and the Ukrainian gymnasium in Buzke. He was also an inspector of Ukrainian schools. He wrote articles on classical philology and on Ukrainian literature. He is the author of school textbooks, among them a reader (1892) and *Vzory poeziï i prozy* (Patterns of Poetry and Prose, 1894; 2nd edn 1909).

Roksoliana Luchakovska: *Madonna*

Luchakovska, Roksoliana [Lučakovs'ka, Roksoljana], b 6 July 1938 in Stanyslaviv (now Ivano-Frankivske). Ukrainian-American painter. A postwar refugee in Philadelphia from 1951, she studied at the Ukrainian Art Studio there and the Pennsylvania Academy of Fine Arts (BFA, 1961). Since 1964 she has lived in Spain with her husband, the sculptor R. Armstrong. Her oeuvre contains landscapes and figural compositions in an impressionist style, frescoes, mosaics, and stained-glass windows. She has had many solo exhibitions in the United States (Philadelphia, New York, Princeton, Washington) and in Spain (Málaga, León, Madrid, and Santander). Her paintings and windows are found in churches, public buildings, and private collections in Europe and the United States.

Luchakovsky, Bohdan [Lučakovs'kyi], b 19 November 1900 in Stanyslaviv county, Galicia, d 11 August 1971 in Spain. Forestry engineer. A graduate of the polytechnical institute in Prague (1925), he was the founder and several times president of the *Union of Ukrainian Foresters and Woodsmen. In 1948–51 he lectured on forestry and forest economy at the Ukrainian Technical and Husbandry Institute in Munich. He was the author of many articles on hunting and forestry. In 1951 he emigrated to the United States.

Luchakovsky, Hryts [Lučakovs'kyj, Hryc'], b 13 September 1892 in Obertyn, Horodenka county, Galicia, d 21 June 1951 in Bathurst, Australia. Judge. While studying law at Lviv University he took part in the campaign for a Ukrainian university and helped found the Ukraina sports society. During the First World War he served as a lieutenant in the Austrian army. After the war he completed his law studies and served as judge in Bolekhiv and Peremyshl. During the 1939–41 Soviet occupation of Western Ukraine he sat on the supreme court of the Generalgouvernement in Cracow and presided over the Labor Alliance of Ukrainian Jurists. When the Germans occupied Galicia he returned to Zolochiv, where he worked as district judge. He helped to organize the Division Galizien and then enlisted in it as a lieutenant. After being interned as a POW by the British he emigrated to Australia.

Volodymyr Luchakovsky   Michael Luchkovich

Luchakovsky, Volodymyr [Lučakovs'kyj], b 1839 in Dovzhanka, Ternopil county, Galicia, d 29 March 1903 in Ternopil. Civic leader, writer, and lawyer. He established a law office in Ternopil in 1862 and became a leading organizer in the local community. He was a founder of various cultural institutions in Ternopil, including the Prosvita society, Ruska Besida, and an amateur theater. In 1884 he helped establish the Prince Ostrozky Foundation, and in 1885, the political organization known as the *People's Council in Lviv. Toward the end of the 1890s he was elected mayor of Ternopil. He collected proverbs and riddles, which eventually were published by I. Franko,

and wrote the study *Prychynok do etnohrafiï halyts'koho Podillia* (Materials on the Ethnography of Galician Podilia, 1883). He wrote poems, stories, comedies for the local theater, and articles on public issues for such papers as *Pravda, Dilo,* and *Zerkalo.* He translated a number of German and Polish plays. In the field of law he translated the Austrian criminal and criminal-procedure codes from German into Ukrainian and compiled notes on legal terminology, which were later used by K. *Levytsky in preparing his legal dictionary.

Luchkai, Mykhailo [Lučkaj, Myxajlo] (Lutskay; né Pop), b 19 November 1789 in Velyki Luchky, Transcarpathia, d 3 December 1843 in Uzhhorod, Transcarpathia. Historian, linguist, and Greek Catholic priest. After graduating from the Barbareum seminary in Vienna, he served as archivist and librarian of the Uzhhorod eparchy and devoted himself to the history, ethnography, and language of Transcarpathia. He wrote *Grammatica Slavo-Ruthena ...* (1830), based on J. Dobrovský's Czech grammar of 1822. It is one of the earliest descriptions of a Ukrainian dialect. It was studied by M. Vozniak (1890), V. Simovych (1930–1), G. Gerovsky (1931), and V. Pogorelov (1939). The grammar was reprinted with an introduction by O. Horbach in 1979. Luchkai argued that Church Slavonic was the oldest form of the Transcarpathian dialect and therefore it should be the literary language of Transcarpathia. Although his six-volume history of Transcarpathia was not published, it was circulated widely and influenced many later historians.

Luchkovich, Michael [Lučkovyč, Myxajlo], b 13 November 1892 in Shamokin, Pennsylvania, d 21 April 1973 in Edmonton. Politician, writer, and teacher, of Ukrainian descent. He moved to Canada in the footsteps of his sisters (who became teachers in Manitoba) and studied at the University of Manitoba (BA, 1916) and the Calgary Normal School (teaching certificate, 1917). He then held a succession of teaching posts in the Ukrainian immigrant communities of east central Alberta until 1926, when he was elected in the Vegreville constituency as the first Canadian member of parliament of Ukrainian origin. He was re-elected in 1930. His parliamentary career was highlighted by his vigorous response to disparaging public comments made by the Anglican bishop of Saskatchewan, G. Lloyd, about 'unpreferred continentals' and by an address to Parliament regarding the violation of minority rights in Poland (following the *Pacification campaign against Ukrainians). After his defeat in 1935, Luchkovich wrote extensively; his works include translations of N. Prychodko's *One in Fifteen Million* (1952), I. Kiriak's *Sons of the Soil* (in abridged form, 1959), and S. Goldeman's *Jewish National Autonomy in Ukraine* (1968). His reminiscences appeared in 1965 as *A Ukrainian Canadian in Parliament.* The Alberta Heritage Scholarship Trust grants a fellowship in his name.

Luchuk, Volodymyr [Lučuk], b 27 August 1934 in Matche, Hrubeshiv county, Kholm region, d 24 September 1992 in Lviv. Poet and translator. He graduated from Lviv University (1958), and worked as poetry editor of the journal *Zhovten'* (1959–63), secretary of the Lviv branch of the Ukrainian Society for the Protection of Historical and Cultural Monuments, and director of the manuscript division of the Lviv Scientific Library. He was the author of the poetry collections *Dovir'ia* (Trust, 1959), *Osonnia* (Sunny Places, 1962), *Maievo* (The Swaying, 1964), *Obrii na krylakh* (The Horizon on Wings, 1965), *Vahomist'* (Weightiness, 1967), *Bratni luny* (Fraternal Echoes, 1974), *Dyvovyd* (Strange View, 1979), *Navstrich* (Toward a Meeting, 1984), and *Kolobih* (Circle Run, 1986). He also wrote over 10 books of verse for children, translated many literary works, and edited a collection of S. Hordynsky's poetry (1990).

Ivan Luchyshyn   Ivan Luchytsky

Luchyshyn, Ivan [Lučyšyn], b 20 May 1895 in Hrushatychi, Peremyshl county, Galicia, d 6 July 1984 in Zurich, Switzerland. Engineer and civic figure. After being arrested and imprisoned in the early 1920s by the Polish authorities for his activity in organizing co-operatives, he left for Czechoslovakia, where he completed his engineering studies in 1926. He returned to Galicia in the late 1920s and became active in the Ukrainian Socialist Radical party, the Kameniari youth association, and the newspaper *Hromads'kyi holos*, while working as an inspector for the Ridna Shkola vocational schools. After the Second World War he emigrated to Germany, where he was active in the Ukrainian National Council, and then to Switzerland.

Luchytska, Kateryna [Lučyc'ka], b 30 September 1889 in Kiev, d 25 January 1971 in Kiev. Stage actress and director. She began her theatrical career in 1908 in the troupe of her father, L. Luchytsky, and then worked in the Ukrainian National Theater in Kiev (1917–18), the Shevchenko First Theater of the Ukrainian Soviet Republic (1920–1), and the Zankovetska Theater (1922–3). From 1923 she worked in various theaters in Kiev, Dnipropetrovske, and Odessa. In 1945–59 she directed the Stryi Ukrainian Music and Drama Theater.

Luchytsky, Borys [Lučyc'kyj], b 7 February 1906 in Ust-Medveditskaia, Don Cossack province, d 6 March 1966 in Chernihiv. Stage actor and director. A pupil of O. Sukhodolsky, in 1923 he began working as an actor and director in various workers' and peasants' theaters, mainly in Chernihiv. In 1933–60 he was artistic director of the Nizhen Ukrainian Music and Drama Theater, and from 1960 he led the Chernihiv Ukrainian Music and Drama Theater.

Luchytsky, Ivan [Lučyc'kyj] (Loutchisky), b 14 June 1845 in Kamianets-Podilskyi, Podilia gubernia, d 22 August 1918 in Kiev. Historian and civic figure; corresponding member of the St Petersburg Academy of Sciences from 1908. He graduated from Kiev University (1866) and served as a professor of history there (1877–1908) and taught at the Higher Courses for Women in St Petersburg. He worked in the Poltava zemstvo administration and was elected to the State Duma as a representative of Kiev and the *Constitutional Democratic party. He was a member of the Old *Hromada of Kiev and a contributor to *Kievskaia starina*. He was one of the cofounders of the *Ukrainian Scientific Society in Kiev. Luchytsky's major works concerned socioeconomic and cultural-religious history; among them are *Katolicheskaia Liga i kalvinisty vo Frantsii* (The Catholic League and Calvinists in France, 1877), *Krest'ianskoe zemlevladenie vo Frantsii nakanune revoliutsii* (1900; repub in French as *La propriété paysanne en France à la veille de la révolution*, 1912), *Rabochee naselenie i ekonomicheskaia politika germanskikh gorodov 15–16 vv.* (Worker Population and the Economic Policy of German Towns in the 15th–16th Centuries, 1894), *Materialy dlia istorii zemlevladeniia v Poltavskoi gubernii v 18 v.* (Materials for the History of Land Holding in Poltava Gubernia in the 18th Century, 1883; on the basis of the Rumiantsev census), and *Etudes sur la propriété communale dans la Petite Russie* (2 vols, 1895, 1899; also pub in *Revue internationale de sociologie*, 1895). His studies of the Ukrainian peasantry are considered the standard in the field.

BIBLIOGRAPHY
Hrushevs'kyi, O. 'Pamiaty profesora I.V. Luchyts'koho,' in *Nashe mynule*, 3 (Kiev 1918)

A. Zhukovsky

Volodymyr Luchytsky

Luchytsky, Volodymyr [Lučyc'kyj], b 2 May 1877 in Kiev, d 20 October 1949 in Kiev. Geologist and petrographer; full member of the AN URSR (now ANU) from 1945; son of I. *Luchytsky. He graduated from Kiev University in 1899 and studied abroad. He then taught at Kiev University, where in 1912 he was appointed a professor of geology. He was head of the Ukrainian Geological Committee (1917–23), which he helped organize. Then he served as a professor at the Moscow Mining Academy

(1923–30) and the Moscow Institute of Geological Prospecting (1930–41). He returned to Kiev, where he was a professor of mineralogy and petrography at Kiev University (1945–9) and became director of the Institute of Geological Sciences (1947–9). Luchytsky's scientific works were devoted to the petrography and mineralogy of the Ukrainian Crystalline Shield, the stratigraphy of Precambrian rocks of the East European Platform, regional hydrogeology, and the mineral resources of Ukraine. He prepared hydrogeological and geological maps of Ukraine. His petrography textbook, first published in 1910, had gone through six editions by 1947. He was editor in chief of the fifth volume of *Geologiia USSR* (Geology of the USSR, 1944).

Luciuk, Lubomyr [Lučjuk, Ljubomyr], b 9 July 1953 in Kingston, Ontario. Geographer and Ukrainian-Canadian community figure. A graduate of Queen's University (MA, 1979) and the University of Alberta (PH D, 1984), he has taught at the Royal Military College in Kingston since 1989. A specialist in historical geography, Luciuk has written a history of Ukrainians in Kingston (1980). He has edited the memoirs of G. Panchuk (1983); and has co-edited documentary collections on Ukrainian-Canadian history (1986), Anglo-American foreign policy vis-à-vis Ukraine in 1938–51 (1987), the documents of the British Foreign Office and the 1932–3 famine in Ukraine (1987), collections of articles on ethnicity and the Canadian state in 1939–45 (1988), and the compendium *Ukrainians in Ontario* (1988). He has coauthored (with B. Kordan) a geography of Ukrainians in Canada (1989).

George Luckyj   Luh society: coat of arms

Luckyj, George Stephen Nestor [Luc'kyj, Yurii], b 11 June 1919 in Yanchyn, Peremyshliany county, Galicia. Literary scholar; member of the Shevchenko Scientific Society and the Ukrainian Academy of Arts and Sciences; son of O. *Lutsky. He was educated at the University of Birmingham and Columbia University (PH D, 1953). He taught at the University of Saskatchewan (1947–9) and the University of Toronto (1952–84), where he occupied the position of chairman of the Department of Slavic Languages and Literatures (1957–61). He was an associate director of the *Canadian Institute of Ukrainian Studies (1976–82) and the first editor of *Canadian Slavonic Papers* (1956–61). He was one of the editors of the two-volume *Ukraine: A Concise Encyclopedia* (1963, 1970) and the English-language editor of the first volume of *Encyclopedia of Ukraine* (1984).

Most of Luckyj's studies are devoted to Ukrainian and Soviet literature. He has edited and introduced a number of volumes, including a documentary study of Vaplite (1957), *Four Ukrainian Poets* (1969), *Modern Ukrainian Short Stories* (1973), *Discordant Voices: The Non-Russian Soviet Literatures* (1975), *Shevchenko and the Critics* (1980), and *Sami pro sebe: Avtobiohrafiï vydatnykh ukraïntsiv XIX-ho stolittia* (About Themselves: Autobiographies of Notable Ukrainians of the 19th Century, 1989). He is the author of *Literary Politics in the Soviet Ukraine, 1917–1934* (1956; 2nd edn 1990), *Between Gogol' and Ševčenko: Polarity in Literary Ukraine, 1798–1847* (1971), *Panteleimon Kulish: A Sketch of His Life and Times* (1983), *Young Ukraine: The Brotherhood of Saints Cyril and Methodius, 1845–1847* (1991), *Lystuvannia z Ievhenom Sverstiukom* (A Correspondence with Yevhen Sverstiuk, 1992), and *Ukrainian Literature in the Twentieth Century: A Readers' Guide* (1992). A prolific translator, he translated (often in co-operation with his wife, Moira) into English works by I. *Bahriany, M. *Khvylovy, and V. *Pidmohylny as well as P. Zaitsev's classic biography of T. Shevchenko (1988). A festschrift in his honor, *In Working Order: Essays presented to G.S.N. Luckyj*, was published as a separate volume of the *Journal of Ukrainian Studies* (1989).

D.H. Struk

Lud (Folk). A Polish ethnographic quarterly published in Lviv from 1895 (as an annual from 1912) by the Polish Ethnographic Society. Its founder and first editor was A. Kalina (1895–1904). In 1945 it was moved to Wrocław. Besides Polish and Slavic ethnographic material *Lud* published a substantial amount in Ukrainian ethnography.

Ludwig, Albert (né Mykhailo Bzovy), b 14 November 1919 in Melfort, Saskatchewan. Lawyer and politician of Ukrainian descent. After serving in the Royal Canadian Air Force during the First World War, Ludwig studied law at the University of Alberta. From a riding in southern Alberta, he was the first Ukrainian elected to the Alberta legislature, as the Social Credit member for Calgary–Mountain View in 1959, 1963, 1967, and 1976. He served as minister of public works from 1969 to 1971, and was appointed a judge in the Athabasca region in 1974.

Luh (Meadow). A paramilitary sports, physical-fitness, and fire-fighting society in Galicia, founded by R. *Dashkevych in Lviv in 1925 after the *Sich society was banned by the Polish government. Luh grew from 163 branches in 1925 to 817 in 1927, and then declined to 750 in 1929 and 598 in 1931, partly as a result of the creation of the *Union of Ukrainian Progressive Youth. The members (8,250 in 1925, 60,000 in 1927, 45,000 in 1931) practiced calisthenics, shooting, and military drills; played organized sports; participated in provincial and county jamborees and community celebrations; and organized amateur theaters. The parent organization (Velykyi Luh) in Lviv owned a sports field and a gymnasium and published a monthly organ, *Visty z Luhu* (1925–39). The Polish government forbade Luh to form branches in Volhynia, Podlachia, and the Kholm and Lemko regions, and in 1932 it placed Luh under the jurisdiction of the state physical education administration and forbade its members to fight fires. The existing branches were split up between those who rejected and those who accepted the new Polish statute imposed on them. In 1934 the former group had 92 branches with 2,000 members, and the latter, 330 branches with 20,000 members. Leading figures in Luh were Dashkevych, V. Fedorchak, O. Kobersky, M. Kozlaniuk, A. Kurdydyk, O. Kurtseba, M., R., and Yu. Mamchak, and O. Pavlova. In 1939, after the Soviet occupation of Galicia, Luh and its 805 branches (50,000 members) were banned.

Luha River. A right-bank tributary of the Buh River. It is 93 km long and drains a basin area of 1,348 sq km. The river flows through Volhynia oblast. It is used by industry, especially the sugar refining industry. The main city located on the river is Volodymyr-Volynskyi.

Luhanchyk River [Luhančyk]. A right-bank tributary of the Donets River. It is 83 km long and drains a basin area of 659 sq km. The river flows through the Donets Ridge within the borders of Luhanske oblast. It is used for irrigation and water supply. Two sluice-gates and several water reservoirs have been built on it.

Luhanka River (also Luhan). A right-bank tributary of the Donets River, which it joins at Stanychno-Luhanske. It is 198 km long and drains a basin area of 3,670 sq km. It flows through the Donets Ridge within the borders of Donetske and Luhanske oblasts. Its waters are used for industry and irrigation. Several water reservoirs and sluice-regulators have been built on it. The main cities located on the river are Pervomaiske, Kirovske, and Luhanske.

Luhanske [Luhans'ke]. V-20, DB II-6. A city (1989 pop 497,000) at the confluence of the Luhan and Vilkhivka rivers and the capital of Luhanske oblast. It is one of the major industrial centers of the country. In 1935–58 and from 1970 until May 1990 it was called Voroshylovhrad.

Luhanske was founded in 1795, when the imperial government decided to build a cannon foundry and ammunition factory for the Black Sea navy there. During the Napoleonic Wars the plant was greatly expanded, and the workers' population increased. The state enterprise stimulated the development of mining in the Donets Basin. After the Crimean War the foundry could not compete with more efficient plants, and in 1887 it was shut down. By then Luhanske was a large industrial center linked by rail to the Dnieper Industrial Region and the ports of the Sea of Azov. In 1882 the county administration was moved from Slavianoserbske to Luhanske, and the town was granted city status. In 1895 the government reopened a munitions factory in Luhanske, and in 1896 a Belgian firm established the largest steam-engine plant in the Russian Empire there. By 1905 the plant was building 21 percent of the steam engines produced in the empire. The city's population grew from 20,400 in 1897 to 34,000 in 1904 and 68,000 in 1914. Much of its population (68.2 percent in 1897) was Russian.

Under the Soviet regime the city grew rapidly in the interwar period. In 1938 it became the administrative center of a new oblast. Today it is an important railway and highway junction and a major industrial center. Its most important industries are machine building and metalworking; it has a diesel-locomotive building consortium, a coal machine-building plant, a motor-vehicle assembly plant, a crankshaft factory, a combustion-engine parts factory, and a tube-rolling mill. The light industry manufactures goods such as fine fabrics, footwear, knitwear, and clothing. The plants of the food industry include meat

Luhanske: view of Kotsiubynsky Street

packers, dairies, and confectionery factories. The building-materials industry produces bricks, tiles, and reinforced concrete. The energy to run the industries is supplied by the Luhanske Power Station in Shchastia.

The city's educational system includes 4 institutions of higher learning – the Agricultural, Pedagogical, Machine-Building, and Medical institutes – as well as 12 specialized secondary schools and 21 vocational schools. The first Ukrainian gymnasium was opened only in 1991. There are about 40 research institutes, including a coal-enrichment institute and a branch of the Institute of the Economics of Industry. The cultural facilities of the city include three theaters (Ukrainian music and drama, Russian drama, and puppet), a circus, a museum of regional studies, and an art museum.

V. Kubijovyč

Luhanske Agricultural Institute (Luhanskyi silskohospodarskyi instytut). An institution of higher learning, until 1991 under the USSR Ministry of Agriculture. It was formed in 1921 out of a secondary agricultural school. In 1991 it consisted of eight faculties, including agronomy, economics, zootechnics, agricultural mechanization, a correspondence school, and a graduate program. The institute maintains an experimental farm. It published the newspaper *Za radians'ki kadry*. At the end of the 1970s its enrollment was almost 5,000.

Luhanske Art Museum (Luhanskyi khudozhnii muzei im. Artema). A collection of paintings, sculptures, graphic art, and decorative art, established in Luhanske in 1945. It was opened to the public in 1963. It is divided into departments of Ukrainian and Russian prerevolutionary art, Soviet art, Ukrainian decorative folk art, and Western European art. The museum contains over 5,000 works. Approx 1,000 of them are exhibited in its 13 exhibition halls. They include works by V. Tropinin, I. Aivazovsky, R. Sudkovsky, A. Kuindzhi, M. Pymonenko, P. Levchenko, O. Murashko, Ye. Bukovetsky, P. Volokidin, S. Svitoslavsky, V. Orlovsky, S. Prokhorov, Ye. Volobuiev, O. Shovkunenko, T. Yablonska, V. Chekaniuk, S. Hryhoriev, Y. Bokshai, and H. Yakutovych.

Luhanske Coal Machine-Building Plant (Luhanskyi zavod vuhilnoho mashynobuduvannia im. O. Parkhomenka). A factory producing mining and mineral-processing equipment. It grew out of a small railway repair shop established in 1878. Since 1930 it has specialized in the production of machines and equipment for mineral enrichment complexes.

Luhanske Diesel-Locomotive Building Consortium (Luhanske vyrobnyche obiednannia teplevozobuduvannia). A consortium created in 1976 and consisting of a diesel-locomotive factory and a branch of the All-Union Scientific Research Institute of Diesel Locomotive Building. The main plant was established in 1896 to produce steam locomotives for freight and passenger trains, boilers, and steel and iron castings. The first locomotive, with a 560-HP capacity, was built in 1900. Since 1957 the plant has specialized in the production of diesel locomotives. By 1980 it was producing almost 95 percent of the diesel locomotives built in the USSR. Many of them were exported. It also produces parts and other railway equipment.

Luhanske Machine-Building Institute (Luhanskyi mashynobudivnyi instytut). An institution of higher learning under Ukraine's Ministry of Higher and Specialized Secondary Education. It was founded in 1960 through the reorganization of the Evening Machine-Building Institute for Workers. It has seven faculties, as well as an evening and correspondence school and a graduate program. The institute's two branches are in Rubizhne and Krasnodon. In 1976–7 the enrollment was about 13,000, in 25 specialties. The interdepartmental collection *Konstruiuvannia i vyrobnytstvo transportnykh mashyn* is published by the institute.

Luhanske Nature Reserve (Luhanskyi zapovidnyk). A nature reserve established in Luhanske oblast for the study and preservation of the natural habitat of floodplain forests, meadows, and multiple grass steppes. The reserve extends over a total area of 1,579.5 ha in three separate divisions: the Striletskyi Steppe (494 ha, est 1936), Stanychno-Luhanske (498 ha, est 1968), and the Provalskyi Steppe (587.5 ha, est 1975 along the Donets Ridge). The aim of the reserve is to preserve in their natural state steppe vegetation and wild fauna, especially the endangered steppe marmot. Over 400 species of flora can be found in the reserve, including tall plants, feather grass vegetation, and brushwoods.

Luhanske oblast. An administrative territory (1989 pop 2,864,000) in eastern Ukraine, formed on 3 June 1938. It has an area of 26,700 sq km and is divided into 18 raions, 37 cities, 109 towns (smt), and 189 rural councils. The capital is *Luhanske.

Physical geography. The Donets River, which flows in a southeasterly direction, divides the oblast into two distinct zones. The northern part consists of a hilly plain rising from the Donets Lowland to spurs of the Central Upland. The southern region consists of the Donets Ridge, an undulating plain with an elevation of up to 200–250 m dissected by river valleys and ravines. That part of the oblast is rich in coal and natural gas deposits as well as limestone, marl, chalk, and clay. The climate is continental: the summers are hot and dry, and the winters are cold and snowless. The average January temperature is –7°C and the average July temperature, 22°C. The annual precipitation ranges from 400–450 mm in the north to 550 mm in the Donets Ridge. The water resources of the oblast are

Luhanske oblast: landscape in Antratsyt raion

limited. The main tributaries of the Donets are the Luhan and the Velyka Kamianka on the right bank and the Krasna, the Borova, the Aidar, and the Derkul on the left. Chernozems cover 81 percent of the surface. Only 8.6 percent of the oblast is forested. In the ravines the prevalent trees are oak, ash, maple, pear, and apple, and in the floodplains, alder, poplar, and willow. Most of the natural steppe vegetation in the oblast has been replaced with cultivated plants; only remnants are left, along riverbanks and in the *Luhanske Nature Reserve.

History. The territory of the oblast has been inhabited since the Paleolithic period. In the 10th to 14th centuries it was occupied by nomadic tribes. In the 16th and 17th centuries Muscovy set up forts and fortifications in the steppes to protect its southern borders from nomadic raiders. The Zaporozhian Cossacks established some outposts in the territory. In the second half of the 17th century runaway peasants from Ukraine and Russia began to form settlements. At the beginning of the 18th century the Russian rulers brought in Serbian, Wallachian, and Moldavian colonists to establish military settlements in the Donets region. The territory became part of Azov gubernia (1775–82) and Katerynoslav vicegerency (1783–1802). In the 19th century the eastern part of the present oblast belonged to Don Cossack province, the southern and western parts to Katerynoslav gubernia, and the northern part to Kharkiv gubernia. After the revolution the territory was incorporated into the Ukrainian SSR.

Population. According to the census of 1989, Ukrainians form a slight majority (51.9 percent) of the oblast's population, followed by Russians (44.8). The rest of the population consists mostly of Belarusians, Tatars, and Jews. The population density is 107 people per sq km and is highest in the southern parts of the oblast. After Donetske oblast, it is the most urbanized oblast in Ukraine: 86 percent of its population is urban. The largest cities are Luhanske, *Komunarske, *Kransyi Luch, *Stakhanov, and *Lysychanske.

Industry. Most of the oblast's output (87.6 percent) is industrial. The main industries are the fuel industry (27.3 percent of the industrial output in 1986), which includes coal (19.2 percent), machine building and metalworking (24 percent), the chemical industry (14 percent), and ferrous metallurgy (12 percent). The energy for those industries is supplied by thermoelectric power plants in Shchastia, Siverskodonetske, and Lysychanske. Coal mining is conducted by 9 consortia, which control 94 mines and 28 enrichment plants. The metallurgical industry imports iron ore from the Kryvyi Rih region for the manufacture of steel (in Komunarske), ferrous alloys (Stakhanov), and tubing (Luhanske). The machine-building and metalworking industries produce transportation vehicles (particularly diesel locomotives in Luhanske), mining machinery (Krasnyi Luch), railway coaches (Stakhanov), and computers (Siverskodonetske). The chemical industry includes a petroleum refinery in Lysychanske, a mineral fertilizers plant in Siverskodonetske, an aniline dyes factory in Rubizhne, and a soda plant in Luhanske. The large building-materials industry produces approx half of the window glass in Ukraine as well as brick, silicate blocks, ceramic plates, and reinforced-concrete products. The main products of light industry are clothing, footwear, and fine fabrics.

Agriculture. In 1986 there were 169 collective and 152 state farms and 8 poultry factories in the oblast. Of the total 1,888,000 ha of farmland 77.2 percent was cultivated, 19.9 percent was pasture, and 1.6 percent was hayfield. Of the farmland 96,400 ha were irrigated. Slightly over half of the sown area (1,352,000 ha) was devoted to grain crops, such as winter wheat (10.7 percent), barley (16.4 percent), and corn (10.3 percent). Feed crops occupied 34.2 percent of the sown area. The main industrial crop was sunflower (10.4 percent). Approx 5 percent of the area was set aside for fruit and vegetable farming. Animal husbandry accounts for 64 percent of the oblast's agricultural output. Most of it consists of beef and dairy cattle farming; hogs, horses, sheep, goats, and poultry are also raised.

Transportation. In 1986 the railway network in the oblast had 1,192 km of track. The main lines crossing the oblast are the Luhanske–Kiev, Luhanske–Moscow, Debaltseve–Luhanske–Millerovo, Kharkiv–Volgograd, and Luhanske–Rostov-na-Donu. There were 5,600 km of highway, 5,300 km of which were paved. The major highways running through the oblast are the Luhanske–Kharkiv, Kharkiv–Rostov-na-Donu, and Luhanske–Donetske. There are two main airports, in Luhanske and Siverskodonetske. The Stavropol–Moscow and Soiuz gas pipelines and the Kuibysheve–Slovianske and Groznyi–Lysychanske oil pipelines cross the oblast.

BIBLIOGRAPHY
Istoriia mist i sil URSR: Luhans'ka oblast (Kiev 1968)

Luhanske Pedagogical Institute (Luhanskyi pedahohichnyi instytut im. T.H. Shevchenka). An institute of higher learning, under the jurisdiction of the Ministry of Education. Originally formed in 1923 as a branch of the Donetske Institute of People's Education, the school was reorganized as a pedagogical institute in 1934 and named after T. Shevchenko in 1939. The institute has six faculties: philology, physics and mathematics, physical geography, history and pedagogy, music education, and physical education. It also operates a research division, branch laboratories, and an agricultural research station. In 1976–7 a total of 5,691 students were enrolled at the institute.

Luhanske Regional Studies Museum (Luhanskyi kraieznavchyi muzei). A museum founded in Luhanske in 1920. Most of its collections were destroyed during the Second World War. After the war the museum was rebuilt. In the late 1970s over 100,000 items were preserved in its natural science, pre-Soviet history, and Soviet history sections. Branches of the museum are also located in Starobilske, Antratsyt, Krasnyi Luch, Sverdlovske, Lysychanske, and Parkhomenko, Krasnodon raion (the Oleksander Parkhomenko Museum). Guides to the museum were published in 1963, 1968, 1977, and 1980.

Luhansky, Mykola [Luhans'kyj], b 8 December 1906 in Kharkiv gubernia, d 29 August 1968 in Kiev. Pharmacologist and toxicologist. A graduate of the Kharkiv Medical Institute (1931), he was director of the Ukrainian Sanitary and Chemical Scientific Research Institute in Kharkiv (1939–41) and the Kiev Scientific Research Institute of Pharmacology and Toxicology (from 1951). From 1942 to 1951 he served as deputy minister of health of the Ukrainian SSR. In his published works he dealt with the mechanism of the action and medicinal properties of thiolic compounds and the combined use of antidotal and pathogenetic therapy.

Luhova Mohyla. See Oleksandropil kurhan.

Maksym Luhovtsov

Luhovtsov, Maksym [Luhovcov], b 11 May 1885 in Yuzivka (now Donetske), Bakhmut county, Katerynoslav gubernia, d 7 June 1956 in Kiev. Metallurgist; full member of the AN URSR (now ANU) from 1939. He graduated from the Katerynoslav Higher School of Mining (1916) and served as director of the AN URSR Institute of Ferrous Metallurgy (1939–51). He did research in the statistical theory of blast furnace processes and sintering and developed methods of improving the quality of cast iron.

Luhovy, Laryssa [Luhova, Larysa], b 23 January 1942 in Ternopil. Ukrainian-Canadian painter. She was raised in Belgium (1943–50) and Montreal, and graduated from George Washington University (MFA, 1969), where she won first prize at the 1969 Annual Art Show. Solo exhibitions of her works have been held in Washington (1970, 1976) and New York (1981). Using oils and acrylics and employing strong hues, nonobjective forms, and highly expressive brush strokes Luhovy has developed her own vocabulary of images.

Laryssa Luhovy: *Composition* (acrylic)

Oleksander Luhovy

Luhovy, Oleksander (pseud of Oleksander Ovrutsky-Shvabe), b 8 January 1904 in Ovruch, Volhynia gubernia, d 30 September 1962 in Chisholm, Alberta. Writer. In 1929 he emigrated to Canada, where he worked as an agricultural and industrial laborer. His dramas and novels, all based on historical topics, include *Vira Babenko* (1936), *Za voliu Ukraïny* (For the Freedom of Ukraine, 1939), *Chorni khmary z-za Prypiati* (Black Clouds from beyond the Prypiat, 1946), and a novel on the life of Ukrainians in Canada, *Bezkhatnyi* (Homeless, 1946). In 1943 he published the historical outline *Vyznachne zhinotstvo Ukraïny* (Outstanding Women of Ukraine), and in 1947 he became publisher and editor of the monthly *Ukraïns'ka rodyna* (Toronto and Edmonton).

Luhyny. II-9. A town smt (1990 pop 5,100) on the Zheriv River and a raion center in Zhytomyr oblast. It is first mentioned in a historical document in 1606. Luhyny received smt status in 1967. A settlement from the early Meolithic period (5th millennium BC) was discovered near the town.

Luka Lake. II-4. A lake located in northwestern Volhynia oblast between the Buh River and the upper part of the Prypiat River. It has an area of 7 sq km and a depth of up to 10 m and is located at an altitude of 162 m. The lake has flat, marshy banks and is fed by surface runoff. Straits connect Luka Lake with Pulemet and Svytiaz lakes.

Luka Zhydiata. See Zhydiata, Luka.

Luka-Raikovetska. An early Slavic settlement of the 7th to 9th century AD, located in the Luka basin on the Hnylopiat River near the present-day village of Raiky, Berdychiv raion, Zhytomyr oblast. The site is approximately 250 m long and 80–120 m wide. It was excavated in 1946–7 by an expedition of the AN URSR Institute of Archeology under the direction of V. Honcharov. Uncovered were the remains of eight semi-pit dwellings which contained stone ovens, hand-molded clay pottery, and iron implements. The material culture found at Luka-Raikovetska was characteristic of the southwestern groups of the East Slavic tribes living along the right bank of the Dnieper River just prior to the emergence of the Kievan Rus' state. In Polisia such groups belonged to the forest-dwelling *Derevliani-ans.

Yevmen Lukasevych   Mykola Lukash

Lukasevych, Yevmen [Lukasevyč, Jevmen], b 26 December 1871 in Bila, Chortkiv county, Galicia, d 20 December 1929 in Warsaw. Physician and civic leader. After completing his medical studies in Zurich (1901) he settled in Kiev, where he worked as a zemstvo physician, was a member of the Ukrainian Scientific Society, helped found the Chas publishing house and the Prosvita society, and was active in the Rodyna club. In 1917–18 he helped organize the Ukrainian Red Cross and the Chief Sanitation Administration and published the monthly *Ukraïns'ki medychni visty*. At the end of 1918 he headed a diplomatic mission of the UNR to Switzerland, and in 1920 he was appointed deputy minister for foreign affairs in V. Prokopovych's cabinet. Having settled in Warsaw after the First World War, he founded and directed a hospital there and financed the daily newspaper *Ukraïns'ka trybuna*. He compiled and published *Anatomichnyi slovnyk* (Anatomical Dictionary, 1926).

Lukash, Mykola [Lukaš], b 19 December 1919 in Krolevets, Chernihiv gubernia, d 29 August 1988 in Kiev. Translator. He graduated from Kiev University (1941) and the Kharkiv Institute of Foreign Languages (1947), and until 1953 he taught German, French, and English in Kharkiv's postsecondary schools. For most of his life Lukash worked as a translator of literature. He translated into Ukrainian from 18 European languages, including J.W. von Goethe's *Faust*, G. Boccaccio's *Decameron*, G. Flaubert's *Madame Bovary*, M. de Cervantes's *Don Quixote*, Lope de Vega's plays, poetry by P. Verlaine, V. Hugo, G. Apollinaire, F. Schiller, H. Heine, R. Burns, A. Mickiewicz, and J. Tuwim, and works by many other writers. He also wrote on lexicographical matters. Through his translations, he restored into use many 17th- and 18th-century words and introduced neologisms into the contemporary Ukrainian literary language. In 1973 he was expelled from the Writers' Union of Ukraine and the editorial board of the journal *Vsesvit* for offering to serve the ailing I. *Dziuba's sentence of political imprisonment.

Lukashevych [Lukaševyč]. A Cossack *starshyna* family in the Pereiaslav region. Lukash (d 1736) was the osaul (1716–33), quartermaster (1735), and acting colonel of Pereiaslav regiment. Hryhorii (1735–52), Mykhailo (1752–67), and Luka (1769–73) were osauls in that regiment. Luka was also the regiment's last quartermaster (1773–9) and the last colonel of Kiev regiment (1779–83). His son was V. *Lukashevych. Other descendants include the ethnographer P. *Lukashevych and the bibliophile I. Lukashevych (1811–60), who was a gubernial secretary (1844–50).

Lukashevych, Antin [Lukaševyč], b 18 February 1870 in Babyn, Bukovyna, d 23 May 1936 in Chernivtsi. Civic and political leader in Bukovyna. A candidate of the National Democratic party, he won a seat in the Bukovynian Diet (1911–18) and in the Austrian parliament (1907–18). In the interwar period he was elected to the Rumanian parliament (1920) and to the Rumanian Senate (1926). In both houses, as well as the minorities department of the League of Nations, he defended the national rights of the Ukrainian people in Bukovyna. In 1922 he helped found the Ukrainian Popular Organization in Bukovyna. In his articles, which appeared in the Ukrainian and Austrian press, he criticized the Rumanian government's discriminatory policies toward Bukovynian Ukrainians.

Lukashevych, Platon [Lukaševyč], b 1806 in Berezan, Pereiaslav county, Kiev gubernia, d 1887 in Berezan. Folklorist. A graduate of Nizhen Lyceum, where he was N. Gogol's classmate, and of the Richelieu Lyceum (1828), he began to collect Ukrainian folklore under J. Kollár's influence. Of the collected materials, he published only four carols and the collection *Malorossiiskie i chervonorusskie narodnye dumy i pesni* (Little Russian and Red Ruthenian Folk Dumas and Songs, 1836), which contained 176 songs of various genres and spells against toothache. Some of the dumas in the collection – on S. Kyshka, the Cossack Holota, and the storm on the Black Sea, and the captives' lament – appeared in print for the first time; others – on I.

Ivas-Konovchenko, I. Nechai, Perebynis, and Morozenko – appeared in a new version. After his death some of Lukashevych's notes were published by V. Horlenko and B. Hrinchenko. His manuscripts are preserved at the Central Scientific Library of the ANU; they include a study of Ukrainian superstitions, a collection of Ukrainian songs written down by him, a collection of folk songs with his commentary, an essay on Ukrainian fables, and his autographs of all the dumas and many of the songs in the 1836 collection.

Lukashevych, Vasyl [Lukaševyč, Vasyl'], b ca 1783 in the Pereiaslav region, d 16 October 1866 in Boryspil, near Kiev. Political activist. After working in St Petersburg at the Collegium of Foreign Affairs (1803–5) and the Ministry of Internal Affairs (1805–7) he settled in Boryspil and founded a county school in Pereiaslav, and from 1811 he served as marshal of the nobility of Pereiaslav county. He was a prominent Ukrainian *Freemason, a member of the Love of Truth Lodge in Poltava and the United Slavs Lodge in Kiev, and in 1818 he joined the *Union of Welfare in St Petersburg. He advocated Ukrainian statehood and political independence, and he organized the *Little Russian Secret Society. In February 1826 he was imprisoned in the Peter and Paul Fortress in St Petersburg and then confined to his estate in Boryspil until the end of his life. According to some historians (eg, M. Petrovsky) Lukashevych was probably the author of *Istoriia Rusov (History of the Rus' Peoples).

Lukashov, Ivan [Lukašov], b 25 October 1901 in Opishnia, Zinkiv county, Poltava gubernia, d 26 May 1970 in Kharkiv. Epizootiologist; corresponding member of the All-Union Academy of Agricultural Sciences from 1956. He graduated from the Kharkiv Veterinary Institute (1926) and from 1931 chaired its epizootiology department. His works are devoted to problems of epizootiology, diagnosis, prophylaxis, and the treatment of chronic infections and viral diseases.

Lukashova, Iraida [Lukašova, Irajida], b 14 January 1938 in Sverdlovsk (now Ekaterinburg) RF. Ballet dancer. After graduating from the Odessa Ballet School (1953) she danced as a soloist with the Odessa (1954) and Kiev (1955–75) opera and ballet theaters, with which she appeared in the roles of Lily in K. Dankevych's *The Lily*, Mavka in M. Skorulsky's *The Forest Song*, Giselle in A. Adam's *Giselle*, Princess Aurora and Masha in P. Tchaikovsky's *Sleeping Beauty* and *The Nutcracker*, and Maria in B. Asafev's *The Fountain of Bakhchesarai*. In 1976 she joined the Kiev Theater of Opera and Ballet as a choreographer and teacher.

Lukavetsky, Zenon [Lukavec'kyj], b 1869, d ? Judge. He served as a judge in Kolomyia and Lviv and sat on the Supreme Court in Warsaw (1929–32). He was a leading member of organizations such as the Ukrainian Invalids' Aid Society, the Ukrainian Catholic Union, and the *Society of Ukrainian Lawyers in Lviv. In 1939 he was deported by the Soviet authorities, and perished without a trace.

Luka-Vrublivetska. A multi-occupational site on the left bank of the Dniester River in Kamianets-Podilskyi raion, Khmelnytskyi oblast. Excavated between 1945 and 1950, the site revealed a Paleolithic occupation, a Trypilian settlement, and *Cherniakhiv culture and Kievan Rus'

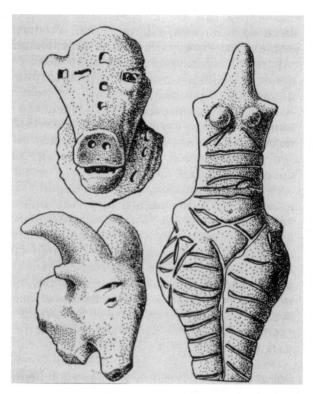

Luka-Vrublivetska: unearthed zoomorphic and anthropomorphic figures

Lev Lukianenko

habitation. The Paleolithic occupation, one of the oldest sites in Ukraine, produced examples of Mousterian flint tools. The Trypilian settlement of the fourth millennium BC revealed seven semi-pit dwellings, the largest being 45 m long and 3–5 m wide, with eleven hearths arranged on the long axis of the building. Faunal remains uncovered indicate the use of domesticated stock (cattle, horses, pigs), as well as wild animals (deer, elk, roebuck, boar, and bear). In addition to the recovery of bone and stone implements (such as sickle blades and bow drills), ceramic vessels (often decorated with curvilinear ornamentation), and approximately 250 terra-cotta effigies of humans and animals, a few copper items (fishing hooks, awls, and small ornaments) were also recovered. These copper items constitute the oldest man-made metal objects found in Ukraine.

Lukianenko, Lev [Lukjanenko], b 24 August 1928 in Khrypivka, Chernihiv okruha. Lawyer, political leader, and dissident. After graduating in law from Moscow University in 1958, he worked as a lawyer in Western Ukraine. Although a Party member, he was a staunch Ukrainian separatist. In 1959 he organized a clandestine group which discussed the possibility of Ukraine's independence and democratization and drafted the program of a projected Ukrainian Workers' and Peasants' Union. The group was uncovered, and in May 1961 Lukianenko was sentenced to be shot, but the sentence was commuted to 15 years' imprisonment. During his 5 years in the Vladimir prison and 10 in strict-regime labor camps in Mordovia and Perm, he was active in protests demanding recognition for political prisoners. Upon completing his term he lived under constant police surveillance in Chernihiv. In 1976 he was a founder of the *Ukrainian Helsinki Group. He was arrested at the end of 1977 and sentenced in July 1978 to 10 years in strict-regime labor camps and 5 years of exile for anti-Soviet agitation and propaganda. After spending 10 years in Mordovian and Perm camps he was exiled to Tomsk oblast and released in December 1988. As head of the Helsinki Group (1988–90) he became active in the political revival in Ukraine and won election to the Supreme Soviet in March 1990. He is a founder and president of the Ukrainian Republican party, the first non-communist party to be registered in Ukraine. In 1992 Lukianenko was appointed the first ambassador of Ukraine to Canada. His letters, petitions, and articles appeared in various underground publications in the USSR and in collections of materials on the Ukrainian human rights movement published in the West.

O. Zinkevych

Lukianivka Prison (Lukianivska tiurma). A fortified prison built in 1863 on Parkhomenko Street in the Lukianivka district of Kiev. In tsarist times V. Vynnychenko, M. Kybalchych, M. Kovalevsky, M. Hrushevsky, S. Bohomolets (a member of the South Russian Workers' Union, who gave birth to the future AN URSR president O. Bohomolets while imprisoned there), Ya. Stefanovych, A. Lunacharsky, and many other political prisoners were held there.

In Soviet times, particularly during the Stalinist terror, myriad Ukrainian political and cultural figures were incarcerated in the prison. They include alleged members of the *Union for the Liberation of Ukraine, such as A. Barbar, V. Chekhivsky, O. Cherniakhivsky, V. Durdukivsky, V. Hantsov, Y. Hermaize, O. Hrebenetsky, H. Kholodny, B. Matushevsky, A. Nikovsky, M. Pavlushkov, L. Starytska-Cherniakhivska, V. Strashkevych, and S. Yefremov; Yu. Bachynsky, Ya. Blachenko, A. Bohdanovych, P. Boretsky, K. Burevii, P. Butuzov, Ye. Dmytriiev, D. Falkivsky, P. Helmer-Didushko, A. Karabuta, I. Khoptiar, H. Kosynka, L. Kovaliv, A. and I. Krushelnytsky, M. Lebedynets, V. Levytsky, A. Liashchenko, L. Lukianov-Svechezarov, S. Matiash, V. Mysyk, M. Oksamyta, V. Piatnytsia, K. Pivnenko, D. Polovy, H. Protsenko, A. Shcherbyna, R. Shevchenko, R. Skazynsky, A. Skrypa-Kozlovska, H. Stupyn, P. Sydorov, I. Tereshchenko, O. Vlyzko, and A. Vynnytsky, who were arrested in connection with the Kirov affair of 1934; the *Neoclassicists M. Zerov, P. Fylypovych, and M. Drai-Khmara; the poets A.

Lebed and M. Vorony; the linguists I. Boikiv, O. Iziumov, and M. Trokhymenko; the physiologist V. Radzymovska; Lesia Ukrainka's sister, I. Kosach-Borysova; and the writers H. Kostiuk, V. Petrovsky, V. Pidmohylny, and Ye. Pluzhnyk.

The prison has held prisoners under investigation in its isolation blocks as well as prisoners in transit. Many prisoners of conscience were held there on fabricated charges. They include O. Feldman (1975), V. Smohytel (1977), M. Horbal (1979–80), and many religious activists, particularly Evangelical Christians.

N. Svitlychna

Lukianova, Olena [Luk'janova], b 13 January 1922 in Blastove, near Mena, Sosnytsia county, Chernihiv gubernia. Pediatrician; corresponding member of the USSR Academy of Medical Sciences from 1978. After graduating from the Kiev Medical Institute (1949) she began working at the Kiev Scientific Research Institute of Pediatrics, Obstetrics, and Gynecology, and in 1979 she became its director. Her works deal with the pathogenesis, prophylaxis, and the treatment of juvenile gastroenteritis and rickets.

Denys Lukiianovych (portrait by V. Kravchenko)   Ivan Lukinov

Lukiianovych, Denys [Lukijanovyč] (pseuds: L. Zhurbenko, Ivan Levytsky, Ivan Makukha), b 13 September 1873 in Horodnytsia, Husiatyn county, Galicia, d 28 January 1965 in Lviv. Writer, literary scholar, publicist, and pedagogue. For many years he worked as a secondary-school teacher in Bukovyna and Galicia. After the Second World War he was appointed professor of Ukrainian literature at Lviv University. His first published book was the collection *Noveli* (Novellas, 1895). In addition to a large number of short stories he wrote several novelettes: *Za Kadyl'nu* (For Kadylna, 1902) and *Vid kryvdy* (From Injustice, 1904), both dealing with peasant life; *Filister* (Philistine, 1909), about teachers and the middle class; *Franko i Berkut* (Franko and Berkut, 1956), a biographical work; and *Ia–z bil'shistiu* (I Am with the Majority, 1934), a satirical novel. As a literary historian he wrote numerous articles and studies, in particular about Yu. Fedkovych, T. Shevchenko, and I. Franko.

Lukiianovych, Stefaniia. See Turkevych-Lukiianovych, Stefaniia.

Lukinov, Ivan, b 5 October 1927 in Popovka, now in Korocha raion, Belgorod oblast, RF. Economist; member of the All-Ukrainian Academy of Agricultural Sciences since 1973 and of the AN URSR (now ANU) since 1976. After graduating from the Kharkiv Agricultural Institute in 1951, he worked at the Institute of Economics and in the apparat of the CC CPU (1956–67). He has served as a department head (1965–7) and director (since 1976) of the Institute of Economics and director of the Ukrainian Scientific Research Institute of the Economics and Organization of Agriculture (1967–76). In 1977 he was appointed editor of *Ekonomika Radians'koï Ukraïny*, and in 1979, vice-president of the AN URSR. He has written numerous works, including monographs on labor productivity in agriculture (1958), pricing and profitability in the production of farm products (1964), and economic relations between the state and the collective farms (1974).

Lukoml [Lukoml']. A fortified medieval town in Pereiaslav principality on the right bank of the Sula River. It is first mentioned in the Hypatian Chronicle under the year 1178. In the 13th century it was destroyed by the Mongols; eventually it revived. In the 16th century it belonged to the Wiśniowiecki princes. During Ya. Ostrianyn's uprising the rebels made camp there (1638). Under the Hetman state Lukoml was a company center of Lubni regiment. Today a small village called Lukimia, in Orzha raion, Poltava oblast, stands at the site of the old town.

Lukomsky, Georgii [Lukomskij, Georgij] (Loukomski, Georges), b 16 March 1884 in Kaluga, Russia, d 1952 in

Georgii Lukomsky: *The Boim Chapel in Lviv* (1915)

southern France. Russian architect, architectural and art historian, and painter. He studied at the St Petersburg Academy of Arts and in Paris and Rome and was curator of the Russian imperial palace in Tsarskoe Selo. He researched and painted, drew, or photographed many architectural monuments in the Russian and Austrian empires, France, and Italy. In 1919 he was curator of the Khanenko Art Museum in Kiev and worked with M. Biliashivsky and M. Makarenko on the restoration of the St Sophia Cathedral. Around 1920 he fled Bolshevik rule and lived as an émigré in Berlin and Paris. During the Second World War he lived in London. His many works on Russian, Ukrainian, French, and Italian architecture and art include books in Russian on the buildings of the Rozumovsky family in Chernihiv gubernia (1911), the ancient Rus' architecture of Chernihiv (1912), the history of the destruction and restoration of the Baturyn Palace (1912), the architecture of 12th- to 18th-century Galicia (1915, containing his own illustrations), and old estates in Kharkiv gubernia (1917). As an émigré he published books in Russian on his friend H. Narbut (1923), Kiev's ancient architecture and the Ukrainian baroque (1923), Kiev's church architecture (1923, containing his own photographs; German trans 1923; French trans 1929), and the Khanenko Museum (1925).

S. Hordynsky

Lukomsky, Stepan [Lukoms'kyj], b 1701 in Uman, Bratslav voivodeship, d ca 1779. Historian. A graduate of the Kievan Mohyla Academy (1730), he served as a scribe in the General Military Chancellery and as captain of the Pryluka (1735–47), Yahotyn (1751–7), and Perevolochna (1757–63) companies and quartermaster of Pryluka regiment (1763). He translated S. Okolski's Polish diary, as *O Ostraninovoi voine z liakhami* (On [Ya.] Ostrianyn's War with the Poles, 1738), and M. Tytlowski's notes on the Polish-Turkish War of 1620–1, which he supplemented with information about events in Ukraine from 1639 to 1648, based on various Cossack chronicles (it appeared in the fourth volume of S. Velychko's chronicle, 1864). From Polish and Ukrainian chronicles Lukomsky compiled *Sobranie istoricheskoe* (Historical Collection, 1770), which covers the history of Ukraine from Gediminas (1299) to the end of the 16th century. It was published as a supplement to the Samovydets Chronicle in 1878 (trans and repub as *The Eyewitness Chronicle* [1972], accompanied by an analysis of Lukomsky's work by O. Levytsky). Lukomsky's autobiography was published in *Kievskaia starina* (vol 9 [1890]), and A. Yershov's analysis of his sources was published in the *Zapysky* of the Nizhen Institute of People's Education (vol 8 [1928]).

Lukomsky, Vladislav [Lukoms'kyj], b 17 July 1882 in Kaluga, Russia, d 11 July 1946 in Moscow. Heraldry scholar of Ukrainian descent. He graduated from St Petersburg University (1905). He became director of the heraldry department of the Imperial Senate (from 1914) and the heraldic museum (1918–28). He wrote, with V. Modzalevsky and H. Narbut, *Malorossiiskii herbovnyk* (Little Russian [Ukrainian] Heraldry Directory, 1914), a study of the printer I. Fedorovych (1935), and articles about Russian and Ukrainian heraldry, including the Myloradovych coat of arms, M. Romanchenko's collection, and K. Ostrozky's medal. He was a member of the Lviv Heraldic Society

(from 1910), the Chernihiv gubernial Scholarly Archival Commission (from 1913), and the Ukrainian Bibliological Society in Kiev (from 1928).

Lukomsky, Volodymyr [Lukoms'kyj], b 24 February 1927 in Bodzentyn, Poland. Architect. A graduate of the Lviv Polytechnical Institute (1950), he has worked in Ivano-Frankivske. His contributions to Ukrainian architecture include the Hutsulshchyna tourist center in Yaremcha (built 1963, expanded 1970) and the airport (1962), the pedagogical institute (1967), a fashion center (1964), the trade tekhnikum (1965), and the main post office (1968) in Ivano-Frankivske.

Lukovsky, Leon [Lukovs'kyj], b 23 April 1903 in Voronezh. Ukrainian otolaryngologist. A graduate of the Faculty of Medicine of Voronezh University (1925), he worked at the Dnipropetrovske Institute for the Upgrading of Physicians (1931–7) and at the Dnipropetrovske Medical Institute (from 1940), where he held the chair of otolaryngology (from 1948) and was deputy academic director (1952–8). A member of the board of the Ukrainian Scientific Society of Otolaryngologists and head of the Dnipropetrovske Scientific Society of Otolaryngologists, he studied acute and chronic tonsillitis, atypical mastoiditis, and sinus thromboses of allergic origin.

Lukych, Vasyl [Lukyč, Vasyl'] (pseud of Volodymyr Levytsky), b 2 September 1856 in Belzka, now Honcharivka, Zolochiv raion, Lviv oblast, d 6 October 1938 in Vynnyky, now a suburb of Lviv. Writer and civic figure; full member of the Shevchenko Scientific Society from 1926; honorary member of the Prosvita society from 1925. His literary activities began in 1875. He coedited the student journal *Druh* and the almanac *Dnistrianka* (1876). He collaborated with I. Franko in compiling an anthology of Ukrainian poetry (1881) and edited many publications, including the almanacs of the Prosvita society for 1880–5, 1890, 1893, and 1916–18; a popular handbook for peasants, *Rus'kyi pravotar domovyi* (The Ruthenian Home Judge, 1885, which he coedited with Yu. Selsky); the almanac *Vatra* (1887); and the journal *Zoria* (1890–6), in which he introduced the phonetic orthography. Under his editorship the journal assumed an all-Ukrainian character. He edited the works of some Ukrainian writers, particularly writers from the Dnieper region. In 1919 he edited the official legislative bulletin *Vistnyk derzhavnykh zakoniv i rozporiadkiv Zakhidnoï oblasty* UNR. He wrote ethnographic studies, surveys of national and cultural life in central Ukraine, short stories, and tales.

Lullabies (*kolysanky, kolyskovi pisni*). A basic form of children's folklore, the examples of which were designed to calm children and put them to sleep. They derive their name, *kolyskovi*, from the fact that they are sung over a crib (*kolyska*) to the accompaniment of gentle rocking (*kolysannia*). In the past they were believed to have magical powers. Lullabies are characterized by caressing words, a special intonation, refrains, and a rhythmic repetition of certain words and sounds. Addressed only to the child and to no other listener, they are meant to convey the deep feeling the parent has for the child. Because of their simple composition they permit wide improvisation. The most frequent images in Ukrainian lullabies are personified Sleepiness (*Drimota*) and Dream (*Son*) and various domestic animals and birds. They express the parent's hope for the child's happiness, expectations of future support from the child, and complaints about the difficulties of raising a child. Lullabies played an important role in the child's upbringing.

The first published text of a Ukrainian lullaby was of 'Oi khodyt' son kolo vikon' (Oh, Dream Walks by the Windows), which appeared in the almanac *Rusalka Dnistrovaia* (1837). The first melody to be transcribed was that of 'Oi ty kote, ne hudy' (Oh, Cat, Don't Purr) in M. Vovchok's collection (1867). A number of lullaby collections, such as those of M. Nahorny and H. Sukhobrus (1939) and H. Sukhobrus and I. Fedas (1973), came out in Soviet Ukraine. The largest of them (933 songs) is H. Dovzhenok and K. Luhanska's *Dytiachyi fol'klor* (Children's Folklore, 1984).

M. Mushynka

Lumber industry. A branch of the forest products industry that cuts timber and prepares sawn lumber for the woodworking, furniture, and chemical industries. The lumber industry in Right-Bank Ukraine began to export timber to Western Europe in the late 15th century. In the 17th century the industry expanded to Left-Bank Ukraine. Until the beginning of the 19th century timber was used as fuel in foundries and smelting furnaces and in the manufacture of potash, tar, furniture, and barrels. As rail transportation developed, coal was substituted for wood as fuel, and it became easier to transport lumber. By the late 1890s approx 2,000 small lumber mills in Ukraine were employing 78 percent of all lumber workers, and 121 larger mills were employing 45,051 workers and producing 2.1 million rubles' worth of lumber. Most of the mills were in Volhynia and Kiev gubernias. In 1913, 27,100 ha of forest were harvested, and 4.5 million cu m of timber were produced. Of that production, 2.7 million cu m were processed in sawmills and woodworking plants, and the rest was used for firewood. There were 185 sawmills in the Ukrainian gubernias of the Russian Empire at the time; they employed about 10,100 workers.

After the 1917 Revolution the industry in Soviet Ukraine developed rapidly under the five-year plans. From 1928 to 1937 the production of industrial timber rose from 1 to 3.9 million cu m, or from 2.4 percent to 3.4 percent of the USSR output. Much of the timber was exported from Ukraine and then imported in the form of finished wood products. Consequently, the output of sawn wood in Ukraine rose only from 0.8 to 1.3 million cu m, and Ukraine's share of the Soviet lumber output declined, from 5.8 percent to 3.8 percent. The rapid expansion of timber cutting depleted Ukraine's forest resources and was not curtailed until 1938.

After the Soviet occupation of Western Ukraine at the end of the Second World War, the forests of the Carpathian Mountains were exploited ruthlessly. Despite severe erosion the average annual wood harvest during the 1950s was twice as high as the theoretical limit for proper forest reproduction. From 1940 to 1950 the output of industrial timber rose from 5.2 to 11.2 million cu m, and of sawn lumber, from 3.0 to 6.2 million cu m. In 1948 Ukraine's share of the Soviet timber output peaked at 8.5

percent, and in 1950 its share of the Soviet lumber output reached a high of 12.4 percent. For the rest of the decade the timber harvest remained stable, and lumber production increased. In 1959, new restrictions on harvesting were introduced. Overcutting had given rise to significant waste through improper felling and logging. When 30 percent of the harvest was fit only for firewood, over 54 percent of the timberland consisted of young forest (1956), and large areas of the Carpathians had been denuded, it became obvious that the industry had to be reorganized. Since 1961 the logging area has been reduced to permit the forests to recover.

In the last 15 years the output of industrial timber rose from 7 million cu m in 1970 to 9 million cu m in 1983, and Ukraine's share of the Soviet output rose from 2 percent to 3.3 percent. The output of lumber continued to decline, however. In 15 years it fell from 10.4 to 7.6 million cu m, and Ukraine's share of the Soviet output declined from 8.9 percent to 7.8 percent.

The Carpathian Mountains provide half of the timber harvested in Ukraine, Polisia a third, and the forest-steppe and steppe regions the rest. Since 1950 the industry has become increasingly mechanized: felling, sorting, and sawing are almost completely mechanized. The transportation of logs is labor-intensive. From 1959 to 1970 employment in the lumber industry declined from 69,720 to 45,241 workers, or from 9.6 percent to 8.7 percent of the Soviet lumber labor force. But there may be up to 100,000 seasonal workers in the industry.

Approx 60 percent of the timber harvested in Ukraine is processed into building materials and other wood products, 25 percent is used as logs in construction, and 13 percent is used by the chemical industry to produce cellulose. Ukraine's lumber industry is unable to meet domestic demand: 67 percent of its timber and 38 percent of its lumber were imported from other republics in 1966. Less than 2 percent of its output, mostly hardwoods, is exported to Belarus and Moldova.

B. Somchynsky

Luna (Echo). A Ukrainian literary almanac published by I. Ilnytsky, with the help of O. Konysky, in Kiev in 1881. In it were published poems by T. Shevchenko, M. Starytsky, Ya. Shchoholev, O. Konysky, and V. Mova, as well as I. Nechui-Levytsky's novel *Pryiateli* (Friends) and essay 'Shevchenkova mohyla ...' (Shevchenko's Grave) and M. Starytsky's vaudeville *Iak kovbasa ta charka* ... (If [There Is] Sausage and a Shot Glass ...). The publication of *Luna* initiated a series of literary-art almanacs in central Ukraine, particularly in Kiev, and stimulated literary activity.

Lunacharsky, Anatolii [Lunačarskij, Anatolij], b 23 November 1875 in Poltava, d 26 December 1933 in Menton, France. Bolshevik revolutionary, the first Soviet people's commissar of education (1917–33), writer, literary critic, and art scholar; full member of the USSR Academy of Sciences from 1930. Lunacharsky was a contributor to the journal *Dzvin* and wrote works on T. Shevchenko (*Velykyi narodnyi poet* [A Great National Poet, 1912], the speech he gave at the commemoration of the 50th anniversary of Shevchenko's death organized by the Ukrainian community in Paris in 1911]), M. Kotsiubynsky, Lesia Ukrainka, and M. Kulish. He also critiqued the performance given by the Ivan Franko Theater when it toured Moscow

(1926). Some of Lunacharsky's plays, such as *Iad* (Poison), were included in the repertoire of Soviet Ukrainian theaters.

Lundin, Aksel, b 1886 in Stockholm, d 1943 ? Actor and film director. He came to Russia in 1905 and completed drama school in Petrograd (1920). In 1912 he joined the Khudozhnii Ekran society in Kiev as an actor. Then he became an agitprop film director for the Chervona Zirka company (1919), the Photo-Cinema Committee in Kharkiv (1920), and the Odessa Film Factory of the All-Ukrainian Photo-Cinema Administration (1924), where he directed the films *Za chorne zoloto* (For Black Gold, 1924), *Lisovyi zvir* (The Forest Beast, 1925), and *Piłsuds'kyi kupyv Petliuru* (Piłsudski Bought Petliura, 1926). Having been criticized for his adaptation of V. Vynnychenko titled *Pryhody poltynnyka* (Adventures of a Half Ruble, 1929) Lundin returned to theater work in the RSFSR.

Lupii, Oles [Lupij, Oles'], b 28 March 1938 in Nova Kamianka, now in Nesterov raion, Lviv oblast. Poet, prosaist, and dramatist. His works include the collections of poems *Vinky iunosti* (The Wreaths of Youth, 1957), *Odnaiedyna* (One and Only, 1984), and *Dovholittia bdzholy* (The Longevity of the Bee, 1987); the novelettes *Persha zyma* (First Winter, 1975) and *Sontse pomizh sosnamy* (The Sun among the Pines, 1979); and the novels *Herts'* (The Duel, 1966), *Hran'* (The Embers, 1968), *Virnist'* (Loyalty, 1976), and *Nikomu tebe ne viddam* (I Will Surrender You to No One, 1984). His poetic and prose works have been published in Russian, Belarusian, Lithuanian, Moldavian, Georgian, Armenian, Polish, German, Vietnamese, and Spanish translations.

Lupii, Yaroslav [Lupij, Jaroslav], b 2 June 1946 in Nova Kamianka, Zhovkva county, Lviv oblast. Film director. After graduating from the Kiev Institute of Theater Arts (1971) he worked at the Odessa Artistic Film Studio, where he directed *Liubi moï* (My Dears, 1975), *Khlib dytynstva moho* (The Bread of My Childhood, 1978), *Bahriani berehy* (The Purple Banks, 1979), the environmental film *Sto radostei, abo knyha velykykh vidkryttiv* (A Hundred Joys, or the Book of Great Discoveries, 1982), and *Zrozumii mene* (Understand Me, 1983).

Lupkiv Pass (Lupkivskyi pereval). IV-2. A mountain pass (elevation, 657 m) in the Middle Beskyds of the eastern Lemko region. Situated along the Polish-Slovak border, the pass provides a thoroughfare for the Peremyshl–Michalovce–Budapest train line.

Lupu, Roksana (Rozanda, Ruxandra), b ?, d 1686. Moldavian princess; daughter of V. *Lupu. She married T. *Khmelnytsky in 1652. After his death in 1653, she lived in Chyhyryn; later she moved to an estate given to her by B. Khmelnytsky, in the town of Rashkiv, in Podilia. In 1666 she returned to Moldavia. The details of her marriage are discussed in A. Horbach's *Tymish Khmel'nyts'kyi v rumans'kii istoriohrafii ta literaturi* (Tymish Khmelnytsky in Rumanian Historiography and Literature, 1969).

Lupu, Vasile, b 1593?, d 1661. Hospodar of Moldavia (1634–54). He was a supporter of Poland and then became an ally of his son-in-law's father, B. *Khmelnytsky, with

whom he made a pact in 1652. Lupu played a key role in Khmelnytsky's plans for creating a Danube League, in which Ukraine was to have a decisive influence. The plans were thwarted when T. *Khmelnytsky died in 1653. During Lupu's reign (1634–54) the Rumanian language was used for the first time in official deeds, and at his request professors from the Kievan Mohyla Academy founded a Slavic-Latin college in Iaşi in 1640 (headed by S. Pochasky). In 1641, with the help of P. *Mohyla, the first Moldavian print shop was established in Iaşi. In 1642 a common synod of the Ukrainian and Moldavian Orthodox churches was held in Iaşi, with the participation of Mohyla's representatives (including I. Kozlovsky-Trofymovych).

Manoly Lupul   Ivan Lutsenko

Lupul, Manoly (Robert), b 14 August 1927 in Willingdon, Alberta. Historian, educator, and community leader. A graduate of the universities of Alberta, Minnesota, and Harvard (PH D, 1963), he taught educational foundations and Canadian educational history at the University of Alberta from 1958. He became a leading figure in the Ukrainian Canadian Professional and Business Federation and played a major role in the establishment of the Ukrainian-English bilingual program in Alberta schools (1974) and the creation of the *Canadian Institute of Ukrainian Studies (CIUS). As the institute's first director (1976–86) he was instrumental in setting the direction of Ukrainian studies in Canada at a critical juncture in its development and in involving CIUS in its most ambitious venture, the preparation of the *Encyclopedia of Ukraine*. He was also active in promoting multicultural policy in Canada as prairie regional chairperson and national vice-chairperson of the Canadian Consultative Council on Multiculturalism (1973–9) and in searching out new directions for Ukrainian-Canadian development as a key member and first chairperson (1982–3) of the *Ukrainian Community Development Committee. He is the author of *The Roman Catholic Church and the North-West School Question, 1875–1905* (1974) and editor of five major collections on Ukrainian–Canadian themes, including *A Heritage in Transition* (1982).

D.H. Struk

Lupynis, Anatolii, b 1937 in Cherkasy oblast. Poet and dissident. In late 1956 he was sentenced to six years in Mordovian labor camps for his nonconformist poetry. In

September 1957 he had his sentence extended by five years for heading a Mordovian camp strike-committee. Lupynis served part of his term in the Vladimir Prison near Moscow. When he was released in 1967, both his legs were paralyzed. For reciting poetry at the Shevchenko monument in Kiev in May 1971, he was sentenced to an indefinite term in psychiatric prisons in Moscow, Dnipropetrovske, Kiev, Alma Ata, Smila, and Orel. His maltreatment there was brought to the attention of the international human rights movement, and his case was brought up at the 1977 International Congress of Psychiatrists in Honolulu. He was finally released in 1987. In 1990 he began publishing the independent periodical *Zoloti vorota* in Kiev.

Lurie, Oleksander [Lur'je], b 3 February 1868 in Kiev, d 17 January 1954 in Kiev. Dermatologist and venereologist. A graduate of the medical faculty of Kiev University (1893), he was department head at the Kiev Institute for the Upgrading of Physicians (1919–49). He specialized in the diagnosis and treatment of fungal skin diseases and syphilis. He set up the first mycological dispensary in the USSR, in Kiev in 1920. For many years he was president of the Kiev Scientific Society of Dermatologists and Venereologists.

Lurie, Oleksander [Lur'je], b 12 October 1897 in Klymovychi, Mahiliou gubernia (Belarus), d 24 May 1958 in Kiev. Obstetrician and gynecologist; corresponding member of the AN URSR (now ANU) from 1939. A graduate of the medical faculty of Moscow University (1921), he headed a department at the Kiev Medical Institute (1938–58) and was chief obstetrician and gynecologist in the Ukrainian SSR Ministry of Health (1948–58). He researched maternal mortality, painless birthing, the prophylaxis and treatment of uterine cancer, and midwifery. The obstetric-gynecology clinic of the Kiev Medical Institute was named after him.

Lusatian culture. An archeological culture of a large group of tribes in the Bronze and early Iron ages (12th–4th century BC). It was widespread in the Oder and Vistula basins and extended as far east as the Buh River. The name is derived from the Sorbian region of Lusatia (Lausitz), now in east Germany, where monuments of the culture were first discovered and studied. Remains of fortifications, settlements, burials with cremations, tools, ornaments, and hoards were excavated. The people of the culture lived in patriarchal clans and practiced land cultivation, herding, hunting, and fishing, and traded with the tribes of the Dnieper basin. Their bronze-casting and iron-working were highly developed. Relics of this culture have been found in Ukraine in the Kholm region and western Volhynia. Most Slavic scholars consider the culture to be proto-Slavic.

Lushpynsky, Oleksander [Lušpyns'kyj], b 1878, d 1943. Architect. A graduate of the Lviv Polytechnic (1904), he was the chief engineer of I. *Levynsky's construction firm in Lviv. He also built wooden churches in the villages of Mykytyntsi, Veldizh, Vorobliachyn, and Tysmenytsia and buildings such as the Basilian convents in Lviv and Stanyslaviv and the People's Home in Drohobych. He is the author of two albums, one on rebuilding the village

(1917), which contains plans in a traditional folk style for village houses and institutions, and one on 16th- to 19th-century Galician wooden churches (1920). Lushpynsky consciously used a 'national' Ukrainian style in his urban designs.

Lustration (*liustratsiia*; Polish: *lustracja*; derived from the Latin *lustrum*, a five-year period or censor's term of office). An inventory of royal lands for tax and military purposes. The first such descriptions were prepared in the Lithuanian-Ruthenian state in the early 16th century. From 1568 until the partitions of Poland they were prepared by Polish officials (*lustratory*) every five years. The lustration contained detailed information about estates and villages, their inhabitants, and the condition of lands, domestic animals, and buildings. After the Polish partitions the tsarist government carried out lustrations in the annexed territories in 1778–9, 1839–63, and 1867. The voluminous data recorded in the lustrations make them an important source for the social and economic history of Ukraine.

Lutherans. Members of Protestant churches based on the Augsburg Confession, the catechism of M. Luther (1528–9), and various writings of the 16th century. Lutheranism is widespread throughout Germany, Scandinavia, Latvia, and Estonia and is closely related to other Protestant and Evangelical Christian churches. Lutheranism was occasionally the subject of early polemical writings in Ukraine, but the movement attracted fewer followers in Ukraine than did Calvinism, which was widespread among the gentry. The number of Lutherans increased considerably with the arrival of the German colonists who settled in southern Ukraine in the 18th century. Lutheran churches were established in Ukrainian cities where there were sizable German communities and in certain German agricultural colonies. They were also established among Czech settlements in Volhynia and by Hungarian and Slovak Lutherans in Transcarpathia. In the interwar period Lutheranism attracted a few thousand followers in Western Ukraine (Galicia and Volhynia), where the *Ukrainian Evangelical Church of the Augsburg Confession was formed. At the outset of the First World War the Russian authorities repressed the church along with all other German institutions in the empire. Under Soviet rule, an attempt to revive the church in 1924 was unsuccessful, and the subsequent antireligious campaigns of the 1930s destroyed almost all organized church life in Ukraine. Lutherans continued to be persecuted through the late 1940s. Today there is no organized Lutheran movement in Ukraine, although the recent liberalization may permit a rebirth of the church. (See *Evangelical Christians.)

Lutsenko, Ivan [Lucenko], b 1864, d 25 March 1919 in Polonne, Novohrad-Volynskyi county, Volhynia gubernia. Physician and political leader in Odessa. During the revolutionary period he was a member of the Central Rada and a leader of the *Ukrainian People's party. He helped organize and chaired the Odessa Military Council, and sat on the Ukrainian General Military Committee. While serving as a military doctor with the UNR Army he was captured and executed by the Bolsheviks.

Lutsenko, Oleksander [Lucenko], b 2 April 1911 in Yelysavethrad, Kherson gubernia. Stage actor. Besides the

Ukrainian heroic repertoire, Zalizniak in T. Shevchenko's *Haidamaky*, Hyria in M. Kulish's *97*, and Svichka in I. Kocherha's *Svichchene vesillia* (Svichka's Wedding), he played the title role in B. Brecht's *Herr Puntila und sein Knecht Matti*. From 1930 he worked in the Odessa Ukrainian Music and Drama Theater.

Luka Lutsiv

Lutsiv, Luka [Luciv] (Luciw, Luke), b 30 October 1895 in Hrushova, Drohobych county, Galicia, d 1 December 1984 in Philadelphia. Literary scholar and critic; member of the Shevchenko Scientific Society. He studied in Prague at the Ukrainian Free University (1921–6) and at Charles University (PH D, diss on T. Shevchenko, 1926). From 1927 to 1944 he worked as a teacher in Galicia. As a postwar refugee he taught in displaced persons camps in Bavaria before settling in New York City in 1949. From 1952 to 1970 he worked as an editor for the daily *Svoboda*. He published literary articles and hundreds of book reviews in Galician and émigré periodicals and scholarly serials and wrote books on the writers M. Shashkevych (1963), O. Kobylianska (1963), T. Shevchenko (1964), I. Franko (1967), and V. Stefanyk (1971). He also edited two books of articles on the Drohobych region (1973, 1978). A selection of his articles and reviews from 1925 to 1975 with a bibliography and autobiography appeared in 1982 as *Literatura i zhyttia* (Literature and Life).

Lutsiv, Volodymyr [Luciv], b 25 June 1929 in Nadvirna, Galicia. Tenor singer and banduryst. After emigrating to

Volodymyr Lutsiv

Yurii Lutsiv

England in 1948, he studied music in Bradford and London and at St Cecilia's Conservatory in Rome (with Bishop I. Buchko's support). He has toured Italy, Germany, the United States, and Canada with his concerts, and has organized tours for Ukrainian choirs in Europe and North America in an effort to popularize Ukrainian music. He commonly sings under the stage name Tino Valdi.

Lutsiv, Yurii [Luciv, Jurij], b 12 May 1931 in Lviv. Conductor. A pupil of M. Kolessa, he graduated from the Lviv Conservatory in 1953 and was directly engaged to conduct the symphony orchestra of the Lviv Philharmonic (1953–4 and 1960). In 1954–9 he worked in Zaporizhia. Since 1960 he has been a conductor with the Lviv Theater of Opera and Ballet (principal conductor during 1963–73) and a lecturer at the Lviv Conservatory. His productions include B. Liatoshynsky's opera *Zolotyi obruch* (The Golden Ring), S. Prokofiev's ballets *Cinderella* and *Romeo and Juliet*, and P. Tchaikovsky's *Nutcracker Suite*. In 1961 he toured Canada (Calgary and Edmonton).

Lutskay, Mykhailo. See Luchkai, Mykhailo.

Lutske: 14th-century castle of Prince Liubartas (rebuilt in the 15th–16th centuries)

Lutske or **Lutsk** [Luc'ke or Luc'k]. III-6. A city (1991 pop 210,000) on the Styr River and the center of Volhynia oblast and Lutske raion. It is first mentioned in the Hypatian Chronicle under the year 1185, but it was probably a tribal center of the Luchanians as early as the 10th century. There is evidence that the area was settled in the Neolithic period. Lutske was the capital of an independent principality from 1154. In 1225 it belonged to Volodymyr-Volynskyi principality and later to Galicia-Volhynia principality. In 1340 it was annexed by Liubartas, who built a large castle there and established Lutske as the capital of an appanage principality (1340–84, 1440–53) within the Lithuanian-Ruthenian state. After the Union of Lublin in 1569, the city came under Polish rule and served as a voivodeship center. In the 15th and 16th centuries it was one of the main trade centers in Ukraine because of its location at the crossroads of major trade routes. Many *Karaites from the Crimea settled there in that period, as Armenians had done earlier. In 1429 Vytautas of Lithuania called a conference of European monarchs in Lutske. The city was also an important Ukrainian religious and cultural center. In the 13th century it was the seat of an eparchy, and the *Zhydychyn St Nicholas's Monastery was established nearby. In 1617 the *Lutske Brotherhood

Lutske: a view of the center

Today Lutske is a center of food production (milling, meat–packing, and sugar refining), smelting, machine building, brick-making, and clothes and footwear manufacturing. It has a pedagogical institute, a drama theater, a philharmonic orchestra, and a regional museum. The old quarter of the city is situated on an elevated section of the bank of the *Styr River, surrounded by swampland on both sides. The city expanded northward, toward the railroad station, and, recently, toward the west and southwest. The most important historic monument is Liubartas's castle, which stands on a small hill between the Styr and the Hlushytsia rivers. It includes remnants of the upper castle built in the 13th century and several towers. The most majestic building is the baroque Roman Catholic church built in 1619–20. Few old Ukrainian churches remain. There are no traces of the cathedral that stood within the fortifications or of St Demetrius's Church (14th century). The Church of the Holy Protectress was reconstructed from its 15th-century ruins, and the Church of the Elevation of the Cross was rebuilt in 1890 from the remains of the brotherhood's church (1619–20). Outside the old quarter is the Orthodox cathedral, built in the baroque style in 1754 on the site of a wooden church (1648).

V. Kubijovyč

Lutske Brotherhood of the Elevation of the Cross

(Lutske khresto-vozdvyzhenske bratstvo). A renowned Orthodox *brotherhood founded in 1617 by H. Mykulych, the hegumen of the Chercha monastery. The Lutske Brotherhood included monks, priests, bishops, nobles, aristocrats, and members of the middle class from Lutske and Volhynia. It received a charter from the Polish king Sigismund III in 1619 and was granted the status of *stauropegion by the Patriarch of Constantinople in 1623. It ran the *Lutske Brotherhood of the Elevation of the Cross School and operated a printing press in the monastery. After the Khmelnytsky era the brotherhood entered a period of steady decline. It was revived in 1896 by the Russian government with the intention that its activities 'strengthen the Russian people.' From 1920 the brotherhood functioned without a charter. In 1931 it was liquidated by the Polish government, only to be granted a new charter in 1935 which recognized the brotherhood's 17th-century

of the Elevation of the Cross was founded, and in 1621 it set up a school. A Jesuit college was added in 1614 to the city's Polish schools. Later in the 17th century Lutske declined. It was annexed by Russia in 1795, and became a county center. The town grew: in 1897 its population was 14,800 (79 percent Jewish), and in 1912, 26,600. Until the First World War there was a Russian fortress in Lutske. In 1917–19 the city belonged to the Ukrainian state. In May 1919 the Polish army overpowered the Ukrainian Kholm Division and took Lutske.

As a voivodeship center under the Polish regime, Lutske grew to 35,600 by 1931. In the interwar period it was the Ukrainian political and cultural center for western Volhynia. It was the center of a network of Prosvita reading rooms (134 of which were closed down by the Polish authorities in 1932) and the seat of a Ukrainian Orthodox eparchy. It had a private Ukrainian gymnasium, a Ridna Khata club, and the Volhynian Ukrainian Theater and was the base of the religious-education Mohyla Society (est 1931). It was also a modest publishing center: periodicals such as *Hromada* and *Volyns'ka hromada* in the 1920s and *Volyns'ka nedilia*, *Ukraïns'ka nyva* (later *Volyns'ke selo*), and *Ridnyi kolos* in the 1930s appeared there. In 1939 Lutske was occupied by the Bolsheviks, who, retreating from the Germans in 1941, murdered about 3,000 Ukrainians in the local prison.

Ruins of the church of the Lutske Brotherhood of the Elevation of the Cross (lithograph of a painting by Strukov, 1867)

roots but not the right to its holdings (they were left under government jurisdiction). The activities of the brotherhood ceased with the Soviet occupation of Lutske.

Lutske Brotherhood of the Elevation of the Cross School (Lutska bratska shkola). A *brotherhood school founded by Volhynian noblemen and townsmen who were members of the *Lutske Brotherhood of the Elevation of the Cross. The most prominent member of this group was the nobleman L. *Drevynsky.

The Lutske School was established between 1617 and 1620. Extant records of its statutes and regulations dating from 1624 testify to the fact that it was modeled on the *Lviv Dormition Brotherhood School. From the beginning its educational program stressed philological training in Greek, Church Slavonic, and Latin within a liberal arts curriculum. Later the teaching of Greek was de-emphasized, and Polish was introduced as the language of instruction. The school attained considerable reputation for the teaching of polyphonic choral music.

In the tradition of brotherhood schools, the Lutske School was open to male children of all estates and from various economic backgrounds. Among its teachers were I. Ilkovsky (school director in 1628), P. Bosynsky (1634), Hegumen A. Slavynsky (instructor in rhetoric, philosophy, and mathematics in the mid-17th century), Z. Sohnykevych, and the famous iconographer and painter Y. *Kondzelevych. Between 1625 and 1628 the school benefited from the services of the peripatetic printing shop run by P. *Liutkovych-Telytsia.

The Lutske school frequently suffered from repressive measures enforced by the Catholic opposition. Its actual decline began after the Khmelnytsky wars.

N. Pylypiuk

Lutske eparchy. An eparchy in Volhynia, with its see in Lutske. The earliest mention of the eparchy dates from ca 1326. From 1495 it was known as Lutske-Ostrih eparchy. In 1595 Bishop K. *Terletsky traveled to Rome to make his confession of faith to the pope and became a leading proponent of the Church Union of *Berestia. Orthodox forces continued to battle for control of the eparchy, however, and Ye. Pochapovsky, Terletsky's successor, was forced to relinquish the eparchy to the Orthodox bishop A. Puzyna

in 1633. From then the remaining Uniate parishes and several monasteries were administered by the archimandrite of the Zhydychyn St Nicholas's Monastery. Orthodox bishops in the 17th century included D. Balaban and H. Sviatopolk-Chetvertynsky. In 1702 Bishop D. *Zhabokrytsky led the eparchy back into the Uniate church, but he was arrested by the Russian authorities, and died in prison.

In the 18th century there was only one Orthodox bishop of Lutske but eight Uniate bishops, including T. and S. Rudnytsky-Liubienitsky. After the partitions of Poland the territory of the eparchy came under Russian rule. At that time a new Orthodox eparchy of Volhynia was created from most of Lutske-Ostrih and Volodymyr-Volynskyi eparchies. Several Uniate bishops were appointed to the Lutske see in the early 19th century, but in 1839 Tsar Nicholas I forcibly liquidated the Uniate church in the Russian Empire, and the Uniate eparchy was dissolved.

During the First World War, Metropolitan A. Sheptytsky appointed Y. Botsian as the Uniate bishop of Lutske. After the war, however, the territory again came under Polish rule, and the Polish authorities and Roman Catholic hierarchy, both opposed to the Uniate presence in Volhynia, forced Botsian to relinquish his post in 1924. In 1932 P. Sikorsky was consecrated bishop of Lutske for the *Polish Autocephalous Orthodox church. After the Second World War the Russian Orthodox church created the Volhynian eparchy, which contained Volhynia (Lutske) and Rivne oblasts. In 1963–72 V. Velychkovsky was bishop of Lutske for the underground Ukrainian Catholic church. With the liberalization of religious life in Ukraine in the early 1990s, the renewed Ukrainian Autocephalous Orthodox church established an eparchy in Lutske.

Lutske Gospel (Lutske yevanheliie). A manuscript of 262 two-column folios transcribed in Ukraine in the 14th century from a south Slavic original. In the 14th and 15th centuries it belonged to the Monastery of the Savior on the outskirts of Lutske. Today it is preserved in the Lenin Public Library in Moscow. The gospel contains many Ukrainianisms, particularly phonetic ones: a new ѣ, e instead of y in unaccented syllables, a prothetic v-, and the confusion of i with ы and u with v. Its language was studied by A. Sobolevsky in *Ocherki iz istorii russkogo iazyka* (Essays on the History of the Russian Language, 1884) and particularly by P. Buzuk in *Zbirnyk Komisiï dlia doslidzhennia istoriï ukraïns'koï movy*, vol 1.

Lutske Pedagogical Institute (Lutskyi pedahohichnyi instytut im. Lesi Ukrainky). A postsecondary institution established in Lutske by the Ministry of Education of the Ukrainian SSR as a teachers' college in 1940. In 1951 it was transformed into a pedagogical institute. During the 1979–80 academic year the institute had eight faculties: physics-mathematics, philologics, history, natural sciences–geography, foreign languages, physical education, pedagogy, and elementary education. During that year the institute had an enrollment of 4,561 students. It has a library (with 340,000 volumes) and a botanical garden and offers extramural courses. In 1964 V. *Moroz taught modern history there.

Lutske Tribunal (Trybunal lutskyi). The highest appellate court for Bratslav, Volhynia, and Kiev voivodeships, created in 1578 by the Great Diet of the Polish-Lithuanian Commonwealth in Warsaw. Modeled on the *Royal Tribunal, it was composed of 13 judges (deputies) elected by the voivodeship dietines: five judges from Volhynia and four each from Kiev and Bratslav. The tribunal heard appeals of decisions of the city, land, and *pidkomorskyi* courts and was governed by the Lithuanian Statute of 1566. The official language of the tribunal was Ukrainian. Because of opposition from the Polish gentry and Roman Catholic hierarchy, the court was merged in 1589 with the Royal Tribunal, which heard appeals from Ukrainian territories at its sessions in Lublin and Lviv. The abolition of the Lutske Tribunal was an important blow to Ukrainian autonomy in the Polish-Lithuanian Commonwealth.

Lutskevych, Marko [Luckevyč], b 26 April 1882 in Kovel, Volhynia gubernia, d 1934. Co-operative and political leader in Volhynia. After completing his studies in Moscow he became involved in co-operative work. In 1922 he was elected to the Polish Sejm, from which he was quickly expelled for attacking the Polish state in his speeches. He fled from the Polish police to Czechoslovakia, and in 1924 he moved to the Ukrainian SSR. Two years later he was arrested by the Soviets and sentenced to forced labor camps in Siberia, where he died.

Lutskevych, Yurii [Luckevyč, Jurij], b 9 September 1934 in Kirovohrad. Painter and graphic artist. A graduate of the Kiev State Art Institute (1959), he continued his studies at the workshops of the USSR Academy of Arts in Kiev (1962–5). His early works (eg, *In the Days of the War* [1965]) were in keeping with *socialist realism. His later work remained figurative, but his subject matter and style changed. He now paints more intimate compositions, using a flickering brush stroke and an abundance of white pigment to create interesting overall effects and surfaces full of light (eg, *Bouquet of Lilies* [1987] and *Small Fountain* [1988]).

Lutsky, Myron [Luc'kyj], b 29 September 1891 in Luka, Sambir county, Galicia, d 10 March 1961 in Toronto. Military and civic leader; brother of O. *Lutsky. After studying law in Lviv and agriculture in Vienna he joined the 41st Chernivtsi Infantry Regiment of the Austrian army and served in it as a lieutenant during the First World War. Having been assigned to the Ukrainian Sich Riflemen at the end of October 1918, he was acting chief of staff of Group East during the siege of Lviv and then chief of staff of the First Brigade of the Ukrainian Sich Riflemen. In 1920 he was appointed chief of the operative department of the Second Brigade of the Red Ukrainian Galician Army. After the war he was active in the Ukrainian National Democratic Alliance and in a number of important economic institutions: he was president of Silskyi Hospodar in Lviv (1936–9), vice-president of the Lviv Agricultural Chamber (1936–9), and director of the sugar trust in Ukraine (1941–3). After emigrating in 1944, he chaired the Ukrainian Relief Committee in Berlin. In 1948 he settled in Canada, where he was active in various Ukrainian organizations.

Lutsky, Oleksander [Luc'kyj] (noms de guerre: Andriienko, B.A. Bohun), b 1910 in Bodnariv, Stanyslaviv county, Galicia, d ? Senior UPA military officer. In 1933 he was sentenced to six years' imprisonment by the Poles for his

OUN activities. After his release he finished the OUN military courses in Cracow (1939–40) and was appointed OUN leader for Stanyslaviv oblast. After service in the *Legion of Ukrainian Nationalists (1941–3), he was appointed as the first commander of the UPA-West (1943–4). In February 1944 he was appointed commander of the UPA front in the southern Kholm region and was captured en route by the Gestapo. He escaped in July 1944 and served briefly as sector commander of the UPA-West. He was captured by the NKVD in 1945 and sentenced to 25 years' hard labor.

Ostap Lutsky

Lutsky, Ostap [Luc'kyj], b 8 November 1883 in Luka, Sambir county, Galicia, d 1941 near Kotlas, RSFSR. Political leader, co-operative organizer, publicist, and poet; father of G.S.N. *Luckyj. While studying liberal arts at Prague and Cracow universities he joined the literary group *Moloda Muza and wrote several collections of poetry – *Bez masky* (Without a Mask, 1903), *Z moïkh dniv* (From My Days, 1905), and *V takii khvyli* (At Such a Moment, 1906). While working in Chernivtsi as an editor of *Bukovyna* (1907–13) he became active in the local co-operative movement and in the Ruska Besida society. During the First World War he served as a lieutenant in the Austrian army, and in 1918 he was appointed aide-de-camp to the young Archduke Wilhelm. With the collapse of the Austrian Empire he joined the Ukrainian Galician Army and served as chief of staff of the Fourth Zolochiv Brigade (1919) and then as S. Petliura's liaison with J. Piłsudski. After the war he settled in the Stryi region and became active in its economic revival: he restored the local branch of Silskyi Hospodar and founded and directed (1926–8) the Stryi County Union of Co-operatives. As supreme director and head of the organizational department of the *Audit Union of Ukrainian Co-operatives (1928–39) he was largely responsible for the success of the co-operative movement in Galicia. His writings in the field included *Kooperatyvna problema* (The Problem of Co-operation, 1937) and *Sil's'ko-hospodars'kyi kredyt* (Agricultural Credit, 1939). He also played a prominent role in Galician politics: he sat on the executive of the Ukrainian National Democratic Alliance (1925–39) and was elected as its candidate to the Polish Sejm in 1928 and 1930 and to the Senate in 1935. As a Sejm member he served on the budget and economic committees, and as senator he sat on the foreign relations committee. On 2 October 1939, shortly after the Soviet occupation of Galicia, Lutsky was arrested. He was deported to a concentration camp in northern European Russia, where he perished.

Lutsky, Yurii. See Luckyj, George Stephen Nestor.

Stepan Lutsyk at his easel (1948)

Lutsyk, Stepan [Lucyk], b 10 October 1906 in Lviv, d 10 October 1963 in St Paul, Minnesota. Painter. He studied at the Novakivsky Art School in Lviv (1926–30) and F. Léger's Modern Academy in Paris (1931). A cofounder of the *RUB artists' group and coauthor of its almanac *Karby* (Notches, 1933), he took part in exhibitions organized by the Association of Independent Ukrainian Artists (1931) and the Society of Friends of Ukrainian Art (which he cofounded) and contributed art reviews to D. Dontsov's *Vistnyk* (1933–9). His impressionist oil paintings of that period include *Hay Harvest in the Hutsul Region* (1931), *Sunday at the Lviv Castle, Ruins of the Maniava Hermitage*, portraits, and many landscapes, enlivened by human figures, of Lviv, its environs, and the Hutsul region. An émigré from 1944, in Munich he was active in the *Ukrainian Association of Artists, coedited its journal *Ukraïns'ke mystetstvo*, painted Alpine landscapes, and took part in German exhibitions. From 1950 he lived in St Paul, where he was active in the Ukrainian community, was a member of the Minneapolis Society of Fine Arts (from 1957), and participated in exhibitions at the Minnesota Institute of Arts and the University of Minnesota. A collection of articles about him, with reproductions of his works, was published in Toronto in 1973.

Lutugin, Leonid, b 21 February 1864 in St Petersburg, d 17 August 1915 in Kolchugino, Tomsk gubernia, Russia. Russian geologist. He graduated from the St Petersburg Mining Institute (1889) and then taught there (as professor from 1897) and worked with the Geological Committee (from 1892). For 22 years he conducted geological research of the Donets Coal Basin. He produced the first geological diagram of the coal-bearing strata of the basin (1911) and together with other geologists surveyed and determined the extent of its deposits. In 1914 he conducted research in the Kuznetsk Coal Basin, where he determined the correlation between the quality of coal and the degree of metamorphism. Lutuhyne, a city in Luhanske oblast, was named after him.

Lutuhyne. V-20, DB III-6. A town smt (1990 pop 18,900) on the Vilkhivka River and a raion center in Luhanske oblast. It was founded in 1896 when a steel-rolling machinery plant was built there. In 1914 a railway station was built, and the settlement was named Shmidtivka. In 1925 it was renamed Lutuhyne. It became an smt in 1960. It has a coal mine and machine-building and metalworking plants.

Hryhorii Luzhnytsky   Rev Leonyd Luzhnytsky

Luzhnytsky, Hryhorii [Lužnyc'kyj, Hryhorij] (Luznycky, Hryhor or Gregory; pseuds: L. Nyhrytsky, Meriiam, B. Polianych), b 27 August 1903 in Lviv, d 3 March 1990 in Philadelphia. Writer, journalist, and literary scholar and critic; member of the AN URSR (now ANU) Lviv branch in 1939–41; full member of the Shevchenko Scientific Society from 1952 and the Free Czecho–Slovak Academy of Arts and Sciences. Luzhnytsky studied Slavic culture at the University of Graz and received his PH D from the University of Vienna in 1926. He was a member of several faculties, at the University of Lviv (1939–41), University of Graz (1945–50), and University of Pennsylvania (1959–68), where he was a visiting professor. He was a literary consultant for the Lviv Ukrainian Drama Theater (1939–44) and the literature editor for Ukrainska Presa publishers (until 1939). From 1959 he worked in the editorial office of the newspaper *Ameryka* (Philadelphia). In addition to numerous articles on historical and cultural themes he wrote several novels, plays, and sketches. His scholarly works include *Ukraïns'ka tserkva mizh Skhodom i Zakhodom* (The Ukrainian Church between East and West, 1954), *Ukrainian Literature within the Framework of World Literature* (1961), and *Persecution and Destruction of the Ukrainian Church by the Russian Bolsheviks* (1964). He is the coauthor of *The Quest for an Ukrainian Catholic Patriarchate* (1971) and coauthor and editor of *P'iatdesiat rokiv ukraïns'koho teatru* (Fifty Years of the Ukrainian Theater, 1975).

D.H. Struk

Luzhnytsky, Leonyd [Lužnyc'kyj], b 25 April 1869 in Sorotsko, Skalat county, Galicia, d 16 October 1951 in Hecksternüst, West Germany. Ukrainian Catholic priest and pedagogue; founding member of the *Ukrainian Theological Scholarly Society. He taught catechism at the Academic Gymnasium of Lviv (1894–1929) and church history at the Greek Catholic Theological Seminary and Academy in Lviv. He wrote several textbooks on dogma, liturgics, ethics, and church history.

Łużny, Ryszard, b 1927 in Vovchkiv, Stanyslaviv county, Galicia. Polish scholar of Ukrainian and Russian baroque literature. He received his doctorate from Cracow University in 1963 and has been director of its Institute of Russian Philology and dean of its Faculty of Philology. He is the author of a monograph in Polish on writers of the Kievan Mohyla Academy circle and Polish literature (1966); of articles about the academy, about T. Prokopovych, S. Polotsky, and S. Yavorsky, and about related topics, which were published in Polish and Soviet scholarly periodicals and collections and in *Harvard Ukrainian Studies*; and of a survey of the history of Ukrainian literature in a 1970 Polish handbook on Ukraine edited by M. Karaś and A. Podraza.

Lva River [L'va] (also Mostva). A left-bank tributary of the Stvyha River. It is 160 km in length and drains a basin area of 2,400 sq km. The river flows through Rivne oblast into Belarus. Its valley, though partially drained, remains fairly marshy.

Lviv [L'viv] (Latin: Leopolis; Polish: Lwów; German: Lemberg; Russian: Lvov). IV–4, 5. A city (1991 pop 803,000) and oblast center, the historical capital of Galicia and Western Ukraine, and, after Kiev, the second cultural, political, and religous center of Ukraine. By population it is the seventh-largest city in Ukraine and the largest in the western oblasts. Standing at the meeting place of three geographical-economic regions – the Roztochia woodlands, the cultivated fields of the Buh Depression, and the fields of Podilia – Lviv has been for centuries a natural exchange center among them. But the main reason for its development was its location at the intersection of natural trade routes – the north–south route from the Baltic Sea to the Black Sea (Kholm–Halych) and the east–west route (Cracow–Kiev). Because of its location Lviv became an important commercial and cultural intermediary between Western and Eastern Europe, a role assumed from the declining cities of Zvenyhorod, Halych, and Kholm. Lviv's influence fluctuated between national and regional, according to historical events, particularly the power of Galicia. Its western location, far from the usual invasion routes of the Tatars, assured it a more peaceful development than Kiev's. Nevertheless, it was the principal arena of Polish-Ukrainian conflict.

Physical geography. The oldest part of Lviv lies in the depression of the Poltva River, which cuts into the Podolian Upland. The plain, 3–4 km wide and 260–270 m above sea level, was once a peat bog. It narrows to 1 km toward the north and slides between the Podolian Upland and Roztochia to the Buh Depression. The northern side of the depression along the Poltva is hemmed in by the western part of the *Holohory, which separates it from the Buh Depression with a thin ridge 100–150 m above the depressions running from the Chortivska Cliff (414 m) in the east to Vysokyi Zamok (413 m) in the northwest. Built of chalk marls and Miocene sand, sandstone, and limestone dissected by wooded ravines, the ridge is the most scenic part of Lviv. In the northwest it is continued by the somewhat lower, forested Roztochia from Kortumivka Hill (374 m) west of the Poltva River to Lysa Hill (380 m) near Briukhovychi.

The depression of the Poltva rises 60–100 m toward the south, southwest, and west to the *Opilia Upland (the so-called Lviv Plateau), which forms part of the European watershed running from the northwest to the southeast. The gently undulating plain, which reaches 350 m above sea level, is covered with loess and chernozem and is not forested. The western outskirts of Lviv have a different landscape. There the Lviv Plateau descends to 310 m above sea level. The meltwaters of a glacier, which reached as far west as Yaniv, once ran along the Bilohorske slope to the Buh Depression. Sand and gravel fields, with moving sand hills, and marshes cover the slope. The northern part of Lviv is a plain 240–280 m above sea level consisting of wide, gentle ridges (Malekhiv) covered with fertile loess and separated by the peat-covered valleys of the Buh's tributaries.

Lviv lies in a moderate, damp climate belt, between a continental and a maritime climate. Its average annual temperature is 7.5°C, with averages of 18.5°C in July and 4.1°C in January. The annual rainfall is 666 mm, most of it in July (102 mm) and least in January (27 mm). The average cloud cover is 66 days (maximum in December, minimum in August).

Since 1841 the Poltva River has been covered up. It is exposed only at its source and at its emergence from the city.

History. Lviv was founded in the mid-13th century by Prince *Danylo Romanovych near *Zvenyhorod, which had been razed by the Tatars, and named after his son Lev. Excavations on Vysokyi Zamok have shown that the site was settled in the 10th century. The city is first mentioned in the Galician-Volhynian Chronicle under the year 1256. The chronicle goes on to recount how the Tatar khan, Burundai, ordered the castle to be destroyed in 1259, and how Khan Telebuh attacked Lviv in 1263 and 1287. In the 1260s, during the reign of Prince *Lev Danylovych, Lviv became the capital of the Principality of *Galicia-Volhynia; it remained its capital until the end (1340s). As Kiev declined, Lviv rose to national stature.

At first Lviv covered a small area (later the Zhovkva suburb) on the right bank of the Poltva and consisted of three parts: the *ditynets* or stronghold on Lysa Hill (today the western plateau of Vysokyi Zamok), the inner town at the foot of the *ditynets*, and the outer town, the least fortified suburb, stretching as far as the Poltva River. The population was 2,000 to 3,000. Besides Ukrainians it included Germans, Armenians, Tatars, Poles, Karaites, Hungarians, and Jews. The names of some streets, such as Virmenska and Tatarska, as well as of Stare Okopyshche (the Old Jewish cemetery) date back to medieval times. There were 10 Orthodox churches, 3 Armenian churches, and 2 Catholic churches.

The Polish period, 1387–1772. After the death of Prince *Yurii II, Galicia was governed by D. Dedko, the vicegerent of Liubartas, until 1349, when Casimir III the Great captured Lviv. After a short period of joint Polish-Hungarian rule (1370–87) Lviv was annexed by Poland. At first it served as the capital of a separate country united with Poland. Called Regnum Russiae, it had its own coat of arms (the lion), currency, laws, and administration dating back to the Princely era. Then it became the capital of the Polish province known as *Rus' voivodeship (1434–1772). In 1356 Casimir granted Lviv the rights of *Magdeburg law, which enabled the German and Polish merchants to take control of the municipal government. The influx of German merchants and tradesmen increased rapidly.

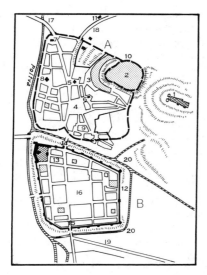

LVIV IN THE 13TH AND 14TH CENTURIES

A. Initial territory of Lviv
B. Territory of Lviv established in 1270

1. High Castle
2. *Ditynets*
3. Dwellings of the princes and boyars
4. Staryi rynok – the city's old market square
5. St Nicholas's Church
6. St John the Baptist Roman Catholic Church
7. Church of the Resurrection
8. St Theodore's Church
9. Virgin of the Snows Roman Catholic Church
10. Probable fortifications of the original territory of the city
11. Church of Good Friday
12. Fortifications of the city as of 1270, built in the second half of the 13th century
13. Low Castle
14. Tatar Gate
15. Halych Gate
16. Market square
17. Volhynian path
18. Podolian path
19. Galician path
20. Moats

In the second half of the 14th century the city center shifted southwest to the wide valley of the Poltva River, which provided a better site for a fortified town on the Western European model. The ramparts and moats ran along today's Pershoho Travnia Street, Danylo Halytskyi Square, Pidvalna Street, and Valova Street and enclosed an area of approx 50 ha. Walls were built within the ramparts; in the 15th century they were expanded and reinforced with 17 towers. Today only one of them, the Porokhova Tower, opposite Lysenko Street, survives. The city's fortifications included two castles, the Low Castle, the residence of the voivode, and the High Castle, an observation post with a magazine and a jail built by Casimir in 1360. The fortified town had two main gates, the Cracow Gate in the north and the Halych Gate in the south. There were two smaller gates for pedestrians, the Jesuit Gate in the west, near the Jesuit church, and the Bosatska

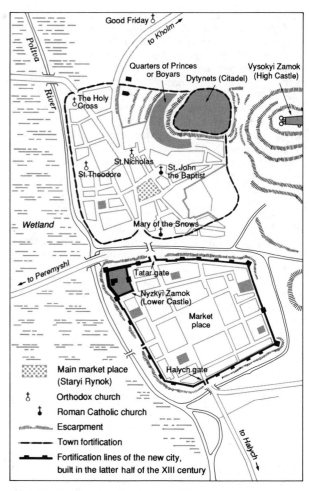

LVIV IN THE 14TH CENTURY

(Barefoot) Gate in the east, opposite Ruska Street, which led to the monastery of the discalced Carmelites. The suburbs, which stretched out along the main roads to the city, were unfortified and vulnerable to enemy attack. In 1438 the Crimean Tatars raided the suburbs, and in 1498 the Turkish army lay siege to the city. Much of the town was destroyed by fires in 1479, 1494, 1511, and 1527.

Cottages of Lviv burghers and estates (called *yurydyky*) of nobles, who did not come under the city courts, sprang up around the city and turned eventually into farming settlements. In the 20th cenutry they became the new suburbs of Zamarstyniv (from the estate of I. Sommerstein, est 1349), Klepariv (from the estate of A. Klopper, 1419), Holosko (1401, near the Olovsko Basin), Kulparkiv (from the estate of P. Goldberg, 1425), Bilohorshcha (1463), and Briukhovychi (1503). There were over 50 churches in the city and its suburbs.

Lviv's economy developed from a farming, manufacturing, and commercial base in the Princely era to a commercial and manufacturing economy with a range of operations extending beyond the frontiers of Poland. Lviv had 'absolute warehousing rights,' which made it a unique trade center. Its renowned trade fairs were held on St Agnes's Day, 3 February (21 January OS), and St Margaret's Day, 30 July (17 July OS), and in later times on St George's Day, 6 May (23 April OS). Banking was in the

Lviv: old fortifications with the campanile of the Bernardine monastery in the background

Lviv: seal of the municipal council depicting the town's coat of arms (16th century)

ter. The Germans had gained control of the city government and judiciary, and German was the official language of the city council. Sermons in the Roman Catholic churches were in German, and the first Catholic bishop was a German. Lviv also attracted many Armenians, Poles, and, later, Jews. By the beginning of the 16th century most of the German and Armenian population had been Polonized, and Lviv to a large extent had assumed the character of a Polish town. Ukranians were in the majority only in the suburbs. Their rights were limited by Magdeburg law, which applied only to Catholics. Thus, Ukrainians were excluded from municipal affairs, their trading rights were limited, and they were shut out from the better residential areas.

Lviv in the 17th century (drawing by A. Passarotti)

Old Lviv: view from Zamkova (Castle) Mountain

hands of Jewish and Armenian merchants. After the first period of development ending in the mid-15th century, Lviv's trade declined because of changes in the trade routes. From the mid-16th to the mid-17th century its trade grew again. Most of the townsmen were craftsmen organized in guilds. The first reference to guilds dates from 1386. By the mid-17th century there were as many as 30 guilds totaling over 500 craftsmen. Lviv's manufactured products had a high reputation, especially its metalware, jewelry, and weapons.

Until the early 16th century Lviv had a German charac-

The name of Ruska Street dates back to that period. Ukrainians suffered not only social but also national and religious discrimination from the ruling Roman Catholic circles. They protested often and organized themselves into *brotherhoods. The most prominent of the 10 brotherhoods in the 16th and 17th centuries was the *Lviv Dormition Brotherhood (est 1439), which was granted the right of *stauropegion in 1586. Through the efforts of the Lviv brotherhoods, the city once again, after the Princely era, became an important Ukrainian cultural and religious center. I. *Fedorovych's publishing activity also contributed to Lviv's prominence.

From the mid-17th century until 1772 the city declined, and the burghers grew poorer as the government favored the nobility. The trade routes changed, and incessant warfare disrupted commerce. B. Khmelnytsky's Cossack army twice besieged Lviv; first on 6–10 October 1648, when it took the Vysokyi Zamok fortress, and again between 25 September and 8 November 1655. The city was attacked several times by Turkish-Tatar armies; in 1672, 1675, 1691, and 1695. The greatest blow was inflicted by the Swedes in 1704: they plundered the city and exacted a

Lviv: buildings of the Lviv Dormition Brotherhood, including the Dormition Church and the Korniakt Tower

heavy tribute from the burghers, especially the Dormition Brotherhood, thereby weakening Lviv for decades.

In the 18th century the guild system disintegrated, and the number of unorganized tradesmen, known as *partachi* (outsiders, from Latin *a parte*), increased. A period of fierce competition between the two groups was followed by general impoverishment and decline. The castle and many buildings fell into ruin. Many merchant and manufacturing shops were empty. Approx 75 percent of the enterprises were taken over by Jews.

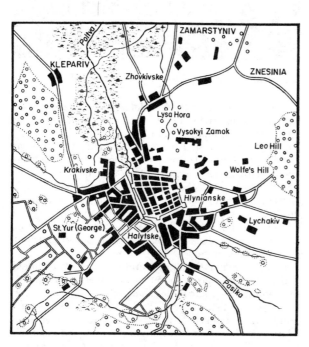

LVIV IN THE LATE 18TH AND EARLY 19TH CENTURIES

The Austrian period, 1772–1918. The transfer of Lviv to Austria (19 August 1772) as the capital of the Crownland of Galicia and Ladomeria opened a new chapter in the city's development. Lviv was inundated with German civil servants, soldiers, merchants, and colonists. After the partitioning of Poland many Polish immigrants poured into Lviv. The city grew into a commercial, administrative, and cultural center. The first newspaper on Ukrainian territory, the French-language *Gazette de Léopol*, came out in Lviv in 1776. The first city theater was founded that year. In 1784 the *Lviv University and an academic gymnasium were set up.

As the population increased, the city had to expand. In 1777 the fortifications, which had lost their military value, were torn down and replaced with tree-shaded boulevards. The Poltva River was walled in and diverted into an underground canal. The suburbs spread along the main roads to the city. First to be built up was Horodok district, on both sides of the paved highway leading to Vienna. The city began to be developed beyond the belt of grand buildings along the city walls, the wooded areas along Copernicus Street, toward Franko Park (Jesuit Garden). Emperor Joseph II closed down 27 Roman Catholic churches and monasteries, 7 Ukrainian churches, and 3 Armenian churches and converted them into public buildings, citadels, and prisons. A new city hall was built in 1835.

Lviv's population grew rapidly. By the mid-19th century it was as large as Kiev's and, among Ukrainian cities, second only to Odessa's. By the turn of the century Lviv was the fifth-largest city in the Austro-Hungarian Empire

Lviv: main railway station

and the fourth-largest city (after Odessa, Kiev, and Kharkiv) in Ukraine.

The spread of railways stimulated the city's growth. The first lines were Lviv–Peremyshl–Cracow (1861), Lviv–Stanyslaviv–Chernivtsi (1866), Lviv–Krasne–Brody (1869), Lviv–Ternopil–Pidvolochyske (1870), and Lviv–Stryi–Lavochne (1873). Another five lines were laid later. Lviv became an important railway junction, one of the largest in Austria-Hungary and Eastern Europe. With the building of the main station and the Pidzamchia freight station the city spread from the valley of the Poltva to the adjacent plateau. In 1871 Lviv was divided for the first time into districts – Halych, Cracow, Zhovkva, Lychakiv, and Central. In 1890 Novyi Svit was added.

In the 19th century Lviv's industry and trades developed rapidly. In 1814 there were 21 guilds, although the guild system had lost its former influence. In 1841 the first steam mill was built in Lviv. The chief industries were food processing, clothes manufacturing, construction, and metalworking. There were 9 major enterprises in 1850, 16 in 1870, and 25 in 1902. The enterprises became larger through the 20th century: in 1900 the 22 largest enterprises, with over 100 workers each, represented approx 8 percent of all the enterprises (278) and employed 5,580 workers, or approx 55 percent of the total work force (10,163). Beginning in 1841 banking and savings and loan institutions appeared as branches of Austrian banks or of local Jewish, Polish, or Ukrainian ventures (Dnister, 1892; Tsentrobank, 1898; Land Mortgage Bank, 1910).

Austria's social reforms and enlightened cultural and educational policies, and a relatively liberal political regime, were favorable to the Ukrainian national revival. Before the Revolution of 1848 Lviv was the center of the national awakening: the *Ruthenian Triad wrote at the beginning of the 1830s and D. Zubrytsky published Kronika miasta Lwowa (Chronicle of the City of Lviv, 1844). During the Spring of Nations the *Supreme Ruthenian Council arose in Lviv and declared the people of Galician Ruthenia to be one nation with the people of central Ukraine. At the same time the *Congress of Ruthenian Scholars and the *People's Home were set up in Lviv. A chair of Ukrainian language and literature was founded at Lviv University. By the end of the 19th and the beginning of the 20th century, owing to the particular historical situation whereby there was a repressive Russian regime in central Ukraine and a liberal Austrian regime in Galicia, Lviv, for the third time in its history, assumed a leading role in Ukrainian national development. That role is evident in the history of the evolution of Ukrainian political thought from populism to Galician autonomy and, finally, to the idea of complete national independence and unity. The headquarters of the major political organizations, such as the National Democratic party, the Ukrainian Radical party, and the Ukrainian Social Democratic party, were in Lviv. The key Ukrainian cultural institutions, such as the *Prosvita society (1868), the Ruska Besida theater (1864; later Ukrainska Besida), the Ridna Shkola society (1881), the *Lysenko Music Society (1903), and the National Museum, were established in Lviv. The head offices of the various Ukrainian co-operatives were located there. As the home of the *Shevchenko Scientific Society (est 1873) Lviv made an enormous contribution to Ukrainian learning. It was also the leading center for Ukrainian publishing: in 1913, of 83 Ukrainian periodical and 410 nonperiodical publications in the world, 65 and 299 respectively were published in Lviv. Important newspapers, such as *Pravda (1867–96), *Dilo (1880–1939), and *Svoboda (1897–1918), and journals, such as *Zoria (1880–97), *Literaturno-naukovyi vistnyk (1898–1906, 1922–32), and Zapysky Naukovoho tovarystva im. Shevchenka (1892–1939), were published in Lviv.

In the 19th century Lviv was also a Polish political and cultural center. Taking advantage of their privileged status in Galicia and political influence with the Austrian government, the Poles strenuously opposed the Ukrainian movement. Lviv became a battleground between Ukrainians and Poles. The struggle sometimes erupted in violence, such as A. *Potocki's assassination in 1908, and finally led to the *Ukrainian-Polish War in Galicia, beginning on 1 November 1918. On 19 October 1918 the Ukrainian National Rada in Lviv had proclaimed a Ukrainian state in the western Ukrainian territories, and on 9 November the Rada named it the Western Ukrainian National Republic (ZUNR). On 21 November the Poles captured Lviv, thereby forcing the ZUNR government to flee to Ternopil.

Interwar period, 1919–39. After the First World War Lviv's importance declined. It was no longer the capital of a large province of the Austro-Hungarian Empire but the center of a voivodeship. The USSR's economic isolation undermined Lviv's role as a trading intermediary between east and west. Attempts to sell Polish goods to the USSR (the eastern trade) were fruitless. Lviv supplied mostly agricultural products from Galicia and Volhynia to the home and Western markets. In 1935, of 6,242 commercial enterprises, 3,022 sold food products, and 1,340 sold confectionery products. Industrial enterprises accounted for only a quarter of the turnover of commercial firms. Compared to Poles and Jews, Ukrainians did not play an important role in Lviv's economy. Nevertheless, Ukrainian provincial co-operatives, such as *Maslosoiuz, *Tsentrosoiuz, and *Narodna Torhovlia, the Union of Ukrainian Merchants and Entrepreneurs, and the Zoria artisans' association, had a great impact on the economic life of Galicia's Ukrainian population.

Polish-Ukrainian hostility increased sharply in the period as Lviv became the center of organized resistance to the Polish occupation of Galicia. On 18 March 1923 40,000 people demonstrated against the decision of the *Conference of Ambassadors to award Galicia to Poland. The Ukrainian Military Organization (UVO) conducted an armed struggle against the regime, in attempting to assassinate J. Piłsudski (25 September 1921) and President S. Wojciechowski (5 September 1924) on their visits to Lviv. On the 10th anniversary of the *November Uprising a massive Ukrainian demonstration was held in the city. In 1929 the national executive of the OUN was set up in Lviv. On 22 October 1933 a staff member of the Soviet consulate in Lviv was assassinated by the OUN in protest against the man-made famine and the terror in Soviet Ukraine. In 1936 the OUN executive for Western Ukraine was put on trial in Lviv. In defiance of Polish discrimination in education, the *Lviv (Underground) Ukrainian University and the *Lviv (Underground) Ukrainian Higher Polytechnical School were set up. The headquarters of Ukrainian political parties, such as the Ukrainian National Democratic Alliance, the Ukrainian Socialist Radical party, the Ukrainian Social Democratic party, the Ukrainian Catholic People's party, and the clandestine Communist Party of Western Ukraine, were in Lviv.

The Second World War. Under the first Soviet occupation

(22 September 1939 to 30 June 1941) Lviv served as an oblast center. Before fleeing the German advance the Soviet occupational regime murdered thousands of Ukrainian civilians, mainly members of the city's intelligentsia. During the three-year German occupation (June 1941 to July 1944) Lviv was the center of the Galicia district within the *Generalgouvernement. In 1942 an executive branch of the *Ukrainian Central Committee headed by K. Pankivsky was set up in Lviv. The city was a center of the Ukrainian resistance movement (OUN, UPA). On 30 June 1941 the *Proclamation of Ukrainian statehood took place there and the *Ukrainian State Administration was formed. The Ukrainian National Council, headed by K. Levytsky, operated in Lviv from July 1941. On 27 July 1944, Soviet forces re-entered Lviv without battle. The city sustained little damage during the war.

Lviv: airport terminal

The Soviet period. After the war Lviv's administrative division was changed a number of times. Today Lviv is divided into five raions: Zaliznychyi, Halytskyi, Shevchenkivskyi, Lychakivskyi, and Frankivskyi. The city's streets, parks, and institutions were given Ukrainian names, and new cultural and scientific institutions, such as the Lviv branch of the AN URSR (3 April 1951, now ANU), were set up. The national composition of its population changed dramatically. Rapid industrial development was accompanied by demographic growth and changes in the social structure of the city. New industrial and residential districts sprang up. With the Sovietization of the economy, civic life, and private life, Lviv lost its historical role as a center of Ukrainian national and religious life and as Ukraine's link with the West. All pre-Soviet cultural institutions and the Ukrainian Catholic church were abolished. The inhabitants resisted the anti-Ukrainian acts of the Soviet authorities, passively and actively. In the 1960s and 1970s a number of Ukrainian intellectuals were arrested and tried in Lviv (see *Dissident movement). The funeral of the murdered (allegedly by the KGB) composer V. *Ivasiuk in 1979 turned into a massive demonstration. In the late 1980s Lviv took the lead in democratic reform and in the revival of national consciousness. The first mass political rallies in Ukraine took place in Lviv in the summer of 1988. In the national and local elections of March 1990, democratic candidates, some of them former dissidents, won large majorities in the Lviv city and oblast councils. After that victory many pre-Soviet Ukrainian institutions

and associations, such as the Ukrainian Catholic church, the Shevchenko Scientific Society, the Prosvita society, and the Plast scouting organization, were revived in Lviv.

Economy. Until 1939 Lviv was a commercial, administrative, and industrial city. Its dominant industry, accounting for 60 percent of the output, was the food industry. Under the Soviet regime its industry was nationalized, some of the older plants were reconstructed, and many new ones were built. Today the main industry is machine building (40 percent of the total output), especially middle- and precision-machine and tool manufacturing, and its largest plants are the *Lviv Bus Plant, the truck-building consortium Avtonavantazhuvach, the conveyor-building consortium Konveier (est 1965), and the locomotive and car repair plant (est 19th century), the bicycle factory, the diamond and diamond instruments manufacturing consortium, and the farm-machinery and chemicals manufacturing consortium Lvivkhimsilhospmash. The chief representatives of the tool and instrument manufacturing industry in Lviv are Lvivprylad, Ternoprylad, and Mikroprylad, the last of which makes electronic measuring devices, automation equipment, and computers. In radioelectronics Kineskop makes color picture tubes and specializes in color (7 models) and black-and-white (15 models) television sets, and Rema makes electronic medical equipment. Lviv's insulator plant was the only plant in the former USSR to produce glass insulators for every type of power transmission.

The food industry accounts for 20 percent of Lviv's industrial output. It includes a bacon packing factory and a poultry packing complex, a liquor distillery, flour mills and bakeries, the Svitoch confectionery consortium, and the Kolos brewing consortium. Light industry is third in importance. Factories of the Promin manufacturing consortium produce cotton thread, cloth, and knitwear. The Prohres consortium makes footwear, and the Vesna, Maiak, and Yunist consortia sew clothes. The building-materials industry is dependent on local sources of materials. Its plants produce bricks and tiles, wall and facing materials, window glass, and reinforced concrete. Lviv also has a woodworking industry that makes furniture, flooring, musical instruments, and plywood and a chemical industry that produces petrochemicals, oxygen, paints and varnishes, pharmaceuticals, and perfumes. Lviv is an important publishing center with a number of large printing enterprises. In 1978 there were 137 large enterprises in Lviv. Of a total work force of 281,000 in 1980, 172,000 people were employed in industry.

Lviv is also an important communication center. It is the junction of nine railroad lines and has five railway stations. A number of national highways converge in Lviv. Its Sknyliv airport connects it by air with the major cities of Eastern Europe.

Population. In the mid-17th century Lviv had a population of 30,000 (Kiev ca 10,000) and was the largest city in Ukraine. By the time Lviv was annexed by Austria, the population had fallen to 20,000. During the Austrian period it grew steadily, from 19,500 in 1776 to 38,700 in 1795, 46,000 in 1820, 70,000 in 1857, 87,000 in 1869, 109,700 in 1880, 159,000 in 1900, and 206,100 in 1910. The First World War interrupted its growth (219,400 in 1921). In 1931 some suburban districts were included in Lviv, and its population jumped from 241,800 to 312,200.

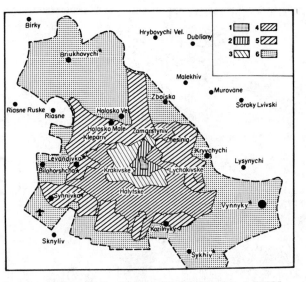

TERRITORIAL EXPANSION OF LVIV

1. Lviv in the 15th century
2. Lviv in the late 17th and early 18th centuries
3. Lviv in the 19th century
4. Lviv in the 20th century
5. Lviv between 1939 and 1941
6. Lviv's present territory

*Briukhovychi has been incorporated into the city's Shevchen-
kivskyi raion, Vynnyky and Sykhiv into Lychakivskyi raion,
Levandivka (Zhovtneve) and Bilohorshcha into Zaliznychyi
raion, and Syhnivka into Frankivskyi raion.

Under Austrian rule Lviv attracted new residents
from eastern and western Galicia, whereas in the interwar
period almost all new residents came from eastern Galicia.
In 1900–10 immigration to the city (28,000) exceeded its
natural growth (18,000); in 1921–31 the respective figures
were 53,000 and 18,000. The expansion occurred mainly in
the suburbs. During the Second World War the population
fluctuated wildly. It jumped by over 100,000 to 430,000
(May 1940) as refugees from Poland poured into the city.
In 1943, during the German occupation, it decreased to
180,000 (discounting the Germans), because of the destruction of the Jews. After the war the population increased rapidly, to 387,000 in 1956, 411,000 in 1959, 553,000
in 1970, 665,000 in 1979, and 787,000 in 1989, mainly be-

cause of industrialization. The ethnic composition of Lviv
changed gradually until the last war. Before 1914 the proportion of Ukrainians increased slowly but steadily because of immigration from the countryside. During the
First World War the proportion of Jews increased because
of their influx from the small towns, and the proportion of
Ukrainians fell because of war casualties and political emigration. In the interwar period the Ukrainian population
increased slightly at the expense of the Poles and Jews. In
the Second World War the number of Jews fell drastically,
and the number of Ukrainians increased. After the war
most of the Poles left Lviv, and their place was taken by
Ukrainians, including inhabitants of the Sian and Lemko
regions, which were annexed by Poland. Thus, the ethnic
composition that had characterized Lviv for centuries
changed radically, and the Ukrainians became by far the
largest group. Then Russians began to settle in Lviv (see
the table).

Science and culture. Lviv is the scientific and cultural
center of western Ukraine. In 1951 a branch of the AN URSR
(now ANU) consisting of the Institutes of Social Sciences,
Machine Building and Automation, the Geology of Useful
Minerals, and Agrobiology was set up in Lviv. In 1971 the
Western Scientific Center of the ANU was opened there.
Besides the academy's institutes there are many research
institutes with high reputation: the *Ukrainian Scientific
Research Institute of the Printing Industry, the *Ukrainian
Scientific Research Institute of Geological Prospecting, the
(until 1991 All-Union) Design and Experimental Institute
of Bus Building, the Lviv Scientific Research Institute of
Epidemiology and Microbiology, and the Lviv Observato-
ry. In the Polish period there were five higher schools in
Lviv: the university, the polytechnic, the Greek Catholic
Theological Academy, the Veterinary Academy, and the
Higher School of Foreign Trade. By the 1980s there were
11, some of them based on the earlier schools: Lviv University, the *Lviv Polytechnical Institute, the *Ukrainian
Printing Institute, the *Lviv Institute of Forest Technology, the *Lviv Agricultural Institute, the *Lviv Medical Institute, the *Lviv Zootechnical-Veterinary Institute, the
*Lviv Trade and Economics Institute, the *Lviv Institute of
Physical Culture, the *Lviv Institute of Applied and Decorative Arts, and the *Lviv Conservatory. Their total
enrollment in 1979 was 62,500. There are also some
30 specialized secondary schools, some 30 vocational
schools, and over 100 general education schools. The largest libraries are the *Lviv Scientific Library of the Academy of Sciences, the Lviv University Library, and the

The ethnic composition of Lviv, 1869–1989 (thousands; percentage of total in parentheses)

Year	Total pop	Ukrainians		Poles		Jews		Others	
1869	87.1	12.4	(14.2)	46.3	(53.2)	26.3	(30.2)	2.1	(2.4)
1890	127.9	21.9	(17.2)	67.3	(52.6)	36.1	(28.1)	2.6	(2.1)
1910	206.1	39.3	(19.2)	105.5	(51.2)	57.4	(27.8)	3.9	(1.8)
1921	219.5	7.3	(12.4)	111.9	(51.0)	76.9	(35.1)	3.4	(1.5)
1931	312.2	50.9	(16.3)	156.0	(50.0)	99.6	(31.9)	5.7	(1.8)
1943	209.1	62.7	(29.9)	131.3	(62.9)	–	–	15.1	(7.2)
1979	665.1	492.2	(74.0)	11.9	(1.8)	18.0	(2.7)	143.0[a]	(21.5)
1989	786.9	622.7	(79.1)	9.7	(1.2)	12.8	(1.6)	141.7[b]	(18.0)

[a]Including 128,300 Russians
[b]Including 126,500 Russians

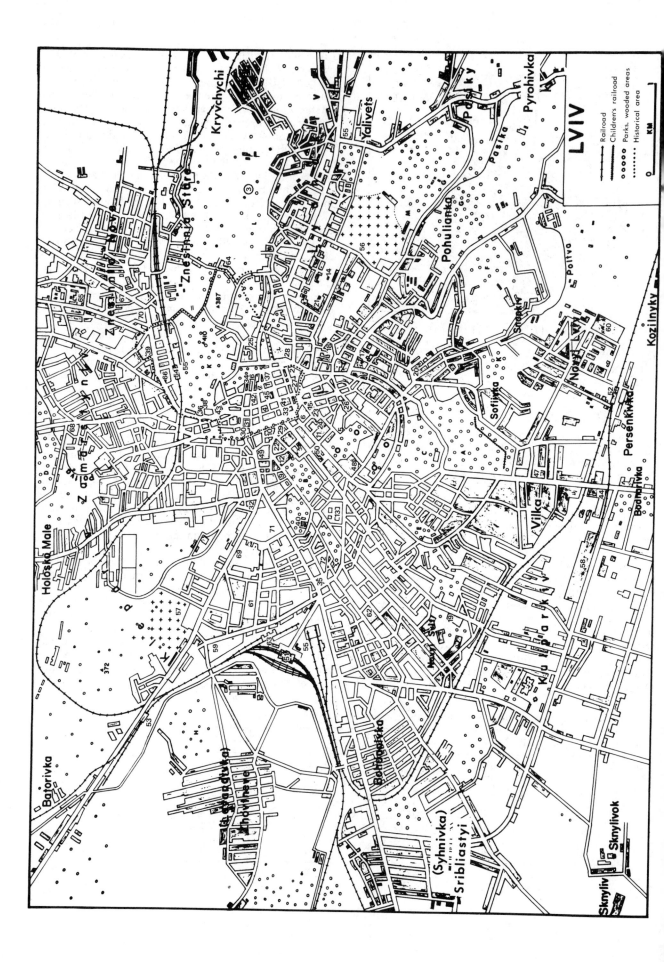

LVIV

1. Lviv Historical Museum
2. Central State Historical Archive of Ukraine
3. Lviv Museum of Folk Architecture and Folkways
4. Natural Science Museum of the ANU
5. National Museum
6. Lviv Art Gallery
7. Pharmacy Museum
8. Lviv Franko Literary Memorial Museum
9. Oleksa Novakivsky Memorial Museum and Olena Kulchytska Memorial Museum
10. Ukrainian State Museum of Ethnography and Crafts
11. Lviv branch of the ANU
12. Lviv University
13. Lviv Polytechnical Institute
14. Lviv Medical Institute
15. Lviv Conservatory
16. Ukrainian Printing Institute
17. Pedagogical Institute
18. Lviv Trade and Economics Institute
19. Lviv Institute of Forest Technology
20. Lviv Institute of Applied and Decorative Arts
21. Lviv Zootechnical-Veterinary Institute
22. Lviv Institute fo Physical Culture
23. Philharmonic Society
24. Lviv Scientific Library of the Academy of Sciences of Ukraine
25. Library of Rare Books
26. Lviv University Library
27. Regional Library
28. Children's Library
29. Scientific-technical Library
30. Lviv Theater of Opera and Ballet
31. Lviv Ukrainian Drama Theater
32. Lviv Russian Drama Theater
33. Lviv Young Spectator's Theater
34. Lviv Puppet Theater
35. Circus
36. Printing Museum
37. Dormition Church
38. St Onuphrius's Church and Monastery
39. Church of Good Friday
40. St George's Cathedral
41. Latin Cathedral
42. Armenian Cathedral
43. St Nicholas's Church
44. Press House
45. City Hall
46. Regional (oblast) soviet
47. Regional (oblast) government
48. Former KGB headquarters
49. Former MVD (former NKVD) headquarters
50. Main Post Office
51. Main Railway Station
52. Persenkivka Railway Station
53. Klepariv Railway Station
54. Pidzamche Railway Station
55. Bus stations
56. Lychakiv Cemetery
57. Yaniv Cemetery
58. Lviv Bus Plant
59. Avtonavantazhuvach Truck-building Consortium
60. Bicycle factory
61. Lviv Elektron Television Plant
62. Electric lamp plant
63. Locomotive and car repair plant
64. Chemical and pharmaceutical factory
65. Metalworking factory
66. Cotton mill
67. Foundry
68. Paints and varnishes factory
69. Knitting factory
70. Printing enterprise
71. Lvivkhimsilhospmash farm machinery and chemicals manufacturing consortium
72. Candy factory

A. Stryi Park
B. Franko Park
C. Khmelnytsky Park
D. Park of the 700-year Anniversary of Lviv
E. Students' Park
F. Friendship Park
G. Pohulianka Park
H. Zhovtneve Park
K. Vysokyi Zamok Park
L. Shevchenkivskyi Hai
M. Botanical garden of Lviv University

Library of the Lviv Polytechnical Institute. There are approx 400 public libraries, with total holdings of over 15 million books. The most important archives in Lviv are the *Central State Historical Archive of Ukraine and the Lviv Oblast State Archive.

In the interwar period the city theater in Lviv was Polish, and the Ukrainian public was served by a number of itinerant troupes. Today there are five main theaters: the *Lviv Theater of Opera and Ballet, the *Lviv Ukrainian Drama Theater, the *Lviv Young Spectator's Theater, the *Lviv Russian Drama Theater, and the Lviv Puppet Theater. There is also a symphony orchestra, the Lviv Oblast Philharmonic, and the *Trembita state choir. Of the 40 or more cinemas in the city, the largest are Myr, Dnipro, Lviv, Kyiv, and Ukraina.

Most of the 10 museums that served Lviv in the interwar period, including the *National Museum and the museums of the Shevchenko Scientific Society and the Stauropegion Institute, were reorganized during the Soviet period. The chief museums today are the *Lviv Historical Museum, the National Museum, the *Natural Science Museum of the Academy of Sciences, the *Lviv Art Gallery, the Ukrainian State Museum of Ethnography and Crafts, the Franko Literary Memorial Museum, the Lviv Museum of Folk Architecture and Folkways, and the Arms Museum (est 1981).

Once a center of Ukrainian publishing (65 papers before 1939), Lviv was reduced in the Soviet period to only one Ukrainian daily (*Vil'na Ukraïna*), one monthly journal (*Zhovten'* [*Dzvin*, as of 1990]), and a young people's magazine (*Lenins'ka molod'*). The chief publishing houses were Kameniar and Vyshcha Shkola. Under the reforms of the late 1980s some new papers appeared, most of them organs of unofficial organizations. After Ukraine's independence many new papers (*Za vil'nu Ukraïnu, Dilo, Moloda Halychyna*) and journals appeared.

Religious life. For several centuries Lviv was a bastion of the Orthodox faith in Western Ukraine. The *Lviv Dormition Brotherhood had an important impact on the religious and cultural life of all Ukraine in the 16th and 17th centuries. The city was the seat of *Lviv eparchy, which was Orthodox until the end of the 17th century and then Uniate, and of *Halych metropoly (est 1807). Through the efforts of Metropolitan A. *Sheptytsky Lviv became the leading center of Ukrainian Catholic theology. It was the home of the *Greek Catholic Theological Seminary, the *Greek Catholic Theological Academy, and the *Ukrainian Theological Scholarly Society, which published the journal *Bohosloviia*. At the same time it was the seat of Polish and Armenian eparchies. After the abolition of the Ukrainian Catholic church by the Soviet authorities in 1946, only the Russian Orthodox church was permitted to maintain an archbishop in Lviv. In 1990 the Ukrainian Catholic church under Metropolitan V. Sterniuk in Lviv was officially recognized, and St George's Cathedral was returned to it. Since early 1991 its head, Cardinal M. *Liubachivsky, has resided in Lviv.

Layout. Today Lviv has an area of 155 sq km. For descriptive purposes Lviv can be divided into three concentric circles: the central core, consisting of the old city in the depression of the Poltva, an architecturally and economically mixed area built up in the 19th and early 20th (to 1930) centuries, and the suburbs that were once villages and are not yet fully built up.

Old Lviv (woodcut by Bohdan Soroka, 1981)

The core is the city of the 14th to 18th centuries. It appears well planned: the rectangular market square and city hall stand at the center of the street grid, which is encircled by broad, green boulevards at the site of the old walls. The core is densely built up with tall stone buildings, many of them in their original style. In the second half of the 19th century the center of the city shifted west and southwest. Shevchenko (formerly Akademichnyi) *prospekt*, Mickiewicz Square, and Horodetska Street became the new axis of the city. That is the most imposing part of Lviv, with many public buildings, hotels (eg, the Inturist, formerly George Hotel), cafés, stores, and banks in 19th- and early 20th-century styles. At one end of the axis stands the opera theater, and off to the sides are Lviv University, the ANU Institute of Social Sciences, and the main post office.

The core is surrounded by several districts: Krakiv, in the west, is a mixed residential and commercial area, with an industrial section near the main railway station; Halych and Novyi Svit, in the south, are residential areas with fine villas; Zhovkva, in the north, is an old manufacturing and trading district, its southern part settled mostly by Jews until the war and its northern edge covered with factories; and Lychakiv, in the east, is residential, with

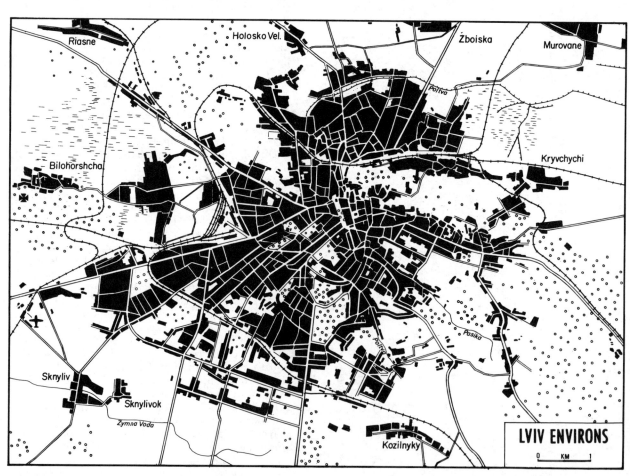

✠Site of military combat against special units of the MVD, where the supreme commander of the UPA, Taras Chuprynka (R. Shukhevych), was killed on 5 March 1950.

A new railroad line was built near Bilohorshcha for military purposes (Warsaw Pact); it links the western, eastern, and northern lines.

Lviv: A) Bernardine church; B) Boim Chapel; C) Transfiguration Church; D) Armenian Cathedral; E) Dominican church; F) Chapel of the Three Saints

hospitals and a cemetery on its outer edge. The third circle consists of the suburbs: to the north, Zamarstyniv and Znesinnia are the most industrialized districts of Lviv, and Male and Velyke Holosko, Zboiska, Kryvchytsi, and Klepariv have preserved some of their agricultural character; to the west, Levandivka, Bohdanivka, and Syhnivka are settled by workers and have some industry; to the south, Kulparkiv has a large psychiatric hospital; and to the southwest, Kozilnyky, Snopkiv, and Pasiky are green residential areas with some farmland.

Lviv is a very green city with a varied vegetation. The largest and most picturesque parks are Stryi (60 ha, est 1887), in the south, Vysokyi Zamok (37 ha, est 1835) and Shevchenkivskyi Hai (84 ha), in the east, and Druzhba (60 ha, est 1959–63). The smaller parks are Zalizna Voda (18.2 ha, est 1905), Franko (the former Jesuit Garden, 12.2 ha, est late 16th century), Lychakiv (8.4 ha), Pohulianka, and Khmelnytsky (25 ha). The Lychakiv Cemetery, which contains some famous monuments to noted Ukrainian and Polish residents of Lviv, and the Yaniv Cemetery, with over 200 graves of fighters for Ukrainian independence, resemble parks.

Architecture and art. The oldest monument in Lviv consists of the foundation and walls of St Nicholas's Church, built by Prince Lev Danylovych in the 13th century. The church burned down in 1623 and 1783 and was rebuilt in 1800. The remnants of Vysokyi Zamok date back to the 13th century. A number of medieval churches, built originally in the Byzantine Romanesque style, have since been reconstructed; among them are *St Onuphrius's Church and Monastery, the Church of *Good Friday (reconstructed in 1643–5), the Roman Catholic churches of St John the Baptist (1260) in the old Market Square and the Virgin of the Snows (14th century), both rebuilt at the end of the 19th century, and St George's Church and Monastery (later St George's Cathedral), built by Prince Lev outside the city. St Theodore's Church, the Church of the Resurrection, and the Church of the Annunciation from medieval times have completely disappeared. The *Armenian Cathedral was restored in the 1920s. The only indubitably medieval piece of art is Dymytrii's bell, poured for St George's Church in 1341. Lviv's Gothic architecture of the 14th and 15th centuries was destroyed by fire in 1527. Only the Latin Cathedral (built 1340, rebuilt 1761–76) survived, and in 1619 the Renaissance chapel of the Kampian family was added to it.

By the end of the 16th century Lviv had the appearance of a Renaissance city. It is the only city in Ukraine that still has some original Renaissance architecture. The finest examples of the style are the *Dormition Church (1591–1629); the Chapel of the Three Saints (1578–91); the central part of the Armenian Cathedral complex; the Boim family chapel (1609–15); the Roman Catholic churches of the Bernardine monks (1600–30), St Lazarus (1620–40), Mary Magdalene (1615–35), St Wojtich (1602), and St Sophia (1574); the Synagogue of the Golden Rose (1582); the residential buildings in Rynok Square, such as the *Black Building (1577–88), *Korniakt building (1580), and Massari building; and the additions to the fortifications, consisting of the city arsenal (1555–6) and the gunpowder tower (1554–6).

The baroque style of the 17th century is characteristic of Kiev rather than Lviv. There are only a few monuments in

that style in Lviv: the Church of SS Peter and Paul (1668), the Church of the Holy Spirit (1722–9, destroyed 1939), the Church of the Transfiguration (1729, restored 1906), the churches of the Jesuit order (1610–30), the Carmelite order (1634), and the Franciscan order (1708), St Anthony's Church (1718), and the General Hospital (formerly the Piarist College, 1748). During a period of decline in the 18th century, several rococo buildings were constructed: *St George's Cathedral (1744–70), the Dominican church (1749–66), the Royal Arsenal, and the façade of the Lubomirski Palace.

The Austrian period was marked by the classical style, which is embodied in the guardhouse on Pidkova Square, the Ossolineum (1823–33, now the Lviv Scientific Library of the Academy of Sciences), the Dzieduszycki Museum (now the Natural Science Museum), and the Baworowski Library (now the Arts Cabinet of the ANU). The City Hall (1827–35) and the four fountains around it are in the Empire style; the Polytechnic Institute (1872–7), University (1877–81), Opera (1897–1900), main railway station, and post office (1921–2) are in the pseudo-Renaissance or Art Nouveau styles. During the Soviet period Khmelnytsky and Tereshkova streets were lined with residential buildings (1962–73). The Gagarin Palace of Culture (1961), the new buildings of the polytechnic institute (1964–72), the Computing Center (1969), the Lviv (1969) and Dnister

The Lviv city hall

Lviv: the Neptune Fountain in Market Square

(1983) hotels, the Museum of the Carpathian Military District (1952), and the bus terminal (1980) were added to the skyline.

The main monuments in the city are to A. Mickiewicz (by M. Parashchuk and A. Popel, 1905–6), I. Franko (1964), V. Stefanyk (1971), and I. Fedorovych (1978); there are also sculptures and an eternal flame (1958) at the Kholm Slavy Memorial Military Cemetery. The Lenin monument (1952) was dismantled in 1990. A monument to Sluvchenko was erected in 1992.

BIBLIOGRAPHY
Zubrzycki, D. *Kronika miasta Lwowa* (Lviv 1844)
Krypiakevych, I. *L'viv: Ioho mynuvshyna i teperishnist'* (Lviv 1910)
Czołowski, A. *Historia Lwowa od założenia do 1600* (Lviv 1925)
– *Historia Lwowa od 1600 do 1772* (Lviv 1927)
Holubets', M. *L'viv* (Lviv 1935)
Nash L'viv: Iuvileinyi zbirnyk, 1252–1952 (New York 1953)
Stepaniv, O. *Suchasnyi L'viv* (Lviv 1943; 2nd rev edn, New York 1953)
Mudryi, A. (ed). *Lviv: A Symposium on Its 700th Anniversary* (New York 1962)
Kis', Ia. *Promyslovist' L'vova u period feodalizmu* (Lviv 1968)
Ovsiichuk, V. *Arkhitekturni pam'iatky L'vova* (Lviv 1969)
Vuitsyk, V. *L'vivs'kyi derzhavnyi istoryko-arkhitekturnyi zapovidnyk* (Lviv 1979)
Ostrovskii, G. *L'vov: Arkhitekturno-khudozhestvennyie pamiatniki XIII–XX vekov* (3rd edn, Leningrad 1982)
Sekretariuk, V. (ed). *Istoriia L'vova* (Kiev 1984)
Trehubova, T.; Mykh, R. *L'viv: Arkhitekturno-istorychnyi narys* (Kiev 1989)

A. Figol, V. Kubijovyč, A. Zhukovsky

Lviv Agricultural Institute (Lvivskyi silskohospodarskyi instytut). A technical school of *higher education in Dubliany, Lviv oblast. It was founded in 1946 on the basis of the agronomy and forestry faculties of the *Lviv Polytechnical Institute. In 1980 it was under the jurisdiction of the USSR Ministry of Agriculture and had faculties of agronomy, economics, surveying, agricultural mechanics, architecture, and upgrading of qualifications (for leading cadres and specialists). Both degree and graduate programs are offered. A total of 6,413 students were registered for courses in 1980, 3,390 of whom studied by correspondence. The institute has a 3,791-ha experimental farm and a 380,000-volume library.

Lviv Almazinstrument Manufacturing Consortium (Lvivske vyrobnyche obiednannia Almazinstrument). An enterprise of the equipment- and instrument-building industry, formed in 1979 out of the Lviv Plant of Diamond Instruments (est 1957), the Boryslav Plant of Artificial Diamonds, and a special technical design office for diamonds. It produces artificial diamonds and diamond instruments.

Lviv Art Gallery (Lvivska kartynna halereia). An art museum in Lviv, established in 1939 on the basis of the nationalized People's Museum in Lviv (1907–39). The core of its collection consists of 300 paintings once owned by a magnate from Podilia, J. Jakowicz, and canvases formerly in Lviv's Museum of Artistic Industry (est 1905), National Museum (1905), Lubomirski Museum (1907), B. Orzechowicz collection (1921), Museum of the Stauropegion Institute, Greek Catholic Theological Seminary, and numerous private collections. During the Second World War hundreds of valuable paintings were removed by the Nazis. Today the gallery's 34 halls have over 1,000 works on permanent display. In 1986 it possessed over 35,000 works – Ukrainian, Russian, Polish, Western and Eastern European, and Soviet paintings, graphic works, sculptures, ceramics, and ornamental and applied art from the 15th century on, ranging from works by Leonardo da Vinci and Titian to those of contemporary Ukrainian painters (L. Medvid, V. Patyk, R. Selsky, O. Shatkivsky, H. Smolsky) and sculptors (T. Bryzh, D. Krvavych, E. Mysko). It has original porcelain from Korets, Meissen, and Vienna, a copy of the Lviv *Apostol* of I. Fedorovych, and other priceless artifacts. Since 1966 departments of 16th- to 18th-century Lviv portraiture and 18th- to 19th-century Oriental art have existed at the gallery. Branches of the gallery are the 17th-century Boim Chapel and the I. Fedorovych Museum (est 1977) in Lviv and the Olesko Castle Museum-Preserve (est 1975) in Buzke raion. Many albums with reproductions of paintings in the gallery have appeared, most recently in 1987, and a guide to the gallery was published in 1975.

S. Yaniv

Lviv Astronomical Observatory. See Astronomy.

Lviv Brigade of the Ukrainian Galician Army (Lvivska [7] brygada UHA). Formed in January 1919 from units of the Southern Group, the brigade consisted of two infantry regiments and an artillery regiment and was part of the Third Corps. Its commanders were Col K. Sliusarchuk and Maj A. Bizanz. In June 1919 the Lviv Brigade spearheaded the Chortkiv offensive against the Polish army. Later it fought successfully in Volhynia and Podilia against Bolshevik and Denikin forces. In February 1920 the brigade was reorganized into the Seventh Infantry Regiment of the First Brigade of the Red Ukrainian Galician Army and was sent into action against the Poles. At the end of April 1920 it left the Red Army and was encircled by the Poles. Some of its units surrendered immediately; others broke out of the encirclement but surrendered two weeks later.

Lviv Brotherhood. See Lviv Dormition Brotherhood.

Lviv Bus Plant (Lvivskyi avtobusnyi zavod). A large enterprise of the automotive industry, built in Lviv in 1946. Until 1957 it built mobile cranes and hitches. In 1957 it began to build the LAZ-695 passenger bus seating 55 people, and in 1958 it became a specialized plant. It built several versions of the basic model: the LAZ-695Ye for urban transportation, the LAZ-695YeE for countries with a temperate climate, the LAZ-695YeYu for countries with a tropical climate, and the LAZ-697Ye Tourist for intercity transportation. Since 1970 those models have been replaced by the LAZ-695M Lviv and the LAZ-695M Tourist. The plant also builds hydraulic transmissions and spare parts for its buses.

Lviv Chronicle (Lvivskyi litopys). A chronicle written in the first half of the 17th century and discovered by D. *Zubrytsky, who named it after the city where he found it. It describes events mostly in western Ukraine (the Kiev region, Podilia, and Galicia) from 1498 to 1649. From 1630 the author of the chronicle deals with events in which he was involved in greater detail. The unidentified author devotes much attention to the causes of the Cossack-Polish wars, to the Cossack rebellions of 1636 and 1637–8, and to B. Khmelnytsky's uprising (up to the Treaty of *Zboriv) and gives a positive evaluation of P. Sahaidachny's, Khmelnytsky's, and P. Mohyla's roles. The language is close to the western Ukrainian dialect. The chronicle was part of M. Hunashevsky's manuscript, and M. Hrushevsky, M. Marchenko, and O. Bevzo consider him to be the author of the chronicle. It was published by A. Petrushevych in his *Naukovyi sbornik* (1868; repr 1971). Today the manuscript is preserved in the Central Scientific Library of the Academy of Sciences of Ukraine.

Lviv Conservatory (Lvivska konservatoriia im. M. Lysenka). A higher school of music, established in Lviv in 1940 by the merger of the *Lysenko Higher Institute of Music (est 1904) and the Polish Lviv Conservatory (est 1830). Its teachers have included V. Barvinsky (director 1940–8), S. Liudkevych, M. Kolessa (director 1953–65), W. Wytwycky, B. Kudryk, Z. Lysko, R. Liubynetsky, R. Savytsky, H. Levytska, and A. Soltys. In 1985–6, there were six faculties (composition, history and theory of music, conducting, and vocal, piano, and orchestra studies), with a total of nearly 500 students, and 16 chairs associated with the conservatory, in addition to a basic course of musical instruction for children. The conservatory's library holds approx 140,000 volumes.

Lviv Dormition Brotherhood (Lvivske uspenske bratstvo, aka Lviv Stauropegion Brotherhood [Lvivske stavropihiiske bratstvo]). An Orthodox religious association founded in the 15th century by Lviv merchants and tradesmen at the Dormition Church. It is the oldest and one of the leading Ukrainian brotherhoods, and it served as an example to other brotherhoods. There are historical references to it dating back to 1463. According to its charter, which was confirmed by Patriarch Joachim of Antioch in 1586 and Patriarch Jeremiah of Constantinople in 1589, the brotherhood was independent of the local bishops (right of stauropegion) and subject directly to the Patriarch of Constantinople. It had the right to oversee the activities not only of secular members of the church but also of the clergy and even the bishops. Its membership was open to all estates and to Orthodox believers from other cities and countries. Membership dues, profits from book sales, donations, and gifts were used to support the Dormition Church and St Onuphrius's Monastery, which were owned by the brotherhood, and to operate a printing press, school, orphanages, hospitals, and homes for elderly members. As the leading cultural and religious institution for Western Ukraine, the Lviv brotherhood played a key role in resisting Polish national and religious oppression and in fighting for equality with the Catholics and the Polish burghers. Owing to its efforts the Lviv eparchy was restored in 1539, and one of the brotherhood's members, M. Tuchapsky, was appointed bishop. For a century it was one of the centers of opposition to the Church Union of *Berestia. On 5 April 1709, after Pope Clement XI guaranteed its rights, the brotherhood accepted the union with Rome and thenceforth limited its activities to church affairs. In 1788, under Austrian rule, the brotherhood was disbanded. It was restored the same year with a different statute as the *Stauropegion Institute, was taken over by Russophiles, and continued to operate until 1939.

As the owner of a printing press the brotherhood developed a wide publishing program. Its earliest surviving publications came out in 1591: the charter of Patriarch Jeremiah of 1589; a collection of verses in honor of Metropolitan M. Rahoza, titled *Prosphonima*; and a Greek grammar known as *Adelphotes*. From 1591 to 1722 the brotherhood press printed 140 titles in 160,000 copies, including liturgical books, school textbooks, and polemical literature. In the first half of the 17th century it published three editions

Lviv Dormition Brotherhood: coat-of-arms

Lviv Dormition Brotherhood Press: coat-of-arms

of the Octoechos (1630, 1639, 1644), the *Apostol* (1634, 1637, 1648), and the *Antolohion* (1632, 1638, 1643) and two editions of the Gospel (1636, 1644). The most important of its later publications were I. Galiatovsky's *Kliuch razumieniia* (The Key of Understanding, 1663 and 1665) and *Nebo novoie* (The New Heaven, 1665) and *Ifika iieropolitika* (1760). The directors of the printing press included Brother Myna and Rev Nykyfor in the 16th century and M. Slozka and A. Skulsky in the 18th century. Its books spread throughout Ukraine and even beyond it, to Belarus, Wallachia, Moldavia, Bulgaria, and Serbia. In Russia the import and sale of Lviv books was prohibited. Peter I permitted them to be sold, but only in Left-Bank Ukraine. The Stauropegion Institute press existed until 1939.

On 8 October 1586 the brotherhood opened a 'Greek and Ruthenian school,' the first brotherhood school in Ukraine. It was governed by a special statute (*Poriadok shkilnyi*), which was worked out by the founders and the first rector of the school, Bishop Arsenii of Elasson. The statute is the oldest document in Ukrainian pedagogical literature. Besides merchants' children boys from the lower classes were admitted. Instruction was conducted in vernacular Ukrainian, and Old Church Slavonic, Greek (until the 1660s), Latin (from 1604), and Polish (occasionally) were studied as subjects. The other subjects were music, astronomy, mathematics, dialectics, poetics, rhetoric, grammar, philosophy, and theology. By training teachers and printing textbooks the school played an important role in the development of education not only in Ukraine but also in Belarus, Russia, Wallachia, and Moldavia. Its rectors and professors included some noted Ukrainian cultural figures, such as L. and S. Zyzanii, K. Stavrovetsky-Tranquillon, Y. Boretsky, O. Mytura, Z. Kopystensky, P. Berynda, F. Sydorovych, and M. Hrek. In the 18th century the school began to decline. The Stauropegion Institute maintained a school and a student residence until 1939.

The Dormition Brotherhood maintained close ties with Orthodox countries in the 16th and 17th centuries. The hospodars and statesmen of Moldavia, such as A. Lopuşnianu (1558–66), J. Movilă (1598–1606), L. Stroici (1598–1606), S. Movilă (1606–7), V. Lupu (1641), M. Movilă (1650–60), A. Movilă-Potocki (1664), G. Duca (1671), and C. Duca (1694), supported the brotherhood and corresponded with it, usually in Ukrainian.

BIBLIOGRAPHY
Krylovskii, A. *L'vovskoe stavropigial'noe bratstvo* (Kiev 1904)
Medyns'kyi, Ie. *Brats'ki shkoly Ukraïny i Bilorusiï v XVI–XVII st.* (Kiev 1958)
Isaievych, Ia. *Bratstva ta ïkh rol' v rozvytku ukraïns'koï kul'tury XVI–XVIII st.* (Kiev 1966)

B. Kravtsiv

Lviv Dormition Brotherhood Press. A press founded by the Lviv Dormition Brotherhood in 1586. With a printing press and other equipment used by I. *Fedorovych, it printed liturgical books, primers, poetry, dramas, and theological, educational, and polemical literature. Its oldest extant publications date from 1591: the 1589 charter of Patriarch Jeremiah granting the brotherhood the right of *stauropegion, a booklet of verses in honor of Metropolitan M. Rahoza titled *Prosphonima*, and the grammar *Adelphotes*. From 1591 to 1722 the press issued 140 books with a total run of some 160,000 copies. They were distributed throughout Polish-ruled Ukraine and Belarus, and even in Wallachia, Moldavia, Serbia, and Bulgaria. They were not, however, permitted to be sold in Russian-ruled Ukraine until 1707. Among the authors published were P. Berynda, A. Skulsky, I. Volkovych, S. Kosiv, A. Zhelyborsky, and M. Kozachynsky. The press's directors and master printers included the monk Myna, P. Kulchych, P. Berynda, Y. Kyrylovych, M. Slozka, A. Skulsky, I. Kunotovych, D. Kulchytsky, S. Polovetsky, S. and V. Stavnytsky, D. Pyniavsky, I. Hrozevsky, and Ya. Paslavsky. The press played an important role in the intellectual life of Ukraine and the defense of the Orthodox church. In 1788 the Lviv brotherhood and its press were succeeded by the *Stauropegion Institute.

Lviv Dormition Brotherhood School (Lvivska bratska shkola). An institution of *secondary education established by the *Lviv Dormition Brotherhood in 1586. It was the first *brotherhood school in Ukraine. Its organizers were Orthodox burghers and noblemen who integrated across estate lines in the defense of their ancestral religion and traditions. One of their main goals was to raise the spiritual and intellectual level of the Orthodox church with the help of a network of urban schools open to children of all estates. Among the better-known activists associated with the early history of the Lviv School were Yu. *Rohatynets, L. Maletsky, I. Krasovsky, and S. Morokhovsky. Their fund-raising efforts were supported by the city's Orthodox bishop, H. *Balaban.

The Lviv School opened at a time when there were only a few Orthodox ecclesiastical schools, none of which offered secondary education. An important stimulus to its creation was a discriminatory ruling of Lviv's municipal government, controlled by Catholic patricians, which had prevented Orthodox children from enrolling in the Catholic cathedral school since 1570.

Following the humanistic patterns of the Western European classical grammar school, the liberal arts curriculum of the Lviv School was divided into separate subjects, and from the outset stressed philological training. In its program, grammar was regarded as the key introductory discipline, from which students would progress through poetics and rhetoric to philosophy and theology. But rather than emphasizing Latin over Greek, as was being done in Protestant and Catholic schools, the Lviv School concentrated on Church Slavonic and Greek, the sacred languages of the Orthodox Slavs, and placed Latin last in the hierarchy. Because of this divergence Lviv teachers and other Ukrainian pedagogues set out to publish their own Greek and Church Slavonic grammars and Slavonic-Ruthenian dictionaries. The first comparative Greek-Slavonic grammar, the *Adelphotes* (1591), was prepared at the Lviv School and published by the Lviv Brotherhood. One of the school's first teachers was L. *Zyzanii, who compiled a Slavonic grammar and a dictionary in 1596. The pedagogical activity of the Lviv School initiated linguistic scholarship among Ukrainians and subsequently among the East Slavs.

Descriptions of the library of the Lviv School attest to the fact that for other curricular needs brotherhood teachers relied on Polish and Western European publications of Greek and Roman authors (Aesop, Aristotle, Demosthenes, Euripides, Isocrates, Pindar, Horace, Virgil, Ovid, Cicero) and of contemporary Greek and Latin grammarians (G. Cnapius, Clenardi, C. Valer, E. Álvarez). A considerable body of poetry and the first Ukrainian religious drama are direct products of this school's linguistic-literary activity. Among the school's holdings were also contemporary European works on music theory. The library houses a collection of manuscripts of polyphonic choral music by various composers which, according to a 1697 list, make up 87 volumes.

Between 1589 and the mid-17th century the Lviv School's curriculum and educational philosophy were instrumental and influential in the establishment of many brotherhood schools in Ukraine and Belarus. A number of Lviv teachers and administrators (among them, the Latin and Greek instructor Y. Boretsky and the famous lexicographer P. Berynda) subsequently moved to Kiev and laid the foundations of the *Kiev Epiphany Brotherhood School. Throughout the 17th and 18th centuries instructors and alumni of the *Kievan-Mohyla Academy and the Lviv School maintained close professional contacts.

BIBLIOGRAPHY
Kharlampovich, K. *Zapadnorusskie pravoslavnye shkoly XVI i nachala XVII veka* (Kazan 1898)
Isaievych, Ia. *Bratstva ta ïx rol' v rozvytku ukraïns'koï kul'tury XVI–XVIII st* (Kiev 1966)
– *Dzherela z istoriï ukraïns'koï kul'tury doby feodalizmu* (Kiev 1972)
N. Pylypiuk

Lviv Elektron Manufacturing Consortium (Lvivske vyrobnyche obiednannia Elektron). A television manufacturing enterprise set up in 1970 on the basis of 10 television plants and 4 research institutes in Lviv and Transcarpathia oblasts. Its largest factory is the Lviv Television Plant (est 1957), which produced 15 models of black-and-white TV sets and 7 models of colored sets, including Ogonek, Elektron, and Elektron-2. The consortium was the first TV manufacturer to introduce an automated production-control system and a complex system of quality monitoring.

Lviv eparchy. A church administrative unit with its see in Lviv. The eparchy had its beginnings as Halych eparchy, founded in the mid-12th century. This eparchy was under the jurisdiction of the Kievan metropolitan, although in 1303 it was elevated to the status of a run metropoly (see *Halych metropoly). It ceased to function as a separate eparchy in the early 15th century and was administered by vicars designated initially by the Kiev metropolitan and later by the Roman Catholic archbishop of Lviv. The Polish king Sigismund I renewed the eparchy in 1539 and named the previous administrator, M. Tuchapsky, as bishop of Halych, Lviv, and Kamianets-Podilskyi, with his see in Lviv. Ordained by the Kievan metropolitan Makarii II in 1540, Tuchapsky (1540–9) was the first in a long uninterrupted line of Lviv bishops that included A. Balaban (1549–69), G. Balaban (1569–1607), Ye. Tyssarovsky (1607–41), Arsenii Zhelyborsky (1641–63), and Atanasii Zhelyborsky (1663–76). In 1700 Bishop Y. Shumliansky (1646–1708) accepted the Church Union of *Berestia, and the eparchy joined the Greek Catholic church. Uniate bishops of Lviv included V. Sheptytsky (1710–15), A. Sheptytsky (1715–46), L. Sheptytsky (1749–79), P. Biliansky (1780–98), and M. Skorodynsky (1798–1805). In 1807 Halych metropoly was re-established with two eparchies, Lviv and Peremyshl. Since then the Lviv bishop (later archbishop) has also been metropolitan of Halych.

In 1885 a portion of Lviv eparchy was established as Stanyslaviv eparchy. In 1936 Lviv eparchy included 1,266 parishes and 1,350,000 faithful. After the Second World War the territory of Lviv eparchy was incorporated into the Ukrainian SSR. The Ukrainian Catholic church was suppressed, and the sham *Lviv Sobor of 1946 proclaimed the conversion of the eparchy to Orthodoxy. The eparchy was enlarged with some parishes from Peremyshl eparchy; its name was changed to the Lviv-Ternopil eparchy; and a bishop of the Russian Orthodox church was installed. The Ukrainian Catholic church survived in the underground, however, and on 1 December 1989 it was legalized. At that time V. Sterniuk was recognized as the ordinary of Lviv archeparchy, assisted by bishops F. Kurchaba, M. Sapryha, and Yu. Voronovsky. In March 1992 the eparchy claimed approx 1,000 parishes. The late 1980s also saw the rebirth of the Ukrainian Autocephalous Orthodox church and the establishment of a Lviv eparchy of that church, under Metropolitan I. Bodnarchuk.

W. Lencyk

Lviv Franko Literary Memorial Museum (Lvivskyi derzhavnyi literaturno-memoriialnyi muzei). It was established on 10 October 1940 by the government of the Ukrainian SSR in the building in Lviv where I. *Franko resided from 1902 to 1916, and where he died. The writer's study has been restored. The museum houses a collection of about 4,000 objects, including Franko's manuscripts, photographs, correspondence, and printed works, almost all of which are first-edition copies.

Lviv Gospel (Lvivske yevanheliie). Monument of the Old Ukrainian language written in 1423. It was preserved in the Church of Tithes in Kiev.

Lviv (2nd) Group of the Ukrainian Insurgent Army (Lvivska [2] hrupa UPA Buh). A division of the UPA-West, organized in 1943 out of UPA units operating in the Second Military District, which consisted of the northern and eastern counties of Lviv oblast. In the spring of 1944 its units fought against the Polish Home Army on the northwestern border of Galicia, and in the autumn of 1944 they joined combat against NKVD troops. The largest battle occurred on 29 August near Kariv, Rava-Ruska county, when two UPA battalions and two training companies successfully fended off an attack by NKVD border guards. At its peak strength in late 1944, the Lviv Group had at least seven battalions and many independently operating companies. In 1945 the Second Military District was expanded to include the First Military District with Lviv city and the surrounding counties. It then encompassed the entire Lviv oblast, along with Rohatyn, Rudky, Mostyska, and (partly) Zhydachiv counties. The new district was divided into 5 tactical sectors, numbered from 11 to 15, but the number of combat units in the region was reduced drastically, and by 1947 only platoon-size units were still operating in it. The Lviv Group ran the last UPA school for noncommisioned officers, which graduated a class on 6 December 1946. Two of its combat units, Pereiaslavy and Halaida-II, were active until the summer of 1947. The UPA Supreme Headquarters was located in the district, and Col O. Hasyn and Brig Gen R. Shukhevych fell in battle there. The group's commanders were Lt O. Lynda (nom de guerre: Yarema, 1943–4) and Maj V. Levkovych (nom de guerre: Vorony, 1944–6).

P. Sodol

Lviv Historical Museum (Lvivskyi istorychnyi muzei). A state museum established in 1940 on the basis of Lviv's Historical Museum (est 1893) and Polish People's Museum (est 1903) and supplemented with collections from the museums of the Shevchenko Scientific Society, the Stauropegion Institute, and the Greek Catholic Theological Academy as well as the National Museum and the Lubomirski Museum. It is housed in three Renaissance buildings (including the Korniakt and Black buildings) in the old market square in the center of the city. Its holdings consist of about 270,000 items, connected mostly with the city's history beginning in the 13th century and with the western oblasts of Ukraine. The museum has four departments: primitive society, feudalism, capitalism, and Soviet society. It has valuable archeological monuments of the Trypilian, Bronze, and Scythian cultures, numismatic and sphragistic collections, and rich collections of weapons, tools, printing presses, manuscripts and incunabula, jewelry, glass, weavings, and prints.

Lviv Institute of Applied and Decorative Art (Lvivskyi institut prykladnoho ta dekoratyvnoho mystetstva). A postsecondary institution, under the jurisdiction of the Ministry of Higher and Specialized Secondary Education, offering a five-year program. It consists of two faculties, applied and decorative arts (with departments of pottery and glassware, and decorative woven textiles and garment designing) and interior decoration (departments of interior and furniture design). Approximately 150 students attend the institute during a given academic year. (In 1961 there were 131 students registered in the day program and 58 in the evening courses.)

The institute was established in 1946 by decrees of the Councils of Ministers of the USSR (13 August 1946) and of the Ukrainian SSR (6 September 1946). Initially the institute fell under the Ministry of Culture of the Ukrainian SSR and consisted of the faculties of applied and decorative arts and applied and graphic arts. The faculty of graphic arts was transferred to the *Kharkiv Industrial Design Institute and the *Kiev Art School. Two sections of the faculty of applied and decorative arts – the departments of monumental decorative painting and of monumental decorative sculpture – were later also transferred to the Kiev Art School. In 1959 a department of garment designing complemented the department of decorative woven textiles. A department of interior design, added in the 1960s, later developed into a faculty. The woodcrafting department was abolished in the late 1970s.

The academic staff of the institute has included the painter V. *Manastyrsky, the painter and graphic artist I. Hutorov, the graphic artist S. Lazeba, and the art historian Ya. Zapasko. Among the graduates of the institute are the ceramist A. Bokotei, the painter Z. Flinta, and the sculptors D. *Krvavych and L. *Terletsky.

B. Medwidsky

Lviv Institute of Forest Technology (Lvivskyi lisotechnichnyi instytut). A technical school of higher education formed in 1945 and until 1992 under the Ukrainian SSR Ministry of Higher and Specialized Secondary Education. It contains departments of forestry, forestry engineering, mechanical engineering, and engineering economics, and a correspondence school, an evening school, preparatory courses, a school of continuing education, and graduate-level studies. As of 1979 the institute had approx 7,000 students and had graduated over 16,000 engineers.

Lviv Institute of Physical Culture (Lvivskyi institut fizychnoi kultury). An institute of higher education founded in 1946 on the basis of the Lviv Tekhnikum of Physical Culture. Until August 1991 it was administered by the Committee on Physical Culture and Sport of the Council of Ministers of the Ukrainian SSR. It also acted as a resource center for sports methodology; it assisted sports teams in Ukraine and other parts of the USSR in training programs and in the study of theoretical and administrative questions regarding physical education. It has sports, pedagogical, and correspondence faculties. In 1980–1 the institute had an enrollment of 1,856 students. One of the most notable graduates of the institute was V. *Chukarin.

Lviv Kineskop Manufacturing Consortium (Lvivske vyrobnyche obiednannia Kineskop). An enterprise formed in 1976 out of the Lviv Electric Lamp Plant (est 1940) and the Yavir Plant. The former began to manufacture picture tubes for TV sets in 1954, the first to do so in the USSR. Its tubes were used in the Lviv, Verkhovyna, Syhnal, Ogonek, Elektron, Horyzont, and Krym television sets. Since 1967 it has manufactured large tubes for colored sets, and since 1977, small tubes for portable colored sets. The Yavir Plant manufactures automated infrared heating equipment and ultraviolet irradiation devices.

Lviv Medical Institute (Lvivskyi medychnyi instytut). A higher teaching institution, until 1992 under the Ministry of Health of the Ukrainian SSR. It was formed in 1939 out of the medical faculty of Lviv University, which was itself established in 1894 out of the Lviv Collegium Medicum (est 1773). The first institute of *medical education in Ukraine, the Collegium Medicum was incorporated into the medical faculty (est 1784) of the university in 1817. Under both Austrian and Polish rule in Galicia, the number of Ukrainian medical students was restricted. The Lviv Medical Institute graduated 495 physicians in its first two years (1939–40). It consists of six faculties – internal medicine, pediatrics, hygiene, stomatology, pharmacology, and continuing medical education – and 74 departments. It has three museums (anatomy, human diseases, and the history of the institute), a large library (500,000 vols), and four dispensaries, and it oversees 5,000 hospital beds. Its faculty has included O. *Makarchenko, D. *Panchenko, and Ya. Parnas. The enrollment is over 5,000.

Lviv Mikroprylad Manufacturing Consortium (Lvivske vyrobnyche obiednannia Mikroprylad). An instrument-building enterprise formed in 1975 out of the Lviv Plant of Electric Measuring Devices (est 1946), the Omega Plant in Sambir, the Vymiriuvach Plant in Ostriv, the Modul Plant in Peremyshliany, the Kvant Plant in Sokal, and a design office for microelectronics and instrument-making. It produces over 150 devices, including electric measuring instruments, parts for automated systems, and computing technology.

Lviv Museum of Folk Architecture and Folkways.
See Museums of folk architecture and folkways.

Lviv Museum of Ukrainian Art. See National Museum.

Lviv oblast.
An administrative territory on the western edge of Ukraine, established by the Soviet regime on 4 December 1939. Its area of 21,800 sq km is divided into 20 raions, 483 rural councils, 41 cities, and 36 towns (smt). Its 1989 population was 2,727,400. The oblast center is *Lviv.

Physical geography. Most of the oblast consists of the rolling hills of the Volhynia-Podilia Upland, which rises toward the northwest to form the Holohory watershed. South of the upland lie the Sian and Dniester lowlands and then the foothills of the Carpathian Mountains. The southern rim of the oblast is occupied by the Middle and High Beskyd of the Carpathians. In the north the soil is mostly degraded chernozems and gray and dark gray forest podzolized soils; in the northeast, deep chernozems; in Subcarpathia, clayey and peat podzolic soils; in the Carpathians, brown soils and mountain meadow soils; and in the river valleys, alluvial bog soils. Forests consisting mainly of beech, fir, and pine in the mountains and oak, beech, and ash in the lowlands cover approx 545,000 ha, or 29 percent of the oblast's territory. The oblast is rich in mineral resources, including oil, natural gas, coal, potassium and rock salt, ozocerite, peat, limestone, sandstone, marl, gypsum, clays, and mineral waters. It is drained by two river systems: the Dniester River, with its right tributaries (the Bystrytsia, the Stryi, and the Svicha) and left tributaries (the Vereshchytsia, the Stryvihor, the Zubra, and the Svirzh), and the Styr River, a tributary of the Prypiat, drain into the Black Sea; the Sian with its tributaries (the Vyshnia and the Shklo) and the Buh, with the Poltva, the Rata, and the Solokiia, drain into the Baltic Sea. There are numerous lakes in the oblast, especially in the Dniester Valley. The climate of the oblast is temperate continental: temperatures in the lowlands average −4°C in January and 18.3°C in July, and in the mountains, −6°C and 12.8°C respectively. The annual precipitation is 700 mm (up to 1,000 mm in the mountains), and the growing season lasts up to 210 days a year.

History. Until the 12th century the territory of the present oblast was part of Kievan Rus'. When the realm splintered into small principalities in the 11th and 12th centuries, the western section of the oblast's territory became part of Peremyshl principality, the eastern section, part of Zvenyhorod principality, and the northern and central sections, part of Volodymyr-Volynskyi principality. In the second half of the 12th century the territory of today's oblast was consolidated within Halych principality and then the Principality of Galicia-Volhynia. In the 13th and 14th centuries the land was ravaged by the Tatars but never completely conquered. It was annexed by the Poles in 1349 and remained under Polish rule until the 18th century. At the first partition of Poland in 1772, the Lviv territory was acquired by Austria. During the First World War it was briefly a part of the Western Ukrainian National Republic, and after the postwar settlement it was again under Poland. In the interwar period the territory consti-

tuted the eastern part of Lviv voivodeship. It was occupied by the Soviet army in 1939, reorganized into Lviv oblast, and recaptured from the Germans in 1944.

Population. The population of the oblast grew by 6.3 percent in 1969–79 and by 6.2 percent in 1979–89. Its density in 1989 was 125.1 persons per sq km. It is the most urbanized of the western oblasts. The proportion of the urban population rose steadily, from 42.4 percent in 1963 to 47.3 percent in 1970, 53.2 percent in 1979, and 59 percent in 1989. The ethnic composition of the population has changed slightly in favor of Ukrainians during the last 30 years: in 1989 (1959 figures in parentheses) Ukrainians accounted for 90.4 percent (86.3) of the population, Russians for 7.2 percent (8.6), and Poles for 1 percent (2.8). In 1989 the four largest cities in the oblast were Lviv (786,900), Drohobych (78,000), Chervonohrad (72,000), and Stryi (67,000).

Industry. Industry accounts for over 80 percent of the goods and services produced by the oblast. Its main branches are machine building and metalworking (43.4 percent of the industrial output in 1988), food processing (16.8 percent), light industry (13 percent), fuel and energy (8.2 percent), chemicals and petrochemicals (7.7 percent), forest products (4.5 percent), and building materials (3 percent). The chief centers of the machine-building and metalworking industries are Lviv (buses, mobile cranes, conveyors, television and radio sets, appliances, diamond instruments, milling machines, and farm machinery), Drohobych (mobile cranes, chisels), Stryi (metalworking presses, locomotive repairs), and Khodoriv (printing presses). The key branches of the food industry are sugar refining (Khodoriv, Sambir, Krasne, Zolochiv, and Radekhiv), meat packing (Lviv, Zolochiv, Boryslav, and Stryi), dairying (Lviv, Chervonohrad, and Drohobych), vegetable-oil and lard processing (Lviv), brewing (Lviv), and confectionery (Lviv). The light industry consists mainly of clothes manufacturing (Lviv, Chervonohrad, Drohobych, Stryi, and Sambir), textiles (Boryslav, Lviv), and footwear (Lviv, Boryslav, Drohobych, and Stryi). For energy the oblast depends on its Dobrotvir Regional Electric Station and the Lviv and Boryslav thermoelectric centers, the wells of the *Subcarpathian Petroleum and Natural Gas Region, and the mines of the *Lviv-Volhynia Coal Basin. The chemical and petrochemical industry produces sulfur (Novyi Rozdol and Novoiavorivske), chemical (Novyi Rozdol) and potassium fertilizers (Stebnyk), synthetic fibers (Sokal), and paint (Lviv and Boryslav). Woodworking and furniture manufacturing are centered in Lviv, Drohobych, Dobromyl, Staryi Sambir, Stryi, Sambir, Skole, and Kamianka-Buzka, and cellulose and paper manufacturing, in Zhydachiv and Lviv. The building-materials industry consists mostly of cement production (Mykolaiv), concrete and reinforced-concrete structures manufacturing (Lviv, Chervonohrad, and Drohobych), and glass- and porcelain-making (Lviv, Pisochne, Nesterov, and Boryslav).

Agriculture. In 1988 the agricultural sector of Lviv oblast was organized into 306 collective farms, 90 state farms, 10 agroindustrial complexes, 8 agroindustrial associations, 2 agroindustrial co-operative associations, 6 agrofirms, and 2 agrocommercial international enterprises. Of the 1,267,000 ha of farmland (in 1987), 861,000 ha were cultivated land, 155,000 ha were hayfields, and 229,000 ha were pasture. The seeded land was devoted mostly to feed crops (371,000 ha) and grains (326,000 ha), but potatoes and vegetables (92,000 ha) and industrial crops (86,000 ha) were raised also. Winter wheat and spring barley are the chief grains, and sugar beets and flax the chief industrial crops, grown in the oblast. The principal fruits are apples, pears, plums, and cherries. Animal husbandry accounts for over 60 percent of the oblasts's agricultural output. It consists mainly of dairy- and beef-cattle farming as well as hog, sheep, and goat raising. Poultry farming, fishing, and beekeeping are practiced widely.

Transportation. In 1989 there were 1,309 km of railway, 763 km of them electrified, in the oblast. The main railway lines are Kiev–Zdolbuniv–Lviv–Stryi–Chop, Kiev–Ternopil–Lviv, Lviv–Sambir–Uzhhorod, Stryi–Drohobych–Sambir, Lviv–Chervonohrad–Volodymyr-Volynskyi, and Lviv–Khodoriv–Ivano-Frankivske. The main junctions are Lviv, Krasne, Sambir, Chervonohrad, and Stryi. There are 8,000 km of motor highways and roads, 7,400 km of which are paved. The main highways are Kiev–Rivne–Lviv–Stryi–Mukachiv, Lviv–Ternopil, Lviv–Sambir–Uzhhorod, Lviv–Mostyska–Peremyshl, and Lviv–Ivano-Frankivske. There is an airport in Lviv. The Druzhba oil pipeline and the Braterstvo gas pipeline run through the oblast to Eastern Europe.

BIBLIOGRAPHY
Rozkvit ekonomiky zakhidnykh oblastei URSR (1939–1964 rr.) (Lviv 1964)
Istoriia mist i sil Ukraïns'koï RSR: Lvivs'ka oblast' (Kiev 1968)

Lviv Oblast Ukrainian Music and Drama Theater

(Lvivskyi oblasnyi ukrainskyi muzychno-dramatychnyi teatr). A theater established in Drohobych in 1939. The cast originally consisted of local amateurs and young actors from eastern Ukraine. In 1941–4 the theater was reorganized into a professional musical-drama theater, with the directors R. Tymchuk and, later, Y. Stadnyk, the musical director B. Piurko, and the administrator Yu. Sherehii, and a varied repertoire, including M. Tsukanov's *Prolisky* (The Snowdrops), Yu. Kosach's *Obloha* (The Siege), F. Lehár's *Land of Smiles,* and M. Arkas's *Kateryna.* Since 1945 its repertoire has been dominated by Soviet Ukrainian and Russian plays. In 1987 its artistic director was F. Makulovych.

Lviv Opera Theater

(Lvivskyi opernyi teatr). A theater that existed during the German occupation in 1941–4 under the management of A. Petrenko, with V. *Blavatsky as principal director. It was installed in the former Municipal Theater and was a virtual successor to the *Lesia Ukrainka Theater. During the short time of its existence, the Lviv Opera Theater was the most eminent theater in Ukraine. Its drama troupe (directed by Blavatsky and Y. *Hirniak) included the renowned Galician actors O. Kryvytska, V. Levytska, S. and S. Stadnyk, H. Sovacheva, M. Stepova-Karpiak, I. Rubchak, and B. Pazdrii. The theater produced W. Shakespeare's *Hamlet* for the first time on a Ukrainian stage (1943); M. Halbe's *The River*; Lesia Ukrainka's *Kaminnyi hospodar* (The Stone Host), *Na poli krovi* (On the Field of Blood), and *Iohanna zhinka Khusova* (Joanna, Wife of Chuza); and M. Kulish's *Myna Mazailo.* The opera troupe (musical director, L. Turkevych; concertmaster, M. Lysenko; choirmaster, Ya. Boshchak; choreographer, Ye. Vigilov; scenery designer, M. Radysh) had considerable success with the European repertoire, including G. Ver-

di's *Aida, La Traviata,* and *Il Trovatore,* G. Bizet's *Carmen,* G. Puccini's *Tosca* and *Madame Butterfly,* R. Leoncavallo's *I Pagliacci,* B. Smetana's *Bartered Bride,* and C. Gounod's *Faust.* Notable soloists included Ye. Pospiieva, L. Chernykh, Z. Dolnytsky, I. Romanovsky, O. Rusnak, and V. Tysiak. The Lviv Opera Theater also produced classical ballets and operettas (musical director, Ya. Barnych). Most of its actors had fled Ukraine by 1944, and continued their work in the Ensemble of Ukrainian Actors in Germany and, after emigrating to the United States, in the *Ukrainian Theater in Philadelphia and the *Theater-Studio of Y. Hirniak and O. Dobrovolska.

W. Wytwycky

Lviv Polytechnical Institute

Lviv Polytechnical Institute

(Lvivskyi politekhnichnyi instytut). The oldest technical school of higher education in Ukraine, founded as a technical academy in 1844 on the basis of an Austrian Realschule. From 1872 it was called the Lviv Higher Polytechnical School and from 1921 the Lviv Polytechnic; in 1939 it acquired its present name. In 1919 the Dubliany Agricultural Academy (est 1891) and the Lviv School of Forestry (est 1874) were incorporated into the institute's Department of Agriculture and Forestry. In 1922–5 the Lviv (Underground) Ukrainian Higher Polytechnical School was run by Ukrainians to counter the discriminatory, anti-Ukrainian educational policies of the Polish authorities.

In 1985 the institute had departments of electrical energy, electromechanics, mechanical engineering, mechanical machine building, automation, electrophysics, construction engineering, geodesics, architecture, radio engineering, chemical technology, heating technology, organic substances technology, engineering economics, and general engineering, as well as a graduate school. It had branches in Ternopil, Lutske, Drohobych, Chervonohrad, and Novovolynske. Its library had approx 1.9 million volumes (1980). In 1985–6 the institute had approx 30,000 students. The main building housing the institute in Lviv was designed (1873–7) by J. Zacharjewicz.

Lviv Prohres Manufacturing Consortium

(Lvivske vyrobnyche obiednannia Prohres). A footwear manufacturing enterprise set up in Lviv in 1961 and known until 1976 as the Prohres footwear plant. In 1980 it consisted of the Lviv Footwear Factory No. 3 and similar factories in Stryi, Boryslav, Kulykiv, Lutske, and Terebovlia. The consortium produces men's and women's footwear for various age-groups and several lines of model footwear. It has a research laboratory and an automated system of quality control.

Lviv Russian Drama Theater (Lvivskyi rosiiskyi dramatychnyi teatr). Established in 1931 in Kiev as the Theater of the Kiev Military District. It was renamed several times. In 1941–4 it performed outside of Ukraine (mainly in Siberia), and in 1944–53 it was the Theater of the Odessa Military District. Since 1954 it has been stationed in Lviv under its present name. All of its performances have been in Russian. Its artistic directors were Yu. Lishansky (1931–40) and V. Lyzohub (1958–63); in 1987 the director was A. Rotenshtein.

Lviv Scientific Library of the Academy of Sciences of Ukraine

Lviv Scientific Library of the Academy of Sciences of Ukraine (Lvivska naukova biblioteka Akademii nauk Ukrainy im. V. Stefanyka). The Lviv branch library of the *Central Scientific Library of the AN URSR (now ANU) in Kiev. It was established in January 1940, after the Soviet occupation of Western Ukraine, by the appropriation of the library collections of the *Shevchenko Scientific Society (207,900 vols, 2,250 geographic and historical charts and maps, and 1,500 manuscripts and individual parchments), the *People's Home in Lviv (120,000 vols and 5,000 manuscripts), the *Ossolineum Institute (297,460 vols and 6,270 manuscripts), the Baworowski Foundation (founded in 1856 on the basis of the Stadnicki family's and D. Zubrytsky's collections, 55,000 vols), the Dzieduszycki collection, the Lviv Jewish Community Library, the St Onuphrius's Church and Monastery, and 76 other state, public, private, and theological libraries. As the Lviv branch library of the AN URSR, it was transformed in 1941–2 by the German occupational authorities into the Lviv State Library (Lemberger Staatsbibliothek). In 1944 the retreating German forces removed a part of the early manuscript collection, some of which was later turned over to various state libraries in Warsaw and Wrocław. In 1944 the library once again became the Lviv Library of the AN URSR; in June 1963 it was renamed the Lviv State Scientific

Library and placed under the jurisdiction of the Ministry of Culture of the Ukrainian SSR; in 1969 it was returned to the jurisdiction of the AN URSR; and in 1971 its name was amended in honor of the Ukrainian writer V. Stefanyk. In January 1971 the Stefanyk Library (as it is popularly known) contained over 5.5 million items (books, letters, journals, posters, maps, incunabula, and graphics, including 100,000 manuscripts dating from the 15th century). With its four branches (all located in Lviv) it has the most complete collection of materials on the sociopolitical, economic, and cultural life of Galicia and represents one of the former Soviet Union's largest libraries. Many of the materials are still housed in their original (pre-Soviet) premises.

BIBLIOGRAPHY
L'vivs'ka naukova biblioteka im. V. Stefanyka (1940–1980 rr): Pokazhchyk vydan' vydany' biblioteky ta literatury pro ii diial'nist' (Lviv 1982)
L'vivs'ka naukova biblioteka im. V. Stefanyka AN URSR: Zbirka naukovykh prats' (Kiev 1985)

L. Szuch

Lviv Sobor of 1946 (Lvivskyi sobor). The central formal event in the annexation of Halych metropoly of the Ukrainian (Greek) Catholic church by the Moscow patriarchate and the Russian Orthodox church following the Soviet occupation of Western Ukraine. Held on 8–10 March 1946 in St George's Cathedral in Lviv, the sobor was the culmination of a lengthy campaign against the church. Some preparatory work – particularly the probing of political, ideological, and personality differences within the Ukrainian Catholic church – had been undertaken by the Soviet authorities during their first occupation of Galicia in 1939–41. The cohesiveness of the Ukrainian Catholic church structure, however, and the exposed strategic location of Galicia on a frontier with German-occupied territories made any campaign of 'reunification' with the Russian Orthodox church politically untenable. Postwar conditions were considerably different. The death of Metropolitan A. *Sheptytsky (1 November 1944), the spiritual leader of Ukrainian Catholics, had left the church without a strong figurehead, and the extension of Soviet influence over the entire Eastern bloc had diminished Galicia's relative strategic significance. Moreover, the Soviet authorities could conveniently employ charges of 'treason to the Fatherland' against the Ukrainian Catholic church because of the moral support it had lent to anti-Soviet Ukrainian groups during the German occupation of Ukraine. Thus the stage was set for a campaign against the church which ultimately led to its formal liquidation in 1946 at the Lviv Sobor.

The Lviv Sobor set the stage for similar actions in Transcarpathia (1949) and Czechoslovakia (1950). The case of the Halych metropoly, however, was of particular significance, partly because of the sheer size of the metropoly, with (according to 1938 statistics) 2,354 diocesan and monastic priests, at least 315 brothers, 929 nuns, and 3.4 million faithful. More significant was the potential political challenge the church represented because of its traditional role as a bulwark of Ukrainian national consciousness in the newly annexed region.

Events immediately following the Soviet occupation seemed to indicate that a modus vivendi might be reached between the church and the Soviet authorities. An elaborate funeral was allowed for Metropolitan A. Sheptytsky after his death on 1 November 1944, and the Soviet press noted the installation of Y. *Slipy as the new metropolitan of Halych. In turn, a Ukrainian Catholic delegation went to Moscow in December 1944 for discussions with Soviet officials about the normalization of the church's status, and also paid a courtesy visit to the Moscow patriarchate. The situation had changed dramatically, however, by the early spring of 1945. In the wake of the church's refusal to partake in Soviet propaganda efforts, particularly those denouncing the Ukrainian nationalist movement, the official press published articles and pamphlets (notably those written by the publicist Ya. *Halan) which attacked the Ukrainian Catholic church and accused it of subversive acts. Soon afterwards (11 April 1945) Metropolitan Slipy and Bishops H. Khomyshyn, M. Charnetsky, N. Budka, and I. Liatyshevsky were arrested, and later (in June 1946) they were sentenced to lengthy terms in forced labor camps for their purported 'traitorous activities and collaboration with the German occupation forces.' At the same time the Soviet authorities took measures to block the election by the Ukrainian Catholic clergy of capitular vicars to administer the vacant sees, thus rendering the church leaderless.

A government-approved 'Sponsoring Group for the Re-Union of the Greek Catholic Church with the Russian Orthodox Church' emerged publicly on 28 May 1945 and proclaimed itself as the only legally constituted leadership of the Ukrainian Catholic church. In spite of a letter of protest from some 300 Ukrainian Catholic clergymen, the sponsoring group was officially given an exclusive jurisdiction over the church by Soviet Ukrainian authorities on 18 June 1945. Likewise, the newly appointed Russian Orthodox bishop for Western Ukraine, Makarii (Oksiiuk), was instructed to 'assist' the group in its efforts. The Sponsoring Group consisted of three priests, representing each of the metropoly's eparchies: H. *Kostelnyk (the Lviv-based chairman and a well-known critic of the Vatican's policy toward the Uniate church), M. Melnyk (vicar-general of Peremyshl eparchy), and A. Pelvetsky (a dean in Stanyslaviv eparchy). The three priests led an intensive campaign to convince the Galician clergy of the benefits of 'reunification,' focusing mainly on the political realities of living under the new Soviet regime and on dissatisfaction with the Latinizing elements within the Uniate church. Priests who were not convinced by these arguments were subjected to less subtle persuasion by Soviet security officials, through direct threats, deportation, or summary sentences to terms in forced labor camps. By March 1946 a total of 986 priests (over 50 per cent of the clergy) had been convinced to support the 'reunification.' Of the remaining 'recalcitrant' priests in Galicia, only 281 were reported to be still at large; others either had been imprisoned or deported or had gone into hiding.

With overt public resistance from the clergy now unlikely, the road was almost clear for completion of the 're-unification' process. The one remaining obstacle was the canonic need for the participation of bishops in convening and conducting a church sobor. Since none of the imprisoned Ukrainian Catholic bishops would succumb to Soviet pressure to convert to Orthodoxy, the Moscow patriarchate undertook the extraordinary action of ordaining two of the Sponsoring Group leaders, Pelvetsky and Melnyk, as Orthodox bishops in February 1946.

The sobor itself was a carefully staged showpiece. Set to coincide with the 350th anniversary of the Union of *Berestia, which had given birth to the Uniate church, its proceedings were covered by Soviet film crews and reporters. A total of 216 clerical and 19 lay delegates were 'invited' to participate. The agenda of the proceedings was not announced until the commencement of the sobor, following the pronouncement by the leaders of the Sponsoring Group that they had appointed themselves as the presidium of the gathering. The first day of the session consisted of the Sponsoring Group's reports and its presentation of a draft resolution abolishing the Union of Berestia and 'returning' the metropoly to the Russian Orthodox church. With no further discussion, the resolution was adopted 'unanimously' by a show of hands. Only then did Kostelnyk reveal to the delegates that Pelvetsky and Melnyk had been ordained as Orthodox bishops. The remaining two days of the sobor were taken up with ceremonial aspects of the 're-union,' the approval of earlier-prepared political messages to state authorities, and a plea to the clergy and faithful of the Ukrainian Catholic church to accept the new state of affairs.

The sobor was followed by a wave of repression against those priests and monks who had refused to accept the 're-union.' The Ukrainian Catholic church, as such, became an illegal, catacomb organization. Extensive popular resistance was demonstrated against the new situation as many parishes refused to allow Russian Orthodox clergymen into their churches. In September 1948 the Sponsoring Group leader, Kostelnyk, was assassinated in Lviv, allegedly by a 'Vatican-nationalist' agent; in fact, all indications are that this act was masterminded by the Soviet authorities. The leading polemicist against the Ukrainian Catholic church, Halan, was killed by Ukrainian nationalists in October 1949. In 1972 the 'reunion' of the Greek Catholic church was ratified by the local sobor of the Russian Orthodox church. In the West the uncanonical nature of the Lviv Sobor was noted, and the liquidation of the church roundly condemned by Catholic authorities, most notably by the papal encyclical *The Oriental Churches* of 15 December 1958 and, later, at the meeting of the synod of the Ukrainian Catholic bishops in Rome in 1980. On 1 December 1989 the Ukrainian Greek Catholic church was legalized by the authorities of the Ukrainian SSR.

BIBLIOGRAPHY
Diiannia soboru hreko-katolyts'koï tserkvy v m. L'vovi 8–10 bereznia 1946 roku (Lviv 1946)
Hryn'okh, I. 'Znyshchennia Ukraïns'koï Katolyts'koï Tserkvy rosiis'ko-bol'shevyts'kym rezhymom,' *Bohosloviia*, XLIV, 1–4 (1980)
Moiseyev, F. *The Lvov Church Council: Documents and Materials, 1946–1981* (Moscow 1983)

B.R. Bociurkiw

Lviv Svitoch Consortium of the Confectionery Industry (Lvivske vyrobnyche obiednannia kondyterskoi promyslovosti Svitoch). An enterprise formed in 1962 out of several confectionery factories in Lviv oblast. It manufactures over 300 varieties of confectionery, including candies, caramels, chocolates, jams, and waffles. Its gross output is 52,000 t per year.

Lviv Synod (Lvivskyi synod). The *synod of the Galician province of the Greek (Ukrainian) Catholic church which took place in Lviv on 22 September to 8 October 1891. It was convened by Metropolitan S. *Sembratovych, and its express intention was to reform church practices that had existed since the *Zamostia Synod of 1720. Under the chairmanship of an apostolic legate, the participants in the Lviv Synod included Sembratovych, bishops Yu. Pelesh (Peremyshl) and Yu. Kuilovsky-Sas (Stanyslaviv), the members of the canonical chapters in all three eparchies, the archimandrite and superiors of the Basilian order, noted theologians, eminent priests, and the senior of the Stauropegion Institute, I. Sharanevych.

The synod determined the number of feast days and fasts during the year and reached agreements on several contentious issues, including church discipline and the manner of conducting the Liturgy. The two main currents in the church – the traditionalist Eastern and reformist Western – disputed the question of a mandatory celibate clergy, which was rejected by the synod. The synod, however, did oblige priests to follow the Latin practice and to recite the priest's breviary in their daily routines.

In spite of losing some minor prerogatives, the Halych metropolitan emerged from the Lviv Synod with powers comparable to those afforded to a Latin rite metropolitan by the Council of Trent. He could determine the manner of ordinations, and supervise the affairs of eparchies in his metropoly. The decisions of the synod were printed in Ukrainian and Latin with a large addendum. They were confirmed by Rome in 1895 with some changes, which were made by Sembratovych himself in response to pressure from Polish and Vatican officials. The decisions of the Lviv Synod were adopted by Ukrainian Catholic church jurisdictions beyond Galicia, including Transcarpathia, the United States, and Canada, as a particular church law.

BIBLIOGRAPHY
Acta et decreta Synodi Provincialis Ruthenorum Galiciae habitae Leopoli an. 1891 (Rome 1896)

W. Lencyk

Lviv Theater of Opera and Ballet

Lviv Theater of Opera and Ballet (Lvivskyi teatr opery ta baletu im. I. Franka). Founded in 1940 in the former Lviv Municipal Theater built in 1900 by the architect Z. Gorgolewski. It functioned until 1941 (see *Lviv Opera Theater), and then was re-established under the new Sovi-

Lviv Theater of Opera and Ballet: view of the balcony and ceiling in the auditorium

et regime in Lviv. The theater staged productions of the classical European repertoire and of Ukrainian and contemporary works, including M. Lysenko's *Taras Bulba* and *Utoplena* (The Drowned Maiden), K. Dankevych's *Bohdan Khmel'nytskyi*, Yu. Meitus's *Moloda Gvardiia* (The Young Guard) and *Ukradene shchastia* (Stolen Happiness), V. Kyreiko's *Lisova Pisnia* (The Forest Song), A. Kos-Anatolsky's *Zahrava* (Incandescence) and his ballet *Soichyne krylo* (The Jay's Wing), and B. Liatoshynsky's *Zolotyi obruch* (The Golden Ring). Opera soloists included P. Duma, P. Karmaliuk, N. Shevchenko, V. Herasymenko, Z. Holovko, M. Popil, and Yu. Lysiansky. Ballet soloists included N. Slobodian, M. Tryhubiv, and O. Stalinsky. The conductors were Ya. Voshchak and Yu. Lutsiv, and the directors were O. Hrechnov and S. Smiian. The scenery designers were F. Nirod and O. Salman.

Lviv Trade and Economics Institute (Lvivskyi torhovelno-ekonomichnyi institut). A higher educational institute administered by the Central Association of Consumer Co-operatives (Tsentrospilka). Founded in 1939, it teaches economists about trade, accounting, finances, and commodity management. In 1979 the institute had 2,700 full-time and 2,980 corresponding students. Its library contains over 500,000 titles.

Lviv Ukrainian Drama Theater (Lvivskyi ukrainskyi dramatychnyi teatr im. M.K. Zankovetskoi). Founded in 1922 as the Zankovetska Theater from the cast of the State *People's Theater in Kiev, it has been one of the foremost drama theaters in Ukraine. In 1923–31 it worked as a *touring theater in the Donets and Poltava regions, and in 1931–41, as the resident drama theater in Zaporizhia. During the war it worked in Tobolsk, Siberia, and since 1944 it has been based in Lviv.

During the 1920s it used renowned Ukrainian actors in the staging of world classics. As a guest director P. *Saksahansky staged F. Schiller's *Die Räuber* (1922) and W. Shakespeare's *Othello* (1926); as well, the theater staged Molière's *Tartuffe*, C. Goldoni's *La Locandiera*, L. de Vega's *Fuenteovejuna*, J. Słowacki's *Mazepa*, and K. Gutzkow's *Uriel Acosta*. From the Ukrainian classics it staged an adaptation of P. Kulish's novel *Chorna rada* (The Black Coun-

Lviv Ukrainian Drama Theater

Lviv Ukrainian Drama
Theater: poster advertising
performances of W. Shake-
speare's *Othello*

cil) and M. Starytsky's *Ostannia nich* (The Last Night). S.
Cherkasenko's *Zemlia* (The Land), V. Vynnychenko's
Chuzhi liudy (The Foreigners), *Memento,* and *Dysharmoniia*
(Disharmony), and Lesia Ukrainka's *U pushchi* (In the Wil-
derness) were staged from the modern Ukrainian reper-
toire; Ya. Mamontov's *Do tretikh pivniv* (Until the Third
Crowing of the Cocks), *Rozheve pavutynnia* (The Pink
Web), *Respublika na kolesakh* (Republic on Wheels), *Kniazhna Viktoriia* (Princess Victoria), and *Ioho vlasnist'* (His
Property), I. Kocherha's *Feia hirkoho myhdaliu* (The Fairy of
the Bitter Almond) and *Marko v pekli* (Marko in Hell), and
M. Irchan's *Rodyna shchitkariv* (The Family of Brush Makers) and *Pidzemna Halychyna* (Underground Galicia), from
the contemporary playwrights; and O. Mirabeau's *Les
Mauvais Bergers*, M. Pagnol and P. Nivoix's *Les Marchands
de gloire*, and J. Synge's *The Playboy of the Western World*,
from the new Western European repertoire. With the beginning of Russification in the 1930s a leading place was
given to dramas by O. Korniichuk, I. Mykytenko, and L.
Pervomaisky and to numerous Soviet Russian playwrights, but to only one play from the non-Soviet repertoire, S. Kingsley's *Men in White.*

In Lviv from 1944, the theater staged Soviet patriotic
productions, such as I. Chabanenko's *Na Ukraïni mylii*
(In Dear Ukraine), L. Smiliansky's *Muzhyts'kyi posol* (The
Peasant Representative), and L. Pervomaisky's *Dovbush.* It
also staged contemporary plays, such as J. Priestley's *They
Came to a City.* Later, notable Ukrainian productions were
an adaptation of I. Franko's novelette *Boryslav smiiet'sia*
(Boryslav Is Laughing, 1951) and his *Son kniazia Sviatosla-
va* (The Dream of Prince Sviatoslav, 1957), adaptations of
T. Shevchenko's poems *Haidamaky* (1963) and *Maryna*
(1964), Lesia Ukrainka's *Blakytna troianda* (The Azure
Rose, 1968), M. Kulish's *Maklena Grasa* (1967), an adapta-
tion of I. Vilde's novel *Sestry Richyns'ki* (The Richynsky
Sisters), O. Levada's *Faust i smert'* (Faust and Death), I.
Riabokliach's *Mariia Zan'kovets'ka*, an adaptation of P.
Kozlaniuk's trilogy *Iurko Kruk*, V. Vrublevska's *Kafedra*
(The Department, 1980), and M. Zarudny's *Obochyna* (The
Roadside). Shakespearean tragedies performed have in-
cluded *Hamlet* (1956), *King Lear* (1969), and *Richard III*
(1974). The theater also staged an adaptation of G. Boccac-
cio's *Decameron* (1982) and, from the modern repertoire, J.

London's *Theft* and F. Molnár's *The Devil.* Recent productions include A. Vakhnianyn's operetta *Eve of Kupalo*, a
*vertep-style *Oi raduisia, zemle* (O Rejoice, Earth), and M.
Kulish's *Narodnii Malakhii* (The People's Malakhii).

The theater's main founders were B. Romanytsky (artis-
tic director until 1948), O. Korolchuk, V. Yaremenko, and
V. Liubart. Its directors have been I. Chabanenko, V.
Kharchenko, B. Tiahno, V. Hrypych, S. Danchenko, A.
Kravchuk, and F. Stryhun (since 1987); its scenery design-
ers, Yu. Stefanchuk, V. Borysovets, and M. Kyprian (since
1963 the main designer); and its actors, D. Dudariv, V.
Danchenko, V. Polinska, N. Dotsenko, F. Haienko, D.
Kozachkivsky, O. Hai, I. Rubchak, O. Kryvytska, B. Stup-
ka, L. Kadyrova, B. Kozak, I. Lytvynenko, M. Hrynko, and
V. Maksymenko.

BIBLIOGRAPHY
Kordiani, L.; Melnychuk-Luchko, L. *Teatr im. Zan'kovets'koï*
(Kiev 1965)
Kulyk, O. *L'vivs'kyi teatr im. M.K. Zan'kovets'koï* (Kiev 1989)
                                                        V. Revutsky

Lviv Ukrainian Independent Theater (Ukrainskyi
nezalezhnyi teatr). Established in May 1920 in Lviv by
members of the Theater of the Supreme Command of the
Ukrainian Galician Army, under the administration of H.
Nychka and artistic directorship of M. Bentsal. Under the
auspices of the Ukrainska Besida society it staged 12 plays
from the modern Ukrainian and Western repertoire. In
August 1921 it joined the cast of the reborn Ukrainska Besida Theater.

Lviv Ukrainian Youth Theater-Studio (Lvivskyi
ukrainskyi molodizhnyi teatr-studiia, or LUMT). A contemporary professional troupe founded in Lviv in March
1988, with V. Kuchynsky as artistic director, A. Matsiak as
director, A. Humeniuk as designer, and a cast composed
mainly of young actors who had left the *Lviv Ukrainian
Drama Theater. LUMT concentrates on teaching and developing the L. *Kurbas method of 'image transformation,'
enhanced by contemporary theatrical approaches, workshop study, and experimentation. The LUMT productions
are expressive; they integrate poetic metaphor, psychological character interpretation, music, mime, and modern
stage design, scenery, and choreography. The repertoire
includes poetic interpretations of the works of V. Stus; L.
Kostenko's *Sad netanuchykh skul'ptur* (The Garden of Un-

melting Sculptures), *Nich u Florentsiï* (A Night in Florence), and *Proshcha* (A Pilgrimage, based on *Marusia Churai*); V. Vynnychenko's *Mizh dvokh syl* (Between Two Powers) and *Zakon* (The Law); S. Mrożek's *Tango*; and Lesia Ukrainka's *Na poli krovi* (In a Field of Blood). Among the leading actors are T. Kaspruk, O. Drach, O. Oleksyshyn, O. Hrechanovsky, and N. Polovynka. The LUMT is Ukraine's only 'uncategorized' theater. In 1989 it was the first recipient of the Vasyl Stus Award.

Lviv (Underground) Ukrainian Higher Polytechnical School

(Lvivska [taiemna] ukrainska vysoka politekhnichna shkola). An institution of higher education established in 1922–3 at the *Lviv (Underground) Ukrainian University. The program consisted of one-year general courses in theoretical subjects, which had to be continued by studies abroad, usually in Danzig (*Gdańsk). There were three departments – general studies, engineering, and forestry – modeled on the Danzig Polytechnic and the Příbram Mining Academy in Czechoslovakia (forestry department). The rector was V. Luchkiv; there were 64 students. In 1925 the school ceased operations in conjunction with the closure of the university.

Building of the Lviv (Underground) Ukrainian University (1921–5) and the Shevchenko Scientific Society (to 1939), now the Institute of Social Sciences of the Academy of Sciences of Ukraine at Lviv University

Lviv (Underground) Ukrainian University

(Lvivskyi [taiemnyi] ukrainskyi universytet). An institution of *higher education established in July 1921 on the basis of university courses initiated in September 1919 by the *Shevchenko Scientific Society, the *Mohyla Scholarly Lectures Society, and the *Stauropegion Institute. The courses were instituted because the Polish authorites had abolished all Ukrainian chairs and teaching positions at *Lviv University in 1919 and had made higher education available exclusively to Polish citizens and citizens of Allied states who served in the Polish or Allied armies. When the government banned Ukrainian courses in 1920, a clandestine program of instruction in the humanities, law, and medicine was undertaken, and a boycott of Polish higher educational institutions was announced. The first rector was V. *Shchurat; he was followed by M. *Panchyshyn and Ye. Davydiuk. There were 54 departments and 1,260 students in 1921, and 65 departments and 1,500 students in 1922–3. The Faculty of Medicine offered only a two-year program; it had to be continued by

studies abroad. Virtually all Ukrainian scholars and professionals living in Lviv taught at the university, which was financed by private donations. The program was recognized by foreign universities.

In February 1923 the Board of Ukrainian Higher Schools was established to supervise the university and the *Lviv (Underground) Ukrainian Higher Polytechnical School. It proposed the legalization of the university, which proposal led to negotiations in 1924–5 involving K. *Studynsky and R. *Smal-Stotsky on the Ukrainian side and S. *Grabski, S. Łoś, and T. Waryński on the Polish. A government commission studied the proposal, but it received scant support and was undermined by the relentless persecution of Ukrainian education in Poland. Denied official recognition, the university ceased operations in late 1925.

BIBLIOGRAPHY
Mudryi, V. *Ukraïns'kyi universytet u L'vovi u rr. 1921–1925* (Nuremberg 1948)
Martynets', V. *Ukraïns'ke pidpillia: vid UVO do OUN: Spohady i materiialy do peredistoriï ta istoriï ukraïns'koho orhanizovanoho natsionalizmu* (Winnipeg 1949)
Bohachevsky-Chomiak, M. 'The Ukrainian University in Galicia: A Pervasive Issue,' *HUS*, 5, no. 4 (December 1981)

M. Yurkevich

Lviv University, main building

Lviv University

(Lvivskyi universytet im. I. Franka). The oldest university in Ukraine, established in 1784 by the emperor of Austria Joseph II with Latin as the language of instruction. Candidates for the priesthood who knew no Latin could study in the vernacular, but only after the establishment of the *Studium Ruthenum in 1787. In 1805 the university was transformed into a *lyceum, and in 1817 the university status was restored, the institution was renamed in honor of Emperor Francis I, and German became the language of instruction. During the Revolution of 1848–9 in the Habsburg monarchy, demands were raised for the introduction of the Ukrainian and Polish languages. In 1849 the chair of Ukrainian language and literature was established (first held by *Ya. Holovatsky). Ukrainian-language instruction was introduced in the second half of the 19th century, first in the Department of Theology and then of Law (1862–72). From 1867 the struggle for the language and character of the university began between Ukrainians and Poles. In 1871 all restrictions in teaching in either Ukrainian or Polish were abolished and it was ordered that only people with the command of either of the two languages could occupy university chairs. In 1879 Polish became the administrative language at the university, and the appointment of Ukrainians to docent positions was obstructed. In 1894 the

Chair of Ukrainian History was established and given to M. *Hrushevsky. In 1900 a separate Chair of Ukrainian Literature was added.

The Ukrainians continued to try to establish their own university in Lviv and to get rid of the Polish domination at the existing one. Ukrainian university students, organized in the secret Committee of Ukrainian Youth (KUM), led the battle. In 1901 they staged a protest secession from Lviv University. In 1910 a member of KUM, A. Kotsko, was killed in a fight with Polish students. In 1912 the Austrian government finally agreed to establish a Ukrainian university in Lviv by 1916, but the realization of the plan was prevented by the outbreak of the First World War.

By 1914 the university consisted of four faculties – theology, philosophy, law, and medicine (est 1894) – with an enrollment of 5,000. After the Polish occupation of eastern Galicia the authorities abolished Ukrainian chairs and docent positions. By the order of 14 September 1919 only those who had served in the Polish army and were Polish citizens were eligible for admission to the university. Since the status of eastern Galicia was not resolved by the victorious Entente until 1923, and Ukrainians refused to consider themselves Polish citizens, they were not permitted to enroll at the university. In 1919 the name of the university was changed to Jan Casimir University in honor of the Polish-Lithuanian king who founded a Polish Jesuit college in Lviv (1661–1763), which the Poles claimed was the predecessor of the university. In 1920 the university was moved to its present site, the building of the former Galician Diet (built in 1877–81). Ukrainians, who continued their demands for a separate Ukrainian university in Lviv, boycotted the university until 1925 and organized the *Lviv (Underground) Ukrainian University and the Department of Theology at the *Greek Catholic Theological Seminary in Lviv to replace the one abolished at Lviv University. In the 1930s the university had 6,000–7,000 students and up to 200 faculty members. There were few Ukrainian lecturers (none in 1928–33). Ukrainian language and literature were taught by the Polish professor J. *Janów. A Ukrainian students' circle was organized among his students.

After the annexation of Western Ukraine by the USSR in 1939, Lviv University was Ukrainianized in language and Sovietized in spirit. The Galician Ukrainian literary scholar K. *Studynsky was appointed its prorector or vice-chancellor. The Faculty of Theology was abolished, and the Faculty of Medicine was reorganized into a separate medical institute, in keeping with the Soviet education system. In 1940 the name of I. *Franko (who had been a student at Lviv University) was conferred upon the university. The Soviets promulgated a false genealogy for the university, one claiming that it originated in 1661 but ignoring its affiliation with the Jesuits. After the retreat of the Soviets at the end of June 1941, the Ukrainian linguist V. *Simovych was elected rector of the university, but it was not allowed to operate under the German occupation. Its main building was occupied by the Gestapo.

The university was reopened in 1944, when the Soviets reoccupied Lviv. The Ukrainianization of 1939 was replaced with a program of Russification. In 1982 the university had departments of philology (for Slavic languages and literatures, including Ukrainian), foreign languages (including classical philology, a feature unique in the Ukrainian SSR), history, law, biology, chemistry,

physics, mathematics, applied mathematics and mechanics, geography, journalism, geology, and economics (with a five-year curriculum), as well as evening and extramural departments (with a curriculum of five or six years). The university had about 11,000 students in 1988–9 (almost 50 percent of whom were enrolled in evening or extramural courses). More than 57,000 students had graduated from the university between 1939 and 1989. The library had approx 2.5 million volumes in 1981. The university has published its journal *Visnyk* since the 1960s.

BIBLIOGRAPHY
Wolf, G. *Geschichte der Lemberger Universität von ihrer Begründung, 1784 bis 1848* (Vienna 1893)
Finkel, L.; Starzyński, S. *Historia Uniwersytetu Lwowskiego*, 2 vols (Lviv 1894)
Barvins'kyi, B. 'Predtecha Universytetu im. Frantsa I u Lvovi,' *ZNTSh*, 75 (Lviv 1918)
Lazarenko, I. *300 lit L'vivskoho universytetu* (Lviv 1961)
Chuhaiov, V.; et al (eds). *L'vivs'kyi universytet* (Lviv 1986)
B. Struminsky

Lviv Workers' Theater (Robitnychyi teatr). A pro-communist theater established in Lviv in 1927. Besides performing and helping to organize drama courses for workers and peasants, it published *Zhyva stsena* as a supplement to the journal *Vikna*. The Polish government restricted its activities in 1932 and suppressed it in 1934.

Lviv Young Spectator's Theater (Lvivskyi teatr yunoho hliadacha). Founded in Kharkiv in 1920 as the Fairytale Theater (Russian), from 1921 it was called the Kharkiv First State Children's Theater (bilingual from 1925), and in 1944 it was transferred to Lviv. In 1945 the director, V. Skliarenko, staged Yu. Kostiuk's *Taras Shevchenko*. From Ukrainian classics the theater staged I. Franko's *Uchytel'* (The Teacher) in 1956. Its repertoire for children has included an adaptation of M. Twain's *The Adventures of Tom Sawyer* and A. Shyian's *Kotyhoroshko* (The Pea Roller) and *Letiuchyi korabel'* (The Flying Ship). Its contemporary Ukrainian repertoire has included M. Irchan's *Rodyna shchitkariv* (The Family of Brush Makers), V. Gzhytsky's *Po zori* (At Dawn), and P. Lubensky's *Neskorena poltavchanka* (The Undefeated Girl from Poltava). It has also staged the Russian plays *Nedorosl'* (The Minor) by D. Fonvizin and *Revizor* (The Inspector General) by N. Gogol. In 1982 the director, V. Kozmenko-Delinde, staged an experimental production of W. Shakespeare's *Hamlet*. The theater's artistic directors have been V. Kharchenko, S. Danchenko, and O. Ripko, and the stage designers, B. Kosariv and I. Deshko.

Lviv Zootechnical-Veterinary Institute (Lvivskyi zooveterynarnyi instytut). A higher institution of learning, until 1992 under the jurisdiction of the USSR Ministry of Agriculture. Located in Lviv, it was formed in 1939 out of the Academy of Veterinary Medicine, which itself was organized in 1897 out of the Lviv Veterinary School (est 1881). The institute consists of zoological engineering and veterinary faculties, a correspondence and graduate school, two experimental farms, two laboratories, a research sector, and a large library. In 1974 the Faculty for Upgrading Zootechnical-Veterinary Specialists was added. The enrollment in 1980 was 3,800, including 1,900 correspondence students. The institute is known for its research in areas such as the prevention of animal sterility, the treatment of metabolic disorders and poisoning, and raising animal productivity.

L'vivs'ki visti (Lviv News). A daily paper published in Lviv from August 1941 to July 1944. It was controlled by the German chief of the press in the German-occupied Distrikt Galizien. The paper superseded the organ of the Lviv municipal government established after the Soviet retreat, the daily *Ukraïns'ki shchodenni visti* (June–July 1941), which had been banned by the Germans. The chief editors were O. Bodnarovych and, from 26 June 1944, M. Semchyshyn. The paper had a circulation of 124,000 copies in 1941, 296,000 in 1942, 238,000 in 1943, and 93,000 in 1944.

Lviv-Volhynia Coal Basin. A major coalfield in western Ukraine, covering almost 8,000 sq km of Lviv and Volhynia oblasts and extending into Poland. Its geological structure is connected with the Galician-Volhynian geosyncline, and contains deposits from the Paleozoic, Mesozoic, and Cenozoic periods. The basin has almost 60 coal seams (of 0.6 to 2 m width) at depths of between 300 m in the north and 600 m in the south. Aquifers hinder mining. The coal has an ash content of 13.7 percent, a sulfur content of 1–4 percent, and a phosphorus content of 1.5 percent. Its thermal value is 6,800–7,500 kcal/kg. In 1986 the recoverable reserves were estimated at 970 million t.

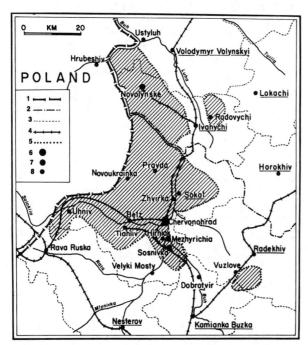

LVIV-VOLHYNIA COAL BASIN

1. State boundaries
2. Oblast boundaries
3. Raion boundaries
4. Railway lines
5. Boundary of the coal deposit
6. Cities with population over 30,000
7. Towns with population over 10,000
8. Settlements with population under 10,000
Raion centers are underlined.

A search for the coal deposits, which were first predicted by the Russian geologist M. Tetiaev in 1910, was conducted in the interwar period by the Polish geologist J. Samsonowicz supported by a large Silesian industrial concern. After the war detailed explorations were carried out, and mining began in 1954. The development of the basin played a major role in the industrialization of Western Ukraine after the war. In the 1960s some 30,000 people, 75 percent of them Ukrainians, were employed in the coal mines. In 1976 their output totaled 15 million t, or about 7 percent of Ukraine's coal output. Coal from the basin is used mainly for fuel. Some 30 percent is exported, primarily to Kaliningrad oblast and the Baltic republics.

LVU. See Canadian League for Ukraine's Liberation.

Lybid River [Lybid']. A right-bank tributary of the Dnieper River. It is 14 km long and drains a basin area of 68 sq km. It flows within the boundaries of Kiev from its source in the western end of the city and joins the Dnieper River in the southeastern part of the city. Its average width is 3–4 m. It is believed that the river was named after Lybid, a sister of Kyi, the legendary founder of Kiev. In the Middle Ages the Lybid formed the southwestern boundary of Kiev, and several dams with watermills were constructed on it. At that time its lower course was navigable. Later the river was silted up. Numerous burial sites dating from the times of the Zarubyntsi culture and the Cherniakhiv culture have been excavated in the river's valley.

Lyceum. A type of secondary school, in some cases also an institution of *higher education. In Russian-ruled Ukraine there were three lyceums resembling institutions of higher learning, the *Kremianets Lyceum (1819–33), the *Richelieu Lyceum in Odessa (1817–65), and the *Nizhen Lyceum (1832–74).

In Galicia lyceums were schools for women that offered incomplete secondary education. From the end of the 19th century until 1918, the *Ukrainian Girl's Institute in Peremyshl was the only Ukrainian lyceum.

Ukrainian lyceums as senior secondary schools appeared in Galicia and Volhynia following the 1932 Polish school reform. By 1939 there were 21 Ukrainian general education lyceums (5 state-supported and 16 private), as well as the Co-operative Lyceum in Lviv of the *Audit Union of Ukrainian Co-operatives, offering a three-year course, and the state agricultural lyceum in Chernelytsia (est 1934).

Since the late 1980s, as a consequence of political changes and the greater flexibility in education administration, lyceums have re-emerged. Lyceums were established in 1989 at the *Odessa Pedagogical Institute and at the Izmail Pedagogical Institute which offer an enriched complete secondary education for selected students at the grade nine level.

Lychakiv Cemetery. A cemetery in the Lychakiv district of Lviv. It is mentioned in historical documents at the end of the 16th century. Until the Austrian authorities moved the cemeteries outside the cities at the end of the 18th century, prominent and rich people were buried within or under the churches, and Lychakiv served as the burial ground of the common people or the victims of epidemics. The present layout of the cemetery dates from 1855–61. Besides many Polish noblemen and cultural fig-

Lychakiv Cemetery: Ivan Franko's burial monument (sculpture by Serhii Lytvynenko)

ures, prominent Ukrainians are buried there, including M. Shashkevych, I. Franko, M. Pavlyk, V. Barvinsky, A. Petrushevych, A. Vakhnianyn, P. Svientsitsky, Yu. Lavrivsky, D. Zubrytsky, V. Shashkevych, I. Levytsky, O. Terletsky, Yu. Tselevych, V. Nahirny, and V. Ivasiuk. A special section is set aside for the Ukrainian soldiers who died in the November Uprising of 1918. In the interwar period commemorative services were held annually at the cemetery for those who had fallen in the struggle for Ukrainian independence. Such commemorations were banned under the Soviet regime and were revived only at the end of the 1980s.

Lykholat, Andrii [Lyxolat, Andrij], b 12 December 1914 in Rozsokhuvatka, near Cherkasy, Kiev gubernia. Historian and Communist party functionary. He worked in the CC of the All-Union Bolshevik Party (1942–61) and in the AN URSR (now ANU) Institute of History. In the 1970s he came to play an important role as official historian of the Soviet rise to power. His works include *Razgrom natsionalisticheskoi kontrrevoliutsii na Ukraine (1917–22 gg.)* (The Defeat of the Nationalist Counterrevolution in Ukraine [1917–22], 1954), *Zhovten' na Ukraïni* ([The] October [Revolution] in Ukraine, 1967), and *Lenins'ka natsional'na polityka partiï v diï* (The Leninist Nationality Policy of the Party in Action, 1977).

Lyman, Leonyd, b 13 August 1922 in Mali Sorochyntsi, now in Myrhorod raion, Poltava oblast. Poet and writer. He began to publish lyric poetry when he was still a student at the Kharkiv Pedagogical Institute. A postwar refugee, in 1949 he settled in New York City and resumed writing. His poetry appeared in various journals and collections. Excerpts from his novels 'Kolhospnyky' (Collective Farmers) and 'Povist' pro Kharkiv' (A Tale about Kharkiv) have been published in several periodicals. He has edited the cultural and political news digest *Notatnyk*

since 1961. Although no collections of his poetry have been published so far, some critics consider Lyman to be one of the best Ukrainian poets of his generation.

Lymanske [Lymans'ke]. VII-10. A town smt (1990 pop 8,700) in Rozdilna raion, Odessa oblast. It is located on the Kuchurhan Estuary on the border between Ukraine and Moldova. It was founded in the late 18th century and was called Zeltsi until 1944. Lymanske has two vineyards with wineries and a branch of the Odessa Furniture Manufacturing Complex.

Lymansky, Vasyl. See Mova, Vasyl.

Lymarenko, Danylo, b 2 January 1895 in Karlivka, Yelysavethrad county, Kherson gubernia, d 14 August 1968 in Philadelphia. Military and community figure. An officer in the tsarist army during the First World War, in December 1917 he became an officer with the Ukrainian Free Cossacks in Kherson gubernia. In 1919–20 he commanded a partisan detachment fighting both the Whites and the Bolsheviks, and then served as captain in the First Zaporozhian Rifle Division. As a postwar refugee in Germany, he was a founding member of the Ukrainian National State Union (UNDS) and the Union of Ukrainian Veterans. After emigrating to the United States he headed the Philadelphia branch of the UNDS (from 1956) and the Union of Ukrainian Veterans in America (from 1967).

Lynnychenko, Ivan [Lynnyčenko], b 24 October 1857 in Kiev, d 9 April 1926. Historian. He graduated from Kiev University (1879), where he studied under V. Antonovych, and became a professor at Odessa (1884–8, 1896–1926) and Moscow (1888–96) universities. His works deal with the history of Kievan Rus' and the sociopolitical history of Galicia in the 14th and 15th centuries. He treated Ukrainian history from a Russian imperial viewpoint, but his studies on Galicia contain valuable source materials.

Lyntsevsky, Hervasii [Lyncevs'kyj, Hervasij], b 1683 near Kiev, d 2 January 1770. Orthodox churchman and missionary. He graduated from and then taught at the Kievan Mohyla Academy before becoming leader of the Peking Orthodox mission (1742–55) and, later, bishop of Pereiaslav (1757–68). He fought against the spread of Uniate Catholicism in Right-Bank Ukraine and supported the Koliivshchyna rebellion.

Lypa, Ivan (pseuds: Petro Shelest, I. Stepovyk), b 24 February 1865 in Kerch, Tavriia gubernia, d 13 November 1923 in Vynnyky, Lviv county, Galicia. Civic and political figure, writer, and physician. As a student at Kharkiv University he helped found the Brotherhood of Taras and was imprisoned (1893) for over a year for his activity in it. After completing his studies at Kazan University he practiced medicine in the Kherson region, Poltava, and then (1902–18) Odessa, where he published the Ukrainian paper *Narodnyi stiah* and organized a Ukrainian club, a Prosvita society, and the Odessa Literary Association. During the revolutionary period he was elected Ukrainian commissioner of Odessa and sat on the CC of the Ukrainian Party of Socialists-Independentists. Under the Directory of the UNR he served as minister of religious affairs in V. Chekhivsky's and S. Ostapenko's cabinets. After emigrating to Tarnów (Poland) in 1921, he chaired the Council of

Ivan Lypa   Yurii Lypa

the Republic and became minister of health in the UNR government-in-exile. In 1922 he settled in Vynnyky, near Lviv. As a writer Lypa is known for his symbolic-philosophical poetry and short stories, which appeared in various journals, such as *Literaturno-naukovyi vistnyk* and *Ukraïns'ka khata*, and various almanacs. They were collected posthumously in *Opovidi pro smert', viinu i liubov* (Stories about Death, War, and Love, 1935) and *Trynadtsiat' prytch* (Thirteen Parables, 1935). His stories for children were published in *Dzvinok*, and his numerous articles, in leading Ukrainian papers, such as *Pravda*, *Dilo*, and *Bukovyna*.

Lypa, Yurii, b 1900 in Odessa, d 1944. Writer and publicist; the son of I. *Lypa. He was a graduate of Poznan University (1929) and a physician by profession. From 1920 he lived in Poland and Galicia. He died serving as a physician with the Ukrainian Insurgent Army. His poetry began to be published in 1919. Several collections of his poetic works appeared: *Svitlist'* (Brightness, 1925), *Suvorist'* (Severity, 1931), *Viruiu* (I Believe, 1938), and *Poeziia* (Poetry, 1967). His prose works include a novel, *Kozaky v Moskoviï* (The Cossacks in Muscovy, 1931, 1942, 1957), three volumes of short stories *Notatnyk* (Note Book, 1936–7, 1955), *Ruban* (1946), and *Kinnotchyk ta inshi opovidannia* (The Horseman and Other Stories, 1946), and a collection of essays, *Bii za ukraïns'ku literaturu* (The Battle for Ukrainian Literature, 1935). He wrote a number of publicistic works which were popular at the time: *Ukraïns'ka doba* (The Ukrainian Age, 1936); a kind of trilogy, consisting of *Pryznachennia Ukraïny* (The Destiny of Ukraine, 1938), *Chornomors'ka doktryna* (The Black Sea Doctrine, 1940, 1942, 1947), and *Rozpodil Rosiï* (The Partition of Russia, 1941, 1954), in which he outlined his so-called Black Sea doctrine; and numerous publicistic articles and essays of literary criticism. Lypa's 'imperial' concept was not well-founded but it was expounded in such a brilliant and stirring style that he became one of the most popular figures of his time in Galicia and among Ukrainian emigrants. His medical works, such as *Fitoterapiia* (Phytotherapy, 1933), *Tsiliushchi roslyny v davnii i suchasnii medytsyni* (Healing Plants in Ancient and Contemporary Medicine, 1937), and *Liky pid nohamy* (Medicines under Foot, 1943), were reprinted several times and enjoyed great popularity.

Lypkivsky, Ivan [Lypkivs'kyj], b 14 September 1892 in Lypovets, Kiev county, Kiev gubernia, d late 1930s. Painter. He studied under M. Boichuk at the Kiev State Art Institute (1921–7) and was a member of the *Association of Revolutionary Art of Ukraine. He perished during the Great Terror. Some of his works, such as *The Red Blast Furnace* (1926), *The Steelworkers* (1929), and *Agreement on Socialist Competition* (1932), have been preserved at the Kiev Museum of Ukrainian Art.

Metropolitan Vasyl Lyp-   Rev Bohdan Lypsky
kivsky

Lypkivsky, Vasyl [Lypkivs'kyj, Vasyl'], b 19 March 1864 in Popudnia, Lypovets county, Kiev gubernia, d 27 November 1937. Church leader; cofounder and metropolitan of the *Ukrainian Autocephalous Orthodox church (UAOC). He studied at the Uman Theological School (1873–9), the Kiev Theological Seminary (1879–84), and the Kiev Theological Academy (1884–9). He was ordained in 1891, and from 1892 to 1903 he was dean of the cathedral in Lypovets and supervisor of the schools in Lypovets county. In 1903–5 he lectured on canon law in the Kiev Church Teachers' School, but he lost this position for his support of a separate Ukrainian church. With the fall of the tsarist regime in 1917, Lypkivsky joined the struggle for the establishment of an independent Ukrainian Orthodox church. He was elected chairman of the Kiev Eparchial Sobor and of the *Brotherhood of the Resurrection, which later became the *All-Ukrainian Orthodox Church Council. In May 1919 he celebrated the first Liturgy in the Ukrainian language – after translating many of the liturgical works into modern Ukrainian – in St Nicholas's Military Cathedral in Kiev. Although this action was opposed by the Russian hierarchy, who defrocked Lypkivsky, it was welcomed by supporters of the emerging Ukrainian national church. In the summer of 1919 Lypkivsky became parish priest of the St Sophia Cathedral in Kiev.

In October 1921 the All-Ukrainian Church Council in Kiev, which had declared the establishment of the UAOC in May 1920, elected Lypkivsky the first metropolitan of the church. When bishops of the official Russian church denounced the election and refused to consecrate the new metropolitan, the sobor revived the ancient Alexandrine tradition of 'the laying of hands' to consecrate Lypkivsky without the participation of other bishops. Without a traditional episcopal ordination, Lypkivsky was constantly vilified by the Russian church as a noncanonical bishop outside the apostolic succession. His legitimacy was also questioned by other churches and some of the Ukrainian faithful. Nonetheless, Lypkivsky devoted himself to organizing the new church. He traveled throughout Ukraine, visiting more than 500 parishes after his election and overseeing the growth of the UAOC (by 1927 the church claimed 36 bishops and over 2,500 priests). Insisting on the active participation of the laity in church affairs, he propagated many church reforms, and he modified many Orthodox canons and traditions, including the absolute celibacy of bishops, with the result that married men were admitted to episcopal ordination. He was also insistent on preserving the independence of the Ukrainian church vis-à-vis Moscow. Lypkivsky's popularity soon earned him the enmity of the Soviet authorities, who, after arresting him a few times, had him dismissed by the All-Ukrainian Orthodox Council in 1927. From 1927 to 1937 he lived in a Kiev suburb, under virtual house arrest and in poverty. He was arrested by the NKVD in November 1937, charged with anti-Soviet activity, and summarily executed (although it was commonly believed that he had survived at least to early 1938).

Lypkivsky wrote prolifically on canon law, church history, and theology, but most of his writings remained in manuscript and were destroyed during the Second World War. Only the last volume of his seven-volume history of Ukrainian Orthodoxy was published (posthumously). This volume, concerning the history of the UAOC, has appeared in three different editions, the most authoritative of them edited and annotated by S. Savchuk as *Vidrodzhennia Ukraïns'koï Tserkvy* (1961). Several of Lypkivsky's articles appeared in postwar periodicals, including 'Ukraïns'ka Avtokefal'na Tserkva i radians'ka komunistychna vlada' (The Ukrainian Autocephalous Church and Soviet Communist Rule) in *Vil'na Ukraïna* (1955–8) and 'Iak Ukraïns'ka Tserkva povernula sobi voliu' (How the Ukrainian Church Regained Its Freedom) in *Ukraïns'ke pravoslavne slovo* (1956). A collection of his sermons, including a short autobiography, *Propovidi na nedili i sviata* (Sermons for Sundays and Holidays, 1969), and a number of his letters to Rev P. Maievsky in 1933–7 also appeared posthumously in the West, and an autobiography appeared in the Warsaw journal *Nasha kul'tura* in 1936.

BIBLIOGRAPHY
Bilanych, J. 'De evolutione Ecclesiae Orthodoxae Ukrainorum annis 1917–1942,' diss (Rome 1943)
Heyer, F. *Die Orthodoxe Kirche in der Ukraine von 1917–1945* (Köln-Braunsfeld 1953)
Lypkivs'kyi, V. *Vidrodzhennia Tserkvy v Ukraïni 1917–1930* (Toronto 1959)
– *Vidrodzhennia Ukraïns'koï Pravoslavnoï Tserkvy* (Winnipeg 1961)
Sadylenko, M. *Sumni naslidky lypkivshchyny v Ukraïns'kii Pravoslavnii Tserkvi* (Toronto 1978)
Armstark, R. *Die Ukrainische Autokephale Orthodoxe Kirche: Erinnerungen des Metropoliten Vasyl' K. Lypkivs'kyj* (Würzburg 1982)

Lypko, Petro, b 1876, d ? Senior UNR Army officer. A graduate of the General Staff Academy in St Petersburg and officer of the Russian army, he joined the UNR Army and served on its General Staff in 1919 as chief of intelligence and then as general quartermaster. In 1920 he became chief of staff and was promoted to brigadier general.

Lypova Dolyna. III-14. A town smt (1990 pop 5,400) on the Khorol River and a raion center in Sumy oblast. It was founded in the first half of the 17th century, and it was part of the estates of J. Wiśniowiecki until 1654. It received the status of smt in 1962. The town has a dairy and a mixed-feed factory.

Lypovets [Lypovec']. IV-10. A town smt (1990 pop 9,400) on the Sob River and a raion center in Vinnytsia oblast. According to a historical document of 1545 Lypovets arose in the 14th century. The Union of Lublin in 1569 assigned the town to Poland. The castle built there at the beginning of the 17th century played an important role in the Cossack-Polish War of 1648–57 and the popular uprisings of 1702–4 and 1737. With the second partition of Poland in 1793, Lypovets was annexed by Russia and turned into a county center of Kiev gubernia. In 1918–19 the UNR Army fought the Red Army near Lypovets on several occasions. In August 1919 the Zaporozhian Division crushed a Bolshevik unit there. Lypovets became an smt in 1925. Today it has a research plant of the Remdetal Scientific and Manufacturing Association.

Lypovetska, Mlada [Lypovec'ka] (Lipovetzka; Norlander; real name: Belman, Taisa), b 1897 in Volhynia, d ? Singer, translator, literary scholar. In 1914 she came to Italy to study singing. She gave concerts and popularized Ukrainian songs. Her articles on T. Shevchenko and her translations of several of his poems appeared in 1919 in the newspaper *La Voce dell' Ucraina* (Rome). In 1926, in collaboration with C. Meano, she prepared a collection of translations of Shevchenko's poetry into Italian, entitled *Taras Scevcenko: Liriche scelte dal 'Cobsar.'* The collection was never published, but some of the poems appeared in 1932 in *Ucraina*, a journal of Ukrainian studies founded by Lypovetska.

Lypovetsky, Ivan [Lypovec'kyj], b 24 March 1897 in Rivne, Volhynia gubernia, d 30 December 1975 in Toronto. Civic leader and journalist. During the struggle for Ukraine's independence Lypovetsky joined the *Sixth Sich Division of the Army of the UNR and edited its journal *Ukraïns'kyi strilets'*. During the division's internment in Poland he worked in the editorial office of its newspaper *Nove zhyttia* and then edited the journal *Na chuzhyni* and represented the Parisian weekly *Tryzub* among the Ukrainian émigrés in Poland. In 1952 he emigrated to Canada, where he cofounded the political party known as the *Ukrainian National State Union in Canada, headed the *Ukrainian War Veterans' League of Canada (1959–70), and edited the journal *Dorohovkaz*.

Lypsky, Bohdan [Lyps'kyj], b 9 April 1903 in Lviv, d 12 October 1969 in Toronto. Ukrainian Catholic priest and professor. After completing his studies at the Pontifical Oriental Institute in Rome, he taught at the Khrystynopil Basilian monastery and then moved to Lviv in 1932 to teach moral theology and dogma at the Greek Catholic Theological Academy. He also served as chaplain (1932–9) of Ukrainian political prisoners in Galicia. In 1940–4 he was a member of the chancery office, in the Lemko region, and in 1946–51 he taught at seminaries in Germany and Holland. He moved to Canada in 1951 to serve as a parish priest at St Nicholas's Church in Toronto. In his pastoral work and in a monograph, *Dukhovist' nashoho obriadu* (The Spirituality of Our Rite, 1974), he stressed the importance of avoiding Latin influences and of maintaining the purity of the Eastern rite in the Ukrainian Catholic church.

Volodymyr Lypsky   V'iacheslav Lypynsky

Lypsky, Volodymyr [Lyps'kyj], b 11 March 1863 in Samostrily, Novhorod-Volynskyi county, Volhynia gubernia, d 24 February 1937 in Odessa. Botanist; full member of the VUAN from 1919 and corresponding member of the USSR Academy of Sciences from 1928. After graduating from Galagan College (1881) and Kiev University (1886) he worked in the university's and the Imperial Botanical Gardens. After the Revolution of 1917 Lypsky helped organize the VUAN, of which he served as vice-president (1921–2) and president (1922–8). From 1928 he was director of the Odessa Botanical Garden. Lypsky conducted many botanical expeditions to Central Asia, the Far East, Africa, and the Americas. He identified 4 new plant genera and over 220 new species and studied marine plants of the Black Sea and radioactive mineral springs of the Zhytomyr region. He published scientific accounts of the flora of Ukraine, Bessarabia, Caucasia, Central Asia, Tunisia, Algeria, and Indonesia, including multivolume works on the flora of Caucasia (1899–1902) and Central Asia (1902–5), as well as *Botanichnyi sad Ukraïns'koï akademiï nauk* (Botanical Garden of the Ukrainian Academy of Sciences, 1922). Lypsky's biography, by A. Barbarych, was published in Kiev in 1958.

Lypynsky, V'iacheslav [Lypyns'kyj, V'jačeslav], (Lipiński, Wacław), b 5 April 1882 in Zaturtsi, Volodymyr-Volynskyi county, Volhynia, d 14 June 1931 near Vienna. Historian, political philosopher, and publicist; full member of the Shevchenko Scientific Society from 1914. After studying history and agronomy at Cracow and Geneva universities he settled on his estate in the Uman region and devoted his energies to reconverting the Polonized nobility to Ukrainian culture. He wrote the brochure *Szlachta ukraińska i jej udział w życiu narodu ukraińskiego* (The Ukrainian Gentry and Its Participation in the Life of the Ukrainian People, 1909) and articles in the biweekly *Przegląd Krajowy*. He accepted some of the ideas of the *khlopomany but wanted the nobility to change into a politically conscious Ukrainian class that would preserve its

corporate character. His efforts were at least partly successful.

His first historical works were articles in the serials *Literaturno-naukovyi vistnyk*, *Zapysky NTSh*, and *Rada*, as well as the monumental *Z dziejów Ukrainy* (From the History of Ukraine, 1912; repr 1959), which was edited and for the most part written by him (particularly the monograph *Stanisław Michał Krzyczewski*). In 1917 he took part in organizing the *Ukrainian Democratic Agrarian party and drafted its program, based on the principle of a sovereign Ukrainian state and the private ownership of land. Under the Hetman government Lypynsky was appointed Ukrainian envoy to Vienna, and he retained that post under the UNR government until June 1919.

Except for a brief stay in Berlin (1926–7), where he held the chair of state history at the Ukrainian Scientific Institute, Lypynsky lived in Austria after the struggle for Ukraine's independence. That was his most creative period; his monograph *Ukraïna na perelomi 1657–1659 ...* (Ukraine at the Turning Point of 1657–1659, 1920, 1991) was published, and at his initiative the *Ukrainian Union of Agrarians-Statists (USKhD) was formed. He drafted its statute and served as president of its board of directors. He became a leader and ideologist of the conservative monarchist movement, which won adherents among Ukrainians abroad and in Western Ukraine. Its ideological journals were the irregular collection *Khliborobs'ka Ukraïna* (1920–5), which published his fundamental political treatise *Lysty do brativ-khliborobiv* (Letters to Brothers-Agrarians) in 1926 (repr 1956). Tactical and ideological disagreements with Hetman P. *Skoropadsky led Lypynsky to dissolve the USKhD in 1930, and with a small group of followers (M. Kochubei, V. Zalozetsky, and V. Kuchabsky) he set up the short-lived Brotherhood of Ukrainian Classocrats-Monarchists. Its organ was *Zbirnyk khliborobs'koï Ukraïny*.

Lypynsky's historical research centered on the Cossack revolution of the mid-17th century. He offered the view, in contrast to the populist interpretations of the B. Khmelnytsky period, that that period represented a fundamental stage in the development of Ukrainian statehood. According to Lypynsky the rebirth of the Ukrainian state was conditioned by the following factors: (1) the consolidation of all social strata around the Cossack nucleus, which in the course of the liberation war absorbed the most active elements of all the other estates; (2) the strong influx of the Ukrainian nobility into the Cossack ranks, which at a decisive moment raised the political culture of the Cossacks and enabled the settled, town Cossacks to control the seminomadic Zaporozhian Cossacks; (3) the victory of the nobility-*starshyna* land tenure system, with its intensive *khutir* farming, over the extensive colonial and parasitic farming practiced by Polish magnates on their latifundia; and (4) the Orthodox church's blessing for the liberation war. Lypynsky paid particular attention to the way in which the essentially military organizations were transformed into a territorial government of a monarchic (hereditary) inclination. He regarded the Treaty of Pereiaslav (1654) as a military alliance of Ukraine and Muscovy. Along with S. Tomashivsky and D. Doroshenko Lypynsky founded a new statist school of Ukrainian historiography.

His Ukrainian political program was based on a universal theory that was influenced by a number of contemporary Western (particularly French) thinkers, such as G.

Sorel, V. Pareto, and G. Lebon. According to Lypynsky states arose by conquest, either external or internal. Regardless of their structure all states had a certain quantity of power and an elite which exercised it. For Lypynsky the three sources of power were military (warriors), economic (producers), and intellectual (intelligentsia), of which various combinations were possible. He attributed special politically creative abilities to the warriors and producers and gave the intelligentsia the auxiliary role of articulating the elemental, unconscious strivings of society. His three main kinds of state were classocracy, democracy, and ochlocracy; they were timeless, and appeared in various periods, at various stages of economic development, and in various cultures. Characteristic of a classocracy was the balance between power and liberty, and between conservative and progressive forces; democracy promoted personal freedom; and ochlocracy, the absolutist rule of warriors-nonproducers, suppressed liberty and civic initiative. The three state types succeeded each other with a certain regularity: the classocracy, spoiled by excessive prosperity, degenerated into democracy, which was then destroyed by ochlocracy, and the struggle against ochlocracy gave rise to classocracy. That historical cycle was not, however, deemed deterministic.

Lypynsky rejected the subordination of the church to the state (cesaropapism) and the striving of the clergy for political power (clericalism). Instead he advocated co-operation between the church and the state as two autonomous and equal institutions. The religious theme was omnipresent in his works; he professed that the ultimate purpose of human activity is to realize, as far as possible, the eternal truth in the life of nations. Lypynsky expressed his views on the historical role of the Ukrainian church in *Relihiia i tserkva v istorii Ukrainy* (Religion and Church in the History of Ukraine, 1925, 1933, 1956).

On those foundations he built his Ukrainian political program. He believed that the Ukrainian nation could best be unified on the basis of territorial patriotism, that is, solidarity among all the permanent inhabitants of Ukrainian territories regardless of their social standing, religious faith, ethnic origin, and even national consciousness. The Ukrainian liberation movement had to depend not only on the intelligentsia, but also on the managers of agriculture, industry, and the military. Ukraine would be a common homeland for all; hence, the reassimilation of the denationalized higher social strata was a necessary condition for the revival of Ukrainian statehood. It was more important to have Ukrainian organic class (professional) structures than Ukrainian political parties. Lypynsky was a severe critic of the democratic wing (the UNR camp) and the ochlocratic wing (the Soviet and nationalist movements) in Ukrainian politics. In his opinion only the classocratic system, based on a hereditary and legal 'labor monarchy' in the traditional form of the hetmanate, could meet the needs of Ukrainian state-building.

BIBLIOGRAPHY
Zabarevs'kyi, M. [Doroshenko, D.]. *V'iacheslav Lypyns'kyi i ioho dumky pro ukrains'ku natsiiu ta derzhavu* (Vienna 1925; Augsburg 1946)
V. Lypyns'kyi iak polityk i ideoloh (Uzhhorod 1931)
Dzvony [commemorative issue], 1932, no. 6
Bosyi, V. *V'iacheslav Lypyns'kyi: Ideoloh ukrains'koi trudovoi monarkhii* (Toronto 1951)
Pyziur, Ie. 'Viacheslav Lypyns'kyi i politychna dumka zakhidn'oho svitu,' *Suchasnist'*, 1969, no. 9
Pelenski, J. (ed). *The Political and Social Ideas of Vjačeslav Lypyns'kyj*, special issue of HUS, 9, no. 3/4 (1985)
Rudnytsky, I. 'Viacheslav Lypynsky: Statesman, Historian, and Political Thinker,' in his *Essays in Modern Ukrainian History*, ed P. Rudnytsky (Edmonton 1987)

I.L. Rudnytsky

Lypynsky East European Research Institute

Lypynsky East European Research Institute (Skhidno-evropeiskyi doslidnyi instytut im. V.K. Lypynskoho). A nonprofit research and publishing institution in Philadelphia, founded in 1963 by E. Zyblikewycz, its first president (1963–86), and headed since 1986 by J. Pelenski. The institute houses the personal papers and library of V. *Lypynsky, a major Ukrainian conservative political theorist, historian, and sociologist, as well as the papers of more than 50 prominent historical figures linked to the history of Ukraine since the turn of the century. The most important of these are the personal papers of Hetman P. Skoropadsky. The institute's library has more than 7,000 volumes relating to the social, economic, and political history of Ukraine. The institute has published important government documents, monographs, and the correspondence of various Ukrainian political leaders from the 1914–40 period, the most significant of which are *Ereignisse in der Ukraine 1914–1922* ... (1966–9), editions of the letters of D. Doroshenko (1973) and O. Nazaruk (1976) to Lypynsky, a parallel Polish-Ukrainian edition of Lypynsky's *Stanisław Michał Krzyczewski* ... (1980), and Lypynsky's *Ukraina na perelomi 1657–1659* ... (1991), all of them with long, scholarly introductions and notes.

Lypytsia culture. An archeological culture of the inhabitants of the upper Dniester region from the 1st century BC to the 3rd century AD. Its name is derived from Verkhnia Lypytsia, now a village in Ivano-Frankivske oblast, where the first burial site of this culture was discovered by I. *Kopernicki in 1889. In the 1930s intensive research on the Lypytsia monuments was begun. The remains of semipit and ground dwellings grouped in unfortified settlements along rivers and burial grounds were excavated. The clay, bronze, and glass ware, iron tools and weapons, and bronze ornaments discovered indicate that the inhabitants had close trade ties with the Roman provinces. They practiced communal farming and herding and some hunting and fishing. The ethnic affiliation of the culture is still unclear, but some scholars assert that its people are the direct ancestors of the *Tivertsians.

Lyric poetry (from Greek *lyra*, 'lyre'; hence, a song sung to the accompaniment of a lyre). A literary genre the main purpose of which is to express emotions, not to depict actions or events as in epic poetry or drama. It is difficult to draw a clear line between lyric poetry and epic poetry or drama, for lyrical elements appear in all literary genres – subjective passages in epic poetry and monologues in dramas. The lyrical element plays an important role in Ukrainian folk songs and dumas as well as in the 'poems' of the 17th century – love poems, religious cantos, and the so-called worldly songs. In the 17th and 18th centuries satirical and epigrammatic lyric poetry became widely known, and lyrical features appeared in monologues of religious dramas and baroque homilies. In the Romantic period lyrical verse was even introduced into epic poems; T. Shevchenko and P. Kulish, for example, inserted lyrical passages into their Byronic poems. It also played an important role in the mixed genre known as the ballad. Furthermore, all the imitations of lyrical folk songs, including poetic montages of excerpts from folk songs, were essentially lyrical works. At the same time the role of political lyric poetry, particularly in poems by Kulish, gained importance. The practice of imitating folk songs continued in the period of realism; the most apparent example is the frequent use of songs in plays. Reflective lyric poetry, in which the expression of feeling is combined with reflection, appears in Ukrainian literature much later than in other European literatures. Although reflective lyrical poems are not infrequent in Shevchenko and Kulish, they become prominent only in the work of I. Franko and Lesia Ukrainka. In the period of modernism, as represented by poets such as M. Vorony, M. Cherniavsky, and O. Oles, the Romantic tradition of imitating folk songs was replaced by the use of formally perfected lyrical genres and styles. In postrevolutionary poetry the current of lyric poetry, represented by the early collections of M. Rylsky, P. Tychyna, and others, was exceptionally strong. The rebirth of Ukrainian poetry in the 1960s was marked by a resurgence of lyricism (L. Kostenko, M. Vinhranovsky, and I. Drach). A lyricism of national and social *engagement* developed in the poetry of the 1970s (I. Kalynets, V. Holoborodko).

Beginning in the 17th century, literary lyrical works were in large measure absorbed by the oral folk tradition. Among contemporary folk songs there is a significant number of lyrical works, often considerably altered, of literary origin. The borrowings are not limited to I. Kotlia-revsky's and T. Shevchenko's verses, but include poems of other classical poets and even of lesser poets, such as S. Pysarevsky, M. Petrenko, Ya. Komarnytsky, S. Hulak-Artemovsky, and P. Nishchynsky. Some works of Polish poets, such as T. Padura and K. Cięglewicz, have made their way into the Ukrainian folk tradition.

BIBLIOGRAPHY
Chubinskii, P. *Trudy etnografichesko-statisticheskoi ekspeditsii v Zapadno-Russkii krai*, 7 vols (St Petersburg 1872–9)
Hrushevs'kyi, M. *Istoriia ukraïns'koï literatury*, vol 1 (Kiev 1923)
Zerov, M. *Nove ukraïns'ke pys'menstvo* (Kiev 1924; 2nd edn, Munich 1960)
Bilets'kyi, O. (ed). *Khrestomatiia davn'oï ukraïns'koï literatury: Lirychna poeziia*, 2nd edn (Kiev 1952)
Nud'ha, H. 'Pisni ukraïns'kykh poetiv ta ïkh narodna pererobka,' in *Pisni ta romansy ukraïns'kykh poetiv*, vol 1 (Kiev 1956)
Shakhovskyi, S. *Liryka i liryky* (Kiev 1960)
                                          D. Chyzhevsky

Lyrical songs. The largest and most popular group of Ukrainian *folk songs, they are songs of relatively recent origin expressing the feelings and moods of individuals. The genre developed out of calendric ritual folk poetry, ballads, and laments and became well established in the 16th century. It includes a broad range of themes, and although there is yet no universally accepted classification scheme, lyrical songs are often divided into two groups, songs about social life and songs about family life. The first includes Cossack and serf songs, *recruits' and soldiers' songs, *chumak songs, wanderers' and migrant laborers' songs, and servants' songs. The second group consists of lullabies, love songs, women's songs, and humorous songs. Lyrical songs are usually built in the form of a monologue or dialogue (a conversation between parents and a son or daughter). Poetic devices, such as psychological parallelism, similes, symbols, epithets, and metaphors, are used extensively. Rhythmically, lyrical songs evolved from a free recitative to a syllabic verse and then to regular syllabo-tonic symmetry.

The oldest examples of lyrical songs date from the 16th century, but these examples of genre were not published until the end of the 18th century. They are assigned a particularly important place in 19th- and 20th-century song collections. The more important collections published in and outside Ukraine are *Lira* (The Lyre, 1945), B. Zarevych's *Velykyi spivannyk* (The Great Songbook, nd), and H. Sydorenko's *Ukraïns'ki narodni pisni* (Ukrainian Folk Songs, 3 vols, 1964–7). The Institute of Fine Arts, Folklore, and Ethnography of the AN URSR published a series of song collections including *Pisni Iavdokhy Zuïkhy* (The Songs of Yavdokha Zuikha, 1965), *Zhartivlyvi pisni* (Humorous Songs, 1967), *Tantsiuval'ni pisni* (Dance Songs, 1970), *Rekruts'ki ta soldats'ki pisni* (Recruits' and Soldiers' Songs, 1974), *Naimyts'ki ta zarobitchans'ki pisni* (Servants' and Laborers' Songs, 1975), *Chumats'ki pisni* (Chumak Songs, 1976), *Vesil'ni pisni* (Wedding Songs, 1982), and *Dytiachyi fol'klor* (Children's Folkore, 1984). The more important regional collections of lyrical songs are L. Yashchenko's *Bukovyns'ki narodni pisni* (Bukovynian Folk Songs, 1964), Z. Vasylenko's *Zakarpats'ki narodni pisni* (Transcarpathian Folk Songs, 1962), V. Goshovsky's *Narodnye pesni Zakarpat'ia* (Folk Songs of Transcarpathia, 1971), N. Prysiazhniuk's *Pisni Podillia* (Songs of Podilia, 1976), and Yu. Kostiuk, Yu. Tsymbor, and A. Duleba's *Ukraïns'ki narodni pisni Skhidnoï Slovachchyny* (Ukrainian Folk Songs of Eastern Slovakia, 3 vols, 1958–77)

M. Mushynka

Lys Mykyta

Yurii Lysan

Lys Mykyta (Fox Mykyta). A magazine of humor and satire published and edited from 1947 to 1990 by E. *Kozak, who was also its principal caricaturist and cartoonist. Its name is taken from I. Franko's famous book of fables in verse about a wily fox. Originally a semimonthly, until March 1949 *Lys Mykyta* was published in Munich. Interrupted during Kozak's emigration to the United States, it reappeared in New York City in 1950 under the abbreviated title *Lys* (until April 1951). From November 1951 *Lys Mykyta* was published in Detroit, first as a semimonthly to the end of 1953, then once every three weeks, and then monthly from 1957. It satirized Ukrainian émigré life and politics and was especially biting in its portrayal of Soviet rule in Ukraine. Among its contributors were I. Kernytsky, B. Nyzhankivsky, S. Ryndyk, M. Ponedilok, M. Levytsky, I. Manylo, O. Smotrych, B. Oleksandriv, and Z. Kohut.

Lysak, Adriane (née Sobchyshyn), b 9 October 1930 in Yavoriv, Galicia. Painter and graphic artist. A postwar refugee, she started her art studies at the School of Applied Arts in Graz, Austria. After emigrating to Canada in 1949, she studied at the Sir George Williams School of Arts (1952–3) and L'Ecole des beaux arts (1963–6) in Montreal. Since 1961 she has participated in over 60 group shows in Canada, the United States, and France, where she received an honorary diploma at the 1973 Salon International des Arts Libres. Solo exhibitions of her works have been held in Toronto (1965), Montreal (1965, 1973, 1974), Detroit (1970, 1974), Winnipeg (1974), and New York (1980). Lysak is a versatile artist who uses many techniques and combines real objects with geometric forms to create sophisticated plays of real and abstract elements.

Lysan, Yurii, b 1874, d 1946. Bukovynian political and civic leader. As mayor (1910–14) of Vashkivtsi he promoted Ukrainian civic life and education and was instrumental in establishing a Realgymnasium there in 1912. A candidate of the National Democratic party, he was elected to the Bukovynian Diet (1911–18). After the First World War he was a founder of the Ukrainian People's Organization (1922) and then of the Ukrainian National party

(1927–8) in Bukovyna. As a member of the Rumanian Senate in 1926–7, he protested against the government's policy of Rumanianization.

Lysenko. A Cossack *starshyna* family in Left-Bank Ukraine in the 17th and 18th centuries. Ivan Lysenko (d 1699) was colonel of Chernihiv regiment (1669–71), envoy of the general *starshyna* to Moscow (1672), general osaul (1672–8) of the Hetman state, colonel of Pereiaslav regiment (1677–8, 1690–2), and a participant in the Chyhyryn (1687), Crimean (1689), and Azov (1696) campaigns. His son, Fedir Lysenko (d 1751), was a general osaul (1728–41) and general judge (1741–51). The composer Mykola *Lysenko was a descendant of the family.

Lysenko, Andrii, b 1851 in Zhovnyne, Zolotonosha county, Poltava gubernia, d 10 June 1910 in Sviatoshyne, Kiev county. Civic and revolutionary figure; brother of Mykola *Lysenko. A physician by profession, he took part in the Revolution of 1905 as a supporter of the Bolshevik Russian Social Democratic Workers' party and was deported to Viatka. He fled abroad and lived in Switzerland and Galicia. He contributed to the Ukrainian press.

Lysenko (Hurevych), Liudmyla, b 20 November 1934 in Taman, Krasnodar krai, RSFSR. Champion runner. A graduate of the Kiev Institute of Physical Culture (1960), in 1960 she set an Olympic and world record in the women's 800-m race. She set two world, two Soviet, and five Ukrainian records in the 800-m in the years 1955–63 and was the USSR champion in women's cross-country in 1960 and 1964.

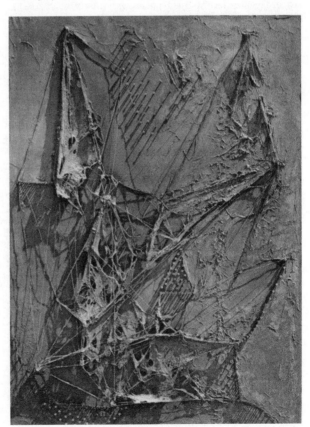

Adriane Lysak: *Cobwebs of Vikings* (relief)

Lysenko, Mariana, 1887–1946. Pianist; daughter of Mykola *Lysenko. She was a lecturer as well as director of the Lysenko Music and Drama Institute in Kiev (1912–8) and concertmaster at the Kiev and Lviv (1939–44) operas. She wrote the textbook *Shkola navchannia na fortepiano* (A School for Teaching Piano).

Mykhailo Lysenko: In *the Torture Chamber of Fascism* (fragment, plaster, 1935)

Lysenko, Mykhailo, b 29 October 1906 in Shpylivka, Sumy county, Kharkiv gubernia, d 8 May 1972 in Kiev. Sculptor; full member of the USSR Academy of Arts from 1970. He studied at the Kharkiv Art Institute (1926–31) and taught there (1938–41) and at the Kiev State Art Institute (1944–72). He executed many sculptural portraits, monuments, and socialist-realist compositions, usually in collaboration with others. They include the high reliefs *Heroism of the Civil War* and *Heroism of Socialist Construction* for the USSR pavilion at the 1939 New York World's Fair; the compositions *China Rises Up* (1933), *Partisan Raid* (1947), and *Loyalty* (1947); monuments to S. Kovpak (1971), V. Lenin (1964), M. Shchors (1954), and other Bolshevik leaders, in various towns; the memorial complex at the Kholm Slavy military cemetery in Lviv (1958); and the Babyn Yar memorial in Kiev (1976). Books about him were published in Kiev in 1958 and 1975.

Lysenko, Mykola, b 22 March 1842 in Hrynky, Kremenchuk county, Poltava gubernia, d 6 November 1912 in Kiev. Composer, ethnomusicologist, conductor, pianist, teacher, and community figure. The descendant of an aristocratic Cossack family, he acquired the rudiments of piano playing from his mother and gained a strong appreciation of Ukrainian music and Cossack lore from his grandparents. From 1860 he studied at Kharkiv and Kiev universities, graduating in 1865 with a degree in natural sciences. His stay in Kiev, his activities in the *Hromada of Kiev, and his close relationships with his cousin M. *Starytsky, and with V. *Antonovych, T. *Rylsky, and others, led Lysenko to make a strong personal commitment to the study and development of Ukrainian music. He worked for two years as an arbitrator in Tarashcha county, then furthered his music studies in Leipzig (1867–9) under K. Reinecke and E. Richter. After returning to Kiev in 1869 to work as a music teacher and conductor, he

Mykola Lysenko

moved to St Petersburg (1874–6) to study orchestration under N. Rimsky-Korsakov; then he returned to Kiev in 1904 to open his own school of music and drama.

At the time, Lysenko was at the center of Ukrainian cultural and musical life in Kiev. He gave piano recitals and organized choirs for performances in Kiev and tours through Ukraine in 1893, 1897, 1899, and 1902. He cultivated an informal network of patriotic Ukrainians, and headed the *Ukrainian Club from 1908. He also maintained close ties with community leaders in Western Ukraine from as early as 1867, most notably with I. Franko.

Lysenko's musical compositions were numerou and varied. His operatic works include the singspiel *Chornomortsi* (Black Sea Cossacks, 1872); the operetta *Natalka from Poltava* (1889); the operas (based on works by N. Gogol) *Christmas Night* (1873–82), *Utoplena* (The Drowned Maiden, 1883), and *Taras Bulba* (1890); the operetta *Aeneid* (1911); the miniature opera *Nocturne*; and three operas for children: *Koza Dereza* (Billy Goat's Bluff, 1888), *Pan Kots'kyi* (Sir Catsky, 1891), and *Winter and Spring* (1892). Other theatrical musical works include *Sappho* (1886–94), which is composed of scenes from life in ancient Greece, and music for W. Shakespeare's *Hamlet*.

An eminent concert pianist, Lysenko wrote many compositions for the piano. These works include a sonata, two rhapsodies, a suite, a scherzo, and a rondo, as well as a long list of smaller forms such as 'Songs without Words,' nocturnes, waltzes, and polonaises. In these works he often uses the melodies and rhythms of Ukrainian folk songs. In some, F. Chopin's influence is noticeable. In the field of chamber music, Lysenko wrote many works for violin and piano as well as a trio for two violins and viola and a string quartet. He also wrote a symphony (unfinished) and a symphonic fantasia.

Settings of words by T. Shevchenko occupy a special place in Lysenko's works. The settings include solo songs, choral works, and cantatas for choir and orchestra, such as *Raduisia nyvo nepolytaia* (Rejoice, Unwatered Field), *Biut' porohy* (The Rapids Roar), and *Na vichnu pam'iat' Kotliarevs'komu* (To the Eternal Memory of Kotliarevsky). Shevchenko's collection *Kobzar* particularly fascinated Lysenko, who composed music for 82 of its texts. He also wrote many vocal solos with piano accompaniment to the poems of I. Franko, Lesia Ukrainka, O. Oles, H. Heine, A. Mickiewicz, and others.

From an early age Lysenko displayed an interest in musical folklore. While still in school he began transcribing Ukrainian folk songs, and when working in Tarashcha

Title page of Mykola Lysenko's cantata, *Jan Hus* (design by Yuliian Pankevych, 1888)

county he recorded the wedding songs of the Pereiaslav region and the dumas and songs performed by the renowned kobzar O. *Veresai. Lysenko's ethnomusicological works include *Kharakterystyka muzychnykh pytomennostei ukraïns'kykh dum i pisen', vykonuvanykh kobzarem O. Veresaiem* (Characterization of the Musical Traits of Ukrainian Dumas and Songs, Performed by the Kobzar O. Veresai, 1874; repr 1955) and *Narodni muzychni instrumenty na Ukraïni* (Folk Musical Instruments in Ukraine, 1894; repr 1955). He also published several collections of folk songs.

Over his lifetime Lysenko arranged approx 500 folk songs, including both solos and choruses with piano accompaniment, and a cappella choruses. He concentrated on tonal and harmonic particularities of Ukrainian folk songs, selecting appropriate means for the arrangement of various types of songs and preserving the folk style of melodizing.

Lysenko was the founder of the national movement in Ukrainian music, based on a specific Ukrainian cultural tradition and the originality of its folk music. His prolific and versatile life's work became the foundation for the further development and expansion of Ukrainian musical culture. Lysenko influenced a large group of Ukrainian composers, including K. Stetsenko, Ya. Stepovy, M. Leontovych, O. Koshyts, S. Liudkevych, L. Revutsky, and M. Verykivsky.

A compilation of Lysenko's works was published in 20 volumes in Kiev in 1950–9.

BIBLIOGRAPHY
Zbirnyk Muzeiu diiachiv nauky ta mystetstva Ukraïny (Kiev 1930)
Lysenko, O. *M.V. Lysenko: Spohady syna* (Kiev 1959, 1966)
Arkhimovych, L.; Hordiichuk, M. *Mykola Vitaliiovych Lysenko: Zhyttia i tvorchist'* (Kiev 1963)
Rudnyts'kyi, A. *Ukraïns'ka muzyka* (Munich 1963)
Zahaikevych, M. (ed). *Mykola Lysenko: Borets' za narodnist' i realizm u mystetstvi* (Kiev 1965)
Lysenko, O. (ed). *M.V. Lysenko u spohadakh suchasnykiv* (Kiev 1968)
Vasylenko, Z. *Fol'klorystychna diial'nist' M.V. Lysenka* (Kiev 1972)
Bulat, T. *M. Lysenko* (Kiev 1973)
Tovstukha, Ie. *Mykola Lysenko: Opovidi pro kompozytora* (Kiev 1988)

W. Wytwycky

Lysenko, Ostap, b 13 July 1885 in Kiev, d 1 October 1968 in Kiev. Musical scholar; son of Mykola *Lysenko. After graduating from the Lysenko Music and Drama Institute in Kiev in 1930, he taught at music schools in Kiev until 1941, when he reorganized the Kiev Conservatory and became its director. He later lectured at the Lviv (1945–51) and Kiev (1951–68) conservatories. He edited the collections *Neopublikovani vokal'ni tvory M. Lysenka* (The Unpublished Vocal Works of M. Lysenko, 1967) and *M.V. Lysenko u spohadakh suchasnykiv* (M.V. Lysenko in the Memoirs of His Contemporaries, 1968) and was instrumental in steering through publication a complete rendition of his father's works during the 1950s. He is also the author of the memoirs *M.V. Lysenko: Spohady syna* (M.V. Lysenko: A Son's Memoirs, 1959, 1966).

Lysenko, Sofiia, b 1865 in the Poltava region, d 10 November 1946 in Baku, Azerbadzhan. Opera singer (soprano). She learned singing by taking private lessons in St Petersburg and Italy. In 1887–91 she appeared in operas in Milan and Venice, and in 1891–3 sang as a soloist with the Kharkiv Opera. She appeared on stage in Moscow, St Petersburg, and Kiev. From 1912 she taught music in St Petersburg and Baku. Her main roles were Tamara in A. Rubinstein's *Demon*, Rosina in G. Rossini's *Barber of Seville*, and Dinorah in G. Meyerbeer's *Dinorah*.

Trokhym Lysenko

Lysenko, Trokhym [Lysenko, Troxym], b 29 September 1898 in Karlivka, Kostiantynohrad county, Poltava gubernia, d 20 November 1976 in Moscow. Agronomist and agrobiologist; full member of the AN URSR (now ANU) from 1934 and the USSR Academy of Sciences from 1939; head of the Michurinist trend in Soviet biology. Lysenko attended horticultural schools in Poltava (1913) and Uman (1917–20) and studied agronomy at the Kiev Agricultural Institute (1921–5). He rose to prominence in 1925–9 while posted in Azerbaidzhan, by publishing an article (1928) on the relationship between cold temperatures and late ripening, suggesting that it was possible to produce desirable characteristics by manipulating growing conditions. He experimented with winter wheat on his father's farm (1928–9) by burying germinating seeds in snow, and this measure reportedly led to greatly increased yields. Lysenko termed this procedure 'vernalization' (*yarovizatsiia*). In 1929 he was given a laboratory in the physiology division of the All-Union Selection and Genetics Institute in Odessa. To popularize his work, in 1931 the USSR Ministry of Agriculture created the journal *Biuleten' iarovizatsii* (renamed *Iarovizatsiia* in 1935 and *Agrobiologiia* in 1946).

During the heyday of Soviet 'vernalization' (1929–35) Lysenko devised similar techniques and applied them to a wide range of vegetables, fruits, and grains. He and his supporters made extravagant claims for the efficacy of his techniques, and 'vernalization' was reportedly used for many millions of hectares of crops in the early 1930s. For this work, in 1934 Lysenko became scientific director of the All-Union Institute of Genetics and Selection in Odessa and a full member of the Ukrainian Academy of Sciences. He led similar campaigns for the summer planting of potatoes (1935) and maize (1956), for grafting or 'vegetative hybridization' (late 1930s), for the 'grassland system' of planting (1939–52) and the 'cluster method' of forestation (1948–52), and for increasing the butterfat content in milk (1958–62).

In 1935 Lysenko joined forces with the Leningrad lawyer and philosopher I. Prezent and began to elaborate his agronomic practices into a theoretical framework with heavy ideological content. In pamphlets the two asserted that, with alteration in the conditions at the end of a developmental stage, the heredity of a plant could be destabilized or 'cracked,' and the plant thereby rendered plastic and malleable. Following the death of the plant breeder I. Michurin in 1935, Lysenko declared himself the heir to Michurin's tradition and named his own approach 'Michurinist biology,' as a contrast to the approach of G. Mendel and A. Weismann's genetics, a 'bourgeois capitalist science.' Lysenko was a member of the USSR government's Central Executive Committee (1935–7) and assistant to the president of the council of the Supreme Soviet (1937–50).

In 1935 N. *Vavilov was removed as president of the All-Union Academy of Agricultural Sciences (VASKhNIL), and Lysenko was elected a full member; the next year he was put in charge of its Odessa Institute. Lysenko assumed the president's post of VASKhNIL in 1938 and held it for almost two decades. With the help of the NKVD he used his position to harass and undermine Vavilov's supporters. After Vavilov's arrest in August 1940, Lysenko left Odessa to replace him as director of the academy's Institute of Genetics in Moscow, a post he held until 1965.

In 1948–9 the massive Soviet reforestation program made use of Lysenko's cluster method of planting and sustained extensive losses. Lysenko was forced to resign as president of VASKhNIL in 1956. By late 1958 he had embraced N. Khrushchev's agricultural policy, and he gained influence in the subsequent development of Khrushchev's agricultural program. In 1961–2 Lysenko was again briefly president of VASKhNIL. After Khrushchev's ouster a joint commission of the Ministry of Agriculture and the two academies investigated Lysenko's Lenin Hills experimental farm. It concluded that his experimental work had been carried out and tested improperly, and that all of his agricultural techniques were either ineffective or harmful. Lysenko was removed as director of the Institute of Genetics (1965), and it was officially disbanded, but he kept control of his Lenin Hills farm until his death.

BIBLIOGRAPHY
Huxley, J. *Heredity East and West* (New York 1949)
Zirkle, C. (ed). *Death of a Science in Russia* (Philadelphia 1949)
Safonov, V. *Land in Bloom* (Moscow 1951)
Zirkle, C. *Evolution, Marxian Biology, and the Social Scene* (Philadelphia 1959)
Medvedev, Zh. *The Rise and Fall of T.D. Lysenko* (New York 1969)
Joravsky, D. *The Lysenko Affair* (Cambridge, Mass 1970)
Lecourt, D. *Lysenko: Histoire réelle d'une 'science prolétarienne'* (Paris 1976)
Buican, D. *L'éternel retour de Lyssenko* (Paris 1978)
Regelmann, J-P. *Die Geschichte des Lyssenkoismus* (Frankfurt 1980)
Popovsky, M. *The Vavilov Affair* (Hamden, Conn 1984)
Roll-Hansen, N. *Onsketenkning som vitenskap: Lysenkos innmarsji sovjetisk biologii, 1927–37* (Oslo 1985)

M. Adams

Vera Lysenko

Lysenko, Vera (pseud of Vera Lesik, who also wrote under the name of Luba Novack), b 7 August 1910 in Winnipeg, d 20 October 1975 in Toronto. Writer; daughter of Ukrainian immigrants from Kiev gubernia. Lysenko graduated from the University of Manitoba (BA, 1930). She moved to eastern Canada in 1936 and worked for *Magazine Digest* in Toronto and for the Windsor *Star*. During and immediately after the Second World War she researched and wrote *Men in Sheepskin Coats: A Study in Assimilation* (1947), a popular examination of Ukrainian-Canadian life from the perspective of the pro-communist *Association of United Ukrainian Canadians. She also wrote two novels, *Yellow Boots* (1954, repub 1992), the story of a Ukrainian-Canadian girl who sacrifices everything for material success, and *Westerly Wild* (1956), a melodramatic tale of life in rural western Canada during the 1930s. She did not publish after 1956.

Lysenko, Yurii (Heorhii), b 21 April 1910 in Valiava, Cherkasy county, Kiev gubernia. Actor and stage and film director. A graduate of the Kiev Institute of Theater Arts (1940), he worked as an actor and the chief stage director in Volhynia, Melitopil, and Poltava theaters. In 1957 he began directing films at the Kiev Artistic Film Studio, where in 1978 he became artistic director of the film actors' theater. Among his films are *Iak by kaminnia hovorylo* (If the Stones Talked, 1957, based on a story by I. Franko), *Tavriia* (1959, based on a novel by O. Honchar), *Hroza nad poliamy* (A Storm over the Fields, 1959, based on a novel by A. Shyian), *Litak vidlitaie o 9-tii* (The Plane Leaves at 9, 1960), *Perevireno – min nemaie* (Confirmed, There Are No Mines, 1965), *Vohon'* (The Fire, 1974), and *Bilyi kruh* (The White Circle, 1975).

Lysenko Chorus. A choir established as the Canadian Ukrainian Opera Chorus in 1974 in Toronto under the auspices of the Canadian Ukrainian Opera Association; it was renamed in 1990. Its artistic director is V. *Kolesnyk, and its choirmaster, Z. *Lawryshyn. A mixed chorus numbering 60 voices, it has performed full and concert versions of operas by Ukrainian and Canadian composers in many North American cities. In 1979 the Lysenko Chorus premiered in the Western world A. Vakhnianyn's opera *Kupalo*. It has also performed world premieres of *Symphony No. 4* and *Concerto-Cantata for Piano and Chorus* by G. Fiala and the North American premiere of S. Liudkevych's symphony-cantata *Kavkaz*. In 1991 it staged a concert version of D. Sichynsky's opera *Roksoliana* in Toronto.

Lysenko Higher Institute of Music (Vyshchyi muzychnyi instytut im. M. Lysenka). A school formed in 1903 by the *Lysenko Music Society in Lviv. An institute from 1907, it was an important training facility for Ukrainian musicians in Galicia. It grew from 6 teachers with 50 pupils in 1907 to 25 teachers with 248 pupils in 1935. Its directors included A. *Vakhnianyn (1903–8), S. *Liudkevych (1908–15), and V. *Barvinsky (1916–40). The institute began establishing branches in 1911 and eventually formed nine of them (Peremyshl, Stanyslaviv, Stryi, Drohobych, Kolomyia, Ternopil, Zolochiv, Drohobych, and Boryslav). In 1935 the branches employed 30 teachers with approx 350 pupils. The institute had its own building in Lviv from 1916 and published *Muzychnyi vistnyk* (The Music Bulletin) bimonthly. In 1940 it was amalgamated with the *Lviv Conservatory, and its branches were turned into independent music schools. Its structures and ethos later provided a model for the establishment of Ukrainian *music education societies in the West after the Second World War.

Lysenko Music and Drama Institute (Muzychno-dramatychnyi instytut im. M. Lysenka). A music school established in 1918 in Kiev, succeeding the *Lysenko Music and Drama School. The institute served as a major training center for many of the most promising musical and stage talents in Soviet Ukraine. It functioned until 1934, when it was restructured as the *Kiev Conservatory and the *Kiev Institute of Theater Arts. Musicians such as K. Stetsenko, M. Leontovych, M. Mykysha, P. Kozytsky, and D. Revutsky, and theater directors such as L. Kurbas, I. Stadnyk, and M. Starytska, taught at the institute.

Lysenko Music and Drama School (Muzychno-dramatychna shkola im. M. Lysenka). A school established in Kiev 1904 by Mykola Lysenko to foster the development of Ukrainian music. Lysenko financed the project with funds originally gathered by his supporters to buy him a country house for his 35th jubilee celebration. The school's curriculum was on the level of a conservatory, and there was a separate drama department and a museum of Ukrainian folk instruments. The school was directed initially by Lysenko and then by his daughter Mariana (1912–18). Teachers included Lysenko, H. Liubomyrsky, O. Myshuha, and M. Starytska. The school was the only Ukrainian higher music school of its day, and its influence in the development of Ukrainian music is reflected in the list of its graduates, which includes K. Stetsenko, O. Koshyts, L. Revutsky, and M. Mykysha. In 1918 the school was reorganized and renamed the *Lysenko Music and Drama Institute.

Lysenko Music Society in Lviv (Muzychne tovarystvo im. M. Lysenka u Lvovi). A society founded in 1903 to promote the development of Ukrainian music in Western Ukraine. Its original name, the Union of Song and Music Societies, was changed in 1907 to honor the work of Mykola *Lysenko. The group's first president was V. Shukhevych. Other leaders included V. Barvinsky, S. Liudkevych, and N. Nyzhankivsky. The society sponsored concerts, competitions, and the publication of music. Its most significant undertaking was the running of a music school that eventually developed into the *Lysenko Higher Institute of Music.

Lysenko String Quartet (Kvartet im. M. Lysenka). A musical instrumental ensemble formed in Kiev in 1951 and named in honor of Mykola Lysenko in 1962. In 1989 members of the ensemble were A. Bazhenov and B. Skvortsov (violins), Yu. Kholodov (viola), and L. Krasnoshchok (cello). The ensemble has recorded works by D. Bortniansky, Lysenko, B. Liatoshynsky, and V. Barvinsky on the Melodiya label and has performed world premieres of works by S. Liudkevych, B. Liatoshynsky, A. Shtoharenko, A. Filipenko, P. Kozytsky, and A. Kos-Anatolsky. The ensemble's large repertoire (more than 250 works) testifies to its creative range and its efforts to familiarize listeners with various schools and styles. The quartet is equally at home with L. van Beethoven, D. Shostakovich, M. Skoryk, Ye. Stankovych, L. Dychko, and V. Sylvestrov.

Lysiak, Mariia [Lysjak, Marija], b 18 July 1916 in Monastyryska, Buchach county, Galicia. Heroic and character actress and singer. She worked in Y. Stadnyk's touring theaters (1935–9), in the Lviv Theater of Opera and Ballet and with Veselyi Lviv (1939–44), and in the Ukrainian theater in Aschaffenburg, Germany (1946–7). Since moving to the United States in 1949, she has appeared in productions of the Veselyi Lviv (1959–66) and Teatr u Piatnytsiu (1968–71) theaters.

Oleh Lysiak

Lysiak, Oleh [Lysjak], b 27 July 1912 in Lviv. Journalist and writer. He was a member of the press corps of the Division Galizien in 1943–5, and after the war he worked in Munich as an editor of the émigré papers *Ukraïns'ka trybuna* (1946–8) and *Ukraïns'kyi samostiinyk* (1950–2) and also edited there *Visti Bratstva kolyshnikh voiakiv I Ukraïns'koï dyviziï Ukraïns'koï Natsional'noï Armiï* (1950–2). After emigrating to Philadelphia in 1953, he worked for the paper *Ameryka* (1953–7) and contributed feuilletons and articles to other Ukrainian émigré periodicals. Lysiak also wrote two novels about his comrades-in-arms and Galician contemporaries, *Za strilets'kyi zvychai* (The Rifleman's Way, 1953) and *Liudy taki, iak my* (People like Us, 1960), and edited a collection of articles about the Division Galizien, *Brody* (1951).

Pavlo Lysiak   Borys Lysiansky

Lysiak, Pavlo [Lysjak], b 10 March 1887 in Uhniv, Rava Ruska county, Galicia, d 8 January 1948 in Wattenscheid, West Germany. Lawyer, civic and political figure, and publicist; husband of M. Rudnytska and father of I. Lysiak Rudnytsky. As a student of law, economics, and political science at Lviv and Berlin universities he was active in the student movement. After the First World War he edited *Ukraïns'kyi prapor* in Vienna (1919–21) and the monthly *Natio* (1926) in Warsaw. Upon his return to Galicia he practiced law in Zhuravno, near Stryi (1927–39), and in 1938 he was elected as a candidate of the Ukrainian National Democratic Alliance to the Polish Sejm. During the Second World War he practiced law in Cracow (1940–4) and then emigrated to Germany, where he served in Goslar as president of the Regional Representation of the Ukrainian Emigration in the British zone. A brilliant editor and journalist, he contributed many articles, particularly on economics and Soviet policy in Ukraine, to such papers as *Dilo, Novyi chas* (which he briefly edited), and *Krakivs'ki visti* and wrote the booklet *Nasha natsional'na polityka i ostannii Narodnii Z'ïzd* (Our Nationality Policy and the Last Popular Congress, 1938).

Lysiak-Rudnytsky, Ivan. See Rudnytsky, Ivan Lysiak.

Lysianka [Lysjanka]. IV-11. A town smt (1990 pop 8,900) on the Hnylyi Tikych River and a raion center in Cherkasy oblast. It is first mentioned in a historical document in 1593. Lysianka was granted the rights of *Magdeburg law in 1622, and a castle was built there afterward. The town played an important role in the Cossack-Polish War of 1648–57, the popular uprisings against the Poles in 1664–5, and the haidamaka revolt of 1768. In 1674 the town was captured and almost razed by the Turks. Today Lysianka has a bakery, a mixed-feed factory, and a regional museum.

Lysiansky, Borys [Lysjans'kyj], b 22 September 1892 on Mezynivka *khutir* in Zvenyhorodka county, Kiev gubernia, d 7 September 1952 in Aulnay-sous-Bois, France. Physicist. An interwar émigré, from 1922 he chaired the physics department and Terminological Commission of the Engineering Faculty at the Ukrainian Husbandry Academy (later Ukrainian Technical Husbandry Institute) in Poděbrady, Bohemia. A specialist in electric and radio technology, he wrote five volumes of lectures (1923, 1925–6) for use by the academy's students, a biography of V. Samiilenko (1926), and articles on civic and political subjects. As a postwar refugee in Germany, he published the poetry collection *Pro patria* (1948). From 1950 he lived in France, where he was secretary of the Metropolitan Council of the Ukrainian Autocephalous Orthodox church.

Lysiansky, Yurii [Lysjans'kyj, Jurij], b 13 August 1773 in Nizhen, d 6 March 1837 in St Petersburg. Explorer and captain in the Russian navy. He completed naval training in the Kronstadt Naval Academy in 1786. In 1788–90 he took part in battles in the Baltic Sea. With the Estonian A. Krusenstern Lysiansky organized the first Russian expedition around the world on the *Neva* and the *Nadezhda* (1830–6). Lysiansky commanded the *Neva*, which followed the route Kronstadt–Cape Horn–Hawaii–Alaska–Canton–Cape of Good Hope–Kronstadt. His numerous oceanographic and ethnographic findings and the navigational charts made by him were published in 1812 as *Puteshestvie vokrug sveta na korable 'Neva' v 1803–1806 godakh* and appeared in English in 1914 as *Voyage round the World on the Ship 'Neva' in 1803–1806*. An island near the shore in the Sea of Okhotsk and a mountain on the island of Sakhalin have been named after Lysiansky.

Lysin, Borys, b 4 August 1883 in Novohrad-Volynskyi, Volhynia gubernia, d 22 November 1970 in Kiev. Chemical engineer; full member of the AN URSR (now ANU) from 1939. He graduated from the Kiev Polytechnical Institute (1909) and taught there until 1956. He studied the methods of processing and the properties of raw silicates, clays, cements, and other building materials and researched the faience industry in Ukraine.

Kalenyk Lysiuk   Zinovii Lysko

Lysiuk, Kalenyk [Lysjuk] (also Lissiuk; real name: Lepykash, Vasyl), b 18 August 1889 in Bubnivka, Haisyn county, Podilia gubernia, d 12 August 1980 in Chicago. Revolutionary, civic leader, and philanthropist. In 1909 he was sentenced to 20 years' imprisonment for participating in an assassination plot, but he escaped within eighteen months. During the First World War he served in the Russian army, and during the revolutionary period (1917–20), in the UNR Army. After emigrating to the United States in 1923, he sold rare postage stamps and later set up a manufacturing and an investment firm. He donated some of his expanding profits to Ukrainian cultural and charitable institutions, such as the Ukrainian Scientific Institute in Berlin, the Ukrainian Husbandry Academy in Poděbrady, the Ukrainian Invalids' Home in Lviv, and the Museum of Ukraine's Struggle for Independence in Prague. In 1954 he founded the Ukrainian National Museum in Ontario, California; he served as its president until it was merged four years later with the Ukrainian National Museum in Chicago. In 1958 he set up the Ukrainian-American Foundation. He published the bilingual journal *Our News* (1940) and the museum quarterly *Na slidakh* (1955–6), compiled three stamp catalogues, and wrote several political pamphlets.

Lysko, Zinovii [Lys'ko, Zinovij], b 11 November 1895 in Rakobovty, Kaminka Strumylova county, Galicia, d 3 June 1969 in New York. Musicologist and composer. A former Sich Rifleman, he studied composition privately in Lviv under V. Barvinsky and in Prague under F. Yakymenko, then musicology under Z. Nejedlý in Prague at Charles University (1926); he completed a doctorate (1929) at the Ukrainian Free University with a dissertation on S. Hulak-Artemovsky's opera *Zaporozhian Cossack beyond the Danube*. He also studied at the Prague Conservatory under J. Suk. He taught at the Kharkiv Conservatory and in Lviv at the Conservatory and the Lysenko Higher Institute of Music. After the Second World War he lived in Germany and (from 1960) the United States, where he taught at and was president of the *Ukrainian Music Institute of America.

Lysko's compositions are in the modern style and include orchestra, chamber, and piano works, as well as works for chorus and arrangements of Ukrainian folk songs. His writings include *Muzychnyi slovnyk* (Music Dictionary, 1933), *Ukraïns'kyi muzychnyi leksykon* (Ukrainian Music Lexicon, 1947), and other reference works, bio-historical studies, textbooks, and articles on folk music. He was editor-in-chief of the journal *Ukraïnska muzyka* (1937–9) and compiler of *Spivanyk Chervonoï kalyny* (The Chervona Kalyna Songbook, 1937), which contained arrangements of Ukrainian songs for chorus. He also edited and published the religious works of O. *Koshyts (1970). Lysko's magnum opus was his collection, analysis, and systematization of 11,447 Ukrainian folk songs in the 10-volume *Ukraïns'ki narodni melodiï* (Ukrainian Folk Melodies, 1967–86 [vols 1–8]), the largest collected body of folk songs from Eastern Europe. This undertaking took nearly 15 years to complete (1947–61) and represents the culmination of Lysko's lifelong interest in Ukrainian folk music.

R. Savytsky

Lysohir, Mariia. See Lesawyer, Mary.

Lysonia. A hill lying approx 4 km southeast of *Berezhany, situated between the valley of the Zolota Lypa River and its left-bank tributary, the Tsenivka. From September 1916 to July 1917 the front line between the Austro-Hungarian and Russian armies ran through this area. On 2–4 September 1916 the Ukrainian Sich Riflemen fought the Russian army there, and on 18 June 1919 the Ukrainian Galician Army defeated the Poles there.

Lysonia (3rd) Group of the Ukrainian Insurgent Army (Ternopilska [3] hrupa UPA Lysonia). A division of the UPA-West comprising combat units operating on the sparsely forested territory of the Third Military District (covering Ternopil oblast). Organized in 1943, units of the Lysonia Group fought their first battle with the Germans on 16 December 1943 in Koropets raion. By 1944 the Lysonia Group numbered at least 12 rifle companies and conducted its own school for noncommissioned officers. In the summer of 1944 most of the group moved temporarily into the Carpathian Mountains to avoid the German-Soviet front line, which came to a halt in the middle of Ternopil oblast. In August some of the returning companies were grouped into battalions and launched a series of raids against the NKVD. In September O. Polovy's brigade, consisting of two UPA battalions, fought several engagements in Berezhany county and then set off on a raid to Volhynia. Along the way it fought pitched battles on 24 September in Pochaiv raion and on 27 September in Zboriv raion. The largest battle in the district occurred on 30 September near Univ, Peremyshliany raion, when D. *Karpenko's battalion pushed back a motorized NKVD brigade. In November 1944 Bystry's battalion set out on a raid from the Berezhany area through southern Galicia into Bukovyna, where it crossed the Dniester River and fought a major battle on 29 November.

In 1945 the Third Military District was restructured and divided into four tactical sectors, numbered from 16 to 19. The number of combat units was reduced, and they were assigned to specific sectors. During the summer of 1947 the last three companies were demobilized, and their soldiers were reassigned to the armed underground. The commanders of the Lysonia Group were Lt O. Polovy (nom de guerre: Ostap, 1943–5) and Maj V. Yakubovsky (nom de guerre: Bondarenko, 1945–7).

P. Sodol

Lysovets, Demian [Lysovec', Dem'jan], b ?, d November 1654. Cossack officer. A close associate of Hetman B. Khmelnytsky, he served as his general osaul (1649–54) and as acting hetman in the Don (1650), Polish (1651), Moldavian, and Podilian (1653) campaigns. In 1654 Khmelnytsky sent him as a diplomatic envoy to Moldavia and Wallachia. He was also an adviser to T. Khmelnytsky.

Lyst. A legal document issued by the grand duke of the Grand Duchy of Lithuania. The *sudebnik* codified under Casimir IV Jagiellończyk in 1468 was called a *lyst*. Along with charters of privilege, *lysty* were a source of private rights. Documents of guaranty were also known as *lysty*: *zaliznyi lyst* was a safe-conduct and *lysty davaty* in the Cossack period meant 'to recommend.' In the Hetman state, *lysty* were the documents issued to regimental *starshyna* confirming their ownership of land.

Lystopad (November). A literary group of young nationalist writers which met in Lviv in 1928–31. Among its members were R. Drahan, V. Kovalchuk, B. Kravtsiv, S. Lenkavsky, R. Olhovych, Ye. Pelensky, Zh. Protsyshyn, and V. Yaniv. The members published a collective volume, *Litavry* (Kettledrums), and contributed to *Literaturno-naukovyi vistnyk*.

Lysty do pryiateliv (Letters to Friends). A journal of politics, history, and culture, published as a monthly

Lysty do pryiateliv

Volodymyr Lysy

Yurii Lytvyn

(March 1953–December 1960), bimonthly (January 1961–April 1965), and trimonthly (May 1965–December 1967) in New York City. Its founder and chief editor was M. *Shlemkevych; after his death in February 1966 the journal was edited by V. Rudko and then by an editorial board consisting of D. Kuzyk, M. Stepanenko, and O. Tarnavsky. *Lysty do pryiateliv* contained essays and reports on a wide range of developments in Ukraine and on Ukrainian émigré life and Western culture, memoirs, and book and art reviews. It was nonpartisan, and frequently criticized the émigré Ukrainian establishment. Its contributors included prominent émigré figures. An index to the journal by R. Sawycky, Jr, was published in two parts (1964, 1969).

Lysy, Alberto [Lysyj], b 11 February 1935 in Buenos Aires, Argentina. Violinist, teacher, and conductor. The product of a musical immigrant family, he won musical awards as a youth that allowed him to study in Paris and London. In 1955 he won first prize at the Queen Elizabeth of Belgium International Competition, and then he went on to study with Y. Menuhin. He has toured extensively in solo recitals and with orchestras in Europe, Japan, India, and North and South America. He formed the Camerata Bariloche in Buenos Aires in 1965 and later became the director of the International Menuhin School in Gstaad, Switzerland, where he established a new chamber orchestra called Camerata Lysy.

Lysy, Illia [Lysyj, Illja], b 1882, d 2 January 1961 in Ternopil. Co-operative activist and civic and political figure. He was executive manager of Silskyi Hospodar in Lviv and was active in the Prosvita society, the Ridna Shkola society, and the credit co-operative movement. A onetime member of the National Democratic party, later he devoted much of his time to the Organization of the Ukrainians of Lviv and the Ukrainian National Democratic Alliance.

Lysy, Volodymyr [Lysyj], b 5 November 1893 in Kopychyntsi, Galicia, d 26 December 1966 in Detroit. Lawyer, publicist, and civic and political leader. In 1917, after studying law at Lviv University, he was drafted into the Austrian army, in which he served as liaison between the Austrian command in Ukraine and the Central Rada. In 1919 he worked in the State Secretariat of Internal Affairs of the Western Province of the Ukrainian National Republic and prepared a draft of the election law (with an extensive commentary) for the Ukrainian National Rada. After

the war he passed his bar examinations and in 1924 opened a law office in Ternopil. He was an active member of local educational and economic organizations and also sat on the executive of the Ukrainian Socialist Radical party (from 1928 as its deputy leader). He left Ukraine in 1944, and in 1949, he settled in Detroit, where he was active in the Ukrainian-American Center and the Self-Reliance Credit Union. A leading figure in the Ukrainian Free Society of America, he edited and managed the journal *Vil'na Ukraïna* for many years. Lysy wrote numerous articles on political and legal issues, some of which (eg, *Derzhavnyi status URSR v 1917–1923 rr.* [The Legal Status of the Ukrainian SSR in 1917–1923, 1963]) were published under separate cover.

Lysychanske [Lysyčans'ke]. V-19, DB II-4. A city (1990 pop 126,600) on the Donets River in Luhanske oblast. Founded in 1795, it is the oldest coal-mining center in the Donets Basin. It received the status of city in 1938. Today Lysychanske has six coal mines, an oil refinery, a soda, rubber, and glass factory, a regional museum, and the V. Sosiura Literary Memorial Museum.

Lysyk, Kenneth, b 1 July 1934 in Weyburn, Saskatchewan. Lawyer, educator, and judge. Educated at McGill University, the University of Saskatchewan (LL B, 1957), the University of Oxford, and Columbia University, Lysyk taught law at the universities of Toronto and British Columbia, where he was dean of the law school (1976–82). He held a number of advisory positions, served as deputy attorney general of Saskatchewan (1972–6), and acted as chairman of the Alaska Highway Pipeline Inquiry (1977). Lysyk was appointed Queen's Counsel in 1973 and appointed to the Supreme Court of British Columbia in 1983.

Lysyk, Yevhen, b 17 September 1930 in Shnyriv, Brody county, Galicia, d August 1991 in Lviv. Theatrical scenery designer. In 1961 he completed study at the Lviv School of Applied and Decorative Arts; since then he has worked as a designer in the Lviv Opera Theater (from 1967 as principal designer). He has also created scenery for productions in the Kiev Theater of Opera and Ballet (eg, B. Liatoshynsky's *Golden Ring*, 1971).

Lysytsia, Ivan [Lysycja], b and d ? Cossack colonel in the Bratslav regiment. A personal aide to Hetmans I. Samoilovych and I. Mazepa, he undertook diplomatic missions on several occasions, most notably in 1685, when he was sent by Samoilovych to Constantinople to obtain from the patriarch confirmation for the election of H. Chetvertynsky as metropolitan of Kiev, and agreement for the transfer of Kiev metropoly to the jurisdiction of the Moscow patriarchate.

Lysytsia, Mykhailo [Lysycja, Myxajlo], b 15 January 1921 in Vysoke, Radomyshl county, Kiev gubernia. Physicist; full AN URSR (now ANU) member since 1982. A graduate of Kiev University (1950), he taught there and was a professor from 1963 to 1976. Since 1961 he has headed a department at the AN URSR Institute of Semiconductors. A highly productive researcher with a wide range of expertise, he has contributed substantially to the fields of molecular spectroscopy, semiconductor phonon modes, nonlinear optics, quantum electronics, thin-film physics, the interaction of laser light with transparent materials, and multiquantum transitions.

Lyta Mohyla. See Melgunov kurhan.

Lytovchenko, Ivan [Lytovčenko], b 8 July 1921 in Buhruvate, Okhtyrka county, Kharkiv gubernia. Decorative artist. A graduate of the Lviv Institute of Applied and Decorative Arts (1954), he was one of the artists that created the mosaic wall panels inside the Kiev River Station (1961) and Boryspil Airport (1965) and the mosaic panel (with O. Kishchenko) at the restaurant of the Khreshchatyk metro station that was covered over by the Soviet authorities in the 1960s. He has created artistic tapestries, such as *Koliivshchyna* (1968), *Earth* (1987), and *Prometheus* (1989), together with his wife, Mariia, or V. Priadka, and the high-relief, mosaic-stone-and-metal compositions *Music* (1976), *To the Light* (1976), *Dawn* (1979), and *Creation* (1982) at the Chornobyl Atomic-Electric Station.

Lytovchenko, Oleksander [Lytovčenko], b 1835 in Kremenchuk, Poltava gubernia, d 28 June 1890 in St Petersburg. Painter. He studied at the St Petersburg Academy of Art until 1863. A cofounder of the St Petersburg Artists' Artel, in 1868 he was elected a member of the academy, and in 1876 he joined the *Peredvizhniki. He painted portraits and historical canvases, among them *Falconer* (1868), *Heavy Thoughts* (1866), *Christ in the Garden of Gethsemane*, and *Tsar Aleksei Mikhailovich and [Archibishop] Nikon* (1886). He painted seven murals in the Moscow Church of Christ the Savior.

Lytvak, Leonid, b 16 April 1899 in Tyraspil, Kherson gubernia, d 20 March 1970 in Kharkiv. Neurologist. A graduate of the Odessa Medical Institute (1924), he served as a professor at the Kharkiv Medical Institute (1941–5) and the Kharkiv Institute for the Upgrading of Physicians (1946–53) and the scientific director of the Ukrainian Psychoneurological Scientific Research Institute in Kharkiv (from 1953). His research dealt with the localization of brain functions, blood circulation within the brain, the circulation of cerebrospinal fluid, and the diagnosis of brain trauma.

Lytvyn, Mykhailo. See Michalon Lithuanus.

Lytvyn, Oleksander, b 21 November 1927 in Sumy. Geologist and mineralogist. He graduated from Kiev University (1952) and since 1969 has worked at the Institute of Geochemistry and the Physics of Minerals of the AN URSR (now ANU, as department head from 1979). His main contributions have been in the areas of mineralogy, crystal chemistry, structural crystallography, and X-ray analysis of crystal structures.

Lytvyn, Stepan, b 10 June 1931 in Holovchyntsi, now Karmaliukove, Zhmerynka raion, Vinnytsia oblast. Poet. Lytvyn graduated from the philological faculty of Kiev University (1954). His poetry began to appear in newspapers and journals in 1950. Since then he has published several collections, including *Sertse ne movchyt'* (The Heart Is Not Silent, 1958), *Pid nebom Krymu* (Under the Skies of the Crimea, 1960), *Bentezhnist'* (Embarrassment, 1966), *Rushnyk i shablia* (The *Rushnyk* and the Saber, 1972), and *Nezdolannist' liubovi* (Invincibility of Love, 1976). He has also translated poetry from Russian, Belarusian, Georgian, and Bulgarian into Ukrainian.

Lytvyn, Vitalii, b 5 February 1937 in Radyslavka, Rivne county, Volhynia. Artist. A graduate of the Lviv Institute of Applied and Decorative Arts (1964), he has done decorative carvings, woodcuts, oils, mosaics, ceramics, and stained glass. His works appeared in group exhibitions in Kiev (1971, 1972), Lviv (1972, 1973), and Yalta (1971). In 1980 he emigrated to Toronto, where he has continued to work as an artist; he has produced woodcuts and the iconostases in the Ukrainian Catholic churches in Niagara Falls and Chatham, Ontario.

Lytvyn, Yurii, b 1934 in Barakhty, Vasylkiv raion, Kiev oblast, d 5 September 1984 in Kuchino, Perm oblast, RSFSR. Journalist, poet, and dissident. He was sentenced on false charges five times and spent a total of 20 years in labor camps. In 1955, after he had served two years of a sentence, the sentence was revoked, but he was imprisoned again that year for allegedly having organized an anti-Soviet group in the labor camp. After being released in 1965, he returned to Ukraine and became active in the human rights movement. In 1974 he was sentenced to three years for 'slandering the state.' He joined the *Ukrainian Helsinki Group in 1978 and contributed articles to its underground bulletin. In spite of a severe stomach ulcer and thrombophlebitis, he was given three years in December 1979 for 'resisting authority' and an additional 10 years' imprisonment and 5 years' exile in 1982 for anti-Soviet agitation and propaganda. He died of unknown causes, probably of illness, in Perm Camp 36–1. His verses on prison life, titled 'Trahichna halereia' (The Tragic Gallery), have not been published. His remains were transferred (with those of V. Stus and O. Tykhy) to Ukraine and interred in Kiev on 19 November 1989.

Lytvynchuk, Ivan [Lytvynčuk] (nom de guerre: Dubovy), b 1917 in Derman, Dubno county, Volhynia gubernia, d 1951 south of Lutske, Volhynia oblast. Revolutionary and senior military officer. In the 1930s he served time in a Polish prison for his OUN activities. In 1942 he became the OUN (Bandera faction) chief leader for Sarny district, and in 1943 an organizer of the UPA and commander of its Zahrava Group (1943–5), which operated in the area between Rivne and Pynske. In 1943 he fought recurrent skirmishes with Soviet partisans, and in 1944 with NKVD troops. In 1945 he was promoted to major and appointed commander of the UPA-North, and in 1949 deputy OUN chief for the northwestern region. Facing imminent capture by the NKVD, he committed suicide.

Lytvynenko, Leonid, b 12 January 1921 in Tahanrih, d 26 October 1983 in Donetske. Chemist; full member of the AN URSR (now ANU) from 1965. A graduate of Kharkiv University, he taught there (1950–65), was rector of Donetske University (1965–8), directed the Donetske branch of the AN URSR Institute of Physical Chemistry (1968–75) and the AN URSR Institute of Physical-Organic Chemistry and Coal Chemistry, and chaired the Ukrainian Section of the Scientific Council of the USSR Academy of Sciences (1982–3). His research covered the structure-reactivity relationship in organic compounds and the kinetics of organic reactions. He studied the mechanism of nucleophilic substitution in unsaturated carbon, sulfur, and phosphorus systems; elucidated the mechanism of organic catalysis in acyl transfer reactions, particularly nucleophilic catalysis in nonaqueous solvents; formulated the rules of bifunctional catalysis; and discovered a number of important organic catalysts.

Lytvynenko, Leonid, b 7 May 1938 in Kharkiv. Radio physicist and radio astronomer; AN URSR (now ANU) corresponding member since 1982. A graduate of Kharkiv University (1959), in 1976 he became a professor there. A specialist in radiation in the millimeter and submillimeter range, including radio astronomy at these wavelengths, he has also contributed to the fields of wave propagation and diffraction at high frequencies.

Lytvynenko, Serhii, b 5 October 1899 in Poltava gubernia, d 20 June 1964 in New York City. Sculptor. An interwar émigré from 1920, he studied at the Cracow Academy of Fine Arts (1924–9) and in Paris (1930), where he exhibited at the Salon des Tuileries. From 1930 he lived in Lviv, where he was an active portrait sculptor; executed many memorial monuments, including those to I. Franko, Metropolitan A. Sheptytsky, V. Pachovsky, and soldiers who died in battle for the liberty of Ukraine; and ran a pottery studio. Until 1941 he took part in the exhibitions of the Society of Friends of Ukrainian Art and the Association of Ukrainian Pictorial Artists. He was a postwar refugee in Germany, and from 1949 he lived in New York, where he cofounded and first headed the *Ukrainian Artists' Association in the USA (1952–7) and chaired the Ukrainian Literature and Art Club (1949–59). He participated in Ukrainian group exhibitions in New York (1953–62), Toronto (1953), and Syracuse (1956) and at the Carnegie Foundation in New York (1956) and the Wayne State University Art Museum in Detroit (1960), and sent his works to be exhibited in Paris at the Salon des Indépendants (1956, 1958, 1961). Three solo exhibitions of his work were held in New York (1957, 1961), and one in Philadelphia. Lytvynenko created many compositions and monuments, and over 100 bronze, plaster, or terra-cotta portraits, mainly of Galician and émigré cultural and political figures (eg, V. Barvinsky, M. Bentsal, M. Kolessa, I. Svientsitsky, K. Hrynevycheva, E. Kozak, O. Harkavenko, O. Hrytsai, Ivan Mazepa, O. Boidunyk, L. Makarushka, F. Dudko, B. Kravtsiv, R. Kupchynsky, I. Kernytsky, Ye. Malaniuk, V. Lesych, E. Andiievska, M. Ponedilok, M. Shlemkevych, V. Kubijovyč, I. Rakovsky, L. Kuzma, V.

Serhii Lytvynenko and his bust of Hetman I. Mazepa

Lasovsky, M. Moroz, L. Morozova, I. Pryima, Gen O. Zahrodsky, V. Hrytsyn, I. Zhukovsky, V. Blavatsky, M. Fomenko). An impressionist of the post-Rodin school, he did not copy his models but tried to capture their emotional traits. A catalog of his works was published in New York in 1963.

S. Hordynsky

Lytvynenko, Valentyn, b 28 August 1908 in Kremenchuk, Poltava gubernia, d 15 December 1979 in Kiev. Graphic artist. He studied under M. Samokysh in Symferopil and at the workers' faculty of the Kharkiv Art Institute (1932–4). From 1941 he worked as a caricaturist for the satirical journal *Perets'* and designed Soviet political posters and leaflets; *lubok* pictures; linocuts, such as *The Jury* (1945), *Hunting Lyrics* (1951), *Hunting Jokes* (1961), and *Spring Silence* (1959); and linocut illustrations for books, including editions of fairy tales by L. Hlibov (1946), Lesia Ukrainka (1962), and I. Franko (1966), O. Vyshnia's stories (1954), and Ukrainian folk tales (1968).

Lytvynenko, Vasyl, b 2 February 1899 in Saratov, Russia, d 14 January 1966 in Moscow. Choreographer, ballet dancer, and singer. A graduate of K. Aleksiutovich's ballet school in Saratov (1918), M. Mordkin's dance studio in Tbilisi (1922), and the Tbilisi Conservatory (1923), he worked as a ballet soloist and choreographer at the opera and ballet theaters of Saratov (1918–21), Tbilisi (1922–6, 1935–44), Kharkiv (1927–31, 1946–56), and Kiev (1932–4). He staged several ballets in which he himself performed, as Yarosh in M. Verykivsky's *The Nobleman Kanovsky* (the first Ukrainian ballet, premiered 1931 in Kharkiv and 1932 in Kiev), Major Campbell in B. Yanovsky's *Ferenji* (1932),

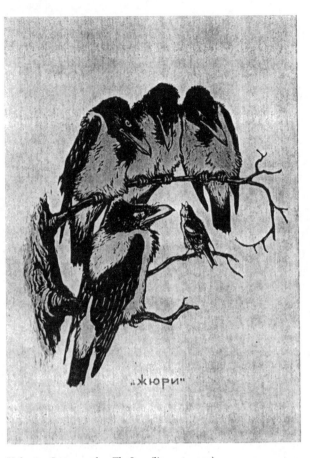

Valentyn Lytvynenko: *The Jury* (linocut, 1945)

and Danko in V. Nakhabin's *Danko* (1948). He also danced the roles of Phoebus in C. Pugni's *La Esmeralda*, Basilio in L. Minkus's *Don Quixote*, and Siegfried in P. Tchaikovsky's *Swan Lake*.

Mariia Lytvynenko-Volgemut

Lytvynenko-Volgemut, Mariia, b 13 February 1892 in Kiev, d 3 April 1966 in Kiev. Opera singer (dramatic soprano). In 1912–14 she performed in Sadovsky's Theater and then was a soloist at the St Petersburg Theater of Musical Drama. She returned to Ukraine in 1917, performed in Kiev, Kharkiv, and Vynnytsia, and was a soloist at the Kharkiv (1923–34) and Kiev (1934–51) operas. Lytvynenko-Volgemut created many classical stage parts

in Ukrainian opera – Odarka in S. Hulak-Artemovsky's *Zaporozhian Cossack beyond the Danube* and Natalka and Terpelykha in *Natalka from Poltava*, the mother in M. Lysenko's *Taras Bulba*, Roksoliana in D. Sichynsky's *Roksoliana*, Oksana in A. Vakhnianyn's *Kupalo*, Varvara in K. Dankevych's *Bohdan Khmelnytsky*, and Hanna in M. Verykivsky's *Naimychka* (The Hired Girl) – and in classical opera – Yaroslavna in A. Borodin's *Prince Igor*, Lisa in P. Tchaikovsky's *Queen of Spades*, and the eponymous roles in S. Moniuszko's *Halka*, G. Verdi's *Aida*, and G. Puccini's *Tosca*. From 1946 Lytvynenko-Volgemut was a professor at the Kiev Conservatory.

Lytvynov, Ivan, b 7 July 1907 in Sumy, d 20 October 1976 in Kiev. Structural engineer; full member and secretary of the Academy of Construction and Architecture of the Ukrainian SSR from 1956. He graduated from the Kharkiv Civil-Engineering Institute (1930) and served as director of the Southern Scientific Research Construction Institute in Kharkiv (1952–7) and head of the academy's Department of Structural Foundations and Soil Mechanics (1963–76). He did research on the strengthening of reinforced concrete thermal structures and the deep stabilization of soils.

Lytvynov, Olimpii, b 5 November 1905 in Beryslav, Kherson county. Civil engineer. He graduated from the Odessa Industrial Institute (1928) and worked on housing construction projects in Artemivske, Kiev, Nykopil, Tbilisi, and Kharkiv. In 1946–63 he worked in Kiev at the Scientific Research Institute of Construction Materials and Products and the Scientific Research Institute of Building Production. In 1963 he joined the Kiev Civil-Engineering Institute. His main contributions are in building technology, particularly the application of stone in building exteriors.

Lytvynov, Volodymyr, b 16 April 1936 in Cherkaske, Slovianske raion, Donetske oblast. Philosopher. A graduate of Lviv University (1963), he taught Latin and classical literature at the Nizhen Pedagogical Institute and headed the Department of Foreign Languages there until 1980. Since obtaining a candidate's degree in philosophy (1974), he has been a senior research associate of the AN URSR (now ANU) Institute of Philosophy. A specialist in 16th- to 18th-century Ukrainian thought, he has written a book in Ukrainian on the ideas of the early Enlightenment in the philosophical thought of Ukraine (1984); cocompiled a collection of descriptions of the philosophy and rhetoric courses of professors at the Kievan Mohyla Academy (1982); translated into Ukrainian Erasmus's *In Praise of Folly* (1981) and Phaedrus's fables (1986); contributed three chapters to the first volume of the ANU history of philosophy in Ukraine (1987); composed a university-level Latin textbook (1990); and coauthored a book on humanistic and Reformation ideas in Ukraine in the 16th and early 17th centuries (1990).

Lytvynova, Pelahiia (née: Bartosh), b 15 October 1833 at Tereben *khutir*, Chernihiv gubernia, d 20 September 1904 in Zemlianka, Hlukhiv county, Chernihiv gubernia. Ethnographer and civic activist. After graduating from the Elisavetskii Institute in Moscow (1852) she worked as a teacher in Zemlianka and collected economic statistics and ethnographic materials. She wrote a school primer (1877), compiled an album of folk designs, *Iuzhnorusskii narodnyi ornament* (South Russian Folk Ornamentation, 1878; 2nd edn 1902), and wrote a study of wedding rituals in Zemlianka (1900).

Metropolitan Spyrydon Lytvynovych

Andrii Lyzohub

Lytvynovych, Spyrydon [Lytvynovyč], b 6 December 1810 in Dryshchiv, Berezhany circle, Galicia, d 4 June 1869 in Lviv. Ukrainian Catholic metropolitan and political activist. After finishing his studies in Vienna with a doctorate in 1839, he delivered sermons at St George's Cathedral in Lviv and served as parish priest of St Barbara's Church in Vienna, and then became rector of the theological seminary in Vienna (1852). He was consecrated auxiliary bishop of Lviv in 1857 and elevated to the office of metropolitan of Halych in 1864. Lytvynovych was a prominent member of the Diet and the Reichsrat, in which he defended Ukrainian interests and fought Polish dominance in Galician affairs. He promoted the interests of the Ukrainian Catholic church by seeing through a *concordat establishing the equality of the Eastern and Latin rite churches in the Habsburg Empire and by gaining formal recognition for canonical chapters in Lviv and Peremyshl eparchies. Opposed to Russophilism, in 1859 he issued instructions to his priests to use Ukrainian in their pastoral work and to ensure its use in local schools. He was loyal to the Habsburg monarchy, and when administrative control of Galicia was granted to the Poles in 1867, he retired from political life.

Lyvchak, Yosyp. See Livchak, Osyp.

Lyzanivsky, Ivan [Lyzanivs'kyj], b 1892 in Zarichia, Zolochiv county, Galicia, d 1934. Civic and political figure and publicist. In 1912 he moved to central Ukraine. He became a member of the Central Rada and of the CC of the Ukrainian Party of Socialist Revolutionaries (UPSR, the so-called central current), as well as one of the founders of the Sich Riflemen. He joined the Committee for the Defense of the Republic (March 1919), directed the Ministry of Press and Propaganda in the government of B. Martos (from April 1919), and was a member of the regional council in Khmilnyk. In 1921 a Bolshevik tribunal convicted Lyza-

nivsky at the show trial of V. Holubovych and the members of the CC of the UPSR. He was later released, and he worked for Knyhospilka publishers and edited the works of I. Franko. In 1934 Lyzanivsky was among those tried by P. Postyshev for espionage and treason; he was probably executed by the NKVD.

Lyzohub. A family line of Cossack *starshyna* from the Pereiaslav region, known from the B. Khmelnytsky period. Ivan Lyzohub (Kobyzenko) was colonel of Kaniv (1659, 1662) and Uman (1659–61) regiments and Hetman I. Vyhovsky's emissary to Moscow (1658). He was shot on Yu. Khmelnytsky's orders in late 1662 or early 1663. His brother was Yakiv *Lyzohub. Yakiv's son, Yukhym (d 1704), was general standard-bearer (1688–90), general flag-bearer (1694–8), colonel of Chernihiv (1698–1704) regiment, and Hetman P. Doroshenko's son-in-law. Yukhym's sons were Yakiv *Lyzohub and Semen Lyzohub (b 1678 or 1680, d 19 April 1734 in Hrodna); Semen graduated from the Kiev Academy in 1699 and was a fellow of the standard in 1715–34. The family also included Illia Lyzohub (b 26 October 1787 in Kulykivka, Horodnia county, d 1867 in Sedniv, Chernihiv county), who was a member of the United Slavs Masonic Lodge in Kiev, and his brother, Andrii *Lyzohub; both were aldermen in Sedniv. Andrii's sons were Dmytro and Fedir *Lyzohub; Fedir was head of the Hetman goverment in 1918.

Lyzohub, Andrii, b 16 June 1804 in Burkivka, Sosnytsia county, Chernihiv gubernia, d 1864 in Sorochyntsi, Myrhorod county, Poltava gubernia. Descendant of a Cossack officer family in the Chernihiv region; father of D. and F. *Lyzohub. He graduated from Moscow University and worked as a civil servant in 1827–38. He owned a large estate in the Chernihiv region, where his close friend T. *Shevchenko visited him in 1846–7. Lyzohub was a good musician and painter, as well as a supporter of Ukrainian language and literature. He was among the few who corresponded with Shevchenko in exile and who sent him material aid.

Lyzohub, Dmytro, b 29 July 1849 in Sedniv, Chernihiv county, d 22 August 1879 in Odessa. Revolutionary and political activist; son of A. *Lyzohub. In 1874 he joined a Kiev group of Russian populists led by I. Fesenko, and in 1877 he was one of the founders of the party *Zemlia i Volia (Land and Freedom). He was convicted of participating in terrorist activities, sentenced in Odessa by a military tribunal, and hanged.

Lyzohub, Fedir, b 6 November 1851 in Sedniv, Chernihiv county, Chernihiv gubernia, d 1928 in Yugoslavia. Civic and political leader; son of A. *Lyzohub. A member of the Chernihiv gubernia zemstvo assembly (1886–1901), he served as executive chairman of the Poltava gubernia zemstvo in 1901–15. He emerged as a defender of Ukrainian cultural interests: he ensured that the Poltava Zemstvo Building was built in a Ukrainian style, founded the Poltava Museum, erected a monument to I. Kotliarevsky in Poltava and published his works, and encouraged Ukrainian handicrafts. In 1915–17 he sat on the council of the Russian vicegerent for Caucasia. In the Hetman government he served as premier (10 May to 14 November 1918) and minister of internal affairs (10 May to 8 July 1918) and

Fedir Lyzohub

conducted a moderate conservative policy which sought a compromise with the Ukrainian National Union. Eventually he emigrated to the Crimea and, later, to the Balkans.

Lyzohub, Oleksander, b 1790 in the Chernihiv region, d 1839. Composer and pianist. He was one of the first Ukrainian composers for piano. His works include nocturnes, mazurkas, romances ('Death in a Foreign Land'), and sets of variations on Ukrainian folk songs ('Oh, There Is a Well in the Field,' 'And I Had a Wife,' and 'Don't Go to the Party, Hryts'). Contemporary sources also refer to some works by Lyzohub that have not survived, including two lyrical nocturnes.

Lyzohub, Yakiv, b ?, d 9 August 1698 in Chernihiv. Cossack *starshyna*. He served as colonel of Kaniv regiment (1666–9), Hetman I. Briukhovetsky's emissary to Moscow (1667), P. Doroshenko's general osaul (1669–74), and acting hetman (1670 and 1673). In 1674 he crossed over to Left-Bank Ukraine. He participated in the general council that signed the *Kolomak Articles and was a candidate for hetman in 1687. Lyzohub was known as a remarkable commander; he took part in the Chyhyryn and Crimean campaigns and served as colonel of Chernihiv regiment (1687–98) and acting hetman at the siege of Oziv (1696). He was buried in the Yeletskyi Dormition Monastery.

Lyzohub, Yakiv, b 22 October 1675, d 24 January 1749 in St Petersburg. Cossack officer; son of Yukhym and grandson of Yakiv *Lyzohub. He was educated at the Kievan Mohyla Academy, and served as general standard-bearer (1713–28), in the course of which service he accompanied Hetman I. Skoropadsky to Moscow in 1718, and general quartermaster (1728–49). He headed the government of the Hetman state in 1723–4, and after the death of Hetman D. Apostol he was senior representative of the *starshyna* in the Russian administration of the Hetmanate (from 1734). He took part in the Polish (1733) and Turkish (1737) campaigns. He is thought by some researchers to be the author of the *Lyzohub Chronicle.

Lyzohub Chronicle. A historical record written in 1742. Of its two sections the first is a chronological compilation of events from the beginning of the 16th century to the end of the 17th century on the basis of Cossack chronicles, and the second is an account of events in which the *Lyzohub family played an important role. The latter begins in the 1690s and covers the years 1725–37 in great detail. The chronicle ends with a description of the Cossack campaign against the Crimean Khanate commanded by Acting Hetman Ya. Lyzohub. Ukraine's past is evaluated in the chronicle from an autonomist standpoint, and its present is seen throught the eyes of a Russian loyalist who is not uncritical of the tsarist policy toward Ukraine. The authorship of the work has been attributed by some (V. Antonovych, P. Klepatsky) to Ya. *Lyzohub; the possibility of his brother Semen's contribution has not been excluded. The chronicle was first published by M. Bilozersky in *Iuzhnorusskie letopisi* (South Russian Chronicles, 1856), and then in another version in V. Antonovych's *Sbornik letopisei, otnosiashchikhsia k istorii Iuzhnoi i Zapadnoi Rossii* (Collection of Chronicles Pertaining to the History of Southern and Western Russia, 1888).

M

Macaronics. Burlesque compositions, usually in verse, in which words of one or more languages are intermixed and hybridized. The form's inventor, the Benedictine monk T. Folengo, applied Latin endings to Italian words to produce the burlesque epic of chivalry *Baldus* (1517). The form spread through medieval Europe in schools, where macaronics were written using Latin or Greek and the vernacular. In Ukraine the form became popular with the wandering preceptors and in the *intermedes. I. *Kotliarevsky gave the form currency in modern Ukrainian literature when he used it in his *Eneïda* (Aeneid, 1798–1809; 'Eneus noster magnus panus / i slavnyi troianorum kniaz''). As Latin and Greek gave way to the vernacular, authors using macaronics began to mix many languages to produce a humorous effect. Kotliarevsky used the technique in creating the character of Voznyi in his operetta *Natalka Poltavka* (Natalka from Poltava, 1819), in which the village scribe speaks a mixture of the learned Church Slavonic and the Ukrainian vernacular.

In that second use by Kotliarevsky macaronics soon lost the prime reason for their existence, the comic, and began to be used as a characterization technique. Many Ukrainian authors used a mixture of two languages to characterize the ethnic (Jewish, Russian, and Polish) and social origins of personages. The plays of the dramatists M. Kropyvnytsky, I. Karpenko-Kary, and M. Starytsky and the works of the prosaists Yu. Fedkovych, I. Franko, V. Vynnychenko, and V. Stefanyk, along with many others, are replete with such characterizations.

Closer to using macaronics in the original way are the works of such émigré writers as Ya. *Maidanyk, whose creation and alter ego Shtif Tabachniuk, with his mixtures of English and Ukrainian, became extremely popular in interwar Canada; Maidanyk's work was published in 1959 as *Vuiko Shtif Tabachniuk i inshi novi korotki opovidannia* (Uncle Shtif Tabachniuk and Other New Short Stories). E. *Kozak's Hryts Zozulia mixes the Pokutia Ukrainian dialect with many languages (German, Polish, Yiddish, and English); the author, like his hero, was displaced by the Second World War, and moved from his native Galicia to Germany and thence to the United States. Hryts Zozulia's macaronics have been the longtime staple of the humorous journal *Lys Mykyta* and have appeared in separate collections as *Hryts' Zozulia* (1973) and *Na khlops'kyi rozum Hrytsia Zozuli* (According to Hryts' Zozulia's Common Sense, 1982).

The rich field of 'Ukeish' (a Ukrainian-English linguistic mixture) is exploited by many Ukrainian-Canadian humorists and comedians (eg, T. Woloshyn, L. Goy) and has found its way into humorous folk songs and *kolomyiky ('Sori, Meri, ia ne khtiv / ia traiuiu azh zipriv') as well as into works by such authors as I. Kernytsky (Iker), Z. Kohut, W. Cap, M. Ponedilok, and M. Koliankivsky (M. Tochylo).

D.H. Struk

Maccabees' Feast (*Makovii*). A church feast observed on 14 August (1 August OS). This day is noted for its ritual blessing of flowers and herbs picked and plaited into wreaths by young girls and women in the early morning before the church service. The blessed flowers and herbs were believed to possess magical and protective qualities, and were dried and hung in homes.

Mace, James, b 18 February 1952 in Muskogee, Oklahoma. Historian. He graduated from the University of Michigan (PH D, 1981). He worked at the Ukrainian Research Institute at Harvard University, where he studied the man-made famine of 1932–3 (1984–6), and directed the US (Congress) Commission on the Ukraine Famine in Washington, DC (1986–90). He wrote the *Report to Congress* (1988) resulting from the commission's research, as well as the monograph *Communism and the Dilemmas of National Liberation: National Communism in Soviet Ukraine, 1918–1933* (1983). He was the founder and chairman of the American Friends of *Memorial.

Macenko, Paul. See Matsenko, Pavlo.

Machine building. A branch of industry that builds machines, machine parts, and equipment for use in other industries. It includes *agricultural machine building, the *automotive, *electrotechnical, *locomotive, *railroad-car, and *construction and road-building machinery industries, and various other branches grouped under either heavy machine building (HMB) or light machine building (LMB). Under the Soviet classification of industry the *metalworking industry was closely related to machine building, and the two were usually grouped together in statistics.

The development of the machine-building industry in Ukraine began in the mid-19th century. The first plants produced agricultural machinery and, later, sugar refining equipment and textile machines. The industry grew rapidly in the second half of the century in response to the demand for machinery and equipment from the metallurgical, mining, and railway industries. Early production, particularly of steam turbines, boilers, and locomotives, was concentrated in the Donets Basin, the Dnieper Industrial Region, and Kharkiv. Initially, much of the industry was developed and owned by foreign firms and syndicates, which imported modern machinery from Western Europe. By 1913 Ukraine accounted for almost one-quarter of all machine building in the Russian Empire (excluding the Baltic regions and Poland). The industry was concentrated in the agricultural machine and locomotive branches; the other branches were poorly developed.

Machine building, along with all other branches of the economy, was severely disrupted by the First World War and the struggle for Ukrainian independence. Only in 1925 were prewar levels of production matched. Some new plants were built in the 1920s, and many older ones were reopened. The greatest growth in the industry came during the industrialization drive of the First Five-Year Plan (1928–32), which stressed the development of heavy industry. Much capital was invested in Ukraine, especially in the Donets Basin. The republic's share of the USSR machine-building industry increased from 6.8 percent in 1925 to 12.1 percent in 1929, 21.6 percent in 1932, and 24.8 percent in 1938. Among the major HMB plants modernized in that period were a mining and railway machinery plant in Kramatorske, transport machine plants in Kharkiv and Luhanske, and metallurgical and mining-equipment factories in Donetske, Horlivka, Slovianske, Debaltseve, Kryvyi Rih, and Druzhkivka. New plants included a machine-building plant in Kramatorske, the Kharkiv turbine plant, and metallurgical plants in Dnipropetrovske. Many of them were the sole producers of specific machines in the USSR. By 1934 the machine-building industry had emerged as the largest and most important industry in Ukraine. In the second half of the 1930s Ukraine's share in the USSR industry declined somewhat, because the development of eastern regions of the RSFSR was given priority. The total number of factories in Ukraine increased from 94 in 1927 to 150 in 1940. The profile of the industry also changed: the importance of agricultural and railway machinery declined in comparison with that of mining, electrotechnical, and chemical machinery. In the interwar and postwar periods little attention was paid to the development of LMB.

At the outset of the Second World War many machine-building plants were evacuated to the east. Most of the physical plant that was left behind was destroyed. Soon after the German armies retreated, most factories were reconstructed. In the 1950s and 1960s Ukraine's machine-building industry expanded rapidly: from 1950 to 1965 the average annual growth rate in the machine-building and metalworking sector combined was 15.5 percent, compared to the industrial average of 11.1 percent. Ukraine's growth rate, however, was lower than that of the USSR: regions less affected by the war recovered more quickly. Since the mid-1970s the industry's growth rate has fallen considerably, to an annual average of 9.5 percent from 1965 to 1985, and much of the physical plant has deteriorated. Nonetheless, machine building has greatly increased its share in Ukraine's overall economy: in 1970 it accounted for 16.3 percent of all industrial production, in 1980 for 25.7 percent, in 1985 for 29.3 percent, and in 1987 for 30.5 percent. From 1980 to 1987 production in machine building and metalworking increased by 53 percent. The largest gains were registered in the instrument-making (87 percent), energy (74 percent), and chemical (70 percent) machine-building branches; the poorest performances were in the gas-processing (21 percent), automotive (16 percent), and cellulose-paper (13 percent) machine-building branches. The output of construction and road-building machines showed a decline of 3 percent in that period.

The machine-building and metalworking industries in Ukraine were subordinated to all-Union ministries in Moscow until the dissolution of the USSR, and most of their plant managers did not report to republican authorities. This industrial organization was introduced in the 1965 economic reform.

Heavy machine building. According to the Soviet classification system HMB referred to the conglomerate of metallurgical, coal-mining, and mining machine building. According to a broader definition HMB includes also machinery for heavy industry, transport, and construction. The development of HMB is closely related to the overall development of *heavy industry.

Since HMB products are made of metals, the machine factories are usually located close to metallurgical plants. Ukrainian HMB benefits from the local availability of high-quality metals and plentiful energy and labor resources. Ukraine produced a wide range of modern machines and equipment for Soviet heavy industry and for export.

The HMB branch of metallurgical equipment turns out blooming rolling mills, equipment for blast furnaces, continuous-operation steel casting machines for cast slabs, oxygen converters, pipe welding and rolling mills, roasters for iron-ore pellets, section bending units, equipment for the vacuum casting of steel, rolling mills for the cold rolling of sheet and pipe, and wide-band sheet mills. Among the largest producers are the *New and *Old Kramatorske Machine-Building plants, the *Slovianske Heavy-Machine-Building Plant, the *Dnipropetrovske Metallurgical Equipment Plant, and the *Mariiupil Heavy-Machine-Building Plant.

The coal-mining machinery branch produces cutter loaders, coal plows, power drills, powered roof supports, entry-driving machines, hydraulic excavators, ventilating and lighting equipment, and water pumps. The largest plants belonging to this branch are in Horlivka, Luhanske, Donetske, Druzhkivka, and Kharkiv.

The mining machinery branch manufactures machines and equipment such as cutter loaders and entry-driving combines, drill bits and drilling rigs, ventilation fans, ore-dressing equipment, rotary excavators with spoil dumpers, shaft and mine winches, shields, and surface equipment. The largest producers are plants in Kryvyi Rih, Konotip, Donetske, and Luhanske.

Oil and gas equipment produced in Ukraine includes turbodrills, turbine pumps, and other devices for deep exploration and exploitation. The largest plants of this branch are located in Drohobych, Chernivtsi, and Ivano-Frankivske. Ukrainian HMB plants accounted for almost one-third of all the chemical and petrochemical machines and equipment manufactured in the USSR. The most important plants are located in Sumy, Kiev, Berdychiv, and Khvastiv. The hoisting and conveying equipment branch in Ukraine manufactures cranes, conveyors, elevators, escalators, loaders, and stacking cranes. Of the many specialized enterprises of this branch the most important are in Kharkiv, Odessa, Kramatorske, and Lviv.

In the late 1980s the development of HMB in Ukraine, especially the growth of the metallurgical, mining, coal-mining, chemical, and transport equipment branches, was emphasized.

Light machine building. This classification refers to the group of machine-building branches that manufacture equipment and machinery for the textile, garment, leather, footwear, food-processing and food services, retail trade, and printing industries. It is also customary to include in LMB the production of consumer durables, even though these are dispersed throughout the entire machine-building sector in Ukraine.

Ukraine is a major manufacturer of food-processing equipment: in 1979 it accounted for almost half of all the USSR output. A variety of pasteurizing, bottling and canning, packing, baking, milling, and other machines are produced in Cherkasy, Melitopil, Odessa, Symferopil, Poltava, and Smila. Production in that branch was worth some 368 million rubles in 1987.

The major centers for producing equipment and machinery for the retail trade and the food services industry are Kharkiv and Luhanske. The output includes refrigerators, steam tables, cash registers, and vending machines. Household goods, such as washing machines, refrigerators, and appliances, are produced in Kiev, Donetske, Melitopil, Kharkiv, and Lviv. The production of those branches was worth 112 million rubles in 1987.

In 1979 almost one-third of all the machinery and equipment for the printing industry in the USSR was made in Ukraine. Duplicating machines and printing presses are made in Kiev, Kharkiv, Romen, and Odessa. Little (only 2 percent of the Soviet total) machinery and equipment for the textile and clothes industries is made in Ukraine.

(See also *Industry, *Heavy industry, and *Light industry.)

BIBLIOGRAPHY

Mashynobudivnytstvo v druhomu p'iatyrichchi: Zbirnyk stattei i materiialiv (Kharkiv 1932)
Prokopenko, M. *Rozvytok khimichnoho mashynobuduvannia na Ukraïni* (Kiev 1961)
Oboznyi, A. *Osnovnye fondy mashinostroeniia i puti uluchsheniia ikh ispol'zovaniia: Na primere stankostroitel'noi promyshlennosti USSR* (Kiev 1962)
Chervanev, D. *Sovershenstvovanie mezhotraslevykh proizvodstv: Na materialakh mashinostroitel'noi promyshlennosti* (Kiev 1974)
Bem, I.; Demidon, B. *Problemy rozvytku i rozmishchennia mashynobuduvannia ta metaloobrobky v Ukraïns'kii RSR* (Kiev 1977)
Lych, N.; Rozenplenter, A.; Fialko, G. *Ekonomika mashinostroitel'noi promyshlennosti* (Kiev 1979)
B. Balan, V. Holubnychy, F. Kushnirsky

Machine science. Machine science was introduced in Ukraine in the latter half of the 19th century by O. Latyshev and H. *Proskura at the Kharkiv Technological Institute, K. Shindler and M. Delone at the Kiev Polytechnical Institute, O. Dynnyk at the Katerynoslav Higher Mining School, and at the Lviv Polytechnical Institute. Until 1917 machine research was concentrated on problems of mechanics (Delone), the resistance of materials, the theory of elasticity and oscillation (Dynnyk and S. *Timoshenko), the theory of mechanisms (V. Kirpichov), metal cutting (K. Zvorykin), and the strength of materials (K. *Siminsky and A. *Vynohradov). M. *Kybalchych sketched the first recorded design of a jet-propelled flying machine, and Proskura designed propeller turbines. From 1918 scientific work on machines was conducted at the Institute of Technical Mechanics at the VUAN in Kiev, initially under the directorship of Timoshenko (1919–20). In the postwar period institutes were set up within the AN URSR (now ANU), with specialties in physical mechanics, electric welding, mechanics, cybernetics, technical thermophysics, electrodynamics, and metal physics. Machine science institutes were established in Kramatorske and Kharkiv, and the Ukrainian Scientific Research Institute of the Machine Tool and Instrument Industry was founded in Odessa. In the 1920s, research on farm machinery was undertaken at experimental stations in Hrushky (Kiev region), in Akyminske (Melitopil region), and at the Kharkiv Institute of Agricultural Machine Science and Machine Building.

Ukrainian scientists, such as D. *Grave, contributed to theoretical machine science. M. *Krylov and N. Bogoliubov developed a theory of nonlinear mechanics that is applied in estimating the efficiency of electric machines and the stability of airplanes. Proskura specialized in the theory of hydraulic machines, A. *Vasylenko in the theory of tilling machines, and V. Dobrovolsky and S. *Serensen in machine parts. Yu. *Kondratiuk developed *rocket technology and wind turbines, and H. Chechet and D. *Hryhorovych contributed to aircraft construction. H. *Savin investigated the concentration of stress around openings in machine elements. H. *Pysarenko studied the strength of materials. A. *Kovalenko developed new methods of assessing the efficiency of turbomachines and thermal elasticity. The theory and construction of thermal engines and power equipment were worked out by I. *Shvets and Ye. Dyban. O. *Penkov, Yu. *Mytropolsky, and V. Kononenko studied the strength, endurance, and oscillation of mechanical systems, and H. Karpenko studied the physicochemical mechanics of materials. K. *Starodubov, V. Danylov, and V. *Svechnikov dealt with metals processing. A. *Filipov and A. *Pidhorny investigated the strength of large power machines. O. *Kukhtenko and O. Ivakhnenko developed the theory of automatic control and the regulation of mechanisms. M. *Kilchevsky examined the problems of impact theory.

Ukrainian specialists have developed advanced gas turbines and jet engines for airplanes (O. *Ivchenko and A. *Liulka), turbines (L. *Shubenko-Shubin), transport and passenger planes (O. *Antonov), welding machines and mechanisms (B. *Paton), farm machines (Shindler, A. Vasylenko, O. *Karpenko, L. *Kramarenko, P. *Vasylenko, Siminsky), and thermal engines (Shvets).

A number of journals in the different fields of machine science are published in Ukraine, all of them in Russian: *Dvigateli vnutrennego sgoraniia, Lokomotivostroenie, Gornye stroitel'nye i dorozhnye mashiny, Tekhnologiia i avtomatizatsiia mashinostroeniia, Stanki i rezhushchie instrumenty, Samoletostroenie i tekhnika vozdushnogo flota, Teplovye napriazheniia v elementakh konstruktsii, Soprotivlenie materialov i teoriia sooruzhenii,* and *Dinamika i prochnost' mashin.* The Institute of Machine Science and Agricultural Mechanics of the AN URSR (now ANU) published its collected papers in 1950–4.
L. Onyshkevych

Machine-tractor stations (*mashyno-traktorni stantsii*, or MTS). State-run institutions that provided machinery, combines, and other heavy equipment for agriculture in the USSR. In the 1920s, co-operatives were set up for the joint purchase and use of expensive farming equipment. They were organized by informal groups of peasants, agricultural *artels, *associations for the joint cultivation of land, and other bodies. The first MTS is considered to be the Shevchenko MTS in Bereziv raion, Odessa county. It was organized in 1927–8 by the agronomist A. Markevych, who proposed a system in which the MTS provided farmers with tractors and other machinery as well as seed and technical expertise (although the peasants did most of the work) in return for a portion of the grain harvest. The relationship between the partners was contractual. The idea spread quickly, and various *state farms and other organizations in Ukraine and the RSFSR began to establish stations. Markevych's initiatives soon gained the attention of the authorities. In 1929 the All-Union Center of Machine-Tractor Stations was established as a joint-stock association to co-ordinate the development of the MTS.

Official support for the movement grew quickly after 1930 and the beginning of the forced *collectivization of agriculture. Then the Party realized the importance of the MTS as an instrument for controlling the peasantry and implementing Party policies, especially in *grain procurement. In 1933, political departments were organized in all the MTS, and personnel were selected according to political criteria. They were usually workers or other city residents who knew little about agriculture, yet they were given great authority over the collective farms. The lack of trained agricultural machine operators and machinery in good repair further diminished the economic impact of the MTS. Such problems were particularly acute in the 1930s. The MTS came under the Ministry of Agriculture, which provided general guidelines for their activities. The stations signed formal contracts with collective farms, setting rates and conditions of work. After the mid-1930s a typical contract gave the MTS up to 22 percent of the crop.

Machine-tractor stations in Ukraine, 1940–57

	1940	1945	1950	1957
Number of MTS	1,227	1,227	1,347	1,367 0
Number of 15-HP tractors (in 1,000s)	77.3	44.4	80.7	118.0
Total power of tractors (in 1,000 HP)	1,371	737	1,832	2,740.8
Number of combines (in 1,000s)	27.9	12.5	26.2	51.6
Number of trucks (in 1,000s)	6.9	3.0	10.2	14.4
Area tilled under contract (in 1,000 ha)	51,472	23,767	71,362	124,632

Despite those problems, the MTS movement in Ukraine continued to grow (see the table). By 1957 the stations were servicing 14,700 collective farms and performing 85 percent of all fieldwork. Forty-three percent of all stations served from 6 to 10 collective farms, and 44 percent served from 11 to 20 farms. Some 610,000 people were employed by the MTS (1956), 48,000 of whom were administrative staff, 32,000, political cadres, and the rest, operators or mechanics.

Under N. Khrushchev the MTS were initially given an expanded role and greater authority over the collective farms. They failed to meet expectations, however, and were abolished in 1958. Their tractors and machinery were transferred to the collective farms, although repair and technical stations were established to provide facilities for major repairs, rent specialized equipment, and distribute spare parts and fuel.

BIBLIOGRAPHY
Miller, R. *One Hundred Thousand Tractors: The MTS and the Development of Controls in Soviet Agriculture* (Cambridge, Mass 1970)
M. Kurakh

Machtet, Grigorii [Mačtet, Grigorij], b 15 November 1852 in Lutske, d 27 August 1901 in Yalta. Russian writer and revolutionary populist of Ukrainian-Polish descent. In 1870–1 he was a teacher in Volhynia, where he became a friend of M. Starytsky. From 1872 to 1874 he worked as a farm laborer in the United States and began publishing stories in Russian journals about his travels and about immigrant life. He was imprisoned in 1876. From 1877 to 1885 he lived in political exile in northern Russia and Siberia and continued publishing stories and novels. While living in Zhytomyr (1896–1900) he contributed to the paper *Volyn'* and befriended M. Kotsiubynsky. Editions of his complete works were published in 1902 (12 vols) and in 1911–13 (10 vols). His novel *I odin v pole voin* (And a Single Warrior in the Field, 1886), about life in a Western Ukrainian village, appeared in a Ukrainian translation in 1929. M. Grebennikov published a book about Machtet in Kiev in 1961.

Machukhy settlement and burial mounds. A Scythian settlement and burial ground of the 6th to 5th century BC near the village of Machukhy, now in Poltava raion. Excavations by M. *Rudynsky in the 1920s and again in 1946 exposed substantial quantitites of ceramic vessels (bowls, jars, ladles, small goblets), iron knives, and the bones of domesticated fauna within the boundaries of the settlement. Excavation of the burial ground in the late sixties and early seventies revealed the existence of two types of burial traditions and a variety of grave goods. Excavations in 1969 uncovered a fragment of a mold for a Scythian-style stag figurine – the first physical evidence of the local production of such ornaments.

Maciej of Miechów (Ukrainian: Matvii z Miekhova; actual surname: Karpiga), b 1457 in Miechów, near Cracow, d 8 September 1523 in Cracow. Polish historian and geographer, and physician by profession. He was a professor (from 1485) and rector (1501–19) of the Cracow Academy and the author of *Tractatus de duabus Sarmatiis Asiana et Europiana et de continentis eis* (1517; Polish trans 1535), a survey of Asian Sarmatia east of the Don River and the European lands from the Vistula to the Don, in which he recognizes the geographic, cultural, and linguistic identity of Ruthenians (Ukrainians). The work was translated into several languages and reprinted 18 times during the 16th century; it became a standard reference work on the subject in Europe.

Maciejowski, Wacław, b 1793, d 9 February 1883 in Warsaw. Polish historian. He was a professor of Roman and universal law at Warsaw University (1818–31) and a proponent of Pan-Slavism. He researched the cultural development and legal history of the Slavic peoples, particularly the customary laws of Ukrainians and Russians. He wrote *Historia prawodawstw słowiańskich* (The History of Slavic Legislations, 4 vols, 1832–5) and *Polska i Ruś aż do pierwszej połowy w. XVII pod względem obyczajów i zwyczajów* (Poland and Rus' up to the First Half of the 17th Century with Respect to Customs and Traditions, 4 vols, 1842).

Mackerel (*Scomber scombrus*; Ukrainian: *skumbriia, makrelia*). A commercially valuable fish of the perch family Scombridae, found in temperate and tropical seas. It grows up to 50 cm in length and approx 1.6 kg in weight. Its back is bluish-green with several curved black stripes, and its belly is silver-white. In Ukraine mackerel is abundant in the Black Sea and rarer in the Sea of Azov.

Mackiw, Theodore [Mac'kiv, Teodor] b 30 May 1918 in Strutyn, Zolochiv county, Galicia. Historian. He studied at

Theodore Mackiw   Vladimir Mackiw

the University of Frankfurt, where he received a PH D (1950) for his dissertation on the Ukrainian Cossacks in German literature of the first half of the 18th century. A resident of the United States since 1950, he also studied at Seton Hall (1953–4) and Yale (1959–61) universities. From 1962 to 1984 he taught at the University of Akron. His major works are *Mazepa in dem Lichte der zeitgenössischen deutschen Quellen (1687–1709)* (1963), *English Reports on Mazepa: Hetman of Ukraine and Prince of the Holy Roman Empire, 1687–1709* (1983), and a book in Ukrainian on Hetman I. Mazepa in Western European sources of the years 1687–1709 (1988).

Mackiw, Vladimir [Mac'kiv, Volodymyr], b 4 September 1923 in Stanyslaviv (now Ivano-Frankivske), Galicia. Metallurgical engineer; fellow of the Chemistry Institute of Canada and the American Institute of Mining and Metallurgical Engineers, and full member of the Shevchenko Scientific Society since 1962. He was educated at universities in Breslau, Erlagen (1946), and Leuven (1948). He emigrated to Canada in 1948, where he joined Sherritt Gordon Mines Ltd (1949) and became a director of research (1952) and executive vice-president (1972). A specialist in the extraction of nickel from ore, he was a member of the National Research Council of Canada (1971–7), an adviser to the Ministry of Energy, Mines, and Resources (1972–9), and chairman of the Nickel Development Institute (1984–6). In 1976 he received an honorary doctorate from the University of Alberta, and in 1977 the Gold Medal of the Institute of Mining and Metallurgy in London, England. In 1991 the Mackiw Materials Center was opened in Fort Saskatchewan, Alberta. Mackiw is the author of numerous scientific publications and the holder of over 50 patents.

Maday, Andrij [Madaj, Andrij], b 26 November 1953 in Philadelphia. Graphic artist and iconographer. A graduate of the Pennsylvania Academy of Fine Arts (1977), he spent a year as resident artist at Manor Junior College (Jenkintown, Pennsylvania) and studied icon painting under Rev Yu. Mokrytsky at St Theodore's Studite Monastery in Castel Gandolfo, Italy. Maday has had 22 solo exhibitions of his woodcuts and drawings and has participated in many group shows. He has also created icons on panels and decorated St Joseph's Church in Chicago.

Madey, Johannes, b 23 April 1933 in Katowice, Silesia, Poland. German Catholic scholar; member of the Shevchenko Scientific Society since 1985. He studied philosophy and theology in Fulda and Munich, and completed a D TH in 1961 with a dissertation on V. Solovev. He has been a professor of Eastern theology at the Johann-Adam-Möhler Ecumenical Institute in Paderborn since 1972, and an honorary professor of the Pontifical Eastern Institute of Religious Studies in Kottayam, the only faculty of Eastern Catholicism in India. He has also served as a special adviser on Eastern Christianity to the Melchite and German Catholic churches. Madey has published several monographs on the history and organization of the Ukrainian Catholic church, including *Kirche zwischen Ost und West* (1969) and *Le Patriarcat Ukrainien vers la perfection de l'état juridique actuelle* (1971), and articles in *Encyclopedia of Ukraine, Bohosloviia,* and other collections and journals.

Madrid. See Spain.

Maeotians (*meoty*). Ancient agricultural tribes inhabiting the eastern shore of the Sea of Azov (Greek: Maeotis) between the Don River and the Kuban River, from the 1st millennium BC to the middle of the 1st millennium AD. The Maeotians are mentioned in old Greek and Roman sources. According to Strabo they included the Sindians, the Dandarii, and the Doschi. Some of the tribes spoke an Iranian language, others a language related to that of the Adygs. In the 4th and 3rd centuries BC the Maeotian tribes were under the *Bosporan Kingdom.

Semen Magalias

Magalias, Semen [Magaljas], b 17 May 1885 in Vynnyky, Lviv county, Galicia, d 1978 in Newark, New Jersey. Civic and military figure. While studying law at Lviv University he became active in the Prosvita society and then worked as an inspector and organizer for the Silskyi Hospodar society. With the collapse of the Austrian Empire he volunteered for service in the Ukrainian Galician Army and was put in charge of arms acquisition. He headed the foreign affairs department of Otaman S. Petliura's general staff and later the mobilization department of the UNR Army (1920–1). After returning to Lviv he served as executive director of the Prosvita society's head office in Lviv from 1922 to 1939. Magalias compiled a list of Ukrainian books that were banned and confiscated by the Polish authorities in the interwar period (1932; 2nd rev edn 1937). Under the German occupation he was secretary of the

Lviv municipal executive. At the close of the war he emigrated to Germany and then to the United States.

Magdalenian culture. The last of the Paleolithic cultures in Europe, named after the rock shelter of La Madeleine in France. It lasted in Ukraine from approx the 20th to the 8th millennium BC. People of the Magdalenian culture engaged in hunting, gathering, and fishing. They lived a seminomadic life in loose tribal groupings with a matriarchal structure. Their dwellings consisted of conical huts made from animal skins placed on a frame of large bones (occasionally wood) and secured by stones and bones. Their flint technology, while still primitive, had become more sophisticated than in earlier eras. Notable artistic developments took place during this time, especially as seen in sculpture (particularly female figurines carved out of mammoth tusks) and (cave) paintings of the period. Important Magdalenian culture sites in Ukraine include Molodove V, Mizyn, and Kyrylivska. (See also *Paleolithic Period.)

Magdeburg law. The legal code adopted in medieval times by the city of Magdeburg and copied by many municipalities in Germany and Eastern and Central Europe, including Ukraine and Belarus. The code was based on the compilations of *Germanic law (the *Sachsenspiegel*) and showed little influence of Roman law. It combined norms of customary law with various municipal regulations.

Magdeburg law (ML) was brought to Ukraine by German colonists. King Danylo Romanovych and his successors granted them the right to establish their own judicial and administrative institutions and to use their own law. When Ukrainian territories were annexed by Lithuania and Poland, the right to use ML was granted by Polish kings or Lithuanian grand dukes. The first cities to receive ML included Volodymyr-Volynskyi (before 1324), Sianik (1339), Lviv (before 1352), Kamianets-Podilskyi (1374), and Berestia (1390). In the 15th and 16th centuries several towns of Right-Bank Ukraine received it, including Kiev (1494). Originally, ML applied only to the German inhabitants of the town. It was extended to all the residents of a town for the first time in Sianik, by Yurii II Boleslav.

Initially, the appointed *viit* (mayor) held much power in cities under ML, but eventually the cities purchased his power for themselves. The *magistrat* from then on was composed of an elected *viit*, two *burmistry*, and a body of *raitsi*. New members of the *magistrat* were co-opted. In a few instances the *viit* and *lava* court members were elected, and then the *magistrat* members were chosen from among the court members. Judicial authority was shared by the *magistrat* and *lava* court: their powers were not always distinctly defined. The *lava* courts were usually responsible for criminal matters. The *magistrat's* unrestricted power often led to an abuse of power by the city oligarchy. To protect the public against abuses, the king sometimes set up competing bodies representing the interests of the general population; eg in 1577 King Stephen Báthory established the *izba gminna* in Lviv to represent the broad spectrum of city residents and to advise the *magistrat*.

According to the first royal charters, the *magistrats* in towns governed by ML were to be composed of both Polish (Catholic) and Ukrainian (Orthodox) representatives. The Poles, however, often pushed the Ukrainians out of the city councils. In Kamianets-Podilskyi there were three separate national jurisdictions: Ukrainian, Polish, and Armenian. Only a few Ukrainian cities, including Lviv, Kiev, and Kamianets-Podilskyi, enjoyed the full rights of ML. Most towns had only partial rights; eg, their *viit* or starosta remained independent of the *magistrat*. In these towns, *magistrat* and *burmistry* were elected. The Lviv *magistrat* acted as an appellate court for other cities of Galicia.

The *Pereiaslav Treaty of 1654 guaranteed the rights of the Ukrainian cities governed by ML. The following cities in the Hetman state enjoyed ML: Kiev, Chernihiv, Pereiaslav, Starodub, Nizhen, Oster, Kozelets, Pohar, Pochep, Mglin, Novhorod-Siverskyi, and Poltava. Most of them received ML during the Polish-Lithuanian period, and the hetmans confirmed their rights. The rest obtained ML from the hetmans or the Russian tsars. The cities of the Hetman state usually had only some of the rights of ML: appeals of the decisions of city courts were heard by regimental courts and from 1730 by the General Court, and the regimental *starshyna* interfered in municipal affairs and limited the autonomy of the cities. However, some towns without ML acquired certain trappings and privileges of ML. Municipal self-government declined at the end of the 18th and the beginning of the 19th century, as Ukraine lost its autonomy and was absorbed into the Russian Empire. In 1831, the tsar finally abolished ML in all the cities except Kiev, where it remained in force until 1835. In Western Ukraine it was abolished by Joseph II in 1786.

The institution of ML in Ukraine promoted the formation of a distinct social estate out of the urban population. Although its influence was not as strong as in Western Europe, ML did introduce certain characteristics of Western city life into Ukraine and played an important role in bringing Ukrainian culture and law closer to European developments.

The main sources of ML in Western Ukraine and the Hetman state were 16th-century Polish translations of German and Latin codes done by P. Szczerbic and B. Groicki. In the second half of the 17th and in the early 18th century these codes were translated into Ukrainian. City courts relied not only on these codes but also on the *Lithuanian Statute and on local customary law. The *Code of Laws of 1743 provided for municipal self-government based on ML, but it did not come into force. ML was increasingly replaced by the Lithuanian Statute in the 18th century.

Many historians and jurists have studied ML in Ukraine, including V. Antonovych, M. Vladimirsky-Budanov, O. Kistiakovsky, O. Lazarevsky, M. Hrushevsky, D. Bahalii, M. Vasylenko, F. Taranovsky, D. Doroshenko, and A. Yakovliv. In general, Hrushevsky and Vladimirsky-Budanov pointed to the negative consequences of ML, while Antonovych, Bahalii, and Yakovliv noted its positive influence on Ukraine's legal and social traditions. Since the 1930s Soviet historians have paid little attention to ML and have usually been critical of its influence on the development of Ukrainian cities. (For further bibliography, see also *Germanic law.)

BIBLIOGRAPHY
Rozvidky pro mista i mishchanstvo na Ukraïni-Rusy v XV–XVIII vv., 2 vols (Lviv 1904)
Klymenko, P. 'Misto i terytoriia na Ukraïni za chasiv Het'manshchyny (1654–1767 rr.),' *ZIFV*, 7–8 (1926)

Padokh, Ia. *Mis'ki sudy na Ukraïni-Het'manshchyni pislia 1648 r.* (Munich 1948)

Kul'chyts'kyi, V. *Kodyfikatsiia prava na Ukraïni u XVIII st.* (Lviv 1958)

Tkach, A. *Istoriia kodyfikatsiï dorevoliutsiinoho prava Ukraïny* (Kiev 1968)

Magic. A set system of notions, rituals, and invocations that are believed to have a mysterious mystical power to influence physical phenomena or natural events. Magical practices can be traced into the distant past. They can be classified by their social function into malefactory, military, love, medical, preventative, productive, and meteorological, or by their psychological mechanism into contact (touching an object), imitative (similarity or mimicry), and sympathetic (substitution of part for the whole).

Magic played an important role in the life of Ukrainians, particularly the peasantry. Not a step could be taken without it. It was used widely in medicine: shamans used spells and charms, often combined with rational practices, employing medicinal plants or psychotherapy. Water, fire, and eggs were held in the highest esteem by Ukrainian sorcerers. Magic was also an important part of calendric folk rituals tied to farming (sowing, harvesting, taking livestock to pasture) and family life (birth, marriage, and death). Wetting with water, leaping over a fire, and the use of fur coats as a symbol of wealth often appear in these rituals. The most common form of malefactory magic was witchcraft. Witches were believed capable of depriving a cow of milk, of harming crops, and of inflicting disease and even death on particular people, but also of charming young men, of protecting people from disease, and of canceling the spells of other witches.

Magic is closely tied to religion. In the Middle Ages white magic, which invoked the saints and angels, and black magic, which turned to 'unclean spirits' such as devils and demons, were practiced widely in Ukraine. The alleged practitioners of black magic were often tried by the community or the courts, but there were no witch hunts comparable to those known in Western Europe.

BIBLIOGRAPHY

Antonovych, V. *Chary na Ukraïni* (Lviv 1905)

Bogatyrev, P. *Actes magiques: Rites et croyances en Russie Subcarpathique* (Paris 1929)

M. Mushynka

Magistrat. An institution of municipal self-government in Ukrainian cities enjoying *Magdeburg law in the 14th to 18th centuries. It was composed of the *viit (mayor), two *burmistry (chairmen of the city council), and two collegia: the city council composed of *raitsi*, and the *lava court. The officers and councilmen were elected by the city's residents or co-opted by sitting members. Sometimes the *viit* was appointed by the crown or landlord. The *magistrat* was responsible for city administration, the courts, the local economy and finances, and the police. This institution spread throughout Right-Bank Ukraine in the 15th to 17th centuries, to most cities of the Left Bank in the first quarter of the 17th century, and to Slobidska Ukraine in the early 18th century. In the Russian Empire *magistraty* were introduced by Peter I in the early 18th century to bring Russian urban administration closer to Western European models. They were abolished as organs of municipal self-government after the urban reforms of the 1780s, but the term was used until the 1860s to describe courts for merchants. In Ukrainian territories under Austrian and then Polish rule, the term was applied to the municipal executive that was elected by the municipal council.

Magner, Yukhym, b 1883, d 1931. Painter and set designer of German origin. In the 1920s he worked in Kharkiv for the Franko Theater (until 1926) and the Chervonozavodskyi Ukrainian Drama Theater. He designed the sets for productions of I. Karpenko-Kary's *Suieta* (Vanity), Ya. Mamontov's *Respublika na kolesakh* (Republic on Wheels), B. Lavrenov's *Rozlom* (The Split), I. Kocherha's *Pisnia v kelykhu* (Song in a Chalice), and M. Starytsky's *Oborona Bushi* (The Defense of Busha). An early victim of the Stalinist terror, he died in a Soviet prison camp.

Paul Magocsi   Sylvester Magura

Magocsi, Paul, b 26 January 1945 in Englewood, New Jersey. Historian. He studied at Rutgers and Princeton (PH D, 1972) universities and worked at the Harvard Ukrainian Research Institute as a scholarly associate and lecturer (1976–80). He has held the Chair of Ukrainian Studies at the University of Toronto since 1980 and became director of the Multicultural History Society of Ontario in 1990. His main scholarly interests include the history of Galicia and Transcarpathia and East Slavic immigration to the United States. He has written *The Shaping of a National Identity: Subcarpathian Rus', 1848–1948* (1978), *Galicia: A Historical Survey and Bibliographic Guide* (1983), and *Our People: Carpatho-Rusyns and Their Descendants in North America* (1984). He also prepared *Ukraine: A Historical Atlas* (1985) and *Carpatho-Rusyn Studies: An Annotated Bibliography* (vol 1 [1975–84], 1988). Magocsi has advocated a 'Rusyn,' as opposed to Ukrainian, identity for the inhabitants of Transcarpathia and the Prešov region. A bibliography of Magocsi's works was published in 1985.

Magura, Sylvester, b 2 January 1897 in Husiane, Lublin gubernia, and d ? Archeologist. He specialized in the Trypilian culture and wrote many scholarly articles during the 1920s and 1930s. In 1934 Magura became a member of the AN URSR (now ANU) Institute of the History of Material Culture. He remained in this position until 1937, when he was arrested in the Stalinist terror and sent to a prison camp, where he died. In 1960 he was rehabilitated.

Magura. The name (derived from a Rumanian word for hill) of several mountains and mountain ridges in the Ukrainian Carpathians. The highest of them is the Magura Ridge (1,362 m in height), located between the Opir and the Myzunka rivers in the High Beskyd. Also of note are Mt Magura (1,015 m) in the Hutsul Beskyd between the Cheremosh and Seret rivers in Bukovyna and Mt Magura in the southern part of the Gorgany.

Magyarone. The term applied, often pejoratively, to members of the Transcarpathian intelligentsia, especially the Greek Catholic clergy and hierarchy, who in the 19th and early 20th centuries consciously Magyarized themselves. Although some Magyarones sympathized with the Transcarpathian Russophiles or with the *tuteishi*, that is, the local patriots with a low level of Ukrainian national consciousness, they believed that Transcarpathia's Ukrainians would be better off if they became linguistically and culturally Magyarized. They actively fostered that assimilationist goal in the church and schools, where they introduced the use of Hungarian, through their Magyar-language periodicals *Kelet* (1888–1901) and *Görögkatholikus Szemle* (1899–1918) and through Budapest-based organizations, such as the National Committee for Magyars of the Greek Catholic Rite (est 1898) and the Union of Magyar Greek Catholics (est 1902). In the 19th century they opposed Transcarpathian 'awakeners' such as Rev O. Dukhnovych, A. Dobriansky, and Rev I. Rakovsky. After 1920, when Transcarpathia was part of Czechoslovakia, they propagated the idea of Transcarpathia's restoration to Hungary, and during the 1939–44 Hungarian occupation of Transcarpathia they supported and collaborated with the M. Horthy regime. Some prominent Magyarones were Bishops S. *Pankovych (I. Pankovics) and A. Papp of Mukachiv and I. Novak of Prešov, the scholars S. *Bonkáló and A. *Hodinka, and the politicians A. *Beskyd, A. *Brodii, M. Demko, S. *Fentsyk, Rev O. *Ilnytsky, Y. *Kaminsky, M. Kutkafalvy (Kutka), and A. Stefan (not to be confused with A. Shtefan).

Mahadyn, Trokhym, b 1801 in Bubny, Lokhvytsia county, Poltava gubernia, d after 1876. Kobzar. His repertoire included the classical dumas, such as those about the flight of the three brothers from Azov, Ivas Konovchenko, and the storm on the Black Sea. In 1876 P. Martynovych wrote down not only Mahadyn's dumas and songs but also his account of the kobzar brotherhood and its initiation rites.

Mahala settlement. A *Noua culture settlement of the late Bronze and early Iron ages, located near the village of Mahala, Chernivtsi oblast. Excavated between 1955 and 1960, this site and the *Ostrivets archeological site are the most illustrative examples of Noua culture in Ukrainian lands.

Mahalevsky, Yurii [Mahalevs'kyj, Jurij], b 1876 in Podilia gubernia, d 29 October 1935 in Lviv. Painter. He studied, at the St Petersburg Academy of Arts, under I. Repin and then in Paris. In 1917–18 he worked in education in the Katerynoslav region. As an émigré, from 1922 he lived in Lviv, where for many years he headed the *Ukrainian Emigrant Aid Society. Mahalevsky painted many portraits of Ukrainian leaders, such as Gen A. Huly-

Hulenko, Gen M. Omelianovych-Pavlenko, I. Lypa, I. Svientsitsky, O. Zaharov, and S. Fedak; painted decorative murals in churches and chapels in Galician villages, such as Holosko Velyke, Uhersko, Stare Selo, Olesko, Rava Ruska, and Kholoiv; and illustrated books. His recollections were published in *Literaturno-naukovyi vistnyk* and the *Dnipro* almanacs.

Mahar, Volodymyr, b 5 July 1900 in Kalnybolota, Zvenyhorodka county, Kiev gubernia, d 11 August 1965 in Zaporizhia. Stage director and actor. In 1934 he completed study at the Lysenko Music and Drama Institute in Kiev. In 1936 he joined the Kiev Oblast Touring Theater as artistic director and actor. He moved in 1938 to Zhytomyr and then in 1944 to Zaporizhia with the theater, of which he remained artistic director until his death.

Mahda, Ivan, b 12 June 1904 in Barvinkove, Izium county, Kharkiv gubernia. Veterinary surgeon. A graduate of the Kharkiv Veterinary Institute (1926), he began working there in 1927 (today the Kharkiv Zootechnical-Veterinary Institute) and became head of the surgery department in 1935. He is the author of scholarly works and textbooks on anesthesiology and veterinary surgery.

Mahdalynivka. V-15. A town smt (1990 pop 7,000) on the Chaplynka River and a raion center in Dnipropetrovske oblast. It was founded in the late 18th century and was made an smt in 1958. The town has a regional museum and several enterprises of the food industry.

Mahomet, Yosyp, b 13 January 1880 in Kornyn, Skvyra county, Kiev gubernia, d 27 September 1973 in Skvyra, Kiev oblast. Horticulturist. A self-educated man, he began working at the Skvyra experimental farm in 1919 and became head of its selection and seed cultivation division in 1946. He developed and refined over 100 fruit, vegetable, and flower varieties, among them the 1-528 onion, the 247-4 carrot, and the Skvyra early melon.

Maiak, Yosyp [Majak, Josyp], b 25 December 1882 in Pidlisnivka, Sumy county, Kharkiv gubernia, d 28 October 1974 in Kiev. Stage actor. Maiak worked in the troupes of M. Yaroshenko, D. Haidamaka, and L. Sabinin in 1908–14 and in the Kharkiv Theater of Miniatures in 1918. He studied at the Kharkiv Theater-Studio under the direction of Ya. Mamontov and I. Yukhymenko in 1920–2 and worked in the Kharkiv Franko Theater (1923–6), the Dnipropetrovske Ukrainian Drama Theater (1926–7), the Kharkiv Chervonozavodskyi Ukrainian Drama Theater (1928–30), and the Odessa Ukrainian Drama Theater (1931–64). He played Shevchenko in S. Holovanivsky's *Poetova dolia* (A Poet's Fate) and the title role in W. Shakespeare's *Othello*.

Maiak. A publishing house founded in Odessa in 1964 on the basis of the Odessa Oblast Newspaper-Journal Publishers (1945–60) and the Odessa Book Publishers (1960–4). It publishes books on a wide range of topics, including regional studies, and tourist guides to Odessa, Mykolaiv, and Vinnytsia oblasts. In the early 1970s it published approx 100 titles annually, with a total run of approx 1.2 to 2.4 million copies.

Maiak (Beacon). An illustrated weekly of culture and civic affairs, published in Kiev from January 1913 to July 1914. Edited by Z. Shevchenko, it published articles on literary and historical topics, political commentaries, prose, and poetry. Contributors included P. Tychyna, Ya. Mamontov, O. Slisarenko, and M. Hodovanets. Special issues were devoted to M. Kotsiubynsky, T. Shevchenko, and Lesia Ukrainka. The journal advocated liberal democratic politics and devoted special attention to the Ukrainian and peasant questions in the Russian Empire. The tsarist government used the pretext of the outbreak of the First World War to close down *Maiak*.

Maiak (Beacon). A Russian literary and cultural monthly published in St Petersburg in the years 1840–5. It was edited by P. Korsakov and S. Burachek, who despite their reactionary, xenophobic views promoted 'Little Russian' literature and published in the journal works by the Ukrainian writers H. Kvitka-Osnovianenko, P. Hulak-Artemovsky, Ye. Hrebinka, O. Korsun, K. Dumytrashko, and T. Shevchenko, and articles by such ethnographers as I. Sreznevsky, M. Kostomarov, A. Metlynsky, and O. Afanasiev-Chuzhbynsky.

Maiakovsky, Vladimir [Majakovs'kij], b 19 July 1893 in Bagdadi (now Maiakovsky), Georgia, d 14 April 1930 in Moscow. Russian futurist poet of Ukrainian descent. His attitude to Ukraine ranged from one of great sympathy for the land of his ancestors and its language, as in 'Dolg Ukraine' (Debt to Ukraine, 1926), to one of Russian chauvinism, as in 'Nashemu iunoshestvu' (To Our Youth, 1927). Many editions of his poetry have appeared in Ukrainian translation, including *Vybrane* (Selections, 1936, 1940) and *Vybrani tvory* (Selected Works, 3 vols, 1953).

Heorhii Maiboroda   Platon Maiboroda

Maiboroda, Heorhii [Majboroda, Heorhij], b 1 December 1913 at Pelekhivshchyna *khutir*, Kremenchuk county, Poltava gubernia, d 7 December 1992 in Kiev. Composer; brother of P. Maiboroda. A student of L. Revutsky, he graduated from (1941; graduate studies, 1949) and taught at (1952–8) the Kiev Conservatory. In 1967–8 he served as head of the Union of Composers of Ukraine, and in 1967, 1971, and 1975 as deputy to the Supreme Soviet of the Ukrainian SSR. His works commonly use heroic and patriotic themes in monumental forms, and have achieved wide recognition among state authorities and the general public. He composed the operas *Mylana* (1957), *Arsenal*

(1960), *Taras Shevchenko* (1964), and *Yaroslav the Wise* (1973); three symphonies (1940, 1952, 1976); a concerto for voice and orchestra (1969); the symphonic poems *Lily* (text by T. Shevchenko, 1939) and *Kameniari* (Stone-cutters, text by I. Franko, 1941); the vocal-symphonic poem *Zaporozhians* (text by L. Zabashta, 1954); and the orchestral *Hutsul Rhapsody* (1949). He also wrote songs to texts by V. Sosiura, T. Masenko, A. Mickiewicz, Lesia Ukrainka, I. Franko, and P. Tychyna, as well as incidental music for W. Shakespeare's *Hamlet* and *King Lear*. Together with L. Revutsky he edited and orchestrated piano and violin concertos by V. Kosenko.

BIBLIOGRAPHY
Hordiichuk, M. *Hryhorii Ilarionovych Maiboroda* (Kiev 1963)
Zin'kevych, O. *Heorhii Maiboroda* (Kiev 1973)
                                                          R. Savytsky

Maiboroda, Platon [Majboroda], b 1 December 1918 at Pelekhivshchyna *khutir*, Kremenchuk county, Poltava gubernia, d 8 August 1989 in Kiev. Composer; brother of H. Maiboroda. He studied under L. Revutsky and graduated (1947) from the Kiev Conservatory. His works include the symphonic overture *Prometheus*, choral works, and the vocal-symphonic poem *Poplar* (text by T. Shevchenko, 1966). He is best known for his popular songs, such as 'The Kiev Waltz,' 'White Chestnuts,' 'Song about the Dnieper,' and the widely familiar 'Rushnychok' (Embroidered Towel, text by A. Malyshko), which is commonly known as 'Ridna maty moia' (Dear Mother Mine). He was awarded the Shevchenko State Prize in 1962.

BIBLIOGRAPHY
Hordiichuk, M. *Platon Ilarionovych Maiboroda* (Kiev 1964)

Maichyk, Ivan [Majčyk], b 1927 in the Lemko region. Folk musicologist, composer, and conductor. He was artistic director of the Trembita Kapelle, which he founded, and the Choir of the Lviv Television and Radio Committee. He has published seven collections of folk music, arranged over 120 Lemko songs for choir, and set over 150 poems to music. His chief works are *Ukraïns'ki narodni pisni v obrobtsi I. Maichyka* (Ukrainian Folk Songs Arranged by I. Maichyk, 1980), *Oi zatsvila cheremshyna* (Oh, the Chokecherry Has Bloomed, 1981), and *Ukraïns'ki narodni pisni z repertuaru O. Vrabelia* (Ukrainian Folk Songs from O. Vrabel's Repertoire, 1982).

Maidansky, Vsevolod [Majdans'kyj] (Kolomiitsev-Maidansky), b 10 December 1927 in Kalisz, Poland. Orthodox bishop. He studied theology at the Warsaw Theological Seminary and at the Dillingen Theological University in Germany, and social work at Yeshiva University in New York (MA, 1964), and worked at the Albert Einstein College of Medicine. In 1985 he was ordained a priest of the Ukrainian Orthodox Church of America, and in 1987 he was consecrated a bishop and head of the church. He has been actively involved in the ecumenical movement, in cultivating close relations with other Ukrainian Orthodox churches and the Ukrainian Catholic church and serving as a member of the Standing Conference of Canonical Orthodox Bishops of America.

Maidanyk, Yakiv [Majdanyk, Jakiv] (Maydanek, Jacob), b 20 October 1891 in Svydova, Chortkiv county, Gali-

Yakiv Maidanyk: title page of his *Vuikova knyha*

Hryhorii Maifet   Ivan Maistrenko

cia, d 3 June 1984 in Winnipeg. Cartoonist and writer. After emigrating to Canada in 1911, he graduated from teachers' college in Brandon and worked as a teacher for a while. His popular caricatures and humorous letters and stories on Ukrainian immigrant life, written in the voice of the loutish cartoon character Shtif Tabachniuk, appeared in the Ukrainian and English press. He also wrote a successful comedy, *Manigrula* (1915). In the 1920s he edited and published the magazine *Vuiko and illustrated calendars of Shtif Tabachniuk. He also published two collections of his drawings and writings, *Vuikova knyha* (Uncle's Book, 1931) and *Vuiko Shtif Tabachniuk i inshi novi korotki opovidannia* (Uncle Shtif Tabachniuk and Other New Short Stories, 1959). H. Kuchmij's film *Laughter in My Soul* (1983) provides a portrait of Maidanyk and his comic creation.

Maievsky, Ivan [Majevs'kyj], b and d ? Political activist and journalist. He appeared in Kiev in 1917; his origin remains a mystery. Some claim he came to Ukraine from the United States. He was elected to the CC of the Ukrainian Party of Socialist Revolutionaries, and represented the party in the Central Rada and the Little Rada. He published the paper *Konfederalist*, which advocated independence for Ukraine. In January 1919 he organized an unsuccessful uprising against the Rumanians in Khotyn. He was last seen in April 1919.

Maifet, Hryhorii [Majfet, Hryhorij], b 1 August 1903 in Romen, Poltava gubernia, d 13 September 1975 in Kanin, near Pechora, RSFSR. Literary scholar and critic. He graduated from the Poltava Institute of People's Education in 1924 and completed postgraduate studies at the Taras Shevchenko Scientific Research Institute in Kharkiv. From 1931 to 1934 he taught Western European literary history at the Poltava Pedagogical Institute. He was arrested in 1934 and was sentenced to 10 years' imprisonment in concentration camps. He was released in 1946 and was ordered to settle in Kanin in the Soviet Arctic. Maifet was fluent in English, German, French, Italian, and Spanish. From 1925 to the time of his arrest he published over 100 articles dealing with the development of Ukrainian and Western literatures and with translations of the works of T. Shevchenko into other languages. Among his works were *Materiialy do kharakterystyky tvorchosty P.H. Tychyny*

(Materials for the Characterization of the Work of P.H. Tychyna, 1926), *Pryroda noveli: Zbirka persha* (The Nature of the Novella: First Collection, 1928), *Pryroda noveli: Zbirka druha* (The Nature of the Novella: Second Collection, 1929), 'Meni odnakovo' ta ioho vidtvorennia v anhliis'komu i nimets'komu perekladakh ([Shevchenko's] 'Meni Odnakovo' and Its Rendering in English and German Translations, 1929).

Maiorov, Mikhail [Majorov, Mixail] (né Biberman), b 10 January 1890 in Skorodnoe, Homel county, Mahiliou gubernia, d 20 January 1938. Bolshevik activist and Soviet official. After the February Revolution in 1917 he was a leader of the Bolshevik faction in the Kiev Council of Workers' Deputies, chairman of the Bolshevik All-Ukrainian Provisional Committee (May–June 1918), and a leader of the Bolshevik underground in Kiev and Katerynoslav. Under Soviet rule he was a candidate (1918–20) and full member (1920–1) of the CC CP(B)U, first secretary of the Party's Odessa Gubernia Committee (1922–3) and Odessa Oblast Committee (1932–3), deputy head of the CP(B)U Central Control Commission (CCC; 1927–30), a member of the All-Union CCC (1927–34), the people's commissar of supply in Ukraine (1930–2), and a candidate member of the CC CP(B)U Politburo (1932–3). He wrote books on the revolutionary struggle in Ukraine in 1914–19 (1922; Ukrainian trans 1928) and the 1905 Revolution in Ukraine (1932). He perished in the Stalinist terror.

Maisky, Mykhailo [Majs'kyj, Myxajlo] (pseud of Mykhailo Bulgakov), b 3 June 1889 in Hraivoron, now in Kursk oblast, RF, d 31 December 1960 in Kharkiv. Writer. Maisky initially wrote in Russian, and was first published in 1920. He then began writing in Ukrainian, joined Hart and Vaplite, and published collections of stories, among which were *Nich* (Night, 1925), *Tvortsi biloho mista* (The Creators of the White City, 1927), *Borh* (Debt, 1930), *Industriial'ni etiudy* (Industrial Etudes, 1930), *Ispyt* (The Test, 1930), *Noveli* (Novellas, 1930), *Zlochyny staroho maistra* (The Crimes of the Old Master, 1931), and *Kosmynyna problema* (Kosmyn's Problem, 1932). He was repressed in the early 1930s, and withdrew from futher literary work.

Maistrenko, Ivan [Majstrenko] (pseuds: Babenko, Daleky, Korsun, Radchenko, Hrebinka, Avgur), b 28 August 1899 in Opishnia, Zinkiv county, Poltava gubernia, d 18 November 1984 in Munich. Political figure and publicist.

In 1919–20 he was a leading member of the *Borotbists' Kobeliaky partisan brigade. In 1920 he entered the CP(B)U together with the Borotbists, but he soon quit it to join the independentist *Ukrainian Communist party (UKP), was elected to its CC, and became a UKP activist in the Donbas (1920–1). When the UKP was forced to dissolve in 1925, he rejoined the CP(B)U and worked as an editor for the republican papers *Selians'ka pravda* and *Komunist*, in the cooperative movement, and as a political lecturer and propagandist. He played an important role in the Ukrainization of Odessa as deputy chief editor of the city paper *Chornomors'ka komuna* (1929–31). From 1931 he was deputy director of the All-Ukrainian Communist Institute of Journalism in Kharkiv. After being expelled from the Party in 1935, he was arrested in December 1936, and he survived over a year in a Kharkiv prison and three years in Siberian labor camps. In 1942–3, under German rule, he managed the Ukrainian Banduryst Kapelle that toured Western Ukraine and entertained Ukrainian *Ostarbeiter* in Germany. As a postwar refugee in Bavaria he led the left faction of the *Ukrainian Revolutionary Democratic party and edited its monthly newspaper *Vpered* (1949–59). He also prepared regular political commentaries and analyses for Radio Liberty and was a professor at and rector (1979–84) of the *Ukrainian Technical and Husbandry Institute. Maistrenko wrote numerous articles and brochures (many under the pseud Babenko) on Soviet politics, economics, and society and on Marxist theoretical issues. His most important works are *Borot'bism: A Chapter in the History of Ukrainian Communism* (1954); books, in Ukrainian, on the nationality policy of the CPSU (1978) and the history of the CPU (1979); and his memoirs, *Istoriia moho pokolinnia* (History of My Generation, 1985).

Maivsky, Dmytro [Majivs'kyj] (nom de guerre: Taras Kosar), b 8 November 1914 in Reklynets, Zhovkva county, Galicia, d 19 December 1945. Revolutionary and OUN leader. He joined the OUN when he was still a secondary-school student, and eventually was placed in charge of its cadres in Zhovkva county. During the Soviet occupation of Galicia (1939–41) he was OUN commander for Sokal okruha and delegate to the Second Great Assembly of the OUN. In May 1943 he was appointed to the three-man OUN Executive Bureau and placed in charge of propaganda. He was editor of *Ideia i chyn* (1942, 1944–5) and one of the organizers of the Third Great Assembly, which made major revisions in the OUN political program. He died in battle against Soviet border guards as he tried to cross the Soviet-Czechoslovak border.

Majer, Józef, b 12 March 1808 in Cracow, d 3 July 1899 in Cracow. Polish anthropologist. A doctor of medicine and a surgeon by profession, he held the Chair of Physiology at Cracow University (1848–56, 1861–77), where he also served as rector (1848–51, 1865–6). Among his numerous works are a study (with I. Kopernicki) of the physical traits of Galicia's population in *Zbiór wiadomości do antropologji krajowej* (vols 1 and 9, 1877, 1885) and articles on the physical traits of Ukrainians in the Dnieper region as compared to those of Ukrainians in Galicia (1879) and on the annual physical growth of Galicia's population (1881). A biography of Majer, by A. Wrzosek, was published in Wrocław in 1957.

Majolica or maiolica. Earthenware made of colored, coarse-grained clay and covered with a white tin glaze. A massive form, brilliant glaze, and sharp color contrast are its typical features. Majolica was introduced in Italy from Moorish Spain through the island of Majorca or Maiolica (hence its name). Introduced in Ukraine as early as the 11th century, majolica tableware was used by the nobility there, and majolica tiles decorated the Church of the Tithes and St Sophia Cathedral in Kiev and other churches in Chernihiv, Halych, and Volodymyr-Volynskyi. In the 17th to 19th centuries majolica tiles, tiled stoves and fireplaces, and tableware were produced in Kiev and in Nizhen, Horodnia, and Ichnia in the Chernihiv region. Today majolica products are made by potters in Opishnia, in Poltava oblast; Ichnia and Nizhen, in Chernihiv oblast; Vasylkiv and Dybyntsi, in Kiev oblast; Hnylets and Holovkivka, in Cherkasy oblast; Bubnivka and Bar, in Vinnytska oblast; Smotrych, in Khmelnytskyi oblast; Kosiv and Kolomyia, in Ivano-Frankivske oblast; and Vilkhivka, in Transcarpathia. A book about contemporary Ukrainian majolica by V. Shcherbak was published in Kiev in 1974.

Major schools (*holovni shkoly*). Public *elementary schools established in cities of the Austrian and Russian empires in the 18th century. In their Austrian variant, major schools (German: *Hauptschulen*) had a four-year program with a teacher for each grade. Clerics were often the instructors at and the administrators of the schools. After completing practical training, graduates of major schools were qualified to teach in the more rudimentary trivium schools. Major schools were established in the larger cities of Galicia and Bukovyna in 1776; instruction was in German and later in Polish. Courses were taught in Ukrainian only at the Basilian major school in Lavriv (1789–1911), which graduated 7,000 students. After the Austrian reorganization of urban public schools in 1863, the major schools were transformed into seven-year public elementary schools (see also *Senior elementary schools).

In 1786 Catherine II issued the Statute for Public Schools in the Russian Empire, which made education a state responsibility and established major schools (Russian: *glavnye narodnye uchilishcha*). Modelled largely on the Austrian model, these schools had a five-year, four-grade program, with the final grade lasting two years. Graduates of the major schools could become teachers at minor schools. Major schools were established only in large cities and towns. The first Ukrainian major school was established in Kiev in 1789. Major schools were abolished in 1804 with Alexander I's school reform and replaced with *county schools.

B. Krawchenko

Mak, Bohdan, b 11 June 1926 in Polivtsi, Chortkiv county, Galicia. Engineer and business executive. He served as an officer in the UPA in 1943–7. Emigrating to the United States in 1950, he completed his education in mechanical engineering and business administration and worked as a research engineer and manager in the fields of rocketry and explosives with the United States Department of Defense. He lectured at the University of Miami and then worked in private industry. In 1972 he was appointed vice-president of Valiant Metal Co. Mak has published numerous papers on subjects such as rocket propellants, valves, and cyclothol explosives.

Olha Mak   Stefan Makar

Volodymyr Makar   Oleksander Makarchenko

Mak, Olha (pseud of O. Hets; née Petrov), b 20 July 1913 in Kamianets-Podilskyi, Podilia gubernia. Emigré writer. A postwar refugee, she emigrated in 1947 to Brazil, where she was active in the Ukrainian Relief Committee (1948–9) in Curitiba. She emigrated to Toronto in 1970, where she became president of the Association of Ukrainian Writers for Young People (1971–6). She has written several widely read works: the memoirs *Z chasiv iezhovshchyny* (From the Time of the Yezhov Terror, 2nd edn, 1954); the adventure novel *Boh vohniu* (The God of Fire, 3 vols, 1955–6) and the historical novel *Zhaïra* (2 vols, 1957–8), which are set in Amazonia; and the novels *Chudasii* (The Strange One, 1956), *Proty perekonan'* (Against One's Convictions, 1959), *Kudy ishla stezhka* (Where the Path Went, 1961), and *Kaminnia pid kosoiu* (Stones beneath the Scythe, 1973), which deal with Stalinist rule in Ukraine. Mak has also published prose, as well as articles and feuilletons, in émigré periodicals.

Makar, Stefan (pen name: Stepan Khlopiv), b 1870 in Bushkovychi, Peremyshl county, Galicia, d 2 January 1915 in Cleveland. Greek Catholic priest and community activist. After emigrating to the United States in 1897, he was elected to the auditing committee of the Ruthenian National Association and became editor of the association's paper *Svoboda* (1897–1900). He contributed sketches, stories, and a survey of Ukrainian immigration to the United States. His plays *Amerykans'kyi shliakhtych* (American Noble) and *Skupar* (Miser) were staged successfully, and a collection of his stories appeared in the early 1900s as *Biznes* (Business). He translated English books into Ukrainian and compiled a Ukrainian–English dictionary (1901). Much of his time was devoted to organizing Ukrainian schools and financial institutions.

Makar, Volodymyr, b 4 January 1911 in Stanyslaviv, Galicia. Political activist and journalist. As a student at Lviv University (1929–32) he became involved in the OUN and was arrested by the Polish authorities in 1932, 1934, and 1936 for his activities. He emerged from prison only after Poland's defeat in 1939 and remained in the OUN underground during the Soviet occupation of Galicia. Under the German occupation he worked in the press and information agency of the OUN (Bandera faction), and in 1943 he joined the staff of its underground radio station, Free Ukraine. After being stricken with typhus in 1944, he was taken to the West. He has served in the OUN network in Austria, Belgium, and Canada. He has written several books of memoirs – *Bereza Kartuz'ka* (1956), *Boiovi druzi* (Comrades in Arms, 1980), and *Proidenyi shliakh* (The Traveled Road, 1983).

Makara, Arsen, b 31 January 1916 in Lubianka, Kiev county, d 17 April 1975 in Kiev. Metallurgist; corresponding member of the AN URSR from 1967. He graduated from the Kiev Polytechnical Institute (1940) and from 1954 to 1970 was deputy director of the AN URSR Institute of Electric Welding. His main technical contributions were in the area of the electric welding of special steels.

Makara, Serhii, b 6 May 1937 in Michalovce, Slovakia. Ukrainian poet in the Prešov region. He began writing in 1953 and has published six collections of poetry, the titles of which reveal the content of his poems: *Osiaiana iunist'* (Illuminated Youth, 1958), *Zrostannia* (Maturing, 1961), *Shukaiu sebe* (I Am Searching for Myself, 1967), *Sovist'* (Conscience, 1970), *Lenin z namy* (Lenin Is with Us, 1980), and *Syvyna torknulas' skron'* (Grayness Has Touched the Temples, 1985). He has also written a collection for children, *Shcho virsh – to zahadka* (Every Poem Is a Riddle, 1982). His poetry is marked by a heavy reliance on simile, a paucity of metaphors, attempts at philosophizing, and a didactic declarative tone.

Makarchenko, Oleksander [Makarčenko], b 22 October 1903 in Mariiupil, Katerynoslav gubernia, d 5 July 1979 in Kiev. Neurophysiologist; full member of the AN URSR (now ANU) from 1961. A graduate of the Kharkiv Medical Institute (1933), he served as director of the Ukrainian Institute for the Upgrading of Physicians in Kharkiv (1937–9) and the Lviv Medical Institute (1939–41). He was deputy health minister of the Tadzhik SSR (1942–4), the Ukrainian SSR (1944–9), and the Russian SFSR (1949–50) and then worked at the Kiev Institute for the Upgrading of Physicians (1950–3) and the Institute of Physiology of the AN URSR (1953–66, from 1955 as director). He served one term (1962–3) as vice-president of the AN URSR. His work dealt with the influence of infections and intoxication on the bioelectrical activity of the cerebral cortex, the interrelations between the cortex and the subcortical regions under normal and pathological conditions, and the effect of manganese poisoning on the nervous system.

Andrii Makarenko

Anton Makarenko

Makarenko, Andrii, b 17 July 1886 in Hadiache, Poltava gubernia, d 28 September 1963 in Houston, Texas. Civic figure. During the revolution, while holding a high position in the railway administration for Ukraine, he used his influence to organize Ukrainian railway workers, and in the summer of 1917 he formed a railway regiment, which became a part of the UNR Army. Under the Hetman government he was appointed chairman of a department in the Ministry of Railways. As a member of the Ukrainian National Union he helped organize P. Skoropadsky's overthrow and then sat on the Directory of the UNR. In the interwar period he lived in Czechoslovakia, where he completed a doctorate at the Ukrainian Higher Pedagogical Institute. After the war he fled from Soviet forces to Germany, where he worked to save Ukrainian refugees from repatriation to the USSR. In 1951 he settled in the United States.

Makarenko, Anton, b 13 March 1888 in Bilopillia, Sumy county, Kharkiv gubernia, d 1 April 1939 in Moscow. Soviet pedagogue and writer. After completing teacher training in Kremenchuk (1905) Makarenko held various teaching positions in Ukraine. He studied at the Poltava Pedagogical Institute (1914–17) and taught at schools in Poltava and Kriukiv. In 1920 he began a new phase of his career by founding and running an institution outside of Poltava for homeless children, the Gorky Labor Colony. From 1927 until 1935 Makarenko headed the Dzerzhynsky Children's Commune, a penal institution for young offenders outside of Kharkiv. The colony held many children left homeless by the man-made famine of 1932–3. Makarenko then worked in Kiev as deputy head of the labor-colony division of the NKVD (1935–6) and also headed a labor colony in Brovary, a village near the mass grave of victims of the NKVD in the Bykivnia forest, on the outskirts of Kiev. In 1937 Makarenko moved to Moscow, where he spent the rest of his life writing literary and pedagogical works.

The central tenet of Makarenko's pedagogical theories was that the education of children should be based upon and accomplished through the collective. Makarenko applied this principle by creating a system of children's brigades and hierarchical structures of self-government that allowed children to participate in the administration of the collective and relied on peer pressure to enforce conformity to the standards of behavior demanded by the collective. Competition among brigades (similar to the Stakhanovite method used in industry), paramilitary uniforms and daily rituals, collective criticism of misbehavior, and the director's exclusive right to punish miscreants served to maintain order in Makarenko's children's collectives. The children were always reminded that their own collective was part of the larger Soviet collective. Makarenko countered the objection that educating children through the collective destroys individuality by maintaining that in a socialist society the interest of the collective and the interest of the individual become the same.

Makarenko's most important works are *Marsh 30 goda* (The March of 1930, 1932), *Pedagogicheskaia poema* (Pedagogical Poem, 3 vols, 1933–5; often titled The Road to Life in English translations), an account of his work at the Gorky Labor Colony, and *Kniga dlia roditelei* (A Book for Parents, 1937). Makarenko wrote only in Russian, but his books have been translated into 58 languages. His collected works (in 7 vols) appeared in Ukrainian (1953–5) and Russian (1957–8). Makarenko's fiction was influenced by M. Gorky. Centers specializing in the study of Makarenko and his pedagogical theories exist in England, Bulgaria, Italy, Germany, Czechoslovakia, and Japan. The Makarenko research center based at Philipps University in Marburg, Germany, is the leader in the field.

BIBLIOGRAPHY
Dadenkov, M. *Zhyttia, diial'nist' i pedahohichni ideï A.S. Makarova* (Kiev 1949)
Lilge, F. *Anton Semyonovitch Makarenko* (Berkeley–Los Angeles 1958)
Bowen, J. *Soviet Education* (Madison, Wis 1962)
Get'manets', M. *A.S. Makarenko i kontseptsiia novogo cheloveka v sovetskoi literature 20–30-kh godov* (Kharkiv 1978)

C. Freeland

Makarenko, Ivan, b 4 January 1884 in the Kuban, d May 1945 in Prague. Kuban civic and political leader; brother of P. *Makarenko. At the outbreak of the revolution in 1917, he was active in the councils that sprang up in the Kuban. He proposed the idea of a union of the various Cossack hosts and mountain peoples that led to the formation of the Southeastern krai, and he served as the union's vice-president. He was the author of the constitution of the Kuban krai, adopted in September 1917, and the republic's general comptroller. After the revolution he emigrated to Czechoslovakia. In April 1945 he was arrested by the Gestapo. He was liberated by the Czech resistance but later the same day was shot in street fighting.

Makarenko, Mykola, b 4 February 1877 in Moskalivka, Romen county, Poltava gubernia, d 1937. Art historian, archeologist, and graphic artist; full member of the Ukrainian Scientific Society (UNT) and Poltava and Chernihiv archival commissions. A graduate of the Shtiglits Technical Art School and Archeological Institute in St Petersburg, from 1902 to 1917 he conducted many digs in Ukraine and Russia for the Russian Archeological Commission and the Moscow Archeological Institute while teaching art history and working as an assistant curator in the Hermitage Museum in St Petersburg. In 1919 he moved to Kiev, where he became chairman of the UNT art section, full member of the *All-Ukrainian Archeological Committee, the first director (1920–5) of the VUAN Museum of Arts (now the *Kiev Museum of Western and Eastern Art), and a member of the Restoration Commission (est 1924). He continued working as an archeologist; he

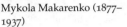

Mykola Makarenko (1877–1937)   Petro Makarenko

excavated settlements near Romen, Olbia, Oster, and Pryluka and oversaw restorations of medieval churches and monasteries in Chernihiv, Kiev, and Pryluka. He wrote many articles; a book in Russian on barrows and fortified settlements in Poltava gubernia (1917); books in Ukrainian on the VUAN Art Museum (1924), 16th- to 18th-century Ukrainian book ornamentation (1926), and the Mariiupil burial site (1933); and long articles on the Chernihiv Transfiguration Cathedral (1928) and sculpture and carving in Kievan Rus' before the Mongol invasion (1930). He was arrested in late 1933 and exiled to Kazan, Russia, where he taught at the university for two years. In 1937 he was rearrested and executed by the NKVD.

Makarenko, Mykola, b 19 December 1912 in Kiev. Stage and film director. After completing study at the Kiev Institute of Theater Arts (1935) he began to work in cinema (1937). In 1942–56 he worked as actor and director in theaters in Zaporizhia, Luhanske, and Vinnytsia. Assisted by the writer M. Stelmakh, Makarenko produced a film trilogy based on Stelmakh's novel *Velyka ridnia* (The Great Family): *Krov liuds'ka – ne vodytsia* (Human Blood Is Not Water, 1960), *Dmytro Horytsvit* (1962), and *Liudy ne vse znaiut* (People Don't Know Everything, 1964).

Makarenko, Petro, b 6 July 1888 in Novoshcherbynivka Stanytsia, Kuban, d 13 April 1970 in Caracas, Venezuela. Political leader, brother of I. *Makarenko. A graduate of the Higher Pedagogical Institute in Moscow (1914), he rose to prominence in the Kuban during the revolutionary period. He was a member of the Kuban Territorial and Legislative councils (1917–19) and headed the Kuban Committee for Propaganda, the Territorial Council's school commission, the Kuban delegation to the General Cossack Congress in Petrograd (mid-1917), and the special mission to Ukraine (1918). On 19 November 1919, after A. Denikin's coup d'état, he was arrested, and a month later he was deported to Turkey. After settling in Prague, Makarenko helped organize the Kuban Hromada, which he headed (1921–39), and the Kuban Historical Archive and Library Abroad (1925). In 1930 he directed a protest campaign against Polish repressions in Galicia. During the Second World War he fled to Germany, and in 1949 he emigrated to Venezuela. In Caracas he founded and di-

rected the Center for Research on Ukrainian Culture and a Ukrainian radio program (1951–9). He edited a number of Ukrainian newspapers in the Kuban and Prague as well as *Kuban': Zbirnyk stattiv pro Kuban' i kubantsiv* (Kuban: A Collection of Articles on the Kuban and Kubanians, 1926). He also wrote the monumental *Tragediia kozachestva* (The Tragedy of Cossackdom, 5 vols, 1933–9) and *Imperialismo, colonialismo y capitalismo en Rusia: Panorama historico, 1462–1962* (1963).

Makarenko, Serhii, b 10 January 1904 in Chernihiv gubernia, d 6 May 1979 in New York. Painter. In the 1920s he studied at the Kiev State Art Institute and became a member of the *Union of Contemporary Artists of Ukraine (1928). After graduating in 1930, he worked as a book illustrator and designer in Kharkiv, supervised an art workshop, and chaired the Department of Art Studies at the Kharkiv Pedagogical Institute. He emigrated to Yugoslavia in 1943, and thence to Italy, Argentina (1949), and the United States (1960). In Argentina he achieved a national reputation as a portraitist. In the United States he created many portraits, of figures such as V. Lypynsky, O. Arkhimovych, S. Smal-Stotsky, M. Shashkevych, T. Shevchenko, and Hetman I. Mazepa, and painted murals and iconostases in Ukrainian churches in Brooklyn, Boston, Long Island, Trenton, Parma, and Cleveland. A monograph on him and his wife, N. *Somko, was published in 1971.

Makarenko, Serhii, b 11 September 1937 in Kryvyi Rih. Canoeing champion. Together with L. Geishtor, he won the 1960 Olympic gold medal in the men's 1,000-m Canadian pairs and the 1961 and 1963 European championships in the men's 10,000-m Canadian pairs. He was also the Canadian singles world champion in 1963 and the Ukrainian and USSR champion several times in 1959–63.

Makarenko, Volodymyr (Makar), b 26 July 1943 in Verkhivtseve, Verkhnodniprovske raion, Dnipropetrovske oblast. Painter and graphic artist. A graduate of the Dnipropetrovske Art School (1963) and Leningrad Institute of Applied Art (1969), he was forced to leave Leningrad in 1973, and settled in Tallinn, Estonia. In 1975 he received first prize at the Biennale of Graphic Art in Ljubljana, Slovenia, and helped to organize the first Ukrainian nonconformist exhibition, which was held in Moscow in a private apartment. In 1976 his first one-man exhibition was held at the Galerie Hardy in Paris. Makarenko emigrated to the West in 1979 and settled in Paris. The subjects of most of his works are highly personal, as are his images and vocabulary, which often reflect his Ukrainian heritage and Ukrainian history and literature. His 'mixed-media' watercolors and oils reveal his childhood dreams (eg, *Souvenir de ma mère*, 1973), nostalgia for his homeland (*Melancholy Evening in Kiev*, 1975), erotic fantasies (*Symbole érotique*, 1975), and interest in the metaphysical (the series 'Buste métaphysique,' 1974–5). Although Makarenko is not a narrative artist, some of his paintings are visual texts with multiple readings; his *My Ukraine* (1975), for example, makes a statement about the lack of freedom in his homeland. Makarenko also paints still lifes and figural compositions, often on religious themes, such as the Annunciation (*La Rencontre*, 1983), *Palm Sunday* (1978, 1983), and the *Holy Trinity* (1982). In works such as *Three Dreams* (1982) he has transformed the traditional composition of

TRAVELS OF MAKARIOS III

Volodymyr Makarenko: *Self-Portrait* (oil, 1990)

icons into a secular, symbolic statement that can be read as that of a woman or of Mother Ukraine. He has successfully synthesized several disparate sources, including V. Kandinsky, Ukrainian icons, surrealism, and abstract art, into an unusual and unique vision. Since 1981 he has had numerous one-man exhibitions in France, Germany, Switzerland, and North America, including Toronto (1982, 1983, 1991) and Chicago (1983).

D. Zelska-Darewych

Makarii I [Makarij], b ?, d 1 May 1497 in Stryholovo, near Mozyr, Belarus. Kievan metropolitan and martyr. The archimandrite of the Trinity Monastery in Vilnius, he was elected metropolitan at a congress of bishops in 1495. He was murdered by Tatars during a journey from Vilnius to Kiev. His remains were transferred to Kiev, where they were placed in the St Sophia Cathedral, and then moved to St Volodymyr's Cathedral. Makarii was canonized in 1621–2.

Makarii II [Makarij], b ? in Moscow, d ? Metropolitan of Kiev (1534–56). He was instrumental in reviving the Halych Orthodox eparchy, with its see in Lviv, and consecrated M. Tuchapsky as bishop. Under his direction a church congress was held in Navahrudak, Belarus, in February 1540, which defined the relationship between the bishop of Lviv and the metropolitan of Kiev and strengthened the authority of the latter.

Makarios (Macarius) III, b and d ? Patriarch of Antioch (1647–72). He traveled on a long journey, in 1652–9, through Wallachia, Moldavia, Ukraine, and Muscovy. His

Patriarch Makarios III

son and companion, *Paul of Aleppo, wrote an account of their trip which included descriptions of their visits with Hetman B. Khmelnytsky and other Cossack and church leaders, and of everyday life in Ukraine. The account remains an important source for the history and culture of 17th-century Ukraine. In 1666 Makarios attended a church sobor in Moscow, where he criticized the reforms of Patriarch Nikon.

Makariv. III-10. A town smt (1990 pop 12,200) on the Zdvyzh River and a raion center in Kiev oblast. At the end of the 16th century the village of Voronine was renamed Makariv, and in the 17th century a castle was built there by Polish landlords. After M. Kryvonis captured the castle in 1648, the town became the center of a Cossack company. Its inhabitants took part in the popular uprisings of 1664–5, 1694, and 1702–4. Makariv became an smt in 1956. Today it has a flax-processing plant, a food industry, and a branch of the Bila Tserkva Clothing and Haberdashery

Consortium. Archeologists have found some tools from the Bronze Age near the town.

Makarov, Anatolii, b 28 January 1939 in the Far East. Literary critic. He graduated from Kiev University and has worked for the paper *Literaturna Ukraïna* and the Radianskyi Pysmennyk publishing house. His criticism and reviews have been published in Ukrainian periodicals and separately as the collections *Rozmaïttia tendentsii* (Variety of Tendencies, 1969), *Barvy Ukraïny* (Colors of Ukraine, coauthor, 1970), and *Svit obrazu* (The World of the Image, 1977) and the award-winning collection *P'iat' etiudiv: Pidsvidomist' i mystetstvo* (Five Studies: The Subconscious and Art, 1990).

Makarovsky, Mykhailo [Makarovs'kyj, Myxaijlo], b 1783, d 19 September 1846 in Hadiache, Poltava gubernia. Poet. He studied at the Poltava Theological Seminary and worked for many years as a tutor and county-school teacher in Hadiache. In the 1840s he wrote epigonic Romantic poetry, which is interesting because of its ethnographic and historical descriptions. It was published posthumously: the long poems 'Natalia ...' and 'Haras'ko ...' appeared in A. Metlynsky's miscellany *Iuzhnyi russkii sbornik* (South Russian Collection) in Kharkiv in 1848 and separately in Lviv in 1899, and a short collection of the poetry was published in Poltava in 1864.

Makarukha, Lidiia [Makaruxa, Lidija], b 23 March 1929 in Peremyshl, Galicia, d 25 April 1972 in Buenos Aires. Community leader. Having emigrated to Argentina in 1930, she completed medical school in 1955 and worked at a Buenos Aires hospital. She was active in community affairs as a member of numerous organizations, president of the Union of Ukrainian Women of Argentina, and an executive member of the World Federation of Ukrainian Women's Organizations.

Liubomyr Makarushka

Ostap Makarushka

Makarushka, Liubomyr [Makaruška, Ljubomyr], b 12 August 1899 in Sivka Voinylivska, Kalush county, Galicia, d 6 February 1986 in Bad Godesberg, Germany. Political and military leader; son of O. and Ye. *Makarushka. After graduating from the Theresa Military Academy in Wiener Neustadt he served briefly in the Austrian army and then as captain in the First (Stanyslaviv) Battalion of the Ukrainian Galician Army. After the war he studied economics at the World Trade Academy in Vienna (PH D, 1927). Upon

his return to Lviv he served as executive director and then general secretary (1927–9) of the Ukrainian National Democratic Alliance (UNDO) and in 1930 was elected as its candidate to the Polish Sejm. As a major of the *Division Galizien he negotiated the unit's surrender to the British at the end of the Second World War. From 1948 he represented the UNDO on the émigré Ukrainian National Council and sat on the council's executive body (1948–51). He also headed the Department for Non-German Refugees at the German Refugee Bank in Bonn (1951–64).

Makarushka, Ostap [Makaruška], b 9 August 1867 in Yavoriv, Galicia, d 24 November 1931 in Lviv. Galician philologist and pedagogue; full member of the Shevchenko Scientific Society from 1919; husband of Y. and father of L. *Makarushka. After graduating from Lviv University (1894) he studied abroad and then obtained a PH D from Chernivtsi University (1904). He taught classical philology at the Ukrainian gymnasium in Kolomyia and the Academic Gymnasium in Lviv (1897–1905). He served as principal of the Ukrainian Pedagogical Society's women teachers' seminary in Lviv (1910–21) and inspector of secondary schools run by the Ridna Shkola society (1921–31). He was also on the faculty of the Lviv (Underground) Ukrainian University. His articles and brochures dealt with topics such as Turkish loanwords (1895), compound participles in the Galician-Volhynian Chronicle (1896), the life and importance of O. *Potebnia (1901), and M. Smotrytsky's grammar (1908). He also wrote five gymnasium textbooks of classical Latin and Greek.

Yevheniia Makarushka

Hryhorii Makhiv

Makarushka, Yevheniia [Makaruška, Jevhenija] (née Mulyk), b 4 August 1880 in Lviv, d 6 July 1977 in New York. Civic leader; wife of O. and mother of L. *Makarushka. An organizer of vocational education for women, she headed the *Union of Ukrainian Women before its formal constitution (1917–21) and was a member of its executive until 1931. Active in the Ukrainian National Democratic Alliance, she ran in the 1928 elections as its candidate to the Polish Sejm. She chaired the organizing committee of the Ukrainian Women's Congress in Stanyslaviv (1934) and the building committee of the Girls' Vocational Residence in Lviv (1935).

Makhiv, Hryhorii [Maxiv, Hryhorij], b 23 August 1887 in Kiev, d 22 August 1952 in Birmingham, Michigan. Soil scientist; full member of the Shevchenko Scientific Society from 1948 and the Ukrainian Academy of Arts and Sciences of the US. He graduated from Kiev University (1913), worked as a soil scientist for the Kiev zemstvo, and then taught at Kiev University (1920) and the Kharkiv Agricultural Institute (1924). He headed the soil research section of the Agricultural Scientific Committee of Ukraine and of the VUAN. After being dismissed from his positions for political reasons in 1927, he worked as a researcher and consultant in Kiev, Odessa, and Kharkiv. A postwar refugee in Germany, he taught at the Ukrainian Technical and Husbandry Institute, and in 1949 he emigrated to the United States, where he helped found the Ukrainian Academy of Arts and Sciences. Makhiv specialized in solonetz soils and their amelioration, soil depletion and erosion, the effectiveness of shelterbelts in the steppe region, and drought control. He wrote numerous works, including the textbook *Gruntoznavstvo* (Soil Science, 1925), *Chetvertynni poklady Ukraïny* (The Quaternary Deposits in Ukraine, 1924), and *Grunty Ukraïny* (Soils of Ukraine, 1930); edited the first seven volumes of *Materialy doslidzhennia gruntiv Ukraïny* (Materials for the Study of Soils in Ukraine, 1923–7); and prepared the first synthetic soil map of Ukraine (1927; pub also in English).

Makhnenko, Volodymyr [Maxnenko], b 27 October 1931 in Cherkasy. Metallurgist; full member of the AN URSR (now ANU) since 1990. He graduated from the Odessa Institute of Naval Engineers (1955) and taught there and has worked at the ANU Institute of Electric Welding since 1964. His main scientific work is in electrical welding and special metallurgical problems.

Nestor Makhno   Leonid Makhnovets

Makhno, Nestor [Maxno], b 27 October 1889 in Huliai-Pole, Katerynoslav gubernia, d 25 July 1934 in Paris Anarchist leader. Because of the injustice he experienced Makhno joined an anarcho-communist group. As a result of the group's terrorist activities Makhno was twice arrested; the second time, in 1910, he was sentenced to death. The death penalty, however, was commuted to life imprisonment. He served his sentence in the Butyrki prison in Moscow. In prison Makhno acquired a general

and political education from the prison library and from other political prisoners. There he became a confirmed anarchist. Makhno was released on 2 March 1917.

Makhno returned to Huliai-Pole, where he organized local peasants, workers, and artisans and headed the local soviet of workers' and peasants' deputies. He also organized peasant bands for the expropriation and redistribution of the manors of the local nobility. In July 1918 he began to mobilize resistance to the Central Powers and Hetman P. Skoropadsky. Makhno led a popular insurrection against the occupying German forces while conducting raids on local estates. As military leader he combined clever and unorthodox tactics with a resolute and well-disciplined army (based for the most part on voluntary enlistment). Instrumental to Makhno's military successes were the light mobile cavalry units he formed, which featured innovative horse-driven carriages (known as *tachanky*) upon which machine guns had been mounted.

The withdrawal of the Central Powers from Ukrainian territory in November 1918 left Makhno in a position of considerable strength in Katerynoslav gubernia. His forces effectively controlled the entire Huliai-Pole region for the first five months of 1919. In the spring of 1919 he was strengthened by the arrival of members of the Nabat Confederation of Anarchist Organizations, which had its headquarters in Kharkiv but maintained branches in the major cities of Ukraine. They assisted in the cultural and ideological work of the anarchist movement by editing its periodicals *Put' k svobode* and *Nabat*.

Makhno concluded a shaky alliance with the Bolsheviks in March 1919 against A. *Denikin but resisted attempts to subordinate his command to the Red Army, and the alliance deteriorated. On 14 June 1919 Bolshevik forces attacked Huliai-Pole and dissolved the existing anarchist communes. In July 1919 Otaman N. *Hryhoriiv, whose army was operating in the vicinity, offered to ally himself with Makhno. Makhno refused, executed Hryhoriiv, and brought a large portion of the otaman's forces into his army's ranks. The alliance with the Bosheviks resumed in the summer of 1919 with the advance of Denikin's Volunteer Army into Ukraine. Makhno's forces were pushed back as far as Uman, where they encountered the Ukrainian Galician Army and S. Petliura's regular UNR Army. A brief pact was concluded with them on 21 September 1919, but Makhno continued to operate against Denikin's forces independently. On 26 September he delivered a major blow to the Whites near Perehonivka, and forced them to retreat while the Bolsheviks inflicted further damage.

With the defeat of Denikin Makhno reached the zenith of his influence in Ukraine, at which time he took the cities of Katerynoslav and Oleksandrivske, in October and November 1919. (In Katerynoslav a Ukrainian-language anarchist newspaper, *Shliakh do voli*, was started.) His troops, numbering approx 40,000, controlled about one-third of the present territory of Ukraine (mainly in Left-Bank and Southern Ukraine) and included a population of roughly 7 million.

In October 1920 in the face of a renewed White threat emerging from the Crimea, the Makhnovites and Bolsheviks concluded a treaty calling for military co-operation and amnesty for all anarchists held in Russian jails. The offensive launched by P. Wrangel's army was dealt with quickly, and afforded the Bolsheviks an opportunity to deal decisively with the Makhnovites. They massacred a group of Makhno's soldiers returning from the Crimean campaign on 25 November 1920 and then turned their troops on Huliai-Pole. Makhno was forced to make a dash for the Rumanian border, and crossed it on 28 August 1921 with a small band. The remnants of his army in Ukraine were soon crushed.

In Rumania Makhno and his band were arrested and interned, but he escaped to Poland, where he was arrested a second time on charges of fomenting rebellion among Galicia's Ukrainians. After being acquitted he moved to Danzig (now Gdańsk), where he was arrested a third time. He escaped to Berlin and from there moved to Paris. There he remained active in anarchist circles and contributed regularly to the international anarchist press (including occasional articles discussing the latest developments in Ukraine). He also wrote his incomplete memoirs (in Russian), dealing with events to 1918.

BIBLIOGRAPHY
Kubanin, M. Makhnovshchina (Leningrad 1927)
Makhno, N. Russkaia revoliutsiia na Ukraine (Paris 1929)
– Pod udarami kontr-revoliutsii (Paris 1936)
– Ukrainskaia revoliutsiia (Paris 1937)
Peters, V. Nestor Makhno: The Life of an Anarchist (Winnipeg 1970)
Arshinov, P. History of the Maknovist Movement (Detroit–Chicago 1974)
Holota, W. 'Le mouvement makhnoviste ukrainien, 1918–1921,' PH D diss, Université des sciences humaines de Strasbourg, 1975
Palij, M. The Anarchism of Nestor Makhno, 1918–1921: An Aspect of the Ukrainian Revolution (Seattle 1976)
Sysyn, F. 'Nestor Makhno and the Ukrainian Revolution,' in Ukraine, 1917–1921: A Study in Revolution, ed T. Hunczak (Cambridge, Mass 1977)

S. Cipko, M. Palij

Makhnovets, Leonid [Maxnovec'], b 31 May 1919 in Ozera, Kiev county. Literary scholar. In 1950 he defended his candidate of sciences diss on I. Franko as a scholar of 16th- to 18th-century Ukrainian literature. He wrote a book on satire and humor in 16th- to 18th-century Ukrainian prose (1964) and large parts of vols 1 and 2 of the AN URSR history of Ukrainian literature (8 vols, 1967–71; he was the editor responsible for vol 1 and a member of the editorial board of the entire history). He compiled vol 1 of the biobibliographical dictionary of Ukrainian writers (1960). He edited, with introductions, annotated compilations of old Ukrainian humor and satire (1959) and fables in 17th- and 18th-century Ukrainian literature (1960), a collection of articles on Ukrainian intermedes (1960), and a book of poetic translations and renderings of the medieval Slovo o polku Ihorevi (The Tale of Ihor's Campaign, 1967). In 1972 he published a popular biography of H. Skovoroda in which he used many new archival sources; his interpretation was condemned by neo-Stalinist critics. His annotated modern translation of the medieval Kiev Chronicle was published in nos 6–8 of the literary monthly Kyïv for 1984, and his annotated translation of the Hypatian Chronicle was published in 1989.

Makhorin, Kostiantyn [Maxorin, Kostjantyn], b 13 August 1928 in Dnipropetrovske. Chemical technologist; AN URSR (now ANU) corresponding member since 1972. A

graduate of the Dnipropetrovske Metallurgical Institute (1950), he has worked at the AN URSR Institute of Gas and served as its deputy director (1961–77). He has researched the chemical transformations of gaseous hydrocarbons and carbonaceous materials, the modeling of fuel-conversion processes, and related areas.

Makhorka. See Tobacco.

Makhov, Gregory. See Makhiv, Hryhorii.

Makiivka [Makijivka]. V-18, DB III-3. A city (1990 pop 426,700) on the Hruzka River in Donetske oblast. Makiivka village was first mentioned in historical documents in 1777. In 1875–7 several small mines were opened there. In 1920 Makiivka and Dmytriievske villages were merged to form the city of Dmytriievske, which in 1931 was renamed Makiivka. During the industrialization drive of the 1930s, the city's population rose from 79,000 (1926) to 242,000 (1939). After the Second World War Makiivka was rebuilt, and by 1959 its population had reached 381,000. Today it is a major coal-mining and metallurgical center and a railway junction. It has 18 coal mines and 4 enrichment plants, a large metallurgical plant, a tube plant, a civil engineering institute, a branch of the Donetske Regional Museum, and a metallurgical museum. Several kurhans from the Bronze Age, the Scythian period, and the 9th to 13th centuries AD have been excavated near Makiivka.

Makiivka Civil-Engineering Institute (Makiivskyi inzhenerno-budivelnyi instytut). A technical institute, until 1992 under the jurisdiction of the Ukrainian SSR Ministry of Higher and Specialized Secondary Education. It was founded in 1972 on the basis of the Makiivka branch of the *Donetske Polytechnical Institute. The institute includes faculties of architecture, institutional and civic construction, metal construction, and sanitation technology. Day, evening, and correspondence courses are offered. In 1980 the library contained approx 280,000 titles, and the institute had an enrollment of 4,500 students.

Makiivka Metallurgical Plant (Makiivskyi metalurhinyi zavod im. S. Kirova). One of the largest metallurgical plants in the Soviet Union, located in Makiivka, Donetske oblast. It was built in 1898 by a French joint-stock company, the General Company of Cast Alloy, Iron, and Steel Factories of Russia. Within two years the plant had one blast furnace, three Martin furnaces, and two blooming mills. It was destroyed during the First World War, reconstructed in 1923, and enlarged in 1926. In 1929 the Soviet Union's first and largest mechanized blast furnace was constructed there. The plant was destroyed again during the Second World War. It reached its prewar output by 1950. Postwar construction included a blast furnace, four open-hearth furnaces, and blooming, rod, and sheet mills. The principal products are cast iron, rolled steel, alloy steels, sheet metal, and pipes.

Makivchuk, Fedir [Makivčuk], b 9 September 1912 in Kordyshivka, Berdychiv county, Kiev gubernia, d 4 December 1988. Journalist and writer. He began his journalistic career in 1931 at *Komuna*, the Starokostiantyniv raion newspaper, and then edited Komsomol newspapers in Kamianets-Podilskyi and Lviv before briefly serving as chief editor of *Molod' Ukraïny* (1944–6). From 1946 to 1986 he was chief editor of the republican humor magazine *Perets'*. He wrote hundreds of feuilletons for *Perets'* and other Soviet magazines, and several books of satire and humor, including *Zdoroven'ki buly!* (How Are You!, 1952), *I smikh, i hrikh* (Both Laughter and Sin, 1957), and *Liubov i parahraf* (Love and the Paragraph, 1966). His anti-American *Reportazh z toho svitu* (Report from the Other World, 1960), which contained vicious attacks on Ukrainian émigrés, earned him official praise and awards.

Stepan Makivka

Makivka, Stepan, b 11 October 1889 in Koden, Tomaszów county, Lublin gubernia, d 24 January 1966. Podlachian civic and political leader. After studying history at Kiev University he served in the sanitation department of the Eighth Russian Army (1915–17). In 1922–8 he was a deputy to the Polish Sejm. In the 1920s he helped found *Sel-Soiuz and *Sel-Rob and then its left wing and published (1925–8) the Kholm newspapers *Nashe zhyttia* and *Nove zhyttia*. In 1929–36 he was imprisoned by the Poles for his political activity. After Poland's collapse he demanded that the Kholm region and Podlachia be annexed to Ukraine. After the war he settled in Soviet Ukraine, where he wrote journalistic and fictional works and several volumes of memoirs, including *Neskoreni kresy* (The Indomitable Borderlands, 1954; 2nd ed 1957).

A trench of the Ukrainian Sich Riflemen on Mt Makivka (1915)

Makivka. A mountain (958 m) in the Carpathian Mountains near the town of Slavske. At this site the first major battle of the *Ukrainian Sich Riflemen (USS) took place, on 29 April to 2 May 1915. The USS victory against the overwhelming forces of the Russian army raised the morale of the Ukrainian people and established the reputation of the USS as an elite fighting force. After the struggle for independence the battle was commemorated annually with pilgrimages to the site and memorial services. This tradition was rekindled in Ukraine in 1989.

Mako, Serhii, b 1885 near Tomsk, Siberia, d 4 June 1953 in Nice, France. Portrait painter. In 1919 he was a member of the UNR diplomatic mission to Italy. As an émigré he lived in Prague, where he was a professor of drawing and painting at the *Ukrainian Studio of Plastic Arts (1924–32) and founded the 'Scythians' artists' group, which tried to create a 'synthesis of the spirit of the East with that of the West.' His impressionist works include a portrait of Ye. Chykalenko. Several of his paintings are in museums in Nice.

Makohin, Yakiv, b 1880 in Ukraine, d 13 January 1956 in Boston. Ukrainian-American political activist. In 1905–21 he served in the US armed forces. Later he married S. Fallon, a wealthy widow. In 1930 he toured Galicia with his wife, and after his tour he informed British parliamentarians and journalists about the *Pacification. He set up and financed the *Ukrainian Bureau in London and then in Geneva and a representation of the bureau in Prague. He and his wife supported the *Museum of Ukraine's Struggle for Independence in Prague and provided scholarships for Ukrainian students and artists. They owned a valuable collection of old Ukrainian icons and paintings and a fine stamp collection.

Makohon, Dmytro (pseuds: Makohonenko, Ivan Halaida, Khorostkivsky), b 28 October 1881 in Khorostkiv, Husiatyn county, Galicia, d 7 October 1961 in Ivano-Frankivske. Writer and teacher; father of I. *Vilde. He was a public school teacher in Bukovyna (1903–14, 1919–22) and in Galicia (1923–56). For a time he also coedited the journal *Kameniari* in Chernivtsi. His publications include a collection of poetry, *Muzhyts'ki idylii* (Peasant Idylls, 1907), and collections of short stories about the hard life of peasants and teachers: *Shkil'ni obrazky* (School Sketches, 1911), *Uchytel's'ki harazdy* (Teachers' Fortunes, 1911), *Proty fyli* (Against the Current, 1914), and *Po nashykh selakh* (In Our Villages, 1914). After 1945 he wrote humorous sketches and fables in the Soviet spirit. A collection of his stories, *Vybrani opovidannia* (Selected Stories), was published in 1959.

Makohon, Ivan, b 26 October 1907 in Hrushuvakha, Izium county, Kharkiv gubernia. Sculptor. He studied at the Kharkiv Art Institute (1926–31) and with I. Severa. After the Second World War he was a member of the Studio of Military Painters (1944–53) and taught at the Kiev State Art Institute (from 1954). His works include M. Hrushevsky's burial monument (with V. Krychevsky), portraits of I. Severyn (1937) and O. Honchar (1971), a bust (1938) and bronze medal (1939) of T. Shevchenko, the compositions *Banner of Victory* (1946) and *Harvest* (1970), the 6-m bas-relief at the Arsenal metro station in Kiev

Ivan Makohon: fragment of the monument to N. Sosnina in Teterivske, Kiev oblast (bronze, 1968)

(with A. Nimenko), a bas-relief of M. Bazhan (1984), and Gen Yu. Shchadenko's (1952) and Yu. Yanovsky's (1961) burial monuments.

Makov, Konstantin, b 7 January 1911 in Voronezh, Russia, d 15 August 1948 in Kiev. Hydrogeologist; corresponding member of the AN URSR (now ANU) in 1948. He graduated from the Kiev Geological Prospecting Course (1933) and was deputy director of the AN URSR Institute of Geological Sciences from 1945. His main technical contributions were studies of underground water, of the hydrology of Ukraine and Bashkiria, and of a method of structural hydrogeological analysis.

Osyp Makovei   Yakiv Makovetsky

Makovei, Osyp [Makovej] (pseuds: ∗∗, ∗∗, Yevmen, M., M∗, Mak, Om., Omikron, Sokolyk, O. Stepanovych, Stefan, Spektator, Yaroshenko), b 23 August 1867 in Yavoriv, Galicia, d 21 August 1925 in Zalishchyky. Writer, journalist, and teacher. He attended Lviv University, from which he graduated in 1893. Varied work as an editorial assistant and a contributor to *Dilo (1891), Narodna chasopys' (1892), and other newspapers prepared him for the position of editor of *Bukovyna (1895–7). He was also one of the editors of *Literaturno-naukovyi vistnyk (1897–9). He was

awarded a scholarship to the University of Vienna in 1899, from which he graduated with a doctorate in 1901. He taught Ukrainian language and literature at the teachers' seminaries in Chernivtsi (1899–1910) and Lviv (1910–13). From 1913 until his death he was director of the teachers' seminary in Zalishchyky. Makovei began his literary career with translations from H. Heine, which were published in *Zoria* (1885). Although he wrote several longer poems and even published a collection of poetry in 1894, Makovei was primarily a writer of short prose, feuilletons, and literary sketches marked by good-natured and at times poignant observation of human life. Besides two longer novelettes – one of village life, *Zalissia* (1897), and one historical novelette, *Iaroshenko* (1905) – and numerous works scattered through contemporary newspapers, his literary output primarily consists of collections of stories, *Nashi znakomi* (Our Acquaintances, 1901), *Opovidannia* (Stories, 1904), *Krovave pole* (A Bloody Field, 1921), and the satiric and humorous *Pryzhmurenym okom* (Through a Squinting Eye, 1923). His output in literary criticism consists of numerous critical articles, introductions to the works of various authors, and three major studies: on P. *Kulish, Pan'ko Kulish: Ohliad ioho diial'nosti* (Pan'ko Kulish: A Survey of His Activities, 1900); on philology, *Try halyts'ki hramatyky* (Three Galician Grammars, 1903); and on Yu. *Fedkovych, Zhyttia Osypa Iuria Fed'kovycha* (The Life of Osyp Yurii Fedkovych, 1911). A selection of his works appeared in 1930, 1954, 1961, and 1979, and a full, two-volume edition appeared in 1990. His poetry collection of 1894 was republished in 1967.

BIBLIOGRAPHY
Kushch, O. *Osyp Makovei: Bibliohrafichnyi pokazhchyk* (Lviv 1958)
Pohrebennyk, F. *Osyp Makovei: Krytyko-biohrafichnyi narys* (Kiev 1960)
Zasenko, O. *Osyp Makovei* (Kiev 1968)
                                                    D.H. Struk

Makovetsky, Yakiv [Makovec'kyj, Jakiv], b 19 May 1909 in Riplyn, Jarosław county, Galicia, d 8 July 1990 in Munich. Civic leader. After moving to France in 1932, in 1939 he interrupted his studies there to join the Carpathian Sich and then the Legion of Ukrainian Nationalists. He switched to civilian work for the remainder of the war, during which he handled resettlement matters in Warsaw and Biała Podlaska. In 1945 he moved to Munich, where he was active in resettling Ukrainian refugees (until 1954) and helped create the *Central Representation of the Ukrainian Emigration in Germany. A leading figure in the Melnyk faction of the OUN, Makovetsky also served on the Ukrainian National Council.

Makovsky, Vladimir [Makovskij], b 7 February 1846 in Moscow, d 21 February 1920 in Petrograd. Russian painter. A member of the *Peredvizhniki society from 1872 and the St Petersburg Academy of Arts from 1873, he painted genre scenes in Ukraine. They include *Waiting for the Teacher* (1881), *Fair in Poltava* (1882), *Ukrainian Girl* (1882), *Horse Fair in Ukraine* (1885), *Mother and Daughter* (1886), *Respite on the Road from Kiev* (1888), *Maiden's Evening* (1888), *Feast Day in Ukraine* (1898), and *Ukrainian Man* (1918). Makovsky's brothers, Konstantin and Nikolai, also painted genre scenes in Ukraine.

Vladimir Makovsky: *Ukrainian Girl* (oil, 1882)

Makovsky, Volodymyr [Makovs'kyj], b 27 July 1870 in Yeiske, Rostov county, Don Cossack province, d 3 January 1941 in Kharkiv. Machine scientist. He studied and worked in Kharkiv. In 1899 he was arrested and exiled for revolutionary activities. He returned to Ukraine in 1904 and taught at the Katerynoslav (later Dnipropetrovske) Mining Institute (1904–30) and the Kharkiv Polytechnical Institute (1930–41), where he organized a department of turbine construction. In 1933 he organized the first turbine laboratory in the USSR, and in 1940 he built a stationary gas turbine with a capacity of 736 kW.

Makovytsia Massif. A group of volcanic mountains located between the Uzh and the Liatorytsia rivers in Transcarpathia oblast. Part of the Vyhorlat-Hutyn Ridge in the Volcanic Ukrainian Carpathians, it consists of two volcanic rings, the Antalovedska Poliana (971 m) and Makovytsia (976 m, the largest ring in the Volcanic Ukrainian Carpathians). The massif is built mainly of andesites, basalts, and tuffs. Its slopes are covered with thick beech and oak forests and are almost uninhabited. At the foot of the mountains is a densely populated agricultural region with numerous vineyards.

Makovytsia region. The historical name for the northwestern part of the Prešov region. The northern part of the former Sáros komitat, the region historically has been inhabited mainly by Ukrainians. Its name is derived from the 13th-century Makovytsia castle, near Zborov, north of Bardejov.

Maksaky Transfiguration Monastery (Maksakivskyi Preobrazhenskyi manastyr). A monastery on the Desna River near Maksaky, now in Mena raion, Chernihiv region. It was founded by A. *Kysil in 1642 as a men's monastery. After 27 years of vacancy it reopened in 1803; in 1829 it was converted into a women's monastery. In the early 20th century it had 20 nuns and 15 novices. The monastery's main church was built in the late 17th to early 18th century. The monastery was dismantled in the 1930s.

Maksymchuk, Juliian [Maksymčuk, Julijan], b 30 August 1890 in Stryi, Galicia, d 13 December 1980 in Chicago. Lawyer and philatelist. A former student activist, Ukrainian Galician Army veteran, and civic official in Drohobych and Boryslav, he emigrated to the United States in 1951. His writings include listings of Ukrainian postage stamps (11 catalogues, 1950–75), non–government issue Ukrainian stamps, foreign stamps with Ukrainian themes, and heraldic stamps and bank notes. The Ukrainian Philatelic and Numismatic Society has recognized his contribution to this field of endeavor by naming an award in his honor.

Maksymeiko, Mykola [Maksymejko], b 17 June 1870 in Batsmany, Romen county, Poltava gubernia, d 14 April 1941 in Kharkiv. Legal historian; from 1926 a corresponding member of the VUAN and AN URSR (now ANU). Having graduated from Kiev University (1892), he lectured at Kharkiv University (1897–1925). After chairing the section on the history of Ukrainian law at the Kharkiv Institute of People's Education (1926–34), he became a senior research associate of the ANU Institute of History. He specialized in Rus' and Lithuanian law. His more important works were *Seimy Litovsko-Russkogo gosudarstva do Liublinskoi unii 1569 goda* (The Diets of the Lithuanian-Ruthenian State up to the Lublin Union of 1569, 1902), *Opyt kriticheskogo issledovaniia Russkoi Pravdy* (An Attempt at a Critical Examination of *Ruskaia Pravda,* 1914), and 'Systema Rus'koï Pravdy v ïï poshyrenii redaktsiï' (The System of the *Ruskaia Pravda* in Its Expanded Edition), *Pratsi Komisiï dlia vyuchuvannia istoriï zakhidnorus'koho ta ukraïns'koho prava,* no. 2, 1926.

Maksymenko, Fedir, b 4 February 1897 in Bilenke, Oleksandrivske county, Katerynoslav gubernia, d 24 November 1983 (reportedly) in Lviv. Bibliographer. He graduated from the Kiev Institute of People's Education (1925) and became director of the regional studies museum in Bakhmut (now Artemivske, 1919–20). He worked from 1921 as a bibliographer in libraries in the Donbas, Kiev, and Lviv (as assistant director of the research library at Lviv University). He compiled a book of bibliographic materials on Ukrainian regional studies in 1847–1929 (1930), a catalog of incunabula at the Lviv University Scientific Library (1958), a book on collections of historical information about Soviet Ukraine's inhabited places (1964, reprinted in *Arkhivy Ukraïny*), and a catalog of Cyrillic books printed in Ukraine in 1574–1800 that are preserved in collections in Lviv (1975).

Maksymenko, Oleksandr, b 18 November 1916 in Luchky (now Vilkhuvatka), Kobeliaky county, Poltava gubernia. Painter. A graduate of the Kiev State Art Institute (1947), he has done mostly genre paintings, portraits, and landscapes. They include *Approaching Autumn* (1948),

Land: Plowed Field (1952), *The Water Has Arrived* (1957), *Meditations of a Farmer* (1963), *Golden Autumn* (1968), *Father's Cares* (1971), *Collective-Farm Market* (1974), *Apple Tree* (1978), and several views of Sedniv. An album with reproductions of his works was published in Kiev in 1982.

Maksymiuk, Stefan [Maksymjuk] (Maksymjuk), b 16 June 1927 in Uzhhorod. Radio producer and discographer. A longtime employee of the Voice of America (1955–87), he has written articles on the discography of soprano S. Krushelnytska (1965), the O. Koshyts Chorus (1966–7), the Lineva expedition (1966), dumas (1969), and renditions during the years 1900–65 of works by T. Shevchenko (1990). His collection of Ukrainian phonograph records contains more than 1,000 78 RPM and approx 1,500 45-RPM and LP items. It includes releases from the early 1900s to the most recent issues from Ukraine, Russia, Austria-Hungary, Poland, Germany, England, the United States, and Canada and covers classical, popular, folk, and religious music. It is considered the largest collection of its kind outside Ukraine.

Maksymiw, Myron [Maksymiv], b 13 May 1946 in Goslar, Germany. Conductor. He grew up in England and came to Canada in 1968, where he completed university degrees in Slavic studies and music at the University of Toronto. In 1981 he founded Canada's first independent professional Ukrainian choral ensemble, *Musicus Bortnianskii, and became its musical and artistic director.

Maksymonko, Leontii [Maksymon'ko, Leontij], b 4 August 1893 in Tseniava, Dolyna county, Galicia, d 5 April 1965 in Toronto. Ophthalmologist. He interrupted his medical studies to serve in the Austrian army and then in the First Corps of the Ukrainian Galician Army as adjutant to its sanitation chief. After graduating from Graz University (1923) he worked at the General Hospital in Lviv and then opened his own practice. For 10 years he served as secretary and in 1934 as president of the Ukrainian Physicians' Society. He was also treasurer of the Narodnia Lichnytsia hospital and lecturer at the Lviv (Underground) Ukrainian University. During the Second World War he was in charge of the eye clinic of the Lviv Medical Institute. In 1944–8 he was a senior clinician at Graz University. Afterward he emigrated to Canada.

Maksymovych [Maksymovyč]. A family of Cossack *starshyna* established by Maksym Vasylkivsky (b in Nizhen, d ca 1694–8), one of the wealthiest men in the Hetmanate. He owned a number of mills and niter sources in the Kiev region, leased lands from the Sapieha family in the Chornobyl area, and conducted significant trade in Right-Bank Ukraine, Poland, and Moldavia. His sons were Ioan (1651–1715), the archbishop of Chernihiv from 1697 and metropolitan of Tobolsk from 1711; Vasyl (d 1698), the acting colonel of Pereiaslav, slain in a battle with the Tatars on the Kodyma River; Petro, a notable military fellow; Hryhorii, the archpriest of Pereiaslav (1680–1711); Mykhailo and Antin, fellows of the standard; and Dmytro *Maksymovych. Dmytro's sons were Fedir, the colonel of Starodub regiment (1741–56), and Ivan *Maksymovych. Fedir's son, Ivan (d ca 1803), was the first colonel of the Starodub Carabineer Regiment (1783–9) and later a Russian major general and a member of the *Novhorod-Si-

verskyi patriotic circle. Their descendants were landed gentry in Chernihiv and Poltava gubernias. Mykhailo *Maksymovych was a descendant of Vasyl, and Yurii *Maksymovych was a descendant of Dmytro.

Maksymovych, Andrii [Maksymovyč, Andrij], b 1865 in Poltava gubernia, d 9 February 1893 in Yalta, Tavriia gubernia. Actor. After studying in the Poltava theological seminary he was a leading character and comic actor in the troupes of M. Kropyvnytsky (1882–3, 1885–8), M. Starytsky (1883–5), and M. Sadovsky (1888–92).

Antin Maksymovych   Borys Maksymovych

Maksymovych, Antin [Maksymovyč], b 1881, d ? Civic and political activist. An employee of the Limanova Co, he was active among the Ukrainian workers in the Boryslav region. In 1928 he was elected to the Polish Sejm as a candidate of the Ukrainian National Democratic Alliance. In 1940 he was deported by the Soviets, and his further fate is unknown.

Maksymovych, Borys [Maksymovyč] (Maximovich), b 1906 in Kiev. Concert pianist and teacher. He graduated from the Kiev Conservatory (1928), where he studied under the virtuosi S. Barere and H. Beklemishev, and then taught at the conservatory. A postwar émigré he appeared as solo pianist in Western Europe and the United States. His repertoire as soloist included D. Scarlatti, L. van Beethoven, F. Chopin, R. Schumann, F. Liszt, and I. Stravinsky. Maksymovych was noted for his performances of P. Tchaikovsky's Piano Concerto no. 1 in B-flat Minor. He also popularized the piano works of L. Revutsky and V. Kosenko.

Maksymovych, Dmytro [Maksymovyč], ?–1732. Cossack official; husband of T. *Sulyma. After gaining access to Hetman I. Mazepa's inner circle through D. Zelensky, he was chancellor of Nizhen regiment (1682–92), military executor responsible for collecting taxes on monopoly goods (from 1694), and general standard-bearer (1703–8) and general osaul of the Hetman state (1708–9). He gave himself up to the Russians after the Battle of Poltava, and in 1710 he was exiled with his family to Arkhangelsk.

Maksymovych, Heorhii [Maksymovyč, Heorhij], b 26 April 1922 in Horostyta, near Lublin, Poland. Scientist in physical chemistry and the mechanics of materials; corresponding member of the AN URSR (now ANU) since 1978.

He graduated from the Lviv Polytechnical Institute (1951). Since 1958 he has been deputy director of the ANU Physical-Mechanical Institute. His main contributions are in the fields of the high-temperature strength of construction materials, microhardness measurements, and alloy properties.

Maksymovych, Ihnatii [Maksymovyč, Ihnatij], b 1730s, d 11 December 1793 in Chernihiv. Writer, educator, and churchman. From 1757 to 1764 he lectured at the Kievan Mohyla Academy, from which he had graduated. From 1768 until his death he served as hegumen of various monasteries. His 'Oda na pervyi den maia 1761 goda' (Ode on the First Day of May in the Year 1761) is the first syllabo-tonic verse in Ukrainian literature.

Maksymovych, Ioan [Maksymovyč, Joan], b 1651 in Nizhen, d 10 July 1751 in Tobolsk, Siberia. Orthodox churchman, missionary, and writer. He graduated (1669) from and then taught at the Kievan Mohyla Academy before entering the Kievan Cave Monastery. A noted preacher, he became hegumen of the Yeletskyi Dormition Monastery in Chernihiv (1696) and then archbishop of Chernihiv (1697). In 1700 he founded *Chernihiv College with the support of I. Mazepa. In 1711 Tsar Peter I named him metropolitan of Siberia, with his see in Tobolsk. From there he conducted missionary work among the various Siberian peoples. While in Chernihiv, he published sermons, epigrams, and poems, including *Alfavit sobrannyi, rifmami slozhennyi ot sviatykh pisanii ...* (An Alphabet Compiled and Rhymed from the Holy Scriptures ..., 1705) and *Bogomyslie v pol'zu pravovernym* (Pious Thoughts for the Benefit of True Believers, 1710, 1711). His biography appeared in *Kievskie eparkhialnye vedomosti* in 1916.

Maksymovych, Ivan [Maksymovyč], b ?, d 1732. Cossack official. After studying at the Kievan Mohyla Academy he became active in Hetman I. Mazepa's administration. He fled from Ukraine with Hetman I. Mazepa after the Battle of Poltava, and then became general chancellor under Hetman P. Orlyk and was instrumental in concluding alliances with the Crimean Tatars and the Ottoman Porte. After returning to Ukraine in 1715, he was exiled to Moscow, where he worked as a clerk and was responsible for cataloging and putting in order the library of the synodal printing house. In 1722–6 he prepared a Latin-Slavonic dictionary based on G. Knapski's Latin-Polish dictionary (1626), but it remained unpublished. He was dismissed in 1728 for political disloyalty.

Maksymovych, Ivan [Maksymovyč], b 1679 in Pyriatyn, Lubni regiment, d 3 March 1745 in Kiev. Monk and church painter. He was in charge of the icon painting studios at the Zolotonosha, Mhar, Pereiaslav, and Kievan Cave (1718–45) monasteries. His mural paintings in these monasteries have not survived (they are known only from archival sources), and his most famous works, in the Dormition Cathedral of the Kievan Cave Monastery, were destroyed in the 19th century. The Kiev Museum of Ukrainian Art has his *Crucifixion*, with a depiction of Col L. Svichka.

Maksymovych, Karlo. See Savrych, Karlo.

Maksymovych, Manasiia [Maksymovyč] (secular name: Mykhailo), b ? in the Myrhorod region, d 13 July 1758 in Kiev. Orthodox churchman. He graduated from the Kievan Mohyla Academy and then taught German, Hebrew, and theology there (1746–9) and served as rector. He was also archimandrate of the Kievan Epiphany Brotherhood Monastery (1755–8). An author and translator, he oversaw the publishing activities of the Kievan Cave Monastery.

Mykhailo Maksymovych

Maksymovych, Mykhailo [Maksymovyč, Myxajlo], b 15 September 1804 at the Tymkivshchyna estate, near Zolotonosha, Poltava gubernia, d 22 November 1873 at the Mykhailova Hora estate, near Prokhorivka, Zolotonosha county, Poltava gubernia. Historian, philologist, ethnographer, botanist, and poet. In 1832 he concluded his studies at Moscow University, and remained at the university for further academic work. He lectured in botany. In 1833 he received his PHD and was named professor for the chair of botany in Moscow University. In 1834 he was appointed professor of Russian folk literature at Kiev University, and that year he became the university's first rector, a post he held until 1835. Owing to ill health he retired in 1845, and he devoted the rest of his life exclusively to scientific and literary work, which he engaged in on his estate, Mykhailova Hora. Notwithstanding his authority as an academic (he was an honorary member of numerous Ukrainian and Russian universities and many scientific societies) he was made a corresponding member of the Russian Academy of Sciences only toward the end of his life, in 1871. Maksymovych's learning was of encyclopedic dimensions and covered an unusually wide range, from botany to history. His scientific work in the field of the natural sciences was published in the 1820s and 1830s. That work, such as *O sistemakh rastitel'nogo tsarstva* (On Systems of the Plant Kingdom, 1827), *Osnovaniia botaniki* (The Foundations of Botany, vols 1–2, 1828, 1831), *Razmyshlenniia o prirode* (Reflections on Nature, 1833), not only met the standards of contemporary science but proposed a new methodology.

As a folklorist Maksymovych published *Malorossiiskie pesni* (Little Russian Songs) in Moscow in 1827 and *Ukrainskie narodnye pesni* (Ukrainian Folk Songs) in 1834. A third anthology, *Sbornik ukrainskikh pesen* (A Collection of Ukrainian Songs, pt 1), was published in Kiev in 1849. Maksymovych's publications on folklore had a major influence on Ukrainian folklore studies, even in Galicia.

They also created interest in Ukrainian folklore in other Slavic nations (especially among Russians, Poles, and Czechs) and also in England and America. In the field of philology Maksymovych published many papers on the classification of Slavic languages (1838, 1845, and 1850), in which he extensively used examples from Ukrainian. He was also the author of an *etymological spelling, guide, the *maksymovychivka. As a literary scholar Maksymovych studied *Slovo o polku Ihorevi* (The Tale of Ihor's Campaign) and transcribed it into contemporary Ukrainian. He wrote *Istoriia drevnei russkoi slovesnosti* (The History of Old Rus' Literature, vol 1, 1839). In addition he translated the Psalms into Ukrainian and wrote several poems (of note is the one dedicated to T. Shevchenko, 'Oi, iak duzhe za Toboiu tuzhyla Vkraïna' [O, How Ukraine Has Longed after You]). Maksymovych published the anthologies and almanacs *Dennitsa* (1830–4), *Kievlianin* (1840–1, 1850), and *Ukrainets* (1859, 1864).

Maksymovych adhered to the then-popular idea of romanticism and identification with the peasant ethnos (*narodnist'*). He defended the theory of the organic link between the Princely and Cossack eras in Ukrainian history, to which he devoted much research and many articles, critical notes on sources, and other writings. In his article 'O mnimom zapustenii Ukrainy' (On the Imaginary Desolation of Ukraine, 1857) and in letters to M. Pogodin, Maksymovych exposed the faulty basis of Pogodin's hypothesis of the 'Great Russian' population of the Kiev region during the Princely era. The works of Maksymovych on the history of Rus', Kiev, and its historic monuments are numerous; among them are *Ocherk Kieva* (Essay on Kiev, 1847) and *Pis'ma o Kieve k M. Pogodinu* (Letters about Kiev to M. Pogodin, 1871). He wrote many articles on the history of the Cossack period, the Hetmanate, and the haidamaka uprisings (on Hetman P. Sahaidachny, for example) and *Istoricheskie pis'ma o kazakakh pridneprovskikh* (Historical Writings on the Dnieper Region Cossacks, 1863–5), *Pis'ma o Bogdane Khmel'nitskom* (Writings about Bohdan Khmelnytsky, 1859), and *Bubnovskaia sotnia* (Bubniv Company, 2 vols, 1848–9). His research in those areas was significant for the development of Ukrainian historiography.

Maksymovych also worked in the field of Ukrainian archeology and was the author of the first archeological report using the typological method in Ukraine, *Ukrainskie strely drevneishikh vremen ...* (Ukrainian Arrows of More Ancient Times ..., 1868). His work in the natural sciences and history found common ground in his philosophical work. Following F. von Schelling's philosophy of nature, Maksymovych claimed that the study of nature and society should be based on scientifically researched facts. Research should be 'rigorously analytical and carefully synthetic, and thus positive' because 'philosophy can be found in every work of the mind,' and 'all learned disciplines should be philosophy.' 'Regarding the various sciences, or various branches of knowledge, one all-encompassing philosophy ought to be used, right down to fine details.' His historical and philological work has been collected in three volumes, edited by O. Kotliarevsky and published in Kiev in 1876–80. His correspondence has been only partially published, in *Kievskaia starina* (1904); his autobiography also appeared there (1904, no. 9). The Maksymovych archival collection is located in the manuscript division of the Central Scientific Library of the Academy of Sciences of Ukraine and, partially, in the Central State Archive of Literature and Art in Moscow.

BIBLIOGRAPHY
Ponomarev, S. *M. Maksimovich* (St Petersburg 1871)
Iubilei M.A. Maksimovicha (Kiev 1871; 2nd edn, St Petersburg 1872)
Hrushevs'kyi, A. 'M.A. Maksimovich,' in *Izvestiia Otdeleniia russkogo iazyka i slovesnosti Imperatorskoi akademii nauk*, vol 1 (St Petersburg 1906)
Popov, P. *M.O. Maksymovych* (Kiev 1954)
Ostrianyn, D. *Svitohliad M.O. Maksymovycha* (Kiev 1960)
Popov, P. *Pershyi zbirnyk ukraïns'kykh narodnykh pisen': Ukraïns'ki pisni, vydani M. Maksymovychem* (Kiev 1962)

O. Ohloblyn

Maksymovych, Mykola [Maksymovyč], b 7 March 1855 in Kiev, d 14 March 1928 in Kiev. Hydraulic engineer and designer. A graduate of the St Petersburg Institute of Road Engineers (1878), he designed and supervised the construction of the river port in Kiev (1896). He was a professor at the Kiev Polytechnical Institute (from 1900) and head of the hydrological section of the Ukrainian Academy of Sciences (from 1919). He wrote important works on the Dnieper and its watershed, electrification of the Kiev region, and regulation of the Dnieper River in Kiev.

Maksymovych, Mykola [Maksymovyč], b 29 April 1914 in Dobratycze, near Lublin, Poland. Electrical engineer. A graduate of the Lviv Polytechnical Institute (1941), he was director there (from 1954) and rector of Lviv University (from 1963). His main technical contributions are in the areas of electrotechnical theory and electric circuit calculations.

Maksymovych, Yurii (Heorhii) [Maksymovyč, Jurij (Heorhij)], b 2 May 1877 in the Chernihiv region, d ? Historian. He studied at Kiev University under M. Dovnar-Zapolsky and was a professor at the Nizhen Historical-Philological Institute, Kiev University (until 1919), and the Crimean Pedagogical Institute in Symferopil (during the 1920s). In the 1920s he was a full member of the Kharkiv Scientific Research Department of the History of Ukrainian Culture. He was imprisoned during the Stalinist terror of the 1930s, but he was later released, and became a professor at the pedagogical institute in Piatigorsk (1954). He wrote studies in the history of the 18th-century Hetman state, including monographs on Count P. Rumiantsev as governor of Little Russia (1913), military exercises in Little Russia in the second half of the 18th century (1913), and elections and mandates in Little Russia to the Legislative Commission of 1767 (1917).

Maksymovych-Ambodyk, Nestor. See Ambodyk-Maksymovych, Nestor.

Maksymovychivka [Maksymovyčivka]. An *etymological spelling first used by M. *Maksymovych in his three editions of Ukrainian folk songs (1827, 1834, 1849). Its principles were set forth in his article on orthography and pronunciation in the 1827 edition and in an 1842 letter to H. Kvitka-Osnovianenko. In order to distinguish the Ukrainian language from Russian and yet make it recognizable to Russian readers, Maksymovych retained the etymological letters ы, и, ѣ, and ъ (eg, *сынъ, robиtи, lѣѣъ* 'son, to work, forest'); rendered the letters *o, e, i,* and *и,* when pronounced as *i,* simply with a diacritical mark (eg, *vônъ, mêdъ, dobrû* 'he, honey, good' pl), and used *ъ* after labial consonants before iotated vowels (eg, *vъъzžae, krovъju* '(s)he drives in, with blood'), *ë* instead of *йo* and *ьo* (eg, *ёho, sëho* 'his, of this'), and *e* for both *e* and *je.* P. Lukashevych used the *maksymovychivka* in his 1836 song collection, and P. Kulish wrote in it for a while, but almost all writers in Russian-ruled Ukraine rejected it. In Galicia, Bukovyna, and Transcarpathia, however, a modified version (mainly with regard to etymological markings and the use of *-l* endings in the past tense [eg, *xodylъ* instead of *xodyv* 'he went']) was adopted by the 1848 *Congress of Ruthenian Scholars in Lviv and was used in the grammars of M. Osadtsa (1862), H. Shashkevych (1865), P. Diachan (1865), O. Partytsky (1873), and O. Ohonovsky (1889). In Galicia and Bukovyna the *maksymovychivka* remained in force in the schools until 1895, and in the Russophile press and books until the 1930s. Ye. *Zhelekhivsky's Ukrainian-German dictionary (1886) and S. *Smal-Stotsky's Ruthenian grammar (1893) played a decisive role in its withdrawal from the schools. In Transcarpathia, however, an etymological spelling based on the *maksymovychivka* was sanctioned by O. *Dukhnovych's grammar (1853), L. *Csopey's primers of the 1880s, and the school questionnaire issued in Uzhhorod in 1920. It remained current there because of the archaic phonetics of the Transcarpathian dialects and the unfamiliarity of Transcarpathian populist writers with literary Ukrainian. I. *Pankevych's (1923, 1927) and A. *Voloshyn's (1907, 1920) grammars were based on this orthography. (See also *Orthography.)

O. Horbach

Ivan Makukh   Ivan Makushenko: *Self-Portrait* (oil, 1907)

Makukh, Ivan [Makux], b 17 September 1872 in Dorozhiv, Sambir county, Galicia, d 18 September 1946 in Salzburg, Austria. Lawyer, civic and political leader, and co-operative organizer. Upon graduating from Lviv University (PH D, 1901) he was active in the *Ukrainian Radical party and edited its paper *Hromads'kyi holos*. In 1907 he opened a law office in Tovmach and became active in the educational and political life of the county: he organized Prosvita reading rooms, Sich branches, and the Selianska Kasa credit union. As deputy to the Galician Diet (1908–18) he demanded reform of the electoral system, which was biased against the Ukrainian population. Dur-

ing the First World War he was a member of the General Ukrainian Council and the Ukrainian National Rada. He served as secretary of public works in the First State Secretariat (1918) and secretary of internal affairs in the Second State Secretariat of the Western Ukrainian National Republic (1919). After the government's evacuation beyond the Zbruch River he became deputy minister of internal affairs of the UNR (1920). Upon returning to Tovmach at the end of 1920, he resumed his law practice and political activity. He headed the Ukrainian Socialist Radical party (1930–9) and was twice elected to the Polish Senate (1928 and 1930). In 1944 he emigrated to Austria, where he wrote his memoirs, which were published posthumously as *Na narodnii sluzhbi* (In the People's Service, 1958).

Makukh, Vasyl [Makuxa, Vasyl'], b 1921 in Kariv, Rava Ruska county, Galicia, d 5 November 1968 in Kiev. Political protester. Having served long terms of imprisonment throughout the 1950s, he set himself on fire on Khreshchatyk Boulevard, the main thoroughfare of Kiev, to protest Soviet political repression and the colonial subjugation of Ukraine. Before his death he was heard to shout 'Colonialism out of Ukraine!' and 'Long live a free Ukraine!' His self-immolation was the first such act of protest in Ukraine.

Makushenko, Ivan [Makušenko] (Makukha), b 30 March 1867 in Lysianka, Zvenyhorodka county, Kiev gubernia, d 7 June 1955 in Kiev. Painter and educator. He studied under I. Repin at the St Petersburg Academy of Arts (1892–7) and then worked in Ukraine, where he taught at the Kiev Art School (1905–19) and the Kiev State Art Institute (1934–55). He is known for his genre paintings, such as *Feast Day in Ukraine* (1900), *Before the Feast Day* (1904), *Lirnyk in the Village* (1911), and *Grandmother with Little Girl* (1936). Some of his works have been preserved at the Kiev and Lviv museums of Ukrainian art.

Mal, b ?, d 946. *Derevlianian prince, also known as Niskinei. According to the Primary Chronicle, *Povist' vremennykh lit*, in 945 Mal led the Derevlianians of Iskorosten (Korosten) in a revolt against the Kievan prince *Ihor. Ihor was killed in the revolt, and the Derevlianians proposed that his widow, *Olha, marry Mal, so that he could lay claim to the Kiev principality. She replied by forcibly suppressing the revolt in 946, at which time Mal was either killed or executed. In certain interpretations of the chronicles it is alleged that Mal was the father of *Malusha (mother of Volodymyr the Great), but that is highly unlikely.

Mala, Liubov, b 13 January 1919 in Kopani, Berdianske county, Tavriia gubernia. Internal medicine specialist; full member of the USSR Academy of Medical Sciences from 1974. A graduate of the Kharkiv Medical Institute (1938), she began working at the institute in 1946. In 1955 she was appointed head of the internal medicine department and scientific head of the cardiology laboratory at the institute's hopital. Her publications deal with the early diagnosis and treatment of arteriosclerosis, arterial hypertension, and ischemia. She wrote *Ishemicheskaia bolezn' serdtsa u molodykh* (Ischemic Heart Disease in Young People, 1978).

Mala Danylivka. III-17. A town smt (1990 pop 8,400) on the Lopan River in Derkachi raion, Kharkiv oblast. It was founded in 1714, and attained smt status in 1938. It is the home of the *Kharkiv Zootechnical-Veterinary Institute and a branch of the Ukrainian Scientific Research Institute of Plant Cultivation, Selection, and Genetics.

Mala Vyska. VI-12. A city (1990 pop 14,900) on the Mala Vys River and a raion center in Kirovohrad oblast. It was founded in the first half of the 18th century, and attained city status in 1957. It has a sugar-refining complex, a distillery, and a powdered-milk plant.

Malakhov, Heorhii [Malaxov, Heorhij], b 29 March 1907 in Bilopillia, Sumy county, Kharkiv gubernia. Mining scientist; full member of the AN URSR (now ANU) since 1967. He graduated from the Dnipropetrovske Mining Institute (1930) and worked in the mining areas of Kryvyi Rih and the Urals. Since 1973 he has been in charge of the Kryvyi Rih division of the ANU Institute of Geological Sciences. His works deal with mining (particularly mining at great depths), prospecting, and geology.

Malakhov, Petro [Malaxov], b 1753 in Chernihiv, d 1807 in Chernihiv. Physician. A graduate of Chernihiv College and the Moscow Medical-Surgical School (1773), he was physician of Chernihiv vicegerency from 1784 and inspector of the Chernihiv Medical Administration from 1797. He compiled the first medico-topographical description of Chernihiv gubernia.

Malakhov, Vasyl [Malaxov, Vasyl'], b 8 March 1779 in Malakhivka, Chernihiv region, d 1856. Physician and surgeon. Educated at Chernihiv Seminary and the St Petersburg Medico-Surgical Academy 1801, he was general staff doctor of the Podilia army from 1813 and a hospital inspector (from 1829). In 1820 he proposed a practical classification scheme for diseases.

Malanchuk, Hryhor. See Malantschuk, Gregor.

Malanchuk, Valentyn [Malančuk] (né Milman), b 13 November 1928 in Proskuriv (now Khmelnytskyi), d 25 April 1984 in Kiev. Stalinist functionary and historian. A graduate of Lviv University (1950), he worked in the Lviv Oblast Komsomol Committee (1950–2) and then in the Lviv Oblast Party Committee (1952–67). He served as deputy minister of higher and specialized secondary education (1967–72), CC CPU ideology secretary (1972–7), and candidate member of the Politburo (1972–81). A protégé of M. Suslov, Malanchuk made his reputation by suppressing 'Ukrainian bourgeois nationalism' in Lviv oblast in the 1960s and purging the CPU and Ukrainian academic and cultural institutions of dissidents after P. Shelest's downfall in 1972. A professor at Kiev University from 1968 and head of the department of CPSU history at the Kiev Polytechnical Institute from 1979, he wrote articles on the history of the Communist Party of Western Ukraine, a book on the Komsomol in Western Ukraine (1959), and a book on Soviet nationality policy (1963), in which he advocated Russification.

Malanchuk, Volodymyr [Malančuk], b 20 August 1904 in Zalishchyky Mali, Buchach county, Galicia, d 29

Bishop Volodymyr   Ira Malaniuk
Malanchuk

September 1990 in Saskatoon, Saskatchewan. Ukrainian Catholic bishop. He graduated from the Redemptorist seminary in Eschen, Belgium, in 1924 and entered the Redemptorist order. He was ordained in 1931, and taught at Redemptorist schools in Galicia and continued his studies at the universities of Lviv and Munich (PH D, 1944). A postwar refugee, he was a lecturer at the Ukrainian Catholic seminaries in Hirschberg, Germany, and Kulemborg, Netherlands, and general vicar in Great Britain (1949–50) before emigrating to Canada. He served as protohegumen of the eastern rite Redemptorists in North America and edited the order's journal *Lohos*. In 1962 he was consecrated bishop and first exarch of the Ukrainian Catholic church in France. After retiring in 1982, he returned to Canada.

Malaniuk, Ira [Malanjuk], b 19 January 1919 in Stanyslaviv (now Ivano-Frankivske), Galicia. Opera and concert singer (mezzo-soprano). She studied under A. Didur in Lviv and at the Vienna Music Academy. In 1941–4 she appeared at the Lviv Opera Theater, and in 1947 at the Municipal Opera in Zurich. From 1952 she was a soloist of the Munich State Opera, and she also sang at the Vienna State Opera, La Scala, the Paris Opera, and Covent Garden, and in Berlin and Stuttgart. She was highly regarded in operas by R. Strauss and was well known at the Salzburg Festivals. In recitals she sang from the Ukrainian repertoire, including works by M. Lysenko, D. Sichynsky, S. Liudkevych, V. Barvinsky, Ya. Stepovy, N. Nyzhankivsky, B. Liatoshynsky, and A. Hnatyshyn. She recorded for many international labels.

Malaniuk, Yevhen [Malanjuk, Jevhen], b 20 January 1897 in the Kherson region, d 16 February 1968 in New York. Poet and political and community activist. He became an officer of the UNR Army in 1917 and was interned in Kalisz, Poland, in 1920. He graduated from the Ukrainian Husbandry Academy in Poděbrady in 1923. Toward the end of the Second World War he resettled in Germany, and then he emigrated to the United States. He founded the literary journal *Veselka* with Yu. Darahan in Kalisz, and he continued to publish it in 1922–3. Published collections of his poetry include *Stylet i stylos* (The Stiletto and the Stylus, 1925), *Herbarii* (Herbarium, 1926), *Zemlia i zalizo* (Earth and Steel, 1930), *Zemna madonna* (The Earthly Madonna, 1934), *Persten' Polikrata* (The Ring of Polycrates,

Yevhen Malaniuk   Gregor Malantschuk

1939), *Vybrani poeziï* (Selected Poetry, 1943), *Vlada* (Power, 1951), *Poeziï* (Poems, 1954), and *Ostannia vesna* (The Last Spring, 1959). He also published a longer poem, *P'iata symfoniia* (The Fifth Symphony, 1953), and a number of collections of essays, including *Narysy z istoriï nashoï kul'-tury* (Essays in the History of Our Culture, 1954), *Do problemy bol'shevyzmu* (On the Problem of Bolshevism, 1956), and *Knyha sposterezhen'* (A Book of Observations, 1962). An edition of his selected works with extensive annotation and a bibliography, *Zemna Madonna* (The Earthly Madonna), was published in 1991 in Prešov.

His poetry is one of the better examples of the literary resurgence of the 1920s and 1930s. He was a member of the *vistnykivtsi*, made up of literary contributors to D. Dontsov's journal **Vistnyk*. His work was influential in émigré circles, in Western Ukraine, and in the Ukrainian SSR, where he was under constant attack by official critics, who called him a Ukrainian fascist.

The style and engaged content of his poetry emerged as a result of his generation's anger and frustration at Ukraine's subjugation, at the defeat of the national revolution, and at the ongoing tragedy caused by Moscow's domination of Ukraine. His anger was directed not only at external forces but also at internal weaknesses, such as the **Little Russian mentality, anarchism, lack of national discipline and organization, and the domination of emotion over intellect. His poetry is accordingly characterized by dynamism, the frequent use of words with shock value, pathos, prophecy, and reflections on the past. He used mostly regular strophes, with classical meter (he favored the energy of iambs) and rhyme schemes, and was inventive in his use of visual imagery. According to V. Derzhavyn, 'Only partially imbued with classicism, his poetry ranges for the most part between symbolism and the baroque (or romanticism) with a preference for the latter.'

Yu. Lavrinenko

Malanka (aka *Melanka*). A Ukrainian folk feast on New Year's Eve corresponding to St Sylvester's Feast in the Latin calendar. The name originates from St Melaniia, whose day falls on 13 January (31 December OS). In central and eastern Ukraine the feast was also known as *Shchedryi vechir* (Generous Eve) or *Shchedra kutia*. Traditionally, Ma-

lanka (a bachelor dressed in women's clothing), with a dressed-up goat, gypsy, old man, old woman, Jew, and other characters and musicians, went from house to house in the village supposedly to put the households in order. But instead of bringing order Malanka played all kinds of pranks. In some locales young men and women brought a plow into the house and pretended to plow a field. The folk play was concluded with caroling. The *Malanka* traditions were most prevalent in the Dnieper region. They combine old agrarian themes with folk theater (the **inter-mede* and **vertep*). After the 1917 Revolution the *Malanka* tradition declined, but it was revived in the early 1930s as part of the New Year celebrations. Today Ukrainians in and outside Ukraine celebrate *Malanka* as the traditional way of inaugurating the Julian-calendar New Year.

Malantschuk, Gregor [Malančuk, Hryhor], b 2 September 1902 in Harbuziv, Zboriv county, Galicia, d 20 August 1978 in Copenhagen. Philosopher; a leading authority on S. Kierkegaard. After studying at Berlin University (PH D, 1934) he moved to Copenhagen, where from 1939 he conducted private study circles in philosophy and psychology, taught Ukrainian language and literature (1948–61), lectured on Kierkegaard (1962–73), and was a research fellow (1966–73) at the University of Copenhagen. His Kierkegaard lectures attracted scholars from around the world, and his works on Kierkegaard have been translated from Danish into several languages. He wrote over five monographs on Kierkegaard, the most important of which are *Dialektik og Existens hos Søren Kierkegaard* (1968; English trans: *Kierkegaard's Thought*, 1971) and *Fra Individ til den Enkelte* (1978). Malantschuk's Kierkegaard collection was acquired by McGill University in Montreal in 1981.

Malaria (Ukrainian: *maliariia*). An acute debilitating disease characterized by periodic recurrences of chills and fever, anemia, enlargement of the spleen, and high mortality. The infection is caused by various organisms of the genus *Plasmodium* that are transmitted by Anopheles mosquitoes. Malaria is most common in tropical and subtropical climates and is therefore not a major illness in Ukraine. Before the revolution 3 percent of the population yearly developed the disease. In 1919 the number of cases rose sharply, mainly as a result of lack of drugs (quinine), generally bad health care, and the suspension of control of the mosquito population. In 1923–4 there were nearly three million sufferers annually in Ukraine; in some regions up to 20 percent of the population was infected. Outbreaks also occurred in 1932–4 (up to two million afflicted) and 1943–5 (approx 5 percent of the population). The Ukrainian Protozoan Institute was founded in Kharkiv in 1923. The People's Commissariat of Health Protection created a department to combat malaria, and 285 antimalarial stations were set up that year. To combat the mosquito population, extensive draining of marshes and aerial spraying were employed.

A global eradication program was launched in 1955 under the auspices of the World Health Organization. These preventive and control measures contributed to the virtual elimination of malaria in Ukraine (32 cases in Ukraine in 1958).

A number of Ukrainian scientists contributed to research on the infection. V. Danylevsky discovered the malaria pathogen in birds (1884); V. *Rubashkin studied the microscopic structure of *Plasmodium*; and F. Favr, K. Selivanov, and M. Morozovska studied its infection patterns.

BIBLIOGRAPHY
Dobreitser, I. *Maliariia v SSSR* (Moscow 1924)

P. Dzul

Malashchuk, Roman [Malaščuk], b 11 November 1913 in Bedrykivtsi, Zalishchyky county, Galicia, d 8 May 1991 in Toronto. Political leader. He joined the OUN as a gymnasium student in Kolomyia and by 1937 had been appointed to its national executive as chief of the student network. In March 1939 he was arrested by the Polish police along with other participants in a student congress. After fleeing from the Soviets to Cracow he helped organize *OUN expeditionary groups. At the outbreak of the German-Soviet War, he returned to Stanyslaviv, where he was arrested in September by the Gestapo. He spent the rest of the war in the Auschwitz concentration camp. From 1945 he played a leading role in the Bandera faction of the OUN in the West. After emigrating to Canada in 1948, he helped to found the Ukrainian Youth Association, the *Canadian League for Ukraine's Liberation (which he headed in 1949–75), and the newspaper *Homin Ukraïny*. Malashchuk headed the presidium of the *Ukrainian Liberation Front in 1967–83 and sat on the Secretariat of the World Congress of Free Ukrainians in 1973–83. His experiences are described in *Z knyhy moho zhyttia: Spomyny* (From the Book of My Life: Memoirs, 2 vols, 1987, 1988).

Malashevych, Ivan [Malaševyč], b ?, d ca 1737. Zaporozhian Cossack leader. He was elected kish otaman nine times in 1714–37, first of the Oleshky Sich and later of the New Sich. He was a leading advocate of returning the Zaporozhian Cossacks to their traditional strongholds (albeit under the suzerainty of the Russian tsar). In 1714, 1716, 1717, 1727, and 1728 he was the emissary of Hetmans I. Skoropadsky and D. Apostol to the tsarist government. In March 1734 they returned from Oleshky and established the New Sich. Malashevych died during the Zaporozhian campaign to Ochakiv.

Malashkin, Leonid [Malaškin], b 1842 near Riazan, Russia, d 11 February 1902 in Moscow. Russian composer, conductor, and pedagogue. After studying music in Berlin, he was appointed conductor of the Kiev Opera in 1877. He also taught singing at the Kiev Theological Academy. While in Kiev, Malashkin composed a cycle of liturgical music based on Kievan chant, premiered his opera *Illia Muromets'* (1879), and composed piano works based on Ukrainian folk songs (including 'Kozachok' and 'Our Ukraine'). In 1888 he returned to Moscow, where he published an anthology of 50 Ukrainian songs arranged for voice and piano.

Malashko, Mykhailo [Malaško, Myxajlo], b 1882, d 1920. Military and political activist. An officer of an infantry school in the Russian army, in June 1917 he was elected to the All-Ukrainian Council of Military Deputies. At the end of the year he was appointed deputy commissioner of the Central Rada for the Donets Basin. As commander of a partisan detachment in 1919–20, he fought the Bolsheviks, N. Makhno's forces, and A. Denikin's troops. He was captured and executed by the Bolsheviks.

Malavsky, Volodymyr [Malavs'kyj], b 1853 in Kamianets-Podilskyi, Podilia gubernia, d 28 March 1886 in Schlüsselburg county, St Petersburg gubernia. Civic activist. He was a political propagandist in Podilian villages from 1874, and he was arrested in 1877 for his role in planning a peasant uprising in Chyhyryn county, Kiev gubernia. He was sentenced to 20 years of hard labor in Siberia in 1880 and had 15 years added to his term after an unsuccessful escape attempt in 1881. For taking part in protests over severe prison conditions he was transferred to the Peter and Paul Fortress in St Petersburg in 1883 and then to the nearby Schlüsselburg Fortress, where he died of consumption.

Malczewski, Antoni, b 3 June 1793 in Kniahynyne, near Dubno, Volhynia, d 2 May 1826 in Warsaw. Polish poet; member of the *Ukrainian school in Polish literature. He completed his education at the Kremianets Lyceum in 1811. His only published work, *Maria, powieść ukraińska* (Maria, A Ukrainian Novelette, 1825), was written under the influence of the Ukrainian oral tradition and contains descriptions of Ukraine's landscape and people.

Malecha, Nestor [Maleča], b 8 November 1887 in Struhovska Buda, Surazh county, Chernihiv gubernia, d 9 August 1979 in Uralsk, Kazakhstan. Philologist and educator. A graduate of the Free Higher School in St Petersburg (1907) and the Kiev Archeological Institute (1925), he compiled the first dictionary of T. Shevchenko's language (1916) and prepared a number of primers and textbooks for adults. He was director of the lexicological office of the VUAN Institute of Linguistics (1930–3). After his arrest and exile he lectured at the Uralsk Pedagogical Institute and compiled a dialectological dictionary of the language of the Ural Cossacks (unpublished). He was a founder of the Ukrainian Ethnographic Society and of the Western Kazakhstan Section of the USSR Geographical Society.

Viktor Malets

Malets, Viktor [Malec'], b 1 October 1894 in Chuhuiv, Zmiiv county, Kharkiv gubernia, d 9 July 1969 in London. Military figure. An officer in the Russian army during the First World War, in December 1917 he joined the UNR Army and became staff captain in the First Serdiuk Division, battalion commander in the Second Zaporozhian Regiment (October 1918), and commander of the 19th Zaporozhian Republican Regiment (April 1919). In 1920 he commanded the 48th Battalion of the Sixth Sich Division and retreated with it into Poland. In the 1920s he studied engineering at the Ukrainian Husbandry Academy in Poděbrady and then served as a major in the Polish army. In 1940 he organized and directed an OUN officer school near Cracow, and in autumn 1941 he served as an officer with the OUN (Melnyk faction) expeditionary groups in central Ukraine. From May 1943 he was in charge of the officers' sector at the Military Board (Division Galizien). After being released from British internment in 1948, for many years he served as a representative of the defense department of the UNR government-in-exile and president of the Ukrainian Combatants' Council and Ukrainian Officers Club in England.

Bishop Volodymyr Malets

Malets, Volodymyr [Malec'], b 23 April 1890 in the Kherson region, d 23 July 1967 in Detroit. Orthodox bishop. He graduated from the historical-philological faculty of Kiev University in 1915 and then taught in postsecondary schools and engaged in scholarly work. In June 1942 he was consecrated bishop of Cherkasy in the renewed Ukrainian Autocephalous Orthodox church (UAOC) in Kiev. In 1944 he emigrated to Warsaw, and then to Germany, where he was made bishop of UAOC faithful in northern Bavaria. From 1946 he was a member of the Ukrainian Orthodox Scholarly Theological Institute and curator of the Theological Academy of the UAOC in Munich (1948–9). In 1951 he emigrated to Detroit, and in 1957 he was elevated to the office of archbishop.

Malevich, Kazimir [Malevič], b 23 February 1878 in Kiev, d 15 May 1935 in Leningrad. Painter, designer, and theorist. He studied at the Kiev Art School (1895–7), the Moscow School of Painting, Sculpture, and Architecture (1904–5), and F. Rerberg's studio in Moscow (1905–10). Influenced at first by the Impressionists and Fauvists, he participated in avant-garde exhibitions in Moscow, at which he displayed paintings in a neoprimitivist style, such as *Peasants in Church* (1910–11) and *The Harvest* (1911); cubo-futurist works, such as *The Knife Grinder* (1912); and paintings, such as *An Englishman in Moscow* (1914) and *Woman beside an Advertising Pillar* (1914), which show the influence of P. Picasso and G. Braque's synthetic cubism. In 1915 Malevich launched the artistic movement of *suprematism in Petrograd. He was the first modern painter to work in a purely geometric, cerebral, nonfigurative manner (eg, his paintings *Black Square* [1913] and *White on White* [1918]). In 1916 he published the journal *Supremus*. Under Soviet rule he was a member of the Division of Visual Arts of the Russian Commissariat of Enlightenment; taught at the Vitsebsk Art Institute in Belarus (1919–22), the Leningrad Academy of Arts (from 1922), and the Kiev State Art Institute (1927–9); and direct-

Kazimir Malevich: *Girls in a Field* (oil, ca 1928–32)

ed the Leningrad Institute of Artistic Culture (1923–6). In the 1920s he began working in a constructivist style, in which he produced urban architectural models and furniture, textile, and china designs. He was a prolific writer and produced various theoretical works, notably *The World as Non-Objectivity* (English trans 1976), developed new educational methods, and established original theoretical frameworks for the analysis of paintings. His works and theories influenced a number of Soviet avant-garde artists, including the Russians I. Chasnik and El Lissitsky and the Ukrainians V. Yermilov, V. Meller, and A. Petrytsky. In the late 1920s, because of growing opposition on the part of the central Soviet government to the avant-garde, Malevich was able to publish 13 articles of his theories only in the Kharkiv journal *Nova generatsiia* (1928–9). Having been forced to return to a figurative style of painting in 1929, he died in poverty and oblivion.

N. Mykytyn

Mali druzi (Little Friends). An illustrated children's monthly published in Lviv (1937–8, 1942–4) and Cracow (1940–4). The magazine was renewed in Augsburg, Germany (1947–8), by the Association of Ukrainian Writers for Young People. It was edited by B. Hoshovsky and illustrated by R. Chornii and O. Sudomora. Contributors included V. Barahura, I. Bahriany, I. Kernytsky, B. Nyzhankivsky, S. Hordynsky, Yu. Tarnovych, L. Poltava, V. Onufriienko, O. Oles, O. Stefanovych, O. Liaturynska, O. Kobets, K. Perelisna, V. Chaplenko, I. Savytska, B. Zaklynsky, and V. Vovk.

Mali Mynky. A village now in Narodychi raion, Zhytomyr oblast. On 17 November 1921 the Volhynia Group of the UNR Army, during the Second Winter Campaign, was surrounded there by Bolshevik forces. Many UNR soldiers died in battle, but the majority were captured and later executed at *Bazar. This marked the end of UNR military operations against the Bolsheviks.

Maliar, Volodymyr [Maljar], b 7 April 1941 in Kharkiv. Actor. In 1962 he completed study at the Kharkiv Theater

Institute, and since then he has worked in the Kharkiv Ukrainian Drama Theater. He has played mainly heroic and character roles, notably the title role in W. Shakespeare's *Richard III* (1976).

Maliarstvo i skul'ptura. See *Obrazotvorche mystetstvo*.

Maliatko (Preschooler). An illustrated monthly children's magazine published in Kiev by the Communist Youth League of Ukraine from 1960 to 1992. It contains poems, folktales, stories, songs, games, riddles, and exercises intended primarily for preschoolers. In 1980 it had a circulation of 611,000.

Maliieva-Tahaieva, Hanna. See Tahaiv, Anna.

Archbishop Kostiantyn Maliushkevych

Antin Maliutsa: *That Way* (charcoal, 1947)

Maliushkevych, Kostiantyn [Maljuškevyč, Kostjantyn], b 2 February 1890 in Zhylyntsi, Zaslav county, Volhynia gubernia, d 1937? Bishop of the Ukrainian Autocephalous Orthodox church (UAOC). A graduate of the Zhytomyr Theological Seminary (1912) and the Kiev Theological Academy (1916), he was ordained in 1915, and worked as a teacher (1916–21). In 1922 he was consecrated bishop of Uman. After serving as bishop of Katerynoslav (1924) he was elected vice-president of the presidium of the All-Ukrainian Orthodox Church Council (1926) and elevated to the office of archbishop of Kiev and vice-metropolitan (1927). After the UAOC was dissolved, he headed the Kiev eparchy of the restructured Ukrainian Orthodox church (1930–4). Harassed constantly by the authorities, he was forced to resign in 1934 and forbidden to deliver sermons or conduct services. Maliushkevych was arrested in 1937, and his subsequent fate is unknown; he was probably shot in 1937 or 1941.

Maliutsa, Antin [Maljuca], b 1908 in Toky, Zbarazh county, Galicia, d 17 June 1970 in New York City. Painter, graphic artist, and critic. He studied at the Novakivsky Art School (1926–30) and State Institute of Plastic Art (1935–9) in Lviv and was a member of the RUB artists' group. A postwar refugee, in 1950 he emigrated to New York, where he was an executive member of the Literary-Artistic Club and the Ukrainian Artists' Association in the USA. He experimented with various printing techniques. He produced two series of drawings, 'Horrors' and 'A Voyage in Darkness,' and oils, engravings, and church murals, and wrote many articles on art for the Ukrainian émigré press.

Rev Mykola Maliuzhynsky

Maliuzhynsky, Mykola [Maljužyns'kyj], b 1903 in Liubar, Novohrad-Volynskyi county, Volhynia gubernia, d 15 October 1943 in Rivne, Volhynia. Priest and Orthodox church activist. He graduated from the Kremianets Theological Seminary and then received an MA in theology from Warsaw University. While serving as a parish priest in various villages in Volhynia, he protested the forced conversion of Orthodox Ukrainians to Catholicism by the Polish authorities in 1937–8, for which action he was persecuted. When the Soviets occupied Volhynia in 1939, he fled to the Kholm region, where he served as general vicar and as member of the Kholm Consistory. In 1941 he joined the administration of the Ukrainian Autocephalous Orthodox church in Lutske as an assistant to Metropolitan P. Sikorsky. He was executed by the Nazis in a Rivne prison.

Mykola Malko

Malko, Mykola [Mal'ko] (Nicolai), b 4 May 1883 in Brailiv, Vinnytsia county, Podilia gubernia, d 23 June 1961 in Sydney, Australia. Conductor. He studied under N. Rimsky-Korsakov, A. Liadov, A. Glazunov, and N. Tcherepnin in St Petersburg, M. Lysenko in Kiev, and F. Mottl in Munich before taking a position with the St Petersburg Opera (1909–18). He then moved between Vitsebsk and Moscow, Kiev, and Kharkiv (1921–4) before returning to Leningrad to teach in the Conservatory and conduct the Philharmonic. From 1928 he toured Western Europe to considerable acclaim, and in 1930 he emigrated permanently to the West. He settled initially in Copenhagen, where he founded the Danish National Orchestra. In 1940 he moved to the United States to teach conducting at Mills College in Oakland and then conducted the Chicago Symphony Orchestra. He subsequently conducted the Yorkshire Symphony Orchestra in England (1954–6) and the Sydney Orchestra in Australia (1956–61). His performances of P. Tchaikovsky, N. Miaskovsky, S. Prokofiev, B. Liatoshynsky, and others were highly regarded for their clarity and balance. Malko conducted many world premieres, including Miaskovsky's Symphony no. 5 (Moscow, 1920) and the first two symphonies of the young D. Shostakovich (Leningrad, 1926 and 1927). He was also the first to conduct in the West the 'Galician Dances' from Liatoshynsky's opera *The Golden Ring*. Widely recorded, Malko earned particularly high regard for his discs with the London Symphony Orchestra. He also wrote a methodological study, *The Conductor and His Baton* (1950), and a memoir about his mentors, *A Certain Age* (1966). A collection of his writings was translated into Russian and published in Leningrad in 1972.

R. Savytsky

Malkovych, Ivan [Malkovyč], b 10 May 1961 in Nyzhnii Bereziv, Kosiv raion, Ivano-Frankivske oblast. Poet. He graduated from Kiev University (1985) and has worked as an editor for the Veselka and Molod publishing houses. Malkovych is the author of two poetry collections, *Bilyi kamin'* (White Stone, 1984) and the avant-garde *Kliuch* (The Key, 1988).

Malorosiistvo. See Little Russian mentality.

Malorossiiskii prikaz. See Little Russian Office.

Malorusskii literaturnyi sbornik (Little Russian Literary Collection). A Ukrainian literary almanac published in 1859 in Saratov by D. *Mordovets. It contained works by Mordovets and M. Kostomarov; over 200 folk songs; the first four Ukrainian folk tales to be published, 'Okh,' 'Koza-dereza' (Billy Goat's Bluff), 'Kazka pro Ivasyka i pro vid'mu' (A Tale about Ivasyk and the Witch), and 'Kazka pro korolevu Katerynu' (A Tale about Queen Catherine); and the first translation of N. Gogol ('Vecher nakanune Ivana Kupala' [St John's Eve]) into Ukrainian. In his introduction to the poem 'Kozaky i more' (The Cossacks and the Sea) Mordovets argued for the use of Ukrainian in the press and the schools.

Malovantsi. A religious sect in the Kiev region that split from the Baptists in the late 19th century. It was founded by K. Malovany, a peasant born in 1844 in Tarashcha, Kiev gubernia. Adherents of the sect believed that the end of the world was approaching, and most stopped working and awaited the Apocalypse. When Malovany's prophecies did not come true, his followers became disillusioned and resumed their normal lives. After Malovany's death in 1913, the sect disappeared.

Malovany, Volodymyr [Mal'ovanyj], b 1848 in Katerynoslav county, d 10 March 1893 in Tomsk, Siberia. Political activist and poet. He was exiled to Balagansk, Irkutsk gubernia, in 1879 for being a member of the Odessa Hromada, but he escaped in 1881 to Geneva, where he became active in M. Drahomanov's circle. He returned to Ukraine in 1883 under the assumed name of Hryhorii Petrov, and in Kharkiv he helped to establish a hromada and developed plans for a Ukrainian radical party. He was arrested a second time in 1883, and died of stomach cancer in Tomsk. His poem 'Ne poturai' (Pay No Heed) was published by I. Franko in the anthology *Akordy* (1903).

Maltsev, Aleksandr [Mal'cev], b 7 April 1855 in Totma county, Vologda gubernia, Russia, d 26 November 1926 in Poltava. Russian physician. A graduate of the St Petersburg Medico-Surgical Academy (1880), he worked under V. Bekhterev at Kazan University. In 1886 he became director of the Poltava Psychiatric Hospital, and in 1890 he organized a psychiatric clinic for Poltava gubernia that provided free treatment. He wrote textbooks in psychiatry and pharmacology.

Malusha [Maluša] (real name: Malfrid), b ?, d ca 1000. Concubine of Sviatoslav I Ihorevych the Conqueror; sister of *Dobrynia of Liubech and mother of *Volodymyr the Great. According to the ancient chronicles, which recorded her name as Malusha, she was the daughter of Malko Liubchanyn and a favorite of Princess Olha, Volodymyr's grandmother. Other sources say she was the daughter of the Derevlianian prince *Mal. The *Zapiski* of the Russian Imperial Academy of Sciences (vol 5) contain articles on Malusha by D. Prozorovsky and I. Sreznevsky.

Malyi Kuialnyk River [Malyj Kujal'nyk]. A river in Odessa oblast. It is 89 km in length and drains a basin area of 1,540 sq km. It empties into the Black Sea at the Khadzhybei Estuary. The river is dammed and used for irrigation. Its flow is intermittent owing to seasonal droughts.

Malyi misionarchyk (Little Missionary). A monthly Catholic children's magazine published in Zhovkva, Galicia, by the Basilian Fathers in 1903–14 and 1920 as a supplement to **Misionar*. It was edited by Revs Ye. Teodorovych and L. Berezovsky, who also edited *Misionar*.

Malyk, Volodymyr (pseud of Volodymyr Sychenko), b 21 February 1921 in Novosilky, Kiev gubernia. Writer of popular fiction. Since 1957 he has published several collections of historical-mythical tales and poetry for children; five children's novels, including *Slid vede do moria* (The Trail Leads to the Sea, 1975), *Kniaz' Kyi* (Prince Kyi, 1982), and *Dvoie nad prirvoiu* (Two above the Abyss, 1983); and several widely read, well-researched novels set in the Cossack and medieval periods: a tetralogy consisting of *Posol Urus-Shaitana* (Urus-Shaitan's Emissary, 1968; English trans: *The Cossack Ambassador*, 1986), *Firman sultana* (The Sultan's Coachman, 1969), *Chornyi vershnyk* (The Black Rider, 1976), and *Shovkovyi shnurok* (The Silk String, 1977), and the novels *Taiemnyi posol* (The Secret Emissary, 2 vols, 1981–2) and *Cherleni shchyty* (Crimson Shields, 1985). A two-volume selection of his works appeared in 1986.

Malyn. III-10. A city (1990 pop 29,700) on the Irsha River and a raion center in Zhytomyr oblast. It was founded in the 11th century, and played an important role in the Cossack-Polish War of 1648–57. It attained city status in 1938. Malyn is an important center of the paper industry and the building-materials industry. Its pride is a large park established in the 19th century.

Malyn. A village in Ostrih district, Volhynia (now in Mlyniv raion, Rivne oblast). On 14 July 1943 German security forces consisting of Poles and Uzbeks forced its Ukrainian and Czech inhabitants, including the pastor, into the village church, school, and barns and set them afire. Eight hundred and fifty people perished.

Malynivka. IV-17. A town smt (1990 pop 7,600) on the Donets River in Chuhuiv raion, Kharkiv oblast. It was founded in 1652 as a Cossack settlement, and attained town status in 1938. Several Scythian settlements from the 5th to 3rd centuries BC have been excavated near Malynivka.

Malynka, Oleksander, b 19 August 1865 in Mryn, Nizhen county, Chernihiv gubernia, d 22 May 1941 in Kiev. Folklorist. A graduate of the Nizhen Historical-Philological Institute (1890), he worked as a teacher in different regions of Ukraine and collected ethnographic materials. In the 1920s he was a research associate of the VUAN Ethnographic Commission. He was interested particularly in the songs of lirnyks and kobzars. His works include studies of the Ukrainian wedding (1897), the Kupalo festival (1898), and baptism (1898); a collection of materials in Ukrainian folklore (1902); and a song collection based on the repertoires of the kobzars O. Vlasko and D. Symonenko and the lirnyk A. Ivanytsky (1929).

Malynkovych, Volodymyr [Malynkovyč], b 1940. Physician and dissident. He joined the Ukrainian Helsinki Group in December 1978 and was harassed by the KGB until he left Ukraine at the end of 1979. He settled in Munich, where he edited *Forum*, a journal dealing with Soviet affairs.

Malynovska, Marharyta [Malynovs'ka], b 22 November 1941 in Uim, Volhynia, d 22 October 1983. Writer and literary critic. She graduated from Kiev University (1966) and worked on the editorial boards of the journals *Vitchyzna* and *Literaturna Ukraïna*. She was appointed secretary responsible for the Dramaturgy Commission of the Writers' Union of Ukraine. She published many articles and two collections of criticism on contemporary Soviet Ukrainian theater, books on O. Honchar (1971) and on L. Leonov and Ukraine (1979), and the novels *Hrymuchi ozera* (Thunderous Lakes, 1977) and *Polissia* (1980).

Malynovsky, Borys [Malynovs'kyj], b 24 August 1921 in Lukh, now in Ivanovo oblast, Russia. Computer scientist; corresponding member of the AN URSR (now ANU) since 1969. He graduated from the Ivanovo Energetics Institute (1950) and worked at the AN URSR Institute of Electrotechnology (1953–7) and the AN URSR Computing Center (since 1962; now ANU Institute of Cybernetics). His main contributions are in computational theory. He was in charge of the Dnipro computer project and developed the design principles for the main line of Soviet microcomputers.

Rev Mykhailo Malynovsky   Rev Oleksander Malynovsky

Malynovsky, Mykhailo [Malynovs'kyj, Myxajlo], b 1812, d 1894. Ukrainian Catholic priest. A canon of the Lviv archeparchy, he also served as its administrator (1869–70) and as a member of the Galician Diet (1861–6). He wrote several works concerning the history of the Ukrainian Catholic church in Ukrainian and German, including *Die Kirchen- und Staats-Satzungen bezüglich des griechisch-katholischen Ritus der Ruthenen in Galizien* (1861). He also arranged for the 1862 publication of the *Annales Ecclesiae Ruthenae* by M. Harasevych.

Malynovsky, Oleksander [Malynovs'kyj], b 12 January 1889 in Zhukiv, Zolochiv county, Galicia, d 18 November 1957 in Bradford, England. Ukrainian Catholic priest. After finishing gymnasium in Peremyshl, he worked and then joined the Austrain army (1911–20); he eventually attained the rank of captain in the Ukrainian Galician Army. After further studies, he was ordained in 1925. He held a number of administrative positions in 1927–40 in Lviv at the Greek Catholic Theological Seminary and Academy. In 1940 he became apolistic administrator of the *Lemko Apostolic Administration (1940–6). After the war he was rector of the Ukrainian Catholic seminaries in Germany and Holland. He moved to England in 1950, where he was the Ukrainian Catholic vicar general for the United Kingdom until his death.

Marshal Rodion Malynovsky   Andrii Malyshko

Malynovsky, Rodion [Malynovs'kyj], b 23 November 1898 in Odessa, d 31 March 1967 in Moscow. Marshal of the Soviet Union. He joined the Red Army in 1919. After graduating from the Frunze Military Academy (1930) he participated in the Spanish Civil War (1937–8). In the Second World War he commanded the Third and then the Second Ukrainian fronts of the Red Army. After the war he was commander in chief of the Soviet forces in the Far East (1947–56) and then served as the USSR minister of defense (1957–67).

Malynovsky, Yoanykii [Malynovs'kyj, Joanykij], b 16 November 1868 in Ostrih, Volhynia gubernia, d March 1932. Historian of law; from 1919 a full member of the VUAN. He taught law at Tomsk and Don universities before moving to Kiev (1924) and becoming chairman of its Commission for the Study of Ukraine's Customary Law and editor of its publications. He was also president of the Society of Ukrainian Jurists. His specialty was the law of Rus' and the Lithuanian-Ruthenian state, customary law, and Soviet law. His more important works were *Uchenie o prestuplenii po Litovskomu Statutu* (The Doctrine of Crime according to the Lithuanian Statute, 1894), *Rada Velikogo Kniazhestva Litovskogo v sviazi s boiarskoi Dumoi drevnei Rusi* (The Council of the Grand Duchy of Lithuania in relation to the Boyar Duma of Ancient Rus', 2 vols, 1903–4, 1912), *Radians'ki popravcho-trudovi ustanovy poriviniuiuchy z burzhuaznymy tiurmamy* (Soviet Corrective-Labor Institutions as Compared to Bourgeois Prisons, 1928), and *Starodavnii derzhavnyi lad skhidnikh slov'ian i ioho piznishi zminy* (The Ancient State System of the Eastern Slavs and Its Later Changes, 1929).

Malyshevsky, Ivan [Malyševskij], b 1828 in Belarus, d 23 January 1897 in Kiev. Church historian. He studied at the Kiev Theological Academy and was later a lecturer

and professor (1861–97) of Russian church history there. A member of the Historical Society of Nestor the Chronicler, he published his research in the society's *Chteniia*, in the academy's *Trudy* (TKDA), and in *Kievskaia starina* (KS). His works in TKDA included studies on the relations of Rus' with the Roman church during the reign of Prince Volodymyr the Great (1863, no. 2), on the legend of St Andrew's visit to Rus' (1866, no. 6), on Jews in Southern Rus' and Kiev in the 10th to 12th centuries (1878), on the identity of the first Kievan metropolitan (1883, no. 10), on Kievan church sobors (1884, no. 12), on SS Cyril and Methodius (1885), and on the Varangians in the initial history of Christianity in Kiev (1887, no. 12); and in KS, on the ancestry of Princess Olha (1889, nos 7–8). His major works are monographs on Patriarch Meletios Pigas and his involvement in the Rus' church (1872) and on western Rus' and its defense of its faith and nationality (2 vols, 1897, 4 edns). He also wrote about Patriarch Jeremiah and Prince K. Ostrozky and an article on the history of the Kiev Theological Academy (TKDA, 1869).

Malysh-Fedorets, Mariia [Malyš-Fedorec', Marija], b 20 January 1885 in Nizhen, Chernihiv gubernia, d 5 April 1960 in Melbourne, Australia. Actress. She was a leading heroic and character actress in Sadovsky's Theater (1907–20) and later toured with M. Sadovsky and P. Saksahansky (1926–32). She also acted in the film *Zaporiz'kyi skarb* (Zaporozhian Treasure, 1913). In 1945 she emigrated to Germany, and in 1951 to Australia.

Malyshko, Andrii [Malyško, Andrij], b 15 November 1912 in Obukhiv, Kiev county, d 17 February 1970 in Kiev. Poet and publicist. He graduated from the Kiev Institute of People's Education in 1932 and then taught in Ovruch. He worked for *Komsomolets' Ukraïny*, *Literaturna hazeta*, and *Molodyi bil'shovyk*. Malyshko's first published works appeared in *Molodniak* in 1930, and his first published collection of poetry was *Bat'kivshchyna* (The Fatherland, 1936). His other prewar collections included *Liryka* (Lyrics, 1938), *Z knyhy zhyttia* (From the Book of Life, 1938), *Narodzhennia syniv* (The Birth of Sons, 1939), *Lysty chervonoarmiitsia Opanasa Baidy* (The Letters of Red Army Serviceman Opanas Baida, 1940), *Berezen'* (March, 1940), *Zorevi dni* (Starry Days, 1940), and *Zhaivoronky* (The Meadow Larks, 1940). During the Second World War he was a correspondent of front-line newspapers and published the collections *Do boiu vstavaite* (Arise to Battle, 1941), *Ukraïno moia* (My Ukraine, 1942), *Ponad pozhary* (Above the Conflagrations, 1942), *Slovo o polku* (A Word about the Regiment, 1943), and *Bytva* (The Battle, 1943). His postwar material, among numerous collections, includes *Za synim morem* (Beyond the Blue Sea, 1950), *Knyha brativ* (The Book of Brothers, 1954), *Sertse moieï materi* (My Mother's Heart, 1959), *Zapovitne dzherelo* (The Source of the Testament, 1960), *Dubovyi tsvit* (Oak Blossoms, 1960), *Taras Shevchenko: Dramatychna pisnia* (Taras Shevchenko: A Dramatic Song, 1964), *Synii litopys* (The Blue Chronicle, 1968), and *Serpen' dushi moieï* (August of My Soul, 1970). He also published collections of critical essays, *Dumky pro poeziiu* (Thoughts on Poetry, 1959) and *Slovo pro poeta: M.T. Ryl's'kyi ta ioho tvorchist'* (A Word about a Poet: M.T. Rylsky and His Work, 1960), and translations of Russian verse. Compilations of his work appeared in 5 vols (1962) and 10 vols (1972–4).

The references to internal and international politics and Party directives throughout Malyshko's voluminous canon made him the recipient of various Soviet awards. His works were held out as models of socialist realism and lauded for their populism and adherence to the Party line. In accordance with the prime directive of socialist realism of 'creating for the people' he employed a simplistic lexicon and poetic form and concentrated on the sentimental and patriotic. Many of his works have been put to music (eg, 'Kyïvs'kyi val's' [Kievan Waltz]).

BIBLIOGRAPHY
Kovalenko, L. *Poet Andrii Malyshko* (Kiev 1957)
Nedil'ko, V. *Vyvchennia tvorchosti A. Malyshka* (Kiev 1977)
I. Koshelivets

Konstantyna Malytska

Malytska, Konstantyna [Malyc'ka] (pseuds: Rastyk, Vira Lebedova, and Chaika Dnistrova), b 30 May 1872 in Kropyvnyk, Kalush county, Galicia, d 17 March 1947 in Lviv. Educator, writer, and women's leader. After graduating from the State Teachers' Seminary in Lviv (1892), she taught elementary school in Halych and Luzhany and at the Shevchenko Girls' School in Lviv. She edited the children's magazine *Dzvinok* (1906–12), in which her stories and plays appeared. She was also active in the Women's Hromada in Lviv. In 1913 she was one of the founders of the Fund for Ukraine's Needs, which provided aid to the Ukrainian Sich Riflemen in 1914. During the Russian occupation she was arrested and deported to Siberia (1915–20). On her return she presided over the Women's Congress of 1921 and then served as president (1923–4) and executive member (1924–8) of the Union of Ukrainian Women. In 1930 she joined the editorial board of *Nova khata*, to which she contributed articles. In 1941 she initiated the relief organization Women's Service to Ukraine (1941). After the Second World War she worked at the Lviv Scientific Library of the AN URSR (now ANU). Some of Malytska's magazine contributions have come out in separate collections – her stories for children in *Mali druzi* (Little Friends, 1899; 2nd edn 1906) and her pedagogical articles in *Maty* (Mother, 1902) and *Z trahedii dytiachykh dush* (From the Tragedies of Children's Souls, 1907). She also wrote children's plays and Sich songs and translated children's literature.

Malytsky, Fedir [Malyc'kyj, Fedir], b 1 March 1900 in Dovobychiv, in the Kholm region, now in Poland, d 21 July 1988. Writer and poet. He graduated from the Kiev Institute of People's Education in 1929. He began publishing his works in 1926, at which time he belonged to the writers' groups Pluh and Zakhidnia Ukraina. He published several collections of poetry: *Kholmshchyna* (The Kholm Region, 1927), *Poeziï* (Poems, 1931), *Hrozy nad smerekamy* (Storms over the Firs, 1966), *Tsvit lomykamenniu* (The Flower of Rockfoil, 1971), and *Obzhynky* (Harvest Festival, 1979). He composed two historico-biographical poems, *Iurii Kotermak*, about Yurii Drohobych, and *Mudrets' z Chornukh* (The Wise Man from Chornukhy), about H. Skovoroda. His prose works consist of novels, such as *Bystryi Buh* (The Fast-flowing Buh, 1931), and short stories, which appeared in such collections as *Zahravy nad Buhom* (Crimson Skies over the Buh, 1970). He was arrested by the GPU in 1933 and imprisoned until 1935. Many of his poems have been set to music.

Malytsky, Mykola [Malyc'kyj], b 1890, d ? Civic leader and philanthropist. A teacher by profession, he served as a lieutenant in the Ukrainian Galician Army and edited *Ukraïns'kyi holos* (1918, renamed *Ukraïns'ki visti* in 1919), the official paper of the Ternopil County National Council. Through marriage with D. *Vikonska he became the owner of an estate in Shliakhtyntsi and a patron of Ukrainian students and artists. He donated a tract of land to the People's Home in Ternopil and helped found the Luh sports society. In 1938 he was elected as a candidate of the Ukrainian National Democratic Alliance to the Polish Senate. During the Soviet occupation of Galicia he was arrested and deported (1940). His subsequent fate is unknown.

Malytsky, Oleksander [Malyc'kyj], b 10 September 1874 in Moscow, d ? Jurist. He served as a professor of law and dean of the law faculty of the Kharkiv Institute of the National Economy, and as assistant to the state procurator of the Ukrainian SSR. He wrote a number of works and textbooks on Soviet state and civil law, including *Cheka i GPU* (Cheka and the GPU, 1923), *Komentari do tsyvil'noho kodeksu USSR* (A Commentary on the Civil Code of the Ukrainian SSR, 1927), and *Radians'ka konstytutsiia* (The Soviet Constitution, 3rd edn 1928). He was arrested during the Yezhov terror, and his further fate is unknown.

Mamonich [Mamonyč]. Two Belarusian merchant brothers, Kuzma (b and d ?) and Luka (?–1606) Mamonich, from the Mahiliou region. In 1575 they established a religious press with P. Mstsislavets in Vilnius. In 1576 the brothers were granted a royal monopoly on the printing and sale of books in Vilnius, and began publishing mainly church texts and religious literature in Belarusian, Ukrainian, and Polish (from 1591). Their works reached a wide market throughout Eastern Europe and contributed to the support of national minorities in the Grand Duchy of Lithuania. The operation assumed a pro-Uniate character when Kuzma's son, Leon Mamonich, became its manager (1601) and then owner (1606). The press was sold to the local church brotherhood in 1622.

Mamontov, Yakiv, b 4 November 1888 in Strilytsia (now Shaposhnykove), Sumy county, Kharkiv gubernia, d 31 January 1940 in Kharkiv. Dramatist, theater scholar, and pedagogue. He began his literary career by writing poetry and prose. He published the story *Pid chornymy khmaramy* (Under Black Clouds) in 1907, and poems, such

Yakiv Mamontov

as 'Koly ia dyvliusia' (When I Look, 1908), which later appeared in the collection *Vinky za vodoiu* (Wreaths on the Water, 1924). The majority of his literary output, however, was plays: *Divchyna z arfoiu* (The Girl with a Harp, 1918), *Veselyi kham* (The Happy Boor, 1921), *Dies Irae* (1922), *Koly narod vyzvoliaiet'sia* (When a Nation Liberates Itself, 1923), *Ave Maria* (1924), *Do tretikh pivniv* (Until the Third Cockcrow, 1924), *Respublika na kolesakh* (The Republic on Wheels, 1928), *Rozheve pavutynnia* (Pink Cobweb, 1928), *Kniazhna Viktoriia* (Princess Victoria, 1928), *Het'manshchyna* (The Hetmanate, 1930–9), and *Svoia liudyna* (A Person One Can Trust, 1936). He also wrote a number of stage adaptations of the works of T. Shevchenko, M. Kotsiubynsky, I. Franko, and others. Most of his plays centered on the revolution and the Ukrainian-Soviet War, in which *otamanshchyna*, or warlordism, is satirized. He wrote operatic librettos, including *Zolotyi obruch* (The Golden Ring), *Turbaïvtsi*, and *Karmeliuk*. He also tried his hand at screenplays and children's plays (*Kho*). Having begun to write before the First World War, he continued to be mainly influenced by Ukrainian *modernism. For that reason, although his plays were popular in the 1920s (of the 27 he wrote, 21 were staged, in many Ukrainian and Russian theaters), and although some of them, such as *Respublika na kolesakh* and *Rozheve pavutynnia*, were written with the Soviet censors in mind, Soviet critics harshly attacked his works. In the early 1930s his plays were barred from theatrical repertoires altogether.

Mamontov also wrote a number of studies in drama, including *Dramatychne pys'menstvo* (Dramatic Writing, 1927–8), *Ukraïns'ka dramaturhiia peredzhovtnevoï doby* (Ukrainian Prerevolutionary Drama, 1931), and *Dramaturhiia I. Tobilevycha* (The Dramaturgy of I. Tobilevych, 1931). Together with O. Biletsky he edited *Khrestomatiia istoriï ukraïns'koho teatru* (An Anthology in Ukrainian Theater History, 1941). He also wrote 'Pedahoh iak mystets'' (The Pedagogue as an Artist, *Suchasni problemy pedahohichnoï tvorchosty*, 1922, no. 1) and taught pedagogy in various postsecondary schools in Kharkiv. A volume of his works was published in 1962.

I. Koshelivets

Mamutov, Valentyn, b 30 January 1928 in Odessa. Jurist; full member of the AN URSR (now ANU) since 1988. A graduate of the Sverdlovsk Juridical Institute (1949), he worked for several government ministries before joining the Donetske branch of the Institute of Economics of the AN URSR in 1966. In 1969 he was appointed assistant director and in 1981 director of the Institute of the Economics of Industry. A specialist in industrial law and administration, he is the author of several books, including *Regional'noe upravlenie: Opyt i problemy* (Regional Administration: Experience and Problems, 1984) and *Pravovaia rabota v narodnom khoziaistve: Sbornik normativnykh aktov* (Legal Work in the National Economy: A Collection of Normative Acts, 1986).

Fedir Manailo: *On St John's Eve* (tempera, 1933)

Manailo, Fedir [Manajlo], b 19 October 1910 in Ivanivka, near Mukachiv, Transcarpathia, d 15 January 1978 in Uzhhorod. Painter. He studied at the Higher Art and Industrial School in Prague (1928–34). He depicted the landscapes and folkways of Transcarpathia on his canvases. His early works, such as *Old Pauper* (1932), *On St John's Eve* (1933), and *Hutsul Girl* (1939), were influenced by expressionism. He also created murals and mosaics (eg, in the Uzhhorod Restaurant in Uzhhorod and the Verkhovyna Restaurant in Kiev). An album of reproductions of his works was published in 1970. A small museum dedicated to his life and works was opened in Uzhhorod.

Manastyrsky, Antin [Manastyrs'kyj], b 2 November 1878 in Zavaliv, Pidhaitsi county, Galicia, d 15 May 1969 in Lviv. Painter and graphic artist; father of V. *Manastyrsky. He studied at the Lviv Art and Industrial School (1895–9) and Cracow Academy of Fine Arts (1900–5).

Antin Manastyrsky:
Self-Portrait (oil, 1919)

Vitold Manastyrsky: *Highland Girl* (1960)

From 1899 he was a member of the *Society for the Advancement of Ruthenian Art, and from 1905 he lived in Lviv. Manastyrsky painted icons, church murals, and many Carpathian landscapes, portraits, historical scenes (particularly from Cossack history), genre paintings, architectural views, still lifes, and works inspired by T. Shevchenko's poems. He also illustrated interwar children's storybooks and primers, a Ukrainian Bible (Lviv 1926), and editions of works by Shevchenko, I. Franko, N. Gogol, A. Pushkin, I. Turgenev, and A. Chekhov. Many of his historical paintings were reproduced on Galician postcards of the 1910s and 1920s. His paintings include *Road* (1900), *Winter in the Carpathians* (1904), *At the Fortune-Teller's* (1910), *Kateryna* (1913), *The Cossacks Rose before Dawn* (1914), *Lirnyk* (1914–16), *At the Watering Spot* (1917), *Willows* (1927), *Portrait of M. Yatskiv* (1929), *Zaporozhian Cossack* (1932), *Gathering Sheaves* (1949), *Prut River Valley* (1953), and *The Scout* (1955). Books about him, with reproductions of his works, have been written by H. Ostrovsky (1958), Ya. Nanovsky (1959), and Kh. Sanotska (1980).

Manastyrsky, Inokentii [Manastyrs'kyj, Inokentij], ?–1697. Orthodox churchman and writer. The hegumen of Lublin (1678–81) and St Cyril's in Kiev (1681–97) monasteries, he was twice (1685 and 1689) sent to Moscow to represent the Ukrainian clergy and defend Ukrainian church interests. In 1690 he headed the church sobor that elected V. Yasynsky as metropolitan of Kiev. He enjoyed the support of Hetman I. Mazepa, who helped him restore the Trinity Cathedral of St Cyril's Monastery and expand the monastery's landholdings.

Manastyrsky, Oleksander [Manastyrs'kyj], b 22 June 1857, d 23 October 1920 in Chernivtsi. Bukovynian Orthodox church and community activist and ethnographer. As an adviser to the consistory (from 1898) and then archimandrite and vicar to the metropolitan, he fought for Ukrainian rights in the Bukovynian Orthodox metropoly. He wrote a religious textbook for elementary schools and the article 'Die Ruthenen' in the collection *Die Österreichisch-Ungarische Monarchie in Wort und Bild – Bukowina* (1899), and coauthored *Die Ruthenen in der Bukowina* (with R. Kaindl, 2 vols, 1889–90). Manastyrsky's ethnographic works include articles, written in Ukrainian and German, on New Year and Easter traditions.

Manastyrsky, Vitold [Manastyrs'kyj, Vitol'd], b 11 January 1915 in Lviv. Painter; son of A. *Manastyrsky. A graduate of the Warsaw Academy of Arts (1939), from 1947 he lectured at the Lviv Institute of Applied and Decorative Arts. He has painted Carpathian, Crimean, and Baltic landscapes, portraits, genre paintings, and still lifes. His works include *Century-old Grandmother* (1935), *Group of Hutsul Folk Musicians* (1951), *Haystacks* (1956), *Highland Girl* (1960), *Mt Chornohora* (1963), *At the Foot of Mt Sokil* (1965), *Blooming Dzembronia* (1967), *Marichka* (1973), and *Happy Childhood* (1979). A book about him by M. Tkachenko was published in 1977.

Manchester. A city in northwestern England (1988 pop 445,900). In the 1920s and 1930s it was home to 15 or 20 Ukrainian families that had remained there while en route to Canada. The community was centered largely around the Ukrainian Social Club. During the Second World War many Ukrainians in Canadian army units stayed in the city and the surrounding area. On 7 January 1943 a local chapter of the Ukrainian Canadian Servicemen's Association was founded, and by midyear it had over 1,000 members. After the war an influx of people from DP camps in Germany and of war prisoners from Italy made it one of the largest Ukrainian communities in Great Britain, with nearly 900 people. A chapter of the *Association of Ukrainians in Great Britain, the *Federation of Ukrainians in Great Britain, and a number of other Ukrainian community and cultural groups (including the Homin choir and the Orlyk dance ensemble) were established. Both the Ukrainian Orthodox and Catholic churches have their own churches and parishes in the area. The community club,

Bukovyna, is also active. The larger concentrations of Ukrainians in the surrounding area include those in Bolton (500), Bury (300), Oldham (800), and Rochdale (600), which together with those in the city proper make up a community of approx 3,000.

Manchuria. See China.

Mandelshtam, Leonid [Mandel'štam], b 4 May 1879 in Mahiliou, Belarus, d 27 November 1944 in Moscow. Physicist; full member of the USSR Academy of Sciences from 1929. A graduate of Strasbourg University, he became a docent at Odessa University in 1915 and a professor at the Odessa Polytechnical Institute in 1918. In 1925 he became a professor of physics at Moscow University, and later he worked concurrently at the Institute of Physics of the USSR Academy. Mandelshtam played a major role in the study of radio physics and optics.

Mandryka. A Cossack *starshyna* family, known from the 16th century. It had several members on the Cossack register of 1649, and it controlled the captaincies of Kobyzhcha company in Kiev regiment during 1672–1781. The Mandryka family was related to the Polubotok, Khanenko, and other *starshyna* families. Matvii Mandryka opposed a Ukrainian treaty with Moscow and was executed in 1705 for speaking out against Hetman I. Mazepa.

Mykyta Mandryka

Mandryka, Mykyta, b 28 September 1886 in Kiev, d 20 August 1979 in Winnipeg. Writer, diplomat, and community leader. A member of the Central Rada in Kiev, Mandryka also served in the diplomatic corps of the Ukrainian National Republic (UNR) in the Far East, Batum, Istanbul, Sofia, and Prague. He attended the Ukrainian Free University in Prague (LL D, 1925), where he became a docent of international law in 1927. He was sent to Canada in 1928 by the *Ukrainian Party of Socialist Revolutionaries to undertake organizational work. Backed by the Ukrainian National Home (UND) in Winnipeg, Mandryka toured extensively on a speaking tour in 1928–9, laying the groundwork for a UND-centered *Union of Ukrainian Community Centres of Canada, the establishment of the newspaper *Pravda i volia*, and the staging of an All-Ukrainian Educational-Economic Conference in Winnipeg (all in 1929). These efforts failed to achieve their desired goals, but provided Mandryka with enough support to establish a Ukrainian Labor Association (Ukrainske trudove obiednannia), which was active for about a decade. He later helped organize the Ukrainian Canadian Committee

(now Congress) and was president of the Ukrainian Free Academy of Sciences in Canada (1970–3). His published collections of poems include *Pisni* (Songs, 1907), *Pisni pro Anemonu* (Songs about the Buttercup, 1917), *Mii sad* (My Orchard, 1941), *Zolota osin'* (Golden Autumn, 1958), *Radist'* (Joy, 1959), the epic poem *Mazepa* (1960), and *Vik Petliury* (The Age of Petliura, 1966). He also wrote a *History of Ukrainian Literature in Canada* (1968). His nonliterary publications include *Natsionalni menshosti v mizhnarodn'omu pravi* (National Minorities in International Law, 1925), *Istoriia konsul's'koho prava i instytutiv* (History of Consular Law and Institutes, 1927), and *Teoriia hospodars'koï demokratiï* (The Theory of Economic Democracy, 1934).

Mandych, Olena [Mandyč] (née Shinali), b 26 September 1902 in Dulafagva, Transylvania, d 12 March 1975 in Košice, Slovakia. Sculptor. A graduate of the Prague Academy of Fine Arts (1925), she won an honorable mention at the academy's exhibition in 1927. She created monuments to O. Dukhnovych in Prešov (1933), Ye. Fentsyk in Uzhhorod (1926), T. Masaryk in Uzhhorod (1927), and A. Dobriansky in Uzhhorod (1929) and Prešov (1933) and sculptural portraits and compositions (eg, *Carpatho-Ruthenian Song*, 1930).

Mandychevsky, Yevsevii [Mandyčevs'kyj, Jevsevij] (Mandyczewski, Eusebius), b 17 August 1857 in Molodiia, Chernivtsi county, Bukovyna, d 13 July 1929 in Vienna. Musicologist, composer, and conductor. He studied under S. Vorobkevych in Chernivtsi and R. Fuchs and M. Nottebohm in Vienna, his home from 1875. In 1880 he became conductor of the Vienna Singakademie and archivist of the Gesellschaft der Musikfreunde. In 1896–1921 he was a professor at the Vienna Academy of Music as well as the Vienna Conservatory, teaching music history, composition, and instrumental science. His students included K. Böhm, G. Szell, and C. Prohaska. Mandychevsky was also engaged as a researcher, editor, and publisher of the collected works of F. Haydn, and worked on collections by F. Schubert, J.S. Bach, and his close personal friend J. Brahms. He also wrote a study of S. Vorobkevych. His musical works included piano pieces, choruses, and songs, a number of which used Ukrainian texts.

Man'dzhurs'kyi vistnyk (Manchurian Herald). A weekly newspaper published in Harbin, Japanese-occupied Manchuria, from September 1932 to July 1937. It reported on developments in Soviet and Western Ukraine – reprinting articles from such periodicals as *Dilo*, *Svoboda*, and *Tryzub* – and in the Ukrainian community in the *Far East, especially *China. In general the newspaper supported the politics of the Government-in-exile of the UNR. Its editor and publisher was I. *Svit. A total of 199 issues appeared.

Mandziuk, Nicholas [Mandzjuk, Mykola], b 13 December 1902 in Kryvche, Borshchiv county, Galicia, d 7 September 1969 in Winnipeg. Lawyer, community leader, and political activist. After coming to Canada with his parents in 1904, he graduated from the University of Manitoba (LL B, 1932) and practiced law in Oakburn. He served as president of the local board of trade, chairman of the board of education, president of the Ukrainian Self-Reliance League, and general secretary of the Ukrainian Canadian Committee (now Congress). For five consecutive terms (1957–68) he was the Progressive Conservative MP for Marquette (Manitoba). In 1968 he was named Queen's Counsel.

Abram Manevich: *Kievan Roofs* (oil)

Manevich, Abram [Manevič], b 25 November 1881 in Mstsislau, Mahiliou gubernia, Belarus, d 30 June 1942 in New York. Painter. A graduate of the Kiev Art School (1905), he studied at the Munich Academy of Arts and was a founder of and professor at the *Ukrainian State Academy of Arts (1917–19). He had two solo exhibitions in Kiev (1910, 1916). Manevich was noted for his impressionistic landscapes, particularly of Kiev, such as *Autumn: The Dnieper* (1913), *Roman Catholic Church in Kiev, Spring in Kiev's Kurenivka District, Urban Landscape* (1914), and *Kievan Roofs*. From 1920 he lived abroad. In 1922 he settled in the United States, where he did the urban landscape series 'Prosaic America' (1925–7), portraits, and landscapes, such as *Winter: Canada* (1932) and *Spring* (1942).

Manevychi [Manevyči]. II-6. A town smt (1990 pop 9,000) and raion center in Volhynia oblast. It was founded in 1892 during the construction of the Kovel–Sarny railway line, and given smt status in 1940. The town has a furniture factory and a food industry.

Manganese industry. A branch of the mining industry that extracts manganese ore and processes it for use in the metallurgical, chemical, ceramics, glass, and pharmaceutical industries. Over 95 percent is used to make ferroalloys, particularly steel. Steels usually contain under 1 percent manganese; alloys containing more are hard and wear-resistant. The Soviet Union has the world's largest manganese reserves, and Ukraine accounts for 40 percent (2.3 billion t) of them. In Ukraine manganese deposits are located in the *Nykopil and Tokmak manganese basins at Inhulets and Khashchuvate, and in the Carpathian Mountains.

The industry arose in the 1860s, when the Bessemer and Martin processes were introduced in the iron and steel industry. Manganese mining in the Nykopil basin began in 1885. By 1895, 42,500 t were being mined, and by 1913, 275,900 t. Over 95 percent of the output was exported. The number of workers employed at Nykopil doubled from 1899 to 1916, from 1,120 to 2,252. Before the First World War Nykopil was producing 22.2 percent of the empire's manganese; it was second only to the Chiatura Basin in Georgia. By the 1920s the Nykopil basin was the Soviet Union's chief producer, with 75.5 percent of its output. Without new investments Nykopil's relative position declined: in 1940 it produced 893,000 t of manganese, or 40 percent of the Soviet production. During the Second World War the Germans exploited the mines at Nykopil before destroying them. The mines were reconstructed soon after the war. In 1952 the first open-pit mines came into operation, at Ordzhonikidze, where lower-grade carbonate ores are found. By 1968 nearly 74 percent of the manganese ore was being mined in that manner.

Since the 1950s Ukraine has regained its leading position as a producer of manganese ore. In 1975 it produced 6,537,000 t, or 77.3 percent of the Soviet output, and in 1985, 7,115,000 t, or 71.9 percent. In 1968, 48 percent of the ore was enriched. The main manganese enrichment plants in Ukraine are the Marhanets and Ordzhonikidze mineral enrichment complexes and the enrichment factories in Chkalove, Bohanivka, and Hrushivka.

BIBLIOGRAPHY
Varentsov, I.; Grasselly, G. (eds). *Geology and Geochemistry of Manganese*, 2 vols (Stuttgart 1980)

B. Somchynsky

Maniak, Volodymyr [Manjak], b 6 November 1934 in Kryshtopivka, Proskuriv okruha, Vinnytsia oblast, d 23 June 1992. Writer. He graduated from Lviv University (1956). He is the author of the poetry collection *Povnolittia* (Maturity, 1957); the prose collections *Zelenyi merydian, Evryka, Misiats' spokiinoho sontsia* (The Green Meridian, Eureka, Month of the Calm Sun, 1967), *Prospekt imeni liudei* (Avenue in the Name of the People, 1970), *Makove pole* (Poppy Field, 1972), and *Kolyska vitriv* (Cradle of the Winds, 1975); and the novels *I ziishov den'* (And the Day Rose, 1974), *Borozny* (Furrows, 1977), *Vysoki berehy zemli* (The High Shores of the Land, 1979), *Plot' tvoia i krov* (Your Flesh and Blood, 1981), *Podillia* (1984), and *Reid* (The Raid, 1986). In recent years he cochaired the *Memorial society and edited collections of eyewitness accounts of Nazi destruction in Ukraine (1988) and the man-made *famine of 1932–3 (1990).

Maniava Hermitage (Maniavskyi Skyt). An Orthodox monastery near Maniava, now in Bohorodchany raion, Ivano-Frankivske oblast. It was founded by Y. *Kniahynytsky when he settled in an isolated wooded area in the Gorgany Mountains on the banks of a tributary of the Bystrytsia-Solotvynska River. Although he planned to live in solitude, he soon began to attract other monks and believers, who built the first cells of the monastery in 1611 and then a wooden church in 1612. Later, additional cells were constructed, and with the patronage of O. Movilă, the daughter of a Moldavian magnate, the main church, of the Elevation of the Cross, was erected. In 1620 the Constantinople patriarch Timothy II granted the monastery stauropegion status, which enabled it to remain Orthodox despite the subsequent conversion of the entire region to the Uniate church.

Maniava Hermitage (reconstruction by Mykola Pavliuk)

The Maniava Hermitage soon came to house nearly 240 residents. It became a model of monastic life throughout Ukraine and maintained close relations with monasteries in Uhornyky, Kolomyia, Tovmachyk, and Suceava (Moldavia). The hermitage was also an important cultural center. Its library contained many rare manuscripts and books, and it was the site of one of the first professional schools of church music in Western Ukraine. Although it was fortified by a defensive wall and three towers (a gate tower, a bell tower, and a defensive tower), the monastery was destroyed by the Turks in 1676. It was rebuilt in 1681. In September 1785 the hermitage was closed by order of the Austrian government, and its monks dispersed to monasteries in Kiev and Bukovyna. The monastery collapsed in ruins, and only the outer walls and the foundations of the main church and bell tower remained.

Throughout its 150-year existence the hermitage was renowned for the asceticism of its monks. Many laymen asked to be buried there, including Hetman I. Vyhovsky. Most of the monastery's important artifacts have not survived, but the iconostasis by Y. *Kondzelevych, painted in 1698–1705, was taken to Bohorodchany after the monastery was closed, and then deposited in 1923 in the National Museum in Lviv. In 1785 the wooden church of the hermitage was transferred to Nadvirna, where it stood until it was destroyed by fire in 1914. In 1972–80 restorations were conducted on the site of the hermitage, and all three main towers, the defensive walls, and the wooden and stone cells were rebuilt, and the frescoes restored. In 1981 it was made into a branch of the Ivano-Frankivske Regional Museum.

The Maniava Hermitage has inspired many literary and artistic works (eg, by I. Mohylnytsky, I. Franko, Ya. Holovatsky, O. Makovei, N. Kobrynska and I. Trush), and I. Vahylevych wrote a historical study of it in 1848.

BIBLIOGRAPHY
Tselevich, Iu. *Istoriia Skitu Maniavs'koho* (Lviv 1887)
I. Korovytsky, A. Zhukovsky

Holy Resurrection Orthodox Church in Sifton, Manitoba

Manitoba. A prairie province (1989 pop 1,026,241), situated near the geographical center of Canada, with an area of 649,947 sq km. Its capital and largest city is *Winnipeg. Formed in 1870, the province experienced large-scale colonization after 1890 when thousands of agriculturalists settled its virgin lands. Between 1870 and 1901 the population grew from 20,000 to 255,000. The first Ukrainian rural settlements were established in 1896 by immigrants from Galicia and Bukovyna at Stuartburn, south of Winnipeg, and at Lake Dauphin (Terebowla), in the northwest. By 1914 a network of Ukrainian homesteads and rural trade centers or railway towns could be found stretching from the American border in the southeast (Senkiw, Zhoda, Sarto, Vita [formerly Shevchenko], Tolstoi, Caliento, Sirko, Rosa) to the peripheries of Winnipeg (Brooklands, Gonor), in the Interlake region (Komarno, Ethelbert, Zbaraz), and from Sandy Lake to Swan River (Halicz, Ukraina, Zoria) in the northwest. A substantial amount of the land settled by Ukrainians in Manitoba, particularly in the southeast and Interlake area, was of substandard quality, and economic progress was in consequence impeded over time.

Manitoba Ukrainians quickly entered the political arena and by 1910 had been absorbed into the Conservative party machine of Premier R. Roblin at the provincial level (until the party's downfall in 1915). The first reeve elected was I. Storoszczuk, in Stuartburn (1908); the first alderman was T. Stefanyk, in Winnipeg (1911); and the first member of the legislative assembly (MLA) was T. Ferley, in the Gimli electoral district (Independent, 1915). By 1939 a total of 10 MLAs had been elected, all from outside Winnipeg. In 1950 N. Bachynsky became the speaker of the assembly, and in 1955 M. Hryhorczuk was appointed the first Manitoba Ukrainian cabinet minister. That same year

W. Wall (Wolokhatiuk) became the first Ukrainian-Canadian senator. Ukrainians achieved a high profile in the New Democratic party administrations of the 1970s and 1980s, with cabinet ministers such as S. Uskiw, B. Uruski, and W. Parasiuk.

Ukrainian-English bilingual schools were established in approx 120 Manitoba localities early in the century. Teachers for them were trained at the *Ruthenian Training School in Brandon, and many of them went on to become community leaders throughout western Canada. The bilingual schools were forcibly abolished in 1916, ostensibly in the course of 'educational reform.' They returned to the province only in 1979 and have been promoted by the Manitoba Parents for Ukrainian Education since 1980. To preserve their culture and language, Ukrainians have maintained their own privately funded evening and Saturday schools.

Dancers at the 1970 Ukrainian Festival in Dauphin, Manitoba

Manitoba (particularly Winnipeg) traditionally has been an important center of Ukrainian community life, and most Ukrainian-Canadian associations have their headquarters or branches in the province. Moreover, Manitoba's landscape is dotted with Ukrainian church architecture and Ukrainian place-names. In 1981 there were 130,285 Ukrainians in the province, of whom 69,351 lived in Winnipeg. In 1991, 39,175 inhabitants claimed Ukrainian as their mother tongue; they represented 19.97 percent of the Canadian total.

BIBLIOGRAPHY
Yuzyk, P. *The Ukrainians in Manitoba* (Toronto 1953)
Marunchak, M. *Studiï do istoriï ukraïntsiv Kanady*, vol 2, *Istoriia suspil'no-kul'turnoho rostu ukraïntsiv Manitoby* (Winnipeg 1966–7)
Morton, W. *Manitoba: A History*, 2nd ed (Toronto 1979)

O. Gerus

Manizer, Matvei, b 17 March 1891 in St Petersburg, d 20 December 1966 in Moscow. Russian sculptor. A graduate of the St Petersburg Academy of Arts (1916), he taught at the Leningrad Academy of Arts (1921–9, 1935–41, 1945–7), Moscow Institute of Applied and Decorative Arts (1946–52), and Moscow Art Institute (1952–66). His works were found throughout the USSR, including Ukraine, where his chief works are the monuments to T. Shevchenko in Kharkiv (1935), Kiev (1938), and Kaniv (1939).

Matvei Manizer: monument to T. Shevchenko in Kharkiv (1935)

Mankin, Valentyn, b 19 August 1938 in Bilokorovychi, Olevske raion, Zhytomyr oblast. Yachting champion. A graduate of the Kiev Civil Engineering Institute, he won Olympic gold medals in yachting in 1968 (Finn class), 1972 (Tempest class), and 1980 (Star class) and a silver medal in 1976 (Tempest class). He was also the European and world Tempest-class champion in 1973, the European Star-class champion in 1978, and a USSR champion in 1959, 1961–3, 1967, 1970, 1972, and 1974–8. Mankin wrote *Bilyi trykutnyk* (The White Triangle, 1976).

Mankivka [Man'kivka]. V-11. A town smt (1990 pop 9,300) on the Mankivka River and a raion center in Cherkasy oblast. It was first mentioned in a historical document in the late 16th century. During Hetman B. Khmelnytsky's rule it was a company center of Uman regiment. Its inhabitants took part in popular uprisings against the Poles in 1664–5 and 1768. In 1672 Mankivka was destroyed by the invading Turks and Tatars. It attained smt status in 1965. The town has a majolica factory and two brick factories. Archeologists have found six settlements of the *Trypilian culture, six Bronze Age settlements, and four settlements of the *Cherniakhiv culture near the town.

Mankivsky, Borys [Man'kivs'kyj], b 23 March 1883 in Kozelets, Chernihiv gubernia, d 24 November 1962 in Kiev. Neurologist; full member of the USSR Academy of Medical Sciences from 1944. A graduate of Kiev University (1910), he was a department head at the Kiev Medical Institute (1922–59), the founding director of the Kiev Psychoneurological Scientific Research Institute, and a department head at the Kiev Institute for the Upgrading of Physicians (1926–60). He also headed the department of gerontologic changes in the nervous system at the Institute of Gerontology of the USSR Academy of Medical Sciences. The founder of the school of neurology in Ukraine, he wrote works dealing with neurological diseases as they affect the reactivity of the whole organism, sclerosis disseminata, neuroinfections, inflammations of the brain, and disorders of the brain vessels. His biography was published in Kiev in 1975.

Manko, Hryhorii [Man'ko, Hryhorij], b 1885, d ? Opera singer (baritone) and actor. He was a soloist with the Kharkiv Opera (1925) and the Kiev Opera (1934–41), with which he performed leading roles in A. Borodin's *Prince Igor*, A. Dargomyzhsky's *Rusalka*, B. Smetana's *The Bartered Bride*, and N. Rimsky-Korsakov's *Christmas Eve*. He acted in the film *Natalka Poltavka* (1936). As a postwar refugee, from 1950 he taught and performed in Toronto under the surname Yaroshevych.

Leonid Manko   Clarence A. Manning

Manko, Leonid [Man'ko], b 29 March 1863 in Poltava, d 16 April 1922 in Yelysavethrad (now Kirovohrad), Kherson gubernia. Actor and playwright. He played character and comic roles in the troupes of M. Kropyvnytsky (1882–3, 1888–92), M. Starytsky (1893–8), H. Derkach (1893–4), P. Myrov-Bediukh (1895–8), O. Suslov (1901–9), and D. Haidamaka (1911–16). Manko is the author of dramas and adaptations, including *Neshchasne kokhannia* (Unrequited Love) and *Krashche svoie latane, nizh chuzhe khvatane* (Better Poor Than Dishonestly Rich).

Mannerism. An artistic style that prevailed in much of Europe in the period between the High Renaissance and the baroque (ca 1525–1600). It has not received any recognition in Ukrainian art history studies. The qualities to which it gave precedence were idealized beauty and elegance, cultured poise, sophistication, and facility rather than truth to nature. Even though there are examples of mannerist art in Lviv from the early 17th century, no attemps have been made to study them separately from the *baroque. According to V. Liubchenko, one of the few Ukrainian scholars to have mentioned mannerism (book on Lviv sculpture, 1981), mannerist tendencies were

present in Western Ukraine in the 1620s. The few examples are the wooden altar attributed to I. Luk (now in the Lviv Art Gallery) and the sculpture *Credence of Thomas* in the Armenian Cathedral in Lviv. In Lviv's architecture mannerism was limited to external decoration and did not affect building design (eg, the treatment of second-story windows and the Archangel Michael over the doorway in the Royal Arsenal Building [1639–46]).

Manning, Clarence Augustus, b 1 April 1893 in New York, d 4 October 1972 in Pleasantville, New York. American Slavist; member of the Shevchenko Scientific Society. He graduated from Columbia University (PH D, 1915) and taught there from 1917 to 1958. He became a professor in 1924 and chairman of the Slavic department in 1940. In 1948 he received an honorary PH D from the Ukrainian Free University. An early promoter of Ukrainian studies and the Ukrainian national cause in American academic circles, he wrote *Ivan Franko* (1938), *Ukrainian Literature: Studies of the Leading Authors* (1944), *Taras Shevchenko, Poet of Ukraine: Selected Poems* (1945, intro and trans), *The Story of Ukraine* (1947), *Outline of Ukrainian History* (1949), *Twentieth-Century Ukraine* (1951), *Ukraine under the Soviets* (1953), *Hetman of Ukraine, Ivan Mazeppa* (1957), and many articles in the *Ukrainian Quarterly*. He was one of the initiators of the project to publish *Ukraine: A Concise Encyclopaedia* and edited collections of I. Franko's selected poems (*Ivan Franko, the Poet of Western Ukraine*, 1948) and Lesia Ukrainka's works (*Spirit of Flame*, 1950) translated by P. Cundy.

Manoilo, Mykola [Manojlo], b 8 December 1927 in Manyly, Kharkiv okruha. Opera singer (baritone). A graduate of the Kharkiv Conservatory (1960), he began performing as a soloist with the Kharkiv Theater of Opera and Ballet in 1958. His notable roles have been Ostap in M. Lysenko's *Taras Bulba*, the Prince in P. Tchaikovsky's *Enchantress*, the Demon in A. Rubinstein's *Demon*, Rigoletto in G. Verdi's *Rigoletto*, and Iago in G. Verdi's *Othello*. He served as a member of the Supreme Soviet of the Ukrainian SSR (1974–84).

Manor Junior College (MJC). A Ukrainian Catholic junior college located in Jenkintown, Pennsylvania, a suburb of Philadelphia. It was founded in 1947 and operated by the *Basilian order of nuns. The college offers two-year associate of arts and associate of science degrees in liberal arts and career-oriented programs. In 1986 MJC had 340 students and 41 faculty members. The college library houses over 28,000 volumes. In 1977 the Ukrainian Heritage Study Center (UHSC) was established at MJC. It consists of four major areas: academics, museum collection, library, and archives. The UHSC library includes over 4,000 Ukrainian books and journals, among them many rare and first-edition books.

Manorial Cossacks (*nadvirni kozaky*). Cossacks who served in the private armies of the great landowning magnates in Ukraine during the 16th to 18th centuries. Wealthy Polish or Ukrainian magnates, such as the Wiśniowiecki, Ostrozky, Zasławski, Korecki, and Potocki families, maintained their own military forces, recruited from among peasants or serfs, who received land grants, cash payments, and exemptions from corvée in return for their services. The armies numbered up to several thousand men. They were used by the magnates to maintain social order on their estates and to repel raids. Occasionally the manorial Cossacks turned against their masters and participated in Cossack and haidamaka rebellions. The best-known examples are Capt *Verlan's rebellion against Prince Lubomirski in 1734 and I. *Gonta's support of M. *Zalizniak in 1768. Manorial armies were disbanded in the Left-Bank Hetman state and in Right-Bank Ukraine after the partitions of Poland in 1772 and 1793.

Manoryk, Andrii, b 1 September 1921 in Verbivka, Lypovets county, Kiev gubernia, d 25 June 1974 in Kiev. Botanist and plant physiologist; AN URSR (now ANU) corresponding member from 1973. A graduate of the Uman Agricultural Institute (1948), he joined the ANU Institute of Plant Physiology and Agrochemistry in 1951, became its associate director in 1957, and served as its director in 1973–4. His major research interests included the use of composts for producing organic fertilizers and nitrogen fixation in leguminous plants.

Manufacturing consortium (*vyrobnyche obiednannia*). A group of manufacturing enterprises in the USSR, including plants, research and design organizations, and construction and planning institutions, that are bound together by production ties and centralized administration. Manufacturing consortia emerged in the 1960s in response to the growing complexity of the production process to improve planning and co-ordination among different organizations contributing to the process. The first such association in the USSR was the Prohres leather firm in Lviv. The industrial reform of 1973, which was to eliminate some of the bureaucratic interference in industry, gave impetus to the movement. By 1975, 2,314 associations had been formed, in various Soviet industries. They accounted for 24.4 percent of the industrial output. A manufacturing consortium was not limited by territory: members could be located in different regions of the USSR. It could vary greatly in size, from as few as 5 to as many as 30 or more enterprises. Its structure also varied: some associations consisted of scientific and technical institutions, some of similar enterprises (eg, mines in a single region), and others of supplier and consumer organizations. Most were headed by a general director, who was responsible to a board of directors composed of the directors of the component enterprises. These consortia were not usually legal entities under Soviet law.

The consortia fulfilled their mandate only partially. Since they were usually formed on orders from a relevant ministry, they were not autonomous but controlled by the ministry. Moreover, the component enterprises were often incompatible or too dispersed for effective central management. Although they were supposed to be somewhat independent of the state, the various state planning bodies continued to dictate production targets and prices. M. Gorbachev's economic reforms tended to reduce state interference in the affairs of manufacturing enterprises.

B. Balan

Manuilovych, Ivan [Manujlovyč], b ?, d 1740. Cossack official. He rose through the ranks as general osaul of the Hetman state (1713–14), captain of Hlukhiv company in Nizhen regiment (1714–28), member of the tribunal in the General Chancellery (1724–7), and general osaul to Hetman D. Apostol (1728–38), to whom he was related.

Sofiia Manuilovych

Manuilovych, Sofiia [Manujlovyč, Sofija], b 13 October 1892 in Ponornytsia, Krolevets county, Chernihiv gubernia, d 12 August 1971 in Odessa. Actress, director, and playwright. After completing study at the Lysenko Music and Drama School in Kiev, she worked in Molodyi Teatr (1916–19), acted in the Zhytomyr Ukrainian Drama Theater (1919–22) and Berezil (1922–6), directed Berezil's Odessa workshop (1925–6), founded and directed the Odessa Children's Theater (1928–30), taught at the Odessa Music and Drama Institute (1926–34), and worked in the Moscow Puppet Theater (1934–6) and the Mykolaiv Young Spectator's Theater (1934–9). She wrote several agitprop dramas.

Manuilsky, Dmytro [Manujil's'kyj], b 3 October 1883 in Sviatets (Manuilske), Kremianets county, Volhynia gubernia, d 22 February 1959 in Kiev. Bolshevik revolutionary and Soviet functionary; full member of the AN URSR from 1945. A member of the Russian Social Democratic Workers' party (RSDRP) from 1903, he studied at St Petersburg University and helped organize the 1906 Kronstadt and Sveaborg mutinies. He was punished with exile to Yakutia, but he escaped and worked in the RSDRP underground in Kiev. After fleeing to Paris in 1907, he belonged to the Vpered group and completed his law studies at the Sorbonne (1911). In 1918 he became a member of the CP(B)U Provisional Bureau and deputy head of the Soviet delegation that negotiated with the Hetman government in Kiev. Then he headed the Political Committee for the Defense of Kiev (July–August 1919) and attended the secret conference of Ukrainian Bolshevik 'federalists' led by Ya. *Lapchynsky (November). Siding with Moscow, he was appointed member of the *All-Ukrainian Revolutionary Committee (1919–20), special delegate to the Soviet-Polish peace negotiations in Riga (1919), member of the CC CP(B)U Politburo (1920–3), people's commissar for agriculture in Ukraine during the famine of 1920–1, and first secretary of the CC CP(B)U and editor of its organ *Kommunist* (1921–2). From 1922 he held senior posts in the *Communist International. As secretary of its Executive Committee (1928–44) he supervised the Stalinist purges and terror in the Comintern apparat and foreign Communist parties, including the Communist Party of Western Ukraine. From 1944 to 1950 he was deputy chairman of Ukraine's Council of People's Commissars (from 1946, Ministers), people's commissar and minister of foreign affairs, and head of the Ukrainian delegation at the United Nations. In 1950 he fell into disfavor and was forced to retire.

R. Senkus

Vadym Manzhelii

Manzhelii, Vadym [Manželij], b 3 May 1933 in Kharkiv. Experimental physicist; AN URSR (now ANU) corresponding member since 1982 and full member since 1990. A graduate of Kharkiv University (1955), he did postgraduate work there until 1960 and then joined the staff of the newly formed AN URSR Physical-Technical Institute of Low Temperatures in Kharkiv. Manzhelii has investigated the thermal properties of molecular crystals and contributed significantly to the understanding of the dynamics of crystal lattices.

Stepan Manzhula   Ivan Manzhura

Manzhula, Stepan [Manžula], b 3 January 1885 in Dinska Stanytsia, Kuban, d ? Civic and political leader. A graduate in agronomy from the Kiev Polytechnical Institute, he was a member of the Revolutionary Ukrainian party and one of the leaders of the Ukrainian independence movement in the Kuban. He became a member of the Kuban Territorial and Legislative councils (1917–20) and a delegate from the Kuban to the Paris Peace Conference. After emigrating to Prague ca 1920, he worked as an agronomist and educator in the Berehove region of Transcarpathia. In 1945 he was deported from Prague by the Soviets. His further fate is unknown.

Manzhura, Ivan [Manžura] (pseud: Ivan Kalichka), b 1 November 1851 in Kharkiv, d 15 May 1893 in Katerynoslav. Poet, folklorist, and ethnographer. He was a full member of the Kharkiv Historical-Philological Society (from 1887) and the Moscow Natural Sciences, Anthropology, and Ethnography Society (from 1891). Manzhura studied at the Kharkiv Veterinary Institute (1870–1), from which he was suspended for 'political bad conduct'; he remained under tsarist police surveillance for the rest of his life. Manzhura's debut as a poet came in 1885 in the weekly *Step'*. In 1889 his first anthology of poetry, *Stepovi dumy ta spivy* (Steppe Dumas and Songs), was published. He subsequently prepared another anthology, *'Nad Dniprom'* (By the Dnieper), and a book of edited folk literature, *'Kazky ta prykazky i take inshe'* (Fables, Proverbs, and Other Such Things), neither of which was published in his lifetime. Manzhura's social and intimate lyric poetry was greatly influenced by folk literature. Finely written and completely original in the context of the literature of its time, his poetry showed the poet's close attention to language and was unencumbered by needless poetic decorative devices. Among Manzhura's longer works are stories in verse, *Tr'omsyn-bohatyr* (Tromsyn the Giant), *Ivan Holyk*, and *Kazka pro khytroho lysovyna ...* (The Tale of the Crafty Fox ...). Two of the more extensive editions of Manzhura's works are *Poeziï* (Poems, ed Ya. Aizenshtok, 1930) and *Tvory* (Works, ed M. Bernshtein, 1961).

BIBLIOGRAPHY
Berezovs'kyi, I. *Ivan Manzhura* (Kiev 1962)
Zaremba, V. *Ivan Manzhura* (Kiev 1972)
Bernshtein, M. *Ivan Manzhura* (Kiev 1977)

I. Koshelivets

Manzii, Volodymyr [Manzij], b 4 April 1884 in Kiev, d 22 April 1954 in Kiev. Opera director. He graduated from the Kiev School of Music (1903; now the Kiev Conservatory) and worked in various theaters from 1917. In 1925 he became director of the Kharkiv Opera, and in 1928 of the Kiev Ukrainian Opera. He directed many operas, among them M. Lysenko's *Taras Bul'ba* and *Utoplena* (The Drowned Maiden), B. Liatoshynsky's *Zolotyi obruch* (The Golden Ring), M. Verykivsky's *Naimychka* (The Hired Girl), and B. Smetana's *Bartered Bride*.

Maple (*Acer*; Ukrainian: *klen, yavir*). A deciduous tree or shrub of the family Aceraceae that grows in mixed and deciduous forests. Pure maple stands are rare. The common maple (*A. campestre*) measures up to 15–20 m in height and 50–60 cm in trunk diameter. It is used as a decorative tree in parks because its leaves turn brilliant colors in autumn. The tree sap contains 2–5 percent sugar; maple flowers yield nectar. Maple wood has many uses in the manufacture of furniture, musical instruments, and millwork. In Ukraine the Norway maple (*A. platanoides*) grows almost everywhere. The sycamore maple (*A. pseudoplatanus*) is concentrated in Western Ukraine and in parks; its wood is used in the production of furniture and musical instruments. The Tatar maple (*A. tataricum*), with smooth, almost black bark, is a hardy tree or shrub that grows in the steppe, forest-steppe, and Caucasia. The American maple, also known as the box elder (*A. negundo*), is used in landscaping.

Maps. See Cartography.

Mara. A female figure in Ukrainian and other Slavic folk mythology who was believed to assume various forms – animal, plant, inanimate, monstrous, or ghostly – and to cause people harm. The name was occasionally used to refer to the devil or to a house demon known as a *domovyk*.

Marakhov, Hryhorii [Maraxov, Hryhorij], b 18 August 1918 in Kevsala, near Ipatovo, Stavropol gubernia. Soviet Ukrainian historian. He graduated from the Krasnodar Pedagogical Institute (1941), taught the history of the CPSU and the USSR at institutions of higher education in Kiev (from 1945), worked at the AN URSR (now ANU) Institute of History (1958–63), chaired the Department of Marxism-Leninism at the Ukrainian Printing Institute in Lviv (1963–70), and lectured at Kiev University (from 1970). He oversaw the compilation of *Suspil'no-politychnyi rukh na Ukraïni v 1856–1864 rr.* (The Sociopolitical Movement in Ukraine in 1856–64, 2 vols, 1963–4) and wrote monographs on the Polish Insurrection of 1863–4 in Right-Bank Ukraine (1967), T. Shevchenko and his contemporaries (1976), sociopolitical movements in Ukraine in 1820–40 (1979) and during the 1850s and 1860s (1981), and 'revolutionary-democratic' movements at Kiev University (1984).

Maramureş Basin (also Khust-Solotvyna Basin or Upper Tysa Basin). A basin in the Transcarpathians along the upper Tysa River. Situated between the Polonynian Beskyds in the northeast and the Volcanic Ukrainian Carpathians in the southwest, it is a continuation of the *Inner Carpathian Valley. In the west the basin connects (by way of the Tysa River valley) with the Tysa Lowland; its southeastern portion lies within Rumania. The basin is over 50 km long and up to 30 km wide; it covers an area of nearly 1,400 sq km, with a population of approx 140,000. It is the main geographic feature of the Maramureş region.

The basin itself is a tectonic depression, filled out by a thick layer of Miocene sedimentary deposits mixed with relatively thin layers of salt and tuff. Its northeastern part consists of gently rolling hills (300–600 m in height) divided by the tributaries of the Tysa, the Rika, the Tereblia, and the Teresva rivers. In the southwest stretches the Tysa River valley (elevation, 160–240 m; width, 6–8 km), with well-defined terraces covered by alluvial sediment. The relief of the Maramureş Basin is also marked by cuestas of Miocene conglomerates, volcanic remains (notably Fortress Hill in Khust), and salt pillars (around Solotvyna). The climate of the region is more continental than that of the rest of Transcarpathia: the average temperature for the city of Khust is –4° C in January and +21.1° C in July, with precipitation of up to 900 mm per year. The soils in the region are of medium quality, with slightly clayey types in the valleys and meadows and light brown forest and clayey types in the hilly regions. The forests in the region are of oak and beech, although most of them have been transformed for agricultural applications. At present the forests make up approx 30 percent of the terrain, pastures and hayfields about 40 percent, and tillage 25 percent.

Because of advantageous natural conditions and a location along transport routes, the Maramureş Basin has long been densely populated, particularly in the Tysa River valley (average, 100 persons/sq km). The main occupation is agriculture, with corn and fruit (apples, pears, apricots, plums, and cherries) the predominant crops. The local industries include food processing, forestry, wood products, and salt industries.

The major cities and towns of the region are on the Tysa River. Until 1918 the main center was Sighetul Marmaţiei (Syhit). Since then that city's role has been taken over in the northern part of the basin by Khust (1987 pop, 34,000). Other notable centers include Tiachiv, Solotvyna, Velykyi Bychkiv (the center of the salt-producing industry), Bushtyna, and Teresva.

V. Kubijovyč

Maramureş region (Ukrainian: Marmaroshchyna, Maramorshchyna; Hungarian: Máramaros). A historical-geographic region in the *Maramureş Basin. Its larger, northern part is Ukrainian ethnic territory (eastern Transcarpathia), the inhabitants of which speak a *Transcarpathian dialect of Ukrainian. The south is settled by Rumanians.

The name Máramaros appears in a Hungarian charter in 1199. Until the 14th century the region was sparsely populated and served mainly as a hunting ground for Hungarian kings and nobles. In the 14th century it was colonized by Ukrainians from Galicia and Vlachs from *Transylvania. At that time it was ruled by a voivode under Hungarian tutelage. In 1385 it became an administrative-territorial *komitat. After the partition of Hungary in 1526, the region was part of Transylvania until 1733, when it was reclaimed by Hungary, and it remained under Hungary's control until 1918. In 1891 Máramaros komitat (10,354 sq km) had a population of 268,281: 122,528 Ukrainians, 64,957 Rumanians, 45,679 Germans, and 33,610 Magyars. In 1910, 45 percent of the region's population of 360,000 was Ukrainian, 24 percent was Rumanian, 17 percent was Jewish, and the rest was German or Magyar. The region's Ukrainians were Greek Catholics and belonged to *Mukachiv eparchy. In the early 20th century a portion of them converted to Orthodoxy and were accused by the Hungarian government of being Russian agents. In the resulting show trials 9 peasants in 1904–6 and 96 in 1913–14 were sentenced to various terms of imprisonment.

After the dissolution of the Austro-Hungarian Empire the northern Maramureş region was annexed by Czechoslovakia and administered as a *župa* (county). The south was annexed by *Rumania. Because the new Czechoslovak-Rumanian border along the Tysa River did not correspond to the ethnic border, much of the region's Ukrainian ethnic territory – 800 sq km – became part of Rumania.

Fourteen Ukrainian villages are now within Rumania: along the Ruskova River, Poliany or Ruska Poliana (Rumanian: Poienile de sub Munte, approx pop 8,000), Kryvyi (Repedea, pop 3,000), and Ruskova (Ruscova, pop 3,000); along the Vyshava (Vişeu) River, Krasnyi (Crasna, pop 2,000), Bystryi (Bistra, pop 3,000), Vyshavska Dolyna (Valea Vişeului, pop 1,200); and on the left bank of the Tysa, Luh (Lunca la Tisa, pop 1,500), Velykyi Bychkiv (Bocicoiul Mare, pop 1,000), Krychuniv (Crăciuneşti, pop 1,500), Vyshnia Rivna (Rona de Sus, pop 4,000), Myhovo (Virişmort, pop 1,000; 300 Ukrainians), Dovhopole (Câmpulung la Tisa, pop 3,000; 550 Ukrainians), Tiachevo (Teceu, pop 700), and Remety (Remeţi, pop 2,000). Outside the territory of compact Ukrainian settlement, Ukrainians also live in the town of Vişeul de Sus (pop 13,000; 500 Ukrainians). In 1960 there were more than 30,000 Ukraini-

Maramureş Komitat
up to 1918 in Hungary

------- Historical boundary of Maramureş Region   ·········· Rumanian-Ukrainian ethnic boundary

Rivna Town inhabited by Ukrainians

Mykovo Town inhabited by Rumanians

0   10   20km

MARAMUREŞ REGION

ans in the Maramureş region. In 1971, 3,500 Ukrainians lived in the border town of *Sighetul Marmaţiei (pop 40,000).

Under interwar Rumanian rule Ukrainian community life in the Maramureş region was poorly developed. In the 1920s and 1930s the region's Ukrainians relied on the cultural influence of the Bukovynian capital of Chernivtsi. The Greek Catholic church was largely responsible for preserving Ukrainian identity against the militant onslaught of Rumanianization, as it had previously preserved it against Magyarization. In the 1930s, 11 Ukrainian Greek Catholic parishes and 3 of their chapters were subordinated to the vicar-general for Ukrainian Catholics in Rumania. In the early 1920s the region's Ukrainians elected two representatives, O. Ilnytsky and T. Bokotei, to the Rumanian parliament. In 1926 Rev A. Sabo founded a Ruthenian party in Sighetul Marmaţiei, but it did not have a significant impact. In 1931 a branch of the Ukrainian National party in Rumania was founded in the region, but it too was largely unsuccessful. The leading Ukrainian cultural and educational figure in the region at that time was the lawyer I. Odovichuk. In March 1939 the region's Ukrainians helped refugees who had fled from the Hungarian occupation of Carpatho-Ukraine.

The *Vienna Arbitration of 1940 granted the Maramureş region to Hungary, which occupied it until 1944. In 1944–5 the region was occupied by the Soviet army. In the winter of 1945 Transcarpathian Ukrainians took over the administration of Sighetul Marmaţiei and the Ukrainian villages. Soon thereafter, however, the region again came

under Rumanian rule, which was confirmed by the Paris Peace Treaty of 1947. The Rumanian administrative reform of 1968 established a province called Maramureş (6,215 sq km, 1980 pop 543,000) in the region.

Ukrainian cultural life in the region improved after 1948, when new educational rights were granted to Rumania's national minorities. The Ukrainian lyceum (est 1948) and Ukrainian pedagogical school (est 1950) created in Sighetul Marmaţiei fostered a new generation of nationally conscious Ukrainian intelligentsia for Rumania as a whole. In all the elementary schools in villages with a Ukrainian majority, teaching was conducted mostly in Ukrainian. Later, however, Rumanian sections were introduced in most of them, and with time the language of instruction became Rumanian. In the 1960s the pedagogical school in Sighetul Marmaţiei was closed down, and the Ukrainian, Rumanian, and Hungarian lyceums there were amalgamated into one lyceum with three sections, the Dragoş Vodă Lyceum, where approx 150 Ukrainian students study each year. In each of the sections instruction is conducted in the native language of the students, but general subjects, such as history and geography, are taught only in Rumanian. Since 1980 the only elementary schools where teaching is conducted in Ukrainian have been those in Krychuniv, Poliany, and Vyshnia Rivna. Elsewhere Ukrainian has only been taught as a subject. Ukrainian reading rooms, clubs, and amateur groups are active in the villages.

In 1948 the Rumanian authorities forced the region's Ukrainian Catholic church and faithful to convert to Orthodoxy. In the churches liturgies are conducted in Old Church Slavonic, but sermons are delivered in Ukrainian. In the 1980s the region's eight Ukrainian parishes and eight priests were placed under the authority of an archpriest of the Ukrainian Orthodox church in Rumania, which is itself subordinated to the Rumanian Transylvanian eparchy.

(See also *Transcarpathia.)

BIBLIOGRAPHY

Wenzel, G. *Kritikai fejtegetések Máramaros megye történetéhez* (Pest 1857)

Bergner, R. *In der Marmaros* (Munich 1885)

Mihalyi, I. *Diplome Maramureşene din secolul XIV şi XV* (Sighetul Marmaţiei 1900)

Várady, G. 'Das Máramaroser Comitat,' in *Die österreichisch-ungarische Monarchie in Wort und Bild: Ungarn*, vol 2, pt 2 (Vienna 1900)

Hadzhega, V. 'Dodatky k istorii rusyniv i rus'kykh tserkvei: Studii istorychno-arkhivni: Marmarosh,' *Naukovyi zbirnyk Tovarystva Prosvita*, 1 (Uzhhorod 1922)

Kubijovyč, V. *Pāstoritul în Maramureş* (Bucharest 1935)

Filipaşcu, A. *Le Maramures* (Sibiu 1944)

Pavliuk, M. 'Do istorii ukraïns'kykh sil Maramoroshchyny,' *Novyi vik* (Bucharest), nos 134–6 (1957)

Pavliuk, M.; Robchuk, I. 'Rehional'nyi atlas ukraïns'kykh hovirok Rumunii,' in *Pratsi XIII Respublikans'koï dialektolohichnoï narady*, ed F. Zhylko (Kiev 1971)

Niculescu, I. (ed.) *Judeţul Maramureş* (Bucharest 1980)

M. Pavliuk, A. Zhukovsky

Maramureş-Bukovynian Upland

(also Maramureş-Bukovynian Massif, Maramures Massif, Rakhiv-Chyvchyn Massif). A crystalline massif in the southeastern part of the Ukrainian Carpathians. The upland stretches beside the Polonynian and the Bukovynian Beskyds from the Chorna Tysa River valley in the northwest, southeast to the headwaters of the Vişeu (Vyshava) and the Bistriţa Aurie (Zolota Bystrytsia) rivers near Prislop Pass, in northern Rumania. The orographic foundation of the upland is a ridge 100 km long, which is the watershed between the Tysa River on one side and the Prut and the Seret rivers on the other.

The core of the anticlinal zone consists of metamorphosed crystalline rocks – gneiss, crystalline schist, and marbleized limestone. The sedimentary rocks that formerly covered the crystalline core, consisting of Triassic and Jurassic formations (limestones, sandstones, porphyrites, and conglomerates) as well as Cretaceous and Paleogene layers, were partly destroyed by erosion. Because of its varied geological composition, significant absolute (average ridge height, 1,600–1,900 m) and relative (approx 1,000 m) elevation, and glacial formations, the Maramureş-Bukovynian Upland is more picturesque than other parts of the Ukrainian Carpathians. That is particularly true of the *Hutsul Alps, in the western reaches of the upland, and the *Chyvchyn Mountains, near its center. Further to the southeast the Bukovynian part of the upland, consisting of crystalline schist formations, is considerably lower in elevation. Only occasionally do peaks of hard limestone or conglomerates rise above the nearly even ridges.

The upland is covered with forests of fir and of beech (in the southwest), which often grow at elevations of 1,500 m, and in places of 1,600 m. At higher elevations there are alpine meadows, although the Hutsul Alps have rocky outcroppings not fit for cultivation. Junipers are found in the eastern part of the upland. The ridges of the middle portion of the upland are covered throughout by alpine meadows, which make up the largest such area in all the Ukrainian Carpathians. Barely 5 percent of the upland is inhabited; the population consists of Ukrainians (see *Hutsuls) and (in the southwest) Rumanians. Foresting and pasturing provide a significant influx of inhabitants on a seasonal basis.

V. Kubijovyč

Marble. Granular metamorphic rock formed as a result of a recrystallization of limestone or, less frequently, dolomites, under the influence of heat, pressure, and aqueous solutions. Pure marble is white; various admixtures result in different colors, such as pink, red, yellow, brown, green, black, gray, and blue. The largest deposits of marble are in Italy and Greece. In Ukraine deposits of marble are located in the Ukrainian Crystalline Shield (mostly gray marble) on the Teteriv River (Koziivka) and the Boh River (Khashchuvate, Zavallia); in Transcarpathia, where deposits of marble in Dilove (white, gray, and dark gray), Rakhiv and Tiachiv (red and pink), and other locations have significant industrial importance; in the Crimean Mountains (mainly pink, red, and brown), near Balaklava, Haspra, and other sites; and in the Donets Basin, where deposits of marblelike limestones are located near Troitsko-Khartsyzke and Novopavlivka and elsewhere.

Marchak, Valerii [Marčak, Valerij], b 1949 in Krasnohirka, Holovanivske raion, Kirovohrad oblast. Painter and muralist. A graduate of the Lviv Institute of Applied and Decorative Arts (1977), he has taught painting there since 1978 and was appointed head of its Faculty of Painting. He created a stylized mural based on Ukrainian folk tales and another using fantasy at the Pioneer Palace in Lviv. At Lviv's House of Children no. 173 he painted the mural *Sounds of Music.*

Marchenko, Andrii [Marčenko, Andrij], b 1908 in Volhynia, d 1943 in Lviv. Political activist. While studying in Lviv in the 1930s, he became active in the OUN and a driving force behind the organization of the OUN underground in Volhynia. He served time in Polish prisons and was murdered in a Gestapo prison. His articles and militant poetry and songs appeared in the nationalist press.

Marchenko, Ivan [Marčenko], b 1 November 1892 in Parichi, Minsk gubernia, Belarus, d 3 March 1968 in Derby, England. Educator and mathematician. After graduating from St Petersburg University (1913) he was wounded in action in the First World War and then taught secondary school in Poltava. From 1925 he taught mathematics in Dnipropetrovske at the electrical sciences tekhnikum and then at the Metallurgical Institute (1930–41). After emigrating to Germany in 1944, he became active in the United Hetman Organization and edited its weekly *Ranok* (1948–54). In 1951 he settled in England, where he became a leading member of the hetmanite movement and the Association of Ukrainians in Great Britain. He was a founder and president (1959–62) of the British Association of Ukrainian Teachers and Educators and the author of two widely used textbooks, *Matematyka v tekhnikumi* (Mathematics in the Tekhnikum, 1930) and *Zadachnyk z* *matematyky dlia tekhnikumiv* (Exercise Book in Mathematics for Tekhnikums, 1932).

Mykhailo Marchenko   Valerii Marchenko

Volodymyr Marchenko

Marchenko, Mykhailo [Marčenko, Myxajlo], b 19 September 1902 in Hatne, Kiev county, d 21 January 1983 in Kiev. Historian; grandfather of V. *Marchenko. A graduate of the Institute of Red Professors in Kiev (1937), he chaired the Department of Feudalism at the AN URSR (now ANU) Institute of History and the USSR History Department at the Kiev Pedagogical Institute (1937–9), was rector of Lviv University (1939–41), and lectured at the pedagogical institutes in Novosibirsk (1941–5) and Kiev (1945–56). From 1956 he taught at Kiev University. He wrote many articles and reviews, and monographs on the struggle between Russia and Poland for Ukraine in 1654–64 (1941), Ukrainian history as depicted in the works of T. Shevchenko (1957), the historian O. Lazarevsky (with L. Polukhin, 1958), Ukrainian historiography up to the mid-19th century (1959), and the history of Ukrainian culture up to the mid-18th century (1961).

Marchenko, Valerii [Marčenko, Valerij], b 16 September 1947 in Kiev, d 7 October 1984 in Leningrad. Literary scholar, writer, and dissident; grandson of M. *Marchenko. After graduating in philology from Kiev University he studied Azerbaijani language and literature at Baku University and wrote a dissertation on A. Krymsky's research and translations of Azerbaijani literature. He translated H. Tiutiunnyk's short story 'Markiian' into Azerbaijani and A. Rzaev's 'Sklianka vody' (Glass of Water) into Ukrainian. In 1970–3 he worked as an editor for *Literaturna Ukraïna*. He was arrested in June 1973 and sentenced to six years' imprisonment and two years' exile for 'Ukrainian and Azerbaijani nationalism.' He was accused of writing three samvydav articles. Having served his time in the Perm concentration camps and his exile in Aktiubinsk, in May 1981 he returned to Ukraine. In 1984 he was tried again and sentenced to 10 years' imprisonment and 5 years' exile for 'anti-Soviet agitation and propaganda.' He died of kidney failure resulting from inadequate medical attention during his incarceration.

Marchenko, Volodymyr [Marčenko], b 7 July 1922 in Kharkiv. Mathematician; full member of the AN URSR (now ANU) since 1969 and of the Russian Academy of Sciences since 1987. A graduate of Kharkiv University (1945), he taught there in 1945–61 (professor from 1953). Since 1961 he has worked at the Physico-Technical Institute of Low Temperatures in Kharkiv. Marchenko's main work is in the theory of differential equations, theory of functions, mathematical physics, and functional analysis. He is well known for his original results in the spectral theory of differential equations, including the discovery of new methods for the study of the asymptotic behavior of spectral functions and the convergence of expansions in terms of eigenfunctions. He also obtained fundamental results in the theory of inverse problems in spectral analysis for the Sturm-Liouville and more general equations. In the periodic case the famous Kordeweg–de Vries equation was solved by Marchenko in 1972 by the use of the method of the inverse problem in the theory of dissipation. In the spectral theory of differential operators he proved a basic theorem on the unique determination of a differential operator by its spectral characteristics. He laid the foundation for the spectral theory of non-self-adjoint singular differential operators and for the theory of boundary value problems with a fine-grained boundary. He also solved many problems in the approximation theory of continuous functions defined on the entire line and the theory of almost periodic functions. Marchenko made significant contributions to the theory of self-adjoint differential operators with infinitely many independent variables and also to the theory of spaces of functions of infinitely many variables as inductive limits of locally convex function spaces.

W. Petryshyn

Marchlewski raion. See Dovbysh.

Marchuk, Ivan [Marčuk], b 12 May 1936 in Moskalivka, Kremianets county, Volhynia voivodeship. Painter and sculptor. He graduated from the Lviv Institute of Applied and Decorative Arts in 1965 and then moved to Kiev. Until 1988 he was denied membership in the Union of Artists of Ukraine because his themes and style did not conform to *socialist realism. In Kiev he created the wall-size ceramic-tile relief compositions (1969–72) in the AN URSR (now ANU) Institute of Theoretical Physics. Marchuk paints fantastic figural and floral compositions with elements of *surrealism, hyperrealist portraits (eg, *R. Selsky*, 1981), enigmatic landscapes, and abstract expressionist compositions (eg, the series 'Colored Preludes' [1978]). His figural tempera paintings of the 'Voice of My Soul' series depict seemingly irrational situations with skeletal, often

Ivan Marchuk: a painting of his Shevchenkiana series (tempera, 1983)

grotesque, persons cut off at the waist and surrounded by sinister objects and creatures set in a vast empty landscape (eg, *Empty Nest* [1975] and *Dialogue without Words* [1976]). Marchuk's palette borders on the monochromatic, and the unreality of the imagery is thereby reinforced. His realistic landscapes have a peculiar, dense texture consisting of weblike layers of pigment that, combined with the dramatic use of light and dark, create an atmosphere of unease and mystery (eg, *Willows in the Embrace of a Moonlit Night* [1978] and *Apple in the Snow* [1979]). After the 1986 Chornobyl nuclear accident Marchuk created nightmarish compositions depicting the total destruction of our planet (eg, *Warning* [1986]). He has had numerous solo exhibitions, starting in Moscow in 1979 and Kiev in 1980. His 43 canvases inspired by the poetry of T. Shevchenko were exhibited at the Shevchenko Museum in Kaniv. Since 1989 he has had several exhibitions in Australia, Canada, and New York City.

D. Zelska-Darewych

Marcinkowski, Antoni (pseuds: Albert Gryf, Antoni Nowosielski), b 29 January 1823 in Mostyshche, Kiev county, Kiev gubernia, d 12 September 1880 in Kiev. Polish writer, literary critic, and ethnographer. After graduating from Kiev University (1844) he worked for the Polish newspaper *Gwiazda* in Kiev (1846–9). He traveled extensively in Ukraine and wrote several works on Ukrainian ethnography and history: *Stepy, morze i góry: Szkice i wospomnienia z podróży* (Steppes, Sea, and Mountains: Sketches and Reminiscences from a Trip, 2 vols, 1854), *Lud Ukraiński* (The Ukrainian People, 2 vols, 1857), and *Pogranicze Naddnieprzańskie* (The Dneiper Frontier, 2 vols, 1863).

Marena. A figure of Ukrainian folk mythology, identified by some scholars as a goddess of spring and of the waters. Marena plays a prominent role in March celebrations and the *Kupalo festival. In the latter she is represented by a wood-and-straw figure decorated with wreaths, flowers, and candles and is either paraded with song or stationed in one spot to be entertained with dances and games. At the end of the festivities she is burned, thrown into the water, or buried in the ground.

Aleksei Marenkov: poster design (1921)

Marenkov, Aleksei, b 25 March 1888 in Orel, Russia, d 1942 in Kiev. Graphic artist and muralist. He studied at the Kiev Art School (1905–12). In the 1920s he belonged to the *Association of Artists of Red Ukraine and designed many posters and book covers, in a style combining formalist simplicity with Cossack-baroque and Ukrainian folk-art motifs. His early posters and book covers show the influence of his teacher, H. *Narbut. Marenkov also painted murals inside the building of the All-Ukrainian Central Executive Committee and the Chervonyi Hotel in Kharkiv and taught at the Kharkiv Art Tekhnikum and Institute (1923–31).

Marenych Trio. A vocal and instrumental group established in Lutske in 1975. It consists of Valerii Marenych (baritone and guitar), his wife Antonina (soprano), and her sister Svitliana (alto, the group's musical director). They accompany themselves on guitar and percussion (drum, castanets, and bongo). The trio, with its distinctive gentle and relaxed style, has become very popular in Ukraine and among Ukrainians in the West. Its repertoire

Marenych Trio

Arnold Margolin and his wife

consists of folk songs arranged by Svitliana. It has toured Ukraine, Eastern Europe, and Canada.

Marfiievych, Mykola [Marfijevyč], b 20 March 1898 in Ispas, Bukovyna, d 2 September 1967 in Kiev. Writer. He graduated from the teachers' institute in Chernivtsi in 1920 and completed graduate studies at the AN URSR (now ANU) Institute of Linguistics in 1933. He published collections of poetry, *Mizh verkhamy* (Between Summits, 1922), *Kvity* (Flowers, 1923), *Mykola Shuhai* (1927), *Halata* (1927), *Povstantsi* (The Rebels, 1930), and *Bukovyni* (For Bukovyna, 1930); a play, *Zbuduiemo Dniprel'stan* (We Shall Build the Dnieper Hydroelectric Station, 1928); and the novelettes *Proty boiar* (Against the Boyars, 1929) and *Krutizh* (The Vortex, 1931). He belonged to the *Zakhidnia Ukraina literary organization and was repressed in the 1930s, but rehabilitated in 1957. His work was republished posthumously in *Cheremoshe, bratku mii* (Cheremosh, My Brother, 1968).

Margolin, Arnold, b 17 November 1877 in Kiev, d 29 October 1956 in Washington, DC. Ukrainian-Jewish political leader, scholar, and lawyer; corresponding member of the Ukrainian Academy of Arts and Sciences in the US. He graduated from the law faculty of Kiev University and studied abroad until 1900. After being called to the bar, he acted as defense counsel in many political trials, including the M. Beilis trial (see *Beilis affair), and headed the South Russian Branch of the Union for Equal Rights for Jews in Russia (1905–17) and the Jewish Territorial Organization (1906–18). A firm believer in national self-determination, during the revolutionary period he joined the *Ukrainian Party of Socialists-Federalists and played a prominent role in the Ukrainian liberation struggle: he sat on the General Court of the UNR and served as deputy minister of foreign affairs in V. Chekhivsky's cabinet, as a member of the UNR delegation to the Paris Peace Conference, and as chief of the UNR mission to London. In 1922 he emigrated to the United States, where he practiced law, lectured at various universities, and promoted Ukrainian-Jewish understanding. He defended Ukraine's right to independence and the reputation of S. *Petliura. He served as a professor at the Ukrainian Technical Institute in New York and contributed to the weekly *Narodna volia*. Besides numerous articles on law and contemporary history, he wrote a number of books: *Ukraïna i politika Antanty* (Ukraine and the Policy of the Entente, 1922; English trans, 1977), *The Jews of Eastern Europe* (1926), and *From a Political Diary: Russia, the Ukraine, and America, 1905–1945* (1946).

Marhanets [Marhanec'] (Marsanets). VI-15. A city (1990 pop 54,500) at the mouth of the Tomakivka River on the right bank of the Kakhivka Reservoir in Dnipropetrovske oblast. At the end of the 19th century a mining settlement was established at the site. In 1938 several settlements were amalgamated to form the city of Marhanets. Today the city is a major mining center of the Nykopil Manganese Basin. It is the home of a manganese mining and enrichment complex, a mining machinery repair plant, and a regional museum.

Maria Theresa, b 13 May 1717 in Vienna, d 29 November 1780 in Vienna. Archduchess of Austria and queen of Hungary and Bohemia from 1740, and the de facto ruler of the Holy Roman Empire from 1745 (the emperor, Francis I, married her in 1736). She was the daughter of Emperor Charles VI, and in 1765 her son (later her successor) *Joseph II became coregent. During Maria Theresa and Joseph's reign Austria annexed Galicia from partitioned Poland (1772) and Bukovyna from the Ottoman Empire (1774). The numerous modernizing administrative, fiscal, economic, judicial, ecclesiastical, educational, and military reforms Maria Theresa had introduced elsewhere in the empire, including Transcarpathia, were implemented in those lands. She introduced a number of reforms that improved the legal status of the peasantry and limited the Polish magnates' powers and privileges, and introduced various measures to stimulate the development of agriculture and commerce. The Ukrainian Greek Catholic clergy had their status raised to that of the Roman Catholic clergy (which they had not under Polish rule), a seminary was founded in Vienna (see *Barbareum), and the Uniate church was entrusted with establishing new elementary schools. Maria Theresa's reforms aimed to lift Galicia and Bukovyna out of the cultural restriction and economic stagnation they had endured under Polish and Ottoman rule.

Marian of Jaśliska's dictionary, 1641. A Slavonic dictionary of Ukrainian recension. The Polish Dominican monk Marian (d 1658) compiled the dictionary at Zhovkva in 1641 under the title *Dictionarium Sclauo-Polonicum: hoc est vocabula quaedam Illyrica seu Dalmatica Polonice explicata ordine alphabetico* (according to popular belief, Church Slavonic had been created by St Jerome in Illyria and Dalmatia in the 4th and 5th centuries). The Slavonic register (ca 4,000 entries in Polish transliteration) was based mostly on P. *Berynda's Slavonic-Ruthenian dictionary of 1627. Definitions were given in Polish and sometimes in Latin.

Marian societies (Mariiski tovarystva; Latin: Sodalitates Marianae). Canonically erected Catholic lay bodies which promote a Christian way of life for their members through a program of spiritual formation and group religious activity centered on the veneration of Mary, the Mother of God. The first body of this type was formed in Rome in 1563 by a Jesuit priest, J. Leunis, and the movement was subsequently introduced into a number of Catholic countries. Approbation to form Marian societies in Ukraine was granted in 1615 by Pope Paul V in response to a request by Metropolitan Y. Rutsky. Promoted mainly by priests and nuns of the Basilian order through their network of schools, approx 30 to 40 societies were established in Ukraine during the 17th and 18th centuries. In spite of some efforts at rejuvenation by I. *Dolnytsky, the movement declined during the 19th century.

In 1920 Rev Y. *Markevych launched a successful campaign to form Marian societies throughout Galicia. His efforts were aided by a vigorous publishing program that included journals for youths and children (*Postup and *Nash pryiatel'), a society bulletin (*Vistnyk Mariis'koho tovarystva*), series of popular books (Biblioteka Nashoho pryiatelia and Tsikavi opovidannia), calendars, and brochures. The number of societies reached 31 in 1926 and continued to grow steadily until 1939. The societies' work was co-ordinated by an organizational center in Lviv that was headed first by Markevych and then by Rev I. *Nazarko. The societies expanded from their initial target groups of secondary and primary school students to include children, the elderly, and even adults. Societal activity centered around semimonthly meetings, corporate participation in the Liturgy at least once a month, the raising of religious consciousness, and various group programs.

The movement was outlawed with the Soviet occupation of Western Ukraine. Marian societies have been established in Ukrainian Catholic parishes in countries such as the United States, Canada, Brazil, and Argentina. Following the easing of religious persecution in Ukraine in the late 1980s, attempts have been made to revive Marian societies there.

BIBLIOGRAPHY
Villaret, E. *Abridged History of the Sodality of Our Lady*, trans W. Young (St Louis 1957)

Marianenko, Ivan [Mar'janenko] (real surname: Petlishenko), b 9 June 1878 at Sochevaniv *khutir*, near Marianivka, Yelysavethrad county, Kherson gubernia, d 4 November 1962 in Kharkiv. Actor of heroic roles, director, and teacher. After completing district school in Kupianka (1895) he worked in the troupe of his uncle, M. Kropyvnytsky, as a stage manager and actor, in O. Suslov's troupe (1899–1906), and in F. Volyk's troupe (1903–4). He was an

Ivan Marianenko in the role of Yaroslav the Wise

actor and director in Sadovsky's Theater in Kiev (1906–14). He led the Society of Ukrainian Actors (1915–16) and the *Ukrainian National Theater in Kiev (1917–18). In 1918 he joined the State Drama Theater (from 1919 the Shevchenko First Theater of the Ukrainian Soviet Republic). He worked in *Berezil (1922–34) and in the Kharkiv Ukrainian Drama Theater (1934–58). Marianenko appeared in nearly 200 roles in a variety of plays ranging from Ukrainian populist-ethnographic plays to world classics. An established actor of the populist-ethnographic theater, he made the transition to Berezil's formally innovative acting style. In 1933, when L. *Kurbas was attacked, Marianenko spoke in his defense. Marianenko's best roles were Gonta in *Haidamaky* (based on T. Shevchenko), Davidson in *Sadie* (based on S. Maugham's *Rain*, Verryna in F. Schiller's *Die Verschwörung des Fiesko zu Genua*, Felix Grandet in *Eugénie Grandet* (based on H. de Balzac), and the title roles in W. Shakespeare's *Macbeth*, O. Korniichuk's *Bohdan Kmel'nyts'kyi*, and I. Kocherha's *Iaroslav Mudryi* (Yaroslav the Wise). He also acted in films: *The Downpour* (1929), *Fata morgana* (1931), *Koliivshchyna* (1933), and *Prometheus* (1936). He taught at the Lysenko Music and Drama School in Kiev (1917–18) and at the Kharkiv Theater Institute (1944–61). Marianenko is the author of *Mynule ukraïns'koho teatru* (The Past of the Ukrainian Theater, 1953). Biographies of him were published in Kiev in 1964 and 1968.

V. Revutsky

Marianivka culture. A Bronze Age culture of the early 2nd to early 1st millennium BC located in Left-Bank Polisia and the northern forest-steppe regions of Ukraine. It was named after the site excavated in 1929 near the village of Marianivka, Sumy oblast. Excavations there and at other sites revealed surface dwellings and shallow pit-houses of a relatively large size, pottery with featherlike and pitted ornamentation, flint and quartz tools, and a small number of bronze items. The tribes of this culture engaged in hunting, fishing, and (later) agriculture and animal husbandry. The culture can be divided into three chronological periods – early Marianivka, middle Studenok, and late *Bondarykha (the latter being regarded as a separate or equal culture). Evidence suggests the origins of the Marianivka culture are linked to the *Pitted-Comb Pottery culture.

Máriapócs Monastery. A Basilian monastery located in an area of northeastern Hungary inhabited mostly by Magyarized Greek Catholic Ukrainians. It was established in 1749 and served as an important religious and cultural center for Transcarpathia. A miraculous icon of the weep-

Máriapócs Monastery

Street In Mariiupil

ing Mother of God was located there. The monastery attracted up to 100,000 pilgrims annually to 1914 and during the Second World War. After the war it was closed; the church was declared a minor basilica in 1948.

Mariinskyi Palace. The tsarist palace in Kiev. Using Count O. Rozumovsky's palace in Perov, near Moscow, as his model, B. *Rastrelli designed it in the rococo style for Empress Elizabeth I. It was built above the Dnieper River in the Pecherske district under the supervision of the architects I. Michurin, P. Neelov, and I. *Hryhorovych-Barsky in the years 1747–55. The palace consisted of a long central section with a stone ground floor and wooden second story (destroyed by a fire in 1819), two stone one-story wings, and a large adjacent park with an orangery and orchards. It was inhabited sporadically by visiting members of the royal family and various governors, including P. Rumiantsev (in 1776), but otherwise stood empty. From 1834 to 1868 it was leased by a mineral-water company. The palace was renovated in 1870 according to K. Maievsky's Louis XVI–style design for the visit of Emperor Alexander II and Empress Maria (hence its name). In 1918 it housed the Hetman government's Ministry of the Interior and the National Guard headquarters, in 1919, the Soviet Council of People's Commissars, and in 1920, the Soviet military-district headquarters. From 1923 to 1925 an agricultural school was located there. Since 1925 the palace has housed an agricultural museum, a permanent industrial exhibit, and various official agencies. After being damaged and looted during the Second World War, it was rebuilt by 1949.

Mariiupil or **Mariupol** [Marijupil' or Mariupol']. VI-18. A port city (1990 pop 519,900) on the Sea of Azov at the mouth of the Kalmiius River in Donetske oblast. A major industrial center, it is the ninth-largest city in Ukraine. From 1948 to 1989 it was called Zhdanov. Its origins date back to the beginning of the 16th century, when the Cossack fortress of Kalmiius was built. By 1611 Kalmiius was the center of a palanka. When Russia annexed the territory in 1775, the fortress was renamed Pavlovsk, and the palanka was reorganized into a county. In 1780 many Greeks from the Crimea were resettled there, and the town was renamed Mariiupil (Mariupol, Marianopol). In the late 19th century Mariiupil was developed as a shipping port for the Donets Basin, in 1882 it was linked with Donetske by rail, and in 1886–9 the port was built. The main exports were coal and grain. By 1900 the port was handling 1 million t of freight, and the tonnage doubled in the next decade. At the turn of the century a tube-rolling and a metallurgical plant were built, and from that time the town's heavy industry grew rapidly. From 1892 to 1897 the population of Mariiupil almost doubled, from 17,000 to 32,000. About half of it was Ukrainian and Russian, 28 percent Greek, and 21 percent Jewish. By the beginning of the First World War it had jumped to 110,000, and by 1921 it had fallen to 30,000. In the late 1920s the port was expanded to handle the Donets Basin's increased output, and the Azovstal Metallurgical Plant, one of the largest in the Soviet Union, was built. The Mariiupil region became, after the Donets Basin and the Dnieper Industrial Region, the third-largest center of heavy industry in Ukraine. By 1939 its population had reached 227,000. The city was heavily damaged during the war, and its population fell to 85,000 in 1943.

Today Mariiupil has many metallurgical and heavy-machine-building plants, a coke refinery, and a large food industry. Its port is second only to Odessa's in Ukraine. The use of icebreakers enables it to remain open year-round. Known as 'the ocean gateway of the Donbas,' Mariiupil is used by Ukraine to export coal, metals, grain, salt, and machines and to import iron ore, manganese ore, and cement. Its importance as a shipping outlet increased with the completion of the Volga–Don Canal, which linked the Sea of Azov with Moscow and the Caspian Sea. After the Second World War the seacoast near Mariiupil was developed into a resort area specializing in climatological and mud therapy. Mariiupil is one of the most polluted cities in Ukraine. Its heavy industry is largely responsible for polluting the Sea of Azov.

Mariiupil Azovstal Metallurgical Plant (Mariiupil-skyi metalurhiinyi zavod Azovstal. One of the largest ferrous metallurgical plants in Ukraine. Located in Mariiupil, it uses iron ore from the Kerch Iron-ore Basin and coal from the Donets Basin. The construction of the plant began in 1930. Most of its machines and equipment were imported from the United States, and American engineers took part in building the plant. The first blast furnace went into operation in 1933, and the first Martin gas furnace in 1935. By 1941 the plant had four blast furnaces and six Martin gas furnaces. After the war the plant was reconstructed. In 1948 a large blooming, rail, and girder mill – the largest mill in Ukraine and one of the largest in the Soviet Union – was opened. As a result the plant could carry out a complete metallurgical cycle. In October 1953 a large rolling mill was added. By 1959 the plant had 6 blast furnaces and 12 Martin furnaces, and in 1961 the Martin furnace shop was reconstructed and expanded. The plant's steel output is still insufficient, and its quality is low because of phosphorus content in the ore. Since 1958 the plant has used a special flux agglomerate delivered in a hot state by sea from the Komysh-Buruny Iron-ore Complex. The plant produces such products as rails, poles, stands, girders, and structural forms for buildings and bridges.

Mariiupil burial site. A late Neolithic tribal burial site from the 3rd or 4th millennium BC, located near the city of Mariiupil. It was excavated in 1930 by M. *Makarenko, who published a monograph about his findings in 1933. The site included approx 120 skeletons buried three-deep with their heads oriented toward the east or west. The grave pits were covered by an elongated wooden vault to which sections were added as needed. Traces of red ocher, evidently used in burial rites, were found on half the skeletons. Stone utensils and adornments made from shells and the teeth of animals were also uncovered. Similar burial sites were found in the lower Dnieper area after the Second World War.

Mariiupil Heavy-Machine-Building Plant (Mariiupilskyi zavod vazhkoho mashynobuduvannia). A major factory of Ukraine's machine-building industry, located in Mariiupil. It was organized in 1958 out of the machine-building division of the Mariiupil Metallurgical Plant, which built railway tankers. It was the only plant in the USSR that made railway tankers for transporting oil, chemicals, natural gas, food products, and other goods. Its also produces machinery and equipment for the metallurgical, shipbuilding, and mining industries and for hydroelectric stations. In the early 1970s the plant employed over 5,500 workers.

Mariiupil Iron-ore Deposit. An ore source in Donetske oblast 20 km west of Mariiupil. The deposit covers an area of approx 150 sq km and consists of iron quartzites (principally magnetite) with an iron content of 20–30 percent. The seams, 20–160 m thick, are found 80–600 m underground and can be mined by open-pit or deep-shaft methods. The ores contain few impurities and are easily concentrated. The deposit was discovered in 1963 but has yet to be exploited. It is a potential source of iron ore for the nearby iron and steel center of Mariiupil.

Mariiupil Metallurgical Institute (Mariiupilskyi metalurhiinyi instytut). A higher educational institution, until 1992 under the Ministry of Higher and Secondary Specialized Education of the Ukrainian SSR. It was established in 1930 as an evening school of metallurgy, and in 1939 it acquired a day division. The institute has seven faculties, including metallurgy, technology, energy, and welding, and an evening and graduate school. In 1979 its enrollment was about 6,000.

Mariiupil Metallurgical Plant (Mariiupilskyi metalurhiinyi zavod). A major factory of the metallurgical industry, located in Mariiupil (until 1989, Zhdanov), Donetske oblast. The factory was built in 1897 by the Nykopil-Mariiupil Mining and Metallurgical Company. A second metallurgical factory, called Providence, was built in Mariiupil in 1899. The two plants were nationalized and merged in 1919 to form the Mariiupil Association of State Metallurgical Plants. The plant received its present name in 1924.

In the interwar period the plant produced extrastrength and ironclad steel, new types of pipes, and the first pipes for boreholes in the USSR. The plant was destroyed during the Second World War and then rebuilt. At first it built railway tankers. In 1958 the Mariiupil Heavy-Machine-Building Plant was founded on the basis of the machine-building division of the metallurgical plant. Now the plant produces cast iron, steel, rolled steel, sheet metal, pipes, and other products. In 1970 it employed almost 5,000 workers and was one of the largest metallurgical plants in Ukraine.

Marine Hydrophysical Institute of the Academy of Sciences of Ukraine (Morskyi hidrofizychnyi instytut ANU). A physical oceanography research institute based in the Crimea since 1963, in Sevastopil and Katsyveli near Simeiz. Its predecessor was the Marine Hydrophysical Station (est 1929), which came under the Marine Hydrophysical Institute of the Academy of Sciences of the USSR in 1948 (transferred to the AN URSR [now ANU] in 1961). The institute consists of 15 departments, an experimental station, and a construction shop. The main areas of study are circulation in the world's oceans, interaction between the atmosphere and the oceans, surface and deep oceanic waves, and ocean turbulences. The institute operates a Black Sea research ship *Muksun* and the far-ranging oceanic research vessels *Akademik Vernadskyi* and *Mikhail Lomonosov*. It also owns various major testing facilities, including a very large wave tank, for the study of storm systems and uses computer modeling to produce oceanic maps. The institute took part in an international project to study the Caribbean Sea and the Gulf of Mexico (MOCARIB) and in a joint project with the United States to study the dynamics of oceans (POLIMODE).

Marinka [Marjinka]. VI-18, DB IV-3. A city (1990 pop 10,900) on the Osykova River and a raion center in Donetske oblast. It was founded in the 1840s, and attained city status in 1977. Marinka has a tire manufacturing and repair plant and a food industry.

Maritchak, Oleksander [Maritčak] (Maritczak), b 18 September 1887 in Stryi, Galicia, d 1 October 1981 in Detroit, Michigan. Lawyer, political figure, and educator; member of the Shevchenko Scientific Society from 1918. A graduate of Lviv University (LL D, 1909), he opened his own law office in Rudky in 1918. During the November

Oleksander Maritchak

uprising he was elected county commissioner and member of the Ukrainian National Rada in Stanyslaviv. With the collapse of the Western Ukrainian National Republic he emigrated to Vienna, where he became secretary of the Western Ukrainian League of Nations Society (1921–4) and studied international law. Upon returning to Lviv in 1923, he resumed his law practice and taught international law at the Lviv (Underground) Ukrainian University. He often acted as defense counsel in political trials. He sat on the presidium of the Ukrainian People's Labor party and then on the presidium and CC of the Ukrainian National Democratic Alliance. During the Soviet occupation of Galicia he headed the department of international law at Lviv University. After emigrating in 1944, he taught international law at the Ukrainian Higher School of Economics in Munich and then (1949) resettled in the United States. He was active in the Ukrainian community in Detroit, where he served as president of the local Self-Reliance Credit Union.

Markelov, Hryhorii (Grigorii), b 7 February 1880 in Perm, Russia, d 8 April 1952 in Odessa. Neurologist; full member of the AN URSR (now ANU) from 1939. A graduate of Odessa University (1906), he taught at the Odessa Medical Institute (from 1918) and in 1927 became chairman of a department there. From 1930 he was director of the Odessa Psychoneurological Scientific Research Institute. His work dealt with the normal and diseased state of the autonomic nervous system, methods for studying patients, the pathology of brain vessels, neurological disorders associated with malaria, and the effect of external factors, such as light, on physiological processes. He wrote *Zabolevaniia vegetativnoi sistemy* (Diseases of the Autonomic System, 1948).

Markevych, Andrii [Markevyč, Andrij], b 21 November 1830 in Poltava gubernia, d 24 March 1907 in St Petersburg. Jurist and music ethnographer; son of M. *Markevych. An official of a juridical department in St Petersburg, he attained the rank of full councillor and the office of senator. He was an assistant of the curator of the Imperial Philanthropic Society and vice-president of the Russian Music Society. He became acquainted with T. Shevchenko in 1858 in Moscow and corresponded with him. From 1898 he presided over the Shevchenko Society in St Petersburg, which supported poor Ukrainians studying in the city. Markevych obtained permission to use Shevchenko's manuscripts in the archives of the police's

Third Section for the first full publication of *Kobzar* (ed V. Domanytsky, 1907). He arranged the music to 25 Ukrainian folk songs, which appeared in P. Kulish's *Zapiski o Iuzhnoi Rusi* (Notes on Southern Rus', vol 2, 1857), and compiled the collection *Narodnye ukrainskie napevy, polozhennye na fortepiano* (Ukrainian Folk Melodies Arranged for Piano, 1860).

Markevych, Hryhorii [Markevyč, Hryhorij], b 1849 in Voronky, Lokhvytsia county, Poltava gubernia, d 1923. Civic leader, educator, and writer. A graduate of the Kiev Theological Academy (1871), he was an inspector at the Poltava Girl's School and served on Poltava's municipal council. He organized a printing press and bookstore in the city, where he published the newspaper *Ridnyi krai*, Ukrainian textbooks, and the works of Ukrainian writers, such as I. Tobilevych, M. Kropyvnytsky, and A. Kashchenko. He was one of the initiators of the Kotliarevsky monument and school in Poltava. His writings include a study of the elective principle in the Ukrainian church and some poetry.

Mykola Markevych (portrait by L. Zhemchuzhnikov, 1861)

Markevych, Mykola [Markevyč] (Markevich, Nikolai), b 7 February 1804 in Dunaiets, Hlukhiv county, Chernihiv gubernia, d 21 June 1860 in Turivka, Pryluka county, Poltava gubernia. Historian, ethnographer, poet, musician, and composer. He studied in St Petersburg at the boarding school of the Pedagogical Institute (1817–20), where he befriended M. Glinka. He served as an officer in the Russian army (1820–4) and later studied piano and composition under J. Field in Moscow. Markevych was close to Decembrist literary circles (eg, A. Pushkin, K. Ryleev). In 1829 his collections *Elegii i evreiskiia melodii* (Elegies and Jewish Melodies) and *Stikhotvoreniia eroticheskiia i Parizina*

(Erotic Poems and [a translation of Byron's poem] *Parisina*) were published in Moscow, and in 1831 his collection of Romantic ballads about Ukraine's heroic past, *Ukrainskiia melodii* (Ukrainian Melodies), was published there. From 1830 Markevych lived on his estate in Turivka and collected materials on the history of Ukraine, particularly those found in archives in Chernihiv and Poltava gubernias, and Ukrainian folklore and folk songs. In 1836 he published the first volume of a historical, mythological, and statistical dictionary of the Russian Empire.

The then unpublished *Istoriia Rusov* had a significant impact on Markevych's major work, the five-volume *Istoriia Malorossii* (History of Little Russia), published in Moscow in 1842–3. Vols 3–5 contain valuable documentary addenda, notes, source descriptions, lists of regiments, the General Officer Staff, and colonels in the Hetman state, of companies at the Zaporozhian Sich, and of the Ukrainian higher clergy, and chronological tables. In his monograph Markevych approached the history of Ukraine as an independent, uninterrupted process from earliest times to the late 18th century. Markevych's history greatly influenced 19th-century Ukrainian historiography and his Romantic contemporaries, particularly his friend T. Shevchenko. Among Markevych's other historical writings the most noteworthy are on Hetman I. Mazepa (*Maiak*, 1841), the hetmancy of Ya. Barabash (*Russkii vestnik*, 1841, no. 2), the first Little Russian hetmans and official documents explaining the history of Little Russia (*Chteniia v Moskovskom obshchestve istorii i drevnostei rossiiskikh*, 1848, no. 8), and the Cossacks (ibid, 1858, no. 4).

Among Markevych's ethnographic writings are a larger work on Little Russian customs, beliefs, cuisine, and beverages (1860) and compilations of Little Russian songs (1840) and 'South Russian' (ie, Ukrainian) songs (1857). Many of Markevych's works have not been published. His personal archive (including his diary) is preserved at the Institute of Russian Literature in St Petersburg. His valuable annotated collection of 6,550 documents from the 16th to 18th centuries is in the State Library in Moscow. Ya. Shchapov and I. Kudriavtseva's annotated bibliography of Markevych's and I. Lukashevych's collections of manuscript books in that library was published in Moscow in 1959. A biography of Markevych by E. Kosachevskaia was published in Leningrad in 1987.

O. Ohloblyn

Markevych, Oleksander [Markevyč], b 9 April 1894 in Troitske, Vasylkiv county, Kiev gubernia, d 5 February 1978 in Kiev. Folk singer and kobzar. After losing his eyesight in the First World War, he learned to play the kobza and bandura and developed an extensive repertoire of dumas, historical songs, psalms, and musical renditions, often his own, of poems by T. Shevchenko, S. Rudansky, and L. Hlibov. In 1939 he took part in the First Republican Conference of Kobzars and Lirnyks and joined the State Kobzar Ensemble. In the 50 years of his career he visited almost every village of the Kiev region.

Markevych, Oleksander [Markevyč], b 19 March 1905 in Ploske, Tarashcha county, Kiev gubernia. Zoologist; full member of the AN URSR (now ANU) since 1957 (corresponding member from 1948). He graduated from the Kiev Institute of People's Education (1930) and worked in Leningrad (1930–5) before becoming an associate of the

Oleksander Markevych   Rev Yosafat Ivan Markevych
(1905–)

ANU Institute of Zoology in 1935 and its director in 1948–50. From 1970 he was affiliated with the ANU Institute of Hydrobiology. Markevych also taught and held several administrative positions at Kiev University (1935–61), and he organized the Ukrainian Parasitology Society in 1945. His principal research was on parasitology, the zoology of invertebrates, the phylogeny of animals, and the history of zoology. His major publications include *Osnovy parazytolohii* (The Principles of Parasitology, 1950) and *Filoheniia tvarynnoho svitu* (The Phylogeny of the Animal World, 1964).

Markevych, Oleksii [Markevyč, Oleksij], b 1847 in Smosh, Pryluka county, Poltava gubernia, d 18 June 1903 in Odessa. Historian and community figure; full member of the Shevchenko Scientific Society (NTSh) from 1901. He studied at the Nizhen Lyceum, graduated from Odessa University (1869), and taught Russian history in gymnasiums in Odessa and Tahanrih before becoming a docent (1880–8) and professor (1888–95) at Odessa University. He was forced to retire from the university after he was accused of spreading Ukrainophile propaganda. He remained an active member of the Odessa Society of History and Antiquities and the Tavriia Scholarly Archival Commission. A specialist on the history of Muscovy and Southern Ukraine, he wrote monographs on the Muscovite service nobility (PH D diss, 1879) and the Rus' chronicles (2 vols, 1883, 1885) and contributed articles to *Kievskaia starina*, *Zapysky NTSh*, and *Zapiski Odesskago obshchestva istorii i drevnostei*, which published a bibliography of his works in vol 26.

Markevych, Yosafat Ivan [Markevyč, Josafat], b 1880 near Kańczuga, Przeworsk county, Galicia, d 31 January 1959 in Chicago. Basilian monk and Catholic activist of Polish descent. He was introduced to the Basilian order while attending a gymnasium in Buchach and then continued his studies at the Jesuit seminary in Innsbruck, where he was ordained in 1904 and completed a DD in 1911. He was a leading organizer of the *Marian societies movement in Galicia and a regular contributor to various Catholic journals for youth (*Postup* and *Nash pryiatel'*). After the Second World War he moved to the United States, where he was less active owing to failing health.

Markina, Valentyna, b 24 December 1910 in Teplivka, Pyriatyn county, Poltava gubernia, d 24 July 1990 in Kiev. Historian. She studied at the Moscow Pedagogical Institute (1933–7) and taught medieval history at the Izhevsk Pedagogical Institute in the Udmurt ASSR (1937–45). In 1945 she received a candidate's degree from Moscow University and began teaching at Kiev University. From 1961 to 1984 she chaired the department of ancient and medieval history, and in 1963 she became a professor. Markina wrote monographs on magnates' estates in Right-Bank Ukraine in the second half of the 18th century (doctoral diss, 1961) and the peasantry of Right-Bank Ukraine from the late 17th century to the 1860s (1971), and over 70 articles.

Markish, Perets [Markiš, Perec], b 7 December 1895 in Polonne, Novohrad-Volynskyi county, Volhynia gubernia, d 12 August 1952 in Moscow. Soviet Yiddish poet, novelist, and playwright. Markish began to publish in Yiddish in 1917 and with D. Hofstein and L. Kvitko formed the so-called Kiev lyric triad of Yiddish poets. His early poetry glorifies the new Soviet revolution. From 1921 to 1926 he lived in Poland and in France, and in 1926 he returned to the USSR. Markish wrote about industrialization, collectivization, and other aspects of life in the Soviet Union. Among his best-known works is the epic poem 'Brider' (Brothers, 1929). Markish was arrested in 1948 during the Zhdanov purge of Jewish culture and sentenced to death with other Yiddish cultural figures by a secret Military Collegium tribunal. He was executed in the Lubianka Prison. He was posthumously rehabilitated.

Markivka. IV-20. A town smt (1990 pop 7,900) on the Derkul River and a raion center in Luhanske oblast. It was founded in 1703 as a Cossack settlement and razed by Russian troops in 1709 for its part in K. Bulavin's uprising. It was rebuilt a generation later. In 1960 it attained smt status. The town has a food industry and a regional museum.

Markov, Dimitrii, b ?, d 26 July 1938 in Bratislava, Czechoslovakia. Lawyer, political leader, and publicist; son of O. and brother of Y. *Markov. A prominent Russophile leader in Galicia, he claimed that there were two Ruthenian peoples in Galicia, Russians and Ukrainians. In 1907 he was elected to the Austrian parliament, and in 1913, to the Galician Diet, where he was the sole Russophile among 31 Ukrainian deputies. In his works, such as *Die russische und ukrainische Idee in Österreich* (1908; 2nd edn 1912; trans into Russian 1915) and *Mémoire sur les aspirations nationales des petits-russiens de l'ancien empire austro-hongrois* (1918), he advocated a 'reunion' of Galicia with Russia. After the war he revised his views and co-operated with Ukrainian émigré circles.

Markov, Mykhailo, b ca 1760, d 1819. Historian and administrator. He was procurator of Chernihiv gubernia (1794–7), director of Ukrainian schools in Little Russia gubernia (1800), and director of the Chernihiv gymnasium (1805–19). His studies of the Chernihiv district were among the first attempts at writing detailed regional histories of Ukraine based on primary sources. His works include *O gorodakh i seleniiakh v Chernigovskoi gubernii, upominaemykh v Nestorovoi letopisi* (About Towns and Settlements in Chernihiv Gubernia, Mentioned in Nestor's Chronicle, 1813), an introduction to Little Russian (Ukrainian) history (published in *Ukrainskii vestnik*, 1817), an article on the important monuments of Chernihiv, and several unpublished items.

Markov, Osyp, b 1849 in Hrushova, Sambir circle, Galicia, d 10 November 1909 in Lviv. Russophile journalist; father of D. and Y. *Markov. As a student at the Academic Gymnasium in Lviv, he became involved with the Russophile press, working for the newspaper *Slovo* under the tutelage of B. Didytsky. In 1881 he started the weekly *Prolom, which eventually became a daily. Because of injunctions by the Ukrainian Catholic church against the publication, it appeared under a variety of names: *Novyi prolom* (1883–7), *Chervonaia Rus'* (1888–91), *Halytskaia Rus'* (1891–2), and *Halychanyn* (1893–1913). Markov also published the popular Russophile weekly *Russkoe slovo* (1890–1914).

Markov, Yosyp, b 25 October 1890 in Lviv, d 27 November 1976 in Bratislava. Jurist, pedagogue, and ethnographer; son of O. and brother of D. *Markov. He studied in Lviv (1913) and Rostov-na-Donu (1917) and worked in Paris, Vienna, and Mukachiv. He was a professor at Prague (from 1931) and Bratislava (1945–50, rector in 1948–9) universities, where his research centered on the legal history of Czechoslovakia, Yugoslavia, and Transcarpathia. His views changed from Russophilism to Ukrainian nationalism, and for that reason he was dismissed from the university. His works, based on extensive archival research, include studies of N. Gogol in Galician-Ruthenian literature (1913), A. Dobriansky (1930), and the social history (1930), customary law (1932), and folk art (1962) of 18th-century Transcarpathia.

Markovsky, Leonid [Markovs'kyj], b 21 November 1939 in Grodekovo, Primorskii krai, RSFSR. Organic chemist; AN URSR (now ANU) corresponding member since 1978 and full member since 1988. A graduate of the Lviv Polytechnical Institute (1961), since 1966 he has worked at the AN URSR Institute of Organic Chemistry. A specialist in organosulfur, organofluorine, and organophosphorus chemistry, he discovered reactions leading to compounds with multiple sulfur-nitrogen bonds and has developed additives to synthetic fibers and leather, foamed polyurethanes, and electrical insulators.

Markovsky, Mykhailo [Markovs'kyj, Myxajlo], b 20 November 1869 in Ksaverivka, Vasylkiv county, Kiev gubernia, d 30 June 1947 in Kiev. Literary scholar and critic. Markovsky lectured on Ukrainian literature and language at higher educational institutions and coedited the publications of the Historical-Philological Division of the VUAN. His most important works are studies on the baroque and modern periods of Ukrainian literature published in *Zapysky Istorychno-filolohichnoho viddilu VUAN*.

Markovsky, Yevhen [Markovs'kyj, Jevhen], b 18 November 1893 in Papuzhyntsi, Uman county, Kiev gubernia, d ? Literary scholar; son of M. *Markovsky. He worked in various VUAN historical institutes and wrote works on I. Kotliarevsky and A. Radyvylovsky, as well as a pioneering book on the Ukrainian *vertep (1929). He was arrested in 1932 during the Stalinist terror, and his further fate is unknown.

Markovych [Markovyč]. A family of Cossack *starshyna* of Jewish origin. It originated with Avraam in the early

17th century. His son, Marko (d 1712), was a wealthy rentier in Pryluka in the 1660s and Pryiatyn in 1683–5. Marko's daughter, Anastasiia (Nastia, 1671 to 30 December 1729), married Hetman I. Skoropadsky. Marko's sons were Andrii *Markovych, a colonel of Lubni regiment (1714–27) and general treasurer (1729–40) of the Hetman state; Ivan (d 30 October 1724), a captain of Pryluka company (1709–19) and judge (1719–24) of Pryluka regiment; and Fedir (d 1737 or 1738), a captain of Pryluka company (1719–24) and a fellow of the standard (1724–7). Andrii's son Yakiv *Markovych began the Chernihiv branch of the family, which includes his grandsons Yakiv *Markovych and Oleksander *Markovych. Semen, Andrii's other son, was a captain of Romen company in Lubni regiment (1731–8). His descendants are the ethnographer Opanas *Markovych and the writer Dmytro *Markovych. Fedir's descendants constituted the Pryluka branch of the family, who in the 19th century changed their name to Markevych. They include the historians Mykola *Markevych and Oleksii *Markevych, and Mykola's son, Andrii *Markevych. Andrii's grandsons are the pianist and composer Igor Markevitch (1912–83), who conducted the Montreal Symphony (1956–60) and several Western European orchestras, and his Swiss-born brother, Dmitry (b 1923), a cellist and the founder and director of the Higher Musical Institute in Montreux.

Markovych, Andrii [Markovyč, Andrij], b ca 1674 in Pryluka, d 23 January 1747 in Poharshchyna, Romen company, Lubni regiment. Senior official in the Hetman state; father of Ya. *Markovych. A captain of Hlukhiv company in Nizhen regiment (1701–14) and a notable military fellow (from 1708), he turned against Hetman I. Mazepa in 1708 and helped A. Menshikov's Russian army to capture Baturyn. In 1709 he was Peter I and Hetman I. Skoropadsky's envoy in Constantinople. For his loyal services he was awarded large estates and appointed colonel of Lubni regiment (1714–27). He was removed after court proceedings were initiated against his extreme maltreatment of his peasants. He was acquitted, however, because of pressure exerted by the Russian government and his sister, Anastasiia, Skoropadsky's wife. Despite opposition from Hetman D. Apostol he was appointed general treasurer (1729–40). He was accepted into the Russian nobility in 1736.

Markovych, Dmytro [Markovyč] (pen name: Olenin), b 8 November 1848 in Poltava, d December 1920 in Vinnytsia, Podilia gubernia. Jurist, civic and co-operative activist, and writer; nephew of Opanas *Markovych. He served as a court official in various localities of the Russian Empire – in Kherson, the Kuban, and Warsaw. In the early 1900s he retired to his estate in Mykhalkivtsi, Volhynia, and devoted himself to community service, co-operative and zemstvo affairs, and political activity. He became a member of the Society of Ukrainian Progressives. After moving to Vinnytsia he edited the weekly *Podil's'ka volia* (1917). During the revolutionary period he served as general procurator under the Central Rada, senator under the Hetman government, and minister of justice in S. Ostapenko's cabinet under the UNR Directory. His stories first appeared in the almanac *Step* in 1886 and were collected later under the title *Po stepakh ta khutorakh* (Through the Steppes and Homesteads, 1898; 2nd edn 1908). His complete works were published in two volumes in 1918–19.

Markovych, Lev [Markovyč], b 1881, d 1930. Civic and political leader in Volhynia; son of D. *Markovych. When his father moved to Vinnytsia in 1912, he managed the family estate in Mykhalkivtsi, near Ostrih. He served as president of the county school and sanitation-epidemic councils and was an honorary member of the Prosvita society. In 1922–8 he represented Ostrih county in the Polish Senate.

Markovych, Oleksander [Markovyč], b 31 July 1790 in Svarkove, Hlukhiv county, Novhorod-Siverskyi vicegerency, d 3 December 1865. Nobleman, historian, and civic figure in the Chernihiv region; brother of Ya. *Markovych. He graduated from Kharkiv University and then worked in Chernihiv gubernia as a registrar (1807–12), county judge in Hlukhiv (1820–1), general justice (1827–30), and marshal of the nobility (1826–7, 1832–8). In 1852 he submitted a proposal to the tsarist government for the emancipation of his 979 serfs and their right freely to purchase his land, but his request was refused. After the abolition of serfdom in 1861, he took an active part in implementing peasant reforms in Chernihiv gubernia. He built and funded a school for the peasants in Svarkove, paid their taxes, and maintained a hospital for syphilitics that was established by his grandfather. Markovych wrote a socioeconomic, historical, and statistical study of the Left-Bank gentry as an estate and their properties in Chernihiv gubernia, based on the archives of the Chernihiv Gentry Assembly (pub in a book of the Ministry of the Interior's materials on the statistics of the Russian Empire [vol 2] in 1841 and separately in 1894); a historical description of Hlukhiv (excerpts pub in O. Lazarevsky's work on Old Little Russia, vol 2, 1893); a history of the Hamaliivka monastery in Hlukhiv county (pub in F. Gumilevsky's history of Chernihiv eparchy, 1873); and a novelette about the 18th-century Cossack *starshyna*, 'Malorossiiskaia svad'ba' (Little Russian Wedding, pub in *Kievskaia starina* in 1897). Markovych also published nine historical documents from his family's archive in *Ukrainskii zhurnal* (1824) and a condensed version of the diary of his grandfather, Ya. *Markovych, in Russian translation (2 vols, 1859).

A. Zhukovsky

Opanas Markovych

Markovych, Opanas [Markovyč], b 8 February 1822 in Kulazhyntsi, Pryiatyn county, Poltava gubernia, d 1 September 1867 in Chernihiv. Ethnographer, composer, and civic figure; husband of M. *Vovchok. After graduating from Kiev University (1846) he was arrested for belonging to the *Cyril and Methodius Brotherhood and exiled to

Orel. Apart from a brief stay in St Petersburg (1860–1), where he worked on the journal *Osnova*, from 1851 he lived in Ukraine and collected folkloric and ethnographic materials. Many of them were published in collections edited by A. Metlynsky, M. Nomys, and V. Antonovych and M. Drahomanov or in journals and almanacs. He scored the music for I. Kotliarevsky's *Natalka Poltavka* (Natalka from Poltava, 1857) and K. Topolia's *Chary* (Charms, 1866) and staged these operettas in Chernihiv and Novhorod-Siverskyi. A collection of the materials gathered by Markovych and his wife, titled *Fol'klorni zapysy Marka Vovchka ta Opanasa Markovycha* (Folklore Notations of Marko Vovchok and Opanas Markovych), came out in 1983.

Markovych, Pavlo [Markovyč], b 19 November 1924 in Habura, Prešov region. Artist, pedagogue, and ethnographer. After completing his art education in Bratislava (1953) he taught art in a Prešov secondary school and then lectured at the pedagogical faculty of Šafařík University. His paintings consist mainly of landscapes and ethnographic sketches (ink, pastels, tempera, oils). He has held solo exhibitions in Svydnyk, Prešov, Bardejov, and Humenné. A specialist in Ukrainian embroidery and Easter eggs, he has written *Ukraïns'ki narodni khrestykovi vyshyvky Skhidnoï Slovachchyny* (Ukrainian Folk Cross-stitch Embroidery of Eastern Slovakia, 1964), *Ukraïns'ki pysanky Skhidnoï Slovachchyny* (Ukrainian Easter Eggs of Eastern Slovakia, 1972), and *Rusyn Easter Eggs from Eastern Slovakia* (1987). He emigrated to the United States in 1991.

Markovych, Petro [Markovyč], b 13 August 1937 in Chornoriky, Krosno county, Galicia. Painter, graphic artist, and ceramist. A graduate of the Lviv Institute of Applied and Decorative Arts (1965), he has experimented with styles such as postimpressionism and surrealism (eg, his paintings *Yellow Trees* [1961] and *Pale Blue Spring* [1971]). In his later compositions he has used images and colors as symbols. He has also produced decorative plates and reliefs (eg, *King Danylo* [1967]).

Markovych, Yakiv [Markovyč, Jakiv], b 17 October 1696 in Pryluka, d 20 November 1770 in Svarkove, Hlukhiv company, Nizhen regiment. Cossack *starshyna* in the Hetman state and writer; son of A. *Markovych. He studied at the Kievan Mohyla Academy, where he was a prize pupil of T. Prokopovych. He became a Cossack fellow of the standard in 1721 and served as acting colonel of Lubni regiment (1723–5) and general judge (1739) and general treasurer (1740, 1762) of the Hetman state. In 1714 he married Olena, the daughter of Hetman P. Polubotok. One of the more learned men of his time, he wrote prose and religious verse, composed valuable genealogical notes, and translated Latin writings. His most outstanding work was his diary of the years 1717–67, which contains a wealth of information about political, socioeconomic, cultural, and daily life in the Hetmanate. Until the 1930s the manuscript was preserved in Kiev in the library of the Historical Museum (vols 2–10) and the State Public Library (vol 1) of the Ukrainian SSR. An abridged version of the diary was published in Russian translation in 2 vols in 1859 by O. Markovych, Yakiv's grandson. A fuller, though incomplete, version for the years 1717–34, edited by O. Lazarevsky, was published in the original language as appendixes to *Kievskaia starina* from April

1891 to December 1896 and reprinted in 3 vols (1893, 1895, 1897). A similar version of the diary for the years 1735–40 was edited by V. Modzalevsky and published by the Archeographic Commission of the Shevchenko Scientific Society as vol 22 of *Zherela do istoriï Ukraïny-Rusy* (1913).

A. Zhukovsky

Markovych, Yakiv [Markovyč, Jakiv], b 27 October 1776 in Pyriatyn company, Lubni regiment, d 1804. Nobleman and historian; brother of O. *Markovych. He studied at the Hlukhiv boarding school and at Moscow University's boarding school. In 1795 he traveled throughout Left-Bank Ukraine, researching its geography and economy. From 1797 he was an interpreter in the College of Foreign Affairs in St Petersburg, where he was part of O. *Bezborodko and D. *Troshchynsky's coterie. On the basis of historical monuments and documents (including those provided by A. *Chepa) and of Slavic, French, Latin, and German sources, he wrote and published in St Petersburg the first part of his pioneering *Zapiski o Malorossii, eia zhiteliakh i proizvedeniiakh* (Notes on Little Russia, Its Inhabitants and Works, 1798). Written with obvious love for his native land, it provides information about the physical geography, folkways, folklore (especially songs), political structure, society, and economy of the 18th-century Hetman state, and about the Ukrainian language, ancient and medieval Ukrainian history and mythology (to the middle of the 11th century), and the origin of the Slavs and Rus'. The completion of Markovych's work, which made a significant impact on his contemporaries, was interrupted by his suicide. His archive has not been preserved.

Vasyl Markus

Markus, Vasyl [Markus', Vasyl'], b 27 December 1922 in Bedevlia, Máramúres county, Transcarpathia. Political scientist and activist; full member of the Shevchenko Scientific Society and the Ukrainian Academy of Arts and Sciences in the US. After studying Slavics at the Ukrainian Free University (PH D, 1948) and law at the University of Paris (PH D, 1956), he taught Russian at Notre Dame University (1959–62) and political science at Loyola University in Chicago (1962–88). He collaborated for many years on *Entsyklopedia ukraïnoznavstva* (Encyclopedia of Ukraine, 10 vols, 1955–84) and was an editor of *Ukraine: A Concise Encyclopedia* (vol 2, 1971) and an associate editor of the first two volumes of *Encyclopedia of Ukraine* (1984–8). He heads the encyclopedia of the Ukrainian diaspora project and is active in the Ukrainian Catholic church and other Ukrainian organizations. Besides numerous articles on current and historical themes he has written the monographs *L'incorporation de l'Ukraine subcarpathique à l'Ukraine soviétique, 1944–5* (1956) and *L' Ukraine soviétique dans les relations internationales et son statut en droit international, 1918–1923* (1959).

Markush, Oleksander [Markuš], b 2 November 1891 in Khust, Transcarpathia, d 27 October 1971 in Khust. Writer and pedagogue. From 1910 to 1939 he worked as an elementary school teacher and then as a school inspector. He was editor of the children's magazine *Nash ridnyi krai* (1922–38) and published many readers and textbooks. His short stories were published in several collections: *Vymirialy zemliu* (They Surveyed the Land, 1925), *Irynu zasvataly* (They Got Iryna Engaged, 1941), *Korovku hnaly* (They Drove the Little Cow, 1943), *Maramors'ki opovidannia* (Maramureş Stories, 1956), and *Lyst materi* (A Letter to Mother, 1963). He also wrote two novels, *Iulyna* (1942) and *Mriinyky* (Daydreamers, 1961).

Marl. A term applied to a great variety of sediments and rocks which contain an earthy mixture of fine-grained minerals. They normally consist of calcium carbonate (calcite) or magnesium carbonate and clayey minerals, and they are commonly used as building material or (in the case of marls with a high carbonate content) in the manufacture of cement. In Ukraine marls occur among sediments from various ages (most frequently from the Upper Cretaceous period) in Volhynia, the Chernihiv region, the Donetske Basin, the Crimea, the Dniester River Basin, and other regions. Marl deposits near Amvrosiivka and Karpivka, in Donetske oblast (one of the largest marl deposits in the world), and near Novorosiiske, in Krasnodar krai, have significant industrial importance, particularly in the cement industry.

Marmarosh region. See Maramureş region.

Marples, David, b 17 October 1952 in Chesterfield, England. Specialist in Soviet Ukrainian energy policy and economics. A graduate of the University of Alberta (1980) and the University of Sheffield (PH D, 1985), he has worked as a research analyst for Radio Liberty in Munich, as a publications editor and research associate of the Canadian Institute of Ukrainian Studies, and as a professor (since 1991) in the department of history at the University of Alberta. He has written *Chernobyl and Nuclear Power in the USSR* (1986), *The Social Impact of the Chernobyl Disaster* (1988), and *Ukraine under Perestroika: Ecology, Economics, and the Workers' Revolt* (1991).

Marriage. The state in which a man and a woman are formally united for the purpose of living together (usually in order to procreate), and by virtue of which they establish legal rights and obligations with respect to each other. In Ukraine, as everywhere in the former USSR, a marriage was considered valid only if it was registered with the *ZAHS, the civil registry. The legal age for marriage in Ukraine is 18 for men and 17 for women. Entrance into marriage is marked by the acceptance of certain moral, social, and economic obligations. Though the rights and obligations of both spouses are not as clearly defined as they are in the marriage contract in Western countries, full equality in rights and obligations (eg, equality in the ownership of property and equal rights in the raising and support of children) is presumed. The principle of the economic equality of spouses becomes apparent during divorce, when the division of property is carried out according to that principle irrespective of actual income. Spouses also have an equal responsibility to render each other and their children financial assistance.

Marriage between close relatives is not permitted, nor is marriage to a mentally ill person who has been declared legally incompetent or to a person already married. In the 1940s and 1950s, marriage to a foreigner was forbidden in the USSR, and such marriages are still hindered by a range of administrative formalities (eg, the need to obtain the necessary certificates and visas). The prevention of a marriage on the grounds of religion, nationality, or race is legally forbidden. Likewise, it is forbidden for parents or the civil authorities to force or prevent a marriage.

Before the Revolution of 1917 civil marriages did not exist. Marriages had to be concluded in religious institutions, usually in a church with a service conducted by a priest. Although divorce was legal, it occurred rarely because it was virtually impermissible in the eyes of the ecclesiastical tribunal that decided such matters. The parents of the bride and groom played a significant role in the conclusion of the marriage by giving their blessing (that is, permitting the marriage) and by taking part in all discussions concerning the household, such as of the bride's dowry and groom's property. As a rule the wife moved into the home of the husband, where she was subservient not only to the husband's parents but to all his relatives.

The Central Rada passed legislation allowing civil marriage and divorce. After the establishment of Soviet rule church weddings were abolished, government registration of marriages was introduced, and divorce was made relatively easy. The first Soviet decrees on marriage in Ukraine were issued on 20 February 1919; they recognized common-law marriages as well as registered marriages. Those laws, together with the quick destruction of the traditions of the old society, resulted in a significant change in the character of marriage, especially in the cities, and also in a noticeable weakening of the marriage bond. Demographic changes in the structure of the population, the increased number of urban dwellers, and the waning influence of religion all gave rise to a decrease in the number of marriages. But the decrease was offset by factors conducive to the growth of the marriage rate, such as the simplification of the procedure for marrying and the increasing economic independence of young people. Thus, whereas between 1911 and 1914 there were 7.9 marriages per 1,000 inhabitants in Ukraine, by 1926 the figure had grown to 12.1 (see table 1). At the same time the length of married life increased as a result of the decrease in mortality. In the 1920s a Ukrainian woman who had reached the age of 15 would spend 29 years, or 58 percent of her remaining life, married. In the 1920s, changes in the marriage law and changing conceptions of morality also resulted in a rapid increase in the number of divorces.

Because of the growth in the number of divorces and the large numbers of male deaths during the terror of the 1930s and the Second World War, the length of time women remained married had decreased to 25.6 years by 1958–9. Thereafter the figure increased gradually, and it had reached 31.3 years by 1979.

TABLE 1
Marriages and divorces in Ukraine (per 1,000 inhabitants), 1886–95 to 1990

Year	Marriages	Divorces
1886–1895	9.0	–
1896–1910	8.5	–
1911–1914	7.9	–
1926	12.1	1.9
1940	7.3	0.9
1950	11.7	0.3
1960	10.7	1.2
1970	9.8	2.9
1980	9.3	3.6
1990	9.3	3.7

In the mid-1930s the Soviet regime took measures to strengthen the stability of the family. The family was assigned an increasingly critical role in sustaining new patterns of authority, maintaining high birthrates, and maximizing the productivity of the labor force by accommodating itself to female employment. While working outside the home, however, wives were still expected to provide a full range of domestic services. The intensification of the state's demands on the family was accompanied by greater state regulation. The state forbade *abortion and made *divorce more difficult to obtain by introducing court proceedings. In 1944 common-law marriage was invalidated.

During the 1960s, limitations on divorce were gradually relaxed, and a fairly rapid rise in the divorce rate ensued. At the same time, as in the West, the age at which people first married increased, to an average of 24 for men and 22 for women. The number of people married, divorced, or widowed has also increased (see table 2), as has the number of births to young parents and of illegitimate births. Premarital relations have increasingly become the norm, and the three-generation patriarchal family has been replaced by the nuclear family.

The integration of Ukraine into the USSR and the consequent large-scale in-migration of Russians have resulted in a rapid rise in ethnic intermarriage, which Soviet authorities encouraged as a way of promoting Russification and hailed as a virtual act of internationalism. Whereas in 1927 ethnically mixed marriages constituted only 6.5 percent of all marriages in Ukraine, in 1979 they constituted 21.9 percent. In 1979, 30 percent of all urban and 9.3 percent of all rural marriages were between members of dif-

TABLE 2
Ukraine's population aged 16 and over by marital state (per 1,000 inhabitants), 1926–89

Year	Married	Never married	Widowed	Divorced
Males				
1926	678	276	41	5
1979	744	201	24	29
1989	743	177	30	46
Females				
1926	613	220	157	10
1979	588	138	205	67
1989	605	119	193	79

ferent nationalities. In 1979, 63 percent of all marriages were between partners both of whom listed Ukrainian as their nationality.

BIBLIOGRAPHY

Pustokhod, P.; Tratsevs'kyi, M. 'Shliubnist' na Ukraïni,' *Demohrafichnyi zbirnyk*, vol 7 (1930)

Hurevych, Z.; Vorozhbyt, A. *Stateve zhyttia selianky* (Kharkiv 1931)

Chuiko, L. *Braki i razvody: Demograficheskoe issledovanie na primere Ukrainskoi SSR* (Moscow 1975)

Ponomarev, A. *Mezhnatsional'nye braki v USSR i protsess internatsionalizatsii* (Kiev 1983)

– *Razvitie sem'i i brachno-semeinykh otnoshenii na Ukraine (etnosotsal'nye problemy)* (Kiev 1989)

A. Babyonyshev, B. Krawchenko

Members of MARS. From left: Borys Antonenko-Davydovych, Hryhorii Kosynka, Mariia Halych, Yevhen Pluzhynyk, Valeriian Pidmohylny, Teodosii Osmachka

MARS (Maisternia revoliutsiinoho slova [Workshop of the Revolutionary Word]). A literary organization established in 1924 in Kiev under the name Lanka; it adopted its new name in 1926. It included a group of talented writers of varying literary predilections who were united by their desire to be independent of official politics in the area of literature. They included B. Antonenko-Davydovych, M. Ivchenko, Ya. Kachura, H. Kosynka, T. Osmachka, V. Pidmohylny, Ye. Pluzhnyk, Ya. Savchenko, and B. Teneta. They were all also members of the editorial board of *Zhyttia i revoliutsiia*. Together with the *Neoclassicists, for a long time they continued their opposition to the politicization of literature. They were forced to disband in 1929. Most of the members were executed during the Stalinist terror; Osmachka managed to emigrate at the end of the Second World War, and B. Antonenko-Davydovych was persecuted until his death in Kiev in 1984. In the late 1980s all of the members were rehabilitated, and their works began to be republished.

Marshal (*marshalok*). The title of several high state officials in the Polish Commonwealth and the Grand Duchy of Lithuania. As early as the 13th century, the royal (*koronnyi*) marshal was the highest minister of the king. His deputy was called court (*nadvornyi*) marshal. From Poland the term spread to the Lithuanian court. The marshal of the land (*marshalok zemskyi*) was the highest official of the grand duke's court. He was in charge of etiquette at the court and in the diet. In the duke's absence he represented the ruler in the Council of Lords. He was assisted by the court (*dvornyi*) marshal, who headed the court servitors. The *hospodarski* marshals were lower government officials who also had some judicial responsibilities. In Russian-ruled Ukraine in the late 18th (after 1785) and in the 19th century, marshals were presidents of elected gubernial or county noble assemblies. They represented the local nobility before the tsar and Senate, and carried out some administrative functions at the local level.

Marshal-commissioner court (*marshalkivsko-komisarskyi sud*). An appellate court in Left-Bank Ukraine that heard appeals of decisions of the **pidkomorski* courts. The courts evolved from the marshal and commissioner courts, which were central state institutions in the Grand Duchy of Lithuania. Their decisions could be appealed directly to the grand duke. Marshal-commissioner courts consisted of the county marshal of the nobility, who presided over the court, and commissioners appointed by the hetman or Little Russian Collegium. According to the Lithuanian Statute, their decisions could not be contested. From 1801 their rulings could be appealed to the General Little Russian Court or the Russian Senate, if the commissioners were appointed without the consent of both parties. The marshal-commissioner courts were abolished in 1861.

Marshall, Joseph, b and d ? 18th-century English traveler and writer. His *Travels through Holland, Flanders, Germany, Denmark, Sweden, Lapland, Russia, the Ukraine, and Poland in the Years 1768, 1769, and 1770* (3 vols, 1772; repr edn of vol 3 as *Travels through Germany, Russia, and Poland in the Years 1769 and 1770*, 1971) provided an account of Ukraine as a particularly rich and fertile region, with a high degree of agricultural productivity.

Marshes. See Wetlands.

Apolinarii Marshynsky   Ivan Martiuk

Marshynsky, Apolinarii [Maršyns'kyj, Apolinarij], b 1865, d 30 July 1929 in Prague. Civic leader, financial expert, and educator. A civil servant in the Russian finance ministry, he worked in St Petersburg, Latvia, and Estonia, where he organized a Ukrainian hromada in Dorpat. In

1917 he was director of the Department of Financial Affairs in the General Secretariat of the Central Rada, and in 1919, UNR deputy minister of finance. From 1924 he lectured at the Ukrainian Pedagogical Institute in Prague. His recollections about the 1880s were published in the 1923 *Dnipro* calendar.

Martel, Antoine, b 2 February 1899 in Baume-les-Dames, Doubs, d 12 October 1931 in Besançon, France. French Slavist. A graduate of the School of Oriental Studies in Paris (1924), from 1927 he taught Russian and Polish languages and literatures at the University of Lille and published a chronicle of Ukrainian publications in *Revue des études slaves*. His posthumously published book, *La Langue polonaise dans le Pays des Ruthènes* (1939), is one of the most important surveys of the history of 16th- and 17th-century literary Ukrainian.

Martel, René, b 23 August 1893 in Baume-les-Dames, Doubs, France, d 6 January 1976 in Paris. French historian and publicist. He taught history in lycées in Sens, Chartres, and Paris (Montaigne) and was a professor at Ljubljana University (1926–9). He cotranslated (with S. Borschak) T. Shevchenko's *Ivan Hus* into French (1930) and wrote *Vie de Mazeppa* (with E. Borschak, 1931; Ukrainian trans 1933), *La question d'Ukraine* (1927), *Les Blancs Russes* (1929), *La France et la Pologne: Réalités de l'Est Européen* (1931, using Ukrainian documents), *La Ruthénie Subcarpathique* (1935), *Le problème de l'Ukraine* (1938), and 'La politique allemande en Ukraine' (in *L'Allemagne contemporaine*, 1939). He also contributed articles to *Le Monde slave* on L. Léger (1929), D. Bahalii (1932), Soviet nationality policy in Ukraine (1934), Ukrainian proverbs (1935), Transcarpathia in the Middle Ages (1936), Ukraine after the Battle of Poltava (1937), and E. Borschak's book on Napoleon and Ukraine (1938).

Martiuk, Ivan [Martjuk], b 19 September 1889 in Skala, Borshchiv county, Galicia, d 26 April 1972 in Świdnica, Wrocław county, Poland. The chief organizer of Sich societies in the Borshchiv region. During the First World War he served in the Austrian army and the Ukrainian Galician Army. After returning to civilian life he was director of the County Union of Co-operatives in Kopychyntsi until 1930 and then a founder and director of **Tsentrosoiuz in Lviv. As the union's chief manager of farm-product export he visited various European countries and served as vice-chairman of the State Exporting Board. His *Tsentrosoiuz: Soiuz kooperatyvnykh soiuziv u L'vovi v rokakh 1924–1944* (Tsentrosoiuz: The Union of Co-operative Unions in Lviv in 1924–1944, 1973) is a valuable historical account based on his recollections.

Marton, Ishtvan, b 24 November 1923 in Sofiia, Bereg county, Transcarpathia. Ukrainian composer of Hungarian descent. He graduated from the Uzhhorod Music School (1949) and subsequently became a lecturer and concertmaster there. From 1975 he was musical director of the Hungarian folk ensemble of the Transcarpathian Philharmonic Orchestra. His works include the musical comedy *Konvaliï tsvitut' dlia tebe* (The Lilies of the Valley Bloom for You, 1963), the vocal suite *Wreath of Immortality* (1963), pieces for choir, and arrangements of Ukrainian and Hungarian folk songs.

Martos. A family of Cossack *starshyna* in the Poltava region. Its Lubni branch originated with the Lokhvytsia Cossack Vasyl in the 17th century. His sons were Martyn (d 1708), a captain of Lokhvytsia company (1693–8) and a judge of Lubni regiment (1698–1706), and Pavlo (d 1745), a captain of Lokhvytsia company (1699–1708, 1710–20) and quartermaster (1712–37) and acting colonel (1728–30) of Lubni regiment, who was imprisoned in 1708–9 for siding with Hetman I. Mazepa against Peter I. Later an Andrii Martos was osaul of Lubni regiment (1772–81), and Petro Martos (b 1809), a noble with estates in Lokhvytsia and Lubni counties, paid for the publication of T. *Shevchenko's *Kobzar* in 1840 (Shevchenko dedicated his poem 'Tarasova nich' [Taras's Night] to him). The Pryluka branch of the Martos family originated with Petro, an otaman of Ichnia company (1756). His son was the sculptor Ivan *Martos, and his grandson was the historian Oleksii *Martos. Other members of the branch included the government official Ivan *Martos and the political leader Borys *Martos.

Borys Martos

Ivan Martos: monument for Hetman Kyrylo Rozumovsky's grave in Baturyn (1803–5)

Martos, Borys, b 1 June 1879 in Horodyshche, Kremenchuk county, Poltava gubernia, d 19 September 1977 in Union, New Jersey. Political leader, co-operative organizer, and educator; full member of the Shevchenko Scientific Society from 1948. As a student at Kharkiv University he was active in the clandestine Ukrainian student hromada and collaborated with the Revolutionary Ukrainian party. For these activities he was arrested three times. In 1905 he joined the Ukrainian Social Democratic Workers' party and became involved in the revolutionary movement in Kharkiv and Liubotyn. He was not permitted to teach after graduating in 1908, so he worked as a co-operative instructor in Volhynia (1910–11), a financial director of the Black Sea–Kuban Railway Board, a director of the Kuban Co-operative Bank, and a co-operative inspector of the Poltava gubernia zemstvo (1913–17). During the revolutionary period he was a member of the Central Rada and the Little Rada and served on its General Secretariat, first

as secretary and then as deputy secretary of agrarian affairs. Under the Hetman government he retired from political life and devoted himself to the co-operative movement: he chaired the executive of the Central Ukrainian Co-operative Committee and the board of directors of Dniprosoiuz, lectured at the Kiev Commercial Institute, and organized the Co-operative Institute in Kiev. Under the UNR Directory he served in V. Chekhivsky's cabinet as minister of food supplies and then as premier and finance minister (April–August 1919). In 1920 he emigrated, and eventually he settled in Prague, where he directed the co-operatives office of the Ukrainian Civic Committee in Czechoslovakia and founded the Society of Ukrainian Co-operative Leaders. He was one of the founders of and a professor (from 1924) at the Ukrainian Husbandry Academy and the director of the *Ukrainian Technical and Husbandry Institute (1936–8). He was elected full member of the Institut pour les études cooperatives. After the Second World War he moved to Munich, where he was founder and rector of the Ukrainian Higher School of Economics (1945–9). A senior associate of the *Institute for the Study of the USSR, he served as president (1954–6), vice-president (1956–7), and secretary (1957–8) of its Learned Council. In 1958 he emigrated to the United States, where he lectured for a time at the Ukrainian Technical Institute in New York. Among his numerous works on co-operation and contemporary history are *Teoriia kooperatsii* (The Theory of Co-operation, 1924), *Kooperatyvna reviziia* (Co-operative Auditing, 1927), and *Hroshi ukraïns'koï derzhavy* (The Currency of the Ukrainian State, 1972, coauthor). A collection of Martos's articles and reminiscences about the Ukrainian national movement was published by the Shevchenko Scientific Society in 1989.

Martos, Ivan, b ca 1752–4 in Ichnia, Pryluka regiment, d 17 April 1835 in St Petersburg. Classicist; sculptor; father of O. *Martos. After studying at the St Petersburg Academy of Arts (1764–73) and in Rome (1774–9) he taught at the academy (1779–1835) and served as its rector (1814–35). He created numerous sculptures in Russia and Ukraine, including the burial monuments of Hetman K. Rozumovsky in Baturyn (1803–5) and Count P. Rumiantsev at the Kievan Cave Monastery (1797–1805) and statues of Count A. de Richelieu in Odessa (1823–8), Emperor Alexander I in Tahanrih (1828–31), and Prince G. Potemkin in Kherson (1829–36). His works are noted for their restrained, lucid form and philosophical depth.

Martos, Ivan, b 1760 in Hlukhiv, Nizhen regiment, d 4 April 1831. Government official. He studied at the Kievan Mohyla Academy and served as Hetman K. Rozumovsky's cabinet secretary. After joining the Russian imperial civil service in 1778, he held posts in Ukraine, Belarus, and St Petersburg, including those of secretary of the Senate Department from 1802 and director of a department in the Ministry of Justice in 1815–16. An active Freemason and a friend of V. *Kapnist, he wrote a study on bath construction as described by Nestor the Chronicler (1809). O. Lazarevsky published Martos's correspondence in *Kievskaia starina* (1896, nos 6, 10–11; 1897, nos 7–8; 1898, nos 6–8) and separately (1898), and his biography of Martos appeared in that journal (1895, no. 10).

Martos, Oleksii, b 12 December 1790 in St Petersburg, d 25 August 1842. Historian; son of the sculptor I. *Martos.

A graduate of the Engineering Corps in St Petersburg (1806), he worked as a military engineer in Kiev and took part in the Russo-Turkish War of 1806–12 and the War of 1812. From 1821 he worked as a civil servant in various places in Russia and Siberia. Martos wrote a five-volume history of Little Russia to the end of the Hetman state. Although the work was esteemed by scholars, its publication was not allowed by the tsarist censors, and the manuscript subsequently was lost. Only two chapters from vol 3 – accounts of the Battle of Berestechko and T. Khmelnytsky's marriage and death – were published, in *Severnyi arkhiv* (1822, nos 13–14; 1823, nos 6, 12–13). Martos's memoirs and diary of the years 1806–16 were published in *Russkii arkhiv* (1893, nos 7–8). O. Lazarevsky's biography of Martos appeared in *Kievskaia starina* (1895, no. 2).

Les Martovych   Oleksander Martynenko

Martovych, Les [Martovyč, Les'], b 12 February 1871 in Torhovytsia, Horodenka county, Galicia, d 11 January 1916 in Poharysko, Rava Ruska county, Galicia. Writer, lawyer, and community activist. He completed his legal studies by correspondence at Lviv University in 1909 and worked as a clerk and legal assistant in various Galician towns. From 1898 he lived in Lviv and edited the radical newspaper *Hromads'kyi holos*. His first published work appeared in 1889, a story entitled 'Nechytal'nyk' (The Illiterate). He later published collections of stories, including *Nechytal'nyk* (1900), *Khytryi Pan'ko* (Clever Panko, 1903), *Strybozhyi darunok* (Gift from Stryboh, 1905), and the novellette *Zabobon* (Superstition, 1917). He depicted the daily life of the Galician peasantry and small-town intelligentsia, particularly that of priests and teachers of the late 19th and early 20th centuries. He wrote in the realist style, with touches of impressionism and with occasional sharp satire directed at the rural bourgeoisie and the bureaucracy. He contributed to *Dilo* and other newspapers and journals. His works were translated many times, and a three-volume compilation of his works, edited by Yu. Hamorak, was published in 1943. Other editions of selected works have appeared in Ukraine since 1949.

Martych, Yukhym [Martyč, Juxym] (pseud of Mordukh Finkelshtain), b 28 June 1910 in Kiev, d 27 July 1981 in Kiev. Writer and theater director. He wrote biographical novels, including *Natalia Uzhvii* (1939), *Oleksander Bohomolets'* (1951), *Polina Kumanchenko* (1964), *Povist' pro narodno-*

ho artysta (Tale about a Folk Artist, 1954), and *Zustrichi bez proshchan'* (Meetings without Farewells, 1970). He also wrote the novel *L'otnyi den'* (Flight Day, 1947), the essay in literary theory *Put' povely* (They Led the Way, 1941), and the autobiography *Pro druziv i pro sebe* (About My Friends and about Myself, 1960).

Martynenko, Ivan, b 21 October 1924 in Khrestyshche, Izium county, Kharkiv gubernia. Agricultural mechanization specialist; member of the All-Union Academy of Agricultural Sciences since 1970. After graduating from the Moscow Institute of Agricultural Mechanization and Electrification (1955) he worked at the Ukrainian Scientific Research Institute of Agricultural Mechanization and Electrification (1957–62) and then at the Ukrainian Agricultural Academy. His research has dealt primarily with farm mechanization.

Martynenko, Oleksander, b 1895 in the Poltava region, d 24 June 1983 in Minneapolis. Opera singer (dramatic baritone). After concluding his studies at the Kiev Conservatory in 1925, he performed in opera theaters in Kharkiv, Odessa, Donetske, and Kiev and in musical drama theaters in Luhanske and Vinnytsia. He fled to Western Europe in 1943 and emigrated to the United States in 1950. His major roles were the title role in V. Kostenko's *Karmeliuk*, Telramund in R. Wagner's *Lohengrin*, Amonasro in G. Verdi's *Aida*, and Scarpia in G. Puccini's *Tosca*.

Martynenko, Volodymyr, b 6 October 1923 in Horbuliv, now in Cherniakhiv raion, Zhytomyr oblast, d 18 April 1988 in Kiev. Soviet diplomat. After serving in the Soviet Army (1941–6), he graduated from the Faculty of International Relations at Kiev University in 1951 and worked in the CC CPU system and the Ukraina Society (1951–61). Upon completing his graduate studies at the CC CPSU Academy of Social Sciences (1964) he served as first secretary of the USSR embassy in Canada (1965–8), deputy minister of foreign affairs for Ukraine (1968–73), and Ukraine's permanent representative to the UN (1973–9). In November 1980 he was appointed minister of foreign affairs of the Ukrainian SSR, and in 1981 he was elected a member of the CC CPU and of Ukraine's Supreme Soviet. His works deal with the history of Canada, the activities of the UN, and Ukraine's role in international relations.

Martynets, Hnat [Martynec'], b 25 June 1882 in Kalush, Galicia, d 9 December 1968 in Munich. Pedagogue and

Hnat Martynets

community leader. In 1915–17 he was the Austro-Hungarian military mayor of Volodymyr-Volynskyi, where he helped organize the Ukrainian school system in Volhynia. He served as commissioner of the Western Ukrainian National Republic in Sniatyn county (1918–19). From 1924 Martynets lived in Sambir, where he was a cultural and educational activist and director (1941–4) of the Sambir Teachers' Seminary. From 1944 he lived in Germany and was active in many Ukrainian community activities, especially the Ukrainian Christian Movement, which he headed from 1954 until his death.

Martynets, Mykhailo [Martynec', Myxajlo], b 1859 in the Boiko region, d 8 June 1919 near Nadvirna, Galicia. Forestry engineer. A graduate of Vienna University, he worked in Sambir as head of a ministry department for the regulation of mountain streams in Galicia (1900–14) and wrote several works on the subject. During the First World War he directed the head office for reconstruction in Lviv (1916–18), and in December 1918 he accepted the portfolio of agrarian affairs in the State Secretariat of the Western Ukrainian National Republic. During his tenure as secretary he helped draft the land reform law. As the Ukrainian Galician Army was retreating, he and his coworkers were captured by Polish troops and executed without trial.

Volodymyr Martynets

Martynets, Volodymyr [Martynec'], b 15 July 1899 in Lviv, d 10 December 1960 in Winnipeg. Political leader and publicist. He served in the Ukrainian Sich Riflemen and the Sich Riflemen and was a gubernial official in the Polisia, Podlachia, and Kholm regions under the Hetman government. After spending seven months in Polish POW camps he resumed his studies in Lviv and became active in the student movement. He was elected secretary of the Academic Hromada, treasurer of the Provincial Student Council, and a trustee of the Lviv (Underground) Ukrainian University and Higher Polytechnic School, which he had helped organize. In 1923 he moved to Prague, where he studied at the Higher Commercial School and played an important role in student organizations, as vice-president of the Central Union of Ukrainian Students (1926–7) and as editor of *Natsional'na dumka* (the organ of the Group of Ukrainian National Youth) and of *Nash shliakh* (the organ of the Ukrainian Student Council). After being summoned by Ye. Konovalets to Berlin in 1927, he became a member of the Supreme Command of the *Ukrainian

Military Organization (1927–31) and chief editor of *Surma* (1927–33) and *Rozbudova natsiï* (1928–34). At the beginning of 1929 he was one of the key organizers and participants in the Congress of Ukrainian Nationalists, which gave birth to the *Organization of Ukrainian Nationalists (OUN). In 1934–40 he lived in Paris, where he edited *Ukraïns'ke slovo*. Upon returning to Lviv Martynets served officially as director of the Literary-Artistic Club and president of the Association of Ukrainian Journalists (1941–4), and secretly as leader of the OUN (Melnyk faction) in Western Ukraine (1941–2). In 1944 he was imprisoned in the Brätz concentration camp by the Germans. After emigrating to Canada in 1949, he became an editor of *Novyi shliakh* in Winnipeg and a member of the presidium of the Ukrainian Canadian Committee. He wrote numerous articles and over a dozen books, of which the most important are *Za zuby i pazuri natsiï* (For the Nation's Teeth and Claws, 1937), *Ukraïns'ke pidpillia: Vid UVO do OUN ...* (The Ukrainian Underground: From UVO to OUN, 1949), and *Ideolohiia orhanizovanoho i t. zv. volevoho natsionalizmu* (The Ideology of Organized and So-Called Voluntarist Nationalism, 1954).

Bishop Yosyp Martynets   Bishop Ivan Martyniak

Martynets, Yosyp [Martynec', Josyp] (Martenetz, José), b 7 February 1903 in Lviv, d 23 February 1989 in Curitiba, Brazil. Basilian priest and Ukrainian Catholic bishop. After moving to Brazil at an early age with his parents, he studied in Rome until his ordination in 1928 and then returned to Brazil to serve with the Basilian order. From 1953 he worked in the Basilian curia in Rome, headed a commission for the publication of the Bible in Ukrainian, and was rector of St Josaphat's Ukrainian Pontifical College. Martynets was consecrated auxiliary bishop to Cardinal J. Câmara for Eastern rite Catholics in 1958. In 1962 he was named exarch, and in 1971 he was appointed bishop of the Ukrainian eparchy of Brazil. He retired in 1978.

Martyniak, Ivan [Martynjak], b 20 June 1939 in Spas, Kaminka Strumilova county, Galicia. Ukrainian Catholic bishop. A graduate of the Warsaw Theological Seminary, he was ordained in 1964. He served as a parish priest among Ukrainians in the Legnica and Szprotawa regions before being appointed vicar-general for Ukrainian Catholics in Poland in 1981. In 1989 Martyniak was consecrated as the first Ukrainian Catholic bishop in Poland since the Second World War. Initially an assistant to the Polish cardinal J. Glemp, in 1991 he was appointed bishop of Peremyshl.

Martynivka hoard: unearthed silver adornments

Porfyrii Martynovych: Michael Marunchak
Self-Portrait (pencil, 1877)

Martynivka hoard. A hoard of Slavic archeological artifacts from the 6th to 7th century found in 1909 in Martynivka, Cherkasy oblast. Fifty-five silver (some gilded) artifacts were uncovered, including clasps, belt ornaments, women's jewelry pieces, and effigy figures of horses and humans. The horse figures were stylized in a Scythian-Sarmatian manner, while those of the humans depicted mustached men wearing long-sleeved shirts and long pants. The collection is now housed in the Historical Museum of Ukraine.

Martynovsky, Volodymyr [Martynovs'kyj], b 22 May 1906 in Moscow, d 2 August 1973 in Odessa. Technical thermodynamics scientist. He graduated from the Odessa Polytechnical Institute (1930) and taught in Odessa and Baku (1933–47). He served as rector of the Odessa Technological Institute of the Refrigeration Industry (1948–73, with interruptions) and led a group of Soviet scientists at the Bombay Technological Institute in India (1956–8). From 1960 to 1964 he was deputy chairman of the Department of Education at UNESCO. His main scientific contributions were in the fields of refrigeration, thermodynamics, and gas cycles.

Martynovych, Porfyrii [Martynovyč, Porfyrij], b 7 March 1856 in Kostiantynivka, Kostiantynohrad county, Poltava gubernia, d 15 December 1933 in Krasnohrad, Kharkiv oblast. Painter and graphic artist. He studied at the St Petersburg Academy of Arts (1873–81) and spent his summer vacations in the Poltava region collecting ethnographic materials and painting or drawing village scenes and portraits of peasants, landlords, stewards, and precentors. From 1881 he lived in Kostiantynohrad (now Krasnohrad) and traveled throughout the Poltava region with O. *Slastion, drawing and painting landscapes and portraits. He and V. Horlenko compiled a register of historical monuments in the region (1888). Martynovych also drew historical and literary figures (eg, B. Khmelnytsky, I. Mazepa, H. Skovoroda, and H. Kvitka-Osnovianenko) and pictures inspired by I. Kotliarevsky's *Eneïda* (Aeneid, 1903), Shevchenko's poems 'Kateryna' and 'Haidamaky,' folk songs, and Cossack dumas. His best-known genre

paintings are *Old Women Baking Bread* (1877–80) and *At the Volost Inspector's Office* (1879). His ethnographic notes were published in *Kievskaia starina* in 1904. O. Slastion wrote recollections of Martynovych (1919, 1931), and P. Zholtovsky (1930) and S. Taranushchenko (1958) wrote books about him.

Marunchak, Michael [Marunčak, Myxajlo], b 4 October 1914 in Dalesheva, Horodenka county, Galicia. Community figure and historian. Marunchak studied at the University of Lviv (1936–40), Ukrainian Free University in Prague (PH D, 1941), and University of Manitoba (1955). He was interned by the Germans during the Second World War. After the war he headed the League of Ukrainian Political Prisoners (1947–8), and he left Germany for Canada in 1948. He has been active in the Ukrainian Canadian Committee (now Congress), the Shevchenko Scientific Society (full member since 1961), and the Ukrainian Academy of Arts and Sciences in Canada (president since 1983). Marunchak compiled a considerable private archive of materials related to Ukrainian-Canadian history and started developing a broad scheme about Ukrainian life in Canada. His magnum opus is the two-volume *Istoriia ukraïntsiv Kanady* (1968, 1974), which appeared in English in a single volume as *The Ukrainian Canadians: A History* (1970; 2nd edn, 1982). His other major Ukrainian-Canadian works include *Studiï do istoriï ukraïntsiv Kanady* (Studies in the History of Ukrainians in Canada, 5 vols, 1964–80) and *Biohrafichnyi dovidnyk do istoriï ukraïntsiv Kanady* (A Biographical Guide to the History of Ukrainians in Canada, 1986). Marunchak also wrote *Systema nimetskykh kontsentratsiinykh taboriv i polityka vynyshchuvannia v Ukraïni* (The System of German Concentration Camps and the Politics of Extermination in Ukraine, 1963) and *Ukraïntsi v SSSR poza kordonamy URSR* (Ukrainians in the USSR outside the Borders of the Ukrainian SSR, 1974).

Maruniak, Volodymyr [Marunjak], b 2 November 1913 in Rozhubovychi, Peremyshl county, Galicia. Community figure, journalist, and scholar. A graduate of the Free School of Political Science in Prague (1936), in 1940 he moved from Prague to Berlin, where he served as the cultural-educational and propaganda representative of the *Ukrainian National Alliance and edited its newspaper

Ukraïns'kyi visnyk. A postwar refugee in Germany, he worked for the Information Section of the Central Representation of the Ukrainian Emigration in Germany (1947–9) and was European secretary of the Ukrainian Canadian Relief Fund (1950–1) and representative of the United Ukrainian American Relief Committee in northwestern West Germany (1954–9). Later he worked as an editor for the newspaper *Ukraïns'ke slovo* in Paris (1964–9) and the Radio Liberty Ukrainian broadcast section in Munich (1972–8). Maruniak edited a book about the Ukrainian Gymnasium in Czechoslovakia (1975) and wrote books on the Ukrainian displaced persons in Germany and Austria after the Second World War (1985) and on the émigré leader O. Boikiv (1986).

Marusia Bohuslavka. The main character in a renowned Ukrainian duma of the same name. The heroine is a priest's daughter from Bohuslav who, enslaved by the Turks, renounces her faith and wins her master's trust. On Holy Saturday, when the pasha is away, she frees 700 Cossacks from the dungeon. There is no evidence that Marusia Bohuslavka existed; she is probably a composite of slave girls who had helped captive Cossacks in some way. Marusia Bohuslavka became a common image in Ukrainian literature and the subject of several novels and plays and a ballet.

Arbishop Myroslav Marusyn

Marusyn, Myroslav, b 26 June 1924 in Kniazhe, Zolochiv county, Galicia. Ukrainian Catholic archbishop; member of the Shevchenko Scientific Society since 1979. He studied theology at the Greek Catholic Theological Academy in Lviv, the Catholic academy in Paderborn, Germany (1944–9), and the Papal Institute for Oriental Studies in Rome (PH D, 1951). He was ordained in 1946 and became secretary and chancellor to Archbishop I. Buchko in Rome in 1949. In 1958 he joined the Liturgical Commission of the Congregation for Eastern Churches, which prepares new editions of liturgical books. In 1963 he became a professor of liturgical studies at the Ukrainian Catholic University. He also served as a priest for parishes in Italy, Switzerland, and Scandinavia, and in 1971 he was made apostolic visitator for Ukrainians in Western Europe. He was consecrated a bishop in 1974, and Pope Paul VI then appointed him deputy head of the commission charged with revising the Eastern canon law. Pope John Paul II made him archbishop on 12 November 1982 and appointed him as secretary of the *Congregation for Eastern Churches. Marusyn has published a history (in German) of the relationship between Lviv and Peremyshl eparchies

and the Vatican (1951), and a number of pamphlets and articles on liturgical, theological, and historical themes.

Marvan, Jiri, b 28 January 1936 in Prague. Linguist, educator, and publicist. He studied at Charles University in Prague (PH D, 1966) and began university teaching in 1966 in Uppsala, Sweden. He later moved to Pennsylvania State University and then Monash University in Sydney, Australia, where he helped to lay the groundwork for a Ukrainian Studies program. His main field of interest is Slavic linguistics.

Marx-Engels-Lenin Institute. See Institute of Party History of the Central Committee of the Communist Party of Ukraine.

Marxism. The set of political, economic, philosophical, and social doctrines developed by K. Marx (1818–83) and F. Engels (1820–95). In Ukraine interest in Marxian ideas appeared as early as the 1870s. The economist M. *Ziber was one of the first interpreters of Marx in the Russian Empire. S. *Podolynsky corresponded with Marx and Engels and attempted to show that the laws of thermodynamics confirmed Marx's theory of surplus labor. In the late 1870s and early 1880s I. *Franko wrote popularizations of Marxist theory and translated portions of *Das Kapital* and Engels's *Anti-Dühring*. In 1875 the first Marxist organization on Ukrainian territory, the *South Russian Union of Workers, was formed in Odessa. Some tendencies in Ukrainian socialism at that time, however, were strongly critical of Marxism. M. *Drahomanov and his disciple M. *Pavlyk criticized Marxism on various grounds. As members of a stateless nation and as anarchists, they opposed the Marxian preference for centralism and the idea of state control of the economy; in particular, they objected to Marx and Engels's call for the restoration of a Polish state within historical boundaries that would include Ukrainian territory. They also felt that Marxism, which identified the urban proletariat as the only revolutionary class in capitalist society, had little to offer a nation whose masses were largely peasant; moreover, Marx and Engels's views of the peasantry as politically and economically backward and on the verge of extinction found few adherents among Ukrainians. Drahomanov, Pavlyk, and, later, Franko developed *radicalism as an alternative to Marxian socialism.

Marx and Engels's views on Ukraine were shaped in relation to their views on Russia and particularly Poland. Both placed great hopes in a Polish revolution against Russia, which they considered the greatest menace to European democracy and the future of socialism. Because of their pro-Polish attitudes they often ignored the fact that the Polish revolutionaries were landowning gentry, and denied the existence of a separate Ukrainian nation. Engels in particular, during the *Revolution of 1848–9, classified Ukrainians among the 'nonhistoric' peoples of East Central Europe who were counterrevolutionary by nature and doomed to extinction. By the 1870s, however, Marx and Engels began to hope for a revolution within Russia itself and consequently became more critical of Polish aspirations to Ukrainian territory.

By the beginning of the 20th century Marxism and Marxist political parties had become a serious force throughout the Russian and Austro-Hungarian empires, including their Ukrainian-inhabited territories. In Galicia in the 1890s the dissident radicals V. *Budzynovsky and Yu. *Bachynsky used a Marxist framework to argue that Ukraine was essentially a colony under imperialist rule and needed to become an independent state. Bachynsky and other dissidents left the Ukrainian Radical party in 1899 to form the avowedly Marxist *Ukrainian Social Democratic party. The latter party's leading theoretician, V. *Levynsky, devoted several works to the Marxist interpretation of the nationality question. In the Russian Empire the Revolutionary Ukrainian party also split in 1904–5 and gave birth to the Marxist *Spilka and *Ukrainian Social Democratic Workers' party. A leader of the latter party, L. *Yurkevych, wrote an important critique of V. Lenin's position on the nationality question with particular reference to the Ukrainian question. The economist M. *Tuhan-Baranovsky was a leading exponent of legal Marxism in the 1890s and wrote a series of revisionist interpretations of Marxist economic theory. In general, prior to 1917, Ukrainian Marxists and Marxist parties inclined to the reformist rather than to the revolutionary wing of Marxism, although L. Yurkevych took a highly radical stand against participation in the First World War.

In Soviet Ukraine the Marxist CP(B)U established its monopoly in political life, and *Marxism-Leninism became the official ideology. Marxist studies were concentrated at the *Ukrainian Institute of Marxism-Leninism (UIML). Some intellectual independence and debate were tolerated until the end of the 1920s, and then a rigid vulgarized version of Marxism-Leninism was imposed by J. Stalin. Most Ukrainian Marxists who had been active in the 1920s were repressed. In 1931 the UIML was accused of harboring national deviationists and was broken up into an association of autonomous institutions, the *All-Ukrainian Association of Marxist-Leninist Scientific Research Institutes (VUAMLIN), which was dissolved in 1937–8 and replaced in 1939 by the Ukrainian branch of the Institute of Marx-Engels-Lenin of the CC of the All-Union Communist Party (Bolshevik).

In Western Ukraine Marxism enjoyed some prestige in the 1920s thanks to its association with *Sovietophilism and the nationally conscious *Communist Party of Western Ukraine (KPZU). In the 1930s the expulsion of the KPZU's leaders for nationalism, the man-made famine of 1932–3, and the terror in Soviet Ukraine ruled out any attraction Marxism might have had for most Western Ukrainians.

In Soviet Ukraine since the Second World War, Marxism has remained largely an instrument of Party policy. Members of the dissident movement, such as I. Dziuba and L. Pliushch, have used Marxism as a tool of critical analysis. M. Rudenko wrote a critique of Marx's economic theory from a physiocratic standpoint. Some Ukrainian scholars outside Ukraine have contributed to our understanding of Marxism. R. *Rozdolsky, a founder of the KPZU, achieved international recognition for his interpretation of Marx's economic thought. V. Holubnychy, B. Levytsky, and I. Maistrenko (all associated with the left wing of the *Ukrainian Revolutionary Democratic party and its newspaper Vpered, 1945–59) as well as J.-P. Himka and B. Krawchenko have been influenced by Marxism or have studied it sympathetically.

BIBLIOGRAPHY
Hrushevs'kyi, M. Z pochyniv ukraïns'koho sotsiialistychnoho rukhu: Mykh. Drahomanov i zhenevs'yi sotsiialistychnyi hurtok (Vienna 1922)
Iurynets', V. Filosofs'ka geneza Marksa (Kharkiv 1933)
Doroshenko, D. Z istoriï ukraïns'koï politychnoï dumky za chasiv svitovoï viiny (Prague 1936)
Holubnychy, V. Soviet Regional Economics: Selected Works (Edmonton 1982)
Mace, J.E. Communism and the Dilemmas of National Liberation: National Communism in Soviet Ukraine, 1918–1933 (Cambridge, Mass 1983)
Rosdolsky, R. Engels and the 'Nonhistoric' Peoples: The National Question in the Revolution of 1848 (Glasgow 1986)
J.-P. Himka

Marxism-Leninism. The official ideology of the CPSU and the USSR. Its advocates have claimed that it is not merely a scientific description of nature, society, and knowledge, but also a practical means for their transformation. The name implies that this ideology is a synthesis of *Marxism and *Leninism. Its basic ontological and epistemological doctrines were, however, elaborated by F. Engels. Marxism-Leninism is usually divided into three parts: (1) a philosophical theory that encompasses dialectical materialism and historical materialism, (2) Marxian economic theory, and (3) a sociopolitical theory known as scientific communism.

Dialectical materialism consists of an ontology that defines matter, the principles and categories of reality, and the three laws of dialectic; an epistemology that deals with the relation of mind and being; and the dialectic method, which treats laws and categories of the dialectic as normative rules of thought. Historical materialism is claimed to be the application of dialectical materialism to history. As a philosophy of history it assumes history to be law-governed, distinguishes the determining factors (base) from the determined factors (superstructure) in social life, and describes the five stages of history and the laws of transition between them. Marxian economic theory deals mostly with the nature of capitalism and its inevitable self-destruction. Scientific communism consists of the Party's pronouncements on the gradual evolution of Soviet society toward communism.

In the first decade of Soviet rule the main task of Soviet philosophers, including those in Ukraine, was to ensure that the ideology of the new regime prevailed throughout society. Although they devoted much energy to developing the synthesis of K. Marx's, F. Engels's, and V. Lenin's views which they called Marxism-Leninism, they concentrated on translating the classics of the official philosophy, preparing popular anthologies and textbooks, and training ideological cadres. Most of the classics were issued in Russian translation, but Engels's Anti-Dühring (1924, 1932), Ludwig Feuerbach ... (1926), and Dialectics of Nature (1932, 1934) and Lenin's Materialism and Empiriocriticism (1932) and collected works in 29 volumes (1936) also came out in Ukrainian. S. Semkovsky compiled a Marxist anthology in Russian (1922); R. Levik and S. Hopner and E. Kviring published Lenin anthologies. The first textbook in Ukraine in historical materialism was written in Russian by M. Perlin (1925). Textbooks in Ukrainian were prepared by V. Boiko (1928), H. Yefymenko (1929), S. Lavrov (1930), and S. Semkovsky (1933). The most notable textbook from the philosophical viewpoint was a collectively written work by O. Bervytsky, R. Levik, T. Stepovy, V. Yurynets, and others (1932), which was condemned and banned for its 'nationalism' a few years later.

In his article on the meaning of militant materialism (1922) Lenin pointed out the main questions to be addressed by Soviet thinkers: the relation of Marxism to the natural sciences and the materialist interpretation of the Hegelian dialectic. Within this framework S. Semkovsky wrote several monographs (1924, 1926) defending the compatibility of dialectical materialism and the theory of relativity. V. Asmus (1924) gave, in Russian, the first Soviet account of the evolution of the dialectic from I. Kant to Lenin and defined the distinctive features of Marx's dialectic. O. Vasyliva, Ya. Bludov, and O. Zahorulko wrote a book in Ukrainian (1930) examining the influence of G. Hegel's dialectic on Marx, and S. Petropavlovsky (1924), S. Semkovsky (1927), T. Stepovy (1929), and M. Lohvyn (1930) wrote articles assessing Lenin's contribution to Marxism. Particular categories were analyzed by P. Demchuk (chance, 1928), T. Stepovy (cause, 1929), and A. Slutskin (quality, 1929). The main controversies centered on (1) the place of the dialectic in the new synthesis, with the supporters of A. Deborin defending the importance of the dialectic against the 'mechanists,' and (2) Lenin's contribution to Marxism-Leninism, with the 'Deborinists' being condemned for underestimating Lenin's philosophical importance and separating theory from practice. In the early 1930s further discussion was suppressed, and in the terror of the following years most of the participants in earlier discussions were arrested. An oversimplified official version of Marxism-Leninism was set down in *A History of the All-Union Communist Party (Bolsheviks): Short Course* (1938).

It was only after J. Stalin's death in 1953 that philosophical discussion of the basic issues in Marxism-Leninism was revived. More attention has been devoted to dialectical materialism than to any other branch of the philosophy. V. Voitko wrote the widely used textbooks in the field in Russian (1962) and Ukrainian (1972). A. Bosenko examined the dialectic as a general theory of development (1966), and others analyzed its particular laws and categories: M. Zolotina (1957) and V. Bosenko (1961), the transformation of quantity into quality; D. Fesenko (1957), the negation of the negation; Ya. Savenko (1959) and V. Hott and N. Depenchuk (1960), the unity and struggle of opposites; V. Melnykov (1959) and, in Russian, M. Bulatov (1980), the nature and function of the categories; V. Nichyk (1960), causality; H. Ivanov (1960), necessity and chance; Yu. Bogdanov, in Russian (1962), essence and appearance; and M. Parniuk, in Russian (1967, 1972), determinism. In the 1980s a group at the AN URSR (now ANU) Institute of Philosophy headed by M. Parniuk produced a series of collectively written books in Russian describing the history and role of the various categories in philosophy, the sciences, and social practice: finitude and infinity (1982), continuity and discontinuity (1983), space and time (1984), reality and appearance (1987), law and chaos (1987), necessity and contingency (1988), connectedness and separateness (1988), and possibility and actuality (1989). The dialectic was presented as a method of knowledge in Russian-language monographs by P. Kopnin (1961), V. Lutai (1970), and V. Shynkaruk (1977, 1979).

In epistemology I. Holovakha wrote, in Russian, on the intelligibility of the world (1955); L. Horbatova, on the theory of reflection (1961); and D. Mykytenko, on sensation (1966). P. Kopnin wrote, in Russian, an introduction to Marxist epistemology (1966) and a study of the dialectic as a logic and theory of knowledge (1978). The subject-object relation in knowledge was discussed by M. Duchenko (1964) and, in Russian, by M. Parniuk (1979). V. Tabachkovsky dealt in Russian with the role of the categories in knowledge and practice (1986).

Marxism-Leninism's claim to scientific status raised the problem of reconciling dialectical materialism with advances in science and, particularly, with the revolutionary changes in physics. Ukrainian philosophers have figured among the leading Soviet authorities in this field. M. Omelianovsky wrote in Russian on the relevance of Lenin's ideas to modern physics (1947), criticized the positivist interpretation of quantum theory (1953, 1956), and edited a collection of articles on philosophical problems of modern physics (1956). Similar collections were edited by D. Ostrianyn and others (1954, 1958) in Ukrainian and by Y. Shtokalo and others (1964) and V. Bazhan et al (1974) in Russian. N. Depenchuk interpreted, in Russian, the principle of complementarity in dialectical terms (1975). P. Dyshlevy wrote a monograph on time and space in the theory of relativity (1959), coauthored, with O. Kravchenko and M. Rozhenko, a book on philosophical issues in physics (1967), and edited Russian collections of articles on A. Einstein's theory of gravitation (1964, 1965, 1966). The methodological role of the materialist dialectic in the natural sciences was analyzed in Ukrainian by I. Holovakha (1961) and in a collection edited by V. Shynkaruk, V. Ivanov, and O. Yatsenko (1973). A Russian-language analysis was written by I. Kravets (1960), I. Holovakha (1971), P. Kopnin (1962), and V. Chornovolenko (1970) and in collections edited by N. Depenchuk and V. Lukianets (1976), P. Dyshlevy (1976), P. Dyshlevy and F. Kanak (1977), N. Depenchuk and L. Ozadovskaia (1980), V. Lutai (1981), P. Dyshlevy and V. Naidysh (1981), M. Duchenko and others (1983), I. Isaev (1984), and N. Kiselev and V. Khmarova (1985). Its role in biology was discussed in a collection edited by P. Dyshlevy and others (1966) and in Russian by N. Depenchuk (1973). Without abandoning epistemological realism, Soviet philosophers have gradually reduced their claims about the objectivity of science and the intelligibility of nature.

Marxism-Leninism constituted the theoretical core of the 'scientific' worldview dominant in Soviet society. V. Shynkaruk and his colleagues at the Institute of Philosophy collectively wrote a series of monographs in Russian on the nature of a worldview and its role in individual existence and social life. While broadening the discussion about the nature and role of philosophy, this approach did not lead to any new discoveries. Much of it consisted of old dogmas dressed up in new terminology.

Some attention was devoted to the methodology and basic concepts of historical materialism, but much more time has been spent on the so-called practical issues of 'developing socialism' and the 'transition to communism.' The methodological function of historical materialism in the social sciences was discussed in Russian in I. Boichenko's monograph (1982) and several collections of articles edited by V. Kutsenko (1972, 1985, 1986, 1987). Under Kutsenko's editorship the Department of Historical Materialism at the Institute of Philosophy prepared collections in Russian in which it tried to apply the laws and concepts of historical materialism to problems of social forecasting (1977) and social management (1979). In Russian, Yu. Pryliuk examined the problem of communication in historical materialism (1985), and M. Bulatov (1982), Bulatov and V. Tabachkovsky (1983), and M. Honcharenko (1980, 1987) applied the dialectic to an analysis of cultural progress.

In the field of 'scientific communism,' a number of 'practical' themes were discussed continuously: the friendship of nationalities (in Ukrainian: O. Bilous et al, 1953; in Russian: I. Kravtsev, 1965, 1966), democratic centralism (in Ukrainian: V. Vasylenko, 1957), the stage of developed socialism (in Russian: V. Kutsenko et al, 1980, 1982; A. Butenko, 1984; N. Kirichenko, 1984, 1985; and V. Pazenok, N. Kirichenko, et al, 1987), the development of the individual within socialist society (in Russian: L. Sokhan, 1966; A. Lysenko, 1976; and V. Kutsenko et al, 1983), scientific-technological progress (in Ukrainian: V. Shynkaruk et al, 1976; in Russian: Ye. Holovakha et al, 1988), and the imminent transition from socialism to communism (in Ukrainian: P. Koval et al, 1965; in Russian: L. Sokhan, 1966, and N. Kirichenko, 1984). From the 1960s this field was extensively revised and developed. But this was not the only area of Marxism-Leninism where discussion and change were permitted.

Despite the appearance of unanimity and changelessness, there was some debate among Soviet philosophers even on the basic doctrines of dialectical and historical materialism. Competing interpretations were offered, and the consensus of philosophical opinion shifted on some points. Yet diversity and change were difficult to detect. They appear to have been concealed intentionally by the avoidance of open confrontation and the adherence to traditional formulas. In spite of the growing disparity between the predictions of Marxism-Leninism and reality, the claim of its scientific nature has not been given up.

BIBLIOGRAPHY
Wetter, G. *Dialectical Materialism: A Historical and Systematic Survey of Philosophy in the Soviet Union*, trans P. Heath (London 1958)
Ievdokymenko, V.; et al (eds). *Rozvytok filosofiï v Ukraïns'kii RSR* (Kiev 1968)
Scanlan, J. *Marxism in the USSR: A Critical Survey of Current Soviet Thought* (Ithaca, NY 1985)

T. Zakydalsky

Mary. The mother of Jesus. Her stature as a Christian cult figure is second only to that of Christ. She has been venerated since apostolic times. Images of her first appeared in the 2nd century, and shrines in her honor were built from the 5th century and named in commemoration of particular events in her life, such as the Annunciation, Assumption (Dormition), Birth, and Presentation at the Temple. The doctrinal recognition of Mary as the Theotokos or Mother of God was finally defined at the Council of Ephesus in 431. Other dogmatic titles were applied to her throughout the early church period, including the Most Holy Virgin, the Ever-Virgin, the Lady, the Protectress of All Christians, the Immaculate, the Pneumatophora (Carrier of the Holy Spirit), and the Triadophora (Carrier of the Trinity).

In the Eastern Christian church her role as the mother of God has always been the main focus of her cult. Her cult was particularly promoted in the East by SS Ephrem the Syrian, John of Damascus, and Andrew of Crete, and St John Chrysostom's theology was revived and popularized in Ukraine in the 17th century by Metropolitan P. Mohyla. In the Western church the Mary cult has empha-

sized her virginity. The major theological differences persisting between the Eastern and Western churches today concern the doctrines of the Immaculate Conception (declared a dogma by Pius IX in 1854) and the Assumption (declared a dogma by Pius XII in 1950), which are not accepted as dogmas in the East. The liturgical veneration of Mary is an older tradition in the East than in the West, and is seen in various prayers, canons, and supplications and especially in *Hymnos Akathistos*. The personal cult of Mary was condemned by the reformers of the 16th century and is not practiced in most non-Catholic Western churches.

The great popularity of the cult of Mary has left its mark on Ukrainian literature, beginning with the apocryphal tales of Kievan Rus' – such as the 'Knyha rozhdestva Divy-Mariï' (The Book of the Nativity of the Virgin Mary), 'Khozhdeniie Bohorodytsi po mukakh' (The Mother of God's Journey through Agony), and 'Son Bohorodytsi' (The Mother of God's Dream) – and continuing through the works of I. Galiatovsky, L. Baranovych, A. Radyvylovsky, D. Tuptalo, I. Maksymovych, T. Shevchenko, Yu. Fedkovych, and P. Tychyna. The motif of Mary has an important place in oral tradition as well, especially in incantations, carols, hymns, and various other pious songs, some of which are of pre-Christian origin and were adapted to Marian devotion. It has also been reflected in toponymy: Bohorodytsia (Mother of God) in the Kholm region, Bohorodchany in Galicia, and Bohorodychne in Kharkiv oblast are among the many place-names associated with her. Even plants have been named after her (eg, *Bohorodchyna kosa* 'the Braid of the Mother of God').

Accounts of miracles associated with Mary abound. The early chronicles attribute the defeat of the Cumans in the 12th century to her intervention, in retribution for their destruction of the Church of the Tithes in Kiev. The account of her appearance at the *Pochaiv Monastery, when she intervened to save the monastery during a Turkish and Tatar attack in the late 17th century, is especially popular and has been immortalized in the famous song 'Oi ziishla zoria vecherovaia' (Lo, the Evening Star Ascended). Over two hundred miraculous *icons of Mary, held in churches in Kiev, Korsun, Kholm, Dobromyl, Hoshiv, Sambir, Zhovkva, Zarvanytsia, and elsewhere, have attracted pilgrims for centuries. The icons of Mary (of Byzantine origin) in the Pochaiv Monastery and in Częstochowa, Poland (brought from Byzantium during the reign of Volodymyr the Great to Belz in Western Ukraine, and then taken in 1382 to Poland), and the Vyshhorod (Vladimir) Theotokos are the most famous icons of her. In addition to icons depicting Mary with the infant Christ, popular images of her in Ukrainian iconography are of the deesis, or her adoration, with St John, of Jesus on the heavenly throne, and of Mary the Protectress. One of the oldest images of Mary in Ukraine is the mosaic Oranta in the main apse of the St Sophia Cathedral in Kiev.

Holidays in Mary's honor occupy an important place in the church calendar; they include the Annunciation (25 March), the Dormition (15 August), the Nativity of Mary (8 September), and the Presentation at the Temple (21 November). In Ukraine, 14 October (1 October OS) is the day of Mary the Protectress. This holiday, which gained great popularity among the Zaporozhian Cossacks, is almost a national celebration (it was not celebrated in the Byzantine church).

Many significant churches and chapels in Ukraine were

dedicated to Mary, including the *Dormition Cathedral of the Kievan Cave Monastery; the Church of the Tithes; and churches in Volodymyr-Volynskyi, Halych, Kholm, Lviv, Chernihiv, and elsewhere.

In the Ukrainian Catholic church, *Marian societies have been particularly active in preserving and furthering the cult of Mary.

BIBLIOGRAPHY
Kondakov, N. *Ikonografiia Bogomateri*, 2 vols (St Petersburg 1914–15)
Gordillo, M. *Mariologia Orientalis* (Rome 1954)
Gharib, G. *La Madonna nell'anno liturgico bizantino* (Rome 1972)
Beinert, W.; Petri, H. *Handbuch der Marienkunde* (Regensburg 1984)

I. Korovytsky

Ukrainian-American veterans in front of St Michael's Ukrainian Catholic Church in Baltimore, Maryland (1945)

Maryland. A state (1990 pop 4,798,622) on the eastern coast of the United States covering an area of 27,400 sq km. Its capital is Annapolis, and its largest city is Baltimore. There are about 16,000 Ukrainians in the state. Most of them (44 percent) live in the Baltimore metropolitan area. Another 20 percent reside in the outskirts of Washington and in the Baltimore–Washington corridor. The rest are scattered in eastern farming counties, such as Worcester, Wicomico, and Cecil, and the western coal-mining counties of Allegheny and Garrett.

Ukrainian immigrants from Galicia, Bukovyna, and Transcarpathia began emigrating to Maryland in the 1890s, with at least 1,100 arriving in 1899–1914. Most of them settled in *Baltimore, where the first Ukrainian parishes and secular associations appeared. Just before the war a small Ukrainian farming community sprang up in Chesapeake City around the Ukrainian Catholic Orphanage. Hundreds of Ukrainians found jobs in the coal mines of western Maryland. The second wave of immigrants from Western Ukraine, in the interwar years, strengthened the existing organizations, and the newcomers founded some others, such as the Ukrainian American Citizens Club (1929) and the Ukrainian National Home (1931) in Baltimore. After the Second World War a large number of Ukrainian refugees and displaced persons en-

tering the United States came to Maryland as farm workers. Within a year most of them headed to the cities. The Ukrainian community in Baltimore more than doubled in numbers at this time, and its level of activity rose sharply. The Ukrainian Education Association of Maryland was founded in 1972 to educate the American public about Ukrainian culture and history. It co-ordinated the publication of *The Ukrainians of Maryland* (1977). A number of Ukrainians have been prominent in state politics, notably P. Dypsky, J. Staszak, C. Yarema, M. Hrabec, and J. Shmorhun.

T. Zakydalsky

Maryniak, Bohdan [Marynjak], b 1844 in Rozdzhalovychi, Sambir circle, Galicia, d 9 June 1912 in Lviv. Machine-building specialist and pedagogue. After completing his studies at the Lviv Technical Academy he taught drafting at the academy (from 1872 the Lviv Higher Polytechnical School). He was elected to chair the department of machine building (the only such department in Galicia). After upgrading his qualifications in Berlin and Belgium, he returned in 1876 to the Polytechnical School and continued to chair the machine-building department. He was a patron of Ukrainian theater and a benefactor of the *Osnova society, as well as an advocate for the creation of a Ukrainian university in Lviv.

Maria Maryniak:
Self-Portrait (pastel, 1981)

Myroslav Marynovych

Maryniak, Maria [Marynjak, Marija] (née Murynets), b 10 May 1939 in Horodok, Galicia. Artist and art instructor. Maryniak arrived in Canada in 1949. She graduated from the University of Alberta in 1979. She creates impressionistic chalk pastel compositions, mostly of Canadian landscapes. Since 1981 Maryniak has had several solo exhibitions in Canada, participated in over 20 group exhibitions, and contributed to *Arts Atlantic* and *Site Sound*. Since 1985 she has lived in London, Ontario. In 1987 she received an award at the International Exhibition of Pastels held in Toronto, and in 1989 she exhibited two works at the International Exhibition of Pastels held in Compiègne, France.

Maryniuk, Viktor [Marynjuk], b 10 April 1939 in Kazavchyn, Haivoron raion, Kirovohrad oblast. Painter and muralist. A graduate of the Odessa Art School (1967), he participated in official and unofficial group exhibitions in Odessa and in the Second Exhibition of Nonconformist Ukrainian Artists (1976), held in a private Moscow apartment. From the representational style of the early 1970s (eg, *Girl with Ribbons*) Maryniuk has moved through several contemporary styles, from partial (*Outside the Town*, 1979) to total abstraction (*Composition*, 1981) to neoexpressionism (*Two Women*, 1988). Most of his compositions contain figures of women. He also painted the murals inside the Odessa Student Palace and the Odessa Book Building.

Marynovych, Mykola [Marynovyč], b 1861, d 1944. Army officer. A colonel in the Austrian army during the First World War, he joined the Ukrainian Galician Army in November 1918 and was briefly its first chief of general staff during the battle for Lviv. He was murdered by Soviet partisans in 1944.

Marynovych, Myroslav [Marynovyč], b 4 January 1949 in Drohobych, Lviv oblast. Dissident. In November 1976 he became one of the cofounders of the *Ukrainian Helsinki Group in Kiev. For his participation in various activities in defense of human rights, he was arrested in April 1977 and sentenced in March 1978 to seven years in strict-regime labor camps and five years' exile. While in a camp in Perm oblast, he took part in hunger strikes and other protest actions of the political prisoners there. He was released from exile in Kazakhstan in 1987, and returned to Ukraine. Since 1987 Marynovych has lived in Drohobych, where he writes for a local paper and teaches at the pedagogical institute.

Marynych, Hryhorii [Marynyč, Hryhorij], b 29 November 1876 in Hupalivka, Novomoskovske county, Katerynoslav gubernia, d 11 April 1961 in Dnipropetrovske. Actor. He began his theatrical career in Saksahansky's Troupe in 1906, and then worked in T. Kolesnychenko's troupe (1910) and in Sadovsky's Theater in Kiev (1911–14). He joined the Shevchenko First Theater of the Ukrainian Soviet Republic in 1920 (with a hiatus with an amateur theater in Kursk in 1921–4) and followed it when it was transferred and renamed the Dnipropetrovske Ukrainian Music and Drama Theater (1925–57).

Marynych, Oleksander [Marynyč], b 4 September 1920 in Subottsi, Oleksandriia county, Kherson gubernia. Geographer and geomorphologist; corresponding member of the AN URSR (now ANU) since 1969. After studying at Kiev University he graduated from Kazan University in 1942. After the war he taught at Kiev University, and he served there as dean of the geography faculty (1956–68) and department head of physical geography (1958–71). In 1964 he was elected president of the Geographical Society of the URSR. He served as Ukraine's minister of education (1971–9), headed the geographical division of the ANU Institute of Geophysics, and was a professor at Kiev University (1989). Marynych specializes in the physical geography and geomorphology of Ukraine and the rational use of the natural environment. He has written two books on the physical geography of Polisia (1962, 1963) and coauthored books on the physical geography of Ukraine (1982), the landscapes of Ukraine (1985), and environmental protection in the Middle Dnieper region (1986). He is the editor in chief of the three-volume *Heo-*

hrafichna entsyklopediia Ukraïny (Geographic Encyclopedia of Ukraine), which began to appear in 1989 in Kiev.

Marzeev, Aleksandr, b 6 April 1883 in Nizhnii-Novgorod, Russia, d 1 February 1956 in Kiev. Russian hygienist; full member of the USSR Academy of Medical Sciences from 1944. A graduate of Moscow University (1911), he headed the sanitation and epidemiology department of the People's Commissariat of Public Health of the Ukrainian SSR (1922–35), directed the Ukrainian Scientific Research Institute of Communal Hygiene (1931–56), and chaired the departments of communal hygiene at the Kharkiv (1934–41) and Kiev (1944–56) medical institutes. He was one of the first organizers of public sanitation in Ukraine.

Masalsky, Volodymyr [Masal's'kyj], b 25 July 1896 in Kiev, d 14 January 1979 in Kiev. Linguist. A graduate of Kiev University (1920), he worked as a teacher in provincial towns. From 1933 he was an associate of the AN URSR (now ANU) Institute of Linguistics, taught (with interruptions) at Kiev University, and chaired its department of Slavic philology (1960–71) as well as the methodology division of the Scientific Research Institute of Pedagogy. From the mid-1930s on he published articles on the methodology of secondary-school teaching of Ukrainian and Russian, on Ukrainian grammar, and on stylistics (T. Shevchenko, M. Kotsiubynsky, P. Tychyna, and I. Kyrylenko).

New extension of the Masandra winery

Masandra. IX-15. A town smt (1990 pop 6,400) on the Black Sea coast in Crimea oblast. Lying only 5 km from Yalta, it is administered by Yalta's municipal council. Masandra was first mentioned in historical documents in the mid-18th century. It attained smt status in 1941. The town is known as a health resort and as the home of the main winery of the Masandra Wine-Making Complex. On its outskirts is the famous *Nikita Botanical Garden. Traces of Taurian burial mounds and ancient settlements, catacombs from the 1st to 3rd centuries, and the ruins of a 12th-to 15th-century monastery are found near Masandra.

Masaryk, Tomáš Garrigue, b 7 March 1850 in Hodonín, Moravia, d 14 September 1937 in Lány, Kladno county, Czechoslovakia. Czech scholar, philosopher, and statesman. A graduate of Vienna University (PH D, 1876), he was a professor of philosophy at Charles University in Prague (1882–1914) and the first president of the Czechoslovak Republic (1918–35). In his scholarly and publicistic works, such as *Russland und Europa* (1913; English edn: *The Spirit of Russia*, 1919), *The New Europe: The Slav Standpoint* (1918), and *The Slavs after the War* (1922; Ukrainian edn 1923), and his memoirs, *Světova revoluce: Za války a ve válce, 1914–1918* (1925; English edn: *The Making of a State: Memories and Observations*, 1927; Ukrainian edn: *Svitova revoliutsiia*, 1930), Masaryk often expressed his opinion on Ukrainian issues. He treated the question of Ukrainian nationhood as an open one and sympathized with Ukrainian aspirations to national emancipation. But he hoped that one day Ukraine would be part of a democratic, federated Russia, which would serve as a counterweight to the German threat.

Masaryk came into contact with Ukrainian issues at various times in his career. He was acquainted with I. Franko, who dedicated a collection of translated verses to him and contributed his recollections about their relations to a festschrift on Masaryk's 60th birthday. He assisted Ukrainian students in Prague after their secession from Lviv University in 1901–2. As a deputy to the Austrian parliament he took part in the 1908 debates on the Ukrainian-Polish conflict in Ukraine, and in a major speech on 25 May he defended the rights of the Galician Ukrainians to develop freely and independently. After the outbreak of the First World War he headed the Czecho-Slovak independence movement within the Entente alliance. During his stay in Russia and Ukraine (1917–18) he organized a legion of Czech and Slovak POWs and negotiated an agreement with the UNR guaranteeing the legion's extraterritorial status in Ukraine and obtaining government support for it. When the UNR declared its independence and concluded the Peace Treaty of Brest-Litovsk, he annulled the agreement. The legion remained neutral in the Soviet-Ukrainian conflict that followed and eventually left Ukraine for the Far East.

During his visit to the United States (May–November 1918) Masaryk organized the Mid-European Democratic Union, an organization of émigré representatives of the various nationalities of the Austro-Hungarian Empire. It included M. Sichynsky and L. Tsehlynsky from the Ukrainian community and H. Zhatkovych from the *American National Council of Uhro-Rusins. On the basis of an agreement between the Uhro-Rusin council and Masaryk, Transcarpathia was incorporated into the new Czechoslovak Republic in 1919.

As president of Czechoslovakia Masaryk supported the use of the local dialect instead of Russian in Transcarpathian educational and administrative institutions. He was sympathethic to the cultural needs of the large émigré community from Russian-ruled Ukraine and helped establish such institutions as the Ukrainian Free University in Prague and the Ukrainian Husbandry Academy in Poděbrady (see *Bohemia and *Czechoslovakia). In spite of his sometimes pro-Soviet and Russophile leanings, Masaryk was popular among Ukrainians.

I.L. Rudnytsky

Masenko, Teren, b 10 November 1903 in Hlodosy, Yelysavethrad county, Kherson gubernia, d 6 August 1970 in Kiev. Poet and journalist. He was a member of the literary organizations *Molodniak and *Prolitfront and first began to publish his work in 1924. He is the author of the anthologies *Stepova mid'* (Copper of the Steppes, 1927), *Pivdenne more* (The Southern Sea, 1929), *Virshi ta poemy* (Verses and Poems, 1939), *Tsvit zemli* (The Earth's Bloom, 1948), *Kyïvs'ki kashtany* (The Chestnut Trees of Kiev, 1954), *Iak pakhne zemlia* (How the Earth Is Fragrant, 1958), and many others, and of a versified novel, *Step* (The Steppe, 1938). Masenko also published collections of articles and essays and the autobiographical *Zhyttia i pisnia* (Life and Song, 1960). He is the author of several books of verses for children. Over 200 of his verses have been set to music by Ukrainian composers.

Mashchenko, Mykola [Maščenko], b 12 January 1929 in Miluvatka, now in Svatove raion, Luhanske oblast. Film director. In 1953 he completed study at the Kharkiv Theater Institute, and from 1957 he has worked in the Kiev Artistic Film Studio (since 1988 as director), where he has directed many films on moral and social problems and the telefilms *Shliakh na Sofiiu* (Road to Sofia, 1978) and *Ovid* (The Gadfly, 1980, based on E. Voinich's novel); he was awarded the Shevchenko Prize in 1982. He has also taught at the Kiev Institute of Theater Arts.

Mashivka [Mašivka]. IV-15. A town smt (1990 pop 4,300) on the Tahamlyk River and a raion center in Poltava oblast. It dates from the mid-19th century. Mashivka attained smt status in 1971. It has a food industry and a regional museum.

Masiuk, Kalenyk [Masjuk], b 1878 in Dybyntsi, Kaniv county, Kiev gubernia, d 3 June 1933 in Dybyntsi. Master potter. He made bowls, pitchers, and tiles, which he decorated with original vegetative motifs and stylized images of animals, birds, and human beings. His design was scratched onto the surface of the clay. Masiuk's works can be found in museums in Kiev, Lviv, Poltava, and St Petersburg. His son, Vasyl, has continued the art.

Masiutko, Mykhailo [Masjutko, Myxajlo] (pseud: Mykhailo Perekop), b 18 November 1918 in Chaplynka, Dnieper county, Tavriia gubernia. Dissident. After studying at the Kherson and Zaporizhia pedagogical institutes he worked as a teacher in the Zhytomyr region. Having been accused of disseminating counterrevolutionary propaganda he was imprisoned in concentration camps in the Soviet Arctic (1937–40) and then exiled to the Khabarovsk region (1940–2). He was arrested in Teodosiia in September 1965 for possessing dissident and émigré literature and sentenced in March 1966 in Lviv to six years in Vladimir Prison and in a strict-regime labor camp in Mordovia. Some of his extant poems, stories, letters, petitions, and documents pertaining to his trial were published in the West in V. *Chornovil's *Lykho z rozumu* (1967; trans: *The Chornovil Papers*, 1968) and in *Ukraïns'ka inteligentsiia pid sudom KGB* (Ukrainian Intellectuals Tried by the KGB, 1970).

Masiutyn, Vasyl [Masjutyn, Vasyl'] (Masjutin, Wassilij), b 29 January 1884 in Riga, Latvia, d 15 December 1955 in West Berlin. Ukrainian engraver, medalist, sculptor, painter, graphic artist, writer, and art scholar. He studied at the Moscow School of Painting, Sculpture, and Architecture (1909–14). His early work consisted of fantastic

Vasyl Masiutyn:
Self-Portrait (1938)

Volodymyr Masliak

symbolist, often grotesque, etchings, such as *Hermaphrodite* and *Woman with Tail*. In 1920 a large solo exhibition of his works was held at the Rumiantsev Museum in Moscow. An émigré in Berlin from 1921, he worked there as a commercial artist and illustrator of Russian books. In the early 1930s he became a member of the Association of Independent Ukrainian Artists and took part in its exhibitions in Lviv. Having turned his attention to Ukrainian themes, he sculpted busts of Hetmans P. Sahaidachny, B. Khmelnytsky, P. Doroshenko, and I. Mazepa and produced a series of 63 bronze historical medallions (10 on Kievan Rus', 47 on the Cossack period, and 7 on the modern period). He also did the print series 'Seven Mortal Sins,' colored woodcuts, illustrations to Aesop's fables and the works of N. Gogol, F. Dostoevsky, A. Pushkin, and H. Balzac, and oils. He wrote *Die Gravüre und die Lithographie* (1922), a study of the English graphic artist T. Bewick (1923), articles on Ukrainian art and artists in Ukrainian and German art journals, and novels in German (eg, *Der Doppelmensch*, 1925), two of which appeared in Ukrainian – *Dva z odnoho* (Two from One, 1936) and *Tsarivna Nefreta* (Queen Nefertiti, 1938).

S. Hordynsky

Maskiewicz, Bogusław Kazimierz (Maszkiewicz), b ca 1625, d 1683. Polish memoirist and officer in the private army of the magnate J. Wiśniowiecki. He maintained a diary in 1643–9 which provided descriptions of manor life, the Kodak fortress and the Dnieper Rapids, and the Khmelnytsky uprising of 1648–9. Although the original has not survived, the memoirs were published in Polish and Russian during the 19th century, and together with those of his father Samuel in *Pamiętniki Samuela i Bogusława Kazimierza Maskiewiczów* (1961).

Masliak, Stepan [Masljak], b 19 November 1895 in Stanyslaviv, d 8 July 1960 in Lviv. Writer. In 1924–5 he lived in Prague, and from 1945, in Lviv. He was a senior lecturer of the chair of Slavic philology of Lviv University. His first published work appeared in 1923, and his writings continued to appear in Lviv's leftist journals *Nova kul'tura* and *Vikna*. Masliak belonged to *Horno. He wrote the epic poem *Prolom* (The Breakthrough, 1934), but he is known primarily as a translator of Polish (A. Mickiewicz, J. Słowacki, M. Konopnicka, A. Asnyk, J. Tuwim), Czech (J.

Hašek's *Good Soldier Schweik* and I. Olbracht's *Nikola Šuhaj loupežnik* [Nikola Šuhaj, the Bandit]), German, French, Italian, and Slovak, including 17 librettos for opera translated into Ukrainian. He also translated Ukrainian works into Polish (T. Shevchenko, L. Hlibov, Yu. Fedkovych, P. Tychyna, V. Sosiura, L. Pervomaisky).

Masliak, Volodymyr [Masljak] (pseud: Volodymyr Zalukvych), b 14 September 1858 in Sernky Seredni, Galicia, d 15 December 1924. Writer, poet, and publicist. He published several collections of poetry, including *Poeziï* (Poems, 1886) and *Z chornoho shliakhu* (From the Black Road, 1897). His best poems are similar to folk songs and have been set to music. In his satirical novel *Kistiaky Hol'dbeina* (Holdbein's Skeletons, 1896) he portrayed the Galician clergy. In 1885 Masliak edited *Nove zerkalo*, a magazine of political satire, and in 1898 he compiled and published *Na velyki rokovyny* (On the Great Anniversary), a literary collection in honor of I. Kotliarevsky.

Masliuchenko-Hubenko, Varvara [Masljučenko], b 1902, d 23 January 1983 in Kiev. Actress; wife of O. *Vyshnia. She mostly played heroic roles in the State Drama Theater (1918–19), the Shevchenko First Theater of the Ukrainian Soviet Republic (1918–19), the Franko New Drama Theater in Kharkiv (1923–6), the Kharkiv Chervonozavodskyi Ukrainian Drama Theater (1927–30), and the Kharkiv Theater of the Revolution (1931–4). She was arrested in 1934 and imprisoned in the Soviet Arctic. After her release she acted in the films *Poema pro more* (A Poem about the Sea, 1958) and *Lisova pisnia* (The Forest Song, 1961, based on Lesia Ukrainka's drama).

Masliukov, Oleksa [Masljukov], b 2 June 1904 in Cherkasy, Kiev gubernia, d 14 April 1962 in Kiev. Film director. In 1929 he completed study at the Odessa State Cinema College; later he worked in the Odessa and Kiev Artistic Film studios (since 1952 in the Kiev studio only). He produced several films on children's education, notably *Pedahohichna poema* (A Pedagogical Poem, 1955, based on A. Makarenko's novel).

Maslosoiuz Provincial Dairy Union (Kraievyi molocharskyi soiuz 'Maslosoiuz'). An association of dairy cooperatives that was founded in Stryi in 1905 by the Stryi branch of the Prosvita society and was first called the Union of Ruthenian Dairy Co-operatives. From 1907 to 1925 it was known as the Provincial Farm and Dairy Union. The organizers and first leaders of Maslosoiuz were Ye. *Olesnytsky, O. Nyzhankivsky, L. Horalevych, and I. Bachynsky. By 1914 it represented about 100 small dairy unions, which together collected some 7.5 million L of milk from peasants and produced about 300,000 kg of butter annually.

The union was reorganized in 1924, after recovering from the First World War. In 1925 it changed its name and statute. Individual members were replaced by corporate members, and new people – mostly former officers of the Ukrainian Galician Army who had graduated from professional schools abroad – took over the management of the union. The main figures in the organization in the interwar period were O. *Bachynska, A. *Mudryk, A. *Palii, M. *Khronoviat, T. Kotyk, and O. Lys. Formally its head office was in Stryi, but its real center was Lviv, where its

A Maslosoiuz store in Lviv

Main Trading Office was located. In 1927 Maslosoiuz began to export its butter to Czechoslovakia and Austria and restored the dairy school that had been founded in Stryi in 1913. Its monthly *Kooperatyvne molocharstvo* appeared in 1926. To improve efficiency and facilitate mechanization, small dairy co-operatives serving single localities were reorganized into larger regional co-operatives called district dairy associations. The first association was set up in Voinyliv in 1926. In 1928 the associations were reorganized into district dairies, each of which served several villages. Almost all of the district dairies had modern equipment and trained technical staff. The growth of Maslosoiuz is summarized in the table.

In 1938 Maslosoiuz had 12 departments, with 26 wholesale and 57 retail stores. Its base consisted of 136 district dairies with a total membership of 205,000 farms, which supplied the milk. Maslosoiuz itself employed about 300 people, and the district dairies employed 150 dairy technicians, 64 farming experts (mostly professional agronomists), and 18 veterinarians. The association was the most vital part of the *co-operative movement in Western Ukraine, and the leading force behind the movement's modernization. Together with the *Silskyi Hospodar society, Maslosoiuz played a major role in modernizing agriculture in Western Ukraine. The Polish authorities, however, restricted its operation to Galicia, where it achieved almost complete control of the butter market, its produce being sold to Poles and Jews as well as to Ukrainians. In Volhynia there was only one department of

The growth of Maslosoiuz, 1925–38

	1925	1931	1935	1938
Number of member dairies	72	224	141	151
Number of district dairies	–	112	113	136
Number of milk-collecting dairies	300	1,259	1,400	2,000
Milk received (in million L)	8.4	65	74.6	115
Butter supplied to Maslosoiuz by district dairies (in thousand kg)	165	2,428	2,810	2,948
Butter exported (in thousand kg)	0.2	842	483	112
Sales (in million zlotys)	0.9	14.7	9.3	12.1

Maslosoiuz, with two stores in Lutske. The few district dairies in Volhynia were not permitted to trade with Maslosoiuz. Another two departments were opened in Silesia.

During the first Soviet occupation of eastern Galicia (1939–41) the dairy co-operatives were brought formally under the control of so-called food co-operatives but in effect were subordinated to state control. Most of Maslosoiuz's managers fled to the Generalgouvernement in German-occupied Poland, where they organized about 50 co-operative dairies and a department of Maslosoiuz in Jarosław, which came under the supervision of the Lublin and Cracow branches of the Audit Union of Ukrainian Co-operatives. When the Germans occupied eastern Galicia in 1941, they permitted Maslosoiuz to resume its operations but limited the union's activities to the new Distrikt Galizien of the Generalgouvernement. All dairy farming was brought under the Provincial Union of Dairy Farming, which also took over technical and organizational responsibilities; Maslosoiuz retained responsibility for commercial operations. As the only central organization of dairy co-operatives in Galicia, Maslosoiuz was one of the few institutions that could defend the interests of Ukrainian peasants before the German authorities. In 1943 there were 181 Ukrainian district dairies in the Generalgouvernement, 137 of which were in Galicia. They processed 220 million L of milk, and their gross sales came to over 100 million zlotys. Maslosoiuz was dissolved when the Soviets occupied Galicia for the second time (1944).

BIBLIOGRAPHY
Kachor, A. *Ukraïns'ka molochars'ka kooperatsiia v Zakhidnii Ukraïni* (Munich 1949)
Vytanovych, I. *Istoriia ukraïns'koho kooperatyvnoho rukhu* (New York 1964)

A. Kachor

Maslov, Leonyd, b 1909, d 1943 in Rivne, Volhynia. Architect; son of Senator M. Maslov. In interwar western Volhynia he researched architectural monuments, particularly old churches, and wrote about them in Ukrainian and Polish periodicals, such as *Nasha bat'kivshchyna* and *Zhyttia i znannia*; he also wrote a book on wooden churches of the Kholm region and Podlachia (1941). He was executed by the Germans.

Maslov, Mykola, b 1880 in Lubni, Poltava gubernia, d 1942 in Kazakhstan. Community figure and politician. He studied law at St Petersburg University, was active in the Ukrainian student hromada there, and practiced law in St Petersburg. After the February Revolution he served as a commissioner of the Central Rada in Borshchiv county, Galicia, and then directed the chancery of the Little Rada in Kiev. Under the UNR Directory he headed a government department in 1919. As an interwar émigré in Polish-ruled Volhynia, he headed the executive of the local government in Lutske, was active in the *Volhynian Ukrainian Alliance and the *Ridna Khata society, administered the state property of the Orthodox Brotherhood of the Elevation of the Cross, and presided over the Ukrainian Theater Society. Maslov was elected to the Polish Senate in 1930 and 1935 and became a deputy senator in 1938. He served as a secretary in the senate and was a member (from 1935) of its Legal Commission. From 1935 on he spoke out in support of educational and agricultural reforms, the eradication of unemployment among the Ukrainian peasantry and intelligentsia, and normalization of the legal status of the Orthodox church. Maslov was arrested during the 1939 Soviet occupation of Western Ukraine and deported to Kazakhstan, where he died or was killed.

Serhii Maslov

Maslov, Serhii, b 28 November 1880 in Ichnia, Chernihiv gubernia, d 11 January 1957 in Kiev. Literary scholar and bibliologist. From 1914 he was a privatdocent and a professor at Kiev University, and from 1939, a corresponding member of the AN URSR (now ANU). Maslov was the author of many works in the history of Ukrainian literature, mainly of the 17th and 18th centuries, and in Ukrainian bibliography, archeography, paleography, ethnography, and other areas. Among his major writings are 'Rukopysy Sofiis'koï katedry v Kyievi' (Manuscripts of the St Sophia Cathedral in Kiev, *ZNTSh*, vol 72, 1906), *Obzor rukopisei biblioteki Imperatorskogo Universiteta sv. Vladimira* (A Survey of Manuscripts in the Library of the [Kiev] Imperial University of St Vladimir, 1910), *Biblioteka Stefana Iavorskogo* (The Library of Stefan Yavorsky, 1914), *Drukarstvo na Ukraïni v XVI–XVIII st.* (Printing in Ukraine in the 16th to 18th Centuries, 1924), *Ukraïns'ka drukovana knyha XVI–XVIII st.* (The Ukrainian Printed Book in the 16th to 18th Centuries, 1925), 'Ukrainische Druck-Kunst des 16 bis 18 Jahrunderts' (*Gutenberg Jahrbuch*, 1926), *Etiudy z istoriï ukraïns'kykh starodrukiv* (Studies in the History of Ukrainian Old Printed Books, 1926–8), *Kul'turno-natsional'ne vidrodzhennia na Ukraïni v kintsi XVI i pershii polovyni XVII st.* (The Cultural-National Rebirth in Ukraine at the End of the 16th Century and the Beginning of the 17th Century, 1943), and *Pochatkovyi period v istoriï ukraïns'koho knyhodrukuvannia* (The Initial Period in the History of Ukrainian Book Printing, 1949). Maslov was the coauthor, with Ye. Kyryliuk, of *Narys istoriï ukraïns'koï literatury* (An Outline of the History of Ukrainian Literature, 1945), which was condemned by the CC CPU for bourgeois nationalism. A biobibliography, *Serhii Maslov, 1902–27*, appeared in 1927.

I. Koshelivets

Maslov, Vasyl (Maslii), b ca 1841, d 12 December 1880 in Moscow. Writer and teacher. In the late 1850s he studied in Kiev, where he became acquainted with T. Shevchenko. He wrote the first Russian popular biography of the poet (1874) and collected materials on the archeology and history of Ukraine.

Maslov, Vasyl, b 2 January 1885 in Ichnia, Chernihiv gubernia, d 22 March 1959 in Kiev. Literary scholar and ethnographer; brother of S. Maslov. After graduating from Kiev University (1909) he taught the history of Russian and Ukrainian literature at the university and at the Kiev Pedagogical Institute. He wrote over 50 works, including studies of Ukrainian ethnography in the first half of the 19th century (1934), agricultural implements and technique in the feudal period (1937), and A. Pushkin and the Decembrists (1951). Some of them (eg, the study of the Decembrist influence in 19th-century Ukrainian literature) remain unpublished.

Maslovsky, Opanas [Maslovs'kyj], b 1739 in Tserkovyshche, near Kozelets, Chernihiv regiment, d 7 October 1804 in Kiev. Physician. A graduate of the Kievan Mohyla Academy and the Moscow Medico-Surgical School (1772), he was appointed physician of the Kiev vicegerency in 1784. He introduced the practice of quarantine, attained the rank of doctor of medicine (1792), served as inspector of the Orel (1797–1801) and Kiev (from 1801) medical administrations, and taught medicine at the Kievan Mohyla Academy (from 1802). He wrote a number of works on obstetrics, infectious diseases, botany, and toxicology.

Maslovych, Vasyl [Maslovyč, Vasyl'], b 1793 in Kharkiv, d 1841 in St Petersburg. Writer and journalist. In 1816 he published and edited the journal **Khar'kovskii Demokrit'',* in which his own satirical poems appeared. After it was closed down by the tsarist authorities, he moved to St Petersburg, where he continued writing, but most of his poetry was never published. His tale of Kharko, the founder of Kharkiv, his daughter, Hapka, and the journeyman Yakiv was published in 1890, and his essay on St Petersburg's Nevskii prospekt appeared in 1928.

Masnyk, Ihor, b 17 September 1930 in Mostyska, Lviv county, Galicia. Organic chemist and civic and cultural activist; member of the Shevchenko Scientific Society. A postwar displaced person, he emigrated to the United States in 1949 and completed his education at the University of Chicago (PH D, 1962). Masnyk worked in the field of predictive indices for early recurrence of breast cancer, and administered and comanaged large screening studies in early detection of lung, breast, and colon cancer. Since 1984 Masnyk has been deputy director of the Division of Cancer Biology, Diagnosis, and Centers of the National Cancer Institute (NCI), National Institutes of Health (NIH), in Bethesda, Maryland. From 1983 to 1988 he was also director of international affairs of NCI–NIH. In 1991–2 he participated in setting up and implementing a study of ophthalmic complications in Ukrainian children after the Chornobyl nuclear accident. In 1990 he was honored as Washington's Ukrainian of the Year. Masnyk is the biology subject editor of vols 3–5 of the *Encyclopedia of Ukraine.*

Masnytsia (aka *masliana* and *maslianytsia* 'butter week'). The last week of fun, games, and good food before Lent. During this week, milk, dairy products, and eggs, but not meat, could be consumed. The *masnytsia* had a special ritual menu, which included cheese dumplings with sour cream and butter and buckwheat pancakes. Its rites included the burning of a straw scarecrow representing winter and the mock fettering of eligible young men and women for not having married during the preceding *miasnytsia* (pre-Lenten or inter-Lenten period, or meat week). The first day of the week (Monday) is called *kolodii* (see **Kolodka*), and the last day (Sunday), *pushchennia* 'farewell' (or *lacte vale*). Under the Soviet regime some traditional elements of butter week were preserved in the officially approved spring festivities.

Petro Masokha   Mykhailo Matchak

Masokha, Petro [Masoxa], b 16 September 1904 in Pliuvaky (now Pervomaiske), near Monastyryshche, Lypovets county, Kiev gubernia, d 28 July 1991 in Kiev. Film and stage actor. He completed study at the Lysenko Music and Drama Institute in Kiev (1923) and then played in Berezil (1923–8) and in the Drohobych Ukrainian Music and Drama Theater (1942–4). He acted in O. Dovzhenko's films *Zemlia* (The Earth, 1930) and *Ivan* (1932; the title role) and in other films. After 1945 he was arrested and imprisoned. After his release he participated in the film *Ie takyi khlopets'* (There Is Such a Boy, 1956) and wrote a memoir of L. Kurbas.

Masol, Vitalii, b 14 November 1928 in Olyshivka, now in Chernihiv raion. Communist party leader and Soviet official. After graduating in mechanical engineering from the Kiev Polytechnical Institute (1951) he worked at the Novokramatorske Machine-Building Plant and eventually became its director (1963–71). In 1972 he was appointed first deputy chairman of Ukraine's State Planning Committee, and in 1979, first deputy chairman of the Council of Ministers and chairman of the State Planning Committee. From 1979 he was also deputy to the Ukrainian SSR Supreme Soviet. In July 1987 he replaced O. Liashko as chairman of Ukraine's Council of Ministers, and three years later he was dismissed from the post at the demand of striking students in Kiev. He was a member of the CC CPU from 1976 and of the Central Auditing Committee of the CPSU in 1981–6.

Masons. See Freemasonry.

Masovyi teatr (Mass Theater). A monthly illustrated sociopolitical arts journal. In 1926–31 it was published as *Sil's'kyi teatr* by the Kharkiv municipal art department of the Administration of Political Education of the Ukrainian

SSR. It contained one-act plays, adaptations, reviews of performances of professional and amateur theaters, and instructions for amateur groups, and organized repertory competitions in villages. In 1929–31 another illustrated journal, *Radians'kyi teatr*, was published in Kharkiv by the arts administration of the People's Commissariat of Education of the Ukrainian SSR. It contained theoretical, practical, and historical analyses of theater arts. In 1931–3 the Kharkiv Narkomos and the CC of the Komsomol of the Ukrainian SSR together published *Masovyi teatr*.

Mass. See Liturgy, Divine.

Matchak, Mykhailo [Matčak, Myxajlo], b 28 February 1895 in Volia Yakubova, Drohobych county, Galicia, d 19 November 1958 in Potma, Mordovian ASSR. Political leader, publicist, and publisher. A volunteer to the Ukrainian Sich Riflemen (1914), he was captured in action by the Russians and in 1917 helped organize the Sich Riflemen in Kiev. After being promoted to the rank of captain he sat on the Sich Council and was in charge of the corps's recruitment and training department. After the war he studied law in Lviv and took part in organizing the Lviv (Underground) Ukrainian University and the Ukrainian Military Organization (UVO). A member of the Supreme Command of the UVO, he was sentenced to two years in prison for his involvement in an attempt on J. Piłsudski's life (1921). After resigning from the UVO he became a member of the Chief Secretariat of the Ukrainian Socialist Radical party and its deputy to the Polish Sejm (1930–5). In 1931 he set up his own publishing house, Izmarahd. After emigrating to Vienna in 1944, he worked for the United Nations Relief and Rehabilitation Administration. On 27 February 1947 he was kidnapped by Soviet agents, and subsequently he was sentenced to 25 years of hard labor in Kazakhstan. He was released from labor camp as an invalid in 1955 but was not permitted to leave the USSR.

Mateiuk, Antonii [Matejiuk, Antonij], b ? in Podlachia, d November 1919 in Zhmerynka, Vinnytsia county, Podilia gubernia. Orthodox priest and political and military activist. In 1917 he organized the All-People's Congress of the Kholm Region in Kiev and served as vice-chairman of the Kholm Gubernia Executive Committee and as one of its representatives to the Central Rada. Later he was chaplain of the Second Serdiuk Guard Division and (under the Directory) head chaplain of the UNR Army. After contracting typhus he was captured and shot by A. Denikin's troops.

Materials science (*materialoznavstvo*). The study of the structure, properties, and applications of all types of materials, including metals, ceramics, glasses, and polymers. The earliest research on materials in Ukraine was done in the second half of the 19th century at Kharkiv University, where N. Beketov did some work in aluminothermia. The strength of materials was studied by M. **Ostrohradsky, whose theory of elasticity achieved world renown. D. **Zhuravsky was the first to establish the existence of shearing stresses (1855), and he derived a formula that is still used in design calculations. F. Yasynsky developed a theory of buckling for stresses below and beyond the elastic limit (1893). Research was conducted at the Ukrainian

Academy of Sciences (est 1918) and at universities and higher educational institutions.

In the early 20th century the wider use of *reinforced-concrete and steel structures and the advent of complex machines and mechanisms gave an impetus to the development of materials science in Ukraine. In the 1920s and 1930s scientists such as G. *Kurdiumov, L. Lysak, L. Khandros, and M. Arbuzov conducted X-ray studies of the tempering and annealing of steel and martensitic transformations in nonferrous alloys which laid the foundation for current theories of the thermal treatment of steels and alloys. Norms governing the structure and formation of solids through crystallization from a liquid under external influences were formulated by V. Danilov, D. Ovsiienko, and others. A. *Vynohradov studied the layered structure of steel. Various metal powders were produced by the electrolysis of metal melts and nonaqueous solutions by V. *Izbekov, V. *Plotnikov, and E. Natanson, and iron powder was obtained by M. Luhovtsov and I. Frantsevych by the renewal of mill scale with natural gas. The fundamental mechanisms of the plastic deformation of crystals were investigated and the difference between the theoretical and the empirical strength of crystals was explained by I. Obreimov, N. Brylliantov, R. Harber, V. Startsev, and Y. Hindin.

After the Second World War materials science institutes were set up within the AN URSR (now ANU), including the Institute of Metal Ceramics and Special Alloys (now the *Institute for Problems of Materials Science), the *Institute of Metal Physics, the Institute of Casting Production (now the Institute for Problems of Casting), the Physical-Technical Institute of Low Temperatures, the Ukrainian Design and Technological Institute of Synthetic Superhard Materials and Instruments (now the *Institute of Superhard Materials), and the *Physical-Technical Institute in Donetske. Materials science research is also conducted at the Kiev and Kharkiv polytechnical institutes, Kiev University, the Kharkiv Aviation Institute, and the Dnipropetrovske Metallurgical Institute.

Theoretical and experimental research in materials science in Ukraine has been concerned with heterogeneous equivalences and physical-chemical analysis (V. *Yeremenko, A. Berezhnoi, P. *Budnikov, L. Lopato), electron theory and the electron structure of metals (I. *Lifshyts) and chemical bonds (G. *Samsonov), the physical theory of the deformation and destruction of solids (V. *Trefilov), the thermodynamics of molten metals and the chemistry of surfaces (Yeremenko, Yu. *Naidych, H. Lukashenko), the theoretical problems of heat proofing and thermal and heat resistance (Frantsevych), and theoretical aspects of the formulation of the properties of porous and composite materials and products (D. Karpynos, V. Skorokhod, P. Kysly). A unique method of heat treating high-carbon steels was developed by V. Hridniev, Trefilov, and Yu. Meshkov. The norms of diffusion and recrystallization processes were studied by S. Hertsriken, Ya. Geguzin, I. Dekhtiar, and L. Larikov. Theories were developed about imperfections in crystal structure and how to detect them (M. *Kryvohlaz, A. *Smirnov, Ye. Nesterenko, Dekhtiar), powder sintering (B. Pines, Geguzin), and the diffusion-dislocation tendency of crystals, the dislocation mechanism of crystal growth, and pore and crack filling under pressure (Lifshyts, A. Kosevych, V. Slozov). The effect of

temperature on the plastic deformation and strengthening of uranium, as well as methods and conditions for the alloying of uranium, was studied by V. *Zelensky, A. Voloshchuk, and A. Stukalov. A dislocation theory for the cold frangibility of refractory materials and bonds was proposed by Trefilov, Yu. Milman, and S. Firstov. Pioneering studies on the plastic deformation of metals and laminated materials produced by vacuum rolling were begun by K. *Synelnykov, V. Ivanov, and V. Amonenko. Descriptions of norms in the appearance of secondary grain boundaries in cast metals and alloys and the properties of the mechanism of intercrystalline destruction in those materials (B. *Movchan) had many practical applications.

The physicochemical approach to materials science was widely developed in Ukraine and was focused on diagramming the states of metal and nonmetal systems, the thermodynamics of metal melts, the interphase interaction and adhesion of diffuse melts, and the internal adsorption in solids (V. *Svechnikov, V. *Arkharov, Yeremenko, Naidych, Yu. Krakovetsky-Kocherzhynsky). A series of experiments was conducted on the synthesis and crystallochemistry of refractory bonds, their physicochemical and mechanical properties, and the technology for producing such materials (Samsonov, T. Kosolapova, V. Obolonchyk, M. Smolin, Ye. Hladyshevsky). Frantsevych and I. *Radomyselsky refined the technology and equipment for producing iron powder.

Methods for producing superthin fibers and preparing porous materials out of discrete fibers were developed. New materials were created, including frictional and frictionless, filter (I. *Fedorchenko), resistant (G. Gnesin, O. Teodorovych), and superhard instrumental materials (V. *Bakul, Frantsevych, H. Kariuk, Kurdiumov, O. *Pyliankevych), materials with special physical properties (O. *Goldman, M. *Lysytsia, K. *Tovstiuk, L. Palatnyk), and superconducting alloys (B. *Lazarev). Yu. *Taran-Zhovnir developed the theory of the multiphase crystallization of eutectic alloys; S. Tresviatsky studied diagrams of the oxide states of rare-earth elements; K. *Starodubov developed the theoretical foundations, technology, and equipment for the strengthening heat treatment of cast products; and B. *Hrozin proposed a complex method of investigating the surface-active layers of metals.

Advances were made in the technological processes of metalization, particularly the gas-detonation method, and in the soldering of nonmetallic materials. Fundamental work was done by O. Aksonov and V. Popov on friction and wear resistance in metals, by K. Bunin on phase transitions in metals, by O. *Romaniv on the mechanics of the corrosive destruction of metals, by V. Trufiakov on the strength of materials and structures, by G. Zemskov on the chemical-thermal treatment of metals and alloys, by D. *Dudko on the plasma treatment of materials, and by M. Braun on new methods of fracture analysis.

Recent materials science research in Ukraine is focused on developing chemical and technological processes for producing new substances and materials with more efficient and environmentally benign properties as well as investigating the real dislocational structure of monocrystals of refractory metals.

Results appear in Russian-language scientific journals, published in Ukraine, such as *Poroshkovaia metallurgiia*, *Sverkhtverdye materialy*, *Metallofizika*, *Fiziko-khimicheskaia mekhanika materialov*, and *Problemy prochnosti*.

BIBLIOGRAPHY
Pisarenko, G.; et al. *Prochnost' metallov pri vysokikh temperaturakh* (Kiev 1966)
Samsonov, G. *Nitridy* (Kiev 1969)
Troshchenko, V. *Ustalost' i neuprugost' metallov* (Kiev 1971)
Trefilov, V.; Mil'man, Iu.; Firstov, S. *Fizicheskie osnovy prochnosti tugoplavkikh metallov* (Kiev 1975)

Materialy z etnohrafiï ta mystetstvoznavstva (Materials in Ethnography and Art Studies). An annual collection of the Ukrainian State Museum of Ethnography and Crafts, published in Kiev from 1954 to 1963 (a total of eight volumes). The first three issues were titled *Materialy z etnohrafiï ta khudozhn'oho promyslu*. The serial published articles on ethnography and the history of Ukrainian culture and art, concentrating on Galicia, Transcarpathia, Polisia, and the Carpathian region. Its chief editors were I. Symonenko, M. Ivasiuta, and Yu. Hoshko.

Materiialy do ukraïns'koï bibliohrafiï (Materials for Ukrainian Bibliography). An irregular serial published in Lviv by the Bibliographic Commission of the Shevchenko Scientific Society from 1909 to 1939. A total of eight volumes appeared. The first three volumes consisted of I. Levytsky's bibliography of Ukrainian publications in the Austro-Hungarian Empire. Many of the subsequent volumes were edited by V. Doroshenko.

Materiialy do ukraïns'koï etnolohiï (Materials on Ukrainian Ethnology). An annual publication of the *Ethnographic Commission of the Shevchenko Scientific Society, published in Lviv in 1899–1928 (a total of 22 volumes). The collection was called first *Materiialy do ukraïns'korus'koï etnolohiï* (16 vols, 1899–1908) and then *Materiialy do ukraïns'koï etnolohiï* (1909–19). In 1928 it reappeared briefly as *Materiialy do etnolohiï i antropolohiï*. It contained articles on Ukrainian and non-Ukrainian ethnography, folklore, culture, and history; book reviews; and surveys of developments in ethnographic studies. The editors of the collection were F. Vovk (1899–1905), I. Franko (1906–15), and V. Hnatiuk. Among its many contributors were F. Kolessa, V. Shukhevych, M. Rusov, S. Liudkevych, I. Rakovsky, V. Domanytsky, and K. Hrushevska.

Mathematics. Mathematics can be defined as the systematic treatment of magnitude, relationships between figures and forms, and relations between quantities expressed symbolically.

Elements of mathematical knowledge are found in the early history of Ukraine. In Kievan Rus' the requirements of commercial transactions, trade, taxation, land measurement, construction, architecture, military fortifications, navigation, the calendar, and other undertakings contributed not only to the development of a specific system of measurement but also to the application of elementary rules of arithmetic and geometry. The Rus' way of counting was used until the introduction of the decimal system at the end of the 17th century. Some explanations of Aristotelian definitions of abstract mathematics is contained in the *Izbornik* of Sviatoslav (1073), and some mathematical problems are contained in *Ruskaia Pravda*. The first textbooks on mathematics appeared in Ukrainian in the 17th century.

One of the most distinguished professors of mathematics and physics at the Kievan Mohyla Academy was T. *Prokopovych. His courses in mathematics at the academy were the first in Ukraine and in the Russian Empire. Although mathematics was taught at Lviv University, it was not a subject of serious study until the second half of the 19th century.

Beginning of the 19th century to 1917. The development of mathematics as a separate science began in Ukraine early in the 19th century with the establishment of universities in Kharkiv (1805) and Kiev (1834). The growth of this discipline by the later 19th century is reflected in the establishment of the *Kharkiv Mathematics Society (1879) and the *Kiev Physics and Mathematics Society (1890). A significant role in the development of mathematics was also played by the founding of universities in Odessa (1865) and Chernivtsi (1875). Since 1897 the mathematical–natural sciences–medical section of the *Shevchenko Scientific Society (NTSh) has published transactions that include articles on mathematics and on Ukrainian mathematical terminology.

One of the first mathematicians and physicists at Kharkiv University was T. *Osipovsky, whose main contribution to mathematics was a three-volume treatise (1801–23) that was a basic university textbook for many years. The first Ukrainian mathematician to gain world renown was M. *Ostrohradsky. In addition to original contributions to number theory, algebra, and geometry, he is best known for his contributions in mathematical analysis and, in particular, for his work on the transformation of multiple integrals, a theory of which he (together with G. Green and K. Gauss) is regarded as the founder. The so-called Green-Ostrohradsky or Gauss-Ostrohradsky theorem forms a basis for the modern study of partial differential equations, variational calculus, theoretical mechanics, and electromagnetism. V. *Buniakovsky is well known for his work in mathematical analysis, number theory, and probability theory. Ostrohradsky's students I. Sokolov and E. Beyer joined the staff of Kharkiv University in 1839 and 1845 respectively. Sokolov's teaching and research were in theoretical mechanics; Beyer was primarily interested in differential equations and the theory of probability. Beyer's course on probability initiated a field of study for which Kharkiv University became well known. In the 1870s and 1880s most mathematics courses were taught by D. Delarue and M. Kovalsky, both graduates of Kharkiv University, and by K. *Andreev, V. Ishmenetsky, and M. *Tykhomandrytsky.

At the end of the 19th and the beginning of the 20th century Kharkiv University played a particularly significant role in the development of mathematics in Ukraine. During that time its faculty was joined by a group of young mathematicians that included A. *Liapunov, V. *Steklov, A. Psheborsky, S. *Bernshtein, and D. *Syntsov. They gained world recognition for fundamental results: Liapunov's stability theory of motion and central limit theorem of probability; Steklov's results in the theories of potential and heat conduction, the existence of Green's function and its analytic representation, the use of eigenfunction expansion, and the notion of completeness in the solvability of boundary value problems in mathematical physics; Psheborsky's results in the theory of elliptic functions and differential geometry; Bernshtein's new method of determining the solvability of ordinary and partial differential equations, constructive function theory, and the axiomatic theory of probability; and Syntsov's theory of conics and the geometry of differential equations.

At Kiev University S. Vyzhevsky, M. *Diachenko, and A. Tykhomandrytsky taught mathematics from its founding in 1834. In the later part of the 19th century important research was conducted by M. *Vashchenko-Zakharchenko (the use of operational calculus in determining the solvability of linear differential equations, theory of probability, history of mathematics), V. *Yermakov (new method of determining the solvability of the canonical system of dynamics, some problems of algebra and the convergence of series, theory of probability), B. *Bukreev (theory and applications of Fuchsian functions of rank zero, projective and non-Euclidean geometry, study of differential invariants and parameters in the theory of surfaces, history of mathematics), and P. Pokrovsky (theory of ultraelliptic functions).

At the beginning of the 20th century the mathematics faculty in Kiev was joined by three talented newcomers, Yu. *Pfeiffer (1900), P. *Voronets (1899), and D. *Grave (1902). Pfeiffer's most important contributions were to the development of the theory of partial differential equations along the lines initiated by the famous Norwegian mathematician S. Lie. Voronets's most important work was done in mechanics when in 1908 he derived the equation of motion for nonholonomic systems. Grave did some work in applied mathematics and mechanics, but his main interest was in algebra and number theory, where he obtained some new results in Galois theory and the theory of ideals. Several of his students (including O. Shmidt, M. Chebotarev, B. Delone, V. Velmin, M. Kravchuk, E. Zhilinsky, and A. Ostrovsky) later became world-class algebraists. With Grave as the founder of the Kiev algebra school, Kiev became by 1917 the leading center of algebraic studies in Ukraine.

Mathematical research at Odessa University in the 1890s was conducted by V. Preobrazhensky (calculus, differential equations), I. *Sleshynsky (method of least squares, mathematical logic, theory of probability), and S. *Yaroshenko (analytic geometry, least squares method). At the turn of the century the mathematics faculty was enlarged by Sleshynsky's promising graduates I. Tymchenko (differential equations, history of mathematics, analytic functions), V. Tsimmerman (variational calculus, projective geometry), and E. Bunitsky (integral equations, ordinary differential equations, construction of Green's functions for nth order equations). This group was further strengthened by the addition of the two talented mathematicians V. Kahan (axiomatic treatment of Euclidean geometry different from Hilbert axiomatics, study of Lobachevsky geometry) and S. *Shatunovsky (algebra, geometry, number theory, analysis, constructive approach to mathematics).

In the later 19th century, mathematical research at Lviv University was conducted by W. Żmurko (analytic geometry, algebra, and mathematical analysis) and later by J. Puzyna (analytic function theory). The basic mathematics courses at the university were taught by Puzyna and J. Rajewski. Important research activity began in 1909, when W. Sierpiński started to teach analytic number theory, theory of functions, and mathematical analysis. In 1913 Z. Janiszewski joined the faculty, and in 1917 Lviv University attracted the talented mathematician H. Steinhauss, thus initiating the famous Lviv school of functional analysis. Mathematics was also taught at the Lviv Polytechnic (today the Lviv Polytechnical Institute).

From 1893 to 1917 the mathematical–natural sciences–medical section of the NTSh published 17 volumes of its *Zapysky*. It provided a valuable forum for Ukrainian mathematicians, such as V. *Levytsky, M. Chaikivsky, and M. *Zarytsky. The major emphasis of the section was to develop Ukrainian terminology in mathematics and the natural sciences. The noted Ukrainian-born mathematician Ya. *Kulyk worked at Charles University in Prague (1826–63).

After 1917. The structure of the Ukrainian Academy of Sciences included a division of physics and mathematics. The entire Ukrainian educational system, however, was now required to have a practical orientation. One result was that in the 1920s D. Grave discontinued the algebra seminar which formed the basis of his famous prerevolutionary Kiev school of algebra, but led a seminar in applied mathematics devoted to various technological problems. The abolition of the university system in Ukraine provided additional difficulties and spurred a wholesale departure of mathematicians from Ukraine for universities in Moscow, Leningrad, and Kazan. Scholars such as Shmidt, Delone, and Chebotarev left and later became founders of different algebraic schools at their respective universities. Kahan left Odessa in 1923 for Moscow University, where he became the founder of a school of tensor differential geometry.

During the 1920s the Academy of Sciences in Kiev and its affiliates – commissions on pure mathematics (chaired by Yu. Pfeiffer), applied mathematics (Grave), and mathematical statistics (Kravchuk), and the chair of mathematical physics (M. *Krylov) – assumed the leading role in mathematical research in Ukraine. Some research was also done at the mathematical chairs of institutes of people's education and of polytechnical and other institutes.

In the 1930s a shift in Soviet policy led to the reorganization of research and educational institutions in Ukraine, but mathematical research continued to be harnessed to the needs of the heavy industrialization program in Ukraine. The academy became an association of 36 branch institutes. The *Institute of Mathematics was established in 1934 out of three mathematical commissions and Grave served as the institute's first director (1934–9). After the Soviet occupation of Galicia in 1939 and Bukovyna in 1940, several distinguished Polish mathematicians of the well-known Lviv school of functional analysis (notably S. *Banach) and some mathematicians from Chernivtsi University became affiliated with the institute. During Yu. *Mytropolsky's directorship (1958–88), the institute experienced a great expansion in research personnel and mathematical disciplines, and an improvement in the quality of research. Until the middle of 1941 the Kiev institute was a co-ordinating center for mathematical work done at the universities in Kiev, Kharkiv, Odessa, Dnipropetrovske, Lviv, and Chernivtsi. At present, mathematical research is conducted at various institutes of the Academy of Sciences, including the institutes of Mathematics (Kiev), Cybernetics (Kiev), Theoretical Physics (Kiev and Kharkiv), Applied Mechanics and Mathematics (Lviv), and Applied Mathematics and Mechanics (Donetske). There is a mathematical section at the Physical-Technical Institute of Low Temperatures (Kharkiv) and there are mathematics chairs at nine universities, at polytechnical institutes, computer centers, and other institutions.

Algebra, geometry, topology. The development of algebra, including number theory, in Ukraine passed through two stages. The first began with the founding of the Kiev school of algebra and number theory by Grave in the early 20th century and ended in the late 1920s when Grave was ordered to shift his research and teaching activities from algebra (including number theory) to mechanics and various problems in applied mathematics. During the second decade of this stage Grave and his former students Shmidt, Delone, and Chebotarev obtained important results in Galois theory and other areas. At the same time fundamental contributions to the theory of semigroups were made by A. Sushkevych, the proponent of a concept known as the Sushkevych kernel. He was also the founder of the theory of quasi-groups. During the 1930s new results in algebra were obtained by Sushkevych, Kravchuk, and M. Krein from Odessa.

The publication of the works of H. Vorony in 1952–3 provided a fresh stimulus, and from the mid-1950s Kiev began to regain its position as a strong center of algebraic studies. In 1955 the noted algebraist L. Kaluzhnin, who worked in the area of group theory, occupied the fledgling chair of algebra at Kiev University. In 1956 V. *Hlushkov joined the AN URSR (now ANU) Institute of Mathematics. He received world recognition for his fundamental work in topological algebras and cybernetics. In the early 1950s V. Velmin returned to Kiev as a professor of algebra and number theory, and in 1952–4 he published his lectures on the theory of algebraic fields. In the mid-1960s an algebra section was established at the Institute of Mathematics of the ANU. Its longtime director, S. Chernikov, obtained results in the study of locally solvable and locally nilpotent groups and other areas and established a useful principle of limiting solutions in the study of the algebraic theory of linear inequalities. In the early 1960s the work of Hlushkov on topological groups was continued by V. Charin, who joined Chernikov, Kaluzhnin, and the talented younger algebraists D. Zaitsev and Ya. Sysak, and later by Yu. Drozd at Kiev University in studying the theory of groups of various types. Work in linear algebra was done by A. Roiter, L. Nazarova, and V. Bondarenko. Sushkevych's work on semigroups was continued in the 1960s by his student L. Hlushkin. The chair of algebra and number theory at Kharkiv University was directed by Yu. Lubich, who led studies of periodic and almost periodic semigroups in Banach and other spaces, while Drozd at Kiev University studied mostly the representation of finite groups.

During the 1920s some important work in tensor differential geometry was initiated in Odessa, and interesting results in kinematic geometry were obtained in Dnipropetrovske. In Kiev, B. Bukreev continued his main research into various geometries and from the 1940s concentrated on aspects of Lobachevsky geometry. During that time interesting results in geometric constructions in the Lobachevsky plane were also obtained by O. Smohorzhevsky of the Kiev Polytechnical Institute. After 1961 geometry was taught at Kiev University by M. Kovantsov, who obtained significant results in nonholonomic and projective differential geometries. Kharkiv, however, emerged as the most important center of geometry studies in Ukraine, the university and the ANU Physical-Technical Institute of Low Temperatures playing a leading role in this regard. The base for a Kharkiv school of geometry was laid by Syntsov and his students (including Ya. Blank

and D. Hordiievsky). O. *Pohorielov, who taught at Kharkiv University from 1947, assumed the leadership of the school and turned it into a leading scientific center. V. Drinfeld, a member of that center, was awarded the Fields Medal in mathematics in 1990 for his contributions to algebraic geometry, number theory, and quantum group theory.

In the 1960s a group of Kiev mathematicians at the ANU Institute of Mathematics began the study of topological properties of functions and transformations, including problems in Morse theory and K-theory. Yu. Trokhymchuk has shown that if the transformation of a domain in an n-dimensional Euclidean space into itself is nullmeasurable and its local degree is defined and positive, except for a certain set, then it is isolated and open on the entire domain, and its local degree is positive everywhere. A series of theorems characterizing holomorphic mappings in terms of local geometric characteristics was proved by A. Bodnar in the study of multidimensional analogues of derivative operators in complex spaces. Using multivalued mappings Yu. Zilinsky obtained the geometrical criteria for strong linear convexity of compacts and domains in multidimensional complex space and solved a number of problems concerning the transformation of domains into manifolds. V. Sharko found necessary and sufficient conditions for the exact Morse function defined on a simply connected manifold to be isotopic, devised a method for the construction of the minimal Morse function on a non-simply-connected manifold, and developed substantially the finite-dimensional Morse theory and its applications. Quite general cover theorems and other results were obtained by P. Tamrazov. Morse functions were also studied by E. Mykhailiuk and I. Solopko.

Theory of functions. The most fruitful development in the theory of functions has been in the theory of approximation of functions of real and complex variables by algebraic or trigonometric polynomials or other simpler functions.

After 1917 S. Bernshtein continued his work at Kharkiv University in constructive function theory, for which he became internationally known in the early 1920s. In the 1920s and early 1930s Bernshtein and members of his school obtained important results in the study of absolutely monotone functions and entire functions with finite degrees. From the many members of the Kharkiv school significant contributions were made by Ya. Geronimus (orthogonal polynomials, studies of extremal properties of trigonometric and rational polynomials), V. Honcharov (approximation and interpolation of functions), B. Levin (theory of entire functions with regular growth), and B. Levitan (study of almost periodic functions defined in all of R). In 1933 N. *Akhiiezer joined the Kharkiv school and soon became its leading member. His most outstanding work consisted of deep approximation results in the constructive function theory, including the solution of the problem of Zolotarev. Outstanding results in the approximation theory were obtained in the 1950s by V. *Marchenko of the Physical-Technical Institute in Kharkiv including the study of almost periodic functions in R. Important contributions for the latter class of functions were also made in the 1930s to 1950s by O. Kovanko and I. Sokolov in Lviv, N. Bogoliubov, M. Kravchuk, and S. Zukhovytsky in Kiev, and M. Krein and B. Korenblium in Odessa. In the mid-1930s Ye. *Remez made a significant contribution to a new aspect of the constructive function theory by developing a rigorous numerical method known as the Remez algorithm. Subsequently a similar algorithm was constructed for the rational approximation of continuous functions defined on a segment.

In the mid-1930s the works of A. Kolmogorov and J. Favard laid the foundation for the study of a new problem (know as the extremal problem on classes of functions). In 1937 Akhiiezer and Krein solved the extremal problem in space c for differentiable periodic functions, and somewhat later Akhiiezer solved it for analytic functions. In 1940 S. Nikolsky of Dnipropetrovske University extended the result of Kolmogorov to other classical methods of approximation (Fejer method, interpolation polmonial, and others), to different classes of functions, and for spaces with integral and other norms. Favard proposed a conjecture known as the Favard problem, which was studied extensively in both the former Soviet Union and Europe, until it was solved completely in 1959 by V. *Dziadyk. A by-product of Dziadyk's work on aspects of the Favard problem provided the best linear approximation on classes of functions with bounded fractional derivatives. The problem of finding the exact least upper bound (l.u.b.) of the errors for the class of Hölder continuous periodic functions when the approximation is given by the linear Favard method was solved in 1961 by M. Korniichuk of Dnipropetrovske University. In 1970 Korniichuk solved that problem in its complete generality by inventing a new method, which was subsequently used by various authors. In the late 1960s and early 1970s Korniichuk, Dziadyk, and A. Stepanets developed a new method for finding asymptotic l.u.b. when smooth functions are approximated by general Fourier summation polynomials. This method was later extended by Stepanets to the multidimensional case.

Korniichuk joined Dziadyk at the ANU Institute of Mathematics in 1974, thereby making Kiev a strong center for the study of the approximation theory of functions. Dziadyk and his students V. Konovalov and L. Shevchuk developed new methods for the solution of extremal problems and found the best conditions to ensure the continuation of a function in a Sobolev space from some plane set to the entire plane. Korniichuk and his school continued to work on the theory of approximation of functions, which led in 1987 to the publication of a monograph on exact constants in the theory of approximation (1987). In 1983 Stepanets developed a new approach in the classification of periodic functions. Yu. Melnyk developed new effective methods for the construction of entire functions with given asymptotic properties, which were then applied to the theory of system representation. V. Havryliuk found necessary and sufficient conditions for the convergence of multiple singular integrals at Lebesgue points of summable functions. These types of results in real function theory were extended by Konovalov, Shevchuk, P. Zaderei, and others. Important work in the real function theory was also carried on in Kharkiv (Y. Ostrovsky, V. Protsenko), Dnipropetrovske (A. Timan), Lviv, Odessa, and other centers.

The development of the theory of functions of a complex variable was influenced by the Moscow mathematician M. *Lavrentev, who was appointed director of the Institute of Mathematics in Kiev (1939–41, 1945–8) during the height of industrialization and hydrotechnical construction in Ukraine. Lavrentev made fundamental contributions to the theory of conformal and quasi-conformal mappings and its diverse application to various fields, including industrial development. His theories were further developed by a number of his students and associates in Ukraine and elsewhere. P. Bilinsky of Lviv University made significant contributions in the 1950s to the differentiability and the behavior theory of quasi-conformal mappings at isolated points and to structure theory. He was the first to introduce the basic variational method into the theory of quasi-conical maps. His students S. Krushkal and P. Biluta continued his work. In the 1960s H. *Suvorov of Donetske extended a number of Lavrentev's results for conformal and quasi-conformal mappings, including stability and differentiability theorems, to more general classes of plane and spatial transformations. Original results in the theory of functions of a complex variable were obtained in the 1950s and 1960s by H. *Polozhii of Kiev, who introduced a new notion of p-analytic functions, defined the notions of derivative and integral for these functions, developed their calculus, obtained a generalized Cauchy formula, and devised a new approximation method for solution of problems in elasticity and filtration. His results were further developed by his students and I. *Liashko, who solved a series of problems in the theory of filtration. P. Filchakov obtained important results in the effective approximate construction of the Riemann function, the determination of constants in the Kristoffel-Schwartz integral, and the development of a method, based on the earlier results of Lavrentev, for the solution of general problems of plane filtration in homogeneous and anisotropic grounds. Efforts of Lavrentev's and his colleagues' research were directed after 1945 toward the development of methods that laid the foundation for the massive hydrotechnical construction of dams, canals, and bridges on the Volga, Dnieper, and Don rivers.

Significant results in the theory of general analytical functions were obtained in the 1960s and 1970s by I. *Danyliuk of Donetske who used them to solve complicated PDEs and singular integral equations. Dziadyk obtained a simple geometrical characterization of analytic functions and their conjugates and introduced new ideas into their study. P. Tamrazov solved an important general problem concerning the limiting behavior of the holomorphic function and also solved a number of extremal problems for conformal mappings. I. Mitiuk obtained new results for univalent and multivalent conformal mappings and developed new methods for their study. Using some topological results of Reshetniak of the late 1960s, Yu. Trokhymchuk showed that the well-known theorems of D. Menshov on conformal mappings are valid in n-dimensional Euclidean space for n larger than two. Earlier V. Zmorovych of Kiev extended significantly the Riesz-Gerglotz theorem to obtain new integral representation theorems for certain classes of univalent and nonunivalent injective holomorphic and meromorphic functions, by means of which theorems he solved many extremal problems. The approach of integral representation used widely by Kiev mathematicians in the theory of univalent functions (1948–66) was later 'rediscovered' and developed anew by Western mathematicians.

Fundamental and multifaceted contributions to the theory of entire and meromorphic functions were made by scholars based in Kharkiv (Bernshtein, Levin, Honcharov,

Akhiiezer, Ostrovsky, and Marchenko), Odessa (Krein, V. Potapov), and Lviv (A. Goldberg), and earlier by Kravchuk and Chebotarev. The problem of approximating various classes of functions of a complex variable by polynomials and rational functions was considered by Lavrentev and Bilinsky. But the constructive theory of functions of complex variables (similar to the one originated by Bernshtein for functions of real variables) arose from the work of Dziadyk in the late 1950s and in new methods he described in a series of outstanding papers in the 1960s and 1970s. Significant results were also obtained in the 1970s and 1980s by his former students Shevchuk, V. Bely, A. Holub, and V. Andriievsky in Donetske and Konovalov, Tamrazov, V. Temlakov, and Zaderei in Kiev.

Functional analysis and its applications. The development of functional analysis and its applications was a fruitful field in Ukraine, especially after 1950, when the renowned Odessa school was joined by strong functional analysis groups in Kiev (N. Bogoliubov, O. Parasiuk, Yu. Berezansky, Yu. Daletsky, M. Horbachuk, and H. Kats), Kharkiv (Akhiiezer, Marchenko, Ostrovsky, I. Glazmann, M. Kadets, L. Pastur, and D. Milman), Donetske (I. Skrypnyk, Danyliuk), Lviv (V. Lantse, A. Plishko), and Chernivtsi (M. Popov).

The first major results in Ukraine were obtained in 1935–7 by Bogoliubov and Krylov, who proved the existence of an invariant measure in dynamical systems that had been simply assumed until then. This proof was essential to the development of a general theory. During the first phase of development (1935–50) M. Krein obtained fundamental and, in some cases, pioneering results in areas such as cones in Banach spaces, eigenvalue problems for positive linear operators, and topology and geometry in Banach spaces. Some of these results are now found in standard books on functional analysis as theorems of Krein, Krein-Rutman, Krein-Shmulian, Krein-Milman, Krein-Krasnoselsky, and so on. The development of functional analysis in Ukraine was enhanced after the annexation of Western Ukraine when one of the founders of its study, S. Banach of Lviv, joined the Ukrainian mathematical community. In the 1950s important topological and geometrical properties of Banach spaces were obtained by Kadets, Milman, and Levin and a series of results on extension of operators (different from Krein's) were obtained by I. Glazmann of Kharkiv and Lantse of Lviv. The first essential step toward studying the spectral theory was taken in the late 1940s by Krein, who later applied his results and the theory of entire operators to the Sturm-Liouville problem on semiaxis. In 1956–65 Berezansky developed a new abstract method in the expansion theory in Hilbert spaces and used it to extend Krein's results to partial differential operators of a certain type in functional Hilbert spaces. He also showed that an abstract self-adjoint operator in Hilbert space admits an expansion in terms of its generalized eigenvectors. Some results of the latter type were also obtained by Kats. In the late 1970s and early 1980s Berezansky further extended his results. The study of differential equations which can be written only in bilinear forms was undertaken by M. Horbachuk and his students in Kiev. In the 1970s and 1980s V. Koshmanenko of Kiev developed a general theory of dissipative operators. During this time Berezansky together with his students H. Usom, Yu. Kondriatev, and Yu. Samoilenko developed a spectral theory of elliptic operators with an infinite number of variables and applied it to some operators in quantum field theory. Further results in this direction were obtained by L. Nizhnyk for nonelliptic operators.

The first basic results on the asymptotic behavior of the spectral measure and of the spectral function for the Sturm-Liouville equation were obtained in the early 1950s by Marchenko, who later obtained similar results for the Schrödinger equation. The so-called inverse problem for Sturm-Liouville was solved independently by different methods in the 1950s by Marchenko, Krein, and by I. Gelfand and B. Levitan in Moscow. Jointly with Y. Ostrovsky, Marchenko also solved the eigenvalue problem for the Hill equation with periodic boundary conditions and summarized the results in his monograph *Sturm-Liouville Operators and Applications* (1986). Berezansky was the first to study the inverse problem for equations involving partial derivatives or partial differences. In the 1960s Nizhnyk began detailed study of direct and inverse problems in nonstationary dissipation and, in particular, the system of Dirac equations. In 1947–8 M. Krein began the study of equations in Banach space involving bounded operator coefficients with emphasis on stability. This work was continued by Daletsky, S. Krein, and others. In 1949 Bogoliubov and B. Khatset showed that some equilibrium problems in statistical mechanics lead to the solvability of an operator equation of the above type in a Banach space of distributions. The case of differential equations whose coefficients are unbounded operators in Hilbert space was studied by Horbachuk and others. The study of spectral properties, completeness of generalized eigenvectors, resolvents, and other properties of non-self-adjoint operators and operator-functions was undertaken in the 1950s to 1980s by Yu. Berezansky, M. Horbachuk, M. Krein, V. Marchenko, V. Lantse and others. In the 1950s to 1970s M. Krein developed the theory of linear operators in spaces with indefinite metric. A. Kuzhel of Kiev dealt with spectral analysis and extensions of various classes of linear operators in the 1960s to 1980s.

Berezansky and Kats introduced and studied the abstract form of Sobolev spaces with positive and negative norms. The application of these spaces disclosed a series of interesting facts about partial differential equations and provided a framework for other work. Berezansky, V. Didenko, Ya. Roitberg, and others studied the Dirichlet boundary value problem for elliptic equations, smoothness of solutions, and properties of Green's functions. O. *Parasiuk used the generalized functions to study the solvability of integral equations. Together with Bogoliubov he proved a fundamental theorem on the possibility of regularization of a matrix of dissipation for any order of the perturbation theory. These results were later applied to the construction of a theory of electromagnetic and weak interactions. Since 1970 I. *Skrypnyk has made fundamental contributions to the development of nonlinear functional analysis, in which he introduced a new class of type (α) nonlinear operators acting from a Banach space to its dual, developed for it a detailed topological degree theory, and applied this theory to obtain new existence theorems for a general class of abstract and concrete nonlinear partial differential equations in mechanics, elasticity, mathematical physics, and other fields. Direct methods of qualitative spectral analysis were applied by Glazmann in the 1960s to singular differential operators.

Mathematical physics and nonlinear mechanics. The first important and new results in mathematical physics in Ukraine were contained in pioneering works published in the late 1920s and early 1930s by Krylov and Bogoliubov, who founded the renowned Krylov-Bogoliubov school. They laid the foundation of nonlinear mechanics, a new branch of mathematical physics that deals with the development of effective mathematical methods in the study of nonlinear oscillations by means of nonlinear differential equations involving a small parameter. Bogoliubov's most important contribution, the so-called method of averaging, was made in 1945. In 1949 Mytropolsky began a sustained and systematic study of this and other asymptotic methods as well as the construction of a general theory of dynamic systems. He developed new asymptotic methods with applications to problems in contemporary physics and technology and, together with Bogoliubov, published (1961) a classic work on asymptotic methods in the theory of nonlinear oscillations. The ideas of Krylov and Bogoliubov were further developed in monographs by O. Lypkova (1973), B. Moseenkov (1976), D. Martyniuk (1979), A. Molchanov (1981), H. Khoma (1983), A. Samoilenko and D. Martyniuk (1985), Samoilenko (1987), and A. Lopatin (1988), all coauthored by Mytropolsky.

The development of mathematical physics in Ukraine after the 1930s was undertaken by Bogoliubov, Parasiuk, V. Fushchych, D. Petryna, L. Pastur, L. Drimfold, and others. Bogoliubov again made pioneering contributions. He was the first to provide the mathematical foundation for a consistent microscopic theory of superfluidity (1947) and constructed a mathematical theory of superconductivity (1958). The latter theory represents a fundamental achievement in theoretical physics. He also derived equations in hydrodynamics and obtained important results in quantum statistics. Together with Parasiuk he provided the mathematical foundation for the method of renormalization in quantum field theory – the so-called Bogoliubov-Parasiuk theorem. Continuing these studies, Parasiuk developed a theorem in the theory of generalized functions analogous to E. Titchmarsh's theorem, and obtained new results in the theory of plasticity, and dynamical systems. Fushchych studied the symmetric properties of equations of mathematical physics and introduced an effective method (distinct from the method of S. Lie) for the study of symmetric properties of solutions of partial differential equations.

Since the 1970s L. Pastur has dealt with the spectral properties of various operators, an area of study which relates to mathematical physics, theoretical physics, and in particular, the theory of disordered condensed systems. In 1964 Petryna obtained important results in the study of analytic properties of the enclosed Feynman diagram. Petryna, V. Garasimenko, and V. Malyshev studied solutions of Bogoliubov equations for an infinite three-dimensional system of particles.

Theory of differential equations. Mathematicians such as Bernshtein, Pfeiffer, Krylov, Bogoliubov, Yu. *Sokolov, M. Krein, Daletsky, Lavrentev, Y. *Shtokalo, Ya. *Lopatynsky, Marchenko, Mytropolsky, Berezansky, Danyliuk, Skrypnyk, A. *Samoilenko, M. Perestiuk, O. *Sharkovsky, and A. Myshkis and their students made some important contributions to the theory of ordinary, functional, and partial differential equations (ODEs, FDEs, and PDEs). Fundamental applications to mechanics, elasticity, hydrodynamics, geometry, and other fields are contained in the works of Krylov, Bogoliubov, Yu. Sokolov, O. Dynnyk, H. Savyn, Pohorielov, L. Pastur, M. Lavrentev, and others. In addition to the well-known Kiev school of nonlinear mechanics and the school of theoretical physics founded by Bogoliubov, the elasticity school founded in the late 1920s by O. Dynnyk in Dnipropetrovske had a considerable influence on the development of the theory of differential equations in Ukraine, especially on the development of asymptotic methods and their application to various types of nonlinear ODEs and FDEs. As well, Yu. Sokolov obtained significant results in the theory of differential equations, which he applied to problems of analytical mechanics, and developed the Sokolov method (averaging method with functional corrections).

In 1955 Bogoliubov and Mytropolsky published a monograph on asymptotic methods in the theory of nonlinear oscillations. It led to further refinements of the theory of asymptotic methods and to new methods of solving nonlinear ODEs and FDEs. In the 1960s the Kiev school of nonlinear mechanics shifted its attention to at least three areas that involve certain classes of ODEs and FDEs: systems of nonlinear ODEs with impulsive action (culminating in A. Samoilenko and M. Perestiuk's monograph in 1987), ODEs with delay and/or deviating argument (A. Myshkis, Mytropolsky, Martyniuk, and A. Samoilenko), and FDEs and related equations (Sharkovsky, E. Romanenko, and H. Pelekh).

Since the mid-1940s the qualitative theory, particularly the stability theory of solutions of systems of linear ODEs, has become a subject of considerable study. Important contributions to linear ODEs with almost-periodic and quasi-periodic coefficients were made in the 1940s and 1950s by Shtokalo, who was the first to extend the applicability of the operational method to linear ODEs with variable coefficients. M. Krein studied the problem of the existence and distributions of stability and instability zones for linear Hamiltonian systems with periodic coefficients, extended Liapunov's results to systems of equations, and established the connection between the eigenvalues of certain differential operators and the boundary of the stability zones. For these systems Krein also obtained important results in the theory of direct and inverse spectral problems. In the 1960s M. Gavrilov and his students in Odessa obtained new and very general criteria for stability in the Liapunov sense of solutions of linear systems and even nonlinear ODEs. Interesting results concerning the asymptotic behavior of solutions of linear ODEs and systems of ODEs were obtained in the 1950 and 1960s by S. Feshchenko, M. Shkil, and I. Rapoport under various conditions on the coefficients.

In the 1960s V. Skorobohatko and E. Bobyk in Lviv found the necessary and sufficient conditions for the solvability of the Vallée-Poussin problem for linear ODEs of the nth order in an arbitrary interval, and the analogous sufficient condition for the solvability of nonlinear ODEs of any order. Fundamental results for direct and inverse spectral problems for one-dimensional Sturm-Liouville equations were obtained by Marchenko. Qualitative studies of and spectral analysis of singular differential operators were done by Glazman in the 1960s.

Although his work at Kharkiv University after 1917 dealt mostly with the theory of probability and constructive function theory, Bernshtein also made qualitative studies of some PDEs. In Kiev Pfeiffer continued his studies of linear systems of PDEs of the first order with one unknown function. While in Ukraine during the 1940s, Lavrentev developed the theory of quasi-conformal mappings that determined a new geometric approach to the theory of PDEs with applications to hydrodynamics, filtration detonation, and other fields. Some of his results in the theory of filtration were extended by Filchakov and his students. The foundation of the general theory of boundary value problems for linear systems of PDEs of elliptic type is contained in the works of Lopatynsky. In addition to making other important contributions to the theory of linear PDEs, he was the first to identify the condition for the compatibility of the coefficients of the elliptic system with the coefficients of the boundary operator, now known as the Lopatynsky condition. In the 1950s Berezansky was the first to develop a method for dealing with the inverse problem of spectral analysis for PDEs. Among other results, he developed the spectral theory for self-adjoint PDEs in unbounded domains. Nizhnyk studied the nature of the spectrum for nonelliptic PDEs. In addition to his work on systems of ODEs with delay in the 1960 and 1970s, Myshkis obtained interesting results for PDEs of hyperbolic and other types. In his work on PDEs Skorobohatko obtained a generalization of the Gerlotz formula, solved the Cauchy problem in case of multiple roots of the characteristic equation, and made a deep study of the solvability of the Dirichlet problem for systems of elliptic PDEs. In the 1970s and 1980s the asymptotic methods of nonlinear mechanics of Krylov, Bogoliubov, and Mytropolsky were extended to PDEs in monographs by Moseenkov, Khoma, A. Bakai, and Yu. Samoilenko, all written jointly with Mytropolsky. The celebrated Stefan problem was studied in the 1980s by several researchers from Donetske, including Danyliuk. The Kordeweg–de Vries equation was solved by V. Marchenko in 1972 and the Cauchy problem for the Kordeweg–de Vries equation was studied in the 1980s by V. Kotliarov and E. Khryslov.

Since the 1960s Danyliuk has made significant contributions to the theory of PDEs and nonlinear problems in mathematical physics with free (unknown) boundaries. He applied his results to various problems of physics (such as the Stefan problem), mechanics, and other fields. Since 1970 deep and systematic studies of abstract and concrete very general nonlinear elliptic PDEs of the higher order of divergence type were conducted by Skrypnyk, who developed and worked with a new topological degree theory for the abstract nonlinear operator of type (α) from a separable Banach space to its dual. He extended his results to some nonelliptic PDEs and to elliptic equations which are not of divergence form.

Probability and statistics. Until 1917 the theory of probability and mathematical statistics was developed in Ukraine by mathematicians in Kharkiv (A. Pavlovsky, M. Tykhomandrytsky, Liapunov, and Bernshtein), Kiev (Vashchenko-Zakharchenko, V. Yermakov, and Ye. Slutsky), and Odessa (Sleshynsky). The development of the theory in Ukraine after 1917 can be divided into two phases, 1917–45 and 1945 to the present. The first phase focused mainly on such related fields as limit theorems in probability, the theory of random processes, and mathematical statistics and has involved such mathematicians as Kravchuk, Slutsky, Bernshtein, Krylov, Bogoliubov, and Y. Hikhman. Kravchuk studied orthogonal polynomials corresponding to discrete probabilistic distributions (now known as Kravchuk's polynomials). Slutsky obtained a series of interesting results in the theory of random functions which contributed to the development of the theory of random processes. Bernshtein extended Liapunov's central limit theorem, made the first attempt at the axiomatic construction of the theory of probability, initiated the study of stochastic equations, and considered a very special case of the Markov process. A different approach to the qualitative study of random processes was proposed by Krylov and Bogoliubov. Hikhman developed the theory of stochastic differential equations.

The second phase of development started in 1945, when B. *Hniedenko joined the Lviv branch of the ANU Institute of Mathematics and immediately organized a section on the theory of probability and mathematical statistics. He wrote a textbook in Ukrainian on probability theory and coauthored a monograph on the boundary resolution for sums of independent random quantities (1949), which explained his ideas on local limit theorems in probability. The latter work had a substantial impact both within and outside the USSR. Further results on local limit theorems were obtained by Parasiuk and E. Rvacheva, who used them to solve problems in statistical mechanics and physics.

In 1949 Hniedenko joined the Institute of Mathematics in Kiev and organized a section on the theory of probability and mathematical statistics. It studied nonparametric problems in mathematical statistics and the theory of massive service. The section attracted talented young mathematicians such as V. Koroliuk, A. Skorokhod, M. Portenko, A. Husak, A. Dorogovtsev, Buldygin, I. Yezhov, A. Turbin, H. Butsan, V. Mykhalevych, and N. Slobodeniuk and constituted the nucleus for the so-called Kiev school of probability theory. Skorokhod's pioneering monograph on random processes and stochastic differential equations (1961) was followed by new results on the martingal problem and equations in infinite-dimensional space. He introduced a number of new notions and methods now called Skorokhod space, Skorokhod topology, Skorokhod versions of weak convergence, the Skorokhod convergence theorem, and the Skorokhod-Wichura-Dudley theorem. Solutions of stochastic differential equations were obtained by Portenko; problems in the stability of solutions of differential with random coefficients were studied by Mytropolsky, A. Samoilenko, and Y. Hikhman. In the early 1970s Hikhman and A. Skorokhod published a three-volume treatise on the theory of stochastic processes. Skorokhod obtained original results in studying various aspects of the Markov processes, one of the main areas of study in the probability and statistics section. He was later joined by younger specialists. Portenko and R. Boiko studied branching processes, while V. Koroliuk and A. Husak worked on boundary problems for random processes.

Semi-Markov processes began to be studied in the USSR in the mid-1960s. In 1965 Koroliuk solved a problem that was a key to various application problems. He also studied the asymptotic analysis of the distribution of functionals related to semi-Markov processes. Together with Turbin he obtained new results for larger classes of Markov and semi-Markov processes and applied them to some problems of statistical physics and hydrodynamics.

In the 1970s A. Skorokhod developed further the theory

of probabilistic measures in infinite-dimensional spaces and established the theory of quasi-invariant measures in Hilbert spaces, which provided the most general conditions for the absolute continuity of measures under nonlinear transformation. Important studies in this area were done also by Buldygin and H. Sytoi.

The study of evolutionary random families represents a new direction in the theory of random processes founded earlier by the members of the institute. In the 1960s A. Skorokhod suggested a new method for describing matrix noncommutative random processes with independent multiplicative increments and obtained new results by means of classical random processes. These studies were continued by Butsan, who introduced a general notion of stochastic subgroups as a random two-parameter family of operators satisfying the evolutionary relation and indicated important classes of stochastic continuous multiplicative semigroups. Further studies in this and other areas were done by A. Skorokhod, V. Koroliuk, and their former students. In the 1980s the Kiev school of probability theory made rapid progress in its work on the theory of probability and mathematical statistics: its members, such as Buldygin, V. Girko, D. Silvestrov, Daletsky, A. Volpert, Husak, and Butsan, published dozens of monographs, many of which were translated into English. It consolidated its international reputation as a leading center of mathematical research.

Approximation methods for solving abstract and differential equations. Starting in the 1920s Krylov, Bogoliubov, and Kravchuk developed new methods for obtaining fundamental results in the areas of approximate solvability of differential equations and abstract operator equations. Krylov first provided a rigorous justification for the use of variational methods and the direct methods of Ritz and least squares for the approximate solvability of self-adjoint problems of mathematical physics. Krylov (later with Bogoliubov) succeeded in obtaining effective error estimates for his approximation methods. Kravchuk studied the existence and convergence of the approximate solutions obtained in Krylov's research when applied to ODEs, PDEs, and integral equations. He obtained good error estimates and characterized the speed of convergence depending on the coefficients of the equations.

In the 1950s M. Polsky in Kiev made a deep study of the abstract projection method (mostly in Hilbert spaces), which included methods of the Ritz-Galerkin type. A number of results for Ritz-Galerkin and projection type methods, dealing mostly with the study of good and effective error estimates, the speed of convergence, and the stability of the methods, were obtained by A. Luchka in Kiev in the late 1960s. From the late 1950s A. Martyniuk in Zhytomyr studied the approximate solvability of odd ODEs, complicated PDEs, and abstract operators in a Hilbert space.

At the end of the 1950s Yu. Sokolov introduced and studied a new and effective method for the approximate solvability of differential and integral equations. Further development of the Sokolov or the averaging method with functional correction was done by Luchka and N. Kurpel. In the late 1950s Polozhii began an intensive effort to construct an effective approximate method for solving boundary value problems in mathematical physics, which led to the development of the method of summary representation.

Dziadyk made a major contribution to the theory of approximation methods for solving operator equations. He examined ways of using the Chebychev theory of the approximation of functions in order to construct new and practically effective methods for the solution of differential and integral equations. His results, as well as those obtained by his students in the 1970s and 1980s, were summarized by Dziadyk in a 1988 monograph on approximation methods for the solution of differential and integral equations.

Mathematicians in the West. Important results have been obtained by mathematicians of Ukrainian ancestry in the West, most of whom worked or are working as professors at various universities in the United States, Canada, Australia, and other countries. They include O. *Andrushkiv, R. Andrushkiv (eigenvalue problems for linear and nonlinear K-symmetric operators, solution of nonlinear parabolic PDEs with application to cryosurgery, theory of hydrodynamics stability), I. Bohachevsky (applied mathematics, stochastic optimization), M. Derzhko (operator theory, PDEs, applied mathematics, operational research), I. Hawryshkewycz (computer sciences, development of new areas of research in computer sciences, structure techniques for analysis of information systems), B. Lawruk (general theory of PDEs, special symplectic spaces, symplectic relations to PDEs, involutory conditions for Riemann invariants), W. Madych (applied mathematics, including certain aspects of signal processing, computerized tomography, classical Fourier theory and approximations), A. Nagurney (applied mathematics, operational research), A. Ostrowski (algebra, geometry, analysis), W. *Petryshyn (iterative and projection methods, fixed point theorems, nonlinear Friedrichs extension, A-proper mapping theory, solvability of ODEs and PDEs, topological degree for multivalued K-set-contractions [with P. Fitzpatrick]), L. *Romankiv (computer sciences, operational research), E. Seneta (theory of probability and mathematical statistics, history of mathematical statistics), M. Skalsky (theory of probability, statistics, applications), W. Vasilaki (new probabilistic approach to the approximation methods for PDEs and boundary layer problems, computerized tomography, nuclear magnetic resonance), and R. Voronka (analysis, applied mathematics, development of effective methods for teaching mathematics).

History of mathematics. Until 1917 the study of the history of mathematics in Ukraine focused mostly on the history of a specific field, institution, or mathematician. Historical research was conducted sporadically by mathematicians in Kharkiv (Pavlovsky, Syntsov), Kiev (Diachenko, Vashchenko-Zakharchenko, Bukreev, Grave), and Odessa (Tymchenko, Kahan, Shatunovsky). In 1917–50 the research became more systematic: Grave studied the history of algebraic analysis; Krylov, the emergence of variational calculus and the role of the minimum principle in contemporary mathematics; Kravchuk, mathematics and mathematicians at Kiev University in 1835–1935, the influence of Euler on the development of mathematics; Marchevsky, history and development of mathematics chairs and the first 75 years of the Kharkiv Mathematics Society; Sushkevych, mathematics at Kharkiv University in 1805–1917 and the history of group theory; Syntsov, detailed study of the works of the faculty of Kharkiv University; Tymchenko, history of logarithms; D. Kryzhanivsky, lectures on the history of mathematics given at Odessa

University; Levytsky, mathematics at the NTSh and the Lviv (Underground) Ukrainian University; Chaikivsky, bibliography of Ukrainian mathematics; and Zarytsky, historical developments in mathematics.

Since the 1950s the history of mathematics has gained increasing attention at Ukrainian universities and the Academy of Sciences in Kiev. In 1956 the Institute of Mathematics established a separate section on the history of mathematics under the supervision of Shtokalo and a special seminar, which quickly became republican in scope. Between 1956 and 1964 the section published 13 volumes, in Ukrainian, on the history of mathematics as well as some special historical books. It also published the collected works of distinguished Ukrainian mathematicians, including Ostrohradsky (3 vols, 1959–61), Krylov (3 vols, 1949–61), H. Vorony (3 vols, 1952–3), Bogoliubov (3 vols, 1964), Grave (1971), and Liapunov (1982). L. Hratsianska and V. Dobrovolsky have written a series of papers on the development of mathematics at Kiev University and biographies of Kiev mathematicians such as Vashchenko-Zakharchenko, Yermakov, Grave, Bukreev, and Pfeiffer. B. Bily studied the contributions of Liapunov, Steklov, and S. Kovalevska, while I. Naumov published a biography of Syntsov and Akhiiezer wrote a book about Bernshtein. A. Bogoliubov wrote a collection of short biographies of Kiev mathematicians (1979) and *Matematiki i mekhaniki* (Mathematicians and Mechanicians, 1983). Book-length biographies of S. Kovalevska (1955), Grave (1940, 1968), Ostrohradsky (1963), Kravchuk (1979), and Krylov (1987) have appeared.

In the 1950s Hikhman and Hniedenko examined the development of the theory of probability in Ukraine. Hniedenko and I. Pohrebynsky published several articles on the development of mathematics in Ukraine. Blank, Hordiievsky, and Pohorielov prepared a history of geometry at Kharkiv University (1956). Shtokalo edited a Russian-Ukrainian mathematical dictionary (1960) and a Ukrainian mathematical bibliography for 1917–60 (1963). In the late 1950s and in the 1960s M. Krein, S. Kiro, and others wrote on the history of mathematics in Odessa. Chaikivsky wrote on the history of mathematics in Lviv. Some historical studies on nonlinear mechanics by Mytropolsky appeared in the 1970s. M. Pavlenko wrote a study of Hlushkov's ideas (1988).

Although some attempts to write a separate history of mathematics in Ukraine have been made, the most informative source for the subject is the four-volume *Istoriia otechestvennoi matematiki* (A History of the Fatherland's Mathematics, 1966–70), edited by Shtokalo, which deals with the development of mathematics in the countries of the former USSR.

W. Petryshyn

Mathematics, Institute of the Academy of Sciences of Ukraine. See Institute of Mathematics of the Academy of Sciences of Ukraine.

Matiiv-Melnyk, Mykola [Matijiv-Mel'nyk], b 1 December 1890 in Yabloniv, Kolomyia county, Galicia, d 28 September 1947 in New Haven, Connecticut. Writer, journalist, and teacher. He was a teacher of Ukrainian and German in gymnasiums in Stanyslaviv and elsewhere in Galicia. He published a collection of poetry and several short novels: *Po toi bik hrebli* (On That Side of the Dam,

1922), *Za ridne hnizdo* (For the Home Nest, 1927), *Kriz' dym i zhar* (Through the Smoke and Ember, 1928), and *Na chornii dorozi* (On the Black Road, 1930). He rendered in Ukrainian *Slovo o polku Ihorevi* (The Tale of Ihor's Campaign, 1936). His best-known poem is *Na rikakh Vavylons'kykh* (On the Rivers of Babylon, 1921). A collection of his poetry, *Horyt' mii svit* (My World Is Burning, 1951), appeared posthumously.

Matiuk, Viktor [Matjuk], b 18 February 1852 in Tudorkovychi, Zhovkva circle, Galicia, d 8 April 1912 in Kariv, Rava Ruska county, Galicia. Composer and musicologist. He studied music and began composing while attending the Peremyshl gymnasium (1873–6) and then had the most fruitful period of his musical activity while at the Lviv seminary (1876–80). Matiuk composed secular and religious choral works; the cantata *Hamaliia* to the poetry of T. Shevchenko; and songs for solo voice, including 'Vesnivka' (Spring Song) to the words by M. Shashkevych. He arranged folk songs and musical games, in addition to scoring melodramas such as 'Kapral Tymko' (Corporal Tymko), 'Neshchasna liubov' (Unlucky Love), 'Invalid' (The Invalid), and 'Nashi poselentsi' (Our Settlers). He also compiled an anthology of the works of Ukrainian composers titled *Boian* (The Troubadour, 1884; 2nd edn 1886), wrote school (1886) and church songbooks, and penned many articles on musical topics, among them a biography of I. Lavrivsky. In his compositions Matiuk continued the musical traditions of the Peremyshl school.

Borys Matiushenko   Zynovii Matla

Matiushenko, Borys [Matjušenko], b 1883 in Kiev, d 25 March 1944. Physician and civic and political leader; full member of the Shevchenko Scientific Society from 1931. A graduate of Kiev University, he was active in the Revolutionary Ukrainian party from 1903 and then in the Ukrainian Social Democratic Workers' party. As head of the Chief Medico-Sanitary Board under the General Secretariat of the Central Rada in 1917, he organized the health care system in Ukraine. During the Hetman government he was director of the health department. In 1919 he was a member of the UNR delegation to the Paris Peace Conference and head of the foreign office of the Ukrainian Red Cross (1919–21). In 1922 he settled in Prague, where he headed the hygienics department at the Ukrainian Free University, and taught at the Ukrainian Husbandry Academy in Poděbrady. He founded and headed (1922–35) the

*Ukrainian Physicians' Association in Czechoslovakia and edited its journal *Ukraïns'kyi medychnyi vistnyk* (1923–5). He was a member of the Ukrainian Scientific Institute in Berlin and of the Czech Eugenics Society. He wrote articles on public hygiene and eugenics and coedited M. Halyn's *Medychnyi latyns'ko-ukraïns'kyi slovnyk* (Latin-Ukrainian Medical Dictionary, 1926).

Matla, Zynovii (nom de guerre: Sviatoslav Vovk), b 1910. Political and military figure. An OUN activist, in 1934 he was sentenced to death by a Polish court, but the sentence was commuted to life imprisonment, and with the collapse of Poland, he was set free. In 1941 he commanded the Southern Expeditionary Group of the OUN (Bandera faction). After being promoted to the faction's leadership (1942–3) he was imprisoned by the Germans. In Germany in 1945, he became a member of the Leadership of the External Units of the OUN. In 1952 he settled in the United States. In 1954 he joined with L. Rebet to form the so-called *dviikari* (the twosome) opposition to the leadership of S. Bandera. In 1956 this opposition formally became the OUN (Abroad). Matla wrote articles on ideological and political questions, using the pseudomyn O. Lvivsky, and a short book of memoirs, *Pivdenna pokhidna hrupa* (The Southern Expeditionary Group, 1952).

Matriarchy. A term designating a social structure in which women hold political and often religious power. Matriarchy is usually understood to subsume matrilineality, or the inheritance of property and position according to the female line, and matrilocality, or a married couple's joining the village or clan of the wife rather than that of the husband. Matriarchy is the opposite of patriarchy, or a social order dominated by men, as is typical of many current, especially Western, societies. Matriarchy is usually assigned to a time in the distant past and thus assumed to be a social order that was supplanted by patriarchy.

For the Slavs, specifically the Ukrainians, the most significant Western archeological study is M. Gimbutas's *The Goddesses and Gods of Old Europe*. Examining artifacts from an area which had major sites in both central Ukraine (the *Trypilian culture) and western Ukraine and Moldavia, Gimbutas found a predominance of female cult statuary (eg, the *stone *baba*), votive figurines, and sacred images. Her finds prompted her to theorize that Neolithic cultures on the territory of Ukraine offered religious devotion to a goddess rather than to a god. The goddess was a mistress of animals; she appeared with wolves and bears or was portrayed alone, zoomorphically, as a woman-bird or a woman-frog. She was connected to water, the snake, and the fertility of crops and other vegetation. She was sculpted with the symbol of a plowed field on her stomach or over her entire body; sometimes marks showed where seeds had been pressed into the clay of the statue, and sometimes the statue was shaped as a vessel containing seeds or clay pellets representing seeds. She was probably also a goddess of human fertility, as evidenced by her depiction in birthing position or holding a child. The various figurines Gimbutas examined are highly stylized and lead one to suspect that they were not representational but symbolic and sacred. Because such female statuary was found in temples and on altars, Gimbutas theorized that the archeological objects portrayed a goddess or a pantheon of goddesses, and the sheer number of female images led her to presume that worship of goddessess was the primary form of early religious activity. The appearance of male figurines in archeological materials from later periods led her to postulate further that worship of a goddess or goddesses was eventually replaced by worship of a male 'year god.'

The psychologists interested in matriarchy have been mostly Jungian, and their work can also be connected to the early theories of a primordial past when women ruled. Studies in Jungian psychology dealing with matriarchy, such as E. Neumann's *The Great Mother*, point to various pictorial and verbal images of the mother archetype from all areas of the world and from all time periods. J. Stalin's strong feelings against psychology resulted in the exclusion of psychological studies of the mother archetype and matriarchy from Soviet scholarship until the M. Gorbachev period.

Matriarchy is important to the Slavs, specifically the Ukrainians, for a number of reasons. First, the Amazons of ancient Greek myth are said to have lived in an area that corresponds to Ukraine, and some of the earliest written sources indicate that primeval Ukrainian social organization was indeed female-dominated. Second, major sites with goddess artifacts are located in Ukraine. Third, the social structure ascribed to the *Cossacks can be seen as a remnant of matriarchy. The pattern whereby women and children live on and farm the land while men (the Cossacks) live in an all-male separate group (the *Zaporozhian Sich) for extended periods of time bears great resemblance to descriptions of matriarchy. Finally, Ukrainian literature, art, and even popular culture contain a plethora of strong, if not dominant, female figures. Powerfully built women appear in the representational arts. Perhaps the most striking is the huge Second World War monument erected in Kiev in 1980; called Fatherland-Mother, its Amazon-like features are unmistakable. D. Richardson noted the importance of the Theotokos (Mother of God) to Byzantine Orthodoxy and traced it to possible ancient goddess beliefs. A similar source can be argued for the figure of *Mary, Mother of God, in Ukrainian Orthodoxy. Certainly the Theotokos and Child dominate in most churches, at least visually. Strong women appear in literature, from N. Gogol's inadvertently destructive heroines and the courageous and long-suffering women in late 19th-century works to the formulaic Communist heroines in socialist-realist prose who lead their men to the correct path.

Evidence of possible earlier matriarchal social organization is even stronger in folklore than in the fine arts. Folk songs and dumas present mothers who are objects of intense longing. These elder women have great power; they aid or kill their offspring with just a prayer or a curse. In folk material culture, wood carving, and especially embroidery the female images are so close to prehistoric goddess images that connections can be made on almost every level. Embroidered female figures appear in 'scenes' surrounded by stylized vegetation, birds, and horses. Water and sun symbols are frequently used for borders. The embroidered figures can therefore be seen as mistresses of crop and animal fertility, much like the Neolithic goddesses. More stylized versions show a woman giving birth or a larger figure with a smaller 'child,' making the embroideries therefore analogous to ancient human fertility artifacts. Curious 'temple' structures are sometimes sewn about the central female figures, as if they were sacred. Even more convincing than the images on the embroidery are the uses to which the embroidered objects are put, especially in ritual. *Rushnyky* embroidered with what can be called goddess figures are used in the home to 'protect' openings such as doors and windows. Similar ones adorn the bride's wedding costume, the crib, and the coffin. A woman in childbirth traditionally held a *rushnyk* to ease labor. The *rushnyky* have the appropriate form of the goddess figure: the one held during labor is embroidered with birth figures; the one worn by the bride, with bird-goddesses and other animals; and the one used for infants and the dead, with goddesses and a tree of life. The use of different symbols indicates that the meanings of the embroideries were, at least partially, consciously continued into the 19th and 20th centuries.

In Ukrainian folk belief there is a water nymph called a *mavka* or *rusalka. She leaves her watery home at night to sit in trees, sing beautiful songs, and seduce men. She also joins her fellow *rusalky* to dance in the fields, where their presence stimulates crop growth. This supernatural female being seems to be associated with water and crops, much like the goddesses of matriarchal times. Like matriarchal women she is the aggressor in sexual relations. The various beliefs connected with the *rusalka* suggest that she is a remnant of matriarchy. She is said to be the ghost of a woman who drowned herself because she became pregnant out of wedlock. She bears and nurses her infant in her watery home, under circumstances which may allude to the matriarchal world being literally submerged by the advent of patriarchy. Traditional Ukrainian wedding rituals include a lamentation by the bride, but no such expressions of sorrow or regret by the groom, because it is the man who imposes marriage on the reluctant woman. Forced matrimony is exactly what scholars such as M. Stone assume occurred when the patriarchal Indo-Europeans conquered the matriarchal clans.

BIBLIOGRAPHY
Neumann, E. *The Great Mother: An Analysis of the Archetype* (Princeton and New York 1963)
Bachofen, J. *Myth, Religion, and Mother-Right: Selected Writings* (Princeton 1967)
Stone, M. *When God Was Woman* (New York 1976)
Richardson, D. 'The Mother Goddess in Minoan Crete and Vestiges in the Contemporary Greek Orthodox Church,' PH D diss, New York University, 1981
Rybakov, B. *Iazychestvo drevnikh slavian* (Moscow 1981)
Gimbutas, M. *The Goddesses and Gods of Old Europe, 6500 to 3500 BC: Myths and Cult Images* (Berkeley 1982)
Berger, P. *The Goddess Obscured: Transformation of the Grain Protectress from Goddess to Saint* (Boston 1985)
Rybakov, B. *Izaychestvo drevnei Rusi* (Moscow 1987)
– (ed.) *Ot doklassovykh obshchestv k ranneklassovym* (Moscow 1987)
Hubbs, J. *Mother Russia: The Feminine Myth in Russian Culture* (Bloomington, Ind 1988)

N. Kononenko Moyle

Matsenko, Pavlo [Macenko] (Macenko, Paul), b 24 December 1897 in Kyrykivka, Okhtyrka county, Kharkiv gubernia, d 8 March 1991 in Winnipeg. Musicologist and pedagogue. After serving in the armies of Imperial Russia and the UNR, Matsenko emigrated to Czechoslovakia via Cyprus in 1924. In Prague he studied at the Ukrainian Higher Pedagogical Institute (1926–8) and at the Conservatory of Music, where he completed a doctorate in musical-pedagogical studies in 1932. He settled in Winnipeg in

Pavlo Matsenko   Kost Matsiievych

1936, where he initiated and co-ordinated higher educational courses for Ukrainian-Canadian cultural activists. A founding member in 1945 of the Ukrainian Cultural and Educational Centre (Oseredok) in Winnipeg, he was affiliated with the Ukrainian National Federation and a strong supporter of the Ukrainian Canadian Committee. He taught at St Andrew's College (University of Manitoba) after 1956, served as rector of St John's Institute in Edmonton (1958–61), and lectured at St Vladimir's College in Roblin, Manitoba (1963–72). His publications include arrangements of the Full Divine Liturgy for mixed choir (1931), the Divine Liturgy for three women's voices (1948), and other religious texts, as well as a wide range of folk songs and carols. He wrote *Narysy do istoriï ukraïns'koï tserkovnoï muzyky* (Studies in the History of Ukrainian Church Music, 1968) and biographies of such composers as F. Yakymenko, D. Bortniansky, and M. Berezovsky. A collection of Matsenko's autobiographical articles, articles about him, and letters to him was published in 1992.

R. Savytsky

Matsiievska, Lidiia [Macijevs'ka, Lidija] (married name: Morenets), b 8 December 1889 in Kashperivka, Tarashcha county, Kiev gubernia, d 24 December 1955 in Odessa. Actress. She grew up in the M. Kropyvnytsky family and studied history at the Odessa Higher Courses for Women (1906–9). She did agitprop performances for the state political education department in 1921–3 and helped organize the First Ukrainian Workers' and Peasants' Theater (1924) and the Odessa Derzhdrama theater (1925), in which she was the leading character and comic actress until her death. During 1935–41 and 1945–52 Matsiievska taught at the Odessa Theater Arts and Technology College.

Matsiievych, Arsenii [Macijevyč, Arsenij] (secular name: Oleksander), b 1697 in Volodymyr-Volynskyi, d 11 March 1772 in Revel (Tallinn), Estonia. Orthodox metropolitan, theologian, preacher, and writer. The son of a Uniate priest, he studied at the Varenytsia and Lviv colleges and, from 1715, at the Kievan Mohyla Academy. In Kiev he converted to Orthodoxy, and in 1716 he was tonsured at the Novhorod-Siverskyi Transfiguration Monastery. He was ordained a hieromonk in 1723. After a brief stay at the Trinity–St Elijah Monastery in Chernihiv, he worked as a missionary in Siberia, there engaging in lengthy polemics with Old Believers. Matsiievych was consecrated metropolitan of Tobolsk and Siberia (1741), and then metropolitan of Rostov and Yaroslavl (1742) and a member of the *Holy Synod. In these positions he was in constant conflict with secular and religious authorities. He protested against secular control of the Synod (which had been essentially reduced to a government department) and advocated the re-establishment of the patriarchal system. He was especially critical of Catherine II's religious policies and her secularization of monastery and church property in Ukraine (in 1763 he even pronounced an anathema on those who wanted to seize church estates). For his actions Matsiievych was stripped of his ecclesiastical rank and exiled to a monastery. When he continued his protests and criticism of Catherine, he was defrocked (1767) and imprisoned in solitary confinement in Revel. The majority of Matsiievych's polemical and theological writings were not published, but a volume of his sermons appeared in the 1740s, and his biography of St D. Tuptalo was published in several editions.

BIBLIOGRAPHY
Ilarion (Ohiienko, I.). *Mytropolyt muchenyk Arsenii Matsiievych* (Winnipeg 1964)

I. Korovytsky

Matsiievych, Kost [Macijevyč, Kost'], b 18 May 1874 in the Kiev region, d 2 April 1942 in Poděbrady. Agronomist, educator, and civic and political leader. A graduate of the agricultural institute in Novo-Aleksandriia (now Puławy), he served as scientific secretary of the Poltava Agricultural Society (1899–1901), gubernial agronomist of the Saratov zemstvo (1901–5), research associate of the Kharkiv Agricultural Society (1907–15), editor of the popular magazine *Khliborob* and the scientific periodical *Agronomicheskii zhurnal*, and a professor of agricultural economics at the Higher Agricultural Courses for Women and the Kamianoostriv Agricultural Courses in Petrograd (1915–17). After returning to Kiev he was active in the Ukrainian Party of Socialists-Federalists. As deputy general secretary of agrarian affairs under the Central Rada, he drafted a land reform bill for Ukraine. He also taught agricultural economy in higher educational institutions, edited *Vistnyk hromads'koï ahronomiï*, and organized farm co-operatives. In 1918–19 he was assigned by the UNR Directory to negotiate with the Entente and was appointed minister of foreign affairs in S. Ostapenko's cabinet. Then he headed the UNR diplomatic mission to Rumania (1919–23). After emigrating to Czechoslovakia he served as a professor at the Ukrainian Husbandry Academy and then at the Ukrainian Technical Husbandry Institute. He continued his political activity as a member of the Ukrainian Radical Democratic party and president of the Ukrainian Democratic Club in Prague.

Matsiievych, Lev [Macijevyč], b 13 January 1877 in Oleksandrivka, Yelysavethrad county, Kherson gubernia, d 7 October 1910 in St Petersburg. Maritime engineer and airplane pilot and civic leader. Matsiievych was active in the Ukrainian student movement, the Revolutionary Ukrainian Party, and the St Petersburg Hromada. He graduated from the Kharkiv Technological Institute (1901) and the Mykolaiv Naval Academy (1906) and worked on the construction of battleships in Sevastopil and at naval installations in St Petersburg. He developed a number of advanced submarine designs and antimine measures, and

Lev Matsiievych

worked on theoretical and design problems in aeronautics, as well as designing a hydroplane (1909). He died in a plane crash. A collection of commemorative articles about him was published in St Petersburg in 1912.

Matskevych, Volodymyr [Mac'kevyč], b 14 December 1909 in Pryvilne, Tavriia gubernia. Soviet government and Party official. After graduating from the Kharkiv Zootechnical Institute in 1931, he was a secondary-school teacher, director of the institute (1939–41, 1943–6), and editor of *Kolkhoznaia proizvodstvennaia entsiklopediia* (Collective-Farm Production Encyclopedia, 1940–50). After serving as deputy minister and minister of animal husbandry and then of agriculture and deputy chairman of the Council of Ministers in the government of Ukraine (1946–52), he was appointed deputy minister (1953–5) and minister of agriculture (1955–60, 1965–71) in the USSR government. He retired after serving as ambassador extraordinary to Czechoslovakia (1973–80). For many years he sat on the CC CPSU (1956–81).

Matskiv, Teodor. See Mackiw, Theodore.

Matskiv, Tymotei [Mac'kiv, Tymotej], b 7 July 1892 in Poberezhe, Stanyslaviv county, Galicia, d 18 January 1972 in Toronto. Galician jurist and émigré civic figure. He completed his studies at Vienna University (LL D, 1921), practiced law in Stanyslaviv, served as civil court judge in Dolyna (1925–37), and served as district court judge in Poznań (1937–40) and Cracow (1940–1). In Cracow he was active in the Ukrainian Relief Committee. Under the German occupation (1942–4) he was deputy chief prosecutor of the Lviv Appellate Court and helped prepare the Ukrainian versions of the criminal, criminal-procedure, and civil-procedure codes. After emigrating to Germany he presided over the court of honor under the *Central Representation of the Ukrainian Emigration in Germany, and represented Ukrainian interests before Allied military and UNRRA authorities. In 1949 he emigrated to Canada, where he served as first president of the Ukrainian Canadian Committee branch in Ottawa. He wrote a book of memoirs, *Z-nad Dnistra na kanads'ki preriï* (From the Dniester to the Canadian Prairies, 1963).

Matskiv, Volodymyr. See Mackiw, Vladimir.

Matskov, Fedir [Mackov], b 21 November 1897 in Ostrohozke, Voronezh gubernia, d 3 February 1977 in Kharkiv.

Plant physiologist; corresponding member of the AN URSR (now ANU) from 1948. After graduating from the Kharkiv Agricultural Institute (1922) he worked at the Kharkiv Institute of Applied Botany (1928–35) and then became a professor at the agricultural institute (1934). He was director of the Ukrainian Scientific Research Institute of Forest Management (1945–9), the research laboratory of the ANU Institute of Genetics and Selection (1949–51), and the Ukrainian Scientific Research Institute of Plant Cultivation, Selection, and Genetics in Kharkiv (1957–61). Matskov specialized in the physiology of the development and mineral alimentation of agricultural plants, particularly non-rootage alimentation. He also researched photoperiodism and hybridization.

Matson, Yulii (Ferdinand) [Macon, Julij], b 1817 in Riga, d 1 January 1886 in Kiev. Pathologist and internal medicine specialist of German descent. After graduating from Tartu University (1843) he worked as a physician in Kiev, taught internal medicine and pathological anatomy at Kiev University (1852–75), and was director of the university's clinic and dean of its medical faculty (1868–70). He was president of the Society of Kiev Physicians (1871–81) and the first director of the Alexandrian Municipal Hospital in Kiev (1875–85).

Matsuka, Hennadii [Macuka, Hennadij], b 5 September 1930 in Prymorske, Donetske oblast. Biochemist; AN URSR (now ANU) corresponding member sine 1976 and full member since 1985. A graduate of the Kiev Veterinary Institute (1955), he has practiced veterinary medicine; worked at the ANU Institute of Biochemistry, where he chaired a department from 1964; and has directed the ANU Institute of Molecular Biology and Genetics since 1973. He has published extensively in the area of structure and function studies of transport ribonucleic acids (tRNA) and aminoacyl-tRNA-synthetases of animals; discovered the adaptation phenomena of these compounds during protein synthesis; and studied inactive tRNA in animal tissues. Matsuka has been academic secretary of the ANU Division of Biochemistry, Physiology, and Theoretical Medicine; vice-president of the Ukrainian Society of Geneticists and Selectionists; editor of the USSR journal *Biopolimery i kletka*; and chairman of the ANU Molecular Biology Problems Council.

Matsurevich, Ippolit [Macurevič], b 8 February 1882 in Hlusk, Babruisk county, Minsk gubernia, d 22 July 1939. Organic chemist; full member of the AN URSR (now ANU) just before his death. He graduated in 1907 from Kiev University, remained there as a researcher, and became a professor in 1935. He studied the synthesis of beta-oxyacids, of alcohols by way of the Grignard reaction, of 1,2,4-triazole derivatives, and of semicarbazides of unsaturated ketones.

Matsynsky, Ivan [Macyns'kyj], b 9 April 1922 in Medzilaborce, Prešov region, d 14 March 1987 in Prešov, Slovakia. Writer and cultural figure in the Prešov region. He worked in Prešov as an editor and literary consultant, a lecturer in political economy (1951–6), director of the *Ukrainian National Theater (UNT, 1956–60), head of the Department of Ukrainian Literature at the Slovak Pedagogical Publishing House (1960–9), the first secretary of

Ivan Matsynsky   Mykola Matusevych

the *Cultural Association of Ukrainian Workers (KSUT, 1969–70), and an editor of Ukrainian literature at the Slovak Pedagogical Press (1970–85). While serving as the external director of the KSUT cultural and educational department he initiated the creation of the Ukrainian Branch of the Slovak Writers' Union and served as its first chairman (1952–5), its secretary, and a member of the editorial board of its journal, *Duklia* (est 1953).

Matsynsky wrote several poetry collections: *Belye oblaka* (White Clouds [in Russian], 1949), *Nasha mova* (Our Language, 1956), *Ivanko ta Olenka* (1958), *Karpats'ki akordy* (Carpathian Chords, 1962), *Prystritnyky* (Sorcerers, 1968), the lyrical *Vinky sonetiv* (Garlands of Sonnets, 1985; his largest and, finest collection), and the posthumous *Merydiany i paraleli* (Meridians and Parallels, 1989). He also wrote literary criticism and reviews; stories (published mostly in *Duklia*); two plays in Russian (in the early 1950s); an anthology of Slovak poetry in Ukrainian translation (1953); a short novel, *Zymova nich* (A Winter's Night, 1961), about collectivization in the Prešov region; a book, *Rozmova storich* (A Discourse of Centuries, 1965), on the sociocultural development of 18th- and 19th-century Transcarpathia; a book on Slovak and Ukrainian literary development and on J. Botto, with Ukrainian translations of Botto's poetry (1981); scholarly studies of the UNT, early Ukrainian primers, the 19th-century Transcarpathian poet V. Dovhovych, and the artist O. Dubai; and materials for a cultural dictionary of Czechoslovakia's Ukrainians (serialized in *Duklia*).

R. Senkus

Matthews, William, b 22 February 1901 in Estonia, d 3 May 1958 in London. British linguist and Slavist. After graduating from Manchester (1923) and London (PH D, 1926; D LITT, 1955) universities, he taught English at the State Institute of English in Riga and the University of Latvia (1926–40). From 1946 he taught Russian language and literature at the School of Slavonic and East European Studies in London, and from 1950 he edited *The Slavonic and East European Review*. His works include *Languages of the USSR* (1951); *The Structure and Development of Russian* (1953) and *Russian Historical Grammar* (1975), in which he discusses Old Ukrainian; articles on the phonetic basis of pleophony in East Slavic and on the Ukrainian system of declension; the brochure *Taras Shevchenko the Man and the Symbol* (1951; repr 1961); and a critical essay in *Taras*

Shevchenko: Song Out of Darkness: Selected Poems (1961). He was elected an honorary member of the Association of Ukrainians in Great Britain in 1955 and the first president of the British Association of Slavists in 1957.

Matusevych, Mykola [Matusevyč], b 19 July 1947 in Matiushi, Bila Tserkva raion, Kiev oblast. Human-rights activist and political prisoner. An editor at the Zdorovia publishing house in Kiev, in November 1976 he became one of the cofounders of the *Ukrainian Helsinki Group. Consequently he was arrested in April 1977 and sentenced in March 1978 to seven years in a strict-regime labor camp in Perm oblast and five years' exile in Chita oblast, Siberia. In the camp he took part in hunger strikes and other protest actions by the political prisoners. In October 1980 he was transferred to the prison in Chistopol in Caucasia. He was released from exile in late 1988.

Olha Matusevych-Heiko   Vira Matushevska

Matusevych-Heiko, Olha [Matusevyč-Hejko, Ol'ha], b 9 September 1953 in Kiev. Philologist and dissident; wife of M. *Matusevych. She joined the *Ukrainian Helsinki Group in May 1977 after her husband's arrest. She was arrested in March 1980 for 'anti-Soviet slander' and sentenced to three years in a women's labor camp near Odessa. On the eve of her release she was charged with 'anti-Soviet agitation and propaganda' and given another three years in a Mordovian camp. In 1986 she returned to Kiev.

Matushevska, Vira [Matuševs'ka] (née Popova), b 1874 in Kharkiv, d 22 April 1944 in Temnikovskii, Mordovian ASSR. Civic activist and physician; wife of F. *Matushevsky. A graduate of the Women's Medical Institute in St Petersburg, she was appointed director of the zemstvo hospital in the Kiev suburb of Boiarka in 1904. A member of the Revolutionary Ukrainian party, she worked during the 1920s in Kiev polyclinics and sat on a language commission of the All-Ukrainian Academy of Sciences formed for the purpose of compiling a medical dictionary. In 1937 she was arrested by the NKVD and sent to a labor camp in Mordovia, where she perished.

Matushevsky, Borys [Matuševs'kyj], b 1907 in Boiarka, Kiev county, Kiev gubernia, d 14 January 1977 in Kiev. Political prisoner; son of F. and V. *Matushevsky. A student at the Kiev Institute of People's Education, he was arrest-

Borys Matushevsky   Fedir Matushevsky

ed in 1929 for purportedly belonging to a clandestine Ukrainian Youth Association (SUM) and was sentenced to five years in prison. He was released in 1934, and he worked at a meteorological station in Kirovske until he was arrested again in 1938. After being released in 1940, he served in the Soviet army (1943–5) and then returned to Kiev, where he worked at a hydrometeorological station.

Matushevsky, Fedir [Matuševs'kyj], b 21 June 1869 in Smila, Cherkasy county, Kiev gubernia, d 21 October 1919 in Athens. Civic and political leader and publicist. After graduating from the law faculty of Dorpat University (1904), where he founded a Ukrainian student hromada, he settled in Kiev and devoted himself to writing and publishing. He was one of the founders of the *Vik publishing house and a contributor to *Rada*, *Kievskaia starina*, *Literaturno-naukovyi vistnyk*, and *Ukrainskaia zhizn'* as well as editor of the first Ukrainian daily in Russian-ruled Ukraine, *Hromads'ka dumka* (1905–6). He organized co-operatives in the villages of Kharkiv and Kiev gubernias and edited the co-operative weekly *Muraveinyk-Komashnia*. A leading member of the Ukrainian Democratic Radical party and the Society of Ukrainian Progressives and, later, of the Ukrainian Party of Socialists-Federalists, he devoted much of his energy to political work. During the revolutionary period he was a member of the Central Rada. In January 1919 he was appointed head of the UNR diplomatic mission to Greece. Particularly notable among his numerous articles were his report on T. Shevchenko's grave, his study of A. Svydnytsky, his biography of V. Antonovych, and his essays on Shevchenko. Excerpts from his diary were published posthumously in the first volume of *Z mynuloho* (From the Past, 1938).

Matveev, Aleksandr, b 2 May 1816 in Orel gubernia, Russia, d 4 June 1882 in Kiev. Russian obstetrician, gynecologist, and pediatrician. A graduate of Moscow University (1841), he taught at Kiev University (from 1844) and served as dean of the medical faculty (1862–5) and rector (1861–71 and 1875–8) of the university. He did research on postnatal diseases and invented the silver nitrate bath for preventing blennorrhea (1853). He wrote two popular obstetrics manuals.

Matveev, Artamon, b 1625 in Moscow, d 25 May 1682. Russian diplomat. In 1653 he and I. Fomin were sent as emissaries to Hetman B. Khmelnytsky to negotiate the terms of the *Pereiaslav Treaty of 1654. In 1655 Matveev commanded Muscovite troops in the battles against the Poles near Kamianets-Podilskyi and Lviv. He later headed the *Little Russian Office (from 1669) and the Diplomatic Office (concurrently from 1671). Matveev was a strong advocate of Russian territorial expansion into Ukrainian lands, and he played a major role in shaping Muscovite policy toward Ukraine.

Nina Matviienko

Matviienko, Nina [Matvijenko], b 10 October 1947 in Nedilyshche, Yemilchyne raion, Zhytomyr oblast. Singer (alto). She graduated from the studio of the Verovka State Chorus in 1968 and from the Kiev University in 1975. From 1968 she has sung as soloist with the Verovka State Chorus. She has also sung as lead vocalist in the Zoloti Kliuchi folk music trio. Her large repertoire consists mostly of Ukrainian folk songs, but she also performs works by contemporary Ukrainian composers. Matviienko has appeared in films and radio. Immensely popular in Ukraine, she was awarded the 1988 Shevchenko Prize.

Mavka (aka *niavka*, *navka*, from Old Slavic *nav* 'the dead'). A mythological female figure, tall, round-faced, long-haired, and sometimes naked. The nymphs known by this term represented the souls of girls who had died unnatural deaths. They were believed to live in groups in forests, mountain caves, or sheds, which they decorated with rugs. They made thread of stolen flax and wove thin transparent cloth for making clothes for themselves. They loved flowers, which they wore in their hair. In the spring they planted flowers in the mountains, to which they enticed young men, whom they tickled to death. On Pentecost (known as *Mavka*'s Easter) they held games, dances, and orgies. A demon accompanied them on a flute or pipes. They are depicted in literature, most notably in Lesia Ukrainka's *Lisova pisnia* (The Forest Song) and M. Kotsiubynsky's *Tini zabutykh predkiv* (Shadows of Forgotten Ancestors).

Maximos, b ?, d 6 December 1305 in Vladimir, on the Kliazma. Greek churchman. The successor to Cyril II, he served as metropolitan of Kiev and all Rus' in 1283–1305. He transferred the see of the metropoly to Vladimir in 1299–1300, thereby prompting demands for the creation of a separate metropoly for the Principality of Galicia-Volhynia.

Maydanek, Jacob. See Maidanyk, Yakiv.

Mayer, Johann, b and d ? Swedish diplomat. While traveling from Bucharest to Stockholm in 1651, he maintained a diary that included a description of his passage through Ukraine. He also provided an account of the Ukrainian Cossacks and assisted W. Hondius in preparing a map of Ukraine.

Mazade, Fernand, b 14 October 1863 near Anduze, France, d 17 June 1939. French poet, critic, and journalist. Sympathetic to the cause of Ukraine's independence, he rendered assistance to the Ukrainian delegation at the Paris Peace Conference (1919–22). He was a cofounder of the French Society of Ukrainian Studies. His translations of two poems by T. Shevchenko were published in the weekly *France et Ukraine* in 1920. He also translated some of M. Rylsky's poetry. M. Tereshchenko translated some of Mazade's poetry into Ukrainian.

Mazapeta. A 17th- to 18th-century gentry family of Greek heritage. Manuil Mazapeta became a member of the Lviv Dormition Brotherhood in 1590, and his son, Kostiantyn (d 1656), was an elder of the same body in 1637–40. His descendants, in turn, settled in Left-Bank Ukraine under Hetman B. Khmelnytsky and became part of the *starshyna* of Chernihiv regiment. The family line died off on the male side in the mid-18th century, and its descendants on the female side maintained the name Mazapeta-Brodovych.

Mazaraki. A Ukrainian and Polish gentry family of Greek heritage. Christos (Krzysztof) Mazaraki (d before 1641) was a Greek merchant who settled in Lviv near the end of the 16th century. His son, Ivan (d before 1667), was nominated for nobility status by Hetman I. Vyhovsky for services rendered to the Zaporozhian army; the status was granted by the Polish Sejm in 1659. Ivan and his son, Ivan (d ca 1690), were marshals of the Lviv Dormition Brotherhood, and the younger led the brotherhood's opposition to Bishop Y. Shumliansky. One of his sons, Demian, settled in the Hetmanate, where his descendants became part of the Cossack *starshyna*. In the 19th and 20th centuries members of the Mazaraki family were estate owners in Poltava gubernia and Southern Ukraine. Serhii Mazaraki (d 1912) was an amateur archeologist and collector who excavated Scythian burial grounds near Romen for the Kiev Historical Museum.

Mazepa (aka Koledynsky). A noble family in the Bila Tserkva region, first mentioned in the 16th century. Mykhailo Mazepa received the *khutir* Kamenets (later called Mazepyntsi) from King Sigismund I in 1544. His son, Mykola, Hetman Ivan *Mazepa's great-grandfather, received confirmation of his right to the estate from Sigismund II in 1572. Another Mazepa (Fedir?), possibly Mykola's brother, was a Cossack leader who was executed in Warsaw in 1596 for his part in S. Nalyvaiko's uprising. Several Mazepas appear in the 1649 Cossack register of Bila Tserkva regiment. One of them, Stepan-Adam *Mazepa, was the hetman's father. The family line was extinguished with the hetman's death in 1709.

Mazepa, Halyna, b 9 February 1910 in St Petersburg. Ukrianian modernist painter, graphic artist, and ceramist; daughter of Isaak *Mazepa. From 1923 she lived in Prague, where she studied at the Ukrainian Studio of

Halyna Mazepa: *Poterchata* (The Unbaptized Dead, oil, 1965)

Plastic Arts, the School of Applied Art (1929–35), and the Academy of Arts. In the 1930s she began painting; illustrating Czech and Ukrainian books, magazines and postcards; and designing theatrical and ballet costumes. In 1947 she resettled in Caracas, Venezuela. Her first solo exhibition was held there in 1948. While working as an animator and as an illustrator for Venezuelan magazines (eg, *Tricolor*) and the publishing house of the Venezuelan Ministry of Education, she devoted her spare time to painting, ceramics, and illustrating Ukrainian books. For her ceramic icon of the Holy Protectress she received a national prize in 1956. Her first solo show in the United States was held in New York in 1970. Her distinctive work is noted for its iconlike simplicity of line and composition and flat planes, gentle stylization, and vibrant, contrasting colors. Many of her paintings and drawings depict female figures and deal with Ukrainian historical, folkloric, or literary themes (eg, T. Shevchenko's poems). An album of her works was published in Munich by the Ukrainian Free University in 1982.

Isaak Mazepa

Mazepa, Isaak, b 16 August 1884 in Kostobobriv, Novhorod-Siverskyi county, Chernihiv gubernia, d 18 March 1952 in Augsburg, West Germany. Political leader and statesman; husband of N. *Synhalevych-Mazepa and father of H. *Mazepa. In 1905, while studying at St Petersburg University (1904–10), he joined the underground *Ukrainian Social Democratic Workers' party (USDRP), and he soon became one of its leading members. He was also active in the *Ukrainian Student Hromada in St Petersburg. After graduation he worked as an agronomist for the gubernial zemstvos in Nizhnii Novgorod (1911–15) and Katerynoslav (1915–18). After the February Revolution of 1917 he was a member of the Katerynoslav City Duma and the Katerynoslav Council of Workers' and Peasants' Deputies. In April 1918 he headed the Katerynoslav Gubernia Revolutionary Council. Under the Hetman regime he coedited the USDRP paper *Nasha sprava*. In January 1919 Mazepa was a delegate at the *Labor Congress in Kiev and was elected secretary of the USDRP CC. On 9 April 1919 he was appointed UNR minister of internal affairs, and from 29 August 1919 to late May 1920 he was prime minister of the UNR and head of the *Council of National Ministers. In May and June 1920 he was the last UNR minister of land affairs.

From late 1920 Mazepa lived as an émigré in Lviv, where he edited the USDRP serial *Vil'na Ukraïna* and the monthly paper *Sotsiialistychna dumka*. In 1923 he emigrated to Prague. From 1927 he was a botany docent at the Ukrainian Husbandry Academy and its successor, the Ukrainian Technical and Husbandry Institute (UTHI), in Poděbrady. Mazepa represented the USDRP and defended Ukrainian interests at many international socialist conferences and was a member of the executive committee of the Labor and Socialist International. As a postwar refugee in Germany he was a professor at the UTHI in Munich from October 1946, cofounded the *Ukrainian National Rada, was the first chairman of its executive organ (July 1948 to January 1952), and was a founding member of the *Ukrainian Socialist party (est 1950).

Mazepa wrote many political articles; the book *Bol'-shevyzm i okupatsiia Ukraïny* (1922; German trans: *Bolschevismus und die russische Okkupation der Ukraine*, 1923); a study, concentrating on the national movement and major Ukrainian historical processes and problems, *Pidstavy nashoho vidrodzhennia* (Foundations of Our Rebirth, 2 vols, 1946); and memoirs of the years 1917–21, *Ukraïna v ohni i buri revoliutsiï* (Ukraine in the Fire and Storm of Revolution, 3 vols, 1941; 2nd edn 1950–2). His major scientific works are a book of lectures on plant morphology (1934) and a monograph on Carpathian mountain pastures (1944).

BIBLIOGRAPHY
Fedenko, P. *Isaak Mazepa – borets' za voliu Ukraïny* (London 1954)
Isaakovi Mazepi na vichnu pam'iat', no. 3 of *Nashe slovo* (Munich and London 1973)

M. Kurakh, A. Zhukovsky

Mazepa, Ivan, b 20 March 1639 in Mazepyntsi, near Bila Tserkva, d 2 October 1709 in Bendery, Bessarabia. Hetman of Ukraine in 1687–1709; son of S.-A. *Mazepa and M. *Mazepa. He studied at the Kievan Mohyla College (Academy) and at the Jesuit college in Warsaw. While a page at the court of Jan II Casimir Vasa in Warsaw, he was sent by the king to study in Holland. In 1656–9 he learned gunnery in Deventer and visited Germany, Italy, France, and the Low Countries. After his return to Warsaw Mazepa continued his service as a royal courtier, and in 1659–63 he was sent on various diplomatic missions to Ukraine. The legend of his affair with Madame Falbowska and his subsequent punishment by being tied to the back of a wild horse was first popularized by the Polish memorialist J.C. Pasek. Although it has no basis in fact, it has in-

Hetman Ivan Mazepa (portrait, late 17th century)

spired a number of European Romantics, including F. Liszt, P. Tchaikovsky, G. Byron, V. Hugo, and A. Pushkin.

In 1663 Mazepa returned to Ukraine to help his ailing father. After his father's death in 1665 he succeeded him as hereditary cupbearer of Chernihiv. In 1669 Mazepa entered the service of Hetman P. *Doroshenko as a squadron commander in the Hetman's Guard, and later he served as Doroshenko's chancellor. He took part in Doroshenko's 1672 campaign against Poland in Galicia and served on diplomatic missions, including ones to the Crimea and Turkey (1673–4). During a mission in 1674 he was captured by the Zaporozhian otaman I. *Sirko, who was forced to hand him over to Doroshenko's rival in Left-Bank Ukraine, I. *Samoilovych. Mazepa quickly gained the confidence of Samoilovych and Tsar Peter I, was made a 'courtier of the hetman,' and was sent on numerous missions to Moscow. Mazepa participated in the *Chyhyryn campaigns of 1677–8. In 1682 he was appointed Samoilovych's general osaul. He was elected the new hetman on 25 July 1687 by the Cossack council that deposed Samoilovych and concluded the disadvantageous *Kolomak Articles with the tsar.

Mazepa's political program had become evident during his service to Doroshenko and Samoilovych. He was a firm supporter of a pan-Ukrainian Hetman state, and his main goal as hetman was to unite all Ukrainian territories in a unitary state that would be modeled on existing European states but would retain the features of the traditional Cossack order. Initially Mazepa believed that Ukraine could coexist with Russia on the basis of the *Pereiaslav Treaty of 1654. Mazepa actively supported Russia's wars with Turkey and the Crimean Khanate and sent his forces

to help those of Peter I. Although the Treaty of Constantinople of 3 July 1700 did not extend Ukrainian dominion to the Black Sea, it temporarily secured Ukrainian lands from Turkish encroachment and Crimean Tatar incursions. Until 1708 Mazepa also supported Peter in the first phase of his Great Northern War with Sweden, by providing the Russians with troops, munitions, money, and supplies in their effort to capture the Baltic lands. Mazepa's participation in the war made it possible for him to take control of Right-Bank Ukraine in 1704, after S. *Palii's Cossack revolt effectively weakened Polish authority there. Mazepa's relations with Palii were not entirely positive, however. Mazepa did not share the Khvastiv colonel's radical social policies, and that difference gave rise to conflicts between them.

Portal and fronton (1690–3) for the church of the Kiev Epiphany Brotherhood funded by Hetman Ivan Mazepa

Mazepa contributed to the development of Ukraine's economy, particularly its industry. He also supported Ukrainian scholarship (history in particular) and education (the transformation of the Kievan Mohyla College into the *Kievan Mohyla Academy, the establishment of *Chernihiv College). Under his hetmancy *literature flourished (see D. *Tuptalo, S. *Yavorsky, I. *Maksymovych, T. *Prokopovych, and Y. *Krokovsky). Mazepa himself wrote some verse. He was a generous patron of painting and *architecture, who funded many churches built in the Cossack *baroque style in Kiev, Chernihiv, Pereiaslav, Baturyn, Pryluka, and other towns. Mazepa was also a patron of the Orthodox church outside Ukraine. He funded the publication of the New Testament in Arabic in Aleppo in 1708, and he donated an Easter shroud and a pure gold chalice for the Tomb of the Lord in Jerusalem.

Although Mazepa was able to establish a new and loyal senior *Cossack starshyna, he also faced considerable opposition from many members of the Cossack elite, and even open rebellion (see P. *Petryk, V. *Kochubei, and I. *Iskra). Mazepa's many attempts to secure the rights of the Cossacks as an estate (the universal of 1691), the burghers (a series of universals protecting their rights), and the peasantry (the universal of 28 November 1701 limiting corvée to two days a week) could not stem the growth of social discontent caused by endless wars, abuse of the population by Russian troops stationed in Ukraine, destruction, and increasing exploitation by the landowning *starshyna*. Mazepa's alliance with Peter also caused onerous responsibilities and losses to be inflicted on the population, in particular as a result of the Northern War and Russian exploitation in Ukraine. Consequently Mazepa was deprived of the popular support he needed at a critical juncture in Ukrainian history.

Peter I not only interfered in the Hetmanate's internal affairs and mercilessly exploited the population in his belligerent pursuits, but embarked on a policy of annihilating Ukrainian autonomy and abolishing the Cossack order and privileges. When Peter's intentions became clear, Mazepa, supported by most of his senior officers, began secret negotiations in 1706 with King *Stanislaus I Leszczyński of Poland and then with Charles XII of Sweden, and forged with them an anti-Russian coalition in 1708. The actual terms of the alliance are unknown, but according to official Russian sources its chief goal was 'that the Little Russian Cossack people be a separate principality and not subjects of a Russian state.' Later the Zaporozhian Host joined the coalition, and on 28 March 1709 Mazepa, Otaman K. *Hordiienko, and Charles XII signed a treaty in which Charles agreed not to sign any peace with Moscow until Ukraine and the Zaporozhian lands were freed of Russian rule.

But the Russo-Swedish War of 1708–9, which was waged on Ukrainian territory, ended in defeat for the allies. Peter's forces captured Mazepa's capital, Baturyn, together with its large armaments depot and artillery, massacred its 6,000 inhabitants, and succeeded in splitting Mazepa's followers by engineering the election of I. *Skoropadsky as a new hetman in Hlukhiv in November 1708. Russian military terror descended on those who remained loyal to Mazepa. Captured Zaporozhian Cossacks were brutally executed, the Zaporozhian Sich was destroyed, and many of Mazepa's followers (eg, D. Maksymovych, Archimandrite H. Odorsky) were executed or exiled to northern Russia. Mazepa's efforts at organizing a broad anti-Russian front in Eastern Europe proved unsuccessful, and his and Charles's defeat at the Battle of *Poltava on 8 July 1709 sealed Ukraine's fate. Mazepa, Charles, and Hordiienko, together with 3,000 followers, fled to Turkish-held territory. Broken by his defeat, old and ill, Mazepa died in Bendery, Moldavia. He was buried at St George's Monastery in Galați, where his tomb was subsequently desecrated.

Peter initially sought Mazepa's extradition from Turkey. Having condemned Mazepa as a traitor he ordered the Russian and Ukrainian churches to anathematize him. Thereafter, imperial, both Russian and Soviet, propagandists and historians did their utmost to vilify the Ukrainian patriot and statesman. Although there have been controversial assessments of Mazepa, he has remained a symbol of Ukrainian independence. The period of his hetmancy has justifiably been known as the Mazepa renaissance.

BIBLIOGRAPHY

Umanets, F. *Getman Mazepa: Istoricheskaia monografiia* (St Petersburg 1897)

Kostomarov, N. 'I. Mazepa,' in *Istoricheskiia mongrafii i issledovaniia*, vol 6 (St Petersburg 1905); repr: *UIZh*, 1988, no. 8ff

Jensen, A. *Mazepa: Historiska bilder från Ukraine och Karl XIIS dagar* (Lund 1909)

Borschak, E.; Martel, R. *Vie de Mazeppa* (Paris 1931)

Andrusiak, M. *Mazepa i Pravoberezhzha* [sic] (Lviv 1938)

Smal'-Stots'kyi, R. (ed). *Mazepa: Zbirnyk*, 2 vols (Warsaw 1938–9)

Krupnyckyj, B. *Hetman Mazepa und seine Zeit (1687–1709)* (Leipzig 1942)

Het'man Ivan Mazepa: Pysannia (Krakiv and Lviv 1943)

Manning, C.A. *Hetman of Ukraine Ivan Mazeppa* (New York 1957)

Nordmann, C.J. *Charles XII et l'Ukraine de Mazepa* (Paris 1958)

Ohloblyn, O. *Het'man Ivan Mazepa ta ioho doba* (New York, Paris, and Toronto 1960)

Kentrschynskyj, B. *Mazepa* (Stockholm 1962)

Mackiw, T. 'Mazepa im Lichte der zeitgenössischen deutschen Quellen,' *ZNTSh*, 174 (1963)

– *Prince Mazepa, Hetman of Ukraine in Contemporary English Publications, 1687–1709* (Chicago 1967)

Babinski, H. *The Mazeppa Legend in European Romanticism* (New York 1974)

Subtelny, O. (ed). *On the Eve of Poltava: The Letters of Mazepa to Adam Sieniawski, 1704–1708* (New York 1975)

– *The Mazepists: Ukrainian Separatism in the Early Eighteenth Century* (New York 1981)

Mackiw, T. *English Reports on Mazepa: Hetman of Ukraine and Prince of the Holy Roman Empire, 1687–1709* (New York, Munich, and Toronto 1983)

Mats'kiv, T. *Het'man Ivan Mazepa v zakhidn'oevropeis'kykh dzherelakh, 1687–1709* (Munich 1988)

O. Ohloblyn

Mazepa, Maryna (née Mokiievska), b ca 1624 in the Bila Tserkva region, d 1707 in Kiev. Mother of Hetman I. Mazepa. After the death of her husband in 1665, she devoted herself to church and community work, joined the *Lutske Brotherhood of the Elevation of the Cross in 1666, and later entered a monastery, where she took the name Mariia Mahdalyna. As superior of the women's Kievan Cave Monastery of the Ascension (ca 1682–1707) and the Transfiguration Monastery in Hlukhiv (1688–1707) she did much to improve their material status and artistic embroidery work. She was a close adviser to her son and actively participated in church politics. In 1687–8 and 1692 she traveled to Moscow to receive alms and charters confirming her monasteries' properties and exemptions from the tsar. She was buried at the Monastery of the Ascension in Kiev.

Mazepa, Stepan-Adam, b ?, d after 12 March 1665. Cossack *starshyna*; father of Hetman I. *Mazepa. He fought in the Cossack-Polish War of 1648–57, from 1654 as otaman of Bila Tserkva regiment. In 1658 he was Hetman I. Vyhovsky's military envoy to King Jan II Casimir Vasa, who confirmed Mazepa's claim to the family estates of Mazepyntsi and Trylisy. In 1662 he was appointed cupbearer of Chernihiv.

Mazlakh, Serhii [Mazlax, Serhij], b ? in Kobyliaky, Poltava gubernia, d ? Journalist and Bolshevik leader of Jewish background. He helped organize the Ukrainian Social Democratic Workers' party in Poltava gubernia for the elections to the Ukrainian Constituent Assembly and took part in the Tahanrih Conference of the Bolsheviks in Ukraine on 18–20 April 1918. With V. *Shakhrai he wrote *Do khvyli! Shcho diiet'sia na Ukraïni i z Ukraïnoiu?* (1919; trans: *On the Current Situation in Ukraine*, 1970), which calls for an independent Ukrainian Bolshevik party and state and criticizes V. Lenin's opposition to both proposals. The authors were expelled from the Party in June 1919, and Mazlakh was reinstated on appeal. In 1920 he became editor of the newspaper *Vserossiiskaia kochegarka* in Luhanske. In the 1920s he was director of the Central Statistical Bureau of the Ukrainian SSR. He disappeared in the terror of the 1930s.

Mazon, André, b 7 September 1881 in Paris, d 13 July 1967 in Paris. French Slavist; member of the Shevchenko Scientific Society from 1927, the USSR Academy of Sciences from 1928, the Académie des inscriptions et belles lettres from 1941, and the Polish Academy of Sciences from 1956. He studied at the Sorbonne and Prague University, taught French at Kharkiv University (1905–8), and was a professor of Slavic philology at the University of Strasbourg (1919–23) and the Collège de France (1924–52). He was the head of the Institute of Slavic Studies at the University of Paris from 1937 and the vice-president of the International Committee of Slavists (1958–67). Among his many works are articles on M. Vovchok in France, N. Gogol, and T. Shevchenko; a book about *Slovo o polku Ihorevi* (*Le Slovo d'Igor* [1940], where he doubted its authenticity); surveys of publications in Ukrainian studies (1921–4) in *Revue des études slaves*, which he cofounded and later edited; and the introduction to A. Martel's book on the Polish language in Ukraine (1939). He cotranslated M. Uspensky's *Quelques données historiques sur 'Le Slovo d'Igor' et Tmutorokan* (1965).

Mazovia (Polish: Mazowsze). A Polish historical-geographic region in the Vistula Basin, of which the major city is Warsaw. Mazovia became part of Poland in the 10th century and a separate appanage in the mid-12th century. After the mid-13th century it was divided into a number of smaller principalities. By the mid-14th century it was a fiefdom of Poland, which finally absorbed it in 1526. In the east Mazovia bordered on Volodymyr-Volynskyi appanage principality and then the Galician-Volhynian principality and maintained friendly relations with them. Prince Danylo Romanovych and his successors supported the Mazovian princes against Poland and acted to some extent as their protectors. The last prince of Galicia-Volhynia, Yurii II Boleslav, was the son of the Mazovian prince Trojden II and Mariia, the daughter of King Yurii Lvovych.

Mazur, Oleksandr, b 30 August 1913 in Popivtsi, Mohyliv county, Podilia gubernia. Greco-Roman wrestler. He was the world champion in 1955 and the Ukrainian and USSR champion in 1944, 1945, 1947, and 1949.

Mazurenko, Halia, b 25 December 1901 in St Petersburg. Poet. Having served in the UNR Army under S. Petliura, she emigrated to Prague in 1920 and resettled in London in 1945. She coedited the journals *Vistnyk* and *Proboiem* and published several collections of poetry: *Akvarely* (Watercolors, 1926), *Stezhka* (The Footpath, 1939), *Vohni* (Fires, 1939), *Snihotsvity* (Snow Flowers, 1941), *Porohy* (The Rapids, 1960), and the larger *Kliuchi* (Keys, 1969), *Skyt poetiv* (Monastery of Poets, 1971), *Zelena iashchirka* (Green Lizard, 1971), *Try misiatsi v literi zhyttia* (Three Months in the Alphabet of Life, 1973), and *Pivnich na vulytsi* (Midnight on the Street, 1980).

Mazurenko, Oleksii, b 20 June 1917 in Yelysavethrad county, Kherson gubernia. Senior Soviet Naval Aviation officer. He joined the Red Army in 1938 and was commissioned in 1940. During the Second World War he com-

Halia Mazurenko   Semen Mazurenko

manded an escort unit of a regiment of the Baltic Fleet and flew more than 300 missions. He was twice decorated Hero of the Soviet Union. After the war he commanded an aviation division. He graduated from a military academy in 1952 and was promoted to brigadier general. He retired in 1972.

Mazurenko, Semen, b 1879, d ? Political activist; brother of V. and Yu. *Mazurenko. An activist of the 1905 Revolution, he helped organize the All-Russian Peasant Union. In 1906 he was arrested and sentenced to imprisonment and internal exile. He returned to Ukraine in 1917 and became active in the Ukrainian Social Democratic Workers' party. At the beginning of 1919 he headed a special diplomatic mission of the UNR to Moscow to normalize relations with Bolshevik-ruled Russia. He was arrested in Ukraine by the Soviets in 1925 and was probably executed.

Mazurenko, Vasyl, b 1877, d ? Engineer and political activist; brother of S. and Yu. *Mazurenko. He was active in the Revolutionary Ukrainian party from 1901 and, later, in the Ukrainian Social Democratic Workers' party. During the revolutionary period he was a member of the Central Rada. In 1917–19 he served as deputy to a number of finance ministers, general secretary of finance (November 1917), and minister of finance in V. Chekhivsky's cabinet (1919). He went to Italy as head of the UNR diplomatic mission. In 1920 he returned to Ukraine and was appointed director of the Chamber of Weights and Measures in Kharkiv. He was arrested by the GPU in the early 1930s, and disappeared. He wrote several works on silicates.

Mazurenko, Yurii, b 1 July 1885 in Kryvorizhia, Don Cossack province, d 3 November 1937. Political and civic leader and jurist; brother of S. and V. *Mazurenko. During the revolutionary period he was one of the leaders of the Ukrainian Social Democratic Workers' party (Independentists), and in 1919 he commanded its insurgent forces against the Bolshevik government in Kiev. In the summer of 1920 he was elected to the CC of the Ukrainian Communist party. After its dissolution he joined the CP(B)U. In the 1920s he chaired the codification department of the People's Commissariat of Justice and taught at the Kharkiv Institute of the National Economy. He presided over the Juridical Society in Kharkiv. In the early 1930s he was president of the Kharkiv Scientific Society of the All-

Ukrainian Academy of Sciences. After being arrested in 1934, he was sentenced to 10 years in prison for belonging to a 'Ukrainian terrorist organization,' and most likely died in a camp or was executed. His publications dealt largely with family law.

St Joseph's Ukrainian Catholic Church in Chicago; architect Zenon Mazurkevich

Mazurkevich, Zenon [Mazurkevyč], b 31 August 1939 in Rozhnitiv, Jarosław county, Galicia. Architect. A graduate of the University of Pennsylvania (1972), he has worked as an architect in Chicago and Philadephia. Although he designs mostly hotels, he renovated St Nicholas's Ukrainian Catholic Cathedral in Chicago and designed St Joseph's Ukrainian Catholic Church in Chicago and St Michael's Ukrainian Catholic Church in Baltimore (1988).

Mazurkevych, Mykhailo. See Mazurki, Mike.

Mazurkevych, Yurii [Mazurkevyč, Jurij], b 6 May 1941 in Lviv. Concert violinist and teacher. He began his musical training in Lviv and then studied (1960–7) with D. Oistrakh at the Moscow Conservatory, completing both graduate and postgraduate courses under him. In 1967–73 he taught at the Kiev Conservatory and recorded for the Melodiya label. Mazurkevych has won prizes at international violin competitions in Helsinki (1962), Munich (1966), and Montreal (1969) and has performed widely in Finland, Poland, Germany, Bulgaria, Czechoslovakia, Switzerland, Canada, and the United States. Mazurkevych emigrated from Ukraine in 1973, teaching at the University of Western Ontario in London, Canada (1975–85), and then Boston University (from 1985).

Mazurki, Mike (né Mazurkevych, Mykhailo; Mazurski), b 25 December 1909 in Ternopil, Galicia, d 9 Decem-

Mike Mazurki

ber 1990 in Glendale, California. Hollywood film actor. A resident of the United States from 1915, he graduated from Manhattan College and was a professional heavyweight wrestler before making his screen debut in *The Shanghai Gesture* (1941). He acted mostly character roles in over 100 films, including *Murder, My Sweet* (1944), *Dick Tracy* (1945), *Samson and Delilah* (1949), *Some Like It Hot* (1959), and *Challenge to Be Free* (1975).

Mazurok, Yurii, b 18 July 1931 in Krasnyk, Poland. Ukrainian opera singer (baritone). In 1960 he graduated from the Moscow Conservatory in the class of S. Migai and A. Sveshnikova. In 1963 he finished postgraduate studies under A. Sveshnikova and began his career as a soloist in the Bolshoi Theater. His main roles include Count di Luna in G. Verdi's *Il Trovatore* and Rodrigo in his *Don Carlos*, and Tsarev in S. Prokofiev's *Simeon Kotko*. He also appears as a concert performer. Since 1962 Mazurok has toured abroad, throughout Europe and in Great Britain, Japan, Canada, and the United States.

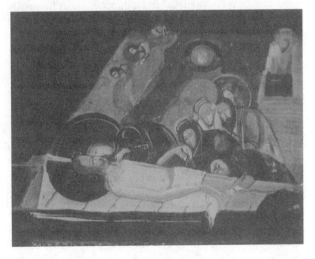

Omelian Mazuryk: *Pieta*

Mazuryk, Omelian, b 2 February 1937 in Brezhava, Dobromyl county, Galicia. Painter and iconographer. A graduate of the Wrocław Art School (1958) and the Cracow Academy of Fine Arts (1964), he came to Paris in 1967 to study at L'Ecole des beaux arts and remained in that city. Since his solo exhibition in 1972 in Paris, he has had many others in France, Belgium, Germany, Italy, Holland, Canada, and the United States. Mazuryk is best known for his neo-Byzantine religious paintings, in which he has synthesized expressionism, Ukrainian-Byzantine traditions, and folk art. He is one of the few Ukrainian artists who have succeeded in creating icons that retain the spirituality of the ancient models but at the same time embody the experiences of the 20th century. Mazuryk's icons for the iconostasis in the St Volodymyr Ukrainian Catholic Church in Paris are a fine example of modern Ukrainian church art. He also painted the iconostases in the chapels of the Shevchenko Scientific Society in Sarcelles, France, and the Ukrainian Catholic Holy Spirit Seminary in Ottawa, Canada. An atmosphere of mystery and unrest often pervades his landscapes, which display a great sensitivity to color gradations and an expressionistic brush stroke. In 1990 he had a solo exhibition in Lviv and was invited to teach icon painting at the Lviv Institute of Applied and Decorative Arts.

D. Zelska-Darewych

Meadowland. A type of grassland consisting mostly of perennial mesophytes. Unlike the vegetation of the steppe, which becomes largely dormant in the dry summer heat, meadowland vegetation develops throughout the vegetative period. The most conducive conditions for the development of natural meadows are in the forest-steppe belt, where temperate, subhumid conditions prevail, and the soils are rich in nutrients. In the steppe zone upland meadows are rare, for the steppe vegetation is dominated by drought-resistant xerophytes and ephemerals. In the forest zone to the north, natural clearings are either dry soil zones or wetlands. Nearly all meadowlands in Ukraine (except those in nature preserves) are now used for agriculture. Where they have not been plowed, they are used as hayfields or pasture. Hayfields and pastures were also created from areas that were not natural meadows. In 1988, hayfields (both natural and cultivated) occupied 2.1 million ha, and pasture (both natural and improved), 4.8 million ha (respectively representing approx 3.5 and 8 percent of the total land area of the Ukrainian SSR). About 60 percent of Ukraine's hayfields are in Polisia and the Carpathian Mountains, where they occupy over 30 percent of the agricultural land. Pastures are found in the mountainous areas and the floodplains as well as on the steep slopes of ravines in the steppe belt of Ukraine.

Measures. See Weights and measures.

Meat-processing industry. A branch of the *food industry that processes fresh meat and various meat products, such as sausages and canned meats. Before the 1920s, meat processing in Ukraine was essentially a cottage industry. There were only four large abattoirs in the nine Ukrainian gubernias of the Russian Empire in 1912. As agriculture was collectivized and the economy centralized in the 1930s, some 40 large meat-packing and -processing facilities were built in cities such as Kiev, Poltava, Vinnytsia, Melitopil, Kremenchuk, Mykolaiv, Dnipropetrovske, Luhanske, and Odessa, and fowl-processing facilities in Koziatyn, Pervomaiske, and Bakhmach. After a sharp decline during the Second World War, the industry was rebuilt. The overall growth of the industry since the war is illustrated in the table.

Meat production in Ukraine, 1960–87 (in 1,000 metric t)

	1960	1970	1980	1987
Meat	911	1,565	2,074	2,615
Beef and veal	416	763	1,111	1,453
Mutton	40.4	24.8	12.9	18.6
Pork	330	563	547	625
Fowl	28.2	73.2	229	317
Other meats and by-products	96.5	141	174	201
Sausages	243.4	436.4	685.5	823.8
Lard	190	245.2	335.5	421.2
Canned meat (in million standard cans)	84.2	145.4	179.6	244.6

The largest meat-processing facilities are now in Kiev, Vinnytsia, Dnipropetrovske, Luhanske, Odessa, and Poltava. The oblasts with the largest meat output (in thousands of metric t, 1987 figures) are Dnipropetrovske (164.6), Donetske (164.5), Kharkiv (150.1), Crimea (132.6), Cherkasy (132.1), Poltava (131), and Vinnytsia (128.6). The smallest output was registered in Western Ukraine, in Transcarpathia (32.2), Chernivtsi (42.8), and Ivano-Frankivske oblasts (55.4). Between 1960 and 1979 Ukraine's share of the USSR meat output increased from 20.7 percent to 23.2 percent for all meat, including by-products but not fowl, and from 18 to 23.3 percent for sausages and smoked meat.

Despite considerable progress in the meat-processing industry, meat, especially good-quality meat, is still in short supply in Ukraine. Moreover, growth rates in the industry have slowed in recent years: meat output increased by 71 percent from 1960 to 1970, but by only 32.5 percent from 1970 to 1980 and 26 percent from 1980 to 1987.

Mechanics. Akin to machine science, a discipline encompassing general machine theory, the mathematical theory of mechanisms, problems of materials, strength and elasticity, friction and wear, manufacturing, reliability, efficiency, and automation. Early research in mechanics was conducted in Ukraine in the 19th century at the universities of Kiev, Kharkiv, and Odessa, where M. *Ostrohradsky, T. Osipovsky, V. Imshenetsky, V. *Steklov, G. Suslov, and P. Vorontsov worked in analytical mechanics. A. *Liapunov's fundamental studies in the theory of stability were published in Kharkiv in 1892. Research in general mechanics was also carried out at the Kiev Polytechnical Institute (V. Kirpichov, S. *Timoshenko, B. Delone, Ye. *Paton) and at the Katerynoslav Higher School of Mining (O. Dynnyk; today the Dnipropetrovske Mining Institute).

In the Soviet period the first scientific work in mathematical mechanics at the AN URSR (now ANU) was directed by D. *Grave, M. *Krylov, and K. *Siminsky in Kiev and Dynnyk in Dnipropetrovske. Advanced research was carried out in analytic and space mechanics, the theory of motion of absolute and deformed solids, and the general theory of motion stability. Dynnyk, M. *Kilchevsky, A. *Kovalenko, H. *Savin, and I. *Shtaierman studied the theory of elasticity; in the postwar period M. *Lavrentev, A. *Ishlinsky, M. Leonov, V. Maizel, and D. Vainberg made important contributions to that field. Today thermal elasticity is researched at the *Institute of Mechanics of the ANU by Kovalenko, A. Ulitko, V. Hrinchenko, I. Motovylovets, and Yu. *Shevchenko and at the *Institute of Applied Mathematics and Mechanics of the ANU by Ya. *Pidstryhach, Ya. Burak, Yu. Koliano, and H. Kit. Mathematical methods for solving problems in the theory of elasticity were developed by scientists such as Savin, Kovalenko, H. *Polozhii, O. *Huz, O. Kosmodamiansky, and Ulitko. Problems in the analytic mechanics of the environment were researched by Shtaierman, V. *Chelomei, I. Rapoport, and Kilchevsky in Kiev in the 1930s. Fundamental data on the dynamics of solids were obtained after the war at the AN URSR Institute of Mathematics by Ishlinsky and V. Koshliakov. Shtaierman, Savin, Ishlinsky, Kilchevsky, Leonov, A. *Filipov, V. *Mossakovsky, and V. *Rvachov wrote on the mechanics of contact interaction between deformed bodies. At the Institute of Applied Mathematics and Mechanics P. Kharlamov solved various problems in the dynamics of solids and the stability of motion. The work of Huz and his students on general problems of the three-dimensional theory of the durability of deformed solids with different materials and structures has been widely applied; the physical and mechanical properties of such materials are studied at the Institute of Mechanics. Lavrentev's research in the mechanics of explosion was further developed in various institutes of the ANU, particularly by O. Vovk at the *Institute of Geophysics.

In the field of plasticity and thermal plasticity Ishlinsky and his students developed a theory of plasticity for materials with linear reinforcement, S. Malashenko devised equipment for measuring the plasticity of materials, and Shevchenko and his students developed a deformation theory of plasticity under variable nonisothermic loading processes. At the ANU *Institute for Problems of the Strength of Materials H. *Pysarenko and V. Kyselevsky studied creep and boundary conditions under complex stress applications within a wide temperature range, as well as problems of forecasting long-term strength and creep under high temperatures, particularly under irradiation. The new branch of fracture mechanics has been developed intensively in Ukraine by Savin, Leonov, V. *Panasiuk, Ulitko, Hrinchenko, and Kit.

The theory of mechanical oscillation is developing today as an independent branch of mechanics. In 1929 Krylov and N. *Bogoliubov founded a scientific school of nonlinear oscillations, later recognized throughout the world. Yu. Mytropolsky investigated nonstationary processes in nonlinear oscillations and developed asymptotic methods for the theory of nonlinear oscillations. Pysarenko developed methods of nonlinear mechanics for solving oscillation problems in machine building, with an energy dispersion factor in cyclically deformed material. The oscillation of tensile systems was also investigated by S. *Serensen, I. Tetelbaum, V. *Kononenko, M. Kornoukhov, P. Varnak, Vainberg, and Filipov. V. *Lazarian studied mechanical vibrations, particularly in reinforced columns. Kilchevsky and his students studied the oscillation of multiphase systems. The dissipation of energy that accompanies oscillation has been researched since the 1950s at the ANU Institute for Problems of Materials Science and since 1966 at the Institute for Problems of the Strength of Materials and the Kiev Polytechnical Institute. In the prewar period Siminsky, Serensen, F. *Bieliankin, M. Afanasiev, and Pysarenko made important contributions to research on the strength of materials under cyclic loading. Research on the fatigue of materials and structures was carried out after the war by Serensen, M. Harf, O. Kramarenko, and Ye. Buhlov; B. *Hrozin and D. Draihor researched contact strength. H. *Karpenko, Panasiuk, and H. *Maksymovych at the ANU Physical-Mechanical Institute researched the influence of corrosive environments on fatigue strength.

In the early 1960s a scientific school devoted to the strength of materials and structural elements in extreme conditions was set up at the Institute for Problems of the Strength of Materials. Among the problems connected with the requirements of new technologies, the strength of materials under high (Pysarenko, V. *Troshchenko, H. Tretiachenko, V. Rudenko) and low (A. *Lebedev, M. *Novykov, V. Stryzhalo) temperatures was studied, as well as fatigue limit and creep at high temperatures (M. Mozharovsky, V. Kovpak), strength of materials and structural elements under high-pressure gas flow (Tretiachenko, L. Kravchuk, R. Kuriat), the effect of neutron irradiation and of corrosive environments on the strength of materials (Kyselevsky, Kravchuk, B. Liashenko), the strength of materials in a wide temperature range (4 to 2,000°K) and under complex stress application (Lebedev, B. Kovalchuk), and impact resistance (H. Stepanov).

Other problems researched include fatigue and thermal fatigue (Troshchenko, V. Kuzmenko, B. Hriaznov), oscillations in *machine building (Pysarenko, V. Matveev, A. Yakovlev, M. Vasylenko, V. Khilchevsky), the structural strength of glass (Yu. Rodychev, K. Amelianovych), and physical aspects of strength (A. Krasovsky, V. Naumenko).

O. *Antonov and V. Kovtunenko contributed to the development of aero- and gas-dynamics; H. *Proskura, I. *Povkh, I. *Shvets, and O. *Shcherban, to industrial aero- and hydrodynamics; and O. Akhiiezer, to magnetic hydrodynamics. Ukrainian scientists also had a major impact on the development of the mining sciences (M. Fedorov, M. *Poliakov, V. *Poturaev, F. *Abramov), construction sciences (Kornoukhov, Bieliankin, B. *Gorbunov), and hydrology and hydrotechnology (Lavrentev, P. Filchakov, I. *Liashko).

Research of mechanics scientists in Ukraine is co-ordinated by scientific councils of the Academy of Sciences of Ukraine. Problems of mechanics are discussed in the Russian-language journals *Prikladnaia mekhanika* and *Problemy prochnosti*.

S. Protsiuk

Mechnikov, Illia [Mečnikov, Illja] (Metchnikoff, Élie) b 15 May 1845 in Ivanivka, Kupianka county, Kharkiv gubernia, d 15 July 1916 in Paris. Biologist, comparative anatomist, and immunologist; Nobel laureate in 1908 for his discovery of phagocytosis. Mechnikov graduated from Kharkiv University (1864) and worked at Odessa (1867–8) and St Petersburg (1868–70) universities. In 1870–82 he held the chair of zoology and comparative anatomy at Odessa University. In 1886 he founded (with M. Hamaliia and Ya. Bardakh) and directed the first bacteriological station in the Russian Empire (today the Scientific Research Institute of Virology and Epidemiology), but he was harassed by the Russian medical fraternity and forced to resign in 1887 by the Odessa Medical Society. In 1888 he was invited to Paris by L. Pasteur, and he headed a laboratory at the Pasteur Institute until his death.

Contrary to then prevailing chemical immunological approaches (championed by P. Ehrlich), Mechnikov's

Illia Mechnikov

phagocytic theory of immunity (1883) emphasized the role of foraging white blood cells (phagocytes) in attacking and digesting pathogens that invade the body. Mechnikov also conducted zoological studies of infusoria and parasites, embryological studies on the origin and development of germinal layers (several undertaken jointly with A. Kovalevsky), and periodicity studies on sugar beet weevil infestations and other epidemics. He discovered antilymphocyte globulin (1889) and with V. *Vysokovych developed a concept of the reticuloendothelial system (1892–1903).

Mechnikov was elected to the American Academy of Arts and Science (1898), the St Petersburg Academy of Sciences (1902), and the Académie des Sciences in Paris (1904). He published two popular books that went through many editions in several languages – *Études sur la nature humaine* (1903) and *The Prolongation of Life* (1907) – in which he expressed the view that most people die prematurely, estimated an attainable longevity of 100 to 120 years, and advocated yogurt as a key to human rejuvenation.

M. Adams

Mechnyk, S. [Mečnyk] (real name: Mudryk, Stepan), b 1919 in Kryve, Radekhiv county, Galicia. Political activist and journalist. As a young man he belonged to the OUN and fought for Ukrainian independence in the Ukrainian Insurgent Army. He settled in West Germany after the war. He has written several volumes of memoirs, including *Pochatok nevidomoho* (The Beginning of the Unknown, 1984) and *Rozdumuiu, pryhaduiu* (I Reflect, I Recall, 1985), and several documentary novels, such as *Neskoreni* (The Undaunted, 1965), *Vid oprychchyny do KGB* (From Oprichnina to the KGB, 1981), and *V zatiazhnii borot'bi* (In a Prolonged Struggle, 1983). He has contributed many articles to *Ukraïns'kyi samostiinyk* and *Shliakh peremohy*.

Mechnyk. In Kievan Rus' an officer of the prince's junior *druzhyna* who along with the *ditskyi* was responsible for various legal functions. The name is derived from *mech* (sword) and means 'sword bearer.' The *mechnyk* was responsible for maintaining order in the courts and for carrying out court sentences. In the Lithuanian-Ruthenian state the *mechnyk* was second last in rank among land officials. In the Polish Commonwealth he was the sword bearer who walked at the head of the king's entourage,

and he also presided over a military court. Eventually the office was reduced to a ceremonial one.

Medals. See Orders, medals, and honorific titles of the Ukrainian SSR.

Medical education. Prior to the end of the 18th century Ukrainian students wishing to pursue a medical career traveled to universities eleswhere in Europe, mostly to Italy, Germany, and Poland. They could also study in the Russian Empire at the Academy of Medicine and Surgery in St Petersburg or at the medical faculty of Moscow University (est 1764).

The first medical school in Ukraine was the Collegium Medicum, founded in Lviv in 1773. It was incorporated into the medical faculty (est 1784) of *Lviv University in 1817; a medical faculty with a full complement of courses was established in 1894. With the installation of Soviet rule in 1939, this faculty was reorganized into the *Lviv Medical Institute. The second school of medicine and surgery in Ukraine existed in Yelysavethrad (now Kirovohrad) in 1787–97. In 1802–17 a two-year medical program was offered at the *Kievan Mohyla Academy; its first lecturer was O. *Maslovsky.

Systematic medical education in Ukraine began with the development of medical faculties at the universities of Kharkiv (1805), Kiev (1841), Lviv (1894), Odessa (1900), and Katerynoslav (now Dnipropetrovske, 1918). By the middle of the 19th century numerous institutions had also been established for the training of nurses and medical assistants. The first faculty of medicine to use Ukrainian as the language of instruction was the Ukrainian State University of Kiev in 1918, during the time of Hetman P. Skoropadsky. In 1921 a medical department with a two-year program was organized by M. *Panchyshyn and M. *Muzyka under the auspices of the *Lviv (Underground) Ukrainian University; it lasted until 1925.

During the Soviet period a system of medical institutions of higher education was established in the Ukrainian SSR under the direction of the Ministry of Health of the USSR. In 1985 there were 14 medical institutes – the Lviv, *Kharkiv, *Kiev, *Odessa, *Poltava, *Dnipropetrovske, Zaporizhia (est 1921), Donetske (1930), Symferopil (1931), Vinnytsia (1932), Chernivtsi (1944), Ivano-Frankivske (1945), Luhanske (1956), and Ternopil (1957) medical institutes – as well as the Kharkiv Pharmaceutical Institute (1921), Kiev Scientific Research Institute of Pharmacology and Toxicology (1934), and the medical faculty at Uzhorod University.

The Kiev, Lviv, Odessa, Kharkiv, Dnipropetrovske, and Donetske institutes also have faculties of general hygiene and pediatrics. The Symferopil institute has a faculty of pediatrics; the Kiev, Odessa, Poltava, and Lviv institutes have faculties of stomatology; and the Lviv institutes have faculties of pharmacology. Medical studies consist of a six-year program, and pharmacology and stomatology studies, a five-year program; postgraduate and specialization programs are also available. In the 1984–5 academic year over 56,000 students were enrolled at the various medical institutes. Degrees for the general practice of medicine are granted at all the medical institutes; specialization requires another two years, and candidacy for a degree in medical sciences may take another three years of study. Postgraduate medical education in Ukraine is obtained at the Donetske, Kharkiv, Zaporizhia, and *Kiev institutes for the upgrading of physicians. There is also a department of continuing medical education at the Lviv Medical Institute.

Intermediary medical personnel, such as medical assistants, obstetricians, laboratory technicians, nurses, dental technicians, x-ray technicians, and opticians, are trained at medical *tekhnikums, where programs of study are two to three and a half years.

BIBLIOGRAPHY

Chistovich, Ia. *Istoriia pervykh meditsinskikh shkol v Rossii* (St Petersburg 1883)

Petrov, B.; Bratus, V.; Duplenko, K. (eds). *Ocherki istorii meditsinskoi nauki i zdravookhraneniia na Ukraine* (Kiev 1954)

Gronek, M. 'The History of Medical Education in Russia,' in *The History of Medical Education*, ed C. O'Malley (Berkeley 1970)

P. Pundii

Medical journals. The first medical journals in Ukraine were published in eastern Ukrainian territories under the Russian Empire in Russian: *Sovremennaia meditsina* (1860–81) and *Vestnik oftalmologii* (1884–1902) in Kiev, *Meditsinskii vestnik* (1862–86) in Teodosiia, *Arkhiv psikhiiatrii, nevrologii i sudebnoi psikho-patologii* (1882–99) in Kharkiv, *Zemskii vrach* (1884–1902) in Chernihiv, and *Akusherka* (1890–1917) in Odessa. Nineteen medical journals were published in Russian-ruled Ukraine in 1890–9, 25 journals in 1900–9, and 50 journals in 1917. The first Ukrainian-language journal in there to treat medical issues was *Zhyttia i znannia* (Poltava 1913–14), edited by H. Kovalenko and geared toward a general public. In the period of the Ukrainian National Republic two medical journals came out in Kiev, *Ukraïns'ki medychni visty*, edited by Ye. *Lukasevych, and *Vistnyk Ministerstva narodn'oho zdorovlia i opikuvannia*, edited by Yu. Melenetsky. In the Soviet period (1920–39), 69 medical journals were published, 22 of them in Ukrainian, including *Kyïvs'kyi medychnyi zhurnal* (1928–30), *Ukraïns'ki medychni visti* (1925–31, in Kiev), *Ukraïns'kyi medychnyi arkhiv* (1927–32, in Kharkiv), *Dnipropetrovs'kyi medychnyi zhurnal* (1922–31, in Dnipropetrovske), and *Profilaktychna medytsyna* (1929, in Kharkiv). After the Second World War the bimonthlies *Pediatriia, akusherstvo i hinekologiia, Farmatsevtychnyi zhurnal, Mikrobiolohichnyi zhurnal*, and *Fiziolohichnyi zhurnal*, as well as four Russian-language journals, have been published.

In Austrian-ruled Galicia scholarly medical journals and articles began to appear sporadically at the end of the 19th century. Among the research topics dealt with was the problem of Ukrainian medical terminology. In 1897 the Medical Commission of the Shevchenko Scientific Society began including medical articles in its *Zapysky Naukovoho tovarystva im. Shevchenka*. Eight issues, edited by Ye. Ozarkevych, had come out by 1901; they were later collected in two volumes. In 1902, articles began appearing in the annals of the mathematical and natural sciences section of the Shevchenko Scientific Society. On the initiative of Ozarkevych and I. Horbachevsky *Zdorovlie* was published in Lviv (20 issues, 1912–14). From 1920 to 1939 *Likars'kyi vistnyk* was published (62 issues). In 1928 S. *Parfanovych initiated the popular journal *Vidrodzhennia* in Lviv. Also published were *Ukraïns'kyi medychnyi vistnyk* in Prague (6 issues, 1922–5) and *Narodne zdorovlia* (1927–34, ed B. Matiushevsky).

In the United States the bilingual Ukrainian-English medical journal *Likars'kyi visnyk* began publication in 1954.

P. Dzul

Medical scientific societies. The Society of Kiev Physicians (est 1840) was the first of its kind in Russian-ruled Ukraine (see *Kiev Medical Society). Among its honorary members were I. Mechnikov, S. Botkin, N. Pirogov, I. Sechenov, and the French scholar L. Pasteur. The society paved the way for the future development of medical research, education, and practice. It was followed by the Odessa Medical Scientific Society (1849) and then by the more specialized Pharmacists' Association in Lviv (1871), the Association of Scientific Medicine and Hygiene in Kharkiv (1872), the Odessa Bacteriological Association (1876), the Gynecology and Obstetrics Association (1886) and the Physico-Medical Association (1896) in Kiev, and the Syphilis Research Association in Kharkiv (1900) and Kiev and Odessa (1902).

During the struggle for independence (1917–20) an All-Ukrainian Physicians' Association was active in Kiev and published *Ukraïns'ki medychni visty*. With the onset of Soviet rule all existing medical scientific societies were abolished and re-established as the Unified Scientific Medical Society. It consisted of various specialized branches that eventually broke off into independent societies. In 1985 there were 38 republican medical scientific societies in the Ukrainian SSR, apart from oblast-level and municipal associations. Their congress sat on the scientific committee of the Ukrainian SSR Ministry of Health and was subordinated to the All-Union Medical Scientific Society.

In Galicia a medical commission, initiated by Ye. *Ozarkevych, was founded in 1897 under the auspices of the Shevchenko Scientific Society. In 1910 it became the *Ukrainian Physicians' Society. By 1937 its membership had reached 289, with branches in Kolomyia, Stanyslaviv, Ternopil, and Peremyshl.

In Prague the *Ukrainian Physicians' Association in Czechoslovakia was founded in 1922 as the central organization of émigré doctors, with a membership of approx 120. It disbanded in 1940. In Germany Ukrainian Medical (Physicians') Societies were established in Munich (1946), Augsburg (1946), Hannover (1946), and Regensburg (1946). They were reorganized in 1952 into the Ukrainian Medical Association in Germany, which ceased its activity in 1958. The Ukrainian Medical Association of West Germany was founded in 1975 (renewed in 1979). Similar societies were also organized in Austria: in Vorarlberg and Tirol (1946), Salzburg (1948), with a total membership of 80; they had ceased activity by 1950 and were revitalized in 1985 as the Ukrainian Austrian Medical Association.

In the United States the Ukrainian Medical Association was founded in 1950; it was later expanded to include Canadian doctors as the *Ukrainian Medical Association of North America. In Australia the Ukrainian Medical Association was founded in 1975. To unite Ukrainian medical societies from around the world, the World Federation of Ukrainian Medical Associations was founded in 1977. It has held world congresses in Munich (1984), Vienna (1988), and Kiev and Lviv (1990).

P. Pundii

Medical technology industry. A branch of light industry that manufactures medical instruments, supplies, and equipment. In Ukraine the first simple medical instruments were made in the first half of the 19th century at the Kherson Instruments Factory. In 1853 a shop for making surgical instruments opened in Kharkiv, and in 1860 two shops for autoclaves and medical and prosthetic devices were set up in Kiev. Later a similar shop was founded in Odessa. These shops were small, and their production was rudimentary.

In Soviet Ukraine a surgical instruments factory was opened in Kharkiv and several factories were started in Kiev. Health care and medical research institutions designed and tested new instruments and equipment. Particular progress was made by V. Filatov and A. Martsynkovsky, who designed special machines used in eye surgery. Factories in Ukraine also produced Soviet-designed x-ray machines, electrocardiograph machines, inhalators, thermostats, and various other instruments and machines. In 1940 there were 16 factories and 18 small workshops, which produced some 300 separate items. But there was a shortage of almost all medical supplies during the interwar period, and the goods that were available were of inferior quality. Most specialized machinery and instrumentation was imported from abroad.

During the Second World War most medical supplies factories were evacuated from Ukraine. After the war the reconstruction of the industry was made a priority. By 1950 most of the prewar factories had been restored. In the 1960s the industry expanded rapidly: major factories were constructed in Izium (optical equipment), Odessa (laboratory apparatus), Lviv (radioelectric equipment), Kharkiv (medical machine-building equipment), and Mariiupil (technical supplies). In 1970 there were 12 enterprises, producing over 560 separate items, and Ukraine accounted for 25 percent of all Soviet production. In the 1970s many of the plants were expanded, and several were linked in manufacturing associations. By 1980 production was up by 81 percent over 1970, and there were 3 manufacturing associations, 8 separate factories, 2 research factories, and 6 special design bureaus, producing over 700 separate items of medical instrumentation, equipment, and supplies. Research in medical technology is conducted at the former All-Union Scientific Research and Design Institute of Radioelectric Medical Instrumentation in Lviv.

Medicinal plants. A great number of plants have been used throughout the world from time immemorial for the prevention or cure of sickness in humans and animals alike. Using plants for scientific or *folk medicine is known as phytotherapy. The medicinal attributes of plants are owing to their constituent components, such as alkaloids, glycosides, saponins, vitamins, organic acids, mineral salts, volatile oils, and antibiotics. The roots, tubers, bulbs, leaves, flowers, seeds, and bark of medicinal plants are selectively used in making teas, infusions, tonics, juices, tinctures, powders, and poultices. About 80 percent of the ingredients in drugs for heart disease, gastrointestinal or nervous disorders, and other grave illnesses are taken from medicinal plants.

During the First World War and the postwar period the disruption of imports resulted in an acute shortage of drugs in Ukraine. Intensive research on medicinal plants was conducted at the Ukrainian Institute of Applied Botany (1927–33; see *Agricultural Scientific Committee of Ukraine), the Kharkiv Institute of Experimental Medicine

(1935–7), and the Kharkiv Pharmaceutical Institute (1937–41). A research station in Lubni (est 1916, reorganized in 1931 as a branch of the All-Union Institute of Medicinal and Aromatic Plants) and the Acclimatization Garden in Kiev (set up by M. *Kashchenko in 1914) were responsible for introducing, testing, and cultivating new plants that eventually saw wide application in medical practice.

Since the Second World War over 20 research institutions connected with medical and pharmaceutical institutes and universities have conducted reseach on medicinal plants in Ukraine. The Kharkiv Pharmaceutical Institute, which concentrates mainly on isolating glucosides and using them in the preparation of new medicines, plays a leading role in this field. The gathering of wild plants and the cultivation of medicinal plants have expanded, and the research on new plants has led to the introduction of many foreign species and the adoption of many plants by official medicine.

Of the approx 12,000 species of medicinal plants worldwide, approx 1,000 are officially recognized as medicinal by the *pharmacology field. In Ukraine there are approx 1,200 species of medicinal plants, including 68 wild and 52 cultivated officially recognized species. Medicinal plants are classified by (1) their chemical components, (2) their effect on the human organism, or (3) the pathogen or symptom of a specific illness. For cardiovascular disorders the medicinal plants commonly used are campion (*Adonis vernalis*; Ukrainian: *horytsvit vesnianyi*), lily of the valley (*Convallaria majalis*; Ukrainian: *konvaliia travneva*), periwinkle (*Vinca*; Ukrainian: *barvinok*), and *belladonna (*Atropa belladonna*; Ukrainian: *beladonna likarska*). Belladonna, *valerian (*Valeriana officinalis*; Ukrainian: *valeriana likarska*), wild *poppy (*Papaver rhoeas*; Ukrainian: *mak dykyi, samosii*), and *jimsonweed (*Datura stramonium*; Ukrainian: *durman*) are utilized as painkillers and sedatives. For skin disorders the medicinal plants applied are shrub aloe (*Aloe arborescens*; Ukrainian: *aloe, stolitnyk*), *juniper (*Juniperus communis*; Ukrainian: *yalivets*), *wormwood (*Artemisia absinthium*; Ukrainian: *polyn*), and *plantain (*Plantago major*; Ukrainian: *podorozhnyk*). Bronchial and lung diseases are treated with thyme (*Thymus vulgaris*; Ukrainian: *chebrets*), *linden (*Tilia cordata*; Ukrainian: *lypa sertseva*), *sage (*Salvia officinalis*; Ukrainian: *shavliia likarska*); *viburnum (*Viburnum opulus*; Ukrainian: *kalyna*), and mint (*Mentha piperita*; Ukrainian: *miata kholodna*). Hepatic and bilious disorders are treated with St-John's-wort (*Hypericum perforatum*; Ukrainian: *zvirobii*; also called 'the herb against 99 maladies'), *yarrow (*Achillea millefolium*; Ukrainian: *derevii*), chicory (*Cichorium intybus*; Ukrainian: *tsykorii*), mint, and caraway (*Carum carvi*; Ukrainian: *kmyn*). *Parsley (*Petroselinum sativum*; Ukrainian: *petrushka*), caraway, and juniper are diuretics. Medicinal plants used in gastrointestinal disorders are mint, caraway, yarrow, wormwood, aloe, and rosemary (*Rosmarinus officinalis*; Ukrainian: *rozmaryn*). Viburnum, yarrow, and nettle (*Urtica dioica*; Ukrainian: *kropyva dvodomna*) are used as coagulants or to stop hemorrhaging.

Medicinal plants are mentioned in Ukrainian folk songs and folktales. Folklore conferred special status and power on the men and women who knew how to use such plants. In the 20th century, medicinal plant lore is available for public use in books such as M. and I. Nosal's *Likars'ki roslyny i sposoby ikh zastosuvannia v narodi* (Medicinal

Plants and Methods of Their Popular Use, 1965) and V. Karkhyt's *Liky navkolo nas* (Medicines around Us, 1975).

Ukraine produced one-half of the medicinal plant harvest of the USSR in 1957, almost a half of which was grown in Khmelnytskyi oblast. Dnipropetrovske oblast and the Crimea were also big producers.

Many wild-growing medicinal plants have been placed on the endangered species list. Efforts are being made by specific agrarian institutions and farm collectives to protect, cultivate, and preserve these valuable plants for posterity.

BIBLIOGRAPHY
Bordzilovs'kyi, Ie. *Dykorosli likars'ki roslyny fl'ory Ukraïny* (Kiev 1935)
Osadcha-Janata, N. *Herbs Used in Ukrainian Folk Medicine* (New York 1952)
Mamchur, F. *Dovidnyk z fitoterapiï* (Kiev 1986)
Likars'ki roslyny: Entsyklopedychnyi dovidnyk (Kiev 1989)
P. Dzul, N. Osadcha-Yanata

Medicine. The science and the art of diagnosis, prevention, and treatment of diseases (see also *Public health, *Hygiene, and *Sanitation).

During the Scythian period (7th–3rd centuries BC), herbal medicine and some surgical procedures were in common use, including tooth-pulling, debridement, suturing with horsehair, the bandaging of wounds, phlebotomy, the reduction of fractures, amputation, trepanation, embalming, and mummification. The physicians Anakharsis Abaris and Toxaris used *medicinal plants to increase blood coagulability, to treat ulcers, and to induce anesthesia. The therapeutic use of bathhouses was widespread. The Scythian ruler Mithridates VI, King of Pontus, was an experimenter in mithridatism.

In Kievan Rus' the profession of physician was officially acknowledged by legal statutes of Grand Princes Volodymyr the Great and Yaroslav the Wise. *Hospitals were regulated by a statute of Volodymyr the Great. The monk-physician St Anthony of the Caves founded the Kievan Cave Monastery, where a hospital was organized in 1070 by St Theodosius of the Caves.

In general, medicine was practiced by folk healers, monk-physicians (Anthony of the Caves, Ahapit, Olimpii, Pymen, and Kozma), and secular physicians (Ivan Smera, Petro Sirianyn, Fevronia, Maryna, Yevfrosyniia, and Danylo Zatochnyk). Princess Yevpraksiia Mstyslavna wrote a scholarly medical treatise on salves (*Allima*, Constantinople 1130; see also *Folk medicine). Kievan physicians were acquainted with many conditions, including itching, jaundice, dermatoses, eye disorders, pleurisy, arthritis, bronchial asthma, angina pectoris, meningocele, epilepsy, stroke, brain contusion, tuberculosis, typhoid fever, malaria, plague, and anthrax. Treatment consisted of the application of medicinal herbs, the use of sedatives and narcotics, hypnosis, massage, hydrotherapy, hygiene, and isolation. Maternal and child care was in the hands of midwives. Barber-surgeons (*tsyrulnyky, rizalnyky,* or *rukodily*) performed bandaging, tooth extractions, cauterizations, removal of lymphatic gland tumors, amputations, and trepanations of the skull (10th–11th centuries).

Knowledge of the natural sciences and of medicine was accumulated in Kievan Rus' in translations of Byzantine medical books, such as Exarch John of Bulgaria's *Shestodnev* (Hexaemeron, 1263) and *Fiziolog* (Physiologist), and

others, and in original local *zilnyky* or *travnyky* (herbaria) that contained descriptions of healing herbs, baths, the treatment of some diseases, and bloodletting. Possibly as early as the 11th to 13th centuries Kievan Rus' herbaria made the transition into *likarstvenni* or *lechebnyky* (medicinal compendiums) that contained both folk and scientific medicine. Segments of *Mefodiivskyi likarstvennyk* have survived.

During the 13th century Ukraine was overrun by the Mongols and Tatars, and progress was halted in all fields of endeavor, including medicine. Nevertheless, Vasylii Ruthenus of Kiev opened the first pharmacy in Lviv (1445), and Yu. *Drohobych wrote *Iudicum prognosticon* (Rome 1483) on astronomy and infectious diseases (plague). M. Bulev translated *Hortus sanitatus* (Lubek 1432) into Old Ukrainian (1534).

Hospitals were founded in Peremyshl (1461), Lviv (1591), Kiev (1629), Chernihiv, and Lutske, as well as homes for the aged, sick, and infirm, pharmacies in Kiev (military in 1715, civilian in 1728), and guilds for *tsyrulnyky* (see *Surgery and *Feldsher) in Kiev and Lviv.

Military medicine developed in the Zaporozhian Sich in the first half of the 16th century. During B. Khmelnytsky's hetmancy (1648–57) every regiment of his army had a physician, and each company had a *tsyrulnyk*. Treatment of wounded Cossacks was carried out in hospitals of the Mezhyhiria Transfiguration and Trakhtemyriv monasteries. With the creation of gubernias in the Russian Empire, the Prikaz of Public Charity (1775–1864) initiated organized medicine, including the establishment of medical schools, hospitals, infirmaries, pharmacies, and public health services.

During the 18th century notable medical scholars, researchers, and practitioners in Ukraine included I. *Poletyka; M. Terekhovsky, whose thesis, *De chao infusorio Linnaei* (1775), concluded that liquorous animalcules represent living organisms which die on heating or cooling; the epidemiologist D. *Samoilovych; the obstetrician and encyclopedist N. *Ambodyk-Maksymovych, who wrote an anatomical-physiological dictionary (1783) and a medical-pathological-surgical dictionary (1785); the organizer of health care in Western Ukraine, A. Krupiński; the histologist O. *Shumliansky; M. Hamaliia, who wrote a monograph on the Siberian plague (1792); the veterinarian S. *Andriievsky, who proved that human and animal anthrax were identical (1786); the anatomist P. *Zahorsky; the physiotherapist E. Mukhin, who pioneered 'nervism' in medicine (reflex theory, 1800) and prescribed resuscitation for victims of drowning, strangulation, and choking (1805); and the scholar I. *Orlai.

During the 19th century in the Russian Empire, medical education was managed by the Ministry of Education, health care by the Ministry of Internal Affairs, and military medicine by the Department of Land and Navy Forces. Zemstvo medicine served rural areas (1864–1917). Among the medical specialists in Ukraine were the anatomist I. Kamensky, who wrote a dissertation on 'squeezing the heart' (1802); the biologist P. *Peremezhko; the anatomist V. *Bets; the ophthalmologist O. *Ivanov, who studied the microanatomy of the eye; O. Kovalevsky, who discovered the neuroenteric (Kovalevsky's) canal; and M. Kulchytsky, who described argentaffine (Kulchytsky's) cells (1897). The physiologist O. Filomafitsky introduced the theory of the cyclical function of the nervous system

(1836–40), performed a gastrostomy (1842), and investigated intravascular administration of ether, chloroform, and benzine for anesthesia (1849); A. *Walter proved the vasoconstrictive effect of the sympathetic nerves on blood vessels (1842) and described the effect of cooling on the safety of an operation (1862) and thus defined hypothermia; I. Sechenov discovered the reflex inhibitory (Sechenov's) center in the medulla oblongata and spinal cord (1862); the physiologist V. *Danylevsky demonstrated the biochemical activity of the cerebral cortex (1876); and B. Veriho (1899) described displacement of the oxyhemoglobin dissociation curve by a change in partial pressure of carbon dioxide or in pH (Veriho-Bohr effect). In biochemistry, O. *Danylevsky isolated amylase and trypsin (1863), observed the hydrolysis of proteins by pancreatic juice, demonstrated the synthesis of proteins from peptones in the presence of ferments (1886), and formulated the theory of protein structure (1888–91); I. *Horbachevsky synthesized uric acid (1882) proving that it derived from cell nuclei (1889) and that it increases in neoplasms (1891–2), thereby introducing a biochemical screening to *oncology; O. *Bakh developed a theory of slow oxygenation and cellular respiration (1897); and F. Selivanov described a test for fructose in the urine (Selivanov's test, 1887). Among microbiologists and immunologists, were G. *Minkh, O. *Mochutkovsky, Nobel laureate I. *Mechnikov, V. Vysokovych, Hamaliia, who discovered bacteriophages (1898), Ya. *Bardakh, and the plague researchers I. *Savchenko and D. *Zabolotny. In *pathology D. *Vellansky approached diseases from a more rationalistic *Naturphilosophie*; the Kievan school of pathologists was organized by V. *Pidvysotsky; and the origin of radiology could be traced, perhaps, to the construction of the cathode ray lamp by I. *Puliui (1882).

In the field of internal medicine (Ukrainian: *terapiia*) a systematic description of clinical symptoms, complications, and treatment of ulcers of the stomach and duodenum was given by F. Uden (1809–22); V. Lambl discovered *Lamblia intestinalis* and lambliosis (1859); F. Loesh discovered *Entamoeba histolytica* and amoebic dysentery; and M. Tolochnikov reported on the interventricular septal defect of the heart (1874). The development of hygiene was promoted by V. *Subbotin; a sign of costovertebral angle tenderness was described by F. Pastenatsky; S. *Podolynsky wrote on protein ferments of the pancreatic glands (1876); and H. Shapiro noted bradycardia in the course of myocarditis (Shapiro sign). An early separation of the epidermis from the basal layer of the skin in pemphigus vulgaris was described by P. Nikolsky (Nikolsky sign, 1896); H. Rossolimo introduced a reflex of plantar flexion of toes (Rossolimo reflex, 1902); and D. Romanovsky developed the prototype of eosin–methylene blue (Romanovsky's stains for blood cells and parasites, 1890–1).

In *surgery I. *Buialsky introduced a method of sectional sawing of frozen cadavers for anatomical dissection (1836); T. *Vanzetti noted that in sciatica with scoliosis the pelvis is always horizontal, but that in other lesions with scoliosis the pelvis is inclined (Vanzetti sign); N. *Pirogov introduced rectal and intravenous anesthesia (1847), performed a mastectomy for breast carcinoma (1847), invented an osteoplastic amputation of the leg at the ankle in which a part of the calcaneus bone is left in the lower end of the stump (Pirogov's amputation, 1852), outlined a

venous (Pirogov's) angle formed by the junction of the internal jugular and subclavian veins and the angles of the teeth (Pirogov's point), and introduced an extraperitoneal approach to the external iliac artery (Pirogov's incision, 1881); O. Karavaiev performed pericardiocentesis (1840) and organized the Clinic of Eye Diseases in Kiev (1844); Yu. Shymanovsky designed a flap reconstruction of the cleft lip and palate, transplanted the cornea, and performed an amputation of the thigh through the knee using a patella as an osteoplastic flap over the end of the femur; O. *Yatsenko introduced blepharoplasty with full-thickness free skin graft (1871) and bouginage of a stenosed esophagus through gastrostomy. N. *Sklifosovsky introduced the compression lock for fixation of fractures complicated by delayed union or nonunion (Sklifosovsky lock, 1875), propagated metalo-osteosynthesis (1893), and resected a prolapsed rectum followed by mucomuscular anastomosis (Sklifosovsky operation); O. *Bohaievsky performed a gastrostomy and removal of echinococcal cysts of the liver, paracentesis, and gastric resection (1888); M. Subbotin designed an artificial urinary bladder and urethra using the anterior portion of the lower rectum (Subbotin operation) and a suction drainage for wounds and abscesses (1902–6); A. *Pidriz closed a bullet wound of the heart (1897); I. *Sabaneev designed an osteoplastic intercondyloidar amputation of the thigh (Sabaneev operation, 1890) and a gastrostomy by pulling a cone of the stomach through an incision in the left rectus muscle (1890); M. *Volkovych founded modern surgery in Ukraine; and A. *Matveev introduced prophylaxis of neonatal blennorhea by the routine subconjuctival application of a 2 percent silver nitrate solution (1853). Child *psychology and psychopathology were developed by I. *Sikorsky.

In the 20th century, contributions to medicine continued to be made by specialists in Ukraine and Ukrainians throughout the world, including the anatomist V. *Vorobiov, who described the subepicardial nervous plexus of the heart; the physiologist V. *Pravdych-Nemynsky, who recorded the electroencephalogram (EEG) in a dog, using a stringed galvanometer (1913); the pathophysiologist O. *Bohomolets, who did pioneering work on the theory of stress and developed the concept of the reticuloendothelial system; G. *Folbort, who established the principles of the physiology of exhaustion and recovery; D. Alpern, who proved the desensitizing and anti-inflammatory action of the hypophyseal cortex (1935); the pathophysiologist M. *Syrotynin, who proposed practical recommendations regarding hypoxia in space medicine (1973); J. Walawski, who discovered enterogastrone in the small bowel (1928) and proposed a theory of the etiology of gastric ulcers based on the function of enterogastrone; and Y. Babsky, who improved ballistography (1956–63).

In biochemistry J. *Parnas discovered the pathway of glucose metabolism (Embden-Mayerhoff-Parnas pathway, 1935); A. *Palladin researched vitamin synthesis (1938), muscle function, and biochemical topography (1965–72); the geneticist S. *Hershenzon demonstrated the mutagenic activity of exogenic DNA (1939); I. Kochan introduced the concept of nutritional immunity (1973); and the pharmacist O. *Hornykiewicz noted the dopamine depletion of the striatum in Parkinson's disease (1960) and introduced L-dopa for its treatment. In microbiology and immunology M. Weinberg developed a complement fixation (Weinberg) test for hydatid disease, introduced culture (Weinberg media) for the growth of anaerobes, and discovered the bacteria causing gas gangrene (*Bacillus oedematicus* and *histolyticus*, 1918); O. Bezredka discovered the Bezredka antivirus (1903), filtered and heated bacteria cultures for local immunity (1925), described a complement deviation test for tuberculosis (Bezredka reaction), and introduced a desensitization (Bezredka) method during immunization with tetanus toxoid or immune globulin (1930); V. *Drobotko formulated the bacterial dissociation theory; and Nobel laureate S. Waxman obtained streptomycin from *Streptomyces griseus* and proved its effectiveness against tuberculosis (1944).

In pathology, work was done by N. *Melnikov-Razvedenkov, who studied the fixation of anatomical preparations (1896), the pathology of alveolar echinococcus, tumors of the brain and stomach, and rhabdomyoma of the heart; P. *Kucherenko; R. *Kavetsky, who applied lasers to oncology (1969); and the immunologist and oncologist L. *Dmochowski. Evolutionary genetics was established by T. Dobzhansky, who applied Mendelian genetics to Darwinian evolution. In radiology E. Zavoisky did pioneering work in nuclear magnetic resonance (1944); and L. Bilaniuk was among the first (1982) to report diagnostic application of magnetic resonance imaging.

In internal medicine V. *Obraztsov and M. *Strazhesko clinically diagnosed acute myocardial infarction due to thrombosis of the coronary artery; the work of F. *Yanovsky centered on the diagnosis of kidney diseases (1927); L. Dmytrenko described a velvety sound in endocarditis; professional and ethical standards of medical practice were created by M. *Panchyshyn; disturbances of bronchial conductivity in bronchitis and bronchial emphysema were found by B. Votchal; V. Vasylenko reported metabolic alkalosis and (with M. Strazhesko) proposed a clinical classification of congestive heart failure (1939); V. *Ivanov contributed to the evaluation of gastric mobility and secretion (1926–8); D. *Panchenko constructed a barometric chamber for the treatment of essential hypertension and neuropsychiatric disorders (Panchenko biotrom, 1960); O. *Hrytsiuk demonstrated a transition of the subendocardial into the transmural myocardial infarction (1973); a Nobel laureate, Y. Chazov introduced intracoronary thrombolysis for acute myocardinal infraction (1975). Anesthesia in Ukraine was developed by A. Treshchynsky and L. Chepky.

In surgery, surgical oncology was founded by H. Bykhovsky, who also described a test for albumin in the urine (Bychovsky test); M. Diederichs invented a transport splint (1932); the cofounder of neurosurgery, N. *Burdenko, advanced military field surgery; the ophthalmologist V. *Filatov coinvented the tubed or pedicle (Filatov-Gillies) flap (1917), advanced keratoplasty, and initiated the use of cadaver corneas (1931); Ya. *Halpern proposed to substitute the esophagus with a greater curvature of the stomach (1911); V. *Shamov employed elecrocoagulation to destroy malignant tumors (1910–11) and initiated the transfusion of cadaver blood (1928); and O. Melnykov developed an anatomical basis for extrapleural approaches to the subphrenic spaces and abscesses (1929–3) and the concept of precancerous lesions of the stomach (1950–4). Neurosurgery was pioneered by I. *Ishchenko; T. Hryntschak introduced suprapubic transurinary prostatectomy with a primary closure of the prostatic bed and

urinary bladder (Hryntschak prostatectomy); Yu. *Vorony described the immunologic character of graft rejection (1929), performed the first human kidney allograft (1933), and introduced the mechanical suture in vascular surgery (1949); M. *Novachenko developed original operations for arthrodesis and for re-construction of the hip joint; V. Kolesov created internal thoracic–coronary artery grafting (1964–8); A. *Arutiunov and A. Romadonov contributed to the diagnosis and surgery of craniocerebral trauma, vascular abnormalities, and tumors of the brain and spinal cord; I. *Shevchenko recommended preoperative radiation for malignant tumors and combined intraoperative roentgen-radium therapy with the resection of lung cancer (1962); M. *Amosov introduced mechanical sutures in thoracic surgery (1957), advanced the use of computers in medicine (1960), simplified the heart-lung machine (1962), and constructed bileaflet and cuffed heart valve prostheses (1962–5); P. Dzul pioneered methods of microsurgery of the middle ear (1960) and introduced the intracavitary treatment of maxillary carcinoma (1967); K. Syvash developed endoprostheses for total hip (1959) and total knee (1978) replacement; W. Bobetchko designed the Toronto braces for Legg-Calve-Perthes disease (1968); H. Knyshov performed the first coronary artery bypass graft in Ukraine using a vein (1973); and L. Kuzmak designed stoma adjustable gastric banding for morbid obesity (1983).

Contributions to *pediatrics and *obstetrics were made by the psychoneurologist K. *Platonov; A. *Nikolaiev, who proposed administering oxygen, glucose, and cardiac stimulants (Nikolaiev's triad, 1952) to alleviate intrauterine asphyxia; and V. Hryshchenko, who applied hypothermia and cryosurgery and used echocardiography for the diagnosis of fetal heart abnormalities (1977–8). The work of O. Khokhol focused on nutritional diseases in infants.

The neurologist O. *Shcherbak developed a clinical classification of psychiatric disorders and introduced a segmental collar and lumbar reflex physiotherapy. The psychiatrist V. *Protopopov introduced physiology and biochemistry in the evaluation of patients. The neurologists V. Hakkebush, T. Heier, and O. Heimanovych defined a senile dementia due to atherosclerosis of the cortical arteries of the brain (Hakkebush-Heier-Heimanovych syndrome, 1912–15). The philosopher-pedagogue S. *Balei was a pioneer of childhood (1931), pedagogic (1938), and social (1959) psychology. One of the founders of forensic medicine, M. *Bokarius, proposed the classic sperm test and methods for examining a strangulation furrow (1925–30). Space medicine originated from the work of the aeronautical engineer S. *Korolov. Biological and medical computers for space technology were developed at the Division of Biological Cybernetics (organized by Amosov in 1960) of the AN URSR (now ANU) Institute of Cybernetics in Kiev (1957) and at the Kiev Scientific Research Institute of Tuberculosis, Pulmonology, and Thoracic Surgery.

The medical library of Ukraine (est 1930), located in a building formerly the property of the Tereshchenko family in Kiev, housed over one million volumes in 1980, and had 24,000 individual and 3,000 group subscribers. The Ukrainian Medical Museum (est 1973 by A. Grando) is located in the former Anatomy Theater of the Kiev Medical Institute.

(For more medical history, see *Health education, *Medical education, *Medical journals, *Medical science societies, *Veterinary science, and *Zemstvo medicine.)

BIBLIOGRAPHY

Garrison, F. *An Introduction to the History of Medicine, with Medical Chronology: Suggestions for Study and Bibliographic Data* (Philadelphia 1929)

Mikhn'ov, A. (ed). *Narysy istoriï terapiï v URSR* (Kiev 1960)

Petrov, B. *Ocherki istorii otchestvennoi meditsiny* (Moscow 1962)

Olearchyk, A.; Olearchyk, R. *Concise History of Medicine*, vol 38, no. 3 (1991) of *Journal of the Ukrainian Medical Association of North America*

A. Olearchyk

Medobory Mountains. See Tovtry.

Medovar, Borys, b 29 March 1916 in Kiev. Metallurgist; full member of the AN URSR (now ANU) since 1973. He graduated in 1940 from the Kiev Polytechnical Institute, and from 1941 he worked at the AN URSR Institute of Electric Welding (from 1946 as department head). His main contributions were in the areas of the electric welding of steel and iron alloys, particularly pipe welding, steel corrosion, specialty steel compositions, the influence of gases on steel joints, and many other areas of ferrous metallurgy. A biography of him was published in Kiev in 1986.

Levko Medved

Medved, Levko [Medved'], b 18 June 1905 in Chorna Hreblia, Olhopil county, Podilia gubernia, d 22 February 1982 in Kiev. Hygienist; full member of the USSR Academy of Medical Sciences from 1969. A graduate of the Vinnytsia Pharmaceutical Institute (1927) and the Kiev Medical Institute (1939), he served in the latter as director (1941–5) and head of the occupational hygiene department (1944–51). He was deputy health minister and health minister (1947–52) of the Ukrainian SSR, director of the Kiev Scientific Research Institute of Occupational Hygiene and Diseases (1952–64), and director of the All-Union Scientific Research Institute of the Hygiene and Toxicology of Pesticides, Polymers, and Plastics (from 1964). His publications, numbering over 250 works, dealt with agricultural and industrial hygiene, pesticide toxicology, and the history of Soviet health care.

Medvedeva, Nina, b 27 December 1899 in Saratov, Russia, d 26 May 1969 in Kiev. Pathophysiologist; corresponding member of the AN URSR (now ANU) from 1939. A graduate of Saratov University (1921), from 1931 she taught and chaired a department at the Institute of Experimental Biology and Pathology in Kiev (from 1953 the AN URSR Institute of Physiology). She researched the biodynamics of proteins and the biological significance of sulfur, and isolated a corticoid hormone.

Medvediev, Fedir [Medvedjev] (Medvedev, Fedor), b 28 May 1912 in Semenovka, Bohuchar county, Voronezh gubernia. Linguist. After graduating from Kharkiv University (1936) he continued his graduate studies under L. Bulakhovsky. After the war he lectured in the department of Ukrainian language at Kharkiv University and served as its chairman (1947–75). He wrote over 450 works in Slavic, Russian, and Ukrainian linguistics, including a textbook of Ukrainian historical grammar (1950) and books on the grammar of Standard Ukrainian (1951), the historical grammar of Ukrainian (1955, 1964), and Ukrainian conjunctions (1962).

Medvediev, Yukhym [Medvedjev, Juxym] (Vedmediv), b 1886 in Bakhmut, Katerynoslav gubernia, d 1938 in Kharkiv. Head of the first Soviet government in Ukraine. A member of the strike committee in Katerynoslav in 1905, after the February Revolution in 1917 he joined the Ukrainian Social Democratic Workers' party. As a delegate of the Kharkiv Executive Committee to the All-Ukrainian Congress of Workers', Soldiers', and Peasants' Deputies in Kiev, he walked out with the Bolshevik minority and attended the First All-Ukrainian Congress of Soviets in Kharkiv, which on 25 December 1917 elected him chairman of the Presidium of the Central Executive Committee in Ukraine. In March 1918 he attended the peace conference at Brest-Litovsk and the Second All-Ukrainian Congress of Soviets, which relieved him of his chairmanship. Later in 1918 he joined the *Borotbists and organized Borotbist partisan units in Katerynoslav gubernia. He joined the CP(B)U with other Borotbists in 1920 and resigned from it in the 1930s. In 1938 he was arrested, accused of organizing a counterrevolutionary terrorist organization, and shot. He was rehabilitated in 1957.

Medvedsky, Yuliian [Medveds'kyj, Julijan] (Niedźwiedski, Julian), b 18 October 1845 in Peremyshl, Galicia, d 7 January 1918 in Lviv. Geologist; full member of the Shevchenko Scientific Society from 1914 and the Polish Academy of Sciences from 1893. He graduated from Vienna University in 1872. He then taught mineralogy and geology at the Lviv Technical Academy (later the Lviv Polytechnical Institute), and he served as its rector in 1879, 1884, and 1887. He was appointed a lecturer at Lviv University in 1887. A supporter of Ukrainian education, he was vice-president of the Prosvita society and left his estate to various educational institutions. His geological studies of mountain regions include several works on the geology of the Carpathian Mountains and the mineralogy of Subcarpathia, particularly the Kalush region. His scientific works were published in German or Polish.

Medvetska, Edita [Medvec'ka], b 22 October 1932 in Mukachiv, Transcarpathia oblast. Painter. A graduate of the Lviv Institute of Applied and Decorative Arts (1958), she has painted genre scenes, Transcarpathian landscapes and folkways, and still lifes in a representational manner, often depicting workers and construction. She does not copy nature but transforms what she sees by means of a bright palette and simplified form.

Liubomyr Medvid: *New Street in the Village of Rudno* (tempera, 1972)

Medvid, Liubomyr [Medvid', Ljubomyr], b 10 July 1941 in Variazh (now Novoukrainka), Sokal raion, Lviv oblast. Painter. A graduate of the Lviv Institute of Applied and Decorative Arts (1965), he taught there until 1970. He experimented with elements of surrealism in the series 'Evacuation' (1965–7), painting distorted, floating figures and deep space. Later he developed a realist style (eg, *A New Street in Rudno* [1972] and *Boundary* [1974]) characterized by unusual points of view, a subdued palette sometimes bordering on the monochromatic, and an enigmatic atmosphere created by the positioning of figures and objects; at times the works echo those of the American realist A. Wyeth. Working mostly in tempera, he has painted interesting portraits of the writers T. Shevchenko (1985) and Lesia Ukrainka (1983), the composer S. Liudkevych (1978), and the violinist O. Krysa (1988). His triptych *Emigrants* (1981) is a powerful close-up image of forlorn figures. Medvid successfully uses the dramatic effects of light and dark to create tension and set up abstract patterns (eg, *Fluidity of Time* [1986] and *A Tone of Pure White*

[1988]). The figures in his most recent works, particularly the 'Yavoriv Region' series, are less structured; spatial dislocations add to the atmosphere of the mysterious. Medvid has had solo exhibitions in Lviv (1972) and Toronto (1990).

Medvid, Mykhailo [Medvid', Myxajlo] (aka Karpovych, Kremianetsky], b 1911? in Tysmennytsia, Tovmach county, Galicia, d 8 June 1945 in Deviatnyky, Novi Strilyshcha raion, Drohobych oblast. Senior UPA officer. After joining the OUN in 1933, he was imprisoned by the Poles for underground activities. In 1942 he became chief of the military department in the Dnipropetrovske Regional Leadership of the OUN (Bandera faction). He was transferred in 1943 to UPA headquarters in the northwestern region, and promoted on 26 January 1944 to captain and appointed chief of staff of the UPA-North. In the summer of 1944 he was reassigned to the UPA General Staff as its chief of communications, and wrote articles for the UPA journal *Povstanets'*. Facing capture by NKVD troops, Medvid shot himself. He was promoted posthumously to lieutenant colonel.

Medvid, Oleksandr [Medvid'] (Medved), b 16 September 1937 in Bila Tserkva, Kiev oblast. Wrestling champion. A graduate of the Minsk Institute of Physical Culture in Belarus, he won Olympic gold medals in freestyle wrestling in 1964 (light heavyweight), 1968 (heavyweight) and 1972 (super-heavyweight). He was also a five-time world champion and three-time European champion in various weight categories in the years 1962–72.

Medzhybizh castle (16th century)

Medzhybizh [Medžybiž] (historical name: Mezhybizh). IV-8. A town smt (1990 pop 2,000) on the Boh River in Letychiv raion, Khmelnytskyi oblast. It was first mentioned in the Hypatian Chronicle under the year 1146. At the end of the 12th century Medzhybizh was an important center in the Principality of Galicia-Volhynia. It was captured by the Tatars in 1241 and was recovered by Prince Danylo Romanovych in 1255. In 1258 his troops crushed the Tatar army near Medzhybizh. The town came under Lithuanian rule in 1362 and was transferred to Poland under the Union of Lublin in 1569. Its wooden castle was rebuilt in stone in the 14th to 16th centuries to protect the town from frequent Tatar attacks. The town was granted the rights of

Magdeburg law in 1593, and became an important cultural center in the 17th century. During the Cossack-Polish War of 1648–57 some major battles (in 1648, 1649, and 1651) were fought near Medzhybizh. In 1666 the town was captured by the Turks, who held it for 27 years. It was involved in the popular revolts against the Polish nobles in 1702–4 and 1734. After being transferred to Russia in 1793, Medzhybizh declined. In 1917 the First Ukrainian Corps commanded by P. Skoropadsky was stationed in Medzhybizh. In the following year several battles between the UNR Army and the Red Army were fought in its vicinity.

Today Medzhybizh has several food-processing plants and a brick factory. Its architectural monuments include the stone castle, which was partly rebuilt in the 19th century, the 16th-century Dormition Church, which contains many old frescoes, the 16th-century Roman Catholic Church of the Holy Trinity, and a 16th-century palace.

Medzilaborce. IV-2. A town (1962 pop 3,000) in the Prešov region of Slovakia, inhabited mostly by Lemkos. In 1918 the town and the surrounding region voted to join Czechoslovakia rather than Poland.

Medzvietsky-Koval, Mykola [Medzviec'kyj-Koval'], b 1868, d 1929 in Warsaw. Senior officer, astronomer, and geodesist. During the First World War he rose to major general in the Russian army. As brigadier general in the Army of the UNR, he was chief of the Main Geodetic Service and a member of the Council of the UNR Ministry of Defense.

Megalithic culture. See Nordic culture.

Megas, Osyp (Joseph), b 1882 in Galicia, d 8 September 1955 in Edmonton. Physician, educator, journalist, and community leader. After emigrating to Canada in 1905, Megas was appointed 'supervisor of Ruthenian schools' by the government of Saskatchewan (1907–17), and helped organize the Training School for Teachers for Foreign Speaking Communities in Regina in 1909. He served as editor of *Kanadiis'kyi farmer* (1906–8) and helped establish the pro–Liberal party paper *Novyi krai* in Rosthern, Saskatchewan (1910–13). In 1916 he was among the founders of the Mohyla Ukrainian Institute in Saskatoon, and in 1919 he was a delegate from the Ukrainian Canadian Citizens' League to the *Paris Peace Conference. After visiting Galicia he published his impressions in *Tragedia halyts'koï Ukraïny* (The Tragedy of Galician Ukraine, 1920). Following studies at the universities of Manitoba and Alberta (MD, 1926) he established a medical practice in Edmonton (1926).

Mehedyniuk, Marko [Mehedynjuk], b 1842 in Richka, Kolomyia circle, Galicia, d 1912 in Richka, Kosiv county. Hutsul folk artist and master of wood inlay. His work, including crosses, plates, chests, candle holders, *tsymbaly, and axes, was distinguished for its fine detail and the use of colored beads and metal. His works were exhibited in Cracow (1887), Lviv (1894, 1905), and Kolomyia (1912) and are preserved today at the Ukrainian State Museum of Ethnography and Crafts in Lviv, the National Museum in Lviv, and the Kosiv School of Applied Art.

Petro Mehyk: *Zinnias* (tempera)

Mehyk, Petro, b 24 June 1899 in Vashkivtsi, Bukovyna, d 26 August 1992 in Philadelphia. Painter and graphic artist. A graduate of the Warsaw Academy of Fine Arts (1928), he taught drawing at secondary technical schools in Warsaw (1928–44), worked as an artist at the medical faculty of Warsaw University (1925–39), was a founding member of the *Spokii art circle in Warsaw, and participated in Ukrainian art exhibitions in interwar Lviv, Warsaw, Prague, and Berlin. A postwar refugee, in 1949 he emigrated to Philadelphia, where he directed the *Ukrainian Art Studio, served on the executive of the Ukrainian Artists' Association in the USA, and edited *Notatky z mystetstva / Ukrainian Art Digest. He has done portraits, landscapes, and still lifes in oil, tempera, and watercolor, but his favorite medium is pencil drawing. He compiled the album *Rysunky* (Drawings, 1962) and wrote studies of fresco painting technique (in Polish) and Ukrainian folk sculpture. A retrospective catalog of his works was published in 1979.

Meihesh, Yurii [Mejheš, Jurij], b 20 January 1925 in Velykyi Rakovets, Transcarpathia. Writer. A former teacher, he is secretary of the Writers' Union of Ukraine in Transcarpathia oblast. Since 1950 he has published 10 novels about life in Transcarpathia, notably *Verkhovyntsi* (Highlanders, 1961), *Kam'ianyi idol* (The Stone Idol, 1966), *Taka liubov* (Such Is Love, 1968), *S'ohodni i zavzhdy* (Today and Forever, 1969), *Nebezpechnyi vik* (A Dangerous Age, 1983), and *Stykhiia* (The Elemental Force, 1985). A volume of his selected works appeared in 1985.

Meitus, Yulii [Mejtus, Julij], b 28 January 1903 in Yelysavethrad (now Kirovohrad). Composer. A graduate of the Kharkiv Music and Drama Institute (1931) in the class of S. Bohatyrov, he has worked as a composer for his entire life. His works include 14 operas, most notably *Perekop* (1939–40) and *Haidamaky* (1940–1) (both composed with V. Rybalchenko and M. Tits), *Abadan* (composed with A. Kuliev, 1942–3), *Star over the Dvina* (1951–5), *Stolen Happiness* (1958–9), and *Yaroslav the Wise* (1973); five orchestral suites; choral and choral-orchestral works on Ukrainian and Turkmen folk themes; songs to texts by T. Shevchenko, I. Franko, and others; and music for the the-

Yulii Meitus

Teofil Melen

ater and films. Fairly modern in style, Meitus is a notable representative of contemporary Ukrainian music.

Mekhanizatsiia sil's'koho hospodarstva (Mechanization of Agriculture). A monthly scientific and technical magazine published in Kiev since 1950 by the Committee for the Technical and Production Needs of Agriculture of Ukraine. It contains articles on economic problems, farm management, the use of machines and tractors in farming, and the mechanization and electrification of the production processes on collective and state farms. Its circulation was approx 15,000 in the 1950s, 26,000 in 1970, 28,500 in 1976, and 25,000 in 1980.

Ukrainian Orthodox Church of the Dormition in Melbourne

Melbourne. The state capital (1989 pop 3,002,300) of Victoria, in southeastern Australia. The Ukrainian community in Melbourne, about 9,000 strong, consists of postwar emigrants and their descendants. Melbourne is the seat of a Ukrainian Catholic eparchy and its former exarchate (1958–82) as well as of the Australian eparchies of the Ukrainian Autocephalous Orthodox church and the Ukrainian Orthodox Church of Canada. The state branch of the Federation of Ukrainian Organizations in Australia

is centered there, and the local branch of the Shevchenko Scientific Society is the most active one in Australia. The city's cultural life is enriched by the Chaika male choir (and its affiliated Korali female quartet and Akord male quartet), the Kurbas theater (est 1950), the Soniashnyi Promin dance group, and the Vasyl Symonenko Literary-Artistic Club. In addition to Ukrainian Saturday schools, the youth organizations Plast Ukrainian Youth Association and Ukrainian Youth Association (SUM) are active there. The Levy Sports Association fields a soccer team. The semimonthly *Ukraïnets' v Avstraliï* has been published there since 1956. The Catholic eparchy publishes *Tserkva i zhyttia* (1960–), and the Lastivka publishers have published *Novyi obrii*, an almanac devoted to literature, art, and culture (six issues by 1980). The economic strength of the community is illustrated by the Dnister credit union (est 1951), with 2,500 members and assets of five million pounds; the Odessa building co-operative, with 400 members and assets of two million pounds; and the Postup trade co-operative, with 370 members and assets of 800,000 pounds. In 1983 the first university-level Ukrainian courses in Australia were initiated at the city's Monash University, and in 1988 the M. Zerov Lectureship in Ukrainian Studies was established at the university through a permanent endowment. The current holder is M. *Pavlyshyn.

Melek-Chesmen kurhan. A large burial mound (8 m tall and 60 m in diameter) of a noble of the *Bosporan Kingdom from the 4th century BC in Kerch (ancient *Panticapaeum), Crimea. Excavated in 1858, the kurhan was found to contain a stone burial chamber with a preceding corridor (*dromos*). The grave was found looted, and contained only the skeletal remains of a child, pottery sherds, and a small bronze bracelet with gold ornamentation.

Melen, Teofil [Melen', Teofil'], b 1879, d 28 May 1915 in Yezupil, Stanyslaviv county, Galicia. Civic and political leader and publicist. As a university student in Lviv he was active in Ukrainian affairs and a contributor to *Moloda Ukraïna*. Upon graduating he became a leading member of the Ukrainian Social Democratic party and editor of its semimonthly *Volia*. He helped organize the *peasant strikes in Galicia in 1902. In 1914–15 he represented his party on the Supreme Ukrainian Council and helped recruit soldiers for the Ukrainian Sich Riflemen. A supporter of the General Ukrainian Council, he contributed articles and reports from the battlefront to its *Vistnyk*. He served as a courier in the Ukrainian Sich Riflemen and was killed in action.

Melenevsky, Mariian [Melenevs'kyj, Marijan] (pseuds: Basok, Ivan Hilka or Hylka, Samoilovych, and others), b 1878 in Fediukivka, Tarashcha county, Kiev gubernia, d ? Political activist; scion of a Polonized gentry family in central Ukraine. He graduated from a Kiev gymnasium (1896) and was expelled from the Agricultural and Forestry Institute in Nova Aleksandriia (Puławy), Lublin gubernia, the same year for participating in student protests. He was one of the first members of the Ukrainian intelligentsia to take an overt Marxist position. He cultivated a social-democratic workers' group on his father's estate, funded the *Ukrainian Socialist party and later the

*Revolutionary Ukrainian party (RUP), edited 12 issues of *Selianyn*, and spread revolutionary propaganda among rural homesteads and villages. In 1899 he was arrested in Kiev for participating in student demonstrations, and in 1901 he was exiled for two years to Vologda gubernia. He emigrated to Lviv and continued his activity in the Foreign Committee of the RUP.

After leaving the RUP in late 1904, Melenevsky founded and led the Ukrainian Social Democratic *Spilka; following its collapse he joined the Ukrainian Social Democratic Workers' party and published the article 'Do roboty cherez iednannia' (To Work through Unification, *Nash holos*, 1911, nos 11–12). He was unable to reconcile his ideals of the 'unity of the international proletariat' with the idea of a free and independent Ukraine, and at the start of the First World War he joined the *Union for the Liberation of Ukraine (SVU). He became a presidium member and represented the SVU in Turkey (1914–15) and on the *General Ukrainian Council in Vienna (1915). In 1923, however, after the imposition of Soviet rule in Ukraine, Melenevsky supported the Bolsheviks; he accounted for his action in an article published in Vienna, 'Kudy ity?' (Where to Go? *Nova hromada*, vol 1 [1923]). He later moved to Soviet Ukraine; his further fate is unknown.

Melensky, Andrei [Melenskij, Andrej], b 1766 in Moscow, d 1833 in Kiev. Architect of the *Empire style. He was trained in the drafting office of the Kremlin Building Expedition in Moscow (1786–7) and the palace design office run by G. Quarenghi in St Petersburg (1787–92). He worked for a time as gubernial architect for Volhynia and

then as chief architect of Kiev (1799–1829) and director of the Kiev gubernial drafting office (1802–32). He helped prepare the general plan for Kiev (1808–9) and rebuilt the Podil district after it was destroyed by fire in 1811. Many government and church buildings in Kiev were designed by Melensky, including the governor's residence and building of the Nobles' Assembly in the Pecherske district (1806–10), the first theater building (1806), the Nativity Church (1814), the buildings of the contract fairs (1800–1817), the rotunda church at Askoldova Mohyla (1810), the new building of the Kiev Theological Academy (1824), the Resurrection Church and hegumen's residence at St Flor's Monastery (1824), and the monument to the restoration of Magdeburg law (1802–8). He also designed buildings in other towns of Kiev gubernia and conducted a survey of architectural monuments in the region.

Meleshkin, Mikhail [Meleškin, Mixail], b 6 August 1918 in Davlekanovo, Bashkiria, d 29 May 1980 in Odessa. Economist; corresponding member of the AN URSR (now ANU) from 1976. A graduate of the Gorky Industrial Institute (1941), he worked in industry before becoming deputy director of the AN URSR Institute of Economics (1964) and director of its Lviv and Odessa sections. In 1975 he was appointed deputy director of the Southern Branch of the AN URSR. He wrote articles and monographs on ways of increasing efficiency in industry and, most notably, on marine economics and ecology, including *Ekonomiko-ekologicheskie problemy morskoi sredy* (Economic and Ecological Problems of the Maritime Environment, 1982) and *Ekonomika i okruzhaiushchaia sreda: Vzaimodeistvie i upravlenie* (The Economy and the Environment: Interaction and Management, 1979).

Meleshko, Fotii [Meleško, Fotij], b 25 August 1889 in Hlodosy, Yelysavethrad county, Kherson gubernia, d 6 December 1970 in New York. Political leader and writer. In 1917 Meleshko was one of the organizers of Ukrainian military units; subsequently he became a political activist for an independent Ukraine. In 1921 he emigrated to Prague, and after the Second World War, to the United States. He is the author of numerous sketches and stories. His best-known works are the dramas *Ponad Dniprom* (Along the Dnieper, 1921) and *Tr'oma shliakhamy* (By Three Roads, 1964) and the novel *Try pokolinnia* (Three Generations, vol 1, 1943; vol 2, 1959).

Meletios Pegas, b 1549 in Crete, d 14 September 1601 in Alexandria. Orthodox Patriarch of Alexandria. He entered the service of the patriarchal courts in Alexandria and Constantinople in 1575 and was consecrated patriarch in 1590. Meletios was well acquainted with church affairs in Ukraine. He opposed the Church Union of *Berestia of 1596; corresponded with leaders of the Orthodox opposition (esp Prince K. Ostrozky); and dispatched his representative, C. Lucaris, to assist them. His letters to Sigismund III Vasa, in which he criticized the union and the notion of papal supremacy, have survived. Meletios also granted stauropegion rights to several church brotherhoods to help them resist conversion. I. Malyshevsky's monograph on Meletios and his relations with the Russian and Ukrainian churches appeared in 1872.

Andrei Melensky: monument to Magdeburg law in Kiev (1802–8)

Melgunov, Aleksei, b 9 February 1722, d 2 July 1788. Russian military figure and administrator. After serving in the courts of Elizabeth I and Peter III Fedorovich (from 1756) he was made commander of New Serbia and governor of New Russia gubernia (1763–5) by Catherine II. In those capacities he organized the *lancer regiments, and he also started the first excavations of Scythian grave sites in Ukraine (including the 1763 unearthing of Lyta Mohyla, known also as the *Melgunov kurhan). From 1777 he was governor-general of Yaroslavl and Vologda gubernias in Russia.

Melgunov kurhan: gold sheath and fragment of sword hilt

Melgunov kurhan. An early 6th-century BC royal Scythian burial, found near the village of Kucherivka, now in Znamianka raion, Kirovohrad oblast. It takes its name from A. Melgunov, governor of New Russia gubernia, who commissioned the excavation of the site in 1763. Known also as Lyta Mohyla, this site contained the remains of a Scythian chieftain and his armor (bronze arrowheads, sword, sheath), a gold crown, and silver adornments. Assyrian and Persian designs on some of the artifacts testify to Scythian contacts with the Middle East. The collection is housed in the Hermitage in St Petersburg.

Melikhov, Heorhii [Melixov, Heorhij], b 24 May 1908 in Kharkiv, d 22 April 1985 in Kiev. Painter; corresponding member of the USSR Academy of Arts from 1979. He graduated from the Kiev State Art Institute (1941), where he studied under P. Volokydin and F. Krychevsky, and later taught there (1945–62). He painted and drew portraits, a series of German-Soviet War scenes (1943–5), still lifes, and landscapes and illustrated editions of literary works. His works include *Young Taras Shevchenko at the Home of the Artist K. Briullov* (1947), *Hutsul Woman from the Village of Yasynia* (1946), *Children* (1952), *In Our Native Ukraine* (1965), and *Mountain Road* (1971). Albums with reproductions of his works were published in 1962 and 1979.

Melitopil or **Melitopol** [Melitopil' or Melitopol']. VII-16. A city (1990 pop 175,800) on the Molochna River and raion center in Zaporizhia oblast. A frontier settlement was established at the site in 1784. In 1816 it was named Novooleksandrivka, and in 1841 renamed Melitopil. From 1841 to 1923 Melitopil was a county center in Tavriia and

Heorhii Melikhov: *Hutsul Woman* (oil, 1947)

then Zaporizhia gubernia. On 18 June 1918 the UNR Army defeated the Red Army near the town. During the Soviet period Melitopil developed into an industrial city. Its chief industries are machine building (automobile engines, refrigerators, tractor parts), metalworking, light industry, and the food industry. Its main educational institutions are the *Melitopil Institute of Agricultural Mechanization and the Melitopil Pedagogical Institute (est 1922). It has a regional museum.

Melitopil Institute of Agricultural Mechanization (Melitopilskyi instytut mekhanizatsii silskoho hospodarstva). A technical school of higher education formed, in 1930, on the basis of an agricultural tekhnikum and until 1992 under the Ukrainian SSR Ministry of Agriculture. Originally known as Zavod-vuz, it was renamed the Institute of Engineers-Mechanics of Agriculture in 1936 and given its present name in 1944. It has departments of the mechanization of agriculture and electrification, graduate-level studies, a correspondence school and preparatory programs, and an experimental farm. In 1980 the institute had over 5,000 regular students and approx 2,600 correspondence students.

Melitopil kurhan. A Scythian royal burial mound from the 4th to 3rd century BC near Melitopil, Zaporizhia oblast.

Melitopil kurhan: gold combination quiver and bow-case decorated with scenes from Achilles' life

It was excavated in 1954. Archeologists uncovered two biers containing the remains of a noble Scythian couple and a slave, as well as approx 4,000 artifacts. Included among the latter were gold and silver ornaments and military gear decorated with animal (eagles, lions, wild boars) or mythological (Athena, Achilles) motifs. Eleven amphorae and a bronze kettle were also found. The collection is now housed at the Museum of Historical Treasures of Ukraine in Kiev.

Meller, Vadym, b 26 April 1884 in St Petersburg, d 4 May 1962 in Kiev. Theatrical designer and painter. While completing a law degree at Kiev University (1908) he took courses at the Kiev Art School (1903–5). In 1908–12 he studied at the Munich Academy of Arts. Then he moved to Paris, where he joined the Société des Artistes Indépendants, and in 1912–14 participated in the 'Free Workshops.' After returning to Kiev in 1917, he worked at easel and monumental painting, graphic design, and costume design. In 1920 Meller began working as a theatrical designer in the Shevchenko First Theater of the Ukrainian Soviet Republic; he soon became the leader of modernist constructivism in Ukrainian theater design. He achieved remarkable results in a synthesis of architecture, painting, and sculpture. He was the main stage designer in *Berezil (1922–34), in the Kharkiv Ukrainian Drama Theater (from 1935), and in the Kiev Ukrainian Drama Theater (1953–61). At the Berezil Meller did his most interesting work in creating the designs for G. Kaiser's *Gas I* (1923 production), an adaptation of U. Sinclair's *Jimmie Higgins* (1923), W. Shakespeare's *Macbeth* (1924), F. Crommelynck's *Tripes d'or* (1926), the revue *Hello on Wavelength 477* (1929), M. Kulish's *Myna Mazailo* (1929) and *Maklena Grassa* (1933), and I. Mykytenko's *Dyktatura* (Dictatorship, 1933). Meller's designs were singled out at the 1925 International Exposition of Decorative Arts in Paris and shown in the 1926 International Theater Exposition in New York. In the 1930s, however, he abandoned his avant-garde style and began to work in a conservative style more consistent with the tenets of socialist realism. Meller's later work included designs for O. Korniichuk's *Bohdan Khmel'nyts'kyi* (1939), O. Levada's *Faust and Death,* and W. Shakespeare's *King Lear.*

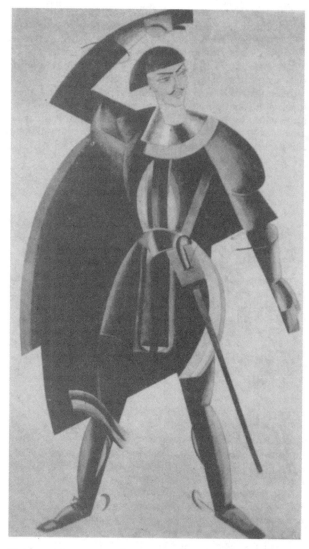

Vadym Meller: drawing of a costume for the production of J. Słowacki's *Mazepa* (1921) by the Shevchenko First Theater of the Ukrainian Soviet Republic (1921)

BIBLIOGRAPHY
Kucherenko, Z. *Vadym Meller* (Kiev 1975)
Mudrak, M. *The New Generation and Artistic Modernism in the Ukraine* (Ann Arbor, Mich 1986)
                                                        V. Revutsky

Melnikov, Leonid [Mel'nikov, Leonid], b 31 May 1906 in Degtiarovka, Briansk county, Orel gubernia, Russia. Soviet official and Party functionary. After graduating from the Donetske Industrial Institute in 1936, he held Party posts in Staline and Karaganda. After the war he served as first secretary of the Donetske Oblast Party Committee and then secretary (1947–9) and first secretary (1949–53) of the CC CP(B)U. After Stalin's death he was criticized for grave errors in his nationality policy, especially for his Russification of Lviv University, and demoted to the office of ambassador to Rumania. From 1955 he held a number of government appointments in Kazakhstan and, later, in Moscow.

Melnikov-Razvedenkov, Mykola [Mel'nikov], b 24 December 1866 in Ust-Medveditskaia, Don Cossack province, d 20 December 1937 in Kharkiv. Pathological anatomist; full member of the VUAN and AN URSR (now ANU) from 1927. A graduate of Moscow University (1889), he served as a professor at Kharkiv (1902–20) and Kuban (1920–2) universities and the Kuban Medical Institute (1922–5). He was director of the Ukrainian Institute of Pathological Anatomy (1925–30) and a department head at the Ukrainian Institute of Experimental Medicine (from 1930) in Kharkiv. His publications deal with anthrax, echinococcosis, periarteritis, the morphology of allergic processes, neuropathology, and the history of pathological anatomy. He proposed a method of fixing anatomical specimens (1896).

Melnychuk, Bohdan [Mel'nyčuk], b 8 December 1922 in Dauphin, Manitoba, d 17 August 1987 in Edmonton. Businessman and bookseller. After serving in the Canadian air force during the Second World War, he began to work for the Ukrainian Book Store in Edmonton. In 1961 he took over the business and developed it into one of the largest operations of its kind outside Ukraine. He was active in the Ukrainian Orthodox church and a founder of the *Ukrainian Canadian Archives and Museum of Alberta.

Melnychuk, Oleksander [Mel'nyčuk], b 12 July 1921 in Pysarivka, Balta county, Podilia gubernia. Linguist; corresponding member of the USSR Academy of Sciences since 1981 and full member of the AN URSR (now ANU) since 1985. A graduate of Kiev University (1947), he joined the staff of the ANU Institute of Linguistics in 1950 and has served as head of its division of general and Slavic linguistics (since 1961), academic secretary of the ANU Section of Literature, Language, and Art Scholarship (1971–8), and a member of the academy's presidium. He proposed an original classification of simple sentences in contemporary Ukrainian, and wrote a book on the development of Slavic sentence structure (1966) and articles on Ukrainian syntax, dialects, and toponymics. He edited the institute's collective monographs on the comparative historical study of Slavic languages (1966), the syntax of modern literary Ukrainian (1972), the historical typology of the Slavic languages (1986), the institute's Ukrainian dictionary of loanwords (1974), and its projected seven-volume Ukrainian etymological dictionary (vol 1, 1982; vol 2, 1985; vol 3, 1989).

Melnychuk, Taras [Mel'nyčuk], b 20 August 1938 in Utoropy, Kolomyia county, Galicia. Poet. He studied at the Gorky Institute of Literature in Moscow, from which he was expelled for 'political bad conduct.' In 1972–5 he was imprisoned in concentration camps in Perm oblast. He was rearrested in 1979 and sentenced to four years' imprisonment in the concentration camp in Vinnytsia. Melnychuk has written the poetry collections *Nesimo liubov planeti* (Let's Bring Love to Our Planet, 1967), *Chaha* (1971, unpublished), *Iz-za grat* (From Behind the Bars, 1982, published in the West), and *Kniaz' rosy* (Prince of Dew, 1990). His verse is terse and his metaphors of humanity and Soviet Ukraine are acerbic.

Melnychuk, Yurii [Mel'nyčuk, Jurij], b 7 May 1921 in Kamianky Mali, Kolomyia county, Galicia, d 12 August 1963 in Lviv. Communist propagandist. After the Second World War he studied at the CC CPU school and at Lviv University. After serving briefly as an editor at the Radianskyi Pysmennyk publishing house he was chief editor of the literary monthly *Zhovten'* from 1951 until his death. Melnychuk published several scurrilous attacks on Ukrainian 'bourgeois nationalists' and the Ukrainian Catholic church, including *Sluhy zhovtoho dyiavola* (Servants of the Yellow Devil, 1958), *Oblychchia bozhoho voïnstva* (The Faces of God's Warriors, 1961), and *Pravdi sluzhyty* (To Serve the Truth, 1962). He also published literary biographies of Ya. Halan (1953) and O. Havryliuk (1955). Melnychuk is the subject of a 1980 biography by Y. Tsokh.

Andrii Melnyk

Melnyk, Andrii [Mel'nyk, Andrij], b 12 December 1890 in Volia Yakubova, Drohobych county, Galicia, d 1 November 1964 in Köln, Germany. Military figure and political activist. His studies at the Higher School of Agriculture in Vienna (1912–14) were interrupted by the outbreak of the First World War, when he volunteered for the Legion of the Ukrainian Sich Riflemen. A company commander, he fought in the battles of Makivka and Lysonia before being taken prisoner in September 1916 by Russian forces and interned in Tsaritsyn and other locations. In captivity Melnyk became a close confidant of Ye. *Konovalets. After escaping imprisonment toward the end of 1917, he was one of the organizers of the Galician-Bukovynian Battalion of Sich Riflemen (the original formation of the *Sich Riflemen) in Kiev and held senior positions in it (from battalion commander to second-in-command). From January 1919 he was chief of staff of the Army of the UNR. After a short period as a Polish prisoner of war, he became a military attaché for the UNR and lived in Prague and Vienna (1920–1), where he finished his forestry studies. From 1922 he lived in Galicia.

Melnyk assumed the home command of the *Ukrainian Military Organization (UVO) in Galicia in 1922, after Konovalets had left the country and set up its command center abroad. In the spring of 1924 Melnyk was arrested and sentenced to five years' imprisonment for his UVO activities. He was freed toward the end of 1928, partly as a result of the efforts of the president of the UNR Directory, A. Livytsky. He served as head of the Orly Catholic Association of Ukrainian Youth in 1933–8, was involved with the Moloda Hromada society, and maintained his underground nationalist connections and activity. After the assassination of Konovalets in 1938, Melnyk went abroad to head the *Organization of Ukrainian Nationalists (OUN). His position was formally ratified in August 1939 at the OUN's Second Grand Assembly in Rome, but he could not retain the allegiance of the entire OUN membership. In 1940 a faction led by S. *Bandera broke from the OUN to pursue a more radical course of action. The respective groups became known as *Melnykites and *Banderites.

From 1941 Melnyk was kept under house arrest by the Germans until he was finally imprisoned in the Sachsenhausen concentration camp, in 1944. During this period Melnyk assigned the co-ordination of OUN activities on Ukrainian soil to his deputy, O. *Olzhych. Together with other leading Ukrainian activists (M. Velychkivsky, Metropolitan A. Sheptytsky, A. Livytsky, Gen M. Omelianovych-Pavlenko), Melnyk submitted a memorandum to A. Hitler in January 1942 demanding an end to German destructiveness in Ukraine. After the war he worked toward a consolidation of Ukrainian political and community life in the West. He was instrumental in the founding of the Ukrainian Co-ordinating Committee in 1946 and the *Ukrainian National Council in 1947. He proposed the idea of a world congress of Ukrainians in 1957; it was realized in 1967 with the founding of the World Congress of Free Ukrainians. Melnyk was also the author of historical articles on the Ukrainian independence struggle. From 1945 he lived in Luxembourg, where he is buried. A memorial book in his honor, edited by M. Antonovych, was published in 1966. A monograph on his life, edited by Z. Knysh, appeared in 1974, and a collection of memoirs about him appeared in 1991 in Lviv.

V. Yaniv

Melnyk, Lubomyr [Mel'nyk, Ljubomyr], b 22 December 1948 in Munich. Composer and pianist. He moved to Canada as a child and studied at the University of Manitoba (BA, 1969) and Queen's University in Kingston (MA, 1971). Melnyk is regarded as the creator of a new ('continuous') technique for playing piano based on incongruent patterns for each hand. He has composed a body of more than 90 works, mostly for piano, which include KMH, *Lund–St Petri Symphony*, *The Song of Galadriel*, and *Islands*. A number of his symphonic and chamber works are based on Ukrainian themes, including *Poslaniie* (lyrics by T. Shevchenko for soprano and chamber ensemble), *Concert-Requiem* for violin and piano (written in commemoration of the victims of the 1932–3 famine), and *A Portrait of Petlura* [sic] (for two violas and two pianos). Melnyk has concertized extensively throughout Canada and in Europe, given lecture-recitals, and recorded for national radio organizations in several countries. He is regarded as one of the fastest piano players in the world, being capable of sustaining arpeggios at over 19 notes per second on each hand. His musical approach is explained in his *Open Time: The Art of Continuous Music* (1981).

Melnyk, Mykhailo [Mel'nyk, Myxajlo], b 21 October 1903 in Sukha Volia, Liubachiv county, Galicia, d 9 October 1955 in Kiev. Church figure. After studying at the Peremyshl Seminary and obtaining his TH D at Innsbruck University, he was a professor of theology at the Peremyshl Seminary from 1932 and then vicar-general for Drohobych from 1944. One of the founders of the so-called Initiating Committee for the Reunification of the Ukrainian Catholic Church with the Russian Orthodox Church,

he was secretly ordained Orthodox bishop of Drohobych and Sambir by the Moscow patriarch Aleksei in February 1946. This initiating committee later convened the *Lviv Sobor of 1946, which disbanded the Ukrainian Catholic church in Western Ukraine.

Melnyk, Mykhailo [Mel'nyk, Myxajlo], b 1944 in Ordyntsi, Pohrebyshche raion, Vinnytsia oblast, d ca 9 March 1979 in Pohreby, Brovary raion, Kiev oblast. Dissident. A graduate student at the AN URSR Institute of History, he was expelled after participating in the commemoration of T. Shevchenko at his monument in Kiev on 22 May 1971. Thereafter he was subjected to constant harassment by the KGB. He was expelled from the CPU and fired from his job as a teacher at a secondary school in 1973, after writing a letter to the authorities protesting the persecution of Ukrainian writers and intellectuals. In 1978 he established close ties with the *Ukrainian Helsinki Group. Unable to stand the persecution that ensued, he committed suicide.

Mykola Melnyk

Melnyk, Mykola [Mel'nyk], b 20 November 1875 in Dovzhanka, Ternopil county, Galicia, d 1956 in Lviv. Botanist and teacher; member of the Shevchenko Scientific Society (NTSh) from 1920. He graduated from Vienna University and then taught in Ternopil and at the Academic Gymnasium in Lviv (from 1907) and the Ukrainian Underground University. He headed the physiography section of the NTSh and edited its *Fiziohrafichnyi zbirnyk* (Physiographic Collection, 7 vols, 1925–39). Following the Soviet occupation of Galicia he taught botany and zoology at Lviv University and prepared secondary-school texts on mineralogy, geology, and botany.

Melnyk, Oksana [Mel'nyk], b 8 May 1932 in Kolodne, Transcarpathia. Ethnomusicologist. After graduating from Uzhhorod University (1957) she finished study at the Lviv Conservatory (1967) and completed a candidate's degree (1970). She has published a number of articles on the folk songs of Transcarpathia and a monograph, *Etnomuzykolohiia skhidnykh slovian* (The Ethnomusicology of the Eastern Slavs, 1991).

Melnyk, Oleksandr [Mel'nyk], b 9 May 1949 in Mala Ofirna, Fastiv raion, Kiev oblast. Painter. A graduate of the Kiev State Art Institute (1974), he paints large-scale canvases in a style reminiscent of Ukrainian-Byzantine art and the 1920s murals of M. Boichuk. In his triptych *We, the*

Idol Worshippers (1988) he portrays pre-Christian times as an allegory of contemporary life.

Melnyk, Serhii [Mel'nyk, Serhij], b 2 April 1898 in Odessa, d 23 July 1968 in Odessa. Viticulturist and wine maker; corresponding member of the All-Union Academy of Agricultural Sciences from 1956. A graduate of the Odessa Agricultural Institute (1920), he became a professor at the institute (1938) and then its director (1959–68). He wrote several works on the biology and agrotechnology of grape cultivation.

Melnyk, Vasyl [Mel'nyk, Vasyl'] (pseud: V. Limnychenko), b 31 December 1899 in Nebyliv, Kalush county, Galicia, d 8 March 1949 in Munich. Poet and Catholic priest. After finishing his studies in Lviv he was ordained in 1923, and served as a parish priest in Zarvanytsia and Zvenyhorod until 1944, when he emigrated to Germany. He first emerged as a poet during the early 1920s as a member of the Logos Catholic writers' group affiliated with the journal *Postup* (Lviv). He wrote a number of poetry collections, including *Klonius'* (I Bow Down, 1926) and the posthumous *Bilii Pani – Lysh ty odna potrapysh nas spasty* (To the White Lady [Mary] – You Alone Can Save Us, 1977). Melnyk's work is infused with religious themes, Ukrainian patriotism, and Boiko regionalism.

Melnyk, Yaroslav [Mel'nyk, Jaroslav] (nom de guerre: Robert), b 1917? in Kalush county, d 31 October 1944 in Stanyslaviv oblast. Senior OUN leader. He rose swiftly in the OUN leadership from raion leader (1938) to Stanyslaviv oblast leader (1942). After the reorganization of the OUN in 1945, he became OUN leader for the Carpathian region. He was one of the few recipients of the Gold Cross of Merit for extraordinary service in the UPA. To avoid capture by MVD troops, Melnyk shot himself.

Melnyk, Yurii [Mel'nyk, Jurij], b 7 August 1931 in Kiev. Geologist; corresponding member of the AN URSR (now ANU) since 1979. He graduated from Kiev University in 1954 and worked in the Institute of Geological Sciences of the ANU. He was appointed department head at the Institute of the Geochemistry and Physics of Minerals of the ANU in 1970. Melnyk has contributed to the theory of the genesis of ferrous and flint rocks and has worked out chemical-physical models of geological processes.

Melnyk, Zinowij [Mel'nyk, Zinovij], b 7 October 1928 in Yabloniv, Kolomyia county, Galicia. Economist; full member of the Ukrainian Academy of Arts and Sciences and the Shevchenko Scientific Society. A postwar refugee, he studied at the Ukrainian Technical and Husbandry Institute in Munich before emigrating to the United States, where he graduated from the University of Michigan (MBA, 1953) and Michigan State University (PH D, 1961). He worked briefly in industry and then taught industrial management at Purdue University (1961–4). He has taught finance at the University of Cincinnati since 1967. He has written several articles on Ukraine's economy and the monograph *Soviet Capital Formation: Ukraine, 1928/29–1932* (1965) and edited (with V. Bandera) *The Soviet Economy in Regional Perspective* (1973) and several collections in management and business finance.

Melnykites (Melnykivtsi). The colloquial name for those members of the *Organization of Ukrainian Nationalists who supported Col A. *Melnyk after the schism in the organization in 1940. They followed the political and ideological program of the Leadership of Ukrainian Nationalists (PUN) as established by the resolutions of the Second Grand Assembly of Ukrainian Nationalists in Rome in 1939. After Melnyk's death O. Shtul, D. Kvitkovsky, and M. Plaviuk assumed the leadership of the faction. Compared to their breakaway rivals, the *Banderites, the Melnykites adhered closely to the initial principles of the OUN and were therefore considered conservative. In 1946 they abandoned their preference for a single-party system and espoused a policy of 'national solidarism' and political pluralism. They subsequently cofounded and were active in the Ukrainian National Council. Major pro-Melnykite organizations include the *Ukrainian National Federation (UNO) in Canada, the *Organization for the Rebirth of Ukraine (ODVU) in the United States, the *Union for Agricultural Education in Brazil, the *Vidrodzhennia society in Argentina, the *Ukrainian National Alliance in France, and the *Federation of Ukrainians in Great Britain.

Melnykov, Heorhii [Mel'nykov, Heorhij], b 22 January 1904 in Chernava, Tambov gubernia, Russia, d 11 May 1973 in Dnipropetrovske. Hydrobiologist. He completed his studies at the Dnipropetrovske Institute of People's Education (1929) and taught at Dnipropetrovske University (from 1941), where he later served as rector (1956–64). He researched hydrobiological systems, zooplankton formation, and fish farm usage in the water reservoirs of southern Ukraine. He also maintained an interest in space biology.

Melnykova, Iryna [Mel'nykova], b 24 October 1918 in Mena, Sosnytsia county, Chernihiv gubernia. Soviet historian; AN URSR (now ANU) corresponding member since 1973. A graduate of Kiev University (1940), she lectured at postsecondary schools in Kazakhstan (1941–7) and worked at the Institute of Slavic Studies of the USSR Academy of Sciences in Moscow (1947–57). From 1957 to 1988 she worked at the ANU Institute of History, where from 1965 she directed the Department of the History of Socialist Countries and Ukraine's International Relations. She has written books on the class struggle in Czechoslovakia in 1924–9 (1962) and foreign participation in the Soviet cause in 1917–20 (1967), as well as articles about interwar Czechoslovakia and Transcarpathia and the communist movement there, and she has contributed to multiauthor monographs on the Ukrainian SSR and the Soviet bloc countries (1965) and Ukraine's co-operation with the European socialist countries in 1966–70 (1974).

Melon. See Muskmelon and Watermelon.

Melosky, Louis [Melovs'kyj, Lev], b 14 July 1930 in Oakburn, Manitoba. Orthodontist and community leader. After graduating from the University of Manitoba (B SC, 1955), University of Alberta (DDS, 1959), and University of Washington (MDS, 1966), he went into private practice and taught dentistry at the University of Manitoba. In 1977 he was appointed to the university's board of governors, and then served as its chairman (1980–3). He has held leading positions in Ukrainian organizations, including the presidency of the *Ukrainian Cultural and Educational Centre, the Ukrainian Professional and Business Club of Winnipeg (1979), and the Canadian Foundation for Ukrainian Studies (1986) and the headship of the Prairie Region and Manitoba sections of the Ukrainian Community Development Committee. In 1984 he was appointed to chair the Canadian Multicultural Council.

Memoir literature (from French *mémoire* 'memory'). A body of recollections written, in a literary, publicistic, or chronicle style, simultaneously with the occurrence of events (as in diaries and notebooks) or subsequently in recollection (as in autobiographies and travelogues).

Ukrainian memoir literature can be divided into two groups, works written in Ukrainian or other languages by Ukrainians, and works written by foreigners about Ukraine. Among the oldest examples of the former group is the passage in *Povist' vremennykh lit* (The Tale of Bygone Years) by Nestor the Chronicler which concerns the transferral of the sacred remains of the founder of the Kievan Cave Monastery, St Theodosius of the Caves, entered into the chronicle in 1091. Early examples of the latter group are the autobiography of Prince Volodymyr Monomakh and a fragment of his *Poucheniie ditiam* (A Teaching for [My] Children), and a Chernihiv memoir, *Zhytiie i khodzheniie Danyla, rus'koï zemli ihumena* (The Life and Pilgrimage of Danylo, Abbot of Rus', ca 1100), of a pilgrimage to the Holy Land.

Memoir literature is particularly rich from the 16th and early 17th centuries. Among the most notable works to have been preserved are the autobiography of the Kievan hierodeacon Yoakym-Isaia, who sojourned in Muscovy in 1560–90; the notes of an unknown Galician of the late 16th or early 17th century concerning a pilgrimage to Jerusalem; the notes of B. Balyk-Bozhko of Kiev about his adventures during the 1612 campaign on Moscow and other events; the notes of Metropolitan P. Mohyla concerning events and meetings with various persons in the 1620s and 1630s; the memoirs of Hieromonk Ihnatii of Liubariv concerning the religious and cultural life of Galicia (*Zhytie i zhizn' prepodobnoho ottsa nasheho Iova* [The Life and Times of Our Worthy Father Yov, 1621]); and the *Diariiush* (Diary) of Hegumen A. Fylypovych of Brest concerning the struggle with the Poles over the Orthodox faith, written in 1637–48.

The Khmelnytsky era had a series of chroniclers, both Ukrainian and Polish. The most renowned among them was S. Zorka, whose *Diariiush* S. Velychko purportedly draws on in his *Skazanie o voini kozatskoi z poliakamy* (Account of the Cossack War with the Poles), but which historians consider to be suspect. The memoirs of the Ukrainian nobleman J. Jerlicz about the events of 1620–73 mention the lost memoirs of the Jerlicz and Butovych families. Hegumen Teodosii Vaskovsky wrote about current events in Kiev of the same period. Other accounts of the late 17th century include the notes of the Lviv merchant P. Kunashchak (or Kunashovych) about the life of a burgher in 1663–96; the *Diariiush* and *Keliini zapysky* (Notes from a Monastic Cell) of Metropolitan D. Tuptalo; the travelogues (journeys to Italy) of Hieromonk T. Kaplonovsky from the year 1697; and those of H. Skybynsky, who explored many Western European countries between 1686 and 1696.

Of the memoirs of the 18th century the more historically important are those of Cossack officers, such as the *Dnevniki* (Diaries) of Gen M. Khanenko, which cover the years 1719–21 and 1727–54; the *Diiariiush: Dnevnyia zapiski* (Diary: Daily Notes) of Ya. Markovych, covering the years 1717–67; the *Diiariiush* of Hetman P. Orlyk of the years 1720–32, which was written in Polish; and the *Dnevnik* (Diary) of Hetman P. Apostol, written in French, covering the period May 1725 to May 1727. The regimental osaul of Pryluka, M. Movchan, provides valuable descriptions of daily life and includes the register of 1727. Movchan's grandson, A. Mazaraki, continued the family chronicle for the period 1732 to 1787. Valuable information is found in the journal of the Pohar chamberlain S. Lashkevych, which covers the years 1768–82. More intimate is the autobiography of the colonel of Pryluka, H. Galagan. Also useful are the memoirs of church leaders, including the biographical notes of Bishop Y. Horlenko (1740–4); the autobiography of A. Matsiievych; the six-volume *Diarium Quotidianum* of M. Ryllo, the bishop of Kholm and Peremyshl, which deals with religious events of 1759–1804; and the memoirs of the traveling priest I. Turchynovsky. Of the travelogues of the 18th century those of V. Hryhorovych-Barsky, of his travels through Europe, Asia, and Africa from 1723 to 1747, are among the most interesting. Daily and cultural life of the last quarter of the 18th century is described in H. Vynsky's *Moë vremia* (My Time) and in the memoirs of M. Hornovsky, V. Hettun, I. Tymkovsky, and others. Slobidska Ukraine is described by the architect V. Yaroslavsky, and Southern Ukraine appears in the memoirs of S. and O. Pyshchevych. The 19th-century memoirs of the former Zaporozhian M. Korzh (*Ustnoe skazanie* [Oral Account]) describe the last days of the Zaporozhian Sich. Right-Bank Ukraine at that time is described in Polish memoirs, particularly those concerning the Koliivshchyna rebellion. The memoirs of the Ukrainian Freemasons M. Antonovsky and V. Lomykovsky are engaging and occasionally fantastic.

Among the many but as yet scantily published memoirs of the 19th century the *Zhurnal* (Journal) and autobiography of T. Shevchenko are particularly important. Also notable are those of M. Markevych (an unpublished diary kept in the Markevych archive in the St Petersburg Pushkin Museum), O. Martos (published in *Russkii arkhiv*, 1893, nos 7–8), A. Skalkovsky (unpublished), O. Kistiakovsky (unpublished), H. Galagan, and V. Hnylosyrov. The autobiographies of M. Kostomarov, M. Drahomanov, V. Antonovych, M. Hrushevsky (two), D. Bahalii, and other leading figures are noteworthy and interesting. Other sources include the notes of O. Mykhailovsky-Danylevsky (military historian), the memoirs of S. Skalon (daughter of V. Kapnist), the family chronicle of A. Kochubei, the notes of A. Storozhenko, M. Lazarevsky's *Pamiati moi* (My Memories), and the memoirs of Ya. Holovatsky, L. Zhemchuzhnikov, I. Sbytnev, M. Chaly, V. Debohorii-Mokriievych, B. Poznansky, K. Mykhalchuk, O. Lazarevsky, O. Barvinsky (*Spohady z moho zhyttia* [Memories of My Life, 2 vols, 1912–13], about community and literary life in Galicia, 1860–88), Ye. Chykalenko (*Spohady, 1861–1907* [Memoirs, 1861–1907, 1955]), S. Rusova, O. Lototsky (*Storinky mynuloho* [Pages from the Past, 4 vols, 1932–4]), M. Slavynsky, V. Shcherbyna, M. Vasylenko (serialized in *Ukraïns'kyi istoryk*), and M. Storozhenko (unpublished). An impressive number of memoirs were published in *Kievskaia starina*, in *Ukraïna*, in the collection *Za sto lit*, and elsewhere. V. Leontovych's *Khronika rodyny Hrechok* (Chronicle of the Hrechka Family, 1932) and *Dytiachi i iunats'ki roky Volodi Hankevycha* (The Childhood and Youthful Years of Volodia Hankevych) are memoiristic. The memoir literature of the 19th and early 20th centuries focused on Right-Bank Ukraine.

The early 20th century and the struggles for Ukrainian statehood are reflected in the memoirs of D. Doroshenko (*Moï spomyny pro davnie-mynule, 1901–1914 roky* [My Memories of the Distant Past, 1901–14, 1949] and *Moï spomyny pro nedavnie mynule, 1914–20* [My Memories of the Recent Past, 1914–20, 1923–4, 1969]), Yu. Kollard, M. Halahan, O. Shulhyn, V. Doroshenko, V. Shcherbakivsky, M. Kovalevsky, A. Zhuk, I. Makukh, O. Stepaniv, A. Chernetsky, M. Tyshkevych, V. Ivanys, O. Skoropys-Yoltukhovsky, F. Dudko, P. Bilon, P. Zaitsev (fragments), and others. For a knowledge of the community and cultural life of that time Chykalenko's *Shchodennyk* (Diary, covering 1901–17) and the diary of V. Modzalevsky (particularly of 1915–17, unpublished) are particularly important. The fate of the notes of H. Narbut's circle in Kiev (1918–20) and S. Yefremov's diary is unknown.

The memoirs of the days of national liberation form a separate group. Notable political accounts include V. Vynnychenko's *Vidrodzhennia natsiï* (Rebirth of a Nation, 3 vols, 1920) and *Shchodennyk* (Diary, of which two volumes [1980, 1983], covering the years 1911 to 1925, have been published to date), I. Mazepa's *Ukraïna v ohni i v buri revoliutsiï* (Ukraine in the Flames and Storm of Revolution), O. Nazaruk's *Rik na Velykii Ukraïni* (A Year in Central Ukraine, 1920), L. Tsehelsky's *Vid legendy do pravdy* (From Legend to Truth, 1960), V. Andriievsky's *Z mynuloho* (From the Past, 2 vols, 1921, 1923), M. Kovalevsky's *Pry dzherelakh borot'by* (At the Source of Struggle, 1961), D. Dontsov's *Rik 1918, Kyïv* (Year 1918, Kiev), and the memoirs of P. Skoropadsky (fragments published in *Khliborobs'ka Ukraïna*), Ye. Konovalets, M. Shapoval, O. Dotsenko, and A. Margolin. Military accounts of the period have been published in *Litopys Chervonoï kalyny*, *Kalendar Chervonoï kalyny*, *Za derzhavnist'*, and other anthologies and periodicals. The more notable ones are those of V. Petrov, V. Zelinsky, S. Shukhevych, A. Krezub (O. Dumyn), Yu. Tiutiunnyk (H. Yurtyk), V. Kedrovsky, O. Kobets (O. Varavva), O. Levytsky, and N. Makhno. Of the Soviet memoirs of the early 1920s those of V. Zatonsky and O. Shlikhter are worthy of mention.

The events of the interwar period have not been well represented in memoir literature. Conditions in the Soviet Union, particularly in the 1930s, were not conducive to the keeping of such records, and those that have been published have largely been the recollections of émigrés. Soviet realities, such as the man-made famine and the terror, were depicted by S. Pidhainy in *Nedostriliani* (Those [Left] Unshot, 2 vols, 1949) and *Ukraïns'ka inteligentsiia na Solovkakh* (The Ukrainian Intelligentsia on the Solovets Islands, 1947), V. Yurchenko, K. Turkalo in *Tortury* (Tortures, 1963), I. Nimchuk in *595 dniv soviets'kym v'iaznem* (595 Days as a Soviet Prisoner, 1959), I. Shkvarka in *Proklynaiu* (I Curse), V. Dubrovsky (fragments), and others. Ukrainian life in Galicia and in the emigration were the subject of the writings of I. Herasymovych, I. Kedryn, I. Makukh, M. Ostroverkha, Ye. Onatsky, and S. Shakh. Since the Second World War the NTSh has produced a

series of Western Ukrainian regional histories that contain much memoiristic material. The experiences of Ukrainians in the Bereza Kartuzka concentration camp were outlined in the memoirs of V. Makar and I. Nahaievsky, among others. Z. Knysh has described the activities of the Ukrainian Military Organization and the Organization of Ukrainian Nationalists (OUN) in Western Ukraine.

K. Pankivsky provides an account of the political situation in Ukraine during the Second World War in *Vid derzhavy do komitetu* (From a State to a Committee, 1957), as do the memoirs of V. Kubijovyč, V. Martynets, Dubrovsky, Knysh, and many others. The life of Ukrainians in the Soviet Army is described by D. Chub and M. Serhiienko. The struggle of the OUN and the UPA is depicted in the accounts of Z. Matla, L. Shankovsky, S. Khrin, and many others, most of which were published in periodicals, such as *Do zbroï*. The history of the Division Galizien of the Ukrainian National Army is the subject of the memoirs of P. Shandruk, Ye. Zahachevsky, and Yu. Krokhmaliuk, most of which were published in *Visti kombatanta*. The role of North American Ukrainians in helping the displaced persons is presented in the memoirs of B. Panchuk and S. Frolick. The experiences of concentration camp survivors have been described by M. Bazhansky (*Mozaïka kvadriv v'iaznychnykh* [A Mosaic of Prison Quarters, 1946], O. Dansky (*Khochu zhyty* [I Want to Live]), P. Mirchuk (*V nimets'kykh mlynakh smerty* [In the German Mills of Death, 1957; published in English translation, 1976]), and others. Memoirs of life in Soviet prisons and camps include A. Kniazhynsky's *Na dni SSSR* (At the Bottom of the USSR, 1959), U. Liubovych's *Rozkazhu Vam pro Kazakhstan* (Let Me Tell You about Kazakhstan, 1969), and D. Shumuk's reminiscences. Numerous memoirs of Soviet partisan warfare have been published, such as those of P. Vershyhora and S. Kovpak.

Accounts depicting the 1920s and 1930s include I. Maistrenko's memoirs (1985), O. Semenenko's *Kharkiv, Kharkiv* (1976), Y. Hirniak's *Spohady* (Memoirs, 1982), I. Koshelivets's *Rozmovy v dorozi do sebe* (Conversations on the Way to Myself, 1985), and H. Kostiuk's *Zustrichi i proshchannia* (Meetings and Partings, 1987). Descriptions of the interwar years include D. Shumuk's *Perezhyte i peredumane* (My Life and Thoughts in Retrospect, 1983; English trans: Life Sentence, 1984). The postwar years are described in L. Pliushch's *V karnavali istoriï* (At the Carnival of History, 1977; published in English translation as *History's Carnival*).

For Ukrainian cultural history the memoirs of and about writers and artists serve as important documents. Some have been collected in anthologies, such as *Spohady pro Shevchenka* (Memories of Shevchenko, 1958), *Ivan Franko v spohadakh suchasnykiv* (Ivan Franko in the Memoirs of His Contemporaries, 1956), and *Spohady pro Lesiu Ukraïnku* (Memories of Lesia Ukrainka, 1963). Franko is discussed in individual accounts by S. Baran, T. Franko, and others. The more important literary memoirs include U. Kravchenko's *Spohady uchytel'ky* (Memoirs of a Teacher, 1935); P. Karmansky's *Ukraïns'ka bohema* (Ukrainian Bohemians, 1935); B. Lepky's *Kazka moho zhyttia* (The Tale of My Life, 1936–41); M. Drai-Khmara's *Bezsmertni* (The Immortals, 1963); the memoirs of O. Vyshnia (fragments published); the diaries, notebooks, and autobiographical fiction (*Zacharovana Desna* [The Enchanted Desna]) of O. Dovzhenko; A. Liubchenko's diary; the memoirs of H.

Zhurba about literary life in Kiev during the civil war and the revolution; and V. Sokil's *Zdaleka do blyz'koho* (From Far Away to Close at Hand, 1987). Other works of autobiographical fiction include M. Rylsky's poem *Mandrivka v molodist'* (A Journey into Youth, 1943) and Zhurba's novellette *Dalekyi svit* (A Distant World, 1955). After a long interval caused by Soviet repressions the following memoirs were published: M. Rudnytsky's *Pys'mennyky zblyz'ka* (Writers at Close Range, 3 vols, 1958–64), Yu. Martych's *Iskry zhyvoho vohniu* (Sparks of Living Fire, 1959), H. Hryhoriev's *U staromu Kyievi* (In Old Kiev, 1961), Ye. Krotevych's *Kyïvs'ki zustrichi* (Kievan Encounters, 1965), and those of Rylsky, V. Mynko, P. Kovalenko, and L. Bilotserkivsky. Particularly valuable are Yu. Smolych's accounts of the 1920s and 1930s, *Rospovid' pro nespokii* (A Tale of Unrest, 1968), *Rozpovid' pro nespokii tryvaie* (The Tale of Unrest Continues, 1969), and *Rozpovidi pro nespokii nemaie kintsia* (The Tale of Unrest Has No End, 1970).

Toward the end of the 1980s, memoirs of the years of Stalinist terror began to be published in Kiev. They include V. Sosiura's *Tretia rota* (The Third Platoon, 1988) and I. Ivanov's *Kolyma 1937–1939* (1988).

Among artists' and musical memoirs of the 19th and 20th centuries are M. Bashkirtseva's *Journal de Marie Bashkirtseff* (1887), O. Hryshchenko's *L'Ukraine de mes jours bleus* (1957; translated into Ukrainian in 1959), *Spohadamy* (Recalled by Memories, 2 vols, 1947–8, about Yu. Narbut), O. Koshyts's *Spohady* (2 vols, 1947–8) and *Z pisneiu cherez svit* (Across the World with a Song, 1952), and O. Lysenko's *Pro bat'ka Mykolu Lysenka* (About My Father, Mykola Lysenko, 1957).

Ukrainian theater memoirs include those of M. Kropyvnytsky, M. Sadovsky (*Moï teatral'ni zhadky* [My Theatrical Recollections, 1930; 2nd edn 1956], P. Saksahansky (*Po shliakhu zhyttia* [On the Path of Life, 1935]), S. Tobilevych (*Moï stezhky i zustrichi* [My Paths and Encounters, 1957]), I. Marianenko (*Mynule ukraïns'koho teatru* [The Past of the Ukrainian Theater, 1953]), M. Donets (*Teatral'ni spohady* [Theatrical Memoirs]), and the many accounts about L. Kurbas written by Hirniak, V. Revutsky, and others.

Memoir literature on émigré life includes the works of Karmansky (*Mizh ridnymy v Pivdennii Amerytsi* [Among Relatives in South America, 1923]), O. Prystai (*Z Truskavtsia u svit khmaroderiv* [From Truskavets to the World of Skyscrapers, 4 vols, 1933–5]), P. Stasiuk, A. Romaniuk, O. Bryk, I. Humeniuk, and S. Parfanovych. Memoirs about Ukrainian community life in North America have been written by numerous people, including V. Chumer, A. Hlynka, M. Luchkovich, M. Surmach, and P. Zvarych.

A large section of important memoir literature consists of foreign impressions of Ukraine. The more important ones, dating from the 16th and 17th centuries, were described by Antonovych in *Memuary, otnosiashchiesia k istorii Iuzhnoi Rusi* (Memoirs Pertaining to the History of Southern Rus') and in the surveys of F. Adelung, S.R. Mintslov, V. Kordt, D. Doroshenko, E. Borschak, and V. Sichynsky.

BIBLIOGRAPHY

Krevets'kyi, I. *Ukraïns'ka memuarystyka* (Kamianets-Podilskyi 1919)

Chaikovs'kyi, I. 'Nasha memuarystyka,' *Naukovi zapysky* UTHI, 11 (1966)

I. Koshelivets, B. Kravtsiv, O. Ohloblyn

Memorial. A Ukrainian historical and public-education society established in Kiev on 4 March 1989. It is dedicated to combating neo-Stalinism and promoting democracy and human rights in Ukraine. The society initially functioned according to the statute and program of the USSR Memorial society, whose honorary president was A. Sakharov and on whose executive L. Taniuk was the Ukrainian representative. Memorial has spearheaded research and publications on Soviet terror, political repression, and the man-made famine of 1932–3; commemorated the victims of Stalinism; and aided former political prisoners and their families. The society has both collective (associations, enterprises, etc) and individual members. Its Co-ordinating Council is composed of representatives of branches throughout Ukraine. The society was initially collectively headed by the writers O. Deko and V. Maniak, the writer and theater director Taniuk, the screenplay writer V. Kuznetsov, the student V. Tsymbaliuk, from Odessa, and the former political prisoners I. Dobroshtan, from Dnipropetrovske, and I. Riznychenko, from Kiev. It is funded by Ukraine's creative workers' unions, the Ukrainian Culture Fund, the ANU Institutes of Literature and History, and the journals *Filosofs'ka i sotsiolohichna dumka* and *Pam'iatky Ukraïny*. The biggest branches of Memorial are in Lviv, Ternopil, Dnipropetrovske, Donetske, Kharkiv, Lutske, Odessa, and Rivne. In July 1989 the North American Society for the Advancement of Ukrainian Memorial was formed in Washington.

L. Taniuk

Memorial museums. In Soviet Ukraine many *museums dedicated to the lives and contributions of prominent figures were created, usually in buildings where the persons so honored had lived or worked. Besides over 25 state-funded *literary memorial museums dedicated to prominent Ukrainian writers, other state-funded museums were established to commemorate (1) scholars and scientists, such as the Danylo Zabolotny Museum in Zabolotne, Kryzhopil raion, Vinnytsia oblast (est 1929), the Nikolai Pirogov Museum in Pyrohove, near Vinnytsia (est 1947), the Anton Makarenko Museum in Kremenchuk (est 1951), the Mykola Kybalchych Museum in Korop, Chernihiv oblast (est 1959), the Dmytro Yavornytsky Museum in Dnipropetrovske (est 1964), the Volodymyr Hnatiuk Museum in Velesniv, Monastyryska raion, Ternopil oblast (est 1969), the Serhii Korolov Museum in Zhytomyr (est 1970), the Volodymyr Zabolotny Museum in Pereiaslav-Khmelnytskyi, Kiev oblast, the Hryhorii Skovoroda museums in Skovorodynivka, Zolochiv raion, Kharkiv oblast, Chornukhy, Poltava oblast, and Pereiaslav-Khmelnytskyi, and the Vasyl Sukhomlynsky Museum in Pavlysh, Onufriivka raion, Kirovohrad oblast; (2) artists, such as the Hryhorii Svitlytsky Museum in Kiev (est 1958, supervised by the Museum of Kiev's History), the Ilia Repin Museum in Chuhuiv, Kharkiv oblast (est 1969), the Olena Kulchytska Museum in Lviv (est 1971), the Oleksa Novakivsky Museum in Lviv (est 1972), and the Ivan Trush Museum in Lviv; (3) composers, such as the Viktor Kosenko Museum in Kiev (est 1964) and the Mykola Lysenko Museum in Kiev (est 1980); (4) actors and performers, such as the Panas Saksahansky Museum in Kamiano-Kostuvate, Bratske raion, Mykolaiv oblast, and the Solomiia Krushelnytska Museum in Bila, Ternopil raion (est 1963) and the Les Kurbas Museum in Staryi Skalat, Ternopil oblast (est 1988); (5) a pioneering Ukrainian printer, the Ivan Fedorov Museum in Lviv (est 1977); (6) Communist party figures, such as the Vladimir Lenin museums in Kiev (est 1938) and Lviv (est 1950), the Kliment Voroshilov Museum in Lysychanske, Luhanske oblast, the Oleksandr Tsiurupa Museum in Tsiurupynske, Kherson oblast, the Maurice Thorez Museum in Torez, Donetske oblast (est 1965), the Ulianov Family Museum in Kiev (est 1977), and the Andrei Zhdanov Museum in Mariiupil (named Zhdanov from 1948 to 1989), Donetske oblast; and (7) Soviet military figures, such as the Mykola Shchors Museum in Shchors, Chernihiv oblast (est 1943), the Mykola Kuznetsov Museum in Rivne, and the Mykhailo Kyrponos Museum in Vertiivka, Nizhen raion, Chernihiv oblast. The Kosyi Kaponir Museum (est 1971 on the grounds of a former tsarist prison) and the Hall No. 19 Memorial Complex of the History of the 1941–5 Great Patriotic War (est 1981) were established as branches of the *Historical Museum of the Ukrainian SSR in Kiev. A few museums were dedicated to prominent Russian cultural figures who were active in Ukraine, such as the Anton Chekhov Museum in Yalta (est 1904); the Vladimir *Korolenko museums in Poltava (est 1928) and Zhytomyr (est 1973); the Alexandr Pushkin and Peter Tchaikovsky Museum in Kamianka, Cherkasy oblast (est 1937), containing a permanent exhibition dedicated to the Decembrists in Ukraine; and the Maksimilian Voloshin Museum in Planerske, Crimea oblast. The Sholom Aleichem Museum in Pereiaslav-Khmelnytskyi was established in 1978. Hundreds of publicly funded 'people's museums' in Ukraine also had memorial rooms dedicated to cultural and Party figures and Soviet partisans.

R. Senkus

Mena. II-13. A town (1990 pop 13,300) on the Mena River and a raion center in Chernihiv oblast. It is mentioned in historical documents as early as 1066. In the 11th to 13th centuries it was an important trade center protected by a large fortress. In the 17th century it was a large fortified town. During B. Khmelnytsky's rule Mena was a company center in Chernihiv regiment. In 1659 Hetman I. Vyhovsky fought several battles against the Russian army near the town. Before the close of the century Mena received the rights of *Magdeburg law. In spite of its small size, in 1966 it attained city status. Most of Mena's enterprises belong to the food industry. It has a regional museum and a zoological park. Archeologists have found several settlements from the Bronze Age, the Yukhnove culture, and the early Slavic period (8th–10th century) in the vicinity.

Menaion (Ukrainian: *minei*, from the Greek for 'moon'). The name for several *liturgical books used in the Orthodox and Eastern Catholic churches. They contain the services with special prayers and chants for the fixed *church holidays. The most comprehensive edition, the Monthly Menaion, consists of 12 volumes containing the services for each month. A smaller edition, the General Menaion, includes services honoring particular groups of saints (such as apostles and martyrs) and for particular holidays. The Abridged Menaion, which contains only services for the major holidays, is known as the Menaion of Holy Days. In Ukraine a special type of menaion, the *chet' menaion* or menaion for daily reading, gained great pop-

ularity. It contained the lives of saints, organized by the calendar, and was used extensively in the education of Orthodox monks and clergy and for popular reading. The most famous was that written by Metropolitan D. *Tuptalo in 1689–1705.

Menaion for Daily Reading of 1489 (Mineia chetiia). A collection of the lives of saints in a calendar order, with added sermons of St John Chrysostom, copied by two Ruthenian scribes at Kamianets, near Berestia, in 1489 and soon thereafter from a Ukrainian model. It is an important example in the history of the Ukrainian language of how Church Slavonic evolved toward the Ruthenian vernacular.

Menchyts, Volodymyr [Menčyc'], b 1837 in Vchoraishe, Skvyra county, Kiev gubernia, d 1916 in Kiev. Civic activist and ethnographer. A student at the Kiev Theological Academy, he was active in the St Petersburg hromada (1860s) and later established bookstores in Kherson, Mykolaiv, and Yelysavethrad. During his life he was an enthusiastic collector of folklore and ethnographic data. Some of his materials were published by M. Drahomanov in *Malorusskie narodnye predaniia i rasskazy* (Little Russian Folk Legends and Tales, 1876), but most remain in manuscript at the Central Scientific Library of the Academy of Sciences of Ukraine.

A Mennonite village on the Dnieper River that was later submerged after the construction of the dam of the Dnieper Hydroelectric Station

Mennonites. A religious-cultural group whose adherents represented a large portion of the settlers colonizing the southern Ukrainian steppe in the late 18th to early 19th century. Founded in the 16th century by Menno Simons as an outgrowth of the Anabaptists, the group was notable for certain social practices, particularly its refusal to swear oaths and its rejection of military service. Until the late 18th century the major concentrations of Mennonites were found in tightly knit rural agrarian communities in southern Germany, the Vistula River basin in Poland, and the Netherlands. The prospect of increased religious persecution in Germany and Poland led the Mennonites to consider the possibilities of settling in the recently opened lands of *southern Ukraine. This prospect was made especially attractive by Catherine II's decree of 1763–4 that guaranteed generous financial incentives, religious freedom, and exemption from military service for foreign settlers in the area. In 1789 the first group of Mennonites in Ukraine settled near the former Cossack stronghold of

Khortytsia, in Katerynoslav gubernia. Subsequent Mennonite settlers established a second colony southeast of Khortytsia near the Molochna River. By 1835 there were approx 1,600 Mennonite families located in 72 colonies in Katerynoslav and Tavriia gubernias. By 1911 there were 104,000 Mennonites in Southern Ukraine, constituting 19.2 percent of the German population in that region. As well, a small number of Mennonite colonies were formed in Samara gubernia and Caucasia.

The Mennonites prospered in Ukraine. They acquired significant landholdings and worked them as model farmers. They also developed extensive milling interests in southern Ukraine as well as the manufacture of agricultural machinery. The Mennonites were not assimilated into Ukrainian society because of both their conscious attempts to maintain a cohesive society of their own and the desire of tsarist authorities to keep them isolated from other social groups. Their most extensive interaction with Ukrainians was as employers of farm laborers. In general Ukrainians regarded the Mennonites as being fair in their business dealings, and they benefited indirectly from the agricultural techniques learned from them.

The Mennonites' political fortunes took a turn for the worse during the 1870s, in part as a result of the souring of relations between the Russian Empire and Germany. In 1871 the codex under which they had colonized Ukraine was revoked. The Mennonites lost their administrative autonomy, were required to use Russian as the language of instruction in schools, and (from 1874) were expected to perform noncombatant military duty. A large portion of the Mennonite population of Ukraine then emigrated to North America; those from the Khortytsia region generally favored Canada, and those from the Molochna valley, the United States. Others moved to more remote regions of the Russian Empire. Mennonites, as other minorities, suffered greatly during the revolutionary upheavals of 1917–20. The major tribulations of the Mennonites, however, occurred after the establishment of the Soviet regime, which took over control of education and closed down Mennonite churches, the basis of their community life. A concerted effort by worldwide Mennonites allowed some of their coreligionists to emigrate from the Soviet Union in the 1920s, most notably a group of nearly 20,000 who settled in western Canada. The Mennonites suffered further losses during the Soviet collectivization campaign (when many were deported to Siberia as kulaks), the great man-made famine of 1932–3, and the Stalinist terror (when many of their religious leaders were imprisoned). The final blow to the community in Ukraine came during the Second World War, when Mennonites were evacuated eastward in 1941 before advancing German troops, and westward in 1943 before the advancing Soviet army. The Mennonite colonies in Ukraine were effectively dismembered in the process and never reconstituted. Some of the Mennonite refugees who found themselves in Germany after the war were resettled in North and South America. The majority, however, were repatriated and either imprisoned or resettled in Western Siberia and Central Asia. Those who survived were released in the mid-1950s but denied permission to return to Ukraine. Most Mennonites had emigrated from the Soviet Union by 1985.

BIBLIOGRAPHY
Rempel, D. 'The Mennonite Colonies in Russia: A Study of Their Settlement and Economic Development from 1789 to 1914' (PH D diss, Stanford University, 1933)
Epp, F. *Mennonite Exodus* (Altona 1962)
Friesen, P. *The Mennonite Brotherhood in Russia, 1789–1910,* trans and ed J. Toews et al (Fresno 1978)
Stumpp, K. *The German-Russians: Two Centuries of Pioneering,* trans J. Height (New York 1978)
Epp, G. 'Mennonite-Ukrainian Relations (1789–1945),' *Journal of Mennonite Studies,* 7 (1989)
Friesen, J. *Mennonites in Russia, 1788–1888* (Winnipeg 1989)
Dyck, H.L. (ed and trans). *A Mennonite in Russia: The Diaries of Jacob D. Epp, 1851–1880* (Toronto 1991)

A. Makuch

Mensheviks. The moderate wing of the *Russian Social Democratic Workers' party (RSDRP), which first emerged at the party's second congress in London in August 1903. The Mensheviks, who emphasized historical gradualism, legal methods of struggle, and a broadly based party, were closer in outlook than the rest of the RSDRP to the European social democratic parties. Adhering to Marxist theory, they recognized the necessity for a bourgeois revolution in Russia and were willing to co-operate with liberal forces to promote such a revolution as a precondition for the proletarian revolution. Although the Mensheviks played an important role in the St Petersburg Soviet during the 1905 Revolution, their position in 1917 was confused. Their alliance with the Constitutional Democrats (until September 1917) in the Russian Provisional Government and their vacillation on the issue of Russia's participation in the First World War undercut their authority.

The Mensheviks had little appreciation of the nationality problem in the Russian Empire. In Ukraine they were urban-oriented, and most of them were Jewish (often from the Jewish Social Democratic Bund) or Russian. They had little or no contact with the Ukrainian peasantry or the Ukrainian intelligentsia. The Ukrainian language was not used in their party activities or their publications. The few Ukrainian Mensheviks included K. Kononenko and D. Chyzhevsky. Led by M. Balabanov, Mensheviks participated in the Central Rada in 1917 and supported demands for Ukrainian autonomy, but not independence, as expressed in the Rada's Third and Fourth universals. The Mensheviks favored the restoration of a unified Russian state. When the Bolsheviks came to power, the Menshevik position became untenable: in advocating reunification with Russia they were strengthening their opponents' regime. By November 1917 the Mensheviks in Ukraine could obtain only 1.3 percent of the popular vote in the Constituent Assembly elections.

BIBLIOGRAPHY
Volin, S. *Men'sheviki na Ukraine, 1917–1921* (New York 1962)
Haimson, L. *The Mensheviks* (Chicago 1974)
Ascher, A. (ed). *The Mensheviks in the Russian Revolution* (London 1976)

J. Reshetar

Menshikov, Aleksandr, b 16 November 1673 in Moscow, d 23 November 1729 in Berezovo, Tobolsk gubernia, Russia. Russian military figure. After humble beginnings in Moscow he became one of the most powerful men in the Russian Empire and a personal favorite of Peter I. In 1708 he was put in charge of co-ordinating military operations in Ukraine with Hetman I. *Mazepa against Charles XII. When Mazepa's alliance with the Swedish king became known, Menshikov razed his stronghold at Baturyn (massacring almost all of its 6,000 men, women, and children) and then instituted a reign of terror in order to dissuade the population from siding with the hetman. At the Battle of *Poltava in May 1709, he commanded a wing of the Russian army.

For his services and loyalty Menshikov was awarded huge tracts of land in Ukraine, as well as positions of power and privilege, including the governorship of St Petersburg province. He used those to amass a large fortune, particularly in Ukraine, where he illegally annexed lands, enserfed Cossacks, and built up his own exploitative economic infrastructure. Whereas in 1704 he had controlled 1,300 serfs, the number surged to 28,000 in 1709 and to over 55,000 in 1725. Menshikov was investigated several times for corruption, and in 1723–4 he was accused of concealing 30,000 serfs who had either hid from military service or fled from their landowners on Mazepa's former estate at Baturyn. After Peter's death in 1725, Menshikov maneuvered his widow onto the throne as Catherine I. Not only did he persuade the empress to drop all investigations against him, he received additional grants of land in Ukraine.

Menshikov changed his long-standing opposition to Ukrainian autonomy when the president of the Little Russian Collegium, S. Veliaminov, implemented a program of increased taxation in Ukraine that included Russian landowners. He suddenly became critical of the collegium and defensive of Ukrainian autonomy, and he used his influence to dismantle the imperial administrative body and to see through the election of a new hetman, D. Apostol.

Menshikov fell from power after the death of Catherine I in 1727 and the ascension of Peter II. In 1728 he was exiled with his family to Siberia, where he died.

Menshov, Dmytro [Men'šov], b 1855 in Slobidska Ukraine, d 1917. General officer and military historian. During the First World War he rose to lieutenant general in the Russian army and was deputy chief of artillery supply for the southwestern front. He joined the UNR Army in 1917 and served as chief of artillery. His articles on Ukraine's military history and the history of Kiev, particularly its fortifications, have appeared in the leading Russian historical journals.

Modest Menzinsky

Menzinsky, Modest [Mencins'kyj] (Mentsinsky, Mentzinsky), b 29 April 1875 in Novosilky, Galicia, d 11 December 1935 in Stockholm. Opera and concert singer (heroic tenor). He studied at the Lviv Conservatory under W. Wysocki and at the Frankfurt Conservatory under J. Stockhausen (1899–1903). He sang first tenor at the Stockholm Royal Opera (1904–10) and the Cologne Opera (1910–26) and toured widely in Western Ukraine, Austria, Germany, Holland, Belgium, and England. A distinguished and versatile artist, Menzinsky performed leading roles in operas of varying style, from W. Mozart to G. Verdi, G. Bizet, and R. Wagner. He performed leading parts in the world premieres of F. Schreker's modern operas *Die Gezeichneten* (Frankfurt, 1918), *Der Schatzgräber* (Frankfurt, 1920), and *Irrelohe* (Cologne, 1924). He was also noted for his performances of lieder, including M. Lysenko's art songs and songs to texts by T. Shevchenko, and arrangements of Ukrainian folk songs by D. Sichynsky, S. Liudkevych, M. Verbytsky, Ya. Yaroslavenko, and A. Jedlicka. Menzinsky was the first to introduce this Ukrainian repertoire to the West, in recitals and numerous recordings for the Gramophone recording company.

BIBLIOGRAPHY
Derkach, I. *Modest Mentsyns'kyi: Heroïchnyi tenor* (Lviv 1969)
Kolessa, H. *Spohad pro Modesta Mentsyns'koho* (Kiev 1976)
R. Savytsky

MEOM. A Ukrainian acronym for *mala elektronna obchysliuvalna mashyna* 'small electronic computing machine.' The MEOM was the first electronic digital computer built in the USSR and anywhere outside the United States. It was designed and constructed in 1950 at the *Institute of Electrodynamics of the AN URSR (now ANU), under the directorship of S. *Lebedev. This general-purpose machine, though small in capacity, incorporated numerous advanced concepts which laid the foundations for many future developments in digital computers in the USSR.

Mercenary regiments (*kompaniiski polky, kompaniitsi*). In the Hetman state free men, including non-Ukrainians, were employed as mercenaries by the hetmans and regimental colonels to serve as their personal guard and to perform various policing duties. Peasants and town Cossacks were excluded from their ranks. Hetman B. Khmelnytsky personally commanded three mercenary cavalry regiments. The 1672 *Konotip Articles abolished such regiments, but in 1687 they were reinstated by Hetman I. Mazepa, who hired two cavalry (*kompaniitsi*) and four infantry regiments (see *Serdiuk regiments), each with approx 500 to 600 men. He placed them under his own direct command and used them to defend his person and his residence, to quell popular unrest, to prevent peasants from fleeing to Zaporizhia and Slobidska Ukraine, and to maintain security on the southern and western borders. The *kompaniitsi* wore distinctive green-and-red coats, tight trousers, low boots, and round hats. They were commanded by colonels appointed by the hetman and later by the Russian tsar. Unlike regular Cossack regiments, the *kompaniitsi* were transferred from place to place, according to need, and local inhabitants were obliged to quarter, feed, and supply them; they were known for their abuses and looting. In 1708 Mazepa had four regiments of *kompaniitsi*. In 1728 the Russian government limited their number to two regiments of 600 men each, and in 1776 it transformed them into the Kiev, Chernihiv, and Novhorod-Siverskyi regular light-cavalry regiments.

Merchants. A social class in precapitalist societies, involved in *trade. Under conditions of modern capitalism merchants are part of the capitalist or entrepreneurial classes.

Ukraine's merchant class first appeared in Kievan Rus',

where domestic trade played an important part in economic life. Merchants sold arms, jewelry, and other items of artisan production made in Kiev, Novgorod, and Chernihiv to all parts of the realm. The southern regions of Kievan Rus' supplied the northern parts with grain. Salt mined in Galicia was also a significant commodity of trade in the period. *Fairs, which existed in most of the larger towns of Kievan Rus', played an important role in the development of trade. Kiev was the most important center of trade, with (according to eyewitness accounts) eight fairs at the beginning of the 11th century. Rus' was also active in foreign trade with Byzantium, Central Europe, Central Asia, and the Far East. Merchants from Armenia, Poland, Moravia and Bohemia, Germany, Italy, France, and Arab lands established a presence in Kiev, and some settled there permanently. In the early 11th century Kiev had colonies of Venetian, German, and Far Eastern merchants.

Until the mid-11th century the Kievan princes and their retainers dominated foreign trade and often combined trade activity with plunder. From the second half of the 11th century, as Kievan society became more developed, professional merchants emerged whose services the princes would use. The largest contingent of merchants in Kievan Rus' in the period, however, consisted of townsmen involved in trade, primarily for the domestic market. Merchants, together with the nobility, dominated Rus' towns. Merchants were often unpopular with urban dwellers since they used their monopoly control of certain commodities to increase prices. In 1113, for example, Kiev's population revolted against the merchants to protest their unfair trade practices.

The Tatar-Mongol invasions in the mid-13th century dealt a serious blow to trade and to the development of Ukraine's merchant class. For a period of time most trade with the East ceased. The subsequent incursion of Ottoman forces and of the Crimean Tatars in the 14th and 15th centuries also served to limit trade. In the 15th and 16th centuries, under Lithuanian and Polish rule, the further development of distinctive social groups and the growth of the urban population (which expanded the domestic market) promoted the development of Ukraine's merchant class. The fact that Ukrainian towns served as intermediaries in trade between Western Europe and the East was also of great significance for the growth of the country's merchant class. Under Polish rule, however, Orthodox (Ukrainian) merchants were the objects of discriminatory policies that strengthened the position of Polish and German merchants in Ukrainian towns. Ukrainian merchants remained a significant force in Western Ukrainian towns, where they were closely interrelated with the region's nobility. The rise of the Cossacks as a social force in the early 16th century served to strengthen the Ukrainian merchant class since many Cossacks were involved in trade.

The last decades of the 17th and first decades of the 18th century were characterized by a large and intensive expansion of trade and Ukrainian merchant prosperity in Left-Bank Ukraine under the Hetmanate, an expansion owing to a number of factors. First, Western Europe had been starved of Ukrainian raw materials because of the disruption of commercial relations during the period of the *Ruin and was eager to resume trade. The Ukrainian market, hitherto denied access to Western European man-

ufactured goods for similar reasons, showed a high demand for imports. Second, because Russian merchants had not been granted a privileged position, Ukrainian merchants were the most active participants in the burgeoning trade with Western Europe. Finally, the development of a money economy, the accumulation of merchant capital, and the increase in the size of landholdings in Left-Bank Ukraine contributed to a growth in production which necessitated the search for new Western markets. Trade involved a significant portion of the population, as is indicated by the fact that approximately 46 percent of the Left-Bank population, that is, roughly 450,000 people, lived in towns. Almost one-third of the urban population was engaged in commerce, approx 10 percent as merchants. Initially the Cossacks, particularly the *starshyna*, were the most important merchants, but as trade developed, merchants arose from among the burghers of Ukrainian towns to play a dominant role.

Because Ukrainian trade was relatively lucrative, it came to the attention of Russian officials, especially when Russian state finances reached a state of crisis as a consequence of Peter I's reforms and wars. Although the tsar attempted to interfere with Ukrainian commerce before the Battle of *Poltava (1709), his efforts were largely unsuccessful because of the Hetmanate's autonomy. After the defeat of Hetman I. Mazepa at Poltava Ukraine's trade and its merchants came under the control of the Russian state and of a few Russian merchant houses which had a privileged relationship to that state. Ukrainian trade routes were ordered redirected to Russian ports; trade in a wide range of commodities was disallowed; and high export duties and new taxes were imposed. Russian commercial institutions and practices were extended into the territory of the Hetmanate, notably the Russian treasury's monopoly of trade in a series of goods and commodities, and the *gosti* ('guests') – privileged Russian merchants who acted as the state's agents in collecting state revenues (customs duties and excises), and through whom the treasury traded in prohibited goods. Those measures sounded the death knell for Ukrainian merchants. The number of merchant bankruptcies increased dramatically in the 1710s and 1720s. Equally fatal for Ukrainian merchants were the bans on imports imposed by Russia.

The new conditions resulted in a penetration of the Ukrainian market by Russians. To avoid paying double duties Ukrainian merchants started hiring Russians to transport their goods and also engaged Russian partners. Since Russian traders were not subjected to the same tax burdens and duties as Ukrainians, many Russian merchants migrated to Ukraine and started competing directly with the local population. Although Ukrainian merchants and hetmans protested against those conditions, they were unable to stop them or their consequences. By the end of the 18th century Russian merchants had conquered the Hetmanate. They also dominated the growing merchant class in Southern Ukraine. The 1832 census showed that of the 32,000 merchants who belonged to the merchants' guild, 22.2 percent were Ukrainians, 52.6 percent were Russians, and 20.9 percent were Jews. There were no Ukrainians in the upper or first guild (involved in foreign trade), only 15 percent in the second, and 26 percent in the third. The third guild largely operated locally, an indication of the thoroughness with which the internal Ukrainian market had been conquered.

In Right-Bank Ukraine, under Polish rule until the end of the 18th century, Ukrainian merchants suffered rapid decline because of Polish policies. The abolition of Cossackdom permanently undermined the juridical and economic position of an important sector of Ukraine's merchant group. The old feudal order was reimposed in Right-Bank Ukraine by Polish nobles, who began to take private ownership of towns and direct control of the most lucrative branches of trade. Discrimination against Orthodox Ukrainian townsmen further undermined the indigenous merchant class. Ukrainian merchants went bankrupt, some escaped to the Left Bank, Moldavia, or the Zaporozhian Sich, and many slipped back into the peasantry.

In Russian-ruled Ukraine merchants were formed into a separate estate and granted their own guild structure by tsarist decrees of 1775 and 1785. The 1897 general population census noted 30,456 members of the merchant estate in Ukraine, of whom only 11.7 percent were Ukrainians. Jews and Russians formed the majority among the merchants. After the abolition of serfdom in 1861 and with the growth of industry, some merchants transformed themselves into manufacturers and became part of the capitalist class. The economic backwardness of the Russian Empire was such, however, that merchant capital never played the leading role in industrialization there that it did in Western Europe. At the beginning of the 20th century merchants continued to dominate foreign trade, but their role in internal trade declined. In 1917, merchant guilds and estates were abolished.

In Western Ukraine under Austrian rule, Ukrainians played an insignificant role in the merchant class. That class was dominated by Jews, Poles, Germans, Hungarians, and Rumanians. In the 1920s and 1930s in Western Ukraine under Polish rule, there developed a small Ukrainian merchant class which had to face many discriminatory economic policies.

BIBLIOGRAPHY
Ohloblyn, O. *A History of Ukrainian Industry* (Munich 1971)
Nestorovych, V. *Ukraïns'ki kuptsi i promyslovtsi v Zakhidnii Ukraïni, 1920–1945* (Toronto–Chicago 1977)
Koropeckyj, I. (ed). *Ukrainian Economic History: Interpretive Essays* (Cambridge, Mass 1990)
Kotliar, M.; et al (eds). *Torhivlia na Ukraïni XIV–seredyna XVII stolittia: Volyn' i Naddniprianshchyna* (Kiev 1990)
B. Krawchenko

Mercury (Ukrainian: *rtut'* or *zhyve sriblo* 'live silver'). A chemical element and liquid metal. Mercury forms alloys with most metals. The *Mykytivka mercury deposit in Ukraine was one of the largest mercury sources in the USSR. Some mercury deposits in Transcarpathia have been exploited since the Second World War, and a processing facility was constructed there in 1971. Before the war Ukraine's mercury reserves were estimated at 4.3 million t, or about 8 percent of total world reserves. Recent statistics on reserves and production are not available, since mercury is considered to be a strategic resource.

Mercury has been known for millennia, and its unique properties as a liquid metal made it the subject of many popular beliefs. In the Carpathian foothills peasants believed that mercury poured into an unsuccessful well hole would produce a water supply. Hutsuls believed that mercury poured into a river would cause rain and end a drought. Hutsul girls wore amulets of nutshells filled with mercury to prevent pregnancy. In the Nadvirna region peasants cut the tips off cows' horns and filled the cavity with mercury to protect the cows from sorcery.

Merefa. IV-17. A city (1990 pop 28,900) on the Merefa River in Kharkiv raion, Kharkiv oblast. It was founded in the 17th century as a Cossack settlement and was a company center in Kharkiv regiment and the probable birthplace of the Zaporozhian otaman I. *Sirko. Merefa played an important role in a popular uprising in 1670. In the early 18th century it was destroyed by the Crimean Tatars a number of times. Merefa attained city status in 1938. It is a railway junction and has several railway-related enterprises. It is the home of the Ukrainian Scientific Research Institute of Vegetable and Melon Cultivation. Archeologists have discovered several settlements from the Neolithic Period and the Bronze Age, a Scythian settlement (5th–3rd century BC), and a settlement of the *Saltiv culture (8th–9th century AD).

Meretyn, Bernard (Merderer, Merettini, Meretynych), b late 17th century, d 1758 in Lviv. Galician architect of German origin. His projects include *St George's Cathedral in Lviv (1745–70), the town hall in Buchach (1751), and a number of Polish churches. His buildings are in the rococo style, with some transitional classicist features and traditional Ukrainian adaptations. They are distinguished by their grace and elegance, attention to detail, and use of sculpture.

Mérimée, Prosper, b 28 September 1803 in Paris, d 23 September 1870 in Cannes, France. French writer, historian, and archeologist. Through the works of N. Gogol and a correspondence with I. Turgenev and S. Sobolevsky he became acquainted with Ukrainian history and developed a fascination with the Cossacks. Having read the works of G. Le Vasseur de Beauplan, P. Chevalier, C.-L. Lesur, J.-B. Scherer, Voltaire, and M. Kostomarov he wrote *Les Cosaques de l'Ukraine et leurs derniers atamans* (1854), a work commissioned by French officials during the Crimean War and focusing particularly on Hetmans B. Khmelnytsky and I. Mazepa. He also published a literary rendition of Kostomarov's monograph on Khmelnytsky in *Journal des savants* (1863); it was republished with an article about S. Razin as *Les Cosaques d'autrefois* (1865). The Cossacks are also mentioned in his *Faux Demetrius* (1852) and the unfinished *Histoire du règne de Pierre le Grand* (1864). Mérimée also translated M. Vovchok's story 'Kozachka' (Servant Girl) into French. He supported Ukrainian aspirations and warned French circles (Napoleon III and Empress Eugénie) about the danger of Polonophilism.

Some of Mérimée's works have been translated into Ukrainian by M. Rudnytsky (a collection of stories, 1925), V. Levytsky-Sofroniv (a collection of stories, 1932), V. Pidmohylny (his *Colomba*, 1927), M. Rylsky (his *La chronique du règne de Charles IX*), B. Tkachenko (his *Carmen*), S. Buda, M. Konstantynopolsky (his *La Jacquerie*, 1936), M. Tereshchenko (1957), Ye. Rzhevutska (his *La carrosse du Saint-Sacrement*, 1958), M. Meshcheriak (1959), A. Yurkevych (1959), M. Lytvynets (his *Tamango*, 1959), and Ya. Kravets (1988). His *La Jacquerie* was staged by the Berezil theater.

BIBLIOGRAPHY
Savchenko, F. 'Kozachchyna u frantsuz'komu pys'menstvi ta
   kozakofil'stvo Merime,' *Ukraïna*, no. 14 (1925)
Rantsova, O.; Lozyns'kyi, I. 'Ukraïna v tvorchii spadshchyni P.
   Merime,' *Vsesvit*, 1961, no. 8
Iankovs'kyi, Iu. *Prosper Merime: Zhyttia i tvorchist'* (Kiev 1976)
Joukovsky [Zhukovsky], A. 'Prosper Mérimée et la question
   ukrainienne,' in *L'Ukraine et la France au XIXe siècle* (Paris 1987)
                                                    A. Zhukovsky

Mering, Friedrich, b 10 March 1822 in Dohna, Saxony,
d 31 October 1887 in Kiev. Internal medicine specialist and
hygienist. A graduate of Leipzig University (1845), he
worked in Poltava and Chernihiv gubernias, directed a
hospital in Buromka, Zolotonosha county, and lectured at
Kiev University (from 1853). During the Crimean War he
studied the typhus epidemic in the Southern Army, and
later he combated the typhus epidemic in Kiev. In 1864 he
was appointed director of the internal medicine clinic at
Kiev University. His publications include courses on hygiene and clinical medicine.

Mering, Sergei, b 1862, d 1920. Industrialist and politician. An owner of sugar refineries in Ukraine, he opposed
Ukrainian independence. A member of the Union of Industry, Trade, Finance, and Agriculture, he served as minister of trade and industry in F. Lyzohub's second cabinet
and in S. Gerbel's cabinet in the Hetman government.

Merlia River

Merlia River [Merlja] (also Merla, Merlo). A left-bank
tributary of the Vorsklo River. It is 116 km long and drains
a basin area of 2,030 sq km. The Merlia has its source in the
Central Upland in Belgorod oblast and flows through
Kharkiv and Poltava oblasts. Its waters are used for domestic consumption and irrigation. The main city on the
river is Bohodukhiv.

Mertvovid River (also Mertvi Vody, Mertvovod). A
left-bank tributary of the Boh River, which it joins at
Voznesenske. It is 114 km long and drains a basin area of
1,820 sq km. The Mertvi Vody flows through Kirovohrad
and Mykolaiv oblasts. Its waters are used for irrigation.

Merzlykin, Mykola, b 1 September 1936 in Kiev. Stage
director. In 1964 he completed study at the Kiev Institute
of Theater Arts. He then worked in the Russian Drama

Theater in Mariiupil (1964–5) and directed the Kiev Young
Spectator's Theater (1967–83, from 1978 as artistic director). In 1970–4 he completed the actor's program at the
Kiev Artistic Film Studio. Since 1985 he has been artistic
director of the Kiev Children's Musical Theater.

Meshcherska, Hanna [Meščers'ka] (real surname: Pashchenko), b 1 June 1876 in Kiev, d 1 April 1951 in Odessa.
Actress. She began her career in a Russian troupe in
Cherkasy in 1895 and remained on the Russian stage until
1918, when she joined the State Drama Theater (later the
Shevchenko First Theater of the Ukrainian Soviet Repub-
lic), with which she toured in 1919–27. In 1927–51 she was
the leading actress in character and heroic roles at the
Odessa Ukrainian Music and Drama Theater. Her exten-
sive repertoire included Hanna in I. Karpenko-Kary's *Bez-
talanna* (The Unfortunate), Shkandybykha in P. Myrny's
Lymerivna (The Saddler's Daughter), and Mrs Alving in H.
Ibsen's *Gengangere*. She acted in the films *Hostra mohyla*
(The Steep Grave, 1934) and *Karmeliuk* (1931).

Oksana Meshko

Meshko, Oksana [Meško], b 31 January 1905 in Stari
Sanzhary (now Reshetnyky), Poltava county, d 22 January
1991 in Kiev. Teacher and dissident. A former Soviet political prisoner (1947–54), in 1970 she sent letters to the
Supreme Soviet and Supreme Court protesting the imprisonment of V. Moroz. In 1972 she led a public campaign for the release of her dissident son, O. *Serhiienko.
A founding member of the *Ukrainian Helsinki Group in
1976, she became its head in March 1979. For her activities
she was persecuted, incarcerated in psychiatric prisons in
1980, and sentenced in January 1981 to six months in a labor camp and five years' exile in the Khabarovsk region of
the Soviet Far East. After being allowed to return to
Ukraine in 1985, she joined the revived Ukrainian Helsinki Union led by V. Chornovil. In 1987 she travelled to Australia for medical treatment. From there she visited the
United States, Australia, and Canada, where she made
many public appearances. In January 1989 she returned to
Ukraine. Her memoirs, *Between Life and Death*, were published in English in 1981, and *The Oksana Meshko Story*, by
N. Strokata and N. Pazuniak, appeared in 1985.

Mesolithic Period. A transitional period of the Stone
Age, between the Paleolithic and Neolithic (ca 8th–5th
millennium BC), also known as the Epipaleolithic. The
start of this historic period coincided with the beginning
of the current geological age, the Holocene. During this
time the earth experienced warmer temperatures and the
glaciers covering large portions of the northern hemi-

sphere retreated, leaving behind the basic geological and hydrological features of modern Ukraine.

Several significant social and technological advances took place during this period. Flint technology developed to the point where small, almost standardized, geometrically shaped pieces could be made. The basic tool and implement inventory of Upper Paleolithic man continued to be used, albeit with an increase in the manufacturing of bone and wood items. The introduction of the bow and arrow and the domestication of the dog led to changes in hunting practices, particularly the smaller size of hunting groups. Fishing expanded as an important sustinence activity, attempts at domesticating animals (pigs) for consumption were made, and there was even some rudimentary agricultural activity. Mesolithic sites have also revealed evidence of the earliest efforts to make pottery in Ukraine.

Three main settlement areas of this period have been identified: southern Ukraine (the steppe and Black Sea regions and Crimea), the forest steppe (particularly the middle Dnieper and Donets basins), and northern Ukraine. Research has also shown that the Mesolithic population of Ukraine was more migratory than its Upper Paleolithic counterparts. One explanation for this is that there was a need to look further afield for game because of the demise of the mammoth, the thinning out of traditional hunting grounds, and an increase in population. Mesolithic peoples commonly constructed winter shelters of a permanent or semipermanent nature and made extensive use of temporary summer shelters. Some sites have shown evidence of rectangular semi-pit winter dwellings with post construction. Presumably the walls would have been made of clay and the structure covered with skins or with locally available vegetation. Caves were also commonly used as winter dwellings.

Studies at Mesolithic sites reveal that full body burials were common. They also supply evidence for other practices, such as tying the hands of the deceased at the time of burial (perhaps to keep their spirit from 'wandering' the earth) and the ritual severance of finger segments.

The artistic activity of Mesolithic peoples was not at all as developed as that of Upper Paleolithic peoples and was limited largely to schematic drawings on rocks and the making of personal adornments from animal and fish teeth.

The earliest cultural-chronological schemes for the Mesolithic period in Ukraine were proposed in the 1920s by P. *Yefymenko and M. *Rudynsky. As research about this period continued, new schemes emerged. Despite considerable progress in this respect, a definite chronology will require more research.

BIBLIOGRAPHY
Arkheolohiia Ukraïns'koï RSR, vol 1 (Kiev 1971)
Telegin, D. Pamiatniki epokhi mezolita na territorii Ukrainskoi SSR (Kiev 1985)

Messianism. A historico-philosophical conception of a mission to redeem all of humanity. Ukrainian messianism found its fullest expression in the ideology of the *Cyril and Methodius Brotherhood (1845–7), particularly in the programmatic text *Knyhy bytiia ukrains'koho narodu (Books of the Genesis of the Ukrainian People), written by M. *Kostomarov, as well as in writings by V. *Bilozersky. They felt that Ukraine alone had preserved true Christianity, which in their view espoused a profound egalitarianism. They particularly idealized the Cossacks, whose deep devotion to Orthodoxy, defense of Christian Europe against Islam, democratic form of organization and self-rule, and opposition to landlords and serfdom heralded a future new order. Because of its very virtues Ukraine had been oppressed by rapacious neighbors, and seemed to be the least among the Slavic nations; in fact it was destined to lead a political and spiritual renewal that would culminate in the establishment of a Slavic federative republic.

Messianism in the strict sense of the term is connected with a religious worldview, but in its wider application it can also refer to conceptions of the nation's mission within a secular framework. In that sense elements of messianism can also be found in the writings of S. *Podolynsky, particularly in his Parova mashyna (Steam Engine) of 1875, in which Ukraine, because of its Cossack and haidamaka past, was assigned the mission of starting the socialist revolution and ushering in the socialist utopia throughout the Russian Empire. In the 1920s M. *Khvylovy and writers close to him also developed a variety of messianism. They predicted that Ukraine, long oppressed and on the boundary of East and West, would be the leader of an 'Asiatic renaissance' that would renew European and indeed world culture. Messianic ideas, placed once again within a religious context, have also been put forward by O. *Berdnyk, particularly in the late 1980s and early 1990s in connection with his Assembly of Spiritual (Holy) Ukraine (Sobor dukhovnoï sviatoï Ukraïny).

BIBLIOGRAPHY
Kozak, S. Ukraińscy spiskowcy i mesjaniści. Bractwo Cyryla i Metodego (Warsaw 1990)

J.-P. Himka

Mest' (vengeance). In medieval Ukraine, the punishment or vengeance exacted for a crime or offense. This legal institution, which was found among ancient tribes, survived in some regions to the beginning of the 20th century. Among the ancient Slavs it was not only the right but the obligation of clan members to avenge wrongs, particularly homicide, done to one of them. Later, *mest'* was replaced by pokora, ie, symbolic retribution. *Ruskaia Pravda permitted mest'* if it was approved by the court. If it was committed without court permission, it had to be justified before the court. In medieval Ukraine mest' was not very severe, and it could be carried out only by the victim's closest relatives, and only within a short period after the crime. The victim's family could substitute vykup (compensation) for mest'.

Meta (Goal). A monthly journal of culture and community affairs published in Lviv from September 1863 to January 1864 by a group of young Populists and edited by K. Klymkovych. One of the first, thick, journals in Ukraine, it contained poetry, prose, articles on historical and ethnographic subjects, a chronicle of current events, and reports on Ukrainian life in Kiev, Kharkiv, and elsewhere. Regular contributors included prominent writers from both Russian-ruled (eg, P. Kulish, D. Mordovets) and Western (Yu. Fedkovych) Ukraine. Meta was renewed in March 1865 and appeared semimonthly and then monthly until December (18 issues). It now devoted less attention to literature and more to politics, and reported on the activities of the *Halytsko-Ruska Matytsia society. Among the con-

Meta (Lviv, 1863–4)

tributors were S. Kachala, Ye. Zharsky, P. Pavlusevych, and M. Vovchok (two reports from Paris).

Meta (Goal). The first Ukrainian socialist feminist journal, published semimonthly in Lviv from March to December 1908. It was edited by D. Starosolska and was closely associated with the *Circle of Ukrainian Women.

Meta (Goal). A weekly organ of the *Ukrainian Catholic Union, published in Lviv from 1931 to 1939. It contained articles on political developments in Western and Soviet Ukraine and throughout the world, written mostly from a liberal Catholic perspective, as well as reports on the activities of the Ukrainian Catholic church. Considerable attention was paid to the role of young people and women in the church, and special sections dealt with culture and literature. The longtime managing editor was P. Kozitsky.

Meta (Goal). A newspaper published by the Ukrainian Information Bureau in Munich (1952–82) and Philadelphia (since 1982). A monthly since the 1970s, it contains news and analyses of developments in Ukraine and in the Ukrainian émigré community, documents, memoirs, and articles on historical topics, particularly the struggle for Ukrainian independence. It was the organ of the *Ukrainian National-State Union, and from 1972 it was the semi-official organ of the *Ukrainian National Council. Among its editors have been M. Shramenko, L. Vasyliv, and V. Biliaiv.

Metallurgical industry. A branch of heavy industry dealing with the extraction of metals from their ores, the refining of them, and the combination of them into alloys. It is divided into ferrous and nonferrous metallurgy.

The *iron industry in Ukraine can be traced as far back as the 5th century BC. It was well developed in Kievan Rus'. The blast furnace was introduced in the mid-18th century, and by 1836 there were 153 small-scale smelting enterprises in Ukraine. In the early 19th century the Russian government built three large smelting plants in southern Ukraine. They were plagued with technical difficulties and high production costs. The first coke-fueled blast furnace was introduced in the Kerch region in the mid-19th century. Railway expansion in the second half of the century increased the demand for iron rails, equipment, and metal in general. When domestic production

could not meet the demand, the government decided to spur the development of private instead of state enterprises. With the construction of a railway link between the Kryvyi Rih Iron-ore Basin and the Donbas, the iron industry expanded rapidly. By the turn of the century there were 17 integrated metallurgical plants in Ukraine: 10 in the Donbas, 3 in the Dnieper, and 4 in the Azov region. All but three or four of them were owned, partially or wholly, by French, Belgian, English, or American investors.

Ukraine's output of ferrous metals and its share in the empire's output rose rapidly during the last two decades of the 19th century (see table 1). Several factors account for the growth, including (1) the industry's superior corporate organization, which provided a better capital base, (2) the relative newness and technical superiority of its fixed capital, (3) its foreign ownership and its use of Western European and American specialists, (4) the heavy demand for rails for the expanding railway system, and (5) state subsidies and protection from foreign competition. Plants in Ukraine were much more efficient than those in the Urals. In 1900, for example, the output of pig iron per worker was 5.8 times greater in Ukraine than in the Urals.

TABLE 1
Output of pig iron and rolled stock in Ukraine, 1880–1917 (in 1,000 metric t; percentage of empire's output in parentheses)

Year	Pig iron		Rolled stock	
1880	21.3	(5.0)	26	(4.5)
1890	219	(24.3)	141	(17.8)
1900	1,500	(51.8)	969	(44.0)
1903	1,367	(55.4)	1,130	(50.7)
1913	3,107	(67.0)	2,309	(57.3)
1917	2,194	(72.3*)	1,572	(61.7*)

NOTE: Figures are for 'southern Russia' and include a small amount of territory outside the current boundaries of Ukraine. *Does not include Poland

The expansion of the iron and steel industry was interrupted by the worldwide economic depression in 1900–4. The Russo-Japanese War, however, stimulated demand. Ukraine's share of rolled stock remained steady, but its share in the manufacture of different types of rolled products varied. In 1912, for instance, Ukraine accounted for 79.3 percent of the rails produced in the Russian Empire (within the 1924 USSR boundaries), 88.8 percent of the beams and girders, 47 percent of the shaped steel, 55 percent of the wire rods, 24 percent of the roofing iron, and 57 percent of the sheet steel. In 1913 Ukraine had 21 metallurgical plants, employing some 90,000 workers. Almost 90 percent of the output was controlled by foreign firms. In 1902 the producers organized a cartel called *Prodamet to reduce competition and stabilize the market. Controlled by French banks, the cartel encompassed the 12 largest corporations, which in 1906 produced 80 percent of Ukraine's ferrous metal and 40–50 percent of the empire's output. By 1914 it controlled 90 percent of the empire's ferrous metal output.

During the First World War and the revolution, the Ukrainian iron industry suffered serious damage: of 63 blast furnaces only 1 was partly operational in 1919. Moreover, 9 of 15 large metallurgical plants, which in 1918 had accounted for 80 percent of the pig iron and steel output, were nationalized in 1919, and by that year all metallurgical plants had come under Soviet control. By 1920 Ukraine's output of pig iron had fallen to a mere 0.5 percent of the 1917 output, its steel output to 1.5 percent, and its rolled-steel output to 1.8 percent. During the 1920s the metallurgical industry was reconstructed, and by 1928 Ukraine had almost returned to its prewar production figures.

In its First Five-Year Plan the Soviet regime emphasized the growth of the metallurgical industry as the foundation of all other branches of industry. In its investment policy the USSR State Planning Committee gave priority to the development of a new metallurgical industry in the Urals and Western Siberia (the Ural-Kuznetsk Industrial Complex) and reduced Ukraine's share of the total investment to less than 30 percent. The Ukrainian State Planning Committee and Ukrainian economists, such as Y. Dimenshtein, argued that on purely economic grounds Ukraine ought to be favored.

Between 1928 and 1940 pig iron production in Ukraine increased by a factor of 4.08, steel by 3.3, and rolled steel by 3.2 (see table 2). The large increases in output were achieved through higher investment. During the First and Second Five-Year Plans fixed capital in the Ukrainian iron industry increased from 415 million rubles in 1928 to 2,681 million rubles in 1938 (in constant prices). During the First Five-Year Plan large enterprises, such as Zaporizhstal in Zaporizhia and Azovstal in Mariiupil, were built, and during the Second Five-Year Plan they went into operation. Some plants were reconstructed, and many new facilities were added, in 1928–40: 28 blast furnaces, 42 open hearth furnaces, 12 electric furnaces, 6 converters, 32 rolled steel and steel pipe mills, 11 iron-ore mines, and a number of auxiliary plants. The number of workers rose from 100,600 in 1929 to 153,000 in 1935. A great deal of capital was spent on foreign technology. There was much waste, a result of poor planning and incompetent management. The productivity of the metallurgical industry as well as the quality of its output was below Western standards.

The metallurgical industry in Ukraine was seriously damaged during the Second World War. Much equipment was evacuated to the east or destroyed so as not to fall into German hands. The retreating Germans systematically destroyed operating facilities. The industry was rebuilt rapidly after the war: by 1950 the output of pig iron, steel, and rolled stock had reached the prewar level. In 1950–70 Ukraine's ferrous metallurgical industry received some 30 percent of the capital invested in the industry throughout the USSR.

TABLE 2
Iron and steel production in Ukraine, 1928–89
(in 1,000 metric t; percentage of USSR total in parentheses)

Year	Pig iron		Steel		Rolled stock	
1928	2,361	(71.5)	2,409	(56.7)	1,995	(58.1)
1932	4,243	(68.8)	3,301	(55.7)	2,668	(60.2)
1937	9,216	(63.6)	8,738	(49.3)	6,468	(49.9)
1940	9,642	(64.7)	8,938	(48.7)	6,520	(49.7)
1950	9,168	(47.8)	8,351	(30.6)	6,929	(33.2)
1960	24,163	(51.7)	26,155	(40.1)	21,105	(41.4)
1970	41,411	(48.2)	46,599	(40.1)	37,519	(46.5)
1987	47,400	(41.5)	56,300	(34.5)	39,300	(34.2)
1989	46,500	(40.8)	54,800	(34.2)	39,900	(34.5)

In 1971-86 capital investment in Ukraine's metallurgical industry totaled 23,400 million rubles. The production of steel pipes rose from 0.6 million t in 1940 and 2.2 million t in 1960 to 7.1 million t in 1988 and 6.9 in 1989. Ukraine accounted for approx one-third of the USSR steel-pipe output. In the 1970s efforts were made to improve the industry's productivity: new technology was introduced; the preconditioning of raw materials was improved; oxygen and economical fuels, such as natural gas, were used more widely; and the pressure and temperature of blast furnaces were increased for higher efficiency.

Although the Ukrainian metallurgical industry has grown, its share of what was the all-Union output declined. It has difficulty securing adequate supplies of energy and iron ore. Because of higher materials and fuel costs, its production costs were higher than those of the Magnitogorsk or Kuznetsk ferrous metallurgical industries. In addition the industry lagged behind in technology: the continuous process for casting steel, for example, and the method of coke processing were used in other countries more widely than in the former USSR, where they were first developed. With the introduction of self-accounting in 1988, the problems of Ukraine's ferrous metallurgical industry were compounded. Eighty percent of its expenditures in 1988 were on raw materials. Finally, the industry must deal with the extensive pollution it has caused.

Prior to the 1930s Ukraine had no nonferrous metallurgical industry to speak of. Metallic mercury was first obtained in 1887 from the *Mykytivka mercury deposits, and no other nonferrous metals were produced. This branch of industry was developed during the First Five-Year Plan. In 1933 the Dnieper Aluminum Plant in Zaporizhia was put into operation. It used electric power from the Dniprohes and bauxites imported from Russia (see *Aluminum industry). A zinc plant started operation in 1931, and the Dnieper Magnesium Plant was built in 1935 in Kostiantynivka (Donbas). Mercury production in the Donbas was expanded. During the war virtually all plants of the industry were destroyed, and their reconstruction after the war proceeded slowly. In 1950 the output of nonferrous metals was 75 percent of the 1940 output. From 1950 to 1966 the output increased by a factor of 21. In 1960 the value of fixed capital in the industry was 137.4 million rubles, or 1 percent of the total fixed capital in Ukrainian industry. From 1976 to 1980 the output of nonferrous metallurgy doubled.

Production data on nonferrous metallurgy are not published because of its military significance. Ukraine's limited deposits of nonferrous metals restrict the industry's potential for growth. Another important restriction is the shortage of electrical power. Bauxite deposits, which have yet to be exploited, are found near Smila (Cherkasy oblast) and in Vysokopillia (Kherson oblast). *Titanium ores in Ukraine are extracted by quarrying; hence, production costs are relatively low. In 1987 Ukraine produced 7.2 million t of magnesium ore and 2.2 million t of magnesium metal. (In 1960 the respective figures were 2.7 and 0.9.) Zirconium, which is important for many technological processes, is extracted in the Samotkan (Dnipropetrovske region) and Azov regions. In the 1930s a zirconium plant was constructed in Kostiantynivka (Donetske oblast). Small deposits of nickel, cobalt, lead, and zinc have been found in the Azov region. Uranium has been discovered near Zhovti Vody, in Dnipropetrovske oblast.

(See also *Coke-chemical industry and *Manganese industry.)

BIBLIOGRAPHY

Sukhov, O. *Ekonomichna heohrafiia Ukraïny* (Odessa 1923)
Seredenko, M. *Chernaia metallurgiia Ukrainy 1917–1957* (Kiev 1957)
Lukinov, I.; et al (eds). *Istoriia narodnoho hospodarstva Ukrains'koï*
    RSR, 3 vols in 4 bks (Kiev 1983–7)

I. Koropeckyj, B. Krawchenko, B. Wynar

Metallurgy. The science and technology of obtaining
metals from their ores and modifying them for use. Those
processes use numerous technologies and include enriching the mined and crushed ores, reducing the separated
minerals to metal, alloying, and subjecting the metal to
various treatments to impart properties required by the
end-use.

From about the 6th century BC the inhabitants of Ukrainian territories developed a practical knowledge of metallurgy; they utilized copper, silver, and gold in the
manufacture of functional and ornamental objects and
produced iron from bog iron ore. From the 9th century
they started practicing ore enrichment, and from the 14th
century they began producing steel in blacksmith foundries. That production continued up to the 18th century in
Galicia, Polisia, and the Kharkiv and Poltava regions. In
industrial metallurgy, toward the end of the 19th century
a center of ferrous metallurgy emerged, based on the *Donets Basin coal seams and the Kerch and Kryvyi Rih iron-
ore deposits. The first industrial production of ferrous
metals commenced in 1872 at the Yuzivka (now the Donetske) Metallurgical Plant; it was followed in 1887 by the
Dnipropetrovske plant. By 1913 there were 21 metallurgical plants in Ukraine (including 42 blast furnaces, 72 Siemens-Martin furnaces, 28 converters, and about 70 rolling
and pipe-forming lines) that produced over half of all pig
iron, steel, and rolling stock in the Russian Empire. About
90 percent of the metallurgical industry was owned by
Western corporations.

The only prewar nonferrous metallurgical industry in
Ukraine was based on the mercury-ore deposits at Mykytivka, which were discovered in 1879. In 1930 a zinc plant
(Ukrtsynk) started operating in Kostiantynivka; it was followed by the first aluminum plant, in Zaporizhia (powered by the Dniprohes), in 1933 and the first magnesium
plant, in Zaporizhia, in 1935. After the Second World War
new industries emerged, based on freshly discovered ore
deposits of nonferrous and rare metals: the Irshanske
Mining and Enrichment Complex, the *Verkhnodni-

METALLURGICAL INDUSTRY

provske Mining and Metallurgical Complex, the Pobuzke Nickel Plant, the Artemivske Plant for Processing Nonferrous Metals, the Zaporizhia Titanium-Magnesium Complex, and others. Ukraine became a large-scale producer of technologically important metals and materials, including aluminum, magnesium, silicon, and semiconductor components, as well as a reliable raw-material base for titanium and zirconium production. The nonferrous metals industry introduced new types of product lines including zirconium, hafnium, refined ferronickel, and other metals.

Scientific studies of metallurgy began in Ukraine toward the end of 19th century. They were carried out primarily at the Kharkiv Technological Institute (A. Moevius), the Kiev Polytechnical Institute (V. *Izhevsky), and the Katerynoslav Higher Mining School (P. Rubin, L. Fortunato, S. Telny, M. Pavlov, A. *Vynohradov). After the revolution departments of metallurgy were organized at the Donetske Industrial Institute, the Dniprodzerzhynske Evening Metallurgical Institute, and the *Mariiupil Metallurgical Institute. The Dnipropetrovske Metallurgical Institute was formed out of part of the *Dnipropetrovske Mining Institute. Among the newly established scientific research institutes for metallurgy were those in Kharkiv (see *Ukrainian Scientific Research Institute of Metals), Dnipropetrovske (which later became the All-Union Pipe Institute), and the institutes of ferrous metallurgy in Kharkiv (1939–53), Dnipropetrovske (est 1953), and Donetske (est 1960).

Blast furnace metallurgy. Fundamental studies of blast-furnace technology commenced in Ukraine at the beginning of the 20th century (Moevius, I. Thieme, M. Kurako, I. Zelentsov, Izhevsky, Yu. and O. Horiainov). Pavlov, Rubin, and A. Pokhvysnev began their research at the only institution of higher learning at that time dealing with mining and metallurgy, the Katerynoslav Higher Mining School (now the Dnipropetrovske Metallurgical Institute). Since the 1940s, issues of blast furnace production have been researched mainly at the institutes of ferrous metallurgy in Kharkiv, Donetske, and Dnipropetrovske. New blast furnaces of up to 5,000 cu m were constructed. The use of natural gas along with oxygen-enriched blowing (up to 30–40 percent) was an innovation introduced by Z. Nekrasov and was adopted worldwide. Issues of the blast furnace industry are discussed in publications such as *Metallurgicheskaia i gornorudnaia promyshlennost'* and *Metallurgiia i koksokhimiia*, as well as in the internal publications of research institutes and academic institutions.

Steel smelting metallurgy. Research in steel smelting began in Ukraine at the beginning of the 20th century at the Kharkiv Technological (now Polytechnical) and Kiev Polytechnical institutes and the Katerynoslav Higher Mining School. The scientific issues of steel production were studied by Moevius, who wrote the first textbook on metallurgy in Ukraine, *Chugunoliteinoe proizvodstvo* (Cast-Iron Production, 1859); the brothers Horiainov, who introduced the ore-based Siemens-Martin process; and Fortunato, who introduced an original modification of the Thomas process. Acceleration of steel production took place in the 1920s and 1930s, and most of the efforts during the early 1940s went into the war effort (armor steel, etc), but major restructuring and modernization of the industry took place in the postwar years and involved extensive research and development at various scientific institutions.

Among the areas studied were the temperature and heat regimes and the physicochemical processes in Siemens-Martin furnaces (V. Lapytsky, S. Levin), oxygen injection into Siemens-Martin furnaces (Ya. Shneierov), the use of natural gas, and the scaling up of processes (M. Medzhybozhsky). The fundamental studies undertaken in those areas pioneered the introduction of the oxygen-converter process into industry, and were applied for the first time at the Dnipropetrovske and Kryvyi Rih plants. Newer continuous processes were developed by V. Baptyzmansky and others, who studied microalloying and modifying the chemical composition of steels and also developed the theoretical and technical basis for its extensive desulfurization (I. Bornatsky). New technology of steel pouring under inert gas and rapid methods of transferring boiling steel were introduced (V. *Yefimov). Other developments included rapid electrothermal treatment of steel and its alloys (V. *Hridniev), new types of semipassivated and specialty steels (I. Uzlov et al), and studies of heat- and mass-exchange processes (Ye. Kapustin).

Currently, research on various problems of steel smelting is carried out at the ANU *Institute of Electric Welding, the ANU Institute for Problems of Casting (both in Kiev), the Institute of Ferrous Metallurgy in Dnipropetrovske, the Ukrainian Scientific Research Institute of Metals in Kharkiv, and the Dnipropetrovske and Mariiupil Metallurgical, Donetske Polytechnical, and Dniprodzerzhynske Industrial institutes.

Casting metallurgy. Practical knowledge of metal casting accumulated over many centuries, beginning in Ukraine in the Bronze Age, but scientific studies in the area did not commence until the end of the 19th century (Moevius, V. Knabbe). Even then, no dedicated research centers for metal casting existed. Only in the early 1930s were institutes, laboratories, and university chairs of casting science established, at the Zaporizhia Machine-Building Institute (1931) and the Odessa Polytechnical Institute (1932). Casting specialists were trained mainly at the Kiev Polytechnical and Dnipropetrovske Metallurgical institutes. Ukrainian scientists studied problems in improving the quality of cast iron and cast-iron objects, specialty steels, tin-free bronzes, and aluminum castings.

After the Second World War the attention of Ukrainian scientists was directed at elaborating the theoretical foundations for casting processes, perfecting casting technology, and developing production methods for casting molds used in metallurgy (K. Vashchenko). The various achievements included the perfection of casting technology (N. Voronova), the improvement of rollers (A. Kryvosheiev), and the development of chemically resistant alloys (V. *Vasyliev) and of new methods for producing superhard iron containing spherical graphite (A. *Vasylenko), including the necessary complex modifying additives (A. Horshkov, M. Voloshchenko). The introduction of the centrifugal casting of ingots from low-melting and exothermic mixtures (A. Shevchenko) increased production efficiency. Ukrainian scientists developed methods for casting steel, utilizing insulating and slag-forming mixtures, modifiers, microcoolers, improved casters, and crystallizers for continuous steel casting (Yefimov). Fundamental research was done in the area of the electromagnetic transport and dosimetry of molten metal (V. *Polishchuk, V. Zlobin). A magnetodynamic device for the casting and distribution of aluminum, zinc, and magnesium alloys was constructed at the ANU Institute of

Casting Production (later the Institute for Problems of Casting). The device was used in many Soviet plants and was patented and exported to most Western countries. Other developments included the casting of alloyed construction steels, corrosion-resistant steels, and thermally stable steels and alloys (M. Braun), a method of casting under controlled low pressure (H. Borysov), and the electro-slag casting method (B. *Medovar). The scientific basis for the use of plasma, induced plasma, and electron beams as heat sources for the melting of high-quality alloys was studied, as was the technology for producing bimetallic materials and reconditioning worn parts. The latter method for the mass production of bimetallic parts from worn ones was introduced throughout the USSR. Dosimetric devices were constructed for casting molten iron into centrifugal molds, with ancillary regulating equipment, digital regulators of casting, and control panels for monitoring the melting conditions in induction furnaces (O. Kryzhanivsky). Alloyed molten-iron thermodynamics was studied by L. Vladimirov. Ukrainian metallurgists also researched the complex mechanization and automation of casting procedures, the creation of advanced cast materials, and low-waste, streamlined casting processes.

Problems of the casting industry are researched primarily at the ANU Institute for Problems of Casting in Kiev, formed in 1958 on the basis of the AN URSR Institute of Machinery and Agricultural Mechanics. Headed by Yefimov, the institute has studied physicochemical phenomena involving the modification and alloying of cast ingots and developed high-productivity processes for the casting of steel, as well as new casting materials, and automated casting methods. More recent research has been directed at the theoretical foundations for casting processes, novel technologies and equipment for the improved production of castings, including studies of external effects on molten metal, metal in the process of crystallization, and novel cast materials that would improve the economy of metal utilization. Other research centers involved in casting research include the Scientific Research Institute of Special Casting Methods in Odessa and the institutes of design and construction. Issues of casting technology are covered in the journal *Tekhnologiia i organizatsiia proizvodstva*, as well as in the collected works of scientific research establishments and academic institutions.

Rolling metallurgy. Studies of rolling stock production commenced in Ukraine toward the end of the 19th century. Centered at the laboratories of the Kharkiv Technological and the Kiev Polytechnical institutes, as well as at the Katerynoslav Higher Mining School, they dealt primarily with making generalizations based on the experience of rolling-mill operators with roller calibration.

The work of A. Vynohradov formed the basis of further development of the calibration theory and became closely integrated with practical considerations. Later research took place at the Ukrainian Scientific Institute of Metals in Kharkiv and the Institute of Ferrous Metallurgy in Kharkiv (since 1953 in Dnipropetrovske). Specialists in rolling stock were trained at the Dnipropetrovske Metallurgical Institute. Ukrainian scientists studied theoretical problems of rolling, particularly the conditions for metal deformation during longitudinal rolling (A. Vynohradov), devised methods for precision rolling, and designed the supporting equipment. After the Second World War they articulated the theoretical foundations of rolling (O.

*Chekmarov, S. Filipov, V. Lykhansky, O. Smolianynov) and the theory and technology of continuous rolling (M. Safian, O. *Shevchenko). The mechanism of external friction was studied, as well as the effect of friction on the stress of rolling; effective technological lubricants were invented for cold and hot rolling (O. Grudev). Theories of roller calibration for solid rolled shapes (D. Starchenko) and precise rolling of thick sheets (V. Klymenko) were introduced. Other important research dealt with the technology of bent rolled sheets (I. Tryshevsky), the rolling of powdered materials (H. Vynohradov), sheet rolling directly from molten metal (Ye. Nykolaienko), and the formation of surface microgeometry in cold rolled sheet (V. Mazur). Also developed was the theory of the simultaneous rolling of two ingots (Chekmarov), which found wide industrial application. Numerous studies were done on pipe rolling production (S. Borysov) and on the hardening thermal treatment of rolling stock (K. *Starodubov).

The problems of rolling stock production are studied at the Donetske Scientific Research Institute of Ferrous Metallurgy, the former All-Union Scientific Research and Design Technology Institute of the Pipe Industry (in Dnipropetrovske), the Ukrainian Scientific Research Institute of Metals (in Kharkiv), and the Dnipropetrovske Metallurgical, Donetske Polytechnical, and Komunarske Mining and Metallurgical institutes, as well as at institutions of the Academy of Sciences. Issues of rolling stock production were discussed in the journals DOMEZ (1925–35), *Teoriia i praktika metallurgii* (1936–40), and *Stal'* (1931–40). Now, articles are published in the scientific and industrial journals *Metallurgicheskaia i gornorudnaia promyshlennost'* and *Metallurgiia i koksokhimiia*, as well as in the internal publications of various academic and scientific research establishments.

Powder metallurgy. The first scientific endeavors in this field were pioneered by P. Sobolevsky and V. Liubarsky, who in 1826 used compression and firing techniques to process platinum powder into various products, and N. *Beketov, who prepared the theoretical basis for the manufacturing of powders from different metals (1865). Systematic research in powder metallurgy commenced in the 1920s and centered during the 1930 and 1940s at the ANURSR (now ANU) Institute of Chemistry in Kiev and the Institute of Ferrous Metallurgy in Kharkiv. Methods of obtaining various types of metallic powders were explored, and powders of bismuth and zirconium were obtained by electrolytic methods (V. *Izbekov, V. *Plotnikov, O. Kudra, I. *Sheka), as were those of beryllium, silver, zinc, cadmium, aluminum, and so forth (Yu. *Delimarsky, B. Markov). Initial studies on obtaining iron powder from ore concentrate were done in the 1930s by reduction with natural gas (M. *Luhovtsov, I. *Frantsevych) and in 1948–51 by the use of a blended reducing agent consisting of natural gas and carbon (this method became commercialized). From 1952, specialists in powder metallurgy were trained at the Kiev Polytechnic Institute.

Research in powder metallurgy was furthered by the establishment of a laboratory for special alloys within the ANU. The laboratory was reorganized in 1955 into the ANU Institute of Metal Ceramics and Special Alloys (now the *Institute for Problems of Materials Science). The institute was the main powder metallurgy research center for the whole USSR and the co-ordinating center for the COMECON countries in the area of powder metallurgy. One of the more important developments at the institute involved the production of high-quality powders of ferrous and nonferrous metals through the atomization of their melts with the aid of gases or water. Jointly with the industrial sector, its scientists developed a commercial technology for the manufacture of frictional discs for buses and tractors. They pioneered the production of durable and slippage-resistant bits for drilling rigs. The institute publishes the monthly *Poroshkovaia metallurgiia* (which is translated into English in the United States) and the periodical compendiums *Adgeziia razplavov i paika materialov* and *Zashchitnye pokrytiia materialov*.

Special electrometallurgy. Research in the area of special electrometallurgy, which permits the production of improved-quality, highly efficient specialty steel alloys, was pioneered in the 1950s at the AN URSR Institute of Electric Welding (see *Welding). The institute is a research and development complex including not only departments of exploratory, theoretical, and experimental studies, but also a department of experimental technological design, an experimental electromechanical plant, an experimental plant of welding materials, and a pilot plant. Its staff has included B. *Paton, K. *Khrenov, D. *Dudko, V. *Lebedev, Medovar, B. Movchan, I. *Pokhodnia, B. Kasatkin, S. *Kuchuk-Yatsenko, V. *Makhnenko, and V. Trufiakov, and it represented the former USSR in the International Welding Institute. Among its significant achievements are fundamental studies of metallurgical and electrophysical processes occurring during arc welding, which became the basis for developing new and more effective welding wires and fluxes; studies of brittle failure in metallic structures, which led to the development of methods to increase resistance to brittle failure, and in particular to the breakthrough invention of very reliable multishell welded pipes for gas transmission mains; the invention of a new class of metallic materials, referred to as reinforced quasi-multilayered or quasi-monolithic, that exhibit high resistance to brittle failure; the establishment of the fundamentals of electro-slag smelting and the construction of the first electro-slag furnace in the world, which was put into operation at the Zaporizhia Dniprospetsstal Electrometallurgical Plant in 1958; the creation of the new field of electro-slag casting; studies of electrical and thermal processes taking place during the rapid electrical heating of contact points between metallic objects, which formed the theoretical basis for improved flash welding; and studies of the physicochemical behavior of electron-beam evaporation and the subsequent condensation of streams of metallic and nonmetallic materials.

The institute collaborates closely with industry, particularly in the areas of the manufacture of large-diameter (up to 1.42 m) multishell gas pipelines and electro-slag welding technology. Its scientists introduced the technology of repairing point defects in oil pipelines without interruption of product flow. More recent research areas include complex studies of physicochemical phenomena in metal welding and the development, on the basis of the studies, of new and improved methods of unbreakable bonding between metals and alloys; tensile strength studies of welded bonds under various types of external loads and the establishment of a scientific basis for designing welded constructions; and the invention of new technological processes of metal processing, including the action of superhard materials.

Problems of special electrometallurgy are also studied at the Ukrainian Scientific Research Institute of Special Steels, Alloys, and Ferroalloys (Zaporizhia), at the Dnipropetrovske and Mariiupil metallurgical institutes, and at the Donetske Polytechnical Institute. The area of special electrometallurgy is covered in the journal *Problemy spetsial'noi electrometallurgii*.

BIBLIOGRAPHY
Seredenko, M. *Chornaia metallurgiia Ukrainy, 1917–1957* (Kiev 1957)
Fedorchenko, I.; Andrievskii, R. *Osnovy poroshkovoi metallurgii* (Kiev 1963)
Razvitie metallurgii v Ukrainskoi SSR (Kiev 1980)
                                                    S. Trofimenko

Metalworking industry. A branch of *heavy industry that manufactures metal products and structures and repairs machinery and equipment for various branches of the economy. In Ukraine it is officially classified as a subbranch of the *machine-building industry.

The industry makes products for industrial use, such as iron and cast-iron building fixtures, shoemaking tools, springs, mesh, chains, anchors, and farm implements, and for consumer use, such as cooking utensils, pots, kettles, razors, scissors, beds, carriages, lamps, and sports equipment. Its metal structures are used in the construction of buildings, bridges, power lines, and water conduits.

Metalworking in Ukraine dates back to ancient times. The craftsmen of Kievan Rus' supplied not only the home market but also the export market with weapons, metal tools, and metalware. In the 19th century metalworking was one of the largest industries in Ukraine. Under the Soviet regime the industry grew rapidly. From 1940 to 1968 its output increased by a factor of 13.7. By 1968 its share in Ukraine's industrial output was 3.7 percent. Of the 795 enterprises belonging to the industry in 1968, 233 made metal products, 47 built metal structures, and 515 repaired machines and equipment. Most of them were located in the Donets, Dnieper, and southwestern regions. The largest metalworking plants are the tableware plants in Kiev and Vilnianske and Metalopobut and Metaloshtamp in Dnipropetrovske, the metal structures plants in Dnipropetrovske, Mariiupil, Zhytomyr, and Donetske, the boat repair docks in Kherson, and the automotive repair plant in Kiev. Research on various aspects of metalworking is conducted at the Ukrainian Steel Structures Design Institute and the Ukrainian Scientific Research Institute of Cultural and Consumer Products.

Metelytsia. A fast Ukrainian folk dance performed by many pairs of dancers formed in a circle with one couple in the center. The dance, accompanied by the folk song 'Metelytsia' in 2/4 time, conveys the impression of a *metelytsia* 'snow flurry.'

Meteorology. See Climatology and meteorology.

Methodius, Saint. See Saint Methodius.

Metiuk, Andrei [Metjuk, Andrej] (secular name: Hryhorii), b 3 January 1898 in Terebin, Hrubeshiv county, Lublin gubernia, d 2 February 1985 in Winnipeg. Orthodox bishop and metropolitan. After studies at the Vilnius Theological Seminary and the theology faculty of Warsaw University (M DIV, 1924), Metiuk was ordained in 1924 and

Metropolitan Andrei Metiuk   Amvrosii Metlynsky

held various church positions in the Kholm region until 1944, when he was forced to emigrate. He resided in Switzerland (1945–8) before coming to Canada (1948). In 1959 he was consecrated bishop of the Ukrainian Orthodox Church of Canada for the eparchy of Edmonton and Western Canada. He was elevated to archbishop in 1963 and designated metropolitan and head of the church in 1975. Among his publications are *Pravoslavna vira* (The Orthodox Faith, 1962, 1976), *Vid Ierusalymu pochynaiuchy* (Beginning in Jerusalem, 1980), and *Ryms'ka uniia ne dlia ukraïntsiv* (The Union with Rome Is Not for Ukrainians, 1984). His biography, by F. Onufriichuk, appeared in 1983.

Metlynsky, Amvrosii [Metlyns'kyj, Amvrosij] (pseud: A. Mohyla), b 1814 in Sary, Hadiache county, Poltava gubernia, d 29 July 1870 in Yalta. Poet, ethnographer, and publisher. He served as a professor at Kharkiv (1843–9, 1854–8) and Kiev (1849–54) universities. He published a collection of poetry, *Dumky i pisni ta shche deshcho* (Thoughts and Songs and Some Other Things, 1839), under his pseudonym. Some of his poetry was reprinted in the almanacs *Snip* and *Molodyk*. He also published an anthology of works by Kharkiv poets, *Iuzhnyi russkii sbornik* (Southern Russian Anthology, 1848), that included his works and those of S. Aleksandrov, M. Petrenko, and H. Kvitka-Osnovianenko. Metlynsky was a member of the so-called *Kharkiv Romantic School; his poetry is suffused with nostalgia for the glories of the Ukrainian past, which he thought were destined never to return. His disbelief in a Ukrainian renaissance led him to embrace ideas of Slavic unity and to place hope in Russia. His nostalgia prompted him to collect Ukrainian folk songs, which he published in *Narodnye iuzhnorusskie pesni* (Southern Russian Folk Songs, 1854), a collection that contained an abundance of previously unpublished material.

Metropolitan. The head of an ecclesiastical province in the Ukrainian Catholic and Orthodox churches. Originally a metropolitan was a bishop residing in the principal city, or a metropolis, of a civil province of the Roman Empire whose authority extended over all the eparchies of the province. This title continues to be used, both in Eastern and Western churches, but the authority of the office and the method of appointment have evolved over time.

From its beginnings the Ukrainian church was headed by the metropolitan (*mytropolyt*) of Kiev, who was initially under the jurisdiction of the Patriarch of Constantinople (see *Kiev metropoly). Most early metropolitans were Greeks appointed and consecrated directly by the patriarch. In reality the early church in Ukraine enjoyed considerable autonomy, and Rus' princes often succeeded in nominating candidates to the office; this was especially true in the cases of the first two native metropolitans, *Ilarion and *Klym Smoliatych. The rights and authority of a metropolitan in the Ukrainian church were defined in apostolic regulations, *canon law, and decrees of the princes of Rus'. The metropolitan was residential bishop of Kiev eparchy, convened and headed synods of bishops of his metropoly (16 eparchies in Kiev metropoly before the Tatar invasions), ensured that synodal decisions were adhered to, and oversaw the appointment of bishops to vacant positions. The metropolitan had the patriarchal right to consecrate and distribute the Holy Myron; he could also confirm and ordain bishops, visit eparchies, sit in judgment in bishop's courts, and remove bishops from office. The metropolitan even had authority (which diminished over time) in certain secular affairs; he represented the church before the highest secular authorities and often influenced affairs of state as an adviser to the prince. During the Tatar occupation of Rus', metropolitans were the official appointees of the khan and would often intercede with him on behalf of the population.

The decline of the Kievan state and the destruction of Kiev by the Tatars led to the disintegration of Kiev metropoly. During the 14th and 15th centuries *Halych, *Lithuanian, and Moscow metropolies all claimed jurisdiction over Ukrainian territories (see church *Hierarchy and history of the Ukrainian *Church). In the mid-15th century Moscow metropoly broke its ties with Kiev before eventually constituting itself as a patriarchate in 1589. After the appointment of H. *Bolharyn as Kievan metropolitan in 1470, the metropoly included eight Ukrainian and two Belarusian eparchies. From then until the end of the 15th century the Kievan metropolitan was chosen by a sobor of Rus' bishops, often with the participation of lay leaders. In 1498, however, the Kievan metropolitan Y. Bolharynovych was appointed by the Lithuanian grand duke Alexander, and not elected by sobor. This was the first overt manifestation of *patronage that placed the church hierarchy in direct dependence on secular authorities. From then the independence of the metropolitan was compromised by Polish kings, Lithuanian princes, newly formed church *brotherhoods, and certain monasteries; the latter two often relied on the support of various patriarchs, who granted them stauropegion (exempt status) to guarantee their independence from local bishops and metropolitans.

At the Church Union of *Berestia in 1596, the Kievan metropolitanate established the Uniate church. In 1620, however, Y. Boretsky was consecrated Orthodox metropolitan of Kiev by the Jerusalem patriarch Theophanes. He had been elected by a sobor, with the participation of the clergy, Cossack officers, and the hetman. This practice continued for several years, although P. Mohyla was elected by Orthodox deputies of the Warsaw Diet in 1632 and confirmed by King Władysław IV Vasa. In all cases the Patriarch of Constantinople ratified these elections.

As Muscovite influence over Ukrainian political and church life grew, Orthodox metropolitans of Kiev rapidly lost their rights and privileges. In 1686 Kiev metropoly was placed under the Patriarch of Moscow, and in 1688 the metropolitan was deprived of the title 'of All Rus'.' In 1721 the Russian *Holy Synod began appointing Kievan hierarchs, who lost the formal rights of provincial metropolitans and became mere bishops of the Russian church. Although the title of metropolitan was revived in 1743, the authority of the Kievan metropolitan was limited to his own eparchy.

After the 1917 Revolution, eparchial sobors sought to remove Ukrainian eparchies from under Muscovite administration and revive the old authority of the metropolitan of Kiev. The Ukrainian government issued a proclamation in 1918 and a statute in 1919 stipulating that the Ukrainian church was autocephalous and headed by the metropolitan of Kiev, but the Bolshevik consolidation of power in Ukraine prevented the practical implementation of this autocephaly. In 1921 the Moscow patriarch created a Ukrainian exarchate headed by a metropolitan who had no specific rights. At the same time Ukrainian national church circles established a separate *Ukrainian Autocephalous Orthodox church (UAOC). When church leaders, mostly members of the clergy, could not convince any bishops to consecrate a new hierarchy for the UAOC, they used a tradition of the church of Alexandria to elevate V. *Lypkivsky to the rank of metropolitan; this ordination was denounced as noncanonical and invalid by the Russian Orthodox church and other churches. Neither the UAOC nor the *Living church (another entity established after the revolution) survived the antireligious terror of the 1930s.

After the Second World War the Moscow patriarch again appointed an exarch for Ukraine with the title of 'Metropolitan of Kiev and Halych,' but he has the powers only of a bishop. The UAOC was revived during the Second World War under the spiritual authority of Metropolitan D. *Valedinsky of the Polish Autocephalous Orthodox church. The UAOC survived in the West as a church with two metropolitanates (Western Europe and the United States with South America), both of which are headed by M. *Skrypnyk. The various churches that split from the UAOC and the Ukrainian Orthodox Church of Canada are also headed by metropolitans. In all of these jurisdictions, church sobors elect the metropolitan. The metropolitan of the Ukrainian Orthodox Church of America (ecumenical patriarchate) is appointed by the ecumenical patriarch in Constantinople.

There have been other Orthodox metropolitans with eparchies in Ukrainian territories. In 1873 an autocephalous Bukovyna-Dalmatia metropoly was established, with its see in Chernivtsi. The metropolitans were chosen by the Austrian emperor. During the Rumanian occupation the metropolitan was placed under the authority of the Patriarch of Rumania. The Polish Autocephalous Orthodox church from 1922 had its own metropolitan, who was nominated by the Polish government and confirmed by the ecumenical patriarchate in Constantinople.

After the Union of Berestia, Pope Clement VIII's 1596 bull *Decet Romanum Pontificem* gave Ukrainian Catholic metropolitans of Kiev the same rights that Kievan metropolitans had under Constantinople. The candidate for metropolitan would be chosen by direct vote of the assembled bishops and Basilian protoarchimandrites. Then he would be nominated by the Polish king and confirmed by

the pope. Only I. Potii and A. Seliava were confirmed as metropolitans by the pope without having served as bishops. After Right-Bank Ukraine and Belarus came completely under Russian control following the partitions of Poland, the powers of the Uniate metropolitan were progressively restricted and then formally abolished in 1838. The partitions also led to the 1807 revival of Halych metropoly. The metropolitan's rights, however, were limited by the Austrian authorities. Soon the title became purely honorific. The archeparchy of Winnipeg and metropolitanate of Canada was erected by Pope Pius XII in 1956, and the archeparchy of Philadelphia in 1958. In 1963 the Halych metropolitan was recognized as the major archbishop of Lviv.

BIBLIOGRAPHY
Petrushevych, A. 'Avtorytet, prava, i pryvileï mytropolyta v ierarkhiï hreko-rus'koï Tserkvy vid pochatku azh do nashykh chasiv,' *Nyva* (1933)
Lotots'kyi, O. *Avtokefaliia*, 2 vols (Warsaw 1935–8)
Vlasovs'kyi, I. *Narys istoriï Ukraïns'koï Pravoslavnoï Tserkvy*, 4 vols (South Bound Brook, NJ 1955–66)
Patrylo, I. *Archiepiscopi-Metropolitani Kievo-Halicienses* (Rome 1962)
Polons'ka-Vasylenko, N. *Istorychni pidvalyny UAPTs* (Rome 1964)
Khoma, I. *Kyïvs'ka mytropoliia v beresteis'kim periodi* (Rome 1979)
Blažejowskyj, D. *Hierarchy of the Kyivan Church (861–1990)* (Rome 1990)
Fedoriv, Iu. *Orhanizatsiina struktura Ukraïns'koï Tserkvy* (Toronto 1990)

W. Lencyk

Metropolitan Ilarion Theological Society (Bohoslovske tovarystvo im. Mytropolyta Ilariona). A Ukrainian theological society based at St Andrew's College in Winnipeg. Established as the Scholarly Theological Society in 1948, the society initially included such churchmen and scholars as Archbishop M. Skypnyk, S. Sawchuk, D. Doroshenko, and I. Vlasovsky. In 1954 Metropolitan I. *Ohiienko assumed leadership of the society and renamed it the Ukrainian Scholarly Theological Society. Under Ohiienko's direction the society published a regular journal, *Vira i kul'tura*, and a number of books on theology and church history, primarily by Ohiienko. After a period of inactivity, the society was revived in 1972, after Ohiienko's death, and renamed in his honor. Since then *Vira i kul'tura* has also been revived as an annual publication.

Mezentsev, Ihor [Mezencev], b 9 September 1915 in Zhytomyr, Volhynia gubernia, d 9 March 1984 in Kiev. Architect. A graduate of the Kiev State Art Institute (1946), he taught there from 1967. He helped design various buildings in Kiev and other cities, including the general plan, main entrance, gate, fountain, and pavilions of the Exhibition of the Economic Achievements of the Ukrainian SSR (1951–7), the Kiev Geophysical Observatory (1947–50), the memorial complex in honor of Soviet soldiers and partisans in Poltava (1968–71), the Ukrainian Museum of the Great Patriotic War (1973–81), and residential complexes in Kiev and Tashkent. He also wrote technical papers on architecture and city planning.

Mezhenko, Yurii [Meženko, Jurij] (pseud of Yurii Ivanov-Mezhenko), b 18 June 1892 in Kharkiv, d 24 November 1969 in Kiev. Bibliographer, literary scholar, and

Yurii Mezhenko (portrait by Mykhailo Zhuk, ink and pencil, 1919)

bibliotek URSR (Concerning the Inventory of Libraries of the Ukrainian SSR, 1926), *Knyzhkova produktsiia na Ukraïni v 1917–1921 rokakh* (Book Production in Ukraine in 1919–21, 1927), and *Materiialy do Shevchenkiiany za roky 1917–29* (Materials on Shevchenkiana in 1917–29, 1930). In the early days of the revolution he wrote philosophical essays, such as *Tvorchist' indyviduuma i kolektyv* (Creativity of the Individual and the Collective, 1919), in which he proposed that the nation was 'permanent and lasting,' and that writers were the purveyors of 'national urges and demands.' Under Soviet rule he was unable to continue writing in that vein, but he managed to produce articles of interest, including 'Pro V. Kobylians'koho' (About V. Kobyliansky, 1920) and 'Tvorchist' M. Khvyl'ovoho' (The Works of M. Khvylovy, 1923).

I. Koshelivets

Mezhlauk, Valerii [Mežlauk, Valerij], b 19 February 1893 in Kharkiv, d 29 July 1938 in Moscow. Bolshevik party leader and Soviet government official. A graduate of Kharkiv University, he joined the Bolshevik party in July 1917 and was active in the Kharkiv Party Committee and Soviet. From February 1918 he was finance commissar of the *Donets–Kryvyi Rih Soviet Republic. In January 1919 he was appointed deputy people's commissar for military affairs in the Ukrainian Soviet government. At the Third All-Ukrainian Congress of Soviets on 6–10 March 1919, he was elected to the All-Ukrainian Central Executive Committee. From May 1919 to March 1920 he served on the revolutionary military soviets in the 2nd Ukrainian Red Army and the 5th, 10th, and 2nd Russian Red armies on the Ukrainian, Tula, and Caucasian fronts. After 1920 he worked in Moscow organizing the railway system, the metalworking industry, and heavy industry. He was a member of the Presidium of the Supreme Council of the National Economy (1924–6), deputy chairman of the council (1926–31), first deputy chairman of the State Planning Committee (1931–4), and deputy chairman of the USSR Council of People's Commissars (1934–7). In 1934 he was promoted to the status of full member of the CC of the All-Union Communist Party (Bolshevik). He was arrested in December 1937 and executed.

J. Koshiw

collector. He graduated from Moscow University in 1917. Mezhenko was head of the Council of the National Library of Ukraine (1919–22), director of the Ukrainian Scientific Institute of Bibliology (1922–31), and editor of the journal *Bibliolohichni visti* (1923–30). After the liquidation of the institute he was accused of nationalism and forced to work outside of Ukraine as a supervisor in the bibliographic section of the State Public Library in Leningrad (1934–45). He subsequently returned to Ukraine and assumed the directorship of the library of the Academy of Sciences of the Ukrainian SSR (1945–8).

From 1911 to 1962 Mezhenko amassed a unique collection of Shevchenkiana, which he bequeathed to the Institute of Literature of the AN URSR (now ANU). He wrote over 150 works, of which most are concerned with library science (including reviews of the literature), and some deal with the history of literature and theater. Among them are *Bibliotechna tekhnika* (Library Science, 1922), *Pro perepys*

Mezhov, Vladimir [Mežov], b 29 May 1830 in Saratov, Russia, d 29 May 1894 in St Petersburg. Considered the first Russian bibliographer, from 1851 to 1866 he worked at the St Petersburg Public Library. The St Petersburg journal *Osnova* published his bibliographies of books and articles about Right-Bank Ukraine in 1858–60 (1861, nos 8, 11, 12) and Galician-Ruthenian literature in 1837–62 (1862, no. 6). His statistical and bibliographic overview of Russian literature in 1859–68 (9 vols, 1861–83) and his Russian historical bibliographies for the years 1800–54 (3 vols, 1892–3) and 1865–76 (8 vols, 1882–90) are valuable reference works for Ukrainian scholars.

Mezhova [Mežova]. V-17. A town smt (1990 pop 8,900) on the Kamianka River and a raion center in Dnipropetrovske oblast. The Mezhova railway station was built in 1884, and several settlements sprang up around it. In 1956 the villages of Hryhorivka, Kamianka, and Novoslovianka were amalgamated to form the town of Mezhova. There is a regional museum in the town.

Mezhyhiria Chronicle (Mezhyhirskyi litopys). A valuable source for events in Ukraine from 1608 to 1700. The manuscript was kept in the Mezhyhiria Transfiguration Monastery near Kiev, and initially belonged to its overseer, I. Koshchakivsky (d 1720). Some scholars (eg, M. Marchenko) consider him to be the compiler, but others ascribe authorship of the chronicle to one of the former Cossacks residing at the monastery. The chronicle consists of 41 narratives, including ones about the rebellions led by Ya. Ostrianyn and P. Pavliuk, the Cossack-Polish War of 1648–57, and Turkish-Tatar invasions of Ukraine. Seven describe natural disasters, such as a locust plague, a solar eclipse, and a fire and earthquake in Kiev. The chronicle was published in Kiev in *Sbornik letopisei, otnosiashchikhsia k istorii Iuzhnoi i Zapadnoi Rusi* (Collection of Chronicles Relating to the History of Southern and Western Rus', 1888), edited by V. Antonovych.

Products of the Mezhyhiria Faience Factory

Mezhyhiria Faience Factory (Mezhyhirska faiansova fabryka). One of the first factories in Ukraine. It was established in 1798 on land belonging to the Mezhyhiria Transfiguration Monastery, near a large deposit of high-quality faience clay. It was owned and administered by the Kiev *magistrat* until 1810, when it burned down. It was rebuilt by the Russian government and from 1822 was overseen by the imperial cabinet.

Initially the factory employed foreign artisans and craftsmen. Later on Ukrainians were trained, and in 1826 a school was established there to train artists and craftsmen. Most of the Ukrainian workers were state peasants from the villages of Novi Petrivtsi and Valky, in Kiev gubernia. The factory produced plates and dishes, church vessels, decorative vases and plates, porcelain Easter eggs and sculptures, and other objects. The early products followed Western classicist styles, but the factory soon developed a unique, Ukrainian style of porcelain design and decoration based on folk motifs. In the second half of the 19th century it also produced plates decorated with portraits of Ukrainian national figures, such as T. Shevchenko, P. Kulish, and M. Kostomarov; scenes of everyday Ukrainian life; landscapes; and historic buildings and monuments. Articles produced by the Mezhyhiria factory were popular throughout Ukraine, Belarus, and Russia. Some were exported and can be found in museums in Western Europe. In the 1850s the factory started to decline, and in 1874 it was closed.

BIBLIOGRAPHY
Kuz'min, E. 'Mezhigorskii faians,' *Iskusstvo*, 1911, nos 6–7
Ohloblyn, O. 'Arkhiv Kyivo-Mezhyhirs'koï faiansovoï fabryky,' *Zapysky Istorychno-filolohichnoho viddilu VUAN*, 9 (1926)
Dolyns'kyi, L. *Ukraïns'kyi khudozhnii farfor* (Kiev 1963)
O. Ohloblyn

Mezhyhiria Transfiguration Monastery (drawing by Taras Shevchenko)

Mezhyhiria Transfiguration Monastery (Mezhyhirskyi Spaso-Preobrazhenskyi manastyr). An orthodox men's monastery located in Novi Petrivtsi (formerly Mezhyhiria), near Vyshhorod, 20 km north of Kiev. According to some accounts, it was founded by Greek monks from Mount Athos who arrived in Kiev at the time of its Christianization in 988. Prince Andrei Bogoliubskii allegedly moved it to a more favorable location (hence its name, which means 'between the hills'). According to these accounts, it was destroyed during the Mongol invasion of 1240.

The first written records of the monastery date from 1523, when it was granted a royal charter. Soon after it ceased to exist, but it was renewed under the Greek monk Athanasius, with the backing of I. Kopynsky. It grew quickly and by the mid-17th century had 150 monks. In 1665 it was partially destroyed by a fire, but its growth resumed soon after. In 1687 it was granted *stauropegion.

The Mezhyhiria monastery was long known as the 'Cossack military monastery' because of its close association with the Cossacks. They were important benefactors, and many of them retired to the monastery. From 1683 all clergymen assigned to the Zaporozhian Sich had to come from there. Supported generously by hetmans (esp I. Mazepa), magnates, metropolitans, and the Zaporozhian Sich (which funded a military hospital there), the monastery became one of the wealthiest in Ukraine. The Mezhyhiria Chronicle, a history of the Volhynia and Kiev regions in the 14th to 17th centuries, was probably written by a monk at the monastery. Monks from Mezhyhiria also assisted in the establishment of other monasteries, notably the *Mhar Transfiguration Monastery and the *Hustynia Trinity Monastery.

The main buildings of the complex were built in the late 17th to early 18th centuries. These included the Church of the Transfiguration (1690), from which the monastery took its name; the Church of SS Peter and Paul (1768–74, funded by P. Kalnyshevsky); the bell tower; and the monks' cells (designed by I. Hryhorovych-Barsky, 1766, rebuilt 1816–17). In 1786 the Russian government closed the monastery and nationalized its extensive landholdings, and in 1787 a massive fire gutted the main buildings. In place of the monastery the *Mezhyhiria Faience Factory was opened in 1798. The monastery was reopened in 1886; in 1908 it housed 14 monks and 23 novices. In the early 1920s the Soviet authorities confiscated its valuables and dispersed its monks, and established an artistic-ceramic technical school in its place. In the 1930s, under the pretext of 'development of the Mezhyhiria area,' the main buildings of the monastery were destroyed, and dachas for Communist party leaders were built in their place.

I. Korovytsky

Mezhyrich Monastery (15th–16th centuries)

Mezhyrich [Mežyrič] (aka Mezhyrichchia). A village (1973 pop 1,700) at the junction of the Zbytynky and the Viliia rivers in Ostrih raion, Rivne oblast. It is first mentioned in a historical document in 1396. In the 15th century the Ostrozky family built a fortified monastery and the Church of the Holy Trinity there. By 1605 the town had the rights of *Magdeburg law. In 1609 Prince K. Ostrozky's grandson granted the church and monastery to the Franciscan order. The church and the towers of the monastery have been preserved. Archeologists have discovered a settlement from the Bronze Age and a fortified settlement from the time of Kievan Rus' near the village.

MGB (Ministerstvo gosudarstvennoi bezopasnosti; Ukrainian: MDB, or Ministerstvo derzhavnoi bezpeky [Ministry of State Security]). A Soviet political police agency formed in February 1941 from parts of the *NKVD and known first as the People's Commissariat of State Security. It was reintegrated into the NKVD in July 1941 and separated from it again from April 1943 to March 1953. In March 1946 it was renamed the MGB. After being merged with the *MVD by L. Beria (March 1953 to March 1954) it was set up as a distinct agency under the name *KGB.

The separation of the state security service from the internal affairs ministry marked a return to earlier Soviet practice, when the *GPU and the *Cheka were distinct organizations. As a Union-republic institution, the MGB was subordinated to both the all-Union and the Ukrainian governments. This meant that in practice Moscow controlled state security in Ukraine. During the war the MGB organized civil defense, enforced the rationing system, rooted out spies, prevented soldiers from deserting, deported the Volga Germans and the Crimean Tatars, and gathered intelligence on anti-Soviet resistance movements in the Baltics and Western Ukraine. After the war its foreign department oversaw security in the Soviet puppet states in Eastern Europe, supervised Soviet trade missions and representatives abroad, and monitored the activities of Soviet émigrés. The operations department was responsible for all internal security and the espionage and antiespionage department took over most of the functions of the wartime Smersh. Its Secret Political Office kept watch over the entire civilian population, and special departments oversaw industrial establishments, universities, schools, and religious affairs. In Ukraine the operation department co-operated with the NKVD and the Soviet armed forces in destroying the Ukrainian partisan and nationalist movement after the war. Besides secret police units the MGB maintained large military forces and border troops in Ukraine. Specially trained MGB agents infiltrated the Ukrainian Insurgent Army and similar partisan outfits in Lithuania, Belarus, Latvia, and Estonia. The ministers for state security were V. Merkulov (February–July 1941, April 1943 to October 1946), V. Abakumov (October 1946 to the beginning of 1952), and S. Ignatiev (1952 to March 1953).

B. Balan, O. Yurchenko

Mglin (Ukrainian: Mhlyn). 0-13. A town (1962 pop 6,000) and raion center in Briansk oblast, RF. It is first mentioned in historical documents in the 14th century. Under the Hetman state the town was a company center in Starodub regiment. In 1802 it became a county center in Chernihiv gubernia.

Mhar Transfiguration Monastery (Mharskyi Spaso-Preobrazhenskyi monastyr). A men's monastery located in Mhar, a village on the Sula River near Lubni, in the Poltava region. It was founded by I. Kopynsky in 1619 with the financial support of Princess R. Vyshnevetska. Later it enjoyed the patronage of hetmans B. Khmelnytsky, I. Mazepa, and others and became one of the wealthiest monasteries in Left-Bank Ukraine. The monastery was also active in political affairs. In the 1720s to 1730s, Hegumen V. *Zahorovsky advocated the unification of Left- and Right-Bank Ukraine under one hetman and opposed Muscovite rule in Ukraine; for this he was arrested in 1733 and taken to Muscovy. In 1737–48 the hegumen was Y. *Horlenko. There is evidence that the monks of the monastery supported I. Mazepa's revolt against Russia.

The central Transfiguration Cathedral was designed by J. Baptist and built in 1682–94 with the assistance of M. Tomashevsky and A. Pyriatynsky. The design combined elements of the traditional Ukrainian cruciform three-nave shrine and the Western European basilica, and stands as one of the finest examples of the Ukrainian baroque. Its construction was funded by Hetmans I. Samoilovych and I. Mazepa. It was rebuilt and expanded in the mid-18th century, and two of the original seven cupolas were removed. A unique feature is its stucco decor. The monastery complex included the archimandrite's residence

Iconostasis of the Mhar Transfiguration Monastery cathedral (artist Sysoi Shalmatov, 1762–5)

(1786), the monks' cells (which have not survived), a baroque bell tower (completed in 1844), a hospice (second half of the 19th century), and the Annunciation Church (built in a pseudo-Byzantine style in 1804). St Athanasius Patellarius, a former Patriarch of Constantinople who died in Mhar, is buried in the monastery. In 1908 the Mhar monastery housed 61 monks and novices. It was closed down in 1926 by the Soviet authorities, and the building and grounds were made into a state architectural preserve. Restoration of the complex was begun in the 1980s.

Miakotin, Venedikt [Mjakotin], b 1867 in Gatchina, St Petersburg county, d 1937 in Prague. Russian historian and political activist. He graduated from St Petersburg University (1891), taught in Kiev (1891–1901), studied the social and economic history of the Hetmanate under the guidance of I. Luchytsky, and worked for the journal *Kievskaia starina*. In 1918, after returning to St Petersburg, he emigrated and became a professor at Sofia University in Bulgaria. His historical writings included *Ocherki sotsial'noi istorii Ukrainy v XVII–XVIII vv.* (Studies of the Social History of Ukraine during the 17th–18th Centuries, 3 vols, 1924–6).

Miaskowski, Wojciech (Miastkowski), b ?, d 1650. Polish administrator and diplomat. As chamberlain of Lviv (from 1637) he accompanied A. Kysil to Pereiaslav in February 1649 to conduct negotiations with Hetman B. Khmelnytsky. The diary he kept of the discussions is a valuable historical source for the period. It was first pub-

lished by J. Nemcewicz (1822), and then in *Zbiorek pamiętników o dawnej Polszcze* (Collection of Monuments of Ancient Poland, vol 4, 1839) and *Vossoedinenie Ukrainy s Rossiei: Dokumenty i materialy* (The Reunification of Ukraine with Russia: Documents and Materials, vol 2, 1954).

Miastkivsky, Andrii [M'jastkivs'kyj, Andrij], b 14 January 1924 in Sokolivka, now in Kryzhopil raion, Vinnytsia oblast. Poet, prose writer, and translator. He graduated from the Vinnytsia Pedagogical Institute (1962) and worked as a teacher and for various journals and publishing houses. Miastkivsky is the author of many collections of poetry, including *Nad Buhom-rikoiu* (By the River Buh, 1955), *Vid zemli* (From the Earth, 1957), *Taiemnytsia vohniu* (The Secret of Fire, 1976), *Ivaniv vohon'* (Ivan's Fire, 1983), and *Piznia raiduha* (The Late Rainbow, 1984), and he has written numerous books for children. Among his novels are *Vyrii* (South, 1965), *Khloptsi z Bubny* (The Boys from Bubna, 1967), and *Cherez vohon'* (Through the Fire, 1971). His plays include *Don'ka biloï berezy* (The Daughter of the White Birch, 1970) and *Benhal's'kyi kylym* (The Bengal Carpet, 1980). He has translated from Belarusian, Moldavian, Hebrew, and Rumanian.

Michał Korybut Wiśniowiecki (Vyshnevetsky, Mykhailo), b 31 July 1640, d 10 November 1673 in Lviv. King of Poland in 1669–73; son of J. *Wiśniowiecki. He was elected following the abdication of Jan II Casimir Vasa, and he faced considerable pressure to regain the Ukrainian territories lost by Poland in earlier struggles. For that reason he refused to consider Muscovite proposals to make the Treaty of *Andrusovo a lasting agreement. In 1672 he faced a joint Cossack-Turkish attack in Right-Bank Ukraine, which resulted in the further ceding of Ukrainian territory under Polish control by the terms of the (never-ratified) *Buchach Peace Treaty. He was succeeded by his rival, Jan III Sobieski. Wiśniowiecki's biography, by N. Baumgarten, was published in *Orientalia Christiana Periodica* (1935, no. 1).

Michalon Lithuanus (Mykhailo Lytvyn), b and d ? Lithuanian diplomat and memoirist. As an emissary to the Crimea in 1548–55, he compiled a somewhat impressionistic diary of the region and the traditions of its Tatar inhabitants, as well as an effusive account of the abundant natural resources in the Kiev region. They were first published in Basel as *De moribus Tartarorum, Lithuanorum, et Moschorum ...* (1615). They were reprinted in Russian translation in Kiev as *Memuary, otnosiashchiesia k istorii Iuzhnoi Rusi* (Memoirs Relating to the History of Southern Rus', 1890).

Michalovce (Ukrainian: Mykhailivtsi). A district center in Czechoslovakia (1970 pop 29,200), situated in the Eastern Slovak Lowland on the Laborets River. It is the former administrative and trading center of the Ruthenians in Zemplén komitat. Until the late 19th century Michalovce was largely an agricultural town owned by Hungarian and German landowners. In 1876 it became a circle center, and in 1919, a *zhupa* center. Its Orthodox inhabitants (Greek Catholic after 1646) belonged to Mukachiv eparchy. From 1951 the town was the seat of one of the four Orthodox eparchies in Czechoslovakia. The Church of the

Holy Trinity was built by V. Sichynsky in 1933–4, and served as the monastery church of the Redemptorist order until 1949. Most of the Ukrainian population has been Slovakized.

St Mary the Protectress Ukrainian Orthodox Church in Southfield, Michigan

Michigan. A north central state (1990 pop 9,328,784) of the United States, with an area of 251,000 sq km. About 44,000 Ukrainians live in the state (1990), most of them in metropolitan *Detroit, and smaller numbers in Grand Rapids, Flint, Saginaw, Lansing, and Muskegon. The first Ukrainian family settled in Detroit in 1895. The community grew rapidly as jobs in the automobile factories attracted new immigrants. By the mid-1930s there were about 25,000 Ukrainians in Detroit proper, 10,000 in Hamtramck, and 2,000 in Dearborn. In 1939 about 50 Ukrainian organizations in the area formed an umbrella body, the Federation of American Ukrainians in Michigan, which co-ordinated cultural and civic activities and represented Ukrainians in the larger community. During the war it helped raise funds for the American Red Cross and sold war savings bonds. To help Ukrainian refugees it set up the Ukrainian War Relief Committee (1944), which soon merged with the United Ukrainian American Relief Committee. The federation was also one of the founders of the Ukrainian Congress Committee of America. Courses in Ukrainian language and literature are offered at the University of Michigan and Wayne State University, and the University of Michigan developed into a center for graduate studies in Ukrainian history and literature.

Mickiewicz, Adam, b 24 December 1798 in Zavosse, Belarus, d 26 November 1855 in Constantinople. Polish poet. In 1823 he was implicated in the trial of an underground students' society in Vilnius and was exiled to St Petersburg (1824) and then Odessa (1825), whence he made brief trips to the Crimea. He traveled to Moscow in 1826 and there met P. Hulak-Artemovsky and M. Maksymovych. Mickiewicz's major works include *Ballady i romanse* (Ballads and Romances, 1822), *Grażyna* (1823), *Dziady* (The Old Men, 1822–3), *Konrad Wallenrod* (1828), *Księgi narodu polskiego i pielgrzymstwa polskiego* (Books of the Polish People and of the Polish Pilgrimage, 1832–3), and *Pan Tadeusz*

(Master Tadeusz, 1834). His works had a marked influence on Ukrainian literature of the 19th century, particularly on T. Shevchenko. His *Księgi* influenced the Cyril and Methodius Brotherhood (see *Knyhy bytiia ukraïns'koho narodu*). His works have been translated into Ukrainian by L. Borovykovsky, P. Kulish, M. Starytsky, I. Franko, Lesia Ukrainka, P. Tychyna, M. Bazhan, A. Malyshko, M. Lukash, and M. Rylsky and are included in *A. Mitskievich. Vybrani tvory* (A. Mickiewicz: Selected Works, 2 vols 1955).

I. Koshelivet

Mickiewicz, Mieczysław, b 1879 in Kamianets-Podilskyi, Podilia gubernia, d ? Polish political leader. He practiced law in Kiev. Under the Central Rada he served as undersecretary of Polish affairs in the General Secretariat (1917) and, at the beginning of 1918, as minister of Polish affairs in V. Vynnychenko's cabinet.

Microbiological industry. A branch of industry that uses microbiological synthesis to produce various items from a wide variety of raw materials and agricultural byproducts. The industry has emerged in recent years and is based on progress made in chemistry, biology, physics, and other sciences. Most of its products, such as animal antibiotics, feed supplements, vitamins, and protein supplements, are used in agriculture. Microbiologically derived substances are used extensively in food preservation and the manufacture of fertilizers, pesticides, and fungicides. Some products have applications in industry (in making molds for brewing, flavorings, extracts, dyes, etc) and in the making of medicinal products.

From 1966 the entire Soviet microbiological industry was under the control of a single body, the Chief Administration of Microbiology of the USSR Council of Ministers. In general the industry is not as developed as it is in Western Europe or North America. In Ukraine there were nine factories of the microbiological industry in 1980. They supplied some 30 percent of all feed antibiotics, 20 percent of all feed supplements, and 35 percent of all fermenting agents produced in the USSR. The largest factories are in Ladyzhyn, Vinnytsia oblast, and Nemishaieve, Kiev oblast. Aspects of the microbiological industry are studied at the ANURSR (now ANU) Institute of Microbiology and Virology and at scientific research institutes of the alcohol, meat, dairy, and food industries.

Microbiology. See Biology.

Middle Beskyd. That part of the *Beskyds lying between the Sian River in the west and Turka and Boryslav in the east and between the Low Beskyd in the northwest and the High Beskyd in the southeast. It has an area of approx 2,800 sq km and is one of the lower and more gently undulating parts of the Carpathians. It rises approx 200–300 m (rarely 400 m) above the surrounding Subcarpathian region. It has a lattice structure, with longitudinal sandstone ridges separated by parallel valleys and depressions carved out of soft schists and clays. The ridges reach elevations of over 1,000 m and are intersected by the Stryvihor, the Dniester, and the Stryi river valleys.

The Middle Beskyd is largely denuded, forests covering only 33 percent of the territory (47 percent is under cultivation, and 16 percent is hayfields and pastures). Before

Middle Beskyd: the Slavske tourist area

1940 it was one of the most settled parts of the Carpathians, with a population density of 80 people per sq km. Most of the inhabitants were *Boikos engaged in agriculture (rye, potatoes, and oats), animal husbandry (mostly sheep raising), forestry, or, in the vicinity of Boryslav, the petroleum industry. Towns and cities in the Middle Beskyd include Peremyshl, Nyzhankovychi, Dobromyl, Khyriv, Staryi Sambir, and Boryslav (on the edges of the Carpathians), and Turka and Ustryky Dolishni (in the mountains). Since 1945 the western part of the Middle Beskyd has been under Polish rule, and in the immediate postwar period the Ukrainian population was forcibly resettled during *Operation Wisła. In recent years, however, some Ukrainians have returned to their former homes.

V. Kubijovyč

Middle-Dnieper culture. A Bronze Age archeological culture of the late 3rd to mid-2nd millennium BC found along the tributaries of the middle and upper Dnieper and the Desna Rivers. It was first identified by V. Gorodtsov in the 1920s. An offshoot of the Corded Ware cultures in Western Ukraine and other parts of Europe, its trademark was pottery with imprints of rope or small etched lines forming horizontal layers of ornamentation. On the basis of changes in pottery style, scholars have divided the culture into early (24th–22nd century BC), middle (22nd–17th century BC), and late (17th–15th century BC) periods of development. Its major economic activities were agriculture and animal husbandry, although it also traded with tribes in the northern Caucasus, the Carpatho-Danube region, and the Baltic region. Houses consisted of surface dwellings with stone hearths. The culture practiced both full body and cremation burials in either dugout graves or kurhans. Material culture remains found at excavation sites included stone querns, flint chisels, arrowheads, copper and amber adornments, stone and bronze tools, and (corded-ware) pottery made from clay with an admixture of fine sand. Notable Middle Dnieper archeological sites

include Iskivshchyna (near Kaniv), *Pekari, and *Mys Ochkynskyi.

Middle-Transcarpathian dialects. See Transcarpathian dialects.

Midwifery. See Obstetrics.

Mieshkovsky, Yevhen. See Myshkivsky, Yevhen.

Migrant workers. Workers who take part in seasonal *migration, usually for a period of from one month to half a year, in search of work elsewhere. Unlike migrant workers in other countries, those in the USSR could seek work only in other oblasts and Soviet republics and were not allowed to leave the USSR.

In Russian-ruled Ukraine prior to 1914, seasonal migration for purposes of work was widespread. Because of agrarian overpopulation peasants from the Right-Bank gubernias headed to the fertile regions of Southern Ukraine and northern Caucasia during the harvest and haymaking seasons. During the winter months masses of idle peasants throughout Ukraine moved to the city to earn money until the spring. The Donbas attracted seasonal migrant workers not only from Ukraine but also from other parts of the Russian Empire. After the abolition of serfdom in 1861, particularly during the period of intensive industrial development in the late 19th and early 20th centuries, the number of migrant workers increased rapidly. During the 1880s in the Russian Empire, an average of 5 million temporary internal passports were issued to peasants each year. In the 1890s, 7.2 million were issued, 1.2 million of them in Ukraine. From 1906 to 1910, 9.4 million passports were issued, 2 million of them in Ukraine (approx 1 million for work in agriculture and 1 million for work in industry). In that period seasonal work involved about 10 percent of Ukraine's total population and 20–25 percent of the working population. In regions of high rural overpopulation (the northern and western gubernias) the proportion of the working population was as high as 40–50 percent.

Migrant workers constituted about 80 percent of all those engaged in agricultural labor in Ukraine in the 1880s. After the introduction of farm machinery into Southern Ukraine and the increase in its population, seasonal migration there decreased. By the 1900s the share of seasonal workers in Ukraine's total agricultural labor force had declined to 70 percent. At that time about 20 percent of migrant workers were women, and over half were young people under the age of 20. The proportion of women and young people in the seasonal work force continued to rise. Approximately one-fifth of the migrant workers in Ukraine came from Russia and Belarus. The overall number of migrants changed markedly from year to year, according to the size of the harvest and the corresponding demand for labor. The principal employers were gentry landowners and, to a lesser degree, rich peasants and German colonists.

The migrants made their way to their place of work on foot or sailed down the Dnieper on ships; they rarely used the railroad. They set out in April or May in order to arrive at their destination before the beginning of the harvest season. The main centers for hiring laborers were Kakhivka, Odessa, Mykolaiv, Katerynoslav (now Dnipropetrovske), Znamianka, Shpola, and Kherson, where workers gathered in the tens of thousands. The search for work required a great deal of effort, because the hiring system was badly organized. Only a minority were able to obtain work contracts in advance. The salary was only 40 to 110 rubles a season in agriculture and even less in industry. By the end of the 19th century, nonagricultural workers accounted for half of all seasonal migration. In 1900, for example, of 147,900 migrants from Kiev gubernia, 66,700 found employment as agricultural laborers, 49,500 in large and small factories, and 52,700 as domestic servants. In 1913, of 210,800 migrants from that gubernia, 71,900 found work in agriculture, 63,800 in factories, and 73,000 as servants.

The *Stolypin agrarian reforms dealt a significant blow to seasonal work. Peasants received the right to leave the commune and sell the land they owned. It was therefore no longer necessary for them to return from temporary work in the city to the village, and many chose to live in urban centers on a permanent basis. In addition, after colonization of the virgin lands in the Russian Far East, southern Siberia, Kazakhstan, and Central Asia intensified, seasonal migration began to be displaced by *emigration.

In Western Ukraine under Austria-Hungary, seasonal migration took place on a smaller scale. In the summer migrants sought agricultural work in Podilia, Transcarpathia, and the Hungarian lowlands, and in both the winter and the summer they took jobs in the lumber industry in the Carpathian Mountains. That industry provided approx 100,000 logging jobs in a given season; most of the labor came from the neighboring regions. A significant number of Ukrainian peasants from Galicia and Bukovyna (in 1907–12 approx 75,000 annually) sought agricultural employment in Germany (chiefly in Prussia), Bohemia, Moravia, and Denmark and in the sugar refineries of Russian-ruled Podilia. In the period between the two world wars seasonal migration declined. Only the Carpathian lumber industry continued hiring significant numbers of Western Ukrainian migrant workers.

There were also itinerant occupations in Ukraine, for the most part those of traveling merchants and tradesmen. Those travelers returned home only for important holidays, to rest, or to take part in agricultural work (if they were also peasants). Often they established their own professional organizations, shared work among themselves, and lived communally. The best-known and largest group of such migrants in central Ukraine were the *chumaks. In Western Ukraine itinerant occupations were widespread in the Carpathian Lemko (pot menders), Boiko (fruit vendors), and Hutsul (building trades) regions. Traveling precentors and barbers were also common. With the development of modern transportation and industry in the second half of the 19th century, the role of traveling merchants greatly diminished.

After the Revolution of 1917 land was distributed equally, and the gentry and rich peasants disappeared. Consequently, seasonal employment in agriculture was sharply curtailed. Calculations based on the 1927 Soviet agricultural census show that only 1 percent of those working in the field were hired workers. The Soviet government tried to protect the rights of seasonal laborers by forcing their employers to conclude special contracts with each of them and, more important, by classifying employ-

ers as 'exploiters of labor.' As political pressure on the more prosperous villagers increased, the number of migrant workers in agriculture diminished. By 1929 they had virtually disappeared. Seasonal work in industry, however, continued to be widespread. The abolition of internal passport regulations restricting freedom of movement and the peasants' need for cash under the conditions of the *New Economic Policy favored the development of seasonal work in the 1920s. In the mid-1920s in Kozelets county, Chernihiv gubernia, for example, 85 per cent of peasant households had a family member working in industry for at least half the year. Peasants found employment usually in light industry, especially food and raw-material processing

*Collectivization gave rise to a complete re-examination of the concept of seasonal work. Peasants seeking employment were required to obtain permission from their collective-farm chairmen and a certificate from the rural soviet. Spontaneous seasonal migration was replaced by organized selection and control. In 1933 the USSR People's Commissariat of Labor issued a series of regulations on seasonal labor that limited it to a period of not longer than six months except in forestry, where the term was eight months.

In the postwar period migrant workers were hired through the official *organized recruitment of labor. The largest number of seasonal workers were employed by state farms (eg, 160,000 in 1970). Many other seasonal workers were employed in construction, peat extraction, and various branches of the forest industry. In the second half of the 1950s hundreds of thousands of young people were recruited to work in the virgin lands of Kazakhstan and on major industrial projects in the RSFSR.

Seasonal migrant workers continue to play a significant role in Ukraine's economy. In the past, however, it was the peasants who traveled from region to region seeking work. Now urban dwellers make up a significant proportion of migrant workers. As before, the main cause of seasonal migration is the shortage of agricultural labor. In 1986, for example, collective and state farms in the USSR hired 1.4 million seasonal workers. In addition employees of enterprises tied to a particular collective farm (under the system of sponsorship or sheftstvo) participated in the harvesting of potatoes and beets and in other fieldwork. In 1986 every factory worker and white-collar employee in Ukraine performed one day of agricultural labor, and every employee of a research institute, two days. Postsecondary students have regularly assisted with the harvest and have been members of construction crews in various rural locales. In 1986 there were 2,823 such crews, with a total of 89,600 people. Aside from the organized dispatching of urban residents to the countryside, work not sanctioned by the government has also been performed by people in search of additional income. By working during the harvest or on construction projects, they have earned considerable sums of money. Such migrant workers have been popularly called shabashnyky (literally 'Sabbath violators'), and the attitude toward them of the local population and the supervisors has not always been positive.

Considerable seasonal migration has taken place within the rural population during the harvest period. When the migrant workers finished the harvest in northwestern Ukraine, they moved to the south and west and ultimately made their way to somewhere in the Altai region of

MIGRATION **401**

Central Asia or Kazakhstan. A large number of migrant workers also worked for traveling geological expeditions, in railroad and highway maintenance and construction projects, and in resorts throughout the USSR. Several hundred thousand people have continued working in the Carpathian lumber industry during the winter months.

Most of Ukraine's migrant workers have come from the southwestern oblasts, where almost 45 percent of the population is concentrated, but where industry is comparatively poorly developed, and where there is a shortage of good agricultural land. Contemporary researchers have noted that seasonal migration is usually a preparatory stage to permanent relocation. Overall, such migration has been declining in Ukraine.

BIBLIOGRAPHY

Shakhovskii, M. *Zemledel'cheskii otkhod krest'ian* (St Petersburg 1903)

Luhova, O. *Sil'skohospodars'kyi proletariat pivdnia Ukraïny v period kapitalizmu* (Kiev 1965)

Regional'nye problemy naseleniia i trudovye resursy SSSR (Moscow 1974)

A. Babyonyshev, V. Kubijovyč

Migration. Permanent or temporary (including seasonal, weekly, and daily) intercontinental, international, or internal change of residence for economic, political, or ecological reasons. Migration has long been part of Ukraine's history. For centuries population groups migrated into previously unsettled territories there. The steppes of *Southern Ukraine were gradually colonized by settlers from the east and north. In the late 19th and early 20th centuries began the mass emigration of Ukrainians living in Russian-ruled Ukraine to other parts of the Russian Empire. A chain of Ukrainian villages stretched across ethnic Russia's Voronezh, Saratov, and Samara gubernias, crossed the Urals, and followed the Trans-Siberian Railway to the shores of the Pacific Ocean. In the years 1896–1914, 1.6 million Ukrainians resettled permanently in regions of the empire east of the Urals. The largest numbers were from Poltava (23 percent) and Chernihiv (17 percent) gubernias, followed by Kiev (12 percent), Kharkiv and Katerynoslav (11 percent), Kherson (9 percent), Tavriia (7 percent), Podilia (4.5 percent), and Volhynia (4 percent) gubernias.

In the late 19th century, mass emigration also began from Western Ukraine under Austria-Hungary. In the years 1895–1913, 413,000 Western Ukrainians emigrated to the New World. The exodus continued in the interwar period and peaked in 1927–9 before diminishing because of the Great Depression.

Under Soviet rule the forced collectivization of the Ukrainian peasantry in 1929–30 was accompanied by the mass deportation and resettlement of so-called *kulak families (approx 1 million people) to Soviet Asia. The enormous population losses caused by the man-made *famine of 1932–3 halted the growth of Soviet Ukraine's cities, exhausted the peasantry's demographic potential, and resulted in a significant decline in the migration of Soviet Ukrainians. During the Stalinist *terror of the late 1930s another wave of mass deportations of Ukrainians occurred.

Mass deportations and population losses and transfers also took place during the Second World War. The evacuation from Ukraine to Soviet Asia alone encompassed 1.9 million people, 1.8 million of them from central and eastern Ukraine. The largest numbers of evacuees (a total of 71 percent) were from Kiev (301,900), Kharkiv (270,100), Dnipropetrovske (209,900), Staline (now Donetske, 182,700), Odessa (182,700), Zaporizhia (122,200), and Luhanske (106,300) oblasts. Between 1941 and 1946 the population of Ukraine's eastern oblasts declined by 19.4 percent, and that of its western oblasts (Lviv, Drohobych, Stanyslaviv [now Ivano-Frankivske], Volhynia, Rivne, and Ternopil) declined by 29 percent. The larger losses of Western Ukraine, from which only 114,700 people were evacuated by the Soviet regime during the German invasion, were the result of longer Nazi occupation and terror, during which the Jewish population was almost totally annihilated; the deportation to Siberia and Soviet Asia of nearly 1 million 'nationalist' Ukrainians and Poles; and the immediate postwar transfer of most of the region's Polish inhabitants to Poland.

In the postwar period migration from and into Ukraine was primarily 'internal,' that is, from and into the other Soviet republics. The principal partner in Ukraine's migration relations was the RSFSR, which supplied more immigrants than Ukraine did out-migrants. Since 1986, however, the number of permanent emigrants from Ukraine, primarily to Israel, Germany, the United States, Canada, and Greece, has grown considerably. In 1987–9 alone 74,400 inhabitants of Ukraine emigrated from the USSR.

From 1945 the migration of Ukrainians from Ukraine to other parts of the USSR significantly influenced Ukraine's population development. In the years 1961–89 Ukraine's urban population increased by 7.6 million people and the rural population decreased by 6.6 million (see table 1). In those years the principal source of formation of the urban population was migration, which accounted for 50 percent of the increase, and more during certain five-year periods. In 1988, 73.2 percent of the increase in Ukraine's urban population resulted from intrarepublican migration. Of that increase, 55.1 percent resulted from intraoblast migration from rural to urban areas, and 18.1 percent resulted from interoblast migration. An additional 8 percent increase in Ukraine's urban population resulted from administrative-territorial changes that turned suburban regions into urban centers (see table 2).

Migration processes have played a determining role in the decline of Ukraine's rural population. In the 1960s and 1970s the natural increase in Ukraine's rural population partly compensated for rural out-migration. But since 1979 – a watershed year in the demographic development of the Ukrainian countryside – rural depopulation has been nationwide and has thereby aggravated the detrimental effect of rural out-migration. The average annual out-migration of Ukraine's rural inhabitants increased from 0.5 percent in 1959–69 to 1.2 percent in the 1970s and 1980s. The general decline in Ukraine's rural population in 1979–88 was 2.1 million people, of which 82.8 percent is attributable to out-migration. Since the mid-1980s, however, because of the exhaustion of Ukraine's human resources, the shortage of urban housing, and growing economic and social crises, there has been a discernible trend toward reduced levels of rural out-migration to the cities.

In-migration into rural areas in Ukraine has also become a widespread phenomenon. In recent decades more

TABLE 1
Population growth/loss in Ukraine, 1961–89 (thousands and percentages)

	1961–89	1961–5	1966–70	1971–5	1976–80	1981–5
Thousands						
Total growth/loss						
General	9,126.6	2,451.0	1,959.0	1,644.0	984.0	859.0
Natural	8,180.4	2,277.9	1,602.3	1,414.7	1,014.6	892.3
Through migration	946.2	173.1	356.7	229.3	–30.6	–33.3
Urban growth						
General	15,156.6	2,711.0	2,886.0	2,869.0	2,310.0	2,266.6
Natural	6,366.3	1,187.2	1,002.7	1,112.1	994.8	976.5
Through migration	7,569.5	1,173.3	1,617.3	1,531.7	1,160.9	1,199.9
Through administrative-territorial changes	1,220.8	350.5	266.0	225.2	154.3	90.2
Rural growth/loss						
General	–6,030.0	–260.0	–927.0	–1,225.0	–1,326.0	–1,407.6
Natural	1,814.1	1,090.7	599.6	302.6	19.8	–84.2
Through migration	–6,623.3	–1,000.2	–1,260.6	–1,302.4	–1,191.5	–1,233.2
Through administrative-territorial changes	–1,220.8	–350.5	–266.0	–225.2	–154.3	–90.2
Percentages						
Total growth/loss						
General	100.0	100.0	100.0	100.0	100.0	100.0
Natural	89.6	92.9	81.8	86.0	103.1	103.9
Through migration	10.4	7.1	18.2	14.0	–3.1	–3.9
Urban growth						
General	100.0	100.0	100.0	100.0	100.0	100.0
Natural	42.0	43.8	34.8	38.8	43.1	43.1
Through migration	50.0	43.3	56.0	53.4	50.2	52.9
Through administrative-territorial changes	8.0	12.9	9.2	7.8	6.7	4.0
Rural growth/loss						
General	–100.0	–100.0	–100.0	–100.0	–100.0	–100.0
Natural	30.0	419.5	64.7	24.7	1.5	–6.0
Through migration	–109.8	–384.7	–136.0	–106.3	–89.9	–87.6
Through administrative-territorial changes	–20.2	–134.8	–28.7	–18.4	–11.6	–6.4

people have migrated into rural areas than into urban centers. Of the total number of rural in-migrants in 1985, 42.3 percent had lived in rural areas for less than 10 years, and 27.7 percent had lived there for more than 25 years. For urban in-migrants, the corresponding figures were 34.8 percent and 30.6 percent (see table 3). Reflected in the disparity are the greater tendency of rural out-migrants to remain in urban centers, the growing migrational mobility within the rural population, and the relative 'youthfulness' of migration processes within rural areas.

Impact on national composition. The growth of Ukraine's urban population has occurred primarily through the in-migration of Ukrainian peasants (67.6 percent). The in-migration of *Russians has also been substantial, however; it has constituted 25.4 percent of the mechanical increase in the urban population. The in-migration of other non-Ukrainians has been insignificant (a total of approx 7 percent) and consists mostly of Belarusians (1.4 percent), Moldavians (1 percent), and Tatars (1.8 percent). Longtime Ukrainian-Russian migration relations have had a substantial impact on Ukraine's national composition. According to the 1989 Soviet census there were 11.4 million Russians, constituting 22.1 percent of the population. In the decade 1979–89 nearly a quarter of the Jews living in Ukraine emigrated. Nonetheless, in 1989 they still constituted the third-largest ethnic group –

486,000, or 0.9 percent of the population. Besides Russians and Jews 110 other ethnic minorities live in Ukraine, where in 1989 they constituted a total of 4.3 percent of the population. Of them the Hungarians, Gagauzy, Greeks, Moldavians, Rumanians, and Bulgarians live compactly. The population of Ukraine's Poles declined in 1979–89 by 15 percent; of Czechs, by 14 percent; of Slovaks, by 9 percent; of Greeks, by 5 percent; of Bulgarians, by 2 percent; and of Hungarians, by 1 percent.

In November 1989, after the Soviet government declared the forced deportation of peoples by the Stalinist regime to have been illegal and criminal in nature and guaranteed the rights of those peoples, the Crimean Tatars, who had been deported to Soviet Asia in May 1944, began returning en masse to their homeland in the Crimea. By 1991 approx 100,000 Crimean Tatars had resettled there.

In 1989 nearly 6.8 million Ukrainians – 15.3 percent of all Ukrainians in the USSR – were living in the USSR outside Ukraine: 4.4 million (9.9 percent) in the RSFSR, 897,000 (2 percent) in Kazakhstan, 600,000 (1.4 percent) in Moldavia, 291,000 (0.7 percent) in Belorussia, 153,000 (0.4 percent) in Uzbekistan, 108,000 (0.2 percent) in Kirgizia, 92,000 (0.2 percent) in Latvia, 52,000 (0.1 percent) in Georgia, 48,000 (0.1 percent) in Estonia, 45,000 (0.1 percent) in Lithuania, 41,000 (0.09 percent) in Tadzhikistan, 36,000 (0.08 percent)

TABLE 2
Population growth/loss in Ukraine, 1979–88 (thousands)

Oblast	General	Natural	Through migration	Through administrative territorial changes
Cherkasy	−15	2	−17	
Chernihiv	−86	−16	−70	
Chernivtsi	48	58	−10	
Crimea	275	143	132	
Dnipropetrovske	242	142	100	
Donetske	171	159	12	
Ivano-Frankivske	91	99	−8	
Kharkiv	139	57	82	
Kherson	77	70	6	1
Khmelnytskyi	−31	25	−56	
Kiev (excluding city of Kiev)	16	50	−11	−23
Kiev (city only)	459	171	265	23
Kirovohrad	−12	4	−16	
Lviv	164	156	8	
Mykolaiv	88	60	29	−1
Odessa	99	74	25	
Poltava	12	−3	15	
Rivne	49	95	−46	
Sumy	−30	−1	−29	
Ternopil	6	39	−33	
Transcarpathia	98	114	−16	
Vinnytsia	−113	3	−116	
Volhynia	45	72	−27	
Voroshylovhrad	76	98	−22	
Zaporizhia	136	78	58	
Zhytomyr	−52	46	−98	
Total	1,952	1,795	157	

resettlement in other regions of Ukraine were only the first stage of the 'ecological' migration from an imperiled region. Because of Chornobyl, plans were made to resettle 14,800 families in 1991 from several other raions in Kiev, Zhytomyr, and Rivne oblasts. It is likely that environmental degradation in other parts of Ukraine, particularly in Zaporizhia, Dnipropetrovske, Dniprodzerzhynske, Kryvyi Rih, Chernivtsi, and other over-polluted cities and surrounding raions, will make migration imperative in the future.

Migration and marginalization. One of the significant consequences of migration processes in Ukraine has been social marginalization. In the years 1960–90 half, and in certain subperiods over half, of urban population growth in Ukraine is attributable to in-migration. In that period 9 out of 10 new urban residents were children of peasants. It is they who have defined the specificity of existing urban social relations. Social marginalization has resulted from the interaction, or lack thereof, between recent in-migrants and established urban dwellers. A distance is constantly maintained between them and is manifested by their different social status and their divergent aspirations, abilities, and potential for realizing their goals. The inequality between the two social groups has frequently resulted in tension and conflict. The pattern is repeated with every new in-migration.

Adaptation by new residents in Ukraine's cities was average for the USSR as a whole and reached 150 per 1,000 new arrivals in 1988. As a rule most in-migrants are young. Pensioners constitute only 6.3 percent of them and 5.8 percent of those who leave the cities. In the urban population in 1988, in-migrants represented 30 per 1,000 persons younger than 16, 51 per 1,000 persons of official working age (women 16 to 54 and men 16 to 59), and 15 per 1,000 officially retired persons (women 55 and older and men 60 and older). The corresponding figures for out-migrants from cities in the three age-groups were 20, 43, and 11 per 1,000. Urban growth through in-migration is thus realized primarily because of young and working-age people. Ukraine's urban population is characterized by a relatively high migration turnover of well-educated people (postsecondary and special-secondary students from other places living in cities only for the duration of their studies and those leaving for employment elsewhere after graduation) and those called up for military service.

in Turkmenistan, 32,000 (0.07 percent) in Azerbaidzhan, and 8,000 (0.02 percent) in Armenia.

Ecological factors. Soviet industrial and agricultural policies have resulted in the *pollution and degradation of Ukraine's natural environment. The degradation culminated in the 1986 accident at the Chornobyl Atomic Energy Station, which has had obvious, if not conclusive, negative effects on the population. The evacuation of the inhabitants in the 30-km zone around Chornobyl and their

TABLE 3
Population of Ukraine changing their place of permanent residence (percentages)*

	Duration of stay in last place of residence						
	Less than 2 yr	2–5 yr	6–9 yr	10–14 yr	15–19 yr	20–4 yr	25+ yr
Total population	10.0	15.3	11.2	13.3	10.3	10.0	29.9
Males	10.5	15.9	11.7	13.7	10.5	10.3	27.4
Females	9.7	14.8	10.9	12.9	10.2	9.8	31.7
Urban population	9.3	14.5	11.0	13.5	10.7	10.4	30.6
Males	9.5	14.8	11.4	13.9	10.9	10.9	28.6
Females	9.3	14.2	10.7	13.2	10.5	10.1	32.0
Rural population	12.3	17.9	12.1	12.5	9.0	8.5	27.7
Males	13.9	19.6	12.8	12.9	9.1	8.1	23.6
Females	11.1	16.7	11.6	12.1	8.9	8.8	30.8

*Based on a selected demographic study of people who have moved since birth, conducted in 1985

Of the in-migrants contributing to urban population growth, 55.3 percent have obtained general secondary education diplomas, 21.4 percent have incomplete secondary educations, and 8.3 percent have only primary educations. Ukraine's cities have a great need for skilled workers. Lack of such workers is one of the economic reasons for the influx of unskilled and semiskilled labor into the cities.

(See also *Displaced persons, *Emigration, *Immigration, *Migrant workers, *National composition, *Organized recruitment of workers, *Peasants, *Population, *Repatriation, *Resettlement, *Social mobility, and *Urbanization.)

BIBLIOGRAPHY

Tovkun, V. 'Mihratsiini protsesy i zv'iazky Ukraïns'koï RSR z soiuznymy respublikamy,' in *Ukraïns'kyi istoryko-heohrafichnyi zbirnyk*, 2 (Kiev 1972)

Zahrobs'ka, A. *Orhanizovani pereselennia v systemi mihratsii naselennia URSR* (Kiev 1974)

Chinn, J. *Manipulating Soviet Population Resources* (London and Basingstoke 1977)

Chumachenko, N. (ed). *Naselenie i trudovye resursy Donbassa* (Kiev 1977)

Kubiiovych, V. 'Migratsiini protsesy v Ukraïns'kii SSR za perepysom 1970 roku,' in *Zbirnyk na poshanu prof. d-ra Oleksanda Ohloblyna*, ed V. Omel'chenko (New York 1977)

Zhuchenko, V. (ed). *Demograficheskoe razvitie Ukrainskoi SSR (1959–1970 gg.)* (Kiev 1977)

Lewis, R.; Rowland, R. *Population Redistribution in the USSR: It's* [sic] *Impact on Society, 1897–1977* (New York 1979)

Taborisskaia, I. *Maiatnikovaia migratsiia naseleniia* (Moscow 1979)

Grandstaff, P. *Interregional Migration in the USSR: Economic Aspects, 1959–1970* (Durham, NC 1980)

Krawchenko, B. *Social Change and National Consciousness in Twentieth-Century Ukraine* (London 1985; Edmonton 1987)

Steshenko, V. (ed). *Demograficheskoe razvitie Ukrainskoi SSR (1970–1979 gg.)* (Kiev 1987)

Buhai, M. 'Deportatsiï naselennia z Ukraïny (30–50-i roky),' *UIZh*, 1990, nos 10–11

Perkovskii, A.; Pirozhkov, S. 'Iz istorii demograficheskogo razvitiia 30–40-kh godov (na primere Ukrainskoi SSR),' *Ekonomika. Demografiia. Statistika* (Moscow 1990)

S. Pirozhkov, I. Pribytkova

Migratory birds (Ukrainian: *pereletni ptytsi*). Migration is a part of the life cycle of some birds. It is an annual phenomenon involving whole populations of birds in long-range displacements from their breeding grounds to wintering sites and back. Migration depends on a complex internal rhythm affecting the whole organism, particularly the endocrine glands. The geographical position of Ukraine and its climatic variations support several patterns of migratory behavior among the more than 150 species of migrating birds found there: seasonal translocation, overflights, mixed sedentary/migratory movements, and vertical movements. Most birds fly south or southwest for the winter, but some prefer eastern directions (finch, willow *warbler). Massive seasonal translocation is typical for *swallows, *storks, geese, glareoles, *sandpipers, *nightingales, and other birds. The birds arrive in April or May and depart in September or October. Hawks, *owls, ducks, Palla's sangrouse, Bohemian *waxwings, and willow ptarmigans arrive from the northern regions to winter in Ukraine. Stifftails (Ukrainian: *savky*), *swans, some golden-eye ducks, and eiders can be seen only in overflights to other areas. Redstarts and rock ptar-

migans move from higher mountain elevations to warmer valleys. Pointed snipes, stone curlews, water *rails, and plovers migrate south from moderate and cold climates but are sedentary in warmer southern Ukraine. Many water birds remain in their breeding areas as long as the lakes and rivers stay ice-free.

I. Masnyk

Mii pryiatel' (My Friend). A monthly illustrated children's magazine published in Winnipeg since 1949 by the Ukrainian Catholic church and edited by Rev S. Izhyk. Since 1968 it has appeared as a supplement to *Postup*.

Volodymyr Miiakovsky (portrait by Liuboslav Hutsaliuk)

Miiakovsky, Volodymyr [Mijakovs'kyj] (pseuds: V. Porsky, B. Stokhid, V. Svitlytsky, V. Varlamov, B. Yanivsky), b 18 July 1888 in Kovel, Volhynia gubernia, d 22 March 1972 in New York City. Literary scholar, historian, and archivist; full member of the Shevchenko Scientific Society from 1947 and the Ukrainian Academy of Arts and Sciences (UVAN) from 1948. He studied at Kiev (1906–7) and St Petersburg (1907–11, 1912–13) universities and then taught in gymnasiums in St Petersburg and did research in the state archive there. After the Revolution of 1917 he collected documents pertaining to Ukrainian studies in the archives of the tsarist censorship administration and published them in the Kievan journal *Nashe mynule*. Miiakovsky moved to Kiev in December 1917 and worked as chief cataloger in the archives and libraries division of the Ministry of Education. He succeeded V. Modzalevsky as director of archival administration and the Kiev Central Historical Archive in 1920. In the 1920s he was a member of the VUAN Commission for the Publication of Monuments of Modern Literature (headed by S. Yefremov), the Kiev branch of the Taras Shevchenko Scientific Research Institute, and the VUAN Archeographic and Archeological commissions. He was also an associate of the Ukrainian Scientific Institute of Bibliology, and from 1926 he administered the Shevchenko House and Museum in Kiev. Miiakovsky contributed to *Nashe mynule, Knyhar, Literaturno-naukovyi vistnyk, Ukraïna, Bibliolohichni visti, Za sto lit, Chervonyi shliakh, Zhyttia i revoliutsiia*, and other journals in the 1920s.

In 1929 Miiakovsky was arrested and sentenced in one of the show trials of the *Union for the Liberation of Ukraine to five years in a labor camp in Karelia, where he worked as a statistician. From 1934 to 1941 he worked in various medical research institutions in Kiev. During the wartime German occupation he attempted to renew the work of the Kiev Central Historical Archive. A postwar refugee in Germany from 1945, he was a founding member of the UVAN and *MUR and was a professor at the Ukrainian Free University in Munich (1948–50). In 1950 he emigrated to New York, where he remained UVAN secretary-general and curator of the UVAN Archives and Museum, which he had founded.

Miiakovsky's research dealt with the history of social, intellectual, and political movements in 19th-century Ukraine (eg, the Decembrists, the Cyril and Methodius Brotherhood, the hromadas) and 19th-century Ukrainian and Russian literature, particularly T. Shevchenko. He was the author of numerous articles and reviews. His major contributions are a biography of A. Radishchev (1918); booklets on revolutionary appeals to the Ukrainian people in 1850–70 (1920), the correspondence of the members of the Cyril and Methodius Brotherhood (1928), the Shevchenko House and Museum (1929), *Bakunin and the Russian Jacobins and Blanquists as Evaluated by Soviet Historiography* (1955), and D. Antonovych (1967); and articles on P. Kulish's educational activity (1919), M. Hulak (1926, 1928), and O. Markovych (1927) and T. Shevchenko (1962) in the Cyril and Methodius Brotherhood. He coedited (with Yefremov) a collection of articles on the Decembrists in Ukraine (1926) and (with V. Bazylevych and L. Dobrovolsky) a collection of archival materials on the Decembrists in Ukraine (1926); wrote biographical notes for vols 3 and 4 of the complete collection of Shevchenko's works, edited by Yefremov (1927, 1929); edited a book on Shevchenko's 'Moskaleva krynytsia' (Soldier's Well, 1930) and *Kostomarov's Book of Genesis of the Ukrainian People* (Yanivsky, 1954); and coedited (with G.Y. Shevelov) *Taras Ševčenko, 1814–61: A Symposium* (1962). A book containing some of his articles and a bibliography of his works, edited by M. Antonovych, was published in New York in 1984.

A. Zhukovsky

Miius River [Mijus] (also Mius). A river that flows through Luhanske, Donetske, and Rostov oblasts. It is 258 km long and drains a basin area of 6,680 sq km. The Miius has its source in the Donets Ridge and empties into a liman at Tahanrih Bay, on the Sea of Azov. The river freezes over in December and thaws in March. Its main tributaries are the Krynka Hlukha (right) and the Naholna Kripenka (left). Several water reservoirs have been built on the Miius. The river is used for water supply and irrigation.

Miiusynske [Mijusyns'ke]. V-19, DB III-5. A city (1989 pop 7,800) on the Miius River under the jurisdiction of the Krasnyi Luch city council in Luhanske oblast. It originated in 1923, when the Shterivka Hydroelectric Station was constructed, and was called Shterhres. In 1965 the settlement was renamed and promoted to city status. It has a workshop of the Donbasenerho machine repair plant and a reinforcement-products plant.

Mikeshin, Mikhail [Mikešin, Mixail], b 21 February 1835 in Platonovo, Smolensk gubernia, d 31 January 1896 in St Petersburg. Belarusian sculptor and graphic artist. A graduate of the St Petersburg Academy of Arts (1858), he created a number of monuments in the Russian Empire, including that of Hetman B. Khmelnytsky in Kiev (1879–

Mikhail Mikeshin: statue of Hetman Bohdan Khmelnytsky (bronze, 1888) in Kiev's Khmelnytsky Square

88), and illustrated editions of T. Shevchenko's *Iliustrovanyi Kobzar* (Illustrated Kobzar, 1896) and N. Gogol's novels (1869–72). In his journal, *Pchela* (1876–8), he published his own articles, recollections, and drawings. In his recollections he mentions Shevchenko, whom he knew personally. A. Savinov's book about Mikeshin appeared in Moscow in 1971.

Mikhnevych, Petro [Mixnevyč], b 22 October 1901 in Berdychiv, Kiev gubernia. Stage and film actor. In 1925 he completed study at the Lysenko Music and Drama Institute in Kiev. Then he worked as an actor in the Kiev Ukrainian Drama Theater (1926–31), the Kharkiv Theater of the Revolution (1931–40; from 1935 the Kharkiv Lenin Komsomol Theater), and, from 1940, the Chernivtsi Oblast Ukrainian Music and Drama Theater. Mikhnevych also acted in many films, including *Kyianka* (The Kiev Girl, 1958).

Mikhnevych, Yosyf. See Mykhnevych, Osyp.

Mikhnov, Anatolii [Mixn'ov, Anatolij], b 1 July 1909 in Radul, Horodnia county, Chernihiv gubernia, d 3 October 1970 in Kiev. Internal medicine specialist. A graduate of the Kiev Medical Institute (1933), he served on its faculty (1944–50) and worked at the Ukrainian Scientific Research Institute of Clinical Medicine (now Cardiology), where he became director in 1952. His work dealt with the effects of liver disorders on metabolism, with rheumatism, and with the approval of new drugs for clinical use.

Mykola Mikhnovsky

Archbishop Yurii Mikhnovsky

Mikhnovsky, Mykola [Mixnovs'kyj], b 1873 in Turivka, Pryluka country, Poltava gubernia, d 3 March 1924 in Kiev. Political and community activist, publicist and lawyer, and ideologue of Ukrainian nationalism. He studied law at Kiev University and during his student years was one of the initiators (1891) of the *Brotherhood of Taras. His speech at the T. Shevchenko anniversary celebrations in Poltava and Kharkiv in 1900, printed in Lviv as *Samostiina Ukraïna* (Independent Ukraine), became the program of the *Revolutionary Ukrainian party (RUP) in its early period. When most of RUP's membership abandoned an independentist platform, he left it to assist in organizing the *Ukrainian People's party (UNP, founded in 1902) and wrote the 'Ten Commandments' and the 'Program' to underscore its commitment to full Ukrainian statehood. A representative of the citizens of Kharkiv during the unveiling of the Kotliarevsky monument in Poltava in 1903, Mikhnovsky insisted in speaking in Ukrainian rather than in Russian and inspired the rest of the delegates at the gathering to follow suit. He popularized independentist ideas in various periodicals (short-lived because of a lack of funds) that he edited or published, including *Samostiina Ukraïna* (Lviv 1905), *Khliborob* (Lubni 1905), *Zaporizhzhia* (Katerynoslav 1906), and *Slobozhanshchyna* (Kharkiv 1906). A somewhat more durable publication was *Snip*, which he published in Kharkiv in 1912–13.

During the Revolution of 1917 Mikhnovsky was in Kiev propagating the idea of Ukrainian independence and the formation of a national army. He organized the *Ukrainian Military Club (which he represented in the Central Rada) as well as the *Khmelnytsky Regiment. A member of the presidium of the First All-Ukrainian Military Congress (18–21 May 1917) and the Ukrainian General Military Committee, he became frustrated by the opposition to his independentist ideas. He was a key figure in the attempt by the *Polubotok Regiment to seize power on 18 July 1917. Early in 1918 he began working with the Ukrainian Democratic Agrarian party. After P. Skoropadsky pronounced the federation of Ukraine with Russia, Mikhnovsky joined the anti-hetman insurrection. With the Bolshevik occupation of Ukraine, Mikhnovsky was imprisoned, and upon his release he fled to the Kuban,

where he worked in co-operatives and as a teacher at the Pedagogical Technical School in Poltava Stanytsia. He returned to Kiev in the spring of 1924, but incessant persecution by the Soviet authorities led him to suicide.

Mikhnovsky was the ideologue of independent Ukrainian statehood. He formulated the principles of Ukrainian nationalism in the 'Ten Commandments' of the UNP and then developed them into a social program that foresaw an inevitable struggle with both capitalism and the internationalist tenets of socialism and communism. He favored 'a single united, free, and independent Ukraine ... from the Carpathians to the Caucasus.' Mikhnovsky ultimately proved intolerant of others and unable to unite a strong following to realize his ideas. Nevertheless, his ideas had a significant impact on the post–First World War generation of the 1920s and 1930s, particularly in Western Ukraine and in the emigration. The nationalist *Ukrainian Student Organization of Mikhnovsky is named in his honor.

BIBLIOGRAPHY
Shemet, S. 'Mykola Mikhnovs'kyi,' *Khliborobs'ka Ukraïna*, 5 (1925)
Andriievs'kyi, V. *Mykola Mikhnovs'kyi* (Munich 1950)
Mirchuk, P. *Mykola Mikhnovs'kyi – Apostol ukraïns'koï derzhavnosty* (London 1960)

V. Yaniv

Mikhnovsky, Yurii [Mixnovs'kyj, Jurij], b 6 May 1868 in Pishchany, Poltava gubernia, d 1937 in Kiev. Archbishop of the Ukrainian Autocephalous Orthodox church (UAOC). He studied at the Poltava Theological Seminary and was ordained in 1894; he then worked as a clergyman in Pereiaslav and Zolotonosha counties. At the first All-Ukrainian Orthodox Church Congress in October 1921, he was consecrated archbishop of Chernihiv, and in 1922 he was transferred to Zolotonosha. In 1923–31 he did not have an eparchial see, and served as a parish priest throughout the Poltava region. In 1931 he moved to Kiev, where he was vicar of the St Sophia Cathedral until the Soviet authorities forced him out, in 1934. In 1937 Mikhnovsky was arrested and shot by the NKVD.

Mikhnovsky Student Association. See Ukrainian Student Organization of Mikhnovsky.

Miklosich, Franz (Miklošič), b 20 November 1813 in Radomerščak, Slovenia, d 7 March 1891 in Vienna. Prominent Slovenian Slavist; member of the Austrian Academy of Sciences from 1851. A graduate of the universities of Graz (PH D, 1838) and Vienna (D JUR, 1841), he was a professor of Slavic philology and literature at Vienna (1850–86), where he established a comparative-historical school of Slavic grammar. Among his students were the Western Ukrainian linguists M. Osadtsa, O. Ohonovsky, and S. Smal-Stotsky. His works *Vergleichende Grammatik der slavischen Sprachen* (4 vols, 1852–75), *Die slavischen Ortsnamen aus Appellativen* (1872–4), *Die türkischen Elemente in den südost- und osteuropäischen Sprachen* (1884–90), *Etymologisches Wörterbuch der slavischen Sprachen* (1886), and *Über die Wanderungen der Rumänen in den Dalmatischen Alpen und den Karpaten* (1879) are rich in factual information, including information about the Ukrainian language. In his *Beiträge zur Kenntnis der Zigeunermundarten* (1872–80) he analyzed the Romani language in Ukraine. Miklosich was one of the first Western linguists to treat Ukrainian as a distinct language. He supported the attempts by Galicia's Ukrainians to develop a literary language based on the vernacular and believed that their alphabet should be Latinized. Miklosich's methodology prevailed among Ukrainian linguists in Galicia and Bukovyna until the advent of structuralism. A book of letters to him from Ukrainian Slavists was published in Kiev in 1988.

O. Horbach

Miklukho-Maklai, Nikolai [Mikluxo-Maklaj, Nikolaj], b 17 July 1846 in Rozhdestvenskoe, Borovichi county, Novgorod gubernia, Russia, d 14 April 1888 in St Petersburg. Anthropologist, ethnographer, and geographer of Ukrainian descent. After studying at St Petersburg (1863), Heidelberg (1864), Leipzig (1865), and Jena (1866–8) universities he made 10 voyages to the Pacific Ocean and spent 15 years (1871–86) exploring the geography and observing the natives of New Guinea, the Philippines, Indonesia, Melanesia, Micronesia, and Australia. He argued for the unity and equality of all races and defended the rights of the native peoples. His travel diaries were published in 1923, and a five-volume collection of his works in 1950–4. E. Webster's *The Moon Man* (1984) is a biography of him and an assessment of his scientific contribution.

Mile. See Weights and measures.

Miliaieva, Liudmyla [Miljajeva, Ljudmyla], b 13 November 1925 in Kharkiv. Art historian. A graduate of Kiev University (1950), since 1962 she has lectured at the Kiev State Art Institute. She has written articles on Ukrainian art history and books on K. Trutovsky (1955), the murals of Potelych (1969), 14th- to 17th-century Ukrainian art (1963, with H. Lohvyn), and medieval Ukrainian painting (1976, with Lohvyn and V. Svientsitska).

Miliakh, Oleksander [Miljax], b 29 August 1906 in Symferopil, Tavriia gubernia, d 25 October 1985 in Kiev. Electrical engineer; corresponding member of the AN URSR (now ANU) from 1964. He graduated from the Kharkiv Electrotechnical (now Polytechnical) Institute (1931) and worked at the ANU Institute of Electrodynamics (from 1947, and as director in 1959–73). His main technical contributions were in the areas of complex circuit analysis, electrodynamics, and electromagnetism. He supervised the design of automatic machinery for spacecraft, stabilizers, inverters, energy converters, frequency converters, and other electric machinery.

Milianych, Atanas [Miljanyč], b 1902, d 30 April 1987 in New York. Economist and civic leader. A graduate in civil engineering at Danzig University, he organized the *Prombank in Lviv to raise capital for new Ukrainian industrial firms and served as one of its directors (1936–9). During the Second World War he worked for the Ukrainian Central Committee as its economic (1940–1) and financial (1944–5) manager, and for the Ukrainian Sugar Board in Kiev as its financial director (1942–3). He fled to Germany in 1944 and served as financial manager on the Central Representation of the Ukrainian Emigration in Germany. After settling in the United States, he was active in the Plast Ukrainian Youth Association and other Ukrainian groups. He was founder and director of the *Ukrainian Center for Social Research in New York and chief editor

Atanas Milianych

of *Ukraïns'ki poselennia: Dovidnyk* (Ukrainian Settlements: A Handbook, 1980).

Military Board of the Division Galizien (Viiskova uprava Dyvizii Halychyna). A committee formed in Lviv in April 1943 to help organize the *Division Galizien. Later its activities included providing care and aid to soldiers' families and satisfying the cultural needs of the division. It published the weekly paper *Do peremohy* (1943–5). The board consisted primarily of former officers of the Ukrainian Galician Army; its chairman was Col A. Bizanz, and its secretary was Capt O. Navrotsky. Its head office moved from Lviv (1943–4) to Luben and finally to Vienna. Besides a head office, it had a representative in each county of Galicia. The board dissolved itself on 22 August 1947 in Munich. A book about the board, by R. Krokhmaliuk, was published in Toronto in 1978.

Military Committee. See Ukrainian Military Committee.

Military congresses. See All-Ukrainian military congresses.

Military decorations. Ukrainian armies of the 1917–20 period did not award military decorations, although regulations governing such awards were approved by the Hetman government in 1918 and the Galician government in 1918–19. Neither the Central Rada nor the UNR Directory established any military decorations. Some Ukrainian officers wore decorations they had earned in the Russian or Austrian army.

The secretary of military affairs of the Western Ukrainian National Republic established a variety of decorations for soldiers of the Ukrainian Galician Army (UHA). In November 1918 the Defender of Lviv decoration, in the form of a cross, was established to be awarded to both military and civilians participating in the campaign of 1–21 November 1918. In April 1919 a more comprehensive regulation established decorations for bravery, meritorious service, and wounds. The Trident (4 classes: gold, silver, bronze, and iron) was the decoration for bravery in action and for exceptional service. These and other decorations, however, were never awarded because of the difficult circumstances in which the UHA found itself. Instead, UHA officers were recognized for bravery by promotion to a higher rank.

In the post-1920 period, the UNR government-in-exile

Military decorations. Clockwise, from top left: the UNR Symon Petliura Cross (est 1932), the UNR Directory Cross (est 1929), the Mazepa Cross of the Ukrainian Sich Riflemen (est 1940), the UNR Military Cross (est 1953), the UNR Order of the Iron Cross (est 1920), and the Cross of the Legion of Ukrainian Sich Riflemen (est 1918)

established and awarded the Iron Cross (1920), for participation in the First Winter Campaign, and the Symon Petliura Cross (1932), for participation in any battles or campaigns of the UNR Army. Commemorative medals or crosses were also issued by various veterans' associations, usually in conjunction with specific anniversaries, such as the Division Galizien's 10th anniversary of the Battle of Brody.

The only military decorations awarded to Ukrainian soldiers in active service were those of the Ukrainian Insurgent Army (UPA). General Order No. 3/44 on 27 January 1944 created seven degrees of recognition for bravery, the highest being the Gold Cross of Combat Merit First Class, followed by three degrees of the Cross of Merit (gold, silver, bronze) and stars for wounds received in action. On 6 June 1948 the Ukrainian Supreme Liberation Council introduced a medal for combat in particularly difficult circumstances. Awards of UPA decorations were regularly announced in military orders and sometimes in underground publications. The actual crosses and medals were not made available until 1951, when a limited number were produced from designs prepared by N. Khasevych. The last UPA awards were made in October 1952.

P. Sodol

Military district (*viiskova okruha*). An organizational unit consisting of the military institutions and bodies located within a specific geographic region. In the Russian Empire, military districts were established in 1862, and Ukraine was divided into the Kiev and Odessa military districts. The old districts remained intact under the Central Rada and were redrawn only in September 1918 by the Hetman government into the following military districts: Kiev, Volhynia, Odessa, Chernihiv, Poltava, Kharkiv, and Katerynoslav. The plan to set up one army corps in each okruha could not be implemented before the Hetman was overthrown. The Ukrainian Galician Army divided Galicia into 13 military districts.

Under the Soviet regime the entire Ukrainian SSR formed one military district. In 1935 it was divided into the Kiev, Odessa, and Kharkiv military districts, and in 1939 the Lviv (renamed the Carpathian in 1946) Military District was added. Later the Tavriia Military District was created. Since 1956, there have been three districts: Kiev, Odessa, and Subcarpathia.

In 1943 the Ukrainian Insurgent Army (UPA) divided its area of operations into military districts, which were about as large as oblasts. The UPA-North (in Volhynia and Polisia) consisted of four, the UPA-South (in central Ukraine) of at least two, and the UPA-West (Galicia) of six military districts. In 1945 the number of military districts was reduced to two in the north and four in the west ('Buh' [Lviv], 'Hoverlia' [Carpathians], 'Lysonia' [Podilia], and 'Sian' [Zakerzonnia]). The military units within a district constituted a group, which was equivalent to an infantry division. In 1949 the UPA military districts ceased to function.

P. Sodol

Military education. From the Middle Ages to the Cossack period young men in Ukraine received practical military training at the courts of princes and nobles or at the Zaporozhian Sich. A young Cossack served as a novice for three years before he received full status. In the late 18th century the nobility of the Russian Empire began to send its sons to military schools. In the 19th century, secondary military schools provided a specialized education for future officers. Admission was weighed in favor of young men who had completed a general secondary education in cadet schools, which were restricted largely to officers' sons. In 1862–82 these cadet schools were replaced by military gymnasiums. Naval officers began their education at the Naval Cadet School.

The first cadet schools in Ukraine were set up in Kiev and Poltava. Later, similar schools were opened in Odessa and Sumy. Infantry schools were established in Kiev, Odessa, and Chuhuiv; a cavalry school in Yelysavethrad; and an engineering school in Odessa. During the First World War, lieutenant schools with an accelerated course were opened. Many officers who later served in the UNR Army were graduates of these schools. Higher military education was provided by academies, such as the Mykolaiv General Staff Academy (est 1832) and the Artillery, Military Engineering, Military Law, Military Medicine, Naval, and Quartermaster academies. Noncommissioned officers (NCOs) were trained in teaching companies attached to army units.

In Austria higher military education was offered by the academy in Wiener-Neustadt, and in Hungary by the academy in Budapest. Specialized secondary education was provided by cadet schools. Lower-ranking officers of the reserve were trained in what were known as one-year volunteer schools.

In the UNR, plans for a system of military education were never realized. The Hetman government, however, managed to set up an Officer Instruction School in Kiev. The UNR Army had its own unified military youth schools for training officers (see *Officer schools of the Army of the UNR). The Ukrainian Galician Army had altogether five schools with accelerated courses (see *Officer schools of the Ukrainian Galician Army). During the interwar period some Ukrainians graduated from military schools in Poland, Hungary, Rumania, and Czechoslovakia.

In the Soviet Ukraine, apart from the many Russian schools for the various branches of the military, Red officer schools were set up in Kharkiv (1921–34) and Sumy, to train professional officers for Ukraine's territorial divisions. Their language of instruction was Ukrainian. Several higher military schools operated in Ukraine, including the Cavalry and Communications academies in Kiev and the Academy of Military Economy in Kharkiv. Other academies were situated in Moscow and Leningrad. In 1943–4, closed secondary schools, known as *Suvorov army cadet schools and Nakhimov navy cadet schools, were introduced. The Soviet network of military schools was constantly reorganized.

During the Second World War young officers of the First Ukrainian Division of the Ukrainian National Army (Division Galizien) were trained at the Junker academies of the German SS. The Ukrainian Insurgent Army had an officer school, which graduated four classes, and several schools and courses for NCOs.

Military estates (*viiskovi maietnosti*). Fields, pastures, mines, buildings, mills, distilleries, and other properties in Left-Bank Ukraine that belonged to the Cossack army in the second half of the 17th and in the 18th century. They were confiscated from the Polish king, magnates, and nobles who were forced out of Ukraine during the Cossack-Polish War (1648–54). Some of these estates were immediately distributed among Cossack *starshyna* (see *rank estates), and the rest were transferred to the Cossack army. All the taxes collected from the *common peasants who lived on these lands were used for the needs of the Cossack army and administration. Eventually, many of these estates fell into the hands of the Cossack *starshyna* or the tsar, who then granted them to Russian nobles or Cossacks. In this manner, Cossack families such as the Apostol, Bezborodko, Galagan, Rozumovsky, and Khanenko families amassed huge estates and became important landowners. With the abolition of Ukrainian autonomy in the late 18th century, the remaining military estates were appropriated by the Russian state, and the peasants on them were reduced to state peasants.

Military formations. During periods of independence, armed forces have been an integral part of the Ukrainian state. In periods of foreign domination Ukrainians served in foreign armies, sometimes in separate ethnic detachments. At the restoration of independence, Ukrainian career soldiers from foreign armies played a leading role in organizing a national army.

Pre-Kievan Rus'. The peoples that inhabited Ukraine before the arrival of the Slavic tribes possessed varying degrees of military skill and organization. Of these, the *Scythians were the most warlike and sophisticated. The Slavic tribes of Ukraine were less militant. In wartime they formed detachments based on tribal or clan structures, commanded by an elected chieftain. For defense they fortified their settlements with walls, stockades, and ditches. According to some estimates, there were 1,300 fortified settlements in northern and central Ukraine in the 5th to 8th centuries. Combatants were usually armed with spears, axes, bows and arrows, slings, and swords. Battle tactics were primitive.

Rus' to the 11th century. A more regular military force emerged during the process of state-building in Ukraine. The core of the army consisted of mercenary Varangian *druzhyny, ranging from 400 to 6,000 men and subdivided into detachments of 40 to 60 men. The typical Varangian fighter was armed with a coat of mail, helmet, sword, ax, spear, and large shield. The Varangians contributed to the development of a naval capacity in Rus', for use against the Byzantine Empire in the Black Sea and against Arab forces in the Caspian Sea. According to contemporary sources, 200 boats took part in the Byzantium campaign of 907, 500 in the campaign of 913, and 1,000 in that of 941.

Rus' in the 11th to 14th centuries. During this period the art of war was influenced not only by the Varangians, Greeks, and Turkic nomads, but also by developments in central Europe. A prince's army consisted of a heavily armed *druzhyna*, lightly armed levies, and subservient steppe hordes. The armed retinue was maintained by the prince from taxes and tributes. Summoned foreign troops were allowed to raise supplies in the towns and countryside. In an emergency a *levy en masse raised poorly equipped troops from among townsmen and peasants. Turkic tribesmen settled on the outskirts of Rus', and loyal to the prince, furnished him with another 15,000–30,000 troops. In a crisis the prince could raise an army of up to 50,000. Besides the arms inherited from the Varangians, the princes adopted the curved saber, light armor, and bow of the steppe horsemen. A heavily armed cavalry on the Byzantine model was added to the infantry-based army.

Polish-Lithuanian period. With the fall of Kievan Rus' and the Principality of Galicia-Volhynia, the security of Ukrainian territories became the responsibility of the occupying powers of Poland, Lithuania, and Hungary. The nucleus of the Lithuanian army consisted of *boyars, who were obliged to do military service. In wartime, recruits were conscripted from the general population.

In Ukrainian lands under Poland in the 14th to 16th centuries, military duty was required of boyars, village heads, and mayors of towns under Magdeburg law. In wartime each landowner provided one to four suitably armed mounted soldiers, and a levy en masse was called. In the mid-16th century a regular army (*kwarciane wojsko*) was established to defend the commonwealth's southeastern frontier (Ukrainian territory) from the Tatars.

Cossack period. In the 15th and 16th centuries a unique military caste, the *Cossacks, was formed on the southern steppe frontier of the Polish Commonwealth. In 1552–4 the Zaporozhian Cossacks established a permanent fortress known as the *Zaporozhian Sich. The Polish authorities tried to bring this force under their control and to use it for protecting the southeastern border of the commonwealth from the Tatars. They engaged a limited number of *registered Cossacks on terms similar to those of the regular frontier army.

The *Cossack-Polish War of 1648–57 led to the rise of the *Hetman state, which was organized and governed according to the *regimental and *company systems. A similar administrative territorial structure was established in Slobidska Ukraine, although it was integrated more closely into the imperial Russian administration. The Cossack fighting units of the Hetman state participated increasingly in Russian campaigns and wars, such as the *Russo-Turkish War and the Northern War launched by Peter I. In the latter part of the 18th century, Ukrainian military units lost their distinctive character and became part of the imperial army.

Ukrainians in the Russian army. With the abolition of the Hetman state in 1764, its ten territorial regiments were reclassified as light-cavalry regiments; in 1784 they were re-formed into carabineer units of the imperial army. In 1765 the five Cossack regiments of Slobidska Ukraine were transformed into hussar regiments of the Russian army. Recruitment to the new regiments was widened to the free peasantry, and their Cossack members were demoted to the status of peasants.

After the destruction of the Zaporozhian Sich (1775) its Cossacks scattered throughout Ukraine or emigrated to Turkish territory, where they set up the *Danubian Sich. Those who stayed behind were eventually organized by the Russian authorities into the *Black Sea Cossacks and the *Boh Cossack Army to defend the empire's southern frontier. In the 19th century the *Azov Cossack Host and the *Kuban Cossack Host were formed from the descendants of the Zaporozhian Cossacks who settled on the Azov coast and the Kuban. The Kuban Host was the only Ukrainian Cossack formation to survive until the dissolution of the Russian Empire.

During the 19th century some territorial Ukrainian military units were formed by the Russian government in response to crises such as the Napoleonic invasion (see *Ukrainian regiments in 1812), the *Polish Insurrection of 1830–1, the *Crimean War, and the *Polish Insurrection of 1863–4. They were disbanded as soon as the crises passed. On the eve of the First World War, Ukraine was divided between 2 (Kiev and Odessa) of the empire's 12 military districts. Two rifle brigades, 8 cavalry divisions, 2 cavalry regiments, and 16 infantry divisions were stationed in Ukraine. Fewer than 40 percent of their soldiers were Ukrainian. In the *Black Sea Fleet, approx 80 percent of the sailors were Ukrainian. Approx 25 percent of the empire's 1.3 million soldiers (prior to the general mobilization) were Ukrainian. A number of high officers of the Russian army, including N. Repnin, M. Myloradovych, Y. Kukharenko, and M. Dragomirov, were of Ukrainian descent.

Austrian army. Before the Revolution of 1848 there were no attempts to set up special Ukrainian units within the Austrian army. Then a short-lived national guard was formed in several towns of eastern Galicia by the Supreme Ruthenian Council. In 1849 it was succeeded by the *Ruthenian Battalion of Mountain Riflemen, which was disbanded in early 1850. With the introduction of universal conscription in Austria-Hungary in 1868, the number of Ukrainians in the army rose sharply. Three of the empire's 12 military districts covered Ukrainian territory. Since military service was based on residency, military units of

the 6th (Košice), 10th (Peremyshl), and 11th (Lviv) districts had a high percentage of Ukrainians. Officers of Ukrainian origin, such as S. Kobyliansky and Y.M. Vitoshynsky-Dobrovolia, were rare exceptions. The *Ukrainian Sich Riflemen, formed in 1914, was the only national Ukrainian legion in the Austrian army.

1917–21 period. As the Russian and Austrian armies disintegrated toward the end of the First World War, large numbers of their Ukrainian soldiers and officers joined the new Ukrainian national armies: the *Army of the Ukrainian National Republic and the *Ukrainian Galician Army (UHA), which defended Ukrainian independence from Russia and Poland in the *Ukrainian-Soviet War (1917–21) and the *Ukrainian-Polish War in Galicia (1918–19). Besides the regular army, a citizens' militia known as the *Free Cossacks supported the newly created UNR. In southern Ukraine, independent insurgent groups led by figures such as N. *Hryhoriiv and N. *Makhno shifted their allegiance among the chief combatants (see *Partisan movement in Ukraine, 1918–22). The Bolshevik forces in Ukraine, commanded by V. *Antonov-Ovsiienko, were largely Russian. Eventually the Poles took control of Western Ukraine, and the Red Army recaptured the Ukrainian territory previously ruled by Russia.

Interwar period. In Western Ukraine, Ukrainian citizens of Poland, Hungary, Rumania, and Czechoslovakia were compelled to serve in the armies of those countries and had no special units of their own. Some former officers of the UNR Army (57 in 1937) received special training and served under contract in the Polish army. Many officers and soldiers of the UHA and the Sich Riflemen joined the *Ukrainian Military Organization, which carried on the fight for independence in the underground. The only Ukrainian military force in this period was the short-lived *Carpathian Sich (1938–9), which defended the independence of *Carpatho-Ukraine.

Soviet Ukraine did not have its own army. As a result of the Ukrainization policy, Ukrainian was used as the language of instruction and command in Ukrainian territorial divisions (10 infantry and 4 cavalry divisions in 1928), which did not belong to the regular army but formed a militia (1922–34). In the unified Soviet military system, Ukraine and the Crimea formed one military district. Its commander sat on Ukraine's Council of People's Commissars, where he represented the Military-Naval People's Commissariat of the Russian SFSR. In 1935 Ukraine was divided into three military districts (Kiev, Odessa, and Kharkiv), and in 1939 the Lviv district was added.

Second World War. Ukrainians fought in the Second World War as members of a number of alien armies. About 4.5 million Ukrainians served in the Red Army. Others joined the ranks of *Soviet partisans in Ukraine. Inhabitants of Western Ukraine could be found in the Rumanian and Hungarian armies, as well as the *Polish Second Corps. Several Ukrainian units were established by the Germans, including the *Legion of Ukrainian Nationalists (the Nachtigall and Roland groups) and the *Division Galizien. Ukrainian leaders, who supported these projects, hoped these units would eventually become the nucleus of an independent Ukrainian army. Ukrainians from eastern Ukraine played a role in the *Russian Liberation Army and the *Ukrainian Liberation Army, which were formed from among Soviet war prisoners by the Germans. Only the *Ukrainian Insurgent Army, which fought both Germans and Soviets, was fully independent and Ukrainian-controlled.

Postwar period. In 1946 the Red Army was renamed the *Soviet Army. Although a Ukrainian commissariat of defense was set up in 1944 (abolished in 1947), the army continues to be centralized and Russian in profile. Ukrainian conscripts serve alongside other nationals in various regions. In its Declaration of State Sovereignty (1990), Ukraine claimed the right to maintain its own armed forces and demanded that its citizens in the Soviet Army serve on Ukrainian territory. In 1991, after the dissolution of the USSR and the proclamation of Ukrainian independence, Soviet formations in Ukraine became part of the newly created Ukrainian armed forces.

A. Makuch

Military ranks. Titles conferred upon officers or soldiers to indicate their military qualifications and professional standing. In most modern armies there are five levels of rank: general officer, field grade officer (major to colonel), company grade officer (lieutenant and captain), noncommissioned officer (corporal and sergeant), and soldier (recruit, private, and private first class). Cadets, officer candidates, and warrant officers are usually ranked just below lieutenants.

During the struggle for Ukrainian independence (1917–20) the rank system of the Ukrainian armies changed several times. Under the Central Rada, in January 1918, instead of regular ranks a functional rank system was instituted, in which rank reflected the individual's position in the organizational structure. The ranks, in ascending order, were *kozak* (soldier), *roiovyi* (squad leader), *chotovyi* (platoon sergeant), *bunchuzhnyi* (company first sergeant), *pidsotennyi* (platoon commander or lieutenant), *sotnyk* (company commander), *kurinnyi* (battalion commander), *polkovnyk* (regimental commander), and *otaman brygady, dyvizii, korpusu,* or *armii* (brigade, division, corps,

or army commander). Theoretically, upon reassignment an individual left his rank with the unit, and his future rank depended on his new position. In July 1918, Hetman P. Skoropadsky established permanent military ranks (see table). After his downfall the UNR Army returned to the functional rank system. It was not until March 1920 that the UNR Army instituted a regular rank system (see table), with rank insignia worn on the collar.

The Ukrainian Galician Army (UHA) had a military rank system from its very beginning. It was formally confirmed in a decree of the secretary of military affairs on 30 April 1919. The rank structure provided for 17 grades (see table), but the highest rank ever attained by an officer (O. Hrekov) was major general. The UHA had relatively strict promotion standards. Given the shortage of officers, it was not unusual for majors or captains to command brigades, and one corps commander started his assignment as a major. Promotions were generally based on merit and service, but in some cases officers were promoted for bravery in combat.

The Ukrainian Insurgent Army (UPA) had a dual rank system. In January 1944 it established a rank system based on functions. There were eight command positions (in descending order): supreme commander, *krai* commander, group commander, *zahin* commander, battalion commander, company commander, platoon commander, and squad commander. The appropriate insignia were worn on the right sleeve. At the same time, the UPA routinely appointed and promoted its officers and soldiers to traditional military ranks (see table), for which no insignias were provided. Promotions in the UPA usually followed a period of service as long as one or two years in a position that required a higher rank. R. Shukhevych, for example, was promoted to brigadier general only after serving as supreme commander for over two years. Officers and soldiers who had been killed in battle were often promoted to a higher rank posthumously.

P. Sodol, Z. Stefaniv

Military ranks in Ukrainian armies (comparative outline)

English-language equivalents	Hetman government army July 1918	Ukrainian Galician Army April 1919	UNR Army March 1920	Ukrainian Insurgent Army January 1945	Ukrainian army 25 March 1992
General	–	–	Holovnyi otaman	(?)	Heneral armii Ukrainy
Lieutenant general	Heneral-bunchuzhnyi	Heneral-sotnyk	Heneral-polkovnyk	(?)	Heneral-polkovnyk
Major general	Heneral-znachkovyi	Heneral-poruchnyk	Heneral-poruchnyk	(?)	Heneral-leitenant
Brigadier general	Heneral-khorunzhyi	Heneral-chetar	Heneral-khorunzhyi	Heneral-khorunzhyi	Heneral-maior
Colonel	Polkovnyk	Polkovnyk	Polkovnyk	Polkovnyk	Polkovnyk
Lieutenant colonel	Viiskovyi starshyna	Pidpolkovnyk	Pidpolkovnyk	Pidpolkovnyk	Pidpolkovnyk
Major	–	Otaman	–	Maior	Maior
Captain	Sotnyk	Sotnyk	Sotnyk	Sotnyk	Kapitan
First lieutenant	Znachkovyi	Poruchnyk	Poruchnyk	Poruchnyk	Starshyi leitenant
(None)	–	Chetar	–	–	Leitenant
Second lieutenant	Khorunzhyi	Khorunzhyi	Khorunzhyi	Khorunzhyi	Molodshyi leitenant
Chief warrant officer	–	–	–	–	Starshyi praporshchyk
Warrant officer	–	–	–	Bunchuzhnyi	Praporshchyk
Officer candidate	–	Pidkhorunzhyi	Pidkhorunzhyi	–	–
Master sergeant	Bunchuzhnyi	Bulavnyi	Bunchuzhnyi	Starshyi bulavnyi	Starshyna
Staff sergeant	Chotovyi	Starshyi desiatnyk	Chotovyi	Bulavnyi	Starshyi serzhant
Sergeant	Roiovyi	Desiatnyk	Roiovyi	Starshyi vistun	Serzhant
Corporal	Hurtkovyi	Vistun	Hurtkovyi	Vistun	Molodshyi serzhant
Private first class	–	Starshyi strilets	Mushtrovyi kozak	Starshyi strilets	Starshyi soldat
Private	Riadovyi	Strilets	Kozak	Strilets	Riadovyi

Military science. Also known as war doctrine. The study of warfare, including strategy, tactics, logistics, and technology, from a theoretical, historical, or biographical viewpoint.

In the medieval and the Cossack periods military knowledge was based largely on personal experience and was transmitted through personal contact. The princes of Rus' adopted the idea of border fortification from the Greeks and Romans, defensive retreat tactics with the use of wagons from steppe nomads, naval tactics from the Varangians, and the concept of guard towers from western neighbors. In the 13th century Danylo's tactics included the integrated use of different weaponry in battle. Cossack tactics were influenced by the tactics of Czech Taborites and by Western siege strategies. B. Khmelnytsky's tactics display a familiarity with the lessons of the Thirty Years' War and an ability to compensate for weaknesses (such as the lack of heavy cavalry) by other factors.

By the time military science began to flourish in the West, Ukraine had lost its military traditions. When military and paramilitary formations were revived (in 1848, 1914, and 1917), the military practices of other countries were adopted, from infantry drills to field operations (the Kuban Cossack Host was the only Ukrainian military formation with a continuous tradition). Ukrainian military leaders served other countries, particularly Russia, with their skills and knowledge. Some studies in Ukrainian military history by Ukrainian scholars appeared in *Vestnik Kievskogo otdela Voenno-istoricheskogo obshchestva* (1909–14). The officers of Ukrainian armies established in the period of Ukrainian statehood (1917–20) inevitably followed the thinking of the Russian (influenced by Prussian theories) or Austrian (in the case of the Ukrainian Galician Army) officer schools. This was most evident in the military statutes they adopted. The rapid development of events in 1917–21 left no time for studying the problems of military science.

Some early Ukrainian works in military science were analyses of the unsuccessful wars for Ukrainian independence written after the First World War by émigrés, mostly by prisoners in internment camps in Tarnów and Kalisz, and published in the quarterly *Tabor*. This work was continued by the *Ukrainian Military History Society in Warsaw, which published the serial *Za derzhavnist'* (1925–39). Particular military operations were analyzed in monographs, such as M. Kapustiansky's *Pokhid ukraïns'kykh armii na Kyïv–Odesu v 1919 rotsi* (The March of the Ukrainian Army on Kiev–Odessa in 1919, 1922; 2nd edn 1946), M. Omelianovych-Pavlenko's *Zymovyi pokhid* (The Winter Campaign, 1934) and *Ukraïns'ko-pol's'ka viina* (The Ukrainian-Polish War, 1929), Yu. Tiutiunnyk's *Zymovyi pokhid 1919–20* (The Winter Campaign of 1919–20, 1923), and A. Krezub's *Narys istoriï ukraïns'ko-pol's'koï viiny 1918–1919* (An Outline of the History of the Ukrainian-Polish War of 1918–19, 1923). Collections of documents were published by O. Dotsenko (*Zymovyi pokhid armiï* UNR [The Winter Campaign of the UNR Army, 1932]) and by V. Salsky and P. Shandruk (*Ukraïns'ko-moskovs'ka viina 1920 roku v dokumentakh* [The Ukrainian-Russian War of 1920 in Documents, 1933]). The principal military histories to come out at the time were *Istoriia ukraïns'koho viis'ka* (History of the Ukrainian Armed Forces, 1936), edited by I. Krypiakevych and B. Hnatevych, and Z. Stefaniv's *Ukraïn-*

s'ki zbroini syly 1917–21 rr. (Ukrainian Armed Forces of 1917–21, 1934–5). V. Petriv and M. Kolodzinsky wrote studies in military geography and V. Kurmanovych wrote a handbook for junior officers (1938). Military memoirs, including those of V. Petriv and S. Shukhevych, were published by the Chervona Kalyna publishing house in Lviv.

In Soviet Ukraine, military science was taught at the School for Red Officers in Kharkiv (1921–34). Y. Yakir's use of airborne troops in maneuvers of the Ukrainian Military Okruha near Kiev in 1928 shows that Ukrainians were not lagging in tactical doctrine. The newspaper *Chervona armiia*, Ukrainian translations of Soviet military statutes, and the classics of European military science were published in Kharkiv. All this was brought to a halt when the Ukrainian units of the Red Army were suppressed.

Nationalist military circles became keenly interested in military science on the eve of the Second World War. Military statutes based on German models were used in Ukrainian formations during the war, particularly by the Ukrainian Insurgent Army (UPA). Subsequently, the UPA used translations of Soviet army manuals. UPA members published textbooks on insurgent tactics, the construction of hideouts, and related matters based on their practical experience. After 1945 some works on insurgent and infantry tactics and infantry training, based on Soviet, German, and US sources, appeared abroad. They also drew on the UPA experience. A number of military histories have been published, including V. Dovzhenok's *Viis'kova sprava v Kyïvs'kii Rusi* (Military Affairs in Kievan Rus', 1950), O. Udovychenko's *Ukraïna u viini za derzhavnist'* (Ukraine in the War for Statehood, 1954), and Yu. Khrokhmaliuk's *Boï Khmel'nyts'koho* (Khmelnytsky's Battles, 1954). Ukrainian military science is now limited to military history.

O. Horbach

Military service. Active duty in a country's armed forces. Recruitment may be voluntary or compulsory. Voluntary recruitment relies either on individuals' perceptions of moral or social duty or on their desire for monetary reward. Compulsory recruitment is implemented through some form of conscription.

In medieval Ukraine there were three forms of military service: that of the warriors of the prince's *druzhyna*, who were landowners owing service in return for their lands; that of the Varangian retinues and steppe tribes, as hired mercenaries; and that of the *levies en masse, called in emergencies. Under Lithuanian and Polish rule military service was limited to landowners, boyars, and certain town officials. From 1578, crown peasants known as the elect (*vybrantsi*) served in the Polish king's army. Mercenaries were often hired. Registered Cossacks served the Polish crown in return for privileges and landholdings. In the Hetman state something like compulsory military service was imposed on certain segments of the population, such as the *Notable military fellows and the Cossacks. *Mercenary regiments of cavalry and infantry troops were also used. In Zaporizhia military service was essential to being a Cossack. In the Hetman state and later in Slobidska Ukraine, the Don region, and the Kuban, peasants bore no military obligations.

In Russian-ruled Ukraine from the end of the 18th century, common soldiers were recruited by force. At first the usual term of service was 20 to 25 years; after 1821 it was reduced to 15 years, and after 1874 to 3 to 5 years. In 1874 universal conscription of all men between the ages of 21 and 43 was introduced. After active service one was assigned to the reserves until age 38, and then to the militia of the second category until age 43. Surplus conscripts were assigned to the militia of the first category.

In Austria-Hungary military recruitment was according to estate: common recruits were conscripted from among serfs and peasants, and members of the higher estates were attracted by the advantages of a professional career. In 1868 universal conscription of all men 20 to 42 years of age was introduced. After two to three years of active service, the conscripts were assigned to the reserves. Forty percent of the draftees served in the imperial army, 40 percent in the regional units, and 20 percent in the reserves.

The Ukrainian Galician Army (UHA) was organized on the basis of the compulsory service of the citizens of the Western Ukrainian National Republic, and the draftees served in the region of their origin. Service in the navy and army of the UNR was voluntary. The Hetman government adopted a law on compulsory service on 24 June 1918, which set a term of two years for infantrymen, three years for cavalry and artillerymen, and five years for sailors. The age limit for recruits was 38 for the reserves, and 45 for the militia. Hetman P. Skoropadsky's universal of 16 October 1918 provided for a semimilitary Cossack estate formed of wealthier peasants who would serve in special Cossack units. This idea was never implemented. When the Directory came to power, service in the UNR Army became voluntary again.

In the Ukrainian SSR and the USSR, military service for the 'working element' was compulsory until 1939; the 'nonworking element' served two years in labor battalions. Ukrainians in territorial divisions served at home, and those in the regular forces, largely outside Ukraine. Draftees were first given three to six months of training, and then spent one to two summer months on maneuvers during the next three to four years. Thereafter they were assigned to one of the two reserve categories. The term in the regular army was initially set at two to four years, and it was usually served outside Ukraine. After 1937 the term was two years for the infantry and cavalry, three years for artillery and tank units, four years for the air force, and five years for the navy. A new conscription law introduced in 1939 abolished the former social restrictions.

Since the Second World War the term of compulsory military service has ranged from two to five years. The draft age is 19. Recruits to the navy, border guard, and MVD army were selected according to special Party criteria. Upon completing their tour of duty, soldiers were assigned to reserves of the first category. Young men who were excused from active duty were placed in reserves of the second category. Each reserve category was divided into three age groups: up to 35, up to 45, and up to 50. Reservists underwent periodic training.

In the interwar period Ukrainians under Polish, Rumanian, and Czechoslovakian rule were subject to the same military obligations as the citizens of those countries. In Poland and Rumania they were barred from serving in special units, and in Poland from cadet schools as well. Service terms were one and one-half to four years, depending on the branch of the armed forces. Ukrainians usually served in units of mixed national composition located outside Ukrainian ethnographic territories. In 1938 Poland introduced alternative service in labor battalions, to which many Ukrainians, particularly politically active ones, were assigned.

V. Markus

Military settlements (*viiskovi poselennia*). In 1817–25, to reduce military expenditures while maintaining a self-sufficient standing army, the tsarist regime settled 36 infantry battalions and 240 cavalry squadrons in state-owned villages in Slobidska Ukraine, Kherson, and Katerynoslav gubernias. The soldiers were allowed to live with their families in carefully planned and reconstructed villages. They supported themselves by farming allotted holdings and operating saw and flour mills, quarries, and stud farms. The peasants already living there were classified as military settlers and placed under a permanent martial law and discipline that combined the worst aspects of serfdom and the most brutal conditions of military life. Although they received better medical care, education, and material benefits than other peasants, they were forced to wear uniforms, to perform military drills and a weekly minimum of three days of corvée (farming and construction) for the state under military command, and to feed and shelter the active soldiers and their families. All aspects of their lives, including marriage and having children, were strictly regimented and monitored by local officers. Violators were severely punished, usually with the knout. From the age of 7 males attended schools and underwent military training, and from the age of 18 to 45 they were kept in military service. From 1831 the military settlers were called farming soldiers. In 1837 the same lot befell peasants living on lands in Kiev and Podilia gubernias confiscated from Polish nobles who had taken part in the Polish Insurrection of 1830–1. The military settlements in Ukraine at that time encompassed an area of 2.4 million desiatins with 554,000 inhabitants (including those of the towns of Yelysavethrad, Olviopil, and Uman). The military settlers repeatedly rebelled against the extraordinarily harsh regime imposed on them. Particularly large and violent were the 1817 rebellion of former Cossacks of the Boh Cossack Army; the 1819 rebellion of Chuhuiv and Tahanrih regiments, in Slobidska Ukraine gubernia, which resulted in the imprisonment of over 2,000 participants, the court-martial and brutal flogging of 273 (who each received 12,000 lashes), and the exile to Siberia of over 400; and the 1829 Shebelynka uprising in Slobidska Ukraine gubernia. Because the military settlements, which constituted one-third to one-half of the Russian military forces, failed to fulfill their political and economic objectives, they were abolished in 1857. The active soldiers were incorporated into regular units, and the farmers were reclassified as state peasants.

Military treasury (*viiskova skarbnytsia, heneralnyi skarb*). The treasury and finance department of the Hetman state. (The Zaporozhian Sich also had a military treasury.) Until 1728 it was part of the private assets of the hetman, who managed it with the help of trusted individuals. Hetman I. Briukhovetsky (1663–8) appointed R. *Rakushka 'supervisor of the military treasury.' Finally, in 1728, the position of *general treasurer was introduced, but the military treasury was ultimately under the control of the Russian government, which assigned three comptrollers to supervise the general treasurer and his chancellery and to watch for irregularities in collecting and spending revenues. The military treasury was abolished along with the Hetman state in 1764.

Military tribunals (*viiskovi sudy*). Courts for hearing criminal cases involving military personnel and, in areas under martial law, civilians as well. Military tribunals operate according to specific statutes of military justice or emergency laws. In the past there was no sharp distinction between military and common criminal law: in the Cossack state military personnel came under the jurisdiction of ordinary courts – regimental, general, or company. At the Zaporozhian Sich cases were heard by the military, palanka, or kurin judge. Graver charges such as treason were heard by the hetman court or at the Sich by the kish otaman or the Sich council.

In Ukrainian territories under Russian and Austrian rule military tribunals were used often before the First World War as instruments of repression against the civilian population. They were particularly active in suppressing peasant unrest in the Russian Empire in 1902–7. During the First World War the civilian population of Galicia was suspected of pro-Russian sympathies and was treated harshly by Austro-Hungarian tribunals.

During the period of Ukrainian independence (1917–20) the UNR Army had military courts in regiments and divisions. The staff of the Operational Army of the UNR had a staff military court. Under the Hetman government in 1918 the highest military court was the General Court and then the General Criminal Court of the State Senate, which assumed the powers of the former Russian Chief Military and Military-Naval Courts. The UNR Directory's law on extraordinary tribunals (26 January 1919) provided for an extraordinary military tribunal to deal with grave crimes. Its sentences had to be approved by the supreme otaman. The military justice system was administered by the Supreme Military Justice Board. The Ukrainian Galician Army adopted the Austrian military law. On 3 December 1918 the Ministry of Military Affairs ordered field military courts to be set up in each military district, and on 18 January 1919 it established the Field Court at Supreme Headquarters. Subsequently, military tribunals were organized in each corps and in subordinate units. They were authorized to try military and civilian personnel. Military judges belonged to a separate branch within the army and were promoted on separate lists. The highest ranking military judges were Lt-Col S. Tysovsky, Maj O. Pidliashevsky, and Maj H. Tsastka.

The Red Army had revolutionary military tribunals at every level. They tried civilians as well as soldiers, and their verdicts were not subject to appeal or annulment. Many Ukrainian intelligentsia and peasants, accused of 'counterrevolutionary activity and banditry,' fell victim to these courts. After the Second World War, military tribunals tried members of the OUN and soldiers of the UPA. The system of Soviet military justice subsequently underwent many changes, and various units of the armed forces, garrisons, and districts had their own military tribunals. The highest court was the Military Collegium of the USSR Supreme Court.

In the UPA, commanders of each independent combat unit (company, battalion) had the authority to field courts

to try serious disciplinary cases. Their sentences were subject to review by the commander.

P. Sodol

Military-defense industry. In the narrower sense, a branch of heavy industry that manufactures weapons, ammunition, and military vehicles, tools, and equipment and, in the broader sense, a set of branches that manufacture goods for the military.

Handcrafted *arms and military equipment have been made in Ukraine since ancient times. It was not until the 18th century, however, that large ordnance factories were built: for example, a gunpowder factory in Shostenske, Chernihiv regiment (1736), a cannon foundry in Luhanske (1795), the Arsenal in Kiev (1782), and naval factories in Kherson and Mykolaiv. By the end of the 19th century there were almost 30 specialized ordnance factories in Ukraine, all run by the state. Most of them produced only gunpowder and light artillery and were technologically backward. Beginning in the 1880s, large warships were constructed by a Belgian company in Mykolaiv and by the state in Sevastopil. During the Russo-Japanese War and the succeeding period some privately owned ordnance factories were set up. The defense industry in Ukraine continued to concentrate on the manufacturing of artillery, warships, and explosives. In 1912 a French and Belgian banking cartel pushed out its German competitors and gained control of the artillery industry in the Russian Empire. The Russian military-defense industry flourished in the years preceding and including the First World War and contributed substantially to the industrialization of the country. In Ukraine, however, the industry was much less developed.

The First World War and the Revolution of 1917 disrupted the military-defense industry in Ukraine. Chronic shortages of ordnance greatly hampered the efforts of the Ukrainian national armies, and the Red Army relied on supplies from Russia. By the end of the Civil War military supplies had been exhausted throughout the USSR. In 1926 the Soviet regime announced a plan to rebuild the defense industry. Development was particularly rapid during the period of the Second Five-Year Plan (1933–7) and the years immediately preceding the Second World War. The character of the industry changed somewhat in that period: ordnance manufacture was transferred from specialized plants to civilian factories (eg, military aircraft were built in ordinary airplane factories, and tanks in tractor factories). Many civilian factories were designed for rapid conversion to military production. Kharkiv became an important center of the defense industry: tank engines were built at its locomotive factory, artillery movers at its tractor factory, and the T tank at another plant. Aircraft engines were assembled in Zaporizhia. In 1938–9 the defense industry in Ukraine expanded by 117 percent (the machine-tool industry as a whole expanded by only 54 percent). In 1939–41 many civilian factories were converted to munitions production, and the output of nonmilitary heavy machinery, such as combines, tractors, and excavators, fell sharply. By mid-1941 Ukraine was producing a third of the USSR munitions. At least 125 factories were involved in arms production: 9 of them belonged to the airplane industry, 14 to the defense industry, 10 to the machine-building industry, and 3 to the shipbuilding industry. On the eve of the war Ukraine's annual ordnance output was approx 1,500 fighter planes, 3,000 tanks, 2,500 cannons, and 15 to 20 warships. In addition almost 150 plants produced ammunition (approx 8 million pieces monthly). Ukraine was also an important supplier of raw materials and semimanufactured products to munitions operations elsewhere in the USSR: over 50 percent of the USSR high-grade steel, pipes, aluminum, magnesium, and explosives.

After the Second World War the defense industry in Ukraine was rebuilt, but because of the rapid development of military production in central Russia and the Urals, Ukraine's share in the USSR's defense industry fell to approx 20–25 percent. The practice of manufacturing ordnance in ordinary metalworking and machine-building plants continued in the 1950s and 1960s. The Ministries of Medium Machine Building (est in 1953), of the Radio Industry (est 1954), and of General Machine Building (est 1965) belonged largely in the defense industry. Because so much of defense production is hidden under civilian manufacturing, accurate data on the defense industry in Ukraine are difficult to obtain. In the postwar period aircraft have been built in Kharkiv and Kiev, tanks in Kharkiv and the Donbas, artillery in the Dnieper region, warships in Mykolaiv and Kherson, and explosives in the Donbas and Dnieper region. In Kharkiv the first Soviet uranium-graphite reactor began producing plutonium for atomic bombs in 1946. Kharkiv is involved in atomic weapons production.

The defense industry in Ukraine and in the rest of the former USSR has grown substantially since the 1970s. Its growth has caused numerous problems in the rest of the economy. First, an unbearably high proportion of the budget – approx 25 percent of the Soviet GNP – was spent on defense. Second, the defense industry had first and, usually, exclusive claim to the most sophisticated technology and resources, desperately needed in the civilian economy to improve the standard of living. Third, the defense industry monopolized the USSR research and development potential. Furthermore, excessive secrecy and rigid compartmentalization prevented any technological spillover from the defense to the civilian sector of the economy. According to information released in 1990, about two-thirds of Ukraine's scientific and technical potential (research establishments, personnel, and funds) was concentrated in the defense sector and made virtually no contribution to the development of the civilian economy.

The USSR's economic crisis in the latter half of the 1980s led to a re-evaluation of the defense industry's place in the national economy. Defense expenditures were reduced, and sections of the defense industry were converted to civilian production. Ukraine's declaration of independence in August 1991 entailed a complete restructuring of the defense industry on Ukrainian territory.

BIBLIOGRAPHY
Kravchenko, G. *Voennaia ekonomika SSSR 1941–1945* (Moscow 1963)
Maddock, R.T. *The Political Economy of Soviet Defence Spending* (New York 1988)
                              D. Goshko, V. Holubnychy, B. Krawchenko

Militia (*militsiia*). The name of the ordinary *police that has been used in Ukraine since 1917. The militia established throughout the Russian Empire in March 1917 differed from the tsarist police in being subject to local government, not to the central Ministry of Internal Affairs. In the UNR the police was placed under the control of the Ministry of Internal Affairs in March 1918. Under the Hetman government it was reorganized into the *National Guard, and then under the UNR Directory it was called a militia and, from 1920, a civil guard.

In Soviet Ukraine the militia at first came under the control of the republic's People's Commissariat of Internal Affairs. For a few years (1930–4) the militia was controlled directly by the republic's Soviet of People's Commissars, and then by both the republic and the Union commissariats of internal affairs, which in 1946 were renamed ministries of internal affairs. Since 1960 it has been under the republic's Ministry of Internal Affairs.

The militia's role is to ensure public order, protect public and communal property, and suppress crime. It oversees the internal passport system and registers automotive vehicles. Its personnel consists of recruits with a two-year term and of career officers. They are assisted by special civilian volunteers, the *narodni druzhyny*, who help patrol neighborhoods, control crowds, and gather information on the activities of civilians. Historically, the militia has been an important part of the state security apparatus. In 1949–53 it was under the operational control of the *MGB. Up to the demise of the USSR in 1991, it co-operated closely with the *KGB in keeping individuals under surveillance and provided a cover of legality for political repression. Each militia station had a KGB staff assigned to it. With the rise of mass demonstrations under M. Gorbachev's regime, the militia set up special riot- and crowd-control units.
                                                        O. Skrypnyk

Miliukov, Pavel [Miljukov], b 15 January 1859 in Moscow, d 31 March 1943 in Aix-les-Bains, France. Russian historian, publicist, and politician. Miliukov was a founding member of the influential *Constitutional Democratic (Kadet) party, and in 1907 he became its leader and was elected a member of the State Duma. In 1912–13 he conferred secretly with the *Society of Ukrainian Progressives. In 1914 he condemned the actions of the tsarist occupational regime in Galicia; in 1915 he protested in the Duma against the tsarist persecution of Ukrainians and defended the right of the Ukrainian movement to exist; and throughout the First World War he was a vocal critic of tsarist military policies.

After the February Revolution of 1917 Miliukov was the first minister of foreign affairs in the Russian Provisional Government. He was a defender of the indivisibility of the Russian Empire and thus an opponent of the Ukrainian Central Rada and of Ukrainian political autonomy. In 1919 he fled to Istanbul, and in 1920 he lived in London. In 1921 he settled in Paris, where he headed the émigré Republican Democratic Alliance and edited its organ, *Poslednie novosti*.

Miliutenko, Dmytro [Miljutenko], b 21 February 1899 in Slovianske, Tahanrih county, Don Cossack province, d 25 January 1966 in Tashkent, Uzbekistan (buried in Kiev). Stage and film actor. He began his stage career in Slovianske (1920–3) and then worked in the Ivan Franko Theater in Kharkiv (1923–6), Berezil (1926–34), the Kharkiv Ukrainian Drama Theater (1934–6), and the Kiev Ukrainian Drama Theater. Miliutenko's extensive repertoire of dra-

matic and comic characters included Taras Shevchenko in
O. Ilchenko's *Peterburz'ka osin'* (Autumn in Petersburg)
and I. Kocherha's *Prorok* (The Prophet) and the Fool in W.
Shakespeare's *King Lear*. In films he portrayed V. Vynnychenko (*Shchors*, 1939), Hetman Potocki (*Bohdan Khmel'-nyts'kyi*, 1941), and Commandant Uskov (*Taras Shevchenko*, 1951).

Milk production. See Dairy industry.

Miller, Dmytro, b 1 October 1862 in Kotelva, Okhtyrka
county, Kharkiv gubernia, d 14 June 1913. Historian. He
graduated from Kharkiv University (1888), where he
studied under D. *Bahalii. From 1887 he worked in
Kharkiv, where he became a librarian at the university
(1895) and an editor of the newspaper *Iuzhnyi krai* (1903).
A specialist on the history of the Hetman state and Slobidska Ukraine, he wrote, in Russian, a monograph on the
land, city, and *pidkomorskyi* courts in 18th-century Ukraine
(2 vols, 1895, 1898), which contained many documentary
materials; a book-length, four-part article on the transformation of the Cossack *starshyna* into Russian nobility
(*Kievskaia starina*, 1897, nos 1–4); and books on the archives
of Kharkiv gubernia (1902) and the history of the first 250
years of Kharkiv (2 vols, 1905, 1912, cowritten with Bahalii).

Mykhailo Miller

Miller, Mykhailo, b 26 November 1883 in Millerovo,
Kamenskaia county, Don Cossack province, d 15 February
1968 in Munich. Archeologist and émigré scholar. Born
into a family of German settlers, Miller grew up in a predominantly Ukrainian section of the Don region. He studied history at Moscow University and then law at
Kharkiv. After working as a judge (1913–20) then a high
school teacher (1921–30) in Tahanrih, he was a lecturer at
the Dnipropetrovske Pedagogical Institute (1931–4) then
taught history and archeology at both the Rostov State
Pedagogical Institute and Rostov State University (1934–
43). Between 1900 and 1942 he led or took part in numerous archeological expeditions in the Volga-Don, Northern
Caucasus, and Dnieper rapids regions and became a specialist in the prehistory of these areas. In 1943 Miller left
for Munich, where he continued his scholarly work. After
the war he was active in the Ukrainian Academy of Arts
and Sciences, the Shevchenko Scientific Society (a full
member from 1950), the Institute for the Study of the USSR,
and the Ukrainian Free University. His émigré writings –
particularly during the 1950s – frequently dealt with the

destruction of historical monuments in Ukraine and with
the fate of Soviet archeology and archeologists during and
after the Stalinist terror. His major work in this regard is
Arkheologiia v SSSR (1954; translated and published in 1956
as *Archeology in the USSR*).

Miller, Oleksander, b 1875 in Millerovo, Kamenskaia
county, Don Cossack province, d 1935. Archeologist;
brother of M. Miller. A professor of archeology at St Petersburg (later Leningrad) University, he was in charge of
the Caucasian section of the Russian Ethnographic Museum in 1907–33. He studied the Bronze Age in Ukraine as
well as archeological sites in the lower Don region. He
was responsible for locating the ancient Greek settlement
of Tanais. Miller was renowned for his methodological
teachings and wrote *Arkheologicheskie razvedki* (Archeological Explorations, 1934). He was arrested in the Stalinist
terror and exiled to Siberia, where he died.

Miller, Vsevolod, b 19 April 1848 in Moscow, d 18 November 1913 in St Petersburg. Russian folklorist, linguist,
and archeologist; member of the St Petersburg Academy
of Sciences from 1911. In his works on the *Tale of Ihor's
Campaign* (1877), *Bylyny* (1893), and the legend of Illia
Muromets (1894) and in *Ocherki russkoi narodnoi slovesnosti*
(Outlines of Russian Folk Literature, 3 vols, 1897, 1910,
1924) he dealt with Ukrainian literature and folklore. His
work had a notable influence on other Ukrainian folklorists, such as I. Franko and A. Krymsky.

Millet (*Panicum*; Ukrainian: *proso*). A genus of grasses of
the cereal family, cultivated in Asia and North Africa for
over 4,000 years. The most widely grown species in
Ukraine is the common millet (*P. miliaceum*), which grows
to 45–200 cm high and, depending on the variety, ripens
in 60–120 days. It is resistant to drought, heat, and salt. Its
small edible seeds are used as livestock and bird feed in
North America and as a food cereal in Eastern Europe and
Asia. It cannot be made into leavened bread and is consumed as flatbread and grits. In the past millet was widely
cultivated, but it has been largely replaced by wheat and
rye. In 1913, 525,000 ha in Ukraine were devoted to millet.
That area represented 15 percent of the total millet area in
the Russian Empire but only 2.1 percent of the grain area
in Ukraine. Millet became more important in the years
following the Second World War, especially during
droughts when the winter wheat crop failed. In 1960,
722,000 ha in Ukraine were seeded to millet, an area representing 5.6 percent of Ukraine's grain acreage and 19
percent of the total USSR millet acreage. Since then millet
has declined in importance: in 1985 only 302,000 ha, or 1.9
percent of the grain area in Ukraine, was devoted to millet. Millet is grown throughout Ukraine, except in the
western regions. The most widely used strains are Veselopodolianske 38, 312, and 367, Podolianske 24, Kharkivske 436, and Myronivske 85.

In Ukrainian folklore millet symbolizes maidens'
braids and fertility. Millet seeds were believed to have
magical protective powers against evil spirits.

B. Somchynsky

Mills. See Flour milling.

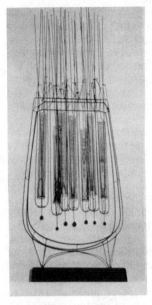

Konstantin Milonadis: *AC-II*
(chromed steel, 1969)

Milonadis, Konstantin, b 5 June 1926 near Kremenchuk, Poltava oblast. Sculptor and art professor. A postwar refugee, he has lived in the United States since 1951 and studied at the School of the Art Institute of Chicago (1953–7) and Tulane University (MFA, 1959). Milonadis has been a professor and artist in residence at numerous universities in the United States and has been active in the Ukrainian Institute of Modern Art in Chicago. His bronze, wood, stone, and steel-wire-and-spring kinetic constructions can be considered sculptures of negative space, and invite contemplation by the viewer. Solo exhibitions of his works have been held in Chicago, Urbana, Binghamton, Valparaiso, and Fort Wayne.

Miloradovich. See Myloradovych.

Milove. IV-21. A town smt (1990 pop 6,000) and raion center in Luhanske oblast. It was founded at the end of the 19th century, and it attained smt status in 1938. It has a vegetable-oil and protein plant and a geological museum.

Mindaugas (Mindove, Mendog, Mindovh), b ?, d 1263. Lithuanian ruler, considered the founder of the Grand Duchy of Lithuania. While consolidating his rule over Lithuanian lands in the 1230s and 1240s, he faced a major revolt by many of his leading nobles, including his brother and nephews. The uprising was supported by the Galician-Volhynian prince *Danylo Romanovych, who was married to a niece of Mindaugas, and who sought to include the *Chorna Rus' lands in his domains. Mindaugas eased his situation in 1251 by accepting Christianity, thereby gaining the backing of the Livonian and the Teutonic Knights. He arranged the marriage of Danylo's son to his own daughter and concluded a peace treaty in 1254 that made Roman Danylovych ruler of Chorna Rus', including the Navahrudak principality. In 1258 Mindaugas broke the treaty and invaded Slavic territories, and by 1260 he had reverted to paganism and routed the Livonian and Teutonic forces near Lake Durbe. He and two of his sons were murdered in 1263 by conspiring Lithuanian feudal lords. A period of internal unrest followed in Lithuania, until the *Gediminas dynasty came into power and ushered in an extended period of territorial expansion.

Mineral fertilizers. Synthesized chemical substances applied to the soil to increase its fertility. The most important elements in the compounds are nitrogen, phosphorus, and potassium, followed by sulfur, magnesium, calcium, and certain trace elements. Nitrogenous fertilizers are produced by treating synthetic ammonia with sulfuric acid, by converting ammonium salts, or by more modern methods of utilizing natural and coking gases. Phosphorus fertilizers most commonly include the soluble compounds of superphosphate and triple superphosphate, obtained by treating calcium phosphate with sulfuric and phosphoric acids respectively. Calcium phosphate is found in phosphorite and apatite ores and in the slag by-product of steel furnaces. Potassium fertilizers are obtained from potash deposits.

The production of mineral fertilizers is one of the older branches of the chemical industry. Potash began to be processed in 1913 in Stebnyk and Kalush, in Galicia. Since then potash has been the main source of potassium in Ukraine. In 1983 the Stebnyk plant was involved in an environmental disaster: the dam of a tailing pond collapsed, and salt brine severely polluted 500 km of the Dniester River. Before the First World War superphosphate plants were established in Odessa and Vinnytsia. After the war a

Mineral fertilizer production in Ukraine, 1928–85 (final processed product; in 1,000 t)

	1928	1940	1965	1970	1975	1980	1985
Total	11	212	1,582	2,498	3,856	4,124	5,073
Nitrogenous			801	1,396	2,222	2,403	3,220
Phosphoric			519	703	1,178	1,344	1,563
Potassic			262	399	456	377	290
Fertilizer application (kg/ha)			38.5	65.1	111.8	112.3	153.4
Ukraine's share in total Soviet production (percentage)		28.0	21.4	19.1	17.5	16.5	15.3

(For mineral fertilizer gross production see Chemical industry.)

new superphosphate plant was built in Kostiantynivka, and the older plants were greatly expanded. During the 1930s synthetic ammonia manufacturing complexes were constructed at Horlivka and Dniprodzerzhynske. In 1928 Ukraine's share of the Soviet gross output of mineral fertilizers was 42 percent. With the construction of large chemical plants outside Ukraine during the 1930s, its share of the output had declined to 26 percent by 1937. Ukraine had a monopoly on superphosphate production until 1940.

By the 1950s Ukraine's phosphorus reserves were inadequate to meet its needs, and fertilizers began to be imported from the Kola Peninsula and Kazakhstan. In recent years slag from the Mariiupil Azovstal Metallurgical Plant has become a source of phosphate fertilizer. The older ammonia plants were reconstructed in the 1950s, and plants utilizing natural and coking gases were built in Rivne and Cherkasy. In the late 1970s mineral fertilizer output fell, with adverse effects on agricultural production. In 1985 nitrogenous fertilizers accounted for 63.5 percent of the fertilizer production, phosphorus fertilizers for 30.6 percent, and potassium fertilizers for 5.7 percent (see the table).

Before 1965 fertilizers did not play an important role in increasing agricultural productivity. In 1960 only 14.6 kg of fertilizer per ha was applied. By 1975 the rate of application had reached 111.8 kg per ha, approaching European and American standards. Much fertilizer was misapplied or wasted because of backward agrotechnology, lack of storage facilities, and a shortage of spreaders. Fertilizer is usually spread in solid form, although the liquid form is more effective. Fertilizer runoff has caused serious harm to rivers and lakes in Ukraine.

B. Somchynsky

Mineral resources. Inert substances, occurring naturally in the earth, which can be used for economic purposes either in their original form or after processing. From the standpoint of their utilization in a national economy, mineral resources are usually classified into three groups: fuels (coal, petroleum, natural gas, peat, oil shale, and uranium), metals (ferrous, nonferrous, and precious metals), and nonmetallic minerals (including raw materials for the chemical industry, precious stones, mineral waters for bathing or drinking, and building materials).

History. Mineral exploitation in Ukraine dates back to the Paleolithic Age, when flint was mined and shaped into tools. Mines (such as that at the Luka-Vrublivetska excavation, near Kamianets-Podilskyi) yielded flint that was traded over considerable distances. In the Bronze Age copper was mined in the present-day Donbas region, in the Kherson area, and in Transcarpathia. During the Iron Age sedimentary deposits of bog iron ore in the forest belt came under exploitation. In addition, use was made of building stone, flint, sandstone, and potter's clay. From ca 500 BC marble was quarried in the Crimea for the construction of the Hellenic cities of Chersonesus and Panticapaeum. Probably even in prehistoric times salt was mined in Subcarpathia, and gold in Transcarpathia. During the Princely era the principal mineral resources were bog iron ore, salt, potter's clay, building stone, and amber. Similar exploitation continued into the periods of the Polish-Lithuanian Commonwealth and the Hetmanate, with the extraction of salt, iron ore, and saltpeter gaining prominence.

Modern exploration and industrial exploitation of min-

eral resources in Ukraine began in the 19th century. Coking coal of the Donets Basin was first mined at the end of the 18th century, and the mining of that resource was widespread by the 1870s. The mining of iron ore in Kryvyi Rih began in 1881, and that of manganese ore in the Nykopil area in 1886. The extraction of petroleum in the Subcarpathian foothills began in the 1850s. By the 1890s the coal and iron-ore mining industries were developing rapidly. Iron ore, manganese, coal, and (since the Second World War) natural gas continued to be the outstanding mineral resources of Ukraine, accounting for nearly 90 percent of the mined resources by value. In addition the extraction of many other mineral resources (including potassium salts, phosphorites, mercury, titanium, and uranium) developed in Ukraine. At present Ukraine is endowed with over 80 kinds of mineral resources, concentrated in over 7,000 deposits, of which more than 4,000 were being exploited in 1984. Ukraine contained over 30 percent of the proven iron-ore reserves of the former USSR, approx 30 percent of the coking coal, some 80 percent of the manganese ores, over 50 percent of the graphite and ozocerite, and some 30 percent of the mineral pigments and kaolin. Ukraine is the world's fourth-largest producer (after China, the United States, and the RF) of bituminous coal, second-largest producer (after China) of iron ore, and largest producer of manganese.

Location. The mineral resources of Ukraine are favorably located with respect to both one another and the marketplace. The location of mineral deposits is closely related to the geological structure of Ukraine. The diversity and the proximity of the various minerals stem from three factors: (1) the presence of three basic structural zones of the earth's crust – the platform (underlain by the Ukrainian Crystalline Shield), the geosyncline (the Dnieper-Donets Trough and the Donets Basin), and the foredeeps (the Subcarpathian foothills and the Black Sea Depression); (2) an exceptional diversity of deposits with respect to origin and structure; and (3) a diversity of strata, representative of all stages of the geological development of the territory. The network of railways and waterways in Ukraine enhances the transportability of the resources to other regions and for export.

The diversity of mineral resources in Ukraine is apparent in each of the three major categories. Among the hydrocarbon-based fuels the most representative are coal (the anthracite and bituminous coal of the Donets Basin, the bituminous coal of the Lviv-Volhynia Coal Basin, and the lignite or soft coal of the Dnieper Lignite Coal Basin), natural gas and petroleum (the Dnieper-Donets Trough, the Subcarpathian foothills, and the Black Sea Depression), peat (mostly in Polisia), ozocerite (Subcarpathian foothills), and the as yet unexploited oil shale (the Podilia Platform). Uranium, though not abundant, is mined near Zhovti Vody, in the Ukrainian Crystalline Shield. Outstanding among the metals are the large, rich deposits of iron ore (concentrated mostly along several elongated structures in the Ukrainian Crystalline Shield, but also in the sedimentaries of the Kerch Peninsula) and manganese ore (in sedimentaries overlying the Shield near the iron-ore deposits). Deposits of titanium mineral (ilmenite) at Irshanske (south of Korosten) and Vilnohirske (west of Dnipropetrovske) have helped make Ukraine one of the world's largest producers of titanium metal. Other metallic ores, such as bauxite, copper, nickel, lead, zinc, and mercury, are scattered in a number of little deposits with

Production of extractable minerals, 1890–1987 (in million t)

	1890	1913	1930	1940	1950	1960	1970	1980	1987
Bituminous coal	1.3	22.5	30.5	83.3	76.4	160.1	196.2	188.2	182.7
Iron ore	0.1	6.9	7.8	20.2	21.0	59.1	111.2	125.5	117.9
Manganese ore	–	0.3	0.3	0.9	0.9	2.7	5.2	6.9	7.2
Natural gas (billion cu m)	–	–	0.4	0.5	1.5	14.3	60.9	56.7	35.6
Petroleum	0.1	1.0	0.5	0.4	0.3	2.2	13.9	7.5	5.6
Lignite	–	–	0.1	0.5	1.6	12.0	10.9	8.9	9.3
Peat	–	–	0.4	3.5	2.9	4.7	4.1	1.6	2.2

small reserves. Raw materials for the chemical industry include the abundant deposits of common salt, potassium salts, phosphorites, gypsum, and chalk. Other large and valuable mineral resources of Ukraine include kaolin, fire clay, graphite, and sulfur. Ukraine possesses rich building-material resources: crystalline rocks, such as granite, basalt, andesite, porphyry, and labradorite; noncrystalline rocks, such as sandstones, limestones, and marble; and various kinds of clays, sands, and gravels. Among the precious and fabricated stones are topaz, rock crystal, garnet, opal, amber, tourmaline, and chalcedony. Of considerable medicinal significance are the large reserves of mineral waters.

Exploitation. The exploitation of mineral resources has increased rapidly in the 20th century. The output of the most important minerals in Ukraine grew in most cases almost continuously until about 1970, after which the major fossil fuels began to indicate some decline (see the table).

Whereas the depressed values of mined output after 1913 or 1940 indicate an incomplete recovery after wartime devastation, the declines following 1970 or 1980 reflect an exhaustion of mineral resources. Only the declines in lignite and peat, by the 1970s, were indicative of their partial replacement for fuel by the cleaner and more efficient oil and natural gas. Oil and natural gas, however, were being withdrawn at a faster rate than new reserves could be found or developed, and their output began to decline in the 1970s. Deposits of bituminous coal, used for generating electricity and the production of coke for iron smelting, likewise have been depleted. Despite deeper mining (which is more difficult and involves a greater danger of methane gas explosions) and the employment of more sophisticated (and more costly) machinery, output has declined since the 1970s. The richest reserves of iron ore, too, have been exhausted, and even with increased concentration and pelletization, the total output has started to decline.

Besides depleting the reserves mining activity has had a negative environmental impact. The underground mining of coal in the Donets Basin has generated high conic mounds of rock wastes near the mine sites, from which toxic substances or acidic waters have seeped into nearby ponds and streams. Cave-ins have damaged surface structures. As well, open-pit surface mining of lignite, iron ore, manganese ore, bauxite, kaolin, sand, gravel, and rock – though lending itself to the use of large machinery and entailing lower labor costs, greater labor safety, and more complete removal of the mined mineral resources – increasingly has accelerated the pollution of water and the loss of agricultural land to mining. In an attempt to counteract the trend, a code concerning the extraction of mineral resources was adopted by Ukraine in 1976, but improvements to date have been minimal.

BIBLIOGRAPHY
Bondarchuk, V. *Heolohiia rodovyshch korysnykh kopalen' Ukraïny* (Kiev 1966)
Bahatstva nadr Ukraïny: Rozvytok heolohorozviduval'noï spravy za roky radians'koï vlady (Kiev 1968)
Kadastr mineral'nykh resursiv Ukraïns'koï RSR: Rudna i nerudna syrovyna dlia chornoï metalurhiï (Kiev 1971)
Kadastr mineral'nykh resursiv Ukraïns'koï RSR: Syrovyna dlia khimichnoï promyslovosti (Kiev 1973)
Romaniuk, A.; Slowikowski, I. 'The Non-Renewable Resources of Ukraine,' in *Ukraine in the Seventies*, ed P.J. Potichnyj (Oakville, Ont 1975)
Padalka, I.; Matsui, V. *Zemni skarby Ukraïny* (Kiev 1978)
Mishchenko, V. *Vykorystannia i okhorona nadr v SRSR* (Kiev 1983)
Palamarchuk, M.; Horlenko, I.; Iasniuk, T. *Heohrafiia mineral'nykh resursiv Ukraïns'koï RSR* (Kiev 1985)
I. Stebelsky

Mineral Resources Institute (Instytut mineralnykh resursiv). A technical research institute devoted to the study of solid mineral resources and underground waters in Ukraine. Formed in 1956 in Symferopil out of the Crimean branch of the AN URSR (now ANU), it was transferred to the Ministry of Geology of the Ukrainian SSR in 1964. It consists of 15 departments and a branch in Dnipropetrovske; its main areas of study are metallogenics, coal geology, hydrogeology, geological engineering, geophysics, and ore enrichment processes.

Mineral waters. Waters (usually underground) that contain a raised concentration of dissolved mineral components and gases. They possess physical and chemical properties that are considered beneficial to the human organism or of therapeutic value for rheumatism, arthritis, skin diseases, and other ailments.

The occurrence of mineral waters in Ukraine is uneven. The greatest concentrations are in the Carpathian Mountains and the Caucasus and their foothills. Smaller concentrations are found in the Ukrainian Crystalline Shield, the Dnieper-Donets Trough, the Lviv Trough and the Podilia Upland, and the Crimean Mountains. The remaining (mostly) lowland areas have few sources of mineral waters, and those that are found are of low mineral concentrations. Of the many mineral water sources in Ukraine, only a small number are used for therapeutic purposes. Naturally carbonated mineral waters are used as table beverages. A few mineral waters have industrial significance, as sources of salts, iodine, or bromine, or have the potential for use as sources of heat.

Radioactive (radon, radium) mineral waters are associated with the Ukrainian Crystalline Shield. Despite their reputed medicinal qualities, they are not widely used and have not been adequately studied. The major developed sources of such waters are located at Khmilnyk, Myroniv-

ka, and Polonne, although other sites, such as Zhytomyr, Znamianka, and Vladyslavivka, are also known.

Carbonated mineral waters are common in the Carpathian Mountains, mostly in Transcarpathia and the Lemko region. In the Lemko region, at Krynytsia and other locations, carbonated mineral waters have been used for a long time. In the Hutsul region, to the southwest of Kolomyia, they are known near Verkhovyna (formerly Zhabie). In Transcarpathia there are nearly 120 sources of mineral waters: soda-carbonated mineral waters, located mostly in western Transcarpathia in the vicinity of Svaliava; alkaline-carbonated mineral waters, located mostly in the central part of the region; carbonated mineral waters of the Narzan type, in the southeast; and carbonated saline mineral waters, in the Uzh River valley.

Hydrogen sulfide mineral waters, though also found in Transcarpathia, are concentrated along the Carpathian foothills and the Dniester River at Morshyn, Truskavets, Nemyriv, and other locations. Sulfur springs are also found, in the Crimea near Teodosiia and at the foot of the Western Caucasus at Matsesta (near Sochi).

Glauber's salt, saline, and alkaline mineral waters are found in the foothills of the Carpathians (at Truskavets, Morshyn, and other places), the Crimean Mountains, the Dnieper-Donets Trough (in Myrhorod and its vicinity and Luhanske), the Black Sea Depression (near Odessa, near Kyrylivka, south of Melitopil, near Berdianske, and across the Azov Sea at Yeiske), and the foothills of the Caucasus (at Horiachyi Kliuch, Khadyzhenske, Naftohorske, and Maikop). Thermal springs are found in the Crimea in two groupings, those rising naturally to the surface on the Kerch Peninsula, and those fed by tube wells at Saky and Yevpatoriia.

As well as being used at resorts, mineral waters are being bottled in increasing quantities for consumption as table beverages. In 1961 more than 30 plants in Ukraine filled 190 million bottles of mineral water. Since then the output has increased fivefold, about one-half of it being lightly mineralized carbonated waters. The most widely distributed bottled carbonated mineral waters of Ukraine are from Zhytomyr, Myrhorod, Truskavets ('Naftusia'), Drahove, Ovidiopil (near Odessa), Berezivka (near Kharkiv), Teodosiia, and Shepetivka.

BIBLIOGRAPHY

Babynets', A. Dzherela mineral'nykh vod v URSR (Kiev 1958)
Babinets, A.; Gordienko, E.; Denisova, V. Lechebnye mineral'nye vody i kurorty Ukrainy (Kiev 1963)
Babinets, A.; Marus, V.; Koinov, I. Mineral'nye i termal'nye vody Sovetskikh Karpat (Kiev 1978)
Bilak, S. Mineral'nye vody Zakarpat'ia (Lviv 1986)

I. Stebelsky

Mineralogicheskii zhurnal (Mineralogy Journal). A bimonthly scientific journal published since 1979 in Kiev by the AN URSR (now ANU) Division of Geology, Geophysics, and Geochemistry. It deals with theoretical, applied, regional, and genetic mineralogy, including topics such as problems of mineral crystallography, crystallochemistry, mineral physics, mineral genesis, and the history of mineralogy. It also includes articles on the methodology of mineralogical studies and on mineralogical methods of exploration and assessment of useful mineral deposits.

Mineralogy. The study of minerals, their formation and occurrence, their properties and composition, and their classification. The development of mineralogy in Ukraine was closely connected with that of geology. Until 1917 research in mineralogy was conducted mainly by the chairs of mineralogy associated with geology at the universities of Kharkiv, Kiev, Lviv, and Odessa, the institutes of technology at Kiev and Lviv, and the Katerynoslav Mining Institute. By the 1920s and 1930s, in addition to being conducted by the geological institutions in the All-Ukrainian Academy of Sciences (now ANU), research in mineralogy was being undertaken by the Ukrainian branches of various all-Union institutes (of the Mineralogy of Raw Materials, of Fertilizers, and others). At present most work in mineralogy in Ukraine is done at the Lviv Geological Society, which also publishes *Mineralogicheskii sbornik*, and at various ANU institutes (of the Geological Sciences, of the Geochemistry and Physics of Minerals). Since 1970 the Ukrainian Mineralogy Society has been active, and since 1979 the ANU has published *Mineralogicheskii zhurnal* in Russian. The most outstanding mineralogist of Ukraine was V. *Vernadsky. Other prominent mineralogists were M. Bezborodko, V. Luchytsky, Ye. Lazarenko, and M. Sydorenko. Current mineralogists of note include A. Povarennykh, M. Semenenko, and M. Shcherbak.

Miniature painting. A term used to describe a picture in an illuminated manuscript, and a classification for all small paintings, particularly portraits that can be mounted and worn as lockets or cameos. The portrait miniature, which was meant for personal and household use, was preceded by the medieval *illumination of manuscripts and the Renaissance portrait medal. In Ukraine portrait miniatures were not widespread and have not been studied adequately. Some of the earliest were of the *panagia* type worn as medallions by clerics. Medallion portraits of the tsar awarded on special occasions gained some currency. In the late 18th and early 19th centuries miniature portraits became popular, particularly among the aristocracy, and galleries of them were founded in the palaces of the Ivanenko, Kochubei, Rodzianko, Kapnist, and Iskrytsky families. These miniature portraits were painted on vellum, wood, metal, ivory, cloth, or porcelain in watercolor, oil, or gouache. They were usually square, oval, or round and were hung on walls, displayed on furniture, or used in rings, medallions, tobacco boxes, and brooches. In the late 18th and early 19th centuries miniature portraits were painted by H. Musiisky and V. Borovykovsky, who painted a miniature of V. Kapnist (1793) and portrait medallions in his large-scale portraits (eg, of H. Bezborodko and his daughters [1803]). Some other interesting ones were by the folk artists I. Pokorsky (portrait of Zhoravko, 1810s) and Ye. Krendovsky, who painted single (V. Martinova-Ostrogradskaia, 1840), double (Shyrynsky-Shakhmatov, 1847), and family portraits (the Mahdenko children, 1848). The self-taught artist S. Rymarenko also painted portraits (1936).

Miniature portraiture declined with the widespread use of photography in the 19th century. In the early 20th century, however, interest was revived in miniature silhouettes; they were created by H. Narbut (his self-portrait with his family, 1915), M. Zhuk, and S. Kononchuk. Although miniature portraits are rarely produced by con-

Miniature painting from the 1073 *Izbornik* of Sviatoslav

temporary artists, some have been done in ceramic, porcelain, and enamel (eg, by O. Borodai).

V. Ruban

Mining science (*hirnycha nauka*). Mining science in Ukraine dates back to the beginning of the 20th century, when mining schools were set up in Lysychanske and Horlivka, and the Higher Mining School was established in Katerynoslav (1899). In 1912 the latter was reorganized into a mining institute; it attracted scientists such as M. *Fedorov, O. Dynnyk, and A. Terpigorev. In the early years of the 20th century the Makiivka Mining Rescue Station was founded to study the technology of shaft reinforcement, ventilation, and fire fighting. In the 1930s the Institute of Mining Mechanics of the AN URSR was set up in Kiev. Mining faculties appeared in higher educational institutions. Today theoretical and experimental research is conducted at the ANU (formerly AN URSR) institutes of Mining Mechanics and Cybernetics in Donetske, the institutes of Mine-Machine-Building, Automation, and Computing Technology in Kharkiv, the (until 1992 All-Union) Scientific Research Institute of Coal in Kharkiv (est 1928), and the Dnipropetrovske and Kryvyi Rih mining institutes.

An institute in Makiivka investigates work safety in the mining industry. These institutions developed the theoretical and practical principles for locating, preparing, and exploiting mineral seams, as well as the theory of cutting coal, the dynamics of cutting-machines, the mechanization of reinforcement, and new forms of shaft transport. Among the researchers were Fedorov (mining mechanics), Dynnyk (mining pressure, hoists, ventilation), O. *Shcherban, V. Cherniak (mining thermodynamics and ventilation in deep shafts), H. *Savin (the dynamics of hoists), V. *Pak (the construction of shaft ventilators), Terpigorev (the exploitation of coal fields and mechanization of mining), K. Borysenko (compressors and pneumatic engines for mining machines), M. *Poliakov and S. Volotkovsky (belt conveyers and underground electric transport), P. Nestorov (the construction of shaft hoists), K. *Tatomyr, B. Lokshyn, O. Naidysh, and D. Ohloblyn (shaft design, beam installation, ventilation), O. *Kukhtenko and O. Kryzhanivsky (automated control of cutting-machines and shaft hoists), M. Zaitsev (mining pressure and coal and gas blowouts), M. *Starykov (developing seams at great depths), M. Ivanov (productive capacity planning), and F. *Abramov and B. Hrentsinger (the theoretical foundations of the dynamics of air and gas in shaft ventilation). Ukrainian scientists, engineers, and builders designed coal-mining combines (the Donbas, Kirovets, and UKR), cutters (the USB), ore-loading machines (the EMP-1 and PLM-5), coal saws, equipment complexes (Don-VUHI and Dondniprovuhlemash), and mechanical hydraulic coal-crushing equipment (Ukrainian Scientific Research Institute of Hydraulic Coal Mining). The Ukrainian Ministry of the Coal Industry has published the monthly Russian-language journal *Ugol' Ukrainy* since 1957.

S. Protsiuk

Ministries of the Ukrainian SSR. The central administrative organs of Soviet Ukraine. Until March 1946 ministries were called *people's commissariats. Central agencies within Ukraine's Council of Ministers, such as the State Planning Committee, the CC CPU Committee for Party-State Control, the KGB, and the Central Statistical Administration, had nonadministrative (development, co-ordinating, and planning) functions. The ministers and heads of state committees and commissions made up the central government, the *Council of Ministers of the Ukrainian SSR.

Until August 1991 there were two types of ministries in Ukraine, Union-republican and republican. The Union-republican ministries were subordinated to both the Council of Ministers and the corresponding USSR Union-republican ministry in Moscow. The republican ministries were constitutionally subordinated directly to the Council of Ministers, although in practice USSR ministries and Union-republican ministries in Moscow interfered in the work of the republican ministries, and the division of responsibilities was unclear. In the 1960s the number of republican ministries was reduced, and some became Union-republican ministries. In 1981 Soviet Ukraine had Union-republican ministries of the construction of heavy-industry enterprises; higher and specialized secondary education; internal affairs; the coal industry; geology; energy and electrification; state purchases (of agricultural products); foreign affairs; communications; culture; light

industry; forest management; the lumber, paper, and woodworking industry; melioration and water management; assembled and special building works; the meat and dairy industry; education; health protection; fruit and vegetable farming; industrial construction; the building-materials industry; state farms; rural construction; the rural economy; trade; finances; the food industry; ferrous metallurgy; and justice. It had only six republican ministries: automobile transportation; auto-route construction and utilization; communal-housing management; local industry; public services; and social security.

Ministries were created, reorganized, and abolished, and their ministers appointed and removed, by Ukraine's Supreme Soviet or, between its sessions, by the Supreme Soviet's Presidium on the recommendation of the chairman of the Council of Ministers subject to subsequent approval by the Supreme Soviet. Ministers were answerable to the Supreme Soviet, its Presidium, and the Council of Ministers; they had to be CPSU members and perform their duties on the basis of the principle of 'one-man management.' A ministry's responsibilities and tasks were defined by the Council of Ministers, and a minister's instructions and decrees could be annulled by the Council of Ministers and, in the case of Union-republican ministries, by corresponding USSR ministers.

Ministry of Internal Affairs. See MVD.

Ministry of State Security. See MGB.

Grigorii Minkh

Minkh, Grigorii [Minx, Grigorij], b 19 September 1836 in Griazi, Lipetsk county, Tambov gubernia, Russia, d 23 December 1896 in Kiev. Russian pathological anatomist and epidemiologist. After graduating from Moscow University (1861) he specialized in pathological anatomy in Germany and taught at Kiev University (1876–95). He presided over the Society of Kiev Physicians (1882–6) and participated in expeditions to Turkestan, Egypt, Palestine, and Southern Ukraine to study the plague, leprosy, and typhus.

Minkivsky, Oleksander [Min'kivs'kyj], b 25 December 1900 in Snizhna, Skvyra county, Kiev gubernia, d 25 April 1979 in Kiev. Conductor and teacher. He completed his studies at the Lysenko Music and Drama Institute in 1930 and taught music at the Kiev Pedagogical Institute and the Music and Drama Tekhnikum. In 1934 he became artistic director and chief conductor of the Ukrainian Radio Committee Choir. Evacuated from Kiev in 1941, he was appointed director of the Verovka State Chorus upon his return and then transferred to the newly created State Banduryst Kapelle of Ukraine as artistic director and chief conductor (1946–72). He also held a position at the Kiev Conservatory (lecturer from 1951, professor from 1960).

Minkovych, Volodymyr [Minkovyč] (Minkowycz, Wolodymyr), b 21 October 1937 in Libukhova, Dobromyl county, Galicia. Mechanical engineer and educator; member of the American Society of Mechanical Engineers. He graduated from the University of Minnesota (PH D, 1965) and worked at the Argonne National Laboratory and as an independent consultant. He also taught at the University of Minnesota and University of Illinois. He was editor of *International Journal of Heat and Mass Transfer*. He has published numerous technical papers and *A Laboratory Manual for Fluid Mechanics* (1973) and edited *Progress in Heat and Mass Transfer* (vol 5, 1972).

St Constantine Ukrainian Catholic Church in Minneapolis

Minneapolis. A midwestern American city, which forms part of the Twin Cities metropolitan area (together with St Paul). In 1980 the population of Minneapolis proper was 370,950, and that of the metropolitan area was 2,113,530, including 7,720 Ukrainians.

The first group of Ukrainians arrived there in the 1870s from the Transcarpathian region of Ukraine and were followed in the early 1900s by immigrants from Galicia. Upon arrival they settled on the land bordering the city in what is now northeast Minneapolis and worked in the forest, factory, sawmill, and railway industries. The largest influx of Ukrainian immigrants came after 1949. Today many Minneapolis Ukrainians are white-collar workers and professionals.

The first church for Ukrainian faithful was St Mary's Greek Catholic Church, built in 1888. A jurisdiction dispute with the local Roman Catholic bishop following the arrival of the church's first priest, Rev A. Toth, in 1889, led the parish to affiliate with the San Francisco–based Russian Orthodox church. Minneapolis subsequently became an important Russian Orthodox center in spite of the fact that its local adherents were predominantly Ukrainian. The first specifically Ukrainian church in Minneapolis (St Constantine's) was built in 1913. In 1971 it was rebuilt, and a new rectory and gallery added. There are two Ukrainian Orthodox parishes in Minneapolis. A Ukrainian Protestant community has existed since the 1940s. There are two Ukrainian Baptist communities, one of which sponsors a Ukrainian-language radio broadcast in the Twin Cities on Sunday afternoons.

Minneapolis remains the center of Ukrainian social and cultural life in the Twin Cities. Among the earliest social and cultural organizations were the Zaporozhian Sich (1918) and an amateur theatrical group (1925), a branch (no. 32) of the Organization for the Rebirth of Ukraine, and a folk ballet and chorus (1934). The most important and prominent social, cultural, and political leader of the Ukrainian community in the Twin Cities was A. *Granovsky. Many new political organizations were founded by the postwar immigrants. In 1980 the Minnesota branch of the Ukrainian Congress Committee of America (UCCA) contained representatives from 29 local bodies, including churches and their allied organizations; independent youth groups; a veterans' association; political organizations, such as the Ukrainian Republican Club and the Ukrainian Democratic Club; the Ukrainian American Center; benevolent associations; and a credit union. The Ukrainian Gift Shop, founded by M. Procai, is well known throughout North America for its Ukrainian Easter eggs. The Immigration History Research Center (1964) at the University of Minnesota in Minneapolis houses the largest collection (founded by A. Granovsky) in the country of materials on Ukrainian immigration to the United States. The two main cultural organizations are the chorus Dnipro and the women's vocal ensemble Yevshan Zillia. The music journal *Muzychni visti* was published in the Twin Cities in 1962–9 before moving to Jersey City. Three English-language publications are the Ukrainian Catholic quarterly *Trident* (1972–), the Ukrainian Orthodox League *Newsletter* (1972–), and *UKADET* (Ukrainian Kadet, 1941–65, 1971–2), published by the Ukrainian Folk Ballet at St Michael's Church.

BIBLIOGRAPHY
Minnesota Ukrainian Bicentennial Committee. *Minnesota Ukrainians Celebrate the Bicentennial of the USA* (Minneapolis 1977)
Dyrud, K. 'East Slavs: Rusins, Ukrainians, and Belorussians,' in *They Chose Minnesota: A Survey of the State's Ethnic Groups*, ed J.D. Holmquist (St Paul 1981)

H. Myroniuk

Minnesota. One of the western north central states of the United States (1990 pop 4,375,099; 10,691 Ukrainians). The 1980 census indicated a total of 4,075,970 inhabitants, with 9,558 Ukrainians identified as a single-ancestry group. In 1976 it was estimated that there were 10,000 Minnesotans of Ukrainian origin, with the largest concentration in the Twin Cities (Minneapolis–St Paul) area. The first immigrants arrived in the 1870s from Transcarpathia and settled on land which is now Northeast *Minneapolis. At the end of the 19th century, Ukrainians from Galicia and Subcarpathia settled in northern Minnesota to work in the iron mines of the Mesabi Range, especially in the Chisholm area. Some Ukrainians from Canada also settled in the northern part of the state after remaining on homestead lands they thought were situated in southern Manitoba. Others settled in the towns of Virginia, Hibbing, and Eveleth. The third wave of immigration, after the Second World War, brought over 100 Ukrainian families to Minnesota.

St Josaphat's Ukrainian Pontifical Minor Seminary

Minor seminary (Mala seminariia). A secondary school that prepares students for further theological pursuits in the Catholic church, in addition to providing a basic course of studies. The first Ukrainian minor seminary, named after St Josaphat, was established in Lviv in 1919; in 1935 it had 172 students. A second, smaller minor seminary (42 students in 1935) was established in Rohatyn in 1931. These schools were closed after the Soviet occupation of Western Ukraine, although the Lviv seminary was briefly reopened under the subsequent German occupation.

Outside Ukraine the first Ukrainian minor seminary was St Basil's Academy in Philadelphia (est 1924), which was later moved to Stamford, Connecticut. In Canada, St Vladimir's College was established in Roblin, Manitoba, under the direction of the Redemptorist Fathers. In South America, minor seminaries are run by the Basilian order in Prudentópolis, Brazil (St Josaphat's), and Apóstoles, Argentina. The only minor seminary in Western Europe in which the language of instruction is Ukrainian is St Josaphat's Ukrainian Pontifical Minor Seminary, in Rome (est 1951 in France, moved to Castel Gandolfo in 1956 and to Rome in 1959).

Minorities. See National minorities.

Mykhailo Minsky

Ivan Mirchuk

Minsky, Mykhailo [Mins'kyj, Myxajlo] (Michael; real name: Spirin), b 20 August 1918 in Ukraine, d 9 October 1988 in Holland. Opera and concert singer (baritone). He studied geography at Kazan University. In a DP camp in Germany after the Second World War, he became one of the main soloists of the Ukrainian Bandurist Chorus. He arrived in the United States with the chorus in 1949 and soon launched a musical career of his own. He sang in operatic and concert appearances in Italy, Germany, Switzerland, France, England, Holland, Belgium, Canada, and the United States. He performed leading baritone parts in *I Pagliacci, Cavalleria rusticana, Il Trovatore, La Traviata, Tosca,* and *Carmen,* as well as songs by M. Mussorgsky and A. Khachaturian. His Ukrainian repertoire included songs by M. Lysenko, Ya. Stepovy, Yu. Meitus, M. Fomenko, V. Hrudyn, and A. Rudnytsky. Minsky's 11 LP recordings of Ukrainian songs have enjoyed considerable popularity since the 1950s.

Mint (*Mentha,* Ukrainian: *miata*). A fragrant, strong-scented perennial herb of the family Lamiaceae, with elongated elliptical leaves and small white, pink, or pale purple flowers arranged in clusters. There are many species, of which commercially the most valuable is the peppermint (*M. piperita;* Ukrainian: *miata kholodna*). Peppermint-541, with a high menthol content, was developed in Ukraine. Mint leaves and flowers contain essential oil which is used to improve the flavor of some medicines, in perfumery and the cosmetic industry as a fragrance, and in the food industry as a spice. Mint drops are used to treat nausea and vomiting. In Ukraine peppermint is planted in fertile lowlands, such as the forest-steppe region.

Mir. See *Obshchina.*

Mirchuk, Ivan [Mirčuk], b 18 June 1891 in Stryi, Galicia, d 2 May 1961 in Munich. Philosopher, cultural historian, and émigré community leader; full member of the Shevchenko Scientific Society from 1938 and the Ukrainian Academy of Arts and Sciences from 1946, and corresponding member of the Bavarian Academy of Sciences from 1949. A graduate of Vienna University (PH D, 1914), after the First World War he was a docent (1921–5), professor (1925–61), and rector (1947–8, 1950–5, 1956–61) at the *Ukrainian Free University in Prague and Munich and a research fellow (1926–30) and director (1931–45) of the *Ukrainian Scientific Institute in Berlin. From 1954 he was a research fellow of the Institute for the Study of the USSR in Munich and editor of its journal *Sowjetstudien.* A member of the émigré hetmanite movement, he was president of the *Ukrainska Hromada association in Berlin. At first he was interested in Greek ethics and epistemology, and published articles on the foundations of Greek ethics (1923), ethics and politics (1923), the implications of metageometry for the Kantian concept of space (1924), and the possibility of synthetic a priori judgment and edited a Ukrainian translation of I. Kant's *Prolegomena zu jeden künftigen Metaphysik* (1930). Turning to ethnopsychology, he attempted to describe the main features of Slavic philosophy (1927 and 1936) in order to isolate, eventually, the unique traits of the Ukrainian mind. He tackled this task in articles on L. Tolstoi and H. Skovoroda as two national types (1929), the Ukrainians' and Russians' different attitudes to the demonic (1936; later elaborated into *Das*

Dämonische bei den Russen und den Ukrainern, 1950), the worldview of the Ukrainian people (1942), and Ukraine as a mediator between the East and West (1941). Calling upon his extensive knowledge of Ukrainian thought and culture he prepared the encyclopedic *Handbuch der Ukraine* (1941; rev English trans: *Ukraine and Its People*, 1949) and *Geschichte der ukrainischen Kultur* (1957). He also wrote the textbook on esthetics (1926) used at the Ukrainian Studio of Plastic Arts in Prague. The festschrift *Symbolae in memoriam Ioannis Mirtschuk*, edited by O. Kulchytsky, appeared in 1974.

T. Zakydalsky

Petro Mirchuk   Zinaida Mirna

Mirchuk, Petro [Mirčuk], b 26 June 1913 in Dobrivliany, Galicia. Political activist, journalist, and historian. While studying law at Lviv University in the 1930s, he was active in the OUN. In 1939 he emigrated to Prague, where he completed his studies at the Ukrainian Free University (LL D, 1941). After the war he was elected president of the Central Union of Ukrainian Students (1945–7) and appointed to the leadership of the OUN (Bandera faction, 1948–52). After settling in the United States in 1950, he taught at a number of colleges and received a PH D in history from the Ukrainian Free University in Munich (1969). Besides numerous political and historical articles in the Ukrainian press, he wrote over 20 books, including *Ukraïns'ka Povstans'ka Armiia, 1941–1952* (The Ukrainian Insurgent Army, 1941–1952, 1953), *Narys istoriï Orhanizatsiï ukraïns'kykh natsionalistiv* (An Outline of the History of the Organization of Ukrainian Nationalists, 1968), and *U nimets'kykh mlynakh smerty* (1957; published in translation in 1976 as *In the German Mills of Death, 1941–1945*).

Mirmekion. An ancient Hellenic settlement 5 km north of present-day Kerch. Founded as an independent city-state in the 6th century BC, Mirmekion grew into a center for trade, manufacturing, agriculture, wine making, and fish preserving. Excavations in 1934 revealed wall fortifications and towers, living quarters, workshops, and fish processing facilities. The city also minted its own coin stamped with the city's symbol of ants ('mirmekion' being the Greek word for 'ant'). Mirmekion became part of the Bosporan Kingdom before collapsing in the 3rd century AD.

Mirna, Zinaida (née Khylchevska), b 1875, d 1 April 1950 in Prague. Civic and political leader; wife of I. *Mirny. After moving to Kiev in 1910, she was active in the Ukrainian women's and education movements. During the First World War she organized relief for deportees from Western Ukraine and played an important role in the independence movement as a member of the Central Rada and the Little Rada. In 1919 she helped found the *National Council of Ukrainian Women in Kamianets-Podilskyi, and she served as its vice-president. Later she headed its Berlin branch. After settling in Prague in 1924, she served as the longtime president of the *Ukrainian Women's Union in Czechoslovakia and gave much of her time to the Museum of Ukraine's Struggle for Independence. In 1937 she was elected to the presidium of the World Union of Ukrainian Women. She was a constant contributor to the Ukrainian press and a translator of French literature into Ukrainian.

Ivan Mirny   Yevheniia Miroshnychenko

Mirny, Ivan [Mirnyj], b 30 August 1872 in Kharkiv gubernia, d 17 March 1937 in Prague. Civic leader; husband of Z. *Mirna. After the February Revolution of 1917 he was a member of the Central Rada and acting commissioner of Kiev gubernia. In October he was appointed undersecretary in the UNR General Secretariat. Under the Hetman government and the UNR Directory he served as chancery director of the Ministry of Foreign Affairs. In 1919 he was a member of the UNR delegation at the Paris Peace Conference, and from 1920 he served in Berlin as the financial representative of the UNR government-in-exile. In 1924 he settled in Prague, where he was secretary of the Ukrainian Civic Committee, a member of the executives of several other émigré organizations, and office manager of the Ukrainian Higher Pedagogical Institute. He wrote a history of the institute (1934) and contributed to Ukrainian émigré periodicals.

Miroshnychenko, Yevheniia [Mirošnyčenko, Jevhenija], b 12 June 1931 in Radianske, now in Kharkiv oblast. Opera singer (lyric-coloratura soprano). She completed her studies at the Kiev Conservatory (1957, pupil of M. Donets-Tesseir), and then performed as a soloist with the Kiev Theater of Opera and Ballet. Her major roles were Violetta in G. Verdi's *La Traviata*, Rosina in G. Rossini's *The Barber of Seville*, Venus in M. Lysenko's *Aeneas*, Martha in N. Rimsky-Korsakov's *The Tsar's Bride*, Iolan in H. Maiboroda's *Mylana*, and the title role in G. Donizetti's *Lucia di Lammermoor*. She received an award at the International Vocal Competition in Toulouse, France (1958), and studied at Milan's La Scala. She has performed as a concert soloist in the Soviet Union and abroad, in Poland, Bulgaria, Yugoslavia, France, Canada, and Japan. She has recorded operatic arias, Ukrainian classical compositions, and folk songs on LPs and in films.

Mirtovsky, Mykola [Mirtovs'kyj], b 8 March 1894 in Saratov, Russia, d 16 April 1959 in Lviv. Neurologist. A graduate of Saratov University (1916), he was a professor at the Dnipropetrovske (1930–55) and Lviv medical institutes (1955–9). His research dealt with the treatment of epilepsy, botulism, and hyperkinesis, disorders of the autonomic nervous system, and circulatory disorders of the brain.

Mirylo pravednoie (Just Measure). A handbook for judges compiled in Kievan Rus' in the 12th to 13th centuries. The work contains instructions on just and unjust sentences in the first part, and on civil and church norms of Byzantine and Rus' law in the second part. The oldest extant redaction, known as the Troitskyi redaction, dates from the late 14th century. It was published in part during the 19th century and in full in 1961 in Moscow as *Merilo pravednoe*.

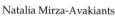
Natalia Mirza-Avakiants   Mykhailo Mishchenko

Mirza-Avakiants, Natalia [Mirza-Avak'janc, Natalja] (née Dvorianska), b 23 October 1889 in Boryspil, Pereiaslav county, Poltava gubernia, d ? Historian. She studied at Kharkiv University under D. Bahalii. In the 1920s and 1930s she was a professor of Ukrainian history at the Kharkiv and Poltava institutes of people's education and at Kiev University (1935–7). One of the founders of the Poltava Society for the Study and Preservation of Monuments and Antiquity and Art (1918–20) and a full member of the Scientific Research Department of the History of Ukrainian Culture in Kharkiv, she wrote articles on the Cossack *starshyna* in the late 17th century (1919), peasant movements in Poltava gubernia in 1902 (1924), and the legal system in Left-Bank Ukraine in the second half of the 17th century (1926); a book on peasant unrest in Ukraine in 1905–7 (1925); a pioneering monograph on the history of Ukraine in relation to the history of Western Europe (1928); and a reader in Ukrainian history. She was arrested in 1937 and sent to a Soviet concentration camp. Her further fate is unknown.

Mishalow, Victor [Mišalov, Viktor], b 4 April 1960 in Sydney, Australia. Banduryst, educator, and musicologist. A graduate in music from the University of Sydney (1985), he established himself as a banduryst of note in the West through concert tours in North America (1979, 1983, 1985), solo appearances with the Ukrainian Bandurist Chorus, and the release of several recordings featuring traditional, classical, and original works. He furthered his studies at the Kiev Conservatory (1979–82) under S. Bashtan and has published over 50 articles on aspects of the bandura's history.

Mishchenko, Dmytro [Miščenko], b 18 November 1921 in Zelene, Melitopil county, Tavriia gubernia. Writer and literary scholar. He completed postgraduate studies at Kiev University in 1954 and was appointed senior editor of the Radianskyi Pysmennyk publishing house and editor in chief in 1964. Several collections of his short stories have appeared: *Syny moria* (Sons of the Sea, 1955), *Bat'kivs'ka liniia* (Father's Line, 1960), *Vesniana povin'* (Spring Flood, 1960), *Dolia poeta* (The Poet's Fate, 1961), and *Ochi divochi* (Girl's Eyes, 1964). Mishchenko has written several novels, including *Siveriany* (The Siverianians, 1959), *Vitry prynosiat' hrozu* (The Winds Bring a Storm, 1968), *Chest' rodu* (The Clan's Honor, 1977), and *Naivyshchyi zakon* (The Highest Law, 1978). His most important scholarly publication is *Rozvytok realizmu v tvorchosti M. Kotsiubyns'koho* (The Development of Realism in the Work of M. Kotsiubynsky, 1957).

Mishchenko, Mykhailo [Miščenko, Myxajlo], b 24 May 1896 in Kharkiv, d 20 May 1974 in Minneapolis. Psychiatrist and neurophysiologist; full member of the Ukrainian Academy of Arts and Sciences in the USA and the Shevchenko Scientific Society (from 1947). In 1917 he joined the Army of the UNR and served as a major at the front. After completing his medical studies in 1929, he taught at the Kharkiv Institute of People's Education and the Kharkiv Medical Institute and conducted research at the All-Ukrainian Psychoneurological Academy. A postwar refugee, he taught briefly at the Ukrainian Free University in Munich and then emigrated to the United States (1949), where he practiced psychiatry and continued his research. His scientific papers, most of them based on his own experiments, were published in Ukrainian, English, German, and Russian; they deal with topics such as the treatment of schizophrenia, the nature of hypnosis and sleep, and psychiatric aspects of heart diseases.

Misiia Ukraïny (Mission of Ukraine). An organ of the émigré Association for the Liberation of Ukraine (SVU), published in Toronto from 1957 to 1974 (a total of 32 issues). The magazine contained organizational documents and news, articles on the history of the struggle for Ukrainian independence and the evils of Russian communism and imperialism, polemics with other émigré political groups, and condemnations of the émigré sympathizers of 'national communism-Khvylovism.' The chief editors were S. Pidkova and V. Koval.

Misionar (Missionary). A religious journal published by the Basilian monastic order, with some interruptions, between 1897 and 1944. It began in Lviv, but soon moved to the Zhovkva monastery, the main center of Basilian activ-

Misionar (1897–1944)

ty. During the First World War it appeared in Zagreb, Croatia, and in 1940–1 it was published in Peremyshl. Initially the journal appeared semimonthly, but later it became a monthly. During 1921–39 it was called *Misionar presviatoho sertsia Isusovoho*. Several supplements to *Misionar* were published, including *Malyi misionarchyk* for children (1903–14, 1939). Among the editors of *Misionar* were P. Filias (1897–8 and 1921–6), L. Berezovsky (1898–1908 and 1916–20), and M. Marysiuk (1927–32 and 1940–1). *Misionar* was one of the most popular journals of its kind and was regularly published in a pressrun of 30,000 to 40,000 copies.

Misionar (Missionary). A monthly journal of the *Basilian order of nuns in the United States, published in Philadelphia from 1917 to June 1990. It contained popular articles on religious topics, prayers, and stories on religious themes. From the 1950s it appeared in a bilingual Ukrainian-English edition.

Misionar (Brazil). See *Ukraïns'kyi misionar*.

Misiones. The northeastern province of Argentina, situated between the river Paraná and Paraguay, with its borders on the east with Brazil, on the northwest with Paraguay, and on the southeast with the province of Corrientes. Its area is 29,800 sq km, and it has 787,514 (1991) inhabitants.

Misiones was the first region of Argentina to be settled by Ukrainians and has the second-largest Ukrainian population in the country (after the Buenos Aires region). The first settlers arrived in 1897, and by 1914 the community had grown to more than 10,000. During the interwar period 20,000 Ukrainians from Volhynia and Polisia and 3,000 Bukovynians and Transcarpathians moved into the earlier-settled *Apóstoles region, in addition to establishing new settlement areas in L.N. Alem and Oberá. The majority of the settlers worked as agriculturists and adapted to local farming methods and crops quite readily. After the Second World War additional immigrants arrived in the province from the displaced persons' camps in Germany as well as from Paraguay. By the 1980s the 70,000 Ukrainians in Misiones constituted 10 percent of the province's total population and approx 25 percent of the country's Ukrainians.

Ukrainians are distributed in almost every place in the province of Misiones as follows: in the district of Apóstoles, Las Tunas, Tres Capones, Capon Bonito, San José, Sierra San José, Tuna; in the department of Posadas, Posadas, Parada Leis, and Fachinal; in the department of Candelaria, Campina; in the department of L.N. Alem, Gob, López, Picada San Javier, Bonpland, Picada Belgrano, Picada Galitsiana, Arroyo del Medio, Cerro Azul, Campi-

MISIONES

nas, and Gen Guemes; in the department of Concepción, Concepción de la Serra and Santa Maria; in the department of San Javier, San Javier, Florentino Ameghino, and Itacaruare; in the department of Oberá, Panambi, Los Helechos, Campo Ramón, Guarani, San Martin, Chopa, Quinta Sección, Campo Viera, and Novena Sección; in the department of San Ignacio, Jardin America and Nacanguazú; and in the department of Cainguas, Campo Grande, Aristobulo del Valle, and Seguin.

Community development in the province began early in the century with the establishment of church parishes, choirs and amateur theater groups, and reading rooms. By 1922 there was a brick church, a school, and a Prosvita society in Apóstoles. In 1948 the Basilian order established a printing press in Apóstoles. The Basilian brothers operate the St Josafat seminary for boys and a junior high school for girls in Apóstoles and a high school in Posadas. During the 1970s monuments to T. Shevchenko were put up in Apóstoles and Oberá. Because of their large numbers and their continuing presence, Ukrainians have been recognized for their contribution to the development of the province. Likewise, the compact nature of their settlement has assisted them in maintaining a group identity. (See *Argentina.)

N. Kerechuk

Miskhor [Misxor]. IX-15. A resort area on the southern coast of the Crimea 13 km southwest of Yalta that is part of the town of *Koreiz. It has 14 sanatoriums and health resorts dealing with respiratory problems, heart and circulatory diseases, and nervous disorders. Its most famous architectural monument is the Swallow's Nest castle (built in 1912).

Misko, Stefan [Mis'ko], b 1912 in Lviv, Ukraine, d 1986. Painter. He was self-taught in landscape, figurative composition, and expressionist and neoimpressionist styles in watercolor and oil. He expressed his feelings in symbolism and abstraction. After arriving in Australia in 1949, he founded the Ukrainian Artists' Society in Australia (SUOMA). He held several one-man exhibitions and is widely represented in private collections in Australia and overseas.

Mitla (Broom; Spanish: La Escoba). An Argentinian-Ukrainian journal of humor and satire. Published monthly and edited from 1949 by Yu. Serediak, *Mitla* was a popular eight-page compilation of short pieces and cartoons that looked whimsically at émigré life, indulged in broadax humor, and occasionally attacked Soviet politics. The name was also used for Serediak's publishing house and for an almanac he published irregularly. *Mitla* did not appear after 1976, although the publishing house continued operating.

Mitrak, Aleksander. See Mytrak, Oleksander.

Ivan Mitrynga

Mitrynga, Ivan (Mitringa; pen names: Serhii Oreliuk and Polyn), b 1909 in Bibrka county, Galicia, d 6 September 1943 at Viliia, near Ostrih, Volhynia. Political leader and publicist. In the 1930s he studied history in Lviv and was active in the OUN, and also formed a group critical of the OUN's fascist tendencies and favoring a progressive ideology and a program with a wider popular appeal. In 1938 he edited the propagandist paper *Het' z bol'shevyzmom*, which first issued the slogan Freedom for Peoples! Freedom for the Individual! After breaking with the OUN (Bandera faction) in 1941, he set up in Polisia the Ukrainian Revolutionary Party of Workers and Peasants, which joined in 1942 with a number of other groups to form the *Ukrainian People's Democratic party. Mitrynga edited the new party's organ *Zemlia i volia*. At the same time he served as chief of the political and propaganda staff in the *Polisian Sich under T. Borovets's command. He was killed in action against Soviet partisans. Besides articles in the nationalist press Mitrynga wrote a number of political pamphlets, including *Hitler i Ukraïna* (Hitler and Ukraine, 1939) and *Nash shliakh borot'by* (Our Path of Struggle, 1940).

Mitsyk, Volodymyr [Micyk], b 25 May 1925 in Piatykhatky (now in Dnipropetrovske oblast). Biologist. A graduate of the Dagestan Agricultural Institute (1950), h worked at the Kiev Veterinary Institute and the Ukrainia Scientific Research institutes of the Physiology and Bic chemistry of Farm Animals and of the Meat and Dairy Ir dustry. In 1974 he became a professor at the Kiev Trad and Economics Institute. His main research is in the are of biochemical processes in meat.

Mittenwald. A health and vacation resort center (197 pop, approx 9,000) on the Isar River near the Austrian bor der in Bavaria. After the war many Ukrainian DPs wer housed at two camps in Mittenwald: 2,900 in Jäger-Kaser ne (1946–51) and 1,200 in Pionier-Kaserne (1947–50). A the time a Ukrainian Autocephalous Orthodox and tw Ukrainian Catholic parishes, Ukrainian nurseries, ele mentary schools and a secondary school, libraries, a teach ers' college and vocational courses, choirs, Y. Hirniak an O. Dobrovolska's Theater Studio (1947–9), and the Plas Ukrainian Youth Organization were active there. Th weekly bulletin *Taborovi budni* (1947), the religious weekl *Khrystyians'kyi shliakh* (1946–7), the Christian monthl *Khrystos nasha syla* (1946–7), and the sports weekly *Zma* (1946) came out in Mittenwald.

Mixed-feed industry. An industry that produces high protein livestock, poultry, and fish feed – roughages, con centrates, and protein-vitamin-antibiotic-mineral supple ments – from cereal grains, grasses, and the by-product and surpluses of the food and chemical industries. Befor 1914 it was only a cottage industry concentrated in Kiev Poltava, Rybnytsia, Berdychiv, Balta, and other cities o Ukraine.

Under Soviet rule the industry developed slowly befor the Second World War. The first feed plant was built i 1930. In 1940 nine plants produced 511,000 t of mixec feed, or 42.5 percent of the USSR production. The industr began to grow rapidly in the 1950s. During the Eight Five-Year Plan (1966–70) feed supplements were first pro duced. The industry produced 2.5 million t of mixed fee in 1965, 3.73 million t in 1969, and 15 million t (as well a 1.3 million t of supplements) in 1979. Mixed feeds are nov produced by over 90 specialized feed plants and larg bakeries, raion food-production complexes, and interfarn mixed-feed plants. The largest enterprises are located ir Mykolaiv, Poltava, Kharkiv, Kiev, Rivne, Odessa, Kirovo hrad, Lutske, Donetske, Luhanske, and Chernihiv.

Mixed-forest zone. A region of natural vegetation characterized by a mixture of broad-leaved and needle leaved forests, that forms a transitional zone between th broad-leaved, deciduous forests to the south and the nee dle-leaved taiga to the north.

The mixed-forest zone of Ukraine forms part of the mixed-forest zone of the East European Plain. It occupies the northern part of Ukraine and corresponds with the physical-geographical region of *Polisia. The southern border of the zone extends from Kholm in the west east ward to Korets, and then drops south to Shepetivka, whence it continues eastward past Zhytomyr, Kiev, Nizhen, Krolevets, and Hlukhiv before swinging north ward toward Sevsk. It also includes *Little Polisia as a nar row southwestern outlier. The southern border of the zone reaches the Central European broad-leaved forest in the west, and east of Ostrih it merges with the *forestteppe zone. Within Ukraine the mixed-forest zone incorporates most raions of Volhynia, Rivne, Zhytomyr, and Chernihiv oblasts and parts of Khmelnytskyi, Kiev, and Sumy oblasts. Its area exceeds 113,000 sq km and represents 19 percent of the territory of Ukraine.

Characteristic of the mixed-forest zone in Ukraine are (1) a temperate continental climate with an average annual precipitation slightly in excess of evaporation, (2) a predominantly lowland topography with periglacial or glacial sandy surface deposits underlying podzolic and organic soils, and (3) a vegetation cover consisting of mixed needle-leaved and broad-leaved forests, meadows, and swamps.

The environment of the mixed-forest zone has been modified by human activity. Today only 30 percent of the zone is forested. Nearly one-third of the zone's area is occupied by cultivated land, an amount which continues to increase with the expansion of wetland drainage. Careless drainage development has resulted in waterlogging and other damage in some areas. In response plans were formulated to meliorate the situation and to proceed with environmentally sensitive development, including improved hydrotechnical construction, agrotechnical measures, and the afforestation of loose sands. Meanwhile the Chornobyl nuclear accident (April 1986) and prolonged radioactive fallout from the ensuing fire contaminated the environment and the food system in much of the mixed-forest zone. The full extent and intensity of the contamination are not yet known.

With its relative abundance of forests the mixed-forest zone has become an important outdoor recreational region in Ukraine. So that the zone's natural landscapes and wildlife would be preserved and studied, there were established in Ukraine the Polisia Nature Reserve, the Dnieper-Teteriv and the Zaliske game preserves (both north of Kiev), and several wildlife refuges. The Shatsk National Park was established in 1983 for both nature preservation and recreation. (See also *Forest, *Flora, and *Vegetation regions.)

I. Stebelsky

Miz, Roman [Myz'], b 14 August 1932 in Drohobych, Galicia. Priest and civic leader. He studied at the Catholic theological faculty in Zagreb (1953–9) and then at the faculties of philosophy in Zagreb, Novi Sad, and the Ukrainian Free University in Munich. In 1958 he was ordained a priest, and he served in Lipovljani (Croatia) and Novi Sad. He headed the Council of Ukrainian Pastors and Catechists in Yugoslavia and was secretary of the Ecumenical Institute of the Catholic theological faculty in Zagreb. In 1978 he established the Center of Theological Culture for Laity in Zagreb. He organized and served as the director of the Ukrainian radio program in Banja Luka (1967–8) and was coeditor of the monthly *Nova dumka*. He has published numerous articles in Ukrainian periodicals on religion, church history, and Ukrainians in Yugoslavia.

Mizhhiria [Mižhirja]. V-4. A town smt (1990 pop 10,200) on the Rika River and a raion center in Transcarpathia oblast. It was founded in the 13th century and was first mentioned in historical documents in 1415. It attained smt status in 1947, and its name was changed from Volove to Mizhhiria in 1953. The town has a forest products complex, a sanatorium, and tourist centers.

Miziun, Hryhorii [Mizjun, Hryhorij], b 7 April 1903 in Kryvushi, Kremenchuk county, Poltava gubernia, d 15 December 1963 in Chernivtsi. Poet and playwright. He was one of the founders of the association of Komsomol writers, Molodniak. Miziun's poems were first published in 1920. He wrote dramas about Soviet life: *Syla na sylu* (Might against Might, 1926), *Novymy stezhkamy* (On New Paths, 1930), *Rekonstruktsiia* (Reconstruction, 1931), *Liubov i druzhba* (Love and Friendship, 1937), and *Tovaryshi* (Comrades, 1938). He was the author of a critical literary study of Yu. Fedkovych titled *Spivets' narodnykh spodivan'* (The Bard of the People's Hopes, 1959).

Mizko, Mykola, b 25 May 1818 in Katerynoslav, d 8 June 1881 in Voronezh, Russia. Ukrainophile journalist. He graduated from Kharkiv University and briefly edited the official semimonthly of Katerynoslav gubernia. He also wrote articles on Russian and Ukrainian literature, social issues, and folklore for prominent Russian journals. From 1868 he lived in Voronezh. In his 1861–2 articles and reviews of Ukrainian literature in the journal *Osnova*, Mizko wrote that Ukrainian literature and theater were distinct from their Russian counterparts, raised the need for a Ukrainian literary bibliography, and published his memoirs of the actor K. Solenyk. His translations into Russian of 12 poems by T. Shevchenko appeared in the Voronezh weekly *Don* in 1869–71.

Mizyn. An Upper Paleolithic site located on the right bank of the Desna River in Chernihiv oblast. Excavated intermittently from 1908 until 1961, the site is one of the better known examples of *Magdalenian culture in Ukraine. The site contained five circular dwellings, the largest being 6 m in diameter. The dwellings were constructed by using wooden poles which were covered with animal skins and reinforced by bones or tusks. The inhabitants hunted mammoths, deer, and other animals. Approximately 113,000 pieces of flint were uncovered, of which 4,500 could be identified as tools; spear tips and needles were also found in considerable quantities. Many artifacts were excavated, including stylized sculptures of women and animals (particularly mammoths). Geometric and meandering decorative motifs were found on the female sculptures as well as on bone bracelets found at the site. Some examples of shell jewelry were also excavated. The collection is now housed in Kiev at the ANU Archeological Museum and the Historical Museum of Ukraine.

Mlaka, Danylo. See Vorobkevych, Sydir.

Mliiv Orcharding Research Station (Mliivska doslidna stantsiia sadivnytstva im. L. Symyrenka). A research station for fruit growing, established in 1921 in the village of Mliiv, now in Horodyshche raion, Cherkasy oblast. It was based on the private orchards and nursery established by L. *Symyrenko, after whom the station was named in 1958. It has a collection of 1,500 fruit and berry plants and over 250,000 hybrids and produced hundreds of thousands of seedlings for fruit farms throughout the USSR. The station has developed new strains of apple, pear, and cherry trees and of gooseberry, currant, and raspberry bushes. It is under the jurisdiction of the *Ukrainian Scientific Research Institute of Orcharding. The station was directed until 1933 by V. *Symyrenko.

Mlotkovska, Liubov [Mlotkovs'ka, Ljubov] (né Kolosova; surname by first marriage: Ostriakova), b ca 1805 in Kursk, d 31 October 1866 in Kiev. Actress on the Ukrainian and Russian stage. She debuted in I. Stein's troupe in 1823 and remained in it until 1832. She was subsequently in her husband L. Mlotkovsky's troupe (1833–43), in the Kharkiv Theatrical Enterprise (1843–50), and in theaters in Odessa (1850–6) and Kiev (1856–66). Her repertoire spanned several genres – vaudeville, melodrama, comedy, and tragedy. She played leading roles in the premieres of the first Ukrainian plays, such as Tetiana in I. Kotliarevsky's *Moskal'-charivnyk* (The Muscovite [Soldier] Sorcerer) and Uliana in H. Kvitka-Osnovianenko's *Svatannia na Honcharivtsi* (Matchmaking at Honcharivka). A biography, by A. Klinchyn, was published in Kiev in 1958.

Mlotkovsky, Liudvig [Mlotkovs'kyj, Ljudvig] (Młatkowski, Molotkovsky), b ca 1795, d 27 March 1855 in Mykolaiv, Kherson gubernia. Stage actor and managing director of Polish origin. He worked in A. Zmiievsky's troupe in Kiev (1816–20) and in I. Stein's troupe (1820–32) and from 1833 had his own troupes in Kursk (until 1836), Kharkiv (until 1837), and Kiev (until 1840). He returned to Kharkiv, where in 1842 he built a new theater, organized a theater school, and staged I. Kotliarevsky's and H. Kvitka-Osnovianenko's plays. He also built a theater in Bobrynets.

Mlyniv. III-6. A town smt (1990 pop 8,700) on the Ikva River and a raion center in Rivne oblast. Mlyniv has been known since the beginning of the 16th century. In the 17th century D. *Bratkovsky sparked some popular uprisings in the town. The fortified settlement of Muravytsi (or Moravytsi), mentioned in a medieval chronicle under the year 1149, has been excavated in Mlyniv.

Mnohohrishny, Demian [Mnohohrišnyj, Dem'jan], b ca 1630 in Korop, Chernihiv region, d after 1701 in Selenginsk Staryi, Trans-Baikal province, Siberia. Hetman of Left-Bank Ukraine. As colonel of Chernihiv regiment (1665–9) he participated in the 1668 anti-Muscovite rebellion led by Hetman I. Briukhovetsky. In June 1668 Hetman P. *Doroshenko appointed Mnohohrishny acting hetman in *Left-Bank Ukraine. In the autumn Mnohohrishny pledged loyalty to the tsar and was recognized as 'Siversk hetman.' On 13 March 1669 he was elected full hetman of Left-Bank Ukraine. Soon thereafter Mnohohrishny signed the *Hlukhiv Articles with Moscow. A staunch supporter of Ukrainian independence, he spoke out against Muscovite encroachments and Muscovy's territorial concessions to Poland, and later he conducted secret negotiations with P. Doroshenko and sent him money and troops to fight the Poles. Mnohohrishny favored autocratic rule by a strong hetman. He did not trust the senior Cossack *starshyna*, and appointed many of his relatives colonels and captains and granted them estates. In 1671 he appointed, with the approval of the Council of Officers, his brother, V. *Mnohohrishny, as acting hetman, possibly to ensure his succession. The act generated much opposition among the already aggrieved *starshyna*, and they engineered a Moscow-supported coup.

Mnohohrishny was arrested in Baturyn on 23 March 1672 and secretly taken with his brother, Vasyl, and nephew, Mykhailo, in chains to Moscow. There he was charged with high treason, tortured, and sentenced to death. The sentence was commuted to exile for life in Siberia. Mnohohrishny was released from the prison in Irkutsk in 1682 and accorded the status of a junior boyar. He was reimprisoned in 1684 at the request of Hetman I. Samoilovych. After being released in 1688, he became commander of the Russian garrison in Selenginsk. He entered a monastery in 1696 and was still alive in 1701. Mnohohrishny's popularity as hetman is reflected in the Cossack chronicles and in *Istoriia Rusov*.

BIBLIOGRAPHY
Antonovich, V.; Bets, V. *Istoricheskiia deiateli Iugo-Zapadnoi Rossii*, 1 (Kiev 1884)
Kostomarov, N. 'Ruina Getmanstva Briukhovetskago, Mnogogreshnago i Samoilovicha,' in his *Sobranie sochinenii*, vol 15, bk 6 (St Petersburg 1905)
A. Zhukovsky

Mnohohrishny, Vasyl [Mnohohrišnyj, Vasyl'], b and d ? Cossack leader; brother of Hetman D. *Mnohohrishny. He served as osaul of Nizhen regiment (1664–8), emissary to Moscow (1668), captain of Chernihiv regiment (1671–2), and acting hetman (1671). In 1672, after the deposition of his brother, he was tortured in Moscow and exiled to Siberia. He later regained official favor and became a junior boyar in Krasnoiarsk and commander of local imperial troops (1682–94).

Mochemordy Society (Obshchestvo mochemordiia; literally: 'society of wet mugs,' ie, boozers). A loose grouping of liberal petty gentry in Pyriatyn county, Poltava gubernia, in the 1840s, whose members (V. and P. Zakrevsky, M. Markevych, Ya. De Balmen, and others) engaged in carousing. T. *Shevchenko is known to have taken part in their revels. At one of T. Volkhovska's balls on her estate in Moisivka in August 1848, the Zakrevskys drunkenly proposed a toast to the French republic. Consequently they and De Balmen were arrested and interrogated by the tsarist police for possible sedition, but they were released. M. Drahomanov and V. Shchurat posited that the Mochemordy were antitsarist, autonomistic freethinkers, and that that is why Shevchenko was attracted to them. M. Novytsky showed, however, that there is inconclusive evidence to support that claim, in his article in *Zhyttia i revoliutsiia* (1930, no. 3).

Mochulsky, Mykhailo [Močul's'kyj, Myxajlo], b 1 November 1875 in Mykolaiv, Zhydachiv county, Galicia,

Mykhailo Mochulsky

14 February 1940 in Lviv. Literary scholar, literary critic, and translator. Among his works are studies in modern Ukrainian literature – *Goshchyns'kyi, Slovats'kyi i Shevchenko, iak spivtsi Koliivshchyny* ([S.] Goszczyński, [J.] Słowacki, and Shevchenko, the Bards of the Koliivshchyna Rebellion, 1936), *Pohruddia z bronzy: Mykola Tsertelev i Ivan Manzhura* (Bust in Bronze: Mykola Tsertelev and Ivan Manzhura, 1938), and *Ivan Franko* (1938) – and studies of the poets of the Ukrainian school in Polish literature. Mohulsky also translated works by V. Stefanyk into Polish and wrote articles on ethnography.

Mochulsky, Teoktyst [Močul's'kyj], b 1732 in Right-Bank Ukraine, d 30 April 1818 in Kursk, Russia. Orthodox churchman and scholar; member of the Russian Imperial Academy of Sciences. A graduate of the Kievan Mohyla Academy, he served as hegumen of the SS Peter and Paul Monastery in Hlukhiv, the St Michael's Golden-Domed Monastery in Kiev, and the Elevation of the Cross Monastery in Poltava (1776–84). In 1784 he was consecrated bishop and made vicar of Moscow eparchy. Later he served as bishop of Bilhorod (1787–99) and of Kursk (1799–1818). He was elevated to the rank of archbishop in 1801. He published sermons, several works on church organization and regulations, theological tracts, a textbook on logic and rhetoric (1789), a curriculum for elementary schools (1808), and advice on educating the children of the clergy. His biography, by F. Titov, appeared in *Trudy Kievskoi dukhovnoi akademii* (1894).

Mochulsky, Vasilii [Močul'skij, Vasilij], b 13 January 1856 in Striukove, Ananiv county, Kherson gubernia, d 21 January 1920 in Odessa. Russian literary historian. Among his works on the history of Russian literature are several studies that deal with the Ukrainian language or Ukrainian literature: *K istorii malorusskogo narechiia* (Toward a History of the Little Russian Dialect, 1894), *Malorossiiskie i peterburgskie povesti N.V. Gogolia* (N.V. Gogol's Little Russian and Petersburg Stories, 1902), and *Otnoshenie iuzhno-russkoi skholastiki 17 v. k psevdoklassitsizmu 18 v.* (The Relation of the South Russian Scholasticism of the 17th Century to the Pseudoclassicism of the 18th Century, 1904).

Mochutkovsky, Yosyp [Močutkovs'kyj, Josyp], b 1845 in Kherson gubernia, d 5 June 1903. Infectious diseases specialist, neuropathologist, and balneologist. A graduate of Kiev University (1869), he worked at the Odessa Municipal Hospital (1870–93) and helped found the medical paper *Iuzhnorusskaia meditsinskaia gazeta* (1892–6) in Odessa. From 1893 he was a consultant and professor of neurology at the St Petersburg Clinical Institute for the Upgrading of Physicians. In a self-experiment he showed that relapsing and typhoid fevers are transmitted through the blood by bloodsucking insects (lice).

Modernism. A tendency in art which rejected traditional styles, primarily scholasticism (in painting and sculpture), and aimed to introduce innovations in form and idea and to use (particularly in architecture and sculpture) nontraditional materials, such as new metal alloys, glass, and and synthetic plastics.

Since the 19th century, modernism has come to encompass *impressionism, *symbolism, *cubism, *futurism, *suprematism, *expressionism, *surrealism, *constructivism, and abstractionism. All of those currents have had some impact on the Ukrainian arts, although to varying degrees. In the graphic arts, painting, and decorative art, the main Ukrainian exponents of modernism were P. *Kovzhun, V. *Krychevsky Sr, M. *Boichuk, M. *Andriienko-Nechytailo, O. *Hryshchenko, M. *Butovych, H. *Mazepa, P. *Kholodny Jr, A. *Petrytsky, and V. *Meller. In sculpture A. *Archipenko was a world leader in the formation of modernist art; his style evolved, from so-called sculpto-painting (*riz'bo-maliarstvo*), through cubism and constructivism, to abstractionism. In architecture the revival of the Ukrainian national style was modernist in the designs of Krychevsky, K. *Zhukov, O. *Tymoshenko, and I. *Levynsky and in the constructivism of V. *Horodetsky, S. Kravets, O. Lipetsky, P. Yurchenko, and others. After the Second World War modernism in Ukrainian émigré art proliferated in the United States and Canada in reaction to the state-sanctioned *socialist realism in Ukraine (eg, L. *Hutsaliuk, B. Bozhemsky, Myron *Levytsky, A. *Olenska-Petryshyn, Ju. *Solovij, *K. Milonadis, and the architect R. *Zuk).

Modernism was also manifested in theater (*Molodyi Teatr; the *Berezil theater, led by L. *Kurbas; the *Mykhailychenko Theater, led by M. *Tereshchenko; the *Zahrava Theater, led by V. *Blavatsky; and the *Theater-Studio of Y. Hirniak and O. Dobrovolska), in cinema, and in music.

In Ukrainian literature modernism made its appearance in the works of M. *Vorony and the members of *Moloda Muza, who propounded the cult of 'pure art.' Vorony was a theoretician of the movement. He believed that modernism consisted of a change in thematic focus from the social to the psychological, of the enrichment of forms of versification, and of greater sophistication of metaphor. Modernism became widely characteristic of Ukrainian poetry, after the publication of *Soniashni kliarnety* (Sunny Clarinets, 1918) by P. *Tychyna, and of prose after the appearance of *Syni etiudy* (Blue Etudes, 1923) by M. *Khvylovy. Modernism, including its most radical manifestations (such as M. Semenko's futurism and V. Polishchuk's Avanhard), rejuvenated Ukrainian literature and brought it closer to trends in world literature. In the early 1930s the Soviet political authorities repressed and eradicated modernism, substituted for it an artificial 'folk' literature, and so produced a general literary decline. Not until the 1960s did a movement (see *shestydesiatnyky) building on the gains of the 1920s re-emerge. In émigré literature modernism is most apparent in the works of the *New York Group of poets.

S. Hordynsky

Modylevsky, Yakiv [Modylevs'kyj, Jakiv], b 28 January 1883 in Kiev, d 8 March 1968 in Kiev. Cytologist and plant embryologist; corresponding member of the AN URSR (now ANU) from 1939. A graduate of Munich (1907) and Kiev (1908) universities, he worked for the ANU (from 1922) and taught at Kiev University and other institutions (1920–49). He joined the ANU Institute of Botany in 1931, and in 1935–41 served as its director.

Modzalevsky, Vadym [Modzalevs'kyj], b 9 April 1882 in Tbilisi, Georgia, d 3 August 1920 in Kiev. Historian, genealogist, and archivist. A descendant of Cossack *starshyna* in the Chernihiv region, he graduated from the Nicholas Engineering School in St Petersburg (1902),

Vadym Modzalevsky

worked as a military engineer in Kiev (1902–6), and then was a training officer of the First Cadet Corps in St Petersburg. From 1911 to 1917 he directed the V. Tarnovsky's Museum of Ukrainian Antiquities in Chernihiv and was administrator and editor of publications of the Chernihiv Gubernia Scholarly Archival Commission. From 1918 he lived in Kiev, where he headed the archives and libraries divisions of the UNR Ministry of Education and the Hetman government's Arts and National Culture Administration. He was also active in the Ukrainian Scientific Society in Kiev and was secretary of the Commission for the Development of a Draft Law on the Creation of the UAN. Under Soviet rule he headed the Archival Administration and the All-Ukrainian Main Archives, was a member of the VUAN Archeological Commission, and directed the VUAN Commission for the Compilation of a Biographical Dictionary of Ukrainian Personalities.

Modzalevsky's research was based extensively on documents he had collected in the archives of Ukraine, Moscow, and St Petersburg. A specialist on the Left-Bank Hetman state, he wrote books on the history of Lokhvytsia, Sencha, Chornukhy, Kurinka, and Varva companies (1906) and on glassworks in the Chernihiv region (1926). He wrote longer articles on Poltava regiment (*Trudy Poltavskoi uchenoi arkhivnoi komissii*, vols 1–2 [1905–6]), the general judge I. Chernysh and his family (*Kievskaia starina*, 1904, nos 4–5), relations between the monks of the Mhar Transfiguration Monastery and the Cossacks of Lubni regiment in 1649–61 (ibid, 1906, nos 3–4), and R. Rakushka, the first military treasurer (1663–9) (*Zapysky Istorychno-filolohichnoho viddilu VUAN*, vols 1–3 [1919, 1923]). He also edited, with introductions, editions of the books of acts of the municipal governments in Poltava in the 17th century (1912) and in Starodub in 1693 (1914), and the 1735–40 diary of Ya. *Markovych (vol 2 of *Zherela do istoriï Ukraïny-Rusy*, 1913).

Modzalevsky's best-known works are his *Malorossiiskii rodoslovnik* (Little Russian Genealogy, 4 vols, 1908–14), the fifth and final volume of which was never published, and *Malorossiiskii gerbovnik* (Little Russian Heraldry, 1914), which he cowrote with V. *Lukomsky, and which was illustrated by H. *Narbut. He also wrote a booklet on the fundamental traits of Ukrainian art (1917) and articles on artistic metalwork in Left-Bank Ukraine and the engraver H. Levytsky. Modzalevsky's diary of the years 1896–1917 and his correspondence are preserved at the Central State Historical Archive of Ukraine in Kiev. His valuable collec-

tion of archival documents pertaining to 17th- and 18th century Left-Bank Ukraine is in the manuscript division of the State Library of Ukraine in Kiev, and his personal library is part of the Central Scientific Library of the Academy of Sciences of Ukraine. An incomplete bibliography of Modzalevsky's works was published in *Zapysky Istorychno-filolohichnoho viddilu VUAN* (vol 1, 1919).

O. Ohloblyn, A. Zhukovsky

Moeller, Johann-Wilhelm, b 1748, d 1806. German doctor and traveler. As personal physician to King Stanislaus II Augustus Poniatowski of Poland he traveled through Ukraine and recorded his observations in *Reise von Wolhynien nach Cherson in Russland im Jahre 1787* (1802) and *Reise von Warschau nach der Ukraine im Jahre 1780 und 1781* (1804).

Mohyla, Andrii (aka Mohylenko and Myhula), b ?, d 1689. Cossack leader from Left-Bank Ukraine. He was colonel of a Cossack infantry regiment during Hetman S. *Kunytsky's 1683 Moldavian campaign and succeeded Kunytsky as hetman in 1684. Mohyla resided in Nemyriv and was pro-Polish. He negotiated with the Vatican concerning Cossack participation in the anti-Turkish coalition (his letter to Pope Innocent XI of 8 May 1684 has been preserved). Mohyla was killed in a Cossack dispute over the division of pay.

Mohyla, Petro (Rumanian: Movilă, Petru), b 10 January 1597 in Moldavia, d 11 January 1647 in Kiev. Ukrainian metropolitan, noble, and cultural figure; son of Simeon, hospodar of Wallachia (1601–2) and Moldavia (1606–7), and the Hungarian princess Margareta; and brother of the Moldavian hospodars Michael (1611), Gabriel (1617–20), and Moses Movilă (1630–2). After his father's murder in 1607, Mohyla and his mother sought refuge with magnate relatives in Western Ukraine. He was tutored by teachers of the Lviv Dormition Brotherhood School, and pursued higher education in theology at the *Zamostia Academy and in Holland and France. After his return to Ukraine he entered the military service of the Polish crown hetman and chancellor S. Żółkiewski and fought as an officer against the Turks in the battles of Cecora (1620) and Khotyn (1621). In 1621–7 he received estates in the Kiev region and, through his friendship with Metropolitan Y. Boretsky, became interested in affairs of the Ukrainian Orthodox church.

In September 1627 a dietine in Zhytomyr chose Mohyla to succeed the late Z. Kopystensky as archimandrite of the influential *Kievan Cave Monastery. As archimandrite and a deputy in the Polish Sejm Mohyla successfully lobbied the Polish government to restore the legality of the Orthodox church in the Polish Commonwealth, which it did in its 1632 'articles of appeasement,' and King Władysław IV Vasa granted the church the right to have its own hierarchs as long as the candidates were ratified by the government. To act upon that right as quickly as possible, in November 1632 the Orthodox deputies in the Polish Sejm nominated Mohyla the metropolitan of Kiev in place of the more radical I. *Kopynsky. Mohyla was consecrated on 7 May 1633 in the Dormition Church in Lviv.

As metropolitan Mohyla improved the organizational structure of the Orthodox church in Ukraine, set strict

Metropolitan Petro Mohyla (resco portrait, Transfigura-on Church in Berestove, 644-5)

Coat of arms of Metropolitan Petro Mohyla

ogmatic guidelines, reformed the monastic orders, and enriched the theological canon. He gathered together a circle of scholars and cultural leaders known as the Mohyla Atheneum (A. Kalnofoisky, Y. Kononovych-Horbatsky, . Kosiv, I. Kozlovsky-Trofymovych, I. Oksenovych-tarushych, S. Pochasky, and Y. Tryzna), which produced an impressive corpus of theological scholarship. Under Mohyla's guidance the circle prepared new editions of the Bible and the Lives of the Saints; elaborated a new catechism, *Orthodoxa Confessio Fidei*, which was ratified by the Orthodox sobor in Kiev in 1640, by the sobor in Iaşi in 1642 (with emendations), and by all of the Greek Orthodox patriarchs in 1643; and issued an important work of dogma, the polemical treatise *Lithos, albo kamien ...* (Lithos, or Stone ..., 1644; repub in *Arkhiv Iugo-Zapadnoi Rossii*, vol 9, no. 1 [1893]), a reply to K. Sakovych in defense of the Orthodox faith and rite, possibly written by Mohyla himself. Mohyla wrote introductions to a nomocanon (1629), a liturgicon (1629), an anthology of prayers (1636), a didactic Gospel (1637), a triodion (1640), and *Evkhologion, al'bo molytvoslov yly trebnyk* (Euchologion, or a Sacramentary or Trebnyk, 1646), also known as the Great *Trebnyk* of Petro Mohyla; and he is the author of *Krest Khrysta Spasytelia i kazhdoho cheloveka ...* (The Cross of Christ the Savior and of Every Man, 1632), which contains an emblematic poem and the text of one of his sermons. Manuscripts from his archive (150 pp) were published in *Arkhiv Iugo-Zapadnoi Rossii* (vol 7, no. 1 [1887]).

In 1631 Mohyla established a school at the Kievan Cave Monastery. In 1632 it was merged with the Kiev Epiphany Brotherhood School to create a college, which eventually became the largest center of scholarship and education in Eastern Europe, the *Kievan Mohyla Academy. Ukrainian printing flourished under Mohyla's guidance, particularly at the *Kievan Cave Monastery Press. Mohyla himself edited several liturgical publications there, and he brought in the best scholars, master printers, and engravers to work at the press. Mohyla donated a substantial portion of his personal fortune to the uncovering and restoration of medieval churches and other religious landmarks in Kiev, including St Sophia Cathedral, the Church of the Tithes (the first archeological excavation in Ukraine), the churches at the Cave Monastery, the Trans-

figuration Church in the Berestove district, St Michael's Church at the Vydubychi Monastery, and the Church of the Three Saints.

Mohyla established close cultural and educational ties with other Orthodox countries, particularly with his native Moldavia and Wallachia. In 1641 he sent printers and a press to Iaşi, where they printed the first Rumanian book, *Cazania lui Varlaam* (The Sermons of [Metropolitan] Varlaam, 1643). Mohyla was instrumental in the founding of a college in Iaşi, to which he sent professors from the Mohyla College led by S. Pochasky. In 1635 he gave Wallachia a press, which was established with the help of Ukrainian printers in Câmpulung, and in 1637 he gave the Govora Monastery a press. They printed church books modeled on the Kievan editions.

Mohyla bequeathed most of his estate to various church institutions, mostly to the Mohyla College. He was buried in the Dormition Cathedral (destroyed in 1941) at the Kievan Cave Monastery.

BIBLIOGRAPHY
Golubev, S. *Kievskii Mitropolit Petr Mogila i ego spodvizhniki (Opyt istoricheskago issledovaniia)*, 2 vols (Kiev 1883, 1898)
Panaitescu, P. 'L'influence de l'oeuvre de Pierre Mogila, archevêque de Kiev, dans les principautés roumaines,' in *Mélanges de l'école roumaine en France*, pt 1 (Paris 1926)
– *Petru Movilă şi românii* (Bucharest 1942)
Ionescu, T. *La vie et l'oeuvre de Pierre Movila* (Paris 1944)
Zhukovs'kyi, A. *Petro Mohyla i pytannia iednosty Tserkov* (Paris 1969)
Jobert, A. *De Luther à Mohila: La Pologne dans la crise de la Chrétienté, 1517–1648* (Paris 1974)
Popivchak, R. *Peter Mohila, Metropolitan of Kiev (1633–47): Translation and Evaluation of His 'Orthodox Confession of Faith' (1640)* (Washington 1975)
The Kiev Mohyla Academy: Commemorating the 350th Anniversary of Its Founding (1632), special issue of *HUS*, 8, no. 1/2 (1984)
                                              O. Ohloblyn, A. Zhukovsky

Mohyla Scholarly Lectures Society (Tovarystvo naukovykh vykladiv im. Petra Mohyly). An organization established in Lviv in 1908 and abolished by the Soviet authorities in 1939. With branches in Lviv, Peremyshl, Rohatyn, Sambir, Sokal, Stanyslaviv, and Ternopil, the society was very active. During its first four years it organized over 400 academic and public lectures. It also helped various professional and tradesmen's societies (eg, Zoria, the burghers' brotherhood, Syla, Rus') to disseminate information and organized, in co-operation with the *Prosvita society, general education courses for the public. The society's founding president was O. *Kolessa; he was succeeded by V. Shchurat, V. Kucher, I. Svientsitsky, and D. Lukiianovych. Through the efforts of S. Okhrymovych the society's Lviv branch was also the legal arm of the *Union of Ukrainian Nationalist Youth from 1929. Under the branch head A. Figol the society successfully promoted the cult of the Battle of *Kruty, and under V. Yaniv it expanded cultural-educational activities in the Prosvita and tradesmen's societies. After Yaniv the Lviv branch was headed by B. Levytsky. Among the society's active female members were Z. Kravtsiv, S. Moiseiovych, and A. Chemerynska.

Mohyla Society (Tovarystvo im. Mytropolyta Petra Mohyly). A religious education society based in Lutske in 1931–9. Dedicated to studying traditional Ukrainian Orthodox religious practice and encouraging religious education, the society published the periodicals *Za sobornist'* (edited by I. *Vlasovsky) and *Shliakh* and organized lectures and seminars. It also published some *liturgical books that were being translated into Ukrainian by a special synodal commission of the Polish Autocephalous Orthodox church. The society was headed by S. *Tymoshenko and M. Khanenko. It was disbanded after the Soviet occupation of Western Ukraine in 1939.

Mohyla Ukrainian Institute

Mohyla Ukrainian Institute (Ukrainskyi instytut im. Petra Mohyla). A student residence and cultural center established in *Saskatoon in 1916. Initially a nonsectarian residence for Ukrainian students from rural areas attending educational institutions in Saskatoon, the institute became the center of a major controversy in 1917, when the Ukrainian Catholic bishop N. Budka demanded that it become a Catholic entity, and that its properties be incorporated with the Ruthenian Greek Catholic Episcopal Corporation. The desire to protect what was regarded as the national integrity of the institute provided a catalyst for the liberal intelligentsia in Canada to break ranks with the Catholics and establish the *Ukrainian Orthodox Church of Canada in Saskatoon in 1918. The institute then became an important symbol of and center for the fledgling church community. It sponsored courses in Ukrainian language, literature, history, choral singing, and folk arts; held concerts, lectures, and debates intermittently throughout Saskatchewan; and sought to develop a sense of Ukrainian patriotism in the students who lived there (approx 100 annually). These activities played an important role in shaping many future Ukrainian community leaders. The institute also provided the first home of the *Ukrainian Museum of Canada, from 1936 (to 1980), and operated a library, whose holdings currently number approx 10,000 volumes. In 1958 the institute began publishing a bilingual newsletter, *Holos instytutu/Voice of the Institute*, and in 1964 it moved to a new building situated closer to the University of Saskatchewan campus. Since 1975 the institute has conducted an annual Ukrainian-immersion summer school. The rectors of the institute include W. Swystun (1917–21), J. Stechishin (1921–9, 1931–3), V. Burianyk (1932–5, 1936–7), I. Syrnyk (1943–7), Rev V. Senyshyn (1956–62), and A. Kachkowski (1970–9). The early years of the institute are described in *Iuvileina knyha*

25-littia ukraïns'koho instytutu im. Petra Mohyly v Saskatu (Twenty-Five Years of the Petro Mohyla Ukrainian Institute in Saskatoon, 1945).

Mohyla-Mechetna [Mohyla Mečetna]. V-19. The high est point (367 m) of the *Donets Ridge, situated on its mai watershed between the Sea of Azov and the Donets Rive in Luhanske oblast.

Mohylianska, Ladia [Mohyljans'ka, Ladja], b 1902 i Chernihiv, d 1937. Neoromantic poet; daughter of M *Mohyliansky and sister of D. *Tas. Her first poem wa published in the Kharkiv monthly *Chervonyi shliakh* i 1923. Several others appeared between 1924 and 1927 i *Zhyttia i revoliutsiia, Nova hromada, Vsesvit, Zoria,* and *Lite raturno-naukovyi vistnyk*. She was accused of belonging t the *Union for the Liberation of Ukraine and from 193 she was imprisoned in labor camps in the Solovets Island and near Moscow, where she was executed by the NKVD.

Mohyliansky, Arsenii [Mohyljans'kyj, Arsenij] (secu lar name: Oleksii), b 17 March 1704 in Reshetylivka Poltava regiment, d 8 June 1770 in Kiev. Orthodox metro politan. He studied at the Kievan Mohyla Academ (1721–7) and the Kharkiv College (1727), where he late taught. In 1741 he became a teacher of catechism and grammar at the Moscow Academy. In 1744 he was ap pointed archimandrite of the Trinity–St Sergius's Monas tery, consecrated a bishop, and appointed to the Hol Synod. In 1748 he was made official court preacher. I 1757–70 he was metropolitan of Kiev. As metropolitan h introduced a number of reforms at the *Kievan Mohyl Academy, including the teaching of arithmetic and geom etry and the choosing of professors and the rector by th faculty council. He also renewed the school's building and enriched its library. Mohyliansky actively defende the traditional rights of the Kievan metropoly against Rus sian centralism. He coauthored a petition to the Legisla tive Commission of 1767–8 that contained a program fo Ukrainian church autonomy, including the retention o the title 'Metropolitan of Kiev, Halych, and Little Russia,' renewal of the custom of electing the metropolitan fron among local candidates, transfer of control of the Ukraini an church from the Holy Synod to the College of Foreig Affairs, and the stipulation that the metropolitan (not th Synod) confirm the appointment of bishops and hegu mens in Ukraine. Several of Mohyliansky's sermons wer published in Moscow and St Petersburg. His biography by N. Shpachinsky, appeared in Kiev in 1907.

A. Zhukovsky

Mohyliansky, Dmytro. See Tas, Dmytro.

Mohyliansky, Mykhailo [Mohyljans'kyj, Myxajlo], b 4 December 1873 in Chernihiv, d 22 March 1942 in Bolshaia Murda, Krasnoiarsk krai, RSFSR. Literary scholar, publicist translator, and writer. In the late 1890s he published un der cryptonyms in the Galician papers *Zhytie i slovo* and *Dilo*. After studying law at St Petersburg University h worked as a lawyer in Kiev and contributed regularly to the paper *Kievskiia otkliki*. After the Revolution of 1905 he practiced law in St Petersburg, was an active member of the Constitutional Democratic party, and contributed arti cles on Ukrainian literature and the Ukrainian question to

Mykhailo Mohyliansky   Rev Antin Mohylnytsky

its organ *Rech'* and to the journals *Russkaia mysl'* and *Ukrainskaia zhizn'*. His Russian translations of the stories of his friend M. Kotsiubynsky were published in Russian journals and in three separate volumes (1910, 1911, and 1914) in St Petersburg. In 1911 he published his first of several stories in the Lviv journal *Literaturno-naukovyi vistnyk*.

After the Revolution of 1917 Mohyliansky lived in Kiev. Under Soviet rule he published articles in literary theory and on Ukrainian literature (particularly on the writers H. Skovoroda, P. Kulish, Kotsiubynsky, and T. Shevchenko) in VUAN serials and in *Knyhar, Zhyttia i revoliutsiia, Nova hromada*, and other Soviet periodicals. From 1923 he supervised the important VUAN Commission for the Compilation of a Biographical Dictionary of Ukraine (the first volume of the dictionary had been completed by 1930, but was never published). He was closely associated with the *Neoclassicists and took part in the famous *Literary Discussion of 1925. In 1926 his story 'Ubyvstvo' (The Murder) was published in *Chervonyi shliakh*; it was seen as condemning the former UNR president M. Hrushevsky's accommodation with the Soviet regime, and the Bolshevik authorities forbade the publication of his works. They continued to appear, however, under various pen names (including P. Chubsky) until the late 1920s. During the Stalinist terror of the 1930s Mohyliansky's daughter, L. *Mohylianska, and son, D. *Tas, were sent to labor camps, and he was purged from the VUAN. He voluntarily moved to northern Russia to be near his daughter, who was executed in 1937. During the Second World War he was evacuated to Krasnoiarsk krai, where he died.

R. Senkus

Mohyliany. An archeological site from the Early Bronze Age located in Mohyliany, Rivne oblast. Excavated in 1955 by M. *Smishko, the site provided evidence of culture which cremated its dead and buried the remains in urns. The nature of this tribal grouping is unknown, although evidence suggests its existence in other areas of western Ukraine.

Mohyliv-Podilskyi [Mohyliv-Podil's'kyj]. V-8. A city (1990 pop 36,300) on the Dniester River and a raion center in Vinnytsia oblast. In 1595 S. *Potocki founded a town at the site of Ivankivtsi village and named it after his father-in-law, B. Mohyla (Movilă), a prince of Moldavia. A few years later a castle was built. In the 17th to 19th centuries the town was known under various names, such as Mohyliv, Mohyliv-na-Dnistri, and Mohyliv-Dnistrovskyi. Located on the trade route from Ukraine to Moldavia, it grew rapidly into an important trading center and the largest town in Podilia. Its inhabitants took part in a number of popular uprisings – that of S. Nalyvaiko in 1595 and others in 1614 and 1637–8. In 1648 Mohyliv-Podilskyi became a regiment center in B. Khmelnytsky's Cossack state. It was destroyed during the Cossack-Polish War in 1649 and 1654. After participating in I. *Sirko's uprisings in 1664 and 1671, it was captured by the Turks (1672–99). The town gained the rights of *Magdeburg law in 1743 and developed into a flourishing economic and cultural center. In 1616 its Orthodox brotherhood set up a press, and in the 18th century printed books in Ukrainian, Russian, Greek, and Moldavian. In 1795 Mohyliv came under Russian rule and was turned into a county center of Podilia gubernia. In the second half of the 19th century it regained its commercial importance as a river port for the exporting of farm products. By 1897 its population had reached 32,440, much of it (17,000) Jewish. During the revolutionary period the town witnessed many battles. In June 1919 the UNR Army defeated the Red Army near Mohyliv. In 1923 the city was officially named Mohyliv-Podilskyi. Today the city's chief industries are machine building and food processing. Its finest architectural monuments are St Nicholas's Cathedral (1757) and St George's Church (1809–19).

Mohyliv-Podilskyi regiment (aka Mohyliv, Podilia, or Dniester regiment). An administrative territory and military formation of the Hetman state. It was formed in the summer of 1648 as soon as Podilia was liberated from Polish rule. The regiment's first commander was Col I. *Bohun, whose headquarters were in Vinnytsia. After the Battle of Zboriv in 1649, most of the regiment was absorbed by Bratslav regiment. In 1656 it was revived under the name of Podilia regiment, with headquarters in Mohyliv (now Mohyliv-Podilskyi). Its territory was ceded to Poland by the Treaty of Andrusovo (1667), but the regiment was not disbanded. It was resettled on the territory of Kiev regiment, and functioned as a separate military force until 1676. During the last period of its existence the regiment was commanded intermittently by Col O. *Hohol.

Mohylnytsky, Antin [Mohyl'nyc'kyj] (Liubych-Mohylnytsky), b 3 March 1811 in Pidhirtsi, near Kalush, Stryi circle, Galicia, d 13 August 1873 (buried in Yablinka, Nadvirna county, Galicia). Romantic poet and civic figure. He graduated from the Greek Catholic Theological Seminary in Lviv (1840), was ordained, and served from 1841 as a priest and teacher in the villages of Khitar, Zbora, Komariv (1845–59), and Babche (from 1859). Inspired by the *Ruthenian Triad, especially M. Shashkevych and his friend Ya. Holovatsky, Mohylnytsky published several poems in the Galician vernacular, including 'Ridna mova' (Native Language, 1839), 'Zhadka staryny' (Memory of Antiquity, 1939), 'Uchenym chlenam Rus'koï Matytsi' (To the Learned Members of [the] Ruska Matytsia [society], 1849), and other patriotic poems about the Ukrainian language; the ballad 'Rusyn-voiak' (Ruthenian Soldier, 1849), about the trials and tribulations of Ukrainian military recruits in the Austrian army on the Italian front; and the first Western Ukrainian epic, the unfinished 'Skyt Maniavs'kyi' (Maniava Hermitage, 1854), based on folk legends. His 1839 seminary address titled 'Obligations of Subjects' appeared in *Vinok rusynam na obzhynky (1847). During the Revolution of 1848–9 Mohylnytsky favored Ukrainian-Polish co-operation. In 1861 he was elected to the Galician Provincial Diet and was a delegate to the State Council in Vienna, where he spoke out for the equality of Ukrainians with the other Slavic peoples in Austria-Hungary. From 1864 he was persecuted by secular and church authorities, and in 1866 he left politics. Editions of his works were published in Lviv in 1885, 1906 (along with works by M. Shashkevych, Ya. Holovatsky, and M. Ustyianovych), and 1913 (with works by Ustyianovych). Mohylnytsky's biography, by K. Luchakivsky, appeared in 1887, and an analysis of his life and works by V. Lev was published in O. Horbatsch's festschrift in 1983.

Rev Ivan Mohylnytsky   Oleksander Mokh

Mohylnytsky, Ivan [Mohyl'nyc'kyj], b 1777, d 1831. Ukrainian Catholic priest and pedagogue. In 1808 he organized a model school in his village parish of Drozdovychi. Later, as the canon of Peremyshl eparchy responsible for education, he undertook (with the active support of the bishop, M. *Levytsky) a major campaign to establish a network of village schools providing instruction in vernacular Ukrainian. He also initiated the founding of a precentors' school in Peremyshl in 1817 and served as its first rector. As a member of a special commission (1816–18) headed by Governor F. Hauer to study the contentious issue of language policy in Galician schools, he was instrumental in bringing about an improvement in the status of Ukrainian-language education. Mohylnytsky wrote a memorandum in 1821 that noted explicitly, for the first time, the distinctiveness of the Ukrainian language from Polish and Russian. He also initiated (1816) the establishment of the Societas Presbyterorum, a publisher of religious and educational materials, and wrote five school textbooks. Mohylnytsky was a leading figure in a Peremyshl group (including I. Snihursky, I. Lavrovsky, Y. Levytsky, and Y. Lozynsky) that greatly influenced the views of subsequent Ukrainian activists in Galicia, particularly the *Ruthenian Triad.

Moiseienko, Fedir [Mojsejenko] (aka Moiseenkov], b 22 November 1754 in Lebedyn, Sumy regiment, Slobidska Ukraine, d 24 November 1781. Mineralogist. After graduating from St Petersburg University in 1775, he studied at the Freiberg Mining Academy in Saxony (1776–9) and then lectured at Berg College in St Petersburg. He proposed a classification of minerals containing lead and defined some characteristics of lead ores useful for prospecting. He first predicted the presence of deposits containing lead in the Ural Mountains and Siberia. Along with M. Lomonosov, Moiseienko is recognized as a founder of the dynamic approach in mineralogy.

Mokh, Oleksander [Mox], b 22 May 1900 in Hlyniany, Peremyshliany county, Galicia, d 15 November 1975 in Toronto. Catholic journalist and publisher. He studied philosophy and theology in Lviv and Innsbruck. In 1920 he established the Dobra Knyzhka publishing house in Lviv. As a postwar refugee in Germany and in Canada, he published (to 1955) 153 books in several series (eg, Historical Figures, Our Religion, For Light [popular brochures], Logos Library [belles lettres], and Library of Theatrical Works), primarily intended to foster a Catholic awareness and Ukrainian national consciousness among youths. He was the editor of Svitlo i tin' in Lviv (1932–9) and Zhyttia i slovo in Innsbruck (1948–9). He also helped edit and was a regular contributor to Postup, Nova rada, Pravda, Nova zoria, Dzvony, Zapysky ChSVV, Nedil'ni visti, Ameryka, Shliakh, and Holos. In Toronto he published the Christian quarterly Pravda (1969–75), which printed his memoirs in 1974–5.

Mokh, Rudolf [Mox, Rudol'f], 1816–91. Galician priest, writer, and community figure. He studied at the Greek Catholic Theological Seminary in Lviv and became involved in circles close to the *Ruthenian Triad. He is the author of Motyl' (The Butterfly, 1841), the second collection of poetry published in the Ukrainian vernacular in Western Ukraine, and of the first Ukrainian-language secular plays staged in Galicia, among them Sprava v seli Klekotyni (The Affair in the Village of Klekotyn, 1849), 'Terpen-spasen' ([He Who] Suffers [Is] Saved, 1849), and 'Opikunstvo' (Guardianship). In 1848 he was a spokesman of the Drohobych committee of the Supreme Ruthenian Council and participated in the *Congress of Ruthenian Scholars in Lviv, where he advocated the abandonment of *etymological spelling.

Mokiievsky, Kostiantyn [Mokijevs'kyj, Kostjantyn], b ? in the Bila Tserkva region, d ca 1709. Cossack officer; relation (possibly cousin) of Hetman I. Mazepa. He was colonel of Kiev (1691–1708) and Chyhyryn (1708–9) regiments, a distinguished field commander in campaigns against Turkey and Sweden, and a patron of the Ukrainian church. He also undertook diplomatic missions for Mazepa to the Crimea and the Zaporizhia in 1708–9, which resulted in a coalition against Peter I.

Mokosh (aka Makosh). A goddess of fertility, water, and women in old Ukrainian mythology. According to folk belief she shears sheep and spins thread. The name itself is derived from the word combination maty kota 'mother of the cat,' that is, 'mother of good fortune.' She is related to Hecate and Aphrodite in classical mythology and to Zhyva and Morena in western Slavic mythology. Mokosh is mentioned in the Primary Chronicle as among the chief gods, which include Perun, Khors, Dazhboh, and Stryboh. Some scholars believe that Mokosh was Perun's wife. She is depicted with a cornucopia on the *Zbruch idol. In the

14th to 16th centuries her cult was transformed into that of St Parasceve, and 10 November (28 October OS) was assigned as her feast day.

Mokra Sura River. A right-bank tributary of the Dnieper River, which it joins south of Dnipropetrovske. It is 138 km long and drains a basin area of 2,830 sq km. It flows through Dnipropetrovske oblast. In the summer the upper reaches of the river dry out. A reservoir has been built on the river, the waters of which are used for irrigation and pisciculture.

Mokrenko, Anatolii, b 22 January 1933 in Terny, near Nedryhailiv (now in Sumy oblast). Opera singer (baritone). A graduate of the Kiev Polytechnical Institute (1956), he studied voice at the Kiev Conservatory and sang in its opera studio (1963–8). In 1968 he was appointed soloist at the Kiev Theater of Opera and Ballet; since then he has performed leading roles in M. Lysenko's *Natalka from Poltava* and *Taras Bulba*, S. Hulak-Artemovsky's *Zaporozhian Cossack beyond the Danube*, B. Liatoshynsky's *The Troop Commander*, H. Maiboroda's *Yaroslav the Wise*, V. Kyreiko's *The Forest Song*, P. Tchaikovsky's *Eugene Onegin*, G. Rossini's *The Barber of Seville*, and G. Bizet's *Carmen*. He starred in a television version of G. Donizetti's *Lucia di Lammermoor* (1980). His biography, by V. Kachkan, was published in 1989.

Mokri Yaly River [Mokri Jaly]. A left-bank tributary of the Vovcha River. It is 147 km long and drains a basin area of 2,660 sq km. The river has its source in the Azov Upland and flows through the western reaches of Donetske oblast. A reservoir has been built on the river, the waters of which are used for irrigation.

Mokriiev, Yurii [Mokrijev, Jurij], b 14 April 1901 in Novomyrhorod, Yelysavethrad county, Kherson gubernia. Playwright and prose writer. He became popular after his first satiric play, *Viddai partkvytok* (Turn in Your Party Membership Card, 1930), which was followed by many others, such as *Soiuz vidvazhnykh* (Union of the Brave, 1935), *Syhnaly z moria* (Signals from the Sea, 1939), *Zhuravli letiat'* (The Cranes Are Flying, 1943), *Veseli zaruchyny* (The Merry Betrothal, 1965), *A mymo prolitaiut' poïzdy* (And the Trains Speed By, 1975), which were performed in theaters across Ukraine. Mokriiev is also the author of collections of humorous stories, including *Usmishky Hordiia Smishky* (The Smiles of Hordii Smishka, 1943), *Veselyi saliut* (The Merry Salute, 1945), and *Sto koliuchok v boky* (A Hundred Thorns in the Side, 1961); of the novels *Plavni palaiut'* (The Floodplains Are Aflame, 1959), *Chorna buria* (The Black Storm, 1961), and *Slid na zemli* (Tracks on the Ground, 1969); and several prose collections. He has also written memoirs, *Take blyz'ke ...* (So Close ..., 1974) and screenplays for films.

Mokriievych [Mokrijevyč] (aka Debohorii-Mokriievych). A family of Cossack *starshyna* in the Chernihiv region. It originated with Karpo Mokriievych (d 1704), the chancellor (1660–1) and quartermaster (1688–90) of Chernihiv regiment and general chancellor of the Hetman state (1669–72). His son, Ivan (Ioannykii), was captain of Liubech company (1690–3). Ivan's son, Mykhailo (d 1738), was osaul of Chernihiv regiment (1723–38), signed the Kolomak Articles, and died while leading the Chernihiv Reg-

iment in battle against the Tatars near Haiman-Dolyna. The revolutionary populists Ivan and Volodymyr *Debohorii-Mokriievych were descendants of Mykhailo. Ivan founded the clandestine American Group in 1871 in the Chernihiv region. Its aim was to organize agrarian communes throughout the world to pave the way for socialism. A branch of the family emigrated to the United States in the second half of the 19th century.

Mokriievych, Samiilo [Mokrijevyč, Samijlo], b?, d ca 1712. Cossack captain of Berezna in Chernihiv regiment (1689–90) and a notable military fellow (1704–9) under Hetman I. Mazepa; son of K. Mokriievych. In honor of Mazepa he wrote *Vynohrad, domovytom blahym nasazhdennyi ...* (Grapes by a Good Husbandsman Grown, 1697), which contains a poetic rendering in Ukrainianized Church Slavonic of the Book of Genesis and the Gospel according to St Matthew, and other religious poems.

Volodymyr Mokry

Mokry, Volodymyr [Mokryj] (Włodzimierz), b 18 April 1949 in Drawia, Olsztyn voivodeship, Poland. Slavist, publicist, Ukrainian community leader, and politician in Poland. A graduate of Cracow University, he has taught Ukrainian language and conducted seminars on Ukrainian history and culture there. Mokry has published scholarly, political, and religious articles in Polish Catholic newspapers and journals, Polish scholarly periodicals, and the Ukrainian-language press in Poland. In 1989–91 he was the first Ukrainian elected to the postwar Polish Sejm. He served in the Sejm committee on national minorities and spearheaded a campaign for official condemnation of *Operation Wisła and for material compensation of its deported victims, their right to return to their ancestral homes, and restitution of their property. Mokry founded in 1989 in Cracow the Foundation of St Volodymyr the Baptizer of Kievan Rus'. He is chairman of this foundation, the aim of which is to promote Ukrainian studies and Ukrainian Christian culture in Poland, and understanding and rapprochement between Poles and Ukrainians.

Mokryi Yelanchyk River [Mokryj Jelančyk] (also Mokryi Yalanchyk). A river that flows through Donetske and Rostov oblasts. It is 105 km long and drains a basin area of 1,390 sq km. It empties into Tahanrih Bay on the Sea of Azov. The river is used for irrigation and water supply.

Mokrytsky, Apollon [Mokryc'kyj], b 12 August 1810 in Pyriatyn, Poltava gubernia, d 8 or 9 March 1870 in Mos-

Apollon Mokrytsky:
Self-Portrait (1840)

cow. Painter; full member of the St Petersburg Academy of Arts from 1849. He studied painting under K. Pavlov at the Nizhen Lyceum and under A. Venetsianov and K. Briullov in St Petersburg (1830–9). After working in Ukraine and visiting Italy he was appointed a professor at the Moscow School of Painting, Sculpture, and Architecture (1851–70). His paintings, including portraits of Ye. Hrebinka (1840) and N. Gogol, a self-portrait (1840), and Italian landscapes, are done in a lucid, realist style. He took part in the purchasing of T. *Shevchenko's freedom and mentioned the poet in his diary (pub 1975).

Mol, Leo. See Molodozhanyn, Leonid.

Molchanivsky, Teodosii [Molčanivs'kyj, Teodosij] (Movchanivsky), b 9 May 1899 in Berestivtsi, Uman county, Kiev guberniia, d ? Archeologist. Educated at the Kiev and Odessa theological seminaries, in 1925–32 he was the director of the Berdychiv Regional Museum. He then worked from 1932 to 1937 for the All-Ukrainian Archeological Committee and its successor, the Institute of the History of Material Culture. He developed a solid reputation for his excavation of the *Raiky fortified settlement as well as his study of archeological sites in and around Kiev; however, his later study stating that the St. Michael's Golden-Domed Monastery had no historical value was used to justify the monastery's destruction. In 1937 Molchanivsky was arrested during the Stalinist purges; his subsequent fate is unknown.

Molchanov, Igor [Molčanov], b 13 September 1929 in Tula, Russia. Mathematician. He completed his studies at the Mykolaiv Pedagogical Institute in 1957, and from 1959 he worked at the Computing Center (since 1962 the AN URSR [now ANU] Institute of Cybernetics) in Kiev. In 1964 he became head of one of the institute's departments. Molchanov's principal contributions are in computer sciences, particularly in the field of the theoretical investigation and development of numerical methods for handling computer translation problems.

Molchanov, Porfyrii [Molčanov, Porfyrij], b 24 February 1863 in Kharkiv, d 13 April 1945 in Odessa. Composer and pedagogue. A graduate of the St Petersburg Conservatory (1887), he studied composition with N. Rimsky-Korsakov and A. Liadov. From 1888 he taught theory at the Odessa Music School, and from 1926 he was professor at the Odessa Institute of Music and Drama (after 1934 the Odessa Conservatory). His works include two sympho-

nies, the orchestral *Scherzo*, a cantata, and a string sextet. In 1891 he edited and orchestrated the piano score of the opera *Kateryna* by M. Arkas.

Molchanovsky, Nykandr [Molčanovs'kyj], b 1858 in Lozuvata, Balta district, Podilia gubernia, d 17 December 1906 in Kiev. Historian and community activist. In 1879 he was expelled from Kiev University for his political activities and exiled for two and a half years to Viatka gubernia. In 1884, after his return to Kiev, he completed his studies under V. Antonovych, and in 1885 he wrote a study of the Podilia land to the year 1434. Because he was a member of the *Hromada of Kiev, he was deemed politically unreliable and barred from becoming a professor. The Kiev Archeographic Commission sent him to do research at archives in Stockholm (1898–9) and Budapest. The materials he collected in the Stockholm State Archive about Ukraine in the second half of the 17th century were published posthumously with his long introduction in *Arkhiv Iugo-Zapadnoi Rossii*, in 1908 (vol 6, no. 3), and in *Ukraïns'kyi arkheohrafichnyi zbirnyk*, in 1930 (vol 3, ed V. Kordt). From 1889 Molchanovsky contributed over 20 articles and archival documents and some 80 reviews (signed mostly 'N.M.') to *Kievskaia starina*. They include articles on the Kiev municipal administration in 1786 (1889, nos 5–7), women at the hetman's court in Chyhyryn (1894, nos 1–2), 15th- to 17th-century Left-Bank Ukraine (1896, nos 4–6), Kiev's budgets in the mid-18th century (1898, no. 1), reports of the Venetian envoy A. Vimina about Hetman B. Khmelnytsky and the Cossacks (1900, no. 1), the origin of the term *katsap (1901, no. 12), and Hetman I. Mazepa's death and his successors (1903, no. 1). From 1902 he directed the chancellery of the governor-general of Kiev, Podilia, and Volhynia gubernias.

Moldavia (Rumanian: Moldova; Ukrainian: Moldaviia, Voloshchyna, from *volokhy* 'Vlachs'). A region (approx area, 90,000 sq km) bordering on southwestern Ukraine. Its natural boundaries are the Carpathian Mountains to the west, the Dniester River to the east, and the Black Sea to the south. Named after the Moldova River, in the 14th century it became a Vlach principality, which ruled *Bukovyna until 1774 and *Bessarabia until 1812. Later the principality was reduced to the territory between the Carpathians and the Prut River, which is now part of *Rumania. In 1859 it was united with Wallachia to form the state of Rumania. After the Second World War Bessarabia became the *Moldavian SSR, and in 1991, Moldova.

In prehistoric times Moldavia was inhabited by *Scythians and Thracian tribes (*Getae, Dacians), who established an independent state there in the 1st century BC. From 106 to 273 AD southern Moldavia was part of the Roman Empire, which built *Trajan's Walls there. From the 3rd century on it was invaded by many nomadic peoples, including the Goths, Huns, Avars, Bulgars, Magyars, Pechenegs, Cumans, and Tatars. From the 4th century on, particularly from the 6th, the East Slavic *Antes settled there. In the 9th and 10th centuries Moldavia was colonized by the proto-Ukrainian *Tivertsians and *Ulychians, who founded the towns of *Peresichen, Tehyn (now *Bendery or Tiaghina), and *Bilhorod-Dnistrovskyi.

In the 10th century the territory of Moldavia came under the domination of Kievan Rus', and from 1200 to 1340 it was ruled by the Principality of *Galicia-Volhynia. Im-

Moldavia: church in Galaţi where Hetman I. Mazepa was buried

portant trade routes from Galicia to the Black Sea passed through Moldavia, and Galician merchants founded the town of Malyi Halych (now *Galaţi) there. In the 12th and early 13th centuries a separate principality populated by fugitives from Galicia-Volhynia called *Berladnyky (named after the Moldavian town of Berlad [Bîrlad]) existed in southern Moldavia. Its most notable ruler was Ivan Rostyslavych *Berladnyk.

After the Tatar invasion of 1241 Galician influence in Moldavia waned, contacts with the Eastern Slavs beyond the Carpathians diminished, and Vlachs from Wallachia began settling there. In 1352 King Louis I of Hungary expelled the Tatars from Moldavia and installed the Vlach Dragoş as its voivode (military governor). Under Dragoş the influx of Vlachs from Transylvania and the Maramureş region intensified. In 1359 the new voivode, Bogdan, overthrew Hungarian rule and founded an independent Moldavian principality dominated by boyars and the Orthodox church. The capital was Suceava. In that period the Lithuanian-Ruthenian prince Yurii Koriiatovych, the nephew of the Lithuanian grand duke Algirdas, served briefly as a Moldavian voivode. In 1387 Moldavia became a Polish vassal state. In the late 14th century it extended its borders to the Carpathians, the

Dniester River, the Danube, and the Black Sea and occupied the northern part of *Shypyntsi land (Bukovyna). In 1456 it became an autonomous tribute-paying vassal state of the Ottoman Empire.

Moldavia prospered during the reigns of its voivodes Alexander the Good (1400–32) and Stephan III the Great (1457–1504). Under Alexander the Patriarch of Constantinople recognized the separate Moldavian metropoly in Suceava (1401), and commercial ties with Lviv were secured, whereby Moldavian merchants were granted privileges. Stephan married Yevdokiia, the daughter of the Kievan prince Olelko Volodymyrovych. He repulsed the Hungarians in 1467, the Turks in 1475–6, and the Poles in 1497, after which Moldavia enjoyed full independence until 1538. Stephan and his successors Bogdan III and Peter Rareş (1527–46) often invaded Pokutia and sought to annex it. During the Polish-Moldavian wars in Pokutia, Ukrainian and Moldavian peasants took part in the *Mukha rebellion (1490–2), and many Galician Ukrainian fugitives settled in Moldavia.

After Moldavia was forced to accept Turkish suzerainty in 1538, the Zaporozhian Cossacks assisted the Moldavians in their struggle against Turkey and intervened in their internal power struggles. In 1541 a Zaporozhian force waged a campaign against Turkish-Tatar garrisons

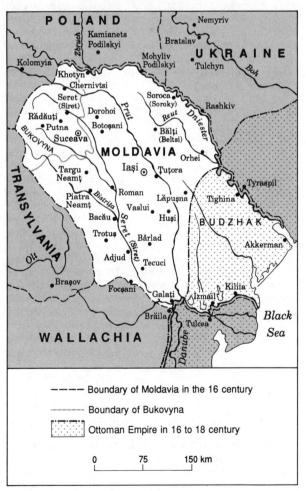

MOLDAVIA IN THE 15TH–18TH CENTURIES

on the lower Dniester. In 1563 Prince D. *Vyshnevetsky led two Zaporozhian campaigns against the Turks in Moldavia. In 1574 a force of 1,200 Cossacks led by Otaman I. Svirchevsky took part in the anti-Turkish rebellion led by the hospodar John the Terrible. In 1577 Otaman I. *Pidkova briefly occupied the Moldavian throne. In 1583 the Cossacks attacked Turkish garrisons in Moldavia and destroyed the fortress in Bendery. In 1594–5 S. Nalyvaiko and H. Loboda led Cossack raids into Moldavia to help anti-Turkish insurgents. In 1600 a force of 7,000 Cossacks fought for Michael the Brave of Wallachia during his war against the Turks in Moldavia and Transylvania. During the Polish-Turkish War of 1620–1 Cossack units led by M. and B. Khmelnytsky were defeated by the Turks at the Battle of *Cecora in Moldavia, but the forces of Hetman P. Sahaidachny played a key role in the Polish victory at the Battle of *Khotyn. In 1635 Zaporozhians led by I. Sulyma plundered the Turkish-held Moldavian port of Kiliia.

Moldavia played an important part in Hetman B. Khmelnytsky's *Cossack-Polish War of 1648–57. Because the Moldavian hospodar V. *Lupu was an ally of Poland, Khmelnytsky led his army against Moldavia in 1650 and forced Lupu into an alliance. After the Cossack defeat at Berestechko in 1651, Lupu broke away, but he was forced back into the alliance by a second Cossack offensive against Moldavia, in 1652. The alliance was sealed by the marriage of Khmelnytsky's son, Tymish, to Lupu's daughter, Rozanda. In 1653 T. Khmelnytsky died defending Suceava from the Poles, and Lupu was overthrown by Gheorghe Ştefan, who signed a peace treaty with B. Khmelnytsky and later maintained good relations with Hetman I. Vyhovsky.

In 1672 Moldavia was allied with Hetman P. Doroshenko and Turkey against Poland. In 1681 the Turkish sultan appointed Gheorghe Duca 'hospodar of Ukraine,' but Gheorghe Duca ruled only Moldavia and only until the following year. At that time many Moldavians began settling in the Ukrainian lands between the Dniester and the Boh rivers. Cossack units led by S. Kunytsky fought in the Polish army that ended the Turkish-Moldavian siege of Vienna in 1683, and they continued the offensive against Turkey in Hungary, Wallachia, and Moldavia. Hetman I. Mazepa and his successor, P. Orlyk, sought refuge in Moldavia after their defeat at the Battle of Poltava in 1709.

After the anti-Ottoman military alliance between the Moldavian prince D. Cantemir and Tsar Peter I was defeated in 1711, Moldavia was governed by Greek Phanariots appointed by Constantinople until 1821. From the late 18th century the Russian, Austrian, and Ottoman empires vied for control of Moldavia. In 1774 Austria occupied Bukovyna, and in 1812 Turkey ceded Bessarabia to Russia. During the Russo-Turkish War of 1828–9 Russia occupied Moldavia, and in the 1829 Treaty of Edirne Turkey recognized Moldavia's autonomy under Russian tutelage. In 1859 the principalities of Moldavia and Wallachia elected A. Cuza as their joint ruler, and their union as the country of Rumania was formally proclaimed on 23 December 1861.

Ukrainians and Moldavians have shared a common history (to the 14th century) and the Byzantine wellspring of culture and Orthodox religion. Ukrainian villages have existed in Moldavia for centuries. The medieval Moldavian state and society were similar to those of Kievan Rus' and the Principality of Galicia-Volhynia, and Ukrainian

was the official language of the Moldavian church and state (see *Moldavian charters). Not until Iaşi became the new capital of Moldavia in 1564 did Rumanian begin supplanting Ukrainian as the official language. The process was completed in the mid-17th century.

Ties between the Moldavian and Ukrainian churches were close. Under Voivode Peter I (1373–7) a Moldavian episcopate subordinated to Halych metropoly was established. Metropolitan G. Tsamblak of Kiev contributed to the cultural development of Moldavia in the early 15th century. The Lviv Dormition Brotherhood and its school and press received ongoing assistance from Moldavian hospodars and boyars from the mid-16th to the late 17th century, and the Moldavian hospodars A. Lăpuşneanu and I. and S. Movilă helped fund the construction of the Lviv Dormition Church. The Lviv Dormition Brotherhood School trained Moldavian leaders, including the chronicler G. Ureche and Metropolitan Dositheus.

The son of S. Movilă, P. *Mohyla, became the most outstanding metropolitan of Kiev, and the famous college he founded in Kiev (see *Kievan Mohyla Academy) was attended by Moldavian students. The college's teachers S. Pochasky and I. Yevlevych founded a similar Latin-Slavonic school in Iaşi in 1640, and Ukrainian printers founded a press there in 1641. Moldavian writers had their works printed in Lviv, Univ, Krekhiv, and Maniava. The Moldavian metropolitans Varlaam (1632–53) and Dositheus (1671–86, who was born in Lviv) translated church books from Ukrainian into Rumanian. The influence of Ukrainian writers, such as Z. Kopystensky, M. Smotrytsky, P. Mohyla, P. Berynda, I. Gizel, L. Baranovych, I. Galiatovsky, and P. Velychkovsky, on Moldavian culture was considerable, and the Ukrainian towns of Kiev, Lviv, Kamianets-Podilskyi, Univ, Zhovkva, and Bar had a cultural impact on Moldavia.

Because the trade route linking Western Ukraine with Constantinople and the Near East passed through Moldavia, Moldavia had close economic ties with Western Ukrainian cities. Those ties became stronger after Alexander the Good conferred special privileges on Lviv's merchants in 1408 but were weakened after Turkish control over Moldavia increased. In the 18th century Ukraine and Moldavia were close trading partners.

Valuable information about Ukrainian-Moldavian relations from 1359 to 1743 can be found in the Moldavian chronicles of G. Ureche, M. and N. Costin, and I. Neculce.

BIBLIOGRAPHY

Korduba, M. 'Moldavs'ko-pol's'ka hranytsia na Pokuttiu do smerty Stefana Velykoho,' Zbirnyk NTSh (Lviv 1906)

Nistor, I. 'Contribuţii la relaţiunile dintre Moldova şi Ucraina în veacul al XVII-lea,' Academia Română, Memoriile secţiunii istorice, ser 3, vol 13 (1932–3)

Zhukovs'kyi, A. 'Istoriia Bukovyny,' in Bukovyna: Ï mynule i suchasne, ed D. Kvitkovs'kyi, T. Bryndzan, and A. Zhukovs'kyi (Paris 1956)

Dan, M. Ştiri privitoare la istoria Ţărilor Romîne in cronicele ucrainene: Studii şi materiale de istorie medie, vol 2 (Bucharest 1957)

Sergievskii, M. Moldavo-slavianskie etiudy (Moscow 1959)

Mokhov, N. Ocherki istorii moldavsko-russko-ukrainskikh sviazei (s drevneishikh vremen do nachala XIX v.) (Kishinev 1961)

Mokhov, N.; Stratievskii, K. Rol' russkogo i ukrainskogo narodov v istoricheskikh sud'bakh Moldavii (Kishinev 1963)

Romanets', O. Dzherela braterstva: Bohdan P. Khashdeu i skhidnoromans'ko-ukraïns'ki vzaiemyny (Lviv 1971)

Ukraina i Moldaviia (Moscow 1972)

Joukovsky, A. 'Les relations culturelles entre l'Ukraine et la Moldavie au XVIIe siècle,' *VIIe Congrès International des Slavistes: Varsovie, 21–27.8.1973* (Paris 1973)

Zelenchuk, V. *Naselenie Moldavii (Demograficheskie protsessy i etnicheskii sostav)* (Kishinev 1973)

Byrnia, P. *Moldavskii srednevekovyi gorod v Dnestrovsko-Prutskom mezhdurech'e (XV–nachalo XVI v.)* (Kishinev 1984)

Spinei, V. *Moldavia in the 11th–14th Centuries* (Bucharest 1986)

Dragnev, D.; et al (eds). *Ocherki vneshnepoliticheskoi istorii Moldavskogo kniazhestva (posledniaia tret' XIV–nachalo XIX v.)* (Kishinev 1987)

A. Zhukovsky

Moldavian charters (Moldavski hramoty). Documents composed from the mid-14th to the mid-17th centuries in Moldavian principality. Written in Middle Ukrainian, which shows the influence of Middle Bulgarian and Rumanian Slavonic spelling, they are important sources for the history of the Ukrainian language. Most of the materials used in *Slovnyk staroukraïns'koï movy XIV–XV st.* (Dictionary of Old Ukrainian of the 14th and 15th centuries, 1977) is drawn from them. From the mid-17th century, Ukrainian was replaced with Rumanian and Greek in Moldavian diplomacy. The language of the charters, particularly those of the 14th and 15th centuries, was studied by A. Yatsimirsky (1904) and O. Yaroshenko (1931).

Moldavian Soviet Socialist Republic. One of the 15 former Soviet republics, situated in the southwestern USSR between Rumania and Ukraine and bounded by the Prut River in the west and, roughly, by the Dniester River in the east. Its area is 33,700 sq km, and its 1989 population was 4,335,000, 47 percent of it urban. The Moldavian SSR was formed on 2 August 1940 out of the Moldavian ASSR and the larger part of Bessarabia, which was occupied by the Soviets on 28 June 1940. The republic is divided into 37 raions, 21 cities, and 44 towns. The capital is Kishinev. In 1991 Moldavia declared its independence and assumed the name of Moldova.

The boundaries of Moldova and Ukraine coincide roughly with the boundaries of Rumanian and Ukrainian ethnic territories, although Moldova includes a few Ukrainian regions on the left bank of the Dniester. According to the 1989 census the national composition of Moldova was as follows: 2,794,700 Rumanians (64.5 percent), 600,400 Ukrainians (13.9 percent), 562,100 Russians (13 percent), 153,500 Gagauzy (3.5 percent), 88,400 Bulgarians (2 percent), and 65,700 Jews (1.5 percent). Most of the Ukrainians live in rural areas. They are concentrated in Lipcani, Edineţi, Răşcani, Beltsi, Făleşti, Bendery, and Căuşani raions. On the left bank of the Dniester, the Ukrainians are concentrated in Rybnytsia and Tyraspil.

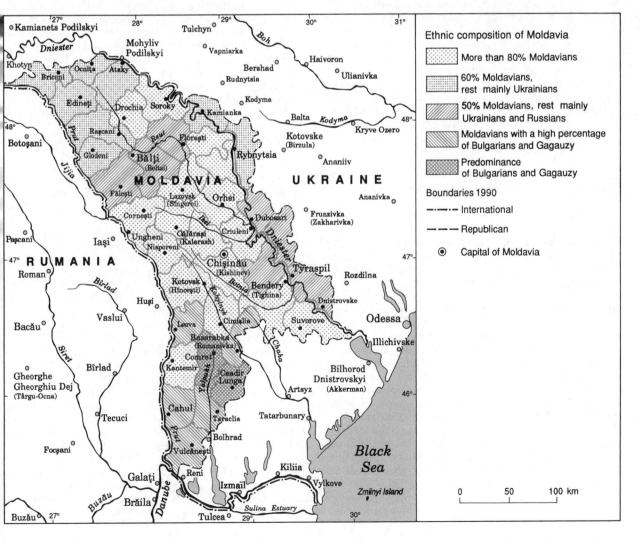

The Soviet authorities made strenuous efforts to Russify the Rumanian and Ukrainian population of the Moldavian SSR by encouraging the in-migration of Russians and the out-migration of the local population and by favoring the Russian language in education and public life. Most of the books and newspapers published in Moldavia were in Russian, not Rumanian, and none were in Ukrainian.

See also *Bessarabia, *Moldavia, *Moldavians.

A. Zhukovsky

Moldavians (Rumanian: *Moldoveni*; Ukrainian: *moldavany*). The predominantly Vlach population of *Moldavia. After the principalities of Moldavia and Wallachia united in 1859 to form Rumania, the term Moldavian, like Wallachian and the southern Rumanian term Munten, became a regional designation. The Soviet regime created a fictional Moldavian nation, language, and literature to justify the existence of the Moldavian ASSR and *Moldavian SSR. In fact the language of the Moldavian SSR and its recent successor state, Moldova, is a Rumanian dialect the lexicon of which has many borrowings from Ukrainian and Russian, and which has been written in the Russian Cyrillic alphabet instead of the Rumanian Latin alphabet. In the Soviet era many Soviet Russian neologisms entered the dialect, and on the basis of those words Soviet scholars (eg, M. Sergievsky) tried unconvincingly to substantiate the idea that Moldavian was a separate language.

In 1989 there were 3,352,352 Moldavians in the USSR. Of those, 2,794,749 lived in the Moldavian SSR, where they made up 64 percent of the population; 324,525 lived in the Ukrainian SSR; and 172,671 lived in the RSFSR. Of the Moldavians in Ukraine in 1989, 44.5 percent lived in Odessa oblast; 26 percent, in Chernivtsi oblast; 5 percent, in Mykolaiv oblast; 4.1 percent, in Donetske oblast; 3.3 percent, in Kirovohrad oblast; 2 percent, in Dnipropetrovske oblast; 2 percent, in Crimea oblast; 1.8 percent, in Luhanske oblast; and 1.7 percent, in Kherson oblast.

(See also *Rumanians.)

Moldova. See Moldavian Soviet Socialist Republic.

Moldova River (or Moldava). A right-bank tributary of the Seret River (which it meets just south of Roman, in Rumania). It is 205 km long and drains a basin area of 4,350 sq km. The river has its source in the Bukovynian Carpathians and runs its entire course in Rumania. It is used for floating logs to lumber mills.

Mole (*Talpa*; Ukrainian: *krit, slipets', slipunets'*). A small (10–25 cm long), often blind, burrowing insectivorous mammal of the family Talpidae. Moles have a short, dense, yet velvet-soft fur. Their habitat in Ukraine is in forests, steppes, and forest-steppes as well as along water conduits and mountain meadows in the Carpathian Mountains and Caucasia. Moles are active during both the day and the night and consume more than their body weight in food daily. Their habit of burrowing just below the surface and feeding on young plants is an annoyance to gardeners. They stir and aerate the soil, however, and control noxious organisms. In Ukraine the common mole (*T. europaea*) is valued by the fur industry; about 2 million skins are processed annually.

Molecular biology. A branch of *biology dealing with the basic biological processes, such as heredity, mutability, growth, protein synthesis, and energy transformation, on a subcellular and molecular level. In Ukraine experiments in the field began in the first half of the 20th century. In 1939 S. *Hershenzon demonstrated the mutagenic activity of exogenic deoxyribonucleic acid (DNA). The discovery was important for practical medicine, which was faced with the task of obtaining vaccines free of nucleic acid. In the 1940s V. *Belitser theorized that the denaturation of proteins consists of the unwinding of the molecule and the rupture of numerous weak bonds (this theory was confirmed by research which established the general principle of conformative changes of protein). The field of molecular biology began to develop rapidly after J. Watson and F. Crick proposed a model of the DNA molecule (1953). The branches of molecular biology in Ukraine researched the relation between the structure and the functioning of proteins and nucleic acids. In the 1950s Belitser showed that the structure of fermenting protein could be viewed as the basic criterion for the catalytic activity and specificity of ferments. He also proved that supramolecular biological structures can be formed, and proposed a model for the transformation of fibrinogen into fibrin that helped to explain the occurrence of thrombosis and cardiovascular disorders.

In the 1960s at the AN URSR (now ANU) Institute of Radio Physics and Electronics, I. Todorov studied the molecular mechanisms of the biosynthesis of the adrenocorticotropic hormone, and V. Maleev investigated the hydration of nucleic acids. In 1973 the molecular biology and genetics section (est 1968) at the ANU was reorganized into the Institute of Molecular Biology and Genetics. S. Serebriany did research on the primary protein structure of viruses. The institute's researchers determined the spectra of absorption and fluorescence of nucleic acids and their components, the nature of the hypochromic effect in the DNA molecule, the electronic mechanism of ultraviolet radiation activity on DNA, and the nature of the stability and hydration of biomolecular associatives (V. Danilov). The functional adaptation of transfer ribonucleic acid (RNA) and aminoacyl-transfer RNA-synthetase to the biosynthesis of specific proteins was discovered there, as well as the structural grounds of the interaction of leucine transfer RNA with synthetases and ribosomes and the role of transfer RNA in insuring effective translation. The structure and function of the components of the translation mechanism in higher organisms is being investigated by H. *Matsuka and H. Yelska. Biologically inactive transport RNA has been discovered in animal tissue, and Matsuka has studied its structural traits and role in the biosynthesis of proteins. The interaction between components of nucleoprotein complexes is being investigated by Matsuka and M. Zheltovsky in relation to the problem of protein-nucleic identification. I. Todorov, K. Platonov, and O. Halkin determined the role of cytoplasmic protein synthesis in controlling the expression of nuclear and mitochondric genomes in the cells of higher organisms. Research is also taking place in Ukraine in quantum biology, a new branch of molecular biology. The institute (through the experiments of V. Kordium) has participated in Soviet and international biological experiments in space.

Chemically modified anomalous nucleosides of various types and related bonds are being studied from different aspects. Some of these substances, studied by V. Chernetsky, proved to be effective antiswelling and antiviral agents. Problems of genetic engineering are also under investigation.

The fermentative synthesis of many structural genes, including the genes of human interferons, globins of various animals, oncornaviruses, plant viruses, and keto immunoglobulin, has been carried out under the international Reverse Transcriptase project. A laboratory was set up at the institute to prepare revertase ferments for many Soviet and foreign institutions. V. Kordium developed a genetic engineering system for supersynthesizing biologically active substances. Bacterial genes have been successfully transplanted into plant cells by S. Maliuta. I. Kok determined the molecular structure and the organizing principle of the genome of bacillo-viruses which affect a number of useful and harmful insects.

The primary structure of some individual transfer RNA of animal origin has been decoded by Matsuka and M. Tukalo. The results of research on the mutagenic action of exogenic DNA and artificially synthesized polynucleotides point to new approaches to one of the chief problems of genetics – directed mutagenesis (S. Hershenzon). The genetic foundations of plant selection have been worked out, and it is possible to design new varieties of agricultural plants.

At the ANU Institute of Biochemistry M. *Huly has studied the initial stages and the regulation of protein biosynthesis under certain extreme states of the organism. The institute's research was conducted in co-operation with branch institutes of the ANU and the academies of sciences of the USSR, Czechoslovakia, and Germany as well as departments within the All-Union Academy of Agricultural Sciences, the Health Ministry of the Ukrainian SSR, and the agriculture ministries of Ukraine and the USSR. Work in the physicochemical biology of membranes is conducted by the ANU at the Institute of Biochemistry under V. *Lishko and the *Institute of Physiology under V. Kostiuk. At the Institute of Botany K. *Sytnyk is overseeing research in genetic engineering. Methods of parasexual hybridization of cells to obtain whole plants are being widely used. An ultrastructural analysis of hybridization has been carried out. At the Institute for Problems of Oncology research is devoted to the molecular basis of carcinro- and leucogenesis and the transcription and translation of RNA in swollen cells (Z. Butenko, N. Berdynsky, V. Shliakhonenko).

Molecular biology research is conducted at institutions outside of the ANU. At Kharkiv University V. *Nikitin oversees research on age-related changes in the genetic mechanism of vertebrates. At Kiev University M. Kucherenko and his colleagues are studying the translation processes under various types of radiation. At the Kiev Scientific Research Institute of Endocrinology and Metabolism V. *Komisarenko oversees research on the molecular mechanisms of the hormonal regulation of protein biosynthesis. Research results in molecular biology appear in the Russian-language periodical *Tsitologiia i genetika*, published by the ANU.

M. Adams

Moleniie Danyla Zatochnyka (Supplication of Danylo the Exile). A collection of political and practical personal advice addressed to an unidentified prince from Pereiaslav. In some redactions the addressee is Prince Yaroslav Vsevolodovych of Pereiaslav (1201–6), in others, Prince Yaroslav Volodymyrovych of Novgorod (1182–99). The work was probably written in the 12th or 13th century; the original has not been preserved. The oldest copies date from the 16th century. At first it was thought that *Moleniie* was a genuine petition from the exiled author to his prince, but later it was shown that the petition is merely a literary form. Many of the themes and ideas that appear in *Moleniie* can be found in other monuments of Old Ukrainian literature. An outstanding edition of *Moleniie* is N. Zarubin's *Slovo Daniila Zatochnika po redaktsiiam XII i XIII vv. i ikh peredelkam* (Danylo Zatochnyk's Supplication in 12th- and 13th-Century Redactions and Their Revisions, 1932).

Molentsky, Antin [Molenc'kyj] (real name: Naibok), b 1843 in Zolochiv, Galicia, d 1874 in Lviv. Stage actor and director. He began his theatrical career in 1864 in K. Lobojiko's mixed Polish-Ukrainian troupe and then worked in the Ruska Besida Theater, as actor in 1864–7 and as artistic director in 1869–71.

Moliavko, Hryhorii [Moljavko, Hryhorij], b 23 January 1901 in Altynivka, Krolevets county, Chernihiv gubernia. Geologist. He graduated from the Kiev Institute of People's Education (1926) and worked as a teacher until joining the AN URSR (now ANU) Institute of Geological Sciences in 1932. He was a department head from 1955 to 1969. In 1951–4 and 1969–71 he also taught at Kiev University. His main scientific works were devoted to the stratigraphy of Neogene and Quaternary sediments in Ukraine, the paleography of Ukraine, and the history of geological scholarship.

Molnar, Larysa [Mol'nar] (née Nahorna), b 14 November 1928 in Plysky, Borzna county, Chernihiv okruha. Ukrainian writer and translator in the Prešov region of Slovakia; wife of M. *Molnar. A graduate of the Kiev Institute of Theater Arts (1952), she has worked as an editor at the Mystetstvo publishing house in Kiev and, since 1960, the Ukrainian literature department of the Slovak Pedagogical Publishing House. She has written a book containing two novelettes, *Voda v mori ochyshchaiet'sia* (Water Is Purified in the Sea, 1969), the story collection *Khvylyny* (Minutes, 1972), and literary criticism, including literary portraits of O. Dovzhenko, Yu. Yanovsky, M. Valek, A. Plavka, Ya. Kostra, and others. Molnar has translated works of Russian, Czech, and Slovak writers into Ukrainian, and has also translated D. Stavrovský's book on the Slovak-Polish-Ukrainian borderland up to the 18th century (1967) and B. Kovačovičová-Puškárová and I. Puškár's book on Ukrainian wooden churches in eastern Slovakia (1971).

Molnar, Mykhailo [Mol'nar, Myxajlo] (Czech: Molnár, Michal), b 4 November 1930 in Velyka Chynhava (now Borzhavske), Transcarpathia. Literary scholar; husband of L. *Molnar. He studied at the Ukrainian gymnasium in Modržany, near Prague (1940–5), Prague University (1950–5), and Kiev University (graduate studies, 1956–60). Since 1960 he has worked at the Slovak Academy of Sciences in Bratislava, where he is director of the Institute of World Literature and Languages. An authority on 19th- and 20th-century Ukrainian-Czechoslovak literary relations, he has edited, with introductions, several books in the field (including the first Soviet anthology of works by Ukrainian writers living in Slovakia's Prešov region, 1960), Slovak translations of Ukrainian literature, Ukrainian translations of Czech and Slovak literature, and editions of works by Ukrainian writers from the Prešov region. He has written books on T. Shevchenko's reception by the Czechs and Slovaks (1961) and on Slovak-Ukrainian literary relations (1965, with relevant documents) and hundreds of articles and reviews. An edition of his selected works (with a bibliography), *Zustrichi kul'-tur* (The Meetings of Cultures), appeared in 1980.

Molochanske [Moločans'ke]. VI-16. A town (1990 pop 9,100) located on the Molochna River in Zaporizhia oblast and administered by the Tokmak municipal council. In 1803 a settlement called Halbstadt was founded at the site by German Mennonites. It was renamed Molochanske in 1915 and granted city status in 1938. The town has several food enterprises, a furniture factory, and a branch of the Prohres metallurgical plant. Archeologists have discovered many kurhans from the Bronze Age (3rd–1st millennium BC) and the Scythian (4th–3rd century BC) and Sarmatian (2nd century BC to 2nd century AD) periods in the vicinity.

Molochna River [Moločna] (also Tokmak). A river in Zaporizhia oblast that flows into Molochne Lake. It is 197 km long and drains a basin area of 3,450 sq km. Three reservoirs have been built on the river. Its waters are used for industrial consumption, irrigation, and pisciculture. The main cities located on the river are Tokmak, Molochanske, and Melitopil.

Molochne Lake

Molochne Lake [Moločne ozero] (Molochnyi lyman). VII-16. A saltwater lake located in the southwestern part of Zaporizhia oblast along the Sea of Azov coast. Molochne Lake was formed as a result of the flooding of the plain at the mouth of the Molochna River by the Sea of Azov. The lake is separated from the sea by a sandy strip of land up to 500 m in width. The lake is 32 km long and up to 8 km wide (168 sq km). Its average depth is 1.5 to 2 m, and the maximum depth is 9 m. The Tashchenak and the Dzhekelnia rivers also flow into the lake. The Kyrylivka health resort is located on the lake and uses its mud and brine for curative applications.

Molod. The publishing house of the Communist Youth League of Ukraine. Established in 1923 in Kharkiv, it was called Molodyi Robitnyk (1923–30), Molodyi Bilshovyk (1930–41), and the State Publishing House of Children's and Young People's Literature (1945–8); it assumed its present name in 1948. Since 1934 it has been located in Kiev. Although Molod published works on social and political subjects, on art, and on other topics, primarily for a younger audience, it is especially known for its publications of prose and poetry by younger authors. Until 1992 each year it issued approx 130 titles with a total run of approx 4.5 million copies. Molod published O. Honchar's first major work, *Praporonostsi* (The Standard Bearers, 1947–8), and, in the 1960s, many of the first books by the *shestydesiatnyky. In 1988 the director of the press was A. Davydov.

Molod' Ukraïny (Youth of Ukraine). An organ of the Communist Youth League of Ukraine CC. It was first published in Kharkiv in June 1920 as a Russian-language weekly but with a Ukrainian title, *Visti TsK Komunistychnoï spilky molodi Ukraïny*. From July 1922 it appeared semiweekly as *Molodoi rabochii*. Renamed *Molodoi leninets* in January 1924, it became a Ukrainian-language daily in December 1925 under the title *Komsomolets' Ukraïny*. From 1934 until the June 1941 German invasion it was published in Kiev. It was revived in Kharkiv in October 1943 under its present name and transferred to Kiev late that year. The paper appeared five times a week. In 1980 it had a circulation of 750,000; its Russian-language counterpart, *Komsomols'koe znamia* (est 1938), had one of 250,000.

Moloda Hromada (Young Community). An association of veterans of the Ukrainian Galician Army and the UNR Army, formed in 1925 in Lviv. Its activities included lectures and discussions on the recent liberation struggle, commemorations of 1 November and 22 January, and organized visits to soldiers' cemeteries. Besides promoting personal contacts among veterans, it provided financial aid to war invalids, veterans, and their families. In 1938 the society organized the funeral of Brig Gen M. *Tarnavsky. Its presidents were Yu. Sheparovych and A. Palii, and its long-term secretary was L. Makarushka. The society's activities ceased in 1939.

Moloda Muza (Young Muse). An informal modernist group of writers and artists in Western Ukraine, founded in 1906. The group's manifesto, as expressed by one of the founders (O. *Lutsky), was 'freedom and liberty in content and form' and an emphasis on the more subtle and gentle experiences of the human soul. To publicize its works the group established a publishing house with the same name, which during its brief existence (1906–9) brought out more than 10 works by the members of the group as well as the extremely ambitious but short-lived periodical *S'vit. The members consisted of the writers B. Lepky, V. Pachovsky, P. Karmansky, M. Yatskiv, S. Charnetsky, Lutsky, S. Tverdokhlib, and V. Birchak, the painter M. Sosenko, the sculptor M. Parashchuk, and the composer S. Liudkevych. Sympathetic to the group were the writer V. Shchurat and the critic M. Yevshan.

Although as in all such loosely organized groups the style and quality of literary production is varied and uneven, there are some common traits which characterize

Some members of Moloda Muza. Sitting, from left: Volodymyr Birchak, Neonilia Pachovska, Ivan Kosynin; standing, Mykhailo Yatskiv, Vasyl Pachovsky, Mykhailo Strutynsky

the group as a whole: a predilection for the esthetic above the utilitarian in life and an affinity for the unease and pessimism of the Western European intelligentsia of the turn of the century. Some members of Moloda Muza were influenced by its Polish counterpart Młoda Polska. But though they were but a pale reflection of their Polish 'modernist' friends, to say nothing of the symbolists and decadents whose works they often translated, the members of Moloda Muza not only did not receive popular support (the newspaper *S'vit* had to give up its international profile and turn to more mundane matters after only nine months of publication), they had to contend with attacks from such notables as S. *Yefremov and I. *Franko. Franko's criticism, despite his sensitivity to their talent, centered on the absence of proper and meaningful purpose in their creativity. At a time when so much still had to be done in the social, national, and political spheres, there was little room for the luxury of esthetics. For Franko literature had more important aims. Their sensitive brooding was labeled destructive pessimism, their attention to form, needless formalism, and their striking imagery, decadence.

Such a climate put an end to the group's fragile attempt to free literature from social purpose. Moloda Muza produced some interesting works (Yatskiv's expressionistic miniatures, Pachovsky's erotic lyrics, and Karmansky's haunting and melancholy pieces) and had some influence on the writers of the 1920s (D. Zahul, V. Kobyliansky, and even the early P. Tychyna). But its elegant publications found little favor among the local intelligentsia. Moloda Muza marks only an interesting interlude in the development of Ukrainian literature in the 20th century since neither the interwar nationalist school of criticism nor the Soviet socialist-realist criticism could see any value in literary activity outside of social and political concerns.

BIBLIOGRAPHY
Rudyk, D. 'Molodomuztsi,' *ZhR*, 1925, no. 12
Stepniak, M. 'Poety Molodoï muzy,' *ChSh*, 1933, no. 1
Karmans'kyi, P. *Ukraïns'ka Bohema* (Lviv 1936)
Rudnyts'kyi, M. 'Shcho take "Moloda muza",' intro to *Chorna Indiia 'Molodoï muzy'* (Lviv 1937)
Romanenchuk, B. 'Modernistic Trends in Ukrainian Literature: 1900–1923,' PH D diss, University of Pennsylvania, 1958

Rubchak, B. 'Probnyi let,' in *Ostap Luts'kyi – Molodomuzets'*, ed Yu. Luts'kyi (New York 1968)

D.H. Struk

Moloda Ukraina (Young Ukraine). A network of student circles in Galicia and Bukovyna in 1899–1903. The groups consisted of secondary-school and university students, who met to exchange ideas and foster intellectual development among themselves. The leading thinkers among them, including L. Tsehelsky, V. Starosolsky, Ye. Kosevych, and T. Melets, articulated an ideology in which the goal of national independence was based on the demand for the social emancipation of the Ukrainian people. The leading members of the organization published the journal *Moloda Ukraïna* (1900–3) and collaborated closely with student hromadas in Kharkiv, Kiev, and Poltava. They helped smuggle revolutionary literature and even arms into Russian-ruled Ukraine. Many members of Moloda Ukraina became active in Ukrainian political parties in Galicia and Bukovyna.

Moloda Ukraïna (Lviv, 1900–3)

Moloda Ukraïna (Young Ukraine). A monthly student journal published, with interruptions, in Lviv from January 1900 to March 1903 (a total of 33 issues); the unofficial organ of the *Academic Hromada. Its editors and publishers included M. Zalitach, V. Starosolsky, Ye. Kosevych, A. Krushelnytsky, A. Hoshovsky, F. Tuziak, V. Tsebrovsky, and S. Baran. Among its contributors were the belletrists l. Martovych, S. Charnetsky, V. Shchurat, M. Yatskiv, and Lesia Ukrainka, and many other young activists who gained prominence in the revolutionary period and interwar years. *Moloda Ukraïna* strongly supported the Ukrainian national movement and the concept of an independent unitary Ukraine. It published articles on Ukrainian history and culture and developments in the student movement – reporting extensively on Ukrainian student activities in Galicia, Bukovyna, Vienna, and Russian-ruled Ukraine – and advocated the establishment of a Ukrainian university in Lviv. The journal also contained commentaries on general political trends, usually from a populist or socialist perspective; book reviews; and a chronicle of current events. It was regularly subjected to censorship by the Austro-Hungarian government. Attempts at reviving the journal in 1905 (4 issues appeared, edited by V. Paneiko) and again in 1910 as the organ of the Ukrainian Students' Union (7 issues edited by M. Vitoshynsky and V. Lototsky) were short-lived.

Moloda Ukraïna (Kiev, 1906–14)

Moloda Ukraïna (Young Ukraine). The first and only Ukrainian-language children's magazine in Russian-ruled Ukraine before the First World War, published in Kiev (1906 [1 issue], 1908–12) and Hadiache (1914 [4 issues]) as a monthly supplement to *Ridnyi krai*. Edited by O. Pchilka, it contained stories and poems by Kh. Alchevska, Lesia Ukrainka, M. Rylsky, T. Shevchenko, S. Rudansky, S. Vasylchenko, and others, and stories translated from Russian (N. Gogol, M. Lermontov, L. Tolstoi), English (J. Swift, C. Dickens, O. Wilde), and other languages. A total of 64 issues appeared.

Moloda Ukraïna (Young Ukraine). A magazine for teenagers published and edited by M. Taranko in Lviv. A total of 66 semimonthly (1923–5) and monthly (1926) issues appeared.

Moloda Ukraïna (Young Ukraine). A monthly organ of the Ukrainian Democratic Youth Association (ODUM), published since November 1951 in Toronto. It contains articles on historical and political subjects and on current developments in Ukraine, émigré and Soviet Ukrainian poetry and prose, cultural reviews, and reports on ODUM activities. It has been edited by an editorial committee, which has included B. Oleksandriv, O. Smoliansky, M. Dalny, I. Pyshkalo, M. Havrysh, Ya. Bilinsky, P. Hursky, Ye. Fedorenko, L. Lishchyna, L. Pavliuk, P. Rodak, O. Poshyvanyk, and O. Kharchenko.

Molode Zhyttia (Young Life). A publishing house established by the *Plast Ukrainian Youth Association in Munich in 1946 to publish the Plast magazines *Molode zhyttia*, *Novak*, and *Plastovyi shliakh* and various Plast books and brochures. It has also published several publications of the Shevchenko Scientific Society, over 25 monographs, and the *Entsyklopediia ukraïnoznavstva* (Encyclopedia of Ukraine, 2 + 10 vols, 1949–84). Its longtime director has been A. Figol.

Molode zhyttia (Young Life). A magazine of the *Plast Ukrainian Youth Association published in Lviv (1921–30) and, after the official suppression of Plast by the Polish government, in Prague (nos 77–80). After the Second World War the journal was renewed and published monthly in Munich (1946–50) and Detroit (1951–9). It contained reports on Plast activities, popular articles on Ukrainian history and culture, articles on scouting, prose, poetry, and directives from the Plast leadership. Its edi-

tors included S. Tysovsky (1921–4), B. Kravtsiv (1924–7, 1946–59), and P. Isaiv (1927–9). A total of 145 issues appeared.

Molodizhne [Molodižne]. A town smt (1990 pop 4,700) in Symferopil raion, Crimea oblast. It was founded in 1929, and attained smt status in 1972. It is the home of an experimental farm of the Crimean Agricultural Institute.

Molodniak (Youth). A literary organization of Komsomol writers, established in 1926 by P. Usenko in Kharkiv and liquidated in 1932 by a decree of the Party's Central Committee, 'On the Reconstruction of Literary and Artistic Organizations.' Members of the Kharkiv branch included V. Kuzmych, D. Hordiienko, L. Pervomaisky, I. Momot, P. Holota, O. Kundzich, and Ya. Hrymailo. B. Kovalenko, M. Sheremet, O. Korniichuk, A. Klochia, P. Kolesnyk, A. Shyian, and others belonged to the Kiev branch. There were also branches active in Dnipropetrovske, Donetske, Kherson, Kremenchuk, Mykolaiv, Zaporizhia, and Uman. Similar to the All-Ukrainian Association of Proletarian Writers, Molodniak contributed to the destruction of Ukrainian culture in the 1920s and early 1930s. B. Kovalenko was its chief ideologue. Pervomaisky and Korniichuk were among those who began their activities within the organization and went on to prominence as leading Soviet writers. The organization's members published in an organ which bore the same name. (See also *Pluh.)

Molodniak (Youth). A literary, cultural, and political monthly journal of the Communist Youth League of Ukraine CC. Published in Kharkiv (1927–35) and Kiev (1935–7) and edited by O. Hromov, B. Daniman, P. Trublaievych, A. Khvylia, and P. Usenko, it published poetry and prose by members of the Komsomol writers' group *Molodniak (until 1932) and the Writers' Union of Ukraine (SPU, from 1932). From July 1936 the journal was also an SPU organ. In August 1937 it was superseded by *Molodyi bil'shovyk*, which appeared until May 1941.

Molodogvardiiske or **Molodohvardiisk** [Molodogvardijs'ke or Molodohvardijs'k]. V-20, DB III-7. A city (1990 pop 31,800) in Luhanske oblast, administered by the Krasnodon municipal council. It was founded in 1955 with the opening of several coal mines, and attained city status in 1961. Its economy rests mostly on four coal mines and an enrichment plant.

Molodove. A multi-occupational Paleolithic site on the right bank of the Dniester River near Molodove, Chernivtsi oblast. Discovered in the 1920s, the site was excavated from 1951 to 1980. While numerous occupational periods have been discovered at Molodove, the most important are Molodove I and Molodove V. Molodove I consists of nine distinct settlements spanning the period from the Middle Paleolithic (the *Mousterian culture) to the Mesolithic. Dwellings of Molodove I utilized mammoth bones to provide a building frame upon which skins were laid. At Molodove V twenty settlements spanning the Middle and Upper Paleolithic periods were uncovered. Many flint, bone, and horn artifacts were uncovered, including primitive flutes made from mammoth tusks.

Leonid Molodozhanyn and former Prime Minister John Diefenbaker admiring Molodozhanyn's work (1975)

Molodozhanyn, Leonid [Molodožanyn] (Mol, Leo), b 15 January 1915 in Volhynia.

Sculptor and stained-glass artist. He studied at the art academies in Berlin and the Hague before emigrating to Winnipeg in 1948. He has created over 90 stained-glass windows, including 30 for the SS Volodymyr and Olha Ukrainian Catholic Cathedral in Winnipeg. Mol has earned an international reputation as one of Canada's leading sculptors. Working in the classical tradition, he has won numerous international competitions, including ones for monuments to T. Shevchenko in Washington, DC (1964), and Buenos Aires (1971), to Queen Elizabeth II in Winnipeg (1970), and to the former Canadian prime minister J. Diefenbaker in Ottawa (1985). He has executed numerous busts of well-known figures, including W. Churchill (1966), D.E. Eisenhower (1965), J.F. Kennedy (1969), Popes Paul VI (1967), John XXIII (1967), and John Paul II (1982), and Cardinal Y. Slipy (1971). To commemorate the millennium of Ukrainian Christianity in 1988, he created bronze monuments of St Volodymyr for the Ukrainian communities in London (England), Winnipeg, and Toronto. A past president of the Manitoba Society of Artists and the Sculptors' Society of Canada and a member of the Royal Canadian Academy of Arts and the Allied Artists of America, for his contribution to Canadian art he was awarded honorary doctorates by the Universities of Winnipeg and Alberta (1985) and was appointed to the Order of Canada (1989). In 1992 the Leo Mol park and museum was established in Winnipeg. A monograph about him has been written by the Canadian art historian P. Duval (1982).

D. Zelska-Darewych

Molodyi bil'shovyk. See *Dnipro* and *Molodniak.*

Molodyi Teatr (Young Theater).

A theatre troupe in Kiev headed by L. Kurbas from 1917 to 1919. The core group of actors consisted of graduates of the Lysenko Music and Drama School. Most of the productions were directed by Kurbas, although H. *Yura, V. Vasilev, and S. Semdor also directed shows. A. Petrytsky was the main stage designer. Kurbas's articles, such as the 'Manifesto' (in *Robitnycha hazeta,* 1917) and 'Molodyi Teatr' (Young Theatre, 1917), called for a new Ukrainian theatre and out-

The Molodyi Teatr troupe after the premiere of Volodymyr Vynnychenko's *Chorna pantera i bilyi vedmid'* (Black Panther and White Bear) in Kiev in 1917. First row, from left: Olha Horodyska (2nd), Sofiia Manuilovych (3rd), Antonina Smereka (4th); second row: Yona Shevchenko, Vasyl Vasylko, Polina Samiilenko, Les Kurbas, Vira Shchepanska, Petro Myloradovych, Halyna Ihrets, and, standing, Hnat Yura and Marko Tereshchenko; third row: Oleksander Yursky (1st), Volodymyr Kalyn (2nd), Valerii Vasyliev (4th), Yakiv Savchenko (5th), Lev Piasetsky (7th), Borys Vasyliev (8th), Olimpiia Dobrovolska (9th), Andrii Shchepansky (11th); last row: Stepan Bondarchuk (in white shirt)

lined the artistic goals of the group. Molodyi Teatr rejected the Ukrainian ethnographic repertoire and presented modern Ukrainian plays and world classics. Kurbas's search for a new form resulted in imaginative uses of rhythm, gesture, music, and design in his productions. The first season included Kurbas's productions of the realistic *Chorna pantera i bilyi vedmid'* (Black Panther and White Bear) by V. Vynnychenko, the naturalistic *Jugend* by M. Halbe, and *Doktor Kerzhentsev,* based on L. Andreev's *Mysl'* (Thought), directed by Yura. These were followed by a stylized presentation of four symbolic études by O. Oles, two of which were directed by Kurbas and one by Yura. Molodyi Teatr concluded its first season with a production of J. Żuławski's impressionistic verse play *Ijola.*

The second season (1918–19) opened with Kurbas's production of Sophocles' *Oedipus Rex,* the first Ukrainian production of a classical Greek play. Kurbas's subsequent productions included Lesia Ukrainka's *U pushchi* (In the Wilderness); F. Grillparzer's *Weh dem, der lügt!* in the commedia dell'arte style; a stylized *Vertep,* which used the conventions of the puppet theater; expressionistic stagings of T. Shevchenko's dramatic poems 'Ivan Hus' and 'Velykyi l'okh' (The Great Vault); and performances of several lyrical poems as choral movement pieces with music, which Kurbas would later see as his first attempt to create 'transformed gestures,' the central concern of his later work. During the season the other directors presented literal stagings of such plays as G. Shaw's *Candida* (directed by Yura), G. Hauptmann's *Die versunkene Glocke* (by Yura) V. Vynnychenko's *Hrikh* (Sin, by Yura), Moliere's *Tartuffe* (by Vasilev), and H. Ibsen's *En folkefiende* (by Semdor).

In the spring of 1919, as the internal artistic conflicts came to a head, Molodyi Teatr was nationalized by the Bolshevik government and forced to merge with the *State Drama Theatre to form the *Shevchenko First Theatre of the Ukrainian Soviet Republic. Although it lasted only two seasons, Molodyi Teatr changed the direction of Ukrainian theatre, and from its ranks came the artistic directors of the major theaters of the 1920s, including Kurbas, Yura, M. Tereshchenko, and V. Vasylko.

BIBLIOGRAPHY
Hirniak, I. 'Birth and Death of the Modern Ukrainian Theater,' in *Soviet Theaters: 1917–1941*, ed M. Bradshaw (New York 1954)
Boiko, Iu. 'Molodyi teatr,' in his *Vybrane*, vol 1 (Munich 1971)
Tkacz, V. 'Les Kurbas and the Creation of a Ukrainian Avant-Garde Theatre: The Early Years,' MA thesis, Columbia University, 1983
Labinsky, M. (ed). *Molodyi Teatr* (Kiev 1991)

V. Revutsky

Molodyk (New Moon). A literary-art almanac published in 1843–4. Four issues in total appeared; three were printed in Kharkiv, and the fourth in St Petersburg. *Molodyk* was published by I. Betsky with the assistance of H. Kvitka-Osnovianenko, M. Kostomarov, and others. It published works by T. Shevchenko, Kvitka-Osnovianenko, Ye. Hrebinka, A. Metlynsky, M. Kostomarov, M. Petrenko, F. Glinka, and others, and articles on history and the history of literature (eg, Kharkiv College, H. Skovoroda). Russian literary critics (especially V. Belinsky) had a hostile attitude to *Molodyk*.

Molokans (Russian: *molokane*). A Russian religious sect formed in the 18th century in Tambov gubernia that later spread to other areas of the Russian Empire. Founded by S. Uklein, a former Doukhobor, the sect rejected a formal church, the ritual of worship, and the sacraments in favor of Bible readings and prayer meetings. Because of their pacifism, sect members frequently came into conflict with state authorities, and during the 19th century Molokan groups were exiled to Caucasia, Siberia, and the Volga and Amur regions. By the beginning of the 20th century there were approx 1.2 million Molokans in the Russian Empire. Some of them settled in Southern Ukraine, most notably a subgroup known as the Jumpers (*pryguny*) because of their practice of jumping during religious services. An undetermined number of Molokans remain in Ukraine today.

Molot (Sledgehammer). A radical literary and political miscellany published in the *drahomanivka* alphabet by M. Pavlyk in Lviv in 1878. Like its predecessors *Dzvin* and *Hromads'kyi druh*, it was confiscated by the Austrian authorities.

Molotov, Viacheslav (né Skriabin), b 9 March 1890 in Kukarka, Viatka gubernia, Russia, d 9 March 1986 near Moscow. Bolshevik party functionary and Soviet diplomat. As secretary of the CP(B)U Donetske Gubernia Committee in 1920, he supervised the suppression of the Workers' Opposition in the Donbas. After being promoted to the office of first secretary of the CP(B)U (November 1920 to March 1921) he implemented Moscow's policy of War Communism, purged the CP(B)U, and waged war on the anti-Soviet partisan movement. He was rewarded with appointments to the CC of the Russian Communist Party (Bolshevik) and its Politburo. A servile supporter of J. Stalin after V. Lenin's death, he became the secretary of the Moscow Party Committee and a full Politburo member in late 1925. After purging the Moscow organization of

Stalin's opponents in 1928–30, he was appointed chairman of the USSR Council of People's Commissars and held the post during the terror and purges until 1941. At the Third CP(B)U Conference in Kharkiv in 1932, he rejected Ukrainian entreaties to lower the excessive grain-delivery quotas which would lead to the man-made famine of 1932–3. In 1937 he played a key role in purging the CC CP(B)U. As commissar of foreign affairs in 1939–49, he negotiated the *Molotov-Ribbentrop Pact and then the Soviet alliances with the United States and Great Britain. At the 1945 Yalta Conference he proposed that Soviet Ukraine become a member of the United Nations. After Stalin's death he again served as foreign minister (1953–6) and as minister of state control until June 1957, when he was stripped of all offices for working with the 'anti-Party group' to depose N. Khrushchev. Later he served as ambassador to Mongolia and Soviet delegate to the International Atomic Energy Agency in Vienna (1960–1). In 1964 he was expelled from the CPSU, and retired from political life.

Molotov-Ribbentrop Pact. The popular name of the German-Soviet Nonaggression Pact signed in Moscow on 23 August 1939 by the foreign ministers of the USSR (V. Molotov) and Nazi Germany (J. von Ribbentrop). The pact was signed immediately after the agreement of 19 August, which granted the USSR 180 million marks for the purchase of German goods. It followed months of unsuccessful negotiations between the USSR on the one side and France and Great Britain on the other, and Soviet failure to organize an anti-Nazi diplomatic coalition.

The Molotov-Ribbentrop Pact was one of the most important diplomatic acts in Soviet history. Its formal section, consisting of seven articles, was made public. It specified that the signatories would refrain from aggression against each other, remain neutral in case of war with other states, exchange information, and resolve disputes peacefully. The pact was to remain in force for 10 years. A secret protocol of four articles which was appended to the formal part divided Poland between Germany and the USSR along the Sian–Buh–Narev rivers (roughly following the *Curzon Line) and thereby handed over most of the Polish-ruled Ukrainian and Belarusian territory to the USSR and assigned Latvia, Estonia, Finland, and Bessarabia to the Soviet sphere of influence and Lithuania to the German sphere. An adjustment on 28 September 1939 transferred Lithuania to the Soviet sphere of influence and redrew the border along the Sian–Buh–Narev rivers, to remove some ethnically Polish territory from the Soviet part.

This pact led directly to the Second World War. Fearing that Great Britain and France would honor their treaty obligations to Poland and come to its defense, Hitler needed a guarantee of Soviet neutrality before he could launch his assault on Poland, for he believed that Germany could not fight on two fronts simultaneously. On 1 September Germany attacked Poland, and on 3 September Britain and France declared war. The USSR invaded Poland from the east on 17 September and occupied the territory assigned to it in the secret protocol. J. Stalin justified the action by citing the need to guarantee the safety of the millions of Ukrainians and Belarusians in eastern Poland. Rigged elections were quickly held, and on 27 October 1939 the new National Assembly of Western Ukraine formally proclaimed Soviet rule and petitioned the USSR to incorporate the territory into Soviet Ukraine. The 'request' was granted on 1 November.

The Baltic states were forced to sign mutual assistance pacts with the USSR, which gradually expanded its influence in their affairs. The Red Army occupied the countries on 15–16 June 1940. As in Western Ukraine, the quickly 'elected' assemblies 'applied' in August 1940 to become Soviet republics. In June 1940 the USSR occupied Bessarabia and northern Bukovyna in the name of 'national liberation.'

The Ukrainian question was an important factor behind the Molotov-Ribbentrop Pact. Stalin was concerned about a possible alliance between Germany and Western Ukrainian nationalists, who wanted to liberate Ukraine from Soviet rule. He probably feared that the short-lived independent *Carpatho-Ukraine would serve as an inspiration to Ukrainians in the USSR. Hence, Stalin aimed to bring all Ukrainians under his rule in order to control them. He also knew that the man-made famine of 1932–3 and terror of the 1930s had alienated the Ukrainian people from his regime, and that they would welcome a German invasion. Hence, he needed Germany's friendship or, at least, its neutrality.

The Molotov-Ribbentrop Pact remained the foundation of Soviet-German relations throughout the first years of the war. Stalin continued to abide by its provisions for cooperation and mutual support. He provided the Germans with much-needed raw materials for their war effort, even as Germany prepared for its invasion of the USSR. The pact entailed a radical change in Soviet foreign policy: the USSR abandoned its criticism of the Nazis and forced the Comintern and its communist allies in Western Europe and elsewhere to do likewise. This about-face greatly undermined the popularity of many Communist parties outside the USSR. In Canada the government suppressed pro-Soviet organizations, such as the *Ukrainian Labour-Farmer Temple Association. It was only the German invasion in June 1941 that put an end to the pact.

For most of the postwar period the official Soviet justification for the Molotov-Ribbentrop Pact was that the USSR needed time to prepare for a war with Germany. Until the late 1980s the Soviet authorities never even admitted the existence of the secret protocol, but stubbornly maintained that the Red Army had occupied Western Ukraine, Belarus, and the Baltic states in response to calls for assistance and protection. A major re-evaluation of the entire Soviet diplomatic record and especially of the pact has begun.

BIBLIOGRAPHY
Ulam, B. *Expansion and Coexistence: The History of Soviet Foreign Policy, 1917–67* (New York–Washington 1968)
Read, A.; Fischer, D. *The Deadly Embrace: Hitler, Stalin, and the Nazi-Soviet Pact, 1939–1941* (New York–London 1988)
Kolasky, J. *Partners in Tyranny: The Nazi-Soviet Nonaggression Pact, August 23, 1939* (Toronto 1990)

B. Balan

Momot, Ivan, b 23 February 1905 in Valky, Kharkiv gubernia, d 27 May 1931 in Kharkiv. Literary critic; member of *Molodniak. Momot published a collection of his articles, *Literaturnyi komsomol* (Literary Komsomol, 1927), and numerous essays on the works of M. Kozhushny, I. Shevchenko, V. Chumak, and others, which appeared in Komsomol newspapers and journals as well as the journal *Pluzhanyn*.

Monarchism. See Conservatism.

Monasteries. Communities and settlements of monks (see *Monasticism) with attendant buildings and estates. Depending on the monastic order that the particular monastery belonged to or the monastic typicon that was followed, life ranged from strictly anchoritic, to semi-communal (where monks lived in individual cells but ate and prayed together), to communal or idiorrythmic. Novices also lived in the monastery before being tonsured. Monasteries were generally formally headed by a council of all the monks or nuns, which chose an abbot or overseer (an *archimandrite or *hegumen). Historically, depending on various political, legal, and economic conditions, monasteries enjoyed differing degrees of autonomy. *Lavry (of which there were two in Ukraine, the *Kievan Cave and *Pochaiv monasteries) and *stauropegion monasteries were subject only to the highest church authority (initially the Patriarch of Constantinople, later the Patriarch of Moscow and the Holy Synod) and were independent of the local bishop. Cathedral monasteries were directly subordinate to the bishop of the eparchy to which they belonged. Other types included self-administering monasteries (the majority) and *hermitages (skyty, skytyky, pustyni) that were dependent on larger monasteries.

Larger monasteries had a main church and bell tower, as well as smaller chapels, baptismal alcoves, and separate refectories. Apart from the shrines and monks' residences (cells), monasteries typically had an array of administrative buildings and workshops and sometimes their own hospitals, schools, and printing presses. The monasteries were often surrounded by fortified walls or palisades, with defensive ramparts, towers, and trenches, and some monasteries even grew into large complexes that served as fortresses (especially in Slobidska Ukraine and in areas bordering the Tatar-controlled steppes).

Monastic life in Ukraine began before the official adoption of Christianity, but the first monasteries were not built until after the baptism of Kiev and its environs in the late 10th century. The first formal monasteries were established under Yaroslav the Wise – the men's St George's and the women's St Irene's monasteries in Kiev (both mentioned in 1037). Other early monasteries included St Demetrius's (later *St Michael's Golden-Domed) Monastery, the *Vydubychi Monastery, and *St Cyril's Monastery. In the 11th to 13th centuries the number of monasteries in the Kiev region rose to 20. Monasteries were founded in other parts of Ukraine, primarily in such princely capitals as Pereiaslav, Chernihiv (the *Yeletskyi and *Trinity–St Elijah monasteries), Novhorod-Siverskyi, Volodymyr-Volynskyi, Halych, Kholm, and Lviv (St George's Monastery). Smaller monasteries were established throughout Ukraine. Although information about these is often incomplete, a partial list of smaller monasteries in the 11th to 13th centuries includes the Zarubskyi Monastery near Kaniv, the SS Borys and Hlib Monastery near Pereiaslav, the Zahoriv Monastery near Volodymyr-Volynskyi, the *Zhydychyn St Nicholas's Monastery in Volhynia, St Daniel's Monastery in Uhrovske (Kholm region), the Synevidsko and Polonynskyi monasteries in the

Carpathians, and the Rata Monastery near Rava Ruska. Other monasteries that were probably established in the Princely era became known only in the late Middle Ages – the *Mezhyhiria Transfiguration Monastery near Kiev, the *Novhorod-Siverskyi Transfiguration Monastery, the Peresopnytsia and Dorohobuzh monasteries in Volhynia, the Byblo Monastery near Peremyshl, the Horodyshche Monastery near Sokal, St *Onuphrius's Monastery in Lviv, and the *Lavriv and Spas monasteries near Sambir.

Monasteries were established mainly by princes and boyars, although some were founded by spiritual leaders and churchmen. Noble patrons oversaw the monasteries: they cared for their growth and development and often donated estates, valuables, and money. They were thereby guaranteed certain rights over the organization and administration of the monasteries, extending to the approval of charters and the appointment of hegumens or hegumenissas. Patrons also maintained family crypts in their monasteries.

In the Princely era, monasteries became firmly established as important centers of religious, educational, scholarly, cultural, and artistic life. Their influence extended throughout Ukraine, and in some cases (eg, the Kievan Cave Monastery) throughout Eastern Europe. Their importance in the economic life of the country was also great, particularly as a result of their colonization of outlying territories. *Church peasants, essentially serfs, worked on the large monastery estates that were the basis of their wealth. Many monasteries owned mills and even workshops and small factories. In addition the defensive fortifications of monasteries made them important military installations, and they did much charitable work. The largest institutions came to exercise considerable authority in state affairs.

The Tatar invasions in the 13th and 14th centuries brought devastation to monasteries. Many were wiped out, and the monks forced to hide in cliff-side monasteries (eg, in Bakota and Bubnyshche). Only a small number (notably the Kievan Cave Monastery) managed to survive. After the annexation of Ukraine by the Grand Duchy of Lithuania and then by Poland, new monasteries began to emerge, particularly in Galicia, where by 1500 there were 44 of them.

The 16th and 17th centuries saw a revival of monastic life in Volhynia and central Ukraine. Through the efforts of metropolitans Y. Boretsky, I. Kopynsky, and P. Mohyla, and with support from the Cossacks, a series of monasteries founded in the Princely era were revived. New monasteries were also established, including the *Kiev Epiphany Brotherhood and *St Nicholas's monasteries in Kiev, the *Hustynia Trinity Monastery near Pryluka, the *Mhar Transfiguration Monastery near Lubni, the Krasnohiria Monastery near Zolotonosha, and the Moshnohiria Monastery near Cherkasy. In the Cossack era, monasteries again played an important role in the religious, cultural, and economic life of the country. The Cossack elite, especially under B. Khmelnytsky and I. Mazepa, assisted in the revival or the establishment of many monasteries, particularly in Left-Bank Ukraine. These included the Krupytskyi St Nicholas's Monastery near Baturyn, the *Maksaky Transfiguration Monastery, the SS Peter and Paul Monastery in Hlukhiv, the Elevation of the Cross Monastery in Poltava, the Ascension and St Michael's monasteries in Pereiaslav, the Annunciation Monastery in Nizhen, and the Nativity of the Mother of God Monastery

in Domnytsia near Mena. The St Mary the Protectress Monastery in Kharkiv and the *Sviati Hory Dormition Monastery on the Donets River were established in Slobidska Ukraine, and the Samara St Michael's Monastery was founded in Zaporizhia. Hetman Mazepa was a generous benefactor of monasteries: he donated much money, valuable religious objects, and estates with rights for industry and trade, and granted the monasteries exemptions from taxes. After the mid-18th century, however, centralist Russian imperial policies led to a decline in the economic position of monasteries, and in 1786 Catherine II issued a ukase confiscating all their assets. Only a few were selected for state support; the rest had to generate their own income. Many smaller monasteries were closed outright.

In the century of the Church Union of Berestia (1596), most monasteries in Right-Bank Ukraine and Belarus accepted the union and joined the *Basilian monastic order, which in the 17th and 18th centuries grew to encompass approx 150 monasteries in the Ukrainian territories under Polish rule. The exceptions were the *Maniava Hermitage and the so-called foreign monasteries of the Kievan Orthodox metropoly. After the partitions of Poland, however, *Joseph II introduced reforms in the Habsburg Empire that confiscated land and property from the orders and closed all but 14 of the Basilian monasteries. In Right-Bank Ukraine, which came under Russian rule, monasteries were either closed or given to the Russian Orthodox church. In 1908 there were 67 men's and 43 women's monasteries in the nine Ukrainian gubernias in the Russian Empire, plus several more in the Kuban and the ethnic Ukrainian territories in neighboring gubernias (see table).

Monasteries in Russian-ruled Ukraine, 1908

Gubernia	Men's	Monks and novices	Women's	Nuns and novices
Volhynia	10	344	4	387
Katerynoslav	3	80	4	640
Kiev	20	2,805	6	2,308
Podilia	5	125	6	518
Poltava	3	128	5	1,164
Tavriia	7	360	4	376
Kharkiv	8	1,033	5	1,021
Kherson	2	95	3	377
Chernihiv	9	322	6	659
Total	67	5,292	43	7,450

In Transcarpathian Ukraine the first monasteries date from the 14th century. *Hrusheve in the Maramureş region and the Chernecha Hora near Mukachiv were important centers, where more than 20 monastic communities of varying size were eventually established. After the Josephine reforms only seven of them remained, including the *Krasný Brod, *Máriapócs, and Imstycheve monasteries. These later joined the Roman Catholic church to form a separate Basilian province. In Bukovyna there were about 30 monastic settlements, including ones in Suceava, Putna, and Drahomirna. In the late 18th century the authorities confiscated all of their holdings and abolished many of them. In Right-Bank Ukraine and, until 1648, Left-Bank Ukraine there were also a number of Roman Catholic monasteries (Bernardine, Dominican, Jesuit, Carmelite, and others) established under Polish rule.

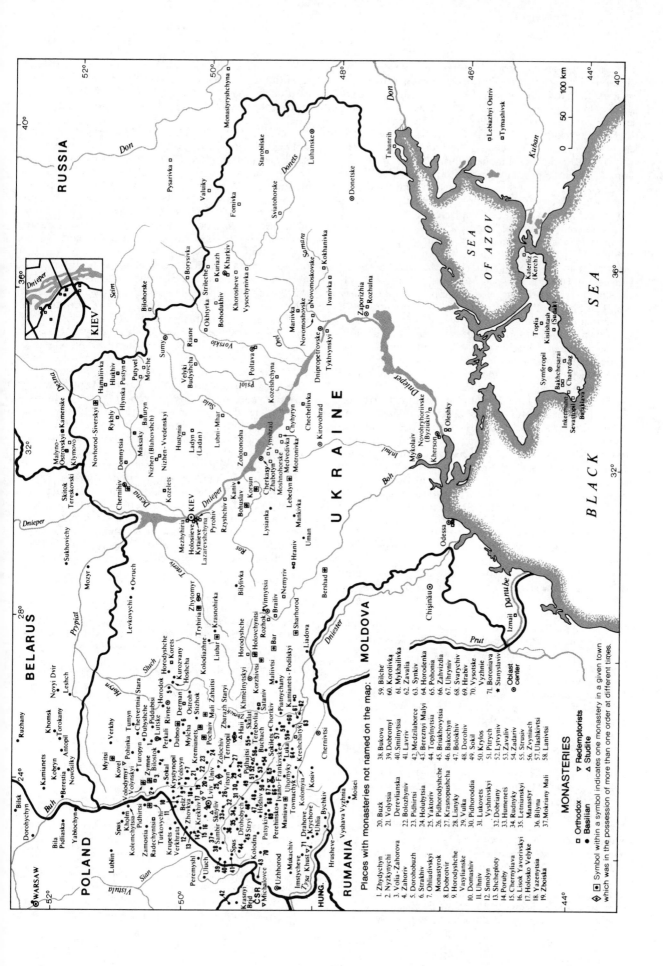

Throughout history monasteries exerted a great influence on Ukrainian culture. In the Middle Ages and Cossack era they were the principal centers of education and scholarship. The *Povist' vremennykh lit*, the *Mezhyhiria and *Hustynia chronicles, and important manuscripts, such as the *Horodyshche *Apostol* and Gospel, the *Byblo *Apostol*, the *Putna Gospel, and the *Peresopnytsia Gospel, were all compiled in monasteries. With the introduction of *printing, many monasteries (especially in *Derman, Chernihiv, Pochaiv, Suprasl, *Univ, Kiev, and Lviv) became the earliest and most important *publishers in Ukraine; they issued secular as well as religious works in a variety of languages. Many of the earliest schools were established at monasteries or in affiliation with them: the *Kiev Epiphany and *Lviv Dormition brotherhood schools; the *Chernihiv, *Pereiaslav, and *Kharkiv colleges; and even the *Kievan Mohyla Academy. Liturgical singing, icon painting (see *Kievan Cave Monastery Icon Painting Studio), the *graphic arts (esp engraving), *fresco painting, embroidery (in women's monasteries), and other art forms flourished in monasteries, and many monasteries maintained important libraries and fostered the development of *historiography and literature.

Churches, bell towers, and other monastery buildings are important examples of Ukrainian *architecture. Shrines of the 11th to 12th centuries – eg, the Dormition and Trinity churches of the Kievan Cave Monastery, the cathedrals of the Vydubychi and St Michael's Golden-Domed monasteries, the Transfiguration Church in Berestove in Kiev, the Yeletskyi Monastery Dormition Cathedral in Chernihiv, and St Panteleimon's Church in Halych – were generally three-nave buildings in the Byzantine style, although the last two show Romanesque influences. Monastery churches of the 12th century (eg, St Elijah's Church in Halych and St Basil's Church in Zymne, near Volodymyr-Volynskyi) often included rotundas; in the 15th to 16th centuries three-conch shrines of the Byzantine Renaissance were common (eg, churches of the Lavriv Monastery and the Trinity Monastery in Kamianets-Podilskyi). Later monasteries were built in various styles: the late Gothic (eg, the Trinity Church in Mezhyrich, near Ostrih; the Dormition Church in Zymne; and the gate tower of the Derman Monastery), Renaissance (16th–17th century; eg, the monastic church in Zaluzhia, near Zbarazh; the reconstructions of monasteries of the Princely era in Kiev made under P. Mohyla; the Church of the Protectress in the Nyzkynychi Monastery), Cossack baroque (17th–18th centuries; eg, the Trinity and ss Peter and Paul churches of the Hustynia Trinity Monastery, the All Saints', Resurrection, and ss Peter and Paul churches of the Kievan Cave Monastery; and other five-domed monastic shrines), and rococo (18th century; eg, the bell tower of the Pochaiv Monastery). The wooden churches and bell towers of the Mezhyhiria Transfiguration Monastery (1611), the Krekhiv Monastery (1658), the Maniava Hermitage (1676), and the Moshnohiria and Medvediv monasteries also had a distinctive style. In the 19th and 20th centuries very few new monasteries were built in Russian-ruled Ukraine, and those were constructed according to local designs or in a Muscovite style (eg, the refectory of the Kievan Cave Monastery, 1900, and the Trinity Cathedral in Pochaiv, 1906) that stood in stark contrast to the style of the older structures. In Galicia and Transcarpathian Ukraine, notable monastery buildings included the Basilian churches in Hoshiv and Zhovkva, the churches of the Basilian women's monasteries in Lviv and Stanyslaviv, and the churches of the *Redemptorist monasteries in Mykhailivtsi and the Prešov region. Generally, Ukrainian Catholic monasteries were smaller than Orthodox ones and much less ornate.

The Bolshevik occupation of Ukraine brought ruin to virtually all monasteries. On the basis of a decree issued in January 1918, all monastic holdings were nationalized, and the monasteries were abolished and liquidated. The artistic valuables they held, including liturgical objects, icons, decorations, and books, were confiscated, and most were destroyed. Many valuable *iconostases were demolished. Even the monastery buildings, of immeasurable historical and artistic value, were razed, particularly in the early 1930s.

During the German occupation of Ukraine in 1941–3, a number of Orthodox monasteries were reopened. After the war, as a result of the new religious policy adopted by the Soviet government, some were allowed to stay open. All Ukrainian Catholic monasteries (over 150 of them) in the newly occupied territories, however, were closed. In 1954 there were approx 39 active monasteries and hermitages in the Ukrainian SSR, as compared with 69 in all of the USSR. Of these, 14 were in Transcarpathia. There were few in central and eastern Ukraine, among them the half-ruined Kievan Cave Monastery, two women's monasteries in Kiev, and the Dormition Monastery in Odessa. In 1954 the antireligious campaign resumed, and most of the remaining monasteries were closed. The Kievan Cave Monastery was closed in 1964, but part of it was returned to the Russian Orthodox church in 1988 on the occasion of the millennium of the Christianization of Ukraine. By 1970 there were only seven monasteries open (two men's and five women's), with a total of approx 800 (mostly elderly) monks and nuns. In the Ukrainian diaspora, there are now over 250 Ukrainian Catholic men's and women's monasteries and monks' communities. The Ukrainian Orthodox church has one in the United States.

BIBLIOGRAPHY

Zverinskii, V. *Materialy dlia istoriko-topograficheskogo issledovaniia o pravoslavnykh monastyriakh v Rossiiskoi Imperii s bibliograficheskim ukazatelem*, 3 vols (St Petersburg 1890–7)

Setsinskii, E. 'Materialy dlia istorii monastyrei Podol'skoi eparkhii,' *Trudy Podol'skogo istoriko-statisticheskogo komiteta*, vol 5 (1891)

Titov, F. 'O zagranichnykh monastyriakh Kievskoi eparkhii XVII–VIII vv.,' *TKDA*, 1905, nos 1–2

Denisov, L. *Pravoslavnye monastyri Rossiiskoi Imperii* (Moscow 1908)

Kryp'iakevych, I. 'Seredn'ovichni manastyri v Halychyni,' *ZChVV*, nos 1–2 (1926)

Lukan', R. *Vasyliians'ki manastyri v Stanyslavivs'kii eparkhiï* (Lviv 1935)

Vavryk, M. *Po vasyliians'kykh manastyriakh* (Toronto 1958)

Zubkovets, V. *Natsionalizatsiia monastyrskikh imushchestv v Sovetskoi Rossii (1917–1922 gg.)* (Moscow 1975)

Libackyj, A. *The Ancient Monasteries of Kiev Rus* (New York 1979)

Senyk, S. *Women's Monasteries in Ukraine and Belorussia to the Period of Suppression* (Rome 1983)

M. Vavryk

Monasticism. A complex of religious institutions and rituals that regulates contemplative religious life. Monks and nuns, having renounced secular life, live in special residences, monasteries, or hermitages or in complete isolation. They devote themselves to the service of God through prayer and penance; some also devote themselves to assisting others. A monk renounces family life and remains celibate (after taking a vow of chastity) and renounces property (after a vow of poverty; see *asceticism). Daily life, duties, and even dress are regulated by the monastic order or by the rules of the monastery. Tonsuring proceeds through three stages that culminate in the adoption of a monastic name, symbolizing a rejection of the former way of life (this is no longer compulsory in Catholic orders). Lay novices, known as *poslushnyky*, live in the monasteries and perform various duties and services (*posluhy*) during liturgies, assist in the upkeep and work of the monastery, and do various tasks. Some monks (in the Catholic church, the majority) remain in contact with the outside world by working actively in parishes, visiting hospitals, teaching in schools, running shelters and orphanages, or involving themselves in scholarship.

Monastic orders do not have ordained clerics, but some monks were ordained to conduct services in the monasteries and their churches (see *clergy). These monks were known as the regular or 'black' clergy. Generally, in monasteries the monks' basic needs are seen to, and they are thereby allowed to work for the good of the institution, although in some Eastern rite monasteries (but not Catholic ones) monks take care of their own daily needs and gather only for common prayers. All monks and nuns farm or work in crafts, schools, or hospitals, and all take an active part in liturgical life and pastoral work. In Ukraine there was always a small number of wandering monks who moved from one monastery to another, seeking either spiritual perfection or better living conditions.

The monastic community elected a *hegumen as head of the monastery. Larger monasteries were headed by an *archimandrite, who was initially chosen by the monks with the participation of the lay authorities; later, he was appointed by the state or by the higher church authorities. In the East, all monasteries were initially independent of one another and subject to the authority of local bishops; only later were some *stauropegion monasteries established.

In Ukraine, monasticism emerged soon after the adoption of Christianity and was modeled on Byzantine practices. Some sources suggest that a monastery had already been established at the Church of the Tithes in the 10th century, and a St Sophia's Monastery is said to have burned down in 1037. By 1062 there was a large community of monks in the Kievan Cave Monastery, and by the 12th century there were some 17 other monasteries in the Kiev region. During the Princely era, all metropolitans and bishops of the Ukrainian church were usually chosen from the monastic orders, and prominent monks had considerable influence in secular affairs. In the 16th and 17th centuries secular authorities began to interfere in monastic life and often appointed hegumens and archimandrites, thereby undermining the authority of the church hierarchy. In some cases monasteries were exploited financially by secular figures. In general, monastic life declined as feuds and conflicts undercut the religiosity and spirituality of many monasteries, although individual communities continued to be important centers of religious and cultural life.

Many outstanding theologians and writers (eg, M. *Smotrytsky) were monks, and Ukrainian monks also contributed to the cultural development in neighboring countries, particularly in the early 18th century. In Russia, for example, S. *Yavorsky and T. *Prokopovych made important contributions to literature and theology. In Ukraine the most important monastic communities were the *Kievan Cave, *Pochaiv, *Derman, *Maniava Hermitage, *Hustynia Trinity, *Kiev Epiphany Brotherhood, and *Mhar Transfiguration monasteries. Members of prominent Ukrainian families, including (in the 16th century) D. Zubrovytsky, O. Sanguszko, and I. Tyshkevych, joined monastic orders. In the 18th century P. *Velychkovsky initiated a major reform in monastic life in Ukraine and throughout Eastern Europe.

In the 19th century, monasticism was Russified in Russian-ruled Ukraine, and Ukrainian monastic traditions were continued in Galicia and Transcarpathian Ukraine by Greek Catholic monasteries, such as the *Zhovkva and *Mukachiv St Nicholas's monasteries. The monasteries in *Lavriv, Drohobych, and Buchach ran schools, and *St Onuphrius's Monastery in Lviv maintained a large library, a collection of valuable manuscripts, the archive of the Basilian order, and a large gallery of paintings.

Monastic orders of the Ukrainian Catholic church acquired their own distinctive features, and a wide range of activities were initiated. Only the *Basilian monastic order and order of nuns, the *Studite Fathers and Sisters, and eastern branches of the Benedictines and Franciscans bear the official title *chyn* ('order'). All others that were established in the last hundred years are known as congregations and are modeled largely on Western orders. Congregations and orders are headed by protoarchimandrites, archimandrites, priors, or other church officials chosen by monastic councils for varying terms. All congregations and orders are divided into provinces overseen by protohegumens or other hierarchs. No archimandrite of a monastery has served for life since the 19th century.

Novices are accepted into monasteries at age 18 and undergo a two- to three-year initial probationary period. A second probationary period lasts three to six years, after which candidates take the so-called eternal vows. After this process they can be ordained. Until the 19th century, only monks could be chosen as bishops of the Ukrainian Catholic church.

(See also *Monasteries and *Churches of Ukraine.)

BIBLIOGRAPHY

Kossak, N. *Shematizm Provintsii sv. Spasitelia China Sv Vasiliia V. v Halytsii i korotkii pohliad na monastyr i na monashestvo rus'ke ot zavedenia na Rusi viry Khristovoi azh po ninishnoe vremia* (Lviv 1867)
Goetz, L. *Das Kiever Höhlenkloster als Kulturzentrum des vormongolischen Russlands* (Passau 1904)
Denisov, L. *Pravoslavnye monastyri Rossiskoi imperii* (Moscow 1908)
Voinar, M. *Vasyliiany v ukraïns'kim narodi* (New York 1955)
Vavryk, M. *Narys rozvytku i stanu Vasyliians'koho Chyna 17–20 st.* (Rome 1979)
Smolytsch, I. *Russisches Mönchtum: Enstehung, Entwicklund und Wesen, 988–1717* (Würzburg 1958)
Oriente Cattolico: Cenni storici e statistiche (Vatican City 1974)
Blažejovskyj, D. *Byzantine Kyivan Rite Metropolitanates, Eparchies, and Exarchates: Nomenclature and Statistics* (Rome 1980)
                                                    I. Korovytsky, I. Patrylo

Monastyryshche [Monastyryšče]. V-10. A city (1990 pop 16,500) on the Konelia River and a raion center in Cherkasy oblast. Its name begins to appear in historical chronicles in the mid-16th century. During the Cossack-

Polish War of 1648–57 I. Bohun defeated S. Czarniecki's troops near Monastyryshche, on 20–21 March 1653. In the 18th century the inhabitants took part in several haidamaka uprisings led by S. Palii and M. Zalizniak. Monastyryshche attained town status in 1811 and city status in 1985. Today the city has a machine-building factory and several food-processing plants. Archeologists have discovered a settlement from the Bronze Age near the city.

Monastyryshche. A Slavic fortified settlement of the 8th to 10th century on the Romen River at the Monastyryshche landmark in Romen, Sumy oblast. Uncovered in 1901 and excavated in 1906 and 1924, the site yielded five semi-pit dwellings with clay ovens. Artifacts recovered in the course of excavations include elaborately decorated pottery, iron knives, bones of domestic and wild animals, and amulets featuring the teeth of animals (particularly bears). Ethnically, the inhabitants of the site are identified as *Siverianians. Similar archeological sites have come to be known as 'Romen fortified settlements,' after the town in which Monastyryshche was found.

Monastyryska [Monastyrys'ka]. IV-6. A town (1990 pop 6,600) on the Koropets River and a raion center in Ternopil oblast. It is first mentioned in a historical document in 1454. By the 16th century it was an important manufacturing and trading center on the route from Podilia to Halych and Lviv. After its destruction by the Turks in 1672, the town declined. In July 1919 the Kolomyia Brigade of the Ukrainian Galician Army defeated the Polish army near Monastyryska. Today it has a tobacco-processing plant and a sewing factory. Archeologists have discovered several burial sites from the 2nd and 3rd centuries and a fortified settlement from the time of Kievan Rus' near the town.

Monde Slave, Le. A French Slavic-studies journal published in Paris in 1917–18 and 1924–38. Edited by J. Legras, L. Eisenmann, and E. Denis, it contained articles on Ukrainian language, scholarship, history, and political affairs by French scholars, such as R. Martel, P. Chasles, and A. Meillet, and by Ukrainians, such as F. Savchenko (among other contributions, a 1918 bibliography of French-language works on Ukraine), O. Shulhyn, M. Korduba, V. Kubijovyč, and especially E. Borschak, and by the Russian historian V. Miakotin. The journal also published some documents concerning Ukrainian affairs. An index to it appeared in 1935.

Mondok, Ivan, b 21 May 1883 in Ruskyi Hrabovets, Transcarpathia, d 8 December 1941. Communist activist in eastern Slovakia. After graduating from a teachers' college in Uzhhorod he taught in rural schools and was conscripted into the Austrian army. After being captured by the Russians in 1916, he participated in the revolution as a member of the Red Guard, the Red Army, and the Party. On his return home at the end of 1918, he became active in the communist movement in Transcarpathia and Hungary. In 1920 he was a founder of the International Socialist Party of Subcarpathian Ruthenia, its first secretary, and editor of its paper *Pravda*. He was a member of the Central Committee of the Communist Party of Czechoslovakia (1923–9) and the Party's deputy to the Czechoslovak parliament (1924–5). In 1930 he emigrated to Soviet Ukraine.

Ivan Mondok

He was arrested during the Stalinist purges, and probably died in a labor camp.

Money. See Currency and coins.

Mongols. A mixture of Asiatic tribes, known also as Tatars, who in the 13th century created an empire extending from China to eastern Europe. They first appeared on the outskirts of Rus' in 1223, and they invaded and conquered Rus' in 1239–41. Then they set up the state of the Golden Horde in the lower Volga region and for over a century exercised hegemony over Ukraine. (See also *Golden Horde and *Tatars.)

Monkevych, Borys [Monkevyč], b 1895, d 7 February 1971 in Montreal. Captain of the UNR Army. During the revolutionary period he fought at Kruty and then served in the Zaporozhian Corps and was active in the Hetman movement. In the 1920s he emigrated to Germany, where he headed the Col Bolbochan Zaporozhian Society. He wrote a number of books based on his recollections: *Slidamy novitnykh zaporozhtsiv: Pokhid Bolbochana na Krym* (In the Footsteps of the New Zaporozhians: Bolbochan's Crimean Campaign, 1928; 2nd edn 1956), *Spomyny z 1918 roku* (Recollections from 1918, 1928), and *Chorni Zaporozhtsi: Zymovyi pokhid i ostannia kampaniia Chornykh Zaporozhtsiv* (The Black Zaporozhians: The Winter March and the Last Campaign of the Black Zaporozhians, 1929).

Monks. See Monasteries and Monasticism.

Monopoly. Exclusive control or ownership of a commodity or service through legal privilege, command of supply, or concerted action, usually for the purpose of controlling prices and thus maximizing profit. A monopoly operates in a given market and can be held by a single private or state enterprise or by an association of enterprises. In the preindustrial period private monopolies were granted by rulers to stimulate trade or the development of some branch of manufacturing in order to guarantee supply, but also to increase state revenues.

In Kievan Rus', the Lithuanian-Ruthenian state, the Polish Commonwealth, and the Hetman state, the respective rulers granted monopolies, such as storage rights, to individual merchants, entrepreneurs, and craftsmen as well as to trading companies, guilds, and local magistrates. In the Polish state the gentry possessed a slew of monopolies. In different periods state monopolies known as *regalii* operated in mining, hunting, and logging as well as in customs, collecting, minting, and the postal service. The *regalii* were an important source of state revenues at a time when there was no regular taxation system. As the state's expenses grew, new monopolies were introduced: a salt-trade *regaliia*, for example, was introduced in the mid-16th century, which survived in Western Ukraine until 1939. Russian state monopolies were extended to Ukraine by Peter I. In the first half of the 19th century, as trade expanded and competition increased, manufacturing and trading monopolies became obsolete. Nevertheless, a number of the larger cities in Russian-ruled Ukraine held a monopoly on the liquor trade within their limits until 1862.

In its first phase industrial capitalism in Ukraine was competitive, but in the last quarter of the 19th century large private industrial and financial monopolies appeared and grew rapidly. They were associations of companies in the same branch of the economy or in the same territory, known as *cartels or syndicates, and they were controlled mainly by French, Belgian, or German capital. They sprang up, usually, in response to frequent economic crises, which they proposed to control by restraining competition, dividing markets, planning production and prices, consolidating small enterprises, and dissolving unprofitable companies. In some cases the intent was to lower costs and expand production. At first the Russian government encouraged the formation of cartels and syndicates and worked closely with them. After 1910, however, fearing that the syndicates in Ukraine would become foreign-controlled trusts, from which Russian capital would be squeezed out, the state took some measures against them. But such actions were unsuccessful, because French and Belgian banks, and even the French government, which had lent huge sums to the Russian government, interceded on behalf of their shareholders who owned the monopolies in Ukraine.

The first cartel in Ukraine was the *Syndicate of Sugar Manufacturers (1887–95), which was revived in 1897 as the All-Russian Society of Sugar Manufacturers. Its head office was in Kiev. In 1890 the government's Metallurgical Committee bought up virtually all the cast iron and rails produced in the Russian Empire. To counteract this monopoly the French bankers of the Société Générale pour l'Industrie en Russie, who controlled most of the coal and metallurgical companies in Ukraine, set up two syndicates, the *Prodamet in 1902 and the *Produgol in 1904. The first represented about 80 percent of the empire's metallurgical factories, but by 1908 its core membership consisted of plants in Ukraine. Defeating other cartels, it established its control of heavy industry in Ukraine. Prodamet was a key player in the *Council of the Conferences of Mining Industrialists in Southern Russia and prompted it to consolidate and defend the interests of industries in Ukraine against competition from the coal and metallurgical centers in Russia and Poland. Produgol represented 60 percent of the mines in the Donbas, the mines owned by French and Belgian shareholders. By 1910 it controlled about 75 percent of the coal and coke production in the Donbas.

A number of local monopolies were established in Ukraine. The Locomotive Union of the Luhanske and Kharkiv plants was formed in 1907. The Urozhai syndicate of farm-machine builders (est 1907) represented 18 companies, which accounted for 72 percent of the farm-machinery output in Ukraine. The Belgian-controlled *Prodarud syndicate (1908–15) commanded at one time over 80 percent of the ore mined in Kryvyi Rih. Other cartels in Ukraine controlled the markets for tobacco (from 1912), salt (in Odessa and Crimea), and flour (in Odessa, Kherson, Mykolaiv). All shipping in the Black and Azov seas came under the Russian Steam Shipping and Trading Society. The Med, Prodvagon, Trubprodazha, Gvozd, Provoloka, and Rockefeller's petroleum sydnicates had an all-Russian status.

The financial monopolies in Ukraine had some distinctive features but were less important than those in Russia, because the shares and obligations of the major industrial companies in Ukraine were usually held by foreigners and their banks, such as Crédit Lyonnais, Banque de Paris et des Pays-Bas, and the Northern Bank in St Petersburg (fully French-owned). The only large bank centered in Ukraine was the *Azov-Don Bank (est 1871), which, although financing grain exports from Ukraine, controlled virtually the entire Ukrainian sugar industry and was an important shareholder in Prodamet and Produgol. Most of the credit and commercial operations in Ukraine, however, apart from industrial financing, were in the hands of the large Russian banks in St Petersburg. The syndicate of insurance companies that operated in Ukraine was an all-Russian one.

It was characteristic of the development of capitalist monopoly in Ukraine that none of the empire's largest monopolies concentrated there were controlled by Russian capital, but by Western European investors. They competed fiercely with monopolies in Russia and the Kingdom of Poland, and opposed controls and interference in their affairs by the Russian goverment. Although multinational in origin, the bourgeoisie in Ukraine, which formed territorial conferences and local syndicates and cartels, became increasingly aware of its common territorial interests. Oriented primarily toward Paris and Brussels, it moved gradually closer to the idea of territorial separatism, although it had no direct ties to the Ukrainian national movement.

In the Russian Empire the state had a monopoly on the postal, telegraph, and telephone services and, from 1895, on the liquor trade. The profit margin on liquor sales until 1914 was 78.8 percent. In 1914–22 all trade in spirits was prohibited by law. In 1923 the Soviet government reimposed a state monopoly on liquor.

Although monopolies were far more extensive in Ukraine than in the rest of the Russian Empire, they did not reach the levels prevalent in Western Europe and the United States. No trusts or concerns arose in Ukraine. In 1914 the monopolies were subordinated to the state, because of the war. During 1914 the Russian government set up a number of special councils, state committees, and commissions to control industry. By 1916 all industry and the wholesale trade came under direct state control. The influence of Prodamet was reduced virtually to nil, and Produgol and Prodarud were dissolved completely. In late 1916 and early 1917, state monopolies in the grain trade and then the cloth, leather, sugar, and coal trades were introduced.

In 1918–21 the Bolsheviks extended state monopoly to almost all branches of the economy and nationalized private property. During the NEP period most state monopolies, except the prewar ones and those involving foreign trade, were abolished. Even nationalized enterprises competed with one another on the market and geared their production to demand. That was monopolistic competition, however, because they were all bound together in branch and territorial trust syndicates. During the NEP 19 state trusts, representing about 800 large industrial concerns, including Donvuhillia, Pivdenstal, Trudtsukor, Sklosoda, and the Leather Trust, were set up. In December 1929 the trusts and syndicates were stripped of their planning and distribution powers, which were transferred to the central government. Competition between firms was halted. The introduction of central all-Union planning meant the restoration of state monopoly in all branches of production and distribution, although the phrase 'state monopoly' was never used by Soviet economists to refer to the Soviet economy. In contrast to previously known forms of monopoly the Soviet system created by J. Stalin can be called total state monopoly. In it the state planned everything from one center, and set all prices and wages without regard to market demand. There was no competition among enterprises, and they worked not to satisfy demand but to fulfill the state plan. The determination of profit margins and prices in the Soviet economy was also monopolistic.

In Western Ukraine monopolies developed relatively quickly, although industrial monopolies remained underdeveloped. Under the Austrian Empire the railway communications, the tobacco industry, and the salt and liquor trade were state monopolies. Under Poland match production was added as a state monopoly. The development of certain local industries, such as sugar refining, was restrained by Austrian cartels so that competition would be stifled. In the late 1880s most sawmills and the entire lumber export trade were in the hands of two German and one Austrian firm, which continued to dominate the industry under the Polish regime. The *petroleum industry was controlled before the First World War by Austrian, British, French, and German concerns, and after the war by Austrian, British, American, and French companies. Under Poland all of the main branches of industry were controlled by cartels. The government made no attempt to restrict the monopolies because they were held by international cartels to which the Polish government was deeply in debt. That state of affairs complicated the industrialization of Western Ukraine, drove down the value of local agricultural output relative to that of the imported industrial products, and impoverished the Ukrainian population. Economic conditions in Transcarpathia were somewhat better.

BIBLIOGRAPHY
Hauptmann, B. *Die russische Eisenindustrie und die Kartellbewegung* (Zurich 1913)
Zagorsky, S. *State Control of Industry in Russia during the War* (New Haven 1928)
Liashchenko, P. *Istoriia narodnogo khoziastva SSSR*, vol 2 (Moscow 1956)
Kononenko, K. *Ukraine and Russia: A History of Economic Relations between the Ukraine and Russia, 1654–1917* (Milwaukee 1958)
Nesterenko, O. *Rozvytok promyslovosti na Ukraïni*, vol 2 (Kiev 1962)

V. Holubnychy

Months of the year. The Ukrainian names of the months reflect a strong consciousness of natural phenomena. January (*sichen'*) is derived from the verb *sikty*, meaning to cut to pieces, to slash. In a similar vein, February (*liutyi*) can be understood to be 'the angry [or fierce] one.' The next three months derive their names from springlike phenomena: March (*berezen'*) from the sprouting of the birch tree (*bereza*), April (*kviten'*) from the emergence of flowers (*kvity*), and May (*traven'*) from the greening of the grass (*trava*). June (*cherven'*) takes its name from larva (*cherviak*), which commonly attacks trees and orchards at this time of year; July (*lypen'*), from the blossoming of the linden tree (*lypa*); and August (*serpen'*), from the sickle (*serp*) used to harvest grain. A type of fern (*veres*) lent its name to September (*veresen'*), and the yellowing of trees (*zhovtinnia*) and the dropping of leaves (*lystia*), to the names for October (*zhovten'*) and November (*lystopad*) respectively. The name for December (*hruden'*) alludes to the return of winter and frozen lumps of earth (*hrudky*). Many of these names for the months were already in use by Kievan Rus' times, although *cherven'* (June) was used for July and *hruden'* (December) for November. Different names were also given to January (*prosynets'*, derived from winter's rousing from sleep, or *prosynannia*, as the days grew longer), February (*snizhen'*, or 'snowy one'), June (*izok*, after a type of steppe horse), August (*zarev*, the time for hunting deer), and December (*studen'*, noting a period of 'cooling' off, from *studyty* 'to cool').

Montreal. The largest city (1981 pop 980,000; metropolitan pop 1,738,000) in Quebec, near the confluence of the St

St Sophia Ukrainian Orthodox Church in Montreal

Lawrence and Ottawa rivers. It is a major industrial, commercial, and financial center of North America. The Ukrainian population of Montreal numbers approx 13,700 (1981) and is the only significant Ukrainian community in a French-Canadian environment.

Ukrainian residence in Montreal dates from 1904. The community grew slowly before the arrival of the second (interwar) and third (post–Second World War) waves of immigrants. The interwar immigrants from Ukraine had been active in the struggle for independence in 1917–20 and were more politically and nationally conscious than the earlier immigrants. The most important organization formed by them was the Ukrainian National Federation. The postwar immigrants were mostly refugees from Galicia. They formed new Ukrainian institutions and organizations, such as credit unions, a Ukrainian section of Radio Canada, a Ukrainian radio program 'Ukrainskyi chas,' and university courses in Ukrainian literature and language. In 1950 an illustrated bimonthly, *Oko svitu*, and in 1979–86 a trilingual monthly, **Oko*, came out in Montreal.

About 65 percent of the Ukrainian population of Montreal is Ukrainian Catholic, 30 percent Ukrainian Orthodox, and 5 percent Protestant. The first Ukrainian church in Montreal was the Catholic St Michael's, built in 1916. Another six were built later, five of them in the late 1950s and early 1960s. There are also three Orthodox parishes. Most of the churches are located in the areas of highest Ukrainian concentration, such as Rosemont, St-Michel, Montreal North, and St-Leonard. In 1991, 5,580 inhabitants of Montreal claimed Ukrainian as their mother tongue.

Monumenta Ucrainae Historica. A collection of over 2,400 documents of the years 1035–1839 pertaining to the history of the Ukrainian church. The collection was conceived and financed by Metropolitan A. Sheptytsky. The documents were transcribed in the Vatican archives by Rev K. Korolevsky, who deposited a copy of his 15-volume typescript at the Oriental Institute in Rome. The typescript was given to Cardinal Y. Slipy after his release from exile, and the collection was edited by him and finally published in 11 volumes (1964–71, 1974) by the Ukrainian Catholic University. Excluded from the publication are documents that had already appeared in the 16 volumes of series 2, section 3 of *Analecta Ordinis S. Basilii Magni* (1953–4, 1956, 1959–65), edited by Rev A. Velyky. Vol 12 of *Monumenta* has yet to be published. Vols 13 and 14 (1973, 1977) consist of documents, compiled and edited by Rev A. Baran, pertaining to the Ukrainian Catholic church in Transcarpathia from 1771 to 1853 and the question of a Ukrainian patriarchate in the 19th century.

Morachevsky, Pylyp [Moračevsʹkyj], b 26 December 1806 in Shestovytsia, Chernihiv county, Chernihiv gubernia, d 26 September 1879. Translator of the Bible into Ukrainian. After graduating in history and philology from Kharkiv University (1823) he worked as a teacher in various towns in Ukraine (Sumy, Lutske, Kamianets-Podilskyi) and then as an inspector for the Nizhen Lyceum (1849–59) in Nizhen; contributed to the first Ukrainian literary miscellany, *Ukrainskii alʹmanakh*; and translated various books of the Old and New Testaments. In 1860 the Holy Synod of the Russian Orthodox church denied him permission to publish his first translations. In 1862, having completed the major books of the New Testament (the Gospels and the Acts of the Apostles), Morachevsky appealed to the Russian Imperial Academy of Sciences; it endorsed the quality of his work and agreed that such a translation was necessary, but again the Synod refused to allow him to publish his work. This refusal was followed by the P. **Valuev circular of 1863 and the *Ems Ukase of 1876, which prohibited the publication in Ukrainian of almost all works, including religious texts, in the Russian Empire. Morachevsky's translation remained unpublished until after restrictions on Ukrainian publications were eased following the 1905 revolution. An editorial commission under Bishop P. Levytsky prepared the first texts for publication in 1907–11, and subsequent editions appeared in 1914, 1917, and later. His translation of the Gospels (with minor linguistic corrections) was printed in the Church Slavonic alphabet in Warsaw in the interwar period, to be used as the great altar Gospel in Liturgies. It was republished in Canada (1948) and in the United States (1966). These editions are still used in liturgies by the Ukrainian Orthodox church in the diaspora.

I. Korovytsky

Moraczewski, Wacław, b 27 November 1867 in Warsaw, d 13 September 1950 in Lviv. Polish chemist, physician, and literary critic; husband of S. **Okunevska-Moraczewska. After the First World War he taught at the Veterinary Medicine Academy in Lviv and served as its rector (1926–8). He published over 180 papers on organic chemistry and animal physiology, and also popularized in Polish journals the works of T. Shevchenko, I. Franko, and particularly his friend V. **Stefanyk, 13 of whose stories he translated, and about whom he wrote several articles and memoirs.

Yakiv Moralevych

Moralevych, Yakiv [Moralevyč, Jakiv], b 30 April 1878 in eastern Podilia, d 1 November 1961 in Denver, Colorado. Economist and civic figure. A graduate of the Kamianets-Podilskyi Theological Seminary, he worked as a teacher and then studied at the Psychoneurological Institute in St Petersburg. From 1914 he worked for the Union of Zemstvos and Cities in Kiev and studied at the Kiev Commercial Institute. He was chief accountant for the UNR Ministry of Trade and Industry and, later, director of the ministry's finance department and the economic ministry's general department. An émigré from 1920, he taught commercial subjects in UNR Army internment camps in

Poland and Bohemia and at the Ukrainian Husbandry Academy (1922–35) and Ukrainian Technical and Husbandry Institute (UTHI, 1932–44) in Poděbrady. The academy published his commercial arithmetic (1924), finance (1924), and general accounting (1925) textbooks. He was also active in the League of Ukrainian Nationalists and the co-operative movement in Transcarpathia and became chief comptroller of the OUN in 1929. A postwar refugee in Bavaria, he continued teaching at the UTHI in Regensburg and then emigrated to the United States (1949), where he taught at the Ukrainian Technical Institute (1954–6) in New York.

Danylo Mordovets

Mordovets, Danylo [Mordovec'] (Mordovtsev, Daniil), b 19 December 1830 in Danylivka *sloboda*, now a town in Volgograd oblast, Russia, d 23 June 1905 in Kislovodsk, Stavropol region. Ukrainian and Russian writer, publicist, and historian. He began his literary career with a versified translation of the Králové Dvůr manuscript from Czech into Ukrainian. He wrote in Ukrainian the romantic poem 'Kozaky i more' (The Cossacks and the Sea, 1854, pub in *Malorusskii literaturnyi sbornik*, 1859); the historical narratives 'Dzvonar' (The Bell Ringer, 1859), 'Soldatka' (The Soldier's Wife, 1859), and 'Startsi' (The Beggars, 1855, pub 1886), the novels *Dvi doli* (Two Fates) and *Semen Palii* (1882); and other works. His novels in Russian on Ukrainian themes include *Sagaidachnyi* (Sahaidachny, 1882) and *Tsar' i getman* (The Tsar and the Hetman). Mordovets was greatly influenced by his two visits to Ukraine, in 1883 and 1886, and by his acquaintance with T. Shevchenko (he reviewed Shevchenko's *Kobzar* in 1860 and described their meetings in his memoirs *Iz proshlogo i perezhytogo* [From the Past and the Experienced, 1902]) and with M. Drahomanov and M. Kostomarov. The more important of Mordovets's historical works are *Haidamachchyna* (Haidamaka Uprisings, 1870) and a publicistic attack on P. Kulish's views on the historical past of Ukraine, *Za krashanku – pysanka: P.O. Kulishevi* (A Pysanka in Exchange for a Krashanka: For P.O. Kulish, 1882). Mordovets did a great deal to help Ukrainian writers in St Petersburg publish their works, and he defended Ukrainian theater from the attacks of the Russian press. The fullest edition of Mordovets's works is *Tvory* (Works, 2 vols, 1958).

I. Koshelivets

Mordovia or **Mordovian Autonomous Republic.** A Finno-Ugric enclave in the RF, covering 26,000 sq km and surrounded by Russian ethnic territory except on the side bordering the Chuvash Autonomous Republic. Its population (965,000 in 1989) is composed mostly of Russians (60 percent) and Mordvinians (34 percent).

Mordvinians, an ancient Finno-Ugric ethnic group, were first mentioned under the name 'Mordens' by the Gothic historian Jordanes in the 6th century AD. In the mid-13th century Mordovia fell to the Golden Horde, and in 1552 it was annexed by Ivan the Terrible along with the rest of the Kazan khanate. Under tsarist rule the Mordovians were deprived of political power and cultural self-expression. It was not until 1928 that the Mordovians as a nation received some degree of political recognition. The USSR government set up the Mordovian national okrug. In 1930 it was reorganized into the Mordovian autonomous oblast, and in 1934, into an ASSR. Formally, the Mordovian ASSR has all the attributes of national autonomy, but in reality the Russian majority determines the form and content of its culture. At the Mordovian State University, which has an enrollment of 4,480, most disciplines are taught in Russian. The dominant Soviet newspapers, *Sovetskaia Mordovia* and *Molodoi leninets*, were published in Russian. Newspapers published in the two Mordovian languages have limited editions.

The first labor camps in the republic originated after the October Revolution. At least eight Gulag camps (Barashevo, Sosnovka, Saransk, Ruzaevka, Lesnoi, Potma, Yavas, and Zubova Polianka) and a prison (Saransk) were located there. Since the Second World War many political prisoners, particularly Ukrainians, have served time in these camps.

J. Borys

Morfill, William, b 17 November 1834 in Maidstone, Kent, d 9 November 1909 in Oxford, England. British Slavist. A graduate of Oxford University, he taught there from 1870 and became the first professor of the Slavic chair in 1900. He visited Lviv and Kiev and corresponded with M. Drahomanov from 1871 to 1895. He was the first British scholar to write about T. Shevchenko, in articles in the *Westminster Review* (1880) and *Macmillan's Magazine* (April 1886). He also reviewed the Ukrainian literary anthology *Vik* (3 vols, 1902) in *Athenaeum* (January 1903), translated several of Shevchenko's poems, and contributed information on Ukrainian literature and folklore to *Encyclopaedia Britannica*.

Morgilevsky, Ippolit [Morgilevskij], b 12 September 1889 in Radovka, Orenburg gubernia, Russia, d 7 December 1942 in Kiev. Architectural historian; corresponding member of the USSR Academy of Architecture from 1941. A graduate of the Kiev Polytechnical Institute (1917), in the 1920s he was a member of the All-Ukrainian Archeological Committee, studied the architectural monuments of medieval Rus' and Caucasia, and lectured at the Kiev Architectural, Civil-Engineering, and State Art institutes. His studies on the St Sophia Cathedral and Chernihiv's Transfiguration Cathedral and Dormition Church were published in VUAN collections on Kiev (1926) and Chernihiv and northern Left-Bank Ukraine (1928).

Morgulis, Naum, b 14 May 1904 in Liatychiv, Podilia gubernia, d 1 September 1976 in Kiev. Physicist; AN URSR (now ANU) corresponding member from 1939. A graduate of the Kiev Institute of People's Education (1926), from 1927 to 1961 he worked at the AN URSR Institute of Physics in Kiev, and from 1934 he taught at Kiev University. Morgulis made substantial contributions to the understanding of electron emission from various metallic surfaces and investigated (together with P. Marchuk in 1949) the possibilities for direct conversion of thermal into electric energy. His book on the thermoelectronic energy converter (Moscow 1961) has been translated into French and Czech.

Morhun, Fedir, b 12 May 1924 in Novooleksandrivka, Donetske gubernia. Soviet official and Party functionary. After graduating from the Dnipropetrovske Agricultural Institute in 1949, he worked as an agronomist and state-farm director in Poltava oblast. From 1954 he served in oblast Party and state organs in Kazakhstan. In 1965 he moved into the CC CPSU apparat, and in 1969 he was appointed first deputy chairman of the Kirgizian Council of Ministers. In the following year he was elected to the USSR Supreme Soviet. As a member of the CC CPSU and CC CPU from 1976, he was a prominent supporter of M. Gorbachev's policies in Ukraine. He served as the chairman of the USSR State Committee for the Protection of Nature (1987–9). Morhun has written several books on Soviet agriculture.

Morhun, Oleksander, b 5 August 1874 in Velykyi Pereviz, Myrhorod county, Poltava gubernia, d 17 January 1961 in Dornstadt, West Germany. Economist; full member of the Ukrainian Academy of Arts and Sciences. As a law student at Kiev University he was persecuted by the authorities for his political activities. He completed his education in Heidelberg (1900) and returned to Ukraine to work in the Myrhorod county and Poltava gubernia zemstvos. He was particularly active in the co-operative movement, as a member of which he promoted handicraft and cottage industries among the peasantry. After the revolution he continued his involvement in the movement until it was suppressed by J. Stalin, and in the 1930s he taught at the Kharkiv Co-operative Institute. Morhun fled from Ukraine during the Second World War and settled in Germany, where he taught at the Ukrainian Higher School of Economics and the Ukrainian Technical and Husbandry Institute in Munich. He wrote economics articles in various journals, and *Narys istorii promyslovoï kooperatsiï Ukraïny* (A Survey of the History of Manufacturing Co-operation in Ukraine, 1966).

Morokhovsky, Yoakym [Moroxovs'kyj, Joakym] (secular name: Illia), b ?, d 1632. Churchman. He studied at the Gregorian College in Rome and then served as secretary to the Polish king Sigismund III Vasa. In 1612 he joined the Basilian order, and in 1613 he was consecrated bishop of Volodymyr-Volynskyi. He worked with Metropolitans I. Potii and Y. Rutsky to extend the Uniate church. Morokhovsky wrote a number of polemical works directed against Orthodoxy, including *Paryhoria* (1612, a response to M. Smotrytsky) and *Dyskurs o początku rozerwania cerkwi greckiej od kościoła rzymskiego* (A Discussion on the Origins of the Separation of the Greek Church from the Roman Church, 1622). He also wrote biographies of Y. Kuntsevych and I. Potii.

Moroz, Anatolii, b 30 January 1928 in Zapsillia, Kremenchuk county, Poltava gubernia. Novelist and literary critic. He graduated form the Faculty of Journalism of Kiev University in 1952. He has been director of the Radianskyi Pysmennyk publishing house and, since 1979, secretary of the board of the Writers' Union of Ukraine. Moroz has written the following novels: *25 storinok odniieï liubovi* (25 Pages of One Love, 1960), *Troie i odna* (Three [Men] and One [Woman], 1963), *Chuzha kokhana* (Someone Else's Sweetheart, 1966), *Kioskerka na perekhresti* (The Kiosk Lady at the Crossroads, 1971), *Dovha-dovha khvylyna ...* (A Long, Long Minute, 1974), *Lehke zavdannia* (An Easy Task, 1976), *Tovaryshi* (Comrades, 1978), *Chetvero na shliakhu* (Four on the Road, 1980; awarded the Shevchenko State Prize in 1982), and *Vash poïzd o dev'iatii* (Your Train Leaves at Nine, 1984). A three-volume edition of his works appeared in 1987, and V. Marko's book about him was published in 1988.

Moroz, Danylo (pseuds: Danylo Kostiantynovych, D. Nedolia, Danylo), b 23 August 1841 in Sakhnivka, Chernihiv gubernia, d 15 January 1894 in Tbilisi, Georgia. Writer. He was a graduate of Kiev University and a member of the Old *Hromada of Kiev. Moroz published an arithmetic textbook for Ukrainian Sunday schools in 1862, the story 'Beztalanna' (The Hapless Girl, *Osnova*, 1862, no. 10), written in the style of M. Vovchok, the comedy *Buv kin', ta z'ïzdyvsia* (There Was a Horse, but He Was Worn Out by Riding, 1864), and the drama *Nesparavona para* (The Mispaired Pair, 1885). His memoirs appeared in *Kievskaia starina* (1895, nos 5–6).

Mykhailo Moroz: *Self-Portrait* (oil)

Moroz, Mykhailo, b 7 July 1904 in Plikhiv, Berezhany county, Galicia, d 27 September 1992 in Staten Island, New York. Painter. He studied at the Novakivsky Art School in Lviv (1923–7) and, with a stipend from Metropolitan A. Sheptytsky, in Paris (1928–30), at the Académie Julien and the Conservatoire national des arts et métiers. After returning to Lviv he worked as O. Novakivsky's assistant and as a portraitist. From 1925 he participated in group exhibitions in Lviv, including those of the Association of Independent Ukrainian Artists. A postwar refugee in Germany, in 1949 he emigrated to New York. Solo exhibitions of his work were held there at the Panoras Gallery (1959–63) and in Toronto (1964), and his works have been shown in other cities in the United States and Canada and in Munich and Paris. He has painted over 3,000 works – portraits (eg, of Metropolitan A. Sheptytsky and Cardinal Y. Slipy), icons, landscapes, and genre paintings – in a style that has evolved from a calm impressionism to expressionism.

Moroz, Myroslav, b 17 January 1923 in Lviv. Bibliographer and literary scholar. He graduated from Lviv University in 1950 and completed graduate studies in 1963. Moroz was a bibliographer at the Lviv Scientific Library of the AN URSR (now ANU) in 1957–73 and a scholarly associate of the ethnography department at the Lviv branch of the ANU Institute of Fine Arts, Folklore, and Ethnography in 1977–88. He is a specialist in 19th- and 20th-century Ukrainian literature and has written approx 300 works, including bibliographic guides to V. Shchurat (1963), M. Kotsiubynsky (1964), P. Hrabovsky (1964), I. Franko (1966, 1987), M. Vozniak (1968), I. Kotliarevsky (1969), Dante in Ukraine (1970), Lesia Ukrainka (1972), I. Franko's works in the languages of the Soviet peoples (1972), W. Shakespeare in Ukraine (1986), and I. Nechui-Levytsky (1988), and a postsecondary textbook on I. Kotliarevsky (1969). He has prepared chronicles of the life and work of Lesia Ukrainka and Franko, bibliographies of Ukrainian folklore, ethnography, and folk art, and a bibliography of M. Drahomanov.

Valentyn Moroz   Kostiantyn Morozov

Moroz, Valentyn, b 15 April 1936 in Kholoniv, Horokhiv county, Volhynia. Dissident. A graduate in history from Lviv University (1958), he taught in 1964–5 at the Lutske and then the Ivano-Frankivske pedagogical institutes. He was arrested in September 1965 for reading and disseminating samvydav and Western literature and was sentenced in January 1966 to four years in the Vladimir prison near Moscow and in labor camps in the Mordovian ASSR. After being released in September 1969, he was rearrested in June 1970 and sentenced to nine years' imprisonment and five years' exile. In July 1974, while in Vladimir prison, he began a five-month hunger strike to protest his maltreatment. The strike attracted international attention and protests and spawned a vigorous movement for his defense among Ukrainians in the West. In 1976 Moroz was transferred to a Mordovian camp and renounced his Soviet citizenship. As a result of an agreement between the US and USSR governments, he and four other Soviet dissidents were exchanged for two Soviet spies on 27 April 1979 and flown to the United States. Once in the West, Moroz came into conflict with a large part of the Ukrainian community, including his erstwhile nationalist supporters. He resides in Canada, where he publishes his own magazine, *Anabazys*, and runs his own weekly radio program. In 1992 he was appointed professor and head of the Ukrainian studies department at the Ukrainian Printing Institute in Lviv.

While a prisoner, Moroz wrote a number of hard-hitting, widely disseminated samvydav essays about his persecution and official Soviet crimes, which were smuggled out and published in the West. They include *Reportazh iz zapovidnyka imeny Beriï* (1968; trans: *Report from the Beria Reserve*, 1974), *Sered snihiv* (1968; trans: *Among the Snows*, 1971), *Bumerang* (1974; trans: *Boomerang*, 1974), *Eseï, lysty i dokumenty* (Essays, Letters, and Documents, 1975), and *Moisei i Datan* (Moses and Dathan, 1978). In the West he published collections of his writings and speeches (1980) and lectures in Ukrainian history (1982).

O. Zinkevych

Moroz, Zakhar, b 12 November 1904 in Nemyriv, Bratslav county, Podilia gubernia, d 29 June 1958 in Kiev. Literary scholar and dramatist. He graduated from the Kharkiv Institute of Professional Education (1930) and the Institute of Red Professors in Moscow (1937). He taught in postsecondary schools in Kharkiv and Kiev and from 1947 to 1958 headed the Department of Pre-Soviet Ukrainian Literature at the Institute of Literature of the AN URSR (now ANU). Moroz published over 30 literary studies (particularly on 19th-century drama), including books on the positive hero in pre-Soviet Ukrainian literature and Lesia Ukrainka's plays (1952). An edition of his collected plays was published in 1959, and books of his selected literary studies appeared in 1961, 1966, and 1971 (2 vols).

Morozenko, Stanyslav (actual surname: Mrozowicki), b ? probably in Spas, Belz voivodeship, d 28 July 1649 in Zbarazh, Galicia. Cossack leader. He studied in Cracow and Padua, and served as a page in the court of Władysław IV Vasa and as a secretary for the Tarnowski, Ossoliński (to 1634), and Leszczyński (to 1638) families. Despite his Roman Catholic faith Morozenko espoused a Ukrainian territorial patriotism, and after reportedly serving as colonel of Chyhyryn regiment (from 1638 or 1645) he joined the 1648 uprising led by Hetman B. Khmelnytsky. As colonel of Korsun regiment (August 1648 to April 1649), he (along with M. Kryvonis and I. Hanzha) played a key role in the liberation of Podilia and distinguished himself at the Battle of *Pyliavtsi. He also took part as a cavalry commander in the battle of Zboriv in July 1649, and was killed during the siege of Zbarazh. A historical song emerged about Morozenko and his heroic exploits; it was later embellished with details from the life of Cossack leader Nestor Morozenko (possibly his son; some Soviet sources confuse the two), who was brutally killed by Turkish janissaries after leading an unsuccessful uprising in Sharhorod in 1675.

Moroz-Khodorovsky, Hryhorii. See Khodorovsky, Hryhorii.

Morozov, Kostiantyn, b 3 June 1944 in Brianka, Luhanske oblast. Defense minister of Ukraine. He graduated from the Kharkiv Higher Military Aviation School in 1967 and then served in the Soviet air force. In 1975 he completed a three-year course at the Gagarin Air Force Academy, and in 1984 he graduated from the two-year General Staff Academy. His assignments have included command of an air regiment, an air division, and an air army. He reached the rank of brigadier general in the Soviet air force. He was in command of the air force of the Kiev Military District when the parliament of Ukraine approved his nomination to be the country's defense minister. In November 1991 he was promoted to the rank of lieutenant general, currently the highest active military rank in the Ukrainian armed forces.

Morozov, Vladimir, b 4 March 1940 in Krasnovodsk, Turkmenia. Canoeist. A graduate of the Kiev Institute of Physical Culture (1971), he was a member of the USSR teams that won Olympic gold medals in the 1,000-m kayak fours (1964, 1972) and pairs (1968), the world championships in the 10,000-m (1966) and 1,000-m (1970–1) kayak fours, and the European championships in the 10,000-m kayak fours (1967) and 1,000-m kayak pairs (1969). He was also the USSR champion in the 500-m (1963, 1965, 1968) and 1,000-m (1964) kayak singles and a member of the teams that won the USSR championships in the 500-m (1967) and 1,000-m (1969) kayak pairs, the 1,000-m (1962, 1964, 1966, 1968–9, 1972) and 10,000-m (1962, 1966, 1971) kayak fours, and the 4 × 500-m relay (1967, 1970).

Liudmyla Morozova: *Portrait of a Girl*

Morozova, Liudmyla, b 6 July 1907 in Kiev. Painter. A graduate of the Kiev State Art Institute (1931), where she studied under M. Kozik and F. Krychevsky, she began exhibiting her works in 1935. A postwar refugee, in 1951 she emigrated to the United States, where she taught at the

Queensboro Art Society. She has painted portraits, landscapes, and still lifes. Solo exhibitions of her work were held in New York, Chicago, Cleveland, Philadelphia, and Washington. Her Hellas collection is on permanent display in her studio in Hunter, New York.

Morozovsky, Noi [Morozovs'kyj, Noj], b 1892 in Oleksandriia, Kherson gubernia, d 14 September 1953 in Kiev. Pulmonary specialist. A graduate of Kiev University (1919), he headed the tuberculosis department of the People's Commissariat of Public Health of the Ukrainian SSR (1920–5). In 1934–53 he worked at the Ukrainian Scientific Research Institute of Tuberculosis in Kiev and chaired a department at the Kiev Institute for the Upgrading of Physicians. In 1940 he was elected president of the Ukrainian Scientific Society of Physicians-Phthisiologists. His publications deal with tuberculosis statistics, epidemiology, and the organization of research on tuberculosis.

Morphology. The part of *grammar dealing with the internal structure of words and their elements (morphemes), inflection (person, tense, and case), and derivation (the formation of new words from existing ones). In the Ukrainian language, morphemes are divided into roots, prefixes, suffixes, and endings. The first three are used in word formation, and the last two are used with words in a sentence. Books on Ukrainian morphology have been written by V. Ilin (prefixes, 1953), M. Ivchenko (numerals, 1955), S. Bevzenko (inflection and word formation, 1960), A. Kolodiazhny (prepositions, 1960), I. Chaplia (adverbs, 1960), I. Kucherenko (1961), I. Matviias (1962), A. Medushevsky (1962), E. Sasynovych (gerunds, 1963), S. Samiilenko (2 vols, 1964, 1970), L. Kots (gerunds, 1964), I. Kernytsky (inflection, 1967), I. Bilodid (ed, 1969), C. Bidwell (1971), M. Zhovtobriukh (ed, 1975), S. Bevzenko, A. Hryshchenko, et al (historical morphology, 1978), H. Arpolenko (numerals, 1980), K. Horodenska (derivation, 1981), M. Hnatiuk (participles, 1982), M. Leonova (morphology textbook, 1983), and O. Bezpoiasko and K. Horodenska (morphemes, 1987).

Morshyn's resort park

Morshyn [Moršyn]. IV-4. A town smt (1990 pop 9,300) on the Berezhnytsia River in Lviv oblast and administered by the Stryi municipal council. It is first mentioned in historical documents in 1482. By the end of the 19th century it was known as a health resort, and in 1948 it was given smt status. Morshyn has eight sanatoriums and a hospital, which treat diseases of the digestive system, liver, joints, and peripheral nervous system using local mineral waters and peat muds. A research group of the Lviv Geological Association is stationed in Morshyn.

Morska, Mariia [Mors'ka, Marija] (real surname: Piet-kevych-Fessing), b 1895 in Ostropil, Novohrad-Volynskyi county, Volhynia gubernia, d 28 November 1932 in Warsaw. Stage actress; wife of O. *Zaharov. She worked in the State Drama Theater (1918–19), the Shevchenko First Theater of the Ukrainian Soviet Republic (1919–20), the Ruska Besida Theater (1921–3), and the Ruthenian Theater of the Prosvita Society (1923–5). She retired from the stage in 1926.

Mortality. See Population.

Mosaic. A method of wall and floor decoration in which small pieces of cut stone, glass (tesserae), and, occasionally, ceramic or other imperishable materials are set into plaster, cement, or waterproof mastic.

The earliest existing examples of mosaics in Ukraine are fragments from the floor of a domestic bath found at the site of the Greek colony of Chersonese Taurica (ca 3rd–2nd century BC). Made of various colored pebbles, the floor depicts two nude figures and decorative motifs.

Mosaic was used to decorate various Rus' churches and palaces in the 10th to 12th centuries, including the Church of the Tithes (989–96), the St Sophia Cathedral (1037 to the late 1040s), the Dormition Cathedral (1078) of the Kievan Cave Monastery, and St Michael's Church (1108–13) of the St Michael's Golden-Domed Monastery. Only fragments of the mosaic floors in the Church of the Tithes have been preserved, and no mosaics from the Dormition Cathedral are extant. St Michael's Church was destroyed in 1934–6, but fragments of its mosaics have been preserved in the Tretiakov Gallery in Moscow or installed in the choir balcony of the *St Sophia Cathedral, which also contains the only in situ extant mosaics from the Kievan Rus' period (260 sq m of 640 sq m of wall space originally decorated). The St Sophia mosaics are made of tesserae of 18 hues in 143 tonal variations and of 25 colors of gold and silver. Because the mosaics show two manners, one strongly reminiscent of the Constantinople school and the other of a local Kievan style, it is likely that the work was carried out by a team of Greek craftsmen with the aid of local masters.

The mosaics of St Michael's Church show the development of a Kievan style that is more dynamic and compositionally less schematic than that of the St Sophia mosaics. In the rendering of the Eucharist in the St Sophia Cathedral the Apostles are uniformly posed and robed in subdued tones. In the St Michael's version of this subject the Apostles are depicted in a variety of more naturalistic poses and garbed in bright colors. The mosaics of St Michael's tend to be linear in style, whereas the St Sophia mosaics are modeled with subtle variations in tone and hue.

Because of high production costs and changing esthetics mosaic was rarely used in large-scale murals after the 13th century. In the 17th, 18th, and 19th centuries it was used as a decorative architectural element.

In 1937 the Mosaics Workshop was formed at the Kiev Art Institute. In keeping with the socialist-realist penchant large-scale mosaics have been extensively used to adorn numerous public sights. Their style ranges from the pedantic realism of such artists as V. Ovchynnykov (*Mother Nursing Her Child*, on an apartment building in Kiev) and S. Kyrychenko and N. Klein (*Harvest*, 1957) to the stylized joint works of A. Rybachuk and V. Melnychenko (mosaic mural in the Kiev Palace of Pioneers and Schoolchildren, 1965) and E. Kotkov, V. Lamakh, and I. Lytovchenko (*Peace, Work, and Happiness*, in the Boryspil Airport, 1965). Many of the large mosaic murals, particularly on the exteriors of buildings, are made from a variety of materials, including ceramic tiles and pieces of sculpted colored cement.

Emigré artists, such as V. Balias, M. Dmytrenko, and P. Kholodny, Sr and Jr, have employed the mosaic medium on a limited scale. The most notable example of mosaic in Ukrainian émigré art is the neo-Byzantine mural in the St Sophia Cathedral in Rome designed by S. Hordynsky.

BIBLIOGRAPHY
Lobanovs'kyi, B. *Mozaïka i freska* (Kiev 1966)
Popova, L. *Ukraïns'kyi radians'kyi monumental'nyi zhyvopys* (Kiev 1973)
Garkusha, N.; et al. *Monumental'noe i dekorativnoe iskusstvo v arkhitekture Ukrainy* (Kiev 1975)

N. Mykytyn

The monument in Moscow to Taras Shevchenko (sculptors: Mykhailo Hrytsiuk, Yurii Synkevych, Anatolii Fuzhenko; bronze and granite, 1964)

Moscow (Russian: Moskva). The principal city and capital of Russia and the former USSR. It was founded as the center of a Rus' appanage principality in 1147 by Prince *Yurii Dolgorukii, of Suzdal, and by the 14th century it was the hub of the Great Muscovite Principality and the seat of the Russian Orthodox metropolitan. From 1478 to 1712 Moscow was the center of the unified Russian state. On 12 March 1918 it became the capital of the RSFSR, and on 30 December 1922, the capital of the USSR. Greater Moscow covers an area of 878.7 sq km and had a population of 8,967,000 in 1989. According to the Soviet censuses, 184,900 Ukrainians lived there in 1970, and 252,670 in 1989. In 1970 only 37.2 percent gave Ukrainian as their mother tongue. Unofficial sources estimate that 600,000 to 1 million Ukrainians live in Moscow today.

Ukrainian cultural, educational, religious, and political figures began appearing in Moscow almost immediately after the dissolution of Kievan Rus' in the late 13th century. Metropolitan *Petro of Kiev and Halych lived and worked in Moscow, and in 1322 he transferred his seat there. In 1389 Metropolitan *Cyprian of Kiev also moved to Moscow and amended church rituals and texts there. In the 14th century Prince Dmytro Bobrok-Volynsky, the son of Koriat-Mykhailo, the Lithuanian prince of Volhynia, married Anna, the sister of Prince Dmitrii Donskoi of Moscow. He distinguished himself as a military leader at the Battle of Kulikovo Pole in 1380 but was killed in 1399 in a clash on the Vorskla River between Vytautas of Lithuania and the Tatar khan Edigei. In 1481 F. Belsky, one of the leaders of a rebellion of Ukrainian princes against Lithuania, fled to Moscow and entered the Muscovite tsar's military service; later he became an influential political figure there. I. *Fedorovych (Fedorov), the first printer in Ukraine, began his publishing activities in Moscow, and from 1586 O. Radyshevsky, a Volhynian printer and binder, worked the state press in Moscow.

In the early 17th century joint Polish and Ukrainian Cossack forces advanced on Moscow numerous times, and in 1610 they captured it and held it briefly. In 1618 Hetman P. Sahaidachny's 20,000-man Cossack army helped Władysław IV Vasa defeat the Russian army near Moscow. In 1620, however, Sahaidachny sent envoys to Moscow to offer Mikhail Fedorovich his services.

In the Cossack Hetman state Moscow exerted political influence until the completion of the new Russian capital of St Petersburg in 1712. In the nonpolitical sphere, however, the reverse was true: the cultural invasion of Moscow by Ukrainians forever altered church life, literature, and education there.

After the *Pereiaslav Treaty of 1654 political relations between Ukraine and Muscovy changed. In 1653 Otaman K. Bulai had been sent to Moscow on a reconnaissance mission, and the treaty was signed there in March 1654. Col A. Zhdanovych of Kiev traveled to Moscow on a diplomatic mission in 1654, after the treaty was signed, and P. Zabila journeyed there several times in 1654–5 as Acting Hetman I. Zolotarenko's envoy, and in 1665 with Hetman I. Briukhovetsky, the first head of the Cossack state to travel to Moscow to petition the tsar. General Quartermaster F. Korobka was sent to Moscow as envoy of Hetmans B. and Yu. Khmelnytsky and I. Vyhovsky. Later the tsars frequently summoned hetmans (eg, I. Mazepa) to Moscow.

As Ukraine's autonomy was eroded, Moscow became a place of exile and even imprisonment of its political leaders. I. Krekhovetsky, the general judge under Hetman P. Teteria, was captured in 1665 by Muscovite forces and exiled to Moscow. Hetman P. *Doroshenko was ordered deported from Ukraine by the tsar and was forced to live in Moscow in 1677–9. After the defeat of Hetman Mazepa many Cossack officers fell into disfavor and were forced to live in Moscow (eg, H. *Hertsyk, I. *Charnysh, I. *Maksymovych, and V. *Zhurakovsky). Others (eg, D. Horlenko) moved there of their own accord.

The *Kievan Mohyla College (later Academy) played a significant role in the development of Muscovite education and church life. In 1649 the college sent Ye. *Slavynetsky and A. *Koretsky-Satanovsky, and later, D. Ptytsky, to Moscow. Slavynetsky worked there as a translator, pedagogue, and lexicographer for 26 years. He founded the first Greco-Latin school in Moscow in 1653

and served as its principal. After the Pereiaslav Treaty increasing numbers of Ukrainians visited or moved to Moscow. Usually they resided in the 'Little Russian quarter,' known as the Maloroseika, the main street of which is now named after B. Khmelnytsky.

In the late 17th century seven monasteries in Moscow were headed by Ukrainians and Belarusians. Ukrainians exerted considerable influence on the city's cultural development and were instrumental in implementing Patriarch Nikon's church reform. In 1665 S. *Polotsky, a graduate of the Mohyla College, initiated a Slavonic-Greco-Latin Academy in Moscow modeled on the Kievan college. H. *Dometsky, who was in constant theological conflict with the Russian church authorities, served as an archimandrite in Moscow.

Under Peter I Ukrainian cultural figures continued to be exiled to Moscow or were invited there or moved there to advance their careers. S. *Yavorsky and T. *Prokopovych moved there and helped Peter to attract other scholars and church figures to Moscow. In his capacity as exarch Yavorsky instructed Metropolitan V. Yasynsky of Kiev to have the Kievan academy send its professors A. Hoskevych, M. Kansky, R. Krasnopolsky, O. Sokolovsky, A. Stresovsky, and Y. Turoboisky to Moscow. Kievan scholars often took senior students along in order to provide a good example for Muscovite students. According to S. Smirnov, between 1701 and 1763, 95 professors of the Kievan academy (18 of 21 rectors and 23 of 25 prefects) transferred to the Moscow academy. Ukrainians who were prominent at the Moscow academy included T. Lopatynsky, I. *Kulchytsky, H. Buzhynsky, G. Vyshnevsky (rector in 1722–8), V. Liashchevsky (rector in 1752–4; author of a Greek grammar used in all theological seminaries in Russia), Ya. Blonytsky (author of a Greek-Slavonic and a Slavonic-Greek-Latin dictionary), A. *Mohyliansky, S. Kalynovsky, and H. *Shcherbatsky.

From the mid-18th century the number of Ukrainian professors in Moscow decreased because of the rise of native scholars and because Catherine II discouraged Ukrainians from traveling to Moscow. Ukrainian scholars who studied or worked in Moscow include the historians M. *Bantysh-Kamensky, Ya. *Markovych, and M. Zahorovsky (author of a topographic description of Kharkiv vicegerency, 1787); the jurist S. *Desnytsky; the philosopher S. *Hamaliia; the medical practitioners I. *Andriievsky, H. Mokrenets (lecturer at the Medical Surgical School from 1787 and chief surgeon at the Moscow hospital in 1790–1800), P. Pohoretsky (a graduate of the Kievan academy who taught at the Moscow Medical Surgical School and developed Russian medical terminology), I. *Rutsky, and Y. Tykhonovych; the architects A. *Melensky, M. Mostsepanov, and I. *Zarudny; the engraver M. *Karnovsky; the sculptor I. *Martos; the painter A. *Mokrytsky; and the conductors and composers Y. *Zahvoisky, M. *Dyletsky, A. *Vedel, and H. *Rachynsky.

Ukrainian cultural influence troubled Muscovite conservative circles, particularly the clergy, who suppressed Ukrainian publications imported by Ukrainian chumaks and sought to eliminate Ukrainian influences in church, music, rites, and homiletics. Extreme prejudice gave rise to the practice of forcing Ukrainian priests and monks in Muscovy to be rebaptized. Ukrainians were readily invited to work in Moscow, but any manifestation of Ukrainian influence was staunchly opposed. In the late 18th and early 19th centuries attitudes changed, and Ukrainian folk songs, legends, and themes introduced by Ukrainian writers and artists (eg, V. Narezhny and N. Gogol) became popular among the Muscovite intelligentsia.

In the 19th century, after the decline of the Kievan academy, many Ukrainians studied at Moscow University and other Muscovite schools. Many later remained there as scholars, bureaucrats, economists, cultural figures, and administrators. In the early 19th century Ukrainians in the city created their own organizations, and Moscow became an important Ukrainian political center. From the 1820s Ukrainian works (eg, H. *Kvitka-Osnovianenko's *Malorossiiskie povesti* [Little Russian Novelettes]) were published there. Notable Ukrainians who worked in Moscow included the historians O. *Bodiansky, M. *Maksymovych, M. *Markevych, V. *Ploshchansky, Yu. *Venelin, and D. *Yavornytsky; the philologists V. *Maslov, A. *Krymsky, and M. *Storozhenko; the pedagogue I. *Derkachov; the journalist and archeologist O. *Hattsuk; V. *Maslov; the economist I. *Myklashevsky; the scientists A. *Prokopovych-Antonsky and V. *Vernadsky; the folklorist M. *Yanchuk; the philosopher P. *Yurkevych; and the art historian O. *Novytsky.

Many Ukrainian actors and singers worked in Moscow's theaters and opera houses, and over 200 worked and performed with the Moscow philharmonic orchestra and at the conservatory. The more outstanding performers included I. Butenko (operatic bass, 1852–7), M. *Shchepkin, S. *Hulak-Artemovsky, M. *Donets, M. *Deisha-Sionytska, P. *Tsesevych, I. *Alchevsky, O. Stepanova (a soloist at the Bolshoi Theater in 1912–44), and the composer P. *Senytsia.

Ukrainian organizational activity in Moscow was initiated by students (see *Students, postsecondary) at Moscow University. They were supported by the Ukrainian professors there. The number of Ukrainian students in the city grew steadily, and by 1908 the 250-member Ukrainian Student Hromada in Moscow was the largest student organization in the city. In the years 1810–60 an average of 15 to 20 Ukrainian students annually studied in Moscow; most had private stipends. In the 1860s the annual number of students rose, to reach 63 in 1865. In the late 1850s the first *zemliatstva*, associations uniting students from the same region, were organized with the aim of providing mutual assistance and promoting cultural activity. From 1859 to 1866 the Ukrainian Student Hromada operated clandestinely and had its own underground library. Its leaders included I. Derkach, P. Kapnist (grandson of V. Kapnist), M. Lazarevsky, I. Rohovych (a privatdocent at Moscow University from 1872), V. Rodzianko, M. Shuhurov, I. Sylych, and F. Volkhovsky. The organization was uncovered and liquidated because of its 'separatist' tendencies, and its 52 members were blackballed as 'unreliable.' The hromada was re-established only in 1898 (by V. *Doroshenko, among others), and it continued to meet secretly until 1905, when it became a legal organization. In 1912 it was headed by M. *Kovalevsky. Each year Ukrainian students gathered to commemorate T. Shevchenko.

In the early 20th century, particularly after the Revolution of 1905, Ukrainian life in Moscow became more dynamic and political. During the period of the so-called Stolypin reaction many members of the Ukrainian intelligentsia avoided persecution in Ukraine by fleeing to Moscow. In the early 1910s there were 18,000 Ukrainians in the city. In 1909 Alchevsky, Donets, S. Khvostov, H. Kozlovsky, N. Nezhdanov, and others organized the Ukrainian Music and Drama Hromada, which was later registered as the Kobzar circle. It was headed by Khvostov and Alchevsky. During the First World War it was banned by the tsarist regime.

Ukrainian scholars in Moscow belonged to the Society of Slavic Culture, led by F. *Korsh, and constituted a Ukrainian section therein. Among its members were B. *Kistiakovsky, V. Khvostov, S. *Petliura, V. *Picheta, O. *Salikovsky, and M. Yanchuk.

The public commemoration of the 50th anniversary of Shevchenko's death in 1911, organized by a committee headed by S. Khvostov, was a major event for the Ukrainian community in Moscow. It was significant because such commemorations were prohibited in Kiev and elsewhere in Russian-ruled Ukraine. Events included an exhibition of Shevchenko's art organized by Novytsky at the Moscow School of Painting, Sculpture, and Architecture; an official gathering at Moscow University, at which F. Korsh, A. Krymsky, Novytsky, and V. Picheta spoke; a celebration at the literary and art club, with speeches by Korsh and L. Yanovska; and performances of excerpts from Shevchenko's play *Nazar Stodolia* and M. Arkas's opera *Kateryna*. Materials from and about the celebrations were published as a collection in Moscow in 1912. Preparations for the celebration of Shevchenko's centenary in 1914 were begun but were called off after such commemorations were banned in Ukraine.

During the revolutionary upheaval in Moscow in 1906, the first Ukrainian illustrated weekly in the Russian Empire, *Zoria*, was established. Ukrainian journalists living in Moscow also contributed to the Russian press: K. Danylenko (*Russkoe slovo*), A. Bondarenko and H. Kozlovsky (*Stolichnaia molva*), O. Salikovsky (*Russkiia vedomosti*), V. Hiliarovsky, M. Levytsky, and V. Panchenko. In 1912–17 the monthly journal *Ukrainskaia zhizn'* was published in Moscow in Russian to inform society in the Russian Empire about the Ukrainian question. Edited by Petliura and Salikovsky, it was the unofficial organ of the Moscow branch (est 1907) of the clandestine *Society of Ukrainian Progressives. Two volumes of *Ukraïns'kyi naukovyi zbirnyk*, three collections of M. *Filiansky's poetry, and a collection of plays were also published in Moscow in that period. During the First World War L. Solohub and V. *Vynnychenko edited the weekly *Promin'* (1916–7) in Moscow, and Ukrainian political life there revolved around *Ukrainskaia zhizn'* and *Promin'*.

During the February Revolution of 1917 Ukrainians in Moscow issued a joint declaration of the Union of Ukrainian Federalists, the Moscow Committee of Ukrainian Socialists, the editorial boards of *Ukrainskaia zhizn'* and *Promin'*, and the Ukrainian section of the Society of Slavic Culture. The declaration demanded the introduction of Ukrainian government institutions, courts, and schools in Ukraine and of the territorial organization of the armed forces. In late May 1917 a Ukrainian Council was founded in Moscow, consisting of Salikovsky (chairman), A. Khrutsky, A. *Pavliuk, and A. *Prykhodko. In the April 1917 elections to the Ukrainian Central Rada M. *Shrah and P. Sikora were elected as delegates from Moscow.

In March 1918 Moscow became the capital of Soviet Russia. That year the first two CP(B)U congresses were held there, and the Hetman government sent a delegation to

Moscow in an attempt to normalize relations with the Soviet state and appointed A. Kryvtsov its consul general here. In early 1919 the UNR Directory sent a diplomatic mission headed by S. Mazurenko to Moscow to negotiate, unsuccessfully, with the Soviet government.

Under Soviet rule Moscow once again became the center of an empire, where all political, economic, and cultural power was concentrated. Thereafter all essential decisions concerning Soviet Ukraine were made in Moscow, and the various official representations of the Ukrainian SSR in Moscow served the interests of Russian imperialism. Until the end of 1922 the Ukrainian SSR had a diplomatic mission in Moscow. Thereafter a Soviet Ukrainian permanent representation was based there.

In the 1920s the Ukrainian community in Moscow continued its cultural activity. The Ukrainian Shevchenko Club organized literary readings, debates, and Shevchenko jubilees in which thousands participated.

In 1924 an association of Ukrainian writers, Selo i Misto (SIM), with branches throughout the RSFSR, was established in Moscow. Headed by V. *Gadzinsky, K. *Burevii, and H. Koliada, SIM also ran a publishing house that issued works by Gadzinsky, Koliada, and A. Harasevych, a two-volume edition of Shevchenko's works, and the journal *Neolif*. SIM was liquidated in 1927.

Under Soviet rule many Ukrainians continued to study and work in the 'imperial' capital. They included literary scholars, such as M. Alekseev (a member of the USSR Academy of Sciences who headed the council on Ukrainian literature of the USSR Writers' Union), S. Bohuslavsky (a professor at Moscow University), M. Gudzii, M. Parkhomenko, M. *Zozulia, and O. Deich, who lived in Moscow from 1925 to 1972, published works there on I. Franko, M. Kulish, Lesia Ukrainka, and Shevchenko, and helped persecuted Ukrainian literary figures, such as M. Rylsky, I. Drach, and L. *Taniuk. Other scholars included the neuropathologist Ye. Benderovych, the soil scientist K. *Gedroits, the translator I. Karabutenko (secretary of the council on Ukrainian literature of the Writers' Union from 1950 to 1985), the metallurgist H. Kashchenko, the chemist V. *Kistiakovsky, the musicologist and ethnographer K. *Kvitka, the economist P. *Liashchenko, and the geologist V. *Luchytsky.

In 1924–34 the *Moscow Ukrainian Theater of the RSFSR was active in Moscow under the direction of H. Behicheva, a former assistant at the Berezil theater in Kharkiv. In 1933 L. *Kurbas worked briefly at the Jewish Theater in Moscow before his arrest. Many graduates of Ukrainian conservatories and theater schools have worked at the Bolshoi Theater in Moscow. They include V. Borysenko, O. Byshevska (from 1934), O. Holoborodko, A. *Ivanov, S. Korkoshko, I. *Kozlovsky, I. and L. Maslennykov, M. *Mykysha, Ye. Nesterenko, B. *Rudenko, and A. Shpiller. The famous director A. Tairov was born in Romen, and studied at Kiev University. He founded the Chamber Theater in Moscow and staged plays there by Ukrainian playwrights, such as O. Korniichuk, M. Kulish, L. Pervomaisky, and Yu. Yanovsky, including the premiere of Kulish's *Patetychna Sonata* (Sonata Pathétique) in 1931.

During the Stalinist period many Ukrainian community, cultural, scholarly, and artistic figures fled from repression in Ukraine or were exiled to Moscow. A few survived the terror, among them S. Buniak, A. Chuzhy (a futurist poet), and Yu. Illina, all of whom continue to write and are published in Ukrainian in Moscow, and I. Stadniuk, the author of *Liudi ne angely* (People Are Not Angels, 1962), a Russian-language novel about the famine in Ukraine.

During the Second World War the writers O. *Dovzhenko, Korniichuk, A. Malyshko, Rylsky, Yu. Smolych, V. Sosiura, and P. Tychyna lived in Moscow, and Ukrvydav, a publisher of materials in Ukrainian destined for the front, functioned there. In 1940 the Ukrainskaia Kniga bookstore was opened in Moscow's Arbat district; many readings by Ukrainian writers have been held there.

From 1936 official 10-day festivals of Ukrainian art and literature were held in Moscow. Reduced to single-day events in the 1970s, they served as vehicles of propaganda promoting the fiction of the 'flowering' of Ukrainian literature and praising Russian-Ukrainian friendship. Standardized commemorations of Ukrainian writers, such as Franko, Lesia Ukrainka, Shevchenko, and H. Skovoroda, were also held.

The postwar Ukrainian theater directors Taniuk and R. Viktiuk have worked in Moscow. Forced to work there were the film directors Dovzhenko (he is buried in Moscow) and I. Savchenko. The Ukrainian-born director S. *Bondarchuk made his career in Moscow and still lives there. Postwar Ukrainian writers who have studied in Moscow include L. Kostenko, P. Movchan, H. Tiutiunnyk, I. Drach, M. Vinhranovsky, and L. Cherevatenko.

In the 1960s the Ukrainian community in Moscow became more active. Ukrainian students there began holding independent Shevchenko celebrations and gatherings, at which they sang Ukrainian songs and read proscribed literary works. They were aided in their efforts by the writer and former political prisoner M. Kutynsky (1890–1974), who compiled a 2,000-page biographical dictionary of 7,000 Ukrainian historical and cultural figures (serialized in the journal *Dnipro* since 1990).

In the last few years of Soviet rule under M. Gorbachev, the Ukrainian community was reactivated. Demonstrations supporting the lifting of the ban on the Ukrainian Catholic and Ukrainian Autocephalous Orthodox churches were held there. In 1988 the Ukrainian community leaders E. Deich, S. Hnidina, O. Ivanchenko, V. Liubun, I. Movchan, I. Shyshov, and A. Siry established the Slavutych Society of Friends of Ukrainian Culture, headed by the former cosmonaut P. *Popovych and L. Taniuk, and organized a Ukrainian library. A Ukrainian Youth Club was also established within the local Komsomol, led by V. Martyniuk and P. Zhovnerenko. In 1989 the Ukrainian Helsinki Association (now Ukrainian Republican party) established an active branch in Moscow, represented by A. Dotsenko, O. Horbatiuk, and M. Muratov; the Society for the Support of the Popular Movement of Ukraine (Rukh) was also founded, headed by Ye. Siary; and an independent journal, *Ukrainskii vopros*, edited by S. Matsko, began appearing. Throughout the Gorbachev period the Ukrainian poet V. *Korotych was editor of the popular Moscow magazine *Ogonëk* and in that capacity was instrumental in promoting glasnost and perestroika throughout the USSR.

Ukrainian landmarks in Moscow include a monument to Shevchenko erected in 1964 (sculptors, A. Fuzhenko, M. Hrytsiuk, and Yu. Synkevych), the Shevchenko Library, the Lesia Ukrainka Library, and the building of the Permanent Representation of the Ukrainian SSR.

BIBLIOGRAPHY
Kharlampovich, K. *Malorossiiskoe vliianie na velikorusskuiu tserkovnuiu zhizn'* (Kazan 1914; The Hague and Paris 1968)
Kozlovs'kyi, H. 'Z zhyttia ukraïns'koï kol'oniï v Moskvi v 1900 r. ("Ukraïns'ka Muzychno-Dramatychna Hromada"),' *Z mynuloho*, 1 (Warsaw 1938)
Doroshenko, V. 'Ukraïns'ka students'ka hromada u Moskvi,' in *Z mynuloho*, vol 2, *Ukraïns'kyi students'kyi rukh u rosiïs'kii shkoli* (Warsaw 1939)
Doroshkevych, O. *Ukraïns'ka kul'tura v dvokh stolytsiakh Rosiï* (Kiev 1945)
Kovalevs'kyi, M. *Pry dzherelakh borot'by: Spomyny, vrazhennia, refleksiï* (Innsbruck 1960)
Stovba, O. 'Ukraïns'ka students'ka hromada v Moskvi 1860-kh rokiv,' in *Zbirnyk na poshanu prof. d-ra Oleksandra Ohloblyna*, ed V. Omel'chenko (New York 1977)

I. Shyshov, A. Zhukovsky

Moscow Articles of 1665 (Moskovski statti). An agreement between Hetman I. *Briukhovetsky and the Muscovite government signed in Moscow on 11 October 1665. It superseded the *Baturyn Articles of 1663. Negotiations were conducted in conditions unfavorable to Briukhovetsky and his government. They were totally dependent on Muscovy because of a belligerent Poland, a discordant Cossack *starshyna*, and a restive population. Briukhovetsky was forced to accept Muscovite demands, which essentially obliterated the sovereignty of the Hetman state and handed all military, administrative, and fiscal power there over to the Muscovite military governors, with the exception that the Cossacks maintained their autonomy as a social estate. The articles increased the number of Muscovite troops stationed in Ukraine and obliged the people to feed and maintain them. Muscovite garrisons and military governors were to be stationed in all major *Left-Bank Ukrainian towns (Chernihiv, Pereiaslav, Nizhen, Poltava, Kremenchuk, Novhorod-Siverskyi, Oster) and in Kiev, Kaniv, and even Kodak, in the Zaporizhia. Taxes were to be collected from the people (except Cossacks) by Muscovite administrators and deposited in the tsar's treasury. In accordance with the articles a property census of the non-Cossack population in Left-Bank Ukraine was conducted in 1666, and the Ukrainian Orthodox church was subordinated to the Patriarch of Moscow. The implementation of the agreement aroused widespread dissatisfaction in Ukraine and was one of the catalysts of the revolt against the Muscovite garrisons and the subsequent murder of Briukhovetsky.

BIBLIOGRAPHY
Iakovliv, A. *Ukraïns'ko-moskovs'ki dohovory v XVII–XVIII vikakh* (Warsaw 1934)

O. Ohloblyn

Moscow Ukrainian Theater of the RSFSR (Ukrainskyi teatr RRFSR). Established as the Ukrainian Theater of Musical Drama in Moscow in 1924, with L. Savinin, D. Oleksiienko, and H. Brahin as the directors. In its repertoire were the works of Ukrainian classical and contemporary playwrights, including I. Kotliarevsky, S. Hulak-Artemovsky, M. Starytsky, M. Kropyvnytsky, and O. Korniichuk. In 1932 it was united with the *Moscow Ukrainian Theater-Studio under its current name. It was active until 1934.

Moscow Ukrainian Theater-Studio (Ukrainska teatralna studiia im. L. Kurbasa). The studio was initiated in 1928 by K. *Burevii and the Society of Friends of Ukrainian Theater in Moscow. L. Kurbas sent V. Inkizhinov from Berezil to work with the studio. Its repertoire consisted of P. Mérimée's short plays from *Le Théâtre de Clara Gazul*, H. Kosynka's *Rodychi* (The Relatives, an adaptation of his story 'Polityka' [Politics]), and the pantomime *Do i pislia* (Before and After) to the music of F. Liszt. In 1932 it was incorporated into the *Moscow Ukrainian Theater of the RSFSR.

Leonid Mosendz   Kostiantyn Moshchenko

Mosendz, Leonid (pseuds: Osyp Liaskovets, Rostyslav Berladnyk), b 20 September 1897 in Mohyliv-Podilskyi, Podilia gubernia, d 13 October 1948 in Blonay, Switzerland. Writer. He studied at the teachers' seminary in Vinnytsia (1911–15) and worked as a teacher in Hnivan (1918–20). A demobilized UNR Army soldier, he fled to Poland in 1920. He returned to Lutske in 1921, whereupon he was arrested by the Poles and sent to an internment camp in Kalisz. After his release he studied chemical engineering at the Ukrainian Husbandry Academy (1923–8) in Poděbrady. There he translated a Czech inorganic chemistry textbook (1924) with M. Vikul, contributed to the student periodicals *Podiebradka* and *Students'kyi visnyk*, worked as an assistant to V. Ivanys, and wrote a brochure in Czech about Ukraine. After two years of graduate studies in Brno he received a doctorate from the academy in 1931 and worked as a civil engineer in Bratislava. In 1937–9 he taught in a commercial school in Sevliush, Transcarpathia. From 1939 to 1945 he was a chemist in Bratislava, whence he fled to the British zone in Austria. He died in a Swiss tuberculosis sanatorium.

From the late 1920s Mosendz contributed poetry, prose, literary criticism, and book reviews to the journals *Literaturno-naukovyi vistnyk*, *Vistnyk*, *Samostiina Ukraïna*, and *Proboiem*. He wrote the drama in verse *Vichnyi korabel'* (The Eternal Ship, 1933); the narrative poems *Kanitfershtan* (from the German *Kann nicht verstehen*, 1945) and *Volyns'kyi rik* (A Volhynian Year, 1948); the poetry collections *Zodiiak* (Zodiac, 1941) and *Dyiabolichni paraboly* (Diabolic Parabolas, 1947, together with Yu. *Klen under the collective pseud Porfyrii Horotak); the autobiographical novelette *Zasiv* (The Sowing, 1936, 1941, 1946); the story collections *Liudyna pokirna* (*Homo lenis*, 1937, 1951), *Vidplata* (Retribution, 1939), and *Pomsta* (Revenge, 1941); and the posthumously published unfinished novel *Ostannii prorok* (The Last Prophet, 1960). He also translated English (eg, E.A. Poe), French, German, and other literary works into

Ukrainian. The principal themes of Mosendz's works, including his publicistic pamphlets about the Prussian statesman Baron K. Stein (1935) and M. Khvylovy (1948), derive from his well-developed sense of Ukrainian patriotism.

R. Senkus

Moshchenko, Kostiantyn [Moščenko, Kostjantyn], b 1876 in the Kharkiv region, d 16 September 1963 in Dornstadt, West Germany. Ethnographer and museologist. After graduating in architecture from the St Petersburg Academy of Arts (1903) he worked on the construction of V. Krychevsky's zemstvo building in Poltava and then turned to collecting applied folk art and studying folk architecture. He worked at the Kiev Historical Museum (1904–7) and then headed the historical-ethnographic section of the Poltava Museum (1907–25) and the painting department of the Kievan Cave Monastery Museum (1926–30). He was arrested and exiled in 1933–7. During the Second World War he emigrated to Germany. He designed house plans based on the folk architecture of the Poltava area and wrote studies of rural architecture in the Kamianets-Podilskyi region (1927) and of H. Galagan's building (1962).

Moshchych, Petro [Moščyč], b 27 April 1928 in Volosate, Lisko county, Galicia. Pediatrician. A graduate of the medical faculty of Uzhhorod University (1952), he joined the department of clinical pediatrics at the Kiev Medical Institute in 1956 and became department head in 1971. In 1973 he was appointed chief pediatrician of the Ministry of Health of the Ukrainian SSR. His works deal with rheumatism, tuberculosis, meningitis, chronic tonsillitis, dysentery, and viral hepatitis.

Mosienko, William (Bill) [Mosijenko], b 2 November 1921 in Winnipeg. Professional hockey player. During 14 seasons in the National Hockey League (NHL) with the Chicago Black Hawks (1941–55), Mosienko played in 711 regular season games, scored 259 goals, and earned 281 assists. In 22 play-off games he recorded 10 goals and 4 assists. He is best known for scoring 3 goals in 21 seconds against the New York Rangers on 21 March 1952, still an NHL record. In the 1944–5 season he won the Lady Byng Trophy as the most sportsmanlike player. He was voted into the NHL Hall of Fame in 1965.

Mosin, Oleksander, b 16 October 1871 in Shestirnia, Kherson county, d 9 September 1929 in Kiev. Opera singer (tenor). A graduate of the Moscow Conservatory (1897), he sang in St Petersburg (1903–5, 1910–16), in Kiev (1905–8), at the Bolshoi Theater in Moscow (1908–10), and in Tbilisi (1923–5). He was a soloist at the Kharkiv (1925–6) and Kiev (1926–9) theaters of opera and ballet and at the same time sang with the Odessa opera. His main roles were Hermann in P. Tchaikovsky's *Queen of Spades*, Vakula in N. Rimsky-Korsakov's *Christmas Eve*, Othello in G. Verdi's *Othello*, and Mykola in M. Lysenko's *Christmas Night*.

Moskal, Robert [Moskal'], b 24 October 1937 in Carnegie, Pennsylvania. Catholic bishop. He studied at St Basil's Seminary in Stamford, Connecticut, and the Catholic University of America in Washington (MA, 1963). He was ordained in 1963, and consecrated auxiliary bishop of

Bishop Robert Moskal

Philadelphia in 1981. In 1983 he was assigned to the newly created eparchy of Parma, Ohio. Moskal has been active in community life, and he heads the Providence Association of Ukrainian Catholics in America.

Moskalenko, Artem, b 2 November 1901 in Hryhorivka, Oleksandrivske county, Katerynoslav gubernia, d 23 October 1990 in Odessa. Linguist and pedagogue. A graduate of the Dnipropetrovske Institute of People's Education (1926), from 1939 he chaired Odessa University's department of Ukrainian language, served as dean of the Faculty of Philology, and also taught at the Odessa Pedagogical Institute and the Odessa Higher Party School. He published nearly 200 works, including a Ukrainian language course conspectus (1929); postsecondary textbooks on Ukrainian historical grammar (1941, 1951), modern phonetics (1947), sentence syntax (1959), historical phonetics (1960), orthography (1971), and historical lexicology (1972); histories of the Ukrainian language (1948), alphabet and orthography (1958), pre-Soviet dialectology (1961), Soviet dialectology (1962), and orthography in the Soviet period (1968); a chrestomathy in the history of the Ukrainian literary language (1954); a dialectal dictionary of Odessa oblast (1958); and a survey history of Ukrainian lexicography (1961). He also prepared several dialectological questionnaires, compiled two issues of a chrestomathy of Ukrainian dialects in Odessa oblast (1965–6), organized several dialectological conferences in Odessa and many dialectological field trips, and prepared bibliographies of Ukrainian dialectology (1966) and orthography (1971), the history of the standardization of the Ukrainian literary language (1974), and lexicology and lexicography (1973).

R. Senkus

Moskalenko, Kyrylo, b 11 May 1902 in Hryshyne, Bakhmut county, Katerynoslav gubernia. Marshal of the Soviet Union. He joined the Red Army in 1920. After graduating from the Dzerzhinsky Artillery Academy (1939) he fought in the Finnish-Soviet War. In the Second World War he commanded the 38th, 1st Tank, and 40th armies. After the war he was in charge of the Moscow Military District (1948–60) and then served as commander of strategic missile forces (1960–2), deputy defense minister, and chief inspector of the defense ministry (1962–83).

Moskalenko, Nadiia, b 20 June 1928 in Dnipropetrovske. Linguist; daughter of A. Moskalenko. After graduating from Odessa University in 1952, she continued her studies at the Kiev Pedagogical Institute (candidate's diss, 1956) and lectured there (1958–60). She taught Ukrainian language at Odessa (1960–85) and Bordeaux (1976–8) universities. She has written a monograph on the history of Ukrainian grammatical terminology (1959) and on the history of Ukrainian punctuation terminology (1959), and articles on stylistics and syntax.

Moskovets, Semen [Moskovec'], b 16 January 1900 in Sanzharivka (now Poltavka), Oleksandrivske county, Katerynoslav gubernia, d 24 September 1971 in Kiev. Virologist; corresponding member of the AN URSR (now ANU) from 1967. A graduate of Kiev University (1929), he worked in Azerbaidzhan (1934–52) and Kherson (1952–60) before becoming department head (1960–2) and director (1962–71) of the ANU Institute of Microbiology and Virology in Kiev. His major research was on viral diseases of agricultural plants (esp cottons), their antigens, and their cellular interaction.

Moskvofily. See Russophiles.

Mosler, Anselm, b ca 1871 in eastern Galicia, d 31 January 1917 in Zakopane, Nowy Targ county, western Galicia. Jewish socialist figure. As a gymnasium student in Stanyslaviv he established ties with the socialist underground in Kiev and helped to smuggle illegal propaganda from Galicia to Russian-ruled Ukraine. He was arrested by the tsarist authorities in 1896, imprisoned for two and a half years in Kiev, and then expelled from the country. After graduating from Vienna University (1900) he practiced law in Buchach and (from 1909) Monastyryska and became a leading member of the left wing of the Polish Social Democratic Party of Galicia (until 1905) and Jewish Social Democratic Party of Galicia (from 1905). He collaborated with members of the Ukrainian Social Democratic party and published the Polish-Ukrainian monthly *Służba Dworska* (1905) for agricultural workers in Galicia. He took part in the campaign for electoral reforms and for the election of Ukrainian representatives to the Austrian parliament in 1907, supported the *Bund and the Social Democracy of the Kingdom of Poland and Lithuania, and assisted in M. *Sichynsky's escape from prison in 1911.

Mospyne. VI-19, DB IV-4. A city (1990 pop 13,400) on the Hruzka River in Donetske oblast. It was founded in 1800 and given city status in 1938, at which time its name was changed from Makhorivka. It is administered by the council of Proletaskyi raion of Donetske. Its chief enterprises are a coal mine and an enrichment plant.

Mossakovsky, Volodymyr [Mossakovs'kyj], b 27 August 1919 in Melitopil, Tavriia gubernia. Mechanics scientist; full member of the AN URSR (now ANU) since 1972. He studied and taught at Dnipropetrovske University and served as rector there (1964–86). His main contributions are in the areas of elasticity theory and the mechanics of membranes.

Mossakovsky, Yevhen [Mossakovs'kyj, Jevhen], b 24 February 1839 in Borovychi, Lutske county, Volhynia gubernia, d ? Political activist. He graduated from the Volhynian Theological Seminary in 1859 and entered Kiev University. While in Kiev, he became involved in the conspiratorial *Kharkiv-Kiev Secret Society, helped organize Sunday schools, and disseminated the works of T. Shevchenko and other proscribed literature. In November 1861 he was arrested for his illegal activities at the Kiev Military School, where he resided and taught. In June 1861, after months of interrogation, he was tried and exiled to Kharkiv, where he was placed under strict police surveillance. He completed his studies at Kharkiv University in 1865 and prepared a full collection of Shevchenko's works, but its publication was not allowed. Nothing else is known about Mossakovsky, except that he wrote an unpublished comparative study of the works of Shevchenko, A. Pushkin, and A. Mickiewicz and worked as an assistant to a state comptroller in Zhytomyr (1865–7) and Kiev (1867–83).

Mostovshchyna. See *Sharvarok.*

Mostovych, Mykola [Mostovyč], b 1915 in Volhynia, d 19 January 1968 near Shelbyville, Kentucky. Physicist, metallurgist, and political activist. He studied at Lviv University. From 1934 he served as the OUN Home Executive's leader in Volhynia and, later, the Kholm region. After two years in Polish prisons (1937–9), he organized Ukrainian schools in the Kholm region and headed the Ukrainian Relief Committee in Kholm (1940–1). He was arrested by the Gestapo in 1941, and was imprisoned in concentration camps until 1945. As a postwar émigré he received a PH D at the Sorbonne and was a research associate of its institute of physics (1947–53) and a member of the Shevchenko Scientific Society. After emigrating to the United States in 1953 he worked as a metallurgist, developed several patents, and was a professor of physics at the University of Louisville (1958–68). He died in an automobile accident.

Mostva River. See Lva River.

Mostyska [Mostys'ka]. IV-4. A town (1990 pop 7,900) on the Sichna River and a raion center in Lviv oblast. It is first mentioned in a historical document in 1244. In 1404 it was granted the rights of *Magdeburg law, and in 1498 and 1524 it was destroyed by the Tatars and Turks. During the Cossack-Polish War of 1648–57 it was captured by the Cossacks, and its castle used as a Cossack stronghold. Under Austrian rule the town flourished as a county administrative and trade center. Today its chief enterprise is a plant of the Elektron Manufacturing Consortium.

Moszyński, Kazimierz, b 5 March 1887 in Warsaw, d 30 March 1959 in Cracow. Polish ethnographer and linguist; member of the Polish Academy of Sciences and the Shevchenko Scientific Society. After studying biology in Switzerland and Cracow, he served as a tutor and collected ethnographic material in the Bila Tserkva region. In 1913 he published a series of articles on Ukraine in *Ziemia*, and in 1914 a study of the folk rituals, beliefs, and stories in the Berezhany region. As a professor of Cracow (1926–34) and Vilnius (1935–9) universities, in 1932 he organized, with F. Kolessa, an expedition to collect folk songs. His chief work, *Kultura ludowa Słowian* (The Folk Culture of the Slavs, 2 vols, 1929, 1939), contains much Ukrainian material.

Motor vehicle transport. One of the basic modes of surface transportation of people or cargo, by means of buses or trucks. It is organized into intracity, intercity, subur-

Truck and bus transportation: basic indexes, 1940–86

Category	1940	1970	1980	1986
Highway network				
1. Paved highways (in 1,000 km)[a]	29.3	90.8	133.7	147.3
2. Highways (per 100 sq km)	4.9	15.0	22.2	24.8
3. Highways (per 1,000 people)	0.71	1.93	2.68	4.1
Freight traffic				
4. Output (in billion Tkm)[b]	1.7	41.6	70.1	74.6
5. Volume (in million t)	187	3,058	4,392.0	4,856.0
Container haul (in 1,000 t)	–	–	3,072.0	7,683.0
Packaged haul (in 1,000 t)	–	–	14,502.0	19,653.0
6. Productivity of 1 truck per year (in 1,000 Tkm)	11.7	29.0	36.3	34.0[e]
7. Average daily truck-run (in hours)	9.0	9.7	9.4	9.3[e]
8. Use-coefficient of a working truck (in % of whole physical plant)	40.3	69.2	69.0	67.0[e]
9. Average trip distance of 1 ton of haul (in km)	9.1	13.0	16.0	15.2
10. Cost of haul per 10 Tkm (in kopecks)	–	56.3	55.3	58.1[e]
Passenger traffic				
11. Output (in billion Pkm)[c]	0.28	46.6	81.7	88.5
Intracity	0.3[d]	15.7	25.3	28.0[e]
Suburban	–	19.1	38.3	37.2[e]
Intercity	–	11.8	18.1	18.8[e]
12. Volume (in million passengers)	29.4	5,060.4	7,801.1	8,228.2
Intracity	27.0[d]	3,030.0	4,104.0	4,373.0[e]
Suburban	–	1,802.0	3,402.0	3,194.0[e]
Intercity	2.0	229.0	295.0	309.0[e]
13. Average trip distance per pass (in km)	9.6	9.2	10.5	10.7[e]
14. Cost of haul per 10 Pkm (in kopecks)	–	8.9	10.7	11.4[e]
Sector's share of overall traffic (in %)				
15. Freight output	2.2	6.8	9.1	9.0
16. Freight volume	47.1	78.0	80.3	80.6
17. Passenger output	1.8	48.5	52.8	51.5
18. Passenger volume	11.8	90.0	91.6	92.2

[a]Includes highways for general use and major city streets
[b]Tkm is the freight volume, in tons multiplied by trip distance in kilometers.
[c]Pkm is the number of passengers multiplied by trip distance in kilometers.
[d]Includes suburban traffic.
[e]In 1983

ban, and international networks. Motor vehicles serve industrial enterprises, commercial organizations, and the general public.

Motor vehicle transport dates back to the turn of the century. Before 1913 the Russian Empire, including Ukraine, had approx 9,000 vehicles, most of which were personal cars or taxis. At the time, the empire had only 24,300 km of paved highways. Its tiny trucking sector carried approx 10 million metric t of freight, or 5 percent of the freight total. There was no bus service. Motor vehicle transportation as an industry developed during the Soviet period. Most of its growth occurred only after the Second World War.

By function, motor vehicle transport is divided into two branches: freight transport, to carry goods, and passenger transport, to carry people. Motor vehicles have significant advantages over trains: they are more accessible and flexible, and their service is cheaper and direct.

Trucks are able to transport almost all goods, but in the USSR their chief role was to transport farm products from the source to the processing plants, warehouses, and stores.

Ukraine is well suited for surface transportation. Most

of its territory consists of plains with gently rolling hills. The Carpathian and Crimean mountains are not particularly difficult to penetrate. The operational potential of the sector depends on the quantity and quality of highways, subsidiary lines, paved accesses to industrial enterprises, maintenance and repair shops, service stations, and personnel. Ukraine's highway network is underdeveloped in comparison with other parts of the USSR (see *Roads and highways).

The output of motor vehicles in Ukraine, in tonne kilometers (Tkm) and passenger kilometers (Pkm), is approx 15 percent and 19 percent of the all-Union output respectively. The share of motor freight in Ukrainian freight traffic is fairly low (9 percent), but the share of motor passenger traffic in passenger traffic is almost 52 percent (see the table). With the exception of beltways around major cities, all Ukrainian highways are two-lane. In the last two decades the growth of the highway network in Ukraine has been rapid but uneven.

The performance of freight and passenger transport would be much higher if the network were denser in certain regions, or if the distribution of activities and the mobility of inhabitants were proportional to the level of economic development.

Three- and four-axle trucks equipped with heavy-duty tires are used widely. Recently the truck/bus productivity has increased significantly because of the greater mechanization of the operation and better servicing and maintenance of the vehicles. Loading and unloading have also become more mechanized with the introduction of powerful modern cranes. Workers are better trained to increase productivity, and more advanced techniques and computers are used in planning traffic flow and setting timetables.

The productivity of a truck (in Tkm) has increased by approx 17 percent from 1975 to 1990, and the cost of production per unit of time increased by only 3.2 percent. However, the coefficient of trucks in use relative to the whole fleet of trucks was still relatively low (67 percent), and the coefficient of an 'effective' use was even lower (approx 60 percent). That means that the rate of 'empty runs,' the number of breakdowns on the road, the time lost in repairs, and the number of other technical lapses, such as lack of fuel, were still much too high by European standards. Ukraine's truck productivity was well above the USSR average (approx 132 percent with respect to tonnage and 102 percent with respect to Tkm per year).

Between 1940 and 1986 the growth of passenger traffic was astronomical: output in Pkm grew by a factor of 313, whereas the volume of passengers grew by a factor of 280. Nevertheless, supply has lagged far behind demand in that sector.

By 1983, 449 Ukrainian cities had a regular bus service besides the older modes of public transport, such as by streetcar and trolley. From 1970 to 1983 passenger output grew by 6.9 percent annually, and volume grew by 4.8 percent annually (see the table). Although not high by Western standards, the growth was higher than the USSR averages. At the same time the average trip distance and mobility increased.

Compared with that of the Baltic republics Ukraine's intercity traffic was particularly low with respect to the finding of new opportunities and the more efficient use of existing potential. In 1975 Ukraine produced 59,900 Pkm per worker compared to Baltic region's 67,800 Pkm. The difference represents the magnitude of Ukraine's relative immobility. Capital investment in the sector in Ukraine was more in line with that in the Baltic region, but the use-coefficient of the physical plant was only 71.1 percent in 1983, close to the former Soviet Union average and much below the Baltic figure. The implication is that in Ukraine physical plant was more obsolete or tied up in repairs longer, since the labor component (6.3 percent of the total labor force) was similar to or even higher than the Union average.

Motor vehicle transport came under a special republican ministry. Such jurisdiction should have insured better traffic distribution and passenger flow, but since capital outlays were determined in Moscow, the effect of local autonomy was minimal.

The major shortcoming of Ukrainian truck/bus transportation lies not in the international branches but in the rural traffic. It lacks an adequate network, uses outdated buses and inept personnel, and provides too few runs.

Ukraine has its own truck-building industry: the KrAZ-256 is built in Kremenchuk, and the LuAZ-969M in Lutske. The bus-building factory in Lviv builds the LAZ695, LAZ697E, and LAZ-699A. The Komunar factory in Zaporizhia and its subsidiary in Lutske build the ZAZ-968 car and the Tavriia. The Ukrainian motor fleet consists also of Russian-built trucks, buses, and personal cars, the Hungarian Icarus buses, and Czechoslovak and Polish trucks.

E. Bej

Motovylivka. A village and railway station near Khvastiv, Kiev oblast, where on 18 October 1918 the Sich Riflemen defeated the Hetman forces. The decisive victory sparked a popular uprising against the *Hetman government and led to Hetman P. Skoropadsky's downfall.

Motronynskyi Trinity Monastery (Motronynskyi troitskyi manastyr; also St Matrona's Monastery). A monastery near Chyhyryn, in Motronynskyi forest, founded sometime before 1568. In the 17th and 18th centuries it was a center of Orthodox life in the southern Kiev region. During the tenure of Hegumen M. *Znachko-Yavorsky (1763–8), it was a center of preparations for the *Koliivshchyna rebellion; Maksym *Zalizniak lived there. The baroque stone Trinity Church (built in 1800–4; depicted in an 1845 watercolor by T. Shevchenko) is still standing. In 1910 the monastery housed 9 monks and 23 novices; it was closed by the Soviet authorities in the 1920s.

Motyl, Alexander [Motyl', Oleksander], b 21 October 1953 in New York. Political scientist. After graduating from Columbia University (PH D, 1984) he joined its political science department. As a student he was editor of the political journal *New Directions* (1972–5). In 1988–92 he served as director of the Nationality and Siberian Studies Program at the Harriman Institute and then as the institute's associate director. He is the author of *The Turn to the Right: The Ideological Origins and Development of Ukrainian Nationalism, 1919–1929* (1980), *Will the Non-Russians Rebel? State, Ethnicity, and Stability in the USSR* (1987), *Sovietology, Rationality, Nationality: Coming to Grips with Nationalism in the USSR* (1990), and *The Dilemmas of Independence: Ukraine and the Politics of Post-Totalitarianism* (1992) and the editor of *Thinking Theoretically about Soviet Nationalities: History and Comparison in the Study of the USSR* (1992) and *The Post-Soviet Nations: Perspectives on the Demise of the USSR* (1992).

Mountain ash (Sorbus; Ukrainian: horobyna, riabyna). A deciduous tree or shrub of the Rosaceae family. Ash grows wild in northern Ukrainian forests, and domesticated species are cultivated as ornamentals in the south and Transcarpathia. The European mountain ash (S. aucuparia) has smooth gray bark, white flowers, and tart red fruit that contains 4–18 percent sugar, carotene, vitamin C, and organic acids. The fruits are used in the preparation of marmalade, preserves, aperitifs, and vinegar. The Old World service tree (S. torminalis; Ukrainian: bereka) grows in the Carpathian Mountains. It has a hard, fine-grained wood excellent for the manufacturing of furniture. Suitable for planting as a protective antierosion measure, it is also used as an ornamental tree. In the Crimea another species named service tree (S. domestica) is cultivated in orchards.

Mountain Brigade of the Ukrainian Galician Army (Persha hirska brygada UHA). Formed out of the Staryi Sambir and Liutovyska groups in January 1919 by Maj V. Chersky, the brigade established its headquarters in Turka and became part of the Third Corps. During the Polish offensive in May 1919, it was cut off from other UHA units and retreated across the border into Czechoslovakia. The Czechs disarmed it and sent it to *Deutsch-Gabel for internment. The Galician government failed to win its release. The brigade remained in POW camps until 1926, when it was dissolved. Its commanders in the camps were Lt Col V. Fedorovych, Col A. Varyvoda, Brig Gen V. Kurmanovych, and Brig Gen A. Wolf.

Bohdan Yatsiv and the Ukrainian flag at the top of Mont Blanc, 1947

Mountaineering (*alpinizm*). Mountain climbing in Ukraine assumed an organized form only after the First World War. Before then, the peaks of the Caucasus and Pamir mountains were tackled by individual climbers. M. Pogrebetsky led several Ukrainian expeditions into the Tien Shan Mountains (1926–36) that conquered a number of peaks for the first time. In the latter half of the 1930s, Kiev, Dnipropetrovske, and Kharkiv mountaineers organized camps in the Caucasus, and in 1938 the Committee on Physical Culture and Sports of the Ukrainian SSR opened the first mountain-climbing school in Adir-Su. By the end of 1939 it had graduated 528 climbers, including 143 instructors. The USSR Mountaineering Federation (est 1936) has held Union-wide competitions since 1949. Ukrainian teams consisting of climbers such as A. Kustovsky, V. Monogarov, M. Oleksiuk, V. Cherevko, B. Syvtsov, and V. Svyrydenko placed first in various categories in 1961, 1965–9, 1972, and 1973. In the Western European Alps and the North American Rockies, mountain climbing has been practiced by members of the Plast Ukrainian Youth Association, especially the 'Burlaky' group, two members of which (B. Yatsiv and I. Sukhoversky) were the first Ukrainians successfully to climb Mont Blanc (1 September 1947) and the Matterhorn (1948). In 1982 M. Turkevych and S. Bershov were the first Ukrainians to conquer Mount Everest and the first climbers ever to reach the summit at night. In May 1991 V. Pastukh, I. Sverhun, and S. Makarov hoisted the blue-yellow Ukrainian flag on Mount Manaslu, one of the highest Himalayan peaks.

Mousterian culture. The final phase of the Lower Paleolithic period, lasting from approx 100,000 BC to 40,000 BC.

Named after Le Moustier, a rock shelter discovered in France, it follows the *Acheulean culture and precedes the Upper Paleolithic Aurignacian culture. The use of stone tools, particularly primitive knives and scrapers, dominated this period. Major technological developments included the discovery of the means of starting fires and the use of bones and antlers for making tools. Food was obtained through hunting (mammoths, cave bears, rhinoceroses, aurochs, and other animals) and gathering. Mousterian man usually lived in caves or makeshift shelters in river valleys. Although archeological evidence is not conclusive, it appears that a matriarchal social order and a rudimentary religious consciousness may have been developing during this period. Mousterian culture sites in Ukraine include Molodove, Kiik-Koba, Starosilia, and Shaitan-Koba. (See also *Paleolithic Period.)

Mova, Denys (real surname: Petrov), b ? in Berdianske, Tavriia gubernia, d 1922 in Odessa. Stage actor, director, and singer (tenor). He completed study at the St Petersburg Conservatory and worked in the troupes of M. Starytsky and M. Kropyvnytsky (1885–9), M. Sadovsky (1889–90 and 1893–5), and P. Saksahansky (1890–3 and 1895–1909). He briefly led his own troupe in 1909 and then abandoned the stage because of illness.

Vasyl Mova

Mova, Vasyl (pseuds: Vasyl Lymansky, Myhutsky, Myhuchenko), b 13 January 1842 at a *khutir* near the Cossack village of Staroderev, iankivska, Kuban, d 13 June 1891 in Katerynodar (now Krasnodar), Kuban. Writer. After graduating from Kharkiv University (1867) he worked in Katerynodar as a teacher, court investigator, and, later, justice of the peace. Because of the critical social content of his writings Mova suffered tsarist persecution. To avoid further harassment he chose to live in Ust-Labinsk and Yeisk in the years 1876–85. In 1886 he returned to Katerynodar.

One of Mova's earliest poems appeared in the St Petersburg Ukrainian journal *Osnova* (1861, no. 4). During his lifetime he published fewer than 15 poems on social themes, most of them after 1880 in the Lviv periodicals *S'vit* and *Zoria* because publishing in Ukrainian was forbidden in the Russian Empire. His narrative poem 'Na stepy' (To the Steppes, 1883) is the first literary depiction of the plight of Ukrainian settlers in the Kuban. Mova's posthumously dramatized novel *Stare hnizdo i molodi ptakhy (Dramatychni obrazy)* (An Old Nest and Young Birds [Dramatic Images], 1907) masterfully portrays the tragedy of denationalization and social and moral degradation among the descendants of the Kuban Cossacks in the

1850s. Mova appears to have been influenced by T. Shevchenko and P. Kulish but is more than their epigone. At a time when ethnographic realism and Romantic idealizations of the Cossacks dominated in Ukrainian literature, he presented sober, critical (yet patriotic) views of the past and present in a unique style marked by macabre, grotesque exaggerations and a novel, expressive poetic lexicon combining folkloric and vernacular elements and daring neologisms. He can be considered the precursor of expressionism in Ukrainian literature. Mova left behind 50 manuscript notebooks of poetry, prose, and drama. The vast majority of his works were never published and have been lost. A bowdlerized edition of his poems appeared in Kiev in 1965. A complete edition of his previously published prose, poetry, and letters was edited by G.Y. Shevelov and published in Munich in 1967.

R. Senkus

Movchan, Borys [Movčan], b 9 January 1928 in Makiivka, Nizhen okruha. Scientist in the fields of metallurgy and the physics of metals; full member of the AN URSR (now ANU) since 1978. He graduated from Kiev University (1951) and worked at the AN URSR Institute of Electric Welding. His main contributions have been in the areas of crystal structure in alloys, the crystallinity of alloys, vacuum condensation, the electron-beam evaporation of metals and other materials, and the etching of metals.

Julian Movchan

Bishop Hryhorii Mozolevsky

Movchan, Julian [Movčan, Julijan], b 19 February 1913 in Zorokiv, Zhytomyr county, Volhynia gubernia. Physician and journalist. After working on several factory newspapers in Kharkiv, he studied medicine at the Kharkiv and Lviv medical institutes (MD, 1943). A postwar refugee in Germany, he emigrated to the United States and went into private practice there. He has contributed numerous articles on public and political issues and medical questions to the Ukrainian press in the United States and Canada and wrote a popular medical handbook (1946), the book of political commentary and recollections *Shcho varto b znaty* (Things Worth Knowing, 1966), the autobiographical collection *Zapysky likaria* (Doctor's Notes, 1970), and *Zbirka opovidan'* (A Collection of Short Stories, 1988).

Movchan, Pavlo [Movčan], b 13 July 1939 in Velyka Vilshanka, Vasylkiv raion, Kiev oblast. Poet, translator,

and screenwriter. He graduated from Moscow's Gorky Institute of Literature (1965) and the Higher Screenwriting and Directing Courses there (1970). In recent years he has been a leading member of the Ukrainian Language Society, and since 1990 he has been a member of the Ukrainian parliament. One of the most popular poets in Ukraine in the 1980s, Movchan is the author of the collections *Nate!* (Take It! 1963), *Kora* (Bark, 1968), *Letiuche derevo* (Flying Tree, 1972), *Zelo* (Herb, 1973), *Pam'iat'* (Memory, 1977), *Dosvid* (Experience, 1980), *Kruhovorot* (Whirl, 1981), *V den' molodoho sontsia* (On the Day of the Young Sun, 1981), *Zholud'* (Acorn, 1983), *Kalendar* (Calendar, 1985), *Svitlo* (Light, 1986), and *Porih* (Threshold, 1988). A large edition of his selected poems, *Sil'* (Salt), was published in 1989.

Movchan, Vasyl [Movčan, Vasyl'], b 14 January 1903 in Nemorozh, near Zvenyhorodka, Kiev gubernia, d 2 July 1964 in Kiev. Ichthyologist; corresponding member of the AN URSR (now ANU) from 1951 and the All-Union Academy of Agricultural Sciences from 1955. A graduate of the Kiev Veterinary-Zootechnical Institute (1929), he was director of the Scientific Research Institute of Pond Fisheries in Kiev (1930–41), a professor at Kiev University (from 1945), director of the ANU Institute of Zoology laboratory (1946–9), and a department head in the ANU Institute of Hydrobiology. He proposed an effective method of intensified inland fish-stocking.

Movchan, Yehor [Movčan, Jehor], b 1 May 1898 in Velyka Pysarivka, Bohodukhiv county, Kharkiv gubernia, d 22 March 1968 in Kiev. Kobzar. Blind at 10 months and orphaned by the age of five, he studied with the kobzar S. Pasiuha, and then set off on his own in 1913. His prerevolutionary repertoire included all major dumas and historical songs, notably 'Nevil'nyts'kyi plach' (The Captives' Lament), 'Duma about the Widow and Her Three Sons,' and 'Duma about the Three Brothers of Samara,' as well as songs to the words of T. Shevchenko. Under Soviet rule he began composing pseudo-folkloric dumas and songs in honor of contemporary leaders and Soviet holidays. He frequently performed on radio and television.

Movchun, Petro [Movčun], b 6 September 1925 in Bilychi (now part of Kiev). Sculptor. A graduate of the Kiev State Art Institute (1950), where he studied under M. Lysenko, he has done sculptural portraits of T. Shevchenko (1962) and I. Franko (1964) and a number of monuments, including ones to T. Shevchenko in Nova Odessa (1967) and Zolotonosha (1976) and to Marko Vovchok in Nemyriv (1971). His favorite medium is marble.

Movoznavstvo (Linguistics). A nonperiodical journal published in Kiev from 1934 to 1939 (14 issues) by the AN URSR Institute of Linguistics. Its editors were N. *Kahanovych (until 1937) and M. Kalynovych. *Movoznavstvo* was an instrument of the Party: it published articles denouncing linguists-purists (S. Smerechynsky, O. Kurylo, D. Sheludko), rejecting the terminological dictionaries of the Institute of Ukrainian Scientific Language, and attacking I. Ohiienko's *Ridna mova*. New terminological material appearing in the journal was edited to promote Russification, and M. Marr's Japhetic theories on language were applied to Ukrainian. Yet some articles on word formation, the dialects of the Chernihiv, Kiev, and eastern Podilia regions, and particularly L. *Bulakhovsky's studies on

ccentology have made important contributions to lin-
uistics.

From 1941 to 1963 a similar nonperiodical journal, *Mo-
oznavstvo: Naukovi zapysky*, was published by the Insti-
ute of Linguistics. The editors were L. Bulakhovsky (until
961, 16 issues) and I. *Bilodid (1962–3, nos 17–18). After
ulakhovsky's death the journal reverted to a predomi-
antly political-propagandistic character.

Since January 1967, a new *Movoznavstvo* has been pub-
ished bimonthly by the ANU Division of Literature, Lan-
uages, and Fine Arts in Kiev. Its editors have been I.
ilodid (1967–82), V. Rusanivsky (1982–8), and O. Melny-
huk (1988–).

J. Hursky

Mozalevsky, Ivan [Mozalevs'kyj], b 24 September 1890
n Wrocław, Poland, d ? Graphic artist. He graduated
rom the Kiev Art School (1912) and audited classes at the
t Petersburg Academy of Arts (1914–15). From 1920 he
ived abroad, in Vienna, Berlin, Prague, where he taught
raphic art at the Ukrainian Studio of Plastic Arts (1923–
), and Paris. In 1947 he returned to Ukraine and settled in
ymferopil. His specialty was book graphics, but he also
ngraved portraits (eg, of C. Baudelaire and I. Repin) and
ther subjects; designed bookplates, Ukrainian currency,
tamps, and government documents; and carved minia-
ures in ivory. A catalog of one of his exhibitions was pub-
ished in 1963.

Mozart, Franz Xaver, b 26 July 1791 in Vienna, d 29 July
844 in Karlovy Vary, Bohemia. Austrian composer, pia-
ist, and conductor; son of W.A. Mozart. He lived in Lviv
n 1808–19 and 1822–38 as a private music instructor. His
fforts in establishing the St Cecilia Society and Choir
1826) and an institute of singing contributed greatly to
he quality of musical instruction in the city. He toured
Kiev and Zhytomyr as a pianist in 1819, and composed a
umber of piano pieces based on Ukrainian folk songs.

Mozolevsky, Hryhorii [Mozolevs'kyj, Hryhorij], b
876 in the Chernihiv region, d 1938? Orthodox bishop.
efore 1917 he taught religion in various secondary
chools in the Chernihiv region. In 1924 he was consecrat-
d bishop of the Ukrainian Autocephalous Orthodox
church for the Konotip region. In 1926–7 he was a parish
priest in Radomyshl, and later in Spask. He was arrested
by the NKVD in 1936, and his subsequent fate is unknown.

Mozyr. I-10. A city (1989 pop 101,000) on the Prypiat River and a raion center in Homel oblast, Belarus. It is on the
border of Ukrainian ethnic territory. In the 12th century
Mozyr was part of Kievan Rus' and, later, of the Grand
Duchy of Lithuania. In the 17th century it belonged to the
Hetman state. In 1793 it became a county center in Minsk
gubernia. In 1918–20 Mozyr was included in the territory
claimed by the UNR.

Mozyra, Lukian (Mozyria, Mazurenko), b ?, d 1652.
Cossack officer. As colonel of Korsun regiment he took
part in battles at Korsun (1648), Zboriv (1649), and Berestechko (1651) and undertook diplomatic missions to Poland (1648) and Moscow (1651). His dissatisfaction with
the Treaty of *Bila Tserkva (1651) led him to conspire with
M. *Hladky against Hetman B. Khmelnytsky, for which he
was executed.

Mriia (Dream). The largest transport plane in the world.
Designed at the Antonov Design Bureau near Kiev, the
six-engine model AN-225 has a maximum 600-tonne take-
off payload and can carry 250 t of cargo over 4,000 km at
an airspeed of 800 km/hr. The first large airplane to be
given a Ukrainian name, the Mriia made its first test flight
on 21 December 1988. It has since then been used to transport heavy cargo and in airlifts of food and medical aid
from North America to victims of the explosion at the
Chornobyl Atomic Power Station.

Mstyslav Danylovych, b ?, d ca 1290–1308. Volhynian
prince; son of King *Danylo Romanovych. After Danylo's
death he inherited Volodymyr-Volynskyi. In 1288 he succeeded his cousin, Volodymyr Vasylkovych, as prince of
the Volodymyr-Volynskyi, Lutske, and Berestia lands. He
took an active part in Polish conflicts and helped Konrad
I of Mazovia to regain the Sandomierz land.

Mstyslav Gospel (Mstyslavove yevanheliie). One of the
most important medieval paleographic monuments. The
manuscript was written in Kiev, probably in 1115–17, at
the request of Prince Mstyslav Volodymyrovych of Kiev,
by Oleksa, the son of Presbyter Lazar of the Novgorod
Church of the Annunciation. It is preserved at the State
Historical Museum in Moscow. The text was published by
P. Simoni in St Petersburg in 1905–10 and by L. Zhukovskaia in 1983. Its language was analyzed by E. Karsky in
Russkii filologicheskii vestnik, 34 (1895).

Mstyslav Hlibovych, b ?, d ca 1239. Prince of Chernihiv. After his cousin, *Mykhail Vsevolodovych, became
grand prince of Kiev in 1235, Mstyslav succeeded him in
Chernihiv. Mstyslav was the first Ukrainian prince to confront directly the Mongol-Tatar army during Batu Khan's
invasion. After the rout of Mstyslav's army in October
1239, Chernihiv was sacked by the Tatars, and Mstyslav
fled to Hungary.

Mstyslav Iziaslavych, b ?, d 19 August 1170 in Volodymyr-Volynskyi. Grand prince of Kiev from 1167; son of
*Iziaslav Mstyslavych and father of *Roman Mstyslavych.
During his father's reign in Kiev, Mstyslav ruled Pere-
iaslav from 1151 and Volodymyr-Volynskyi from 1154.
Together with his father he fought against the *Olhovych
princes of Chernihiv and his granduncle, *Yurii
Dolgorukii. Yurii's ally, Yaroslav Osmomysl, routed
Mstyslav's army at Terebovlia in 1151. In 1152 Mstyslav
twice defeated invading Cuman armies. In 1160 he gained
control of Kiev and placed his uncle, *Rostyslav
Mstyslavych of Smolensk, on the Kievan throne. After
Rostyslav's death in 1167, Mstyslav succeeded him in
Kiev. Like his great-grandfather, Volodymyr Monomakh,
Mstyslav drew together the forces of all the Ukrainian
princes against the Cumans, and defeated them at the Orel
River in 1168. He struggled against the princes of
Vladimir-Suzdal for supreme rule in Rus'. In 1169 he
failed to repulse the attack on Kiev by Dolgorukii's son,
*Andrei Bogoliubskii, and fled to Volhynia. Shortly before
his death he briefly recaptured Kiev but was forced to re-
treat to Volhynia. Mstyslav was buried in Volodymyr-
Volynskyi's Dormition Cathedral, which he had built in
1160.

Mstyslav Mstyslavych, known as the Successful (*Udatnyi*), b before 1176, d 1228 in Torcheske, in the Kiev land. Senior Rus' prince; grandson of *Rostyslav Mstyslavych. He ruled Trypilia (1193–1203), Torcheske (1203–7, 1227–8), Toropets (1207–8), and the lands of Novgorod (1208–15, 1216–18) and Halych (1219–27). In 1193 and 1203 he waged successful campaigns against the Cumans. In 1212 he and his cousin, *Mstyslav Romanovych, drove *Vsevolod Sviatoslavych Chermny from Kiev. From 1219 he battled Hungarian and Polish princes to gain control of the Halych land. In 1221, with the help of the Cuman khan *Kotian (his father-in-law) and Mstyslav Romanovych, he defeated a Polish-Hungarian army and finally captured Halych. Both Mstyslavs organized the large military expedition of the southern Rus' princes against the Tatars that ended in the debacle at the Kalka River and the death of nine princes in June 1223. Later, with the help of his son-in-law *Danylo Romanovych of Volhynia (husband of his daughter Anna), Mstyslav fought against Hungarian encroachments in Galicia and with various Galician boyars. Nevertheless he gave Peremyshl to his son-in-law Andrew, the son of Andrew II of Hungary, and bequeathed Halych to him.

Mstyslav Romanovych, known as the Good and the Old, b ?, d 6 June 1223. Grand prince of Kiev from 1212; grandson of *Rostyslav Mstyslavych and nephew of *Riuryk Rostyslavych. Until 1212 he was prince of Pskov, Drutske, Bilhorod, and the Smolensk land (1197–1212). In 1212 he and his cousin, *Mstyslav Mstyslavych, drove *Vsevolod Sviatoslavych Chermny from Kiev, and soon afterward Mstyslav Romanovych became prince of Kiev. Both Mstyslavs organized the large 1223 expedition of southern Rus' princes against the Tatars that ended in the debacle at the Kalka River. Mstyslav Romanovych and his two sons-in-law were captured and crushed to death beneath a platform on which the Tatars held their victory banquet.

Mstyslav Volodymyrovych (Christian name: Konstantyn), known as the Fair (*Krasnyi*) and the Brave, b ?, d 1034 or 1036 in Chernihiv. First prince of *Tmutorokan principality from 988 and prince of *Chernihiv principality from 1024; son of *Volodymyr the Great and half-brother of *Yaroslav the Wise, *Sviatopolk I, and *Saints Borys and Hlib. Mstyslav received Tmutorokan as a fiefdom from his father in 988. He waged successful wars against the *Khazars (1016) and the Kasogians (he killed the Kasogian khan Rededia in a duel in 1022). Mstyslav opposed the attempt of Yaroslav the Wise to gain supreme rule of Rus'. He tried to take Kiev in 1023, took Chernihiv, and defeated Yaroslav's army in the 1024 Battle of Lystven near Chernihiv. Thereafter Mstyslav ruled all of Left-Bank Ukraine except Pereiaslav principality, which remained in Yaroslav's hands, and from 1026 the two brothers lived in harmony. In 1029 Yaroslav's forces took part in Mstyslav's offensive against the *Yasians, and in 1031 Mstyslav helped Yaroslav to regain the *Cherven towns from Poland. During Mstyslav's reign a stone cathedral in Tmutorokan and the Cathedral of the *Transfiguration in Chernihiv, in which he was buried, were built.

Mstyslav I Volodymyrovych (Christian name: Havryil), known as the Great, b 5 June 1076 in Turiv, d 20 April 1132 in Kiev. Grand prince of Kiev from 1125; eldest son of *Volodymyr Monomakh and *Gytha, daughter of Harold II of England; brother of *Yaropolk II Volodymyrovych, *Viacheslav Volodymyrovych, and *Yurii Dolgorukii. As prince of Novgorod (1088–93, 1095–1117) and Rostov and Smolensk (1093–5) Mstyslav took part in the 1093, 1107, and 1111 Rus' campaigns against the Cumans. He drove his godfather, *Oleh Sviatoslavych, out of Murom, Rostov, and Suzdal in 1096 and forced him to attend the *Liubech congress of princes in 1097. From 1117 to 1125 Mstyslav was prince of Bilhorod, near Kiev, and coruled his father's realm. After Monomakh's death in May 1125, he ascended the Kievan throne. With the help of his six sons (among them *Iziaslav, *Rostyslav, and *Volodymyr Mstyslavych), his brothers, and his cousins he controlled virtually all of Kievan Rus'. He subdued the rebellious Polatsk princes in 1128 and gave Polatsk principality to Iziaslav, pushed the Cumans beyond the Volga and the Don rivers in 1129, defeated the Lithuanians in 1130 and 1131, and had his sons restore dominion over the Chud in 1131. Continuing the Riurykide tradition of dynastic ties he married as his first wife Kristina, the daughter of King Ingi of Sweden. He gave his daughter Malfrid in marriage to King Sigurd I of Norway, his daughter Ingeborg to the Danish duke Knud Lavard, and his daughter Iryna Dobrodeia to the Byzantine prince (later emperor) Andronicus Comnenus. After Mstyslav's death his daughter Yevfrosyniia married the Hungarian king Géza II.

Mud volcano. A cone-shaped or flattened mound of mud heaved up through overlying sediments with a funnel-shaped crater on its top through which mud, water, and gases are erupted. In Ukraine there are mud volcanoes on the Kerch Peninsula. The best known are the Bulhanak and the Tarkhan. They can also be found in the Taman Peninsula. In some cases (especially on the Kerch Peninsula) salt springs and iron-ore deposits are formed in the vicinity of mud volcanoes.

Mudrak, Myroslava (née Tsishkevych), b 19 July 1950 in Cleveland, Ohio. Art historian specializing in Ukrainian modernism. A graduate of the University of Texas at Austin (PHD, 1984) and an associate professor at Ohio State University in Columbus, she is the author of *The New Generation and Artistic Modernism in the Ukraine* (1986), a monograph on Soviet Ukrainian art of the 1920s.

Mudrak, Yuliian, b 18 April 1878 in Skopiv, Peremyshl county, Galicia, d 27 May 1950 in New York. Economist and civic leader. After completing his studies in mining engineering in Czechoslovakia and Austria, he worked as an engineer for the Post and Telegraph Directorate (1901–34), whose jurisdiction included much of Western Ukraine. He was one of the founders of the Plai hiking society, president of Silskyi Hospodar, member of the board of directors of the Dnister bank and Narodna Torhovlia, director of I. Levynsky's building company, a member of the Dilo publishing company, and an executive member of the Shevchenko Scientific Society, the Prosvita society, and the Ukrainian Technical Society. He was also publisher of the monthly *Polityka* (1926–8). In 1944 he left Ukraine for Germany, and in 1949 he emigrated to the United States.

Vasyl Mudry   Andrii Mudryk

Mudry, Vasyl [Mudryj, Vasyl'], b 19 March 1893 in Vik-no, Skalat county, Galicia, d 19 March 1966 in New York. Civic and political leader, and journalist; full member of the Shevchenko Scientific Society from 1958. As a student at Lviv University he was an executive member of the Ukrainian Student Union and the Academic Hromada. Having been elected to the Proskuriv zemstvo executive in 1918, he was in charge of education in the county and in the fall of 1920 was county head. After returning to Lviv in 1921, he helped organize the Lviv (Underground) Ukrainian University, of which he served as finance offic-er and secretary (1921–5). He joined the editorial board of the daily *Dilo* in 1926 and soon became its chief editor (1927–35). He was also active in the Prosvita society as a member of its central executive (from 1921), general secre-tary (1925–31), and first vice-president (1932–9). In 1931–3 he chaired the Franko Monument Committee and, in 1933, the Committee to Save Ukraine, which organized famine relief for Soviet Ukraine. As one of the founders of the *Ukrainian National Democratic Alliance (UNDO) he draft-ed the party program that was adopted in 1926 and served as the party's first vice-president (1928–35) and president (1935–9). He was elected to the Polish Sejm in 1935 and 1938, and there he was the chief proponent of the policy of *Normalization and served as leader of the *Ukrainian Parliamentary Representation and vice-marshal of the Sejm. After leaving Ukraine in 1944, he served as a vice-president of the Ukrainian Supreme Liberation Council (1944–7), executive chairman of the *Ukrainian National Council, and the first president (1945–9) of the *Central Representation of the Ukrainian Emigration in Germany. In 1949 he emigrated to the United States, where he be-came executive director of the *Ukrainian Congress Com-mittee of America and an executive member of the Shevchenko Scientific Society and the United Ukrainian American Relief Committee. In addition to numerous ar-ticles on political and cultural topics in the press, he wrote several pamphlets, on the man-made famine of 1933, the Prosvita society, the UNDO, and the underground univer-sity in Lviv, and a book on the campaign to establish a Ukrainian university in Lviv titled *Borot'ba za ohnyshche ukraïns'koï kul'tury v zakhidnykh zemliakh Ukraïny* (The Struggle for the Hearth of Ukrainian Culture in Ukraine's Western Lands, 1923). He also edited *Lviv: A Symposium on Its 700th Anniversary* (1962).

Mudryk, Andrii, b 12 August 1893 in Pavlokoma, Be-reziv (Brzozów) county, Galicia, d 8 January 1969 in Tor-onto. Co-operative and civic leader. He fought in the First World War as a lieutenant of the Ukrainian Galician Army. In 1923 he returned to Galicia from internment in Czechoslovakia and began working as an organizer of dairy co-operatives. He became organizational director for all Galicia of Maslosoiuz (1924–39, 1941–4), an instruc-tor of dairying in the union's dairy schools in Stryi and Lviv, and a coeditor of the monthly *Kooperatyvne molo-charstvo* (1926–39). He was also active in Tsentrobank, the Audit Union of Ukrainian Co-operatives, and Ridna Shkola. He left Ukraine in 1944 and eventually settled in Brazil, where he was vice-president of the Society of Friends of Ukrainian Culture in Curitiba. He later moved to Canada, where he remained active in credit union activ-ities. In addition to numerous articles on co-operation, he wrote *Kooperatyvnyi katekhyzm* (The Co-operative Cate-chism, 1939).

Mukachiv castle

Mukachiv or **Mukacheve** [Mukačiv or Mukačeve]. V-3. A city (1990 pop 86,200) on the Liatorytsia River and a raion center in Transcarpathia oblast. The site has been settled since prehistoric times. Archeologists have discov-ered settlements in the vicinity from the Neolithic Period, the Bronze Age, the Iron Age, and the Slavic period (8th–9th century AD). In the 10th century Mukachiv belonged to Kievan Rus', and in the 11th century, to Hungary. The for-tress, rising high above the town, was destroyed by the Cumans in 1086 and by the Tatars in 1241. It was rebuilt by F. *Koriiatovych, who also built St Nicholas's Monas-tery. By the end of the 14th century Mukachiv was an im-portant manufacturing and trading center on a trade route between Hungary and Galicia. In 1445 it was granted the rights of *Magdeburg law. Because of the monastery the town became a cultural and religious center in the 15th century, and until the end of the 18th century it was the seat of an eparchy. Owing to its strategic location Muka-chiv was contested frequently by the Habsburg and Tran-sylvanian dynasties in the 16th and 17th centuries. At the end of the 17th century the town was annexed by Austria. It flourished in the 18th century and became the chief trade center in Transcarpathia. A gymnasium was established in 1746. Mukachiv played an important role in the revolutionary movement of 1848–9. After the First World War the city belonged to Czechoslovakia. Its importance diminished whereas that of Uzhhorod grew. In 1938 Mukachiv came under Hungarian rule. By a Soviet-Czechoslovak treaty of June 1945 Transcarpathia became part of Soviet Ukraine.

In 1921 Mukachiv had a population of 21,000, consisting mostly of Jews (48 percent), who began to settle there in the late 17th century, Ukrainians (24 percent), and Hungarians (22 percent). In 1925 the first Hebrew gymnasium on Ukrainian territory was established in Mukachiv. By 1966 the city's population had risen to 50,500. It consisted mostly of Ukrainians (60 percent), followed by Hungarians (18 percent), Russians (10 percent), and Jews (6 percent).

Mukachiv has several machine-building plants, a furniture factory, and a food industry. A branch of the Ukrainian Scientific Research Institute of Forest Management and Agroforest Amelioration is located in the city. Its chief architectural monuments are the castle (rebuilt in the 18th century), a Gothic chapel (14th century), the White Building (a baroque monument of the 17th century rebuilt in 1746), the arsenal (now the regional museum, built in 1624), St Nicholas's Monastery (Cathedral from 1806), and the wooden church moved there from Shelestove village (1777).

Mukachiv eparchy. A Ukrainian Catholic eparchy in Transcarpathia, with its see in Mukachiv (to 1780) and then Uzhhorod. The first mention of a bishop in Transcarpathia is from 1491, when the Hungarian king Ulászló (Władysław) II confirmed Ivan of St Nicholas's Monastery in Mukachiv as bishop. The first Uniate bishop of Mukachiv was P. Petrovych, who assumed the post in 1664. Previously, 63 priests in the eparchy had declared their union with Rome (1646), and Bishop V. *Tarasovych had personally converted to Catholicism, although he was not permitted to participate in the 1646 sobor. In 1725, Uniate territories were expanded, and the Maramureş region was added to the eparchy. Because there were no surviving documents concerning the founding of the eparchy or the establishment of the union there by the Vatican, the Hungarian Roman Catholic bishops of Eger in the 17th and 18th centuries claimed jurisdiction over the eparchy and attempted to annex it. In response Bishop M. Olshavsky worked, from 1749, to gain recognition of the eparchy's independence; it was finally granted by the pope in 1771. A. *Bachynsky reorganized the eparchy, established several institutions, and moved its see to Uzhhorod.

Initially all the Greek Catholic parishes of northeastern Hungary belonged to the Mukachiv eparchy. Later the *Prešov (1818), Gerlia (1853), and *Hajdúdorog (1912) eparchies were separated from it. When the eparchy was recognized by Rome, it was placed under the jurisdiction of the Esztergom Hungarian Catholic metropolitan. Bishop Bachynsky's attempts to place it under the Uniate metropolitan of Halych in the late 18th century were unsuccessful. In 1937 the Vatican announced its intention to establish a Mukachiv metropoly with eparchies in Prešov, Uzhhorod, and Khust, but the outbreak of the Second World War prevented the implementation of the plan.

Situated on the border separating Ukrainians, Slovaks, and Hungarians, Mukachiv eparchy was exposed to a variety of cultural and political influences. In the 17th century many Hungarian magnates adopted Protestantism and attempted to introduce it throughout the eparchy. Later, Roman Catholicism was espoused by the local elite and supported by the state. In response to these pressures confessional strife was common. In the interwar period many inhabitants returned to Orthodoxy, and the Mukachiv-Prešov Orthodox eparchy was established in 1929. This eparchy, with its see in Mukachiv, claimed 121,000 followers in 1930.

The Soviet occupation of Transcarpathia in 1944 resulted in the martyrdom of Mukachiv eparchy's Uniate bishop, T. *Romzha; the exile to Kazakhstan of his successor, O. *Khira; and the formal liquidation of the Greek Catholic eparchy in August 1949. From then until the late 1980s only the Orthodox Mukachiv-Uzhhorod eparchy under the Russian Orthodox church, with its see in Mukachiv, was officially sanctioned. The Greek Catholic church survived in the underground, however, and emerged again during the period of liberalization after 1985. (See also *Ukrainian Catholic church.)

BIBLIOGRAPHY
Pekar, A. *Narysy istoriï Tserkvy Zakarpattia* (Rome 1967)
– *The Bishops of the Eparchy of Mukachevo, with Historical Outlines* (Pittsburgh 1979)

W. Lencyk, A. Pekar

Mukachiv Saint Nicholas's Monastery

Mukachiv Saint Nicholas's Monastery (Mukachivskyi Sviatomykolaivskyi manastyr). A men's monastery located on Chernecha Hora (literally 'monk's hill') near Mukachiv. Believed to have been founded in the late 11th century, the monastery was revived and expanded considerably in the late 14th century, when it enjoyed the patronage of F. *Koriiatovych. In 1491 it became the residence of the bishop of Mukachiv, whose jurisdiction covered all of Transcarpathia. The monastery's monks led efforts to establish church union in 1646, when the monastery joined the Basilian order; from then the archimandrite also served as superior general of the order in Transcarpathia. The monastery's school and library played important roles in the cultural and religious life of the region; A. *Kralytsky, a hegumen of the monastery, was one of the most prominent Transcarpathian writers of the 19th century. The monk's cells and refectory were constructed in 1766–72 in place of an earlier wooden structure. The large

St Nicholas's Church was built in 1798–1804 in a classical style. It is rectangular and has a single apse and bell tower.

The bishop's residence was transferred to Mukachiv in 1751, but the monastery remained the administrative center for the Basilians. During the 1920s the order was thoroughly reformed. An active missionary program was begun, and a press was established at the monastery to publish religious books and journals. After the Soviet occupation of Transcarpathia the monastery was handed over to the Russian Orthodox church, and the monks, all of whom refused to covert, were exiled. At the same time the monastery's valuable collection of over 6,000 rare books and manuscripts and its archives were transferred to local museums and archives. It now houses a community of nuns.

Mukha rebellion. One of the first popular rebellions against the oppressive rule of Polish magnates. Named after its leader Petro Mukha, the revolt erupted in Pokutia in 1490 and soon spread throughout most of southeastern Galicia. It was supported by the Moldavian voivode Stephan. The 10,000-man rebel army (mostly Ukrainian and Moldavian peasants, but also burghers and Orthodox petty nobles from Pokutia) took the fortified towns of Sniatyn, Kolomyia, and Halych and killed many Polish nobles and burghers. Their advance on Lviv was halted by a combined force of the Galician magnates' levy en masse, a Polish royal army, and Prussian mercenaries. Many of the rebels died in battle near Rohatyn, and Mukha and the survivors fled to Moldavia. In 1492 Mukha returned to Galicia to revive the rebellion. He was captured near Kolomyia, and died, according to one account, in a Cracow prison. V. Hrabovetsky's book about the rebellion was published in Kiev in 1979.

Mukhavets River [Muxavec']. A right-bank tributary of the Buh River, which it joins near Brest. It is 130 km long and drains a basin area of 6,200 sq km. The river flows through Polisia, in Brest oblast. It is navigable and forms part of the Dnieper-Buh Canal–Pyna-Prypiat waterway. The city of Kobryn is situated on its banks.

Mykhailo Mukhyn

Mukhyn, Mykhailo [Muxyn, Myxajlo], b 1894 in Kiev, d 7 September 1974 in Altan, Germany. Literary scholar and publicist. After the First World War he emigrated to Prague, and after the Second World War, to Germany. He was a regular contributor to *Samostiina dumka* (Chernivtsi) and D. Dontsov's *Vistnyk. Among his major works are

critiques of M. Drahomanov's ideas (eg, 'Drahomanov bez masky' [Drahomanov without a Mask], *Vistnyk*, 1934) and essays on Ukraine in contemporary Polish, Russian, and French literature (*Knyholiub*, 1927–32).

Mykola (Bohdan) Mukhyn: *Zaporozhian Cossack*

Mukhyn, Mykola (Bohdan) [Muxyn], b 24 May 1916 in Zaitseve, Bakhmut county, Katerynoslav gubernia, d 8 May 1962 in Philadelphia. Sculptor; brother of V. *Mukhyn. In the 1930s he studied at the Kharkiv, Odessa, and Kiev art institutes. During the 1941–4 German occupation he headed the department of sculpture at the Lviv Art School. A postwar refugee in Germany, in 1949 he emigrated to the United States. Mukhyn worked in various techniques and materials (wax, stone, plaster, silver, and bronze). In a Romantic impressionist style he depicted historical figures (eg, *Prince Ihor, Drinking Cossack, Otaman, Glory, Chumaks in the Steppe*) and female figures (*Nude, Praying Woman*, and *Night*). His works were exhibited in Moscow, Leningrad, Lviv, New York, and Philadelphia.

Mukhyn, Viktor [Muxyn], b 28 September 1914 in Zaitseve, Bakhmut county, Katerynoslav gubernia, d 9 February 1977 in Voroshylovhrad (Luhanske). Sculptor; brother of M.(B.) *Mukhyn. He began his studies at the Kharkiv Art Institute (1931–2) and completed them at the Kiev State Art Institute (1938). He sculpted many Soviet monuments, such as those to fallen Soviet soldiers in Voroshylovhrad (1944) and Kadiivka (1946); portraits (eg, *P. Tchaikovsky*); and female figures (eg, *Woman with An Ear of Grain*). An exhibition catalog of his works was published in 1968.

Müller, Gerhard Friedrich, b 29 October 1705 in Herford, Westphalia, d 22 October 1783 in Moscow. German and Russian historian and archeographer. A graduate of Leipzig University, from 1725 he lived in St Petersburg, where he worked as a gymnasium teacher and adjunct of the Imperial Academy of Sciences, edited *Sankt-Peterburgskiia vedomosti*, and was a history professor at the academy from 1731. After exploring Siberia (1733–43) he was appointed the imperial academy's historiographer (1748) and conference secretary (1754). From 1766 he directed the Moscow Archive of the Russian College of Foreign Affairs. Müller wrote many works on the history, archeology, and ethnography of Russia, Siberia, and Ukraine and compiled *Sammlung russischer Geschichte* (9 vols, 1732–65). Among his works are articles in *Ezhemesiachnyia sochineniia, k pol'ze i uveseleniiu sluzhashchiia* on the beginnings and origins of the Cossacks (1760) and what is known about the Zaporozhian Cossacks (1760) and the first detailed account of the Little Russian people and the Zaporizhia (1775–6). Some of his manuscripts were later published by O. Bodiansky in *Chteniia v Imperatorskom obshchestve istorii i drevnostei rossiiskikh* in 1846–8 and separately as *Istoricheskiia sochineniia o Malorossii i malorossiianakh* (Historical Works about Little Russia and the Little Russians, 1847). In his 1749 doctoral lecture at the imperial academy on the origin of the Russian people and their name, Müller first advocated the *Norman theory of the origin of Rus'. It met with indignation and harsh criticism and was banned from publication. It was eventually published abroad as 'Origines Rossicae' in *Allgemeine historische Bibliothek* (vol 4, 1768). J.L. Black's *G.F. Müller and the Imperial Russian Academy* was published in Montreal in 1986.

A. Zhukovsky

Multicylindrical-Pottery culture. A Bronze Age culture that existed primarily along the Dnieper and the major rivers of Left-Bank Ukraine in the 16th to 15th century BC. Although remains of this culture had been discovered by the turn of the century, it was considered a late phase of the *Catacomb culture until the 1950s, when excavations at Babyne III and Volyntseve led to the conclusion that it was actually a distinct successor culture. The culture's trademark was biconical pottery decorated with cylindrical strips of clay in rings or geometric patterns (usually treelike or triangular). Research at sites revealed semi-pit and surface dwellings and indications of cattle-raising, agriculture, and fishing. Remains of flints arrowheads, bronze knives, bone items, and querns were also found. Burials were commonly in kurhans, with the deceased placed in a flexed position. Common grave goods included pottery and flint and bronze implements.

Mumm von Schwarzenstein, Philip Alfons, b 19 March 1859 in Frankfurt, d 1924. German diplomat. Having been educated in law and previously posted in London, Tokyo, Washington, and other locations, he was sent to Ukraine in 1918 following its occupation by the Central Powers. Although immediately concerned with the orderly procurement of foodstuffs for Germany, he also contributed to the establishment of Ukraine as a viable client state. He became involved in the overthrow of the *Central Rada by P. *Skoropadsky, attempted to persuade the *Hetman government to moderate its ultraconservative character and pro-Russian leadership by adopting more liberal policies and including more Ukrainophiles in the cabinet, and engineered diplomatic gestures, such as the visit by Skoropadsky to William II, to provide the fledgling Hetman government with a greater political profile. His closest associate in those undertakings was W. *Groener, the German military chief of staff in Ukraine.

MUN. See Young Ukrainian Nationalists.

SS Peter and Paul Ukrainian Catholic Church in Mundare

Mundare. A town in Alberta originally named Beaverlake, situated approx 70 km east of Edmonton. Most of its inhabitants are of Ukrainian origin. In 1902 the first Basilian missionary station, which included four Sisters Servants of Mary Immaculate, was established there under the leadership of Rev P. Filias. The present monastery was built by Rev N. Kryzhanovsky in 1923. It houses the Basilian novitiate, press, and school. Until 1948 Mundare was the seat of the Basilian protohegumen for Canada and the United States. The Sisters Servants likewise established a novitiate and operated a school, orphanage, and hospital. The town is the chief Ukrainian Catholic pilgrimage site in Canada. The monastery's library has over 20,000 volumes. Its museum and archive (est 1957) contains valuable collections of old Ukrainian manuscripts and incunabulae (much of it collected by Rev J. *Jean), such as the Ostrih Bible, old maps of Ukraine, rare stamps, old coins and bank notes, medals, pioneer implements, and samples of Ukrainian folk arts and crafts.

Munich (German: München). The capital of the German state of Bavaria (1989 pop 1,211,617). Prior to 1914 a number of Ukrainians studied at the arts academy, including D. Horniatkevych, M. Ivasiuk, E. Lipetsky, O. Murashko, Yu. Narbut, M. Parashchuk, M. Sosenko, and I. Trush. Parashchuk lived in the city in 1909–15 and founded the Ukrainian Art Society there. Metropolitan A. Sheptytsky studied at Munich University in 1889–90, as did R. Smal-Stotsky (PH D, 1914). V. Orenchuk headed the UNR consulate in 1918–23. After 1940 many Ukrainians arrived in Munich to study, and after June 1941 many were brought as forced laborers (*Ostarbeiter) to work in heavy industry.

Munich. Clockwise, from top left: the residence of the apostolic exarch, the mosaic behind the altar in the Ukrainian Catholic cathedral, the parish center, the cathedral, the Ukrainian Free University, and the Ukrainian student residence

At that time a Ukrainian Catholic parish was established, as was the students' society Baturyn.

In the immediate postwar period Munich became the largest center of Ukrainian life in Western Europe. In 1945–9 there were approx 15,000 to 20,000 Ukrainians living in the city and its immediate environs, mainly in *displaced persons' camps. Over 2,000 were enrolled either in German schools or in Ukrainian educational institutions that had been moved to or established there, including the *Ukrainian Free University (UVU), the Ukrainian Technical and Husbandry Institute (UTHI), the *Ukrainian Higher School of Economics, and the Ukrainian Orthodox Theological Academy. The *Shevchenko Scientific Society (NTSh) and the *Ukrainian Academy of Arts and Sciences (UVAN) were re-established in the city during this time, and three Ukrainian gymnasiums and a teachers' college were active. The city also served as the major center of Ukrainian émigré political life in Western Europe (notably the external units of the OUN – OUN leaders S. Bandera and L. Rebet were assassinated there by a KGB agent) and the headquarters of the *Ukrainian National Council. Publishing activity was extensive, particularly in the immediate postwar period, when 74 newspaper and journal titles were issued there.

Munich also developed into a major center of Ukrainian academic and intellectual life. Its three major Ukrainian scholarly institutions (UVU, UTHI, and NTSh) established the Society for the Advancement of Ukrainian Scholarship (in 1962), which has published the *Jahrbuch der Ukrainekunde* since 1965. Ukrainian language courses were taught briefly at the University of Munich in 1914 and 1920 by J. Berkener and have been part of the curriculum since 1945, taught by H. Nakonechna (1945–65), B. Mykytiuk (1965–73), M. Antokhii (1973–88), and N. Pliushch (since 1988). Yu. Boiko taught courses in the history of Ukrainian literature (1962–88). The *Institute for the Study of the USSR was active in 1950–72, and produced a variety of studies about Ukraine. The flagship publication of the Ukrainian émigrés in the West, *Suchasnist'*, was issued in the city in 1961–90. *Radio Liberty, established in 1953, transmits a daily Ukrainian program and prepares regular research reports about current events in Ukraine.

A mass exodus of Ukrainians from Munich began in 1948, and now (1988) only a community of approx 1,000 remains. Nevertheless, Munich continues to be an important Ukrainian organizational center. Groups found there include the *Central Representation of the Ukrainian Emigration in Germany, the Ukrainian Medical and Charitable Service, the Ukrainian Women's Alliance, societies of former Ukrainian political prisoners in Germany, the Ukrainian Christian Workers' Movement, the Ridna Shkola Society (which runs a students' residence), the

Union of Ukrainian Veterans, the Association of Ukrainian Combatants, the Union of Ukrainian War Invalids, the Union of Ukrainian Students in Germany, and branches of the Plast Ukrainian Youth Association and the Ukrainian Youth Association (SUM). The *Anti-Bolshevik Bloc of Nations is also centered there.

The current Ukrainian press includes the weeklies *Khrystyians'kyi holos* and *Shliakh peremohy* and the monthly ABN-*Korrespondenz*. Local publishing and printing houses include Suchasnist, Ukrainske Vydavnytstvo, Molode Zhyttia, Logos, Cicero, and P. Belei's academic publishing house.

Artists who have resided in Munich include S. Burachok, H. Kruk, M. Moroz, L. Kachurovska, V. Sazonov, and V. Strelnikov. Writers who have lived there include E. Andiievska, O. Hrytsai, and L. Semaka.

BIBLIOGRAPHY

Prokoptschuk, G. (ed). *Ukrainer in München und in der Bundesrepublik*, 2 vols, (Munich 1958–9)

M. Antokhii, H. Prokopchuk

Munich Agreement. A settlement of the crisis over Czechoslovakia, signed by Britain, France, Germany, and Italy on 29 September 1938, commonly regarded as the culmination of the Western democracies' policy of appeasement of the Nazis. It ceded the Czechoslovak territory of the Sudetenland to Germany and provided for frontier adjustments for Poland and Hungary at the expense of Czechoslovakia. The four powers then guaranteed the rump of Czechoslovakia against unprovoked aggression. The agreement precipitated an internal crisis which enabled Slovakia to achieve autonomy within Czechoslovakia on 8 October 1938, a status demanded by and granted to Ukrainian Transcarpathia on 11 October. The frontier adjustments promised in the agreement were regulated by the *Vienna Arbitration of 2 November 1938.

Municipal government. A unit of local government that administers the affairs of an urban area. (For its history before the 19th century see *Cities and towns, *Magdeburg law, *Magistrat, *Burmister, *Viit, and *Ratusha.)

Russian-ruled Ukraine. With the abolition of Magdeburg law in 1831 (1835 in Kiev), the municipal self-government was severely limited in Ukraine. Although the most important city bodies continued to be elected, the interference of centrally appointed governors in city affairs increased sharply. Eventually city administration became totally subservient to the imperial government. In general the governors sought to replace traditional Ukrainian forms of municipal government with Russian ones. In the second half of the 19th century, thanks to the influence of liberal ideas from the West, municipal self-government was introduced in St Petersburg and then in Odessa (1864). A municipal code for the entire empire was adopted in 1870 and began to be introduced in Ukraine in 1875. It established the city council or duma as the highest organ of municipal government. Council members were elected for four years on the basis of a limited franchise: the vote was restricted to city residents, dwellers who owned real estate or a business in the city and paid municipal taxes. The voters were divided into three categories, and the wealthiest had the greatest voice. Jews had only a limited franchise, and in Kiev they were completely disen-

franchised. The executive arm of the council was the municipal board, which was composed of a chairman and two to six members, depending on the size of the city. The board's responsibilities included administering municipal proper-ties, providing health care and public education, and regulating trade and industry in the city. State authorities only made sure that the municipal officials complied with the law. A new law in 1892 limited the number of voters (by excluding small tradesmen and merchants) and increased the state's review powers over the local administration.

During the revolutionary period (1917–20) municipal government in Ukraine was greatly democratized. City councils and boards were elected by all adult city residents. The Provisional Government and the Ukrainian national governments generally refrained from interfering in municipal affairs, although occasionally they dissolved city councils that were controlled by the enemy.

Western Ukraine. Before the introduction of the 1881 Constitution in Austria-Hungary, municipal self-government in Galicia and Bukovyna was limited. Only in 1862 was a unified system of municipal self-government established throughout the empire, and old local privileges abolished. Further improvements in the system were made by the Galician Diet in 1866, 1889, and 1896. The city council, elected under a curial electoral system, was the highest governing body. Its executive branch was the *magistrat*, which consisted of the *burmister*, his deputy, and delegates from the city council. The municipal government was responsibile for municipal services, finances, police, and for responding to social problems. Some of these responsibilities belonged to the cities by law and came under their exclusive jurisdiction; others were assigned to them by the state. For carrying out the latter duties, city authorities were responsible to the county *starostas or county boards.

The Austrian system of municipal government was retained by the Polish state in the interwar period, except that universal suffrage was introduced by the decrees of 1918 and 1927. In territories that had been under Russian rule up to 1918 the law on cities of February 1919 established a municipal system similar to Galicia's. The administration of the larger cities came under the supervision of the voivodeship authorities; the smaller cities came under the county authorities. These authorities could intervene in municipal affairs, annul local decisions, change the composition of municipal organs, and even dissolve city councils. The law of 23 March 1933 established a uniform system of municipal government: city councils were enlarged to 12 to 72 members (depending on the size of the city) elected by an electoral college (not by direct voting), and the powers of the *burmister* were increased. Moreover, municipalities with fewer than 3,000 inhabitants lost their rights to self-government. Like the *curial system under the Habsburgs the electoral colleges severely restricted Ukrainian participation in municipal affairs.

In Transcarpathia under Hungarian rule the system of municipal government was similar to that in the Austrian-controlled territories, although major changes were introduced in 1886. In particular the central government exerted greater control over cities, and notaries public, who were civil servants, served as municipal secretaries. In general this system was retained in Czechoslovakia, except that general universal suffrage was introduced. The organs of municipal government were the city council (elected for four years), the *magistrat*, city notaries, and the elected head of the city, known as the starosta. In Bukovyna under Rumanian rule cities lost much of their autonomy to the central government.

Ukrainian SSR. In the Soviet system municipal governments came under the authority of the state apparatus, which was organized according to the principle of democratic centralism. The structure of local governments was regulated by statutes on city councils, which, according to the constitution, were passed by the republican governments. The local soviet of people's deputies with its executive committee was the highest organ of municipal self-government. The deputies were elected through direct balloting for two and a half years. They were nominated by civic organizations, or more precisely, by the Party. The soviet held at least six sessions a year and was responsible for local affairs and for implementing the decisions of the oblast and republican soviets that pertain to the cities. In addition they were responsible for the activities of the lower soviets (eg, in specific city raions). The executive committee of each soviet had a large apparatus that functioned in tandem with the soviet's permanent commissions.

BIBLIOGRAPHY
Nemirovskii, A. *Reforma gorodskogo samoupravleniia* (St Petersburg 1912)
Terlets'kyi, V. (ed). *Mistsevi rady URSR* (Kiev 1970)
Taubman, W. *Governing Soviet Cities: Bureaucratic Politics and Urban Development in the USSR* (New York 1973)
                                                          A. Bilynsky

Municipal schools (*horozhanski shkoly*). Lower three-year and then four-year secondary schools in Transcarpathia. Graduates of municipal schools were admitted to teachers' colleges, to trade schools, and, after an admission examination, to gymnasiums. In 1938–9 there were 23 Ukrainian municipal schools, with an enrollment of 6,485, in Transcarpathia and 2 municipal schools in the Prešov region.

Municipal services. A set of services under the control of municipal councils that meet the material and social needs of residents of a given city or town, including public housing, public transit, road maintenance, garbage collection and sewage, street lighting, water, gas, and power supply, policing, and fire protection. In the West some of those services are provided by public utilities. In the former USSR many municipal services were run jointly by municipal departments and republican or Union ministries. In the smaller towns some of the services (eg, water supply) were not under local control. In 1991, 436 cities and 925 towns (smt) in Ukraine, with a total of 35 million residents (67.6 percent of the total population), provided such services, and about 806,000 people were employed in them.

Public housing is one of the main departments of municipal administration. Municipalities control about an eighth of Ukraine's housing fund. The total fund of urban housing for 1940–90 is given in the table. In 1991 only 36.7 percent (or 210.5 million sq m) of the urban housing fund was under the control of municipal councils. The rest belonged to enterprises and ministry organizations (25.6 percent), housing co-operatives (6.2 percent), and individuals (31.1 percent). Not all of the housing stock is equipped with standard utilities, but public housing is better equipped than co-operative or private housing. In 1990, 95.1 percent of public housing had running water, 94.4 had sewage, 89.8 had central heating, 90.3 had a bath or shower, and 92.9 was supplied with gas. There is an acute housing shortage in Ukraine: about one-fifth of the urban residents are inadequately housed.

Urban housing fund in Ukraine (in million sq m), 1940–90

	1940	1960	1970	1980	1990
Residential units	97.0	203.7	313.1	440.7	574.3
Average sq m/person	6.7	9.9	12.1	14.2	16.5

Practically all cities and towns in Ukraine are supplied with natural gas. In 1990, 431 cities and 902 towns were supplied with natural gas either by pipeline or by tank (liquefied gas). In these municipalities 7,125,000 living units (apartments or houses) used piped-in gas, and 2,932,000 units used liquefied gas. In 1990 private consumption used 4 billion cu m of natural and 19,000 t of liquefied gas.

In 1990, 434 cities and 803 towns in Ukraine were equipped with a water-supply system. The total length of the network was 21,410 km, of which 20,438 km belonged to cities. About 54 percent of the network was controlled by municipal authorities; the rest came under republican or Union ministries. In 1989, 1,416 million cu m of water were consumed by urban residents. (See also *Water management.)

By 1990, 308 cities and 431 towns had sewage systems. The length of the sewage network in the cities and towns was 9,553,000 km. The total sewage-processing capacity of the network was 13,174,000 cu m per day.

For public transportation in cities and towns see *Urban transit and for power consumption see *Electric power.
                                                          A. Revenko

Münster, Sebastian, b 1489 in Ingelheim, Germany, d 23 May 1552 in Basel, Switzerland. Hebrew scholar, mathematician, cartographer, and cosmographer. His *Cosmographia* (1544) was the first German description of the world and a major contribution to the development of geography in Europe. In the fourth volume of the work he describes western Ukraine, including Galicia and Right-Bank Ukraine, which he calls Ruthenia, and clearly distinguishes it from Muscovy. He also compiled a Latin-Greek-Hebrew dictionary entitled *Dictionarium trilingue* (1530) and prepared *Mappa Europae* (1536).

MUR (Mystetskyi ukrainskyi rukh [The Artistic Ukrainian Movement]). An artistic-literary organization of Ukrainian émigrés in Europe. It was founded on 25 September 1945 in Fürth, Germany, on the initiative of a committee consisting of I. Bahriany, V. Domontovych (Petrov), Yu. Kosach, I. Kostetsky, I. Maistrenko, and Yu. Sherekh (Shevelov). MUR organized three writers' congresses (1945, 1947, and 1948) as well as three conferences devoted to various aspects of literary activity (28–29 January 1946, general theory; 4–5 October 1946, criticism; and 5–6 November 1947, drama). The head of the organization for its duration was U. *Samchuk, and its membership (both full and candidate members) numbered 61.

The objectives of MUR were to gather Ukrainian writers scattered by the Second World War, to organize the pub-

Title page of the MUR almanac

lication of their works, and to become a center, within a comprehensive national ideology, for creative dialogues among members representing various styles and literary aims. MUR played a positive role in that it managed to organize almost all of the noted émigré writers and provide them with a forum for discussion while it stimulated an interest in literature among the public at large. But despite various attempts during the difficult times in postwar Germany, MUR did not succeed at establishing its own printing house or a permanent journal, nor was it really successful in transforming into a united body the writers of various ideologies and disparate Ukrainian backgrounds. Although there were plans to continue the organization in the New World (see *Slovo Association of Ukrainian Writers in Exile), with Samchuk's departure for Canada in 1948 the organization, for all practical purposes, ceased to exist.

Despite its inability to establish a printing house, MUR published three miscellanies (MUR Zbirnyk I, April 1946; MUR Zbirnyk II, September 1946; MUR Zbirnyk III, early 1947), one almanac (MUR Al'manakh, late 1946), and several editions of the series Mala biblioteka MUR-u. It also formed its own publishing firm, Zolota Brama, whose name was used by many of the member authors to show sponsorship of MUR. Some books of Bahriany, V. Barka, Domontovych, D. Humenna, Yu. Klen, Kosach, Kostetsky, B. Kravtsiv, T. Osmachka, Samchuk, Ya. Slavutych, S. Parfanovych, and other writers appeared with that imprint.

BIBLIOGRAPHY
Sherekh, Iu. 'Ukraïns'ka emigratsiina literatura v Evropi 1945–1949,' in Iu. Sherekh, Ne dlia ditei (Munich 1964)
Kostiuk, H. Z litopysu literaturnoho zhyttia v diiaspori (Munich 1971)
Samchuk, U. Plianeta Di–Pi (Winnipeg 1979)
Struk, D.H. 'Organizational Aspects of D.P. Literary Activity,' in The Refugee Experience: Ukrainian Displaced Persons after World War II, ed W. Isajiw et al (Edmonton 1992)
                                        G.Y. Shevelov, D.H. Struk

Murafa River. A left-bank tributary of the Dniester River, which it joins at Yampil. It is 163 km long and drains a basin area of 2,410 sq km. The river flows through Vinnytsia oblast. Its largest tributaries are the Murashka and the Lozova rivers. It is used for water supply and irrigation.

Mural. A large-scale artistic work created as a permanent part of an architectural structure with the use of media such as buon fresco or fresco secco, mosaic, egg tempera, or various glue, oil, or polymer paints.

The earliest existing examples of murals in Ukraine are fragments of *fresco paintings from the Greek colonies on the northern Black Sea coast. *Mosaics and frescoes were used in the mural decorations of churches in Kievan Rus'.

The most spectacular and complete extant mural cycles from that period are found in the *St Sophia Cathedral in Kiev. Most of the major mosaics there have been preserved, including the grand, 5.45-m Orante, in the apse, and the Deesis, in the main dome. Apart from the fine mosaic the Eucharist and fresco renderings of the sacrifice of Abraham, and of numerous saints, St Sophia also houses fresco portraits of the family of Grand Prince Yaroslav the Wise and numerous secular subjects (hunting scenes, court musicians, and jesters).

Though the murals of Kievan Rus' were strongly influenced by *Byzantine art, they chronicle the development of an indigenous style. By the 13th century frescoes had replaced mosaics as the preferred media in mural decoration. The preserved fresco cycles of the *Armenian Cathedral in Lviv (14th century) attest to stylistic changes in mural painting based on a synthesis of Byzantine and Western art.

By the 17th century the use of fresco in mural painting had markedly declined. Examples of frescoes from this period have been preserved in Kiev, in the Church of the Transfiguration in the Berestove district (1644–6). Many mural cycles from this period were painted with egg tempera on gesso, which was applied directly to the wooden structure of the church. The murals of the *Potelych Church of the Holy Ghost (1620) and the Church of the Elevation of the Cross in Drohobych (ca 1636) differ greatly in style from those in the Kievan Church of the Transfiguration. Whereas in the latter naturalistic renderings show Renaissance influences, in the Drohobych and Potelych churches the linear murals show the influence of indigenous folk-art styles.

From the late 17th century a new Kievan school of monumental painting flourished. By the third decade of the 18th century, when this school reached its apex, many churches in Kiev, Chernihiv, Poltava, and Pereiaslav had been decorated by its members. Of the Cossack baroque murals of this period only those in the Holy Trinity Church above the main gate of the Kievan Cave Monastery have survived in good condition. They were painted in the 1720s and 1730s by artists with a solid knowledge of illusionistic figurative methods, who adapted standard Western baroque methods of depicting space and modeling form to conform to more Byzantine standards, and depicted figures with fully modeled heads and hands who are clothed in heavily gilded, ornamented, and flattened robes.

This tension between foreign art and indigenous traditions became a central problem during the revival of large-scale fresco painting in the 20th century. In the 1900s and 1910s the prominent mural painters were S. *Vasylkivsky and M. *Samokysh in Russian-ruled Ukraine and M. *Sosenko in Galicia. In Soviet Ukraine in the 1920s, M. *Boichuk and his students (including O. *Pavlenko, I. *Padalka, V. *Sedliar, M. *Rokytsky, K. *Hvozdyk, and M. *Shekhtman) at the Workshop of Monumental Painting in the Kiev State Art Institute worked to revive traditional mural painting as well as to synthesize modern formalist ideas with indigenous folk and icon traditions. These art-

MURALS AND MOSAICS 1) V. Marchak: *Fairy Tales* (tempera, 1985; Palace of Young Pioneers, Lviv). 2) An Angel Rolling up Heaven (12th century; fresco, St Cyril's Church, Kiev). 3) O. Dubovyk: *Feast of Knowledge* (mosaic, 1984; Crystal Factory, Kiev). 4) M. Levytsky: *Holy Eucharist* (apse mural, 1979–80; St Andrew's Church, Lidcombe, Australia). 5) The Apostles (12th century; detail from the mosaic of the Holy Eucharist, St Michael's Golden-Domed Cathedral, Kiev). 6) The Pantocrator and Archangels (11th century; main cupola mosaic, St Sophia Cathedral, Kiev). 7) S. Kyrychenko and N. Klein: *Harvest* (mosaic, 1957). 8) O. Kyrychenko: *Folk Art* (mosaic, 1980; village of Lysianka). 9) V. Pasyvenko and V. Priadka: *Tryvoha* (Alarm), detail from *Pain of the Earth* (cold encaustic, 1986–9).

sts composed numerous murals for various public buildings (see *Fresco painting). Apart from the 'Boichukists,' V. *Yermilov, L. *Kramarenko, M. *Pavliuk, and H. Dovzhenko extensively worked on murals combining indigenous and modernist styles. After the imposition of socialist-realist dicta in the 1930s, most of these works were destroyed.

The new stylistic imperatives of socialist realism encourage the creation of propagandistic forms of large-scale mural art. Works such as the ceiling in the vestibule of the Supreme Soviet in Kiev (1936–41, by V. and B. Shcherbakov), which drew on the grandiose decorative traditions of baroque painting, became popular. Apart from works apotheosizing the communist state, many monumental works with more mundane subjects, such as *Mother Nursing Her Child* (by V. Ovchynnykov) and *Harvest* (by S. *Kyrychenko and N. Klein, 1957), were commissioned for public buildings.

Outside Soviet Ukraine most mural painting has been done in churches. In interwar Galicia P. *Kholodny, Sr, M. *Osinchuk, P. *Kovzhun, and Yu. *Mahalevsky painted neo-Byzantine murals using traditional tempera techniques. In Transcarpathia, church murals were executed by Yu. *Virah, I. *Roshkovych, and Y. *Bokshai. Emigré artists who have worked in the large-scale format include P. *Kholodny, Jr, M. *Dmytrenko, G. *Kozak, M. *Levytsky, I. *Dyky, R. Kowal, and S. *Hordynsky. One of the best examples of mural decorations in Ukrainian émigré art is Hordynsky's mosaics in the St Sophia Cathedral in Rome.

BIBLIOGRAPHY
Kholotenko, Ie. *Monumental'ne maliarstvo Radians'koï Ukraïny* (Kiev 1932)
Lobanovs'kyi, B. *Mozaïka i freska* (Kiev 1966)
Bazhan, M.; et al (eds). *Istoriia ukraïns'koho mystetstva*, 6 vols (Kiev 1966–70)
Garkusha, N.; et al. *Monumental'noe i dekorativnoe iskusstvo v arkhitekture Ukrainy* (Kiev 1975)
Zholtovs'kyi, P. *Monumental'nyi zhyvopys na Ukraïni XVII–XVIII st.* (Kiev 1988)

N. Mykytyn

Rev Mykola Muranii

Mykola Murashko: *Self-Portrait* (lithograph, 1868)

Muranii, Mykola [Muranij], b 11 May 1911 in Berezove, Transcarpathia, d 12 January 1979 in Uzhhorod. Catholic priest. He completed his studies in Strasbourg and returned to Uzhhorod to become the bishop's personal secretary. He was general vicar of Mukachiv eparchy when the Soviets occupied Transcarpathia in 1945. In 1947, after Bishop T. Romzha was murdered, Muranii was elected as eparchial administrator. In 1949, after extensive interrogations, he was arrested and sentenced to 25 years in a labor camp. He was amnestied in 1956 after Stalin's death but rearrested early in 1957. After serving eight months of a new 10-year sentence, he was again released. He returned to Uzhhorod, where he continued as administrator of the underground Mukachiv eparchy until his death.

Murashko, Andrii [Muraško, Andrij], b ? in the Liubech region, d 1674. Cossack officer. In 1658 he became colonel of Chausy regiment in Belarus, and later, colonel of a volunteer regiment under Hetmans D. Mnohohrishny and I. Samoilovych. He was captured and killed by the Turks after an unsuccessful defense of Ladyzhyn.

Murashko, Mykola [Muraško], b 20 May 1844 in Hlukhiv, Chernihiv gubernia, d 22 September 1909 in Bucha, near Kiev. Painter, graphic artist, and pedagogue. After graduating from the St Petersburg Academy of Arts (1868) he worked in Kiev as a secondary-school art teacher and in 1875 founded the influential *Kiev Drawing School, which he ran until 1901. As an art critic he defended the realist tradition of the *Peredvizhniki and rejected modernism. His paintings and drawings consist of landscapes (eg, *Autumn, Above the Dnieper, View of the Dnieper*) and portraits (*N. Ge*). He did a series of lithograph portraits, including ones of T. Shevchenko (1867) and P. Mohyla and a self-portrait (1868), and illustrated a Ukrainian edition of H.C. Andersen's tales (1873) and other books. At the end of his life he published his memoirs (3 vols, 1907–9; Ukrainian trans 1964). Yu. Turchenko's book about him was published in Kiev in 1956.

Mykola Murashko (1891–1949)

Murashko, Mykola [Muraško] (Muraszko, Nicholas), b 15 December 1891 in Sviate, Jarosław county, Galicia, d 3 August 1949 in New Brunswick, New Jersey. Community leader. He emigrated to the United States in 1907 and became active in Ukrainian organizations. For many years he served as president of the Ukrainian National Association (1929–49), and he was the first president of the Ukrainian Congress Committee of America (1940–4) in addition to working as a business manager for the newspapers *Svoboda* and *Ukrainian Weekly*. As vice-president of the United Ukrainian American Relief Committee (1947–9) he devoted much of his time to organizing relief for Ukrainian émigrés in Europe.

Oleksander Murashko: *Self-Portrait* (oil, 1918)

Murashko, Oleksander [Muraško], b 7 September 1875 in Kiev, d 14 June 1919 in Kiev. Painter. He studied at the Kiev Drawing School (1891–4), under I. *Repin at the St Petersburg Academy of Arts (1894–1900), and in Munich and Paris (1902–4). He belonged to the New Society of Artists in St Petersburg and participated in its annual exhibitions (1904–14). In 1907 he settled in Kiev, where he taught painting at the Kiev Art School (1909–12) and at his own studio (1912–17). In 1909 he exhibited his canvases in Paris, Munich, and Amsterdam, and in 1910 at the international exhibition in Venice and at one-man shows in Berlin, Köln, and Düsseldorf. From 1911 he exhibited with the Munich Sezession group. In 1916 he joined the *Peredvizhniki society and became a founding member of the Kiev Society of Artists. He was a cofounder of the *Ukrainian State Academy of Arts in 1917 and served there as a professor and rector. Murashko's style evolved from the realism of the Peredvizhniki school into a vivid, colorful impressionism. His paintings and portraits possess psychological depth. They include *Burial of a Kish Otaman* (1900), *Girl with a Red Hat* (1902–3), portraits of H. Tsyss (late 1890s), T. Yazera (1901–4), M. Murashko (1904), and J. Stanisławski (1906), *Day at Rest* (1911), *By the Pond* (1913), *Peasant Family* (1914), *Washerwoman* (1914), *Flower Sellers* (1917), and *Woman with Nasturtiums* (1918). Murashko established an international reputation and had a strong influence on the development of Ukrainian portrait painting in the 20th century. He was murdered in Kiev by unknown assailants.

BIBLIOGRAPHY
Kataloh posmertnoï vystavky kartyn prof. Ukraïns'koï akademiï mystetstv Oleksandra Oleksandrovycha Murashka (1875–1919), ed with intro by F. Ernst (Kiev 1923)
Shpakov, A. *Oleksandr Oleksandrovych Murashko* (Kiev 1959)
Chlenova, L. (ed). *Oleksandr Murashko* (Kiev 1980)

Murashko, Pavlo [Muraško], b 22 October 1939 in Prague. Scholar. He studied Ukrainian language and literature at the universities of Prešov and Prague, and received a PH D for his work on the life and works of O. Oles. He taught at the Ukrainian gymnasium in Prešov and served as an editor of *Duklia* (also in Prešov). He arranged the publication of a number of works of Ukrainian samvydav in the West, including *Ukraïns'kyi visnyk* and I. Dziuba's *Internatsionalizm chy rusyfikatsiia* (Internationalism or Russification), for which action he was arrested and imprisoned in 1972 for three years. After his release he remained in Czechoslovakia, working as a laborer and taking part in activities of the Charter 77 human-rights defense group. He compiled *Bibliohrafiia ukraïns'koï ta slov'ians'koï periodyky u praz'kii slov'ians'kii bibliotetsi* (Bibliography of Ukrainian and Slavic Periodicals in the Slavic Library of Prague, 1990) and has contributed to Ukrainian periodicals in Czechoslovakia.

Muratov, Ihor, b 29 July 1912 in Kharkiv, d 29 March 1973 in Kharkiv. Writer and playwright. His first published work appeared in 1925. In the 1950s he worked with the Return to the Homeland Committee in Berlin and was editor of its official propaganda organ, *Za povernennia na bat'kivshchynu.* He published a large number of collections of verse written in the official tone, including *Kosmohrafik* (Cosmographer, 1933), *Zahybel' syn'oï ptytsi* (Death of the Blue Bird, 1934), *Dvadtsiatyi polk* (The Twelfth Regiment, 1941), *Bytva za sontse* (The Struggle for the Sun, 1962), *Ochi* (The Eyes, 1962), and *Myt' i vichnist'* (A Moment and Eternity, 1973). Muratov's prose includes *Bukovyns'ka povist'* (Bukovynian Novelette, 1951), *Doroha do syna* (The Road to the Son, 1967), *Spovid' na vershyni* (Confession on the Summit, 1971), and the novel *U sorochtsi narodzhenyi* (Born in a Shirt, 1964). He also wrote plays and publicistic articles. A compilation of his works, *Tvory* (Works, 4 vols, 1982–3), was published posthumously.

Murava Road (Muravskyi shliakh). A principal trade and military route in 16th- to 18th-century Southern and Left-Bank Ukraine. Originating in Perekop in northern Crimea, it passed northeastward through southern Left-Bank Ukraine between the sources of the Molochni Vody and the Kinski Vody rivers, crossed the Vovchi Vody, the Samara, and the Orel rivers, and traversed Slobidska Ukraine by way of Kolomak, Valky, and Okhtyrka before entering Muscovy and ending in Tula. In the upper reaches of the Donets, the Oskil, the Vorskla, the Psol, and the Seim rivers the road merged with the *Izium Road. Much of the trade between the Crimean Khanate and Slobidska Ukraine and Muscovy was conducted along the road, and until the early 18th century it was used by the Crimean Tatars during their raids on Ukraine and Muscovy.

Muraveinyk-Komashnia (Anthill). A weekly organ of the Kiev Association of Credit Unions, published in Kiev in 1913–19. Initially it appeared in both Ukrainian and Russian, but official pressure in 1914–16 forced the publishers to use Russian only. After the Revolution of 1917 it appeared only in Ukrainian (as *Komashnia* and then as *Kooperatyvnyi kredyt [Komashnia]*). The paper published articles on developments in the *co-operative movement in Ukraine and abroad. Its editors were Kh. Baranovsky (1913–16), V. Melnykov, and, later, F. Matushevsky.

Muravev, Mikhail, b 25 September 1880 in Burdokovo, Kostroma gubernia, Russia, d 11 July 1918 in Simbirsk (now Ulianovsk). Russian military commander during the revolutionary period. He was an experienced colonel in the tsarist army, and he joined the Russian Socialist Revolutionary party in 1917. He went on to serve the new Soviet regime and was chosen by V. *Antonov-Ovsiienko to be field commander of the 1917–18 Bolshevik offensive into Ukraine. After quickly taking over Kharkiv and Poltava he advanced on Kiev with approx 4,000 men, most of them Russians. En route he encountered and destroyed a considerably smaller Ukrainian force at the Battle of *Kruty (29 January 1918). His occupation of Kiev on 9 February

918, after five days of fighting, was followed by orders or the mass execution of supporters of Ukrainian independence. Muravev was killed by Bolsheviks during an attempted Socialist Revolutionary coup d'état (some sources cite suicide).

Muravev-Apostol. A noble family in Poltava gubernia, descended on the female side from Hetman D. *Apostol. In 1801 the diplomat, senator, and writer Ivan Muravev (1765–1851), Apostol's grandson, was allowed to use the name Muravev-Apostol and to take over the Apostol estates in Myrhorod county. His sons, Matvei (1793–1886), Sergei (1796–1826), and Ippolit (1805–26), were involved in the *Decembrist movement. Matvei was exiled to Siberia, Sergei was hanged, and Ippolit shot himself during the revolt of the Chernihiv Regiment. The male side of the family disappeared at the end of the 19th century.

Muravev-Apostol, Sergei, b 9 October 1796 in St Petersburg, d 25 July 1826 in St Petersburg. Leader of the *Decembrist movement. A lieutenant colonel in the Russian army, he was one of the organizers of the clandestine *Union of Salvation and *Union of Welfare and headed the Vasylkiv council of the *Southern Society. He advocated centralizing the Decembrist forces, and in 1824–5 he conducted negotiations with the Polish Patriotic Society that led to the fusion of the Southern Society and the *Society of United Slavs. He was, however, hostile to the *Little Russian Secret Society. Muravev-Apostol compiled (together with M. Bestuzhev-Riumin) a revolutionary 'Orthodox catechism.' He led the revolt of the Chernihiv Regiment in January 1826 and was seriously wounded in a battle near Kovalivka, in Vasylkiv county, Kiev gubernia. He was imprisoned and hanged in the Peter and Paul Fortress in St Petersburg. A book about Muravev-Apostol by L. Medvedska was published in Kiev in 1961.

Muravin, Lev, b 5 November 1906 in Belgorod, Kursk gubernia, d 25 November 1974 in Moscow. Sculptor. A graduate of the Kharkiv Art Institute (1929), he later taught sculpture there (1940–3) and at the Kiev State Art Institute. From 1951 he worked in Moscow. He took part in creating the sculptures at the USSR pavilion at the 1939 New York World's Fair and did portraits of the academicians O. Bohomolets (1945) and A. Palladin (1946), a statue of Lesia Ukrainka (1947) in Lutske, and many statues of Soviet leaders.

Muraviov, Volodymyr [Muravjov], b 15 June 1885 in Kherson, d 23 May 1963 in Kiev. Plant pathologist; corresponding member of the AN URSR (now ANU) from 1951. A graduate of Kiev University (1910), he was director of the laboratories at the Myronivka Experimental Selection Station (1924–9) and the Ukrainian Scientific Research Institute of the Sugar Industry (1929–46) and then worked at the ANU Institute of Entomology and Phytopathology (as director in 1950–63). He was also a professor at the Maslivka Institute of Selection and Seed Cultivation (1925–31) and Kiev University (1932–5).

Muravsky, Pavlo [Muravs'kyj], b 30 July 1914 in Dmytrashkivka, Olhopil county, Podilia gubernia. Conductor and teacher. In 1941 he graduated from the Kiev Conservatory in the class of H. Taranov. He subsequently conducted the Dumka chorus (1941, 1946–8, and 1964–9) and was artistic director and main conductor of the *Trembita chorus in Lviv (1948–64). In 1949–55 he taught at the Lviv Conservatory and since 1969 has been a lecturer and professor at the Kiev Conservatory.

Murovani Kurylivtsi [Murovani Kurylivci]. V-8. A town smt (1990 pop 6,700) on the Zhvan River and a raion center in Vinnytsia oblast. It is first mentioned in historical documents in 1493. It was recognized as a town in 1775 and as an smt in 1956. Its chief industry is food processing. Some architectural monuments, among them an 18th-century palace and park and several 19th-century mansions, have been preserved.

Volodymyr Mursky

Mursky, Volodymyr [Murs'kyj], b 10 November 1888 in Lviv, d 19 July 1935 in Istanbul. Civic and political activist and publicist. A teacher by profession, he was deported from Galicia by Russian forces during the First World War. In the revolutionary period he was an adviser to the UNR Ministry of Foreign Affairs and director of the press and propaganda department. In 1921 he became a member of the Council of the Republic in Poland. After emigrating to Austria he served the UNR government-in-exile as its envoy to Turkey. In addition to journalistic articles in Ukrainian, Polish, and Turkish, he wrote two books on Ukraine in Turkish, as well as several translations.

Murzak-Koba. A Mesolithic settlement of the *Tardenoisian culture on the left bank of the Chorna River, Crimea. Excavations in 1936 and 1938 revealed a number of stone tools (cutters, scrapers), bone and horn items (needles), and animal bones (deer, boar, bear). The site is best known for the recovery of a burial in which the women's skeletal remains indicated that her phalangies (little fingers) had been severed.

Murzakevich, Nikolai [Murzakevič, Nikolaj], b 3 May 1806 in Smolensk, d 28 October 1883 in Odessa. Historian and archeologist of Belarusian descent. He studied in Smolensk and Moscow before becoming a professor of Russian history and director of the Richelieu Lyceum in Odessa. He was a founding member of the *Odessa Society of History and Antiquities, and he edited and contributed numerous articles to its *Zapiski.* His area of specialization was the archeology of Southern Ukraine.

Murzakevich's autobiography was published posthumously in 1886 and in the serial *Russkaia starina* (1887–9).

Murzhenko, Oleksii [Muržcenko, Oleksij], b 23 November 1942 in Kharkiv oblast. Dissident. In March 1962, while studying at the Moscow Institute of Finance, he was arrested for founding the Freedom of Thought student organization and sentenced to six years in the Vladimir prison near Moscow, and in labor camps in the Mordovian ASSR. After his release he lived in Lozova, Kharkiv oblast, where he was subjected to constant KGB harassment. In June 1970 he, Yu. Fedorov, and 10 Jewish dissidents (E. Kuznetsov, M. Dimshits, and others) were arrested for attempting to hijack a plane in Leningrad to Sweden. Murzhenko was sentenced to 14 years in special-regime labor camps in the Mordovian ASSR and Perm oblast. He was rearrested in June 1985 and sentenced to two years' imprisonment. Upon his release in 1987 he was allowed to emigrate to the West with his family.

Muscovy. See Russia.

Museology. See Museums.

Museum of Anthropology and Ethnology (Muzei antropolohii i etnolohii im. F. Vovka). An ethnographic museum established in 1921 by the VUAN in Kiev as an extension of the *Cabinet of Anthropology and Ethnology. F. *Vovk's collection, archives, and library, brought from Leningrad according to Vovk's will, formed the museum's core. Later the collection of the museum of the Ukrainian Scientific Society was added to its holdings. O. Alesho served as the museum's first director and was succeeded by A. Onyshchuk. In 1934 both the cabinet and the museum were closed down, and many of the workers were persecuted by the state.

Museum of Ethnography and Handicrafts. See Ukrainian State Museum of Ethnography and Crafts.

Museum of Historical Treasures of Ukraine (Muzei istorychnykh koshtovnostei Ukrainy). A state museum established in Kiev in 1969 as a branch of the *Historical Museum of the Ukrainian SSR (custodian, V. Bondar). Located on the grounds of the Kievan Cave Historical-Cultural Preserve, the museum is the major Ukrainian repository (approx 130,000 objects) of artifacts made from precious metals and stones by the *Scythians (20,000 gold objects, exhibited in three halls), ancient Slavs (one hall), Kievan Rus' artisans (one hall), 14th- to 19th-century Ukrainian goldsmiths (one hall), 17th- to 19th-century Russian jewelers (one hall), and modern Ukrainian jewelers (two halls). It also has a numismatic collection dating as far back as the 6th century BC and a collection of Russian and European medals. Several photo albums of the museum's Scythian objects have been published.

Museum of Kiev's History (Muzei istorii Kyieva). A museum opened in Kiev in May 1982 during the celebrations of Kiev's 1,500th anniversary. It is housed in 19 halls in the upper two stories of the former Klov Palace (designed by J. Schädel and built in 1756 by P. Neelov and S. Kovnir). About 8,000 exhibits dealing with Kiev's archeology, history, and current life, based on holdings of over 100,000 items, are on display. The museum sponsors the Experts on Kiev club (Kyievoznavtsi) and public lectures and supervises the rotunda in Kiev's Askoldova Mohyla Park, the Pecherske Gate in Independence Square (formerly October Revolution Square), a house in Kiev where Peter I stayed, and the Hryhorii Svitlytsky Memorial Museum. An illustrated guidebook to the museum was published in Russian in 1988, and the Experts on Kiev club has published numerous bibliographic guides to various aspects of the city's history and historiography.

Museum of Literature of Ukraine (Derzhavnyi muzei literatury Ukrainy). The main museum of literature in Ukraine. It was opened in Kiev in July 1986 in the building which once housed Galagan College. Over 35,000 books (including old, rare, and first editions), manuscripts, photographs, posters, newspapers, and writers' personal items are in its inventory; 5,000 of them are displayed in 15 rooms. Memorial corners for the writers P. Tychyna, M. Rylsky, Yu. Yanovsky, A. Malyshko, M. Bazhan, and Yu. Smolych have been created there.

Museum of Slobidska Ukraine (Muzei Slobidskoi Ukrainy im. H. Skovorody). A museum founded in Kharkiv in January 1920, on the premises of the former Kharkiv Museum of Art and Industry. With historical, fine art, and ethnographic divisions, as well as a library, the museum had an all-Ukrainian profile (despite its name) and was considered one of the finest in Ukraine. Its stated mandate was to study Ukrainian folkways, primarily of *Slobidska Ukraine, by collecting, restoring, and classifying its cultural artifacts. The museum focused particularly on Ukrainian architecture, tiled stoves, folk musical instruments, woodcraft, women's headdresses, embroidery, kilims, and guilds. After three years of difficult circumstances, including relocation, the confiscation of the artifacts in two of its divisions, and the death of its first director, M. *Sumtsov, the museum revived and began to renew its activity. The exhibits of its historical division were based on the collections of the former Museum of Fine Art and Antiquity at Kharkiv University, the Kharkiv Historical-Philological Society, and the Church Museum at the Kharkiv Eparchial Consistory, as well as on new acquisitions. They included maps, paintings, and photographs of 18th- and 19th-century Kharkiv, portraits of the hetmans and political activists of 18th-century Slobidska Ukraine, and memorabilia of Ukraine's literary giants. The fine art division received the estate of S. *Vasylkivsky, who originated the idea of a museum of Slobidska Ukraine in Kharkiv. Besides 500 of his own paintings, the collection included the works of I. Aivazovsky, M. Berkos, O. Kulchytska, S. Mako, L. Pozen, O. Sudomora, K. Trutovsky, M. Uvarov, and T. Shevchenko. The ethnographic division incorporated the holdings of the former Ethnographic Museum of the Kharkiv Historical-Philological Society, which had acquired the exhibits of the Twelfth Archeological Conference (Kharkiv, 1902). It was subdivided into seven groups, covering dwellings, dress, diet, measuring instruments, artisanship, art, and children's toys. The museum's most important collectors, researchers, and activists were M. Sumtsov, D. Zelenin, D. Bahalii, O. Nikolaiev, R. Dankovska, M. Riedin, Yu. Zelinsky, I. Yerofeiv, and M. Horban. The museum was closed down during the Stalinist terror of the 1930s. It was suceeded after the Second World War by the Kharkiv Historical Museum.

O. Maryniak

Museum of Sports Fame of Ukraine (Muzei sportyvnoi slavy Ukrainy). The first museum devoted solely to the history of physical education and sports in the Russian Empire and the USSR, opened in May 1970. Its exhibits (over 3,000) include photographs of the first USSR champions and record holders, of the opening of the Central Stadium in Kiev, and of the graduates of the first Institute of Physical Culture in Ukraine; portraits of all Soviet Olympic champions; the medals of the first All-Russian Olympiad in Kiev (1913); the first soccer Ukraine Cup; and prizes and medals won by Ukrainian athletes in Soviet, Olympic, and other international competitions.

Museum of the Book and Book Printing of Ukraine (Muzei knyhy i knyhodrukuvannia Ukrainy). A state museum established in Kiev in 1972 (International Year of the Book) and opened to the public in 1975. A precursor to the museum, the Museum of Ukrainian Writing and Printing, was founded in 1924 and shut down by the Stalinist authorities in 1934. It was housed in a former building of the Kievan Cave Monastery Press that was built in the early 17th century. The museum's 3,000 exhibits in five halls chronicle the development of book writing and printing in Ukraine. Facsimiles and original copies of rare medieval manuscripts, old printed books, and incunabula, examples of early and modern printing technology, first editions of 19th- and 20th-century Ukrainian books and other publications, and original book illustrations and bookplates are on display. An illustrated guidebook to the museum was published in 1981. A new exhibition of *bookplate art (over 1,000 works by more than 200 artists, including H. Narbut, O. Kulchytska, Ya. Muzyka, and S. Hebus-Baranetska) was opened in 1987.

Museum of Ukraine's Struggle for Independence: military exhibit, including pottery made by Ukrainian internees in the German POW camp in Rastatt

Museum of Ukraine's Struggle for Independence (Muzei vyzvolnoi borotby Ukrainy). A repository in Prague of books, artworks, artifacts, and archives of the 1917–21 struggle for Ukrainian independence voluntarily deposited by Ukrainian émigré figures and organizations. The museum was founded in 1925 by a group of Ukrainian war veterans and professors at the Ukrainian Free University. It was funded solely by donations, mostly from the United States (particularly by K. *Lysiuk), Canada, and the Ukrainian Bureau in London. The museum was owned by a society (140 members in 1943) headed by I. Horbachevsky (1925–35), S. Smal-Stotsky (1935–8), A. Yakovliv (1939–?), and D. Doroshenko (?–1945). Until 1945 the museum's director was D. *Antonovych, and the assistant director was S. *Narizhny. The museum had about 1 million items. They were exhibited in three and then six rented rooms and kept in three garages. A building to house the museum was bought only after enough money had been raised, in 1938. It opened in 1939.

The museum had invaluable archival holdings, including the archives of various UNR diplomatic missions, the *Union for the Liberation of Ukraine, the Ukrainian Sich Riflemen, Ukrainian POW camps in Germany during the First World War, Ukrainian internment camps in Poland and Czechoslovakia after the war, and the Ukrainian Republican Kapelle, literary manuscripts, and the correspondence of figures such as O. Barvinsky, M. Yevshan, B. Lepky, Ya. Vesolovsky, and Metropolitan V. Lypkivsky. It had an impressive art collection (paintings and over 1,400 engravings donated by émigré artists and collectors); sets of approx 1,200 Ukrainian periodicals; a Ukrainian numismatic and currency collection; a collection of Ukrainian military uniforms, weapons, army photos, documents, and reports; and a large library consisting of over 70 book collections (including those of Antonovych, A. Artymovych, V. Bidnov, S. Cherkasenko, B. Lepky, K. Matsiievych, I. Mirny, O. Kolessa, and Smal-Stotsky), antique maps of Ukraine, J.B. Homann's *Atlas Novus* (1716), and a collection of calendars. The museum published its own bulletin, *Visty*, irregularly in 1925–36 and then quarterly.

In February 1945 the museum was hit by an Allied bomb, and its offices and a large part of its holdings were destroyed. During the Soviet military occupation of Prague access to the remainder was restricted. From November 1945 the museum functioned minimally and was called the Ukrainian Museum. At that time its executive council was headed by Yu. Dobrylovsky and K. Zaklynsky, and its director was Narizhny. In March 1948 the Czechoslovak government closed down the museum and confiscated its remaining holdings. Part of the archive was taken to Moscow, and the rest was deposited in the state archive in Prague. The Slavonic Library in Prague received most of the museum's library holdings.

A. Zhukovsky

Museum of Ukrainian Culture in Svydnyk. See Svydnyk Museum of Ukrainian Culture.

Museums. Institutions for art objects, antiquities, and other cultural goods that have been divested of their sacred and functional qualities. In museums they serve the secondary purposes of preservation, classification, and education. Private collections are the most reliable sources for replenishing damaged or destroyed museum collections.

Ukraine before Soviet rule. In the period of Kievan Rus' valuable private collections belonged to the Kievan, Galician-Volhynian, and appanage princes. The only artifacts that could be seen by the general public were the artworks gracing cathedrals and monasteries and those held in sacristies. Many churches in Ukraine amassed large collections of artifacts. The sacristes of the St Sophia Cathedral, the Kievan Cave Monastery, the St Michael's Golden-Domed Monastery, and the Cathedral of the Transfiguration in Chernihiv are known to have contained priceless collections. Incursions by nomadic tribes and internecine fighting among the princes caused considerable damage to those holdings. Also, much was lost during the sacking of Kiev by Andrei Bogoliubskii in 1169. The greatest losses were sustained during the Mongol-Tatar invasions of the 13th century, which only individual artifacts survived. They are still being found in archeological excavations. Some are housed in Russian and other museums. The Lithuanian-Polish state-sponsored private collections suffered a similar fate. In the 14th to 17th centuries countless ornamented implements and artworks (probably similar to those of Western Europe) were assembled in the castles of magnates and on the estates of lords. Many of them were destroyed in the uprisings of the mid-17th century.

For subsequent times, lists of holdings in the collections of various palaces, including paintings, furniture, and decorative tableware, are extant. Diaries of Ukrainian Cossack officials also catalog their acquisition of jewelry and folk musical instruments. The renewed accumulation of artifacts was a reflection of the Ukrainian national and cultural revival in the 18th century. The most distinguished patron of the time was Hetman I. Mazepa.

Russian-ruled Ukraine. In the late 18th century a numismatic collection already existed at the Basilian school in Uman (eventually transferred to the Kremianets Lyceum). In 1809 an archeological collection was opened at the Hydrographic Bureau in Mykolaiv. Similar museums were opened in Teodosiia (1811), Odessa (1825), and Kerch (1826). Of them the Odessa Municipal Museum of Antiquities had the most valuable collection; it later became the first public museum in the Russian Empire. Formal schools of museology were established in the late 18th and early 19th century.

M. Berlynsky, K. Lokhvytsky, and M. Maksymovych were central figures in the development of museums in Kiev. The first to be established was the Archeological Museum at Kiev University (est 1835). Part of its exhibitions were formed from archeological digs conducted by Lokhvytsky, V. Antonovych, M. Ivanyshev, D. Samokvasov, O. Stavrovsky, and Ya. Voloshynsky; the collection of the archeological museum of the Higher Courses for Women was donated to it in 1916. The Numismatics Cabinet was opened in the university's library in 1835 (overseen by Antonovych in 1872–1908), with its exhibits drawn from the collections of the Kremianets and Vilnius lyceums.

The Kiev Society of Church Archeology at the Kiev Theological Academy organized a museum, headed by M. Petrov, with a large and valuable collection of artifacts (approx 20,000) in 1872. The collection included Palestinian and Cypriot treasures (gathered by Archimandrite A. Kapustin), Byzantine icons of the 4th to 15th centuries, particularly encaustic icons (Bishop P. Uspensky), eastern shrines (A. Muravev), and church relics (M. Leopardov). Similar societies in Chernihiv, Kamianets-Podilskyi, Poltava, and Zhytomyr founded treasuries of antiquities from the local eparchies.

Independent museums were organized in central Ukraine by various groups of enthusiasts, community institutions, and local administration officials. Among them were the Museum of the Odessa Society of History and Antiquities (founded in 1843, based on the municipal museum), the Yelysavethrad Museum at the Realschule (1883), the Historical Museum of the Chernihiv Scientific Archival Commission (1896), and the Volhynian Museum (1900, founded by the Volhynia Research Society). The Kiev Museum of Art and Industry was founded by the Kiev Society of Art and Antiquities in 1904, with the collections of O. Bobrynsky, K. Bolsunovsky, B. and V. Khanenko, S. Mazarka, M. Tarnovsky, and S. Znosko-Borovsky. The *Kiev Society for the Preservation of Ancient and Artistic Monuments (est 1910) was active throughout the central gubernias. As well, private collectors devoted considerable effort to establishing museums, including V. Tarnovsky in Chernihiv (the museum opened in 1901, with exhibits relating to the Cossack-Hetman state), O. Pol in Katerynoslav (1902, reorganized as a museum of Zaporozhian Cossack history by D. Yavornytsky), B. and V. Khanenko (1919, the *Kiev Museum of Western and Eastern Art), V. Babenko in Vovchanske (1911, artifacts from his archeological digs), and K. Skarzhynska in Lubni (folk art).

During that time many unique and valuable artifacts, including Scythian and ancient treasures, Cossack standards, and items from I. Zabelin's excavations, were transported en masse to imperial holdings in St Petersburg and Moscow.

Western Ukraine under Austrian rule. Exhibits were opened of the collections of the Lubomirski (1823) and Dzieduszycki (1871) families, and the first public archeological exhibition in Lviv was held in 1861. In the 1870s an endowment was established for the first Ukrainian museum at the *People's Home in Lviv, and it was formally opened in 1901. The Lviv Pharmacy Museum, located in the three-story premises of the original pharmacy (est 1735) on Rynok Square, is one of the city's oldest extant museums.

Priceless collections of icons, old manuscripts (see *Paleography), tapestries (see *Weaving), coins, archeological artifacts, and folk art were assembled by the Shevchenko Scientific Society (founded in 1873, its collection opened as an independent museum in 1914), the *Stauropegion Institute (founded in 1788, its collection opened as a museum in 1889), and the *National Museum in Lviv (reorganized in 1908 from the church museum of Metropolitan A. Sheptytsky). These collections were also displayed in museums in Peremyshl, Chernivtsi, and Ternopil.

Ukraine under Soviet rule. The Revolution of 1917 brought about vast changes in the way private and community cultural goods were preserved. It resulted in the massive destruction of countless ornamented implements from aristocratic estates, religious items, and peasants' tools. A considerable share of individual artifacts and collections held privately (eg, by M. Hrushevsky, V. Krychevsky) was lost. Ukraine also lost various items of Polish origin as a result of the Peace Treaty of Riga between the USSR and Poland. The Soviet Ukrainian government in Kharkiv created the All-Ukrainian Committee for the Preservation of Ancient and Artistic Monuments (1919), with sweeping powers at the county, raion, volost, and village levels, in order to nationalize all museums, private historical and art collections, public monuments, and other cultural and scientific treasures. The stated purpose of 'systematizing cultural property and preventing its theft, destruction, or exportation' was in fact a pretext that allowed the committee itself to steal, destroy, and export: museum funds were plundered, campaigns of expropriation of church valuables were conducted (1922), public burnings of icons were held (1931), and priceless artifacts from museums were sold abroad for foreign currency. Many items also disappeared during the course of the transfer and reorganization of institutions.

The efforts of Ukrainian museum officials, such as F. Ernst, D. Shcherbakivsky, and S. Taranushenko, rescued many collections from destruction. The Tereshchenko and Hansen family collections were the foundation of the Kiev Picture Gallery (see *Kiev Museum of Russian Art, 1922), and the Branicki family holdings went into the Bila Tserkva Archeological and Ethnographic Museum. Other artifacts provided the basis for the *Sumy Art Museum (1920, drawn largely from O. Hansen's collection), the Konotip Regional Museum (1920, drawn from S. Ponomarev's collection), and other *regional studies museums.

Ukrainian museum development reached its zenith in the 1920s. The country's museums consolidated, organized, and exhibited perhaps the finest examples of Ukraine's cultural heritage. In 1923 the *Kiev Museum of Church Antiquities was transferred to the Kievan Cave Monastery, and the collection of the Numismatic Cabinet at Kiev University was used to establish the holdings of the All-Ukrainian Museum Quarter's numismatic department. A new category of museum came into being, the Museum of the Revolution, with the express purpose of explaining and propagandizing the history of communism and the revolutionary movement. In 1926 the All-Ukrainian Museum Quarter was established on the site of the Kievan Cave Monastery, and was later reorganized as the *Kievan Cave Historical-Cultural Preserve (director, P. Kurinny). The site housed the Lavra Museum of Religious Cults and Folkways, the Museum of Architecture, the Potocki Museum of Ukrainian Antiquity, the VUAN Theater Museum (see *Kiev Museum of Theater, Music, and Cinema Arts), the Museum of Archeology of the Cabinet of Anthropology and Ethnology of the VUAN, the All-Ukrainian Restoration Workshop, and the archives and library of the monastery. The monastery's shrines and churches were also opened as museums.

A Party commission oversaw the return of many artifacts which had been taken to Russia. In 1927 the academic journal Ukraïns'kyi muzei began publication. The role of a national Ukrainian museum was assumed by the All-Ukrainian Museum of History, founded in 1925 with the collections of the Kiev Museum of Art and Industry (director M. Biliashivsky). Other prominent museums included the Kharkiv Museum of Ukrainian Art (see *Kharkiv Art Museum), founded on the basis of the collection of the Museum of Church History (director, S. Taranushenko), and the VUAN Museum of Ukraine's Figures in Scholarship and Art (custodian, Ye. Rudynska).

In the Stalinist terror of the 1930s all the aforementioned institutions, as well as a substantial number of lesser ones, were liquidated, and their employees were persecuted and arrested. On 25 September 1937 Pravda in Moscow reported that more than 20 museums had been looted, their holdings sold, and an untold number of priceless artifacts destroyed. Among the institutions that perished was the Museum of the Myrhorod Ceramic School, which had been active for 35 years and had amassed an impressive collection of European and Asian ceramic works. The Museum of Agriculture in Kiev was despoiled, as was the Tarnovsky Collection in Chernihiv and the Potocki Museum at the Kievan Cave Monastery. The Museum of Archeology and History in Odessa (see *Odessa Archeological Museum) was closed. The fate of the collections of the museums in Cherkasy, Shepetivka, Zvenyhorod, Kupianka, and Nizhen is unknown.

During that period exhibitions in museums were created to illustrate basic Marxist-Leninist dogma and to serve as antireligious propaganda. Special 'antireligious museums' or 'museums of atheism' were established in churches and shrines, the largest of them in St Volodymyr's Cathedral in Kiev and in the Poltava Museum. Original artifacts were removed and were replaced primarily by displays of diagrams, quotations, and slogans written in huge letters. Virtually all of the museums in Ukraine lost their true character as depositories of valuable cultural and historical property. Of the 120 museums which existed during 1917–32, 95 remained: 13 museums of the Revolution, 6 historical museums, 46 regional museums, 16 art museums, 7 literary memorial museums, 3 antireligious museums, and 1 museum of Hebrew culture. Ukrainian materials were virtually excluded from exhibits, or (as in the case of art museums) they were displayed only alongside Russian materials, with a heavy preponderance of the latter. Among museum employees only a few were Ukrainian.

Ukrainian cultural property suffered incalculable and massive damage during the Second World War. Artifacts were evacuated into the depths of the USSR, or detonated in booby traps set by the retreating Soviet army and security organs, or confiscated or destroyed by the German occupational forces. Among the museums annihilated outright were the Archeological Museum and the *Museum of Slobidska Ukraine in Kharkiv and the Poltava Museum.

Interwar Western Ukraine and the émigré community. Ukrainian museums were maintained systematically and continued to develop in interwar Western Ukraine. Central to the effort was the work of I. *Svientsitsky, the director of the National Museum in Lviv. Western Ukrainian scholars established a network of regional museums, encompassing the Hutsul (in Kolomyia, est 1926 by V. Kobrynsky), Boiko (in Sambir, est 1927 by V. Kobilnyk), Lemko (est 1930, see *Lemkivshchyna Museum), and Sokal (in Sokal, est 1937 by B. Chaikovsky) regions. In Prague D. Antonovych was the director of the *Museum of Ukraine's Struggle for Independence, founded in 1925. Its holdings included diplomatic and military material, as well as material on the history of the Ukrainian emigration. The collection was transported into the USSR after the Second World War. In 1952, 1,743 exhibits of the National Museum (including paintings by H. Narbut, M. Boichuk, P. Kholodny, and P. Kovzhun) were destroyed at the *spetsfond of the *Lviv Scientific Library of the AN URSR.

Postwar Soviet Ukraine. Whereas in 1940 there was a total of 174 museums in Ukraine (counting the ones nationalized when the Soviets invaded Western Ukraine), only 119 museums survived the war. By 1950 their number had increased to 137 (compared to 542 in the RSFSR, 937 in the USSR). Newly established museums were for the most part named after events or figures of the 'Great Patriotic War.' As in the fields of history and historiography, exhibits concentrated on recent years and decades (eg, the *Exhibition of Economic Achievements of the Ukrainian SSR) and treated earlier periods in a cursory or distorted fashion. All museums came under the jurisdiction of the Administration of Museums and Preservation of Cultural Landmarks, an organ of the Ministry of Culture of the Ukrainian SSR. Among them were nearly 1,000 'people's museums,' supposedly maintained and staffed entirely by volunteers, which were supervised by local Party and Soviet organizations.

Museums in postwar Soviet Ukraine had several common characteristics: (1) they were headed by Party functionaries who knew little or nothing about the material they oversaw; (2) their budgets and salaries were miserly, the result being a scarcity of qualified workers (especially in art *restoration) and an extremely high rate of turnover; (3) their collections were housed in poorly maintained structures, often entirely unsuited for conservation and exhibition; (4) they contributed to the repression of Ukrainian culture by confiscating artifacts, rewriting history, and serving as propaganda vehicles for the state; and (5) their holdings (particularly the Lviv museums, the Kievan Cave Historical-Cultural Preserve, and the Lubni Regional Studies Museum) were often misappropriated by directors and employees out of various motives (for personal gain, or in the interest of preserving certain artifacts).

Nevertheless, a few notable museums emerged in Ukraine in the 1960s to 1980s, including the *Museum of Historical Treasures of Ukraine, the *Museum of Kiev's History, and the *Pereiaslav-Khmelnytskyi Historical Museum. In 1988 there were 201 museums in the Ukrainian SSR (compared to 1,130 in the RSFSR and 2,207 in the entire USSR). According to official attendance figures the most popular museums were in Kiev – the award-winning *St Sophia Museum, the Kievan Cave Historical-Cultural Preserve, the Central Scientific Natural History Museum, the Ukrainian State Museum of the History of the Great Patriotic War, and the branch of the Central Lenin Museum – and in Sevastopil – the Museum of the Heroic Defense and Salvation of Sevastopil and the Aquarium-Museum.

The number of objects (in millions) inventoried in Ukrainian museums increased from 3.6 in 1970 (30 in the RSFSR, 43 in the USSR) to 5.6 in 1980 (35, 56) and 8.1 in 1987 (41, 68). The number of employees working in Ukrainian museums increased from 3,950 in 1970 to 8,700 in 1980 and 10,750 in 1987. It is noteworthy, however, that the floor space officially allotted to museums in Ukraine decreased by over one-half (2.1 million sq m in 1985 to 1 million sq m in 1987), whereas it increased in every other Soviet republic during the same period. The proportion of floor space in Ukrainian museums allocated for exhibition space (25 percent vs 35–65 percent elsewhere in the USSR) and storage space (5 percent vs 8–18 percent) was lower than in all other Soviet republics (except the Tadzhik SSR).

The West. Ukrainian museums of various kinds, organized by scholarly, religious, and community groups, are to be found on every continent where Ukrainians live. Among the most notable are the *Ukrainian Cultural and Educational Centre 'Oseredok' (Winnipeg), the *Niagara Falls Art Gallery and Museum, the *Ukrainian Museum of

Canada, the *Ukrainian Museum (New York), the *Ukrainian Museum-Archives (Cleveland), the *Ukrainian National Museum (Chicago), the Ukrainian-American Archives, Museum, and Library (Detroit), the *Petliura Ukrainian Library (Paris), and the *Svydnyk Museum of Ukrainian Culture. An exhibition of Ukrainian ethnography was opened at the Canadian Museum of Civilization in Ottawa in 1991. Many Ukrainian exhibits are also to be found in Poland, in the Silesian Museum in Wrocław, the Poznań and Warsaw ethnographic museums, and the Polish Military Museum in Warsaw.

(See also *Literary memorial museums, *Memorial museums, and *Museums of folk architecture and folkways.)

BIBLIOGRAPHY
Naukovi ustanovy ta orhanizatsiï USRR (Kharkiv 1930)
Mikorskii, B. *Razrushenie kul'turno-istoricheskikh pamiatnikov v Kieve v 1934 do 1936 gg.* (Munich 1951)
Miller, M. 'Ruïnatsiia bil'shovykamy pam'iatok istoriï, kul'tury ta mystetstva v Ukraïni,' *Novyi shliakh*, 9, nos 6–13 (1952)
– Muzei v sisteme sovetskoi propagandy,' *Vestnik Instituta po izucheniiu SSSR*, no. 5 (1953)
Mezentseva, G. *Muzei Ukrainy* (Kiev 1959)
Legkoduh, V.; et al. 'Museums in the Ukraine,' *Museum*, 19, no. 3 (1966)
Danyliuk, A. 'Muzeï na Ukraïni,' in *Ukraïns'kyi kalendar* (Warsaw 1974)
Vasylenko, A. *Litopys slavy narodnoï: Z istoriï stanovlennia i rozvytku narodnykh muzeïv na Ukraïni* (Kiev 1974)
Bulanyi, I.; Iavtushenko, I. *Hromads'ki muzeï Ukraïny: Istoriia, dosvid, problemy* (Kiev 1979)
Mezentseva, H. *Muzeieznavstvo* (Kiev 1980)
Iavtushenko, I.; et al. 'Museums of Kiev,' *Museum*, 34, no. 3 (1982)
Varine, H. de. 'The Rape and Plunder of Cultures,' *Museum*, 35, no. 3 (1983)
Bouianovskaya, A. (ed). *Museums of Kiev* (Moscow 1984)
Grimsted, P. *Archives and Manuscript Repositories in the USSR: Ukraine and Moldavia*, 2 vols (Princeton, NJ 1988)
Muzei Akademii nauk SSSR i akademii nauk soiuznykh respublik (Moscow 1989)

S. Bilokin

Museums of folk architecture and folkways. The name of skansens or open-air museums in Ukraine. Open-air museums were introduced in Sweden in 1891 as offering an effective way of preserving folk architecture. By 1982, they had spread from there, and numbered more than 2,000 in Europe alone. In Ukraine there are 5 central and over 20 local and regional open-air museums. Most of them were built in the 1970s and 1980s on the model of foreign museums. Considered an important educational source, they are state-supported. Ukrainian open-air museums are devoted mostly to peasant cottages, with their furnishings and farm buildings, from the 19th and early 20th century. The 'class' differentiation within the preevolutionary village in Ukraine was stressed in the displays. Churches, bell towers, schools, artisans' workshops, mills, and related structures occupy an important place in the museums. Virtually all of the buildings are original; replicas or reconstructions are the exception. The farms are stocked with livestock and fowl, and fields are planted with the local grains and vegetables. Trees and wild plants typical of the region are maintained.

Women in regional folk costumes take care of the artifacts on display, and craftsmen, such as weavers, smiths, potters, and shingle makers, demonstrate old techniques in the workshops. These activities convey an impression

Buildings at the Museum of Folk Architecture and Folkways of Ukraine in Kiev

of daily life. The museums often host concerts, festivals, souvenir markets, and thematic exhibits. They also have designated rest and recreation areas.

The largest museum of folk architecture and folkways in the former USSR is in Kiev. When completed, it will be the largest such museum in the world. Its construction began in 1971 on a 150-ha site in a forest and park zone of the Pyrohiv district near the Exhibition of Economic Achievements of the Ukrainian SSR. By the summer of 1976 the first part had been opened to visitors. By 1985 the museum included 250 buildings and about 50,000 artifacts, such as costumes, woven products, implements, ceramic and wooden objects, and over 700 musical instruments. The museum site is divided into seven zones that correspond to the architectural-ethnographic regions of Ukraine at the beginning of the 20th century: the Middle-Dnieper region, the Poltava region, Slobidska Ukraine, Polisia, Podilia, the Carpathian region, and southern Ukraine. In each zone a typical village was reconstructed; the Middle Dnieper village, for example, is laid out along a main road with a central square, the Polisian village is scattered unevenly around a main road, and the Carpathian village is a set of unconnected farmsteads. The church is the dominant building in almost every zone. Some rare old churches have been moved here: St Michael's Church (built in 1612) from Dorohynka, Kiev region; one built in 1742 from Zarubyntsi, Cherkasy region; a 17th-century church from Kysorychi, Volhynia; a Podilian church from Zelene (1817); and a Transcarpathian church from Ploske (1742). A group of windmills is assembled in a separate area.

In 1979 an eight-zone (12-ha) site was opened devoted to the socialist village. It exhibits the typical buildings of contemporary collective farms in Ukraine and is divided into six architectural-ethnographic regions: Polisia, the western forest-steppe, the eastern forest-steppe, the central forest-steppe, the steppe, and the Carpathians. Each subzone contains one or two farms and four or five buildings typical of the region. The farm cottages are furnished with contemporary, often factory-made, furniture, homemade articles, and folk handicrafts (embroidery, weavings, ceramics, engraved or embossed wooden articles, and painted artifacts). There are also religious items. In the future an archeological department, a prerevolution-

ary rural settlement, restoration and souvenir workshops, and an administrative and scientific building are to be added to the museum.

The Lviv Museum of Folk Architecture and Folkways occupies 67 ha of the Shevchenko Park. The idea of an open-air museum in Lviv was proposed first by I. *Svientsitsky in the 1930s, but only one wooden church (built in 1763) was moved to the site, from Kryvka near Turka. The church now serves as the museum's centerpiece. Construction of the skansen began in 1967, and the first part of its exhibition was opened in 1972. The original plan was to relocate 150 buildings, excluding minor structures, at the site. By 1980, 74 buildings had been moved and over 10,000 artifacts assembled at the museum. The Lviv open-air museum presents the folk architecture of Western Ukraine. Its territory is divided into eight historical-ethnographic zones: the Boiko, Hutsul, Lemko, and Lviv regions and Podilia, Polisia, Bukovyna, and Volhynia, and one area represents the old town. Each zone includes 15 to 20 buildings which constitute a distinctive miniature village. The Boiko zone has been completed; the others are still under construction.

The more outstanding stuctures in the Lviv open-air museum are a church (built in 1778) from Sokoliv, Ternopil region; St Michael's Church (1863), with a belfry from Tysovets, Lviv region; the Church of the Holy Trinity (1774), with a belfry from Chernivtsi; a chapel (1752) from Yalynkuvate; a belfry (1887) from Komarivka, near Brody; a school (1880) from Busovysko; a Lemko cottage from Zaricheve, in Transcarpathia; a Hutsul *grazhda from Kryvorivnia; a chicken coop (1860) from Oriavchyk; an oil press (1811) from Holovetske, a water mill from Lybokhora; windmills from Shyrivtsi (Bukovyna) and Pidsynivka (Volhynia); a felt press from Pylypets, in Transcarpathia; smithies from Turie (1870) and Krasnoiliv; a Boiko sawmill from Velykosillia; Hutsul beehives from Kuzmynets and Zamahoriv; a shepherd's shed from Krynychna meadow; and a granary (1880s) from Pidlyssia.

Construction of the Pereiaslav-Khmelnytskyi Museum of Folk Architecture and Folkways began in 1965 on Tatar Hill, within the city. By 1980 it contained 140 structures from various oblasts, spread over a 30-ha site. The archeological department has preserved or reconstructed some ancient buildings, such as a house from the 11th century and the Cherniakhiv culture, a 10th-century pottery oven, wooden frame walls from 10th-century Kiev, a square and pagan altar from the Trypilian period, and an early-14th-century house. There is also a wooden Cossack church (built in the 17th century) from Ostriiky, Bila Tserkva raion, a church from Andrushi (1767), and one from Viunyshche (1833), in Pereiaslav-Khmelnytskyi raion.

The collection consists of several peasant cottages of the 19th century, representing the landless, middle, and wealthy peasantry, and the houses of rural artisans (potter, oil maker, carpenter, weaver, tanner, cooper, and miller). The museum also has a collection of 14 windmills, 2 water mills, a parish school, a rural tavern, a community granary, a drying house, a village council hall with a jail, a large (8-ton) oil press, a hunting lodge, an arbor, and the upper structures of wells. In late 1982 a beekeeping museum based on F. Khvostyk's apiary in Pomokli, near Pereiaslav-Khmelnytskyi, was added. It is the only museum of its kind in Ukraine.

The Transcarpathian Museum of Folk Architecture and

Folkways in Uzhhorod was established in 1965 and opened in 1970 on the slopes of Zamkova Hill. The relatively small site (3.5 ha) includes 13 rural houses, a *grazhda*, water mill, smithy, sawmill, felt press, lumbermen's cabin, shepherd's shed, tavern, schoolhouse, and beehives. St Michael's Church, from Shelestove (18th century), hovers over the village. One-half of the exhibition is devoted to the architecture of the Transcarpathian lowlands (Ukrainian, Rumanian, Hungarian), and the other half to the buildings of the Transcarpathian highlands (Boiko and Hutsul).

The Chernivtsi Museum of Folk Architecture and Folkways was opened in 1983 in the tourist area, not far from the city center. It contains monuments of Bukovynian folk architecture.

A network of smaller local museums based on the Uzhhorod open-air museum was established in Transcarpathia. They consist of houses, churches, belfries, and sometimes farm or industrial buildings which have been preserved in their original locations or have been moved to a different place within their villages. Ethnographic museums housed in single cottages were formed in Antonivka, Buklyve, Horyncheve, Neresnytsia, Osii, Ternove, Vilnytsia, and Zubivka. There is an interesting milling complex in Monastyrets and a restored wooden dam (of the mid-19th century) and a log-driving, lumbering museum on the Chorna River, near Synevyr Lake. The wooden churches in Steblivka (built in 1780), Krainykove (1688), Danylove (1709), Neresnytsia (1798), Oleksandrivka (17th century), and Sokyrnytsia (18th century) have been converted into museums. A few wooden churches from Ukrainian villages in Transcarpathia were transferred to Czechoslovakia in the interwar period. In Bronka and Dovhe peasant cottages have been reconstructed and turned into museums; in Petrove a whole complex of old rural buildings has been erected.

In the late 1970s or early 1980s regional museums of folk architecture and folkways were built in Kamianets-Podilskyi (representing Podilia), Kharkiv (Slobidska Ukraine), Lutske (western Polisia), Chernihiv (eastern Polisia), and Korosten (central Polisia).

Artifacts of Ukrainian folk architecture have been preserved in museums outside the country, in Czechoslovakia, Poland, Rumania, and Canada. In 1975 construction of an open-air exhibition at Svydnyk, the *Svydnyk Museum of Ukrainian Culture, was started. The first section (10 structures) was opened in 1981. The 7-ha site will include 45 buildings from Ukrainian villages in the Prešov region.

In 1963 an open-air museum was set up in Bardejovské Kúpele. It has over 30 buildings, virtually all of them from Ukrainian villages of the Prešov region. In 1977 construction of similar museums began in Stará L'ubovňa and Humenné. Most of the buildings in them are Ukrainian. A few Ukrainian peasant houses and farm buildings are part of the Slovak Village Museum in Martin. Some 27 wooden churches in the Prešov region were designated national monuments of Slovakia in 1968, and in 1979 the easternmost Ukrainian village, Osturňa, with its 236 houses and 1,100 inhabitants, was declared a state reservation of folk architecture.

The Sianik Museum of Folk Architecture contains the largest number of Ukrainian buildings in Poland. It was opened in 1968 and is now the largest Polish museum of its kind (103 structures in 1979). It includes a church from Grąziowa (1730), many Lemko and Boiko houses and farm buildings, and a large collection of Ukrainian icons and ethnographic materials. Much attention is devoted to the Ukrainian exhibits in the museum's official publications, *Materiały Muzeum budownictwa ludowego w Sanoku* and *Acta scansenologica*. Ukrainian folk architecture can be found also in the Ethnographic Park in Nowy Sącz, the Folk Building Center in Szembark, and other museums. A museum of Lemko culture was opened in Zyndranowa in the 1960s.

Rumanian open-air museums, such as the Muzeul Satului in Bucharest and similar museums in Suceava, Tulcea, and Sighetul Marmaţiei, have holdings from Ukrainian villages.

In 1975 the *Ukrainian Cultural Heritage Village near Edmonton was set up. Sponsored by the provincial government of Alberta, it includes pioneer artifacts and buildings and features re-enactments of daily life in rural Alberta before 1930.

BIBLIOGRAPHY

Materiały Muzeum budownictwa ludowego w Sanoku, no. 24 (1978)
Danyliuk, A.; Krasovs'kyi I.; Rybak, B.; Ianov, V. *Muzei narodnoï arkhitektury i pobutu u L'vovi: Putivnyk* (Lviv 1980)
Hudchenko, Z. *Muzeï narodnoï arkhitektury Ukraïny* (Kiev 1981)
Czajkowski, J. *Muzea na wolnym powietrzu w Europie* (Rzeszów–Sanok 1984)
Bairak, Ia.; Fedaka, P. *Zakarpats'kyi muzei narodnoï arkhitektury i pobutu* (Uzhhorod 1986)

M. Mushynka

Yurii Mushketyk   Mykola Mushynka

Mushketyk, Yurii [Mušketyk, Jurij], b 21 March 1929 in Vertiivka, Nizhen raion, now in Chernihiv oblast. Writer and community activist. He graduated from the philological faculty at Kiev University (1953) and received his candidate's degree there. For many years he was editor of the journal *Dnipro* and headed the Kiev oblast writers' organization and in 1986 he became the first secretary of the executive of the *Writers' Union of Ukraine. He is the author of numerous novels and novelettes, many of them on historical subjects, such as *Semen Palii* (1954), *Haidamaky* (Haidamakas, 1957), and *Iasa* (1987), and many about contemporary life, such as *Den' prolitaie nad namy* (The Day Flies above Us, 1967), *Bila tin'* (White Shadow, 1977), and *Vernysia v dim svii* (Return to Your Home, 1981). Of particular note is the finely written satirical novel *Obval* (The Crumbling Away, 1985). Mushketyk has also written novels for children, the documentary novel *Na kruti hory* (Onto Steep Mountains, 1976), the play *Ne kydai mene v dorozi* (Don't Forsake Me on the Way, 1969), the critical biography *Anatolii Shyian* (1960), and other works. As first secretary of the Writers' Union of Ukraine Mushketyk has taken an active role in the struggle for the rebirth of the Ukrainian language and Ukrainian culture.

Mushrooms (Ukrainian: *hryby*). A popular name for nonflowering, fleshy fungi of the order Agaricales, mostly of the class Basidiomycetes, also Ascomycetes. Mushrooms have a spore-producing, umbrella-shaped fruiting body which emerges from an extensive underground network of threadlike mycelia. As long as nourishment is available and temperature and moisture are suitable, a mycelium will provide a new crop of mushrooms each year.

Composed of 90 percent water and less than 3 percent protein, mushrooms have low nutritional value but are prized for their taste. A few kinds are considered as choice edibles. Mushrooms have been an important component of the daily diet and traditional *foods of Ukrainians from time immemorial, especially in the regions of Volhynia, Polisia, the Carpathian Mountains, and Subcaucasia. The harvesting and processing of mushrooms (drying, curing, marinating, or salting) represent an important segment of local commercial activity. Early commercial ventures in the Carpathian region, based in Lviv and managed by *Tsentrosoiuz, date from 1939.

By far the largest group of mushrooms found in Ukraine is the Boletaceae family (genus *Boletus*). They include the king bolete (*B. edulis*; Ukrainian: *bilyi hryb, pravdyvyi, borovyk*), edible bolete (*B. scaber*; Ukrainian: *berezovyk, pidbereznyk, babka temna*), mossy mushroom (*B. variegatus*; Ukrainian: *mokhovyk zhovto-buryi*), butter mushroom (*B. elegans*; Ukrainian: *masliuk modrynovyi*), orange cup (*B. versipellis*; Ukrainian: *osykovyk, babka chervona*), *B. granulatus* (Ukrainian: *masliuk zernystyi*), slippery jack (*B. luteus*; Ukrainian: *masliuk, sosnak*), and *B. subtomentosus* (Ukrainian: *mokhovyk zelenyi, reshitka*). Found during summer and autumn months in both deciduous and coniferous forests, all these boletes are edible. Other species common in Ukraine are from the Agaricaceae family. Among them are the meadow/field mushroom (*Agaricus campestris/arvensis*; Ukrainian: *pecherytsia stepova/polova*), honey mushroom (*Armillaria mellea*; Ukrainian: *openok osinnii spravzhnii, pidpenok*), common milk cap (*Lactarius deliciosus*; Ukrainian: *ryzhyk smachnyi*), chanterelle (*Cantharellus cibarius*; Ukrainian: *lysychka, kurka*), and russula (*Russula delica/xerampelina/vesca*; Ukrainian: *syroizhka bila/voniucha/istyvna, holubinka*). A favorite mushroom in North America, the morel (*Morchella esculenta/conica*; Ukrainian: *smorzh, zmorshok*), is considered conditionally edible in Ukraine.

Among the most toxic mushrooms are representatives of the genus *Amanita* (Ukrainian: *mukhomory*), including the destroying angel (*A. virosa*; Ukrainian: *mukhomor bilyi voniuchyi*), death cap (*A. phalloides*; Ukrainian: *mukhomor zelenyi, blida pohanka*), fly agaric (*A. muscaria*; Ukrainian: *mukhomor chervonyi*), and the panther and lemon *Amanitas*. Almost 90 percent of all mushroom poisonings are caused by the pale greenish death cap. These species grow from June to mid-October. Among other poisonous mushrooms in Ukraine are the sulfur tuft (*Naematoloma fasciculare*; Ukrainian: *openok nespravzhnii*), lorchel or false morel (*Gyromitra/Helvella esculenta*; Ukrainian: *strochok zvychainyi*), and *Entoloma lividum* (Ukrainian: *rozhevoplastynyk otruinyi*).

Along with berries and herbs mushrooms are extremely susceptible to contamination by radiation (esp cesium-137). Even in 1991, five years after the nuclear explosion at the Chornobyl Atomic Energy Station, mushroom picking was forbidden in Kiev and Zhytomyr oblasts in the area above the Kiev–Korosten line.

BIBLIOGRAPHY
Zerova, M. *Istivni ta otruini hryby Ukraïny*, 2nd edn (Kiev 1970)
Dudka, I.; Vasser, S. *Griby: Spravochnik mikologa i gribnika* (Kiev 1987)

I. Masnyk

Mushynka, Mykola [Mušynka] (Mušinka, Mikulaš; pseud: M. Hnatiukivsky), b 20 February 1936 in Kuriv, Bardejov county, Czechoslovakia. Ukrainian folklorist. After graduating from Prague University (1959) he completed his graduate studies in Kiev and Prague (1967) universities and worked in the department of Ukrainian studies at the Prešov campus of Košice University (1966–71). He founded and edited *Naukovyi zbirnyk Muzeiu ukraïns'koï kul'tury u Svydnyku* (1965–70). Because of his contacts with Ukrainian dissidents and Ukrainian émigrés he was expelled from his job and forbidden to publish. He was not reinstated in a research position until 1990. Mushynka has written over 300 studies, articles, and reviews, mainly on folklore and the culture of Ukrainians in Czechoslovakia. He compiled two anthologies of Ukrainian folklore in eastern Slovakia (1963 and 1967) and a collection of the folk songs sung by A. Yabur (1970). Besides a study of the folklore of the Ruthenians of Vojvodina (1976) and a biography of O. Zilynsky (1983) he has published several monographs on V. *Hnatiuk: *Volodymyr Hnatiuk-doslidnyk folkl'oru Zakarpattia* (Volodymyr Hnatiuk: Researcher in the Folklore of Transcarpathia, 1975), *Volodymyr Hnatiuk: Bibliohrafiia drukovanykh prats'* (Volodymyr Hnatiuk: Bibliography of Printed Works, 1987), and *Volodymyr Hnatiuk: Zhyttia ta ioho diial'nist' v haluzi folkl'orystyky, literaturoznavstva ta movoznavstva* (Volodymyr Hnatiuk: His Life and His Work in the Field of Folklore Studies, Literary Scholarship, and Linguistics, 1987). Mushynka has contributed numerous articles to and served as subject editor of ethnography for the *Encyclopedia of Ukraine*.

D.H. Struk

Musianovych, Yaroslav [Musjanovyč, Jaroslav], b 31 January 1915 in Yavoriv, Galicia. Émigré community leader in France. He studied medicine in Grenoble and Lyon and then practiced in Lyon and Paris. He headed the Ukrainian National Alliance in France (1949–61) and the *Ukrainian Central Civic Committee in France (1979–87). After 1961 he headed the Ukrainian Movement for a Federated Europe (consisting of Ukrainian members of the federalist European Movement) for many years, as well as the Society of Former Combatants of the Ukrainian Republican Democratic Army in France (1979–82).

Music. Ukrainians are known popularly as a musical people with a remarkable legacy of folk songs and talented performers.

Medieval Ukraine. During the Middle Ages in Ukraine, three kinds of music developed. The first was music-making at the courts of the princes and boyars. Groups of musicians, local and foreign, resided at the princely courts and performed during festivals and banquets, praising the prince and entertaining the guests. Wandering musicians and actors, the *skomorokhy, entertained their listeners with songs and acrobatic tricks. Many musical instruments were in use at that time in Ukraine, including stringed harps, metal and wooden trumpets and horns, wooden pipes, drums, and kettledrums.

The first *church music and its performers came from Byzantium and Bulgaria. These foreign musicians were the earliest conductors of local choirs and the first music teachers. Local influences began to be felt, however, with the increasing numbers of local musicians and performers of religious music. In the second half of the 11th century, the Kievan Cave Monastery became the center for the development of religious music in Ukraine. The chief characteristics of religious music at that time were a cappella singing and monophony. The melodies were recorded in a nonlinear notation, called *znamenna*, written in above the words of the liturgical services. Another type of nonlinear notation was the *kondakarna* notation, which was used to note down liturgical singing, specifically the kontakia.

The third major type of music consisted of *folk songs. These accompanied all significant events in a person's life and reflected the spiritual characteristics and the worldview of the Ukrainian people. Songs which were connected with ritual calendar changes figured prominently: the New Year *carols (*koliadky* and *shchedrivky*), the rich cycle of spring *rusalka songs, songs of the midsummer *Kupalo festival, and so on. A large part of the repertoire was made up of songs associated with family and everyday life, as well as love songs and historical songs.

14th to 17th centuries. Church *brotherhoods had an influential role in the development of music in Ukraine during this period. The brotherhoods in Lviv, Peremyshl, Ostrih, Lutske, and Kiev were particularly active in their religious educational work and founded schools in which prime importance was given to the study of church music and music theory. A significant innovation was the introduction of *polyphonic singing, leading to the development of the five-line notation called *kyïvske znamia* that replaced the non-linear notation. The 'musical grammar' written by the musicologist and composer M. *Dyletsky in 1675, was a complete description of the theory of polyphonic music. This work was rewritten and republished many times and in the 17th and 18th centuries became one of the basic texts of music theory throughout Eastern Europe. A favorite musical form of the time was the *partesnyi* concert, an a cappella composition for choir, consisting of one movement written to a religious text. Two music registers belonging to the Lviv Dormition Brotherhood in 1697 record 398 works by Ukrainian composers for 3 to 12 voices. Most of the works (120) are for 8 voices.

18th and 19th centuries. The 18th century witnessed a paradoxical situation in which Ukrianian music started to reach a higher level of maturity and sophistication that was ultimately absorbed by Russian musical develop-

ment. The bases for developing a talented core of Ukrainian musical talent were expanding at this time. The Kievan Mohyla Academy had an orchestra and choir comprising up to 100 musicians and 300 singers. The *Hlukhiv Singing School, founded in 1738, provided thorough education for future musicians. Cossack *starshyna* families supported musical ensembles, if not whole orchestras, the most notable of which was found at the court of K. *Rozumovsky.

But the musical talents of Ukraine usually did not remain in Ukraine; they were being drawn into the developing Russian musical life on an ever-increasing scale. The start of this trend could be seen already in the late 17th century, when Dyletsky was summoned to Moscow by the tsar to teach the rudiments of polyphonic singing, and in the early 18th century with the appointment of I. *Popovsky as the precentor of the imperial court choir (and his subsequent recruitment of singers from Ukraine). This tendency became particularly pronounced after the Rozumovsky family had established itself at the St Petersburg court in the 1740s and began seeking out talented musicians from Ukraine, such as M. *Poltoratsky, for service in the imperial capital. Likewise, the most talented graduates of the Hlukhiv school were routinely brought to St Petersburg to further their musical education.

The outcome of these practices can be seen by the late 18th century, when a trio of the most talented Ukrainian musicians of the age – M. *Berezovsky, D. *Bortniansky, and A. *Vedel – composed exceptional works that became commonly regarded as 'Russian' music in the West. By the 19th century, Ukrainians, while still providing a source of recruits for musicians in Russia, had lost the dominant position (outside the Italian opera) they had earlier held in the Russian musical life of the St Petersburg court. In Ukraine itself musical life failed to develop much further than the level of traveling theater companies performing operettas or operas with broad thematic appeals (most notably S. Hulak-Artemovsky's *Zaporozhian Cossack beyond the Danube* and M. Arkas's *Kateryna*). Another area of indistinction between the two musical cultures was evident in folk music. The first compilations of Russian folk music, undertaken in the later 18th century by V. *Trutovsky and I. *Prach, include Ukrainian songs. Over time these 'Little Russian' numbers were increasingly accepted as an integral part of the Russian musical heritage and employed by Russian composers (notably M. Mussorgsky and P. Tchaikovsky) in their works.

The provincial state of Ukrainian musical life began to change only in the late 19th and early 20th centuries. Ironically one of the main instruments of this renewed development of Ukrainian musical life was the *Russian Music Society, which established music schools (that later became conservatories) in Kiev, Kharkiv, and Odessa. The society restored a certain level of music training in Ukraine and cultivated a taste for refined music at least among certain segment of the population, providing the rudiments of an institutional and social base for later Ukrainian musical development.

Western Ukraine to the mid-19th century. Ukrainian musical life in Galicia saw some significant developments in the early 19th century. The main focus of Ukrainian musical life was in Peremyshl, where a distinctive school of music was initiated by M. *Verbytsky and I. *Lavrivsky. The group had close connections with the Peremyshl

Choir (est 1829) and the Peremyshl Music School, and influenced the work of subsequent composers, such as V. *Matiuk, S. *Vorobkevych, and A. *Vakhnianyn. A second trend in Ukrainian musical life of this period was the development of an interest in Ukrainian folk music. In part this came about under the rubric of a general interest in the music of the peoples of the former Polish Commonwealth, which was studied by musicologists such as W. *Zaleski and K. *Lipiński. Folk music was also studied by Ukrainians (eg, the members of the *Ruthenian Triad). The general level of musical life in Western Ukraine was raised by the establishment of a singing school in Lviv, initially through the St Cecilia Society begun in 1826 through the efforts of F.X. Mozart, and then with the founding of the Lviv Conservatory in 1830. The latter school, however, functioned largely as a Polish institution and did not actively foster Ukrainian musical devlopment.

Late 19th and early 20th centuries. Considerable efforts were made in this period to develop a Ukrainian national school of music comparable to those established among the Poles, Czechs, Russians, and Norwegians. The key figure in this process was M. *Lysenko, who collected and arranged a large number of Ukrainian folk songs and studied them in order to establish their cultural specificity. By 1904 Lysenko was able to found a school of music in Kiev that served as a major center for the fostering of Ukrainian music and musicians. He also toured through Ukraine with choruses under his baton in order to spread the sound of Ukrainian music.

Lysenko's work had a marked influence in Western Ukraine, where Ukrainians had not been subject to the same sort of state strictures as those under Russian rule. The study of Ukrainian folk music there had been able to develop at a considerable pace, Ukrainian music activists had been able to establish printing houses for the publication of music, and the *Boian music society had built an effective network throughout Galicia. In this milieu composers such as F. *Kolessa, O. *Nyzhankivsky, D. *Sichynsky, H. Topolnytsky, and (later) S. *Liudkevych were able to come to the fore and establish a degree of professionalism in all aspects of musical culture. As well, the *Lysenko Higher Institute of Music was established in Lviv in 1903 to foster futher Ukrainian musical development.

A high-water mark for the development of a Ukrainian national school of music was reached in 1917–22, when the Lysenko Music and Drama School in Kiev was expanded into an institute, a state *Ukrainian Republican Kapelle was formed, and a group of composers (including M. *Leontovych, K. *Stetsenko, and Ya. *Stepovy) was recruited to come to Kiev to work for the new state institutions of Ukrainian musical life. These advances were short-lived, however. Leontovych, Stetsenko, and Stepovy all met early deaths (by 1922), the Republican Kapelle fled to the West, and the institutional base for Ukrainian musical development was unable to develop fully. The situation in Western Ukraine remained somewhat more promising, as musical life was allowed to develop without overt state interference, and the Lysenko Higher Institute of Music was able to establish a full network throughout Galicia before it was dismantled with the Soviet invasion of 1939.

Soviet Ukraine. The establishment of Soviet power in Ukraine has proved to be a mixed blessing for musical development. State support for the art has strengthened the *music education system, underwritten the printing of musical journals and scores, and provided steady employment for musicians, composers, and music critics. The state, however, has often fostered mediocre work in its demand for ideological conformity and in its effort to maintain socialist realism as a cultural policy. Consequently, a large repertoire of lackluster works dedicated to Lenin, the glory of the Party, the memory of the Second World War, heroic women workers, and like themes has been commissioned over the years. In spite of these constrictions, composers such as L. *Revutsky, B. *Liatoshynsky, V. *Barvinsky, S. *Liudkevych, V. *Kosenko, V. *Kostenko, B. *Yanovsky, A. *Shtoharenko, K. *Dankevych, Yu. *Meitus, P. *Maiboroda, and A. *Kos-Anatolsky have produced interesting and challenging works.

Four Ukrainian composers in Lviv in 1927. From left: Antin Rudnytsky, Vasyl Barvinsky, Stanyslav Liudkevych, Pylyp Kozytsky

The most open period for musical composition in Soviet Ukraine was the 1920s, before the onset of Stalinism. A major body for the promotion of Ukrainian musical development at that time was the *Leontovych Music Society, which was formed in 1922 and sponsored the flagship music journal *Muzyka*. The Lysenko society was dissolved in 1928 as a result of government pressure and restructured as a more pliable body, the All-Ukrainian Society of Revolutionary Musicians (Ukrainian acronym: VUTORM), which itself was renamed Proletmuz in 1931 and replaced by the *Union of Composers of Ukraine in 1932. In the 1930s the Soviet regime established the concept of socialist realism as a norm for artistic activity, and the result was a wholesale retreat from the sort of composing done in the 1920s.

The ideological pressure eased somewhat only in the 1960s. The relaxation allowed for a whole group of young composers to use the newest means of musical expression. The members of this group, who went by the name 'Kiev Avant-Garde,' were L. *Hrabovsky, V. *Sylvestrov, V. Hodziatsky, V. Zahortsev, and V. Huba. The appearance of this group created much interest abroad, especially in the United States, although in Kiev their achievements did not reach beyond a narrow circle of listeners. The composers M. *Skoryk, L. *Dychko, and, among the younger generation, Ye. *Stankovych, I. *Karabyts, and others have created original syntheses of the traditional with the modern.

A lighter musical form that developed in 20th-century Ukraine was stage music (*estradna muzyka*) or, in a more general sense, popular music. The art songs written by composers such as P. Maiboroda constituted an early form of this genre. Popular stage music, however, came into its own in Ukraine only in the late 1960s and early 1970s, with the development of a musical style based largely on North American rock and Europop models mixed with folk themes. The *estradna* style was emulated by many Ukrainian youth bands outside Ukraine.

Outside Ukraine. A small number of Ukrainian composers have worked outside Ukraine, although financial constraints have usually rendered it impossible to develop a full career from the writing of Ukrainian scores. The most notable of these figures have worked in Canada and the United States; they include M. *Haivoronsky, R. *Prydatkevych, O. *Koshyts, and P. *Pecheniha-Uhlytsky before the Second World War and A. *Rudnytsky, V. *Hrudyn, M. *Fomenko, G. *Fiala, and I. *Sonevytsky after it. A number of Ukrainians within the general realm of the North American musical world, most notably L. *Melnyk and V. *Baley, have also composed works.

BIBLIOGRAPHY
Hrinchenko, M. *Istoriia ukraïns'koï muzyky* (Kiev 1922)
Barvins'kyi, V. 'Ohliad istoriï ukraïns'koï muzyky,' *Istoriia ukraïns'koï kul'tury*, ed I. Kryp'iakevych (Lviv 1937)
Kudryk, B. *Ohliad istoriï ukraïns'koï tserkovnoï muzyky* (Lviv 1937)
Wytwycky, W. 'Music,' in *Ukrainian Arts*, ed O. Dmytriv (New York 1952)
Dovzhenko, V. *Narysy z istoriï ukraïns'koï radians'koï muzyky*, 2 vols (Kiev 1957, 1967)
Rudnyts'kyi, A. *Ukraïns'ka muzyka: Istorychno-krytychnyi ohliad* (Munich 1963)
Arkhimovych, L.; Karysheva, T.; Sheffer, T.; Shreier-Tkachenko, O. *Narysy z istoriï ukraïns'koï muzyky*, 2 vols (Kiev 1964)
Shreier-Tkachenko, O. (ed) *Istoriia ukraïns'koï dozhovtnevoï muzyky* (Kiev 1969)
– *Istoriia ukraïns'koï muzyky* (Kiev 1980)
Hordiichuk, M.; et al (eds). *Istoriia ukraïns'koï muzyky*, 6 vols (Kiev 1989–)

W. Wytwycky

Music criticism. A branch of musicology that provides readers of periodical publications with a professional opinion about musical events and phenomena. The first Ukrainian music critics appeared in the early decades of the 20th century; among them were S. Liudkevych, V. Barvinsky, P. Kozytsky, and, later, A. Rudnytsky and N. Nyzhankivsky. The development of music criticism benefited from the founding of the music periodicals *Muzyka*, *Muzyka masam*, and, later, *Ukraïns'ka muzyka* and the growth of musical institutions throughout Ukraine. Subsequently, new critics began to publish their work, among them I. Belza, M. Mykhailov, M. Hordiichuk, V. Hoshovsky, and M. Zahaikevych. In émigré publications, the most prominent critics are P. Matsenko, R. Prydatkevych, A. Rudnytsky, M. Fomenko, V. Hrudyn, A. Olkhovsky, W. Wytwycky, R. Savytsky Jr, A. Vyrsta, and T. Yuskiv. Many articles of music criticism have appeared in *Visti* (Minneapolis, 1962–71), *Suchasnist'*, and other émigé periodicals.

Music education. Until the 19th century, music education in Ukraine was conducted largely in an ecclesiastical setting, in a small number of higher educational institutions, and through private teaching. Of major importance were the singing schools at various monasteries and cathedral churches in the 15th to 17th centuries. The musical training given at these was extended by the training offered in brotherhood schools as well as at the *Kievan Mohyla Academy. Music education in Ukraine was expanded further in the 18th and 19th centuries. The first professional music school in Ukraine, the *Hlukhiv Singing School, was established in 1738, although it actually functioned largely as a training center for musicians to be recruited into the imperial Russian service. Vocal and instrumental classes were taught at Kharkiv College from 1773, lectures in music theory took place at Kharkiv University from the time of its establishment in 1805, and music courses continued to be taught at the Kievan academy after it was turned into a theological institute. Music was also taught by members of music guilds, seminaries, teachers' colleges, and music schools attached to serf, army, and municipal orchestras (most notably in Kiev). Advanced music education was commonly obtained by travel abroad. Private music tuition, usually by foreign music teachers, was also widespread.

Civic music societies increasingly became concerned with music education during the late 19th century. The *Russian Music Society (RMS), which had branches in Kiev, Kharkiv, and Odessa, was particularly significant in this regard, although it functioned largely as an all-empire institution rather than one dedicated to specifically Ukrainian needs. The other most notable music associations of the period were centered in Kiev and included the Amateur Choir Society (conducted by M. Lysenko in the 1870s–1890s), the choir of the St Sophia Cathedral, the Kiev Society of Music Lovers, and the student choir of Kiev University. The *Boian music society also established branches in Kiev and Poltava. The *Lysenko Music and Drama School, established in 1904, operated as an institution primarily dedicated to developing Ukrainian music. Within the Russian Empire, however, the most advanced musical training was available at the Moscow and St Petersburg conservatories. This situation changed only in 1913, when the RMS music schools in Kiev and Odessa were converted into conservatories.

Music education increasingly became a state concern in Ukraine after 1917. The Lysenko school was combined with the Kiev Conservatory in 1918 to become the *Lysenko Music and Drama Institute (until it reverted to the *Kiev Conservatory in 1934); the *Kharkiv Conservatory was established in 1917; and the *Odessa Conservatory was maintained in various guises until it reverted to its original form in 1934. Music education was further expanded with the creation of seven-year elementary music schools, high schools specializing in music education, and the postsecondary Kharkiv Music Institute and Donetske Musical Pedagogy Institute.

Music education in Western Ukraine underwent a separate development. Until the 20th century it was closely tied to churches and precentor schools. The most important of these was located in Peremyshl, with others situated in Lviv, Stanyslaviv, Uzhhorod, and Chernivtsi. A conservatory was located in Lviv, but it existed as a Polish rather than a Ukrainian institution. The first Ukrainian music school was established in 1903 by the Union of Song and Music Societies and became in 1907 the *Lysenko Higher Institute of Music. The school developed a network of branches in several Galician towns and was active until 1939. The Prosvita Society was also active in music education by organizing courses for conductors. After the Soviet occupation of Western Ukraine, the Lysenko institute was replaced by the *Lviv Conservatory.

Ukrainian music education outside Ukraine first took the form of courses offered in Prague at the Ukrainian Free University and the Ukrainian Higher Pedagogical Institute during the interwar years. A short-lived attempt to establish a Ukrainian conservatory in New York was made in 1924 by M. Haivoronsky and R. Prydatkevych. Music courses were offered in Canada on an irregular basis through the 'higher education courses' for the training of cultural activists, sponsored by associations such as the Ukrainian Labor Farmer Temple Association and the Ukrainian National Federation. From 1953 to 1985 the Lysenko Music Institute, under the directorship of I. Kovaliv, was active in Toronto. The most developed organization for music education, however, remains the *Ukrainian Music Institute of America, which was founded in 1952 and has branches in several American cities. In more recent times the Ukrainian Choral Federation of Canada and other music associations have begun sponsoring advanced workshops for music specialists.

W. Wytwycky

Music journals. Periodical publications dedicated to Ukrainian music developed only in the 20th century. The earliest publications of this type were short-lived efforts that appeared in Galicia. The first was *Muzychnyi kalendar-al'manakh*, published in Lviv in 1904–7 by R. Zarytsky. The 10 issues of the Lviv-based *Artystychnyi vistnyk* that appeared in 1905–7 contained a music section edited by S. Liudkevych. Later attempts included *Muzychnyi lystok* (1925), *Boian* (1929–30), and *Muzychni visty* (1934). In 1937–9 the monthly *Ukraïns'ka muzyka* was published as the official medium of the Union of Ukrainian Professional Musicians in Lviv.

In Soviet Ukraine, the monthly *Muzyka* started publication in Kiev in April 1923 and proved to be very influential. It continued to appear under various titles until 1941. *Muzyka* started publication once more in Kiev in 1970 as the bimonthly organ of the Ministry of Culture of the Ukrainian SSR, the Union of Composers of Ukraine, and the Music Society of the Ukrainian SSR. It is an important chronicle of Ukrainian musical scholarship and events (within the parameters afforded by state control), with M. Hordiichuk, A. Shtoharenko, and others on its editorial board.

A number of small or short-lived émigré Ukrainian musical journals were established after the Second World War. The Dnipro choir in Twin Cities, Minnesota, published *Visti* in 1962–71. Its editor–in–chief was O. Kostiuk, and some of its contributors were P. Matsenko, Z. Lysko, R. Prydatkevych, O. Zalesky, and O. Bryn. It was succeeded briefly in 1971 by *Muzychni visti*, published in Jersey City. Since 1981 the New York School of Bandura has published the bilingual (Ukrainian-English) journal *Bandura*. The journal is dedicated to the art, repertoire, history, and construction of the instrument, and to literary works featuring the bandura or bandurysts; its managing editor is N. Czorny. *Bandura* has printed or reprinted articles by H. Khotkevych, H. Kytasty, Z. Shtokalko, L. Maistrenko,

R. Levytsky, V. Lutsiv, A. Hornjatkevyč, and V. Mishalow.

W. Wytwycky

Music societies. Associations whose purpose was to provide a strong civic base for musical performance and development began appearing in Ukraine in the 19th century. The first such formations were the St Cecilia Music Society (1826) and the Society for the Advancement of Music (1838) in Lviv, which were created through the efforts of F. *Mozart; and the *Torban society, which was active in Lviv and other Galician centers in 1869–71. In the 1890s a series of *Boian music and song societies were established in Western Ukraine, which created the *Union of Song and Music Societies in 1903. The union was renamed the *Lysenko Music Society in 1907. It played a vital role in Western Ukrainian musical life until it was dissolved in 1939. In Russian-ruled Ukraine the most active civic musical association was the *Russian Music Society, which formed branches in Kiev (1863), Kharkiv (1871), and Odessa (1884) and sponsored music schools. After the revolution the most active Ukrainian music association was the *Leontovych Music Society. Formed in 1922, the group was active until 1928, when it was supplanted by the All-Ukrainian Society of Revolutionary Musicians, which in turn became Proletmuz in 1931 and the *Union of Composers in Ukraine in 1932. It was not until 1959, with the formation of the *Music Society of Ukraine, that a music association with a significant civic base again existed in Ukraine.

W. Wytwycky

Music Society of the Ukrainian SSR (Muzychne tovarystvo Ukrainy). A voluntary association of professional musicians and amateurs. Founded in 1959 as the Choral Society of the Ukrainian SSR, it became the Music and Choral Society of the Ukrainian SSR in 1967, Music Society of the Ukrainian SSR in 1975, and was renamed in 1990 as the All-Ukrainian Musical Association. The society organizes music competitions, festivals, master classes, and training seminars for the conductors of amateur choirs and instrumental ensembles. In 1984, its membership included 3,584 groups with over 128,500 individuals. It has been headed by P. Kozytsky (1959–60), S. Kozak (1960–73), M. Kondratiuk (1973–85), and D. Hnatiuk (since 1985). In 1992 it had 500 members, and its president was A. Avdiievsky.

Musical instruments. See Folk musical instruments.

Musical instruments industry. A branch of industry that manufactures various string and wind instruments. In Ukraine some *folk musical instruments, such as *banduras and *tsymbaly*, are mass-produced in factories in Lviv and Chernihiv; others are made by hand in small numbers. Before the 1920s there was little manufacturing of musical instruments in Ukraine. By 1980 there were 12 instrument factories, located in Kiev (wind instruments), Odessa (pianos, bow instruments), Zhytomyr (accordions), Lviv (folk instruments), Poltava (accordions and electric accordions), Chernihiv (pianos, string instruments), and Izmail (guitars). The output of instruments in Ukraine has dropped considerably, from 32,000 pianos and 191,000 accordions in 1970 to 17,000 and 32,000 respectively in 1987.

Musicians' guilds (*muzykantski tsekhy* or *muzychni bratstva*). Professional associations of musicians existing in the larger cities of Ukraine in the 16th to 19th centuries. With the introduction of Magdeburg law in the 14th century, Ukrainian craftsmen and merchants began to organize themselves into *guilds. The earliest-known Ukrainian musicians' guilds appeared in Kamianets-Podilskyi (1578) and Lviv (1580). In 1652 Hetman B. Khmelnytsky organized all musicians of Left-Bank Ukraine into a regional guild with H. Illiashenko-Makushenko as guild master. Other musicians' guilds appeared in Poltava (1662), Kiev (1677), Pryluka (1686), Starodub (1705), Nizhen (1729), Chernihiv (1734), Kharkiv (1780), and other places. Guild members reserved the right to perform in towns, villages, market squares, and inns, at weddings, funerals, and other social occasions. In addition to providing services for their members and undertaking certain civic duties, they maintained equitable fee structures and offered musical training for young musicians. The most important guild was in Kiev, which formed the Kiev City Orchestra in the 17th century and provided the basis for the Kiev Music School (1768). Competition from the growing numbers of city orchestras and serf instrumental ensembles and the overall decline of the guild system caused the musicians' guilds to disappear by the end of the 19th century.

BIBLIOGRAPHY
Fil'ts, B. 'Muzykants'ki tsekhy,' in *Istoriia ukraïns'koï muzyky*, vol 1, ed M. Hordiichuk et al (Kiev 1989)

W. Sydorenko

Musicology. Most of the early writings on Ukrainian musicological themes have dealt with the description or compilation of Ukrainian folk music. Later writings dealt with the history of Ukrainian musical development. Many primary texts and monographs have been published on these subjects, and several overview histories were undertaken.

The study of musical *folklore developed intensively during the 19th century. An important starting point was the publication of a large collection of Ukrainian folk song texts edited by M. *Maksymovych (1827), who, in a detailed introduction, emphasized the differences between Russian and Ukrainian folk songs. Further ethnomusicological studies were carried out in the second half of the 19th century by P. *Sokalsky, M. *Lysenko, and O. *Rubets, and in the early 20th century by F. *Kolessa, S. *Liudkevych, and V. *Shukhevych. Their work was later continued by K. *Kvitka, D. *Revutsky, M. *Hrinchenko, Z. *Lysko, and others. The musicological articles and reports resulting from this work commonly appeared in periodicals such as *Kievskaia starina*, *Literaturno-naukovyi vistnyk*, *Artystychnyi vistnyk*, and *Muzychnyi kalendar-al'-manakh*.

The interwar period saw some significant undertakings in Ukrainian musicology. In 1922 M. Hrinchenko published the first significant history of Ukrainian musical development to the 20th century. The Lysenko Music Society enlivened the musicological field by publishing the journal *Muzyka* from 1923. In Western Ukraine a musicological commission headed by S. Liudkevych was formed in the 1930s, the journal *Ukraïns'ka muzyka* (1937–9) provided some valuable articles on musicological themes, and B. *Kudryk published a survey of Ukrainian church music (1937). In Soviet Ukraine musicological work was severely curtailed by the Stalinist repressions of the 1930s. Some research was still undertaken in the field, notably by A. Olkhovsky at the Kiev Conservatory. But the monograph resulting from his work, *Narys istoriï ukraïns'koï muzyky* (An Outline of the History of Ukrainian Music), was confiscated and destroyed shortly after its publication in 1941.

Since 1945 the conservatories and the AN URSR Institute of Fine Arts, Folklore, and Ethnography (IMFE) have been responsible for work in Ukrainian musicology. Some notable research has been undertaken by I. Belza, M. Hordiichuk, O. Dovzhenko, O. Shreier-Tkachenko, L. Arkhimovych, M. Zahaikevych, and others. Since 1964 the annual *Ukraïns'ke muzykoznavstvo* has carried articles on the theory and history of music as well as on performance and folklore. The bimonthly periodical *Muzyka*, printed in Kiev since 1970, has also published musicological articles. Numerous brochures and monographs have been written on Ukrainian composers, among them M. Lysenko (by L. Arkhimovych and M. Hordiichuk), S. Hulak-Artemovsky (L. Kaufman), K. Stetsenko (L. Parkhomenko), M. Leontovych (M. Hordiichuk), S. Liudkevych (M. Zahaikevych), F. Kolessa (S. Hrytsa), B. Liatoshynsky (N. Zaporozhets), A. Shtoharenko (M. Borovyk), and H. Maiboroda (M. Hordiichuk). Monographs on great Ukrainian performers, such as S. Krushelnytska, O. Myshuha, M. Mentsinsky, and B. Hmyria, have also been published.

Some notable works on Ukrainian musicology have appeared in the West. They include O. Koshyts's *Spohady* (Memoirs, 1947–8) and *Z pisneiu cherez svit* (Around the World with Song, 3 vols, 1952–74). Monographs have been published about composers such as D. Bortniansky, M. Berezovsky, F. Yakymenko, A. Vedel, O. Koshyts, and M. Haivoronsky. Other noteworthy publications include P. *Matsenko's *Narysy do istoriï ukraïns'koï tserkovnoi muzyky* (Studies in the History of Ukrainian Church Music, 1968) and *Konspekt istoriï ukraïns'koï tserkovnoï muzyky* (A Synopsis of the History of Ukrainian Church Music, 1973); A. *Rudnytsky's *Ukraïns'ka muzyka: Istorychno-krytychnyi ohliad* (Ukrainian Music: A Historical and Critical Survey, 1963) and *Pro muzyku i muzyk* (On Music and Musicians, 1980); and M. *Antonowycz's *Chants from Ukrainian Heirmologia* (1974). Some musicological essays are found in *Zbirnyk na poshanu H. Kytastoho ...* (Anthology in Honor of H. Kytasty ..., 1980). In the field of musical folklore, *Ukraïns'ki narodni melodiï* (Ukrainian Folk Melodies), a projected 10-volume collection edited by Z. *Lysko, is of particular significance.

Starting in the 1950s there have been some attempts to write broader histories of Ukrainian music. Notable efforts include V. *Dovzhenko's two-volume *Narysy z istoriï ukraïns'koï radians'koï muzyky* (Essays on the History of Soviet Ukrainian Music, 1957, 1967), the collectively authored *Narysy z istoriï ukraïns'koï muzyky* (Essays on the History of Ukrainian Music, 1964), the collectively authored *Istoriia ukraïns'koï dozhovtnevoï muzyky* (The History of Ukrainian Prerevolutionary Music, 1969), and O. Shreier-Tkachenko's *Istoriia ukraïns'koï muzyky* (1980). While adding to the knowledge of Ukrainian musical development, these works are hampered by the shortcomings of Soviet Ukrainian scholarship, particularly in overstating Russian influences on Ukrainian culture (without acknowledging reciprocal Ukrainian influences on Russian cultural development) and in expounding upon the benevolence and brilliance of the Soviet system and state. In addition, these works tend to be more narrative than analytical in style. Such shortcomings are also evident in the first volumes of the six-volume *Istoriia ukraïns'koï muzyky* published by IMFE under the editorship of M. *Hordiichuk since 1989.

BIBLIOGRAPHY
Ol'khovs'kyi, A. *Music under the Soviets: The Agony of an Art* (New York 1955)
Hrinchenko, M. *Vybrane* (Kiev 1959)
Liudkevych, S. *Doslidzhennia, statti, retsenziï* (Kiev 1973)
Hordiichuk, M. *Na muzychnykh dorohakh* (Kiev 1973)
W. Wytwytcky

Musicus Bortnianskii. An independent professional Ukrainian-Canadian choral ensemble. Founded in Toronto in June 1981 by M. *Maksymiw, the group collects, researches, performs, and publishes classical Ukrainian choral music. Its repertoire includes baroque masterpieces, operatic selections, folk song arrangements, and new works by contemporary Ukrainian composers. The choir has issued the complete 35 sacred concertos of D. *Bortniansky and M. Fedoriv's *Jerusalem Matins* on its own recording label.

Musiichuk, Stepan [Musijčuk], b 1896 in Korshiv, Kolomyia county, Galicia, d 2 October 1952 in Youngstown, Ohio. Community leader and clergyman. Having emigrated to the United States in 1911, he became active in the Sich movement and after the First World War edited the newspaper *Sich* (1920–3). Opposed to the hetmanite takeover of the movement, he joined the Organization of Democratic Siches. He was active also in the Ukrainian National Association, the United Ukrainian Organizations in America, and the Organization for the Rebirth of Ukraine. In the 1930s he was ordained in the Orthodox church. He was the author of the official songs of several Ukrainian organizations; his verses came out in two collections, *Na krylakh v Ukraïnu* (On Wings to Ukraine, 1946) and *Vichnym dukhom Ukraïny* (With Ukraine's Eternal Spirit, 1948).

Musiiko, Oleksander [Musijko], b 30 August 1903 in Musiiky, near Reshetylivka, Poltava county, d 30 November 1980 in Odessa. Plant breeder; corresponding member of the All-Union Academy of Agricultural Sciences from 1956. A graduate of the Poltava Agricultural Institute (1927), in 1939–71 he worked in the All-Union Selection and Genetics Institute in Odessa (as its director from 1958). His specialty was the selection and seed cultivation of agricultural plants. He produced new (Odessa) hybrids of corn, buckwheat, and rye.

Muskmelon (*Cucumis melo*; Ukrainian: *dynia*). A warm-climate, herbaceous annual plant of the gourd or squash family Cucurbitaceae, including the cantaloupe and the honeydew melon. The nutritious fruit is large and sweet, weighs 1–5 kg, and contains vitamin C, carotene, pectins, minerals, and 15–17 percent sugar. In Ukraine melons are grown in the steppes, the central chernozem zone, Transcarpathia, and even the north. Melons are picked selectively as they mature; late varieties may be picked green and allowed to ripen in storage. They are eaten fresh, baked, roasted, marinated, and candied; they are also used to feed farm animals. Many Ukrainian varieties of melon have been developed and popularized.

Mussorgsky, Modest [Mussorgskij], b 21 March 1839 in Karevo, Pskov gubernia, Russia, d 28 March 1881 in St Petersburg. Russian composer and pianist. Regarded as one of the leading Russian musicians of the 19th century, he used Ukrainian themes and melodies in a number of his works. His symphonic picture *Night on Bald Mountain* (1867) was conceived on Kievan legends and displayed influences of the Ukrainian folk melos. Two of his songs for solo voice with piano, 'Hopak' and 'On the Dnieper' (Song of Yarema), were faithful Russian remakes of texts in T. Shevchenko's poem *Haidamaky* that reflected some modal characteristics of Ukrainian folk music. His comic opera *Sorochyntsi Fair* (based on Gogol's tale) utilized several Ukrainian folk songs and Ukrainian vocabulary, including Shevchenko's verse 'Utoptala stezhechku cherez iar' (I Trod a Path through the Gully). In this opera Mussorgsky used the jocose folk tune 'Na berezhku u stavka' (On the Pond's Bank), originally titled 'Hopak' and scored for mixed chorus and orchestra. In time this number became transcribed extensively for concert use, eg by F. Kreisler for violin and orchestra and by S. Rachmaninoff for piano solo and for symphony orchestra. Mussorgsky traveled through Ukraine in 1879 as an accompanist to a touring soloist.

BIBLIOGRAPHY
Iefremova, L. *Mussorhs'kyi i Ukraïna* (Kiev 1958)
R. Savytsky

Mutual Benefit Association of St Nicholas of Canada. See Ukrainian Mutual Benefit Association of Saint Nicholas.

Muzahet

Muzahet (from Greek, meaning 'leader of muses'). A symbolist literary and artistic group and journal founded in 1919. Some of the more important members and/or contributors to *Muzahet* were P. Tychyna, D. Zahul, K. Polishchuk, P. Fylypovych, Yu. Mezhenko, Ya. Savchenko, O. Slisarenko, V. Kobyliansky, P. Kovzhun, and M. Zhuk. Although many of the works written by its members reflect more the modernism of *Moloda Muza or *Ukraïns'ka khata* than Western symbolism, they represent an attempt at Europeanization and a departure from the populist tendencies of the 19th century. The journal had only one issue (nos 1–3, 1919), which contained some important articles of literary theory and criticism by Zahul, Savchenko, and, especially, Mezhenko. It was primarily owing to Mezhenko's programmatic article ('Tvorchist' individuma i kolektyv' [The Creativity of the Individual and the Collective]), in which he argued for a nationally conscious artistic elite 'above the masses,' that *Muzahet* was outlawed by the authorities, and that both the journal and the organization ceased to exist. In pursuit of apolitical and artistic literary aims some of the members formed *Hrono, others joined *Aspys and then *Vaplite, and some (Savchenko) even joined the proletarian *Hart. Most, however, perished in the Soviet terror of the 1930s.

Muzhylovsky, Andrii [Mužylovs'kyj, Andrij], b and d ? Churchman and polemicist of the first half of the 17th century. He was an Orthodox priest in Slutsk, Belarus, and then a hieromonk of the Kievan Cave Monastery (1631). In 1631 he was the Cossack candidate for the office of metropolitan of Kiev, but he was opposed by King Sigismund III Vasa, who sent a letter to the voivode of Kiev to block the candidacy. He participated in the Kiev church council of 1628 that condemned M. *Smotrytsky's conversion to Catholicism, and he wrote the polemic *Antidot ...* (Antidote ..., 1629), in which he repudiated Smotrytsky's *Apologia* and defended the Orthodox leaders K. Ostrozky and S. Zyzanii.

Muzhylovsky, Syluian [Mužylovs'kyj, Sylujan] (Samuil), b ?, d 1654. Cossack *starshyna* and diplomat; son of A. *Muzhylovsky. He was one of the students at the Kievan Cave Monastery School who delivered the panegyric 'Eucharisterion' to Metropolitan P. Mohyla on Easter Sunday in 1632. During the Cossack-Polish War he was Hetman B. Khmelnytsky's envoy in Moscow (with K. Burliai, 1649, 1653), Lithuania (1649), Turkey (1651), and the Crimean Khanate (1653). In 1649 he toured Ukraine as Khmelnytsky's representative with the Patriarch of Jerusalem, who greeted Khmelnytsky at the gates of Kiev. In 1654, as judge of Nizhen and Belarusian regiments, he participated in the Belarusian campaign of the acting hetman I. Zolotarenko, who killed him during a heated argument. While in Moscow in 1649, Muzhylovsky kept historically valuable notes; they were published in *Ukraïna* (1914, no. 2).

Muzychenko, Oleksander [Muzyčenko], b 18 August 1875 in Stanyslav, Kherson county, d 1940. Pedagogue. After graduating from Odessa University he taught pedagogy at the *Nizhen Lyceum until 1917. After the Revolution of 1917 he was a leading member of the *All-Ukrainian Teachers' Association and campaigned actively for the establishment of *labor schools. Many of his ideas can be found in his monograph *Suchasni pedahohichni techiï v Zakhidnii Ievropi i Amerytsi* (Contemporary Pedagogical Trends in Western Europe and America, 1919). Under the Central Rada he was the chief instructor of teachers for the Ministry of Education and a proponent of the Ukrainization of the educational system. He was also a member of the faculty of the Ukrainian Pedagogical Academy. In the 1920s he was a professor of pedagogy at the *Kiev Institute of People's Education and director of a local labor school. Renowned as an expert on elementary education, Muzychenko wrote several works about methodology in *Vil'na ukraïns'ka shkola* and elsewhere, and the mono-

graphs *Chtenie i kul'tura slova v sovremennoi shkole* (Reading and the Culture of Language in Contemporary Schools, 1930) and *Chto takoe pedagogika i chemu ona uchit?* (What Is Pedagogy and What Does It Teach? 1912).

Andrii Muzychka   Maksym Muzyka

Muzychka, Andrii [Muzyčka, Andrij], b 6 December 1886 in Dobrovody, Zbarazh county, Galicia, d 8 September 1966 in Semipalatinsk, Kazakhstan. Literary scholar. During the First World War he graduated from Lviv University and taught in gymnasiums in Zbarazh and Ternopil. In 1918–19 he was in the Ukrainian Galician Army. In the 1920s he taught at the Odessa Institute of People's Education and wrote books on the beginnings of modern Ukrainian literature (1925), Lesia Ukrainka (1925), I. Franko's poetry (1927), and M. Cheremshyna (1928), and articles on other writers in VUAN serials and in the journal *Chervonyi shliakh*. During the Stalinist terror of the mid-1930s Muzychka was deported to Kazakhstan. There he taught at the Semipalatinsk Pedagogical Institute. The AN URSR published his booklet on Lesia Ukrainka in Russian in 1956.

Muzychka, Ivan [Muzyčka], b 15 November 1921 in Pukiv, Rohatyn county, Galicia. Catholic priest and pedagogue; member of the Shevchenko Scientific Society since 1985. He graduated from St Josaphat's Ukrainian Pontifical College and the Urbanianum University (D TH, 1953) in Rome. He was ordained in 1951 and served as a priest in Great Britain in 1953–75. He became a professor of practical theology at the Ukrainian Catholic University in Rome in 1970 and served also as rector of the university (1980–5) and then rector of its St Sophia's College. Since 1975 he has been a member of the editorial board of the theological quarterly *Bohosloviia*, in which he has published several articles.

Muzychna Drama (Musical Drama). The first Ukrainian opera theater. It was established in Kiev in 1919 by the All-Ukrainian Music Committee (headed by L. Sobinov) and the All-Ukrainian Theater Committee (headed by K. Mardzhanishvili) with the active support of S. Bondarchuk, S. Butovsky, and L. Kurbas. Its chief conductor was Ya. Stepovy; chief opera director, M. Bonch-Tomashevsky; chief designer, A. Petrytsky; and chief ballet master, M. Mordkin. L. Kurbas and V. Haievsky worked at the theater as directors, O. Khvostenko-Khvostov as scenery designer, and L. Sobinov, M. Lytvynenko-Volgemut, O. Petliash-Bariotti, and P. Tsesevych as soloists. The theater prepared M. Lysenko's *Utoplena* (The Drowned Maiden), Hutel's *Aziade*, S. Moniuszko's *Halka*, and M. Lysenko's *Taras Bulba*, but performed only the first two operas before Kiev was invaded by A. Denikin's army and the theater was dissolved.

Muzychna Ukraina (Musical Ukraine). A publishing house established in Kiev in 1966 which developed out of the music division of Mystetstvo publishers. The major producer of music editions in Ukraine, it has five editorial departments (musicology, Soviet songs and vocal music, instrumental music, textbook editions, and esthetic appreciation for children and youth). It publishes the series 'Ukraïns'ka symfonichna muzyka' (Ukrainian Symphonic Music), 'Perlyny svitovoï muzyky' (Pearls of World Music), and 'Symfonichna muzyka XX stolittia' (Symphonic Music of the 20th Century), as well as the learner series 'Skrypka' (The Violin) and 'Fortepiano' (The Pianoforte). It also publishes the musicological series 'Tvorchi portrety ukraïns'kykh kompozytoriv' (Portraits of Ukrainian Composers and Their Work), the annual *Ukraïns'ke muzykoznavstvo*, the bimonthly periodical *Muzyka*, and *Muzychni vechory* (Musical Evenings), a monthly compilation of works for amateur ensembles.

Muzychni visti (Music News). A quarterly journal of music and the performing arts. Published by the Dnipro Choir in St Paul, Minnesota, under the name *Visti* from 1962, the journal was edited by O. Kostiuk. It contained articles on Ukrainian music and the performing arts and included P. Macenko, Z. Lysko, and R. Prydatkevych among its contributors. It moved briefly to Jersey City, New Jersey, in 1971–2, where it changed its name and was published and edited by M. Kots.

Muzychnyi kalendar-al'manakh (Musical Calendar-Almanac). A short-lived annual miscellany published in 1904–7 in Lviv by R. Zarytsky. Its premier issue was dedicated to M. Lysenko. It represents the first attempt by Ukrainians to publish a musical serial.

Muzyka, Maksym, b 15 July 1889 in Lviv, d 24 May 1972 in Lviv. Physician, bacteriologist, and civic leader; full member of the Shevchenko Scientific Society (NTSh) from 1933. A graduate of Lviv University (MD, 1913), he was president of the Medical Hromada (1911–12), founded and headed the Bacteriological-Chemical Institute of the NTSh, and taught at the Lviv (Underground) Ukrainian University (1921–5), which he helped organize. He was president of the Ukrainian Physicians' Society in 1925, 1927, and 1930, a member of the editorial board of *Likars'kyi vistnyk* (1922–39), and a member of the *Ukrainian Physicians' and *Narodnia Lichnytsia societies. He was deputy director of the Lviv Medical Institute (1939–41), head of its microbiology department (1940–1, 1949–69), and its director (1944–9). His publications include articles on bacteriology, epidemiology, and the history of medicine in Ukraine.

Muzyka, Yaroslava (née Stefanovych), b 10 January 1898 in Zalistsi, Zboriv county, Galicia, d 24 November 1973 in Lviv. Painter, graphic artist, and restorer; wife of M. *Muzyka and niece of S. *Krushelnytska. She studied

Yaroslava Muzyka: *Hetman Bohdan Khmelnytsky's Arrival in Kiev* (appliqué and embroidery, 1968)

painting under S. Batowski in Lviv, restoration under M. Kasperovych in Kiev and I. Hrabar in Moscow, and in Paris (1935). An icon restorer at the National Museum from 1928 and a founding member of the *Association of Independent Ukrainian Artists in interwar Lviv, she was best known for her book graphics, bookplates, and iconlike engravings. She painted still lifes, portraits, such as *Princess Olha* (1925), *Hutsul with a Pipe* (1928), *Portrait of a Woman* (1933), and *Beatrice* (1968), and paintings on glass, such as *Shepherdess* and *Anna Yaroslavna* (1965–8); produced over 350 prints, including the series 'Creatures' (1932–65), 'Nature' (1958–61), and 'H. Skovoroda's Symbols' (1972); and created glass bowls, enamel portraits of T. Shevchenko and Lesia Ukrainka, the enamel series 'Hutsul Folk Beliefs,' and the mosaic *Princess Olha* (1968). After the Second World War she was deported to Kazakhstan, and spent eight years there. Her works were exhibited in Lviv, Prague, Berlin, Chicago, Naples, and Los Angeles. A catalog of her last show in Lviv was published in 1968. Muzyka bequeathed her valuable collection of folk art and her own works to the Lviv Art Gallery.

Muzyka (Music). The foremost Ukrainian music periodical. Established as the official publication of the *Leontovych Music Society, it was published monthly in Kiev in 1923–6 and semimonthly in 1927 (the last three issues were published in Kharkiv). *Muzyka* contained articles on the history of Ukrainian music, and musical ethnography, reviews of the musical life, biographies, and bibliographical material. M. Hrinchenko, K. Kvitka, P. Klymko, M. Verykivsky, P. Kozytsky, and Ya. Yurmas worked on the periodical. *Muzyka* was renamed *Ukraïns'ka muzychna hazeta* in 1926. In 1928, after the dissolution of the Leontovych society, the journal was replaced by the monthly *Muzyka masam*, renamed *Muzyka mas* in 1931. In 1933–4 and in 1936–41 it appeared bimonthly in Kiev under the title *Radians'ka muzyka*. In 1970 *Muzyka* was revived in Kiev as a bimonthly publication sponsored by the Ukrainian SSR Ministry of Culture, the Union of Composers of Ukraine, and the Music Society of the Ukrainian SSR.

Muzyka masam. See *Muzyka*.

MVD (Ministerstvo vnutrennikh del; Ukrainian: MVS, or Ministerstvo vnutrishnikh sprav [Ministry of Internal Affairs]). A ministry of the Soviet government established on 19 March 1946 as a successor to the *NKVD. The MVD was a Union-republican ministry, which included a number of central agencies, branches in the national republics, and local units. Its bodies were under dual subordination; that is, they were responsible to both higher-level MVD organs and corresponding local soviets. The MVD oversaw and administered the uniformed police (*militia); fire fighters; prisons and labor camps; internal troops (though the *KGB may actually have controlled these troops); the internal passport system; city residence permits; the licensing of firearms, motor vehicles, printing/copying facilities; and state archives. Structurally, it was divided into a number of main administrations and administrations organized along functional lines.

The institutional status and responsibilities of the MVD underwent numerous changes from 1946. At first the *MGB, which was responsible for state security, was separate from the MVD. Then, after J. Stalin's death, from March 1953 to March 1954, the two ministries were merged to form a powerful MVD under the control of L. Beria. He was arrested in June 1953 and executed in December. S. Kruglov was reinstated as minister of internal affairs, and Beria's supporters in the top positions were purged. To avoid another challenge to its authority the Party leadership reduced the might of the MVD by transferring some of its functions to other ministries and by setting up an independent agency, the KGB, to handle state security. In the course of N. Khrushchev's campaign for 'socialist legality' the economic power of the ministry was trimmed: it lost administrative control over various enterprises (ie, construction, coal mining, oil extraction, and gold mining and processing), and its captive labor force was cut drastically by amnesties to political prisoners. In 1957 control of the border guards was handed over to the KGB. The MVD was weakened further in 1960, when the Union or central ministry was abolished, and only republican ministries and their local branches remained. In 1962 the institutional name was changed from MVD to the Ministry for the Protection of Public Order (MOOP), a designation which symbolically severed the ministry's link with its past.

Under L. Brezhnev, however, the ministry's institutional status was upgraded: its Union status and its name were restored in 1966 and 1968 respectively. It received more funds and better training for its personnel. During Yu. Andropov's and M. Gorbachev's regimes charges of high-level corruption and inefficiency in the MVD became common. As a result Brezhnev's supporters in the ministry's higher levels were dismissed, including N. Shchelokov, long-term head of the MVD/MOOP, and I. Churbanov, former first deputy chairman of the Union MVD and Brezhnev's son-in-law. Shchelokov committed suicide, and Churbanov was sentenced in December 1988 to 12 years' imprisonment. During his tenure as minister of internal affairs (December 1982 to February 1986) V. *Fedorchuk conducted a major purge of the ministry. He was succeeded by A. Vlasov (from 26 January 1986), V. Bakatin (from 22 October 1988), and B. Pugo (1 December 1990 to 22 August 1991).

J. Bilocerkowycz

My (We). A journal of literature and art published in Warsaw from 1933 to 1939 by the Variah publishing house. It was founded by supporters of the UNR Government-in-exile who were opposed to the ultranationalism of D. Dontsov's journal *Vistnyk. Until 1938 it was a quarterly; then it became a bimonthly. *My* was edited by A. Kryzhanivsky, I. Dubytsky, and B. Olkhivsky (in 1939). Among its contributors were B.I. Antonych, I. Cherniava, Yu. Kosach, H. Lazarevsky, V. Lesych, N. and P. Kholodny, M. Rudnytsky, and P. Zaitsev.

My i svit (We and the World). An illustrated popular journal published irregularly in Mittenwald (1950) and Paris (1951–5), and then monthly (later bimonthly) in Toronto and Niagara Falls (to 1985). Modeled in style and format on *Reader's Digest*, the journal contained reprinted and original articles on cultural, political, historical, and other topics. It also published literary works by Soviet Ukrainian and émigré writers. The journal devoted considerable attention to contemporary developments in Ukraine and frequently criticized émigré Ukrainian institutions and political parties. For this it was denounced by many émigrés as pro-Soviet. The editor and publisher of *My i svit* was M. *Koliankivsky.

Mycology. A branch of *botany dealing with the study of *mushrooms and fungi in general. Mycological research was undertaken in Ukraine before 1917 by individual botanists (A. Pitra, I. Borshchov, Ya. Walz, A. Yanovych) and emerged as a systematic study during the 1920s and 1930s, led by the VUAN, AN URSR (now ANU) *Institute of Botany and the ANU Institute of Microbiology and Epidemiology (later Virology). Much of the initial work of identifying, classifying, and studying the characteristics of fungi in Ukraine was undertaken by M. *Pidoplichko, V. *Bilai, S. Morokhovsky, and M. Zerova. One of the outstanding results of the efforts of Ukrainian mycologists is the five-volume *Vyznachnyk hrybiv Ukraïny* (Field Guide to Mushrooms of Ukraine, 1967–79). More recently mycological research in Ukraine has addressed experimental mycology and the commercial production of mushrooms.

Mydlovsky, Isydor [Mydlovs'kyj], b 4 February 1854 in Sadzhavka, Nadvirna county, Galicia, d 18 July 1916 in Lviv. Stage actor, playwright, and theatrical organizer. He played in the Ruska Besida Theater (1869–72) and was stage director of the Ternopil amateur theater (1890–1910). His populist dramas *Kapral Tymko* (Corporal Tymko, 1875) and *Invalid* (1881) were staged by the Ruska Besida Theater.

Myhal, Ivanna [Myhal'], b 6 July 1937 in Lviv, d 17 September 1983 in Toronto. Operatic mezzo-soprano. She emigrated as a refugee from Germany to Canada in 1949 and studied at the Royal Conservatory of Music in Toronto, the University of Toronto Faculty of Music's Opera School, the Summer Music School in Aspen, Colorado, and the New York Metropolitan Opera Studio. From 1969 she was a soloist at the Metropolitan Opera and also performed in operas and recitals in Miami, Newport (Rhode Island), and Toronto, on CBC Radio, and with 16 American and Canadian orchestras. A phonographic record of Ukrainian songs sung by Myhal was released in 1978.

Myhal, Taras [Myhal'], b 19 July 1920 in Rusiv, Sniatyn county, Galicia, d 13 August 1982 in Lviv. Prose writer and publicist. He contributed to many provincial newspapers in Lviv and was editor of publicistic literature in the journal *Zhovten'*. His collections of short stories and essays include *Na bystryni* (On the White Water, 1960), *Zustrich lita* (The Welcome of Summer, 1963), and *Bilyi hutsul* (The White Hutsul, 1964). His novels include *Shynok 'Oseledets' na lantsiuhu'* (The Herring on a Chain Tavern, 1966), *Vohon' i chad* (Fire and Fumes, 1970), *Probudzhene misto* (The Awakened City, 1976), and *Ostannyi parol'* (The Last Password, 1979). He was acclaimed and given an award for his collections of pamphlets directed against the Ukrainian liberation movement, opposition activists, and political émigrés. The pamphlets included *Zhyvym i mertvym* (To the Living and to the Dead, 1967), *ABN* (1967), *Znaide vas kometa-meta* (A Comet-Goal Will Find You, 1973), *Z-pid hanebnoho stovpa* (From under the Shameful Post, 1974), and *Strakh pered pravdoiu* (Fear of Truth, 1978).

Myhulin, Oleksii, b 20 September 1893 in Dvorichnyi Kut, near Derhachi, Kharkiv gubernia, d ? Zoologist. A graduate of Moscow University (1917), he was a director at the Kharkiv Plant Conservation Station (1925–9), teacher at the Ukrainian Agricultural Academy (1940–3), and professor at the Kharkiv Agricultural Institute (1943–75). He initiated the movement to conserve indigenous plant species in Ukraine and wrote the first survey of the mammals of Ukraine (1938).

Myhulko, Viktor [Myhyl'ko], b 11 December 1924 in Hubnyk, Haisyn county, Podilia gubernia. Film and theatrical designer. In 1940–7 he completed study at the Odessa Art School, and in 1947–53 at the State Institute for Cinema Arts in Moscow. In 1953 he began working in the Kiev Artistic Film Studio as art director for films and telefilms, among them *Ivan Franko* (1956), *Oleksa Dovbush* (1959), and *Doshch u chuzhomu misti* (Rain in a Strange City, 1980). He has done theatrical scenery for the Kiev Russian Drama Theater.

Myhura, Ivan (Mihura; monastic name: Ilarion), b and d ? Early-18th-century engraver. He was educated at the Kievan Mohyla College and became an archdeacon at the Kievan Cave Monastery and hegumen of St Nicholas's Monastery in Baturyn (1709–12). He made over 20 panegyric engravings, consisting of portraits and verses in honor of such notables as Hetmans I. Mazepa, P. Sahaidachny, I. Skoropadsky, and D. Apostol, Metropolitan S. Yavorsky, V. Kochubei, and I. Lomykovsky; prints of St John Chrysostom and St Nicholas; and printed portraits of A. Voinarovsky and Metropolitan V. Yasynsky and a self-portrait. A virtually complete collection of his printing blocks has been preserved at the Kievan Cave Monastery Museum.

Myketei, Hryhorii [Myketej, Hryhorij], b 1888, d 1945 in Austria. Educator and civic and political leader. In 1919 he was chief of the press bureau of the Supreme Command of the Ukrainian Galician Army and editor of *Strilets'*. After serving as envoy of the Western Ukrainian National Republic (ZUNR) to the kingdom of the Serbs, Croats, and Slovenes (later Yugoslavia) in 1919–20, he worked in the ZUNR Secretariat of Foreign Affairs in Vienna (1920–3).

Ivan Myhura: *Apotheosis of Hetman Ivan Mazepa* (engraving, 1700)

Upon his return to Lviv in 1924, he taught secondary school and edited the Lviv weekly *Rada and the pedagogical journal *Ukraïns'ka shkola*.

Hryhorii Myketei

Mykhail Vsevolodovych [Myxajil Vsevolodovyč], b August 1179, d 20 September 1246 in Sarai, near Astrakhan. Kievan Rus' prince of Chernihiv; son of Vsevolod Sviatoslavych Chermny and an Olhovych by lineage. After the death of Volodymyr Sviatoslavych at the Battle of

Kalka in 1223, Mykhail assumed the throne of Chernihiv and began a campaign of territorial aggrandizement. He gained control of Novgorod and waged an ongoing struggle for Kiev and Halych, particularly against *Danylo Romanovych. With the help of Iziaslav Volodymyrovych, Mykhail succeeded in taking Kiev in 1236, but his tenure was short-lived. He fled to Hungary after the Mongols captured Chernihiv in 1239, thereby escaping the sack of Kiev in 1240. He returned to Rus' in 1241 in an attempt to regain his possessions, and went to Sarai in 1246 to obtain a patent to rule from *Batu Khan. The Mongol leader had Mykhail executed, probably for not surrendering Kiev and possibly (according to some chronicles) for ordering the death of Mongol envoys sent in 1239 to negotiate a peace with him. Popular perception attributed his execution to a refusal to participate in pagan rites, and a cult developed around Mykhail as a staunch defender of Orthodoxy. The veneration accorded him eventually brought about his canonization by the Russian Orthodox church and the transfer of his remains to Moscow during the 16th century, an act that was also motivated by the intention to propagandize the political and religious continuity between Kievan Rus' and Muscovy. A book about Mykhail, by M. Dimnik, was published in Toronto in 1981.

Mykhailiuk, Andrii [Myxajljuk, Andrij], b 30 November 1911 in Hermanivka, Kiev county, d 24 October 1937 in Kiev. Socialist-realist poet. He wrote three poetry collections, *Virshi* (Poems, 1932), *Kinets' idylii* (End of an Idyll, 1933), and *Soniachnyi den'* (A Sunny Day, 1936). Mykhailiuk was sentenced to death by firing squad during the Stalinist terror. He was rehabilitated under N. Khrushchev, and a selection of his verse was published in 1959.

Mykhailiv, Leonyd [Myxajliv], b 1884, d ? Political leader. A member of the Ukrainian Social Democratic Workers' party, he served as UNR minister of labor in V. Holubovych's cabinet (February–April 1918). In 1919 he was appointed deputy chief of the UNR diplomatic mission to Poland. In 1921 he returned to Lutske, where he worked for Ukrainbank. In 1939 he was deported by the Soviets, and his later fate is unknown.

Mykhailiv, Yukhym [Myxajliv, Jukhym], b 27 October 1885 in Oleshky (now Tsiurupynske], Tavriia gubernia, d 15 July 1935 in Kotlas, Arkhangelsk oblast, RSFSR. Symbolist painter, graphic artist, and art scholar. He studied in Moscow at the Stroganov Applied Arts School (1902–6) and School of Painting, Sculpture, and Architecture (1906–10). In the 1910s he began contributing poetry to Ukrainian journals and designing book and magazine covers and illustrations. From 1917 he lived in Kiev, where he was active in the Ukrainian Scientific Society, directed an arts and crafts school (from 1923), and headed the All-Ukrainian Committee for the Preservation of Monuments of Antiquity and Art, the Leontovych Music Society (1921–4), and the Kiev branch of the Association of Artists of Red Ukraine. He contributed articles on Ukrainian art and artists to *Mystetstvo*, *Zhyttia i revoliutsiia*, and *Bibliolohichni visti* and wrote books on weaving (1919) and earthenware ceramics (1921) in Ukraine and on the artists M. Zhuk (1930) and H. Diadchenko (1931). Mykhailiv painted or drew over 300 works. Among them there are

Yukhym Mykhailiv: *Behind the Curtain of Life* (pastel, 1923)

three prominent themes: the Ukrainian national revival (*Music of the Stars* [1919], the triptych *Moonlight Sonata* [1925]), the Ukrainian past (*To the Goddess Lada* [1915], the triptych *God's Creator* [1916], *Stone Babas* [1919], *Yaroslavna's Grief* [1925]), and death (*On the Edge of Eternity* [1926]). Mykhailiv was arrested in 1934 by the NKVD and exiled to the Soviet Arctic, where he died. A book about him (ed Yu. Chaplenko), with reproductions of his works, was published in New York in 1988.

Mykhailivka [Myxajlivka]. VI-16. A town smt (1990 pop 15,100) and a raion center in Zaporizhia oblast. It was founded at the beginning of the 19th century, and attained smt status in 1965. It has several enterprises of the food industry and a regional museum.

Mykhailivka settlement. A multi-occupational settlement of the 3rd to 2nd millennium BC, near the present-day village of Mykhailivka, Kherson oblast. Excavations in 1952–5 and 1960–3 identified the existence of an earlier copper age settlement and a later *Pit-Grave occupation.

Mykhailivka Virgin Soil Preserve. See Ukrainian Steppe Nature Reserve.

Mykhailo Olelkovych [Myxajlo Olel'kovyč], b ?, d 30 August 1481 in Vilnius. Lithuanian-Ruthenian appanage prince of Slutsk and Kopyl, in Belarus; son of Prince *Olelko of Kiev and Anastasiia, daughter of Grand Prince Vasilii Dimitrovich of Moscow. In 1470–1 he served as King Casimir IV Jagiellończyk's viceroy in Novgorod the Great. When he did not succeed his late brother, *Semen Olelkovych, as appanage prince and voivode of Kiev, Mykhailo and Princes Fedir *Bilsky (his cousin) and Ivan Holshansky organized a conspiracy to assassinate Casimir IV. The conspiracy was uncovered, and Mykhailo was executed for treason.

Mykhailov, Kostiantyn [Myxajlov, Kostjantyn], b 29 December 1882 in Krolevets, Chernihiv gubernia, d 3 April 1961 in Kiev. Pedagogue and pianist. A graduate of the Kiev School of Music (1907) and the St Petersburg Conservatory (1913), he studied piano with V. Pukhalsky. He was a cofounder and professor of the *Kiev Conservatory as well as its director (1922–6) and prorector (1934–53). He also headed the Kiev Opera College (1920–1), and the Lysenko Music and Drama Institute (1927–33) and co-founded the Kiev Philharmonic (1934). In 1939–40 he was sent to Western Ukraine as an organizer of music education. His pupils include the pianists L. Weintraub and I. Zettel.

Mykhailova Hora. An estate near Prokhorivka, Zolotonosha county, Poltava gubernia (now Kaniv raion, Cherkasy oblast). It was the location of the orchards of Mykhailo *Maksymovych, where he lived for nearly 30 years. His main residence has been preserved. It is of particular interest because of its famous visitors. T. *Shevchenko stayed there in June 1859 and there wrote the poem 'Mariia' and painted portraits of Maksymovych and his wife. N. *Gogol was another visitor; the local church, built by Zaporozhians in 1774, appears in his story *Vii*. Today the residence is a memorial museum dedicated to Maksymovych, and a rest resort has been built on the grounds.

Mykhailovsky, Oleksander [Myxajlovs'kyj], b 1882, d 1932 in Poděbrady, Czechoslovakia. Engineer and civic activist. As a young man he was active in the Revolutionary Ukrainian party. In 1918–19 he was vice-chairman of the Poltava gubernia zemstvo executive and then director of the UNR Department of Land Reform. After emigrating to Czechoslovakia he lectured at the Ukrainian Husbandry Academy in Poděbrady. His publications include a mathematics textbook (1922) and several works on milling in the Poltava region.

Mykhailovsky, Volodymyr [Myxajlovs'kyj], b 15 August 1914 in Konstiantynohrad (now Krasnohrad), Poltava gubernia, d 13 December 1978 in Lviv. Scientist in the fields of automation, telemechanics, and measurement technology; corresponding member of the AN URSR (now ANU) from 1961. He graduated from the Moscow Energy Institute (1939) and headed a department at the AN URSR Institute of Machinery and Automation from 1952. His main contributions were in designing measuring devices and the manipulation and transmission of information, particularly in mining and prospecting applications.

Mykhailychenko, Hnat [Myxajlyčenko] (pseud: Ihnatii Mykhailych), b 27 September 1892 in Studenok, Kursk gubernia (now Myropillia, Krasnopillia raion, Sumy oblast), d 21 November 1919 in Kiev. Writer, revolutionary, and cultural activist. He was arrested in 1915 and sentenced to six years of hard labor for his Socialist Revolutionary activity. He served two years of his sentence and returned to Ukraine in 1917, during the February Revolution. A member of the *Borotbists, he became people's commissar of education of the new Communist government in Kiev in 1919. He remained in Kiev during A. Denikin's advance on the city, was captured by the White forces, and was executed.

The relatively small canon of Mykhailychenko's writings includes the symbolic and allegorical *Blakytnyi roman* (The Azure Novel, 1921), the short story 'Istoriia odnoho zamakhu' (The Story of One Assassination Attempt), and a number of lyrical, free-form prose miniatures published in the journal *Mystetstvo*, which he coedited with M. Semenko, and in the almanacs *Chervonyi vinok* and *Muzahet*

Hnat Mykhailychenko   Kostiantyn Mykhalchuk

and the journal *Shliakhy mystetstva*. Two collections of his works were published posthumously, *Noveli* (Novellas, 1922) and *Tvory* (Works, 1929).

The official criticism of the period, particularly that of V. Koriak, considered Mykhailychenko and other Borotbist writers to be the 'first wave of the brave,' that is, the originators of Ukrainian Soviet literature. After 1930, however, those writers were declared counterrevolutionary and were banned. There was no talk of rehabilitating Mykhailychenko until 1987.

I. Koshelivets

Mykhailychenko Theater (Teatr im. H. Mykhailychenka). A leftist experimental theater-studio founded in 1920 in Kiev as Tsentrostudiia under the leadership of Marko *Tereshchenko. A former member of *Molodyi Teatr, Tereshchenko denied the importance of the playwright, the director, and the actor as individuals and proclaimed Tsentrostudiia's creative platform of *mystetstvo diistva* 'the art of the performance.' Members of the theater worked out a so-called *zaduma* (conception), which essentially followed the ideals of the *Proletkult. In May 1921 Tsentrostudiia was renamed in honor of the writer H. Mykhailychenko. Its first production, *Pershyi budynok novoho svitu* (The First Building in the New World, 1921), portrayed a struggle between the proletariat and capitalists, and its second one, *Nebo horyt'* (The Sky Is Burning, 1922), portrayed a miners' uprising. Both performances were staged without scenery or dialogue and attempted to create a 'theater of the collective art.' The performance of *Carnival* (1923) included some episodes from contemporary life. Tereshchenko's attempts to adapt prose and drama works to the demands of the theater's cultural platform did not succeed, and early in 1926 the Mykhailychenko Theater ended its performances.

Mykhalchuk, Kostiantyn [Myxal'čuk, Kostjantyn], b 2 January 1841 in Zozulyntsi, Berdychiv county, Kiev gubernia, d 20 April 1914 in Kiev. Linguist; member of the Ukrainian Scientific Society in Kiev (UNTK), the Historical Society of Nestor the Chronicler, and the Shevchenko Scientific Society (from 1911). He studied at Kiev University (1859–61), was active in the university's Ukrainian hromada, and taught at the first Ukrainian Sunday school in Kiev. Persecuted by the authorities for his Ukrainophile activities, he was kept under house arrest on his mother's homestead in 1863–6. From 1873 he worked as an office manager of the Kiev Brewing Company, was active in the Old Hromada of Kiev, and contributed publicistic articles under various pseudonyms (eg, Kh[okho]-l) to *Kievskii telegraf, Trud,* and *Zaria* in Kiev, and *Dilo* and *Pravda* in Lviv. In *Trudy etnografichesko-statisticheskoi ekspeditsii v Zapadno-russkii krai,* edited by his friend P. *Chubynsky, he published an ethnographic study of the Poles in Right-Bank Ukraine and the first scholarly descriptive and genetic study of Ukrainian dialects (1872). In the latter monograph he conceptualized the still-accepted tripartite (northern, southwestern, and southeastern) division of the dialects and described subdialects within them. He also prepared the first Ukrainian dialectal map (1871). Although Mykhalchuk did not produce a systematic history of the Ukrainian language, in several articles and reviews published from 1893 on in *Kievskaia starina, Zapysky* UNTK (of which he became a coeditor in 1909), and *Ukrainskaia zhizn'* he examined the main questions of the historical phonetics, morphology, and origins of Ukrainian. In some of his concepts he was a precursor of structuralism. With Ye. *Tymchenko he prepared a program for the collection of Ukrainian dialectal features (publ 1908) and was elected a corresponding member of the Russian Academy of Sciences. His 1886 open letter to A. Pypin in defense of the Ukrainian language was published as a brochure in 1909, and another defense, written in 1898 in reply to attacks in *Kievlianin,* was published only in 1929 in the VUAN *Ukraïns'kyi diialektolohichnyi zbirnyk* (vol 2). A collection of philological articles dedicated to his memory was published in Kiev in 1915. His selected works appeared in 1991.

R. Senkus

Mykhalevych, Mykhailo [Myxalevyč, Myxajlo], b 22 July 1906 in Kiev, d 9 February 1984 in Philadelphia. Artist and political figure; grandson of O. *Mykhalevych. He studied at the Kiev State Art Institute (1924–8). After escaping from the USSR he continued his studies at the Art and Crafts School (1934–6) and State Academy of Arts (1937–8) in Prague. After joining the OUN he headed its art department (1934–42) and the art workshop of the Supreme Command of the Carpathian Sich in Carpatho-Ukraine (1939). After being released from a Hungarian concentration camp he went to Kiev with an OUN expeditionary group in 1941. From 1942 he worked in Lviv in the cultural department of the Ukrainian Central Committee and oversaw the art cabinet at the Institute of Folk Creativity there (1942–4). As a postwar refugee in Germany, he taught commercial art in a DP camp and painted iconostases. He was appointed cultural officer of the OUN Leadership (Melnyk faction) in 1947 and, after emigrating to the United States, head of the OUN there in 1950. His graphic art (mostly book graphics) was exhibited in Lviv, Naples, Canada, and the United States.

Mykhalevych, Opanas [Myxalevyč] (pseud: Panas Oberezhny), b 17 July 1848 in Skulyn, Kovel county, Volhynia gubernia, d 1 February 1925 in Zinovivske (now Kirovohrad). Community figure. A physician in the Kiev University clinic and a member of the *Hromada of Kiev from 1873, he was banished from Kiev by the tsarist authorities because of his Ukrainophile and socialist activism (he shared the ideas of M. *Drahomanov). He worked as a zemstvo physician in Myrhorod county, served in the

Russo-Turkish War of 1877, and worked at a Nizhen hospital before settling in Yelysavethrad (Kirovohrad) in 1878. There he practiced medicine and revived a clandestine Ukrainophile circle, which included Ye. Chykalenko, I. Karpenko-Kary, M. Kropyvnytsky, M. Levytsky, D. Markovych, O. Rusov, S. Rusova, and M. Sadovsky. In January 1885 he was arrested for circulating banned books, and in 1887, after two years in an Odessa prison, he was exiled to the village of Tunka, in Irkutsk gubernia, Siberia. In 1892 he was allowed to return with his family to Yelysavethrad, where he again practiced medicine. Mykhalevych collected folklore and translated into Ukrainian A. Smith's *Wealth of Nations,* which he paid to have published by the Prosvita society in Lviv in 1913.

Volodymyr Mykhalevych

Mykhalevych, Volodymyr [Myxalevyč], b 10 March 1930 in Chernihiv. Mathematician and cyberneticist; full member of the AN URSR (now ANU) since 1973 and of the USSR Academy of Sciences from 1984. He completed his studies at the University of Kiev in 1952, and since 1958 has worked at the Computing Center (later the ANU Institute of Cybernetics) in Kiev (serving as its director from 1982). He is known for his research in cybernetics, particularly in optimization theory and economic cybernetics. He invented the method of serial analysis for numerical solutions of problems of optimization.

Mykhalkiv hoard. A large hoard of gold artifacts, including a goblet, two crowns, bracelets, clasps, and decorative items believed to be Thracian-Cimmerian in origin. These items were recovered during the excavation of an 8th- to 7th-century BC settlement in Mykhalkiv, Ternopil oblast, in 1878 and 1897.

Mykhnevych, Osyp [Myxnevyč] (Mikhnevych, Yosyf), b 1809 in Lokachi, Volodymyr-Volynskyi county, Volhynia gubernia, d 2 November 1885 in Odessa. Philosopher. A graduate of the Kiev Theological Academy (1835), he lectured there (1836–9) and was a professor of philosophy (1839–49) at the Richelieu Lyceum in Odessa and an assistant curator of the Kiev (1859–67) and Warsaw (1867–71) school districts. In his philosophical outlook he was an idealist, influenced by F. Schelling and to some extent by G. Hegel, yet he stubbornly defended revelation as a source of philosophical knowledge about God and man. He wrote a biography of Duke A.E. du Plessis de Richelieu (1849), a history of the Richelieu Lyceum (1857), articles on Greek philosophy (1839) and the nature of philosophy (1840, 1842), a logic textbook (1847; 2nd edn 1874), and a popular exposition of Schelling's philosophy (1850).

Myklashevsky [Myklaševs'kyj]. A family of Cossack *starshyna* and Russian nobility in the Chernihiv region. It originated most likely with Andrii (aka Andrushko Myklashechko), a registered Cossack of Chyhyryn company in Right-Bank Ukraine in 1649. His son, Mykhailo *Myklashevsky, was colonel of Starodub regiment in 1689–1706. Mykhailo's sons, Andrii (d 1752), Stepan (d 1750), and Ivan (1740), began the family's senior and junior Starodub lines and the Hlukhiv line. The senior Starodub line included the economists Ivan *Myklashevsky and Oleksander *Myklashevsky and their brother, Mykola (13 July 1860 to 9 June 1909), a member of the first Russian State Duma from Chernihiv gubernia. The Hlukhiv line included Andrii (19 July 1801 to 1895), the owner of a porcelain factory in Volokytyne, Hlukhiv county, that was famous for its artistic wares. Prominent members of the junior Starodub line were Gov Mykhailo *Myklashevsky and the musicologist Yosyp *Myklashevsky. Mykhailo's son Oleksander (1798–1831) was a lieutenant colonel of a Russian guard regiment who was exiled for his involvement in the Decembrist movement to the Caucasus, where he died in battle in Dagestan. Mykhailo's younger sons and their descendants owned large estates in Chernihiv and Katerynoslav gubernias in the 19th and early 20th centuries. They established a line of the family in Katerynoslav.

O. Ohloblyn

Myklashevsky, Ivan [Myklaševs'kyj], b 22 September 1858 in Bilyi Kolodiaz, Vovchanske county, Kharkiv gubernia, d 2 December 1901 in Kharkiv. Economist, historian, and statistician; brother of O. *Myklashevsky. A graduate of Odessa University (1882), he taught at Moscow University and then held the chair of political economy and statistics at Kharkiv University (1896–1901). He wrote some 30 works on agrarian history, especially that of Southern and Slobidska Ukraine, including *K istorii sel'-skokhoziaistvennogo byta Moskovskogo gosudarstva: Zaselenie i sel'skoe khoziaistvo iuzhnoi okrainy XVII v.* (On the History of the Agricultural Life of the Muscovite State: The Settlement and Agriculture of the Southern Borderland in the 17th Century, 1894), which was one of the first works on agriculture in the Russian Empire based on archival documents, and 'Ocherki krest'ianskogo khoziaistva v Malorossii' (Essays on Peasant Agriculture in Little Russia, in *Izvestiia* of the Imperial Academy of Sciences, 1887).

Myklashevsky, Mykhailo [Myklaševs'kyj, Myxajlo], b in the 1640s, d 30 March 1706 in Niasvizh, Belarus. Cossack statesman. An adjutant (1671) and close adviser to Hetman D. Mnohohrishny (1672), after the 1672 Baturyn revolt against Mnohohrishny he served in the governments of Hetmans I. Samoilovych and I. Mazepa and became town otaman of Hlukhiv (1675) and osaul of Nizhen regiment (1679–82). He participated in the 1677–8 Chyhyryn campaigns and served on various diplomatic missions, particularly to Moscow. As general flag-bearer (1682) and general osaul of the Hetman state (1683–90) and colonel of Starodub regiment (1689–1706) he owned

Col Mykhailo Myklashevsky (portrait) (1640s–1706)   Gov Mykhailo Myklashevsky (ca 1756–1847)

large estates, glassworks, and iron-ore mines in Starodub and Nizhen regiments. A benefactor of Ukrainian art, churches, and monasteries, he funded the construction of St George's Cathedral at the Vydubychi Monastery in Kiev. Myklashevsky opposed the pro-Muscovite policy of Mazepa's government. In 1703 he conducted secret negotiations with Polish and Lithuanian magnates with the aim of uniting Ukraine with the Polish Commonwealth on the basis of the provisions of the 1658 Union of Hadiache and thereby creating a Great Ruthenian principality. He was killed during the Swedish siege of Niasvizh.

Myklashevsky, Mykhailo [Myklaševs'kyj, Myxajlo], b ca 1756 in Demenka, Topal company, Starodub regiment, d 26 August 1847 in Ponurivka, Starodub county, Chernihiv gubernia. Military figure and statesman; great-grandson of M. *Myklashevsky. He served in a guard regiment in St Petersburg (1775–89), was colonel of the Starodub Carabineer Regiment (1789–92), and commanded regiments along the Dnieper Line (1792–7), from 1795 as a brigadier. In 1797 Emperor Paul I appointed him governor of Volhynia and Little Russia gubernias, but in 1800 he removed him. Alexander I appointed him governor of *New Russia gubernia in 1801 and a senator in 1808.

Myklashevsky was a Ukrainian autonomist who defended Ukrainian interests in St Petersburg and kept contact with the *Novhorod-Siverskyi patriotic circle. In 1812 he submitted a controversial proposal for the reintroduction of Cossack regiments in Left-Bank Ukraine that would include state peasants in their ranks. He was forced to retire in 1818, and settled on his Ponurivka estate. There he created a center of Ukrainian culture, politics, and historical study (*Istoriia Rusov* was written there) and established a profitable woolens factory. Myklashevsky was opposed to serfdom and drafted a number of proposals aimed at bettering the lot of the peasantry.

Myklashevsky, Oleksander [Myklaševs'kyj], b 8 December 1864 in Bilyi Kolodiaz, Vovchanske county, Kharkiv gubernia, d 1917. Economist; brother of I. Myklashevsky. After completing his master's dissertation on the classical theory of money (pub 1895) at Moscow University, he taught political economy there and at Tartu University. He was one of the leading specialists in monetary theory in the Russian Empire. Besides articles he wrote *Rabochyi vopros i sotsial'noe zakonodatel'stvo v Germanii* (The Labor Question and Social Legislation in Germany, 1896) and *Denezhnyi vopros v literature i v iavleniiakh deistvitel'noi zhizni* (The Monetary Question in Literature and in the Phenomena of Real Life, 1896).

Myklashevsky, Yosyp [Myklaševs'kyj, Josyp], b 16 April 1882 in St Petersburg, d 21 September 1959 in Kharkiv. Musicologist, pianist, and educator. He graduated from the Kiev School of Music in the piano class of V. Pukhalsky and theory class of Ye. Ryb (1911) and from the St Petersburg Conservatory (1913). He became editor of the journal *V mire iskusstva* and then director of the St Petersburg Music Institute (1913–18). As a pianist he popularized the works of M. *Lysenko and authored one of the earliest attempts to analyze Lysenko's style. In 1919–47 he taught in a number of music schools in Kharkiv, including the Conservatory. Among his main writings are *Ocherk deiatel'nosti Kievskogo otdeleniia Imperatorskogo Russkogo muzykal'nogo obshchestva za 50 let* (A Sketch of the Activity of the Kiev Branch of the Imperial Russian Music Society for the Last 50 Years, 1913) and *Muzychna i teatral'na kul'tura Kharkova kintsia xvii–pershoï polovyny xix st.* (Kharkiv's Musical Culture from the Late 17th to the Mid-19th Century, 1967).

Ivan Mykolaichuk (in *Shadows of Forgotten Ancestors*)

Mykolaichuk, Ivan [Mykolajčuk], b 15 June 1941 in Chortoryia, Bukovyna, d 3 August 1987 in Kiev. Film actor, screenwriter, and director. In 1957 he completed drama studies at the Chernivtsi Oblast Ukrainian Music and Drama Theater, and in 1965 he graduated from the Kiev Institute of Theater Arts. From 1965 he worked in the Kiev Artistic Film Studio. Following the esthetic traditions of O. Dovzhenko, he gave intense, realistic portrayals of archetypal and historical characters in films such as *Son* (The Dream, based on T. Shevchenko's poem, 1964), *Tini zabutykh predkiv* (Shadows of Forgotten Ancestors, 1964), *Zakhar Berkut* (1972), *Bilyi ptakh z chornoiu oznakoiu* (A White Bird with a Black Mark, 1972, written with Yu. Illienko), and *Vavilon–xx* (Babylon–xx, 1979), which he directed. On the basis of Mykolaichuk's script Illienko directed the film *Mriiaty i zhyty* (To Dream and Live, 1975). Mykolaichuk also directed the film *Taka piznia, taka, tepla osin'* (Such a Late, Such a Warm Autumn, 1982, written with V. Korotych). A book of memoirs about Mykolaichuk, interviews with him, and his scenarios was published in Kiev in 1991.

Mykolaiv

Mykolaiv [Mykolajiv]. VII-12. A city (1991 pop 513,000) at the confluence of the Boh and the Inhul rivers, oblast capital, raion center, sea and river port, and industrial center. Archeologists have found several settlements from the Neolithic Period, the Bronze Age, and the early Slavic period (3rd–5th century AD) in the vicinity of the city. The region was uninhabited until a fort (1784) and a shipbuilding wharf (1788) were built during the Russo-Turkish War of 1787–91. A settlement, which was named Mykolaiv, sprang up around them. In 1802 it became the capital of a gubernia, and in 1861, a county center of Kherson gubernia. Until 1862 it was an exclusively military port, where sailing ships and steamships (beginning in the 1820s) were built, and where the first iron ship on the Black Sea was constructed, in 1853. During the Crimean War and again in 1870–1900 the command of the Black Sea navy was located in Mykolaiv. In the second half of the 19th century Mykolaiv developed into the third-largest port in the Russian Empire and an important industrial center and railway junction. Its population grew from 3,300 in 1792 to 32,500 in 1860, 92,000 in 1897, and 104,000 in 1914. During the revolutionary period Mykolaiv changed hands frequently, and much of its industry was destroyed. The population decreased to 84,000 in 1923 and then rose steadily to 105,000 in 1926 and 169,000 in 1939. The city was designated an oblast capital in 1937. During the Second World War it was devastated. After the war it was rebuilt, and it expanded as its population grew, to 242,000 in 1961. The population has become ethnically more diverse. In 1926, Russians accounted for 44.5 percent of the population, Ukrainians for 29.9 percent, and Jews for 21 percent, but by 1959 the proportion of Ukrainians had risen to 60 percent.

Today Mykolaiv is an important industrial center. Its major industries are machine building, food processing, light industry, and building-materials manufacturing. Of its 250 enterprises, the largest are the *Black Sea Shipyard, the *Mykolaiv Okean Shipyard, the *Mykolaiv Shipyard, the Mykolaiv Reinforced-Concrete Plant, and the Mykolaiv Cotton Manufacturing Complex. It is the home of a number of research institutions, such as the *Mykolaiv Shipbuilding Institute and the *Mykolaiv Pedagogical Institute, three theaters (Ukrainian, Russian, and puppet), a regional museum, and an observatory. Mykolaiv boasts a number of architectural monuments, including the building of the Black Sea Naval Command (1793), the Black Sea Naval Observatory (1827), St Nicholas's Church (1817), and the Naval Officers' Building (1824).

BIBLIOGRAPHY
Istoriia mist i sil Ukraïns'koï RSR: Mykolaïvs'ka oblast' (Kiev 1971)
Mykolaïv (Kiev 1981)

Mykolaiv [Mykolajiv]. IV-4. A city (1988 pop 13,600) and raion center in Lviv oblast. It was founded before 1570, and received the rights of *Magdeburg law in 1578. In 1917 Mykolaiv was a training center of the Ukrainian Sich Riflemen. In 1919 the Lviv Brigade of the Ukrainian Galician Army fought a battle with the Polish army nearby. The town's chief enterprises are a cement-mining complex and a building-materials factory.

Mykolaiv Art Museum (Mykolaivskyi khudozhnii muzei im. V.V. Vereshchagina). An art museum established in Mykolaiv in 1914. Its collection contains over 6,000 works by Ukrainian, Russian, and Western European artists, among them I. Aivazovsky, V. Vereshchagin, V. Tropinin, L. Borovykovsky, K. Trutovsky, R. Sudkovsky, K. Briullov, L. Pozen, A. Kuindzhi, M. Yaroshenko, K. Kostandi, Z. Serebriakova, O. Murashko, S. Vasylkivsky, P. Nilus, Ye. Bukovetsky, M. Manizer, A. Kotska, V. Mykyta, and T. Yablonska. Branches of the museum are located in Voznesenske and Ochakiv. Since 1986 the museum has been housed in a new building with 10 exhibition halls. A guide to it was published in 1986.

Mykolaiv Astronomical Observatory. See Astronomy.

Mykolaiv gubernia. See Kherson gubernia.

Mykolaiv oblast. An administrative territory (1990 pop 1,336,200) in Southern Ukraine with an area of 24,600 sq km. It is divided into 19 raions, 253 rural councils, 9 cities, and 20 towns (smt). The capital is Mykolaiv. The oblast was formed on 22 September 1937.

Physical geography. Most of the oblast lies in the steppe of the Black Sea Lowland on both banks of the Boh River directly north of the Black Sea. The land is flat and slopes gently from the north toward the Black Sea. The northern part of the oblast covers the fringe of the Dnieper Upland and is dissected by ravines and river valleys. The jagged coastline is dotted with shallow saltwater lakes, limans, bays, spits, and sandy islands. In the north the soils are mostly low-humus chernozems; in the south, mostly chernozems and dark chestnut alkaline soils. In the floodplains of the river valleys the soils are alluvial. Virgin steppe flora and fauna have been preserved only in ravines and nature preserves. Some forests, consisting mostly of oak, maple, acacia, and elm, have survived in the south. The oblast is rich in granite, limestone, marl, kaolin, graphite, and gypsum deposits. Salt, mineral waters, and curative muds are extracted from the coastal lakes. The principal rivers in Mykolaiv oblast are the Boh and its tributaries – the Inhul, the Kodyma, the Chychykliia, and the Hnylyi Yelanets. In the northeast the main river is the Inhulets, a tributary of the Dnieper. The rivers are used mostly for irrigation. The climate is temperate-continental: the average January temperature is –5°C and the average July temperature is 23°C. The average annual precipitation is 300–350 mm in the south and 450 mm in the north. Winters are mild, and there is little snowfall. Summers are hot, dry, and windy. There are frequent dust storms and droughts.

History. According to archeological evidence the territory of the oblast has been inhabited since the Paleolithic period, as early as the 15th millennium BC. In the 8th to 3rd centuries BC the area was settled by Scythians and Sarmatians. The first Greek settlement on the northern Black Sea coast was established on Berezan Island in the 7th century BC. Later the territory belonged nominally to Kievan Rus', the Grand Duchy of Lithuania, and the Crimean Tatars. It was annexed by Turkey in 1475 and transferred to Russia after the Russo-Turkish War (1768–74). The territory of the present oblast was a part of New Russia gubernia (1774–95, 1796–1803), Voznesenske gubernia (1795–6), and Kherson gubernia (1803–1920). Mykolaiv gubernia, formed by the Soviet authorities in 1920, was incorporated into Odessa gubernia in 1922 and then divided among Mykolaiv, Odessa, Pervomaiske, and Kherson okruhas in 1925. The territory was reintegrated into Odessa oblast in 1932.

Population. The population of the oblast increased from 941,000 in 1940 to 1,148,000 in 1970 and 1,242,000 in 1979. The share of the urban population rose from 26 percent in 1940 to 66 percent in 1989. The average population density in 1990 was 54.3 inhabitants per sq km. The percentage of Ukrainians in the total population dropped from 81.2 percent in 1959 to 75.6 percent in 1989, and that of Russians rose from 13.8 to 19.4 percent. The oblast's largest cities are Mykolaiv, Pervomaiske, Voznesenske, and Ochakiv.

Industry. Industrial production accounts for 65.3 percent of the oblast's gross product. Its main industries are machine building and metalworking (42 percent of the industrial output in 1988), food processing, light industry (12 percent), and the building-materials industry. Mykolaiv's shipyards build and repair freighters, tankers, and other seacraft, and its giant plants build road-construction machines, cranes, food-processing machinery, and mining equipment. Irrigation equipment and diesel engines are built in Pervomaiske. The food industry consists of meat-packaging plants in Mykolaiv, Voznesenske, and Pervomaiske; dairies in Pervomaiske, Veselynove, and Nova Odessa; fruit- and vegetable-canning plants in Voznesenske and Snihurivka; a sugar refinery in Pervomaiske; a mineral-water bottling factory in Snihurivka, and a fish-processing plant in Ochakiv. The largest plants of the light industry are the sewing factories in Mykolaiv and Pervomaiske and the footwear and leather goods factories in Mykolaiv and Voznesenske. The building-materials industry is based on local resources. Cement is produced in Olshanske, and reinforced-concrete structures in Mykolaiv and Oleksandrivka. Power for the oblast's industries is provided by the Mykolaiv Thermoelectric Center, the Oleksandrivka, Pervomaiske, and Konstiantynivka hydroelectric stations, and the Southern Ukraine nuclear power plant.

Agriculture. In 1989 there were 224 collective farms and 155 state farms in Mykolaiv oblast. The total area of agricultural land in the oblast was 2,003,300 ha, of which 1,715,600 ha were cultivated, 238,400 ha were pasture, and 5,800 ha were hayfields. Of the seeded area 52.6 percent was devoted to grains, 30.5 percent to feed crops, and 13.3 percent to industrial crops. The main crops were winter wheat (28.8 percent of the seeded area), spring barley (8.9 percent), corn (18.9 percent), sunflower (8.9 percent), and sugar beet (4.2 percent). In 1979, vineyards occupied 17,700 ha, and fruit orchards (apples, pears, cherries, apricots, and plums), 27,800 ha. Animal husbandry accounts for 56 percent of the agricultural output and consists mostly of dairy- and beef-cattle farming. Some hog, sheep, poultry, rabbit, fish, and silkworm farming is practiced also. Fishing in the Black Sea and the limans contributes to the oblast's food production.

Transportation. In 1989 there were 753 km of railroad track in the oblast, 143 km of it electrified. The main lines crossing the oblast are the Mykolaiv–Znamianka–Kiev–Moscow, Odessa–Voznesenske–Bakhmach–Moscow, Mykolaiv–Odessa, and Mykolaiv–Kherson lines. The main railway junctions are Mykolaiv, Voznesenske, Pervomaiske, and Snihurivka. There were 5,300 km of highways, 4,700 km of which were paved. The main highways in the oblast are Mykolaiv–Odessa–Kishinev, Mykolaiv–Kherson–Symferopil, Mykolaiv–Kryvyi Rih, and Mykolaiv–Kirovohrad. Mykolaiv has an airport. Mykolaiv and Ochakiv are important seaports, and Oleksandrivka and Voznesenske are large river ports.

BIBLIOGRAPHY
Istoriia mist i sil Ukraïns'koï RSR: Mykolaïvs'ka oblast' (Kiev 1971)

Mykolaiv Okean Shipyard (Mykolaivskyi sudnobudivnyi zavod Okean). A shipbuilding plant in Mykolaiv, built from 1946 to 1951. In 1951–6 it built barges and sea vessels. Then it built 5,500-t refrigerated transport ships, 6,400-t refrigerated processing ships, and lumber carriers. In 1970 the shipyard changed to building larger dry-goods carriers and multipurpose ships. In the 1970s several oil tankers (130,000 t), supertrawlers (8,850 t), and ore carriers (62,500 t) were assembled there.

Mykolaiv Pedagogical Institute (Mykolaivskyi pedahohichnyi instytut im. V. Bielinskoho). An institute of higher education under the jurisdiction of the Ministry of Education of Ukraine. Founded in 1913 as a *teachers' institute, in 1920 it became an institute of people's education. In 1930 it was transformed into one of the *institutes of social education, and in 1933 it became a pedagogical institute. In 1986–7 the institute consisted of five faculties: history, philology, physics-mathematics, the pedagogy and methodology of elementary education, and physical education. The institute also trained instructors in Russian language and literature for the Uzbek SSR. In 1987 the student enrollment was 4,800.

Mykolaiv Regional Studies Museum (Mykolaivskyi kraieznavchyi muzei). A museum established in Mykolaiv in 1950 on the basis of the Mykolaiv City Natural Science and Regional Museum (est 1913) and the Mykolaiv Historical-Archeological Museum, which had been destroyed during the Second World War. The museum's exhibitions, based on holdings of over 68,000 items, pertain to the natural environment, archeology, and history of Mykolaiv and Mykolaiv oblast. The museum also has a sizable collection of minerals, stuffed animals, and butterflies and moths from around the world. It administers two other museums, the Ochakiv Military History Museum (est 1966) and the Mykolaiv Shipbuilding and Naval Museum (est 1978). Guidebooks to the museum have been published in Ukrainian (1962) and Russian (1979, 1980).

Mykolaiv Shipbuilding Institute (Mykolaivskyi korablebudivnyi instytut). A technical school of higher education under the Ukrainian Ministry of Higher and Specialized Secondary Education. Organized in 1920 as a polytechnical institution, in 1929 it was renamed the Mykolaiv Machine-Building Institute and in 1930 given its present name. It has departments of shipbuilding, machine building, and electrical instrumentation, two evening sections, postgraduate studies, and a branch in Kherson. In 1985 the institute had over 7,000 students.

Mykolaiv Shipyard (Mykolaivskyi sudnobudivnyi zavod im. 61 komunara). A shipbuilding plant in Mykolaiv. It was founded in 1788 as a dockyard of the Russian Admiralty. It built sailing and metal-hulled ships. In 1900 the famous battleship *Potemkin* was built there. Now the plant builds mainly refrigerated transport ships and self-propelled barges.

Mykolaiv Ukrainian Theater of Drama and Musical Comedy (Mykolaivskyi ukrainskyi teatr dramy i muzychnoi komedii). A theater established in 1959 as an oblast musical-drama theater on the basis of the oblast Shevchenko Ukrainian Drama Touring Theater and the local Young Spectator's Theater. Its repertoire has consisted of Ukrainian, Russian, and world classics, and contemporary plays, such as O. Korniichuk's *Storinka shchodennyka* (Page from a Diary) and V. Lukashov's musical comedy *Volodymyrs'ka hirka* (St Volodymyr's Hill). In 1979 its artistic director was V. Bezlepko.

Mykolaivka [Mykolajivka]. V-18, DB II-3. A town smt (1990 pop 16,300) on the Donets River in Donetske oblast. It is administered by the Slovianske municipal council. Mykolaivka was founded in the first half of the 18th century, and attained smt status in 1956. It is the home of the Slovianske Raion Electric Power Station.

Mykolaivka [Mykolajivka]. VII-11. A town smt (1990 pop 4,200) on the Chychykliia River and a raion center in Odessa oblast. It was founded in the late 18th century, and attained smt status in 1965. It has several food enterprises.

Mykulyntsi [Mykulynci]. IV–6. A town smt (1990 pop 3,800) on the Seret River in Terebovlia raion, Ternopil oblast. It was first mentioned in a historical document in 1096 under the name of Mykulyn. In the 12th and 13th centuries it belonged to Halych and Galicia-Volhynia principalities. It was annexed by Poland in 1387 and renamed Mykulyntsi in 1389. A castle was built in 1550 to protect the town from the Tatars. By 1595 Mykulyntsi had attained town status. After being destroyed by the Turks in 1672, the town never regained its prosperity. Today it has several food enterprises and a furniture and brick factory. Its architectural monuments include the ruins of the castle, a palace (18th–19th century), and a Roman Catholic church in the baroque style (18th century).

Mykysha, Mykhailo [Mykyša, Myxajlo], b 6 June 1885 in Myrhorod, Poltava gubernia, d 20 November 1971 in Kiev. Opera and concert singer (heroic tenor). He studied at the Lysenko Music and Drama School in the class of O. Myshuha. In 1910 he joined Sadovsky's Theater, and in subsequent years he was a soloist of the Kiev Opera (1914–22), the Bolshoi Theater, and the Kharkiv Opera (1932–4). He taught in the Kharkiv (from 1937) and the Kiev (from 1944) conservatories. His better-known opera roles include Vakula in P. Tchaikovsky's *Cherevichki* (Little Shoes) and Hermann in his *The Queen of Spades*, Herod in R. Strauss's *Salome*, and Raoul de Nangis in G. Meyerbeer's *Les Huguenots*. He was also an outstanding performer of Ukrainian songs. He compiled the methodological study *Praktychni osnovy vokal'noho mystetstva* (Practical Bases of Vocal Art) as retold and edited by M. Holovashchenko (Kiev 1971). Mykysha's biography, by M. Sheliubsky, was published in Kiev in 1947.

Taras Mykysha

Mykysha, Taras [Mykyša], b 2 February 1913 in Pryimivka (now Pryimivshchyna), Lubni county, Poltava gubernia, d 15 March 1958 in Buenos Aires. Pianist, teacher, and composer; son of M. *Mykysha. He studied initially in Kiev and Moscow; his formative years of 1927–33, however, were spent in Vienna, where he studied at the Academy of Music with J. Marx (composition) and others (graduating in 1930), and at the Klavier Meisterschule under P. Weingarten (finishing both theory and piano classes in 1933). In 1932 he won the first of several prizes at international music competitions and in 1933 started appearing as a soloist. Renouncing his Soviet citizenship in 1935, he remained in the West and toured extensively (appearing also with orchestras) in Hungary, Rumania, Austria, Czechoslovakia, Yugoslavia, Holland, and Sweden. From 1947 he worked in Buenos Aires as a piano teacher. His Ukrainian concert repertoire included works by V. Barvinsky, V. Kosenko, L. Revutsky, and M. Kolessa. Mykysha also composed a number of piano works based on Ukrainian folk melodies. These include *Ukrainian Rhapsody*, six sonatas, seven fugues, variations, preludes, dances, and chamber music.

Mykyta, Irenei, b 11 October 1936 in Peremyshl, Galicia. Stage director and teacher. He arrived in Adelaide, South Australia, in 1949 and started professional theater activity in 1955. He has worked with local Ukrainian and Australian theater groups as stage manager, director, and set constructor. He was a founding member and the vicepresident of Ethnic Broadcasters Inc (1975–8) and has taught drama and performing arts at the South Australian Institute of Technology (in Adelaide) since 1975.

Mykyta, Volodymyr, b 1 February 1931 in Rakoshyn, near Mukachiv, Transcarpathia. Painter. He studied under A. Erdeli, Y. Bokshai, and F. Manailo at the Uzhhorod School of Applied Art (1947–50). The influence of modernism is evident in his work, which consists of portraits, landscapes, still lifes, and genre paintings, such as *Collec-*

Volodymyr Mykyta: *Celebration in the Village Club* (1972)

tive-Farm Shepherd (1960), *Old Hutsul* (1966), *From Peak to Peak* (1973), *Good Morning* (1976), *Ivan Chendei* (1979), and *Apple Gathering* (1984). An album of his works was published in 1983.

Mykytas, Vasyl [Mykytas', Vasyl'], b 23 October 1924 in Zhovte, Verkhnodniprovske county, Katerynoslav gubernia. Literary critic and scholar. He graduated from Dnipropetrovske University in 1951. Among his numerous works are the critical survey *O.V. Dukhnovych* (1959), the monograph *Ukraïns'kyi pys'mennyk-polemist Mykhailo Andrella* (The Ukrainian Writer-Polemicist M. Andrella, 1960), *Pravda pro Vasylia Stefanyka* (The Truth about V. Stefanyk, 1975), *Davnia ukraïns'ka literatura* (Old Ukrainian Literature, coauthor, 1978), and *Ivan Franko – Doslidnyk ukraïns'koï polemichnoï literatury* (I. Franko, Researcher of Ukrainian Polemical Literature, 1983). Mykytas also coedited *Poety Zakarpattia: Antolohiia zakarpatoukraïns'koï poeziï XVI st.–1945* (Poets of Transcarpathia from the 16th Century to 1945, 1965).

Mykytchuk, Anastasiia [Mykytčuk, Anastasija] (née Pavliuk), b 19 September 1889 in Vyzhnytsia, Bukovyna, d 17 November 1977 in Hamilton, Ontario. Educator and political activist; wife of V. *Mykytchuk. A graduate of the Chernivtsi teachers' seminary, she was active in the radical movement in the Kolomyia district, where she organized rural women's groups and served as an executive member of the Ukrainian Radical party. In 1924 she helped to found the women's newspaper *Zhinocha dolia*, and in 1930–5 she assisted in the preparation of *Ukraïns'ka zahal'na entsyklopediia* (The Ukrainian General Encyclopedia, 1930–5). She left Ukraine in 1944 for Austria and Italy, and then Argentina, where she took an active part in organized Ukrainian life. In 1957 she settled in Canada.

Mykytchuk, Vasyl [Mykytčuk, Vasyl'], b 26 January 1887 in Prykmyshche, Kolomyia county, Galicia, d 7 August 1986 in Toronto. Educator and publisher. He initiated, spearheaded, and largely financed (with great personal sacrifice) the publishing of *Ukraïns'ka zahal'na entsyklopediia* (The Ukrainian General Encyclopedia,

1935), the first reference work of its kind (see *Encyclopedias of Ukraine). In 1936 he was a cofounder of the *Ukrainian Publishing Institute in Lviv. After the Second World War he emigrated, eventually to Canada.

Ivan Mykytenko   Dmytro Mykytiuk

Mykytenko, Ivan, b 6 October 1897 in Rivne, Yelysavethrad county, Kherson gubernia, d 18 October 1937. Writer, publicist, playwright, and Soviet activist. He was one of the leading organizers of Soviet literature in the 1920s and 1930s. Mykytenko headed the Odessa branch of *Hart while he was a student at the Odessa Medical Institute. In 1927 he moved to Kharkiv, where he finished his studies at the Kharkiv Medical Institute. From 1932 to 1934 he was an organizer of the founding committee of the Writers' Union of the USSR. In 1934 he became a member of the executive of the *Writers' Union of Ukraine. Mykytenko began writing poetry and publicistic works in 1922, while still a student in Odessa. His first published collection of stories was *Na soniashnykh honakh* (On Sunny Tilled Fields, 1926), and his first novel was *Braty* (Brothers, 1927). He also wrote humorous works for children, including 'Havryïl Kyrychenko – Shkoliar' (Havryil Kyrychenko, the Schoolboy). His more notable works, such as *Vurkahany* (1928) and *Ranok* (Morning, 1933), were about the homeless in Soviet society. Mykytenko's first plays, *Na rodiuchii zemli* (On Fertile Ground, 1925) and *Idu* (I Am Going, 1925), were unsuccessful. His play *Dyktatura* (Dictatorship, 1929) was on the collectivization of the Ukrainian village; its superficial symbolism, use of pathos, and occasionally deft humor endeared it to Party activists, and Mykytenko's plays became part of the repertoire of many Ukrainian and other Soviet theaters. The rest of his plays were written on commission, and served to illustrate the latest Party decisions. Among them were *Kadry* (or *Svitit' nam zori*) (Cadres [or Shine for Us, Stars], 1930), *Sprava chesty* (or *Vuhillia*) (A Matter of Honor [or Coal], 1931), and *Divchata nashoï kraïny* (The Girls of Our Country, 1932). His later plays *Bastyliia Bozhoï materi* (The Bastille of the Mother of God, 1933), *Dni iunosty* (Days of Youth, 1935–6), and *Marusia Churai* (1935) were less popular. His best play with respect to artistic quality was *Sol'o na fleiti* (Flute Solo, 1933–6), which was conceived as an official satire on a deposed grandee, but came to be staged as a satire on the entire Soviet system and was therefore banned. Despite the fact that Mykytenko never strayed from the Party line, in October 1937 he was removed from the executive of the Writ-

ers' Union of Ukraine, dismissed from his position as editor in chief of *Radians'ka literatura*, and expelled from the Party. Recent sources indicate that he committed suicide. After his death his works were proscribed. He was rehabilitated after 1956, and most of his works have been republished.

BIBLIOGRAPHY
Syrotiuk, M. *Ivan Mykytenko: Zhyttia i tvorchist'* (Kiev 1959)
Rod'ko, M. *Proza Ivana Mykytenka* (Kiev 1960)

I. Koshelivets

Mykytenko, Oleh, b 22 December 1928 in Kharkiv. Literary critic and translator; son of I. *Mykytenko. He graduated with a degree in philology from Kiev University in 1952 and completed a doctorate in 1957. He has written articles on Ukrainian and other Slavic literature. He has translated from Czech and Slovak. In 1986 he became chief editor of *Vsesvit*, after serving as its assistant editor for many years.

Mykytiuk, Dmytro [Mykytjuk], b 8 August 1899 in Rakivchyk, Kolomyia county, Galicia, d 8 March 1983 in Winnipeg. Publisher. In 1914–18 he served in the ranks of the Ukrainian Sich Riflemen and then in the Ukrainian Galician Army. After emigrating to Canada in 1930, he collected materials on the war of independence in Ukraine and published them at his own expense in a five-volume collection titled *Ukraïns'ka Halyts'ka Armiia* (The Ukrainian Galician Army, 1958–76). He also published other books on Ukrainian military topics and donated generous sums to Ukrainian scholarly institutions.

Mykytivka mercury deposit. The oldest and largest mercury deposit in Ukraine and one of the largest in the former USSR. It is located in the Donets Basin, near Horlivka (formerly the village of Mykytivka). Mercury was first discovered there in 1879 and began to be extracted in 1886. The mercury is found in dolomites, limestone, and quartziferous sandstone found under schistose rocks. Multiveined deposits extend to a depth of 2,000 m. The Mykytivka Mercury Refining Complex processes the mercury. The refinery constructed in 1886 was completely rebuilt after the Second World War. Because mercury was considered a strategic resource in the USSR, no precise data on the reserves and on the output of mercury were published.

Gen Osyp Mykytka   Count Hryhorii Myloradovych

Mykytka, Osyp, b 21 February 1878 in Zeleniv, Rohatyn county, Galicia, d August 1920 in Moscow. General officer of the Ukrainian Galician Army (UHA). Commissioned in the Austrian army in 1902, by the start of the First World War he held the rank of captain. In January 1918 he served briefly as commander of the Legion of Ukrainian Sich Riflemen. After joining the UHA he took command of its Stare Selo Group, in December 1918, and then, at the rank of major, of the First Corps of the UHA (formerly the Northern Group), in January 1919. In May he was promoted to lieutenant colonel and in June to colonel. On 7 November 1919 he became brigadier general and replaced M. Tarnavsky as the commander in chief of the UHA. Arrested by the UHA Revolutionary Committee, he was turned over to the Bolsheviks on 6 February 1920 and held for several months in a concentration camp near Moscow. After repeatedly turning down posts in the Red Army, Mykytka was executed.

Mykytovych, Roman [Mykytovyč] (Mykytowycz), b 15 July 1921 in Lviv. Biologist; full member of the Shevchenko Scientific Society and its president in Australia since 1981. A graduate of Munich University (D Vet Med, 1948), he emigrated to Australia in 1949, where he worked (1950–86) with the Commonwealth Scientific and Industrial Research Organization in the Division of Wildlife Research. His publications deal largely with various aspects of the biology of Australian mammals and birds. He was also engaged in early studies of myxomatosis, a viral disease used to control populations of wild rabbits (*Oryctolagus cuniculus*) considered to be agricultural pests.

Myleshko, Yakiv [Myleško, Jakiv], b 16 January 1898 in Popivka (now Smyrnove), Berdianske county, Tavriia gubernia, d 23 June 1978 in Odessa. Operatic stage director. In 1934 he completed study at the Leningrad Theatrical Institute. In 1934–41 and 1945–7 Myleshko worked as stage director in the Kirov Opera and Ballet Theater in Leningrad, and from 1948 to 1962 as stage director (and since 1954 principal stage director) in the Odessa Opera and Ballet Theater.

Myletsky, Avram [Mylec'kyj], b 10 March 1918 in Kiev. Architect. He graduated from the Kiev Civil-Engineering Institute (1941), where he studied under Y. Karakis and V. Zabolotny. Since 1962 he has taught at the Civil-Engineering Institute and the Kiev State Art Institute. He has designed or helped design a number of war memorials, including the memorial to the meeting of American and Soviet armies in Torgau on the Elbe (1945) and the Slava park and memorial in Kiev (1957), the bus terminal in Kiev (1959–60), the Pioneer and Student Palace in Kiev (1964), the memorial and burial complex of the Kiev Crematorium (1968), and Red Square in Kiev (1972).

Mylohrad-Pidhirtsi culture. An *Iron Age culture that existed in northern Ukraine during the 5th to 3rd century BC and in southern Belarus during the 7th to late 2nd century BC. It was named after sites near Homel and Kiev where the culture was discovered in the 1950s. Settlements of this culture were built usually on raised floodlands. The inhabitants lived in semi-pit or surface dwellings with post construction. Pottery (some with convex sides), bronze pins, iron adzes and other tools, bronze arrowheads (both locally made and imported from the Scythians), numerous horse trappings, personal adornments (including bronze pins, bracelets, pendants, clasps, and glass jewelry), molds for iron work, crucibles, and earthenware figurines of animals were found at excavation sites. The dead were buried in a supine position but not in kurhans. Some scholars believe the people of the Mylohrad-Pidhirtsi culture to be proto-Slavs, while others regard them as Balts.

Myloradovych [Myloradovyč] (Miloradovich). A family of Cossack *starshyna* and Russian nobility of Serbian origin. The progenitor was a 17th-century Herzegovinian, Rodion Miloradovich. His grandsons, Mihajlo, Gavrilo, and Aleksandar Miloradovich, went over to the Russian side during the Russo-Turkish War of 1711, and Peter I rewarded them with high posts and estates in Left-Bank Ukraine. Mihajlo (d 25 September 1726) served as colonel of Hadiache regiment (1715–26) and signed the Kolomak Petitions of 1723. Gavrilo (d 1730) succeeded him as colonel (1727–9) but was removed because of his excesses and rapacity. Several lines of the Myloradovych family stemmed from the three brothers and included many Ukrainian and Russian statesmen, military leaders, and cultural figures.

Aleksandar's son, Mykhailo, was colonel of Izium regiment in Slobidska Ukraine (1759–61), and Mykhailo's grandson, also Mykhailo, was a Ukrainian autonomist and marshal of the nobility in Poltava gubernia in 1807. Mihajlo's grandson Petro (1723 to 18 January 1799) studied at the Kievan Mohyla Academy and was the last colonel of Chernihiv regiment (1762–83). Petro's son, Hryhorii (19 January 1765 to 30 May 1828), was general judge of Chernihiv (1799) and governor of Tavriia gubernia (1802–3). Hryhorii's grandsons were the historian Hryhorii *Myloradovych and Leonid (1841–1908), who was a diplomat, secretary of the Russian embassy in Stuttgart (1862), deputy governor of Kiev gubernia (1878), and governor of Podilia gubernia (1879–82). Petro's brother Andrii (1726 to 13 June 1796) also studied at the Kievan Mohyla Academy, was a fellow of the standard (1747–9), and fought in the Seven Years' War and the Russo-Turkish War of 1769–74, from 1771 as lieutenant general. He served as governor of Little Russia (1779) and Chernihiv vicegerency (from 1781) and directed the writing of a description of Left-Bank Ukraine in 1779–81. Andrii's son, Mykhailo (Mikhail, 12 October 1771 to 27 December 1825), became a Russian general and count, the military governor of Kiev (1810–12), a member of the Russian State Council and the Committee of Ministers, and the military governor of St Petersburg (from 1818). He was killed during the Decembrist uprising in St Petersburg. The ethnographer Vasyl Myloradovych is descended from the family line begun by Gavrilo.

BIBLIOGRAPHY
Miloradovich, G. *O rode dvorian i grafa Miloradovich* (Kiev 1871)
Lazarevskii, A. 'Liudi staroi Malorossii, Miloradovichi,' *KS*, 1882, no. 3
Skazaniia o rode dvorian i grafov Miloradovichei (Kiev 1884)
Modzalevskii, V. 'Miloradovichi,' in *Malorossiiskii rodoslovnik*, vol 3 (Kiev 1912)

O. Ohloblyn

Myloradovych, Hryhorii [Myloradovyč, Hryhorij] (Miloradovich, Grigorii), b 6 October 1839 in Chernihiv, d 26 August 1905 in Chernihiv. Historian, genealogist, and

Russian count from 1873. A nobleman of Serbian descent, he was educated at the Page Corps in St Petersburg, served as an officer in a guard regiment, and fought in the Russo-Turkish War of 1877–8. In 1890 he was promoted to the rank of lieutenant general and was elected marshal of the nobility in Chernihiv gubernia (to 1896). In 1898 he became a member of the Council of the Ministry of Agriculture and State Property. He organized and was the first president of the Chernihiv Learned Archival Commission.

Myloradovych wrote many historical studies of Left-Bank Ukraine and Ukrainian genealogy and heraldry, which were published in *Kievskaia starina*, *Chteniia Moskovskago obshchestva istorii i drevnostei rossiiskikh*, *Chernigovskiia gubernskiia vedomosti*, and other periodicals. His major works are a guide to sources for the study of Little Russia (1858); a book of materials on the history of 'Southern Russia' (1858); a guide to foreign sources on the history of Little Russia (1859); a biography of Gov A. Myloradovych (1877); a booklet on the Polubotok family's documents of 1669–1734 (1889); a description of Chernihiv cathedrals of the Transfiguration and SS Borys and Hlib (1889); studies on the Little Russian nobility (1890) and the heraldic crests of Little Russian noble families (1892); a history of the town of Liubech (1898), which his family owned; and a genealogical guidebook to Chernihiv gubernia's nobility (2 vols, 1901). Documents from Myloradovych's family archive in Liubech were edited by O. Lazarevsky and published as supplements to *Kievskaia starina* in 1896 and 1898 and separately in 1898. Myloradovych kept a diary from 1875 on. It is a valuable source for the study of Ukrainian conservatism in the second half of the 19th century.

O. Ohloblyn

Myloradovych, Vasyl [Myloradovyč, Vasyl'], b 1 January 1846 in Tokari, Lokhvytsia county, Poltava gubernia, d 1911 in Lytvianky, Lubni county, Poltava gubernia. Ethnographer and folklorist. After graduating in law from Kharkiv University (1869) he served for many years as a justice of the peace in Lubni county. In his free time he studied the folklore and folkways of the local population. His more important articles, which were published in *Kievskaia starina*, deal with workers' songs of Lubni county (1985), recruits' songs of Lubni county (1897), Sniatyn antiquities (1897–1900), folk medicine in Lubni county (1900), the daily life of a Lubni peasant (1902–4), the central Lubni region (1903), and the steppe Lubni region (1904). His unpublished manuscripts include collections of party and love songs, spring songs, and St Peter's Feast songs. He also translated H. Heine's, A. Maikov's, and A. Fet's poems.

Myloradovych, Yelysaveta [Myloradovyč, Jelysaveta], b 12 January 1832 in Trostianets, Pryluka county, Poltava gubernia, d 27 March 1890 in Poltava. Community leader and benefactor; aunt of P. *Skoropadsky. The daughter of I. Skoropadsky, a marshal of Poltava gubernia's nobility, she married H. Myloradovych's son, Lev, in 1856. In the 1860s she was active in the Poltava Hromada and contributed generously to Ukrainian publishing ventures and to local Sunday schools and the Poltava women's gymnasium. She personally funded the village school in Rybtsi, near Poltava. She also supported the Ukrainian move-

Yelysaveta Myloradovych   Dezyderii Myly: *Self-Portrait* (oil, 1934)

ment in Galicia, by giving generously to the Prosvita society and the journal *Pravda*. She donated 20,000 Austrian kronen for the founding of the Lviv Shevchenko Society in 1873; it became the *Shevchenko Scientific Society in 1893. From 1878 Myloradovych headed the Poltava Philanthropic Society. Her activities were investigated by the tsarist authorities, who suspected her of heading an organization whose aim was the restoration of the Hetmanate.

Mylost' Bozhiia Ukrainu ... svobodyvshaia (Divine Grace Which Has Liberated Ukraine ...). One of the masterpieces of Ukrainian baroque drama. The play was staged in 1728 at the Kievan Mohyla Academy. It was dedicated to Hetman D. *Apostol and was probably written by T. *Prokopovych. Its subject is Hetman B. Khmelnytsky and the Cossack-Polish War of 1648–57, and it abounds in lofty patriotic monologues. The language of the play is refined yet fresh and vivid. The text was first published by O. Bodiansky in Moscow University's *Chteniia v Imperatorskom obshchestve istorii i drevnostei rossiiskikh* (1858, vol 1). The play was analyzed by Ya. Hordynsky in *Zapysky NTSh* (vols 136–7, 146).

Myluvannia [Myluvannja] (aka Mylovanie). A village in Ivano-Frankivske raion, Ivano-Frankivske oblast. In 1911 the Prosvita society established the first Ukrainian agricultural school there. The school, which contributed to the improvement of farming methods and agricultural technology in Galicia, was dissolved by the Soviet occupational authorities in 1939.

Myly, Dezyderii [Mylyj, Dezyderij] (Dezider Milly), b 7 August 1906 in Kyjov, Sabinov county, Slovakia, d 1 September 1971 in Bratislava. Ukrainian artist. He studied at the Prešov Teachers' Seminary (1922–6) and the Prague Higher Applied Arts School (1926–33) and taught art at the village school in Orlov (1935–43), Slovak University in Bratislava (1947–9), and the Bratislava Higher School of Fine Arts (1949–71), where he served as rector in 1953–7. He produced lithographs, woodcuts, charcoals, watercolors, and oils. His works include genre paintings and landscapes of the Prešov region, such as *Peasants* (1934), *Without a Job* (1939), *Funeral* (1942), *Easter Monday* (1948), and *Rocks in the Country* (1969). An exhibition catalog of his works was published in Bratislava in 1971. A gallery of his works was opened at the Museum of Ukrainian Culture in Svydnyk in 1983.

Oleh Mynko: *Portrait of My Daughter* (tempera, 1980)

Mynko, Oleh [Myn'ko], b 3 August 1938 in Makiiivka, Donetske oblast. A graduate of the Lviv Institute of Applied and Decorative Arts (1965), in the 1960s he experimented with abstraction (eg, *Composition II* [1959–65] and *Card Game* [1959–65]). His paintings, such as *Death of a Kish Otaman* (1969) and *Poem about the Old Steppe* (1969), combine amazing simplification of form with bold composition and make a statement about Ukrainian history. Since the 1970s he has painted portraits, still lifes, landscapes, and figural compositions characterized by hazy outlines and panoramic views over water (eg, *Village of Vytiaz* [1982] and *By the Lake* [1985]). Mynko participated in several group exhibitions with L. Medvid and O. Flinta in Lviv (1982), Kiev and Vilnius (1983), and Moscow (1986). His first solo exhibition was held in Lviv in 1988.

Mynko, Vasyl, b 14 January 1902 in Mynkivka, Valky county, Kharkiv gubernia, d 30 January 1989. Writer, journalist, and dramatist. His first published work was the 1924 play *Kupala*. From 1926 to 1932 he belonged to the peasant writers' group *Pluh. Mynko wrote several story collections, including *Belladonna* (1929) and *Na perepravi* (At the Crossing, 1933); the novels *Shturmivtsi* (The Storm Troops, 1931), *Iaryna Cherkas* (1936), *Nad richkoiu Khorolom* (At the Khorol River, 1949), *Iasni zori* (Bright Stars, 1951); and the autobiographical novels *Moia Mynkivka* (My Mynkivka, 2 vols, 1962, 1970), *Chervonyi Parnas* (Red Parnassus, 1972), and *Ïkhav kozak na viinon'ku* (A Cossack Was Riding Off to War, 1979). He wrote many plays, notably

Ne nazyvaiuchy prizvyshch (Without Naming Names, 1953), *Komediia z dvoma infarktamy* (Comedy with Two Heart Attacks, 1967), and *Uvaha, kakadu!* (Attention, Cockatoo!, 1972). Editions of his travel sketches (1957, 1958), selected works (1962), comedies (1968), and plays (1959, 1977) have also been published. His memoirs, *Z perom, iak z bahnetom* (With a Pen, As If with a Bayonet), appeared in 1981.

Mynyk, Teodor, b 3 October 1896 in Tershiv, Staryi Sambir county, Galicia, d 10 July 1975 in Scranton, Pennsylvania. Ukrainian community activist in the United States. After emigrating to the United States in 1912, he joined the Ukrainian Workingmen's Association (1919) and served as its chief secretary (1927–74) and first vice-president (1959–74). He was also its representative in the Ukrainian Congress Committee of America, where he served as acting president in 1961–2.

Myr (World). A newspaper published in *yazychiie three times a week from March 1885 to mid-1887 (a total of 333 issues) in Lviv by Rev Y. Komarnytsky. Edited by him and I. Levytsky, it devoted considerable attention to church, political, economic, and cultural affairs (providing regular reports on the activities of the Galician and Viennese diets and reports from correspondents in various Galician towns) and published literary works by writers such as M. Vovchok, M. Kostomarov, and V. Masliak. In 1887 *Dushpastyr* began appearing as a supplement to *Myr*.

Myrhorod. IV-14. A city (1990 pop 47,100) on the Khorol River and a raion center in Poltava oblast. It was founded in the mid-16th century, and in 1575 was granted town status and selected as a Cossack regimental center by King Stephen Báthory of Poland. Because of its role in the 1637–8 Cossack uprising the Myrhorod regiment was abolished. The town belonged to J. Wiśniowiecki until 1648, when it was captured by the Cossacks and restored as a regimental center. Myrhorod played an important role in the Cossack-Polish War of 1648–57. In 1650 Hetman B. Khmelnytsky conducted negotiations with Russian envoys there. In 1690–1 the Myrhorod regiment revolted against Hetman I. Mazepa. Under Russian rule Myrhorod became a county center of Poltava gubernia in 1802 and a prosperous trade center. Its economic development was strongly affected by the founding of a health resort in 1912–14 and the extraction of oil and natural gas in the 1950s. Today Myrhorod has several large enterprises of the building-materials industry and the food industry. Its mineral springs support seven balneological sanatoriums, which treat disorders of the digestive system, liver, and stomach. For centuries Myrhorod has been famous for its handicrafts, particularly its ceramics, embroideries, and folk dress. In 1896 the Gogol Handicrafts School and in 1912 the first Ukrainian ceramics manufacturing association were set up in Myrhorod. Today a ceramics tekhnikum and factory operate there. In its vicinity two settlements of the Cherniakhiv culture (2nd–4th century) have been excavated. N. *Gogol immortalized the town by naming his second volume of Ukrainian stories *Mirgorod* (Myrhorod, 1835).

Myrhorod regiment (Myrhorodskyi polk). An administrative territory and military formation of the Hetman state. The regiment was first established in 1630 and was merged with Pereiaslav regiment in 1638. It was re-established in 1648 after the Cossacks overthrew Polish rule. With its administrative center in Myrhorod, the regiment consisted of 16 companies and 2,630 registered Cossacks. The territory was well populated: in 1657 it had 30,000 inhabitants. For supporting M. *Pushkar's rebellion the regiment was devastated by Hetman I. Vyhovsky in 1658. Most of its companies were transferred to Lubni regiment, and it was left with only four. In the 1670s six companies from Poltava and five from Chyhyryn regiments were added to it. By 1723 Myrhorod regiment's 15 companies had a population of 16,500, including 4,800 Cossacks. Its commanders included some prominent statesmen, such as Col M. *Hladky (1648–52) and D. *Apostol (1683–1727). The regiment was abolished by the Russian authorities in 1782, and its territory was incorporated into Kiev vicegerency.

Myrivske [Myrivs'ke]. VI-14. A town smt (1986 pop 7,600) under the administration of the Terny raion council of the city of Kryvyi Rih, Dnipropetrovske oblast. Myrivske was established in 1958. Several manufacturing enterprises related to the Kryvorizhzalizbeton manufacturing association as well as a manufacturing base of the Kryvyi Rih house-building complex and other enterprises are located in Myrivske.

Panas Myrny   Dmytro Myron

Myrny, Panas [Myrnyj] (pseud of Atanas Rudchenko), b 13 May 1849 in Myrhorod, d 28 January 1920 in Poltava. Writer. He worked in various government offices and eventually achieved the rank of full government councillor (1914). The works of T. Shevchenko had the greatest influence on the formation of Myrny's worldview, artistic preferences, and ideology. His early literary attempts included poems, dramas, and short stories. In 1872 the short story 'Lykhyi poputav' (The Evil One Did It), written in the style of M. *Vovchok, was printed in the Lviv journal Pravda. In 1877 appeared his novel Lykhi liudy (Evil People), about the life of the intelligentsia. His best-known work is the novel Propashcha syla (The Ruined Strength), also titled Khiba revut' voly, iak iasla povni? (Do the Oxen Bellow, When Their Mangers Are Full?, 1880),

which he coauthored with his brother, I. *Rudchenko (pseud: I. Bilyk). The work can be characterized as a socio-psychological novel-chronicle; it covers almost a hundred years in the history of a Ukrainian village, from serfdom to the postreform era. In it Myrny depicts social oppression, internal strife between different social groups, the tsarist legal system, the harsh life of a soldier during the time of Tsar Nicholas I, police violence, and spontaneous protests against lies and injustice. Myrny's second important sociopsychological novel, Poviia (Loose Woman, 1884), describes new social processes brought about by the reforms of 1861. Myrny also portrayed the changed social dynamics of the village after the abolition of serfdom in the stories 'Lykho davnie i s'ohochasne' (Ancient and Contemporary Evil, 1903) and 'Sered stepiv' (Among the Steppes, 1903). Myrny also wrote some dramatic works, the comedies Peremudryv (He Outsmarted [Them], 1886) and Zhuba (Loss, 1896), and the dramas U chernytsiakh (Among the Nuns, 1884) and Spokusa (Temptation, 1901). The most popular drama was Lymerivna (The Daughter of the Harness Maker, 1883), which was first published in 1892 in the journal Zoria (Lviv). He is also known as the translator of H.W. Longfellow's poem The Song of Hiawatha and of W. Shakespeare's King Lear. Myrny markedly expanded the lexicon of the Ukrainian literary language and with his talent for rhythmic and melodious phrasing enriched Ukrainian syntax.

BIBLIOGRAPHY
Ievdokymenko, V. Suspil'no-politychni pohliady Panasa Myrnoho (Kiev 1955)
Syvachenko, M. Istoriia stvorennia romana 'Khiba revut' voly, iak iasla povni' (Kiev 1957)
Hrytsiutenko, I. Mova ta styl' khudozhnikh tvoriv Panasa Myrnoho (Kiev 1959)
Pyvovarov, M. Maisternist' psykholohichnoho analizu: (Roman 'Poviia' Panasa Myrnoho) (Kiev 1960)
Cherkas'kyi, V. Khudozhnii svit Panasa Myrnoho (Kiev 1989)
                                                     P. Odarchenko

Myron, Dmytro (pseud: Orlyk), b 5 November 1911 in Rai, Berezhany county, Galicia, d 25 July 1942 in Kiev. Nationalist revolutionary leader. In the 1930s he studied law at Lviv University and was active in the OUN. As secretary of youth on the national executive of the OUN (1932–3) he was arrested by the Polish authorities and sentenced to five years in prison. In 1941 he led the Southeastern Expeditionary Group of the OUN (Bandera faction), and upon reaching Kiev in October of that year he became regional commander for central Ukraine. He was arrested by the Germans and killed during an escape attempt. He wrote a number of articles on ideological questions, including 'Ideia i chyn' (Idea and Deed, 1940).

Myronenko, Vasyl, b 9 January 1911 in Orikhivka, Lubni county, Poltava gubernia, d 10 April 1964 in Kharkiv. Graphic artist. After graduating from the Kharkiv Art Institute (1936) he taught there until his death. He did aquatint etchings, mostly of rural and industrial landscapes. His better-known print series are 'Ukrainian Landscapes' (1936–41), 'Ukraine' (1941–3), 'My Ukraine,' and 'The Azov Coast.'

Myroniuk, Lavro [Myronjuk], b 1887 in Rakhnivka, Haisyn county, Podilia gubernia, d ? Poet. In 1921 he studed at Charles University and at the Ukrainian Free University in Prague. From 1923 he lived in Vienna. He succumbed to a mental illness and was most likely murdered by the Nazis after their occupation of Austria. Myroniuk published a few dozen poems in émigré periodicals, such as *Veselka* and *Students'kyi visnyk*. He apparently wrote some 800 poems, 300 of which he gave to D. *Stefanovych. Only 61 have been preserved.

Myronivka. IV-11. A city (1990 pop 16,100) on the Rosava River and a raion center in Kiev oblast. It was founded in the first half of the 17th century and was annexed in 1793 by Russia. Its city status dates from 1968. It is the home of the famous *Myronivka Institute of Wheat Selection and Seed Cultivation.

Myronivka Institute of Wheat Selection and Seed Cultivation (Myronivskyi naukovo-doslidnyi instytut selektsii i nasinnytstva pshenytsi). An important scientific research institute, subordinate to the formerly All-Union Academy of Agricultural Sciences, located in Myronivka raion, Kiev oblast. It was created in 1968 on the basis of the Myronivka Selection Research Station (est 1911 as the Central Research Station of Sugar Beet Cultivation, in 1956 renamed and subordinated to the Scientific Institute of Corn). Its divisions do scientific work on selection and seed development, the agrotechnology and mechanization of corn production, agriculture, and plant protection. It also has a laboratory of agrochemistry and a laboratory of flour-milling and bread-baking technologies. The research on selection and seed cultivation encompasses winter wheat, corn, peas, and fodder grasses. The institute has developed highly productive winter wheat varieties, including Ukrainka, Myronivka 264, Myronivka 808, and Illich.

Myronivskyi [Myronivs'kyj]. DB III-4. A town smt (1990 pop 9,800) on the Luhanka River, under the Debaltseve city council in Donetske oblast. Myronivskyi was established in 1950 in conjunction with the building of the thermoelectric station there (see *Electric power).

Myronosytsi sisterhood. A women's society named in memory of the women who brought balsam to anoint Christ's dead body. The group was set up in 1886 at the Greek Catholic church in Chernivtsi to maintain the building and raise funds for the parish. It later extended its activity to charitable work, particularly among poor children. In 1896–7 the society organized the first Ukrainian kindergarten in Chernivtsi, which it maintained until 1940. In the 1920s it provided aid to refugees from Soviet Ukraine. Its leading members were E. Kaluzhniatska, K. Kostetska, M. Bilynkevych, and O. Siretska. The society was dissolved in 1940.

Myropil [Myropil']. III-8. A town smt (1986 pop 5,700) on the Sluch River in Dzerzhynske raion, Zhytomyr oblast. It is first mentioned in historical documents of the early 16th century. Today it has a paper factory, silicate, asphalt, and baking plants, a forestry industry, and a hydroelectric station.

Myrovych [Myrovyč]. A family of Cossack *starshyna* in Pereiaslav regiment that was significant during the het-

mancies of I. *Mazepa and P. Orlyk. It was established by Ivan *Myrovych, the colonel of Pereiaslav regiment in 1692–1706. His son, Fedir *Myrovych, was Mazepa's general standard-bearer (1708–9) and fled abroad with Mazepa after the Russian victory at Poltava in 1708. All of the Myrovych estates were confiscated by the Russian government. Fedir's mother, Pelahiia (née Holub, a relative of Hetman I. Samoilovych), was deported to Moscow with other members of the family. She was exiled to Tobolsk in 1716 and was not allowed to return to Ukraine until 1745, and then only on the condition that she not communicate with Fedir or her other renegade son, Ivan *Myrovych. Her third son, Vasyl (d 1736), who had also been deported to Moscow, was accused in 1715–16 of contacts with the Swedes and his brother Fedir and of attempting to escape abroad. After many tortures he was exiled to forced labor in Siberia, where he died. His sister, Anna, married A. *Voinarovsky and lived for a time in Bendery. After the Russians captured her husband, she and her children sought refuge in Sweden. Fedir's sons, Yakiv and Petro, were taken to St Petersburg for schooling. For contacting their father they were exiled in 1732 to Siberia, where they were both appointed military governors in 1742, Yakiv in Kuznetsk and Petro in Eniseisk. Yakiv's son, Vasyl (1740 to 26 September 1764), was a second lieutenant in the Russian army. He was executed for taking part in a foiled plot to liberate the former tsar Ivan VI from the Schlüsselburg Fortress.

O. Ohloblyn

Myrovych, Fedir [Myrovyč], b ?, d 1758 in the Crimea. Cossack leader; son of I. *Myrovych. A graduate of the Kievan Mohyla Academy, he became a fellow of the standard and served as general standard-bearer of the Hetman state in 1708–9. He fled abroad with Hetman I. Mazepa after the Russian victory at Poltava in 1709. In 1710–11 he was general osaul to the émigré hetman P. Orlyk. He lived abroad in the Crimean Khanate, the Ottoman Empire, Sweden (1715–19), and Poland (1719–54) before returning to the Crimea. He was entrusted with many political tasks by Orlyk, particularly that of maintaining a liaison with the Zaporozhian Sich. The tsarist regime responded to Myrovych's 'treasonous' activities by exiling his mother, brother, and children and confiscating all of their estates and assets (see *Myrovych). He remained an unrelenting enemy of Moscow and a defender of the Ukrainian right to statehood as set forth in the 1710 Constitution of *Bendery.

Myrovych, Ivan [Myrovyč], b ?, d 1709. Cossack leader. A notable military fellow from 1689, he was appointed colonel of Pereiaslav regiment (1691–1706) by Hetman I. Mazepa. He took part in numerous campaigns, particularly against the Tatars. During the Great Northern War he was acting hetman of a 10,000-man Cossack army in Volhynia. He was taken prisoner by the Swedes near Liakhavichy, in Belarus, in the spring of 1706, and died in Swedish captivity. He was a patron of Ukrainian church art and funded the construction (1704–9) of the Church of the Holy Protectress in Pereiaslav.

Myrovych, Ivan [Myrovyč], b ?, d 1753. Political prisoner and émigré figure. Because of the role his brother, F. *Myrovych, played in Hetman I. Mazepa's revolt against

Peter I, Ivan was exiled to Moscow in 1712 and to Siberia in 1716, where he served as a captain in mining factories from 1728 on. In 1730 he was sent to St Petersburg with a shipment of iron, but he escaped to the Crimea and served as an interpreter to the Crimean khan. He and his brother served as Hetman P. Orlyk's liaison officers with the Zaporozhian Cossacks (to 1734) and the Crimean Khanate. In 1735 he was Orlyk's envoy to the Polish king Stanislaus I Leszczyński in France, and in 1736 he served as Orlyk's representative at Turkish army headquarters.

Mys Ochkynskyi. A Neolithic settlement on the left bank of the Desna River near the village of Ochkyne, Seredyna-Buda raion, Sumy oblast. Excavation in 1947 uncovered a large number of flint tools (axes, wedges, knives, scrapers, awls, chisels) as well as pottery that had combed or pitted ornamentation. The burial practice of the settlement was typical of the *Middle-Dnieper culture.

Myshakov, Oleksandr [Myšakov], b 1913 in Kharkiv. Gymnastics coach. A graduate of the Kharkiv Institute of Physical Culture before the Second World War, after the war he taught at the Kiev Institute of Physical Culture and trained many Ukrainian world and Olympic champions in *gymnastics.

Myshanych, Oleksa [Myšanyč], b 1 April 1933 in Liakhovets, near Mizhhiria, in Transcarpathia. Literary scholar. After graduating from Uzhhorod University (1956) he completed his graduate studies at the AN URSR (now ANU) Institute of Literature (1961) and joined its staff as a research associate. In 1985 he became head of the Department of Old Ukrainian Literature. He has written over 100 articles in the history of Ukrainian literature, folklore, Ukrainian literature in Transcarpathia and Yugoslavia, and inter-Slavic literary relations and has edited a number of anthologies and scholarly collections. His more important monographs are *Literatura Zakarpattia 17–18 st.* (The Literature of Transcarpathia of the 17th to 18th Century, 1964), *Hryhorii Skovoroda i usna narodna tvorchist'* (Hryhorii Skovoroda and the Oral Folk Tradition, 1976), and *Ukraïns'ka literatura druhoï polovyny 18-oho st. i usna narodna tvorchist'* (Ukrainian Literature of the Second Half of the 18th Century and the Oral Folk Tradition, 1980).

Myshchenko, Fedir [Myščenko] (Mishchenko, Fedor), b 29 February 1847 in Pryluka, Poltava gubernia, d 1906 in Kiev. Classical scholar. While a student (1866–70) and a docent (1872–84) at Kiev University, he was active in the Hromada of Kiev, was a member of the Historical Society of Nestor the Chronicler (from 1874), and served on the editorial board of *Kievskaia starina*. His Ukrainophile sympathies, correspondence with M. Drahomanov, and critical articles in the press cost him his job at Kiev University and earned him administrative exile from Kiev. From 1889 to 1903 he was a professor of classics at Kazan University. His articles on Greek literature, writers, history, and historians and on the Scythian world were published in *Universitetskiia izvestiia* (Kiev), *Zhurnal Ministerstva narodnago prosveshcheniia*, and *Filologicheskoe obozrenie* and in the Brockhaus and Efron Russian encyclopedia. His biography, by A. Shorman, was published in Kazan in 1974.

Myshchenko, Fedir [Myščenko], b 11 August 1874 in Poltava gubernia, d ? Byzantologist; VUAN full member

from 1919. Before the Revolution of 1917 he was a professor at the Kiev Theological Academy. Under the 1918 Hetman government he was a professor at Kiev University and a member of the Learned Committee of the Ministry of Religious Denominations. From 1919 he headed the VUANCommission for the Study of Byzantine Literature and Its Impact on Ukraine. He and K. Kharlampovych were dismissed in 1928 by order of the People's Commissariat of Education because of their earlier affiliation with the Theological Academy. Further details of his life are unknown. Among his works is a booklet on Byzantine marriage and kinship (1927).

Myshchenko, Mykola [Myščenko] (Mishchenko), b 1895 in Kharkiv, d 30 July 1960 in Kiev. Painter and graphic artist. A graduate of the Kharkiv Art School (1919), he was a member of the Union of Seven cubo-futurist artists' group in Kharkiv from 1915 and submitted works to their album *Sem' plius tri* (Seven Plus Three, 1918). His *Musical Window* (1917) and *Departure* (1918) illustrate the group's intuitive approach to dynamism. From the 1930s on he painted stylistically traditional figures and landscapes.

Myshetsky, Semen [Myšeckij], b 1716, d ? Russian nobleman and military engineer. After living at the *Sich from 1736 to 1740, he wrote *Istoriia o kazakakh zaporozhskikh ...* (A History of the Zaporozhian Cossacks ..., 1740). The work remained in manuscript form until it was published in the proceedings of the Moscow-based Imperial Society of History and Antiquities (1847) and then in a superior form in the proceedings of the Odessa Society of History and Antiquities (1852). Together with the writings of A. *Rigelman, Myshetsky's history remains one of the most valuable primary sources about the Zaporozhians in the 18th century, particularly in its portrayal of their social order and daily life.

Gen Yevhen Myshkivsky   Luka Myshuha

Myshkivsky, Yevhen [Myškivs'kyj, Jevhen], b 12 April 1882 in Poltava gubernia, d 9 July 1920 in Ternopil, Galicia. Senior officer of the UNR Army. A graduate of the General Staff Academy in St Petersburg (1912), he served in the Russian army during the First World War and attained the rank of colonel. In 1918 he joined the UNR Army and was assigned to the operations branch of the General Staff. On 10 December 1918 he became chief of the General Staff of the Ukrainian Galician Army (UHA); he is credited with preparing its organizational scheme. From February 1919 he served as chief of staff of the Eastern Group of the UNR

Army, then of the Volhynian Group, and finally of the UNR Army itself. In 1920 he was appointed general quartermaster on the General Staff of the UNR Army. He was mortally wounded in action against the Bolsheviks. He was promoted posthumously to brigadier general.

Myshko, Dmytro [Myško], b 9 November 1907 in Karpylivka, Lubni county, Poltava gubernia, d after 1976. Historian. A graduate of the Kharkiv Pedagogical Institute (1937) and a senior associate of the AN URSR (now ANU) Institute of History from 1943, he wrote books about the Cossack leaders I. Bohun (1956) and S. Nalyvaiko (1962), Ukrainian-Russian relations in the 14th to 16th centuries (1959), and the peasantry and antifeudal movements in 15th- and 16th-century Ukraine (1963).

Myshkovsky, Tyt [Myškovs'kyj], b 4 October 1861 in Perehrymka, Sianik circle, Galicia, d 4 February 1939 in Lviv. Theologian, biblical scholar, and priest. He was ordained in Peremyshl in 1885, and he completed his TH D in Vienna in 1889 and then became prefect of the Greek Catholic Theological Seminary (1889–94) in Lviv. He began lecturing at Lviv University in 1899 and became a full professor of biblical studies in 1908. When he refused to swear an oath of allegiance to the new Polish state in 1918, he was dismissed from the university. From 1920 he taught at the Greek Catholic Theological Seminary in Lviv, and in 1928 he became a full professor, and later dean and vice-rector, of the Lviv Greek Catholic Theological Academy. In 1923–39 he also served as president of the *Halytsko-Ruska Matytsia. In addition to several articles in Ukrainian for religious journals, Myshkovsky published the following works in Latin: *Chronologico-historica introductio in Novum Testamentum* (1892), *De ratione litterarum A.T. in Cantico Mariae conspicua* (1901), and *Isaiae liber in versionibus Graeca LXX et Latina Vulgata et Paleoslavica exhibitus et explicatur* (1909).

Myshuha, Luka [Myšuha], b 30 October 1887 in Novyi Vytkiv, Radekhiv county, Galicia, d 8 February 1955 in New York. Civic and political leader and journalist; nephew of O. *Myshuha. A graduate (1911) of the law faculty of Vienna University, he joined the Ukrainian Sich Riflemen in 1915 and served as a community organizer in Volodymyr-Volynskyi. With the collapse of the Austrian Empire he set up a Ukrainian local government in the town. Upon returning to Galicia he was assigned as a commissioner of the Western Ukrainian National Republic (ZUNR) to Radekhiv and then as a lieutenant to Otaman S. Petliura's general staff in Kamianets-Podilskyi. At the end of 1919 he moved to Vienna with the ZUNR government and thenceforth carried out special assignments for it: he was secretary of a mission to Riga (1921) and head of a mission in Washington, DC, which, besides maintaining diplomatic ties, raised loans for the ZUNR government-in-exile (1921–3). He organized the *United Ukrainian Organizations in America and served as its general secretary (1923–40), helped found the Ukrainian Congress Committee of America (1940) and sat on its political council, and helped organize the *United Ukrainian American Relief Committee (1944), which he headed (1953–5). He also worked as an editor (1926–33) and chief editor (1933–55) of *Svoboda. He wrote many brochures on political, historical, and literary subjects, including *Iaki teper sudy na Ukraïni?* (What Are the Courts Like Today in Ukraine?,

1919), *Ukraine and American Democracy* (1939), and *Shevchenko and Women* (1940), and edited *Propamiatna knyha Ukraïns'koho narodnoho soiuzu* (Jubilee Book of the Ukrainian National Association, 1936), *Ukraïntsi u vil'nomu sviti* (Ukrainians in the Free World, 1954), and the annual almanacs and calendars of *Svoboda* and the Ukrainian National Association. He encouraged scholarly publications on Ukraine and inspired the preparation of *Ukraine: A Concise Encyclopaedia* (1963).

Oleksander Myshuha

Myshuha, Oleksander [Myšuha] (stage name: Filippi), b 20 June 1853 in Novyi Vytkiv, Radekhiv county, Galicia, d 9 March 1922 in Freiburg, Germany (buried in Novyi Vytkiv). Opera and concert singer (lyric tenor), teacher, and benefactor. He studied in Nice and Milan and under W. Wysocki at the Lviv Conservatory and made his debut in Lviv (1880) in S. Moniuszko's *The Haunted Castle*. Myshuha was highly successful as first tenor of the Warsaw Grand Theater (1884–92), especially in operas by Moniuszko. In 1885 he appeared as a guest performer at the Vienna Imperial Opera. In addition he toured Lviv, Kiev, St Petersburg, Italy, France, Berlin, and London. His recordings of songs by F. Mendelssohn and F. Tosti and of arias from Moniuszko's and C. Gounod's operas executed for the Gramophone and Zonophone labels (ca 1911–12) are today extremely rare and highly valued collector's items. In later years Myshuha taught at the Lysenko Music and Drama School in Kiev (1904–11), the Chopin Higher Music School in Warsaw (1911–14), the Moniuszko Music Institute in Warsaw (1912–13), and in Stockholm (from 1919). His students included M. Mykysha, S. Myrovych, and M. Donets-Tesseir. A friend of I. Franko, Myshuha assisted in the publication of his collection *Ziviale lystia* (Withered Leaves). Myshuha funded the publication of *Ukraïns'ke mystetstvo* (Ukrainian Art) in Kiev, actively supported Sadovsky's Theater, and left his entire estate to the Lysenko Higher Institute of Music in Lviv.

BIBLIOGRAPHY
Derkach, I. (ed). *Vydatnyi spivak Oleksander Myshuha* (Lviv 1964)
Holovashchenko, M. (ed). *Oleksander Myshuha: Spohady, materialy, lysty* (Kiev 1971)

R. Savytsky

Mysko, Emmanuil [Mys'ko, Emmanujil], b 21 May 1929 in Ustryky Dolishni, Lisko county, Galicia. Sculptor. A graduate of the Lviv Institute of Applied and Decorative Arts (1956), he has taught there since 1981 and became its rector in 1988. He has sculpted portraits of artists, such as O. Kulchytska (1957–60), O. Novakivsky (1960), and L. Levytsky (1966), and of writers, such as V. Gzhytsky (1970), R. Ivanychuk (1970), and V. Stefanyk (1971), and collaborated on the monuments to I. Franko in Lviv (1964) and Drohobych (1967) and to the Soviet Armed Forces in Lviv (1970). An album of his works came out in 1978.

Myslavsky, Samuil [Myslavs'kyj, Samujil] (secular name: Semen), b 24 May 1731 in Poloshky, Hlukhiv region, d 5 January 1796 in Kiev. Orthodox churchman and scholar. After graduating from the *Kievan Mohyla Academy in 1754, he became a monk, and professor and rector (1761–8) of the academy. He also wrote a brief history of the academy (1766). He was consecrated bishop of Belgorod in 1768 and served as administrator of Moscow eparchy (1771–6) and bishop of Rostov and Yaroslavl (1776–83). He was appointed to the Holy Synod in 1775 and elected archbishop in 1777. In 1783–96 Myslavsky was metropolitan of Kiev. Although he attempted to preserve some of the prerogatives of the Kievan metropolitan, he soon became an influential proponent of Russian centralization and control over Ukrainian church affairs. He insisted on the introduction of literary Russian as the only language of instruction at the academy, which he reformed to emphasize its role as a seminary, and to which he limited the admission of lay students. He also oversaw the secularization of monasteries and church property in the Hetmanite under Catherine II, and he sought to end the Ukrainian tradition whereby each parish chose its own priest, and replaced it with the episcopal appointment of clergy. A member of the Russian Imperial Academy of Sciences, he oversaw the publication of T. Prokopovych's works and wrote a history of the Kievan Cave Monastery (published posthumously in 1817). His biography, by T. Rozhdestvensky, appeared in *Trudy Kievskoi dukhovnoi akademii* (1876–7).

A. Zhukovsky

Mystery plays (*misterii*). Medieval religious allegorical plays. They originated in France and then spread throughout Europe. In Ukraine Y. Boretsky began staging 'passions' (a form of liturgy with elements of mystery plays) in 1626. Later a multitude of allegorical baroque plays were written, among which were D. Tuptalo's *Komediia na den' rozhdestva Khristova* (A Comedy on the Day of Christ's Birth) and Yu. Konysky's *Voskresenie mertvykh* (Resurrection of the Dead). During the Romantic period of the 19th century, mystery plays once again became fashionable. A typical example is T. Shevchenko's satiric poem 'Velykyi l'okh' (The Great Vault).

Mystets'ka trybuna (Art Tribune). A semimonthly illustrated art journal published by the All-Ukrainian Committee of Art Workers in Kharkiv in 1930–1 (a total of 33 issues). *Mystets'ka trybuna* published art and film criticism and theoretical articles. It devoted special attention to art education and the debates on the development of Soviet Ukrainian art. Its contributors included many prominent artists, critics, and writers, among them L. Kurbas, A. Petrytsky, O. Dovzhenko, M. Krushelnytsky, and D. Hrudyna.

Mystetskyi ukrainskyi rukh. See MUR.

Mystetstvo. A publishing house founded in Kharkiv in February 1932. Since 1935 (except in 1941–4) it has been located in Kiev, where from 1956 to 1963 it was called the Publishing House of the Pictorial Arts and Musical Literature. Mystetstvo has been the principal publisher in Ukraine of books in art theory, the fine arts, theater, and film and of art books, catalogs, posters, and calendars. Each year it publishes at least 100 titles with a total run of at least 2 million.

Mystetstvo (cover design by Heorhii Narbut)   Vasyl Mysyk

Mystetstvo (Art). A literature and art journal, of which only eight issues appeared in Kiev: six between May and July 1919, one later in 1919, and one in April 1920. The journal was edited by H. *Mykhailychenko and M. *Semenko and was the organ of the Ukrainian Section of the All-Ukrainian Literary Committee and, with issue no. 3, the Division of Arts of the People's Commissariat of Education. The direction that the new Soviet Ukrainian literature, art, and theater should take was discussed on its pages. Among its contributors were the editors and V. Blakytny, M. Burachek, V. Chumak, V. Koriak, H. Kotsiuba, I. Kulyk, L. Kurbas, O. Murashko, H. Narbut, A. Petrytsky, K. Polishchuk, Ya. Savchenko, O. Slisarenko, M. Tereshchenko, P. Tychyna, V. Yaroshenko, and D. Zahul.

Mystetstvo (Art). An illustrated organ of the *Association of Independent Ukrainian Artists, five issues of which appeared in Lviv in 1932–6. The journal contained art reproductions, criticism, articles on the history of Ukrainian art, and reviews. It was edited by P. Kovzhun and S. Hordynsky.

Mystetstvo (Art). A bimonthly illustrated arts magazine published in Kiev from January 1959 to December 1969. The organ of Ukraine's Ministry of Culture and unions of composers and artists, it was edited by a board headed by I. Chabanenko (1954–8) and I. Korniienko (1958–69). The magazine published popular articles on Ukrainian, Soviet, and Soviet-bloc art, music, dance, opera, theater, and film. Among the contributors were prominent Soviet Ukrainian figures in the arts. In 1970 *Mystetstvo* was succeeded by three journals: *Obrazotvorche mystetstvo*, *Muzyka*, and *Ukraïns'kyi teatr*.

Mystetstvo kino (Art of Cinema). An annual scholarly serial published since 1979 by the Kiev Institute of Theater Arts. It discusses problems and issues in cinema and profiles leading cinema personalities.

Mysyk, Vasyl, b 24 July 1907 in Novopavlivka, Katerynoslav gubernia, d 3 March 1983 in Kharkiv. Writer and translator. He debuted as a poet in *Chervonyi shliakh* in 1923. From 1924 he lived in Kharkiv, where he belonged to the writers' groups *Pluh and *Prolitfront, contributed to *Literaturnyi iarmarok*, studied English, German, and Persian, and published the poetry collections *Travy* (Grasses, 1927), *Blakytnyi mist* (The Azure Bridge, 1929), *Chotyry vitry* (The Four Winds, 1930), *Turksyb* (1932), and *Budivnyky* (Builders, 1933) and the story collection *Galaganiv son* (Galagan's Dream, 1930). After visiting Central Asia he wrote the essay collections *Tysiachi kilometriv* (Thousands of Kilometers, 1931) and *Kazakhstans'ka magistral'* (The Kazakhstan Trunk Line, 1931). He was arrested during the Stalinist terror in December 1934 and was imprisoned in labor camps in the Soviet Arctic until 1940. From 1942 to 1945 he was in a German concentration camp for Soviet prisoners of war. After being rehabilitated in 1956, he published editions of his selected works (1958, 1967, 1977), the new collections *Borozny* (Furrows, 1962), *Verkhovittia* (Top Branches, 1963), *Chornotrop* (The Snow-free Way, 1966), *Lan* (The Farmland, 1970), and *Bereh* (The Shore, 1972), and the story collection *Brians'kyi lis* (Briansk Forest, 1978). He became a leading translator of English, American, German, and Persian literature. Published separately were his translations of the poetry of R. Burns (1932), Rudaki (1962), Omar Khayyam (1965), J. Keats (1968), Hafez (1971), and Firdousi (1975). A book of his articles and essays was published in 1982, and a collection of memoirs about him and V. Khytruk's literary biography appeared in 1987.

R. Senkus

Mythology. A body of myths or stories dealing with the gods, demigods, and heroes of a given people. The earliest historical record of pre-Christian religious beliefs in Ukrainian territory belongs to the 6th-century Byzantine historian Procopius of Caesarea. According to him the Sclaveni and *Antes were monotheist. They believed in a god of lightning and thunder and sacrificed cattle and other animals to him. Procopius does not give the god's name. M. Hrushevsky and other scholars assumed it was *Svaroh. These peoples also venerated rivers, water nymphs, and other spirits, offered sacrifices to them, and foretold the future from the offerings.

Two periods are distinguished in the evolution of eastern Slavic mythology: an earlier one, marked by Svaroh's supremacy, and a later one, dominated by *Perun. The legends about the *Scythians as having originated from one father and three sons and about the founding of Kiev by the three brothers Kyi, Shchek, and Khoryv, as well as 12th-century data on the pagan pantheon of Kievan Rus', suggest that the chief god of the Sclaveni and Antes was named Troian, which in Ukrainian suggests 'father of three sons.' A reference to the deity in *Slovo o polku Ihorevi has led some scholars to the conclusion that Troian was at one time the ruling god of Rus'. In the 12th-century apocryphal work 'Khozhdeniie Bohorodytsi po mukakh' (The Mother of God's Journey through the Agony) Troian is listed first among the deities and is followed by *Khors, *Veles, and Perun. The grouping of father and three sons was observed in the pantheon of Volodymyr the Great, in which Perun was elevated to first place and was followed by Khors, *Dazhboh, and *Stryboh. By function and importance Svaroh or Troian corresponds to *Sviatovyt (Svitovyt), the god of the sun and later of war and plenty in the western Slavic pantheon.

The main deities of the early period of Kievan Rus' were Perun, the god of rain, lightning, and thunder, and Veles (Volos), the god of livestock. As the tribal society evolved into a more organized state, the functions of both deities expanded: Perun became the god of war, and Veles, the god of prosperity and commerce, and they were adopted by the prince as the official gods of the state. At first Volodymyr the Great tried to create a unified state religion by incorporating all common and tribal deities of his realm into one pantheon. According to the Primary Chronicle (for 980 AD) Volodymyr set up idols of Perun, Khors, Dazhboh, Stryboh, Symarhl, and *Mokosh outside the palace at Berestove. The chief god in this pantheon was Perun. Khors, a sun god borrowed from the Persians, was second in rank. Dazhboh's functions were similar to Khors's. Some scholars held that the two names referred to the same god. Next in rank was Stryboh, the god of wind and water. The nature of Symarhl has been the subject of much speculation. Some scholars identify Mokosh with *Marena, the Slavic goddess of spring and water; others define her as a goddess of birth. Volodymyr's pantheon was short-lived; in 988 Christianity became the state religion.

The cults of *Kupalo, *Koliada, Tur, *Yarylo, Kostrub, *Lada, and Marena of the early Slavic and Princely periods survived for several centuries after the introduction of Christianity and then were absorbed into Christian ritual or folk customs. Their memory lingers in popular superstition and folklore. Mythological figures such as Lado, Lel, Polel, and Podaha, who appear in 16th- and 17th-century monuments and later literature, are mostly of literary origin.

The mythological figures of *Rod and the *rozhanytsi*, who are mentioned in many literary monuments, date back to prehistoric times. The *rozhanytsi* are similar in function to the Roman Parcae, whose name is derived from the Latin *parcere* 'to give birth.' The names Rod and Rozhanytsia are related to the Ukrainian (and Slavic) words *rid* 'clan,' *narod* 'people,' *rodyty* 'to give birth,' and *pryroda* 'nature.' The belief in Rod and the *rozhanytsi* influenced folk ideas of death, the dead, and the afterworld and folk wedding and birth rituals. The church struggled for many centuries against the cults of these deities.

During Christian times the ancient mythology of Ukraine's inhabitants survived to some extent in the folklore and *demonology of the Ukrainian people. Many elements of ancient religious belief were absorbed also by church rites and ritual.

BIBLIOGRAPHY
Leger, L. *La Mythologie slave* (Paris 1901)
Niederle, L. *Život starých Slovanů*, 2 (Prague 1916; 2nd edn 1924)
Mansikka, V. *Die Religionen der Ostslaven* (Helsinki 1922)
Hrushevs'kyi, M. *Z istorii relihiinoi dumky na Ukraïni* (Lviv 1925; 2nd edn, Munich 1962)
Rybakov, B. *Iazychestvo drevnei Rusi* (Moscow 1987)
B. Kravtsiw, B. Medwidsky

Mytiukov, Kalenyk [Mytjukov] (aka Mytiuk), b 3 August 1823 in Kiev, d 1885. Scholar. After graduating from Kiev University (1845) he taught Roman law there (1846–81) and served as dean of the law faculty (1861–3, 1865–7) and rector of the university (1865–9). For many years he presided over the Kiev Juridical Society, which he helped found. His main work is *Kurs rimskogo prava* (A Course in Roman Law, 1883–4).

Rev Oleksander Mytrak   Yurii Mytropolsky

Mytrak, Oleksander (Mitrak, Alexander; pseud: Materyn), b 16 October 1837 in Ploske, Transcarpathia, d 17 March 1913 in Rosvyhove, near Mukachiv, Transcarpathia. Orthodox priest, writer, ethnographer, folklorist, and lexicologist of Russophile orientation. His ethnographic studies appeared in some Transcarpathian papers, such as *Slovo*, *Listok*, and *Karpaty*. He collected folk songs, some of which were published in Ya. Holovatsky's *Narodnye pesni Galitskoi i Ugorskoi Rusi* (Folk Songs of Galician and Hungarian Ruthenia, 1878). His elegies and patriotic verses appeared under his pseudonym. He compiled and published at his own expense a Russian-Hungarian dictionary of almost 70,000 words, including over a thousand middle-Transcarpathian dialectisms (1881). His Hungarian-Russian dictionary was published only in 1922.

Mytrofanov, Syla, b ?, d 1772. Physician. After being educated at the Kievan Mohyla Academy and the medical schools of the Moscow and St Petersburg general hospitals, he received a PH D from Leyden University in 1765. As chief physician of the Kiev Military Hospital, from 1770 he directed the fight against the plague in Podilia, and eventually became infected himself. His publications include a study of spontaneous pneumothorax.

Mytropolsky, Yurii [Mytropol's'kyj, Jurijl, b 3 January 1917 in Shyshaky, Myrhorod county, Poltava gubernia. Mathematician; full member of the AN URSR (now ANU) since 1961 and of the USSR Academy of Sciences from 1984. After graduating from Kazakh University in Alma-Ata (1942), he worked at the Institute of Constructive Mechanics of the ANU (1946–50) and the Institute of Mathematics of the ANU (1951–88). He also taught at Kiev University from 1949. Under his directorship (1958–88) the institute expanded greatly and improved the quality of its work. Mytropolsky has made major contributions to the theory of oscillations and nonlinear mechanics as well as to the qualitative theory of differential equations. He further developed asymptotic methods and applied them to the so-lution of practical problems. He extended the Krylov-Bogoliubov symbolical method to nonlinear systems and extended asymptotic methods in the theory of nonlinear oscillations, and later applied these to many equations of nonlinear mechanics. Using a method of successive substitutes, he constructed a general solution for a system of nonlinear equations and studied its behavior in the neighborhood of the quasi-periodic solution. He also successfully applied the averaging method to the study of oscillating systems with slowly varying parameters.

W. Petryshyn

Oleksander Mytsiuk

Mytsiuk, Oleksander [Mycjuk], b 21 June 1883 in Novooleksandrivka, Katerynoslav gubernia, d 30 December 1943 in Prague. Economist, sociologist, and political activist; full member of the Shevchenko Scientific Society. A supporter of the Revolutionary Ukrainian party in the early 1900s, he was arrested and exiled for organizing a peasant alliance. After his release he joined the Ukrainian Party of Socialist Revolutionaries. During the struggle for Ukrainian independence he served under the UNR Directory as minister of internal affairs and deputy minister of the national economy. After fleeing to Czechoslovakia he was a professor at the Ukrainian Husbandry Academy and then a professor and rector of the Ukrainian Free University in Prague (1938–9, 1940–1). Mytsiuk published articles and monographs in economics, including the textbooks *Istoriia politychnoï ekonomiï* (A History of Political Economy, 2 vols, 1922, 1923) and *Agrarna polityka, 1800–1925* (Agrarian Politics, 1800–1925, 2 vols, 1925), *Agraryzatsiia zhydivstva Ukraïny na tli zahal'noï ekonomiky* (The Agrarianization of the Jews of Ukraine against the Background of the General Economy, 1933), *Narysy z sotsiial'nohospodars'koï istoriï b. Uhors'koï, nyni Pidkarpats'koï, Rusy* (Essays in the Socioeconomic History of the Former Hungarian, Now Subcarpathian, Ruthenia, 2 vols, 1936, 1938), and biographies of T. Rylsky (1933) and S. Podolynsky (1933).

Mytsyk, Ivan [Mycyk] (nom de guerre: Askold), b 1913 in Synevydsko Vyzhnie, Stryi county, Galicia, d spring 1941 near Yezupil, Stanyslaviv county, Galicia. Nationalist revolutionary. An OUN member, he was sentenced in 1931 by a special Polish court to 20 years in prison for killing a provocateur. When Poland fell in 1939, he was released from prison and appointed deputy chief of the OUN (Melnyk faction) for Western Ukraine (1940–1). He was allegedly killed by the rival Bandera faction.

Mytusa. A modernist monthly of literature and art edited by the poets V. *Bobynsky and R. *Kupchynsky and the artist P. *Kovzhun, four issues of which were published in Lviv from January to April 1922. The periodical was named after a medieval Galician bard and had a symbolist profile. Among its contributors (many of them Ukrainian Sich Riflemen veterans) were the writers O. Babii, Yu. Shkrumeliak, A. Pavliuk, M. Obidny, B. Homzyn, Yu. Lypa, and D. Zahul, the critic M. Rudnytsky, and the scholar V. Sichynsky. Works by H. Narbut, A. Archipenko, and Kovzhun were reproduced in the journal.

Myzin, Oleksandr, b 23 July 1900 in Kharkiv, d 26 July 1986 in Moscow. Decorative artist. He graduated from the Kiev State Art Institute (1928), where he studied under M. Boichuk, and from 1936 taught at the Moscow Art Institute. He has painted frescoes and designed mosaics, tapestries, and stained-glass windows. The Kiev Ring station of the Moscow metro is decorated with his mosaic panels (1952–4). He designed the stained-glass window *Friendship of Peoples* (1954) for the palace of culture in Nova Kakhivka, the tapestry *Soviet Ukraine* (1956), and the murals of the palace of culture at the Kremenchuk Hydroelectric Station (1959–60).

N

Na finansovomu fronti (On the Financial Front). A semimonthly magazine of the People's Commissariat of Finances, the USSR State Bank, and the Union of Financial and Banking Employees. Published in Kharkiv (1930–4) and Kiev (1935–41, 1945–6), it contained official decrees and information about the Ukrainian banking system. It was succeeded by *Na dopomohu finansovomu pratsivnyku* (1947–9).

Na Hori (On the Mountain). A publishing venture in West Germany established by I. *Kostetsky and his wife, E. Kottmeier. Unique in its devotion to the enrichment of Ukrainian literature through translations, it published editions in Ukrainian translation of T.S. Eliot's selected poems (1956, trans Kostetsky) and *Murder in the Cathedral* (1963, trans Z. Tarnavsky); O. Wilde's *Salome* (1957, trans B. Lepky); W. Shakespeare's *Romeo and Juliet* (1957, trans Kostetsky), sonnets (1958, trans Kostetsky), *Macbeth* and *Henry IV* (1961, trans T. Osmachka), and *King Lear* (1969, trans V. Barka); P. Claudel's *L'Annonce faite à Marie* (1962, trans M. Kalytovska); J. Anouilh's *Antigone* (1962, trans Zh. Vasylkivska); a collection of Japanese tankas compiled by Fujiwara no Sadaie in 1235 (1966, trans I. Shankovsky); and the selected poetry of F. Garcia Lorca (1958, various trans), E. Pound (1960, trans Kostetsky et al), S. George (1971, trans Kostetsky, O. Zuievsky, and M. Orest), R.M. Rilke (1971, trans Kostetsky), C. Beaudelaire (1979, trans V. Vovk), and P. Verlaine (1979, trans Kostetsky). It also published Kottmeier's German translations of V. Barka's *Troiandnyi roman* (*Trojanden-Roman*, 1956), the anthology *Weinstock der Wiedegeburt: Moderne ukrainische Lyrik* (1957), and V. Vovk's poetry collection *Liebesbriefe der Fürstin Veronika an den Kardinal Giovannibattista* (1967); collections of poems and translations by O. Zuievsky (*Pid znakom feniksa* [Under the Sign of the Phoenix], 1958), M. Kalytovska (*Rymy i ne-rymy* [Rhymes and Non-Rhymes], 1959), and V. Lesych (*Kreidiane kolo* [Chalk Circle], 1960); and V. Vovk's poetry collection *Chorni akatsiï* (Black Acacias, 1961) and novel *Vitrazhi* (Stained-Glass Windows, 1961).

R. Senkus

Na shakhti (At the Mine). A weekly newspaper for Ukrainians working in Germany's mines during the Second World War. It was published in Berlin in 1942–5 and edited by B. Kravtsiv.

Na slidi (On the Trail). A monthly magazine for teenagers, published in Lviv in 1936–9 and edited by R. Olesnytsky. It was renewed under the editorship of B. Kravtsiv in Bayreuth, Germany, and published in 1947–8 as a supplement to the émigré newspaper *Chas*.

Na varti (On Guard). A Ukrainian Orthodox religious journal published monthly and then semimonthly in Vo-lodymyr-Volynskyi in 1925–6 and briefly in 1929. Financed and edited by A. *Richynsky, *Na varti* promoted the Ukrainianization of the Russified Orthodox church in Volhynia.

Na vichnu pam'iat'
Kotliarevs'komu

Na vichnu pam'iat' Kotliarevs'komu (In Eternal Memory of Kotliarevsky). A 510-page literary miscellany issued by the *Vik publishing house in Kiev in 1904 to commemorate the unveiling of a monument to I. *Kotliarevsky in Poltava. Among its contributors were T. Borduliak, V. Domanytsky, M. Cherniavsky, I. Franko, H. Barvinok, P. Hrabovsky, B. Hrinchenko, H. Hryhorenko, I. Karpenko-Kary, N. Kobrynska, O. Konysky, M. Kotsiubynsky, A. Krymsky, Lesia Ukrainka, M. Levytsky, O. Makovei, L. Martovych, D. Mordovets, P. Myrny, V. Prokopovych, P. Radchenko, V. Samiilenko, V. Stefanyk, P. Stebnytsky, M. Vorony, and L. Yanovska. A bibliography of works by and about Kotliarevsky was prepared by M. Komarov. The miscellany was illustrated by V. Korniienko, L. Pozen, and O. Slastion, and the cover was designed by F. Krasytsky.

Naboikin, Yurii [Nabojkin, Jurij], b 24 November 1923 in Bohodukhiv, Kharkiv gubernia. Physicist. A graduate of the Kharkiv Polytechnical Institute (1952), since 1960 he has worked at the AN URSR (now ANU) Physical-Technical Institute of Low Temperatures in Kharkiv, where he has contributed to the development of tuned lasers and conducted research in quantum electronics and molecular spectroscopy, particularly on the properties of highly excited molecular crystals at low temperatures.

Naboka, Serhii, b 26 April 1955 in Tula, RSFSR. Journalist and dissident. In 1981 he was sentenced to three years' imprisonment in a labor camp in Khmelnytskyi oblast for distributing political leaflets. In 1987 he organized and headed the Ukrainian Culturological Club, an unofficial organization in Kiev. In 1990 he became director of the Respublika information agency in Kiev of the newly founded Ukrainian Republican party, and the editor of the party's organ, *Holos vidrodzhennia*.

Nachtigall. See Legion of Ukrainian Nationalists.

Nad, Havryil [Nad', Havryjil], b 17 April 1913 in Stari Vrbas, Bačka, Serbia, d 16 October 1983 in Koćura, Bačka. Cultural and civic figure in the *Bačka region. He graduated from Belgrade University in 1936 and worked as a teacher in Subotica. After the Second World War he was a member of the Yugoslav Constituent Assembly and became the first director of the Ruthenian gymnasium in Ruski Krstur. From 1954 he lived in Koćura. He translated children's literature and wrote poetry, songs, and linguistic articles in the Bačka dialect of Ukrainian.

Naddniprians'ka pravda (Dnieper Truth). The chief daily organ of the CPU in Kherson oblast. It was published in Russian as *Soldat i rabochii* (1917–18), *Khersonskaia pravda* (1919), *Izvestiia* (1919–21), and *Khersonskii kommunar* (1922–5). It was first published in Ukrainian as *Kherson-s'kyi komunar* in May 1925, and later that year it became two separate newspapers – the Ukrainian-language semi-weekly *Chervonyi selianyn* and the Russian-language daily *Rabochii* – which were merged in March 1928 as *Naddniprians'ka pravda*. The paper was not published during the German occupation of 1941–4. In 1944 it became the principal oblast organ. It initially was published five days a week but from 1970 was published six days a week. In 1980 the paper had a daily circulation of 141,000.

Mykola Nademsky

Nademsky, Mykola [Nadems'kyj], b 27 September 1892 in Kiev, d 27 December 1937. Stage and film actor. After completing study at the Kiev Art School he worked in the Franko New Drama Theater in Kharkiv (1923–5) and was an actor in the Odessa Ukrainian Drama Theater (1925–6) and the Odessa Artistic Film Studio (1926–35). He is best known for his roles in O. Dovzhenko's films *Zvenyhora* (1928), *Arsenal* (1929), and *Ivan* (1932). He was arrested in 1935 and died in a concentration camp or was executed by the NKVD.

Nadenenko, Fedir, b 26 February 1902 in L'gov, Kursk gubernia, Russia, d 2 December 1963 in Kiev. Composer, pianist, and editor. A graduate of the Lysenko Music and Drama School (1914), Kiev Conservatory (1921), and University of Kiev (1924), he studied composition and piano

with B. Yavorsky. He was the concertmaster and choirmaster of the Kiev Opera (1926–35) and the Leningrad Opera (1935–7) before becoming the artistic director of the Kiev Philharmonic (1938–40). He later headed the music department of the Mystetstvo publishing house and edited the complete works of M. Lysenko. His compositions include *My Homeland* (1950) for choir; nearly 80 piano pieces; folk song arrangements; and songs to words of T. Shevchenko, Lesia Ukrainka, and I. Franko.

Nadiin, Dmytro [Nadijin], b 1907 in Volodymyrivka, Kherson county, d January 1942. Poet. He graduated from the Mykolaiv Pedagogical Institute. From 1933 he was secretary of the Odessa journal *Literaturnyi Zhovten'* and taught at the Odessa Pedagogical Institute. He began publishing in 1927 and wrote three small collections of poetry (1929, 1931, 1933). Posthumous editions of his works appeared in 1958, 1960, 1966, and 1972.

Nadlymanske settlement. A Scythian fortified settlement of the 4th to 3rd century BC, on the Dniester estuary near Nadlymanske, Ovidiopil raion, Odessa oblast. Excavated intermittently from 1957 to 1966, the site revealed clay dwellings with stone foundations, grain storage pits, milling facilities, and artisans' wares. The inhabitants engaged primarily in agriculture and craftsmanship, and they also traded with Greek settlements in the region.

Nadraga, Oleksander, b 15 October 1885 in Berezhany, Galicia, d 3 April 1962 in Sambir, Galicia. Jurist; member of the Shevchenko Scientific Society. After graduating in law and political science from Lviv University (1911) he worked in the Austrian civil service in Stanyslaviv. During the period of Ukrainian independence he was a commissary of Stanyslaviv county. After the war he went into private practice in Lviv and taught Roman and civil law at the Lviv (Underground) Ukrainian University (1921–4), the Greek Catholic Theological Academy (1932–9), and Lviv University (1940–1). In 1944 he and his family were arrested and deported to Siberia by the Soviets. They returned to Galicia only in 1960.

Nadvirna. V-5. A city (1990 pop 20,500) on the Bystrytsia Nadvirnianska River and a raion center in Ivano-Frankivske oblast. It was first mentioned in historical documents in 1595. After the first partition of Poland in 1772 it was annexed by Austria. In 1939 it was occupied by the Soviets and granted city status. The Nadvirna region is rich in natural resources, such as oil, natural gas, potassium salts, and forests. Petroleum refining is a major source of the city's income.

Nadvirna Petroleum Refinery (Nadvirnianskyi nafto-pererobnyi zavod). A refinery located in Nadvirna, Ivano-Frankivske oblast. It was founded in 1897 as a seasonal operation. After the Second World War it was extensively modernized and automated. Now it produces some 20 petroleum products, including petroleum-coke, paraffin, and gasoline.

Nadvirni kozaky. See Manorial Cossacks.

Nagurski, Bronko [Nagurs'kyj, Bronislav], b 3 November 1908 in Rainy River, Ontario, d 7 January 1990 in International Falls, Minnesota. Professional American football player of Ukrainian origin. Having moved to the United States with his parents in 1912, he began his career as a tackle and fullback with the University of Minnesota football team (1927–9). He was the only player to be selected to two positions on a single all-American team (1929). A versatile player, he distinguished himself as a fullback with the Chicago Bears (1930–8, 1943–4) and was renowned for his sheer physical strength. In 1932 he began to wrestle professionally, and he won the world heavyweight title in 1937 and again in 1939. In 1951 he was inducted into the National Football Hall of Fame.

Nahaichynskyi kurhan. A *Sarmatian burial mound from the 1st century BC located near Nyzhnohirskyi, Crimea. Excavation in 1974 uncovered a Sarmatian noblewoman buried in a wooden sarcophagus. She wore a gold-link crown, bracelets adorned with human figures on her hands and legs, and a brooch on her chest. Other artifacts found in the grave included alabaster earthenware, a bronze mirror, 570 adornments made of gold and precious stones, and a case containing perfume, jewelry, silver spoons, and a rock-crystal dolphin figurine with gold inlay.

Nahaievsky, Isydor [Nahajevs'kyj] (Nahayewsky, Isidore), b 21 June 1908 in Polivtsi, Chortkiv county, Galicia, d 7 May 1989 in Parma, Ohio. Ukrainian Catholic priest and historian. In 1939 he was a political prisoner in the Polish concentration camp in Bereza Kartuzka. During the Second World War he was imprisoned by the NKVD and the Gestapo. From 1943 to 1945 he served as a chaplain with the Division Galizien, and from 1945–7, in a POW camp; subsequently he emigrated to the United States. Nahaievsky received his PH D from the Ukrainian Free University in 1953 and was a professor at the Ukrainian Catholic University in Rome. He wrote books in Ukrainian on the mission and impact of SS Cyril and Methodius in Rus'-Ukraine (1954), Rome and Byzantium (1956), Prince Iziaslav Yaroslavych and the papal see (1957), ancient Ukraine as reflected in historical monuments (1961), the history of the Roman Catholic pontiffs (3 vols, 1964, 1967, 1979), and the origin and significance of patriarchates (1973). He also wrote *History of Ukraine* (1962), *History of the Modern Ukrainian State, 1917–1923* (1966), and memoirs of Bereza Kartuzka (1957), the interwar years (1960), and the Division Galizien (1985).

Nahiriany settlement. An early Scythian settlement of the late 7th to early 6th century BC near Nahiriany, Kelmentsi raion, Chernivtsi oblast. Excavated by I. *Shovkoplias in 1950, the site yielded three triangular semi-pit dwellings with both open fireplaces and stone ovens. Also recovered were flint and bone tools, pottery, and bones of domestic animals.

Nahirna, Kateryna (née Kuryshko), b 12 April 1949 in Vepryk, Hadiache raion, Poltava oblast. Canoeist. She was a member of the USSR women's teams that won the 1971 world and European championships in the kayak fours and the 1972 Olympic gold medal in the 500-m kayak pairs. She was also a USSR champion in 1970–2 and 1975.

Nahirny, Vasyl [Nahirnyj, Vasyl'], b 11 January 1847 in Hirne, Stryi circle, Galicia, d 25 February 1921 in Lviv. Ar-

Vasyl Nahirny

chitect and populist civic figure. He studied architecture at the Zürich Institute of Technology (1871–5) and then worked in Zürich, where he became involved with Western European co-operative movements (which he described in articles sent to *Pravda* and *Dilo* in Lviv) and Russian and Ukrainian émigré circles. From 1882 he lived in Lviv. Nahirny designed and built (from 1906 with his son, Yevhen) many Galician churches and buildings. In 1883 he presented a program for the socioeconomic revival of Galicia's Ukrainians at the Second Public Assembly (*viche*) and initiated, with A. Nychai, the creation of the *Narodna Torhovlia wholesalers' co-operative. He served as its director for many years, and was also the founder and chief organizer of the Zoria artisans' association, the Dnister insurance company, the Sokil society (president, 1894–1900), the Trud women's manufacturing association, the Society for the Advancement of Ruthenian Art (chairman, 1898–1904), and the Narodna Hostynnytsia hotel. He was a member of the chief executive of the Prosvita society; editor and publisher of the humorous journal *Nove zerkalo* (1883–4), the weekly *Bat'kivshchyna* (1885–90), and the semimonthly *Hospodar i promyshlennyk* (1886–7); and a contributor on social and economic problems to *Dilo*. His memoirs were published posthumously, in 1935.

Nahirny, Volodymyr (Vladimir) [Nahirnyj], b 9 August 1927 in Halych, Galicia. Sociologist. A graduate of Marquette (1952) and Harvard (1954) universities and the University of Chicago (PH D, 1960), he became a professor of sociology at Hunter College in 1962. A specialist on the sociology of intellectuals and of ethnicity in the United States, he has written scholarly articles, *Language Loyalty in the United States* (coauthor, 1966), and *The Russian Intelligentsia: From Torment to Silence* (1983).

Nahirny, Yevhen [Nahirnyj, Jevhen], b 25 August 1885 in Rudno, Lviv county, Galicia, d 8 June 1951 in Lviv. Architect. After graduating from the Lviv Polytechnic (1912) he worked as an architect with his father, V. *Nahirny. After 1921, working independently, he designed over 300 residential, public, and church buildings in Western Ukraine. From 1946 he taught in higher educational institutions in Lviv. His church in Stebnyk (Drohobych county, 1935) is representative of his style, which is based on Ukrainian baroque and folk traditions. The influence of constructivism is evident in his later work.

Church in Stebnyk (architect: Yevhen Nahirny)

Nahnybida, Mykola, b 20 September 1911 in Popivka, now Smyrnove, Kuibysheve raion, Zaporizhia oblast, d 16 September 1985 in Kiev. Poet. He began his writing career in the early 1930s as a member of *Prolitfront. His first poetry collections, *Dniprovs'ka vesna* (Spring on the Dnieper, 1932), *Zerna* (Seed, 1933), and *Poeziï* (Poems, 1934), were written mainly on the theme of the Komsomol. During the Second World War he worked at the radio station Radianska Ukraina and wrote for the front-line press. He has written the following collections on the theme of war: *Zdrastui, Kharkiv* (Hello, Kharkiv, 1943), *Lialia Ubyivovk* (1946), and *Nezabutnie* (The Unforgettable, 1946). A number of his books of postwar lyric poetry have been partially republished in the collected editions *Vybrani poeziï* (Selected Poems, 2 vols, 1961) and *Vybrane* (A Selection, 2 vols, 1971).

Naholnyi Ridge. A section of the main plateau of the *Donets Ridge. Situated in the southeastern part of the ridge, it runs from the Miius River in the west to the Kundriucha River in the east at an average elevation of 290–320 m. Its highest point is Mechetna Mohyla (367 m).

Nahorny, Oleksander [Nahornyj], b 10 September 1887 in Kharkiv, d 11 May 1953 in Kharkiv. Physiologist; corresponding member of the AN URSR (now ANU) from 1948. He graduated from Kharkiv University (1912) and worked there (as a professor from 1924), researching insect respiration, the hysteresis of hydrophilic colloids, and the physiology of aging (esp the role of the nervous system).

Naidych, Yurii [Najdyč, Jurij], b 6 August 1929 in Kharkiv. Materials scientist; full member of the AN URSR (now ANU) since 1988. He graduated from the Kiev Polytechnical Institute (1953) and has worked at the ANU Institute for Problems of Materials Science (since 1954). He has made important contributions in the areas of metal alloys, solid state physics, welding technology, the metallization of materials, and composites.

Naive art. See Primitive art.

Nakhabin, Volodymyr [Naxabin], b 21 April 1910 in Sharivka, Bohodukhiv county, Kharkiv gubernia, d 20 October 1967 in Kharkiv. Composer, pedagogue, and conductor. A graduate of the Kharkiv Music and Drama Institute (1932), he studied composition with S. Bohatyrov. From 1945 he was the conductor and artistic director of the Kharkiv Theater of Opera and Ballet, and from 1952 a lecturer at the Kharkiv Conservatory, where he also served as rector (1963–7) when it became the Kharkiv Institute of the Arts. He was a member of the committee of composers responsible for writing a national anthem for the Ukrainian SSR (1949). His works include the ballets *Mariika* (1939), *Danko* (1948), and *Tavriia* (1960); musical comedies; three symphonies (1932, 1945, and 1959); symphonic poems; a piano concerto; and numerous film scores.

Nakhman of Bratslav, b 1772 in Medzhybizh, d 1810 in Uman. Founder of the Breslover (Bratslavite) dynasty of Jewish Hasids. A great-grandson of the founder of *Hasidism, Nakhman of Bratslav developed a deeply mystical form of Hasidism which has thousands of followers to this day, mainly in Jerusalem. He was known for his disturbing allegorical tales, which he would improvise and recite to crowds of admirers. These stories, told exclusively in the Yiddish vernacular (rather than Hebrew, the language of the educated elite), freely borrowed motifs from Ukrainian folktales. With some interruptions enforced by the Soviet government, his grave at Uman has been the site of yearly pilgrimages for many Bratslavite Hasidim.

BIBLIOGRAPHY
Buber, M. *The Tales of Rabbi Nachman* (New York 1956)

Nakhodkin, Mykola [Naxodkin], b 25 January 1925 in Prokhorivka, Zolotonosha okruha, Poltava gubernia. Radio physicist; AN URSR (now ANU) corresponding member since 1973 and full member since 1990. A graduate of Kiev University (1950), he has taught there and was promoted to professor in 1972. He specializes in physical electronics and thermoplastic information storage; his major contributions are in the study of semiconductor surfaces by means of ionization spectroscopy.

Nakhymovsky, Fedir [Naxymovs'kyj], b ?, d 1758. Cossack diplomat of Jewish origin. He undertook numerous diplomatic missions for Hetmans I. Mazepa and P. *Orlyk, including representations to Stanislaus I Leszczyński (1708–9) and to the Zaporozhian Cossacks, the Crimean Tatars, and the Ottoman Porte (1720–1). Orlyk's son described Nakhymovsky as a valued and trustworthy assistant, particularly in Mazepa's negotiations with the Swedish king Charles XII. He followed Orlyk into exile in Bendery (under Turkish rule, 1709–14) and Sweden (1714–20) and then lived in Poland (from 1720) and the Crimea (from 1754), where he associated with F. Myrovych.

Nakonechna, Hanna [Nakonečna] (Nakonetschna), b 5 May 1896 in Pluhiv, Zolochiv county, Galicia, d ? Linguist. In the interwar period she was an associate of the Research Institute of Phonetics and the Ukrainian Scientific

Institute in Berlin. After the Second World War she taught Ukrainian at Munich University. She compiled a German-Ukrainian pocket dictionary (1939, 5th edn 1944), cowrote (with J. Rudnyckyj, 1940) *Ukrainische Mundarten: Südkarpatoukrainisch (Lemkisch, Bojkisch und Huzulisch)*, and wrote a short German grammar in Ukrainian (1941) and a few articles in German on the linguistic geography of Ukrainian dialects.

Nakonechny, Mykola [Nakonečnyj], b 6 September 1900 in Novyi Tahamlyk, Poltava gubernia, d 11 November 1981 in Kharkiv. Linguist and Slavist. After graduating from the Poltava Institute of People's Education (1923) he was a graduate student (1925–8) and a research associate (1928–32) at the Kharkiv Pedagogical Institute of Professional Education. Accused of nationalism, he was dismissed from his teaching position at Kharkiv University in 1934 (to 1939) and 1948 (to 1958). In 1943 he was head of the Ukrainian language department. Because of political persecution his scholarly output was limited to the practical Russian-Ukrainian dictionary (1926) which he coauthored with M. Yohansen, K. Nimchynov, and B. Tkachenko; the Russian-Ukrainian phraseological dictionary (published in *Prapor*, 1963–7) which he edited; a teacher's handbook on the Ukrainian language (1928); a university program in Ukrainian dialectology (1941, 1949); and a chapter on Ukrainian phonetics in *Kurs suchasnoï ukraïns'koï literaturnoï movy* (A Course in Contemporary Literary Ukrainian, 1951).

Vasyl Nakonechny

Nakonechny, Vasyl (Basil) [Nakonečnyj, Vasyl'], b 22 August 1918 in Luka Voinylivska, Kalush county, Galicia. Naval architect and mechanical engineer; member of the American Society of Naval Engineers, the Royal Institute of Naval Architects, the Shevchenko Scientific Society, and the Ukrainian Engineers' Society of America. He studied in Lviv, Graz, Vienna, and Leuven and at the Catholic University of America (PH D, 1963). He worked in Belgium and Canada as a naval architect, and in the United States as director of research and technology applications at the David Taylor Research Center in Bethesda, Maryland. His research, published in numerous technical papers, centers on surface ship powering and maneuvering models, propellers, cavitation phenomena, and ship-systems studies.

Sofiia Nalepinska: illustration to Stepan Vasylchenko's novelette *Olyv'ianyi persten'* (wood engraving, 1930)

Nalepinska, Sofiia [Nalepins'ka] (Nalepińska, Zofia) b 30 July 1884 in Łódź, Poland, d 11 December 1937. Graphic artist and xylographer of Polish origin; wife of M. *Boichuk (from 1917) and sister of the Polish poet T. Nalepiński. She studied at the St Petersburg Academy of Arts, in Munich (1906–7), and in Paris (1909–11), where she first met Boichuk. She taught at the Myrhorod Art and Ceramics Tekhnikum (1918–21) and the Kiev Art and Industrial Tekhnikum (1921–2) and then headed the xylographic workshop at the Kiev Institute of Plastic Arts (1922–4), taught at the Kiev State Art Institute (1924–35), and belonged to the *Association of Revolutionary Art of Ukraine (1925–31). Nalepinska created many xylographs, which were used as book illustrations, covers, and posters. Her approach was influenced by Ukrainian folk art, icons, 17th- and 18th-century engraving, H. Narbut, and formalist theory, and in turn, she influenced I. *Padalka and O. *Sakhnovska. In 1928–32 her works were exhibited in over 35 group shows of Soviet art. She and Boichuk were arrested by the Soviet secret police in November 1936 and later executed. She was posthumously rehabilitated in 1958.

Nalotova, Kateryna [Nal'otova], b 1787, d 1869. Actress. In 1813 she began acting in an amateur group in Poltava with I. Kotliarevsky (from 1917 the Poltava Free Theater). In 1819 she played the title role in the premiere of his *Natalka Poltavka* (Natalka from Poltava). In 1821–2 Nalotova worked in M. Shchepkin's troupe in Kiev.

Yuliian Nalysnyk   Vasyl Nalyvaiko

Nalysnyk, Yuliian, b 1 July 1890 in Krasna, Krosno county, Galicia, d 22 April 1960 in New York. Lawyer and civic leader. Interrupting his law studies in 1914, he joined the Ukrainian Sich Riflemen, and in 1916 he was deported by the Russians as a POW to Siberia. In 1917 he escaped to Kiev, where he served in the Ministry of Foreign Affairs. On O. Shulhyn's invitation he joined the UNR mission to Bulgaria. After returning to Galicia in 1921, he completed his law studies in Cracow and in 1931 opened a law office in Dukla. He became a prominent activist in the Lemko region, where he organized the Ukrainian People's Home and Silskyi Hospodar in Krasna and was persecuted by both the Poles and the Germans. He fled to Austria in 1944 and then emigrated to the United States, where he revived the *Organization for the Defense of Lemkivshchyna and from 1958 served as its first president.

Nalyvaiko, Demian [Nalyvajko, Dem'jan], b in the 1550s in Husiatyn, Galicia, d 1627 in Ostrih, Volhynia. Orthodox priest and cultural figure. He studied at the Ostrih Academy and in Vilnius and was taught printing by I. *Fedorovych. He served as the private priest and confessor of Prince K. *Ostrozky from 1589 and taught at the *Ostrih Academy. In 1594–6 he took part in the rebellion led by his brother, S. *Nalyvaiko, and in 1596 he participated in the Orthodox synod that proclaimed the Church Union of Berestia to be illegal. Later he directed Ostrozky's presses at the Derman Monastery (1602–5) and in Ostrih (1607, 1612), wrote verses and prefaces in the Derman Octoechos (1604) and Ostrih Horologion (1612), and contributed the introduction, an emblematic verse dedicated to Ostrozky, and translations of St John Chrysostom's homilies to an Ostrih collection (1607).

Nalyvaiko, Severyn [Nalyvajko], b ca 1560 in Husiatyn, Galicia, d 21 April 1597 in Warsaw. Cossack leader; brother of D. *Nalyvaiko. He participated in Zaporozhian Cossack campaigns against Turkey and the Crimean Tatars and then served as a captain in Prince K. Ostrozky's private army. In 1594 he became otaman of an independent Cossack force in the Bratslav region and led it on a campaign into Moldavia, where it defeated the Crimean Tatars advancing against Hungary. In the spring of 1595, together with H. *Loboda and M. *Shaula, he successfully engaged the Turks in Moldavia and Transylvania, thereby halting their advance on Austria.

After Nalyvaiko returned to Ukraine, he led a popular rebellion against the Poles that spread from the Bratslav region throughout Right-Bank Ukraine and into Belarus. With the help of local burghers the rebels captured Bratslav, Husiatyn, Bar, Lutske, Kaniv, Cherkasy, and Slutsk, Babruisk, and Mahiliou in Belarus. In late 1595 the Polish government sent Hetman S. Żółkiewski and the royal army to suppress the rebellion. Having retreated from Belarus, in April 1596 Nalyvaiko's force united with Shaula's Zaporozhians and successfully engaged the Poles at Bila Tserkva before retreating to Pereiaslav. There Nalyvaiko was elected hetman in place of the wounded Shaula. On 26 May 1596 the rebels were surrounded by a superior Polish force near Lubni. After a two-week Polish siege a mutiny arose among the rebels. Loboda was lynched, and on 7 July 1596 Nalyvaiko and Shaula were handed over to the Poles. During peace negotiations Żółkiewski's army caught the rebels off guard and slaughtered several thousand Cossacks. Nalyvaiko was taken to Warsaw, where he was cruelly tortured before being beheaded, quartered, and put on public display. After the rebellion all Cossack lands and enterprises were legally confiscated and redistributed among Polish magnates. Nalyvaiko was portrayed as a hero in folk stories, songs, and legends. T. Shevchenko and K. Ryleev glorified him, and the Soviet writer I. Le wrote a novel about him.

BIBLIOGRAPHY

Antonovych, M. *Studiï z chasiv Nalyvaika* (Prague 1941)
Rozner, I. *Severin Nalivaiko: Rukovoditel' krest'iansko-kazatskogo vosstaniia 1594–1596 gg. na Ukraine* (Moscow 1961)
Myshko, D. *Severyn Nalyvaiko* (Kiev 1962)
Gordon, L. *Cossack Rebellions: Social Turmoil in the Sixteenth-Century Ukraine* (Albany, NY 1983)

Nalyvaiko, Vasyl [Nalyvajko, Vasyl'], b 14 January 1887 in Severynivka, Bratslav county, Podilia gubernia, d 24 August 1938 in Prague. Physician. He obtained his medical education at Tomsk and Odessa universities and served as a doctor in the UNR Army (1918–20). An émigré in Poland and then Czechoslovakia, he was active in the Ukrainian Physicians' Association in Czechoslovakia. Besides scientific articles on surgery he published *Po sviatii zemli* (Through the Holy Land, 1937) and helped compile and edit M. Halyn's *Medychnyi latyns'ko-ukraïns'kyi slovnyk* (Medical Latin-Ukrainian Dictionary, 1926).

Namoradze, Georgii, b 14 October 1882, d 12 February 1965. Georgian poet and translator. From 1907 to 1936 he lived in Ukraine. In the 1920s he became head of the periodicals division of the State Publishing House of Ukraine. He was repressed in the mid-1930s and later rehabilitated. He translated Georgian literature into Ukrainian and Ukrainian into Georgian, and contributed to Georgian periodicals articles about Ukrainian writers, such as T. Shevchenko, M. Kotsiubynsky, Lesia Ukrainka, and M. Lysenko.

Nanovsky, Yaroslav [Nanovs'kyi, Jaroslav], b 1 September 1908 in Pecheniia, Peremyshliany county, Galicia, d 5 October 1992 in Lviv. Art historian and critic. A graduate of Lviv University (1939), he worked as a curator at the Lviv Museum of Ukrainian Art from 1942 and taught at the Lviv Art School (1945–52) and Lviv Institute of Applied and Decorative Arts (1947–52). He wrote many articles on Western Ukrainian art and books about K. Ustyianovych (1963), I. Trush (1967), and Yu. Pankevych (1986) and compiled albums of the paintings of A. Manastyrsky (1959) and the Lviv Museum of Ukrainian Art (1963).

Nansen, Fridtjof, b 10 October 1861 in Store-Froen, Norway, d 13 May 1930 in Lysaker, Norway. Explorer, oceanographer, statesman, and philanthropist; honorary member of the Russian (later USSR) Academy of Sciences from 1898. Nansen served as head of the Norwegian delegation to the League of Nations General Assembly (1920). In the league's assembly and its Political Commission he spoke out on behalf of national minorities. As the league's high commissioner (1920–2) he oversaw the repatriation of 500,000 prisoners of war from the USSR. In 1921–3 he served as high commissioner of the International Committee of the Red Cross which provided relief to famine-stricken Ukraine and Russia. In 1922 he initiated the international agreement that created a 'Nansen Office' to care for political refugees from the USSR, including thousands of Ukrainians, who were issued 'Nansen certificates' recognized by over 50 governments in lieu of passports. The Geneva-based Nansen International Office for Refugees aided refugees and issued certificates until 1951.

Naperedodni (On the Eve). A literary and art biweekly published in Lviv from October 1937 to December 1938. Its editor was B. *Kravtsiv.

Napoleon Bonaparte, b 15 August 1769 in Ajaccio, Corsica, d 5 May 1821 in St Helena Island. French statesman.

Napoleon's government (like those of the 18th-century French kings) took an interest in Ukraine's economic potential, particularly vis-à-vis commerce in the Black Sea ports, and it commissioned several studies on that subject (eg, *Essai historique sur le commerce et la navigation de la mer Noire* by A. de Saint-Joseph, 1805). Ukraine became a factor in Napoleon's political designs after his vassal state, the Grand Duchy of *Warsaw (est 1807), laid claim to the Ukrainian lands that had been a part of Poland before the partition. He did not immediately agree to the Polish claims, but he did not deny them. Ukraine acquired more political significance for Napoleon when he began planning his invasion of Russia. Having received frequent reports from his diplomats and spies in Eastern Europe about antitsarist sentiments in Ukraine and the growth of peasant unrest and pro-French, pro-Napoleon sympathies there, Napoleon requested from his foreign ministry detailed information about Ukraine and scenarios for the dismemberment of the Russian Empire. In 1812 Counts A.-M. Blanc de la Naulte d'Hauterive and J.-G.-M. de Montgaillard submitted memorandums proposing the return of Right-Bank Ukraine (without Volhynia, which Napoleon had promised to Austria for military support in his war against Russia) to Poland, and the creation of two French puppet states in Left-Bank and Southern Ukraine that would isolate Russia from Europe and block its access to the Black Sea. One state would have consisted of the territories of Chernihiv and Poltava gubernias and adjacent lands as far north as Orel, and the other, to have been called Napoléonida, the territories of Katerynoslav gubernia, the Donets valley, and Tavriia gubernia (including the Crimea).

Because Napoleon's 1812 invasion of Russia was directed at the conquest of Moscow, western Volhynia was the only Ukrainian region occupied by his Grande Armée. There Napoleon's Austrian, Saxon, and Polish allies engaged the Russian Third Army commanded by A. Tormasov. During the Napoleonic invasion Ukraine supplied to the Russian military much of its grain, fodder, and horses, and 22 Ukrainian Cossack cavalry regiments and a huge Ukrainian *levy en masse (nearly 75,000 men) fought in the Russian ranks. The Ukrainian gentry, however, organized the levy reluctantly. At their assemblies in Chernihiv and Poltava they resolved to lower the number of recruits from 4 to 1 per 100 inhabitants, and they unwillingly donated money to Russia's military cause. Other Ukrainian notables (eg, Archbishop V. *Shyshatsky) even openly supported Napoleon's invasion and were later punished as a result. During the ill-fated winter retreat of Napoleon's army, attempts to penetrate from Belarus into the gubernias of Left-Bank Ukraine were effectively thwarted by Ukrainian forces. The Ukrainian gentry became alarmed at Napoleon's Polish plans and in the end remained loyal to Russia. Napoleon's interest in Ukraine (which prompted the commissioning of C.-L. *Lesur's 1813 history of the Cossacks) and plans for a second invasion of Russia were laid to rest after the rout of his army by Russia, Prussia, Austria, and Britain in 1813–15 and his forced abdication and exile.

BIBLIOGRAPHY
Borschak, E. [Borshchak, I.]. 'Napoléon et l'Ukraine,' *Revue des études Napoléoniennes,* 19 (July–December 1922)
Lazarevs'ka, K. 'Kyïvs'ka reiestrova khorohva ta napoleonovs'ki viiny v Evropi,' *Iuvileinyi Zbirnyk na poshanu akad. M.S. Hrushevs'koho,* vol 1 (1928)
Borshchak, I. *Napoleon i Ukraïna* (Lviv 1937)
Butsyk, A.; Strel's'kyi, V. *Velykyi patriotychnyi podvyh (Uchast' ukraïns'koho narodu u Vitchyznianii viini 1812 r.)* (Kiev 1962)
                                                                    V. Kosyk

Naranovych, Pavlo [Naranovyč], b 1801 in Chapliivka, Krolevets county, Chernihiv gubernia, d 14 January 1874 in Tsarskoe Selo, near St Petersburg. Physician; brother of Petro *Naranovych. A graduate of the St Petersburg Medico-Surgical Academy (1824), he was a professor of anatomy at the academy (from 1839), chairman of descriptive anatomy (1844), and director of the academy (1867–9). He edited *Voenno-meditsinskii zhurnal* (1839–40), served as vice-president of the Society of Russian Physicians in St Petersburg (1852–66), and helped found the Society for the Care of Sick and Wounded Soldiers (1867), which eventually became the Russian Red Cross Society. He translated medical books from German and wrote articles on anatomy, surgery, and military sanitation.

Naranovych, Petro [Naranovyč], b 1805 in Chapliivka, Krolevets county, Chernihiv gubernia, d 20 May 1858 in Kharkiv. Physician; brother of Pavlo *Naranovych. A graduate of the St Petersburg Medico-Surgical Academy (1826), he worked at the St Petersburg Military Hospital, where he attained the rank of surgeon and obstetrician (1834). He was a professor of anatomy (from 1837) and of surgery (from 1843) at Kharkiv University. His work dealt with locomotion in humans, and new surgical procedures. He invented a number of surgical instruments.

Narbut, Danylo, b 22 January 1916 in Petrograd. Scenery painter; son of H. *Narbut. He completed the All-Union Courses for Theater Artists at the All-Russian Academy of Arts in 1935. He has worked for various theaters in Ukraine, including the Chernivtsi Oblast Ukrainian Music and Drama Theater in the 1940s, the Ivano-Frankivske Ukrainian Music and Drama Theater in the 1950s, and the Cherkasy Music and Drama Theater since the 1960s.

Heorhii Narbut: frontispiece for the journal *Mystetstvo* (1919)

Heorhii Narbut: illustration for the letters *y* and *i* of the Ukrainian alphabet (1917)

Narbut, Heorhii (Yurii), b 9 March 1886 in Narbutivka, Hlukhiv county, Chernihiv gubernia, d 23 May 1920 in Kiev. Painter and graphic artist. From 1906 he lived in St Petersburg, where he learned to draw from I. Bilibin and M. Dobuzhinsky. After studying art in Munich for several months in 1909, he returned to St Petersburg and became part of the Mir Iskusstva circle and gained prominence through his book covers and book illustrations (eg, for I. Krylov's fables [1912] and several stories by H.C. Andersen) and his neoclassical and symbolist watercolors. Having developed a keen interest in heraldry and the silhouette he illustrated and designed Russian-language editions of V. Lukomsky and V. Modzalevsky's book on 'Little Russian' heraldry (1914), the coats of arms of the Cossack hetmans of 'Little Russia' (1915), H. Lukomsky's book on ancient Galician architecture (1915), and a book on the old estates of Kharkiv gubernia (1917). After the February Revolution of 1917 Narbut returned to Ukraine. In September 1917 he was appointed a professor at the *Ukrainian State Academy of Arts in Kiev, and in February 1918 he became its rector. There he laid the foundations for advanced art education and fostered a pleiad of graphic artists, including L. Lozovsky, P. Kovzhun, and R. Lisovsky. Through his covers and graphics for postrevolutionary books and journals (*Nashe mynule, Zori, Solntse truda, Narodnoe khoziaistvo Ukrainy, Mystetstvo*); his graphic designs for UNR *currency, postage stamps, seals, and charters; and his bookplates and series of drawings and initials illustrating the Ukrainian alphabet (1917, 1919) with Cossack, Ukrainian baroque, and folk motifs, he initiated, with M. Boichuk and V. Krychevsky, the rebirth of Ukrainian art. His finest work after 1917 was his gouache frontispiece for a 1919 edition of I. Kotliarevsky's *Eneïda* (Aeneid). Narbut died prematurely from typhus.

BIBLIOGRAPHY

Ernst, F.; Steshenko, Ia. *Heorhii Narbut: Posmertna vystavka tvoriv* (Kiev 1926)
Karmazyn-Kakovs'kyj, V. 'Die schöpferischen Interessen Narbuts,' *Jahrbuch der Ukrainekunde 1982* (Munich 1982)
Bilets'kyi, P. *Heorhii Narbut: Al'bom* (Kiev 1983)
Beletskii, P. *Georgii Ivanovich Narbut* (Leningrad 1985, 1987)
Bilokin', S. (comp). *Heorhii Narbut v ekslibrisi* (Sumy 1988)

S. Bilokin

Narcissus (*Narcissus*; Ukrainian: *nartsyz*). A bulbous, often fragrant ornamental plant of the family Amaryllidaceae. The leaves are linear, the flowers generally white or yellow. Single-flowered species, including the daffodil (*N. pseudonarcissus*) and the poet's narcissus (*N. poeticus*), are cultivated as decorative flowers. Of its approx 40 species, only the narrow-leaved narcissus (*N. angustiformis*) grows wild in Ukraine, in the mountains of Transcarpathia. It is now so rare that it has been put on the list of endangered species (in the so-called red book). Narcissus bulbs are poisonous and contain a number of alkaloids, used in *folk medicine as emetics and cathartics.

Narcotics. Criminal law in the USSR and the Ukrainian SSR provided for punishment of the makers and suppliers of illicit narcotics and other toxic substances by imprisonment for up to 10 years, with or without the confiscation of their property. Criminal responsibility was also specified for planting opium poppy, Indian hemp, and southern Manchurian or southern Chu hemp without appropriate permits. Penalties existed for violating laws concerning the storage, distribution, registration, transportation, and sending of narcotics, and for involving minors in the use of narcotics.

Drug abuse in Ukraine emerged as a serious problem in the 1970s and 1980s, especially after the return of Soviet troops from Afghanistan, where many of them used opium, hashish, and other drugs and developed addictions. The main area in the former USSR where narcotic plants have been grown is Central Asia. There opium has served as a traditional medicine. Recent press reports indicate that a kilogram of opium costs 8,000 rubles on the black market in Turkmenia and tens of thousands in the large cities of Russia and Ukraine. The number of drug addicts in what was the USSR has risen in recent years. According to official data there were 52,000 registered drug addicts in 1988, but the real figure is much higher. In 1986 the first large-scale public information campaign against drug abuse was launched. In 1987 the Soviet government began limiting and controlling the areas where hemp and opium poppies were cultivated, and tried to find a means of destroying wild hemp. In the large cities special centers for the study of drug addiction registered addicts, and police-run rehabilitation centers treated addicts who were there either voluntarily or by court order. Studies indicate that most drug addicts are urban males under the age of 35. The majority have completed their secondary education, hold jobs, and are married and have children; half, however, admit to being from families where alcoholism, drug abuse, mental illness, or crime was present. Most abusers begin using drugs in their late teens or early twenties.

Narcotics and substance abuse is more widespread in Ukraine than in other former republics of the USSR, except Kirgizia and Turkmenistan in Central Asia. In 1988, 37.4 of every 100,000 persons in Ukraine were treated for narcotic or substance abuse, compared to 24.3 in the USSR as a

Persons receiving medical treatment for narcotic and substance abuse, 1984–8 (per 100,000 inhabitants)

	1984	1986	1987	1988
Ukraine	14.9	24.9	32.4	37.4
USSR	13.7	17.1	21.5	24.3
Russia	11.2	13.4	17.9	20.6
Belarus	1.4	3.2	4.8	5.9
Lithuania	5.9	7.2	10.1	11.2

whole and 20.6 in Russia. Moreover, there has been a significant increase in the number of people treated (see the table). In Ukraine the number of persons treated grew from 8.5 to 43.5 per 100,000 inhabitants between 1980 and 1990.

The abuse of various other substances has been common in the Soviet republics and their successor states. Novocaine, codeine, morphine, and other pain relievers are frequently stolen from medical pharmacies and hospitals and sold on the black market. The press has also reported the existence of a number of synthetic drugs prepared in secret chemical laboratories and other methods of inducing euphoria, such as glue sniffing.

Unlike in the West, drug addiction in the former Soviet republics has not yet become a mass phenomenon, and the social functions of escaping reality and finding relaxation are fulfilled primarily by alcohol in the youth subculture. Nonetheless, drug abuse has become a growing problem, especially since international contacts have increased, and greater freedom of movement has become possible.

A. Babyonyshev, D. Goshko, B. Krawchenko

Narezhny, Vasilii [Narežnyj, Vasilij] (Narizhny, Vasyl), b 1780 in Ustyvytsia, New Russia gubernia, d 3 July 1825 in St Petersburg. Russian writer of Ukrainian descent, and a representative of the Ukrainian school in Russian literature at the beginning of the 19th century. He first published his work in 1804 (the tragedy *Dimitrii Samozvanets* [Dimitrii the Impostor]). His most noteworthy work on a Russian theme was *Rossiiskii Zhil' Blaz* (The Russian Gil Blas, 1814). But Narezhny wrote mainly on Ukrainian themes: *Aristion* (1824), *Zaporozhets* (The Zaporozhian, 1824), *Bursak* (The Seminarist, 1824; Ukrainian translation by V. Doroshenko published in 1928), *Dva Ivana* (Two Ivans, 1825; Ukrainian translation by H. Bili, 1931), and *Garkusha* (1825; Ukrainian translation by P. Nimchenko, 1931). Narezhny's works, characterized by an interest in social problems and rich in Ukrainian folklore, inspired the work of N. *Gogol.

Narid (The People). A weekly newspaper published in Warsaw in 1926–8 and edited by V. Ostrovsky. It supported the newly founded Ukrainian National Democratic Alliance (UNDO) and was especially popular in Volhynia and the Kholm region.

Narizhny, Oleksander [Narižnyj] (pen name: Maksym Slyvka), b 1884 in Sokilka, Kobeliaky county, Poltava gubernia, d 6 January 1965 in Zurich. Civic and co-operative leader and journalist; brother of S. *Narizhny. In 1917 he was elected vice-president of the All-Ukrainian Council of Military Deputies. In 1921 he emigrated to Czechoslovakia, where he studied at the Czech Technical School in Prague and presided over its Ukrainian students' club (1922). Subsequently, in Transcarpathia, he organized co-operative dairies and then his own private dairies. In 1931 he edited *Svoboda* in Uzhhorod. His humorous sketches and political satires appeared in the Ukrainian émigré press.

Narizhny, Symon [Narižnyj], b 30 January 1898 in Sokilka, Kobeliaky county, Poltava gubernia, d 23 July 1983 in Sydney, Australia. Émigré historian and community figure. He studied at the Poltava Historical and Philological Faculty (1918–21). As an émigré in Prague he studied at the Ukrainian Free University (UVU, 1922–7; PH D, 1927) under D. Doroshenko and taught medieval and modern world history at the Ukrainian Higher Pedagogical Institute (1928–32) before becoming a docent and professor (1933–45) of Ukrainian and Eastern European history at the UVU. Narizhny also served as deputy director (1925–45) and director (1945–8) of the *Museum of Ukraine's Struggle for Independence and secretary of the *Ukrainian Historical-Philological Society (1929–44). A postwar refugee in Germany, in 1951 he emigrated to Australia, where he taught at the University of Adelaide.

Narizhny wrote articles about Hetman I. Vyhovsky (1929), the Treaty of Hadiache in Ukrainian historiography (1930), Poltava University (1930), V. Antonovych (1934), V. Bidnov (1934), justice and punishment in the Zaporizhia (1939), the Hrabianka Chronicle (1939), the Ukrainian Historical-Philological Society (1939), the Odessa Society of History and Antiquities (1941), and the Kharkiv Historical-Philological Society (1944). Most of them appeared in Ukrainian scholarly serials and collections published in Prague and Lviv. He also wrote a booklet about M. Vasylenko and his scholarly work (1936) and a book on the medieval Muslim world (1931), but he is best known for his pioneering survey, *Ukraïns'ka emigratsiia: Kul'turna pratsia ukraïns'koï emigratsiï mizh dvoma svitovymy viinamy* (Ukrainian Emigration: The Cultural Work of the Interwar Ukrainian Emigration, 1942). Later he wrote three booklets about the Museum of Ukraine's Struggle for Independence (1957–9) and an article about the Historical Society of Nestor the Chronicler (1975–6).

M. Antonovych

Narod (The People). A semimonthly socialist magazine published in Lviv (January 1890 to October 1892), Kolomyia (to August 1894), and again in Lviv (to August 1895). It was edited by I. Franko and M. Pavlyk (the main contributors) and supported by a group of young Ukrainian socialists (eg, V. Okhrymovych, M. Hankevych, and Ye. Levytsky). From October 1890 to August 1893 *Narod* was the organ of the Ruthenian-Ukrainian (later *Ukrainian) Radical party. At first it devoted some space to literature (eg, Franko's poems and stories), culture, and the arts, but from 1892 it was primarily a political journal. *Narod* strongly criticized the Galician status quo and extensively covered the socialist movement in Europe, the women's question in Ukraine, and oppression in the Russian Empire. Its politics were greatly influenced by M. *Drahomanov; it first published his 'Chudats'ki dumky pro ukraïns'ku natsional'nu spravu' (Eccentric Thoughts on the Ukrainian National Problem, 1892), 'Lysty na Naddniprians'ku Ukraïnu' (Letters to Dnieper Ukraine, 1893), and many of his other articles, and devoted a special issue to him in 1894. Other contributors included esia Ukrainka, P. Hrabovsky, V. Budzynovsky, A. Krymsky, S. Danylovych, V. Stefanyk, N. Kobrynska, L. Marovych, O. Kobylianska, and Yu. Bachynsky (the first chapters of his *Ukraïna Irredenta*). A systematic index to *Narod* (comp P. Babiak) was published in Lviv in 1970.

Narod (The People). An organ of the Ukrainian Radical party published in Stanyslaviv (now Ivano-Frankivske) in 1919. It was edited by M. Balytsky. Among the contributors were M. Yevshan and Mykyta Shapoval. The paper appeared weekly (nos 1–8) and then daily (nos 9–33, 24 April–25 May).

Narod (The People). A weekly organ of the Subcarpathian Social Democratic party published in 1920–1 in Uzhhorod and edited by S. Klochurak and Ye. Puza. It was succeeded by *Vpered*.

Narodna chasopys' (People's Periodical). A Ukrainian-language supplement to *Gazeta Lwowska*, the Polish-language organ of the Austro-Hungarian government in Galicia, published daily except Sundays and holidays from December 1890 until the outbreak of the First World War and in 1918. It contained extensive reports on government activities, excerpts from speeches in the Viennese parliament and Galician Diet, reprints from Austrian and other newspapers, and numerous articles on international affairs. Some articles on historical and cultural topics and some poetry and prose were also published. Among its editors were A. Krechowiecki (who also edited *Gazeta Lwowska*), V. Berezovsky, and K. Kakhnykevych.

Narodna hazeta (People's Newspaper). A pro-Communist newspaper and organ of the *Ukrainian Labour-Farmer Temple Association, published daily in Winnipeg from September 1937 to July 1940 as the successor to *Ukraïns'ki robitnychi visti*. The paper published articles on the labor movement and laudatory reports on developments in the USSR as well as especially strident attacks on Ukrainian 'bourgeois nationalists' in Canada. Editors of the paper included many of the most prominent Ukrainian-Canadian communists, among them P. Krawchuk, M. Hrynyshyn, I. Navizivsky, M. Shatulsky, and A. Bilecki. *Narodna hazeta* was closed down by the Canadian government for its pro-Soviet positions. From December 1940 to April 1941 Ukrainian nationalists in Canada (M. Mandryka, O. Hykavy, V. Bosy, and others) published *Narodnia gazeta*, an anti-Soviet weekly sent to former subscribers to *Narodna hazeta* in a bid to win their sympathies.

Narodna Hostynnytsia (People's Hotel). A co-operative in Lviv, established in 1899 by V. Nahirny. It owned a hotel and restaurant, which were popular centers of Ukrainian social life in the city. The co-operative's property was nationalized by the Soviet authorities in 1939.

Narodna Lichnytsia. See Narodnia Lichnytsia.

Narodna shkola (Public School). A semimonthly newspaper for teachers and others interested in education, published in Kolomyia in 1875 (a total of 21 issues). It was edited by I. Shyshkovsky and then I. Levytsky, with the assistance of F. Miskevych.

Narodna Torhovlia (People's Trade). The first large Ukrainian consumer co-operative in Western Ukraine. It was established in 1883 on the initiative of V. Nahirny and A. Nychai, who headed the organization for many years. With its headquarters in Lviv, it served as a wholesaler to private and community-owned stores in villages and small towns throughout Galicia, as a training network for their workers, and as a retailer in the larger cities. In 1907 it changed its charter to become a central association of Rochdale-type consumer co-operatives, which were created from the better-organized community stores. By 1914 the organization had 19 of its own stores-warehouses and 1,244 members (including 93 co-operative members). Its share capital was 215,000 Austrian crowns, its reserve funds 61,000 crowns, and its annual turnover over 2.5 million crowns. A total of 831 small stores were associated with the organization.

The First World War caused great disruption in the *co-operative movement in Galicia. Much of Narodna Torhovlia's physical plant was destroyed, postwar inflation and currency reform by the new Polish regime wiped out much of the organization's capital, and many of its contacts were broken. As a result the entire co-operative structure was reorganized. Responsibility for rural consumer co-operatives was transferred to *Tsentrosoiuz in 1926, and Narodna Torhovlia retained responsibility for consumer co-operatives in the cities. It also assumed the task of maintaining relations with co-operatives in Western Europe and individual producers, for importing goods to be sold in Ukrainian co-operative stores (particularly coffee, tea, and fruits), for selling goods produced by Ukrainian co-operatives and manufacturers, and for training co-operative workers. By 1937 Narodna Torhovlia owned 31 stores and warehouses (including 3 in Volhynia). It had a membership of 6,443, including 5,837 individuals and 86 urban consumer co-operatives, and a share capital of 224,000 zlotys, almost half of which was owed by county co-operative associations and Tsentrosoiuz. The total turnover of almost 5 million zlotys was considerably under the 16-million turnover in the peak years of 1929 and 1930. The decline was due primarily to the Great Depression, which caused a large drop in prices. Moreover, in 1934 the Polish government introduced new restrictions on the activities of the *Audit Union of Ukrainian Co-operatives, of which Narodna Torhovlia was a member. Over 60 percent of the goods handled by Narodna Torhovlia were sold through the organization's own stores. In the interwar period the leading figures in the co-operative included M. *Zaiachkivsky, M. Lazorko, Yu. *Pavlykovsky, and O. Baryliak.

In 1939 the Soviet authorities nationalized all of Narodna Torhovlia's assets and merged the organization with the state bodies responsible for retail and wholesale trade. During the German occupation of Galicia the organization was partially revived to handle the distribution of rationed consumer goods in the cities. When the Red Army returned in 1944, Narodna Torhovlia was finally dissolved.

I. Vytanovych

Narodna tvorchist' ta etnohrafiia (Folk Creativity and Ethnography). A scholarly journal of the AN URSR (now ANU) Institute of Fine Arts, Folklore, and Ethnography and of the Ministry of Culture of Ukraine. It dates back to 1925, when it came out as *Etnohrafichnyi visnyk (to 1932). Later it appeared under the names *Ukraïns'kyi fol'k-

Narodna tvorchist' ta etnohrafiia

lor (1937–9), *Narodna tvorchist'* (1939–41), and *Naukovi zapysky* (1947–54). In 1957 it got its present name and appeared quarterly. In 1964 it became a bimonthly. Its main sections are the history of science, culture, everyday life, the criticism of 'bourgeois' and 'bourgeois-nationalist' ideological concepts, folklorists in the 'brotherly' republics, a young researchers' forum, surveys, reviews and annotations, and a chronicle of current events. Its main focus, until 1991, was political events, anniversaries, and the current 'Soviet way of life.' There are relatively few academic papers devoted to traditional ethnography and folklore. Its editors have been M. Rylsky (1957–66), O. Dei (1966–74), S. Zubkov (1974–88), and H. Kostiuk.

Narodna volia

Narodna volia (Popular Will). An organ of the *Ukrainian Fraternal Association (UFA), published since June 1911. Preceded by the newspaper *Shershen'* (est 1909), it appeared weekly until 1914 and then two or three times a week before again becoming a weekly in 1950. Until 1913, when the paper moved to Scranton, it was published in Olyphant, Pennsylvania. Initially *Narodna volia* had a strong socialist orientation and generally supported the positions of the *Ukrainian Radical party in Western Ukraine. Since the Second World War, however, the paper has moved, along with the UFA, toward the mainstream of Ukrainian national political life. It contains articles on political affairs, on cultural and historical topics, and on Ukrainian life in the United States and elsewhere, as well

as reports on the activities of the UFA. The first editor of *Narodna volia* was Ye. Hvozdyk. He was succeeded by O. Kosovy, I. Ardan, M. Stechyshyn, D. Borysko, M. Repen, Ya. Chyzh (1924–42, at times as head of an editorial board), M. Tsehlynsky, V. Lototsky, D. Korbutiak, I. Hundiak, M. Stakhiv (1949–71), V. Verhun, I. Smolii, R. Rychok, V. Polishchuk, and finally M. Dupliak (1987–). Since 1947 the paper has included an English-language section, *The Fraternal Voice*, which was edited for many years by J. Pronko. It also publishes an annual almanac.

Narodnaia shkola (Public School). A monthly journal for teachers, published by the Russophile *Teachers' Society of Subcarpathian Ruthenia in Mukachiv in 1921–38. It published articles on education and teaching methodology and pressed for the use of the Russian language and the teaching of Russian culture in Transcarpathian schools. The editors included D. Antalovsky and M. Vasylenkov. The journal was published irregularly during the Hungarian occupation of Transcarpathia in 1939–44, under the editorship of P. Fedor.

Narodnaia Volia (People's Will). A conspiratorial Russian revolutionary populist organization that was formed in the summer of 1879 following a split in the organization *Zemlia i Volia. Advocates of political struggle through the use of terror formed Narodnaia Volia, and those opposed to it formed Chernyi Peredel (Black Repartition). Narodnaia Volia never grew to be a large organization; it probably had no more than several dozen members at any given time. As its immediate aim the organization sought the destruction of autocracy, and the assassination of high-ranking government officials was chosen as a means of achieving that goal. The killing of the tsar soon became an idée fixe of the group, and on 1 March 1881, after numerous attempts, they succeeded.

Much of Narodnaia Volia's activities took place in Ukraine. Groups existed at one time or another in Kiev, Kharkiv, Odessa, Mykolaiv, Nizhen, Romny, Yelyzavethrad, and Kamianets-Podilskyi. Despite the heavy concentration of activities in Ukraine Narodnaia Volia was a Russian organization and did not consider the rights of non-Russian nations important (although some of its manifestos and declarations were written in Ukrainian). A number of Ukrainians belonged to Narodnaia Volia, among them A. *Zheliabov, O. *Bakh, and M. *Kybalchych, who made the bomb that killed Alexander II.

Representatives of the Ukrainian national populist movement did not generally support Narodnaia Volia, although in the early 1880s V. Malovany, M. Kotsiubynsky, and I. Karpenko-Kary (I. Tobilevych) maintained ties with or helped Narodnaia Volia groups. M. *Drahomanov wrote several articles and a major work, *Istoricheskaia Pol'sha i velikorusskaia demokratiia* (Historical Poland and Great Russian Democracy, 1881–2), in which he strongly criticized the Russian revolutionaries' use of terror. He also disapproved of their centralist tendencies, accused them of Jacobinism, and condemned them for disregarding the national rights of non-Russian nations.

BIBLIOGRAPHY
Volk, S. *Narodnaia Volia 1879–1882* (Moscow–Leningrad 1966)
Rud'ko, M. *Revoliutsiini narodnyky na Ukraïni* (Kiev 1973)
Voloshchenko, A. *Narysy z suspil'no-politychnoho rukhu na Ukraïni v 70-kh–na pochatku 80-kh rokiv XIX st.* (Kiev 1974)

Ulam, A. *In the Name of the People: Prophets and Conspirators in Pre-revolutionary Russia* (New York 1977)

Naimark, N.M. *Terrorists and Social Democrats: The Russian Revolutionary Movement under Alexander III* (Cambridge, Mass 1983)

Offord, D. *The Russian Revolutionary Movement in the 1880s* (New York 1986)

Katrenko, A. *V bor'be za probuzhdenie narodnoi revoliutsii: Iz istorii revoliutsionno-demokraticheskogo dvizheniia* (Kiev 1988)

B. Klid

Narodne slovo (People's Word). An illustrated newspaper published three times a week in Lviv from December 1907 to late 1911 (a total of almost 600 issues). A popular publication intended for a broad readership, it published articles on political developments in Galicia and Russian-ruled Ukraine, international affairs, and historical and cultural topics. The chief editors were A. Shostak (1907–8), A. Veretelnyk (1908, 1909), Ye. Turbatsky (1908), A. Kryshtalovych (1909), and M. Kurtseba (1909–11).

Narodne slovo. See *Ukraïns'ke narodne slovo.*

Narodne zdorov'ia (Public Health). A popular illustrated monthly published by the *Ukrainian Hygienic Society and the Vidrodzhennia society in Lviv from 1937 to 1939 as *Narodne zdorovlia*. It was founded and edited by R. *Osinchuk. The journal was revived in January 1991 as a weekly, edited by O. Kitsera and published by the Ukrainian Medical Association of Lviv.

The Metropolitan Sheptytsky Hospital of the Narodnia Lichnytsia society in Lviv

Narodnia Lichnytsia (People's Clinic). A society established in Lviv in 1902 to provide free medical care to residents of Lviv and all Galicia regardless of their religious or national affiliation. Its chief founder was Ye. *Ozarkevych, and its patron and main financial supporter was Metropolitan A. Sheptytsky. The society operated an outpatient clinic (est 1903) that consisted of four departments, internal medicine and pediatrics, surgery, ophthalmology, and gynecology. In 1905 a dermatology department was added; it was followed by dental, ear, and urology departments. The clinic's operation was disrupted by the First World War and revived by I. Kurovets. In 1937 its staff of 17 doctors treated 41,000 patients. During the 1930s the society built a 100-bed hospital, financed through public donations, with the assistance of the *Ukrainian Physicians' Society. Known as the Ukrainian

Hospital of the Narodnia Lichnytsia in Honor of Metropolitan Sheptytsky, the facility was opened officially in 1938. Besides providing medical care, it served as a research and specialization center for Ukrainian doctors, whose access to university clinics and state hospitals was severely restricted by the Polish government. The directors of the Narodnia Lichnytsia hospital were Ye. Ozarkevych (1903–14), B. Ovcharsky (1918–21), S. *Drymalyk (1921–3), I. Kurovets (1923–31), and T. Burachynsky (1931–9). In 1944 the society was dissolved by the Soviet authorities, and its hospital was integrated into the state health system.

Narodnia prosvita (Popular Enlightenment). A monthly organ of the Prosvita society in Lviv in 1923–7, edited by O. Terletsky and I. Bryk. A successor to *Pys'mo z Prosvity*, it promoted learning among the general population and extracurricular education.

Narodnia sprava (People's Cause). A weekly organ of the Kiev Gubernia People's Administration, published in Kiev in 1918–19 under the editorship of B. Doroshkevych. It published news; articles on political, economic, historical, and cultural topics; and translations. Among its many contributors were S. Petliura, V. Sadovsky, and N. Hryhoriiv.

Narodnia sprava (People's Cause). An illustrated weekly newspaper for peasants, published by I. Tyktor in Lviv in 1928–39 and edited by Yu. Shkrumeliak and then V. Bachynsky. It generally supported the Ukrainian National Democratic Alliance (UNDO) and was popular among the peasantry. By 1938 it had reached a circulation of 40,000, at least partly because of its policy of financially aiding subscribers whose properties had been destroyed by fire or whose cattle had died. The annual calendar-almanac *Zolotyi kolos* (from 1929) and a series of 18 popular booklets (1929–34) were published by the newspaper.

Narodnia syla (People's Power). A semimonthly organ of the *Ukrainian Peasants' and Workers' Party of Subcarpathian Ruthenia, published in 1936–8 in Uzhhorod. It was edited by M. Tulek and I. Nevytska.

Narodnia Torhovlia. See Narodna Torhovlia.

Narodnia trybuna (People's Tribune). An organ of the Ukrainian Peasant Alliance, a legal front organization of *Sel-Rob, published from November 1930 to September 1932 in Sambir and Lviv (a total of 53 issues). The pro-Soviet newspaper strongly criticized both the Polish government and the Ukrainian nationalist movement. It was frequently censored and eventually closed down by the Polish authorities.

Narodnia volia (People's Will). A daily published by the Ukrainian Central Co-operative Committee in Kiev from May 1917 to February 1919. The chief editor was M. Kovalevsky and the secretary was P. Khrystiuk. It was the most widely read Ukrainian newspaper of the time (with a circulation of up to 200,000) and an important supporter of the Central Rada. A large group of correspondents submitted reports on developments throughout Ukraine, and contributors such as M. Hrushevsky, Kh. Baranovsky, M. Tuhan-Baranovsky, A. Stepanenko, and O. Shumsky provided political commentaries and analyses. Prose, poetry, and literary criticism by M. Zerov, H. Chuprynka, V. Samiilenko, M. Vorony, O. Oles, H. Zhurba, and others were also published in *Narodna volia*. The paper served as the national organ of the *Peasant Association and the mouthpiece of the majority in the Central Rada.

Narodniki. See Populism, Russian and Ukrainian.

Narodnyi dim. See People's Home in Lviv.

Narodnyi holos (People's Voice). A weekly newspaper published in Chernivtsi from December 1909 to 1915 and briefly in 1921 and 1923. The organ of the *Ruska Rada society and then the *National Democratic party, it covered political developments in the Austro-Hungarian Empire and abroad and devoted considerable attention to the activities of Ukrainian deputies in the Bukovynian Diet and Viennese parliament. In 1910 it published a literary supplement. It was edited by a committee headed by, among others, A. Veretelnyk (1909–11), O. Lutsky (1911), O. Dik (1912–13), and Yu. Dobrovolsky (1914–15).

Narodnyi uchytel' (Public School Teacher). A weekly newspaper of the All-Ukrainian Committee of the Union of Education Workers, published in Kharkiv in 1925–30. It was one of the best Ukrainian pedagogic newspapers of the time and one of the most popular, with a pressrun of 13,000. It contained articles on teaching methodology, sample curricula, book reviews, bibliographies, and discussions on contemporary issues, especially the Ukrainization of the education system. The paper supported the creation of a Ukrainian system of *labor schools. *Narodnyi uchytel'* was edited by N. Kaliuzhny, O. Mizernytsky, and others, and its contributors included M. Popiv, Ya. Chepiha, and O. Shumsky. Several supplements were published with the paper, including *Samonavchannia* (1928), *Literatura i pobut* (1928–9), and *Vyrobnycha dumka*. The newspaper was suppressed by the authorities; it was succeeded by *Za kul'turnu revoliutsiiu* (1931–5), which more closely toed the Stalinist line in education.

Narodovishchaniie (Folk Enlightenment). A collection of catechismal and literary instructions and teachings prepared by Basilian priests in the mid-18th century. Intended for distribution in the Kremianets region, the collection was first published at the Pochaiv Monastery Press in 1756. It was reprinted in 1768, 1778, and (in Lviv) 1886. The first section contained numerous short stories and legends taken from the collections written by D. *Tuptalo. The second portion consisted of an 'instruction about Christian rites,' in which papal decrees were cited in support of the prohibition of Ukrainian Catholics changing from the Byzantine or Eastern rite to the Latin rite.

Narodovtsi. See Populism, Western Ukrainian.

Narodychi [Narodyči]. II-10. A town smt (1990 pop 6,100) on the Uzh River and a raion center in Zhytomyr oblast. It is first mentioned in historical documents in 1545. After the Union of Lublin (1569) Narodychi belonged to Poland. With the partition of Poland in 1793, it became part of the Russian Empire. Narodychi attained smt status in 1958. It has a small textile industry. Lying only 80 km west of Chornobyl, it is polluted with radio-active material from the 1986 explosion of a nuclear reactor at the Chornobyl power plant.

Nash holos (Our Voice). A monthly organ of the *Ukrainian Social Democratic party and *Ukrainian Social Democratic Workers' party, published in Lviv from November 1910 to the end of 1911 (a total of 12 issues). It was funded and edited by L. Yurkevych. Among its contributors were Yu. Bachynsky, V. Vynnychenko, D. Dontsov, V. Levynsky, V. Stepankivsky, O. Nazariiv, M. Melenevsky, and A. Chernetsky.

Nash holos (Our Voice). A monthly organ of the Ukrainian American Association, published since June 1968 in Trenton, then Irvington, and finally Union, New Jersey. Until 1972 it was called *Biuleten' Asotsiiatsiï ukraïntsiv Amerytsi*. The journal publishes book reviews, memoirs, and articles on political and historical affairs by a wide range of contributors from North America and Europe. It is especially noteworthy for its commentary on Ukrainian political affairs, in which it often criticizes leading émigré institutions and parties from a liberal-democratic perspective. The founder of *Nash holos* and editor until his death in 1982 was D. Kuzyk. Since then the journal has been edited by a board headed by E. Pereima. It has a circulation (1988) of approx 2,500.

Nash klych

Nash klych (Our Call). A pro-OUN weekly of political and community affairs, published in Lviv in 1933 and edited by V. Yaniv. In May 1933 it published a single issue of the supplement *Probii* edited by D. Myron. *Nash klych* was banned by the Polish authorities and was succeeded by the monthly *Nash front* (1933), two issues of which appeared before it too was banned.

Nash klych (Our Call; Spanish: Nuestra Llamada). An Argentinian-Ukrainian newspaper published weekly in Buenos Aires since 1934. The publication was initially the organ of the Ukrainian Riflemen's Hromada, which reorganized into the Organization for the Rebirth of Ukraine (1938) and finally became the *Vidrodzhennia society (1939). The paper has an overtly nationalistic tone. It carries pages dedicated to women's issues, young people, and co-operatives, as well as a Spanish section. Its editors have included M. Prymak, N. Blavatny, N. Velechovsky, I. Kryvy, Ye. Onatsky, and M. Fesylovych.

Nash kontakt (Our Contact). A journal devoted to the Ukrainian co-operative and credit union movement in North America, published in Detroit in 1954–9. It appeared every two months under the editorship of V. Nestorovych. In 1959 it merged with *Novyi svit* to form *Nash svit*.

Nash lemko

Nash lemko (Our Lemko). A semimonthly paper of community and cultural affairs, established in Lviv by the Ukrainska Presa publishing house in January 1934. Distributed in the Lemko region, it promoted Ukrainian national consciousness there and countered the influence of the Russophile *Łemko* (Krynytsia, 1934–9), which was subsidized by the Polish government, and *Karpatskii zvon* (1937–9), the semimonthly organ of the Polish-controlled Lemko Apostolic Administration. *Nash lemko* was edited by P. Smerekanych and then Yu. Tarnovych. From 1936 until the German invasion in 1939 it was published by the so-called Lemko Committee.

Nash postup (Our Progress). A weekly newspaper published in Edmonton from November 1922 to 1929 (with some interruptions). Published by T. Tomashevsky and edited by him and T. Datskiv, the paper was populist in orientation and dedicated to raising the cultural, economic, and political level of awareness of the Ukrainian population of Canada. It strongly supported the Canadian farmers' movement and was instrumental in the campaign to elect M. *Luchkovich as member of parliament for the Vegreville constituency district in 1926.

Nash prapor (Our Flag). A daily organ of the left, 'independent' faction in the *Ukrainian Labor party, which supported the government-in-exile of the Western Ukrainian National Republic led by Ye. Petrushevych. It was published in Lviv from December 1923 under the editorship of A. Maletsky; from May to November 1924 it was called *Prapor* and was edited by M. Strutynsky. It was succeeded in November 1924 by the weekly organ of the Ukrainian Party of Labor's *Ukraïns'ka rada*, which in August 1925 was renamed *Rada*.

Nash prapor (Our Flag). A popular illustrated newspaper published in Lviv by the Ukrainska Presa publishing house as a semiweekly (December 1932 to 1935) and then three times a week (1936–9). The editors were H. Stetsiuk, V. Kachmar, and I. Kernytsky. In late 1938 it had a circulation of 12,000 copies. The newspaper also published the supplements *Amators'kyi teatr* (1935–9), edited by H.

Luzhnytsky, and *Muzhychna biblioteka* (1937–9). Its subscribers received free copies of the *Ukrainska biblioteka book series. The paper was widely read in both Galicia and Transcarpathia.

Nash pryiatel' (Our Friend). A monthly Catholic children's magazine published by the Marian Youth Society in Lviv in 1922–39. It was edited by Basilian priests, among them Y. Markevych, T. Hornykevych, and I. Nazarko, and illustrated by J. Hnizdovsky, P. Andrusiv, and Yu. Kyryienko. In 1930 it had a circulation of 8,000 copies. The magazine also published a book series featuring works by Catholic writers.

Nash ridnyi krai (Our Native Land). A children's magazine published monthly (except July and August) in 1922–38 in Tiachiv, Transcarpathia, by the *Pedagogical Society of Subcarpathian Ruthenia. Edited by O. Markush, it contained much local folklore and helped inculcate Ukrainian national consciousness among its readers. In 1924 *Vinochok dlia podkarpats'kykh ditochok appeared as a supplement to the magazine.

Nash shliakh (Our Path). A daily newspaper published in Kamianets-Podilskyi in 1919–20. Edited by I. Kosenko, it was not aligned with any political party in the UNR.

Nash stiah (Our Banner). An organ of the pro-hetmanite *Sich society in the United States, published in Chicago in 1934–41. It succeeded *Sich and continued its conservative line and support for P. Skoropadsky. It also reported on political developments and the affairs of the Sich movement. The editor of *Nash stiah* was O. *Shapoval.

Nash svit (Our World). An illustrated weekly journal of literature, culture, and popular science, published in Warsaw in 1924–5 by V. *Ostrovsky and distributed in Volhynia, the Kholm region, and Podlachia. Ostrovsky revived the journal as a monthly in Lutske in 1935 and published it there until 1936. Among the contributors were Ye. Lukasevych, V. Zaikin, I. Ohiienko, K. Polishchuk, S. Khrutsky, Ya. Voitiuk, H. Orlivna, S. Siropolko, and Ye. Malaniuk.

Nash svit (Our World). An organ of the *Self-Reliance Association of American Ukrainians, published monthly and then every two months in New York since 1959. It was established through the merger of two earlier journals, *Nash kontakt and *Novyi svit. It publishes articles on the co-operative and credit union movements and on political and economic affairs. Among its editors have been R. Ilnytsky, V. Nestorovych, and M. Ostroverkha. The journal's circulation was approx 2,650 in 1986.

Nasha bat'kivshchyna (Our Homeland). A monthly illustrated journal published by the *Plai society in Lviv in 1937–9. Edited by S. Shchurat, it contained articles on hiking, sports, and especially regional history and ethnography by I. Svientsitsky, Ya. Pasternak, and others. The journal also published a series of regional studies brochures.

Nasha bat'kivshchyna (Our Homeland). A magazine of political thought, literature, and scholarship, published biweekly from 1962 to 1971, bimonthly in 1972, once in 1973, and three times in 1974 by S. Kravets in New York City and, from 1972, in Mountain Dale, New York.

Nasha derzhava (Our State). A semimonthly conservative newspaper published in Toronto from July 1952 to 1955. It was founded after a split in the *United Hetman Organization by M. Hetman, who earlier had edited *Ukraïns'kyi robitnyk*, the organization's organ. *Nasha derzhava* was pro-hetmanite in orientation but also stressed its loyalty to Canada. It was succeeded by *Bat'kivshchyna*.

Nasha dolia (Our Fate). The title of three miscellanies published in Stryi in 1893 and in Lviv in 1895 and 1896 by N. *Kobrynska. They consisted of articles on issues relevant to the Ukrainian women's movement, Ukrainian and translated literary works, and reviews of Western European literature. Among the contributors were Kobrynska, O. Kobylianska, M. Damian (W. Moraczewski), H. Barvinok, H. Shukhevych, and I. Petryshyn.

Nasha Kooperatsiia (Our Co-operation). An organization of activists in the Ukrainian co-operative movement, established in Kiev in 1912. Although the organization was opposed by the Russian authorities, its membership grew quickly to 150 throughout Russian-ruled Ukraine. It emerged as the ideological center of the co-operative movement and an important base for the development of Ukrainian national consciousness. The society published the weekly journal *Nasha kooperatsiia* from January 1913 to December 1914 and popular booklets and pamphlets on the co-operative movement. It was banned by the authorities at the end of 1914. Attempts in 1913 to establish a similar organization with the same goals and name in Lviv were cut short by the outbreak of the First World War.

Nasha kul'tura (Our Culture). A monthly journal of scholarly, literary, and cultural affairs, published and edited by I. Ohiienko in Warsaw from April 1935 to December 1937 (a total of 32 issues). It contained articles on Ukrainian cultural history, belles lettres, memoirs (primarily from the 1917–20 period of Ukrainian independence), book reviews, and surveys of cultural and scholarly developments in Soviet Ukraine and abroad.

Nasha kul'tura. See *Vira i kul'tura*.

Nasha meta (Our Goal). A women's journal in Lviv, published semimonthly and then weekly in February and March 1919. It was closed down by the Polish authorities, was revived as a semimonthly in August 1919, and continued (later as a monthly) to the end of 1920. In 1920 it served as an organ of the *Ukrainian Social Democratic party for working women. A total of 30 issues appeared before the journal folded because of a lack of support. It was edited by D. Starosolska.

Nasha meta (Our Goal). A Catholic newspaper published weekly in Toronto since October 1949 as the organ of the Eastern eparchy of the Ukrainian Catholic church in Canada. Besides articles on religious and cultural topics and church developments, it devotes regular sections to the Ukrainian Catholic Women's League and the Ukrainian Catholic Brotherhood of Canada. The chief editor from

1951 until 1983 was P. Khomyn. He was assisted at various times by Ya. Chumak, M. Koliankivsky, M. Syrotynsky, and others. Since the mid-1980s the chief editors have been M. Davosyr and M. Poroniuk. In 1989 the paper's circulation was approx 2,000.

Nasha pravda (Our Truth). A weekly newspaper of the underground Communist Party of Eastern Galicia, published in Vienna from April 1921 to August 1923 (122 issues). Published under the same title was the principal theoretical journal of the *Communist Party of Western Ukraine; it was printed in Berlin and later Czechoslovakia from December 1923 to November 1935 (a total of 82 issues). Both periodicals were smuggled into Western Ukraine.

Nasha shkola (Our School). A pedagogical journal published in Lviv by the Galician *Teachers' Hromada society and the Bukovynian *Skovoroda Society of Higher School Teachers. It appeared quarterly in 1909–13 but then bimonthly in 1914 and 1916–18. *Nasha shkola* published articles on pedagogy and the history of Ukrainian education. It devoted particular attention to contemporary developments in Ukrainian education and remains an excellent source of information on 19th- and early 20th-century education in Western and Russian-ruled Ukraine. It also published book and journal reviews and reports on the activities of the Teachers' Hromada and Provincial School Union in Galicia and Bukovyna. It was edited by I. Krevetsky and M. Hrushevsky (1909–12), S. Tomashivsky, M. Chaikivsky, and Yu. Rudnytsky (1916–18). Among its contributors were V. Simovych, I. Krypiakevych, V. Shchurat, M. Vozniak, and V. Doroshenko.

Nasha shkola (Our School). A monthly pedagogical journal published in 1935–8 by the Teachers' Hromada of Subcarpathian Ruthenia in Mukachiv. It was edited by I. Vasko.

Nasha zahradka (Our Kindergarten). A children's magazine published in Ruski Krstur, Yugoslavia, in 1937–41. It appeared in the local Bačka dialect but was Ukrainophile in spirit. It was edited by M. *Kovach and illustrated by J. Hnizdovsky and published for a school-age audience. A total of 37 issues appeared. In 1947 it was succeeded by *Pyonerska zahradka*.

Nasha zemlia (Our Land). A pro-Soviet Ukrainophile political and literary monthly published in Uzhhorod from February 1927 to January 1929 (a total of 23 issues). Edited by V. *Grendzha-Donsky and published in standard Ukrainian, it did much to promote Ukrainian national consciousness in Transcarpathia before it was closed down by the Czechoslovak authorities.

Nasha zemlia (Our Land). An irregular unofficial organ of the Communist Party of Western Ukraine, published in Lviv from March 1930 to September 1932 (a total of 60 issues). Its editors included O. Yurkevych, A. Hoshovsky, and V. Ohonovsky. In 1930 it had a circulation of 1,000. The paper was closed down by the Polish authorities.

Nashchynsky, Davyd (Danylo) [Naščyns'kyj], b ca 1721 in the Poltava region, d 1793. Scholar and churchman. A graduate of the Kievan Mohyla Academy, he served as professor of philosophy and theology, prefect (1752–8), and rector (1758–61) there. He revised the academy's philosophy curriculum, replacing its Aristotelian textbooks with C. Baumeister's textbook based on C. Wolff's system, and collected and published works by T. Prokopovych (1743, 1745). Later he served as archimandrite of several monasteries in Ukraine and Belarus. He was a friend of O. *Lobysevych and had close contacts with the *Novhorod-Siverskyi patriotic circle. Influenced by Wolff's views, he defended the use of the vernacular in literature and always stressed his national origin.

Nashe mynule (Our Past). A literary and scholarly journal published in Kiev in 1918 (three issues) and 1919 (a double issue). Edited by P. Zaitsev, it contained articles by prominent cultural figures of the time – eg, V. Modzalevsky, P. Fylypovych, S. Yefremov, and O. Slastion – on the history of Ukrainian culture, art, the Ukrainian national movement, and literature (especially on T. Shevchenko); memoirs of community leaders of the 19th and early 20th centuries; and archival documents (eg, the first full publication of *Knyhy bytiia ukraïns'koho narodu*). H. Narbut designed the journal's cover.

Nashe selo (Our Village). A weekly newspaper for peasants, published in Odessa in 1918–19 by the Selianska Samoosvita society. The editor was Yu. Hryshchenko.

Nashe slovo (Our Word). The weekly and later irregular central organ of *Sel-Rob, the legal front organization of the Communist Party of Western Ukraine, published in Lviv in 1927–30 (a total of 103 issues) and edited by I. Kalynovych (1927), V. Pashnytsky (1928), and P. Kraikivsky, the secretary-general of Sel-Rob. After the split in the organization the journal was aligned with the Shumskyist 'right' faction. In 1930 its circulation was 3,750.

Nashe slovo (Our Word). A weekly organ of the *Ukrainian Social and Cultural Society (USKT; since 1990 the Alliance of Ukrainians in Poland [OUP]) in Poland, published since 1956 in Warsaw. It contains articles on developments in the Ukrainian community in Poland – focusing

Nashe slovo

on the activities of the OUP – and Ukraine, regular reviews of Ucrainica published in Poland, prose, poetry, and political commentary. Although its content was closely monitored by the Polish authorities, the newspaper enjoyed considerable autonomy in its coverage of cultural affairs. It devoted special attention to the folklore and ethnography of Ukrainians in Poland and included special sections devoted to the Lemko community, its history and culture in Poland, and women's issues. It also publishes the semimonthly supplement *Svitanok* (Dawn) for children and the literary and scholarly supplement *Nasha kul'tura* (Our Culture), which appeared monthly until 1988 and, after an interruption, resumed publication on an irregular basis in March 1988. The editors of the newspaper have been M. Shchyrba, A. Hoshovsky, H. Boiarsky, and M. Verbovy, and its regular contributors have included most of the prominent Ukrainian cultural and community figures in Poland. In 1988 the circulation of *Nashe slovo* was approx 10,000.

Nashe zhyttia (Our Life). An irregular mimeographed organ of the Petrograd Committee of the clandestine Ukrainian Social Democratic Workers' party, published from 1915 to May 1917 in Petrograd (St Petersburg). Edited by P. Fedenko and L. Chykalenko, it became legal only in March 1917. The paper exhorted workers to oppose Russia's involvement in the First World War and to rebel against and overthrow tsarism.

Nashe zhyttia (Our Life). A socialist weekly newspaper of political, cultural, and community affairs in the Kholm region, published in 1920 and 1922–8 in Kholm. The newspaper was founded by the brothers A. and P. Vasynchuk, and its editors included M. Vavrysevych, V. Kozlovsky, S. Kozachuk, Ya. Voitiuk, and S. Makivka. It was the organ of *Sel-Soiuz in 1924–6 and then came under the control of the more radical faction that joined *Sel-Rob. The paper's editors were persecuted by the Polish authorities. In 1928 it was succeeded by *Nove zhyttia*.

Nashe zhyttia (Our Life). A weekly newspaper published in Bucharest in 1940–2. After the suppression of the Ukrainian press in Bukovyna, it was the only Ukrainian-language newspaper in Rumania. The newspaper was constantly harassed by the Rumanian authorities, and it was forced to change its name frequently; its titles included *Nove zhyttia* and *Ukraïns'ke zhyttia*. It was edited by M. Kovalevsky and O. Turushanko.

Nashe zhyttia (Our Life). A weekly and later semimonthly democratic-socialist newspaper for displaced persons, published by P. Kotovych in Augsburg, Germany, from September 1945 to March 1948. The editors were V. Chaplenko and P. Fedenko. Contributors included S. Dovhal, M. Dolnytsky, S. Drahomanov, and N. Kebaliuk. In 1947–8 it sublicensed the co-operative monthly *Hospodars'ko-kooperatyvne zhyttia*, the pedagogical paper *Ukraïns'ka shkola na emigratsiï*, the children's monthly *Mali druzi*, and the literary paper *S'ohodni* and published them as supplements. *Nashe zhyttia* folded after Kotovych's death.

Nashe zhyttia/Our Life. A monthly organ of the *Ukrainian National Women's League of America, published in Philadelphia and then New York since 1944. The successor to an insert dealing with organizational issues in the newspaper *Ameryka*, the journal publishes articles on the women's movement, the league's activities, home economics, the arts, and other topics. It also contains belles lettres, children's stories, and poems. An English-language section has been included in the journal since its beginnings. It was launched in a newspaper format, but in 1951 it changed over to a 32-page journal format. Its circulation in the 1970s and 1980s was approx 4,600 to 5,000. Its editors have included K. Olesnytska (1944–6), O. Lototska (1946–51), L. Burachynska (1951–72), U. Starosolska (1972–84 and 1987–90), O. Liskivska (1985–6), and I. Chaban.

Nashi dni (Our Days). An illustrated monthly of literature, art, and culture, edited by M. *Strutynska with the help of S. *Hordynsky and M. *Shlemkevych. It was published in Lviv by the Ukrainske Vydavnytstvo publishers in 1941 (1 issue), 1942 (12), 1943 (12), and 1944 (1). Among the contributors were I. Bahriany, D. Humenna, P. Kovaliv, L. Kovalenko, E. Kozak, N. Koroleva, Yu. Kosach, Yu. Lypa, A. Liubchenko, V. Miiakovsky, O. Ohloblyn, T. Osmachka, O. Povstenko, O. Tarnavsky, and Yu. Sherekh (G.Y. Shevelov).

Nastup (Attack). A newspaper published semiweekly in 1938–9 in Uzhhorod and then Khust as the organ of the *Ukrainian National Defense and *Carpathian Sich. The editor was S. *Rosokha. After the occupation of Carpatho-Ukraine by the Hungarians, it was published weekly in Prague (1940 to January 1944), and supported the OUN (Melnyk faction). It had a pressrun of 5,700. It also published the separate biweekly supplements *Narodnia volia* (1938–9) and *Natsionalist* (1940–2). *Nastup* was closed down by the Gestapo, and Rosokha was sent to a concentration camp.

Nasturtium (*Tropaeolum*; Ukrainian: *nasturtsiia*). A perennial plant of the family Tropaeolaceae, with brilliant yellow, orange, and red funnel-shaped flowers. Only the medicinal nasturtium exists in Ukraine; its leaves contain vitamin C, carotene, and iodine.

Natiiv, O. [Natijiv], b ?, d 1919. Senior officer in UNR Army. An Ossetian by origin, he was a general officer in the Russian army during the First World War and joined the UNR Army in 1917. In March–April 1918 he commanded the Separate Zaporozhian Division, which cleared Left-Bank Ukraine and the Crimea of Bolshevik forces. In 1919 he organized the Transcaucasian Volunteer Battalion in Batumi. He was murdered by the Bolsheviks.

National Anthem. See Anthem.

National communism. A current within the Communist movement or Communist parties that attempted to reconcile national interests with Marxist-Leninist doctrine in order to sanction a national road to socialism. National communism emerged as a political phenomenon in Ukraine in 1918 and has had many counterparts elsewhere.

The first Bolshevik to state a national-communist position was V. *Shakhrai, a leader of the Poltava Bolshevik organization. In the latter half of 1918 he wrote a pamphlet under the pseudonym Skorovstansky, *Revoliutsiia na Ukraïni* (Revolution in Ukraine), in which he argued that the national question had to be solved in tandem with social problems. In January 1919 Shakhrai and S. *Mazlakh published *Do khvyli: Shcho diietsia na Ukraïni i z Ukraïnoiu* (Concerning the Moment: What Is Happening in and to Ukraine), in which they argued that the CP(B)U should be replaced by a separate Ukrainian Bolshevik party that would affirm Ukraine's language, culture, and rights as a state.

Shortly before the collapse of the second Soviet republic in Ukraine in July 1919, a group of disaffected Bolsheviks led by Yu. *Lapchynsky and P. Slynko formed in Kiev. Later known as the Federalist Opposition, it advocated an independent Soviet Ukraine led by a new Ukrainian party that would select its own leadership and control its own military and economic resources. In subsequent months the group modified its position, in calling for a Russo-Ukrainian federation but insisting on equal rights. It also believed local Bolsheviks should merge with local pro-Soviet parties, notably the *Borotbists, to form a new *Ukrainian Communist party (UKP). Founded in January 1920, the UKP held views that had much in common with those of later Third World Marxist thinkers. It held that whereas imperialism threatened oppressed peoples with the loss of their national culture, it also promoted their economic development and thereby stimulated them to economic consolidation and national liberation. In the early 1920s the UKP spokesmen were the most consistent critics of the economic exploitation of Soviet Ukraine by the rest of the USSR. Consequently the UKP was dissolved by the Comintern in 1925. Its members were allowed to join the CP(B)U, and helped carry out the *Ukrainization policy.

Not only disillusioned Bolsheviks became national communists; so did Ukrainian leftists who became disenchanted with the policies of the dominant Ukrainian socialist parties. The Borotbists favored federation with Soviet Russia but refused any subordination of Soviet Ukraine to Russia and believed Soviet Ukraine should be led by Ukrainians. In March 1919 they were admitted into the Soviet government in Ukraine led by Kh. Rakovsky, but had little authority. They then petitioned the Comintern to admit them as the legitimate representative of Ukrainian communism on the grounds that the CP(B)U was alien to the Ukrainian revolutionary process and, through hostility to everything rural and Ukrainian, had distorted and hindered the natural course of Ukraine's revolutionary development. Recognizing their usefulness, in November 1919 V. Lenin forced the Russian-dominated CP(B)U leadership to begin negotiations with the Borotbists on merging with the CP(B)U. At the same time Lenin and L. Trotsky issued statements promising to respect the Ukrainians' right to cultural self-assertion and promised Ukrainians 'the right to rule their own country,' albeit in a federation with Russia. The CP(B)U and the Borotbists merged in March 1920, and the Borotbist leaders O. *Shumsky and V. *Blakytny were elected to the CP(B)U CC. Of about 5,000 Borotbists about 4,000 were admitted into the CP(B)U. All but 102 were purged during the following year.

The successes of Ukrainization fostered the myth that Ukrainians had achieved a measure of national liberation within the Soviet framework, and led a number of prominent Ukrainian Communists to believe their national-communist views had been legitimized. Thus, as Ukraine's commissar of education in 1925, Shumsky urged J. Stalin to replace the CP(B)U first secretary, L. Kaganovich, with an ethnic Ukrainian, V. Chubar, and called for faster implementation of Ukrainization so as to de-Russify Ukraine's cities and proletariat. Shumsky also defended M. *Khvylovy, who argued that Ukrainian culture should take its models from Western Europe and reject Russian influence in order to liberate itself from the legacy of colonialism.

Stalin, however, condemned both 'Shumskyism' and 'Khvylovyism' in April 1926. Because Shumsky was supported by the majority of the leadership of the *Communist Party of Western Ukraine (KPZU), the Comintern 'deposed' that leadership, thereby splitting the KPZU and ending its role as an influential force in Western Ukrainian political life. In 1927 Shumsky was removed from his Ukrainian post and transferred to Moscow. He was arrested in 1933, and died in a labor camp in 1946.

Another casualty of Shumsky's downfall was the national-communist view of Ukrainian Party history, which portrayed the CP(B)U as an amalgam of Russian Bolshevism and Ukrainian socialism, culminating in the Borotbist-Bolshevik merger. That 'two roots' theory, which was first enunciated in 1923 by the historian M. Ravich-Cherkassky (Rabinovich), was condemned in 1927, and a new, Stalinist, official history of the CP(B)U, by N. *Popov, was published in 1928.

M. *Skrypnyk, who replaced Shumsky as commissar of education, was until 1933 the Soviet regime's and the Comintern's most authoritative spokesman on nationality policy and a defender of Soviet republican prerogatives as formulated in the 1923 Soviet Constitution. He consistently advocated policies that would make the Soviet system attractive to oppressed peoples living on the USSR's periphery. Skrypnyk also continued to lobby for Ukraine's economic interests with respect to both republican control over establishments located in the Ukrainian SSR and new construction. In February 1928 M. *Volobuiev, Skrypnyk's subordinate in charge of political education, popularized findings of the economist V. Dobrohaiev demonstrating that Ukraine was being exploited fiscally by the USSR just as it had been exploited by the tsarist government. Volobuiev also criticized the Russian chauvinism of economic decision-makers in Moscow, argued that their centralized control distorted Ukraine's economic development and had harmful consequences for Ukraine's national and cultural life, and called for the Ukrainian SSR to strive for economic self-sufficiency. He was condemned for providing Ukrainian 'bourgeois nationalism' with an economic basis.

In 1928–9 a campaign was initiated against the leading official Soviet Ukrainian historian, M. *Yavorsky, whose views reflected Skrypnyk's orthodox national communism. Although he was criticized for many alleged errors, the most significant charges leveled against him were his overemphasis on Ukrainian ideas and figures in the Ukrainian revolutionary process, his having adopted many ideas from the writings of M. Hrushevsky, and his portraying Ukrainian history as distinct from Russian history.

On 14 December 1932 Moscow ordered the CP(B)U to halt the 'mechanistic' implementation of Ukrainization and root out 'national deviations' from the Party line. The 1933 Party purge singled out 'national communists' as primary targets. Stalin appointed P. *Postyshev as CP(B)U second secretary on 12 January 1933, and over the course of several months Skrypnyk and his views were condemned,

and his followers were accused of spying and treason. The suicide of Khvylovy in May 1933 and that of Skrypnyk in July 1933 mark the end of openly expressed national-communist ideas in Ukraine.

Modest attempts to reconcile Ukrainian aspirations with communism, however, continued to arise. In 1965 the literary critic I. *Dziuba wrote a major restatement of national-communist ideas in his critique of Soviet nationality policy, *Internationalism or Russification*, and the Ukrainian dissident movement of the 1960s and 1970s had other national-communist thinkers (eg, Yu. *Badzo). Moscow's continuous opposition to national-communist ideas resulted in the 1972 removal of the CPU first secretary, P. *Shelest, on the grounds of 'bourgeois nationalism.' After the advent of glasnost in the mid-1980s, greater tolerance for national-communist ideas became evident, and the Party press published articles favorable to major national-communist figures of the past, including Shumsky, Khvylovy, and Shakhrai.

In the Soviet Union outside Ukraine, national communism was most often associated with Mir Said Sultan-Galiev (1880–193?), a prominent Volga Tatar Communist who became disillusioned with Lenin's nationality policy toward the Moslem peoples and evolved his own variant of national communism. From 1929 to 1939 thousands of Communists of Moslem origin were arrested for 'Sultan-Galievism.' In addition the Jewish Communist party, an offshoot of the Poale Zion party that upheld a fusion of communism and left-wing Zionism, was allowed to exist until 1924.

National communism had more success outside the Soviet Union. Under J. Tito Yugoslavia broke with Stalin on national grounds in 1947. In 1956 both Poland under W. Gomulka and Hungary under I. Nagy sought national roads to socialism. Hungary's attempt was crushed by Soviet military intervention, but Poland's achieved some successes before sinking into political stagnation. In breaking with the Soviet Union in the early 1960s, China was able to create a communist state relatively free from outside influence, the basic goal of national communism. Czechoslovakia under A. Dubček also sought its own national road to socialism, but its attempt too was aborted by Soviet military intervention in 1968.

BIBLIOGRAPHY

Girchak, E. *Na dva fronta v bor'be s natsionalizmom* (Moscow–Leningrad 1930)

Maistrenko, I. *Borot'bism: A Chapter in the History of Ukrainian Communism* (New York 1954)

Dokumenty ukraïns'koho komunizmu (New York 1962)

Mazlakh, I.; Shakhrai, V. *On the Current Situation in the Ukraine*, trans and ed P. Potichnyj (Ann Arbor 1970)

Koshelivets', I. (ed). *Mykola Skrypnyk: Statti i promovy* (Munich 1974)

Bilinsky, Y. 'Mykola Skrypnyk and Petro Shelest: An Essay on the Limits of National Communism,' in *Soviet Nationality Policies and Practices*, ed J. Azrael (New York 1978)

Mace, J. *Communism and the Dilemmas of National Liberation: National Communism in Soviet Ukraine, 1918–1933* (Cambridge, Mass 1983)

Khvylovy, M. *The Cultural Renaissance in Ukraine: Political Pamphlets, 1925–1926*, ed and trans with an intro by M. Shkandrij (Edmonton 1986)

Somchynsky, B. 'National Communism and the Politics of Industrialization in Ukraine, 1923–1928,' *JUS*, Winter 1988

J. Mace

National composition of Ukraine. Changes in the population share of Ukrainians and *national minorities in Ukraine have been effected by border changes, *emigration, *immigration, and natural increase. The lack of independent statehood has played a decisive role. Coupled with the persecution of the Ukrainian language and Ukrainian culture by the occupying powers of tsarist and Soviet Russia, Poland, Hungary, and Rumania, it resulted in the *Russification, Polonization, Magyarization, and Rumanianization of many Ukrainians and the extensive colonization of Ukraine by the ruling nations. The major sources for the study of the national composition of Ukraine have been the various *censuses conducted by the occupying regimes. They have, however, varied in degrees of accuracy.

The national composition of eastern and central Ukraine was dramatically altered as a result of their occupation by tsarist and Soviet Russia. An important factor contributing to Russia's capacity to hold on to Ukraine lay in colonization. Throughout the 18th century Russian nobles, bureaucrats, merchants, and peasants immigrated to Ukraine. In addition, under Catherine II, colonists from Central and Eastern Europe were granted tracts of land and allowed to establish colonies in *Southern Ukraine. The development of industry in the *Donets Basin in the second half of the 19th century spurred further immigration. The extent of colonization can be gauged by comparing the demographic data of the late 18th century with those of the late 19th century. According to the fifth tsarist enumeration of 1795, Ukrainians constituted 89 percent of the population of Russian-ruled Ukraine. By 1897 the Ukrainians' share of the population there had dropped to 77 percent.

By 1926, despite the loss of life during the First World War and the Ukrainian-Soviet War, the Ukrainians' share of the total population of Soviet Ukraine had increased, as a result of a high rate of natural population increase and of *Ukrainization policies, which partly reversed the trend of Russification. The 1926 Soviet census was much more precise than previous censuses in establishing the nationality of respondents. Some national minorities registered significant declines in their share of Ukraine's population as a result of emigration, out-migration, and population losses during recent wars (see table 1). The massive depor-

TABLE 1
Changes in the national composition of Ukraine, 1897–1926[a] (percentage of total in parentheses)

	1897		1926	
Total population	20,649,848	(100.0)	28,026,427	(100.0)
Ukrainians	15,824,764	(76.7)	22,646,620	(80.8)
Russians	2,085,382	(10.0)	2,318,361	(8.4)
Jews	1,644,488	(8.0)	1,565,494	(5.6)
Germans	377,956	(1.8)	375,824	(1.3)
Poles	267,972	(1.3)	461,047	(1.6)
Moldavians[b]	185,549	(0.9)	257,745	(0.9)
Greeks	58,284	(0.3)	103,587	(0.4)
Bulgarians	59,844	(0.3)	91,856	(0.3)
Belarusians	67,055	(0.3)	71,566	(0.2)
Czechs	11,445	(0.1)	15,186	(0.1)
Others	67,109	(0.3)	119,141	(0.4)

[a]Within the 1926 boundaries of the Ukrainian SSR
[b]Rumanians

TABLE 2
Changes in the national composition of Ukraine, 1926–37[a] (percentage of total in parentheses)

	1926		1937		1937 as % of 1926
Total population	28,026,432	(100.0)	28,397,658	(100.0)	101.3
Ukrainians	22,646,620	(80.8)	22,212,525	(78.2)	98.1
Russians	2,318,361	(8.4)	3,221,898	(11.3)	139.0
Jews	1,565,494	(5.6)	1,470,484	(5.2)	93.9
Poles	461,047	(1.6)	417,613	(1.5)	90.6
Germans	375,824	(1.3)	401,880	(1.4)	106.9
Moldavians[b]	257,745	(0.9)	221,831	(0.8)	86.1
Belarusians	71,566	(0.2)	106,325	(0.4)	148.6
Greeks	103,587	(0.4)	102,257	(0.4)	98.7
Bulgarians	91,856	(0.3)	74,862	(0.2)	81.5
Czechs	15,186	(0.1)	11,516	(0.1)	75.8
Others	119,146	(0.4)	156,467	(0.5)	131.3

[a]Within the 1926 boundaries of the Ukrainian SSR
[b]Rumanians

tations of peasants (*kulaks) during collectivization, the man-made *famine of 1932–3, and large-scale repression during the Stalinist *terror resulted in a decline of the Ukrainians' share of the population of Soviet Ukraine. Between 1926 and 1937 their total number decreased. Meanwhile, because of intensive in-migration during the 1930s, the number of Russians in Ukraine increased by almost 40 percent. A number of minorities, particularly the Jews and Poles, also registered a drop in their number because of Soviet policies of the 1930s (see table 2).

Before its incorporation into Soviet Ukraine in 1939, Western Ukraine was characterized by a complex national composition. In the 1790s, Ukrainians made up 80 percent of the population of eastern Galicia, 74 percent of Bukovyna, and 31 percent of Transcarpathia. Polish, Hungarian, Rumanian, and German colonization, national oppression, and the ensuing assimilation of Ukrainians had resulted by the 1850s in the decline of the Ukrainians' share of the population to 66 percent in eastern Galicia, 41 percent in Bukovyna, and 24 percent in Transcarpathia. In 1900, Ukrainians constituted 60 percent of the population of that part of Western Ukraine within the latest boundaries of Ukraine. The partition of the region among Poland, Rumania, and Czechoslovakia after the First World War was followed by a sizable in-migration of civil servants and colonists from the ruling nations (see table 3).

The 1959 Soviet census was the first to provide data on the national composition of postwar Ukraine. It revealed a marked increase in the Russian population of Ukraine as a result of large-scale in-migration. The Nazi Holocaust, postwar border changes, and the postwar *resettlement of people also altered Ukraine's national composition. Between 1926 and 1959 a threefold decline in the number of Jews and a sixfold decline in the number of Poles occurred (see table 4).

Since 1959 the share of Russians in Ukraine's population has continued to increase as a result of the ongoing large-scale in-migration of Russians and the Russification of Ukrainians and other nationalities in the republic see table 5).

The present distribution of national minorities in Ukraine is represented, by percentage composition, in

TABLE 3
Changes in the national composition of Western Ukraine,
1900–31[a] (percentage of total in parentheses)

	1900[b]		1930–1		1930–1 as % of 1900
Total population	7,415,700	(100.0)	9,073,800	(100.0)	122.4
Ukrainians	4,483,100	(60.5)	5,385,300	(59.4)	120.1
Poles	975,000	(13.2)	1,715,000	(18.9)	175.9
Jews	941,000	(12.7)	893,000	(9.8)	94.9
Rumanians[c]	223,900	(3.0)	309,100	(3.4)	138.1
Russians	214,400	(2.9)	214,600	(2.4)	100.1
Germans	220,400	(3.0)	194,200	(2.1)	88.1
Bulgarians	125,500	(1.7)	125,600	(1.4)	100.1
Hungarians	108,300	(1.5)	123,400	(1.4)	113.9
Czechs and Slovaks	22,000	(0.3)	67,200	(0.7)	305.5
Gagauzy	22,100	(0.3)	22,100	(0.2)	100.0
Belarusians	51,800	(0.7)	6,000	(0.1)	11.6
Others	28,200	(0.4)	18,300	(0.2)	64.9

[a]Within the current boundaries of the western Ukrainian oblasts
  of Volhynia, Rivne, Lviv, Ivano-Frankivske, Ternopil,
  Chernivtsi, Transcarpathia, and Odessa (including parts of
  former Bessarabia)
[b]1897 data used for Volhynia
[c]Moldavians

TABLE 4
Changes in the national composition of Ukraine, 1926–59[a]
(percentage of total in parentheses)

	1926[b]		1959		1959 as % of 1926[b]
Total population	38,569,000	(100.0)	41,869,000	(100.0)	108.6
Ukrainians	28,625,600	(74.2)	32,158,500	(76.8)	112.3
Russians	3,164,800	(8.2)	7,091,300	(16.9)	224.1
Jews	2,491,900	(6.5)	840,300	(2.0)	33.7
Poles	2,193,800	(5.7)	363,300	(0.9)	16.6
Germans	624,900	(1.6)	23,100	(0.1)	3.7
Moldavians[c]	454,400	(1.2)	342,500	(0.8)	75.4
Bulgarians	223,100	(0.6)	219,400	(0.5)	98.3
Hungarians	124,300	(0.3)	149,200	(0.4)	120.0
Greeks	120,700	(0.3)	104,400	(0.2)	86.5
Belarusians	85,700	(0.2)	290,900	(0.7)	339.4
Czechs and Slovaks	84,200	(0.2)	28,500	(0.1)	33.8
Tatars	22,300	(0.1)	60,900	(0.1)	273.1
Gagauzy	22,100	(0.1)	23,500	(0.1)	106.3
Armenians	21,100	(0.1)	28,000	(0.1)	132.7
Others	310,100	(0.7)	145,200	(0.3)	46.8

[a]Within contemporary boundaries of Ukraine
[b]Adjusted to 1959 boundaries to include parts of Poland,
  Czechoslovakia, Rumania, and the Crimea
[c] Rumanians

table 6. Russians, the largest minority, are found in all cities but are concentrated in the Donets-Dnieper industrial belt, Kharkiv, and the industrial and port cities of the south. Russians are a majority in the Crimea, a strategic peninsula from which the Crimean Tatars were deported

TABLE 5
Changes in the national composition of Ukraine, 1970–89
(thousands; percentage of total in parentheses)

	1970		1979		1989	
Total population	47,127	(100.0)	49,609	(100.0)	51,452	(100.0)
Ukrainians	35,284	(74.9)	36,489	(73.6)	37,419	(72.7)
Russians	9,126	(19.4)	10,472	(21.1)	11,356	(22.1)
Jews	777	(1.7)	634	(1.3)	486	(0.9)
Belarusians	386	(0.8)	406	(0.8)	440	(0.9)
Moldavians*	378	(0.8)	416	(0.8)	460	(0.9)
Poles	295	(0.6)	258	(0.5)	219	(0.4)
Bulgarians	234	(0.5)	238	(0.5)	234	(0.5)
Hungarians	158	(0.3)	164	(0.3)	163	(0.3)
Greeks	107	(0.2)	104	(0.2)	99	(0.2)
Tatars	76	(0.1)	91	(0.2)	134	(0.3)
Others	306	(0.7)	337	(0.7)	442	(0.9)

* Rumanians

TABLE 6
National composition of Ukraine's oblasts, the city of Kiev, and
the Crimea in 1989 (percentages)

Oblast	Ukrainians	Russians	Others
Ternopil	96.8	2.3	0.9
Ivano-Frankivske	95.0	4.0	1.0
Volhynia	94.7	4.3	1.0
Rivne	93.3	4.6	2.1
Vinnytsia	91.5	5.9	2.6
Chernihiv	91.5	6.8	1.7
Cherkasy	90.5	8.0	1.5
Lviv	90.4	7.2	2.4
Khmelnytskyi	90.3	5.8	3.9
Kiev (excluding the city of Kiev)	89.4	8.7	1.9
Poltava	87.9	10.2	1.9
Sumy	85.5	13.3	1.2
Kirovohrad	85.3	11.7	3.0
Zhytomyr	84.9	7.9	7.2
Transcarpathia	78.4	4.0	17.6
Kherson	75.7	20.2	4.1
Mykolaiv	75.6	19.4	5.0
Kiev (city only)	72.4	20.9	6.7
Dnipropetrovske	71.6	24.2	4.2
Chernivtsi	70.8	6.7	22.5
Zaporizhia	63.1	32.0	4.9
Kharkiv	62.8	33.2	4.0
Odessa	54.6	27.4	18.0
Luhanske	51.9	44.8	3.3
Donetske	50.7	43.6	5.7
Crimea	25.7	67.0	7.3

following the Second World War (and to which they are now returning), and where the numbers of Ukrainians have been consistently understated at each census. Some oblasts along the southwestern border of Ukraine contain significant non-Russian minorities: Hungarians (12.5 percent of the oblast population) in Transcarpathia, Rumanians (19.6 percent) in Chernivtsi, and a collage of Bulgarians (6.3 percent), (Rumanians (Moldavians, 5.5 percent), Jews (2.6 percent), and Gagauzy (1.0 percent) in Odessa oblast. Moreover, the Jews remain a significant minority in major urban areas throughout most of Ukraine, the Belarusians have recently become significant in the Donets-Dnieper area, as have the Volga Tatars, and the Poles retain some significance in Zhytomyr, Khmelnytskyi, Lviv, and Kiev oblasts, and the Greeks in Donetske oblast near the Sea of Azov.

(See also *Population.)

BIBLIOGRAPHY
Kordouba, M. *Le Territoire et la population de l'Ukraine: Contribution géographique et statistique* (Bern 1919)
Smal'-Stots'kyi, R. (ed). *Ukraïns'ka liudnist' SSSR* (Warsaw 1931)
Naulko, V. *Etnichnyi sklad Ukraïns'koï RSR* (Kiev 1965)
Natsional'nyi sostav naseleniia SSSR (Moscow 1991)

B. Krawchenko, I. Stebelsky

National Council of Ukrainian Women (Natsionalna rada ukrainskykh zhinok; also Ukrainska zhinocha natsionalna rada). A women's organization established in Kamianets-Podilskyi in 1919 to provide a focal point for Ukrainian women's groups in various parts of Europe and to inform international women's bodies about Ukraine's struggle for independence. It was admitted to the International Council of Women at that council's congress in Oslo in 1920, but as a representative of a stateless nation it lost its membership eight years later. Branches of the council were organized in Berlin, Bern, Vienna, Rome, Paris, and Prague, the location of its head office from 1924. The council participated in conferences of a number of international women's organizations and submitted memorandums to them on issues such as the *Pacification. The first executive of the council consisted of S. *Rusova as president, M. Hrushevska, K. Malytska, Z. Mirna, and L. Starytska-Cherniakhivska as vice-presidents, and H. Chykalenko-Keller and N. Surovtsova as secretaries. B. Baran, Kh. Kononenko, O. Lototska, N. Makarenko, and M. Rudnytska were among the most active members. In 1938 the council's executive resolved to dissolve the organization.

National Democratic party (Natsionalno-Demokratychna partiia, or NDP; also known as the Ruthenian National Democratic party, Ukrainian-Ruthenian National Democratic party, and [from 1914] Ukrainian National Democratic party). A centrist Galician political party founded on 26 December 1899 in Lviv by members of the right wing of the Ukrainian Radical party (V. *Okhrymovych, Ye. Levytsky, V. Budzynovsky, and I. *Franko) and the majority of the Galician populists (particularly members of the People's Council in Lviv), including Yu. Romanchuk, K. Levytsky, M. *Hrushevsky, Ye. Olesnytsky, and T. Okunevsky. The party was headed by the People's Committee, consisting of Hrushevsky, K. *Levytsky, Okhrymovych, D. *Savchak, and Franko. Its first congress, on 5 January 1900, adopted a platform of national unity and independence. The party quickly gained a dominant position in Ukrainian political life in Galicia; it relegated the Radical party largely to the role of a permanent opposition and substantially curtailed the influence of Galician Russophiles. In the first direct Galician elections to the Austrian parliament based on universal male suffrage, in 1907 and 1911, it won the support of most Ukrainian voters. In 1907, 17 of the 27 deputies elected by Ukrainian and Russophile Galicians were National Democrats. In 1918 the party played a leading role in setting up the Ukrainian state.

The presidents of the National Democratic party were

Yu. Romanchuk (1899–1907) and K. Levytsky. Its secretaries were K. Levytsky (1899–1907), V. Bachynsky (1907–13), and S. Baran. It published the weekly *Svoboda, and its platform was supported by *Dilo* and *Bukovyna*.

At a party conference in Stanyslaviv in April 1919 the NDP changed its name to the *Ukrainian Labor party, and in 1923 the party split into two groups. On 11 July 1925 the two groups and the Ukrainian Party of National Work formed the *Ukrainian National Democratic Alliance, which dominated mainstream Ukrainian political life in the interwar Polish state.

V. Mudry

National emblem. See Coat of arms.

National flag. See Flag.

National Guard (Narodnia gvardiia; German: Nationalgarde). Territorial militias established in the Austrian Empire during the Revolution of 1848. Ferdinand I declared their creation on 14 March 1848, and his decree of 8 April empowered them to defend the constitutional monarchy and preserve law and order. The Poles of western Galicia formed a force of 20,000 men. In eastern Galicia the units were to include both Ukrainians and Poles, but such formations were never created. Ukrainian units were organized after appeals were issued by the Supreme Ruthenian Council in September, but only in Berezhany, Lviv, Stanyslaviv, Stryi, Ternopil, Yavoriv, and Zhovkva. They had their own Ukrainian commanders, distinct uniforms, and flags depicting a golden lion on an azure background. The first drill manual in Ukrainian was published at that time in Kolomyia. Because of government opposition the Ukrainian units never fully developed, except in Yavoriv, which had 300 uniformed members. The National Guard was abolished as an institution on 10 January 1849. National Guard units were re-established in 1991 after Ukraine declared its sovereignty.

National Guard (Derzhavna varta). The state security and intelligence services in Ukraine under the *Hetman government, formed under the law of 18 May 1918. Controlled by a separate department in the Ministry of Internal Affairs, the National Guard was subordinated on the local level to gubernial and county heads (starostas). In urban centers there was one guardsman for every 400 civilians; thus there were approx 2,000 guardsmen in each of Kiev and Odessa. In Kiev, Kharkiv, Odessa, and Mykolaiv there were additional reserve cavalry units of 260 men each, and in every county there was a reserve company (100 men). A separate corps guarded the national railways.

National income. A macroeconomic concept used as an indicator of the productive capacity of an economy. It is the net national product for a year, that is, the gross national product less the expenditure for a given year. Unlike the Western concept, the Soviet concept of national income was restricted to the material product (consumer goods and means of production). It excluded most services, such as government, education, defense, and health care. In Soviet statistics three variants of the concept were used: (1) the net material product (NMP), which is the sum of the differences between the gross output and the material expenditure in all the sectors of material production;

TABLE 1
Ukraine's national income (in billion rubles in real prices), 1923–24 to 1929–30

Year	Income	Year	Income
1923–24	2.4	1927–28	5.0
1924–25	3.1	1928–29	5.5
1925–26	4.7	1929–30	7.4
1926–27	4.6		

TABLE 2
Ukraine's national income in 1923–4 by sector and its share in the USSR income

Sector	Million rubles	Percentage of total	Percentage of USSR total
Agriculture	1,194.0	55.7	24.6
Industry	532.0	24.8	20.0
Transport (rail)	76.3	3.6	21.8
Commerce	340.5	15.9	22.9
Total	2,142.8	100.0	22.9

(2) the national income produced (NIP), which is the sum of the net outputs of the various sectors plus (a) the balance of the turnover tax and government subsidies and (b) payments from foreign countries; and (3) the national income utilized (NIU), which is the part of the NIP available for consumption and capital accumulation, that is, what remains of the income after losses, foreign aid, and balance-of-trade payments have been deducted. The first variant is close to the Western concept of national income.

In the former USSR national income began to be calculated in the mid-1920s. V. Myshkis calculated Ukraine's national income in the 1920s (see table 1). In 1923–6, on the average 84 percent of the national income was apportioned to consumption, 11 percent to capital accumulation, and 5 percent to the Union budget for general needs and the redistribution of national incomes, and so forth.

The republic's national income by sectors and its share in the USSR total in 1923–4, according to the People's Commissariat of Finance of the Ukrainian SSR, is shown in table 2. Although Ukraine had only 19.8 percent of the USSR population (1926), it accounted for almost 23 percent of the USSR income (in 1923–4). By 1928–30, according to Myshkis, Ukraine's share in the USSR income fell to 17.9 percent. After 1931 national income and other macroeco-

nomic indicators were no longer computed for Ukraine, only for the USSR.

The system of estimating the national income of the USSR and its constituent republics was put into place in 1956–8. Ukraine's NIP has been published since 1956, and its NIU since 1961. The system remained practically unchanged until the late 1980s. Before then, detailed information about national income, apart from general and, usually, indexed indicators (not absolute), was hardly ever published. In 1990 all restrictions were lifted, and Western methods of computing the gross national product (GNP) were adopted.

In 1988 national income began to be calculated also by oblast. In 1989 Ukraine's GNP was estimated at 154.9 billion rubles. Basic macroeconomic data on Ukraine are given in table 3. It should be noted that the official figures based on constant prices are exaggerated by a factor of two and can be used only to indicated the relative weight of the different indicators.

Ukraine was second only to the RSFSR in the Soviet Union in the absolute size of its national income. In 1989 Ukraine generated 16.2 percent and the RSFSR 59.5 percent of the USSR income. After 1970 Ukraine's share in the total social product and the NIP of the USSR declined steadily (see table 4). The decline was the result of many factors, but particularly of the redistribution of resources for the economic development of new regions of the USSR. The decline of Ukraine's share in the total population of the USSR from 20.1 percent in 1956 to 18.0 percent in 1989 must also be taken into account.

In these circumstances Ukraine's standing among the other republics in terms of national income per capita (in actual prices) was deteriorating. After 1970 Ukraine no longer belonged to the top five republics, although its position improved slightly in later years (see table 5).

Ukraine's position by per capita income is influenced particularly by its high share of heavy and extraction industries and lower share of light industry (which generates a significant turnover tax) as well as the large and growing subsidies for agriculture. In 1989 Ukraine was 9th among the 15 republics in regard to the average worker's and office worker's wage (90.6 percent of the Union average), and 11th in regard to the average collective farmer's wage (91.8 percent of the Union average). Of course, the cost of living and the cost of construction were lower in Ukraine than the Union average. Nevertheless, the relative decline in Ukraine's per capita income, from 96.9 percent of the Union average in 1970 to 94.1 percent in 1976, 89.0 percent in 1980, and 88.6 percent in 1985

TABLE 3
Basic macroeconomic indicators of Ukraine's development (real prices in billion rubles), 1956–89

Indicator	1956	1960	1970	1980	1985	1989
Total social product	39.89	55.70	122.06	191.08	241.55	275.90
Material expenditure	19.67	28.65	67.30	113.58	147.55	166.99
National income produced	20.22	27.05	54.76	77.50	94.00	108.91
Net material product	15.18	21.12	46.53	60.74	80.25	103.68
Constant prices as percentage of 1960 prices						
Total social product	71.2	100.0	193.3	300.8	353.6	394.5
Material expenditure	71.1	100.0	192.2	312.7	366.3	404.8
National income produced	71.2	100.0	194.4	287.1	339.2	391.1
Net material product	70.9	100.0	189.8	263.4	305.9	365.2

TABLE 4
Ukraine's share in the USSR's total social product and national income produced in actual prices, 1956–89 (percentages)

Indicator	1956	1960	1970	1980	1985	1989
Total social product	18.8	18.7	19.0	17.7	17.6	17.3
National income produced *including*	18.9	18.7	18.9	16.8	16.7	16.2
Industry	18.0	17.1	18.5	16.3	15.8	17.2
Construction	18.3	19.0	16.7	14.5	15.2	13.5
Agriculture	22.1	23.7	22.0	20.5	20.0	17.9
Transport and communications	14.2	15.2	16.4	15.5	15.4	13.8
Commerce	18.4	18.5	17.9	17.5	16.8	17.2

TABLE 5
Ranking of former Soviet republics by per capita income, 1970–89

1970	1975	1980	1985	1989
Estonia	Latvia	Latvia	RSFSR	Latvia
Latvia	Estonia	Estonia	Latvia	RSFSR
Lithuania	Lithuania	RSFSR	Estonia	Estonia
RSFSR	RSFSR	Belorussia	Belorussia	Ukraine
Belorussia	Belorussia	Lithuania	Lithuania	
Ukraine	Ukraine	Armenia	Georgia	
		Georgia	Ukraine	
		Ukraine		

TABLE 6
The structure of Ukraine's national income produced in 1960–89 in real prices (percentages)

Sector	1960	1970	1980	1985	1989
Industry	47.9	50.0	50.0	44.3	42.6
Construction	10.2	9.2	8.9	10.1	10.4
Agriculture	26.0	25.3	18.2	24.0	28.1
Transport and communications	4.3	4.8	5.4	5.7	5.1
Commerce	6.4	5.9	7.3	6.6	6.9

(though with a slight rise to 89.7 percent in 1989), is cause for concern. It is all the more disturbing when Ukraine's performance is compared with Belarus's: in 1970 Ukraine's average per capita income was 106.0 percent of Belarus's, but then it plummeted to 89.7 percent in 1975, to 81.2 percent in 1980, to 79.5 percent in 1985, and to 75.8 percent in 1989.

In the last 30 years the structural changes in the various sectors of the Ukrainian economy have been insignificant. Industry's share in the output has increased slightly, the construction industry's share has declined significantly, and the agricultural sector's contribution has decreased slightly. The share of other sectors has remained practically unchanged (see table 6). These figures are close to the shares of the various sectors in the USSR income. The structure and the growth rate of the total social product and the NIP are affected substantially by the turnover tax, state subsidies, and foreign payments. According to some indicators the turnover tax in Ukraine is much higher than in Western countries. In 1984 (ie, prior to the antialcoholism campaign) it stood at 17.5 percent of the NIP (or about 13 percent of the GNP, compared to 8 percent in the United States).

In 1970 the turnover tax in Ukraine constituted 16–17.5 percent of the NIP, and by 1984 it had declined to 14–14.5 percent. This indicator was about two points below the Union average. Both in the USSR as a whole and in Ukraine, the share of the turnover tax in retail prices was very high (before the price increases of April 1991): 94 percent of the price of alcohol, 64 percent of that of cars, 61 percent of that of carpets, 47 percent of that of synthetic fibers, and 39 percent of that of refrigerators. In the years before the dissolution of the Union subsidies increased

sharply. Twenty-five to 30 years ago they accounted for only 5–7 percent of the turnover tax. Then, as state purchasing prices on animal products rose repeatedly, while state retail prices remained practically unchanged (before April 1991), the subsidies increased year by year. They grew to match the turnover tax, and in 1989 they even surpassed it, by 1.1 billion rubles. The major part of the subsidies was allocated for two products, milk and meat. Coal also had been subsidized, in the amount of three to five billion rubles.

Another peculiarity of Soviet macroeconomic statistics was that the total social product and the NIP included the trade balance. So far only the trade among the Union republics had been taken into account by the USSR State Statistical Committee. The weight of certain supplementary components in the national income and the connection between the NIP and the NMP are given in table 7. It should be noted that in 1980 and 1985 Ukraine's NIP increased

TABLE 7
The structural relation between the national income produced and the net material product in Ukraine in 1960–89 in real prices (percentages)

Indicator	1960	1970	1980	1985	1989
1. National income produced	100.00	100.00	100.00	100.00	100.00
2. Turnover tax	–	15.80	17.54	15.45	–
3. Subsidies	–	4.51	5.53	9.42	–
4. Balance (2 – 3)	18.88	11.29	12.01	6.03	–1.05
5. External trade balance	3.03	3.74	9.60	8.60	6.22
6. Deductions (4 + 5)	21.91	15.03	21.61	14.63	5.17
7. Net material product (1 – 6)	78.09	84.97	78.39	85.37	94.83

only because of the increase in the balance of external trade.

Until recently there was practically no significant information about the value structure of the national income. The classical relationship between the necessary and the surplus product is of social interest (see table 8). In Soviet statistics the outlays for social security and insurance as well as for wages in the nonproduction sector (education, health, etc) were included in the surplus product. In 22 years the surplus product has increased 0.94 percentage points relative to the necessary product (see table 9).

TABLE 8
The value structure of Ukraine's national income produced in 1966–88 in real prices (percentages)

Components of NIP	1966	1972	1977	1982	1988
Necessary product (labor cost of material production)	52.30	52.59	51.31	51.71	51.36
Wages & salaries	29.12	29.61	31.15	30.18	30.80
Bonuses (not incl in wages)	0.37	2.14	1.57	2.31	2.93
Other cash payments	1.00	1.19	1.19	1.25	1.33
Collective-farm wages	9.27	7.64	7.09	6.48	6.64
Net production of private plots	2.54	11.71	10.31	11.48	9.66
Surplus product	47.70	47.41	48.69	48.29	48.64
Sales profits	17.48	23.81	22.37	19.44	31.10
Turnover tax less subsidies	16.06	10.65	10.13	10.68	1.07
Social security & insurance	2.56	2.71	2.88	3.73	4.30
Net income of collective farms	6.46	3.36	3.28	1.25	4.20
External trade balance	2.80	4.30	6.92	10.49	6.41
Other elements of surplus product	2.34	2.88	3.11	2.70	2.12

The ratios were very low in agriculture (particularly in 1982, before the increases in purchase prices) and in construction. They were related to the relatively low share of profits, which could not ensure normal social reproduction and accumulation in the sectors. NIU had been calculated in the Ukrainian SSR since 1961. A breakdown of its principal components is given in table 10. The share of personal consumption in the total NIU increased from 65.2 percent in 1961 to 69.8 percent in 1989, and the share of ba-

TABLE 9
The ratio of the surplus to the necessary product in real prices in the chief sectors of the economy, 1966–88

Sector	1966	1972	1977	1982	1988
General economy	0.912	0.912	0.949	0.934	0.947
Industry	1.655	1.743	1.556	1.434	1.291
Agriculture	0.402	0.223	0.344	0.097	0.403
Construction	0.194	0.223	0.263	0.154	0.447

TABLE 10
Ukraine's national income utilized in real prices, 1961–89 (in billion rubles)

	1961	1970	1980	1985	1989
Total	27.22	49.98	74.10	91.77	107.95
including					
Consumption	19.25	36.57	60.70	72.03	85.72
Personal	17.76	32.98	53.75	63.80	78.36
Material expenditures on consumer services	1.24	2.89	5.47	6.65	7.94
Material expenditures on research & management	0.25	0.70	1.48	1.58	2.42
Accumulation & other expenditures	7.97	13.41	13.40	19.74	22.23
Growth of reserves	4.70	8.37	7.94	9.42	12.15
Production	3.38	5.70	5.36	5.03	5.29
Nonproduction	1.32	2.67	2.58	4.39	6.86
Growth of material turnover costs & reserves	3.27	5.04	5.46	10.32	10.08

sic reserves growth decreased from 17.3 percent to 11.3 percent. In the basic reserves growth the share of nonproduction reserves growth doubled from 28 percent in 1961 to 56 percent in 1989.

Changes in the basic components of personal consumption are given in table 11. Since many services are excluded from personal consumption, food supplies account for the largest share of consumer spending. Although their share has decreased steadily, from 61.0 percent in 1966 to 50.42 percent in 1989, it remains high. The share of light-industry products also went down, but within that category the share of spending on clothing rose from 7.40 percent in 1966 to 8.38 percent in 1989, and on knitwear, from 3.68 percent to 4.47 percent.

National income began to be computed by oblast only

TABLE 11
The structure of personal consumption in Ukraine, 1966–89

	1966	1972	1977	1982	1987	1989
Total (in billion rubles)	25.18	36.65	43.97	57.75	66.44	75.36
including (in percentages)						
Food	61.00	57.65	59.09	55.06	54.68	50.42
Agricultural output	19.95	16.51	16.53	16.47	17.82	17.78
Other goods	34.39	38.58	37.39	41.56	41.78	46.44
Light-industry products (cloth, clothing, footwear, etc)	21.41	22.78	23.65	22.93	20.95	20.70
Fuel, natural gas, electric power	1.31	1.45	1.59	1.68	1.90	2.52
Machines & metal products	4.10	5.89	7.12	5.40	7.48	7.56
Furniture	1.75	1.81	2.07	2.08	2.24	2.26
Housing amortization	4.61	3.77	3.52	3.38	3.54	3.14

TABLE 12
National income in 1989 by oblast, the city of Kiev, and the Crimea in real prices (ranked by NIP; personal consumption as % of total consumption in parentheses)

Oblast	National income produced		National income utilized (in %)	
	in billion rubles	rubles per capita	Total consumption	Savings and other expenditures
Ukrainian SSR	108.91	2,104	79.4 (69.8)	20.6
1. Zaporizhia	5.54	2,655	74.0 (65.4)	26.0
2. Kiev (city only)	6.46	2,471	90.0 (72.2)	10.0
3. Dnipropetrovske	9.45	2,428	85.2 (75.4)	14.8
4. Kharkiv	7.64	2,390	82.4 (72.0)	17.6
5. Poltava	4.14	2,357	78.8 (68.4)	21.2
6. Odessa	6.06	2,296	75.9 (65.5)	24.1
7. Sumy	3.27	2,287	77.9 (70.3)	22.1
8. Lviv	6.11	2,221	76.8 (68.5)	23.2
9. Chernihiv	3.07	2,171	73.9 (66.4)	26.1
10. Kiev	4.01	2,065	70.8 (62.0)	29.2
11. Kherson	2.57	2,064	69.7 (63.7)	30.3
12. Cherkasy	3.10	2,024	78.2 (70.6)	21.8
13. Kirovohrad	2.47	1,994	71.2 (64.3)	28.8
14. Donetske	10.54	1,976	83.4 (73.6)	16.6
15. Luhanske	5.59	1,951	89.6 (78.9)	10.4
16. Mykolaiv	2.56	1,917	79.9 (71.2)	20.1
17. Zhytomyr	2.94	1,904	72.6 (65.1)	27.4
18. Vinnytsia	3.62	1,878	75.4 (67.7)	24.5
19. Volhynia	1.98	1,861	68.6 (62.5)	31.3
20. Chernivtsi	1.72	1,835	72.5 (65.2)	27.5
21. Ivano-Frankivske	2.59	1,816	83.1 (74.0)	16.9
22. Ternopil	2.12	1,815	73.2 (65.1)	26.8
23. Crimea	4.50	1,813	83.5 (71.9)	16.5
24. Khmelnytskyi	2.75	1,801	77.6 (70.3)	22.4
25. Rivne	2.11	1,801	75.8 (68.4)	24.2
26. Transcarpathia	2.00	1,597	83.5 (73.7)	16.5

in 1988 (see table 12). Analysis of the figures must take into account that the NIP has been influenced by uneven shares of the turnover tax and subsidies; the coal subsidies to Donetske and Luhanske oblasts, for example, lowered their figures. In contrast, the NIU of the Crimea and Kiev City was exaggerated, because many people from other oblasts purchased goods there (see table 12).

Unfortunately, no comparative data on the gross internal product (GIP) are available. But use of the per capita comparative data for Hungary and the former USSR, and then for Hungary and other countries, gives rise to the inference that in 1985 the per capita GIP of Ukraine was one-quarter that of the United States and Canada, and that the per capita personal consumption was about one-fifth. Since then the figures have become even smaller.

BIBLIOGRAPHY
Grinshtein, A. (ed). *Kapitaly i natsional'nyi dokhod Ukrainy v 1923–24 g.* (Kharkiv 1926)
Myshkis, V. *Opyt sostavleniia balansa narodnogo khoziaistva Ukrainy za 1923–4 i 1924–5 gg.* (Kharkiv 1927)
Kontrol'ni tsyfry rozvytku narodnoho hospodarstva URSR na 1929–30 (Kharkiv 1929)
Natsional'nyi dokhod Ukraïns'koï RSR (Kiev 1963)
Koropeckyj, I. *Development in the Shadow: Studies in Ukrainian Economics* (Edmonton 1990)

A. Revenko

National Library of Ukraine. See Central Scientific Library of the Academy of Sciences of the Ukrainian SSR.

National minorities. Distinct groups of the population in a state that differ from the dominant nation in their language and culture and express a desire to form a national community. The term 'national minority' is largely European in usage. It usually signifies a group that lives in compact settlements or has inhabited a territory for centuries. Numerous border changes connected with the growth of large European empires often produced national minorities. Their political and legal conceptualization emerged in the 19th century, although some earlier international accords guaranteed the rights of religious and ethnocultural groups. Because for several centuries Ukrainians did not have their own state, and Ukrainian ethnographic territories were part of large empires, Ukrainians were during that time treated as a national minority in their own homeland. Only with the establishment of a Ukrainian state in 1917 were Ukrainians recognized as a nation with a defined territory.

The tsarist regime did not consider Ukrainians in the Russian Empire a separate nation, and denied them the limited cultural and national rights granted to the Baltic, Polish, and Moslem nations in the empire. In the Austro-Hungarian Empire, in contrast, Ukrainians were recognized as a distinct nation, and shared in the rights established by the empire's multinational policies. Ukrainians living in territories in the Hungarian part of the empire were, however, discriminated against.

After the First World War Western Ukraine was divided among Poland, Rumania, and Czechoslovakia, and the

Western Ukrainians became national minorities in those states. In 1933 there were 6.2 million Ukrainians in Poland, 1.2 million in Rumania, and 600,000 in Czechoslovakia. Over 40,000 Ukrainians lived in Yugoslavia. Unlike the Ukrainian immigrants in Western Europe and the Americas, Ukrainians living in the Eastern European states formed compact settlements. Moreover, in Poland, Rumania, and Czechoslovakia they constituted majorities in the territories they inhabited, and considered those territories their ancestral lands.

Poland, Rumania, Czechoslovakia, and Yugoslavia were bound by international treaties to respect the linguistic, educational, religious, and political rights of their national minorities. The Treaty of *Versailles (1919) bound Poland in that respect, and the treaties of *St-Germain (1919), Neuilly (1919), and Sèvres (1920) bound Rumania. Czechoslovakia and Yugoslavia were committed to such policies by the Treaty of St-Germain. Poland had special obligations to protect the rights of its Ukrainians and Belarusians under the terms of the Peace Treaty of *Riga (1921), concluded with the RSFSR and Ukrainian SSR; it was also bound to grant Galicia regional autonomy and to recognize the political and cultural rights of the Ukrainians by decisions reached at the 1923 Conference of Ambassadors. Czechoslovakia, in addition to guaranteeing the rights of all national minorities, committed itself to granting territorial and administrative autonomy to the Ukrainian national territory of Transcarpathia (Subcarpathian Ruthenia). Both Poland and Czechoslovakia included the provision of minority rights in their legislation. Overall, however, only Czechoslovakia to some extent honored its obligations, by granting Ukrainians living on a limited territory distinctive administrative status. That was far short of the autonomy envisaged by the Treaty of St-Germain. Far worse violations of international accords were committed by Poland, which refused to respect its own legislation of 1922 granting Galicia provincial self-government, and in 1934 openly abrogated international provisions for the protection of national minorities, with the claim that such protection was an internal matter. Similarly, Rumania reneged on its commitment to protect its national minorities, and in a 1938 government decree it excluded national minorities from the protection and guarantees of the conventions of the League of Nations.

Protection of the rights of national minorities in the interwar period was a concern of the *League of Nations. It established its Minorities Commission to receive petitions from aggrieved minorities, and the Council of the league was empowered to create committees to investigate problems and work out a basis of settlement. Representatives of the Ukrainian minorities in Poland, Rumania, and Czechoslovakia filed petitions with the commission, but the league lacked the authority and the mechanisms to deal with them effectively. Apart from giving publicity to minority grievances, it produced no concrete results.

The treatment of Ukrainian national minorities varied in the interwar period. Under Polish rule the Ukrainians of Galicia had more rights than the Ukrainians of Volhynia, and the Ukrainians of Polisia, the Kholm region, and Podlachia had virtually no rights. The Czechoslovakian government separated the Prešov region from the province of Subcarpathian Ruthenia and incorporated it into Slovakia. Under Slovak rule the Ukrainians were subject to highly discriminatory policies. Under Rumanian rule the Ukrainians of Bukovyna and Bessarabia were denied elementary rights. The Ukrainians often joined forces with Poland's, Czechoslovakia's, and Rumania's other national minorities to defend their interests. In Poland, for instance, Ukrainians formed electoral blocs in the 1922 and 1928 elections with the Jews, Germans, Lithuanians, and Belarusians.

Border changes after the Second World War radically altered the fate of the Western Ukrainians. Most of them now lived in territories annexed by the Ukrainian SSR. Significant Ukrainian minorities, however, remained in Czechoslovakia (the *Prešov region) and Rumania (the *Maramureş region), where they continued living in compact settlements in what were historically Ukrainian ethnographic territories. In Poland Ukrainians were deported from their traditional homelands in the Lemko and Sian regions (see *Operation Wisła) and were dispersed throughout parts of western and northern Poland annexed from Germany.

In the postwar period international agreements for the protection of national minorities lost the little force they had had. Only Rumania was obliged under the terms of the 1946 Paris Peace Conference to treat its national minorities fairly. Equitable treatment of national minorities was increasingly rooted in concepts of human rights, and the constitutions of the newly established socialist regimes in Eastern Europe included declarations on respecting the cultural and linguistic rights of their national minorities. In practice, however, those regimes paid scant attention to such rights and discriminated against their minorities. Communist Czechoslovakia and Yugoslavia had the most liberal policies toward their minorities and granted Ukrainians official minority status and attendant rights. Poland (especially until 1956) and Rumania pursued the most discriminatory policies. The new Eastern European governments that in 1989 and 1990 replaced the communist regimes have committed themselves to respecting minority rights.

With the establishment of Ukrainian statehood in 1917, the Central Rada and UNR and Hetman governments pursued liberal policies toward Ukraine's national minorities. In July 1917, 25 percent of the seats in the Central Rada were allocated to three of Ukraine's principal minorities, the Russians, Jews, and Poles. Those groups were also represented in the Rada's General Secretariat and all UNR ministries. All laws promulgated by the Central Rada were published in the languages of those minorities. The Rada's Third Universal recognized the rights of national minorities to free national and cultural development. A statute granting *national-personal autonomy was adopted on 22 January 1918 and later incorporated into the UNR Constitution. The turbulent revolutionary period and the wars of 1918–20 allowed for only a partial implementation of such rights. The Jewish and Polish national minorities managed to organize their own briefly functioning national conventions and secretariats. The Russians in Ukraine, however, refused to recognize Ukrainian independence and resisted the idea that they were a national minority. Under the Hetman government they tried to reassert their dominance. The chaos of 1919–20, which resulted in *pogroms against Jewish communities, did much to cloud the positive record of 1917–18.

The Western Ukrainian National Republic of 1918–19 also adopted legislation guaranteeing the free development of its national minorities and the protection of their educational and cultural institutions.

With the consolidation of Soviet Ukraine in 1920, Ukrainians formally ceased to be a national minority there. In practice, however, until the mid-1920s they were treated as such in the Bolsheviks' *nationality policy. From the mid-1920s on, after the adoption of *Ukrainization policies, the designation of national minority in the Ukrainian SSR was applied to non-Ukrainians. According to the 1926 Soviet census the minorities numbered 5.4 million, or 19.2 percent of the total population of the republic. Russians constituted the largest group (2.3 million, or 8.4 percent of the population); they were followed by Jews (1.6 million, or 5.6 percent), Poles (461,000, or 1.6 percent), Germans (376,000, or 1.3 percent), and Rumanians (258,000, or 0.9 percent).

Soviet policies toward national minorities in Ukraine at first focused on propaganda and the organization of support for the regime among the groups. Bureaus or sections of the CC CP(B)U and gubernial Party committees were established to carry out propaganda in Yiddish, Polish, German, and Rumanian. The Central Commission on National Minorities of the All-Ukrainian Central Executive Committee was created and was charged with ensuring the economic, cultural, and educational development of the national minorities, and with publishing propaganda in the minority languages. The People's Commissariats of Internal Affairs and Education established national-minority sections or bureaus at the central and local level. Newspapers and journals were published in the minority languages. Areas where minorities lived in compact settlements and represented a sizable proportion of the population were designated national raions and allowed to have organs of local self-government that functioned in the minority languages. Prior to 1930 there were 9 Russian national raions, 7 German, 3 Bulgarian, 3 Greek, 3 Jewish, and 1 Polish. In addition, the Moldavian ASSR, where Moldavians (Rumanians) constituted 30.1 percent of the total population, was created within Soviet Ukraine's boundaries in 1924. Outside the territories of the national raions, 1,097 national-minority soviets were created: 450 Russian (41 urban), 254 German, 156 Jewish (68 urban), 151 Polish, 14 Moldavian (outside the Moldavian ASSR), 12 Czech, 4 Belarusian, and 3 Albanian. There were also 28 courts where proceedings were held in various minority languages. In 1927, 2,616 of 18,412 elementary schools in Soviet Ukraine were minority-language schools: 1,310 were Russian, 496 German, 393 Jewish (Yiddish), 281 Polish, 69 Moldavian, and 44 Bulgarian; 23 other schools taught in the languages of other minorities. Soviet Ukraine's publishing industry also serviced the needs of minorities: in 1928, for example, out of 5,695 books published, 2,216 were in Russian, 96 in Yiddish, 77 in German, 50 in Polish, 38 in Bulgarian, and 12 in other languages.

The 1929 Constitution of the Ukrainian SSR guaranteed national minorities their own raions and rural soviets, the right to use their native language, and protection against discrimination.

In the 1930s, after the liquidation of the achievements of Ukrainization and during the Stalinist terror and offensive against Ukrainian cultural development, the rights of national minorities, except the Russians, were also violated. Their raions and village soviets were abolished, restrictions were placed on the publication of newspapers and books in minority languages and on the school network, and the staffs of cultural and educational institutions serving the needs of the national minorities were purged. Institutions serving the Russian minority, however, were greatly expanded, and the Russians in Ukraine ceased to be considered a national minority and became a privileged group vis-à-vis the Ukrainian majority.

As a consequence of the Second World War and the incorporation of Western Ukraine into the Ukrainian SSR, Ukraine's *national composition changed dramatically. Most of the Jewish population had been annihilated during the Nazi occupation, Germans and Crimean Tatars were deported to the east by the Soviets, and many Poles were repatriated to Poland after the war. At the same time new significant minorities (eg, the Hungarians) emerged. In the postwar period *Russification was accelerated, and Russian became the dominant language, in the bureaucracy, mass media, and education, especially in urban centers. National minorities were encouraged to assimilate into Russian culture and were, as a rule, denied their own schools, newspapers, and theaters. Only schools for Hungarians, Rumanians, and Poles living in areas bordering on their home country were maintained, for purposes of foreign policy. In 1962 there were 144 Rumanian (Moldavian) schools (with 31,700 pupils), 96 Hungarian schools (20,100 pupils), and 3 Polish schools (6,000 pupils) in those areas.

The growth of the Ukrainian national movement and democratization of Ukrainian society that began in the late 1980s has resulted in a new emphasis on minority rights. The Popular Movement of Ukraine (Rukh) and other democratic Ukrainian organizations have actively campaigned in their favor, and new freedoms have allowed national minorities to establish their own organizations, publications, schools, and theaters.

Sizable Ukrainian minorities lived in the Russian Empire and in the USSR outside the boundaries of Ukraine. In the 1920s, during Ukrainization, the authorities tried to serve the cultural and educational needs of those communities. Ukrainian schools and institutions were established in the Kuban, Slobidska Ukraine, and even the Soviet Far East, and national-communist leaders, such as O. Shumsky and M. Skrypnyk, demanded protection of the national and cultural rights of Ukrainians living outside the republic. The Stalinist offensive against Ukrainian culture begun in 1933 resulted in the total liquidation of all Ukrainian institutions in the USSR outside Soviet Ukraine. Consequently, until the late 1980s, Ukrainians living in the USSR outside Ukraine (5.1 million in 1959, 5.9 million in 1979, 6.8 million in 1989 [V. Kubijovyč estimated the figure to be 8 million]) had no community infrastructures of any kind. In 1988–9, however, in connection with the general changes occurring in the USSR, those Ukrainian minorities began organizing their own community organizations. Among the most active are those in Lithuania and Moscow. Moscow's Slavutych club has launched a campaign to organize the sizable Ukrainian minority living in the Russian republic. Throughout 1989 and 1990 many new Ukrainian periodicals were established by the organizations, and Ukrainian-language instruction was begun in several centers, including ones in the Far East. The organizations have campaigned, with little success to date, for public policies to protect the rights of national minorities.

BIBLIOGRAPHY
Natsional'ni menshosti Radians'koï Ukraïny (Kiev 1931)
Janowsky, O. *Nationalities and National Minorities (with Special Reference to East-Central Europe)* (New York 1945)
Horak, S. *Poland and Her National Minorities, 1919–39: A Case Study* (New York 1961)
Chyrko, B. 'Natsional'ni menshosti na Ukraïni v 20–30-kh rr.,' *UIZh*, 1990, no. 1
– 'Do istoriï mizhnatsional'nykh protsesiv na Ukraïni,' *UIZh*, 1990, nos 6, 8, 11; 1991, nos 1–2
Hontar, O. 'Deiaki pytannia mizhnatsional'nykh vidnosyn na Ukraïni v 20-tykh rokakh,' *UIZh*, 1991, no. 7
                                        B. Krawchenko, V. Markus

National Museum (Natsionalnyi muzei). A museum in Lviv, founded as a church museum in 1905 by Metropolitan A. Sheptytsky at his consistory. It was expanded, named the National Museum in 1909, placed under the authority of independent curators, and moved in 1911 to the building (bought by Sheptytsky) where it is currently housed. In 1939 to 1990 it was called the Lviv Museum of Ukrainian Art. The National Museum had departments of archeology, folk art, church antiquities, modern Ukrainian art, monuments of cultural history, numismatics, and sphragistics; a major library; and an invaluable collection of over 1,600 manuscript books, 2,400 early printed books, and more than 5,000 archival documents pertaining to the cultural and church history of Galicia.

The folk-art department boasted a valuable collection of 17th- and 18th-century kilims, Easter eggs, tapestries, and embroidery. The church antiquities department housed the largest extant collection of 14th- to 18th-century Galician icons, wooden engraved crosses, vestments, candelabras, chalices, and iconostases. The modern Ukrainian art department possessed works of 19th- and early 20th-century painters, such as A. Archipenko, M. Boichuk, L. Gets, M. Hlushchenko, M. Ivasiuk, I. Izhakevych, O. Kulchytska, T. Kopystynsky, F. Krasytsky, V. Krychevsky, K. Kryzhytsky, O. Kurylas, P. Levchenko, A. and V. Manastyrsky, P. Martynovych, M. and O. Murashko, O. Novakivsky, Nykyfor, V. Orlovsky, Yu. Pankevych, Yu. Pihuliak, M. Pymonenko, M. Rokytsky, T. Romanchuk, O. Shatkivsky, O. Skrutok, M. Sosenko, S. Svitoslavsky, S. Tomasevych, I. Trush, K. Ustyianovych, S. Vasylkivsky, and M. Yablonsky, and sculptors, such as H. Kuznevych, M. Parashchuk, I. Severa, and P. Viitovych. The cultural history department housed portraits of notable figures of the 16th to 18th centuries, a collection of Shevchenkiana (including a self-portrait), and artifacts from the 1917–20 Ukrainian revolution. The library held 30,000 titles on Ukraine and Ukrainians, with a particular emphasis on art and museology. The collection of 14th- to 18th-century incunabula, books, and manuscripts includes the first printed works issued by S. Fiol and F. Skoryna, I. Fedorovych's *Apostol*, the Zabludiv Psalter (1569), the Kievan Cave Patericon (1703), various early maps and engravings, and Ukrainian and other Slavic manuscripts. These exhibits showed the development of Ukrainian ornamentation and book miniatures (eg, by O. and L. Tarasevych and N. Zubrytsky). The National Museum possessed over 80,000 objects. Under the longtime curator and director (1905–52) I. *Svientsitsky the staff were engaged in research, which was published in 16 vols of *Zbirky Natsional'noho muzeiu*, containing various archival catalogs and icons, oil printed books, and church art

The National Museum

and architecture, and in the journal *Litopys Natsional'noho muzeiu* (1934–9). The museum held close to 70 exhibitions.

Under Soviet rule, until 1990, it was called the Lviv Museum of Ukrainian Art; it had seven departments, including a Soviet art department (est 1947). Today it contains nearly 100,000 objects, including paintings by Y. Bokshai, M. Burachek, A. Erdeli, Z. Flinta, M. Hlushchenko, S. Hryhoriev, V. Kostetsky, O. Lishchynsky, V. Manastyrsky, L. Medvid, V. Patyk, M. Selska, R. Selsky, H. Smolsky, O. Shovkunenko, and T. Yablonska; graphic works by M. Derehus, S. Gebus-Baranetska, S. Karaffa-Korbut, V. Kasiian, Z. Ketsalo, O. Kulchytska, V. Kutkin, L. Levytsky, P. Obal, I. Ostafiichuk, O. Sakhnovska, I. Selivanov and H. Yakutovych; and sculptures by V. Borysenko, M. Brynsky, Ya. Chaika, Ye. Dzyndra, H. Kalchenko, D. Krvavych, E. Mysko, and V. Odrekhivsky. In the 1940s, the National Museum's historical, numismatic, sphragistic, and archeological collections were transferred to the *Lviv Historical Museum; part of its folk-art collection was transferred to the *Ukrainian State Museum of Ethnography and Crafts; and the collection of paintings by Western European masters was transferred to the *Lviv Art Gallery. In 1952 over 2,100 artworks and 4,500 books were confiscated as 'ideologically harmful' by local Party officials. Part of them were placed in *spetsfondy*; most were unlawfully destroyed, sold abroad, or misappropriated. Separate branches of the museum include smaller museums devoted to the life and work of O. Kulchytska (est 1971), O. Novakivsky (est 1972), L. Levytsky, I. Trush, and A. Manastyrsky, and there is also a branch in Chervonohrad. Its current director is A. Novakivsky. Several albums of art reproductions from the museum have been published, the most recent in 1987.

BIBLIOGRAPHY
Svientsits'kyi, I. (ed). *Dvadsiat'piat'littia Natsional'noho muzeiu u L'vovi: Zbirnyk* (Lviv 1930)

Nanovs'kyi, Ia.; Otkovych, V.; Oshurkevych, L.; et al (comps). *L'vivs'kyi muzei ukraïns'koho mystetstva: Putivnyk* (Lviv 1978)

S. Yaniv

National parks. See Park and Wildlife refuge.

National territory. See Territory, national and ethnic.

National Union of Ukrainian Student Organizations in Germany. See Union of Ukrainian Student Organizations in Germany and Danzig.

Nationalism. In the Ukrainian political consciousness of the late 19th century nationalism was usually equated broadly with national consciousness and patriotism. Over time it developed a significantly narrower meaning. Prior to the First World War and during the Ukrainian Revolution it was equated with an independentist mind-set. Then, in the 1920s, an ideological current emerged that adopted the name 'nationalism' and developed a political and literary movement around the concept. Since that time the idea of Ukrainian nationalism has centered around readily identifiable groups or parties.

Nationalism is defined differently in different political systems. In the USSR it was commonly labeled 'bourgeois nationalism,' a term used indiscriminately to smear national groups opposed to Russian centralism. Continuous repressions by the communist regime in its struggle against 'nationalism' actually inspired varying degrees of popularity for the concept, albeit without specific ideological, social, or constitutional-political content. In the earliest years of the Ukrainian SSR *national communism emerged in part as an attempt at securing a degree of independence for Ukraine from Moscow's rule (within the parameters of a Soviet political system). In Anglo-American terminology nationalism is a very broad concept. It includes national consciousness, the principle of national sovereignty, and the principle of national self-determination or liberation. By and large English-language literature on Ukraine considers nationalism to be the province not only of the fervent few, but of all patriots regardless of party affiliation. The term, however, generally used to differentiate a specific ideology of nationalism that pertains to a political movement from the wider understanding of patriotism or independentism is 'integral nationalism.'

Genesis and early development. M. *Mikhnovsky is commonly referred to as the father of Ukrainian nationalism, although that designation is not entirely accurate. Mikhnovsky was one of the cofounders of modern Ukrainian independentist thought, but the historical and legal underpinnings of his ideology (such as a project for the restoration of the 'Pereiaslav Constitution') were foreign to the tenor of later integral nationalism, which cared little for constitutional or legal argumentation. The same is true for such prerevolutionary proponents of independentism as Yu. Bachynsky, I. Franko, V. *Lypynsky, and L. Tsehelsky (and even D. *Dontsov in his early writings).

Integral nationalism emerged only later in reaction to the events of the Ukrainian struggle for *independence. It first appeared in the 1920s as the spiritual ferment of a young generation protesting the collapse of Ukrainian statehood and searching for direction in the postwar world. The first attempts at establishing nationalist organizations came out of student circles in Galicia and the emigration – the Group of Ukrainian National Youth (Prague), the *League of Ukrainian Nationalists (Poděbrady), and the *Union of Ukrainian Nationalist Youth (Lviv). The *Ukrainian Party of National Work, led by Dontsov, D. *Paliiv, and V. *Kuzmovych, and its organ *Zahrava* (1923–4) had nationalist leanings. It was the publicist Dontsov who finally crystallized Ukrainian nationalist ideology, particularly with his widely influential work *Natsionalizm* (Nationalism, 1926). Other major ideologists of the movement, whose works commonly appeared in the Prague-based *Rozbudova natsiï*, included D. *Andriievsky, V. *Martynets, M. *Stsiborsky, and Yu. *Vassyian.

The *Ukrainian Military Organization (UVO) was established in 1920 by a group of former officers of the Sich Riflemen (Ya. *Chyzh, Ye. *Konovalets, V. *Kuchabsky, M. *Matchak, A. *Melnyk, R. *Sushko, Ye. *Zyblikevych, and others) and Ukrainian Galician Army (Yu. *Holovinsky, O. *Navrotsky, M. *Saievych, O. *Senyk, and others). In 1929 the UVO joined ranks with the rising generation of young nationalists to create the *Organization of Ukrainian Nationalists (OUN) under the leadership of Konovalets. From that time the OUN served as the vanguard of the nationalist movement, which now had a broader base and included a large number of supporters.

Ideology. Integral nationalists professed themselves to be the harbingers of an 'idealistic' worldview, which they understood not only as the antithesis to the materialist philosophy of Marxist-Leninism but also as a remedy for the positivism of leading figures of Ukrainian democratic thought (including V. Antonovych, M. Drahomanov, I. Franko, and M. Hrushevsky). In their search for causes of the failure of the Ukrainian revolution of 1917–21 nationalists became convinced that the masses had sought an independent state but had been frustrated and disillusioned by weak governmental leadership. Criticism of individual failings grew into a systematic rejection of the democratic and socialist principles that had been the hallmark of the Ukrainian national movement in the late 19th and early 20th centuries. The humanist traditions of the prerevolutionary Ukrainian leadership were characterized as naive and lacking in national conviction. Nationalists believed that their era demanded new forms of revolutionary action that could match the ruthlessness and determination shown by Ukraine's enemies.

The nationalists insisted on the primacy of will over reason, action over thought, and practice over theory. Their doctrine of nationalism was infused with aspects of the irrational, voluntaristic, and vitalistic theories popularized in Western Europe by such philosophers as H. Bergson, F. Nietzsche, G. Le Bon, G. Sorel, and O. Spengler. In the place of objective scientific discovery the nationalists propagated myths and favored an ideologically 'correct' image of the Ukrainian past. They promoted a cult of the struggle and reverence for national martyrs with the building of ceremonial grave mounds and commemoration of anniversaries, such as that of the Battle of *Kruty.

The nationalist worldview also embraced a form of ethical idealism that spurned individual happiness (in the eudaemonic sense) and celebrated the heroic virtues of courage, fidelity, and self-sacrifice. That idealism was in keeping with a pragmatic relativism in regard to traditional moral values, which were subject to the demands of political expediency – as, for example, in the end's justifying the means. Some publicists even openly advocated

Machiavellianism. The nationalists sought to develop a new type of Ukrainian – a 'strong man' of 'unbending' character, fanatically devoted to the ideals of the movement and ready to sacrifice self and others for the cause.

The nationalists regarded the nation as the ultimate ideal. One of the resolutions of the 1929 Congress of Ukrainian Nationalists stated: 'The Ukrainian nation is the starting point for all activity and the end goal of every undertaking by a Ukrainian nationalist; the nation is the highest form of human society.' Integral nationalism rejected political values that did not relate to the national interest. In contrast to the majority of those involved in creating the first modern Ukrainian state, who viewed national independence in the context of universal notions of liberty and justice, integral nationalists considered international relations as a 'struggle for existence' that was decided purely by force. They believed that a continual succession of sabotage and terrorist actions would prevent foreign powers from entrenching their control over Ukrainian lands and keep the masses in a constant state of revolutionary fervor. Such individual revolutionary deeds would eventually blossom into full-blown national revolution that would culminate in the rebirth of a Ukrainian state. They were vehemently opposed to the existing political order in Ukrainian lands under the USSR. Within the interwar Polish state they rejected any attempts at furthering the Ukrainian cause through so-called organic or evolutionary methods of political action and had a poor opinion of attempts at 'realpolitik.' Those efforts were judged as 'opportunism' or 'minimalism,' and were countered with statements of the need for 'principalism.'

Ukrainian integral nationalism resembled a totalitarian movement. The all-encompassing character of the movement was reflected in the complete and unqualified submission of its followers to nationalist ideology and organizational discipline. The movement did not restrict itself to political affairs, but sought to control cultural matters also, particularly in regard to literature, which was considered an important means of shaping society's worldview. The nationalist milieu produced a literary school known as the Visnykivtsi (around Dontsov's *Vist-nyk) that included such writers as B. *Kravtsiv, Ye. *Malaniuk, L. *Mosendz, O. *Olzhych, U. *Samchuk, O. *Teliha, and Yu. *Lypa. Nationalists rejected the concept of independent esthetic criteria and opposed 'art for art's sake' with calls for an engaged literature. Nationalists also sought to extend their influence over the Ukrainian institutions and organizations outside the USSR – in effect, to bring all community activity under the control of their movement. They were ill disposed to other political parties, camps, and centers, and their occasional co-operation or agreements with them were commonly tactical in nature.

Nationalist doctrine devoted little attention to socio-economic problems, but certain tendencies were evident. Its hostility to socialism was clear and unequivocal. Moreover the nationalists did not differentiate between the totalitarian communist and democratic variants of socialism: they presented Ukrainian socialist democratic parties (such as the Galician radicals) as demi-communists. They rejected liberal capitalism but were markedly supportive of the co-operative movement (as reflected in Stsiborsky's *Natsiokratiia* [Natiocracy]). Some nationalist publicists propagated the doctrine of so-called national solidarism, the exact formulation of which remained rather vague.

Political program. The political order of the future Ukrainian state was to consist of a one-party system and would be based on a principle of supreme leadership (*vozhdyzm*). There would be only one political organization (OUN), which would consist of a supraclass of 'better people.' The state structure would be formed from a hierarchy of leaders under the supreme leader (*vozhd*), who would function both as leader of the movement and head of state. Propaganda and educational materials for young cadres would consistently underline the role and authority of the leader. Konovalets and then Melnyk and S. *Bandera were accorded a kind of charismatic aura. A type of populist 'demophilia,' marked by the idea of 'the will of the masses' as the ultimate authority, also entered nationalist thinking.

The nationalists mastered successful methods of mass organization and inspired large numbers of people to action through emotional appeals. They gained influence in various segments of society, including the poorer peasantry and young tradespeople (notably in Lviv). The movement's leading cadres in Galicia in the 1930s consisted largely of students.

The motivating factor of Ukrainian nationalism was the pathos of the Ukrainian liberation struggle. Its main success lay in its ability to arouse dynamism in postrevolutionary Ukrainian society and to secure the continuation of the independence struggle after the failure to maintain statehood. The closest relatives of Ukrainian nationalism were not German Nazism and Italian fascism, which were the product of industrialized and urbanized societies, but similar ideologies of parties among agrarian peoples in less-developed countries of Eastern Europe, including the Ustaše (Ustashi) of Croatia, the Rumanian Iron Guards, the Slovak L'udaks (supporters of A. Hlinka's Slovak People's party), and the Polish National-Radical Camp. Ukrainian nationalism was a uniquely generated phenomenon, although its development was decisively influenced by foreign models. The Ukrainian movement also adopted certain symbolic paraphernalia (such as forms of greeting). Racist theory, in particular anti-Semitism, was not an intrinsic part of Ukrainian integral nationalism, although in the 1930s some publicists touched on anti-Semitic themes, and others began to examine the issue of the 'Ukrainian race.'

The origins and development of Ukrainian nationalism were particularly influenced by the dire political circumstances of the Ukrainian people in the 1920s and 1930s. Stalinist policies in the USSR threatened the very physical existence of the Ukrainian people, and under Polish domination the Ukrainian population was shut out from positions of authority and subject to arbitrary rule. That situation was compounded by the poor economic conditions prevalent in Western Ukraine – general economic stagnation, rural overpopulation, and high unemployment among the intelligentsia. The conditions undermined faith in legal efforts to produce change, radicalized the general population, and gave credence to extremist tendencies. The obvious crisis that beset many European parliamentary democracies at that time also undermined the prestige of democracy among the Ukrainian citizenry. Ukrainians obviously could not support the post-Versailles status quo, and they sympathized with revisionist tendencies. In spite of their credo to rely on their 'own strengths,' Ukrainian nationalists looked to Germany for support in their cause; certain circles in the Reich, in turn, encouraged those expectations and calculations.

1929–39. From the founding of the OUN to the outbreak of the Second World War nationalism grew to become the most dynamic political force in the Ukrainian world outside the Soviet Union. It managed to transcend regional boundaries and extend its influence among Ukrainians in Poland, Rumania, and Czechoslovakia, among the political émigrés in Western Europe, and even among those in North America. It nevertheless remained centered in Galicia and, despite repeated efforts, did not manage to spread into Soviet Ukraine.

Nationalist doctrine stressed the need to wage a revolutionary struggle against all occupiers of Ukrainian lands, but until 1939 OUN-directed sabotage and terrorism was focused exclusively against Poland. Anti-Russian action largely took the form of combating *Sovietophilism (regarded by nationalists as a new form of Russophilism) and assassinating Soviet diplomats.

The nationalist dynamic proved so strong that other currents in Ukrainian political life were willingly or unwillingly influenced by it. The effect was most strongly felt among supporters of the former Hetman state, who, despite the warnings of Lypynsky, increasingly began to change their conception of the Hetman from one of a constitutional monarch to one of a dictator. Some members of the UNR government-in-exile also began to lean in that direction. Nationalism even attracted some supporters from the ranks of the Ukrainian National Democratic Alliance (UNDO). Nationalist ideology was not actively opposed by the Greek Catholic church. Some younger priests were even active members of the movement; a group of 'Christian nationalists' (K. *Chekhovych, V. *Hlibovytsky, and others) emerged from their ranks.

All the same, nationalism did not go unchallenged. In the 1930s Paliiv established a party known as the *Front of National Unity that espoused 'creative nationalism' (formulated by M. *Shlemkevych) and hoped to compete ideologically with the OUN. Others who opposed integral nationalism on ideological grounds included Galician radicals and social democrats (K. *Kobersky and V. *Starosolsky), some national-democrats (S. *Baran, M. *Rudnytska), some Catholic activists (O. *Nazaruk), and supporters of the democratic traditions of the UNR in Prague (I. Mazepa, P. Federenko). Moreover the revolutionary nature of integral nationalism made it, by definition, inimical to UNDO (the mainstream Galician Ukrainian political party) as a whole and brought it into conflict with the Ukrainian Catholic authorities, notably Metropolitan A. Sheptytsky.

Neither the criticisms of other Ukrainians nor the repressions of the Polish authorities could stem the growth of nationalism. Nevertheless the movement itself had begun to show signs of internal crisis by the 1930s. The OUN, simultaneously an underground army and a political movement (even an unofficial party), was hard-pressed to reconcile the imperative of strict organizational discipline and secrecy demanded by its revolutionary posture with the need to generate mass appeal as a political movement: mass participation rendered the organization vulnerable to penetration by informers and provocateurs. Many nationalists also found it difficult to discriminate between

the tactics and methods used to combat the 'occupational regime' and the way in which they dealt with their Ukrainian political opponents. The moral and political capital amassed in the struggle against an external enemy became the basis of efforts to establish their hegemony over Ukrainian civic life. Internal political motivations, conscious and unconscious, came to influence OUN strategies. A new social type now emerged in Western Ukraine, the 'professional revolutionaries,' who were usually motivated by the noblest ideals but commonly exhausted themselves and their potential contributions after several years of feverish activity.

The irrational underpinnings of integral nationalism confounded sober critical analysis and rendered perspective and appropriate decision-making, as well as the rectification of mistakes, very difficult. In the 1920s, nationalist groups were often centers of discussion and spiritual quest; by the 1930s the intellectual level of the nationalist environment had declined sharply. Young dilettante publicists self-confidently began tackling so-called global problems. Their writings were characterized by pathos, inflated rhetoric, and a penchant for poetic clichés drawn from the works of national bards or the articles of Dontsov. The aim of that kind of writing was to create an emotive atmosphere. Thus, while serving to strengthen the collective resolve of Ukrainians outside the Ukrainian SSR, nationalism lowered the level of Ukrainian political culture.

The Second World War. The war was the period of nationalism's greatest heights and most fundamental organizational and ideological crisis. With the Soviet occupation of Galicia and Volhynia in 1939 and the expansion of Nazi control over most of the European continent, the activity of other political parties and groupings in Western Ukraine ground to a complete halt. Only the nationalists continued to function. In Soviet-controlled territories they maintained their underground network, and under Germany they benefited (until 1941) from a semilegal status, even in Poland and Czechoslovakia. Three major developments influenced the subsequent development of Ukrainian nationalism: a schism in the OUN, the German occupation of Ukraine in 1941–4, and direct contact with eastern Ukraine and the Soviet system.

In 1940 the OUN broke into two hostile factions, the *Banderites and the *Melnykites. The conflict was the result of differences in personality and tactical preference. In many respects it was caused by a lack of understanding between émigré nationalist circles, who considered Melnyk to be the successor of Konovalets, and the more extremist elements on Ukrainian territory (headed by Bandera), who, motivated by their achievements in the armed struggle and by their personal suffering, sought the leadership of the organization. After their split into two factions in 1940, each continued to use the OUN name and claimed adherence to the same ideology. The schism not only weakened the capability of the nationalist movement to deal with external problems but also resulted in a bloody internecine struggle that compromised fundamentally nationalism's moral prestige.

The colonial policies of Nazi Germany's occupational authorities in Ukraine did not coincide with the foreign policy adopted by the nationalist movement. German unwillingness to enter into partnership with the Ukrainians, however, freed nationalists from roles comparable to those played by the Croatian Ustaše or the Slovak L'udaks.

The Soviet annexation of Western Ukraine in the fall of 1939 meant a shift for the nationalists from an anti-Polish to an anti-Soviet orientation. It also opened the way to central and eastern Ukraine for the nationalist movement, which previously had been restricted to Galicia and Volhynia. The movement displayed extraordinary initiative and great daring in its dealings with a hitherto unknown Soviet reality, and the patriotism and self-sacrifice of its representatives attracted sympathy and trust as well as a desire by nationally conscious Ukrainians in those regions to participate in the cause. The movement's weakness in socioeconomic issues, however, and its streak of totalitarianism proved to be major stumbling blocks to greater popularity among a population whose experiences under the Soviet regime had given it a revulsion to any form of dictatorship.

Wartime proved to be the supreme test of the nationalist movement. Despite the movement's internal difficulties it was the strongest Ukrainian political force of the day, and it managed to lead a resistance movement against both a Hitlerite Germany and a Stalinist Soviet Union. In 1942–3 the resistance took concrete form in the *Ukrainian Insurgent Army, a body that kept alive Ukrainian aspirations to statehood in even the most adverse circumstances.

The forerunner of revisionist currents in OUN ideology was I. *Mitrynga, who had sought to make the nationalist movement deal with Soviet realities and turn its ideology more to the left. The process of ideological revisionism affected the various branches of the movement in different ways. Members of *OUN expeditionary groups that worked with the underground in central Ukraine were the most susceptible. The resolutions of the Third Great Congress of the OUN, held in 1943 (by the Bandera faction), and the platform of the Ukrainian Supreme Liberation Council (UHVR) of 1944 contained significant changes in ideology. Some of the fundamental revisions were the abandonment of compulsory idealism, and the toleration of pluralism both in the liberation movement and in the future Ukrainian state; the rejection of racism and ethnic exclusivity, and the recognition of the legal equality of all citizens of Ukraine regardless of ethnic background; and the adoption of a detailed socioeconomic program, which favored a mix of nationalized, co-operative, and private sectors. When it came to the question of the future political order, however, the changes offered were vague and inconclusive.

Postwar developments. The anticommunist underground in the Ukrainian SSR fought on until the early 1950s. Sources available in the West indicate that by that time the Ukrainian resistance movement, although tied to the earlier OUN, had completely purged itself of the characteristics of integral nationalism and had adopted democratic independentism. The writings of such publicists as P. *Poltava and O. *Hornovy in the late 1940s and early 1950s clearly illustrate such an evolution.

Emigré nationalism was still represented by the factions of the OUN, but there were now three of them. In the late 1940s a splinter group broke off from the Bandera faction because of the faction's apparent reversion to the old tenets of integral nationalism. The new group consisted of UHVR members and other OUN revisionists. The group,

which actually stepped outside the bounds of traditionally nationalist organizations, was initially led by L. *Rebet and was known as the OUN (Abroad).

The Melnyk faction kept the OUN name after the war. By means of its work with other émigré parties in the Ukrainian National Council it proved that it had abandoned the old tenets of party exclusivity. The faction, right-wing and conservative but largely moderate in orientation, included most of the intellectuals of the nationalist movement. The traditional mentality and ideology of integral nationalism were best preserved in the emigration by the OUN Bandera faction.

Before the changes in Ukraine in 1991, as a political movement and an ideology Ukrainian nationalism could be active only in the emigration. Even in its splintered form it remained an explosive and vibrant force. It had great ideological difficulties, however, because of its confrontation with Western democracy, its inability to deal fully with the question of the political beliefs of Ukrainians in Ukraine, and its lack of contact with political processes there. Nevertheless it left an indelible mark on Ukrainian history, both as a sign of the people's life and as a revolutionary force in the struggle for self-determination.

BIBLIOGRAPHY
Rudnyts'kyi, S. *Do osnov ukraïns'koho natsionalizmu* (Vienna 1920)
Dontsov, D. *Natsionalizm* (Lviv 1926; rev edns, Munich 1951 and Toronto 1966)
Stsibors'kyi, M. *Natsiokratiia*, 2nd edn (Prague 1942)
Pozytsiï ukraïns'koho vyzvol'noho rukhu (Munich 1948)
Martynets', V. *Ukraïns'ke pidpillia vid UVO do OUN: Spohady i materiialy do peredistoriï ta istoriï ukraïns'koho orhanizovanoho natsionalizmu* (np 1949)
Lisovyi, R. *Rozlam v OUN* (Neu-Ulm 1949)
Mirchuk, P. *Za chystotu pozytsiï ukraïns'koho vyzvol'noho rukhu* (Munich–London 1955)
OUN v svitli postanov Velykykh Zboriv, konferentsii, ta inshykh dokumentiv z borot'by 1929–55 (np 1955)
Zhdanovych, O. (ed). *Orhanizatsiia Ukraïns'kykh Natsionalistiv. Zbirka stattei* (Paris 1955)
Shankovs'kyi, L. *Pokhidni hrupy OUN* (Munich 1958)
Poltava, P. *Zbirnyk pidpil'nykh pysan'* (Munich 1959)
Knysh, Z. *Rozbrat: Spohady i materiialy do rozkolu OUN u 1940–1941 rokakh* (Toronto 1960)
Krychevs'kyi, R. *OUN v Ukraïni, OUNz, i ZCh OUN: Prychynok do istoriï ukraïns'koho natsionalistychnoho rukhu* (New York–Toronto 1962)
Lapychak, T. *Ukraïns'kyi natsionalizm* (New York 1962)
Rebet, L. *Svitla i tini OUN* (Munich 1964)
Pan'kivs'kyi, K. *Roky nimets'koï okupatsiï 1941–1944* (New York–Toronto 1965)
Armstrong, J.A. *Ukrainian Nationalism*, 2nd edn (Littleton, Colo 1980)
Motyl, A. *The Turn to the Right: The Ideological Origins and Development of Ukrainian Nationalism, 1919–1929* (New York 1980)
Lashchenko, O.; Mel'nyk, K.; Veryha, V. (eds). *Na zov Kyieva: Ukraïns'kyi natsionalizm u II svitovii viini* (Toronto–New York 1985)

I. Lysiak-Rudnytsky

Nationalist Organization of Ukrainian Students in Germany (Natsionalistychna orhanizatsiia ukrainskykh studentiv v Nimechchyni, or NOUS). A student umbrella organization centered in Berlin that co-ordinated the activities of Ukrainian émigré student societies and branches of NOUS in Central Europe in 1941–5. It succeeded the

*Union of Ukrainian Student Organizations in Germany and Danzig, which dissolved in the wake of the schism in the OUN in 1940. In 1944 NOUS had 662 members – 285 in Vienna, 46 in Graz, 135 in Prague, 83 in Berlin, 40 in Breslau, 23 in Danzig, 24 in Leipzig, and smaller numbers in Munich, Göttingen, Freiburg, Dresden, Innsbruck, and Leoben. Thirty percent of them were medical students, and 20 percent were technological students. In January 1945 NOUS changed its name from 'Nationalist' to 'National.' Its official organ was *Biuleten' NOUS-a* (15 issues, 1942–3). NOUS was headed by V. Rudko (1941–4) and Ye. Pyziur (1945–7). Notable members included A. Kozak, I. Lysiak-Rudnytsky, B. Plaskach, O. Pritsak, and B. Tsymbalisty.

Nationality policy. A government's treatment of nationalities in a multiethnic state. Soviet nationality policy determined Ukraine's national development and defined its relationship with the all-Union center in Moscow. The goal of the policy was to obliterate Ukrainian national identity and to subordinate Ukrainian to Russian interests.

The nationality policy of the USSR was referred to as the 'Leninist policy on the national question.' As recently as 1986 the CPSU Program claimed that 'the nationalities question, which was inherited from the past, has been successfully resolved in the Soviet Union,' implying that interethnic harmony and equality had been achieved, and that national allegiance had been subordinated to communist internationalism. In fact the Leninist approach was a strategy to suppress national consciousness. It has failed not only to eradicate national distinctions but even to overcome ethnic conflict.

Impressed by the revolutions of 1848, K. Marx and F. Engels realized the value of harnessing the growing aspirations of national groups in support of the proletarian socialist revolution. They advocated the 'self-determination' of nations but did not explain what would happen to nations after the revolution. Nor did they treat all nations as equals; nonhistoric nations, according to them, had no future. For F. Engels the question of national independence for the Ruthenians (Ukrainians) and other peoples was absurd.

V. Lenin inherited the Marxian conception of national consciousness as an epiphenomenon of the economic processes associated with the bourgeois period in history and as a propellant for the communist revolution. In addition he inherited a fundamental ambivalence toward nationalism: he spoke of it as secondary to the class struggle but treated it as a primary political force.

Lenin had little appreciation of the nationalism of the dominant nationality (the Russians), although from time to time he inveighed against its 'great-nation chauvinism.' He saw nationalism mainly as a response to prejudice and oppression. Once these were lifted, nationalism would disappear. Meanwhile it could be used to promote the revolution. His strategy for dealing with nationalism can be summarized in three rules: (1) before taking power, promise ethnic minorities self-determination and equality; (2) on assuming power, terminate the prospect of self-determination altogether and assimilate the minorities; and (3) the Party must be organizationally centralized and ethnically undifferentiated. This approach may appear opportunistic, but it is consistent with Lenin's understanding of nationalism.

Bolshevik promises of self-determination and the right

of secession for the various nationalities of the Russian Empire were critical to the outcome of the 1917 Revolution and the Civil War. But their implementation was conditional: if the interests of the proletarian revolution and the socialist state demanded it, self-determination for the national minorities would have to be set aside by the Party. Instead of appealing to the principle of voluntary association the Bolsheviks turned to military force to reassemble the Russian Empire, which they had sworn to dismantle. Having established their control of the former Russian Empire, Lenin and the Bolsheviks encouraged the 'flourishing' of national cultures, which they expected would then 'draw together.' It was assumed that important components of nationhood, such as language and statehood, were mere 'forms' that could be separated from the national content and filled with international and communist content. In 1925 J. Stalin introduced the concept 'national in form, socialist in content,' which has served as the cornerstone of Soviet cultural policy. Although equality of nationalities was enshrined in the Constitution of 1936, there was never any equality in real life. By its discriminatory nationality policy the Party imposed on Ukrainians and Belarusians the status of 'younger brothers' to the dominant Russians and promoted the assimilation of the various nationalities into the Russian culture.

In spite of considering language to be national in form, Stalin and his successors gradually reduced the language rights of minorities in the Soviet Union. Following the brief period of *indigenization or nativization of cadres and communications in the republics, the non-Russian languages were restricted first to their own territories. Then, in 1938, Russian was made a compulsory subject in the schools of the national republics. In 1958 N. Khrushchev permitted parents to decide whether their children would be instructed in their native language or in Russian. In L. *Brezhnev's Constitution of 1977 the right to education in one's native language was reduced to a mere 'opportunity.' As a practical consequence of this policy the percentage of Ukrainians in Ukraine claiming Ukrainian as their native language declined from 93.5 in 1959 to 89.1 in 1979 and 87.7 in 1989, whereas the use of Russian as the second language increased from 35.8 in 1970 to 51.8 percent in 1979. In 1988 one-half of Ukraine's schoolchildren were being taught in Russian. Increasing limitations on non-Russian languages resulted in a clear trend toward monolingualism.

The selection of the leadership of the national republics was left neither to chance nor to history. Appreciating the strategic value of nationalized cadres, Lenin believed that a national elite was essential to bring the masses of a given nationality into the socialist society, but that its power should be entirely cosmetic. Accordingly, in the 1920s and early 1930s the Party and government bureaucracy of the non-Russian republics was subjected to indigenization. In Ukraine the leading proponents of this policy (see *Ukrainization) were O. *Shumsky, M. *Khvylovy, and M. *Skrypnyk. Beginning in 1928, however, Stalin reversed the policy and dispatched first L. Kaganovich, then P. Postyshev, and finally Khrushchev to Ukraine to destroy its national cadres. While all Union republics were affected, Ukraine was treated with special severity: its intellectual and cultural elite was wiped out in the terror, and its political cadres were decimated in the purges. Stalin's successors continued to distrust the native leadership of the national republics. To keep the native cadres under surveillance the second secretary (in charge of cadres) in each republic was usually Russian. Members of national minorities in the armed forces were posted outside their homelands. The command of security and military formations was entrusted mostly to Russians. The 1961 CPSU Program endorsed the principle of 'exchange of cadres' between republics, thus discarding the facade of national leadership. In practice this exchange of administrative personnel was one-directional, and any murmur against its pro-Russian bias was treated as treasonous. From time to time the native cadres of the Party and state were purged for nationalism. In spite of these measures republic leaders, such as P. *Shelest, occasionally spoke up in defense of their native culture and language.

To obliterate national distinctions and create a homogeneous Soviet people the authorities manipulated national borders and resettled ethnic groups. Ethnically related peoples were split into separate nationalities. Boundaries of national republics were drawn to exclude significant irredenta as well as to include unrelated ethnic groups. Indigenes were deported, sometimes en masse (eg, the Volga Germans, Crimean Tatars, Chechens, Ingushi, Balkars, and Karachai), and nonindigenes, especially Russians, settled on their territories. According to Khrushchev, Stalin would have deported the entire population of Ukraine during the Second World War had he had enough boxcars. The so-called sovereign republics did not control their own immigration policies.

Given Lenin's flexibility and ambiguity on the issue, his successors might have pursued a subtle nationality policy varied in tempo and attuned to the state's needs. This was not the case. Except for the 1920s, when 'great-nation chauvinism' (ie, Russian nationalism) was identified as the chief danger, 'local nationalism' was held up as the gravest threat to the Soviet state. While pride and even interest in non-Russian traditions or history was branded as nationalism, the Great Russians were glorified for staging the revolution, building the USSR, and winning the war against A. Hitler. From the 1960s there was wide discussion on the 'growing together' (*sblizhenie*) and 'fusion' (*slianie*) of nationalities and the development of a *Soviet people. The Russian language was singled out as the medium of inter-national communication and the key to scientific knowledge and higher culture. Rapid Russification was thus the order of the day under Khrushchev and, after a brief respite, under Brezhnev and his successors.

The failure of the Leninist nationality policy in the Soviet Union was not acknowledged officially until 1989. The policy had neither eradicated national distinctions nor established equality (political, economic, or social) or harmony among the nationalities of the USSR. In fact it had legitimized national identity by emphasizing language, symbols of statehood, borders, and institutions and had exacerbated ethnic resentments and hostilities by discriminating against the non-Russian nations and suppressing them. The various nationalities of the Union and their supreme soviets came to life in the wake of the 1989–90 elections, demanding sovereignty and then secession from the USSR. Adhering to the traditional centralist policy of the CPSU, M. Gorbachev offered the republics a new deal but resorted to small concessions to preserve the Union and the dominant position of the Russians. His efforts were superseded by the dissolution of the USSR in 1991.

BIBLIOGRAPHY

Smal-Stocki, R. *The Nationality Problem of the Soviet Union and Russian Communist Imperialism* (Milwaukee 1952)

Dzyuba, I. *Internationalism or Russification? A Study of the Soviet Nationalities Problem* (London 1968)

Connor, W. *The National Question in Marxist-Leninist Theory and Strategy* (Princeton 1984)

Krawchenko, B. *Social Change and National Conciousness in Twentieth-Century Ukraine* (London 1985)

B. Harasymiw

Nationalization. A national government's act of assuming control or ownership over the means of production and other property. The terms of nationalization may vary from full compensation for the original owner to outright confiscation.

In the second half of the 19th century the socialist movement in Europe and in Ukraine demanded that the largest industries and banks be nationalized. There was little agreement within the movement on the extent of nationalization and on the degree of compensation to the former owners. During the 1917 Revolution the demand for nationalization as a means of asserting control over key sectors of the economy became widespread. The *Central Rada moved toward nationalizing certain sectors of the economy. In its Third Universal it abolished private land ownership by nonpeasants and empowered land committees to redistribute the lands concerned. The Fourth Universal and the Land Law of 31 January 1918 invested the Central Rada with supreme control over all land, abolished private ownership of land, and entrusted land committees with redistributing the land according to a consumption and labor formula. In their decrees the Central Rada and the Directory of the UNR proclaimed state and workers' control of production, trade, and banking but stopped short of full nationalization. Neither the Rada nor the Directory had the power to implement the acts, especially those dealing with industry and banking. In general, Ukrainian leaders accepted social democratic principles and intended to build a mixed economy.

Widespread nationalization without compensation was implemented by the Bolshevik regime in Ukraine. The policy was motivated in part by communist ideology, which rejected the market and money mechanism in deference to planning in terms of physical targets. It was also a response to the economic dislocation brought on by revolution and civil strife. The Provisional Government under A. Kerensky had established a centralized system headed by the Economic Council and its executive branch, the Supreme Executive Committee. After taking power the Bolsheviks transformed this committee into the Supreme Economic Council. V. Lenin toyed with schemes of a mixed economy and co-operatives until workers' control committees posed a political threat to the local Bolshevik-controlled soviets and compelled Lenin to nationalize industry, on 28 June 1918. Many of the measures taken by the Bolsheviks in Russia were applied automatically to Ukraine.

Industry in Ukraine began to be nationalized in Donetske, in January 1918. Nationalization was carried out in stages and was not always orderly. In the first period *workers' control over many enterprises was asserted. Although encouraged at first by the Bolsheviks, that development was resisted later, and enterprises were placed under the control of regional soviets and organs of the state, such as the Supreme Council of the National Economy of Ukraine. The various sectors of industry were not nationalized at the same time, and since Bolshevik power in Ukraine was unstable, not all areas were affected equally. By 1920, however, all the main branches of industry were owned by the state. The need for supplies during the struggle for Ukraine was a major factor in the Soviet government's decision to institute complete nationalization. By 1920, 11,000 enterprises, employing 82 percent of Ukraine's industrial workers, had become the property of the state. In 1939–40, when Western Ukraine came under Soviet occupation, all its industry was nationalized.

The first Soviet government of Ukraine, formed in December 1917, nationalized all land and allocated it for use by the peasantry. When *collectivization was launched in 1929, the peasantry lost the right to individual use of the land. They retained the right to the use of small plots, which were the property of the state. The nationalization of land in Western Ukraine was implemented by the Soviet regime in 1939 and 1940.

Forests and all natural resources were nationalized in 1918 and, more extensively, in 1923. Similar measures were carried out in Western Ukraine in 1939–40. Banks and all other credit institutions were nationalized in Central Ukraine in 1919 and in Western Ukraine in 1939. All large retail and wholesale trade companies were nationalized as early as 1918.

During the period of the *New Economic Policy small private enterprises (primarily in trade and commerce) were allowed to operate. In 1925–6 private capital in Ukraine accounted for only 6 percent of the total industrial output and 23 percent of trade. With the introduction of the First Five-Year Plan the drive to nationalization was resumed. Since the 1930s private ownership in the USSR has been restricted to housing and to articles of personal use.

In the few years before the dissolution of the USSR, the economic crisis spurred efforts to revive private property. In 1990 a law establishing the right to private property was under consideration, and private companies, called co-operatives, were encouraged by the government. The sale of nationalized industry to its employees, and of smaller retail concerns to private individuals, was being contemplated. But the denationalization of the economy failed to materialize before the USSR ceased to exist.

B. Krawchenko

National-personal autonomy. The right to self-government of national minorities in Ukraine, recognized in the legislation of the UNR and put into practice to some extent during the period of Ukrainian independence in 1917–20. This autonomy was based not on the territorial principle but on the nationwide association of all the members of a given minority. Minority members gained cultural national rights as a group, regardless of where they lived. These rights included primarily the right to have laws published in the minority's language (Yiddish and Polish), the right to enjoy state support for religious and educational institutions, limited veto rights with respect to all laws impacting on the minority, and the right to have the minority's language appear on the state currency. This solution of the nationality question in multinational states was developed by the Austrian socialists O. Bauer and K. Renner before the First World War and was generally favored by Jewish political parties (especially

the Folkspartey and Faraynigte) and Ukrainian socialist circles.

The *All-Ukrainian National Congress on 19–21 April 1917 recognized the rights of national minorities in Ukraine. After representatives of the Russian, Polish, and Jewish communities joined the Central Rada in July 1917, and a general secretariat of nationalities, with undersecretaries for Jewish, Polish, and Russian affairs, was formed (see *General Secretariat), work on an autonomy law was begun. The Third Universal (20 November 1917) of the Central Rada unequivocally endorsed the concept of national-personal autonomy and called for legislative proposals to define the concept. Finally, on 24 January 1918 the Little Rada passed, together with the Fourth Universal, the Law on National-Personal Autonomy. It granted all the minorities of Ukraine (referred to in the law as 'nations') the right to govern, through national unions, their own affairs in the spheres of culture and community organization. This right was granted to the Jewish, Russian, and Polish minorities. The Belarusians, Czechs, Rumanians, Germans, Tatars, Greeks, and Bulgarians could also gain this right by presenting a petition signed by at least 10,000 members of the given nationality to the General Court.

The law provided for the compilation, on a voluntary basis, of national registers listing the members of each national union. The national unions had the right to elect their own autonomous organs: a constituent national assembly, national councils, etc. All of these autonomous organs were to be state organs of the UNR. The national unions were to be funded by the state and by taxation of their members. This law eventually became an integral part (sec 7) of the Constitution of the UNR (28 April 1918).

According to the Law on National-Personal Autonomy, a hierarchy of institutions for minority self-government was to be established. Only the Jewish community undertook to organize the full system of self-government; the Russians and Poles merely established national ministries. Before a Jewish constituent assembly was called, an advisory 50-member Nationality Council, based on equal representation of major Jewish political parties (Bund, Poale-Zion, Zionists, Faraynigte, and Folkspartey), was created (10 October 1917) under the Department (later Ministry) of Jewish Affairs. When the Bolsheviks occupied Kiev (February 1918), all Jewish institutions were abolished. They were renewed when the UNR government returned to Kiev.

The Hetman government under P. Skoropadsky did not favor minority rights, and on 9 July 1918 it rescinded the Law on National-Personal Autonomy. But the Jewish minority set up its representative bodies and convened the Zionist-dominated Provisional Jewish Parliament in early November 1918. The UNR Directory restored the Law on National-Personal Autonomy (10 December 1918), but only for the Jewish minority; the Polish and Russian minorities were excluded. Jewish government organs were abolished again in Kiev when it was captured by the Bolsheviks in March 1919, but they continued to function until November 1920 in territories held by the UNR Army.

Because of shifting fronts and political instability, national-personal autonomy could not be fully implemented in Ukraine. Nonetheless, this was the first serious attempt to resolve the problem of international relations in a multinational state. In the 1920s a similar policy was followed by Latvia, Lithuania, and Estonia.

IBLIOGRAPHY
Khrystiuk, P. *Zamitky i materiialy do istoriï ukraïns'koï revoliutsiï 1917–1920*, vol 2 (Vienna 1921; New York 1969)
Doroshenko, D. *Istoriia Ukraïny 1917–1923 rr.*, vol 1, *Doba Tsentral'noï Rady* (Uzhhorod 1932; New York 1954)
Goldelman, S. *Jewish National Autonomy in Ukraïne 1917–1920* (Chicago 1968)

V. Markus

Natsionalist

Natsionalist (Nationalist). An organ of the *Organization for the Rebirth of Ukraine. It began to appear in June 1935 as the continuation of *Vistnyk ODVU*. It was published weekly in Philadelphia and then New York and edited by T. Svystun and V. Dushnyk. In 1939 its name was changed to *Ukraïna*. The journal continued to come out weekly and then monthly in the early 1940s.

Natsional'na dumka (National Thought). A monthly organ of the *Group of Ukrainian National Youth, published in Prague from April 1924 to December 1927. Partly financed by the *Ukrainian Military Organization from 1926, it was the first periodical to espouse a radical nationalist ideology. Its editors were I. Gyzha, M. Konovalets, S. Nyzhankivsky, I. Olkhovy, O. Boidunyk, O. Babii, V. Martynets, and O. Boikiv. Contributors included Yu. Vassyan, V. Galan, O. Hrytsai, R. Sushko, M. Omelianovych-Pavlenko, A. Kravs, and D. Andriievsky. The journal was succeeded by *Rozbudova natsiï*.

Natsional'na trybuna (National Tribune). A weekly newspaper published in New York since 1982; the unofficial organ of the *Ukrainian Congress Committee of America. It contains American and international news and articles about Ukrainian life in the United States, Ukraine, and elsewhere. The paper has a circulation of approx 5,000.

Natural gas deposits. In Ukraine natural gas deposits are located in three petroleum-and-natural-gas–bearing regions, the Carpathian, the Dnieper-Donets, and the Black Sea–Crimean–Caucasian. The Carpathian region, which has the longest history of gas extraction, extends along the northeastern flank of the Carpathian Mountains. Gas deposits located mostly along the northeastern (platform) side of the inner zone of the Subcarpathian Depression constitute what is known as the Subcarpathian Petroleum and Natural Gas Region. Overlain in places by the Stebnyk Nappe, the deposits are found in lenses and layers of sandstone between impervious layers of Miocene clays (at depths of 100–1,200 m), in Upper Cretaceous sandstones (1,200–2,600 m), and in Upper Jurassic porous limestone (2,600–4,800 m). Gas deposits are concentrated in three zones of accumulation, the Rudky-Liubachiv zone (which includes the Rudky natural gas field), the Dashava zone, and the Kosiv zone. In 1986 there were 29 gas deposits, producing either dry gas or gas with small admixtures of heavier hydrocarbons. In addition there were eight deposits producing a mixture of petroleum and gas.

Recent exploration in the Volhynian-Podolian subregion of the Carpathian region has revealed the presence of petroleum and natural gas around the eastern perimeter of the Lviv-Volhynia Coal Basin, where natural gas was released from Paleozoic formations at depths ranging from 1,600 to 8,000 m. At present gas is being exploited from a small deposit east of Novovolynske.

The Dnieper-Donets region contains the largest and the most productive (since 1958) gas deposits in Ukraine. The fields were discovered in the early 1950s and had entered production by mid-decade. Gas deposits, as well as gas-petroleum deposits, are located within a graben about 150–200 km wide and 800 km long that extends northwest to southeast through the central part of the Dnieper-Donets Trough. It contains over 60 gas and gas condensate deposits in Jurassic, Triassic, Permian, and Carboniferous sandstones, at depths of 940 m to over 5,000 m. The petroleum deposits tend to be located in the northwestern half of the graben (mostly west of Poltava), whereas the gas deposits are concentrated in the eastern half, along the central axis of the graben. Gas-petroleum deposits (nearly 40) are commonly found in intermediate locations (around Poltava and westward toward Pyriatyn). The largest commercial natural gas deposit, Shebelynka (now virtually exhausted), is located in the central axis of the graben southwest of Kharkiv. Other major deposits along that axis include those at Radchenko Khutir and Sahaidak in the west (near the Sula River, both associated with petroleum), Runivshchyna, Kehychivka, Spivakivka, and Yefremivka in the middle (southwest and south of Kharkiv), and Khrestyshche (near Slovianske) and other deposits near Luhanske in the east.

The Black Sea–Crimean–Caucasian region is associated with the Black Sea Depression. A fragmented graben extends along the east–west axis of the depression from just north of the Danube Delta, under the northwest embayment of the Black Sea, through the northern part of the Crimea, and then under the Sea of Azov to the Kuban Lowland. It contains most of the deposits of natural gas in the region. Small quantities of natural gas were tapped on estates before the Revolution of 1917 near Melitopil and Pryozivske. Large-scale commercial developments occurred only after the Second World War (since 1954 in Krasnodar krai and since 1966 in the Crimea).

In the Crimea the main gas fields are concentrated on the Tarkhankut Peninsula (northwest of Yevpatoriia) in the Lower Cretaceous deposits along the southern edge of the Tarkhankut Graben at depths of 100–4,600 m. Moreover, there are several small deposits to the east, along the graben at Dzhankoi and under the Arabat Spit south of Henicheske. Recent exploration has also uncovered offshore deposits west of Cape Tarkhankut in Tertiary and Cretaceous rocks. Small quantities of associated gas are found with oil in the Miocene limestones of the Kerch Peninsula. In Krasnodar krai natural gas was first extracted at petroleum and gas fields along the southern edge of the Azov-Kuban Depression. Exploration and extraction then expanded into the Kuban Delta, with gas fields at Krasnoarmiiske and Hryvenska. Subsequent discoveries brought the development of gas fields in the platform (graben) zone. They consisted of about 20 fields in five groupings extending in a double arc from Maikop and Labinsk in the southeast toward Prymorsko-Akhtarske and Yeiske on the coast of the Sea of Azov.

BIBLIOGRAPHY
Vitenko, V.; et al. *Naftovi ta hazovi rodovyshcha Ukraïny* (Kiev 1961)
Glushko, V.; et al. *Geologiia neftianykh i gazovykh mestorozhdenii Ukrainskoi ssr* (Moscow 1963)
Geolologicheskie formatsii neftegazonosnykh provintsii Ukrainy (Kiev 1984)

I. Stebelsky

Natural gas industry. A branch of the *fuel industry dealing with the extraction and processing of natural gas. In Ukraine it developed first in the Subcarpathian region. The first gas well, drilled in Kalush in 1910, had a small yield and did not spur further development in the area. Commercial extraction of natural gas began in 1924 in the Dashava gas field in the Lviv region. This small-scale operation supplied the town of Stryi. Although Subcarpathia

had substantial reserves of natural gas, the industry remained underdeveloped: in 1938 its output was merely 150 million cu m. After the Soviet occupation of Western Ukraine Subcarpathia's gas industry expanded rapidly, and by 1940 it was producing 450 million cu m of gas. In 1940 the Opari gas field began commercial production, and the Dashava–Lviv gas pipeline was opened. In 194 the Uhersko and other Subcarpathian gas fields began to be exploited commercially. That year the Dashava–Kiev pipeline was opened, and in 1951 it was extended to Moscow.

Intensive gas exploration in central and eastern Ukraine after the Second World War resulted in the discovery of the *Shebelynka gas field in Kharkiv oblast. With estimated reserves of 500,000 million cu m, it was the largest gas field in Europe. In 1965 the Shebelynka field accounted for 68 percent of Ukraine's gas output, and by the end of the 1960s, for 30 percent of the Soviet output. As more attention was given to the development of natural gas, new fields were discovered. In 1960–75 Ukraine was the backbone of Soviet gas production. Ukraine's natural gas output rose from 495 million cu m in 1940 to 14 billion in 1960 and 69 billion in 1975 (45 percent of the Soviet output; see table 1).

Gas pipelines from Shebelynka to Ukrainian urban centers and to the Russian cities of Kursk, Orel, Briansk, and Moscow were constructed in the 1960s. Gas from the Sub

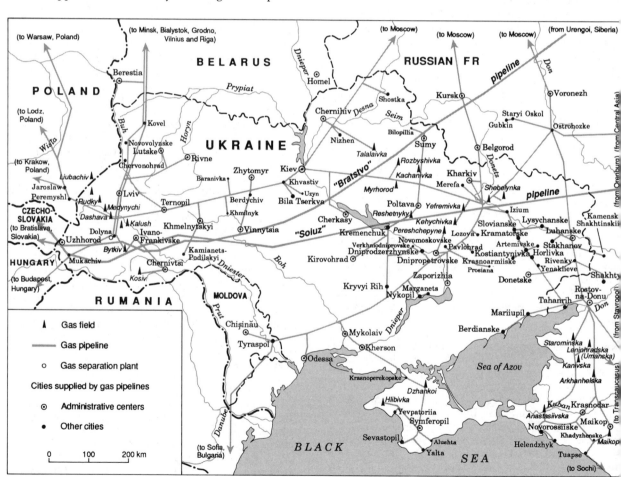

NATURAL GAS PIPELINES

TABLE 1
Ukraine's natural gas output, 1940–87

Year	Output in billion cu m	Percentage of former USSR output
1940	0.5	–
1950	1.5	26
1960	14.3	32
1970	60.9	31
1980	56.7	–
1987	35.6	–

carpathian fields was piped to cities in western Ukraine, to Kiev, and to urban centers in Belarus and Russia.

In the mid-1970s natural gas output in Ukraine began to decline, because of rising production costs, falling output per unit of capital, and the development of natural gas fields east of the Urals. By 1980 gas output had fallen to 56.7 billion cu m, and by 1988 to 32.4 billion cu m. In 1976 Ukraine's natural gas reserves were estimated at 950 billion cu m. That figure represented only 4 percent of the former USSR's known reserves. Current trends suggest that a rapid decline in production cannot be avoided in the future.

Natural gas represented 31 percent of Ukraine's fuel output in 1970. By 1988 that share had declined to 18 percent. Ukraine's household consumption of gas in 1984 was 10 billion cu m. By 1990 practically all cities and towns (smt) and most rural settlements were supplied with natural gas, whether it was brought in by pipeline or in tanks as liquefied gas. Most cities were connected to the pipeline network, but most towns and the vast majority of the villages were not, and had to use the more expensive liquefied gas (see table 2).

TABLE 2
Settlements in Ukraine supplied with natural gas, 1990

Form of delivery	Cities	Towns smt	Villages
Pipeline	42	33	545
Pipeline & tank	264	276	1,883
Tank only	125	593	24,104
Total	431	902	26,532

BIBLIOGRAPHY
Toplivaia baza Ukrainskoi SSR (Kiev 1978)
Stern, J. *Soviet Natural Gas Development to 1990* (Lexington, Mass–Toronto 1990)

B. Krawchenko

Natural resources. Those elements of the natural environment that are used to fill human needs and are valued for their potential to do so. Ukraine possesses a rich, diverse, functionally complementary, and conveniently located complex of natural resources. In the Soviet quantitative assessment by republics and economic regions, by T. Runova, Ukraine accounted for over 13 percent of the combined mineral, hydroelectric, forest, and agricultural land resources of the USSR. In that assessment another 5 percent of the USSR's natural resources were estimated for the North Caucasian economic region, which includes the Kuban, Subcaucasia, and Stavropol krai

(ethnically mixed territories). Soviet assessments used constant values for each unit of natural resource, such as standard coal-equivalent tons of fossil fuel, iron-equivalent tons of iron ore, hectares of nonirrigated cultivated land, and hectares of irrigated cultivated land. The location of a deposit with respect to the market or other complementary resources, the labor force or existing infrastructure, the degree of knowledge about a deposit, and the variation with respect to soil and climate for cultivated land were not considered in determining the value of each resource. Had they been considered, a significantly higher value for Ukraine's share would have been obtained.

Nevertheless, Soviet assessments of natural resources were indicative of approximate regional distribution and mix, especially within Ukraine (see tables 1 and 2). Nearly 60 percent of the republic's natural resources are concentrated in the Donets-Dnieper Basin, one of the three economic regions of Ukraine, mostly because nearly 90 percent of the republic's industrial resources are found there: the Donets coalfield, the Kryvyi Rih Iron-ore Basin, and the gas and oil fields of eastern Ukraine. Yet the agricultural base of the Donets-Dnieper economic region is also formidable, for it exceeds 40 percent of the republic's agricultural land resources. The Southwest economic region, although slightly larger than the Donets-Dnieper, accounts for only a little over one-quarter of the natural resources of the republic. It contains nearly 40 percent of the republic's agricultural resources, but a mere 8 percent of its industrial resources (a diverse mix consisting of oil and gas in Subcarpathia, the Lviv Basin coalfield, hydroelectric power, and forests). Smallest both in area and in its resource base is the South economic region, which accounts for nearly 13 percent of all the republic's resources. It consists largely of cultivated land, a significant proportion of which is under irrigation. The most important industrial resources in the region are deposits of ferrous ores along the Boh River and south of Kryvyi Rih, which represent slightly less than 3 percent of the republic's endowment.

A better perspective on the natural resources of Ukraine is obtained when their values are divided by the area of the territory in question. Such a calculation shows that the area concentration of natural resources in Ukraine exceeds those of the former USSR by 4.8 times. The position is attained mostly as a result of the enormous area concentration of natural resources within the Donets-Dnieper economic region, the value of which exceeds the mean of the former USSR 7.8 times.

A different picture emerges when the value of natural resources is divided by the population. The resulting quotient, representing the per capita supply of natural resources, places Ukraine below (or at 72 percent of) the mean of the former USSR and far below those of the West Siberia, the East Siberia, and the Far East economic regions and of Kazakhstan. Because of its high endowment of natural resources the Donets-Dnieper economic region retains a per capita supply equivalent to the mean of the former USSR. The South economic region has a level equivalent to 64 percent of the mean of the former USSR, but the more densely peopled Southwest economic region is equivalent to only 44 percent of the former USSR's mean.

Ukraine possesses considerable land-based (agricultural, forestry) natural resources. Those were appropriated by the government of the USSR after the Revolution of 1917 and then reallocated, through all-Union and Union-re-

TABLE 1
Natural resource endowment of Ukraine and its economic regions (former USSR total in parentheses)*

	Ukraine	Donets-Dnieper	South	Southwest
All resources	100.0 (13.0)	59.7 (7.7)	12.9 (1.7)	27.4 (3.6)
Agricultural resources	100.0 (18.2)	41.7 (7.6)	19.3 (3.5)	39.0 (7.1)
Industrial resources	100.0 (8.6)	89.5 (7.7)	2.3 (0.2)	8.2 (0.7)

*According to T. Runova (1986)

publican ministries, to government organizations, public bodies, groups, and individuals for a specified period of time or in perpetuity. Peasants were initially allowed to hold land individually, but they were later collectivized, and a state management system was imposed on their operations. Other natural resources, usually called common property resources, such as water and air, were not owned at all. Such common property resources attracted users, each of whom tried to maximize benefits from them and so contributed to their rapid degradation through *pollution or exhaustion. Common property resources therefore raised special management problems that still remain to be solved by various levels of government or intergovernmental agencies.

TABLE 2
Resource composition of Ukraine and its regions*

Resource	Ukraine	Donets-Dnieper	South	Southwest
Coal	23.8	39.1	0.0	1.6
Oil and gas	3.2	3.1	0.7	4.8
Iron ore	8.0	12.3	5.9	0.0
Hydroelectric power	1.3	0.9	2.1	1.8
Forest	0.4	0.0	0.1	1.3
Plowland	61.2	43.3	89.1	86.7
Pastures and hayfields	2.1	1.3	2.1	3.8
Total	100.0	100.0	100.0	100.0

*According to A. Mints and T. Kakhanovskaia (1973)

Over time, stock or nonrenewable natural resources have been depleted. The most accessible and thickest coal seams of the Donbas have been mined out. The remaining seams are deep, thin, and steeply inclined and therefore difficult and hazardous to mine. The depletion of oil and natural gas has been even faster and more dramatic; it has converted Ukraine from a net exporter to a net importer of hydrocarbons. Only the large iron-ore reserves still represent a significant export base, although the richest ores have been removed, and the low-quality ores require concentration and beneficiation. Soils, too, have been depleted as a result of increased erosion, chemical and radioactive pollution, and their removal from agriculture for municipal, industrial, and other uses, or inundation by water reservoirs of the Dnieper Cascade.

Some depletion is an inevitable result of the decision to exploit a given natural resource. Depletion commonly increases in proportion to the growing demand for the products of that resource. In Ukraine, however, there has been excessive depletion owing to careless or inefficient exploitation. Such wasteful use of natural resources was prompted mostly by ambitious Soviet *five-year plans, which called for massive mobilization of labor and the acceleration of basic production processes for the sake of catching up with and surpassing industrialized 'capitalist' countries. Short-term results outweighed the long-term benefits of greater efficiency, slower overall depletion, less pollution, and, above all, lower human cost. For reasons of ideology natural resources, such as land, water, or minerals in the ground, were considered 'free,' an attitude that promoted disregard for their intrinsic value and made it more difficult for managers to arrive at economically rational decisions. The shortcomings of such an approach have increasingly been recognized since the mid-1980s, but the problems stemming from it have by no means been eliminated.

BIBLIOGRAPHY
Kantsebovskaia, I.; Komar, I.; et al (eds). *Resursy, sreda, rasselenie* (Moscow 1974)
Mints, A.; Kakhanovskaia, T. 'An Attempt at a Quantitative Evaluation of the Natural Resource Potential of Regions in the USSR,' *Soviet Geography: Review and Translation*, 25, no. 9 (November 1974)
Runova, T. 'Prirodno-resursnyi potentsial osnovnykh ekonomicheskikh raionov SSSR,' in *Osnovy konstruktivnoi geografii*, ed I. Gerasimov and V. Preobrazhenskii (Moscow 1986)
Sakhaev, V.; Shcherbitskii, B. *Ekonomika prirodopol'zovaniia i okhrana okruzhaiushchei sredy* (Kiev 1987)

I. Stebelsky

Natural Science Museum of the Academy of Sciences of Ukraine (Pryrodoznavchyi muzei ANU). A museum and study facility located in Lviv. Established in 1940 as the Lviv Scientific Natural Studies Museum of the AN URSR (now ANU) following the merger of the natural studies collections of the Dzieduszycki Museum of Prehistory, Ethnography, and Nature and the Shevchenko Scientific Society Museum, it became a separate division within the AN URSR in 1954. The museum holds over 300,000 items, of which approx 9,000 are on public display. It has a research department specializing in the study of western Ukrainian flora and fauna, a zoology and botany laboratory, and a scientific library. Its permanent galleries feature exhibits on the development of the natural world, the plants and animals of Ukraine, and the origins of man.

Naturalism. A literary and artistic style of the late 19th century. In literature it was a current that opposed idealism and romanticism, and that aimed to depict comprehensively and photographically life in all of its biological aspects. The tendency existed in Ukrainian prose toward the end of the 19th and beginning of the 20th century, particularly in the works of V. *Vynnychenko and to a certain extent in those of V. *Pidmohylny. Soviet criticism considered naturalism an entirely bourgeois phenomenon, even though the officially sanctioned *socialist realism was strongly reminiscent of it, particularly in the so-called industrial novels. The tendencies of naturalism flow into those of realism, and it is difficult to distinguish between the two. For example, the early prose of Valerii *Shevchuk is marked by a kind of neonaturalism.

In the theater naturalism appeared in the coarse psychological portrayal of character. It was a feature of the productions of certain Ukrainian itinerant theaters (D. Haidamaka's, V. Sukhodolsky's, L. Sabinin's) as well as those of H. Yura's company, which aimed to counterbalance L. Kurbas's neoromantic theater.

In painting naturalism aimed at truth to nature and rebelled against idealization, stylization, and modernism in art. The works of P. *Levchenko, M. *Pymonenko, I. *Izhakevych, and M. *Bashkirtseva are typical of naturalism. Naturalism is also reflected strongly in the Soviet Ukrainian socialist-realist art of M. Bozhii, V. Ovchynnykov, S. Hryhoriev, M. Khmelko, and to a certain extent V. *Kasiian.

S. Hordynsky

Naturalists' societies. Learned societies active in the fostering of knowledge in the natural sciences. Societies of naturalists were first formed in Ukraine in the mid-19th century on a regional basis. The *Kiev Society of Naturalists and the *Kharkiv Society of Naturalists were formed in 1869; they were followed by a comparable group in Odessa in 1870. Regional naturalists groups were established at later dates in Podilia, Volhynia, the Crimea, and the Kuban. Commonly affiliated with a local university, the groups organized conferences, published scholarly collections, and established scientific research institutions. They were active until the late 1920s, when their functions were taken over by republican or all-Union institutions, such as the *Ukrainian Botanical Society, and placed under the jurisdiction of the Academy of Sciences. In Western Ukraine a Polish naturalist society (named after Copernicus) was active in Lviv from 1886, and the Shevchenko Scientific Society's mathematical–natural sciences–medical section engaged in natural studies until the Second World War.

Naturalization. The legal process of conferring citizenship upon an alien. The preconditions and procedures for naturalization are defined in law. The ease or difficulty of obtaining citizenship depends on the immigration policies of a given country. Naturalization is a voluntary, individual act, in contrast to the collective change in citizenship that occurs when a territory is annexed by another state. In Ukrainian territories the process of naturalization was defined at different times by the law of the Russian Empire, Austria-Hungary, Czechoslovakia, Poland, and Rumania, which ruled various parts of Ukraine. During the short-lived period of Ukrainian independence, the UNR and Hetman governments passed *citizenship acts. Until 1938 Soviet Ukraine had its own citizenship and naturalization laws (decree on aliens of 28 March 1922 and sec 7, arts 231–46 of the Administrative Code of 1927). Since then the acquisition of all-Union citizenship through naturalization was followed automatically by the conferring of republican citizenship by the Supreme Soviet of the republic. Republican citizenship merely indicated one's place of residence. The number of people acquiring Soviet citizenship through naturalization was quite low.

Naturalization is an important means for integrating immigrants into the social and political structure of their adopted country. Before the First World War relatively few (20–25 percent) of the Ukrainian immigrants in Canada, the United States, and South America were naturalized. This changed dramatically during and immediately after the war, when many immigrants acquired citizenship to ensure their political, social, and economic security. After the Second World War most Ukrainian immigrants to the New World (see *displaced persons) became naturalized. The desire to participate fully in the political process was an important factor in their decision. In the United States most Ukrainians were naturalized under the terms of the McCarren-Walter Act of 1952, which was much more liberal than earlier policies. The immigrant was required to reside in the country for five years, to make a formal application for citizenship, and to demonstrate a knowledge of English and of the American political system. Illiterate, handicapped, criminal, and politically undesirable people (eg, Communists) were denied citizenship. The five-year residency requirement could be shortened for individuals serving in the armed forces: in the 1950s many young Ukrainians took advantage of this loophole. In the United States the naturalization process culminates in an oath of allegiance sworn before a judge. Canada's requirements for naturalization are similar: some knowledge of English or French and of Canadian history and political life is required. A judge administers the oath of allegiance. In the US, unlike in Canada, naturalized citizens do not have the same rights as native-born citizens: they are barred from the highest political offices and their citizenship can be revoked for treason, living outside the country for a long period, or lying during the naturalization process. In Canada, the extraordinary War Times Election Act of 1917 (rescinded in 1920) stripped thousands of naturalized Canadians, including many Ukrainians, of their right to vote.

European countries have more stringent requirements for naturalization. In the interwar period very few Ukrainian émigrés gained citizenship in Czechoslovakia, Poland, Germany, Austria, France, and the other countries in which they settled. Most remained 'stateless,' living on so-called Nansen Passports. Even today, many older Ukrainians have not been naturalized. Immigrants' children born in Great Britain are automatically citizens, while those born in France become citizens by taking an oath of allegiance upon reaching maturity. In Germany, Austria, and Belgium, in contrast, citizenship is difficult to attain for immigrants' children born there. (See also *Emigration.)

V. Markus

Nature preserves (*zapovidnyky*). Territories recognized as having intrinsic value that are designated for protection from commercial exploitation so that their natural characteristics will be maintained. In Ukraine a system of different kinds of nature preserves has evolved. The preserves differ in the scope of their protection activities, the jurisdiction under which they serve, the size of the territory

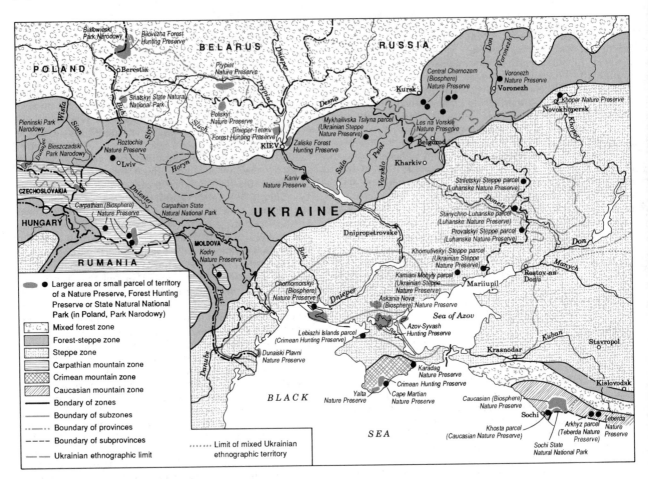

NATURE PRESERVES

they control, and the extent to which they are open to the public for popular education and outdoor recreation. The need for establishing a system of natural preserves and parks in Ukraine emerged as a result of the widespread and increasingly intensive use of land for agriculture, the growth of large-scale exploitation of forests and minerals, and rapid industrialization and urbanization. The total area of all kinds of nature preserves and parks is over 1 million ha, an area representing about 1.5 percent of the total land area of Ukraine, significantly smaller than the preserved area in countries such as the United Kingdom (4 percent) or Canada (5 percent). Green space for public outdoor recreation is also maintained in the form of parks and gardens (see *Park).

Nature preserves represent the principal focus of Ukraine's nature preservation effort. The system was initiated in the former Soviet Union shortly after the Revolution of 1917, and by 1988 it encompassed more than 150 nature preserves, of which 12 were in Ukraine. They were the *Askaniia-Nova Nature Reserve, *Black Sea Nature Reserve, Danube Shoals Nature Reserve, *Kaniv Nature and Historical Preserve, *Kara-Dag Nature Reserve, *Carpathian Nature Reserve, *Luhanske Nature Reserve, Cape Martian Nature Reserve, *Polisia Nature Reserve, Roztochia Nature Reserve, Ukrainian Steppe Nature Reserve, and *Yalta Mountain and Forest Nature Reserve. Their total area (1985) was approx 140,000 ha. Other nature re-

serves established on Ukrainian ethnographic territory beyond the borders of Ukraine were the Caucasian (in Krasnodar krai), the Les na Vorskle (in Belgorod oblast), and the Prypiat (in Homel oblast, Belarus).

Preserves were established primarily to function as scientific research facilities and to promote biosphere conservation activities. They also preserve representative portions of a particular type of landscape or biome, such as steppe, estuary, or forest ecosystems, and are sometimes called 'standards of nature' (etalony). Some nature preserves, such as Ukrainian Steppe, are made up of several discontiguous sections so that isolated remnant exclaves of biotic importance will be preserved. The nature preserves are not intended to have any significant tourist function; that role is assigned to the national parks.

A few nature preserves have been given a supplemental title, that of a biosphere reserve, under the United Nations' Man and the Biosphere program. In Ukraine the Askaniia-Nova and Black Sea preserves are so designated.

Game (hunting) preserves (zapovidno-myslyvski hospodarstva) are a companion category of partially preserved areas. In Ukraine there are four such units: the *Azov-Syvash (mostly for protecting migratory birds and providing wintering sites), the *Crimean (for protecting the forests and their fauna – the deer, the roe, and the mouflon), the Dnieper-Teteriv, and the Zaliske (both within short driving distance of Kiev). In addition the *Bilovezha

Nature preserves and parks in Ukraine, 1985

Type of preserve or park	Number	Total area (ha)
Nature preserves (*derzhavni zapovidnyky*)	12	139,800
Hunting preserves (*derzhavni zapovidno-myslyvski hospodarstva*)	4	142,700
Wildlife refuges (*derzhavni zakaznyky*)	1,490	597,600
Monuments of nature (*derzhavni pamiatnyky pryrody*)	2,621	15,900
Preserved sites (*derzhavni zapovidni urochyshcha*)	533	60,300
National parks (*derzhavni pryrodni natsionalni parky*)	2	82,800
Botanical gardens (*derzhavni botanichni sady*)	13	1,500
Dendrological parks (*derzhavni dendrolohichni parky*)		1,200
Zoological gardens (*derzhavni zoolohichni parky*)	6	100
Monuments of garden-park art (*derzhavni parky-pamiatnyky sadovo-parkovoho mystetstva*)	497	13,800
Total	5,178	1,055,700

Forest hunting preserve (for protecting European bison, deer, wild boar, and elk) is located near the Ukrainian border in Brest oblast, Belarus.

*Wildlife refuges (*zakaznyky*) constitute a category of smaller parcels of land or bodies of water designated for the purpose of protecting some elements of nature (usually an endangered plant or animal species) but not the entire natural complex (as in the case of the nature preserves). The most common wildlife refuges are established for the purpose of protecting valuable animals and birds by disallowing hunting for 10 years or more. Fishing refuges are established for the protection of spawning grounds or young fish. A landscape *zakaznyk* may serve to protect a picturesque river valley or a lake with scenic shores. Small plots of forest, steppe, or wetlands may be designated *zakaznyky* for the protection of their unique complex of plants.

Regulations that govern human activities on wildlife refuge sites are determined by the government of Ukraine, the regional departments responsible for the protection of nature, and the local executive committees. Activities incompatible with the purpose of the refuge, such as hunting, fishing, logging, grazing, hay cutting, and mining, are usually forbidden on the territory of a *zakaznyk*.

Monuments of nature (*pamiatnyky pryrody*) are a subcategory of landscape preserve; the term is usually applied to a specific feature, such as a cave or a waterfall. They are more commonly of local rather than state significance. Either the broader regulations of the *zapovidnyk* or the narrower restrictions of the *zakaznyk* apply to a monument of nature, according to the requirements of the feature to be protected.

Preserved sites (*zapovidni urochyshcha*) are also a subcategory of landscape preserve; the term is applied to somewhat larger features, such as riverbanks and small lakes. Again, the restrictions of either the broader *zapovidnyk* or the narrower *zakaznyk* type apply. (See also *Wildlife refuge.)

BIBLIOGRAPHY
Lavrynenko, E. *Okhorona pryrody na Ukraïni* (Kharkiv 1922)
Okhorona pam'iatok pryrody na Ukraïni, 2 vols (Kharkiv 1927–8)
Shalyt, M. *Zapovedniki i pamiatniki prirody Ukrainy* (Kharkiv 1932)
Okhorona pryrody na Ukraïni (Kiev 1957)
Chervona knyha Ukraïns'koï RSR (Kiev 1980)
Pryrodookhoronni terytoriï Ukraïns'koï RSR (Kiev 1983)
Zaretskii, V. *Territorial'nye aspekty okhrany okruzhaiushchei sredy* (Lviv 1985)
Zapovedniki Ukrainy i Moldavii (Moscow 1987)

P. Pryde, I. Stebelsky

Nauka (Learning). A popular Russophile journal published in Kolomyia (December 1871 to 1876), Lviv (1877–86), Vienna (1886–1900, after it was banned in Galicia by Metropolitan S. Sembratovych), Chernivtsi (1902–6), and again in Lviv (1906–14, 1924–39). Founded by Rev I. *Naumovych, it was published and edited by him (1871–86), F. Drozdovsky (1872), and D. Kozaryshchuk (1886–1900). From 1873 *Nauka* was a monthly. In 1892 it appeared only until May, and from 1893 to 1900 it was published, with interruptions, in double and triple issues. *Nauka* published excerpts from the Scriptures, sermons, religious articles, news, commentaries on Galician affairs, prose and poetry, folklore, and articles on farming, medicine, science, other lands (eg, Africa), the 'Ruthenian' language, and historical subjects. It was initially published in the Galician vernacular, but Naumovych soon switched over to the use of the *yazychiie. From 1924 it was an organ of the *Kachkovsky Society.

Nauka (Learning). A religious and educational Catholic newspaper published semimonthly (1897–1903), weekly (1904–12), monthly (1912–14), and again weekly (1918–22) in Uzhhorod. The organ of the *Society of St Basil the Great to 1902 and the only populist periodical in Transcarpathia before the First World War, it was printed in the Transcarpathian dialect using *etymological spelling. Its editors were the Greek Catholic priests and community figures Yu. Chuchka, V. Hadzhega, P. Gebei, Ye. Sabov, A. Voloshyn (1903–14, 1918–22), and V. Zheltvai. Much local folklore appeared in *Nauka*. The paper also published a bimonthly supplement of Sunday sermons, *Slovo Bozhe* (1905–6); a monthly illustrated supplement for the peasantry, *Selo* (1911–12); and a series of monthly booklets containing didactic readings. *Nauka* appeared under the titles *Tserkov*, *Narod*, and *Eparkhiia* in 1918 and as *Rus'ka kraina* in 1919. In 1922 it was succeeded by the newspaper *Svoboda.

Nauka i suspil'stvo (Science and Society). A popular journal published monthly in Kiev since April 1951 (until July 1965 under the title *Nauka i zhyttia*) by the *Znannia Society. Since 1970 the chief editor has been Yu. Romaniuk. The journal contains articles on scientific developments, nature, ecology, technology, historical and cultural topics, and the socioeconomic development of the USSR. It also publishes science fiction. Its monthly pressrun was increased from 22,000 in 1960 to 57,000 in 1970 and 72,000 in 1979, but then reduced to 57,000 in 1980.

Naukova Dumka (Scientific Thought). The publishing house of the AN URSR (now ANU) and State Publishing,

Printing, and Book Trade Committee in Kiev. Founded in 1922 as part of the VUAN Editorial-Publishing Commission, in 1927 it became the Publishing House of the VUAN (from 1936, AN URSR). In 1964 it assumed its present name. The most important scholarly and academic publishing house in Ukraine, each year it issues hundreds of monographs in the humanities and social, technical, and pure sciences; journals (52 in 1989); and serial publications (81 in 1989). It has released many important publications, including histories of the Ukrainian SSR (10 vols, 1977–9) and Ukrainian literature (8 vols, 1967–71); a major Ukrainian dictionary (11 vols, 1970–80); academic editions of the collected works of T. Shevchenko (10 vols, 1939–64; 12 vols, 1989–) and I. Franko (50 vols, 1976–86); *Fauna Ukraïny* (40 vols, 1956–); and *Flora URSR* (12 vols, 1936–65). Officially, as the publishing house of the AN URSR, Naukova Dumka was not subject to the usual Soviet censorship. In practice this meant little, and works issued by it generally conformed to the Party line and official dictates on scholarship. In the decades preceding the 1980s it was subject to increasing Russification, and most of its publications, especially in the natural and applied sciences, appeared in Russian. In the 1980s it published approx 700 titles each year, written by staff members of over 80 ANU institutes. Naukova Dumka had over 500 employees.

Naukovi zapysky Instytutu movoznavstva AN URSR. See *Movoznavstvo.*

Vsevolod Naulko   Volodymyr Naumenko

Naulko, Vsevolod, b 8 December 1933 in Tarashcha, Kiev oblast. Ethnographer. A graduate of Kiev University (1956), he received a candidate's degree from the USSR Institute of Ethnography in Moscow (1964) and worked as a research associate of the AN URSR (now ANU) Institute of Fine Arts, Folklore, and Ethnography. He has taught at Kiev University since 1971; he received his doctorate there in 1977 and became a professor in 1978. In 1982 he was elected to the presidium of the European Association of Ethnography and Folklore. Naulko is the author of over 170 works, including a book on Ukraine's ethnic composition (1965), a map of Ukraine's ethnic groups with an accompanying text on their geographic distribution (1966), and books on the development of interethnic relations in Ukraine (1975) and Ukrainian culture and folkways (with

V. Mironov, 1977). He has contributed to many scholarly compendiums, including ones on the ethnography of the Eastern Slavs (1987) and Ukrainian-Moldavian ethnocultural relations (1987), and a new postsecondary textbook on Ukrainian folk culture and folkways (editor in chief 1991).

Naum, Nataliia, b 14 January 1933 in Staryi Mizun, Dolyna county, Galicia. Film actress. She began acting in cinema in 1953. In 1958 she completed study at the Kiev Institute of Theater Arts; since then she has worked in the Kiev Artistic Film Studio, where she has played heroic and character roles in films and telefilms.

Naumenko, Ivan, b 1856, d 1913. Actor. He worked in M. Sadovsky's (1888–93), M. Kropyvnytsky's (1894–1900) and O. Suslov's (1902–7) troupes, in which he played character and comic roles. In 1907–11 he toured with his own troupe outside Ukraine, their tour including St Petersburg and Rostov. Naumenko wrote the play *Chervoni cherevychky* (The Red Shoes), based on N. Gogol's story *Rizdviana nich* (Christmas Night).

Naumenko, Volodymyr, b 7 July 1852 in Novhorod-Siverskyi, Chernihiv gubernia, d 8 July 1919 in Kiev. Civic figure, educator, ethnographer, and philologist. He graduated from Kiev University in 1873 and taught in Kiev's secondary schools until 1903. From 1905 to 1914 he was director of a gymnasium in Kiev founded by him. Naumenko was a member of the Old *Hromada of Kiev; he was elected its treasurer in 1875, and maintained contact between it and M. Drahomanov in Geneva. He regularly contributed to *Kievskaia starina*, in which he published over 90 articles on Ukrainian history, literature and writers, education, and ethnography, and of which he served as the last editor (1893–1906). In addition to contributing to other Ukrainian periodicals he wrote a survey (in Russian) of the phonetic traits of 'Little Russian' (1889) and discovered a collection of folk songs compiled by Z. *Dołęga-Chodakowski. From 1914 to 1917 he was president of the *Ukrainian Scientific Society in Kiev. After the February Revolution of 1917 he temporarily headed the newly created Central Rada in Kiev until M. Hrushevsky's arrival. In 1917 he quit the Russian Constitutional Democratic party and became a founding member of the conservative Ukrainian Federative Democratic party (est December 1917). He served as the last minister of education (November–December) of the 1918 Hetman government, and after its downfall he worked at the newly founded Ukrainian Academy of Sciences, where he collected new materials on the history of 19th-century Ukrainian literature (pub 1919, 1924). He was executed by the Bolsheviks and went unmentioned in Soviet publications.

R. Senkus

Naumets, Volodymyr [Naumec'], b 5 February 1945 in Lviv. Painter. Naumets studied at the Odessa Art School and graduated from the Moscow Higher Applied Art School (1970). In 1976 he participated in the Second Exhibition of Ukrainian Nonconformist Artists in a private apartment in Moscow. In his works he experimented with surrealism and abstraction before discovering Christian symbolism and religious themes, the result being semiabstract compositions, such as *Icon* (1979). More recently his paintings have become highly expressive (eg, the series

'Crucifixion'). Naumets's works have been exhibited in New York, Copenhagen, and Munich. In 1988 he was invited to work at Studio Central in Bern, Switzerland, and in 1989 he had solo exhibitions in Warsaw, Hamburg, and Köln.

Naumovets, Anton [Naumovec'], b 2 January 1936 in Rudka, Pinsk raion, Brest oblast, Belarus. Physicist. A graduate of Kiev University (1957), he joined the AN URSR (now ANU) Institute of Physics, where since 1981 he has headed the Division of Physical Electronics. Since 1984 he has also been a professor at Kiev University. Naumovets has made substantive contributions to the understanding of electronic phenomena involved in absorption and surface diffusion.

Rev Ivan Naumovych   Ivan Navizivsky

Naumovych, Ivan [Naumovyč] (pseuds: I.N. Buzhanenko, Reb-Chaim), b 26 January 1826 in Kizliv, Zolochiv circle, Galicia, d 16 August 1891 in Novorossiisk, Kuban oblast. Writer and cultural and political figure. He graduated from the Greek Catholic Theological Seminary in Lviv (1851) and was ordained. While serving as a priest in Galician villages he established reading clubs and temperance societies and promoted peasants' savings banks, communal stores, and rational husbandry. He was a prominent *Russophile spokesman (he saw Galicia's union with Russia as the only alternative to Polonization) and an active member of the *Halytsko–Ruska Matytsia society. He was elected to the Galician Provincial Diet (1861–6) and the State Council in Vienna (1873–9). In Kolomyia he founded the first Galician beekeepers' association (1868), the Russophile *Kachkovsky Society (1874), and the Russophile periodicals *Nauka (editor, 1871–2, 1874–6) and *Russkaia rada (editor, 1871–80). For encouraging a parish in Hnylychky, Zbarazh county, to convert to Russian Orthodoxy he was imprisoned for eight months in 1883–4 and then excommunicated. After his release he emigrated to Russian-ruled Ukraine. From 1886 he served as an Orthodox missionary in Kiev, where he led a campaign against Stundism, and then as a parish priest in Borshchahivka, Skvyra county, Kiev gubernia.

Naumovych published articles, prose, and poems in Galician periodicals (eg, Zoria halytska, Slovo, Lastivka,

Nauka, Russkaia rada, Prolom, Novyi prolom) from 1849. His didactic novelettes, stories, and plays, written in the vernacular, were popular, especially in Galicia. An edition of his complete works (3 vols, 1926–7) was published in Lviv. Biographies of him have been written by O. Monchalovsky (1899) and V. Vavrik (1926).

Navizivsky, Ivan [Navizivs'kyj] (Navis, John), b 29 September 1888 in Vorvulyntsi, Zalishchyky county, Galicia, d 25 April 1954 at sea. Communist political organizer, press editor, and community leader. In 1908, after completing study at the teachers' seminary in Galicia, Navizivsky emigrated as a laborer to the United States and joined the Socialist Party of America. In 1911 he moved to Winnipeg and worked for Robochyi narod, the weekly organ of the Ukrainian Social Democratic party in Canada. He later espoused an openly communist position; he helped form the Communist Party of Canada (CPC) and served on its Central Committee for many years, attended the Sixth Congress of the Comintern in 1928 as a delegate, and served (from 1943) on the politburo of the Labor Progressive party. He was closely associated with the *Ukrainian Labour-Farmer Temple Association (ULFTA) and the Workers' Benevolent Association, both of which he helped to establish. Navizivsky was reprimanded by Party officials in 1930 for his defense of the autonomy of the ULFTA vis-à-vis the CPC. By 1931 he had submitted to Party discipline and remained loyal thereafter. In April 1931 he led a 'labor-farmer delegation' to the Ukrainian SSR that returned with glowing reports about conditions there. In 1940 he was arrested together with other prominent Communists and interned for two years. After the Second World War he oversaw the printing of Ukraïns'ke zhyttia and The Ukrainian Canadian. He died at sea while returning from the USSR.

M. Lupul

Navrotsky, Borys [Navroc'kyj], b 8 May 1894 in Kiev, d 10 February 1943. Shevchenko scholar and literary theoretician. Using the methodology of O. *Potebnia's literary school, he wrote the study Mova ta poeziia (Language and Poetry, 1925) and many articles on T. *Shevchenko's poetics, prose, themes, and creative method; they appeared in journals, such as Zhyttia i revoliutsiia, Chervonyi shliakh, Hlobus, and Literaturnyi arkhiv, and in the annuals Shevchenko (1928, 1930). Seven articles made up the collection Shevchenkova tvorchist' (Shevchenko's Creativity, 1931). Navrotsky also wrote a monograph on the sources, style, and composition of Shevchenko's 'Haidamaky' (1928). He was critical of Western idealist and experimental esthetics. Navrotsky was arrested during the Yezhov terror, and most likely died in a labor camp.

Navrotsky, Oleksander [Navroc'kyj], b 9 August 1823 in Antypivka, Zolotonosha county, Poltava gubernia, d 22 October 1892 in Temir-Khan-Shura (now Buinaksk), Dagestan. Revolutionary figure, poet, and translator. He graduated from Kiev University in 1847. Through his cousin, M. Hulak, he joined the *Cyril and Methodius Brotherhood; he was arrested in Poltava in 1847, imprisoned for six months in Viatka, and then exiled to Elabuga, Viatka gubernia, and Kursk, Russia. From the time of his release in 1853 until the end of his life he worked as a tsarist functionary, mostly outside Ukraine, in St Petersburg, Novocherkassk, Mykolaiv, Yerevan, and Temir-Khan-Shura. Inspired by his friend T. Shevchenko, he began writing Romantic poems in 1847; a few were published in the journals *Osnova* (1861), *Russkii arkhiv* (1892), and *Kievskaia starina* (1900, 1902) and in M.(N.) Petrov's history of 19th-century Ukrainian literature (1884); all 20 extant poems appeared in a Soviet anthology of poetry of the post-Shevchenko period (1961). Navrotsky translated into Ukrainian around 140 literary works, including Homer's *Iliad* and *Odyssey* and the poetry of S. Rustaveli, H. Heine (the first Ukrainian translations), J.W. von Goethe, F. Schiller, G. Byron, J. Milton, P.B. Shelley, A. Mickiewicz, A. Pushkin, and M. Lermontov.

Osyp Navrotsky

Volodymyr Navrotsky

Navrotsky, Osyp [Navroc'kyj], b 24 March 1890 in Holhochi, Pidhaitsi county, Galicia, d 6 August 1972 in Winnipeg. Lawyer and military and civic leader. While studying law at Lviv University he was president of the Ukrainian Student Union (1912–13) and a member of the chief executive of the Ukrainian Radical party (1912–33). During the First World War he fought with the Ukrainian Sich Riflemen in the Carpathians and then served as quartermaster of the Kolomyia Brigade and assistant quartermaster of the Third Corps of the Ukrainian Galician Army and quartermaster of the Kherson Division of the UNR Army. In 1920 he helped found the *Ukrainian Military Organization (UVO) and served as chief (1920–1) and member (1920–6) of its supreme collegium. He was imprisoned in 1921–2 and 1922–3 in connection with UVO actions. He was an executive member of the Chervona Kalyna publishing house (1920–39), the Prosvita society, and the Ridna Shkola society (1923–6). During the Second World War he headed the Ukrainian Relief Committee in Krynytsia (1940–2) and was executive director of the *Military Board of the Division Galizien (1943–5). After arriving in Canada in 1948, he worked at the head office of the Ukrainian Canadian Committee until 1962. His recollections of the liberation struggle were published in the Ukrainian press.

Navrotsky, Stepan [Navroc'kyj], b 1895, d 1960. Lawyer and civic leader. He practiced law in Peremyshl and was elected as a candidate of the Ukrainian National Democratic Alliance to the Polish Sejm in 1938. He emigrated to Canada in 1949.

Navrotsky, Vasyl [Navroc'kyj, Vasyl'], b 11 February 1897 in Dzednae, Babruisk county, Minsk gubernia, d 6 October 1975 in Kharkiv. Hygienist; full member of the USSR Academy of Medical Sciences from 1960. A graduate of the Kharkiv Medical Academy (1921), he was a sanitation inspector in the Donbas, worked at the Kharkiv Scientific Research Institute of Occupational Hygiene and Diseases (1927–53), and taught at the Ukrainian Institute for the Upgrading of Physicians (1944–72). His publications deal with safety and health problems in industry, experimental industrial toxicology, silicosis, and the effects of low-concentration pollutants on the body's immune system.

Navrotsky, Volodymyr [Navroc'kyj] (pseud: Onysym), b 18 November 1847 in Kotuziv, Berezhany circle, Galicia, d 16 March 1882 in Rzeszów, Poland. Economist, statistician, and publicist. As a gymnasium student in Stanyslaviv he led a Ukrainophile student hromada with O. Terletsky. While studying law at Lviv University (1866–71) he was active among Lviv Populists and in the Prosvita society (secretary of its chief executive, 1870–2) and contributed to *Pravda* in Lviv. The Polish authorities banished him to Rzeszów in 1871. From there he contributed to *Pravda* and *Dilo* in Lviv and to liberal Russian-language periodicals, such as *Kievskii telegraf*, *Odesskii vestnik*, and *Vestnik Evropy*. His largest work, on drunkenness and propination in Galicia, appeared in M. Drahomanov's *Hromada* (Geneva 1882). Navrotsky and his articles significantly influenced the decision of many young Ukrainians to devote themselves to 'organic work on behalf of the people.' Of a projected multivolume edition of his collected works, only the first volume, containing his satire, ethnographic studies, and poetry, was published (1884, ed I. Franko). Navrotsky's diary was published by Franko in *Zhytie i slovo* (1894, no. 6), and I. Vytanovych's book about him appeared in Lviv in 1934.

Navy. See Black Sea Fleet.

Nazarenko, Ivan, b 16 August 1908 in Birky, Khorol county, Poltava gubernia, d 9 June 1985. Communist party functionary. In the 1930s, after graduating from the Kharkiv Institute of Red Professors, he lectured in philosophy. After the war he was chief of the propaganda department of the CC CP(B)U (1945), a secretary of the CC CP(B)U (1946–7, 1949–56), a member of its Politburo (1950–6), and director of its Institute of Party History (1956–74). He wrote some works on Party history and on T. Shevchenko's worldview (1959).

Nazarenko, Vasyl, b 24 August 1908 in Chyhyryn, Kiev gubernia. Analytical chemist; AN URSR (now ANU) corresponding member since 1972. A graduate of the Odessa Chemical-Pharmaceutical Institute (1931), he headed the laboratory divisions of the ANU Institute of General and Inorganic Chemistry (1957–77) and Institute of Physical Chemistry (from 1977). He researched the analytical chemistry of rare elements, ultrapure substances, and semiconductor materials; introduced new quality-control methods in the production of germanium, niobium, and tantalum; and developed methods to determine the mechanism in analytical reactions. His monograph *Analytical Chemistry of Germanium* (1974) was published in English translation.

Nazarevsky, Oleksander [Nazarevs'kyj], b 12 December 1887 in Zlatopil (now Novomyrhorod), Chyhyryn county, Kiev gubernia, d 30 September 1977 in Kiev. Literary scholar. He graduated from Kiev University in 1910 (where he studied under V. Peretts) and taught there from 1914. From 1928 to 1950 he was also a senior associate of the VUAN and AN URSR (now ANU). He wrote over 100 works on old and modern Ukrainian and Russian literatures. They include books on N. Gogol and art (1910), the historical course of Ukrainian literature (1930), the early 17th-century Russian historical narrative (1958), the literary aspects of early 17th-century Muscovite charters and other documents (1961), and Russian-Ukrainian literary relations (1963); a bibliography on the ancient Rus' narrative (1955); and many articles in Ukrainian and Russian serials. He was also involved in preparing the academic editions of the works of Gogol and T. Shevchenko.

Oleksa Nazariiv

Rev Irynei Nazarko

Nazariiv, Oleksa [Nazarijiv], b 1880, d 1918. Political activist. A native of the Poltava region, he was involved in the clandestine gymnasium in Pryluka and became active in student organizations (including the St Petersburg hromada), the Revolutionary Ukrainian party, and the Ukrainian Social Democratic Workers' party. In 1908 he moved to Lviv, where he worked as a librarian for the Shevchenko Scientific Society (1912–13) and contributed to the press. He was a member of the Union for the Liberation of Ukraine from 1914 until his return to eastern Ukraine.

Nazarko, Irynei, b 7 July 1905 in Tovstoluh, Ternopil county, Galicia, d 20 April 1976 in Ottawa. Basilian priest, church activist, and scholar; full member of the Shevchenko Scientific Society from 1956. He entered the Krekhiv Monastery in 1922 and was ordained in 1930 after completing his education in Basilian schools. In 1932–44 he headed the *Marian societies movement in Galicia and helped edit several of its publications. He was hegumen of St Onuphrius's Monastery in Lviv (1941–4) until he emigrated, first to Germany and then to Canada. There he edited the journal *Svitlo* (1946–8), obtained a doctoral degree in philosophy from Ottawa University (1951), and was a visiting professor at universities in Ottawa and Montreal (1949–53). He moved to Rome and in 1955 became general counselor for the Basilian order and rector of St Josaphat's Ukrainian Pontifical College. He returned to Canada in the late 1960s and became a spiritual adviser to Basilian students at the University of Ottawa. Nazarko was a prolific writer; his publications include *Sviatyi Volodymyr Velykyi* ... (St Volodymyr the Great, 1954) and *Kyïvs'ki i halyts'ki mytropolyty* (Kievan and Halych Metropolitans, 1962).

Nazarova, Tetiana, b 21 November 1933 in Kiev, d 18 April 1976 in Kiev. Linguist. A graduate of Kiev University (1956), from 1958 she was an associate of the AN URSR (now ANU) Institute of Linguistics. She specialized in Ukrainian and East Slavic dialectology, publishing about 60 scholarly articles on the Polisia dialects, Belarusian-Ukrainian dialectal contacts, and Ukrainian dialects in the Far East. She was instrumental in putting together the atlas of the Ukrainian language (1984–8).

Osyp Nazaruk

Nazaruk, Osyp, b 31 August 1883 in Nahirianka, Buchach county, Galicia, d 31 March 1940 in Cracow. Lawyer, publicist, and civic and political leader. As a law student at Vienna and Lviv universities he was active in student organizations. He was an executive member of the Ukrainian Radical party (1905–19) and editor of its semimonthly *Hromads'kyi holos* (1916–18). At the outbreak of war he enlisted with the Ukrainian Sich Riflemen (USS). In 1915 he directed its press bureau, and in 1918 he presided over its commissariat in Podilia. A member of the Ukrainian National Rada, he was sent with a delegation to Hetman P. Skoropadsky in November 1918 to obtain military aid for the Western Ukrainian National Republic (ZUNR). He remained in central Ukraine and sat on the council of the Sich Riflemen, and later took part in the hetman's overthrow. His positions under the UNR Directory included those of minister of the press and propaganda in V. Chekhivsky's cabinet and director of the press and propaganda board during S. Ostapenko's premiership. From the middle of 1919 he collaborated closely with Ye. Petrushevych and edited the military magazine *Strilets'*. After moving to Vienna with the ZUNR government he contributed to its organs *Ukraïns'kyi prapor* and *Volia*. At the end of 1922 he was sent to Canada to raise loans for the government-in-exile. After undergoing a conversion from socialism to Catholicism and hetmanite conservatism he moved to the United States, where he edited the weekly *Sich* in Chicago, infused the Sich organization there with a hetmanite ideology, organized new Sich branches, and coedited *Ameryka* in Philadelphia. In 1926 he returned to Lviv, where he was active in the Ukrainian Christian Organization and edited its organ *Nova zoria*. In 1937–9 he represented Bishop H. Khomyshyn on the Ukrainian Coordinating Committee.

Nazaruk wrote a great many articles on political and historical questions and many books in several genres: memoirs, such as *Slidamy USS* (In the Footsteps of the Ukrainian Sich Riflemen, 1916), *Nad Zolotoiu Lypoiu* (On the Banks of the Zolota Lypa, 1916), and *Rik na Velykii Ukraïni* (A Year in Central Ukraine, 1920); historical novelettes, such as *Kniaz' Iaroslav Osmomysl* (Prince Yaroslav Osmomysl, 1920; repr 1959) and *Roksoliana* (1930; repr 1955); brochures on topics such as the class struggle (1913), the student movement (1921), government corruption (1921), and the workers' movement and religion (1926); and accounts of his travels in Ukraine, Canada, the United States, and Scandinavia.

Nazaruk, Serhii, b 4 October 1896 in Volodymyr-Volynskyi, Volhynia gubernia, d ? After serving in the Russian army as an engineer and sapper, he established a Ukrainian sapper regiment, which was attached to the Army of the UNR. He returned after the revolution to Volodymyr-Volynskyi, where he became active in the Prosvita society. In 1923 he was sent to the Polish Sejm as a replacement for V. Komarevych. He moved his support from the Ukrainian Club to the *Sel-Soiuz faction. He did not support the group's merger into Sel-Rob, however, and in 1926 he broke ranks with the latter, together with P. Vasynchuk, in order to re-establish Sel-Soiuz.

Nazi war crimes in Ukraine. The International Military Tribunal that tried 22 Nazi defendants in Nuremberg in 1945–6 defined war crimes in traditional fashion as 'violations of the laws or customs of war,' including murder, the ill-treatment or deportation of civilians to slave labor, the murder or ill-treatment of prisoners of war, the killing of hostages, and the plunder or destruction of property. It also introduced the unprecedented charge of 'crimes against humanity,' encompassing 'inhumane acts committed against any civilian population, before or during the war; or persecutions on political, racial, or religious grounds.'

On all those counts Nazi war crimes took a staggering toll during the occupation of Ukraine in 1941–4. A. *Hitler, who regarded Jews and Slavs as subhuman, considered Ukraine and its people as resources to be exploited ruthlessly in the interests of German eastward expansion and world domination. His views were enthusiastically supported by top Nazi officials, notably E. Koch, head of the *Reichskommissariat Ukraine. Those officials overrode the objections of others, such as A. *Rosenberg, head of the Ministry for the Occupied Eastern Territories, who favored the establishment of German dominance by means of concessions to the non-Russian Slavs. Nazi racial theory, the ideological basis for the criminal mistreatment of the Eastern European peoples, was openly expressed in such publications as the SS pamphlet *Der Untermensch* (1942).

Following the invasion of the USSR in June 1941, the Germans took approximately 5.8 million prisoners of war, whom they held in open-air camps. Some 3.3 million perished as a result of deliberate starvation, neglect, physical abuse, and lack of international protection. More than 1.3 million POWs died in approximately 160 concentration camps throughout Ukraine. Some escaped death by recruitment as concentration camp guards and, after the defeat at Stalingrad, in military and other formations.

In occupying Ukraine the Germans were particularly concerned to exploit the country's agriculture and raw materials for the war effort, to recruit slave labor, and to crush popular support for Soviet or Ukrainian nationalist partisans. Numerous war crimes were committed in the effort to achieve those goals. By the autumn of 1941, serious food shortages were being reported in Kiev and Lviv, but nothing was done to alleviate them: the provision of food to the army and the German population was seen as the overriding priority. General W. von Reichenau wrote in November 1941 that feeding locals and POWs was an 'unnecessary humanitarian gesture,' and a report of the German Economic Armament Staff dated 2 December 1941 advocated the 'elimination of superfluous eaters (Jews and inhabitants of large Ukrainian cities such as Kiev, which get no food rations at all).' Urban dwellers were forbidden to change their places of residence or buy food in villages on pain of arrest and fine. Kiev lost about 60 percent of its population, and Kharkiv lost about 80,000 persons to starvation. High-calorie foods were reserved for Germans. Ultimately more than 80 percent of the food that Germany took from the eastern territories came from Ukraine.

The Soviet collective-farm system was left virtually unchanged under Nazi rule, with work norms and delivery quotas rigorously enforced. Draconian penalties, including execution, were inflicted on those who failed to deliver food to the occupation authorities. Village officials were held responsible for prompt fulfillment. According to a decree issued in Lubni on 8 April 1943, the penalty for delivering watered milk was confiscation of all the offending peasant's property. When Hitler demanded 3 million t of Ukrainian grain in 1943, Koch ordered that the task be carried out 'without regard for losses,' since the feeding of the Ukrainian civilian population was 'of absolutely no concern.'

In late 1941, when it became clear that the conflict would be protracted, the Germans began to recruit workers (initially volunteers) from the local population for work in Germany. According to Rosenberg's decree of 17 July 1941 all inhabitants of the eastern territories aged 18 to 45 were obliged to work according to their abilities. By 20 October 1941 the Chernihiv city government was forcing men aged 16 to 60 and women aged 16 to 50 to register with the labor board on pain of being dealt with as saboteurs. By early 1942, concentration camps had been established for those avoiding labor, and the death penalty had been proclaimed for those refusing to work. As the war intensified, local officials were told to deliver specified numbers of workers, and the army was ordered to assist in roundups. In order to meet quotas policemen took to rounding up people at random on the streets as well as in workplaces and institutions. The standard punishment for those refusing to work was arrest and confiscation of property; by 1943, men and women aged 16 to 55 were being ordered to report to labor boards on pain of execution. Those transported to Germany were herded onto cattle cars with insufficient food and drink. Once there, they were underfed and exploited so mercilessly that, as a rupp official noted in 1942, they lacked the strength to do their jobs. Of the total 2.8 million *Ostarbeiter* from he eastern territories, more than 2 million came from Ukraine.

For those who assisted partisans (officially called bands' after August 1942 and so deprived of combatant tatus) the death penalty was proclaimed on 14 August 941. In a circular of 16 September 1941 the commander in hief of the armed forces, Gen W. Keitel, ordered the 'immediate use of the most severe measures' to establish the uthority of the occupation forces and prevent the spread of resistance. It became common practice for the Germans o take scores of civilian hostages, changed at intervals, in order to ensure the safety of their troops and prevent sabotage. Civilians were also shot in reprisal. In Dnipropetrovske in December 1941, for example, 100 were killed for he attempted assassination of a German officer, and in he same month the Zhytomyr *Generalkommissar* ordered he shooting of 100 men and women for every killing of a *Volksdeutsche*. During the winter of 1941–2 in Kharkiv, 40 to 70 citizens were hanged every few days because of sightings of Soviet partisans; the corpses hung from balconies for days at a time. When dealing with villages suspected of harboring or assisting partisans, whether voluntarily or not, the Germans showed no mercy. Eyewitness testimony on the fate of Ukrainian villages during the occupation relates hundreds of instances of depredations carried out by punishment details. Typically the Germans would surround a village, shoot the inhabitants indiscriminately, drive some of them into buildings to be burned alive, subject others to public torture, and then loot and burn the village.

As part of their systematic effort to exterminate the Jews of Europe the Nazis rounded up and killed Jews living in Ukraine. Since no extermination camps were built on Ukrainian territory (although 50 ghettos were established), the killings typically took place in the open. Among the sites in Ukraine where Jews were killed the most infamous was *Babyn Yar in Kiev. The city's Jewish population of almost 70,000 was machine-gunned there in the autumn of 1941, and the ravine was then used as a mass grave for two more years. In Lviv about 200,000 Jews perished in the Yaniv concentration camp during the occupation. The Germans' Rumanian allies, who occupied Transnistria, also committed war crimes: some 200,000 residents of Odessa and the surrounding region were murdered in December 1941.

In addition to human losses there was great destruction of Ukraine's cultural monuments and institutions during the German occupation. The losses suffered by the Academy of Sciences alone are estimated at 126 million rubles. The Germans destroyed 116 institutions of higher learning along with 8,104 schools (another 10,052 schools were partially destroyed). Many architectural monuments were leveled, as were 151 museums – museum exhibits commonly being either plundered or damaged beyond repair. More than 50 million books were burned or stolen; 634 print shops (77 percent of the Ukrainian SSR total) were ruined; and more than 200 theaters were destroyed. During their retreat from Ukraine the Germans followed a 'scorched earth' policy and destroyed everything useful to their enemies.

According to recent Soviet figures a total of more than 5,265,000 civilians and POWs were killed during the occu-

pation of Ukraine. The figure presumably includes the 900,000 Ukrainian Jews whom Western scholars estimate to have been murdered. The Germans destroyed 714 towns and urban areas and 28,000 villages and farmsteads, and left approximately 10,000,000 people homeless. Total material losses have been estimated at a value of some 1.2 trillion prewar rubles.

BIBLIOGRAPHY
International Military Tribunal. *Trial of the Major War Criminals* (Nuremberg 1947–9)
Kamenetsky, I. *Hitler's Occupation of Ukraine, 1941–1944: A Study of Totalitarian Imperialism* (Milwaukee 1956)
Hilberg, R. *The Destruction of the European Jews* (Chicago 1961)
Kamenetsky, I. *Secret Nazi Plans for Eastern Europe: A Study of Lebensraum Policies* (New York 1961)
Nimets'ko-fashysts'kyi okupatsiinyi rezhym na Ukraïni: Zbirnyk dokumentiv i materialiv (Kiev 1963)
Wytwycky, B. *The Other Holocaust: Many Circles of Hell* (Washington 1980)
Ueberschär, G.R.; Wette, W. (eds). '*Unternehmen Barbarossa': Der deutsche Überfall auf die Sowjetunion, 1941* (Paderborn 1984)
Fedorov, O. et al. (eds). *Vinok bezsmertia: Knyha-memorial* (Kiev 1988)

M. Yurkevich

Nazustrich (Rendezvous). A bimonthly journal of literature and the arts, published in Lviv in 1934–9. It published art reproductions, literary and art criticism, articles on the history of Ukrainian art, reviews, prose, and poetry. The contributors and editors included some of the most prominent young Galician cultural figures of the time, O. Bodnarovych, V. Simovych, M. Rudnytsky, S. Hordynsky, and B.I. Antonych.

Neapolis frescoes

Neapolis. A Scythian city located on the Salhyr River southeast of Symferopil, Crimea. Digging began as early as 1827, but systematic exploration began in 1945. Founded in the 3rd century BC, Neapolis quickly grew into a substantial trade and crafts center. The *Scythians established their capital there in the 3rd century BC after being forced south from the Pontic steppe by the Sarmatians. Neapolis reached the zenith of its influence in the 2nd century BC under kings Skhilouros and Palakhos. The Scythians' power was checked in the 2nd and 3rd centuries AD by the *Bosporan Kingdom and during the 3rd and 4th centuries

Neapolis fell under attacks by Goths and Huns, and the city was abandoned.

The city covered an area of approx 20 hectares. It was surrounded by thick walls (up to 12 m) with towers. Inside the walls were stone buildings (some covered with tiles and frescoes), warehouses, and private homes. Round semi-pit dwellings resembling nomads' tents were also found. Scythians formed a majority of the city's population, but there were also numerous Sarmatians, Taurians, and Greeks who in particular exerted a strong cultural influence on the city. The most striking remains of Neapolis are the mausoleums of the Scythian rulers and burial chambers dug into rock formations.

Nebaba, Martyn, b ? in Korostyshiv, d 1651. Cossack officer. He became colonel of Chernihiv regiment in 1648. He was killed in a battle near Loev against the Lithuanian army of J. Radziwiłł.

Nebeliuk, Myroslav [Nebeljuk] (pseuds: Roman Nemyr, Nechypir Gava), b 30 September 1914 in Rosilna, Nadvirna county, Galicia. Journalist, civic leader, and veterinarian; full member of the Ukrainian Academy of Arts and Sciences. In 1937 he emigrated to France, where he joined the editorial board of *Ukraïns'ke slovo* and completed his studies as a veterinarian in 1951. In 1952 he emigrated to Canada, where he served as president of the Ukrainian Veterinary Medical Association (1971–5) and edited the association's journal *Informatyvnyi lystok OUVL* (1964–7). Since 1985 he has been editor of the journal *Hutsul'shchyna*. Nebeliuk is the author of several publicistic articles and translations of French authors into Ukrainian.

Nebera, Volodymyr, b 2 July 1924 in Kiev. Film director and pedagogue. He completed study at the Kiev Institute of Theater Arts (1949) and then worked as a director at the Ukrainian Studio of Chronicle-Documentary Films (1950–72) and taught at the Kiev Institute of Theater Arts (from 1966). He coauthored the screenplays *My z Ukraïny* (We Are from Ukraine, 1961) and *Polum'ia festyvaliu* (The Flames of the Festival, 1985).

Nebesnaia tsaritsa (Queen of Heaven). A semiofficial monthly organ of the Byzantine Ruthenian Greek Catholic diocese of Pittsburgh, published in McKeesport, Pennsylvania, from January 1927 to August 1955. Intended for Eastern rite Catholic immigrants from Transcarpathia, it was published in a mixture of Transcarpathian dialect, Church Slavonic, and Russian. It contained articles on church affairs and on religious and historical topics. Editors of *Nebesnaia tsaritsa* included P. Dolynai and V. Shereghy (Shereghy).

Nečas, Jaromir, b 17 November 1888 in Nové Město na Moravé, Czechoslovakia, d 1944. Czech political leader and Ukrainophile. In 1919 he was a secretary of the Directorate of Subcarpathian Ruthenia, and in 1924, a deputy (of the Social Democratic party) from Transcarpathia to the Czechoslovak parliament. Eventually he became minister of public health. He supported Ukrainian national aspirations in Transcarpathia and wrote popular works about the Ukrainian cause, such as *Východoevropská tragedie a Ukrajina* (The East European Tragedy and Ukraine, 1919).

Nechai, Danylo [Nečaj], b ?, d 21 February 1651 in Krasne, Podilia. Cossack leader during the Cossack-Polish War; brother of I. *Nechai. The first colonel of Bratslav regiment (1648–51), he came from a noble family and distinguished himself in the battles of Pyliavtsi in 1648 and Medzhybizh, Zbarazh, and Zboriv in 1649. After the Treaty of Zboriv he protected the peasantry from the Polish nobility. Together with T. Khmelnytsky he took part in the campaign against Moldavia, during which he captured Iaşi in September 1650. During the war of 1651 he defended the southwest sector of the front and died in battle against a numerically superior Polish force led by M. Kalinowski. Nechai was glorified in Ukrainian historical songs and dumas. Books about him by L. Polukhin (1954) and O. Lola (1956) have been published in Kiev.

Nechai, Ivan [Nečaj], b and d ? Cossack leader; brother of D. *Nechai and husband of Hetman B. Khmelnytsky's daughter, Stepanyda. He was Khmelnytsky's consul in the Crimean Khanate (1650–3) and was acting hetman of Belarus in command of the Belarusian regiment (1656–9) after I. Zolotarenko's death. Continuous Muscovite attempts to annex southern Belarus resulted in conflict with his troops. Nechai supported the Treaty of *Hadiache. He was captured during the Ukrainian-Muscovite War of 1659 and exiled to Tobolsk until 1663. His subsequent fate is unknown.

Nechai, Mykhailo [Nečaj, Myxajlo], b 8 November 1919 in Volodymyrivka, Oleksandrivske county, Katerynoslav gubernia. Socialist-realist writer; former secretary responsible for the Dnipropetrovske branch of the Writers' Union of Ukraine. He has written several collections of literary sketches; the novels *Virnist'* (Fidelity, 1958), *Diti zemli* (Children of the Earth, 1960), *Liudyna zhyve liubov'iu* (A Person Lives by Love, 1961), *Nebo dushi tvoiei* (The Sky of Your Soul, 1963), *Bili lebedi* (White Swans, 1970), *Skhidnyi bastion* (The Eastern Bastion, 1972), *Liubov i pam'iat* (Love and Memory, 1977, 1984), *Shumiv suvoro okean* (Grimly the Ocean Groaned, 1982), and *Tryvozhni nashi dni* (Troubling Are Our Days, 1987); and the novelette collection *Sotvory svoiu doliu* (Create Your Own Fate, 1981).

Nechai, Pavlo [Nečaj], b and d ? Writer. In the 1920s and early 1930s he was a member of the peasant writers' group Pluh. He wrote the humor collections *Safatova dolyna* (Safatova [Josaphat's] Valley, 1926) and *Zacharovane kolo* (The Enchanted Circle, 1929) and the trilogy *Kalynovyi lyst* (The Viburnum Leaf, 1931). In 1933 he was condemned as a 'kulak' writer and repressed. His fate is unknown.

Necherda, Borys [Nečerda], b 11 July 1939 in Yareshky, Andrushivka raion, Zhytomyr oblast. Poet of the *shestydesiatnyky* generation; secretary responsible for the Odessa branch of the Writers' Union of Ukraine. His early seafaring poems are reminiscent of those of O. *Vlyzko written in the 1920s. He has written the collections *Materyk* (The Mainland, 1963), *Lada* (1965), *Barel'iefy* (Bas-reliefs, 1967), *Poeziï* (Poems, 1970), *Litak u krapli burshtynu* (An Airplane in a Drop of Amber, 1972), *Tanets' pid doshchem* (A Dance in the Rain, 1978), *Vezha* (The Tower, 1980), *Udvokh iz matir'iu* (Alone with Mother, 1983), and *Poeziï* (1984).

Ivan Nechui-Levytsky (portrait by Ivan Trush, 1909)

Nechui-Levytsky, Ivan [Nečuj-Levyc'kyj] (pseud of Ivan Levytsky; other pseuds: I. Nechui, I. Bashtovy, Hr. Hetmanets, O. Krynytsky), b 25 November 1838 in Stebliv, Kaniv county, Kiev gubernia, d 15 April 1918 in Kiev. Writer. Upon graduating from the Kiev Theological Academy (1865) he taught Russian language, history, and geography in the Poltava Theological Seminary (1865–6) and, later, in the gymnasiums in Kalisz, Siedlce (1867–72), and Kishinev (1873–4). He began writing in 1865, but because of Russian imperial censorship his works appeared only in Galician periodicals, such as *Dilo*, *Pravda*, and *Zoria*. The first to be published were two stories, 'Dvi moskovky' (Two Muscovite Women) and 'Horyslavs'ka nich, abo Rybalka Panas Krut'' (A Night in Horyslav, or Panas Krut the Fisherman), both of which appeared in *Pravda* in 1868. He mainly wrote stories, in which he combined the styles of the novel and the folkloric narrative. His works about the lives of peasants and laborers established him as a master of Ukrainian classical prose and as the creator of the Ukrainian realist narrative. They include *Mykola Dzheria* (1878), *Kaidasheva sim'ia* (Kaidash's Family, 1879), *Burlachka* (The Wandering Girl, 1880), *Ne toi stav* ([He] Changed, 1896), and the cycle of short stories *Baba Paraska ta baba Palazhka* (Granny Paraska and Granny Palazhka, 1874–1908). The Ukrainian clergy was described and satirized in *Starosvits'ki batiushky ta matushky* (Old-World Priests and Their Wives, 1888), *Pomizh vorohamy* (In the Midst of Enemies, 1893), and *Afons'kyi proidysvit* (The Vagabond from Athos, 1890). The Polish aristocracy and the Polonized Ukrainian middle class are portrayed in *Prychepa* (The Hanger-on, 1869) and *Zhyvtsem pokhovani* (Buried Alive, 1898). Nechui-Levytsky was the first to provide fictional characterizations of various classes of the Ukrainian intelligentsia, ranging from students and teachers to high-ranking members of the Russian civil service. Against a background of colonial repression and thoroughgoing Russification Nechui-Levytsky sought to depict the stirrings of national consciousness in the Ukrainian intelligentsia and their attempts to 'place first on the agenda the inevitability of national liberation' (O. Biletsky). Those attempts on the part of his protagonists usually bring about their downfall. Such is the theme of *Khmary* (Clouds, 1874), the first Ukrainian work of fiction to address the problem, of *Nad Chornym Morem* (On the Black Sea Coast, 1890), of *Navizhena* (The Madwoman, 1891), and of many other works. Nechui-Levytsky also wrote historical fiction (mainly under the influence of M. Kostomarov), including *Zaporozhtsi* (The Zaporozhians, 1873),

Kniaz' Ieremiia Vyshnevets'kyi (Prince Jeremi Wiśniowiecki, 1897, first pub 1932), and *Het'man Ivan Vyhovs'kyi* (1899). His plays included the historical dramas *Marusia Bohuslavka* (1875) and *V dymu ta polum'i* (In the Smoke and the Flames, 1911), the comedies *Na Kozhum'iakakh* (In Kozhumiaky; adapted by M. Starytsky in 1875 and published as *Za dvoma zaitsiamy* [Chasing After Two Hares]) and *Holodnomu i open'ky m'iaso* (For a Starving Man Even Mushrooms Are Meat, 1887), and children's interludes.

Nechui-Levytsky also wrote popular works on Ukrainian mythology, history, and ethnography, and numerous articles about Ukrainian theater and the various people active in it. In his articles on Ukrainian literature, such as 'S'ohochasne literaturne priamuvannia' (The Contemporary Literary Trend, 1878, 1884) and 'Ukraïnstvo na literaturnykh pozvakh z Moskovshchynoiu' (The Ukrainian Community in Literary Litigation with Russia, 1891), he championed the idea of a national literature formed independently of outside influences, and asserted that 'Russian literature is useless [as a model] for Ukraine.'

In the field of linguistics Nechui-Levytsky was categorically opposed to the dissemination of the Galician variant of the literary language and to the orthography adopted in Galicia in the 1890s and 1900s. His polemical brochures *S'ohochasna chasopysna mova na Ukraïni* (Contemporary Language of the Press in Ukraine, 1907) and *Kryve dzerkalo ukraïns'koï movy* (The Distorted Mirror of the Ukrainian Language, 1912) were written in the spirit of conservative romanticism. He argued for a pure national lexicon and phraseology that was to be kept clean of all neologisms and foreign expressions. In his own works, however, he frequently used the grammatical and lexical dialectal forms of the nearby Russian territories, and he refused to allow any corrections. His inconsistency is most evident in his amateurish *Hramatyka ukraïns'koho iazyka* (A Grammar of the Ukrainian Language, 1914).

BIBLIOGRAPHY
'Zhyttiepys' Ivana Levyts'koho (Nechuia), napysana nym samym,' *S'vit*, no. 7 (1888)
Iefremov, S. *Nechui-Levyts'kyi* (Kiev 1924)
Mezhenko, Iu. 'Ivan Semenovych Nechui-Levyts'kyi,' *Tvory*, 1 (Kiev 1926)
Bilets'kyi, O. 'Ivan Semenovych Levyts'kyi (Nechui),' *Tvory v chotyr'okh tomakh*, 1 (Kiev 1956)
Pokhodzilo, M. *Ivan Nechui-Levyts'kyi* (Kiev 1960)
Krutikova, N. *Tvorchist' I.S. Nechuia-Levyts'koho* (Kiev 1961)
                                    B. Kravtsiv, O. Horbach

Nechyporenko, Prokip [Nečyporenko], b and d ? Historian. In the 1920s he was a graduate student in the Kiev Scientific Research Department of the History of Ukraine. Several of his articles on the socioeconomic history of the 18th-century Hetmanate (particularly during the hetmancy of K. Rozumovsky) were published in the VUAN serials *Ukraïna* (1926–7), *Zapysky Istorychno-filolohichnoho viddilu* (1927–8), *Naukovyi zbirnyk* (1927), *Istorychno-heohrafichnyi zbirnyk* (1927), and *Studiï z istoriï Ukraïny* (1929). He was repressed in the early 1930s, and his further fate is unknown.

Nechytailo-Andriienko, Mykhailo. See Andriienko-Nechytailo, Mykhailo.

Nedbailo, Petro [Nedbajlo], b 12 July 1907 in Novonovytske, Surazh county, Chernihiv gubernia, d 31 October 1974 in Kiev. Lawyer and jurist; corresponding member of the AN URSR (now ANU) from 1969. A graduate of the Kharkiv Juridical Institute (1930), he chaired the law department at Lviv (1940–1, 1946–59) and Kiev (from 1959) universities. He served on several delegations from the Ukrainian SSR to the United Nations before becoming, in 1958, a permanent representative to the UN Commission on Human Rights. A specialist in human rights, legal and state theory, and the theory of socialist law, he authored over 70 works, including *Osnovy teoriï derzhavy i prava* (The Foundations of the Theory of the State and Law, 1959), *Sovetskie sotsialisticheskie pravovye normy* (Soviet Socialist Legal Norms, 1959), and *Primenenie sovetskikh pravovykh norm* (The Application of Soviet Legal Norms, 1960).

Nedilia (Sunday). A periodical published in Lviv, weekly in 1865 (50 issues) and semimonthly in 1866 (23 issues). It contained Gospel readings, catechism lessons, poetry, prose, folklore, and popular articles on religion, history, culture, farming, crafts, trade, and hygiene. The editor was M. Popel. Among the contributors were A. Dobriansky, V. Ilnytsky, H. Lehin, I. Naumovych, and S. Kachala.

Nedilia (Sunday). The name of three weekly papers for the 'Ruthenian' peasants of Transcarpathia. The first was funded by the Hungarian Ministry of Agriculture and published in Budapest from 1897 to 1918. Edited by K. Demko (1897–9) and M. Vrabel (1899–1918), it was published in the Transcarpathian dialect. From 1916 to 1918 it was forced to appear in the Hungarian alphabet. The second *Nedilia* was funded by Bishop O. Stoika of Mukachiv. Published in Uzhhorod from October 1935 to 1938 and edited by E. Bokshai, it appeared in an artificial language based on the Transcarpathian dialect and promoted a non-Russophile, non-Ukrainian, 'Ruthenian' identity, Greek Catholicism, and loyalty to the Czechoslovak Republic. The third *Nedilia* was published in Uzhhorod after the defeat and occupation of the Carpatho-Ukrainian state by Hungary. Edited by O. Ilnytsky under the title *Karpatska nedilia* (1939–41) and by A. Nemet as *Nedilia* (1941–4), it was the unofficial organ of Mukachiv eparchy and promoted a pro-Hungarian 'Ugro-Ruthenian' identity. It was closed down after the Soviet occupation of Transcarpathia.

Nedilia (Sunday). A popular illustrated weekly of culture and community affairs, published from January 1911 to the end of 1912 in Lviv as a supplement to the newspaper *Dilo*. It was edited by V. Shchurat and Ya. Vesolovsky (from the 18th issue). Its numerous contributors included I. Franko, I. Krypiakevych, M. Vozniak, S. Tomashivsky, Yu. Romanchuk, and V. Pachovsky. *Nedilia* did much to popularize Ukrainian history and culture and published many translations of Western European literature.

Nedilia (Sunday). A popular illustrated weekly published in Lviv from 1928 to 1939. It carried articles on cultural and literary topics and popular enlightenment. Initially published by M. Holubets and R. Holiian, it was bought by the *Ukrainian Catholic Union in 1931. In 1930 its circulation was 8,000. *Nedilia* published a parallel edition for Ukrainians in Volhynia with coverage of events there, *Volyns'ka nedilia* (ed S. Vyshnivsky), in Lviv (1928–34) and Lutske (1935–9); a monthly supplement, *Svit*

(1931); books of new Ukrainian prose and poetry, translated literature, and regional studies; and the annual almanac *Krynytsia* (1934–9). A. *Kurdydyk contributed regularly to the paper.

Nedilia (Sunday). A weekly (with interruptions) newspaper for Ukrainian displaced persons, published from December 1945 to 1949 in Schweinfurt and Aschaffenburg, Germany, and edited by H. Kotorovych. During its first year it was printed in the Latin alphabet. Among its contributors were A. Kurdydyk, T. Lapychak, M. Livytsky, S. Pidhainy, S. Rosokha, M. Stakhiv, O. Shtul-Zhdanovych, and A. Zhyvotko. From 1950 to 1956 it was published irregularly in Augsburg.

Mykola Nedilko: *On the Dniester* (oil, 1942)

Nedilko, Mykola, b 23 November 1902 in Yushchenivka, Sumy county, Kharkiv gubernia, d 12 May 1979 in Glen Cove, New York. Artist. While studying at the Kiev State Art Institute (1922–8) under F. Krychevsky and M. Boichuk he joined the *Association of Revolutionary Art of Ukraine. In 1940 he came with M. Azovsky and M. Dmytrenko to Soviet-occupied Lviv. He remained there after the 1941 Soviet evacuation, joined the *Labor Association of Ukrainian Pictorial Artists, and exhibited at its shows. A postwar refugee in Germany, he emigrated in 1948 to Buenos Aires and in 1961 to New York. Solo exhibitions of his works were held in New York (1962, 1965, 1966, 1980), Paris (1965), Philadelphia (1966, 1982), and Edmonton (1983). He is best known for his landscapes, painted usually *en plein air*. They include *On the Dniester* (1942), *Bodensee* (1948), *The Andes* (1958), and *Lake George* (1966). His postimpressionist oils are built on strong contrasts of light and shadow, and color. A book about Nedilko (ed B. Pevny), with 60 color plates, was published in New York in 1983.

Nedilsky, Ivan [Nedil's'kyj], b 25 July 1895 in Potik Zolotyi, Buchach county, Galicia, d 5 June 1970 in New York. Composer and teacher. He graduated from the Stern Conservatory in Berlin in 1924 and then worked for the Stanyslaviv branch of the Lysenko Higher Music Institute as a teacher of cello and music theory and as director (1930–9). He continued to serve as the music school director in

Stanyslaviv under the Soviet and German occupations until 1944, subsequently emigrating to the United States via Germany. In 1952 he cofounded the *Ukrainian Music Institute of America and began teaching in its New York school. His works and arrangements are mainly for chorus and include the popular march 'Zasialo sontse zolote' (The Golden Sun Shone Forth) and a *Divine Liturgy* (1948). His collection *Selected Works for Mixed Chorus a Cappella* was published in 1982 by the Ukrainian Music Foundation. Nedilsky also wrote solo songs and theater, chamber, and piano music.

Sofron Nedilsky

Nedilsky, Sofron [Nedil's'kyj], b 10 January 1857, d 8 August 1917 in Bielsko-Biała, Poland. Galician lexicographer and educator. While teaching at the Ukrainian gymnasium in Stanyslaviv, he helped found the *Ruska Besida society and completed vol 2 of Ye. *Zhelekhivsky's Ukrainian-German dictionary (1886). Later he was the first principal of the Ukrainian gymnasium in Kolomyia (1894–1914). In 1914 he became a representative on the Provincial School Council and was evacuated to Poland.

Nedolia, Leonyd [Nedolja] (pseud of Lukian Honcharenko), b 19 September 1897 in Tsysarska Sloboda (now Chervona Sloboda), Cherkasy county, Kiev gubernia, d 5 July 1963 in Cherkasy. Writer, journalist, and political activist. He was exiled to Siberia for his revolutionary activities during the First World War, and returned to Ukraine after the establishment of Soviet rule there. After the Second World War he worked as a journalist in Cherkasy. Nedolia is the author of numerous collections of short stories and studies, including *Smert' pryvatnii kukhni* (Death to the Private Kitchen, 1925), *Zhyvi braty: Kriz' Khiny* (Real Brothers: Through China, 1929), *Ponevoleni khintsi* (The Oppressed Chinese, 1931), and *Na kytais'kii zemli* (In Chinese Territory, 1934), and the poem 'Svoï prava' (One's Own Rights, 1931).

Nedoshytko, Oleh [Nedošytko], b 27 January 1950 in Odessa. Painter and teacher. After graduating from the Odessa Pedagogical Institute's Faculty of Art in 1977, he worked as an instructor there until 1985. His early work consists of landscapes of the environs of Odessa executed in an impressionist manner, full of sunlight and displaying a great sensitivity for color tonalities (eg, *Cossack Church*, 1980). Since the mid-1980s his paintings have been more expressionistic, executed in a slashing brush stroke with a high-intensity palette (eg, *Forgotten Melody* and *Festival Evening*, 1988).

Nedrigailov, Viktor [Nedrigajlov], b 8 November 1865 in Kursk, Russia, d 27 April 1923 in Petrograd. Microbiologist. After graduating from Kharkiv University in 1893, he worked at the Kharkiv Bacteriological Institute, from 1908 as its director. He organized the large-scale production of antidiphtheria serum and edited *Kharkovskii meditsinskii zhurnal*. From 1914 he was a department head at the Institute of Experimental Medicine and lecturer at the Women's Medical Institute in Petrograd. He discovered a laboratory method of diagnosing cholera and a vaccination method against gas gangrene.

Nedryhailiv [Nedryhajliv]. III-14. A town smt (1990 pop 6,700) on the Sula River and a raion center in Sumy oblast. It was founded in the 1640s, and served as a fortress defending Slobidska Ukraine and as a company center in Sumy regiment. In 1780–96 it was a county center in Kharkiv vicegerency. It attained smt status in 1958. Its main enterprises are a dairy and a canning factory.

Nedzvedsky, Mykola [Nedzveds'kyj], b 12 December 1891 in Kiev, d 3 September 1977 in Washington, DC. Composer, musicologist, and pedagogue. A graduate of the Kiev Music and Drama Institute (1927), he studied composition with H. Liubomyrsky, R. Glière, and B. Liatoshynsky. He was a lecturer at the Kiev Workers' Conservatory (1929–31) and from 1936 a professor at the Kiev Conservatory. In 1943 he emigrated to the West. He continued teaching in Bavaria, Morocco, and the United States and became a professor at the Ukrainian Music Institute in Washington, DC. Among his pupils were the composers I. Bilohrud and G. Fiala. His works include the symphonic overture *Dorian Gray*, the orchestral suite *Tini zabutykh predkiv* (Shadows of Forgotten Ancestors), the symphonies *Ashkhabad* and *Fez*, and the piano quintet *Testament*.

Nefelin, Vasyl (pseud of Vasyl Nahorsky), b 13 March 1907 in Svaromia, Kiev county, d 11 June 1968 in Oster, Chernihiv oblast. Writer and journalist. He graduated form the teachers' institute in Chernihiv and worked on the editorial board of the journal *Pluh and for the newspapers *Bil'shovyk* and *Kolhospne zhyttia*. He began his literary career in the 1920s. His first short stories and poems were published in *Pluh*. He published the short story collections *Iz hlybyny* (From the Depths, 1930, compiled by S. Pylypenko), *Sulons'ki opovidannia* (Sulon Stories, 1959), *Zolote vidertse* (The Golden Pail, 1962), and *Liubov* (Love, 1965), the novel *Budni* (Ordinary Days, 1930), and the autobiographical *Ranok ioho zhyttia* (The Morning of His Life, 1960). He was imprisoned in Stalinist labor camps (1937–44).

Neformaly. Groups, associations, and political organizations that emerged in the USSR during the M. Gorbachev period. Such groups were called informal (*neformalni*) or unofficial because they were not part of CPSU or state structures and had no juridical status under Soviet law. Of the hundreds of such organizations that came into being, only a few were officially registered in 1990 (with all the attendant rights to nominate candidates in elections and have a bank account). Among the most significant are the *Memorial society, which is dedicated to chronicling and rehabilitating the millions of victims of Soviet repression, the Zelenyi Svit Ukrainian Ecological Association, the Ukrainian Language Society, and the Popular Movement of Ukraine (Rukh). Zelenyi Svit and the Ukrainian Language Society each have approximately three-quarters of a million members.

The amnesty of *political prisoners, many of whom were hardened political activists, in the early part of 1987 was the catalyst that launched the wide-scale growth of unofficial groups. The amnesty also coincided with the launching of the policy of glasnost, which led to a general liberalization and democratization of Soviet society. Under glasnost the number of people willing to participate in activities hitherto subject to severe repression increased dramatically.

The first large organization to be established was the Ukrainian Language Society, headed by D. *Pavlychko. Its founding congress was held on 11–12 February 1989 in Kiev. The society promotes the use and development of the Ukrainian language and actively campaigns against Russification. It publishes two newspapers, Slovo (Kiev) and Prosvita (Lviv). Soviet officialdom had hoped that the emerging Ukrainian national movement would confine itself to promoting the Ukrainian language and culture and not pursue more political goals. By granting the society official recognition, however, the state in fact created a legal framework for political opposition to the state. The society provided office space for Rukh and nominated its own oppositional candidates in elections.

The largest and most important organization in Ukraine in the early 1990s was Rukh. It was formed on the initiative of members of the ANU Institute of Literature and the large Kiev branch of the Writers' Union of Ukraine. Rukh's draft program was published in Literaturna Ukraïna in mid-February 1989. Between February and September 1989 the CPU engaged in a counterproductive media campaign against Rukh. The campaign backfired: its effect was to attract many new members to Rukh and thereby increase its influence. Rukh is a coalition of all the main unofficial groups in Ukraine. Its founding congress in Kiev on 8–10 September 1989 was attended by 1,200 delegates, who elected I. *Drach their head. Rukh sponsored numerous initiatives designed to break the monopoly of the Party and state apparats and campaigned for the adoption of a more democratic electoral law. On 21 January 1990 it held its most successful event – a human chain of some one million people holding hands from Ivano-Frankivske to Lviv and on to Kiev – to commemorate the 1919 proclamation of the union of the UNR with the Western Ukrainian National Republic. Rukh was not registered in time to field candidates for the 4 March 1990 elections to the Ukrainian Supreme Council. It was, however, the main force behind the Democratic Bloc that won almost a quarter of the seats in the Supreme Council. Immediately after the elections (which were marked by large-scale fraud and irregularities) prominent Rukh members, including Drach and Pavlychko, called for the transformation of Rukh into a political party that would advocate Ukraine's independence and a multiparty system. On 24 March 1990 the Great Council of Rukh meeting voted against the proposal, considering it inadvisable to trans-

form a large coalition of diverse forces into a political party.

The largest number of independent newspapers and bulletins in Ukraine has been published by Rukh (over 30 titles from every region of Ukraine). The CPU leadership, though tolerating Rukh's existence, did everything in its power to block Rukh's growth. Thus, Rukh was not registered by the Council of Ministers or allowed to publish its official organ, Narodna hazeta, until February 1990. Because supplies of newsprint were restricted, the circulation of the newspaper was limited to 10,000 copies.

Two of the first neformaly to be established in Ukraine were the *Ukrainian Helsinki Group (UHG) and the Ukrainian Association of Independent Creative Intelligentsia. In August 1987 V. Chornovil, the dissident and former political prisoner (who was elected in 1990 to Ukraine's Supreme Council, and who also held the chairmanship of the Lviv Oblast Council), signaled the launching of the Ukrainian unofficial movement with his open letter to Gorbachev. The open letter announced the re-establishment on 30 December 1987 of the journal *Ukraïns'kyi visnyk, which he had edited as a *samvydav publication in 1970–2. The UHG was renamed the Ukrainian Helsinki Association in 1988, and attracted approx 600 members. At its congress in Kiev on 29–30 April 1990 the association was dissolved and replaced by the new Ukrainian Republican party. Headed by L. *Lukianenko, the party was the first non-Communist party registered in Ukraine.

The Ukrainian Association of Independent Creative Intelligentsia was formed in October 1987 as an unofficial writers' and cultural-workers' union. It has published the journal Kafedra, edited by M. Osadchy in Lviv, and four other literary journals: Ievshan zillia (Lviv), Skarby hir (Ivano-Frankivske), Porohy (Dnipropetrovske), and Snip (Kharkiv). One of the first neformaly formed in Kiev was the Ukrainian Culturological Club, in September 1987. With the increased politicization of the population, the club disbanded at the beginning of 1989, and its members joined the Helsinki Association and other groups. Among the most active cultural and educational groups in Ukraine has been Lviv's *Lev Society (est 1987).

The Memorial society held its founding congress on 4 March 1989 in Kiev. Its most active branches are in Lviv (which publishes Poklyk sumlinnia) and Ternopil (which publishes Dzvin) oblasts. The western branches of Memorial have undertaken to document the scope of repression carried out by Soviet occupational forces after the absorption of Western Ukraine into the Soviet Union.

Zelenyi Svit, which publishes a newspaper of the same name, held its founding congress in Kiev on 28–29 October 1989. It began as a purely ecological and anti–nuclear power group, but under the leadership of Yu. *Shcherbak it has become increasingly politicized. It joined the Democratic Bloc formed in November 1989 as an umbrella group of all neformaly during the Supreme Soviet election campaign, and a few days before the fourth anniversary of the Chornobyl nuclear accident on 22 April 1990, it launched the Green Party of Ukraine.

One of the first student neformaly was the Hromada society at Kiev University, formed in the spring of 1988. It represented the new generation of radical student activists brought to the fore under glasnost. Hromada published the uncensored journal Dzvin and organized numerous meetings in Kiev, including the first large student demonstration in November 1988, and a boycott of military education classes. By the middle of 1989 Hromada had ceased to exist. Most of its members joined new, more overtly political organizations.

Other youth and student *neformaly* were created in most Ukrainian cities and postsecondary schools. In February 1990 the western Ukrainian Student Brotherhood (which published the newspaper *Bratstvo* and the journal *Vikno)* and the Ukrainian Student Association in central and eastern Ukraine (which published the newspaper *Svoboda)* joined together to form the Confederation of Ukrainian Students and organized political mass strikes at universities and polytechnical institutes. A 1989 survey published in the Soviet Ukrainian press showed that over 800 new sociopolitical clubs were operating in Ukraine's postsecondary institutions. Some of the more significant youth groups created in the late 1980s were the nationalist Association of Independent Ukrainian Youth (the youth wing of the Ukrainian Helsinki Union), which published *Moloda Ukraïna* in Lviv and *Rada* in Kiev, and the revived scouting *Plast Ukrainian Youth Association. Over 20 new noncommunist political parties also emerged.

Ukrainians living in other Soviet republics also formed *neformaly*. The Moscow-based Slavutych Society, founded in 1988 and headed by the former cosmonaut P. Popovych, is among the most active. National minorities in Ukraine (Jews, Poles, Greeks, Hungarians, and Crimean Tatars) have also organized independent associations and published their own bulletins.

The *neformaly* and their publications attracted a mass following and readership and challenged the Communist monopoly of power. From the late 1980s they published some 200 independent, uncensored periodicals, with circulations ranging from 500 to 10,000. Although they were harassed by the authorities, the *neformaly* persevered and were the harbingers of a renewed civil society and national movement. The abolition of article 6 of the Constitution of the USSR (which enshrined the leading role of the CPSU in all spheres of life) allowed the possibility of a multiparty system and served to stimulate autonomous political activity and the articulation of bold political demands. The end result was the collapse of the Communist regime and the proclamation of Ukraine's independence in 1991.

T. Kuzio

Negrich, Ivan [Negryč] (Negrych), b 1876 in Bereziv, Kolomyia county, Galicia, d 25 October 1946 in Winnipeg.

Ivan Negrich

Teacher, community leader, and journalist. Active in the Galician Ukrainian radical movement, Negrich emigrated to Canada in 1897, where he attended Manitoba College (Presbyterian) in Winnipeg in 1900 and taught school in rural Manitoba. One of the initiators of the *Independent Greek church in 1903, and briefly a priest in it, he embraced the Russian Orthodox faith in 1908. He was also the first editor (1903–5) of *Kanadiis'ky farmer, the first Ukrainian newspaper in Canada. In 1916 he served as a member of the Ukrainian delegation that lobbied the government of Manitoba to retain the bilingual school system.

Nehalevsky Gospel (Nehalevskoho yevanheliie). A 16th-century literary monument, preserved at one time at St Michael's Monastery in Kiev. It is a translation of the four Gospels into vernacular Ukrainian made by V. Nehalevsky in 1581 in Khoroshiv, near Ostrih, on the basis of M. Czechowicz'z Polish translation of the New Testament (1577). The language is almost free of Church Slavonicisms, and its syntax and lexicon are strongly influenced by Polish. In places the Polish version has been transcribed in the Cyrillic alphabet. The gospel's language was analyzed by O. Nazarevsky (*Kievskiia universitetskiia izvestiia*, 1911, nos 8, 11–12), O. Nazariiv (*Zapysky NTSh*, vol 110 [1912]), and I. Ohiienko (1922).

Nehrebetsky, Ivan [Nehrebec'kyj], b 1853, d 25 May 1927 in Yasenytsia Silna, Drohobych county, Galicia. Greek Catholic priest and civic leader. He published and edited (1898–1905) the paper *Hospodar in Peremyshl and wrote popular books on farming (published by the Prosvita society) as well as articles in the press.

Nehrovets Ridge [Nehrovec']. A mountain ridge of the Carpathian Mountains in Transcarpathia oblast. The ridge stretches along the left bank of the Tereblia River and is bordered by the Gorgany Mountains in the north and the Krasna Ridge of the Polonynian Beskyd in the south. It rises to a height of 1,707 m. Conifers and beech trees grow on the lower slopes of the ridge; higher up there are thickets of mountain pines, alders, and Siberian junipers as well as patches of meadowlands. The ridge sits in an avalanche zone.

Neimark, Izrail [Nejmark, Izrajil], b 21 August 1907 in Pidhorodne, Novomoskovske county, Katerynoslav gubernia. Chemist. A graduate of the Dnipropetrovske Institute (1931), from 1933 he worked at the AN URSR (now ANU) Institute of Physical Chemistry, where he became a department head (1957–75) and a scientific consultant (from 1975). He studied the synthesis, structure determination, and surface chemistry of mineral adsorbents and catalyst carriers, and worked on theories of gas and water adsorption. He was the first in the USSR to synthesize molecular sieves (zeolites).

Nejedlý, Zdeněk, b 10 February 1878 in Litomyšl, Moravia, d 9 March 1962 in Prague. Czechoslovak statesman, historian, and music and literary critic; member of the Czech Academy of Sciences and Arts from 1907, full member of the Shevchenko Scientific Society from 1923, and founder and president (from 1952) of the Czechoslovak Academy of Sciences. A graduate of Prague University, he was a professor there (1909–39, 1945–62) and at

Moscow University (1939–45). In the interwar period he published a book (1920) about the Ukrainian Republican Kapelle and articles about the plight of Transcarpathia's Ukrainians, the Ukrainian question, T. Shevchenko, and O. Korniichuk. During the Second World War his articles on Transcarpathian history, Shevchenko, and Czech-Ukrainian relations appeared in periodicals published in Moscow. His archive contains book-length manuscripts on Galicia's Ukrainians under Austrian rule and on the history of Western Ukraine.

Nekhoda, Ivan [Nexoda], b 24 June 1910 in Oleksiivka, Bohodukhiv county, Kharkiv gubernia, d 17 October 1963 in Kiev. Socialist-realist poet and screenwriter. He completed studies at the Kharkiv Institute of People's Education in 1932 and later worked as a teacher on the editorial staff of the newspaper *Na zminu*. He was chief editor of the Molod publishing house (1945–57) and headed the Crimean branch of the Writers' Union of Ukraine (1957–63). A prolific poet, from 1931 on Nekhoda published some three dozen collections, many of them for children. He also wrote a novel in verse about the Second World War, *Khto siie viter* (Who Sows the Wind, 1959). Editions of his selected works appeared in 1949, 1956, 1960, and 1980.

Nekrashevych, Ivan [Nekraševyč], b 1742 in Vyshenky, Chernihiv regiment, d after 1796 in Vyshenky. Writer. He graduated from the Kiev Academy (1763) and returned to his native village to serve as a priest. He wrote a number of works of epistolary verse, the theological poem 'Spor dushi i tila' (The Struggle of the Soul and the Flesh, 1773 [published in 1873]), the versified dialogue 'Ispovid'' (Confession, 1789), and 'Iarmarok' (The Marketplace, 1790). Many scholars also attribute to him the dialogue 'Zamysl na popa' (A Design against the Priest). His humorous and satirical works were based on folk (mainly Chernihiv) dialect and were written in syllabo-tonic verse.

Nekrasov, Ihnat (Nekras), b ca 1660, d 1737. Don Cossack leader. He took over the Bulavin revolt in 1708 after the death of its leader and solicited the aid of the Zaporozhian Cossacks and other groups. The insurgency was suppressed, and Nekrasov led a group of followers into the Kuban, where he established and led a Cossack republic, continued to raid Russian-controlled territories, and maintained connections with figures such as Charles XII and P. Orlyk. In 1740 the so-called Nekrasovites resettled in Turkey, where they were granted a host of special privileges.

Nekrasov, Viktor, b 17 June 1911 in Kiev, d 3 September 1987 in Paris. Writer. After graduating from the Kiev Construction Institute (1936) and the actors' studio at the Kiev Russian Drama Theater (1937) he worked as an actor and set designer in Kiev. He wrote one of the best Russian-language novels about the war, *V okopakh Stalingrada* (In the Trenches of Stalingrad, 1946), for which he was awarded the 1947 Stalin Prize and was elected a member of the Presidium of the Writers' Union of Ukraine. His novel *V rodnom gorode* (In the Home Town, 1954) and various stories about the war and its social consequences were some of the earliest works of the post-Stalin thaw. His anti-Stalinist novel *Kira Georgievna* (1961) and collection of essays about his visit to Western Europe and the United States,

Po obe storony okeana (On Both Sides of the Ocean, 1962), were condemned by the Soviet authorities, including N. Khrushchev. In the late 1960s and 1970s he spoke out against the persecution of Russian and Ukrainian dissidents (eg, A. Solzhenitsyn, V. Chornovil). In 1973 he was expelled from the CPSU. He was granted permission to emigrate to France in 1974, where he worked as associate editor of the émigré-dissident journal *Kontinent*.

Nekrasov, Zot, b 8 January 1908 in Melitopil, Tavriia gubernia, d 1 December 1990 in Dnipropetrovske. Metallurgist; full member of the AN URSR (now ANU) from 1961. He graduated from the Dnipropetrovske Metallurgical Institute (1930), and in 1952–78 he headed the ANU Institute of Ferrous Metallurgy (until 1992 under the USSR Ministry of Ferrous Metallurgy). He made fundamental contributions in the fields of ferrous metallurgy, blast furnaces, and ores processing.

Nelepo, Boris, b 15 August 1932 in Moscow. Oceanographer; AN URSR (now ANU) corresponding member since 1976 and full member since 1978. A graduate of Moscow University (1955), since 1963 he has worked at the ANU *Marine Hydrophysical Institute in Sevastopil and served as its director (1974–85). In 1980 he was elected a member and an academic secretary of the ANU presidium. He has contributed to the fields of ocean dynamics and nuclear hydrophysics, studied hydrophysics via satellites and the automation of oceanographic measurements, invented devices for measuring oceanic radioactivity, and written a monograph on nuclear hydrophysics (1970).

Metropolitan Yosyf Neliubovych-Tukalsky

Neliubovych-Tukalsky, Yosyf [Neljubovyč-Tukal'-s'kyj, Josyf], b ?, d 26 July 1675 in Chyhyryn. Orthodox churchman. He served as archimandrite of the Holy Ghost Monastery in Vilnius (1657–8) and participated in the 1657 church sobor in Kiev, where he was nominated as metropolitan. In 1661 he was consecrated bishop of Orsha and Mstsislau, and in 1663 a sobor of clergy, nobility, and Cossack officers in Korsun elected him metropolitan of Kiev. When this election was not confirmed by the Polish king (who supported the candidacy of Bishop A. *Vynnytsky), an administrative schism erupted in the church, and Tukalsky retained authority over only a part of the Ukrainian church province: Right-Bank Ukraine, Belarus, and Lithuania (but not Galicia, Volhynia, and Podilia). An opponent of Hetman P. Teteria and the Polish government, he was arrested in 1664 and imprisoned in the Marienburg fortress for two years. After Hetman P. *Doroshenko secured his release, Tukalsky resumed the metropolitan's post and settled near the hetman's residence in Chyhyryn; the Patriarch of Constantinople confirmed his election as metropolitan and exarch in 1668. He served as Doroshenko's close adviser and supported his pro-Turkish and anti-Polish and -Russian policies. In church affairs he opposed any rapprochement with the Moscow patriarchate, which stance brought him in opposition to the representative of the Moscow patriarch in Kiev, M. *Fylymonovych. After Tukalsky's death his remains were moved to the Mhar Transfiguration Monastery, and his archives were stored at the Kievan Cave Monastery.

I. Korovytsky

Nemet, Myroslav, b 14 June 1943 in Malyi Bereznyi, Transcarpathia. Ukrainian writer in the Prešov region of Slovakia. He graduated from the Prešov division of Košice University in 1966 and since then has worked as an editor with the Ukrainian literature department of the Slovak Pedagogical Publishing House in Prešov. He is the author of three collections of lyrical, love, and didactic poetry – *Poliusy sertsia* (The Poles of the Heart, 1968), *Pryboï* (Breakers, 1975), and *Svit v zeleni* (The World in Verdure, 1978) – and of the story collections *Opovidannia z-pid hory* (Stories from beneath the Mountain, 1984) and *Ostannie vesillia* (The Last Wedding, 1989).

Nemoshkalenko, Volodymyr [Nemoškalenko], b 26 March 1933 in Stalingrad (now Volgograd), Russia. Physicist; full AN URSR (now ANU) member since 1982. After graduating from the Kiev Polytechnical Institute (1956) he joined the ANU Institute of Metal Physics, where he became a department head in 1963 and deputy director in 1973. Using X-ray spectroscopy, he has investigated the electronic structure of real solids, particularly transition metals and their alloys, and contributed significantly to the understanding of the changes in electronic structure that occur in the transition of solids from a crystalline to an amorphous state.

Nemyriv. III-4. A town smt (1990 pop 2,100) in Yavoriv raion, Lviv oblast. In 1580 it was granted the rights of *Magdeburg law. Because of its hydrogen sulfide springs a balneological health resort was established there in 1815. The town is still known for its mineral baths, which are used to treat cardiovascular, skin, and nerve disorders.

Nemyriv. V-9. A city (1990 pop 11,400) and raion center in Vinnytsia oblast. It was founded at the end of the 14th century, and came under Polish rule after the Union of Lublin (1569), under Turkish rule (1672–99), and under Russian rule after the partition of Poland in 1793. It attained city status in 1985. Nemyriv has several enterprises of the food industry. Its architectural monuments include a 19th-century palace and park and two churches, built in 1801 and 1881.

Nemyriv fortified settlement. An Early Scythian (7th–6th century BC) fortified settlement on both banks of a tributary of the Boh River near Sazhky, Nemyriv raion, Vinnytsia oblast. Excavations from 1909 to 1948 identified the remains of defensive earthen walls and trenches. It was found that the inhabitants lived in large (up to 6 m in diameter) pit dwellings. Clay ovens, earthenware, and bronze arrowheads were among the artifacts recovered at the site.

Nemyrovsky, Yevhen [Nemyrovs'kyj, Jevhen], b 24 April 1925 in Zinovivske (now Kirovohrad). Library scientist. He graduated from the Moscow Correspondence Printing Institute (1950) and headed a department at the State Library of the USSR from 1974 (professor from 1979). His works deal with the history of Slavic book printing in Cyrillic; among them are three studies of I. Fedorovych (1964, 1974, 1979).

Nemyrovych, Ivan [Nemyrovyč], b 20 February 1928 in Nyzhnodniprovske (now part of Dnipropetrovske), d 17 June 1986 in Kiev. Writer and banduryst. He played with the Dnipropetrovske Philharmonic after the Second World War and with the State Bandurist Kapelle of the Ukrainian SSR from 1953. From 1959 to 1964 he was assistant director and then director of the Republican Building of Litterateurs in Kiev. He graduated from the Faculty of Journalism of Kiev University in 1965 and later worked for the satirical magazine *Perets'*. From 1956 on he published over 30 books of poetry and humor and satire. Nemyrovych also wrote a book about the composer O. Bilash (1979), the novel *Na bilomu koni* (On a White Horse, 1979), and a book of essays about contemporary Ukrainian kobzars and bandurysts (1986). Published posthumously were selections of his humorous novelettes (1987) and poetry (1988).

Nemyrych [Nemyryč] (Polish: Niemirycz). Originally an Orthodox noble family in Right-Bank Ukraine, known from 1528. Yosyf was the judge of the Kiev land court (1580–90). His son Andrii (d 1610) replaced him and began a branch of the family in Cherniakhiv, north of Zhytomyr. Andrii's son, Stefan (d 1630), studied before 1610 at the Altdorf Academy and Basel University in Switzerland, converted to *Socinianism, and established a Socinian center in Cherniakhiv and other congregations in Volhynia. He served as chamberlain of Kiev (ca 1623–30) and was a member of the Polish commission that negotiated the 1625 Treaty of *Kurukove with the Cossacks. At the end of his life he owned 12 towns and 75 villages in Volhynia and the Kiev region. Yurii *Nemyrych and Stefan *Nemyrych were his sons. Stefan's heirs continued a Polonized line of the family into the 20th century. A second line of the family, in Olevske, was descended from Yosyf's son Matvii, the founder of the Lublin Orthodox Brotherhood. It became Polonized and Catholic in the second half of the 17th century and died out in the 18th.

Nemyrych, Stefan [Nemyryč] (Polish: Niemirycz), b ca 1626–30, d 22 February 1684. Ukrainian magnate and religious and military leader; brother of Yu. *Nemyrych. He studied at the Socinian academy in Kyselyn, Volhynia, and abroad (1646–8), in Amsterdam, Orléans, and Geneva. During the Cossack-Polish War he was appointed standard-bearer of Kiev and, in 1656, a Polish cavalry commander. Under his brother's influence he switched to the Cossack side and was a delegate at the Sejm of 1659 that ratified the Treaty of Hadiache. Under Hetman I. Vyhovsky he was general of the artillery of the Grand Duchy of Ruthenia from 11 June 1659. In 1661 he was elected Polish chamberlain of Kiev. In 1663 he emigrated to Silesia because of Polish persecution of the Socinians and became a general of the artillery in the army of Frederick William of Brandenburg-Prussia. He returned to Poland in 1680, converted to Catholicism, and served as castellan (1680–2) and voivode (1682–4) of Kiev.

Nemyrych, Yurii [Nemyryč, Jurij] (Polish: Niemirycz, Jerzy), b 1612, d August 1659. Ukrainian magnate and political and military leader. He studied at the Arian academy in Raków and, in 1630–4, at Leiden and Basel universities and in England, France, and Italy. He led a private army during Poland's wars with Muscovy and Sweden in the 1630s. In 1641 he was elected chamberlain of Kiev. As the recognized leader of the Ukrainian *Socinians he defended their rights at the 1636 Lublin Tribunal and the 1637–9 sejms. He took part in public debates with the Jesuits and was one of the founders of the Arian academy in Kyselyn, Volhynia. By 1648 Nemyrych owned an immense latifundium consisting of 14 towns and over 50 villages in Volhynia and the Kiev region and huge tracts of land in Left-Bank Ukraine between the Psol and the Orel rivers. During the Cossack-Polish War of 1648–57 and the Polish-Muscovite War of 1654 he was the Polish colonel general of Kiev voivodeship.

From 1648 Nemyrych supported the candidacy of the Transylvanian prince György Rákóczi I for the Polish throne. In 1655 he joined the side of King Charles X Gustav of Sweden, received the rank of major general in the cavalry, and acted as a Swedish envoy to Transylvania, the Hetman state, and Poland. In the summer of 1657 he switched to the Ukrainian side, converted to Orthodoxy, was appointed a colonel, and reclaimed his Left-Bank holdings. Nemyrych represented Sweden at the Cossack *Korsun Council, which elected I. Vyhovsky hetman, and in October 1657 he signed the Swedish-Ukrainian military alliance against Poland. He conceived the idea of the creation of the autonomous Grand Duchy of Ruthenia within the Polish Commonwealth and wrote the expanded draft of the Treaty of *Hadiache and the Hetmanate government's 1658 manifesto to the European states. As chancellor of the grand duchy in 1659, he headed the Ukrainian delegation to the Sejm that ratified the Treaty of Hadiache, and he fought in the Battle of Konotip (1659). During the Cossack uprising against Hetman Vyhovsky he commanded a detachment loyal to Vyhovsky and was slain by insurgents near Kobyzhcha, in the Chernihiv region.

Nemyrych wrote the historical treatise *Discursus de bello Moscovitico anno 1632* (1632), a Polish poem on the duties of a Christian knight, *Panoplia ...* (Panoply, 1653), Arian prayers in Polish, and a famous speech, delivered in the Sejm on 23 April 1659.

BIBLIOGRAPHY
Kot, S. *Georges Niemirycz et la lutte contre l'intolérance au 17e siècle* (The Hague 1960)
Tazbir, J. 'The Political Reversals of Jurij Nemyryč,' HUS, 5, no. 3 (September 1981)

O. Ohloblyn

Nenadkevych, Lidiia [Nenadkevyč, Lidija] (née Huguenin), b 1892 in Geneva, d 25 June 1956 in Poughkeepsie, New York. Collector of and specialist in em-broidery. She was raised in Zhytomyr, and studied applied art in Kiev and taught courses in embroidery. Her unique collection of 90 embroidered blouses, 48 ceremonial towels, kilims, wraparound skirts, belts, and over 300 transcriptions of embroidery designs, which she had amassed over many years, was destroyed in Berlin in 1945. As a postwar refugee in the United States, she contributed articles on Ukrainian embroidery to journals such as *Nashe zhyttia* and *Zhinochyi svit*.

Nenadkevych, Yevhen [Nenadkevyč, Jevhen], b 29 December 1882 in Dovhalivka, Dubno county, Volhynia gubernia, d 30 September 1966 in Zhytomyr. Literary scholar and pedagogue. A professor at the Zhytomyr (1920–9) and Nizhen (1930–3) institutes of people's education, he was arrested in 1933 and exiled. He worked at the Mordovian and Perm pedagogical institutes until his return to Zhytomyr in 1947. He wrote studies of the works of V. Stefanyk, I. Franko, Lesia Ukrainka, and T. Shevchenko, including *Tvorchist' T. Shevchenka pislia zaslannia, 1857–8* (The Post-Exile Works of T. Shevchenko, 1857–8, 1956) and *Z tvorchoï laboratoriï T. Shevchenka* (From the Creative Laboratory of T. Shevchenko, 1959).

Nenasytets Rapid [Nenasytec'kyj porih]. The fifth and largest of the *Dnieper Rapids before the construction of the Dnieper Hydroelectric Station. Also known as Did, Revuchyi, or Rozbiinyk, it was the most dangerous section of the waterway, with a drop of 5.8 m over its 1,750-m length and a water flow that reached up to 4.1 m/second. It was also the only one of the nine rapids that did not freeze over during the winter.

Neo-Byzantinism. A term for numerous modern variants of art which are influenced, to various degrees, by *Byzantine art. In 1910 G. Apollinaire applied the term to the art of M. *Boichuk. In the 1920s Boichuk and members of his school revived the use of ancient techniques, such as fresco and egg tempera, in their murals. The style prevailing in modern Ukrainian church art, particularly in the West, since the 1950s has been called neo-Byzantine. Among the first artists to work in this style in Western Ukraine were P. Kholodny, Sr, M. Sosenko, and V. Kryzhanivsky. Other artists whose work can be considered neo-Byzantine are S. Hordynsky, I. Dyky, Yu. Mokrytsky, V. Konash-Konashevych, P. Kholodny, Jr, and S. Zarytska.

Neoclassicism. A term designating the revival of interest in classical art and architecture in the 20th century. (For earlier revivals see *Classicism.) It has been most visible in architecture, where an eclectic combination of classical styles has been used. Neoclassicism has been popular under totalitarian regimes, such as those of Nazi Germany, Fascist Italy, and the USSR, where the construction of massive public buildings with neoclassical colonnades, arches, and exaggerated decorations was characteristic of most architecture built in the Stalin era and became known as Stalinist architecture. Neoclassical buildings in Kiev include those of the Council of Ministers (architects, I. Fomin and P. Abrosimov, 1936–8), the Supreme Soviet (architect, V. Zabolotny, 1936–9), and the CC CPU (architect, J. Langbard, 1936–9) and the pavilions of the Exhibition of Economic Achievements (1951–7). Examples of

Stalinist architecture of the 1950s can be seen throughout Ukraine.

Members of the Neoclassicists. Sitting, from left: Oswald Burghardt, Pavlo Fylypovych, Borys Yakubsky, and Maksym Rylsky; standing: Viktor Petrov and Mykola Zerov

Neoclassicists (*neokliasyky*). A literary movement of the 1920s. The nucleus of the group consisted of M. *Zerov, M. *Rylsky, P. *Fylypovych, M. *Drai-Khmara, and O. Burghardt (Yu. *Klen) – the *piatirne grono* (cluster of five), as Drai-Khmara called them in his sonnet 'Lebedi' (The Swans). They never established a formal organization or program, but they shared cultural and esthetic interests. M. *Mohyliansky, V. *Petrov, and others are also included in this loose grouping. The group's name is derived from their use of themes and images of antiquity and was given to them by their opponents in the *Literary Discussion of 1925–8. The Neoclassicists were self-consciously concerned with the production of high art and disdained 'mass art,' didactic writing, and propagandistic work. Their opponents, in contrast, organized themselves around writers who were supported by the Communist party, and viewed literature in a primarily utilitarian fashion, that is, as a means of strengthening Soviet rule in Ukraine.

The works of the Neoclassicists were anti-Romantic and antifolkloric. They sought universal themes and considered Ukrainian culture to be an organic part of Western European culture. The closest to what could be considered their program is clearly set out in Zerov's *Do dzherel* (To the Sources, 1926). 'We should,' he wrote, 'assimilate the highest culture of our times, not only in its latest manifestations, but also in its original forms.' From that commitment stemmed the demands the Neoclassicists made of a writer: (1) a comprehensive knowledge of the best works of Ukrainian literature; (2) a comprehensive knowledge of the achievements of world literature; and (3) poetic craftsmanship of the highest level. High art, in their view, could be conveyed only through clarity of thought and mastery

of form. Their poetry, therefore, is characterized by balance, plasticity of image, and logical ordering of subject and composition. The main purpose of literature, as they perceived it, was esthetic; they rejected the tendentiousness, agitation, and moralizing of their contemporaries. In order to gain a knowledge of world literature most of them translated into Ukrainian selected works, ranging from those of antiquity to those of the Parnassians in France. Individual Neoclassicists gravitated toward particular styles: Rylsky and Fylypovych to symbolism, Klen (Burghardt) to neoromanticism.

In the 1930s Zerov, Fylypovych, and Drai-Khmara were sent to Soviet concentration camps and executed. Rylsky was forced to publish socialist-realist works, and Burghardt emigrated to the West, where he wrote under the pseudonym Yu. Klen. The tradition of the Neoclassicists was continued among émigré poets, most notably by M. *Orest.

In the 1960s the Neoclassicists were partially rehabilitated. After 20 years of stagnation, a slow movement to full rehabilitation began in the late 1980s.

BIBLIOGRAPHY
Dosvitnii, O. 'Neokliasyky,' *Vaplite*, 1 (1926)
Klen, Iu. *Spohady pro neokliasykiv* (Munich 1947)
Hordynsky, S. 'The Fivefold Cluster of Unvanquished Bards,' *Ukrainian Quarterly*, 1949, no. 3
Sherekh, Iu. 'Legenda pro ukraïns'kyi neokliasytsyzm,' in his *Ne dlia ditei* (Munich 1964)
Struk, D. 'The Kievan Neoclassicists.' MA thesis, University of Alberta, 1964

S. Hordynsky

Neolithic Period. The closing phase of the Stone Age, lasting in Ukraine from ca 5000 to 2500 BC. The Neolithic Period was characterized by the development of agriculture and pottery manufacturing, the establishment of sedentary agriculturally based settlements, the use of polishing techniques for stone tools, the emergence of increasingly complex systems of religious belief, and the growth of tribal social orders. This epoch was also marked by the existence of a greater diversity of cultures than in either the Paleolithic or Mesolithic periods. By far the most developed culture was the agrarian *Trypilian culture, which existed throughout most of Right-Bank Ukraine until the Bronze Age. Other groups that existed during this period include the *Pitted-Comb Pottery, *Serednii Stih, *Boh-Dniester, and *Tisza cultures. The Neolithic Period ended with the introduction of metal technology during the *Eneolithic Period or the *Bronze Age.

BIBLIOGRAPHY
Danilenko, V. *Neolit Ukrainy* (Kiev 1969)
Arkheolohiia Ukraïns'koï RSR, vol 1 (Kiev 1971)

Neounion (*Neouniia*). The unofficial name for the campaign to spread Eastern rite Catholicism among the Ukrainian and Belarusian Orthodox population in territories occupied by Poland during the interwar period. Structured around a body known as the Parishes of the Eastern Slavic Rite Catholic Church (Polish: Parafje Kościoła Katolickiego Wschodnio-Słowiańskiego Obrzędu), neounionism was conceived to attract converts to the Catholic church in Eastern Europe. The action was focused on Volhynia, the Kholm region, and western Belarus, the areas of interwar

Poland with a significant Orthodox population. It did not involve the Ukrainian Catholic church, whose jurisdiction was limited by the *Concordat of 1925 to Galicia.

In spite of its promotion of the Eastern rite, the neounion campaign was infused with a strong Latin orientation. The movement was conceived and promoted by a group of Jesuit priests which included J. Urban, the editor of the journal *Oriens*. Neounion priests were trained almost exclusively in the Latin rite seminaries in Lublin, Pynske, and Vilnius, which offered supplementary courses in Eastern Christianity (the new church also attracted some Ukrainian Orthodox priests). Neounion parishes were placed directly under the jurisdiction of Roman Catholic bishops.

The neounion experiment received papal approval in 1924, and work commenced immediately thereafter to establish parishes. The effort was generally greeted with suspicion by the local Orthodox population, which derisively dubbed it 'the government union' (*zhondova uniia*). Although it gained adherents, it failed to establish itself as a mass movement. Some attempts were made to strengthen the effort with the appointment in 1931 of an apostolic visitator for the fledgling church body, M. *Charnetsky, who was elevated to the position of bishop of Kovel (although never granted the full authority of a bishop), and the opening (1931) of an Eastern rite seminary in the Volhynian city of Dubno. These actions, however, brought little benefit. The neounion experiment lasted until the outbreak of the Second World War, at which time it had (according to official estimates) approx 25,000 adherents and 46 priests.

Nepmen. Private entrepreneurs during the period of the *New Economic Policy (NEP), introduced in 1921 in the USSR. The nepmen were not a large group in Soviet Ukraine. In late 1926, at the height of the NEP, they and their dependents constituted some 6 percent of the population. The largest contingent consisted of 325,000 self-employed persons in the cottage industry, construction, and transportation, and 99,000 self-employed in retail trade. A smaller number hired labor: 381 large and small factory owners (1,512 people if family members are included); 20,000 in the cottage industry, construction, and transportation; and 3,800 retailers. Nepmen who were employers represented 0.3 percent of the urban population. Farmers who hired labor were usually called *kulaks; they constituted about 1 percent of the population. (Those who employed hired labor were officially classified as exploiters, whereas people working alone or with members of their families were also often considered nepmen.)

Almost immediately after the introduction of the NEP the Soviet government began a struggle against the 'bourgeois' nepmen, which intensified after V. Lenin's death, particularly under J. Stalin's rule. The campaign classified them as social enemies, deprived them of the right to vote, and did not allow their children to enter institutions of higher learning. Nepmen were also subjected to a higher tax rate, which was often entirely arbitrary and in excess of their income. Finally, they were the first victims in the campaign to expropriate gold and valuables that was carried out in the late 1920s and early 1930s. All persons suspected of holding gold or foreign currency were arrested for an indefinite period, subjected to cruel interrogation, and occasionally tortured until they agreed to turn over

their valuables to the government for free.

After the industrialization policy was introduced, the tax rate imposed on nepmen grew rapidly, and they were effectively squeezed out of the economic life of the country, sometimes completely bankrupted, and exiled from the large cities as antisocial elements. Retailers and wholesalers of agricultural products were subjected to even greater persecution, and few of them escaped arrest and imprisonment. The only nepmen who survived industrialization were artisans, who were permitted to form *artels and continue their work on a co-operative basis.

BIBLIOGRAPHY
Ocherki razvitiia narodnogo khoziastva Ukrainskoi SSR (Moscow 1954)
Morozov, L. *Reshaiushchii etap bor'by s nepmanskoi burzhuaziei (1926–1929)* (Moscow 1960)
Novaia ekonomicheskaia politika: Voprosy teorii i istorii (Moscow 1974)
Ball, A.M. *Russia's Last Capitalists: The Nepmen, 1921–1929* (Berkeley, Los Angeles, and London 1987)

A. Babyonyshev

***Nepokhozhi* peasants** (*nepokhozhi seliany, nepokhozhi liudy*). A major category of manorial peasants in the 14th- to 16th-century Lithuanian-Ruthenian state. Unlike the *pokhozhi peasants, they did not have the right to move from one feudal lord to another. The lord owned the land they used, as well as their tools and domestic possessions, and had the right to judge, punish, sell, trade, or give them away. The peasants had to pay *quitrents and perform corvée and other obligations for the lord. Free peasants became *nepokhozhi* ('immobile') if the land they lived on belonged to the grand duke and he awarded or sold it to a lord, if they became personally indebted to a lord and could not repay their debts, or 10 years after they voluntarily settled on land owned by a lord. The *nepokhozhi* peasants' dependent status was ratified in a privilege issued by Casimir IV Jagiellończyk in 1447. Their sale and purchase with or without land was legalized by the 1529 Lithuanian Statute. After the 1569 Union of Lublin the term *nepokhozhi* fell out of use, but the institution of dependent manorial peasants (called *kholopy, otchychi, panski liudy*) remained, and in the 1588 Lithuanian Statute they were all enserfed.

Neporozhnii, Petro [Neporožnij], b 13 July 1910 in Tuzhylivka (now part of Yahotyn), Pyriatyn county, Poltava gubernia. Engineer and electrical power construction administrator; member of the Ukrainian SSR and USSR Academies of Construction and Architecture (1956–63) and corresponding member of the USSR Academy of Sciences from 1979. He graduated from the Leningrad Institute of Water Transport Engineers (1933) and worked on the construction of major hydroelectric stations in Svirsk and Kakhivka. He was deputy head of the Ukrainian SSR Council of Ministers, head of the State Building Committee (1954–9), and USSR minister of energy and electrification (1962–85).

Neprytsky-Hranovsky, Oleksander. See Granovsky, Alexander.

Nepyipyvo, Vasyl [Nepyjpyvo, Vasyl'], b 10 January 1916 in Kamianka, Poltava county. Painter. A self-taught

Vasyl Nepyipyvo: *The Nativity Church* (oil)

artist, he is known for his lyrical landscapes, such as *Koncha-Zaspa* (1959), *Vorskla River* (1960), *Wheat* (1967), and *Dnieper Slopes* (1968). An album of his paintings was published in 1986. He has created some 700 works.

Neronovych, Yevhen [Neronovyč, Jevhen], b 1888 in Sorochyntsi, Myrhorod county, Poltava gubernia, d April 1918 in Sorochyntsi. Political leader. Before the First World War he was a student activist in St Petersburg and an editor of *Ukraïns'kyi student* (1913). After the February Revolution he was active in the Ukrainian Social Democratic Workers' party (USDRP) and was a member of the Central Rada and its Little Rada. He was a member of the organizing committee of the Third All-Ukrainian Military Congress, held in Kiev in November 1917. Soon after the congress he left the Rada and came to lead the *Ukrainian Social Democratic Workers' party (Independentists), which supported co-operation with the Bolsheviks. In March 1918 he briefly served as people's secretary of war in M. Skrypnyk's Bolshevik government in Poltava, but soon thereafter he left the government over political differences. He was captured and shot as a traitor by UNR soldiers. In 1925 Sorochyntsi (now Velyki Sorochyntsi) was renamed Neronovychi in his honor, but the name was rescinded in 1931.

Nerovetsky, Oleksander [Nerovec'kyj], b 17 March 1884 in Cherkasy, Kiev gubernia, d 31 December 1950 in Kiev. Construction technologist and organizer; member of the Academy of Architecture of the Ukrainian SSR from 1945 and corresponding member of the USSR Academy of Architecture from 1941. He graduated from the Kiev Polytechnical Institute (1907) and worked on major construction projects, including the Kharkiv Tractor Factory and the Kramatorske Machine-Building Plant. He was a professor at the Kharkiv (from 1934) and Kiev (from 1944) civil-engineering institutes and headed the Ukrainian Scientific Research Institute of Buildings in Kharkiv (1936–9), the Institute of Construction Technology in Kiev (1945–8), and the Department of Civil Engineering at the Ukrainian SSR Academy of Architecture (1947–50).

Nerunovych, Inokentii [Nerunovyč, Inokentij], b ? in Kiev, d 26 July 1747 in Irkutsk, Siberia. Churchman, mis-

sionary, and pedagogue. A graduate of the Kievan Mohyla Academy (1721), he taught rhetoric and poetics there before becoming a professor at (1728) and prefect of (1731–2) the Slavonic-Greek-Latin Academy in Moscow. From 1732 he served as bishop of Irkutsk, and he gained fame as one of the greatest missionaries of Siberia. Some scholars (M. Vozniak, L. Makhnovets) attribute to him the drama *Mylost' Bozhiia* (God's Mercy).

Neshchadymenko, Marko [Neščadymenko], b 15 May 1869 in Serdehivka, Zvenyhorodka county, Kiev gubernia, d 1 October 1942. Microbiologist. A graduate of Kiev University (1896), he worked at the Kiev Bacteriological Institute and chaired the microbiology department at the university (1919–41). His publications deal with problems in immunology and bacteriology, such as the action of the diphtheria toxin, the properties of streptococci, and the preventive role of tuberculosis vaccines.

Ryta Neshchadymenko

Neshchadymenko, Ryta [Neščadymenko] (Kharytyna), b 13 April 1890 in Serdehivka, Zvenyhorodka county, Kiev gubernia, d 25 April 1926 in Kiev. Actress. In 1914–15 she studied at F. Komissarzhevsky's studio in Moscow. In 1918 she joined Molodyi Teatr and became a supporter of L. *Kurbas's method. She worked with him in the Shevchenko First Theater of the Ukrainian Soviet Republic (1919–20), in Kyidramte (1920–2), and in Berezil (1922–6).

Neshcheretove kurhans. Burial mounds located on the Bila River near Neshcheretove, Bilokurakyne raion, Luhanske oblast. Excavations in 1928–9 uncovered nine mounds, most of them from the Bronze Age. Two particularly interesting kurhans from the 2nd to 3rd century AD revealed Sarmatian corpses with deformed craniums. Earthenware, a section of an iron sword, and elaborate silver buckles were also found.

Neslukhiv settlement. A multi-occupational settlement on the Buh River near Neslukhiv, Kamianka-Buzka raion, Lviv oblast. Excavations in 1898–1903 and 1946 uncovered evidence of settlements from the *Bronze Age, the *Cherniakhiv culture, the 7th to 9th centuries, and the 12th to 13th centuries. Semi-pit or surface dwellings and storage pits from each era were uncovered. The site also contained remains of kilns, hand-built and thrown pottery, amphoras, and decorative glass, as well as bone, iron, and bronze items.

Nestaiko, Vsevolod [Nestajko], b 30 January 1930 in Berdychiv, Zhytomyr oblast. Children's writer. He has worked on the editorial staff of the journals *Dnipro* and *Barvinok* and the publishing houses Molod and Veselka (from 1956). He has written numerous books for children, including *Shurka i Shurko* (Shurka and Shurko, 1956), *Kosmo-Natka* (Cosmo-Nat, 1963), *Nadzvychaini pryhody Robinzona Kukuruzo ...* (The Extraordinary Adventures of Robinson Cucurusoe ..., 1964), *Taiemnytsia tr'okh nevidomykh* (The Secret of the Three Strangers, 1970), *Pryhody zhuravlyka* (Adventures of a Little Crane, 1979), and *Zahadka staroho klouna* (The Enigma of the Old Clown, 1982). Nestaiko's TV film *Toreadory z Vasiukivky* (Toreadors from Vasiukivka) received the grand prize at an international festival in Munich in 1968, and his novelette of the same name (1973) was placed on the H.C. Andersen List of Distinction by the International Board on Books for Young People (Basel) in 1979. An edition of his selected novelettes appeared in 1986.

Nesterenko, Anatolii, b 6 April 1899 in Blahodatne, Yelysavethrad county, Kherson gubernia, d 30 May 1975 in Kiev. Electrical engineer; corresponding member of the AN URSR (now ANU) from 1951. He studied and taught at the Kiev Polytechnical Institute and worked in the field of electrical technology. He headed a laboratory at the Institute of Energetics of the USSR Academy of Sciences (1936–8) and managed the construction of an electrical instruments factory. He directed the ANU Institute of Electrodynamics (1951–9). His main technical contributions were in the field of electrical instrumentation and measurement.

Nesterenko, Dmytro, b ?, d November 1708 in Hlukhiv, Nizhen regiment. Captain of Baturyn company in Nizhen regiment (1691–1708). One of Hetman I. Mazepa's closest aides, he took part in peace negotiations with Turkey in Constantinople in 1699 and conducted talks on Mazepa's behalf at the Zaporozhian Sich concerning the Bulavin rebellion in 1708. Along with D. Chechel and F. von Königsek he commanded the defense of Baturyn during the Russian offensive in 1708. He was taken prisoner and executed.

Nesterenko, Ivan, b 18 May 1950 in Brovarky, Zolotonosha raion, Cherkasy oblast. Painter and sculptor. He studied at the Lviv Institute of Applied and Decorative Arts. He paints ornamental symmetrical designs and figurative compositions. Nesterenko's paintings on glass (eg, *My Brother Mykola*, 1970s) convey the charm of folk art through simplified shapes and the hieratic use of space. The sophisticated primitivistic figures in his oils and gouaches are rendered with little modeling (eg, *Cold Summer*, 1973–6). His sculptures, constructed of found objects, metal, and wood, are more in tune with the whimsical three-dimensional works of P. Klee and J. Miró than with socialist realism. A combination of folk-art motifs and often humorous cutout figural silhouettes adorns Nesterenko's weather vanes (eg, *Kozak*, 1980s). His first solo show was held in 1988 in Kiev.

Nesterenko, Maksym, b and d ? Cossack leader and diplomat. In 1637 he took part in the uprising led by P. Pavliuk and K. Skydan and became colonel of the Korsun Regiment of registered Cossacks (1637–8). In 1646, togeth-

Ivan Nesterenko: *Goat* (wood sculpture at the Pereiaslav-Khmelnytskyi Museum of Folk Architecture and Folkways)

er with B. Khmelnytsky, he took part in secret negotiations with King Władysław IV Vasa regarding a Cossack offensive against Turkey. From December 1649 to March 1650 he headed Hetman Khmelnytsky's mission in Warsaw that negotiated ratification of the Treaty of Zboriv. He served as colonel of Korsun regiment in 1653. In 1655 he and I. Bohun led a Cossack detachment that defended the Bratslav region from the Crimean Tatars

Nesterenko, Oleksii, b 4 March 1904 in Prystan, Okhtyrka county, Kharkiv gubernia. Economist; corresponding member of the AN URSR (now ANU) since 1958. After graduating from the Kharkiv Institute of Communist Education (1930) he worked for the Ministry of Education of the Ukrainian SSR. He chaired the department of political economy at Kiev University (1946–8), directed the ANU Institute of Social Sciences in Lviv (1951–3) and the Institute of Economics (1953–65), and then served as a professor of political economy at the Kiev Trade and Economics Institute. His works deal with the development of Ukrainian industry and the working class and include *Rozvytok promyslovosti na Ukraïni* (The Development of Industry in Ukraine, 3 vols, 1959–66), *Ocherki istorii promyshlennosti i polozheniia proletariata Ukrainy* (Outlines of the History of Industry and the Condition of the Proletariat of Ukraine, 1954), *Zakonomernosti sotsial'no-ekonomicheskogo razvitiia goroda i derevni* (The Patterns of the Socioeconomic Development of the City and Countryside, 1975), and *Vozvyshenie potrebnostei v usloviiakh razvitogo sotsializma* (Rising Expectations under the Conditions of Developed Socialism, 1981).

Nesterov, Pavel, b 23 February 1903 in Tula, Russia, d 17 October 1978 in Kharkiv. Mining mechanics specialist; corresponding member of the AN URSR (now ANU) from 1948. He graduated from the Moscow Mining Institute (1932), and from 1948 he worked in the Kharkiv Mining Institute (now the Kharkiv Institute of Radioelectronics). His main contributions were in the design and development of mining machinery and apparatus.

A 17th-century street arcade in Nesterov

Nesterov. III-4. A city (1990 pop 12,900) on the Svynia River and a raion center in Lviv oblast. In 1951 its name was changed from Zhovkva to Nesterov in honor of P. *Nesterov. According to archeological evidence the site was inhabited as early as the 3rd or 2nd century BC. A settlement at the location is first mentioned in historical documents in 1368. In 1603 the town was named Zhovkva and was granted the rights of *Magdeburg law. A castle was built to protect the town from Tatar raids, and King Jan III Sobieski established a residence there. Zhovkva developed into a trade and manufacturing center. It was noted for its talented craftsmen and artists, who at the beginning of the 18th century formed the *Zhovkva School of Artists. The town was also an important religious center, with many churches and monasteries. .The *Zhovkva Monastery of the Basilian order, which was built in the 17th century, developed into an important publishing center at the end of the 19th century. Nesterov's architectural monuments include the large, well-preserved castle, a Dominican church and monastery from the 17th century, a synagogue, two wooden churches from the beginning of the 18th century, the Basilian church and monastery, which were restored in 1907, the remnants of the brick defensive walls and two city gates, and the old market square with some original buildings. The oldest and most important industry in Nesterov is glass-making, but there are also a canning and a brick factory.

Nestor the Chronicler (Nestor litopysets), b ca 1056, d ca 27 October 1114 in Kiev. Famous medieval hagiographer and chronicler; saint in the Ukrainian church. The

Nestor the Chronicler (engraving by Leontii Tarasevych, 1702)

date of his canonization is uncertain. He entered the Kievan Cave Monastery at 17 and was a hierodeacon under Hegumen Stefan (1074–8). He participated in the ceremonial disinterment of the relics of St Theodosius of the Caves in 1091. The earliest biography of Nestor appeared in the Kievan Cave Patericon (pub 1661). He was one of the most educated men in late 11th- and early 12th-century Rus', renowned for his knowledge of theology, history, literature, and Greek. Nestor wrote the lives of SS Borys and Hlib and St Theodosius of the Caves in the 1080s, and he supplemented and continued the text of the Rus' Primary Chronicle (written in 1093), and completed its redaction, known as *Povist' vremennykh lit (The Tale of Bygone Years), ca 1111–13. The original has not been preserved. Most scholars (eg, D. Abramovych, M. Braichevsky, D. Chyzhevsky, M. Hrushevsky, D. Likhachev, M. Priselkov, O. Pritsak, A. Shakhmatov, M. Vozniak) consider Nestor the Hagiographer and Nestor the Chronicler to be one person. Some (eg, E. Golubinsky, P. Kazansky, A. Sobolevsky), however, believe they are different persons. Some Western scholars of the *Povist'* (eg, L. Leger, L. Müller) have referred to it as the Nestor Chronicle.

BIBLIOGRAPHY

Abramovich, D. 'Nestor Letopisets,' in *Izsledovanie o Kievo-Pecherskom paterike, kak istoriko-literaturnom pamiatnike* (St Petersburg 1902)

Shakhmatov, A. 'Letopisets Nestor,' *ZNTSh*, 117–18 (1914)

Priselkov, M. *Nestor-letopisets: Opyt istoriko-literaturnoi kharakteristiki* (Petrograd 1923)

Scheffler, L. *Textkritischer Apparat zur Nestorchronik* (Munich 1977)

A. Zhukovsky

Volodymyr Nestorovych

Nestorovych, Volodymyr [Nestorovyč] (pseud: V. Sever), b 23 January 1895 in Lviv, d 5 February 1980 in Detroit. Economist, publicist, and civic leader. After being conscripted into the Austrian army in 1915, he was captured in battle and deported by the Russians to the Far East. In Nikolsk-Ussuriiskii he became a leading member of the Ukrainian hromada and the district council and edited *Nasha dolia* for Ukrainian POWs. At the end of 1920 he reached Vienna and enrolled in the Higher School of International Trade, from which he graduated in 1924. In the 1930s he taught economics and bookkeeping at the Ridna Shkola commerce school and the business gymnasium. He contributed economic and political articles to various Ukrainian papers and edited the economics section of *Dilo* (1932–9) and the semimonthly *Torhovlia i promysl* (1934–9). He left Austria for Germany in 1944 and then moved to the United States, where he was active in Ukrainian credit unions in Detroit and edited their magazine *Nash kontakt* (1954–9). He was president of the Literary-Artistic Club (1952–9) and a member of the editorial board of *Nash svit* (1959–62). His novel *Sertsia i burevii* (Hearts and Storms, 1965) is based on his recollections of Siberia and the Far East. He also wrote *Ukraïns'ki kuptsi i promyslovtsi v Zakhidnii Ukraïni* (Ukrainian Merchants and Manufacturers in Western Ukraine, 1977).

Nesturkh, Fedir [Nesturx], b 22 June 1857 in Odessa, d 1 May 1936 in Odessa. Architect. After graduating from the St Petersburg Academy of Arts (1887) he worked as the chief architect of Odessa (1900–17) and was a professor at the Odessa Art Institute (1928–33). He designed many buildings in Odessa, including the emergency hospital (1903–5), the city library (1904–7), and the psychiatric hospital (1910–12).

Nesvitsky, Yakiv [Nesvits'kyj, Jakiv], b 10 May 1911 in Potapka, Kaniv county, Kiev gubernia, d 28 April 1974 in Kiev. Specialist in the field of automotive transport. He graduated from the Institute of Agricultural Mechanization in Kharkiv (1936) and worked in various institutes of the AN URSR (now ANU) in the Ukrainian SSR Ministry of Agriculture, and in the Kiev Automobiles and Roads Institute (from 1948). His main contributions were in the field of automobile reliability, and he wrote a widely used handbook on the technical applications of automobile transport.

Netherlands. A western European state (1990 pop 14,934,000) covering an area of 41,863 sq km. Its capital is Amsterdam. Up to the 17th century, Ukrainian relations with the Netherlands (as well as with Belgium, with which the Netherlands was united at the time) were primarily economic and were conducted mainly through Amsterdam. Ukrainian students attended Dutch institutions of higher learning, including Leiden University (Yu Nemyrych), in the 17th century. In the same period Dutch cartographers (H. Gerritsz, W. Hondius, J. Blaeu) drew and published the first maps of Ukraine as plotted by T Makovsky and G. Le Vasseur de Beauplan. C. Cruys, who later served as an admiral in the Russian navy, was the author of an atlas of the Don River and the Black Sea, published in Amsterdam in 1703. Dutch engravers took up Ukrainian subjects in their work. A. van Westerfeldt made a drawing of Kiev (published in 1653); views of many Ukrainian cities were published in atlases assembled by J Jansson and others; and W. Hondius engraved a portrait of B. Khmelnytsky. Dutch scholars of the 17th and 18th centuries, such as A. Cellarius and T. Salmon, included descriptions of Ukraine in their works on geography and history.

Contacts between the Netherlands and Ukraine grew significantly after the First World War. In 1919–23 there was a UNR mission to the Netherlands and Belgium, headed by A. Yakovliv, in The Hague and then in Brussels. In 1920 O. Koshyts led the Ukrainian Republican Kapelle on a concert tour of the Netherlands. In 1921 Metropolitan A Sheptytsky visited the country and set in motion the establishment of an apostolate for local Ukrainians. In 1948–50 the apostolate funded the establishment of a Ukrainian Catholic seminary in Culemborg, and in 1951 it contributed to the founding of the Byzantine Choir of Utrecht (whose members were all Dutch) under the direction of M. *Antonowycz. In the 1950s and 1960s Antonowycz taught music at the state university in Utrecht, and O Kushpeta taught economics at the Catholic university in Tilburg.

After the Second World War there were about 800 Ukrainians living in Holland, mainly women who had worked as forced laborers in Germany and were then resettled in the Netherlands. For the most part they married Dutch men and were assimilated. Today there are about 460 Ukrainians in the Netherlands, who mainly live in Amsterdam, Utrecht, and the province of Overijssel, near the German border. In 1948 the Association of Ukrainians in Holland (Bond van Oekraïners in Nederland) was formed. It was headed successively by O. Kushpeta, M. Bryk, M. Skrypnyk, M. Berskers, and O. Berskers; it now has around 100 members. Colonel Ye. Konovalets is buried in Rotterdam, where he was assassinated on 23 May 1938.

BIBLIOGRAPHY
Bryk, M. *Ukraïntsi Holliandiï* (Losser–Munich 1979)
A. Zhukovsky

Netishyn [Netišyn]. A city (1989 pop 26,500) on the Horyn River in Slavuta raion, Khmelnytskyi oblast. The village is first mentioned in a historical document in 1648. It expanded rapidly in the 1980s, when the Khmelnytskyi Nuclear Power Station was built there. In 1984 it was granted city status. Most of its residents work at the power station.

Nettle (*Urtica*; Ukrainian: *kropyva*). A coarse, prickly herb of the nettle family Urticaceae, armed with stinging hairs and green, tufted flowers. Of its 50 species, 6 grow in Ukraine. The most common are the annual weed *U. urens* (Ukrainian: *kropyva zhalka*), which grows to 60 cm in height, and the perennial weed *U. dioica* (Ukrainian: *kropyva dvodomna*), which grows to 150 cm. Nettles are rich in vitamins B, K, and C, carotene, and tannins; young plants are eaten in salads and are used to feed animals. The plant is medicinal: extracts and infusions are used to stem blood flow.

Neubauer, Ernst Rudolf, b 14 April 1822 in Iglau (now Jihlava), Moravia, d 4 or 5 May 1890 in Rădăuți, Bukovyna. German writer and historian. He studied at Vienna University (1838–42). From 1850 to 1872 he was a gymnasium teacher in Chernivtsi. There he associated with Ukrainians and in 1862–9 published the newspapers *Bukowina* and *Czernowitzer Zeitung*, which printed articles on Ukrainian history and culture. From 1872 to 1883 he directed the gymnasium in Rădăuți. He wrote the poetry collection *Lieder aus der Bukowina* (1855); the historical and ethnographic studies *Illustrierte Bukowina* (1857) and *Grundzüge zur Geschichte von Serethland* (1874); the historical prose collection *Erzählungen aus der Bukowina* (1868); the drama *Mädchen aus Kaliczanka* (1865), set in Kalichanka, the Ukrainian district of Chernivtsi; and the epic *Nogaja oder die Steppenschlacht, ein Gedenklied aus Sereth* (1876). Yu. Fedkovych's poems 'Shypits'ki berezy' (The Birches of Shypit) and 'Yurii Hinda' were written on the basis of Neubauer's reworkings of Bukovynian legends. A. Klug's *Ernst Rudolf Neubauer: Der Mann und das Werk* (2 vols, 1931, 1939) was published in Chernivtsi.

Neurology. That medical specialty which deals with the structure, function, and diseases of the nervous system. In Ukraine neurologists are called neuropathologists. Historically, illness of the brain was considered to be the work of evil spirits, and its sufferers were subjected to magic, incantations, exorcising, and incarceration in dungeons or asylums for the insane. In Russian-ruled Ukraine, at the end of the 19th century neurology was practiced only at university centers. In Western Ukraine under Austro-Hungarian rule, neurology was taught at Lviv University. After the Second World War there was marked development in this branch of *medicine, particularly in general awareness of psychiatric disorders and better diagnostic and treatment facilities. Neurology centers in Ukraine include the departments of diseases of the nervous system at the institutes of *medical education, the institutes for the upgrading of physicians in Zaporizhia, Kiev, and Kharkiv, and the Scientific Research Institute of Neurology and Psychiatry in Kharkiv (est 1922) and the Scientific Research Institute of Neurosurgery in Kiev (est 1950).

BIBLIOGRAPHY
Man'kovs'kyi, B. 'Osnovni pidsumky rozvytku nevropatolohiï v URSR,' in *Dosiahnennia okhorony zdorov'ia v URSR* (Kiev 1958)

Neurosurgery. That branch of medicine which deals with the surgical treatment of the nervous system, including brain surgery. As an independent branch of *medicine

related to *psychiatry and *neurology, neurosurgery emerged only at the beginning of the 20th century.

In Ukraine in the 1890s and early 1900s, several surgeons made progress in neurosurgery: K. *Sapiezhko and B. Kozlovsky established surgical methods to alleviate internal brain-swelling, O. *Shymanovsky worked on surgical techniques, and P. Volkovych, O. Tykhonovych, O. Rava, and others developed methods for the surgical treatment of trauma and prenatal nervous system disorders. Pioneering work in neurosurgery was done in Russia by N. *Burdenko, who was of Ukrainian descent.

The first centers of neurosurgery in Ukraine were established at clinics of the Scientific Research Institute of Psychoneurology in Kharkiv (1931, with Z. Heimanovych) and in Kiev (1935, with P. Babytsky). A neurosurgical clinic headed by V. *Shamov was established in 1935 at the *Kharkiv Medical Institute. O. *Krymov and I. *Ishchenko did research in Kiev, and F. Roze worked in Kharkiv. In 1950 the neurosurgical clinic at the Psychoneurology Institute in Kiev was reorganized as the Kiev Scientific Research Institute of Neurosurgery under the directorship of A. *Arutiunov, the founder of the school of neurosurgeons in Ukraine. Today there are neurosurgical sections in all oblast-level hospitals and neurotrauma centers in the larger cities. The organization of teaching, training, clinical work, research, and accreditation is headed by the Kiev Scientific Research Institute of Neurosurgery and carried out by the neurology departments of the *medical education institutes for the upgrading of physicians in Kiev, Donetske, Zaporizhia, and Kharkiv. The *Kiev Institute for the Upgrading of Physicians is particularly strong in this field. The journal *Neirokhirurgiia* is published in Russian in Kiev. Neurosurgery in Ukraine is hampered by the chronic shortage of modern equipment and drugs, as well as by the poor *hygienic conditions that exist in medical institutions throughout the former USSR.

P. Dzul

Nevolin, Konstantin, b 1806 in Orlov (now Khalturin), Viatka gubernia, Russia, d 18 October 1855 in Bruck, Austria. Russian historian; corresponding member of the St Petersburg Academy of Sciences from 1853. He graduated from the theological seminary in Moscow (1827) and then served as a professor of law at (from 1833) and rector of (1837–43) Kiev University, and as prorector and dean of law at St Petersburg University. His *Entsiklopediia zakonovedeniia* (Encyclopedia of Jurisprudence, 2 vols, 1839–40), published in Kiev, was a ground-breaking work in its field and was instrumental in the subsequent development of legal studies in the Russian Empire.

Nevrlý, Mikuláš (Nevrli, Mykola), b 15 November 1916 in Rostov-na-Donu, Russia. Ukrainian literature specialist and literary critic in postwar Czechoslovakia. From the early 1920s he lived in Poltava, where his father taught at the Institute of People's Education. He emigrated to Czechoslovakia with his parents in 1933 and taught in a Transcarpathian village school (1936–9). He graduated from the teachers' seminary in Uzhhorod (1939), and subsequently studied in Prague at Charles University and the Ukrainian Free University (1940–5) and received two doctorates (1945 [Prague]; 1949 [Brno University]). Nevrlý has written over 575 works, mostly in Czech and Ukrainian: books on I. Franko (1952), T. Shevchenko (1954, 1960),

Mikuláš Nevrlý

and the history of Czechoslovak-Ukrainian literary relations (coeditor, 1957); a bibliography of Ukrainian studies in Slovakia in the years 1945–64 (1965); hundreds of articles published in Eastern European and Soviet Ukrainian periodicals and encyclopedias; and introductions to Czech translations of novels by Franko (1951), P. Myrny (1953), and V. Sobko (1953). He has also edited a Czech anthology of Ukrainian poetry (1951, with O. Zilynsky), Prešov editions of the poetry of B.I. Antonych (1966) and D. Falkivsky (1969), the Slovak edition of Shevchenko's works (2 vols, 1959, 1962, with M. Molnar), and P. Bunhanych's Slovak-Ukrainian dictionary (1986). His doctoral diss (1945) on O. Oles's poetry and his candidate's diss (1966) on Soviet Ukrainian poetry of the 1920s have not been published.

Nevytska, Iryna [Nevyc'ka] (née Buryk), b 10 December 1886 in Zbudská Belá, Zemplén komitat, Slovakia, d 21 November 1965 in Prešov, Slovakia. Ukrainophile writer and community figure in interwar Transcarpathia; wife of O. *Nevytsky. Her first poems, stories, and articles appeared under the pen names Anna Novak and Anna Horiak in Transcarpathian periodicals in 1905. In the interwar years she was the only writer in Ukrainian in the Prešov region. In 1922 she founded the Union of Ruthenian Women of the Prešov Region. In 1929 she moved to Uzhhorod, where she headed the women's section of the Prosvita society, chaired the organizing committee of the First Congress of Ukrainian Women in Transcarpathia (1934), and was a leading member of the Society of Ukrainian Writers and Journalists. She edited the biweekly *Slovo naroda* (Prešov 1931–2), the first periodical in the Prešov region published in modern literary Ukrainian. In 1936 she became leader of the new nationalist *Ukrainian Peasants' and Workers' Party of Subcarpathian Ruthenia and editor of its biweekly organ *Narodnia syla* (Uzhhorod 1936–8). In 1939 she was an active member of the Ukrainian National Alliance in Khust. After the Hungarian occupation of Transcarpathia in 1939, she moved to Prešov and thereafter was inactive. Among her works are the first Transcarpathian Ukrainian novel, *Pravda pobidyla* (The Truth Triumphed, 1924), the story collection *Darunok* (The Gift, 1929), several plays, and stories and poetry for children. A posthumous edition of her novelette *Matii Kukolka* was published in Prešov in 1968.

Nevytsky, Omelian [Nevyc'kyj, Omeljan], b 1878, d 30 January 1939 in Minersville, Pennsylvania. Greek Catholic priest and civic leader. After teaching at the Prešov Teachers' College he served as a parish priest at Ujak, in the Prešov region. In 1918 he and his wife, I. Nevytska, organized the Ruthenian National Council in Stará L'ubovňa. Under his chairmanship (1918–19) it became the first such council to declare itself in favor of Transcarpathia's union with Ukraine. In 1921 he emigrated to the United States, where he served as a priest in the Pittsburgh Ruthenian exarchy and was an active community organizer. In 1938 he founded and headed the Committee for the Defense of Carpatho-Ukraine.

New Economic Policy (NEP). A policy, announced by the 10th Congress of the Russian Communist Party (Bolshevik) in March 1921, aimed at reinstating a market system. It replaced the system of *War Communism, which had brought the economy to ruin. The Kronstadt rebellion, peasant uprisings in Ukraine, and other threats to Bolshevik dictatorship forced V. Lenin to reconsider his economic policy. The NEP established a mixed socialist market economy, in which industry was largely nationalized, but private enterprises with up to 25 workers were allowed; agriculture was predominantly private, but large estates were connected to state farms; and retail and wholesale trade was predominantly co-operative.

Economic and social rights and obligations were codified. In Ukraine the system accommodated geographic and national peculiarities. The Union government monopolized the 'commanding heights' of the economy – that is, heavy industry, transportation, banking and the allocation of capital, taxes, government spending, foreign trade, and natural resources. In Ukraine co-operatives under local control and private farming grew rapidly. The budgetary system and other policy instruments, however, were used by the center to exploit the republic. In 1928 the economist M. Volobuiev argued that Moscow's fiscal and other policies returned Ukraine to its former colonial status.

Consolidating its political control, the regime allowed socioeconomic and cultural innovation. The policy of *Ukrainization promoted the Ukrainian language in administration, education, and business. Overall the NEP elicited support from the peasantry and the technical and administrative cadres. Historians generally agree that the NEP period was favorable to the formation of modern Ukrainian nationhood.

In his quest for power J. Stalin aligned himself with the *Left Opposition in claiming that the NEP encouraged capitalist elements, and that it would impede rapid industrialization. Beginning in 1927 the legal guarantees of private ownership and enterprise were increasingly violated. A campaign was launched to eliminate private businessmen, known as *nepmen, and successful farmers, known as kulaks. Ukrainian Communist leaders, such as M. Khvylovy, O. Shumsky, and M. Skrypnyk, protested strongly against the violations of Ukraine's autonomy. Forced collectivization and grain requisitions resulted in the tragic man-made famine of 1932–3. The NEP market system was replaced by the Stalinist planned command economy.

Some Western economists regard the NEP system as a viable mixed economy, similar to that of Yugoslavia and Hungary in the 1980s. In official Soviet historiography the NEP period was treated as a tactical retreat from communist principles and a transitional phase in the establishment of a planned Soviet model.

BIBLIOGRAPHY

Dmytryshyn, B. *Moscow and the Ukraine, 1918–1953*: A Study of Russian Bolshevik Nationality Policy (New York 1956)

Kononenko, K. *Ukraïna i Rosiia: Sotsiial'no-ekonomichni pidstavy ukraïns'koï natsional'noï ideï, 1917–1960* (Munich 1965)

Dereviankin, T. (ed). *Istoriia narodnoho hospodarstva Ukraïns'koï RSR*, vol 2, *Stvorennia sotsialistychnoï ekonomiky (1917–1937 rr.)* (Kiev 1984)

V. Bandera

New Era (Nova era). An attempt to establish a rapprochement between Galician Ukrainians and Poles in Austria-Hungary in 1890–4. Spurred by growing tensions between the Austro-Hungarian and Russian empires, the Austrian minister of foreign affairs, Count G. Kálnoky, pressured his government to try to satisfy the Ukrainians' demands and secure their loyalty (the likely battleground for the seemingly imminent hostilities being Galicia). Since the government had come to an agreement concerning Galicia that gave the Poles effective administrative control over the crownland, Kálnoky was forced to hand the matter over to the governor of Galicia, K. Badeni. The marshal of the Galician Diet, E. Sanguszko, and A. Chamiec assisted Badeni. The Ukrainian leaders associated with the effort included Metropolitan S. Sembratovych and several moderate populists, such as O. Barvinsky, Yu. Romanchuk, and K. Telishevsky. Representatives of the Hromada of Kiev, led by V. Antonovych, also took part in the ensuing negotiations. But the New Era had little chance of success. The Ukrainians hoped to ensure a better climate for Ukrainian social and cultural development in Galicia; Badeni was willing to try to appease Ukrainians only with limited concessions in education and language rights.

The Ruthenian-Ukrainian Radical party immediately came out against the policies of the New Era, but spokesmen of populist groups offered their support at the parliamentary sessions in November 1890. On behalf of the government Badeni promised that Ukrainians would be allowed free national development based on the principles of the Austrian constitution.

The positive consequences of the New Era for Ukrainians included the wider use of Ukrainian in administrative affairs and in the courts; the introduction of a phonetic orthography in Ukrainian textbooks; bilingualism in teachers' seminaries; the establishment of a state gymnasium in Kolomyia; the creation of chairs of Eastern European (essentially Ukrainian) history and Ukrainian literature at Lviv University; the setting up of Ukrainian financial institutions, such as Dnister in Lviv and the Ukrainian Savings Bank in Peremyshl; and the publication of a Ukrainian-language government daily, *Narodna chasopys'*. The broader political changes Ukrainians believed would be forthcoming, however, never materialized, and Ukrainian support for the New Era dwindled. In 1894, led by Romanchuk, the populists rejected the New Era and joined the ranks of its opponents. Sembratovych and a small number of populists, led by Barvinsky and A. Vakhnianyn, continued to support the policy and centered their activities on the daily *Ruslan* (est 1897).

The failure of the New Era sharpened the tone of Galician politics. The 1895 provincial election to the Diet and the 1897 election to the national parliament were fraught with administrative abuses unusual even for Galicia. Far from cowing them, those assaults on their political work strengthened the resolve of Ukrainians to develop their political strengths and provided an impetus for a major restructuring of Ukrainian political parties in the late 1890s (notably with the establishment of the National Democratic party).

St Andrew's Memorial Church at the Ukrainian Orthodox Center in South Bound Brook, New Jersey

New Jersey. A middle Atlantic state (1990 pop 7,748,630) of the United States, covering an area of 20,300 sq km. Its capital is Trenton. In the 1960 census 13,000 inhabitants gave Ukrainian as their mother tongue, and in the 1980 census 80,800 declared Ukrainian origin. By 1990 their number had fallen to 74,000. The largest Ukrainian communities are in Jersey City, Elizabeth, *Newark, New Brunswick, *Passaic, Patterson, and *Trenton.

The first wave of Ukrainian immigrants to New Jersey (1870–1914) consisted mostly of poor peasants from Galicia, Bukovyna, and Transcarpathia, who worked as unskilled farm laborers or factory workers. After a few years some of them had raised enough capital to buy their land or to set up small businesses. In about 1908 the first Ukrainian rural settlement was established near Great Meadows. Later, Ukrainian farm colonies arose in Millville, Woodbine, Williamstown, New Market–Nova Ukraina,

Newton, and Blairsville in southern New Jersey. The earliest forms of community life were church parishes. The first Ukrainian Catholic parishes were organized in Jersey City (1888), Elizabeth (1905), Newark (1907), Perth Amboy (1908), and Passaic (1910). A Ukrainian Presbyterian church was founded in Newark in 1909. Reading groups were formed for adults and evening schools for children to pass on a basic knowledge of Ukrainian language, literature, and history. The earliest schools were organized in Jersey City (1894), Newark (1895), and Passaic (1899). In the absence of social welfare, mutual aid societies were organized: the first sisterhood, St Olha's, was established in Jersey City in 1897, and 35 branches of the Ruthenian (later Ukrainian) National Association (UNA) had been set up by 1914. Community halls were commonly built in the larger communities to stage concerts and plays and to hold meetings. By 1914 about 50,000 Ukrainians lived in New Jersey.

The second wave of Ukrainian immigration (1920–39) included more people with education. Some newcomers and American-educated children of earlier immigrants entered the professions and local politics. By 1935 there were about 60,000 Ukrainians in New Jersey.

The postwar immigration (1945–60) of political refugees and displaced persons included a high proportion of educated men and women, who strengthened existing Ukrainian institutions and formed some new ones. Rutgers University introduced courses in Ukrainian language, literature, and history. By 1975 the UNA had 59 branches with 12,000 members in New Jersey. The Ukrainian Catholic church has 19 parishes with about 22,000 members in the state, and the Ukrainian Orthodox Church in the USA, centered in South Bound Brook, has 8 parishes with about 10,000 members. National political organizations, such as the Ukrainian Congress Committee of America, the Organization for the Defense of Four Freedoms for Ukraine, and the Ukrainian National Women's League of America, have branches in many of the state's cities. Jersey City, the site of the UNA's head office, is a major publishing center for the daily *Svoboda*, the *Ukrainian Weekly*, and the children's monthly magazine *Veselka*. By 1976 there were six Ukrainian credit unions in New Jersey, all founded after the Second World War.

New Kramatorske Machine-Building Plant (Novokramatorskyi mashynobudivnyi zavod). A heavy-machine-building plant located in Krama-torske, Donetske oblast. The plant was constructed in 1929–34. Before the Second World War it produced slab and strip mills, cranes, mining machinery, and other machines. The plant was evacuated at the outbreak of the war and completely rebuilt afterward. By 1948 production had reached the prewar level. Now the plant produces equipment for rolling mills, mining hoists, metalworking machines, and presses. It is one of the largest producers of specialized forges and casts for the electrotechnical and mill-building industries. In 1971 over 10,000 people worked at the plant.

New Kryvyi Rih Mineral Enrichment Complex (Novokryvorizkyi hirnycho-zbahachuvalnyi kombinat). A concern of the mining industry, located in Kryvyi Rih, Dnipropetrovske oblast. It was constructed in 1956–9 to process the ferruginous quartzite iron ores found on the left bank of the Inhulets River. Agglomeration plants were opened in 1961 and 1962. Its planned production capacity was 9,090,000 t of raw ore with an iron content of 36.2 percent, 4,540,000 t of concentrate with an iron content of 62 percent, and 8,050,000 t of agglomerates with a basicity of 1.1 percent and iron content of 52 percent per year. The complex includes three quarries and a pulverizing, enriching, and agglomerating plant.

New Lviv Theater (Novyi lvivskyi teatr). A society of actors under the artistic triumvirate of V. *Kalyn, A. *Buchma, and M. *Bentsal, established on the initiative of F. Lopatynsky and Kalyn in Ternopil in December 1918 by a union of the Ternopil Ukrainian Drama Theater (1918–19) and the actors from the Ruska Besida Theater. In 1919 it performed under the auspices of the Ukrainian Galician Army in Chortkiv, Kamianets-Podilskyi, Proskuriv, and Vinnytsia. That summer it split into two groups; one, led by M. Bentsal, continued touring and was interned by Polish authorities in May 1920, and the other joined with a faction of the former Molodyi Teatr under H. Yura to form the touring Franko New Drama Theater (see *Kiev Ukrainian Drama Theater).

New Russia (Novorosiia, Novorosiiskyi krai). The tsarist designation for the lands of *Southern Ukraine annexed from the Zaporozhian Cossacks, the Crimean Khanate, and Ottoman Turkey. From 1764 the lands constituted a large part of *New Russia gubernia, which in 1802 was divided to create *Katerynoslav, *Kherson, and *Tavriia gubernias. From 1812 the newly annexed province of *Bessarabia, and from the early 20th century to 1917 the *Stavropol region (gubernia) and the province of the *Don Cossacks, were also considered part of New Russia.

New Russia Cossack Army (Novorosiiske kozatske viisko). A tsarist military formation created in December 1806 from among Cossacks and Ukrainian and Russian fugitives from serfdom living along the Danubian frontier. Originally called the Ust-Danubian Budzhak Army, it was supposed to prevent the flight of peasants from Podilia and Kherson gubernias to the *Danubian Sich and Ottoman-held territory along the lower Danube. Its failure to do so and its absorption of many such fugitives into its ranks resulted in its demobilization by tsarist punitive forces in September 1807. Approx 500 Cossacks were transported to the Kuban, where they became part of the Black Sea Cossack Army, and the majority dispersed into the Danubian steppes. During the Russo-Turkish War of 1828–9 a similar Danubian Cossack Army was constituted from among former Cossacks and Balkan volunteers. During the Crimean War it fought in the Dobrudja and the Caucasus and took part in the 1854 defense of Odessa. The rank-and-file soldiers mutinied against the harsh treatment by their officers in 1843–5, 1849, 1855, and 1857. In 1857 the army was renamed the New Russia Cossack Army. In 1858 it consisted of 12,085 men, living in 10 military settlements. The army's 13,150 soldiers were demobilized in 1868.

New Russia gubernia (Russian: Novorossiiskaia guberniia). The administrative-territorial designation from 1764 for the region in *Southern Ukraine annexed by the Russian Empire from the Zaporozhian Cossacks, the Hetnan state, the Crimean Khanate, and the Ottoman Empire. The gubernia encompassed the frontier territories of New Serbia, *Slobidskyi regiment, *Sloviano-Serbia, the Ukrainian Line, and 39 companies of the abolished Hetman office's Poltava, Myrhorod, Lubni, and Pereiaslav regiments. From 1765 the gubernial center was Kremenchuk. The gubernia was governed according to the Russian Senate's 'Plan for the Colonization of New Russia Gubernia,' and the military colonists and Cossacks there were transformed against their will into regular hussar and lancer regiments. The gubernia was divided into the Elizabethan province, with five regiments west of the Dnieper River, and the Catherinian province and Bakhmut county, with four regiments east of the Dnieper. It was the first region in the Russian Empire in which Catherine II allowed foreign Jews to settle.

The gubernia bordered on the Zaporizhia, the 'free lands' of the Zaporozhian Cossacks, who opposed tsarist encroachments onto their lands and repeatedly attacked and destroyed new settlements. Consequently the gubernia's administration had a semimilitary character. It was governed consecutively by the 'supreme commanders' A. Melgunov, J. von Brandt, M. Leontev, F. Voeikov, and, from 1774, G. Potemkin. The regimental commanders under them had both military and civil authority.

Each settler in the gubernia received a subsidy and 26–30 desiatins of land. Those who also enlisted in the cavalry regiments received larger subsidies and did not have to pay taxes. Any military officer (including a member of the Cossack *starshyna*) who settled in the gubernia received noble status and a rank estate. Nobles and recruiting agents could establish and own a hereditary free village (*sloboda*) of no more than 48 households and recruit settlers, usually from among Ukrainian peasants who had fled Polish and Russian serfdom, but also from among Russian Old Believers and state peasants. If the village owner did not populate his land within three years, he forfeited it. Foreigners (mostly Moldavians and Wallachians, but also Germans, Serbs, Bulgarians, Armenians, Georgians, and Greeks) received the largest subsidies; those who brought 300 colonists with them received the rank of major, those who brought 150 became captains, and those who brought 30 became sergeant majors. In the northern part of the Catherinian province much of the land was already owned by the wealthy Cossack *starshyna*. Because most of the peasants there were enserfed, several thousand fled to the free villages and to the lands of the Zaporozhian Cossacks.

In the gubernia's towns Greeks and Old Believers controlled commerce. Unlike elsewhere in the Russian Empire merchants (65.1 percent Russian, 24.5 percent Ukrainian, and 10.4 percent foreign in the 1770s), not landed gentry, owned the factories. During the Russian-Turkish War of 1768–74 the gubernia's inhabitants bore the brunt of maintaining the Russian forces. In 1769–70 the gubernia's Donets, Dnieper, and Luhan *lancer regiments rebelled against tsarist rule and were brutally repressed. Also in 1769, Crimean Tatars invaded the Elizabethan province, destroyed over 50 villages, and took away the inhabitants and cattle.

In 1774 the gubernia absorbed new lands annexed from Turkey between the Dnieper and the Boh rivers and along the Black Sea littoral. In 1775 the free lands of the Zaporizhia were confiscated and divided between New Russia

gubernia and the newly created *Azov gubernia, and in 1776 Bakhmut county and the Catherinian province were transferred to Azov gubernia. Thereafter New Russia gubernia consisted of Kremenchuk county and the provinces of Yelysavethrad (3 counties), Poltava (2 counties), Slovianske (renamed Nykopil in 1781; 3 counties), and Kherson (3 counties). After the Russian annexation of the Crimea in 1783, New Russia and Azov gubernias were replaced by Katerynoslav vicegerency. In 1791 the vicegerency absorbed lands annexed from Turkey between the Boh and the Dniester. In 1797 most of the vicegerency's territory became part of a new New Russia gubernia, with its capital in Novorossiisk (Katerynoslav). In 1802 the gubernia's lands were divided among the new Mykolaiv (from 1803, *Kherson), *Katerynoslav, and *Tavriia gubernias.

R. Senkus

New Russia University. See Odessa University.

New Serbia (Nova Serbiia). A Russian administrative and military territorial unit in Southern Ukraine, created by Empress Elizabeth Petrovna in January 1752 out of the northwestern lands of the Zaporizhia (ie, the northern parts of Kodak and Boh-Hard palankas) between the Syniukha River to the west and the Dnieper to the east. Although the officially stated purpose of the new territory was defense of the Russian Empire from Turkish and Crimean Tatar attack, the territory also gave Russia a base from which it could control the Zaporozhian Cossacks, isolate the Zaporizhia from Right-Bank Ukraine and part of the Left Bank, and facilitate Russia's expansionist designs in the Ukrainian steppe frontier. New Serbia had an area of 1,421,000 desiatins. The Russian government evacuated all of its inhabitants (according to A. Schmidt, 4,008 Cossack and peasant households), despite the protests of Hetman K. *Rozumovsky and the Zaporozhian Sich. In their place it imported Serbian military colonists from Austrian-ruled Slavonia and Hungary led by Col I. Horvat and, later, similar Bulgarian, Vlach, Greek, and other Orthodox colonists who had fled from Turkish rule.

The colonists were subject to military rule and were divided between a hussar regiment based in Novomyrhorod and a pandour regiment based in Krylov, which together constituted the New Serbia Corps. A medal commemorating the creation of New Serbia was struck in 1754. That year the *Slobidskyi Regiment of Cossack colonists mostly from Left-Bank and Slobidska Ukraine was organized on the southern frontier of New Serbia, and the St Elizabeth Fortress was built to serve as the administrative center of the territory. (In 1775 the fortress became the center of the new town of Yelysavethrad [Kirovohrad].) Two-thirds of New Serbia's population was Ukrainian. The colonists clashed repeatedly with the neighboring Zaporozhian Cossacks and inhabitants of Polish-ruled Right-Bank Ukraine. The Serbian officers often abused their positions and their subordinates. In 1764 Horvat was removed from his post and exiled to Vologda. That year New Serbia was abolished, and its territory became part of the new *New Russia gubernia.

BIBLIOGRAPHY
Bahalii, D.I. *Zaselennia pivdennoï Ukraïny (Zaporozhzhia i Novorosiis'koho kraiu) i pershi pochatky ïï kul'turnoho rozvytku* (Kharkiv 1920)

Polons'ka-Vasylenko, N. *The Settlement of the Southern Ukraine (1750–1775)*, special issue of AUA, 4–5 (Summer–Fall 1955)
Dyck, H.L. 'New Serbia and the Origins of the Eastern Question, 1751–55: A Habsburg Perspective,' RR, January 1981

A. Zhukovsky

New Sich (Nova Sich, aka Pokrovska Sich). The last *Zaporozhian Sich. It was founded in 1734 by Cossacks who returned to Russian-ruled Ukraine from the *Oleshky Sich. The fortress was built 3–5 km from the earlier *Chortomlyk Sich on land jutting into the Pidpilna River, a tributary of the Dnieper, near what is today the village of Pokrovske, in Nykopil raion, Dnipropetrovske oblast. The large territory of the *Zaporizhia belonging to the New Sich was divided among eight *palankas. A total of nearly 100,000 people (Cossacks, Cossack helpers, and peasants) lived in the Sich and over 100 free villages (*slobody*) and 4,000 *zymivnyky. On 16 June 1775 a Russian army commanded by Gen P. Tekeli destroyed the Sich on the orders of Catherine II.

New Year. The first day of the yearly cycle, marked with religious and traditional festivities. Before its Christianization in 988 Rus' followed the ancient Roman calendar, which began the year on 1 March. With Christianity came the Byzantine calendar, which began the new year on 1 September and followed a chronology which set the date of creation at 5508 BC. The common people, however, continued to use the Roman calendar. In the 14th and 15th centuries, under Polish and Lithuanian influence, the Julian *calendar, which began the year on 1 January, was adopted in Ukraine. In Russia this change came only in 1700, under Peter I. The more accurate Gregorian calendar was adopted in Western Europe in 1582, but neither the Ukrainian people nor the church accepted this calendar. Today Ukrainians in and outside Ukraine celebrate the New Year twice: officially on 1 January, according to the Gregorian calendar, and unofficially on 14 January (1 January according to the Julian calendar).

The New Year, particularly New Year's Eve, was celebrated with a rich repertoire of folk rituals. Their primary purpose was to secure a bountiful harvest and the family's health and happiness. The key rituals were the eating of *kutia*, children's caroling, the *polaz* (bringing cattle into the house), walking *Malanka around the village, fortune-telling and forecasting the weather for the next year, and the symbolic sowing of wheat. According to popular superstition, on New Year's Eve domestic animals are able to speak in human language, and buried treasures burn with a blue flame. Garbage was to be burnt at sunrise in the garden or the orchard to ensure good crops, and people washed in river water with coins in it to guarantee good health. There were many other customs connected with the New Year.

The Soviet authorities banned the traditional rituals of the New Year, considering them to be part of a religious cult. Thereafter they became confined to the family circle. All public celebrations were arranged by the officials. In the early 1930s the New Year's tree was introduced in clubs, palaces of culture, schools, factories, and public places. At New Year meetings Party and government officials rewarded workers for their performance and delivered speeches, reports, pledges, and toasts. The meetings were followed usually with a dance, a carnival, a contest, or the appearance of Grandfather Frost and the Snow Nymph. In 1960 some students in Kiev made the first attempt to revive the traditional New Year's celebrations by caroling. The practice began to spread through Ukraine and was prohibited by the authorities in the 1970s. Since the mid-1980s the traditional New Year's customs, however, have been revived by many voluntary groups.

M. Mushynka

St George's Ukrainian Catholic Church in Manhattan

New York City. A major city (1980 pop 7,071,000; metropolitan pop 9,119,700) situated at the mouth of the Hudson River on the eastern seaboard of the United States, with a Ukrainian population (the largest community in the country) of between 34,400 (according to the 1980 census) and 56,340 (estimated). In 1930, 7,200 identified themselves as Ukrainians, and in 1960, 13,000 New Yorkers listed Ukrainian as their mother tongue.

From the late 1870s Ukrainian emigrants landed at the port of New York on their way to the mining towns of Pennsylvania or the industrial cities of the interior. A few stayed in New York to work at unskilled jobs, but they did not form organizations. At the turn of the century Ukrainians began to settle there in large numbers; they were joined in the interwar period by immigrants moving to New York from other cities. After the Second World War a large number of political émigrés settled in New York.

The earliest immigrants usually took hard, low-paying jobs. Eventually the more enterprising among them set up their own small businesses, mostly grocery stores, and by the end of the 1930s there were several hundred Ukrainian businesses in New York. At first few immigrants had higher education. The number of intellectuals and professional people increased in the early 1920s and particularly after the Second World War.

Ukrainians settled in lower east-side Manhattan, where they replaced German, Czech, Hungarian, Irish, and Italian immigrants who had moved into other areas of the city at the beginning of the century. This section remains the main Ukrainian area of New York. Other areas of Ukrainian concentration include the Williamsburg, South Brooklyn, and Green Point districts in Brooklyn and the Astoria area of Queens. In recent years Ukrainians have moved into more upscale districts of the city or into the suburbs.

The first Ukrainian organizations in New York were mutual benefit societies founded by Transcarpathian immigrants. Their central association, the *Greek Catholic Union of the USA, moved its central office to New York in 1896 and published its biweekly *Amerikanskii russkii viestnik* there until 1901. Other fraternal societies organized under the Ruthenian National Association were established in New York at the beginning of the century. With the founding of a Greek Catholic parish and the calling of the first Ruthenian Popular Meeting in 1905, the Ukrainian community began to develop rapidly. By 1907 there were 14 Ukrainian societies and institutions in New York, including the socialist organization *Haidamaky, which had its own periodical, and the National Aid Association (est 1907). In 1908 the Prosvita society was founded. In 1912–14 the *Providence Association of Ukrainian Catholics in America maintained its head office in New York.

During and after the First World War various political organizations appeared in the city, including the Ukrainian Council (1914) and the Ukrainian Assembly of America, which founded the Federation of Ukrainians in the United States at its meeting in New York on 30–31 October 1915. The Ukrainian National Committee (1918–22) and the Sich Organization of Ukrainians (1919) were also formed in New York. By 1935 about 50 local and central organizations were active in the city. To co-ordinate their programs the Ukrainian Popular Hromada was established in 1917; it was followed by the Union of Ukrainian Popular Societies and the Central Committee of Ukrainian National Societies of New York City (est 1930).

During the Second World War New York became the home of the *Ukrainian Congress Committee of America (UKKA), the Ukrainian umbrella organization for the United States. The local UKKA branch, the Committee of United Ukrainian Organizations of New York City, had 73 member organizations by 1966. In addition, representations of the Ukrainian National Council and the Ukrainian Supreme Liberation Council and the head offices of social and political organizations, such as the Organization for the Defense of Four Freedoms for Ukraine, the Organization for the Rebirth of Ukraine, and the *Self-Reliance Association of American Ukrainians, located themselves in New York shortly after the war. The city also had a number of Ukrainian professional, student, and sports associations. The *Self-Reliance Federal Credit Union was organized in 1951, and by 1978 its membership had reached 5,300 and its assets 22,895,000 dollars.

The first Ukrainian evening or Saturday schools were set up at the beginning of the century at the Ukrainian People's Home and the parish churches. Today a regular elementary (est 1941) and high school (est 1946) are operated at St George's Catholic Church (enrollment over 800), and Ukrainian courses are offered by a number of Catholic and Orthodox parishes, the Self-Reliance Association, and other organizations (over 600 students in the 1960s).

The New York Ukrainian community has been entertained by a number of amateur and semiprofessional drama and music groups, such as the Ruthenian Popular Theater (est 1909), the Ukrainian Theater (1922–6), several drama groups organized by Jews from Ukraine, the American Boian singing society (1905), the choir of Ukrainska Besida (1911), and church choirs. A part of the Ukrainian Republican Kapelle stayed in New York in 1922 and formed the core of O. Koshyts's United Ukrainian Choir of New York in 1926. V. Avramenko set up a school

of Ukrainian dance in New York in 1929. After the Second World War the Dumka, the Boian, and various church choirs were active. Recently the Homin Stepiv Bandura Ensemble was founded. In the 1950s the *Theater-Studio of Y. Hirniak and O. Dobrovolska continued its career in New York, and the New Theater was founded in 1966. The *Ukrainian Music Institute of America, the *Ukrainian Artists' Association in the USA, and the Slovo Association of Ukrainian Writers in Exile have their head offices in New York. The *New York Group of poets is based there. The cultural needs of the local community are served by the Literary-Artistic Club, which owns its own building, the Ukrainian People's Home (est 1954), the Sonevytsky art gallery (est 1963), and the *Ukrainian Institute of America (est 1955). Since 1979 the Ukrainian community has staged a spring street fair, known as the Ukrainian Festival, on Seventh Street.

Two learned societies, the Shevchenko Scientific Society and the Ukrainian Academy of Arts and Sciences, with their own buildings, libraries, archives, and publishing houses, were established after the war. The *Ukrainian Museum, which has a large ethnographic and art collection, publishes books on Ukrainian art history.

Many periodicals came out briefly in New York, including *Svoboda* (1906–11), *Sichovi visty* (1918–23), *Ukraïns'kyi visnyk* (1927–8), *Natsional'na trybuna* (1950–1), and *Prometei* (1959). *Visnyk OOChSU, Holos Lemkivshchyny, Ukrainian Bulletin, Ukrainian Quarterly*, and the communist weekly *Ukraïns'ki visti* and monthly *Hromads'kyi holos* have been published in the postwar period. The main Ukrainian publishers and bookstores have been Knyhospilka, Prolog, Chervona Kalyna, Surma, and Hoverlia.

Religious life is organized around parishes and religious societies. The largest Ukrainian Catholic parish is St George's in Manhattan (est 1905), which is run by the Basilian monastic order. There are two Catholic churches in Brooklyn (est 1912 and 1916), one in Astoria (est 1943), one in the Bronx (est 1943), one in Queens (est 1957), and one in Staten Island. Besides the Orthodox Cathedral of St Volodymyr, there are six Orthodox churches in Manhattan and Brooklyn. The Transcarpathian community has three churches, two Catholic and one Orthodox. There are also Evangelical, Baptist, and Pentecostal Ukrainian congregations. In 1935 Brooklyn became the seat of B. Shpylka, the bishop and, later, metropolitan of the Ukrainian Orthodox Church of America, and then the home of Bishop A. Kushchak and Archbishop P. Vydybida-Rudenko of the Ukrainian Autocephalous Orthodox Church in Exile.

BIBLIOGRAPHY
Zolota iuvileina knyha z nahody 50-littia zorhanizovanoho ukraïns'koho hromads'koho zhyttia v N'iu-Iorku, 1905–1955 (New York 1956)

B. Kravtsiv

New York Group (Niu-Iorkska hrupa). A group of poets and artists, which developed spontaneously in the mid-1950s from informal friendships and discussions around the *Students'ke slovo* (Student Word) supplement to the newspaper *Svoboda*. The initiating core consisted of B. *Boychuk, B. *Pevny, and G. *Tarnawsky. The group grew to include the writers E. Andiievska, Zh. Vasylkivska, V. Vovk, B. Rubchak, and P. Kylyna (P. Warren) and the artists Ya. Gerulak and Ju. Solovij. The name, chosen because the majority of members lived in the New York area, was applied to the group from 1959, when they decided to start a serial publication, *Novi poezii*. The name was also used for a publishing house, which published many of the collections of the individual members.

The New York Group was never united by any artistic credo or manifesto. More a grouping of friends than an organization, it embraced Ukrainians who began their period of creativity in North America, and who happened to be living in New York. In form their poetry ranged from the surrealism of Andiievska and the depoeticized verse of Tarnawsky to the more traditional quatrains of Boychuk and Rubchak, although all the members had experienced similar influences (J.-P. Sartre, F.G. Lorca, A. Camus, F. Kafka, P. Neruda), had a common émigré heritage, which at times encouraged in them an excessive preoccupation with the purity of the Ukrainian language, and were united in a desire to distance themselves from the overly nationalistic poetry of the previous generation. Their creativity provided a much-needed revitalization of émigré Ukrainian literature after the Second World War and probably served also as an impetus for the *shestydesiatnyky* in Ukraine. The group has never officially ceased to exist, although since the dispersal of its members, who remain active individually, its activity has been limited to sporadic publications.

BIBLIOGRAPHY
Boichuk, B. 'Iak i poshcho narodylasia N'iu-Iorks'ka hrupa,' *Terem*, 2, no. 2 (1966)
Pytlowany, M. 'Continuity and Innovation in the Poetry of the New York Group,' *Journal of Ukrainian Studies*, 2, no. 1 (1977)
Efimov-Schneider, L. 'Poetry of the New York Group: Ukrainian Poets in an American Setting,' *Canadian Slavonic Papers*, 23, no. 3 (September 1981)

D.H. Struk

St John the Baptist Ukrainian Catholic Church in Hunter, New York

New York State. A northeastern state (1990 pop 18,044,505) of the United States, covering 128,400 sq km. Its capital is Albany. By 1930, 62,200 Ukrainian Americans lived in the state. In the 1960 census 26,800 inhabitants listed Ukrainian as their mother tongue, and in the 1980 census 127,700 declared Ukrainian origin. By 1990 their number had dropped to 121,100. The largest Ukrainian communities in the state are found in New York City, Buffalo, Rochester, Binghamton, and Syracuse. Popular

Ukrainian resort areas in the Catskill Mountains region include Hunter, Kerhonkson, and Glen Spey.

New Zealand. A country (1990 pop 3,389,000) in the southeastern Pacific, covering an area of 270,000 sq km on two main islands and a group of smaller ones. After the Second World War about 250 Ukrainian displaced persons went to New Zealand. Having fulfilled their two-year contracts at assigned jobs, they settled in the large cities. There were over 400 Ukrainians in the country: 120 in Auckland, 75 in Wellington, 190 in Christchurch, and 4 in Dunedin. Ukrainian clubs in Wellington (est 1949) and Auckland (est 1951) organize cultural activities, such as choir concerts, dance performances, and national festivals. Ukrainian Saturday schools were set up in the 1960 in Wellington and Christchurch. Ukrainian Catholics are under the jurisdiction of the apostolic exarch in Australia but do not have their own priest. They are organized into church brotherhoods. The Orthodox belong to the Ukrainian Autocephalous Orthodox Church in Australia and have one parish and a priest in Wellington.

Newark. A port city (1989 pop 313,839) on the west bank of the Passaic River and Newark Bay in northeastern New Jersey. An important industrial, trading, and financial center, it is the largest city in the state. A large job market and its proximity to New York City made Newark attractive to Ukrainian immigrants: in 1930 there were about 1,400 Ukrainian residents, and by 1980 approx 13,600. Community organizations began in the city with the St Nicholas Brotherhood in 1900. In 1906 the first Ukrainian public meeting was held. A Ukrainian Catholic parish was set up in 1907 by Rev I. Dorozhynsky, and an Orthodox parish in 1918. The Ukrainian People's Home was incorporated in 1915, and bought its own building two years later. In 1921 the American-Ukrainian Building and Loan Association was formed; 10 years later its assets reached 750,000 dollars. Newark's Trident Savings and Loan Association (est 1921) survived the depression and had reached assets of 18 million dollars by the 1960s. In 1924 the Black Sea (Chornomorska) Sich sports club was founded, and over time it developed a reputation for its prowess in soccer. In the interwar period there were over 30 organizations in Newark. The Self-Reliance Credit Union was set up in 1959; by 1978 it had almost 3,000 members and assets of 7.2 million dollars. Among the various Ukrainian organizations in Newark, the Ukrainian Center and the Black Sea Sich sports club are the most active.

News from Ukraine. A weekly paper published in Kiev since June 1964 by the *Ukraina Society: Association for Cultural Relations with Ukrainians Abroad. A Ukrainian-language version, *Visti z Ukraïny*, has appeared since November 1960. Both papers published propagandistic articles promoting Soviet Ukrainian cultural, economic, and political achievements and Soviet foreign policy. They refuted charges of Russification and criticism of human rights abuses in Ukraine. They regularly published diatribes against Ukrainian 'bourgeois nationalists' in the West, including 'exposés' of alleged war criminals and of relations between leading figures in the émigré nationalist community and 'imperialist' intelligence agencies and fascism in the West. In the late 1980s, in the spirit of M. Gorbachev's policy of glasnost, the papers muted their attacks and concentrated instead on presenting more objective reports on developments in Ukraine and on the 'blank spots' in Ukrainian history; in the early 1990s the papers supported the new political order in Ukraine and adopted pro-independence profiles. They have been widely distributed (often free of charge) among Ukrainians and pro-Soviet activists in the West, as well as in the developing world. Until very recently they were not available in Ukraine and were rarely mentioned in official sources. In 1990 the editor in chief of *News from Ukraine* was V. Kanash. The editorial board has included prominent writers (eg, I. Drach, D. Pavlychko, and V. Brovchenko), scholars (I. Khmil), and athletes (V. Borzov).

Newspapers. See Press.

Neyman, Czesław, b 1852, d 1906. Ukrainian folklorist and historian of Polish origin. While serving as a notary in Vinnytsia, he studied Ukrainian folklore and became friends with M. Kotsiubynsky (1880s). He contributed articles on Ukrainian songs (1883, 1884), dumas (1885), and the history of the Bratslav region (1889) to *Kievskaia starina* and wrote a study of dumas for the Polish journal *Atheneum* (1885).

Nezabytovsky, Vasyl [Nezabytovs'kyj, Vasyl'], b 1824 in Radomyshl, Kiev gubernia, d 26 June 1883. Jurist. After graduating from the law faculty of Kiev University in 1846, he taught at a gymnasium in Kiev and then held the law chair at Nizhen Lyceum (1850–3) and Kiev University (1853–83). He served as dean of the law faculty (1863–5, 1870–3, 1876–9) and prorector of the university (1865–7). His main interests were financial law, international law, and legal history. He developed an original theory that the state's authority is based not only on ownership or control of a territory, but also on certain legal and public elements. His collected works appeared in Kiev in 1884.

Nezalezhnyky. See Ukrainian Social Democratic Workers' party (Independentists).

Nezamozhnyky (poor peasants). A term used in the early years of Soviet rule to describe peasants who did not own livestock or agricultural equipment or who owned relatively small plots of land. *Nezamozhnyky* constituted one of the three categories introduced by the Soviet authorities in the 1920s to classify the rural population. (The other two were middle peasants [*seredniaky*] and *kulaks, or rich peasants.)

During War Communism Bolshevik rule in the Ukrainian countryside was based not on the soviets but on groups of *nezamozhnyky* organized into *Committees of Poor Peasants, which were easier to control than the soviets. With the introduction of the *New Economic Policy, the administrative powers of the committees were greatly reduced, and in 1925 they were completely removed.

After 1925 the term *nezamozhnyky* was more a political and social category than one indicating the size of property holding. It was usually applied to supporters of the Soviet regime who had comparatively little land, but who were by no means always poor. The budgets of the Committees of Poor Peasants for 1924–5 in Ukraine show that people without land under cultivation had an annual net income of 52 rubles per capita, which was only slightly

less than the average for the republic (60.3 rubles); and their per capita purchases even exceeded those of peasants who were cultivating 4–6 desiatins. *Nezamozhnyky* headed the entire agricultural administration and enjoyed many privileges, including the right to pay dues to their co-operatives in installments, a discount in renting agricultural equipment from the government, and relief from paying taxes.

The role of the *nezamozhnyky* grew sharply with the beginning of *collectivization. Meetings of *nezamozhnyky* carried out individual tax assessments and occasionally confirmed the list of kulaks to be dispossessed. Of course, only a minority became village activists. Any *nezamozhnyk* who refused to support Party policy was immediately reclassified as a 'kulak henchman.' With the completion of collectivization the concept of *nezamozhnyk* disappeared. Although millions of *nezamozhnyky* starved to death in the man-made *famine of 1932–3, they did not fall into the category of the population to which the government rendered economic and social aid.

A. Babyonyshev

Nezhdanova, Antonina [Neždanova], b 29 July 1873 in Kryva Balka, Akkerman county, Bessarabia gubernia, d 26 June 1950 in Moscow. Opera singer (soprano) of Russian, Ukrainian, and Polish descent. Equally successful as a lyric, dramatic, and coloratura singer, she knew M. Kropyvnytsky, P. Saksahansky, and M. Zankovetska from their appearances in Odessa. She popularized Ukrainian music in Moscow (from ca 1909), where she worked with the tenor I. Alchevsky in his Kobzar Association. Nezhdanova recorded for the Gramophone label some items of her Ukrainian repertoire. Her concert repertoire included songs by M. Lysenko, M. Kropyvnytsky, and K. Stetsenko; a number of Ukrainian folk songs; fragments from S. Hulak-Artemovsky's opera *Zaporozhian Cossack beyond the Danube*; and operas on Ukrainian themes by M. Mussorgsky, P. Tchaikovsky, and N. Rimsky-Korsakov. From the 1920s Nezhdanova appeared in Ukrainian opera theaters in Kharkiv, Kiev, and Odessa, where the conservatory now bears her name.

Nezhyvy, Semen [Neživyj] (actual surname: Musiienko), b 1744 in Melnyky, Chyhyryn region, d ? Haidamaka leader. He was a peasant hired hand and a potter by trade. After the outbreak of the *Koliivshchyna rebellion in the spring of 1768, he proclaimed himself the Zaporozhian otaman of Uman kurin. He banded local peasants into a rebel detachment and led raids of Polish estates in the Smila, Cherkasy, Krylov, Kaniv, and Medvedivka districts. Nezhyvy's rebel detachment was attacked by Russian troops while he consulted with the hussar colonel Chorba, and later in Kiev he was sentenced to the lash and to lifelong hard labor in Nerchinsk, Siberia. His subsequent fate is unknown.

Nezvysko settlement. A multi-occupational settlement of the 4th to 3rd millennium BC on the right bank of the Dniester River near Nezvysko, Horodenka raion, Ivano-Frankivske oblast. Excavated in 1926 and in the 1950s, the site yielded early agricultural implements and plates of the *Linear Spiral-Meander Pottery culture. The Trypilian component of the site produced numerous tool forms, small bronze items, and pottery with monochromatic or polychromous ornamentation. The inhabitants of the various settlements at Nezvysko practiced agriculture and animal husbandry.

The Niagara Falls Art Gallery and Museum

Niagara Falls Art Gallery and Museum. A repository of Ukrainian art founded in 1971 by O. and M. *Koliankivsky, the previous owners of the W & W Galleries in Toronto (1958–70). The centerpiece of the new gallery is W. Kurelek's 'Passion of Christ,' a series of 160 panels purchased from the painter in March 1970. The other major part of its collection consists of 70 oils and watercolors by M. Krychevsky. Other valuable artworks include the Okhtyrka Icon (1739), landscapes by painters such as M. Hlushchenko, S. Shyshko, A. Kashshai, V. Manastyrsky, T. Yablonska, and V. Patyk, a *stone *baba*, and 20 sculptures by E. Koniuszy. The collection is housed in a five-level building designed by R. *Zuk especially for the 'Passion of Christ' series and completed in 1971. The gallery has published two Kurelek albums, *The Passion of Christ* (1974) and *The Ukrainian Pioneer* (1980).

Bishop Dionisii Niaradi   Polina Niatko

Niaradi, Dionisii [Njaradi, Dionisij], b 10 October 1874 in Ruski Krstur, Bačka region, Serbia, d 4 April 1940 in Mrzlo Polje, Bačka region. Ukrainian Catholic bishop in Yugoslavia. He was ordained in 1889 and was rector of the

Greek Catholic theological seminary in Zagreb in 1902–14. In 1915 he was consecrated as the first locally born bishop of *Križevci eparchy. Active in supporting Ukrainian causes, he ensured that his priests were trained as conscious Ukrainians, and he maintained close relations with Metropolitan A. Sheptytsky and church circles in Galicia. Niaradi also served the church in Transcarpathia during various crises: he acted as apostolic administrator for Prešov eparchy in 1922–7 and apostolic visitator for Mukachiv eparchy in 1938–9.

Niatko, Polina [Njatko] (real surname: Omelchenko), b 21 October 1900 in Karabachyn, Radomyshl county, Kiev gubernia, d ? Stage and film actress and pedagogue. After completing study at the Lysenko Music and Drama School in Kiev (1916–18) Niatko acted in Molodyi Teatr (1918–19), Berezil (1923–4), the Odessa Derzhdrama (1925–35, with interruptions), and the Kiev Ukrainian Drama Theater (1940–60) and taught at the Kiev Institute of Theater Arts (until 1960). Her notable roles in theater were Mavka in Lesia Ukrainka's *Lisova pisnia* (The Forest Song) and Diiana in V. Mynko's *Ne nazyvaiuchy prizvyshch* (Without Naming Names), and in films, Oksana in *Koliivshchyna* (1933) and Kateryna in *Prometheus* (1936).

Nicephorus (Nykyfor), b ?, d 1121 in Kiev. Metropolitan of Kiev in 1104–21. A Greek by origin, he was assigned to the metropoly from Constantinople in 1104. He is best known for his writings, including epistles to *Volodymyr Monomakh and the Volhynian prince Yaroslav Sviatopolkovych, a sermon on fasting, and a letter to Volodymyr Monomakh on morality. All were originally written in Greek and later translated into Church Slavonic.

Nicephorus, b ?, d 1597. Greek envoy of the Patriarch of Constantinople to the sobor called to discuss the Church Union of *Berestia. He taught at Padua University and was a preacher in Venice before entering the service of the patriarch as a protosyncellus. In 1595 he conducted a mission in Moldavia. Because of his familiarity with the political situation in the region, Nicephorus was invited by Prince K. Ostrozky to participate in the sobor and to provide the Orthodox forces with a powerful symbolic ally. He was detained on the way by Polish authorities, but he arrived in time to participate in the October 1596 meeting of anti-union forces, where he spoke out openly against the union. Nicephorus was later detained again and charged with being a Turkish spy. He died in prison.

Nichlava River [Ničlava]. A left-bank tributary of the Dniester River. It is 83 km long and drains a basin area of 871 sq km. The river flows through the Podolian Upland in Ternopil oblast and the town of Kopychyntsi. It has a drop of 2.1 m/km.

Nicholas I (Nikolai Pavlovich Romanov), b 6 July 1796 in Tsarskoe Selo (now Pushkin), St Petersburg gubernia, d 2 March 1855 in St Petersburg. Russian emperor from 1825. Nicholas ruled as a consistently reactionary anti-Enlightenment and anti-Western autocrat. He suppressed all revolutionary manifestations (eg, the Decembrist movement), centralized the bureaucracy, introduced a secret police (the Third Section) and gendarmerie, and imposed strict censorship throughout the Russian Empire. Externally, his regime supported the status quo in Europe and participated in the suppression of the Polish Insurrection of 1830–1 and the Hungarian Revolution of 1848–9. Its policies vis-à-vis Ukraine (exemplified in the person of Governor-General D. Bibikov) were aimed at the obliteration of Ukrainian national particularities, rights, and traditions. *Magdeburg law in Kiev and the *Lithuanian Statute were abolished, the Uniate church in Right-Bank Ukraine was forcibly liquidated, Russification was intensified, and a full-fledged struggle was waged against any organized national-political activity (eg, the suppression of the *Cyril and Methodius Brotherhood and the exile of T. *Shevchenko). Ukraine's indigenous economic growth (especially in the sugar industry) and the penetration of Ukrainians into the large cities were hindered by a policy of intensive Russian colonization. Nicholas's curtailment of the influence of the Polish landed gentry in Right-Bank Ukraine did not attenuate the plight and oppression of the enserfed Ukrainian peasantry, and peasant unrest erupted in the 1840s and 1850s (eg, the peasant rebellions led by U. Karmaliuk in 1830–5 and the rebellion of the *Kiev Cossacks in 1855). The only positive developments in Ukraine during Nicholas's rule were in belles lettres (eg, by N. Gogol and Shevchenko) and higher education and scholarship (eg, the establishment of St Vladimir [Kiev] University, the Central Archive of Old Documents there, the Kiev Archeographic Commission, the Odessa Society of History and Antiquities, and the Nizhen Lyceum), but even they were undermined by his rigid policies. The defeat of the Russian Empire in the Crimean War exposed the social, economic, and moral bankruptcy of Nicholas's rule.

BIBLIOGRAPHY
Presniakov, A. Apogei samoderzhaviia: Nikolai I (Leningrad 1925); English trans pub as Emperor Nicholas I of Russia: The Apogee of Autocracy, 1825–1855, ed J. Zacek (Gulf Breeze, Fla 1974)
Lencyk, W. The Eastern Catholic Church and Czar Nicholas I (Rome–New York 1968)
Lincoln, W. Nicholas I: Emperor and Autocrat of All the Russias (Bloomington, Ill–London 1978)

O. Ohloblyn

Nicholas II (Nikolai Aleksandrovich Romanov), b 18 May 1868 in Tsarskoe Selo (now Pushkin), St Petersburg gubernia, d 17 July 1918 in Ekaterinburg, Perm gubernia. The last Russian emperor (1894–1917). Nicholas continued the reactionary policies of his father, *Alexander III, which were aimed at the maintenance of autocratic order in the Russian Empire and the political status quo in Europe, imperialistic expansion in Asia (particularly in the Far East), and domination over the empire's non-Russian peoples. Police repression failed, however, to check the growth of peasant unrest, workers' strikes, revolutionary parties, terrorism, national-liberation movements (particularly in Ukraine), and political opposition by the intelligentsia and bourgeoisie (which increasingly took the form of mass petitions, protests, and demonstrations) throughout the empire. The civil strife, combined with Russia's defeat in the Russo-Japanese War of 1904–5, culminated in the *Revolution of 1905. Nicholas was forced to introduce constitutional reforms and a State *Duma with limited legislative powers and to guarantee basic civil liberties. The restrictions against the Ukrainian language lapsed; the language began to be used, and there occurred a rebirth of Ukrainian literary, scholarly, civic, and cultural

activity. The *Stolypin agrarian reforms introduced under Nicholas strengthened the economic influence of the wealthier strata of the Ukrainian peasantry.

But Nicholas subsequently reverted to his reactionary policies. He dissolved the first two dumas, restricted the rights of non-Russian peoples, and patronized the extreme-right *Black Hundreds. After Russia entered the First World War, all Ukrainian-language institutions, publications, and periodicals were banned, and many Ukrainian leaders, including M. *Hrushevsky, were arrested and sent into exile outside Ukraine. During the 1915 Russian occupation of Galicia and Bukovyna Ukrainian institutions there suffered the same repressions. Civic leaders and hundreds of Greek Catholic clergy, including Metropolitan A. Sheptytsky, were deported to Russia and Siberia; publishing in Ukrainian was forbidden; all Ukrainian institutions were closed down; and all manifestations of organized Ukrainian activity were suppressed. Popular dissatisfaction with the war and Nicholas's inept rule gave rise to the February Revolution of 1917 and his abdication, house arrest, and removal by the Provisional Government to Tobolsk, Siberia. He and his wife and five children were executed by the Bolsheviks to prevent their rescue by White forces.

Nichyk, Valeriia [Ničyk, Valerija], b 3 October 1928 in Antonivka, Varva raion, now in Chernihiv oblast. Philosopher. A graduate of Kiev University (1951), since 1952 she has worked at the AN URSR (now ANU) Institute of Philosophy. She has been a candidate of sciences since 1958 and a doctor of philosophy since 1979, and she has directed the institute's Sector of the History of Philosophy in Ukraine since 1984. Nichyk is the leading specialist on philosophy in 17th- and 18th-century Ukraine. She has written numerous articles in this field and books on T. Prokopovych (1977) and on the main themes of philosophy courses at the Kievan Mohyla Academy, titled Iz istorii otechestvennoi filosofii kontsa XVII–nachala XVIII v. (From the History of the Fatherland's Philosophy from the End of the 17th to the Beginning of the 18th Century, 1978); coedited the institute's edition of T. Prokopovych's philosophical works in (3 vols, 1979–81) and the writings of the brotherhood schools (1988); was chief editor of a collection of articles on philosophy from I. Vyshensky to H. Skovoroda (1972) and of the first volume of the ANU history of philosophy in Ukraine (1987); and cowrote a book on humanist and Reformation ideas in Ukraine (1990). She has also done some work in the philosophy of science: she has written books on the philosophical foundations of O. Bohomolet's scientific works (1958) and on causality as a category of dialectical materialism (1960).

Nickel ores. Unrefined mineral deposits of a ferromagnetic metal with varied domestic and industrial applications. The first nickel deposits in Ukraine were mined in 1937 in Dnipropetrovske oblast. Additional finds in the region of the Ukrainian Crystalline Shield have brought the number of known deposits to 10 – 6 in the Boh River region and 4 in the Middle Dnieper area. The nickel content of the ores varies from 0.3 to 2.5 percent, with an average of 0.9 to 1.0 percent.

Niederle, Lubor, b 20 September 1865 in Klatovy, Bohemia, d 14 June 1944 in Prague. Czech Slavist, archeologist, anthropologist, and ethnographer. A graduate of Prague

University (1887), he began lecturing there in 1891. He visited Ukraine in 1893. In 1898 he was promoted to the position of professor of archeology and ethnography. He was a member of the Shevchenko Scientific Society in Lviv and the Ukrainian Scientific Society in Kiev and maintained contacts with Ukrainian scholars, such as M. Hrushevsky and V. Hnatiuk. His chief works on the origin of the Slavs are *Slovanské starožitnosti* (Slavic Antiquities, 4 vols, 1902–25; Russian translation of vol 4, 1904), *Život starých Slovanů* (The Life of the Ancient Slavs, 1909; Russian translation 1909; French translation 1923–6), and *Rukovět' slovanské archeologie* (Handbook in Slavic Archeology, 1931). He wrote extensively about Transcarpathia, which he considered to be the cradle of the Slavs.

Niedźwiedski, Julian. See Medvedsky, Yuliian.

Oleh Niemets

Niemets, Oleh [Njemec'], b 13 February 1922 in Kiev. Physicist; member of the AN URSR (now ANU) since 1978. He graduated from the Kiev Polytechnical Institute in 1947 and from 1949 to 1970 was deputy director of the ANU Institute of Physics and from 1974 to 1982 director of the Institute for Nuclear Research. Since 1956 he has been a professor of physics at Kiev University. His main fields of research are nuclear structure, properties of nuclear forces, and mechanisms of nuclear reactions. He identified the irregular change of deuteron break-up cross section resulting from a decrease in diffuseness, the 'Nemets effect.' Among his monographs are *Poliarizatsiini doslidzhennia v iadernii fizytsi* (Investigation of Polarization in Nuclear Physics, 1980), *Nuklonni asotsiiatsiï v atomnykh iadrakh ta iaderni reaktsiï bahatonuklonnykh peredach* (Nucleon Associations in Atomic Nuclei and Many Particle Transfer Nuclear Reactions, 1988), and *Elektromahnitni momenty zbudzhenykh ta radioaktyvnykh iader* (Electromagnetic Moments of Excited and Radioactive Nuclei, 1989).

Nieuważny, Florian, b 30 April 1929 in Żywiec, Cracow voivodeship, Poland. Polish literary scholar and translator. He completed postgraduate studies at Kiev University (1959) and became a lecturer at and, later, head (1971) of the Department of Ukrainian Philology at Warsaw University. He coedited *Antologia poezji ukraińskiej* (Anthology of Ukrainian Poetry, 1977) and has edited collections of Polish translations of works of 20th-century Ukrainian poets, including P. Tychyna (1969), M. Rylsky (1965), and V. Korotych (1974). His articles on Ukrainian writers and literature have appeared in *Slavia Orientalis*, *Mały słownik pisarzy europejskich narodów ZSRR* (A Concise Dictionary of Writers of the European Nations of the USSR, 1966), *Ukraïns'kyi kalendar*, and *Nasha kul'tura*.

Nightingale (*Luscinia*; Ukrainian: *soloveiko*). A small (approx 14–17 cm long) Eurasian bird of the thrush family Turdidae, renowned for its singing ability. In Ukraine the western or southern nightingale (*L. megarhynchos*) is found primarily in the Crimea but also in Transcarpathia, Polisia, and the western regions of the forest-steppe; the eastern or common nightingale (*L. luscinia*) is found throughout Ukraine; and the blue-throated nightingale (*L. svecica*) is found everywhere except the Crimea, the Carpathians, and the steppe. The nightingale is commonly invoked in Ukrainian *folk songs and *folklore in the image of a creator of sweet sounds, a builder of homes, and a harbinger of spring. The word *soloveiko* is a term of personal endearment.

Nightshade (*Solanum*; Ukrainian: *paslyna, paslin*). Annual and perennial creeping shrubs of the family Solanaceae. About 2,000 species of *Solanum* are known, 6 of which are found in Ukraine. The most common are the black nightshade (*S. nigrum*), with black, poisonous berries, and the bittersweet or woody nightshade (*S. dulcamara*), with foliage and egg-shaped red berries that are poisonous and capable of causing convulsions and death. The closely related deadly nightshade, or *belladonna (*Atropa belladonna*), is a tall, bushy herb, which is the source of a number of alkaloid drugs. Nightshades have been used in *folk medicine to treat rheumatism, respiratory disease, and skin ailments.

Entrance to the Nikita Botanical Garden

Nikita Botanical Garden (Nikitskyi botanichnyi sad). A scientific research complex located near Botanichne (formerly Nikita), a few kilometers east of Yalta, in the Crimea. Its founder and first director was C. Steven (1812–26), a Swedish botanist and the chief inspector of silkworm farming in the southern Russian Empire. Under the sponsorship of Duke A-E. du Plessis de Richelieu, the governor of New Russia, he created the garden as an imperial repository of all useful and decorative Mediterranean and Asian plants, with the purpose of subsequently cultivating them throughout the region. The first Russian pomological collection (1817), a horticultural school (1823, closed down in 1921), vineyards and a wine-making school (1828), medicinal-plant and tobacco plantations, and a botanical cabinet and meteorological station (1908) were established there. In 1890 the garden began publishing its own collection, *Zapiski* (later renamed *Trudy*). In 1920 it had an area of approx 136 ha. In 1924 the garden was designated an all-Union scientific institution. It began publishing a research bulletin in 1929, and research in plant selection and hybridization began there in the 1930s. Under the USSR Ministry of Agriculture and part of the All-Union Academy of Agricultural Sciences, it covered an area of nearly 1,000 ha, employed 1,300 people, and consisted of 15 research departments and laboratories, a museum, archives, printing press, 4 parks, 4 experimental farms (near Yalta, Frunzenske, Gvardiiske, and Medvedivka), and the Cape Martian Nature Preserve (est 1973). Over 15,000 plant species, varieties, sorts, and hybrids were cultivated there. Its library, the oldest and one of the best Ukrainian repositories of biological and agricultural literature, had holdings of over 207,700 books and periodicals; and its herbarium of Crimean flora had over 121,446 pages. The garden's scientists (approx 120) study the Earth's flora and introduce, acclimatize, and select decorative, fruit- and nut-bearing, medicinal, essential-oil, and industrial plants for widespread use and production in southern Ukraine, Moldova, Caucasia, and Central Asia. The garden has about 700,000 visitors annually. An illustrated Ukrainian-French book about it was published in 1987.

R. Senkus

Nikitin, Andrii, b 23 June 1927 in Bohuslav, Bila Tserkva okruha. Cyberneticist and computer scientist. He graduated from Kazan University (1957), and since 1958 he has worked at the AN URSR (now ANU) Institute of Cybernetics in Kiev. He made significant contributions in the areas of operating systems in computers, computer networking, and intercomputer protocols.

Nikitin, Volodymyr, b 7 August 1907 in Arkhangelsk, Russia. Physiologist; full member of the AN URSR (now ANU) from 1967. A graduate of the Kharkiv Institute of People's Education (1929), he worked at the Kharkiv Zootechnical Institute (1930–53) and at Kharkiv University as department head and director of its biology research institute. He wrote over 500 articles and 8 monographs dealing with the physiology and biochemistry of animals, ontogenesis, endocrinology, hematology, and gerontology. He introduced the concept of the endocrine formula of aging and proposed the theory of genome breakdown as the leading factor in cell aging.

Nikitska Yaila

Nikitska Yaila [Nikits'ka Jajla]. A massif in the southwestern part of the main range of the *Crimean Mountains that divides the Yalta and Hurzuf coastal regions. The peaks in the mountain cluster are approx 1,300–1,400 m high, with the tallest, Mount Avinda, reaching 1,473 m. They contain a variety of karst formations. Crimean pine forests are located on the mountains' limestone inclines. Nikitska Yaila forms part of the *Crimean Game Preserve.

Nikolaev, Lev, b 10 February 1898 in Tahanrih, Don Cossack province, d 10 December 1955 in Kharkiv. Anthropologist and orthopedist. A graduate of Paris University (1916) and the medical faculty of Kharkiv University (1920), he chaired the anatomy department at the Kharkiv Institute of People's Education (1924–30) and headed the anthropology subdepartment of the Ukrainian Scientific Research Institute of Orthopedics and Traumatology (1928–34). At the latter institute he organized and chaired (from 1934) the first department of biomechanics in the USSR. His papers appeared in *Materialy po antropologii Ukrainy* (vols 1–3, 1926–7), and he wrote *Antropometricheskie materialy dlia izgotovleniia standartnoi obuvi* (Anthropometric Materials for the Manufacture of Standard Footwear, 1931) and *Biomekhanicheskie osnovy protezirovaniia* (Biomechanical Foundations of Prosthetics, 1954).

Nikolaev, Vladimir, b 1847 in Tsarskoe Selo, Russia, d 11 November 1911 in Kiev. Architect. After graduating from the St Petersburg Academy of Arts (1870) he worked as an architect in Kiev. In 1892 he was elected a member of the Academy of Arts. He was a founder and director of the Kiev Art School (1901–11). He designed many residential and public buildings in Kiev, including the Bergonier Theater (now the Kiev Russian Drama Theater, 1873), the Merchants' Assembly building (now the Philharmonic building, 1882), the Refectory Church at the Kievan Cave Monastery (1893–5), and St Nicholas's Cathedral at the Holy Protectress Monastery (1902). He also took part in the construction of St Volodymyr's Cathedral (1862–96), the Opera Theater (1898–1901), and the City Museum (1897–1900) and designed the base of M. Mikeshin's monument to B. Khmelnytsky.

Nikolaevsk. III-26. A town smt (1959 pop 11,000) on the left bank of the Volgograd Reservoir and a raion center in Volgograd oblast, RF. It was founded as a *sloboda in 1794 and was the largest Ukrainian colony in the Volga Lowland. According to the Soviet census of 1926, Ukrainians represented 77.4 percent of the population in and around Nikolaevsk.

Nikolaiev, Anatolii [Nikolajev, Anatolij], b 5 February 1896 in Tarashcha, Kiev gubernia, d 6 July 1972 in Kiev. Obstetrician and gynecologist; full member of the USSR Academy of Medical Sciences from 1952. A graduate of Kiev University (1917), he practiced medicine in Kiev, Poltava, and Donetske (1922–41), held executive positions at the academy's institutes of obstetrics and gynecology (1944–54), and was assistant scientific director of the Institute of Maternity and Childhood Care in Kiev. He published over 165 papers on the birth process, the prevention of intrauterine asphyxiation, painless childbirth through psychological preparation, and toxicoses due to pregnancy.

Nikolenko, Dmytro, b 7 November 1899 in Zhabotyn, Cherkasy county, Kiev gubernia. Psychologist. He graduated from the Kiev Institute of People's Education (1924) and worked in his specialty in Kiev. In 1930 he began to teach at the Kiev Pedagogical Institute, where in 1952 he was appointed to the chair of psychology. His publications deal mostly with child psychology, educational psychology, occupational psychology, and the history of psychology.

Nikolsky, Oleksander [Nikol's'kyj], b 4 March 1858 in Astrakhan, d 8 July 1942 in Kharkiv. Zoologist; full member of the VUAN and AN URSR (now ANU) from 1919. He completed his studies at St Petersburg University in 1881, and then headed the fish, amphibian, and reptile department of the Zoological Museum of the Academy of Sciences in St Petersburg (from 1896), taught at Kharkiv University (1903–20), headed the zoology research division of the Kharkiv Institute of People's Education (1921–31), and taught at the Kharkiv Medical Institute (1921–6). He led numerous research expeditions in Russia, Ukraine, and particularly the Crimea, during which he identified 69 new species and 16 subspecies of vertebrates. His writings include *Pozvonochnye zhivotnye Kryma* (Vertebrate Animals of the Crimea, 1891) and *Vyznachnyk ryb Ukraïny* (A Guide to the Fish of Ukraine, 1930).

Nikolsky, Volodymyr [Nikols'kyj], b 15 August 1906 in Kvashonki, Tver gubernia, Russia, d 4 April 1979 in Kiev. Microbiologist and virologist. A graduate of the Leningrad Veterinary Institute (1929), he was director of the microbiology and virology department of the Ukrainian Agricultural Academy in Kiev (1956–79).

Nikopol. See Nykopil.

Andrii Nikovsky   Ivan Nimchuk

Nikovsky, Andrii [Nikovs'kyj, Andrij], b 14 October 1885 in Malyi Buialyk (now Sverdlove), Odessa county, Kherson gubernia, d 1942. Political leader, literary scholar, and journalist. He edited the newspapers *Rada* (1913–14) and *Nova rada* (1917–19) in Kiev and the journal *Osnova* (1915) in Odessa. During the revolutionary period he served as the first president of the *Ukrainian National Union (1918) and as minister of foreign affairs in V. Prokopovych's cabinet (1920). After returning to Ukraine in 1924, he worked as a research associate of the Commis-

sion for the Compilation of a Dictionary of the Ukrainian Vernacular and of the historical-philological division at the All-Ukrainian Academy of Sciences. He was sentenced at the *Union for the Liberation of Ukraine show trial to a 10-year term in a prison camp, which he served in the Solovets Islands. He wrote a book of critical essays, *Vita Nuova* (1919), a Ukrainian-Russian dictionary (1927), introductions to works by Lesia Ukrainka, I. Nechui-Levytsky, O. Kobylianska, H. Kvitka-Osnovianenko, and T. Borduliak, and a translation of W. Shakespeare's *Hamlet* (1928–9). He also translated works by N. Gogol and J. London into Ukrainian.

Nilus, Petro (né Slovetsky), b 21 February 1869 on the Busheny estate, Podilia gubernia, d 23 May 1942 in Paris. Painter. He studied under K. Kostandi at the Odessa Painting School (1883–9) and the St Petersburg Academy of Arts and was active in the *Society of South Russian Artists and the *Peredvizhniki society. From 1920 he lived abroad. Although he did some landscapes, he is best known for his large genre paintings, such as *Doing the Rounds* (1891), *In the Tavern* (1894), *On the Boulevard* (1895), *At the Theater Box Office* (1901), and *In the Artist's Studio* (1903). After 1910 he diverged from his earlier realism and began using stronger colors and simpler lines, as in *Golden Dreams, A Paris Street* (1930), and *Metro Exit* (1942). V. Afanasiev's monograph about him was published in Kiev in 1963.

Nimchuk, Dmytro [Nimčuk], b 1897, d 1944. Political leader and publicist. He was active in the Social Democratic Party of Transcarpathia and edited its paper *Vpered (1926–32). He was president of the Public Health Insurance Institution in Khust. In January 1939 he became a member of the executive of the Ukrainian National Alliance. In the following month he was elected in the Khust district to the Diet of Carpatho-Ukraine, where he served as sergeant at arms. After the occupation of Transcarpathia by the Hungarians, he fled to Bratislava, where he was arrested and murdered by the Gestapo.

Nimchuk, Ivan [Nimčuk], b 12 February 1891 in Dzhuryn, Chortkiv county, Galicia, d 1 May 1956 in Edmonton. Civic and political leader and journalist; member of the Shevchenko Scientific Society from 1948. While studying at Lviv University he helped edit the daily *Nove slovo* (1912–14). After recovering from wounds sustained on the Serbian front he moved to Vienna, where he edited *Vidrodzhennia Ukraïny* (1918) and *Ukraïns'kyi prapor* (1921–3) and completed his studies in history (PH D, 1924). In 1925 he joined the editorial board of *Dilo*, and in 1935 he became managing and technical editor of the paper. He also served as a member of the Central Committee of the Ukrainian National Democratic Alliance. After being held by the Soviets in the Lubianka prison in Moscow (1939–41) he returned to Lviv, where he worked as a correspondent and editor of *Krakivs'ki visti* (1942–4) and chief editor of *Nashi dni. After leaving Ukraine he was chief editor of the weekly *Khrystyians'kyi shliakh* (1946–7) in Germany and *Ukraïns'ki visti* (1949–56) in Edmonton. During his career he edited many books and almanacs. His special interests were military history, the growth of populism, and the history of the Ukrainian press, and he wrote many articles on these subjects. His writings include *595 dniv soviets'kym v'iaznem* (595 Days as a Soviet Prisoner, 1950).

Nimchuk, Vasyl [Nimčuk, Vasyl'], b 6 July 1933 in Dovhe, Transcarpathia. Linguist; corresponding member of the ANU (formerly AN URSR) since 1990. Since graduating from Uzhhorod University in 1955 and completing graduate studies there in 1958, Nimchuk has been on the staff of the ANU Institute of Linguistics. His works deal with dialectology, the history of the Ukrainian language, language contacts, onomastics, and the Old Rus' and Old Church Slavonic languages. Among his major publications are *Slovoobrazovanie imennykh chastei rechi v zakarpatskikh verkhnenadborzhavskikh govorakh* (Word Formation of the Nominal Parts of Speech in the Transcarpathian Upper Borzhava Dialects, 1962), *Slovnyk hidronimiv Ukraïny* (Dictionary of the Hydronyms of Ukraine, 1979), *Staroukraïns'ka leksykohrafiia v iï zv'iazkakh z rosiis'koiu ta bilorus'koiu* (Old Ukrainian Lexicography in Its Relations to Russian and Belarusian, 1980), *Kyïvs'ki hlaholychni lystky* (Kiev Glagolitic Folia, 1983), and entries in *Etymolohichnyi slovnyk ukraïns'koï movy* (Etymological Dictionary of the Ukrainian Language, 1983–5) as well as *Movoznavstvo na Ukraïni v XIV–XVII st.* (Linguistics in Ukraine in the 14th–17th Centuries, 1985).

Nimchynov, Kostiantyn [Nimčynov, Kostjantyn], b 3 January 1899 in Andriivka, Zmiiv county, Kharkiv gubernia, d ? Linguist. A professor at Kharkiv University in the 1920s and 1930s and a member of the State Commission for the Formulation of Rules for the Orthography of the Ukrainian Language (1925–6), he helped compile a Russian-Ukrainian dictionary (1926) and two advanced course books of Ukrainian (1929, 1931), and wrote a booklet on the Ukrainian language in the past and present (1925, 1926) and articles on Ukrainian historical morphology, syntax, and etymology. He agreed with S. Smal-Stotsky's rejection of the theory of one proto-Rus' nation. In 1934 he published a brochure attacking 'nationalist sabotage' in Ukrainian syntax, but this Stalinist diatribe did not forestall his arrest in 1937. His further fate is unknown.

Nimenko, Andrii, b 20 June 1925 in Inhulo-Kamianka, Zinovivske okruha. Sculptor, graphic artist, art scholar, and poet. A graduate of the Kiev State Art Institute (1951), he has done portraits of P. Voronko (1951) and T. Shevchenko (1964) and the relief in the Enei café in the Kiev Building of Litterateurs, and collaborated on the reliefs in the Arsenal station of the Kiev metro (1960) and on monuments, such as that to D. Guramishvili in Myrhorod (1969). He has illustrated books and has written several, on M. Lysenko (1958), I. Kavaleridze (1967), Ukrainian sculpture from the mid-19th to the early 20th century (1963), and monuments to Shevchenko (1964). Since 1969 he has published several poetry collections and written documentary film scripts.

Niniowskyi, Wasyl [Nin'ovs'kyj, Vasyl'], b 9 February 1914 in Zhukotyn, Turka county, Galicia. Lexicographer, educator, and graphic artist. In the interwar period he was a community organizer in the Kolomyia region, and was persecuted by Polish and then Soviet and German authorities. Having emigrated to Canada from Western Europe in 1950, he completed his higher education at the universities of Alberta (MA, 1967) and Ottawa (PH D, 1973) and lectured in Slavic languages at the universities of Alberta (1967–9) and Saskatchewan (1972). He has written over 200 articles on historical, literary, artistic, and political topics and two books on the poetic form of Hutsul carols (1967, 1968), and has compiled a Ukrainian inverse dictionary (1969) and a Ukrainian-English and English-Ukrainian dictionary (1985). Several exhibits of his graphic works have been held.

Nirod, Fedir, b 31 April 1907 in St Petersburg. Theatrical designer. He completed study at the Kiev State Art Institute in 1930, and in 1934–45 he worked as stage designer in the Zankovetska Theater (from 1944 the Lviv Ukrainian Drama Theater). In 1950 he started working for the Lviv Opera Theater, and in 1961 he became principal designer of the Kiev Opera and Ballet Theater. In all, he created scenery for over 150 productions, combining elements of constructivism and productionism in his designs (as in K. Gutzkow's *Uriel Akosta* for the Zankovetska Theater). Later he became more conservative (as in P. Tchaikovsky's ballet *Swan Lake*). A biography, by M. Pamfilova, was published in Kiev in 1969.

Nis, Stepan (pseud: S. Voloshyn), b 6 May 1829 in Ponory, Konotip county, Chernihiv gubernia, d 19 December 1900 in Horodnia, Chernihiv gubernia. Ethnographer and writer. After graduating from Kiev University (1854) he served as a physician in Chernihiv and was exiled in 1863 to Novgorod gubernia for 'distributing Little Russian propaganda.' In 1871 he settled in Horodnia, where he practiced medicine and devoted himself to ethnographic studies. His folkloric materials were published in *Chernigovskie gubernskie vedomosti* and A. Metlynsky's, P. Chubynsky's, and M. Nomys's collections. Only some of his short stories, about serfs and Cossacks, appeared in his lifetime, in *Osnova, Chernigovskii listok,* and *Kievskaia starina.* Nis also wrote several popular brochures on home medical care (1874) and folk remedies (1875).

Petro Nishchynsky

Nishchynsky, Petro [Niščyns'kyj] (pseud: P. Baida), b 21 September 1832 in Nemenka, Lypovets county, Kiev gubernia, d 16 March 1896 in Voroshylivka, Vinnytsia county, Podilia gubernia. Hellenist, composer, and translator. He studied music and theory at the Kiev Theological Academy and in 1850 moved to Athens to conduct the Russian embassy's church choir. While there he studied philology and theology at the University of Athens (MA 1856). Nishchynsky was the first to translate Sophocles' *Antigone* (1883) and Homer's *Odyssey* (1889, 1892) from the original Greek into modern Ukrainian. He also translated *Slovo o polku Ihorevi* into Greek, undertook a study of Greek music, and wrote a school text for Greek language study. His musical works include the dramatic scene *Vechornytsi* (Evening Pastimes, 1875) opening the second act of T. Shevchenko's drama *Nazar Stodolia*, which features the popular 'Zakuvala ta syva zozulia' (The Gray Cuckoo Began Cuckooing), and arrangements of historic Ukrainian folk songs.

BIBLIOGRAPHY
Dovzhenko, V. *P.I. Nishchyns'kyi* (Kiev 1955)
Parkhomenko, L. *Petro Nishchyns'kyi* (Kiev 1989)

W. Sydorenko

Nitsch, Kazimierz, b 1 February 1874 in Cracow, d 26 September 1958 in Cracow. Polish linguist. A graduate of Cracow University (PH D, 1898), he was a professor there (1911–17, 1920–39, 1945–52) and at Lviv University (1917–20), and a member of the Polish Academy of Science from 1911, its president from 1946, and secretary of its philological division in 1924–36. He was also a member of the Bulgarian, Serbian, Slovenian, and USSR academies of sciences, the Académie des inscriptions et belles-lettres, and, from 1937, the Shevchenko Scientific Society. In 1952 he became the vice-president of the Polish Academy of Sciences and chairman of its Linguistics Committee. He was a founding member of the Polish Linguistic Society (1925) and the initiator (1913) and chief editor (1919–58) of *Język Polski*. At Cracow University he established (in 1924) a Slavic studies center with chairs of Ukrainian language (held by I. Zilynsky) and literature (B. Lepky) and was the guardian of the Ukrainian Student Hromada. He laid the foundations of Polish historical dialectology, producing the first studies on the history of Polish dialectal lexicography and the first monographic syntheses of Polish dialects. He wrote over 700 works, including studies of the impact of Ukrainian on the Polish literary language and dialects and a linguistic atlas of Subcarpathia (with M. Małecki, 2 parts, 500 maps, 1934). An edition of his selected writings (4 vols, 1954–5, 1958), his memoirs (1960), and a book about him by A. Gruszecka-Nitschowa (1977) have appeared.

Nizhen or **Nizhyn** [Nižen or Nižyn]. II-12. A city (1990 pop 81,300) on the Oster River and a raion center in Chernihiv oblast. It is first mentioned as Unenezh or Unenizh under the year 1147 in the Hypatian Chronicle. The town was destroyed by the Tatars in 1239, and it recovered slowly. In the mid-14th century it came under Lithuanian rule, and in 1514 it was renamed Nizhen. In 1618 it was taken by Poland, and in 1625 it was granted the rights of *Magdeburg law. In the Hetman state it was a regiment center of Nizhen regiment (1648–1782) and then a county center of Chernihiv vicegerency and Chernihiv gubernia (1802–1917). The *chorna rada* in Nizhen in 1663 elected I. Briukhovetsky hetman. By the Treaty of Andrusovo in 1667 Nizhen was handed over to Russia. Situated at the junction of several major trade routes, Nizhen developed into an important manufacturing and trade center in the 17th and 18th centuries. A large Greek merchant colony sprang up in the second half of the 17th century and received special privileges from Hetman B. Khmelnytsky. In 1785 a Greek brotherhood and a Greek municipal council were set up. In 1696 the Greeks organized their

Nizhen. Clockwise, from upper left: the Nizhen Pedagogical Institute (formerly Lyceum), Annunciation Cathedral (early 18th century), Church of the Holy Protectress (2nd half of the 18th century), monument to Nikolai Gogol (sculptor: Parmen Zabila, 1881), and St Nicholas's Cathedral (2nd half of the 17th century)

own school. When Russia gained a foothold on the Black Sea, the trade routes shifted to the Black Sea and Azov Sea ports, and the Greek merchants moved to Odessa, Mariiupil, and Tahanrih. The town's commercial importance declined, but its cultural influence grew. In 1820 a gymnasium was opened, which in 1832 was reorganized into the Nizhen Lyceum (now the Nizhen Pedagogical Institute). In the mid-19th century the town became a railway junction. Today Nizhen's plants build farm machinery, household chemicals, rubber products, clothes, and building materials. The city is known for its vegetable trade. Nizhen has three museums – the Gogol Memorial Museum, a rare books museum, and a regional museum – and an art gallery. There are over 20 architectural monuments in the city, including the cathedrals of St Nicholas (1668), the Annunciation (1702), and the Presentation at the Temple (1778), the churches of St John Chrysostom (1752), the Holy Trinity (1733), and the Transfiguration (1757), the Greek churches of All Saints (1780s) and St Michael (1731), the lyceum building (1807–20), and 18th-century residential buildings. Many architectural monuments were destroyed by the Soviet authorities in the 1930s.

Nizhen Lyceum (Nizhenskyi or Bezborodkivskyi litsei). One of the older institutions of higher learning in Ukraine, located in Nizhen. Founded as the Bezborodko Gymnasium of Higher Education in 1820 with an endowment of 210,000 rubles from Count I. Bezborodko, it emphasized umanities and was initially a gymnasium for the sons of he gentry. Its nine-year program offered a classical education with instruction in religion, classical and modern anguages, geography, history, physics and mathematics, political economy, military science, and the arts. The first director was V. *Kukolnyk. By 1832 the gymnasium had graduated over 100 students, including the writers N. Gogol and Ye. Hrebinka and the ethnographer V. Tarnovsky.

In 1832 the gymnasium was transformed into a technical (physico-mathematical) lyceum for the training of military officers, and in 1840 it became a law school preparing officials for the juridical bureaucracy. Its broad curriculum was replaced by a narrow one, and the general level of education fell. Nonetheless, in this period the lyceum graduated over 1,000 students, including O. Lazarevsky and L. Hlibov. The school returned to prominence after 1875, when it was reorganized as the Prince Oleksander Bezborodko Historico-Philological Institute, named after the brother of its founder. The institute taught classical languages, Russian language, and history and prepared teachers for the secondary-school system. The program also included courses in psychology and pedagogy. From 1876 to 1921 *Izvestiia Istoriko-filologicheskogo instituta*, which contained many original works on Ukrainian and general history by professors and students at the institute, was published there. The first rector of the institute was M. Lavrovsky. Professors at the lyceum or institute included M. Bunge, A. Lynnychenko, P. Morachevsky, M. Grot, and M. Sokolov.

After the revolution the institute was transformed into the Nizhen Institute of People's Education (1922) and then the Institute of Social Education (1930) before becoming the *Nizhen Pedagogical Institute in 1934.

O. Skrypnyk

Nizhen Pedagogical Institute (Nizhenskyi pedahohichnyi instytut im. M.V. Hoholia). An institution of higher learning in Nizhen, Chernihiv oblast. It was founded in 1934 in place of the Nizhen Institute of People's Education (1920–30) and Institute of Social Education (1930–4) as the successor to the *Nizhen Lyceum. In 1939 it was named after N. *Gogol, who had studied at the lyceum during the 1820s. The institute is under the jurisdiction of the Ukrainian Ministry of Education. It consists of five faculties: philology, natural sciences, physics-mathematics, instrumental and vocal music, and English and German. It has a library of over 500,000 volumes and a museum devoted to Gogol. The student enrollment in 1986–7 was 3,300. Among its alumni are many writers (eg, Ye. Hutsalo, Yu. Zbanatsky) and scholars (P. Bohach).

Nizhen regiment (Nizhenskyi polk). An administrative territory and military formation of the Hetman state. Formed in 1648, Nizhen was one of the largest and most important of the Cossack regiments. In 1653–4 the regiment's male population numbered over 20,000, almost 12,000 of whom were Cossacks. It consisted of about 40 companies. The regiment was reorganized in 1663: eight northern companies were separated into Starodub regiment, some companies were transferred to Kiev and Chernihiv regiments, and the eastern part was formed into Hlukhiv regiment. For the next 60 years Nizhen regiment consisted of 20 companies. From 1668 to 1782 the

capital of the Hetmanate, Baturyn and, later, Hlukhiv, was situated on Nizhen territory. Six of its companies formed the hetman guard and did not come under the regiment's command. In the early 1720s the male population of Nizhen regiment was approx 16,300, including 10,000 Cossacks. By 1764 the male population had increased to 141,800, including 21,700 *elect Cossacks and 42,800 Cossack helpers. Many of its officers came from powerful Cossack families, and some of its colonels, such as I. Zolotarenko (1652–5), H. Hulianytsky (1656–9), and I. Obydovsky (1695–1701), attained high office in the Hetmanate. The regiment was abolished by the Russian authorities in 1782, and its territory was absorbed into Chernihiv vicegerency.

Nizhen Ukrainian Drama Theater (Nizhenskyi ukrainskyi dramatychnyi teatr im. M. Kotsiubynskoho). Established in Kiev in 1927 as the Kotsiubynsky Oblast Theater of the Council of Trade Unions under the artistic directorship of B. Luchytsky, and located in Nizhen since 1934. Although officially a resident theater, it has no permanent home and in practice continues to be a touring workers' and peasants' theater, with a repertoire of Ukrainian and Russian classics and contemporary Soviet plays. Its present director is O. Horbenko.

NKVD (Russian: Narodnyi komissariat vnutrennikh del; Ukrainian: NKVS, or Narodnyi komisariiat vnutrishnikh sprav [People's Commissariat for Internal Affairs]). A ministry of the Soviet government responsible for security and law enforcement that was set up on 7 November 1917 and reorganized as the *MVD on 19 March 1946. During its history the NKVD underwent numerous organizational and functional changes: sometimes, as in 1922–3, 1934–41, and 1941–3, it encompassed not only the secret political police and foreign intelligence but also the regular police force, the border guards, and the prison system. At other times, as in 1917–22, 1923–34, 1941, and 1943–6, it was divided into two separate agencies, one responsible for state security and the other for law enforcement. These changes were due to political rather than administrative factors. The NKVD's notoriety as an instrument of terror belongs to the periods when the state security apparatus came under its jurisdiction (July 1934 to April 1943, except for February–July 1941).

At first the *Cheka and the NKVD were independent and often competing institutions. When F. Dzerzhinsky, the founder and chief of the Cheka, replaced H. *Petrovsky as head of the NKVD, in March 1919, the institutional friction between the two agencies subsided. Petrovsky's predecessor was A. Rykov, who headed the NKVD only briefly, in 1917. The new permanent state security organ, the *GPU, which replaced the ad hoc and temporary Cheka in February 1922, came under the NKVD. The Unified State Political Administration (OGPU), which succeeded the GPU in November 1923, was separated from the NKVD until July 1934, when it was renamed the Main Administration of State Security (GUGB) and subordinated to the NKVD. Republican commissariats of internal affairs had been abolished in 1930. After F. Dzerzhinsky's death (1926) the NKVD was headed by V. Menzhinsky until May 1934.

The unified NKVD (1934–41) consisted of numerous main administrations and departments of Union, republic, and lower levels. The main administrations were state security (GUGB), the corrective labor camps (GULAG), the border and internal troops (GUPVO), the worker-peasant militia, and the fire service (GUPO), all of which were established in July 1934. Later the main administrations of state surveying and cartography, highways, and weights and measures were added to the NKVD. The commissariat also had an administrative-economic administration, a department of acts of civil status, and a department of colonization. It is evident from its structure that the NKVD was much more than an organ of state security. In fact in the 1930s and 1940s its economic role was most conspicuous. Because it ran a vast network of labor camps, prisons, and other economic enterprises, the NKVD has been called the USSR's largest employer. Its slave-labor reserves were used in numerous large-scale construction projects, lumbering, and gold mining, and its contribution to the Soviet economy was factored into the five-year plans.

In the 1930s the Main Administration of State Security constituted the central agency of the NKVD. The GUGB was subdivided into six major departments: special, economic, operative, foreign, transport, and political. The first kept the military under surveillance and was a key source of information on anti-Soviet groups. The economic department was responsible for combating economic sabotage in industry and agriculture. The operative department guarded the top leaders, including J. Stalin, and key installations. Foreign espionage and the use of terror abroad came under the foreign department. The transport department protected the transportation network and important shipments in transit. Finally, the political department dealt with political opposition groups and oversaw all organizations. Besides these departments, the GUGB included some technical sections.

The consolidated NKVD was directed by G. Yagoda (July 1934 to September 1936), N. Yezhov (to December 1938), and L. Beria (to February 1941, and July 1941 to April 1943). The NKVD played the dominant role in the terror of the 1930s, in which it carried out countless arrests, interrogations, and executions. Its special boards were empowered to sentence people for up to five years' imprisonment without judicial process. The secret police became the primary pillar of Stalin's personal dictatorship: it was deployed not only against the general population and the intelligentsia, but also against the Party, the military, and the government. The CP(B)U and Ukrainian government leaders, who had shown a reluctance to extend the purge, were decimated by arrests and executions in 1937–8. From September 1937 the republic was virtually governed by the NKVD. The NKVD played a central role in the show trials of old Bolsheviks, such as N. Bukharin, L. Kamenev, and G. Zinoviev, and in L. Trotsky's assassination. It was responsible for the massacre of over 9,000 people in Vinnytsia in 1937–8 and of some 4,000 Polish officers in Katyn Forest in 1940. Ironically, Stalin turned the NKVD upon itself: its last three chiefs along with thousands of their followers were destroyed in the great terror of the late 1930s or in the succession struggle after Stalin's death.

During the Second World War the NKVD and the People's Commissariat of State Security (NKGB) were involved separately in various phases of state security. They provided military assistance to the armed forces, organized Soviet partisans, and engaged in intelligence and counterintelligence activities. At the start of the German offensive in 1941, they brutally executed thousands of political prisoners held in their prisons in Western Ukraine. After the war they administered mass deportations of Ukrainians, Balts, and other non-Russians from the newly annexed territories and suppressed anti-Soviet underground organizations and the Ukrainian Insurgent Army. In January 1946 L. Beria was replaced by S. Kruglov as head of the NKVD, and in March the NKVD was renamed the *MVD. The general substitution of 'ministry' for 'commissariat' was meant to de-emphasize the revolutionary character of the Soviet government.

BIBLIOGRAPHY
Conquest, R. *The Soviet Police System* (New York 1968)
Levytsky, B. *The Uses of Terror: The Soviet Secret Police, 1917–1970* (New York 1972)
Conquest, R. *Inside Stalin's Secret Police: NKVD Politics, 1936–1939* (London 1985)
Dziak, J. *Chekisty: A History of the KGB* (New York 1988)
J. Bilocerkowycz

Nobel [Nobel']. II-6. A village (1971 pop 500) on Nobel Lake in Zarichne raion, Rivne oblast. It is first mentioned under the year 1158 in the Hypatian Chronicle. Nobel is the site of a settlement dating back to the Mesolithic or early Neolithic Period, the oldest settlement in the Prypiat Polisia region.

Nobility (*shliakhta*; Polish: *szlachta*; derived from Old German *Slahta*, 'gender'). The privileged and titled elite class of society. The concept of a noble class (or aristocracy) is largely a European one that developed out of the feudal experience. In Eastern Europe the nobility as a social elite with inherent rights established itself most strongly in the Polish-Lithuanian Commonwealth. In Muscovy and then the Russian Empire the status of the nobility was more closely tied to state service. In Ukraine, after the Princely era, the existence of a distinctive elite class of native nobles was largely pre-empted by the country's domination first by Poland and then by the Russian Empire (which prompted the considerable assimilation of Ukraine's upper class by foreign aristocracies). The notable exceptions to that long-standing state of affairs could be found in the Lithuanian-Ruthenian state, where Orthodox Ukrainian nobles constituted a distinctive subgroup of the aristocracy, and in the Hetmanate, where the Cossack *starshyna* was developing into a noble class. As a result of the assimilation, the social structure of Ukraine was truncated for many years, and Ukrainian society was left without a leading element. Nevertheless, individual noblemen emerged at various times as key figures in the defence of Ukrainian social, religious, and political rights.

Polish and Lithuanian rule. The nobility in the Ukrainian and Belarusian territories originated with knights who established themselves as a class (*nobilis*) first through military service (*jus militare*) and then heredity (*jus hereditarium*). Initially that nobility had a lesser stature than magnates and lords and (in Ukrainian territories) the *prince and *boyars. The members of the nobility were obliged to perform military service, for which they were accorded various privileges, including exemption from taxation and autonomy from local authorities. It was not a closed caste, and it took in new members from the peasantry and clergy.

The nobility steadily expanded its influence in state affairs, by using changing political and social circumstances to its advantage. Polish kings sought its assistance in their own struggle to establish a centralized state in opposition to the atomizing influence of the great landowners. In return the nobility was rewarded with a host of further privileges. King Louis of Anjou conferred the Košice privilege (1374) on those who served in his armies. It exempted noblemen from all duties other than the land tax of two *Groschen* per field (*lan*), extended immunity from arbitrary seizure of property and person, limited the terms of military service, and offered the right to state offices, such as voivode, castellan, justice, and chamberlain. The privilege proved a critical development in the transformation of the nobility from a warrior brotherhood into a social and economic class, consisting of lords and barons, knights (*rycerzy, milites*), and middle and small landowners, who set themselves apart from the rest of the population by their claim to a coat of arms. In time the nobility came to command considerable influence in parliamentary bodies. It extended its powers with the Cracow privilege (1433) and the Cerekwica privilege, which was later confirmed by the Nieszawa statute (1454). By then the nobility had gained legislative powers in matters of war and peace and exemption from the royal court. The Nieszawa statute also struck down the exclusive right of magnates to hold higher governmental positions and limited the rights of towns. King Jan Olbracht's Piotrków statute (1496) bound the peasantry to the land and exempted the nobility from paying duties on imported goods.

Galician boyars were granted equal status with the Polish nobility in 1430. Subsequently some of them were Polonized, and others moved to Volhynia and Podilia. By the 16th century there were no Ukrainian boyar families left in Galicia; only some petty gentry regarded themselves as Ukrainians.

Through the 16th to 18th centuries the nobility progressively increased its influence in the Polish Commonwealth, although its constitutional battles weakened the state. The *szlachta* disregarded that weakening in the defense of what it regarded as its 'golden freedoms.' It developed a corporate sense as the '*szlachta* nation.' It also established an ideology of sorts for itself, based on the belief that the *szlachta* had descended from the ancient *Sarmatians and was imbued with a purity of purpose that had been lost by the nobility of other European nations. In 1573 (under Henry of Valois) the nobles obtained the right to the election of the king by direct vote. That right effectively transformed the Polish state into an aristocratic republic and made the regal position an increasingly ineffectual one. The parliamentary body, the Sejm, was also rendered largely ineffectual after the invocation (from 1652) of the *liberum veto*, which allowed for the passage of legislation only by the complete unanimity of all of its delegates (a single veto could stop deliberations altogether). The resulting chaos initiated Poland's decline until its partition by other European powers in the late 18th century.

The nobility in Ukrainian territories in the Grand Duchy of Lithuania led a separate existence from that in Poland, but it was nevertheless influenced by sociopolitical developments there. A Polish-style aristocratic order was introduced by Polish kings or grand dukes through similar privileges or legal codes. Lithuania, however, contained two strata of nobility: the Lithuanian, which had rapidly been Catholicized, and the Belarusian-Ukrainian,

which remained Orthodox. Both Polish and Lithuanian rulers tended to favor the Lithuanian nobility and usually granted privileges to Belarusian and Ukrainian nobles only when their assistance was required or a rebellion was threatening. The titles used in those areas, such as prince and boyar, were carried over from Kievan Rus', although others (used mainly by Poles) were added, including *barones, nobiles, ziemianie,* and *szlachta*.

After the Union of *Krevo in 1385, Grand Duke Jagiełło converted to Catholicism. In 1387 he officially made his realm Catholic and conferred privileges on those boyars who adopted that faith. The Union of *Horodlo between Poland and Lithuania in 1413 granted the Lithuanian Catholic boyars equal rights with their Polish counterparts and transformed them into a hereditary elite. At the same time it relegated the Orthodox (including Ukrainian) nobility to secondary status. Only in 1432, after civil strife between religious factions, were the rights of the Orthodox and Catholic nobility placed on an equal footing. That equality was legally affirmed in 1447 (*principibus et boiaris tam Lithuanis quam Ruthenis*). The rights of the Lithuanian-Ruthenian nobility were supplemented and expanded in 1492 and 1506. In 1501 and 1509, local privileges were conferred on the Volhynian nobility. Among that group were notable noble families, including the Ostrih, Sanguszko, Czartoryski, and Zbaraski, who possessed massive estates. Until the late 16th century the majority of the Volhynian magnates were Ukrainian; they were largely Polonized in the 17th and 18th centuries.

The rights and privileges of the nobility were codified in the *Lithuanian Statute and confirmed by its three editions. In 1529 the conditions for acceptance into the aristocracy (which favored magnates) were outlined; in 1566 the rights of the regular nobility were expanded, and their representatives were accepted into parliament; in 1588 the rights of the nobility were entrenched, and the peasantry was enserfed. The last edition of the statute underscored that the nobles' claims to estates were based not on the fact of settlement but on notable military service against the enemy.

The Union of *Lublin in 1569 brought Volhynia, Podlachia, the Kiev region, and the Bratslav region under direct Polish control. At the same time the rights of the local nobility were brought into line with those of Poland. The newly acquired territories soon saw an influx of Polish magnates, including the Żółkiewski, Potocki, Koniecpolski, and Kalinowski families. It also set in motion a long process of Polonization that became a feature of Right-Bank Ukraine: by the early 19th century little non-Polonized Ukrainian nobility remained.

Polonization began after the Lublin union and was particularly enforced under Jan Casimir, who in 1649 forbade non-Catholic representation in the Senate and starosta councils. In 1712 the Polish parliament outlawed the non-Catholic nobility altogether. Nevertheless there were Ukrainian nobles who continued to adhere to Orthodoxy, as borne out by the provisions of a treaty signed by Russia and Poland in 1775 that guaranteed to Orthodox nobles the same rights as Catholics. In Right-Bank Ukraine (Volhynia, Podilia, the Kiev region) Polonization of the Ukrainian gentry continued even after the partitions of Poland. After the Polish Insurrection of 1830–1, however, the tsarist authorities actively began trying to counter Polish influence in the region by Russifying its institutions and inhabitants. According to a study of the Right-Bank nobility undertaken by the *Kiev Archeographic Commission only one-tenth of the Right-Bank nobility of the 1860s was of Polish origin. The rest consisted almost entirely of Ukrainian converts to Catholicism. The commission uncovered 711 Ukrainian noble family lines and supplied exact dates of conversion for 140 cases (1 before 1569, 10 in 1569–1600, 48 in 1600–50, 40 in 1650–1700, and 41 in 1700–67).

Galician families that maintained their Ukrainian identity included the Balaban, Cholhansky, Demydetsky, Drahomyretsky, Hoshovsky, Kulchytsky, and Yavorsky lines. In the early 17th century there were 628 Ukrainian noblemen in the Lviv region and 1,000 in the Peremyshl region. Most of them were so impoverished that they did not have their own horses when they came to serve in the army. In the Kholm, Podilia, and Podlachia regions Polonization had set in during the 15th century, and it continued until the 20th century. The Ukrainian aristocracy of the Kiev and Bratslav regions was subject to a general process of Polonization.

After 1569 the significance of the nobility as a Ukrainian social elite diminished. Nevertheless it continued to play a role in judicial affairs (notably with the Lutske Tribunal) and in the defense of the Orthodox church. Ukrainian nobles spoke out for the Orthodox church in legislative councils and influenced the selection of the bishop of Lviv (5 April 1641) and of S. Kosiv as metropolitan of Kiev (25 February 1647). Among the defenders of the Ukrainian Orthodox church were L. Drevynsky, M. Kropyvnytsky, and A. Kysil; those who were otherwise active in cultural and church affairs included the Balaban line, A. Kalnofoisky, M. and Z. Kopystensky, and Ye. Pletenetsky.

The Cossack era. Ukrainian noblemen played a significant role in the emergence of the Cossack state. They were commonly found in the higher ranks of the registered Cossacks, and later provided the impetus and direction required to transform the Cossacks from an amorphous social class into the creators and administrators of a new polity, the Hetmanate. Some notable Cossack leaders drawn from the nobility were D. *Vyshnevetsky, K. *Kosynsky, M. *Khmelnytsky, P. *Sahaidachny, and B. *Khmelnytsky.

The profound changes effected in Ukraine by the Cossacks and the B. Khmelnytsky uprising in 1648 did not include the elimination of a landed social elite. In fact one of the key changes consisted of the replacement of the largely foreign *szlachta* with an indigenous ruling class, the Cossack *starshyna*. A portion of the nobility in Ukraine, although largely Polonized, supported Kmelnytsky's revolution and tied itself to the process of establishing a Cossack state. In the early stages of the Cossack-Polish War the aristocracy, both Ukrainian and non-Ukrainian, was forced off its lands in numerous local uprisings. But Khmelnytsky established instructions through universals for the restoration of property rights for those supporting the new order, namely 'noblemen who will eat bread with us ... and recognize the authority of the Zaporozhian army' (1649). The pro-Cossack nobility, which had had experience in matters of state under the Polish regime, now served the new Hetman state apparatus in the diplomatic corps, military posts, and administrative and judicial offices. The leaders of Khmelnytsky's state drawn from the nobility included H. *Hulianytsky, M. *Krychevsky,

S. *Morozenko, D. *Nechai, I. *Vyhovsky, and A. *Zhdanovych. The Cossack register, drawn up after the Treaty of Zboriv in 1649, included 750 aristocratic families and more than 1,500 individuals. Other accounts (V. Lypynsky, A. Rolle) estimate the number at 2,500, and the figure for nobles active in the Cossack army at between 6,000 and 7,000.

With the establishment of the Hetmanate in Left-Bank Ukraine and the return to relative peace and order in the wake of the Ruin, the Cossack *starshyna* emerged as a social elite that fulfilled many of the roles of a nobility. It was composed largely of members of old, registered Cossack families, but also incorporated Orthodox landowners who supported the Hetmanate as well as common Cossacks who had risen through the ranks. During the reigns of Hetmans I. Samoilovych (1672–87) and I. Mazepa (1687–1709) the *starshyna* began developing the attributes of a noble class. It managed to circumvent the Cossack principle of election to all offices by gradually turning the voting procedure into a pro-forma affair; although the members of the *starshyna* did not establish hereditary rights, they monopolized the offices of the Hetmanate. They also made room for a second tier of *starshyna* by establishing categories within a society of military fellows (fellows of the standard, military fellows, and fellows of the banner) that were tied to no specific military or administrative posts. With position also came privileges, and the members of the *starshyna* were able to demand services from the peasantry by virtue of their office. The higher *starshyna* also established the right to be tried by its peers, another common trait of nobility. Finally the *starshyna* collectively expanded its landholdings through land grants, purchase, and, occasionally, simple seizure.

In the 18th century, while the Cossack *starshyna* established itself as a gentry elite in Left-Bank Ukraine, the Right-Bank region saw the restoration of a Polish or Polonized nobility to a position of pre-eminence. At the same time, however, resentment against the nobility and landowners (often one and the same) in the region grew and gave rise to a series of *haidamaka uprisings.

As the status of the *starshyna* became entrenched, its aspiration to continue in the tradition of the *szlachta* grew. That aspiration was increased in 1743, when a legal compendium entitled *Prava, po kotorym suditsia malorossiiskii narod* (The Laws by Which the Little Russian People Are Judged) established that descendants of appointed or hereditary nobles registered under the former state were entitled to nobility within the Russian Empire. It was further augmented in 1763, when the *pidkomorskyi court was reintroduced. That year a major gathering of *starshyna* representatives met at the hetman's residence in Hlukhiv and proposed, among other things, the transformation of the Cossack officers' council into a diet of the nobility. The most articulate argument for the establishment of *starshyna* rule in Ukraine as a type of *szlachta* democracy was made in 1767 by H. *Poletyka at Catherine II's Legislative Council.

Russian rule. In spite of the fact that Russia and then the Russian Empire had continually expanded its influence over the administration of Ukraine, the *starshyna* and regimental structure of the Hetmanate had been left intact. That state of affairs changed quickly and completely under *Catherine II. She abolished the office of the hetman

(1764), had the Zaporozhian Sich destroyed (1775), and dismantled the regimental system in favor of provincial administration (1782). Notwithstanding the fact that its autonomy and territorial base had been taken away, the Ukrainian elite did not protest the changes. Instead it moved quickly to adapt itself to the new circumstances. The smoothness of the transition was aided by several factors. The governor-general of Ukraine, P. *Rumiantsev, had made specific efforts to prevent overt dissent from manifesting itself and had opened numerous governmental positions to noblemen or their sons in Ukraine. The institution of provincial administration was followed in 1783 by a ukase that established the complete serfdom of the Ukrainian peasantry. Finally Catherine proclaimed a new Charter of the Nobility in 1785 that allowed for the incorporation of the *starshyna* into the Russian nobility. The *starshyna* had long sought legal recognition of its social status but had been hesitant to incorporate itself with the less privileged Russian nobility. The 1785 charter brought the privileges of Russian nobles (*dvorianstvo*) much in line with those of the *szlachta*. A wholesale quest for patents of nobility, sometimes with the aid of fabricated documentation, followed.

The *starshyna* gentry generally benefited materially from its integration into the *dvorianstvo* system, particularly the petty gentry, which found considerable opportunity for advancement in the imperial service. At the same time Ukrainians experienced some unique problems in defining themselves within the broader context of the empire. Some chose total assimilation to the implicitly Russian culture and language. In its extreme form that response took the form of oversubscribing to the values of the dominant culture, in effect becoming 'more Russian than the Russians' and sometimes developing an outright disdain for Ukrainian traditions. Less dramatically, some developed a sense that Ukraine was in fact culturally inferior to Russia, the so-called *Little Russian mentality, which implied deference to Great Russians. A more common response was a desire to integrate into the imperial system but to maintain certain institutional vestiges of the Hetmanate. That response was a sentiment rather than a structured movement, and it focused on matters such as Ukraine's distinct legal code and a desire to have separate Ukrainian Cossack military units. The nobility's reverence for Ukraine's Cossack heritage was challenged by the difficulties many experienced in obtaining their patents, in that the imperial Heraldic Office commonly questioned the validity of Ukrainian titles. The result was protests from the former *starshyna* gentry and a wide search for documents related to Ukraine's past, which ultimately served only to reinforce a sense of local patriotism.

In Right-Bank Ukraine, acquired by the Russian Empire through the partitioning of Poland, the rights of the local gentry were made equal with those of its Russian counterparts, although its *szlachta* privileges were limited. Initially the nobility retained its social status as a ruling class and contributed significantly to culture and education (eg, by establishing the Kremianets Lyceum). The Polish nobility consisted of a small number of magnates, independent landowners, and impoverished lessee aristocrats who were commonly employed as administrators or stewards on larger estates. In general the magnates integrated themselves quickly into the *dvorianstvo* system and were

loyal to the empire, whereas the lesser nobility maintained a sense of Polish patriotism and hoped to restore Poland to its status before the partitions.

After the Polish Insurrection of 1830–1 Russian policy toward the nobility changed significantly. Nearly 10,000 participants in the revolt were prosecuted and had their holdings confiscated. A campaign was begun to verify aristocratic status, aimed at destroying the *szlachta* nobility as a foreign element within the Russian system. Lasting approx 20 years under the direction of the governor-general, D. *Bibikov, the action stripped 340,000 individuals of their status as nobles: 72,000 in 1832–3, 93,000 in 1834–9, 160,000 in 1840–6, and 15,000 in 1846–53. The lesser, poor, and generally, landless nobility suffered. After the verification some 70,000 Poles (nearly 17,500 families) entrenched their claims to nobility. They were primarily large to middle landowners (*szlachta ziemiańska*), who controlled nearly three million serfs. The majority of the legally recognized nobility supported the Russian government, forsook its persecuted countrymen, and was indifferent to all revolutionary movements. Later it sought to integrate itself into Russian society. After the Polish Insurrection of 1863, in which a section of the nobility once again took part, further limitations on noble participation in political, community, and cultural life were imposed.

In spite of the Polish domination of the Right-Bank nobility several pro-Ukrainian movements developed. The *khlopoman* movement emerged in the late 1850s, and a Ukrainophile movement headed by V. *Lypynsky emerged among the Polonized Ukrainian gentry at the end of the 19th century. But the position of the nobility in Right-Bank Ukraine did not change until after the Revolution of 1917. At that time Polish efforts to guarantee special rights for Polish landowners in Ukraine resulted in special provisions in the Treaty of *Warsaw. Those provisions, however, were abrogated with the establishment of Soviet power in Ukraine and the end of the nobility as a class.

Western Ukraine. In Ukrainian territories under the Austrian Empire the nobility on Ukrainian territory enjoyed the same rights as its counterparts elsewhere in Austria. Initially, Joseph II's reforms limited the rights of the Polish aristocracy. After his death in 1790, however, the nobility gradually came to control large sectors of the empire's administrative structure and was able to influence highly placed Austrian officials. The Polish nobility's influence increased even more during the tenure of the Galician vicegerent, A. *Gołuchowski (1849–75, with interruptions). In the interwar Polish state (with Ukrainian territories in its eastern reaches) the nobility as a social class was legislated out of existence (1921). Nevertheless the landed aristocracy maintained its extensive political and economic influence.

In Bukovyna the Ukrainian nobility over time assimilated with the Moldavian-Rumanian elite of the region. Under Austria (from 1774) the administrative structure was controlled by Rumanian boyars, who later complained about Bukovyna's reconstitution into an administrative unit of Galicia (1787–1849). A government decree of 14 March 1787 gave the Bukovynian and Galician nobilities equal status. Even after the establishment of a constitutional monarchy in 1848, the Rumanian nobility continued to have great influence in Bukovyna as a result of the curial electoral system.

A feudal order started developing in Transcarpathia in the wake of the Tatar invasion of 1241 and the establishment of a network of stone fortresses. Most of the nobility in the region consisted of Hungarians. Prince F. *Koriiatovych, a late 14th- to early 15th-century ruler of the Mukachiv region, was the most notable Ukrainian (or Ukrainianized) nobleman in the area. From the 16th century the aristocracy of Transcarpathia was largely without Ukrainians.

BIBLIOGRAPHY

'Akty o proiskhozhdenii shliakhetskikh rodov v Iugo-Zapadnoi Rossii,' *Arkhiv Iugo-Zapadnoi Rossii* no. 4, vol 1 (Kiev 1867)

Antonovich, V. *Ob okolichnoi shliakhte* (Kiev 1867)

Romanovich-Slavatinskii, A. *Dvorianstvo v Rossii ot nachala XVIII veka do otmeny krepostnogo prava* (St Petersburg 1870; 2nd edn, Kiev 1912)

Lipiński, W. *Szlachta na Ukrainie: Udział jej w życiu narodu ukraińskiego na tle jego dziejów* (Cracow 1909)

Hruszewski, M. *Szlachta ukraińska na przełomie XVI i XVII wieku* (Kiev–Cracow 1912)

Lipiński, W. (ed). *Z dziejów Ukrainy* (Kiev–Cracow 1912)

Okinshevych, L. 'Znachne viis'kove tovarystvo v Ukraïni-Het'-manshchyni xvii–xviii st,' *ZNTSh*, 157 (Munich 1948)

Backus, O. *Motives of West Russian Nobles in Deserting Lithuania for Moscow, 1377–1514* (Lawrence, Kans 1957)

Grodziski, S. *Obywatelstwo w szlacheckiej Rzeczypospolitej* (Cracow 1963)

Masiszewski, J. *Szlachta polska i jej państwo* (Warsaw 1969)

Kohut, Z. 'Problems in Studying the Post-Khmelnytsky Ukrainian Elite (1650s to 1830s),' in *Rethinking Ukrainian History*, ed I.L. Rudnytsky (Edmonton 1981)

Sysyn, F. 'The Problem of Nobilities in the Ukrainian Past: The Polish Period, 1569–1648,' in *Rethinking Ukrainian History*, ed I.L. Rudnytsky (Edmonton 1981)

Kamiński, A. 'The *Szlachta* of the Polish-Lithuanian Commonwealth and Their Government,' in *The Nobility in Russian and Eastern Europe*, ed I. Banac and P. Bushkovitch (New Haven 1983)

Kohut, Z. 'The Ukrainian Elite in the Eighteenth Century and Its Integration into the Russian Nobility,' in *The Nobility in Russian and Eastern Europe*, ed I. Banac and P. Bushkovitch (New Haven 1983)

Beauvois, A. *Le noble, le serf, et le revisor: La noblesse polonaise entre le tsarisme et les masses ukrainiennes (1831–1863)* (Paris 1986)

Subtelny, O. *Domination of Eastern Europe: Native Nobilities and Foreign Absolutism, 1500–1715* (Kingston, Ont–Montreal 1986)

Rosman, M. *The Lord's Jews: Magnate-Jewish Relations in the Polish-Lithuanian Commonwealth* (Cambridge, Mass 1990)

LeDonne, J. *Absolutism and Ruling Class: The Formation of the Russian Political Order, 1700–1825* (New York–Oxford 1991)

Šlusarek, K. 'Szlachta w Galicji Wschodniej na przełomie XVIII i XIX wieku: Rozmieszczenie terytorialne i liczebność,' *Studia Historyczne*, 34, no. 2 (1991)

A. Zhukovsky

Nogata or **nohata** (from Arabic *nakd* 'small coin'). A type of Arab silver dirham that, together with the *kuna, circulated in Kievan Rus' from the late 9th century on as a basic form of metal *currency. Valued at 1/20th of a marten collar, it originally weighed 3.41 g; the weight of 20 *nogaty* equaled 1 silver *hryvnia. Later there were two types: a 2.56-g coin in northern Rus' and a 4.09-g coin in southern Rus', where the *nogata* remained a medium of exchange until the early 12th century.

Nogay Tatars. A formerly large horde of *Tatars who derived their name from Nogay (d 1300), a prominent military leader of the Golden Horde. Until the 16th century they inhabited the steppe between northern Kazakhstan and southern Siberia. In the mid-16th century the Nogays split into the Great Horde, which came under Russian rule on the lower Volga, and the Little Horde, which migrated into the southern Ukrainian steppe and became a nominal vassal of the Crimean Khanate, constituting 40 percent of its population. The two hordes were reunited in the 1630s after the Great Horde fled from the Siberian Kalmyks. The Nogays pillaged Ukrainian settlements and were consequently in constant conflict with the Zaporozhian Cossacks. In the 18th century they consisted of four hordes: the *Bilhorod (Budzhak) Horde, between the Dniester and the Danube; the Yedisan Horde, between the Dniester and the Dnieper; and the Yedichkul and Dzhambuiluk hordes, north of the Crimea between the Dnieper and the Sea of Azov. In the 1770s, after the Russian conquest of Southern Ukraine, approx 120,000 Nogays were forcibly resettled between the Don and the Kuban rivers and then in the Caspian steppe but were soon allowed to return to the Azov region. After the Crimean War some 180,000 Nogays emigrated to Ottoman-ruled southern Bessarabia, and a minority remained in Subcaucasia. According to the 1989 census there were 75,181 Nogays in the USSR. Most of them live in Stavropol krai, the Dagestan and Chechen-Ingush autonomous republics, and the Karachai-Cherkess autonomous oblast of the Russian Federation. B. Kochekaev's book about 16th- to 18th-century Nogay-Russian relations was published in Alma Ata in 1988.

Nohaiske. See Prymorske.

Nomenklatura. A Party-controlled political patronage system and crucial instrument of Soviet Communist rule. An essential feature of the Stalinist model of politics, it began to be challenged only in M. Gorbachev's perestroika. It was so entrenched bureaucratically that no frontal assault was able to dislodge it. The term *nomenklatura* referred to a list of positions and names of the people filling them. Every institution in the USSR had its *nomenklatura*, which consisted of all the positions of authority, no matter how petty, and all their holders. In 1985 there were 9.3 million such posts throughout the USSR, some 2 million of which belonged to the CPSU *nomenklatura*. Usually the term *nomenklatura* had a narrower sense: it referred only to the Party's list of positions and personnel. Having evolved from the personnel records introduced by the Uchraspred department (est 1919) of the CC of the Russian Communist Party (Bolshevik), the *nomenklatura* was established formally by 1923. Through it J. Stalin controlled the Party, and the Party controlled the country.

From the 1920s the *nomenklatura* was divided into three basic components. The basic list (*osnovna nomenklatura*) consisted of the most important positions, which could be filled only by the Party. The secondary list (*zvitno-kontrol'na nomenklatura*) contained positions of lesser importance, the filling of which required merely Party approval. Many secondary positions were on the primary institutional list of non-Party organizations. In late 1989 the Party leadership considered abolishing the secondary *nomenklatura*. The Party's third list, called the 'reserve for promotion,' was a pool from which future appointments to the other two lists were made. The appointees-in-waiting were already in some lower-level *nomenklatura*, perhaps as members of elected bodies or as political activists, and were being groomed for promotion into the elite. Outside these lists there was no other route to political power in the Soviet Union.

In 1988 the *nomenklatura* of the CC CPU contained some 35,000 positions. The *nomenklatura* of an oblast Party committee embraced not more than 2,000 positions; for example, the lists of Donetske oblast had 1,203 positions (1973), of Lviv oblast, 1,719 (1981), of Vinnytsia oblast, 1,400 (1978), of Voroshylovhrad oblast, 1,684 (1950), and of Zhytomyr oblast, 572 (1989). A city or raion Party committee *nomenklatura* had from a few hundred to a thousand positions of the lowest level: secretaries of primary Party organizations, upper and middle management of local institutions and enterprises, and local government officials. The Balakliia Raion Party Committee, for example, had 464 positions in its *nomenklatura* in 1968.

Soviet published sources were reticent about these matters. Their silence reinforced suspicions that the political elite of the *nomenklatura* was highly unrepresentative of Soviet society. Some data for Ukraine support the suspicion. In 1950 only 122 of the 1,684 positions in Voroshylovhrad Oblast Party Committee *nomenklatura* were occupied by women. Nationality was one of the most politically sensitive features of the composition of the *nomenklatura*, and there was hardly any official information on the subject. We know only that in 1951, 71.4 percent of the 'leading cadres' (a Soviet euphemism for *nomenklatura* personnel) in the republic were Ukrainians. This figure was at least 5 percentage points lower than the proportion of Ukrainians in the population. By 1981 Ukrainians accounted for only 70.4 percent of the 'leading cadres,' still 3 points below the figure for the population. It is believed that the percentage of Ukrainians decreased as one ascended the hierarchy, and that it varied regionally: it was probably lowest (for demographic and historical reasons) in the western and eastern extremities of the republic. The *nomenklatura* had a definite and, probably, inhibiting effect on the formation of an indigenous Ukrainian political elite. It was an essential device for centralizing political power and maintaining Moscow's control over the national republics. By controlling appointments the CC CPSU extended its power through all the administrative levels of the republics and severely reduced their autonomy.

BIBLIOGRAPHY
Harasymiw, B. *Political Elite Recruitment in the Soviet Union* (London 1984)

B. Harasymiw

Nomocanon. See Canon law.

Nomys, Matvii (pseud of Matvii Symonov), b 17 November 1823 in Zarih, Lubni county, Poltava gubernia, d 26 December 1900 in Lubni, Poltava gubernia. Ethnographer, writer, and educator. Upon graduating from Kiev University in 1848, he taught in the Nizhen and Nemyriv gymnasiums and worked as a government auditor. In 1873 he became principal of the Lubni gymnasium, and in 1877 he was elected president of the Lubni zemstvo. Throughout his life Nomys collected Ukrainian folklore. His first publications were childhood recollections (1858) and short stories (1859), which later came out in a single volume, *Razskazy M.T. Simonova* (Stories by M.T. Symonov, 1900). His most important work is *Ukraïns'ki prykazky, prysliv'ia i take inshe* (Ukrainian Sayings, Prov-

Matvii Nomys

erbs, and the Like, 1864; repr 1985; manuscript facsimile 1928), a collection of 14,339 proverbs and sayings (not including the variants) and 505 riddles. In spite of censor's excisions, the collection was the finest achievement in Slavic paroemiology of its time. It included proverbs collected not only by Nomys but also by M. Bilozersky, V. Bilozersky, P. Kulish, V. Lazarevsky, O. Markovych, S. Rudansky, and M. Vovchok. Nomys left his estate to charitable organizations of Lubni county and to the Shevchenko Scientific Society.

Nonconformist or unofficial art. A term for art created in the USSR that, until the period of glasnost and perestroika in the 1980s, did not meet official approval and recognition. The creators of this art did not adhere to the prescribed program of *socialist realism formulated at the First All-Union Congress of Soviet Writers in 1934. They did not, however, constitute a movement, nor did they represent one style, ideology, or worldview. In most cases their art was not an expression of political dissent. What unified them was their belief in and insistence on the freedom of creative individual expression. Strictly speaking, nonconformist art was not forbidden as long as it was kept private; when it was shown publicly, however, its creators were often subjected to reprisals and persecution. This state of affairs forced nonconformist artists to work in solitude and without official recognition.

Ukrainian nonconformist art had its beginnings in the Khrushchev 'thaw' of the mid-1950s. At that time the socialist-realist framework was widened, and Ukrainian ethnographic and folk-art themes became popular. Artists began exploring hitherto forbidden styles and trends in Western art and Eastern philosophy, as well as Ukrainian art of the 1920s, and developing their individual visions and means of expression. In the 1960s some artists became part of the growing *dissident movement, and O. *Zalyvakha and S. *Shabatura were arrested for their involvement and imprisoned.

Unlike their colleagues in Kiev and in western Ukraine who signed petitions and attended political trials, the Odessa nonconformists pursued only artistic concerns. In 1967, long before the infamous bulldozing of the exhibition of nonconformist art in Moscow in September 1974, two Odessa artists, S. Sychov and V. Khrushch, displayed their art outside the Odessa Opera and Ballet Theater. Even though their exhibition lasted only a few hours before it was closed down by the police, it brought artists' disenchantment with officially sanctioned art into the open and made public the distinction between official and nonconformist art.

During the crackdown on the dissident movement in Ukraine in 1965 and again in 1972, nonconformist art went underground. Thereafter, some artists led a double existence, earning a living by creating socialist-realist art while continuing to paint nonconformist works in private.

In 1975 the First Exhibition of Ukrainian Nonconformist Artists was held in Moscow in a private apartment. Of the five participants, F. *Humeniuk from Leningrad, V. *Makarenko from Tallinn, V. *Sazonov and N. Pavlenko from Moscow, and V. *Strelnikov from Odessa, four had been forced to live and work outside their homelands. In the Second Exhibition of Ukrainian Nonconformist Art, which was held in Moscow in March 1976, 16 artists participated. These exhibitions gave an opportunity for Ukrainian nonconformist artists living in different parts of the USSR to join forces. They could do so only in the Russian capital, however – the only place in the USSR where such a gathering was possible, and where their work would be seen by foreign diplomats and correspondents.

Works by some Ukrainian nonconformist artists eventually made their way to the West, as did three of the artists themselves (V. Strelnikov, V. Makarenko, V. Sazonov). The first traveling group exhibition of such art in the West was organized by the Ukrainian American I. Ciszkewych and mounted in Munich, London, New York, Cleveland, and Washington, DC, in 1979–80. A second exhibition was organized by D. Zelska-Darewych in Toronto in 1982, and traveled to Winnipeg, Chicago, Detroit, Cleveland, and New York. This show included works done by V. Makarenko, V. Sazonov, A. *Solomukha, and V. Strelnikov in the USSR and after their emigration to the West, and its opening was attended by three of the artists.

Ukrainian nonconformist artists who remained in the USSR were unable to exhibit their work publicly until the early 1980s. At that time shows by some more prominent nonconformists, such as I. *Marchuk, were sponsored by official organizations, such as the Writers' Union of Ukraine. By 1987 many unofficial artists had been invited to exhibit in alternative spaces. By 1988 many of them, including Humeniuk and Marchuk, had been accepted as members by the Union of Artists. Articles about O. Zalyvakha and V. *Loboda as well as others appeared in the official press. Because national exhibitions organized by the Union of Artists since the late 1980s have included artworks which formerly would have been labeled decadent, the distinction between official and nonconformist art became blurred and has ceased to exist.

D. Zelska-Darewych

Nonmetallic-ore industry. A branch of the *building-materials industry that extracts and processes natural minerals, such as graphite, kaolin, talcum, dolomite, and pegmatite, the chemical, metallurgical, and ceramics industries. Only small amounts of *kaolin and *graphite were mined in Ukraine in the past. Today they are Ukraine's chief nonmetallic ores. In the 1950s many nonmetallic-ore deposits began to be exploited. Feldspar began to be mined in 1958. Pegmatite and mica are extracted in Zhytomyr, Rivne, and Zaporizhia oblasts, and andesite in Transcarpathia.

Nordic culture. A Bronze Age culture of tribesmen who migrated into Ukrainian lands in the second half of the 3rd millennium BC, probably from the Baltic region near Denmark. It is commonly known as the Funnel Beaker culture. Two waves of migration are included in this culture. The first settled in northern Galicia and was notable for its funnel-shaped beakers. The second wave settled as far east in Ukraine as Kiev and as far south as Bukovyna. Its most distinctive trait was the construction of large stone structures as burial vaults. Nordic culture settlements were usually built on easily defended high terrain. Their inhabitants engaged in animal husbandry, fishing, hunting, and some agriculture. The Nordic culture people were part of a major migration from the Baltic region that dispersed widely across Europe. The culture has occasionally also been referred to as the Megalithic culture, after large stone burial structures discovered in Volhynia and Podilia; or as the Hrybovychi culture, in reference to the 1933–4 discovery of a settlement in Mali Hrybovychi near Lviv. In Ukraine, the members of the Nordic culture eventually were assimilated by the local population.

Normal school (*normalna shkola*). A training institution for primary-school teachers. The first six-grade school of this type in eastern Galicia was established in 1777 in Lviv; another followed shortly afterward in Chernivtsi. German was the principal language of instruction. The normal schools were reorganized into *teachers' seminaries by the school reform of 1869.

Normalization (*normalizatsiia*). A 1935 agreement between the *Ukrainian National Democratic Alliance (UNDO) and the Polish government, designed as a rapprochement between Ukrainians and the *Sanacja regime. The term is said to have been coined by O. *Lutsky. Normalization came about as a result of growing Ukrainian anxieties about the deterioration of international relations (anti-Ukrainian repression in the Soviet Union, the growing affinity between Poland and Germany), the weakening of UNDO's political position as a result of the *Pacification in 1930 and new electoral ordinances threatening the Ukrainians with fewer seats in the Polish parliament, growing dissatisfaction from the nationalist wing of UNDO and the secession of D. Paliiv's Front of National Unity group, and an increase in dealings with the Polish government. Discussions were held in July 1935 in Lviv between UNDO leaders and the minister of internal affairs, M. Zyndram-Kościałkowski. An electoral compromise reached at that time guaranteed the Ukrainians 14 seats in the Sejm and 5 in the Senate, the position of vice-marshal in both chambers, and the elimination of Russophile representation. The government made a proposal for an amnesty, which some OUN activists took advantage of; it also extended credit to several Ukrainian economic organizations in Galicia and made assurances to the Ukrainians for the maintenance of the status quo in schooling. In return the UNDO delegates in the Sejm supported government proposals for 'state necessities' (the budget, military matters, and the like). Normalization did not encompass Ukrainian territories north of the *Sokal border, which omission sparked D. Levytsky's protest and resignation as UNDO leader. The new leader and spokesman for normalization policies became V. Mudry, who was also vice-marshal of the Sejm.

UNDO began to press the government for more substantial changes – the introduction of cultural autonomy for eastern Galicia, concessions in elementary and secondary schooling, a Ukrainian university, territorial self-government, an end to colonization, the introduction of the term 'Ukrainian' into the official language, access to administrative postings for Ukrainians, the regulation of rivers, and measures against starvation in the mountain regions. The government, apart from satisfying a few minor demands, ignored the overtures. The only positive effects were arrangements for material goods to be supplied to invalids of the former Ukrainian army, an increase in the enrollment of Ukrainian students at university, equal status for the terms 'Ukrainian' and 'Ruthenian' in bureaucratic usage, bilingual signs on public service buildings in eastern Galicia, and the acceptance of Ukrainian representatives into government committees. Demands for the elimination of bilingualism in schools, the dismantling of the Bereza Kartuzka concentration camp, higher numbers of Ukrainian teachers in the Galicia region, and the extending of credits to Ukrainian farmers were rejected.

At the same time that the Sanacja regime was backing away from any substantial measures to meet Ukrainian demands, an increasingly strident posture toward Ukrainians was being adopted by Polish politicians, local state administrative offices, and military circles. The accord lost almost all its credibility and support as a result. The fiasco, meanwhile, had led to a substantial split in the UNDO ranks as early as 1936, which included such critics of the policy as Levytsky, V. Kuzmovych, I. Kedryn, and Lutsky (who grouped around the newspaper *Dilo*).

A. Zięba

Norman (Normanist) theory. A historical theory about the origin of states in Eastern Europe, particularly of Kievan Rus', and of the name *'Rus'.' Drawing on the last redaction of the Rus' Primary Chronicle (1118) and various linguistic data, the theory's adherents maintain that the creators of the Kievan state and its culture were Normans (ie, Norsemen or *Varangians) who arrived in Eastern Europe from Scandinavia in the 9th century, and that 'Rus'' is a word of Norman origin. The theory's first proponents were 18th-century German historians of Russia – G. Bayer, G.F. *Müller, and A. Schlözer – and other German historians, such as F. Krug and J. Thunmann. Their views were elaborated in the 19th century by the Russian historians N. Karamzin and S. Solovev and in works dealing specifically with the theory by E. Kunik, M. *Pogodin, and the Danish Slavist V. Thomsen.

The first 'anti-Normanist' response was articulated by the 18th-century Russian scholar M. Lomonosov. Anti-Normanist views were expressed in the 19th century by the Decembrists and the Slavophiles, and a number of professional historians (eg, J. Ewers) posited theories about the Baltic-Slav, Lithuanian, and Gothic origin of Rus' and its name. Their theories received little recognition in historical circles, however. The first serious critiques of the Normanists came from late 19th-century Russian historians, such as S. Gedeonov, D. Ilovaisky, and V. Vasilevsky, but they failed to present well-substantiated alternatives. Consequently the popularity of the Normanist theory was revived at the turn of the 20th century, as reflected in the works of F. Braun, S. Rożniecki, A. Shakhmatov, K. Tiander, and F. Westberg. Besides the traditional conception of Norman conquest, neo-Normanist theories of Norman commercial and ethnic-agrarian colo-

nization, of the social domination of the Slavs by Norman elites, and of continuous domination of the Slavs by foreigners (from the Scythians to the Normans) were presented.

In its various forms the Norman theory prevails to this day among Western historians, particularly those of Germany and the Scandinavian countries (eg, H. Arbman, T. Arne, O. Hötzsch, K. Rahbek Schmidt, A. Stender-Petersen, G. Stöckl), among Russian émigré historians (eg, N. Beliaev, V. Kiparsky, V. Moshin, P. Struve, M. Taube, A. Vasiliev, and G. Vernadsky), and among Polish historians (eg, H. Paszkiewicz). Most Western textbooks present the Normanist interpretation.

Soviet historiography, on the other hand, tended to be anti-Normanist. Although in the 1920s Normanist influences could still be found in the works of the prominent Soviet Russian historians M. Pokrovsky and A. Presniakov, from the 1930s anti-Normanist views were officially sanctioned. They were expressed in the works of Soviet historians of Rus' such as B. Grekov, V. Mavrodin, A. Nasonov, and M. Tikhomirov, the archeologists M. Artamonov and B. Rybakov, and the literary scholar D. Likhachev. All of them denounced the Normanist theory as unscientific, as did historians in other Soviet-bloc countries, particularly in Poland (eg, H. Łowmiański).

Since its inception the Norman theory has been unpopular among Ukrainian historians. In the late 18th century the anonymous author(s) of *Istoriia Rusov* contended that the Kievan state and the name 'Rus'' were of local, Slavic origin. The leading 19th-century Ukrainian anti-Normanists were M. *Maksymovych, who polemicized with Pogodin; M. *Kostomarov, the author of the theory of the Lithuanian origin of Rus'; and V. *Antonovych and members of his historical school in Kiev, who either rejected the Norman legend of the Rus' chronicles outright or denied its historical significance. In the early 20th century M. *Hrushevsky contended that the Norman theory has no historical basis and is simply unnecessary for explicating the origin of the Ukrainian Rus' state. He did not, however, reject the fact that the Varangians contributed in some measure to the creation of the Kievan empire. The literary scholar M. *Vozniak held similar views, as did D. *Bahalii and other historians of Hrushevsky's generation.

The Norman theory had adherents among Ukrainian historians in interwar Galicia and the émigré community. Its influence is particularly evident in the works of S. *Tomashivsky, but also in those of M. *Chubaty, M. *Korduba, and B. *Krupnytsky (a 'critical Normanist'). S. *Shelukhyn's attempt at supplanting the Norman theory with a Celtic one was not successful. Soviet Ukrainian historians by and large adhered to the anti-Normanist positions articulated by Hrushevsky, Bahalii, and V. *Parkhomenko. Most postwar Ukrainian émigré historians (eg, N. *Polonska-Vasylenko, O. *Pritsak) have rejected the classical Norman theory and its various neo-Normanist modifications. Like Hrushevsky, however, they have not denied the Varangian influence in the political and economic life of the Kievan state as it evolved into the Rus' empire of the 10th and 11th centuries.

BIBLIOGRAPHY
Maksimovich [Maksymovych], M. *Otkudi idet russkaia zemlia, po skazaniiu Nestorovoi povesti i po drugim starinnym pisaniiam russkim* (Kiev 1837)
Pogodin, M. *Normanskii period russkoi istorii* (Moscow 1859)

Thomsen, V. *The Relations between Ancient Russia and Scandinavia and the Origin of the Russian State* (Oxford and London 1877)

Hrushevs'kyi, M. *Istoriia Ukraïny-Rusy*, vol 1 (Kiev 1913; repr, New York 1954)

Arne, T. *La Suède et l'Orient: Etudes archéologiques sur les relations de la Suède et de l'Orient pendant l'age des Vikings* (Uppsala 1914)

Parkhomenko, V. *U istokov russkoi gosudarstvennosti VIII–XI vv.* (Leningrad 1924)

Tomasziwskyj [Tomashivs'kyi], S. 'Nowa teorja o początkach Rusi,' *Kwartalnik Historyczny*, 43 (Lviv 1929)

Korduba, M. 'Les théories le plus récentes sur les origines de la Ruthénie,' *Le Monde slave*, 2, no. 2 (1931)

Stender-Petersen, A. *Varangica* (Aarhus 1953)

Paszkiewicz, H. *The Origin of Russia* (New York and London 1954)

Łowmiański, H. *Zagadnienie roli normanów w genezie państw słowiańskich* (Warsaw 1957)

Grekov, B. *Kiev Rus* (Moscow 1959)

Vernadsky, G. *The Origins of Russia* (Oxford 1959)

Shaskol'skii, I.P. *Normanskaia teoriia v sovremennoi burzhuaznoi nauke* (Moscow and Leningrad 1965)

Pritsak, O. *The Origin of Rus': An Inaugural Lecture, October 24, 1975* (Cambridge, Mass 1976)

Stöckl, G. *Der russische Staat in Mittelalter und früher Neuzeit* (Wiesbaden 1981)

O. Ohloblyn

Normans (*normany*). A term used by medieval chroniclers for the Germanic tribes inhabiting Scandinavia and Jutland; a common alternative name for the seafaring brigands, mercenaries, and traders known as Vikings in Western Europe and *Varangians in Rus' and the Byzantine Empire. The theory of the Varangian origin of Rus' is known as the *Norman theory.

North Crimean Canal. A long canal system in Kherson and Crimea oblasts, running from the Kakhivka Reservoir on the Dnieper River through the Perekop Isthmus to the Crimean city of Kerch. Its main sluice, near New Kakhivka, was built in 1956 at the same time as the reservoir. Construction of the canal bed began in 1957 and was accomplished in two stages, from Kakhivka to the Crimea by 1963 and through the Crimea by 1975. The length of the canal system is 400.5 km, the maximum width is 60 m, and the depth varies from 6 to 13 m. The main canal consists of an undivided 200-km stretch from Kakhivka to Dzhankoi and then four sections with locks that raise the water 103 m. The maximum water flow is 300 cu m/sec. There are 24 regulating stations along the length of the canal, including 5 reservoirs, and 118 escape gates and pumping stations. The canal supplies an irrigation network in the steppes of Kherson oblast and the Crimea covering an area of over 100,000 ha and projected to cover 540,000 ha. It also supplies fresh water to Kerch and Feodosiia and many settlements in the Crimea.

North Dakota. A western north central state of the United States (1990 pop 641,364). The 1980 census revealed 1,574 persons in North Dakota reporting a Ukrainian ancestry for both parents, and 1,638 persons who claimed Ukrainian ancestry of at least one parent. By 1990 their total number had risen to 3,643.

The first Ukrainian settlers to North Dakota arrived in 1896 and 1897 by way of Canada. Most were from the region southeast of Borshchiv in Galicia. From 1898 until 1912 a steady stream of immigrants settled in eastern Billings county; in the Snow, Gorham, and Ukraina areas; and in the Belfield region of Stark county. Ukrainian Protes-

tants from eastern Ukraine settled in McHenry and McLean counties in the communities of Max, Butte, and Kief. The majority of Ukrainian immigrants took up farming; others took up ranching, mining, railway work, or common laboring. By the 1930s an estimated 5,000 Ukrainians were living in North Dakota. During the depression a large out-migration of Ukrainians from the state occurred. A period of general social mobility and assimilation into mainstream American society followed, after the Second World War. At the same time the rural areas began to be depopulated, as people moved to nearby towns either to retire or to take up urban occupations. The results can be seen in eastern Billings county, which in 1930 had the greatest concentration of Ukrainians. In 1980 there were only 166 persons of sole Ukrainian ancestry, and another 125 persons with one Ukrainian parent. At the same time Stark county (including Dickinson) contained 360 persons of sole Ukrainian ancestry and 255 persons claiming Ukrainian ancestry of one parent. The postwar wave of Ukrainian immigrants did not have a major impact on the community, as many, dissatisfied with their jobs, left to find more suitable employment in other states. The mid-1960s saw a small but significant influx of medical professionals from Canada.

The first two Ukrainian Catholic churches were built in Belfield (1906) and Wilton (1907). A third church was built in Gorham (1911). From 1921 to 1953 the Wilton parish was a mission church served on an itinerant basis by priests from Belfield. Mission parishes were later established in both Bismarck (1979) and Minot (1981) to accommodate urban residents of Ukrainian background. In 1939 a residence for nuns was built near the Belfield church. The first Ukrainian Orthodox church was founded in 1913 after a split in the Catholic Wilton parish. A similar occurrence took place in Belfield, where in 1917 an Orthodox church was built across from the original Catholic St Demetrius church. In 1944 a new parish, the Ukrainian Catholic Church of St John the Baptist, was established in Belfield.

Ukrainian Stundists erected their first sanctuary, the Russian Baptist Church of Liberty, in the town of Kief in 1901 and a church near Max in 1908. They were largely served by unpaid community elders. The Ukrainian settlements in and around northern McLean county (consisting largely of Evangelical eastern Ukrainian immigrants)

SS Peter and Paul Ukrainian Orthodox Church and St Demetrius's Ukrainian Catholic Church in Belfield, North Dakota (1917)

The postmark of Ukraina, North Dakota

continued to be Protestant in orientation through the generations. Baptist, Congregational, and Seventh Day Adventist congregations are still present.

Ukrainian fraternal and benevolent associations have had a small impact on the Ukrainian communities in North Dakota. In 1955 a North Dakota chapter of the Ukrainian Congress Committee of America was finally incorporated. In 1975 the Ukrainian community organized a Pioneer Days Celebration (commemorating the 75th anniversary of the arrival of the first immigrants), and in 1980 the Ukrainian Cultural Institute was established at Dickinson State College (under the leadership of A. Palanuk). The institute is dedicated to preserving and promoting the Ukrainian heritage through education and cultural events and publishes a quarterly newsletter titled *Ukrainian Cultural Institute* (1980–).

BIBLIOGRAPHY
Pedeliski, T. 'Slavic Peoples,' in *Plains Folk: North Dakota's Ethnic History*, ed W. Sherman et al (Fargo 1988)

H. Myroniuk

North Ossetian Autonomous Republic. An autonomous republic (1989 pop 632,000) within the Russian Federation, covering 8,000 sq km in northern Caucasia. It lies within the basin of the Terek River and its tributaries, the Urukh, Ardon, and Gizeldon. Its capital is Ordzhonikidze. According to the 1989 census there were 335,000 Ossetians, 189,000 Russians, 33,000 Chechens, 12,000 Armenians, and 10,000 Ukrainians in the republic. Since the Ukrainian statistic was deflated, the true figure, in fact, could be as high as 50,000. Only about half of the Ukrainian inhabitants listed Ukrainian as their mother tongue. Ukrainians and Russians inhabit the plain in the northern part of the republic.

North Ukrainian Trough. See Dnieper-Donets Trough.

Northern Caucasia (aka Northern Caucasian krai). A part of the RSFSR set up in 1924. It encompasses the northern slopes of the Caucasus Mountains, Subcaucasia, and the southern Don region. Specifically, it consists of Krasnodar and Stavropol krais, Rostov oblast, and the autonomous republics of Dagestan, Kabardin-Balkar, North Ossetia, and Chechen-Ingush. Its area is 355,100 sq km, and its population is 16.9 million (1990). Thirty percent of the USSR's petroleum and natural gas was extracted there in the 1960s. The southwestern part of Northern Caucasia lies within Ukrainian ethnic territory.

Northern dialects. A group of dialects in the Ukrainian language. They are distributed north of the *southwestern and *southeastern dialects, with which they share a broad zone of transitional dialects. With the Belarusian language to their north they share transitional (eastern and mixed) Ukrainian-Belarusian dialects as a result of the ancient, unequal northwestward diffusion of Ukrainian traits and the later southeastern expansion of Belarusian. The northern dialects consist of the *Podlachian and *Polisian dialects and have the following characteristics: (1) an archaic vocalism (diphthongs) in the stressed position, or monophthongs in place of the stressed *o* and *e* (which were once followed by a weak-jer syllable) *ĕ* that differ from *o*, *e*, and *ĕ*; eg, *pječ*, *duom*, *djed* (Standard Ukrainian [SU]: *pič*, *dim*, *did*) 'oven, home, grandfather'; and (2) the change of *a* (< *ę*) after a palatalized consonant into *e* in an unstressed position; eg, *déset'*, *des'áty* (SU: *désjat'*, *desjátyj*) 'ten, tenth'. Except for some of the Podlachian dialects, in their lexicon and simplified morphology the northern dialects are similar to the southeastern dialects, in whose formation they, together with the Podilian and Volhynian dialects, played a decisive role in the 14th to 17th centuries. (See the map in *Dialects.)

Northern Group of the Ukrainian Galician Army (Pivnichna hrupa UHA). A grouping of *Ukrainian Galician Army (UHA) units located northwest of Lviv in December 1918. In January 1919 this group was reorganized into the First Corps of the UHA, which consisted of four brigades (Sokal, Rava, Belz, and Yaniv) and the First Cavalry Regiment. During 1919 the First Corps held the right wing of the front against the Polish army. Its commanders were Lt Col V. Kurmanovych, Col O. Mykytka, and Col A. Shamanek. When the UHA was incorporated into the Red Army, the First Corps was re-formed as the Second Brigade of the Red Ukrainian Galician Army. Its commanders were Maj O. Lesniak and Capt Yu. Holovinsky. On 23 April 1920 the unit deserted the Red Army and attempted to join the UNR Army, but it was disarmed and interned by the Poles.

Northern Mineral Enrichment Complex (Pivnichnyi hirnychozbahachuvalnyi kombinat). A concern of the mining industry, located in Kryvyi Rih, Dnipropetrovske oblast. It processes ore from the *Kryvyi Rih Iron-ore Basin. The first plant, with an annual capacity of 13.5 million t of ore and 5.9 million t of concentrate, was opened in 1964. A second plant, with a capacity of 33 million t of ore and 14.2 million t of concentrate, was completed in 1970. The complex includes two quarries as well as pulverizing and enrichment plants.

Northwestern Ukrainian lands (Pivnichno-zakhidni ukrainski zemli). The common unofficial designation used by Ukrainians during the interwar period for the northwestern Ukrainian ethnic territories (outside Galicia) that had come under Polish control, including Volhynia, Polisia, Podlachia, and the Kholm region.

Noryn River. A left-bank tributary of the Uzh River, which it joins near Narodychi. It is 84 km long and drains a basin area of 832 sq km. It flows through Zhytomyr oblast, including the town of Ovruch. Its waters are used for irrigation.

Nosach, Pavlo [Nosač], b 22 September 1890 in Bovkun, Tarashcha county, Kiev gubernia, d 20 October 1966 in Kiev. Kobzar. Orphaned as a child, he was wounded in

Pavlo Nosach

Oleksander Nosalevych

battle in 1915 and lost his sight. He learned to play the kobza in 1928 from O. Markevych. His repertoire included folk songs, songs set to the verses of T. Shevchenko, and his own compositions, such as 'A Duma about the Great Kobzar.' During the Second World War his itinerant minstreling helped to strengthen patriotic feelings in Ukraine as well as the resolve to resist the occupying Germans.

Nosachov, Andrii [Nosačov, Andrij], b 13 December 1913 in Hirzhove, Tyraspil county, Kherson gubernia, d January 1990 in Sumy. Actor. In 1933 he completed drama studies in Donetske as a pupil of D. Kozachkivsky. He has worked in the Kryvbas Theater (1933–4), the Dnipropetrovske Oblast Workers' and Collective-Farm Theater (1934–8), the Uralsk Ukrainian Music and Drama Theater in Kazakhstan (1938–41), and the Sumy Ukrainian Music and Drama Theater (since 1941).

Nosalevych, Oleksander [Nosalevyč], b 21 March 1874 in Bylychi, Sambir county, Galicia, d 19 January 1959 in Wiesbaden, Germany. Opera and concert singer (bass-baritone). He graduated from the Vienna Conservatory with distinction (1898) and also studied in Milan under F. Guarino. He was a soloist in theaters in Lviv, Vienna (under G. Mahler), Czechoslovakia, France, England, and especially Germany. Nosalevych also toured in Galicia. His main roles included Rocco in L. van Beethoven's *Fidelio*, Figaro in G. Rossini's *Il Barbiere di Siviglia*, and Mephistopheles in C. Gounod's *Faust*. In concert he sang works by W. Mozart, F. Weber, B. Smetana, J. Brahms, and R. Strauss; art songs by D. Sichynsky and M. Lysenko to texts by T. Shevchenko and I. Franko; and Ukrainian folk songs. In 1930 the artist left the stage and organized his own vocal school in Wiesbaden. Nosalevych's art is preserved in rare recordings.

Nosenko, Ivan, b 26 September 1920 in Aleksandrovka, Orel gubernia, Russia. Sculptor. A graduate of the Dnipropetrovske Art School (1941), he has done a number of monuments, including one to marines in Berdianske (1972), and many smaller sculptures, such as *Zaporozhian Cossacks* (1961) and *Metallurgist* (1967).

Nosiv, Anatolii, b 23 July 1883 in Poltava, d 1941? Anthropologist and archeologist. A student of F. Vovk, he be-

came head of the anthropology and prehistory department of the VUAN Museum of Anthropology and Ethnology in Kiev and a member of the VUAN Archeological Committee. In the 1920s he published several articles in anthropology, coedited (with M. Rudynsky) the annual collection *Antropolohiia* (1927–30), and compiled *Slovnyk antropoheohrafichoï terminolohiï* (A Dictionary of Anthropogeographical Terminology, 1930). In the mid-1930s he was arrested by the NKVD and imprisoned, but was released and managed to find a position at the Yalta Regional Studies Museum. His subsequent fate is unknown.

Nosivka. III-12. A town (1990 pop 18,500) on the Nosivochka River and a raion center in Chernihiv oblast. It is first mentioned, as Nosiv, in the Hypatian Chronicle under the year 1147. An ancient burial ground dating back to Kievan Rus' has been discovered in the vicinity. Under the Hetman state Nosivka was a company center of Chernihiv regiment. Today the town has a food industry and an agricultural research station.

Notable military fellows (Znachne viiskove tovarystvo). The collective name of those Cossacks constituting the ruling estate in the 17th- and 18th-century Hetmanate. It was applied particularly to those members of the elite who had no permanent positions of authority and were therefore not members of the *Cossack starshyna, but were former *registered Cossacks, former Ukrainian noblemen who had fought on the Cossack side in the Cossack-Polish War, or Cossacks who had distinguished themselves in the field. In the late 17th century two categories of fellows were established: *fellows of the standard, who were designated by the hetman's decree, and the lower-ranking *fellows of the banner, who were appointed by the regimental colonels. In the early 18th century an intermediate category of military fellows designated by the *General Military Chancellery was established.

A 1734 tsarist decree placed a limit on the number of notable military fellows in each regiment, thereby artificially arresting the growth of the Ukrainian elite. The restriction was circumvented by the creation of a new category of persons not under general Cossack jurisdiction, the 'appointees to the fellows of the banner' (*asygnovani u znachkovi tovaryshi*).

The notable military fellows' legal status was based on their obligation to perform special administrative or military duties and personal military service (or to provide several armed proxies therefor). Their privileges included the ownership of settled estates and the right to part of the labor of their inhabitants. From 1672, representatives of the fellows participated in the *councils of officers and thus in legislative deliberations. They were exempt from prosecution by general courts. Fellows of the standard could be tried only by the Hetman's Court or, in the 18th century, the *General Military Court. Fellows of the banner could be tried only by regimental courts. After the reintroduction of *land and *pidkomorskyi courts in 1763, they shared the nobles' and starshyna's privilege of being tried by them.

During the 18th century the notable military fellows became a kind of closed hereditary caste. In 1768 the Russian governor-general of the Hetmanate, P. Rumiantsev, decreed that only children of notable military fellows or of Cossack starshyna could become fellows of the banner. In 1785 the notable military fellows were abolished altogether, and a group of them were inducted into the Russian imperial *nobility.

BIBLIOGRAPHY
Okinshevych, L. *Znachne viis'kove tovarystvo v Ukraïni-Het'man-shchyni XVII–XVIII st.* (Munich 1948)
Apanovych, O. *Zbroini syly Ukraïny pershoï polovyny XVIII st.* (Kiev 1969)

L. Okinshevych

Notary public. A public official who authenticates legal acts or documents, and thereby gives them a public status. In most countries notaries are not civil servants, but their activity and organizations are regulated by law. In the Russian Empire notaries were introduced in 1729, and by the late 19th century they had spread throughout the empire. In the Austro-Hungarian Empire notaries were under the jurisdiction of the provincial courts and were organized into professional chambers, one in Lviv and one in Chernivtsi. In the interwar period a similar system existed in Ukrainian territories under Polish and Rumanian rule. The term 'notary' was used in Transcarpathia under both Hungarian and Czechoslovak rule to refer to an administrative office of municipal self-government. Notaries were civil servants who worked for 'notarial districts,' which included several villages.

In the Ukrainian SSR notaries are civil servants. Notary offices are found in all raion centers and larger settlements. In oblast capitals they are headed by senior notaries. Their work is overseen by oblast courts. Appointees have some legal training or considerable legal experience. Their function is to authenticate certain contracts, wills, and trust agreements by affixing an appropriate seal and signature to the original documents.

Notatky z mystetstva / Ukrainian Art Digest. A Ukrainian-language illustrated art journal published by the Philadelphia branch of the Ukrainian Artists' Association in the USA since 1963. It contains theoretical articles, materials on the history of Ukrainian art, biographies of Ukrainian artists, reviews of book designs and exhibitions, and a chronicle of important events in the Ukrainian art world. Since its origin the journal has almost doubled in size and circulation (from 500 to 1,000). By 1990, 29 issues had been published. The managing editor until 1992 was P. Mehyk.

Noua culture. A Bronze Age archeological culture of the 13th to 11th century BC that existed in southwestern Ukraine, northern Rumania, and northern Moldavia. It was identified and named in the 1930s by I. Nestor, a Rumanian archeologist. The people of this culture lived in surface dwellings around which ash-pits and outbuildings were located. They engaged in agriculture, animal husbandry, and bronze working. Studies of their sites revealed earthenware pottery, bone arrowheads, leaflike bronze spearheads, mirrors, and pins. Burial grounds with up to 200 graves in which the deceased were placed in a flexed position have also been uncovered. Notable Noua culture sites in Ukraine include the *Mahala and *Ostrivets archeological sites.

Nova Borova. III-9. A town smt (1990 pop 6,200) on the Irsha River in Volodarske-Volynske raion, Zhytomyr oblast. It arose in the second half of the 17th century. The town has a fruit-drying plant and a reinforced-concrete plant. Its water reservoir is surrounded by a resort area.

Nova Bukovyna. See *Bukovyna.*

Nova Dmytrivka lignite deposit. One of the largest lignite deposits in Ukraine, located near the village of Nova Dmytrivka, Barvinkove raion, Kharkiv oblast. It was discovered in 1950, and covers almost 12 sq km. In 1981 its total reserves were estimated at 536.7 million t, of which 390 million t were extractable. The deposit contains 25 seams of ore, 1–74 m in width, at depths of 86–404 m. The ore has an average ash content of 14.2–24.5 percent, a sulfur content of 1.04–5.5 percent, and a moisture content of 42–64 percent. Its heat value is 1,412–2,560 kcal/kg. The lignite is used for making fuel briquettes and mineral wax and for fuel.

Nova doba (New Era). A weekly journal of politics, economics, and culture, published in Vienna from February 1920 to October 1921 as the organ of the Foreign Group of the *Ukrainian Communist party. It was edited by V. Levynsky with the assistance of V. Vynnychenko.

Nova doba (New Era). A weekly newspaper for Ukrainian Red Army soldiers in German POW camps, published in Berlin from 1941 to 1945. It was edited by H. Kotorovych.

Nova dumka

Nova dumka (New Thought). The official press organ of the Union of Ruthenians and Ukrainians of Croatia, established in 1971 in Vukovar with V. Kostelnyk as editor. It published four to six issues of 50 to 150 pages annually. By 1990, 84 issues had been published. The content is in Ukrainian, the *Bačka dialect, and Serbo-Croatian and deals with regional concerns as well as the history of Transcarpathian and Galician Ukrainians.

Nova Generatsiia (New Generation). A literary organization of futurists, established in Kharkiv in 1927 by former members of the *Association of Panfuturists, M. Semenko, G. Shkurupii, O. Poltoratsky, A. Chuzhy, M. Skuba, and others. Its program embraced the propagandistic slogans of internationalism and proletarian culture and was combined with an imperative to modernize Ukrainian literature by putting it in touch with contemporary literary currents in the West. The organization's official organ bore the same name. In 1929 the name was changed to the All-Ukrainian Association of Workers of

Communist Culture, and in 1930, to the Union of Proletarian Writers in Ukraine. In 1931 the organization was forced to disband. Most of its members were executed during the Stalinist terror, although some, such as O. Poltoratsky, succumbed to pressure and adopted the Party line.

Nova generatsiia (cover design by Pavlo Kovzhun)

Nova generatsiia (New Generation). A monthly journal issued by the organization of the same name, published in Kharkiv from October 1927 to December 1930, under the editorship of M. *Semenko. Much of its contents were devoted to contemporary literary polemics and to the popularization of currents in literature and art in the West (eg, G. Apollinaire, Le Corbusier, W. Baumeister). Among the more frequent contributors were A. Buchma, V. Ver, O. Vlyzko, H. Koliada, F. Lopatynsky, S. Skliarenko, E. Strikha (K. Burevii), and L. Chernov.

Nova hromada (New Community). A literary and scholarly monthly published in Kiev in 1906. A total of 12 issues appeared. It was funded by V. *Leontovych and Ye. *Chykalenko and edited by them and by B. *Hrinchenko and S. *Yefremov. Among the contributors were Kh. Alchevska, S. Cherkasenko, P. Kapelhorodsky, M. Kotsiubynsky, A. Krymsky, M. Kropyvnytsky, V. Kushnir, M. Lozynsky, F. Matushevsky, V. Samiilenko, A. Teslenko, I. Truba, Lesia Ukrainka, M. Vorony, V. Vynnychenko, L. Yanovska, and B.-V. Yaroshevsky. T. Shevchenko's poems 'Sova' (The Owl) and 'Try lita' (Three Years) were first published in the journal. Ukrainian translations of works by H. Heine, V. Hugo, P.-J. de Béranger, M. Maeterlinck, and A. France were also included. The monthly ceased publication with the transfer of *Literaturno-naukovyi vistnyk* from Lviv to Kiev.

Nova hromada (New Community). A weekly organ of the *Federation of Ukrainian Socialists in Canada after its split from the *Federation of Ukrainian Social Democrats in Canada (FUSD). It appeared in Edmonton from February 1911 to September 1912 (a total of 67 issues). It published articles on political affairs, especially concerning the workers' and socialist movements, and some works on Ukrainian history and culture. It strongly criticized *Robochyi narod*, the organ of the FUSD, which was more leftist in orientation. *Nova hromada* was edited by R. Kremar, T. Tomashevsky, I. Semotiuk, and I. Kiriak.

Nova hromada (New Community). A journal published by the *All-Ukrainian Association of Consumer Co-oper-

ative Organizations and Knyhospilka publishing house in Kiev and Kharkiv from 1922 to 1933. Originally called *Biuleten' Kyïvs'koï filiï Vukoopspilky* (1922) and *Pravoberezhnyi kooperator* (1922–3), in 1932 it was renamed *Sotsialistychna hromada*. The journal was aimed primarily at a peasant readership and contained articles on the co-operative movement and scientific, literary, and cultural topics, and prose and poetry. It was edited by O. Kobets and N. Rudenko, and among its contributors were the prominent writers B. Antonenko-Davydovych, M. Zerov, M. Rylsky, S. Vasylchenko, O. Vyshnia, P. Tychyna, and H. Kosynka. The journal appeared 8 times in 1922, 16 times in 1923, 21 times in 1924, 24 times per year from 1925 to 1932, and once in January 1933.

Nova hromada (New Community). A pro-Soviet monthly journal of political and community affairs, published in Vienna from July 1923 to 1925. Edited by S. Vityk with the assistance of A. Krushelnytsky and M. Melenevsky, it reprinted articles from major Soviet Ukrainian periodicals, such as *Visti VUTsVK* and *Chervonyi shliakh*.

Nova Kakhivka [Nova Kaxivka]. VII-14. A port city (1990 pop 57,700) on the left bank of the Dnieper River in Kherson oblast. It was founded in 1951, when the *Kakhivka Hydroelectric Station was built. The city was built on the site of Klisheve village (est 1891). Nova Kakhivka is a modern, planned city with wide streets laid out on a grid and lined with greenery. Its industries produce asphalt, reinforced-concrete structures, and hydroelectric machinery and equipment.

Nova khata (New Home). A monthly (1925–34) and semimonthly (1935–9) magazine for women, published in Lviv by the *Ukrainske Narodnie Mystetstvo co-operative. The chief editors were M. Furtak, M. Hromnytska, and, from 1930, L. Burachynska. *Nova khata* contained articles on folk art, co-operative and educational subjects, fashion, interior decorating, housekeeping, cultural history, and the women's movement; biographies and memoirs of prominent Ukrainian women; and prose and poetry. It was noted for its design and artwork, by artists such as O. Kulchytska, M. Butovych, and S. Hordynsky.

Nova knyha (New Book). A monthly journal of bibliography, library science, literary criticism, book reviews, publishing affairs, and book design, production, and trade, published in Kharkiv in late 1924 and in 1925. It succeeded the journal *Knyha* (five issues, 1923–4). Ten issues appeared under the editorship of S. Pylypenko and M. Hodkevych. Prominent contributors included I. Aizenshtok, D. Bahalii, O. Biletsky, M. Dolengo, V. Ihnatiienko, E. Kagarov, O. Korshakov, Yu. Mezhenko, M. Pakul, M. Plevako, P. Tutkovsky, and M. Yashek.

Nova kul'tura. See *Kul'tura*.

Nova Maiachka [Nova Majačka]. VII-14. A town smt (1990 pop 7,200) in Tsiurupynske raion, Kherson oblast. It was founded at the beginning of the 19th century by serfs who had fled from Kursk, Chernihiv, and Poltava gubernias, and it was given smt status in 1958. Archeologists have discovered artifacts from the 4th and 5th centuries in the town's territory.

Nova Odessa. VI-12. A city (1990 pop 14,900) on the left bank of the Buh River and a raion center in Mykolaiv oblast. The site has been settled since ancient times. Artifacts dating from the Bronze Age and the 1st century AD as well as Scythian kurhans have been discovered there. In 1776 Fedorivka village, named after the Zaporozhian Cossack Fedir Osadchy, was built by Cossacks of the Kherson Pikeman Regiment to defend the territory against Turkish and Tatar raids. When the regiment was abolished in 1783, the region was put under the administration of the Boh Cossack Army. The Odessa Cossack Regiment was stationed in Fedorivka; the village was renamed Nova Odessa in 1832. By 1859 Nova Odessa, which was then part of Kherson gubernia, had a population of 2,190. It attained city status in 1976. Today the town has a cheese factory and a building-materials plant.

Nova Praha. V-13. A town smt (1990 pop 8,100) on the Beshka River in Oleksandriia raion, Kirovohrad oblast. In 1730 the Zaporozhian Cossack P. Petryk established a settlement there, which in 1821 was named Nova Praha. By the middle of the 18th century it had become a prosperous trade and cultural center in Southern Ukraine. In the 1850s Serbs, Montenegrins, and Old Believers settled there. The population in the 1880s was over 9,000. Today the town's industries produce asphalt, bricks, milk products, and canned foods.

Nova rada (New Council). A 490-page literary miscellany published in 1908 by the Kiev Literary-Artistic Society. It was edited by O. Kosach (O. *Pchilka), L. *Starytska-Cherniakhivska, M. *Starytsky, and Ivan *Steshenko. Among the contributors were S. Charnetsky, M. Cherniavsky, R. Hordynsky, H. Hryhorenko, P. Karmansky, H. Khotkevych, B. Lepky, M. Levytsky, M. Lozynsky, P. Myrny, Pchilka, O. Romanova, Starytska-Cherniakhivska, Starytsky, M. Storozhenko, Lesia Ukrainka, V. O'Connor-Vilinska, and M. Vorony.

Nova rada (New Council). A daily newspaper that appeared in Kiev from March 1917 to January 1919 as the continuation of *Rada. Published initially by the Society for the Support of Ukrainian Scholarship, Literature, and Art, it later became the organ of the *Ukrainian Party of Socialists-Federalists. In addition to detailed news reports and extensive reviews of the press, the newspaper published commentary on political and economic developments by prominent figures, such as M. Hrushevsky, Ye. Chykalenko, V. Prokopovych, F. Matushevsky, L. Starytska-Cherniakivska, S. Shelukhyn, S. Rusova, M. Levytsky, and P. Khrystiuk. The editors of *Nova rada* were A. Nikovsky and S. Yefremov.

Nova rada (New Council). A conservative, Catholic daily published in Lviv in 1919–20. The paper was founded by Rev Y. Zastyrets; after the first few issues it was taken over by a public committee consisting of Rev T. Halushchynsky, Rev L. Kunytsky, Rev H. Kostelnyk, Rev O. Malytsky, M. Chubaty, and O. Makarushka. Among the contributors to *Nova rada* were V. Budzynovsky, I. Svientsitsky, M. Halushchynsky, and Revs Ya. Levytsky (the chief editor) and O. Stefanovych. In 1920 the public committee also published *Pravda,* a more popular weekly edited by M. Chubaty. Neither paper recognized the Polish occupation of Galicia. Both were frequently censored, had issues confiscated, and were eventually closed down by the Polish authorities.

Nova Stsena (New Stage). A musical-drama theater in Transcarpathia, organized in 1934 by the brothers Ye. and Yu. *Sherehii, the first theater there led by local artists. At first a drama circle, from 1936 it was affiliated with the Prosvita society in Khust, and later with the Prosvita society in Uzhhorod. Mobilization in March 1938 interrupted its activities, and in November of that year it was reconstituted as the State Ukrainian Theater Nova Stsena, under which name it continued its work until March 1939. The artistic directors of the theater were Yu. Sherehii, M. Arkas, Jr, and V. Libovicki (also the choreographer), and the stage designer was M. Ruda-Tushytska. The repertoire of Nova Stsena consisted primarily of Yu. Sherehii's dramas (pseudonym: Yu. Hrom), based on the ethnographical material of Transcarpathia. The theater also staged M. Arkas Jr's operetta *Moon and Star* (libretto by M. Chyrsky), O. Oles's drama *At the Dnieper* (music by Ye. Sherehii), S. Hulak-Artemovsky's opera *Zaporozhian Cossack beyond the Danube,* and M. Starytsky's populist-ethnographical plays *Marusia Bohuslavka* and *Oi, ne khody, Hrytsiu* ... (Don't Go to Parties, Hryts ...).

Nova svoboda

Nova svoboda (New Freedom). The only daily newspaper in the Carpatho-Ukrainian state of 1938–9, published in Uzhhorod, Khust, and, briefly, Sevliush (now Vynohradiv). Edited by S. Dovhal and then V. Grendzha-Donsky, in 1939 it was the organ of the *Ukrainian National Alliance.

Nova Ukraïna (New Ukraine). A daily organ of the Press Office of Staff of the Army of the UNR, published in Kamianets-Podilskyi from August to November 1919.

Nova Ukraïna (New Ukraine). A monthly and later irregular journal of literature, politics, scholarship, and

Nova Ukraïna

community affairs, published in Prague in 1922–8. A major émigré journal of the 1920s, it contained a chronicle of developments in Soviet Ukraine, Galicia, and abroad, and extensive book reviews and notes. *Nova Ukraïna* was closely allied with the Ukrainian democratic socialist movement and was avowedly anti-Soviet and pro–Ukrainian independence. The founder and chief editor was M. Shapoval; he was assisted by P. Bohatsky (1922), V. Vynnychenko (1923–4), M. Halahan, N. Hryhoriiv (1925–6), S. Dovhal, B. Zalievsky, and M. Mandryka (1927–8).

Nova Ukraïna

Nova Ukraïna (New Ukraine). A daily Ukrainian paper published from November 1941 to February 1943 in Kharkiv, Poltava, and then, with interruptions, Vinnytsia. It was one of the best newspapers to appear in German-occupied Ukraine, at least partly because it was published so close to the German-Soviet front and was subject only to military censorship, which was not as restrictive as the Nazi censorship practiced elsewhere in the Reichskommissariat Ukraine. It was edited by P. Sahaidachny and V. Tsarynnyk. A total of 402 issues appeared, each with a circulation of 25,000 to 50,000 copies.

Nova Ushytsia [Nova Ušycja]. V-8. A town smt (1990 pop 4,900) on the Kalius River and a raion center in Khmelnytskyi oblast. Litnivtsi, the town's original name, is first mentioned in a charter of 1439. In the early 1700s the inhabitants revolted against their Polish overlords. In the mid-18th century Litnivtsi was granted the rights of *Magdeburg law, whereupon its economy flourished. In 1793 the town became a part of Podilia gubernia. In 1829 it was promoted to the status of a county center and renamed Nova Ushytsia. During the revolutionary period, in July 1919 and May–June 1920, the Third Iron Rifle Division of the UNR Army battled the Red Army near Nova Ushytsia. Today the town has a small food industry.

Nova Vodolaha. IV-16. A town smt (1990 pop 14,900) on the Vilkhovatka River and a raion center in Kharkiv oblast. Its name is derived from that of the Vodolaha River, which first appears in documents in 1572. Nova Vodolaha was founded ca 1675 on the *Murava Road by peasants and Cossacks of Kharkiv regiment. Its economy flourished, and by the 18th century Nova Vodolaha had become an important silk trading center in Slobidska Ukraine. Because of its vulnerability to Turkish and Tatar attacks, it served as a fortified outpost. Today the town produces asphalt and building materials.

Nova zoria (New Star). A newspaper of religious and social affairs published weekly in 1926–7 and then semiweekly to 1938 in Lviv and to 1939 in Stanyslaviv. It was the organ of the Ukrainian Christian Organization and then of the Ukrainian Catholic People's party (from 1930).

Nova zoria

The journal supported the 'Westernizing' factions in the Greek Catholic church that advocated the Latinization of the rite. The editors of *Nova zoria* were T. Halushchynsky and O. *Nazaruk (from 1928). In 1930 the paper had a circulation of 2,000.

Nova zoria (New Star). A semimonthly (originally weekly) organ of the Ukrainian Catholic eparchy of St Nicholas, published in Chicago since 1965. It contains articles on religious topics, culture, and education, and it reports on the activities of the church. It is edited by a board headed by Rev Ya. Svyshchuk.

Novachenko, Mykola [Novačenko], b 17 December 1898 in Buryn, Putyvl county, Kursk gubernia, d 1966 in Kharkiv. Orthopedist and traumatologist; corresponding member of the USSR Academy of Medical Sciences from 1957. A graduate of the Kharkiv Medical Institute (1922), he worked at the Ukrainian Scientific Research Institute of Orthopedics and Traumatology and in 1940 became its director. He published over 90 papers on the regeneration of bone tissue, the treatment of bone fractures, and the use of prostheses, and invented a number of prosthetic devices.

Apolinarii Novak

Novak, Apolinarii, b 24 April 1885 in Serafyntsi, Horodenka county, Galicia, d 30 October 1955 in Winnipeg. Journalist and writer. After emigrating to Canada in 1901, Novak was editor of *Kanadiis'kyi farmer* (1909–13) and a longtime staff writer for *Ukraïns'kyi holos* (1922–55). His short stories on Ukrainian pioneer themes were published in the latter journal and in *Khata* (Winnipeg, 1911–12), *Literaturno-naukovyi vistnyk* (Lviv), and *Svoboda* (Jersey City, New Jersey).

Novak, Hryhorii, b 5 March 1919 in Chornobyl, Radomyshl county, Kiev gubernia, d 10 June 1980 in Moscow. Soviet Ukrainian weight lifter of Jewish origin. In

1946 he became the first Soviet athlete to win a world championship. He also won the 1947 European Cup in weight lifting and the 1952 Olympic silver medal in the middleweight class, and set 69 world records and over 100 Soviet records.

Novak, Vilen, b 3 January 1938 in Hlezne, Liubar raion, Zhytomyr oblast. Film director. In 1972 he completed study at the Kiev Institute of Theater Arts; since then he has worked in the Odessa Artistic Film Studio. He has staged films and telefilms, among them *Chervoni dypku-riery* (The Red Diplomatic Couriers, 1977) and *Kamerton* (A Tuning Fork, 1978).

Halyna Novakivska: *Streetcar Stop* (oil)

Novakivska, Halyna [Novakivs'ka] (née Molodetska), b 4 April 1923 in Peremyshl, Galicia. Painter. She studied at the Cracow Academy of Fine Arts and the Cracow Institute of Plastic Art (1939–43). In 1942–4 she worked as a scenery designer at the Theater of Small Forms at the Institute of Folk Creativity in Lviv and at the Ukrainian Theater in Stanyslaviv. A postwar refugee, she emigrated to Canada in 1949 and has lived in Toronto since then. Novakivska has explored textural effects and flattened spatial relationships. Her landscapes, still-life and figural compositions, close-up views of nature, and images of Ontario and Ukraine abound with rich textural surfaces, sophisticated tonal patterns, multiple overlays of several hues, and radiant areas of color, as in *Early Spring* (1985). A member of the Society of Canadian Artists and the Ukrainian Artists' Association, she has had solo exhibitions at

the University of Western Ontario in London (1963) and in Toronto (1964, 1971, 1972, 1980, 1991), Chicago (1974, 1981), Detroit (1976), Ottawa (1978), and Edmonton (1979). Her work was included in the Biennale of Ukrainian Art in Lviv (1991).

Oleksa Novakivsky: *Self-Portrait* (oil, 1911)

Novakivsky, Oleksa [Novakivs'kyj], b 14 March 1872 in Slobodo-Obodivka (now Nova Obodivka), Olhopil county, Podilia gubernia, d 29 August 1935 in Lviv. Painter and educator. He studied painting under F. Klymenko in Odessa (1888–92) and at the Cracow Academy of Fine Arts (1892–3, 1895–1900). After graduating with a gold medal he lived in Mogiła (now Nowa Huta), near Cracow, where he devoted himself to landscape painting. Having attracted Metropolitan A. *Sheptytsky as his patron he moved to Lviv in 1913 and founded the *Novakivsky Art School there in 1923. Solo exhibitions of his works were held in Cracow in 1911 and in Lviv in 1920 and 1921. Novakivsky also exhibited at shows of the Society of Friends of Ukrainian Art, the Association of Independent Ukrainian Artists, and his school. During his Cracow period he painted portraits, landscapes, still lifes, and genre scenes in a naturalistic, impressionist style (eg, *Spring* [1900], *Liberation* [1903], *Caroling* [1907], and *Awakening* [1912]) that resembled that of Polish contemporaries, such as J. Stanisławski, J. Malczewski, and S. Wyspiański. During his early Lviv period his style evolved under the impact of the First World War to become more symbolic and expressionist, as in works such as *The War Madonna* (1916), *St George's Cathedral* (1919), and *Self-Caricature* (1919). He did many portraits, including ones of Metropolitan Sheptytsky, Moses, Prince Yaroslav the Wise, Prince Yaroslav Osmomysl, O. Dovbush, and O. Barvinsky. In the 1920s his colors grew more vivid, and his lines more dynamic. Landscapes such as *St George's Cathedral* (1921–2) and *Fairy Tale about the Hutsul Region* (1926), the canvas *Moloch of War* (1923), his self-portraits, and portraits such as *Dovbush* (1931) and *O. Barvinsky* (1931) are fully expressionist in style. Novakivsky's oeuvre consists of over 500 oils, many of them unfinished. A museum dedicated to him and his works was opened in Lviv in 1972.

BIBLIOGRAPHY
Zalozets'kyi, V. *Oleksa Novakivs'kyi* (Lviv 1934)
Ostrovs'kyi, V. *Oleksa Novakivs'kyi* (Kiev 1964)
Oleksa Novakivs'kyi: Al'bom (Kiev 1973)
Arofikina, V.; Leshchenko-Novakivs'ka, M. *Khudozhn'o-memorial'nyi muzei Oleksy Novakivs'koho u L'vovi: Putivnyk* (Lviv 1983)
Mushynka, M. 'Nevidomyi Oleksa Novakivs'kyi,' *Suchasnist'*, 1990, no. 3

S. Hordynsky

Novakivsky, Yaroslav [Novakivs'kyj, Jaroslav], b 4 January 1920 in Lviv, d 21 May 1982 in Lviv. Architect; son of O. *Novakivsky. A graduate of the Lviv Polytechnical Institute (1950), he taught architecture in Lviv and designed the Dynamo Sports Complex (1953–6) and the telecenter complex (1956–7) there; planned suburban developments in Chernivtsi (1963–5), Uzhhorod, and Lviv (1964–6); and took part in the renovation of the historical center of Lviv and in projecting the general plans for the development of Lviv, Lutske, Chernivtski, Uzhhorod, Drohobych, Boryslav, Truskavets, and Morshyn. He wrote over 20 articles in the history of architecture.

Students of the Novakivsky Art School in 1926. Sitting, from left: Stefaniia Gebus-Baranetska, M. Karpiuk, Oleksa Novakivsky and sons, Olha Pleshkan, and Hryhorii Smolsky; standing: Stepan Lutsyk, Antin Maliutsa, V. Bulyk, Volodymyr Hodys, Sviatoslav Hordynsky, Mykhailo Moroz, V. Hrytsenko, O. Patsurkevych, and Leonyd Papara

Novakivsky Art School (Mystetska shkola O. Novakivskoho). A school of drawing and painting founded in February 1923 by O. *Novakivsky at his studio in Lviv. Although it lacked a formal curriculum and awarded no diplomas, the school's enrollment expanded rapidly. Besides practical training its students were offered lectures (1925–9) on artistic styles and color chemistry by V. Pe-

shchansky, Ukrainian art history by I. Svientsitsky, drawing by O. Kurylas, anatomy by S. Balei, cultural history by I. Rakovsky, and perspective by Ye. Nahirny. In 1926, 1928–9, 1930, 1932, and 1934 exhibitions of student work were held. Around 1932 the school was dissolved because of insufficient community support and declining student interest. About 60 young people attended the school for various periods of time. Among them were later distinguished artists, such as R. Selsky, L. Perfetsky, S. Zarytska, H. Smolsky, Mykhailo Moroz, V. Diadyniuk, A. Maliutsa, S. Hordynsky, S. Gebus-Baranetska, I. Vynnykiv, O. Pleshkan, S. Lutsyk, V. Lasovsky, E. Kozak, and Myron Levytsky.

Novakovsky, Mykhailo [Novakovs'kyj, Myxajlo], b 1872, d 1941. Lawyer and political and civic leader; brother of S. *Novakovsky. While practicing law in Bohorodchany (Galicia) before the First World War, he was active in the Ukrainian Radical party, then in the Ukrainian Social Democratic party, and finally in the National Democratic party. With the outbreak of the war he enlisted in the Ukrainian Sich Riflemen and collaborated with the Union for the Liberation of Ukraine. When the Western Ukrainian National Republic (ZUNR) was formed, he was appointed commissioner of Skalat county and a member of the executive of the Ukrainian National Rada. He went to Warsaw in 1919 as a member of a special diplomatic mission. With the defeat of the ZUNR he emigrated to Prague, and in 1920 he settled in Transcarpathia. In 1939 he moved to Slovakia.

Novakovsky, Stepan [Novakovs'kyj], b 1863, d 1936. Peasant and civic and political activist in Galicia; brother of M. *Novakovsky. He was a noted organizer of the Ukrainian Radical party in the Peremyshl region. In 1895–1901 he served as a deputy to the Galician Diet. Later he supported the Ukrainian Social Democratic party.

Nove Klynove settlement. A settlement and major iron manufacturing center of the late 1st century BC near Nove Klynove, Vynohradiv raion, Transcarpathia oblast. Excavations in 1962–6 revealed iron forges, as well as slag and other remnants of metal production. Located on a major trade route connecting central and eastern Europe, Nove Klynove supplied iron goods throughout the Carpathian region.

Nove Misto. IV-3. A village (1968 pop 709) on the Vyrva River in Staryi Sambir raion, Lviv oblast. It is first mentioned in a document in 1361. Archeologists have discovered stone tools, arrowheads, and Roman and Hungarian coins at the site of the village. On 4 February 1919 the Ukrainian Galician Army fought the Polish army near Nove Misto. The village's most valuable architectural monuments are the Church of St John the Baptist, built in 1529 and rebuilt in 1756, and a Roman Catholic church built in 1512.

Nove mystetstvo (New Art). An illustrated journal of the arts, published in Kharkiv in 1925–8 (a total of 89 issues). An organ of the Chief Ukrainian Administration of Political Education, it contained articles on literary and artistic developments in Ukraine and abroad, on political affairs (especially Ukrainization), criticism, and reviews and devoted considerable attention to the Ukrainian the-

Nove mystetstvo (cover design, with self-portrait, by Anatol Petrytsky)

ater. It was edited by M. Khrystovy and V. Khmury. O. Dovzhenko was one of its illustrators.

Nove selo (New Village). A weekly newspaper for peasants published in Lviv from 1930 to 1939. Founded by a small group of Sovietophile agronomists headed by V. Vorobets, who became chief editor, and published by a cooperative, in 1935 it became pro-OUN. Members of the editorial board in the latter period were Ya. Starukh and B. Levytsky. With the change in political orientation, *Nove selo* became one of the most popular papers in Galicia and reached a circulation of over 20,000.

Nove slovo (New Word). A daily newspaper published in Lviv from the autumn of 1912 to 3 September 1914. Subsidized by Rev T. Voinarovsky-Stolobut and edited by a committee headed by M. Kurtseba and including M. Nyskoklon, S. Biliak, V. Kozak, and I. Nimchuk, it contained articles on political developments and historical and cultural topics, belles lettres, and translations from foreign newspapers, and was one of the most widely read Ukrainian newspapers of its day (reaching a circulation of some 12,000). *Nove slovo* was closed down after the Russian occupation of Lviv, but was briefly revived in June–July 1915, after Lviv had been recaptured by Austro-Hungarian forces, and edited by F. Fedortsiv. It was succeeded by *Ukraïns'ke slovo*.

Nove ukraïns'ke slovo (New Ukrainian Word). A daily newspaper published in German-occupied Kiev from December 1941 to 1943 (a total of 531 issues). Edited by K. Shtepa, it replaced the suppressed *Ukraïns'ke slovo* and was avowedly pro-Nazi and anti-OUN. Some articles on Ukrainian cultural and historical topics were published in it.

Nove zerkalo. See *Zerkalo*.

Nove zhytie (New Life). A weekly and then semimonthly organ of the *Covenant of Brotherhoods fraternal organization, published in Olyphant, Pennsylvania, from 1912 to 1938. The paper's first editor was P. Kyryliuk.

Nove zhyttia (New Life). A daily newspaper published in Stanyslaviv (now Ivano-Frankivske) from November 1918 to April 1919 (a total of 89 issues) by Z. Kozlovsky. It was edited by I. Rybchyn and R. Zaklynsky. Its politics were influenced by the views of the Ukrainian Party of Socialist Revolutionaries, and it openly criticized the policies of the Western Ukrainian National Republic's government.

Nove zhyttia (New Life). A semimonthly organ of *Sel-Rob, published from April 1928 to February 1930 in Kholm as the successor to *Nashe zhyttia*. Edited by S. Makivka and P. Shcherbak, it published articles on political and economic developments written from a pro-Soviet, socialist perspective. The paper was closed down by the Polish authorities, and its editors were arrested.

Nove zhyttia

Nove zhyttia (New Life). A Ukrainian weekly newspaper published in Prešov, Slovakia, since August 1951. At first it was the organ of the Regional Committee of the Slovak Communist party and was largely a translation of the Slovak weekly *Nový život*. In January 1959 the paper became the organ of the *Cultural Association of Ukrainian Workers. Its language, style, and content improved. In the late 1960s it published a series of articles criticizing the nationality policy in Czechoslovakia and Ukraine. As a result some of the paper's staff were dismissed. In the late 1980s the articles became much more interesting. Since mid-1989, 1,000 copies of the paper have been regularly sold in Ukraine. The editors have been V. Kopchak (1959–64), Yu. Datsko (1965–71), L. Halushka (1971–88), and O. Zozuliak (1989–). Today the paper is published by the Union of Ruthenian-Ukrainians of Slovakia.

Novel. See Prose.

November Uprising in Lviv, 1918 (Lystopadovyi zryv). The first stage of armed conflict in the *Ukrainian-Polish War of 1918–19. The proclamation of the *Ukrainian National Rada (UNR) on 18 October 1918 concerning the founding of an independent Ukrainian state initiated preparations on the part of Ukrainians for taking power in eastern Galicia. The UNR originally hoped to establish a Ukrainian administration with the support of the Austrian authorities (Viceroy K. Huyn), but when those hopes were only partially fulfilled, it decided to act unilaterally. It then empowered the *Ukrainian Military Committee under Capt D. Vitovsky to oversee the entire operation. The seizure of Lviv was planned originally for 3 November 1918. It was to be carried out by the Ukrainian soldiers who constituted the majority of the Austrian troops garrisoned in the city as well as by a brigade of the Ukrainian Sich Riflemen (USS) garrisoned in Bukovyna. The creation in Cracow of the *Polish Liquidation Committee (28 Octo-

Proclamation of the November Uprising in Lviv

ber 1918), which announced that it would transfer to Lviv, compelled the Ukrainian politicians to move up the date of the operation.

On 1 November 1918 between 3:30 and 4:00 a.m. the Ukrainian soldiers occupied the public utility buildings and military objectives in Lviv without bloodshed. Ukrainian flags were raised, and proclamations issued announcing the emergence of a Ukrainian state. The Austrian authorities were interned, and Huyn handed power over to V. Detsykevych, the vice-director of the governor-generalship, who recognized the supreme authority of the UNR. The Austrian military commander of the city called on his subordinates to recognize the Rada. Col M. Marynovych now became commandant of Lviv, and the newly promoted Col Vitovsky became commander in chief of the Ukrainian force (numbering 60 officers and 1,200 soldiers).

The Ukrainian uprising met with armed resistance from the city's Polish residents, who constituted about 60 percent of its population. Polish activity before noon on 1 November 1918 was spontaneous and unorganized. Groups of young people assembled in various parts of the city and were directed by members of Polish paramilitary associations. In the afternoon Capt C. Mączyński assumed control of the opposition forces. The Poles managed to obtain arms and ammunition from a police garrison in the Horodok suburb, and in the evening a Polish detachment over 100 strong captured part of the Novyi Svit district.

On the night of 2 November the Poles captured a large ammunition depot in the railway station. At the same time the Ukrainian General Command (from 18 November known as the High Command) was unable to bring into the city detachments of the Sich Riflemen: the detachments encountered strong Polish resistance in the Klepariv suburb and only partly managed to break through into Lviv, on 3 November. The failure brought about a crisis in the Ukrainian command, and Vitovsky was replaced by Col Marynovych.

Until 4 November, battles were waged in different parts of the city, notably near the Sienkiewicz School, the Technician's Center, the Uhlan barracks in Vilka, Hora Strachennia, the post office, and St George's Cathedral, as well as in the Klepariv and Zamarstyniv suburbs. During that time the Poles (numbering approx 1,000) were able to consolidate gains in the western parts of the city and establish, by 5 November, a north–south dividing line.

The outbreak of combat in Lviv mobilized Ukrainian public opinion in Dnieper Ukraine under German occupation and the Hetman government of P. Skoropadsky. Local political organizations (the Ukrainian National Union, the Kiev-based Batkivshchyna society) issued appeals for rapid assistance for their Galician brethren. The first Dnieper detachments arrived in Lviv on 12 November 1918.

On 5 November the function of chief commander was taken over by H. Kossak, who initiated attacks to oust the Poles from the center of the city. The fiercest battles were conducted around the barracks in Vilka. On 9 November the Poles initiated their only offensive, in the area of St George's Cathedral. It was unsuccessful, and the Poles remained largely in defensive positions from that time.

On 9 November another change occurred within the Ukrainian high command, which was now entrusted to Col H. Stefaniv. He delivered a series of blows in the northern and southern parts of the city in order to break through the Polish front line. On 10 November the Ukrainian detachments attacked the building of the railway directory and then occupied the Ferdinand barracks. From 11 to 13 November a battle was waged for the village of Sokilnyky, and on 13 November the Ukrainian forces commenced an assault along the Vilka road. On 14 November an effective Ukrainian offensive on Zamarstyniv and Klepariv pressed hard on the Polish positions in the north. On 15 November another attack was launched against the Cadet School, and two days later the Polish front line in that region was temporarily broken.

In spite of local victories in such skirmishes the line of the front essentially did not change. On 18 November an armistice was signed, originally for two and then for three days. The Ukrainians tried to bring in auxiliary troops from Stanyslaviv, Ternopil, and Stryi, and the Polish authorities in Warsaw made final preparations for an operation intended to seize Lviv. That operation was entrusted to an assault group led by Major J. Stachiewicz, which on 11 November captured Peremyshl. On 20 November a Polish detachment commanded by Col M. Karaszewicz-Tokarzewski (consisting of 140 officers, 1,228 soldiers, and 8 artillery guns) reached Lviv. On 21 November it began an assault with the intention of encircling the Ukrainians. Though repelled, the assault persuaded Col Stefaniv to order a retreat, and most of the detachments left town at night. The next day Lviv was in Polish hands, although Ukrainians surrounded the city on three sides.

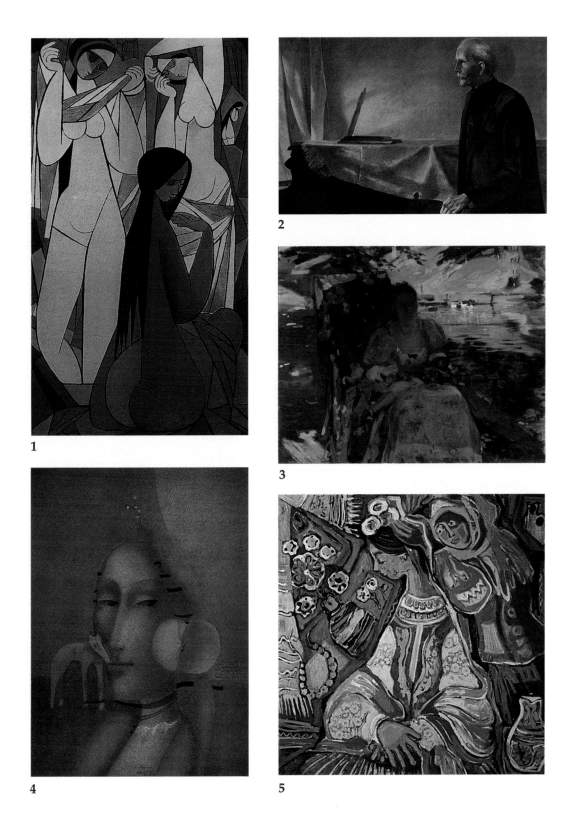

ART 1) H. Mazepa: *Bathers* (oil, 1961; private collection). 2) L. Medvid: *Composer Stanyslav Liudkevych* (tempera, 1978). 3) O. Murashko: *By a Pond* (oil, 1913; Kiev Museum of Ukrainian Art; photo courtesy of the Winnipeg Art Gallery). 4) V. Makarenko: *Roxolana* (mixed media, 1983; courtesy of R. Curkowsky). 5) H. Novakivska: *Prenuptial Party for the Bride, Lemko Region* (oil, 1980; private collection).

BIBLIOGRAPHY
Próchnik, A. *Obrona Lwowa od 1 do 22 listopada 1918 roku* (Zamość 1919)
Kuz'ma, O. *Lystopadovi dni 1918 r.* (Lviv 1931; 2nd edn, New York 1960)
Skrzypek, J. *Ukraińcy w Austrii podczas wielkiej wojny i geneza zamachu na Lwów* (Warsaw 1939)
Hutsuliak, M. *Pershyi Lystopad 1918 roku na zakhidnikh zemliakh Ukraïny zi spohadamy i zhyttiespysamy chleniv komitetu vykonavtsiv lystopadovoho chyna* (New York 1973)
Kozłowski, M. *Między Sanem a Zbruczem: Walki o Lwów i Galicję Wschodnią 1918–1919* (Cracow 1990)

A. Chojnowski

Novgorod the Great (Novgorod Velikii). A city-state in northern Rus' from the 12th to the 15th century. According to some scholars (most notably M. Kostomarov) the town of Novgorod was established by local Slavs (the Ilmen Slovenes) who had migrated to the north from the middle Dnieper Basin. According to the Primary Chronicle *Varangians led by *Riuryk arrived there in 862. Novgorod's location on the *Varangian route to Byzantium determined its political and economic importance vis-à-vis Kiev and its relationship with the capital of the Rus' state. Traders from Novgorod did extensive business in Kiev and had their own district and church there. Kiev's architecture was copied in Novgorod, as is most evident in the similarity of the St Sophia cathedrals in the two cities. The style of the Novgorod chronicles, distinctive in its own right, also displays obvious Kievan influences. Christianity was introduced in Novgorod via Kiev. In spite of initial resistance by the local population to the new religion Novgorod soon became an important religious center and eparchial see (the most notable bishop was Luka Zhydiata) within Kiev metropoly. From 1156 it had its own archbishop.

For the first few centuries Novgorod was ruled by Prince *Ihor and his dynasty. Before they became grand princes of Kiev, both *Volodymyr the Great and his son *Yaroslav the Wise were princes of Novgorod. Yaroslav was succeeded in Novgorod by his son, Volodymyr. Eventually Novgorod principality came to be ruled by the descendants of Volodymyr Monomakh. Novgorod's political and economic interests, rapid growth, and distance from Kiev gradually brought about local opposition to Kievan rule. Such opposition was evident in the 11th century, when Yaroslav the Wise refused to pay tribute to his father in Kiev and Kosniatin (Kostiantin) Dobrynich (Yaroslav's cousin and the viceroy in Novgorod) pursued an obviously anti-Kievan course of action. Vsevolod Mstyslavych, Monomakh's grandson and the son of Mstyslav I Volodymyrovych the Great, was the last prince of the Kievan dynasty in Novgorod (1118–36) to interfere in Novgorod's affairs. The city revolted against his rule and achieved its political independence as a feudal republic in 1136. The supreme governing authority of the city became the *veche* (Ukrainian: *viche*), and the *posadnik* became an elected mayor rather than a viceroy appointed by the prince. In practice the city was run by the local boyars and wealthy merchants. The arrangement was formalized in the 14th century, when a council of representatives of the most powerful boyar families chaired by the archbishop was established to administer the city.

The Tatar invasion of Europe in 1239–40 did not reach Novgorod the Great, but the city was compelled to recognize the suzerainty of the Golden Horde and to pay tribute to its khan. Relative independence from the Tatar yoke allowed the city to develop and prosper considerably by exploiting the neighboring satellites and colonies and engaging in European trade, particularly with the Hanseatic League. A greater threat to the republic in the long term emerged with the rise of Muscovy. Novgorod attempted to stem the growing Muscovite influence and encroachments by allying itself with the Grand Duchy of Lithuania and even electing a Lithuanian-Ruthenian appanage prince from Kiev, *Mykhailo Olelkovych, as its prince in 1470. Those efforts ultimately proved fruitless, as the Muscovite prince Ivan III annexed much of the republic's territory in 1471 and then forced the city, through sheer terror, to recognize Moscow's suzerainty.

BIBLIOGRAPHY
The Chronicle of Novgorod, 1016–1471, trans R. Michell and N. Forbes (London 1914; 2nd edn, Hattiesburg, Miss 1970)
Likhachev, D. *Novgorod Velikii: Ocherk istorii kul'tury Novgoroda XI–XVII vv.* (Moscow–Leningrad 1961)
Ianin, V. *Novgorodskie posadniki* (Moscow 1962)
Podvigina, N. *Ocherki sotsial'no-ekonomicheskoi i politicheskoi istorii Novgoroda Velikogo v XII–XIII vv.* (Moscow 1976)
Birnbaum, H. *Lord Novgorod the Great: Essays in the History and Culture of a Medieval City-State* (Columbus, Ohio 1981)
Rybakov, B. *Kievskaia Rus' i russkie kniazhestva XII–XIII vv.* (Moscow 1982)

M. Zhdan

Novhorodka. V-13. A town smt (1990 pop 7,100) and raion center on the Kamianka River in Kirovohrad oblast. A settlement known as Kutsivka *khutir* was founded in 1770 on the territory that belonged at that time to the Zaporozhian Sich. Most of its inhabitants were former serfs from the Poltava region. In 1822 Kutsivka was renamed Novhorodka. Today the town has a mineral-water bottling factory, a mixed-feed factory, and a granite quarry.

Novhorod-Siverskyi [Novhorod-Sivers'kyj]. I-14. A city (1990 pop 15,600) on the Desna River and a raion center in Chernihiv oblast. According to archeological evidence it was founded in the 980s. It is first mentioned in the chronicles under the year 1044, and the Laurentian Chronicle lists it as the center of the Siversk principality in Kievan Rus'. One of its rulers was *Ihor Sviatoslavych, the central figure of *Slovo o polku Ihorevi* (The Tale of Ihor's Campaign). In 1356 Novhorod-Siverskyi was annexed by Lithuania, and in 1503 by Russia. In 1620, while under Polish rule (1618–54), it obtained the rights of *Magdeburg law. Under the Hetman state it was a company center in Nizhen (until 1663) and then Starodub (until 1781) regiments. Within the Russian Empire it was the capital of Novhorod-Siverskyi vicegerency (1782–96) and then a county center in Little Russia and Chernihiv gubernias. In the 17th and 18th centuries the Novhorod-Siverskyi Transfiguration Monastery and the town's gymnasium played an influential role in Ukraine's religious and cultural life. Today the city is a railway junction and a river port. It produces asphalt, construction materials, dairy products, and cotton fabric. Its many architectural monuments include the Dormition Church (1671–1715) and its bell tower (1820), the wooden St Nicholas's Church (1760), the monastery complex (11th–17th centuries), and the Transfiguration Cathedral (1791–6), which stands on the ruins of the 12th- to 13th-century cathedral. There are also

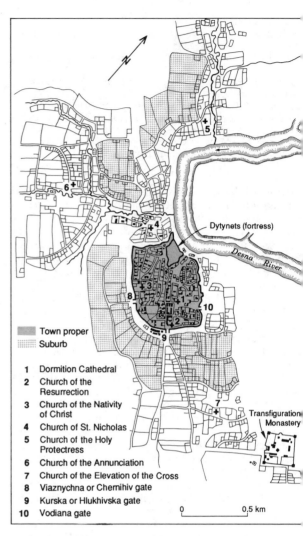

Novhorod-Siverskyi. Clockwise, from upper left: the Dormition Cathedral (late 17th to early 18th century), building of the former gymnasium for women, market stalls and warehouses (late 18th to early 19th century), 19th-century building, and St Nicholas's Church (mid-18th century)

Town proper
Suburb

1   Dormition Cathedral
2   Church of the Resurrection
3   Church of the Nativity of Christ
4   Church of St. Nicholas
5   Church of the Holy Protectress
6   Church of the Annunciation
7   Church of the Elevation of the Cross
8   Viaznychna or Chernihiv gate
9   Kurska or Hlukhivska gate
10   Vodiana gate

Dytynets (fortress)

Desna River

Transfiguration Monastery

0   0.5 km

NOVHOROD-SIVERSKYI

several buildings in the classical style: the triumphal arch (1786), the gymnasium (1808), and an early 19th-century trading mall.

Novhorod-Siverskyi archeological site. An Upper Paleolithic rock shelter located on the banks of the Desna River in Novhorod-Siverskyi, Chernihiv oblast. Discovered in 1933 and excavated in 1935–8 and 1954, the site revealed a typical Upper Paleolithic flint tool assemblage. Three unusually large (33.9, 44, and 45.4 cm) pieces are believed to have been used to cut animal bones. Also recovered were a large mammoth rib (59.5 cm) decorated with linear inscriptions, skull fragments, and animal bones.

Novhorod-Siverskyi Gymnasium (Novhorod-Siverska himnaziia). One of the older institutions of secondary education in Ukraine, located in Novhorod-Siverskyi, now in Chernihiv oblast. It was founded in 1804 on the basis of the main public school, which had been opened in 1789. The gymnasium was opened on the initiative of the Novhorod-Siverskyi patriotic circle, a group of Ukrainian autonomists in Novhorod-Siverskyi in the late 18th century whose agenda highlighted education. The gymnasium was a center of advanced learning for Chernihiv gubernia for many years. Its first director, I. Khalansky, was succeeded by I. Tymkovsky. The gymnasium produced many important graduates, including M. Maksymovych,

K. Ushinsky, P. Zabolotsky-Desiatovsky, P. Kulish, and M. Kybalchych. After the Revolution of 1917 the gymnasium was transformed into a regular secondary school.

Novhorod-Siverskyi patriotic circle. A network of Ukrainian noble autonomists in Novhorod-Siverskyi vicegerency in the late 18th century. Its members and associates included A. Hudovych, T. *Kalynsky, I. *Khalansky, A. *Khudorba, P. *Koropchevsky, O. *Lobysevych (one of the leaders), *M. Myklashevsky, H. *Poletyka, A. *Rachynsky, Bishop V. *Shyshatsky, F. *Tumansky, M. *Znachko-Yavorsky, H. Dolynsky, S. Shyrai, and A. Pryhara. Most were graduates of the Kievan Mohyla Academy and foreign universities. The circle's goals were the revival of an autonomous Ukrainian state and the rebirth of Ukrainian culture.

The activities of the members have not been thoroughly researched, but they were far-reaching. The members propagated the idea of Ukrainian independence, disseminated publicistic works (eg, the speeches of Hetmans P. Polubotok and I. Mazepa), and supplied foreign scholars (eg, N.-G. *Le Clerc and J.-B. *Scherer) with information about Ukrainian history and concerns. They championed he rights of the Ukrainian nobility and Cossacks, engaged in foreign diplomacy (V. *Kapnist's secret mission n Berlin in 1791 was probably connected with their aims), nd took an interest in organizing Ukrainian armed forces involvement in the Ukrainian carabineer regiments and V. Kapnist's 1788 proposal for reviving the Cossack regiments) with the ultimate goal of fighting Russian domination.

The members also took an interest in education (plans o establish a gymnasium and a proposal for a university n Novhorod-Siverskyi) and scholarship (Tumansky's proposal for a Ukrainian academy of sciences – the 'Academic Convention') and collected and prepared for publication materials and writings on the Hetman state (by Poletyka, Tumansky, Khudorba, and Pryhara, and Ya. *Markovych's *Zapiski o Malorossii* [Notes on Little Russia]), the Ukrainian language (Tumansky's 1793 dictionary), and Ukrainian literature (Lobysevych's poetry and plans to publish Ukrainian baroque works).

Few of the circle's plans and projects were realized. Their ideas and activities, however, had an influence in Ukraine in the first quarter of the 19th century even beyond the Novhorod-Siverskyi region.

O. Ohloblyn

Novhorod-Siverskyi Press (Novhorod-Siverska drukarnia). An imprimery founded and funded by Archbishop L. Baranovych in 1674 at the Novhorod-Siverskyi Transfiguration Monastery. It published the polemic and moralizing works of L. Baranovych and I. Galiatovsky, the *Antolohion*, O. Buchynsky's poem 'Chyhyryn ...' (1677), about the heroic defense of the city from Turkish and Tatar armies, and primers and other educational texts. In 1679 it was moved to Chernihiv and was reorganized into the *Chernihiv printing press.

Novhorod-Siverskyi principality. See Siversk principality.

Novhorod-Siverskyi Transfiguration Monastery (Novhorod-Siverskyi Spaso-Preobrazhenskyi manastyr). A men's monastery on the bank of the Desna River in southeastern Novhorod-Siverskyi, believed to have been founded in 1033 by Prince Mstyslav Volodymyrovych of Tmutorokan. The first mention of the monastery is found in a 1552 charter of Ivan the Terrible, written when the city was under Muscovite rule. From the first half of the 17th century the monastery was headed by an archimandrite. In 1635, under Polish rule, it was given to the Jesuit order, but it reverted to Orthodoxy following the outbreak of the Cossack-Polish War in 1648. From 1657 to 1672, while serving as the archbishop of Chernihiv, L. Baranovych resided at the monastery. He had new buildings erected and established the *Novhorod-Siverskyi Press. Baranovych also acquired more properties for the monastery, so that in the 18th century it owned approx 6,000 serfs. From 1785 to 1799 I. Kondratkovsky, the bishop of Novhorod-Siverskyi and Hlukhiv, resided at the monastery. He closed down *Pereiaslav College and in its place created a theological seminary at the monastery. The seminary's first rector was V. *Shyshatsky. In 1908 the monastery housed 38 monks.

Under Soviet rule the monastery was secularized and transformed into a cultural-historical preserve. Its central attractions are the monastery's second Transfiguration

Entrance and campanile of the Novhorod-Siverskyi Transfiguration Monastery

Cathedral, designed in the classical style by G. Quarenghi and built with five cupolas in 1791–6; the 16th- to 17th-century cruciform, one-cupola SS Peter and Paul Church; and the monastery's main gate, with three entrances, arches, and an octagonal belfry, built in the baroque style in the late 17th century. Many prominent 18th- and 19th-century statesmen and cultural figures (eg, Count O. Rozumovsky, Archbishop Shyshatsky) were buried at the monastery.

O. Ohloblyn

Novhorod-Siverskyi vicegerency (Novhorod-Siverske namisnytstvo). One of three Russian *vicegerencies created in Left-Bank Ukraine in 1782 after the abolition of the administrative-territorial regiments of the Hetman state. The vicegerency's capital was Novhorod-Siverskyi. Its territory replaced that of *Starodub regiment and parts of Chernihiv and *Nizhen regiments. It was divided into 11 counties: Hlukhiv, Konotip, Korop, Krolevets, Mglin, Novhorod-Siverskyi, Novoe Mesto, Pohar, Starodub, Sosnytsia, and Surazh. In 1782 the vicegerency had 11 cities, 22 towns, and 2,186 villages and other settlements, with a total male population of 371,046. In 1797 it was abolished, and its territory became part of *Little Russia gubernia. A detailed description of the vicegerency's population and settlements, prepared in 1779–81 by a commission headed by A. Myloradovych, was edited by P. Fedorenko and published by the VUAN Archeographic Commission in 1931.

Novhorodske [Novohorods'ke]. V-18, DB III-3. A town smt (1990 pop 13,200) on the Kryvyi Torets River in Donetske oblast, under the administration of the Dzerzhynske municipal council. It arose at the end of the 18th century and was called Niu Iork (New York) until 1951. Novhorodske is the home of an erosion research station, a machine-building plant, and a brick factory.

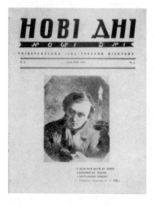

Novi dni

Novi dni (New Days). A monthly magazine established in Toronto in 1950 by P. *Volyniak. It was edited by him until his death in 1969, and since that time it has been edited by an editorial board headed by D. Kyslytsia (1969–76), V. Svaroh (1977–8), and M. Dalny (since 1978). Prose, poetry, literary reviews, publicism, obituaries, memoirs, biographical notes, and news and analyses of developments in Ukraine and among Ukrainian émigrés have appeared in each issue. The magazine's polemical articles have been critical of both the USSR and undemocratic tendencies in the Ukrainian émigré community. Many prominent émigré writers living in Canada, the United States, and Australia have been contributors.

Novi poezii

Novi shliakhy

Novi poezii (New Poetry). An annual publication of the *New York Group of writers which appeared from 1959 to 1979. It contained original and reprinted poetry, mostly by members of the group and other émigré writers (such as V. Lesych, Yu. Kolomyiets, V. Barka, and M. Carynnyk), which was illustrated by member artists. The journal also published translations from English, German, Italian, and especially Spanish, including poems by M. Hernandez, F.G. Lorca, L. Simpson, P. Neruda, J. Jiménez, and others.

Novi Sad. The capital (1981 pop 170,000) of the autonomous region of Vojvodina in Serbia, and the leading cultural center (1971 Ukrainian pop over 6,000) for the Ukrainians in Bačka and Srem. Ukrainians began to settle in Novi Sad in 1765, many of them from Ruski Krstur and Lоćura. In 1780 a Greek Catholic parish was established there, and in 1817 work began on the SS Peter and Paul Church. Novi Sad's Ukrainian cultural and enlightenment society has been active since 1919. Today it boasts a choir, a dance ensemble, and a nationally recognized drama group, Diadia. The weekly *Ruske slovo*, the literary and artistic quarterly *Shvetlosts*, and the children's monthly *Pyonerska zahradka* have been published in Novi Sad since 1967. A program in the Bačka-Ukrainian dialect has been broadcast by local radio since 1949. The library of the Serbian Matica has a Ukrainian-Bačka department. The Sisters Servants of Mary Immaculate founded a convent in Novi Sad in 1956, which was followed by one for the Basilian order of nuns in 1961. As the Ukrainian community expanded after the Second World War, the city replaced Ruski Krstur as the major Ukrainian cultural and educational center in the region.

Novi Sanzhary [Novi Sanžary]. IV-15. A town smt (1990 pop 9,200) on the Vorskla River and a raion center in Poltava oblast. Archeologists have uncovered the remains of a Scythian settlement from the 3rd to 4th centuries BC at the site of the town. The name Sanzhary is of Turkish origin. Novi Sanzhary was founded in the first half of the 17th century. It grew rapidly when B. Khmelnytsky allowed peasants from Right-Bank Ukraine to settle on the hetman's properties along the banks of the Psol, the Sula, and the Vorskla rivers. Novi Sanzhary witnessed many battles during the Cossack-Polish War. Historically the town was a center of the tanning industry. By 1699 a gunpowder factory had been built there. Today the town produces leather, furniture, and bricks.

Novi shliakhy (New Roads). A Sovietophile literary, cultural, and political monthly published in Lviv from 1929 to 1932 and edited by A. *Krushelnytsky. Among the contributors were the Western Ukrainian writers A. and I. Krushelnytsky, V. Bobynsky, P. Derkach, F. Fedortsiv, Ya. Halan, Ya. Kondra, Yu. Kosach, S. Levynsky, and I. Mykhailiuk and the Soviet Ukrainian writers M. Burachek, P. Kozytsky, Y. Shevchenko, and M. Smuzhka (A. Ryndiuh). The journal contained Soviet literary works in both Ukrainian and Russian (translated mostly by S. Shchurat). In 1930 it had a print run of 2,500 copies. It was subject to severe censorship, and issues were often confiscated by the Polish authorities. After the journal was closed down by them, Krushelnytsky published four issues of a journal called *Krytyka* (April–July 1933).

Novi vydannia URSR (New Publications of the Ukrainian SSR). A bibliographic bulletin published three times a month in Kharkiv by the Book Chamber of the Ukrainian SSR from 1958. Until 1974 it was called *Novi knyhy URSR*. It lists all new books, booklets, musical scores, posters, photo albums, and postcards published in Ukraine and provides separate indexes to them. In 1983 it had a circulation of approx 18,000.

Novikov, Mikhail, b 1777, d ca 1822–5. Participant in the *Decembrist movement. After a career of military serice he became (1816) chancery director for the governor-general of Little Russia, N. Repnin, in Poltava. He helped to establish a regional branch of the Union of Salvation and later headed its successor body, the Union of Welfare. He was the author of the first republican-minded constitution of the Decembrist movement. Novikov also established the Love of Truth Masonic lodge in Poltava in 1818.

Novikov, Mykola, b 17 May 1925 in Kiev. Ballet dancer, ballet master, and pedagogue. In 1948 he completed study in the ballet studio at the Kiev Theater of Opera and Ballet; he then worked there as a soloist and, from 1972, the ballet master. In 1967 he began teaching at the Kiev Institute of Theater Arts.

Novikov, Sergei, b 15 December 1949 in Moscow. Judo champion. A member of the Kiev Dynamo sports society, he won the 1976 Olympic gold medal in judo (heavyweight class) and was the 1973 New York, 1976 European, and 1974–8 USSR champion.

Noviny (News). One of the first Ukrainian-language newspapers, published semiweekly in Lviv from January to April 1849. Edited by I. *Hushalevych, it devoted considerable attention to political developments in the Austrian Empire and abroad. Twenty-six issues appeared before Hushalevych closed the paper and began to publish *Pchola.

Novoaidar [Novoajdar]. V-20, DB II-6. A town smt (1990 pop 8,400) on the Aidar River and a raion center in Luhanske oblast. It was founded in the second half of the 17th century by the Don Cossacks. Its inhabitants took part in K. Bulavin's popular revolt in the early 18th century. Today the town has a food industry.

Novoarkhanhelske [Novoarxanhel's'ke]. V-11. A town smt (1990 pop 8,300) on the Syniukha River and a raion center in Kirovohrad oblast. The settlement was founded in 1742 and was called Arkhanhel-horodok until 1764. Today the town has a cheese factory, a brick factory, and a hydroelectric station.

Novoazovsk. See Novoozivske.

Novocherkassk [Novočerkassk]. VI-21. A city (1989 pop 187,000) on the Tuzliv River in Rostov oblast, RF. It was founded in 1805 as an administrative center of Don Cossack province. According to the census of 1926, Ukrainians represented 12 percent of the city's population.

Novodarivka [Novodarjivka]. A town smt (1990 pop 5,200) in Luhanske oblast, under the administration of the Rivenky municipal council. The town was founded ca 1877 and called Darivka until 1932. Today it has a gas compression station, an asphalt plant, and an aggregate factory.

Novodonetske [Novodonec'ke]. V-18, DB II-2. A town smt (1990 pop 6,800) in Dobropillia raion, Donetske oblast. It was founded in 1956 and granted smt status in 1960. Coal mining and furniture making are the major industries there.

Novodruzheske [Novodružes'ke]. V-19, DB II-4. A city (1990 pop 11,200) on the Donets River in Luhanske oblast, administered by the Lysychanske municipal council. It was founded in 1935 with the opening of a coal mine, and attained city status in 1963. Today two coal mines and a brewery are located there.

Novodvorsky, Ivan [Novodvors'kyj], b 1890, d 1942? Lawyer and civic and political leader. He practiced law in Kolomyia and was active in the Ukrainian Radical party, where he held executive positions (including that of vice-president) from 1924. He was arrested by the Soviets in 1939, and disappeared in prison.

Novoekonomichne. See Dymytrov.

Novoheorhiievske. See Svitlovodske.

Novohrad-Volynskyi [Novohrad-Volyns'kyj]. III-8. A city (1990 pop 56,500) on the Sluch River and a raion center in Zhytomyr oblast. It is first mentioned in the Hypatian Chronicle under the year 1257 as the town of Zviahel (Vzviahl, Vozviahl). In 1340 it was annexed by Lithuania, and in 1569, transferred to Poland. In 1793 it was taken by Russia, and in 1795 it was given its present name. Today the city produces agricultural machinery, building materials, beer, and furniture. Lesia *Ukrainka was born and spent her childhood in Novhorad-Volynskyi. A memorial museum has been established there in her honor. Of the castle built by K. Ostrozky in 1507, only remnants of the walls and one tower are left.

Novohrodivka. V-18, DB III-2. A city (1990 pop 19,400) in Donetske oblast, under the administration of the Selydove municipal council. It was founded as a coal-mining settlement in 1939, and attained city status in 1958. It has four coal mines and an enrichment plant.

Novoiavorivske [Novojavorivs'ke]. IV-4. A city (1990 pop 25,200) in Yavoriv raion, Lviv oblast. It was founded in 1965, and attained city status in 1986. It produces reinforced-concrete structures. Nearby is the Sirka manufacturing consortium.

Novokhopersk [Novoxopersk]. II-22. A town and raion center (1959 pop 8,900) in Voronezh oblast, RF. A fortress was built at the site in 1710, and the town became a county center in Tambov vicegerency in 1779 and Voronezh gubernia in 1802. According to the census of 1926, Ukrainians accounted for 45 percent of the raion population.

Novokursnyky. See Russophiles.

Novolypivske settlement. A *Cherniakhiv culture settlement near Chapaivka, Zolotonosha raion, Cherkasy oblast. The site was excavated in 1957–8, then flooded by the Kremenchuk Reservoir in 1959. Eighteen surface structures (including both living quarters with clay ovens and storage facilities), four semi-pit storage structures, an iron-making workshop, and thrown pottery were found at this site. Remains of early Slavic storage pits were also unearthed.

Novomoskovske [Novomoskovs'ke]. V-16. A city (1990 pop 76,200) on the Samara River and a raion center in Dni-

The Trinity Cathedral in Novomoskovske

propetrovske oblast. A Cossack settlement was established at the site in the second half of the 16th century, and eventually it became known as Novoselytsia (or Samarchyk). In 1784 the village was raised to city status and renamed Novomoskovske. From 1796 it was a county town in New Russia gubernia, and from 1802 it was part of Katerynoslav gubernia. Today it manufactures large pipes used for gas and oil pipelines, reinforced-concrete structures, and furniture. It is the home of the famous nine-domed Trinity Cathedral, constructed of wood by Ya. *Pohrebniak in 1773–81.

Novomoskovske Pipe Plant (Novomoskovskyi trubnyi zavod). An enterprise of the metallurgical industry in Novomoskovske, Dnipropetrovske oblast. Built in 1932–5, it produced sheet tin and steel and galvanized plating before the Second World War. The machinery was evacuated at the outset of the war, and the plant was completely rebuilt afterward. Since 1961 it has specialized in the making of electroplated pipes and enameled and galvanized plates.

Novomykolaivka [Novomykolajivka]. VII-16. A town smt (1990 pop 6,100) on the Verkhnia Tersa River and a raion center in Zaporizhia oblast. It was founded in the last quarter of the 18th century and was called Kocherezhky until 1813. Today it has several enterprises of the food industry.

Novomyrhorod. V-12. A city (1990 pop 16,200) on the Velyka Vys River and a raion center in Kirovohrad oblast. It was founded in 1740 by Zaporozhian Cossacks of the Myrhorod Regiment at the site of an ancient settlement from the Bronze Age. Then it was settled by peasants mostly from the Myrhorod region. In 1752–64 Novomyrhorod was a center of New Serbia, and from 1803 it was part of Kherson gubernia. In 1959 the town of Zlatopil and the villages of Vynohradivka and Katerynivka were amalgamated with Novomyrhorod. Today the city manufactures bricks, ceramics, leather, preserves, furniture, and construction materials. It has a coal mine. Its famous St Elijah's Church, built in 1786, is a tourist attraction.

Novooleksiivka [Novooleksijivka]. VII-15. A town smt (1990 pop 10,700) in Henicheske raion, Kherson oblast. It sprang up in the 1890s during the construction of the Lozova–Symferopil railway line and attained smt status in 1938. Today the town has a fruit-canning factory, bakery, and corn research station.

Novoozivske [Novoozivs'ke] (aka Novoazovske). VI-19. A city (1990 pop 13,000) at the mouth of the Hruzky Yelanchyk River and a raion center in Donetske oblast. It was founded in 1849 as a Cossack outpost named Novomykolaivske. From 1923 to 1959 the town was called Budonnivka. In 1963, after being renamed, it was granted city status. Today Novoozivske produces dairy products, asphalt, concrete, and bricks.

Novopokrovka settlement and burial site. A *Cherniakhiv culture settlement and burial ground located near Novopokrovka, Chuhuiv raion, Kharkiv oblast. Excavations in 1936 and 1949 revealed approximately 20 cremated burials as well as the remains of wood-frame clay dwellings and a forge.

Novopskov. IV-20. A town smt (1990 pop 9,100) and raion center at the confluence of the Aidar and the Kamianka rivers in Luhanske oblast. Until 1829 it was called Zakamianka. It arose in the first half of the 17th century and was populated by Ukrainian and Russian serfs who had escaped from their landlords. In 1707 an army detachment was sent there to capture them and return them to their masters, and in 1708 Peter I ordered the town to be burned down. The town participated in K. Bulavin's rebellion, after which it became part of Ostrohozke regiment. From 1802 the town was part of Voronezh gubernia. Today Novopskov produces butter, bread, and animal feed.

Novopylypivka kurhans. A group of 13 burial mounds near Novopylypivka, Melitopil raion, Zaporizhia oblast. Excavations in 1934–5 and 1951–2 produced evidence of 70 burials. The majority of the burials were identified as *Pit-Grave culture but examples of Catacomb, *Timber-Grave, and Sarmatian burial practices, also were uncovered.

Novoraiske refractory-clay deposit. A clay field located in Kostiantynivka and Slovianske raions, in Donetske oblast, covering an area of 32 sq km. With reserves of 60 million t, it is the largest such deposit in Ukraine. It was discovered in 1930 and has been exploited by open-pit mining since 1959. The clay seams are 0.1–6.5 m wide and 0.2–56 m deep and are composed primarily of kaolinite, quartz, and silicates. The clay is resistant to temperatures of 1,580–1,750°C. It is used in the metallurgical, porcelain and white ware, glass, petroleum, and other industries.

Novorossiisk [Novorossijsk]. IX-18. A city (1989 pop 186,000) on Tsemeska Bay in the Black Sea, in Krasnodar krai, RF. It was founded in 1838 as a fortress, and with the development of a cement industry later in the century it gained economic importance. Until the revolution its port was second only to the one in Odessa; the main exports were grain and naphtha. According to the census of 1926, Ukrainians accounted for 22.8 percent of the city's population.

Novorozanivka kurhan. A Scythian burial ground from the 5th century BC near Novorozanivka, Novyi Buh raion, Mykolaiv oblast. Excavations in 1967 revealed the remains of a Scythian warrior in full armor with his sword, quiver, arrows, spear tips, and bone-handled knife present beside him. The remains of a horse were also recovered in the chamber.

Novoselivka glass-sand deposit. A major sand deposit, located near Novoselivka, Nova Vodolaha raion, Kharkiv oblast. It was surveyed in 1932 and has been exploited since 1936. The sand is 6.8 to 17.5 m deep. It is considered to be the best sand in Ukraine and is used in the glass industry in Ukraine and elsewhere in the former USSR.

Novoselytsia [Novoselycja]. V-7. A town (1990 pop 8,400) on the Prut River and a raion center in Chernivtsi oblast. It was first mentioned in historical documents in 1456, as Shyshkivtsi; it was renamed in 1617. Under the Peace Treaty of *Küçük Kaynarca, Novoselytsia was divided between Austria and Turkey. With the signing of the *Bucharest Peace Treaty of 1812 the Turkish (eastern) part of the town, along with Khotyn county, was acquired by Russia. As a border town Novoselytsia became an important trade and transportation center, especially after the construction of a railway line in 1884. By 1870 the town had steam mills, a distillery, and a leather and a paint factory. In the interwar period Novoselytsia was occupied by Rumania, and in 1940 it was annexed by the Ukrainian SSR. Today it produces liquor, canned food, furniture, and reinforced-concrete structures.

Novoselytsia kaolin deposit. A major kaolin deposit, located near Novoselytsia, Katerynopil raion, Cherkasy oblast. Kaolin has been mined there since the early 20th century. The deposit was surveyed in 1936. The kaolin is found at a depth of 25–63 m. It is used for making refractory products and in porcelain ware.

Novosiletsky, Roman [Novosilec'kyj], b 8 March 1926 in Potylych, Rava Ruska county, Galicia. Geologist. He graduated from the Lviv Polytechnical Institute in 1953. He then joined the Ukrainian Scientific Research Institute of Geological Prospecting and was appointed department head in 1971. His work deals with the genesis of natural gas and petroleum and the geological conditions under which they are formed.

Novosilka Kostiukova. A multi-occupational archeological site near Novosilka, Zalishchyky raion, Ternopil oblast. Excavated in 1925–31 by T. Sulimirski, Ya. Paster-

nak, and others, it revealed Upper Paleolithic, Trypilian, Bilohrudivka, Cherniakhiv, and early Slavic remains.

Novosivsky, Ivan [Novosivs'kyj], b 28 August 1902 in Ispas, Vyzhnytsia county, Bukovyna, d 12 February 1988 in New York. Jurist; member of the Shevchenko Scientific Society and the Ukrainian Academy of Arts and Sciences. After graduating in law from Chernivtsi University (1925) he served as a district judge in Rumanian-ruled Bessarabia and Bukovyna. Having left Ukraine after the Second World War, he received an LLD from the Ukrainian Free University in Munich (1949) and settled in New York, where he worked as a notary public. He was active in the Association of Ukrainian Lawyers and the Association of Ukrainian Bukovynians in America. In addition to legal articles he wrote two chapters for *Bukovyna: Ïi mynule i suchasne* (Bukovyna: Its Past and Present, 1956).

Novotroitske [Novotrojic'ke]. VI-18, DB IV-3. A town smt (1990 pop 9,900) on the Sukha Volnovakha River in Volnovakha raion, Donetske oblast. It was founded in 1773 by settlers from the Don and Poltava regions and it was granted smt status in 1938. Today limestone and chalk are extracted and processed there. Fragments of Scythian sculptures have been found in the vicinity.

Novotroitske [Novotrojic'ke]. VII-15. A town smt (1990 pop 12,600) and raion center in Kherson oblast. The town was founded in the 1860s at the site of Sarabulat village. It was referred to by both names until the early 20th century. The town has a beautiful central quarter.

Novotroitske fortified settlement. An early Slavic fortified settlement of the 8th to 10th century AD along the Psol River near Novotroitske (now part of Prystailove), Lebedyn raion, Sumy oblast. Excavations by I. Liapushkin in 1952–4 uncovered the remains of a settlement which had been razed by the Pechenegs early in the 10th century. The remains of 50 semi-pit dwellings with clay exteriors were found at the site, along with approx 100 agricultural structures and workshops. Excavations also revealed a wide range of agricultural implements, forestry, fishing, and trapping equipment, pottery (mainly hand-thrown), bronze and silver jewelry, and a cache of Arab coins.

Novoukrainka [Novoukrajinka]. V-12. A city (1990 pop 20,500) on the Chornyi Tashlyk River and a raion center in Kirovohrad oblast. In 1754 the Russian fortress of Pavlovsk (Novopavlovsk in 1764–73) was built on territory belonging to the Zaporozhian Sich. In 1769 the fortress and the settlement around it were destroyed by the Tatars. The rebuilt settlement was renamed Novoukrainka in 1830 and was granted city status in 1938. Today it has several large enterprises of the food and building-materials industries.

Novovolynske [Novovolyns'ke]. III-5. A city (1990 pop 55,800) of oblast subordination in Volhynia oblast. It was founded in 1950 as an industrial center of the *Lviv-Volhynia Coal Basin and was granted city status in 1957. It has six coal-processing plants, a specialized equipment-building factory, three construction-materials plants, several food-processing enterprises, and a cotton mill.

Novovorontsovka [Novovoroncovka]. VI-14. A town smt (1990 pop 7,300) on the right bank of the Kakhivka Reservoir and a raion center in Kherson oblast. It was founded ca 1895 by Zaporozhian Cossacks and was known first as Mykolaivka. In 1821 the village was acquired by Prince M. Vorontsov and renamed Vorontsovka. Because of its location on the Dnieper River it became a local trading center in the 19th century. Today there are several enterprises of the food industry in the town.

Novozybkov. I-12. A city (1959 pop 24,700) and raion center in Briansk oblast, RF. It was founded in 1701 as Zybkaia settlement in the territory of Starodub regiment. According to the census of 1926, 13.9 percent of the city's population was Ukrainian.

Leonid Novychenko

Novychenko, Leonid [Novyčenko], b 31 March 1914 in Rusanivka, Hadiache county, Poltava gubernia. Literary scholar and critic; full member of the AN URSR (now ANU). He graduated from Kiev University in 1939 and worked in an editorial capacity on various literary journals. He was secretary of the executive of the Writers' Union of the USSR (1959–86) and of the Writers' Union of Ukraine (elected in 1966). Since 1949 he has worked at the Institute of Literature of the ANU. He began publishing in his field in 1939. His works include *Pavlo Tychyna* (1941), *Povist' pro poeta: Liryka M. Ryl's'koho* (The Story of a Poet: The Lyric Poetry of M. Rylsky, 1942), *Tvorchist' Pavla Tychyny* (The Works of P. Tychyna, 1949), *Poeziia i revoliutsiia* (Poetry and Revolution, 1956), *Shevchenko i suchasnist'* (Shevchenko and the Present, 1964), *Poetychnyi svit Maksyma Ryl's'koho, 1910–1941* (The Poetical World of M. Rylsky, 1910–41, 1980), and *T. Shevchenko – poet, borets', liudyna* (T. Shevchenko, Poet, Fighter, Human Being, 1982). Novychenko also wrote studies of the work of M. Irchan, L. Pervomaisky, and others, assisted in the preparation of curricula for Ukrainian literary history, and wrote in the official vein a number of works on the theory of *socialist realism. They include *Pro riznomanitnist' khudozhnikh form i styliv u literaturi sotsialistychnoho realizmu* (On the Many Different Artistic Forms and Styles in Socialist-Realist Literature, 1959) and *Ne iliustratsiia – vidkryttia!* (Not Illustration, Revelation!, 1967). In the 1950s and 1960s he welcomed the works of the *shestydesiatnyky* but came out against the rehabilitation of victims of the Stalinist terror of the 1930s, particularly that of M. Khvylovy and M. Ze-

rov. Editions of his selected works have appeared in Ukrainian (1974; 1983; 2 vols, 1984) and Russian (1985).

I. Koshelivets

Novyi Buh [Novyj Buh]. VI-13. A city (1990 pop 17,600) and raion center in Mykolaiv oblast. In the second half of the 18th century a settlement arose known as Kutsa Balka, after the Cossack Ya. Kutsy. In the early 19th century it was merged with several other settlements to form a town called Semenivka, Novapavlivka, and finally (in 1832) Novyi Buh. Today the city's factories produce cheese, canned goods, bread, mixed feed, footwear, furniture, and clothes.

Novyi chas (New Time). A newspaper published from October 1923 to September 1939 in Lviv. It appeared twice a week to 1925, three times a week from 1926, and daily except Sundays from 1932. Initially funded by the underground Ukrainian Military Organization, from the mid-1920s it was aligned with the Ukrainian National Democratic Alliance. From 1934 it was published by the Ukrainska Presa publishing house, owned by the longtime manager of *Novyi chas*, I. Tyktor. The newspaper became the most widely read Ukrainian daily in Galicia; in 1938 it had a circulation of 16,000. It published several supplements, a library of popular books, and an annual almanac (from 1931) and conducted fund-raising campaigns on behalf of Ukrainian children, the Hutsuls, and community institutions. The editors were D. Paliiv, M. Matchak, M. Konovalets, O. Bodnarovych, P. Sahaidachny, and Z. Pelensky. Its foreign correspondents included Yu. Strutynsky, L. Mydlovsky, D. Katamai, and V. Kysilevsky.

Novyi krai

Novyi krai (New Country). An organ of the *Association of Canadian Ruthenian Farmers, published three times a month and then weekly in Rosthern, Saskatchewan, from August 1910 to February 1913. The paper provided practical advice for farmers and encouraged Ukrainian-Canadian farmers to form co-operatives. It also published reports on developments in Canada and Ukraine, in which it paid particular attention to the plight of the peasantry in Western Ukraine, and encouraged Ukrainian farmers to participate in the Canadian political process and support the Liberal party. *Novyi krai* was published by P. Shvydky and edited by O. *Megas.

Novyi litopys (New Chronicle). A quarterly journal published in Winnipeg in 1961–5. It was closely aligned with the Ukrainian Orthodox Church of Canada and carried articles on religious topics and church history. It also ublished book reviews and articles on a wide variety of istorical, political, and cultural topics by D. Solovei, R. Klymkevych, P. Macenko, P. Kovaliv, S. Paramonov, V. vanys, V. Trembitsky, P. Odarchenko, L. Bykovsky, S. awchuk, and others. The editor of *Novyi litopys* was Yu. Mulyk-Lutsyk.

Novyi Oskol [Novyj Oskol]. III-18. A town (1979 pop 7,700) on the Oskil River and a raion center in Belgorod oblast, RF. It was founded in 1637 as a defensive outpost against Tatar invasion. It was named Tsareve Alekseeve n 1647 and was renamed Novyi Oskol in 1655. In 1779 it ecame a county center in Kursk gubernia. According to he Soviet census of 1926, Ukrainians accounted for 51 ercent of the population of Novyi Oskol raion.

Novyi prolom (New Breakthrough). A Russophile newspaper published in Lviv twice a week in 1883–7 (a total of 564 issues). It was edited by Y. Markov and O. Avdykovsky (1883–4) and I. Pelekh (1884–7). A successor to *Prolom*, it contained articles on political, community, religious, economic, and educational affairs in Galicia. Because of their political content, nearly 90 issues of the paper were confiscated by the Austrian authorities. A similar fate befell *Chervonaia Rus'*, a paper that Markov published instead of *Novyi prolom* three times a week in 1888–91 (a total of 794 issues) and edited with Pelekh. It folded in April 1891 after a ban was imposed on it by Metropolitan S. Sembratovych. Instead, Avdykovsky began publishing the daily *Halytskaia Rus'*.

Novyi Rozdil [Novyj Rozdil]. IV-5. A city (1990 pop 29,700) in Mykolaiv raion, Lviv oblast. It was founded in 1953, when sulfur began to be mined in the area, and was granted city status in 1965. The city is the home of the Sirka Manufacturing Consortium and was one of the largest sulfur-mining centers in the USSR.

Novyi shliakh (New Pathway). A daily newspaper published in Kamianets-Podilskyi in 1919. It was edited by L. Biletsky and S. Shyshkivsky.

Novyi shliakh (New Pathway). A newspaper published since October 1930 in Edmonton, Saskatoon (1933–42),

Novyi shliakh

Winnipeg, and then Toronto (since 1974); the organ of the *Ukrainian National Federation of Canada (UNF). The paper appears weekly, although it was published three times and then twice a week from 1941 to the early 1950s. It contains articles on political affairs and on cultural and historical topics, and reports on the activities of the UNF and Ukrainian affairs in Canada. Generally it supports the positions of the OUN (Melnyk faction). The founder and longtime editor of *Novyi shliakh* was M. *Pohoretsky. V. Martynets, O. Ivakh, D. Kyslytsia, S. Rosokha, R. Malanchuk, P. Matsenko, A. Kurdydyk, V. Levytsky, A. Dobriansky, V. Skorupsky, Yu. Karmanin, and others have also served as editors or been regular contributors. At various times the paper included supplements devoted to the various constituent organizations of the UNF – the Ukrainian War Veterans' Association, the Ukrainian Women's Organization of Canada, and the Ukrainian National Youth Federation – some of which later became separate publications (eg, *Holos molodi* and *Zhinochyi svit*). Since 1977 the paper has also included the English-language monthly supplement *New Perspectives*. Its circulation is approx 7,000 (1988).

Novyi Svit [Novyj Svit]. DB IV-4. A town smt (1990 pop 9,900) on the Starobesheve Reservoir of the Kalmiius River in Starobesheve raion, Donetske oblast. The town arose in 1954 with the construction of the Starobesheve Raion Power Station. It attained smt status in 1956. The town has a small food industry and a building-materials plant.

Novyi svit (New World). A monthly organ of the Self-Reliance Association of Ukrainian Americans, published in New York in 1950–9. It published articles on the co-operative and credit union movements and reports on the activity of the association. Its editors included P. Sahaidachny, V. Mudry, and R. Ilnytsky. In 1959 it merged with *Nash kontakt* to form *Nash svit*.

Novyi vik (New Era). The only Ukrainian newspaper in postwar Rumania, published in Bucharest monthly and then semimonthly from 1949 to 1989. Initially a relatively objective paper with articles on Ukrainian history and ethnography and developments in the Ukrainian community in Rumania and in Ukraine, it was subjected to increasingly strict censorship. Its first editor was V. Bilivsky, who was removed from his post in 1959 and sentenced to seven years' imprisonment for 'Ukrainian nationalism'; he was succeeded by M. Bodnia and then I. Kolesnyk. From 1979 a monthly supplement featuring works by Ukrainian writers in Rumania was published. The paper's pressrun was decreased steadily, from approx 7,000 in the 1960s to about 4,000 in the 1980s. After the overthrow of the Ceauşescu regime, *Novyi vik* was succeeded in January 1990 by *Vil'ne slovo*, the organ of the new Union of Ukrainians of Rumania, edited by I. Petretska-Kovach and Yu. Lazarchuk.

Novyk, Kateryna, b 14 December 1898 in Katerynoslav, d 1 November 1984 in Kiev. Geologist and paleobotanist; corresponding member of the AN URSR (now ANU) from 1951. She graduated from the Dnipropetrovske Institute of People's Education in 1923 and then worked as a teacher. She joined the geology department of the Dnipropetrovske Mining Institute in 1928, and from 1934 she worked at the ANU Institute of Geological Sciences, where she chaired a department (1945–70). She wrote several monographs and numerous articles dealing mostly with the stratigraphy and paleobotany of coal deposits in the European part of the former Soviet Union and the history of the geological sciences.

Novykov, Mykola, b 10 April 1932 in Kiev. Scientist in the areas of mechanics and the strength of materials; full member of the AN URSR (now ANU) since 1985. He graduated from the Kiev Polytechnical Institute (1954) and was appointed to the position of director of the ANU Institute of Superhard Materials (1977). He has made contributions in the areas of the strength of materials in mechanical oscillations at low temperatures, crystallography, composites, and superhard materials.

Novynska, Vira [Novyns'ka], b 1 August 1900 in Kiev, d 15 January 1982 in Kiev. Operetta actress (soprano). She grew up in an acting family and appeared on stage at the age of eight in D. Haidamaka's troupe. After working in Russian operetta theaters outside Ukraine, she joined the first Ukrainian operetta troupe in Kharkiv (1929) and then the Kiev Theater of Musical Comedy (1935; since 1967 the Kiev Operetta Theater). Among her roles were Sofiia in O. Riabov's *Vesillia v Malynivtsi* (The Wedding in Malynivka) and Parasia in Yu. Miliutin's *Trembita*.

Novyny (News). A newspaper published in Edmonton in 1913–22. It began to appear in January 1913 as the weekly organ of the National Association of Alberta. It later appeared twice and then three times a week before folding in late 1915. The paper was renewed in December 1917 by the People's Home in Edmonton. It appeared weekly and then semiweekly before expiring in January 1922. Perhaps the most professional Ukrainian-Canadian paper of the time, *Novyny* reported on world-wide political developments, concentrating on Ukraine and Canada. It strongly supported the bilingual schools in the prairie provinces and devoted considerable attention to the practical problems facing Ukrainian-Canadian farmers. The paper did much to encourage the development of Ukrainian consciousness. It criticized Russophiles in Canada and very early stopped using the term 'Ruthenian' in favor of 'Ukrainian.' The publisher and editor of *Novyny* was R. *Kremar.

Novyny (News). A daily organ of the UNR Ministry of Press and Propaganda, published in Kamianets-Podilskyi in 1919.

Novyny (News). A daily organ of the Kolomyia branch of the Central Bureau of the Directory of the UNR, published in 1919 in Kolomyia.

Novyny kinoekranu (Film Screen News). A semimonthly magazine, published in 1925–31 in Kharkiv and edited by M. Bazhan, Yu. Yanovsky, D. Falkivsky, and O. Dovzhenko. It reappeared briefly in 1936–8. In 1961 it was revived as a monthly supplement to *Mystetstvo* in Kiev with a pressrun of 20,000 copies. By the end of the 1960s its pressrun had reached 700,000 copies, but the figure had declined to 410,000 by 1990. The magazine's editor is L. Cherevatenko. Until 1992 it was published by the USSR State Cinema Committee and the Union of Cinematographers of Ukraine.

Novytsky, Hryhorii [Novyc'kyj, Hryhorij], b ?, d ca 1720–5 (some sources cite 1727) in Kondinskoe volost, Siberia. Cossack officer and ethnographer; son of I. *Novytsky. He was educated at the Kievan Mohyla Academy and later became colonel of a volunteer cavalry regiment (1704–8) and a representative of Hetman I. Mazepa to the Polish voivode, A. Sieniawski. After abandoning the anti-Petrine coalition in 1709, he was restricted to Moscow by Peter I and then sent to Tobolsk, Siberia (1712), where he became active in missionary work. His observations of the Khante (Khanty) peoples were recorded in *Kratkoe opisanie o narode ostiatskom* (A Short Description of the Ostiak People, 1715), one of the world's first specialized ethnographic studies. It was published in German as *Das Leben und die Gewohnheiten der Ostaken* (in *Das veränderte Russland*, 1721), without accreditation to the author, and in Russian in 1884 (in *Kievskaia starina*) and separately in 1941.

Novytsky, Illia [Novyc'kyj, Ilija], b ?, d 1704. Cossack leader; father of H. *Novytsky. He was colonel of volunteer cavalry regiments under Hetmans I. Samoilovych and I. Mazepa (1673–1700), and he distinguished himself in wars against the Ottoman Empire and the Crimean Porte. He assumed the post of acting hetman when Mazepa went to Moscow in 1689.

Novytsky, Ivan [Novyc'kyj], b 1844 in Tarashcha, Kiev gubernia, d 12 August 1890 in Kiev. Historian, ethnographer, and journalist. He graduated from Kiev University and was an associate of the Kiev Central Archive of Old Documents, the Kiev Archeographic Commission, the Kiev Statistical Committee, and the Southwestern Branch of the Imperial Russian Geographic Society. He contributed articles on the social and legal history of Ukraine under Lithuanian and Polish rule and on Ukrainian folk songs to *Kievskaia starina*, *Trudy Kievskago iuridicheskago obshchestva*, and Kiev University's *Universitetskiia izvestiia*. His major contributions are the introduction on the history of the peasantry in 15th- to 18th-century Right-Bank Ukraine in pt 6, vol 1 of *Arkhiv Iugo-Zapadnoi Rossii* (1876), a 31-page reference dictionary of 465 legal terms in the Ukrainian chancery language under Lithuanian and Polish rule (1871), and indexes of personal names (1878) and place-names (1882) in the publications of the Kiev Archeographic Commission. Novytsky participated in P. Chubynsky's ethnographic expedition and wrote down nearly 5,000 Ukrainian folk songs, which were published in *Trudy Etnografichesko-statisticheskoi ekspeditsii v Zapadno-Russkom krae* (vol 5, 1872). He also published ethnographic notes and texts of folk songs in *Kievlianin* and *Kievskiia gubernskiia vedomosti*.

Novytsky, Mykhailo [Novyc'kyj, Myxajlo], b 20 September 1892 in Nizhen, Chernihiv gubernia, d 29 March 1964 in Kiev. A scholar of T. *Shevchenko. He graduated from Petrograd University (1919) and in 1921 became director of the textual studies seminar and cabinet of Shevchenko's biography at the Kiev branch of the *Taras Shevchenko Scientific Research Institute. He took part in the editing and/or annotation of approx 30 Soviet editions of Shevchenko's works and discovered many of the poet's manuscripts and letters and materials about him. Together with S. Yefremov and P. Fylypovych he coedited the collection *Shevchenko ta ioho doba* (Shevchenko and His Era, 2 vols, 1925–6). Novytsky wrote pioneering articles about Shevchenko's life, including Shevchenko's arrest in 1859 (1924), his trial in 1847 (1925), and his arrest in 1850 (1925). He also edited P. Kulish's memoirs about Shevchenko (1930). Novytsky was arrested in 1933 and sent to a labor camp in the Solovets Islands in 1937. He was released after J. Stalin's death in 1956 and rehabilitated. During his last years he worked at the Kiev Shevchenko Museum and helped to compile a book of memoirs about Shevchenko (1958).

Novytsky, Mykola [Novyc'kyj], b 1833, d 14 March 1906. Revolutionary figure. A Russian army lieutenant general, he befriended T. *Shevchenko in St Petersburg after Shevchenko's return from exile. In 1860 he negotiated, on behalf of the Society for the Relief of Impoverished Litterateurs and Scholars, the redemption of Shevchenko's relatives from serfdom. He belonged to the revolutionary group Zemlia i Volia and had ties with the Old Hromada of Kiev. In 1889 he published his memoirs of Shevchenko in *Kievskaia starina*.

Novytsky, Mykola [Novyc'kyj], b 1884, d ? Communist journalist. He was exiled to Siberia for his activities during the Revolution of 1905. In 1915–25 he was involved in Party work in the Far East and then in Ukraine, where he served as assistant editor of *Visti VUTsVK* and contributed articles and feuilletons to *Komunist*, often under the pseudonym Iona Vochrevisushchy. He also edited the *Visti VUTsVK* supplement *Literatura i mystetstvo*. In 1938 Novytsky was arrested in the Stalinist terror; his further fate is unknown.

Novytsky, Oleksa [Novyc'kyj], b 20 April 1914 in Pii, Kaniv county, Kiev gubernia. Poet, songwriter, and translator. From 1933 he worked as a journalist for several newspapers and journals in Ukraine. He began publishing poetry in 1930 and has written poetry collections (1942, 1943, 1966, 1978), a collection of songs (1966), and many articles about literary relations between Ukraine and other nations in the former USSR. He has also translated many poems from Russian, Belarusian, Georgian, and other languages of the former USSR and has edited several Ukrainian anthologies of non-Ukrainian Soviet poetry.

Novytsky, Oleksander [Novyc'kyj], b 1905 in Volhynia gubernia, d 12 February 1970 in Chicago. Orthodox bishop; father of S. *Nowytski. After graduating from the theological faculty of Warsaw University, he was ordained and appointed to a parish in Volhynia (1934–40). During the Second World War he was a member of the consistory of the Polish Autocephalous Orthodox church and a chaplain in the *Division Galizien. He emigrated in 1945 and served as a parish priest in Landshut, Germany, and in Paris before arriving in Canada (1950) to take up parishes in Dauphin and Fort William, Manitoba. In 1965 he was appointed pastor of St Sophia's Church in Chicago, and then, being a widower (1966), he was consecrated a bishop of the Ukrainian Orthodox Church in the USA.

Oleksii Novytsky

Novytsky, Oleksii [Novyc'kyj, Oleksij], b 19 April 1862 in Simbirsk, Russia, d 24 September 1934 in Kiev. Art historian; full member of the Shevchenko Scientific Society from 1914 and full member of the VUAN from 1922. After graduating from Moscow University (1887) he worked as a librarian at the Moscow School of Painting, Sculpture, and Architecture (1898–1918) and was active in the Moscow Ukrainian Hromada. He organized the jubilee exhibition of T. Shevchenko's paintings and graphic works in Moscow (1911) and contributed to *Ukrainskaia zhizn'* (1912–17) and *Promin'* (1917). From 1922 he worked in Kiev, where he chaired the *All-Ukrainian Archeological Committee (1924–33) and headed the VUAN art section and Department of the History of Ukrainian Art. He wrote books on the art of the Peredvizhniki group (1897), the history of Russian art (2 vols, 1902–3), and wooden architecture in Ukraine (1927). He devoted himself to studying the art of Shevchenko, wrote many articles and a book about him as a painter (1914), and organized an exhibition of his works in Moscow in 1911. He was also editor and annotator of vol 8 of the VUAN edition of Shevchenko's works (his art), which was printed but destroyed by the censors before its release, in 1932.

Novytsky, Orest [Novyc'kyj], b 6 February 1806 in Pylypy, Zhytomyr county, Volhynia gubernia, d 16 June 1884 in Kiev. Philosopher. After graduating from the Kiev Theological Academy in 1831, he taught philosophy at the theological seminary in Pereiaslav and then at the Kiev Theological Academy (1834–5) and Kiev University (1834–50), where he became a full professor in 1837 and served as dean of the philosophy faculty (1838–9, 1840–1, 1845–6, 1846–50). At the same time he served as an official censor of Polish-language and, later, foreign publications (1837–69). He wrote, in Russian, a book on the Doukhobors (1832; rev edn 1892); textbooks for his courses on experimental psychology (1840) and logic (1841, 1844), all of them based largely on F. Fischer's German textbooks; and a monograph on the gradual development of philosophical doctrines in relation to the development of pagan beliefs (4 vols, 1860–1). His views on philosophy, expressed in several articles, owed much to those of G. Hegel.

Novytsky, Viktor [Novyc'kyj], b 15 February 1884 in Dvinsk, Vitsebsk gubernia (now Daugavpils, Latvia), d ? Legal historian and archivist; grandson of the philosopher Orest *Novytsky. An associate of the Kiev Central Archive of Old Documents (1920–32) and the VUAN Commission for the Study of the History of Western-Ruthenian and Ukrainian Law, he contributed a few articles to VUAN serials, such as *Zapysky Istorychno-filolohichnoho viddilu*, *Ukraïna*, and the commission's *Pratsi*. He was imprisoned during the Stalinist terror in 1933 and sent into internal exile in 1938. His subsequent fate is unknown.

Yakiv Novytsky   Slavko Nowytski

Novytsky, Yakiv [Novyc'kyj, Jakiv], b 14 October 1847 in Auly, Katerynoslav county, Katerynoslav gubernia, d 19 May 1929 in Zaporizhia. Ethnographer, historian, and educator. While teaching in rural schools in the Oleksandrivske region (1869–77) he collected Ukrainian folklore. He was dismissed for his Ukrainophile sympathies but a few years later was appointed school inspector. On the basis of the materials he gathered he published collections of Ukrainian historical songs (1894), of Zaporozhian traditions and stories (1907), of Ukrainian folk traditions, beliefs, and stories (1907), of Ukrainian historical songs gathered in the Katerynoslav region from 1874 to 1903 (1908), of popular recollections of Zaporozhian historical figures (1909) and Zaporizhia (1911), and of Ukrainian folk charms, spells, prayers, and remedies (1913). He also prepared a history of the city of Oleksandrivske (1905).

Nowosielski, Jerzy, b 7 January 1923 in Cracow, Poland. Polish painter of Ukrainian origin. A graduate of the Cracow Academy of Fine Arts (1947), he taught there in 1962. He studied icon painting under I. Svientsitsky in Lviv in 1942–3. His works have been exhibited in Poland since 1945. Most of his works are figural and abstract compositions displaying the influence of Byzantine and Ukrainian icons. He has painted murals in the Ukrainian Catholic Church in Lourdes, France, and in Polish churches and designed scenery for Polish theaters and the iconostasis (1972) in the Orthodox church in Cracow. Solo exhibitions of his works have been held in Berlin (1958), Paris (1963), London (1963), Vienna (1966), Karlskrona, Sweden (1978), and Stockholm (1978). J. Madeyski's book about him was published in Cracow in 1973.

Nowy Sącz. IV-1. A city (1989 pop 76,700) on the Dunajec River and a voivodeship center in Poland. In 1939 Ukrainians represented 71 percent of the county's population, and the Ukrainian community in Nowy Sącz provided

economic and cultural leadership for the western Lemko region. V. *Kubijovyč was born there. There was a Ukrainian Catholic church and a branch of the Prosvita society in the city. In 1946 the southern part of the county was transferred by the USSR to Poland. The museum in Nowy Sącz exhibits samples of Lemko church decoration and the works of the Lemko artist *Nykyfor.

Nowy Targ. A town (1989 pop 32,200) on the Dunajec River in Nowy Sącz voivodeship, Poland. Before 1946, the eastern part of Nowy Targ county was part of Ukrainian ethnic territory of the Lemko region. Over 90 percent of the population was Ukrainian.

Nowytski, Slavko [Novyc'kyj], b 19 October 1935 in Torchyn, Lutske county, Volhynia. Film director, producer, actor, and cameraman. A resident of the United States since the end of the Second World War, he completed study at the Pasadena Playhouse College (1955–6) and Columbia University (MFA 1964) and then worked as an actor in theater and TV and as a cameraman. Since 1971 he has owned Filmart Productions. He has directed the award-winning films *Pysanka* (1977), *Kung-Fu Master: Gin Foi Mark* (1978), *Immortal Image* (about L. Mol), *Grass on the Roof* (1979), *The Helm of Destiny* (1987, documentary on Ukrainians in the United States), and *Harvest of Despair* (1984, documentary on the man-made famine in Ukraine in 1932–3).

Nuclear power industry. In the 1970s the Soviet Union embarked on an ambitious program of constructing nuclear power plants, particularly in its European part. Much of the development was concentrated in Ukraine. By 1985 the republic's total capacity was 8,880 MW. The ostensible goal was to use nuclear power to meet the increasing demand for power up to the end of the century. By then nuclear power was to have accounted for 60 percent of Ukraine's power output, or approx 50,000 MW. It was considered essential to provide Ukraine with a guaranteed source of electricity that was not subject to the whims of the transportation system or the slumps in the output of raw materials. Traditionally, Ukraine depended for its power on coal- and oil-based thermal power stations (accounting for 70 percent of the power output in 1985) and hydroelectric stations (17 percent of the output). The output in the Donetske coalfield, the largest supplier of Ukrainian energy, was declining.

By the end of 1985 Ukraine had four nuclear power plants, with capacity as follows: Chornobyl (opened in 1977 in Prypiat city), 4,000 MW; Rivne (opened in 1979 in Kuznetsovske), 880 MW; South Ukraine (opened in 1982 in Kostiantynivka), 2,000 MW; and Zaporizhia (opened in 1984 in Enerhodar), 2,000 MW. In 1985 new reactors were under construction or in the planning stage in Chornobyl, Chyhyryn, Khmelnytskyi, and the Crimea.

Apart from the first, all the new reactors were water-pressurized and manufactured in Volgodonsk and Czechoslovakia (VVER). The capacity of a VVER reactor was raised from the initial 440 MW at Rivne to 1,000 MW. There were also plans to bring into operation reactors known from their Russian initials as ATETs that would provide both electricity and heating for the major Ukrainian cities. The project in Odessa was practically ready for operation by the spring of 1986. Construction work had begun on the Kharkiv ATETs; the Kiev station was only at the planning stage.

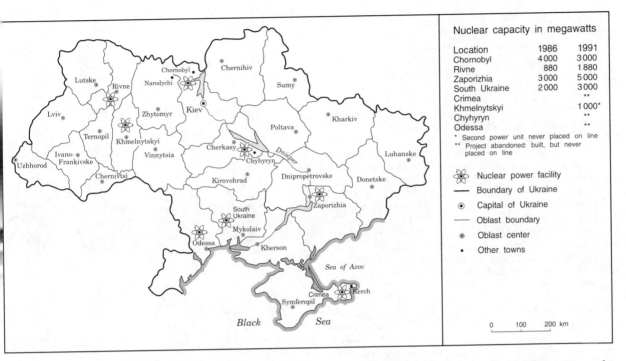

Nuclear capacity in megawatts		
Location	1986	1991
Chornobyl	4 000	3 000
Rivne	880	1 880
Zaporizhia	3 000	5 000
South Ukraine	2 000	3 000
Crimea		**
Khmelnytskyi		1 000*
Chyhyryn		**
Odessa		**

* Second power unit never placed on line
** Project abandoned: built, but never placed on line

Nuclear power facility
Boundary of Ukraine
Capital of Ukraine
Oblast boundary
Oblast center
Other towns

0   100   200 km

The disaster at the Chornobyl plant on 26 April 1986 brought into question the entire Soviet nuclear power program. In 10 days over 450 radionuclides were dispersed into the atmosphere, whence they contaminated a vast area inhabited by over 250 million people. Kiev, Zhytomyr, Rivne, and Chernihiv oblasts were badly contaminated with cesium, strontium, iodine, and other isotopic elements. More than 33 people died immediately after the explosion, and up to 250,000 were evacuated from the 30-km zone. By November 1986 the first two reactors at Chornobyl had been returned to service, and a year later the third reactor, which shared a control room with the damaged fourth reactor, had become operational.

But the construction of a fifth and a sixth graphite-moderated reactor (RBMK) at Chornobyl was suspended in April 1987, and by 1988 the two reactors had been abandoned permanently.

A growing anti–nuclear power movement, spearheaded by the Writers' Union of Ukraine, developed in Ukraine. By December 1987 Yu. *Shcherbak and D. Hrodzynsky had founded the Zelenyi Svit ecological movement, whose aim is to stop the construction of environmentally damaging industrial plants.

Public concern was expressed over the building of plants in geologically or physically unsuited regions (Rivne, Crimea) or on historical landmarks (Chyhyryn). A vigorous protest was mounted against plans of the USSR Ministry of Nuclear Power to raise the capacity of the South Ukraine, Rivne, and Khmelnytskyi plants over the original 4,000-MW limit. There was wide public demand to close down the Chornobyl plant, immediately and permanently. At the 19th Party Conference in Moscow in June 1988, B. Oliinyk demanded a moratorium on the building of new reactors in Ukraine and a review of the entire Ukrainian nuclear energy program. In March 1989 a number of Ukrainian critics of the nuclear power program, such as Yu. Shcherbak and V. Yavorivsky, were elected along with Oliinyk to the USSR Congress of People's Deputies.

Because of the public opposition the Ukrainian nuclear power program, though never officially curtailed, has been thrown into disarray. By early 1988 all three cogenerational nuclear power and heating plants had been abandoned, because they would have been too close to large cities. In the summer of 1988 a team of scientists from the USSR Academy of Sciences concluded that because of its seismic activity the Crimea was unsuitable for a nuclear power plant. In May 1989 the USSR Council of Ministers announced that the Chyhyryn station would not be constructed. At the same time another review of the RBMK raised doubts about the future of the Chornobyl plant. Protests against the building of the South Ukraine and the Zaporizhia stations had grown to mass proportions. By June 1989 the target of the protests in Ukraine, the USSR Ministry of Nuclear Power, had itself finally fallen into question. The USSR Supreme Soviet discussed an alternative administration for the industry: it appeared likely that the responsibility for locating and operating nuclear plants would be shared between a central ministry and the local authorities. Ukraine's declaration of full independence in August 1991 calls for a new solution to the problem of control. In the long term the nuclear power program in Ukraine cannot reach its stated production goals; hence, there is likely to be an intense search for alternative sources of energy.

(See also *Electric power.)

BIBLIOGRAPHY
Marples, D. Chernobyl and Nuclear Power in the USSR (London–Edmonton 1986)
Haynes, V.; Bojcun, M. The Chernobyl Disaster (London 1988)
Marples, D. The Social Impact of the Chernobyl Disaster (London 1988)
Medvedev, G. The Truth about Chernobyl (New York 1991)
                                                          D. Marples

Nuclear Research Institute of the Academy of Sciences of Ukraine. See Institute for Nuclear Research of the Academy of Sciences of the Ukrainian SSR.

Nudha, Hryhorii [Nud'ha, Hryhorij], b 21 January 1913 in Artiukhivka, Romen county, Poltava gubernia. Literary scholar, critic, and researcher of folk literature. He graduated from the philological faculty of Kiev University (1938). He has written numerous studies, including *Ukraïns'ka pisnia sered narodiv svitu* (Ukrainian Song among the World's Peoples, 1960), *Parodiia v ukraïns'kii literaturi* (Parody in Ukrainian Literature, 1961), *Zapovit T.H. Shevchenka* (T.H. Shevchenko's Testament, 1962), *Lystuvannia zaporozhtsiv z turets'kym sultanom* (The Correspondence of the Zaporozhian Cossacks with the Turkish Sultan, 1963), *Teren' Masenko* (1965), *Ukraïns'kyi poetychnyi epos: Dumy* (The Ukrainian Poetic Epos: Dumas, 1971), *Slovo i pisnia* (Word and Song, 1985), and *Na literaturnykh shliakhakh: Doslidzhennia, poshuky, znakhidky* (On Literary Paths: Explorations, Investigations, Findings, 1990). The collection of essays *Ukraïns'ka pisnia v sviti* (Ukrainian Song and the World, 1989) is one of Nudha's more valuable publications. His work is important primarily for having pioneered the study of areas which had previously received inadequate scholarly attention.

Numismatics. An auxiliary historical discipline, and also a layperson's hobby, the object of which is the study of coins (see *Currency and coins) and medals (see *Orders and medals); it generally excludes the study of seals, which falls under the discipline of *sphragistics. A coin may be defined as a piece of metal stamped with a device, with or without an inscription, signifying its issue by an authority that guarantees its value. Paper money, which serves the same purpose, is considered a separate field of numismatics.

Recorded interest in numismatics first began on Ukrainian territories in the 18th century, in conjunction with the unearthing of coin hoards (eg, the discovery of Arab coins in Kiev during the reign of Hetman I. Mazepa) and the creation of numismatic collections at the estates of various nobles or at church institutes (eg, the Kievan Cave Monastery and the Basilian school in Uman).

At the beginning of the 19th century the collecting of coins became more popular, and numismatic discussions and investigations began to take on a scientific and systematic character, particularly in relation to the collections in Kharkiv and those at the Kremianets Lyceum, based on the collection of King Stanislaus II Augustus Poniatowski (described and researched by J. Albertrandy). Kiev University received the Kremianets Lyceum collection in 1834 and assiduously added to it, so that by 1884 its holdings consisted of 34,520 coins and medals. Other large collections were established at the universities in Chernivtsi and Odessa, the latter becoming prominent for its collection and description of ancient coins of former Greek colonies on Ukrainian territories.

The late 19th and early 20th centuries saw the discovery of many large, spectacular hoards in Ukraine. Coins of Kievan Rus' from the 10th and 11th centuries were unearthed at Nizhen (1852) and Kiev (1876). Genoese-Tatar coins, used in the Crimea during the 14th and 15th centuries, were brought to light in Kerch and the Kuban (1909). A vast cache of coins of the 17th and early 18th centuries was found bricked up behind a wall in the Kievan Cave Monastery in 1898. Research on those finds in Ukraine was hindered by an 1866 imperial Russian decree which stated that all hoard materials found within the empire

Numismatic discoveries in Ukraine: a) bronze coin of the Scythian king Skhilouros minted in Olbia (2nd century BC); b) silver dirhem (9th century AD); c) silver Byzantine miliarensis (10th century); d) gold coin of Grand Prince Volodymyr the Great (10th century); e) silver coin of Grand Prince Volodymyr the Great (10th century); f) silver coin of Grand Prince Sviatopolk I (11th century); g) silver coin of Grand Prince Yaroslav the Wise (11th century); h) silver Genoese coin from Kaffa (now Teodosiia) in the Crimea (15th century)

were to be transferred to the Hermitage Museum in St Petersburg. That museum quickly became the premier center for numismatic research.

Many of the numismatic studies in Ukraine during that time focused on delineating through coins the extent of Roman and Arabic influence in Ukraine. With the unearthing of the coin hoards, pioneering classification schemes were compiled by I. Tolstoi (Kievan Rus' coins) and O. Retowski (Genoese-Tatar coins) that for the most part are still in use today. In the bulletin *Zapiski* of Kharkiv University, V. *Danylevych published an article on the significance of numismatics in the study of Ukrainian history (1903).

After the First World War numismatic studies broadened to include the topic of coinage during the Cossack-Hetman era of the 17th and 18th centuries. The leading researchers of the period were V. *Shuhaievsky, the director of the numismatic division at the Kievan Cave Monastery and the All-Ukrainian Institute of Museums in Kiev, and A. *Yershov, M. *Petrovsky, M. *Slabchenko, and I. *Krypiakevych. The main centers for the study of ancient coins found in Ukraine remained in Russia, at the Hermitage and the State Historical Museum (Moscow), where during the 1930s and 1940s various works were released. Only from the 1950s did Ukrainian researchers join Russian numismatists to contribute significantly to the field. Roman coins on Ukrainian territories were researched by M.

*Braichevsky and V. Kropotkin; coins of Kievan Rus' by the Russian scholars I. Spassky, M. Sotnikova, and V. Yanin (Ukrainian numismatists and historians were discouraged from researching and writing about the Kievan period); coins of Chervona Rus' and Lviv of the 14th and 15th centuries by M. Kotliar; and the history of Ukrainian coin terminology by Ye. Chernov.

Numismatic research in Ukraine was centered at the numismatic divisions of the historical museums in Kiev, Odessa, and Lviv. The collection of the Lviv Historical Museum contains some 70,000 specimens. Numismatics was also taught at the universities of Kiev and Odessa. Contributions of researchers were published in archeological journals and in the Russian journal *Numizmatika–Epigrafika*. An outline history of Ukrainian numismatics by I. Spassky was published in that journal in 1955. The only numismatic release in Ukraine was the irregular publication *Numizmatika–Sfragistika*, published in Russian by the AN URSR (now ANU) Institute of Archeology. Numismatic works also appeared in the short-lived historical journal *Istorychni dzherela ta ïkh vykorystannia*. Occasional numismatic articles dealing with or touching upon Ukrainian themes appeared in the Russian collectors' journal *Sovetskii kollekstioner*.

In the diaspora the useful Ukrainian-language *Numismatychnyi slovnyk* (Numismatic Dictionary, 1972) was compiled by V. Zvarych. The international *Ukrainian Philatelic and Numismatic Society (with headquarters in the United States) covers Ukrainian numismatics in its journal *Ukraïns'kyi filatelist / Ukrainian Philatelist*.

I. Kuzych-Berezovsky

Nuns. See Monasticism.

Nuremberg trials. A series of trials of 24 former Nazi leaders, conducted in Nuremberg, Germany, from 18 October 1945 to 1 October 1946. Among the defendants tried by the International Military Tribunal were two who bore considerable responsibility for crimes against humanity perpetrated on Ukrainian territory: H. *Frank, the former governor-general of German-occupied Poland and Galicia, and A. *Rosenberg, the former Nazi minister for the occupied Eastern territories. Both were sentenced to death by hanging. The trial brought to light a great deal of information about *Nazi war crimes in Ukraine. The documents in evidence at the trial were subsequently published; many refer to Ukraine and depict plunder of the economy, forced labor, resettlements, collective punishment, and mass executions as commonplace under Nazi rule. A long memorandum (dated 23 February 1943) of V. *Kubijovyč, head of the Ukrainian Central Committee in Cracow, to Governor-General Frank, for example, provided a documented and detailed description of German outrages against the Ukrainian population in Galicia.

Nurseries. See Preschool education.

Nursery Teachers' Seminary (Zakhoronkarska seminariia sester Vasylianok u Lvovi). A school for the training of nursery-school teachers in Lviv, operated in 1935–9 by the Basilian nuns. Its director was N. Lytvynenko. The program lasted three years. Sixty teachers graduated before the school was closed following the Soviet occupation of Lviv.

Nurzec River (Nurets). A right-bank tributary of the Buh River. It is 100 km long and drains a basin area of 2,037 sq km. The Nurzec flows through eastern Poland in Podlachia and is thus situated within Ukrainian ethnic territory.

Nutria (*Myocastor coypus*; Ukrainian: *nutriia*). A semi-aquatic nocturnal rodent, also known as coypu or swamp beaver, belonging to the family Capromyideae. The nutria is a robust animal, weighing up to 8 kg, with a body 50–85 cm long and a tail 30–45 cm long. Its fur is reddish brown and consists of coarse guard hairs over a soft undercoat. Nutrias were introduced in Ukraine from South America in the 1930s. They live in shallow burrows along ponds or riverbanks, where they feed on reeds and other aquatic plants. Nutria fur is valued in the fur trade. Persistent hunting in the past has caused a decline in nutria populations. Hunting nutria is now forbidden in Ukraine. The animal is bred in semi-captivity for commercial purposes.

Nutrition (*kharchuvannia*). The study of the processes by which food materials taken in by living organisms maintain life and sustain activity. The functions of foods in nutrition may be considered in terms of energy, proteins, minerals, and vitamins. In the former USSR the recommended daily caloric intake was calculated at 2,200–2,800 Cal for sedentary adults, 3,000 Cal for mechanized industry and service workers, 3,200 Cal for physical laborers, and 3,700–4,300 Cal for steelworkers, foresters, and other workers at hard labor. The recommended proportion of proteins to fats to carbohydrates was (in percentages) approx 12:33:55. The accepted ideal norm for adults was to take food four times daily: breakfast (25 percent of the daily ration), lunch (35 percent), afternoon snack (15 percent), and supper (25 percent), with four-hour intervals in between and with supper no later than two to three hours prior to sleep.

In fact, the actual diet of the ordinary adult in the former USSR was simple, monotonous, and usually lacking in proteins, vitamins, and minerals. Although Ukraine is a rich producer of food materials, more than capable of sustaining its own population on a healthy, balanced diet, a woefully inadequate, mismanaged, and corrupt distribution system, as well as the forced export of its food products to other parts of the former USSR and former satellite countries, has resulted in a poorly nourished population. The staple food items are heavy 'black' rye bread, potatoes, various cereals (including buckwheat kasha), flour, and cabbage. Poultry, meat, and dairy products are expensive and scarce; vegetables and fruit are mostly seasonal. Coffee is considered a luxury. In many instances confectionery items are used to compensate for general undernourishment. The effects of malnourishment have had evident consequences on the physical (esp dental), mental, and social well-being of Ukrainians.

Nutrition education is provided by the public health system, and research is carried out at the Kiev Scientific Research Institute of the Hygiene of Nutrition, as well as in specific departments of the Kiev, Kharkiv, and Lviv medical institutes.

BIBLIOGRAPHY
Schroeder, G. 'Consumption in the USSR: A Survey,' *Studies on the Soviet Union*, 1970, no. 4

Artiukh, L. *Narodne kharchuvannia ukraïntsiv ta rosiian pivnichno-skhidnykh raioniv Ukraïny* (Kiev 1982)

P. Dzul

Nychai, Appolon [Nyčaj], b 1846, d 1918. Co-operative activist in Galicia. A teacher by profession, he published the newspaper **Hospodar i promyshlennyk* in Stanyslaviv and Lviv in 1879–85. Together with V. Nahirny, in 1883 he initiated the founding of **Narodna Torhovlia*, which he headed for many years.

Nataliia Nychka   Dmytro Nykolyshyn

Nychka, Nataliia [Nyčka, Natalija] (née Levytska), b 1 March 1893 in Stanyslaviv, Galicia, d 16 January 1964 in New York. Actress. In 1912 she began her theatrical career in the Ruska Besida Theater. Then she worked in the Theater of the Legion of the Ukrainian Sich Riflemen (1916–18), the Lviv Ukrainian Independent Theater (1920–1), the Ukrainska Besida Theater (1921–3), and V. Blavatsky's Ukrainskyi Liudovyi Teatr (1926–7). In 1927 Nychka abandoned her stage career for health reasons.

Nychyporenko, Ivan [Nyčyporenko], b 8 October 1842 in Mezhyhiria (now part of Vyshhorod, Kiev oblast), d 25 January 1910 in Kiev. Pedagogue; member of the **Hromada* of Kiev. He graduated from Kiev University in 1863. From 1879 to 1890 he was director of **Galagan College* in Kiev. An innovator in educational methodology, he encouraged independent study by students.

Nychyporenko, Serhii [Nyčyporenko, Serhij], b 8 October 1900 in Volodymyr-Volynskyi. Colloid chemist. A graduate of the Volhynia Industrial Polytechnic (1928), from 1944 to 1955 he held managerial positions in the Ukrainian Ministry of the Building-Materials Industry and the Scientific Research Institute of Building Materials of the Academy of Construction and Architecture of the Ukrainian SSR. In 1959 he joined the AN URSR (now ANU) Institute of General and Inorganic Chemistry, and in 1968 he moved to the ANU Institute of Colloidal Chemistry and Hydrochemistry. He investigated the physical-chemical behavior of dispersed structures and applied it to industrial problems.

Nykolaichuk, Mykola [Nykolajčuk], b 1890, d ? Lawyer and civic leader in Galicia. He was active in the community and co-operative organizations of the Nadvirna region. He was a member of the Central Committee of the Ukrainian National Democratic Alliance. He was arrested by the Soviets in 1939, and disappeared in a prison camp.

Nykolaichyk, Fedir [Nykolajčyk], b 1857, d ? Historian and pedagogue. In *Kievskaia starina* (KS), *Zoria*, and other publications he wrote about the early history of the Cossacks and about the history of the Hetmanate, Siversk principality, and Left-Bank Ukraine. He also compiled a bibliography of the works of M. Kostomarov (KS, 1885).

Nykolyshyn, Dmytro [Nykolyšyn], b 1884 in Ivankiv, Borshchiv county, Galicia, d 1943. Writer, publisher, literary critic, and pedagogue. From 1914 to 1935 he owned and operated the **Zahalna Knyhozbirnia* publishing house in Kolomyia. He also taught at the Ukrainian gymnasium in Kolomyia and conducted the Boian choir there. He wrote a long introduction and notes to a book of T. Shevchenko's historical poems (1914); the plays *Rozladdie* (Disorder, 1911), *Taina* (The Secret, 1923), *Samson* (1928), *Maty* (Mother, 1929), and *Irod Velykyi* (Herod the Great, 1936); and poetry collections, such as *Svitannia i sutinky* (Dawns and Dusks, 1936) and *Lystopadova symfoniia* (November Symphony, 1937). He also translated Latin and German poetry into Ukrainian.

Nykon, b ?, d 1088. Monk and chronicler. He was ordained, and then entered the Kievan Cave Monastery (before 1058), where he became a close associate of St Anthony of the Caves. He was forced to leave for Tmutorokan (possibly because of a conflict with Prince Iziaslav Yaroslavych), where he established a monastery. He returned to Kiev in 1068, where he assisted St Theodosius of the Caves in compiling and binding manuscripts before the internecine struggle for power in Kiev again forced him to flee to Tmutorokan in 1073. After returning to Kiev in 1077, he served as hegumen of the Kievan Cave Monastery, from 1078 until his death. As hegumen he oversaw the completion of the ornamentation of the monastery's Dormition Cathedral and distinguished himself as a preacher. Nykon is believed to have continued the first Kievan chronicle of 1037 and edited the Kievan Cave Compilation of 1073, on which the **Povist' vremennykh lit* was based. These accomplishments earned him the title 'Great.' Some scholars believe that he and Ilarion, the first native metropolitan of Kiev, were the same person. The major source of information on Nykon's life is the Kievan Cave Patericon.

Nykonenko, Arkhyp, b ? in Orzhytsia, Lubni county, Poltava gubernia, d before 1856 in Orzhytsia. Lirnyk. His repertoire included six or seven dumas, of which P. Kulish transcribed and published five, along with some biographical information on Nykonenko, in the first volume of *Zapiski o Iuzhnoi Rusi* (Notes on Southern Rus', 1856). The most significant of these was an outstanding rendition of 'The Cossack Holota.'

Nykopil [Nykopil'] (aka Nikopol). VI-15. A city (1990 pop 158,000) on the right bank of the Kakhivka Reservoir and a raion center in Dnipropetrovske oblast. In the 16th century there was a portage named Mykytyn Rih at the site, and in the early 17th century the settlement of Mykytyne was established there. After the Russian army destroyed the Zaporozhian Sich in 1775, a fortified town called Sloviansk was built near Mykytyne. In 1782 it was renamed Nykopil. The *chumaks passed through Nykopil on their way to the Crimea. As the Nykopil Manganese Basin began to be developed at the end of the 19th century, Nykopil's metallurgical and machine-building industries grew rapidly. Besides cranes, pipes, and metal alloys the city manufactures building materials, clothes, and food. It is an important river port and railway junction.

Nykopil Crane Plant (Nykopilskyi kranobudivnyi zavod). A major heavy-industry plant located in Nykopil, Dnipropetrovske oblast. It was built in 1885 as an agricultural machinery and implements factory. In the interwar period it began to produce various types of loaders, trucks, and transports. At the beginning of the Second World War the plant was evacuated beyond the Urals, and it returned to operation only in 1944. In 1950 it began producing tower cranes. Now it makes tower and self-propelled hydraulic cranes, machine parts, elevators, tractor treads, and other products.

Nykopil Ferroalloys Plant (Nykopilskyi zavod ferosplaviv). A metallurgical factory in Nykopil, Dnipropetrovske oblast, built in 1962–6. Its products include manganese-silicon and ferromanganese alloys and fluxes for mechanized welding and electroscorification. The plant is equipped with special electric ovens and scrubbers.

Nykopil Manganese Basin. One of the world's largest formations of manganese ore. It is part of a larger manganoferrous basin stretching from Bulgaria through southern Ukraine to Georgia and containing 70 percent of the world's continental reserves of manganese ore. The Nykopil Basin extends from the small deposits at Inhulets to two large deposits north of Nykopil and then southeast of the Dnieper River to Tokmak. The ore deposit is 1–20 km wide and on average 2–3.5 m thick. The total reserves amount to 2.3 billion t.

The ores consist of high-grade oxides, mixed, and lower-grade carbonates with an average manganese content of 23–26 percent, 11–35 percent, and 15–17 percent respectively. The mining of high-grade ores began at Marhanets, northeast of Nykopil, in 1886. Production was greatly expanded in the 1950s, when open-pit mining of carbonate ores began at Ordzhonikidze, northwest of Nykopil. In 1980 the basin included seven mines, two quarries, and five enrichment plants. As the Nykopil Basin proper becomes exhausted, the Tokmak Basin assumes greater economic importance.

(See also *Manganese industry.)

Nykopil Regional Studies Museum (Nykopilskyi kraieznavchyi muzei). A museum established in Nykopil in 1919 as the Nykopil Museum of Art. In the 1920s the museum's staff excavated Hellenic barrows in Nykopil raion and participated in digs around the Dnieper Hydroelectric Station. The museum's holdings of over 20,000 items (of which 6,000 are on display) pertain to the natural environment, archeology, and history of Nykopil and its vicinity. The museum has a local archival collection and published a brochure on Nykopil under Soviet rule (1958). A guide to the museum's exhibits by M. Lytvyn appeared in 1968.

Nykopil Southern Pipe Plant (Nykopilskyi pivdenno-trubnyi zavod). A factory of the metallurgical industry, located in Nykopil, Dnipropetrovske oblast. Built in 1931–5, it produced seamless pipes. The plant was evacuated at the outset of the war and then rebuilt in 1944–7. Today it produces hot-, cold-, and warm-rolled seamless pipes; arc-welded carbon steel, rustproof and stainless steel, and steel alloy pipes of 0.1–920 mm diameter; and other goods. Its pipes are exported widely.

Nykorovych, Sylvestr [Nykorovyč, Syl'vestr], b 15 January 1905 in Kostyntsi, Vashkivtsi county, Bukovyna. Civic and political leader, and journalist. The first OUN liaison officer for Bukovyna, he edited the monthly *Samostiina dumka* in 1931–7 in Chernivtsi. In 1942–5 he published *Zemlia*, a newspaper for Ukrainian workers in Germany. He emigrated to Canada in 1953 and was active in the Ukrainian National Federation.

Nykorovych-Hnidevych, Oleksandra [Nykorovyč-Hnidevyč], b 1913, d 1941 in Chernivtsi. Civic activist; wife of S. *Nykorovych. She was active as a leader in Plast (early 1930s) and then as OUN liaison officer for Bukovyna. She was executed by the Soviets on the eve of the German invasion in 1941.

Nykorovych-Hnidy, Sydoniia [Nykorovyč-Hnidyj, Sydonija], b 1888, d 1957 in Arad, Rumania. Bukovynian writer and publicist. In 1931–3 she edited two supplements of the journal *Samostiina dumka*: *Samostiina dumka ukraïns'koï materi* and *Derzhavno-tvorcha trybuna Ukraïny*. Then she worked with the antinationalist paper *Khliborobs'ka pravda* as editor of its literary-scientific supplement and women's page (1935–7). Her articles on women's issues and short stories about the common people appeared in both periodicals.

Nykyfor: *Architectural Landscape*

Nykyfor (real name: Drovniak, Epifanii), b 21 May 1895 in Krynytsia, Nowy Sącz county, Galicia, d 10 October 1968 in Krynytsia. Lemko naive painter. A deaf son of a beggar woman, he supported himself from his teens by begging for food or a few coins in exchange for his small drawings and watercolors. He was discovered by Ukrainian and Polish artistic circles in the 1930s. With the help of R. Turyn, one of his earliest discoverers, his works were exhibited in Paris in 1932. Over 100 of his works were included in an exhibition of self-taught artists held by the Association of Independent Ukrainian Artists in Lviv in 1938. Like other Lemkos, he was deported to northern Poland by the Polish authorities after the Second World War. He returned illegally twice to Krynytsia before he was allowed to stay. In the 1950s and 1960s his works were exhibited in London, Rome, Belgrade, Amsterdam, Paris, Brussels, Florence, Liège, Haifa, Vienna, Frankfurt am Main, Chicago, Basel, Rotterdam, Lviv, Kiev, and New York. In his lifetime Nykyfor produced over 30,000 small color drawings or watercolors depicting existing and imaginary Lemko buildings, churches, landscapes, saints, and individuals (often himself). In style some of his works belong to the Lemko tradition of folk icon painting on glass; others are typical of naive art in general.

BIBLIOGRAPHY
Kataloh vystavky mysttsiv-samoukiv ANUM (Lviv 1938)
Banach, A.; Banach, E. *Historia o Nikiforze* (Cracow 1966)
Lesych, V. *Nykyfor z Krynytsi* (Munich 1971)

S. Hordynsky

Sava Nykyforiak   Dmytro Nytchenko

Nykyforiak, Sava [Nykyforjak], b 21 December 1886 in Rozhnevi Polia, Sniatyn county, Galicia, d 25 February 1973 in New York. Pedagogue and community activist. After completing university he taught at Ukrainian gymnasiums in Lviv, Chortkiv, and Stanyslaviv (now Ivano-Frankivske), where he was director in 1921–4. Upon the outbreak of the First World War he joined the Sich Riflemen, with which he served until the end of the Ukrainian liberation struggle. After the Second World War he emigrated to Austria, and in 1949 to the United States. He was a leading member of various veterans' organizations and a director of the Chervona Kalyna publishing society.

Nymphaeum. An ancient Greek city in the Crimea, 17 km south of present-day Kerch. Nymphaeum was founded in the 6th century BC at the site of a Scythian settlement. It exported wheat to Greece and manufactured pottery. In the 5th century BC it was briefly a colony of Athens and then belonged to the Bosporan Kingdom. In the 3rd century AD it was destroyed by the Goths. Excavations carried out at the site since 1939 have uncovered the remains of fortifications, public and private buildings, pottery workshops, and a temple of Demeter.

Nytchenko, Dmytro [Nytčenko] (pseuds: D. Chub, Ostap Zirchasty), b 21 February 1905 in Zinkiv, Poltava gubernia. Writer and community figure; member of the Shevchenko Scientific Society. In the 1920s he worked as a journalist, and in the 1930s he graduated from the Kharkiv Pedagogical Institute and then taught in secondary schools. He was a member of the writers' groups Hart and Prolitfront and began publishing under the name Nitsenko in 1922. Nytchenko wrote the collections *Poeziï industriï* (Poems of Industry, 1931) and *Sklepinnia* (The Vault, 1933) and the essay collection *Na prykordonni* (In the Border Area, 1932). In 1942–3 he was literary editor of the Kharkiv daily *Nova Ukraïna*. As a postwar émigré in Germany he worked for the newspaper *Ukraïns'ki visti* and wrote the book *Shevchenko v zhytti* (1947; 2nd rev edn: *Zhyvyi Shevchenko*, 1963; English trans: *Shevchenko the Man*, 1985). He emigrated to Australia in 1949 and played a central role in Ukrainian life there. He founded the Lastivka publishing house in the early 1950s, taught in Ukrainian schools, and headed the Ukrainian Central School Council (1954–62), the Australian branches of the *Slovo Association of Ukrainian Writers in Exile and the Association of Ukrainian Writers for Young People, and the Ukrainian Literary and Arts Club in Melbourne. Under the pseudonym D. Chub he wrote stories for children, memoirs of the Second World War, *V lisakh pid Viaz'moiu* (In the Forests near Viazma, 1958; 2nd rev edn 1983; English trans: *West of Moscow*, 1983), and the story collection *Stezhkamy pryhod* (On the Paths of Adventures, 1975). He also compiled a Ukrainian orthographic dictionary (1968) and wrote a book on the elements of literary theory and stylistics (1975) for Ukrainian schools. He contributed many articles and humorous poems and sketches (under the pseudonym Ostap Zirchasty) to Ukrainian émigré periodicals and edited over 20 Ukrainian-Australian books, the almanacs *Novyi obrii* (New Horizon, 1954–88), and a book of 200 of B. Antonenko-Davydovych's letters (1986). Collections of his selected literary articles appeared in 1981 and 1982.

R. Senkus

Nyva (Sown Field). A populist scholarly and literary journal published three times a month in Lviv in 1865; 20 issues appeared under the editorship of K. Horbal. It published the works of Yu. Fedkovych, T. Shevchenko, M. Starytsky, O. Storozhenko, and M. Vovchok; translations of I. Krylov (by M. Starytsky), A. Mickiewicz (by O. Navrotsky), and W. Shakespeare (by P. Svientsitsky); folklore studies; theater reviews; and literary surveys.

Nyva (Sown Field). A 208-page literary miscellany published by M. Borovsky and D. Markovych in Odessa in 1885. Among its contributors were I. Nechui-Levytsky (the story 'Chortiacha spokusa' [The Devil's Temptation]), M. Starytsky (the operetta 'Utoplena' [The Drowned Maiden]), A. Bobenko, Dniprova Chaika, B. Hrinchenko, P. Nishchynsky (a translation of part of Homer's *Odyssey*), P. Panchenko, and K. Ukhach.

Nyva (Sown Field). A journal of religious and social affairs published semimonthly in 1904–14 and then monthly in 1916–39 in Lviv. The journal supported the traditional Eastern orientation of Ukrainian Catholicism. For a time it was published by the Society of St Paul the Apostle. *Nyva* was edited by Revs Ya. Levytsky (1904–7, 1910–18), O. Voliansky (1908–10), H. Kostelnyk (1920–9), and P. Khomyn.

The journal issued the supplements *Katekhytychnyi misiachnyk* and *Propovidi* and a separate series of books and pamphlets. In 1930 the journal had a circulation of 1,500.

Antin Nyvynsky

Bohdan Nyzhankivsky

Nyvynsky, Antin [Nyvyns'kyj] (pen name: Chekmanovsky), b 1890, d 1945? Volhynian civic leader, journalist, and writer; husband of H. *Zhurba. He helped found the Prosvita society in Rivne and served as its president. He was active in politics as a member of the executive of the Ukrainian Party of Socialist Revolutionaries in Volhynia (1922–6) and its successor, the Ukrainian Socialist Radical party (1926–7). Defrauded of victory in 1928, he won a by-election to the Polish Sejm ordered in the Rivne district by the Supreme Court of Poland in 1930. He edited the weekly *Hromada* in Lutske (1922–4), the monthly organ of the Union of Ukrainian Private Office Employees, *Sluzhbovyk*, and the literary supplement to *Hromads'kyi holos*, titled *Snip* (1937–8). Writing under his pen name, he contributed short stories to Ukrainian journals and published the novelette *Viky plyvut' nad Kyievom* (The Centuries Flow over Kiev, 1938; repr 1964).

Nyzhankivska, Lada-Ariana [Nyžankivs'ka] (Nyzankovsky), b 3 October 1962 in Geneva. Artist; daughter of Z. *Lisovska and Oleh *Nyzhankivsky. She completed her art studies at the University of Geneva and the Geneva Academy of Fine Art (1985). She works as an art teacher in Geneva and specializes in painting and graphic art. She has participated in group shows in Switzerland (1985–90) and since 1986 has had numerous personal shows: in Geneva in 1986, 1987, 1989, and 1990; in New York, Washington, and Philadelphia in 1989; and jointly with her mother in London and Lviv in 1990.

Nyzhankivska, Melaniia [Nyžankivs'ka, Melanija], b 7 March 1898 in Radivtsi, Bukovyna, d 1 June 1973 in Blaugies, Belgium. Writer; daughter of I. *Semaka. She lived in Prague and Lviv with her husband, N. *Nyzhankivsky, who put many of her poems to music. After being imprisoned for several months in Prague by the Soviets at the end of the Second World War, she managed to emigrate to Belgium. She wrote the biographical novel *Na zelenii Bukovyni* (In Green Bukovyna) and stories and articles on literature and music in the postwar émigré press.

Nyzhankivska-Snihurovych, Dariia [Nyžankivs'ka-Snihurovyč, Darija], b 18 August 1916 in Lviv, d 23 July 1980 in Winnipeg. Ballerina, choreographer, and pedagogue; daughter of A. Nyzhankivsky. A pupil of M. Slovenska (Prague) and V. Pereiaslavets (Lviv), in 1939–44 she was the soloist in the Lviv Theater of Opera and Ballet. In 1944–7 she led a ballet studio in Innsbruck, Austria. Then she emigrated to Winnipeg (1950), where she organized the ballet school of Ukrainian dance at the Royal Winnipeg Ballet.

Nyzhankivsky, Amvrosii [Nyžankivs'kyj, Amvrosij] (Bronyslav), b 8 April 1873 in Kolomyia, Galicia, d 7 February 1943 in Kolomyia. Actor and ballet master. He began his stage career in 1892 as a choir member in the Ruska Besida Theater, continued there as a leading actor until 1914 (with a hiatus in 1896–8), and then acted in V. Kossak's troupe (1916–22), the Ukrainska Besida Theater (1923–4), Y. Stadnyk's troupe (1924–8), and the Tobilevych Theater (1929–32). Nyzhankivsky's repertoire of Ukrainian and non-Ukrainian character roles varied from Khoma in M. Starytsky's *Oi ne khody, Hrytsiu ...* (Don't Go to Parties, Hryts ...) to Gesler in F. Schiller's *Wilhelm Tell*.

Nyzhankivsky, Andrii [Nyžankivs'kyj, Andrij] (Niżankowski, Andrzej), b 1592 in Galicia, d 3 April 1655 in Cracow. Organist. A Dominican, he studied the organ in Italy with G. Frescobaldi and then emerged as a virtuoso in his own right. He served as an organist at Santa Maria sopra Minerva Church in Rome and the Dominican church in Cracow, and he probably composed a number of works which have not survived.

Nyzhankivsky, Bohdan [Nyžankivs'kyj] (pseud: Babai), b 24 November 1909 in Zolochiv, Galicia, d 18 January 1986 in Detroit. Writer. After graduating from a commercial school (1929) he worked for the Tsentrosoiuz union of co-operatives and contributed to *Novyi chas, Dilo, Nedilia, Nazustrich, Ukraïns'ki visti, Sluzhbovyk*, and other Lviv periodicals. He worked for Lviv Radio (1940–1) and then, until 1944, was an editor in the Lviv office of *Krakivs'ki visti* and wrote scripts for the *Veselyi Lviv theater. As a postwar refugee in Munich he was an editor of *Ukraïns'ka trybuna* and *Arka*. After emigrating to Detroit he contributed regularly to the satirical magazine *Lys Mykyta*, under his pseudonym, and acquired a reputation as a master of satirical, ironic, and humorous poetry. He wrote a book of anecdotes about his father, A. Nyzhankivsky, called *Aktor hovoryt'* (The Actor Speaks, 1936); two story collections about urban life, *Vulytsia* (The Street, 1936, about Lviv's 'street people') and *Novely* (Novellas, 1941); three poetry collections, *Terpke vyno* (Bitter Wine, 1942), *Shchedrist'* (Generosity, 1947), and *Vahota* (Gravity, 1953); a humorous novelette about émigré life, *Sviato na oseli* (The Celebration at the Resort, 1975); and, under his pseudonym, the poetry collections *Virshi ironichni, satyrychni i komichni* (Verses Ironic, Satiric, and Comic, 1959), *Karuselia virshiv* (Carousel of Verses, 1976), and *Martsypany i vytreben'ky* (Marzipans and Caprices, 1983). Some of his stories and poems appeared in *Arka, Kyïv, Suchasnist', Slovo: Zbirnyk*, and other émigré periodicals. An issue of *Terem (4 [1971]) was devoted to Nyzhankivky.

R. Senkus

Nyzhankivsky, Nestor [Nyžankivs'kyj], b 31 August 1893 in Berezhany, Galicia, d 2 April 1940 in Łódź, Poland.

Nestor Nyzhankivsky   Ostap Nyzhankivsky

Composer, pianist, teacher, and music critic. He received a PH D in history from Vienna University (1923) and graduated from the Prague State Conservatory (1927) in the master class of V. Novak. He returned to Galicia to teach piano and theory at the Lysenko Higher Institute of Music in Lviv (1931–9) and became one of the founders (and first chairman) of the *Union of Ukrainian Professional Musicians (SUPROM). He died after falling ill during his emigration from Soviet-occupied Galicia. His compositions include 'Piano Trio in E Minor'; for piano solo, 'Prelude and Fugue on a Ukrainian Theme in C Minor,' *Little Suite*, 'Intermezzo in D Minor,' and *Variations on a Ukrainian Theme in F Sharp Minor*; approx 20 art songs for voice and piano, among them 'Zasumui trembito' (Trembita's Dirge, text by R. Kupchynsky), 'Zhyta' (Wheat Fields, text by O. Oles), and 'Ty liubchyku za horoiu' (My Beloved beyond the Mountain, text by U. Kravchenko); 13 compositions for chorus, including 'Naimyt' (The Hireling, text by I. Franko) and 'Halochka' (text by M. Obidny); and arrangements of folk songs for chorus, published in the 1937 Chervona Kalyna collection.

BIBLIOGRAPHY
Bulka, Iu. *Nestor Nyzhankivs'kyi* (Kiev 1972)
I. Sonevytsky

Nyzhankivsky, Oleh [Nyžankivs'kyj], b 25 July 1924 in Vienna. Opera and concert singer (baritone). Educated in Belgium and Milan (where in 1957 he studied voice under F. Carpi), he graduated from the Geneva Conservatory, and then began performing in Swiss opera theaters (from 1963 at the Grand Theater of Geneva; from 1966 at the Collegium Academicum) as well as on Geneva radio and television. He performed in the world premiere of F. Martin's opera *Monsieur de Pourceaugnac* (after Molière), staged in Geneva in April 1963 and broadcast live. His repertoire includes songs by his father, N. *Nyzhankivsky, and his uncle, Omelian *Nyzhankivsky, by S. *Turkevych-Lukiianovych, and by A. Rudnytsky.

Nyzhankivsky, Omelian [Nyžankivs'kyj, Omeljan], b 20 August 1895 in Rohatyn, Galicia, d 18 July 1973 in Bern,

Switzerland. Pianist, organist, composer, musicologist, conductor, and pedagogue; cousin of N. *Nyzhankivsky. He was an officer in the Ukrainian Galician Army, and then studied music at Vienna University. Tuberculosis forced him to go to Egypt, where he began teaching at the conservatory in Cairo (1924–8). Later he moved to Switzerland, completed his musical training, and taught at the conservatory in Bern. His compositions include scores for three divine liturgies and numerous sacred works for organ, choir, and voice.

Nyzhankivsky, Ostap [Nyžankivs'kyj], b 24 January 1862 in Drohobych, Galicia, d 22 May 1919 near Stryi, Galicia. Priest, composer, conductor, and civic leader. He dedicated much of his energy to developing musical life in Galicia. He initiated and organized choral concert tours throughout Galicia in 1885, 1889, and 1892, organized and conducted the *Boian Society choir in Berezhany (1892) and conducted the Boian choir in Lviv (1895–6) and in Stryi (1900–14). He founded the music publishing house Muzykalna Biblioteka (1885) and compiled *Ukraïns'ko-rus'kyi spivanyk* (Ukrainian-Ruthenian Songbook, 1907). His works for choir 'Hulialy' (They Danced) and 'Z Okrushkiv' (From Crumbs, text by Yu. Fedkovych) became very popular. He also wrote songs for solo voice with piano accompaniment, including 'Mynuly lita molodii' (The Years of Youth Have Passed By); arrangements of folk songs for solo voice or choir; and *Vitrohony*, a cycle of *kolomyika* melodies for piano.

At the urging of Ye. *Olesnytsky, Nyzhankivsky brought comparable energies to bear in the economic field. He founded the first co-operative dairy (in Zavadiv) and cofounded the Provincial Home and Dairy Union (later renamed *Maslosoiuz) in 1907 in Stryi. His work as the first director of the organization was critical during its initial expansion. Nyzhankivsky was also elected to the Galician Diet in 1908–13. In 1919 he was summarily shot by the Polish authorities.

W. Wytwycky

Nyzhni Sirohozy [Nyžni Sirohozy]. VII-15. A town smt (1990 pop 6,700) on the Velyki Sirohozy River and a raion center in Kherson oblast. It was founded at the beginning of the 19th century by settlers from Kharkiv gubernia. In 1833 the village became a county center in Kherson gubernia. Today food processing is the town's main industry.

Nyzhnia Krynka [Nyžnja Krynka]. V-19, DB III-4. A town smt (1990 pop 16,800) on the Krynka River near Makiivka, Donetske oblast. The town is administered by the council of one of the city raions of Makiivka. Its origin goes back to 1788. The town is known for its coal mine.

Nyzhnohirskyi [Nyžn'ohirs'kyj]. VIII-15. A town smt (1990 pop 10,700) on the Salhyr River and a raion center in Crimea oblast. It was first mentioned in historical documents in the 17th century, as Seitler (Sehydler, Salhyr). In 1783 it was annexed by Russia, and in 1945 it was renamed. The town has a canning plant, a winery, and a dairy.

O

O vospitanii chad (On the Education of Children). One of the first handbooks for parents, 200 engraved copies of which were printed at the Lviv Dormition Brotherhood Press in 1609. Much of it consists of the teachings of St John Chrysostom. In his introduction the compiler (according to scholars, Y. Boretsky, the rector of the Lviv Dormition Brotherhood School at the time) stresses the value of formal education from an early age in shaping a child's character and morals. Two copies of the book have been preserved, one at the Lviv Museum of Ukrainian Art and the other at the National Library in Sofia, Bulgaria. The text is reprinted in *Pam'iatky brats'kykh shkil na Ukraïni, kinets' XVI–pochatok XVII st.* (Monuments of Brotherhood Schools in Ukraine, from the End of the 16th to the Beginning of the 17th Century, 1988).

Oak (*Quercus*; Ukrainian: *dub*). A deciduous or evergreen tree of the family Fagaceae. Oaks grow slowly and have deep root systems, but live long and begin to produce seeds only after 15 to 60 years of growth. After 80 years they increase mainly in circumference. Oak wood is hard and durable and has a pleasing texture. It is used in building ships, underwater installations, railway cars and ties, furniture, and houses, and its tannin is used to tan hides and in the manufacture of ink. Acorns provide food for small game animals and are used to fatten pigs and poultry. In times of war imitation coffee was made from acorns.

Oak is the most common deciduous tree in Ukraine; 20 percent of all trees there are oak. The common oak (*Q. robur*) grows throughout Ukraine; the rock oak (*Q. petracaea*) grows in western regions of Ukraine, in Caucasia, and along the Dniester River. A 700-year-old oak with a trunk circumference of 6.3 m grows in the village of Verkhnia Khortytsia, near Zaporizhia. Oak groves are common in the forest-steppe region. Other trees often found with oak are *beech, *hornbeam, *pine, and *linden. Oak is often used in Ukrainian songs and proverbs to symbolize strength.

Oats (*Avena*; Ukrainian: *oves*). A cereal of the family Gramineae, which includes *A. euavena*, an annual species, and *A. avenastrum*, a perennial steppe and meadow grass. The plants have a fibrous root system, linear leaves, and a one-seeded fruit. Oats may be a spring or a winter crop. Perennial oats is used as fodder; annual oats includes the cultivated oat plant (*A. sativa*). Although oats is used chiefly as livestock feed, some is processed for human consumption (oatmeal). Oats is a source of calcium, iron, vitamin B, and nicotinic acid, and in Ukraine it is a basic grain food. Owing to the use of more productive feed plants in recent years (corn, peas, sugar beets), acreage planted with oats has gradually been diminishing in Ukraine.

Petro Obal: *Hutsul Fields* (oil on plywood, 1930s)

Obal, Petro [Obal'], b 19 April 1900 in Obodivka, Zbarazh county, Galicia, d 27 May 1987 in Stryi, Lviv oblast. Painter and graphic artist. A graduate of the Cracow Academy of Fine Arts (1926), he taught painting in secondary schools in Pomerania (until 1939), the Lemko region (1939–42), and Stryi (1942–56). He exhibited his work in Lviv at shows of the Circle of Contributors to Ukrainian Art (1923), the Association of Independent Ukrainian Artists (from 1934), and the Labor Association of Ukrainian Pictorial Artists (1942). In 1932–3 he took part in graphic art exhibitions in Berlin, Prague, and Chicago. Solo exhibitions of his works were held in Bromberg (1935), Sianik (1940), and Lviv (1966). Most of his paintings are impressionist landscapes; eg, *Golden Podilia* (1931), *Sunset*, and *Hutsul Fields* (1930s). He also did woodcuts and a woodcut album of Ukrainian writers (1930).

Oberuchev, Konstantin [Oberučev], b 1865 in Kiev, d November 1929 in the United States. Russian commander of the Kiev Military District (KMD). In 1905 he was relieved of his post as an artillery officer in the Russian army for revolutionary activity and was forced to emigrate. He returned to Ukraine from Switzerland on the eve of the revolution, was arrested in Kiev, and was freed after the outbreak of the revolution. In May 1917 he became commander of the KMD for the Provisional Government. He was a member of the Russian Social Revolutionary party. His views opposing separate Ukrainian military formations were published in *Kievskaia mysl'*. After the demise of the Provisional Government Oberuchev emigrated to the United States, where he wrote *V dni revoliutsii* (In the Days of the Revolution, 1919) and *Vospominaniia* (Memoirs, 1930).

Mykhailo Obidny

Obidny, Mykhailo [Obidnyj, Myxajlo] (pseud: Mochar-sky), b 24 June 1889 in Myrhorod, Poltava gubernia, d 7 January 1938 in Mukachiv, Transcarpathia. Ethnographer, múseologist, and poet. Until 1910 he taught school in the Kuban region. Upon returning to central Ukraine he worked in a number of museums in Katerynoslav and Kiev, and he published three poetry collections in 1917–18. After the war he studied at the Ukrainian Higher Ped-agogical Institute in Prague, and in 1933 he moved to Transcarpathia, where he helped found the *Ethnographic Society of Subcarpathian Ruthenia and directed the Eth-nographic Museum of Transcarpathia. He wrote some ar-ticles on Ukrainian ethnography and several collections of poetry, including *Pid siaivom voli* (Under the Gleam of Freedom, 1917) and *Neroztsvili ranky* (Unblossomed Mornings, 1923)

Oblast (*oblast'*). An administrative territorial unit of the USSR, introduced in 1931–2 in place of *okruhas. The term was used earlier, in the Russian Empire, for some territo-rial units, such as the *Oblast of the Don Cossack Host, the oblast of the Kuban Cossack Host, and (briefly) Bessarabia oblast. In 1932 the Ukrainian SSR was divided into 5 oblasts. By early 1939 the number had increased to 15, and by the end of the year 6 more oblasts had been added, when Western Ukraine was incorporated into the Ukrai-nian SSR. Two more oblasts were set up in 1940, 1 in 1944, and 1 in 1946. In 1954 Cherkasy oblast was added, the Crimean ASSR was incorporated into Ukraine as an oblast, and 4 oblasts were merged into 2. Since then Ukraine has been divided into 25 oblasts.

The oblasts were under republican jurisdiction. The

UKRAINE

– – Boundary of Ukraine

⊚ Capital of Ukraine

—— Oblast boundary

⊙ Oblast center

Except where noted, names of oblasts are the same as those of their centres

0   100   200 Km

OBLASTS IN UKRAINE

most important political organ in each oblast was the oblast Party committee, which was under the CC CPU. The highest representative body was the oblast soviet (now council), and the highest administrative body was the soviet's executive committee. The administrative apparatus of the oblast executive committee was under the dual jurisdiction of the oblast soviet and the appropriate republican ministries. The only exception was the KGB: its oblast agents were controlled from the center, although formally there were committees of state security at the oblast soviets. Until 1956 this exception also applied to the militia and the oblast courts.

The powers of the oblast administrative organs have varied, depending on the state's overall policies on economic management. In the 1930s oblast soviets were elected according to a system of oblast congresses, at which raion- and city-soviet delegates nominated and voted for candidates. Since 1937, however, oblast-soviet members have been elected to a two-year term by direct election. Until 1934 the administrative apparatus was organized on a collegial principle. Since then the organs have been headed by a chairman and various deputies and secretaries. The legal foundations of the oblast soviets are specified in the 1980 Statute of the Ukrainian SSR on the Oblast Soviet of People's Deputies. (See also *Administrative territorial division.)

A. Bilynsky

Oblast court. A court of the middle level that deals in the first instance with more serious criminal and civil matters, such as treason, first-degree murder, and divorce; oversees the work of the lower *people's courts; and hears appeals against the decisions of the lower courts. In addition, oblast courts handle the administration of the lower courts and oblast notaries, which before 1962 was handled by the territorial organs of the Ministry of Justice of the Ukrainian SSR. The oblast court consists of a chairman, deputy chairman, court members, and *people's assessors, all of whom are elected for five years by the oblast soviets of people's deputies. Oblast courts are divided into civil and criminal collegia, a presidium, a secretariat, and the respective administrative bodies. The structure and functions of the oblast courts are defined by the Law Concerning the Judiciary (1960).

In the 1930s the oblast courts played a key role in Stalin's terror. In 1934 a collegium of three professional judges called a *troika* was set up under each oblast court to hear political cases investigated by the NKVD. The proceedings of these extrajudicial courts were secret, and the accused were denied any civil rights. The *troiki* sentenced hundreds of thousands of innocent people to long imprisonment, exile, and death. From 1940 to 1959 political crimes were tried mostly by military courts and then were reassigned to the oblast courts. Conducting closed trials, these courts sentenced hundreds of Ukrainian dissidents, human rights activists, and defenders of Ukrainian culture to hard labor for up to 15 years and in some cases to death. The courts were tightly controlled by the KGB and the Party. (See also *Court system.)

A. Bilynsky

Oblast of the Don Cossack Host. An administrative-territorial unit in the Russian Empire, situated in the basin of the middle and lower reaches of the Don River and incorporating most of the *Don region. The area was settled primarily by Don Cossacks, though Ukrainians were concentrated in its western and northern parts. In 1914 the territory encompassed an area of 164,000 sq km and contained a population of 3.9 million. The Oblast of the Don Cossack Host (until 1870 known as the Don Cossack Land) was formally constituted in 1792; in 1887 it was enlarged to include Rostov county (from Katerynoslav gubernia) and the city and district of Tahanrih. Its administrative capital was Novocherkassk. The oblast was dismantled under Soviet rule in 1924, and the area now forms part of Rostov and Volgograd oblasts in Russia and Donetske and Luhanske oblasts in Ukraine.

Obmiński, Tadeusz, b 16 April 1874 in Lviv, d 18 July 1932 in Lviv. Architect. A graduate of the Lviv Polytechnic (1898), he later taught there. Until 1914 he worked periodically for the firm of I. *Levynsky. He designed residential and public buildings in Lviv, including the Narodnyi Hotel (1909), in which he blended elements of wooden folk architecture with the Moderne style, and the Scientific-Technical Library of the Lviv Polytechnic (1932).

Obninsky, Viktor [Obnins'kyj], b 1867, d 1916. Russian politician and journalist. He was a representative of Kaluga gubernia to the First State Duma and a leading figure in the autonomist-federalist parliamentary faction, which later became the Autonomists' Union. He was an associate of *Ukrainskaia zhizn'* and maintained close contact with the Society of Ukrainian Progressives during his regular visits to Kiev.

Obnova Society of Ukrainian Catholic Students (Tovarystvo ukrainskykh studentiv-katolykiv Obnova). A religious student organization established in Lviv in 1930. It formed part of the larger *Catholic Action movement and derived its name (*obnova*, meaning renewal) from the movement's motto, To Renew All Things in Christ. In the 1930s its membership was close to 100. Its first president was P. *Isaiv. With the Soviet occupation of Galicia Obnova was dissolved; it was revived only in 1946 in Munich as the Obnova Federation of Societies of Ukrainian Catholic Students. The new president was Ye. Pereima. By 1949 the federation's membership had reached 427. Also in 1946 the Obnova Ukrainian Catholic Academic Alliance was established, by a group of senior Obnova members. The first president of the alliance was V. Hlibovytsky; he was followed in 1951 by R. Danylevych. Both organizations had branches in many cities in Europe, the United States, Canada, and Australia. Obnova is a member of the Pax Romana international Catholic student movement. Its activities have included public lectures and readings, workshops, and conferences. It has also published information bulletins, brochures, the journal *Obnova*, a special page in the Chicago newspaper *Nova zoria*, and several volumes of the collection *Obnov'ianyn*.

Obodovska, Raisa [Obodovs'ka, Rajisa], b 6 August 1948 in Starovirivka, Kharkiv oblast. Cyclist. She won the 1968 and 1969 world championships in the 3,000-m women's individual pursuit and was the women's champion of Ukraine and the USSR in this event many times.

Obolonsky [Obolons'kyj]. A family of Cossack *starshyna* and Russian nobility in Left-Bank Ukraine. It was established by the Cossack Ivan at the end of the 17th century. His son, Vasyl, was captain of Sosnytsia company in 1715–16. Vasyl's son, Demian, (d 1758), was general standard-bearer of the Hetman state in 1741–58. At the Hlukhiv Council of 1750 that elected Hetman K. Rozumovsky Demian was chosen to head the Cossack delegation that thanked Empress Elizabeth I for allowing the election of a hetman. Demian received many landed estates from Elizabeth, and his son, also named Demian, owned 7,330 serfs in the late 18th century. The younger Demian's son was Oleksander *Obolonsky, whose son, Mykola (1856–?), was a professor of forensic medicine at Kiev University from 1889.

Obolonsky, Oleksander [Obolons'kyj], b 1825, d 23 October 1877. Editor and publisher. He met T. Shevchenko (1858) and published his works (in both the original and in Russian translation), as well as those of other Ukrainian writers, such as P. Kulish, Ya. Shchoholiv, and M. Vovchok, in his journal *Narodnoe chtenie*. In 1860 he also printed a renowned autobiographical letter from Shevchenko. After the journal closed down, Obolonsky worked in Poltava gubernia as a county marshal and zemstvo official.

Oborona Ukrainy (Defense of Ukraine). A Ukrainian political organization of a radical socialist profile, established in 1920 in the United States to assist the political and military struggles for independence in Western Ukraine. Until 1923 it was a small, clandestine organization; then it became a wider, public one with individual branches and an official newspaper, *Ukraïns'ka hromada*. Its members dominated the leadership of the Ukrainian Workingmen's Association and worked closely with the Ukrainian Socialist Radical party in Western Ukraine. The group also fought with Ukrainian-American Communists on ideological matters and their efforts to expand their influence by infiltrating other Ukrainian community groups. Its leading activists included M. Sichynsky, M. Tsehlynsky, and Ya. Chyzh. During the 1940s some of its leaders, most notably Sichynsky and V. Levytsky, rejected the organization's program and adopted a pro-Soviet policy. The resulting crisis led to the dissolution of the association after its 1947 convention. Tsehlynsky's group published the journals *Oborona Ukraïny* and *Oborona* for a brief period thereafter and gained the co-operation of new émigrés who belonged to the left wing of the Ukrainian Revolutionary Democratic party, thereby laying the groundwork for the establishment of the *Ukrainian Free Society of America in 1949. The faction led by Sichynsky and Levytsky soon dissipated.

Oboznyi. A high-ranking elected position in the administrative and military hierarchy of the Cossack army and the Hetman state. The general *oboznyi* (see *general quartermaster) and the regimental *obozni* were second in command in their respective officer staffs. They were in charge of supplies and commanded the artillery. In 1835 the imperial government granted those officers and their families the status of hereditary nobility.

Obrazotvorche mystetstvo (Pictorial Art). An illustrated fine arts journal published in Kiev in 1935–41 (a total of 61 issues). Until 1939 it was called *Maliarstvo i skul'ptura*

and was the organ of the Ukrainian Union of Soviet Artists and Sculptors. From 1939 it was called *Obrazotvorche mystetstvo* and was published by the Administration of Artistic Affairs of the Council of People's Commissars of the Ukrainian SSR and the Ukrainian Union of Soviet Artists. The journal propagated the official style of *socialist realism.

Obrazotvorche mystetstvo (Pictorial Art). An illustrated journal published six times a year in Kiev since 1970 by the Ministry of Culture of Ukraine and the Union of Artists of Ukraine. It contains articles on the history of Ukrainian and Russian art, Ukrainian and other artists, and developments in art, as well as art news, criticism, and reviews. The journal was initially published in a pressrun of 16,700, but by 1991 only 3,800 copies were being printed. Its chief editors have been P. Hovdia, O. Zhuravel, and since 1992 M. Marychevsky.

Vasilii Obraztsov

Obraztsov, Vasilii [Obrazcov, Vasilij], b 13 January 1849 (or 1851) in Griazovets (or Vologda), Vologda gubernia, Russia, d 14 December 1920 in Kiev. Russian internal medicine specialist. A graduate of the St Petersburg Medico-Surgical Academy (1875), he was a professor at Kiev University, where he also directed the internal medicine clinic (1904–18), and president of the Kiev Physico-Medical Society and the Society of Kiev Physicians. In his doctoral dissertation (1880) he demonstrated the existence of intermediary stages in the development of red blood cells, which demonstration led to the unitarian theory of blood formation. He developed a method of testing the organs of the abdominal cavity and a technique of sounding the chest. Obraztsov was the founder of the Kiev school of internal medicine, which had an important influence on the development of medicine in the Soviet Union.

Obrii (Horizons). A nationalist literature and art weekly published in Lviv in 1936–7. Its editor was B. *Kravtsiv.

Obrist, Johann Georg, b 26 May 1843 in Jenbach, Tirol, d 18 April 1901 in Innsbruck. Austrian literary scholar and journalist. From 1868 to 1873 he taught in Chernivtsi. He was one of the first ethnic Germans to write about and translate the poetry of T. Shevchenko. His critical biography *Taras Grigoriewicz Szewczenko, ein kleinrussischer Dichter* (1870) included his free translations of 14 poems. His translations also appeared in the collection *Taras Schewtschenko, der grösste Dichter der Ukraine* (Vienna 1914).

Observatories. Scientific research institutions in the field of astronomy. Their chief purpose is to observe light sources in outer space and to interpret the observations. The work of all observatories in the USSR was co-ordinated by the Astronomical Council of the USSR Academy of Sciences. In Ukraine the *Crimean Astrophysical Observatory belonged to the USSR Academy of Sciences until 1992; the Main *Astronomical Observatory and the *Poltava Gravimetric Observatory came under the AN URSR (now ANU). Other astronomical observatories are found in Kiev, Lviv, Kharkiv, Mykolaiv, and Odessa. (See also *Astronomy.)

Obshchina. The Russian word for an agricultural commune, the dominant institution of ethnic Russian peasant agriculture until the Revolution of 1917. Arable land, meadows, and pastures were held communally by the *obshchina*. Fields were divided into sections whose size varied with the quality of the soil and distance from the village. Each peasant household had the right in every section to cultivate one or more strips according to the number of its adult members. Since households grew or diminished over time, every 9 to 15 years the commune took its own census, on the basis of which it carried out an equalized reallocation of the strips.

In Ukraine there were various forms of agricultural associations (see *Hromada and *Land tenure system). The *obshchina* system began developing there only in the second half of the 18th century, after it was introduced by certain landowners during the settlement of Southern Ukraine. The *obshchina* became more widespread as a result of the agrarian reforms that accompanied the emancipation of the peasantry in 1861. The reforms granted village communes, but not individual peasants, the right to redeem land from the gentry landowners. Although the majority of peasant households received land as full-fledged owners, in the steppe gubernias of Katerynoslav, Kharkiv, and Kherson land awarded to the peasants was, for the most part, placed at the disposal of peasant communes on the pattern of the *obshchina*. In those gubernias 89–95 percent of all land was distributed through the communes. In contrast, in Chernihiv gubernia the figure was 52 percent, and in the Right-Bank gubernias and Poltava gubernia only 5–7 percent of land was distributed through the communes. The fiscal needs of the state, namely the tradition of holding all members of the *obshchina* collectively responsible for tax collection, were the main factor behind the introduction of the *obshchina* in Russian-ruled Ukraine. In the Ukrainian gubernias that were formally under the rule of communal land ownership, however, 80.2 percent of the communes did not periodically reallocate land, whereas the typical *obshchina* in Russia proper did. The movement to leave the *obshchina* and pursue private farming initiated in 1906 by the *Stolypin agrarian reforms was particularly strong in Ukraine. There 42 percent of peasant households belonging to peasant communes in Southern Ukraine, 16.5 percent in Left-Bank Ukraine, and 48 percent in Right-Bank Ukraine seceded. That trend accelerated during the years 1906–17 and became almost universal in Ukraine after the February Revolution.

BIBLIOGRAPHY
Kononenko, K. *Ukraine and Russia: A History of the Economic Relations between Ukraine and Russia (1654–1917)* (Milwaukee 1958)
Robinson, G.T. *Rural Russia under the Old Regime: A History of the Landlord-Peasant World and a Prologue to the Peasant Revolution of 1917* (Berkeley and Los Angeles 1967)
Watters, F.M. 'The Peasant and the Village Commune,' in *The Peasant in Nineteenth-Century Russia*, ed W.S. Vucinich (Stanford 1968)
Aleksandrov, V. *Sel'skaia obshchina v Rossii (XVII–XIX v.)* (Moscow 1976)
Atkinson, D. *The End of the Russian Land Commune, 1905–1930* (Stanford 1983)
I. Vytanovych

Obstetrics (*akusherstvo*). The medical specialty that deals with pregnancy, labor, birth, and puerperium. Midwifery from time immemorial was almost exclusively a women's field. The Ukrainian N. *Ambodyk-Maksymovych was the founder of medical obstetrics in the Russian Empire. The level of maternal mortality is still significantly higher in the former USSR than in other European countries. In Ukraine maternal mortality due to complications of pregnancy, birth, or the postnatal period was (per 100,000 births) 68 in 1980, 54 in 1985, and 50 in 1988. The instances of perinatal mortality (per 1,000 births) in Ukraine in 1988 numbered 14.3, including 9 stillbirths.

At present the Institute of Pediatrics, Obstetrics, and Gynecology in Kiev is the most important scientific research center of this branch of medicine in Ukraine. Founded in 1929 as the Ukrainian Scientific Research Institute of Maternity and Childhood Care, it was renamed in 1965 and today is under the Ministry of Health. In 1981 the institute initiated the creation of the Ukrainian Republican Center for Mother and Child Health Care. In Lviv the Institute of Pediatrics, Obstetrics, and Gynecology, also under the Ministry of Health, was founded in 1940 as the Lviv Scientific Research Institute of Motherhood and Childhood Care and renamed in 1983. Scientific societies of obstetricians have held conferences and workshops to deal with the prophylaxis and treatment of complications stemming from pregnancy, labor, and puerperium, as well as the care of the newborn and other gynecological matters. The journal *Pediatriia, akusherstvo i hinekolohiia* is published bimonthly in Kiev by the Ministry of Health.

BIBLIOGRAPHY
Konius, Ie. *Puti razvitiia sovetskoi okhrany materinstva i mladenchestva* (Moscow 1954)

Obukhiv [Obuxiv]. III-11. A city (1990 pop 31,800) and raion center in Kiev oblast. It was first mentioned in historical documents of the 14th century under its original name of Lukavytsia. The town was the site of several battles during B. Khmelnytsky's uprising against the Poles. In the Hetman state it was a company center of Kiev regiment. By 1845 it was known for its textile and brick manufactures. In 1872 a distillery was built. Today Obukhiv produces paper and cardboard, bricks, and dairy products.

Obydovsky, Ivan [Obydovs'kyj], b 1676, d 1701. Cossack officer; nephew of Hetman I. *Mazepa. He graduated from the Kiev Academy, served as colonel of Nizhen regiment (1695–1701), and participated as acting hetman in wars against Turkey (1695) and Sweden (1700–1). Obydovsky was Mazepa's heir presumptive; he received the high administrative rank of *stolnyk*, obtained substantial land grants in Russia and Slobidska Ukraine, and married the daughter of V. *Kochubei. He died prematurely, however, and in 1701 Mazepa chose another nephew, A. Voinarovsky, as a potential successor.

Obytochna River [Obytočna]. A waterway in Zaporizhia oblast. It is 100 km long and drains a basin area of 1,430 sq km. The river flows into the Sea of Azov at Obytochna Bay. It has a reservoir, and its waters are used for industry, irrigation, and pisciculture.

Obytochna Spit

Obytochna Spit [Obytočna kosa]. VII-17. A crustose sand spit on the northern littoral of the Azov Sea. It extends approx 30 km into the sea between Obytochna and Berdianske bays. During the autumn and spring the narrowest stretch of the spit, which is approx 8 m wide, is flooded. It provides a large spawning area for ocean fish and a nesting ground for water birds. Obytochna Spit has been designated a wildlife refuge.

Oceanology or **oceanography.** The study of the oceans and seas in all their aspects, including their physical, geological, and biological properties. Before 1917 only marine biology and marine chemistry were developed in Ukraine, mostly under the auspices of the Imperial Russian Academy of Sciences (M. Andrusiv, N. Zelinsky, and S. Zernov). The research was concentrated at the Sevastopil Biological Station (SBS, est 1872) and was focused principally on the Black Sea.

In 1963 the SBS was reorganized into the *Institute of the Biology of Southern Seas of the AN URSR (now ANU). Later that year, two smaller biological research stations, at Kara-Dag, near Teodosiia (est 1914), and at Odessa (est 1954), were turned into branches of the institute. Field studies at the institute expanded in scope and diversity when two new research vessels, the *A. Kovalevsky* and the *N. Miklukho-Maklai*, were commissioned. The Marine Hydrophysical Institute was transferred in 1961 from the USSR Academy of Sciences in Moscow to the ANU and moved to Sevastopil. Its large research vessel, the *M. Lomonosov*, was capable of all-weather ocean research. The institute's branch at Katsiveli, west of Alupka, continued to serve as an experimental station for testing new equipment. A second branch was opened in Odessa in 1986 to study economic issues of ocean exploration and human-induced phenomena in the coastal seas. In 1973 the USSR Oceanographic Institute in Moscow, which came under the State Committee on Hydrometeorology and Environmental

Monitoring and had branches in Odessa and Sevastopil, launched a major program in marine geology, ocean dynamics, and pollution. The Azov-Black Sea Scientific Research Institute of Fishery and Oceanography in Kerch expanded its global explorations for ocean fisheries.

In its quest for rapid economic and military growth the Soviet government in the 1960s and 1970s increased funding for theoretical and field research in oceanography. By the end of the 1970s more than 20 large ocean-going research vessels were operating from Ukrainian ports. Highest priority was given to, and vast funds channeled into, programs that had some application to submarine warfare (acoustics, subtle ocean structures, sea-ocean connections), a rapid increase in food resources (marine biology), the assimilation of Western technology, and the spreading of propaganda abroad. As a result Soviet oceanographers made unprecedented progress in areas such as oceanic turbulence, vertical water structure, the interaction between inanimate and living matter, sedimentation, oxic-anoxic microbial processes, and underwater acoustics. In an effort to prevent the rapid degradation of the coastal waters and estuaries the effects of pollution in the regions concerned were studied at the Institute of the Biology of Southern Seas and the ANU *Institute of Hydrobiology in Kiev.

In the 1980s, however, Soviet oceanography fell behind the achievements in the West, because of the general technological gap between the two societies. Space oceanography, free suspended floats, completely automated instrumentation, new methods in chemistry and biology, and new drilling techniques in the West could not be matched by Soviet science. The economic restructuring in the late 1980s signified a virtual end to large-scale research in oceanography. The large fleet of research vessels has become obsolete. Funds for oceanographic research have been channeled into other programs. The emphasis has shifted to methods of improving coastal marine systems, conserving water, exploring the adjacent seas prudently, and halting the degradation of the landlocked seas.

BIBLIOGRAPHY
Vinogradov, K. *Ocherki po istorii otechestvennykh gidrobiologicheskikh issledovanii na Chernom more* (Kiev 1955)
Dobrovol'skii, A.; Zalogin, B. *Moria SSSR* (Moscow 1965)
Deriugin, K. *Istoriia okeanograficheskikh issledovanii* (Leningrad 1972)
Tolmazin, D. *Elements of Dynamic Oceanography* (London 1985)
Doronin, Iu. *Regional'naia okeanografiia* (Leningrad 1986)
D. Tolmazin

Ochakiv [Očakiv]. VII-12. A city (1990 pop 19,400) at the mouth of the Dnieper Estuary and a raion center in Mykolaiv oblast. It is believed that a Greek colony existed at the site of present-day Ochakiv in the 7th and 6th centuries BC. In the 14th century the Lithuanian grand duke Vytautas built a fortress called Dashiv there. At the end of the 15th century the territory along the northern coast of the Black Sea came under Crimean Tatar control, and the Tatars erected a fortress on the site. Soon the Turks established their power over the Tatars and the Black Sea steppe. The name Ochakiv is derived from the Turkish name of the fortified settlement, Achi-Kale. In the 16th and 17th centuries the Zaporozhian Cossacks stormed Ochakiv many times. After Russia acquired the territory from Turkey in 1791, Ochakiv grew rapidly. As a port it

Ochakiv (1737 German engraving)

Valeriia O'Connor-Vilinska

has always been an important trade and fishing center. Today it has a fish-canning complex, wineries, and sewing factories. There are several museums and many sanatoriums in the vicinity.

Ocher. An earthy iron ore, usually red or yellow; also any of the ferruginous clays. It is used extensively as a pigment in ceramics and paint-making. In Ukraine ocher is found in the Boh River valley, in the Donets Basin, and on the Kerch Peninsula. In prehistorical times ocher had an important cult function. In the Trypilian culture, corpses that were being buried were stained with ocher. The substance was also used as a pigment for the distinctive Trypilian earthenware.

Ochkove. A tax in kind on honey in 16th- and 17th-century Ukraine. Peasant beekeepers were taxed according to the number of hives they kept. The tax varied at different times from 25 to 50 percent of the honey harvest. Its name was derived from *ochko* (the entrance to a hive).

Ochrymovych, Ariadne [Oxrymovyč, Arijadna], b 21 June 1947 in Wels, Austria. Film director and producer of Ukrainian origin. Ochrymovych came with her parents to Canada in 1949. A graduate in literature of Carleton University (MA, 1974) and in motion picture production of Ryerson Polytechnical Institute (1976), she has produced and directed a number of CBC television dramas, such as *Billy Goat's Bluff* (1982) and *The Juggler* (1983), the National Film Board of Canada series *The Feminization of Poverty* (1986), and the documentary *Playing for Keeps* (1989), and directed a film production on drug abuse (1990). Her own company is called Black Sea Productions.

O'Connor-Vilinska, Valeriia [Vilins'ka, Valerija], b 21 December 1867 in Mykolaivka, Kremenchuk county, Poltava gubernia, d 19 December 1930 in Poděbrady, Bohemia. Writer and community figure; sister-in-law of M. *Lysenko and niece of M. *Starytsky. As a young woman she ran a Ukrainian school and folk theater in Mykolaivka. Later she taught at the Kharkiv eparchial school, was a member of the Publishing Committee of the Kharkiv Literacy Society, and wrote educational pamphlets and feuilletons in the local newspaper. After the Revolution of 1905

she lived in Kiev, where she wrote the plays *Instytutka* (The Girls' School Pupil) and *Storinka mynuloho* (A Page from the Past). In 1917 she was in the first executive committee (later Little Rada) of the Ukrainian Central Rada and in the presidium of the Ukrainian National Theater society. In 1919 she emigrated with her husband, O. *Vilinsky, to Vienna and then Poděbrady, where she wrote the novelette *Skarb* (The Treasure, 1924), parts of a long novel-chronicle, *Na emigratsiï* (In the Emigration), and memoirs of the Lysenko and Starytsky families (1936). Her works and translations of French literature appeared in *Literaturno-naukovyi vistnyk* (Kiev), *Siaivo* (Kiev), *Volia* (Vienna), *Nova Ukraïna* (Prague), and other periodicals. She committed suicide.

October Revolution of 1917 (Zhovtneva revoliutsiia). The Bolshevik coup staged on 25 October (7 November NS) 1917 in Petrograd (formerly St Petersburg) precipitated a full-scale revolution in Russia and the outlying territories that had formerly constituted parts of its empire. After the fall of the tsarist regime following the *February Revolution of 1917 the *Provisional Government assumed power. It was unable, however, to control the volatile social and political conditions in the former empire. As their immediate goal the majority of the population wanted Russia to pull out of the First World War. As a broader goal they demanded wide-ranging social reforms and the redistribution of land. The non-Russian peoples of the empire wanted national autonomy and equality. Meanwhile the Bolsheviks and other left-wing groups, whose power base consisted of workers' and soldiers' councils (soviets), pressed for a continuation of the revolution. The ineffectiveness and growing unpopularity of the Provisional Government made it feasible for them to consider continuing it through force of arms.

The principal organizer of the October Revolution was the *Russian Social Democratic Workers' party (Bolshevik), whose chief ideologue was V. *Lenin. On the eve of the revolution L. *Trotsky, the head of the Military Revolutionary Committee of Petrograd, had almost all of the locally stationed troops and a large part of the workers under his control. On the night of 7 November he mounted an armed insurrection and arrested the members of the Provisional Government. The Second All-Russian Congress of Workers' and Soldiers' Deputies, in which the Bolsheviks had a majority, then announced that the soviets had taken power. They formed the first Soviet government, the Council of People's Commissars (Sovnarkom). It was headed by Lenin, and included Trotsky, A. Lunacharsky, A. Rykov, and J. Stalin. The Sovnarkom issued a series of decrees concerning peace, land, the establishment of workers' control, and the nationalization of all heavy industry. It also issued the Declaration on the Rights of the Peoples of Russia on 15 November 1917, in which the equality of all peoples was proclaimed, and in which the 'right of self-determination, even unto separation' was formally recognized.

By early 1918 the Bolsheviks had managed to seize power fairly easily in most cities and gubernias of Russia. They attempted to stage a similar coup in Ukraine but found considerably stronger opposition. The support for the Bolsheviks was much weaker there, where there were only 5,000 members of Bolshevik organizations (almost exclusively located in the cities). They consisted primarily of Russian or Russified working-class elements in the Donbas region, Katerynoslav, and Kharkiv. Moreover the *Central Rada managed to consolidate its hold on power and on support among the Ukrainian masses through its national and socialist policies.

In the early stages of the October Revolution there was also a third force in Ukraine, the Russian administration of the Provisional Government and the Army Staff of the Kievan Military District, which supported the Russian administration. Under threat of Russian right-wing elements in Kiev, the Central Rada, together with socialist groups of national minorities, established the National Committee for the Defense of the Revolution, in which the Bolsheviks initially also participated. The Bolsheviks left to form their own revolutionary committee after the Rada refused to recognize the Soviet government in Petrograd. The initial round of fighting between the three forces resulted in a victory for the Central Rada and the proclamation of the *Ukrainian National Republic (UNR) on 20 November 1917.

Although the Bolsheviks' attempts to seize power in Ukraine as a whole failed at first, they managed to gain control of Kharkiv and some Russified cities in the Donbas region through their workers' and soldiers' soviets. They hoped to achieve a formal proclamation of soviet power at an *All-Ukrainian Congress of Workers', Soldiers', and Peasants' Deputies, which they convened on 17–19 December in Kiev. The peasant-dominated congress failed to support the Bolsheviks (fewer than 100 of the more than 2,000 delegates were Bolshevik supporters), however, and even gave the Rada a vote of confidence. The pro-Bolshevik delegates reconvened a week later in Kharkiv at an All-Ukrainian Congress of Soviets that included a greater number of deputies from the Donets and Kryvyi Rih regions. On 25 December 1917 that congress proclaimed Soviet rule in Ukraine and elected a central executive committee of Ukraine and a government body, the *People's Secretariat. That body contended for legitimacy with the Central Rada and its General Secretariat.

The creation of a rival Soviet government in Ukraine made it possible for the subsequent armed intervention by Bolshevik troops from Russia during the *Ukrainian-Soviet War to be presented as a class rather than a national struggle. It also marked an important turning point in Ukraine's struggle for *independence, as the Bolsheviks demonstrated their willingness to force their state structure onto Ukraine in spite of the almost total absence of popular support.

BIBLIOGRAPHY
Vynnychenko, V. *Vidrodzhennia natsiï*, 3 vols (Vienna 1920)
Khrystiuk, P. *Zamitky i materiialy do istoriï ukraïns'koï revoliutsiï 1917–1920 rr.*, 4 vols (Vienna 1921–2; New York 1969)
Antonov-Ovseenko, V. *Zapiski o grazhdanskoi voine*, 4 vols (Moscow 1924–33)
Velikaia Oktiabr'skaia Sotsialisticheskaia revoliutsiia na Ukraine, 3 vols (Kiev 1957)
Mazlakh, S.; Shakhrai, V. *On the Current Situation in the Ukraine*, ed. P.J. Potichnyi (Ann Arbor 1970)
Musiienko, V. *Bil'shovyky Ukraïny v Zhovtneviï revoliutsiï* (Kiev 1976)
Borys, J. *The Sovietization of Ukraine, 1917–1923: The Communist Doctrine and Practice of National Self-Determination*, rev edn (Edmonton 1980)
                                                              V. Holubnychy

Octoechos (Ukrainian: *oktoikh* or *os'mohlasnyk*), from the Greek for 'eight' and 'voice.' A *liturgical book used in the Eastern Catholic and Orthodox churches. It contains the texts and notes sung by precentors or the faithful for matins, vespers, and the Divine Liturgy. Each week in the liturgical cycle has a specific tone or mode, used to sing the troparion, kondakion or canticle, and other melodies. In total there are eight tones that alternate throughout the year. The first Octoechos was translated from Greek into Church Slavonic by SS Cyril and Methodius, and the first printed Eastern Slavic Octoechos was published in Cracow in 1491.

Serhii Odainyk: *Hutsul Wedding* (1970)

Odainyk, Serhii [Odajnyk, Serhij], b 16 November 1949 in Kiev. Painter. Odainyk graduated from the Kiev State Art Institute in 1973. His seemingly realistic depictions often suggest an atmosphere of mystery (eg, *Sounds of Summer*, 1980). Odainyk participated in the Young Artists from Ukraine exhibition held in Moscow in 1985. There his figural compositions, such as *Inspiration* (1980) and *Memory* (1983), conveyed a restlessness and sense of impending drama.

Petro Odarchenko

Odessa's skyline

Odarchenko, Petro [Odarčenko], b 20 August 1903 in Rymarivka, Hadiache county, Poltava gubernia. Literary scholar and folklorist; full member of the Ukrainian Academy of Arts and Sciences since 1962 and the Shevchenko Scientific Society since 1975. He studied at the Nizhen Institute of People's Education (1923–6) and then taught there (1928–9), did graduate work at the Nizhen Research Department of the History of Culture and Language (1926–9), and collected materials for the VUAN Ethnographic Commission. In October 1929 he was imprisoned for six months as a counterrevolutionary and then exiled to Alma-Ata in Kazakhstan, and in December 1933 he was imprisoned for another six months and then exiled to Uralsk. From 1938 to 1941 he taught in Kursk, Russia. In 1943–4 he taught at the Orthodox Seminary in Warsaw. As a postwar émigré he taught at the Theological Academy of the Ukrainian Autocephalous Orthodox church in Munich and edited Ukrainian books and periodicals. He settled in the United States in 1950 and worked as a translator and editor for the Voice of America in Washington (1954–73). He has written numerous articles, encyclopedia entries, and reviews on Ukrainian literature (particularly on Lesia Ukrainka and T. Shevchenko), ethnography, language, and orthography, and publicistic articles about Soviet Ukraine. His biobibliography was published in 1973.

Odess. An ancient Greek settlement on the coast of the Black Sea somewhere between the Boh and the Dniester rivers. It is mentioned in the works of F. Arrian and, as Ordess, in Pliny and C. Ptolemy. Various sites have been proposed by modern scholars, among them the shore of Berezan Liman or Tylihul Estuary and Morske village in Berezanka raion, Mykolaiv oblast.

Odessa (Ukrainian: Odesa). VII-11. The fourth-largest city (1990 pop 1,106,000) in Ukraine and the capital of Odessa oblast. It is a major port on the Black Sea, a commercial, industrial, cultural, and administrative center, and a transportation terminal.

Geography. Odessa is situated on a large, virtually ice-free bay on the Black Sea, near the mouths of the Danube, Dniester, Boh, and Dnieper rivers, which link it with the interior of the country. Most of the city stands on a plateau built of Pleistocene strata of clay and chalk, which are covered with brown clays and loess. The plateau rises 50 m above the Black Sea Lowland and falls abruptly in the east to the sea. The edge of the plateau is pushed back by sea erosion, which causes massive landslides. The mining of local chalk for building purposes has produced a labyrinth of underground tunnels. The Odessa Plateau is divided by the Karantynna, Voienna, and Vodiana ravines, which connect the upper parts of the city with the low-lying port. The northern district of Odessa, known as Peresyp, is situated between the sea and the Kuialnyk and Khadzhybei estuaries, on a plain only a few meters above and in some places a meter below sea level. A sea wall has been built to protect that area from flooding.

Odessa lies in a zone with a steppe climate, which is moderated by the sea. The average annual temperature is 9.6°C, the average July temperature 22.1°C, and the average January temperature –2.8°C. The annual precipitation is 351 mm, most of which (236 mm) falls during the warm season. There are 285 sunny days per year. Odessa's port freezes over for only 15 days a year, but the thin ice does not impede shipping. Because of the absence of large sources of fresh water nearby, an aqueduct had to be built from the Dniester River to the city (1873).

History. In prehistoric and early historical times the site of present-day Odessa was settled by various peoples and tribes, among them the Cimmerians, Scythians, Sarmatians, and Greeks. During the time of Kievan Rus' the territory was inhabited by the Ulychians and Tivertsians. In the 14th century Kachybei (Haczbei) settlement and harbor arose. They were fortified at the beginning of the 15th century by the Lithuanian grand duke Vytautas. In 1480 the fortress was captured by the Turks and renamed Hadzhybei or Khadzhybei. In 1764 the Turks reinforced their position by building the Yeni-Dunya fortress nearby. In 1789, during the Russo-Turkish War, the Russian army and the Zaporozhian Cossacks led by A. Holovaty and Ž. Chepiha took the fortress and settlement, and in 1792 the territory was transferred to Russia under the terms of the Treaty of Iaşi. In 1792–4 Hadzhybei was rebuilt under the supervision of Field Marshal A. Suvorov as a fortress and naval port. In 1795 it was renamed Odessa under the mistaken assumption that the Greek colony of Odess had occupied the site from the 4th century BC to the 4th century AD. In 1795 the population of Odessa was 2,300.

Because of Odessa's geographical location and the rapid colonization of the steppes, Catherine II decided to develop the town into a large port and trade center. In 1797–1802 Odessa belonged to New Russia gubernia. In 1803 the town and its vicinity were turned into an autonomous administrative unit, the Odessa *gradonachalstvo*, which with the rest of Odessa county formed part of Kherson gubernia. At the same time Odessa was the seat of the governor-general of New Russia krai (1805–74). The governor-generals of the krai, Duke A.E. de Richelieu (1803–14), Count L.-A. Langeron (1816–23), and Prince M. Vorontsov (1823–45), served as the first chiefs of the *gradonachalstvo*. By 1815 Odessa was already handling more than half of all the freight passing through the Black Sea and Azov Sea ports. Most of it consisted of wheat and, to a lesser extent, wool exports. Odessa's status as a duty-free port from 1819 to 1849 encouraged trade, especially imports. From the 1830s to the 1850s Odessa became the largest wheat exporter on the Black Sea and in the Russian Empire, and by 1874, in all Europe. Its trade volume increased dramatically, from 5.7 million rubles (3.7 export, 2 import) in 1822 to 10.1 million (6.4 and 3.7 respectively) in 1832, 26.4 million (19.3 and 7.1) in 1852, and 38.9 million (28.3 and 10.6) in 1862. At the same time the city's population grew, from 3,700 in 1800 to 12,500 in 1808, 35,000 in 1815, 53,000 in 1829, 73,000 in 1837, and 116,000 in 1861. In the 1830s Odessa was already the largest city in Ukraine, and it retained that position until 1918. Its ethnic composition was diverse: in 1861 fewer than 50 percent of its inhabitants were Ukrainian or Russian, about 25 percent were Jewish, and over 25 percent were Bulgarian, Greek, French, Italian, German, Polish, and Moldavian.

Regarding Odessa as the 'southern window to Europe,' the Russian authorities paid a great deal of attention to its appearance. Odessa is one of the few planned cities in Ukraine. F. de Voland's plan of 1794 was the basis of the general plan for development adopted in 1803. The streets were laid out in a grid. Prymorskyi Boulevard, built up in 1826–9, was the administrative district. The great staircase (1837–41) descended from it to the port. The building ensembles were constructed in the classical style by architects such as A. Melnikov, T. de Tomon, F. Boffo, and E. Kozlov. The city's development was interrupted briefly by the Crimean War (1853–6). In 1854 Odessa was bombarded by the British and the French, who attempted to land their troops there.

The quickened pace of development in the 1860s and 1870s was spurred by the construction of railways connecting Odessa with the hinterland. The first lines extended to Balta (1865) and Yelysavethrad (1869). The Suez Canal, constructed in 1869, linked Odessa by sea with India, eastern Asia, and the Far East. Before the Trans-Siberian Railway was built, the Odessa–Vladivostok shipping line was the primary means of communication between European Russia and the far eastern reaches of the empire. The volume of trade in Odessa climbed steeply, to reach 129 million rubles in 1893 and peak at 174 million rubles in 1903. After St Petersburg, Odessa became the second most important port in the Russian Empire. It handled 20–25 percent of the empire's exports and 8–10 percent of its imports. As in the previous period, Odessa exported mostly grain, followed by sugar and other agricultural products. The main imports were colonial commodities, such as tea, and in the years before the First World War,

Odessa's port

petroleum products, coal, and cement. The port was reconstructed and modernized to handle the increased volume of freight. In the 20th century Odessa's volume of freight decreased, because of competition from other Black Sea ports, such as Mykolaiv, Kherson, and Novorossiisk, particularly in the export of wheat. Yet Odessa retained its position as the largest port of the Black Sea–Azov Sea Basin and the most important trade center in Ukraine.

An increasing proportion of the city's economy consisted of processing agricultural products and imported raw materials. The food industry developed first and accounted (by the end of the 19th century) for 66 percent of the city's industrial output (by value). Its main branches were flour milling (by 1869, 12 steam mills were producing 3.6 million rubles' worth of flour), tobacco processing (by 1869, 15 factories were producing 1.9 million rubles' worth of goods), and sugar refining (a large refinery was built in 1879). By the beginning of the 20th century sugar refining was the chief branch of the food industry, followed by tea packing and flour milling. The metallurgical and metalworking industries developed later and by the late 1890s accounted for 12 percent of the value of industrial output and 24 percent of the labor force. The more important plants in that sector were the Restel Pig Iron Foundry (est 1844), the Ghen Agricultural Machinery Factory (est 1854), the Russian Steam Navigation and Trading Company (est 1858; 800 workers), the Bellino-Fenderikh Machine Works (est 1875), the railway repair yards (est 1864; 1,000 workers), the New Russia Machine-Building

An arch of the former quarantine building in Odessa , with cranes of the port in the background

The Potemkin stairs in Odessa (1841)

Company (est 1884), and the Shpoliansky Metallurgical Plant (1885). In light industry the largest firms were the Novikov Cable Company, the jute factory (1,200 workers in 1908), and the Arps Cork Plant (1,000 workers in 1912). The other important industries in Odessa were the construction industry and the chemical industry (varnish, paint, and superphosphates). From 1859 to 1914 the number of factories in Odessa increased from 53 to 420, the number of factory workers, from 1,000 to 30,000, and the value of industrial output, from 4 million to 100 million rubles.

Odessa's economic development was accompanied by rapid population growth. In 1875 the city had 193,000 inhabitants, in 1897, 404,000, and in 1914, 669,000. Odessa was the fourth-largest city in the Russian Empire (after St Petersburg, Moscow, and Warsaw). The number of Jews rose sharply. Of the major cities in Ukraine Odessa had the smallest proportion of Ukrainian residents. In 1897 Ukrainians (by native language) accounted for only 5.7 percent of the city's population, compared to Russians at 50.8 percent, Jews (Yiddish speakers) at 32.5 percent, Poles at 4.5 percent, Germans at 2.6 percent, and Greeks at 1.3 percent.

The city grew rapidly in the second half of the 19th century. In the central district population density increased, and a number of imposing buildings were added – the opera house (burned down in 1873 and rebuilt in 1883–7), the stock exchange (1898), and the research library. A number of industrial and working-class suburbs arose – Peresyp in the north and Slobidka, Romanivka, and Moldavanka in the west. Along the coast south of the port some villas and cottages with much greenery sprang up. In 1873 an aqueduct carrying potable water from the Dniester River and in 1877 a sewage system (the first in the Russian Empire) were built. A horse-drawn tram (1880) and omnibus (1899) were not replaced by an electric streetcar system until 1910. Gas street lighting was introduced in 1866 and was supplemented with electric lighting in 1880. Almost all buildings were built of stone, and many (40 percent) were three or more stories high. The well-designed and maintained city center contrasted sharply with the slums of the industrial suburbs.

During the first few decades of its history Odessa be-

came the leading cultural center of Southern Ukraine. The dominant culture and language of the city were Russian, but in the second half of the 19th century a Ukrainian cultural movement gathered momentum. The city's sizable Jewish and German communities developed their own distinctive cultural forms, which spread widely through Ukraine.

The *Richelieu Lyceum was founded in 1817 and was reorganized, eventually, into *Odessa University (est 1865). In 1825 the first municipal museum of antiquities in Ukraine (later the *Odessa Archeological Museum) was founded, and in 1839 the *Odessa Society of History and Antiquities was organized. The Odessa Public Library was opened in 1829. The Odessa Society of Naturalists became active in 1869. In 1871 an astronomical observatory and in 1886 the first bacteriological laboratory in the Russian Empire were set up. The City Museum of Fine Arts (now the *Odessa Art Museum) was founded in 1899. The *Odessa Bibliographic Society, the first of its kind in Ukraine, was active in 1911–22. The more noted scholars who lived and worked in Odessa were M. Andrusiv, M. Hamaliia, V. Hryhorovych, O. Zahorovsky, N. Kondakov, A. Kovalevsky, M. Komarov, A. Kochubinsky, I. Lynnychenko, O. Markevych, I. Mechnikov, D. Ovsianiko-Kulikovsky, M. Pirogov, L. Symyrenko, A. Skalkovsky, V. Filatov, and V. Jagić.

Odessa was an important musical center. Its opera house was built in 1810 (see *Odessa Opera and Ballet Theater). A philharmonic society, formed in 1839, organized concerts. In 1897 a school was set up by the Russian Music Society; it was later reorganized as the *Odessa

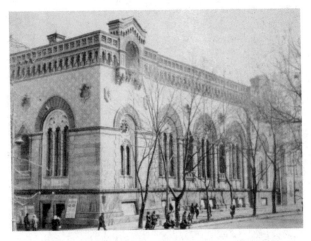

Building of the Odessa Oblast Philharmonic

Conservatory. In the late 19th and early 20th centuries the prominent musicians or composers P. Sokalsky, P. Nishchynsky, and M. Arkas lived and worked in Odessa. In 1803 the first amateur theatrical productions were staged. In 1827–43 the Ukrainian-Russian companies of I. Shtein, K. Zelinsky, and P. Rekanovsky, as well as Italian and French companies, performed there. In 1871 M. Kropyvnytsky made his theatrical debut in Odessa, and in 1883 his troupe established its base there. M. Starytsky's and P. Saksahansky's troupes also visited Odessa.

Odessa painters contributed to the development of painting in Ukraine. The Odessa Society of the Advancement of the Fine Arts set up a drawing school in 1865, which was converted in 1885 into a secondary school and in 1899 into an art school under the St Petersburg Academy of Arts. V. Pavlovsky, K. Kostandi, and G. Ladyzhensky were active in the society and the school. The *Society of South Russian Artists, which included P. Nilus and B. Edvards, was active in 1890–1922.

Odessa developed into an important publishing center. In 1828–60 about 700 books were published there, 530 of them in Russian and only one, *Marusia: Kazka* (Marusia: A Story, 1853), in Ukrainian. In 1864 the Russian-language newspaper *Odesskii vestnik* (1827–93) became the first daily to come out in Ukraine. Ukrainian publishing developed late in the 19th century. In 1883–7 some 44 Ukrainian titles were published in Odessa, including the almanac *Nyva* (1885). Some almanacs, such as *Z-nad khmar i dolyn* (edited by M. Vorony, 1903) and *Bahattia* (edited by I. *Lypa, 1905), came out before the war. The poetry anthology *Vinok T. Shevchenkovi* (A Wreath for T. Shevchenko) appeared in 1912. The *Literaturno-naukovyi vistnyk* in Kiev, which was banned by the Russian authorities, was replaced by the journal *Osnova* in Odessa (1915).

The development of publishing was closely connected with the development of Ukrainian cultural and educational life. The Odessa Hromada sprang up in the late 1860s and maintained strong links with the Hromada of Kiev and M. Drahomanov's circle in Geneva (see *Hromadas). Komarov headed the local Prosvita society (est 1906), whose executive council included Lypa, S. Shelukhyn, A. Nikovsky, and M. Slabchenko. It maintained a library and bookstore and published books and two newspapers, *Narodna sprava* and *Visti*. Thanks to its initiative the first

Ukrainian-language lectures at Odessa University were delivered, by O. Hrushevsky in Ukrainian history. After the Prosvita society was disbanded by the Russian authorities in 1910, its activities were continued by the Ukrainian Club, until 1914.

In the 1870s Odessa was one of the centers of the populist movement. In 1905 the crew of the battleship *Potemkin* staged a mutiny, and workers' demonstrations in Odessa were ruthlessly suppressed.

After the February Revolution of 1917 the Ukrainian Revolutionary Committee took control of Odessa, and Lypa was appointed the city's commissar. In November 1917 the Ukrainian Haidamaka Battalion clashed with the Bolsheviks. In January 1918 Bolshevized units from the Rumanian front took Odessa and were joined by M. Muravev's detachments. In March Odessa was occupied by the Germans and Austrians, who were allies of the UNR. The supreme command of the Austrian army made its headquarters in the city. In 1918, three Ukrainian dailies were published there, *Vil'ne slovo*, *Vistnyk Odesy*, and *Moloda Ukraïna*. In December 1918 Odessa came under the UNR Directory's control, and the municipal government was headed by I. Lutsenko. By year's end the city had been captured by British, French, and Greek expeditionary forces, supported by local Whites. The Russians took over the municipal administration. In April 1919 the allies were expelled by N. Hryhoriiv, who had gone over from the Directory to the Bolsheviks. From August 1919 to February 1920 Odessa was held by A. Denikin, except for a brief interval at the end of 1919 and the beginning of 1920, when the rear guard of the Ukrainian Galician Army was stationed in the city. Having established their power in Odessa by February 1920, the Bolsheviks turned it into a gubernia capital. Odessa suffered heavier losses in 1917–20 than any other city in Ukraine. All foreign trade was suspended because of the war. The suburbs were scarred by the fighting, and many factories were completely destroyed. Many of the residents fled from the city, and some of them emigrated in order to escape from the Bolsheviks. By 1920 the city's population was only 428,000. The famine of 1921–2 caused further loss of life: in 1923 the population stood at 324,000, or half of the prewar figure.

Under the Soviet regime the structure of Odessa's economy changed: trade, particularly foreign trade, lost its importance, and metalworking and machine building assumed priority. Over 30 new factories were built, and many old ones were reconstructed. By 1940 Odessa's industrial output was eight times that of 1913. As the economy improved, the city's population rose: by 1926 it had reached 420,900. Only 17.4 percent of the population were Ukrainians. The majority were Russians (38.7 percent) or Jews (36.5 percent). Significant minorities of Poles (2.4 percent) and Germans (1.3 percent) remained in the city.

In the 1920s Odessa developed into a center of Ukrainian academic and cultural life. Apart from the university, which was reorganized into an institute of people's education, and other higher schools, there were a number of medical, technical, and agricultural research institutes, 13 research chairs, 3 observatories (geodesic, seismic, and astronomical), a branch of the Ukrainian Meteorological Service, and a hydrometeorological bureau. The city's largest research library, the Odessa Scientific Library, was formed out of the university library, the public library, and several other libraries. In 1932 it held 2.3 million volumes. Some new museums were added to the prerevolutionary ones – the *Odessa Museum of Western and Oriental Art (1920), the Museum of Military History (1921), the All-Ukrainian Import-Export Museum (1927), and the Odessa Naval Museum (1928). New scientific associations, such as the *Odessa Scientific Society of the All-Ukrainian Academy of Sciences (1926) and the *Odessa Regional Studies Commission (1923–31), supplemented the established ones. M. Slabchenko headed a center of Ukrainian history, which attracted economists and historians, such as B. Varneke, I. Brover, M. Rubinshtein, T. Slabchenko, O. Pohrebynsky, S. Kovbasiuk, Ye. Zahorovsky, O. Riabinin-Skliarevsky, F. Petrun, and S. Borovy. The literary scholars K. Koperzhynsky, A. Muzychka, V. Lazursky, and V. Herasymenko, the linguists A. Tomson, P. Buzuk, and M. Semeniv (Markevych), and the archeologists S. Dlozhevsky and M. Boltenko worked in Odessa. During the period of Ukrainization Odessa's schools and research institutions were Ukrainized.

A naval school in Odessa

In the 1920s Odessa also became a vibrant artistic center. The *Odessa Artistic Film Studio (est 1919) made Odessa the leading filmmaking center in Ukraine. In 1920 the Physico-Technical Institute of the Film Industry was founded, under the directorship of E. Kurylov. The opera theater was turned into the Ukrainian Opera Theater in 1926 and, eventually, into the Odessa Opera and Ballet Theater. The three other chief theaters were the Odessa Ukrainian Music and Drama Theater (est 1925), the Odessa Russian Drama Theater (est 1927), and the Odessa Young Spectator's Theater (est 1930).

As the city became Ukrainized, its Ukrainian press and book publishing expanded. One of the largest newspapers in the USSR, *Odesskie izvestiia* (*Odesskii listok* before the revolution), was Ukrainized and renamed *Chornomors'ka komuna*. The Ukrainian-language newspaper for the rural population, *Chervonyi step*, the Ukrainized *Moloda gvardiia*, and the literary monthly *Metalevi dni* were published in Odessa. A number of factory bulletins with a sizable circulation were published in Ukrainian. The only remaining Russian newspaper was *Vechernie izvestiia*. The Ukrainian press played an important role in the Ukrainization of Odessa. The circulation of *Chornomors'ka komuna* reached 120,000 in 1931, thereby surpassing that of its Russian predecessor. The Odessa branch of the State Publishing House of Ukraine issued many titles.

After the show trial of the *Union for the Liberation of Ukraine in 1930, the Bolshevik authorities organized a terror campaign against the Ukrainian intelligentsia and an assault on Ukrainian culture. In the early 1930s the activities of the Ukrainian research center in Odessa ceased.

During the Second World War Odessa was besieged by German and Rumanian forces, from August to mid-October 1941. Upon being captured it was made the capital of *Transnistria and administered by the Rumanians. In April 1944 it was recaptured by the Soviet army. During the war Odessa suffered a heavy loss of life and property. Much of the port, industrial plant, and housing (over 1 million of 4 million sq m of living area) was destroyed. By 1948 most of the industrial and port facilities had been rebuilt, and later, new ones were added. The 1939 population figure of 604,000 was reached only in 1956. By 1967 it had increased to 776,000, and by 1979, to 1,115,000. After the war the national composition of the city's population shifted significantly in favor of Ukrainians, as the inhabitants of the surrounding rural regions flooded into Odessa in search of a better life. In 1959, 273,000 of the city residents were Ukrainian (41 percent), 254,000, Russian (38 percent), and 107,000, Jewish (16 percent). Although the Jews had suffered a disproportionate loss during the war, Odessa's Jewish community remains the largest in Ukraine.

Economy. During the Soviet period Odessa became an important industrial center. The leading industries are metalworking and machine building; they account for over one-third of the industrial output. The largest enterprises in those industries are the *Odessa Plow and Harrow Manufacturing Consortium, the *Odessa Radial-boring Lathe Plant, the *Odessa Presmash Manufacturing Consortium, the *Odessa Heavy-Crane Plant, the *Odessa Heavy-Scales Plant, the Odessa Agricultural-Machine-Building Plant, a ship repair yeard, an autocrane assembly plant, a canning equipment plant, and a refrigerator plant. The KINAP factory specializes in building filming equipment for the film industry. The food industry accounts for about a quarter of the industrial output. Its main products are flour, dairy products, sugar, meat, confectionery, beer, wine, liquor, tobacco products, and packaged tea. The chemical industry produces superphosphates, paints and lacquers, petroleum products, plastics, and pharmaceuticals. Some large enterprises of light industry specialize in jute, clothing, footwear, leather goods, cork, and linoleum.

Odessa is an important junction for various modes of transportation. It is the largest port in Ukraine and in the Black Sea–Azov Sea Basin. It (together with Illichivske)

Odessa Sea Terminal

handles almost half of the freight moving through Ukrainian ports and a quarter of that handled by ports of the Black Sea–Azov Sea Basin. In the 1960s it handled 15 million t of freight annually. Of that, 74 percent was foreign trade (64 percent exports, 10 percent imports). The chief exports are petroleum and petroleum products, followed by metals, machines, grain, and sugar. Imports include petroleum (from Batumi and Tuapse), metals (from Kerch and Mariiupil), building materials (from Novorossiisk), and agricultural products. Most of the exports from Odessa were destined for Cuba, Italy, Bulgaria, and Greece. Odessa also served as a base for the Antarctic whaling fleet. Despite some modernizations and expansion Odessa's port is technologically outdated and overused. To relieve Odessa, a new port was built at *Illichivske, 20 km to the southwest, in 1957–8.

Odessa is an important health resort center. The first resorts were opened there in the 1820s. In 1961 there were 12 resorts, 41 sanatoriums, 17 rest homes, and 3 health pensions. The resorts dot the coast for 70 km south from Fontanka. They include the Khadzhybei, Kuialnyk, and Malodolynske mud-bathing resorts, Arkadiia, Velykyi Fontan, Chornomorka, and Luzanivka.

Odessa continues to be one of the leading cultural and scientific centers in Ukraine. It is the home of the Southern Scientific Center of the Academy of Sciences of Ukraine. Some of the state's institutes, such as the Ukrainian Scientific Research Institute of Viticulture and Wine-Making, or branches are located in Odessa. The Odessa Scientific Research Institute of Health Resorts was founded in 1982. There are 14 higher educational institutions in the city, including the university, the polytechnical institute, the conservatory, the Medical Institute, the Institute of Naval Engineers, the Technological Institute of the Food Industry, the Hydrometeorological Institute, the Pedagogical Institute, and the Civil-Engineering Institute. There are also 25 secondary schools and 21 vocational schools in the city. Cultural life is organized around six major theaters, a film studio, a philharmonic orchestra, a circus, two art museums, and an archeological and regional museum. The almanac *Literaturna Odesa* was published at irregular intervals in 1948–58. Three oblast newspapers were published in the city, including *Chornomors'ka komuna*, which appeared in Russian and Ukrainian. The *Maiak publish-

ing house has been publishing Ukrainian and Russian books since 1945.

Layout and appearance. Odessa can be divided into four historical districts: the central core, the port, the coastal area, and the industrial area.

The oldest and most beautiful part of the city is elevated on a plateau, which drops steeply to the port in the east and to Peresyp district in the north. It is bounded in the south and southwest by Staro-Portofrankivska Street and the main railway station. The larger, eastern part of the core is laid out on a grid. The streets of the smaller, western part meet the former Soviet Army Street at a sharp angle. The wide avenues of the central district are paved with granite slabs and lined with acacia trees. The buildings are mostly two-story structures built of limestone. The more important scientific and cultural institutions, the municipal and oblast government offices, and the finest architectural monuments are found in the area. Prymorskyi Boulevard with the semicircular Karl Marx Square and the monumental staircase known as the Potemkin Stairs (built by Boffo, 1837–41) serves as a grand entrance to the city. At the top of the steps stand the monument to Richelieu by I. Martos (1828) and the Pioneers' Palace (formerly Prince M. Vorontsov's Palace, designed by Boffo, 1824–9). The boulevard is also graced by the Old Stock Exchange (1834, later the Municipal Duma and until 1991 the Oblast Committee of the CPU), the Seamen's Palace of Culture (formerly Naryshkina's Palace, built by

Zhukovsky Street in Odessa

Boffo, 1830), and the Literary Museum (former residence of Count Gagarin, built by L. Otton, 1842). All those buildings are in the classical style. Some of them were damaged in the Second World War and restored in 1946–9. Just off the boulevard stands the Odessa Opera and Ballet Theater, which was designed in the Viennese neo-Renaissance style by F. Fellner and H. Helmer (1883–7, restored 1926 and 1965–6). The main commercial artery is Schmidt prospekt (Oleksander prospekt), which cuts through Kirov Square (the Old Bazaar) and Martynovskyi Square (the Greek Bazaar). The other main streets are Derybasivska, Pushkin, and (formerly) Soviet Army. The more important architectural monuments are the Odessa Art Museum (formerly Count S. Potocki's Palace, 1805–10), the old hospital (built by de Tomon, 1806–8) on Pasteur Street, the Philharmonic Hall (formerly the New Stock Exchange, designed by A. Bernardazzi and G. Lonsky, 1899), the Odessa Scientific Library (designed by F. Nestrukh, 1905–7), the Odessa Archeological Museum (formerly the Municipal Public Library, built by F. Gonsiorovsky, 1882), the Odessa Museum of Western and Oriental Art (formerly Abaza's residence built by Otton, 1856), the university building (designed by M. Tolvynsky, restored 1908), and the main railway station (built in the late 19th century by V. Shreter, destroyed in 1944, and rebuilt in 1952 by L. Chuprin).

Monument to Taras Shevchenko in Odessa

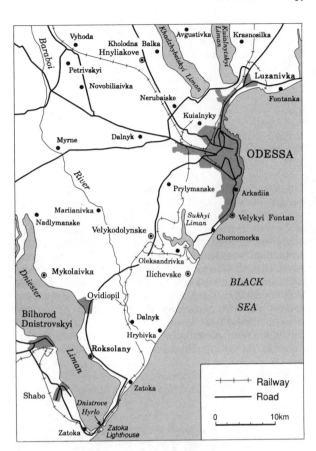

ODESSA AND ENVIRONS

To the northeast lies the port district, which widens in the north into the Peresyp district. That 8-kilometer strip contains a dense network of railway and tram lines, repair yards, docks, factories, and warehouses.

North of Peresyp lie flat sandy beaches and, beyond them, Lyzanivka suburb, with the Ukrainskyi Artek children's resort. The Kuialnyk and Khadzhybei resorts are further on. The plateau to the south and southwest of the port is covered with gardens and parks. Shevchenko Park (formerly Alexander Park) contains the poet's monument, a sports stadium, an open-air theater, and the observatory. Along Proletarskyi Boulevard stand sanatoriums, rest homes, hospitals, educational institutions, and the botanical gardens. On the coast south of the city lie the famous resorts of Malyi Fontan, Velykyi Fontan, Arkadiia, and Chornomorka.

The industrial district of Odessa lies west of the center along the railway line. It consists of the former workers' suburbs of Slobidka, Romanivka, Moldavanka, Buhaivka, Daleki Mlyny, Blyzki Mlyny, and Vorontsivka, which were incorporated into Odessa in the postwar period. In the 1930s and particularly after 1944 the industrial district expanded to the southwest (Novoarkadiiskyi and Velykyi Fontan raions) and to the north (Zhevakhova Hora).

Odessa, containing (1964) 734 ha of greenery, is one of the greenest cities in Ukraine.

BIBLIOGRAPHY
Skal'kovskii, A. Pervoe tridtsatiletie istorii goroda Odessy, 1793–1823 (Odessa 1837)

– *Istoricheskii-statisticheskii opyt o torgovykh i promyshlennykh silakh Odessy* (Odessa 1839)
Smol'ianinov, K. *Istoriia Odessy* (Odessa 1853)
Nadler, V. *K izucheniiu istorii goroda Odessy* (Odessa 1893)
Odessa, 1794–1894: K stoletiiu goroda (Odessa 1895)
Ribas, A. *Staraia Odessa* (Odessa 1913)
Stara Odesa: Arkhitektura Prychornomoria (Odessa 1927)
Kotkov, I.; Ushakov, A. *Arkhitektura Odessy* (Odessa 1967)
Timofeenko, V. *Odessa: Arkhitekturno-istoricheskii ocherk* (Kiev 1983)
Herlihy, P. *Odessa: A History, 1794–1914* (Cambridge, Mass 1986)

B. Kravtsiv, V. Kubijovyč

Odessa Agricultural Institute (Odeskyi silskohospodarskyi instytut). An institution of higher learning, until 1992 under the jurisdiction of the Ministry of Agriculture of the USSR. It was founded in 1918 on the basis of the natural sciences departments of Odessa University and the agricultural courses offered by the Agricultural Society of South Russia. The institute has six departments – agronomy, orcharding and viticulture, veterinary medicine, bioengineering, economics, and economic cybernetics – and an extension and correspondence school. It also has two experimental farms, encompassing a total of 5,780 ha, and a library of 300,000 volumes. In 1985–6 the student enrollment was 5,200. The institute publishes scholarly works.

Odessa Archeological Museum

Odessa Archeological Museum (Odeskyi arkheolohichnyi muzei). A major archeological museum administered by the ANU. Founded in 1825 by I. *Stempkovsky as the Odessa Municipal Museum of Antiquities, the museum was run from 1858 to 1922 by the *Odessa Society of History and Antiquities. In 1959 the *Odessa Archeological Society was formed as an extension body and in 1971 the museum came under the jurisdiction of the ANU. The museum's collection numbers more than 150,000 items, including findings from regional archeological expeditions, a large coin inventory, Egyptian, Greek, and Roman artifacts, and the private collections of D. Kniazhevich and N. Murzakevich. The approx 14,000 items on public display include Trypilian and late Bronze Age artifacts, sculptures from Black Sea Hellenic city-states, findings from Sarmatian-Scythian kurhans, and coins from a wide variety of times and places. The museum sponsors annual field expeditions and since 1957 has published occasional collections of essays about regional archeological activity.

Odessa Archeological Society (Odeske arkheolohichne tovarystvo). A scholarly organization formed in 1959 as an extension of the *Odessa Archeological Museum. With a membership of approx 500 archeologists and regional studies specialists from Odessa, Kiev, St Petersburg, Symferopil, and Kishinev, the society was formed to help coordinate and popularize archeological work in the northern Black Sea region. To this end it has sponsored conferences, published proceedings and serials, and undertaken annual archeological expeditions.

Odessa Art Museum

Odessa Art Museum (Odeskyi khudozhnii muzei). A museum in Odessa, founded as the City Museum of Fine Arts in 1899 by teachers of the Odessa Drawing School and the *Society of South Russian Artists, among them A. Pavlovsky, K. Kostandi, A. Popov, P. Nilus, B. Edvards, and G. Ladyzhensky. Under Soviet rule it was called the People's Art Museum (until 1945), the Odessa Oblast Picture Gallery (1945–50), and the Odessa Picture Gallery (1950–65). In 1918–19 its collection was enriched with the acquisition of several private collections, including O. Rusov's and M. Braikevych's. The museum has departments of medieval art, prerevolutionary art (18th–20th centuries), Soviet art, and decorative and applied art. It contains works by Ukrainian and Russian prerevolutionary painters, such as H. Levytsky, D. Levytsky, V. Borovykovsky, I. Aivazovsky, I. Kramskoi, I. Repin, N. Ge, V. Makovsky, V. Tropinin, M. Yaroshenko, H. Svitlytsky, M. Vrubel, K. Kryzhytsky, S. Vasylkivsky, O. Murashko, I. Trush, and M. Pymonenko; the works of the Odessa painters K. Kostandi, G. Ladyzhensky, and P. Nilus and the Odessa sculptor B. Edvards; and works of So-iet painters, such as Z. Serebriakova, V. Kasiian, Y. okshai, M. Zhuk, M. Bozhii, A. Deineka, O. Shovkunen-o, A. Kotska, M. Derehus, O. Kulchytska, and V. Ly-rynenko. Albums of works at the museum were ublished in 1980 and 1986.

Odessa Art School (Odeske khudozhnie uchylyshche n. M.B. Hrekova). An art school, until 1992 under the ju-isdiction of the Ministry of Culture of the Ukrainian SSR. t was founded in 1865 as the Drawing School of the Odes-a Society for the Advancement of the Fine Arts. In 1885 it ecame an official secondary school, and in 1899 an art chool under the supervision of the St Petersburg Acade-ny of Arts. Under Soviet rule it became a postsecondary chool and then a state artistic handicrafts workshop, an cademy of arts (1921), a polytechnic (1922–8), and an art nstitute (1928–34) before reverting to its present name. Its rt-education, sculpture, and ceramics departments pre-are professional artists and art instructors for secondary chools.

Odessa Artistic Film Studio (Odeska kinostudiia khu-lozhnikh filmiv). Established in 1919 on the basis of everal private film ateliers. It became the Odessa Depart-nent of the All-Ukrainian Film Committee (1920), the Odessa Film Factory of the All-Ukrainian Photo-Cinema Administration (1922), and the Odessa Film Factory Jkrainfilm (1929) and has had its current name since 1938. t was evacuated to Central Asia in 1941 and then reap-peared as the Black Sea Film Factory (actually a branch of Mosfilm), its name until 1955. In the 1920s it was the key enter of development of Ukrainian cinema art and pro-luced artistic films, newsreels, cinema journals, docu-nentaries of historical events, and screen versions of iterary works. In the 1930s its importance declined as the Ukrainian content was forcibly restricted, and since 1945 t has produced only a few Ukrainian films, such as *Ba-riani berehy* (The Scarlet Shores, 1979). The Odessa Artis-cic Film Studio trained such notable Ukrainian film lirectors as O. Dovzhenko, H. Stabovyi, A. Kordium, and I. Kavaleridze and the cameramen D. Demutsky and Yo. Rona.

Odessa Astronomical Observatory (Odeska astro-nomichna observatoriia). A research institution of Odessa University, established in 1871. It has two observation sta-tions, in Maiaky and Kryzhanivka, which are equipped with five reflectors, five refractors, a catadioptrical tele-scope, a Schmidt camera, two meteor patrols, and a seven-chamber astrograph. In 1981 the decameter radiotelescope URAN-4 was put into operation at Maiaky. The Odessa Ob-servatory deals mainly with the determination of the ce-lestial co-ordinates of stars and meteors, research into the nature of mutating stars and meteors, and the develop-ment of new telescoping and electronic systems. Scientists such as O. *Kononovych, A. *Orlov, and V. *Tsesevych have been associated with the observatory.

Odessa Bibliographic Society (Odeske bibliohra-fichne tovarystvo; Russian: Odesskoe bibliograficheskoe obshchestvo). A scholarly society established at Odessa University in 1911 to organize bibliographic research in Ukraine, especially in the field of regional studies. It held lectures and published the monthly (1911–15) and bi-

monthly (1916) journal *Izvestiia Odesskogo bibliogra-ficheskogo obshchestva*, which contained bibliographies, book reviews, and reports on the society. The society ceased to exist in 1922. M. *Komarov was a leading mem-ber.

Odessa Biostymuliator Chemical and Pharmaceu-tical Manufacturing Consortium (Odeske vyrob-nyche khimiko-farmatsevtychne obiednannia 'Biosty-muliator'). A manufacturing consortium created in 1977 by a number of pharmaceutical enterprises. Its key mem-bers are a chemical and pharmaceutical factory founded in 1921 and a vitamin factory founded in 1944. It produces 52 different medicinal products, including vitamins and stimulants.

Odessa Civil-Engineering Institute (Odeskyi inzhe-nerno-budivelnyi instytut). An institution of higher learn-ing, until 1992 under the jurisdiction of the Ministry of Higher and Specialized Secondary Education of the Ukrainian SSR. It was formed in 1930 from the civil engi-neering department of the Odessa Industrial Institute and the architecture department of the Odessa Art Institute. In 1951–7 it was known as the Odessa Institute of Hydraulic Engineering. The institute has seven departments – archi-tecture, industrial and civil engineering construction, in-dustrial and civil engineering design, energetics of engineering, construction technology, sanitation engi-neering, and general technology – and a graduate section. It also has a correspondence department, a branch in Mykolaiv, and a library of over 500,000 volumes. In 1985–6 the student enrollment was 7,000.

Odessa Clothing Manufacturing Consortium (Odeske vyrobnyche shveine obiednannia im. V.V. Vorovskoho). A consortium established in 1965 by the Odessa, Balta, Bolhrad, and Izmail clothing factories. It produces primarily overwear, children's clothing, and bedding. In 1969 it produced approx 1 million coats, 741,000 suits, 1.7 million dresses, 1.3 million pairs of trou-sers, 2.5 million shirts and blouses, and 2.3 million hats. In 1970 the consortium employed 5,700 workers.

Odessa Conservatory (Odeska derzhavna konserva-toriia im. A.V. Nezhdanovoi). A school of advanced music education, until 1992 under the jurisdiction of the Minis-try of Culture of the Ukrainian SSR. Founded in 1913 on the basis of the Russian Music Society's school (est 1897) in Odessa, it was divided in 1923 into the Odessa Institute of Music and the Odessa Music Tekhnikum. In 1928 the schools were combined as the Beethoven Music and Dra-ma Institute, and in 1934 the Odessa Conservatory was re-established in its original form. Today the school has five faculties: piano performance, orchestral technique, vocal and choral training, opera, and musicology. Its graduates include the composer K. Dankevych, the singers M. Hry-shko, O. Kryvchenia, H. Oliinychenko, B. Rudenko, and Ye. Chavdar, the violinist D. Oistrakh, and the pianist E. Gilels. Its notable teachers include K. Dankevych, P. Movchaniuk, J. Perlman, K. Pihrov, J. Přibik, P. Stoliarsky, M. Vilinsky, and V. Zolotarev.

Odessa Derzhdrama. See Odessa Ukrainian Music and Drama Theater.

Odessa Electrotechnical Institute of Communications (Odeskyi elektrotekhnichnyi instytut zviazku im. O.S. Popova). An institution of higher learning, until 1992 under the jurisdiction of the Ministry of Communications of the USSR. Founded in 1930, it has departments of automated electronic communications, multichannel electronic communications, and radio communications and broadcasting, and evening and correspondence programs. The institute has a branch in Kiev and had a consulting office in Kishinev (Chişinau), Moldova. The library contains 748,000 volumes. In 1985–6 the student enrollment was over 8,000.

Odessa Factory of Industrial Textiles (Odeska fabryka tekhnichnykh tkanyn). A factory of the jute-hemp industry, built in 1887 and originally called the Odessa Jute Factory. Before 1917 it produced linen from Indian jute. In the interwar period hemp replaced jute as the factory's main raw material. The Odessa factory accounted for some 27 percent of all the production of the *jute-hemp industry in the USSR. It produces sacks for various industries and is the sole manufacturer of textiles used in linoleum production.

Odessa gubernia. See Kherson gubernia.

Odessa Heavy-Crane Plant (Odeskyi zavod vazhkoho kranobuduvannia im. Sichnevoho povstannia). A plant built in 1863 as a locomotive- and coach-repair shop. In 1930 it was converted to building steam-driven and self-propelled motorized cranes. In 1960 it began to specialize in the production of heavy (25–100-t) pneumatic cranes. Since 1975 the enterprise has been the key member of the Odessa Heavy–Crane-Building Consortium.

Odessa Heavy-Scales Plant (Odeskyi zavod vazhkoho vahobuduvannia im. P.I. Starostina). An enterprise of the heavy-machine-building industry. The factory was set up in 1882 to build wagon, cart, baggage, and other scales. In the interwar period it produced scales for weighing molds used in the metallurgical industry. In 1956 it was converted to the production of heavy scales used in the metallurgical, chemical, mining, and other industries. Its scales are also used to weigh vehicles, trains, and cranes.

Odessa Historical-Philological Society (Russian: Istoriko-filologicheskoe obshchestvo pri Novorossiiskom universitete). An influential research society founded in 1889 at Odessa University to study the history of the region. Among its members were the historians O. Kyrpichnikov, O. Kochubynsky, and F. Uspensky. The society published the serial *Letopis' Istoriko-filologicheskogo obshchestva pri Novorossiiskom universitete* (25 vols, 1890–1916). It ceased activity in 1917.

Odessa Hydrometeorological Institute (Odeskyi hidrometeorolohichnyi instytut). An institution of higher learning, until 1992 under the jurisdiction of the Ministry of Higher and Specialized Secondary Education of the Ukrainian SSR. Founded in Kharkiv in 1932, in 1941 it was evacuated to Ashkhabad, Turkmenistan, and in 1944 relocated to Odessa. It trains engineer-meteorologists, hydrologists, oceanographers, and agrometeorologists. The institute has departments of meteorology, hydrology, and agrometeorology, and a correspondence section. The student enrollment in 1980–1 was 2,250. Research at the institute focuses on problems in hydrometeorology, especially ecological issues, the exploitation of natural resources, and meteorology.

Odessa Institute of Naval Engineers (Odeskyi instytut inzheneriv morskoho flotu). An institution of higher learning, until 1992 under the jurisdiction of the Ministry of the Maritime Fleet of the USSR. Founded in 1930 on the basis of the shipbuilding department of the Odessa Polytechnical Institute as the Odessa Institute of Water Transportation Engineers, it received its present name in 1945. It has departments of shipping management, ship mechanics, economics, shipbuilding, port mechanization, and hydrological engineering, an evening study and correspondence section, and a program for the upgrading of qualifications of workers of the merchant marine. The institute had branches in Baku and Mariiupil. In 1985–6 the student enrollment was 6,500.

Odessa Institute of the National Economy (Odeskyi instytut narodnoho hospodarstva). An institution of higher education, under the jurisdiction of the Ukrainian Ministry of Higher and Secondary Specialized Education. It was established in 1921 on the basis of the economics department of Odessa University. It was reorganized in 1931 into the Odessa Credit and Economics Institute and in 1966 into its present form. The institute is divided into faculties of economic planning, finance, credit, labor economics, and accounting. It offers preparatory, evening, and correspondence courses, upgrading programs for technical workers, and graduate courses. It also maintains a computing center. In 1980 a special upgrading faculty for workers of the Ukrainian Ministry of Finance was established. In 1985–6 the enrollment was almost 10,000.

Odessa Jute Factory. See Odessa Factory of Industrial Textiles.

Odessa Linoleum Plant (Odeskyi linoleumovyi zavod). A factory founded in Odessa in 1913 to produce cork for bottling. The by-products from the cork were used for manufacturing linoleum. In the interwar period the factory produced various types of linoleum. It was evacuated at the outset of the Second World War and rebuilt in 1944–53. It uses cork to produce various types of linoleum and other floor coverings, bottle corks, flotation devices, packaging materials, and other products.

Odessa Medical Institute (Odeskyi medychnyi instytut im. M. Pyrohova). Founded in 1900 as the medical department of Odessa University, it was restructured as an independent institute under the Ukrainian SSR Ministry of Health in 1920. Scientists who have worked at the institute include I. *Mechnikov (professor of zoology and comparative anatomy), V. *Filatov (director of the department for research on eye disease), and I. Sechenov (director of the department of physiology). There are four faculties at the institute, internal clinical medicine, pediatrics, stomatology, and postgraduate studies, as well as a library with 700,000 vols (1984). In the 1980s there were 5,000 students enrolled annually in studies and internships; by 1981 the institute had graduated over 27,000 physicians.

Odessa Museum of Western and Oriental Art (Odeskyi muzei zakhidnoho ta skhidnoho mystetstva). A museum founded in Odessa in 1920 on the basis of the naonalized collections of the City Museum of Fine Arts, Odessa University, and private collectors. It was known as the Odessa Gallery of Old European Painting until 1945. It has departments of ancient art (est 1947; Greek and Roman sculpture, pottery, and glass), Western European art (works by L. van Leyden, F. Hals, Fra Filippo Lippi, F. Bartolomeo, P. Veronese, Tintoretto, M. da Caravaggio, Canaletto, G. Reni, B. Strozzi, F. Guardi, H. Holbein, P. Bruegel the Elder, P. Rubens, D. Teniers, and N. Poussin), Oriental art (est 1951; Chinese, Japanese, Persian, Tibetan, and Indian artists), and applied art (porcelain, glass, tapestries). Altogether its collection contains about 6,000 objects, many of them transferred to it from the Hermitage in Leningrad, the Museum of Oriental Cultures and the Pushkin Museum in Moscow, and the Kiev Museum of Russian Art. An album about the museum, with 150 plates, was published in English in Leningrad in 1985.

Odessa Musical Comedy Theater (Odeskyi teatr muzychnoi komedii). A theater established in Lviv in 1947 and located in Odessa since 1954. Its repertoire consists of the works of Soviet Ukrainian and Russian composers, including O. Riabov's *Vesillia v Malynivtsi* (The Wedding in Malynivka) and O. Sandler's *Na svitanku* (At Daybreak), as well as those of composers of other former Soviet republics, and Russian and classical operettas. In 1981 its artistic director was M. Vodianoi, its conductors, I. Kilberg and O. Vinnytsky, and its set designer, M. Ivnytsky.

Odessa oblast. An administrative-territorial unit (1990 pop 2,638,200) in southwestern Ukraine, formed on 27 February 1932. It covers an area of 33,300 sq km and is divided into 26 raions, 393 rural councils, 17 cities, and 33 towns (smt). Its capital is *Odessa.

Physical geography. Most of the oblast lies in the Black Sea Lowland along the north coast of the Black Sea. Its shoreline is marked by large estuaries, such as the Dniester, the Khadzhybei, the Kuialnyk, and the Tylihul. Spurs of the Podolian Upland, dissected by ravines and gorges, reach its northwestern corner, and the Dnieper Upland forms its northeastern part. Most of the oblast's landscape is a rolling plain sloping toward the Black Sea. The soils are mostly chernozems. The natural vegetation is mainly mixed-grass-fescue steppe. Small oak, beech, linden, and ash forests are found in river valleys and ravines, and cover an area of 204,000 ha. Shelterbelts are common. Although it lacks mineral resources, Odessa oblast is rich in granite, gneiss, limestone, and sand, which are used for building materials.

The major rivers in the oblast are the Danube (along the southern boundary), the Dniester, the Kodyma, and the Savranka (two tributaries of the Boh). Many of the oblast's 225 streams dry up during the summer season. There are several freshwater lakes and some saltwater lakes along the Black Sea coast. The moderate continental climate is characterized by hot summers and mild winters. The average January temperature is –2°C in the south and –5°C in the north. The respective July averages are 21°C and 23°C. The rainfall varies from 380 to 500 mm per year and occurs mostly in the warm season.

History. The territory of the oblast was inhabited as early as the Upper Paleolithic Period. In the 9th century AD it was the home of the Ulychians and the Tivertsians. In the 10th to 12th centuries the region was dominated by Kievan Rus', and in the 14th and 15th centuries by the

Grand Duchy of Lithuania. The Bilhorod (Budzhak) Horde, vassals of the Crimean Khanate, ruled the territory from the mid-15th century. Russian control was established in the second half of the 18th century and confirmed in 1791. The territory was part of New Russia gubernia in 1797–1802 and then of Kherson gubernia. In the 19th century it was colonized intensively, and developed into a major agricultural and industrial region. In 1919 Odessa gubernia was separated from the rest of Kherson gubernia, and in 1925 it was abolished with all the other gubernias. In 1932 Odessa oblast was created out of Odessa, Pervomaiske, Zinovivske, Mykolaiv, and Kherson okruhas. Later the oblast was divided among a smaller Odessa oblast and the new Mykolaiv (est 1937) and Korovohrad (1939) oblasts. In 1954 Odessa oblast absorbed Izmail oblast, which had been created in southern Bessarabia from lands annexed from Rumania in 1940 and again in 1944.

Population. According to the 1989 census Ukrainians constitute a majority (54.6 percent) in the oblast; they are followed by Russians (27.4 percent), Bulgarians (6.3 percent), Moldavians (5.5 percent), and Jews (over 4 percent). Most of the population (66 percent) is urban. The major cities are Odessa, *Izmail, *Bilhorod-Dnistrovskyi, *Illichivske, and *Kotovske.

Industry. Industry accounted for 51.5 percent of the oblast's domestic product in 1988. The main industries are machine building and metalworking (25 percent of the industrial output), food processing (38 percent), light industry (13 percent), and the chemical industry (5 percent). The machine-building industry is concentrated mostly in Odessa. Its major products are farm machinery, construction cranes, printing equipment, industrial scales, refrigerators, and filmmaking equipment. The food industry includes canning (Odessa, Izmail, Kodyma), flour milling (Odessa, Bilhorod-Dnistrovskyi), sugar refining (Odessa, Kotovske), fish processing (Odessa, Izmail, Bilhorod-Dnistrovskyi), meat packing (Odessa, Izmail, Kotovske, Bilhorod-Dnistrovskyi), and wine-making. Light industry manufactures textiles (Odessa, Tatarbunary), footwear (Odessa), clothes (Odessa, Balta, Bilhorod-Dnistrovskyi), and jute products (Odessa). The chemical industry uses imported raw materials to make superphosphates, linoleum, plastics, dyes, and polyethylene film. Building materials, such as reinforced concrete, bricks, facing tiles, roofing materials, and lime, are produced in Odessa, Illichivske, Bilhorod-Dnistrovskyi, Izmail, and Kodyma. Almost 60 percent of the industrial plant is concentrated in Odessa.

Agriculture. The oblast contributes over 5 percent of Ukraine's agricultural output. In 1988 there were 377 collective farms (16 engaged in fish farming) and 153 state farms in the oblast. Of the 2,562,700 ha of farmland 2,081,000 ha were cultivated and 361,800 ha were used for pasture and hayfields. The major crops of the oblast are grains (52.8 percent), including winter wheat (22.4 percent) and corn (11.8 percent), feed (30.4 percent), sunflowers and sugar beets (12 percent), and potatoes, vegetables, and melons (5 percent). A small part of the land is devoted to other fruits and berries. Grapes are grown in the southwestern part of the oblast. Only 10 percent of the farmland is irrigated. The largest irrigation works are at Tatarbunary, the lower Dniester, Kiliia, and Suvorove.

Transport. The oblast has 1,153 km of railroads (1988). The main lines are Odessa–Kiev, Odessa–Kharkiv, Odessa–Moscow, and Odessa–St Petersburg. There are 8,000

km of highway, of which 7,500 km are paved. The main highways are Odessa–Kiev–St Petersburg, Odessa–Kishinev, Reni–Odessa–Mykolaiv–Rostov-na-Donu, and Odessa–Izmail. There are eight major seaports, including Odessa, Illichivske, Kiliia, Reni, and Bilhorod-Dnistrovskyi. Odessa is a terminal of the gas pipeline from Shebelinka and of an ammonia pipeline from Togliatti. There are two airports in Odessa.

BIBLIOGRAPHY
Narodnoe khoziaistvo odesskoi oblasti: Statisticheskii sbornik (Odessa 1960)
Istoriia mist i sil URSR: Odes'ka oblast' (Kiev 1969)

Odessa Opera and Ballet Theater

Odessa Opera and Ballet Theater (Odeskyi teatr opery ta baletu).
A theater established in 1926 on the basis of an existing municipal opera theater that had been founded in 1810. Soon after its founding the Odessa Theater became one of the leading opera theaters in Ukraine, along with those in Kiev and Kharkiv. Its repertoire included operas, operettas, and ballets by Ukrainian, Russian, and Western European composers. Among the works of Ukrainian composers performed by the theater are V. Femelidi's *Rozlom* (The Schism, 1929), B. Yanovsky's *Duma Chornomors'ka* (Black Sea Duma, 1929), B. Liatoshynsky's *Zolotyi obruch* (The Golden Ring, 1930), B. Kostenko's *Karmeliuk* (1930), O. Chyshka's *Iablunevyi polon* (The Apple Tree Captivity, 1931), M. Verykivsky's *Sotnyk* (The Captain), E. Yutsevych's *Kyrylo Kozhumiaka*, and K. Dankevych's *Nazar Stodolia* and *Bohdan Khmelnytsky*. Dankevych's *Lileia* (The Lily) and V. Skorulsky's *Lisova pisnia* (The Forest Song) are among the ballets staged.

Odessa Pedagogical Institute (Odeskyi pedahohichnyi instytut im. K.D. Ushynskoho).
An institution of higher learning, until 1992 under the jurisdiction of the Ministry of Education of the Ukrainian SSR. It was formed in 1920 as a faculty of social education at the Odessa Institute of People's Education. In 1932 it became a pedagogical institute, and in 1946 it was named after K. Ushinsky. The institute has departments of physics and mathematics, physical education, music education, art and graphics, and early childhood education, and correspondence and preparatory sections. It trains teachers for the elementary

and secondary school system. It has four experimental laboratories and a library of 364,000 volumes. The student enrollment in 1986–7 was 4,900.

Odessa Picture Gallery.
The name of the *Odessa Art Museum from 1950 to 1965.

Odessa Plow and Harrow Manufacturing Consortium (Odeske vyrobnyche obiednannia po pluhakh i boronakh 'Odesahruntomash').
A consortium of farm-machine-building enterprises, established in 1973 in Odessa. Its main members are the Odessa Agricultural Machinery Plant (built in 1854) and similar factories in Mariiupil and Kamianets-Podilskyi. The consortium now produces general and special-purpose tractor plows, harrows, scarifiers, machinery used in orcharding, spare parts, and other products. It produced up to 70 percent of all general-purpose and almost all special-purpose plows in the USSR.

Odessa Polytechnical Institute (Odeskyi politekhnichnyi instytut).
An institution of higher learning, until 1992 under the jurisdiction of the Ministry of Higher and Specialized Secondary Education of the Ukrainian SSR. Founded in 1918 as a workers' technical school, it was transformed in 1933 into an industrial institute. In 1945 it became a polytechnical institute. The institute's 13 departments include machine building, mechanical engineering, chemical engineering, thermal-power engineering, atomic energy, the automation and electrification of industry, radio technology and computing sciences, and economics. It also has evening and correspondence programs, a graduate program, and six special laboratories. The library has 1.5 million volumes. In 1985–6 the student enrollment was over 10,000.

Odessa Presmash Manufacturing Consortium (Odeske vyrobnyche obiednannia 'Presmash').
A consortium of seven enterprises in Odessa and Mykolaiv oblasts, formed in 1976. It produces heavy and specialized presses, casting machines for plastics and metals, stamping machines, paper and cardboard presses, and other products. In 1970 its main plant, established in Odessa in 1952, employed 1,300 workers.

Odessa Radial-boring Lathe Plant (Odeskyi zavod radialno-sverdylnykh verstativ).
A factory of the machine-building industry, built in 1944–6. It produces honing, radial-boring, deep-drilling, and various specialized lathes. Many of the models are programmable and are used in automated production. The plant was the only one in the USSR to produce lathes on an automated production line. Since 1976 it has been the chief partner in the Odessa Lathe Manufacturing Consortium.

Odessa Railroad.
See Railroad transportation.

Odessa Regional Studies Commission (Odeska komisiia kraieznavstva pry VUAN).
A research institution affiliated with the VUAN that existed in Odessa from 1923 to 1931. Its president was S. Dlozhevsky, and its secretary was I. Faas. The society's 105 members were grouped into sections that studied southern Ukraine's natural resources, archeology, society and history, and ethnography and dialects; there was also a German section. The society pub-

shed P. Buzuk's brief history of the Ukrainian language 924) and its own bulletin, *Visnyk* (5 vols [10 issues], 24–6, 1929–30), edited by Dlozhevsky, Faas, G. Tanfilev, . Volkov, E. Trifilev, I. Khmelnytsky, N. Lignau, R. Mickitz, and V. Selinov.

Odessa Research Canning Plant (Odeskyi doslidnyi onservnyi zavod). One of the chief specialized plants of he former USSR food industry. It grew out of a small caning and sausage factory established in 1867. Since 1959 it as specialized in canned baby food. In 1980 it produced different products, including canned meats, vegetables, nd fruit.

Odessa Russian Drama Theater (Odeskyi rosiiskyi ramatychnyi teatr im. A. Ivanova). A theater established 1927. It did not function during the Second World War, nd renewed its activity in 1945. Its Ukrainian repertoire as been limited to I. Karpenko-Kary's *Zhyteiske more* (The ea of Life) and O. Korniichuk's plays, including *Platon rechet* and *Bohdan Khmel'nyts'ky*; it mainly stages Russian lassical and Soviet works, as well as world classics. In 987 its artistic director was V. Terentev.

Odessa Scientific Society (Odeske naukove tovarytvo pry VUAN). A scholarly association of the VUAN, ounded in 1926. Until the early 1930s, when it was suppressed, the society was the center of scholarly life in Odessa. In 1928 it had 140 members grouped into socioconomic, historical-philological, natural science–mathenatical, pedagogical, and medical sections, with M. Iordiievsky as president and V. Herasymenko as secreary. The society published its own serial called *Zapysky* 18 issues, 1927–30), K. Koperzhynsky's study of harvest ituals (1926), an edition of M. Kropyvnytsky's letters 1927), V. Kysilov's Russian-Ukrainian medical dictionary 1928), a Ukrainian edition of J. Pestalozzi's selected vorks (1928), and O. Sikyrynsky's book on the correspondence of H. Barvinok (1928).

Odessa Society of History and Antiquities (Imperaorskoe odesskoe obshchestvo istorii i drevnostei). A cholarly society established in Odessa in 1839 to collect, describe, and protect all archeological monuments and nistorical documents pertaining to Southern Ukraine (including the Zaporozhian Cossacks), the Crimea, and Bessarabia; to prepare and publish historical studies of hose regions; and to compile statistical and geographical data about them. The society conducted excavations at the sites of ancient Hellenic colonies and kurhans; created a large library, archive, and museum (est 1840, merged with the Odessa Municipal Museum of Antiquities [now the Odessa Archeological Museum] in 1858); supervised museums in Teodosiia (from 1850), Kerch, and Symferopil (today the Khersones Historical-Archeological Museum) and the Genoese fortresses at Sudak and Bilhorod-Dnistrovskyi; and published its own scholarly *Zapiski* (33 vols, 1844–1919), monographs, catalogs, and indexes. In 1893 the society had 16 honorary members, 122 full members, and 40 corresponding members and associates. Prominent members included Oleksii Andriievsky, O. Berthier-Delagarde, F. Brun, A. Florovsky, D. Kniazhevich (the first president), V. Latyshev, N. Murzakevich (the first secretary), M. Popruzhenko, A. Skalkovsky, E. von Stern, V. Varneke, and V. Yurgevich. The society was

abolished under Soviet rule in 1922. Its traditions have been carried on by the *Odessa Archeological Society (est 1959).

Odessa Sugar Refinery (Odeskyi tsukrorafinadnyi zavod). A sugar refinery built in Odessa in 1896. Its initial capacity was 100 t of sugar a day. It was expanded in the interwar period, destroyed during the Second World War, and rebuilt in 1947–9. It produces granular, cube, and loose sugar, syrup, and other products. Since 1963 it has also refined sugar cane imported from Cuba. In 1980 the plant had a daily capacity of 920 t of unrefined and 866 t of refined sugar.

Odessa Technological Institute of the Food Industry (Odeskyi tekhnolohichnyi instytut kharchovoi promyslovosti im. M.V. Lomonosova). An institution of higher learning, until 1992 under the jurisdiction of the Ministry of Higher and Specialized Secondary Education of the Ukrainian SSR. Formed in 1922 on the basis of the Odessa School of Milling Technology (est 1902), the institute trains workers and specialists for the food-processing industry. It has departments of grain technology, biochemical and nutrient products, food-packaging and -preserving technology, meat and dairy products processing, mechanics, mechanical engineering and automation, and engineering economics, and evening and correspondence programs. The institute has a library of 550,000 volumes. The enrollment for 1985–6 was over 8,000.

Odessa Technological Institute of the Refrigeration Industry (Odeskyi tekhnolohichnyi instytut kholodylnoi promyslovosti). An institution of higher learning, until 1992 under the jurisdiction of the Ministry of Higher and Specialized Secondary Education of the Ukrainian SSR. Founded in 1930 as the Odessa Food Institute, it was called the Odessa Technological Institute of the Canning Industry (1931–50) and then the Odessa Technological Institute of the Food and Refrigeration Industry (1950–70) before receiving its present name in 1970. It prepares specialists and works for the refrigeration industry and has departments of refrigeration engineering, cryogenic engineering, air-conditioning, heat sensing, and refrigeration machinery. It has evening-study and correspondence sections. In 1985–6 the student enrollment was 6,000.

Odessa Theater of the Revolution. See Odessa Ukrainian Music and Drama Theater.

Odessa Ukrainian Music and Drama Theater (Odeskyi ukrainskyi muzychno-dramatychnyi teatr). A theater established in 1925 from the cast of the Mykhailychenko Theater and the Odessa First Ukrainian Workers' and Peasants' Theater. Its founders were I. Zamychkovsky, M. Tinsky, Ye. Khutorna, N. Uzhvii, L. Matsiievska, P. Niatko, Yu. Shumsky, and M. *Tereshchenko, who was also its first director. Originally called the Odessa Derzhdrama, in 1930 it was renamed the Odessa Theater of the Revolution, and in 1940 it acquired its present name. Tereshchenko directed G. Kaufman and M. Connelly's *Merton of the Movies* as a experiment in bright stylization. His successor, V. Vasylko, repeated his *Berezil production *Za dvoma zaitsiamy* (After Two Hares, based on M. Starytsky). Also staged were I. Kocherha's *Feia hirkoho myhdaliu* (The Fairy of the Bitter Almond), V. Vynnychenko's *Nad* (Nad[ia]), Ya. Mamontov's *Kniazhna Viktoriia* (The Princess Victoria), and W. Shakespeare's *The Taming of the Shrew*. In 1929 Tereshchenko directed I. Mykytenko's *Dyktatura* (Dictatorship), and I. Yukhymenko directed O. Korniichuk's *Zahybel' eskadry* (The Destruction of the Squadron), both premieres in Ukrainian theater. The theater has also staged productions based on the works of T. Shevchenko, O. Kobylianska, M. Kulish, O. Dovzhenko, V. Mynko, and B. Brecht. The directors since 1945 have been B. Tiahno, V. Vasylko, V. Miahky, B. Meshkis, and K. Pyvovarov (since 1986).

BIBLIOGRAPHY
Duz', I. *Teatr imeni Zhovtnevoï revoliutsiï* (Kiev 1975)
V. Revutsky

Odessa University (Odeskyi derzhavnyi universytet im. I. Mechnikova). A higher educational institution, under the jurisdiction of the Ministry of Higher and Specialized Secondary Education of Ukraine. It was opened in 1865 as New Russia University on the basis of the *Richelieu Lyceum, on the initiative of N. *Pirogov, the head of the Odessa school district. The tsarist officials initially opposed the founding of a university in Odessa, since they considered the city to be a hotbed of unrest, and offered instead Mykolaiv as a site. Under pressure from the local nobility and merchants, Tsar Alexander II granted the lyceum university status on 10 June 1862.

New Russia University initially had three faculties, history and philology, physics and mathematics, and law. The initial enrollment was 175 students; by 1880 there were 346 students and 45 professors. Almost half of the students were children of the clergy; 70 percent of the students received either scholarships or bursaries. Most of the students came from Southern Ukraine, the Don region, or Caucasia, although the school also attracted students from the Slavic countries in the Balkans. A faculty of medicine was created in 1900. In 1908 the total student enrollment was 3,100. All instruction was in Russian, although in 1906 there was an attempt to initiate a Ukrainian history course to be offered in Ukrainian by O. Hrushevsky. The university published its *Zapiski* from 1867 to 1914.

During the 1917 Revolution attempts were made to Ukrainianize the university. Under Soviet rule New Russia University was dissolved, and the various faculties were separated from the university to form research institutes in 1920. Later that year most of these institutes were combined to form the Odessa Institute of People's Education. In 1925 the institute had 603 students, and Ukrainian was introduced as a language of instruction in many courses. In 1933 several other institutes were merged again, to form Odessa University, which in 1945 was named in honor of the biologist I. Mechnikov. The student enrollment rose from 8,180 in 1960–1 to 12,000 in 1980–1, but it has since then fallen to 10,230 (1988–9). The university has nine faculties (mechanics-mathematics, physics, chemistry, biology, geology-geography, history, law, philology, and Romance and Germanic philology). It also has evening and correspondence sections and a postgraduate program. Virtually all instruction has been in Russian. The university has a library of some 2 million volumes, a botanical garden (opened in 1867), and an astronomical observatory (built in 1817).

BIBLIOGRAPHY
Markevich, A. *25-letie imp. Novorosiiskogo universiteta* (Odessa 1890)
Dobroliubskii, K. (ed). *Odesskii universitet za 75 let (1865–1940)* (Odessa 1940)
N. Freeland, B. Krawchenko

Odessa Young Spectator's Theater (Odeskyi teatr yunoho hliadacha im. M. Ostrovskoho). A theater established in 1931 as the Odessa Children's Theater. In 1941 it assumed its present name. The theater specializes in productions of colorful adventures in a heroic-romantic or lyric-comical style. They are planned according to the age-group of the spectators – preschool (Ye. Shvarts's *Snizhna koroleva* [The Snow Queen, adapted from H.C. Andersen]), primary school (L. Smiliansky's *Lastivka* [The Swallow]), secondary school (S. Larionov's *Vin ishov na Odesu* [He Advanced toward Odessa]), and so on. Its artistic directors have been S. Manuilovych, M. Zaitsiv, V. Miahky, and V. Tomanov (since 1980).

Odesskii vestnik (Odessa Herald). A Russian-language newspaper published from April 1827 to 1893 in Odessa, twice a week at first and daily from 1864. Until 1830 a French section, *Journal d'Odessa*, was also published. Among the editors were Ukrainians, such as M. Sokalsky (1857–71); his brother, P. *Sokalsky (1871–6), who also contributed theater and concert reviews and articles on culture to the newspaper for over 20 years, and defended the use of the Ukrainian language and popularized Ukrainian culture and literature; and P. Zeleny (1877–87). Many articles on the economy and regional history of Southern Ukraine were published in the paper.

Odnodvirtsi (Russian: *odnodvortsy*). A special group of *state peasants in the Russian Empire who came from the lesser service people (*deti boiarskie*). They originated in the 16th century as settlers and defenders of the southern and northeastern frontiers of Muscovy. Some later owned serfs, but the majority ran only one household (*odin dvorets*, hence their name). Military registers show that from 1662 to 1672 there were 28,325 male *odnodvirtsi* in Russian-ruled Slobidska Ukraine. Peter I changed their status: like Cossacks and other petty servitors, they were classified as free peasants and had to pay the *poll tax. In the 18th century, *odnodvirtsi* were settled in Kharkiv, Poltava, Katerynoslav, Kherson, and Tavriia gubernias, where by 1835 they numbered 50,430 males. In 1866 their legal status was made equivalent to that of the rest of the peasantry. Because the *odnodvirtsi* did not live in villages as a rule, they did not merge with the ordinary peasants, but instead constituted a group of more prosperous homesteaders (*khutoriany*).

Odnoosibnyk (individual farmer). The name given to a Soviet peasant who did not join a *collective farm and instead worked his landholding on an individual basis. In 1929 *odnoosibnyky* represented 94.4 percent of peasant households in Soviet Ukraine. During *collectivization repressive measures were applied to ensure that all peasants joined collective farms. Higher quotas for the requisition of grain and other foodstuffs were imposed on *odnoosibnyky* than on collective farmers. They were also taxed more than collective farmers, and all restrictions on the confiscation of their property were removed in cases

f nonpayment. Because the taxes and other payments
ere usually several times higher than their annual in-
omes, most *odnoosibnyky* joined collective farms or fled to
e cities. Many of them were imprisoned or deported to
iberia during the terror. As a result, by 1937, *odnoosibnyky*
epresented only 3.9 percent of peasant households in So-
iet Ukraine. Their farms tended to be located in isolated
reas where it was not always practical to have collective
arms (eg, in hilly, heavily wooded, or marshy regions).
y 1939 only 3 percent of rural households were *odnoosib-*
yky. That year the state took away their right to own land
nd allocated them small parcels of not more than 0.2 ha.
hey continued to pay high taxes, however, and had to
ulfill other obligations, such as helping to build roads.
Vhen Western Ukraine was occupied by the Soviet re-
;ime, collectivization was also carried out there, and by
950 only 9 percent of rural households were made up of
dnoosibnyky. By 1969 they represented a mere 0.1 percent
f rural households throughout Ukraine, farming a total
f only 9,300 ha.

As a result of the serious agricultural crisis in the USSR
ttempts were made in the late 1980s to increase individ-
al family farming by allowing individuals opting out of
he collective farm or willing urban residents to establish
ndividual farms. Such farmers are no longer called *od-*
oosibnyky. As of January 1990 only 43 new private farms
ad been established. An important obstacle was the ab-
ence of legislation establishing the private ownership of
and. The land law of 7 March 1990 granted the right of
ossession to those farming the land and the right of suc-
ession to their children. It did not, however, acknowl-
dge inalienable property rights, and demands for
egislation allowing for the private ownership of land con-
inued to be voiced.

A. Babyonyshev, B. Krawchenko

Odorsky, Hedeon [Odors'kyj], b and d ? Orthodox
churchman. He studied in Olomouc, Bohemia, and then
became a preacher in Kiev in 1680 and served as a professor at and rector of the Kievan Mohyla Academy (1702–5).
It was during his tenure that the academy was enlarged
and a new complex built with the support of Hetman I.
Mazepa. Odorsky served as archimandrite of the Baturyn
Monastery in 1705–12. He was exiled to the Solovets Islands in 1712 for his support of Mazepa and P. Orlyk. He
later served as rector of a seminary in Arkhangelsk (1715–
16).

Odrach, Fedir [Odrač] (pseud of Fedir Sholomitsky), b
13 March 1912 in Misiatyn, Polisia, d 7 October 1964 in
Toronto. Writer. During the Second World War he fought
in the ranks of the Polisian Sich and the Ukrainian Insurgent Army. As a postwar émigré in Canada he wrote
about interwar and wartime Polisia. Among his works are
the novels *V dorozi* (On the Road, 1954), *Shchebetun* (The
Chatterbox, 1957), and *Voshchad* (Incipient Dawn, 1972),
the story collections *Pivstanok za selom* (The Whistle-Stop
outside the Village, 1959) and *Pokynuta oselia* (The Abandoned Settlement, 1960), and the regional study *Nashe Po-*
lissia (Our Polisia, 1955).

Odrekhivsky [Odrexivs'kyj]. A family of folk artists
from Vilka, in the Sian region of Galicia (now in Poland).
Pavlo (b 5 July 1899, d 31 March 1973 in Lviv) was a master
of decorative carving on wooden plates, boxes, and canes.
His son Vasyl (b 18 February 1921), a graduate of the Lviv
Institute of Applied and Decorative Arts (1957), specializes in thematic sculpture and portraits in wood, such as *To
the Market* (1946), *Grape Harvesting* (1949), *Yurii Shkribliak*
(1957), and *The Composer S. Liudkevych* (1967). He helped
create the monuments to I. Franko in Lviv (1964) and Drohobych (1967). Pavlo's second son, Ivan (b 10 October
1923), is a master of thematic sculpture in wood. His
works include *Woodcutter* (1949), *Shepherd* (1956), and
Dovbush (1965). Vasyl's son Volodymyr does lyrical monumental sculptures, such as *Daydreamer* and *The Baiko Sis-*
ters, and his other son, Roman, specializes in artistic glass.
The works of these masters are preserved in art museums
in Kiev and Lviv.

Dmytro Odryna

Odryna, Dmytro, b 1892 in Teleshivka, Vasylkiv county, Kiev gubernia, d 16 November 1919 in Kamianets-
Podilskyi, Podilia gubernia. Physician and political leader. After graduating from Kiev University (1916) he was
active in the Ukrainian Party of Socialist Revolutionaries.
A member of the Central Rada, he was arrested by the
Hetman government for protesting against German atrocities. In January 1919 he was elected vice-chairman of the
Labor Congress. As a leading organizer of medical and
sanitary services for the military and of the Ukrainian Red
Cross, he was invited to join B. *Martos's cabinet as health
minister and deputy premier on 9 June 1919. He directed
a vigorous campaign against typhus, of which he himself
became a victim.

Odudko, Tymish [Odud'ko, Tymiš], b 24 September
1912 in Khorovets, Iziaslav county, Volhynia gubernia, d
25 July 1982 in Lviv. Poet and songwriter. He completed
studies at the Vinnytsia Pedagogical Institute (1939) and
worked as a correspondent for various front-line newspapers during the Second World War. Later he settled in
Lviv, where he became editor of the newspaper *L'vovskaia
pravda*, director of the Kameniar publishing house in Lviv,
and, finally, head of the Lviv Oblast Publishing, Printing,
and Book Trade Administration. Between the years 1950
and 1982 he published 11 poetry collections.

ODUM. See Ukrainian Democratic Youth Association.

ODVU. See Organization for the Rebirth of Ukraine.

Odyntsiv, Oleksander [Odynciv], b 1895 in Vypovziv, Oster county, Chernihiv gubernia, d 1930s. Bolshevik revolutionary and Soviet official. A law student at Kiev University, he joined the Bolshevik party in 1917 and served on the Revolutionary Military Committee. He held important government posts, such as deputy commissar of agriculture for Ukraine and the USSR, member of the Collegium of the USSR Agriculture Commissariat, people's commissar of agriculture for Ukraine, and from 1934, chief of the agricultural administration of the Azov–Black Sea region. From October 1932 he was a member of the CC CP(B)U. He perished in the Stalinist terror.

Officer schools of the Army of the Ukrainian National Republic (Starshynski shkoly Armii UNR). In the summer of 1917 the First Khmelnytsky Cadet School was formed by Ukrainianizing one of the two Russian army cadet schools in Kiev. Under Capt Nosenko's command, its 600 students were organized into a battalion of four companies. Its senior class, commanded by Capt A. Honcharenko, suffered heavy losses in the Battle of *Kruty, and its junior cadets participated in the fighting in Kiev in late January 1918. The surviving cadets were enlisted in the *Haidamaka Battalion of Slobidska Ukraine.

In the spring of 1918 the Officer Instruction School, under Gen O. Ostapura-Stepovy, was opened. It had several departments (infantry, machine gun, engineering, artillery, and cavalry) and produced a total of approx 1,400 officers. In September 1918 the Supreme School Board of the defense ministry, chaired by Gen M. Yunakiv, drew up a plan for a Ukrainian military education system: basic schools were to offer a one-year program, and professional schools a two-year program. Nine schools were to be set up, and admission was to be open to secondary-school graduates.

On 14 January 1919 a unified military youth school was opened in Zhytomyr, under the directorship of Col V. Petriv. From March to July its cadets participated in combat; then they resumed regular training in Kamianets-Podilskyi under the directorship of Col O. Puchkivsky. In October the school graduated its first 300 second lieutenants, and a month later it was again reorganized into a combat unit, which participated in the First Winter Campaign.

In January 1920 another unified military youth school was organized in Kamianets-Podilskyi, under the directorship of Col M. Shapoval. It carried on its work in Polish internment camps, and graduated several classes of officer candidates in different specialties.

Officer schools of the Ukrainian Galician Army. In January 1919 each corps (Zolochiv, Sambir, and Kolomyia) of the Ukrainian Galician Army set up its own infantry officer candidate school. An artillery officer candidate school and a signal officer candidate school were also organized in Stanyslaviv. Each school offered a three-month course patterned on Austrian army courses. Most of the students were veteran noncommissioned officers aged 18 to 24 years. The infantry schools had 78 to 95 students each, and the artillery and signal schools had 42 to 50 students. Besides the first class of officer candidates, two more classes (one infantry and one artillery) were graduated in the fall of 1919 in central Ukraine, for a total of approx 440 officer candidates. The commanders of the schools were Maj F. Rimal, Maj Y. Feshchuk, First Lieut D. Kulchytsky, Capt I. Sitnytsky, Capt L. Sheparovych, Capt O. Dragan, and S. Leshchii.

Ofinor. A press agency established by M. *Yeremiiv to supply the Western press with information on the Ukrainian question and the activities of the Government-in-exile of the UNR. Based in Geneva, it published French-, German-, and Ukrainian-language bulletins there during the years 1928–44. It also issued bulletins in French (1929–39) and Spanish (1932–6) in Paris, and in Italian in Rome (1929–43); the Italian-language bulletins were edited by B. Randone and Ye. Onatsky.

Oghuz (aka Oğuz, Ohuz, Ghuzz, Huz, Uz). A federation of nomadic Turkic tribes, which arose in the Aral Sea region in the first half of the 10th century and established a state on the lower Syr Darya River. Some of their detachments helped Volodymyr the Great in his campaign against the Volga Bulgars in 985. Pressed by the Kipchaks, in the mid-11th century some of the Oghuz moved into the Volga-Don region, thereby forcing the Pechenegs to move into the Black Sea steppes, and others, under the leadership of the Seljuks, conquered Byzantine Anatolia.

OGPU. See GPU.

Ohiichuk, Hryhorii [Ohijčuk, Hryhorij], b 25 January 1893 in Trubiivka, Skvyra county, Kiev gubernia, d 13 February 1985 in Chicago. Orthodox metropolitan. He was ordained in 1919 and joined the new Ukrainian Autocephalous Orthodox church (UAOC) in 1921. He served as a priest in the Kiev region until 1927, when he was made overseer of the Dormition Cathedral in Berdychiv. He was arrested in 1932 and served three years at hard labor in the Kuzbas. He returned to Ukraine but did not resume his pastoral work until the German occupation. In May 1942 he was consecrated bishop (later archbishop) of Zhytomyr of the renewed UAOC. From September 1942 to March 1943 he was imprisoned by the Germans. Upon his release he moved to Westphalia, Germany. After the split in the UAOC in October 1947, he became head of the *Ukrainian Autocephalous Orthodox Church (Conciliar), which rejected the leadership of Metropolitan P. Sikorsky and advocated authority of the church sobor over the episcopate in church affairs. Ohiichuk emigrated to the United States in 1950 and settled in Chicago. He organized a number of parishes in the United States and published the church's organ, *Pravoslavnyi ukraïnets'. In 1971 he was elevated to metropolitan.

Ohiienko, Ivan [Ohijenko] (monastic name: Ilarion), b 14 January 1882 in Brusyliv, Radomyshl county, Kiev gubernia, d 29 March 1972 in Winnipeg. Orthodox metropolitan, linguist, church historian, and cultural figure; full member of the Shevchenko Scientific Society from 1923. He studied Slavic philology and literature under V. Peretts at Kiev University and graduated in 1909 after completing a thesis on I. Galiatovsky's *Kliuch razumieniia*. In 1912 he completed the Higher Pedagogical Courses and began to teach at the Kiev Commercial Institute, and in 1915 at Kiev University.

Following the Revolution of 1917, Ohiienko played an important role in the Ukrainianization of higher education and scholarship. He became a professor of the history of Ukrainian culture at the new Ukrainian State University in Kiev in 1918. Forced to leave the city following the Bolshevik seizure of power there, he helped organize and became the first rector of the *Kamianets-Podilskyi Ukrai-

Metropolitan Ivan (Ilarion)
Ohiienko

nian State University. As a member of the Ukrainian Party of Socialists-Federalists he served as minister of education (early 1919) and then minister of religious affairs (from August 1919) in the Council of Ministers of the Ukrainian National Republic.

With the defeat of the UNR, Ohiienko settled in Tarnów (Poland) in 1920, where he participated in the *Council of the Republic and resumed his functions as minister of religion in the government-in-exile of the UNR (to 1924). He taught at a Lviv gymnasium (1924–6) before becoming professor of Church Slavonic and paleography at the Orthodox Faculty of Theology at Warsaw University (1926). After being removed from his post in 1932 in the anti-Ukrainian campaign initiated by the Polish authorities, he worked as a private scholar and published the journals *Ridna mova and *Nasha kul'tura. He also resumed work on the translation of the Bible into Ukrainian (which he had begun in the early 1920s). His translation of the Gospels appeared in 1937, followed by the New Testament, including the Psalms, in 1939. He finished most of the Bible in 1940 but was not able to publish it because of the war. After revisions and other changes, his complete translation appeared in 1962.

In October 1940 Ohiienko was tonsured and then consecrated bishop of Kholm and Podlachia by Metropolitan D. Valedinsky of the Polish Autocephalous Orthodox church in the wartime Generalgouvernement. He began to Ukrainianize the church in the Kholm region, by introducing Ukrainian practices in the church rite and the use of Ukrainian in services and ordaining several Ukrainian priests. After being elevated to the rank of metropolitan by Valedinsky in March 1944, he was soon forced to flee the advancing Soviet army to Austria and then Switzerland. In September 1947 he was invited to Canada by the parish of St Mary the Protectress in Winnipeg. In August 1951 he was elected metropolitan of Winnipeg and head of the *Ukrainian Orthodox Church of Canada (UOCC). He established the theological journal *Vira i kul'tura and revived *Nasha kul'tura, founded a theological society (now the Metropolitan Ilarion Theological Society), and lectured and served as dean of theology at *St Andrew's College.

A prolific writer, Ohiienko published scores of monographs and articles on a variety of topics. His first major publication, 'Ohliad ukraïns'koho iazykoznavstva' (Sur-

vey of Ukrainian Linguistics, in *ZNTSh*, vols 79–80, 1907), was followed by several articles on I. Galiatovsky, the subject of his MA thesis. In 1918 he published *Ukraïns'ka kul'tura* (Ukrainian Culture). Other works in cultural history included *Istoriia ukraïns'koho drukarstva* (A History of Ukrainian Printing, 1925), *Dokhrystyians'ki viruvannia ukraïns'koho narodu: Istorychno-relihiina monohrafiia* (Pre-Christian Beliefs of the Ukrainian Nation: A Historical-Religious Monograph, 1965), *Kniaz' Kostiantyn Ostroz'kyi i ioho kul'turna pratsia* (Prince Kostiantyn Ostrozky and his Cultural Work, 1958), and *Fortetsia pravoslaviia na Volyni: Sviata Pochaïvs'ka Lavra* (The Fortress of Orthodoxy in Volhynia: The Holy Pochaiv Monastery, 1961). In the 1920s he initiated a series of works on the history of the Slavic languages, beginning with *Kostiantyn i Mefodii: ïkh zhyttia ta diial'nist'* (Constantine and Methodius: Their Lives and Activity, 2 vols, 1927–8), and continuing with monographs on the phonetics of Church Slavonic (1927), the origins of Slavic alphabets and literary languages (1928), Slavic documents of the 10th and 11th centuries (1929), and old Slavic paleography (1928). He also examined the history of Ukrainian and Russian accents (1914) and accents in historical and geographical names (1912). He devoted more attention to this problem in several articles and in many general surveys of Ukrainian linguistics and stylistics, eg, *Kurs ukrainskogo iazyka* (A Course in the Ukrainian Language, 1918), *Ukraïns'kyi stylistychnyi slovnyk* (A Ukrainian Stylistics Dictionary, 1924), *Chystota i pravyl'nist' ukraïns'koï movy* (The Purity and Correctness of the Ukrainian Language, 1925), and *Suchasna ukraïns'ka literaturna mova* (The Contemporary Ukrainian Literary Language, 1935). A representative of the 'ethnographic' school in Ukrainian linguistics, he was particularly concerned with popularizing norms of literary Ukrainian and narrowing the gap between the literary and spoken language; many of his monographs were intended as textbooks, and his journal *Ridna mova* was almost exclusively devoted to this concern. He also made several contributions to Ukrainian etymology and lexicography, including dictionaries of little-used place-names (1934) and words (1973); *Skladnia ukraïns'koï movy* (A Treasury of the Ukrainian Language, 1937–8); and *Etymolohichnyi-semantychnyi slovnyk ukraïns'koï movy* (Etymological-Semantic Dictionary of the Ukrainian Language), three volumes of which have appeared posthumously. His translations were important in the development of modern Ukrainian religious terminology and *liturgical language.

Ohiienko's most important works on the history of Ukrainian were *Ukraïns'ka mova XVI-ho stolittia i Krekhivs'kyi apostol 1560-ykh rokiv* (The Ukrainian Language of the 16th Century and the Krekhiv *Apostol* of the 1560s, 1930), *Narysy z istoriï ukraïns'koï movy* (Surveys of the History of the Ukrainian Language, 1927), and *Istoriia ukraïns'koï literaturnoï movy* (History of the Ukrainian Literary Language, 1950). As a historian of the Ukrainian church, Ohiienko wrote such monographs as *Kanonizatsiia sviatykh v ukraïns'kii Tserkvi* (The Canonization of Saints in the Ukrainian Church, 1965), *Ukraïns'ka Tserkva za Bohdana Khmel'nyts'koho, 1647–1657* (The Ukrainian Church during the Period of Bohdan Khmelnytsky, 1647–57, 1955), and *Ukraïns'ka Tserkva za chas ruïny* (The Ukrainian Church during the Period of the Ruin, 1956). His survey history of the Ukrainian church, originally published in 1942, appeared in English translation in 1986. A collection of his sermons appeared in 1973.

BIBLIOGRAPHY
Zaïkin, V. *Professor Ivan Ohiienko iak tserkovnyi ta hromads'kyi diiach i iak uchenyi* (Warsaw 1925)
Naukovyi zbirnyk v 30 richnytsiu naukovoï pratsi prof. d-ra Ivana Ohiienka (Warsaw 1937)
Iuvileina knyha na poshanu Mytropolyta Ilariona u 75-littia ioho zhyttia i pratsi, 1882–1957 (Winnipeg 1958)
Zhalobna knyha v pam'iat' Mytropolyta Ilariona (Winnipeg 1973)
I. Korovytsky

Ohiievsky, Anatolii [Ohijevs'kyj, Anatolij], b 31 August 1894 in Starodub, Chernihiv gubernia, d 3 April 1952 in Kiev. Hydrologist. He graduated from the Kiev Polytechnical Institute (1922), worked at the Dniprobud organization, and was director of the Kiev Scientific Research Hydrological Observatory (1944–7). He made significant contributions to the understanding of watersheds and water currents in rivers and developed quantitative methods of predicting runoff. A biography of him was published in Leningrad in 1973.

Ohiievsky, Vasyl [Ohijevs'kyj, Vasyl'], b 11 February 1861 in Krolevets, Chernihiv gubernia, d 1 June 1921 in Kiev. Forester and one of the founders of forest research in the Russian Empire. He graduated from the St Petersburg Forestry Institute (1886) and was appointed professor at that institute in 1912 and professor at the Kiev Polytechnical Institute in 1919. Most of his research, which dealt with the fertility and growth rate of pine trees and the seeding and planting methods for pine and oak trees, was done at the Sobych and Mykilske forest stations in Chernihiv gubernia and the forest-cutting areas of the Tula region. In 1909 he set up in St Petersburg the first forest seed control and research station in Russia. Pines of various geographic origin planted by Ohiievsky can be found even today at Sobych. The nest method of seeding oak introduced by Ohiievsky is still used.

Ohiievsky, Volodymyr [Ohijevs'kyj], b 10 May 1890 in Krapivna, Tula gubernia, Russia, d 26 February 1979 in Kiev. Radio technology scientist. Under his leadership the first regularly scheduled radio station was formed, and started operations in 1924 in Kiev. He also did experimental work on radio transmissions, electromagnetic measurements, and various theoretical questions of radio technology.

Ohiievsky-Okhotsky, Petro [Ohijevs'kyj-Oxoc'kyj], b ca 1814, d ca 1888. Ethnographer and writer. While serving as a priest in the Chernihiv region, he collected ethnographic material and folkore. Some of this material appeared in his article on folk customs (1873), and some was used by B. Hrinchenko in his publications. Ohiievsky-Okhotsky also wrote poems, which came out as the collection *Dumky na mohyli* (Thoughts at a Grave, 1854), and fables.

Ohilevich, Pakhomii [Ohilevič, Paxomij], b 12 June 1624 in Minsk, Belarus, d 1690. Basilian writer and liturgist. He entered the Basilian monastery in Byten, and completed a D TH in Rome in 1652. He returned to occupy several posts in the Basilian order in Belarus and Ukraine, including that of protoarchimandrite (1675–9). In 1671 he published a textbook on liturgies, which was reprinted several times.

Ohio. An eastern north central state (1990 pop 10,887,325) of the United States, covering an area of 108,800 sq km south of Lake Erie. Its capital is Columbus. Ukrainians began to settle in Ohio at the turn of the century. By 1930 over 10,000 Ukrainian immigrants had come to the state. According to the 1960 census, 8,500 inhabitants considered Ukrainian their mother tongue. In 1990, 43,600 Ohio residents were listed as Ukrainian by origin. The largest Ukrainian communities are in Cleveland, Parma, Akron, Youngstown, Lorain, Canton, and Toledo.

Ohloblyn, Mykola (Ogloblin, Nikolai), b 1814, d 1877. Orthodox archpriest and church historian; father of M. *Ohloblyn. He had a master's degree from the Kiev Theological Academy and taught at Kiev's theological seminary and institute for daughters of the nobility. His articles on Ukrainian church history and church archeology (particularly of the St Sophia Cathedral, where he was sacristan) were published mostly in *Trudy Kievskoi dukhovnoi akademii* and Kiev's *Eparkhial'nyia vedomosti*. Published separately was his textbook on church liturgy (1862).

Ohloblyn, Mykola (Ogloblin, Nikolai), b 1852 in Kiev, d 1906? Historian and archeographer; son of M. *Ohloblyn. He studied at the Kiev Theological Academy and St Petersburg Archeological Institute and then worked as an archivist at the Moscow Archive of the Ministry of Justice. A member of the Historical Society of Nestor the Chronicler in Kiev and an authority on the archives of Siberia, he produced a pioneering review of the rolls and books of the Russian government's Siberian Office (4 vols, 1895, 1900–1) and a review of historical and geographical materials of the 17th and early 18th centuries (1884). He also contributed several articles to *Kievskaia starina*, among them ones on 17th-century Russian military governors' reports on Ukraine (1885), the Kiev branch of the Russian Military Office (1886), the conversion of Uniates in Kiev (1889), life in late 17th-century Ukraine (1887), and the 1666 investigation of Muscovite soldiers' abuses in Ukraine (1895).

Ohloblyn, Mykola. See Hlobenko, Mykola.

Oleksander Ohloblyn

Ohloblyn, Oleksander, b 6 December 1899 in Kiev, d 16 February 1992 in Ludlow, Massachusetts. Historian, historiographer, and archeographer; member of the Shevchenko Scientific Society from 1947 (honorary member from 1988) and the *Ukrainian Academy of Arts and

Sciences (UVAN) from 1948. He graduated from Kiev University in 1919 and obtained doctorates in Ukrainian cultural history (Odessa, 1926) and historical sciences (Moscow, 1941). He was a professor of Ukrainian economic history at the Kiev Archeological Institute (1920–1), the Kiev Institute of People's Education (1921–33), the Kiev Institute of the National Economy (1927–30), Kiev University (1938–41), and Odessa University (1938–41); a full member of the Kharkiv-based Scientific Research Institute of the History of Ukrainian Culture (1926–31); a senior research associate at the VUAN (1926–33) and AN URSR (now ANU, 1935–41); deputy director of the All-Ukrainian Historical Museum in Kiev (1931–2); director of the Kiev Central Archive of Old Documents (1932–3); chairman of the department of capitalism at the ANU Institute of the History of Ukraine (1937–41); and chairman of the department of Ukrainian history at Odessa University (1939). He was imprisoned for several months in 1930–1 and forced to recant his 'bourgeois nationalist' scholarship. From 1933 to 1935 he was relieved of all academic positions and suffered persecution by the GPU. In the autumn of 1941, during the German occupation of Ukraine, he headed the Kiev municipal administration and was a member of the *Ukrainian National Council there. He lived in Lviv in 1943 and Prague in 1944.

A postwar émigré, Ohloblyn was a professor in Munich at the Ukrainian Free University and the Theological Academy of the Ukrainian Autocephalous Orthodox Church from 1946 to 1951. He emigrated to the United States in 1951. There he chaired the UVAN Historical Section (1951–84) and was a contributing editor of *Entsyklopediia ukraïnoznavstva* and *Encyclopedia of Ukraine*. He also contributed to *Ukraine: A Concise Encyclopaedia* and chaired the scholarly council of the *Lypynsky East European Research Institute (from 1964). He was president of the Ukrainian Genealogy and Heraldry Society (1963–74), the *Ukrainian Historical Association (1965–80), and the UVAN (1970–9, honorary president from 1988); was a visiting history professor (1968–70) and thesis adviser (1970–3) at Harvard University; and was elected an honorary member of the Harvard Ukrainian Research Institute in 1973.

Ohloblyn is the author of over 700 publications (monographs, articles, and reviews) on Ukrainian history, historiography, genealogy, and other historical disciplines. They include monographs on manufacturing in the Hetman state (1925), the precapitalist factory in Ukraine (1925), and the peasant factory in 18th- and 19th-century Ukraine (1931), all of which were reprinted in Munich in a volume titled *A History of Ukrainian Industry* (1971); a textbook on the history of the Ukrainian economy (1929); books of essays on P. Petryk's rebellion (1929) and the history of capitalism in Ukraine (1931); a book on the Muscovite theory of the Third Rome in the 16th and 17th centuries (1951), *The Treaty of Pereiaslav, 1654* (1954), and a book on Ukraine during the hetmancy of B. Khmelnytsky (1957); a book-length article, 'Ukrainian Historiography, 1917–1956,' in *The Annals of the Ukrainian Academy of Arts and Sciences in the US* (1957); monographs on the late 18th- and early 19th-century elite in the Novhorod-Siverskyi region (*Liudy staroï Ukraïny* [People of Old Ukraine], 1959) and Hetman I. Mazepa and his era (1960); and shorter books on O. Lobysevych (1966) and contemporary Soviet Ukrainian historiography (1963).

Ohloblyn's autobiography, articles about him, and a bibliography of his works appeared in a VUAN collection of essays in his honor published in 1977 (ed V. Omelchenko).

L. Wynar

Ohloblyn, Volodymyr, b 11 July 1915 in Vilshany, Kharkiv county. Stage director and actor. A pupil of the psychological-realistic school (of B. Nord, I. Chuzhoi, K. Khokhlov), he completed drama studies at the Kiev Russian Drama Theater in 1939 and then worked in various theaters (Odessa, Lviv, Mykolaiv, Drohobych, Sumy, Symferopil) as stage director until 1952. Nord and he were then assigned to replace M. Krushelnytsky at the Kharkiv Ukrainian Drama Theater; Ohloblyn worked there in 1952–8 and 1967–71 as artistic director. In 1958–67 and 1979–88 he was director of the Kiev Ukrainian Drama Theater. In 1988 he became artistic director of the Kiev Young Spectator's Theater.

Ohnievoi, Kostiantyn [Ohnjevoj, Kostjantyn], b 30 September 1926 in Dnipropetrovske. Opera singer (tenor). A graduate of the Moscow Conservatory (1955) studying with M. Gukova, he was a soloist of the Kiev Theater of Opera and Ballet (1955–73) and the Kiev Philharmonic (1973–8). His operatic roles include Lensky in P. Tchaikovsky's *Eugene Onegin*, Sinodal in A. Rubinstein's *Demon*, the Idiot in M. Mussorgsky's *Boris Godunov*, Alfredo in G. Verdi's *La Traviata*, and Tamino in W. Mozart's *Magic Flute*. He has appeared in concert in Europe, Canada, India, and Pakistan. Since 1965 he has taught at the Kiev Conservatory.

Ohnyshchanyn. The chief administrator of a prince's court in Kievan Rus'. He oversaw the running of the household, the collection of fees, and the management of the prince's herds and stables. His relative importance is reflected in the high penalty of 80 *hryvni* for killing an *ohnyshchanyn* (compared to 40 for killing a free man).

Ohonovsky, Ilarii [Ohonovs'kyj, Ilarij], b 6 December 1854 in Chahriv, Stanyslaviv circle, Galicia, d 10 July 1929 in Lviv. Classical philologist and educator; brother of Omelian, Oleksander, and Petro Ohonovsky. After graduating from Lviv University (1884) he was ordained a Greek Catholic priest, and taught at the Academic Gymnasium in Lviv (1884–1914). He compiled a Greek-Ukrainian dictionary of 13,000 words and names in Homer's *Odyssey* and *Iliad* (1900); wrote a Ukrainian grammar (with V. Kotsovsky, 1894), a Latin syntax and Latin exercise books for gymnasium students, and articles in classical philology (eg, on Virgil and Demosthenes); and translated classical Greek and Latin works into Ukrainian.

Ohonovsky, Oleksander [Ohonovs'kyj], b 17 March 1848 in Bukachivtsi, Rohatyn county, Galicia, d 10 February 1891 in Lviv. Lawyer, legal scholar, and civic leader; brother of Ilarii, Omelian, and Petro Ohonovsky. After graduating from Lviv University (LLD, 1871), he practiced law and, from 1878, taught law at Lviv University. He was the first law professor to lecture in Ukrainian at the university, and he made an important contribution to the development of Ukrainian legal terminology, even though he did not manage to publish the Ukrainian legal diction-

Oleksander Ohonovsky   Rev Omelian Ohonovsky

ary he compiled. In 1886 he was appointed dean of the law faculty. Ohonovsky was a specialist in Austrian civil law and wrote the monographs *Die Geschäftsführung ohne Auftrag nach dem österreichischen Rechte* (1877) and *Österreichisches Ehengüterrecht* (1880). He was active in Ukrainian civic organizations and helped to found a number of societies, such as Druzhnyi Lykhvar, Prosvita, the Shevchenko Scientific Society, and Ridna Shkola. He was editor of the political journal *Pravda* (1872–6) and cofounder and first president of the *People's Council.

Ohonovsky, Omelian [Ohonovs'kyj, Omeljan], b 3 August 1833 in Hryhoriv, Stanyslaviv circle, d 28 October 1894 in Lviv. Philologist and populist; brother of Ilarii, Oleksander, and Petro Ohonovsky. He was ordained after graduating from the Greek Catholic Theological Seminary in Lviv (1857), and he taught religion and (from 1863) Ukrainian language and literature at the *Academic Gymnasium in Lviv. Continuing his studies at Lviv (PH D, 1865) and Vienna (1869–70) universities, he replaced Ya. Holovatsky as docent (1867) and then professor (1870) of Ruthenian (Ukrainian) language and literature at Lviv University. In 1881 he was elected corresponding member of the Polish Academy of Sciences.

Ohonovsky was the compiler of a Church Slavonic (1871) and an Old Ruthenian (1881) anthology; a Ukrainian rendition, with commentary, of *Slovo o polku Ihorevi (1876); Prosvita society booklets about T. Shevchenko (1876), SS Borys and Hlib (1876), St Panteleimon (1882), and M. Shashkevych (1886); *Studien auf dem Gebiete der ruthenischen Sprache* (1880) and a monograph using F. *Miklosich's approach on the etymology of Church Slavonic, Ukrainian, and Polish prepositions (both containing a great deal of material on Ukrainian historical grammar and dialects); a secondary-school Ruthenian grammar (1889) based on the Western Ukrainian vernacular and written according to the *etymological spelling; articles in *Pravda* on several of T. Shevchenko's narrative poems; a long biographical introduction to the two-volume 1893 Lviv edition of T. Shevchenko's *Kobzar; Polish articles on the main traits of the Ukrainian language and on Church Slavonic, Ukrainian, and Polish prepositions; a German encyclopedia article on the Ruthenians; and German articles on Ruthenian literature and on the language of the

Queen Zofia Bible. He also wrote the narrative poem 'Krest' (The Cross, in the almanac *Zoria Halytskaia* [The Galician Star], 1860); the story 'Dolia-machukha' (Fate-Stepmother, *Otechestvennyi sbornik*, 1866, nos 20–27); the dramas *Fed'ko Ostrozhs'kyi* (1861), *Nastasia* (1872), and *Hal'shka Ostrozhs'ka* (1887); and a collection of stories for children (1876).

Ohonovsky's most famous work was his unfinished history of Ruthenian literature serialized in *Zoria* (1887–94) and published separately in four parts (6 vols, 1887, 1889, 1891, 1893–4). Although its approach was somewhat chaotic and uncritical, it contains a great deal of biographical and bibliographic information and was for many years a fundamental source on Ukrainian writers and ethnographers. Ohonovsky's consistently developed concept of the Ukrainian nation, language, and literature as separate from the Russian was vehemently rejected by Russian critics (eg, A. *Pypin in 1890). His reply to Pypin (1890) and other Russian critics elicited a passionate debate and much support for his views (eg, by I. Nechui-Levytsky and M. Kostomarov). He was a founding member of the *Prosvita society, serving as its pre-eminent president from 1877 to his death, of the Shevchenko Scientific Society, and of the populist *People's Council. He was an outspoken opponent of Polonization.

BIBLIOGRAPHY
Kokorudz, I. 'Profesor dr. Omelian Ohonovs'kyi: Ohliad ieho zhyttia i naukovoï ta literaturnoï diial'nosty,' *ZNTSh*, 5 (1895)
Makarushka, O. *Omelian Ohonovs'kyi: Ieho zhyttiia i diial'nist'* (Lviv 1895)
Bryk, I. *Omelian Ohonovs'kyi: U stolittia narodyn velykoho hromadianyna* (Lviv 1933)
Bilets'kyi, L. *Omelian Ohonovs'kyi* (Winnipeg 1950)
V. Radzykevych, R. Senkus

Petro Ohonovsky

Ohonovsky, Petro [Ohonovs'kyj], b 20 July 1853 in Rohatyn county, Galicia, d 9 February 1917 in Ukraine. Pedagogue and civic activist; full member of the Shevchenko Scientific Society (NTSh) from 1899; brother of Omelian, Oleksander, and Ilarii Ohonovsky. He graduated from Lviv University and then taught mathematics and physics at the Academic Gymnasium of Lviv (1885–1914). He was head of the Prosvita society (1906–10) and an active member of the NTSh. Ohonovsky also wrote mathematics and physics textbooks.

Volodymyr Ohonovsky

Ohonovsky, Volodymyr [Ohonovs'kyj], b 9 June 1895 in Nyzhniv, Tovmach county, Galicia, d 16 March 1970 in Lviv. Geographer and political activist; full member of the Shevchenko Scientific Society from 1936. After graduating from Charles University in Prague in 1926, he returned to Galicia and headed the Knyzhka publishing house of the Communist Party of Western Ukraine. He was imprisoned by the Polish authorities for his political activities in 1931–4. After the war he worked at the AN URSR Institute of Social Sciences in Lviv and taught at the Lviv Trade and Economics Institute. He wrote *Skhidn'o-evropeis'kyi step* (The East European Steppe, 1935) and numerous works on the economic geography of Western Ukraine.

Ohrenych, Mykola [Ohrenyč], b 8 December 1937 in Ivanivka, Odessa oblast. Opera singer (tenor). A graduate of the Odessa Conservatory (1968), he played on stage with the Odessa Musical Comedy Theater (1962–5) and then joined the Odessa Opera and Ballet Theater as a soloist (1966). His main roles have included Petro in M. Lysenko's *Natalka from Poltava*, Andrii in S. Hulak-Artemovsky's *Zaporozhian Cossack beyond the Danube*, Lensky in P. Tchaikovsky's *Eugene Onegin*, José in G. Bizet's *Carmen*, and Ottavio in W. Mozart's *Don Giovanni*.

Ohrin Peninsula. A multi-occupational archeological site on the Dnieper Rapids, now flooded by the Dnieper Hydroelectric Station. Excavated during 1927–32 by M. *Miller, the site yielded Neolithic burials, Saltiv culture pottery, and the remains of early Slavic farmsteads.

Ohuz kurhan. A Royal Scythian burial mound from the 4th century BC near Nyzhni Sirohozy, Kherson oblast. The site was excavated in 1891–4, in 1902, and intermittently since 1972. The kurhan, surrounded by an earthen embankment and moat (125 m in diameter), contained three burial vaults. The main chamber, one of which is the largest Scythian burial room found to date, was built of stone. While the central chamber had been looted previously, in the corridors leading to it numerous gold and silver articles of horse equipment were found. A looted noblewoman's grave was located adjacent to the central chamber in which the remains of three horses were encountered. The third chamber was not looted and contained approx 6,000 decorative gold items, including earrings in the shape of a sphinx, pendants with animal forms, plates decorated with mythological figures (Athena, Achilles, Hercules)

and the remains of a decorated sarcophagus. The collection is now housed at the Hermitage in St Petersburg and the Museum of Historical Treasures of Ukraine in Kiev.

Oil plants. Plants used to produce edible and other oil products by pressing the plant's seeds or fruits. They are used in the *vegetable-oil industry. The crushed seeds and other by-products are used extensively as feed and fertilizer. The oldest oil plants in Ukraine are *flax and *hemp. *Sunflower and mustard were introduced in the 18th century, false flax and *rape in the 19th century, and *castor bean, *peanut, *perilla, and others in the 20th century. The most widespread oil plants in Ukraine today are sunflower, flax, hemp, castor bean, and rape; 1.75 million ha of land were devoted to the first three crops in 1987. Some peanuts, perilla, mustard, and mint are also cultivated, and some corn is used to produce oil. Attempts to cultivate *cotton, a good source of oil, in Ukraine were unsuccessful.

Oistrakh, David [Ojstrax], b 30 September 1908 in Odessa, d 24 October 1974 in Amsterdam, Holland (buried in Moscow). Jewish-Russian virtuoso violinist and teacher. He graduated from the Odessa Institute of Music (later Conservatory) in 1926 in the class of P. Stoliarsky. He went on to win numerous international music competitions and gain world renown as a talented musician. Besides his appearances in Paris, London, and the United States, he performed in Kiev, Kharkiv, Odessa, Dnipropetrovske, Kherson, Mykolaiv, Kirovohrad, and other cities of Ukraine, often as a soloist in symphonic concerts. From 1934 he taught at the Moscow Conservatory. His Ukrainian pupils included O. Krysa, O. Parkhomenko, and Yu. Mazurkevych.

OKA. A publishing house in Kolomyia. Directed by O. Kuzma, it issued popular books and literature from 1921 to 1939.

Okanenko, Arkadii, b 16 March 1894 in Smila, Kiev gubernia, d 27 September 1982 in Kiev. Plant physiologist and biochemist; corresponding member of the AN URSR (now ANU) from 1967. A graduate of the Kiev Agricultural Institute (1926), he worked in Kiev at the All-Union Scientific Research Institute of Sugar Beets until 1950 (from 1937 as laboratory director) and then became a department head at the ANU Institute of Plant Physiology. He researched the mechanisms of sugar accumulation and storage in sugar beets (particularly the role of the root system and leaves) and the role of potassium in photosynthesis.

Oke or *oka* (Ukrainian: *oko*). A Turkish measure of weight that was commonly used in the Middle East and the Balkans. It was usually equal to approx 1.3 kg. It was used also to measure fluid volumes (equivalent to 1.28 L). The *oke* was used in southwestern Ukraine, where Turkish influence was strong in the 16th and 17th centuries.

Okhmativ, Battle of. A battle during the *Cossack-Polish War. From 29 January to 1 February 1655, near the village of Okhmativ (now in Zhashkiv raion, Cherkasy oblast), an army of 60,000 Cossacks commanded by Hetman B. Khmelnytsky and 6,000 to 10,000 Russian troops under the command of V. Buturlin and V. Sheremetev engaged a Polish-Tatar force commanded by S. Potocki, S. Lanckoroński, and S. Czarniecki. Although the battle was inconclusive, the Poles and Tatars halted their offensive and retreated from Right-Bank Ukraine. The Vinnytsia Regiment commanded by Col I. Bohun particularly distinguished itself during the conflict.

Okhrana or **Okhranka.** The popular name ('Protection') of the political police of the Russian Empire; it was formally subordinated to the minister of internal affairs and the chief of police. In 1881 Alexander III broadened police powers, restricted civil liberties, and introduced special police units to combat the revolutionary underground and political terrorism in the Russian Empire, and to investigate political crime in St Petersburg, Moscow, and Warsaw. The police units were named Sections for the Protection of Public Security and Order and, from 1903, Protective Sections (Okhrannye otdeleniia). The Okhrana operated an extensive network of secret agents, informants, spies, infiltrators, and provocateurs. Special bureaus at post offices intercepted and read and deciphered the correspondence of suspected revolutionaries. Arrests of suspects were made by the gendarmerie and regular municipal and county police. In Ukraine Okhrana branches were established in Kiev, Odessa, Kharkiv, Mykolaiv, and Katerynoslav in 1902. After the February Revolution of 1917 the Okhrana was abolished by the Provisional Government.

Okhrymovych, Ivan [Oxrymovyč], b 1894 in Veldizh, Dolyna county, Galicia, d ca 1943 in Lviv. Choir conductor. From his early years he organized and conducted student choirs in Lviv. In the 1920s and 1930s he conducted the male student choir Bandaryst, the St George Cathedral choir, and the male choir Surma. With Surma he recorded approx 50 songs for the Syrena-Electro label during the 1930s.

Stepan Okhrymovych   Volodymyr Okhrymovych
                            (portrait by Ivan Trush)

Okhrymovych, Stepan [Oxrymovyč], b 18 September 1905 in Skolie, Stryi county, Galicia, d 10 April 1931 in Zavadiv, Stryi county. Student leader and political activist; nephew of Yu. *Okhrymovych. While studying at the Lviv (Underground) Ukrainian University he was active

in the Plast Ukrainian Youth Association, the Ukrainian Military Organization, and the Union of Ukrainian Nationalist Youth. He attended the Congress of Ukrainian Nationalists in Vienna at which the OUN was founded (1929), and in the following year he was appointed to the OUN leadership for Western Ukrainian territories as organizational chief and then propaganda chief and editor of the OUN bulletin. He helped edit *Iunatstvo* and *V dorohu*. His repeated incarceration by the Polish police worsened his already frail health and led to his death a few days after his release from prison.

Okhrymovych, Vasyl [Oxrymovyč, Vasyl'], b 1914, d 1954. Nationalist leader. An OUN activist and political prisoner in the 1930s, he was appointed regional chief of the Ternopil region in 1941 and OUN western regional leader in Ukraine in 1943. He helped organize the *Ukrainian Insurgent Army and in 1944 became a member of the Ukrainian Supreme Liberation Council. He left Ukraine in 1946 but returned in 1953 to take part in underground operations. He was captured by the Soviets and sentenced to death by a military tribunal in Kiev in May 1954.

Okhrymovych, Volodymyr [Oxrymovyč], b 27 May 1870 in Veldizh, Dolyna county, Galicia, d 6 November 1931 in Lviv. Political figure, ethnographer, and journalist; full member of the Shevchenko Scientific Society (NTSh) from 1899 and corresponding member of the Russian Academy of Sciences. He was active in the *Ukrainian Radical party and contributed to its organs *Narod* and *Zhytie i slovo*. He studied law at Lviv University (1889–93; doctorate, 1897) and headed the university's *Academic Brotherhood. He was a founding member of the *National Democratic party (1899) and edited its organ *Dilo* (1902, 1906–7, 1924–5), in which he introduced a phonetic orthography. He edited (1900) and published (1907) the Lviv weekly *Svoboda*. In 1907–8 he was a member of the Austrian parliament. After being deported by the tsarist occupational authorities to Siberia (1915–17) he underwent a change in his religious and philosophical views (described in his pamphlet *Iak ia navernuvsia do Boha: Pryliudna spovid'* [How I Turned to God: A Public Confession, 1920]). After his return to Lviv in 1918, he was a member of the *Ukrainian National Rada of the Western Ukrainian National Republic (1918–19) and a founding member of the *Ukrainian Labor party (1919–25, its leader in 1923) and *Ukrainian National Democratic Alliance (from 1925). He was also a vice-president of the NTSh and head of its Statistical Commission, and a professor and dean of law at the Lviv (Underground) Ukrainian University (1921–5).

Among Okhrymovych's works are a study of the importance of Ukrainian wedding rituals and songs in the historical development of the family (in *Etnograficheskoe obozrenie*, vols 11, 15 [1891–2]); an article on stress in literary Galician Ukrainian (in *Zapysky NTSh*, vol 33 [1900]); shorter articles on Boiko ethnography, folk rituals, and views of customary law (in *Zhytie i slovo*, 1895), on his impressions of Hungarian-ruled Transcarpathia (in *Narod*, 1985, no. 6), and on primitive communism among the Boikos (in *Zapysky NTSh*, vols 31–32 [1899]); a booklet on Ukrainian proverbs about justice with legal explications (1912); and statistical booklets on Galicia's national composition (1909), the Galician *latynnyky (1912), and factual and fictitious Ukrainian losses in Galicia's demographic balance in the decade 1900–10 (1912). V. Malanchuk's book about Okhrymovych's ethnographic activity was published in Kiev in 1972.

Yuliian Okhrymovych   Lev Okinshevych

Okhrymovych, Yuliian [Oxrymovyč, Julijan], b 1893 in Stryi, Galicia, d 10 October 1921 in Kiev. Political and civic leader; brother of Volodymyr *Okhrymovych. A radical influenced by M. Drahomanov's ideas, he studied philosophy and the social sciences at Lviv University from 1911 and was active in the Ukrainian Student Union and editor of its monthly *Shliakhy* (1913–14). At the outbreak of the First World War he crossed the border into Russian-ruled Ukraine to propagate national revolutionary ideas among students. In 1917–18 he served as a secretary of the Central Committee of the Ukrainian Party of Socialist Revolutionaries and as a deputy of student organizations on the Central Rada. He was one of the leaders of the party's central faction and an influential contributor to its organ *Borot'ba*. He refused to leave Ukraine with the UNR government and found work at the Rukh publishing house in Kharkiv. He was executed by the Bolsheviks for his connection with the Central Insurgent Committee in Kiev. He completed only the first part (up to M. Drahomanov) of his *Rozvytok ukraïns'koï natsional'no-politychnoï dumky* (The Development of Ukrainian National-Political Thought, 1918; repr 1922 and 1965).

Okhtyrka [Oxtyrka]. III-15. A city (1990 pop 51,400) at the junction of the Okhtyrka and Vorskla rivers and a raion center in Sumy oblast. The city was founded in 1641 and was an administrative center of Okhtyrka regiment in 1655–1765. Today it has a machine-building industry, a light industry, and a food industry. Its architectural monuments include the Church of the Holy Protectress (1753). It is the birthplace of Ya. *Shchoholev.

Okhtyrka regiment. An administrative territory and military formation established in 1655–8 in Slobidska Ukraine to protect Muscovy's southern frontier from raids by the Crimean and Nogay Tatars. Its first settlers were 456 peasant and Cossack families from Right-Bank Ukraine. By 1732 the regiment had 20 companies. Its male population was over 41,000, including 7,200 elected Cossacks and 17,100 Cossack helpers. In the administrative reform of Slobidska Ukraine in 1765, the Cossack regi-

The Church of the Holy Protectress in Okhtyrka

ment was replaced by a hussar regiment, and the lands of Okhtyrka regiment were incorporated into the gubernia of Slobidska Ukraine.

Okinshevych, Lev [Okinševyč] (Okinshevich, Leo; pseud: Leo Yaresh), b 6 February 1898 in St Petersburg, d 7 November 1980 in Hillcrest Heights, Maryland. Legal historian and bibliographer, of Belarusian and Czech descent. He graduated from Galagan College in Kiev (1916), studied law at Kiev University, and graduated from the Kiev Institute of the National Economy (1921). From 1921 to 1933 he was a research associate of the VUAN and the Kiev Scientific Research Department of the History of Ukraine and served as secretary of the VUAN Commission for the Study of Western Ruthenian and Ukrainian Law. In 1933 he was briefly a professor at the Nizhen Pedagogical Institute before being expelled as a 'class enemy' and forced to move to Kazakhstan. There and in Smolensk oblast (1937–41) he worked as a legal consultant. A postwar émigré, from 1945 to 1949 he was a professor and dean at the Ukrainian Free University (UVU) in Munich. He emigrated to the United States in 1949 and joined the staff of the Library of Congress in 1954.

Okinshevych published works in Ukrainian, Belarusian, and English. They include books in Ukrainian on the Hetman state's General Officer Staff in Left-Bank Ukraine (1926), General Council (1929), central institutions (2 vols, 1929–30; English trans: *Ukrainian Society and Government, 1648–1781* [1978]), and *notable military fellows (1948), and UVU textbooks on the legal structure of the Hetman state (1947; 2nd edn 1954), the history of legal philosophy (1948), and scholarship about law and the state (1987). Okinshevych also compiled *The Law of the Grand Duchy of Lithuania: Background and Bibliography* (1953), *Latin America in Soviet Writings, 1945–1958* (with C. Gorokhoff, 1958), and *U.S. History and Historiography in Post-War Soviet Writings, 1945–1970: A Bibliography* (1976). He also contributed articles on legal history to *Encyclopedia of Ukraine*.

A. Zhukovsky

Oko (Eye). A trilingual (Ukrainian–English–French) monthly newspaper published in Montreal from January 1979 to January 1986 (a total of 68 issues). It reported extensively on Ukrainian life in Montreal. It also devoted attention to general Ukrainian-Canadian issues and affairs in Soviet Ukraine, particularly the dissident movement. The paper was not aligned with any Ukrainian political party or institution and did not refrain from criticizing official community leaders and organizations. The first editor, R. *Serbyn, was succeeded by V. Lewyckyj (April 1979 to December 1981). From January 1982 the paper was edited by a board. At the height of its popularity, *Oko* had a circulation of approx 2,000.

Okolitenko, Natalia, b 6 September 1939 in Kiev. Writer and journalist. She graduated from Kiev University in 1962. She is a former writer for the weekly magazine *Ukraïna* and the author of the prose collections *Intehral Pifahora* (Pythagoras' Integral, 1967), *Snizhni iahody* (Snow Berries, 1970), *Velyka richka* (The Big River, 1973), *Misiats' aktyvnoho sontsia* (Month of the Active Sun, 1979), *Naikorotsha nich roku* (The Shortest Night of the Year, 1983), *Kazka pro syn'oho ptakha* (Tale of the Blue Bird, 1985), and *Hodynnyk zhyttia* (The Clock of Life, 1985) and of the science fiction collection *Krok vikinha* (The Viking's Step, 1990). Many of her works depict the problems facing the modern Ukrainian woman.

Okolski, Szymon, b 1580 in Kamianets-Podilskyi, d 10 June 1653 in Lviv. Polish historian and heraldist. He was a Dominican monk, and in 1637–8 served as the chaplain for M. Potocki's Polish forces which suppressed the Cossack rebellion of P. Pavliuk, K. Skydan, Ya. Ostrianyn, and D. Hunia. Okolski's two diaries of this period provided a detailed record of the Polish campaign and of Cossack tactics. Published in Zamostia (a 1638 printing of the 1637 diary) and Cracow (a 1639 printing of the 1638 diary), they were translated into Ukrainian and used in works by S. *Velychko and S. *Lukomsky during the 18th century. Later they appeared in *Memuary, otnosiashchiesia k istorii Iuzhnoi Rusi* (Memoirs Relating to the History of Southern Rus', vol 2, 1896).

Okopenko, Andrii, b 1 May 1874 in Kharkiv, d 10 November 1965 in Moscow. Medical and military figure. Having studied medicine in Kharkiv and St Petersburg, he served as a physician in the Russo-Japanese War and in 1912 was put in charge of public health in the Don Cossack province. A senior army surgeon during the First World War, in May–October 1918 he was chief physician of the Hetman government's railway army. After being promoted to general he was appointed the Ukrainian Red Cross plenipotentiary for all Ukrainian POWs in foreign countries (April 1919) and chief of the UNR Military Mission for Central and Southern Europe (May 1919). From then to April 1922 he headed the official Ukrainian mission in Vienna that repatriated thousands of Ukrainian POWs, demobilized soldiers, and refugees in Central Europe. From 1922 he worked as a physician and cultural-educational organizer in Ust Chorna, Transcarpathia. After fleeing the Hungarian occupation of Carpatho-Ukraine, in March 1939 he settled in Vienna, where in February 1942 he founded, under the *Ukrainian Institution of Trust and the German Red Cross, the Ukrainian Committee for the Welfare of Prisoners of War in the Ostmark Lands. During the Soviet occupation of Vienna in 1945, he was persecuted and finally deported to the Borovsk labor camp in the Urals. After being amnestied in 1952 and rehabilitated in 1956, he moved to Moscow in 1958.

Okruha (Russian: okrug). An administrative-territorial unit formed in the Ukrainian SSR in 1923, when *counties were abolished and replaced with 53 okruhas. In 1925 a consolidation took place, and the number of okruhas was lowered to 41. In 1930–2 okruhas were abolished and, after a further consolidation, replaced by *oblasts. After the Second World War okruhas existed in Transcarpathia oblast until 1953. (See *Administrative-territorial division.)

Oksenovych-Starushych, Ihnatii [Oksenovyč-Starušyč, Ihnatij], b ?, d 30 October 1651 in Kiev. Orthodox theologian and churchman. He served as hegumen of the monastery and rector of the college in Hoshcha, Volhynia (1639–40); archimandrite of the Kievan Cave Monastery (1640); professor at and rector of the Kievan Mohyla College (later Academy); and hegumen of the Kiev Epiphany Brotherhood Monastery (1640–2). Together with I. Kozlovsky-Trofymovych and Y. Kononovych-Horbatsky, he represented the Ukrainian Orthodox church at the 1642 church council in Iași that ratified P. Mohyla's confession of the faith. He published a eulogy for Prince I. Sviatopolk-Chetvertynsky in 1641.

Oksiiuk, Yosyf [Oksijuk, Josyf], b 9 September 1894 in Lukovychi, Volodymyr-Volynskyi county, Volhynia gubernia, d 24 April 1991 in Kiev. Orthodox bishop. He graduated from the Kholm Theological Seminary (1914) and the Kiev Theological Academy (1917), where he later taught patrology. During the brief period of Ukrainian statehood he was a member of the Brotherhood of Cyril and Methodius in Kiev. In 1919 he taught church history at Kamianets-Podilskyi Ukrainian State University and translated theological books into Ukrainian. In 1920–2 he was a lecturer in history at the Kamianets-Podilskyi Institute of People's Education. After being consecrated a bishop of the *Ukrainian Autocephalous Orthodox church (UAOC) in 1922, he served as bishop of Kamianets-Podilskyi and then, until 1929, archbishop of Lubni and Poltava and of Myrhorod. In October 1927 he was chosen as second deputy to the metropolitan of Kiev and a member of the presidium of the All-Ukrainian Orthodox Church Council. He was persecuted by the Soviet authorities, and in 1933 he was forced to withdraw from the church. He was arrested in 1935, imprisoned, and exiled. He returned to Ukraine in 1950 and acted as secretary to his brother Makarii, the archbishop of the Russian Orthodox church

Archbishop Yosyf Oksiiuk   Sofiia Okunevska-Moraczewska

Teofil Okunevsky   Yaroslav Okunevsky

in Lviv, who later became metropolitan of the Polish Autocephalous Orthodox church.

Oksiutyntsi kurhans. Scythian burial mounds from the mid-1st century BC, on the Sula River near Oksiutyntsi (now Pustoviitivka), Sumy oblast. Excavated in the late 19th century, the site revealed several hundred kurhans, some up to 10–20 m high. Among the grave goods interred with the dead were armor, horse equipment, ceramic wares, and decorative items.

Oksner, Alfred, b 15 February 1898 in Yelysavethrad (now Kirovohrad), Kherson gubernia, d 20 November 1973 in Kiev. Botanist and lichenologist; corresponding member of the AN URSR (now ANU) from 1972. A graduate of the Kiev Institute of People's Education (1924), he worked in the ANU Institute of Botany in 1931–73 (as director in 1968–70), headed a department in the Kiev Institute of Hydromelioration, and taught at Kiev University. He carried out regular expeditions to study lichens in Ukraine (1926–40), founded a herbarium that became an experimental center for lichenology, and established the Ukrainian school of lichenologists. He is the author of *Vyznachnyk lyshainykiv URSR* (Field Guide to Lichens of the Ukrainian SSR, 1937) and *Flora lyshainykiv Ukraïny* (The Flora of Lichens of Ukraine, 2 vols, 1956, 1968).

Okunevska-Moraczewska, Sofiia [Okunevs'ka, Sofija], b 12 May 1865 in Storozhynets, Bukovyna, d 25 February 1926 in Lviv. Physician and writer; wife of W. *Moraczewski. After completing her medical studies in Zurich (1894) she became the first female physician in Austria-Hungary. In 1897 she opened a private practice in Lviv. A friend of O. Kobylianska, N. Kobrynska, and V. Stefanyk, she was active in the women's movement and contributed to *Pershyi vinok* under the pseudonym Yeryna.

Okunevsky, Teofil [Okunevs'kyj, Teofil'], b 7 December 1858 in Yavoriv, Kolomyia circle, Galicia, d 19 July 1937 in Horodenka, Galicia. Lawyer and civic and political leader of the Kolomyia-Horodenka region. After graduating in law from Vienna University (1885) he became active in Galician politics and helped found the Ukrainian Radical party (1890) and the National Democratic party

(1899). He was elected to the Galician Diet (1889–1900 and 1913–14) and to the Austrian parliament (1897–1900 and 1907–18). In 1890 he established a law office in Horodenka and helped organize and finance various economic, educational, and cultural organizations. For many years (until 1930) he was president of the Prosvita branch in Horodenka. He acted as defense counsel at many political trials, including that of M. *Sichynsky (1908). When the Western Ukrainian National Republic was established, he served as a member of the Ukrainian National Rada, commissioner of Horodenka county, and appeals court judge in Stanyslaviv. His correspondence with M. Drahomanov was published by M. Pavlyk in 1905.

Okunevsky, Yaroslav [Okunevs'kyj, Jaroslav], b 1860 in Radivtsi (Rădăuţi), Bukovyna, d 24 October 1929 in Horodenka, Galicia. Physician and civic leader; brother of T. *Okunevsky. After graduating in medicine from Vienna University he served as general physician in the Austrian navy. When the Western Ukrainian National Republic was established, he founded and headed the Ukrainian sanitary mission to Vienna. After the war he settled in Horodenka and practiced medicine. He contributed articles to many papers and almanacs and published an account of his travels as a naval doctor as *Lysty z chuzhyny* (Letters from Abroad, 2 vols, 1898, 1902).

Olaf I Tryggvason, b ca 966–8, d 9 September 1000 or 1002. King of Norway; son of a chieftain and great-grandson of King Harald I Fairhair of Norway. According to medieval sources, after his father's murder he fled from Norway with his mother, Astrid. After six years' captivity in Estonia, he made his way to the court of Volodymyr the Great, then prince of Novgorod, and served as a leader of Volodymyr's Varangian forces there and in Kiev. Already a Christian at that time, he reportedly played a part in Volodymyr's conversion in 987 and was sent by him to negotiate the treaty with Constantinople. Returning to Norway in the early 990s, Olaf succeeded Haakon the Great as king (995) and imposed Christianity in Norway, the Shetland, Faeroe, and Orkney islands, Iceland, and Greenland. The Norse rune (saga) about Olaf remains a valuable historical resource about Kievan Rus'.

Olbia. A major ancient Greek settlement located on the Boh Estuary near Parutyne, Ochakiv raion, Mykolaiv oblast. The site was discovered in the late 18th century and researched intermittently throughout the 19th century. Extensive excavations beginning in the late 19th century were carried out under the direction of V. Latyshev, B. Farmakovsky, L. Slavin, and others. Since 1920 Olbia has been under official protection and it is at present a state historical site administered by the ANU Institute of Archeology.

Excavated ruins of Olbia

Founded in the early 6th century BC by Greek settlers from Miletus and other Ionian cities, Olbia soon became a prominent trading center on the northern Black Sea coast. Its inhabitants engaged in agriculture, animal husbandry, fishing, viticulture, various trades (metalworking, pottery, woodworking, stone cutting, weaving), and trade with the Greek metropolis. Olbia imported wine, olive oil, fine dishes, cloth, art objects, and glassware both for itself and for trade (together with local goods and services) with Scythians, Sarmatians, and other tribes on the Pontic steppe in exchange for grain, cattle, wool, fish, and slaves. In order to facilitate trade, the city minted its own bronze, silver, and (occasionally) gold coins.

Olbia reached the height of its prosperity and importance in the 5th to 3rd centuries BC as a city-state covering an area of approx 50 ha. It was strong enough to withstand a major siege by one of Alexander the Great's armies in 331 BC. Subsequent attacks in the 2nd to 1st centuries BC by hostile tribesmen weakened the city, and it was forced to accept the suzerainty of Scythian chieftains and then of Mithridates VI Eupator, ruler of the Pontic Kingdom. In the mid-1st century BC, the city was sacked thoroughly by Getae invaders. Olbia was rebuilt in the 1st century AD as a thriving trade center, but it never regained its former size or prosperity. Its population now included a large and influential Scythian element. Olbia fell under Roman influence, and in the mid-2nd to mid-3rd century a Roman garrison was posted there. With the garrison's departure the city fell prey to Goths and other invaders and finally collapsed in the 4th century.

The remains of Olbia reflect a prosperous and well-planned city. It was built in a triangular shape along a north–south axis. The lower town, the area initially settled by the Greek colonists, was located along the estuary and was well suited for port facilities. With Olbia's rapid growth, the settlement expanded to an upper town on the adjacent bluffs. The main square, or *agora*, was situated precisely in the middle of the city, with the principal civic structures, a gymnasium, a theater, a hippodrome, and a temple complex nearby. The city is laid out on an orthogonal grid typical of Greek (Miletian) colonial cities, with a main thoroughfare running the length of the upper town. Statues of gods, heroes, and prominent civic figures lined the main streets. Streets and a stairway connected the upper and lower towns. Aqueducts supplied the city with water, though cisterns finished with waterproof plaster were also numerous. The apogee of building technique came in the 5th to 4th century BC, with carefully laid masonry walls, often rusticated for effect. Stone basements and ground stories topped with one story (or sometimes two) in mud brick were common throughout all periods. Public buildings and wealthy homes were further enhanced with columns and capitals of the Ionic and Doric orders, and other architectural ornaments which developed a specific regional character.

Olbia was fortified by thick masonry walls with towers. Outside the walls stretched extensive (500 ha) burial grounds. Olbia's rural hinterland was thickly studded with hundreds of estates and settlements which remained unfortified until Roman times.

Artifacts from Olbia can be found in St Petersburg's Hermitage, Moscow's Museum of History, Kiev's Historical Museum of Ukraine, the Odessa Archeological Museum, the Mykolaiv and Kherson regional studies museums, and a number of Western European and North American museums.

BIBLIOGRAPHY
Slavin, L. *Zdes' byl gorod Ol'viia* (Kiev 1967)
Belin de Ballu, E. *Olbia: Cité antique du littoral nord de la Mer Noire* (Leiden 1972)
Levi, E. *Ol'viia: Gorod epokhi ellinizma* (Leningrad 1985)
                                                        A. Makuch

Olbracht, Ivan (pseud of Kamil Zeman), b 6 January 1882 in Semily, Bohemia, d 30 December 1952 in Prague. Czech writer and Communist figure. He spent the summers of 1931–3 in the Transcarpathian village of Kolochava. Life in Transcarpathia was the subject of his historical novel *Nikola Šuhaj loupežník* (Nikola Šuhaj, the Robber, 1933; Ukrainian trans 1934, 1960; English trans 1954), his essay collection *Hory a staletí* (Mountains and Centuries, 1935), and the story collection *Golet v údolí* (Exile in the Valley, 1937).

Old Believers (Russian: *starovery* or *staroobriadtsy* ['Old Ritualists']). A grass-roots religious movement that emerged in 17th-century Russia as a reaction against the centralist policies of the Russian Orthodox church under Patriarch Nikon (1652–67). Nikon reformed Russian religious rites, customs, and particularly liturgical books, which he had amended with the aid of the Ukrainian scholars A. Koretsky-Satanovsky, T. Safonovych, and Ye. Slavynetsky to conform to Greek texts. Many Russian parish priests and faithful defended the old rites and texts and rejected the new, despite the support the latter were given by Tsar Aleksei Mikhailovich and the Russian government. Led by A. Petrovich, I. Neronov, and other archpriests, the Old Believers grew into a mass movement even though the Orthodox sobor of 1666–7 anathematized them and the government and church officials persecuted them as schismatics and state criminals. In the 17th century many Old Believers had chiliastic views, and over 20,000 committed suicide by self-immolation instead of waiting for the apocalypse.

The Old Believers took part in political and social movements directed against the tsarist regime, such as the 1668–76 rebellion at the monastery on the Solovets Island in the White Sea, the 1670–1 peasant uprising in southern Russia led by S. Razin, and the 1682 Khovanshchina rebellion around Moscow. Fleeing from brutal persecution, they founded communities in Russia's borderlands in the north, the Urals, and the Don and Volga regions, and beyond in the Left-Bank Hetman state, Polish-ruled Belarus (Vetka in the Homel region), Right-Bank Ukraine, Bukovyna, and Moldavia.

In 1683 the Old Believers split into a moderate majority called *popovtsy* ('Priestists'), who had priests (and, from the mid-19th century, bishops) and administered the Sacraments, and a radical minority called *bespopovtsy* ('Priestless'), who celebrated liturgies without priests and rejected all Sacraments except baptism. The latter group underwent further sectarian splits.

The *popovtsy* who settled in the Left-Bank Hetman state in the 1660s formed, with the approval of Hetman D. Mnohohrishny, 'schismatic free settlements' (*rozkolnychi slobody*) in the territories of Starodub and Chernihiv regiments. Their colonization increased under hetmans I. Mazepa and I. Skoropadsky largely with the permission of local authorities (Cossack *starshyna* and monastic superiors, including the archimandrite of the Kievan Cave Monastery), who expected that they would be able to turn the *popovtsy* into vassals after their eight-year dispensation ended. The economic strength of the free settlements, however, and Russian centralist politics to 1709 helped the Old Believers avoid subjugation. Peter I's 1716 ukase legalized their status in the Hetmanate and confirmed their rights and landholdings. According to the enumeration of 1715–8 there were 586 households in the 17 schismatic free settlements in the northern Hetmanate. The settlements' autonomy, prosperity, and commercial and manufacturing successes resulted in further repressions, this time by the Hetmanate government. In 1716 and 1719 Hetman I. Skoropadsky forbade the Old Believers to trade in the Hetmanate, but this prohibition was not enforced and his petitions to the tsar to have the Old Believers deported from the Hetmanate were in vain. In the second half of the 18th century the free settlement of *Klintsy in the northern Chernihiv region became the Old Believers' cultural and publishing center; from the late 18th century it was an important woolen manufacturing center, which grew to be the largest in Ukraine by the turn of the 20th century.

The free settlements' economic and population growth and constant conflicts with local officials and the Ukrainian government (particularly over increased taxation) caused many Old Believers in the Chernihiv and neighboring Homel regions to move to the sparsely populated lands of Southern Ukraine. There they colonized *New Serbia and *Sloviano-Serbia, and later Kherson and Tavriia gubernias, particularly Beryslav and Melitopil counties. By 1832 over 7,000 Old Believers lived in Southern Ukraine. The tsarist government supported their efforts to settle Ukraine's southern steppes and granted them various exemptions. In 1858, 10 percent of the registered Old Believers in the Russian Empire – 88,762 individuals –

lived in the nine Ukrainian gubernias; by far the largest concentration was in Chernihiv gubernia (51,643), followed by Podilia (9,913) and Kherson (7,105) gubernias. By 1904 their number in the nine gubernias had nearly doubled, to 166,648. In the mid-18th century Old Believers also settled in southern Bessarabia, where they were known as *lipovany*, and near the Danube Delta (eg, the village [now town] of Vylkove). Their in-migration increased after Bessarabia was annexed by the Russian Empire in 1812, and by the late 19th century nearly 30,000 Old Believers were living in southern and northern (Khotyn county) Bessarabia.

From the 1760s to the 1780s *lipovany* who had emigrated to Ottoman-ruled Moldavia, Wallachia, and Bessarabia resettled in Bukovyna and Podilia with the support of Austrian authorities. In 1783 Joseph II exempted them from taxes and guaranteed their religious freedom. In Bila Krynytsia (now in Hlyboka raion, Chernivtsi oblast) the Old Believers built a monastery and a cathedral with the financial support of their coreligionists in the Russian Empire. In 1844 the settlement became the Old Believers' episcopal see. Later a hierarchy headed by a metropolitan was established there and ordained priests and bishops for Old Believers throughout the Russian Empire. After the tsarist edict of toleration was proclaimed in 1905, the center of the *popovtsy* in the Russian Empire was established in Moscow at their church in the Rogozhskoe Cemetery. In 1784 there were 400 Old Believers in Bukovyna; in 1844, 2,000; in 1900, 3,110; and in 1930, 3,200. Most were *popovtsy*. In the 1880s and 1890s they published in Kolomyia the journals *Staroobriadets* and *Davniaia Rus'*, which were edited by N. Chernichev.

In Ukraine, as elsewhere, the Old Believers lived in separate settlements and ghettos. They considered outsiders to be unclean and thus kept contact with them to a minimum. They differed from their Ukrainian neighbors in virtually all aspects: in religion and rite, language (they spoke Russian), the construction and internal arrangement of their houses, and folkways. They wore traditional Russian clothing and did not shave, smoke, or drink alcohol, coffee, or tea. They had strict prohibitions against taverns in their settlements and rejected theater, music, and dance. Their refusal to serve in the military, to take oaths in court, and to register births, deaths, and marriages brought them into constant conflict with the authorities. The Old Believers were engaged primarily in grain and vegetable farming, orcharding, various trades, and manufacturing. Many of those living in towns were prosperous merchants and factory owners. The Old Believers facilitated the Russification of certain parts of Ukraine, particularly the northern Chernihiv region, which is now part of Briansk oblast in Russia.

Under tsarist rule in the 19th and 20th centuries, there was a special department of the history of the 'schism' at the Kiev Theological Academy; it was headed by S. Golubev.

BIBLIOGRAPHY

Makarii [Bulgakov, M.]. *Istoriia russkago raskola, izvestnago pod nazvaniiem staroobriadchestva*, 3rd edn (St Petersburg 1889)

Lileev, M. *Iz istorii raskola na Vetke i v Starodube XVIIX–XVIII vv.* (Kiev 1895)

Smirnov, P. *Istoriia russkago raskola staroobriadstva*, 2nd edn (St Petersburg 1895; repr Westmead, Hants 1971)

Kaindl, F.R. *Das Entstehen und die Entwicklung der Lippowaner-Colonie in der Bukowina* (Vienna 1896)

Polek, J. *Die Lippowaner in der Bukowina* (Chernivtsi 1899)

Zen'kovskii, S. *Russkoe staroobriadchestvo: Dukhovnye dvizheniia semnadtsatogo veka* (Munich 1970)

Naulko, V. *Razvitie mezhetnicheskikh sviazei na Ukraine (istoriko-etnograficheskii ocherk)* (Kiev 1975)

Poliakov, L. *L'Epopée des Vieux-Croyants: Une histoire de la Russie authentique* (Paris 1991)

I. Korovytsky, A. Zhukovsky

Old Kramatorske Machine-Building Plant (Starokramatorskyi mashynobudivnyi zavod). A heavy-machine-building plant in Kramatorske, Donetske oblast, founded in 1896 by a German firm. The plant produced steam engines, compressors, power hammers, and other mining tools and equipment. Its machinery was evacuated at the outset of the Second World War, and the plant was completely rebuilt after 1943. It continues to produce mining equipment and metalworking machinery, including ore transporters, cold-rolling mills, and assembly lines for sheet-metal works and pipe factories. In 1970 the plant employed over 2,700 workers.

Old Ruthenians (*starorusyny or sviatoiurtsi.*) Representatives of a clerical, anti-Polish, pro-Austrian social-political current dominant in Galicia in the mid–19th century. During the *Revolution of 1848–9 in the Habsburg monarchy the higher clergy of the Greek Catholic church in Galicia (Bishop H. *Yakhymovych, M. *Kuzemsky, M. Malynovsky) played a very important role in the Ukrainian movement, especially in the executive of its most representative organization, the *Supreme Ruthenian Council. They remained loyal to the emperor throughout the revolution, partly out of a traditional gratitude to the Habsburg dynasty for numerous improvements it had introduced in Greek Catholic ecclesiastical life, but also because in the imperial court they hoped to find protection against Polish pretensions to rule Galicia. After the defeat of the revolution in 1849, which inaugurated a decade of neoabsolutism in the Habsburg monarchy, the Supreme Ruthenian Council and other Ukrainian institutions either ceased or radically scaled down their activities. Such leadership of the Ukrainian movement as existed was concentrated almost entirely in the hands of the Greek Catholic hierarchy (including Metropolitan S. *Lytvynovych, Bishop and later Metropolitan Yakhymovych) and the canons of the Lviv cathedral chapter (including Kuzemsky and Malynovsky). Thus, during the 1850s the leadership of the Ukrainian movement was dubbed 'the St George party' (*sviatoiurtsi*), after St George's Greek Catholic cathedral in Lviv. The St George party and those who subscribed to its views were also known as Old Ruthenians, especially by the 1860s, when the political situation of Ukrainians in the monarchy changed markedly and younger activists became *Russophiles or embraced Western Ukrainian *populism.

Characteristic of the Old Ruthenians was strong pro-Austrian feeling, relative conservatism in social and political questions, and attachment to the Greek rite, the Cyrillic alphabet, and the etymological orthography (over which they engaged in the *alphabet war of 1859–61). They had no clear conception of national identity. During the revolution of 1848–9 they mainly identified themselves as part of the Ukrainian nation, although already by

then some considered themselves closely related to or even a part of the Russian nation. The Russian idea became more important in Old Ruthenian thinking as time passed. Many Old Ruthenians also thought of themselves as part of a separate Ruthenian or Rusyn nation, restricted to the Ukrainian population of the Habsburg monarchy.

In the 1860s Austria received a constitution and parliament and the crownland of Galicia became autonomous under the domination of the Polish gentry. The new situation called forth new political currents that were much more dynamic than those of the Old Ruthenians. Most Old Ruthenians then sided with the Russophile camp, which attracted them by its social and linguistic conservatism as well as by its Easternizing religious orientation; many of them, however, were never able to adopt Russophile views thoroughly, being unwilling to abandon their loyalty to either the Habsburg emperor or Catholic church. Some Old Ruthenians, such as S. *Kachala, entered the populist movement, bringing with them their conservative views. An incident in 1870 may be considered the last stand of Old Ruthenianism: Metropolitan Y. *Sembratovych and canon Malynovsky tried unsuccessfully to reconcile the Russophile and populist parties on the basis of recognizing a separate Ruthenian nation of three million. Some epigones of Old Ruthenianism survived into the late 19th century, an outstanding example being the bibliographer I. *Levytsky.

J.P. Himka, O. Sereda

Andrew Olearchyk

Olearchyk, Andrew [Olearčyk, Andrij], b 3 December 1935 in Peremyshl. Cardiothoracic and vascular surgeon. A graduate of the Medical Academy in Warsaw (1961). He practices in New Jersey and Philadelphia (since 1982). Olearchyk contributed to anesthesia, and to general, cardiac, and vascular surgery. His publications include the monographs *Subphrenic Abscesses* (1972), *Ulcers of the Stomach and Duodenum in Children* (1974), *Coronary Revascularization: Past, Present and Future* (1988), a 'Concise History of Medicine' (with R. Olearchyk) in *Likars'kyi visnyk* (1991), and medical articles in *Encyclopedia of Ukraine* (vols 3–5).

Oleh (Russian: Oleg; Norse: Helgi), b ?, d autumn 912 (according to the Laurentian Chronicle) or 922 (according to the Novgorod First Chronicle). Semilegendary Varangian prince of Rus'. A relative of *Riuryk, he was Prince *Ihor's guardian and regent in Novgorod. According to the Rus' chronicles, in 882 Oleh sailed down the Dnieper with a force of Varangians, Slavs, and Finns and captured Smolensk, Liubech, and finally Kiev. He had Kiev's rulers *Askold and Dyr murdered, and proclaimed himself prince of Kiev. By 885 Oleh had extended his rule over the *Derevlianians, *Siverianians, *Radimichians, and *Polianians, but he did not succeed in turning the *Ulychians and *Tivertsians into tributaries. Oleh's campaigns against the Khazars were less successful, but they ended Khazar domination in the middle Dnieper region. The Primary Chronicle describes Oleh's successful land and sea campaign against Byzantium in 907, which resulted in the acquisition of extensive commercial privileges for Rus' merchants in the Byzantine Empire. A second treaty, signed in 911 by 15 of Oleh's envoys and the Byzantine emperors Leo VI, Alexander, and Constantine VII, regulated the noncommercial aspects of Rus'-Byzantine relations.

Some scholars (eg, R.H. Dolley, H. Grégoire, O. Pritsak) consider Oleh's Byzantine campaign and Oleh himself to be an invention of the chroniclers, but they concede the likelihood that a treaty was signed by a Kievan prince and Byzantium in 911. The reliability of the Primary Chronicle has been accepted by most scholars. Contemporary historiographers, however, differentiate between the legendary Oleh the Seer of the Primary Chronicle and the Oleh of Rus' who negotiated a favorable treaty with Byzantium. In oral folk literature the legend of Oleh as a ruler with supernatural powers (therefore 'the Seer') endured.

BIBLIOGRAPHY

Vasiliev, A. 'The Second Russian Attack on Constantinople,' *Dumbarton Oaks Papers,* 6 (1951)
The Russian Primary Chronicle: Laurentian Text, trans and ed S.H. Cross and O.P. Sherbowitz-Wetzor (Cambridge, Mass 1953)
Sakharov, A. *Diplomatiia drevnei Rusi: IX–pervaia polovina X v.* (Moscow 1980)
Pritsak, O. *The Origin of Rus'. 1: Old Scandinavian Sources Other than the Sagas* (Cambridge, Mass 1981)

M. Zhdan, A. Zhukovsky

Oleh Sviatoslavych [Svjatoslavyč], b ?, d 977 in Ovruch, Volhynia. Appanage prince; son of Grand Prince *Sviatoslav I Ihorevych. He received the Derevlianian land from Sviatoslav. After Sviatoslav's death Oleh's half-brother, *Yaropolk I Sviatoslavych, sought to annex all Ukrainian territories and moved against him. Oleh died during a battle after falling off his horse into a moat. In 1044 Oleh's nephew, Yaroslav the Wise, had Oleh's remains exhumed, baptized, and reburied in the Church of the Tithes in Kiev.

Oleh Sviatoslavych [Svjatoslavyč], b ca 1050 [in Chernihiv?], d 6 or 24 August 1115 in Novhorod-Siverskyi. Son of *Sviatoslav II Yaroslavych and father of *Vsevolod and *Ihor Olhovych. After his father's death in 1076, Oleh inherited Chernihiv, but the new grand prince, Oleh's uncle *Iziaslav Yaroslavych, gave Chernihiv to another uncle, *Vsevolod Yaroslavych. Instead Oleh ruled Volodymyr-Volynskyi, but he was driven out in 1078 by Iziaslav and sought refuge with his brother, Roman (d 1079), in *Tmutorokan. In 1078 Oleh and his cousin Borys Viacheslavych tried, with Cuman help, to regain his patrimony in Chernihiv, but they were defeated by Iziaslav and Vsevolod's army at Nezhatyna Nyva. Oleh returned to Tmutorokan, where he was captured by the Khazars in

1079 and handed over to the Byzantines. He lived in exile on Rhodes until 1083, when he returned to Tmutorokan and regained it from his cousin Davyd Ihorevych.

In 1094 Oleh took Chernihiv, after his Cuman allies had ravaged it, from his cousin Volodymyr Monomakh. He was driven out by Monomakh in 1096, fled to Starodub, and then took Murom and Rostov from Monomakh's son Iziaslav. Oleh then attacked Iziaslav's brother, *Mstyslav I Volodymyrovych of Novgorod, but was defeated and forced to attend the *Liubech congress of princes in 1097. There Oleh forfeited Chernihiv, Murom, and Riazan but was given Novhorod-Siverskyi and the lands of Kursk, which he ruled until his death. Because of his enduring ties with the Cumans (he also married a Cuman princess) Oleh refused to join Rus' military expeditions against them. In the epic *Slovo o polku Ihorevi* and folk legends he is referred to as the Son of Grief (Horyslavych). Oleh's descendants, the *Olhovych house of Chernihiv, struggled for control of the Kievan state against the descendants of Monomakh.

A. Zhukovsky

Oleh Yaroslavych [Jaroslavyč], b ?, d 1188 in princely Halych. Son of Galician prince *Yaroslav Osmomysl and Nastasiia Charhova. In 1187 he succeeded Yaroslav on the Galician throne, but he was soon driven out by boyars, who installed his half-brother, *Volodymyr Yaroslavych, in his place. Oleh fled to Poland, whence he returned to regain Halych with the help of King Casimir II the Just. He died soon afterward, having been poisoned by boyars.

Oleksandriia [Oleksandrija]. V-14. A city (1990 pop 103,800) on the Inhulets River and a raion center in Kirovohrad oblast. It was founded in the early 18th century as the settlement Usivka, and it was renamed Becheiu (Becha, Bechka) in the 1750s. In 1784 it was renamed Oleksandriisk and later Oleksandriia and chosen as a county center of Kherson gubernia. The city is the center of the *Oleksandriia Lignite Coal Basin: it has three strip mines, two mine shafts, and two briquette factories. It also has a machine-building and a food industry.

Oleksandriia [Oleksandrija]. A dendrological park located in Bila Tserkva, Kiev oblast. At present under the auspices of the Academy of Sciences of Ukraine (ANU), the

Oleksandriia park

park is spread out over 201.5 ha on the bank of the Ros River. Work was started on the project in 1793–7 with a Western European landscaping plan, and continued until 1850. The park was named after O. Branicki, the initiator of the project and the owner of the property on which it was built. It features approx 1,800 species or varieties of local, regional, and imported flora in a setting with architectural features such as the Branicki mansion, pavilions, and quaint bridges. Oleksandriia was damaged during conflicts in 1918–20 and 1941–3. In 1922 it was nationalized, and in 1946 turned over to the AN URSR (now ANU), which restored the park to its former state. The site is now an important center for the academy's scientific research in plant introduction and acclimatization.

Oleksandriia Lignite Coal Region. The richest source in the *Dnieper Lignite Coal Basin. Located in the upper reaches of the Inhulets River near the city of Oleksandriia, in Kirovohrad oblast, it is noted for its wide seams (up to 25 m) of high-grade coal near the surface of the ground (depth of approx 40–45 m), readily extractable by open-pit mining. The coal is processed into briquettes at nearby factories. The region has been mined since 1915.

Oleksandriia settlement. A Copper Age settlement along the Oskil River near Oleksandriia, Borove raion, Kharkiv oblast. Excavation in 1956–7 revealed multiple occupations. The site is best known for the recovery of 33 burials which were sprinkled with red ochre.

Oleksandriv, Borys (pseud of B. Hrybinsky), b 21 July 1921 in Ruzhyn, Skvyra county, Kiev gubernia, d 21 December 1979 in Toronto. Writer. A postwar émigré, in 1948 he settled in Toronto. There he founded and headed the Toronto branch of the *Slovo Association of Ukrainian Writers in Exile and was chief editor of the youth magazine *Moloda Ukraïna* (1951–60). He wrote five collections of lyrical poetry: *Moï dni* (My Days, 1946), *Tuha za sontsem: Poeziï 1945–1965* (Longing for the Sun: Poetry, 1945–65, 1967), *Kolokruh* (a neologism, literally 'Circle-Round,' 1972), *Kaminnyi bereh: Poeziï pro liubov, pro zhyttia i pro smert' 1972–1975* (The Rocky Shore: Poems about Love, Life, and Death, 1972–5, 1975), and *Povorot po slidu: Vybrani poeziï 1939–1979* (Retracing the Path: Selected Poems, 1939–79, 1980). Under the pen name Svyryd Lomachka he also wrote humorous and satiric sketches and poems; they appeared in the émigré press and as the collections *Svyryd Lomachka v Kanadi* (Svyryd Lomachka in Canada, 1951) and *Liubov do blyzhn'oho* (Love for One's Neighbor, 1961). He also translated foreign poetry into Ukrainian; notable examples are his translations of A. Akhmatova's *Requiem* (1973) and of Quebec poetry in the anthology *Poeziia/Kvebek* (Poetry/Quebec, 1972).

Oleksandrivka. V-14. A town smt (1990 pop 12,400) on the Tiasmyn River and a raion center in Kirovohrad oblast. It was founded in the first half of the 17th century, and became part of the Russian Empire at the end of the 18th century. There is a sugar-refining complex and a gas-pipeline construction firm in the town.

Oleksandrivka. VI-12. A town smt (1990 pop 6,300) on the left bank of the Boh River in Voznesenske raion, Mykolaiv oblast. It was founded at the beginning of the

18th century, and attained smt status in 1968. Its factories produce building materials, such as silicate bricks, reinforced-concrete structures, and asphalt, and its two quarries produce granite. There is a bird and a fish sanctuary near the town.

Oleksandrivka. V-17, DB II-1. A town smt (1990 pop 4,900) on the Samara River and a raion center in Donetske oblast. The town, which was first called Bakhmetieve, was founded in 1762 and granted smt status in 1965. It has a brick factory and an experimental fish farm.

Oleksandrivka. VI-18, DB IV-3. A town smt (1990 pop 4,800) in Marinka raion, Donetske oblast. It was founded in 1841 and called Kremina until 1903. It attained smt status in 1938. Its economy since 1890 has depended on a nearby coal mine and on jobs in Donetske.

Oleksandrivka settlement. A Trypilian settlement of the early 3rd millennium BC near Tymkove, Kodyma raion, Odessa oblast. Excavations in 1950–3 uncovered remains of clay dwellings, storage pits, large amounts of pottery (adorned with either paint or geometric incisions), and flint, stone, and bone tools. Of particular interest were approx 100 earthenware cult figurines of women sitting in chairs.

Oleksandrivske. V-20, DB II-6. A city (1990 pop 7,800) on the Luhan River in Luhanske oblast. It was founded in the 1770s. Its name was changed from Oleksandrivka and the town raised to city status in 1961. It is administered by the Artemivske city raion council of Luhanske. Oleksandrivske manufactures electrical appliances.

Oleksandrivske. See Zaporizhia.

Oleksandropil kurhan (engraving)

Oleksandropil kurhan. A Royal Scythian burial site of the 4th to 3rd century BC near Oleksandropil, Nykopil raion, Dnipropetrovske oblast. Excavated in 1852–6, this site, also known as Luhova mohyla, is one of the largest (some 20 m high) of the Royal Scythian burial mounds found in Ukraine. Although extensively looted, the main burial chamber produced the remains of a sarcophagus. In a side chamber the remains of slaves, 15 horses (and their elaborately decorated equipment), and a funeral chariot were recovered.

Oleksandrovych, Mytrofan. See Aleksandrovych, Mytrofan.

Oleksandrovych, Tykhon [Oleksandrovyč, Tyxon], b ?, d 1746. Pedagogue and author. From 1743 he was prefect and a professor of poetics and rhetoric at the Kievan Mohyla Academy. He wrote Latin textbooks on poetics, rhetoric, and Aristotelian philosophy used at the academy.

Oleksenko, Stepan, b 22 October 1941 in Mykhailivka, Volgograd oblast, Russia. Actor. After completing study at the Kiev Institute of Theater Arts in 1964, he worked in the Kiev Ukrainian Drama Theater and acted in the films *Hamlet* (1965) and *Platon meni druh* (Platon Is My Friend, 1980).

Oleksii [Oleksij], b and d ? Painter of the 16th century. He painted icons, some of which have been preserved: *Dormition of the Theotokos* (1547, National Museum in Lviv), *Theotokos*, the *Mandylion*, and the large *Theotokos* from Roven.

Oleksiienko, Oleksa [Oleksijenko] (real surname: Alekseev), b 1876 in Kharkiv, d 31 January 1942. Film director and stage actor. He was an actor in D. Haidamaka's troupe (1897–1907) and then directed five Ukrainian romantic-populist vaudevilles in D. Kharitonov's private film studio in 1909–11, including I. Kotliarevsky's *Moskal'-charivnyk* (The Muscovite [Soldier]-Sorcerer) and V. Dmytrenko's *Kum-miroshnyk* (The Godfather-Miller). The films created a basis for theatrical productions in O. Sukhodolsky's troupe. Oleksiienko quit his cinema activities in the 1920s.

Oleksiievo-Druzhkivka [Oleksijevo-Družkivka]. V-18, DB II-3. A town smt (1990 pop 8,000) on the Kryvyi Torets River in Donetske oblast. It was formed by the merging of two settlements, Oleksiievo, founded in the 1830s, and Druzhkivka, a Cossack outpost founded over a century earlier. The town is administered by the Druzhkivka municipal council. There is a food-processing plant and a firebrick factory in the town.

Oleksiiv, Mykhailo [Oleksijiv, Myxajlo], b 1891, d 8 October 1952. Educator and civic and political activist. He took part in the struggle for Ukrainian independence in 1917–20 as a delegate to the First and the Third All-Ukrainian Military congresses and as a soldier in the Winter campaigns. In the interwar period he worked as a teacher in Dnipropetrovske. Under the German occupation he was a community organizer in that city. After emigrating to Germany he helped found the *Ukrainian National State Union and served as chairman of its Central Committee (1947–50). He later emigrated to the United States.

Oleksyn, Ivan, b 26 June 1922 in Verbylivtsi, Rohatyn county, Galicia. Community leader. After the Second World War he emigrated to the United States, where he settled in Rochester, New York, and completed his civil-engineering education. He was active in community af-

Ivan Oleksyn   Ivan Oleksyshyn

fairs and organized a Ukrainian student club and a sports club. Starting as secretary of the local branch (1957–69), he rose through the ranks of the Ukrainian Fraternal Association to become its president (1973). He was one of the founders of the *Ukrainian American Coordinating Council and has served as its vice-president since 1983.

Oleksyshyn, Ivan [Oleksyšyn], b 1 September 1901 in Khreniv, Kaminka-Strumylova county, Galicia, d 19 December 1987 in Philadelphia. Geologist; member of the Shevchenko Scientific Society. He graduated from Lviv University and the University of Innsbruck (PH D, 1947). He taught in gymnasiums in Ternopil and Lviv (1929–39) and then lectured at Lviv University. He was a senior research associate in the geology division of the Lviv branch of the AN URSR (now ANU) and from 1942 a lecturer at the Lviv Polytechnical Institute. A postwar refugee in Austria, he emigrated to the United States (1949), where he taught at Boston University (1956–67). Oleksyshyn wrote several works on the geology of Western Ukraine, particularly on the Miocene period.

Olelko Volodymyrovych, b ?, d 1455. Prince of Kiev; grandson of Grand Duke *Algirdas of Lithuania. He married Anastasiia, the daughter of the Muscovite prince Vasilii Dmitrievich. An appanage prince in the Lithuanian-Ruthenian state (ca 1443–55), Olelko sought to develop *Kiev principality into an autonomous entity. He fostered the development of the Ukrainian church and culture, and he strengthened the southern frontiers of his lands against Tatar attacks. He was succeeded by *Semen Olelkovych.

Olelkovych [Olel'kovyč] (Polish: Olelkowicz). A family of Orthodox appanage princes in the Lithuanian-Ruthenian state. They were descended from *Volodymyr, the son of Grand Duke Algirdas of Lithuania. His son, *Olelko Volodymyrovych, from whom the family name is derived, and grandson, *Semen Olelkovych, were the last Ruthenian princes of Kiev. Olelko's other son, *Mykhailo Olelkovych, became the prince of *Slutsk principality in Belarus and conspired to assassinate King Casimir IV. Mykhailo's son, Semen (d 14 November 1505), was an unsuccessful candidate for the Lithuanian throne after the death of Casimir IV in 1492. Semen's son, Yurii (b ca 1492, d 17 April 1542), was a member of the *Council of Lords and supported Prince K. Ostrozky, who married his sister, Aleksandra, ca 1524. Yurii was close to King Sigismund II Augustus, married Princess Helena Radziwiłł in 1530, and owned enormous latifundia in Belarus, with over 40,000 peasants. Yurii's son, Yurii (b ca 1531, d 9 November 1578), was also a member of the Council of Lords and became a Polish senator in 1577. He transformed Slutsk into a center of Orthodox culture and was buried at the Kievan Cave Monastery. His son, also Yurii (b 17 August 1559, d 6 May 1586), was also buried there. His orphaned daughter, Sofiia (b 1 May 1585, d 9 March 1612), married Prince Janusz Radziwiłł in 1600, after which Slutsk principality was ruled by the Radziwiłłs.

Olelkovych, Mytro. See Aleksandrovych, Mytrofan.

Olenivka. VI-18, DB IV-3. A town smt (1990 pop 5,200) in Volnovakha raion, Donetske oblast. It was founded in 1840 and granted smt status in 1938. It has a truck and railway depot and a bakery.

Olenivka flux limestone deposit. A flux limestone deposit located near the village of Olenivka, Donetske oblast. It was discovered in 1930 and surveyed irregularly between 1932 and 1975. Covering a territory of some 30 sq km and with estimated reserves of 820 million t (1980), it was the largest such deposit in the USSR. The limestone is found in seams of 50–70 m width and at depths of 10–60 m. The high-quality limestone contains only a little sulfur and phosphorus and is used as flux in the metallurgical industry.

Olenska, Chrystya [Olens'ka, Xrystja], b 17 April 1941 in Rottenburg, Germany, d 29 September 1979 in New York. Painter and sculptor; sister of A. *Olenska-Petryshyn. A graduate of New York University (1965), in the early 1960s she attracted attention with her works in papier-mâché. Her colorful papier-mâché jewelry was exhibited at the Museum of Modern Art (1967–9), Expo '67 in Montreal, and the Museum of Contemporary Crafts in Philadelphia (1967). Olenska devoted the last years of her life to papier-mâché bas-reliefs (eg, *Dreams*) and life-size grotesque figures, such as *Old Woman* and *Flasher*. She also painted landscapes and still lifes, including *Still Life with Flowers*, *Still Life with Fruit*, and *Patio View*, which conveyed a peaceful, contemplative mood. A catalog of her retrospective exhibition at the Ukrainian Institute of Modern Art in Chicago in 1982 was published.

Olenska-Petryshyn, Arcadia [Olens'ka-Petryšyn, Arkadija], b 19 June 1934 in Zbarazh, Galicia. Painter and critic; sister of C. *Olenska and wife of W. *Petryshyn. An émigré in the United States since 1950, she completed her studies at Hunter College (1963) and the University of Chicago (MFA, 1967). Most of her work consists of lithographs, graphics, and oils. Her early works were abstract. Later she concentrated on depicting human figures with expressionless faces. In recent years she has produced paintings of cacti and prints of plants and trees. Her works have been displayed at many group shows and solo exhibitions, in New York (1963, 1964, 1968, 1974, 1978), Chicago (1975, 1980), Toronto (1972), Edmonton (1981, 1985), Antwerp and Brussels (1984), Shenyang, China (1990),

Arcadia Olenska-Petryshyn: *Two Girls* (etching)

Lviv (1990), Kiev (1991), and several cities in New Jersey (Woodbridge [1980], Highland Park [1981], Trenton [1982], Princeton [1983]). She has served as art editor of *Suchasnist'*.

Oleksander Oles

Oles, Oleksander [Oles'] (pseud of Oleksander Kandyba), b 5 December 1878 in Bilopillia, Sumy county, Kharkiv gubernia, d 22 July 1944 in Prague. Poet. He studied at the Kharkiv Institute of Veterinary Science and worked in the Kharkiv zemstvo as a veterinarian. From 1911 he worked on the editorial board of *Literaturno-naukovyi vistnyk* in Kiev and for the Lan publishing house. He emigrated in 1919, first to Budapest and then to Vienna, where in 1920 he was editor of the journal *Na perelomi* and headed the Union of Ukrainian Journalists and Writers Abroad. From 1924 he lived in Prague. He began to publish his work in 1903, and his first collection, *Z zhurboiu radist' obnialas'* (Joy and Sorrow Embraced, 1907), gained him enormous popularity. His second collection, *Poeziï* (Poems, 1909), shared many of the themes and moods of the first. In the poems there is a duality of concern: hopes for national liberation and disappointment at the defeat of the Revolution of 1905. Those themes continue in his next collection, *Tvory* (Works, 1910), and in *Poeziï* (Poems, 1917), a poetic cycle on the national revolution in Ukraine in 1917. Oles also wrote dramatic poems and études, among them 'Po dorozi v kazku' (On the Way to a Fairy Tale, 1910) and 'Nad Dniprom' (By the Dnieper, 1911), which were published in the collections *Dramatychni etiudy* (Dramatic Etudes, 1914) and *Khves'ko Andyber* (1917).

The collections that Oles wrote as an émigré resound with longing for his native land: *Chuzhynoiu* (In Foreign Lands, 1919), *Poeziï* (Poems, 1931), and *Komu povim pechal' moiu* (Whom Can I Tell of My Sorrow, 1931). The collection of historical poems *Mynule Ukraïny v pisniakh: Kniazhi chasy* (Ukraine's Past in Song: The Era of Princes, 1930) holds a special place among his works. Oles's satirical poems on the subject of émigré life were written under the pseudo-nym V. Valentyn, and only the first part of the collection, *Perezva* (Postwedding Party, 1921), was published. Many of his works were not published during his lifetime, such as the satirical comedies 'Revizor z Kam'iantsia' (The Inspector from Kamianets), 'Vlada za kordonom' (The Authority beyond the Border), and 'Narodnyi sud' (The People's Court).

In children's literature Oles translated into Ukrainian *Kazky* (*Märchen*, 1911), by W. Hauff and 'Arabs'ki kazky' (Arabian Tales, 1917). He also wrote original versified stories and plays, such as 'Zlydni' (Hard Times, 1927), 'Solom'ianyi bychok' (The Little Straw Bull, 1927), 'Mykyta Kozhum'iaka' (1929), 'Myslyvets' Khrin ta ioho psy' (The Hunter Khrin and His Dogs, 1944), and 'Babusyna pryhoda' (Grandma's Adventure, 1959).

The poetry of Oles is characterized by its form, which often imitates the structure of the folk song, by its slogan-like lexicon, frequent repetition, and anaphora, and by its facile rhythm, masterfully captured images of nature, and subtle mood. Those qualities, as well as the poetry's deeply patriotic motifs and sincerity of expression, ensured its popularity and its inclusion in many anthologies. Composers such as M. Lysenko, Ya. Stepovy, and K. Stetsenko wrote music to the words of the poems. Oles was popular in the Ukrainian SSR until the 1930s, by which time there were three editions of his *Vybrani tvory* (Selected Works, 1925, 1929, 1930). His works were subsequently banned for over 20 years; although the ban was lifted in the late 1950s, until 1991 his works were interpreted according to the prevailing Party policy and published with restrictions, as *Vybrane* (Selections, 1958) and *Poeziï* (Poems, 1964). Preliminary work on a more complete publication of Oles's works was started in the mid-1980s. A two-volume edition appeared in 1990.

I. Koshelivets, B. Kravtsiv

Oleshia [Oleššja]. A medieval port near the mouth of the Dnieper River, probably at the site of present-day Tsiurupynske. According to 11th- to 13th-century chronicles Oleshia was a major trading center on the Kiev–Constantinople route. Fishing also played an important role in its economy. The town's population was mixed, but the largest group of merchants was Greek. Until the 10th century the town belonged to the Byzantine sphere of influence, and then it became a client of Kievan Rus'. Eventually Oleshia became a Genoese trading colony. In the mid-15th century it was destroyed by the Turks, who established Ochakiv to control access to the Dnieper River.

Oleshia Sands [Oleššja] (Oleshivski pisky). A sandy region on the left bank of the lower Dnieper south of Kherson, extending roughly from Kakhivka in the east to the Kinburn Spit in the west. Once the delta of the Dnieper, the area takes its name from its proximity to the town of Oleshky (now Tsiurupynske). The sandy soil was formed by alluvial deposits. The region is covered with sand dunes 8–15 m in height and small saltwater lakes and bogs (but no rivers). The surface vegetation of the sands is generally poor, and attempts to seed Crimean pines and other trees in the area have generally had disappointing results. Grape growing and fruit cultivation have met with greater success.

Oleshky. See Tsiurupynske.

Oleshky Sich. The second-last *Zaporozhian Sich. It was located above the Dnieper Estuary near what later became the town of Oleshky (now Tsiurupynske, in Kherson oblast). After Russian forces razed the *Chortomlyk Sich in May 1709, the Zaporozhian Cossacks, who had sided with Hetman I. Mazepa against Peter I, resettled along the Kamianka River. In 1711 a Russian offensive forced them to flee, and the Crimean khan permitted them to establish a Sich on the territory belonging to the khanate. Under the provisions of the Russian-Turkish Treaty of 1713 the rights of the Zaporozhian Cossacks and their commercial contacts with the Hetman state were restricted. Ukrainian peasants and other fugitives were prevented from fleeing to the Sich by the Nogay and Crimean Tatars. The Cossacks themselves were not allowed to build fortifications or have artillery, were frequently raided by the Nogays, and were forced to perform arduous construction labor for the khanate and to fight its enemies in the Kuban and Circassia. The Cossacks rebelled in 1728 and began returning to Russian-ruled territory, and in 1734 Empress Anna Ivanovna allowed them to establish the *New Sich there. The kish otamans of the Oleshky Sich were K. Hordiienko and I. Malashevych.

Olesiiuk, Tymish [Olesijuk, Tymiš] (pseud: T. Olesevych), b 21 February 1895 in Dovholiska, near Volodava, Podlachia, d 14 September 1978 in Los Angeles. Physician and civic and political leader; member of the Shevchenko Scientific Society. He interrupted his university studies during the struggle for Ukraine's independence to serve as deputy of the Kholm and Podlachia regions to the Central Rada, secretary of the Kholm Gubernia Executive Committee (1917–18), officer of the UNR Army, deputy commissioner of education for the gubernia (1918–19), and attaché of the UNR diplomatic mission to Warsaw. He was sent in 1920 as a UNR observer to the Polish-Soviet peace negotiations in Riga. After the war he resumed his studies in Warsaw and Prague (MD, 1929). He

Tymish Olesiiuk   Osyp Oleskiv

was active in the Union of Ukrainian Student Organizations under Poland and helped to establish the Central Union of Ukrainian Students. In 1932–44 he practiced medicine in Podlachia. After emigrating to Germany in 1944, he became a member of the UNR government-in-exile and a founder and first president (1946–7) of the *Ukrainian National State Union. In 1947 he settled in the United States, where he resumed medical practice and served on the executive of the Union of Ukrainian National Democrats (1950–2), which he helped found. Besides demographic studies in compendiums, articles on politics and education, and recollections, which were published in journals, he wrote five books, including *Statystychni tablytsi ukraïns'koho naselennia SSSR* (Statistical Tables of the Ukrainian Population of the USSR, 1930) and *Sira Ukraïna* (Gray Ukraine [that is, Ukrainians in Central Asia], 1947).

Oleskiv, Osyp [Oles'kiv] (Oleskow or Oleskiw, Josef), b 28 September 1860 in Skvariava Nova, Zhovkva circle, Galicia, d 18 October 1903 in Sokal. Agronomist and civic figure. After graduating from Lviv University with a PH D in botany he continued his studies in Germany and then taught at a Realschule in Dubliany near Lviv and at the teachers' seminary in Lviv. A populist in orientation, he became concerned with what he considered to be the ruinous emigration of Ukrainians to Brazil. He published *Pro vil'ni zemli* (About Free Lands) in 1895 in an effort to stem emigration, if only briefly, while he traveled to Canada to assess its potential for Ukrainian settlement. He was favorably impressed and published his findings and advice as *O emigratsiï* (About Emigration, 1895). In 1896 he helped to organize the first major wave of Ukrainian immigration to Canada and sought to establish an orderly means for guiding emigration to that country by creating an emigrant aid society and obtaining a commission as an agent. He was superseded by events, however, and received no commissions or financial assistance for his work. He withdrew from the entire process and became director of a teachers' seminary in Sokal. Oleskiv's pivotal role in directing emigration became obscured with time, but it was brought to light again with the publication of V. Kaye's *Early Ukrainian Settlements in Canada, 1895–1900: Dr. Josef Oleskow's Role in the Settlement of the Canadian Northwest* (1964).

M. Lupul

Oleskiv, Vasyl [Oles'kiv, Vasyl'], b 12 October 1924 in the Ternopil region. Emigré political leader. He studied at the University of London in 1946–51. In 1946 he became a member of the OUN (Bandera faction) in Great Britain (which he headed in 1955–63), and in 1952 a member of the faction's general executive. After the death of Ya. Stetsko in 1986, he served as acting head of the executive until formally elected leader in 1987–1991 at the Seventh Greater OUN Congress. Oleskiv has been active in Great Britain and throughout the Ukrainian diaspora in community politics; social, educational, religious, and economic affairs; and publishing. He has been among the leaders of various organizations, such as the Anti-Bolshevik Bloc of Nations, Ukrainian State Administration, Association of Ukrainians in Great Britain, Ukrainian Former Combatants in Great Britain, Ukrainian Publishers Limited, and Ukrainian Information Service.

Oleskiw, Josef. See Oleskiv, Osyp.

Olesko castle

Olesko [Oles'ko]. IV-5. A town smt (1990 pop 1,900) in Busk raion, Lviv oblast. Traces of settlements dating from the Bronze Age and the 12th and 13th centuries have been uncovered at the site. Olesko is first mentioned in historical documents in the mid-14th century, when it was under Polish rule. In 1370–7 it belonged to the Lithuanian prince Liubartas. The Poles occupied the castle in 1432 and granted the town the rights of *Magdeburg law in 1441. Located on the *Kuchmanskyi Route, Olesko was often attacked by the Tatars. In 1507 and 1512 it was destroyed. The Cossacks took control of the town during B. Khmelnytsky's uprising in 1648. In 1711 it was occupied by Russian troops. The town's flourishing economy of the 14th century began to deteriorate around the end of the 15th century, as the trade routes changed. In the 1680s the Polish king Ian III Sobieski, who had been born in Olesko, rebuilt the castle and tried unsuccessfully to revive the town's economy. The town's architectural monuments include a Roman Catholic church from the 15th century, a castle from the 14th to 17th centuries, and a baroque monastery from the 18th century. In 1975 the castle was restored and turned into a historical preserve. It houses a fine collection of Ukrainian art.

Yaroslav Olesnytsky   Yevhen Olesnytsky

Olesnytsky, Yaroslav [Olesnyc'kyj, Jaroslav], b 1875, d 15 July 1933 in Zolochiv, Galicia. Lawyer and civic and political leader. A practicing lawyer in Drohobych and Lviv, he was the founder of the Zemlia society and a leading member of various civic organizations. When the Western Ukrainian National Republic was established, he became counsel of the State Secretariat of Foreign Affairs and a delegate of the Ukrainian National Rada to Kiev for the drafting of the legislation for unification (22 January 1919). In 1919–21 he served as chief counsel and then head of the UNR diplomatic mission to London. After returning to Lviv he taught at the Lviv (Underground) Ukrainian University and was active in the Union of Ukrainian Lawyers. In 1924 he opened a law office in Zolochiv. A member of the Ukrainian National Democratic Alliance, he was elected to the Polish Sejm in 1930. In the following year he submitted a memorandum on the *Pacification from the Ukrainian Parliamentary Representation to the League of Nations. In addition to articles on political and legal issues, he wrote a study of minority rights according to international law.

Olesnytsky, Yevhen [Olesnyc'kyj, Jevhen], b 5 March 1860 in Velykyi Hovyliv, Terebovlia circle, Galicia, d 26 October 1917 in Vienna. Lawyer, civic and political leader, economist, publicist, and translator; member of the Shevchenko Scientific Society from 1899; brother of Yu. *Olesnytsky. A graduate of Lviv University, he opened a law office in Stryi (1891) and set up various institutions in Stryi and branches in the surrounding villages, such as a branch of the Prosvita society (1892), a savings and loan association (1894), the Union of Ruthenian Dairy Associa-

tions (a predecessor of Maslosoiuz, 1905), and the People's Home. After moving to Lviv in 1909, he reorganized the *Silskyi Hospodar society into a strong province-wide institution and established the Provincial Union of Farming and Trading Associations, the paper *Hospodars'ka chasopys*, and the Library of Silskyi Hospodar as adjuncts. He helped found important economic organizations, such as the Dnister insurance company, the Land Bank, and the Provincial Credit Society. He founded a number of magazines and papers, including *Chasopys' pravnycha*. A strong opponent of the *New Era policy of accommodation with the Poles, he worked to consolidate Ukrainian political organizations and played an important role in the founding of the National Democratic party in 1899 and served on the party's Popular Committee until the end of his life. Having been elected to the Galician Diet in 1900–10 (where he headed the Ukrainian caucus) and the Austrian parliament in 1907–17, he fought for electoral reform, land reform, Ukrainian autonomy in eastern Galicia, and educational reform. In 1915 he became a member of the General Ukrainian Council. A lover of theater, he supported the Ruska Besida Theater and translated many plays for it. His memoirs, *Storinky z moho zhyttia* (Pages from My Life, 2 vols, 1935), were never completed, and end with the year 1897.

Yulii Olesnytsky

Olesnytsky, Yulii [Olesnyc'kyj, Julij], b 3 June 1878 in Stanyslaviv, Galicia, d ? Lawyer and civic and political leader of the Stanyslaviv region; brother of Ye. *Olesnytsky. A student of Lviv and Vienna (LLD, 1902) universities, he opened his own law office in Stanyslaviv in 1911. During the First World War he served as a lieutenant in the Austrian army and in the Ukrainian Galician Army. He was active in Ukrainian civic organizations in Stanyslaviv and served as president of the local branch of Prosvita and the Union of Ukrainian Lawyers. In politics he was a strong supporter of the Ukrainian National Democratic Alliance until it adopted the *Normalization policy. In September 1939 he was arrested by the Soviets. He was kept in Lubianka prison in Moscow until his deportation to Sama, Ivdel raion, Sverdlovsk oblast, and was last heard from in June 1941.

Olevske [Olevs'ke]. II-8. A town smt (1990 pop 12,200) on the Ubort River and a raion center in Zhytomyr oblast. The town is first mentioned in historical documents in 1488. After the Union of Lublin in 1569, Olevske was annexed by Poland and in 1641 it was granted the rights of *Magdeburg law. After the second partition of Poland in 1793, it was acquired by Russia. The town's industries include porcelain manufacturing, food processing, and flax processing. Its most valuable architectural monument is St Michael's Church, built in 1596. During the Second World War the town was a center of the activities of the *Polisian Sich of T. Bulba-Borovets.

Olha [Ol'ha] (Olga; Norse: Helga; Christian name: Elena [Helen]), b ca 890, d 11 July 969 in Kiev. Rus' princess and Orthodox saint; wife of Prince *Ihor and mother of *Sviatoslav I Ihorevych. Olha was Sviatoslav's regent during his minority (945–57) and his later military campaigns. After Ihor's death she subdued the rebellious *Derevlianians and avenged his slaying. She expanded and strengthened the central power of Kiev, defined hunting areas, and replaced the annual journey (*poliudie*) to collect tribute (during one of which Ihor had been slain) by a system of local financial-administrative centers (*pogosti*) that collected uniform taxes for Kiev. In foreign affairs she was mainly concerned with political relations with Constantinople and with Rus'-Byzantine commercial relations.

Olha was the first Rus' ruler to become a Christian. Some scholars, relying on the Primary Chronicle, claim she was baptized in 955 in Constantinople. Others contend she was baptized in Kiev before her trip to Constantinople in 957, on which she was accompanied by the priest Hryhorii. Olha urged Sviatoslav to become a Christian, but he remained a pagan. He allowed a Christian community to develop in Kiev, however, thereby paving the way for the *Christianization of Ukraine by his son and Olha's grandson, Volodymyr the Great. In 959 Olha sent a mission to the German king Otto I requesting a bishop and priests to be sent to Rus'. Otto responded by sending the monk Adalbert to serve as bishop in Kiev, where he remained only briefly.

Volodymyr the Great had Olha's remains reburied in Kiev's Church of the Tithes. Metropolitan Ilarion initiated the Christian cult of Olha in the 11th century, and the church canonized her during the first half of the 13th century. In the Ukrainian church Olha is considered an equal of the Apostles. Her feast day is 24 July (11 July OS).

BIBLIOGRAPHY
The Russian Primary Chronicle: Laurentian Text, trans and ed S.H. Cross and O.P. Sherbowitz-Wetzor (Cambridge, Mass 1953)
Sakharov, A. *Diplomatiia drevnei Rusi: IX–pervaia polovina X v.* (Moscow 1980)
Pritsak, O. 'When and Where Was Ol'ga Baptized?' *HUS*, 9 (1985)
M. Zhdan, A. Zhukovsky

Olhopil [Ol'hopil']. V-10. A village (1972 pop 5,600) on the Sarvanka River in Chechelnyk raion, Vinnytsia oblast. In the 18th century it belonged to the estates of the Lubomirski family. Until 1795 the village was called Rohuzka-Chechelnytska. Under Russian rule it was assigned to Voznesenske vicegerency and was renamed in honor of Catherine II's granddaughter Olga. In 1798 Olhopil became a county center in Podilia gubernia. During the 19th century its population grew to 10,000.

Olhovych [Ol'hovyč]. A house of the *Riurykide dynasty in *Chernihiv principality, descended from Prince *Oleh Sviatoslavych (d 1115). It was noted for its family cohesiveness and political strength until the 1237–40 Mongol invasion. The Olhovychi were successful in maintaining control over Chernihiv principality and fought for

control of Kiev and primacy in Rus' with the princely house descended from Volodymyr Monomakh, often with the military backing of the Cumans. Olhovychi who became grand princes of Kiev included *Vsevolod Olhovych, *Ihor Olhovych, *Sviatoslav III Vsevolodych, *Vsevolod Sviatoslavych Chermny, and *Mykhail Vsevolodovych. Other notable Olhovychi were *Yaroslav Vsevolodovych; *Ihor Sviatoslavych and *Vsevolod Sviatoslavych, the heroes of the epic *Slovo o polku Ihorevi*; *Volodymyr Ihorevych and *Roman Ihorevych; *Iziaslav Volodymyrovych; and Roman Mykhailovych and *Rostyslav Mykhailovych.

Domet Olianchyn

Olianchyn, Domet [Oljančyn], b 6 August 1891 in Viitivtsi, Bratslav county, Podilia gubernia, d 25 June 1970 in Stuttgart. Historian; full member of the Ukrainian Historical-Philological Society in Prague and, from 1948, the Shevchenko Scientific Society. He studied at Kiev University (1918–20) and, as an émigré, at the universities of Berlin (1923–6; PHD, 1928) and Münster (1932–5). As an associate of the Ukrainian Scientific Institute in Berlin he collected documents pertaining to 17th- and 18th-century Ukrainian history in the archives of Berlin, Breslau, Dresden, Leipzig, Königsberg, Halle, Jena, and Göttingen. From 1937 he lived in Stuttgart and worked there at the Ausland-Institut and, from 1950, the Landesbibliothek. From 1961 he was a professor at the Ukrainian Free University in Munich. Olianchyn is the author of a German-language monograph about H. Skovoroda (1928, his PHD diss), of several articles about 17th- and 18th-century Ukrainian-German political and commercial relations, and of articles about Prince Iziaslav Yaroslavych, the symbols on the coins of Volodymyr the Great and his successors, and Ukrainian students at Western European universities, which were published in Ukrainian émigré and German periodicals.

Oliinychenko, Halyna [Olijnyčenko], b 23 February 1928 in Hradenytsi, now in Biliaivka raion, Odessa oblast. Opera singer (lyric-coloratura soprano). A graduate of the Odessa Conservatory (1953), she was a soloist of the Odessa Theater of Opera and Ballet (1952–5), the Kiev Theater of Opera and Ballet (1955–7), and the Bolshoi Theater in Moscow (from 1957). Her operatic roles include Marfa in N. Rimsky-Korsakov's *The Tsar's Bride*, Violetta in G. Verdi's *La Traviata*, and Titania in B. Britten's *A Midsummer Night's Dream*. She has appeared in concert in Western Europe and China.

Oliinychuk, Semen [Olijnyčuk], b 1798 in Antonopil, Vinnytsia county, Podilia gubernia, d 8 August 1852 in Schlüsselburg Fortress, St Petersburg gubernia. Antiserfdom activist. He was a serf of the landowner F. Sobieszczański. He surreptitiously obtained an education at the Vinnytsia gymnasium, and then fled and, living under an assumed name, taught in schools in Right-Bank Ukraine and Belarus (1834–9). After returning to Ukraine he was arrested and imprisoned until 1845, when he was freed from serfdom. In 1847 he wrote to Nicholas I in the name of the peasants of Ostrih county, Volhynia gubernia, proposing that the system of serfdom be changed to one of land rental. His strongly critical 'Istoricheskii rasskaz prirodnykh ili korennykh zhitelei Malorossii Zadneprovskoi, t.e. Kievskoi, Kamenets-Podol'skoi i Zhitomirsko-Volynskoi gubernii pro svoe zhit'e-byt'e' (A Historical Account by the Native or Indigenous Inhabitants of Little Russia beyond the Dnieper, ie, Kiev, Kamianets-Podilskyi, and Zhytomyr-Volhynia Gubernias, about Their Lives and Living Conditions) was never completed. He was arrested for his views again in 1849, and transferred from the Kiev to the Schlüsselburg Fortress, where he died.

Oliinyk, Borys [Olijnyk], b 22 October 1935 in Zachepylivka, Novi Sanzhary raion, Poltava oblast. Poet and former Soviet government official. He graduated from Kiev University in 1958 with a degree in journalism and worked on the editorial boards of the journals *Ranok*, *Dnipro*, and *Vitchyzna* and the newspaper *Molod' Ukraïny*. He also became active in the administration of the Writers' Union of Ukraine and served as one of the secretaries of the Writers' Union of the USSR. As a result of his Party activities and the continued publication of his works he became one of the better-known poets in Ukraine. Collections of his work include *B'iut' u krytsiu kovali* (Smiths Hammer the Steel, 1962), *Dvadtsiatyi val* (The Twentieth Rampart, 1964), *Poeziï* (Poems, 1966), *Vidlunnia* (The Echo, 1970), *Na liniï tyshi* (On the Line of Silence, 1972), *Zaklynannia vohniu* (The Conjuring of Fire, 1978), *Poemy* (Poems, 1983), *Sim* (Seven, 1988), and a compilation, *Vybrani tvory* (Selected Works, 2 vols, 1985). He has also published a collection of essays in literary criticism, *Planeta Poeziia* (The Planet Poetry, 1983). In the Ukrainian cultural and linguistic revival of the late 1980s he adopted an ambiguous position. On the one hand he supported the new movement, and on the other he attempted to reconcile the Ukrainian revival with a Party line that was obviously inimical to it.

Oliinyk, Ivan [Olijnyk], b ca 1876, d 1933 in Chiklent, Soviet Central Asia. Agronomist. He was one of the founders of the Kamianets-Podilskyi Agricultural Institute and head of its agricultural economy department. During his term at the institute he published a number of studies in its *Naukovi zapysky*, on crop rotation in Podilia, on the economics of farming in Podilia, on the organizational problems of peasant farming in Right-Bank Ukraine, and on the differentiation of peasant farms in Ukraine. He was arrested by the GPU in the spring of 1931 and imprisoned in Kharkiv for a year before being sent to a labor camp, where he died or was executed.

Oliinyk, Leonid [Olijnyk], b 28 May 1913 in Velyki Derevychi, Novohrad-Volynskyi county, Volhynia gubernia. Stage director and pedagogue. In 1940 he completed study at the Kiev Institute of Theater Arts, and in 1940–1 he worked in the Lutske Ukrainian Music and Drama Theater as stage director and actor. In 1946 he began teaching in the Kiev Institute of Theater Arts, from 1965 as professor.

Oliinyk, Mykola [Olijnyk], b 9 March 1923 in Byshiv, Kiev county. Writer. He has worked as a newspaper and journal editor in Lutske and Kiev. Oliinyk has written two novels about Lesia Ukrainka, *Lesia* (2 vols, 1957, 1960) and *Oderzhyma* (A Woman Possessed, 1962), both of which also appeared together as *Dochka Prometeia* (The Daughter of Prometheus, 1966); other novels, such as *Za zhyttia* (For Life, 1962), *Za krasoiu* (After Beauty, 1967), *Zerna* (Kernels, 1977), *Svitankovi rosy* (Dawn Dews, 1980), *Sudnyi den'* (Judgment Day, 1982), and *Vid svitu ts'oho* (From This World, 1987); the trilogies *Zhyliuky* (The Zhyliuks, 1965, 1968, 1982) and *Proloh* (Prologue, 1971, 1973); the story collections *Volyns'ki opovidannia* (Volhynian Tales, 1955), *Chuiesh, brate mii?* (Do You Hear, My Brother? 1959), *Snihotsvit* (Snow Blossoms, 1964), *Terpkyi zapakh zhyvytsi* (The Sharp Scent of Resin, 1980), and *Nezryma nyt'* (The Invisible Thread, 1983); and the play *Onovlennia* (Renewal, 1957).

Oliinyk, Oleksander [Olijnyk], b 25 November 1929 in Vyshhorod, Kiev okruha. Hydromechanics and hydraulics scientist, corresponding member of the AN URSR (now ANU) since 1973. He graduated from the Kiev Hydromelioration Institute (1953) and worked at the ANU Institutes of Hydrology and Hydrotechnology (1956–64), Mathematics (1964–71), and Hydromechanics (since 1972, and director in 1972–81). He specializes in such areas as groundwaters, water tables, the management of water resources, and hydrodynamics.

Oliinyk, Oleksii [Olijnyk, Oleksij], b 14 March 1914 in Ivanivka, Novomoskovske county, Katerynoslav gubernia, d 11 November 1977 in Kiev. Sculptor. After graduating from the Kiev State Art Institute (1947) he taught there for many years. He created the monuments to Shevchenko in Palermo, Ontario (1951), to S. Korolov in Zhytomyr (1970), and to Bolshevik leaders in several cities, all in the socialist realist manner.

Oliinyk, Petro [Olijnyk], b 15 April 1914 in Ternopil, Galicia, d February 1942 in Kiev. Journalist and community and political activist. He graduated from the Greek Catholic Theological Academy in Lviv in 1939 and studied philosophy at Berlin University in 1940–1. A member of OUN expeditionary groups and a coeditor of *Ukraïns'ke slovo* in Kiev in 1941, he was shot by the Germans at Babyn Yar for his independentist activities. He wrote a number of publicistic works, including *Lystopadovyi zryv* (The November Uprising, 1941), *Den' 22 sichnia 1919 roku* (The Day of 22 January 1919, 1941), and *Za spravzhnie oblychchia stolytsi* (For the True Face of a Capital, 1941), and some historical studies, including *Iak pol'shchyly Posiannia* (How the Sian Region Was Polonized, 1941) and *Lykholittia Kholmshchyny i Pidliashshia* (Years of Woe in the Kholm and Podlachia Regions, 1941).

Oliinyk, Roman. See Rakhmanny, Roman.

Oliinyk, Stepan [Olijnyk], b 3 April 1908 in Pasytsely, Ananiv county, Kherson gubernia, d 11 January 1982 in Kiev. Poet, humorist, and satirist. He graduated from the

Odessa Pedagogical Institute in 1934 and worked on the editorial boards of the newspapers *Moloda gvardiia*, *Chornomors'ka komuna*, and *Stalingradskaia pravda* and the satirical journal *Perets'*. His first collection of poetry was published in 1947. He received the Stalin Prize for his *Nashi znaiomi* (Our Acquaintances, 1948). Subsequently Oliinyk published many collections of humoristic verse, including *Oznaky vesny* (Signs of Spring, 1950), *Za prykladom starshoho brata* (By the Example of the Older Brother, 1954), *Hotov pochaty vse spochatku* (Ready to Begin All Over Again, 1974), *De Ivan?* (Where's Ivan?, 1982), and a compilation, *Tvory* (Works, 4 vols, 1978). He also published a collection of biographical stories, *Z knyhy zhyttia* (From the Book of Life, 1964). He wrote in accordance with the official line and frequently inveighed against 'bourgeois nationalism'; the Soviet literary establishment therefore created for his books a degree of 'popularity' not commensurate with their quality.

Oliinyk, Yurii [Olijnyk, Jurij], b 1 December 1931 in Ternopil, Galicia. Composer, pianist, and pedagogue. A postwar émigré, he graduated from the Cleveland Institute of Music (1956) and Case Western Reserve University (MA, 1959). He has taught piano, theory, and composition privately and at the Cleveland Music School Settlement (1956–9), the Sacramento Extension of the San Francisco Conservatory of Music (1960–7), and California State University in Sacramento (1985–7). His compositions include *Five Etudes for Piano* (1969), *Sonata for Piano* (1977), *Concerto for Bandura and Orchestra* (1987), *Sonata for Bandura* (1988), and *Concerto for Piano and Orchestra* (1988). He has given numerous piano recitals in the United States with a repertoire that includes his own works as well as those of V. Barvinsky, M. Kolessa, V. Kosenko, S. Liudkevych, L. Revutsky, and R. Savytsky.

Olimpii [Olimpij] (Alimpii), b ?, d 17 August 1114 in Kiev. Icon painter. From 1084 he worked under Constantinople masters on the mosaics of the Dormition Cathedral at the Kievan Cave Monastery and learned to paint from them. He is credited with painting the famous icon *Great Panagia* now in the Tretiakov Gallery in Moscow. Some scholars (O. Antonova and H. Lohvyn) attribute the mosaics of Kiev's St Michael's Golden-Domed Monastery to him. Olimpii's works mark the beginning of a distinctive Ukrainian tradition in icon painting. The Kievan Cave Patericon gives an account of his life and miracles.

Olive (*Olea*; Ukrainian: *olyva*, *maslyna*). A genus of *oil plants (family Oleaceae) of almost 60 species. Only one is commercially important, the cultured olive *O. europaea*. It is a subtropical evergreen tree, found in Ukraine only in the southern Crimea. It grows to up to 4–12 m and can live for hundreds of years (a 500-year-old olive tree grows in the Nikita Botanical Garden). Each tree yields 20–40 kg of olives, usually every other year. Olives are used fresh, pickled, or canned, and to produce oil (ripe olives contain 25–90 percent oil). The first extracted oil from a cold pressing is called virgin or provence oil; it is used in cooking, canning, and medicinal production. After cold pressing the residue is heated and then pressed again to yield technical oil. The residual olive cake is fed to livestock. (See *Vegetable-oil industry.)

Olizarenko, Nadiia (née Mushta), b 1953 in Briansk, Russia. Runner. While living in Zaporizhia she developed into a record-setting runner. At the 1980 Olympics she set a world and Olympic record in the women's 800-m race and took third place in the 1,500- m race.

Olizarowski, Tomasz August, b 1811 in Voislavychi, now Volynske, Sokal raion, Lviv oblast, d 3 May 1879 in Ivry-sur-Seine, France. Polish Romantic poet of the *Ukrainian school in Polish literature. He grew up in Volhynia and studied at the Kremianets Lyceum. After participating in the Polish Insurrection of 1830–1 he lived in Galicia. He was exiled for his political activity by the Austrian regime, and lived in London (1836–45), Paris (1845–8, 1858–79), Dresden (1848), Poznań (1848–50), and Belgium. His works on Ukrainian themes include the narrative poems 'Sonia' (1839), 'Zawerucha' ([The Cossack Zaverukha, 1836) and 'Topir-góra' (Topir Mountain, 1852). His longing and love for Volhynia is expressed in many of his lyric poems. Certain of his other poems are reworkings of Ukrainian folk ballads. Kievan Rus' is also depicted in his poetic dramas 'Rognieda' (Rohnida, 1872) and 'Pomsta Rogniedy' (Rohnida's Revenge, 1874).

Olkhivka River [Ol'xivka] (aka Vilhivka). A right-bank tributary of the Luhanka River, which it joins at Luhanske. It is 83 km long and drains a basin area of 814 sq km. The river begins in the Donets Ridge and flows through the southern part of Luhanske oblast. A sluice has been constructed on the river, which is used for irrigation and water supply.

Olkhivsky, Borys [Ol'xivs'kyj], b 1908, d 1944. Journalist and writer from Polisia. From 1931 he lived in Warsaw. He coedited and contributed to several literary and cultural journals, including *Nazustrich*; *My*, which he edited in 1939; and *Nashi dni*. He also edited a page for young people in the Paris journal *Tryzub*. Olkhivsky wrote the book *Vol'nyi narid* (A Free People, 1937) and articles and essays about Polisia and the Kholm region.

Olkhovsky, Andrii [Ol'xovs'kyj, Andrij], b 28 August 1899 in Huty, Bohodukhiv county, Kharkiv gubernia, d 1 February 1969 in Washington, DC. Musicologist, composer, and pedagogue. He studied at the Kharkiv and Leningrad conservatories (graduating with a composer's diploma), then taught history and theory of music at the Kharkiv Conservatory (1929–34) and at the Kiev Conservatory (1934–41), where he headed the history and theory department. He fled from the USSR in 1943 and served as a professor at the Ukrainian Free University in Munich from 1947 until his departure for the United States in 1949. Olkhovsky's first major monograph, *Narys istoriï ukraïns'koï muzyky* (An Outline of the History of Ukrainian Music), was destroyed during a German bombing raid in 1941. He later wrote *Music under the Soviets: The Agony of an Art* (1955), which includes material on Ukrainian music. He also wrote a variety of articles on musical topics. His compositions include the oratorio *Garden of Gethsemane* (in English, after a poem by D. Prudhomme) for mixed chorus, orchestra, soloists, and narrator (1956), four symphonies, two symphonettes, and music to the dramatic poem *Orgy* by Lesia Ukrainka, as well as a cycle of songs for solo voice to texts by her.

Olkhovy, Ilarii [Ol'xovyj, Ilarij], b 1896, d 20 November 1953 in New York. Co-operative organizer in Galicia. He was a specialist on credit co-operation and was in charge of the audit department for credit co-operatives in the Audit Union of Ukrainian Co-operatives. Later he was director of *Tsentrobank (1937–44) in Lviv. After emigrating to the United States he worked at the head office of the Ukrainian National Association.

Olshanivsky, Ihor [Ol'šanivs'kyj] (Olshaniwsky), b 4 February 1930 in Halych, Stanyslaviv county, Galicia, d 8 May 1986 in Livingston, New Jersey. Human-rights activist and community organizer. After emigrating to the United States in 1950, he served with the US armed forces in Korea and then studied civil engineering at New York University. In the 1970s he became an active defender of Ukrainian political prisoners: he chaired the Committee for the Defense of Valentyn Moroz in New Jersey and co-ordinated the activities of Ukrainian human-rights committees in North America. He was the chief founder (1979) and president of Americans for Human Rights in Ukraine, which has lobbied the US Congress for support of the human-rights movement in Ukraine and for the establishment of the Congressional Commission on the Ukraine Famine.

Olshansky, Mykhailo [Ol'šans'kyj, Myxajlo] (Olszański), b ca 1863 in Lviv, d 25 May 1908 in Chernivtsi, Bukovyna. Actor, singer (tenor), and stage director of Polish origin. He debuted in A. Kattner's troupe in 1879 and worked in O. Bachynsky's Ukrainian-Polish troupe in 1892–4 and in the Ruska Besida Theater in 1889–92, 1894–1900, and 1905–8 (in 1897 as administrative director). Olshansky played character roles and sang heroic ones, notably Vakula in M. Lysenko's *Rizdviana nich* (Christmas Night) and Gaspar in R. Planquette's *Les Cloches de Corneville*.

Olshavsky, Mykhailo [Ol'šavs'kyj, Myxajlo] (monastic name: Manuil), b ca 1700 in Olshavytsia, Szepes komitat, Transcarpathia, d 5 November 1767. Uniate bishop. He studied philosophy at Levice and completed a D TH in Tarnov, Czechoslovakia, before being ordained in 1725. In 1743 he was named apostolic vicar of Mukachiv and consecrated a bishop. He organized schools in Transcarpathia and founded a theological school in Mukachiv in 1744. In 1756 he oversaw the completion of the church in Máriapócs and the establishment of a Basilian monastery and school there. He also had a new episcopal residence built in Mukachiv. In 1769 he published in Pochaiv *Slovo o sviatom mezhdu vostochnoi i zapadnoi Tserkvi soiedinenii* (A Word on the Holy Union of the Eastern and Western Church), a polemical brochure on the church union. Written in Latin and Slavonic, it was later published in several other languages. He also published a textbook on teaching Latin (1746). Selections of Olshavsky's correspondence were published by A. Hodinka (in *Zapysky Chyna sv. Vasyliia Velykoho*, vol 6, 1935), and documents concerning his activities were published by M. Lacko (in *Extracta ex Orientalia Christiana Periodica*, vol 25). A monograph on him by B. Boysak appeared in English in 1967.

Olshevska, Halyna [Ol'ševs'ka], b 29 November 1898 in Budylivka, Radomyshl county, Kiev gubernia, d 7 No-

vember 1972 in Chernihiv. Stage actress. From 1915 she worked in various Ukrainian touring theaters, and then in the Chernihiv Ukrainian Drama Theater (1930–41 and 1946–72) and the Kharkiv Ukrainian Drama Theater (1944–6).

Olshevsky, Martyn [Ol'ševs'kyj], b and d ? Foundry master in the 19th century. He was famous for designing and casting bells in Galicia, notably those in Zhukhiv (1824), Svilcha (1832), Korosno (1834, 1835), and Peredilnytsia (1851). On bells and other castings he used ornamental elements of the contemporary Empire style, as well as elements of Ukrainian folkloric ornamentation.

Olshevsky, Volodymyr [Ol'ševs'kyj], b 1880? d 7 July 1933 in Poznań, Poland. Army officer. Having attained the rank of colonel in the Russian army, he joined the UNR Army in 1917 and was one of the organizers of the *Third Iron Rifle Division. During 1919 he commanded an infantry battalion of the division and then became deputy division commander. In 1920 he briefly commanded the Ninth Brigade in the reactivated Iron Division before again assuming the post of deputy division commander. He was promoted to brigadier general in the UNR Army.

Olsztyn (German: Allenstein). A city (1989 pop 161,200) in northern Poland on the Łyna river and a voivodeship center (1989 pop 741,300). There is an active branch of the Ukrainian Social and Cultural Society (since 1990 called Alliance of Ukrainians in Poland) with approx 100 members, and an active group of Ukrainian students. In 1958 local radio began broadcasting a half-hour Ukrainian program directed by S. Demchuk (pseud Maksym Zaporozhets) once or twice a month. The city also serves as the dissemination point for various imported publications in Ukrainian throughout Poland. The surrounding voivodeship has the highest number (estimated at 50,000–60,000) and concentration of Ukrainians in Poland, most of whom went there as a result of forced resettlement during *Operation Wisła in 1947. They live mainly in or around Bartoszyce, Biskupiec, Górowo, Iława, Kętrzyn, Lidzbark, and Morąg.

Olviopil. See Pervomaiske.

Olyka. III-6. A town smt (1990 pop 3,700) situated on the Putylivka River in Kivertsi raion, Volhynia oblast. It was first mentioned in the Hypatian Chronicle under the year 1149. In the 13th and 14th centuries Olyka was part of the Principality of Galicia-Volhynia and the Grand Duchy of Lithuania. At the end of the 15th century the town was acquired by the Radziwiłł family. In 1564 a fortress was built, and the town was granted the rights of *Magdeburg law. During the Cossack-Polish War Olyka was the site of many battles. Its architectural monuments include the fortress, the Lutske gate, which was part of the town wall from 1630, a Roman Catholic church built in 1635, and the Church of the Presentation at the Temple, built in the late 18th century. Today Olyka has a branch of the Kivertsi Canning Factory and a regional museum.

Olympic Games. International sports and athletics competitions held since 1896 every four years (except in 1916, 1940, and 1944) in the summer, and since 1924 also

The Church of the Presentation at the Temple in Olyka (1784)

in the winter. The games are conducted in accordance with the Olympic charter. The charter, however, has been contravened since its inception with regard to the participation of particular countries. Ukraine has not been represented as an individual country at any Olympic Games, although efforts were made to secure Ukraine's membership in the International Olympic Committee and participation in the 1920 games in Antwerp. More recently, this cause has been championed by the *Ukrainian World Committee for Sport Affairs.

Prior to 1917, in 1908 and 1912, teams from the Russian Empire competed in the Olympic Games. In 1920–45 the USSR boycotted the games as 'capitalistic.' The first Soviet Olympic team was fielded for the 1952 games; it included 25 athletes from the Ukrainian SSR. Thirty-four athletes from the Ukrainian SSR were on the Soviet Olympic team in 1956, 35 in 1960, 34 in 1964, 51 in 1968, 71 in 1972, 94 in 1976, 93 in 1980, and 92 in 1988. Athletes from the Ukrainian SSR on Soviet teams first competed in Winter Olympic Games in 1976; from 1976 to 1988 only 11 in all competed in the Winter Games. The USSR boycotted the 1984 Olympic Games in Los Angeles.

In the Olympic Games from 1952 to 1980, Soviet teams won 340 gold medals, 80 of them at the 1980 games in Moscow. Of the 340 medals, 142 were won by athletes from the Ukrainian SSR, 38 of them at the 1980 games. Up to and including the 1988 Olympic Games, athletes from the Ukrainian SSR set 8 world records (WR) and 27 Olympic

records (OR), and many have participated in record-setting or medal-winning team events. The gymnast L Latynina won 9 gold, 5 silver, and 4 bronze medals, more than any other athlete in Olympic history.

In individual track-and-field sports, Olympic gold medalists from the Ukrainian SSR are V. Kuts (1956, 5,000-m OR, 13:39.6; 10,000-m OR, 28:45.6), V. Holubnychy (1960 and 1968, 20,000-m walk, 1:34:07.2 and 1:33:58.4), V. Krepkina (1960, women's long jump OR, 6.37 m), L. Lysenko (1960, women's 800-m WR/OR, 2:04.3), I. Press (1960, 80-m hurdles, 10.8 [semifinals OR, 10.6]; 1964, pentathlon WR 5,246 points), T. Press (1960, women's shot put, 17.32 m 1964, shot put OR, 18.14 m; 1964, discus throw OR, 57.27 m) V. Tsybulenko (1960, men's javelin throw, 84.64 m), V Brumel (1964, men's high jump OR, 2.18 m), M. Avilov (1972, decathlon WR/OR, 8,454 points), A. Bondarchuk (1972, hammer throw OR, 75.5 m), V. Borzov (1972, men's 100-m, 10.14; 200 m, 20.00), F. Melnyk (1972, women's discus throw OR, 66.62 m), Yu. Sedykh (1976, hammer throw 77.52 m; 1980, hammer throw WR/OR, 81.80 m), V. Kyselov (1980, men's shot put OR, 21.35 m), N. Olizarenko (1980, women's 800-m WR/OR, 1:53.50), N. Tkachenko (1980, pentathlon WR/OR, 5,083 points), H. Avdiienko (1988 men's high jump OR, 2.38 m), O. Bryzhina (1988, women's 400-m OR, 48.65), S. Bubka (1988, pole vault OR, 5.90 m) and T. Samolenko (1988, 3,000-m OR, 8:26.53).

In individual gymnastics competition, gold medalists are N. Bocharova (1952, balance beam), V. Chukarin (1952 men's all-around, long horse vault, pommel horse; 1956 all-around, parallel bars), M. Horokhovska (1952, women's all-around), L. Latynina (1956, women's all-around floor exercises, side horse vault; 1960, all-around, floor exercises; 1964, floor exercises), B. Shakhlin (1956, pommel horse; 1960, all-around, long horse vault, parallel bars pommel horse; 1964, horizontal bar), P. Astakhova (1960 and 1964, uneven bars), M. Nikolaeva (1960, side horse vault), and V. Klymenko (1972, pommel horse).

In freestyle wrestling, gold medalists are O. Ivanytsky (1964, heavyweight), O. Medvid (1964, light heavyweight 1968, heavyweight; 1972, super-heavyweight), B Hurevych (1968, middleweight), P. Pinigin (1976, light-weight), A. Beloglazov (1980, flyweight), S. Beloglazov (1980 and 1988, bantamweight), and I. Mate (1980, heavy-weight). In Greco-Roman wrestling, gold medalists are B Hurevych (1952, flyweight), Ya. Punkin (1952, feather-weight), I. Bohdan (1960, heavyweight), and O. Kolchynsky (1976 and 1980, super-heavyweight).

In weight lifting, gold medalists are I. Rybak (1956 lightweight OR, 380 kg), Yu. Vlasov (1960, super-heavy-weight WR/OR, 537.5 kg), L. Zhabotynsky (1964 and 1968 super-heavyweight OR, 572.5 kg), P. Korol (1976, light-weight [disqualified]), and S. Rakhmanov (1980, super-heavyweight OR, 440 kg).

In swimming, gold medalists are G. Prozumenshchiko-va (1964, women's 200-m breaststroke OR, 2:46.4), Ye. Vai-tsekhovska (1976, women's platform diving), S. Fesenko (1980, men's 200-m butterfly, 1:59.76), and O. Sydorenko (1980, men's 400-m individual medley OR, 4:22.89).

In canoeing, gold medalists are S. Makarenko (1960, Canadian pairs 1,000 m), A. Khymych (1964, Canadian pairs 1,000 m), L. Khvedosiuk (1964 and 1968, women's kayak singles 500 m; 1972, kayak pairs 500 m), V. Morozov (1964, 1972, and 1976, kayak fours 1,000 m; 1968, kayak pairs 1000 m), O. Shaparenko (1968, kayak pairs 1,000 m; 1972 kayak singles 1,000 m), K. Kuryshko (1972, women's kay-ak pairs 500 m), Yu. Riabchynska (1972, women's kayak singles 500 m), Yu. Stetsenko (1972, kayak fours 1,000 m), Yu. Filatov (1972 and 1976, kayak fours 1,000 m), S. Na-horny (1976, kayak pairs 1,000 m), S. Petrenko (1976, Ca-nadian pairs 500 m and 1,000 m), S. Chukhrai (1976, kayak fours 1,000 m; 1980, kayak pairs 500 m and 1,000 m), and S. Postriekhin (1980, Canadian singles 500 m). In yachting, gold medalists are V. Mankin (1968, Finn; 1972, Tempest; 1980, Star), V. Dyrdyra (1972, Tempest), and A. Muzy-chenko (1980, Star).

Athletes from the Ukrainian SSR on Soviet teams have also won Olympic gold medals in men's shooting – V. Bo-rysov (1956, free rifle OR, 1,138 points [prone WR, 396 points]), V. Romanenko (1956, running-deer shooting OR, 441 points), Ya. Zheliezniak (1972, moving-target WR, 569 points), and D. Monakov (1988, trapshooting); in fencing – H. Kryss (1964, épée), V. Sydiak (1972, saber), and V. Smirnov (1980, foil); in cycling – V. Semenets and I. Tselovalnikov (1972, 2,000-m tandem), and O. Kyrychen-ko (1988, 1,000-m time trial, 1:04.499); and in judo – S. No-vikov (1976, heavyweight). The Kiev men's volleyball team won the gold medal in 1968. The Kiev Spartak wom-en's handball team won gold medals at the 1976 and 1980 Olympics.

After Ukraine regained its independence in 1991, Ukraine's athletes participated in the 1992 Winter and Summer Games as members of the 'Unified Team' of the former Soviet republics. At the Winter Games V. Petrenko won the gold medal in men's figure skating. At the Sum-mer Games, for the first time in Olympic history, the Ukrainian contingent of the Unified Team marched under the blue-and-yellow Ukrainian national flag and the Ukrainian national anthem was played at the official pre-sentations of gold medals to Ukrainian champions. Ukrai-nians won 40 medals at the Summer Games – 17 gold, 14 silver, and 9 bronze. Individual gold medalists were T. Gutsu (Hutsu, women's all-around gymnastics), T. Lysen-ko (women's balance beam), O. Tymoshenko (women's floor exercises), and O. Kucherenko (Greco-Roman wres-tling).

BIBLIOGRAPHY
Pushkar'ov, K. *Nashi zemliaky olimpiitsi* (Kiev 1978)
Shelukha, Yu. *Ukrainian Athletes in the Olympics* (Kiev 1979)
Sunyk, O. *Vid Olimpiï do Moskvy* (Kiev 1980)
Karpeliuk, V.; Nartovskii, B. (eds). *Olimpiiskie dni Ukrainy* (Kiev 1982)
Zinkewych, O. *Ukrainian Olympic Champions*, 3rd rev edn (Balti-more–Toronto 1984)
O. Zinkevych

Olynyk, Roman. See Rakhmanny, Roman.

Olyzar (Polish: Olizar). A Ukrainian noble family in the Kiev region and Volhynia. The progenitor was Olyzar Volchkevych, the starosta of Chornobyl (1533–45) and one of the organizers of the 1569 Union of *Lublin. The family became Polonized in the late 16th century. Adam Olizar (ca 1572 to 1624), a Polish cavalry commander who con-verted from Orthodoxy to Roman Catholicism, owned large landholdings (7 towns and 33 villages) around Ko-rostyshiv, near Zhytomyr. He and his son, Ludwik (d 1645), developed iron-ore mining there. Ludwik's son, Jan (d ca 1700), was elected marshal of Kiev voivodeship in

1665. Jan's son, Adam (ca 1657 to 1713), was a petty noble-man in Ovruch in Volhynia. One of Jan's descendants, Fi-lip (ca 1750 to 1816), the son of the Kiev functionary Onufry (ca 1722 to 3 April 1753), was the Polish royal chamberlain from 1774 and cupbearer of Lithuania (1780–94). He increased the family's landholdings and built the first iron smelter in the Kiev region, in the early 1780s near Horodske, Zhytomyr county. Under Russian rule he be-came president of the chief court of Podilia gubernia and, in 1807, a member of the Educational Commission of Vol-hynia, Podilia, and Kiev gubernias. Filip's son Gustaw (1798–1868) served as marshal of the nobility in Kiev gu-bernia (1821–6), and was a Polish poet, translator, and publicist. He was imprisoned for participating in the De-cembrist movement. Gustaw helped German colonists to establish a woolens factory in Korostyshiv. His memoirs were published under the pseudonym A. Filipowicz in Lviv in 1892. Gustaw's brother, Narcyz (1794–1862), was also a Polish poet, memoirist, and émigré publicist and was a Volhynian leader of the Polish Insurrection of 1830–1. In 1832 he fled abroad. A few other members of the Olizar family were marshals, starostas, and Sejm dele-gates.

Oleh Olzhych

Olzhych, Oleh [Ol'žyč] (pseud of Oleh Kandyba; other pseuds: O. Leleka, M. Zapotochny, D. Kardash, K. Kos-tiantyn), b 8 July 1907 in Zhytomyr, Volhynia, d 9 June 1944 in the Sachsenhausen concentration camp. Archeolo-gist, poet, and nationalist leader; son of O. *Oles. Olzhych emigrated from Ukraine in 1923 and lived in Prague, where he graduated with a degree in archeology from Charles University in 1929. Besides his doctoral disserta-tion on Neolithic painted ceramics in Galicia and numer-ous articles, his main scholarly work in archeology was *Schipenitz – Kunst und Geräte neolittischen Dorfes* (1937). After a brief lecture tour at Harvard University Olzhych helped found the short-lived Ukrainian Research Institute in America (St Paul, Minnesota) and edited its first collec-tion of papers (1939). In 1929 Olzhych joined the OUN and headed its cultural and educational branch. After the split in the OUN in 1940, he sided with the *Melnykites. As sec-ond-in-command to A. Melnyk he represented the OUN-leadership in Carpatho-Ukraine (1938–9) and took part in forming the *Ukrainian National Council in Kiev in 1941. Until his arrest and execution by the Gestapo in 1944, he directed Melnykite underground activities in Ukraine.

Often relying on historical themes to illustrate the inalienable right of Ukraine to independent statehood, Olzhych's verse typifies the nationalist poetry between the two world wars. Sparse, strict, and forceful, it is consciously devoid of sentimentality or lyrical weakness and exhorts to action and fulfillment of duty. Only two collections appeared during his lifetime, *Rin'* (Gravel, 1935) and *Vezhi* (Towers, 1940). *Pidzamche* (Near the Castle) appeared posthumously, in 1946, and was followed by *Poeziï* (Poems, 1956) and *Velychnist'* (Majesty, 1969). The latter book includes the collections as well as extant poems published in various newspapers. In 1991 M. Nevrlý edited and published in Prešov a complete editon of Olzhych's works with a biobibliography.

D.H. Struk

Omelchenko, Fedir [Omel'čenko], b 21 February 1865 in Krolevets, Chernihiv gubernia, d 4 February 1924 in Kiev. Pathomorphologist and microbiologist; full member of the VUAN from 1921. A graduate in medicine from Kiev University (1890), he was an army doctor and taught pathological anatomy and bacteriology in Kiev, Warsaw, and St Petersburg. He donated his laboratory to the Ukrainian Scientific Society and helped establish the ANU Institute of Biology, where he served as director in 1921–2. He was also a professor and rector of the Kiev Veterinary Zootechnical Institute (from 1922). Omelchenko researched spermatogenesis, cytology, and the anthropological characteristics of Ukrainians.

Omelchenko, Mariia [Omel'čenko, Marija], b 1874, d 1946. Educator and civic leader. While working in the Kuban during the revolutionary period of 1917–19, she was active politically and was a member of the Kuban Territorial Council. In 1920 she settled in Prague, where she served as president of the Ukrainian Women's Union in Czechoslovakia (1926–7) and maintained contacts with southern Slavic women's organizations. In 1933 she was a coeditor of the journal *La femme slave*. She wrote books about her 1934 visit to Yugoslavia (1935) and T. Masaryk (1929) as well as a number of pamphlets.

Omelchenko, Petro [Omel'čenko], b 3 October 1894 in Khorol, Poltava gubernia, d 21 February 1952 in Villejuif, France. Artist; husband of S. *Zarytska. From 1920 an émigré in Poland and then Czechoslovakia, he studied painting at the Prague Academy of Arts (1923–8) and graphic art at the Ukrainian Studio of Plastic Arts in Prague. From 1928 he worked in Paris in various forms of printmaking and engraving on glass. His work was exhibited at the Salon des Artistes Indépendants, at a show of the Association of Independent Ukrainian Artists in Lviv (1932), and at a show of Ukrainian prints in Berlin (1933). While working as a laborer in France during the Second World War, he drew scenes of daily life. His graphic works are distinguished by precision and clear lines and often include Ukrainian themes. His monograph on paints, materials, and techniques was published in Kiev in 1930.

Omelchenko, Tymish [Omel'čenko, Tymiš], b 21 February 1893 in Verbky, Khorol county, Poltava gubernia, d 6 September 1955 in Toronto. Military and civic leader, journalist. In 1914 he was sent to the front from the Kiev military school and was captured by the Germans. He

Petro Omelchenko: *Woman* (color silk screen)

Tymish Omelchenko

helped organize the *Bluecoats in 1918 and served in various posts in the UNR Army, in which he eventually attained the rank of lieutenant colonel. After the war he emigrated to Germany, where for many years he headed the *Ukrainian National Alliance (1937–45) and published its *Ukraïns'kyi visnyk*. In 1950 he resettled in Canada.

Omelchuk, Oleksii [Omel'čuk, Oleksij], b 25 March 1911 in Ustyluh, Volodymyr-Volynskyi county, Volhynia gubernia, d 22 January 1981 in Kiev. Stage actor. In 1935 he completed study at the Kiev Institute of Theater Arts. Then he worked in the Kiev Young Spectator's Theater (1936–41) and the Kiev Ukrainian Drama Theater (1946–81). Among his roles were Ivan Nepokryty in M. Kropyvnytsky's *Dai sertsiu voliu ...* (Give the Heart Freedom ...), Petr in M. Gorky's *Meshchane* (The Bourgeoisie), and Lenin in various Soviet plays.

Omelianovsky, Mykhailo [Omeljanovs'kyj, Myxajlo], b 19 January 1904 in Kiev, d 1 December 1979 in Moscow. Philosopher; full member of the AN URSR (now ANU) from 1948 and corresponding member of the USSR Academy of Sciences (now the Russian Academy of Sciences) from 1968. A Party activist and graduate of the Institute of Red Professorship in Moscow (1931), he headed the Department of Dialectical Materialism at the Voronezh Chemical-Technological Institute of the Food Industry (1931–44) and spent two years as a senior researcher at the USSR academy's Institute of Philosophy in Moscow before he was sent to Kiev to help set up the ANU Institute of Philosophy and serve as its first director (1946–52). He also headed the ANU Section of Social Sciences (1950–1) and chaired the institute's Department of Philosophical Problems of Science (1952–5). In 1955 he returned to Moscow to serve as deputy director of the Institute of Philosophy there (1955–65) and then headed its Department of Philosophical Problems of Science (1955–79). Omelianovsky published over 250 works in the philosophy of science; over 50 have been translated into various languages. His chief contributions are monographs in Russian on the philosophical questions of quantum mechanics (1956) and *Dialectics in Modern Physics* (1973; English trans 1979). A posthumous collection of his works was published in 1984 and a biobibliography in 1985.

Gen Ivan Omelianovych-Pavlenko

Gen Mykhailo Omelianovych-Pavlenko

Omelianovych-Pavlenko, Ivan [Omeljanovyč-Pavlenko], b 31 August 1881 in Baku, Transcaucasian krai, d 8 September 1962 in Chicago. Senior UNR Army field commander; brother of Mykhailo. From 1901 he was a regular officer in the Russian army. In 1917 he commanded the Russian Eighth Hussar Regiment, which he Ukrainianized as the Lubni 22nd Cavalry (Hetman Sahaidachny) Regiment. During 1918 he was commander of the Kharkiv Cossack Battalion and then of the Navariia Group of the Ukrainian Galician Army on the Polish front (December 1918–February 1919). After returning to the UNR Army he became chief cavalry staff officer, and in the spring of 1920 he took command of the *Separate Cavalry Division. In October 1920 he was promoted to brigadier general. In the interwar period he lived in Poland and Czechoslovakia. After the war he emigrated to the United States.

Omelianovych-Pavlenko, Mykhailo [Omeljanovyč-Pavlenko, Myxajlo], b 8 December 1878 in Tbilisi, d 29 May 1952 in Paris. Supreme commander of the *Ukrainian Galician Army (UHA) and the *Army of the UNR; brother of Ivan. Having commanded a company in the Russo-Japanese War and graduated from general staff school (1910), he served during the First World War as a regiment commander, corps chief of staff, and director of an officer candidate school in Odessa. From 1917 he commanded a Ukrainian brigade in Katerynoslav, the Third Rifle Division in Poltava (1918), the Zaporozhian Kish, and the UHA (10 December 1918 to 7 June 1919). After returning to the UNR Army he took command of the Zaporozhian Corps and then of the entire army (December 1919–November 1920) during and after the *Winter campaign. During the interwar years he lived in Prague, where he headed the Alliance of Ukrainian Veterans' Organizations. After the Second World War he served as defense minister in the UNR government-in-exile (1945–8), which promoted him from major general to lieutenant general, and continued to be active in veterans' affairs in West Germany and France. He is the author of *Ukraïns'ko-pol's'ka viina 1918–1919 rr.* (The Ukrainian-Polish War of 1918–19, 1929), *Zymovyi pokhid* (The Winter Campaign, 1934), and two books of memoirs (1930, 1935).

Gen Mykola Omeliusik

Omeliusik, Mykola [Omeljusik], b 1889 in Polisia, d 6 August 1970 in Philadelphia. Senior army officer. An officer of the Russian army during the First World War, he joined the UNR Army in 1918 and commanded an artillery brigade. In 1919, as a lieutenant colonel, he served at the headquarters of the Volhynian Group. During the Second World War he was chief of operations in the UPA-North (1943–4). His memoirs of 1943 were published in *Litopys UPA*, vol 1. The government-in-exile promoted him to brigadier general.

Omsk. An oblast center (1989 pop 1,148,000) of the RF situated at the junction of the Irtysh and Om rivers in southwestern Siberia. Founded in 1716 as a fortress, it had developed into a city by 1782 and the capital of a general gubernia by 1939. With the construction of the Trans-Siberian Railway in the 1890s, it became an important trade center, and its population grew from 37,500 in 1897 to 161,700 in 1926, 288,900 in 1939, 581,100 in 1959, and 1,044,000 in 1981. The main industries are machine building, petrochemical and textile manufacturing, and food processing. A Ukrainian colony has existed in Omsk for many generations. According to the 1926 census, there were 6,700 Ukrainians (3.7 percent of the residents) in the city, and according to the 1959 census, 31,000 (5.5 percent). The actual figures likely were higher.

OMUS. See Ukrainian Theater-Artists' Association.

Nina Onatska

Mykola Onatsky

Onatska, Nina [Onac'ka], b 1895 in Kiev gubernia, d 16 July 1983 in Buenos Aires. Civic and women's activist; wife of Ye. *Onatsky. She emigrated with her husband to Rome (1919) and Buenos Aires (1947). She belonged to the Ukrainian Women of the Vidrodzhennia society and to the Chief Council of the Ukrainian Central Representation in Argentina (from 1948), and served as president of the Ukrainian Women's Association in Argentina and vice-president of the South American branch of the World Federation of Ukrainian Women's Organizations (1951–9). She chaired the Interorganizational Women's Committee (from 1961).

Onatsky, Mykola [Onac'kyj], b 1878, d ? Civic activist. A peasant deputy from the Poltava region to the First Russian State Duma, he emerged as a leading figure in the *Ukrainian caucus. He was a striking and charismatic figure and was instrumental in generating support for the caucus. He was also noted for addressing the Duma in Ukrainian.

Onatsky, Nykanor [Onac'kyj], b 9 January 1875 in Khomenkove, Hadiache county, Poltava gubernia, d 1 July 1940. Painter and poet. After studying at the Odessa Art School (1900–5) and under I. Repin at the Higher Art School of the St Petersburg Academy of Arts (1905) he taught painting in gymnasiums in Lebedyn (1906–13) and Sumy. He founded and directed the *Sumy Art Museum (1920–33) and ran the Poltava Regional Museum (1933–7). In 1929 he joined the Association of Artists of Red Ukraine. His colorful realist paintings consist mostly of landscapes (eg, *Moonlit Night* [1908], *Sunflowers* [1916], and *Haystacks* [1933]) and still lifes (eg, *Lilacs* [1935]). His poetry was published in the paper *Ridnyi krai* and in miscellanies, such as *Ternovyi vinok* (Wreath of Thorns, 1908), *Z nevoli* (From Prison, 1908), and *Ukraïns'ka muza* (Ukrainian Muse, 1908). He also wrote several plays and bro-

Nykanor Onatsky (self-portrait, 1909)

Yevhen Onatsky

chures on Mezhyhiria faience and Ukrainian art glass and porcelain. Onatsky was arrested by the NKVD in 1934 and again in 1935 and 1937. He perished in a prison camp.

Onatsky, Yevhen [Onac'kyj, Jevhen], b 13 January 1894 in Hlukhiv, Chernihiv gubernia, d 27 October 1979 in Buenos Aires. Civic leader, journalist, and scholar; full member of the Shevchenko Scientific Society from 1947 and of the Ukrainian Academy of Arts and Sciences from 1949. While studying at Kiev University (1912–17), he was active in clandestine student societies. After joining the Ukrainian Party of Socialist Revolutionaries in 1917, he was elected to the Central Rada and its presidium and took part in negotiations with the Don and Kuban Cossacks. Having resigned from the party and the Rada in March 1918, he worked in the library of the Kiev Municipal Museum of Antiquities and Art. In January 1919 he was sent as a journalist to the Paris Peace Conference, after which he ended up in Rome, where he directed the press bureau of the UNR diplomatic mission and edited its *La voce del Ucraina*. Eventually he became head of the mission and Italian representative of the Organization of Ukrainian Nationalists (1929–43). In the interwar period he worked as a correspondent for various Ukrainian papers, such as *Dilo, Svoboda, Novyi shliakh, Novyi klych*, and *Ukraïns'ke slovo*, and lectured at the Higher Oriental Institute in Naples (1936–40) and Rome University (1940–3). He then spent a year in a German prison (1943–4). After settling in Buenos Aires in 1947, he helped to organize the Association of Ukrainian Scholars, Writers, and Artists and the Central Ukrainian Representation in Argentina, which he served as president (1953–60) and chairman of the Supreme Council (1960–3). He edited (1947–64) the Vidrodzhennia society's weekly *Nash klych* as well as its almanacs and the monthly *Dzvin*.

Onatsky's publications include *Grammatica ucraina: teoretico-practica* (1937), *Studi di storia e di cultura Ucraina* (1939), a Ukrainian-Italian dictionary (1941; repr 1977) and an Italian-Ukrainian dictionary (1977), *Osnovy suspil'noho ladu* (The Foundations of Social Order, 1941; repr 1949), a collection of essays, *Zavziattia chy spokusa samovypravdannia* (Determination or the Temptation of Self-Justification, 1956), *Po pokhylii ploshchi: Zapysky ukraïns'koho zhurnalista i dyplomata* (On a Sloping Plane: Notes of a Ukrainian Journalist and Diplomat, 2 vols, 1964, 1969), and *U vichnomu misti: Zapysky ukraïns'koho zhurnalista* (In the Eternal City: Notes of a Ukrainian Journalist, 3 vols, 1954, 1981, 1985). He also prepared the four-volume *Ukraïns'ka mala entsyklopediia* (The Little Ukrainian Encyclopedia, 1957, 1959, 1962–3). His life and work are summarized in L. Wynar's *Ievhen Onats'kyi – Chesnist' z natsiieiu* (Yevhen Onatsky: Honesty toward the Nation, 1981).

Onchul, Petro [Ončul], b 30 December 1936 in Korytne, near Vyzhnytsia, Bukovyna. Opera singer (baritone). After graduating from the Lviv Conservatory in 1966, he joined the Donetske Opera and Ballet Theater as a soloist. His main roles include the Sultan in S. Hulak-Artemovsky's *Zaporozhian Cossack beyond the Danube*, Mykyta in Yu. Meitus's *Yaroslav the Wise*, Rigoletto in G. Verdi's *Rigoletto*, and Scarpia in G. Puccini's *Tosca*.

Oncology. A branch of medicine, dedicated to the study and treatment of neoplastic diseases. Malignant tumors with unlimited growth potential are called cancers (Ukrainian: *zloiakisni novoutvorennia, rak, pistriak*). Neoplasms are second only to cardiovascular diseases as the cause of death in most industrialized countries. Experimental oncology studies the etiology and characteristics of tumor growth and evaluates the methods of therapy. In the late 19th century important experimental contributions to the study of tumors were made by the Ukrainian scientists V. *Vysokovych, V. *Pidvysotsky, and M. *Rudniev.

Medical advances in the study of chemical substances, ionizing radiation, viruses, and hormonal imbalances during the second half of the 20th century have paved the way for a better understanding of the etiology of the neoplastic process. Other scientists that have advanced the development of experimental oncology include O. *Repriev, O. *Krontovsky, O. *Bohomolets, Ye. *Tatarynov, Z. Uspenska, and J. Neiman. The founder of the Ukrainian school of oncologists-pathologists was R. *Kavetsky. A number of Ukrainian surgeons, among them I. *Ishchenko, O. *Arutiunov, I. *Shevchenko, M. *Amosov, O. *Shalimov, and A. Romodanov, improved and perfected surgical procedures used in treating malignant tumors of the brain and internal organs. Oncological research in Ukraine has resulted in a line of preparations for the treatment of malignant tumors, new methods of immunotherapy, the autovaccination of patients to prevent relapse or metastases, and chemotherapy and radiotherapy methods using x-rays, cobalt guns, betatrons, and linear accelerators.

Second only to diseases of the circulatory system, neoplasms are the major cause of death for men in the former USSR (along with accidents, poisoning, and traumas). The rate is 50 percent higher than the composite rate of the United States, Germany, France, Great Britain, and Japan. Along with diseases of the circulatory system, neoplasms are the major cause of death for women in what was the USSR, a rate roughly in line with that of other countries (though in other countries it is by far the major cause of death for women). Whereas mortality rates in the former USSR are declining, the number of deaths due to neoplasms is steadily increasing. In Ukraine mortality in men due to neoplasms (per 100,000 age-standardized pop) was 223 in 1980, 268 in 1987, and 276 in 1988. Mortality in women due to neoplasms was 117 in 1980, 128 in 1987, and 131 in 1988.

The combined rate was 194 in 1989 and 197 in 1990. The proportion of patients suffering from cancer in Ukraine from 1980 has been 20–30 percent higher than the USSR average, and it is increasing every year.

The centers of oncological research in Ukraine are the AN URSR (now ANU) Institute for Problems of Oncology (est 1971 by Kavetsky on the basis of the Kiev Institute of Experimental and Clinical Oncology) and the Ministry of Health's Roentgenological and Oncological Scientific Research Institute (est 1920), both in Kiev. The latter institute published the journal *Voprosy onkologii* in Kharkiv in 1928–37. The ANU Council on Malignant Neoplasms coordinates oncological research and publishes the journal *Eksperimental'naia onkologiia* (since 1979). Since the nuclear explosion at the Chornobyl Atomic Energy Station much emphasis has been placed on greater attention to preserving the ecological balance in nature as well as eliminating carcinogenic substances in industry and food production.

BIBLIOGRAPHY
Govorov, A. *Materialy k statistiki rakovykh zabolevanii v Rossii* (St Petersburg 1914)
Morozovskii, N. *Smertnost' ot raka na Ukraine* (Kharkiv 1926)
Peterson, B. *Sovremennoe sostoianie onkologii* (Moscow 1980)
P. Dzul

Ondava River. A right-bank tributary of the Bodrog River in the Danube Basin. It is 112 km long and drains a basin area of 3,400 sq km. The river originates in the Low Beskyd area and flows south through the Prešov region of Czechoslovakia for almost its entire course.

Onion (*Allium*; Ukrainian: *tsybulia*). Biennial or perennial bulbous plants of the family Liliaceae. More than 400 species are known in the Northern Hemisphere, of which 40 are found in Ukraine. Onion has strong bactericidal and antiscurvy properties and is reported to protect against stomach cancer. The following species are cultivated on a wide scale in Ukraine: the common or garden onion (*A. fistolosum*; Ukrainian: *tsybulia*), chive (*A. schoenoprasum*; Ukrainian: *tsybulia siianka* or *tsybulynka*), leek (*A. porrum*; Ukrainian: *tsybulia-porei*), and *garlic (*A. sativum*; Ukrainian: *chasnyk*). The garden onion is the most common species; it is eaten raw, cooked, fried, or dried, and it represents a staple ingredient in Ukrainian traditional *foods. Onions have high nutritional value; they contain 2.4 to 14 percent sugar, 1.7 to 2.5 percent nitrogen, and 0.65 percent minerals as well as pungency-imparting essential oils. The leaves contain vitamin C, vitamin B_1, vitamin B_2, and carotene. Onions also contain a number of volatile compounds. Several Ukrainian varieties have been developed and popularized.

Oniongrass (*Melica*; Ukrainian: *perlivka*). A perennial grass of the family Gramineae that grows in forests and thickets and on mountain slopes in the temperate zones of both hemispheres. Eight species are found in Ukraine, of which the two most common are mountain or nodding oniongrass (*M. nutans*) and *M. picta*. *M. taurica* is found in the Crimean Mountains. *M. transsilvanica* is used as fodder.

Onomastics. The study of names. In Ukraine, the study of place-names (*toponymy) continues to be the most developed branch of onomastics. In the less developed branch dealing with Ukrainian personal and family names (anthroponymy), the earliest contributions were articles by A. Stepovych (1882), M. Sumtsov (1885), and V. Yastrebov (1893) in Russian-ruled Ukraine; by V. Okhrymovych (1895), I. Franko (1906), I. Krypiakevych (1907), and M. Zubrytsky (1907) in Galicia; and by the Polish historian J. Rolle (1889–92). A 16-page dictionary of Ukrainian baptismal names was appended to B. Hrinchenko's Ukrainian-Russian dictionary (vol 4, 1909). In the interwar period only a few articles in anthroponymy appeared, notably by M. Kornylovych (1926, 1930) in Kiev, V. Simovych (1929, 1930) in Prague, and I. Ohiienko (1935) in Warsaw. In 1937 J. Rudnyckyj began publishing a bibliography of Ukrainian onomastics in *Zeitschrift für Namenforschung* (Berlin).

Postwar onomastic studies have been written by Ukrainian scholars in the West, such as J.B. Rudnyckyj (in *Onoma*, Louvain 1952–), E. Borschak, M. Borovsky, V. Hrabets, I. Gerus-Tarnawecky, J. Hursky, A. Bojcun, W. Zyla, Ya. Slavutych, J. Pauls, S. Holutiak-Hallick, J. Rozumnyj, and B. Struminsky. Many of them were published in the series Onomastica (50 issues, Winnipeg, 1951–75), begun and edited by J.B. Rudnyckyj. The series included Rudnyckyj's studies of the names 'Ukraine,' 'Galicia,' 'Volhynia,' and 'Slav,' I. Gerus-Tarnawecky's study of anthoponymy in the 1484 *Pomianyk* of Horodyshche, and F. Bohdan's dictionary of Ukrainian surnames in Canada (1974). V. Simovych's articles were reprinted in one volume in Ottawa in 1981. In Australia dictionaries appeared of Ukrainian Christian (R. Gauk, 1961) and family (S. Radion, 1981) names. Non-Ukrainian Western scholars who have done work in Ukrainian anthroponymy include B. Unbegaun, A. de Vincenz (*Traité d'anthroponymie houtzoule*, 1970), R. Weischedel (*Eine Untersuchung ukrainischer Personennamen des XVIII. Jahrhunderts: Kiever Regiment*, 1974), and S. Luber (*Die Herkunft von Zaporoger Kosaken des 17. Jahrhunderts nach Personennamen* (1983). In postwar Poland, articles on Ukrainian anthroponymy have been written by S. Hrabec, W. Witkowski, E. Wolnicz-Pawłowska, and M. Łesiów (Lesiv); books on the names of rural people in the 15th-century Sianik and Peremyshl land, by J. Rieger (1977); and books on 18th-century Ukrainian names in Rus' voivodeship, by E. Wolnicz-Pawłowska (1978). At the International Committee of Onomastic Sciences in Louvain, Ukraine was represented in 1952–72 by J.B. Rudnyckyj and later by Yu. Karpenko and I. Tsiluiko.

Onomastics in Soviet Ukraine grew significantly under the influence of the work done by Ukrainian scholars abroad. This growth led to the establishment of the Ukrainian Onomastic Commission in 1959. Since that time many works in Ukrainian toponymy have appeared; and articles in Ukrainian anthroponymy by L. Humetska, I. Varchenko, Yu. Redko, I. Sukhomlyn, V. Vashchenko, O. Tkachenko, R. Kersta, M. Khudash, V. Nimchuk, A. Zalesky, O. Kupchynsky, O. Nedilko, N. Stets, V. Horpynych, I. Kovalyk, Z. Nikolaienko, P. Chuchka, S. Bevzenko, K. Lukianiuk, Yu. Karpenko, I. Zheliezniak, L. Krakaliia, L. Masenko, Yu. Tsymbaliuk, O. Palamarchuk, Y. Dzendzelivsky, H. Pivtorak, V. Rusanivsky, and R. Ostash have appeared in linguistic, historical, ethnographic, and archeological journals, several collections of onomastic studies, and *Povidomlennia Ukraïns'koï onomastychnoï komisiï* (15 issues, 1966–76). V. Petrov, B. Kobyliansky, V. Pokalchuk, A. Hensiorsky, O. Seniuk, O. Stryzhak, M. Khudash, and A. Nepokupny have written on ethnonyms in Ukraine. Published separately (in addi-

tion to works in toponymy) have been a Ukrainian-Russian dictionary of personal names by S. Levchenko, L. Skrypnyk, and N. Dziatkivska (1954; rev edns 1961, 1967, 1972, 1976); L. Humetska's chapter on personal names in her book on the word-formation system of the language of 14th- and 15th-century Ukrainian charters (1958); V. Vynnyk's book on the Ukrainian names of units of measurement and weight (1966); Yu. Redko's study (1966) and handbook (1969) of Ukrainian surnames; I. Zheliezniak's book on 12th- to 15th-century suffixes in Serbo-Croatian surnames (1969); O. Dei's dictionary of Ukrainian pseudonyms and cryptonyms (1969); P. Chuchka's book on the anthroponyms of Transcarpathia (1970); I. Sukhomlyn's textbook on Ukrainian anthroponymy (1975); M. Khudash's history of 14th- to 18th-century Ukrainian anthroponyms (1977); V. Horpynych, V. Loboda, and L. Masenko's book on personal names and names formed from toponyms in the Inhul-Boh watershed (1977); R. Kersta's book on 16th-century Ukrainian male names (1984); and L. Skrypnyk and N. Dziatkivska's dictionary-handbook of personal names (1986).

R. Senkus

Ontario. The most populous (1990 pop 9,747,600) and the second-largest (1,069,000 sq km) province of Canada, situated between the Great Lakes and Hudson Bay. Its capital is Toronto.

According to the 1981 census, there were approx 203,000 Ukrainians in Ontario, representing 26.9 percent of the Ukrainian population in Canada. Ontario's Ukrainian community differs socially and culturally from the Ukrainian communities in the other provinces, particularly in the prairie provinces. Ontario Ukrainians are concentrated in the most populated industrial centers of the pro ce: *Toronto, *Thunder Bay, *Hamilton, *St Catharines, *Windsor, *Oshawa, London, *Ottawa, *Sudbury, and Kitchener. This distribution can be explained by the history of Ukrainian settlement in Ontario.

During the first wave of immigration (1891–1914) most newcomers from Galicia and Bukovyna settled in the prairies. Some came as seasonal or migrant workers to Ontar-

The Ukrainian Catholic Church of the Holy Protectress in Thorold, Ontario (architect: Lonhyn Pencak)

io, many of them hoping to accumulate enough capital to buy land back in their homeland or in the prairies. They took jobs in the mines of Sudbury, Timmins, and Kirkland Lake; the lumber and paper mills of northwestern Ontario; the factories of Windsor and Oshawa; the foundries and plants of Hamilton; the railway yards and docks of Port Arthur and Fort William (later combined into Thunder Bay); and the food processing and manufacturing industries of Toronto. Some of them stayed in Ontario, where they set up cultural organizations and small parishes. The second wave of immigration in the interwar period was driven, again, by land hunger in Galicia and Volhynia. After fulfilling an obligatory stint at farm labor, most of the newcomers headed for industrial centers offering better job opportunities and participation in Ukrainian cultural life. Some prairie homesteaders moved to Ontario looking for better wages and educational opportunities for their children. Ukrainian communities in Ontario multiplied and expanded rapidly. The new immigrants, who frequently were more politically conscious than their predecessors, set up a multitude of political and cultural organizations with branches in local Ukrainian communities. The last wave of immigration (1947–52) consisted of displaced persons or refugees. About 75 percent of the Ukrainian newcomers to Canada, who were better educated than their predecessors and of an urban background, settled in Ontario. After fulfilling their one-year contracts on farms or in mines or forests, most moved to the cities and swelled the ranks of existing Ukrainian communities. With their experience of political persecution and war, their nationalist ideology, and their commitment to Ukrainian culture and language, they had a determining influence on the Ukrainian community in Ontario. They revitalized some of the old organizations, such as the Ukrainian National Federation, and founded many of the most influential ones, including the Canadian League for Ukraine's Liberation and the Plast Ukrainian Youth Association.

Ontario is a multicultural province: barely half of its population is of British origin. To preserve their culture and language, Ukrainians have maintained their own privately funded evening and Saturday schools and have taken advantage of the provincially funded heritage language programs in public and Catholic elementary schools. Courses in Ukrainian language and literature have been taught at the University of Toronto since the 1950s, and in the late 1970s the Ukrainian community raised money for a chair of Ukrainian studies at the university and courses in Ukrainian language, literature, and history at York University; courses in Ukrainian studies are also taught at universities in Hamilton and Ottawa. In 1981, 74,000 Ontario residents of Ukrainian origin listed Ukrainian as their mother tongue (language first learned and still understood), the highest proportion in any of the provinces. Of this group 41 percent used Ukrainian as a means of communication in the home, a higher percentage than in any other province. By 1991 the number of residents with Ukrainian as their mother tongue had fallen to 57,220; they represented 29.17 percent of the Canadian total.

Ontario constitutes the main part of the Canadian eastern eparchies of both the Ukrainian Catholic church and the Ukrainian Orthodox church, and Toronto is the seat of these eparchies. The two traditional Ukrainian churches have steadily lost ground to other denominations.

An umbrella organization for Ukrainian organizations in Ontario, the Ontario Council of the Ukrainian Canadian Committee (now Congress), was established in 1970. Its presidents have included B. Hlibovych and B. Maksymets.

BIBLIOGRAPHY
Luciuk, L; Wynnyckyj, I. (eds). *Ukrainians in Ontario*, vol 10 of *Polyphony* (Toronto 1988)

Onufriivka [Onufrijivka]. V-14. A town smt (1990 pop 5,000) on the Omelnyk River and a raion center in Kirovohrad oblast. It originated as a Cossack winter settlement, at the beginning of the 17th century. In the mid-18th century it was a military settlement in New Serbia. It was granted smt status in 1968. The town has a horse-breeding farm, a branch of the Svitlovodske Radio Plant, and a regional studies museum. Its fine dendrological park dates back to 1884.

Onut. A Bukovynian village near the Dniester River, now in Zastavna raion, Chernivtsi oblast. It was first mentioned in the Hypatian Chronicle under the year 1219. Archeological excavations have uncovered a settlement of the *Trypilian culture (3rd millennium BC) on Mt Turetska near the village; closer to the Dniester an early Slavic settlement of the *Cherniakhiv culture (2nd–5th centuries AD) and silver Roman coins have been discovered.

Onypko, Semen, b 31 January 1913 in Osmachky, Poltava county, d 1 March 1975 in Ternopil. Stage actor. He worked in the Poltava, Donetske, Vinnytsia, and Ternopil Ukrainian music and drama theaters. Among his roles were Zadorozhny in I. Franko's *Ukradene shchastia* (Stolen Happiness), Lopata in *Zemlia* (The Land, based on the novel by O. Kobylianska), and Lenin in various Soviet plays.

Antin Onyshchuk

Onyshchuk, Antin [Onyščuk], b 1885, d 1930s. Ethnographer. Before the First World War he was a research associate of the Ethnographic Commission of the Shevchenko Scientific Society in Lviv, where he specialized in the culture of the Hutsuls and in folk pottery. After the war he moved to Kiev, where he worked at the All-Ukrainian Historical Museum and served as director of the VUAN *Cabinet of Anthropology and Ethnology. He was arrested during the Stalinist terror in 1934, and died in a labor camp or was executed by the NKVD.

Onyshkevych, Hnat (Ihnatii) [Onyškevyč, Ihnatij], b 1847 in Uhniv, Zhovkva circle, Galicia, d 26 March 1883 in Vienna. Slavist. After studying at the universities of Lviv and Vienna (under F. Miklosich), he was ordained in the Greek Catholic church. In 1877 he was appointed professor of Ukrainian language and literature at Chernivtsi University. He published the works of I. Kotliarevsky, H. Kvitka-Osnovianenko, M. Shashkevych, I. Vahylevych, and Ya. Holovatsky in the series Rus'ka biblioteka (The Ruthenian Library, 3 vols, 1877–8, 1884); edited with O. Lepky the third edition of M. Osadtsa's Ruthenian grammar for secondary schools (1876); and contributed several articles to periodicals, such as *Rodimyi listok*, *Archiv für slavische Philologie*, *S'vit*, and *Misiatseslov bukovyns'kyi*.

Onyshkevych, Larissa [Onyškevyč, Larysa] (née Zaleska), b 12 May 1935 in Stryi, Galicia. Literary scholar, pedagogue, and community figure in the United States; member of the Shevchenko Scientific Society (NTSh); wife of Lubomyr *Onyshkevych. She graduated from the University of Pennsylvania (PH D, 1973). She has taught Ukrainian literature at Rutgers University and engaged in research at the Institute of Advanced Study in Princeton. She has held executive positions in the NTSh and the Plast Ukrainian Youth Association and has edited a number of Plast periodicals. In 1988 she became literary editor of the monthly journal *Suchasnist'*. She has written articles and reviews on Ukrainian literature and drama.

Onyshkevych, Lubomyr [Onyškevyč, Ljubomyr], b 3 February 1933 in Lviv. Ukrainian-American scientist in the field of electronics and electronic materials; full member of the Shevchenko Scientific Society; husband of Larissa *Onyshkevych. He obtained two graduate degrees from the Massachusetts Institute of Technology and began working at the RCA Laboratories in Princeton, New Jersey, in 1957 (as a group leader in 1979). In 1987 he became a technical manager at SRI International. He has written numerous technical papers and holds about 15 US patents. His main contributions have been in the areas of thin and thick films, microelectronics, computer memory, electronic packaging, special electronic substrates, materials for electronic applications, and acoustic surface waves. An active member of the Plast Ukrainian Youth Association, he cofounded its magazine *Iunak* and edited many Plast publications. Onyshkevych has written numerous entries on technology for *Encyclopedia of Ukraine*.

Onyshkevych, Mykhailo [Onyškevyč, Myxajlo], b 25 March 1906 in Biskovychi, Sambir county, Galicia, d 13 March 1971 in Lviv. Slavic linguist. A graduate of Lviv University (MA, 1935), he taught Polish linguistics there (1940–1, 1945–71), chaired its department of Slavic philology (1956–68), and was an associate of the Lviv branch of the AN URSR (now ANU) Institute of Linguistics (from 1945). He developed the teaching program in Polish descriptive and historical grammar for Soviet universities, wrote many articles in Polish and Ukrainian linguistics (especially the Boiko dialect), and was a coeditor of the ANU Polish-Ukrainian dictionary (2 vols in 3 books, 1958–60). His most important work was a two-volume dictionary of the Boiko dialect, published posthumously in 1984.

Myroslav Onyshkevych

Onyshkevych, Myroslav [Onyškevyč] (nom de guerre: Orest, Bohdan), b 26 January 1911 in Uhniv, Rava Ruska county, Galicia, d 3 June 1950 in Warsaw. Senior UPA commander. In the 1930s he was a member of the OUN and was arrested several times by the Polish police. In the fall of 1943 he organized the Ukrainian People's Self-Defense in the Lviv region, and in 1944 he commanded a UPA battalion which fought the Germans, Poles, and Russians. In late 1944 he became deputy commander of the Second Military District, the territory of the Buh Group of UPA-West, and in October 1945, commander of Sian Group in the Sixth Military District. At this post he was promoted to major. When the Sian Group was demobilized in the fall of 1947, he moved to western Poland, where he was captured on 2 March 1948 by Polish security forces. After more than two years of incarceration and torture he was executed.

Onyshkevych, Stepan [Onyškevyč], b 1861 in Galicia, d 1945. Greek Catholic priest and civic and political leader. He was one of the founders of the National Democratic party and a member of its Popular Committee. He was elected to the Austrian parliament twice (1907 and 1911) and sat on the Ukrainian National Rada in 1918–19. He helped Ye. Olesnytsky reorganize *Silskyi Hospodar (1909–17) and played an important role in other Galician economic institutions, such as the Dnister insurance company and the Karpatiia life insurance company. In the interwar period he supported the Ukrainian National Democratic Alliance.

Onyshkewych, Zenowij [Onyškevyč, Zenovij], b 8 December 1929 in Lviv, Galicia. Painter. A postwar émigré in the United States, he studied at the Art Students' League of New York under R. Marsh (1949–51), the National Academy of Fine Arts, and the Pratt Institute (BFA, 1958). He has taught drawing from life at Fairfield University (1977–84) and has painted oil and watercolor portraits, including ones of Pope Paul VI (1967) and Cardinal Y. Slipy, and American, French, and Italian landscapes. Solo shows of his work have been held in New York, Washington, Chicago, Rome, Toronto, and Philadelphia. He has also done illustrations for the *New York Times*, *Reader's Digest*, and American publishing houses.

OOChSU. See Organization for the Defense of Four Freedoms for Ukraine.

Opara, Stepan, b ?, d ca 1665. Cossack leader. In 1661 he was captain of Medvedytsia company in Chyhyryn regi-

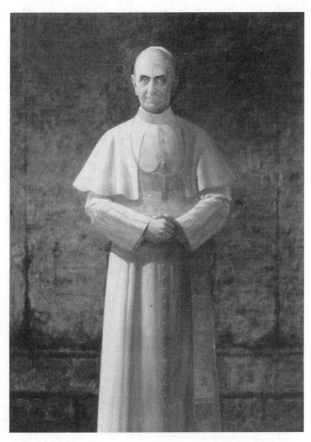

Zenowij Onyshkewych: *Portrait of Pope Paul VI* (1967) in the Vatican

ment and Hetman Yu. Khmelnytsky's envoy in Warsaw. With the support of the Crimean Tatar army, operating in Right-Bank Ukraine as Poland's ally, he proclaimed himself hetman of Right-Bank Ukraine in Uman in June 1665. He appointed P. Doroshenko as his general quartermaster. Opara proved incapable of mastering the complex political and military situation, however, and he quickly lost the support of his *starshyna* and the confidence of the Tatars, who arrested him in late August. Doroshenko, who succeeded Opara as hetman, handed him over to the Poles, who imprisoned him in the Malbork fortress and possibly executed him.

Opatovych, Stefan [Opatovyč], b 15 December 1831 in Horynhrad, Rivne county, Volhynia gubernia, d 12 April 1892. Orthodox priest and writer. He graduated from the theological seminary in Kremianets (1853) and from the St Petersburg Theological Academy (1857). From 1858 he was a priest in St Petersburg, where he was active in the Ukrainian community and assisted students from Ukraine. Opatovych wrote the Russian-language works *Sviatyni Kieva* (The Churches of Kiev, 1873) and *Pervye veka khristianstva i rasprostranenie ego na Rusi* (The First Centuries of Christianity and Its Spread through Rus', 1873). He also published, in Ukrainian, *Opovidannia z sviatoho pysannia* (Stories from the Holy Scriptures), a book of religious instruction that appeared in 1863; planned subsequent volumes were not published owing to the ban in the Russian Empire on Ukrainian-language publications.

OPDL. See Association of Ukrainian Writers for Young People.

Opera. The earliest operatic works by Ukrainian composers were written in the 18th century. M. Berezovsky's *Demofoonte* (1773) and D. Bortniansky's *Creonte* (1776), *Alcides* (1778), and *Quinto Fabio* (1779) were written to Italian librettos. Bortniansky also composed two French comic operas – *Le Faucon* (1786) and *Le Fils rival* (1787) – that were performed at the Russian imperial court. Notable Ukrainian opera singers of the 18th century include O. Rozumovsky, H. Holovnia, and M. Poltoratsky.

Among the notable Ukrainian operas of the 19th century is S. *Hulak-Artemovsky's *Zaporozhian Cossack beyond the Danube*, the music of which is strongly influenced by Ukrainian folk songs. This opera premiered in St Petersburg in 1863 with the composer himself performing the title role of Karas. Since then it has become one of the most popular Ukrainian operas and has been staged by theaters in Ukraine and in the diaspora. Its roles have been sung by some of the finest Ukrainian artists, including M. Sadovsky, P. Saksahansky, M. Kropyvnytsky, I. Patorzhynsky, M. Donets, M. Donets-Tesseir, M. Lytvynenko-Volgemut, M. Sadovska-Barilotti, and M. Zankovetska.

Other Ukrainian operas of the late 19th and early 20th centuries include P. Sokalsky's *Mazepa*, *Obloha Dubna* (The Siege of Dubno), and *May Night*; M. Arkas's *Kateryna* (1890); B. Pidhoretsky's *Kupal'na iskra* (The Spark of Kupalo); A. Vakhnianyn's *Kupalo* (1892); D. Sichynsky's *Roksoliana* (1909); and Heorhii Kozachenko's *Pan sotnyk* (The Noble Captain, 1902).

The most significant Ukrainian operatic works of this period were composed by M. *Lysenko: *Rizdviana nich* (Christmas Night, 1882), *Utoplena* (The Drowned Maiden, 1884), *Chornomortsi* (The Black Sea Cossacks, 1872), the comic opera *Eneïda* (Aeneid, 1910), the chamber opera *Nocturne* (1912), the operetta *Natalka from Poltava* (1889), and children's operas. Outstanding among Lysenko's repertoire is the opera *Taras Bulba* (1891; based on Gogol, libretto by M. Starytsky). It was premiered, after the composer's death, in the Kharkiv State Opera (1924).

In the late 1920s, opera in Ukraine developed rapidly. This was partially because of the significant performing talent centered at the Kiev, Kharkiv, and Odessa opera theaters. Among the works staged were V. Femelidi's *Rozlom* (The Schism), O. *Chyshko's *Iablunevyi polon* (The Apple Tree Captivity), B. *Liatoshynsky's *Zolotyi obruch* (The Golden Ring, 1929; based on I. Franko's *Zakhar Berkut*), V. *Kostenko's *Karmeliuk*, P. *Kozytsky's *Nevidomi soldaty* (The Unknown Soldiers), and M. *Verykivsky's *Captain* and *Naimychka* (The Hired Girl, 1943). This growth did not last, however. With the Stalinist repression of Ukrainian culture, opera was forced to adhere to the principles of socialist realism. It was required that it appeal to a mass audience, reject the influences of Western European modernism, and become a medium for ideology and propaganda.

It was not until the 1960s that the Communist party's ideological pressure somewhat abated. The relaxation led to the creation of a number of works of musical theater, characterized by an increased range of expression and a greater diversity in theme and genre. These operas include Yu. Meitus's *Young Guard* and *Stolen Happiness*, V. Kyreiko's *Forest Song*, K. Dankevych's *Nazar Stodolia*, H.

Maiboroda's *Arsenal* and *Zahybel' eskadry* (The Destruction of the Squadron), H. Zhukovsky's *First Spring*, and others by I. Karabyts, V. Hubarenko, Ye. Stankovych, and V. Zahortsev.

Ukraine has six major opera and ballet theaters, in Kiev, Odessa, Lviv, Kharkiv, Donetske, and Dnipropetrovske. Important conductors of these opera theaters have been V. Piradov, K. Symeonov, V. Tolba, Ya. Voshchak, S. Turchak, A. Pazovsky, S. Zak, V. Kolesnyk, B. Chystiakov, O. Klymov, Yu. Lutsiv, M. Malko, and M. Pokrovsky. The theaters have staged relatively few full-scale productions of Ukrainian operas, compared with those of Russian or European composers.

Acclaimed Ukrainian female opera singers of the 20th century include Ye. Miroshnychenko, O. Petrusenko, B. and L. Rudenko, Ye. Chavdar, Z. Haidai, M. Sokil, Ye. Zarytska, I. Malaniuk, C. Ordassy-Baransky, and S. *Krushelnytska, who premiered G. Puccini's *Madame Butterfly* in Italy in 1904. Notable Ukrainian male opera singers include D. Hnatiuk, O. Myshuha, M. Menzinsky, A. Didur, B. Hmyria, M. Hryshko, M. Romensky, P. Karmaliuk, S. Kozak, Yu. Kyporenko-Domansky, V. Kozeratsky, and M. Skala-Starytsky.

Active émigré Ukrainian composers of opera include A. Rudnytsky (*Dovbush* and *Anna Iaroslavna*), P. Pecheniha-Uhlytsky (*The Witch*), and M. Fomenko (*Marusia Bohuslavka*). The Canadian Ukrainian Opera Association (est 1974; see *Lysenko Chorus) has staged full and concert versions of Ukrainian operas in Canada and the United States.

BIBLIOGRAPHY
Iurmas, Ia. 'Ukraïns'ka opera,' *Zhyttia i revoliutsiia*, 1930, no. 5
Arkhimovych, L. *Ukraïns'ka klasychna opera* (Kiev 1951)
Stanishevs'kyi, Iu. *Opernyi teatr Radians'koï Ukraïny: Istoriia i suchasnist'* (Kiev 1988)

W. Wytwycky

Operation Wisła (Polish: Akcja 'Wisła' or Akcja 'W'). The code name of the military operation, by Polish military and security units (28 April to 31 July 1947), that resulted in the deportation of 150,000 Ukrainians from their autochthonous territories (the *Lemko, *Sian, and *Kholm regions) in southeastern Poland to Poland's 'regained territories' (Ziemie Odzyskane), newly acquired from Germany, in the north and northwest.

Officially the purpose of Operation Wisła was to destroy UPA units active in the *Lemko region as well as to deprive them of a base of support among the local population. On 17 April 1947 the Polish State Committee on Public Security issued an order for the implementation of Operation Wisła, and it was sanctioned by a decree of the Presidium of the Council of Ministers of Poland dated 24 April 1947.

Most Polish sources claim the decision was provoked by the death of Gen K. Świerczewski, the Polish deputy minister of defence, in a UPA ambush on 28 March 1947. In reality it probably had been prepared well in advance, and represented the last of several measures taken by the Soviet and Polish authorities during and after the Second World War to 'solve' Poland's 'Ukrainian problem.' Earlier, on the basis of a Soviet-Polish agreement, signed on 19 September 1944, to 'repatriate' Poles in the Ukrainian SSR and Ukrainians in Poland, almost half a million Ukrainians in Poland had been resettled in the Ukrainian SSR.

Gen S. Mossor headed Operational Group Wisła,

which included approx 20,000 regular Polish troops as well as internal security troops, members of the militia, and armed civilians. The principle of collective responsibility was applied, and all Ukrainians in the affected territories, regardless of their political views and affiliations, were deported. The deportation process was swift and brutal: deportees were often given only a few hours to prepare themselves, could take only limited belongings, and were transported to their destination in crowded boxcars. The food supply was irregular, sanitary conditions were poor, there were many delays en route, and the deportation process was accompanied by considerable violence. Some deportees died in transit; those who resisted deportation, or were suspected of aiding the UPA, were imprisoned in the Jaworzno prison camp in Silesia.

The deportees were dispersed over a wide area, primarily in the provinces of *Olsztyn, *Szczecin, Wrocław, and *Gdańsk. They were to constitute no more than 10 percent of the population in any one location, and the eventual goal of government policy was their assimilation into the Polish majority.

Living conditions were harsh, since the deportees were not properly compensated for their lost property, and the best land and buildings in the 'regained territories' were already occupied by Poles who had been 'repatriated' from Soviet-occupied Western Ukraine (Galicia and Volhynia).

Operation Wisła succeeded in atomizing the Ukrainian community in postwar *Poland, and the existence of the community was not recognized by the Polish government until 1956, when limited organizational activity was permitted. Before 1957, deportees who tried to return home were imprisoned in the Jaworzno prison camp, and after 1957 only a few thousand were allowed to resettle in their ancestral homeland. Attempts to attract Polish settlers to that area were largely unsuccessful. It continues to be underpopulated, and many distinctive Ukrainian wooden churches and other cultural monuments have been vandalized or destroyed or have fallen into disrepair.

A number of popular Polish novels dealing with Operation Wisła (notably J. Gerhard's *Łuna w Bieszczadach* [The Glow in the Beskyds]), have contributed to a generally negative Polish stereotype of Ukrainians by depicting them in a crude and hostile fashion. Recently, however, a number of articles in Polish publications have discussed Operation Wisła in a more forthright and objective fashion. On 3 August 1990 the Polish Senate passed a resolution condemning Operation Wisła.

BIBLIOGRAPHY
Szcześniak, A.B.; Szota, W.Z. *Droga do nikąd: Działalność Organizacji Ukraińskich Nacjonalistów i jej likwidacja w Polsce* (Warsaw 1973)
Trukhan, M. 'Aktsiia "Visla",' *Vidnova*, 3 (Summer–Fall 1985)
Jaworsky, I. l'*Akcja Wisla* [sic] and Polish-Ukrainian Relations,' *Studium Papers*, 12 (April 1988)

J. Jaworsky

Operetta. Early Ukrainian operettas include M. *Verbytsky's *Pidhiriany* (The Foothill Dwellers, 1864) and M. *Lysenko's *Chornomortsi* (The Black Sea Cossacks, 1872). In the 20th century they were followed by K. *Stetsenko's *Svatannia na Honcharivtsi* (Matchmaking at Honcharivka, 1909), Y. Lopatynsky's *Enei na mandrivtsi* (Aeneas in His Wanderings, 1911), and Y. Barnych's *Hutsulka Ksenia*

(Ksenia the Hutsul Girl). The Stalinist crackdown which began in the 1930s stifled the development of Ukrainian culture, including *opera and operetta. Restrictions and the binding conformity to *socialist realism eased only after Stalin's death. Since then Ukrainian operettas have been written by O. Bilash, H. Finarsky, V. Homoliaka, A. Kos-Anatolsky, V. Lukashov, O. Riabov, O. Sandler, and Ya. Tsehliar. In Ukraine the leading operetta theaters are the *Kiev Operetta Theater and the *Odessa Musical Comedy Theater.

Ophthalmology. A branch of medicine that pertains to the structure, functions, diseases, and disorders of the eye. Ophthalmology began to be treated as a separate branch of medicine at the beginning of the 19th century. It was taught at Kharkiv University from 1811 and at Kiev University from 1841. Independent departments of ophthalmology were established at Kharkiv (1868), Kiev (1869), and Odessa (1903) universities. The Kiev surgeon V. *Karavaiv perfected the excision of eye cataracts; he performed about 3,000 operations in the mid-19th century. The first ophthalmological journal, *Vestnik oftal'mologii*, was published by A. Khodin in Kiev from 1884 (now published in Moscow). O. *Shymanovsky of Kiev pioneered the surgical method of transplanting the cornea of the eye. He advanced the teaching of ophthalmology by including compulsory practical courses in the curriculum. The noted Ukrainian ophthalmologist V. *Filatov founded the first glaucoma clinic in the USSR (1931) and established the Institute of Eye Diseases and Tissue Therapy in Odessa (1936), as well as its Russian-language journal *Oftal'mologicheskii zhurnal*. From 1956 the institute's director and the editor of the journal was N. *Puchkivska, a Ukrainian pioneer of cornea transplants and eye-burn treatment. There are departments of ophthalmology at all medical institutes as well as at the postgraduate institutes for the upgrading of physicians. Persistent shortages of instruments, drugs, and eyeglasses, however, as well as questionable hygienic practices in the polyclinics in Ukraine, detract from the ophthalmological services available to the average citizen.

BIBLIOGRAPHY
Rukin, V. *Do istorii vitchyznianoï oftal'molohiï* (Kiev 1957)
P. Dzul

Opilia Upland [Opillja]. The western portion of the *Podolian Upland. Located to the west of the Upper Zolota Lypa River, Opilia has a general elevation of 350–400 m and a maximum elevation of 470 m. In contrast to that of Podilia in general, the landscape is smooth and gentle and notable for its underlying soft chalky rock. A number of left-bank tributaries of the Dniester, among them the Zubra, the Svirzh, and the Hnyla Lypa, run through Opilia. Their watersheds are cut by secondary valleys which provide the region with a hilly terrain. The slopes of the hills are covered with forests (generally beeches, oaks, and elms), and the watersheds with fields and meadows. Some of the larger towns in Opilia are Berezhany, Rohatyn, and Pidhaitsi.

Opilsky, Yuliian [Opil's'kyj, Julijan] (pseud of Yurii Rudnytsky), b 8 December 1884 in Ternopil, Galicia, d 9 February 1937 in Lviv. Teacher and writer; brother of S.

Yuliian Opilsky

*Rudnytsky. He studied at Lviv University and graduated from Graz University (1907). He taught at the Academic Gymnasium of Lviv, was on the district school council (from 1917), and edited the journal *Ukraïns'ka shkola* and various German textbooks for schools. His first literary attempts in lyrical poetry remained unpublished. Opilsky's novels on Ukraine's historical past include *Idu na vas* (Beware! We Shall Attack! 1918), *V tsarstvi zolotoï svobody* (In the Kingdom of Golden Freedom, 1920), *Zolotyi lev* (The Golden Lion, 1926), and *Idoly padut'* (The Idols Are Falling, 1928). Opilsky is also the author of novelettes dealing with various subjects from world history, among them *Tanechnytsia z Pibastu* (A Dancer from Pibast, 1921), *Potsilunok Ishtary* (The Kiss of Ishtar, 1923), and *Shkoliar z Memfisu* (The Schoolboy from Memphis, 1927).

Opishnia [Opišnja]. IV-15. A town smt (1990 pop 7,100) on the Vorskla River in Zinkiv raion, Poltava oblast. Its history goes back to the 17th century. In the Hetman state it was a company town in Hadiache and then Poltava,

Opilia Upland

Yevhen Oppokiv

A glazed clay toy whistle from Opishnia (early 20th century)

Zinkiv, and again Hadiache regiments. Since the 18th century Opishnia has been known for its handicrafts, especially weaving, pottery, and ceramics. Today its ceramics factory makes animal figures, tableware with traditional decorations, and clay toys.

Opishnia fortified settlement. A *Romen-Borshcheve culture settlement of the late 8th to 9th century located in Opishnia, Poltava oblast. Excavations in 1940 and 1957 uncovered fourteen semi-pit dwellings with clay ovens, 20 agricultural buildings and workshops, tools, personal effects, and dishes.

Opolchenie. See Levy en masse.

Oppokiv, Yevhen (Oppokov, Evgenii), b 1 February 1869 in Ruda, Vasylkiv county, Kiev gubernia, d 1 November 1938. Hydrologist and hydrogeologist; full member of the AN URSR (now ANU) from 1929. He studied in Kiev and completed a course at the technology institute in St Petersburg. He went on hydrological expeditions through Belarus and Left-Bank Ukraine from 1894. In 1913 he began to research the wetlands of Polisia, and in 1915 he became a professor at the Kiev Polytechnical Institute. He organized the department of hydrology there (1926), which became the first scientific research institute in Ukraine dedicated specifically to hydrology. Oppokiv headed the new institute as well as the hydrometeorological branch of the *Ukrainian Meteorological Service. His main research interests included watersheds and methods for the drainage of wetlands.

Opryshoks (*opryshky*). Groups of social brigands active in the Ukrainian regions of the Carpathian Mountains from the 16th century to the early 19th century. Opryshoks were similar to the 'noble highwaymen' of other countries and have been idealized in Ukrainian folklore and romantic literature. They consisted mainly of former peasants, servants of noblemen, and (in a later period) resisters of conscription. They usually formed small groups with individual leaders and attacked estates, keeps, tax farmers, tavern keepers, merchants, and wealthy peasants. They commonly kept most of their booty for themselves, but some of them distributed a portion among the poorer peasantry. Many peasants considered them heroes and avengers and often harbored them or gave them other assistance. During times of greater upheaval they also joined them to form insurrectionist forces (notably during the Cossack-Polish War). The opryshoks enjoyed particularly advantageous conditions, in that they worked in a mountainous borderland between three states (Poland, Hungary, and Moldavia).

The first documented reference to activity similar to that of the opryshoks dates from the mid-15th century. The term 'opryshoks' came into use in the early 16th century. The zenith of their activity was in 1738–59, when they were led by the legendary O. *Dovbush, V. Baiurak, and I. Boichuk and were active throughout the Hutsul and Boiko regions, Bukovyna, and Transcarpathia. In the late 18th and early 19th centuries their number increased dramatically because of rising taxes and forced conscription. A noted opryshok leader in the Hutsul region during that period was M. *Shtoliuk. The Austrian government sent out special punitive military detachments to combat the renegades. The disappearance of the opryshoks was due largely to such repressions and to the abolition of serfdom in the mid-19th century.

A wealth of folkloric material concerning the opryshoks was gathered and published by V. Hnatiuk, Ya. Holovatsky, V. Shukhevych, and others. Literature also derived considerable inspiration from the opryshoks, who appear in the works of Yu. Fedkovych, I. Franko, V. Gzhytsky, H. Khotkevych, M. Pavlyk, M. Shashkevych, and I. Vahylevych, as well as in those of the Polish writers J. Korzeniowski and S. Vincenz, the Austrian writer L. Sacher-Masoch, and the Czech writer I. Olbracht. In the Carpathians many mountains, lowlands, and rivers are named after prominent opryshoks, particularly Dovbush.

BIBLIOGRAPHY
Tselevych, Iu. *Opryshky* (Lviv 1897)
Hrabovets'kyi, V. *Antyfeodal'na borot'ba karpats'koho opryshkivstva XVI–XIX st.* (Lviv 1966)
Stavrovs'kyi, O. *Slovats'ko-pol's'ko-ukraïns'ke prykordonnia do 18-oho st.* (Prešov 1967)

Ya. Isaievych

Option. The right to choose one's citizenship, conferred by either international or national law, especially when a territory is transferred from one state to another. Option is usually connected with resettlement in the country of one's chosen citizenship. Peace treaties and other international agreements that involve the transfer of territory contain provisions for option. The Peace Treaty of Riga and the 1921 agreements between the Ukrainian SSR and Estonia, Lithuania, and Latvia, for example, specified the option procedure for inhabitants of the Baltic countries who preferred to be Ukrainian citizens, and vice versa. There was some population exchange between Poland, Ukraine, and the Baltic states as a result.

The resettlement and exchange of populations between Nazi Germany and the USSR in 1939–40 and between Poland and the USSR in 1945–6 was not based on voluntary option, but on force. In 1946 an agreement between the USSR and Czechoslovakia allowed Czechs and Slovaks living mostly in Volhynia and Transcarpathia to opt for

Czechoslovakian citizenship and Ukrainians, Russians, and Belarusians in Czechoslovakia to choose USSR citizenship. As a result, almost 10,000 Ukrainians moved to Ukraine in 1946–7. By the late 1950s many of them wanted to return to Czechoslovakia, but they did not obtain Czechoslovak citizenship until 1968.

Oransky, George [Orans'kyj, Jurij], b 30 January 1917 in Kharkiv. Conductor, musicologist, and pedagogue. His musical education took place at the Kharkiv Conservatory (1935–43) in the class of opera and symphonic conducting and at the Hochschule für Musik in Freiburg, West Germany (1945–9). He began his conductorial activity while still a student at the conservatory and has led choirs in Kharkiv (1942–3), Kiev (1943), Kolomyia (1943–4), and Drohobych (1944), as well as the Philadelphia-based Opera Ensemble of the Ukrainian Music Institute of America (1964–74). Oransky has collaborated with M. Fomenko and V. Ovcharenko on a number of works and has edited, arranged, and orchestrated works by classical and contemporary Ukrainian composers. He has published articles and papers about Ukrainian composers and their music. He has also toured the United States with opera productions and chamber and symphonic groups, and given audiovisual presentations.

Oransky-Voina, Parkhomii [Orans'kyj-Vojna, Parxomij], b ?, d 23 June 1653. Uniate churchman. He studied in Rome and then served as archimandrite of the Basilian Zhydychyn St Nicholas's Monastery before being consecrated bishop of Turiv-Pynske (1637–53). A writer and publicist, he is known for his 1645 rebuttal in Polish to views put forth by K. *Sakovych.

Orations of Gregory of Nazianzus (Slova Hryhoriia Bohoslova Naziianzyna). A collection of 13 sermons by an early Byzantine church father and bishop of Constantinople (379–81) which were translated into Church Slavonic, probably in Kiev. An 11th-century copy of the Orations offers valuable insights into the evolution of the Church Slavonic language and into contemporary Slavic religious practices. Scholars believe that local clergymen, particularly Cyril of Turiv, may have modeled their sermons on the Orations.

Orativ. IV-10. A town smt (1990 pop 3,200) and raion center in Vinnytsia oblast. It was first mentioned in historical documents in 1545. Orativ was involved in the haidamaka rebellion in 1768. In 1793 it was annexed by Russia. In 1919 it was the site of a battle between the UNR and Ukrainian Galician armies and the White forces. Today the town has a dairy.

Oratorio. A nontheatrical setting of a dramatic text on a sacred or semisacred theme for chorus, soloists, and orchestra. The earliest known oratorio in Ukraine was written by I. Vitkovsky and performed at the opening of Kharkiv University. The genre did not develop in Ukraine until the 20th century, when it was used as a monumental art form for the masses and a vehicle for Communist party propaganda. Notable titles include K. Dankevych's *October*, A. Shtoharenko's *Along the Paths of October*, and M. Skorulsky's *A Mother's Voice*. Some contemporary Ukrainian oratorios have managed to avoid blatant politicization, among them M. Verykivsky's *Duma pro divku-branku*

Marusiu Bohuslavku (Duma about the Captive-Girl Marusia Bohuslavka) and P. Kozytsky's *Spring Oratorio* for children's choir. Outside of Ukraine, S. Kouzan's *Neophytes* (to the words of T. Shevchenko) were written for the commemoration of the millennium of Christianity in Rus'-Ukraine (1988).

Orcharding and fruit farming. A major branch of agriculture, devoted to the cultivation of fruits and berries. As a source of many trace minerals, vitamins, acids, oils (up to 70 percent in nuts), and albumen (up to 22 percent in nuts), fruits and berries play an important nutritional role. Because these foods are relatively costly, their consumption is a good indicator of the economic well-being of a population. In Ukraine fruit growing is an important source of revenue for collective farms and private plots: in 1983, 48.1 percent of all orchards were on private plots, and 27.9 percent belonged to collective farms. Thanks to a favorable climate, orcharding has been practiced in Ukraine since ancient times, although prior to the 15th century fruit farming was subsidiary to wild fruit and berry gathering. The Greeks cultivated fruits and berries along the Black Sea coast, especially in the Crimea. In the Princely era horticulture was concentrated in Kiev and its outskirts. As early as the 9th century orchards were cultivated, and selection was used to improve varieties. Later, monasteries, such as the Kievan Cave Monastery, became important centers for the development of horticulture. Apples, pears, cherries, black cherries, plums, and walnuts were the principal crops grown in the medieval period.

In the 18th century orcharding developed rapidly and became widely practiced. Monasteries, the gentry, and the Cossack *starshyna* kept extensive orchards. New varieties and cultivation methods were introduced by German, Bulgarian, and Czech colonists. For the first time peasants became involved in horticulture, although most of their crops were not sold but consumed at home. Peasant fruit farming for commercial purposes began only in the 19th century.

The first significant contributions to scientific horticulture were made by the *Symyrenko family – Platon, Levko, and Volodymyr – and V. *Kashchenko. Horticultural schools and research insitutions, such as the *Nikita Botanical Garden, arose in the 19th century. In 1887 there were 209,000 ha of orchards in the nine Ukrainian gubernias under Russian rule. By 1913 the figure had increased to 293,000, or 44.5 percent of all of the orchards in the Russian Empire. Ukraine produced 557,000 t of fruit (primarily apples, black cherries, cherries, plums, and pears; apricots and walnuts in the southern regions), and its average productivity was 24.8 centners per ha. About 60 percent of the orchards were owned by peasants: they were small and crudely cultivated, and produced a random assortment of fruits. The largest commercial orchards were in the Podilia-Bessarabia region and the Crimea.

In the early 20th century horticulture went through a cycle of destruction (during the First World War), recovery (by 1927 the prewar level had been reached), and destruction (during collectivization). By 1940, 612,000 ha in Ukraine were devoted to fruit farming, with private plots accounting for 52.3 percent of the total area. That figure represented 2 percent of the republic's arable land and 34.2 percent of the orchard area in the USSR.

In Western Ukraine horticulture was less developed

than in Soviet Ukraine. In Transcarpathia, for example, horticulture accounted for less than 1 per cent of the arable land in 1935. In the postwar period horticulture reached a peak in 1965, when 1.3 million ha were devoted to fruit farming. Since then the emphasis has been on intensifying rather than expanding horticulture.

In 1983 1.1 million ha were devoted to orchards, or 3.3 percent of the arable land in Ukraine. That area represented 35.1 percent of the orchard area of the former USSR. The main crops were apple (72.2 percent), plum (10.1 percent), pear (7.5 percent), and red and black cherries (5.8 percent). Polisia had 18.8 percent of the orchards, the forest-steppe region 40.1 percent, and the steppe region 41.1 percent. Private plots with a productivity of 47.9 centners per ha accounted for 48.1 percent of the horticultural land, or 524,000 ha; collective farms with a productivity of 23.4 centners per ha represented 27.9 percent, or 304,000 ha; and state farms with a productivity of 63.9 centners per ha represented 24.0 percent, or 231,000 ha. By 1990 the area of arable land taken up by orchards had decreased to 851,000 ha. Their total harvest amounted to 2.9 million t, and their productivity had risen to 42.3 centners per ha.

Because horticulture demands intensive labor and sophisticated techniques, it continues to experience serious difficulties in Ukraine. In 1970, 20 percent of the fruit was left to rot in the fields for lack of transportation. As a result horticultural produce is in short supply, especially outside the growing season. In 1976 the per capita fruit consumption in the USSR was 20 percent of that in the United States. Scientific research in horticulture is conducted at the *Ukrainian Scientific Research Institute of Orcharding and its research stations as well as in the departments of horticulture in agricultural institutes. (See also *Viticulture.)

BIBLIOGRAPHY

Shcherbyna, M. *Sadivnytstvo plodove ta iahidne* (Kiev 1926)
Sadivnytstvo i vynohradarstvo (Kiev 1959)
Chukhno, D. *Ekonomika sadovodstva* (Kiev 1961)
Iurchyshyn, V. *Ekonomichna efektyvnist' porid i sortiv plodovykh kul'tur* (Kiev 1968)

M. Borovsky, C. Freeland

Orchestra. A unified performing ensemble of musical instruments. Performing ensembles have been part of the Ukrainian musical tradition for at least a millennium. An 11th-century fresco in the St Sophia Cathedral in Kiev depicts a group of *skomorokhy (court musician-entertainers) playing contemporary instruments as an ensemble. Other records indicate that the Rus' armies went into battle with ensembles of drummers and trumpeters, as did those of the Zaporozhian Cossacks several centuries later. The development of the *vertep (puppet theater) and *school drama in the 16th and 17th centuries established a need for some more permanent form of instrumental ensembles, which grew out of the tradition of folk trio ensembles (*troisti muzyky). With the growth of *musicians' guilds from the 16th century and the gradual development of city orchestras, a stronger base was laid for more permanent forms of musical ensembles. At the same time, musical training became more common with the establishment of school orchestras at the Kievan Academy, the Hlukhiv Singing School, and Kharkiv College.

Chamber and symphonic orchestras dedicated specifically to classical music were established on the estates of 18th-century hetmans, such as I. Briukhovetsky, I. Skoropadsky, D. Apostol, and K. Rozumovsky. With the introduction of serfdom after 1785, wealthy landowners, such as the Lyzohub, Galagan, and Boliubash families, set up private serf orchestras. The 19th century saw the establishment of civic societies dedicated to musical performance and development in Ukraine. With them came a growing number of municipal orchestras, concert tours, and opera troupes, all contributing to the evolution of professional orchestras. This trend was extended in the 20th century after the formation of the Ukrainian SSR, when a host of state-sponsored instrumental ensembles were established for public performances and for use in radio broadcasts and movie productions.

At present in Ukraine there are nine symphony orchestras (including the *Symphony Orchestra of Ukraine), seven chamber orchestras, two pop orchestras, and numerous theater orchestras, army bands, and semiprofessional ensembles. In addition, the State Banduryst Kapelle of Ukraine and a number of folk music and dance ensembles that include folk instrument orchestras have been established in Ukraine during the 20th century (most notably the *Verovka State Chorus).

Important composers of orchestral music in Ukraine are S. Liudkevych, L. Revutsky, B. Liatoshynsky, A. Shtoharenko, R. Simovych, R. Prydatkevych, M. Skoryk, and V. Sylvestrov. Prominent conductors in Ukraine include M. Verykivsky, N. Rakhlin, O. Klymiv, A. Rudnytsky, Turkevych, M. Kolessa, I. Blazhkov, V. Kozhukhar, and Turchak.

W. Sydorenko

Orchis (Ukrainian: *zozulyntsi*). A genus of orchids (family Orchidaceae) containing about 100 species, some cultivated as ornamentals. The *Orchis* is a perennial herb with a straight, leafy stem; each plant bears a single flower-spike with many flowers. The root tubers of some species are used as food. Most widespread in Ukraine is *O. maculata*, which grows in boggy meadows and brushwood. Salep, prepared from dried orchid tubers, is taken orally or by enema to treat inflammations of the digestive tract.

Orchyk River [Orčyk]. A right-bank tributary of the Orel River. It is 108 km long and drains a basin area of 1,460 sq km. It flows through Kharkiv and Poltava oblasts and is fed mainly by meltwater. The town of Karlivka is situated on the river, the waters of which are used for irrigation.

Carlotta Ordassy-Baransky

Ordassy-Baransky, Carlotta, b 2 May 1921 in Budapest. Opera singer (soprano). She studied music at the Liszt Academy in Budapest and at the La Scala School for Young Artists in Milan (under G. Cigna). She debuted as Second Lady in W. Mozart's *Die Zauberflöte* at La Scala and continued singing there under W. Furtwängler. In 1950 she moved to New York, where she sang in the Metropolitan Opera as a soloist (1955–77) and as a guest soloist with the Dumka Chorus. She also performed in Salzburg under H. von Karajan and recorded R. Wagner's *Die Walküre* with him and *Das Rheingold* with L. Stokowski.

Order of Saint Basil the Great. See Basilian monastic order.

Orders, medals, and honorific titles of the Ukrainian SSR. Official awards or honors for outstanding service to the state, or exceptional achievement in the building of socialism or in military service. The awards used in the Ukrainian SSR lack a distinctive Ukrainian character. The first Soviet award was the Order of the Red Banner, instituted in 1918 by the Soviet Russia for distinguished service in the Red Army. In 1920 Soviet Russia introduced the Order of the Red Banner of Labor for outstanding workers, and this was adopted by the Ukrainian SSR in 1921. Several orders, including those of the Red Banner (1924), the Red Banner of Labor (1928), Lenin (1930), and the Red Star (1930), were established at an all-Union level. During this period the Ukrainian SSR could bestow its national awards, as well as all-Union orders, on its citizens. This changed in 1933, when Moscow assumed control over the awarding of all orders and medals.

A full system of orders and medals was developed in the Soviet Union during J. Stalin's regime. In 1935 the Order of the Mark of Honor was established, and in 1938 medals were awarded for valor, military service, prowess in work, and distinguished service in work. The honorific titles of Hero of the Soviet Union and Hero of Socialist Labor were established in 1934 and 1938, and were supplemented in 1939 with the medals of the Gold Star and the Gold Hammer and Sickle, respectively. The honorific titles of People's Artist (for both theater and fine arts), Merited Artist, Creator of Art, and Scientific Worker were established at both the republic and all-Union levels. Physicians and teachers were added to the list of potential winners in 1940. These developments reflected the penetration of the state structure into every walk of life and its constant striving for political legitimation among the people.

The Second World War led to a proliferation of orders and medals in the Soviet Union. New orders included the Great Fatherland War (2 classes), Suvorov (3 classes), Kutuzov (3 classes), Aleksandr Nevsky, Bohdan Khmelnytsky (3 classes), Victory, Glory (3 classes), Ushakov (2 classes), Nakhimov (2 classes), Mother Hero, and Maternal Glory (3 classes). Medals were issued for partisans (2 classes), motherhood (2 classes), the defense of cities (including Odessa, Sevastopil, and Kiev), the capture of strategic centers in Eastern and Central Europe (including Budapest, Prague, and Warsaw), and the eventual victories over Germany and Japan.

After the Second World War no new orders were created until the Brezhnev regime instituted the orders of the October Revolution (1967), the Friendship of Nations (1972), Worker's Glory (3 classes, 1974), and Service to the Homeland in the Armed Forces of the USSR (3 classes, 1974). The orders of St Olga, St Daniel, and St Andrew were created in the 1980s. Medals were awarded for meritorious work in postwar reconstruction (ferrous metallurgy, Donbas coalfields), outstanding service in dangerous or essential professions (guarding borders, army service, maintenance of public order, fire fighting, and lifesaving), meritorious work performance, and participation in priority economic projects (such as the reclamation of virgin lands or the building of the Baikal-Amur trunkline). The honorific title 'merited' was extended to a wide variety of occupational categories, among them scientists (such as agronomists, amelioration specialists, geologists), technical personnel (pilots, engineers, agricultural machinery specialists, construction workers), and professionals (jurists, postsecondary teachers, architects. (See also *Prizes and awards.)

BIBLIOGRAPHY
Kolesnikov, G.; Rozhkov, A. *Ordena i medali SSSR*, 3rd edn (Moscow 1983)
Gosudarstvennye nagrady SSSR (Moscow 1987)

A. Makuch

Ordzhonikidze, Grigorii [Ordžonikidze, Grigorij] (pseud: Sergo), b 27 October 1886 in Goresha, Georgia, d 18 February 1937 in Moscow. Georgian Bolshevik and Soviet official. In December 1917 he was appointed extraordinary commissar for Ukraine, and during the first Bolshevik offensive in Ukraine he procured grain and coal for Russia and organized Bolshevik resistance against the German forces, including the flooding of the Donbas mines. In 1919 he helped organize A. Denikin's defeat in Left-Bank Ukraine, and in 1921–2 he took part in the reconstruction of the Donbas industry. As first secretary of the Party's Transcaucasian Krai Committee (1921–6) he established Soviet power in Georgia and brutally suppressed any national resistance. As chairman of the Party's Central Control Commission and commissar of the Workers' and Peasants' Inspectorate he carried out purges of Trotskyists and Ukrainian national communists in the Party. In the spring of 1930 he was sent to Ukraine to speed up collectivization and the antikulak campaign. As head of the USSR Supreme Council for the National Economy (1930) and the USSR commissar for heavy industry he directed the industrialization drive, especially the electrification of the Donbas and Dnieper regions of Ukraine. Opposed to the rapid pace of industralization and the mass terror in the 1930s, he committed suicide.

K. Hohol

Ordzhonikidze [Ordžonikidze]. VI-15. A city (1990 pop 46,200) under oblast jurisdiction on the Bazavluk River in Dnipropetrovske oblast. It was founded as a mining town in 1934 and was amalgamated with the Kalinin and No. 1 settlements and Oleksandrivka village in 1956. A center of the Nykopil Manganese Basin, it has an enrichment complex and machinery-repair plants. The Krasnokutskyi kurhan is nearby.

Ordzhonikidze Mineral Enrichment Complex (Ordzhonikidzevskyi hirnycho-zbahachuvalnyi kombinat). A complex of the manganese industry, founded in 1970 in Ordzhonikidze, Dnipropetrovske oblast. It consists of six open quarries, a mine, and three enrichment and agglomeration factories and produces manganese concentrate. In 1970 it employed 3,500 workers.

Orel, Artem, b 2 November 1897 in Saksahan, Verkhnodniprovske county, Katerynoslav gubernia, d 19 July 1972 in Perth Amboy, New Jersey. Linguist. He studied at the Kharkiv Institute of People's Education (1926–30) and worked as a book editor and translator. In the 1930s he was persecuted and in 1938–9 imprisoned. During the German occupation of Ukraine he was literary editor of the Kharkiv paper *Nova Ukraïna* and an editor of the Division Galizien's paper *Do peremohy*. As a postwar refugee he worked for the journal *Pu-hu* in Augsburg and published an orthographic dictionary (1946). After emigrating to the United States in 1950, he compiled a Ukrainian dictionary of foreign loanwords (3 vols, 1963–6) and contributed articles to émigré periodicals, such as *Svoboda*, *Ukraïns'ki visti, Nasha bat'kivshchyna*, and *Novi dni*.

Vasyl Orel

Vasyl Orenchuk

Orel, Vasyl, b 10 January 1928 in Vasiurynska Stanytsia, Plastunivska (now Dinska) county, Kuban, d 31 August 1987 in Mykolaiv. Community activist and specialist in regional studies. He graduated from the Krasnodar Pedagogical Institute with a degree in philology in 1950. In 1963, together with his wife, L. Orel, he established a regional museum in honor of T. Shevchenko in Malo-Tenhynske, in the Otrado-Olhynske region of Krasnodar krai. He also established the only Ukrainian library in the Kuban, but it was destroyed after he left the area for Mykolaiv in 1965. He studied the Ukrainian press in the Kuban and collected biographical data on M. Dykarenko, I. Kotliarevsky, V. Mova, V. Potapenko, M. Pymonenko, and M. Vorony. During his stay in the Kuban he wrote studies of the works of H. Dobroskok, P. Kapelhorodsky, V. Samiilenko, and Ya. Zharko. He has published more than 300 articles on literary topics.

Orel River [Orel'] (also Oril). A left-bank tributary of the Dnieper River, which it joins at Dnipropetrovske. It is 346 km long and drains a basin area of 9,800 sq km. The river originates in Kharkiv oblast, and part of its course runs along the border between Kharkiv and Dnipropetrovske oblasts and between Poltava and Dnipropetrovske oblasts. Its main tributaries are the Bahata, Berestova, Orchyk, and Orelka rivers. The Dnieper-Donbas Canal runs

along the Orel's floodplains. The river is fed mostly by rain and snow, and its waters are used for irrigation and water supply.

Oreletsky, Vasyl [Orelec'kyj, Vasyl'], b 30 January 189? in Luzhany, Chernivtsi county, Bukovyna, d 9 January 1976 in Munich. Legal scholar. Interrupting his law studies at Chernivtsi University during the First World War he served in the Austrian and then Ukrainian Galician armies. After the war he completed his studies at Charles University and the Ukrainian Free University (LLD, 1932). As a student he was president of the *Central Union of Ukrainian Students (1925–6, 1927–33). From 1939 he taught international law at the *Ukrainian Free University, in Prague and then in Munich, and served as dean of the law faculty and as rector of the university (1963–4, 1965–8). He wrote articles on international law, politics and the student movement. As a leading member of the OUN (Bandera faction), Oreletsky edited or contributed to its publications *ABN Correspondence, The Ukrainian Review, Vyzvol'nyi shliakh*, and *Shliakh peremohy*. A festschrift in his honor was published by the Ukrainian Free University in 1982.

Orelka River [Orel'ka] (also Orilka). A left-bank tributary of the Orel River. It is 95 km long and drains a basin area of 805 sq km. The river runs through the southwestern part of Kharkiv oblast. It is fed mainly by meltwater and tends to dry out in the summer. Its waters are used in industry and agriculture. The Dnieper-Donbas Canal passes through its valley.

Orenchuk, Vasyl [Orenčuk, Vasyl'], b 13 January 189? in Stoianiv, Radekhiv county, Galicia, d 9 March 1958 in Munich. Businessman, journalist, and political leader. After completing his law studies at Lviv and Vienna (LLD, 1913) universities he was drafted into the Austrian army and captured in action by the Russians. In 1917 he escaped from internment and took part in the political events in Kiev. He served as assistant director of the general department at the Ministry of Foreign Affairs and then as UNR consul in Germany (1919–22). In the interwar period he set up a successful import-export firm in Munich and devoted his free time to journalism.

Orenshtain, Yakiv [Orenštajn, Jakiv], b 1875, d? Jewish-Ukrainian owner of the *Ukrainska (originally Halytska Nakladnia publishing house in Kolomyia (from 1903) and Berlin (1919–32), which published hundreds of Ukrainian books. In 1933 Orenshtain moved to Warsaw, where he ran a bookstore. He disappeared in 1939 after the Germans occupied Warsaw, and probably died in the Warsaw ghetto or a Nazi concentration camp.

Oreshkevych, Fedir [Oreškevyč], b 6 May 1872 in Odessa, Kherson gubernia, d 2 October 1932 in Kiev. Opera singer (tenor). He studied at the St Petersburg Conservatory under F. Gushchin (1897–1900) and then was a soloist at the Mariinsky Opera Theater (1901–4), the Warsaw Opera (1904–6), and the Kiev Opera (1906–25). In 1914–15 he also appeared at the Bolshoi Opera in Moscow. In the 1920s he was a professor at the Kiev Conservatory and the Kiev Institute of Music and Drama. His operatic roles included Hermann in P. Tchaikovsky's *The Queen*

Fedir Oreshkevych   Mykhailo Orest

Spades and the name-part in J. Massenet's *Werther*. In recital he often performed Ukrainian folk songs.

Orest, Mykhailo (pseud of Mykhailo Zerov), b 27 November 1901 in Zinkiv, Poltava gubernia, d 12 March 1963 in Augsburg. Poet and translator; brother of M. *Zerov. He graduated from the Kiev Institute of People's Education. He began to publish his poetry after he emigrated to Germany in 1944. The published collections include *Luny lit* (Echoes of the Ages, 1944), *Dusha i dolia* (The Soul and Fate, 1946), *Derzhava slova* (The Dominion of Words, 1952), *Hist' i hospoda* (The Guest and the Inn, 1952), and the posthumously published *Pizni vruna* (Late Sprouts, 1965). His works are said to continue the work of the *Neoclassicist school of the 1920s. His translations too have classical qualities; most have been published as collections, including the translations of S. George (1952), M. Dauthenday (1953), R.M. Rilke, H. von Hofmannsthal, and C.-M.-R. Leconte de Lisle (1956). Anthologies of translations Orest has published include *Antolohiia nimets'koï poeziï* (Anthology of German Poetry, 1954), *Antolohiia frantsuz'koï poeziï* (Anthology of French Poetry, 1954), *More i mushlia* (The Sea and the Shell, an anthology of European poetry, including Italian, English, Spanish, Portuguese, Russian, and Polish, 1959), and *Sim nimets'kykh novel'* (Seven German Novellas, 1962). He also printed unpublished or rare collections of his brother's works, including *Sonnetarium* (1948), *Catalepton* (1952), *Corollarium* (1958), and *Nove ukraïns'ke pys'menstvo* (New Ukrainian Writing, 1960). Orest also edited a collection of memoirs, *Bezsmertni* (The Immortals, 1963), about M. Zerov, P. Fylypovych, and M. Drai-Khmara.

I. Koshelivets

Orfe (*Leuciscus idus*; Ukrainian: *viaz*). An edible sport and commercial fish of the carp family Cyprinidae, growing up to 50 cm in length and 1.0–2.5 kg in weight. It is an elongated, rather fatty fish with a small mouth, dark back, and silvery sides and belly. In Ukraine it is commonly found in the Dnieper, Desna, and Dniester rivers and is bred on fish farms. Golden ide, a reddish brown variety, is kept in pools, park lakes, and aquariums as a decorative fish.

Organization for the Defense of Four Freedoms for Ukraine (Orhanizatsiia oborony chotyrokh svobid Ukrainy, or OOChSU). A sociopolitical organization in the United States, dedicated to defending Ukraine's right to freedom of speech, freedom of religious worship, freedom from want, and freedom from fear. It is linked ideologically with the Bandera faction of the OUN and the *Canadian League for Ukraine's Liberation. The first two branches of the organization sprang up in Newark and New York in 1946, and by August 1947 the organization had been incorporated, with a head office in New York. In 1955 OOChSU had 29 branches and 2,280 members. By the end of 1967 it had 48 branches and 9 representations, and its membership had reached 8,400. Besides the sociopolitical monthly *Visnyk* (est 1947), the organization publishes information about Ukraine and its history in Ukrainian and English and the works of émigré writers. It also organizes lectures and courses. Its founder and first president was Ye. *Liakhovych (1946–8). His successors have included I. Bilynsky, I. Vovchuk, M. Chyrovsky, Ye. Lozynsky, and I. Vynnyk. In 1967 the Women's Association of the OOChSU was founded. It had 16 branches and 1,200 members. Its presidents have been U. Tselevych and D. Protsyk.

Organization for the Defense of Lemkivshchyna (Orhanizatsiia oborony Lemkivshchyny, or OOL). A national organization founded in June 1936 in Philadelphia to resist the Polish government's policy of Polonization and colonization of the Lemko region. The founding convention brought together 26 local Lemko defense committees, many of them formed a year or two earlier through the organizing efforts of M. Dudra. The OOL then started a monthly magazine named *Lemkivs'kyi dzvin* (1936–40). By 1937–9 the organization had reached a high of 53 branches, only to decline considerably during the Second World War. The group was revived in 1958 in Yonkers, New York, for the purpose of aiding Lemkos and other Ukrainians in Poland who had been uprooted from their homes by *Operation Wisła. It held demonstrations, appealed to government agencies, published historical materials, and provided financial help to compatriots who returned to the Lemko region. It published the annual *Lemkivs'kyi kalendar* and the monthly *Lemkivs'ki visti* (Yonkers, Toronto, Passaic 1958–79). Today it also welcomes and helps Ukrainian immigrants from Poland. The OOL has 17 branches and about 1,500 members in the United States and Canada. It maintains a museum in Stamford, Connecticut, and a research center, which publishes books as well as the illustrated magazine *Lemkivshchyna* (1979–). The presidents of the organization have included V. Karbovnyk, V. Levchyk, Yu. Nalysnyk, I. Skvirtniansky, Yu. Kotliar, I. Hvozda, M. Mytso, and M. Dupliak. In 1975 the Canadian branches formed their own national association, the Alliance of Lemkos in Canada (OLK).

Organization for the Rebirth of Ukraine (Orhanizatsiia derzhavnoho vidrodzhennia Ukrainy, or ODVU; acronym also commonly given in English as ODWU). A nationalist political organization established in the United States in 1931. Connected ideologically with the OUN, the group propagated Ukrainian nationalism and supported the liberation struggle in Ukraine. Its groundwork was established in 1930–1 by O. *Senyk, an OUN operative who helped found 35 ODVU branches. The group was particularly popular in the 1930s and developed 78 branches with young people's (*Young Ukrainian Nationalists) and women's (*Ukrainian Gold Cross) affiliates; its combined membership (1938) was approx 10,000. Investigations by the (Congressional) Dies Committee and the FBI for perceived pro-Nazi sympathies after 1939 affected the group seriously (the number of branches had fallen to 27 by 1942), but it was cleared, and it recovered some of its former strength after the war. In the postwar period it has been affiliated with the Melnyk faction of the OUN. ODVU publications include the monthly *Vistnyk ODVU* (1932–4), *Natsionalist* (1935–7), *Ukraïna* (1939–41), all published in New York, and *Samostiina Ukraïna* (1948–). The first president of ODVU was H. Herman. He was followed by A. Granovsky (1935–63), V. Riznyk, B. Hnatiuk, and B. Shebunchak (1982–).

Organization of the Ukrainians of Lviv (Orhanizatsiia ukraintsiv mista Lvova). A nonpartisan organization established at the beginning of the 1920s, mostly through the efforts of S. Biliak, for the purpose of promoting national consciousness among Ukrainian workers and uniting the city's Ukrainian residents in one structure. Its activities consisted mostly of demonstrations and campaigning for Ukrainian Sejm and Senate candidates. After Biliak it was headed by I. Lishchynsky and A. Berezovsky. For many years its secretary was A. Dobriansky. Some efforts were made to politicize the organization, especially by the Ukrainian National Democratic Alliance during the period of *Normalization to turn it into an affiliated group.

Participants at the OUN founding congress (1929)

Organization of Ukrainian Nationalists (Orhanizatsiia ukrainskykh natsionalistiv, or OUN). A Ukrainian political movement dedicated to the establishment of an independent Ukrainian state. The OUN arose from the merger of the *Ukrainian Military Organization (UVO) and several nationalist student associations – the *Group of Ukrainian National Youth, the *League of Ukrainian Nationalists, and the *Union of Ukrainian Nationalist Youth. Two conferences of Ukrainian Nationalists – one on 3–7 November 1927 in Berlin and the other on 8–9 April 1928 in Prague – paved the way for the founding congress, which was held in Vienna from 28 January to 3 February 1929. It elected a nine-man Leadership of Ukrainian Nationalists (PUN) headed by Ye. *Konovalets and including M. *Stsiborsky, V. *Martynets, D. *Andriievsky, M. *Kapustiansky, and Yu. *Vassyian; adopted a statute; and set forth its basic policy. According to its initial declaration the OUN's goal was to establish an independent, unit-

ed national state on Ukrainian ethnic territory. This was to be achieved by a national revolution led by a d torship that would drive out the occupying powers set up a government representing all regions and s groups. The economy was to be a mixture of private (ership, nationalization, and co-operation. The OUN r ed all party and class divisions and presented itself a dominant force in Ukrainian life at home and abroad fining itself as a movement, not a party, it condemne legal Ukrainian parties in Galicia as collaboratic Blaming the socialist and liberal camps for the failu the Ukrainian Revolution of 1917–20, the OUN stresse importance of a strong political elite, national solida and reliance on 'our own forces.' It was attracted Mussolini's fascist regime, which appeared to have s Italy from anarchy. By the 1930s differences in out had appeared in the OUN: Ye. Konovalets and most o PUN were pragmatic realists who thought in terms of ditional militaristic authoritarianism, whereas the yo er members were integral nationalists who espous romantic, irrational devotion to the nation. These idec ical differences contributed ultimately to the split in organization.

The OUN accepted violence as a political tool ag; foreign and home enemies of the cause. Most of its act was directed against the Polish regime. Under the (mand of the Western Ukrainian Territorial Executive February 1929) the OUN carried out in Galicia and hynia hundreds of acts of sabotage, including an ince ary campaign against Polish landowners (which he provoke the *Pacification of 1930), boycotts of s schools and of Polish tobacco and liquor monopolies, ens of expropriation attacks on government institutio obtain funds for its activities, and some 60 assassinati Its most prominent victims included the Polish officia *Hołówko and B. *Pieracki, the Soviet consular offici. Mailov (killed in retaliation for the man-made famir 1932–3 in Soviet Ukraine), and I. *Babii, the director o Ukrainian Academic Gymnasium in Lviv (a Ukrainiar cused of collaboration with the Polish police).

The OUN's membership consisted overwhelmingl students and young people. There are no reliable figu but estimates range as high as 20,000 (1939). Yet the O influence greatly exceeded its size. Its spirit of self even fanatical dedication to the national cause proved mendously attractive to young people. The OUN ca; said to have shaped the political outlook of an entire ; eration of Western Ukrainians.

The OUN's major publications were the legal jou *Rozbudova natsiï and the illegal *Biuleten' Kraiovoï ekz tyvy OUN na ZUZ, *Surma, Iunak, Natsionalist,* and *Ukr s'kyi natsionalist.* A number of legal newspapers Western Ukraine were under strong nationalist influe

Many Galician and Volhynian OUN activists were tenced by Polish courts in the 1930s, and there were trials in Bukovyna in 1937. In 1934 the Polish police ar ed the OUN's leading activists, including S. *Bandera, head of the Western Ukrainian Territorial Executive, kept them in prison until the outbreak of the Sec World War. In spite of these setbacks, the OUN rebuil organizational network. It did not succeed in penetra Soviet Ukraine, but J. Stalin's regime was concer enough about the OUN's potential to order the assass tion of Konovalets in Rotterdam in 1938.

Konovalets's death led to a succession crisis, which

ealed fundamental differences between the OUN members in Western Ukraine and members of PUN, who lived abroad. Underlying the power struggle were generational and ideological divisions. The home cadres, who bore the brunt of the underground struggle, were younger men with an aspiration to leadership and an uncritical acceptance of fascist ideas and methods. Their outlook was influenced strongly by D. *Dontsov, who propounded a cult of will and power and indiscriminately praised fascist and Nazi leaders. The older OUN leaders tended to be more conservative; Ye. *Onatsky and M. Stsiborsky, for example, stressed the positive features of Italian fascism but condemned Nazism.

The Second Grand Assembly of the OUN, held in Rome on 27 August 1939, elected A. *Melnyk to head the organization and adopted the title *vozhd* (equivalent to *Führer*) for its leader, declaring him responsible only to 'God, the Nation, and his own conscience.' By this abrupt departure from its conservative orientation PUN tried to head off any challenge to Melnyk's authority from the home cadres. The measure backfired: Bandera and his followers, who had emerged from prison after Poland's collapse in 1939, formed the Revolutionary Leadership on 10 February 1940 and claimed the right of succession. Melnyk tried in vain to resolve the crisis by negotiation. In April 1941 the Bandera faction held its own Second Extraordinary Congress in Cracow, which declared the Rome assembly illegal, elected Bandera leader, and adopted a program that reaffirmed the basic resolutions of 1929. Most of the home members accepted Bandera's authority, and the rift soon became irreversible. The two factions became known as the OUN(B), 'Banderites,' and OUN(M), 'Melnykites,' after their leaders. During the war the OUN(B) adopted the name Revolutionary OUN (OUN[R]).

Both factions expected that in the impending conflict between Germany and the USSR they would establish an independent Ukrainian state. Hence, each sought a tactical alliance with the Germans. A. Hitler's abandonment of *Carpatho-Ukraine (where younger OUN members had helped create a defense force) to the Hungarians in 1939 aroused misgivings about the German alliance but did not discourage either faction. With German approval the OUN(B) formed two battalions of about 600 men, Nachtigall and Roland, which were intended as the nucleus of a future army (see *Legion of Ukrainian Nationalists). Following the German invasion of the USSR the OUN(B) proclaimed Ukrainian independence in Lviv on 30 June 1941, with Ya. *Stetsko as premier (see *Proclamation of Ukrainian Statehood, 1941). The Germans, needing Ukrainian assistance against Russia, were expected to acquiesce in the fait accompli. Although elements of the German military were inclined to do so, they were overruled by Hitler, whose racial prejudice against Ukrainians precluded co-operation. Bandera and some of his associates were arrested and imprisoned by the Gestapo. Many OUN(B) members were killed outright, or perished in jails and concentration camps. M. *Lebed assumed control of the organization and in May 1943 transferred his powers to R. *Shukhevych. Determined to build an independent state, both factions sent clandestine *OUN expeditionary groups into Ukraine to set up local administrations with nationally conscious Ukrainians. Estimated at 2,000 men (mostly OUN(B) members), the groups were active in the larger cities. An OUN(M) group, which reached Kiev in September 1941, published the newspaper *Ukraïns'ke slovo* and

formed the *Ukrainian National Council, consisting mostly of eastern Ukrainians and headed by M. *Velychkivsky. Its members were arrested in December 1941, and over 40 of them, including O. *Teliha and their leader, O. *Olzhych, were killed immediately or later, some of them in Babyn Yar. Melnyk was kept under house arrest in Berlin until January 1944, when he and other principal OUN(M) figures were arrested and taken to the Sachsenhausen concentration camp.

Anti-German resistance began with the formation of the *Polisian Sich led by T. *Borovets, who co-operated with the OUN(M). In the autumn of 1942 both OUN factions organized armed detachments in Volhynia and Polisia to fight the Germans and Soviet partisans. The *Ukrainian Insurgent Army (UPA) under the control of the Bandera faction disarmed the Polisian Sich and the Melnyk detachments in 1943 and absorbed many of their members. Relations between the two nationalist factions were extremely hostile. Although the UPA was controlled by the OUN(B), it included people of various political and ideological convictions. Furthermore, it needed the support of the broad masses against both the Germans and the Soviets. Much of the nationalist ideology, including the concept of dictatorship, did not appeal to former Soviet citizens who had experienced the dictatorship of the Party. Hence, a revision of the OUN(B) ideology and political program was imperative. At its Third Extraordinary Grand Assembly on 21–25 August 1943, the OUN(B) condemned 'internationalist and fascist national-socialist programs and political concepts' as well as 'Russian-Bolshevik communism' and proposed a 'system of free peoples and independent states [as] the single best solution to the problem of world order.' Its social program did not differ essentially from earlier ones, but it emphasized a wide range of social services, worker participation in management, a mixed economy, choice of profession and workplace, and free trade unions. The OUN(B) affirmed that it was fighting for freedom of the press, speech, and thought. Its earlier nationality policy, encapsuled in the slogan 'Ukraine for Ukrainians,' was dropped in favor of the rights of national minorities. The OUN's command structure was modified: one-man rule was replaced by collegial leadership. A three-man Leadership Bureau consisting of R. Shukhevych, Z. *Matla, and D. *Maivsky was elected. After the congress an all-Ukrainian representative body, the Ukrainian *Supreme Liberation Council (UHVR), was formed, in July 1944. Most of its members were Banderites, and its General Secretariat was headed by Shukhevych. The OUN(M) conducted a similar policy and set up the All-Ukrainian National Council in Lviv in the spring of 1944.

In the autumn of 1944 the Germans released Bandera, Melnyk, and other nationalist leaders in a belated attempt to win support for their war effort. At the end of the war Melnyk resumed his leadership of the OUN(M); Bandera and Ya. *Stetsko were elected to the leadership in Ukraine. In February 1946 the External Units of the OUN (ZCh OUN) were formed in Munich under Bandera's leadership, and in April the *Anti-Bolshevik Bloc of Nations was set up by Stetsko to unify non-Russian nationalities opposed to the Soviet regime. A conflict over the ideological revisions of 1943 arose between a group of OUN(B) emissaries from Ukraine (M. Lebed et al) and Bandera's organization abroad. The latter was accused of resisting the changes and their necessary consequences – the democratization of the OUN(B), the autonomous status of the UPA and UHVR, and the renunciation of dogmatism and elitism. The emissaries voiced their criticism in *Ukraïns'ka trybuna*. In their principal organ, *Vyzvol'na polityka*, Bandera and his group argued that the revision brought the OUN too close to socialism and communism. The controversy culminated in the expulsion of the opposition at the ZCh OUN conference in Mittenwald on 28–31 August 1948. In 1953–4 the OUN(B) leadership in Ukraine reaffirmed the ideological revisions and instructed Bandera, Z. *Matla, and L. *Rebet to form a new ZCh OUN leadership. Negotiations proved fruitless, and in 1956 two of the triumvirate leadership, Matla and Rebet, set up a new organization known as the OUN (Abroad), or *dviikari* ('twosome' for the two leaders). Its activists established the *Prolog Research Corporation, published *Ukraïns'kyi samostiinyk*, and sponsored the monthly *Suchasnist'*. After Rebet's assassination in 1957, the organization was led by B. *Kordiuk and, later, by Rebet's widow, D. *Rebet.

The OUN(M) after the war developed a conservative corporatist ideology purged of fascist trappings. At its Third Grand Assembly on 30 August 1947, it limited the leader's power by making him responsible to a congress that had to be convoked every three years, and introduced into its program the principles of equality before the law, judicial independence, and freedom of conscience, speech, the press, and political opposition. O. *Boidunyk's *Natsional'nyi solidaryzm* (National Solidarism, 1945), which updated the organization's ideology, advocated a Ukrainian nation-state based on the solidarity of corporate social groups.

Strife between the two OUN factions continued in Germany immediately after the war: they fought for dominance in the DP camps and in the émigré *Ukrainian National Council. The OUN(M) and its allies won control of the council, and the ZCh OUN withdrew from it. The OUN factions have had a decisive impact on the Ukrainian émigré community. The community's identity and public image have been shaped largely by the nationalist commitment to Ukraine's liberation. Soviet propaganda aimed at discrediting the OUN as a Nazi collaborator and a hireling of Western intelligence agencies. Claiming to be the vanguard of the struggle against Russian imperialism, the OUN(B) has tried to dominate émigré life. Its umbrella organization, the World Ukrainian Liberation Front (est 1973), includes the *Organization for the Defense of Four Freedoms for Ukraine (United States), the *Canadian League for the Liberation of Ukraine, the *Association of Ukrainians in Great Britain, the *Union of Ukrainians of France, Prosvita (Argentina), the League for the Liberation of Ukraine in Australia and New Zealand, and their affiliated organizations. Its major publications are *Shliakh peremohy* (Munich), *Vyzvol'nyi shliakh*, *Ukraïns'ka dumka*, and *Ukrainian Review* (all in London), *Visnyk OOChSU* and *Natsional'na trybuna* (both in New York), and *Homin Ukraïny* (Toronto). Bandera led the OUN(B) until his assassination in 1959; he was succeeded by S. *Lenkavsky, Stetsko (1968–86), V. *Oleskiv (1987–91), and S. Stetsko (Ya. Stetsko's widow; since 1991).

Nationalist émigré organizations founded in the 1930s, such as the *Organization for the Rebirth of Ukraine (United States), the *Ukrainian National Federation (Canada), and the *Ukrainian National Alliance in France, sided with the OUN(M) after 1940. The *Federation of Ukrainians in Great Britain was established in 1949 as a rival to the Association of Ukrainians in Great Britain. All these orga-

nizations belong to a co-ordinating body known as Ideologically Related Nationalist Organizations. The major OUN(M) publications have been *Ukraïns'ke slovo (Paris), *Samostiina Ukraïna (Chicago), *Novyi shliakh (Toronto), *Nash klych (Buenos Aires), and *Khliborob (Curitiba). Since Melnyk's death in 1964 the OUN(M) has been led by O. *Shtul-Zhdanovych, D. *Kvitkovsky (1977–9), and M. *Plaviuk (since 1981). In the last two decades political groupings opposed to the OUN(B) have tended toward closer co-operation and consolidation and have formed broader associations, such as the *Ukrainian Democratic Alliance (1976) and the Conference of Ukrainian Political Parties and Organizations (1979).

Rivalry among the OUN factions has long divided and sapped the strength of émigré umbrella organizations. To accommodate the nationalist factions the *World Congress of Free Ukrainians has had to sacrifice the principle of majority vote and an efficient decision procedure. In 1980 the *Ukrainian Congress Committee of America was taken over by the OUN(B) and thus ceased to represent the Ukrainian community as a whole. The power and influence of the OUN factions have been declining steadily, because of assimilatory pressures, ideological incompatibility with the Western liberal-democratic ethos, and the increasing tendency of political groups in Ukraine to move away from integral *nationalism.

BIBLIOGRAPHY
Lisovyi, R. *Rozlam v OUN* (Neu-Ulm 1949)
Martynets', V. *Ukraïns'ke pidpillia: Vid UVO do OUN* (np 1949)
Armstrong, J. *Ukrainian Nationalism* (New York 1955; 2nd edn, 1963; 3rd edn, Englewood, Colo 1990)
Orhanizatsiia Ukraïns'kykh Natsionalistiv, 1929–1954 (Paris 1955)
OUN v svitli postanov velykykh zboriv, konferentsii ta inshykh dokumentiv z borot'by 1929–1955 r. (np 1955)
Shankovs'kyi, L. *Pokhidni hrupy OUN* (Munich 1958)
Krychevs'kyi, R. (R. Il'nyts'kyj). *OUN v Ukraïni, OUNz i ZCh OUN: Prychynok do istorii ukraïns'koho natsionalistychnoho rukhu* (New York–Toronto 1962)
Knysh, Z. *Rozbrat* (Toronto nd)
– *B'ie dvanadtsiata* (Toronto nd)
– *Pered pokhodom na skhid*, 2 vols (Toronto nd)
Rebet, L. *Svitla i tini OUN* (Munich 1964)
Mirchuk, P. *Narys istorii Orhanizatsii ukraïns'kykh natsionalistiv, 1929–1939* (Munich–London–New York 1968)
Stets'ko, Ia. *30 chervnia 1941: Proholoshennia vidnovlennia derzhavnosty Ukraïny* (Toronto–New York–London 1968)
Torzecki, R. *Kwestia ukraińska w polityce III Rzeszy (1933–1945)* (Warsaw 1972)
Szcześniak, A; Szota, W. *Droga do nikąd: Działalność Organizacji Ukraińskich Nacjonalistów i jej likwidacja w Polsce* (Warsaw 1973)
Ievhen Konovalets' ta ioho doba (Munich 1974)
Bandera, S. *Perspektyvy ukraïns'koï revoliutsiï* (Munich 1978)
Motyl, A. *The Turn to the Right: The Ideological Origins and Development of Ukrainian Nationalism, 1919–1929* (Boulder, Colo 1980)
Melnyk, K.; et al., (eds), *Na zov Kyieva: Ukraïns'kyi natsionalizm u II svitovii viini* (Toronto–New York 1985)
Kosyk, W. *L'Allemagne national-socialiste et l'Ukraine* (Paris 1986)
Potichnyj, P.; Ye. Shtendera (eds). *Political Thought of the Ukrainian Underground, 1943–1951* (Edmonton 1986)

M. Yurkevich

Organization of Ukrainian Socialists (Orhanizatsiia ukrainskykh sotsiialistiv, or OUS). An association of democratic socialists in the United States, established in 1950 by new émigrés who had an ideological affinity with the Ukrainian Socialist party. OUS co-operated with the

*Ukrainian Free Society of America (UFSA) and other organizations which supported the UNR government-in-exile. It also assisted the UFSA journal *Vil'na Ukraïna*. Among the main activists of OUS have been S. Ripetsky, V. Lysy, I. Palyvoda, Ya. Zozulia, V. Dibert, H. Nychka, M. Halii, and M. Kucher.

Organization of Ukrainian Women in Brazil (Orhanizatsiia ukrainskykh zhinok Brazilii). A women's civic society in Brazil. Women who had been active in the work of the *Union for Agricultural Education (KhOS) organized themselves in 1924 into women's sections of KhOS branches in Porto Union and Curitiba. Inspired by the example of the Union of Ukrainian Women in Galicia, they undertook cultural work, welfare activity, and Ukrainian Saturday school organization. After being closed down for several years in the 1940s by the Brazilian dictatorship, the group resumed activity. In 1948 they established a central organization which had four branches in 1952 when the organization became a charter member of the *World Federation of Ukrainian Women's Organizations. It also started publishing a page of organizational and other news in the KhOS newspaper, *Khliborob*. In 1959 the organization adopted its present name (while retaining the KhOS affiliation), and in 1964 it organized a 40th anniversary celebration of the Ukrainian women's movement in Brazil and published *Ukraïns'ke zhinotstvo u Brazilii* (Ukrainian Women in Brazil). While maintaining its initial activities, the organization (450 members in 7 branches in 1987) recently has become particularly active in the promotion of Ukrainian folk arts. Presidents of the organization have included Z. Yashchynska, N. Felyk, O. Horachuk, T. Bashchyn, L. Yedyn, and O. Borushenko.

Organization of Ukrainian Youth in France (Orhanizatsiia ukrainskoi molodi u Frantsii; French: Jeunes Amis de l'Ukraine). An organization founded in 1956 through the efforts of the Ukrainian National Alliance in France and centered in Paris, it developed 10 branches. It runs Ukrainian courses, publishes the *Bulletin Franco-Ukrainien*, works with the Ukrainian National Union in France, and belongs to the Ukrainian Central Civic Committee in France. Its leading members have included V. Genyk, T. Horishny, K. Huzar-Uhryn, B. Kamianetsky, K. Lazovinska, A. Osnovych, O. Repetylo, and Kh. Sluzhyk.

Organization of Ukrainians of Revolutionary Democratic Convictions (Obiednannia ukraintsiv revoliutsiino-demokratychnykh perekonan). A social-political organization founded in the United States in 1950 with headquarters in New York. Its members were primarily émigrés from Soviet Ukraine. The organization was closely allied with the Ukrainian Revolutionary Democratic party and supported the Ukrainian National Council. Its founders and most prominent members included V. Hryshko, M. Stepanenko, and M. Voskobiinyk. The organization lapsed into inactivity in the 1980s.

Organized recruitment of workers (*organizovannyi nabor rabochikh* or *orgnabor*). A system of recruiting unskilled labor for industry, construction, transportation, and farming in the USSR. It was introduced by the decree On Migration of 30 June 1931 as a way of providing rapidly developing industry with labor from the collective farms. Industrial enterprises were authorized to conclude manpower contracts with collective farms. For releasing their members for industrial employment collective farms received machines and special allocations of supplies from the state. The 'voluntary' recruits were rewarded with privileges for themselves and their families. Lacking any planning and central control, the system was inefficient and open to abuse. In 1938 special recruitment planning groups were set up in the Union, and republican state planning committees and commissions for organized recruitment were formed in the Union and republican economic councils to supervise the system. In 1953 the system was reorganized, and thereafter it was run by a hierarchy of chief administration for organized recruitment of labor attached to the Union and republican councils of ministers. The purpose of the system changed radically: instead of drafting labor from the farms into the urban centers, it resettled surplus urban labor from the western part of the USSR to the underdeveloped regions of the northern and eastern frontier. In 1957 the agencies running the system were renamed chief administrations for the resettlement and organized recruitment of labor. Although by law recruitment was to be voluntary, pressure and force were applied widely.

In the immediate postwar period some 50,000 workers annually were transferred to the Donets-Dnieper Industrial Region, and up to 10,000 families, mostly from Western Ukraine, were relocated in southern Ukraine under the organized recruitment system. In 1946–62 over 2.2 million workers were recruited in Ukraine, and 812,000 were placed in jobs outside their homeland. Of the 277,000 families resettled on collective and state farms, 88,000 were sent outside Ukraine. Massive propaganda for Ukrainian resettlement in the Far East was unsuccessful. By the mid-1960s the importance of the system in providing industrial labor had diminished greatly. It continued to supply seasonal labor, mostly to construction projects. In 1976–80 it placed only 100,000 workers in full-time jobs and 150,000 in seasonal jobs. Efforts to plan labor recruitment have not been successful.

BIBLIOGRAPHY
Conquest, R. (ed). *Industrial Workers in the USSR* (London 1967)
B. Levytsky, B. Krawchenko

Oriekhov, Volodymyr [Orjexov], b 16 August 1904 in Kharkiv, d 17 November 1979 in Kiev. Architect. After graduating from the Kharkiv Art Institute (1929) he worked in architectural agencies in Kiev and taught at the Kharkiv Institute of Communal Building Engineers (1934–41, 1943–5), the Kiev State Art Institute (1945–50), and the Kiev Civil-Engineering Institute (1954–64). He codesigned the Building of Oblast Organizations in Kharkiv (1949–54), the town center of Moryntsi, Cherkasy oblast (1963), the Museum of Folk Architecture and Folkways of Ukraine in Kiev (1970–1), and the left bank districts of Dniprodzerzhynske (1970–1).

Oriental studies (*oriientalistyka*). The study of the languages, history, and culture of the peoples of the East (Asia and Africa). Knowledge of Oriental languages and countries was applied in the Princely era to establish close political, dynastic, economic, and military relations with the Altaic peoples – Turkic (*Khazars, *Torks, *Cumans), Hunno-Bulgars (*Huns, *Pechenegs, Danube and *Volga Bulgars), and *Mongols – as well as the *Iranian peoples

(Sogdians, *Alans, *Yasians), *Caucasian mountain peoples (Georgians and Cherkess), *Armenians, *Jews, and other peoples. Merchants from Rus' traveled to Baghdad, and pilgrims visited Palestine (Hegumen *Danylo). A school for translating ancient Hebrew was active in the 11th century in Kiev. Cossack diplomats, as well as some hetmans (B. Khmelnytsky), had a command of the Tatar (Turkic Mongolian) and Ottoman (Turkish) languages. Ukrainian and Armenian merchants spoke fluent Turkish. One such merchant was Yu. *Kulchytsky, who worked as a translator for the Eastern Company in Vienna. V. *Hryhorovych-Barsky was fluent in Arabic and traveled to many countries of the Near East. Ukrainian Orthodox metropolitans and bishops in Siberia studied the Turkic, Mongol, and Tunguz languages (F. Leshchynsky, I. Kulchytsky, and I. Nerunovych).

Formal academic Oriental studies were initiated at the Kharkiv College, where a large library on the subject was assembled. In 1804 a chair in Oriental studies (Hebrew and other Semitic studies) was established at Kharkiv University and headed briefly by Y. Barendt. In 1829–32 B. Dorn, an authority on Arab and Iranian studies, worked at Kharkiv University. The chair was closed in 1855, after the Russian Empire established an Oriental studies center in St Petersburg; it was re-established in 1870 as the chair of Indology and comparative linguistics. It was headed initially by the Czech professor V. Schertzl, who published a Sanskrit grammar in 1873, and then by the Scot E. Dillon (from 1874), D. *Ovsianiko-Kulikovsky (from 1889), and P. Ritter (from 1905).

Kiev became another center for Oriental studies in Ukraine. S. Todorsky, a professor at the Kievan Mohyla Academy in the 18th century, studied under the German Semitist J.-H. Michaelis. A. and O. Olesnytsky and V. *Rybynsky taught Hebrew language and culture at the Kiev Theological Academy from 1819. Kiev University had a chair in Sanskrit and comparative *linguistics. F. Knauer established the Kiev school of Indology and published a textbook on Sanskrit and a book of Vedic ritual texts. Among his students were O. *Barannykov and M. *Kalynovych.

A chair of Sanskrit and comparative linguistics was also established at Odessa University, where Schertzl (1884–96) and Ovsianiko-Kulikovsky also worked. A number of articles on relations between Ukraine and the East appeared in the Zapiski of the *Odessa Society of History and Antiquities (1844–1919).

The first Ukrainian-language Oriental studies textbook was written by Lesia Ukrainka. It was titled Starodavnia istoriia skhidnikh narodiv (Ancient History of the Eastern Peoples); the manuscript (dated 1890) is preserved at the ANU Institute of Literature. It was published by her sister, O. Kosach-Kryvyniuk, in Katerynoslav in 1918, and a second edition was published the same year.

In Western Ukraine Hebrew studies were established at Lviv University in the faculties of theology and of comparative linguistics in the late 19th century. In 1903 the biblical scholar T. *Myshkovsky taught there. In 1920–39 Polish Oriental studies were centered at the departments of Near and Far Eastern studies and Indology at Lviv University. Among the specialists working there were W. Kotwicz (Altaic and Mongol studies), J. Kuryłowicz (Iranian studies), A. Gawroński (Sanskrit), and S. Stasiak (Indology). The Polish Oriental Studies Society in Lviv (1922–39) published the journal Rocznik Orientalistyczny. In 1939–41

there was a chair of Indology at Lviv University, with Stasiak as director and Ye. Zavalynsky and V. Shaian as lecturers. Oriental studies in Lviv came to a halt after Kuryłowicz emigrated to Poland in 1946, except that M. Knorozov provided language instruction in Chinese and Sanskrit.

In 1918 the Near Eastern Institute was established in Kiev to train diplomats and trade officials of the Ukrainian state. Its directors were Ye. *Stashevsky and I. Babat. It was incorporated into the Institute of Foreign Affairs of the Ukrainian SSR in 1920.

A. *Krymsky and O. *Lazarevsky initiated the wider development of Oriental studies in Ukraine in 1920, particularly at the Chair of Arabic and Iranian Philology, the Turkic Studies Commission, and the Jewish Historical and Archeographic Commission of the VUAN Department of History and Philology. Krymsky's coworkers included I. Galant, T. Grunin (who published the first Turkic grammar in Ukrainian and studied the Cuman dialect of Armenians in Ukraine), V. Ivanytsky, T. Kezma (an Arab), and P. Lozeev. In 1931–2 all those institutions were liquidated, and many scholars were imprisoned or exiled. Krymsky was forbidden to publish his prepared monographs, among them Istoriia khozariv (History of the Khazars) and Istoriia novo-arabs'koï literatury (History of Modern Arabic Literature). He was partially rehabilitated in 1939 and allowed to teach graduate students, including O. *Pritsak (Turkic and Islamic studies), A. Robinson (Semitic studies), and G. Egris (Yakutian studies).

In 1924 a group of former students of the Near Eastern Institute (I. Falkovych, L. Levytsky, L. Velychko) formed the Seminar in Near Eastern Studies. In 1925 the seminar was combined with others conducted at the Kiev Institute of the National Economy and the Kiev Eastern Peoples' House to form the All-Ukrainian Center for Scientific Eastern Studies. In 1926 the center was joined with the Eastern Studies group of the Kharkiv Scientific Society (P. Ritter, A. Kovalivsky, P. Tychyna) to form the *All-Ukrainian Learned Association of Oriental Studies (VUNAS). By 1929 it had 193 full members (83 in Kiev, 60 in Kharkiv, and 50 in Odessa) and 158 supporting members. O. *Shlikhter was the president, with O. Hladstern (a specialist in Turkish law) and L. Velychko (Turkish economy) as deputies and L. Levytsky (natural resources) as scholarly secretary. Many researchers in Ukraine and the diaspora contributed to the association's work, including Turkic specialists O. Samoilovych (in Leningrad) and V. *Dubrovsky, the Iranologists M. Kostiantynopolsky and M. Levchenko, the Indologist O. Barannykov, and the Japanese specialist F. Pushchenko. Other collaborators included V. *Levytsky and Ye. Berliand (economy), V. *Buzeskul, M. *Horban, B. Kurts, O. Ohloblyn, V. *Parkhomenko, F. Petrun, and I. Tryhubov (history), and O. Fedorovsky, D. Hordiiv, T. Ivanovska, and V. Zummer (art history).

In 1926 VUNAS organized state courses in Oriental studies, with three departments in Kharkiv (Persian, Turkish, and Japanese; directed by P. Ritter), and three in Kiev (Arabic, Persian, and Turkish; directed by P. Lozeev). In 1930 the courses were reorganized into the Ukrainian Scientific Research Institute of Eastern Studies, under the deputy people's commissar of education of the Ukrainian SSR, A. Polotsky.

In 1927–8, VUNAS organized two All-Ukrainian Eastern Studies congresses in Kharkiv, in which scholars from

Turkey and Persia participated, and sent representatives to the 17th International Congress of Orientologists at Oxford and to Turkey. In 1929 it worked with the dean of Istanbul University to establish commissions on Ukrainian-Turkish relations.

VUNAS published *Biuleten' VUNAS* (5 issues, 1926–8) and *Skhidnii svit* (17 issues, 1927–31). It also prepared dictionaries for publication, including Azerbaidzhani-Ukrainian (ed V. Dubrovsky), Armenian-Ukrainian (ed P. Tychyna), and Georgian-Ukrainian (ed G. *Namoradze) dictionaries. In 1933 VUNAS and all of its affiliates were liquidated, and the dictionaries were never published. A textbook in Osman paleography prepared by O. Dubrovsky was also destroyed. The development of Oriental studies in Ukraine was repressed until the end of the 1960s, and apart from lectures on certain Eastern languages, there were no active chairs in Eastern studies.

The leading Ukrainian Orientologist at that time, A. Kovalivsky, returned from exile in 1944 and assumed the directorship of a chair of medieval history at Kharkiv University. He attracted a new generation of Oriental scholars, including A. Alekberli (Turkish history), S. Averbukh (ancient Eastern history), V. Badian (Indonesian studies), Yu. Lytvynenko (Indian history), Ya. Pobilenky (Japanese studies), H. Pohosivna Pinhirian (Armenian history), N. Rashba (Turkish history), B. Shramko (the archeology of Central Asia and China), V. Tychyna-Berest (the Ossetian and Armenian languages), and B. Vetrov (Chinese history). He also published an annotated Russian edition of A. *Ibn-Faḍlān's works (1956) and *Antolohiia literatur Skhodu* (Anthology of Eastern Literatures, 1961). Oriental studies as a discipline was completely neglected by the AN URSR. The Department of Foreign Eastern Countries at its Institute of History (1964) was short-lived.

Individual scholars included Ya. Dashkevych (Armenian history and culture), I. Chernykov (Turkey), I. Chyrko (Chinese and Japanese literature), and Yu. Kochubei (Arabic literature), a member of the diplomatic corps. F. Danylenko (Sinology) and B. Vobly (Japanese studies) studied at the Oriental Institute in Vladivostok (est 1899). D. Varchenko (Sinology) studied at the Oriental Institute in Harbin, as did A. Dibrova (Japanese studies) and V. Odynets, who later taught Eastern European history at the university in Hsinking (capital of Manchukuo). S. *Levynsky, a writer and Japanese scholar, lived in Peking in 1935–46. In 1936 an anthology of Japanese and Chinese works in Ukrainian translation, *Dalekyi Skhid* (Far East), was published in Harbin. A. Dibrova and V. Odynets published the *Ukraïns'ko-nipons'kyi slovnyk* (Ukrainian-Japanese Dictionary, 1944). A Ukrainian-Chinese dictionary was compiled by the Lexicography Institute of Heilongjiang University and published in Peking in 1990.

Ukrainian émigrés in Oriental studies include O. Baranovych (Indologist), O. Samoilovych (Turkish studies), S. Rudenko (Scythian and Hun burial grounds in Asia, the ethnographic study of Bashkiria), L. Symonivska (Chinese history), M. Fedorenko (diplomat; Chinese literary history), P. Topekha (Japanese history), V. Fylonenko (Turkish studies; in Piatagorsk), and A. Stanyshevsky (a student of Krymsky; in Tashkent). D. *Doroshenko coauthored studies on Ukrainian relations with Turkey and Tatar Crimea with J. Rypka (published in 1933 and 1936). At Warsaw University D. *Valedinsky studied biblical and Christian archeology, and I. Ohiienko translated the Bible from ancient Hebrew. In 1946–51 a Commission for Eastern Studies was active at the Ukrainian Academy of Arts and Sciences in Augsburg. Its members included two former members of VUNAS, V. *Derzhavyn (who studied ancient Egypt and Africa) and V. Dubrovsky (Crimean history), as well as P. *Kurinny (Eastern archeology), O. Pritsak (Turkish studies), and Marko *Antonovych (ancient Eastern history). M. Brynovsky (Turkic studies and Tatar languages) worked at Berlin University until 1945. In the United States, J. Stetkevych has worked at the University of Chicago (since 1962) as a specialist in Arabic literature, and O. Pritsak worked at Harvard University (from 1964 to 1989) as a specialist in Altaic and Turkic studies and Eurasian history. Pritsak was put in charge of the ANU Institute of Eastern Studies established in Kiev in 1991.

In the 1970s and 1980s a few North American Orientalists of Ukrainian origin completed their PH Ds at Harvard University. They include R. Holod, an Islamic art historian now at the University of Pennsylvania; M. Subtelny, a specialist in medieval Iran and Central Asia, who has taught at the University of Toronto since 1984; and the Ottoman historians L. Hajda and V. Ostapchuk at Harvard.

Ukrainian translations of Eastern literary works influenced the development of Ukrainian Oriental studies. P. Hrabovsky translated poetry from Armenian and Georgian. Krymsky's translations of works from the classical canon of Near Eastern literature were published in his collections *Pal'move hillia* (Palm Fronds, 3 vols, 1901–22). Ritter and Barannykov translated modern Indian literature. H. Khotkevych made translations from Sanskrit. In the 1920s the number of translations of Eastern works increased substantially, particularly from the Semitic, Iranian, Caucasian, Turkic, and Far Eastern languages. Some of them were published, but most were not because of the wave of repressions in the 1930s. After the death of J. Stalin Ukrainian translations of Armenian, Chinese, Japanese, Jewish, Hungarian, Georgian, Kirghiz, Ossetian, Tatar, and Uzbek works began to be published again. The most notable postwar translators have been M. *Lukash (18 Western and Eastern languages), I. Chyrko (Chinese and Japanese), and M. *Bazhan (Georgian). Emigré translators in the field have included L. Holubnycha (Chinese), V. Shaian (Sanskrit and other Indian languages), and Ye. Zavalynsky (Turkic).

BIBLIOGRAPHY
Krachkovskii, I. *Ocherki po istorii russkoi arabistiki* (Moscow–Leningrad 1950)
– (ed). *Skhidnyi svit – Chervonyi skhid: Systematychnyi pokazhchyk* (Kharkiv 1964)
Fal'kovich, I. 'K istorii sovetskogo vostokovedeniia na Ukraine,' *Narody Azii i Afriki*, 1966, no. 4
Zakharova, I.; Sarbei, V. 'Pershyi ukraïns'kyi pidruchnyk iz starodavn'oho skhodoznavstva,' *UIZh*, 1991, no. 2

O. Pritsak

Orikhiv [Orixiv]. VI-16. A city (1990 pop 21,200) on the Konka River and a raion center in Zaporizhia oblast. It sprang up ca 1783 and attained city status in 1938. The city produces clothes, machinery, and building materials. It has a regional museum.

Orikhove Lake [Orixove]. II-5. A lake located in the northern part of Volhynia oblast. It has an area of 5.5 sq km, a length of 3.9 km, a width of 2.1 km, and a depth of up to 3.6 km. The lake is fed by rain and meltwater and is surrounded by bogs and marshes. It supports fishing.

Orkan, Władysław (pseud of Franciszek Smreczyński; other pseud: Smaciarz), b 27 November 1875 in Poręba Wielka, Poland, d 4 May 1930 in Cracow. Polish writer; member of the Polish modernist group Młoda Polska. Orkan wrote stories capturing the life of poor mountain folk in a naturalistic manner. He befriended the Ukrainian writers B. *Lepky and V. *Stefanyk and was instrumental in furthering good relations between Ukrainian and Polish writers. Together with Lepky and V. Yarosh he translated Ukrainian prose into Polish and published it in a collection entitled *Młoda Ukraina* (Young Ukraine, 1908). He helped to publish and wrote the introductions to an anthology of Ukrainian poetry translated into Polish by S. Tverdokhlib, *Antologia współczesnych poetów ukraińskich* (An Anthology of Contemporary Ukrainian Poets, 1911), and M. Yatskiv's collection of short stories, *Wieczorne psoty* (Evening Pranks, 1910). Some of his works were also translated into Ukrainian. H. Verves wrote a monograph on Orkan, *Vladyslav Orkan i ukraïns'ka literatura* (Władysław Orkan and Ukrainian Literature, 1962).

Orlai, Ivan [Orlaj], b 1770 in Palad, Transcarpathia, d 11 March 1829 in Odessa. Medical scholar and educator. He studied in Lviv, Budapest, and Vienna, graduated from the St Petersburg Medico-Surgical Academy (1793), and then practiced medicine, served as scientific secretary of the academy (1808–17), and helped edit its *Pharmacopea castrensis Ruthenica*. He directed the Bezborodko (*Nizhen) Lyceum (1821–6) and the *Richelieu Lyceum (1826–9). A man of the Enlightenment, he believed in education as the key to social and moral progress and advocated a unified system of general education for all the estates in Russia. His biography, by T. Baitsura, was published in 1977.

Orlenko, Leonid, b 2 May 1925 in Tarasivka, Zaporizhia okruha. Muralist and mosaicist. He graduated from the Leningrad Higher Applied Arts School (1958). While living in Zaporizhia he painted the murals in the vestibule of the Pioneer Palace (1959), collaborated on the mosaic panel *Radioelectronics in the Service of Man* at the Radio Tekhnikum (1965), created three mosaic panels at the Regional Museum, and did the tryptich *Union of Workers and Peasants* (1970) and the copper relief *Steelworker's Family* (1979).

Orlenko, Roman (né Prokopovych), b 11 October 1883 in Chyzhykiv, Lviv county, Galicia, d 24 July 1962 in Lviv. Opera singer (bass-baritone) and educator. After graduating from Vienna University in 1907, he sang as soloist with the Vienna Opera 1907–15), the Ostrava Opera (1915–16), and the Ukrainska Besida Theater in Lviv (1918–20). After the war he taught at the Lysenko Higher Institute of Music (1920–5), gymnasiums in Lviv (1925–38), and the Lviv Conservatory (1939–48). His main roles included the Sultan in S. Hulak-Artemovsky's *Zaporozhian Cossack beyond the Danube*, Taras in M. Lysenko's *Taras Bulba*, the Demon in A. Rubinstein's *Demon*, and Wotan in R. Wagner's *Rhinegold* and *Valkyrie*.

Orlivka hoard. A cache of ancient Greek coins found in 1967 in Orlivka, Reni raion, Odessa oblast. The coins, made from a silver-gold blend, were minted in Cyzicus, a Greek trading center on the Sea of Marmara. They date from approx 500–330 BC and were probably hidden around the latter date by a person anxious about the turbulent military situation in Greece and the Pontic steppe. Forty-four types of coins were found, including two previously not known. They were hidden in a bronze vessel dated to the 5th century BC. The collection is now housed in the Odessa Archeological Museum.

Orlivna, Halyna, b 1895 in Lubni, Poltava gubernia, d 1955. Writer and actress; wife of K. *Polishchuk. In 1918–19 she acted with Molodyi Teatr. Her first collections of short stories, *Shliakhom chuttia* (The Path of Feeling, 1921) and *Pered bramoiu* (Before the Gate, 1922), were published in Galicia. In 1925 she returned to the Ukrainian SSR where she published her work in the journals *Chervonyi shliakh*, *Zhyttia i revoliutsiia*, *Hlobus*, and *Vsesvit* and was a member of the literary organization *Pluh. Her work was also published separately in Kharkiv, including the collection of novelettes *Emigranty* (The Emigrants, 1929) and the collections of short stories *Babs'kyi bunt* (The Women's Revolt, 1930) and *Zhaha* (Yearning, 1930). From 1931 Orlivna lived in exile in Kazakhstan. The circumstances of her death are unknown.

Aleksandr Orlov

Orlov, Aleksandr (Oleksandr), b 6 April 1880 in Smolensk, Russia, d 28 January 1954 in Moscow. Astronomer; full member of the AN URSR (now ANU) from 1939 and corresponding member of the Academy of Sciences of the USSR from 1927. A graduate of St Petersburg University, he served as director of the *Odessa Astronomical Observatory (1912–24), the *Poltava Gravimetric Observatory (1926–34, 1938–51), and the Main *Astronomical Observatory of the ANU near Kiev (1944–8, 1950–1). He made important scientific contributions in the areas of theoretical astronomy, the study of comets, geodesy, seismometry, and the study of the migration of magnetic poles, and directed wide-ranging gravimetric studies of Ukraine.

Orlov, Georgii, b 8 April 1901 in Kursk, Russia, d 16 April 1985 in Moscow. Russian architect; full member of the USSR Academy of Arts from 1979. A graduate of the Moscow Higher Technical School (1926), he taught at the Moscow Architectural Institute for many years (1933–8, 1966–70). In 1972 he was elected president of the International Association of Architects. Orlov helped to design and build the Dnieper (1927–32), Kakhivka (1951–4), and Kremenchuk hydroelectric stations as well as residential districts (1930–6, 1938), a summer theater (1938), and residential apartments and cottages (1947–8) in Zaporizhia. After the Second World War he was in charge of the reconstruction of the Dnieper Hydroelectric Station (1944–52).

Orlov, Mykhailo, b 7 January 1900 in Kiev, d 17 October 1936 in Kiev. Mathematician; corresponding member of the VUAN from 1934. A graduate of the Kiev Institute of People's Education, he served as director of the Scientific Research Institute of Mathematics in 1931–4. In 1934–6 he was a professor at Kiev University. His major scholarly contributions were in the areas of equilibrium shapes of rotating fluids and approximate methods in the solution of differential and integral equations.

Orlov, Oleksander, b 1899, d 1960. Geographer; member of the Shevchenko Scientific Society. He was a specialist in geology and mineralogy. He taught in Prague at the Ukrainian Free University (1921–45) and at Charles University (1926–45). His main scholarly interest was the petrography of Czechoslovakia. He was also a contributor to the *Ukraïns'ka zahal'na entsyklopediia* (The Ukrainian General Encyclopedia, 1935).

Orlov, Yakiv, b 17 May 1923 in Ternuvatka, Kryvyi Rih okruha, d 26 February 1981 in Kiev. Conductor. After graduating from the Kiev Conservatory in 1954, he directed and conducted the orchestra of the Verovka State Chorus (1955–67) and the orchestra of the army ensemble (1967–9). He established (1970) and then directed and conducted the Kiev Orchestra of Folk Instruments. In 1980–1 he lectured at the music education faculty of the Kiev Pedagogical Institute.

Orlovsky, Mykhailo [Orlovs'kyj, Myxajlo], b 1873, d February 1918 in Kiev. Physician and civic leader. During the revival of Ukrainian independence he served as a military sanitation inspector and was executed by the Bolsheviks.

Orlovsky, Mykola [Orlovs'kyj], b 15 May 1900 in Shapovalivka, Borzna county, Chernihiv gubernia, d 21 February 1974 in Kiev. Agriculturist. A graduate of the Kiev Institute of Agronomy (1924), he taught at the Kiev Agricultural Institute (1930–41) and worked at the All-Union Scientific Research Institute of Sugar Beets in Kiev. An expert in the selection of sugar beets, Orlovsky wrote *Osnovy biolohiï tsukrovykh buriakiv* (Principles of the Biology of Sugar Beets, 1937; 3rd edn 1961).

Orlovsky, Petro [Orlovs'kyj], b 1825, d 1913 in Kiev. Church historian and Orthodox priest. A graduate of the Kiev Theological Academy, he served as a priest in Warsaw and was later an archpriest at the St Sophia Cathedral in Kiev. His studies and documents of 17th- and 18th-century Ukrainian church history appeared in *Kievskaia starina* (KS), *Trudy Kievskoi dukhovnoi akademii* (TKDA), and Kiev's *Eparkhial'nyia vedomosti*. They include articles in KS on Archbishop V. Sadkovsky (1897, no. 7) and the plague epidemic in Kiev in 1770–1 (1897, no. 6), and in TKDA on the participation of the Zaporozhian Cossacks in the creation of an Orthodox hierarchy in Ukraine by Patriarch Theophanes of Jerusalem in 1620 (1905), the Kiev synod

of 1629 (1905), and a legend about Metropolitan R. Zaborovsky (1908).

Volodymyr Orlovsky: *Village* (1879)

Orlovsky, Volodymyr [Orlovs'kyj], b 1 February 1842 in Kiev, d 19 February 1914 in Nervi, Italy. Landscape and genre painter. He studied under I. Soshenko in Kiev (1855–60) and on T. Shevchenko's recommendation was admitted to the St Petersburg Academy of Arts (1861–8). In 1869–72 he lived and painted in France, Italy, Switzerland, and Germany. He became a member of the academy in St Petersburg in 1874 and a professor there in 1878. In 1886 he returned to Ukraine, where he taught at the *Kiev Drawing School and helped found the Kiev Art School. As Orlovsky gradually freed himself from *academism, his works acquired a more natural composition, more confident lines, and a finer coloration. His famous depictions of the Ukrainian and Crimean countryside include *In Alushta* (1870), *In the Steppe* (1874), *The Sowing* (1874), *Hay Gathering* (1878), *Peasant Houses on a Summer Day* (late 1870s), *Village* (1879), *Harvest* (1882), *Birch Grove* (1884, 1886), *Sudak Coast* (1889), and *Haven* (1890). In the 1900s he painted seascapes almost exclusively. An album of his works was published in Kiev in 1968.

Orly Catholic Association of Ukrainian Youth (Katolytska asotsiiatsiia ukrainskoi molodi 'Orly'). A Catholic youth association (whose name means 'eagles') that was active in 1933–9 in the Lviv archeparchy. Established in the wake of the 1933 Ukrainian Youth for Christ festival, the group functioned under the direct auspices of the Lviv archeparchy until 1937, when it was established as a separate entity. Centered in Lviv, Orly was headed by A. Melnyk in 1933–8 and then by V. Hlibovytsky. It had nearly 450 men's and women's branches with a combined membership of approx 30,000. Before 1937 the women's groups were separately organized and headed by K. Yanovych. The group resembled the Plast scouting organization in several ways and included beginner, junior, youth, and senior levels in its structure. It sponsored summer camps and published the monthly *Ukraïns'ke iunatstvo*, which had a supplement called *Hotovs'* that provided activity materials for small groups.

Orlyhora, Lev. See Sylenko, Lev.

Orlyk, Hryhor (Hryhorii), b 16 November 1702 in Baturyn, Nizhen regiment, d 14 November 1759 near Minden, Germany. Political leader and French diplomat, count, and general; eldest son of Hetman P. *Orlyk and godson of Hetman I. Mazepa. Orlyk emigrated from Ukraine with his parents in 1709, studied at Lund University in Sweden (1716–18), and served as an officer in the Swedish (1715–16, 1718–20), Saxon (1721–6), and Polish (1726–9) armies before entering the French diplomatic corps in 1730. He became a mobile and effective representative of his father's interests and 'the cause of Cossack liberties' in royal courts throughout Europe, from Stockholm to Istanbul and from Paris to Bakhchesarai. In 1732 and 1734 the French government sent him on secret missions to convince the Crimean khan Kaplan-Girei to support the Cossacks against Russia. In 1733 he helped *Stanislaus I Leszczyński to get back to Poland and regain the throne. In 1734 he went on a secret mission to the Hetman state, where he deliberated in Nizhen with members of the Cossack *starshyna* opposed to Russian rule.

Orlyk was particularly active as a diplomat during the Russo-Turkish (1735–9) and Russo-Swedish (1741) wars, during which he sent many memorandums to the French and Swedish governments warning of the dangers of Russian expansionism and stressing that only Ukraine's liberation could halt it and ensure stability in Europe. He drew up a proposal for an anti-Russian coalition consisting of France, Sweden, Prussia, Poland, the Ottoman Empire, the Crimean Khanate, and the Zaporozhian Host. He passed on documents about Ukraine, obtained from his father, to Voltaire, who used them in *L'Histoire de Charles XII* (1731), where he writes that 'l'Ukraine a toujours aspiré à être libre.' Orlyk was the leader of the Ukrainian émigré community after his father's death. He was appointed a French general in 1748 and a count and member of Louis XV's privy council in 1750. In April 1759, during the Seven Years' War, he was severely wounded in the Battle of Bergen, and later died of complications.

BIBLIOGRAPHY
Mémoires d'Argençon, 5 vols (Paris 1857–8)
Borshchak, I. 'Het'man Pylyp Orlyk i Frantsiia (storinky dyplomatychnoï istoriï),' *ZNTSh*, 134–5 (1924); repr *UIZh*, 1991, nos 8–9, 11
Spuler, B. 'Europäische Diplomaten in Konstantinopol bis zum 1739,' *Jahrbücher für Geschichte Osteuropas*, 5 (1936)
Borschak, E. *Hryhor Orlyk: France's Cossack General* (Toronto 1956)
Subtelny, O. *The Mazepists: Ukrainian Separatism in the Early Eighteenth Century* (New York 1981)

T. Mackiw

Orlyk, Pylyp, b 11 October 1672 in Kosuta, Ashmiany county, Wilno (Vilnius) voivodeship, Lithuania, d 26 May 1742 in Iaşi, Moldavia. Cossack statesman and hetman-in-exile. A nobleman of Bohemian ancestry, he studied at the Jesuit college in Vilnius and until 1694 at the Kievan Mohyla College. In 1698 he was appointed secretary of the consistory of Kiev metropoly. In 1699, after marrying Anna, the daughter of Col P. Hertsyk of Poltava regiment, he became a senior member of the Hetman state's General Military Chancellery. In 1706 Hetman I. Mazepa appointed Orlyk general chancellor. In that capacity he was Mazepa's closest aide, facilitated Mazepa's secret correspondence with the Poles and Swedes, and assisted Mazepa in his efforts to form an anti-Russian coalition in Eastern Europe. After the defeat at the Battle of *Poltava in June 1709, Orlyk fled abroad with Mazepa and became a leader of the first Ukrainian political emigration.

After Mazepa's death, on 16 April 1710, Orlyk was elected hetman, with the backing of Charles XII of Sweden, in Bendery. The chief author of the Constitution of *Bendery, he pursued policies aimed at liberating Ukraine from Russian rule. He gained the support of the Zaporozhian Host, concluded a treaty with Charles XII in May 1710, and sought to make the Ukrainian question a matter of international concern by continuing Mazepa's attempts at establishing an anti-Russian coalition. Orlyk signed a treaty with the Crimean khan Devlet-Girei in February 1711, negotiated with the Ottoman Porte, which formally recognized his authority over Right-Bank Ukraine and the Zaporizhia in 1712, conducted talks with the Don Cossack participants in the Bulavin revolt who had fled to the Kuban, and even contacted the Kazan Tatars and the Bashkirs. In 1711–14 he led Cossack campaigns against the Russians in Right-Bank Ukraine. Despite initial victories they ultimately failed, because of Turkish vacillation and because the pillaging, raping, and taking of many civilian captives by Orlyk's Crimean Tatar allies resulted in the loss of public and military support on the Right Bank.

Orlyk and a part of his general officer staff emigrated in 1714 to Sweden, in 1720 to Silesia, and in 1721 to Poland. From 1722 until his death he was interned in Turkish-controlled territories – in Salonika until 1734, then in the Budzhak, and finally in Moldavia. During that period Orlyk sought, in vain, the support of Sweden, Poland, Saxony, Great Britain, Hannover, Holstein, the Vatican, and, through his son, H. *Orlyk, France. He also continued trying to organize, without success, a personal army and to incite the Zaporozhian Host to rise against Russian rule.

Orlyk wrote verses in Latin, the panegyrics *Alcides Rossyiski* (The Russian Alcides [Heracles], 1695) to Mazepa and *Hippomenes Sarmacki* (The Sarmatian Hippomenes, 1698) to Col I. Obidovsky, the political treatise 'Vyvid prav Ukraïny' (Devolution of Ukraine's Rights, 1712), a manifesto to European governments justifying his alliance with the Porte (1712), and numerous memorandums to European rulers and government leaders. His diary of 1720–32 (5 vols) is preserved at the Archives of the Ministry of Foreign Affairs in Paris.

BIBLIOGRAPHY
[Rawita-]Gawroński, F. 'Filip Orlyk, nieuznany hetman kozacki,' in *Studya i szkice historyczne*, ser 2 (Lviv 1900)
Holiichuk, F. 'Fylyp Orlyk u Halychyni,' *Naukovyi zbirnyk prysviachenyi M. Hrushevs'komu* (Lviv 1906)
Iensen [Jensen], A. 'Orlyk u Shvetsiï,' *ZNTSh*, 92 (1909)
Kordt, V.A. (ed). 'Dokumenty ob Andree Voinarovskom i Filippe Orlike,' *Sbornik statei i materialov po istorii Iugo-Zapadnoi Rossii*, 2 (Kiev 1916)
Borshchak, I. 'Het'man Pylyp Orlyk i Frantsiia (storinky dyplomatychnoï istoriï),' *ZNTSh*, 134–5 (1924); repr *UIZh*, 1991, nos 8–9, 11
Krupnyts'kyi, B. *Het'man Pylyp Orlyk (1672–1742): Ohliad ioho politychnoï diial'nosty* (Warsaw 1938)
Borschak, E. 'Pylyp Orlyk's Devolution of the Ukraine's Rights,' *AUA*, 6, nos 3–4 (1958)
Subtelny, O. *The Mazepists: Ukrainian Separatism in the Early Eighteenth Century* (New York 1981)
The Diariusz podróżny of Pylyp Orlyk (1727–1731), intro by O. Pritsak (Cambridge, Mass 1988)

T. Mackiw

Archbishop Stepan Orlyk

Orlyk, Stepan, b 9 January 1891 in Volhynia, d ca 1939 in Zhytomyr. Archbishop of the *Ukrainian Autocephalous Orthodox church (UAOC). He graduated from the theological academy in Paris, and was ordained in 1916 in Volhynia. He served as a priest in Tbilisi, Georgia (1917–21). He returned to Ukraine and was active in the rebirth of the Ukrainian church. At the first sobor of the UAOC (October 1921) he was consecrated bishop and appointed archbishop of Volhynia okruha (1921–3), with his see in Zhytomyr. Orlyk organized nearly 50 parishes of the UAOC in the region and then was appointed to Berdychiv okruha (Berdychiv and Shepetivka, 1925–7). In the course of his work he continually battled the Soviet regime and the clergy of the Moscow patriarchate. In 1927 the authorities demanded that he be removed, and in 1928 he was arrested and exiled for 10 years to the Solovets Islands. After completing his sentence he returned to Zhytomyr, where he was once again arrested. He became blind from maltreatment, and eventually died in prison in Zhytomyr.

Orlyk. A monthly journal of cultural and community affairs published in the displaced persons' camp in Berchtesgaden, Germany, from June 1946 to March 1948 (a total of 22 issues). One of only 10 Ukrainian periodicals granted licenses by the US military authorities, it was edited by T. Lapychak.

Ornament. A decorative design, which is usually symmetrical and rhythmical. It is based on a developed semantic system derived from the repetition of symbols or signs with or without a compositional center.

In Ukraine the oldest examples of ornament are found on Paleolithic bracelets and other artifacts made of mammoth bones discovered at the Mizyn archeological site in the Chernihiv region. Extant Neolithic artifacts reveal a greater variety of geometric ornament. The use of parallel and intersecting lines, spirals, waves, triangles, and comb shapes was characteristic of the Linear Spiral-Meander Pottery, Boh-Dniester, Dnieper-Donets, and Surskyi-Dnieper cultures. The creation of the last remaining principal elements of geometric ornament was attained in the Aeneolithic period, particularly by inhabitants of the Trypilian culture, who used zoo- and anthropomorphic motifs. Ancient ritual ornament was based on a series of geometric archetypes and generalized, stylized, or fragmentary depictions of flora and fauna. Generally they ex-

pressed the conceptualization of cosmic phenomena and concretized ritual semantic signs.

Isomorphic motifs became widespread during the Bronze and Iron ages in the ornament of the Scythians and Sarmatians and the Hellenic states on the northern Black Sea coast. The Greek artisans of the coastal colonies ornamented their creations in the style of their own metropolis but adapted them to indigenous tastes, and Scythian craftsmen borrowed Greek motifs in addition to making objects that were typical of their culture.

In Kievan Rus' the manuscripts, architecture, and implements produced for the higher classes were ornamented with Byzantine motifs and sophisticated drawings depicting mythical beasts (eg, griffins, centaurs, sirens, mermaids) and monograms of Jesus Christ. Ukrainian artisans of the late Middle Ages and early modern times often used motifs borrowed from the widespread European Gothic, Renaissance, baroque, and classicist styles. The kilims and church vestments manufactured in 17th- and 18th-century Stanyslaviv, Korets, and Buchach were at times ornamented with Oriental (especially Persian) floral motifs. Peasant artisans also creatively adapted European styles. Renaissance floral patterns in backgrounds and borders in particular became popular. The influence of baroque ornament can be seen in the *Petrykivka murals, the luxuriant embroidery of the Poltava region, and the lush floral motifs on the Easter eggs of the Chernihiv region. Heraldic eagles and Empire vase shapes were among the most popular motifs used in the woven textiles and embroidery of Left-Bank Ukraine.

Until the end of the 19th century Ukrainian peasant ornament preserved ancient geometric motifs reflecting pre-Christian beliefs and their abstract-associative and logico-symbolic polysemantic imagery. A rhomboid, for example, could symbolize the sun, or a goddess, fertility, ripe grain, a sowed field, or marriage; rhomboid rows on opposite ends of an embroidered towel, the rising and setting sun; and a rosette of eight rhomboids, virginity.

Ukrainian folk ornament has traditionally been associated with sacral and ritual objects. Like other components of the national folkloric universe (fairy tales, legends, carols, ritual folk songs, historical songs, folk painting), it has served as an expression of the ontological origins of human life, the earth, and the universe and has retained vestiges of the belief in its protective functions.

The folkways and spiritual life of the Ukrainian peasantry, which were organically tied to natural cycles (seasons) and rites of passage (marriage, birth, death), were reflected not only in ornament in general but also in its technique and the materials used. Folk ornament has had regional and local traits, which have been manifested through the use of varied motifs, rhythms, and colors. Carpathian (particularly Hutsul) textiles, Easter eggs, and works in metal and wood, for example, have been characterized by their complex geometric, polychromatic designs and multiple local variants. Textiles and embroidery from Polisia have been characterized by their age-old use of red and white. In the Middle Dnieper Basin blue was used in embroidery until the late 19th century, when, because of the noticeable deterioration in the quality of blue dyes, it was replaced by black. Embroidery in the Poltava region has been characterized by white geometric ornament on white or gray in shirts and the use of soft, muted colors. From the Dnieper River to Podilia the contrasts in polychromatic embroidery, textiles, Easter eggs, and porcelain have been progressively more pronounced. Yellows and, less often, green highlights appear in addition to the usual red-black harmonies. The range of colors is supplemented with browns and blues in Galicia and becomes most varied in Bukovyna. In the ornament of Bessarabia and Southern and Slobidska Ukraine, which were settled relatively late and not only by Ukrainians, a complex interaction of various ethnic influences can be observed.

In Ukrainian ornament there are forms that have been particular to a specific locality and others that have been more common and even universal, in both form and name. The most widespread are spiral 'ram's horns,' 'periwinkle' leaves, infinity circles, square 'windows,' crosses, crosslike 'windmills,' rhomboidal 'wafers' and 'loaves,' various 'branches' and 'combs' with parallel teeth, 'roses,' 'oak leaves,' zigzagging 'snakes,' 'grape clusters,' 'laurels,' centrifugal 'spiders,' eight-faceted 'stars,' 'teeth,' and 'wedges.'

The basic universal cosmological image in Ukrainian folk ornament has been the pre-Christian 'Tree of Life' or 'Tree of the World' found in ancient legends and medieval apocrypha. It includes solar signs and symbols of natural phenomena, animals, and birds that appear on Easter eggs, wagons, sleighs, embroidered towels, and pottery as ideograms of the creation and ordering of the world. These ideograms convey the spatial and temporal simultaneity of the union of humans and nature and nature and the cosmos. As a rule they constitute a tripartite, symmetrical composition consisting of the *vazon* (flower pot) motif and 'branches,' 'paws,' 'laurel,' and 'shamrock.' Although their various semantic meanings have been largely forgotten, their traditional significance has been preserved as an esthetic criterion in the world of folk culture.

One of the traits of Ukrainian folk ornament has been its conceptualization of motifs, even the most geometric or abstract ones, in terms of the plant world. There have been few animal or architectural motifs, which appear mainly as associative names rather than isomorphic elements.

In the early 20th century, eclecticism in folk ornament became more pronounced. The mass distribution of printed, stylized embroidery patterns squeezed out ancient local techniques and designs. Traditional motifs in engraving, ceramics, and metalwork were continued, however. Ornament became more detailed, and its rhythms became more frequent and more uniform. The use of multiple colors and tonal dispersion increased.

The gradual turn of Ukrainian folk artisans to the urban and foreign markets gave rise to the appearance of professional instructors who taught how to cater to consumer tastes. Thenceforth ornament has evolved not as a result of internal development but under pressure from external conditions. At times this state of affairs has produced the retrostylization of new works through the copying of museum artifacts, or, conversely, examples of 'folkloric moderne' or 'folkloric academism.'

In the 19th and 20th centuries the creators of folk art that has not been mass-produced introduced designs from published sources, isomorphic depictions, migrating motifs, and polychromatics in ornament. Efforts to revive ornament in the early 20th century were often accompanied by the mechanical magnification (infrequently, diminu-

tion) of the dimensions of elements and motifs. When such innovations have exhausted their variational possibilities or lost their attractiveness as novelty, interest in local classical ornament has been revived, and ancient models have been reproduced.

BIBLIOGRAPHY
Kosacheva, O. *Ukrainskii narodnyi ornament* (Kiev 1876)
Pavluts'kyi, H. *Istoriia ukraïns'koho ornamentu* (Kiev 1927)
Sichyns'kyi, V. *Ukraïns'kyi istorychnyi ornament* (Prague 1943)
                                        O. Naiden, M. Selivachov

Ornowski, Jan (Ornovsky, Yan). A late 17th-century poet from Chernihiv. He is the author of panegyrics, written in Polish, to the Cossack *starshyna*: *Niebeski Merkurjusz* (Heavenly Mercury, 1686), *Muza Roxolańska o tryumfalney sławie i fortunie hetmana Mazepy* (Roxolanian Muse on the Triumphal Fame and Fortune of Hetman [I.] Mazepa, 1688), *Bogata drogich kamieniy speza ...* (A Rich Expenditure of Precious Stones, 1693), *Apollo Sauromacki przy weselnym akcie ... Simeona Lizohuba ... z Iriną corą ... Iana Szkoropackiego ...* (Sauromatian Apollo at the Wedding Ceremony ... of Symon Lyzohub ... with Iryna, the Daughter ... of Ivan Skoropadsky, 1703), and *Bogaty wirydarz* (The Lush Viridarium, 1705).

Orobko, Vasyl, b 1882 in Bukovyna, d 1932. Senior officer of the Ukrainian Galician Army (UHA). He commanded the Chortkiv Military District and then, at the rank of major, the 14th Brigade (June–October 1919). In November 1919 he was reassigned to command the UHA collection point in Odessa.

Orovetsky, Pavlo [Orovec'kyj], b 17 March 1905 in Yelyzavetivka, Novomoskovske county, Katerynoslav gubernia, d 20 February 1976 in Kiev. Socialist-realist writer. From 1930 he wrote over 12 collections of literary sketches and the novels *Sertse soldata* (A Soldier's Heart, 1958), *Druha zustrich* (The Second Encounter, 1960), *Hlyboka rozvidka* (A Penetrating Investigation, 1963), *Rubinovyi promin'* (The Ruby Ray, 1965), *Zahybel' Poloza* (Poloz's Demise, 1969), *Berehy zhyttia* (The Shores of Life, 1971), and *Partyzans'ka povist'* (A Partisan's Tale, 1972).

Orphan's court (*syritskyi sud*). A special court that appeared in the Russian Empire in 1775 to care for the orphans and widows of city residents (merchants, burghers, and tradesmen). In 1781 orphan's courts began to spread through the cities of Russian-ruled Ukraine. They appointed wards for orphans, reviewed the reports of trustees, and handled other legal and financial matters involving orphans and widows. In 1818 they became responsible for the survivors of nobles as well. Attached to *magistraty* and, after 1864, to circuit courts, the orphan's courts consisted of the head of the municipal council, two members of the *magistrat*, and a city starosta. They were abolished in 1917.

Ort (Ukrainian: *vurt, urt, vert*). A silver coin that was used in several European countries in the 16th to 18th centuries. The origin of the word is German. The coin was initially used to designate one-quarter of a larger denomination, usually a **taler*. The coins were used in Gdańsk from 1608. At that time a *taler* was worth 40 *groszy*, and an *ort* 10 *groszy*. Its value later increased to 16 and then 18 *groszy*. In

ORNAMENT 1) Late Paleolithic zigzag ornament in red ochre on a mammoth shoulder bone (excavated in Mizyn, Chernihiv oblast). 2) Polychromatic meander pattern on a clay vessel of the Trypilian culture (Historical Museum of Ukraine, Kiev). 3) Stylized deer on Scythian gold plaques (6th century BC; Museum of Historical Treasures of Ukraine, Kiev). 4) Geometric and floral motifs (11th century) of the mosaic in the central apse of the St Sophia Cathedral in Kiev. 5) Stylized bird on a pendant earring (gold and enamel, 12th- to 13th-century Kiev). 6) Vine and grape motifs on the Royal Gates (gilded wood, 17th century) in the village church of Voinyliv, near Kalush, Galicia. 7) Silver cup with filigree (18th-century Kiev). 8) Tree of Life on embroidered *rushnyk* (early 20th century) from the Kirovohrad region. 9) Flower and vase motifs embroidered with silk and metallic thread on linen (18th-century Slobidska Ukraine).

the 17th century an *ort* was worth 12 kopecks. The *ort* was coined in the Polish Commonwealth until 1766.

Orthodox Academy (Pravoslavna akademiia). A scholarly society of theology students at Chernivtsi University established in 1907. It published D. Yeremiichuk's lectures *Pastyrs'ke bohoslov'ia* (Pastoral Theology, 1920) and the almanac *Nazustrich voli* (Welcoming Freedom, 1922). Its presidents were P. Kateryniuk, M. Kopachuk, H. Revutsky, I. Vynnytsky, and I. Tsurkan. At the end of 1923 the society was dissolved by the Rumanian authorities.

Orthography. The system of rules regulating the written and printed representation of the sounds of a language, the spelling of words, and punctuation. The basis of modern Ukrainian orthography is phonemic and morphemic, although some historical forms unrelated to its phonemic or morphemic structure have been retained.

The first orthography in Ukraine was the Cyrillic Old *Church Slavonic (CS) orthography adopted along with the Christian faith in the 10th century. Some of its features (eg, the written representation of nasal vowels that no longer existed in Ukrainian speech) had only an etymological basis. As the Ukrainian language developed, its orthography increasingly diverged from its phonetics. In the late 14th century Patriarch Euthymius of Tirnovo (or Túrnovo, Bulgaria) introduced a far-reaching CS orthographic reform for all Orthodox Slavs, which restored archaic CS features such as nasal vowel letters (ѫ and ѧ instead of *u* and *ja*), the absence of intervocal iotization (eg, *dobraa*, *-roe*, *ruu* 'good'), the etymological spelling of Greek words (eg, *ahhlъ* instead of *janhol* 'angel'), and under Serbian influence the use of *-ъ* instead of *-ь* (eg, *vѣkъ*, *aminъ* 'age, amen'). The reform was disseminated by Bulgarian, Serbian, and Byzantine monks, monasteries in Bukovyna and Moldavia, and even Metropolitan Cyprian of Kiev. Different chanceries from the 14th to 18th centuries introduced their own orthographic peculiarities.

The orthographic norms in M. Smotrytsky's Slavonic grammar (1619) had a determining impact on the printing of chronicles. His rules (eg, on using *e* or *ie*, *o* or *ω*, *y* or *i*, *kh* or *g*) were retained with certain modifications in the 1648 and 1721 Moscow editions of his grammar and are observed in CS church books to this day. Reinforced by Russian etymological norms based on the 1708 *hrazhdanka* script this historical orthography influenced the use and theoretical justification of etymological orthography in Ukraine (eg, the *maksymovychivka* script, which was widely used in 19th-century Galicia, and the *pankevychivka* script, which dominated in interwar Transcarpathia). Etymological orthography was imprecise (ie, it did not draw a clear line between the vernacular and CS, Old Ukrainian, and Russian) and difficult to master; hence, several attempts, based on the Serbian example, were made to devise a Ukrainian phonetic orthography. They included O. Pavlovsky's grammar (1818); P. Kulish's *kulishivka* script, which was used in populist publications in the 1860s and 1870s; M. Drahomanov's *drahomanivka* script, used in his émigré publications from 1877 and by his Galician supporters; and Ye. Zhelekhivsky's *zhelekhivka* script, used officially in Galicia from 1893. The struggle for a phonetic orthography was linked to the demand for a new vernacular-based (not an archaic book-based) literary language and had important political im-

plications. In the 1880s the *kulishivka* script was banned in Russian-ruled Ukraine, and a modified version of the Russian alphabet, the *yaryzhka* alphabet, was imposed on Ukrainians. During the liberal period 1905–14 most Ukrainian publications in this territory adopted the *kulishivka* script.

It was only after the February Revolution of 1917 that the second tsarist ban (1914) on the *kulishivka* was lifted, and a modern Ukrainian orthography was developed, based on it, the *zhelekhivka* script, and Ye. *Zhelekhivsky's and B. *Hrinchenko's dictionaries. Since 1918 many orthographic dictionaries and handbooks have been published (see *Lexicography). In January 1919 the Orthographic Commission of the UNR Ministry of Education introduced official orthographic rules. Under Soviet rule, similar rules were confirmed by the VUAN in 1920 and the People's Commissariat of Education in 1921. In 1925 a State Commission for the Regulation of Orthography was created. The commission's proposals and the orthographic differences that existed between Soviet (formerly Russian-ruled) Ukraine and Western (formerly Austrian-ruled) Ukraine were debated and resolved at an All-Ukrainian Orthographic Conference held from 26 May to 6 June 1927 in Kharkiv. The new, standardized orthography was adopted in September 1928 by the Council of People's Commissars, in 1929 by the Shevchenko Scientific Society in Lviv, and subsequently by Ukrainians outside Ukraine.

By 1930, however, the Stalinist regime began to modify this orthography. It restricted the use of *g* and *l'*, and in 1933 it banned entirely the use of *g*, *l'o*, *lja*, and *lju* in foreign names and loanwords. It introduced etymological spelling forms (eg, *-ia-* instead of *-ija-*) to align Ukrainian orthography with the Russian. The new, so-called Kiev orthography (published in 1936 and revised in 1945 and again in 1960) was not accepted by most Ukrainians in interwar Western Ukraine or in the West. In 1987 an Orthographic Commission was created at the AN URSR (now ANU) Institute of Linguistics to prepare a new, more contemporary official orthography. The 1990 orthography once again restored the letter *g* in a restricted number of words.

In Austrian-ruled Western Ukraine, attempts in the 19th century to introduce a Ukrainian orthography based on the Polish Latin alphabet by Polonophile circles in Podilia and Volhynia and Polish governing circles (see *Alphabet war) did not succeed. The Latin alphabet was used only by semiliterate peasants in Galicia, Podlachia, and the Kholm region and in popular publications for them. The Latin alphabet in printed Ukrainian was imposed by the governments of Rumania (in Bukovyna, Bessarabia, and Dobrudja), Hungary (in Transcarpathia to 1918), and Slovakia (in church publications in the Prešov region from the 1920s) and was widespread at one time among certain groups of immigrants from these regions in the United States.

(See also *Cyrillic alphabet, Ukrainian *Language, and *Standard Ukrainian.)

BIBLIOGRAPHY
Kryms'kyi, A. 'Narys istoriï ukraïns'koho pravopysu do 1927 r.,' ZIFV, 25 (1929); repr in his *Tvory v p'iaty tomakh*, 3 (Kiev 1973)
Syniavs'kyi, O. 'Korotka istoriia "Ukraïns'koho pravopysu",' in *Kul'tura ukraïns'koho slova*, 1 (Kharkiv–Kiev 1931); repr in *Suchasnist'*, 1982, nos 1–2

Zhovtobriukh, M. 'Do istorii ukraïns'koho pravopysu,' *Movoznavstvo*, nos 11–12 (1937)

Kysilevs'kyi, K. 'Istoriia ukraïns'koho pravopysnoho pytannia: Sproba syntezy,' *ZNTSh*, 165 (1957)

Ilarion [Ohiienko, I.]. *Nasha literaturna mova: Iak pysaty i hovoryty po-literaturnomu: Movni narysy* (Winnipeg 1958)

Moskalenko, A. *Narys istorii ukraïns'koho alfavitu i pravopysu* (Odessa 1958)

Karpova, V. 'Z istorii ukraïns'koho pravopysu v Halychyni (1917–1939 rr.),' *Doslidzhennia i materialy z ukraïns'koï movy*, 2 (Kiev 1960)

Rusanivs'kyi, V. 'Stanovlennia i rozvytok systemy pravopysu,' in *Movoznavstvo na Ukraïni za p'iatdesiat rokiv*, ed I. Bahmut (Kiev 1967)

Shtets', M. 'Rozvytok ukraïns'koho pravopysu na Zakarpatti i v Skhidnii Slovachchyni,' *Naukovyi zbirnyk Muzeiu ukraïns'koï kul'tury v Svydnyku*, 4, bk 1 (1969)

O. Horbach

Liubomyr Ortynsky   Bishop Soter Ortynsky

Orthopedics. A specialty of medicine that deals with the diseases of the skeletal system (bones and joints). The development of orthopedics in Ukraine began with the publication of Ye. Mukhin's *Pervyie nachala kostopravnoi nauki* (The First Beginnings of Bone-Healing Science, 1806). The first orthopedic school in Ukraine was founded by M. *Sytenko at the Medical-Mechanical Institute in Kharkiv (1907). Today it is the Scientific Research Institute of Orthopedics and Traumatology, where prostheses, artificial limbs, and orthopedic equipment are made and tested; there are similar institutes in Kiev and Donetske. The journal *Ortopediia, travmatologiia i protezirovaniie* was published in Kharkiv (from 1926), and a collection with the same title (both in Russian) was published in Kiev (from 1971). Orthopedics and traumatology departments exist at all medical institutes, and orthopedic assistance is given at special treatment clinics throughout Ukraine. The Ukrainian Scientific Association of Orthopedists co-ordinates and aids its members in their work.

BIBLIOGRAPHY
Ternovoi, K.; Shumada, I. *Razvitie travmatologo-ortopedicheskoi nauki v USSR* (Kiev 1978)

Ortynsky, Ilarion [Ortyns'kyj] (Hiliarii), b 29 August 1907 in Sambir, Galicia, d 20 June 1974 in Oviedo, Spain. He graduated from the Cracow Mining Academy (1930) and worked in the petroleum industry in Iraq (until 1939) and for a French geological exploration company in the Algerian Sahara Desert (1947–65). In 1949 he discovered a new oil field in Mesuda. From 1967 he helped organize and taught at a mining school in Oviedo, Spain, under the auspices of UNESCO. He published scientific articles on the geology of the northern Sahara Desert.

Ortynsky, Liubomyr [Ortyns'kyj, Ljubomyr], b 7 June 1919 in Mykhailevychi, Drohobych county, Galicia, d 22 July 1961 in Hunter, New York. Military and political activist and journalist. While studying at Warsaw University he was active in the OUN and was arrested twice by the Polish authorities. During the Second World War he served in the Legion of Ukrainian Nationalists and the Division Galizien. He was in Munich after the war, and emigrated to the United States in 1956 and took up work at the Prolog Research Corporation. He contributed to *Svoboda, Suchasna Ukraïna*, and other publications and took a particular interest in Ukraine's role at the United Nations.

From 1958 he was a member of the External Representation of the Ukrainian Supreme Liberation Council. He was a founder and president of the Brotherhood of Former Soldiers of the First Ukrainian Division of the UNA and coeditor of *Visti kombatanta*.

Ortynsky, Soter [Ortyns'kyj], b 26 January 1866 in Ortynychi, Sambir county, Galicia, d 24 March 1916 in Philadelphia. Ukrainian Catholic bishop and church leader. He entered the Basilian order in 1884 and studied at various Basilian schools before completing his TH D in Cracow. He was ordained in 1891. On the recommendation of Metropolitan A. Sheptytsky, Pope Pius X appointed him bishop of all Greek Catholics in the United States in March 1907. He was officially consecrated and arrived in the United States in August 1907. He was the first Uniate bishop in the country, and his jurisdiction was initially limited: he was under the authority of the Roman Catholic hierarchy until 1913, when the Vatican issued a decree (confirmed by the pope in 1914) naming him full exarch, responsible directly to the pope and with his see in Philadelphia. Ortynsky presided over the rapid growth of the Greek Catholic church in the United States. He founded an orphanage in Philadelphia in 1911, introduced the Basilian order of nuns, organized night schools for deacons, and set up and headed a branch of the Prosvita society. He also founded several church organs, including *Eparkhiial'ni visty, Dushpastyr, Misionar*, and *Ameryka*. Ortynsky's attempts to extend his episcopal authority over almost all aspects of Ukrainian life in the United States often led to conflicts. His desire to assert church control over the *Ukrainian National Association led to a split in the organization; when his efforts failed, he established the rival *Providence Association of Ukrainian Catholics in America, in 1912. Ortynsky was the only Greek Catholic bishop to include under his jurisdiction Ukrainian (Ruthenian) immigrants from Transcarpathia; later they became the faithful of *Pittsburgh metropoly.

W. Lencyk

Oryszowski, Jan (Oryszewski), b ca 1535 in Oryshiv Liatskyi, Belz voivodeship, d 1605, most likely in Haisyn. Polish nobleman. One of the organizers of the *registered Cossacks, in 1578 he was appointed an aide to Prince *Michał Korybut Wiśniowiecki, the starosta of Cherkasy and Kaniv, and commander of a detachment of registered Cossacks. From 1580 to 1591 he served as hetman of the

Zaporozhian Host. He led a Cossack force during the Starodub campaign in the 1580 Muscovite-Polish War and against the Crimean Tatars in 1585. In 1581 a Cossack register was compiled under his supervision. He represented the Zaporozhian Host in the Polish Sejm of 1587 that elected King Sigismund III Vasa, and in 1600 he mediated in negotiations between Poland and the Cossacks. The chapter on the Cossacks in M. Bielski's chronicle of Poland (1597) is based on Oryszowski's oral account.

Orzeszkowa, Eliza, b 6 June 1841 in Milkoushchizna, near Hrodna, Belarus, d 18 May 1910 in Hrodna. Polish writer and feminist. In her novels and stories she depicted the life of Belarusian peasants, the Polish gentry, and small-town Jews in western Belarus and of poor artisans and the intelligentsia in Warsaw. Her novels *Niziny* (Lowlands, 1885), *Dziurdziowie* (The Dziurdzes, 1888), and *Cham* (The Boor, 1888) dealt with the problems of the Ukrainian peasantry in western Polisia. She corresponded with I. Franko, and translated some of his, T. Shevchenko's, M. Vovchok's, and M. Starytsky's works into Polish. Her feminist publicism influenced N. *Kobrynska and U. *Kravchenko. Ukrainian translations of her selected works were published in 1930, 1950, 1952, 1956, and 1966.

Roman Orzhentsky   Mykhailo Osadchy

Orzhentsky, Roman [Orženc'kyj], b 28 February 1863 in Zhytomyr, Volhynia gubernia, d 24 May 1923 in Warsaw. Economist and statistician; full member of the VUAN from 1919. After graduating from Odessa University in 1887, he worked in various institutions in Odessa and in the Yaroslavl gubernia zemstvo. In 1919 he returned to Ukraine, where he was appointed to the VUAN chair of theoretical economics and then made head of its social-economic division (1921–2). Orzhentsky specialized in the theory of value and prices and was the first Ukrainian mathematical economist. As a representative of the psychological school of marginal utility theory, he defended the subjective theory of value and the feasibility of measuring and comparing consumer preferences. He consistently criticized K. Marx's labor theory of value. In his statistical works he developed a new method for measuring sets of multifaceted phenomena with the help of relative variables and probability. He also studied the movement of market prices in Kiev under conditions of monetary inflation. Orzhentsky's major works are

Poleznost' i tsena (Utility and Price, 1895), his master's dissertation on the concept of economic phenomenon (1903), *Politicheskaia ekonomika* (Political Economy, 1909), *Svodnye priznaki* (Summary Indicators, 1910), a texbook in mathematical statistics (1914), and *Elementarnaia teoriia statisticheskikh velichin i vycheslenii* (An Elementary Theory of Statistical Magnitudes and Computations, 1921).

Orzhytsia [Oržycja]. IV-13. A town smt (1990 pop 4,200) on the Orzhytsia River and a raion center in Poltava oblast. It is first mentioned in historical documents in the 16th century. In 1648–58 Orzhytsia was a company center in Kropyvna regiment, and in 1659–1781, in Lubni regiment. Today it has a mixed-feed factory and a peat-processing plant.

Orzhytsia River [Oržycja]. A right-bank tributary of the Sula River. It is 117 km long and drains a basin area of 2,190 sq km (much of it swampy). Its waters are used for consumption and irrigation. Resorts are situated along the river's middle reaches.

Osada, Yakiv, b 30 September 1920 in Zhovta Rika, Verkhnodniprovske county, Katerynoslav gubernia, d 3 November 1979 in Moscow. Scientist in the field of ferrous metallurgy. He graduated from the Dnipropetrovske Metallurgical Institute (1941). He worked in Magnitogorsk and Pervouralsk, and in Dnipropetrovske at the All-Union Scientific Research and Construction Technology Institute of the Pipe Industry (1944–62, from 1950 as director). From 1962 he held industrial management positions in the State Planning Committee of the Ukrainian SSR and the USSR Ministry of Ferrous Metallurgy. His scientific contributions were in the areas of pipe manufacturing and stress analysis in steel pipes.

Osadca, Apollinare. See Osadtsa, Apolinarii.

Osadchuk, Bohdan [Osadčuk] (pseuds: O. Korab, Yu. Chornomorsky), b 1 August 1920 in Kolomyia, Galicia. Journalist and Sovietologist; member of the Shevchenko Scientific Society since 1985. Osadchuk studied at Berlin University (1941–5) and the Ukrainian Free University (UVU). He has been a regular contributor to several Ukrainian (eg, *Ukraïns'ki visti*) and non-Ukrainian newspapers in Western Europe, including the German *Die Neue Zeitung* and *Der Tagesspiegel* and the Swiss *Die Neue Zürcher Zeitung,* for which paper he served for many years as East European expert. His articles on the USSR and its satellite states gained him a reputation as a leading analyst of developments there, particularly the Polish crises of the 1970s and 1980s. Since 1958 he has taught Eastern European modern history at the Free University of Berlin, where he became a professor and director of its Institute of East European Studies in 1978. Osadchuk has also taught at the UVU and served as its dean of law and social sciences (1983–5) and prorector (since 1985). He is the author of *Die Entwicklung der Kommunistischen Parteien Ostmitteleuropas* (1962) and coeditor of *Der Sowjet-Kommunismus* (1964).

Osadchy, Mykhailo [Osadčyj, Myxajlo], b 22 March 1936 in Kurmany, now in Nedryhailiv raion, Sumy oblast. Poet, prose writer, and dissident; honorary member of the Swiss section of the PEN International Association of Poets,

Playwrights, Editors, Essayists, and Novelists since 1979. He graduated with a degree in journalism from Lviv University (1958), where he taught (1960–5) and then completed postgraduate studies (1965). He became active in the Ukrainian *dissident movement in the mid-1960s. Osadchy was arrested in 1965 for anti-Soviet activity and sentenced in 1966 to two years' imprisonment. In 1972 he was arrested again and sentenced to seven years of strict-regime labor camp and three years of exile. He served his term in camps in the Mordovian ASSR and was exiled to the Komi ASSR. His first collection of poetry, *Misiachne pole* (The Moonlit Field, 1965), was published before his arrest. His works were subsequently proscribed in the Ukrainian SSR, but his account of life in Soviet prisons, *Bil'mo* (Cataract, 1971), was published in the West and was translated into English (1976), French, and German. Other collections of his poetry include *Quos ego* (1979) and *Skyts'kyi oltar* (The Scythian Altar, 1990).

Tykhon Osadchy

Osadchy, Tykhon [Osadčyj, Tyxon], b 30 June 1866 in Budyshche, Zvenyhorodka county, Kiev gubernia, d 24 December 1945. Economist, statistician, and co-operative leader. Before the Revolution of 1917 he worked as a statistician with the Kherson and Simbirsk zemstvos (1890–7), served as secretary of an agricultural society in Kiev (1897–1904), and then taught school in the Kiev and Chernihiv regions. He was also active in community affairs, in organizing credit unions and co-operatives and teaching farming techniques. After 1917 he was a member of the central committee of the Peasant Association, a delegate to the Central Rada, and one of the organizers of the Tsentral union of agricultural co-operatives. His economic works included detailed studies of agriculture of the Shchyrbanivska volost in Kherson gubernia and the publicistic *Ukraïns'ke selianstvo ta ioho istorychna dolia* (The Ukrainian Peasantry and Its Historical Fate, 1912). Osadchy also wrote fiction idealizing the populist Ukrainian intelligentsia.

Osadtsa, Apolinarii [Osadca, Apolinarij] (Apollinare), b 12 November 1916 in Voloshchyna, Pidhaitsi county, Galicia. Architect and community figure. He studied at the Lviv Polytechnical Institute (1935–41) and worked as an architect in Lviv (to 1944) and New York City (from 1950). He designed many buildings in the United States, including Ukrainian Catholic churches in New York City, Astoria, Glen Spey (New York), and Passaic (New Jersey); the Sacred Heart Convent in Astoria; the Ukrainian Na-

St Volodymyr's Ukrainian Catholic Church in Glen Spey, New York (architect: Apolinarii Osadtsa)

tional Association building in Jersey City; the Ukrainian National Home and St Joseph's Roman Catholic Cathedral in Hartford, Connecticut; and numerous buildings at the University of Indiana in Bloomington. He has been active in various Ukrainian organizations, including the World Congress of Free Ukrainians, the Ukrainian Engineers' Society of America (vice-president), and the Dumka Chorus in New York (president, 1952–8).

Irma Osadtsa: *Talisman* (oil)

Osadtsa, Irma [Osadca], b 17 January 1949 in Erlangen, Germany. Painter of Ukrainian origin. Since 1950 she has lived in the United States, where she graduated from the Cleveland Institute of Art (1972) and the Yale University School of Art and Architecture (MFA, 1974). Since 1975 she has lived in Canada. She specializes in oil, acrylic, and watercolor abstract paintings. In the 1970s her compositions were marked by complex interlocking shapes of color. For the 'Talisman' series she borrowed from the rich symbolic vocabulary of the Ukrainian Easter egg. Solo exhibitions of her work have been held at Yale University (1974), the Ukrainian Institute of Modern Art in Chicago (1975), and in New York (1981) and Toronto (1981, 1983).

Rev Mykhailo Osadtsa

Gen Oleksander Osetsky

Osadtsa, Mykhailo [Osadca, Myxajlo], b 1836, d 1865. Greek Catholic priest and philologist. He studied under F. Miklosich at Vienna University and taught religion at the Academic Gymnasium in Lviv. He wrote in the *etymological spelling a Ruthenian (ie, Ukrainian) grammar for secondary schools (1862; 2nd edn 1864; 3rd 'Russophile' edn 1876, ed O. Lepky and H. Onyshkevych) based on the Galician vernacular.

Osaul or **osavul** (aide-de-camp). A military and administrative official in the *Hetman state. The hetman usually appointed two *general osauls as his closest military aides. Each Cossack regiment had two osauls who oversaw all regimental military matters (except the artillery), such as training, armaments, and supplies. In peacetime they took part in the civil administration of the regiment's territory. Company osauls had the same responsibilities on the company level. There were also osauls with special functions, such as the osaul of the state's General Artillery, who assisted the *general quartermaster, and the osauls of mercenary infantry regiments and companies. The *starshyna* of the Zaporozhian Host also included an osaul. After the abolition of the Hetman state and the Zaporozhian Sich the osauls of the Cossack regiments incorporated into the Russian imperial army were equal in rank to infantry captains and cavalry troop commanders.

Oselivka archeological site. A multi-occupational Stone Age settlement located on the Dniester River near Oselivka, Kelmentsi raion, Chernivtsi oblast. Excavations in the 1920s by Rumanian archeologists and in 1966–8 uncovered two Paleolithic settlements and a single Mesolithic occupation. In all three strata a wide variety of animal bones (mammoth, horses, deer) and flint pieces were found.

Osetsky, Oleksander [Osec'kyj], b 24 June 1873 in Kremianets, Volhynia gubernia, d 26 February 1937 in Paris. Senior UNR Army officer. In the First World War he commanded a regiment in the Russian army and reached the rank of brigadier general. In 1917 he joined the UNR Army, and he served as corps commander in the Poltava region,

commander of the Railroad Guard Corps under the Hetman regime, and commander of the Kholm Group on the Polish front in 1919. He was briefly (December 1918–January 1919) UNR minister of defense, and then acting UNR Army otaman. In 1920 he headed a UNR military-diplomatic mission to Belgium.

Oshawa. A city (1986 pop 204,000) on Lake Ontario 52 km east of Toronto. In 1986 there were 4,000 residents of Ukrainian origin in Oshawa. General Motors Corp has been the major employer there since 1918. Ukrainians were attracted to Oshawa by jobs in the automobile industry. A Prosvita reading society was established on the initiative of Yu. Kalynka in 1917, and by 1921 it had bought its own hall. In 1934 the society was reorganized into a branch of the Ukrainian National Federation (UNF). In the following year two affiliates of the federation were formed, the Ukrainian National Youth Federation, which set up a flying school (1937–9), and the Ukrainian Women's Organization. The UNF is still active in Oshawa and comes under the local branch of the Ukrainian Canadian Congress. There are two Ukrainian parishes, one Catholic and the other Orthodox, each with its own church.

Osherowitch, Mendl [Ošerovič] (Osherovitsch), b 1888 in Trostianets, Yampil county, Podilia gubernia, d 16 April 1965 in New York. Yiddish writer and journalist. He emigrated to the United States in 1909. From 1914 he was a staff member of the New York *Jewish Daily Forward*, in which he published many of his stories, articles, and criticism. A Ukrainophile, he headed the Association to Perpetuate the Memory of Ukrainian Jews and the Relief Committee for Jews in Ukraine. He wrote three novels in Yiddish, numerous plays, memoirs, and several works on Jewish history, including a book on the history of urban Jews in Ukraine (1948). He also edited a three-volume encyclopedic study of Jews in Ukraine (vol 1, 1961).

Osichny, Dmytro [Osičnyj], b 20 September 1885 in Kobaky, Kosiv county, Galicia, d 26 November 1962 in Kobaky. Writer. He began publishing in 1909. In the 1920s and early 1930s he contributed poetry to the Lviv Sovietophile journals *Vikna* and *Novi shliakhy*. Soviet editions of his poetry and prose were published in 1957, 1962, and 1973.

Osinchuk, Juliana [Osinčuk, Julijana], b 17 May 1953 in New York. Concert pianist, musicologist, and teacher; daughter of R. *Osinchuk. Her early musical training in-

Juliana Osinchuk

cluded instruction from R. Savytsky, N. Boulanger, and L. Talma. She later studied with R. Lhevinne and N. Reisenberg and completed a PHD in music from the Julliard School with a dissertation on V. *Kosenko. She has appeared as both soloist and chamber musician and on radio throughout Europe and the United States, notably at Lincoln Center's Alice Tully Hall (New York). She appears with symphony orchestras performing concertos by F. Liszt (no. 1), S. Rachmaninoff (no. 1), C. Saint-Saëns (no. 2), and G. Gershwin. Her Ukrainian repertoire consists of contemporary piano works, particularly by V. Kosenko. A number of these are featured on a phonodisc she released on the Orion label (1985).

Mykhailo Osinchuk: *Self-Portrait* (1958)   Roman Osinchuk

Osinchuk, Mykhailo [Osinčuk, Myxajlo], b 16 September 1890 in Holoshyntsi, Zbarazh county, Galicia, d 13 February 1969 in New York City. Painter and graphic artist; member of the Shevchenko Scientific Society; brother of R. *Osinchuk. A graduate of the Cracow Academy of Fine Arts and Cracow University (1914), he taught drawing at the Academic Gymnasium of Lviv (1921–6) and painted the murals in over 20 Galician churches (some with P. Kovzhun) and 10 iconostases in the neo-Byzantine style. He was a founding member and the first president of the *Association of Independent Ukrainian Artists and coedited its journal *Mystetstvo*. His book illustrations, woodcuts, and bookplates were similar in style to icons. During the Second World War he was a professor at the Academy of Arts in Lviv. A postwar émigré, from 1947 he lived in the United States, where he painted 4 Ukrainian churches and 10 iconostases. He also painted two churches in Toronto. He was an honorary member of the Ukrainian Artists' Association in the USA. He wrote several art monographs, including one on the icon.

Osinchuk, Roman [Osinčuk], b 5 July 1902 in Holoshyntsi, Zbarazh county, Galicia, d 11 February 1991 in New York. Physician and civic leader; brother of M. *Osinchuk; member of the Shevchenko Scientific Society and full member of the Ukrainian Academy of Arts and Sciences from 1942. A graduate of the Lviv (Underground) Ukrainian University and Lviv University (MD, 1931), he worked at the General Hospital, the Narodnia Lichnytsia hospital, and the Sheptytsky Ukrainian Hospi-

tal and ran an electrocardiograph station in Lviv. He was active in the Ukrainian Physicians' Society, a founding member of the Ukrainian Hygienic Society, and an editor of *Narodne zdorovlia*. During the Soviet occupation he was a section chief at the oblast health department and lectured at the Lviv Medical Institute. Under the Germans he was a member of the Ukrainian National Council and director of the State Medical Institute in Lviv (1941–2). After leaving Ukraine in 1944, he worked as a physician in Germany, and in 1947 he emigrated to the United States. He established his own office in New York and became active in various Ukrainian organizations, particularly medical ones. He founded the *Ukrainian Medical Association of North America and served as its president (1950–5) and editor of its journal *Likars'kyi visnyk*, which he founded in 1954. He was the first president of the World Federation of Ukrainian Medical Associations, which he also helped organize. His publications consist of over 250 popular articles on health care, over 40 scientific articles in clinical medicine, and a dozen articles on the history of Ukrainian medicine.

Osinsky, Valeriian [Osins'kij, Valerijan], b 10 November 1852 in Tahanrih, Don Cossack province, d 26 May 1879 in Kiev. Russian revolutionary. He studied at the St Petersburg Institute of Railway Engineers (1871–2) and worked as a zemstvo administrator. In 1875 he became active in the populist movement of P. Lavrov, but he was already an advocate of terrorism and soon became one of the leading members of Zemlia i Volia. He headed the (Southern) Executive Committee (a fictitious organization composed of himself and a few followers) of the Socialist Revolutionary party which directed terrorist attacks against tsarist officials in Kiev (including the procurator M. Kotliarevsky) and conducted the successful rescue of leading revolutionary activists (L. Deich, Ya. Stefanovych, and V. Bokhanovsky) from Lukianivka Prison in 1878. Osinsky was arrested in February 1879, sentenced by the court of the Kiev Military District, and hanged.

Osipovsky, Timofei [Osipovskij, Timofej], b 2 February 1765 in Osipovo, Vladimir gubernia, Russia, d 24 June 1832 in Moscow. Russian mathematician. After graduating from the St Petersburg Teachers' Seminary, he lectured at Kharkiv University (from 1805) and served as rector (1813–20). He was the author of a three-volume treatise *Kurs matematiki* (A Course in Mathematics, 1801–23), which covered function theory, differential equations, and variational calculus and was a basic university textbook for many years. He also worked in the fields of physics, astronomy, and philosophy. One of his students was M. *Ostrohradsky.

Oskil River (also Oskol). A left-bank tributary of the Donets River. It is 472 km long and drains a basin area of 14,800 sq km. The river flows through Kursk and Belgorod oblasts in the RF before running southward across the eastern end of Kharkiv oblast. It is generally 30–40 m wide and 2.5–3 m deep (maximum depth, approx 10 m). It is fed largely by meltwater and is frozen from November to March. A hydroelectric station is located on the lower course of the river together with the artificial lake, Chervonooskil Reservoir, created by the station. The largest Ukrainian center located along the river is the city of Kupianka.

Oskil River

Otaman Volodymyr Oskilko   Teodosii Osmachka

Oskilko, Volodymyr [Oskil'ko], b 1892 in Volhynia gubernia, d 26 May 1926 in Rivne, Volhynia. Civic leader and army officer. A school teacher by profession, he emerged in November 1918 as the chief organizer of anti-Hetman insurgency in Volhynia. At the beginning of 1919 he was appointed commander of the Northern Group of the UNR Army on the Bolshevik-Polish front. On 29 April 1919 he attempted an unsuccessful coup d'état against the UNR government in Rivne and fled to Poland. After returning to Rivne in the early 1920s, he edited the semiweekly *Dzvin* (1924–5), the organ of the Ukrainian People's party, which propagated a pro-Polish line, and wrote his memoirs, *Mizh dvoma svitamy* (Between Two Worlds, 1924). He was killed by unknown assassins.

Osmachka, Teodosii [Os'mačka, Teodosij], b 3 May 1895 in the village of Kutsivka, Cherkasy county, Kiev gubernia, d 7 September 1962 in Long Island, New York. Poet, novelist, and translator. Although his first poems were written in 1916, Osmachka began his literary career while he was a student at the Kiev Institute of People's Education from 1920 to 1923. He belonged to the literary organizations Aspys and Lanka (see *MARS), and published his first collection of poetry, *Krucha* (The Precipice), in 1922; it was followed by two more collections, *Skyts'ki vohni* (The Scythian Fires, 1925) and *Klekit* ([Crane's]

Clacking, 1929). Like other members of MARS he was attacked and arrested for his 'unpolitical' literary works, but managed to save himself from execution by feigning insanity. During the 1930s he faced constant persecution by the authorities and was unable to publish any works. During the Second World War he fled to Western Ukraine, then to DP camps in Germany, and finally to the United States. Osmachka's personal ordeal had lasting effects on him, and until his death he suffered from a persecution complex. Nonetheless he resumed his literary career in 1943 in Lviv with the publication of his fourth collection of poetry, *Suchasnykam* (To My Contemporaries). In the DP camps he published his epic poem, written in octaves, *Poet* (Poet, 1946), as well as his first prose work, *Starshyi boiaryn* (The Best Man, 1946). *Kytytsi chasu* (Bouquets of Time, 1953) and selected poems published as *Iz-pid svitu: poetychni tvory* (From under the World: Poetic Works, 1954) completed his poetic oeuvre, which is characterized by expressionistic imagery, frequent dumalike rhythms, and a ponderous tone. In his later prose Osmachka devoted himself to the portrayal of the meticulously planned genocidal destruction of Ukraine by the Soviet regime. *Plan do dvoru* (Annihilation, 1951) deals with the liquidation of the independent Ukrainian farmer, and Osmachka's most famous and powerful autobiographical work, *Rotonda dushohubtsiv* (The Rotunda of Assassins, 1956; published in English as *Red Assassins*, 1959), describes the destructive state – a machine for spiritual and physical annihilation – and shows that often the individual's only avenues of escape are death and madness. Besides some poems of G. Byron Osmachka translated O. Wilde's *The Ballad of Reading Gaol* (1958) and W. Shakespeare's *Macbeth* and *Henry IV* (1961). An edition of Osmachka's selected poetry appeared in Kiev in 1991.

D.H. Struk

Osmak, Vasyl [Os'mak, Vasyl'], b 1870 in Hoholiv, Oster county, Chernihiv gubernia, d 1942 in Kiev. Architect. A graduate of the St Petersburg Institute of Civil Engineering (1895), from 1899 he taught at the Kiev Polytechnical Institute. He codesigned important projects in Kiev, such as the Sadovsky Theater (1905, now the Kiev Operetta Theater), the buildings of the university library (1914–15, now the ANU Central Scientific Library), the humanities building at Kiev University (1932), the Dynamo Stadium (1934–5), and the landscaping of the Dnieper bank (1935–8).

Osmialovska, Kateryna [Osmjalovs'ka], b 26 November 1904 in Poltava. Stage and film actress. In 1921 she completed study at the Lysenko Music and Drama Institute in Kiev. Then she worked as an actress in the Shevchenko First Theater of the Ukrainian Soviet Republic (1920–5), the Donetske Ukrainian Drama Theater (1925–6), the Odessa Ukrainian Drama Theater (1926–30), and the Kiev Ukrainian Drama Theater (1930–63). She also acted in the films *Perekop* (1930) and *Natalka Poltavka* (Natalka from Poltava, 1936–45; voice by M. Lytvynenko-Volgemut).

Osnova (Foundation). A society of Ukrainian students attending the Lviv Polytechnic, organized by V. Dydynsky in 1897. Its presidents included Dydynsky, T. Melen, P. Durbak, and P. Volosenko. Its activities declined during the First World War and were restricted afterwards. From

1921 to 1925 the society operated without legal status at the Lviv (Underground) Ukrainian University and Lviv (Underground) Ukrainian Higher Polytechnical School. In 1926–7 it obtained legal status at the Lviv Polytechnic. In 1928 its membership exceeded 300. With the Soviet invasion of Galicia in 1939, its activities ceased. Under the German occupation the society functioned as a section of the Labor Alliance of Ukrainian Students.

Osnova (St Petersburg)

Osnova (Foundation). A Ukrainian journal published in St Petersburg from January 1861 to October 1862 (a total of 22 issues) by V. *Bilozersky. It had a major influence on the development of Ukrainian national consciousness and Ukrainian literature in the 1860s. Bilozersky, his brother-in-law, P. *Kulish, and M. *Kostomarov were the editors; O. Kistiakovsky was the assistant editor and secretary; and D. Kamenetsky (the director of P. Kulish's printery, which printed Osnova) and M. Shcherbak were the managers. Osnova united Ukrainophile writers and scholars in the common goal of substantiating the Ukrainians' right to develop fully and independently as a people. It published prose, poetry, folklore, and ethnographic studies in Ukrainian and historical, literary, polemical, economic, pedagogical, and musicological articles, memoirs, diaries, correspondence, news, bibliographies, and reviews mostly in Russian.

Works by over 40 belletrists appeared in Osnova, notably T. Shevchenko (over 70 poems, including the narratives 'Ivan Hus' [Jan Hus] and 'Neofity' [Neophytes], and the play 'Nazar Stodolia'), L. Hlibov, P. Hulak-Artemovsky, O. Storozhenko, S. Rudansky, O. Konysky, O. Afanasiev-Chuzhbynsky, S. Pysarevsky, D. Mordovets, H. Barvinok, M. Vovchok, Ya. Kukharenko, M. Aleksandrovych, V. Kokhovsky, O. Navrotsky, V. Kulyk, P. Kuzmenko, D. Moroz, B. Poznansky, and M. Verbytsky. M. Kostomarov, P. Kulish, A. Svydnytsky, M. Nomys, S. Nis, P. Yefymenko, and I. Rudchenko, besides their own work, provided ethnographic materials. M. Maksymovych, P. Lavrovsky, O. Kotliarevsky, and M. Hattsuk contributed essays on the Ukrainian language. The right to public education in Ukrainian and the need for a broad network of Ukrainian-language elementary schools and textbooks and educational literature in Ukrainian were advocated by P. Chubynsky, B. Poznansky, M. Levchenko, and particularly Kulish.

Kulish wrote most of the literary criticism and critically evaluated the Cossack era in an essay that was planned as the preface to a book on the history of Ukraine. He also wrote articles on the hetmancies of B. Khmelnytsky and I. Vyhovsky, and in five 'Letters from the Khutir' he condemned the culture of Ukraine's Russified towns and idealized the Ukrainian peasants' ways of life. In a historical essay on the traits of the 'South Russian' people, Kostomarov elaborated a new approach to Ukrainian historiography and a methodology for studying the history of the Ukrainian people. In essays entitled 'The Federative Principle in Ancient Rus'' and 'Two Rus' Peoples' he delineated the Ukrainians' independent historical and cultural development vis-à-vis that of the Russians and Poles.

Kulish, Kostomarov, O. Lazarevsky, T. Rylsky, P. Zhytetsky, and H. Ge contributed polemical articles in which they discussed concepts such as the family, kinship, the nation and the state, the social estates, the Ukrainian national psyche, Ukrainian-Russian and Ukrainian-Polish relations, the peasant emancipation and reforms, and other current issues. V. Antonovych contributed a 'confession' in which he elaborated the principles of the *khlopomany. Articles on Ukrainian folk music were written by A. Serov. Kulish, V. Mezhov, and M. Mizko contributed to the bibliographic section. Osnova also published valuable historical documents and T. Shevchenko's diary, some of his correspondence, and memoirs of him. A news section provided information on attitudes among the peasantry and on economic matters. An album of L. Zhemchuzhnikov's engravings of Ukrainian scenes was published as a separate appendix.

The Russian press (except for Otechestvennye zapiski and Sovremennik) reacted antagonistically to Osnova, particularly to Kulish's and Kostomarov's claim that the Ukrainians have a distinct language and should have their own literature. Plagued by disagreements, denunciations for fomenting separatism, police harassment, censorship, a drop in subscriptions, and financial difficulties, the editors were forced to cease publication.

BIBLIOGRAPHY
Zhyvotko, A. Zhurnal 'Osnova' 1861–1862 (Kiev 1938)
Bernshtein, M. Zhurnal 'Osnova' i ukraïn'kyi literaturnyi protses kintsia 50-kh–60-kh rokiv XIX st. (Kiev 1959)

Osnova (Foundation). A populist newspaper published semiweekly in Lviv from October 1870 to December 1872 (a total of 90 issues). Founded by Yu. Lavrivsky and edited by T. Leontovych and then K. Klymkovych, it promoted political co-operation between the Poles and Ukrainians in Galicia. Regular contributors were S. Kachala, Yu. Lavrivsky, V. Shashkevych, O. Partytsky, and N. Vakhnianyn.

Osnova (Foundation). A semimonthly illustrated journal published in 1906–13 in Lviv. Until July 1908 it was a journal of politics, education, and economics intended for a broad peasant readership. The editors were Rev Ya. Levytsky and A. Veretelnyk. After a brief interruption it reappeared in January 1909 as a 'Christian periodical' devoting considerable attention to church affairs in addition to politics and popular education. Levytsky remained publisher and editor until 1913, when the Society of St Paul the Apostle became the publisher and Rev M. Hornykevych became editor.

Osnova (Foundation). A monthly journal of literature, scholarship, and community affairs, published in Odessa in August–October 1915 in place of *Literaturno-naukovyi vistnyk*, which was banned by the military authorities. Three issues appeared before it too was closed down. The managing editor was I. Havryliuk, and the journal's contributors were prominent Ukrainian cultural and scholarly figures.

Osnova Union of Ukrainian Students in Danzig (Soiuz ukrainskykh studentiv 'Osnova' v Dantsigu). An organization founded in October 1922 by Ukrainians studying at the Polytechnical Institute in Danzig (see *Gdańsk). In 1924 Osnova had 123 members. It was soon eclipsed by new Ukrainian student fraternities (Halych, Zarevo, and Chornomore), and functioned largely as a loose federation of those groups and local political student groups. Osnova ran a student center and refectory and remained active until March 1945. It was affiliated with the *Central Union of Ukrainian Students (it hosted its first congress in 1923), the *Union of Ukrainian Student Organizations in Germany and Danzig, and the *Nationalist Organization of Ukrainian Students in Germany (from 1942). Osnova's presidents were, in chronological order, Yu. Yaremkevych, I. Trach, M. Yarymovych, M. Bukoiemsky, S. Pyndus, S. Shmatera, Ya. Mokhnatsky, T. Hrushkevych, M. Rakovsky, R. Zahaikevych, S. Genyk-Berezovsky, Ya. Yendyk, D. Borynets, R. Stakhiv, and M. Vykrykach.

Osnovianenko, Hrytsko. See Kvitka-Osnovianenko, Hryhorii.

Ossetes (Osetyntsi). A nation numbering 598,000, according to the 1989 Soviet census. Most Ossetes live in the North Ossetian AR (335,000) of the RF and the South Ossetian Autonomous Oblast (65,000) in Georgia. Many live in Stavropol krai (especially the Karachai-Cherkess Autonomous Oblast), and a few live in Ukraine (6,300). The Ossetes are descended from a mixture of aboriginal peoples, Scythians, Sarmatians, and Alans. Their language belongs to the Iranian group of the Indo-European family and is descended from the Scythian and Alanian languages. The oldest record of the language is from 941. The Ossetes have a rich oral tradition, which encompasses heroic fables, stories, songs, proverbs, and anecdotes. Literary ties between the Ossetes and Ukrainians date from the 19th century. Ossetian works have been translated into Ukrainian; the works of T. Shevchenko, I. Franko, M. Kotsiubynsky, P. Tychyna, and V. Sosiura have been published in Ossetian.

Ossolineum Institute. A library and publishing house situated in Lviv (1827–1940) and then (after 1946) Wrocław. It was established as a result of a bequest by J. Ossoliński (d 1817), who donated his private library and set aside funds for the creation of a public institution in Lviv. It served as a regional scholarly library for Galicia. In addition to Polish, German, and other collections it had valuable material on the history and culture of Ukraine (including antiquarian manuscripts, archival materials on the history of Ukrainian cities, and original copies of universals issued by Ukrainian hetmans). In 1940 the Ossolineum collection was incorporated into the library of the

Ossolineum Institute (lithograph by K. Auer, 1846–7)

ANURSR (now ANU) along with those of several other libraries. In 1946 the Ukrainian SSR handed over the main portion of the Ossolineum collection to Poland. It provided the basis for the creation of a new Ossolineum library in Wrocław, which collects books and manuscripts in the humanities that pertain to Poland, particularly Silesia. By an oversight, a mistake, or malicious intent the most valuable sources for Ukrainian history were also passed on to Wrocław. The publishing house has become a separate institution and is run by the Polish Academy of Sciences.

Ossoliński, Jerzy, b 15 December 1595 in Sandomierz, Poland, d 9 August 1650 in Warsaw. Polish statesman and diplomat. After completing his studies in France and Italy, he was a court functionary, adviser to Władysław IV Vasa, and vice-chancellor (1638) and chancellor (1643) of the Polish Commonwealth. Throughout the 1640s he maintained a relationship with the Ukrainian statesman A. *Kysil, whom he provided with access to his inner circles of power while benefiting from his knowledge of Ukrainian affairs and status as an acceptable mediator in disputes. Ossoliński was involved in negotiations to establish a new (Uniate) church union, as well as a scheme to create a broad-based coalition against the Turks and Tatars, in which the Ukrainian Cossacks were to play a vital role. In May 1648 Ossoliński assumed effective interregnum control of the Commonwealth and became a key figure in determining the Polish strategy in the *Cossack-Polish War. Although his efforts in obtaining a negotiated settlement initially failed, in the spring of 1649 he managed to sever the alliance between Hetman B. Khmelnytsky and the Tatar khan Girei and thus brought about the Treaty of *Zboriv.

Ossowski, Gotfryd, b 1835 in Kozarynivka, Kiev gubernia, d 1897 in Tomsk, Siberia. Polish geologist and archeologist. A founding member of the Volhynia Research Society, he worked in Volhynia gubernia and wrote a geological survey of it (1867) and a travel account of Zhytomyr and Ovruch counties (1868). He also prepared a geological (1880) and an archeological (1881) map of Volhynia. He identified the location of various useful minerals. After moving to Cracow he conducted a number of expeditions in western Podilia and wrote a geological and paleontological description of the caves in Volhynia and Galicia (1892). In 1892 he began to study Siberia, where he died during an expedition.

Ostafiichuk, Ivan [Ostafijčuk], b 28 July 1940 in Trostianets, now in Sniatyn raion, Ivano-Frankivske oblast. Graphic artist and painter. A graduate of the Lviv Insti-

Ivan Ostafiichuk: *To Each His Own* (ink drawing, 1977)

Emily Ostapchuk   Yatsko Ostapchuk

tute of Applied and Decorative Arts (1966), he has worked in a variety of print techniques. Linearity and decorativeness predominate in his early linocuts (eg, his series inspired by the writings of V. Stefanyk, 1969). Partially modeled areas and images of the fantastic dominate in his lithograph series 'Hutsul Legends.' The Ukrainian roots of his art are seen in his themes and in the way he has transformed Ukrainian folk and artistic traditions and enriched them with elements of contemporary art. In 1979 his 'Ukrainian Folk Songs' monoprint series received the gold medal at the 9th Biennale of Graphic Art in Brno, Czechoslovakia. Since 1982 Ostafiichuk has worked in an expressionist manner (eg, his paintings *Summer* [1985] and *Self-Portrait* [1986]). He has illustrated poetry collections by D. Pavlychko (1987), L. Kostenko (1987), and I. Drach (1988). Since emigrating to Toronto in 1988, he has had solo exhibitions in Canada and the United States and has illustrated a poetry collection by S. Sapeliak (1989) and the story collection *The Parcel from Chicken Street* (1989) by L. Bereshko (pseud of F. Ponomarenko).

D. Zelska-Darewych

Ostanni novyny (Latest News). A daily newspaper for Ukrainian displaced persons published in Salzburg, Austria, from September 1945 to 1949. It was edited by P. Sahaidachny with the assistance of Yu. Klen and L. Mosendz, and carried a weekly literary addition, *Novi dni*.

Ostapchuk, Emily [Ostapčuk, Emelija] (née Andrusiv), b 13 December 1919 in Radway, Alberta, d 16 November 1984 in St Catharines, Ontario. Community and civic leader; wife of P. Ostapchuk. A popular figure on the Ukrainian stages of Canada, she studied commerce at Ryerson College in Toronto in the 1950s and then moved to Vancouver. She organized community activities in that city, served as the longtime head of the provincial representation of the Ukrainian Canadian Committee (now Congress), and involved herself extensively in civic affairs. In 1976 she was awarded the Order of Canada.

Ostapchuk, Pylyp [Ostapčuk] (pseud: P. Pylypenko), b 29 October 1899 in Vinnytsia, Podilia gubernia, d 1965 in Toronto. Stage actor, director, and playwright. From 1928 he lived in Winnipeg, where he worked as a stage director

at the Winnipeg Prosvita and toured (from 1952) with his troupe, performing Ukrainian plays. He is the author of several plays, among them *Smert' komisara Skrypnyka, abo Holod na Ukraïni* (The Death of Commissar Skrypnyk, or Famine in Ukraine), *Halychyna v ohni (Patsyfikatsiia)* (Galicia in Flames [Pacification]), and *V pazurakh Cheka* (In the Claws of the Cheka). He also published a book, *Narodne mystetstvo Zakarpattia* (Folk Art of Transcarpathian Ukraine).

Ostapchuk, Yatsko [Ostapčuk, Jacko], b 4 January 1873 in Lubianky Nyzhchi, Zbarazh county, Galicia, d 30 January 1959 in Uzhhorod, Transcarpathia oblast. Civic and political leader. A member of the Ukrainian Radical party and then of the Ukrainian Social Democratic party, he was a deputy to the Austrian parliament (1907–11). In 1912 he moved to Transcarpathia. During the First World War he was active in the Union for the Liberation of Ukraine at the POW internment camp in Freistadt (Austria). In 1918–19 he was a member of the Ukrainian National Rada. In 1920 he helped found the Ukrainian Social Democratic party in Transcarpathia and served as its president. With the Hungarian invasion of the region he fled to Czechoslovakia.

Ostapenko, Petro, b 9 July 1922 in Myroliubivka, Skvyra county, Kiev gubernia. Sculptor. He studied under Yu. Bilostotsky and E. Fridman. His works include portraits of M. Rylsky (1936), K. Briullov (1960–1), and O. Shlikhter (1970); the monument to T. Shevchenko in Zvenyhorodka, Cherkasy oblast (1964, cocreator); and Rylsky's burial monument (1969, cocreator).

Ostapenko, Serhii, b and d ? Economist and political leader from Volhynia. Until 1917 he was a lecturer at the Kiev Commercial Institute. After the Revolution of 1917 he was a delegate to the Central Rada from the Ukrainian Party of Socialist Revolutionaries, an economic adviser to the UNR delegation at the negotiations of the Peace Treaty of Brest-Litovsk (1918), minister of trade and industry in the Council of National Ministers of the UNR under the Directory (December 1918 to February 1919), and prime minister of the UNR (February–April 1919). Under his leadership the UNR government was less partisan than under other prime ministers, and tried, albeit unsuccessfully,

Serhii Ostapenko

o negotiate with the Entente powers. After the victory of he Bolsheviks Ostapenko remained in Ukraine. He was probably arrested in 1931, but his fate is unknown. His economic writings deal mostly with foreign trade, especially trade in agricultural products. He wrote mostly popular and publicistic works, including textbooks on the economic geography of Ukraine and political economy.

Ostarbeiter (eastern workers). The German term for several million civilians from the 'conquered eastern territories' taken to Germany for forced labor during the Second World War. The recruitment of workers was not part of the Germans' preinvasion planning, but it began, in November 1941, when it had become apparent that there would be no quick victory on the eastern front. The head of the Nazi Four-Year Plan, H. Göring, issued instructions in that month to the effect that 'Russian' workers should be used for Germany's benefit. In the same month the labor office of the Distrikt Galizien reported that 60,709 workers had been sent to Germany. At the beginning of 1942 a campaign was instituted under the auspices of the Four-Year Plan to supply 380,000 laborers for German agriculture and 247,000 for German industry. On 21 March F. Sauckel was appointed plenipotentiary general for labor allocation (Generalbevollmächtigter für den Arbeitseinsatz, or GBA); he became Göring's subordinate in charge of recruiting 'all available manpower, including foreigners and prisoners of war,' to work in German industry and thereby allow the release of Germans for the war effort. Ukraine was by far the most important source of *Ostarbeiter*: of the approx 2.8 million civilians deported to Germany in 1941–4, about 2.2 million were from Ukraine.

Initially many Ukrainians greeted the Germans as liberators from Soviet rule, and 80 percent of the first labor quotas were filled by volunteers. But the brutal treatment of the volunteers, who were packed into freight cars without food or sanitary facilities, soon became known in Ukraine. By the summer of 1942 there were no more volunteers. With their increasing appetite for manpower, the Germans resorted to forcible means of recruitment. People were rounded up arbitrarily to make up the quotas imposed by the GBA. Towns and villages were ordered to register the able-bodied and to supply quotas of workers; those who failed to report for duty were subject to confiscation of grain and property, the burning down of their houses and villages, and incarceration in concentration camps. Official reports and German soldiers' letters to rel-

atives described the beatings and mistreatment of *Ostarbeiter* as everyday occurrences in Ukraine. Families were often separated, and relatives who tried to give departing workers food and clothing were brutally thrust aside. All that helped to turn popular sentiment decisively against the Germans and encouraged those who faced deportation to join the Soviet partisans or the Ukrainian Insurgent Army. The return of disabled *Ostarbeiter* to Ukraine – the seriously ill, injured, or undernourished, who could not usefully contribute to the war effort – intensified anti-German feelings. Throughout 1942 and 1943 the forced requisition of workers in Ukraine took a dreadful toll in manpower. In Kiev, for example, instructions were given in April 1942 to round up 20,000 workers aged 16 to 55. In September 1942 part of the city was cordoned off, and all unemployed able-bodied inhabitants were pressed into service. By the summer of 1943, 440,000 workers had been deported from the greater Kiev area, with the result that German security police protested there were not enough workers left to gather the harvest.

Irrational aspects of Nazi policy lessened the effectiveness of *Ostarbeiter* recruitment. Tens of thousands of workers were brought to Germany only to be sent back when they were found unsuitable for employment. A report from Kharkiv dated October 1942 pointed out that specialist workers were being forced to leave Ukraine without proper clothing and were being beaten so severely that they were unfit for work. A. Hitler's scheme of recruiting half a million Ukrainian women 'capable of being Germanized' as domestic workers failed to yield the expected results: Sauckel was able to bring in only 15,000. In Germany *Ostarbeiter* were treated worse than forced laborers from other German-occupied countries. Ukrainians from the *Reichskommissariat Ukraine were not recognized as Ukrainian nationals, a status accorded only to those from the Distrikt Galizien. Every effort was made to isolate the *Ostarbeiter* from the German population and from workers of other nationalities by placing them in closed residences. So great was the fear of 'pollution' by the easterners, whom Nazi propaganda described as subhuman, that the death penalty was instituted for sexual intercourse with them, and for numerous other offenses. Every article of clothing *Ostarbeiter* wore had to be be identified with an 'Ost' badge. Whereas the average German industrial worker earned 3.50 reichsmarks (RM) per day, an *Ostarbeiter* earned 2.30, 1.50 of which was deducted for room and board; *Ostarbeiter* working in agriculture averaged a net wage of 3 RM per week. *Ostarbeiter* received smaller food rations than other foreign workers. German maternity laws did not apply to female *Ostarbeiter*, and their children received half the rations allocated to German children. Most *Ostarbeiter* worked in private enterprises but were kept under close surveillance by the German police and the SS. Those caught trying to escape were sent to *concentration camps or killed. In the autumn of 1942, officials of the Ostministerium began to complain that the brutal treatment of *Ostarbeiter* was turning the population against the Germans, and military officers warned that it was leading to an increase in the number of anti-German partisans. The criticism resulted in a slight improvement in the status of the *Ostarbeiter*: their take-home wages were raised to 1.14 RM, a 20 percent rebate of taxes on wages was accorded for excellent work, and a central inspection agency was created to supervise working conditions.

Despite official rhetoric urging better treatment of *Ost-arbeiter* and a growing tendency to equalize their status with that of other foreign workers, measures designed to assist them depended on the goodwill of German employers and were hampered by wartime conditions. The productivity of *Ostarbeiter* labor was strikingly high. According to a comprehensive survey conducted in 1944, the productivity of male workers was 60–80 percent of that of their German counterparts, and that of female workers attained a level of 90–100 percent. After the war most Ukrainian *Ostarbeiter* in occupied Germany were forcibly repatriated to the USSR, where many were victimized for having 'betrayed the Fatherland' by allowing themselves to be captured. (See also *Nazi war crimes in Ukraine and *Repatriation.)

BIBLIOGRAPHY
Dallin, A. *German Rule in Russia, 1941–1945: A Study of Occupation Policies* (London and New York 1957; London 1981)
Homze, E. *Foreign Labor in Nazi Germany* (Princeton 1967)
Herbert, U. *A History of Foreign Labor in Germany, 1880–1980: Seasonal Workers/Forced Laborers/Guest Workers* (Ann Arbor 1990)
                                                        M. Yurkevich

Ostashchenko-Kudriavtsev, Borys [Ostaščenko-Kudrjavcev], b 9 January 1877 in St Petersburg, d 1 October 1956 in Kharkiv. Astronomer and geodesist. He graduated from St Petersburg University (1898) and worked as an astronomer at the Pulkovo Observatory until 1909, when he became a research associate at the Mykolaiv Observatory. From 1923 he worked at the Kharkiv Observatory and taught at institutes of higher learning in that city. His contributions were in the areas of astronomy and geodesy, particularly the application of projection methods in cartography.

Roman Ostashewsky   Yakiv Ostrianyn

Ostashewsky, Roman [Ostaševs'kyj], b 19 April 1924 in Kurnyky, Ternopil county, Galicia, d 26 February 1983 in Edmonton. Museum director and community leader. Ostashewsky was educated at the University of Rome (B PHIL, 1947; B TH, 1950), McGill University (BLS, 1963), and the University of Denver (Dip in Archival Adm, 1967). After emigrating to Canada in 1951, he worked in the Edmonton Public Library (1959–66) and was a senior archivist in the provincial archives of Alberta. In 1975 he

was appointed director of the *Ukrainian Cultural Heritage Village. He was on the national executive of the Ukrainian National Federation (UNO) after 1975, organized and participated in plays and literary readings, and produced and hosted the weekly Ukrainian television program 'Kontakt' in Edmonton. He was awarded the Order of Canada in 1979.

Ostaszewski, Spirydion, b 1797 in Antonivka, Lypovets county, Kiev gubernia, d 25 April 1875 in Avratyn, Zhytomyr county, Volhynia gubernia. Polish Ukrainophile writer. He devoted himself to collecting and studying local folklore and folkways. Influenced by the burlesque writings of I. Kotliarevsky and P. Hulak-Artemovsky, he wrote and published in the Polish alphabet a collection of 29 Ukrainian versified folk fables, *Piw kop kazok ... dla wesełoho myra* (A Score and a Half Tales ... for a Merry World, 1850; pub in Cyrillic by V. Shchurat in 1910). Using the *hrazhdanka alphabet, he published a revised version, *Piw sotni kazok dlia veselykh liudei* (One Half Hundred Tales for Merry People, 1869). A posthumous Ukrainian version, *Sto baiok ... dlia ruskoho myra ...* (One Hundred Fables ... for the Ruthenian World), appeared in Lviv in 1888. He also translated Polish poetry into Ukrainian and wrote on girls' education and Polish history.

Oster. III-11. A town (1990 pop 8,400) on the Desna River in Kozelets raion, Chernihiv oblast. It is first mentioned in the chronicles under the year 1098 as a fortress belonging to Pereiaslav principality. It was built by Volodymyr Monomakh and called Horodets. In 1240 it was destroyed by the Tatars, and it remained in ruins for a century. In 1569 the town was transferred from Lithuanian to Polish rule. In 1648 it became a company center of Pereiaslav regiment. In 1662 Oster obtained the rights of *Magdeburg law, and in 1803 it became a county center of Chernihiv gubernia. Today Oster is a river port with a cotton-textile factory and a food industry. Some parts of the old fortress and St Michael's Church (aka Yurii's Temple), built in 1098, have been preserved.

Oster Drainage System. A canal system covering 34,200 ha of the Oster River floodplains in Chernihiv oblast. It was built in three stages in 1928–55 and was reconstructed in 1960–1 and 1964–8. The system consists of the regulated riverbed of the Oster River itself (207 km), 673 km of open canals, and 246 locks. Excess water is pumped into the Trubizh Drainage and Irrigation System. The drained lands are cultivated or used as pasture.

Oster River. A left-bank tributary of the Desna River. It is 199 km long and drains a basin area of 2,970 sq km. It flows westward through the south-central part of Chernihiv oblast. A drainage system has been built along the marshy waterway. The river, which is fed mainly by meltwater, freezes at the end of November and thaws in March. The settlements located along the Oster include Nizhen, Kozelets, and Oster.

Osteuropäische Korrespondenz. A German-language bulletin published semimonthly and weekly in Berlin in 1924–30. Edited by V. Kuchabsky and then Z. Kuzelia (1926–30), it informed the German public and media about Ukrainian affairs. The bulletin was funded by the

German government and the clandestine Ukrainian Military Organization.

Ostrenko, Viktor, b 10 April 1917 in Katerynoslav (now Dnipropetrovske). Metallurgist; corresponding member of the AN URSR (now ANU) since 1978. He graduated from the Dnipropetrovske Metallurgical Institute (1941), and since 1947 he has worked at the All-Union (until 1992) Scientific Research and Construction Technology Institute of the Pipe Industry in Dnipropetrovske. His main contributions are in the development of the theory and production of seamless pipes.

Ostrianyn, Danylo [Ostrjanyn], b 30 December 1906 in Bilske, Zinkiv county, Poltava gubernia, d 17 May 1988 in Kiev. Philosopher; corresponding member of the AN URSR (now ANU) from 1957. After graduating from the Ukrainian Institute of Communist Education in Kharkiv (1929) he lectured on Marxism-Leninism at postsecondary schools in Kharkiv. In 1952 he moved to Kiev to direct the ANU Institute of Philosophy (to 1962); he chaired its Department of the History of Ukrainian Philosophical and Sociological Thought (1955–63) and the departments of philosophy (1963–69) and the history of philosophy (1969–75) at Kiev University. He wrote numerous works in the history of philosophy in Ukraine, the history of science, and the philosophy of science; edited over 60 monographs and collections of essays; and produced books in Ukrainian on religion and its 'reactionary role' (1955), M. Maksymovych's worldview (1960), and materialist philosophy in Ukraine (1971), and books in Russian on I. Mechnikov (2 vols, 1953) and materialism and dialectics in Russian imperial natural science in the 18th and 19th centuries (1984). He oversimplified the development of philosophy as a struggle between idealism and materialism and exaggerated the materialistic elements in the thought of many thinkers. A biobibliography appeared in 1987.

Ostrianyn, Yakiv [Ostrjanyn, Jakiv], b ?, d ca 6 May 1641. Zaporozhian hetman and leader of the Cossack rebellion of 1638. During the Polish-Muscovite War of 1634 he took part in battles in the Novhorod-Siverskyi region as a colonel of registered Cossacks. He participated in the 1637 rebellion led by P. *Pavliuk, and after the Battle of *Kumeiky he fled to the Zaporozhian Sich, where he was elected hetman of the nonregistered Cossacks in the spring of 1638. Ostrianyn, K. *Skydan, and D. *Hunia renewed the anti-Polish rebellion in Right- and Left-Bank Ukraine. On 15 May 1638 Ostrianyn's forces routed S. Potocki's Polish army at Hovtva, between Kremenchuk and Poltava. The Poles retreated and then regrouped and attacked the encamped rebels on 13 June at Zhovnyne. Ostrianyn and some 1,000 of his followers fled to Slobidska Ukraine, and left Hunia to continue the battle for several weeks. Ostrianyn settled near Chuhuiv. He was murdered by former supporters.

Ostrih or **Ostroh.** III-7. A city (1990 pop 13,100) at the junction of the Viliia and the Horyn rivers and a raion center in Rivne oblast. It is first mentioned in the Hypatian Chronicle under the year 1100. In the second half of the 14th century it came under Lithuanian rule. From 1386 Ostrih belonged to the Ostrozky family, who built a castle and the Church of the Epiphany and established Ostrih as

Castle ruins and the Epiphany Church in Ostrih

an important cultural, religious, and economic center. In 1528 it was granted the rights of *Magdeburg law. Until 1630 the town was a leading center of Ukrainian Orthodoxy: in the 1570s an academy and a printing press were set up, and in 1581 an improved translation of the Bible was published there. As the Roman Catholic movement and the state's policy of Polonization increased in strength, Ostrih lost its cultural and religious role. It was captured by B. Khmelnytsky in 1648, and the castle and church were destroyed in the process. In the second half of the 17th century Ostrih became the property of the Zaslawski, the Wiśniowiecki (in 1673), and finally the Sanguszko (in 1700) families. In 1793, with the partition of Poland, it was transferred to Russia, and became a county center in Volhynia gubernia. Today the town has a dairy, a sugar refinery, a cannery, a brewery, an asphalt and brick factory, and a railway-track repair plant. Its architectural monuments include the remains of the castle (14th–16th century), the 15th-century Church of the Epiphany (rebuilt in the 16th and restored in the 19th century), a 17th-century synagogue, and a 19th-century academy complex.

Ostrih Academy (Ostrozka shkola or Ostrozka akademiia). A postsecondary institution founded in Ostrih, Volhynia, ca 1576 by Prince K. *Ostrozky. At a time when Catholicism was making inroads into Western Ukraine, the academy was a bastion of Orthodoxy and maintained the traditional orientation toward Constantipole. Though the Ostrih Academy did not develop into a Western European–style university, as Ostrozky had hoped, it was the foremost Orthodox academy of its time. The curriculum consisted of Church Slavonic, Greek, Latin, theology, philosophy, medicine, natural science, and the classical free studies (mathematics, astronomy, grammar, rhetoric, and logic). In addition the academy was renowned for choral singing, and developed the *ostrozkyi napiv*. The academy was closely affiliated with the *Ostrih Press. The first rector of the academy was the writer H. *Smotrytsky. The instructors, many of whom had been invited from Constantinople, included the pseudonymous *Ostrozkyi Kliryk, the Greek C. *Lucaris, J. Latos, a philosopher and mathematician from Cracow University, and Y. *Boretsky, who later became rector of the Lviv Dormition Brotherhood School and then metropolitan of Kiev. Hetman P. Sahaidachny, the writer and scholar M. Smotrytsky, and several other prominent political and cultural leaders studied at the academy. With the founding of a rival Jesuit college in Ostrih in 1624, the academy went into decline, and by 1636 it had ceased to exist. The example set by the Ostrih Academy had an enduring influence on pedagogical thought and the organization of schools in Ukraine and provided a model for the *brotherhood schools that were later founded in Lviv, Lutske, Volodymyr-Volynskyi, Vilnius, and Brest.

BIBLIOGRAPHY
Myts'ko, I. (comp). *Materialy do istoriï Ostroz'koï akademiï (1576–1636): Biobibliohrafichnyi dovidnyk* (Kiev 1990)
Myts'ko, I. *Ostroz'ka slov'iano-hreko-latyns'ka akademiia (1576–1636)* (Kiev 1990)

C. Freeland

Ostrih Bible (frontispiece)

Ostrih Bible (Ostrozka Bibliia). The first full Church Slavonic edition of the canonical Old and New Testaments and the first three books of the Maccabees, printed in Ostrih in 1580–1 by I. *Fedorovych (Fedorov) in 1,500–2,000 copies. The preparation of the text and the printing were funded by Prince K. *Ostrozky. With close to 1,400 headpieces, initials, and tailpieces, the 628-folio book is one of the finest examples of printing in late 16th-century Ukraine. The text was based on all the Church Slavonic and Greek sources of the Bible (including the complete 1499 Bible of Archbishop Gennadii of Novgorod) collected by Ostrozky. The Old Testament sources were verified against the Septuagint or translated anew (sometimes incorrectly) by scholars directed by H. *Smotrytsky at the Ostrih Academy. The Bible includes Ostrozky's and Smotrytsky's prefaces, Smotrytsky's heraldic verses dedicated to Ostrozky, and Fedorovych's postscript. Its orthography, phonetics, and morphology are a mixture of Middle Bulgarian and East Slavic. The Russian stresses in its vocabulary were most likely introduced by Fedorovych. The Bible was reprinted with minor revisions in a unified orthography in Moscow in 1663. The text was later corrected by a group of scholars under the direction of Ye. Slavynetsky and then by Ya. Blonnitsky and V. Liashchevsky, and served after the abolition of Vulgata textual elements as the basis of the Synodal (Elizabethan) Bible of 1751 and many subsequent Church Slavonic printings. P. Berynda

studied the text of the Ostrih Bible and used material from it for his lexicon (1627). Initial psalms from it were transliterated to the Latin alphabet as examples of Old Slavonic by the Czech M. Filonomos-Benešovský (1587) and the Pole L. Górnicki (1594). A photofacsimile of the Bible was published in Winnipeg in 1983.

Ostrih Chronicle (Ostroz'kyi litopysets'). A chronicle of the years 1500–1636 in Galicia and Volhynia, compiled in the late 1630s. Events up to 1598 were taken from M. *Bielski's Polish chronicle, but the events of 1599–1636 are based on the observations of an unknown author and other eyewitness accounts. The chronicle describes various Cossack wars, Turkish and Tatar attacks on Ukraine, and significant cultural and religious events during the period of struggle between the Orthodox and Uniate churches. Because much attention is devoted to the Ostrozky princely family and to events in Ostrih, the chronicle was dubbed the Ostrih Chronicle by M. Tikhomirov, who discovered it and published it in *Istoricheskii arkhiv* (vol 7, 1951). The chronicle was written in the Ukrainian vernacular of its time.

BIBLIOGRAPHY
Bevzo, O. *L'vivs'kyi litopys i Ostroz'kyi litopysets': Dzhereloznavche doslidzhennia*, 2nd edn (Kiev 1971)

Ostrih Press. The second oldest printer in Ukraine, founded in 1578 by I. *Fedorovych with the financial backing of Prince K. *Ostrozky at the prince's castle in Ostrih, Volhynia. Its first publications were *Azbuka* (Alphabet, 1578), a collection of prayers in Greek and Church Slavonic; the second impression of Fedorovych's *Bukvar* (1578), the first Ukrainian primer; the first Ukrainian edition of the New Testament and an alphabetical index to it (1580); the *Ostrih Bible (1581); and the first poetic work printed in Cyrillic, A. Rymsha's *Khronolohiia* (Chronology, 1581). It also printed pro-Orthodox, anti-Uniate *polemical literature, including works by H. Smotrytsky, V. Surazky, Ostrozky, Kh. Filalet, and the pseudonymous Ostrozkyi Kliryk; a book (1598) containing eight epistles by M. Pigas and one by I. *Vyshensky (his only work published during his lifetime); several liturgical books; and works by SS Basil the Great and John Chrysostom in Church Slavonic translation. It issued some 30 titles, some of which were later reprinted in Moscow. The press functioned, with some interruptions, until 1612; from 1602 to 1605 it operated at the Derman Monastery.

BIBLIOGRAPHY
Boiko, M. (ed). *Ostroz'ka ta dermans'ka drukarni* (Bloomington 1980)
Zapaska, Ia.; Isaievych, Ia. *Pam'iatky knyzhkovoho mystetstva: Kataloh starodrukiv, vydanykh na Ukraïni*, vol 1 (Lviv 1981)

Ostrivets archeological site. A multi-occupational archeological site located near Ostrivets, Horodenka raion, Ivano-Frankivske oblast. Excavations by M. *Smishko in 1958–60 revealed a settlement of the 13th to 11th century BC and a Sarmatian burial site of the 2nd to 3rd century AD. The site is best known for the recovery of a stone mold for pouring bronze axes and spear tips.

Ostrogoths. See Goths.

Ostrohozke [Ostrohoz'ke] (Russian: Ostrogozhsk). III-
20. A city (1979 pop 34,000) on the Tikhaia Sosna River
and a raion center in Voronezh oblast, RF. It was founded
by Ukrainian Cossacks and fortified in 1652. In 1662 it
became the center of Ostrohozke regiment in Slobidska
Ukraine. A century later the Cossack regiment was reorganized into a hussar regiment, and in 1802 the town
became as a county center in Voronezh gubernia. By the
end of the 19th century its population was 7,000, most of
whom were engaged in trade. According to the census of
1926, Ukrainians accounted for 74.1 percent of the town's
and 69.6 percent of the county's inhabitants.

Ostrohozke regiment. An administrative territory and
military formation established in 1652 in Slobidska
Ukraine and originally known as Rybne regiment. It was
settled by approx 2,000 peasant and Cossack families from
Chernihiv and Nizhen regiments, led by Col I. Dzykovsky. Its purpose was to protect Muscovy's southern
frontier from Tatar raids. By 1732 the regiment consisted
of 18 companies, with 3,100 elect Cossacks and 16,300 Cossack helpers. It took part in Dzykovsky's revolt of 1670,
the Azov campaigns of 1695–6, the Northern War (1700–
21), and the Seven Years' War (1756–63). In 1765 it was
abolished along with the other regiments of Slobidska
Ukraine and reorganized into a hussar regiment. Its territory was incorporated into the gubernia of Slobidska
Ukraine.

Ostrohradsky [Ostrohrads'kyj]. A family of Cossack
starshyna and, later, Russian imperial nobility in the Poltava region. The progenitor was Ivan, a 17th-century fellow
of the standard. His son, Matvii *Ostrohradsky, was judge
of Myrhorod regiment (1715–34). Matvii's sons were
Fedir, the captain of Hovtva company (1723–35) and
judge (1735–52) and colonel (1752–68) of Myrhorod regiment; Hryhorii, the captain of Omelnyk company (1729–
60); and Ivan, a fellow of the standard until ca 1760. The
family produced many captains of Hovtva company, the
last being Volodymyr (1770–83). Notable Ostrohradskys
after the abolition of the Hetman state included Matvii
(ca 1786 to 1849), a lieutenant colonel and marshal of the
nobility in Kremenchuk (1838–41); the mathematician
Mykhailo *Ostrohradsky (1801–62); Vsevolod (b 1843), a
Russian cavalry colonel and inspector general; Vasyl (b
1857), the Russian deputy minister of trade and commerce
in 1906–10; Vasyl (b 1865), a representative of Poltava gubernia in the Third Russian State Duma (1907–12); Oleksander (1852–1907), a pedagogue and director of the
school for the deaf and mute in St Petersburg; Orest (b
1868), a professor of financial law from 1895 at Dorpat
(Tartu) University; and Mykhailo *Ostrohradsky (1870–
1921), a rear admiral of the Black Sea Fleet.

O. Ohloblyn

Ostrohradsky, Matvii [Ostrohrads'kyj, Matvij], b and
d ? Cossack officer; patriarch of the *Ostrohradsky family.
He was captain of the Hovtva company (1691–1715) and a
judge in Myrhorod regiment (1715–34). He was arrested
with P. Polubotok and other senior officers for signing the
*Kolomak Petitions, and released in 1725. Ostrohradsky
took part in numerous military campaigns, from the Chyhyryn campaigns (1677–8) to the Russo-Turkish War
(1735–9).

Mykhailo Ostrohradsky
(1801–62)

Ostrohradsky, Mykhailo [Ostrohrads'kyj, Myxajlo]
(Ostrogradsky, Mikhail), b 24 September 1801 in Pashen-
na (now Pashenivka), Kobeliaky county, Poltava gubernia, d 1 January 1862 in Poltava. Mathematician (student
of T. Osipovsky); member of the Academy of Sciences in
St Petersburg (from 1831), New York (from 1834), Turin
(from 1841), Rome (from 1853), and Paris (from 1856). He
graduated from Kharkiv University (1820). He continued
his studies in Paris at the Collège de France in 1822. From
1828 he taught mathematics in St Petersburg at the Naval
Academy, the Institute of Roads and Communications,
the Main Pedagogical Institute, the Main Engineering
School, and the Main Artillery Academy. He wrote textbooks on analytical mechanics, algebra, differential and
integral calculus, and analytical geometry. Most of his essays (written in French) appeared in the proceedings and
annals of the St Petersburg Academy of Sciences. He contributed to diverse fields of applied mathematics, including ballistics, hydromechanics, hydrodynamics, potential
theory, heat, elasticity, and astronomy.

His most famous theorem is on the reduction of an integral over an n-dimensional space to one over its boundary. A special case for this theorem for three-dimensional space is known as Gauss's theorem (aka théorème
d'Ostrogradsky in French). He was also the first to prove
a theorem in linear differential equations known as Abel's
theorem. Ostrohradsky was a friend of T. Shevchenko,
who mentioned him in his diary and in his novel Khudozh-
nik (The Artist, 1887), in which he called Ostrohradsky a
mathematical genius. In 1952 B. Hniedenko wrote a
monograph about Ostrohradsky.

R. Voronka

Ostrohradsky, Mykhailo [Ostrohrads'kyj, Myxajlo], b
1870, d 1921. Naval commander. He was a rear admiral in
the Imperial Russian navy. Under the Hetman government (1918) he served as the Sevastopil commander of
Black Sea Fleet. From 1919 he worked in the Ministry of
Naval Affairs of the UNR.

Ostromir Gospel (Ostromirove yevanheliie). The oldest
extant East Slavic manuscript and the most important Old
Church Slavonic literary monument in the East Slavic redaction. It was transcribed by the precentor Grigorii in
1056–7 for Ostromir, the vicegerent of Novgorod. The
monument is a copy of an Old Church Slavonic original of
Bulgarian provenence, translated from Greek. Most of it
(parchment folios 25–294) was preserved at the St Sophia

Ostromir Gospel: miniature painting of St Luke the Evangelist

Cathedral in Novgorod and was transferred in 1806 to the St Petersburg Public Library. The gospel was written in two columns using the Cyrillic *ustav* script and was embellished with headpieces, initials, and miniatures of the evangelists Mark, Luke, and John. Its generally pure Old Church Slavonic language has few East Slavic traits. An annotated parallel Slavonic-Greek edition was first published by A. Vostokov (1843; repr Wiesbaden 1964), and photofacsimiles of the original were published by I. Savinkov (1883, 1889). Its language and contents were studied by Vostokov (1843), M. Kozlovsky (1885), V. Shchepkin and A. Shakhmatov (1890), N. Volkov (1897), N. Karinsky (1903, 1920), F. Fortunatov (1908), and L. Zhukovskaia (1961). Some scholars (N. Karinsky, N. Volkov, P. Lavrov [1928]) have speculated that the text was prepared in Kiev, but most favor Novgorod.

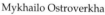

Mykhailo Ostroverkha   Oleh Ostrowsky

Ostroverkha, Mykhailo [Ostroverxa, Myxajlo], b 7 October 1897 in Buchach, Galicia, d 17 April 1979 in Brooklyn, New York. Writer and journalist. In 1923 his poetry appeared under the pen name M. Osyka together with that of Ye. Malaniuk and M. Selehii in the collection *Ozymyna* (Winter Grain). In the years 1926–39 he contributed to various Lviv journals and newspapers. In 1934–9 he wrote books about Italy and its figures. During the Second World War he worked in the *Military Board (Division Galizien) in Lviv and was chief editor (1943–5) of its weekly, *Do peremohy*. As a postwar émigré (from 1948 in the United States) he contributed to the daily *Svoboda* and published several collections of essays on literature, art, and politics – *Z ryms'koho shchodennyka* (From a Roman Journal, 1946), *Nihil novi* (1946), *Bez dokoru* (Without Reproach, 1948), *Homin z daleka* (An Echo from Afar, 1953), *Chornoknyzhnyk iz Zubrivky: Khvyl'ovyi i khvyl'ovyzm* (The

Sorcerer from Zubrivka: Khvylovy and Khvylovis 1955) – and the memoiristic essay collections *Obnizhka na bytyi shliakh* (Towards the Main Road, 1957), *Na zakr Osin' 1939 roku* (At the Turn: The Autumn of 1939, 195 *Hrona kalyny USS* (Viburnum Clusters of the Ukraini Sich Riflemen, 1962), and *Blysky i temriavy* (Flashes a Glooms, 1966). He also translated Italian literary wor (G. Deledda, A. Negri, N. Machiavelli's *The Prince*) in Ukrainian. A selection of his works was published in 198

Ostroverkhivka settlement. An early *Iron Age sett ment near Ostroverkhivka, Zmiiv raion, Kharkiv obla Excavation in 1951–3 by B. Shramko revealed 60 ash p and the remains of earthenware cult figures of anima Greek pottery, and bronze and iron tools. Six kurha were found nearby.

Ostrovska, Lidiia [Ostrovs'ka, Lidija], b 18 March 19 in Kiev. Film actress and director. She completed study the Lysenko Music and Drama Institute in Kiev (1928) a played in the films *Dzhal'ma* (1929), *Mirabeau* (1930), a *Viter z porohiv* (Wind from the Rapids, 1931). In 1945– she worked as a director in the studio of popular scien films at the Kiev Artistic Film Studio.

Ostrovska, Liudmyla [Ostrovs'ka, Ljudmyla], b 30 A gust 1913 in Kiev. Biochemist and plant physiologist. graduate of Kiev University (1940), she became a profe sor there in 1966. She studied the biochemical problems nitrogen assimilation, the biochemical role of trace el ments, the structure of chloroplasts involved in photosy thesis, and the molecular organization of photosyste centers at the AN URSR (now ANU) Institute of Plant Phys ology.

Ostrovsky, Dmytro [Ostrovs'kyj], b 23 July 1911 Yelysavethrad (now Kirovohrad), Kherson gubernia, d July 1979 in Odessa. Stage actor. After studying at th State Institute of Theater Arts in Moscow, he worked in Donetske touring theater (1928–32), the Kharkiv Worker and Collective-Farm Theater (1932–8), the Sumy Theat of Drama and Musical Comedy (1939–43), the Chernivt Oblast Ukrainian Music and Drama Theater (1943–6), an the Odessa Musical Comedy Theater (1946–79).

Ostrovsky, Isaak [Ostrovs'kyj], b 25 March 1909 in K stiantynohrad (now Krasnohrad), Poltava gubernia. R dio physicist. He graduated from the Kharkiv Physic Chemistry, and Mathematics Institute (1932, now part Kharkiv University) and worked at the Kharkiv Chemic Technology Institute (1932–52, from 1950 a part of th Kharkiv Polytechnical Institute) and the Physical-Techn cal Institute of the AN URSR (now ANU) (1944–55). He hea ed a department at the Institute of Radio Physics an Electronics of the ANU. His main contributions were in th field of the propagation and dispersion of millimet waves.

Ostrovsky, Nikolai [Ostrovs'kyj], b 20 September 190 in Viliia, Ostrih county, Volhynia gubernia, d 22 Decem ber 1936 in Sochi, Kuban. Russian writer who lived i Ukraine. In 1927, bedridden as a result of illness, he bega his literary career. Ostrovsky's novels, *Kak zakalialas' sta* (How the Steel Was Tempered, 1934) and *Rozhdennye bure* (Born by a Storm, 1936), were based on the Bolshevik in

terpretation of the events of the revolution and the period following the war in Ukraine. They were published many times in large editions, both in the Russian original and in Ukrainian translation, as models of heroic socialist-realist prose works and were propagandistically used in other art forms, such as film, opera, and ballet. Ostrovsky's hostile attitude to the Ukrainian liberation struggle of 1917–20 became the main reason for his official promotion to the status of a cult figure in the Ukrainian SSR: a museum was established in his honor in Shepetivka in 1946, and from 1958 the republic's literary prize of the Komsomol and the Writers' Union of Ukraine was named after him.

Ostrovsky, Olelko [Ostrovs'kyj, Olel'ko], b ca 1880, d 1920. Writer. In 1917–18 he published several historical stories – 'Ruinuvannia Baturyna' (The Destruction of Baturyn), 'Berestechko,' 'Atakuvannia Novoï Sichi' (The Attack on the New Sich), 'Ruinuvannia Chortomlyts'koï Sichi' (The Destruction of the Chortomlyk Sich), 'Zhovti Vody,' 'Ivan Bohun,' 'Petryk,' and 'Poltava' – and the historical plays *Het'man Ivan Mazepa*, *Nirvana*, and *Stril'tsi* (The Riflemen). He was executed by the Bolsheviks.

Ostrovsky, Volodymyr [Ostrovs'kyj], b 1881 in Reiovets, near Kholm, d 1944. Educator, journalist, and civic leader. After graduating from the Kholm Teachers' Seminary (1901) he taught elementary school in and around Kholm and in Warsaw. In 1917 he taught at a Ukrainian school in Vinnytsia and edited the daily *Shliakh* (1919). In 1921 he moved to Warsaw, where he published the daily *Ukraïns'ka trybuna* and edited the biweekly *Dukhovna besida* and his own papers, *Nash svit*, *Nasha besida*, and *Narid*. After settling in Lutske in 1928, he was active in many Ukrainian organizations and was president of the local Prosvita and Silskyi Hospodar societies and the People's Home co-operative. He also edited *Ukrïns'ka hromada*, *Nash svit*, and *Nova doba* and contributed to several Lviv papers. He was a member of the Central Committee of the Ukrainian National Democratic Alliance. His short stories about life in the Kholm region appeared in the press and in separate collections, such as *Kholms'ki opovidannia* (Kholm Short Stories, 1923) and *Blakytni ochi* (Azure Eyes, 1936). He wrote many novelettes, historical and contemporary, including *Khrest ottsia Vasylia* (Father Vasyl's Cross, 1926) and *Kniaz' Syla-Tur* (Prince Syla-Tur, 1938). After the Soviet occupation of Volhynia in 1939, he fled to the Gorlice region in the Generalgouvernement.

Ostrovsky, Volodymyr [Ostrovs'kyj], b 15 April 1908 in Lviv, d 14 April 1980 in Australia. Civic leader. A teacher and an active member of Prosvita, he emigrated to Australia after the Second World War and settled in Sydney. There he took a leading part in Ukrainian civic, cultural, and educational life, including the building of the first Ukrainian school in Sydney. He was president of the Ukrainian Council of New South Wales in 1963–71.

Ostrovsky, Yosyp [Ostrovs'kyj, Josyp], b 6 April 1934 in Dnipropetrovske. Mathematician; corresponding member of the AN URSR (now ANU) since 1978. After graduating from Kharkiv University in 1956, he has taught there (professor since 1967) and worked at the Physical-Technical Institute of Low Temperatures in Kharkiv since 1969. Ostrovsky's basic research is in the theory of functions and the theory of probability. Among other results, he ex-plained the connection between the asymptotic behavior of the menomorphic function and its distribution of values.

Ostrowsky, Oleh [Ostrovs'kyj], b 16 April 1925 in Chernyliv, Ternopil county, Galicia. Engineer, educator, and artist. After emigrating to England following the Second World War, he worked as an engineer and did advanced studies at Nottingham University (MSE, 1970) and North London Polytechnic (PG Dip Eng Design, 1975). He has lectured in engineering design at the People's College for Engineering and Science in Nottingham and at Nottingham Polytechnic, and has written two textbooks in the field, *Engineering Drawing for Technicians* (2 vols, 1979, 1981) and *Engineering Drawing with Computer-Aided Design Applications* (1989). In 1988 he received a special award from the Institution of Engineering Designers for his contribution to education. His artistic activities include oil painting, designing Ukrainian Christmas and Easter cards, graphics, and book designing.

Ostrozhs'ka narodnia hazeta (Ostrih Popular Gazette). A semiweekly newspaper published in Ostrih, Volhynia, by the local Prosvita society in 1919.

Ostrozky [Ostroz'kyj] (Polish: Ostrogski). A prominent family of Ukrainian Orthodox princes under Lithuanian and Polish rule. Most scholars believe it is descended from the Turiv-Pynske line of the Riurykide dynasty. The progenitor was Prince Danylo Dmytrovych (d after 1366), who fought against Casimir III the Great and built a castle in his town of Ostrih (whence the family name). His son, Fedir (1360–1446), was a supporter of King Jagiełło, who appointed him viceroy of Lutske in 1387. In addition to Ostrih Fedir became owner of Korets, Iziaslav, and other towns. In the 1430s he supported Grand Duke Švitrigaila and fought the Poles in Right-Bank Ukraine. He died as a monk at the Kievan Cave Monastery under the name Teodosii and was later canonized (his feast day is 24 August [11 August OS]). Fedir's son, Vasyl (d ca 1450), was loyal to Casimir IV Jagiellończyk, who appointed him viceroy of Turiv in 1448. He built churches in Ostrih and the *Derman Monastery. After Vasyl's death his son Yurii (d ca 1500) inherited Iziaslav and originated the *Zasławski noble family. Vasyl's son Ivan (d 1465) inherited Ostrih.

Ivan's son, Kostiantyn (ca 1460 to 1530), was grand hetman of Lithuania and starosta of Bratslav, Zvenyhorod, and Vinnytsia from 1497, starosta of Lutske and marshal of Volhynia from 1507, castellan of Wilno (Vilnius) from 1511, and voivode of Troki (Trakai) from 1522. He fought many battles against the Crimean Tatars in Right-Bank Ukraine and defeated the Muscovites at the Battle of Orsha in 1514. One of the five wealthiest magnates in the Lithuanian-Ruthenian state, he was a defender and patron of the Orthodox church and generously supported the Kievan Cave Monastery, where he was buried.

Kostiantyn's son Illia (1510–39) was starosta of Bratslav and Vinnytsia from 1530. He was also a patron of the Orthodox church and was buried at the Kievan Cave Monastery. Illia's brother Kostiantyn *Ostrozky (ca 1526 to 1608) was the most notable member of the family. Kostiantyn's son Oleksander (1570–1603) was voivode of Volhynia from 1597 and, like his father, a defender of Orthodoxy. Another son, Yanush (Janusz, ca 1554 to 1620), converted to Catholicism in 1579. He became voivode of Volhynia in

1584 and castellan of Cracow in 1593, and was also starosta of Kaniv, Pereiaslav, Cherkasy, Bohuslav, and Bila Tserkva. With his death the family name disappeared, and the huge Ostrozky latifundia – 24 towns, 10 smaller towns, and several hundred villages, mostly in Right-Bank Ukraine – were inherited by the sons of his sister, Eufrozyna Zasławska, and subsequently by members of the *Sanguszko and other magnate families.

BIBLIOGRAPHY
Iarushevich, A. *Revnitel' Pravoslaviia kniaz' Konstantin Ivanovich Ostrozhskii i pravoslavnaia litovskaia Rus' v ego vremia* (Smolensk 1897)
Bykov, N. *Kniaz'ia Ostrozhskie i Volyn'* (Petrograd 1915)
L. Wynar

Prince Kostiantyn Ostrozky
(portrait by J. Kosiński, 1620)

Yaroslava Ostruk

Ostrozky, Kostiantyn [Ostroz'kyj, Kostjantyn] (Polish: Ostrogski, Konstantyn), b 1526 or 1527 in Dubno, Volhynia, d 23 February 1608 in Ostrih, Volhynia. Ukrainian nobleman and political and cultural figure; starosta of Volodymyr-Volynskyi and marshal of Volhynia from 1550, voivode of Kiev from 1559, and senator from 1569; the most powerful magnate in Volhynia and one of the most influential figures in the Lithuanian-Ruthenian state and Polish-Lithuanian Commonwealth. He was a candidate for the Polish throne after the death of Sigismund II Augustus (the last Jagiellon) in 1572, and for the Muscovite throne after the death of Tsar Fedor Ivanovich (the last Riurykide) in 1598. Ostrozky defended Ruthenian (Ukrainian and Belarusian) political rights and was the de facto leader of Ukraine in the negotiations leading up to the 1569 Union of *Lublin, during which he demanded that Ruthenia be treated as an equal partner of Poland and Lithuania. A generous patron of Ukrainian culture and an ardent defender of the Orthodox faith, he organized and led the resistance to the 1596 Church Union of *Berestia. Although he was not opposed in principle to Orthodox-Catholic unification, he felt that it had to be an open, ecumenical process involving secular church patrons, not just a secret clerical accord.

Ostrozky was an important figure in the 16th-century Ukrainian cultural and national rebirth. He established schools in Turiv (1572), Volodymyr-Volynskyi (1577), and Ostrih (1590), but is best known for founding the *Ostrih Academy (ca 1576), the *Ostrih Press (ca 1578), and the press at the *Derman Monastery (1602). The *Ostrih Bible (1580–1) was printed under his patronage by I. Fedo-

rovych. Ostrozky had close contacts and corresponded regularly with leading defenders of the Orthodox faith, such as the Lviv Dormition Brotherhood, Prince A. Kurbsky, and Bishop H. Balaban. Although he helped to suppress the popular uprising led by K. Kosynsky in 1593, he did little to contain the uprising led by S. Nalyvaiko in 1594–6, and he maintained relations with the Ukrainian Cossacks; for those reasons he was condemned by the Polish nobility.

BIBLIOGRAPHY
Metropolitan Ilarion [Ohiienko]. *Kniaz' Kostiantyn Ostroz'kyi i ioho kul'turna pratsia* (Winnipeg 1958)
Krajcar, J. 'Konstantin Basil Ostrožskij and Rome in 1582–1584,' *Orientalia Christiana Periodica*, 35 (1969)
Gordon, L. *Cossack Rebellions: Social Turmoil in the Sixteenth-Century Ukraine* (Albany 1983)
L. Wynar

Ostrozkyi Kliryk (Ostrih Cleric). The pen name of an unidentified Orthodox polemicist. An opponent of the Church Union of *Berestia, in 1598 he published a tract criticizing the 1438–45 Council of Ferrara-Florence (1598) and a reply to Metropolitan I. Potii, *Otpys na lyst ... Potiia* (Reply to the Letter ... of Potii, 1598–9). The works exhibit the author's erudition and oratorical skills. Scholars have postulated that the author was M. Smotrytsky, Y. Boretsky, or H. Dorofeievych.

Ostrozky-Lokhvytsky, Ivan [Ostroz'kyj-Loxvyc'kyj], b 1749, d 6 November 1845. Court official of Cossack descent. In the 1790s he was several times elected assessor of the Novyi Oskol land court. His memoirs of the period 1771–1825 were extended to 1846 by his son Petro and were published in *Kievskaia starina* (1886). They are an important source for the history of the Ukrainian gentry and the legal profession.

Ostruk, Yaroslava (pseud of Yaroslava Sosenko), b 1908 in Bosnia, d 5 April 1973 in Philadelphia. Writer. Her novels are set in interwar and wartime Galicia, where she lived. They include *Provallia* (The Abyss, 1961), *Olia* (1962), *Rodyna Gol'div* (The Gold Family, 1964), *Khurtovyna hriade* (The Impending Tempest, 1967), *Te, shcho roz'iednuie* (That Which Divides, 1969), and *Koly merknut' zori* (When the Stars Fade, 1972). Her short stories appeared in émigré periodicals.

Oświęcim, Stanisław, b after 1605, d September 1657. Polish memoirist. As marshal of the court of Grand Hetman S. Koniecpolski and an attendant at the court of King Władysław IV he took part in Polish diplomatic missions and military campaigns against the Crimean Tatars, Cossacks, and Swedes. He kept a daily diary, of which fragments for the years 1643–7 and 1650–1 have been preserved. Excerpts were published in *Kievskaia starina* (1882, nos 1–2, 5–6, 9, 11–12).

Oświęcim Concentration Camp (German: Auschwitz; aka Auschwitz-Birkenau). Nazi Germany's largest concentration and extermination camp, located approx 60 km west of Cracow near the Polish town of Oświęcim. The camp was established by order of the SS chief H. Himmler on 27 April 1940 and was operational by June 1940. It was later expanded and divided into three sections: Auschwitz I, the original camp, reserved for political prisoners; Auschwitz II (Birkenau), a huge extermination complex established in October 1941 approx 3 km from the original camp; and Auschwitz III, which in May 1942 became a slave labor camp.

The major focus of activity in Oświęcim was the mass extermination of Jews. It is estimated that up to a quarter (1.5 million) of the Jews who were murdered in the Nazi quest for a so-called Final Solution died there. Several gas chambers (each capable of killing up to 6,000 people daily) and crematoriums were set up in the Birkenau complex for that purpose. Many of the Jews in the camp originated in Ukraine. In addition to the Jews, Gypsies, Poles, Ukrainians, and other people were interned at the camp.

The first Ukrainians in Oświęcim came from the western regions of Ukraine, often brought in with Polish prisoners. From mid-1941 they were joined by Soviet Ukrainian POWs and political prisoners, including members of the Organization of Ukrainian Nationalists (OUN). A total of more than 15,000 Ukrainians were interned in the camp; most of them perished as a result of multiple privations, epidemics, ill treatment, or murder.

In spite of protests by inmates Ukrainians were generally registered not according to their nationality, but according to what the camp administration considered to be their citizenship. Those from the Soviet Union were given the letter 'R' to wear as a badge of identification, those from Poland the letter 'P,' from Czechoslovakia the letter 'C,' and from Rumania the letters 'Ru.' There were exceptions to the rule: some Ukrainian women were allowed to wear the letter 'U' in correspondence with their nationality, as was later a small group of males in one section of the camp.

Soviet nationals (including Ukrainians) and Jews were denied mail and parcels from home. The camp administration also forbade the Ukrainian Red Cross to come to the assistance of their compatriots in the camp.

Ukrainians, especially those from Soviet territories, were subjected to the crudest forms of humiliation and torture. According to the Nazi racial hierarchy they ranked above the Jews and Gypsies, who were ahead in the order of extermination, but below most other ethnic groups. Most of the Soviet Ukrainian POWs died shortly after their arrival. Between October 1941 and February 1942 approx 8,320 Soviet POWs were put to death by what is believed to have been phenol injections to the heart. Although plans to sterilize all inmates of Slavic origin were not realized, Ukrainians were used, along with other Slavs, in experiments to test sterilization methods. Ukrainians were also among those selected for other Nazi experiments, including the September 1941 tests on the Zyklon B gas that was later used for mass killings. Although most Ukrainians were used as slave labor, a small number served in auxiliary camp administration posts, as overseers and guards, for example. Ukrainian camp guards in Oświęcim staged an insurrection against their masters on the night of 3 July 1943. It proved unsuccessful, and all the rebels were killed. Ukrainians were also involved in other forms of sporadic resistance carried out during the course of 1944. A number of Ukrainians managed to escape from Oświęcim. In 1943–4 the harsh treatment of non-Jewish inmates eased somewhat when the Germans began considering them an invaluable source of slave labor for the war economy.

As the Red Army advanced into Poland, most of the inmates in Oświęcim were evacuated to other concentration camps in Nazi-occupied territory. When the Red Army arrived at the camp in January 1945, they found 7,650 prisoners remaining.

The background of Oświęcim's Ukrainian inmates was mixed. Most were POWs, especially from central and eastern Ukraine, or former political activists. Among the latter group were B. *Kordiuk and R. *Rozdolsky. V. and O. Bandera, brothers of the OUN leader S. *Bandera, were killed in the camp. Several former Ukrainian inmates have written or illustrated their memoirs of the camp. Ukrainian survivors of Oświęcim later joined other former concentration camp inmates to form the League of Former Ukrainian Political Prisoners.

BIBLIOGRAPHY
Osynka, P. *Albom politv'iazna* (Munich 1946)
Marunchak, M. *Systema nimets'kykh kontstaboriv i polityka vynyshchuvannia v Ukraïni* (Winnipeg 1963)
Mirchuk, P. *In the German Mills of Death, 1941–1945* (New York 1976)
Pawelczynska, A. *Values and Violence in Auschwitz: A Sociological Analysis* (London 1979)
Dunin-Wąsowicz, K. *Resistance in the Nazi Concentration Camps, 1933–1945* (Warsaw 1982)
Rosdolsky, R. 'A Memoir of Auschwitz and Birkenau,' *Monthly Review*, 39, no. 8 (January 1988)

S. Cipko

Leonid Osyka

Osyka, Leonid, b 8 March 1940 in Kiev. Film producer. He graduated from the State Institute of Cinema Arts in Moscow (1966). Among his films are a poetic cinema version of V. Stefanyk's novellas called *Kaminnyi khrest* (The Stone Cross, 1968) and the heroic epic cinema version of I. Franko's *Zakhar Berkut* (1972), as well as *Tryvozhnyi misiats' veresen'* (The Alarming Month of September, 1977) and *More* (The Sea, 1978).

Osypenko. See Berdianske.

Osypiv, Mykola, b and d ? Linguist of the 1920s and 1930s in Kharkiv. He wrote a practical Russian-Ukrainian dictionary of words most often used in administrative circles (1926), a booklet of lexical and syntactic reminders for teachers (1928), a booklet about the main changes in the new Ukrainian orthography (1929), a small orthographic dictionary of loanwords in the Ukrainian language (1930), and a few lexicological articles. He disappeared during the terror of the 1930s.

Osypovycheva, Antonyna [Osypovyčeva] (née Skřivan; stage name: Tanska), b 5 May 1855 in Prague, Bohemia, d 22 November 1926 in Lviv. Actress and singer (soprano) of Czech origin. She began her career in the Polish touring troupes of J. Piasecka (1877) and W. Antoniewski (1894–5) and then became a leading actress in the Ruska Besida Theater (1882–1914), the Theater of the Legion of Ukrainian Sich Riflemen (1915), Ternopilski Teatralni Vechory (1916–17), and the Chernivtsi Ukrainian Theater (1918–19). With an extensive repertoire of earlier heroic roles and later character roles, Osypovycheva performed well in drama, comedy, and operettas. Her roles included Vustia in M. Starytsky's *Oi ne khody, Hrytsiu ...* (Don't Go to the Party, Hryts ...), Hetman Doroshenko's mother in V. Pachovsky's *Sontse Ruïny* (The Sun of Ruin), and Czipra in J. Strauss's *Der Zigeunerbaron*.

Otaman (from Turkic origin). The leader (usually elected) of all or parts of the Zaporozhian Host. In the Zaporizhia the *kish otaman was the chief executive officer, and each Cossack *kurin at the Sich was headed by a kurin (*kurinnyi*) otaman. If an otaman was not elected but appointed, for instance during a military campaign, he was called acting (*nakaznyi*) otaman. In the Hetman state the company (*sotennyi*) and regimental town (*horodovyi*) otaman was the captain's lieutenant. A village's kurin otaman commanded its military unit, and the village (*sil's'kyi*) otaman was the civil authority. There were also otamans of the Hetman state's general artillery, regimental artilleries, volunteer regiments and companies, and mercenary cavalry (*zholdak*) troops.

In the Army of the UNR of 1917–19 an otaman was a division, corps, or army group commander. The rank was replaced by that of general in 1920. In the Legion of Ukrainian Sich Riflemen and the Ukrainian Galician Army an otaman was equal in rank to a major. As commander in chief of the UNR Army the head of the UNR Directory (later the president of the UNR) was called the supreme otaman (*holovnyi otaman*). The commanders of the various partisan groups and units that operated during the Ukrainian-Soviet War were also called otamans, and their often arbitrary and even anarchic rule came to be known as *otamanshchyna*.

Valentyn Otamanovsky   Polina Otava

Otamanovsky, Valentyn [Otamanovs'kyj], b 26 February 1893 in Zlatopil, Chyhyryn county, Kiev gubernia, d 1964 in Kharkiv. Historian, bibliographer, and community figure. In 1917 he was a member of the Central Rada representing the Ukrainian Party of Socialists-Independentists. He was a cofounder of the *Vernyhora publishing house and wrote a popular novel for youth, *Syn*

Ukraïny (Son of Ukraine, 1919), under the pseudonym Zlotopolets. In the 1920s he was an associate of the VUAN, a member of its Commission for the Study of the History of Western Ruthenian and Ukrainian Law, and director of the Vinnytsia branch of the National Library of Ukraine and its Research Cabinet for the Study of Podilia. He was arrested and sentenced during the Union for the Liberation of Ukraine show trials of 1930. In the 1940s and 1950s, after his release from a labor camp, he worked in Leningrad. He edited a collection of articles about Vinnytsia okruha (1926) and wrote a brochure about the tasks and needs of regional studies in Podilia (1926), an article about S. Rudansky's roots (1929), and books in Russian about the towns of Right-Bank Ukraine under Polish noble rule from the mid-17th to the late 18th century (1954) and Vinnytsia as a Ukrainian city type in 14th- to 17th-century southern Right-Bank Ukraine (1964).

Otava, Polina, b 1899, d 1937? Stage and film actress; wife of K. Koshevsky. She worked in the Kiev Ukrainian Drama Theater (1924–37). In 1928 she acted in the films *Zvenyhora* and *Za stinoiu* (Behind the Wall). In 1937 she fell victim to the Stalinist terror and disappeared.

Otchychi. A special category of peasants in 15th- and 16th-century Ukraine, Russia, and Lithuania. They were peasants who had lived on the same parcel of land for many generations. With the introduction of serfdom they were often the peasants who were enserfed first, by being deprived of the right to move from their land.

Otchyna. See Seignory.

Otechestvennye zapiski (Notes of the Fatherland). A Russian literary and intellectual journal established in St Petersburg from 1820 to 1884. With V. Belinsky as literary editor until 1846, it became the pre-eminent Russian 'thick' journal of its day. Ukrainian literary and scholarly works were reviewed on its pages. In April 1884 the tsarist police arrested some of its contributors as revolutionaries, and the journal was closed down. Among its Ukrainian contributors were Ye. Hrebinka, M. Kostomarov, H. Kvitka-Osnovianenko, M. Vovchok, D. Mordovets, and M. Ziber. V. Bograd's three-volume index of its contents appeared in Moscow in 1959, 1971, and 1985.

Otechestvennyi sbornik (Fatherland Collection). A weekly and later semimonthly supplement to the newspaper *Vistnyk, published in Vienna in 1853–9, 1861–2, and 1866 (a total of almost 300 issues). Edited by V. Zborovsky (pseud of Yu. Vyslobotsky), it contained prose, poetry, and articles on historical and economic topics. Among the regular contributors were A. Metlynsky, M. Ustyianovych, B. Didytsky, I. Hushalevych, and M. Kozanovych. Initially it was published in the Cyrillic alphabet, but later the *hrazhdanka script was frequently used, especially in literary pieces.

Otkalenko, Nina (née Pletneva), b 23 May 1928 in Kozhlia, Kursk oblast, RSFSR. Runner. From 1948 she represented Ukraine at USSR meets. She was the 1954 European women's champion in the 800-m run; set five world records in the 800-m and in the 880-yd run; achieved impressive results in the 500-m, 100-m, and 1,500-m runs; and won many Ukrainian and USSR championships.

Col Yurii Otmarshtain

Otmarshtain, Yurii [Otmarštajn, Jurij], b 10 April 1890 in Tyraspil, Kherson gubernia, d 2 May 1922 in Szczepiórno, Poland. UNR Army officer. After graduating from the Nikolai Military Academy of the General Staff in St Petersburg (1916) he served in the Russian army. In 1918 he joined the Lubni Cavalry Regiment and soon assumed command of it. After taking part in the anti-Hetman coup, he was appointed chief of staff of the Siege Corps of Sich Riflemen in early 1919, and of the Second Division of Sich Riflemen in July 1919. In 1921, as a colonel, he was chief of staff of the Ukrainian army that conducted the Second Winter Campaign. He was killed by unknown assailants in a Polish internment camp.

Otolaryngology. A branch of clinical medicine dealing with ear, nose, and throat diseases. At the end of the 18th century in the Russian Empire, N. *Ambodyk-Maksymovych developed a fairly precise terminology for diseases of the ear, nose, and throat system. By the end of the 19th century Ukrainian scientists in the field included V. *Karavaiv, V. *Pokrovsky, L. Marovsky, M. Zhuk, and M. Lomykovsky. The first department of otolaryngology was established at Odessa University in 1895 (O. Heshelin, director); it was followed by similar departments at Kiev and Kharkiv universities. In 1907 a clinic was established at Kiev University. After 1922 otolaryngology was taught in all medical institutes as a compulsory subject. Ukrainian scientists who have contributed to the field include M. *Volkovych, M. Trofimov, S. Kompaniiets, O. *Puchkivsky, Ye. Kharshak, O. Skrypt, O. *Kolomiichenko, L. Zarytsky, and S. Mostovy. The Research Institute of Otolaryngology in Kiev was opened in 1960 to co-ordinate the research and development of this specialty. Regional scientific societies of otolaryngologists are co-ordinated by the Ukrainian Otolaryngological Association. The Russian-language journal *Zhurnal ushnykh, nosovykh i gorlovykh boleznei* has been published in Kiev since 1959.

BIBLIOGRAPHY
Otolaringologiia na Ukraine (Kiev 1967)

P. Dzul

Otrok, b and d ? 12th-century Cuman khan; son of Khan *Sharukan and father of Khan *Konchak. As a result of Sharukan's losses along the northern Donets River to a succession of Rus' princes (in 1109, 1111, and 1116) Otrok was forced to retreat with his federation to northern Caucasia, where he entered the service of Georgian rulers. The

Cumans reappeared in the steppe region of Ukraine toward the middle of the century. Otrok is portrayed as the hero of a popular Ukrainian tale about *yevshan-zillia* (wormwood).

Otrok. A junior member of the prince's *druzhyna* in Kievan Rus'. The *otroky* served as the prince's bodyguard, took part in military campaigns, and performed personal services for the prince. By the 12th century they were serving as lower officials in the administration and the courts. They tried cases, collected duties and taxes, and performed ambassadorial functions. A prince could retain several hundred *otroky*. Boyars and metropolitans had their own guard of *otroky*.

Otrokovsky, Volodymyr [Otrokovs'kyj], b 25 October 1892 in Kudryntsi, Kamianets-Podilskyi county, Podilia gubernia, d 26 April 1918 in Kiev. Literary historian and poet. He graduated from Galagan College (1910) and worked in V. Peretts's philological seminar at Kiev University, where he studied Old Ukrainian literature and Ukrainian dialects. Seventeen of his symbolist poems appeared in Kiev's Russian periodicals (mostly in 1918–19). His study of T. Zemka appeared in 1921.

Otroshchenko, Serhii [Otroščenko, Serhij], b 2 April 1910 in Omsk, Siberia, d 6 September 1988 in Moscow. Painter and graphic artist. He studied at the Odessa (1930–5) and Kiev (1935–40) art institutes. Since 1969 he has worked in Moscow. He has painted socialist-realist industrial landscapes and genre paintings and decorative murals. His easel paintings include *Partisans* (1947), *Avengers* (1958), *Shepherd* (1961), *Hutsul Girl* (1972), and the series 'Kiev' (1976–7). He cocreated three wall panels in the lobby of the Ukraine pavilion at the Exhibition of the Economic Achievements of the USSR in Moscow (1951–3) and did the panel *Song from the Time of the Civil War* in the Noty music store on the Khreshchatyk in Kiev (1959). He has also designed scenery for the Odessa and Kiev opera and ballet theaters.

Ottawa. The capital (1986 pop 819,263) of Canada, located on the Ottawa River on Ontario's eastern border with

St John the Baptist Ukrainian Catholic National Shrine in Ottawa

Quebec. In the 1981 census approx 8,400 residents gave Ukrainian as their national origin.. The first Ukrainian immigrants settled in Ottawa in 1905. They were mostly single men who worked on the railways, on farms, and in the forests. The earliest community organizations were the Prosvita society (1908), a branch of the Ukrainian Social Democratic party (1912), and the SS Cyril and Methodius Ruthenian National Organization (1913). St John the Baptist Ukrainian Catholic parish was established in 1914, and the Bukovynian Orthodox Church of the Holy Trinity was consecrated in 1918. By 1914 there were over 200 Ukrainians in Ottawa. After the war a branch of the Ukrainian Labour-Farmer Temple Association was organized. Few newcomers were attracted to Ottawa in the interwar period, because there was little industry there. During the war the expanding federal government attracted educated and professional Ukrainian Canadians from across the country, and a local branch of the Ukrainian Canadian Committee (now Congress) was formed.

After the war the Ukrainian community grew (1,760 in 1951, 2,950 in 1961, 5,200 in 1971). Local branches of national organizations were established in Ottawa: the Plast Ukrainian Youth Association (1949), the Ukrainian Youth Association (1953), the Canadian League for the Liberation of Ukraine (1957), and the Ukrainian National Federation (1957). Another Orthodox parish was organized in 1949, and the Catholic parish built a new church, the Cathedral of St John the Baptist Ukrainian Catholic National Shrine (1987), as a project to commemorate the millennium of Christianity in Ukraine. A Basilian monastery was opened in Ottawa in 1962, and Holy Spirit Seminary was established at the monastery in 1982. The latter moved to its own building in 1984. The Sheptytsky Institute was established at St Paul University in 1990 as a center for scholarship related to Ukrainian Christianity. A Ukrainian language and literature program was introduced at the University of Ottawa in 1952 by C. Bida.

As the capital of Canada, Ottawa has been the home of numerous Ukrainian politicians and civil servants of note, including M. Starr, P. Yuzyk, V. Kaye-Kisilewsky, and Gov Gen R. Hnatyshyn. It also became the site of the Ukrainian Information Office, established by the national office of the Ukrainian Canadian Congress, in 1987. The city houses valuable archival collections pertaining to Ukrainian and Ukrainian-Canadian studies at the National Archives of Canada and Carleton University (the Batchinsky Collection). The Canadian Museum of Civilization contains a collection of Ukrainian-Canadian artifacts.

Otter, European (*Lutra lutra*; Ukrainian: *vydra*). A predatory mammal of the weasel family Mustelidae. The otter has a lithe, slender body, long neck, flattened head, small ears, and short, webbed paws. It grows to up to 70 cm in length and weighs up to 10 kg. Its waterproof fur is shiny, dense, and short, dark brown on the outside and grayish inside. Otters are intelligent, inquisitive, and playful animals. They swim easily and travel considerable distances under water without surfacing for air. They feed on small aquatic animals and live in burrows along riverbanks and lakeshores. They can be found throughout Ukraine, with the exception of the Crimea. The otter's valuable fur makes it a commercially important animal. Because of widespread extermination in the past, hunting for otters is licensed.

Ottoman Empire. See Turkey.

OUN. See Organization of Ukrainian Nationalists.

OUN expeditionary groups (Pokhidni hrupy OUN). Secret groups of organizers and propagandists formed by both the Bandera (OUN[B]) and Melnyk (OUN[M]) factions of the *Organization of Ukrainian Nationalists from among their members in German-occupied Galicia, Rumanian-occupied Bukovyna, and Central and Western Europe. They went into Soviet Ukraine after the outbreak of the Soviet-German War in June 1941 to organize local sovereign Ukrainian administrations that took power after the Bolshevik authorities had fled and before the Germans had established control. Plans to send in such groups were developed in early 1941, before the German invasion of the USSR, and were contingent upon a quick German victory.

The OUN(B) formed and trained three expeditionary groups in the Sian and Lemko regions. Group North, commanded by M. Klymyshyn and then D. Myron and P. Sak, penetrated into Right-Bank Ukraine toward Kiev; Group South, commanded by Z. Matla and T. Semchyshyn, into southern Ukraine toward Dnipropetrovske and the Donbas; and Group East, commanded M. Lemyk and O. Mashchak, into Left-Bank Ukraine toward Kharkiv. A month after the German invasion began, those groups had reached (mostly by bicycle and wagon) as far east as the cities of Vinnytsia, Berdychiv, Zhytomyr, and Kryvyi Rih and had avoided contacts with German units. By that time, however, only a third remained of the approx 1,500 men who had set out on the campaign. They organized Ukrainian national activity on the local level, recruited new members, and spread integral-nationalist propaganda and news of the *proclamation of Ukrainian statehood made in Lviv on 30 June 1941.

In early September 1941 the Gestapo conducted mass arrests of the groups' members active in Zhytomyr, Vasylkiv, Berdychiv, Vinnytsia, Mykolaiv, and Kherson. Some were executed, and the remainder were sent to concentration camps. In mid-September, at the same time that the Gestapo conducted mass arrests of OUN(B) members in Western Ukraine (including S. Bandera and other leaders), SS Einsatzgruppen smashed Group East in Myrhorod and part of Group North. Members of Group South in Dnipropetrovske, Zaporizhia, Balta, Mykolaiv, Kherson, and Dzhankoi (in the Crimea) were arrested and executed. In response to the German repressions, terror, and deportation and extermination policies the OUN(B) leadership still at large (headed by M. Lebed) ordered the remaining members of the expeditionary groups to develop an anti-Nazi and anti-Soviet partisan underground. The resistance was co-ordinated from two centers: from Kiev by Myron, with the assistance of D. Maivsky, M. Prokop, P. Sak, and Ya. Khomov; and from Dnipropetrovske by Matla and, from May 1942, V. Kuk, with the assistance of M. Richka, O. Logush, P. Duzhy, T. Semchyshyn, and Ye. Stakhiv. The resistance attracted many local recruits (it totaled some 5,000 men and women) and remained active in the Dnipropetrovske, Kryvyi Rih, Zaporizhia, Mykolaiv, Vinnytsia, Odessa, Kirovohrad, Chernihiv, Poltava, Kharkiv, Donbas, Mariiupil, and Crimea regions until the Germans' retreat. Most of its leaders and members did not survive, however.

The OUN(M) expeditionary groups were assembled in

Penetration of Nationalists Groups into the East Ukraine in summer and autumn 1941

Routes of principal expeditionary groups

– – – – –   OUN-B (Bandera)

–·–·–·–   Wehrmacht auxiliary under influence of OUN-B ("Roland" and "Nachtigall")

—————   OUN-M (Mel'nyk) groups

··············   Bukovinian groups adhering to the OUN-M

Lviv   Main centers of expeditionary groups (Pokhidni hrupy)

Boundaries of States
- ————— January 1939
- ————— June 1941

Boundaries of Soviet Republics
- – ·· – January 1939
- – – – June 1941

OUN EXPEDITIONARY GROUPS

Hrubeshiv and Krystynopil (led by I. Nebolia), Jarosław and Radymno (led by I. Maly), and Sianik (led by T. Bak-Boichuk). From there 500 of their members penetrated in July 1941 into Volhynia, Subcarpathia, and, from there, Bukovyna, as far east as Kiev, and as far south as Odessa and Mykolaiv. Their activity was concentrated in the Zhytomyr region and, from September 1941, Kiev, where they openly organized municipal administrations, civic and community institutions, schools, and newspapers and initiated the creation of the *Ukrainian National Council. During the first few weeks of the German occupation of Kiev the 200 OUN(M) members there were joined by 1,000 more, who arrived with the *Bukovynian Battalion. The supreme commanders of the OUN(M) groups were at first O. Senyk and M. Stsiborsky. After their assassination in Zhytomyr their duties were assumed in Kiev by O. Olzhych, Ya. Haivas, Ya. Shumelda, M. Antonovych, O. Boidunyk, and M. Kapustiansky. Other prominent members active in Kiev were P. Oliinyk, I. Rohach, O. Chemerynsky, B. Yakhno, R. Gordon-Bida, R. Zakhvalynsky, M. Kuzmyk, O. Zybachynsky, O. Zhdanovych, and Z. Domazar. Units of the expeditionary groups were sent from Kiev to Kharkiv (led there by B. Konyk), Poltava, Dnipropetrovske (B. Mykytchak), Zaporizhia and Mykolaiv (O. Masikevych), the Donbas, and the Crimea (B. Sukhoversky).

The OUN(M) expeditionary groups also suffered German repressions. In the Zhytomyr region several dozen members were arrested by the Gestapo in late November 1941 together with 700 other Ukrainians who had gathered to commemorate the 1921 Winter Campaign of the UNR Army and the massacre at Bazar. Many were subsequently shot. Further arrests took place in Kiev in December 1941 and February 1942, and dozens of leading OUN(M) members (eg, M. and O. Teliha, I. Rohach, I. Irliavsky, I. Koshyk, O. Chemerynsky, D. Huzar-Chemerynska) were executed. Others were shot in Mykolaiv (eg, B. Siretsky, V. Baranetsky, V. Antoniuk, V. Maliarchuk), Lubni, Kremenchuk, Kamianets-Podilskyi, Chernihiv, and Poltava. Part of the leadership and some members went underground, mostly in Western Ukraine and espe-

cially in Volhynia, where they joined the anti-German, anti-Soviet resistance headed by T. *Borovets.

BIBLIOGRAPHY

S[ydor].-Chartoryis'kyi, M. *Vid Sianu po Krym (Spomyny uchasnyka III Pokhidnoï Grupy-Pivden'* (New York 1951)

Matla, Z. *Pivnichna pokhidna hrupa* (Munich 1952)

Shankovs'kyi, L. *Pokhidni hrupy OUN (Prychynky do istoriï pokhidnykh hrup OUN na tsentral'nykh i skhidnikh zemliakh Ukraïny v 1941–1943 rr.)* (Munich 1958)

Armstrong, J. *Ukrainian Nationalism*, 2nd edn (New York 1963; repr, Littleton, Colo 1980)

Melnyk, K.; Lashchenko, O.; Veryha, V. (eds). *Na zov Kyieva: Ukraïns'kyi natsionalizm u II svitovii viini: Zbirnyk stattei, spohadiv i dokumentiv* (Toronto and New York 1985)

O. Shtul, Ye. Stakhiv

Ovcharenko, Anatolii [Ovčarenko, Anatolij], b 10 April 1937 in Ihren, now within the city limits of Dnipropetrovske. Stage actor. His repertoire ranges from classics to contemporary Soviet plays. Since completing study at the Kiev Institute of Theater Arts in the 1960s he has worked in the Vinnytsia Ukrainian Music and Drama Theater. Among his roles have been Hryts in *V nediliu rano zillia kopala* (On Sunday Morn She Picked Herbs, based on O. Kobylianska's novelette) and Oleksii in V. Vyshnevsky's *Optymistychna trahediia* (Optimistic Tragedy).

Ovcharenko, Dmytro [Ovčarenko], b 1 November 1906 in Merefa, Kharkiv county, d 10 November 1976 in Kharkiv. Scenery designer. In 1929 he completed study at the Kharkiv Art Institute (pupil of O. Khvostenko-Khvostov and M. Burachek). He worked as a designer in the Kharkiv Ukrainian Drama Theater, in the Kharkiv Theater of Opera and Ballet, and in the Donetske Ukrainian Music and Drama Theater. From 1931 he taught at the Kharkiv Art Institute.

Ovcharenko, Fedir [Ovčarenko], b 8 February 1913 in Vasylivshchyna, Sumy county, Kharkiv gubernia. Chemist and CPU figure; AN URSR (now ANU) full member since

Fedir Ovcharenko

1961. A graduate of the Hlukhiv Pedagogical Institute (1934), he taught there and at the Kiev Veterinary Institute (1937–41, 1945–9) and worked at the ANU Institute of General and Inorganic Chemistry (1949–67), where he headed the Department of Chemical and Geological Sciences (1959–62), and Institute of Colloidal Chemistry and Hydrochemistry (1967–73), where he headed the Department of Colloidal Chemistry and served as the institute's director (1967–8). He also directed the CC CPU Secretariat's science and culture department (1956–8), was appointed by P. Shelest as CC CPU ideological secretary (1968–72), and was elected a CC CPU member and Politburo candidate member (1968–75). Ovcharenko researched the periodicity of sedimentation; the structure of mineral dispersions; and their adsorptive, ion-exchange, and electrokinetic properties. He pioneered new approaches to the study of the lyophilicity of dispersed minerals and established the interaction mechanism of polar and nonpolar substances with their surface. He wrote over 200 papers, coauthored several monographs, and edited over a dozen books and collections.

Ovcharenko, Mariia. See Pshepiurska-Ovcharenko, Mariia.

Ovcharenko, Vasyl [Ovčarenko, Vasyl'], b 1 August 1889 in Nizhen, Chernihiv gubernia, d 4 October 1974 in Miami. Composer, French horn player, pedagogue, and conductor. After studying at the Kharkiv and Moscow conservatories, he conducted the St Sophia Cathedral Choir in Kiev and then worked in Kharkiv. He fled to Germany in 1944 and emigrated to the United States in 1950. His works include a symphony, a symphonic suite, the *Overture on Ukrainian Folk Themes* (1931), the march 'Western Ukraine' on folk themes (1929), a fantasy on themes from M. Lysenko's opera *Taras Bulba* (1929), 'Dumka' (Thought) in memory of M. Lysenko for string orchestra (1962), arrangements of folk songs, and art songs to texts by T. Shevchenko, O. Varavva, K. Perelisna, and L. Poltava. He also prepared new editions and orchestrations of scores by M. Lysenko (including the opera *Pan Kots'kyi* [Sir Catsky]), K. Stetsenko, M. Koliada, and M. Fomenko. His opera *Fox Mykyta* premiered in 1970 in Philadelphia.

Ovcharenko, Vasyl [Ovčarenko, Vasyl'], b 1 December 1899 in Drabivtsi, Zolotonosha county, Poltava gubernia, d 14 April 1978 in Dnipropetrovske. Stage actor and direc-

tor. He began his theatrical career in 1923 in Ukrainian touring theaters and then completed study at the theatrical college in Dnipropetrovske in 1933. In 1933–74 he was a leading actor in the Dnipropetrovske Ukrainian Music and Drama Theater.

Ovcharov, Hryhorii [Ovčarov, Hryhorij], b 8 February 1904 in Mohyliv, Verkhnodniprovske county, Katerynoslav gubernia. Literary critic. He was a Komsomol activist (1921–6), was editor of the journal *Krytyka* (1929–32), and worked for the chair of literature of the All-Ukrainian Association of Marxist-Leninist Scientific Research Institutes. After M. *Skrypnyk's suicide Ovcharov was persecuted because he had been Skrypnyk's protégé and personal secretary. Ovcharov's main works stress loyalty to Party ideology: *Narysy suchasnoï ukraïns'koï literatury* (An Outline of Contemporary Ukrainian Literature, 1931), *Za bil'shovizatsiiu proletars'koï literatury* (For the Bolshevization of Proletarian Literature, 1931), *Bil'she neprymyrennosty do vorozhykh vystupiv* (More Implacability toward the Enemy's Appearances, 1932 [a critique of V. Vynnychenko's *Soniashna mashyna* [Solar Machine]), and *Mykola Skrypnyk i radians'ka literatura* (Mykola Skrypnyk and Soviet Literature, 1933). He was rehabilitated in 1956, and published *Volodymyr Maiakovs'kyi – spivets' druzhby narodiv* (Vladimir Maiakovsky, the Praiser of the Friendship of Nations, 1956).

Ovchynnyk, Mykhailo [Ovčynnyk, Myxajlo], b 19 September 1901 in Hlukhiv, Chernihiv gubernia, d 3 December 1970 in Detroit. Zoologist; member of the AN URSR (now ANU) from 1932 and of the Ukrainian Free Academy of Sciences. A graduate of Kiev University (1926), he worked at the Experimental Station for Pisciculture and the Ukrainian Scientific Research Institute of Fish Management, took part in numerous hydrobiological expeditions, and taught in Kiev and Zhytomyr. He was imprisoned in a Soviet concentration camp (1938–41). In 1943–8 he taught at the *Ukrainian Free University and in 1949 he moved to the United States, where he taught ichthyology at Michigan State University and was curator at its natural history museum. He researched the fishes of Ecuador in conjunction with the Latin American Studies Center.

Ovchynnykov, Vasyl [Ovčynnykov, Vasyl'], b 25 December 1907 in Kamianske (now Dniprodzerzhynske), d 5 April 1978 in Kiev. Painter and muralist. In 1928–32 he studied at the Kharkiv Art Institute under V. Palmov, O. Bohomazov, and M. Rokytsky. Works such as *The Typist* (ca 1929) show his concern for depicting urban life in a thoroughly modern style. During the government repressions of the 1930s he abandoned his innovations and began working in a realist style (eg, *Love*, 1931).

Overtime work. Work in excess of the standard day or week and, usually, paid at a higher rate (see *work). In the 19th century long working hours were normal: the average industrial worker in the 1870s and 1880s worked 12 to 14 hours a day, not including lunch breaks, travel time, or overtime. In the Russian Empire the average overtime during that period was 20 to 30 minutes per day. The emerging trade-union and workers' movement demanded, among other things, restrictions on compulsory overtime and additional payment for overtime. In 1897 a law on overtime restricted compulsory overtime to 120 hours per year and to cases where the existing technology made overtime necessary. Voluntary overtime was not regulated by law. The laws, however, were violated with impunity. In Kharkiv gubernia in 1899 and 1917, 19 percent of the industrial workers surveyed had worked 166 hours of compulsory overtime per year. The rate of pay was the same as for regular work.

After the revolution the 1922 Labor Code prohibited overtime as a general rule. Exceptions were for defense projects, public emergencies, essential social services (water supply, transport, telephone services), and pressing repair and maintenance work. Originally overtime had to be sanctioned by the Rates and Conflicts Commission; later, only by the factory trade union. The code prohibited anyone from working more than 120 overtime hours per year and for more than 4 overtime hours on two consecutive days, except in seasonal work. In practice, however, the law was widely ignored, especially after the five-year plans were introduced. The law made no provision for overtime as a means of meeting production plans on time, yet such became the most common reason for overtime, especially at the end of the month. With legislation in 1940, workers in most branches of industry received a bonus of 50 percent of the regular rate for the first two hours of overtime and a bonus of 100 percent for all subsequent hours. Piece-rate workers received in addition to their regular wage a bonus of 50 percent of the tariff-wage for time-rate workers in the same tariff class for the first two hours and a bonus of 100 percent for all subsequent hours. Compulsory overtime for young workers under 16, nursing mothers, and pregnant women was prohibited. Overtime was limited to 120 hours per annum and 4 hours in any 48-hour period. In practice the rules were widely ignored – a state of affairs that gave rise to workers' protests in the 1960s and 1970s, especially in the Donbas region, where miners protested against compulsory work on Sundays. The current labor legislation is largely the same as that of 1940. Since the rise of independent trade unions in 1988–9, violations of the labor code have become less frequent.

BIBLIOGRAPHY
Bjork, L. *Wages, Prices, and Social Legislation in the Soviet Union* (London 1953)
Conquest, R. (ed). *Industrial Workers in the USSR* (London 1967)
Kir'ianov, Iu. *Zhiznennyi uroven' rabochikh Rossii: Konets XIX–nachalo XX v* (Moscow 1979)
Trud i zarabotnaia plata v SSSR (Moscow 1989)
B. Krawchenko

Ovidiopil or **Ovidiopol** [Ovidiopil' or Ovidiopol']. VII-11. A town smt (1990 pop 10,600) on the left bank of the Dniester Estuary and a raion center in Odessa oblast. At the beginning of the 18th century the Turkish fortress of Khadzhy-Dere stood at the site. It was seized by Russia in 1791, completely rebuilt in 1793, and renamed. Today Ovidiopil is a port and railway terminal. It has a canning and a brick factory and an automatic-press-building plant.

Ovruch [Ovruč]. II-9. A city (1990 pop 18,900) on the high left bank of the Noryn River and a raion center in Zhytomyr oblast. It is first mentioned in the chronicles under the year 946 as Vruchyi, a *Derevlianian settlement. In 977 the princes Oleh and Yaropolk I Sviatoslavych fought there; *Oleh is purportedly buried in a large grave nearby. In the second half of the 12th century Ovruch was part of Riuryk

St Basil's Church (late 12th century) in Ovruch

Rostyslavych's principality. In 1362 it came under Lithuanian rule, and in 1569 it was transferred to Poland and made a center of Ovruch starostvo. After the partition of Poland in 1793, it was annexed by Russia and became a county town in Volhynia gubernia. Today the town has a dairy, a canning factory, and a winery, as well as railway enterprises. Its architectural monuments include St Basil's Church (12th–13th century, restored 1908–12) and monastery buildings (1907–9).

Ovruch Ridge. An upland in the central portion of Polisia in northern Zhytomyr oblast. Nearly 50 km in length and 5–12 km in width, it stretches in an east–west direction from the town of Ovruch, with elevations ranging from 185 to 316 m. It consists mainly of Proterozoic quartzes, shales, and sandstones covered by a loamy soil and, in some locations, loess. The ridge has forests (mainly pines and oaks), which cover about one-quarter of its total area, and is strongly dissected by ravines.

Ovrutska, Mariia [Ovruc'ka, Marija], b 9 April 1895 in Kiev, d 7 September 1986 in Kiev. Translator. She worked as an editor and manager of the foreign literature department at the Radianska Shkola publishing house. From 1930 on she translated works by M. Kotsiubynsky, I. Franko, Yu. Yanovsky, A. Holovko, O. Vyshnia, I. Le, O. Korniichuk, and S. Skliarenko into German, and works by G.B. Shaw, A.C. Doyle, R. Rolland, F. von Schiller, L. Feuchtwanger, H. de Balzac, and other British, French, and German writers into Ukrainian.

Ovsianiko-Kulikovsky, Dmitrii [Ovsjaniko-Kulikovskij, Dmitrij], b 4 February 1853 in Kakhivka, Tavriia gubernia, d 9 October 1920 in Odessa. Russian literary scholar and theorist, linguist, and Sanskritologist; honorary member of the Russian Imperial Academy of Sciences from 1907. He studied comparative Indo-European gram-

Dmitrii Ovsianiko-Kulikovsky   Vasyl Ovsiienko

mar, Greek, and Sanskrit at the Universities of St Petersburg (1870–3, 1876–7) and Odessa (1873–6; PH D, 1887). In
Odessa he became a Ukrainophile and joined the local
Hromada. From 1877 to 1882 he lived abroad. In Geneva
he became a disciple of M. Drahomanov, who published
anonymously his pamphlet *Zapiski iuzhno-russkago sotsi-
alista* (Notes of a South Russian Socialist, 1877). After his
return he was a privatdocent in Odessa (1883–7) and
wrote for *Odesskiia novosti*. He became a professor at the
Universities of Kazan (1887–8) and Kharkiv (1888–1905)
and at the St Petersburg Higher Courses for Women
(1905–18). From 1894 to 1904 he edited Kharkiv University's *Zapiski*, and from 1912 to 1918, the influential Russian
journal *Vestnik Evropy*. In 1911 he delivered a lecture (pub
Kiev 1914) on T. Shevchenko's poetry at a session of the
Academy of Sciences in St Petersburg.

From 1890 on Ovsianiko-Kulikovsky was an adherent
of O. *Potebnia's psychological school in linguistics and
literature. He wrote many newspaper articles and scholarly studies and books in the fields of Sanskrit, Vedic
mythology and religion, philosophy, psychopathology,
linguistics, and Russian literature. In his memoirs (1923)
there are chapters on M. Drahomanov, M. Ziber, M. Kovalevsky, and O. Potebnia. A book about him by N. Osma-
kov was published in Moscow in 1981.

R. Senkus

Ovsiichuk, Volodymyr [Ovsijčuk], b 28 July 1924 in
Malyi Sknyt, Shepetivka okruha. Art historian at the Lviv
branch of the ANU Institute of Fine Arts, Folklore, and Ethnography. A graduate of Lviv University (1952), he did
postgraduate work at the Hermitage in Leningrad. A specialist in Renaissance and Baroque art and the artists of
Lviv, he has published many articles and a book on Ukrainian art of the 14th to mid-17th centuries and is a coauthor
of a book on the postwar art of the western Ukrainian
oblasts (1979) and *Maistry ukraïns'koho barokko* (Masters of
Ukrainian Baroque, 1991).

Ovsiienko, Vasyl [Ovsijenko, Vasyl'], b 8 May 1949 in
Lenine, Radomyshl raion, Zhytomyr oblast. Dissident. A
high school teacher of Ukrainian language and literature
in Kiev oblast, he was arrested in March 1973 for allegedly
having coedited the samvydav periodical *Ukraïns'kyi visnyk*, and sentenced to four years in labor camps in the
Mordovian ASSR. After his release he lived in Lenine,

where he was denied work and was subjected to administrative surveillance and KGB harassment. He joined the
*Ukrainian Helsinki Group in March 1977. Consequently
in February 1979 he was rearrested on fabricated charges
and sentenced in Radomyshl to three years in a camp in
Zaporizhia oblast. Before his scheduled release in 1981,
his term was extended to 10 years in severe-regime labor
camps in Perm oblast and 5 years' exile. He was amnestied in 1988.

Ovyd (Horizon). An illustrated journal of culture, politics, and the arts, published in Buenos Aires (1949–55) and
Chicago (1957–76), monthly to 1961 and then quarterly, by
M. Denysiuk. It included a section devoted to the Ukrainian Librarians' Association of America.

Owl (Ukrainian: *sova, puhach, spliushka, supukha, sych,
sira*). A nocturnal bird belonging to the order Strigiformes,
including the families Strigidae (typical owls), Tytonidae
(barn and grass owls), and Phodilidae (bay owls). Its body
length ranges from 17 to 74 cm, its weight, from 50 g to
3.25 kg, and its wingspan, from 40 cm to 1.8 m. In Ukraine
there are 13 known species, including both local and migratory. Sedentary owls include the long-eared owl (*Asio
otus*), the short-eared owl (*A. flammens*), which lives in
open areas and avoides forests, the barn owl (*Tyto alba*),
which inhabits abandoned structures, and the little owl
(*Athene noctua*), which settles near empty dwellings and in
dry steppe areas in burrows or rock piles. Irregular winter
flights into Ukraine from the north and northwest are
made by the migratory tawny owl (*Strix aluco*), the Ural or
long-tailed owl (*S. uralensis*), and the great or Lapp owl,
also known as the bearded owl (*S. nebulosa*). Because owls
are beneficial to agriculture and forestry, they are now a
protected species in Ukraine. The owl features prominently as a wise character in Ukrainian *folklore and *children's literature; it has also been known as a harbinger of
doom.

Rev Ivan Ozarkevych   Rev Ivan Ozarkevych
(1794–1854)   (1826–1903)

Ozarkevych, Ivan [Ozarkevyč], b 1794, d 1854 in Kolomyia, Galicia. Ukrainian Catholic priest, community figure, and writer in Galicia. He contributed to *Zoria halytska*.
In 1848 he was the first to stage Ukrainian plays in Kolomyia and Lviv – *Divka na viddanniu, abo Na myluvannia
nema syluvannia* (A Nubile Maiden, or Affection Cannot
Be Forced, his adaptation of I. Kotliarevsky's *Natalka Pol-

tavka [Natalka from Poltava] in the Pokutian dialect) and *Zhovniar-charivnyk* (his adaptation of I. Kotliarevsky's *Moskal'-charivnyk* [The Soldier-Sorcerer]). In 1850 he staged *Svatannia, abo Zhenykh navizhenyi* (Matchmaking, or the Crazy Bridegroom, his adaptation of H. Kvitka-Osnovianenko's *Svatannia na Honcharivtsi* [Matchmaking at Honcharivka]) and *Vesillia, abo Nad tsyhana Shmahaila nema rozumnishoho* (The Wedding, or There's No One Smarter Than the Gypsy Shmahailo, his adaptation of S. Pysarevsky's *Kupala na Ivana* [On St John's Eve]). He also translated a book of Aesop's fables into Ukrainian (1852) and wrote the historical plays *Dary predkiv* (The Ancestors' Gifts) and *Rozvida* (Reconnaissance) and a collection of poetry.

Ozarkevych, Ivan [Ozarkevyč], b 1826, d 8 February 1903 in Bolekhiv, Dolyna county, Galicia. Priest and civic leader; son of I. *Ozarkevych and father of N. *Kobrynska. A moderate populist, he was a deputy to the Galician Diet (1867–76) and the Austrian parliament (1873–91). He was opposed to the New Era policy and in 1895 headed a large Ukrainian delegation to Vienna to protest before the emperor the widespread abuse of power in the recent election in Galicia. He wrote occasional sermons and poems.

Yevhen Ozarkevych

Ozarkevych, Yevhen [Ozarkevyč, Jevhen], b 8 June 1861 in Beleluia, Sniatyn county, Galicia, d 21 September 1916 in Vienna. Physician and civic leader; full member of the Shevchenko Scientific Society (NTSh) and head of its Medical Commission from 1899. A graduate of Vienna University (1891), he worked as a county doctor in Bosnia, Rozhnitiv, Stryi, and Lviv and was an activist of burgher brotherhoods. In Stryi he organized the Mishchanska Besida society, and in Lviv the *Narodnia Lichnytsia society, whose clinic he directed (1903–14), and the Ukrainian Physicians' Society (1910). He edited the short-lived NTSh scientific collection *Likars'kyi zbirnyk* (1898–1901), in which he published his articles and reviews, particularly of Ukrainian medical terminology, and *Zdorovlie* (1912–14). He was vice-president of the Prosvita society and president of its Lviv branch. During the First World War he served as a doctor in a Ukrainian internment camp in Wolfsberg.

Ozaryntsi settlement. A *Trypilian settlement of the late 4th to early 3rd millennium BC near Ozaryntsi, Mohyliv-Podilskyi raion, Vinnytsia oblast. Excavations in 1927 by M. Rudynsky unearthed dwellings, pottery, flint tools, a sculpture of a human head, and earthenware figurines of animals.

Ozeriany Ridge. A distinctive ridge near Ozeriany, in the northwestern corner of Zhytomyr oblast. Nearly 8.5 km in length, between 0.5 and 1 km in width, and up to 190 m in height, the ridge is situated at the edge of the Ukrainian Shield. It runs like a thread in an east–west direction and consists of quartz and sandstones covered mainly by sandy or claylike soils. Pine forests constitute much of its vegetation.

Ozersky, Yurii [Ozers'kyi, Jurij] (pseud of Zebnytsky, Y.), b ca 1886, d after 1933. Pedagogue and political activist. A member of the Ukrainian Party of Socialist Revolutionaries–Borotbists (Communists), he headed the political education section of the People's Commissariat of Education of the Ukrainian SSR under M. Skrypnyk. He was also deputy chief of the agitation and propaganda section of the CC CP(B)U. He taught and wrote articles on pedagogical topics, especially on political education. After the fall of Skrypnyk in 1933, Ozersky was a victim of the Stalinist terror.

Oziv or **Azov.** VI-20. A city (1985 pop 76,000) and port on the Don River and a raion center in Rostov oblast, RF. Founded on the site of the Greek colony of Tanais, Oziv is one of the oldest settlements on the Sea of Azov. In the 10th and 11th centuries it was part of the Tmutorokan principality of Kievan Rus'. In 1067 it was captured by the Cumans, who renamed it Azak and brought it under the control of the Golden Horde. During the 13th to 15th centuries an Italian (Genoaesen) settlement called Tana stood at the site. Azov was captured by Turkey in 1471, and a fortress was built there. During 1637–42 it was held by the Don and the Zaporozhian Cossacks. In the late 17th century the Russians fought the Turks for possession of Azov. It was captured by Russia in 1774 and turned into the capital of Azov gubernia (1775–82). From 1810 it was part of Katerynoslav gubernia, and from 1888, of Don Cossack province. According to the census of 1926, Ukrainians accounted for 83.6 percent of the Azov raion population.

Ozokerite. A naturally occurring, light yellow to dark brown waxy mineral composed primarily of solid paraffinic hydrocarbons. It usually occurs as thin veins in rock fractures in mountain-building areas, where it probably separates from paraffin-base petroleum. It is purified by boiling in water and used widely in the manufacture of carbon paper, leather polishes, cosmetics, electrical insulators, waxes, and candles.

Ukraine's ozokerite deposits are among the largest in the world. They are located in the *Drohobych-Boryslav Industrial Region. Ozokerite has been mined there since the 1860s. By 1873 there were 4,000 operating mines, producing some 20,000 t of the mineral. The mining technology was primitive and inefficient. When the most accessible deposits were depleted, output dropped to 10,000 t in 1880, 1,000 t in 1914, and 300 t in 1938. For many purposes ozokerite has been replaced by paraffin wax. After the Second World War, mining techniques improved, and ozokerite output rose to its current level of 800–1,000 t annually.

P

Pachovsky, Borys [Pačovs'kyj] (Patchowsky), b 28 March 1931 in Peremyshl, Galicia. Graphic artist; son of V. *Pachovsky. A postwar émigré in the United States since 1950, he graduated from City College in New York in 1956. He is a member of the Ukrainian Artists Association in the USA. Pachovsky has taken part in group exhibitions in New York, Detroit, and Chicago. In 1966 he had a solo exhibition at the Ukrainian Institute of America in New York.

Pachovsky, Mykhailo [Pačovs'kyj, Myxajlo] (pseud: Mykhan Lopach), b 20 September 1861 in Dobrostany, Horodok county, Galicia, d 13 March 1933. Pedagogue. He graduated from Vienna University (1887) and worked as a teacher, primarily at the Academic Gymnasium of Lviv. He received his PH D from Chernivtsi University in 1895 and was director of the private Ukrainian gymnasium in Dolyna (1911–22). In 1918–19 he was a member of the Ukrainian National Rada of the Western Ukrainian National Republic. His first story, 'Vechernytsi' (The Evening Party), appeared in *Zerna*, the 1888 literary supplement to the Chernivtsi newspaper *Bukovyna*. He wrote schoolbooks on Ukrainian literature (1909, 1911), several songs, books on Ukrainian *bylyny* and dumas (1893) and Ukrainian burial rites (1903), and articles on Ukrainian folklore and writers in such periodicals as *Uchytel'* and *Pravda*.

Pachovsky, Roman [Pačovs'kyj], b 11 November 1911 in Rava Ruska, Galicia, d 6 February 1968 in New York. Painter; son of V. *Pachovsky. A postwar émigré in the United States from 1950, he studied art at the National Academy and the Art Students' League School and was active in the Ukrainian Artists' Association in the USA. He did landscapes, portraits (eg, *Marusia Bohuslavka* and *Baida Vyshnevetsky*), and historical paintings (eg, *The Escape of the Three Brothers from Azov* and *Duma about a Storm on the Black Sea*). Seven solo exhibitions of his works were held in New York. He wrote articles on art and compiled a collection of his father's literary works.

Pachovsky, Teoktyst [Pačovs'kyj], b 18 February 1907 in Strutyn Vyzhnii, Dolyna county, Galicia, d 30 December 1984 in Lviv. Slavist. He graduated from Lviv University (PH D, 1938), where he taught from 1933. He wrote articles on Old Ukrainian literature and on Ukrainian-Polish literary relations (particularly vis-à-vis T. Shevchenko and I. Franko).

Pachovsky, Vasyl [Pačovs'kyj, Vasyl'], b 12 January 1878 in Zhulychi, Zolochiv county, Galicia, d 5 April 1942 in Lviv. Poet, dramatist, publicist, and teacher. Pachovsky studied at Lviv University (medicine) and Vienna University (history) and completed his studies with a teacher's certificate in 1909. He taught in the high schools of Trans-

Vasyl Pachovsky

carpathian Ukraine (Uzhhorod) and in Galicia (Lviv and Peremyshl). Pachovsky worked as a cultural representative of the *Union for the Liberation of Ukraine in the internment camp at Knittelfeld, Austria (1914–15), edited *Strilets'* (1918–19) while serving in the Ukrainian Galician Army, edited the weekly *Narod* in Uzhhorod in the 1920s, and contributed to various journals throughout his life.

Pachkovsky was a prominent member of *Moloda Muza and made his literary debut in 1901 with a collection of lyrical poetry, *Rozsypani perly* (Scattered Pearls). It was followed by *Na stotsi hir* (On the Mountain Slopes, 1907) and *Ladi i Mareni ternovyi ohon' mii* (To Lada and Marena My Thorny Fire, 1912). His lyrical poetry is marked by a highly melodic line and folk-song stylizations. His dramas, written more in the modernist manner as highly lyrical allegories, at times too publicistic, are stylized patriotic visions of Ukraine in its quest for freedom: *Son ukraïns'koï nochi* (A Dream of a Ukrainian Night, 1903), *Sontse ruïny* (Sun of the Ruin, 1911), *Sfinks Evropy* (The Sphinx of Europe, 1914), *Roman Velykyi* (Prince Roman the Great, 1918), and *Het'man Mazepa* (1933). Similar in style to his plays is Pachovsky's epic poem, *Zoloti vorota* (The Golden Gates), of which only two of the projected four volumes were finished, *Peklo Ukraïny* (Ukraine's Hell, 1937) and *Preispodnia* (The Underworld, pub in 1985 as *Chystylyshche Ukaïny* [Ukraine's Purgatory]). *Zoloti vorota* forms vol 2 of the two-volume collection *Zibrani tvory* (Collected [Poetic] Works, 1984, 1985), of which vol 1 consists of Pachovsky's lyrical poetry, including previously unpublished poems and collections. Pachovsky's historical studies, as well as his *Narys istoriï miniiatury po rukopysiam* (A Survey of the History of Illuminations, 1913), were devoted primarily to Transcarpathia, and consist of *Istoriia Podkarpatskoi Rusy* (History of Subcarpathian Rus', 1921), *Sribna zemlia: Tysiacholittia Karpats'koï Ukraïny* (The Silver Land: A Millennium of Carpathian Ukraine, 1938), and the posthumous *Istoriia Zakarpattia* (History of Transcarpathia, 1946).

D.H. Struk

A co-operative in Kadovbyshchi, Brody county, after the Pacification

Pacification. A campaign of repressions conducted by the Polish authorities against the Ukrainian population of Galicia in the summer and autumn of 1930. They were part of an operation intended to break up and intimidate opposition to the *Sanacja regime on the eve of the parliamentary elections planned for November 1930. The ostensible rationale for the Pacification was the sabotage being carried out by the Ukrainian Military Organization (UVO), which began in July and reached a peak in September and October 1930. The scope of the operations and the manner in which they were carried out, however, made it clear that the Polish government was responding to more than just the UVO threat. In effect the Pacification was comparable to a pogrom against Ukrainians initiated, sanctioned, and executed by the Polish state authorities.

On 1 September Prime Minister J. Piłsudski ordered the minister of the interior to send the police and army into the region affected by the actions. The security forces were supervised by B. *Pieracki (deputy minister), H. Suchenek-Suchecki (head of the nationalities department), and the voivode of Lviv, B. Nakonieczników-Klukowski. In the first week of September intensified control was introduced in Galicia, together with the checking of documents and searches and arrests among people suspected of UVO membership. About 20 leaders of the organization were detained at that time, including Ya. Nestor, B. *Kravtsiv, and Z. *Knysh. On the night of 9 September the authorities imprisoned up to 20 leading members of the parliamentary opposition in an army fort in Brest, together with 5 Ukrainian deputies: V. Tselevych, D. Paliiv, I. Lishchynsky, O. Kohut, and O. Vyslotsky. On 20 September the regional commander of the UVO, Yu. Holovinsky, was arrested outside the Ukrainian National Democratic Alliance (UNDO) offices in Lviv; he was shot on 30 September by the police, purportedly while attempting to escape.

On 21 September the Pacification proper was inaugurated. It lasted until 16 October and encompassed 28 counties of Galicia, where it focused on those villages regarded as sympathetic to the UVO. Security forces commonly surrounded a given village and carried out a detailed search of all its buildings. In the course of many of their actions they devastated the interiors as well as entire houses, removed Ukrainian signs, and indiscriminately destroyed Ukrainian cultural objects (including books, stage wardrobes, folk dress, native needlework, and the like). The army engaged in what it referred to as heavy quartering (compulsory requisitions for food and grain). The population was often forced to sign declarations of loyalty to Poland and to renounce their affiliation to the Ukrainian nation; prominent local leaders were publicly ridiculed. Whippings were widely administered, and seven people died as a result of beatings (Polish sources claimed two victims).

Polish Ministry of the Interior files note that 144 rifles, 156 pistols, 40 kg of dynamite, and 39 kg of gunpowder, as well as other explosives and UVO propaganda literature, were found during the searches. By the end of 1930, 970 persons had been arrested, of whom 538 were released and 432 turned over to the courts. The courts set free 330 persons and proved UVO membership in the case of 42 persons. The detainees included peasants (550), secondary school pupils (135), and students (124). Official Polish reports at that time claimed a larger amount of arms and a greater number of arrests.

The Pacification campaign also affected mainstream Ukrainian political groups and institutions. After the discovery of contacts between the UVO and the UNDO leadership the offices of the UNDO in Lviv were searched, and on 30 September several UNDO members were arrested – D. Levytsky, L. Makarushka, and V. Mudry. On 24 September the authorities closed the Ukrainian secondary schools in Ternopil, Drohobych, and Rohatyn and delegalized the organization *Plast. In village raids Ukrainian reading rooms and co-operative stores were among the buildings specifically targeted for searches (and damage).

The Pacification met with public condemnation in many countries (including Great Britain, France, and Germany). A protest was voiced by Metropolitan A. Sheptytsky, who came to Warsaw on 3 October in an unsuccessful attempt to meet with Piłsudski; his pastoral letter on the matter was subsequently confiscated. Ukrainian émigré groups published accounts of the Polish action in several languages. In December 1930 the Ukrainian Parliamentary Representation in the Sejm moved for examination of the events surrounding the Pacification and the punishment of those guilty of the acts of terror. It was rejected by the Polish majority. Ukrainian representations to the League of Nations on the issue of the Pacification began in November 1930. Although sympathetic hearing was given to various memorandums submitted and circulated among committees and state missions, the Council of the league issued a statement as late as January 1932 in which it stated that the Polish actions could be justified because of Ukrainian sabotage activities.

BIBLIOGRAPHY
Na vichnu han'bu Pol'shchi (Prague 1931)
Revyuk, E. (ed). *Polish Atrocities in Ukraine* (New York 1931)
Knysh, Z. *Dryzhyt' pidzemnyi huk: Spohady z 1930 i 1931 rokiv u Halychyni* (Winnipeg 1953)
Chojnowski, A. *Koncepcje polityki narodowościowej rządów polskich w latach 1921–1939* (Wrocław 1979)
Klymyshyn, M. *V pokhodi do voli: Spomyny*, vol 1 (Detroit 1987)
                                                    A. Chojnowski

Paczoski, Józef, b 8 December 1864 in Bilohorodka, Iziaslav county, Volhynia gubernia, d 14 February 1942 near Poznań, Poland. Botanist of Polish descent. After studying and working as a laboratory assistant at Kiev

University (1888–94) he was director of the Kherson Museum of Natural History (1897–1920) and a professor at the Kherson Polytechnical Institute (1918–22). He worked as an associate of the Askaniia-Nova Nature Reserve (1922–3) and then became a professor at Poznań University (1925). A specialist in the flora and fauna of Ukraine (particularly Polisia and the southern steppe regions) and eastern Poland, he wrote *Flora Poles'ia i prilezhashchikh mestnostei* (The Flora of Polisia and Its Adjacent Areas, 3 parts, 1897–1900) and *Opisanie rastitel'nosti Khersonskoi gubernii* (A Description of the Vegetation of Kherson Gubernia, 3 parts, 1915–27), and, in Ukrainian, *Osnovy fitosotsiologii* (Fundamentals of Phytosociology, 1921).

Ivan Padalka: *Cossacks* (woodcut)

Padalka, Ivan, b 27 October 1894 in Zhornoklovy, Zolotonosha county, Poltava gubernia, d 13 July 1937. Painter, muralist, and graphic artist. He studied at the Myrhorod Applied Arts School (1909–12), the Kiev Art School (1913–17), and under M. *Boichuk and V. Krychevsky at the Ukrainian State Academy of Arts (1917–20). A member of the *Association of Revolutionary Art of Ukraine in the 1920s, he taught at the Myrhorod (1920–1) and Mezhyhiria (1921–5) ceramics tekhnikums, the Kharkiv Art Institute (1925–34), and the Kiev State Art Institute (1934–6). Under M. Boichuk's direction he took part in creating the 14 murals at the Lutske army barracks in Kiev (1919) and the fresco *Rest* at the Chervonozavodskyi Theater in Kharkiv (1933–5). He also did woodcuts, portraits of P. Panch and O. Pavlenko, and genre paintings, such as *Miners, Gather-*

ing Eggplants (early 1930s), *Hay Gathering, Attack of the Red Cavalry* (1927), and *Photographer in the Village* (1927). His prints include *Apple* (1926), *Insurgents*, and the series 'Dnieper Hydroelectric Station' (1928). He illustrated many children's books, including the collection *Barvinok* (Periwinkle, with T. Boichuk, 1919), O. Donchenko's *Ha-la-hal*, and *Slovo o polku Ihorevi* (The Tale of Ihor's Campaign, 1928), and designed posters, bookplates, and covers for editions of works by T. Shevchenko, I. Franko, O. Dosvitnii, I. Kotliarevsky, M. Yohansen, V. Polishchuk, and S. Taranushenko. His paintings and prints were influenced by the icon and *lubok* traditions. Padalka was arrested by the NKVD in September 1936 and later executed.

S. Hordynsky

Padalka, Lev, b 1859 in Chornukhy, Lokhvytsia county, Poltava gubernia, d 1922? Historian and statistician. He graduated from Kiev University (1884) and worked as a statistician for the Poltava and Kherson gubernial zemstvos, the city of Kharkiv, and the government of Poltava gubernia. A member of the Poltava Learned Archival Commission, he wrote, in Russian, studies on the Poltava region's past and colonization (1914), on the maps of Cossack regiments in the Poltava region (1914), on G. Le Vasseur de Beauplan's map of the colonization of the Poltava region in the second quarter of the 17th century (1914), and on the history of Poltava eparchy (1916). He also contributed several articles to *Kievskaia starina* on the history of the Zaporozhian Sich and wrote statistical studies on the lands of Romen county, Poltava gubernia (1904), and the application of the territorial principle in zemstvo statistics (1900). In 1918 he participated in a special commission of the Hetman government that defined the Ukrainian ethnic territories on Ukraine's border with the Don region.

Yaroslav Padokh   Omelian Paduchak

Padokh, Yaroslav [Padox, Jaroslav], b 14 December 1908 in Buchach, Galicia. Lawyer, legal scholar, and civic leader; since 1949 full member of the Shevchenko Scientific Society (NTSh) and the Ukrainian Academy of Arts and Sciences. A graduate of Cracow University (LLM, 1931), he began to practice law in 1937. Upon obtaining an LLD degree from the Ukrainian Free University (UVU) in Prague (1940) he taught law there until 1948, when he emigrated to the United States. He returned to law school at St John's University (LLB, 1956) and opened his own law office. He has been a leading member of many Ukrainian organizations, such as Plast, the Ukrainian National Association, the Ukrainian Congress Committee of America, and the Association of Ukrainian Lawyers. Since 1977 he has headed the US branch of the NTSh, and since 1983 he has been the president of the Executive Council of the NTSh in the diaspora. Padokh has written several books on legal history, including textbooks on the history of Western European law (1947) and of old Ukrainian procedural law (1949), an outline of the history of Ukrainian criminal law (1951), *Mis'ki sudy na Ukraïni pislia 1648 r.* (City Courts in Ukraine after 1648, 1948), and *Sudy i sudovyi protses staroï Ukraïny* (Courts and Legal Procedure of Old Ukraine, 1990).

Paduchak, Omelian Illia [Padučak, Omeljan Illja], b 15 August 1885 in Lypytsia Horishnia, Rohatyn county, Galicia, d 3 May 1961 in Asunción, Paraguay. Civic leader. To avoid arrest for participating in strikes, he emigrated to Germany (1904) and then South America. He was the first Ukrainian known to settle in Paraguay (1910), and preceded the start of regular Ukrainian immigration by 12 years. In 1937 he helped found the Prosvita society in Encarnación and served as its president. Immediately after the Second World War he organized the Ukrainian Relief Committee for War Victims, which became affiliated with the Paraguayan Red Cross in 1946. Paduchak's extensive lobbying efforts, organizing, and legal work helped settle hundreds of Ukrainian *displaced persons in Paraguay. From its inception he served as president of the Ukrainian Center in Paraguay (1949–61) and as an executive member of the Pan-American Ukrainian Conference. He left a valuable archive on the history of Ukrainian settlement in South America.

Padun, Volodymyr, b 25 June 1942 in Plavni, Vasylivka raion, Zaporizhia oblast. Painter. He is a graduate of the Dnipropetrovske Art School (1968). His work has been influenced by Ukrainian folk art, particularly *Petrykivka painting. Using tempera, Padun paints highly ornamental flowers and landscapes in intense, bright colors (eg, *On the River Kilchen* [1978] and *Sunflowers* [1983]).

Padura, Tymko (Tomasz), b 21 December 1801 in Illintsi, Radomyshl county, Kiev gubernia, d 20 September 1871 in Koziatyn, Berdychiv county, Kiev gubernia. Poet and musician of Polish descent; member of the *Ukrainian school in Polish literature. He graduated from the Kremianets Lyceum (1825). He maintained contact with the Decembrists and for that reason was imprisoned by the Russian authorities (1830–2). Padura was influenced by Ukrainian folklore and by J. Niemcewicz, G. Byron, and Ossian. He wrote (in Ukrainian using the Latin script) lyrical poems and songs with a Slavophile and Polonophile interpretation of Ukrainian history ('Lirnyk' [The Lyrist], 'Zaporozhets'' [The Zaporozhian], 'Het'mantsi' [The Hetman's Men], 'Pisniar' [The Songmaker], 'Do Dnipra' [To the Dnieper]) and set some of them to music. His poems were also set to music by composers such as M. Lysenko ('Lirnyk') and K. Lipiński. Padura also wrote poems in Polish.

Paganism (from the Latin *paganus* 'country dweller'; Ukrainian: *pohanstvo*). A general designation for pre-Christian polytheistic religions, the term came into common use in Europe after Constantine adopted Christianity as the state religion of the Roman Empire in 313. In the medieval period even non-Christian monotheistic religions, such as Judaism and Islam, were considered pagan. The earliest reference to paganism in Ukraine appears in Procopius (6th century AD). Paganism survived long after the official Christianization of Rus' in 988. Traces of it can be found even in the 20th century.

Paganism in Ukraine constantly evolved and changed. The oldest form was animism, which accepted the existence of good (*berehyni*) and evil (*upyry, demony*) spirits. Later, fertility gods (*Rod and the *rozhanytsi*) and ancestral spirits were worshiped, and then a supreme deity, Svaroh, the god of heaven and fire. At the start of the rule of *Volodymyr the Great the idols of the chief gods – *Perun, *Khors, *Dazhboh, *Stryboh, Symarhl, and Mokosh – stood on a hill near his palace. Plant, animal, and occasionally human sacrifices were brought before them. Upon adopting Christianity he destroyed the idols and built St Basil's Church at the site. Most of the common people continued to worship the pagan deities (see *Mythology) and nature and household spirits (see *Demonology in Ukraine).

The pagans did not build special shrines but worshiped in the open at altars on sacred sites. According to a Greek chronicler of the 10th century an altar was built under a great oak on Khortytsia Island, and Kiev merchants sailing down the Dnieper stopped to offer sacrifice there. V. *Khvoika excavated a site with a large sacrificial altar in Kiev. Sacred sites of the first few centuries AD were found on vestal hills on the Dnieper, near the village of Trypilia, and on the Ros, near Sakhnivka. There were also several such sites on so-called Bald hills in Ukraine. In the Christian era these locales were believed to be the gathering places of witches and sorceresses. The pagans did not have a separate priestly caste, only soothsayers, known as *volkhvy*. Sacrifices on behalf of particular persons were brought by the persons themselves or their relatives; those for the benefit of a family, by the family head; and those for the country's sake, by the prince.

Pagans in Ukraine believed in the afterlife and viewed it as an extension of this life. According to foreign writers they preferred death to captivity out of the fear of remaining slaves after death. They were buried with their favorite objects and with symbols of their social status. The dead were usually buried, but some were cremated. Funerals involved various rituals and songs. (See *Burial rites and *Laments.) A year after a funeral a commemorative banquet was held. Weddings also were highly ritualized. Paganism tolerated polygamy, although most people, particularly the lower classes, practiced monogamy.

The Christian church actively opposed paganism. It supplanted the more popular cults with Christian ones: Perun with St Elijah, Veles with St George, Kupalo with John the Baptist. The seasonal agricultural festivals were also modified and associated with Christian holidays: the winter equinox became Christmas, the 'Great Day' (*Velykden'*) became Easter, and the *Rosalia became the Descent of the Holy Spirit. Each of these festivals retains to this day elements of pagan rites. Gradually the church introduced its sacraments into everyday life – first into baptism and burial, then, finally, into marriage. Some pagan customs (caroling, the blessing of wells and fields) that could not be suppressed were simply adopted by the church. The expected result, however, was not always achieved: in most cases, Christian and pagan rituals with the same function were practiced side by side. Other pagan customs, such as the *harvest rituals, were converted from religious into folkloric practices. Soothsaying was incorporated into the games of *St Andrew's Eve.

The people often interpreted church festivals in pagan terms; the Virgin Mary's Presentation at the Temple, for example, was viewed as a festival of the dead in Ukraine (the dead were said to 'see' their bodies on this day), and Christ's Presentation at the Temple celebrated the encounter between winter and spring.

Traces of paganism were preserved longest in various seasonal *folk customs and rites, such as the Christmas Eve dinner, caroling, the Easter *vesnianky-hahilky, the transfer of livestock to the pasture in the springtime, the *Kupalo festival, the harvest rituals, and *pomynky (see *Calendric ritual folk poetry). A number of pagan rites have been retained in the wedding ceremonies. The oldest forms of the Ukrainian oral tradition, including tales, legends, and aphorisms, originated in the pagan era.

BIBLIOGRAPHY
Anichkov, E. Iazychestvo i drevniaia Rus' (St Petersburg 1914)
Gal'kovskii, N. Bor'ba khristianstva s ostatkami iazychestva v drevnei Rusi, 2 vols (Kharkiv 1916)
Hrushevs'kyi, M. Z istoriï relihiinoï dumky na Ukraïni (Lviv 1925; 2nd edn, Munich 1962)
Rybakov, B. Iazychestvo drevnikh slavian (Kiev 1981)
– Iazychestvo drevnei Rusi (Moscow 1987)

M. Mushynka

Painting. The portrayal or rendering of pictures on a flat surface with a variety of pigments in such media as tempera, oils, watercolors, and acrylics. In Ukraine the oldest surviving paintings are frescoes and murals found at archeological sites of ancient Hellenic colonies on the northern Black Sea coast, where they were preserved on the walls of tombs. One of the earliest portraits is a head of a young man (4th century AD) on a stone slab in the encaustic technique found at the ruins of Chersonese Taurica. Some early (3rd century) Christian frescoes have been preserved in the Crimea.

Fragments of frescoes from the medieval Rus' period have been found in the Church of the Tithes in Kiev (late 10th century), the Cathedral of the Transfiguration in Chernihiv (11th century), and the St Sophia Cathedral in Kiev (early 11th century). Some of the frescoes of St Michael's Golden-Domed Monastery in Kiev, which was demolished by the Soviet authorities in 1934–5, are preserved at the St Sophia Museum in Kiev. In style these 11th-century frescoes are similar to those of the middle period of Byzantine art. The frescoes in the Church of St Cyril's Monastery in Kiev (mid-12th century) are more realistic and display Balkan influences.

According to the Primary Chronicle portable icons were already being painted in the 10th and 11th centuries, but none so old have survived to our time. The oldest extant icon from Kiev, The Vyshhorod (Vladimir) Mother of God (12th century), which was of Greek origin, is now in the Tretiakov Gallery in Moscow, as are three other icons once in Kiev, the Great Panagia, St Demetrius of Thessalonica, and The Mother of God of the Caves (ca 1288), which also depicts SS Anthony and Theodosius of the Caves. Examples of me-

dieval Ukrainian painting can also be found in illuminated manuscripts (see *Illumination).

With the decline of Kievan Rus' the center of political power and culture shifted to the Principality of Galicia-Volhynia, and only a few paintings (mostly in Western Ukraine) survived the turbulent years of the 13th-century Mongol invasion – the frescoes in the rotunda chapel in Horiany, in Transcarpathia, and in the Armenian Cathedral in Lviv, built in 1363. Two of the better-known surviving icons are St George from Stanylia and The Mother of God from Lutske (late 13th to early 14th century), both rendered in the Byzantine-Ukrainian tradition of icon painting. Ukrainian iconographers were commissioned by Kings Casimir III and Władysław II Jagiełło to decorate churches in the Wawel royal castle in Cracow and the Holy Cross Church in Łysa Góra (1393–4).

In the 15th and 16th centuries there emerged a Galician school of icon painting, in which adherence to Byzantine iconography was tempered by personal interpretations, individual variations, and Western influences. In The Mother of God Hodegetria from Krasiv (second half of the 15th century), for example, Mary's face is considerably rounder and more in keeping with those of local models, and Jesus wears an embroidered shirt. Gothic influences may be seen in the architecture of some icons, such as SS George and Parasceve from Korchyn (late 15th century). During the Renaissance icons gradually lost their rigidity and became more realistic. The development was first apparent in the modeling of facial features, as in Christ Pantocrator (late 15th century) from Starychi, in the Lviv region, and in the use of local landscapes, as in Transfiguration (1575) from Yabluniv. It was not until the 17th century, however, that Byzantine traditions began giving way to the *baroque, which introduced secular themes, three-dimensional forms, and movement in icons (eg, the iconostases in Velyki Hrybovychi [1638], near Zhovkva in Galicia, and in Velyki Sorochyntsi, near Myrhorod [early 18th century]). Two of the better-known icon painters at the time were I. *Rutkovych and Y. *Kondzelevych, whose work was influenced by Western religious painting and iconography. The influence is evident in the theme, composition, and realistic rendering of Christ by the Well (1696–9) in the iconostasis painted by Rutkovych in the Church of the Nativity in Skvariava Nova, near Zhovkva.

In Ukraine portrait painting as a separate genre emerged during the Renaissance (16th century) and was strongly influenced by the icon tradition. The first portraits were those of benefactors (Jan Herburt, ca 1578), which were hung in churches, and memorial likenesses painted on wood or metal panels for coffins (Varvara Larbysh, 1635). Portraits not used for religious purposes did not emerge until the 17th century. They included official portrayals of nobles and Cossack hetmans and officers, known as 'parsunnyi' (personal) portraits, as well as more intimate portraits of nobles and burghers.

The secular themes, illusionistic space, local colors, and realistic representations that the baroque brought from Western Europe remained strong in Ukrainian art until the imposition of socialist realism in the 1930s. Painting expanded thematically to include a variety of portraits, battle scenes, genre depictions, and presentations of historical compositions.

As Ukrainian Cossack autonomy was eroded by the tsars in the 18th century, opportunities for Ukrainian

PAINTING 1) M. Petrakhnovych: *Resurrection of Lazarus* (1638) in the Dormition Church of Velyki Hrybovychi, near Nesterov, Lviv oblast. 2) Anonymous folk painting of *Kozak-Mamai* (oil, 18th century; Chernihiv Historical Museum). 3) A. Mokrytsky: *Portrait of the Artist's Wife* (oil, 1853; Kiev Museum of Ukrainian Art; photo courtesy of the Winnipeg Art Gallery). 4) S. Vasylkivsky: *A Cossack Picket* (oil, 1888; Kharkiv Art Museum). 5) M. Pymonenko: *Going Off to Battle* (oil, 1902). 6) A. Ekster: *Bridge* (oil, 1912; Kiev Museum of Ukrainian Art). 7) V. Yermilov: *Composition* (oil, 1923). 8) V. Kostetsky: *Return Home* (oil, 1947; Kiev Museum of Ukrainian Art). 9) O. Hryshchenko: *Landscape* (oil, 1960s; courtesy of I. Moroz).

painters to have their talents recognized locally became increasingly limited. Consequently, many were attracted to the newly established Academy of Arts in St Petersburg (est 1757), which cultivated the classicist style of painting then popular in Europe. Better-known Ukrainian artists who pursued their careers at the academy and contributed significantly to the development of art in Russia were A. *Losenko, K. Holovachevsky, I. *Sablukov (Sabluchok), D. *Levytsky (one of the greatest portraitists in the Russian Empire), and V. *Borovykovsky.

The emigration of Ukrainian artists to St Petersburg deprived Ukrainian painting of its most creative talents. The exception was T. *Shevchenko, who devoted most of his painting (like his writing) to Ukrainian interests and has been considered the father of modern Ukrainian painting. Shevchenko painted numerous portraits, self-portraits, and landscapes which recorded the architectural monuments of Ukraine. While in exile he depicted Kirgiz folkways and the surrounding countryside, as well as the degradation of tsarist prisons and the first pictorial indictments of the horrors of Russian army life and punishment. Shevchenko was also concerned with formal problems of the effects of light and dark.

During the 19th century landscape painting appeared as a separate genre, and not only in the work of Shevchenko. Inspired by romanticism, I. *Soshenko recorded the pastoral settings of rural scenery, and A. *Kuindzhi, I. *Aivazovsky, S. *Vasylkivsky, I. *Pokhytonov, and S. *Svitoslavsky devoted their efforts to depicting rural scenery at its most beautiful.

A Romantic idealism was reflected in the portraits of A. *Mokrytsky, particularly in that of his wife (1853), as well as in H. *Vasko's *Youth from the Tomariv Family* (1847) and P. *Shleifer's portrait of his wife (1853).

In the last few decades of the 19th century Ukrainian painters studying art in Russia were influenced by the *Peredvizhniki society, formed in 1870 in St Petersburg by artists who were opposed to the classicist traditions of the Academy of Arts. Artists of Ukrainian origin who became active in the society were I. *Repin, N. *Ge, I. *Kramskoi, A. Kuindzhi, M. *Kuznetsov, K. *Kostandi, P. *Levchenko, P. *Martynovych, O. *Murashko, P. *Nilus, L. *Pozen, M. *Pymonenko, and S. Svitoslavsky. Not all of them remained committed to it. Many other artists were influenced by its ideas to paint realistic genre pictures, including F. *Krasytsky, S. *Kyshynivsky, and S. *Vasylkivsky. M. *Samokysh was primarily known for his Cossack and battle scenes, and I. *Izhakevych depicted peasant life.

In Austrian-ruled Western Ukraine artists adapted to European trends, particularly those prevalent in Vienna and Cracow, where some of them had studied. Among them were L. *Dolynsky, K. *Ustyianovych, and T. *Kopystynsky, all of whom depicted rural life through a romanticized ethnographic prism and were active in decorating churches. Both M. *Ivasiuk, who was known for his panoramic historical canvases, and A. *Manastyrsky remained dedicated realists.

*Impressionism made itself felt in the work of several Kiev artists who had worked in Paris, including P. *Levchenko, A. *Manevich, M. *Burachek, O. Murashko, and the exceptionally versatile V. Krychevsky. The new style stimulated an interest in intimate glimpses of ordinary events and urban scenery (eg, Levchenko's *Reading a Letter* and Murashko's *Flower Vendors*). Above all else it altered the palette of most artists for many years to come. In Western Ukraine impressionism influenced the work of I. *Trush (although for the most part he remained a realist), O. *Kurylas, and O. *Kulchytska. Artists who worked in the impressionist style included M. *Sosenko and Ya. *Pstrak.

Whereas the artists in Western Ukraine for the most part remained under the influence of Western European art movements, those working in Kiev, Kharkiv, and Odessa developed close ties with Moscow and Leningrad. Thus P. *Volokidin was influenced by the World of Art movement, and P. *Kholodny and M. Sapozhnikov created symbolist paintings. The early 20th-century avant-garde movement had a direct impact on Ukrainian painting. Artists born in Ukraine, as well as those who considered themselves Ukrainian by nationality, were in its vanguard. The most prominent of them were K. *Malevich, D. and V. Burliuk, A. Ekster, L. Baranoff-Rossiné, and V. *Tatlin. Ekster introduced *futurism to Kiev and helped bring avant-garde exhibitions to Ukraine.

During the brief period of Ukrainian independence the *Ukrainian State Academy of Arts (1917–22) was established in Kiev. It and its successor, the Kiev State Art Institute, made it possible for Ukrainian painters to pursue advanced art training in their homeland. V. Krychevsky was its first rector, and one of the most influential teachers was M. *Boichuk, who revived fresco painting and aspired to develop an art for the masses based on a combination of Ukrainian traditions and Western models instead of the Peredvizhniki. Subsequently Boichuk and his followers (the 'Boichukists') – his brother, T. *Boichuk, his wife, S. *Nalepinska, O. *Pavlenko, V. *Sedliar, I. *Padalka, I. *Lypkivsky, P. Ivanchenko, A. Ivanova, S. Kolos, K. *Hvozdyk, E. *Shekhtman, and M. *Rokytsky – were victims of the Stalinist terror of the 1930s.

F. *Krychevsky, who also taught at the academy and the Kiev State Art Institute, was influenced by impressionist colors, but remained a realist in his modeling of form and space (eg, *Self-Portrait in a Sheepskin Coat*, 1926). Others who adhered to realism included M. *Kozyk, H. *Svitlytsky, S. *Kyshynivsky, S. *Prokhorov, M. *Sharonov, and I. *Shulha.

During the relatively liberal period of the 1920s in Soviet Ukraine, a variety of styles flourished. Cubo-futurist paintings were produced by V. *Yermilov in Kharkiv and O. *Bohomazov, V. *Palmov, and A. *Petrytsky in Kiev. Petrytsky painted over a hundred portraits of Ukrainian personalities, most of which disappeared or were destroyed during the terror. V. *Meller and K. Sikorsky experimented with abstraction; Yu. *Mykhailiv, who was fascinated with mythology, continued the traditions of the symbolists.

In interwar Western Ukraine under Polish rule, the most prominent Lviv painter was O. *Novakivsky, who began as an impressionist and was attracted by French postimpressionism and expressionism. He painted portraits and landscapes, and through his art school he influenced an entire generation of future artists, including I. *Vynnykiv, S. *Hordynsky, and Myron *Levytsky, who went on to explore modern trends in art. R. *Selsky experimented with surrealism; M. *Butovych, P. *Kovzhun, and R. *Lisovsky explored cubism and abstraction. The revival of the Byzantine style of church mural painting and decoration in Western Ukraine was encouraged by Metropolitan A. Sheptytsky, a great patron of the arts. It was practiced by O. *Kurylas, M. *Osinchuk, V. *Diadyniuk, and Yu. *Butsmaniuk.

Artists working in Transcarpathia under interwar Czechoslovak rule, including Yu. *Virah, Y. *Bokshai, A. *Erdeli, and E. *Hrabovsky, had ties with Central and Western European art movements and used bold, vibrant colors. Later A. *Kotska, Z. *Sholtes, F. *Manailo, E. Kondratovych, and H. Hliuk continued the coloristic traditions.

In the 1930s all avant-garde activities in Soviet Ukraine came to a halt with the introduction of *socialist realism as the only literary and artistic method permitted by the communist regime. Painting was limited to naturalistically rendered thematic canvases of the Bolshevik Revolution and its champions, glorification of the Soviet state and its leaders, portraits and genre scenes of happy workers and peasants, and romanticized depictions of war and its heroes. Landscapes and still-life compositions were discouraged and all departures from the socialist-realist canon were condemned as 'formalist,' and their creators were discriminated against and sometimes persecuted. Among the more prominent socialist-realist artists were V. *Kostetsky, M. *Bozhii, S. *Hryhoriev, D. *Shavykin, O. *Shovkunenko, O. *Lopukhov, and O. Khmelnytsky.

The narrow confines of socialist realism were widened somewhat after the death of J. Stalin, particularly during N. Khrushchev's cultural thaw. Artists such as R. *Selsky, M. *Selska, V. *Manastyrsky, T. *Yablonska, and V. *Zaretsky turned to Ukrainian folk themes, more vibrant colors, and a flattened rendering. Younger artists, such as K. *Zvirynsky, V. Basanets, V. Sumar, and V. Lamakh, experimented with abstraction; L. *Medvid, I. *Zavadovsky, P. *Markovych, and I. *Marchuk, with surrealism; and V. *Patyk and V. *Loboda, with expressionism.

The curtailing of artistic freedom in 1965 and again in 1972, as well as the arrest and sentencing of prominent Ukrainian writers and artists, including O. *Zalyvakha and S. *Shabatura, gave rise to nonconformism. In the 1970s Ukrainian artists participating in the exhibitions of nonconformist art in Moscow and Leningrad included N. Haiduk, F. *Humeniuk, V. *Makarenko, V. *Naumets, V. *Sazonov, V. *Strelnikov, and L. *Yastreb. Other artists, such as K. Zvirynsky in Lviv and O. Dubovyk, I. Marchuk, and Ye. *Petrenko in Kiev, stopped exhibiting.

After the failure of the Ukrainian revolution in 1919–20, a good number of Ukrainian painters became émigrés. Among those working in Warsaw were P. Kholodny, Jr, P. Mehyk, and P. *Andrusiv. In Prague I. *Kulets and H. *Mazepa explored cubism and abstraction, and K. *Antonovych was inspired by Boichuk and impressionism. Of the more prominent painters who settled in France S. Levytska worked in a postimpressionist manner and later took part in cubist exhibitions, and O. Hryshchenko (A. Gritchenko) and V. *Khmeliuk painted in an expressionist manner. M. *Andriienko-Nechytailo used constructivist elements in his abstractions. Others who worked in Paris in a variety of figurative styles included S. *Borachok, M. *Hlushchenko, S. *Zarytska, M. *Krychevsky, P. *Omelchenko, V. *Perebyinis, V. Palisadiv, and O. Savchenko-Bilsky. After the Second World War they were joined by I. *Vynnykiv, Yu. *Kulchytsky, A. *Solohub, A. *Yablonsky, and T. *Vyrsta. O. *Mazuryk, who works in an expression-

ist manner inspired by Byzantine-Ukrainian icons, came to Paris from Poland in 1968; A. *Solomukha from Kiev, who has taken a postmodern approach to painting, came in 1978; and V. *Makarenko, whose work is stylized and often symbolic, arrived there in 1980.

After the Second World War many Ukrainian artists fled from communist rule and settled in the West: R. *Lisovsky and R. Hluvko in Great Britain, B. *Kriukov and V. *Lasovsky in Argentina, V. *Krychevsky, Jr, and H. Mazepa in Venezuela, and M. *Kmit in Australia. Of the artists who settled in Canada K. Antonovych, I. Belsky-Stetsenko, and Yu. Butsmaniuk painted in a realist manner, and M. Levytsky and H. *Novakivska pursued a variety of semiabstract styles. Of those who settled in the United States, including M. Butovych, M. *Dmytrenko, S. Hordynsky, L. *Hutsaliuk, P. Kholodny, E. *Kozak, P. Mehyk, Mykhailo *Moroz, M. *Nedilko, M. *Radysh, Ju. *Solovij, and V. *Tsymbal, most worked in a variety of figurative styles and usually exhibited within the Ukrainian community. J. *Hnizdovsky, who is known internationally for his wood engravings, was also an accomplished neorealist painter.

Some Ukrainian artists working in the United States were born in Ukraine, but matured and received their training mostly in America (R. Baranyk, B. Borzemsky, A. *Kolomyiets, S. *Lada, C. *Olenska, and A. *Olenska-Petryshyn). American-born artists of Ukrainian origin who have participated in exhibitions of Ukrainian art include Ya. *Surmach-Mills, J. Gaboda, and L. Bodnar-Balahutrak.

Of the artists born in Canada W. *Kurelek gained international prominence for his convincing depictions of Ukrainian pioneers and other ethnic groups in Canada. Other more prominent artists on the Canadian art scene include L. *Luhovy, A. *Lysak, L. Sarafinchan, M. *Styranka, K. Kulyk, P. *Shostak, N. *Husar, and A. *Prychodko.

Changes brought about by glasnost and perestroika in the USSR resulted in greater creative freedom and a proliferation of styles and manners of depiction in Soviet Ukrainian art of the late 1980s and early 1990s. Artists whose work had been suppressed (eg, O. Zalyvakha, A. Antoniuk, O. Dubovyk, I. Marchuk, and F. Humeniuk) have had solo exhibitions. Many painters have shown great inventiveness, including P. Hulyn from Uzhhorod, R. *Romanyshyn and R. Zhuk from Lviv, M. *Popov from Kharkiv, O. *Tkachenko from Dnipropetrovske, O. *Nedoshytko and L. Diulfan from Odessa, and F. Tetianych, T. Silvashi, V. Budnykov, Ye. Hordiits, M. Heiko, B. Plaksii, and O. Babak from Kiev. After decades of restraint and isolation artists in Ukraine are now free to continue the development of various artistic traditions and have prospects of rejoining the international artistic mainstream.

(See also *Fresco painting, *Genre painting, *Icon, *Landscape art, *Miniature painting, *Modernism, *Mural, *Nonconformist art, *Portraiture, *Primitive art, and *Realism.)

BIBLIOGRAPHY

Zatenats'kyi, Ia. (comp). Ukraïns'ke obrazotvorche mystetstvo: Zhyvopys, skul'ptura, hrafika (Kiev 1956, 1957)
Sichyns'kyi, V. Istoriia ukraïns'koho mystetstva (New York 1956)
Zatenats'kyi, Ia. Ukraïns'kyi radians'kyi zhyvopys (Kiev 1958)
Bazhan, M.; et al (eds). Istoriia ukraïns'koho mystetstva, 6 vols in 7 bks (Kiev 1966–70)
Zabolotnyi, V. (ed). Narysy z istoriï ukraïns'koho mystetstva (Kiev 1966)

Afanasiev, V. *Stanovlennia sotsialistychnoho realizmu v ukraïns'komu obrazotvorchomu mystetstvi* (Kiev 1967)

Belichko, Iu. *Tema. Ideia. Obraz: Tendentsiï rozvytku suchasnoho ukraïns'koho obrazotvorchoho mystetstva (1945–1972)* (Kiev 1975)

Lohvyn, H.; Miliaieva, L.; Svientsits'ka, V. (comps). *Ukraïns'kyi seredn'ovichnyi zhyvopys: Al'bom* (Kiev 1976)

Pavlov, V. *Suchasna ukraïns'ka akvarel'* (Kiev 1978)

Zholtovs'kyi, P. *Ukraïns'ka zhyvopys XVII–XVIII st.* (Kiev 1978)

Pavlov, V. *Ukraïns'ke radians'ke mystetstvo 1920–1930-kh rokiv* (Kiev 1983)

Mudrak, M. *The New Generation and Artistic Modernism in the Ukraine* (Ann Arbor 1986)

Zhaboriuk, A. *Ukraïns'kyi zhyvopys ostannoï tretyny XIX–pochatku XX st.* (Kiev 1990)

Pelens'ka, O. (comp). *Biienale ukraïns'koho obrazotvorchoho mystetstva 'L'viv '91 – Vidrodzhennia': Maliarstvo, hrafika, skul'ptura* (Lviv 1991)

Marko, O.; Shkandrij, M.; Tracz, O.; Walsh, M. (eds). *Spirit of Ukraine: 500 Years of Painting: Selections from the State Museum of Ukrainian Art, Kiev* (Winnipeg 1992)

D. Zelska-Darewych

Pak, Vitold, b 22 August 1888 near Kazlu-Ruda, Lithuania, d 30 May 1965 in Donetske. Mining mechanics scientist; full member of the AN URSR (now ANU) from 1951. He studied in Tomsk and from 1934 worked and taught at the Artem Mining (now Donetske Polytechnical) Institute. He also worked (from 1951) at the ANU Mining Institute (now the Institute of Mining Mechanics). His main contributions were in the areas of ventilation, drainage, and ore transport in mines.

Pakharevsky, Leonyd [Paxarevs'kyj], b 16 September 1883 in Shcherbashyntsi, Kaniv county, Kiev gubernia, d ? Writer, actor, director, and translator. He graduated from Kiev University and the Lysenko Music and Drama School. He began to publish his work in 1905; the short story collections *Budenni opovidannia* (Everyday Stories, 1910) and *Opvidannia* (Stories, 1913) and the plays *Nekhai zhyve zhyttia!* (Long Live Life! 1907) and *Todi, iak lypy tsvily* (When the Linden Trees Blossomed, 1914) were published. Pakharevsky translated from G. Hauptmann and A. Schnitzler. He did not take part in the literary life of the Soviet period, and the details of his own life at that time are unknown. He likely fell victim to the Soviet terror of the 1930s.

Pakhlovska, Oksana [Paxl'ovs'ka], b 18 September 1956 in Kiev. Literary scholar, poet, and translator; daughter of L. *Kostenko. She graduated with a degree in Italian literature from Moscow State University and works at the ANU Institute of Literature. She has published a collection of poetry, *Dolyna khramiv* (The Valley of Shrines, 1988); a monograph, *Italiis'ko-ukraïns'ki literaturni zv'iazky XV–XX st.* (Italian-Ukrainian Literary Relations in the 15th to 20th Centuries, 1990); a book of translations of M. Grasso's poetry, *Holos antychnoho moria* (Voice of the Ancient Sea, 1989); translations of individual works by F.G. Lorca, A. Gatto, J.R. Jiménez, M. Luzi, E. Montale, S. Quasimodo, V. Sereni, and other Romance poets; and numerous articles on the history of Italian classical and modern poetry and on contemporary problems of Ukrainian culture.

Pakhomov, Yurii [Paxomov, Jurij], b 15 July 1928 in Kungur, Perm oblast, RSFSR. Economist; full member of the AN URSR (now ANU) since 1988. After graduating from Kiev University (1953) he lectured at the Slovianske Pedagogical Institute (1955–60) and the Kiev Institute of the National Economy (1964–6, 1975–9), where he became rector in 1980. He headed a department of the ANU Institute of Economics (1970–5). His works deal with relations of production and the relationship between economic interest and the law in a socialist context. His monographs include *Proizvodstvennye otnosheniia razvitogo sotsializma* (Relations of Production in Developed Socialism, 1976) and *Gumanizatsiia sotsialisticheskoi ekonomiki* (The Humanization of the Socialist Economy, 1987).

Paklonski, Konstantin (Poklonsky), b and d ? Belarusian Cossack leader from the Mahiliou region. He lived in Ukraine and knew B. Khmelnytsky and I. Vyhovsky well. In the 1650s he aspired to create a Belarusian state comparable to the Hetmanate. In 1654 he fought against Polish-Lithuanian forces, at first allied with I. Zolotarenko and then with Muscovy (which granted him the rank of colonel). Having lost the support of the Hetmanate and been provoked by the Russian exploitation of Belarusians, Paklonski joined the Lithuanian forces in 1655 (with the backing of the higher Belarusian Orthodox clergy) in a campaign against Muscovy.

Pakul, Mykola [Pakul'], b 28 February 1880 in Belarus, d 27 May 1953. Soviet Ukrainian historian. He graduated from Kharkiv University (1910) and then taught medieval history and chaired the history faculty there from 1920. He researched the origins of feudalism and wrote *Niderlandskaia revoliutsiia* (The Netherlands Revolution, 1929) and *Lektsii po istorii srednikh vekov* (Lectures in the History of the Middle Ages, 2 vols, 1939).

Palace. An elaborate residence built by a monarch or noble. Palaces of the Kievan Rus' period have not survived. Remains of one built near the Church of the Tithes in Kiev were excavated in the 1930s. During the 13th to 16th centuries many castles but few palaces were built. It was only in the 17th century that members of the Cossack *starshyna*, particularly hetmans, began commissioning them. Most of the palaces built during the Hetman era have not survived. All that remains of Hetman B. Khmelnytsky's palaces in Chyhyryn and Subotiv are written descriptions and drawings of the ruins. Only one drawing of Hetman P. Doroshenko's Chyhyryn palace has survived. All traces of Hetman I. Mazepa's imposing baroque palace in Baturyn were destroyed on the orders of Peter I in 1708, and Hetman D. Apostol's palace in Hlukhiv was destroyed by fire. The palaces built by Polish nobles in Right-Bank Ukraine fared much better, including the Renaissance-baroque one in Pidhirtsi (1654) and others in Zbarazh, Berezhany, and Bar.

Most of the surviving palaces in Ukraine date from the late 18th and early 19th centuries. They were constructed in the classical style then popular in the Russian Empire. The most elaborate was the Zavadovsky palace in Lialychi (1794), built by G. *Quarenghi with a Palladian rotunda, a cupola, and a complex semicircular structure of 100 rooms. Two of the finest palaces were Hetman K. Rozumovsky's in Pochep (1796) and Baturyn (1799). Designed by the Scottish architect C. Cameron, the Baturyn palace was built in the Palladian style with Louis XVI interior decoration and some Ukrainian ornamental detailing. It was partially destroyed in 1923 by the Bolshevik regime and is now being rebuilt. Other examples in the classical style include the Galagan palace in Sokryntsi (1829), designed by P. Dubrovsky, and the Vorontsov palace and park (1826) near Odessa, designed by F. Boffo, an Odessa architect originally from Sardinia. Because most of the architects were foreigners, and all buildings had to be approved by the authorities in St Petersburg, Ukrainian traditions were not incorporated in their architecture.

D. Zelska-Darewych

Palaces and houses of culture. Cultural centers located throughout the former USSR and Ukraine. In big cities and commercial centers they are funded and administered mostly by enterprises and trade unions; in rural areas they are operated by the government. The palaces and buildings of culture house various group activities, such as sports and games, recreational activities, and courses of instruction for professional qualification. They also host lessons, lectures, theatrical productions, concerts, film screenings, exhibitions of amateur art, and receptions in honor of political and cultural figures. Most have libraries, reading rooms, and laboratories. Some are intended for use by specific groups, such as scholars, teachers, writers, or railway workers. The first palaces and houses of culture in Ukraine were built in the 1920s.

Roman Paladiichuk   Maksym Palamarchuk

Paladiichuk, Roman [Paladijčuk], b 22 April 1911 in Bilche Zolote, Borshchiv county, Galicia. Journalist, publisher, and political activist. Before completing secondary school he became active in the nationalist movement. By 1928 he was regional leader for Ternopil in the Union of Ukrainian Nationalist Youth. In the OUN he belonged to the oppositionist group headed by I. *Mitrynga and edited its journals *Nash front* (1932–3) and *Proboiem* (1933). He organized the Desheva Knyzhka publishing house in Lviv (1935–9) and edited its popular monthlies *Samoosvitnyk* (1937–9) and *Molodniak* (1937–9). Having left for Germany in 1944, he established the Prometei publishing house in Neu Ulm and joined I. Maistrenko's left-faction of the *Ukrainian Revolutionary Democratic party. In 1949 he settled in Toronto. He is the author of *Vil'ne kozatstvo* (The Free Cossacks, 1936).

Palamarchuk, Hlafira [Palamarčuk], b 16 March 1908 in Fedorivka, now in Vinnytsia oblast. Art historian. A

graduate of Kiev University (1937), she has specialized in the art of T. Shevchenko and edited albums of his watercolors (1963) and self-portraits (1963), written a monograph about him as an artist (1968), and participated in the preparation of several editions of his works.

Palamarchuk, Leonid [Palamarčuk], b 9 August 1922 in Musiivka, Skvyra county, Kiev gubernia. Linguist. After graduating from the Kiev Pedagogical Institute (1949) he joined the research staff of the AN URSR (now ANU) Institute of Linguistics and eventually chaired its Department of Lexicology and Lexicography. In 1978 he became the institute's deputy director. He is the author of numerous articles and of books on synonyms in M. Kotsiubynsky's works (1957) and on Soviet Ukrainian lexicography (1978), coauthor of two orthographic handbooks (1964, 1973), coeditor of the ANU Ukrainian-Russian dictionary (vols 3–6, 1961–3) and dictionary of the Ukrainian language (11 vols, 1970–80), and editor of several collections of articles on lexicology and lexicography (1965, 1966, 1969, 1985).

Palamarchuk, Luka [Palamarčuk], b 19 September 1906 in Troshcha, Lypovets county, Kiev gubernia. Soviet journalist and official. The former head of the Soviet Ukrainian Radio Committee (1941–2) and editor in chief of *Radians'ka Ukraïna* (1943–52), he graduated from Kiev University (1949) and the CC CPU Higher Party School (1950). As Ukrainian deputy minister (1952–4) and minister (1954–65) of foreign affairs he headed the Soviet Ukrainian delegations at the United Nations and then served as Soviet ambassador to Morocco (1965–72). During this time he was a candidate member of the CC CPU (1956–9, 1960–6).

Palamarchuk, Maksym [Palamarčuk], b 22 October 1916 in Vorobiivka, Novohrad-Volynskyi county, Volhynia gubernia. Economist and geographer; full member of the AN URSR (now ANU) from 1973. He graduated from Kiev University (1939). He lectured and headed a department at the Lviv Trade and Economics Institute (1946–62) and then returned to Kiev to work at the ANU Institute of Geological Sciences, the Council for the Study of the Productive Resources of Ukraine, and the geography division of the ANU. In 1975 he was appointed a professor at Kiev University. Palamarchuk's works deal with the distribution of economic resources and development in Ukraine and include *Ekonomichna heohrafiia Ukraïns'koï RSR* (The Economic Geography of the Ukrainian SSR, 1975).

Palamarenko, Anatolii, b 12 July 1939 in Makariv, Kiev oblast. Reciter and actor. In 1961 he completed study at the Kiev Institute of Theater Arts. In 1961–2 he worked as an actor in the Khmelnytskyi Ukrainian Music and Drama Theater, and since 1962 he has been a reciter in the Kiev Philharmonic Society. In his repertoire are works of Ukrainian classical and contemporary writers. He wrote *Kobzareva duma* (The Kobzar's Duma, 1980).

Palance, Jack (né Palahniuk, Walter [Volodymyr]), b 18 February 1920 in Lattimer, Pennsylvania. Hollywood film actor of Ukrainian descent. After studying at the University of North Carolina and Stanford University he was a professional boxer before appearing on Broadway in 1948. He was invited to perform in the film *Panic in the Streets*

Jack Palance

(1950) by E. Kazan. Palance was nominated for Academy awards for his supporting roles in *Sudden Fear* (1952) and *Shane* (1953) and was awarded an Oscar for his supporting role in *City Slickers* (1991). He has appeared in over 50 films, among them *House of Numbers* (1957), *Barrabas* (1962), *Baghdad Café* (where he speaks some Ukrainian, 1988), and *Batman* (1989), and on television in the series *The Greatest Show on Earth* (1963) and *Bronk* (1975–6).

Seals of the Zaporozhian Cossack palankas

Palanka (from Italian *palanca* and Latin *phalanx*). An administrative territorial unit in the *Zaporizhia, corresponding to the *regiment in the Hetman state. A large fortified settlement defended by a Cossack garrison served as its center. In the 1770s there were eight palankas: Kodak (named after a frontier fort), Boh-Hard (named after the Boh River and a frontier town), and Inhul (named after a river) in Right-Bank Ukraine; and Protovch, Orel, Samara, Kalmiius, and Prohnii (all named after rivers) in Left-Bank Ukraine. The full palanka system was introduced during the period of the *New Sich (1734–75), when the increase in the Zaporizhia's population made it necessary to introduce local administrations.

A Cossack colonel had supreme judicial, administrative, financial, and military authority over all Cossacks and peasants living on the territory of each palanka. With the aid of his *starshyna* he supervised the local administration, made up of the otamans and secretaries of the free settlements (*slobody*). The colonel and other palanka officials were not elected, but appointed by the *kish otaman of the Zaporozhian Sich.

Palashchuk, Fedir [Palaščuk] (pseud: Bohdan Konar), b 1895 in Rohatyn county, Galicia, d ca 1933. Revolutionary figure and Soviet official. A Ukrainian Sich Rifleman during the First World War, in 1918 he worked for the Ukrainian administration in Podlachia. In early 1920 he was a member of the Revolutionary Committee of the Red Ukrainian Galician Army in Vinnytsia and the commissar of finance in the *Galician Revolutionary Committee. In the 1920s he held various official posts in Moscow, including deputy director of state publishing and the USSR Industrial Bank and USSR deputy people's commissar of agriculture. About 75 senior agriculture officials in Moscow and Kharkiv, including Palashchuk, were arrested in March 1933 and accused of spying and agricultural sabotage causing the famine in Ukraine, the Kuban, and Belarus. He and 34 others were executed without trial by the Unified State Political Administration (OGPU); the remaining were sent to concentration camps.

Palatinate. See Voivodeship.

Palatine. See Voivode.

Pale of Settlement (*smuha osilosti*; Russian: *cherta osedlosti*; derived from the Latin *palus*, or stake, indicating a fixed territory or district under a particular jurisdiction). The term applied to the area within the Russian Empire to which Jewish settlement was restricted. The region was established as part of the imperial Russian structure after the introduction of a large number of Jews into the realm as a result of territorial acquisitions following the three partitions of Poland (1772, 1793, 1795). Earlier attempts to regulate Jewish settlements in Ukrainian territories included the Treaty of Zboriv (1649), which barred Jews and Jesuits from Kiev, Bratslav, and Chernihiv voievodeships, and a series of early 18th-century ukases (1721, 1727, 1738, 1740, 1742) that prohibited Jews from living in Left-Bank Ukraine.

The Pale covered an area from the Baltic Sea to the Black Sea and included much of Ukraine, Bessarabia, Belarus, and Lithuania. According to the census of 1897 it encompassed 4,899,300 Jews (94 percent of the total Jewish population of the Russian Empire), representing 11.6 percent of the general population of that area. Although they were a minority in every province, 82 percent of Jews lived in the towns and hamlets (shtetls) of the Pale and made up 36.9 percent of the urban population of the region. Just prior to the First World War the Pale included 15 gubernias: Bessarabia, Chernihiv, Hrodna, Katerynoslav, Kaunas, Kherson, Kiev, Mahiliou, Minsk, Podilia, Poltava, Tavriia, Vilnius, Vitsebsk, and Volhynia.

In 1764 and 1783 commercial rights were granted the Jews in the territories of New Russia gubernia, which had been annexed from Turkey. In 1785 the Jews were granted equal rights with other inhabitants of the region. Subsequently those areas were included in the Pale.

In 1791 it was decided to permit the presence of the Jews in their former regions of residence. In 1794 the earlier decree was also applied to the regions which had been annexed with the second partition of Poland, namely, Minsk, Volhynia, and Podilia, as well as lands east of the Dnieper in the Chernihiv and Poltava regions. In 1795, with the third partition of Poland, the law was extended to the provinces of Vilnius and Hrodna.

Occasionally, various territories or districts were closed to Jews, including Courland (1829), Astrakhan and northern Caucasia, Sevastopil, Mykolaiv, and Kiev (1835), some villages in Mahiliou and Vitsebsk gubernias, and crown lands and Cossack villages in Chernihiv and Poltava gubernias (1835). As a result of further restriction ('Temporary Laws' in 1881, of Aleksander III), Rostov and Tahanrih (1887), the city and province of Moscow (from which thousands of Jewish craftsmen and their families were expelled in 1891–2), and Yalta (1893) were closed to Jews. The laws of 1881 also prohibited any new settlement by Jews outside towns and shtetls in the Pale, with the exception of the 10 Polish provinces (the Vistula region). Those Jews who lived in villages prior to 1881 were allowed to reside in them, although the local peasantry was granted the right of demanding expulsion of the Jews who lived among them. At the end of the 19th and the beginning of the 20th centuries the Jews of the Pale experienced widespread and bloody *pogroms.

The Pale of Settlement was abolished by the Provisional Government by the law of 2 April 1917, 'On the Abolition of Religious and National Restrictions.'

BIBLIOGRAPHY
Bikerman, I.M. *Cherta evreiskoi osedlosti* (St Petersburg 1911)
Pipes, R. 'Catherine II and the Jews: The Origins of the Pale of Settlement,' *Soviet Jewish Affairs*, 5, no. 2 (1975)

P. Potichnyj

Paleobotany. The study of plant life of the past, covering the description, classification, occurrence, and distribution of fossil plants, their origins, and their evolutionary trends through geological time. In Eastern Europe Ya. *Zembnytsky was the first to describe fossil plants. One of the foremost researchers of paleobotany in Ukraine was I. *Schmalhausen. Research on the evolution of morphological structures, which led to various generalizations in plant morphology and phylogeny, began in the early 20th century. A. *Kryshtofovych elaborated a number of important theoretical problems while studying the paleoflora from the Devonian to the Quaternary period. The first paleobotanical laboratory in Ukraine was at the AN URSR (now ANU) *Institute of Geological Sciences. Other Ukrainian paleobotanists include D. *Zerov, I. *Shmalhauzen, V. Prynada, O. Karpinsky (paleontology and paleogeography), and O. *Rohovych.

BIBLIOGRAPHY
Zerov, D.; Novyk, K.; et al. *Do storichchia paleobotanichnykh doslidzhen' na Ukraïni: Bibliohrafichnyi pokazhchyk* (Kiev 1972)

Paleography. The study of writing, writing materials, and manuscript ornamentation and illustration. An ancillary discipline of philology and history, Ukrainian paleography focuses on the study of ancient documents and manuscripts written in Ukrainian; in a wider sense it includes all written artifacts created in Ukraine. The related disciplines of *epigraphy, *sphragistics, and *numismatics focus on ancient inscriptions on materials or buildings (graffiti). Ukrainian paleography is concerned with various aspects of the evolution of the graphic form of the letters of the Ukrainian alphabet and other written symbols, including their constituent elements, systems of abbreviation, and graphic delineation. It also concerns the materials and instruments used in writing. Scholars of practical paleography examine manuscripts and establish the time and place of their composition. They are sometimes able to establish the authorship of a document.

Paleographic study of manuscripts also involves charting the history of *orthography (abbreviations, punctuation, diacritical marks, the use of particular letters). Slavic paleography is divided into the study of Glagolitic and Cyrillic (and Latinate for Catholic Slavs) texts. Successive forms of the *Cyrillic alphabet were the *ustav script (uncial, 11th–16th centuries), large and small *pivustav script (14th–18th centuries), and *skoropys* (shorthand, 16th–18th centuries), as well as ornamental *viazi* (ligatures) and relatively rare cryptograms. Since the 1950s the writing of recent decades has also become an object of paleographic research.

The oldest manuscripts were written on parchment. When paper was introduced in the 14th century (initially a cotton rag, *bombitsyna*), each paper factory imprinted its products with distinguishing watermarks (*filigrany*); the study of these made the dating of manuscripts easier. In the 11th to 15th centuries confidential memorandums were written (particularly in Novgorod and Belarus) on birch bark. Ornamented and illuminated manuscripts can be dated according to the designs they bear. Depictions of fantastic or monstrous beasts, for example, were in vogue in the 13th century, geometric designs and more naturalistic images of flora and fauna in the late 14th century, and woven and plaited floral designs in the 15th century.

Slavic paleographic scholarship began to develop in the late 18th century and emerged in institutions devoted to archeography and the collection and description of manuscripts. In the late 19th and early 20th centuries descriptions of collections of Ukrainian manuscripts were published, including outlines by M. Petrov (1875–9) and A. Lebedev (1916) on the collection of the Kiev Theological Academy; by M. Lileev on that of the Chernihiv Theological Academy; V. Berezin, that of the Pochaiv Monastery (1881); M. Popruzhenko, that of the Odessa Municipal Library (1890); H. Kryzhanivsky, that of the Volhynia eparchial depository of ancient manuscripts (1896) and V. Trypilsky, that of the Poltava eparchial depository (1909); M. *Speransky, that of the Nizhen Lyceum (1900, 1905); I. *Svientsitsky, those of the People's Home (1904) and Stauropegion Institute in Lviv (1908); S. *Maslov, that of Kiev University (1910); O. Rystenko, that of the Odessa Association of History and Antiquities (1910); S. Shchehlova (1916) and D. *Shcherbakivsky (1923), that of the Kiev Municipal Museum; M. Heppener, that of the Central Scientific Library of the AN URSR (now ANU; 1969); and Ya. Dashkevych, that of the Lviv branch of the Central State Historical Archive (1972).

V. *Mochulsky (1890) and F. *Petrun (1927) researched the collections of V. Hryhorovych, and I. Svientsitsky, those of A. Petrushevych (1906–11); O. *Bodiansky (1838) and O. *Hruzynsky (1911–12) studied the Peresopnytsia Gospel.

D. *Zubrytsky, one of the founders of Ukrainian paleography, published an album of autographs of Ukrainian historical figures. I. *Kamanin was the first to apply the decimal system of classification, particularly for dating manuscripts (1905). P. Vladimirov and I. Ohiienko published studies of Ukrainian manuscripts from the 11th to 17th centuries (1890). V. *Peretts established a school of archeography and collected materials for a catalog of Ukrainian manuscripts. Scholars of regional script included K. *Lazarevska (Kiev, 1926), P. Bohdan (Bukovyna, 1956), P. Zakharchyshyna (Lviv, 1964), Z. Khomutetska and V. Chuntulova (Kremianets, 1964), and I. Ivanytska (Slobidska Ukraine, 1965, 1968).

General studies of the development of the graphics of Ukrainian writing were published by F. Tytov (1911), O. Maslova (1925), Ye. *Tymchenko (1927), V. *Diadychenko (1963), V. Panashenko (1974), and M. *Boiko (1982). Monographs on the ornamentation and *illumination of Ukrainian manuscripts were published by I. Svientsitsky (1922–3, 1933), D. Shcherbakivsky (1926), Ya. *Zapasko (1960), V. Siverska (1966), and H. *Lohvyn (1974). Watermarks on Ukrainian manuscripts were researched by I. Kamanin and O. Vytvytska (1923), O. Heraklitov (1963), and O. Matsiuk (1974).

BIBLIOGRAPHY

Sreznevskii, I. Slavianorusskaia paleografiia XI–XIV vv. (St Petersburg 1885)

Vladimirov, P. Obzor iuzhno-russkikh i zapadnorusskikh pamiatnikov pis'mennosti ot XI do XVII st. (Kiev 1890)

Kamanin, I. Paleograficheskii izbornik (Kiev 1899)

Beliaev, I. Prakticheskii kurs izucheniia drevnei russkoi skoropisi dlia chteniia rukopisei XV–XVIII st., 2nd edn (Moscow 1911)

Matsiuk, O. Papir ta filigrani na ukraïns'kykh zemliakh (XVI–pochatok XX st.) (Kiev 1974)

Panashenko, V. Paleohrafiia ukraïns'koho skoropysu druhoï polovyny XVII st. (Na materialakh Livoberezhnoï Ukraïny) (Kiev 1974)

Riznyk, M. Pys'mo i shryft (Kiev 1978)

Boiko, M. Paleography and Paper-Mills in Volhynia (Bloomington, Ind 1979)

– Paleographical Outline (Bloomington, Ind 1982)
S. Bilokin, O. Horbach

Paleolithic Period. The earliest period of human development, lasting until approx 8000 BC. In Western archeology the Paleolithic Period (or Old Stone Age) is divided into two epochs: the Lower Paleolithic (to 40,000 BC) and the Upper Paleolithic (40,000–8000 BC). These, in turn, consist of several eras or cultures. Notwithstanding some significant differences between Ukrainian and (Western) European Paleolithic cultures, Ukrainian archeological studies follow this basic scheme.

The Paleolithic period coincides with the geological age known as the Pleistocene, which is marked by a general cooling of the earth's temperature and the corresponding expansion and retreat of glaciers. The three successive waves of glaciations (known as the Mindel, Riss, and Würm glaciations in Western European nomenclature and by other names in Central and Northern European and Soviet classification schemata) that occurred in Europe from approx 600,000 BC are of particular interest to

the study of human development. The Pleistocene epoch ends at the same time as the historical Paleolithic period (ca 10,000–8000 BC) with the final retreat of glaciation over most of Europe and the coming of a new, warmer geological age, the Holocene.

The oldest evidence of human presence in Ukraine (found in *Luka-Vrublivetska) has been dated to as early as 300,000 BC. A small number of other *Acheulean culture (ca 300,000–100,000 BC) sites have been excavated in Ukraine, providing evidence that early humans lived there in hunter-gatherer bands. However, evidence of substantial settlement in Ukraine begins only with the onset of the *Mousterian culture (100,000–40,000 BC), occasionally referred to as the Middle Paleolithic. This period began with the mild temperatures of the Riss-Würm interglacial and then continued with the Würm glaciation, which caused temperatures to fluctuate as it moved back and forth in three phases lasting to 10,000–8000 BC. The population growth experienced in such a glacial period resulted partly from the early humans' increasing ability to adapt to cold conditions. More important was the large number of game animals that could be hunted and the abundant vegetation cover which could be gathered in spite of the colder climate.

Mousterian sites have been discovered in Ukraine mainly in the middle-Dniester and Dnieper-rapids regions and in the hills of southern Crimea. Such locations offered the shelter of river terraces or caves. Evidence indicates that surface dwellings were constructed somewhat similar in appearance to igloos, using animal skins and some form of posts on a foundation of animal bones (particularly mammoths). Remains of cave dwellings, temporary camping grounds, flint extraction locations, and flint workshops have also been found. The ubiquity of hearths in all forms of Mousterian shelters indicates that the ability to make fire had become widespread. A variety of locally made flint tools (particularly side-scrapers and points) have been unearthed at Mousterian sites, indicating a varied usage. Nevertheless, flint technology was not particularly well-developed in this period.

Mousterian humans lived by hunting and gathering. The game during this period included mammoths, the woolly rhinoceros, bison, deer, wolves, and bears. Foods gathered included fruits, leaves, roots, bird eggs, and mollusks.

The Mousterian inhabitants of Ukraine were Neanderthals who lived in small groups that scholars believe may have been matriarchal and matrilineal. The fact that they buried their dead in a ritualized manner on their sides in a flexed position indicated that these people had probably developed at least a rudimentary religious consciousness.

A major change took place ca 40,000 BC when the Mousterian culture was supplanted by a series of Upper Paleolithic cultures. Although a direct causal link cannot be established, this was probably owing to the appearance of the (modern) Cro-Magnons and the demise of the Neanderthals. The genesis of Cro-Magnons in Ukraine is a subject of debate, with some (mainly Soviet) scholars viewing this as an indigenous evolutionary process and others deducing that they migrated into Ukrainian lands. Origins notwithstanding, significant developments took place during this period.

One of the most obvious changes during the Upper Paleolithic was a remarkable increase in the variety of implements used and the quality of their manufacture. End-scrapers and burins became particularly widespread at this time. The manner in which flint was worked from cores was improved. Different types of raw materials, including bone, antler, and ivory, were commonly used. High-quality flint was actively sought and transported over long distances (possibly as a barter item).

Upper Paleolithic settlements tended to be more permanent than their Mousterian counterparts. They became also more widespread throughout Ukraine (with a concentration in the previously settled Dniester and Dnieper areas) as the population increased during this period. Hunting and gathering remained primary occupations, with evidence indicating considerable improvements in hunting technology and organization. Fishing became common during this time.

A fundamental change occurred in the Upper Paleolithic with the emergence of an esthetic consciousness. Whereas the remains of art objects are unknown at Mousterian sites, Upper Paleolithic discoveries include decorated bone, ivory, and antler objects, shell pendants, ivory bracelets, and ivory figurines of women, mammoths, and birds. Remains of flutes and bone percussion instruments indicate that Upper Paleolithic man also created music.

BIBLIOGRAPHY
Efimenko, P. Pervobytnoe obshchestvo (Kiev 1953)
Arkheolohiia Ukraïns'koï RSR, vol 1 (Kiev 1971)
Klein, R. Ice-Age Hunters of the Ukraine (Chicago 1973)

A. Makuch

Paleontology. The scientific study of all aspects of life in the geological past, based on examination of fossil materials. It is commonly divided into paleozoology and paleobotany, but also includes subareas, such as micropaleontology, paleoecology, paleobiogeography, biostratigraphy, and paleoichnology. Although some paleontological activity took place in Ukraine in the second half of the 17th century (eg, the unearthing of the remains of a mammoth in the Kharkiv area), systematic paleonotological research commenced only in the early 19th century. I. *Kalenychenko, who explored the Sumy region, erected a unique structure depicting a mammoth in the village of Kulishivka. O. *Rohovych studied fish fossils.

The mid-19th-century treatises on the paleontology of Russia (E. Eichwald), Poland (G. Pusch), and southern Russia (A. von Nordmann) included all data known at that time on paleontological finds from deposits in Ukraine. The theories of Darwin resulted in intensified paleontological exploration in Ukraine during the late 19th and early 20th centuries. The intensification of geological prospecting and exploration for useful geological deposits underscored the need for research in applied paleontology, particularly in stratigraphy. Early paleobotanical research in Ukraine was done by I. *Shmalhauzen, M. Zalesky, and A. *Kryshtofovych, who studied coal deposits as well as Paleogenic and Neogenic flora. Paleozoological studies done by M. *Andrusiv, G. Sintsov (paleomalacology), and P. *Tutkovsky (micropaleontology) were of importance for biostratigraphy and paleogeography. The work of O. Alekseev, O. *Borysiak, N. Sokolov, and I. *Khomenko laid the foundation for the studies of Neogenic vertebrate fauna. E. Niezabitowski-

Lubicz and M. *Łomnicki studied the Pleistocene vertebrate fauna of Western Ukraine. Paleontological research centers arose at Kiev and Odessa universities, and the first paleontological museums in Ukraine were established in Odessa and Lviv.

From the 1920s, paleontological studies were based at academic institutions, in particular at the zoological and geological museums, and later within newly created departments at the AN URSR (now ANU) institutes of Geological Sciences, Zoology, and Botany. In 1935 the separate Paleontological Museum evolved from the Zoological Museum. Besides the paleontology departments at Kiev and Odessa universities, new centers of paleontological studies emerged at Kharkiv (D. *Soboliev) and Dnipropetrovske (B. *Chernyshov) universities. At that time paleobotanical studies, which included floras of the Neogene, Paleogene, and Mesozoic (N. Pimenova), and Paleozoic (K. *Novyk) periods, laid the foundations for spore-pollen studies of anthropogenic flora (D. *Zerov). Paleozoological studies included invertebrate families, especially the simplest ones, cephalopods, and mollusks (P. Tutkovsky, B. Chernyshov, V. *Bondarchuk, L. Lunsgershauzen, V. Pchelintsev). There was an intensification in the studies of Neogenic and anthropogenic vertebrate fauna, mainly mammals and birds (I. Khomenko, I. *Pidoplichko, V. *Krokos, M. Pavlova, M. Burchak-Abramovych). In 1931 a paleozoological texbook was published by Krokos.

After the Second World War more scientists joined the research centers of the ANU, and new paleontology departments were founded at Lviv, Donetske, and Dnipropetrovske universities. There was an increase in studies dealing with biostratigraphy, paleogeography, and evolutionary paleontology, as well as paleofloristics (K. Novyk, F. Stanisławski, O. Shchogolev), especially in conjunction with spore-pollen analysis (D. Zerov, O. Artiushenko, A. Ishchenko, N. Shchekina). Extensive paleozoological studies of almost all invertebrates were carried out, including the simplest ones (O. *Kaptarenko-Chornousova, I. Vetlinsky), cephalopods (O. Rotai, V. Makrydin), mollusks (B. Chernyshov, V. Sobetsky, D. Makarenko, B. Zhyzhchenko, H. *Moliavko, A. Eberzin, L. Neverska, I. Yatsko), crustaceans (S. Horak, V. Sheremeta), insects (Ye. Savchenko, Pidoplichko), and graptolites (O. *Vialov, O. Obut). A series of paleontological reference books was published, containing data on the fauna of Cenozoic and Mesozoic fossils. Vialov's 1966 monograph on life-activity traces of organisms and their paleontological significance clarified points of the nomenclature and classification of fossils with problematic origin. Substantial accomplishments were achieved in studies of Neogene anthropogenic mammals (Pidoplichko, V. *Topachevsky, O. Korotkevych), Paleozoic agnates and fishes (B. Balabai), and Neogene anthropogenic birds (M. Voinstvensky). The Ukrainian Paleontological Society was founded in 1977 in Kiev by Vialov, with six chapters throughout Ukraine.

BIBLIOGRAPHY
Pidoplichko, I. 'Razvitie paleontologii na Ukraine,' in Trudy Odesskogo gosudarstvennogo universiteta (Kiev–Odessa 1954)
Moliavko, G.; Pidoplichko, I. 'Paleozoologicheskaia nauka na Ukraine za 50 let sovetskoi vlasti,' Paleontologicheskii sbornik, no. 4 (1967)
Paleontologicheskie issledovaniia na Ukraine (Kiev 1980)

Palfii, Fedir [Palfij], b 3 March 1925 in Koroleve, Transcarpathia. Biochemist; corresponding member of the USSR Academy of Agricultural Sciences since 1970. A graduate of the Lviv Zootechnical-Veterinary Institute (1950), in 1954 he joined the AN URSR (now ANU) Institute of Agrobiology, which in 1956 became the Scientific Research Institute of Land Cultivation and Animal Husbandry in the Western Regions of the Ukrainian SSR. He became a professor in 1966 and the institute's director in 1969. He has researched feed biochemistry and fodder storage techniques.

Andrii Palii

Palii, Andrii [Palij, Andrij], b 1 December 1893 in Kryvotuly, Tovmach county, Galicia, d 10 May 1961 in Edmonton. Co-operative and civic leader. He served as a lieutenant in the Austrian army and then in the Ukrainian Galician Army. After the First World War he graduated in agronomy from the Prague Polytechnic (1922) and returned to Stanyslaviv, where he helped revive the *Maslosoiuz dairy union. By 1924 he had been elected to the union's board of directors; he was then appointed executive and trade director (1925–44) and coeditor of its monthly *Kooperatyvne molocharstvo* (1926–39). Under his management Maslosoiuz developed into one of the largest co-operatives in Western Ukraine. He also served on the board of directors of the Audit Union of Ukrainian Co-operatives and of Silskyi Hospodar and was president of the Moloda Hromada veterans' association and vice-president of Sokil-Batko. Under the German occupation he continued to manage Maslosoiuz and became a member of the Military Board of the Division Galizien in charge of family welfare. After leaving Ukraine in 1944, he settled in Toronto in 1948, where he managed the M-C Dairy (1952–7).

Palii, Lida [Palij], b 11 April 1926 in Stryi, Galicia. Graphic artist, literary activist, and writer; daughter of A. *Palii. After moving to Canada (1948) she graduated from the Ontario College of Art (1953) and from the University of Toronto (1967). She has designed posters, books, and bookplates. Palii is engaged in promoting Ukrainian literature in the PEN International Association and has authored a collection of verse, *Dyvovyzhni ptytsi* (Strange Birds, 1989), and two collections of travel reminiscences, *Mandrivky v chasi i prostori* (Trips in Time and Space, 1973) and *Svitla na vodi* (Lights on Water, 1985). In 1988 some of her poems appeared with those of two other poets in an English translation, *Land of Silent Sundays* (1988).

Palii, Mykola [Palij] (Paley, Nicholas) (pseuds: Mykola Hurko, Tibursio), b 7 December 1911 in Bohdanivka, Skalat county, Galicia. Writer, literary scholar, and translator. In the 1930s he contributed feuilletons and articles on Italian literature and Ukrainian ethnography to Lviv periodicals and wrote the brochure *Moloda Italiia* (Young Italy, 1937). After completing medical studies in Rome (1940) he emigrated to the United States. He studied Romance languages at Ohio State University (MA, 1944). From 1944 he was an assistant professor at that university, and from 1950 to 1977 he was a professor at Beloit College in Wisconsin. He contributed humorous and satirical sketches and publicistic articles to *Mitla* (Buenos Aires) and *Ukraïns'ke zhyttia* (Chicago) and published separately the story collections *Nadiini dni* (Hopeful Days, 1949) and *Dud'o i ia* (Dudo and I, 1980), the poetry collection *Etcetera* (1970), the humor and satire collections *Sentymental'na Ukraïna* (Sentimental Ukraine, 1974) and *Romantychna Ukraïna* (Romantic Ukraine, 1980), a novelette, *Mari, Mari* (1975), the scholarly works *Tesis profesionales* (1969) and *Dos novellas de la tierra* (1972), and Ukrainian translations of *La vida de Lazarillo de Tormes* (1970), M. Tamayo y Baus's *Un drama nuevo* (1972), and a selection of Spanish short stories, *Palkoiu liubov'iu* (With Ardent Love, 1978).

Palii, Semen [Palij] (actual surname: Hurko), b early 1640s in Borzna, Chernihiv region, d between 24 January and 13 May 1710 in Kiev. Cossack leader. He studied at the Kievan Mohyla College and became a registered Cossack of Nizhen regiment. In the 1670s he joined the Zaporozhian Host and distinguished himself as a soldier and administrator. He served as a volunteer colonel in King Jan III Sobieski's army and, according to some sources, took part in the rout of the Turks and Crimean Tatars at Vienna in 1683. In 1685 the Polish Sejm adopted a constitution confirming the rights and freedoms given to the Cossacks by the Polish kings, and Cossack regiments were established in Khvastiv and Bohuslav and revived in Korsun and Bratslav. In 1684–5 Palii lived with his regiment around Khvastiv and soon became the de facto ruler of the Bila Tserkva region. In the 1680s and 1690s Palii led successful campaigns against the Turks and Tatars as an ally of Poland and of Hetman I. Mazepa. He concentrated his efforts, however, on recolonizing the Right-Bank territories that had been devastated by the Tatars, liberating them from Polish rule, and uniting them with the Left-Bank Hetmanate. In 1689 his forces attacked Nemyriv, where he was captured by the Poles and imprisoned. He was freed after the intervention of Jan Sobieski in 1690.

Palii's relations with Poland deteriorated after the Sejm ordered the liquidation of all Right-Bank Cossack regiments by force in 1699. In 1702 he and other Right-Bank Cossack leaders under Hetman S. *Samus led an uprising against Polish rule that quickly spread throughout Kiev, Bratslav, and Podilia voivodeships and even affected Galicia. The rebels did not manage, however, to gain the support of the Left-Bank Hetmanate and Russia, which did not want to annex the Right Bank. In 1703 the rebellion was crushed by a large Polish army, and its participants were brutally punished (10,000 were executed). Palii then turned for support to pro-Swedish Polish magnates.

Mazepa, who opposed Palii's radical social policies and feared his popularity among the Zaporozhian Cossacks, sent troops into Right-Bank Ukraine to help the Poles suppress the uprising and had Palii arrested. Palii was deported to Moscow and exiled in 1705 to Siberia. After Mazepa broke with Moscow, Palii was allowed to return to Ukraine. After the Battle of Poltava he resumed command of Bila Tserkva regiment. He was buried at the Mezhyhiria Transfiguration Monastery in Kiev.

BIBLIOGRAPHY
Andrusiak, M. 'Do istoriï pravobichnykh kozakiv v 1689–1690 rr.,' *ZNTSh*, 100 (1930)
– *Mazepa i Pravoberezhzha* [sic] (Lviv 1938)
Diadychenko, V. *Semen Palii* (Saratov 1942)
Perdenia, J. *Stanowisko Rzeczypospolitej szlacheckiej wobec sprawy Ukrainy na przełomie XVII–XVIII w.* (Wrocław 1963)
Serhiienko, H. *Vyzvol'nyi rukh na Pravoberezhnii Ukraïni v kintsi XVII i na pochatku XVIII st.* (Kiev 1963)

O. Ohloblyn

Palii rebellion. See Palii, Semen.

Mykola Paliienko (1869–1937)   Mykola Paliienko (1896–1944)

Paliienko, Mykola [Palijenko], b 7 December 1869 in Kiev, d 11 November 1937. Jurist and legal scholar; full member of the AN URSR (now ANU) from 1930. After graduating in law from Kiev University (1892) he studied for two years at the universities of Paris, Heidelberg, and Strasbourg, and then taught at the Demidov Lyceum in Yaroslavl (1903–6) and Kharkiv University (1906–30). In 1930 he was appointed to the chair of state law at the ANU. Paliienko wrote many books, including a monograph on his own psychological theory of law (1900) and monographs on normative positivism (1902) and the law-governed state and constitutionalism (1906). Later he became interested in the issue of federalism and wrote *Konfederatsii, federatsii i Soiuz Sotsialisticheskikh Sovetskikh Respublik* (Confederations, Federations, and the USSR, 1923), *Pravo hromadianstva v suchasnykh federatsiiakh i v Soiuzi RSR* (The Right of Citizenship in Contemporary Federations and in the USSR, 1926), and *Problema suverenitetu suchasnoï derzhavy* (The Problem of the Sovereignty of the Contemporary State, 1929).

Paliienko, Mykola [Palijenko], b 30 September 1896 in Skvyra, Kiev gubernia, d 21 July 1944 near Khylchychi,

Zolochiv county, Galicia. Army officer. During the First World War he completed training at an artillery officer school and served in Russian artillery units on the Austrian front. In 1918–21 he commanded artillery units of the UNR Army. In 1928 he was selected to serve under contract with the Polish army, and in 1932–4 he attended the Polish Higher Military School in Warsaw. A major in the Polish 26th Artillery Regiment, he fought in the German-Polish War in September 1939. After joining the Division Galizien in July 1943, he commanded a noncommissioned officer school and eventually a heavy artillery battalion. He was killed in the Battle of Brody.

Dmytro Paliiv   Kekyliia Paliiv

Paliiv, Dmytro [Palijiv], b 17 May 1896 in Perevozets, Kalush county, Galicia, d 19 or 20 July 1944 in Brody, Galicia. Political and military leader and journalist. During the First World War he was an officer in the Ukrainian Sich Riflemen. As organizational officer of the Ukrainian Military Committee he was largely responsible for the success of the *November Uprising in Lviv in 1918. After the war he was a founding member of the clandestine *Ukrainian Military Organization (UVO) and became a member of its supreme command (1921–6). He was one of the founding members of the *Ukrainian Party of National Work (UPNR), an UVO front organization, and coedited its journal *Zahrava*. He was also chief editor of *Novyi chas* (1923–33, with some interruptions). After breaking with the UVO he led the UPNR into the new *Ukrainian National Democratic Alliance (UNDO). He sat on the CC of the UNDO (1925–33) and was elected as a candidate of the Bloc of National Minorities to the Polish Sejm in 1928. When the Sejm was dissolved in 1930, Paliiv was arrested along with other Ukrainian deputies, and spent three years in prison. A leading opponent of the *Normalization policy, he was expelled from the UNDO in 1933 and founded the *Front of National Unity. Paliiv edited its newspapers *Bat'kivshchyna* (1934–9) and *Ukraïns'ki visty* (1935–9). During the 1939 Soviet invasion of Galicia he escaped to Krynytsia in the German-occupied Lemko region and remained aloof from political life until 1943, when he helped organize the *Division Galizien. He served as captain and political adjutant to the division's commander and was killed in the Battle of Brody.

Paliiv, Kekyliia [Palijiv, Kekylija] (nickname: Tsiopa), b 6 January 1906 in Perevozets, Kalush county, Galicia, d 11

November 1969 in Toronto. Educator and civic leader; sister of D. *Paliiv. A leading organizer of the *Plast Ukrainian Youth Association in Galicia, she served on its national executive (1926–30) and, after its dissolution by the Polish authorities, worked with the Vohni co-operative publishing house and the Commission for Youth Camps and Excursions, which carried on Plast's work. In 1942–4 she served as youth secretary on the Ukrainian Central Committee and chief organizer of Ukrainian educational societies for youth. After the war she was commandant of Plast girls' units in Germany (1947–9), chief of the Plast movement in Britain (1949–52), and head of the national executive of Plast in Canada (1953–9, 1962–5). She was president of the Ukrainian Teachers' Federation of Canada (1965–9), a founder and vice-president of the Ukrainian Educational Council of the World Congress of Free Ukrainians (1967–9), and the initiator of the patrons' network of the émigré *Entsyklopediia ukraïnoznavstva* (Encyclopedia of Ukraine) being prepared by the Shevchenko Scientific Society in Sarcelles, France.

Palij, Michael [Palij, Myxajlo], b 22 December 1913 in Khorostkiv, Husiatyn county, Galicia. Historian and librarian; corresponding member of the Shevchenko Scientific Society. A postwar refugee, he studied at the universities of Göttingen, Minnesota, Denver (library science), and Kansas (PH D, 1971). He worked as a librarian at the universities of Oklahoma and Kansas and developed their Ukrainian collections. He is the author of *The Anarchism of Nestor Makhno, 1918–1921: An Aspect of the Ukrainian Revolution* (1976) and articles on modern Ukrainian history.

Wasyl Palijczuk: *Contemplation* (mezzotint dry point)

Palijczuk, Wasyl [Palijčuk, Vasyl'], b 10 July 1934 in Tuchapy, Galicia. Painter, sculptor, and educator. A postwar refugee in the United States since 1950, he studied at the University of Maryland and the Maryland Institute of Art MFA, 1965). Since 1967 he has taught art at Western Maryland College, where he has also served as gallery director. He is a member of the Ukrainian Artists' Association in the USA and former president of the Maryland Artists' Equity Association (1982–3). His modernist oils, watercolors, and wood, stone, bronze, and plastic sculptures have been displayed at over 25 solo exhibitions.

Palinodiia ... (Palinode ...). An important Orthodox polemical work written by Z. *Kopystensky in 1619–21. Subtitled 'A Book in Defense of the Catholic Holy Apostolic Eastern Church and the Holy Patriarchs, and about the Greeks, and about the Ruthenian Christians [*rossokh khristianekh*],' it is a defense of the Orthodox faith written in response to a 1617 Polish book by L. Krevza, the archimandrite of the Uniate monastery in Vilnius. The erudite author cited over 100 works in his theological tract and embellished it with baroque pathos, satire, witticisms, proverbs, panegyrics (to Prince K. Ostrozky), and J. Herburt's speech to the Polish Sejm. *Palinodiia* circulated in manuscript form among Orthodox polemicists until 1876, when it was finally published in vol 1 of the series Pamiatniki polemicheskoi literatury v Zapadnoi Rusi. It has been the subject of a book in Russian by V. Zavitnevych (Warsaw 1883) and of an article in Latin by A. Ishchak in *Bohosloviia* (1930–2).

Aleksandr Palladin

Palladin, Aleksandr (Oleksandr), b 10 September 1885 in Moscow, d 6 December 1972 in Kiev. Biochemist; corresponding member of the VUAN/AN URSR (now ANU) from 1926 and full member from 1929; full member of the Belarusian Academy of Sciences from 1934, the USSR Academy of Sciences from 1942, and the USSR Academy of Medical Sciences from 1944. A graduate of St Petersburg (later Petrograd) University (1908; M SC, 1917), he was a professor at the Kharkiv Institute of Agriculture and Forestry (1916–21), taught at Kharkiv University (1917–21), and was a professor in and chairman of the biochemistry departments at the Kharkiv Medical Institute (1921–31) and Kiev University (1934–54). He founded and directed the Ukrainian Biochemical Institute in Kharkiv (1925–31) and the ANU Institute of Biochemistry in Kiev (1931–69); founded (1926) and edited *Ukraïns'kyi biokhimichnyi zhurnal*; founded and headed the Ukrainian Physiological Society (1928–58); was a member of the VUAN/AN URSR presidium (from 1930), its secretary (1934–8), first vice-president (1939–46), and president (1946–62); served as a member of the Ukrainian Supreme Soviet's Presidium

(1947–63) and the CC CPU (1954–66); and headed the Ukrainian (1958–72) and USSR (1964–72) Biochemical societies.

The main subjects of Palladin's research were the biochemistry of vitamins, of muscle activity, and of the nervous system in general. He pioneered Soviet biochemical research of vitamins and of metabolic disorders during avitaminosis; synthesized the K vitamin analog Vicasol; developed the concept of functional biochemistry relating to fatigue, rest, and muscle training; established the biochemical topography of nerve tissue; did radioactive tracer studies on the metabolism of proteins, nucleic acids, and phosphocarbohydrates in nerve tissue; and studied ionic transport processes in the nervous system. Palladin published over 240 works, including monographs on the biochemistry of the nervous system (1965) and on albumins of the brain and their exchange (1972), and textbooks on nutrition (1919, 1922, 1926) and biochemistry (1924; 12th edn 1946). His biobibliography by A. Utevsky was published in Kiev in 1959, 1961, and 1979. The ANU Palladin Biochemistry Prize was established in 1974.

S. Trofimenko

Pallas, Peter, b 22 September 1741 in Berlin, d 8 September 1811 in Berlin. German naturalist and explorer. In 1766, after being educated in Germany, Holland, and England, he was elected an inaugurate member of the St Petersburg Academy of Sciences. In 1793–4 he traveled in the Volga region, northern Caucasia, and the Crimea. On his travels he collected geological, paleontological, geographical, botanical, zoological, and ethnographic data, which he later published. Pallas's major works include the three-volume *Reise durch verschiedene Provinzen des Russischen Reichs in den Jahren 1768–73* (1771–6), which was translated into Russian (1773–88), *Flora Rossica* (2 vols, 1774, 1788), and a comparative dictionary of all languages and dialects (2 vols, 1787, 1789). His works contained the best information at that time on Ukraine's flora and fauna.

Palmetto (*Sabal*; Ukrainian: *sabal*). A palm tree of the family Palmae that grows to a height of 30 m and trunk thickness of 60 cm. In Ukraine the common palmetto (*S. palmetto*) and the short-stemmed bush palmetto (*S. minor* or *S. adansonii*) grow on the Black Sea shores in the Crimea and Caucasia. Their wood serves as a strong, nonrotting building material especially suitable for underwater construction. The leaf fiber is used in the manufacturing of mats, coarse fabrics, and brushes.

Palmov, Viktor [Pal'mov], b 10 October 1888 in Samara, Russia, d 7 July 1929 in Kiev. Painter. A graduate of the Moscow School of Painting, Sculpture, and Architecture (1914), from 1925 he lived in Ukraine and taught at the Kiev State Art Institute and belonged to the Association of Revolutionary Art of Ukraine. In 1927 he founded the leftwing *Union of Contemporary Artists of Ukraine. He contributed articles on art theory to the futurist journal *Nova generatsiia*. In his oils the subject and objects were subordinated to color and its associative effect. Inspired by folk and children's art, they included works such as *Amour* (1926), *For Power of the Soviets* (1927), *Kiev Beach* (1927), *Mother* (1927), *Breaking the Horse* (1927), *Night* (1928), *Fisherman* (1928), and *May 1* (1929). In the 1930s most of his canvases were destroyed by the Stalinist authorities. A retrospective exhibition of his extant works was held at the Kiev Museum of Ukrainian Art in 1988.

Viktor Palmov: *Mother* (oil, 1927)

Palytsyn, Oleksander, b 1741, d 1816 on the Popivka *khutir* (now part of Zalizniak), near Sumy, Slobidska Ukraine. Poet, architect, and patron of the arts. After serving in the army in St Petersburg he settled on his estate, where he drew together a circle of literati (dubbed the Popivka Academy), including the writers V. Kapnist, I. Bohdanovych, and S. Hlynka, the artist M. Alferov, and the architect V. Yaroslavsky. The 'Academy' was also visited by H. Skovoroda and V. Karazyn. Palytsyn donated his collection of paintings to Kharkiv University (it later formed the basis of the Kharkiv Art Museum), and in 1810 he became an honorary member of the university's presidium. He designed several buildings and churches in the Sumy region and published a poetic translation of *Slovo o polku Ihorevi* (The Tale of Ihor's Campaign, 1807), as well as translations of French authors, such as Voltaire, J.-J. Rousseau, and J. Delisle.

Ivan Palyvoda

Palyvoda, Ivan, b 1885 in Poltava gubernia, d 30 January 1985 in Somerset, New Jersey. Educator, political leader, and painter. A member of the Ukrainian Party of Socialist Revolutionaries, he was a delegate to the Labor Congress and served as UNR minister of postal and telegraph services in B. Martos's cabinet in 1919. After the First World War he emigrated to Czechoslovakia. After the Second World War he was a refugee in Germany and then emigrated to the United States. He served as president of the Ukrainian Free Society of America and of the Society of Friends of the Ukrainian National Council (1958–66). For many years he managed the library of the Ukrainian Orthodox Center in South Bound Brook, New Jersey. He participated in exhibitions of the Ukrainian Artists' Association in the United States.

Pam'iatky ukraïns'ko-rus'koï movy i literatury (Monuments of Ukrainian-Ruthenian Language and Literature). The title of a series published by the Archeographic Commission of the Shevchenko Scientific Society. Eight volumes appeared: vols 1–4 and 6 (1896–1910) consisted of I. Franko's study and annotated collection of apocrypha and legends from Ukrainian manuscripts; vol 5 (1906), of K. Studynsky's study of monuments of late 16th- and early 17th-century polemical literature; vol 7 (1912), of V. Peretts's introduction to and collection of the poems of Klymentii, Zynovii's son; and vol 8 (1930), of Ya. Hordynsky's annotated texts and study of 17th- and 18th-century Ukrainian dramatic literature.

Pam'iatky Ukraïny (Monuments of Ukraine). A quarterly magazine of the *Ukrainian Society for the Protection of Historical and Cultural Monuments, published in Kiev since 1969. Until 1988 it was called *Pam'iatnyky Ukraïny* and edited by P. Tronko. After the name change in 1989, under the editorship of A. Sierykov it began to champion openly for the preservation of Ukraine's historical and cultural achievements. In the late 1980s *Pam'iatky Ukraïny* became one of the most popular and influential organs of the Ukrainian cultural revival. It publishes popular articles by historians, archeologists, museum workers, ethnographers, and architects on Ukrainian history and culture and architectural and historical monuments. From 1984 to 1988 its pressrun was increased from 35,000 to 80,000 copies. In 1989 it became a founding member of the *Memorial society.

Pamiatniki, izdannye Vremennoi komisiei dlia razbora drevnikh aktov (Monuments Published by the Temporary Commission for the Analysis of Ancient Acts), aka *Pamiatniki, izdannye Kievskoiu komissieiu dlia razbora drevnikh aktov*. A collection of archival documents, acts, and materials pertaining to the history of 16th- and 17th-century Ukraine, published by the *Kiev Archeographic Commission. The collection was compiled using church and monastery archives, the *Lithuanian Register, books of city and land acts, the private archives of the Sanguszko princely family, the manuscript library of the Chreptowicz family, and the collections of the Matsiievych and Świdziński families.

Vols 1–4 of *Pamiatniki* were compiled by M. Maksymovych and M. Ivanyshev and published in 1845, 1846, 1852, and 1859 (vol 1 was republished in 1848). Each volume has three sections. The first contains the records of various Orthodox church brotherhoods and monasteries,

such as the Lutske Brotherhood of the Elevation of the Cross (vol 1), the Kiev Epiphany Brotherhood (vol 2), the Lviv Dormition Brotherhood (vol 3), and the Derman and Pochaiv monasteries (vol 4). The second section contains acts describing landholdings and the rights and obligations of landowners vis-à-vis the peasantry in 1490–1596 (vol 1), the 1557 *voloka* land reform of King Sigismund II Augustus (vol 2), a description of properties and inventory of various estates in 1566–98 (vol 3), and descriptions of the Kremianets, Volodymyr-Volynskyi, and Lutske castles (vol 4). The third section contains documents of the Cossack-Polish War of 1648–9 (vol 1), 1650–1 (vol 2), and 1652–60 (vol 3), and historical documents of 1660–4 (vol 4).

A revised edition of *Pamiatniki* was edited by O. Levytsky and published in 1897–8. The Church Slavonic alphabet of the original edition was replaced by the Russian; translations of documents in Latin and Polish were omitted (they were provided in the first edition); and the illustrations in the first edition were left out, except for two panoramas of Kiev done in 1651. Eighteen new documents were added to vol 1, 11 to vol 2, and 49 to vol 3. An index of personal and place-names to all three volumes appeared at the end of vol 3.

A. Zhukovsky

The Presidium of the Pan-American Ukrainian Conference, 4th Session (Winnipeg, 1951)

Pan-American Ukrainian Conference (Pan-amerykanska ukrainska konferentsiia, or PAUK). A political umbrella organization representing Ukrainians in North and South America. It was founded on 18–22 November 1947 in New York by delegates of the Ukrainian Congress Committee of America, the Ukrainian Canadian Committee (now Congress, which initiated the gathering), the Society of Friends of Ukrainian Culture in Brazil, and the United Ukrainian Committee in Argentina, Paraguay, and Uruguay. Its purpose was to encourage and co-ordinate support for Ukraine's struggle for independence and to resist the spread of communism. Eventually the Ukrainian organizations in Venezuela and Chile joined PAUK. The presidium of the conference sat initially in Winnipeg and then in New York. PAUK organized the founding conference of the *World Congress of Free Ukrainians in 1967 and then transferred its functions to the congress. Rev V. *Kushnir was repeatedly elected president of PAUK.

Volodymyr Panasiuk

Petro Panch

Panasiuk, Volodymyr [Panasjuk], b 27 February 1926 in Krasne, Lublin voivodeship, Poland. Scientist in the fields of mechanics and strength of materials; full member of the AN URSR (now ANU) since 1978. He graduated from Lviv University (1951), and has worked at the ANU Physical-Mechanical Institute, as its director since 1971. He has made significant contributions in the areas of elasticity theory, brittle fracture theory, and the strength of materials. His mathematical models for calculating equilibrium conditions of stresses in solids with microcracks are now widely applied in calculations of the load-bearing capacity of various structures.

Panch, Petro [Panč] (pseud of Petro Panchenko), b 4 July 1891 in Valky, Kharkiv gubernia, d 1 December 1978 in Kiev. Writer. He was a soldier during the First World War and during the revolutionary period in Ukraine, first in the UNR Army and then with the Bolshevik forces. In the 1920s he was a member of the literary organizations Pluh, Vaplite, and the All-Ukrainian Alliance of Proletarian Writers. From 1923 he worked in Kharkiv as an editor (1923–32 at the journal *Chervonyi shliakh*), and from 1934, in Kiev. During the Second World War Panch worked in the AN URSR (now ANU) and at the radio station Radianska Ukraina. His first collections of novelettes and short stories, *Tam, de verby nad stavom* (Where the Willows Grow by the Pond, 1923), *Solom'ianyi dym* (Straw Fire, 1925), and *Myshachi nory* (Mouse Holes, 1926), dealt with the events of the civil war and the early years of the NEP in Ukraine. The cycle of novelettes consisting of *Z moria* (From the Sea), *Bez kozyria* (Without a Trump), *Holubi eshelony* (The Sky Blue Echelons, 1926), and *Povist' nashykh dniv* (A Tale of Our Days, 1927) describes events in Ukraine from the Revolution of 1905 to the rebuilding of the economy after the war and the Revolution of 1917. *Povist' nashykh dniv* was one of the first works in Ukrainian Soviet literature on the 'industrial' theme. From 1930 the main subject in Panch's works was collectivization, such as in the cycle *Mukha Makar* (1930–4). Panch is also the author of novels on the history of the revolutionary period, such as *Obloha nochi* (The Siege of Night, 1935) and *Oleksander Parkhomenko* (1939), the historical novel *Homonila Ukraïna* (Ukraine Was Humming, 1954), the memoirs *Na kalynovim mosti* (On the Viburnum Bridge [ie, In Old Age], 1965), a large number of stories and novels for children, and other works. His works have been published in collected edi-

tions of 5 vols (1971), 4 vols (1973), and 6 vols (1981). Panch's realistic style, free of any leaning toward formalism, and his loyalty to the Soviet regime earned him a place among those who had contributed nothing new to literature, but who were nevertheless hailed as the founding creators of Ukrainian Soviet prose.

I. Koshelivets

Panchenko, Dmytro [Pančenko], b 24 February 1906 in Novhorodka, Oleksandriia county, Kherson gubernia. Neurologist. A graduate of the Military Medical Academy (1932), he served as a professor (1946–51, director from 1949) at the Lviv Medical Institute and the Kiev Institute for the Upgrading of Physicians (1951–78). From 1960 he was also editor in chief of the Kiev medical journal *Vrachebnoe delo*. His publications deal with ischemic nerve disorders, nerve regeneration, and vascular diseases of the nervous system. At his initiative the first biotron laboratory was constructed in Kiev.

Panchenko, Mykhailo [Pančenko, Myxajlo], b ca 1884 in Poltava, d 1930s. Revolutionary figure and writer. After the February Revolution he was a member of the CC of the *Ukrainian Party of Socialist Revolutionaries, a member of the Presidium of the All-Ukrainian Council of Military Deputies, and a delegate to the Central Rada. In December 1917 he sat in the Presidium of the All-Ukrainian Congress of Workers', Soldiers', and Peasants' Deputies in Kiev. In 1919 he served briefly as people's commissar of education in the Bolshevik government in Kharkiv. As a *Borotbist from 1918, he opposed the party's merger with the CP(B)U and did not join the latter. In the 1920s he worked as an editor, wrote the script for P. Chardynin's films *Taras Shevchenko* and *Malyi Taras* (Little Taras, 1926, with D. Buzko) and the play *Koliïvshchyna* (1927), and headed the Ukrainian Collective of Directors, Writers, and Scenarists. He was arrested with other former Borotbists during the Stalinist terror of the 1930s, and perished in a concentration camp.

Panchenko, Mykola [Pančenko], b 6 November 1924 in Oleksandrivka, Kostiantynohrad okruha, Poltava gubernia. Economist. A graduate of the Lviv Trade and Economics Institute (1948), he has been a professor at Kiev University since 1954. A specialist on consumption and economic management, he has cowritten *Proizvodstvo i lichnoe potreblenie: Vzaimosviaz' i tselevaia napravlennost'* (Production and Personal Consumption: Their Interrelation and Purposive Direction, 1985) and written *Ekonomicheskaia otvetstvennost' v sisteme sotsialisticheskogo khoziaistvovaniia* (Economic Responsibility in the System of Socialist Management, 1977).

Panchenko, Platon [Pančenko] (pseud: P. Taisych), b 28 February 1856 in Kamenka, Orel gubernia, Russia, d 1911 in Rostov, Russia. Poet. He studied at Riga University and worked as a tutor in Astrakhan and Katerynodar. From the 1880s he contributed poetry to *Zoria, Literaturno-naukovyi vistnyk*, and various Ukrainian literary miscellanies and anthologies. A separate collection, *Z vil'nykh chasiv* (From Free Times), was published in 1910.

Panchenko-Yurevych, Volodymyr [Pančenko-Jurevyč], b 1907, d 1942. Chemist, journalist, and civic leader.

n 1925 he settled in Berlin, from where he contributed articles to *Novyi chas*, *Meta*, and *Vistnyk* and for a time edited *Ukraïns'kyi vistnyk*. His articles on topics such as Ukrainian nationalism and the problem of Western Ukraine appeared in the German press in the 1930s. He also published articles in organic chemistry. He was a founder and general secretary of the Committee of Foreign Students in Berlin.

Bohdan Gordon Panchuk   John Panchuk

Panchuk, Bohdan Gordon [Pančuk], b 8 February 1915 near Peterson, Saskatchewan, d 20 June 1987 in Montreal. Community leader. In 1940 he enlisted in the Royal Canadian Air Force and was posted in the United Kingdom, where he founded the *Ukrainian Canadian Servicemen's Association (UCSA) in 1943. Panchuk became aware of the dimensions of the Ukrainian *displaced persons and refugee problem in Europe while serving on the Continent, and mobilized the UCSA's resources for their assistance. To this end he helped establish the *Central Ukrainian Relief Bureau in 1945 and secured Ukrainian support in North America for refugee relief. After serving in the Ukrainian-language section of the Canadian Broadcasting Corporation's foreign service (1952–5) he taught high school in Montreal (1955–80). His memoirs appeared in 1983 as *Heroes of Their Day*.

Panchuk, John [Pančuk, Ivan], b 4 April 1904 in Gardenton, Manitoba, d 4 November 1981 in Battle Creek, Michigan. Lawyer and community leader. After moving to the United States with his parents (1916) he graduated from the University of Michigan law school (1928) and went into private practice. He served as assistant attorney general for Michigan (1937–40) and then as legal counsel for the Federal Home Life Insurance Co (1941–69). He devoted much of his time to the Ukrainian community: he was a founder and president (1936–7) of the *Ukrainian Youth League of North America, chairman of the committee for reorganizing the Ukrainian Congress Committee of America in 1943, and president of the Ukrainian Graduates Club of Detroit and Windsor (1951). A leading figure in the *United Ukrainian American Relief Committee (president in 1947–53), he played a key role in helping Ukrainian war refugees and resettling displaced persons in the United States. He was also active in American political life for many years as a prominent state member of the Democratic party. Panchuk wrote several books on Ukrai-

nian subjects, including *Shevchenko's Testament: Annotated Commentaries* (1965), *Bukovinian Settlements in Canada* (1971), *Persha ukraïns'ka tserkva v Kanadi* (The First Ukrainian Church in Canada, 1974), and *Descendants of Michelo Panchuk* (1975).

Mariian Panchyshyn

Panchyshyn, Mariian [Pančyšyn, Marijan], b 6 September 1882 in Lviv, d 9 October 1943 in Lviv. Physician specializing in internal medicine and roentgenology, and civic leader; full member of the Shevchenko Scientific Society from 1920. After graduating from Lviv University in 1909, he worked at its clinic of internal medicine and by 1912 had become head of the roentgenology department. During the First World War he organized field hospitals in the Austrian army. In 1918–21 he was a leading member of the Ukrainian Citizens' Committee in Lviv and an organizer of medical care for wounded and captured soldiers. After the war he helped organize the *Lviv (Underground) Ukrainian University, at which he served as a professor of anatomy (1920–5), dean of the medical faculty, and rector (1922–5). He was president of the *Ukrainian Physicians' Society for many years and a coeditor of *Likars'kyi vistnyk*. He donated his services to the *Narodnia Lichnytsia society and helped found its hospital. He founded the *Ukrainian Hygienic Society in 1929, organized its outpatient clinics and tuberculosis dispensaries, built a sanatorium in Pidliute, and financed popular pamphlets on hygiene. He was active in various civic organizations in Lviv, such as the Ridna Shkola society. During the Soviet occupation of Galicia (1939–41) Panchyshyn was elected deputy to the People's Congress of Western Ukraine and to the Supreme Soviet of the USSR. He was the first director of the Lviv oblast public health department. As head of clinical therapy at the Lviv Medical Institute, he promoted the Ukrainization of medical studies. He was a member of the Ukrainian National Council in Lviv (1941–2). He published about 25 scientific works, dealing particularly with stomach, intestinal, and kidney disorders.

Pandects of Antiochus. A collection of teachings on Christian morality written ca 620 by the Byzantine monk Antiochus at St Sava's Monastery, near Jerusalem. The earliest extant East Slavic translation, based on three 10th-century South Slavic translations, was made in the *ustav* script in Rus' in the 11th century. The 308-folio parchment manuscript (held at one time in the Stauropegion Monastery of the Resurrection in Moscow gubernia and now at the Moscow Historical Museum) was first studied by Archimandrite Amphilochius and I. Sreznevsky (1858). The longest excerpts were published by O. Bodiansky (1912). Most scholars (including A. Krymsky) believed that the translation was done in Novgorod the Great; A. Sobolevsky held it was done in Kiev. Another translation from the South Slavic (306 folios) was transcribed in the *ustav* script by the monk Marko at the Monastery of the Mother of God, probably in Volodymyr-Volynskyi, in 1307. The southwestern Rus' linguistic traits of the manuscript (preserved at the time at the National Museum in Lviv) were analyzed by I. Pankevych in *ZNTSh* (vols 123–124 [1917]). The *Pandects* were very popular in Rus', and many of the teachings were included in the **Prolog*.

Vasyl Paneiko   Yurii Paneiko

Oleksander Paneiko

Paneiko, Oleksander [Panejko], b 31 May 1891 in Zolochiv, Galicia, d 4 February 1950 in Munich. Galician pedagogue; brother of V. and Yu. Paneiko. He taught Ukrainian language and shorthand at the Academic Gymnasium and Ukrainian trade schools in Lviv (1912–14, 1916–25, 1928–39, 1941–2) and at gymnasiums in Kolomyia (1925) and Ternopil (1925–8). During the Soviet occupation of Western Ukraine he taught at Lviv University (1940–1), and during the German occupation he edited a column about language in the paper *L'vivs'ki visti* (1943). A member of the Shevchenko Scientific Society's Language Commission, he wrote the first Ukrainian stenography textbook (1922; based on the Gabelsberger shorthand system), edited Ukrainian textbooks, and prepared a revised edition of O. Iziumov's Ukrainian orthographic dictionary (1941) that included Western Ukrainian dialectal words. His Ukrainian grammar textbook (1950) was based on O. *Syniavsky's language norms and Polish grammatical traditions.

Paneiko, Vasyl [Panejko, Vasyl'], b 1883 in Zolochiv county, Galicia, d 29 May 1956 in Caracas, Venezuela. Journalist and civic and political leader; brother of O. and Yu. Paneiko. An active supporter of the National Democratic party, he attempted unsuccessfully to revive the monthly *Moloda Ukraïna* in 1905. He contributed to **Dilo* (1907–12) and *Literaturno-naukovyi vistnyk* (1908–14) and then served as chief editor of *Dilo* (1912–18). He was also one of the editors of *Ukrainische Korrespondenz*. In 1919 he was appointed state secretary of foreign affairs of the Western Ukrainian National Republic (ZUNR). He attended the Paris Peace Conference, first as vice-chairman of the UNR delegation and then (1920) as chairman of the

ZUNR delegation. To gain Entente support for Ukrainian independence he advocated an eastern European federation encompassing Ukraine (with Galicia) and Russia. The idea, which he presented in the brochure *Z'iedyneni derzhavy Skhidn'oï Evropy* (The United States of Eastern Europe, 1922), failed to gain support in Ukrainian political circles. After a brief stay in Lviv, where he edited *Dilo* and *Polityka* (1925), Paneiko returned to Paris and worked as a correspondent for *Dilo*. In the 1930s he was no longer active in Ukrainian political life. After the war he emigrated to the United States (1945) and then to Venezuela.

Paneiko, Yurii [Panejko, Jurij], b 3 April 1886 in Zolochiv, Galicia, d 18 August 1973 in Munich. Jurist and legal scholar; full member of the Shevchenko Scientific Society (from 1942) and the Ukrainian Academy of Arts and Sciences; brother of O. and V. Paneiko. While working as a civil servant he completed his law studies at Lviv University (LLD, 1910) and then conducted research at Halle, Vienna, and St Petersburg universities. After the First World War he lectured at Jagiełłonian University in Cracow (1926–8) and Vilnius University (1928–39), and served on the Competency Tribunal in Warsaw (1934–9), settling disputes between the Polish judiciary and government. After the Second World War he emigrated to Vienna and then Germany, where he served as professor and rector of the Ukrainian Free University in Munich (1948–73). He wrote many articles in Polish, Ukrainian, and German on various legal subjects, but his specialty was administrative law. In this area he wrote *Geneza i podstawy samorządu europejskiego* (The Genesis and Foundations of European Self-Government, 1926), a major survey of Polish administrative law (coauthor, 1929), and *Teoretychni osnovy samovriaduvannia* (The Theoretical Foundations of Self-Government, 1963). A list of his works is given in *Studien zu Nationalitätenfragen* (no. 4, 1988).

Panfuturism. See Futurism and Association of Panfuturists.

Paniutyn, Vasyl [Panjutyn, Vasyl'], b 1788 in the Chernihiv region, d 31 December 1855 in Katerynivka, Pavlohrad county, Katerynoslav gubernia. Philanthropist and major general. After enlisting in the Russian army in 1812, he fought against the French and then made his career in the military. He founded hospitals for the poor in

Romen, Novoheorhiievske (Kherson gubernia), and Slovianske (Kharkiv gubernia) by raising money through public subscription. As a member of the prison committee for Kherson gubernia he worked to improve penal conditions. He devoted the income from his estates to charity.

Paniutyne [Panjutyne]. V-17. A town smt (1986 pop 8,300) in Lozova raion, Kharkiv oblast. It arose in 1869 during the construction of the Kursk–Kharkiv–Sevastopil railway line and was first called Lozova-Azovska. Its main employer has been the railway-car repair yard.

Andrii Paniv

Ivan Pankevych

Paniv, Andrii, b 30 September 1899 in Prorub, Kharkiv gubernia, now in Sumy oblast, d 9 October 1937. Poet, prose writer, and teacher; research associate with the Institute of Literature of the AN URSR (now ANU). In 1925 he graduated from the Kharkiv Institute of People's Education, and subsequently he worked at the institute as a lecturer in Ukrainian literature. Paniv was cofounder of the literary organization *Pluh, its executive secretary, and a member of the editorial board of the journal *Pluh*. He began to publish his work in 1921. The main subject of Paniv's writings is village life. His works include the short story collections *Selo* (The Village, 1925), *Iak zviri khatu buduvaly* (How the Animals Built a House, 1925), and *Khrystia* (1928) and the poetry collections *Vechirni tini* (Evening Shadows, 1927) and *Bez mezh* (Without Bounds, 1933). Paniv was arrested on 5 December 1934 and sentenced in 1935 to 10 years in labor camps. In 1937 he was retried again by a special NKVD tribunal and sentenced to be shot.

Pankevych, Ivan [Pan'kevyč], b 6 October 1887 in Tseperiv, Lviv county, d 25 February 1958 in Prague. Linguist, pedagogue, ethnographer, and community figure in Transcarpathia; member of the Shevchenko Scientific Society from 1924. While studying at Lviv University (1907–9), he taught at the boarding school of the *Ridna Shkola society and was secretary of the *Prosvita society in Lviv. He organized 120 Prosvita reading houses in Lviv county. After graduating from Vienna University (PH D, 1912) he taught Russian at the Theresian Consular Academy in Vienna (1912–19). Assuming Czechoslovak citizenship, he was sent to Uzhhorod as the Czechoslovak official responsible for regulating the use of Ukrainian in Transcarpathia's schools and public institutions (1920–4). There he edited the educational journal *Uchytel'* (1920–2), the

children's magazine *Vinochok dlia podkarpats'kykh ditochok* (1920–4), and the regional studies monthly *Pidkarpats'ka Rus'* (1924–36) and taught at the Uzhhorod Gymnasium (1920–38). He was also a founding member of the Uzhhorod Prosvita society, its first secretary (1920–5), a member of its presidium (to 1938), head of its scholarly section, and managing editor of its annual, *Naukovyi zbornyk* (13 vols). He played a key role in the creation and development of the society's publications, library, museum, theater, and network of village reading houses. From 1939 he lived in Prague, where he served as docent at the *Ukrainian Free University (1939–45) and taught Ukrainian language and literature at Charles University (1947–51, 1954–8). From 1951 to 1954 he was persecuted as a 'Ukrainian bourgeois nationalist,' and from 1952 to 1963 his name was not mentioned in Ukrainian periodicals of the Prešov region.

Pankevych studied the phonetics and morphology of the 1307 translation of the *Pandects of Antiochus, the 17th-century *Ladomyrova and Kapishovsky gospels, the 18th-century Tyshiv 'Aleksandriia' and A. Kotsak's Slavonic grammar, notes in the margins of Transcarpathian church books, and other Transcarpathian 16th- to 19th-century manuscripts and charters. His 'Ruthenian' grammar (1922; rev edns 1927, 1936), which used an etymological orthography (*pankevychivka), was a standard secondary-school textbook in interwar Transcarpathia. His extensive research on the Transcarpathian dialects and experimental analysis of their phonetics culminated in the monograph *Ukraïns'ki hovory Pidkarpats'koï Rusy i sumezhnykh oblastei* (The Ukrainian Dialects of Subcarpathian Ruthenia and Adjacent Regions, 1938) and in his study of the history of Ukrainian Transcarpathian dialects in *Acta Universitatis Carolinae: Philologica* (vol 1, 1958). He also wrote on the Lemko dialects (proposing his own hypothesis of their origin, 1958); Galician dialects, literature, and folklore; and Transcarpathian folk rituals and songs, material culture, history, literature, onomastics, and pedagogical concerns. He published a booklet of Ukrainian orthographic rules for use in the Prešov region (1952) and a large anthology of Ukrainian literary texts (1954). Pankevych's activities and publications played a major role in spreading the vernacular-based Ukrainian literary language in Transcarpathia and in overcoming Russophile tendencies there. His massive compilation of Transcarpathian carols and his Transcarpathian dialectal dictionary (approx 130,000 words) have not been published. His autobiography and correspondence with V. Hnatiuk and F. Kolessa, a bibliography of his works, and a selection of articles by and about him were published in *Naukovyi zbirnyk Muzeiu ukraïns'koï kul'tury v Svydnyku* (vols 3 [1967] and 4 [2 books, 1969–70]).

R. Senkus

Pankevych, Yuliian [Pan'kevyč, Julijan] (pseud: Prosten Dobromysl), b 4 July 1863 in Ustia Zelene, Stanyslaviv district, Galicia, d 1933 in Kharkiv. Painter, graphic artist, and writer. He studied at the Cracow and Vienna academies of art and was a founding member of the *Society for the Advancement of Ruthenian Art in Lviv and one of the pioneers of the Ukrainian 'native' style in Galicia. He painted Christ, the Mother of God, and saints in Ukrainian folk costume; portraits of M. Kostomarov, T. Shevchenko (1904), and I. Franko (1910); landscapes, such as *Waterfall* and *The Dniester*; and genre and historical

Yuliian Pankevych: *Peasant Madonna* (oil, 1900s)

paintings, such as *Groups of People by a Fence*, *The Defense of Zvenyhorod*, and *Dovbush's Rock*. He also illustrated editions of S. Rudansky's and Ya. Shchoholev's poetry, ornamented the poetry anthology *Akordy* (Chords, 1903), and contributed poems, fables, stories, articles, and translations to Galician periodicals. Just before his death he moved to Kharkiv, where he worked at the Skovoroda Museum and painted the canvases *In the Carpathians* and *Road into the Mountains*. A book about Pankevych by Ya. Nanovsky was published in Kiev in 1986.

Pankevychivka. An etymological orthography created by I. *Pankevych in 1922 for use in Transcarpathian schools. It was based on the **maksymovychivka* orthography and O. *Ohonovsky's 1885 Galician school grammar. Its rules, which were approved at the 1923 Transcarpathian Teachers' Conference after H. *Strypsky forbade the use of his own orthography, were elaborated in Pankevych's 1922 school grammar and remained in official use in Transcarpathia until 1945. The orthography reflected the local spelling traditions and the pronunciation of the Boiko (Verkhovynets) and Maramureş dialects. It rendered *i* as *ô* in closed syllables and retained the etymological *y* and *ѣ* ('jat''), but did not use the hard sign (*ъ*) or *ê*.

Pankiv, Mykola [Pan'kiv], b 26 August 1894 in Bilche Zolote, Borshchiv county, Galicia, d 17 October 1967 in Dufrost, Manitoba. Agronomist, beekeeper, and pomologist. After emigrating to Canada in 1912, he completed his education and began farming. He developed several frost-resistant varieties of apple, plum, and gooseberry and a variety of feed millet. He kept a large apiary and improved some nectar-bearing plants. At one time (1924) he edited and published a beekeeping monthly in Winnipeg called *Pasika*. He received many awards for his research and served as president of the Manitoba Beekeepers Association (1946).

Pankivska, Yosypa [Pan'kivs'ka, Josypa] (née Fedak), b 1866 in Yavoriv, Galicia, d 10 December 1934 in Lviv. Educator and civic activist; wife of K. *Pankivsky. For many years she worked as a teacher in Lviv. She was a founder of the Vacation Resort Society and was active in the Ukrainian Citizens' Committee and the Ukrainian Society of Aid to Emigrants from Eastern Ukraine.

Kost Pankivsky (1855–1915)   Kost Pankivsky (1897–1973)

Pankivsky, Kost [Pan'kivs'kyj, Kost'], b 15 April 1855 in Ryshkova Volia, Jarosław county, Galicia, d 16 November 1915 in Kiev. Economist, co-operative leader, publisher, and civic leader; founding member of the Shevchenko Scientific Society. A graduate of the Higher Agricultural School in Vienna, he was active in populist student circles. In the 1880s he worked as business manager and news editor of *Dilo* and as director of St Nicholas's Institute (1888–1906). He sat on the board of directors of many leading Ukrainian societies, such as Prosvita, Ruska Besida, and the Ruthenian Pedagogical Society. He edited Prosvita's calendars, books, and journal *Chytal'nia-Pys'mo z Prosvity* (1894–6) as well as the humor magazine *Zerkalo* (1891–3), and helped edit the newspaper *Bat'kivshchyna* (1896), the children's magazine *Dzvinok* (1899–1900), and the literary and scholarly journal *Zoria*. His publishing firm, Dribna Biblioteka (1893–7), published popular works of literature. Pankivsky was a pioneer of the Galician co-operative movement, as a director (1898–1904) of the Provincial Credit Union and a member of the board of directors (1904–14) and managing director (1912–14) of the Provincial Audit Union (KSR). He was chief editor of *Ekonomist*, the official magazine of the KSR (1905–8), and its Ekonomichna Biblioteka (Economic Library) series. He maintained close contacts with leading Ukrainian intellectuals and activists in Russian-ruled Ukraine and with the Prosvita society in Kiev. In his numerous articles he formulated the ideological principles of the Ukrainian co-operative movement. In June 1915 he was deported to Kiev by the occupational Russian authorities.

Pankivsky, Kost [Pan'kivs'kyj, Kost'], b 6 December 1897 in Lviv, d 20 January 1973 in Livingstone, New Jersey. Lawyer and civic and political leader; son of K. and Y. Pankivsky. While studying law in Prague (LLD, 1924) he was president of the Group of Ukrainian Progressive Youth. After opening his own law office in Lviv (1924) he often served as defense counsel at political trials and was active in charitable societies, such as the Ukrainian Invalids' Aid Society and the Child Protection and Youth Care

Society, and served as president of the Plai hiking society. In 1941 he was general secretary of the Ukrainian National Council in Lviv and president of the *Ukrainian Regional Committee. He served as vice-president of the *Ukrainian Central Committee (1942–5). After the war he engaged in émigré politics. In Germany (1945–9) he belonged to the *Ukrainian National State Union and served as vice-president of the UNR government-in-exile. After emigrating to the United States in 1949, he became president of the Union of Ukrainian National Democrats, chairman of the Representation of the Executive Organ of the Ukrainian National Council, and president of the American branch of the League of the Captive Peoples of Russia. He wrote three books of memoirs: *Vid derzhavy do komitetu* (From State to Committee, 1957; 2nd edn 1970), *Roky nimets'koï okupatsiï* (The Years of the German Occupation, 1965; 2nd edn 1983), and *Vid komitetu do derzhavnoho tsentru* (From Committee to State Center, 1968).

Severyn Pankivsky

Pankivsky, Severyn [Pan'kivs'kyj], b 24 April 1872 in Ryshkova Volia, Jarosław county, Galicia, d 10 January 1943 in Lviv. Stage actor, director, and translator. He acted in the troupes of M. Kropyvnytsky (1897–8, 1900–3), M. Starytsky (1898), and P. Saksahansky (1903–5) and in the Ruthenian People's Theater in Lviv (1905–6). He directed and acted in Sadovsky's Theater (1906–17), the State Drama Theater (1918–19), the Shevchenko First Theater of the Ukrainian Soviet Republic (1919–21), and the Romen Ukrainian Theater (1921–3). He acted in the films *Koliivshchyna* (1933) and *Prometheus* (1936). He translated plays by H. Heijermans, G. Zapolska, E. Rostand, and W. Shakespeare and in the 1930s wrote the memoir *Shliakhamy zaviianymy za synioiu ptashkoiu* (Following Snowed-over Paths in Pursuit of a Blue Bird).

Pankovych, Stepan [Pankovyč], b 29 October 1820 in Veliatyn, near Khust, Transcarpathia, d 29 August 1874. Greek Catholic bishop of Mukachiv (1867–74). He studied at Tarnov in Czechoslovakia and in Uzhhorod and then served as a tutor of children of the nobility. As bishop he actively Latinized and Magyarized the eparchy. In 1873 he made a section of the eparchy into a separate Hungarian Greek Catholic vicariate, which later became *Hajdúdorog eparchy.

Pankratiev, Oleksii [Pankrat'jev, Oleksij], b 26 November 1903 in Kiev, d 8 August 1983 in Kiev. Cameraman. He completed study at the Odessa College of Cinema Art (1927) and then worked in the Odessa (1925–7) and Kiev

(from 1928) Artistic Film studios, in the latter of which he led the Scientific Research Laboratory and Department of Combined Filming (1934–40). He taught at the Kiev Institute of Cinematography (1931–2 and 1935–7).

Panshchyna. See Serfdom.

Panske Lake [Pans'ke ozero]. A saltwater lake in the Crimea. Located on the Tarkhankut Peninsula, the lake is separated from the sea by sandbars. It is fed by groundwater and the seepage of seawater. Its salinity ranges from 12 to 28 per cent. The muds on its bottom are noted for their medicinal qualities.

Pan-Slavism. A cultural and political movement among Slavic peoples, prevalent in the 19th century, whose adherents believed that their lineal and linguistic ties should bring about a union of all Slavs. Pan-Slavism was formulated as a theory in the early 19th century, the term itself being established by the Slovak J. Herkel in a linguistic treatise in 1826. The initial stages of the movement were devoted to praising a common Slavic past and studying Slavic languages. Pan-Slavism was pursued in particular by western Slavs as an offshoot of their national awakening. The political subjugation of the majority of Slavic peoples, the ideas of the French Revolution and German romanticism, and concurrent national awakenings resulted in the adoption of a historical and philosophical doctrine of Pan-Slavism, which not only sought the unity and federation of Slavic peoples, but envisioned the establishment of an ideal balance of power in Europe and a rejuvenation of European civilization as a result of their efforts. In the second half of the 19th century the concept was adopted by Russian circles, who quickly came to dominate the movement and developed it as a means of extending Russian influence over other Slavic peoples.

The ideas and writings of German Romantics, such as F. Schelling, H. Hegel, and particularly J. Herder (who praised the Slavic *Volksgeist*), had a great influence on the Slavic cultural milieu in the early 19th century, notably on Czechs, such as J. Dobrovský and V. Durič. P. *Šafařík (a Slovak, 1795–1861) was among the first to publish statistics on Slavs with his *Geschichte der slavischen Sprache und Literatur nach allen Mundarten* (1826), which also mentioned Ukrainians (Little Russians) as a distinct people. Another Slovak, J. Kollár (1793–1852), wrote the epic poem *Slávy dcera* (Slava's Daughter), in which he idealized the past of the 'Slavic people' (believing the many Slavic tribes constituted a single race). Pan-Slavic ideas also promoted the establishment of Slavic studies centers in Prague, Zagreb, Moscow, Berlin, Paris, Vienna, and other cities (both Slavic and not), which later played a central role in many national revivals.

Slavic cultural figures, such as F. *Čelakovský, Dobrovský, L. Gaj, and J. Jungmann, believed that Russia would assist other Slavic peoples in their struggles against pan-Germanism and Turkish domination and dreamed of a political and linguistic union under Russia. Some later came to change their views (including Gaj, L. Štúr, and K. Havlíček-Borovský). Other Pan-Slavists had an Austrophile orientation. The father of Austro-Slavism (as that variant of Pan-Slavism was known) was the Slovene philologist J. Kopitar. The concept was further developed by the Czech F. Palacký (1785–1876), who during the Revolution of 1848–9 supported the preservation of the Austrian

Empire in the form of a federation of Slavs, Austrians, and Hungarians. Palacký, however, did not foresee any granting of rights to Galician Ukrainians, whom he considered Poles. After the transformation of the Austrian Empire into the Austro-Hungarian Empire he shifted his orientation to Russia and participated in the Moscow Slavic Congress of 1867.

Pan-Slavism did not command much support among the Poles, who were swayed more by Romantic patriotism and dreams of renewing the Polish state in its pre-1772 boundaries. At the same time the so-called Polish Question provided a vexing dilemma for Russian Pan-Slavists, who could easily condone the acquisition of Ukrainian lands (the 'western provinces') by the empire but were troubled by the implication that Polish ethnic lands could be incorporated. Nevertheless, within Poland pro-Russian and anti-Russian camps developed, the latter camp believing that the leading role in any Slavic union should be Poland's. Like their Russian counterparts the Polish proponents of Pan-Slavism did not recognize any right of the Ukrainian people to self-determination or to a separate existence.

In the late 19th century Russians came to dominate the debate over the goals and the rationale of Pan-Slavism. Even though one of the earliest proponents of Pan-Slavism, the Croatian priest J. Križanić (1618–83), had formulated the idea of a political union of Slavs under the Muscovite tsar as a form of protection from the perceived German and Turkish menace, the idea of pan-Slavism remained at first weakly developed in Muscovy. With the rise of the *Slavophiles in the 1840s a growing interest began to be shown in Pan-Slavism together with the idea that Russia should be the most prominent figure in any Slavic union. It was the Crimean War, however, in particular the shock of the empire's diplomatic isolation, that raised the profile of Pan-Slavism: a Slavic union was seen as a guarantee that Russia would never again stand alone. The Slavic Benevolent Committee was established in Moscow in 1858, and in 1859 Križanić's manuscript was unearthed and published. Benevolent committees were also established later in St Petersburg (1868), Kiev (1869), and Odessa (1870). The most identifiable figures in the movement included M. Pogodin and M. Katkov. The tone of the Russian Pan-Slavists became increasingly political as Russia moved from a fraternal role to a political one, particularly after the Polish Insurrection of 1863–4. The heyday of Pan-Slavism in Russia lasted from the staging of the Second Slavic Congress in Moscow in 1867 (in which no Poles or Ukrainians, other than two Russophile Bukovynians, took part) until shortly after the Russo-Turkish War of 1877–8. Its most broadly formulated program was prepared by N. Danilevsky in a work serialized in 1869 as *Rossiia i Evropa* (Russia and Europe), which foresaw the future addition of Galicia, Transcarpathia, and Bukovyna to the Russian Empire. Changed political circumstances in the 1880s undercut the tacit political support Pan-Slavism had enjoyed as a semiofficial policy, and it declined in popularity. Nevertheless Russian Pan-Slavism continued in a muted form with state subsidies for Russophiles outside the borders of the empire.

In Ukraine certain notions of Pan-Slavism were evident relatively early in the 19th century. Such ideas were disseminated mainly by Freemasons (notably the United Slavs Lodge in Kiev, 1818–19) and by Decembrists (the Society of United Slavs, 1823–5). The political program of the *Cyril and Methodius Brotherhood (1845–7) was deeply influenced by Pan-Slavism, which was also popular among Ukrainian scholars (O. Bodiansky, M. Maksymovych, and others) and the liberal nobility (H. Galagan, M. Rigelman, and others). Many of the liberal nobility joined the benevolent committees active in Kiev and Odessa.

In Western Ukraine the idea of Pan-Slavism initially fostered but later impeded the development of a Ukrainian national consciousness. In the first half of the 19th century people such as Šafařík and Kollár inspired key representatives of the Ukrainian national revival (notably the *Ruthenian Triad) to search out their Slavic heritage. The *Slavic Congress in Prague of 1848 provided the setting for an unprecedented demand by Ukrainians for national recognition and political rights. That year the *Halytsko-Ruska Matytsia was established as an institution of national 'enlightenment' along the lines of Czech and Serbian institutions. In the later part of the century, following a political reconciliation between Austria and Hungary at the expense of most of the Slavic peoples in the empire, the Ukrainian intelligentsia increasingly consisted of *Russophiles, who were supported morally and financially by Pan-Slavist circles in Russia. They increasingly became a minority party as they were superseded in the 1880s and 1890s by Ukrainophile national populists.

In the early part of the 20th century Pan-Slavism saw a limited revival. Slavic congresses were held in Prague (1908) and Sofia (1910), and a new face was put on the movement by its being dubbed 'Neo-Slavism.' As war became increasingly more likely, patriotic circles in Russia again began to make claims of kinship with other Slavic peoples. One of their activities was the establishment of groups to provide help in laying the groundwork for possible territorial acquisitions in Western Ukraine. The groups included the Galician Russian Committee in St Petersburg and the Committee for the Liberation of Carpathian Ruthenia in Kiev, both of which provided support for regional Russophile activity.

Pan-Slavism largely lost its appeal after the First World War. A concerted effort was made by the Soviet authorities in the 1940s to revive Pan-Slavic sentiments, and in 1941 they backed the creation of the All-Slavic Committee and staged the All-Slavic Congress in Moscow. Similarly, All-Slavic Committees were established in the West as CP front organizations. Those efforts were more an extension of Soviet foreign policy than reflections of popular sentiment. The Pan-Slavic thrust was dropped by the Soviets after their rupture with J. Tito's Yugoslavia in 1948.

BIBLIOGRAPHY

Hrushevs'kyi, M. 'Na ukraïns'ki temy: Ukraïnstvo i vseslovianstvo,' *LNV*, no. 6 (Lviv 1908)

Pypin, A. *Panslavizm v proshlom i nastoiashchem* (St Petersburg 1913)

Leger, L. *Le panslavisme* (Paris 1917)

Hryshko, V. *Panslavizm u sov'iets'kii istoriohrafiï i polityntsi* (New York 1956)

Petrovich, M. *The Emergence of Russian Panslavism, 1856–1870* (New York 1956)

Kohn, H. *Pan-Slavism: Its History and Ideology*, 2nd edn (New York 1960)

Fadner, F. *Seventy Years of Pan-Slavism in Russia: Karazin to Danilevskii, 1800–1870* (Washington 1962)

V. Kosyk

Panteleimonivka [Pantelejmonivka]. DB III-3. A town smt (1986 pop 8,700) in Yasynuvata raion, Donetske oblast. It arose around the railway station built there in 1876 and attained smt status in 1938. The town produces refractory products, bricks, and reinforced concrete.

Panticapaeum. An ancient Greek colony founded in the early 6th century BC at the site of present-day Kerch, in the Crimea. Strategically located on the western shore of Kerch Strait, the city grew quickly; before the end of the century it was minting its own coins. As the leading trade, manufacturing, and cultural center on the northern coast of the Black Sea it became the capital of the *Bosporan Kingdom, which arose in the 5th century. It was heavily damaged in Saumacus' revolt and Diophantus' capture of the city at the end of the 2nd century BC and by an earthquake ca 70 BC. Panticapaeum was rebuilt under Roman rule, and by the 1st century AD had regained its commercial importance. It began to decline in the 3rd century as tribal raids disrupted the trade in the Black Sea and the Mediterranean Basin. Panticapaeum was destroyed by the Huns ca 370. Later a small town arose at the site, which in the Middle Ages became known as Bosphorus.

The city was dominated by Mt Mithridates, on which the temples and civic buildings were placed. The slopes were terraced and covered with private villas. The large bay provided an excellent port. At its apogee the city occupied approx 100 ha. Beyond the city walls was a large necropolis, which has been excavated since the end of the 19th century. It included a number of famous kurhans, such as Melek-Chesmen, Tsarskyi, Zolota Mohyla, and

Panticapaeum: mural painting of Persephone being carried off by Hades (1st century AD)

Yuz Oba. The city itself has been excavated systematically since the Second World War.

BIBLIOGRAPHY
Blavatskii, V. *Pantikapei: Ocherki istorii stolitsy Bospora* (Moscow 1964)
Marchenko, I. *Gorod Pantikapei* (Symferopil 1974)

Pantiukhov, Ivan [Pantjuxov], b 31 July 1836 in Novhorod-Siverskyi, Chernihiv gubernia, d 28 June 1911 in Kiev. Physician. A graduate of Kiev University (1862), from 1872 he worked at the Kiev Military Hospital. He wrote about anthropological questions, the history of medicine, and sanitation statistics. He compiled *Statisticheskie i sanitarnye ocherki Kieva* (Statistical and Sanitary Studies of Kiev, 1875) and wrote popular brochures on medicine, such as *Besedy o zdorove* (Conversations on Health, 1876).

Pantsyrni **boyars.** Impoverished nobles, free peasants, and liberated slaves in the 15th- and 16th-century Lithuanian-Ruthenian state who served in the grand duke's cavalry in heavy armor (*pantsyr*, from the German *panzer*). They lived on ducal lands and were exempted from taxes and other feudal obligations. Their status was between that of the petty nobility and that of the peasantry. In 1528 both the *pantsyrni* and the *putni* boyars were officially abolished. Some were promoted to the status of petty nobles; others were demoted to that of *state peasants. Both categories of boyars continued to exist unofficially until the end of the 16th century. At that time some of those stationed in Ukraine became *registered Cossacks.

Pap, Michael, b 24 July 1920 in Transcarpathia. Ukrainian-American historian. After graduating from Mukachiv-Bratislava State College, Vienna, and Heidelberg University (PH D, 1948) he moved to the United States, where he taught at Notre Dame College and John Carroll University (JCU) in Cleveland. A specialist in Soviet-American relations and the nationalities problem in the USSR, he directed the Institute for Soviet and East European Studies at JCU (from 1961) and edited the book *The Russian Empire: Some Aspects of Tsarist and Soviet Colonial Practices* (1985).

Pap, Oleksandr, b 2 July 1910 in Dashynka, Zhytomyr county, Volhynia gubernia, d 14 September 1979 in Kiev. Obstetrician and gynecologist. A graduate of the Kiev Medical Institute (1937), he served as director of the Kiev Scientific Research Institute of Pediatrics, Obstetrics, and Gynecology (1945–79) and president of the Society of Obstetricians and Gynecologists of the Ukrainian SSR (1979). His work dealt with the particulars of pregnancy, childbirth, and postnatality in women with diseases of the internal organs, the nutrition of pregnant women, and the organization of medical care for pregnant women.

Paper industry. A branch of industry that produces cardboard, paper, various fiber products, and semifinished products such as cellulose. The main raw material used by the cellulose and paper industry is pine and deciduous trees, the straw of grain cereals, hemp, recycled waste paper, and rags. The development of the chemical industry made possible the manufacture of paper and cardboard out of cellulose and wood pulp.

The first paper mills appeared at the beginning of the

Output of the paper industry in Ukraine, 1913–87
(in 1,000 tonnes)

Production	1913	1940	1965	1970	1980	1987
Paper	26.9	27.9	134.3	187.4	209.0	320.4
Cardboard	–	20.6	227.0	326.0	347.5	549.0
Cellulose	2.0	2.8	14.4	131.2	105.7	108.6

16th century in Galicia and Volhynia. The production of paper expanded considerably in the Hetman state of the 18th century. At the beginning of the 19th century the first large paper manufactories were built, and in the second half of the century machines were introduced into the manufacturing process. At the beginning of the 20th century there were 43 paper factories in Ukrainian territories, producing 38,000 t of paper and cardboard. The rate of production growth for cellulose products was even higher under the Soviet regime (see the table). The largest paper and cellulose factories in Ukraine are the Zhydachiv Cellulose and Cardboard Plant, the Poninka Cellulose and Paper Industrial Complex, the Kherson Cellulose Plant, the Malyn Paper Factory, and the Koriukivka Industrial Paper Factory. Ukraine produced scarcely 4 percent of the paper produced by the former USSR and only half the paper and cardboard used in Ukraine. The rest of the paper and some of the raw material for the paper plants were imported from Russia. Paper was one of the so-called subsidized products; hence, its distribution in Ukraine was controlled centrally in Moscow. Through its distribution policy the government in Moscow controlled printing and publishing in Ukraine (see *Printing industry and *Publishers and publishing).

V. Holubnychy

Paprocki, Bartłomiej (Bartosz), b ca 1543 in Paprocka Wola (now Płock), Mazovia region, Poland, d 27 December 1614 in Lviv. Polish writer and heraldist. He studied at Cracow Academy and traveled widely. His *Herby rycerstwa polskiego* (Coats of Arms of the Polish Knighthood, 1584) included portrayals of contemporary Ukrainian gentry families, Tatar and Turkish attacks on Ukraine, and the life and ways of the Cossacks. He described in detail the Moldavian campaign of the early 1580s, which was led by one of his friends, S. *Zborowski.

Paproski, Steve [Paproc'kyj, Stefan], b 23 September 1928 in Lviv. Business manager and politician. At an early age Paproski emigrated to Canada and settled in Edmonton. After attending the University of North Dakota, University of Arizona, and Banff School of Advanced Management, he was elected to the Canadian House of Commons in 1968 as the Progressive Conservative member for Edmonton Centre constituency (now Edmonton North). He was re-elected in 1972, 1974, 1979, 1980, 1984, and 1988. He served as chief Opposition whip in 1976–9 and then minister of state for fitness and amateur sports with responsibility for multiculturalism in the short-lived Clark government of 1979–80.

Parachuting (*parashutnyi sport*). Parachuting was introduced in Soviet Ukraine in the early 1930s. The sport was supervised from 1933 to 1947 by the Society for the Advancement of Defense and Aviation and Chemical Construction. Soviet parachutists had their own organization

from 1948 and their own federation from 1966. From 1954 they took part in biennial world championships sponsored by the International Aeronautic Federation and placed first in the team events many times. Since that year several Ukrainians have been individual world champions: I. Fedchyshyn (1954), P. Ostrovsky (1958), Ye. Tkachenko (1968), H. Surabko (1976), and I. Terlo (1978) among the men, and V. Zakoretska (1976) and L. Koricheva (1982) among the women.

Paradysky, Oleksa [Paradys'kyj], b 1891 in Ananiv, Kherson gubernia, d 1949 in Aschaffenburg, West Germany. Literary scholar. In the interwar years he taught courses in Ukrainian literature at several postsecondary institutions in Kharkiv. In the mid-1930s he became head of the chair of the history of Ukrainian literature at Kharkiv University. He wrote articles on 17th- to 19th-century Ukrainian literature and introductions to many interwar editions of Ukrainian literary classics. He also edited the last volume (the diary) of the 1939 Soviet edition of T. Shevchenko's complete works (5 vols). He survived the Stalinist terror and managed to emigrate during the Second World War.

Serhii Paradzhanov

Paradzhanov, Serhii [Paradžanov, Serhij] (Paradzhanian, Sarkis), b 9 January 1924 in Georgia, d 21 July 1990 in Yerevan. Armenian film director of Ukrainian films. He graduated from the State Institute of Cinema Arts in Moscow (1951, pupil of I. Savchenko) and began working at the Kiev Artistic Film Studio, where he created several short films and musicals, including *Nataliia Uzhvii* (1957), *Ukraïns'ka rapsodiia* (Ukrainian Rhapsody, 1961), and *Duma* (1964). International acclaim came to Paradzhanov in 1964 after the screening of *Tini zabutykh predkiv* (Shadows of Forgotten Ancestors, based on M. *Kotsiubynsky's novella of the same title). It was awarded 16 prizes in all at international film festivals for its magnificent combination of camera work with atonal music and bright colors. In 1965–8 Paradzhanov was harassed for writing letters of protest against the unlawful arrests of intellectuals and for demanding free expression in the press. He moved to Armenia and experimented in a new cinema technique of superimposition of different colors (*The Color of Pomegranates*, 1969). In 1971 he returned to Kiev and began working on the film *Kyïvs'ki fresky* (Kievan Frescoes), but the filming was stopped, and he was arrested in 1973 on spurious charges of currency speculation and homosexuality and sentenced to 15 years' imprisonment. In 1977, after international pressure was applied (petition signed by F. Truffaut, J.-L. Godard, L. Malle, F. Fellini, L. Visconti, R.

Rosselini, and M. Antonioni), Paradzhanov was released from prison, only to be arrested again in Tbilisi in 1982 (charged with 'associating with undesirable persons'). His work was restricted as a result of the arrest; nevertheless, in 1984 he produced the film *Legend of Surami Fortress* and coauthored the screenplay *Swan Lake: The Zone*, which was directed by Yu. *Illienko (1989). His plan to produce a film version of T. Shevchenko's *Mariia* was not realized.

V. Revutsky

St George's Ukrainian Orthodox Church in Encarnación, Paraguay

Paraguay. A country in South America (1990 pop 4,279,500) with an area of 406,752 sq km. Asunción is its capital city. Ukrainian immigration into Paraguay can be traced back to 1922, when a group from neighboring Argentina established itself in Urú Sapucai (now Colonia Carlos A. López), in the department of Itapúa. They were joined in 1926–32 by more Ukrainians, chiefly from Argentina, who were encouraged by the availability of land. From 1927 the lumber company of P. Christophersen had made available approx 71,000 ha of land for sale. The immigrants established settlements in Fram (colonies nos 2, 4, and 12, and later nos 5, 7, and 9) and nearby in Santo Domingo, Capitan Miranda, and Carlos A. López, and bought lots of up to 10 ha. Between 1935 and 1939 a special contract between the Paraguayan and Polish governments brought approximately 3,000 Ukrainian families from Polish-ruled Ukraine to Paraguay. A further influx occurred in 1946–50, when several hundred Ukrainians arrived from displaced persons' camps in Europe or in the Philippines (accommodating Ukrainian refugees from the Far East). The Ukrainian immigrants in Paraguay emanated from all regions in Ukraine, from Transcarpathia to the Kuban, with Volhynians forming the largest single regional group.

No accurate figures exist regarding the number of Ukrainians in Paraguay. It has been estimated that up to 35,000 Slavic immigrants came into the country in 1928–39, including many Ukrainians. The community probably numbered approx 15,000 at this time. Subsequent political instability in the late 1940s and the 1950s impelled a large out-migration, mainly to Argentina, which has left the number of Ukrainians in Paraguay today at between 8,000 and 10,000. The majority continue to reside in the department of Itapúa (a region located in the southeast of the republic, which adjoins the Argentine province of *Misiones), especially in or around the cities of Encarnación and Carmen del Paraná. Some of the colonies, particularly those in the Fram district, are distinguished by their Ukrainian names: Bohdanivka, Polkovnyk Bohun, Nova Volyn, Nova Ukraina, Tarasivka, Perevertivka, and Morozenka. The same is true of colonies around Coronel Bogado (Zelenyi Klyn, Sybir, Persha Sotnia, Kavkaz), Alborada (Symon Petliura), Itangva (Bohdan Khmelnytsky), and Capitan Miranda (Taras Shevchenko). This Ukrainian nomenclature may be credited in large measure to the efforts of Rev T. Hnatiuk. In addition a small number of Ukrainians have settled in Asunción.

The majority of Ukrainians in Paraguay, originally peasants or artisans, are agriculturists who cultivate cotton, rice, corn, yerba maté (Paraguayan tea), and wheat for export, as well as garden vegetables for personal consumption. Other Ukrainians are engaged in the livestock economy (particularly those living around Coronel Bogado), in the lumber industry, or as apiarists. Those who have settled in the cities are employed as artisans and workers, or in commerce, the civil service, and the liberal arts.

Organized Ukrainian community life began when a Ukrainian Orthodox missionary priest from Argentina, Rev T. Hnatiuk, visited Encarnación in 1925 and established a church parish. In 1929 he initiated Paraguay's first Ukrainian People's Home in Urú Sapucai, which later provided the premises for a daily Ukrainian school and an amateur drama troupe. Another Ukrainian People's Home was founded in the colony of Sandova.

These early efforts were soon consolidated with the 1937 founding of a Prosvita society in Encarnación. Between 1937 and 1945 some 10 branches were founded. Today, Prosvita has its headquarters in Encarnación and maintains five branches. In 1948 the Prosvita society formed a youth section (with seven branches) that was later transformed into the *Ukrainian Youth Association (SUM). In 1945 the Ukrainian community founded the Ukrainian Relief Committee as an auxiliary of the Paraguayan Red Cross to lobby for and assist in the resettlement of refugees in Paraguay. The Relief Committee and Prosvita established the Ukrainian Center in Paraguay (Ukrainskyi oseredok v Paragvaiu) in 1949 as a representative umbrella organization. A member of the *Pan-American Conference, the association was headed by O. *Paduchak, A. Kushchynsky, and I. Lytvynovych until it became largely moribund in the 1960s. In the early 1980s its archives were transferred to the central Prosvita. Since 1961 an hour-long Ukrainian program, hosted until 1987 by S. Khudyk, has been broadcast from the local Encarnación radio station.

Some Ukrainians joined organizations which were pro-Soviet, Russophile, or Pan-Slavic in character. They founded the Ukrainian-Belarusian Reading Club in Domingo Bado and, in 1941, the Ukrainian-Belarusian Committee to Aid the Fatherland in Carmen del Paraná. As a result of the strong anticommunist attitude of the Stroessner regime, the pro-Soviet influence has been negligible since the 1950s, and today there is no pro-Soviet organization. The Russophile contingent is organized around the Russian Orthodox church; those of a quasi–Pan-Slavic orientation can be found in the Christian Orthodox church and the Slavic Evangelical-Baptist church. The Baptists conduct services in Ukrainian and Russian and have their own hour-long radio program.

Paraguay is the only country of Ukrainian settlement in the West where the majority (over 60 percent) of Ukrainians are of Orthodox background. The *Ukrainian Autocephalous Orthodox church today has six parishes, which are administered by Archpriest M. Shcherbak. The Ukrainian Orthodox community in Paraguay experiences a chronic shortage of priests. The Ukrainian Catholic church has six parishes served by a priest of German origin, J. Reisinger. The remainder of Ukrainians in Paraguay are largely of Baptist, Stundist, or Mennonite faith.

Partly because of their fairly compact settlement pattern, Ukrainians in Paraguay have not been assimilated to the degree of their counterparts in Argentina and especially Uruguay. The community, however, has not developed an infrastructure comparable to that of its counterparts in North America, Australia, and Europe. It has no press of its own, for instance, and publishing activity from the inception of settlement in 1922 has been negligible.

S. Cipko

Parakhoniak, Oleksandra. See Liubych-Parakhoniak, Oleksandra.

Parakoniev, Kostiantyn [Parakon'jev, Kostjantyn], b 8 September 1920 in Volodymyrivka, Kherson county, d March 1987 in Zaporizhia. Heroic and character stage and film actor and director. In 1945 he completed study at the Kiev Institute of Theater Arts. Then he worked at the Kirovohrad Ukrainian Theater of Music and Drama and, from 1967, the Zaporizhia Ukrainian Music and Drama Theater. He also acted in the film *Son* (The Dream, 1964).

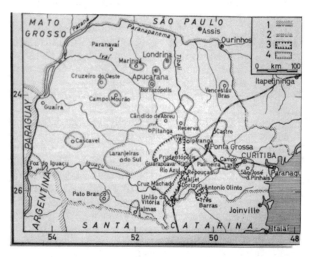

Ukrainians in Paraná: 1, national border; 2, border fo Paraná; 3, areas with a Ukrainian majority; 4, areas with a Ukrainian minority

Paraná. One of the three southern states of Brazil, with an area of 199,324 sq km and an estimated population of 9,137,700 (1990). The climate is subtropical. The state capital is Curitiba. Paraná is an ethnocultural and ethnolinguistic mosaic in consequence of the colonization policy started by Z. de Goes e Vasconcelos, the first president of the province. Faced with the task of developing a huge territory of 200,000 sq km with only 60,626 inhabitants, he initiated a policy of colonization with foreign immigrants in 1855. The subsequent recruiting efforts provided Ukrainians in Galicia and Bukovyna with specific information about settlement in Brazil and stimulated emigration to that country. Three waves of Ukrainian immigration followed, the first starting in earnest in 1895–7 and lasting until 1914.

The earliest areas of settlement included Água Amarela (Antonio Olinto today), Uniao da Vitória and district, Iracema, Mallet, Dorizon, and Prudentópolis district. By 1914 an estimated 45,000 Ukrainians were living in Paraná. Their numbers had increased to at least 61,000 by the end of the Second World War as a result of an interwar wave of immigration from Western Ukraine. They were joined in the post–Second World War period by a numerically small but influential third wave of immigration, a significant portion of which subsequently resettled in North America.

Relatively recent estimates put the number of Ukrainians in the state at 130,000 to 150,000, or approx 80 to 85 percent of the country's total Ukrainian population. Within the state itself Ukrainians represent slightly less than 2 percent of the population. They are concentrated in several regions where they are numerically significant, however. The most notable of these is the so-called Brazilian Ukraine area in and around the city of *Prudentópolis, where Ukrainians constitute approx 75 per cent of the local population. Other small bloc-settlement regions are scattered throughout the state.

Ukrainians played a key role in introducing crops unknown in that part of Brazil, such as wheat, rye, buckwheat, and European potatoes. They also introduced and spread apiculture as well as milling and co-operative economic enterprises. Individual Ukrainians have occupied important government posts and academic positions, and Ukrainian writers and artists have helped shape the cultural profile of the state.

Paraná occupies a central place in the political, educational, organizational, and religious affairs of Ukrainians in Brazil. The country's earliest community structures began to appear there in the early 1900s, and many of the central community institutions of Brazil's Ukrainians are located in either Curitiba or Prudentópolis. In recent times some of the more significant developments affecting Brazilian Ukrainians have taken place in the state. The *Ukrainian Brazilian Central Representation was established in 1985 as an umbrella body for community interests. That same year the Brazilian Center for Ukrainian Studies was revived, and subsequently it has promoted Ukrainian education in the state. Notable developments include efforts to extend the Ukrainian studies program at the Federal University of Paraná in Curitiba from its extension status into the regular program of the department of foreign languages, and the adoption in 1989 of legislation allowing for the introduction of minority-language (including Ukrainian-language) instruction in the state's school curriculum in 1991. A student residence was opened in 1987 in Curitiba under the auspices of the Ukrainian Catholic eparchy. The Community Committee of the Land Fund of ZUADAK (Comitê Social de Aajudas do Fundo Agrário de UUARC) was set up in 1986 in Prudentópolis by a coalition of churches and community groups as a self-help association to assist the landless in purchasing farmsteads. (See *Brazil.)

N. Kerechuk

Parashchuk, Mykhailo [Paraščuk, Myxajlo], b 16 November 1878 in Varvaryntsi, Terebovlia county, Galicia, d 24 December 1963 in Bania, Plovdiv province, Bulgaria. Sculptor and political figure. He studied at the Cracow and Vienna academies of art, the Lviv Polytechnic, and R. Julien's academy and A. Rodin's studio in Paris. In 1908–11 he taught sculpture at the Munich Institute of Applied Arts. In 1911–13 he lived in Kiev and took part in a competition to design a monument in honor of T. Shevchenko. While crossing the border between the Russian and Austro-Hungarian empires in 1913, he was detained on suspicion of espionage and imprisoned by the Austrians in the *Thalerhof concentration camp in Styria. He escaped in 1914 and during the First World War was active in the *Union for the Liberation of Ukraine in Vienna and organized wood-carving, sculpture, and pottery courses for Ukrainians in the Russian army interned in the German POW camps in Rastatt and Wetzlar. In 1918 he returned to Ukraine. In 1920 he was appointed secretary and then head of the UNR diplomatic mission in Tallinn, Estonia, and an adviser to the UNR mission in Latvia. He was sent to the Balkans as a member of an International Red Cross mission, and from 1923 until the end of his life he lived in Bulgaria. There he was an active member of the Ukrainian Hromada in Sofia and the founder and first president of the Ukrainian-Bulgarian Society (1930s to early 1940s).

Mykhailo Parashchuk: *Portrait of Symon Petliura* (plaster, 1936)

Parashchuk created several commemorative monuments: to A. Mickiewicz in Lviv (1905, with A. *Popel); to the Ukrainians who died in the Wetzlar camp; to L. Kalcheva and to M. Drahomanov in Sofia; to Jews killed by the Nazis in Sofia and Plovdiv; and to A. Konstantinov in Pazardzhik. He also sculpted busts of Shevchenko, I. Franko, V. Stefanyk, S. Liudkevych, M. Lysenko, Drahomanov, M. Yatskiv, V. Pachovsky, M. Hrushevsky, S. Petliura, Metropolitan S. Sheptytsky, O. Oles, B. Lepky, S. Cherkasenko, Ye. Petrushevych, M. Livytsky, and many Bulgarian figures; created decorations for over 100 buildings in Ukraine, and for many in Poland and Bulgaria; and created many figure sculptures. In many of his works he gave new expression to the Ukrainian baroque style of the 17th and 18th centuries. Some of his works show the influence of Rodin (eg, the portrait *Old Man* and series 'The Enslaved') and symbolism (eg, the series 'Love'). Parashchuk is buried next to Drahomanov in a cemetery in Sofia.

D. Stepovyk

Parashka, Mount [Paraška]. V-4. A mountain (elevation, 1,268 m) in the High Beskyd region of the Carpathians. Situated in Lviv oblast, the mountain is formed from layered sandstones and shales. Pine and beech forests cover its slopes. It is a popular site for tourists.

Parasitology. The study of animal and plant parasitism, including medical, veterinary, and agricultural parasitology, with the aim of controlling or eradicating the parasites most harmful to human life and well-being. In Ukraine departments of parasitology are active at some of the medical institutes and universities, as well as at the AN URSR (now ANU) institutes of Zoology, Hydrobiology, and the Biology of Southern Seas and the Scientific Research Institute of Epidemiology, Microbiology, and Parasitology in Kiev. There are also many institutions of applied science which treat the veterinary and agricultural aspects of the parasitology question, stressing also the importance of ecology. Scientists who have contributed to the field in Ukraine include I. *Andriievsky, D. Lambl, who discovered the pathogen *Giardia lamblia* (causative agent of lambliosis), V. Danylevsky, who was the first to study hemoparasites in birds, M. Melnikov-Razvedenkov, and O. *Markevych, who wrote the first textbook in Ukrainian, *Osnovy parazytolohii* (Basics of Parasitology, 1950). The Ukrainian Republican Scientific Society of Parasitologists was founded in 1945 in Kiev.

Parasiuk, Ostap [Parasjuk], b 20 December 1921 in Bilka, Peremyshliany county, Galicia. Mathematician and theoretical physicist; full member of the AN URSR (now ANU) since 1964. He graduated from Lviv University (1947) and in 1949–66 worked at the ANU Institute of Mathematics (1956–66 as deputy director). Since 1966 he has worked at the ANU Institute of Theoretical Physics, where he heads the section of mathematical methods in theoretical physics. Since 1956 he has taught at Kiev University, and in 1966–9 he was a member of the Presidium of the ANU and academic secretary of the physics division.

Parasiuk's main work deals with quantum field theory, although he has also made significant contributions to the theories of elasticity and plasticity, the theory of probability, the theory of dynamical systems, functional analysis, function theory, and other fields. He developed a rigorous

Ostap Parasiuk   Sofiia Parfanovych

theory for calculating infinities in quantum field theory and solved completely the problem of regularization of divergent integrals in the theory. Jointly with N. Bogoliubov he worked out the theory of multiplication of special generalized functions in quantum field theory. Parasiuk proposed a new method for the study of Feynman diagrams, generalized the methods of analytical regularization (now known as the Bogoliubov-Parasiuk-Hepp method), and deduced a general theorem about analytic and asymptotic properties of the amplitude of dissipation from the classical theorems of power series. In the theory of analytic continuation of generalized functions he obtained a theorem analogous to that of E. Titchmarsh and applied it to the solvability of coupled integral equations in the class of generalized functions.

W. Petryshyn

Parasiuk, Wilson, b 6 May 1943 in Stenen, Saskatchewan. Politician. Parasiuk was educated at the University of Manitoba (1965) and St John's College, Oxford (MA, 1968), on a Rhodes scholarship. A civil servant, he was elected to the provincial legislature of Manitoba in 1977 as the New Democratic party member for Transcona. He was re-elected in 1981 and 1986, and he served as minister of crown investments in 1982–3, minister of energy and mines responsible for Manitoba Hydro in 1981–7, and minister of health in 1988.

Parasunko, Onufrii [Parasun'ko, Onufrij], b 12 June 1913 in Ozaryntsi, Mohyliv-Podilskyi county, Podilia gubernia. Historian. A graduate of Kiev University (1940), he was vice-rector of Chernivtsi University (1940–1), lectured at Kiev University (1946–9), and was an associate of the AN URSR (now ANU) Institute of History (1949–71), a department chairman there (1963–7), and a department chairman at Kiev University (1971–?). He wrote books on the political mass strike in Kiev in 1903 (1953) and Ukraine's working class from the 1860s to the 1890s (doctoral diss, 1963). He also contributed to ANU multiauthor histories of the Ukrainian SSR (vol 1, 1953, 1967), of Kiev (vol 1, 1959), and of the working class of the Ukrainian SSR (vol 1, 1967) and coedited a collection of documents and materials about Ukraine's workers' movement of 1885–94 (1990).

Parfanovych, Sofiia [Parfanovyč, Sofija] (married name: Volchuk), b 1898 in Lviv, d 26 December 1968 in

Detroit. Gynecologist and writer; full member of the Shevchenko Scientific Society from 1942. A graduate of Lviv University (1926), she worked at the Lviv General Hospital and the Narodnia Lichnytsia clinic. She was active in the Ukrainian Hygienic Society and the Vidrodzhennia society and wrote a number of books on hygiene, proper nourishment, and temperance, including the popular *Hihiiena zhynky* (Hygiene of a Woman, 1939). In 1949 she emigrated to the United States. Her short stories, based on her experiences as a doctor, appeared in the collections *Tsina zhyttia* (The Price of Life, 1936) and *Inshi dni* (Other Days, 1948). She also wrote the collections of short stories *U lisnychivtsi* (At the Forest Reserve, 1954), *Liubliu Dibrovu* (I Love Dibrova [a holiday resort near Detroit], 1959), and *Charivna Dibrova* (Enchanting Dibrova, 1964) and the novels *Virnyi pryiatel'* (Faithful Friend, 1961) and *Takyi vin buv* (The Way He Was, 1964).

Paris. The capital of France and one of the world's political, cultural, and economic centers (1990 pop 2,152,000; metropolitan area, 10,200,000). Paris is one of the destinations of migrants of all countries, and small groups of Ukrainians have resided there since the Middle Ages. It is estimated that in the 20th century between 600 and 1,200 have lived in Paris at any given time.

The first mention of Ukrainians in Paris dates from the mid-11th century, with the marriage of Anna Yaroslavna to Henry I. In the 14th and, increasingly, through the 15th to 17th centuries Ukrainians began arriving in the city to study at the Sorbonne. Some manuscripts written by these students have survived, including the *Hrammatyka slovenskaia / Grammatica sclavonica* (Slavonic Grammar, 1643, 1645) of I. Uzhevych.

The first Ukrainian political émigrés in Paris were H. *Orlyk and the supporters of Hetman I. Mazepa who followed him. In 1765 Hetman K. Rozumovsky visited Paris and was received at the royal court. In 1761–5 the painter A. Losenko studied in Paris. In the late 19th century a number of Ukrainian cultural figures lived in the city, including M. *Vovchok (1860–7), M. *Bashkirtseva (1860–4), and F. *Vovk (who studied and worked in the School of Anthropology in Paris in 1887–1900). M. Drahomanov visited Paris in the 1870s and 1890s and took part in an international literary congress in Paris in 1878. In 1903 M. Hrushevsky stayed in Paris and taught at the Russian higher school of social sciences.

There was no organized Ukrainian presence in Paris until the 20th century, when the *Circle of Ukrainians in Paris became active in 1908–14. Its membership (120) consisted largely of post-1905 emigrants from Russian-ruled Ukraine and Galician students, and it issued a number of French-language publications about Ukraine. The initiator and head of the circle was Ya. Fedorchuk.

After the First World War, Ukrainian members of the expeditionary corps of the Russian army as well as a number of diplomatic delegations of the UNR and the Western Ukrainian National Republic (ZUNR) arrived to take part in the *Paris Peace Conference. The Ukrainian delegations established a press bureau and published the *Bulletin d'informations* (edited by F. Savchenko).

Paris became an important Ukrainian center in the interwar period, as its community grew with an influx of economic immigrants from Western Ukraine (particularly Galicia) in 1923. The following year political émigrés started arriving, among them I. Kosenko, S. Petliura, V.

Prokopovych, O. Shulhyn, M. Shumytsky, former officers and soldiers of the UNR army (M. Kapustiansky, Mykola Shapoval, O. Udovchenko, and others), and members of O. Koshyts's Ukrainian Republican Kapelle (O. Chekhivsky, K. Mykolaichuk). V. *Vynnychenko lived in Paris for a time, in the 1930s, as did M. Stsiborsky and V. Martynets. The major Ukrainian organizations of the period were centered in Paris and included the *Ukrainian Hromada in France (1924–76), the *Ukrainian National Union (1932–44), the *Union of Ukrainian Emigré Organizations in France (1925–40), the Society of Former Combatants of the UNR Army in France (est 1927), the *Union of Ukrainian Citizens in France (1925–32), the Ukrainian Students' Hromada (est 1924), and the *Petliura Ukrainian Library (est 1929). Paris was also the site of S. *Petliura's assassination in 1926 and the subsequent *Schwartzbard Trial.

Eight Ukrainian periodicals were published in Paris during the interwar period, including *Tryzub* (1925–40), *Ukraïns'ke slovo* (est 1933), *Vistnyk Ukraïns'koï Hromady u Frantsiï* (1929–38), *Ukraïns'ki visty* (1926–9), *Prométhée* (1926–38, in French), and *La Revue de Prométhée* (1938–40, in French).

During the German occupation, most Ukrainian organizations halted their activities. Only the Ukrainian Institution of Trust (headed by I. Stasiv), which oversaw the general social and cultural welfare of Ukrainian émigrés and refugees in 1942–4, was officially sanctioned. The Kobzar publishing house was also active. Some Ukrainians in Paris were arrested, including O. Boikiv, E. *Borschak, M. Shapoval, and O. Shulhyn.

Symon Petliura's grave monument at the Montparnasse Cemetery in Paris

More Ukrainian immigrants in Paris arrived at the end of the Second World War from the displaced persons' camps in Germany and Austria. A number of prewar organizations resumed their activities during this period, including the Ukrainian National Union (reconstituted as the Ukrainian National Alliance in France in 1949), the UNR Army Veterans' Society, and the Ukrainian Students'

Hromada. New organizations were also established, including the Union of Ukrainian Workers in France (1945), the Union of Ukrainians of France (1948), Ukrainian Community Aid in France (est 1946), the Ukrainian Academic Society in Paris (1946), the Ukrainian Christian Movement (1954), the Ukrainian Women's Association of France (1945), the Ukrainian Youth Association (1949), and the Organization of Ukrainian Youth in France (1956). In 1951–4 the headquarters of the Central Union of Ukrainian Students was located in Paris. The Ukrainian Central Civic Committee, an umbrella organization established in 1948, co-ordinated the activities of all of these groups. In 1985 the *Ukrainian Central Representation in France was formed as a rival umbrella group.

Postwar periodicals included *Ukraïns'ke slovo* (re-established in 1948), *Ukraïnets'-Chas* (1945–60), *Hromada* (1948–9), *Soborna Ukraïna* (1950–1), and *Ukraïna* (1949–53). Six journals were published in French: ABN *Correspondance* (1952–4), *L'Ukraine libre* (1953–4), *Bulletin franco-ukrainien* (1958–70), *L'Est européen* (est 1962 as a monthly), *Echos d'Ukraine* (1962–9), and *Echanges* (est 1971). Only the weekly *Ukraïns'ke slovo* has continued publishing to this day.

There are two Ukrainian churches in Paris. The Orthodox one was consecrated in 1925; it was presided over by Metropolitan P. *Sikorsky in 1949–53. The Catholic church was consecrated in 1937; it served as the seat for Bishop V. *Malanchuk in 1961–83 and has been the seat of Bishop M. *Hrynchyshyn since then.

Paris is an important center of Ukrainian academic life. The Shevchenko Scientific Society (NTSh) in Europe has its headquarters and a major library in the nearby suburb of *Sarcelles. The Petliura Ukrainian Library contains a valuable library, museum, and archives. Interest in Ukrainian scholarship was fostered by the Franco-Ukrainian Cercle des Etudes Ukrainiennes (est 1930). The Institut National des Langues et Civilisations Orientales has had Ukrainian language and culture as part of its curriculum since 1939. E. Borschak (1939–59), M. Scherrer (1959–72), and E. Kruba (since 1972) have been language instructors; A. Zhukovsky has taught Ukrainian cultural history since 1960. The Institut d'Etudes Slaves, the Institut National des Langues et Civilisations Orientales the Bibliothèque de Documentation Internationale Contemporaine à Nanterre, the Bibliothèque Nationale, and the Bibliothèque Slave also have substantial collections of Ukrainian materials.

The following are some of the artists who have been active in Paris: M. Andriienko-Nechytailo, A. Archipenko, M. Bashkirtseva, M. Boichuk, S. Borachok, S. Hordynsky, O. Hryshchenko, L. Hutsaliuk, V. Khmeliuk, M. Krychevsky, P. Levchenko, S. Levytska, A. Losenko, V. Makarenko, O. Mazuryk, O. Murashko, P. Omelchenko, V. Perebyinis, O. Savchenko-Bilsky, A. Solohub, A. Solomukha, T. Vyrsta, and S. Zarytska. Among the many Ukrainian composers and musicians who resided in Paris have been D. Drohomyretska, V. Hrudyna, M. Kouzan, Yu. Ponomarenko, I. Vovk, A. Vyrsta, F. Yakymenko, and the singers U. Chaikivska, M. Skala-Starytsky, and Ye. Zarytska. Theater productions were staged in the city by amateur groups sponsored by the Ukrainian Hromada in France in 1925–32 and in the 1950s under the direction of N. Pylypenko.

Paris is an an important international political center.

Parisian Ukrainians have been active in the Friendship Committee of Peoples of the Caucasus, Turkestan, and Ukraine; the Anti-Bolshevik Bloc of Nations; the Paris Bloc; and the International Free Academy. The dissident mathematician and thinker L. *Pliushch has resided near Paris since his release from the Soviet Union in 1975 and has frequently championed human rights and Ukraine's cause in the international arena. UNESCO, which has its headquarters in Paris, has occasionally been the site of international exhibitions sponsored by the Ukrainian SSR.

A bust of T. Shevchenko (donated by Soviet authorities) stands in Taras Shevchenko Square near the Ukrainian Catholic church. In the church of St-Germain-des-Prés there is a bas-relief depiction of the Battle of Berestechko between the Ukrainians and the Poles. S. Petliura lies buried in the Montparnasse cemetery, and the graves of Metropolitan Sikorsky, Gen M. Omelianovych-Pavlenko, and N. Makhno are in the Père Lachaise cemetery. (See also *France.)

BIBLIOGRAPHY
Lazovins'kyi, V. *Paryzh (Providnyk)* (Paris 1973)
De Ponfilly, R. *Guide russe, ukrainien, biélorusse de France* (Paris 1987)

A. Zhukovsky

Paris Bloc. The popular name of the League for the Liberation of the Peoples of the USSR, an organization of the captive nations of the Soviet Union. Founded in Paris in March 1953 through the initiative of Ukrainian National Council supporters, the group functioned as a coalition of anti-Soviet forces and included national organizations representing Armenia, Azerbaidzhan, Belarus, the Crimea, Georgia, Idel-Ural, Caucasian peoples, Turkestan, and Ukraine. Its most active Ukrainian members were D. Andriievsky, S. Dovhal, and M. Livytsky. Its purpose was to co-ordinate the independence struggle of the captive nations against Soviet occupation. It sought contacts with international organizations sympathetic to those political aspirations, organized press conferences and demonstrations, published declarations, and submitted memorandums to Western governments. It had branches in Munich, Paris, New York, and Istanbul. In 1958–67 it published the journal *Problems of the Peoples of the USSR*, which was edited by S. Dovhal. By the 1970s the coalition was a spent force and had become inactive.

Paris Peace Conference. The meeting that arranged the international settlement after the First World War. It opened on 18 January 1919 and was dominated by the victorious *Entente powers of the United States, France, the British Empire, and Italy and presided over by Premier M. Clemenceau. The new republics of Poland, Czechoslovakia, and Rumania were each allowed two representatives, but Soviet Russia was not recognized and was excluded. The government of the UNR Directory sent a delegation headed by H. *Sydorenko (replaced in August by M. *Tyshkevych) to lobby for admission to the conference, recognition of Ukraine's independence, the withdrawal of Polish, Rumanian, and Allied forces from Ukraine, and support for its war against Soviet Russia. The delegation, which included V. Paneiko, A. Margolin, O. Shulhyn, S. Shelukhyn, B. Matiushenko, A. Halip, M. Kushnir, S. Tomashivsky, S. Zarkhii, A. Petrushevych, O. Kulchytsky, D. Isaievych, P. Didushok, S. Tymoshenko, V. Kolosovsky,

Members of the UNR delegation at the Paris Peace Conference. From left: Oleksander Shulhyn, Arnold Margolin, and Vasyl Paneiko

M. Levytsky, O. Sevriuk, and F. Savchenko, submitted memorandums to the conference's General Secretariat. The delegation's extraordinary members, M. Lozynsky and D. Vitovsky, lobbied for a Ukrainian-Polish armistice on behalf of the Western Province of the UNR. Ukrainian representatives from Canada and the United States (O. Megas, I. Petrushevych, K. Bilyk, J. Hamil) aided the delegation. From December a separate Western Ukrainian National Republic delegation headed by Paneiko lobbied for Western Ukrainian independence. It submitted memorandums and documents, and protests against the Polish occupation written by Lozynsky, Vitovsky, Ye. Levytsky, Tomashivsky, V. Temnytsky, and O. Burachynsky. Transcarpathian leaders (eg, A. Beskyd, H. Zhatkovych) submitted memorandums to the conference supporting the incorporation of Transcarpathia into Czechoslovakia.

The conference produced the Covenant of the League of Nations and the treaties of *Versailles (with Germany), *Saint-Germain (with Austria), and Neuilly (with Bulgaria). Before it was brought to an end with the formal inauguration of the *League of Nations on 16 January 1920, it also designated the *Curzon Line as Poland's eastern border and laid the groundwork for the 1920 treaties of *Trianon (with Hungary) and *Sèvres (with Turkey) and the work of the *Conference of Ambassadors. Although national self-determination was one of its basic principles, the conference did not officially recognize the Ukrainian delegations or Ukraine's independence, but favored instead (under Russian anti-Bolshevik and American influence) the preservation of the territorial integrity of the Russian Empire. It did not undo the occupation of the Western Ukrainian lands by Poland, Czechoslovakia, and

Rumania, although it tried to put an end to the Ukrainian-Polish, Ukrainian-Soviet, and Russian civil wars (see *Berthélemy Mission, L. *Botha). Under pressure from the pro-Polish French and American delegates (including Clemenceau and Pres W. Wilson), the conference sanctioned the Polish occupation of Galicia.

BIBLIOGRAPHY
Décisions du Conseil Suprême sur la Galicie Orientale: Les plus importants documents, intro M. Lozynsky (Paris 1919)
Notes présentées par la Délégation de la République Ukrainienne à la Conférence de la Paix à Paris (Paris 1919)
Lozyns'kyi, M. *Halychyna v rr. 1918–1920* (Vienna 1922; repr, New York 1970)
Thompson, J.M. *Russia, Bolshevism, and the Versailles Peace* (Princeton 1966)
Lundgreen-Nielsen, K. *The Polish Problem at the Paris Peace Conference: A Study of the Policies of the Great Powers and the Poles, 1918–1919* (Odense 1979)

R. Senkus

Paris Peace Treaties of 1947. Treaties defining boundaries and war reparations of the European states that had supported Nazi Germany and been defeated in the Second World War. A preliminary peace conference was held in Paris between 29 July and 15 October 1946 to discuss the draft treaties for peace with Italy, Rumania, Hungary, Bulgaria, and Finland that had been prepared by the foreign ministries of the Four Powers (Great Britain, France, the United States, and the USSR). Delegates attended from 21 states, including the Ukrainian SSR (represented by D. *Manuilsky, O. Voina, M. Petrovsky, V. Koretsky, M. Ptukha, A. Baranovsky, O. Kasymenko, and others). The Ukrainian SSR was among the signatories to the five treaties signed in Paris on 10 February 1947. Among matters settled were the Ukrainian SSR's boundaries with Rumania and Hungary. Rumania recognized the 1940 cession of Bessarabia and northern Bukovyna to the USSR, and Hungary accepted its 1938 boundaries, except for a minor frontier rectification in favor of Czechoslovakia. Italy and Finland were required to pay reparations valued at 100 million US dollars and 300 million US dollars respectively to the USSR; Bulgaria, Hungary, and Rumania were also required to compensate the USSR for losses incurred during the war. The Ukrainian SSR, however, was not awarded any direct reparation payments. The treaties also made provisions to guarantee the cultural rights of national minorities and general civil rights, but Bulgaria, Rumania, and Hungary subsequently ignored the provisions. Ukrainian émigré organizations used the opportunity of the peace talks in Paris to raise their concern with the delegates as to whether or not the delegates for the Ukrainian SSR were truly representing the interests of the republic's citizens.

S. Cipko, J.-P. Himka

Parish (*parafiia*). The lowest administrative unit in the church that has its own church and priest, and which, as a constituent part of an eparchy, directly serves the faithful. Although most serve a specific locality, some parishes are extraterritorial (eg, for soldiers or a group of émigrés). The term *parafiia* came into use in the 16th century and became entrenched in the 18th and 19th centuries. At the same time *parokh* became an accepted term for a pastor or parish priest (sometimes even for an administrator).

The ways in which parishes were established, churches and parish buildings were built, and parish priests and precentors were supported have changed over time. In the Princely era and in the Hetmanate, churches were funded by princes, hetmans, magnates, nobles, and Cossack officers. They donated land, easements, and sometimes even part of their incomes (eg, for the Church of the *Tithes in Kiev) to parishes. This material support, together with donations from private individuals and the government, enabled the parish *clergy (priests, deacons, precentors, sextons, etc) to minister to the needs of the parishioners, and gave the clergy security as a class. At the Synod of *Zamostia in 1720, Ukrainian and Belarusian Catholics were forbidden to establish parishes without such *patronage. In the Orthodox church under Russian rule, the sole criterion for the opening of a parish was the number of faithful to be served. According to a church regulation of 1841, parishes with small congregations were to be assigned only one priest and one precentor. In an 1869 reform, small church communities were consolidated into larger parishes, and many churches were closed or subordinated to a single parish.

Land was owned by the parish and worked for the benefit of the local church throughout Ukraine until the consolidation of Soviet power (1917–20 in Russian-ruled Ukraine and 1939–46 in Western Ukraine), when all church property was nationalized. Earlier some church lands had been confiscated by the Austro-Hungarian, Russian, or Polish authorities in Ukraine, but in these instances the parishes were compensated for their loss. Now the parishes pay their clergy with contributions from the congregation, such as membership dues, Sunday and other collections, and bequests. Parish clergymen are also paid for special church services (*treby*), including the performance of sacraments and rites (baptism, marriage, funerals, blessing of water, blessing of homes, etc). Clergymen are responsible for pastoral affairs in the parish and for keeping a *church register of vital statistics (*metrykal'na knyha*), a record formerly considered to be an official government document. They teach religion in parish schools or in the church and care for the church's liquid and fixed assets.

Initially parishes chose their own priests (most often from the family of the previous pastor) and the priest's position was confirmed by a bishop. As a centralized church system emerged, this tradition faded, although the recommendation of the parishioners is still important in the Orthodox church. For a time the church patrons who supported the parish financially also had the authority to choose priests; in periods of church decline this authority resulted in abuses by individual clergymen, who held their office with the support of patrons but without the consent of local bishops. Later the right to appoint parish priests came to belong exclusively to bishops and their consistories. In the Russian Empire this had the effect of accelerating the Russification of the Ukrainian church.

Parishes are usually headed by one priest, but larger parishes may include more clerics. Traditionally a priest is permanently assigned to a parish, which he cannot leave of his own volition; neither can a bishop remove a priest from a parish without the approval of the parish. In the Catholic church a canonical process was necessary to make such a change.

Precentors (who usually conducted the church choir) and sextons played an important role in parish life, as did various parish leaders: the sacristan (*tytar*), the church elder (*tserkovnyi starosta*), and the head of the parish council. Church elders, who were confirmed by the bishop, were particularly influential in the Orthodox church. In general, lay influence in parish affairs was more pronounced in the Orthodox church than in the Catholic church, where episcopal authority was supreme. In the Catholic church nuns were often responsible for the upkeep of the church and the teaching of catechism.

Administratively, several proximate parishes were often organized as a deanery or protopresbytery, headed by a dean or protopresbyter. Above these was an *eparchy; the number of parishes or deaneries in an eparchy was never standardized.

In the Ukrainian churches, parishes were always the main center of spiritual and educational life in the community. Before the establishment of similar government institutions, parishes had their own schools, asylums, orphanages, hospitals and clinics, and, in some cases, printing presses. Thus they played an important role in the preservation of national and religious consciousness in the people. Among Ukrainian immigrants, particularly in North and South America, Orthodox and Catholic parishes were for many years the main centers of Ukrainian secular community life as well, and they remain among the best organized and strongest institutions in the diaspora.

I. Korovytsky, I. Patrylo

Park. A tract of wild or cultivated ground set aside for recreation. Larger parks, such as *nature preserves, *wildlife refuges, and national parks, are set aside by the state for the purpose of conservation and scientific research. Smaller parks or gardens are maintained by municipalities for decorative and recreational purposes. Specialized *botanical and *zoological gardens usually belong to scientific institutions and serve scientific ends.

The earliest parks in Ukraine, dating back to the Princely era, were either royal hunting preserves or gardens cultivated by monasteries and princes. Private parks with a decorative purpose appeared only in the first half of the 18th century. They were designed in the Italian baroque or the French style, with a regular geometric plan, symmetrical composition, and a clearly defined center. The most outstanding example of a French garden is Pershotravnevyi Park (formerly Tsarskyi Sad and Municipal Park) in Kiev, which was designed by B. Rastrelli in 1743. A large number of parks were established in the second half of the 18th and at the beginning of the 19th century. Almost all of them were of the landscape or English type, based on the principle of free planning with the fullest utilization of natural conditions. They were usually in picturesque settings, although occasionally, as in Trostianets, natural relief was altered. The natural vegetation was supplemented with trees and shrubs from other biogeographic regions and with decorative structures, such as fountains, grottoes, greenhouses, pavilions, bowers, columns, and obelisks. Most of the parks were established by wealthy landowners and designed by foreign architects. The most famous landscape parks are Oleksandriia Park in Bila Tserkva (est 1793), *Sofiivka Park in Uman (est in 1796–1800), the *Trostianets Dendrological Park (est 1834), the *Veseli Bokovenky dendrological park (est 1893), and Sokyryntsi Park (est 1763). One of the first public parks in Ukraine was Stryi Park in Lviv (est 1877). In the second half of the 19th and at the beginning of the 20th

century many urban and resort parks were established. They were usually small, and their plant composition was not original. Until 1914, except for the industrial cities of the Donbas, Ukrainian cities were adequately supplied with parks and greenery.

Parks and gardens suffered considerable damage during the First World War and neglect during the early years of Soviet rule. Conditions improved somewhat, after Ukraine adopted a law on the preservation of the cultural and natural heritage (16 June 1926). The larger parks were turned into nature preserves or wildlife refuges. In the second half of the 20th century existing parks have been enlarged, and a wide variety of new ones have been established, especially in cities and industrial regions.

National parks are large, mostly forested tracts that are set aside for both conservation and outdoor recreation. Nature preserves, which date back to the 1920s, were not accessible to large numbers of visitors. As the urban population increased and its living standard rose, the need for outdoor recreation in a natural environment became acute. Two parks were set up in Ukraine, the *Carpathian National Park (est 1980, 47,300 ha) and the *Shatsk National Park (est 1983, 32,500 ha). More were proposed as part of a comprehensive national park system.

Forest parks are large, protected forested areas on the outskirts of large cities. Set up in the Soviet period, the parks serve the urban population by offering sites for recreational activities, such as picnicking, swimming, mushroom picking, hiking, and cross-country skiing. The largest forest parks are the Komsomol Forest Park, near Kharkiv (2,383 ha), Holosiieve Park, south of Kiev (1,463 ha), and Briukhovychi Park, northwest of Lviv. Hydroparks on natural or artificial bodies of water provide the public with beaches and boating facilities. The largest hydropark (2,000 ha, including 500 ha of water) is in Kiev, on the left bank of the Dnieper River.

In 1985 there were 16 *dendrological parks, with a combined area of 1,200 ha, 13 *botanical gardens, with an area of 1,500 ha, and 6 *zoological gardens and parks, with an area of 100 ha. Natural monuments, such as waterfalls, rock formations, exposed geological layers, and old trees, have a special status and number close to 500 (total area, 14,000 ha). Special *parks of culture and recreation were developed in the Soviet period to provide urban residents with recreational facilities.

BIBLIOGRAPHY
Rubtsov, L. *Sadovo-parkovyi landshaft* (Kiev 1956)
Lypa, O. *Vyznachni sady i parky Ukraïny ta ikh okhorona* (Kiev 1960)
Korasevs'kyi, I. *Parky Ukraïny* (Kiev 1961)
Perspektivnaia set' zapovednykh ob'ektov Ukrainy (Kiev 1987)
I. Stebelsky

Park of culture and recreation (*park kultury i vidpochynku*). A Soviet designation for an urban park with gardens, wooded areas, and a cultural, educational, and recreational program. The largest have theaters (some outdoors), lecture halls, reading rooms, amusement areas, dance halls, sporting and other equipment rental shops, skating rinks, playing fields, one-day houses of rest, and children's playgrounds. The number of parks of culture and recreation in Ukraine grew from 107 in 1980 to 124 in 1985 and 184 in 1988. The largest are located in Kiev (on the right bank of the Dnieper), Kharkiv, and Lviv.

Parkhomchuk, Stanislav [Parxomčuk], b 30 November 1925 in Chornova, Volodarske-Volynske raion, Zhytomyr okruha, d 2 July 1975 in Kiev. Soviet historian and bureaucrat. A graduate in international relations of Kiev University (1949) and the Higher Diplomatic School of the USSR Ministry of Foreign Affairs (1953), he worked as a senior associate of the AN URSR (now ANU) Institute of History (1958–62, 1966–70) and from 1970 headed its Department of the History of Foreign Oriental Countries. He assumed various functions in the Council of Ministers of the Ukrainian SSR and was a counsel at the European headquarters of the United Nations in Geneva (1963–5). He is the author of books on the birth of modern Rumania (1961) and the October Revolution and revolutionary upheaval in Rumania in 1917–21 (1967).

Parkhomenko, Mykhailo [Parxomenko, Myxajlo], b 22 September 1910 in Shkurativka, Sumy county, Kharkiv gubernia. Literary scholar. He graduated from the Moscow Pedagogical Institute, and in 1960 he became a professor at the CC CPSU Academy of Social Sciences in Moscow. Among his many works are articles on Ukrainian-Russian literary relations, books in Ukrainian on M. Gorky and Western Ukraine (1946) and I. Franko (1956), and books in Russian on O. Korniichuk (1952), I. Franko (1954, 1957, 1966), T. Shevchenko (1964), the image of the positive hero (1962), the national and international in literature and art (1964), the multinational Soviet novel (1966), socialist realism (1975, 1977), and the new literatures of the peoples of the Soviet Arctic and Far East (1982). A selection of his articles on Ukrainian and other Soviet writers, *Gorizonty realizma* (The Horizons of Realism), was published in 1982.

Parkhomenko, Mykola [Parxomenko], b 23 July 1902 in Karavan, Katerynoslav gubernia, d 3 June 1964 in Elista, Kalmyk ASSR. Composer, violinist, and pedagogue. After graduating from the Rostov Conservatory (1924) he taught in a variety of music schools, including the Lviv Conservatory (1946–9). Among his works are the children's operettas *Tale about the Fisherman and the Fish* (1936) and *Alladin's Lamp* (1941), the ballet *Scheherezade* (1925), four symphonies (1930, 1933, 1943, 1947), short violin pieces, and songs.

Parkhomenko, Oleksander [Parxomenko], b 24 December 1886 in Makariv Yar, Slovianoserbske county, Katerynoslav gubernia, d 3 January 1921 in Buzivka, Uman county, Kiev gubernia. Bolshevik revolutionary and military figure. From 1904 he was active in the Bolshevik party in the Donbas. After the February Revolution he helped organize the Red Guard in Luhanske. As commander of the Luhanske Red Army detachment (1918–19) he fought White, UNR, and German forces in eastern Ukraine and the Don region. In January 1919 he was appointed military commissar of Kharkiv gubernia; in December 1919, special official of the Revolutionary Military Soviet of the First Cavalry Army; and in April 1920, commander of its 14th Division in Volhynia, Galicia, and southern Ukraine. He was killed in combat with N. Makhno's forces. P. Panch and V. Ivanov have written novels, and L. Lukov has made a film, about him. D. Myshko (1957), V. Sheludchenko (1956), and G. Tolokolnikov (1962) have published biographies of him.

Parkhomenko, Olha [Parxomenko, Ol'ha], b 7 April 1928 in Kiev. Violinist. She graduated from the Moscow Conservatory (1953) in the class of D. Oistrakh, and since 1954 she has been the soloist with the Kiev Philharmonic. In 1956 she won first prize at the International Mozart Competition in Salzburg, and since 1963 she has taught at the Kiev Conservatory (from 1977 as a professor). Her repertoire includes pieces by B. Liatoshynsky, M. Verykivsky, and A. Shtoharenko.

Terentii Parkhomenko

Parkhomenko, Terentii [Parxomenko, Terentij], b 28 October 1872 in Voloskivtsi, Sosnytsia county, Chernihiv gubernia, d 23 March 1910 in Voloskivtsi. Kobzar. Having lost his sight at 10 he studied the kobza under A. Hoidenko and others and then for five years wandered with Hoidenko through Ukraine. At 30 he began to teach the kobza. Some of his students (P. Tkachenko, Serdiuk-Pereliub, and O. Hrebin) became noted folk singers. He corresponded with M. Lysenko, O. Slastion, A. Malynka, M. Serpansky, Lesia Ukrainka, I. Franko, and V. Hnatiuk. In 1902 he performed for the 12th Archeological Congress in Kharkiv and was invited to appear in Lviv and Drohobych. He gave concerts in Kiev, Poltava, Nizhyn, Mohyliv-Podilskyi, Uman, Vinnytsia, Yelysavethrad, and Warsaw. His repertoire included dumas, historical songs, psalms, lyrical songs, and satires. Because his songs awakened national consciousness among the peasants, he was harassed by the authorities. He died as a result of a police beating.

Parkhomenko, Volodymyr [Parxomenko], b 21 September 1880 in Smile, Romen county, Poltava gubernia, d 1942 in Leningrad. Historian. After graduating from the St Petersburg Theological Academy in 1905, he taught church history at the Poltava Theological Seminary and was the first chairman of the Poltava Church-Archeological Committee. Later he was a privatdocent and, from 1918, docent at Kiev University and the Kiev Institute of People's Education. In the 1920s he was a professor at the Dnipropetrovske Institute of People's Education, director of a department at the Dnipropetrovske Regional Historical and Archeological Museum, a research associate of the VUAN (from 1926), president of the Dnipropetrovske Scientific Society of the VUAN, and a member of the VUAN Commission of Ukraine's Ancient History. He was swept up in 1929 during the arrests of members of the fictitious *Union for the Liberation of Ukraine and exiled from Ukraine. From the late 1930s he was a professor at Leningrad University.

Parkhomenko initially studied Ukrainian church history. He contributed some 20 articles on 18th-century Ukrainian church and secular history to *Kievskaia starina* and wrote a book on the history of the Pereiaslav-Boryspil eparchy in 1733–85 (1910), a booklet on the question of when Princess Olga of Rus' was baptized (1911), and books on the beginnings of Christianity in Rus' in the 9th and 10th centuries (1913) and the origin of the Rus' state (1916). A supporter of the theory of the southeastern (ie, Ukrainian) origins of Rus', in the Soviet period he wrote a book on the 8th- to 11th-century Rus' state (1924) and some dozen articles, including ones on Rus' and the Khazars (1927) and Pechenegs (1929), Princes Oleh and Ihor (1923), the politics of Hetman I. Samoilovych (1928), Rus', the steppe, and the Varangians (1929), and the character and significance of the reign of Prince Volodymyr the Great (1941).

A. Zhukovsky

Parliament. A term commonly used for legislative councils or assemblies. The name parliament and its development are linked with medieval England, where it began its evolution in the 13th century. Whereas at first the parliament fulfilled an advisory or co-operative function, it gradually acquired the independent prerogatives of a legislative entity.

The Ukrainian experience with a parliamentary system was curtailed by several factors. First, the extended periods of Ukrainian statelessness resulted in a scarcity of national institutions. Accordingly, Ukrainians could participate only in foreign councils or assemblies, in which they had no controlling role. They commonly formed a separate caucus or club in those bodies. Second, the legislative assemblies which held jurisdiction over Ukrainian territories usually consisted (until the later 19th century) almost exclusively of representatives of the ruling elite. The nobility of Ukraine took part in the dealings of those bodies, but because in most cases they had assimilated to the norms of the dominant foreign power, they usually did not represent broad Ukrainian interests. Finally, the establishment of Soviet power in Ukraine in the 20th century wholly subverted the principles upon which parliamentary systems are based.

During the Princely era of Ukraine the *Boyar Council fulfilled to a certain extent the functions of a parliament. It was a particularly influential body in the Principality of Galicia-Volhynia. Under the Grand Duchy of Lithuania the main legislative bodies were the *Council of Lords and the *Diet (Sejm); the former constituted an upper chamber, and the latter incorporated a wider-ranging representation, albeit by estate. Among its participants were Ukrainian princes, magnates, members of the nobility, and the higher clergy, and burghers. After the Union of Lublin in 1569 a single diet served the entire Commonwealth. It had two houses, a senate that consisted of the highest-ranking civic and ecclesiastical figures and a chamber of deputies made up of representatives of the nobility. *Dietines acted as agencies of territorial self-government in the voivodeships. They also elected representatives to the Diet.

During the Hetmanate certain parliamentary functions were fulfilled by the *Council of Officers, although the *General Military Council rendered the extent of its jurisdiction somewhat unclear. P. Orlyk drafted a plan for a Cossack parliament – essentially an expanded Council of Officers with regular sittings – in the Constitution of *Bendery in 1710. The plan was never realized. Similarly a late 18th-century plan by H. Poletyka to restore dietines was not realized.

A parliamentary institution was established in the Russian Empire only after the Revolution of 1905. Elected through a curial system, the State *Duma possessed limited legislative power. A *Ukrainian caucus in the Russian State Duma was active from the sitting of the First Duma in 1906.

In the Austro-Hungarian Empire a parliamentary system was created only in 1867 (in spite of earlier efforts, during the Revolution of 1848–9). The Reichsrat consisted of an upper house (Herrenhaus) and a lower house (Abgeordnetenhaus). The Herrenhaus was made up of hereditary nobles, social notables, and appointees of the emperor. The Greek Catholic metropoly was assured of a seat in the upper house, filled for a period by O. Barvinsky and I. Horbachevsky. The chamber of deputies was initially a forum for the provincial diets; then, from 1873, it was elected on a curial basis and, from 1907, on the basis of universal male suffrage. Single-chamber provincial diets were also elected on a curial system in Galicia and Bukovyna.

During the period of Ukrainian independence (1917–20) a parliamentary role was played by the *Central Rada, the *Labor Congress, and the *Ukrainian National Rada in Galicia. Plans were established for elections to a representative *Constituent Assembly of Ukraine, but they were only partially realized because of the precarious military situation. The constitution of the Ukrainian National Republic foresaw a one-house parliament. The Labor Congress, although modeled on labor-class principles, expressed approval of a national, democratically elected Ukrainian parliament. Some of the pronouncements of Hetman P. Skoropadsky indicate that he foresaw the creation of a Ukrainian Diet as the parliament of the Hetman State.

During the interwar period in Poland the two legislative bodies were the Senate and the Sejm, both chosen through open elections. After an initial boycott by Galician politicians of elections under Poland (1922) Ukrainian members established the *Ukrainian Parliamentary Representation. Not all Ukrainians, however, joined the caucus.

Until 1918, Transcarpathian Ukrainians (such as A. Dobriansky, A. Beskyd, K. Hrabar) were elected from time to time, by the curial system, to the Hungarian Diet (Országgyűlés). In the years between the two world wars Ukrainians were also represented in the parliamentary institutions of Czechoslovakia and Rumania. In 1939–44 Transcarpathian representatives were appointed to the Hungarian legislature. The diet of the short-lived Carpatho-Ukrainian state had one chamber and sat in session only once.

The main legislative body of the Ukrainian SSR was the *All-Ukrainian Congress of Soviets (1917–37). Ukrainians were also elected to the corresponding all-Union structure. From 1937 the role of a parliament was played by the *Supreme Soviet of the Ukrainian SSR and its USSR counterpart. In spite of their formal structures the Soviet assemblies functioned not as independent entities that debated and enacted legislation, but as a formal means of approving state plans for the country. They were completely dominated by the Communist party, which determined nominations for (uncontested) elections and controlled their proceedings. Changes in electoral law in 1989 paved the way for establishing an opposition bloc in the Supreme Soviet (renamed the Supreme Council) and making it a more representative parliamentary forum. Since the declaration of Ukrainian independence in 1991 it has remained the highest legislative body in Ukraine.

The Ukrainian minority in the socialist countries of Eastern Europe since 1945 has had fair representation in regional and federal legislative institutions, especially in Czechoslovakia and Yugoslavia. The Ukrainian National Council, created in exile in 1947 as a representative body of the political parties of the Ukrainian National Republic, was based on parliamentary principles. (See also *Elections, *Legislation, *Constitution.)

V. Markus

Parnas, Jakub (Yakov), b 28 January 1884 in Mokriany, Sambir county, Galicia, d 29 January 1949 in Moscow. Biochemist; full member of the Polish Academy of Learning from 1931, the USSR Academy of Sciences from 1942, and the USSR Academy of Medical Sciences from 1944. A graduate of the Berlin Technological Institute (1904), he also studied at Strasbourg (1905) and Zurich (1906–7) universities, was a professor at Warsaw University (1916–19), directed the Medical Chemistry Institute at Lviv University (1920–41) and the Biochemistry Institute of the USSR Academy of Medical Sciences in Moscow (1944–8), and organized and directed the Laboratory of Physiological Chemistry of the USSR Academy of Sciences (1943–9). Parnas studied carbohydrate metabolism and enzymic reactions as key factors in muscle contraction, established the pathway of glycogen formation from glyceraldehyde in the liver, and investigated ammonia formation in blood. In 1935 he codiscovered glycogen cleavage by phosphoric acid. In 1937 he proposed, jointly with Danish physicists, the use of the phosphorus-32 isotope as a marker in biological research; this advance led biochemists to a detailed understanding of carbohydrate metabolism in muscle – the Embden-Meyerhof-Parnas or EMP scheme. Parnas wrote 120 works, including a Polish physiological chemistry textbook (1922). He was arrested by the MVD in 1949, and died in prison.

Parniuk, Mykhailo [Parnjuk, Myxajlo], b 2 October 1921 in Musiivka, Khorol county, Kremenchuk gubernia.

Mykhailo Parniuk

Philosopher. A graduate of Kiev University (1951), since 1955 he has taught in the AN URSR (now ANU) Department of Philosophy. He received a doctorate in 1970 and became chairman of the department in 1973. He has written a book, in Russian, on the principle of determinism in the system of the materialist dialectic (1973) and contributed to and edited multiauthor books on gnoseological, social, and methodological problems and on materialist-dialectical categories.

Parochial schools (*parafiialni shkoly*). Elementary schools that existed in Ukraine in various forms from the 11th century until the 1917 Revolution. They were founded and operated by the church at the parish level.

The instructors at these schools were usually *precentors. The enrollment was made up of children of peasant and other lower classes. The curriculum was rudimentary, with emphasis placed on catechism, Church Slavonic reading and works, and church music.

Parochial schools were the principal educational institutions in Ukraine in the 15th to 18th centuries. In Left-Bank Ukraine in the first half of the 18th century, they existed in almost every parish and educated adults as well as children. In 1740–7 a total of 766 schools (most of them parochial) existed in seven Hetmanate regions, which consisted of 1,099 villages, towns, and cities. In 1738, 129 schools existed in *Slobidska Ukraine. In Polish-controlled Right-Bank Ukraine there were fewer of the so-called Ruthenian church schools than in the Hetmanate.

Toward the end of the 18th and the beginning of the 19th century centralization and Russification resulted in a decrease in the number of parochial schools in eastern and central Ukraine. With Alexander I's 1804 school reform they came under official supervision and were formally designated *parafiialni shkoly*. A number of one-class parochial schools were opened. In 1828 a second statute called for the foundation of two-class parochial schools in larger cities. The system was thus a three-tiered one: there were basic parochial grammar schools, with 1 year of instruction; one-class schools, with 2–3 years of instruction; and two-class schools, with 4–5 years of instruction. The system of centrally administered parochial schools was ineffective. By 1835 the number of formal parochial schools in Russian-ruled Ukraine was down to 100. Children were more likely to be educated through private, informal arrangements made with local clerics.

The number of parochial schools increased considerably with the emancipation of the serfs and following an 1864 statute which made parochial schools an official type of elementary education. In 1884 and 1896, parochial schools were granted additional rights and were redesignated parochial schools (*tserkovno-parafiialni shkoly* or *tserkovno-prykhodski shkoly*). Nevertheless parochial schools were not particularly successful in comparison with other schools, especially in zemstvo gubernias, where the local authorities organized the popular *zemstvo schools. In 1893, in six zemstvo gubernias in Ukraine, parochial schools accounted for only 25 percent of all elementary schools and taught only 14.6 percent of the children in the region. In contrast, in Volhynia, Kiev, and Podilia (non-zemstvo gubernias), 69 percent of elementary schools were parochial, and 64 percent of students attended them. In 1897, parochial schools accounted for 55 percent of all elementary schools in Russian-ruled

Ukraine. Almost half of the school day was devoted to religious instruction at the schools. In 1908, as part of the progressive educational policies adopted after the *Revolution of 1905, general education schools were opened, and the number of parochial schools declined. In 1911 the Kiev school district, which contained five gubernias, had 6,628 parochial schools, or 59.6 percent of the total number of schools in the region. In 1917, parochial schools were reorganized into secular elementary schools.

In Austrian-ruled Galicia and Bukovyna the number of parochial schools began to increase with the introduction of Joseph II's educational reforms. In 1821 there were 1,226 schools in Western Ukraine, of which 834 (68 percent) were parochial. In 1863, parochial schools were reorganized into secular elementary public schools.

In Transcarpathia there were many parochial schools in the late 18th and early 19th centuries: in 1793 there were almost 300 in the region. Later, Hungarian educational policy resulted in a steady decrease in the number of parochial schools: by 1907, 107 of them remained, and by 1918, only 34 were still operating. The language of instruction was Hungarian, Ukrainian being taught only as a subject. In Carpathian Ukraine under Czechoslovakia, very few parochial schools existed. There were more parochial schools in the Prešov region, and they continued to operate until 1948.

Since 19 January 1919, in accordance with article 7 of the Constitution of the USSR, all education in Soviet Ukraine was secular. (See *Secular schools.)

N. Freeland

Parody (from Greek *para* 'against' and *ode* 'song'; hence, a 'song in reverse'). A literary genre based on a humorous-satiric imitation of the content or style of a given literary work, or works, of one author or of a whole literary school, usually with the intention of emphasizing the most negative features in form or content of the work thus parodied. Parody was known in ancient Greece (Hipponax, Aristophanes) and reappeared in European literature during the Middle Ages (various parodies of church liturgies, the poetry of the troubadours). The oldest examples of parody in Ukrainian literature can be found in folk literature (the first mention of it occurs in the manuscript compilation of a certain Kondratsky, ca 1684). In Ukrainian literature parody was codified by H. Konysky in his *Praecepta de arte poetica* (1746) as a literary mode for serious replication of a given work (the model being T. Prokopovych's 'Elegia Alexii' [1698]), although in practice it already had its present-day meaning in the works of the wandering *precentors, especially in the parodying of church services and folk songs and dumas.

In modern Ukrainian literature parody appears in I. Kotliarevsky's *Eneïda* (Aeneid), although the work as a whole belongs to the *burlesque tradition, and in *Natalka Poltavka* (Natalka from Poltava, 1819), especially in the masterful parody of 'learned' speech in the part of the character Vozny. Of the numerous epigones of Kotliarevsky mention must be made of K. Dumytrashko's *Zhabomyshodrakivka* (Frog Mouse Fight, 1847–59), itself a parody-travesty of the ancient Greek parody *Batrachomyomachia*. Owing to the various prohibitions on the development of Ukrainian literature, however, parody could not develop fully during the 19th century. It appeared again toward the end of the 19th and in the early 20th cen-

tury in works of authors such as I. Franko (parodies of I. Hushalevych, M. Ustyianovych), V. Samiilenko, M. Cherniavsky, I. Nechui-Levytsky, and O. Lutsky (parodies of Franko), and in parodies of the works of such modernist poets as P. Karmansky, M. Vorony, and V. Pachovsky (in the journals *Komar* and *Zerkalo*). Parody developed markedly in the 1920s, during which there was a general escalation of literary activity. It was found especially useful in the intensified struggle for hegemony among various literary groups. K. *Burevii was probably the most outstanding parodist of the day. Others who deserve note were V. Blakytny (*Vybrani satyry i baiky* [Selected Satires and Tales, 1930]), O. Vyshnia (various parodies of M. Khvylovy, H. Kosynka, V. Koriak, and others in *Chervonyi shliakh*), V. Chechviansky (*Parodiï* [Parodies, 1930]), Yu. Vukhnal, V. Yaroshenko, and O. Slisarenko.

Parody declined during the terror of the 1930s and became more a forum for publicist indictments than a genre based on artistic caricature, as evidenced in such works as T. Orysio's *Literaturni parodiï, sharzhi, epihramy* (Literary Parodies, Caricatures, and Epigrams, 1932) and O. Khazin's *Literaturni parodiï* (Literary Parodies, 1934). Parody became popular again in the 1950s through the works of S. Voskrekasenko, P. Slipchuk, Yu. Kruhliak, B. Chaly, O. Zholdak, M. Bilkun, and many others, but their parodies on the whole are lackluster. Notable exceptions are the parodies of Yu. Shcherbak and Yu. Ivakin. Sporadic attempts at parody have also occurred among the émigrés. Although most parodies appear in newspapers or journals, some separate collections have been published, namely T. Kurpita's *Karykatury z literatury* (Caricatures from Literature, 1947) and Porfyrii Horotak's (joint pseudonym of Yu. Klen and L. Mosendz) *Dyiabolichni paraboly* (Diabolic Parables, 1947).

BIBLIOGRAPHY
Literaturni parodiï, sharzhi, epihramy, akrostykhy, feleitony, humoresky, aforyzmy i karykatury (Kiev 1927)
Adriianova-Peretts, V. 'Do istoriï parodiï na Ukraïni v XVIII vitsi,' *ZIFV*, 18 (1928)
Pelens'kyi, Ie. *Ukraïns'ka literaturna parodiia* (Lviv 1934)
Literaturni pryparky: Parodiï ta epihramy (Kiev 1956)
Nud'ha, H. *Parodiia v ukraïns'kii literaturi* (Kiev 1961)
I. Koshelivets, D.H. Struk

Parpura, Maksym, b ca 1763 in Konotip company, Nizhen regiment, d 23 June 1828 in Kharkiv gubernia. Cultural and educational activist. He was educated in medicine at the Kiev Academy and in St Petersburg, and he worked as a translator for the St Petersburg Medical College. From 1793 (or 1803) he was director of the college's print shop. In 1798 he published I. Kotliarevsky's *Eneïda* (Aeneid) at his own cost; it was the first book printed in modern literary Ukrainian. Parpura bequeathed considerable sums to hospitals and schools and to Kharkiv University.

Parsehov, Valerii, b 23 March 1936 in Kiev. Ballet dancer and pedagogue. In 1955 he completed study at the Kiev Choreography School. In 1956 he became a soloist in the Kiev Theater of Opera and Ballet. He was the first performer of Ivan in V. Kyreiko's ballet *Tini zabutykh predkiv* (Shadows of Forgotten Ancestors, 1961). From 1965 he taught at the Kiev Choreography School. He received the V. Nijinsky Prize (Paris, 1964).

Parsley (*Petroselinum crispum* or *P. sativum*; Ukrainian: *petrushka*). A hardy biennial herb of the carrot family Umbelliferae, forming a rosette of leaves and a root in the first year and a flower stalk and seeds in the second. Both root (var. *tuberosum*) and leaf (var. *latifolium*) parsley are used in fresh or dried form to garnish and flavor foods. All parts of parsley contain a pungent essential oil consisting primarily of apiol and pinene. The root and leaves are rich in vitamins C and A and in mineral salts. In Ukraine root or Hamburg parsley is planted preferentially over leaf parsley, and it is a staple ingredient in Ukrainian traditional *foods. In *folk medicine parsley extracts and powders were used as diuretics and carminatives.

Parsnip, garden (*Pastinaca sativa*; Ukrainian: *pasternak*). A member of the carrot family Umbelliferae, cultivated in Ukraine and throughout the world for its distinct-flavored edible root. At the end of the summer, the root consists primarily of starch. Parsnip also contains vitamins A, B, and C. It tastes sweetish and is usually served as a cooked vegetable; it is also used to flavor soups and meat and is canned for distribution. Two varieties of *P. sativa* are cultivated in Ukraine. Two wild species of parsnip are found growing in pastures, along roads, and in gardens as weeds.

Partenit. A medieval Greek town on the southern coast of the Crimea at the site of present-day Frunzenske, 16 km from Alushta. The settlement is mentioned in Gothic, Khazar, and Arabic documents of the 8th to 12th centuries. In the 8th century a large three-nave stone basilica was built there. It was destroyed by fire in the 10th century, and it was rebuilt in 1427 and destroyed by the Turks in 1479. Its ruins were excavated in 1871 and 1907.

Parties, political. Political parties in Ukraine have reflected the complexity of the country's social and ethnic stratification. Major nationalities, such as the Ukrainians, Russians, Poles, and Jews, have organized their own political parties. The influence of the national idea was strong enough to fragment even the proletarian movement along national lines.

The basic difference between Ukrainian and national-minority parties in Ukraine lay in their attitude toward self-determination. Whereas Ukrainian parties emphasized national liberation as the first step toward the solution of other problems, the minority parties tended to oppose it or to ignore the issue. Russian parties acted in unison as custodians of Russian imperial interests and opposed Ukraine's separation from Russia. Polish political parties recognized in principle the demand for an independent Ukraine. Almost all Jewish political parties supported the idea of an autonomous Ukraine within the Russian Empire but categorically rejected demands for independence. The Russian Communist Party (Bolshevik) and its instrument, the CP(B)U, recognized the 'abstract right of the Ukrainian people to self-determination' but did everything to prevent its realization.

Modern Ukrainian political parties sprang from the national movement that developed in the late 19th century in reaction to national oppression. After centuries of Russification the Ukrainian national movement was preoccupied mostly with cultural renascence and national awareness. In a sense this so-called Ukrainophile movement was apolitical: beyond protesting against Russification, it raised no objection to the tsarist regime. The Old *Hromada of Kiev attracted mostly moderate intellectuals who cherished the country's romantic past but did not advocate separatism. At most they demanded autonomy for Ukraine. Yet the Hromada's contribution to the education and national awakening of the common people had a profound influence on the future political development of Ukraine.

In Russian-ruled Ukraine the first political parties sprang up only at the turn of the century. In February 1900 a clandestine political organization known as the *Revolutionary Ukrainian party (RUP) was founded in Kharkiv. That year a small *Ukrainian Socialist party (USP) emerged in Kiev, and in 1903 it merged for a brief while with the RUP. In 1902 M. Mikhnovsky formed the *Ukrainian People's party (UNP), which was the most nationalistic of the early Ukrainian parties. The leftist elements of the RUP broke away in 1904 and formed the Ukrainian Social Democratic Association, generally known as *Spilka, which accepted the position of the Russian Social Democratic Workers' party (RSDWP) vis-à-vis the nationalities and party unity. In 1905 the remaining members of the RUP renamed the party the *Ukrainian Social Democratic Workers' party (USDRP). Ideologically, the USDRP was close to the Russian Mensheviks and other social democratic parties in Western Europe. It was not a popular mass party: its social base consisted of Ukrainian workers and radical intelligentsia. It elected only two deputies in the election to the All-Russian Constituent Assembly in 1917. At the beginning of 1919 it split on the issue of independence from the RSDWP, and its leftist faction set up the USDRP (Independentists), which a year later became the *Ukrainian Communist party (UKP).

At the end of 1905 the *Ukrainian Democratic Radical party (UDRP) came into being in Kiev. This was a nonsocialist, liberal party, resembling in many respects the Russian Constitutional Democrats (Kadets). It demanded constitutional monarchy, a federal system instead of an empire, and autonomy for Ukraine. Over 30 of the 40 Ukrainian deputies in the Second State Duma were Democratic Radicals. When the party disintegrated early in 1908, its moderate elements formed a clandestine nonparty organization, the *Society of Ukrainian Progressives (TUP), to combat Russian chauvinism.

Although cells of Ukrainian Socialist Revolutionaries had been active in many Ukrainian gubernias since 1905, they did not form the national party known as the *Ukrainian Party of Socialist Revolutionaries (UPSR) until April 1917. This was an agrarian party that advocated the socialization of land and autonomy for Ukraine. In the 1917 election to the All-Russian Constituent Assembly the UPSR won over 45 percent of the votes in Ukraine. It had the largest caucus in the Central Rada and played a leading role in the General Secretariat and the Council of Ministers of the UNR. At its secret congress in May 1918, the party split, and it was dissolved soon afterward. Its left wing formed the *Borotbists in March 1919; its right and center wings restored the UPSR. The small *Ukrainian Labor party (est October 1917) was close to the UPSR ideologically.

The *Ukrainian Party of Socialists-Federalists (UPSF) was founded in April 1917 by members of the TUP, and built on the program of the earlier UDRP. Its members held important portfolios in the General Secretariat and the

UNR Council of Ministers. The *Ukrainian Party of Socialists-Independentists (UPSS), established in Kiev in December 1917, was composed mainly of Ukrainian military officers and former members of the Ukrainian People's party. The *Ukrainian People's Republican party (est 1918) was antisocialist and a major supporter of V. Oskilko's attempted coup in Rivne on 29 April 1919. On the conservative side the former members of the Old Hromada of Kiev organized the *Ukrainian Federative Democratic party at the end of 1917. The *Ukrainian Democratic Agrarian party (UDKhP), established in Lubni in June 1917, was perhaps the most conservative of all Ukrainian parties. It supported the Hetman coup against the Central Rada but later became critical of P. Skoropadsky's regime.

The chief Russian political parties active in Ukraine in the early part of the 20th century were the Russian Party of *Socialist Revolutionaries, which ideologically resembled its mother party in Russia and differed from it only administratively; the *Russian Social Democratic Workers' party (or Mensheviks), which was the Ukrainian section of the all-Russian Menshevik party and shared its ideological position; the Russian People's Socialists, which represented petit-bourgeois groups with a liberal democratic ideology but had very little influence; the *Constitutional Democratic party (or Kadets), whose ideology and social base were the same as those of P. Miliukov's All-Russian party; and the Bloc of the Nonpartisan Russians, which was a coalition of Russian monarchists and reactionary chauvinists. The Communist Party (Bolshevik) of Ukraine (est 1918) was not an independent political entity but a branch of the single Russian Communist Party (Bolshevik).

The UNR was the first state in modern times to recognize and implement *national-personal autonomy. Hence, representatives of Jewish and Polish parties were admitted to the Central Rada and the General Secretariat. The General Jewish Workers' Union, or *Bund, which had 175 local organizations in Ukraine, supported Ukrainian autonomy but not independence. The United Jewish Socialist party belonged to the socialist revolutionary bloc but disagreed with the Russian Party of Socialist Revolutionaries on the nationality question and supported Ukrainian autonomy. After a split in 1918, its left wing joined the Bund in forming the Jewish Communist Union. The Jewish Social Democratic Workers' party, or *Poale Zion, was the smallest and most conservative socialist group. The most conservative and nationalistic Jewish party, the Zionist party, which promoted the idea of a separate autonomous Jewish territory, co-operated with the Central Rada.

The Polish minority resembled the Russian. Conservative elements of the landed aristocracy could not accept the idea that the Ukrainian 'peasants' were an independent nation. Polish moderates regarded Ukrainians as natural allies against Russian imperialism. The Polish Socialist Party (Center) was the equivalent of the Russian Mensheviks and the Ukrainian Social Democrats. It supported an independent Ukrainian republic. The Polish Socialist Party (Left) differed from the Russian Social Democratic Workers' party only on the national question. It supported independent Polish and Ukrainian republics. The Polish Democratic Center party represented Polish landowners in Ukraine and opposed the agrarian policy of the Rada. Favoring an independent Poland, it wavered on Ukrainian self-determination.

In Russia political parties ceased to exist with V. Lenin's dispersal of the Constituent Assembly on 5 January 1918. In Ukraine they disappeared in the early 1920s with the final victory of the Red Army.

In Austrian-held Ukrainian territories – Galicia and Bukovyna – Ukrainians began to organize their own political parties at the end of 19th century. The first political party in the full sense of the term was the *Ukrainian Radical party (URP), founded in Lviv in 1890. By 1895 three political trends had emerged in the party: a socialist-populist, a Marxist-socialist, and a radical-populist trend. When the groups associated with the latter two trends broke away in 1899 and formed their own parties, the *Ukrainian Social Democratic party (USDP) and the *National Democratic party (NDP), the URP became a peasants' party. At first the USDP was merely a branch of the Austrian Social Democratic party and won little support among Ukrainian voters. The NDP, with its emphasis on national unity and independence, quickly became the dominant party in Galician and Bukovynian political life. In 1918 it played the leading role in building an independent Ukrainian state. At its congress in Stanyslaviv in April 1919, the NDP changed its name to the *Ukrainian Labor party. The URP was the second-strongest Ukrainian party in Galicia before the war. In 1918 it took part in the Ukrainian National Rada.

After the downfall of the Western Ukrainian National Republic, the Ukrainians in Galicia continued the struggle for independence by political means. Their political parties played an important role in raising political consciousness and defending the constitutional rights of Ukrainians against the Polish authorities. The URP refused to co-operate with the USDP because of its pro-Soviet policy, and condemned the imperialist attitude of the Bolshevik party toward Ukraine. In 1926 a group of Socialist Revolutionaries from Volhynia joined the URP, and the party changed its name to the Ukrainian Socialist Radical party. The Ukrainian Labor party split into three factions in 1923, one of which formed the *Ukrainian Party of National Work. The three reached an agreement in 1925 and together set up the *Ukrainian National Democratic Alliance (UNDO), which continued the program of the NDP. It assumed the leading position in Galician political life and expanded its network into Volhynia. A group of Sovietophiles resigned from the alliance and formed the *Ukrainian Party of Labor in 1927. When UNDO's policy of *Normalization was discredited by the behavior of the Polish authorities, some of its members left, and in 1933 they set up the *Front of National Unity, which rejected Normalization on the one hand and the revolutionary terror of the OUN on the other. The *Ukrainian Agrarian party (est 1922) lost popular support because of its appeasement policy, and soon disappeared. Another party that advocated loyalty to the Polish state was the *Ukrainian Catholic People's party. Its constituency was limited to Stanyslaviv eparchy, and its political influence was insignificant. The socialist end of the Ukrainian political spectrum was represented by *Sel-Soiuz (est 1924), which was active in Volhynia and the Kholm region, and the Marxist *People's Will party (est 1923), which was active in Galicia. In 1926 the two parties merged to form the *Sel-Rob, which acted as the legal front of the *Communist Party of Western Ukraine (KPZU). Because of its close ties with the CP(B)U, the KPZU enjoyed an autonomous status within the

Communist Party of Poland. In 1927 the party split, and the majority faction defending O. Shumsky was expelled from the Comintern. The KPZU leadership was subjected to several purges in the 1930s, and the party was dissolved in 1938. In its struggle for independence the OUN rejected lawful political methods as ineffectual and regarded itself as a movement above the ordinary political parties. As extremism and political violence rose throughout Europe and particularly in Poland, its renunciation of parliamentary democracy and law-governed political competition seemed justified.

The non-Ukrainian parties with a significant constituency in Galicia during the interwar period were the Polish Socialist party, the Polish Popular Party–Liberation, the Radical Peasant party, the Peasant Alliance, the Polish Popular Party–Piast, the Christian Democrats, the Popular National Union, the Jewish Bund, and the Jewish Popular Union.

Some of the parties active in Ukraine during the liberation struggle (1917–20) resumed their activities abroad. The Ukrainian Radical Democratic party was the main supporter of the UNR *Government-in-exile during the interwar period. The USDRP recognized the government but refused to participate in it; the UPSR and the *Ukrainian Union of Agrarians-Statists, which was founded in Vienna in 1920, withheld recognition. After the Second World War the government-in-exile set up the *Ukrainian National Council, a quasi-parliament, in which the older émigré parties, such as the UPSR and USDRP, were joined by parties that had been active in Ukraine during the interwar and the war period, such as the UNDO and the two OUN factions, or had sprung up recently outside Ukraine (the *Ukrainian National-State Union, the *Ukrainian Revolutionary Democratic party, the *Union of Lands of United Ukraine, the Ukrainian Peasant party, the *Ukrainian Socialist party, and the OUN [Abroad]).

In Soviet Ukraine political parties other than the CPSU were banned by the constitution and severely suppressed. A few small clandestine groups, such as the *Ukrainian Workers' and Peasants' Union, tried to form alternative political parties but managed at most to draft a party program before they were uncovered and arrested. It was only after the election of a number of former dissidents to the Supreme Soviet of the Ukrainian SSR (March 1990) and the lifting of the CPSU's monopoly on political power (early 1990) that new parties began to proliferate in Ukraine. Within a year over a dozen parties had held their founding conventions: the Ukrainian Republican party (UREP), the Republican Party of Ukraine, the Ukrainian National party, the Democratic Party of Ukraine (DPU), the Social Democratic Party of Ukraine, the United Social Democratic Party of Ukraine, the Ukrainian Christian Democratic party, the Party of the Democratic Rebirth of Ukraine, the Ukrainian Popular Democratic party, the Ukrainian Party of Democratic Consensus, the Ukrainian Peasant Association, the Ukrainian Peasant Democratic party (UPDP), the Popular Party of Ukraine, the Green Party of Ukraine (PZU), the Liberal Democratic Party of Ukraine, and the Party of Slavic Rebirth. By the end of June 1991 only four of them – the UREP, DPU, UPDP, and PZU – had been legally registered.

BIBLIOGRAPHY
Haidalemivs'kyi, P. Ukraïns'ki politychni partiï: Ïkh rozvytok i prohramy (Salzwedel 1919)
Stakhiv, M. Ukraïns'ki politychni partiï v sotsiolohichnim nasvitlenni (Scranton, Penn 1954)
Borys, J. The Sovietization of Ukraine, 1917–1923: The Communist Doctrine and Practice of National Self-Determination, rev edn (Edmonton 1980)
Motyl, A. The Turn to the Right: The Ideological Origins and Development of Ukrainian Nationalism, 1919–1929 (New York 1980)
Markus', V. 'Ukraïns'ki politychni partiï na emigratsiï v 1945–1955 rokakh,' Suchasnist', 1984, nos 10, 12
Haran', O. (ed). Ukraïna bahatopartiina: Prohramni dokumenty novykh partii (Kiev 1991)

J. Borys

Partisan movement in Ukraine, 1918–22. As government and public order in the Russian Empire dissolved after the February Revolution, a host of partisan groups sprang up in Ukraine. Differing in size and political orientation, they never formed a unified force behind a single leader or program and often switched their support from one to another of the major contenders for control of Ukraine. Formed mostly from among the Ukrainian peasantry, the movement defended the broad social and political goals of the revolution and sided increasingly with the national aspirations of the Ukrainian people. After the defeat of the UNR Army, the partisan movement became the chief opponent of Bolshevik power in Ukraine.

The first partisan groups were formed in 1917 in the Kiev region to defend the local population from roving bands of soldiers returning from the front. The peasant brigades that arose from some of these groups, such as the Tarashcha, Zvenyhorod, and Uman brigades, took part in resisting the Bolshevik offensive on Kiev in January–February 1918. Maintaining contact with army units loyal to the Central Rada, these brigades operated in the rear of the Bolshevik forces until April.

During 1918 numerous peasant revolts broke out against the German occupational authorities and the Hetman government in Ukraine. The peasants reacted with violence to forced food requisitions and the return of estates to their former owners. The largest rebellion flared up in the summer in the southern part of Kiev gubernia (Tarashcha, Zvenyhorod, Skvyra, Uman, and Kaniv counties) and was put down only with the help of a German corps (see *Tarashcha uprising). Some partisan operations against the Hetman were instigated by Bolshevik agitators, but they failed to attract wide peasant support. In November–December over 100,000 peasant partisans took part in the overthrow of the Hetman government, which was organized by the *Ukrainian National Union.

The partisan movement in Ukraine grew rapidly in 1919. Some partisan units reached sufficient strength to have a decisive influence on the struggle for power among the main protagonists. N. *Hryhoriïv's support of the Red Army in February–April was a key factor in its successful offensive against the Whites and the Allies in southern Ukraine. D. *Zeleny's revolt against the Directory of the UNR impaired its control of the Kiev, Chernihiv, and Poltava regions. N. *Makhno, who established a brief and uneasy alliance with the Bolsheviks in March, inflicted six months later a harsh defeat on A. Denikin's army, which forced the Whites to abandon their planned offensive on Moscow and to retreat before the Red Army. At the height of his power Makhno commanded a force of 40,000 men and controlled about a third of Ukraine's present territory.

The Bolshevik occupation of Ukraine met with considerable popular resistance in March–June 1919. Heavy requisition of food destined for Russia, Cheka terror, and the Bolshevik land policy provoked widespread revolts. Later, Bolshevik leaders admitted the extent of partisan opposition: according to Kh. Rakovsky, between 1 April and 15 June there were 328 anti-Bolshevik revolts in Ukraine, and according to V. Antonov-Ovsiienko, in April and May peasant unrest in Kiev, Chernihiv, Podilia, and Volhynia gubernias tied down 21,000 Red Army troops. Large anti-Bolshevik detachments were led by otamans, such as A. *Volynets, I. Romashko, and P. Sokolovsky. Many of the instigators of the peasant unrest were Socialist Revolutionaries (SRs) and Social Democrats (Independentists), who wanted an independent socialist Ukrainian republic. In April these parties established in Skvyra the *All-Ukrainian Revolutionary Committee, the Supreme Insurgent Council, and the Supreme Insurgent Staff to co-ordinate the anti-Bolshevik insurrection. The committee was dissolved in July to allow the Bolsheviks to concentrate their forces against Denikin's offensive. Many of the committee's insurgent groups transferred their support to the UNR Army. A regiment of Hryhoriiv's partisans (3,600 men) after his death broke through the Bolshevik front and under Yu. Tiutiunnyk's command formed the Kiev Group of the UNR Army. In September, Otaman Zeleny recognized the authority of the Directory. At the beginning of the month the UNR government set up in Kamianets-Podilskyi the Central Ukrainian Insurgent Committee to co-ordinate partisan activity. The committee was chaired by N. *Petrenko and supported by the SRs, the Ukrainian Social Democratic Workers' party, and the Peasant Association.

In the summer and fall of 1919, as Bolshevik power in Ukraine declined, the partisan movement turned against Denikin's forces, which occupied the territories abandoned by the Bolsheviks. The reactionary social policies of the Whites, their exploitation of the peasants, and their repression of Ukrainian activists provoked spontaneous and uncoordinated mass insurrection. Some of the partisan bands were organized by the Bolsheviks or their sympathizers. The larger and more powerful groups were led by Zeleny, A. *Huly-Hulenko, and Makhno. Partisan activity in his rear undermined Denikin's offensive and enabled the Red Army to score a decisive blow against him at the end of 1919.

The re-established Bolshevik regime was regarded as foreign by most of the population and encountered strong resistance. Generally, the countryside was controlled by partisan bands, and Soviet power remained confined to the towns. During its First Winter Campaign (December 1919–May 1920) the UNR Army tried to unite the various partisan groups in a common uprising against the Bolsheviks. It made contact with Otaman Chuchupaka's forces in Kholodnyi Yar, Otaman Zabolotny's detachments at Balta, and the larger, well-disciplined units of Huly-Hulenko in the Yelysavethrad region. There were many other sizable bands besides these, including A. Bondarenko's in the Zvenyhorodka region, Kuzmenko-Tytarenko's around Tarashcha, F. Meleshko's around Yelysavethrad, and I. Sokil's near Cherkasy. In the summer of 1920 the Cheka chief F. Dzerzhinsky was sent from Moscow with 6,000 special Cheka troops to deal with the partisan problem. In Kiev gubernia there were 11 peasant revolts in June, 51 in July, and 106 in August, and in Poltava gubernia there were 76, 99, and 98, respectively. V. Lenin admitted as late as October 1920 that Soviet control of Ukraine was formal rather than real.

At the beginning of 1921 there were about 40,000 partisans in Ukraine. The largest force was Makhno's in southern Ukraine, but several bands numbered 500 or more men: those under Struk, Sirko, and Mordalevych (in Kiev gubernia), Loshyn (Chernihiv gubernia), Tiutiunnyk (Volhynia gubernia), Holub (Podilia), Shuba (Poltava gubernia), and Burlaka and Siroshapka (Kharkiv gubernia). In March 1921 the Bolshevik regime offered amnesty to insurgents who surrendered voluntarily. By September 1922, 200 otamans and 10,000 men had surrendered. With the suspension of Soviet-Polish hostilities and the defeat of P. Wrangel's army, the Bolsheviks redirected their forces in early 1921 against the partisan movement. Using M. Frunze's tactics of ruthless executions, they launched a wide clearing campaign. In 87 operations during April and May they reportedly killed 5,000 and captured 4,200 partisans, and destroyed 28 bands. In June they eliminated the All-Ukrainian Insurgent Committee headed by Bondarenko in the Bratslav region and the Ukrainian Central Insurgent Committee headed by I. Andrukh in Kiev. By the end of the summer the main partisan groups were crushed, although small, sporadic revolts continued to break out. The UNR government's last attempt to spark a general insurrection against the Bolshevik regime – the Second Winter Campaign, led by Yu. Tiutiunnyk in October and November 1921 – ended tragically, with the execution of 359 soldiers at Bazar.

The partisan movement in Ukraine demonstrated the deep hostility of the Ukrainian peasantry to any foreign invader and particularly to the Bolshevik regime. It also made the Soviet rulers permanently suspicious about Ukraine's loyalty.

BIBLIOGRAPHY
Khrystiuk, P. Zamitky i materiialy do istorii ukraïns'koï revoliutsiï, vols 3–4 (Vienna 1921; repr, New York 1969)
Tiutiunnyk, Iu. Zymovyi pokhid 1919–1920 rr. (Kolomyia 1923)
Antonov-Ovseenko, V. Zapiski o grazhdanskoi voine, vols 2–4 (Moscow 1928–32)
Mazepa, I. Ukraïna v ohni i buri revoliutsiï, 1917–21, vols 1–2 (Prague 1942), vol 3 (Neu-Ulm 1951)
Likholat, A. Razgrom natsionalisticheskoi kontrrevoliutsii na Ukraine, 1917–1922 gg. (Moscow 1954)
Adams, A.E. Bolsheviks in the Ukraine: The Second Campaign, 1918–1919 (New Haven–London 1963)
Kucher, O. Rozhrom zbroinoï vnutrishnoï kontrrevoliutsiï na Ukraïni u 1921–1923 rr. (Kharkiv 1971)
Borys, J. The Sovietization of Ukraine, 1917–1923: The Communist Doctrine and Practice of National Self-Determination, rev edn (Edmonton 1980)
Malet, M. Nestor Makhno in the Russian Civil War (London 1982)
S. Ripetsky

Party and state control. A set of institutions and organs in the USSR that oversaw the work of institutions, enterprises, and collective and state farms to ensure compliance with Party and state directives. Generally they were all-Union bodies directed by the central Party and state authorities in Moscow.

The first control agency for enforcing Party discipline and fighting bureaucratism and administrative wrongdoing was established in 1920. Initially called the Worker-Peasant Inspectorate, it was set up as a government body under the All-Russian Congress of Soviets. Its Ukrainian section was created in February 1920. Both were reorganized into people's commissariats later that year. In 1921 the Central Control Commission of the Russian Communist Party (Bolshevik) was set up, and two years later the state and Party agencies were merged into one people's commissariat, which came under the joint control of the Ukrainian and All-Union councils of people's commissars. In 1934 the commissariat was again split into two bodies: the first became the Commission of Party Control under the CC of the All-Union Communist Party (Bolshevik), and the second became the Commission of Soviet Control under the Council of People's Commissars, then a people's commissariat, and finally the Ministry of State Control. In 1952 the Commission of Party Control was renamed the Committee of Party Control. All of these organs played an important role in the periodic purges of the Party and government under J. Stalin's regime.

In the major reforms of 1962 a single body – the Committee of Party-State Control under the CC CPSU and the USSR Council of Ministers – was formed again to monitor both Party and state activities. It was short-lived, however, for in 1965 the two functions were split up between the Committee of People's Control under the Council of Ministers and the Committee of Party Control under the CC CPSU. The division of roles continued to 1991. The Committee of People's Control, which had bureaus in every republic, oblast, raion, and city and in most villages, was supposed to promote popular participation in government and the accountability of the state bureaucracy; in practice, however, its work had the opposite result.

Party education. See Communist party education.

Party of Agrarian Democrats. See Ukrainian Democratic Agrarian party.

Party of National Work. See Ukrainian Party of National Work.

Omelian Partytsky

Partytsky, Omelian [Partyc'kyj, Omeljan], b 1840 in Teisariv, Stryi circle, Galicia, d 20 January 1895 in Lviv. Linguist, ethnographer, historian, educator, and civic figure. After graduating from Lviv University (1864) he taught at the Ternopil gymnasium (1864–8), the Academic Gymnasium of Lviv (1868–71), and the Lviv Teachers' Seminary (1871–95). An ardent supporter of the national populist movement, Partytsky was an executive member of the Prosvita society, editor of its calendars and books, a writer of textbooks in language and literature, and an editor of newspapers, including *Hazeta shkol'na* (1875–9) and *Zoria* (1880–5). He compiled a substantive German-Ruthe-

nian dictionary (1867), translated *Slovo o polku Ihorevi (1884), and wrote *Starynna istoriia Halychyny* (The Ancient History of Galicia, 1894).

Pashchenko, Dmytro [Paščenko], b 1759, d 1809. Administrator and historian. He worked as a chancellor in Hadiache regiment (from 1774) and for the Little Russian Collegium (from 1777) and became a member of the commission conducting an imperial survey and census of the Hetmanate. He wrote *Opisanie Chernigovskogo namestnichestva* (A Description of Chernihiv Viceregency, 1779–81; parts of it were published by A. Lazarevsky in 1868). Pashchenko later served as a regimental scribe (1783) and as a court chamberlain in Horodnia county, Chernihiv gubernia (from 1802).

Oleksandr Pashchenko: *Flood on the Dnieper: Trukhaniv Island* (color linocut, 1937)

Pashchenko, Oleksandr [Paščenko], b 14 September 1906 in Luka, Bratslav county, Podilia gubernia, d 13 June 1963 in Kiev. Printmaker; corresponding member of the USSR Academy of Art from 1954. As an art student he belonged to the Union of Young Artists of Ukraine. A graduate of the Kiev State Art Institute (1932), he later served as professor (1947–63) and rector (1955–63) there. He worked mostly in color linocut, etching, and watercolor and produced print series such as 'Kiev Suite' (1936–60), 'Kiev' (1944–5), 'Kievan Cave Monastery' (1944–5), 'Reconstruction of the Dnieper Hydroelectric Station' (1945–6), and 'Kiev-Dnieper' (1951) and *With Metallurgists of the Dnieper Region* (1952). Monographs about him have been written by L. Vladych (1957) and P. Hovdia (1964).

Pashchenko, Oleksandr [Paščenko], b 12 April 1929 in Lokhvytsia, Romen okruha, d 1990. Technological chemist; AN URSR (now ANU) corresponding member from 1976. After graduating from the Kiev Technological Institute of Silicates (1954) he joined the Kiev Polytechnical Institute and served there as a department chairman (from 1970) and as prorector (1971–4). His research dealt with the theoretical and practical aspects of the synthesis and curing of cements and with problems of formation and stability in organic element–based coatings. He developed many high-performance adhesives derived from organosilicon and other resins.

Pashchenko-Shulminska, Olimpiia [Paščenko-Šul'-mins'ka, Olimpija], b 1879 in Serby, Mohyliv county, Podilia gubernia, d 10 September 1972 in Lviv. Educator and civic leader. She completed her pedagogical training in Tbilisi. She worked there as a teacher, volunteered as a nurse in Manchuria during the Russo-Japanese War, and in 1909 returned to Kamianets-Podilskyi, where she gained a reputation as an educator. During the period 1917–18 she headed the city's school council, and in April 1917 she was delegated to the All-Ukrainian National Congress in Kiev, where she was elected to the Central Rada. In 1919 she was one of the founders of the Kamianets-Podilskyi Ukrainian State University. In the interwar period she lived in western Volhynia, and after the Second World War she moved to Lviv.

Andrii Pashchuk

Pashchuk, Andrii [Paščuk, Andrij], b 1891, d ? Civic and political leader in western Volhynia. In 1918 he served as the first president of the Prosvita branch in Lutske. A member of the Ukrainian Social Democratic party, he was elected to the Polish Sejm in 1922. Two years later he left the Ukrainian caucus to join the communist one, and in 1928 he moved to Soviet Ukraine. There he was arrested in 1933. He disappeared in a prison camp.

Stefaniia Pashkevych   Mytrofan Pasichnyk

Pashkevych, Stefaniia [Paškevyč, Stefanija], b 3 November 1889 in Sambir, Galicia, d 11 October 1953 in Lviv. Educator and geographer. She graduated from Lviv University in 1913 and then taught geography at a teachers' seminary and a primary school in Lviv. She was also an organizer of the Plast Ukrainian Youth Association and a

coeditor of the daily *Vpered* (1918–22) and the magazine *Nasha meta* (1919–22). An associate of the mathematics and science section of the Shevchenko Scientific Society, she contributed a chapter on Ukraine's landscapes to V. Kubijovyč's *Heohrafiia Ukraïny i sumezhnykh zemel'* (A Geography of Ukraine and Adjacent Lands, 1938). When the Soviets occupied Galicia in 1939, Pashkevych was deported to Siberia (1941–5). Upon returning to Lviv she lectured at the university and wrote a number of morphological studies of Western Ukraine.

Pashkivsky, Roman [Paškivs'kyj], b 1898 in Borshchiv county, Galicia, d 17 August 1971 in Montreal, Canada. Journalist. A former officer in the UNR Army in interwar Lviv, he coedited *Svoboda*, the organ of the Ukrainian National Democratic Alliance (1922–39), *Zyz* (1923–33), and *Komar* (1935–9), and edited the humor magazine *Zhorna* (1933–4). He also organized the first Ukrainian-language radio broadcasts in Lviv.

Pashkovsky, Ivan [Paškovs'kyj], b and d ? A middle to late 18th-century poet and priest in the Ternopil region. He wrote Christmas carols ('Kheruvymy sviat' [Cherubims Holy] was particularly popular in Galicia at one time), religious songs (published in the collection *Bohohlasnyk), and acrostics and secular songs in which rural poverty and the peasants' plight are commented upon.

Pashuk, Andrii [Pašuk, Andrij], b 30 May 1927 in Skoryky, Zbarazh county, Galicia. Philosopher. Since graduating from Lviv University (1950) he has taught philosophy there; he became a candidate of sciences in 1954 and a doctor of philosophy in 1967. A specialist in the history of philosophy, particularly in Ukraine, he is the author of books on S. Podolynsky (1965), the problems of social development in the ideology of the revolutionary democrats in Ukraine (1982), and I. Vyshensky (1990).

Pasichnyk, Mytrofan [Pasičnyk], b 17 June 1912 in Zhyrkivka, Kostiantynohrad county, Poltava gubernia. Physicist; full member of the AN URSR (now ANU) since 1961. He graduated from the Poltava Institute of Social Education (1931) and studied at the ANU Institute of Physics (1932–5), where he worked during 1935–40 and 1946–70 (1949–65 as director). He was head of the physics chair at the Kiev Medical Institute (1938–40) and Chernivtsi University (1940–1), and the chair of nuclear physics at Kiev University (1947–61). He was the founder and first director (1970–3) of the ANU Institute for Nuclear Research, where he is working at present. His fields of research are physics of metals, nuclear physics, and atomic reactors. He discovered the shell effects in nuclei under intermediate- and high-energy excitation. His publications include the monographs *Pytannia neitronnoï fizyky serednikh enerhii* (Problems of Middle-Energy Neutron Physics, 1962), *Neitronna fizyka* (Neutron Physics, 1969), and *Iadra i radiiatsiina stiikist' konstruktsiinykh materialiv* (Nuclei and Radiation Resistance of Structural Materials, 1973).

Pasichnyk, Trokhym [Pasičnyk, Troxym], b 1896 in Podilia, d 29 June 1968 in Woonsocket, Rhode Island. Poet and teacher. As an interwar émigré (from 1921) he taught at the Ukrainian Gymnasium in Czechoslovakia. In 1951 he settled in the United States. He wrote *Po vsii Ukraïni* (Throughout All of Ukraine, 1944; 2nd edn 1957), a narrative poem about the revolutionary period in Ukraine, and 'Petro Hordiienko,' an epopee in seven parts about the Ukrainian nation (only pts 1–2, *V dorozi* [On the Road, 1944; 2nd edn 1964] and *Ridnyi homin* [A Native Echo, 1957], were published).

Pasichynsky, Sydir [Pasičyns'kyj] (Isydor), b 1853 in Krasne, Sambir circle, d 1930 in Zadilsko, Turka county, Galicia. Writer. From 1870 his articles on ethnography and many of his poems appeared in Western Ukrainian papers and journals (eg, *Lastivka, Uchytel', Bukovyna, Rus'ke slovo*). His poem *Beztalannyi* (The Hapless One) was published separately in 1872.

Pasichynsky, Teodor [Pasičyns'kyj] (Pasiczynskyj, Theodore), b 14 October 1916 in Nahachiv, Yavoriv county, Galicia. Civic leader. He arrived in Australia in 1949 and settled in Adelaide. In 1951 he organized the Ukrainian Community School in Adelaide. He served as head of the Australian-Ukrainian Association in South Australia (1967–77); as chairperson of the Ethnic Schools Association in South Australia, the Homin choir, and the Captive Nations Council; and as an executive member of the Ethnic Communities Council of South Australia and the Ukrainian Educational Council of Australia. He became a justice of the peace (1973) and was awarded the Order of Australia Medal in 1981.

Pasiuha, Stepan [Pasjuha], b 11 December 1862 in Velyka Pysarivka, Bohodukhiv county, Kharkiv gubernia, d 1933 in Velyka Pysarivka. Kobzar. His repertoire included the dumas about the widow and her three sons, the captives' lament, and the flight of the three brothers from Azov. In 1911–12 he gave concerts in Kiev, Poltava, Myrhorod, and other towns. His repertoire was written down by F. Kolessa. Pasiuha's students included I. Kucherenko-Kuchuhura and Ye. Movchan.

Paskevych [Paskevyč] (Russian: Paskevich). A family of nobility from the Poltava region. The first to use the name was the Cossack Ivan Paskevych, the grandson of Fedir Tsalenko, a notable military fellow (1698) in Poltava regiment. In the second half of the 18th century some members of the family studied at German universities. One of them, Petro (1738–91), became a fellow of the standard in 1787 and founded the first bookstore in Poltava. Several family members attained high Russian imperial ranks. Ivan's grandson, Fedir (d 26 April 1832 in Kharkiv), was chairman of the Supreme Land Court of Voznesensk gubernia and a collegial adviser. Fedir's son Ivan (b 20 May 1782 in Poltava, d 13 February 1856 in Warsaw) was a brigadier from 1811, a division commander from 1814, commander of the First Army Corps from 1821, and adjutant general from 1825. Appointed commander in chief of the Russian forces in Poland in 1831, for his role in suppressing the Polish Insurrection of 1830–1 he received the title of prince of Warsaw and until the 1850s served as vicegerent of the Congress Kingdom of Poland, where he governed by martial law and imposed Russification. He commanded the Russian army that suppressed the 1849 revolution in Hungary. Ivan's brother Stepan (b 1785, d 21 April 1840) was a colonel from 1816 and served as vice-governor of Slobidska Ukraine (1827–31), governor of Tambov (1831–2), Kursk (1834–5), and Vladimir (1835–6) gubernias, and a member of the Council of the Ministry of Internal Affairs (1837–40). Their brother, Yosyf (1784–1844), attained the rank of major general. Ivan's son, Fedir (1823–1903), was a lieutenant general from 1854. Another Paskevych, Kostiantyn (1790–1836), was a colonel from 1828.

A. Zhukovsky

Paskhaver, Yosyp [Pasxaver, Josyp], b 14 December 1907 in Kryve Ozero, Balta county, Podilia gubernia, d 1981 in Kiev. Statistician and economist. A graduate of the Kharkiv Institute of the National Economy (1930), he taught at the Kiev Institute of the National Economy from 1930 and was appointed to the chair of statistics in 1945. He wrote several works in statistics, including *Zakon bol'shikh chisel i zakonomernosti massovogo protsessa* (The Law of Larger Numbers and the Regularities of Mass Processes, 1966), *Balans trudovykh resursov kolkhozov* (The Balance of Collective-Farm Labor Resources, 1972), and *Serednie velichiny v statistike* (Mean Values in Statistics, 1979), and several articles on agriculture in Ukraine.

Passaic. A city (1980 pop 52,000) on the Passaic River in northern New Jersey, with a Ukrainian population (1980) of 600. Its textile industry attracted many immigrants in the 19th century, including Ukrainians from Transcarpathia and the Lemko region (from 1885) and Galicia (from 1895). The first Ukrainian organization, the St Nicholas Mutual Aid Society, was formed there in 1900. Catholic (1910) and Orthodox (1925) churches were built in the city, as well as a Ukrainian People's Home (est 1913). By 1925 approx 20 Ukrainian organizations, including branches of the four major fraternal societies, could be found in the city. In the 1930s its Ukrainian population reached 2,000. Passaic is the seat of a 'Carpatho-Ruthenian' Catholic eparchy and the site of the head office of the *Organization for the Defense of Lemkivshchyna. One of the parks in the city was named after T. Shevchenko in 1964.

Passek. A Belarusian noble family of Czech origin. The Passeks were related to Cossack *starshyna* families of the Hetman state. Bogdan Passek (d ca 1758) was a Russian member of the Hetmanate's General Military Court until 1734 and served as adviser to the governor of Belgorod gubernia (1739–42) and as its vice-governor (1742). His son, Vasyl (d 1778), served as a lieutenant colonel in Slobidska Ukraine, and his descendants lived there. One of them was Vadim *Passek. Vadim's brother Vasilii (b 26 July 1816, d May 1864) lived on his estate in Izium county and in Kharkiv; he is the author of a posthumously published collection of studies on Kievan Rus' history (1870). Another brother, Diomid (b 1808, d 23 July 1845), died fighting the forces of Shamil in Dagestan with the rank of major general. The first part of his study comparing Charles XII and Peter I as military leaders was published by Vadim in his *Ocherki Rossii* (Studies of Russia, vol 4 [1840]). The archeologist Tatiana *Passek is descended from the same branch of the family.

Passek, Tatiana, b 15 August 1903 in St Petersburg, d 4 August 1968 in Moscow. Russian archeologist. Passek studied at Leningrad University, then worked at the State Academy for the History of Art and the USSR Academy of Sciences' Institute of Archeology. From 1934 she took part in or led archeological expeditions in Ukraine and Molda-

Tatiana Passek

via on sites from the Trypilian era, most notably *Kolomyishchyna. Passek put forth a scheme for the periodization of *Trypilian culture that gained and has retained broad acceptance. Her major works include *Periodizatsiia tripol'skikh poselenii* (A Periodization of Trypilian Settlements, 1949) and *Rannezemledel'cheskie (tripol'skie) plemena Podnestrov'ia* (Early Agricultural [Trypilian] Tribes of the Dniester Region, 1961). She also published *Trypil's'ka kul'tura: Naukovo-populiarnyi narys* (Trypilian Culture: A Scholarly-Popular Survey, 1941).

Passek, Vadim, b 2 July 1808 in Tobolsk, Siberia, d 6 November 1842 in Moscow. Historian, ethnographer, and archeologist. He grew up in Siberia, where his father had been exiled. While studying at Moscow University (1826–30) he became involved with A. Herzen and N. Ogarev's revolutionary circle. He was prevented from occupying the chair of Russian history at Kharkiv University because of his links with Herzen. He settled on his family's estate in Kharkiv gubernia and did ethnographic fieldwork, as well as statistical research for the Ministry of Internal Affairs. He is the author of historical and statistical descriptions of Kharkiv gubernia and its towns (with maps, plans, and coats of arms), which were published in *Materialy dlia statistiki Rossiiskoi imperii* (vol 1, 1839), of descriptions of excavated ancient fortified settlements and kurhans in Valky and Izium counties, and of articles on Ukrainian folk songs, marriage customs, folk beliefs, and locales. In his *Putevyia zametki Vadima* (Vadim's Travel Notes, 1834) Passek expressed his Romantic attachment to Ukraine (Little Russia) and its past. He compiled and published *Ocherki Rossii* (Studies of Russia, 1838–42), which includes valuable Ukrainian ethnographic and historical contributions by I. *Sreznevsky and others. In 1839 he returned to Moscow, where he was active in Slavophile circles. Passek died prematurely of tuberculosis.

Passport system. In most democratic countries a passport is a document used for identification outside the home country. It identifies the holder by name, photograph, and date and place of birth, and sometimes also by height and color of eyes and hair. For identification within one's country a birth certificate or driver's license is sufficient. In the Soviet Union, however, there were two types of passport: one for internal use and the other for external use. The external or 'international' (*zagranichnyi*) passport was of three kinds: diplomatic, official (*sluzhebnyi*), and normal (*obshchegrazhdanskii*). The third type, which was equivalent to an ordinary passport in other countries, was

especially difficult to obtain, since Soviet authorities treated travel abroad as a privilege rather than a right. The international passport had to be handed in to the authorities on one's return from abroad.

The internal passport was issued to every Soviet citizen who had attained 16 years of age. It was uniform throughout the USSR. Printed in two languages, Russian and the language of the republic where it was issued, it listed the holder's surname, given name along with the Russian form of the patronymic, place and date of birth, nationality, children, family status, military service, and place of residence. Social status was dropped in 1974 on the pretense that the USSR had achieved social unity. Three pages of the passport were reserved for photographs taken at the ages of 16, 25, and 45.

Such passports were issued at one's place of residence by the militia (police), which maintained strict control over the system. When citizens traveled outside their area of residence, they had to register with the police in the locality they were visiting within 3 days if in a border city or area (7 days in a city elsewhere) and 30 days in a village. There were various other restrictions on free movement in the passport system. To move permanently one required a special residence permit (*propiska*) from the police. Violations of the passport system were punished by various penalties, depending on the infraction. In addition employees in state enterprises were required to carry a special work passbook or 'booklet,' which contained a complete record of one's positions, awards, dismissals, and transfers. Upon taking a job employees submitted their passbooks at the plant office and picked them up when they moved to another plant. It was a criminal offense to make false entries in the passports of employees or tenants.

Some items in the passport were not entirely accurate. Nationality, for example, was determined by that of one's parents. Children of mixed marriages could choose between the nationalities of their parents. The nationality first entered in the passport was final; no changes were allowed later. Census statistics on the national composition of the Soviet population differed from passport data. The former were based on self-identification and could vary in the course of one's life; the latter were permanent.

The internal passport system that had been in force under the tsarist regime was abolished in 1917. The Soviet system had been introduced in December 1932, at the peak of collectivization. The official justification was that it would 'protect public order and state security,' but the real purpose had been to stop peasants, particularly those on collective farms, from moving freely into the cities and towns. Peasants were not issued passports until August 1974; hence, their movement was restricted even more severely than that of passport holders. Introduced at the time of the man-made famine in Ukraine (1932–3), the passport system contributed to the destruction of the Ukrainian peasantry by reducing the peasants' chances of finding relief in the urban areas.

J. Borys

Pasta industry. A branch of the food industry that produces various forms of pasta. The first pasta factory in Ukraine and the entire Russian Empire was established in 1797 in Odessa. With a large supply of high-quality wheat in Ukraine, the industry grew quickly in the 19th century, although production methods were primitive. In the interwar period the Soviet government gave priority to raising the output of inexpensive, nutritious food. The output of pasta in the Ukrainian SSR increased from 79.4 million t in 1940 to 185.2 million t in 1960, 219.5 million t in 1970, 308.6 million t in 1980, and 343.5 million t in 1987. In 1979 Ukraine accounted for over 20 percent of the pasta produced in the USSR.

Pastelii, Ivan [Pastelij] (secular name: Ivan Kovach), b 27 January 1741 in Transcarpathia, d 1799 in Uzhhorod. Ukrainian Catholic priest, scholar, and writer. After being educated in Uzhhorod, Budapest, and Eger he became (1765) a professor of ethics at the Mukachiv Theological Seminary and later a parish priest in several locations throughout Transcarpathia. In 1787 he became a canon of Mukachiv eparchy and then vicar-general of the newly established Košice vicariate (later Prešov eparchy). Pastelii left a number of poems and a history of Mukachiv eparchy in manuscript.

Ivan Pasternak

Mariia Pasternak

Pasternak, Ivan, b 1876 in Pavliv, Podlachia, d 25 May 1943 in Biała Podlaska, Podlachia. Educator, civic leader, and a pioneer of the Ukrainian revival in Podlachia. He worked as a public school teacher and in 1922 was elected to the Polish Senate. He was president of the Ridna Khata society in Kholm (1923–7). During the Second World War he served as the first president of the Ukrainian Relief Committee and as chairman of the auditing committee of the Podlachian Union of Ukrainian Co-operatives in Biała Podlaska. He was murdered by Polish partisans.

Pasternak, Mariia, b 1897 in Lviv, d 26 August 1983 in Toronto. Pedagogue and expert on folk and artistic dance; wife of Ya. *Pasternak. In the 1930s she taught at the Ridna Shkola school in Lviv, was in charge of preschool education for the Ukrainska Zakhoronka Society (1934–9), and coedited the journal *Ukraïns'ke doshkilia* (1937–9). In 1941–4 she was responsible for preschool education in the Ukrainian Central Committee in Lviv. After the war she emigrated to Germany and then to Canada. She is the author of the textbook *Zainiattia v dytiachomu sadku* (Activities in the Nursery School, 1959) and of *Ukraïns'ka zhinka v khoreohrafii* (The Ukrainian Woman in Choreography, 1963), as well as numerous articles on preschool education and dance.

Pasternak, Severyn, b 1899 in the Drohobych region, d ? Geologist; full member of the Shevchenko Scientific Society (NTSh) from 1934; brother of Ya. *Pasternak. He was a research associate of the NTSh's Museum of Natural History in Lviv (1927–39). Under the Soviet regime he served as director (1954–6 and 1958–60) of the paleontology department of the Natural Science Museum of the AN URSR (now ANU) in Lviv. His major research interests included the minerals of Western Ukraine and the chalk deposits of the Podilia and Volhynia regions.

Yaroslav Pasternak

Pasternak, Yaroslav, b 2 January 1892 in Khyriv, Staryi Sambir county, Galicia, d 30 November 1969 in Toronto. Archeologist; full member of the Shevchenko Scientific Society (NTSh) from 1929. He studied archeology at Lviv University (1910–14). He continued his studies and obtained a doctorate at Charles University in Prague (1922–6). He worked at the National Museum in Lviv (1913–14) and the State Archeological Institute in Prague before becoming the director of the NTSh Cultural-Historical Museum in Lviv (1928–39). He also lectured at the Lviv Theological Academy (1932–9 and 1942–4). During the first Soviet occupation of Western Ukraine (1939–41) he was a professor at Lviv University and a member of the AN URSR (now ANU) Institute of Archeology. He emigrated to Germany in 1944 before the second Soviet occupation.

While in Ukraine and Czechoslovakia Pasternak took part in over 60 archeological expeditions, the most important being in princely *Halych (1939–41). He published three studies about the prehistory of Western Ukraine – *Ruské Karpaty v archeologii* (The Archeology of the Ruthenian Carpathians, 1928, based on his diss [in Czech]), *Korotka arkheolohiia zakhidno-ukraïns'kykh zemel'* (A Brief Survey of Western Ukrainian Archeology, 1932), and *Staryi Halych: arkheolohichno-istorychni doslidy u 1850–1943 rr.* (Old Halych: Archeological-Historical Studies in 1850–1943, 1944) – and numerous scholarly and popular articles in Ukrainian, Czech, German, and Polish.

In Germany he lectured at Friedrich Wilhelm University in Bonn (1946–9) and the Ukrainian Free University in Munich. He emigrated to Canada in 1950, where he remained active in scholarship and publishing. His major undertaking there was a survey, *Arkheolohiia Ukraïny* (The Archeology of Ukraine, 1961), in which he wished to provide a synthesis of the archeology of Ukraine to date and to challenge Soviet (and Western) interpretations in the field. A complete bibliography of his works by I. Luchkiv, listing 290 titles in archeology, regional studies, history, ethnography, and museum studies, appeared in *Iuvileinyi zbirnyk naukovykh prats' z nahody storichchia NTSh i dvadtsiatypia-tyrichchia NTSh u Kanadi* (Jubilee Collection of Scholarly Works on the Occasion of the 100th Anniversary of NTSh and the 25th Anniversary of NTSh in Canada, 1977).

Pasternak, Yevhen, b 24 January 1907 in Vyhnanka, Biała Podlaska county, Podlachia, d 22 November 1980 in Toronto. Community leader and historian; son of I. *Pasternak and husband of Ye. *Pasternak. He graduated from the Danzig Polytechnic (1937) and worked as a civil engineer in Lviv and Lublin. During the Second World War he headed the Union of Ukrainian Co-operatives in Podlachia and the Ukrainian Relief Committee in Biała Podlaska. In 1948 Pasternak emigrated as a refugee from Germany to Toronto. He was a founding member of the Society of Ukrainian Engineers and Associates in Canada and served as its president, cofounded and built the Ivan Franko Ukrainian Home for the Aged in Toronto, contributed to the Ukrainian émigré press, and wrote a history of the Kholm region and Podlachia (1969) and a book on Ukraine under Bolshevik rule (1980).

Yevheniia Pasternak

Pasternak, Yevheniia (née Novakivska), b 8 January 1919 in Fashchivka, Skalat county, Galicia. Administrator. After obtaining a teacher's degree in Lviv (1938) she taught art and music and obtained an administration degree at McMaster University (1971; she had emigrated to Canada in 1948). Since 1964 she has served as director of the Ivan Franko Ukrainian Home for the Aged in Toronto. In 1984 she received the Order of Canada, and in 1987 she was appointed deputy director general of the International Biographical Centre in Cambridge, England.

Pasteur station. The common name for a bacteriological station for the prevention of rabies. Pasteur stations inoculate patients who have been bitten by rabid animals, and undertake measures to reduce rabies among animals, improve sanitary conditions, and educate the public about rabies. The first Pasteur station in Ukraine, second in the world only to the one in Paris, was set up by I. Mechnikov and M. *Hamaliia in Odessa in 1886. It was the only facility that prepared the antirabies vaccine. By the First World War there was a Pasteur station in every gubernia capital in Ukraine. Today there is a network of Pasteur stations and Pasteur depots at therapeutic-prophylactic and sanitary institutions in the cities and raion centers of Ukraine. Some *sanitary-epidemiological stations have special Pasteur departments.

Pastrnek, František, b 4 October 1853 in Kelč, Moravia, d 17 February 1940 in Prague. Czech Slavic philologist; member of the Shevchenko and Bohemian scientific societies and corresponding member of the Russian and Bulgarian academies of sciences. He studied at Vienna University (1873–8; PH D, 1886) under F. Miklosich and V. Jagić and taught there (1888–1902) and at Prague University (from 1902). In Czech scholarly periodicals he published articles in the fields of Church Slavonic and Slovak linguistic history and dialectology. He wrote a history of SS Cyril and Methodius (1902) and a monograph on Church Slavonic (2 vols, 1909, 1912) and engaged in a polemic with V. *Hnatiuk regarding the nationality of the 'Ruthenians' of the Prešov and Bačka regions.

Pastur, Leonid, b 21 August 1937 in Udych, in Teplyk raion, Vinnytsia oblast. Mathematician; full member of the ANU (formerly AN URSR) since 1991. Since graduating from the Kharkiv Polytechnical Institute (1961) he has worked at the ANU Physical-Technical Institute of Low Temperatures in Kharkiv and taught at Kharkiv University. Pastur's major work is in the spectral theory of operators. He is one of the founders of the spectral theory of differential and finite-difference operators with random and almost periodic coefficients. His abstract results have been applied in optics, radiophysics, and solid-state theory. Pastur has written seminal papers on eigenvalue distributions of random matrices with independent entries. He has studied the spectral properties of almost periodic operators and has solved completely the inverse problem of spectral analysis for the one-dimensional Schrödinger operator with limit periodic potential. He has also made substantial contributions to mathematical physics, especially to the study of disordered spin systems.

Pasture. Land covered with various grasses and used for livestock grazing. The grasses, predominantly cereal grasses, can be natural or sown, and the soil is usually poor. Pastures are an important part of the *feed base in Ukraine, although their importance has diminished as more feed crops have been introduced. Most pastures are now found in marginal farming areas, such as the Carpathian Mountains, and in the steppe, especially in the Crimea. In the forest-steppe, pastures account for less than 4 percent of all arable land. In the late 18th century pastures accounted for as much as one-third of all arable land, but as the steppe was brought under cultivation, the figure decreased drastically. In 1965 pastures covered some 4.7 million ha, or 10 percent of all arable land, in Ukraine.

Pastyrske fortified settlement. A multi-occupational site near Pastyrske, Smila raion, Cherkasy oblast. Excavations in 1892–1901 and 1949–55 by V. Khvoika and M. Braichevsky, among others, produced the remains of two settlements, one from the 6th to 4th century BC and the other from the 7th to 8th century AD.

Paszkowski, Marcin, b ? in the Cracow region, d 1620. Polish writer. He wrote several anti-Turkish brochures. On the basis of various documents, he described in verse the Poles' and Cossacks' wars with the Turks and Crimean Tatars during the reign of King Sigismund III Vasa. His works include *Ukraina od Tatarów trapiona o ratunek prosi*

(Ukraine Afflicted by the Tatars Begs for Deliverance, 1608), *Dzieje tureckie i utarczki Tatarów z Kozakami* (History of the Turks and the Conflicts of the Tatars with the Cossacks, 1615), and *Rozmowa Kozaka Zaporoskiego z Perskim gońcem* (Conversation of a Zaporozhian Cossack with a Persian Messenger, 1617).

Tetiana Pata: *Cuckoo on a Viburnum* (gouache and watercolor, 1950)

Pata, Tetiana, b 4 March 1884 in Petrykivka, Novomoskovske county, Katerynoslav gubernia, d 7 July 1976 in Petrykivka. Master of *Petrykivka painting. She decorated houses and chests with plant patterns, painted murals for commercial buildings, and designed kilims, books, and postcards. Among her best-known decorative panels are *Red Viburnum* (1919), *Rushnyk* (1930), *Pepper* (1937), *Peacocks among Flowers* (1949), *Cuckoo on a Viburnum* (1950), and *Bird and Grapes* (1958). She also taught at the Petrykivka School of Decorative Art and trained many Petrykivka painters. An album of her work was published in 1973.

Patent law. The set of legal norms regulating the production, use, and sale of new and useful products or processes. Inventors in Ukraine can obtain either an 'author's certificate' or a patent for their inventions. A certificate, which is valid for the entire USSR, is granted by the USSR Council of Ministers upon proof of novelty to the state patent office. The state reserves control over the invention and its use, and the inventor is eligible for a royalty based on the savings that can be realized through the invention. Extra incentives include better housing or a partial tax exemption on the royalty earnings. The more conventional form of inventor protection, the patent, gives the inventor or his descendants control over the use of the invention, usually for a period of 15 years. In the USSR, however, restrictions on free enterprise made a patent less desirable than an author's certificate. Moreover, patents of inventions that proved to be particularly important could simply be taken over by the state. Patents and author's certificates were regulated by section 6 of the Civil Code of the Ukrainian SSR and by the Statute on Discoveries, Inventions, and Innovational Proposals (1973).

Patericon (Ukrainian: *pateryk*). A collection of edifying tales, anecdotes, and apothegms about saints, the Church Fathers, and prominent monks. Patericons originated in the Byzantine Empire in the 4th century. In the 11th and 12th centuries Church Slavonic translations of the so-called Egyptian, Sinaitic, Roman, Jerusalem, and Skete patericons spread from Bulgaria and Moravia into Kievan Rus'. The *Kievan Cave Patericon was modeled on the translations.

Pathological anatomy. A branch of *pathology that determines the cause of death by observing the effects of disease on the body and its organs; it can also establish the sequences of changes and thus the mechanism and evolution of disease. In Ukraine pathological anatomy began in the early 18th century, after Peter I legalized the dissection of dead bodies (1704). In the 19th century chairs of pathological anatomy were established at Kharkiv (1867) and Kiev (1876) universities and continued to develop in two distinct directions. A clinical-anatomical branch of pathological anatomy was founded by G. Minkh, and an experimental-physiological branch was started by V. *Vysokovych. Other notable scientists in the field included M. *Melnikov-Razvedenkov, P. *Kucherenko, and Ye. *Chaika. The first textbook of pathological anatomy in Ukrainian was written by Kucherenko in 1936. At present, chairs of pathological anatomy are found at all the medical research and education institutes in Ukraine. Autopsies must be performed on all persons who die in hospitals.

Pathology. A medical specialty concerned with the essential nature of disease, especially the structural and functional changes produced in cells, tissues, and organs by disease. Some of the first notable pathologists in the Russian Empire were the Ukrainians H. Bazylevych, O. *Shumliansky, M. Terekhovsky, O. Zviriaka, Ye. Mukhin, D. *Samoilovych, and S. Andriievsky; they lectured at the medical schools and universities of St Petersburg, Moscow, and Yelysavethrad in the late 18th and early 19th centuries. More recent Ukrainian pathologists include I. *Mechnikov, V. *Vysokovych, V. *Pidvysotsky, G. *Minkh, D. *Zabolotny, O. *Bohomolets, and M. *Melnikov-Razvedenkov. The Ukrainian Scientific Society of Pathologists was founded in Kharkiv in 1926. The Institute of Experimental Biology and Pathology in Kiev was founded by Bohomolets in 1930 (see *Institute of Physiology of the AN URSR).

Pathophysiology. The *physiology of abnormal states, specifically the study of the functional changes that accompany a particular disease. Pathophysiology existed under the general name *pathology and began to be differentiated in the middle of the 19th century. At that time a school of pathophysiology was founded in Kiev by N. *Khrzhonshchevsky. By 1925 pathophysiology had become an independent science in Ukraine, where it developed in Kharkiv under O. Repriev and in Kiev and Odessa under V. *Pidvysotsky along with D. *Zabolotny, Lev *Tarasevych, Ivan *Savchenko, and O. *Bohomolets. At the AN URSR (now ANU) *Institute of Physiology (est 1930), Bohomolets and his students researched the development of tumors (R. *Kavetsky), endocrinology (V. *Komisarenko), blood circulation (M. *Horiev), and immunology and allergy (M. *Syrotynin). There are a number of scientific societies of pathophysiologists in Ukraine.

Borys Paton   Yevhen (Evgenii) Paton

Paton, Borys, b 27 November 1918 in Kiev. Metallurgist; son of Ye. *Paton, full member (since 1958) and president (since 1962) of the AN URSR (now ANU). He graduated from the Kiev Industrial Institute (1940) and since 1942 has worked at the ANU Institute of Electric Welding, where in 1953 he became director. His scientific contributions are in modern welding methods, including electric-arc, electron-beam, and plasma welding, welding in space, and seamless pipes. He was active politically, particularly in the 'politics' of science and technology in the USSR, and was a deputy to republican and all-Union CP congresses and supreme soviets. A biography of him was published in Moscow in 1979.

Paton, Yevhen (Evgenii), b 4 March 1870 in Nice, France, d 12 August 1953 in Kiev. Welding scientist and construction technologist; full member of the AN URSR (now ANU) from 1929. He graduated from the Dresden Polytechnical Institute (1894) and the St Petersburg Institute of Civil Engineers (1896) and was a professor at the Kiev Polytechnical Institute (1904–39, with interruptions). While heading the Kiev Bridge-Testing Laboratory (1921–31) he formulated fundamental scientific principles of bridge design and developed a scientific bridge-testing methodology. He published basic textbooks and monographs in the field and designed over 35 bridges and viaducts in 1896–1929, including a major bridge across the Dnieper River (1924). Paton is also considered to be the father of electric *welding in the USSR. In 1929 he organized at the VUAN a laboratory of electric welding technology, which in 1934 became the ANU Institute of Electric Welding. He served as director of the laboratory and institute until his death; today the institute bears his name. His contributions in the field of electric welding include arc welding and automation, welding apparatus design, and strength calculations of welded joints. He helped introduce electric welding technology into Soviet industry and founded the journal *Avtomaticheskaia svarka*, which has appeared in Kiev since 1948.

Paton served as vice-president of the ANU from 1945 to 1952. He served on numerous scientific and political committees and published many books and technical articles on bridge building and welding. His selected works were published in Kiev in 1970, and a biography of him was published there in 1961. In 1964 the ANU established the

Paton Prize for outstanding contributions in the field of materials science, particularly welding technology.

L. Onyshkevych

Ivan Patorzhynsky

Patorzhynsky, Ivan [Patoržyns'kyj], b 3 March 1896 in Petro-Svystunove, Oleksandrivske county, Katerynoslav gubernia, d 22 February 1960 in Kiev. Opera singer (bass) and voice teacher. A graduate of the Katerynoslav Conservatory (1922), he studied singing under Z. Maliutina and was the soloist at the Kharkiv (1925–35) and Kiev (from 1935) opera and ballet theaters. His singing style was representative of the contemporary Ukrainian vocal school. His operatic roles included Karas in S. Hulak-Artemovsky's *Zaporozhian Cossack beyond the Danube*, Vybornyi and Taras Bulba in M. Lysenko's *Natalka from Poltava* and *Taras Bulba*, Deacon Havrylo in K. Dankevych's *Bohdan Khmelnytsky*, Kochubei in P. Tchaikovsky's *Mazepa*, the Miller in A. Dargomyzhsky's *Rusalka*, and Mephistopheles in C. Gounod's *Faust*. In concert he performed Ukrainian folk songs and romances by M. Lysenko, Ya. Stepovy, and M. Verykivsky. He toured in Italy, Germany, and North America. From 1946 he was a professor at the Kiev Conservatory; his pupils included D. *Hnatiuk, A. *Kikot, and Ye. Chervoniuk. In 1945–54 he was the first director of the *Ukrainian Theatrical Society. Biographies of him were written by V. Chahovets (1946) and E. Grosheva (1976).

Patraeus. A Bosporan city that existed from the 6th century BC to the early Middle Ages on the north shore of Taman Bay near Kerch Strait. Archeological excavations at the site revealed extensive fortifications (brick walls surrounded by moats), large buildings, several large wineries, and two caches of coins of the 1st to 3rd centuries (the period of the city's greatest prosperity).

Patriarch. Initially an honorific title in the early church for distinguished bishops of any rank. By the 6th century it was accorded to the bishops of Rome, Constantinople, Alexandria, Antioch, and Jerusalem. Traditionally the pope or patriarch of Rome was recognized as the first or highest patriarch, and the patriarch in Constantinople as the 'ecumenical' patriarch, or patriarch of the entire Eastern Roman Empire. The term patriarch was later applied also to the chief bishops of churches which did not concur with the Council of Chalcedon (451), that is, the Nestorian and Monophysite. Since the Middle Ages various Eastern Christian churches have become patriarchates, and their head bishops patriarchs.

The church of Kiev enjoyed quasi-patriarchal autonomy under a metropolitan, but was dependent on the ecumenical patriarch of Constantinople until 1686, when he transferred this authority to the patriarch of Moscow.

In 1583, while traveling to Moscow, the papal representative A. Possevino met with Ukrainian princes in Cracow to discuss the possibility of the establishment of a patriarchate in Kiev by Pope Gregory XIII. Even though it was supported by Roman and Polish forces, nothing came of this initiative. After the Church Union of *Berestia a plan to establish a patriarchate in Kiev was prepared in 1635–6 by the Uniate metropolitan Y. *Rutsky. The patriarch of Kiev would accept the dogmatic teaching of the Roman Catholic church, which it was agreed would be identical with that of the Orthodox church, but would be free to govern according to Eastern canon law, which gave recognition to the pope and the patriarch in Constantinople in accordance with the ecumenical councils and the Council of Florence (1439). Rutsky proposed the Orthodox metropolitan of Kiev, P. *Mohyla, as candidate.

In the 19th century, after the suppression of the Ruthenian (Ukrainian-Belarusian) Catholic church in the Russian Empire and the flourishing of the same church under Austria, Popes Gregory XVI, Pius IX, and Leo XIII considered the possibility of establishing a patriarchate for all the Slavic 'Greek Catholic' dioceses of Austria-Hungary. The combined opposition of the Hungarians and Poles, however, doomed these proposals from the outset.

When a Ukrainian state was formed in 1918, the idea of creating a Ukrainian patriarchate under the Greek Catholic metropolitan A. Sheptytsky was proposed. Sheptytsky's condition – that he could accept only if the church would unite itself with the Catholic church – was unacceptable to most Orthodox Ukrainians.

In 1963, at the Second Vatican Council, Metropolitan Y. *Slipy, as major archbishop of Lviv and head of the Ukrainian Catholic church, proposed the creation of a Ukrainian patriarchate under Rome. Although supported by most Ukrainian and some Latin church bishops, this proposal was not realized. Later Slipy approached Popes Paul VI and John Paul II with the same request, but it was rejected as untimely. Nonetheless, in 1975 Slipy declared the Ukrainian Catholic church a patriarchate with himself as its patriarch. In this action he was supported by only a minority of his bishops; others followed the instruction of the Vatican, based on the Decree for Eastern Catholic Churches of the Second Vatican Council, that only an ecumenical council or the pope can establish a patriarchate. The Ukrainian Major Archiepiscopate of Lviv-Halych is now recognized by the Vatican as an autonomous (sui juris) church, and is administered as a patriarchal church (can. 152).

The *Ukrainian Patriarchal Society in the United States and the *Ukrainian Patriarchal World Federation for Unity of Church and People were formed to work toward the creation of a Ukrainian Catholic patriarchate. The Vatican Council did make efforts to restore the dignity of the Eastern Catholic patriarchs within the framework of the Catholic church. Still, the codification of the Eastern Catholic canon law, the Codex Canonum Ecclesiarum Orientalium, promulgated on 18 October 1990, has not re-established the patriarchates in their full ancient role. It has also denied all Eastern Catholic churches direct jurisdiction over their own faithful outside the historical boundaries of their churches.

The revival of the *Ukrainian Autocephalous Orthodox church (UAOC) in Ukraine in the late 1980s raised the issue of an Orthodox Ukrainian patriarchate. At a sobor held in Kiev in 1990, Metropolitan M. *Skrypnyk, head of the UAOC in the West, was elected Patriarch of Kiev and all Ukraine; he was formally installed in Kiev in November 1990.

BIBLIOGRAPHY
Andrusiak, M. 'Sprawa Patriarchatu Kijowskiego za Władysława IV,' Prace Historyczne w 30-lecie działalnosci profesorskiej S. Zakrzeskiego (Lviv 1934)
Tanczuk, D. 'Quaestio Patriarchatus Kioviensis tempore conaminum Unionis Ruthenorum (1582–1682),' AOBM, 1 (7) (1949)
de Vries, W. Rom und die Patriarchate des Ostens (Freiburg 1963)
Krajcar, J. 'The Ruthenian Patriarchate: Some Remarks on the Project for Its Establishment in the 17th Century,' Orientalia Christian Periodica, 30, nos 1–2 (1964)
Parlato, V. L'ufficio patriarcale nelle chiese orientali dal IV al X secolo (Padova 1969)
Madey, J. Le Patriarcat Ukrainien vers la perfection de l'état juridique actuel (Rome 1971)
Pospishil, V.; Luzhnycky, H. (eds). The Quest for an Ukrainian Catholic Patriarchate (Philadelphia 1971)
Nahaievs'kyi, I. Patriiarkhaty, ïkh pochatok i znachennia v Tserkvi ta ukraïns'kyi patriiarkhat (New York–Munich–Toronto 1973)
Bilaniuk, P.B.T. Patriiarkhal'nyi ustrii pomisnoï (particularis) Ukraïns'koï Katolyts'koï Tserkvy: Tekst i komentar (Toronto 1974)
Popishil, V. Ex Occidente Lex: From the West – the Law: The Eastern Catholic Churches under the Tutelage of the Holy See of Rome (Carteret 1978)

Patriiarkhat (Patriarchate). An organ of the Ukrainian Patriarchal Society in the United States (formerly Society for the Promotion of the Patriarchal System in the Ukrainian Catholic Church) and, since 1977, the Ukrainian Patriarchal World Federation for Unity of Church and People. It was published in Philadelphia and New York as a quarterly from May 1967 to April 1973; since then it has appeared monthly. Until May 1978 it was called Za patriiarkhat. The magazine has been edited by S. Protsyk (1967–74), V. Pasichnyk (1974–7), and M. Haliv (since 1977). Members of the editorial board have included Z. Gil, B. Yasinsky, M. Toporovych, L. Rudnytsky, P. Zeleny, V. Kachmar, B. Klymovsky, V. Markus, L. Shankovsky, Ya. Klym, D. Kuzyk, B. Lonchyna, and M. Marunchak. The magazine promotes the creation of a Ukrainian Catholic patriarchate and contains articles on religious and theological issues and on the persecution and state of the church in Ukraine, documents, a chronicle of events, organizational news and information, and biographies of religious figures.

Patriot Bat'kivshchyny (Patriot of the Fatherland). A weekly organ of the *Voluntary Society for Assistance to the Army, Air Force, and Navy of the Ukrainian SSR (DTSAAF), published in Kiev from January 1959. It reported on the Ukrainian and all-Union activities of the DTSAAF, promoted knowledge of military affairs and developments, and devoted special attention to promoting Soviet patriotism and communist ideology.

Patronage (patronat). The right or practice that allows the founder (ktytor) or overseer of a church, monastery, or other religious institution to nominate a clergyman to fill a vacant position. In the Byzantine church it included the right of the founder to use church property, and this form of patronage was adopted by the early Ukrainian church. In the Polish-Lithuanian Commonwealth, patronage developed parallel to changes in the Roman Catholic church and became, under Casimir Jagiellończyk, a system for passing on 'church wealth.' Magnates and civil officials began interfering in the spiritual as well as the legal and administrative affairs of churches and monasteries. The appointment of Yosyf I *Bolharynovych as metropolitan of Kiev by Grand Duke Alexander in 1498 was a particularly blatant example of patronage. Subsequently Polish kings reserved the right to appoint metropolitans, bishops, archimandrites, and other church officials in crown territories; magnates and landowners had the same right on their own estates. The practice often led to abuses, as individuals not suited to the vocation were appointed to prominent positions, and members of the aristocracy monopolized almost all the higher positions in the church. Magnates in some areas (eg, Peremyshl) even forbade the appointment of anyone from outside their voivodeship or territory. The various forms of patronage were of some benefit to the church as long as the patrons were of 'Rus' faith,' but with the Polonization of much of the aristocracy and their conversion to Roman Catholicism or Protestantism, their activities frequently came into conflict with the interests of the Orthodox or Uniate churches and the people. Throughout the 16th century patronage degenerated to the point that it involved the virtual sale of bishoprics and other important posts, the acquisition of church estates and churches themselves by the aristocracy, the purchase of priesthoods and churches for various priestly families, and the trade and leasing of shrines and cemeteries. The church struggled against the abuse of patronage through various decrees issued at synods and through edicts issued by the king, but these measures (particularly in the 17th and 18th centuries) proved to be in vain. The Vatican protested against the abuses in the Catholic church, and the Orthodox church in Right-Bank Ukraine appointed *tytari* (sextons) who oversaw the use of church property (but only in free communities). Under Catherine II all church property in the Russian Empire was confiscated, and the clergy was considered to be in the state service. In the Austro-Hungarian Empire, Joseph II nationalized the monasteries in 1782 and transformed the clergy into state employees, paid out of the *religious fund. Patronage was limited to the appointment of parish priests from a list approved by the church administration, and to the conferring of places of honor at services. In more recent times the right of patronage has, for all practical purposes, ceased to exist.

I. Patrylo

Patrons of Agricultural Associations (Patronat khliborobskykh spilok). A body created in 1899 to organize and oversee *Raiffeisen credit co-operatives in Galicia. The body was established by the Galician Diet, which provided credit from government funds. The main organizer of the association was a Pole, F. Stefczyk. Ukrainian leaders, such as D. Savchak, K. Levytsky, and K. Pankivsky, initially supported it. Under Stefczyk, however, the Patrons favored the development of credit co-operatives in Polish localities and encouraged Polish control of co-operatives in Ukrainian localities. Ukrainians reacted to that policy by establishing the *Audit Union of Ukrainian Co-operatives to promote an independent Ukrainian co-operative movement. In 1912 there were 1,575 Raiffeisen co-

operatives in Galicia, some 400 of which were Ukrainian. The Patrons published *Chasopys dlia spilok ril'nychykh* (1904–21) for Ukrainians. The Raiffeisen co-operatives continued to operate through the interwar period, but their role was limited to offering long-term farm credit.

Patronymic. A secondary name derived from the name of a father or ancestor usually by the addition of a suffix or prefix indicating descent. In Ukrainian the suffix is -*Ovych* for men and -*ivna* for women: Ivan Ivanovych is Ivan, the son of Ivan; and Lesia Petrivna is Lesia, the daughter of Petro. The patronymic appears in Rus' chronicles and in *Slovo o polku Ihorevi* (The Tale of Ihor's Campaign). Later, in 16th- and 17th-century documents and incunabula, it stands alongside the surname. In the Cossack period it was often used; according to V. Lypynsky its use without the surname during B. Khmelnytsky's reign had a conspiratorial purpose. The use of the patronymic has been preserved by Ukrainians within the Russian Empire and Soviet Ukraine as a result of Russification. In Western Ukraine, which was more accessible to Western influences, the practice had disappeared by the 19th century.

Patrus-Karpatsky, Andrii [Patrus-Karpats'kyj, Andrij] (pseud of Andrii Patrus), b 29 March 1917 in Tereblia, near Tiachiv, Transcarpathia, d 29 April 1980 in Kiev. Transcarpathian poet. He debuted as a poet in 1934 in Sovietophile Russian-language periodicals in Transcarpathia. In the Carpatho-Ukrainian state of 1938–9 he published his first Ukrainian collection, *Ridnyi krai klyche* (The Native Land Calls, 1938), contributed to the nationalist paper *Nova svoboda*, and belonged to the writers' and artists' group Hoverlia. He fled from Hungarian rule to the USSR in 1939 and returned to Transcarpathia after the Second World War, where he wrote many collections of socialist-realist verse in Ukrainian.

Protoarchimandrite Isydor Patrylo

Patrylo, Isydor, b 30 November 1919 in Zahorody, Mostyska county, Galicia. Catholic priest, Basilian monk, and church historian; a full member of the Shevchenko Scientific Society since 1979 and of the Ukrainian Theological Scholarly Society. He entered the Basilian order in 1933 and studied at Basilian schools in Lavriv, Dobromyl, and Krystynopil (now Chervonohrad, 1935–41). He then studied at Charles University and the Ukrainian Free University in Prague (1942–4), where he completed a PH D dissertation on pedagogy in the Kievan Mohyla Academy. He later obtained doctorates in theology from the Pontifical Angelicum University (1953) and in canon law from the Pontifical Lateran University (1961) in Rome.

He was ordained in 1943 and he served in parishes in Peremyshl (1944), Münster (1944–8), Leeds (1948–9), and various places in Argentina (1949–52, 1953–5). He was summoned to Rome and became director of the Ukrainian section of Vatican Radio (1952–3). He then joined the central administration of the Basilian order in Rome (1955), where he has served as treasurer (1955–62), general secretary (1962–76), and protoarchimandrite of the order (since 1976) and director of its publishing house (since 1962). He was a member of the editorial commission that prepared a Ukrainian translation of the Bible (1957–63); a consultant to the Congregation for Eastern Churches; and head of its Liturgical Commission, which is preparing translations of several liturgical books.

Patrylo is the author of a number of works in Ukrainian church history, including *Dzherela i bibliohrafiia istoriï Ukraïns'koï Tserkvy* (Sources and Bibliography on the History of the Ukrainian Church, 1975–88), *Archiepiscopi-Metropolitani Kievo-Halicienses* (1962), 'Narys istoriï Halyts'koï Provintsiï Vasyliians'koho Chynu' (An Outline History of the Galician Province of the Basilian Order, *ZChVV*, 1982), and 'Narys istoriï Vasyliian vid 1743 do 1839 r.' (An Outline History of the Basilians from 1743 to 1839, *ZChVV*, 1988).

W. Lencyk

Patslavsky, Viktor [Paclavs'kyj], b 1884 in Brody, Galicia, d 31 December 1974 in Yonkers, New York. Lawyer and civic activist. A graduate of Lviv University (LLD, 1909), he established a law office in Drohobych in 1919 and was active in many local organizations, including the Ridna Shkola society, the Lysenko Music Society, and the Boian choir. He was counsel of the wealthy Christian Hromada in Boryslav and an adviser to the Pidoima society of oil-well owners. In politics he was a supporter of the Ukrainian National Democratic Alliance. After emigrating to the United States he taught at a Ukrainian school and ran a music studio of the Ukrainian Music Institute of America.

Patyk, Volodymyr, b 9 October 1929 in Chornyi Ostriv, Bibrka county, Galicia. Painter and muralist. A graduate

Volodymyr Patyk: *Autumn in the Hutsul Region* (oil, 1984)

of the Lviv Institute of Applied and Decorative Arts (1953), he has worked in Lviv. In the 1960s he incorporated ethnographic themes and elements into paintings such as *Korovai* (1964) and *Girl from Bukovyna* (1966). Although most of his work is figurative, he has painted several canvases using Easter egg symbols as the basis of the compositions. Patyk is best known for his expressionist landscapes painted energetically in brilliant, high-intensity colors that convey his emotional response to nature and love of his homeland. *The Green Carpathians* (1970) and *Autumn in the Carpathians* (1986) are examples of the many paintings of the Carpathian Mountains created by the artist. Patyk has also painted thematic canvases, such as *Dovbush – Our Glory* (1967) and the funereal *The Last Journey* (1987), in which he used a dark, brooding palette in keeping with the subject.

Paul I (Pavel Petrovich), b 1 October 1754 in St Petersburg, d 23 March 1801 in St Petersburg. Russian emperor from 1796 to 1801; son of *Peter III and *Catherine II and father of *Alexander I. During his reign Paul facilitated the expansion of gentry landownership in Ukraine, where he gave hundreds of thousands of desiatins and some 150,000 state peasants to the gentry and, in December 1796, enserfed the hitherto free peasantry in Southern Ukraine. At the same time he limited corvée to three days a week and forbade the sale of household serfs and the breakup of peasant families. Paul reversed many of Catherine's reforms. In Ukraine he replaced the vicegerencies with gubernias, partially restored the *court system that had existed in the Hetmanate in 1760–70, and put an end to the persecution of the Uniate church. He also, however, increased bureaucratic control in local government, restricted the political and taxation privileges of the nobility, and introduced a brutal police regime, harsh discipline in the army, strict censorship, and the persecution of all and any free thinkers. As a result there was widespread popular discontent. Many peasant rebellions erupted, which were especially violent in the Ukrainian and neighboring Russian gubernias in 1798, and army officers and members of the nobility organized a number of conspiracies, notably the 'Smolensk conspiracy' of 1798, in which Ukrainians took part, and the guard regiments' conspiracy of 1800–1. During Paul's reign highly placed Ukrainians, such as Prince O. *Bezborodko, D. Troshchynsky, V. Kochubei, and A. and I. Hudovych, were influential in government. Paul was assassinated by disgruntled nobles.

BIBLIOGRAPHY
Ragsdale, H. (ed). *Paul I: A Reassessment of His Life and Reign* (Pittsburgh 1979)

O. Ohloblyn

Paul of Aleppo, b ca 1627 in Aleppo, Syria, d ca 1669. Syrian archdeacon, traveler, and writer. He accompanied his father, Patriarch *Makarios III of Antioch, on a journey from Aleppo to Istanbul, Wallachia, Moldavia, Ukraine, and Muscovy in 1652–9. Paul's journal of the journey provides valuable eyewitness details about the history, geography, culture, folkways, architecture, and religious life of the indigenous population. In Ukraine their route went from Rashkiv on the Dniester (10 June 1654) to Zhabokrychi, Uman, Lysianka, Bohuslav (where they met with Hetman B. Khmelnytsky on 21 June 1654), Trypilia, Vasylkiv,

Kiev (26 June to 10 July; there Paul visited the Kievan Cave Monastery and St Sophia Cathedral), Pryluka, and Putyvl (20 July 1654). The journey home is described in less detail. On their way back from their long stay in Muscovy (July 1654 to 28 May 1656) the travelers passed through Putyvl, Kiev, Boryspil, Pereiaslav, Cherkasy, Chyhyryn (where Khmelnytsky visited Makarios on 2 August 1656), Medvedivka, Zhabotyn, and Smila before arriving in Iaşi on 21 August 1656. Paul described Ukraine as a highly cultured land: 'In the entire land of the Ruthenians, that is, the Cossacks [Paul referred to the Russians as Muscovites], we noticed something strange but wonderful: all of them, with minor exceptions, even the majority of wives and daughters, know how to read and know the order of the church services and church songs.'

The original text of Paul's account is not extant, but several partial and complete Arabic manuscript copies have survived. The most complete copy is preserved at the National Library in Paris. Extracts from the account were freely condensed and translated into English by F.C. Belfour as *The Travels of Macarius, Patriarch of Antioch, Written by His Attendant Archdeacon, Paul of Aleppo* (2 vols, 1829, 1836; a selected version was published in 1936 and reprinted in 1971). A fuller Russian translation was done by G. Murkos and published in Moscow (4 vols, 1896–1900). B. Radu's French translation of the account was published in *Patrologia Orientalis* (vols 22 [1930], 24–5 [1933–4], 26 [1949]).

BIBLIOGRAPHY

Murkos, G. *Arabskaia rukopis' Puteshestviia Antiokhiiskago patriarkha Makariia v Rossii v polovine XVII veka* (Moscow 1899)

Kordt, V. *Chuzhozemni podorozhni po Skhidnii Evropi do 1700 r.* (Kiev 1926)

Radu, B. *Voyage du patriarche Macaire: Etude préliminaire* (Paris 1927)

Kowalska, M. *Ukraina w połowie XVII wieku w relacji arabskiego podróżnika Pawła, syna Makarego z Aleppo: Wstęp, przekład, komentarz* (Warsaw 1986)

A. Zhukovsky

Pauli, Żegota, b 1 July 1814 in Nowy Sącz, Galicia, d 21 October 1895 in Cracow. Polish ethnographer and historian. As a student at Lviv University in the 1830s he was acquainted with members of the Ruthenian Triad and collected folk songs. In 1838 he published a collection of Polish folk songs and then the two-volume *Pieśni ludu ruskiego w Galicji* (Songs of the Ruthenian People in Galicia, 1839–40). The Ukrainian song collection contained ritual and historical songs in the first volume and lyrical songs, dance songs, and *kolomyiky* in the second. From 1844 he worked at the Jagiellonian Library in Cracow.

Pauls, John (pseuds: Ivan Sydoruk, John Sydoruk), b 28 April 1916 in Pavlopol, Kobryn county, Polisia. Emigré Slavist; member of the Shevchenko Scientific Society. He graduated from Warsaw University (1939) and the Ukrainian Free University (PHD, 1947) and taught at the University of Cincinnati (1959–81). He wrote the booklets *Ideology of Cyrillo-Methodians and Its Origin* (1954) and *Pushkin's 'Poltava'* (1962), and articles on I. Mazepa in literature and art, I. Franko, J. Herder and the Slavs, Polisian folk songs and wedding rituals, the Ukrainian-Belarusian linguistic boundary, and Russian-Ukrainian literary relations, in serials such as *Slavistyka*, *Zapysky NTSh*, *Ukrainian Review*, and *Ukrainian Quarterly*.

Paventsky, Antin [Pavenc'kyj], b 24 November 1818 in Nyzhniv, Tovmach county, Stanyslaviv circle, Galicia, d 6 April 1889 in Lviv. Journalist. He graduated from Lviv University and became a member of the Stauropegion Institute. He was the first editor of *Zoria halytska* (1848–50). Frustrated with the Austrian authorities and the Supreme Ruthenian Council, he resigned and worked as a court official and a notary public (1858). In 1861 he was elected to the Galician provincial diet as a representative of Rava Ruska county.

Pavlenko, Nina, b 29 April 1932 in Cherevky, Yahotyn raion, Kiev oblast. Banduryst. After graduating from the Kiev Conservatory in 1958, she joined the Kiev Philharmonic. In 1961 she formed a banduryst trio with V. Tretiakov and N. Moskvyn, which performs Ukrainian folk songs, works by Ukrainian and foreign composers, and folk music of various nations.

Oksana Pavlenko: *Self-Portrait* (oil, 1968) Gen Viktor Pavlenko

Pavlenko, Oksana, b 30 January 1895 in Valiava, Cherkasy county, Kiev gubernia, d 25 April 1991 in Moscow. Painter. She studied at the Ukrainian State Academy of Arts under F. *Krychevsky (1917) and in M. *Boichuk's Workshop of Monumental Painting at the Kiev Institute of Plastic Arts (1918–22). In 1919 she was part of M. Boichuk's team that decorated the Lutske regimental army barracks in Kiev. While teaching painting, drawing, and ceramics at the Mezhyhiria Tekhnikum (1923–9) she painted the frescoes there, titled *Consultation in the Village* (1925). She taught in the ceramics faculty of the Moscow Higher State Artistic and Technical Institute (1929–31) and, with M. Boichuk, V. Sedliar, and I. Padalka, painted the frescoes, later destroyed, in the Chervonozavodskyi Theater in Kharkiv (1933–5). Although Pavlenko continued painting her style became more naturalistic and lost the attributes typical of the Boichuk school.

Pavlenko, Paraskeviia, b 19 January 1881 in Petrykivka, Novomoskovske county, Katerynoslav gubernia, d 30 May 1983 in Kiev. Master of *Petrykivka painting; mother of H. *Pavlenko-Chernychenko. She painted decorative designs on paper and walls, including works such as *Decorative Motif* (1964), *Frieze* (1964), and *Flower Bouquet in a Vase* (1980).

Pavlenko, Viktor, b 1888, d 1932 in the Kuban. Senior aviation officer. During the First World War he served as a regular aviation officer in the Russian army. In 1917 he was a member of the Central Rada and the Ukrainian General Military Committee, and a delegate to the First All-Ukrainian Military Congress. In November–December 1917 he commanded the Kiev Military District, and in 1918 he served in staff positions. For almost two years (December 1918–November 1920) he was chief of aviation in the UNR Army, during which time he was promoted to brigadier general. In 1926 he returned to the USSR. He died during the famine.

Pavlenko, Yurii (Heorhii), b 25 March 1898 in Lebiazhe, Zmiiv county, Kharkiv gubernia, d 4 March 1970 in Kiev. Scientist in the fields of hydromechanics and the mechanics of ships; full member of the AN URSR (now ANU) from 1961. He graduated from the Leningrad Polytechnical Institute (1924) and served as a scientific adviser during the siege of Leningrad in the Second World War. He worked at the Odessa Institute of Naval Engineers (1944–58) and the ANU Institute of Hydromechanics (1958–62) and as a shipbuilding consultant in the Odessa region. His main contributions were in the fields of hydrostatics and hydrodynamics, particularly water friction on hulls, marine power plants, naval automation, and ship safety.

Pavlenko-Chernychenko, Hanna [Pavlenko-Černyčenko], b 8 December 1919 in Petrykivka, Novomoskovske county, Katerynoslav gubernia. Master of *Petrykivka painting; daughter of P. *Pavlenko. She was trained by T. *Pata and studied at the Kiev School of Folk Masters (1937–9). Since 1944 she has worked at the Kiev Experimental Ceramics and Art Plant, where she has created decorative designs for tableware, vases, and bowls. She has also painted wall panels (eg, *Blue Bird* [1970]), designed postcards and books, and made decorative prints.

Pavliuchenko, Serhii [Pavljučenko, Serhij], b 18 October 1902 in Kursk, Russia. Composer, musicologist, and pedagogue. He graduated from (1931) and then taught at (1932–47) the Leningrad Conservatory before becoming the director of the Lviv Conservatory (1947–53) and a professor at the Kiev Conservatory (1954–74). His musical works include *Preludes and Fugues* (1959) for piano, *Etudes* (1972) for chorus, and *Variations and Etudes* (1974) for voice. His musicological works include *Elementarnaia teoriia muzyki* (Elementary Music Theory, 1938), *Kratkii muzykal'nyi slovar'-spravochnik* (A Concise Music Reference Dictionary, 1950), and the reference dictionary *Muzykantu-liubiteliu* (For the Amateur Musician, 1965).

Pavliuk, Antin [Pavljuk], b 1875 in Plavanychi, Kholm county, Lublin gubernia, d 1945 in Germany. Lawyer and political leader. In 1917–18 he was a member of the Central Rada and the Kholm Gubernia Executive Committee. He served as a representative of the UNR Ministry of Justice in the Kholm, Podlachia, Polisia, and western Volhynia regions. During the Second World War he was the first chairman of the Central Kholm Committee (later known as the Kholm Relief Committee).

Pavliuk, Antin [Pavljuk], b 1899 in Volhynia, d ? Writer. From 1922 he lived in Prague, where he edited the literary

Antin Pavliuk (1875–1945)   Ilarion Pavliuk

miscellany *Sterni* (The Stubble Fields), headed the left-wing writers' group Zhovtneve Kolo, and contributed to Western Ukrainian and Soviet Ukrainian literary periodicals. Having emigrated to the USSR in 1932 as a member of the Zakhidnia Ukraina writers' group, he disappeared in the Soviet terror. He wrote several poetry collections: *Sumna radist'* (Sad Joy, 1919), *Zhyttia* (Life, 1925), *Osinni vyry* (Autumn Vortices, 1926), *Bil'* (Pain, 1926), *Pustelia liubovy* (The Wasteland of Love, 1928), *Polyn* (Wormwood, 1930), *Reliquaire* (1931), and *Vatra* (The Bonfire, 1931). He also wrote *Neznaioma (Uryvky iz zapysnyka)* (The Unknown Woman [Excerpts from a Notebook], 1922; dedicated to K. *Polishchuk) and translated the poetry of G. Apollinaire into Ukrainian and Ukrainian poetry into Russian.

Pavliuk, Ilarion [Pavljuk], b 27 May 1887 in Kolesnyky, Ostrih county, Volhynia gubernia, d ? Agronomist and political activist. After 1917, having studied and worked in Moscow, he served in several UNR administrative posts in Ostrih. He was interned by the Poles, and returned to Volhynia, where he worked as an agronomist. In 1922 he was elected to the Polish Sejm. He sat with the Ukrainian caucus but resigned in 1924 and went on to support the Ukrainian National Democratic Alliance. He was also a supporter of the Ukrainian Free Cossacks.

Pavliuk, Mykola [Pavljuk], b 19 December 1901 in Haisyn, Podilia gubernia, d 8 March 1984 in Odessa. Painter. A graduate of the Odessa Art Institute (1930), in the 1920s he was a member of the *Association of Revolutionary Art of Ukraine and a follower of M. *Boichuk. He participated in painting the murals at the Peasant Sanatorium (1929) and the Press Building (1929–30; the mural *The Tsar's Will: 1905* and fresco *Under the Tsarist Yoke*) in Odessa. In the 1930s he painted themes from Soviet history, such as in *End of the Imperialist War* (1935) and *Kotovsky at the Head of a Partisan Detachment* (1937). After the Second World War he created genre paintings, such as *Collective-Farm Agronomist* (1952) and *Family* (1970).

Pavliuk, Mykola [Pavljuk] (Pavliuc, Nicolae), b 11 December 1927 in Lunca la Tisa, Maramureş region, Rumania. Linguist and educator. After graduating from Kharkiv University (PH D, 1958) he taught Ukrainian language and literature at the University of Bucharest. In 1975 he emigrated to Canada, where he has taught Ukrainian at the University of Toronto since 1976. Author of *Limba Ucraineana: Curs practic* (Ukrainian Language:

A Practical Course, 1963) and *Curs de gramatică istorică a limbii ucrainene* (A Historical Grammar of the Ukrainian Language, 1964), he has also written over 50 articles on Ukrainian dialects, language, literature, and pedagogy, as well as other grammars and textbooks.

Pavliuk, Pavlo [Pavljuk] (Pavlo But and Pavlo Mikhnovych), b ?, d 19 April 1638 in Warsaw. Zaporozhian Cossack leader. In 1635 he participated in the Cossack rebellion led by I. *Sulyma that destroyed the Polish fortress of Kodak. In early 1637 Pavliuk led several thousand Cossacks who fought on the side of the Crimean khan Inayet-Girei against the Ottoman appointee. In the summer of 1637 he led an anti-Polish revolt of Zaporozhian Cossacks. After capturing Korsun in August, Pavliuk issued a universal exhorting the Ukrainian people to rise up, and the rebels were soon joined by large numbers of peasants from both banks of Ukraine. In December 1637 his army was routed by the Polish army at the Battle of *Kumeiky. Pavliuk was handed over to the Poles, who took him to Warsaw and had him executed despite A. *Kysil's promise to the contrary.

Ostap Pavliv-Bilozersky

Pavliv-Bilozersky, Ostap [Pavliv-Bilozers'kyj], b 1892, d 7 October 1955 in Scranton, Pennsylvania. Political and civic leader, journalist, and writer. He was a noted member of the Ukrainian Radical party and from 1922 was repeatedly elected to its secretariat. In 1925 he became secretary of the Central Council of the Union of Peasant Associations in Lviv. He was active in the Sich movement and the Union of Ukrainian Progressive Youth. From 1922 to 1928 he edited the Radical party's weekly *Hromads'kyi holos* and then a number of the magazine's monthly supplements – *Molodi kameniari* (1928–32), *Pluh i hart* (1928–9), and *Snip* (1936–7). He served several terms in Polish prisons for his political activities. After the Second World War he coedited the newspaper *Ukraïns'ke slovo* in Germany (1948–9) before emigrating to the United States in 1949. There he contributed to *Narodna volia* and *Vil'na Ukraïna*. As a writer he is known for his short stories and historical novels, including *Naperedodni* (On the Eve, 1935), *Komakha* (Insect, 1939), and *Dyiavol pohnoblenyi* (The Devil Oppressed, 2 vols, 1948). He also translated Polish, German, and Russian literature into Ukrainian.

Pavlivsky, Borys [Pavlivs'kyj], b 21 September 1906 at Podobriivka *khutir*, near Iskryskivshchyna, Sumy county, Kharkiv gubernia. Poet and journalist. From 1925 he worked as an accountant in Artemivske and began to publish verses in the paper *Kocheharka* and the journal *Zaboi*. In 1929 his poem 'Makhnovtsi' (Makhno's Men) appeared in *Novyi shliakh* in Lviv. After enrolling at the Kharkiv Institute of People's Education (1930), he came under political persecution: in 1933 he was sentenced to 5 years of hard labor, in 1939, again to 5 years, and in 1946, to 13 years of imprisonment and 5 years of exile. He returned to Ukraine in 1957, but his articles began to appear in the press only in 1991.

Pavlohrad. V-16. A city (1989 pop 131,000) on the Vovcha River and a raion center in Dnipropetrovske oblast. A settlement called Matviivka arose at the site in the 18th century. In 1779 it was renamed Luhanske, and in 1780 a fortified settlement called Pavlohrad was set up nearby. With their merger Pavlohrad became a county center of Katerynoslav vicegerency (1783–96), New Russia gubernia (1797–1802), and Katerynoslav gubernia (1802–1923). By 1896 the town had a population of 19,000. Today Pavlohrad is an important industrial center in the western Donbas. Its factories produce casting machines, bituminous concrete, food products, building materials, light fittings, leather goods, furniture, and textiles. There are 10 mines and an enrichment factory nearby.

Antin Pavlos: *Evening* (terracotta)

Pavlos, Antin [Pavlos'], b 1905 in Hostynne, Hrubeshiv county, Lublin gubernia, d 4 September 1954 in St Paul, Minnesota. Sculptor. A graduate of the Lviv Applied Arts School (1935), he began exhibiting his work in 1933 at shows organized by the Ukrainian Society of Friends of Art. In the 1930s he created small terra-cotta busts, nudes, and animal figures (mostly horses) and worked on monuments; in that genre he prepared several projects (B. Khmelnytsky, King Danylo, Prince Roman, and Hetman I. Mazepa) but completed only the gravestone of V. Matiuk.

His small nudes are among his better works. A postwar refugee in Germany, in 1949 he emigrated to the United States. In Minneapolis he created sculptures now found in Roman Catholic churches in the United States and a bas-relief of T. Shevchenko. Pavlos also painted impressionist landscapes.

Pavlov, Kapiton, b 1792 in Revel (now Tallinn), Estonia, d 1 February 1852 in Kiev. Russian painter. After studying at the St Petersburg Academy of Arts (1800–15) he settled in Ukraine and taught at the Nizhen Lyceum (1820–39) and Kiev University (1839–46). In Nizhen he taught N. Gogol, Ya. de Balmen, Ye. Hrebinka, and A. Mokrytsky. He was acquainted with T. Shevchenko and is mentioned in Shevchenko's novel *Bliznetsy* (The Twins). His work consists of portraits, such as *B. Lyzohub* (1835) and *Self-Portrait* (1830s); genre paintings, such as *Children Building a House of Cards* (1837); and landscapes, such as *The Transfiguration Church in Poltava* (1830s).

Pavlovsk (Pavlovskoe). III-21. A town (1979 pop 20,100) on the Don River and a raion center in Voronezh oblast, RF. It was founded by Zaporozhian Cossacks ca 1685, and belonged to Ostrohozke regiment. At the beginning of the 18th century Peter I fortified the town and added a shipyard. In 1779 Pavlovsk became a county center of Voronezh vicegerency, and subsequently, of Voronezh gubernia. By 1896 its population was 6,600. According to the Soviet census of 1926, Ukrainians accounted for 36.6 percent of the town's and 71.1 percent of the raion's population.

Pavlovska, Oleksandra [Pavlovs'ka], b 11 December 1928 in Kiev. Graphic artist. A graduate of the Kiev State Art Institute (1954), where she studied under V. Kasiian, I. Pleshchynsky, and S. Hryhoriev, she has designed posters and illustrated many children's books, using mostly watercolor and ink. The latter include *Koza-dereza* (Billy Goat's Bluff, 1957) and *Kyrylo Kozhumiaka* (1958). Her illustrations are reminiscent of the engravings of old Kiev masters.

Pavlovsky, Aleksandr [Pavlovskij], b 13 October 1857 in Chufarovo, Yaroslavl gubernia, Russia, d 18 October 1944 in Bessarabia. Russian bacteriologist and surgeon. A graduate of the Military Medical Academy (1881), he was a professor at Kiev University (1889–1912) and helped organize the Kiev Bacteriological Institute, where he headed the serum department (to 1909). In 1893 he advocated the preparation of anticholera serum, and in 1895 he set up the facilities to prepare and apply an antidiphtheria serum. He founded the Kiev Society for Infectious Diseases and the Kiev Pasteur Station (1894). His publications dealt with atmospheric microbiology, infectious diseases, surgical infections, and tissue cytology.

Pavlovsky, Andrii [Pavlovs'kyj, Andrij], b 19 November 1789 in Valky, Kharkiv vicegerency, d 24 January 1857 in Kharkiv. Mathematician. A graduate of Kharkiv University (1809), he taught there from 1810, was a full professor from 1826, and served as rector in 1837–8. He was noted for his work in partial differential equations, algebra, and probability theory. His most famous student was M. *Ostrohradsky.

Pavlovsky, Hryhorii [Pavlovs'kyj, Hryhorij], b 1884 in Kiev, d 1967 in the United States. Singer (bass), composer, priest, and teacher. He appeared on stage with the Sadovsky theater in Kiev and the Kiev Opera in 1910–18, and then became a member of the Ukrainian Republican Kapelle under O. Koshyts. In 1922 he moved to the United States, where he became a cofounder of and professor of singing at the short-lived Ukrainian Conservatory of Music in New York (1924–9). He had his own music school in the 1930s. A supporter of the Ukrainian Orthodox church in the USA, he edited the Philadelphia-based journal *Dnipro* during the 1940s. His compositions include a liturgical score, sacred songs, carols, and folk-song arrangements.

Pavlovsky, Ivan [Pavlovs'kyj], b 21 January 1851 in Bobrova, Kaluga gubernia, Russia, d 27 May 1922 in Poltava. Historian and archivist. A graduate of Kiev University (1874), he taught history at the Poltava Cadet Corps (1874–1913), was secretary of the Poltava Learned Archival Commission (PUAK, 1903–7), and organized and directed the Museum of the Battle of Poltava (1909–18). Over 90 of Pavlovsky's contributions were published in *Trudy Poltavskoi uchenoi arkhivnoi komissii* and *Kievskaia starina*. He wrote pioneering works on the history and culture of the Poltava region, including a biographical dictionary of scholars and writers of Poltava gubernia from the mid-18th century on (1912) and a supplement (1913); a compilation of statistical data about Poltava gubernia 100 years earlier (1906); books about the nobility of Poltava gubernia (2 vols, 1907), the 1709 Battle of Poltava and its monuments (1908), Poltava gubernia and its environs (1910), Poltava's hierarchs, statesmen, and public figures (1914), A. Kurakin as governor-general of Little Russia gubernia (1914), and Poltava's past (1918); a description of Poltava gubernia and its environs in 1810 (1917); and articles about Poltava in the 19th century (1902, 1905), the Masonic lodge in Poltava (1909), and the Decembrist movement in the Poltava region (1918). Among his many other articles are ones on the Little Russian Cossack levy en masse during the Crimean War (1910) and the Cyril and Methodius Brotherhood (1911), a biography of V. Kapnist (1915), and a description of the archives of Poltava gubernia (1915). Pavlovsky was one of the compilers of the systematic bibliographic guide and index to *Kievskaia starina* (1911) published by the PUAK.

A. Zhukovsky

Pavlovsky, Ivan [Pavlovs'kyj], b 20 May 1890 in Chernihiv county, d ca 1938. Metropolitan of the *Ukrainian Autocephalous Orthodox church (UAOC). He graduated from the Chernihiv Theological Academy in 1914 and was ordained; he then organized Ukrainian parishes in Chernihiv county (1920–1). In November 1921 he was consecrated bishop of the UAOC for Cherkasy-Chyhyryn. From December 1926 he was archbishop of Kharkiv, where he also edited the UAOC organ *Tserkva i zhyttia*. He participated in the extraordinary council of January 1930, at which the Soviet authorities dissolved the UAOC, and in the second extraordinary council of December 1930, at which the Ukrainian Orthodox Church was founded as the successor to the UAOC. At this council he was also made 'metropolitan of Kharkiv and of all Ukraine' (1930–6). When the capital of Ukraine was transferred to Kiev, he moved there. In 1936 he was arrested by the NKVD and de-

Metropolitan Ivan Pavlovsky   Metodii Pavlovsky

ported, at first to Voronezh and then to Kazakhstan, where he died.

Pavlovsky, Metodii [Pavlovs'kyj, Metodij], b 1877 in the Kiev region, d 1957. Journalist and co-operative and civic leader; brother of H. *Pavlovsky. He was secretary (1906) of the newspaper *Hromads'ka dumka* and editor (1907–13) of the daily *Rada* in Kiev, to which he contributed theater and music reviews under various pseudonyms. He compiled and published a collection of Ukrainian folk songs under the pseudonym M. Lisovytsky.

Pavlovsky, Oleksander [Pavlovs'kyj], b 27 June 1927 in Zaporizhia. Experimental physicist; corresponding member of the AN URSR (now ANU) since 1979. A graduate of Kharkiv University (1950), he is a specialist in physics of high energy densities and has major achievements in the development of high-intensity neutron sources, high-current accelerators, and hyperstrong impulsive magnetic fields.

Pavlovsky, Oleksii [Pavlovs'kyj, Oleksij], b 1773 in Shutivka (now Sosnivka), near Hlukhiv, Nizhen regiment, d after 1822. Ukrainian philologist. A graduate of the Kievan Mohyla Academy (1789) and the St Petersburg Teachers' Seminary (1793), he had ties with the *Novhorod-Siverskyi patriotic circle and probably worked in the civil service under Prince O. Bezborodko in St Petersburg. In the 1790s he began writing a survey of the Ukrainian language. Completed in 1805 and published in St Petersburg in 1818 as a 114-page 'grammar' of the 'Little Russian dialect,' it was the first work describing the basic phonetics and morphology of vernacular Ukrainian based on the northern Left-Bank dialects. It was also the first work to render the voiced *i* in a phonetic orthography as the letter 'i', and provided a valuable dictionary of 1,130 words and phrases taken from proverbs, maxims, and poetic works. Its description of the Ukrainian people and their history, language, and literature linked the ideas in *Istoriia Rusov* with those of Ukrainian pre-Romanticism. In 1822 Pavlovsky published a brochure in reply to N. Tsertelev's review of his book.

BIBLIOGRAPHY
Shevel'ov Iu. "'Hramatyka", shcho nalezhyt' do istoriï literatury,' *Slovo: Zbirnyk*, 2 (New York 1964)
Nimchuk, V. (ed.) *Z istoriï ukraïns'koï movy: Do 150-richchia 'Gramatiki' O. Pavlovs'koho* (Kiev 1972)

Pavlovsky, Teoktyst [Pavlovs'kyj], b 1706 in Liutenka, Hadiache regiment, d 28 November 1744. Painter. A graduate of the Kievan Mohyla Academy, he worked from 1730 under I. Maksymovych at the *Kievan Cave Monastery Icon Painting Studio. Eventually he took monastic vows and was appointed director of the studio. He took part in painting the icons in the monastery's Dormition Cathedral and St Nicholas's Cathedral (eg, the portrait of V. Vatanovych). He also painted landscapes and portraits and designed the poetic thesis of S. Kuliabka (1744, engraved in Berlin). His paintings and icon sketches have been preserved in the studio's albums.

Pavlovsky, Vadym [Pavlovs'kyj], b 4 October 1907 in Kiev, d 10 February 1986 in New York. Historian and art scholar. A chemist by profession, he emigrated to the United States after the Second World War. He contributed to *Ukraine: A Concise Encyclopaedia* (vol 2, 1971) and *Encyclopedia of Ukraine* (vols 1–2, 1984, 1988), wrote a monograph on the artist V. Krychevsky (1974), compiled a book about monuments to T. Shevchenko (1966), and coedited (with K. Tserkevych) a reference book on the Ukrainian language (1982) and a Russian-Ukrainian dictionary of legal terms (1984).

Pavlovsky, Viktor [Pavlovs'kyi], b 23 November 1893 in Ananiv, Kherson gubernia, d ? Pedagogue. A professor at the Kharkiv Institute of People's Education and a research associate at the Kharkiv Pedagogical Institute, he wrote on the planning, methodology, and organization of systematic teaching in schools. He disappeared during the terror of the mid-1930s.

Pavlovych, Oleksander [Pavlovyč] (pseud: Chernian Makovytsky) b 19 September 1819 in Šarišské Čierné (Sharyske Chorne), d 25 December 1900 in Svydnyk, in the Prešov region. Writer and cultural figure. He studied at gymnasiums in Bardejov, in the Prešov region, and Miskolc and Eger, in Hungary, and at the Trnava Catholic Seminary (1843–7). He was ordained a Uniate priest in 1848, and worked as secretary of the episcopal chancery in Prešov, where he became a close associate of O. *Dukhnovych and the *Prešov Literary Society. He then ministered in the village of Beloveža (1851–63). From 1864 until the end of his life he lived in Svydnyk. Greatly influenced by the Czech national revival and the Galician Russophiles, from the 1850s on he wrote, in the *yazychiie and later in the Transcarpathian dialect, social, patriotic, historical, and didactic poetry, which appeared in Viennese, Prešov, Uzhhorod, and Lviv miscellanies and periodicals and as the collection *Pesnik dlia makovitskoi russkoi detvy* (Songbook for Ruthenian Children in the Makovytsia [Prešov] Region, 1860). He also wrote fables and collected and published ethnographic and historical materials on the Prešov region. His collected works were published in Uzhhorod in 1942 and in Prešov in 1955. Books about him have been written by S. Voskresensky (1947) and A. Shlepetsky (1982).

Pavlovych, Petro. See Trembovetsky, Apollon.

Pavlovych, Yurii [Pavlovyč, Jurij], b 1906, d ? Scenery designer. He completed study at the Kiev State Art Institute and from 1925 worked in the Odessa Ukrainian Drama Theater, where he created scenery for I. Kocherha's

Feia hirkoho myhdaliu (The Fairy of the Bitter Almond, 1927), and the Odessa Opera and Ballet Theater. A constructivist, he was criticized for formalism, and disappeared during the Stalinist terror of the early 1930s.

Pavlusevych, Volodymyr [Pavlusevyč], b 1887, d 18 May 1958 in Cleveland, Ohio. Writer. He taught in gymnasiums in Galicia (1912–44) and in Germany (1945–50). He wrote a collection of lyrical poems, *Z pisen' kokhannia* (From Songs of Love, 1921), the plays *Amerykanka* (The American Girl, 1928) and *Dobrodii liudstva* (The Benefactor of Mankind, 1934), and the librettos to the operettas *Div–cha z Maslosoiuzu* (Girl from the Maslosoiuz, 1936) and *Sviat Vechir* (Christmas Eve, 1958), among other works.

Tymish Pavlychenko   Dmytro Pavlychko

Mykola Pavlushkov   Hryhorii Pavlutsky (portrait
                           by Fedir Krychevsky, 1922)

Pavlushkov, Mykola [Pavluškov], b 1904 in Tula, Russia, d 3 November 1937. Student activist; nephew of S. *Yefremov. In the 1920s he studied at the Kiev Institute of People's Education. At the show trial of the Union for the Liberation of Ukraine (SVU) in 1930 he was accused of organizing a Ukrainian Youth Association in 1925 and sentenced to 10 years of imprisonment. Broken during his incarceration, he offered testimony which was used to support the fabricated accusations in the SVU trial. He was subsequently shot by order of a tribunal.

Pavlutsky, Hryhorii [Pavluc'kyj, Hryhorij], b 1861 in Kiev, d 15 March 1924 in Kiev. Art scholar. A graduate of Kiev University (1886), he lectured there on the history of art (from 1888). He headed the Ukrainian Scientific Society's art history section and in the 1920s was a professor at the Ukrainian State Academy of Arts. He wrote monographs on the Corinthian order in classical architecture (1891), genre subjects in Hellenic art (1897), and the history of Ukrainian ornamentation (1927); studies on medieval churches in Ukraine in *Drevnosti Ukrainy* (Antiquities of Ukraine, 1905) and *Trudy XIV arkheologicheskago s"ezda v Chernigove* (Works of the XIV Archeological Conference in Chernihiv, 1911); and articles on Ukrainian book decoration.

Pavlychenko, Tymish [Pavlyčenko], b 7 March 1892 in Vinnytsia county, Podilia gubernia, d 5 August 1958 in Saskatoon. Botanical engineer and community leader. Pavlychenko was educated at the Ukrainian State University in Kamianets-Podilskyi (1918–19), the Husbandry

Academy in Cracow (1920–1), Prague University (1927), the University of Saskatchewan (M SC, 1932), and the University of Nebraska (PH D, 1937). In 1917–18 he was a member of the Central Rada and the Ukrainian Constituent Assembly. He left Ukraine in 1920 and emigrated to Canada in 1927; there he worked for the National Research Council of Canada (1932–8). His studies of plant root systems resulted in his appointment in 1938 as chairman of Canada's first department of plant ecology, at the University of Saskatchewan. He was the first professor of Ukrainian origin in Canada and taught the first course on the Ukrainian language in Canada, at the University of Saskatchewan in 1943. In 1948 he left the academy for private industry. An initiator and national executive member of the *Ukrainian National Federation (UNO), he served as one of that association's major ideologues. He also helped establish the *Ukrainian Cultural and Educational Centre (Oseredok) in Winnipeg and served as its president (1950–8). He headed the Representative Committee of Ukrainian Canadians from 1939 until it merged into the Ukrainian Canadian Committee (now Congress) in 1940.

Pavlychko, Dmytro [Pavlyčko], b 28 September 1929 in Stopchativ, now in Ivano-Frankivske oblast. Poet and activist of the Ukrainian renaissance in the 1980s. He graduated from the philological faculty at Lviv University (1953) and worked for the journal *Zhovten'*. From 1971 to 1978 he was editor in chief of the journal *Vsesvit*, and since 1986 he has been secretary of the *Writers' Union of the USSR and the Writers' Union of Ukraine. Since 1989 he has also been head of the Shevchenko Ukrainian Language Society. He was elected to the Supreme Soviet and in 1990 he became chairman of the Foreign Affairs Commission of the Supreme Soviet of the Ukrainian SSR. Pavlychko has published many poetry collections, including *Liubov i nenavyst'* (Love and Hate, 1953), *Pal'mova vit'* (Palm Branch, 1962), *Hranoslov* (The Edge of Words, 1968), *Sonety podil's'koï oseni* (Sonnets of a Podilia Autumn, 1973), *Poemy i prytchi* (Poems and Parables, 1986), *Vybrani virshi* (Selected Verse, 1986), and *Rubaï* (Lumberjacks, 1987). He has also published a collection of articles on literary criticism, *Magistraliamy slova* (On the Highways of the Word, 1977); scenarios for (art) film; and literature for children, such as *Zolotorohyi Olen'* (The Golden-Horned Deer, 1970), *Smerichka* (The Fir Tree, 1982), and *Pleso* (The Water Surface, 1984). He has translated from J. Martí, Kh. Botev, Hviezdoslav, and other writers. Pavlychko's poems are notable for their adherence to form, richness of vocabulary, and finely honed language, especially the sonnets (eg, 'Svitovyi sonet' [The World Sonnet, 1983]). Since the late 1980s, as an activist and publicist, Pavlychko has aided the rebirth of Ukrainian culture and the Ukrainian language and has opposed Russification.

I. Koshelivets

Pavlychko, Solomiia [Pavlyčko, Solomija], b 15 December 1958 in Lviv. Literary scholar and translator; daughter of D. *Pavlychko. Pavlychko completed her studies at Kiev University in American and Western European literature (1984). In addition to articles on American and English literature and feminism in Ukrainian scholarship and culture, she has written monographs on transcendental American poetry (1988) and on G. Byron (1989) and introductions to translations of T.S. Eliot (1989) and E. Dickinson (1991). She has translated into Ukrainian W. Golding's *Lord of the Flies* (1988), D.H. Lawrence's *Lady Chatterley's Lover* (1989), and G. *Grabowicz's study of T. Shevchenko, *The Poet as Mythmaker* (1991).

Anna Pavlyk   Mykhailo Pavlyk

Pavlyk, Anna, b 26 January 1855 in Monastyrske, Kosiv county, Galicia, d 13 October 1928 in Lviv. Civic leader and pioneer of the women's movement; sister of M. *Pavlyk. Her brother's constant helpmate, she propagated socialist ideas among the peasants of Kosiv county and was arrested for her activity several times. She also demanded equality for women. Her articles began to appear in 1881 in *Hromada*.

Pavlyk, Mykhailo (pseuds: M. Halytsky, M. Ivaniv, Khmara, M. Kolomyichuk, Maksym, Mykhailo, M. Pokutsky, M. Tkachenko), b 17 September 1853 in Monastyrske (now part of Kosiv), Kolomyia circle, Galicia, d 26 January 1915 in Lviv. Galician socialist figure and publicist; full member of the Shevchenko Scientific Society (NTSh) from 1900. He and I. *Franko became close friends as students at Lviv University. Both of them contributed to the Academic Circle's organ, *Druh* (1874–7), and both became Ukrainophile socialists under the influence of M. *Drahomanov's letters to *Druh* and the Polish-language *Praca*. Through his writings Pavlyk remained the principal Galician propagator of Drahomanov's ideas, which brought about his persecution (he was tried in court nearly 30 times), imprisonment (in 1877, 1878, 1882, 1885–6, and 1889), and ostracism. In 1876 he played a key role in

the Academic Circle's change in orientation from a Russophile to a Ukrainophile body and in the creation of an unofficial student ethnographic society in Lviv. He became involved in smuggling proscribed Ukrainian literature into the Russian Empire. With Franko he edited (1878) the socialist journal *Hromads'kyi druh* and miscellanies *Dzvin* and *Molot*, all of which outraged the conservative Galician public and were confiscated by the police. In them he published his story 'Rebenshchukova Tetiana' (Rebenshchuk's Tetiana), portraying the evils of forced marriage and peasant brutality; the antiwar, anticonscription story 'Iurko Kulykiv'; and the anticlerical, anti-Russophile novelette 'Propashchyi cholovik' (A Doomed Man).

In 1879 Pavlyk avoided a six-month prison term, which he received for writing 'Rebenshchukova Tetiana,' by fleeing to Geneva, where he worked with Drahomanov and S. Podolynsky on the journal *Hromada*. In 1882 he returned to Lviv and served his sentence. In 1887–8 he lived in Cracow, where he cataloged the library of the Polish writer J. Kraszewski. In 1889 he was the editor of the Lviv paper *Bat'kivshchyna*, but he was forced to resign over political differences. Pavlyk and Franko founded the *Ukrainian Radical party (URP) in 1890 and edited its organs *Narod* (1890–5; in 1892–4 in Kolomyia) and *Khliborob* (1891–5). Pavlyk then worked in Lviv as the first NTSh librarian (1897–1904), headed the URP (1898–1914), and edited its newspaper *Hromads'kyi holos* (1898–1903). In 1914 he was elected vice-chairman of the *Supreme Ukrainian Council in Lviv and served briefly as editor of *Dilo*.

Pavlyk devoted most of his time to editing periodicals and books and to political journalism. Most of his articles and critiques appeared in *Narod* and *Hromads'kyi holos*. He advocated humane anarcho-socialism, the separation of church and state, and national and sexual freedom and equality; and he condemned Polish domination of the Western Ukrainians, capitalist exploitation, and the reactionary Russophiles and Galician clergy, and criticized orthodox Marxists (especially their views on the national question) and the Galician populists. He wrote a book on the development of Western Ukrainian community organizations (1887); translated into Ukrainian works by G. Uspensky, N. Leskov, A. Tolstoi, and H. Ibsen, J.W. Draper's *History of the Conflict between Religion and Science*, G. Hauptmann's *Die Weber* (1898), A. Ostrovsky's *Groza* (The Storm, 1900), and W. Reymont's novel *Chłopi* (Peasants, 1909); and edited and published a jubilee compendium on Drahomanov (1896) and, in *Zhytie i slovo* (1896–7), Drahomanov's correspondence with various Galician figures. He compiled a bibliography of Franko's writings (1898); wrote scholarly articles on J. Gawatowicz (the author of the first Ukrainian intermede, 1900), and Drahomanov's study of incest (1907), a booklet on the Galician Russophiles and Ukrainophiles (1906), and two books about Drahomanov (1907, 1911); and edited publications of his own correspondence with Drahomanov (vols 2–8, 1910–12), Drahomanov's folkloristic studies (1907), and Drahomanov's correspondence with T. Okunevsky (1905) and M. Buchynsky (1910).

An edition of Pavlyk's stories was published in 1909. Soviet editions of his selected works were published in 1955, 1959 (including the first full version of his novelette about Hutsul life, 'Vykhora' [The Whirlwind]), and 1985. A book commemorating 30 years of his public activity appeared in 1905; an edition of folk songs he collected and transcribed appeared in 1974; and P. Babiak and V. Poliek's bibliography of works by and about him was published in 1986 by the Lviv Scientific Library of the AN URSR (now ANU). Books about Pavlyk have also been written by P. Yashchuk (1959), M. Denysiuk (1960), M. Manzenko (1962), and V. Kachkan (1986).

R. Senkus

Pavlyk, Mykola, b 13 April 1896 in Bushkovychi, Peremyshl county, Galicia, d 12 July 1977 in Lviv. Political activist. While working in railway shops in Peremyshl he joined the Communist Party of Western Ukraine and advanced through its ranks to the positions of secretary of its Peremyshl and Stryi district committees, member of its CC, and, finally (1930), general secretary. He was arrested in 1930 by the Polish authorities and sentenced in 1934 at the so-called Lutske Trial of 57 to an eight-year term. After the Second World War he held senior administrative positions in Lviv.

Pavlykiv, Mariia, b 1 June 1865 in Lviv, d ca 1930 in Lviv. Opera singer (dramatic soprano). After graduating from a singing school in Lviv in 1888, she performed at the Lviv Opera until 1897 (and irregularly thereafter). At the same time she appeared in Ukrainian and Polish concerts in Lviv and Cracow. Her main roles were Odarka in A. Vakhnianyn's *Kupalo*, Halka in S. Moniuszko's *Halka*, Aida in G. Verdi's *Aida*, and Marguerite in C. Gounod's *Faust*. In 1909–10 she taught voice at the Lysenko Higher Institute of Music in Lviv.

Pavlykiv, Teofil, b 1821, d 1905. Galician civic leader and Greek Catholic priest. He served as curate of the Dormition Church in Lviv and honorary canon of the metropolitan chapter. A Russophile, he was one of the leaders of the Ruthenian Council in Lviv. He was elected to the Galician Diet in 1861, 1868, and 1873.

Iryna Pavlykovska   Yuliian Pavlykovsky

Pavlykovska, Iryna [Pavlykovs'ka], b 26 February 1901 in Lviv, d 25 September 1975 in Edmonton. Civic leader; daughter of I. *Makukh and wife of Yu. *Pavlykovsky. A music teacher by vocation, she was active in various women's and educational organizations in Lviv: she was a member of the national executive of the Union of Ukrainian Women (1923–8), a founder and director of the Ukrainske Narodne Mystetstvo co-operative (1925–39), a member of the board of directors of the Ukrainska Zakhoronka society (1926–39), and a member of the national

executive of the women's section of Silskyi Hospodar (1935–9). Having left Ukraine after the Second World War, she organized and headed the Ukrainian Women's Alliance in Germany (1945–50) and served on the executive of the World Federation of Ukrainian Women's Organizations, which she helped found. After settling in Canada in 1950, she held various offices on the executive of the Ukrainian Catholic Women's League of Canada, including the presidency (1964–8).

Pavlykovsky, Yuliian [Pavlykovs'kyj, Julijan], b 20 July 1888 in Senkiv, Radekhiv county, Galicia, d 28 December 1949 in Munich. Agronomist, economist, co-operative and political leader, and journalist; full member of the Shevchenko Scientific Society from 1935; husband of I. *Pavlykovska. From 1915, after graduating in law from Lviv University and in agronomy from the Higher Agricultural School in Vienna, he worked in the Silskyi Hospodar society in Lviv as inspector, chief of economic reconstruction, organizer, president (1924–9), and vice-president. He served as chairman of the Provincial Committee for Organizing Co-operatives (1920–1), president of the Provincial Co-operative Union and the Audit Union of Ukrainian Co-operatives (1922–44), and chief director of Narodna Torhovlia (1923–39). He was also a member of the board of directors of various Ukrainian institutions, including Maslosoiuz (1926–39). As the leading organizer and ideologist of the co-operative movement in Galicia he represented Ukrainian co-operatives at international conferences and on Polish national bodies, such as the State Agricultural Council, the State Co-operative Council in Warsaw, and the Council of the Agricultural Chamber in Lviv. He was active in the National Democratic party and a member of its Popular Committee from 1917. He was also deputy leader of the Ukrainian National Democratic Alliance (1930–9), which he helped found, and as its candidate was elected to the Polish Senate in 1930 and 1935. In 1944 he emigrated to Germany, where he headed the Alliance of Ukrainian Co-operatives and taught at the Ukrainian Technical and Husbandry Institute and the Ukrainian Free University. He wrote numerous articles on agronomy, economic conditions in Galicia, the history and ideology of co-operation, and Polish agrarian policy, as well as a number of important monographs, such as *Zemel'na sprava u Skhidnii Halychyni* (The Land Issue in Eastern Galicia, 1922), *V oboroni ridnoï zemli* (In Defense of the Native Land, 1925), and *Narodnia Torhovlia na porozi druhoho stolittia* (Narodna Torhovlia at the Threshold of Its Second Century, 1936).

Pavlysh [Pavlyš]. V-14. A town smt (1986 pop 5,800) in the Omelnyk River valley in Onufriivka raion, Kirovohrad oblast. The town, which was founded at the beginning of the 17th century by peasants from Right-Bank Ukraine, was called Butivka until the 1770s. Pavlysh has a food and a building-materials industry.

Pavlyshyn, Marko [Pavlyšyn], b 7 July 1955 in Brisbane, Australia. Ukrainian literary scholar and community figure; son of R. *Pavlyshyn. He graduated from Monash University (PH D, 1983), where he has been the Mykola Zerov lecturer in Ukrainian since 1983. His articles on German and Ukrainian literature (eg, H. Hesse, E.T.A. Hoffman, A. von Chamisso, I. Kotliarevsky, T. Shevchenko, V. Vynnychenko, O. Berdnyk, P. Zahrebelny, Valerii

Marko Pavlyshyn   Bohdan Pazdrii

Shevchuk, and Ukrainian writers in Australia) have been published in Western scholarly serials and collections. Pavlyshyn is the editor of *Ukrainian Settlement in Australia* (1986), *Glasnost in Context: On the Recurrence of Liberalizations in Central and East European Literatures and Cultures* (1990), *Ukraine in the 1990s: Proceedings of the First Conference of the Association of Ukrainian Studies in Australia* (1992), and *Stus iak tekst* ([Vasyl] Stus as Text, 1992).

Pavlyshyn, Roman [Pavlyšyn], b 3 October 1922 in Chernykhiv, Ternopil county, Galicia. Architect and civic leader. In 1948, after studies in Vienna and Darmstadt, he emigrated to Australia. As director of building for the Queensland government (1969–85) he was responsible for the construction of major public buildings in Brisbane, including the Supreme Court, Parliament House, and the Queensland Cultural Centre. A cofounder (1949) and president (1951–67, 1980–2) of the Ukrainian Association of Queensland, he was also active in the Plast Ukrainian Youth Association and the Ukrainian co-operative movement.

Pavlyshyn, Stefaniia [Pavlyšyn, Stefanija], b 20 May 1930 in Kolomyia, Galicia. Musicologist. She studied at the Lviv and Kiev conservatories (doctorate in musicology, 1955) and has taught at the Lviv Conservatory since 1955 (full professor, 1983). In addition to major works about C. Ives (1979) and 20th-century music in the West (1980), she has published studies on Ukrainian composers, such as D. Sichynsky (1956), S. Liudkevych (1974), V. Sylvestrov (1989), and V. Barvinsky (1990). She has contributed to several journals in the Soviet Union and abroad and has written for radio and television.

Pavoloch [Pavoloč]. IV-10. A village (1973 pop 3,000) on the Rostavytsia River in Popilnia raion, Zhytomyr oblast. In the early 16th century it was part of O. Dashkevych's estate. By the mid-17th century it was a well-fortified stronghold and a regimental center in the Hetman state. In 1663 I. Popovych, the Pavoloch colonel, rebelled against the Poles. After the partition of Poland in 1793, Pavoloch came under Russian rule and was made part of Skvyra county in Kiev gubernia.

Pavoloch regiment. An administrative territory and military formation established in 1648 in Right-Bank Ukraine. In 1649 it became part of Bila Tserkva regiment, and in 1651 it was separated again. Its territory included

14 towns. Its most famous commander was I. Bohun. In 1674, after Right-Bank Ukraine was returned to Poland by the Treaty of Andrusovo (1667), the regiment was abolished. Many of its inhabitants resettled in Left-Bank Ukraine.

Pazdrii, Bohdan [Pazdrij], b 8 February 1904 in Nove Selo, Zbarazh county, Galicia, d 30 March 1975 in Philadelphia. Actor and stage director. He began acting in the Stanyslaviv Ukrainian Touring Theater (1926–8) and the Tobilevych Theater (1929–33) and then directed and acted in the Zahrava and Kotliarevsky theaters (1933–39), the Lesia Ukrainka Theater (1939–41), the Lviv Opera Theater (1941–4), the Ensemble of Ukrainian Actors in West Germany (1945–9), and Teatr u Piatnytsiu in Philadelphia (1950–70). His repertoire spanned over 130 roles in drama, comedy, and operetta.

Nataliia Pazuniak   Olena Pchilka

Pazuniak, Nataliia [Pazunjak, Natalija] (née Ishchuk-Shulhyn), b 24 February 1922 in Kiev. Educator and civic activist; full member of the Ukrainian Academy of Arts and Sciences since 1989. Displaced by the Second World War, she graduated in Slavic studies from the Ukrainian Free University (1949) and the University of Pennsylvania (PHD, 1956) and then taught at Manor Junior College (1956–68), the University of Pennsylvania (1963–83), and Macquarie University in Sydney, Australia. She has been active in the *World Federation of Ukrainian Women's Organizations, and in 1971–3 she served as its vice-president.

Pchela (The Bee). The Slavic title for books of quotations and parables from Christian and classical literature. Its prototypes were the *Theological Chapters* of St Maximus the Confessor and the *Sacred Parallels* of St John of Damascus, which made up a large part of the didactic anthology *Melissa* (The Bee), compiled by the Byzantine monk Anthony Melissa in the 11th century. *Melissa* was translated from Greek into Old Ukrainian at the beginning of the 13th century. *Pchely* were an abundant source of ancient aphorisms and anecdotes, many of which were incorporated into Ukrainian folklore. Later, revised copies replaced many ancient sections with original Rus' parables, proverbs, and maxims. In 1599, scholars of the Ostrih circle produced a new translation, the so-called Derman *Pchola*. The oldest extant manuscript (15th century) was published by V. Semenov in 1893, and several later Ukrainian transcriptions were published by S. Shcheglova in 1910. I. Franko used *pchela* motifs in his literary works.

Pchilka, Olena [Pčilka] (pseud of Olha Kosach), b 29 June 1849 in Hadiache, Poltava gubernia, d 4 October 1930 in Kiev. Writer, community leader, and ethnographer; mother of Lesia *Ukrainka and sister of M. Drahomanov; corresponding member of the All-Ukrainian Academy of Sciences from 1925. She recorded songs, folk rituals, and customs and collected folk embroideries in Volhynia. She published her research as *Ukraïns'kyi ornament* (Ukrainian Ornamentation, 1876). She also funded the publication of S. Rudansky's *Spivomovky* (Singing Rhymes, 1880). In 1883 Pchilka began to publish her own verse and short stories in the Lviv journal *Zoria*. Her first collection was titled *Dumky – merezhanky* (Thoughts – Embroideries, 1886). Pchilka was also an active participant in the women's movement, who edited and published, with N. Kobrynska, the first feminist almanac, *Pershyi vinok* (The First Wreath, 1887). In the 1890s Pchilka lived in Kiev, and from 1906 to 1914 she was editor and publisher of the journal *Ridnyi krai* and the *Moloda Ukraïna* supplement (1908–14). Besides her many poems, tales, and stories for children Pchilka wrote numerous plays: *Vesnianyi ranok Tarasovyi* (Taras's Spring Morning, 1914), *Kazka zelenoho haiu* (The Tale of the Green Wood, 1914), *Shchaslyvyi den' Tarasyka Kravchenka* (Little Taras Kravchenko's Lucky Day, 1920), *Skarb* (The Treasure, 1921), *Myr myrom* (Peace through Peace, 1921), *Kobzarevi dity* (The Kobzar's Children), and others. Pchilka translated and reworked many classics of world literature, by Ovid, A. Mickiewicz, A. Pushkin, J.W. von Goethe, N. Gogol, H.C. Andersen, and V. Hugo. She also wrote publicistic prose, essays of literary criticism, biographies, and an autobiography: *M.P. Savyts'kyi* (1904), *Marko Kropyvnyts'kyi iako artyst i avtor* (Marko Kropyvnytsky as Actor and Author, 1910), *Ievhen Hrebinka i ioho chas* (Yevhen Hrebinka and His Times, 1912), *Mykola Lysenko* (1913), *Spohady pro Mykhaila Drahomanova* (Recollections about Mykhailo Drahomanov, 1926), and *Avtobiohrafiia* (Autobiography, 1930). Pchilka's most significant works in ethnography and folklore are *Ukraïns'ki uzory* (Ukrainian Ornamental Designs, 1912, 1927), *Pro legendy i pisni* (About Legends and Songs), and *Ukraïns'ki selians'ki maliuvannia na stinakh* (Ukrainian Peasant Wall Paintings). Her collected works have been published as *Opovidannia* (Stories, 3 vols, 1907, 1909, 1911) and *Opovidannia* (Stories, including her autobiography, 1930).

P. Odarchenko

Pchilka (Little Bee). A popular children's magazine in interwar Transcarpathia. It was published and edited by P. Kukuruza in Uzhhorod as a supplement to the beekeeping magazine *Podkarpats'ke pcholiarstvo* from July 1922 to August 1923, and independently from September 1923 to June 1932. Its circulation grew from 1,000 in 1922 to 2,500 in 1925 and 5,000 in 1930. The Provincial School Board paid for subscriptions for all schools in Transcarpathia. Among the contributors were prominent Transcarpathian and émigré writers and figures. Illustrations were provided by well-known artists, such as Y. Bokshai, M. Butovych, M. Krychevsky, V. Tsymbal, and Yu. Vovk. *Pchilka* also published a library of children's books by authors such as S. Cherkasenko, M. Levytsky, and V. O'Connor-Vilinska.

Pchola (Bee). The first Ukrainian literary and scholarly journal published in Galicia. Nineteen weekly issues appeared in the Galician dialect and in the *yazychiie* in Lviv between 7 May and 3 September 1849. The editor and publisher was I. Hushalevych. Among the contributors were Ya. Holovatsky, B. Didytsky, Y. Lozynsky, I. Naumovych, A. Petrushevych, and A. Mohylnytsky.

Pea (Ukrainian: *horokh*). A number of herbaceous annuals of the Fabaceae family, grown for their edible seeds. The favorite market pea in Ukraine is a variety of the *Pisum sativum*. Peas contain starch (20–48 percent), sugar (4–10 percent), fat, cellulose, carotene, vitamins B_1, B_2, C, and other nutrients. They are consumed fresh, cooked, and canned, dried and used in soup, and sometimes ground into flour. In Ukraine they are also used extensively as feed. Average yields are 18–25 centners per ha, but in some regions yields reach 30–40 centners per ha. The area devoted to peas in the Ukrainian SSR rose from 358,000 ha in 1940 to 419,000 in 1960, had more than doubled (975,000 ha) by 1970, and then increased slowly to 1,033,000 ha in 1980 and 1,438,000 ha in 1987.

Peace movement. The peace movement before and during the First World War was led by the social democratic workers' movement. Prior to 1914 it was confined largely to declarations opposing war by international socialist congresses, in which the main workers' parties active in Ukraine took part. When the war broke out, however, and patriotic fervor swept the cities of the Russian Empire, the Menshevik wing of the Russian Social Democratic Workers' party and a majority of the Jewish General Workers' Bund backed the imperial war effort and took a leading role in the government's war production committees. For their declaration in the Russian State Duma opposing Russia's entry into the war, five Bolshevik deputies were arrested and exiled to Siberia.

A majority of the Ukrainian Social Democratic Workers' party (USDRP) opposed the war. The newspaper *Borot'ba*, published in Geneva by L. Yurkevych, declared that 'the main task facing Ukrainian Social Democracy is anti-war propaganda.' At the end of 1916, members of the party active in Katerynoslav attempted unsuccessfully to mount a general strike against the government's war effort. S. Petliura was the only notable USDRP leader to declare support for the war effort, which he did in the Moscow newspaper *Ukrainskaia zhizn'*.

Following widespread initial enthusiasm for the war, pacifist sentiments emerged in 1915, when the Russian army invaded Galicia, and grew stronger in 1916, as the death toll at the front mounted. Such sentiments were most evident in the army, where Ukrainian soldiers voiced demands for an end to the war and their reorganization into separate Ukrainian regiments committed solely to the defense of their national territory.

All the soldiers', peasants', and workers' congresses in 1917 that supported the Central Rada called for an end to the war without indemnities or annexations. The more the Rada acquired authority as a provisional government in the Ukrainian gubernias of the former Russian Empire, the more it faced demands from its supporters to sue for a separate peace with the Central Powers. The Rada's failure to do so immediately upon seizing power in Kiev in October explains in part its subsequent failure to withstand the first Bolshevik military offensive from Russia in January 1918.

There was no peace movement during the interwar period, either in Soviet Ukraine or the Ukrainian territories under Polish rule. The widespread economic ruin and war weariness across Europe that resulted from the First World War temporarily removed the prospect of new international hostilities. In the 1930s, however, when Germany rearmed under the Nazis, the Soviet Union's leaders sought to avert war by mobilizing an antifascist movement through the Comintern, by diplomatic means in the League of Nations, and eventually by concluding the *Molotov-Ribbentrop Pact with Nazi Germany.

The Stalinist terror of the 1930s prevented any independent peace movement from emerging in Soviet Ukraine. The evidence of the terror, the purges, and the 1932–3 man-made famine destroyed practically all desire on the part of Western Ukrainians under Polish rule to support the Soviet government's diplomatic efforts at averting war. And given the failure of the League of Nations to defend Ukrainian cultural autonomy in Poland, in the late 1930s a significant proportion of Western Ukrainian young people viewed the prospect of another war favorably, as an opportunity to throw off their national oppression.

Only since the end of the Second World War has a movement dedicated solely to the preservation of peace emerged in Ukraine. The years 1945–90 were dominated by sustained periods of cold war between the superpowers, a rapid buildup of nuclear arsenals on both sides, and the maintenance of peace through a balance of terror based on parity in destructive military capabilities.

An important part of the Soviet government's strategy with respect to the threat of renewed international conflict was to sponsor a peace movement in the Soviet Union and abroad that supported its policy on disarmament. In August 1949 a Soviet Peace Committee was founded in Moscow to co-ordinate all government-approved peace actions across the Soviet Union. Its Ukrainian branch, the Ukrainian Republican Peace Committee (URPC), was founded in September 1951. The URPC built up a sizable membership, raised funds (often through direct deductions from workers' pay packets), staged demonstrations to support the government's diplomatic initiatives, and hosted visits to the republic by member organizations of the World Peace Council, the umbrella organization of the international pro-Soviet peace movement. It did not, however, express criticism of the postwar Soviet military buildup, which was particularly rapid during the years under L. Brezhnev, or of the military interventions in Hungary in 1956, Czechoslovakia in 1968, and Afghanistan in 1979.

Several independent peace initiatives and actions occurred in Ukraine during the 1980s. They included the establishment in Odessa, Lviv, and Rivne of the Groups to Establish Trust between the USA and USSR. Formed in 1982, the Odessa Trust Group called for the Black Sea to be turned into a sea of trust and for Odessa oblast to be declared a nuclear-free zone jointly with the US state of Maryland. The Lviv Trust Group, established by young workers and students, organized demonstrations and issued declarations in support of disarmament by the USSR and the United States, against the war in Afghanistan, and against US military intervention in Central America. The independent Ukrainian Peace Committee, which was

founded in 1987 in London, England, and campaigned throughout Europe for a nuclear-free Ukraine, was designated the external representative of the Lviv Trust Group. In May 1988 a Trust Group was formed in Rivne.

Independent peace initiatives came also from the unregistered Christian congregations. The proscribed Ukrainian Catholic church declared its opposition to the war in Afghanistan in 1984. Young Pentecostals, Baptists, and Jehovah's Witnesses refused conscription on the grounds of conscientious objection. Widespread discontent over the deaths of Soviet soldiers in Afghanistan strengthened the general sentiment in favor of peace in Ukraine throughout the 1980s.

M. Bojcun

Peach (*Prunus persica*; Ukrainian: *persyk, broskvyna*). A fruit tree of the family Rosaceae, native to China. The most widely cultivated variety is the common peach (*P. persica vulgaris*), which grows to about 8 m high. The fruit contains 6–14 percent sugar, 0.5–1.2 percent pectins, and 0.08–1.02 percent acids such as malic, tartaric, and citric acid, as well as vitamin C and carotene. In Ukraine peaches are grown primarily in the south, although several northern varieties were developed – Kiev Early, Kiev Earliest, and Kiev Famous. The average peach tree grown in Ukraine yields 40 kg of fruit; in the Crimea some trees produce up to 100 kg. Fuzzy peaches are considered to be true peaches; peaches with smooth skin are properly nectarines, almost unknown in Ukraine.

Peanut (*Arachis hypogaea*; Ukrainian: *zemlianyi horikh, arakhis*). An annual *oil plant of the family Fabaceae. Native to South America, peanuts were first grown in Ukraine at the Odessa Botanical Garden in 1792. They were introduced for wide-scale cultivation in the 1920s in Zaporizhia, Dnipropetrovske, Odessa, and Kherson oblasts. Recently peanut production in Ukraine has declined (see *Vegetable-oil industry) and given way to imported peanuts from Africa and Asia.

Pear (*Pyrus communis*; Ukrainian: *hrusha*). A fruit tree of the family Rosaceae. In Ukraine it grows wild and in cultivation. Pear fruit contains 6–15 percent sugars, 0.6 percent organic acids, and vitamins A, B, and C. It is consumed fresh, dried, canned, and in marmalades, preserves, and liqueurs. In Ukraine 200–400 kg of pears can be obtained from a single tree. Several Ukrainian varieties have been developed and popularized. Pear wood is hard and strong; it is used in the manufacture of furniture, musical instruments, and milled-wood articles.

Peasant Association (Selianska spilka or Ukrainska selianska spilka). An economic-professional organization of the nationally conscious Ukrainian peasantry, established in Ukraine in April 1917 through the efforts of the *Ukrainian Party of Socialist Revolutionaries (UPSR) and politically dominated by it. The association was initially led by M. *Stasiuk. Organized democratically into village, rural district, county, gubernia, and all-Ukrainian committees, it acted as the mouthpiece of the Ukrainian peasantry and officially supported the Central Rada. The co-operative daily *Narodnia volia served as its national organ, and regional papers were published by it in Kiev, Poltava, Podilia, Chernihiv, and Katerynoslav gubernias. The association was particularly strong in Kiev and Poltava gubernias. The April 1917 congress of its members in Poltava gubernia was the first manifestation by peasants demanding that the Russian Provisional Government recognize Ukraine's national rights. The May 1917 congress of its members in Kiev gubernia called for Ukrainian autonomy, the creation of a national parliament, and Ukrainianization of the army. The association organized and conducted the First (June 1917) and the secret Second (May 1918) *All-Ukrainian peasant congresses, controlled the *All-Ukrainian Council of Peasants' Deputies, and through the latter influenced the actions and decisions of the Central Rada and its cabinet, the General Secretariat (renamed the UNR Council of Ministers). Its representatives in the Rada pushed for the nationalization of land privately owned by the state, church, and gentry and its public distribution among individual farmers. The association advanced its own candidates in the November–December 1917 elections to the Constituent Assembly of Ukraine, often jointly with the UPSR. It did not recognize the authority of the Hetman government after April 1918. After the May 1918 split in the UPSR the association sided with the centrist faction led by N. Hryhoriv against the left faction of the Borotbists. It had three representatives in the Ukrainian National Union that co-ordinated opposition to the Hetman government and the November 1918 uprising against it. In the Directory of the UNR that subsequently took power it was represented by F. Shvets. At that time the association was headed by O. Yanko, who was also in charge of the UPSR Organizational Bureau.

Peasant community. See *Hromada*, *Obshchina*, and *Verv*.

Peasant house. See Folk architecture.

Peasant Land Bank (Selianskyi pozemelnyi bank). A state mortgage bank in the Russian Empire, established in 1882 with capital from the State Bank to provide peasants with loans for purchasing land from the gentry. Branches had been established in every Ukrainian gubernia by the end of 1885. Initially almost all loans were made to peasant communes or co-operatives, which purchased the land jointly. Annual repayments of principal and interest varied from 7.5 to 8.5 percent of the original loan (by comparison, annual repayments by nobles to the analogous Noble Land Bank averaged 4.5 percent). The Peasant Land Bank could finance only 75 percent of the purchase price for land; thus, the commune or co-operative had to provide a large down payment. Those conditions limited the effectiveness of the bank, which helped buy only one-quarter of all the land bought by peasants. From 1883 to the end of 1894 it lent a total of 76 million rubles, which purchased 2.42 million ha of land. The bank's activity in Ukraine in the early period is summarized in the table.

Eventually several changes in the bank's operation in-

creased its effectiveness. In 1895 the bank was permitted to buy land on its own account and resell it later to peasants. At the same time, the maximum repayment term for loans was extended from 36.5 to 55.5 years. In 1895–1905 the bank acquired over 1 million ha itself and financed the purchase of another 5.7 million ha by the peasantry.

After the Revolution of 1905 the bank was reformed even further. Its capital was increased, the average annual repayment price was reduced to 4.5 percent of the original loan, and the bank was permitted to finance 90 percent and even 100 percent of the purchase price of the land. Other major changes followed the introduction of the *Stolypin agrarian reforms, which stressed the development of private farming in the Russian Empire. The bank was encouraged to make loans to individual peasants and peasant households. In 1906 the state also began to sell off much of its own land, and the bank lowered its interest rates. In 1906 to 1915, 11.3 million ha of land were purchased from or through the bank. Much of that land was purchased by peasants who had previously owned little or no land. By the end of 1914 the bank was owed nearly 1.25 billion rubles, and arrears amounted to some 18.5 million rubles.

After the Revolution of 1917 the new Soviet authorities liquidated the Peasant Land Bank and abolished the outstanding loans.

BIBLIOGRAPHY
Robinson, G. *Rural Russia under the Old Regime* (New York 1932)
Yaney, G. *The Urge to Mobilize: Agrarian Reform in Russia, 1861–1930* (Urbana 1982)

B. Balan

Peasant Militia. See People's Militia.

Peasant party. See Union of Lands of United Ukraine.

Peasant strikes in Galicia and Bukovyna. In the first years of the 20th century Ukrainian peasants in Galicia and Bukovyna who hired themselves out as agricultural laborers on landlords' estates participated in a series of mass strikes accompanied by other forms of agrarian unrest. Members of the *Ukrainian Radical party, particularly I. *Franko and V. *Budzynovsky, had begun to propagate the idea of agrarian strikes, which they took from the example of Irish populists in the mid-1890s. Sporadic strikes of agricultural laborers broke out in Bukovyna and Galicia in 1897 and 1898, but the first large-scale strike occurred in Borshchiv county, in Galicia, in 1900. In 1902 a wave of agrarian strikes of unprecedented magnitude encompassed some 400 villages in eastern Galicia. In Husiatyn and Terebovlia counties over two-thirds of the landlords' estates faced work stoppages. Another strike wave of roughly equal magnitude broke out in eastern Galicia in 1906; in 1905–7 over 20 agrarian strikes took

Land purchases in Ukraine financed by the Peasant Land Bank, 1883–94

	No. of loans	No. of ha	No. of individual purchases	No. of ha purchased	
				per loan	per individual
Left-Bank gubernias	2,374	234,800	130,300	98.9	1.8
Right-Bank gubernias	1,020	156,100	94,800	153.0	1.6
Steppe gubernias	635	325,800	130,600	224.1	2.5

place in Bukovyna. The outbreak of the *Revolution of 1905 across the border in the Russian Empire helped to motivate the latter wave of strikes, especially since neighboring Right-Bank Ukraine was also the scene of massive agrarian unrest.

The strikes were precipitated by low wages, the maltreatment of laborers, and disputes over access to forests and pastures. In the course of the strikes the peasants sometimes engaged in violent confrontations with strikebreakers and occupied seignorial land, especially pastures. County authorities called in the military to quell strikes and related unrest and made the village communities quarter the soldiers at their own expense. Hundreds of peasants were arrested in 1902, and dozens in 1906. The backbone of the strike movement tended to be small-holding peasants; landless agricultural laborers, who were traditionally excluded from collective decision-making in the village, and who were also much more dependent on their daily wages, tended to stay in the background. As a result of the strikes agricultural wages rose throughout almost all of Ukrainian Galicia and Bukovyna.

Although the strikes arose primarily in response to socioeconomic conditions, they were not without political and national dimensions. The major strike waves broke out spontaneously, without prior organization. But once under way the strikes were supported by activists of the major Ukrainian political parties. Among the most prominent activists in the strike movement was the social democrat S. *Vityk. Members of the Ukrainian Radical and *Ukrainian Social Democratic parties emphasized the social aspects of the strikes, but the *National Democratic party pointed out that they had a strong national component as well, since, in the main, Ukrainian peasants were using the strikes against Polish landlords. Most Polish political parties in Galicia, with the prominent exception of the Polish Social Democratic party, condemned the strikes as a threat to Polish hegemony in the region. The strikes contributed to the exacerbation of Polish-Ukrainian tension in Galicia. They also demonstrated that the Ukrainian village was capable of co-ordinating effective actions in pursuit of its interests.

BIBLIOGRAPHY

Najdus, W. Szkice z historii Galicji, 2 vols (Warsaw 1958, 1960)
Franko, I. 'Bauernstreiks in Ostgalizien,' in Beiträge zur Geschichte und Kultur der Ukraine: Ausgewählte deutsche Schriften des revolutionären Demokraten, 1882–1915 (Berlin 1963)
Botushans'kyi, V.M. 'Pidnesennia straikovoï borot'by selian Pivnichnoï Bukovyny na pochatku XX st. (1900–1907 rr.),' Mynule i suchasne Pivnichnoï Bukovyny, no. 1 (1972)

                                                        J.-P. Himka

Peasant Union. See Sel-Soiuz.

Peasants. A social class engaged largely in subsistence agriculture. Peasants have played an unusually important part in Ukrainian history. Not only did they make up the overwhelming majority of the Ukrainian population until the 1930s, but they also contributed much to the preservation and development of Ukrainian culture. One of the peculiarities of the peasants as a social stratum is the stability of their way of life and a conservative attitude toward traditions, language, and faith – in short, their fostering of national and ethnic characteristics, some of which extend back to pre-Christian times and even to Indo-European

roots. That peculiarity of the peasants and their cultural life was particularly important for the Ukrainian nation, which had been subdued by powerful neighbors and, particularly in the case of the upper classes and the urban strata, exposed to assimilatory influences. The peasants served as a major source for regeneration in the 19th century, when the Ukrainian literary language was reconstructed on the basis of the peasant vernacular, and the traditions of village life were mined for the components of a national culture.

The peasants of Kievan Rus' arose in conjunction with the new state system that replaced the disintegrating ancestral social structure of the Slavic tribes. The peasants of Rus' were grouped in relatively autonomous settlements, where they worked together to cultivate land using slash-and-burn techniques. The vast majority of peasants fell into the category of *smerds. The smerds were of two types, either entirely free or dependent. The free peasants formed the largest group and enjoyed the rights of free persons. The dependent smerds, whose numbers grew with princely gifts of land to servitors, lived on princely and boyar lands, paying rents primarily in kind (see *quit-rent), but money and labor rents (corvée) were also known. The smerds were not, however, serfs or slaves. A smerd could become a *zakup, that is, an indentured laborer to a lord. That status was temporary, however; once the zakupy had paid off their debts, they were free again.

After the Mongol invasion (1240) and the passage of Ukrainian lands under Polish and Lithuanian rule (mid-14th century) the peasants' rights were further restricted and their rents increased, until they lost their personal freedom and became serfs wholly dependent on the *landowners. That enserfment was part of the so-called second *serfdom that characterized the economy of Eastern Europe beginning in the late 15th century, precisely when serfdom was dying out in Western Europe. Surveyors divided up the arable land and established demesnal estates (see *Filvarok) on which the peasants had to labor as a form of rent to the landlords; peasants also had their own, much smaller plots, from which they eked out their sustenance. Ukrainian peasants resisted enserfment (eg, the *Mukha rebellion in 1490–2), but they were forced to submit. After the Union of Lublin (1569), when all Ukrainian lands formerly under Lithuanian rule passed to the jurisdiction of the Polish Crown, the Ukrainian peasants were encouraged to colonize the relatively empty southwestern and eastern territories of Ukraine. Oppression in Ukraine's heavily populated west led to a great eastward movement of population. The burdens of serfdom were much reduced in eastern Ukraine, both as a natural result of the population (and hence labor) shortage and as part of a deliberate policy to attract colonists. At the end of the 16th century, for example, peasants with one lan of land in Red Rus' (Galicia) owed four or five days' labor on the filvarok; in Volhynia and the region west of Kiev they owed two or three days; and in Left-Bank Ukraine and the Bratslav region they paid money rent only. Peasant obligations were steadily increased, however, and by the 1640s, peasants in Volhynia and the Kiev region worked five days on the lord's estate, and peasants in Left-Bank Ukraine and in the Bratslav region worked one or two days.

Ukrainian serfs sometimes ran away illegally from their owners' estates and headed for the steppe of *Southern and *Slobidska Ukraine, which were in immediate danger of Tatar raids. There they became *Cossacks. Cossack uprisings in the early 17th century often expressed opposition to serfdom. The *Cossack-Polish War of 1648–57, in which peasants joined the Cossack forces, resulted in the abolition of serfdom in the emergent Hetman state. But the *Cossack *starshyna* began appropriating freeholders' land and reimposing labor and other rents on the rank-and-file Cossacks. Around 1700 about a quarter of the population of Left-Bank and Slobidska Ukraine, and by the 1730s about half, consisted of peasant serfs. The reintroduction of serfdom, albeit in mitigated form, engendered conflicts between the *starshyna* and rank-and-file Cossacks and contributed to the instability in Ukraine in the late 17th and early 18th centuries and to the ability of the Muscovite authorities to intervene in the internal affairs of the Hetman state.

In Right-Bank Ukraine, where the Cossack movement had been entirely suppressed by the early 18th century, serfdom was fully reinstituted. But because war and civil strife had depopulated that territory, the obligations of the serfs were not onerous in the first two decades of the 18th century. By the 1760s, however, the position of the Right-Bank peasantry had declined to perhaps its lowest point in history. The great discontent in the countryside fueled the *haidamaka rebellions of the mid-18th century.

The Russian empress Catherine II formally reinstituted serfdom in Left-Bank and Slobidska Ukraine in 1783. The conquest of the northern Black Sea littoral allowed her to extend serfdom to Southern Ukraine as well. Almost simultaneously with the reinstitution of serfdom Catherine dismantled the vestiges of Cossack autonomy, destroyed the Zaporozhian Sich, and resettled part of the Slobidska Cossack population in the *Kuban. Her government also attracted foreign colonists, for the most part Germans and Serbs, to Southern Ukraine, where they formed a free and prosperous peasantry of the Western European type.

In the first half of the 19th century the serfs were the most abject, most oppressed class in the Russian Empire. Although the peasant commune elected its own elders, who dealt with the bailiff and landowner, the gentry landowner had the right to try serfs, exile them to Siberia, send them to the army, and subject them to corporal punishment. Serfs could not marry without his permission, he could sell an entire family of serfs or individual family members, and he set the amount of work that the serf was obligated to perform. Laws limited his exercise of the last two powers. Paul I limited corvée obligations to three days a week and prohibited the sale of serfs without land in Ukraine. Naturally, abuses occurred, but only when he was exceptionally cruel or committed murder could a landowner be deprived of the right to his human property. The land was also considered to be entirely his property, and he had the right to decide all agricultural questions. The burdens of serfdom were greatest in Right-Bank Ukraine, where the majority of peasants were owned by landlords and corvée prevailed. In Left-Bank and Slobidska Ukraine *state peasants, who were mainly descendants of Cossacks, predominated; they paid taxes, generally in money or in kind, to the state (see *Poll tax). Serfdom was weakest in Southern Ukraine, which was newly conquered from the Crimean Tatars and relatively uncultivated; because of a labor shortage rents were less burdensome than elsewhere in Ukraine, and landlords of-

ten leased out land to tenant farmers. The prolonged existence of serfdom in the Russian Empire retarded its economic and social development, a situation that became obvious even to the ruling class after Russia's defeat in the Crimean War in 1856. Against the background of massive social unrest in the Russian and Ukrainian countryside, serfdom was abolished in the Russian Empire in 1861.

In Galicia, which passed under Austrian rule in 1772, the position of the peasantry improved as a result of the reforms of Empress Maria Theresa and Emperor Joseph II. The imperial authorities formally limited corvée to three days a week (although landlords found ways to circumvent the restriction), prohibited some particularly onerous forms of rent, took steps to make the peasants legal owners of the so-called *rustical lands from which they supported themselves, restricted the traditional right of the noble landowner to inflict corporal punishment, permitted the peasants to lodge formal complaints against abuses by the landlords, and abolished personal servitude (*Leibeigenschaft*). The impact of those far-reaching reforms was undermined, however, by the entrenched power of the local Polish nobility and by the conservative reaction that gripped Austria after the outbreak of the French Revolution and the defeat of Napoleon. Peasant resistance to serfdom, often taking the form of refusal to perform labor obligations, mounted in the first half of the 19th century, and soon after the *Revolution of 1848–9 broke out, serfdom was abolished.

Serfdom was also abolished in Habsburg-ruled Bukovyna and Transcarpathia in 1848. Peasant discontent in those regions had been great in the early 19th century, because the position of the serfs had declined tremendously in spite of the reforms of Joseph II. The reason for the decline was Austria's annexation of Galicia; the intense exploitation of the peasantry, characteristic of the Polish nobility there, proved an attractive model for the Magyar and Rumanian gentry of Transcarpathia and Bukovyna. Bukovyna, which was administratively part of Galicia, had been the scene of mass peasant rebellion in the 1840s.

As a result of emancipation in Russian-ruled Ukraine, the peasants received their personal freedom, and part of the land was sold to the village communes (see *Hromada*), to be paid in installments over the course of 49.5 years at a rate of 5 percent a year. The reform was undoubtedly favorable to the peasantry, but because the peasants still did not become landowners, and because of antiquated farming techniques, agricultural production was retarded. Peasant holdings were small. The average size of a peasant household's landholding in Ukraine in 1905 was 7.3 ha. Holdings were largest in the less populated south (8.6 ha in Kherson gubernia, 10.2 in Katerynoslav gubernia, 16.2 in Tavriia gubernia), small in Left-Bank and Slobidska Ukraine (5.4 ha in Poltava gubernia, 6.9 ha in Chernihiv gubernia, 8.0 in Kharkiv gubernia), and smallest in Right-Bank Ukraine (3.6 ha in Podilia gubernia, 4.2 in Kiev gubernia, 3.6 in Volhynia gubernia). To satisfy their hunger for land about 1.6 million Ukrainian peasants emigrated to the Russian *Far East between 1896 and 1914. Because of such a land shortage the villagers who remained in Ukraine started eyeing the disproportionate holdings of the gentry. Peasants cut wood from the landlords' forests without permission, allowed their livestock to graze on the meadows of the gentry, burned estates, and occasionally carried out attacks on the gentry and their representatives. The number of peasant riots recorded in the late 19th and early 20th century was greater than under serfdom. Populist revolutionaries supported the peasantry's acts of defiance and demanded the nationalization of land and its transfer to those who worked it. The idea found favor even among the prosperous elements of the peasantry, who could not buy land because of its high price. It was clear that the peasantry was being impoverished as a result of landlessness, direct and indirect taxes, and the *redemption payments for land that remained from the time of emancipation. The *Revolution of 1905 demonstrated that it was impossible to continue without radical changes.

The changes came in the form of the *Stolypin agrarian reforms, which were introduced by the decree of 9 November 1906 and became law on 14 June 1910. The reforms gave great impetus to peasant migration to *Siberia and Kazakhstan, where settlers were offered financial assistance, land, and exemption from taxes. At the same time remnants of serfdom were abolished in the village, including collective responsibility for repairing roads and billeting troops and the restrictions on the right of peasants to receive passports. The Stolypin reforms led to differentiation by economic status in the peasant population. The more active, prosperous segment of the population, some 10 to 15 percent, received the opportunity to improve their farms, consolidate their landholdings, use modern equipment, and broaden their market. Ukraine, which did not have a tradition of the repartitional commune (see *Obshchina), adapted relatively well to the reforms, and individual peasant farms independent of the communes proliferated.

As a result of the emancipation in Austrian-ruled Ukraine, the peasants became free and owners of their rustical plots. They paid an indemnity to the landowners for the loss of labor and other rents until 1898. The decade following emancipation was marked by the struggle over *servitudes, or rights to forests and pastures, but by the 1860s most of Galicia's and Bukovyna's forests and pastures had been awarded to the gentry. Throughout Habsburg-ruled Ukraine the peasantry faced land hunger. The size of the rustical plots had been reduced by the nobility in the decades preceding and during the abolition of serfdom, and because Ukrainian peasants customarily divided their land among all children, the average size of peasant landholdings declined inexorably. According to official statistics, at the beginning of the 20th century almost half the peasant holdings in Galicia and over half in Bukovyna were 2 ha or smaller. The land shortage was one of the factors motivating the large-scale *emigration of peasants from Transcarpathia, Galicia, and Bukovyna to North America and elsewhere in the decades before the First World War. In the 1860s and 1870s the Austrian government introduced compulsory education in Galicia and Bukovyna; that measure, combined with the efforts of the Ukrainian national movement (particularly organizations such as *Prosvita), raised the cultural level of the West Ukrainian peasantry. In Transcarpathia, however, the Magyar gentry restricted educational opportunities, in particular education in Ukrainian, and prevented the formation of a Ukrainian national movement with its own voluntary associations.

During the years of revolutionary upheaval, 1917–21, armed peasants on the former territory of tsarist-ruled Ukraine liquidated gentry estates, and those lands, as well as land owned by the government and sugar refineries, were redistributed among the peasantry. Peasants refurbished and improved their farms and increased their livestock. For the first time in many years Ukraine did not export huge quantities of grain. As a result, from 1916 to the spring of 1921 the number of livestock in Ukraine increased from 23.9 million to 31.1 million. Raids by Soviet *surplus appropriation detachments disturbed peasant agriculture as soldiers confiscated, without payment, grain and other produce that fell into their hands to feed the urban populations and the Red Army. In such circumstances the peasants did not rush to expand production, and in 1921 a catastrophe struck: the now stronger Soviet regime announced a higher demand for grain, and at the same time a drought hit southern Ukraine and destroyed the harvest. Much of Soviet Ukraine (and Soviet Russia) suffered from *famine. In the same year the government recognized the need to change its agrarian policy and instituted the *New Economic Policy, which amounted to a truce with the peasantry. The main point of the accord was the cessation of unpaid expropriations and the establishment of taxes, after the payment of which peasants could sell the products of their labor. The taxes were substantial, exceeding prerevolutionary ones, and they were supplemented by an indirect tax created by the price gap between industrial and agricultural goods. Nonetheless, the peasantry soon raised agricultural production to prewar levels. In that period peasants were permitted to lease land or equipment and to hire labor for productive purposes. The co-operative movement, especially consumer co-operatives, proliferated. The government put tax and political pressure only on the more prosperous peasants and on people connected with groups that had opposed the Soviets, such as the Ukrainian Party of Socialist Revolutionaries, the partisan movement, the Army of the UNR, and the anarchist forces of N. Makhno. Those people paid higher taxes and could not take part in the management of co-operatives, vote in elections, or be elected to village soviets. Many supplementary responsibilities also fell to their lot.

The social position of the peasantry changed fundamentally from what it had been in prerevolutionary times. Large farms virtually disappeared, and the number of landless peasants decreased. The peasantry became a uniform mass of agricultural producers and, to a degree, landowners. Their independence inspired a certain discomfort in the Bolshevik rulers. The Soviet government laid claim to absolute control over both production and ideology and distrusted the peasants both as petty independent producers and as keepers of national traditions. Its hostility to the peasants was manifested in the cruel manner in which *collectivization was imposed in Ukraine in the late 1920s and early 1930s.

The goal of collectivization was the complete transformation of the economic and social circumstances of the peasantry. The peasants were deprived of the right to own land and the instruments of production; for a while they were also deprived of freedom of movement and were obliged to work in the fields without pay for fear of punishment. The most active and wealthy peasants were arrested and deported with their families to the north, and their property was confiscated. Collectivization took the form of unexpected attacks on the prosperous portion of the peasantry by detachments of workers, Komsomol members, Party members, and activists of the *committees of poor peasants. Everyone else was forced to enter the collective farms under threat of being repressed as *kulaks. Collective farming turned out to be extremely inefficient; the inefficiency was exacerbated by the peasants' passive mass resistance to collectivization, a resistance that included slaughtering their own animals. In 1932–3 the Soviet government created a famine in Ukraine to quell resistance. All grain and most remaining livestock were taken from the peasants, and the confiscation was accompanied by a law proclaiming the death penalty for any theft of food from a collective or government farm. By the summer of 1934, 54 percent of the villagers of Ukraine were without livestock, 64.7 percent had no cows, and 95.4 percent had no pigs. Several million peasants died, and the rest were forced to submit.

Collectivization and the famine destroyed the peasantry as a social stratum. The peasants lost not only their land but their personal freedom and were forced to labor out of fear of punishment and death by starvation. Material incentives were eliminated, and the productivity of labor naturally fell. As a result of collectivization not only the means of agricultural production but also the social position and psychology of the rural inhabitants changed. To a significant degree they lost their love for the land and their habit of working on it.

The peasants in interwar Western Ukraine, divided among Poland, Czechoslovakia, and Rumania, escaped collectivization in the 1930s and the accompanying famine. Under Polish and Rumanian rule their position seems to have declined relatively from the late Austrian period. The Polish and Rumanian regimes undertook *land reforms that did nothing to improve the peasants' position. Estates that were divided in Ukrainian-inhabited areas were generally distributed among ethnic Polish and Rumanian colonists. Because of immigration quotas in the United States and Canada, the traditional solution to rural overpopulation, emigration to North America, virtually ceased to play a role. The Great Depression of the 1930s increased the misery of the peasantry. The only positive development was the rapid growth of the *co-operative movement, which provided increased and better opportunities for the peasantry to market surplus agricultural produce, particularly dairy products and eggs. In Transcarpathia the Ukrainian peasantry remained very poor, but the reformist Czechoslovak regime introduced elementary education in the local language for peasant children and implemented a land reform that, although slow and modest, benefited Ukrainian peasants rather than non-Ukrainian colonists. As a result of the Second World War Western Ukraine passed under Soviet rule, and by the mid-1950s the peasant farms there were completely collectivized.

In the postwar period the production of grain and nonfood crops (eg, cotton and flax) and, to some extent, animal husbandry were the responsibility of the collective farms. A portion of the animals, however, remained the personal property of the collective farmers. In addition each village household had a minute *private plot around its house, which fed its members and provided potatoes and vegetables not only for the villagers but for the city as well. From that plot the peasant was supposed to supply the government with milk and meat and pay taxes. For a while it seemed that the system was producing foodstuffs successfully. N. Khrushchev improved the collective farmers' lot by substantially raising their pay, by gradually restoring their right to move about the country, and by introducing at least a small level of retirement benefits for collective farmers. At the same time huge expanses of virgin lands were colonized, and agricultural production actually rose somewhat. In the 1970s and 1980s, however, the food supply worsened noticeably, because the collective farms could no longer feed the population. One of the main causes of that circumstance was the fall in labor productivity on the private plots. The new generation of peasants raised solely in the collective-farm system turned out to be incapable of productive labor. Young people went off to study or moved away after their military service to work in the cities. The collective-farm peasantry has even taken on the characteristics of an age cohort, consisting more and more of the elderly.

(See also *Agriculture, *Feudalism, *Land tenure system, *Peasant strikes in Galicia and Bukovyna, and *Slavery. For various peasant categories in the feudal era, see *Common peasants, *Economic peasants, *Horodnyk, *Khalupnyk, *Kholop, *Komornyk, *Landless peasants, *Nepokhozhi peasants, *Otchychi, *Pokhozhi peasants, *Poplechnyk, *Possessional peasants, *Pripisnye peasants, *Rank peasants, *Siabr, *Smerd, *Starostvo peasants, and *Tributary peasants.)

BIBLIOGRAPHY

Slabchenko, M. *Khoziaistvo Get'manshchiny v xviiх–xviii stoletiiakh*, 2 vols (Odessa 1922–3)

Iurkevych, V. *Emigratsiia na skhid i zaliudnennia Slobozhanshchyny za B. Khmel'nyts'koho* (Kiev 1932)

Mytsiuk, O. *Narysy z sotsiial'no-hospodars'koï istoriï Pidkarpats'koï Rusy*, 2 vols (Prague 1936, 1938)

Grekov, B. *Krest'iane na Rusi s drevneishikh vremen do xvii veka*, 2nd rev edn, vol 1 (Moscow 1952)

Herasymenko, M. *Ahrarni vidnosyny v Halychyni v period kryzy panshchynnoho hospodarstva* (Kiev 1959)

Leshchenko, N. *Krest'ianskoe dvizhenie na Ukraine v sviazi s provedeniem reformy 1861 goda (60-e gody xix st.)* (Kiev 1959)

Blum, J. *Lord and Peasant in Russia from the Ninth to the Nineteenth Century* (Princeton 1961)

Markina, V. *Magnatskoe pomest'e Pravoberezhnoi Ukrainy vtoroi poloviny xviii v. (sotsial'no-ekonomicheskoe razvitie)* (Kiev 1961)

Rozdolski, R. *Stosunki poddańcze w dawnej Galicji*, 2 vols (Warsaw 1962)

Boiko, I. *Selianstvo Ukraïny v druhii polovyni xvi–pershii polovyni xvii st.* (Kiev 1963)

Myshko, D. *Sotsial'no-ekonomichni umovy formuvannia ukraïns'koï narodnosti (stanovyshche selian i antyfeodal'ni rukhy na Ukraïni v xv–pershii polovyni xvi st.)* (Kiev 1963)

Diadychenko, V.; Kompaniiets', I; et al (eds). *Istoriia selianstva Ukraïns'koï RSR*, 2 vols (Kiev 1967)

Robinson, G.T. *Rural Russia under the Old Regime: A History of the Landlord-Peasant World and a Prologue to the Peasant Revolution of 1917* (Berkeley and Los Angeles 1967)

Stashevskii, E. *Istoriia dokapitalisticheskoi renty na Pravoberezhnoi Ukraine v xviii–pervoi polovine xix v.* (Moscow 1968)

Markina, V. *Krest'iane Pravoberezhnoi Ukrainy: Konets xvii–60-e gody xviii st.* (Kiev 1971)

Leshchenko, M.; et al (eds). *Selians'kyi rukh na Ukraïni, seredyna xviii–persha chvert' xix st.: Zbirnyk dokumentiv i materialiv* (Kiev 1978)

Beauvois, D. *Le noble, le serf, et le revizor: La noblesse polonaise entre le tsarisme et les masses ukrainiennes, 1831–1863* (Paris 1986)

Edelman, R. *Proletarian Peasants: The Revolution of 1905 in Russia's Southwest* (Ithaca, NY 1987)

Himka, J.-P. *Galician Villagers and the Ukrainian National Movement in the Nineteenth Century* (Edmonton 1988)

Hryniuk, S. *Peasants with Promise: Ukrainians in Southeastern Galicia, 1880–1900* (Edmonton 1991)

A. Babyonyshev, J.-P. Himka

Peat industry. A branch of the *fuel industry that extracts and processes peat, mainly for home-heating but also for use in the chemical, construction, and other industries. Peat was first used in Ukraine in the 17th century. The major peat deposits are in Irdyn (Cherkasy oblast), Bucha (Kiev oblast), Zamhlai (Chernihiv oblast), Shostka (Sumy oblast), and Radekhiv (Lviv oblast). The peat is dried and pressed into briquettes in plants in Zhytomyr, Sumy, Chernihiv, and Lviv oblasts. The briquettes output rose from 75,000 in 1958 to approx 800,000 in 1975. Their use increased dramatically during the industrialization drive of the 1920s and 1930s. Peat output has declined, from 4.7 million t in 1960 to 4.1 million t in 1970, 1.6 million t in 1980, and 2.2 million t in 1987. The industry's share in the fuel industry has also diminished. The industry was not a priority in Soviet economic planning.

Peat moss (*Sphagnum*; Ukrainian: *sfagnum*). A perennial plant of the family Sphagnaceae, including 300 species of the single genus. The plants grow to up to 30 m from their roots and form dense hydroscopic thickets in ponds and swamps and on lakeshores. Every year the lower stems die off and form peat, while other branches continue to grow and develop. In Ukraine peat moss is used as fuel and stable litter, in the production of heat insulation sheets, and as packaging material for the protection of fruit and flowers during shipping. Dried sphagnum has also been used for surgical dressings, bedding, diapers, and wicks.

Pechenegs (*pechenihy*). The name of a Turkic tribal federation that dominated the southern steppe region of what is today Ukraine from the late 9th to the mid-11th century. The Turkic appellation *be-ča-nag* ('brother-in-law') was first used in the 8th century to refer to members of the Pecheneg ruling clan. The Pechenegs (Patzinaks in Byzantine sources) originated beyond the Aral Sea near the midstream of the Syr Darya River in Central Asia. Their center was near present-day Tashkent. The sedentary ruling stratum (the Kangar) was of Iranian origin. In the early 9th century the Pechenegs were defeated by the Oghuz (*Torks) and forced to migrate from Central Asia to the lands between the Ural and the Volga rivers, where they warred continuously with the Khazars. In the 880s the Khazars and Oghuz jointly defeated the Pechenegs and again forced them to flee westward. In 889 the Pechenegs attacked the nomadic Magyars living between the Don and the Dnieper and forced them west of the Dnieper. Later they drove the Magyars across the Danube and themselves occupied the steppe between the Don and the Danube.

The Pecheneg domain was divided into two wings separated by the Dnieper River and ruled by the two highest-ranking leaders. The ruler of the western wing was the senior of the two and bore the imperial title of kagan. Each wing had four provinces subdivided into five districts. Each of the 40 districts provided a division of 10,000 mounted warriors. They were masters of lightning mounted maneuvers and were renowned for their art of fighting from fortified wagon encampments. The Pecheneg regime was a kind of military democracy, in which all important decisions were made by a general council. The kagan's seat and the council's meeting place were probably located in the Ros Valley.

Until 1036 the Pechenegs had an estimated population of 2.8 to 3 million. By 1048, when their domain was left with only 11 districts west of the Dnieper, their population had been reduced to approx 800,000. Like all nomadic societies the Pechenegs were not ethnically homogeneous or unilingual. The ruling elite spoke Iranian, whereas most of the population spoke Turkic with a significant admixture of Hunno-Bulgar elements. By the time the Pechenegs had arrived in Ukraine, they were familiar with various religions, including Christianity, Buddhism, and Islam. They were most attracted to Manicheism, and Archbishop Bruno of Querfurt's mission to convert them (ca 1007), which was aided by Grand Prince Volodymyr the Great of Kiev, was unsuccessful. Islamic missionaries, however, had managed to convert most of the Pechenegs by 1010.

The Pechenegs' economy was based on trade and livestock. Their main trading partners were Rus', which bought their cattle, sheep, and horses, and the Byzantine colony of Chersonese Taurica in the Crimea, which bought their hides and wax. The Pechenegs also served as intermediaries in trade with Asia and ensured the safety of the international trade routes. They did not practice slavery.

To retain their mediating role among their neighbors the Pechenegs entered into coalitions with Byzantium (in 914, 968, and 972), Rus' (in 944), and other states, usually against former allies. They often invaded Rus' with the encouragement of Byzantium. In 968 they attacked Kiev, thereby forcing Grand Prince *Sviatoslav I Ihorevych to cut short his campaign against Bulgaria. In 972 a Pecheneg force led by Kagan Kuria routed Sviatoslav's army at the Dnieper Rapids and killed the prince. During Volodymyr the Great's reign the Pechenegs attacked Pereiaslav in 988 and 993, Vasylkiv in 996, and Bilhorod in 997. To defend his realm Volodymyr had lines of fortifications built along the Stuhna River in Right-Bank Ukraine and along the Desna, the Oster, the Trubizh, and the Sula rivers in the Left Bank. He also hired Tork and Oghuz mercenaries and began recruiting the Torks as military settlers (later known as *Chorni Klobuky) to defend his frontier against the Pechenegs. The Pechenegs were often used by the Rus' princes in internecine conflicts, until 1036, when the army of Grand Prince Yaroslav the Wise crushed them near Kiev.

From the early 1040s the Pechenegs were constantly confronted by the Torks, who themselves had been forced to migrate by the Cumans. In the late 1050s the Pechenegs lost control of the entire Left-Bank steppe and later the Right Bank and were forced by the Cumans to migrate west into the Danubian Byzantine territories or across the Carpathians into Hungary. In 1091 Byzantium was saved from the Pecheneg threat by the unexpected arrival and support of the Cumans, which enabled Emperor Alexius I Comnenus to rout the Pechenegs. After another defeat in 1122, the Pechenegs disappeared as an independent force and were assimilated among the Cumans and Bulgars. Some of them entered the service of Rus' princes (documented for the years 1097–1169); most of those later migrated to Hungary, where they managed to remain autonomous until the 14th century, when they were assimilated. Geographic traces of their presence in Ukraine include Pechenihy, in Chuhuiv raion, Kharkiv oblast, where archeologists discovered a 9th-century fortified settlement (possibly a political center); Pecheniuhy, in Novhorod-Siverskyi raion, Chernihiv oblast; and Pechenizhyn, in Kolomyia raion, Ivano-Frankivske oblast.

BIBLIOGRAPHY

Golubovskii, P. *Pechenegi, torki i polovtsy do nashestviia tatar: Istoriia iuzhnorusskikh stepei*, IX–XIII vv. (Kiev 1884)

Vasil'evskii, V. 'Vizantiia i Pechenegi,' in *Trudy*, vol 1 (St Petersburg 1908)

Rasovskii, D. 'Pechenegi, torki i berendei na Rusi i v Ugrii,' *Seminarium Kondakovianum*, 6 (Prague 1933)

Pletneva, S. 'Pechenegi, torki i polovtsy v iuzhnorusskikh stepiakh,' *Materialy i issledovaniia po arkheologii SSSR*, 62 (1958)

Fedorov-Davydov, G. *Kochevniki Vostochnoi Evropy pod vlast'iu zolotoordynskikh khanov: Arkheologicheskie pamiatniki* (Moscow 1966)

Pritsak, O. 'The Pečenegs: A Case of Social and Economic Transformation,' *Archivum Eurasiae Medii Aevi*, 1 (1975)

O. Pritsak

Pavlo Pecheniha-Uhlytsky

Pecheniha-Uhlytsky, Pavlo [Pečeniha-Uhlyts'kyj] (Pecheniha-Ouglitzky, Paul), b 20 June 1892 in Pechenihy, Vovchanske county, Kharkiv gubernia, d 2 July 1948 in New York. Composer, conductor, double-bass player, and teacher. He attended the Russian Musical Society school in Kharkiv, studied (1912–14) at the St Petersburg Conservatory under F. Yakymenko, A. Glazunov, and A. Tcherepnin, and then taught theory and composition (1914–20) at the conservatories in St Petersburg, Rostov, and Yalta. He settled in New York in 1922 and worked for the National Broadcasting Corporation as a composer, orchestrator, and conductor. From the mid-1930s he was an important organizer of Ukrainian musical life in New York City. On 8 January 1939 his compositions were performed by the NBC Radio Chorus and Philharmonic Symphony Society Orchestra at Carnegie Hall in the first Ukrainian symphonic concert in North America. His major works include the opera *The Witch* (after Ye. Hrebinka, libretto by S. Charnetsky, 1936–40), the ballet *Legin'* (Young Lad; libretto by D. Chutro, 1938), the tone poem *Ukraïna* (after T. Shevchenko's *Haidamaky*), three string quartets, and the cantata *Biut' porohy* (The Rapids Roar; text by T. Shevchenko) for mixed chorus and orchestra. He also wrote a score for the *Liturgy of St John Chrysostom* and other works for chorus, solo songs to texts by T. Shevchenko and others, and arrangements of Ukrainian folk songs for chorus and solo voice.

R. Savytsky

Pechenihy [Pečenihy]. IV-17. A town smt (1986 pop 6,700) on the Donets River in Chuhuiv raion, Kharkiv oblast. In the mid-17th century the town was fortified, and became a company center in Izium regiment. In the 19th century it was part of Vovchanske county in Kharkiv gubernia. By 1896 its population had reached 6,600. Today it has a food-processing plant and a fishery. The Pechenihy Reservoir is located nearby.

Pechenihy Reservoir. A body of water created in 1962 on the Dinets River in Kharkiv oblast. It covers 86.2 sq km and has a length of 65 km and a maximum width of 3 km. Its capacity is 384 million cu m. The reservoir supplies Kharkiv with potable water and the surrounding area with water for irrigation and fish farming.

Pechenizhyn [Pečenižyn]. V-5. A town smt (1986 pop 5,400) in the Carpathian foothills of Kolomyia raion, Ivano-Frankivske oblast. It was first mentioned in historical documents in 1443. It has a furniture manufacturing complex and a building-materials factory. Its regional museum is dedicated to O. *Dovbush, who was born in the town.

Pecherska Lavra. See Kievan Cave Monastery.

Pedagogical education. A system for acquiring the theoretical and practical knowledge and skills required to teach others in an educational institution. Until the end of the 18th century there were no schools in Ukraine that provided a systematic course of pedagogical studies. Elementary-school teachers of the day usually received a general education in monasteries or in parish and *brotherhood schools; some were even self-taught precentors or *itinerant tutors. Most teachers in secondary schools or institutions of higher learning were (from the late 16th century) graduates of the *Lviv Dormition Brotherhood School, the *Ostrih Academy, the *Zamostia Academy, the *Kievan Mohyla Academy, and similar institutions, in which many of the instructors had been trained in other Slavic countries or Western Europe.

Central and eastern Ukraine to 1921. A new development in the early 19th century was the establishment of pedagogical institutes for training teachers of *schools for children of the clergy, *county schools, and *gymnasiums at Kharkiv University (1811) and Kiev University (1834); some instruction in the field of pedagogy was also provided by the Kiev Theological Academy. Institutions for training teachers of general education schools were formed only in the latter 19th century, starting with the Provisional Pedagogical School in Kiev (1862). Four-year *teachers' seminaries were formed later in Korostyshiv (1869), Kherson (1872), Pereiaslav (1878), and other locations; by 1917 there were 26 such institutions in Ukraine (out of a total of 171 in the Russian Empire).

These seminaries prepared only a small portion of the total number of teachers in Ukraine. A more significant number received their training through supplementary pedagogical classes, which were added on as an eighth year of study at women's gymnasiums in 1870 (in 1892 some schools expanded the classes to a two-year term); pedagogical classes were also added to the curriculum of *eparchial schools in 1900 as a supplementary seventh year of study. Students graduated from the pedagogical classes with the right to teach in primary schools or in the junior levels of women's gymnasiums. Teachers of *parochial schools received training at teachers' schools under the jurisdiction of the Holy Synod, which also oversaw a two-year school program for teachers of literacy schools. Teachers could upgrade their skills at four-to-six-week summer pedagogical courses organized (from the 1860s) by zemstvos, town councils, and literacy societies.

The training of teachers for *municipal schools (established in 1872 and reorganized as upper elementary schools in 1912) took place in *teachers' institutes under the jurisdiction of the Ministry of Education. These schools, with a three-year course of studies, had a higher educational standard than the teachers' seminaries. The first such institute was established in 1874 in Hlukhiv, and by 1917 there were 11 of them in Ukraine (out of 47 in the Russian Empire). Advanced training for female teachers at kindergartens and the junior levels of gymnasiums was available (from 1908) at the Froebel Institute in Kiev and through Froebel courses offered in Kharkiv. Secondary-school teachers were trained at Kiev, Kharkiv, and Odessa universities, the Kiev Theological Academy, the *Nizhen Lyceum, and advanced pedagogical courses offered in Kiev, Kharkiv, and Odessa.

During the revolutionary period (1917–21) the efforts of pedagogical institutions were supplemented by the founding of the Ukrainian Pedagogical Academy in Kiev (1917), the establishment of new universities (with pedagogical faculties), and the organization of private and public pedagogical courses (the Ministry of Education alone sponsored 64 such courses during the summer of 1918).

Western Ukraine to 1945. Educational reform in the Austrian Empire in 1877 demanded that teachers in lower-level state (trivium) schools be graduates of six-grade *normal schools (located in Lviv and Chernivtsi). The teachers of state primary schools received their training at two-year courses in teacher preparatory schools (five of these were established in Galicia). Precentors normally taught at parish schools. Only a small number, mainly those who had attended a precentors' institute established in Peremyshl in 1823, had any formal pedagogical education. A major overhaul of the education system in 1869 centralized pedagogical education into four-year teachers' seminaries, including some in which the language of instruction was Ukrainian and Polish. The first such institution in eastern Galicia was established in Lviv in 1871, and by the end of the 19th century there were eight of them in the region (six for men, two for women). In addition four private Ukrainian seminaries were established in 1903–12. In Bukovyna a state-run teachers' seminary was established in Chernivtsi in 1871 (a separate division for teaching women was added in 1872). The instruction there was almost totally in German until 1909, when separate instruction in Ukrainian was made available for men. Plans for Ukrainian instruction for women did not materialize, and consequently the *Ukrainska Shkola society established a private Ukrainian teacher training seminary for women in 1910 (Ukrainian instruction for women subsequently was made available at the state teachers' seminary). Three teachers' seminaries were located in Transcarpathia. Secondary-school teachers could obtain their training at universities in Lviv, Chernivtsi, Vienna, Budapest, or elsewhere.

During the interwar period a number of formerly bilingual Polish-Ukrainian teachers' seminaries in eastern Galicia were totally Polonized. In the Lviv school district in 1930, a total of 10 Ukrainian-Polish teachers' seminaries existed (of which 8 were privately run), in comparison with 43 in which the language of instruction was exclusively Polish. In Bukovyna, state policy aggressively pushed for the total Rumanization of education and brought about the close of the private Ukrainian teachers' seminary and the end of Ukrainian-language instruction at the state school (1923–4). During the Second World War nine teachers' seminaries (each with a separate section for early childhood education training) were operating in the Western Ukrainian lands under German occupation.

Ukrainian SSR. With the establishment of Soviet rule the system of pedagogical education was overhauled, starting with the formation of *institutes of people's education in 1920. These institutes were formed from a combination of university-level pedagogical courses, advanced courses for women studying education, and teachers' institutes. They prepared teachers for the upper levels of seven-year schools as well as vocational schools. Three-year *pedagogical tekhnikums were also established in 1920, mainly on the basis of teachers' seminaries. They prepared teachers for primary classes and early childhood education. Underlying these efforts was the desire on the part of the Ukrainian authorities to broaden the base of literacy in the Ukrainian SSR quickly, extensively, and in the Ukrainian language, despite a chronic shortage of teachers (in 1923 approx 45,000 teachers were available to fill an estimated 100,000 positions needed).

The Ukrainian educational structure was brought under the control of a uniform USSR-wide model starting in 1930. The institutes of people's education were reorganized that same year into specialized components, such as *institutes of professional education and *institutes of social education; further changes in 1933 placed the former within the structure of the university system and saw the latter reorganized into *pedagogical institutes. With the advent of compulsory education measures in 1935, two-year teachers' institutes were added to the pedagogical education structure. In 1937 the pedagogical tekhnikums were restructured as *pedagogical schools, with a two-year program for secondary-school graduates and four-year programs for others. By 1940 there were 20 pedagogical institutes (with 15,860 students), 47 teachers' institutes (15,430 students), and 56 pedagogical schools (20,120 students); in 1950 the numbers of these institutions stood at 25, 33, and 82 respectively. Administrative changes in the early 1950s redistributed students from the teachers' institutes to the pedagogical institutes and schools. Since that time the structure has not seen major changes, although pedagogical faculties have been established in conjunction with specialized institutions (eg, polytechnical institutes, conservatories, physical culture institutes, the Kiev Art Institute). Correspondence courses, first initiated in 1927, have also become a common feature of pedagogical education. Statistics for 1989 indicate that there were 29 pedagogical institutes, with an enrollment of approx 146,700, and 50 pedagogical schools, with an enrollment of approx 77,600.

Outside Ukraine. In the interwar period the number of Ukrainian schools in Transcarpathia (then under Czechoslovak rule) greatly increased, and the number of teacher training facilities grew from three to four. In addition Prague emerged as an important center of Ukrainian education, including pedagogy. A chair of Ukrainian language and literature was established at Charles University in Prague to instruct high-school teachers, and the *Ukrainian Free University (UVU) in Prague offered courses in pedagogical history and methodology. Transcarpathia was annexed by the USSR after the Second World War, and its educational institutions were brought into line with Soviet ones; UVU transferred its operations to Munich, where it continued its courses in pedagogical education.

In the absence of Ukrainian school systems or an extensive network of Ukrainian general education schools in the West, Ukrainian pedagogical education there has by and large focused on developing materials and language-instruction methodologies (together with some teacher training) for community-based *ridna shkola* (native school [self-run]) programs, which frequently supplement the education of Ukrainian children in state-run or regulated school systems. In 1967 an attempt was made to co-ordinate such efforts under the World Social-Educational Co-ordinating Council of the World Congress of Free Ukrainians. In those countries in which Ukrainian has been integrated into the public school system or where private Ukrainian schools have been established, more systematic and substantial activity in the area of Ukrainian pedagogical education has taken place.

BIBLIOGRAPHY
Zotin, M. *Pedahohichna osvita na Ukraïni* (Kharkiv 1926)
Siropolko, S. *Istoriia osvity na Ukraïni* (Lviv 1937)
Bondar, A.; et al (eds). *Narodna osvita i pedahohichna nauka v Ukraïns'kii RSR* (Kiev 1967)

Pedagogical institutes (*pedahohichni instytuty*). Institutions of higher learning which train teachers for all types of schools and specialized secondary or professional-technical institutions. In the first half of the 19th century in Russian-ruled Ukraine, there were pedagogical institutes located at the universities of Kharkiv (founded in 1811) and Kiev (founded in 1834). The four-year course of study at these institutes prepared teachers for the gymnasiums and district schools. In 1858 the pedagogical institutes were abolished, and in 1860 pedagogical courses were introduced at universities. These courses were liquidated by the university reform of 1863, the result being a shortage of qualified teachers for secondary schools. The need for pedagogical training in the empire was fulfilled by two historico-philological institutes, one of them the *Nizhen Lyceum in Ukraine.

After the Revolution of 1917 only a few higher-level schools were designated as pedagogical institutes. It was not until 1933 that pedagogical institutes, formed on the basis of the *institutes of social education, became the main type of higher-level pedagogical institution. In 1940 there were 20 such institutes in the Ukrainian SSR, with a total of 15,860 students. The number of institutes in Ukraine increased in the 1950s, when the *teachers' institutes were closed, and a number of them were converted into pedagogical institutes. In 1968 there were 32 pedagogical institutes in Ukraine. In 1989 there were 29, including 2 foreign-language institutes, with a total enrollment of 146,700 and 24,600 students respectively.

Pedagogical institutes are under the jurisdiction of the Ukrainian Ministry of Education. Their program of study lasts 5 years for the training of teachers with 2 or more areas of specialization, and 4 years for students with only 1 area of specialization. Some institutes have graduate research departments for the training of instructors for higher institutions of learning in pedagogical and other specialized disciplines. Institutes prepare textbooks and other educational materials for schools. In Ukraine pedagogical institutes train teachers in 38 specializations.

I. Bakalo, N. Freeland

Pedagogical periodicals. Publications addressing questions and issues of upbringing and education. Because of the political, social, and national implications of education, pedagogical periodicals have often played a role in the larger historical struggles of Ukraine and have always been affected by their outcome.

The first Ukrainian-language pedagogical journal to be published was the quarterly *Dom i shkola*, edited by I. Hushalevych. Published in Lviv in 1864–5, the journal advocated co-operation between school and church and discussed contemporary social, cultural, and economic issues in addition to purely pedagogical and religious topics. The same range of subjects was covered in the Lviv weekly *Uchytel'*, edited by M. Klemertovych (1869–74, 1880). Educational topics were covered extensively in the newspaper *Pys'mo do hromady. Other fortnightly pedagogical journals in Galicia included *Hazeta shkol'na* (Lviv 1875–9), which advocated the use of Ukrainian in schools and was edited by O. Partytsky, *Shkol'na chasopys'* (Lviv 1880–9), edited by H. Vretsona, and *Narodna shkola* (Kolomyia 1875).

The first Ukrainian pedagogical periodical in Transcarpathia was the weekly *Uchytel'* (Uzhhorod 1867), edited by A. Ripai. From 1868 to 1873 the Hungarian Ministry of Education published the weekly *Hazeta dlia narodnykh uchytelei. Both newspapers addressed national, political, economic, and cultural questions as well as strictly educational issues.

Two issues of a pedagogical journal edited by S. Smal-Stotsky and published by the Ruska Shkola society appeared in Chernivtsi in 1888 and 1891.

The fortnightly journal *Uchytel'*, which succeeded *Shkol'na chasopys'*, was published by the Ruthenian Pedagogical Society (later Ridna Shkola) in Lviv in 1889–1914. It became the leading journal of its kind and played an important role in the later development of the pedagogical press. The Ukrainian Teachers' Mutal Aid Society published the journal *Uchytel'ske slovo* in 1912–39. Other pedagogical journals published in the first two decades of the 20th century included the following: in Bukovyna, the fortnightlies *Promin'* (1904–7) and *Kameniari* (1908–14); in Lviv, two short-lived periodicals, *Luna*, a semiofficial organ of the Ukrainian Teachers' Mutual Aid Society, edited by Yu. Lovytsky in the first half of 1907, and *Nashe slovo*, which appeared in the latter half of 1907, edited by P. Kyrchiv and O. Vlasiichuk; *Prapor (1908–12), published in Lviv and then Kolomyia; and *Ukraïns'kyi uchytel'* with the insert *Ridna shkola*, published in 1911 in Stanyslaviv, under the editorship of I. Butsmaniuk. *Nasha shkola was a scholarly journal published quarterly in Lviv by the *Teachers' Hromada, an organization of elementary-school teachers in Galicia and Bukovyna.

The first pedagogical journals in Russian-ruled Ukraine – *Pedagogicheskii vestnik* (Yelysavethrad [now Kirovohrad] 1881–3) and *Shkolnoe obrazovanie* (Odessa 1889–92) – appeared in Russian. The first Ukrainian-language pedagogical journal was *Svitlo, published in Kiev (1910–14) by the

Ukrainskyi Uchytel Publishing House under the editorship of H. Sherstiuk and then V. Prokopovych. The nationally conscious teachers who gravitated toward *Svitlo*, which advocated the use of Ukrainian in schools, formed the All-Ukrainian Teachers' Union in 1917. This group published *Vil'na ukraïns'ka shkola* in 1917–19. Other pedagogical journals in eastern Ukraine were *Nova shkola* (Poltava, 1917–18) and *Osvita* (Kamianets-Podilskyi, 1919).

In Western Ukraine two journals were published irregularly by teachers' societies in 1919, *Nova shkola*, in Drohobych, and *Uchytel's'kyi holos*, in Kolomyia. *Uchytel's'ke slovo* remained the most influential journal of its kind in the interwar period and published the supplements *Shliakh vykhovannia i navchannia* and *Metodyka i shkil'na praktyka* (1930–9). The Teachers' Hromada society published the monthly *Svitlo* (1920–1), edited by M. Halushchynsky, and *Ukraïns'ka shkola* (1925–39). Both journals were in effect continuations of *Nasha shkola*. *Ridna shkola*, published in 1927 and 1932–9, was the organ of the private Ukrainian school society of the same name. In 1938–9 the *Ukrainska Zakhoronka* society published a journal devoted to preschool education, *Ukraïns'ke doshkillia*.

Four monthly pedagogical journals were published in Uzhhorod and Mukachiv in Transcarpathia in the interwar period: *Uchytel'* (1920–36), the organ of the School Administration of Subcarpathian Ruthenia, the Russophile *Narodnaia shkola* (1921–38), and *Uchytel's'kyi holos* (1930–9) and *Nasha shkola* (1935–8), both organs of the *Teachers' Hromada of Subcarpathian Ruthenia.

Pedagogical periodicals in Soviet Ukraine in the 1920s reflected the polemical battle being waged among three pedagogical camps. The first camp advocated the creation of *labor schools with a national basis but adapted to Soviet conditions. Journals that supported this policy included *Osvita* (1920), published in Kiev; the newspaper *Narodnyi uchytel'* (1925–30), published in Kharkiv; the Kharkiv journal *Narodnyi uchytel'* (1926–7); and *Kuznia osvity* (1928–9), published in Kiev. Numerous bulletins also expressed the positions of this group. The second camp espoused modern Western pedagogical theories. Its approach was championed by *Ukraïns'kyi visnyk eksperymental'noï pedahohiky ta refleksolohiï* (1925–30).

The positions of the third camp, represented in the educational policy of the Ukrainian SSR Commissariat of Education, faithful to Marxist-Leninist precepts but independent of the policy of the RSFSR, were advanced in several journals: *Narodna osvita* (1919), published in Ukrainian and Russian in Kiev; *Proletars'ka osvita* (1920–1), published in Kiev; and the official organs of the People's Commissariat of Education of the Ukrainian SSR, *Shliakh osvity* (1922–30) and *Radians'ka osvita* (1923–31), both published in Kharkiv.

With the onset of Stalinism and the official condemnation of all three of these approaches to education, most of the pedagogical press of the 1920s and early 1930s was suppressed and replaced by orthodox Stalinist publications – *Za markso-lenins'ku pedahohiku* (1931–2) and *Za masovu komunistychnu osvitu* (1931–3). In this period the Commissariat of Education also established three new organs: *Komunistychna osvita* (in place of *Shliakh osvity*) and *Za komunistychne vykhovannia doshkil'nyka*, both published in 1931–41, initially in Kharkiv and later in Kiev, and *Pedahohika i metodychna literatura* (Pedagogy and Methodological Literature), published in 1938–41 in Kiev.

During the Second World War pedagogical periodicals in Soviet Ukraine ceased publication, and after the war they were replaced by new journals. The Ministry of Education of the Ukrainian SSR published three monthlies: the scholarly journal *Radians'ka shkola*; (now *Ridna shkola*) since 1945; the methodological journal *Doshkil'ne vykhovannia* (founded in 1951); and the methodological journal *Ukraïns'ka mova i literatura v shkoli*, established in 1963 through the merger of the monthly *Ukraïns'ka mova v shkoli* and the bimonthly *Literatura v shkoli*. *Radians'ka osvita* (now *Osvita*), a newspaper for teachers, has been published since 1940. In addition, since 1962, nine specialized serials dealing with problems of pedagogical methodology have been founded.

Ukrainian pedagogical periodicals have also been published by émigré Ukrainians. The Ukrainian Teachers' Labor Alliance published *Ukraïns'ka shkola* in 1942–3 in Cracow, under the editorship of P. Isaiv. Isaiv also edited a journal of the same name in Augsburg, Germany (1947–8). In New York *Ridna shkola* (1918) and *Uchytel's'ki visty* (1928–9) were both intended primarily for precentors-teachers. In Toronto and later in the United States V. Lutsiv edited and published *Zhyttia i shkola*, a journal for parents and teachers, and *Uchytel's'ke slovo* (1955–8), a methodological journal. In 1969 the Saskatchewan Teachers of Ukrainian started publishing *Tema*, a quarterly magazine devoted to problems of Ukrainian language education. In 1979 the School Council of the Ukrainian Canadian Committee launched the magazine *Ukraïns'kyi uchytel' v Kanadi*. The school boards of the provinces of Alberta, Saskatchewan, and Manitoba all have publications related to their Ukrainian-English bilingual school programs, and parents' organizations in those provinces publish various bulletins and newsletters in support of bilingual education. In 1976 *Informatyvno-metodychnyi lystok* was founded in Melbourne by the Ukrainian Central School Council of Australia.

C. Freeland, S. Yaniv, B. Krawchenko

Pedagogical schools (*pedahohichni shkoly* or *uchylyshcha*). Specialized secondary schools for the training of general elementary-school and preschool teachers. They were established in 1937 on the basis of the pedagogical tekhnikums (est 1920).

These institutions train general teachers for grades one to four of elementary schools, senior Pioneer leaders (until 1991), art, music and singing, preschool, and physical education teachers, and industrial arts and drafting instructors for grades four to eight. Students who have completed only the first 8 years of education before entering the schools enroll for a 3- or 4-year program, which completes their general education; those with a complete secondary education enroll for 2 years. Much time is devoted to training in practical teaching and work experience. The program of instruction revolves around three cycles of learning, social-political, pedagogical, and specialization. Study of at least one musical instrument is compulsory.

In 1966–7 there were 38 pedagogical schools in Ukraine, with a total enrollment of 33,000. In 1988–9 the number of such schools stood at 50, with a total enrollment of 77,600.

Pedagogical societies (*pedahohichni tovarystva*). Volunteer community organizations of teachers, public education activists, and pedagogical scholars that aim to broaden pedagogical knowledge and understanding, foster the development of solutions to existing problems, and address questions and issues in the theory and practice of education and upbringing.

These societies first appeared in Western Ukraine in the 19th century: the Ukrainian Pedagogical Society (est 1881 and renamed the *Ridna Shkola society in 1926), the Ruska Shkola society in Chernivtsi (est 1887 and renamed *Ukrainska Shkola in 1908), the Ukrainian Teachers' Mutual Aid Society in Lviv (est 1905), and the *Skovoroda Society of Higher School Teachers (est 1908). The *Pedagogical Society of Subcarpathian Ruthenia existed in Transcarpathia in 1923–34. In 1941–4 the *Ukrainian Teachers' Labor Alliance operated under the auspices of the Ukrainian Central Committee in Cracow and Lviv.

In Russian-ruled Ukraine the earliest societies were the Ushinsky Kiev Pedagogical Society (est 1899), the Froebel Kiev Pedagogical Society (est 1908), and the Kiev District Pedagogical Society (est 1916).

A number of new pedagogical societies were formed in Ukraine in the wake of the 1917 Revolution. In 1917–20 the *Society of School Education functioned in Kiev. Also in Kiev a Pedagogical Society functioned as a part of the All-Ukrainian Academy of Sciences from 1925; it had a branch in Kharkiv. This society was liquidated in the early 1930s. From 1929 to 1935 the Society of Marxist Pedagogues had a branch in Kharkiv. In 1960 the Pedagogical Society of the Ukrainian SSR was organized. In 1962 it had some 40,000 members. In addition the *Znannia Society of the Ukrainian SSR has a pedagogical division. Before the disintegration of the USSR in 1991, several independent organizations were established that include pedagogical activity in their programs. Among the most important is the Taras Shevchenko Ukrainian Language Society, founded in 1988.

Of the Ukrainian pedagogical societies outside Ukraine, the most active have been the *Ukrainian Pedagogical Society in Prague (1923–45), the *Ukrainian Teachers' Federation of Canada (since 1949), the Ukrainian Educational Council in the United States, and the Union of Ukrainian Teachers and Educators in Great Britain. In the 1980s the Manitoba Parents for Ukrainian Education group and the Alberta Parents for Ukrainian Education group were formed to promote Ukrainian-language education.

N. Freeland, B. Krawchenko

Pedagogical Society of Subcarpathian Ruthenia

(Pedahohichne tovarystvo Pidkarpatskoi Rusy). A pedagogical society with a Ukrainophile orientation, established in Uzhhorod in 1924 and transferred to Khust in 1938. It published a series of elementary- and secondary-school textbooks, by educators such as O. Markush, Yu. Revai, F. Ahii, and A. Voloshyn, as well as the children's magazine Nash ridnyi krai (1922–38) and a journal of regional studies, Pidkarpats'ka Rus' (1923–36). The president of the society was A. Voloshyn. It was suppressed when the Hungarians annexed Carpatho-Ukraine in 1939.

Pedagogical tekhnikums (pedahohichni tekhnikumy). Institutions of secondary learning in Ukraine, established in 1920. They trained teachers for grades one to four of the general elementary-school system, preschool teachers, and instructors in political education institutions, such as clubs and libraries. Tekhnikum students were graduates of seven-year elementary schools. Social, general educational, and pedagogical courses were taught at the tekhnikums. The three-year program of the tekhnikums also included some practical pedagogical training. In 1927 there were 61 pedagogical tekhnikums in Ukraine, with 8,990 students (of which 7,620 were Ukrainian) and 920 staff. In over two-thirds of the tekhnikums, Ukrainian was the language of instruction. In 1937 the tekhnikums were reorganized into *pedagogical schools.

Pedagogy. The discipline which studies education, learning, and child-rearing.

The earliest expression of pedagogical ideas is found in the oral folklore (epic folk songs, folktales, proverbs) of Kievan Rus'. Some pedagogical notions were subsequently expressed in the Testament of Prince Volodymyr Monomakh, Poucheniie ditiam (An Instruction for [My] Children, ca 1117). In the 11th and 12th centuries several collections appeared featuring native Kievan Rus' writing, as well as translations of classical and Byzantine authors on the moral and religious rearing of children.

After the collapse of Kievan Rus', centers of education and culture shifted to the *brotherhood schools in Lviv, Lutske, Ostrih, and later, Kiev. The emergence of printing in the mid-16th century was a powerful impetus to the development of educational and didactic literature. The need to defend the Ukrainian Orthodox brotherhood schools and the values they upheld from encroachments from Polish Catholic institutions served as a further stimulus to pedagogical thought in this period. Major figures of the brotherhood schools, such as Y. *Boretsky, M. *Smotrytsky, K. *Stavrovetsky-Tranquillon, I. *Vyshensky, and L. *Zyzanii, published works which dealt with the principles, form, and methods of instruction, and which extolled the benefits of education.

The Kievan Mohyla College (transformed into an academy in 1701) was the center of pedagogical study in Ukraine, beginning in the second half of the 17th and continuing through the 18th century. Its professors and graduates played an important role in the development of pedagogical thought in Ukraine. Noteworthy among them were I. *Galiatovsky, I. *Gizel, whose work Sinopsis (1674) was the first textbook to be published in Ukraine, and S. *Polotsky, who emphasized the importance of learning and supported the principle of visual methods of instruction.

The educational ideas of H. *Skovoroda had a considerable influence on the development of pedagogical thought in the second half of the 18th century. He defended the principle of the development of a person's natural abilities and demanded that education be made available to all classes of society, including women.

The rise of *populism, a movement which stressed popular enlightenment, brought the question of education to the forefront. But, the development of pedagogy as a discipline and research on the history of education began on a significant scale in Russian-ruled Ukraine only in the 19th century. A chair of pedagogy was created at Kiev University in 1850 and was occupied in 1851 by S. *Hohotsky, a philosopher and the author of works on the theory and history of education. Important figures in the development of pedagogical thought in the second half of the 19th century were F. Bemer, an advocate of humanist and purposeful instruction; M. *Levytsky, who developed a methodology for elementary education; and most important, K. *Ushinsky, who wrote prolifically on the theory of education and instruction and played a leading role in the establishment of pedagogy as a separate discipline. Notable contributions were also made by the Russian physician and educator N. Pirogov, who was active in Ukraine and advocated the idea of a uniform system of general education; Baron N. Korf, an organizer of *zemstvo schools in Ukraine; and I. Derkachov (Derkach), a Ukrainian follower of Ushinsky and the author of over 50 school textbooks. Toward the end of the 19th century Khrystyna *Alchevska developed ideas on adult education, T. *Lubenets wrote on elementary education, and S. *Rusova wrote on public education.

Important questions of pedagogy, such as the organization of schools, instruction in the native language, improvement of the content and method of instruction, the education of women, and professional and technical training, were discussed in various periodicals which appeared in the second half of the 19th century, such as *Osnova, the weekly *Chernigovskii listok, the journal Pedagogicheskii vestnik (published in 1881–3 in Yelysavethrad), the newspaper Shkolnoe obrazovanie (Odessa 1889–92), and the journal *Kievskaia starina. (See also *Pedagogical periodicals.)

Research on the history of education and schools in Ukraine also began in the second half of the 19th century. Significant contributions were made by N. Lavrovsky, O. Lazarevsky, M. Drahomanov, and B. Hrinchenko.

The chairs of pedagogy at Kiev, Kharkiv, and Odessa universities became increasingly active in the early 20th century under the influence of modern trends and methods of education initiated in Western Europe. S. Ananin, a professor of pedagogy at Kiev University and the author of numerous treatises on education, was the chief exponent of these trends and methods. The Pedagogical Museum in Kiev (1901–17) became an important center of educational research.

Pedagogical thought in Russian-ruled Ukraine from the beginning of the 20th century until the 1917 Revolution focused primarily on problems of public education, in particular on the use of Ukrainian in the elementary schools. Works on this subject were written by Hrinchenko, V. Prokopovych, S. Siropolko, M. Chaly, Ya. Chepiha-Zelenkevych, S. Cherkasenko, and H. Sherstiuk. After 1910 the Ukrainskyi Uchytel society became the leading center of educational research; it published *Svitlo, the first Ukrainian-language pedagogical journal in Russian-ruled Ukraine.

In that period there appeared important works on the history of education. An account of education from the earliest times was written by M. *Hrushevsky in the first volumes of his Istoriia Ukraïny-Rusy (History of Ukraine-Rus'). K. *Kharlampovych wrote a broad analytical study of the history of education from its beginnings to the mid-18th century.

In Western Ukraine (under Austrian rule) questions of education and child-rearing occupied an important place in the work of the *Ruthenian Triad in the 1820s and 1830s. The first major work in Western Ukrainian educational literature was O. *Dukhnovych's Narodnaia pedahohiia v pol'zu uchylyshch i uchytelei sel'skikh (Public Pedagogy for the Use of Village Schools and Teachers, 1857). Toward the end of the 19th and in the early 20th century, research

on the theory and history of education was pursued by O. Makarushka, V. Biletsky, I. Demianchuk, K. Malytska, I. Yushchyshyn, and others. The development of educational theory and practice was spurred with the founding of the Ruthenian (subsequently, Ukrainian) Pedagogical Society in 1881 (see *Ridna Shkola society) and the publication of its semimonthly periodical *Uchytel'. Other organizations, such as the *Ukrainian Teachers' Mutual Aid Society, established in 1905, as well as the society's journal *Uchytel's'ke slovo, also contributed to the development of pedagogical thought. The Ukrainska Shkola society was the principal educational center in Bukovyna, and in Transcarpathia the journal Uchytel', founded in 1867, was the venue of pedagogical thought.

In the wake of the collapse of the tsarist regime in March 1917, Ukraine witnessed the large-scale development of *elementary and *secondary schools, as well as of institutions of *higher education. Because much of the growth occurred spontaneously at the local level, it also highlighted the need for a more systematic approach to educational reform. Consequently, practical considerations, notably the drafting of plans and programs for a uniform system of education (the *unified labor school), spurred the development of pedagogical thought. The *Society of School Education, committees of the General Secretariat of Education of the Central Rada and later of the Ministry of Education of the Ukrainian National Republic, as well as individuals such as Rusova, V. Durdukivsky, H. Ivanytsia, Siropolko, and O. Muzychenko, played major roles in the elaboration of new models of education. The journal *Vil'na ukraïns'ka shkola was an important forum for discussion, as were congresses of the *All-Ukrainian Teachers' Association. The Ukrainian Pedagogical Academy, founded in 1917, became a center for research in education and teacher training.

In the first years of Soviet rule in Ukraine, the elaboration of the model of a unified labor school was continued by a group of pedagogues centered in the pedagogical section of the Ukrainian Scientific Society in Kiev, and from 1921 in the Scientific-Pedagogical Commission of the historical-philosophical section of the All-Ukrainian Academy of Sciences (O. Korchak-Chepurkivsky, O. Doroshkevych, and others).

The first half of the 1920s in Soviet Ukraine was characterized by the rise of several competing schools of pedagogical thought, many of which borrowed freely from advanced Western educational theory. Chepiha-Zelenkevych advocated the principles of a liberal education; Ya. Mamontov was a prominent theorist of esthetic education; O. Muzychenko developed an approach which emphasized the comprehensive development of individuals; A. Volodymyrsky and his group stressed the natural development of children and adapted the principles of reflexology to pedagogy; O. Skovoroda-Zachyniaiev, director of the Laboratory of Reflexology and Experimental Pedagogy at the physico-mathematical division of the All-Ukrainian Academy of Sciences, also played a major part in advancing new educational ideas.

Authorities, however, chose a different course in the development of education. A unified system of education was implemented, which stressed social education and professional training. The theorists of this system (which was unique to Ukraine) were H. *Hrynko and Ya. *Riappo. An important center of pedagogical thought in the period was the *Scientific Research Institute of Pedagogy of the Ukrainian SSR founded in 1926. Among the leading journals were *Shliakh osvity and *Radians'ka osvita. During the 1920s important research was done on the history of education by scholars such as A. Savych, T. Titov, A. Gotalov-Gotlib, and D. Krakhovetsky.

The pluralism which characterized pedagogical thought throughout much of the 1920s came to an abrupt halt with the consolidation of Stalinism in the 1930s. Most of the individuals, research centers, and journals active in the 1920s were silenced in the early 1930s. The unified system of social education was radically reorganized. Theories of labor and collective education as advanced by A. *Makarenko, N. Dadenkov, and S. *Chavdarov became the established orthodoxy in pedagogy. The development of pedagogical thought in Ukraine in the 1930s was also stymied by the centralization of educational decision-making. Soviet Ukraine's distinctive system of education was abolished, and a unified model was imposed by Moscow. School curricula, textbooks, and programs were now decided upon centrally. Emblematic of this development was the establishment in 1943 of the Academy of Pedagogical Sciences of the RSFSR. During the 1920s Ukrainian educationalists attempted to establish an academy of pedagogical sciences in Ukraine but were denied permission. The Russian Academy of Pedagogical Sciences became a fundamental formulator of Soviet educational plans and pedagogical methods for the entire USSR.

In Polish-ruled Western Ukraine in the interwar period, the most important center of pedagogical thought was the Ridna Shkola society, which also published a journal by that name. Among those who addressed questions of methodology were P. Bilaniuk, Ya. Bilenky, I. Levytsky, N. Matviichuk, and B. Zaklynsky. Contributions to the history of education were made by I. Krypiakevych, A. Androkhovych, I. Fylypchak, and Ye. Hrytsak.

In the immediate post–Second World War period pedagogy in Ukraine focused on the ideological and political education of pupils. N. Khrushchev's educational reform of 1959 unleashed a debate on pedagogy in Ukraine, and the science was criticized for its lack of innovative thinking. In the 1960s and early 1970s significant research was done by V. *Sukhomlynsky, I. Fusenko, M. *Marchenko, and M. *Hryshchenko.

In Soviet Ukraine pedagogical research was carried out by the Scientific Research Institute of Pedagogy of Ukraine, *pedagogical institutes, and at 10 universities. Several pedagogical periodicals were published in Ukraine. A large-scale debate on questions of pedagogy was opened in Ukraine in 1987, as a result of the political changes taking place. Since then there has been growing public pressure for less authoritarian, more innovative approaches to education.

An important center of pedagogical research outside Ukraine in the interwar period was the *Ukrainian Higher Pedagogical Institute and the *Ukrainian Pedagogical Society in Prague. The leading scholars there were Rusova, V. *Simovych, and Siropolko. After the Second World War a chair of pedagogy was established at the *Ukrainian Free University in Munich, and the post was held by H. *Vashchenko. Questions of methodology have been addressed by various *pedagogical societies in Canada, the United States, and Australia. In Canada, with the development of the *Ukrainian bilingual program, innovative re-

search into second-language acquisition and language instruction methodology has been conducted at the University of Alberta by O. Bilash, and by the curriculum branch of the province of Alberta's Ministry of Education. A Ukrainian Language Education Centre exists at the Canadian Institute of Ukrainian Studies, University of Alberta.

BIBLIOGRAPHY
Siropolko, S. Istoriia osvity na Ukraïni (Lviv 1937)
Narodna osvita i pedahohika v Ukraïns'kii RSR 1917–1967 (Kiev 1967)
Mitiurov, B. Razvitie pedagogicheskoi mysli na Ukraine v XVI–XVII vv. (Kiev 1968)
Rozvytok narodnoï osvity i pedahohichnoï nauky na Ukraïni, 2 vols (Kiev 1987)

B. Kravtsiv, B. Krawchenko

Pediatrics. A branch of medicine dealing with the organismic singularities of the child and the prevention and cure of childhood diseases. The Ukrainian obstetrician N. *Ambodyk-Maksymovych, the author of Iskusstvo spovivaniia, ili nauka o babich'em dele (The Art of Swaddling, or the Science of Women's Matters, 1781), made an important contribution to the development of pediatrics in the Russian Empire. S. *Khotovytsky was the first professor of pediatrics at the Academy of Medicine and Surgery in St Petersburg (1836), as well as the author of the empire's first textbook on childhood diseases (1847). A. Matveev began lecturing on childhood diseases at Kiev University in 1844. The first department of pediatrics was established at Kiev University in 1889; it was followed by one at Kharkiv University in 1892. The first society of pediatricians in Ukraine was founded in 1900 in Kiev.

With the onset of Soviet rule the People's Commissariat of Public Health created a state system of 'maternity and childhood care' in 1920, which was incorporated in 1924 into the system of *medical education (called pediatrics faculties from 1932). Within the pediatrics field there developed several subspecializations, including pediatric surgery, neurology, physiology, cardiology, allergy, as well as age-specific anatomy and neonatal pediatrics. Infant mortality (death of infants under the age of one year) is one of the most important indicators of the health of a nation. The lowest infant mortality rates in the world – fewer than 6 infant deaths per 1,000 live births – are reported from Japan, Sweden, and Finland. In Ukraine the rate was 19.7 (30.6 in the USSR) in 1975, 15.7 (26.0) in 1985, 14.2 (24.7) in 1988, and 12.8 in 1990. The lowest infant mortality rates in Ukraine are in Chernihiv, Vinnytsia, and Cherkasy oblasts, and the highest are in Ivano-Frankivske, Chernivtsi, Luhanske, Kherson, and Zhytomyr oblasts. The rate in Kiev oblast showed a leap from 9.7 in 1989 to 13.0 in 1990, a clear indication of the disastrous medium-term health consequences of the nuclear explosion at the Chornobyl Atomic Energy Station in 1986. Investigations by the state statistical service in 1989 attested to the practice of concealing infant deaths by classifying them as miscarriages and other nonviable pregnancies, in up to 50 percent of the cases in the RSFSR and up to 20 percent of those in Ukraine.

The development of pediatrics strongly influenced *public health in the USSR. Besides the departments of pediatrics at medical institutes in Ukraine, two scientific research institutes of pediatrics, *obstetrics, and *gynecology operate in Kiev and Lviv, and the Scientific Research

Institute for the Health Care of Children and Teenagers (est 1922 as the All-Ukrainian Institute of Maternity and Childhood Care, renamed in 1965) operates in Kharkiv. The journal *Pediatriia, akusherstvo i hinekolohiia* is published bimonthly in Kiev.

P. Dzul

Pediatriia, akusherstvo i hinekolohiia (Pediatrics, Obstetrics, and Gynecology). A scientific bimonthly; founded in 1936 in Kiev and published by the Ukrainian Ministry of Health. It contains papers on clinical problems, improved diagnostic methods, new ways of treating childhood diseases and gynecological disorders, and organizational questions of providing health care for children and women. Its circulation was approx 8,200 in 1980.

Pekalytsky, Semen [Pekalyc'kyj], b ca 1630, d ? Singer, choirmaster, and composer. He was a precentor in the kapelle of Archbishop L. Baranovsky in Chernihiv (1660s), the kapelle of Bishop Y. Shumliansky in Lviv (1667–73), and then the court kapelle in Moscow. In the 1680s he served as a priest in Novhorod-Siverskyi and directed the local choir. His Liturgy in A Minor is a masterpiece of 17th-century Ukrainian church music.

Rev Atanasii Pekar

Pekar, Atanasii (secular name: Vasyl), b 1 March 1922 in Perechyn, Transcarpathia. Basilian priest and church historian; full member of the Shevchenko Scientific Society. After obtaining a PH D at the Pontifical Urbaniana University in Rome (1942) and being ordained (1946), he moved to the United States (1948). He has taught at various theological seminaries and novitiates and has written various works on the history of the Ukrainian Catholic church, including *Narysy istorii tserkvy Zakarpattia* (Surveys of the History of the Church in Transcarpathia, 1967); *Our Past and Present: Historical Outlines of the Byzantine Ruthenian Metropolitan Province* (1974); *The Bishops of the Eparchy of Mukachevo* (1979); and *You Shall Be Witness to Me* (1985), a martyrology of the church in Transcarpathia.

Pekar, Solomon, b 16 March 1917 in Kiev, d 8 July 1985 in Kiev. Theoretical physicist; full AN URSR (now ANU) member from 1961. After graduating from Kiev University (1938) he worked at the ANU Institute of Physics, where he created the Department of Theoretical Physics. From 1960 he headed the same department at the ANU *Institute of Semiconductors, which was formed on his and V. *Lashkarov's initiative. From 1944 he was also a professor

at Kiev University, where he organized the chair of theoretical physics. A highly productive researcher, Pekar made major contributions to applied solid-state physics by elaborating a quantitative theory of semiconductor rectification (1939) and introducing and developing the concepts of polarons (1946–9) and deformation potential (1951). As a result of his investigations of excitons, Pekar proposed and developed a new quantum mechanical theory of the optical properties of crystals (1957–60).

Pekari. A multi-occupational site in Kaniv raion, Cherkasy oblast. Excavations in 1891–2, 1947–8, and 1958–65 uncovered the remains of *Trypilian and *Catacomb culture settlements, as well as a 9th- to 10th-century Rus' occupation. Among the artifacts recovered was a plate bearing a gold-encrusted image of three warriors in front of a fortress.

Pelahiivka [Pelahijivka]. V-19, DB III-5. A town smt (1986 pop 16,600) in Donetske oblast. It was founded as a mining settlement in 1915 and granted smt status in 1938. It has three coal mines and an enrichment plant. The town is run by the Torez city council.

Pelchytsky, Leontii [Pelčyc'kyj, Leontij] (secular name: Levko Zenkovych or Zakhariievych), b ?, d 1595. Bishop of Kholm (1577–85) and Turiv–Pynske (1585–95). The son of a bishop and a nobleman, he was installed as bishop in 1577 and ordained as a priest only in 1580. He is best known for taking part in the initial planning, in 1590, of the Church Union of *Berestia. He died before the realization of church union.

Pelekh, Ivan [Pelex], b 8 February 1859 in Pomoriany, Zboriv county, Galicia, d 23 July 1914 in Lviv. Russophile journalist. Upon graduating from Lviv University in 1881, he worked for the biweekly paper *Prolom*. Then he was a coeditor of the paper *Chervonaia Rus'* (1888–91) and editor of *Russkoe slovo* and *Halychanyn* (1909–13). He contributed to *Strakhopud* and published the Russkaia Biblioteka (Russian Library) series (1887–1905), which included masterpieces of Russian literature. Active in a number of Russophile groups, he served for 25 years on the executive of the Kachkovsky Society.

Pelekh, Petro [Pelex], b 12 March 1887 in Dobrochyn, Sokal county, Galicia, d 15 October 1961 in Kiev. Psychologist. He graduated from Lviv University (1913) and taught secondary school in Ternopil. From 1917 he worked in Kiev teaching Latin, Ukrainian, philosophy, and psychology at the university and other institutions of higher learning. After the Second World War, as a research associate of the Scientific Research Institute of Psychology of the Ukrainian SSR, (1945–59), he did research in occupational psychology, personality development, and the history of psychology. He wrote a number of articles on the lectures in philosophical psychology at the Kievan Mohyla Academy in the 17th and 18th centuries.

Pelekhaty, Demian [Pelexatyj, Demjan], b 1 July 1926 in Lviv. Conductor and pedagogue. He studied conducting and composition at the Lviv Conservatory (graduating in 1951) and taught there in 1952–7 and 1966–71. Since 1951 he has been conductor of the Lviv Symphony Orchestra, and since 1964 its principal conductor. He has premiered numerous works of 20th-century Ukrainian composers, including S. Liudkevych and R. Simovych. He is a well-known interpreter of D. Shostakovich, S. Prokofiev, D. Kabalevsky, and R. Shchedrin.

Pelekhaty, Kuzma [Pelexatyj, Kuz'ma], b 11 November 1886 in Opory, Drohobych county, Galicia, d 28 March 1952 in Lviv. Journalist and political activist. After graduating from the Higher Institute of Journalism in Vienna he worked for the Galician Russophile newspapers *Halychanyn* (1910–13) and *Prikarpatskaia Rus'* (1913–15) and the Russian-language journal *Novaia zhizn'*. After the First World War he was the managing editor of the Sovietophile newspapers *Volia naroda* (1921–7) and *Sel'-Rob* (1927–8), to which he contributed feuilletons under the pen names Kuzma Bezrodny and Maksym Strikha. He adhered faithfully to Comintern policies and attacked the national-communist opposition in the Communist Party of Western Ukraine. Under the Soviet regime, in 1939–41 he worked on the staff of *Vil'na Ukraïna* in Lviv, and in 1949 he was appointed chairman of the Lviv Oblast Executive Committee. A collection of his articles was published in 1959.

Pelekhin, Pavlo [Pelexin], b 1842 in St Petersburg, d 1917. Surgeon; son of Petro *Pelekhin. He taught at the Military Medical Academy in St Petersburg (1868–89, as full professor from 1877). His publications dealt with the treatment of wounds, the resection of joints, ovariotomy, and pyemia. He was a pioneer in the use of antiseptics in the Russian Empire. In 1898 he made a significant donation of 90,000 Austrian kronen to the Shevchenko Scientific Society (NTSh) in Lviv for the foundation of a medical section, for surgical scholarships, and for the purchase of an NTSh building.

Pelekhin, Petro [Pelexin], b 1789 in Makiivka, Cherkasy county, Kiev gubernia, d 3 October 1871 in Kiev. Physician. A graduate of the Kievan Mohyla Academy (1811) and the St Petersburg Medico-Surgical Academy (1824), he taught physiology and pathology at the academy and presented a doctoral thesis on neurosis at Edinburgh University (1829). He did research on cholera in Astrakhan and taught medicine at the Kiev Theological Academy (from 1849).

Pelenska, Iryna [Pelens'ka] (pseud: Iryna Vynnytska), b 6 November 1906 in Hrabovets, Stryi county, Galicia, d 4 January 1990 in Detroit. Writer and community figure; wife of Ye. *Pelensky. She studied at Lviv University (1933). In the years 1925–39 she was active in the Plast Ukrainian Youth Association, student organizations, and the Prosvita society in Galicia. She contributed prose, literary essays, and articles to periodicals there and wrote the novelettes *Khrystyna* (1940) and *Muzyka* (Music, 1944; 2nd edn 1954). As a postwar émigré in Germany she published the novelette *Kam'iana sokyra* (The Stone Ax, 1947; rev edn 1967) and the story collection *Horikhove lushpynnia* (Nutshells, 1948). After emigrating to Sydney in the late 1940s, she became a founding member and the president of the *Ukrainian Women's Association in Australia (1949–56, 1959–62), a member of the executive of the Federation of Ukrainians in Australia (1951–62), and vice-

Iryna Pelenska   Yevhen Yulii Pelensky

president of the Australian chapter of the Shevchenko Scientific Society (1956–62). She also owned and ran a publishing company (1956–62) and contributed prose to Ukrainian-Australian periodicals. After moving to the United States in 1962, she was secretary of the Ukrainian National Women's League of America, a member of the executive of the World Federation of Ukrainian Women's Organizations (SFUZhO), and, until 1982, editor of the SFUZhO organ *Ukraïnka v sviti*. From 1970 she headed the World Preschool Council of the World Congress of Free Ukrainians.

R. Senkus

Pelenski, Jaroslaw [Pelens'kyj, Jaroslav], b 12 April 1929 in Warsaw. Ukrainian historian; foreign member of the Academy of Sciences of Ukraine since 1992. He studied at Würzburg (1948–9), Munich (PH D, 1957), and Columbia (PH D, 1968) universities and has taught Russian, Soviet, Eastern European, and Ukrainian political and intellectual history at the American University (Washington, DC, 1964–7), and, since 1967, the University of Iowa. He is the author of *Russia and Kazan: Conquest and Imperial Ideology, 1438–1560s* (1974) and many scholarly articles. He has edited several books and a special issue of *Harvard Ukrainian Studies* titled *The Political and Social Ideas of Vjačeslav Lypyns'kyj* (1985) and was the editor in chief of the Ukrainian sociopolitical journal *Vidnova* (est 1984). In 1987 he was elected president of the *Lypynsky East European Research Institute in Philadelphia.

Pelensky, Yevhen Yulii [Pelens'kyj, Jevhen Julij], b 3 January 1908 in Koniukhiv, Stryi county, Galicia, d 29 September 1956 in Sydney, Australia. Literary scholar, bibliographer, teacher, and publisher; full member of the Shevchenko Scientific Society (NTSh) from 1937; husband of I. *Pelenska. He received his PH D in Ukrainian literature and Slavic ethnology from Lviv University in 1930. He cofounded and later headed the Society of Ukrainian Bibliophiles, and in the 1930s he was secretary and vice-chairman of the NTSh Ethnological Commission. He was also editor of the literary journal *Dazhboh* (1932–4) and the bibliographic monthly *Ukraïns'ka knyha*. During the Second World War he was executive director of the *Ukrainske Vydavnytstvo (1939–40) and Bystrytsia publishing companies in Cracow. He became a docent at the Ukrainian Free University in Prague (1943–5) and Munich (1946–9). After emigrating to Australia in 1949, he founded and then headed the NTSh branch there and established the Slovo publishing house in Sydney.

Pelensky wrote over 250 works, including books on B. Lepky (1932, 1943), the development of Ukrainian literary parody (1935), R.M. Rilke and Ukraine (1935), Western Ukrainian literature in the years 1930–5 (1935), Ovid in Ukrainian literature (1937, 1943), the period of *Rusalka Dnistrovaia* (1938), M. Cheremshyna (1938), T. Shevchenko (1942), and a history of the NTSh (1949). As a bibliographer he compiled *Bibliohrafiia ukraïns'koï bibliohrafiï* (Bibliography of Ukrainian Bibliography, 1934) and *Ucrainica: Ausgewählte Bibliographie über die Ukraine in west-europäischen Sprachen* (1948). He wrote several dozen Ukrainian language textbooks and primers for Galician schools, published many editions of Ukrainian classics with his own scholarly introductions, and edited an anthology of contemporary Ukrainian poetry (1936). His articles appeared in NTSh serials and various Galician periodicals, including *Literaturno-naukovyi vistnyk* and *Bohosloviia*.

R. Senkus

Pelensky, Yosyp [Pelens'kyj, Josyp], b 31 December 1879 in Komarno, Rudky county, Galicia, d 29 November 1957 in Lviv. Art scholar and conservator; full member of the Shevchenko Scientific Society from 1917. A graduate of Cracow University (PH D, 1914), he specialized in Byzantine art, Ukrainian wooden architecture, and Halych's antiquities. He wrote a Polish-language book on medieval art in Halych (1914) and was a professor at the Kamianets-Podilskyi Ukrainian State University (1918–20).

Zenon Pelensky   Zynovii Pelensky

Pelensky, Zenon [Pelens'kyj], b 26 July 1902 in Tulyholovy, Rudky county, Galicia, d 30 October 1979 in Munich. Journalist and political activist. In interwar Galicia he was a founding member of the OUN and an active member of the Ukrainian National Democratic Alliance (UNDO). He served as the Berlin correspondent of the Lviv daily *Dilo* (1926–8) and was a regular contributor to *Rozbudova natsiï* (1928–35), the OUN journal published in Prague. He also served as chief editor of *Ukraïns'kyi holos* in Peremyshl (1929–32), the UNDO organ *Svoboda* (1936–8), and the Lviv daily *Novyi chas* (1938–9). As a postwar refugee in Munich, he edited the weekly *Ukraïns'ka trybuna* (1946–7) and *Ukraïns'kyi samostiinyk* (1950) and worked for the Ukrainian broadcast section at Radio Liberty (1955–67).

Pelensky, Zynovii [Pelens'kyj, Zynovij], b 1890 in Lysiatychi, Stryi county, Galicia, d October 1943 in Lviv.

Co-operative and political leader. After graduating from the Export Trade Academy in Vienna he worked in the Audit Union of Ukrainian Co-operatives in Lviv, first as editor of its paper *Hospodars'ko-kooperatyvnyi chasopys* (1927–30) and then as head of its co-operative propaganda department. He often represented the union at international co-operative conferences. He helped organize the Vlasna Khata building co-operative in Lviv. In 1929 he became a member of the Central Committee of the Ukrainian National Democratic Alliance. A deputy to the Polish Sejm (1930–8), he was sent by the Ukrainian Parliamentary Representation as its delegate to congresses of national minorities and served on the presidium of the Council of National Minorities in Geneva. During the Soviet occupation of Western Ukraine he lived in Lublin, where he was a commissioner of the Agrarian Bank (1940–1). He then returned to Lviv to become director of the same institution.

Bishop Yuliian Pelesh   Sergei Peletminsky

Pelesh, Yuliian [Peleš, Julijan], b 15 January 1843 in Smerekovets, Jasło circle, Galicia, d 22 April 1896 in Lypovets, Sianik county, Galicia. Uniate bishop and church historian. After graduating from the Vienna Theological Seminary and being ordained (1867) he completed a TH D in Vienna and was appointed prefect of the Greek Catholic Theological Seminary in Lviv (1870). He was a professor at the Peremyshl seminary (1872) and then curate of St Barbara's Church in Vienna and rector of the Ruthenian boarding school there (1874–83). In 1885 he was consecrated as the first bishop of Stanyslaviv eparchy, and in 1891 he became bishop of Peremyshl. Pelesh was one of the initiators of the Lviv Synod of 1891. In addition to textbooks on pastoral theology and catechism, he published *Geschichte der Union der ruthenischen Kirche mit Rom von den ältesten Zeiten bis auf die Gegenwart* (2 vols, 1878, 1880).

Peleshok, Kateryna [Pelešok] (née Shumeiko), b 26 August 1898 in Birky Velyki, Ternopil county, Galicia, d 20 July 1981 in New York. Community activist. After emigrating to the United States in 1921, she settled in New York. During the war she joined the *Ukrainian National Women's League of America and served as president of its New York branch (1945–66) and vice-president on the national executive (1950–9). She collected funds for the United Ukrainian American Relief Committee and was a member of its board of directors (1949–72). At the same time she served on the board of directors of the Ukrainian Congress Committee of America (1946–58) and on its political council (1963–9).

Peletminsky, Sergei (Peletminskij, Sergej), b 14 February 1931 in Tetkino, Glushkovo raion, Kursk oblast, Russia. Theoretical physicist; AN URSR (now ANU) corresponding member since 1978 and full member since 1990. A graduate of Kharkiv University (1953), since 1957 he has worked at the ANU Institute of Physics. Peletminsky has made substantial contributions to statistical mechanics and the quantum theory of fields, particularly by developing a theory of high-frequency relaxation processes in magnetic materials. In 1956, together with O. Akhiiezer and V. Bariakhtar, he discovered the magnetoacoustic resonance phenomenon.

Pellikh, Volodymyr [Pellix], b 17 October 1886 in Lysovychi, Stryi county, Galicia, d 28 December 1981 in Philadelphia. Greek Catholic priest and civic leader. A graduate of Lviv and Vienna (PH D, 1913) universities, he served as pastor at St Barbara's Church in Vienna (1912–16) before becoming a parish priest in Radekhiv (1918–32). There he was active in educational and cultural organizations, such as Prosvita, and was elected to the Polish Sejm in 1928. In 1944 he left for Germany, and three years later, for the United States, where he continued his pastoral work.

PEN. An acronym for the International Association of Poets, Playwrights, Editors, Essayists, and Novelists. The Ukrainian PEN, with headquarters in Kiev, was accepted as a member of the International Association at its 54th World Congress in Canada in 1989. M. *Vinhranovsky was elected president of the Ukrainian PEN, and Ye. *Sverstiuk and P. Movchan became vice-presidents. In the first two years the membership of the Ukrainian PEN grew to 85, including 11 members from the United States, 5 from Canada, 3 from Rumania, and 1 each from Germany, Belgium, Brazil, Poland, Czechoslovakia, Australia, and Israel. Several members in Ukraine who were former Soviet prisoners of conscience and *dissidents have been made honorary members of the International PEN.

Penck, Albrecht, b 1858, d 1945. German geographer and geologist; member of the Shevchenko Scientific Society. He was a professor at Vienna and Berlin universities and one of the first geographers to treat Ukraine as a geographic and sociopolitical entity distinct from Russia. His article on Ukraine, which appeared in *Zeitschrift der Gesellschaft für Erdkunde* (1916), was reprinted separately and distributed during the negotiations leading to the Peace Treaty of Brest-Litovsk.

Penitentiary system. A set of institutions for punishing criminal behavior by means of imprisonment and corrective labor. Imprisonment has been used as a form of punishment in the past; what distinguishes the modern penitentiary system is its scale and its declared purpose to reform the criminal. Modern penitentiaries emerged only in the early 19th century in the United States and Western Europe.

There is little information about the use of imprisonment in Kievan Rus'. Princes or boyars were imprisoned for political reasons in so-called *poruby*, and church people and offenders against the faith were locked up in special cells in monasteries. Other offenders were held under guard in various places. Eventually, towers became the preferred place of incarceration. Prisoners were called

kolodnyky, because they were usually in chains (*kolodky*). During the Cossack period the regimental towns of the Hetman state had prisons for detaining suspects who were under investigation. The main forms of punishment were fines, infliction of pain, and death. Incarceration was rarely used as punishment: only offenses such as harboring thieves, betraying a lover, refusing to return a stolen object, and making a false legal appeal were punishable by imprisonment from 12 weeks to two years, depending on the offense.

In the Russian Empire imprisonment was used only during investigation, until the mid-17th century, when it became accepted as a form of punishment. Even in the 18th century the government did not feed prisoners: sometimes they were allowed to go begging, and sometimes they starved to death. In the 19th century the use of imprisonment increased until it became the chief form of punishment, although *exile and hard labor continued to be used widely. One of the first jurists to espouse the modern concept of penitentiary was M. *Chubynsky. Prison reforms were introduced only in the second half of the century: a law on prison administration was adopted in 1879, and prisons were reorganized into various categories. The prison system was developed in a planned manner. By the turn of the century every town in Russia had a prison building and often more than one. In Kiev, besides the large *Lukianivka Prison, there was a smaller jail on Bibikov Boulevard. In Kharkiv the main prison was on Kholodna Hora. In the 18th and the first half of the 19th century political prisoners were held in the cells of the Kievan Cave Monastery and, later, in the Kievan Cave Fortress.

After the Revolution of 1917 the Bolsheviks tried to develop their own corrective-labor system, different from the conventional penitentiary system. Assuming that honest labor would reform criminals and turn them into constructive, law-abiding citizens, the authorities established *labor camps or colonies, whose inmates worked in state enterprises and received regular wages. The first *Corrective Labor Code was adopted in 1925. The corrective-labor camps quickly developed into a vast system of *concentration camps, which provided the state with *forced labor.

Prisons inherited from the tsarist regime were used to hold suspects under investigation before they were shipped off to concentration camps or executed. As the dimensions of political terror grew, the prisons became terribly overcrowded. Many prisoners died under torture during investigation or were executed in the prisons. Mass executions took place in the prisons of Vinnytsia (1937–8), Lviv, Kiev, Drohobych, Ternopil, Dubno, and other towns in June 1941.

In Western Ukraine under Austrian rule, the penitentiary system evolved to a relatively humane system as the brutal law of Joseph II (1787) was replaced by the more liberal decree of 1790, the criminal code of 1810, and the criminal code of 1852, which remained in force in Galicia until 1932. That code provided for detention for 24 hours to six months for minor offenses, and for imprisonment for six months to 20 years or even life for serious crimes.

Under Polish rule (1918–39) Austrian penal practices were continued until new Polish laws were passed – a prison statute in 1931 and a criminal code in 1932. Petty crimes were punishable with detention for seven days to five years, and serious crimes with imprisonment for six months to 15 years. A 'progressive system' was applied to inmates sentenced to over three years: they were segregated in special prisons according to several factors, such as age, motive of their crime, and criminal record, and were grouped further into classes with different regimes according to their readiness to reform. All prisoners had to work. There were no special jails for political prisoners. Ukrainians convicted of crimes against the state served time in prisons within Poland proper, not in Galicia. The largest prison of a general type was in Lviv and was called Brygidky. In 1934 a concentration camp was set up in *Bereza Kartuzka.

BIBLIOGRAPHY
Gernet, M. *Istoriia tsarskoi tiurmy*, 5 vols (Moscow 1961)

Penkivka settlements. A group of 6th- to 8th-century early Slavic settlements near Penkivka, Kirovohrad oblast. Excavations in 1955–60, previous to flooding by the Kremenchuk Reservoir, uncovered extensive dwelling remains. Pottery recovered from the 7th- and 8th-century occupation was very similar to that found at the neighboring *Pastyrske fortified settlement.

Penkov, Oleksander [Pen'kov], b 11 April 1906 in Katerynoslav, d 24 September 1968 in Kiev. Mechanics scientist; corresponding member of the AN URSR (now ANU) from 1951. He studied at the Dnipropetrovske Mining Institute. He worked at various institutes of the ANU and taught at universities in Kiev and Dnipropetrovske. His main contributions were in various areas of theoretical and applied mechanics: the theory of oscillations, the stability and reliability of structures, the design of machines and structures. His models and equations are widely used by design engineers.

Pennsylvania. A middle Atlantic state (1990 pop 11,924,710) of the United States, covering an area of 177,000 sq km. Its capital is Harrisburg. In 1990, 129,753 of its inhabitants were of Ukrainian origin.

Pennsylvania was the initial focal point of the mass immigration of Ukrainians to the United States, which began in 1877–8 when Pennsylvania mining companies began to recruit workers in Transcarpathia. The first recruits were joined soon by volunteers from the neighboring Lemko region and in the 1890s by peasants from eastern Galicia and Bukovyna. Before the First World War Pennsylvania attracted about 75 percent of the Ukrainian immigrants to the United States. Most of them settled in the coal region, in towns such as Shenandoah, Shamokin, Mount Carmel, Hazleton, Lansford, Freeland, Olyphant, and Mayfield. The first organized Ukrainian community in the United States arose in Shenandoah. By 1884 it had acquired the services of a priest, Rev I. Voliansky, and then it built the first church (1886). Before returning to Ukraine Voliansky established another five churches in the region as well as the first Ukrainian-American newspaper, *Ameryka; the Little Russian Drama Club; a library and reading room; Saturday and Sunday schools; and co-operative stores. The Ruthenian (now Ukrainian) National Association was founded in Shamokin in 1894 and adopted *Svoboda* as its organ. To counteract the influence of the Russian Orthodox church among the predominantly Catholic immigrants, the Association of Ruthenian Church Communities in the United States and Canada was organized in 1901. In 1907 S. Ortynsky was consecrated bishop and

St Michael's, the first Ukrainian Catholic church in the United States, founded in Shenandoah, Pennsylvania, in 1886

apostolic visitor for the Ukrainians and Ruthenians in the United States, and in 1913 was made exarch. His seat was Philadelphia, where the Providence Association of Ukrainian Catholics in America and the weekly *Ameryka* were set up. Just before the war a large number of Ukrainian immigrants joined the work force in the industrial and mining towns of western Pennsylvania. To help the newcomers adjust and establish themselves in the new land, the Ukrainian Workingmen's Association was founded in Scranton in 1910, and the Ukrainian National Aid Association in Pittsburgh in 1913.

During the war Ukrainians in Pennsylvania supported the struggle for independence in Ukraine. In 1916 the Ukrainian National Alliance was formed to publicize Ukrainian political demands, gain official support for them in Washington, and provide relief to war victims.

In the interwar period restrictive laws reduced immigration from Eastern Europe, but the Ukrainian community grew and developed. In 1924 the Ukrainian Catholic exarchy was reorganized into two separate exarchies, a Ukrainian one with its seat in Philadelphia and a Ruthenian (Carpatho-Rusyn) one with its seat in Pittsburgh. At the same time Archbishop I. Teodorovych moved the seat of the Ukrainian Orthodox church to Philadelphia. The Basilian order of nuns built their motherhouse in Fox Chase (1931) and set up the first Ukrainian academy for girls there. The Ukrainian Catholic Youth League, formed in 1933, had its head office in Philadelphia. The first Ukrainian state representative, I. Malena, was elected in Philadelphia.

After the Second World War a large number of new Ukrainian immigrants, including many professionals and others with higher education, came to Pennsylvania. Having settled mostly in Philadelphia, they strengthened the existing Ukrainian institutions and founded new ones: political organizations such as the Organization for the Defense of Four Freedoms for Ukraine; youth organizations, such as the Plast Ukrainian Youth Association and the Ukrainian Youth Association (SUM); and regional associations, such as the Lemkivshchyna and Boikivshchyna societies. Ukrainian language and literature courses were introduced at the University of Pennsylvania in 1959.

Eventually its relative share of the Ukrainian-American population fell, to only 17.5 percent in 1990, but Pennsylvania remains the state most heavily populated by Ukrainians. Its largest Ukrainian communities are found in *Philadelphia, *Pittsburgh, *Scranton, Chester, and Allentown.

BIBLIOGRAPHY
Lushnycky, A. (ed). *Ukrainians in Pennsylvania* (Philadelphia 1976)

M. Kuropas

Pension. A regular monetary payment from state, social, or private insurance funds to elderly or disabled people and their dependents or offspring. In the USSR some high officials and distinguished individuals received special pensions also.

Voluntary mutual insurance programs that provided pensions to blue- and white-collar workers were established in Ukrainian territories under Austro-Hungarian rule in the 1890s. Similar schemes were introduced in the Russian Empire in the early 20th century. In 1912 the Russian government introduced a pension plan covering workers disabled by industrial accidents. Complete invalids received a maximum of two-thirds of the regular wage.

The Ukrainian SSR adopted a state pension plan in 1922. It covered disabled people and their dependents or orphans. Later, pensions were granted to persons who had attained a certain age and had worked a specified number of years. In 1925 the pensions were extended to teachers and doctors, in 1929 to workers in heavy industry and transport, in 1932 to all blue-collar workers, and in 1937 to all white-collar workers and students. Until 1937, pensions were paid from funds raised by mandatory deductions from workers' wages, and in 1931–7 almost all pensions were run by the trade unions. When the state assumed responsibility for the pension system (through the USSR Ministry of Social Security) in 1937, it accepted the entire cost of the program, which it covered from tax revenues. Pensions in that period were very low, and rapid inflation diminished their buying power even further.

A major reform of the pension system was introduced in 1956, and its basic statutes are still in force. Partial pensions were granted to elderly people who had not attained retirement age. In 1964 a pension system was finally established for collective farmers: heads of collective farms, agronomists, and mechanics became eligible for state pensions, and collective farmers were paid pensions from a fund created by the state and supported by the collective farms.

In the 1980s persons qualified for a full pension after reaching 60 years of age (55 for women) and working for 25 years (20 for women). The value of a pension was based upon the worker's earnings in the last 12 months of employment. For workers with a low base pay upon retirement, the pension was equal to the monthly wage or a minimum of 50 rubles a month. The ratio of pension to earnings fell in stages to 55 percent for workers who earned from 100 to 120 rubles a month. Once a pension was granted, the rate remained fixed until the pensioner's death; only small adjustments were made to keep pensions above the escalating minimum. In the early 1990s, however, pensions were raised to ease the devastation caused by spiraling inflation. Pensioners received supplements of 10–15 percent for dependents and 3–5 percent for uninterrupted service at a single job. The pension was reduced by 15 percent if the pensioner lived in a rural area. Because of the low pension levels in the USSR, many people continued to work after they reached retirement age. They were permitted to do so, and in most cases pensions were not affected by other income. Workers in mining, some heavy industries, and other hard and dangerous jobs could retire earlier at full pension.

Pensions for people disabled on the job or suffering from occupational diseases depended on the degree of incapacity, the length of service, and the pensioner's age at the time of injury. In general the levels were slightly lower than for old age pensions. Since 1970 collective-farm workers have also been eligible for disability pensions. Disabled army veterans were paid a pension directly by the state. Supplements for dependents were available to disabled pensioners. Orphans (to age 16 or 18 if they were students) and widows over 55 (widowers over 60) with children of pensioners continued to receive the pension, but the pension was paid to the family as a whole, not to individuals. Some categories of workers, such as teachers, academicians, and health care workers, were eligible for a pension only after a specific length of service (usually 25 years), regardless of age. The maximum pension for those people was higher than for others, up to 240 rubles a month. Army veterans qualified for pensions after age 40 and 20 years of service. Their pensions were even higher and were paid directly from the budgets of the Ministry of Defense, KGB, or Ministry of Internal Affairs.

From 1928 there had been a special category of 'personal pensioners.' Those were individuals who were rewarded for special services to the state or 'revolution.' The special pensions were usually reserved for leading members of the Party. They were given only to men over 55 or women over 50, but without regard for length of service. Personal pensions were all-Union, republican, or local depending on the government awarding them. The first carried a value of 200 or more rubles a month and included such perquisites as free housing and a car.

The lowest pensions were received by collective-farm workers. They bore most of the pension costs through payments by the collective farms. Their pensions ranged from a minimum of 40 rubles a month to a maximum of 120 rubles. Initially, pensions were restricted to men from age 65 and after 25 years of work and to women from age 60 and after 20 years of work. Since 1967, however, farm workers have been treated on a par with workers in other branches of the economy. For many years farmers in Western Ukraine, which was annexed by the USSR after the Second World War, had been eligible for a pension only if they had been original members of a collective farm.

The number of pensioners in Ukraine has been increasing in recent years both in absolute numbers and as a proportion of the entire population. The number of people receiving pensions increased from 3.52 million in 1959 to 6.87 million in 1967 (of these, 1.08 million were veterans, and 2.51 million were collective farmers). There were 8.88 million pensioners in 1971, 10.72 million in 1981, and 13.08 million in 1990 (over 25 percent of the total population), including old age, disability, and long-service pensioners. In 1987, 3.39 million pensioners were collective farmers. During the recent period average pensions have risen, from 30.4 rubles in 1970 to 53.3 in 1980 and 103.6 in 1990. The average pension for state pensioners was 81.7 rubles, and the average old age pension was 90.8 rubles (1987). By contrast, the average pension for collective farmers was 51.3 rubles. Only 3.6 percent of all blue- and white-collar workers received the minimum pension, whereas 59.7 percent of all collective farmers received the minimum. On 1 October 1990 the 1.4 million war veterans and invalids had their average pension raised to 145 rubles.

BIBLIOGRAPHY
US Department of Health, Education, and Welfare, Social Security Administration. *A Report on Social Security Programs in the Soviet Union* (Washington 1960)
Sovetskoe sotsial'noe strakhovanie: Uchebnoe posobie dlia vysshikh profsoiuznykh shkol, 2nd edn (Moscow 1985)
Andreev, V. *Pravo sotsial'nogo obespecheniia v SSSR*, 2nd edn (Moscow 1987)
Korotkova, Z.; Naumov, V. *Sotsial'noe strakhovanie i pensionnoe obespechenie rabotnikov sel'skogo khoziaistva*, 2nd edn (Moscow 1987)

V. Holubnychy , O. Rohach

Pentecost. A church calendar feast day, celebrated fifty days after Good Friday; the first major event of the summer cycle in the Ukrainian ritual calendar. The feast of Pentecost (*piatedesiatnytsia*), known in Ukraine as *Zeleni sviata* (Green Holidays), consisted of several days of ritual observances. Before the main day of the celebration (Sunday), houses were whitewashed and cleaned, and their earthen floors were worked over with an aromatic grass or herb. In addition, houses and churches were decorated both inside and out with tree branches sporting greenery. On Pentecost Sunday young people entertained themselves with song-games, the decorating and ritual undressing a day later of a small birch tree, the plaiting of wreaths that were later floated in water, and the playing of games. In some parts of Ukraine it was also common for farmyards, outbuildings, and fields to be blessed by a priest leading a procession.

The commemoration of the dead had an important role in Pentecost celebrations. Graveyards were decorated with tree boughs and in some cases with lit candles. In some parts of Ukraine a feast would take place in the cemetery in honor of the ancestor there. Among Ukrainians in the West, the blessing of graves commonly takes place on this day.

People's Assembly of Western Ukraine (Narodni zbory Zakhidnoi Ukrainy). A purportedly representative body established in October 1939 by the Soviet occupational authorities to provide a legal basis for the USSR's annexation of Western Ukrainian territories formerly ruled by Poland. Its close to 1,500 deputies were elected on 22 October 1939 in fixed, strictly controlled elections. The assembly convened in Lviv on 26–28 October and formally approved the proclamation of Soviet rule and the 'reunion' of Western Ukraine with the Ukrainian SSR and the USSR. A special commission of 66 deputies presented the decision to the supreme soviets of the USSR and of the Ukrainian SSR. Having served its purpose, the assembly was dissolved.

People's assessor (*narodnyi zasidatel*). A lay judge elected to serve alongside a professional judge at every level of the USSR justice system. Introduced in 1917 by the Soviets in place of juries, assessors (usually two per court) represented a form of popular participation in the judicial process. They had all the rights of judges: they participated in forming the verdict and selecting the punishment. They were elected for two and a half years by people's assemblies at their workplaces or residences. Assessors of military tribunals were elected by soldiers at their military units. An assessor had to be at least 25 years of age but did not need to have any legal training or experience. Each court district kept a list of several hundred assessors, who were rotated to serve about one day a month in court.

People's Commissariat for Nationality Affairs (Narodnyi komisariat po delam natsionalnostei RSFSR, or Narkomnats). A central government department set up on 26 October 1917 by decree of the Central Executive Committee of the RSFSR. Officially its purpose was to implement V. Lenin's nationality policy, as it was outlined in the Declaration of the Rights of the Nations of Russia. In fact its main task was to restore Russian rule over the various nations that had come under the Russian Empire. Its sole chief was J. *Stalin, who had written a theoretical treatise on the nationality question. His aim was to unite the different nations under one centralized, Soviet government and to prevent the outlying countries from separating from Russia. The central Narkomnats worked through 18 national narkomnats or departments, which together formed a collegium and then (19 May 1920) a Council of Nationalities consisting of the chiefs of the national departments and chaired by Stalin. The Ukrainian Narkomnats was created in May 1918 'to assist the Ukrainian people in its liberation from German occupation.' In reality it assisted the Russian Red Army to overthrow the UNR *Directory and to install the Soviet regime, and later on it eradicated vestiges of nationalism within the Communist party and the Soviet government in Ukraine. The Narkomnats was also responsible for invading Georgia and crushing its independent government in early 1921. The Narkomnats played a key role in setting up Soviet national republics and integrating them into the USSR. Having fulfilled its mission the Narkomnats was dismantled in May 1924.

J. Borys

People's commissariats of the Ukrainian SSR (*narodni komisariiaty*). The central and executive organs in Soviet Ukraine, modeled after the commissariats (initially called commissions) established in the RSFSR at the end of 1917. Until January 1919 they were called people's secretariats in Ukraine. The people's commissars had powers analogous to those of government ministers in a parliamentary system. They were invariably members of the

Communist party and were appointed by, and responsible to, the *All-Ukrainian Central Executive Committee. The commissars and heads of various state committees and councils constituted the central government of the republic – the *Council of People's Commissars.

Initially there were 12 commissariats in Ukraine: foreign affairs, defense, Soviet propaganda, internal affairs, education, agriculture, justice, supplies, labor, finance, transportation, and public health. Most of them were subordinated to their Russian counterparts under the terms of special treaties, and the Russian commissars were represented by deputies in Ukraine. After the USSR was formed, the 1924 Constitution defined three types of commissariats in Ukraine: unified (renamed 'Union-republic' in 1936), republican, and Union. Those in the first category, which included the commissariats of finance, labor, worker-peasant inspection, and supplies, were formally under the joint control of the Ukrainian and the USSR governments. Another six commissariats – justice, internal affairs, education, social security, land affairs, and public health – were under republican control. The Union commissariats – foreign affairs, military and naval affairs, foreign trade, roads and highways, and postal and telegraph services – were under the sole authority of the central Soviet authorities in Moscow. This basic system remained in place after the Constitution of 1936 was adopted. The people's commissariats were replaced by *ministries of the Ukrainian SSR in 1946.

People's Council (Narodna rada). A Galician populist political organization founded on 24 October 1885 in Lviv under the leadership of Yu. *Romanchuk with the goal of continuing the traditions of the *Supreme Ruthenian Council of 1848. The council was formed as a counterpoise to the Ruthenian Council, which had been taken over by Russophiles. The People's Council issued a proclamation to 'Ruthenians of the Galician lands' and had its first general meeting on 2 February 1888. The unofficial organs of the People's Council included *Bat'kivshchyna* and *Dilo*. A creation of the populist intelligentsia, the council took a position for the unity of Galician Ukrainians with Ukrainians under Russian rule and separation from the Polish and Russian nations. Its goals included defending the constitutional rights of Galician Ukrainians and establishing their equality with the other peoples in Austria-Hungary as well as the division of Galicia into Ukrainian and Polish territories. The People's Council was not a party, and it had no (formal) branches. In 1899 it joined with the right wing of the Ukrainian Radical party to form the *National Democratic party.

People's Council of Transcarpathian Ukraine (Narodna rada Zakarpatskoii Ukrainy). A representative body in Transcarpathia that assumed certain state functions in the transition period between Czechoslovak and Soviet rule. The group was formed in Mukachiv on 26 November 1944 as the co-ordinating body for the 'people's committees' (at the okruha and municipal levels) in the region and was conceived of and controlled by the Communist party and the Soviet occupational forces. The council, consisting of 17 members, appropriated legislative and executive power in Transcarpathian Ukraine from the outgoing Czechoslovak government. It also introduced the first Sovietization measures in the region and spear-

headed the campaign to unite Transcarpathia with the Ukrainian SSR. The council was based in Uzhhorod and headed by a local Communist, I. *Turianytsia. After the creation of Transcarpathia oblast within the Ukrainian SSR the council continued functioning before being replaced by oblast administrative organizations.

People's court (narodnyi sud). The lowest level of the Soviet court system and the court of first instance for a raion or city. Such courts tried almost all civil and criminal cases, except for very complex civil matters or grave crimes, and some administrative cases. They consisted of one people's judge and two people's assessors. Their decisions could be appealed to an oblast court.

People's Guard. See National Guard.

The People's Home in Lviv

People's Home in Lviv (Ruskyi narodnyi instytut Narodnyi dim u Lvovi). The oldest and wealthiest Ukrainian cultural-educational institution in Galicia. The People's Home was established in 1849 by the *Supreme Ruthenian Council (at the initiative of L. *Treshchakivsky) with the express purpose of developing Ukrainian national and cultural life throughout Galicia. The institution was based on a Czech model. The Austrian government granted it land near Lviv University, on which a building (financed through private donations) was erected in 1851–64. Over time it amassed a substantial number of assets, including several buildings and a church in Lviv, two villages in the Peremyshl region, a museum, a library, and a publishing house.

The People's Home provided a spiritual haven and organizational center for various organizations and causes, most notably the *Halytsko-Ruska Matytsia society (which undertook cultural-educational work and published school textbooks). Until the 1860s its work was conducted in the conservative and clerical-minded spirit of the *Old Ruthenians, and the body was run by a commission set up by the Supreme Ruthenian Council before it disbanded in 1851. The leadership of the People's Home then fell into the hands of *Russophiles, who took it over completely in 1872 with the enactment of a new constitution. Ukrainophile cultural and political activists were excluded from membership in the People's Home, and the institution virtually ceased to be active in promoting Ukrainian national interests. Following the outbreak of the First World War the Austrian government banned the activity of the People's Home and, in 1917, liquidated it and placed its assets under the control of a group of trustees. Under Polish occupation the trustees were replaced by a commissioner, M. Bachynsky, who turned the People's Home over to a group of conservative Russophiles loyal to the Polish state.

Much of the activity of the People's Home from approx 1900 consisted of maintaining a museum and archives. By 1924 it had amassed a library of approx 120,000 items (including 5,000 manuscripts and documents as well as the personal library of A. *Petrushevych) and established archeological-historical and natural science museums. Part of the library was transported to Russia during the First World War and never returned. In 1918 the numismatic collection was lost. The official publication of the People's Home was *Vistnyk Narodnoho doma, printed in 1882–1914 as a monthly publication and from 1921 irregularly. Written initially in the *yazychiie and later in Russian, the publication printed scholarly articles and essays (from a Russophile point of view) in addition to internal organizational news. The People's Home was liquidated in 1939 after the Soviet occupation of Western Ukraine, and its collections were transferred to the Lviv Scientific Library of the Academy of Sciences of Ukraine and various museums in Lviv.

People's homes were established in cities and towns throughout Galicia (as well as in other Ukrainian areas) with the People's Home in Lviv as an institutional model.

B. Kravtsiv

People's homes (*narodni domy* or *narodni budynky*). Community centers that provide a venue for cultural, educational, and sometimes political activities. People's homes, called people's buildings in Russian-ruled Ukraine, housed everything from libraries, theaters, and tearooms to rudimentary collections of newspapers and books. Plays, lecture series, and social events were often held in urban people's homes. In the villages people's homes housed reading rooms and provided space for social and political activities. Collectively people's homes provided an infrastructure for Ukrainian community life independent of church and state.

People's homes were built first in Western Ukraine. The *People's Home in Lviv (1849–1939), founded by the Supreme Ruthenian Council, with its 120,000-volume library and natural science, historical, archeological, and fine art museums, was one of the most ambitious people's homes and the model for homes throughout Ukraine. In Bukovyna people's homes were established later. The most important people's home in that region was founded in 1887 in Chernivtsi. In Transcarpathia people's homes were not established until the 1920s. Alongside those community centers formally called people's homes, similar facilities were often organized spontaneously by local groups. By 1939 the *Prosvita society had built 1,475 community cen-

ters in Galicia. Even more numerous were the rudimentary *public libraries and reading rooms.

In Russian-ruled Ukraine people's buildings were established at the beginning of the 20th century. Often constructed by zemstvo authorities, people's buildings were more closely tied to the state than were the people's homes in Western Ukraine. Even so, they provided an important social infrastructure for populist and social-democratic activists, sometimes to the dismay of the buildings' founders, who usually limited their agenda to educational and cultural issues. The Kiev Trinity People's Building, today the Kiev Operetta Theater, was built in 1902 through the efforts of the Kiev Literacy Society. Staging theater productions for the enlightenment of workers, who were offered free tickets, was a central function of this people's building. Between October 1903 and March 1904, 13,100 workers attended plays at the Kiev People's Building. Another people's building was built in the Kiev suburb of Lukianivka in 1904.

Founded in 1903 by the Kharkiv Literacy Society, the Kharkiv People's Building was reputedly one of the best in the Russian Empire. In 1903 alone 54 plays (attended by 42,126 people), 7 concerts (attended by 2,590 people), and 4 literary-musical evenings, 3 of which were organized by workers (attended by 2,927 people), were held there. In 1901 a people's building was founded in Poltava by the local literacy society, whose ranks included such luminaries as M. Kotsiubynsky and P. Myrny. There were also people's buildings in Odessa, Zhytomyr, Lokhvytsia, Pryluka, and other cities in central and eastern Ukraine.

In the initial period of Soviet rule people's homes were actively supported and constructed by the regime. In June 1921 in Ukraine there were 4,322 people's buildings and Prosvitas, 5,620 reading rooms and *selbudy* (village buildings), and 1,298 workers' clubs. In 1924, people's buildings were reorganized into workers' and village clubs and *palaces and houses of culture. A similar reorganization took place in Western Ukraine after 1945.

Numerous people's homes have been built by Ukrainians in the diaspora. The oldest and most active people's home in Canada is the Winnipeg Ukrainian National Home, built in 1916. Ukrainian-Canadian people's homes co-ordinated their activities through the Union of People's Homes. Ukrainian-American people's homes are found in all major US cities. The first American people's home was founded in New York. Ukrainian people's homes exist in all other areas of Ukrainian emigration, throughout Latin America, Australia, and Europe. In the interwar period a people's home was even established in Harbin, Manchuria.

B. Kravtsiv, C. Freeland

People's judge (*narodnyi suddia*). The presiding official in a people's court, the lowest court of the USSR justice system. Judges were elected to five-year terms by residents of a raion or city, usually on the nomination of the Communist party, although, in theory, other community and professional groups had the right to nominate candidates. Candidates had to be at least 25 years of age but were not formally required to have any legal training. Immediately after the revolution few people's judges had any legal education. Later most had a higher law degree. The people's judge presided over a court that included two *people's assessors, but could hear some cases (eg, administrative wrongdoings) alone. The people's judge could also initiate charges and legal proceedings. People's judges were supposed to be independent of any external pressures and could not be charged with crimes, arrested, or dismissed except on the approval of the presidium of their republic's Supreme Soviet. In reality, however, their decisions, particularly in political cases, were influenced strongly by Party and state authorities.

People's Militia (Narodna samooborona; German: Landsturm). A peasant levy en masse organized by the Austrian government in November 1848 in the Subcarpathian Galician districts of Kolomyia, Sambir, Sianik, Stanyslaviv, and Stryi to protect the population from raids by Hungarian revolutionaries. All Ukrainian men aged 18 to 50 were conscripted. The militia was divided into districts made up of 10 to 14 villages. A district was under the control of a commander and each village had its own commander as well as captains and sergeants if the number of armed men was large enough, and it maintained a continuous armed watch and an armed communication team. Effigies surrounding the village were set on fire to signal the approach of the enemy. Some districts had their own cavalry. Stanyslaviv district also had an artillery unit, whose men wore blue jackets with yellow epaulets and sheepskin hats with yellow tops. The unit forced the Polish National Guard to leave Stanyslaviv in November 1848. Altogether there were some 50,000 militiamen. Stanyslaviv district had the largest number, over 17,000. After the Hungarian revolution was suppressed at the end of 1849, the Austrian government disbanded the militia.

BIBLIOGRAPHY
Shankovskii, A. 'Vospominaniia,' *Rodimyi listok* (Chernivtsi), 1881–3
Krevets'kyi, I. 'Oboronna organizatsiia rus'kykh selian na halyts'ko-uhors'kim pohranychu v 1848–1849 rr.,' *ZNTSh*, 63–4 (1905)

L. Shankovsky

People's Secretariat (Narodnyi sekretariiat). The executive body of the Provisional Central Executive Committee of the Soviets of Workers' and Soldiers' Deputies of Ukraine, established in Kharkiv on 30 December 1917 by Russian and local Bolsheviks. It was set up as a rival (Soviet) government in opposition to the Central Rada and its General Secretariat in Kiev. The first People's Secretariat consisted of S. Bakinsky (a representative of the Soviet of People's Commissars of Russia) as secretary of nationalities, V. Shakhrai (military affairs), Ye. Bosh (internal affairs), F. Artem-Sergeev (industry and trade), E. Luganovsky (food supplies), V. Aussem (finance), V. Liuksemburg (justice), Ye. Terletsky (agrarian affairs), and V. Zatonsky (education). Terletsky was a left-wing Russian Social Revolutionary; all other members were Bolsheviks. Only Shakhrai and Zatonsky were nationally conscious Ukrainians. At first Yu. Medvediev (a Ukrainian Social Democrat who became a Bolshevik), as chairman of the Provisional Central Executive Committee, headed the secretariat. Later the secretariat was joined by M. Skrypnyk (labor, and then industry and trade), Ya. Martianov, and I. Kulyk and Yu. Kotsiubynsky (military affairs). At first the People's Secretariat was located in Kharkiv. On 12 February 1918 it moved to Kiev, on 27 February to Poltava, and in March–April to Katerynoslav and Tahanrih.

The secretariat had little power: representatives of the Petrograd Soviet and the Party watched its activities and even ignored the authority of the Ukrainian Soviet government (notably the Supreme Soviet of the National Economy and the departments of certain industrial oblasts of Ukraine) in a number of areas. The commander of all Soviet armed forces, V. Antonov-Ovsieenko, as member of the Soviet of the People's Commissars of Russia at that time, was responsible only to the Russian center. Shakhrai protested strongly against that state of affairs. But the secretariat was in crisis: its governmental role and powers were unclear, and there were personal conflicts. Those difficulties resulted in its disintegration by the end of February. Then Skrypnyk, who became its chairman, reorganized it and brought in more Ukrainians, such as Ye. Neronovych, a left-wing Ukrainian Social Democrat (military affairs), H. Lapchynsky, a Ukrainian Communist, I. Klymenko, a Ukrainian Social Democrat, and I. Kulyk. Zatonsky, the representative of the secretariat to the Russian Soviet government, assumed the provisional portfolio of foreign affairs. On 7 March 1918 Antonov-Ovsieenko was appointed secretary of military affairs and 'supreme chief commander of the Ukrainian Soviet armed forces.'

The signing of the Peace Treaty of Brest-Litovsk by the Russian Soviet government resulted in the proclamation of the 'independence' of Soviet Ukraine from Soviet Russia by the Second All-Ukrainian Congress of Soviets in Katerynoslav on 17–19 March 1918. At the same time the People's Secretariat was reorganized: Skrypnyk remained chairman, but two new members, A. Bubnov and S. Kosior, both so-called left Communists, were added. The new secretariat could not resist the advancement of Ukrainian, German, and Austrian troops into eastern Ukraine; Russia, in turn, respected the terms of the peace treaty and could offer it no assistance. Hence, on instructions from the Russian authorities the Central Executive Committee and the People's Secretariat were dissolved on 18 April 1918 in Tahanrih. They were replaced by the Bureau for Directing the Partisan Resistance in Ukraine.

The primary purpose of maintaining the secretariat as a separate Soviet government in Ukraine was to cover up the direct aggression of the Russian Bolshevik forces against the UNR and to create a diversion at the peace negotiations in Brest-Litovsk. For that reason a name similar to that of the General Secretatiat of the Central Rada was chosen for the executive body, and the Soviet regime also called itself the Ukrainian National Republic. Its organ was titled *Vestnik UNR*.

BIBLIOGRAPHY
Bosh, E. *Natsional'noe pravitel'stvo i sovetskaia vlast' na Ukraine* (Moscow 1919)
Khmil', I. *Z praporom myru kriz' polum'ia viiny* (Kiev 1962)
Mazlakh, S.; Shakhrai, V. *On the Current Situation in Ukraine*, ed P.J. Potichnyj (Ann Arbor 1970)

V. Holubnychy

People's Theater (Narodnyi teatr). A theater established in Kiev in August 1918 as the State People's Theater under the artistic directorship of P. *Saksahansky. The People's Theater concentrated on moving away from the traditional ethnographic to the Western European repertoire. It also staged I. Karpenko-Kary's historical plays, F. Schiller's *Die Räuber*, and K. Gutzkow's *Uriel Acosta*. In early 1919 Soviet authorities ordered the theater to cease its activities. Its main cast continued to work as the touring People's Theater with Saksahansky. Other members joined the *Shevchenko First Theater of the USR; some of them eventually became the nucleus of the Zankovetska Theater.

People's Ukrainian Council (Narodnia ukrainska rada).

An émigré political center founded in January 1929 in Prague by representatives of the *Ukrainian Party of Socialist Revolutionaries, Ukrainian Peasant Association, Ukrainian Workers' Union in the Czechoslovak Republic, and Ukrainian Socialist Radical party and by nonpartisan scholars. Mykyta *Shapoval was elected its president, S. Shelukhyn vice-president, and N. Hryhoriiv general secretary. The Council of Elders consisted of P. Bohatsky, S. Dovhal, L. Kononenko, V. Petriv, S. Rusova, and A. Zhyvotko. The council set itself the task of co-ordinating émigré efforts to renew Ukrainian statehood in all the émigré ethnic territories. It viewed the 1920 Treaty of Warsaw between the UNR and Poland as illegal because it was unsanctioned by the Ukrainian people, and it regarded the Polish military occupation of Western Ukraine as a blatant violation and conquest. The council was also opposed to the *Government-in-exile of the UNR. In 1929 it began publishing *Vistnyk Narodn'oï ukraïns'koï rady*. After Shapoval's death in 1932, the council's activities were insignificant; it ceased to exist in 1939.

People's universities (narodni universytety).

Community adult-education centers offering anything from technical training to popular lectures on history, literature, the arts, science, and other subjects. In Russian-ruled Ukraine various forms of *extramural education developed from the mid-19th century. They were usually organized by the liberal intelligentsia, often through such groups as *literacy societies, and without the support of the state or official agencies (in fact, these initiatives were usually opposed by reactionary bureaucrats, who feared the centers would become hotbeds of national consciousness or political opposition). Although they were not formally called such, these various *Sunday schools, *public readings, and *zemstvo schools filled a function similar to that of a people's university, in providing broad access to higher education for the masses.

A more formal system of people's universities, modeled on the system of university extension schools that emerged in Western Europe and the United States in the late 19th century, began to develop in the Russian Empire after the 1890s, especially after the Revolution of 1905. Prominent intellectuals and professors (eg, M. Tuhan-Baranovsky and M. Kovalevsky) often taught at these schools, each of which attracted thousands of students to hundreds of lectures over the course of the year. By 1917 they had been established in some 40 cities in the empire, including Kiev, Poltava, Yalta, Kherson, and Odessa in Ukraine. Curricula varied greatly but usually included a broad range of courses in the arts and sciences as well as in vocational skills such as bookkeeping, stenography, and machine operating. Graduates, who received formal degrees, were often eagerly recruited by businesses. Every

university was totally autonomous and relied on local sources for funding. In the revolutionary period between 1917 and 1920, people's universities flourished, and some, notably those in Kiev, Kherson, and Zhytomyr, effectively became schools of higher learning.

In Western Ukraine mass organizations, such as the *Prosvita society, the Mohyla Scholarly Lectures Society, and various *pedagogical societies, provided the services that people's universities offered in Russian-ruled Ukraine. The People's Self-Education University, founded in 1930 in Lviv, offered correspondence courses until 1939. In some respects the *Lviv (Underground) Ukrainian University also operated as a people's university.

After the consolidation of Soviet rule people's universities no longer existed in their original form. In part they were replaced by evening *workers' universities and other institutions for adult education. Some local universities of culture were established in Ukrainian cities in the 1920s and 1930s mostly on the initiative of local Party committees. They offered instruction in culture and the arts, as well as political indoctrination. A more formal system was established after 1958 under the control of the USSR Ministry of Culture and especially the *Znannia Society. After concentrating initially on culture, the system soon expanded to include universities of pedagogy, medicine, science and technology, agriculture, Soviet trade, philosophy, history, and other disciplines. Intended at first to provide a broad education with much emphasis on communist ideology, in the late 1960s the universities changed their emphasis, to focus on developing practical skills and job-related knowledge. People's universities do not charge tuition. Courses, taught during a seven- or eight-month academic year, are scheduled to allow students to work fulltime. In Soviet Ukraine the universities were administered by the Znannia Society, the All-Union Central Council of Trade Unions, the Communist Youth League, and the ministries of education, health, and culture. In 1968, people's universities throughout the USSR were placed under the control of the Moscow-based Central Soviet of People's Universities. In 1964 there were 438,000 students, studying at 2,049 people's universities in Ukraine; 88 percent of all students were urban residents. By 1987 there were 4,354,000 students, studying at 8,868 people's universities (8,014 were located in cities). Universities offering social and political studies accounted for 18 percent of the total number of universities; medical and health studies, 16 percent; culture, 15 percent; pedagogy, 14 percent; law, 9 percent; science and technology, 7 percent; administration, 5 percent; theoretical sciences, 5 percent; and general studies, 2 percent. The highest concentration of people's universities was in the industrial eastern regions of Ukraine, with 10 percent of all Ukrainian people's universities located in Donetske oblast.

BIBLIOGRAPHY
Lee, D. *The People's Universities of the USSR* (New York 1988)
                                    B. Balan, C. Freeland, B. Kravtsiv

People's Will party (Partiia Narodnoi Voli, or PNV).

A pro-communist Russophile political party in interwar Galicia. The origins of the party go back to 1908, when left-leaning Russophiles in Lviv began to publish the newspaper *Volia naroda* (Will of the People). The leaders of the group then as later were K. Valnytsky, K. Pelekhaty, and

M. Zaiats. On 1 May 1924 the group formally took the name People's Will party and drafted a program that was adopted in essentials at the party's first congress, on 25 April 1926. Under the influence of the *Communist Party of Western Ukraine the PNV renounced its Russophile past, took up a Ukrainian orientation, and merged with the Volhynian *Sel-Soiuz to form the pro-Soviet *Sel-Rob party (10 October 1926). When Sel-Rob split in September 1927, the former People's Will party became Sel-Rob Left.

Pepper (*Capsicum*; Ukrainian: *perets struchkovyi*). A plant genus of the family Solanaceae that grows in subtropical areas as a perennial shrub and is cultivated as an annual vegetable plant. In Ukraine, the principal producer of pepper in the former USSR, the *C. annuum* species is grown. There are sweet and sharp varieties, the sharpness being caused by the alkaloid capsaicin. Sweet peppers are used in cooking and canning; sharp peppers are used as a spice. Mature pepper fruit contains 2–8.5 percent sugar (sharp peppers are more sweet), about 1.5 percent proteins, up to 14 mg per 100 g carotene, and 125–300 mg per 100 g vitamins. Pepper extracts are used as a skin irritant and medicinally to improve appetite and digestion. Aqueous extracts also have insecticidal properties.

Perebyinis, Petro [Perebyjnis], b 6 June 1937 in Sloboda-Sharhorodska, Sharhorod raion, Vinnytsia oblast. Poet. He began publishing in 1955, but his first collection, *Chervonyi akord* (The Red Chord), appeared only in 1971. His other collections are *Vysoki raiduhy* (High Rainbows, 1973), *Peredchuttia dorohy* (Premonition of the Road, 1975), *Rankovi surmy* (Morning Trumpets, 1976), *Hrono vohniu* (Cluster of Fire, 1977), *Chervonyi kolir* (Red Color, 1977), *Nebo tvoie i zemlia* (Thy Heaven and Earth, 1979), *Maidan revoliutsiï* (Square of the Revolution, 1980), *Svitlovyi rik* (Light Year, 1982), *Tretia sproba* (Third Attempt, 1983), *Pisnia pam'iati* (Song of Memory, 1984), and *Prysiahaiu Dniprom!* (I Swear by the Dnieper!, 1985).

Perebyinis, Vasyl [Perebyjnis, Vasyl'], b 1 January 1898 in Mali Puzyrky, Iziaslav county, Volhynia gubernia, d 13 November 1966 in London. Artist. He studied at the St Petersburg and Cracow academies of art. An interwar émigré, from 1926 he lived in Paris, where he designed stage scenery and costumes and took part in many exhibitions. In 1931 he participated in the show of the Association of Independent Ukrainian Artists in Lviv. He illustrated many interwar books and almanacs published in Lviv and painted landscapes (many of Normandy), Paris street scenes, portraits, and still lifes, in which postimpressionist influences competed with realist and surrealist ones. From 1946 he lived in London.

Perechyn [Perečyn]. V-3. A town smt (1986 pop 6,900) on the Uzh River and a raion center in Transcarpathia oblast. It was first mentioned in historical documents in 1427, when it was under Hungarian rule. The town has a wood-chemistry and a woodworking complex. In 1925 Ya. Pasternak excavated an Eneolithic burial ground nearby.

Perederii, Vitalii [Perederij, Vitalij], b 24 March 1928 in Artemivka, Staline okruha. Philosopher. A graduate of the Kiev Pedagogical Institute (1948), he worked at the Kiev Institute of National Economy. In 1961 he became a lectur-er at the Kiev Conservatory and eventually the chairman of its Marxism-Leninism department. He has written over 80 works in the history of esthetics in Ukraine and on problems in Marxist-Leninist esthetics, including books on Ukrainian revolutionary-democratic esthetics in the late 19th and early 20th centuries (1964) and Soviet artistic culture (1985).

Peredove. A village near Sevastopil in the Crimea near which a Taurian grave site of the 4th to 3rd century BC was found. Excavations in 1956–7 uncovered two grave grounds, each containing a number of stone burial vaults. Silver jewelry, bronze arrowheads, and pottery fragments were recovered from inside the vaults.

Peredvizhniki (Itinerants). A name applied to members of the Russian Society of Itinerant Art Exhibitions. It was founded in 1870 by I. *Kramskoi, N. *Ge, and 13 other artists who had left the St Petersburg Academy of Arts in protest against its rigid neoclassical dicta. In order to reach the widest audience possible, the society organized regular traveling exhibitions throughout the Russian Empire, including Kiev, Kharkiv, and Odessa in their tours. Over the years the society attracted artists from various parts of Russia, Belarus, and Ukraine. Among the Ukrainians who joined it were K. *Kostandi, A. *Kuindzhi, M. *Kuznetsov, O. *Murashko, L. *Pozen, M. *Pymonenko, P. *Nilus, I. *Repin, S. *Svitoslavsky, and M. *Yaroshenko. Ukrainians who took part in the society's exhibitions but were not members were P. *Levchenko, S. *Kyshynivsky, and Ye. *Bukovetsky. The Peredvizhniki worked in realistic and naturalistic styles and concentrated on landscapes, portraits, and genre themes. Typical of the society's Ukrainian offshoot are works such as Kostandi's *Among the People* (1885) and *Early Spring* (1892) and Pymonenko's *Wedding (The Kiev Gubernia)* (1891) and *Young Men (At the Well)* (1909). The Peredvizhniki were more concerned with realistic portrayals than with stylistic innovation. Consequently, in the wake of formalist experimentation the society, originally radical in nature, became a bastion of conservatism. In 1923 the society amalgamated with the Association of Artists of Revolutionary Russia. The naturalistic styles advocated by its members were later used as the basis of *socialist realism.

BIBLIOGRAPHY
Lebedev, A. (comp). *The Itinerants* (Leningrad 1974)
Valkenier, E. *Russian Realist Art: The State and Society: The Peredvizhniki and Their Tradition* (Ann Arbor 1977)
Hovdia, P.; Kovalenko, O. *Peredvyzhnyky i Ukraïna* (Kiev 1978)
Kovalenko, A. *Peredvizhniki i Ukraina: Stranitsy russko-ukrainskikh kul'turnykh sviazei* (Kiev 1979)
Ezerskaia, N. *Peredvizhniki i natsional'nye khudozhestvennye shkoly narodov Rossii* (Moscow 1987)

N. Mykytyn

Perehinets, Mykola [Perehinec'], b 1897, d 1947. Linguist. In the 1920s and 1930s he taught in postsecondary schools in Kharkiv. He published a few articles on Ukrainian word order and syntactic forms using F. de Saussure's and K. Vossler's approaches and was the coauthor of two course books on the Ukrainian language (1929, 1930). He spent many years in Soviet concentration camps (1938–45). After his release he taught at the Lviv Pedagogical Institute.

Perehinsko or **Perehinske** [Perehins'ko or Perehins'ke]. V-5. A town smt (1986 pop 11,700) on the Limnytsia River in Rozhniativ raion, Ivano-Frankivske oblast. The town was founded in the first half of the 13th century. It has a furniture factory and a forest industry.

Pereiaslav. See Pereiaslav-Khmelnytskyi.

Pereiaslav Articles of 1659 (Pereiaslavski statti). An agreement between the Hetman state and Muscovy concluded in Pereiaslav in October 1659 by Hetman Yu. *Khmelnytsky and the Muscovite representative, A. Trubetskoi. After Khmelnytsky's election as hetman his government drafted a modified version of the *Pereiaslav Treaty of 1654 that was more advantageous to Ukraine (the Zherdev Articles). Taking advantage of the hetman's difficult position (Pereiaslav was surrounded by a 40,000-man Muscovite army), the Muscovite government rejected the new version and imposed a falsified version of the 1654 treaty and 14 'New Articles' that considerably restricted Ukraine's sovereignty.

The articles forbade Ukraine to conduct an independent foreign policy, to enter into international accords (particularly military alliances), and to declare war on neighboring states without the prior consent of the Muscovite government. Muscovite military governors and garrisons thenceforth had the right to be not only in Kiev (where they had been since the 1654 treaty), but also in Bratslav, Chernihiv, Nizhen, Pereiaslav, and Uman. Cossack forces were to be withdrawn from Belarus, and the Zaporozhian Host was deprived of the right to depose and elect hetmans. The hetman himself was forbidden to appoint or remove members of the General Officer Staff and regimental colonels, and that authority was given exclusively to the Cossacks' General Military Council. Cossack leaders thenceforth who attempted to break Ukraine away from Muscovy were to be executed, and the Ukrainian Orthodox church was subordinated to the Moscow patriarch.

The text of the articles was printed by the Kievan Cave Monastery Press by order of Trubetskoi and sent to all of the regiments in the Hetman state. The articles provoked popular indignation in Ukraine and influenced Khmelnytsky's decision to turn to Poland in 1660. The text was published in *Istochniki malorossiiskoi istorii* (Sources for Little Russian History, pt 1, 1858).

A. Zhukovsky

Pereiaslav College (Pereiaslavskyi kolehium). A secondary school founded in 1738 by Bishop A. Berlo. It was located on the territory of the Resurrection Monastery in Pereiaslav, now Pereiaslav-Khmelnytskyi, Kiev oblast. It was founded to prepare Orthodox clergy. The program of study lasted six years and closely followed that of the Kievan Mohyla Academy. The students at the college were mainly children of the clergy and of Cossack officers, although some were the children of burghers and villagers. The college also boarded students. The courses of instruction included Polish, Russian, Greek, Latin, poetics, dialectics, rhetoric, history, vocal music, geometry, and arithmetic. Courses in philosophy (1774) and theology (in the late 1770s) were introduced, and in 1785 a branch of the college was transferred to Novhorod-Siverskyi and reorganized into a seminary. The Pereiaslav College subse-

quently curtailed all secular instruction and became a theological seminary. In 1862 this seminary was transferred to Poltava. In 1972 a memorial museum dedicated to H. Skorovoda, who taught poetics at the college in 1753, was opened on the grounds of the college. Other prominent teachers at the college included I. Kozlovych, I. Levanda, and V. Shyshatsky.

Pereiaslav eparchy. One of the oldest eparchies of the Orthodox church in Ukraine. Established soon after the Christianization of Ukraine, it was one of only three original eparchies in Left-Bank Ukraine. After the city of Pereiaslav was razed during the Mongol invasion and went into decline, the eparchy ceased to exist. In 1702 a vicar bishop to the Kiev metropolitan was established in Pereiaslav, but in 1733 the Pereiaslav eparchy was transferred to the jurisdiction of the Holy Synod. From 1701 to 1795 twelve hierarchs occupied the see, including A. Mohyliansky. After the abolition of the Hetmanate and the creation of gubernias in Ukraine, the territory of the eparchy was included in *Poltava gubernia and the new Poltava eparchy.

Pereiaslav principality. In Ukraine's early history the territory of northern Left-Bank Ukraine was inhabited by the Slavic tribes of the *Siverianians and, closer to the Dnieper, *Polianians and was ruled by the grand princes of Kiev. In his will Prince Yaroslav the Wise designated an appanage principality with its capital in Pereiaslav (now *Pereiaslav-Khmelnytskyi) and bequeathed it to his son, *Vsevolod Yaroslavych, who ruled it from 1054. When Vsevolod ascended the Kievan throne in 1078, he continued ruling Pereiaslav principality as well.

While it was independent, the principality bordered on Kiev principality along the Dnieper and the Desna rivers to the west, and was separated from Chernihiv principality to the north and northeast by the Oster River, the inaccessible marshes of the Smolynka, a tributary of the Seim River, and the Romen and the Sula rivers. Until the first half of the 12th century the principality also controlled the Seim Basin (the Poseimia) as far east as Kursk. Its southern and eastern borders reached at times as far as the Sosna, a right tributary of the Don, and the upper reaches of the Oskil and the Orel rivers, but fluctuated because of constant Pecheneg, Tork, and Cuman incursions. In favorable times Ukrainian colonization of that frontier moved along the Vorskla and the Sula rivers. Apart from Pereiaslav the principality's important fortified towns were Lukoml, Osterskyi Horodets (now Oster), Pryluka, Pyriatyn, and *Voin.

The principality bore the brunt of repeated Cuman attacks on Kievan Rus', and its princes, notably Vsevolod and his son *Volodymyr Monomakh, who ruled the principality from 1094 to 1113, waged war against the *Cumans, often together with other princes. Subsequent partitions of the Ukrainian lands among the princely dynasties reduced the principality to a second-rate appanage that was repeatedly annexed by the more powerful princes. To relieve that unfavorable situation the principality's inhabitants tried to find a dynasty who would help them fight the marauding nomads but not interfere too much in their internal affairs. In the end they chose the northern Rus' Monomakhovych princes of Suzdal, who ruled from the late 12th century on. The rulers of the principality included Monomakh's brother, Rostyslav; Monomakh's sons, Sviatoslav, *Yaropolk II Volodymyrovych, *Yurii Dolgorukii, Andrii, and *Viacheslav Volodymyrovych; Vsevolod and *Iziaslav Mstyslavych, and Iziaslav's son, *Mstyslav Iziaslavych; Dolgorukii's sons, *Rostyslav Yuriievych, *Hlib Yuriievych, and Vsevolod Velyke Hnizdo; Hlib's son, Volodymyr; the Olhovych prince *Sviatoslav III Vsevolodovych and his grandson, *Mykhail Vsevolodovych; Mstyslav Iziaslavych's cousin, *Riuryk Rostyslavych, and Riuryk's son, Volodymyr; and Vsevolod Velyke Hnizdo's sons, Konstantyn, Yaroslav, Volodymyr, and Sviatoslav.

During and after the Mongol-Tatar invasion of 1239–40 the principality suffered greatly at the hands of the invaders. It lost its political independence and was reduced to being a vassal of the Golden Horde. Ca 1360 the region came under Lithuanian rule, and in 1569 it became part of the Polish state. Hostilities between Poland and the Crimean Khanate exposed the region to ongoing Tatar raids, which halted Ukrainian colonization southeastward until the emergence of the Zaporozhian Cossacks.

BIBLIOGRAPHY
Storozhenko, A. *Ocherki pereiaslavl'skoi stariny* (Kiev 1900)
Liaskoronskii, V. *Istoriia Pereiaslavl'skoi zemli s drevneishikh vremen do poloviny XIII stoletiia* (Kiev 1903)
Kuchera, M. 'Pereiaslavskoe kniazhestvo,' in *Drevnerusskie kniazhestva X–XIII vv.*, ed L. Beskrovnyi (Moscow 1975)
Korinnyi, M. 'Pereiaslavs'ka zemlia v X–pershii tretyni XIII st.,' *UIZh*, 1981, no. 7

M. Zhdan

A company flag of Pereiaslav regiment (1762)

Pereiaslav regiment. An administrative territory and military formation in the Hetman state. Mentioned in historical documents from the 1570s, Pereiaslav was one of the oldest regiments in Ukraine. In 1649 it consisted of 19 companies, numbering 2,900 Cossacks. In 1654 it had 11 companies, and in 1665 it had 13. After the Treaty of Andrusovo (1667) it was reorganized: seven companies from the Right-Bank regiments of Cherkasy and Kaniv, two from Kropyvna regiment, and two new companies were added, and five were transferred to Kiev regiment. The regiment took part in the Khmelnytsky uprising, the Chyhyryn campaigns (1667–8), the Northern War (1700–21),

the Russo-Turkish Wars (1735–9 and 1768–74), and the Seven Years' War (1756–63). Two of its commanders, P. Teteria (1653–8) and Ya. Somko (1660–2), became hetmans, and several others – F. Loboda (1649–53), V. Serbyn (1675–7, 1679–83), I. Lysenko (1677–9, 1690–2), and L. Polubotok (1683–7, 1689–90) – served on the General Staff of the Hetmanate. The regiment was abolished in 1781, and its territory was incorporated into Kiev vicegerency.

Pereiaslav Treaty of 1630 (Pereiaslavska uhoda). An agreement between the Cossacks and Poland, signed on 8 June 1630 by the Polish hetman S. *Koniecpolski after a successful Cossack and peasant uprising led by T. *Fedorovych routed the Polish army at Pereiaslav on 25 May. The treaty amended the *Kurukove Treaty of 1625 by increasing the allowable number of *registered Cossacks from 6,000 to 8,000. The additional 2,000 were to be chosen by a commission made up of existing registered Cossacks and participants in the uprising, and the Cossacks were granted the right to elect their own hetman. Nonregistered Cossacks were granted amnesty but had to return to their homes on the nobles' estates. The Cossacks refused the Poles' request to hand over Fedorovych and elected T. Orendarenko as their hetman. The treaty was no more than a temporary compromise, for soon new Cossack-Polish conflicts erupted that resulted in the revolts led by P. *Pavliuk in 1637 and Ya. *Ostrianyn in 1638. Fedorovych's uprising and the treaty are described in a study by Mykhailo Antonovych (1944).

Pereiaslav Treaty of 1654 (Pereiaslavska uhoda). A fateful alliance the Hetman state under B. *Khmelnytsky concluded with Tsar Aleksei Mikhailovich during the *Cossack-Polish War. After the Crimean Tatar army betrayed the Cossacks for the third time during the siege of Zhvanets in 1653, and Khmelnytsky realized he could no longer rely on Ottoman support against Poland, the hetman was forced to turn to Muscovy for help. Moscow responded favorably to an alliance with Ukraine because it would prevent closer Ukrainian-Turkish ties. Negotiations began in January 1654 in Pereiaslav between Khmelnytsky and his General Military Council on one side and Muscovite envoys led by V. *Buturlin on the other. They were concluded in April in Moscow by the Ukrainians S. Bohdanovych-Zarudny (general judge of the Hetman state) and P. Teteria (then colonel of Pereiaslav regiment) and by A. Trubetskoi, V. Buturlin, and other Muscovite boyars.

The treaty consisted of two main documents modeled on the 1649 Treaty of *Zboriv: the tsar's patent to the Zaporozhian Host of 6 April (patents were also granted to other Ukrainian estates), and 11 articles concerning military, political, and technical details. The original documents have not been preserved, but translations and drafts of the tsar's patents have survived. The treaty's form and character were imperfect; some articles were not formulated systematically, and their content was rather vague. (English translations of the treaty appear in Ohloblyn's and Basarab's books [see bibliography].)

As a result of the treaty Ukraine became a protectorate of the Muscovite tsar, thenceforth also the 'tsar of Little Russia,' who in turn recognized the hetman and the Zaporozhian Host as the only representatives of the Hetman state and its government. Ukraine, headed by a freely elected hetman, retained its independence and autonomy in both foreign and internal policy. The rights and freedoms of the Cossacks, nobility, burghers, and clergy were guaranteed. Muscovy was obligated to defend Ukraine militarily, to launch immediately an offensive against Poland, and to send troops and a military governor to defend Kiev. The *registered Cossacks of Khmelnytsky's army were to be paid by the tsar from taxes gathered by local governments in Ukraine, and their number was fixed at 60,000. In view of the state of war the Ukrainian government agreed not to conduct negotiations with either Poland or Turkey without the tsar's permission. (That last provision and the one about collecting taxes in Ukraine for the tsar's treasury were never enforced.)

The treaty's limitations and formal character led to differing interpretations of it on both sides. The Ukrainian government, particularly under Khmelnytsky, considered it to be a temporary political and military alliance. Muscovy, however, particularly after Khmelnytsky's death, used it to justify its increasing interference in Ukraine's internal affairs, whereby it limited Ukraine's sovereignty and eventually nullified the treaty's provisions. Soon after the treaty was concluded, Muscovite officials visited 117 Ukrainian towns, and over 127,300 Ukrainian men swore an oath of loyalty to the tsar.

Historians and legal specialists have not been unanimous in their evaluation of the treaty, particularly its legal aspects and the relations it established between Ukraine and Russia. Some (mostly Russian) scholars believe that it formalized the voluntary incorporation of Ukraine into Russia, either in full or in part (D. Odinets, I. Rozenfeld, V. Miakotin) or Ukraine's autonomy within the Muscovite tsardom and later the Russian Empire (B. Nolde and others). Other historians, both Russian and Ukrainian, considered it to be an act of real union of the two states (N. Diakonov, A. Filippov, A. Popov); or a personal union with the tsar as sovereign of both countries (R. Lashchenko, V. Sergeevich); or the formalization of Ukraine's vassalage (M. Hrushevsky, N. Korkunov, I. Krypiakevych, Miakotin, L. Okinshevych, M. Pokrovsky, M. Slabchenko, A. Yakovliv in his early works) or its status as a protectorate (Hrushevsky, D. Doroshenko, B. Krupnytsky, Krypiakevych, Yakovliv in his later works) or pseudo- or quasi-protectorate (B. Halaichuk); or a temporary military alliance, solidified by the tsar's protection (V. Lypynsky, E. Borschak, Yakovliv in his later works, S. Ivanytsky). Modern Ukrainian historians have been divided: a minority have interpreted the treaty as the formalization of Ukraine's status as a vassal state or protectorate (Okinshevych, Yakovliv), whereas others have viewed it as a military and political alliance (Lypynsky, O. Ohloblyn). Soviet historians generally disputed that it was a treaty at all, and described it as the culmination of the desire of two 'fraternal peoples' to unite in a unitary Russian state.

(See also *Pereiaslav Articles of 1659.)

BIBLIOGRAPHY
Hrushevs'kyi, M. *Istoriia Ukraïny-Rusy*, vol 9, bk 1 (Kiev 1928; New York 1957)
Iakovliv, A. *Ukraïns'ko-moskovs'ki dohovory v XVII–XVIII vikakh* (Warsaw 1934)
– *Dohovir het'mana Bohdana Khmel'nyts'koho z moskovs'kym tsarem Oleksiiem Mykhailovychem* (New York 1954)
Ohloblyn, A. *Treaty of Pereyaslav, 1654* (Toronto and New York 1954)
Prokopovych, V. 'The Problem of the Juridical Nature of the Ukraine's Union with Muscovy,' *AUA*, 4 (Winter–Spring 1955)
O'Brien, C.B. *Muscovy and the Ukraine: From the Pereiaslavl Agreement to the Truce of Andrusovo, 1654–1667* (Berkeley and Los Angeles 1963)
Braichevsky, M. *Annexation or Unification?: Critical Notes on One Conception*, ed and trans G. Kulchycky (Munich 1974)
Basarab, J. *Pereiaslav 1654: A Historiographical Study* (Edmonton 1982)

O. Ohloblyn

Valentyna Pereiaslavets

Pereiaslavets, Valentyna [Perejaslavec'], b 10 February 1907. Ballet dancer, choreographer, and pedagogue. After completing study at the Kharkiv Choreography School (1926) she performed as a soloist in the Kharkiv, Kiev, and Sverdlovsk theaters of opera and ballet and in the Leningrad Choreography School under A. Vaganova. In 1940–4 she was the first soloist dancer in the Lviv Theater of Opera and Ballet. In 1945–8 she led a ballet school in West Germany. In 1949 she moved to New York and worked in T. Semenova's studio at Carnegie Hall. From 1951 she taught in the American Ballet Theater. Among her students were R. Nureyev, E. Bruhn, M. Fonteyn, and C. Fracci.

Pereiaslavets [Perejaslavec'] (aka Malyi Pereiaslavets). The name in the Rus' Primary Chronicle of the medieval Bulgarian town of Malyi Preslav, on the right bank of the lower Danube River. In the 10th century it was situated at the intersection of the trade routes between Rus' and the Danubian lands and Rus' and Byzantium. In 967 Grand Prince *Sviatoslav I Ihorevych captured the town during his first Bulgarian campaign and planned to move his capital there. In 971 the town was taken by the Byzantine troops of John Tzimisces, who slaughtered the Rus' garrison and put an end to Sviatoslav's plans.

Pereiaslav-Khmelnytskyi [Perejaslav-Xmel'nyc'kyj]. III-12. A city (1989 pop 30,000) on the Trubezh River and a raion center in Kiev oblast. In the medieval period it was known as Pereiaslavl, and then as Pereiaslav until 1943. It is one of the oldest cities of Ukraine: it is first mentioned in 907, in a treaty between Prince Oleh and the Greeks, where it is ranked third in importance after Kiev and Chernihiv. Pereiaslav was a strategically important fortress that defended Kievan Rus' against the steppe nomads. According to the chronicles, Volodymyr the Great built up its fortifications in 992, after his victory over the Pechenegs. The city also played an important political, religious, and economic role. From the mid-11th to the early

Pereiaslav-Khmelnytskyi in the 19th century

13th century it was the center of *Pereiaslav principality and the seat of Pereiaslav eparchy. A number of monumental buildings were erected in the period – the five-nave St Michael's Church (built in 1090 under Bishop Yefrem), the Dormition Church (built in 1098 by Volodymyr Monomakh), a three-nave shrine outside the fortress, St Theodore's Church, and St Andrew's Church. The citadel was encircled with walls and a stone gate surmounted by a chapel. In 1239 Pereiaslav was destroyed by the Tatars, and none of the medieval architecture survived.

Pereiaslav began to revive only in the mid-16th century, as a Cossack center in Kiev voivodeship. In 1630 T. Fedorovych's Cossack army defeated the Poles near the town. Ya. Ostrianyn's rebellion in 1638 was centered in Pereiaslav. In 1648 the town became a regimental center in the Cossack state established by B. Khmelnytsky (see *Pereiaslav regiment). It was the site of the negotiations culminating in the *Pereiaslav Treaty of 1654. A number of fine buildings erected in the 17th and 18th centuries have been preserved. Although Pereiaslav lost its political significance, it retained its religious and educational role, as the home of a college (1738–85) and then of a theological seminary (until 1862). H. *Skovoroda taught at the college in 1753. After the abolition of the Hetman state Pereiaslav again entered a period of decline. It became a county center of Kiev vicegerency (1781–96) and then of Little Russia (1797–1802) and Poltava (1802–1922) gubernias. By 1896 its population had reached 15,600. In 1923 it became a raion center.

Today Pereiaslav-Khmelnytskyi is a museum town, with little industry (a clothing, a footwear, and a handicrafts factory) but with 17 museums and many architectural monuments. The most important buildings of the baroque period are St Michael's Church (built in 1646–66 on the site of the medieval church, restored in 1711–19, and painted in 1715), the Ascension Cathedral (built by I. Mazepa in 1695–1700) and its bell tower (1760–70), the college building (1753–7), and the Church of the Holy Protectress (1704–9, financed by Col I. Myrovych). Remnants of the 10th-century fortifications and the foundations of the Church of the Transfiguration (11th century) have been uncovered. Most of the city's museums, including the open-air museum of architecture and folkways, the H. Skovoroda Museum (est 1972), the Archeological Museum, the V. Zabolotny Museum, the Folk-Art Museum of

the Kiev Region, the Museum of Kobza Playing, the Sholom Aleichem Museum, the Beekeeping Museum, and the Bread Museum, were founded by M. *Sikorsky. The A. Kozachkovsky Museum contains memorabilia of T. Shevchenko, who visited the town in 1845 and 1859. In the last few years the local branch of the Kiev Pedagogical Institute has been expanded greatly.

Pereiaslav-Khmelnytskyi burial site. A *Cherniakhiv culture burial ground in the northwestern part of Pereiaslav-Khmelnytskyi, Kiev oblast. Uncovered in 1951 and excavated in 1952–4, the site yielded 42 graves of which 23 were cremations. Pottery shards, glass cubes, bronze clasps, and jewelry were the most frequently recovered grave goods. The wealthiest of the graves contained arrowheads, spurs, and glass game pieces.

Pereiaslav-Khmelnytskyi Historical Museum (Pereiaslav-Khmelnytskyi istorychnyi muzei). A museum founded in Pereiaslav-Khmelnytskyi in 1946 as a historical and regional studies museum; it was given its present name in 1954. The Pereiaslav-Khmelnytskyi Archeological Museum, the Hryhorii Skovoroda and Volodymyr Zabolotny memorial museums, and the diorama of the Battles for the Dnieper in the Pereiaslav-Khmelnytskyi Region in 1943 are its branches. Since 1979 the museum has been part of the Pereiaslav-Khmelnytskyi Historical-Cultural Preserve. In 1988 it had 150,000 archeological, historical, ethnographic, artistic, printed, and numismatic objects in its collections, including items such as a 2nd- to 4th-century chess set, the world's only extant 11th-century candelabra with more than 12 candlesticks, and Hetman B. Khmelnytsky's sword. In the 1960s the museum published two scholarly collections called *Naukovi zapysky*. Since 1951 the museum's (and since 1979 the preserve's) director has been M. Sikorsky. A guidebook was published in Russian and German in 1972.

Pereiaslav-Khmelnytskyi Museum of Folk Architecture and Folkways. See Museums of folk architecture and folkways.

Perekop. VII-14. A village on the Perekop Isthmus in Krasnoperekopske raion, Crimea oblast. In the past it was the departure point for Tatar raids into Ukraine. At the end of the 15th century Mengli-Girei built the fortress of Or-Khap at the site. P. Sahaidachny defeated the Tatars there in 1620. In 1736 and 1738 the Russians captured and destroyed the fortress, but it was rebuilt by the Tatars in 1754. In 1783 Russia annexed the territory and turned Perekop into a county center of Tavriia gubernia. After the Crimean War many Tatars emigrated from the region to Turkey, and Ukrainian settlers moved in. With the building of the Lozova–Sevastopil railway line the town lost its commercial importance. By 1896 its population was only 7,400. According to the census of 1926, Ukrainians accounted for 43.6 percent of the region's population.

Perekop Isthmus. A thin tract of land connecting the Crimean Peninsula with the Ukrainian mainland. Located between Karkinitska Bay, in the Black Sea, and Syvash Lake, toward the Sea of Azov, the isthmus is approx 30 km long and 8–23 km wide, with elevations reaching up to 20 m. It consists of poor, saline soils, some steppe, and a desertlike vegetation cover. Several natural salt lakes (see

*Perekop lakes) are located on its southern reaches. Because it provided the only land link between the Ukrainian mainland and the Crimea, the isthmus has long had great economic importance. It was used as a trade route by Greek and Genoese colonies and from the late 18th century by salt-trading chumaks. The building of the Kharkiv–Symferopil train line over Syvash Lake in the 1870s diminished the importance of the isthmus considerably, although the construction of the Kherson–Dzhankoi line and the North Crimean Canal once more raised its fortunes. Because of its strategic significance the isthmus has been protected by fortified towns with defensive walls and moats (*perekopani rovy*, hence the name Perekop). The ancient Greeks built the town of Tafros there, and the Crimean Tatars had the fortress-town Or-Khap and later Ferk-Ferech-Kermen. In the 15th and 16th centuries the Turks built fortifications (known as the Turkish Wall) across the entire isthmus, which was the scene of major battles during the Russo-Turkish wars of the 18th century. Soviet forces fought their way through the isthmus's fortifications in 1920 during the Perekop-Chouhar Operation to take control of the Crimea. Fighting erupted in the isthmus during the Second World War, in 1941 and 1943.

Perekop lakes. A group of nine saltwater lakes located in the southern portion of the Perekop Isthmus. They are divided into chloric and sulfate-chloric categories. They range in area from 0.7 to 2.8 sq km, the largest lakes being Aihulske, Chervone (Krasne), Kyrleutske, Kyiatske, and Stare. Their banks are generally quite high (reaching 8–13 m), although the water in the lakes is actually 0.1 to 4.5 m below sea level. Some of the lakes have a salinity level of 21–28 per cent during the summer. Their shorelines often recede at that time and leave behind a dense layer of salt; salt extraction was a key economic activity around the lakes until the 20th century. A plant for extracting bromide, magnesium oxide, and magnesium chloride from the brine of the Perekop lakes is now located at Krasnoperekopske.

Perelesnyk (aka *litavets*). A figure in Ukrainian folk mythology akin to an incubus. He was believed to fly in the shape of a fiery dragon or young man, to enter homes through chimneys, doors, or windows, and to seduce women by assuming the appearance of a deceased spouse or lover. The *perelesnyk* has a female counterpart, *perelesnytsia*, but she rarely appears in Ukrainian folk mythology.

Perelisna, Kateryna (pseud of K. Hlianko), b 2 December 1902 in Kharkiv. Children's writer and pedagogue. From 1919 to 1931 she published poems, stories, articles, and reviews in the Kharkiv press and worked for publishers of children's folklore and literature. In 1931 her husband, O. Popov, the director of the Ukrainian Scientific Institute of Pedagogy and editor of *Radians'ka osvita*, was arrested and imprisoned, and she lost her job as a teacher and was harassed. She stopped publishing until 1941, when she fled to Lviv during the German occupation and contributed there to several children's magazines. In 1943 her poems won first prize in a children's literature competition sponsored by the Ukrainian Central Committee and the Ukrainske Vydavnytstvo publishers. After the war she was a displaced person in Germany and then emigrated to

Kateryna Perelisna   Petro Peremezhko

the United States. She is the author of the children's books *Odarka* (1927), *Ievshan zillia* (Homesickness, 1946), *Dlia maliat pro zviriat* (For Youngsters about Animals, 1952), *Oi, khto tam?* (Hey, Who's There?, 1954), *Try pravdy* (Three Truths, 1967), *Moï matusi* (For My Mommy, 1967), and *Kotykova pryhoda* (The Kitten's Adventure, 1973). Many of her works have appeared in émigré periodicals and miscellanies for children, and some of her poems and stories have been put to music as songs and miniature children's operas by composers such as O. Zalesky, M. Fomenko, H. Kytasty, and I. Nedilsky.

Peremezhko, Petro [Peremežko], b 24 July 1833 in Rybotyn, Krolevets county, Chernihiv gubernia, d 8 January 1894 in Kiev. Histologist. A graduate of Kiev University (1859), he worked in Kazan, was a professor of histology, embryology, and comparative anatomy at Kiev University (1868–91), and served as dean of the medical faculty (1872–5) and president of the Society of Kiev Physicians (1882–3). He set up the first histology department in Ukraine and discovered the process of karyokinesis in animal cells (1878), thereby becoming one of the founders of karyology. He first described the nerves which later came to be called proprioceptors. His publications also dealt with the development and regeneration of striated muscles, the structure of the hypophysis, gerontological changes in the thyroid gland, and the development and structure of the spleen. He built the first microtome in Russia and contributed to the first Russian textbook in microscopic anatomy.

Peremoha. An Argentinian-Ukrainian publishing house and bookshop in Buenos Aires, owned by S. Kravets and M. Pareniuk (1947–57). It was founded on the basis of the Promin Publishing House of 1942 and published approx 50 books and 79 issues of the literary journal *Porohy*.

Peremoha (Victory). An ideological organ of the *Front of National Unity, published in Lviv by the Batkivshchyna publishing house, semimonthly from February 1933 to 1936 and then quarterly to 1939. It was edited by M. Shlemkevych, and regular contributors included D. Paliiv, I. Hladylovych, and S. Volynets.

Peremyshl [Peremyšl'] (Polish: Przemyśl). IV-3. A city (1989 pop 68,100) on the Sian River between the Car-

Peremyshl's coat of arms

Peremyshl in 1618 (engraving by F. Hogenberg)

pathian foothills and the Sian Lowland. It has been a county center and, since the mid-1970s, a voivodeship center in Poland. One of the oldest cities in Galicia, it has been throughout its history a major Ukrainian political, cultural, and religious center.

History. Peremyshl is first mentioned in the chronicles under the year 981, but the area has been inhabited almost continuously since the Paleolithic Period. The numerous Roman coins found in the vicinity show that by the 1st century AD Peremyshl was a significant trading post on the route between the Dniester and the Vistula. The discovery of a large hoard of medieval Arab coins from the 9th and 10th centuries confirmed the town's continued commercial importance. Excavations conducted in 1958–60 on Zamkova Hill support the hypothesis that as early as the 9th century Peremyshl was a capital of White Croatian princes and Slavonic-rite bishops: the uncovered foundations of a round chapel and a palace were built of cut stone according to the Galician-Volhynian practice, not of brick (according to the Cracow practice). Because of its border location Kievan Rus' and Poland, and sometimes Hungary, fought over Peremyshl. In 981 Volodymyr the Great annexed it to the Kievan state. In 1018–31 and 1071–9 it was held by the Poles. In the late 11th century it became the seat of a separate principality ruled by *Riuryk Rostyslavych (1087–92), *Volodar Rostyslavych (1094–1124), and Volodar's sons, Rostyslav (1124–30) and *Volodymyrko (1131–52). Volodymyrko brought all the Galician lands under his rule and in 1141 moved the capital to Halych. In the early 13th century some rulers of Peremyshl, such as Sviatoslav Ihorevych (1206–11) and Oleksii Vsevolodovych (1231), claimed independence, until Danylo Romanovych finally incorporated the whole Peremyshl territory into Galicia. During Danylo's and Lev's reigns, German merchants and tradesmen settled in the town and received the right to municipal self-government. At that time the town lay between Zamkova Hill and the Sian River.

Polish period, 1349–1772. In 1349 Peremyshl was captured by the Polish king Casimir III the Great, who built a new castle there. Under Władysław Opolczyk, the viceroy of Louis the Great of Hungary, a Roman Catholic diocese was established in Peremyshl (1375). In 1387 the town returned to Polish rule, and in 1389 King Jagiełło granted it the rights of *Magdeburg law. When Polish law and administration were introduced and Rus' voivodeship was set up in 1434, Peremyshl became a starostvo center in the new province. In 1458 it gained all the rights of a crown city.

In the late 14th century the core of the town shifted east of the old town. A large new market square and a grid of eight streets were enclosed by walls and a moat. In the early 16th century the town's area was 50 ha (similar to Lviv's). Beyond the walls lay the suburbs and, farther on, the gentry estates. Peremyshl prospered from the mid-15th to the mid-17th century. Its residents were engaged mostly in trades, such as leather-working, brewing, and weaving. Some made their living in local and transit trade. By the mid-17th century the town's population had reached 4,000. Apart from Ukrainians and Poles there were Germans (who were quickly Polonized), Armenians, and Jews, who in 1559 were given special privileges by the king. Each ethnic group lived in a different area of the town. Ukrainians lived mostly in Vladyche district and the suburbs. Ukrainian burghers had to struggle for equal rights with the Poles and organized themselves into a brotherhood. In 1592 they founded a school, and later, a hospital. The brotherhood eventually expanded from the Orthodox cathedral to the Church of the Holy Trinity, and in 1633 it set up a printing press, which it sold in the late 17th century to the Lviv Dormition Brotherhood. By the end of the 17th century the Ukrainian community in Peremyshl was in decline, owing partly to Polish discrimination and oppression and partly to religious strife between the Orthodox and the Uniates. The strife lasted throughout the 17th century and ended in the Uniates' victory in 1691 (see *Peremyshl eparchy). The city became an important Polish cultural center, in which the Polish diocese, the cathedral school (later the Jesuit College), and the educated magnates played the leading role. In the 16th and early 17th centuries the Peremyshl region played a prominent role in the Polish renaissance and reformation. The town was also an important Jewish religious and cultural center.

In the late 17th and the 18th centuries Peremyshl declined. At the beginning of the 18th century its population fell to 1,700. Changing trade routes were partly responsible, but the chief cause was Poland's incessant warfare and social conflicts.

Austrian period, 1772–1918. At the first partition of Poland in 1772, Peremyshl was transferred to Austria, which sold it to Count I. Zetner in 1778. At the request of the burghers, however, Joseph II restored all the town's rights and privileges in 1789, and the town became a county center. Civil servants and tradesmen, mostly German and

Main entrance of the former Ukrainian Catholic cathedral (1630; now a Polish Catholic church) in Peremyshl

Members of the Ukrainian girls' team Spartanky in Peremyshl (1927)

Czech, settled in Peremyshl. The old ramparts were leveled, and the town was allowed to expand. It grew at a slow pace: in 1860 the population reached only 10,000 (compared to 70,000 in Lviv). The rate of growth increased in the later part of the 19th century as new railway lines linked Peremyshl with Cracow (1859), Lviv (1861), and Hungary (1872); railway yards and agricultural machinery factories were set up in the town, and the local fortress and garrison were expanded after 1876. In 1880 the population reached 20,700, in 1900, 46,300, and in 1910, 54,700 (including 7,500 military personnel).

Under Austrian rule new opportunities opened before the Ukrainian community in Peremyshl. Thanks to the efforts of I. *Mohylnytsky and the support of Bishops M. *Levytsky and I. *Snihursky the city became, in the first half of the 19th century, an important Ukrainian educational center. The Societas Presbyterorum, a clerical association for publishing educational materials (est 1816), a precentors' school (est 1817), and the chapter library (later also an archive and museum) took the initiative in the educational movement. A number of Ukrainian textbooks and two grammars were published in Peremyshl. By the 1880s Peremyshl had become, after Lviv, the second-largest center for Ukrainian secondary education in Galicia. It was the home of the Peremyshl Greek Catholic Theological Seminary (revived in 1845), a bilingual women teachers' seminary (est 1870), the *Ukrainian Girls' Institute (est 1881), the *Peremyshl State Gymnasium (est 1888), and a number of vocational schools, elementary schools, and boarding schools. Peremyshl was less important as a publishing center, yet an impressive list of periodicals as well as some religious books and school texts appeared there: the first calendars in Galicia, *Peremyshlianyn and Peremyshlianka, the monthly Vistnyk Peremys'koï eparkhiï (1889–

1918), the literary journal Novyi halychanyn (1889), the religious monthly Poslannyk (1895–1907), the monthly *Prapor (1897–1900), the farmers' monthly *Hospodar (1898–1913), the weekly Selians'ka rada (1907–9), and the biweekly *Peremys'kyi vistnyk (1909–14). The influence of its successful Ukrainian economic institutions, such as the Vira co-operative bank (est 1894), the Narodnyi Dim credit union (est 1906), the Ruthenian Savings Bank, and the Burghers' Bank, was felt far beyond the town. The noted community leaders of the period were Bishops H. Yakhymovych, T. Poliansky, I. Stupnytsky, Yu. Pelesh, and K. Chekhovych, the lawyers T. Kormosh and V. Zahaikevych, the businessman I. Borys, and the writer H. Tsehlynsky.

During the First World War the city surrendered after the second siege to the Russian army and was recaptured two months later, in June 1915, by Austrian and German forces.

Interwar period. After the dissolution of Austria-Hungary in 1918, Peremyshl became an arena of the Ukrainian-Polish War. It was controlled briefly (3–12 November 1918) by the Ukrainian authorities. In 1919–21 a Polish internment camp for soldiers of the UNR Army and the Ukrainian Galician Army was located nearby, in *Pykulychi. After the war Peremyshl did not grow: from 1921 to 1931 its population increased only from 48,100 to 51,000. The garrison stationed there was a burden rather than an economic advantage. The city's metallurgical and forest industries developed slowly. It remained a Ukrainian religious center: it was the seat of Bishop Y. Kotsylovsky and the home of the revived Greek Catholic Theological Seminary and of the Peremyshl Eparchy Aid Association.

The population of Peremyshl, 1880–1931 (thousands; percentage of total in parentheses)

	1880	1900	1910	1921	1931
Total	22.0	46.3	54.7	48.0	51.0
Greek Catholics	4.7 (21.4)	10.4 (22.5)	12.3 (22.5)	7.5 (15.6)	8.3 (16.3)
Roman Catholics	9.6 (43.6)	21.3 (46.0)	25.5 (46.6)	21.9 (45.6)	25.1 (49.2)
Jews	7.6 (34.5)	14.1 (30.5)	16.1 (29.4)	18.4 (38.3)	17.3 (33.9)
Others	0.1 (0.5)	0.5 (1.1)	0.8 (1.5)	0.2 (0.4)	0.3 (0.6)

The Peremyshl Greek Catholic Theological Seminary

A Basilian monastery was built in the vicinity. A number of new cultural institutions, such as the *Stryvihor Museum, and young people's and sporting organizations, such as Berkut (1922) and Sian (1929), were set up. Some new co-operatives and private enterprises were organized. The weeklies *Ukraïns'kyi holos* (1919–32) and *Beskyd* (1928–33, later *Ukraïns'kyi Beskyd*) appeared.

After 1939. With the Polish military collapse in the summer of 1939, the Sian River became the dividing line between the German-occupied and the Soviet-occupied territories. The city was cut into two parts. Many Ukrainians and Poles fled from the Soviet side of the river to the German side. Of those who stayed behind many were deported or shot by the Bolsheviks. Toward the end of June 1941 the whole city came under German rule.

In 1939, of 54,200 residents in Peremyshl, 8,600 (15.8 percent) were Ukrainians (2,000 of whom spoke only Polish), 27,100 (50 percent) were Poles, and 18,400 (34 percent) were Jews. According to the German census of 1942, of 34,000 city residents, 8,100 (23.9 percent) were Ukrainians, 20,200 (59.5 percent) were Poles, 3,800 (11.2 percent) were Jews, and 1,800 (5.3 percent) were Germans.

Peremyshl was recaptured by Soviet forces on 27 July 1944, and 40 percent of it was destroyed in the process. According to the Polish-Soviet agreement of 1945 Poland retained Peremyshl, and its Ukrainian population was resettled either in the Ukrainian SSR or the newly acquired territories in western Poland. All Ukrainian schools and organizations were dissolved. Bishops Kotsylovsky and H. Lakota, along with a group of Ukrainian priests, were arrested by the Poles and handed over to the Soviets. The Ukrainian cathedral and chapter buildings were confiscated by the state. The residence of the Ukrainian bishop was converted into the People's Museum of the Przemyśl Land, and most of the holdings of the Stryvihor Museum and the eparchy archives were transferred to it. During the brief political thaw in 1956–60 some Ukrainian cultural activity was permitted. The Ukrainian Social and Cultural Society was formed, parallel Ukrainian-language instruction was introduced in the Polish lyceum, and a Ukrainian boarding school was opened. The last two measures were soon revoked. Peremyshl entered the 1990s with a Ukrainian Orthodox parish. Ukrainian Catholics, however, attend services in a Polish church.

Cut off by the new border from its natural hinterland to the east and south, Peremyshl stagnated for a decade after the war. From 1946 to 1953 its population increased only from 36,800 to 38,000. Then it began to grow, mostly because of industrial investment. It has a well-developed food industry, a building-materials industry, a metallurgical industry, a woodworking industry, and a confectionery industry. Standing at the junction of the main highways and railways, it has been an important center of Polish-Soviet trade.

Culture. The city's contribution to Ukrainian culture was largely connected with the Ukrainian Catholic eparchy of Peremyshl. In the early 19th century most of the scholars who worked in Peremyshl, including A. Dobriansky, H. Hynylevych, Yu. Zhelekhivsky, Y. Levytsky, and I. Mohylnytsky, were priests. In more recent times researchers, such as I. Bryk, Ye. Hrytsak, I. Zilynsky, Bishop Lakota, S. Shakh, and V. Shchurat, worked there. Writers such as O. Avdykovych, P. Karmansky, U. Kravchenko, P. Leontovych, D. Lukianovych, V. Masliak, V. Pachovsky, O. Turiansky, Tsehlynsky, and S. Yarychevsky lived and worked in the city. Its regional and diocesan museums contain many monuments of Ukrainian culture.

Peremyshl is known for its artistic traditions. The German painter Heil, who decorated Wawel Castle in Cracow in the 15th century, received an estate in Peremyshl from King Jagiełło. During Bishop A. Brylynsky's tenure (1581–91) an icon painting school was established in nearby Rybotychi (Rybotycze). In recent times the painters T. Kopystynsky, A. Pylykhovsky, O. Skrutok, Olena and Olha Kulchytska, and S. Chekhovych worked in Peremyshl.

Ukrainian music was cultivated in Peremyshl. The Galician-Volhynian Chronicle under the year 1241 mentions the poet-singer Mytusa, who served at the bishop's court. In the 18th century, a musicians' guild was active in the town. In 1829 Rev Y. Levytsky organized a choir at the Greek Catholic Cathedral, which influenced the development of choral music in the 19th century. It was conducted by the Czech composers A. Nanke, V. Sersavý, and L. Sedlák. The Ukrainian composers I. Lavrivsky and M. Verbytsky lived and worked in the city. The Boian society (est 1891) and the local branch (est 1924) of the Lysenko Music Society fostered Ukrainian musical culture.

Layout and appearance. Old Peremyshl – now the city center with the Market Square – lies on the right bank of the Sian River. It has preserved some of its original character. The northern part of the old town served as the Jewish district until 1942. Today the old town is the administrative and commercial district of Peremyshl. In the 19th and early 20th centuries the city spread eastward toward Lviv along the railway line and Mickiewicz Street. It also expanded, though not as much, southeastward along Słowacki Street. Northeast of the center lies Harbari district. Today most of the industrial buildings and factories are located on the eastern outskirts of the city, in the former villages of Bakonchytsi (Bakończyce), Perekopana (Przekopana), and Korovnyky (Krówniki). A large district arose on the left bank of the Sian, known as Zasiannia (Zasanie). In the southwestern section, on the slopes of the Carpathian foothills, lies a large municipal park.

Most of the noted architectural monuments in Peremyshl are churches. The Ukrainian Cathedral of St John the Baptist (a Carmelite church until 1784), which was built in the baroque style (1625–30) and restored in 1876–

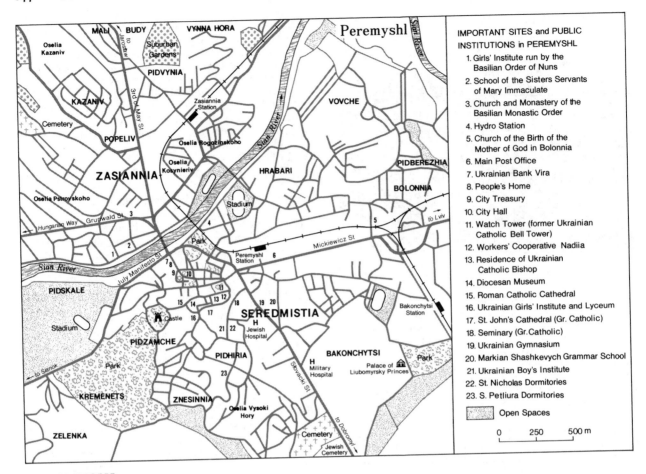

Peremyshl

IMPORTANT SITES and PUBLIC INSTITUTIONS in PEREMYSHL

1. Girls' Institute run by the Basilian Order of Nuns
2. School of the Sisters Servants of Mary Immaculate
3. Church and Monastery of the Basilian Monastic Order
4. Hydro Station
5. Church of the Birth of the Mother of God in Bolonnia
6. Main Post Office
7. Ukrainian Bank Vira
8. People's Home
9. City Treasury
10. City Hall
11. Watch Tower (former Ukrainian Catholic Bell Tower)
12. Workers' Cooperative Nadiia
13. Residence of Ukrainian Catholic Bishop
14. Diocesan Museum
15. Roman Catholic Cathedral
16. Ukrainian Girls' Institute and Lyceum
17. St. John's Cathedral (Gr. Catholic)
18. Seminary (Gr.Catholic)
19. Ukrainian Gymnasium
20. Markian Shashkevych Grammar School
21. Ukrainian Boy's Institute
22. St. Nicholas Dormitories
23. S. Petliura Dormitories

Open Spaces

0   250   500 m

PEREMYSHL

84, is now a Polish Catholic church. The Roman Catholic Cathedral, built in 1460–1571 in the Gothic style at the site of St Nicholas's Church (11th–13th century), was reconstructed in 1724–44 in the baroque style. The oldest Roman Catholic churches include the baroque Jesuit Church (1622–37), the late baroque Franciscan Church (built in the gothic style in 1379, rebuilt in 1754–78 with classical elements, renovated in 1848 and 1875), and the Reformers' Church (1627, rebuilt in 1657), which contains remnants of the town wall. The Old Synagogue, built in 1579 in the Renaissance style and renovated in 1910, was active until 1942. Other architectural landmarks include the Old (or Clock) Tower (1775–7), which was to have served as the bell tower of the planned Greek Catholic Cathedral, the remains of the ramparts in Władycze district, several Renaissance and baroque buildings in the Market Square (partly destroyed in 1944 and restored), and the remnants of the 14th-century castle, which was rebuilt in the Renaissance style in 1612–30, torn down by the Austrian authorities, and then partly rebuilt in 1867, 1887, and 1912. The churches of more recent construction include the Church of the Birth of the Theotokos (1880s), painted by O. Skrutko in 1906, the Church of John the Theologian (1901) in Perekopana, and the church of the Basilian monastery (1935) in Zasiannia.

BIBLIOGRAPHY

Lewicki, A. *Obrazki z najdawniejszych dziejów Przemyśla* (Peremyshl 1881)

Hauser, L. *Monografia miasta Przemyśla* (Peremyshl 1883)

Orłowicz, M. *Ilustrowany przewodnik po Peremyślu i okolicy* (Lviv 1917)

Smolka, J. *Historia miasta Przemyśla* (Peremyshl 1924, 1936)

Hrytsak, Ie. *Peremyshl' tomu sto lit* (Peremyshl 1936)

Al'manakh: De sribnolentyi Sian plyve (Peremyshl 1938)

Wolski, K. *Przemyśl i okolice* (Peremyshl 1957)

Shakh, S. *Mizh Sianom i Dunaitsem*, pt 1 (Munich 1960)

Tysiąc lat Przemyśla (Peremyshl 1961)

Zahaikevych, B. (ed). *Peremyshl': Zakhidnyi bastion Ukraïny* (New York–Philadelphia 1961)

Ziemia Przemyska (Cracow 1963)

Pasternak, Ia. *Kniazhyi horod Peremyshl' u svitli novykh arkheolohichnykh doslidzhen'* (Chicago 1964)

Kunysz, A. *Przemyśl w starożytności i średniowieczu* (Rzeszów 1966)

P. Isaiv, V. Kubijovyč

Peremyshl eparchy. One of the oldest church administrative districts in Ukraine. The eparchy was established at the latest in the 11th century, and possibly as early as the late 9th or early 10th century. The earliest known bishop was A. Dobrynia Yadreikovych (1218–25). The eparchy initially included all of Galicia and Transcarpathia, until the formation of the separate eparchies of Halych (mid-12th century) and Mukachiv (1491). Occasionally the bishops of Peremyshl have also been known as the bishops of Sambir (from 1422) or Sianik (from the latter half of the 17th century). For this reason the eparchy in the Ukrainian Catholic church is officially known as the 'unified eparchies of Peremyshl, Sambir, and Sianik.'

Prominent bishops in the 15th and 16th centuries included Y. Biretsky (1467–76), A. Onykii (1498–1521), and A. Radylovsky (1549–81). In 1596 Bishop M. *Kopystensky did not support the Church Union of *Berestia and remained Orthodox. This action initiated nearly a century of rivalry in the region, with Orthodox and Catholic bishops competing for control over the eparchy. In this period the more prominent Orthodox hierarchs included I. *Kopynsky and A. *Vynnytsky; Uniate hierarchs included A. *Krupetsky, P. *Khmilevsky (who was never allowed to occupy his see), and I. Malakhovsky. The matter was resolved in 1692, when the Orthodox bishop I. *Vynnytsky adopted Catholicism, and the eparchy joined the Uniate church. The eparchy then remained Catholic until 1946. Bishops during that time included Yu. Vynnytsky, O. Shumliansky, A. Sheptytsky, A. Anhelovych, M. Ryllo, M. Levytsky, I. Snihursky, and Y. Kotsylovsky. An eparchial seminary functioned briefly in 1780–3 and regularly from 1845; it published an eparchial organ (called *Vistnyk Peremys'koï eparkhiï* [1889–1914] and then *Peremys'ki eparkhial'ni vidomosty* [to 1939]), which featured church news, sermons, a church calendar, and articles on church history, and copublished the quarterly *Dobryi pastyr*.

In 1934 a portion of Peremyshl eparchy became part of the separate *Lemko Apostolic Administration. This left the eparchy (in 1936) with 578 parishes, 45 deaneries, 695 priests, 8 Basilian men's (with 48 monks) and 8 women's monasteries, 34 residences of the Sisters Servants of Mary Immaculate and 8 of the Sisters of St Joseph, and approx 1,131,000 faithful. During the Soviet occupation of Western Ukraine (1939–41) the western part of the eparchy fell under German control and was administered by the auxiliary bishop, H. Lakota.

After the Second World War the eparchy again was divided, this time between the Ukrainian SSR and Poland. In the eastern portion the Soviet authorities suppressed the Catholic church, and the sham *Lviv Sobor of 1946 announced the formal incorporation of the eparchy into the Russian Orthodox church. At the same time Bishops Kotsylovsky and Lakota were exiled to Central Asia, where they died in labor camps. Meanwhile, most Ukrainians in the western portion were forcibly resettled by the Polish authorities in the north and west of Poland. The few remaining Ukrainians in the region were forced to switch to either Roman Catholicism or Orthodoxy. After 1957 Ukrainians were again permitted to practice the Eastern rite, and in 1989 the Polish cardinal J. Glemp consecrated I. Martyniak as bishop for Ukrainians, but he was not appointed until January 1991 to the eparchy of Peremyshl (see *Ukrainian Catholic church).

In 1983 the Polish Autocephalous Orthodox church revived an Orthodox eparchy of Peremyshl–Nowy Sącz, with its see in Sianik, under the Ukrainian bishop A. Dubets. In the late 1980s the Ukrainian Catholic church emerged from the underground in Soviet Ukraine; the territories of the former Peremyshl eparchy within present-day Ukraine have been incorporated into the revived Lviv archeparchy.

BIBLIOGRAPHY
Skhymatizm vseho klyra rusko-katolicheskoho eparkhiï Peremyshlskoi na hod 1879 (Peremyshl 1879)
Dobrianskii, A. Istoriia episkopov trekh soedinennykh eparkhii, Peremyshl'skoi, Samborskoi i Sanotskoi, ot naidavnyshikh vremen do 1794 (Lviv 1893)
Isaïv, P. Istoriia Peremys'koho iepyskopstva (Philadelphia 1970)
Bendza, M. Prawosławna Diecezja Przemyska w latach 1596–1681 (Warsaw 1982)
Sonevyts'kyi, L. 'Ukraïns'kyi iepyskopat Peremys'koï i Kholms'koï ieparkhii v XV–XVI st.,' in his Studiï z istoriï Ukraïny (Paris–New York–Sydney–Toronto 1982)

W. Lencyk

Peremyshl Greek Catholic Theological Seminary

(Peremyska hreko-katolytska dukhovna seminariia). The training center for priests in Peremyshl eparchy. After a brief existence in 1780–3, the seminary was closed by Joseph II, and theology students forced once again to go to Lviv to study. It was partially reopened in 1845 to accommodate theology students completing their fourth year of study. Only in 1921–39 and 1942–4 was the seminary again fully operational. During this time a fifth year of study was added to the curriculum; the student enrollment grew to over 150, and the staff to 12 (1937); and the students organized religious societies, a co-operative, and an academic society, which in 1937 published a jubilee almanac for theology students in the eparchy. For the last decade of the seminary's existence, I. Kuzych served as rector, and V. Holynsky as assistant rector.

Peremyshl State Gymnasium

(Peremyska derzhavna himnaziia). The second Ukrainian-language gymnasium to be opened in Galicia, preceded only by the *Academic Gymnasium in Lviv. Founded in 1888 as a Ukrainian-language division of a Polish gymnasium, in 1895 it became an independent classical gymnasium, called the Second Imperial Gymnasium in Peremyshl, with a full eight classes. After the First World War, under Polish rule, the gymnasium was renamed the State Gymnasium in Peremyshl with the Ruthenian (Ukrainian) Language of Instruction. After the school reforms of 1932 the gymnasium was reorganized into a four-year general education gymnasium and a two-year lyceum with two faculties, of humanities and of natural sciences and mathematics. The gymnasium was closed shortly after the Soviet occupation of Western Ukraine.

The gymnasium's students came mostly from the Ukrainian-Polish borderlands and from the Lemko region. Some students were also from Poland proper, although (in the interwar period) they were usually the children of refugees from Soviet-occupied Ukraine. Throughout its history the institution was one of the largest and most important Ukrainian-language gymnasiums in Galicia. The gymnasium opened with 329 students in 1895; by 1912 its 1,013 students were being taught by 41 teachers. By the First World War the gymnasium had graduated 912 students. In its first 40 years of operation (1896–1936), 2,452 students, including 114 Jews, graduated from the school, almost all of them men.

The gymnasium's directors included H. Tsehlynsky (1888–1910), A. Alyskevych (1910–17), R. Hamchykevych (1919–24), and S. Shakh (1932–9); instructors included prominent scientists, authors, artists, and community and political activists.

Peremyshliany

[Peremyšljany]. IV-5. A city (1989 pop 7,600) on the Hnyla Lypa River and a raion center in Lviv oblast. According to archeological evidence the site was settled as early as the 2nd century BC. The town is first mentioned in historical documents in 1473. It was granted the rights of *Magdeburg law in 1623. After the partition of Poland in 1772, Peremyshliany was acquired by Austria, and in 1918 it belonged briefly to the Western Ukrainian National Republic. In June 1919 the Ukrainian Galician Army defeated the Polish forces in the vicinity. In 1939 Peremyshliany was occupied by Soviet troops and was granted city status. Today its main industries are food processing and furniture-making. Its architectural monuments include a Roman Catholic church from 1645 and the remnants of a 16th- to 17th-century Dominican monastery in the baroque style.

Peremyshlianyn (The Peremyshlian). An annual church and literary almanac published in Peremyshl in 1850–63. It contained a chronology of holy days, prose, poetry, and historical articles, especially on the history of the Peremyshl region and the Greek Catholic church. It was edited by Rev A. Dobriansky and, from 1857, Ya. Velychko; frequent contributors included I. Ozarkevych, O. Zavadsky, and D. Petrytsky.

Peremys'kyi vistnyk (Peremyshl Herald). A semi-monthly newspaper of the Peremyshl People's Organization, published from January 1909 to 1914. It succeeded the weekly *Selians'ka rada* (1907–8) and published popular articles on politics, economics, and culture. Its chief editors included V. Kitsyla, V. Zahaikevych, and S. Hubchak.

Perepeliuk, Volodymyr [Perepeljuk], b 21 November 1910 in Boryshkivtsi, Kamianets-Podilskyi county, Podilia gubernia. Kobza and bandura player. He learned the art from the bandura trio of the Vinnytsia Philharmonic. In 1941 he joined the new Ukrainian Ethnographic Ensemble of Folk Singers and Kobza Players at the Kiev Philharmonic and composed for it a number of dumas about Semen Palii and about the war with the Poles. In 1944 he became a kobza soloist with the *Verovka State Chorus, with which he performed his own as well as folk dumas. He described his travels abroad in *Povist' pro narodnyi khor* (The Story of the [Verovka] State Chorus, 1970).

Perepelytsia, Stepan [Perepelycja], b 1884, d 1932. Economist and political leader. A specialist in finance cooperation and a sympathizer of the Ukrainian Party of Socialist Revolutionaries, he served as UNR finance minister in V. Holubovych's cabinet (February–March 1918).

Perepiatykha and Perepiat kurhans. A forest-steppe settlement and burial ground of the 6th century BC near Marianivka, Vasylkiv raion, Kiev oblast. Excavations by M. Ivanyshev in 1845 revealed that the mounds of earth covered wooden burial vaults. Artifacts recovered included tulip-shaped pottery (for storing cremated remains), earthenware ladles, jewelry, an iron ax, a bronze mirror, and 24 gold plates decorated with griffin motifs. M. Maksymovych participated in the excavations and T. Shevchenko worked as a draftsman on the project.

Peresada-Sukhodolsky, Mykhailo [Peresada-Suxodol's'kyj, Myxajlo], b 1883 in the Kharkiv region, d 1938 in Galicia. Senior staff officer. A general staff officer in the Russian army, in 1917 he joined the UNR Army as a colonel. During 1918–20 he served as chief of staff of the Fourth Reserve Brigade and the Third Iron Rifle Division,

Gen Mykhailo Peresada-Sukhodolsky

and chief of the quartermaster department of the General Staff. In 1921 he was a deputy chief of staff of the Ukrainian forces in the Second Winter Campaign, and was promoted to brigadier general.

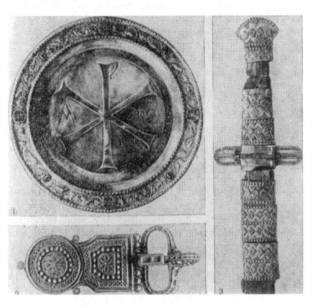

A silver plate, gold sword handle, and gold buckle from the Pereshchepyna hoard

Pereshchepyna hoard. One of the richest finds in Ukraine, discovered near Mala Pereshchepyna, now in Novi Sanzhary raion, Poltava oblast, in 1912. Nearly 25 kg of gold and 50 kg of silver artifacts – including 5th- to 7th-century Byzantine and Iranian art objects, gold and silver dishes, 7th-century Byzantine coins, jewelry, a plate bearing the emblem of the bishop of the Greek colony Tomis, now Constanţa in Rumania, and a Sasanian plate with a portrait of Shapur II – were found. Scholars believe the hoard to be booty from raids into Byzantine territory. The collection is now housed at the Hermitage in St Petersburg.

Pereshchepyne [Pereščepyne]. IV-16. A town smt (1986 pop 10,500) on the Orel River in Novomoskovske raion, Dnipropetrovske oblast. By 1764 it was an important frontier settlement in Orel palanka of the territory held by the Zaporozhian Sich. Today the Dnieper-Donbas Canal runs through the town. The oil and natural gas discovered at

Pereshchypyne began to be extracted in the mid-1960s. A kurhan nearby dates back to the Bronze Age.

Peresichen [Peresičen'] (aka Peresichyn, Peresichna). The main town of the Slavic tribe of the *Ulychians. It was first mentioned in the Novgorod First Chronicle, in connection with the attempt of the Kievan prince Oleh to conquer the Ulychians. Ca 940, after a three-year siege, Peresichen was captured by Prince Ihor's military commander, Sveneld, and was annexed by Kievan Rus'. The exact location of the town has not been determined. Most scholars place it between the Dniester and the Prut rivers, and some point to the present-day town of Peresecina, in Orhei raion, Moldova.

Peresichna [Peresična]. III-16. A town smt (1986 pop 8,400) on the Udy River in Derkachi raion, Kharkiv oblast. The town was founded in 1650. In 1926 a health resort was built around local mineral springs. Poultry farming and feed production contribute to the town's economy. A Scythian settlement of the 5th to 3rd century BC and a burial ground of the Cherniakhiv culture (2nd–4th century AD) have been discovered nearby.

Peresopnytsia [Peresopnycja]. III-7. A medieval Volhynian town on the Stubla River. Now a village in Rivne raion, Peresopnytsia was first mentioned in a Rus' chronicle under the year 1147, as a town in Turiv-Pynske principality belonging to Prince Iziaslav Mstyslavych. In the 12th and 13th centuries it and Dorohobuzh were the chief towns in the so-called Pohoryna domain along the Horyn River. Prince Yurii Dolgorukii captured the Pohoryna in 1149 and installed his sons, Hlib and Andrii, in Dorohobuzh and Peresopnytsia. Prince Yaroslav Mstyslavych of Lutske gained control of the Pohoryna in 1171 and gave part of it, along with Peresopnytsia, to his son, Mstyslav the Mute. Mstyslav's son, Ivan, ceded the town to Danylo Romanovych of Galicia. From 1227 it belonged to the Lutske appanage principality, and its previous significance was lost. Control over it was consolidated by Danylo's brother, Vasylko Romanovych. In the early 14th century the town came under Lithuanian rule. From the late 15th century to 1773 it belonged to the Czartoryski princely family. The town had the Monastery of the Mother of God (built by Mstyslav the Mute), where the translation of the *Peresopnytsia Gospel was completed in 1561.

Archeological excavations have revealed that Peresopnytsia's fortified inner town and castle were built in the Stubla valley amid marshes in the 10th century. A nearby cemetery across the river dates from the 11th and 12th centuries. Twenty medieval earthen dwellings have been excavated near the village. On the village outskirts 170 medieval kurhans, a Neolithic flint-fashioning workshop, a late Neolithic Nordic settlement, and a Bronze Age burial site have been uncovered. K. Antonovych-Melnyk (1898) and O. Tsynkalovsky (1936–8) conducted archeological excavations in the area.

A. Zhukovsky

Peresopnytsia Gospel (Peresopnytske yevanheliie). An ornamented manuscript of the four books of the New Testament translated ca 1556–61, partly in the Monastery of the Holy Trinity in Dvirtsi, Lviv region, and partly in the Monastery of the Mother of God in Peresopnytsia, Vol-

The Peresopnytsia Gospel

hynia. The scribe was probably Mykhailo Vasylovych from Sianik, and the translator was Hryhorii, the archimandrite of the Peresopnytsia monastery. The gospel was discovered in 1837 by O. *Bodiansky and is preserved at the ANU Central Scientific Library in Kiev. It is an interest-ing example of a vernacular Ukrainian translation of the Scriptures from the Polish and Czech (the names of chap-ters are translated from the Czech) using the Bulgarian-Serbian orthography. Its language has western Boiko and, to a lesser extent, southern Volhynian dialectal traits, and many lexical Church Slavonicisms, Polonisms, and lexical synonyms from various dialects (eg, *kolodjaz'*/ *studnja*/ *krynytsja* 'well', *žytnycja*/*klunja*/*stodola* 'barn'). P. Zhytetsky studied its language and published from it the Gospel according to St Luke (*Trudy* III *arkheologicheskogo s"ezda*, vol 2 [1878]). Its paleographic and Renaissance artistic features were analyzed by O. Hruzynsky (1911, 1912) and H. Pavlutsky (*Iskusstvo*, 1911, no. 2).

Perestoroha (A Warning). An anonymously written antiUniate polemical tract. It was written in 1605 or 1606 in Lviv, and contained a cultural and educational program that influenced M. Smotrytsky. Authorship has been attributed to the Lviv priest A. Voznesensky (by D. Zubrytsky, A. Popov, and P. Yaremenko), to Yu. *Rohatynets (by I. Franko, K. Studynsky, M. Vasylenko, and H. Koliada), and to Y. *Boretsky (by M. Vozniak, O. Biletsky, and P. Zahaiko). The tract was first published in 1851 in *Akty, otnosiashchiesia k istorii Zapadnoi Rossii* (Documents on the History of Western Russia, vol 4) from a manuscript found by Zubrytsky in the library of the Stauropegion Institute in Lviv. It was republished by Vozniak in 1954. P. Yaremenko's book about it appeared in 1963. The tract is of interest to historians and literary scholars.

Peretiatkovych, Heorhii [Peretjatkovyč, Heorhij], b 8 December 1840 in Odessa, d 20 August 1908 in Odessa. Historian. After graduating from Moscow University (1877) he lectured at New Russia University in Odessa, where he became a professor in 1886. He is the author of monographs on the colonization of the Volga region in the 15th and 16th centuries (1877) and 17th and early 18th centuries (1882) and of a study of the Little Russians in Orenburg krai at the beginning of its colonization (*Trudy* VI *arkheologicheskago s"ezda*, vol 2 [1888]).

Perets' (Pepper). An illustrated humor magazine published in Kiev in 1941 (nine issues) and semimonthly since 1944 as the successor to **Chervonyi perets'*. During the Second World War it was published in Kharkiv and Moscow. In 1944–50 a separate edition (monthly in 1946–50, with a pressrun of 20,000 copies) was published for newly annexed Western Ukraine. *Perets'* has been noted for its attacks on capitalism, religion, and 'Western imperialism'; its anti-Zionism; and its criticism of Ukrainian 'bourgeois nationalism' and the Ukrainian émigré community. It has also satirized Soviet social and economic ills and the Soviet bureaucracy, but without overstepping the Party line. The editors have been F. Makivchuk (1946–86), O. Chornohuz (1986), and Yu. Prokopenko (1987–). *Perets'* was the most popular magazine of its day in Soviet Ukraine. In 1984 it had a pressrun of 2.3 million copies.

Volodymyr Peretts

Peretts, Volodymyr [Peretc], b 31 January 1870 in St Petersburg, d 24 September 1935 in Saratov, Russia. Philologist and historian of Ukrainian and Russian literature; member of the Shevchenko Scientific Society (NTSh) from 1914, honorary member of the Russian Bibliographical Society from 1915, and full member of the VUAN from 1919. After completing his studies at St Petersburg University and lecturing there (1896–1903) he moved to Kiev, and until 1914 he was a professor at Kiev University, head of the philological section of the Ukrainian Scientific Society in Kiev, and editor of its publication, *Zapysky Ukaïns'koho naukovoho tovarystva v Kyievi*. Peretts was the founder and director of the Seminar of Russian Philology, in 1907–14 at Kiev University and from 1914 at St Petersburg University. The seminar produced many eminent scholars of early and modern Ukrainian and Russian literatures: V. Adrianova-Peretts (Peretts's wife), O. Bahrii, S. Balukhaty, L. Biletsky, S. Bohuslavsky, O. Doroshkevych, M. Drai-Khmara, P. Fylypovych, M. Gudzii, S. Haievsky, O. Hruzynsky, B. Yakubsky, S. and V. Maslov, O. Nazarevsky, I. Ohiienko, V. Otrokovsky, P. Popov, S. Shcheglova, S. Shevchenko, and I. Eremin. In Kiev Peretts held the chair and headed the commission of Old Ukrainian literature of the historical-philological division of the VUAN. The **Leningrad Society of Researchers of Ukrainian History, Literature, and Language was active under his leadership between 1921 and 1933. His opposition to Party intervention in scholarship as well as his defense of his thesis on the Ukrainian character of the early literature and traditions of princely Kiev resulted in repressions. Eventually he was exiled to Saratov, where he died.

In his scholarly research Peretts adhered to the principles of the philological school, which concentrated on the form and structure of early literature and insisted upon a solid knowledge and interpretation of the texts. He published over 300 scholarly works; over 100 of them were published in Kiev in Ukrainian. Worthy of note are his publications and research on early Ukrainian literature in verse, early Ukrainian drama, and the early Ukrainian tale: *Kukol'nyi teatr na Rusi* (Puppet Theater in Rus', 1895), *Materialy k istorii apokrifa i legendy* (Sources for the History of Apocrypha and Legends, 2 vols, 1899, 1901), *Malorusskie vershi i pesni v zapisiakh XVI–XVIII vv.* (Little Russian Poems and Songs in Records of the 16th to 18th Centuries, 1899), *Ocherki starinnoi malorusskoi poezii* (Outlines of Ancient Little Russian Poetry, 1903), *Iz istorii starinnoi russkoi povesti* (From the History of the Ancient Rus' Narrative, 1907), *Novye dannye dlia istorii starinnoi ukrainskoi liriki* (New Data toward the History of Ancient Ukrainian Lyric Poetry, 1907), *Virshi iieromonakha Klymentiia Zinov'ieva syna* (The Poems of the Priest-Monk Klymentii, Zynovii's Son, 1912), and *Issledovaniia i materialy po istorii starinnoi ukrainskoi literatury XVI–XVIII vekov* (Research and Sources on the History of Ancient Ukrainian Literature in the 16th to 18th Centuries, 4 vols, 1926–9, 1962). Of special note are Peretts's synthetic works, *Iz lektsii po istorii drevnerusskoi literatury* (From Lectures on the History of the Literature of Ancient Rus', 1912–13) and the monograph *Slovo o polku Ihorevim: Pam'iatka feodal'noï Ukraïny-Rusy XII viku* (The Tale of Ihor's Campaign: A Monument of Feudal Rus'-Ukraine of the 12th Century, 1926). In his scholarly studies, publications, and lectures Peretts viewed the Princely era in Ukrainian literature and the period of the 14th to 18th centuries as an organic whole. Peretts was also the author of studies of modern Ukrainian literature, bibliography, paleography, textology, and archeology.

B. Kravtsiv

Perevalske [Pereval's'ke]. V19, DB III-5. A city (1989 pop 33,500) and raion center in Luhanske oblast. It arose at the end of the 19th century as the Seleznivka mining settlement. In 1964 several mining settlements were amalgamated into one city, which was named Perevalske. The city's main industry is coal mining.

Perevalsky, Vasyl [Pereval's'kyj, Vasyl'], b 13 June 1938 in Bubnivska Slobidka, Zolotonosha raion, Poltava oblast. Graphic artist. He studied under V. Kasiian at the Kiev State Art Institute (to 1965) and under M. Derehus in the workshops of the USSR Academy of Arts (1965–7). He has engraved many bookplates and illustrations for books, such as *Ukraïns'ki narodni pisni pro kokhannia* (Ukrainian Folk Songs about Love, 1971), *Ukraïns'ki narodni pisni v zapysakh V. Hnatiuka* (Ukrainian Folk Songs Transcribed by V. Hnatiuk, 1971), *Vesnianky* (1984), and editions of works by Lesia Ukrainka, I. Franko, P. Hrabovsky, I. Nechui-Levytsky, M. Rylsky, P. Tychyna, V. Sosiura, O. Honchar, B. Oliinyk, P. Zahrebelny, V. Zemliak, and other writers. His larger wood engravings include *Two Poplars in the Field* (1967) and *What Use Are My Black Brows?* (1968). He also designed a large stained-glass window at Kiev University with V. Zadorozhny and F. Hlushchuk depicting T. Shevchenko. His graphic works continue the 'national' traditions of H. Narbut and V. Krychevsky.

Vasyl Perevalsky: a woodcut illustration for a collection of Ukrainian folk songs about love (1971)

Pereverziv, Dmytro, b 1868, d 1928. UNR Army colonel. A regular officer in the Russian Army, in 1917 he commanded the Fifth Grenadier Regiment in Kiev. In December 1917, as an officer of the UNR, he distinguished himself defending Chernihiv against Bolshevik forces. During 1918–20 he served in the Zaporozhian Corps as chief logistics officer in the First Zaporozhian Rifle Division and as a brigade commander.

Perevod River. A right-bank tributary of the Udai River. It is 65 km long and drains a basin area of 1,260 sq km. It flows through Kiev, Chernihiv, and Poltava oblasts and is regulated by a series of dams.

Perevolochna [Perevoločna]. A village on the left bank of the Dnieper River near the Vorskla River in Kobeliaky raion, Poltava oblast. From the 1660s to 1764 it was a company center of Poltava regiment, which defended the southern borders of the Hetman state against the Crimean Tatars. After the Battle of Poltava was concluded there on 30 June 1709, Hetman I. Mazepa crossed the Dnieper River and fled with his Swedish allies to Turkish territory. In 1802 Perevolochna became a part of Kobeliaky county in Poltava gubernia. When the Dniprodzerzhynske Hydroelectric Station was built in 1962, Perevolochna was inundated, and its residents were moved to the new village of Svitlohirske.

Perevuznyk, Yurii, b 1903 in Serednie, near Uzhhorod, d 17 September 1966 in Prague. Transcarpathian civic and political leader. After graduating in law from Charles University in Prague, he practiced law in Mukachiv. A supporter of Ukrainian culture, he organized Prosvita reading rooms. He became active in politics and set up the Ukrainian section of the Czechoslovak Agrarian party. In 1939 he was appointed state secretary and minister of internal affairs for the newly established Carpatho-Ukraine. Having been arrested by the Hungarians, he was forced to emigrate to Prague, where he served as a judge. In 1945 he was arrested and imprisoned by the Soviets, but later he returned to Prague.

Aka Pereyma: *Stag* (watercolor, 1989)

Pereyma, Aka [Perejma] (née Klym), b 30 September 1927 in Siedlce, Poland. Ukrainian sculptor and painter. A postwar refugee in the United States since 1949, she completed her studies at the Chicago (1963–4) and the Dayton (1966) institutes of art. A versatile artist, she has won recognition for her metal and wood sculptures, ceramics, oils, watercolors, Easter eggs, and ink drawings. She has created abstract geometric sculptures (eg, *Hetman* and *Slave*) and abstract 'birds' (eg, *Omega*). The forms and ornamentation of her ceramic creations are influenced strongly by Ukrainian folk art. Much of her painting is inspired by folk motifs (eg, the watercolor series 'Songs'), and the egg form frequently plays a prominent role (eg, *Windmill*). Solo shows of her works have been held in various cities of Ohio, as well as in Chicago, New York, Buffalo, Toronto, Kiev, and Lviv. A 25-year retrospective exhibition was held in Oxford, Ohio, in 1986.

Perezva. An archaic wedding ritual by which the relatives of a bridegroom, often accompanied by the bridegroom, informed the bride's parents the day after the wedding night (*komora*) of her virginity. After carrying a blood-stained shirt through the village, they greeted the bride's relatives with ritual songs and red liquor with viburnum berries, and invite (*perezyvaty*) them over to the groom's house to continue the celebrations. The parents were thanked in song for bringing up their daughter, were seated in places of honor, and were served the best food and drink. The bride's hair was arranged ceremonially into the form reserved for married women. The ritual was accompanied with erotic songs and tests of the bride's domestic skills. If a bride could not provide evidence of virginity, both she and her parents were ridiculed. In some locales the ritual was known as *propii*, from *propyty* 'to drink away' (the bride's virginity). The oldest description of this ritual appears in G. Le Vasseur de Beauplan's *Description des contrées du Royaume de Pologne* (1650). (See also *Wedding.)

Perfecky, George [Perfec'kyj, Jurij], b 27 May 1940 in Piotrków, Poland. Slavic linguist; member of the Shevchenko Scientific Society. A graduate of Columbia University (PH D, 1970), he has taught Russian since 1965 at La Salle University in Philadelphia. He is the author of an annotated translation (1973) of the Galician-Volhynian Chronicle, of articles on the chronicle and on linguistic Russification and the status of the Ukrainian language in Soviet Ukraine, and of reviews of Soviet Ukrainian dictionaries.

Roman Perfetsky   Yevhen Perfetsky

Leonid Perfetsky: *Defense of the Kruty Station in 1918* (watercolor)

Perfetsky, Leonid [Perfec'kyj] (Perfecky), b 23 February 1901 in Ladyzhyntsi, Galicia, d 25 October 1977 in Montreal. Painter. He studied at the Novakivsky Art School in Lviv, the Cracow Academy of Fine Arts, and A. Lhote's school in Paris. From 1922 on he took part in group exhibitions in Lviv and Paris. Perfetsky specialized in historical battle scenes, such as *The Cossacks at Trabizond*, *Cossack Surprise Attack*, *Black Zaporozhians*, *Attack*, and *Battery in Danger*, and depictions of the 1918–21 Ukrainian-Soviet and Ukrainian-Polish wars (eg, *Kruty*). In Paris he did portraits of prominent Frenchmen and began painting in a constructivist style. A postwar émigré in Canada from 1950, he painted murals in the Holy Ghost Ukrainian Catholic Church, St Elezar's Catholic Church, and St Joseph's Oratory in Montreal. A book about Perfetsky (ed S. Hordynsky) was published in New York City in 1990.

Perfetsky, Roman [Perfec'kyj], b 1880, d 1944. Lawyer and political leader in Galicia. While practicing law in Bibrka he was active in various Ukrainian organizations in the region, and in 1913 he was elected to the Galician Diet. He represented the Union for the Liberation of Ukraine in the POW camp at Wetzlar. In 1918–19 he was a member of the Ukrainian National Rada and deputy state secretary of internal affairs of the Western Ukrainian National Republic (ZUNR). In 1920 he headed a delegation of the Ukrainian National Rada in Lviv and then joined the ZUNR government-in-exile and became president of the Western Ukrainian League of Nations Society (1921–4). After returning to Western Ukraine he became active in politics as a member of the Ukrainian National Democratic Alliance and in 1935 was elected to the Polish Sejm. In 1939 he fled from the Soviets to the Zamość region in the Generalgouvernement, where he worked as a notary public.

Perfetsky, Yevhen [Perfec'kyj, Jevhen] (Perfeckij, Jevgenij), b 11 April 1888 in Nosiv, Kostiantyniv county, Siedlce gubernia, d 18 August 1947 in Bardejov, Slovakia. Historian; cousin of R. *Perfetsky. As a young man he took part in the Ukrainian national revival in Podlachia and founded a branch of the Prosvita society in Kobyliany, Bielsk Podlaski county. He graduated from St Petersburg University (1912). In 1919–21 he was a privatdocent at Kiev University. An émigré from August 1921, from 1922 he taught Eastern European (especially Transcarpathian) history at Bratislava University, where he became a professor in 1935 and a dean in 1946–7, and continued his archival and ethnographic research in Transcarpathia.

Perfetsky's works written in Russian include a survey of 'Ugro-Russian' (Transcarpathian) historiography (1914), a book on the Rus' chronicle compilations and their interrelationship (1922), and a long article on the 17th- and 18th-century religious movement in Transcarpathia (1915). He also wrote articles in Ukrainian about Transcarpathia in the 17th century (1917), Nestor the Chronicler (1918), Y. Bazylovych and his *Brevis Notitia* ... (1918, 1919), Bishop V. Tarasevych of Mukachiv (1923), the Novgorod Chronicle and its relation to the 12th-century Ukrainian chronicles (1924), and the Peremyshl codex as part of J. Długosz's chronicle (1927, 1928, 1931). In Czech he wrote on Prince Fedir Koriiatovych (1922), Transcarpathian and Galician tales and legends about King Mathias Corvinus (1926), Transcarpathian church history, and Russian Slavophilism. Also published in Czech were his pioneering monograph on socioeconomic conditions in 13th- to 15th-century Transcarpathia (1924) and a book on Długosz's history of Poland and the Rus' chronicles (1932).

A. Zhukovsky

Perfume and cosmetics industry. A branch of industry that uses natural and artificial oils, fragrances, animal products, and alcohol to manufacture beauty aids and hygienic preparations, such as makeup, perfume, bath oil, powder, skin cream, toothpaste, and shaving cream. Perfumes and cosmetics began to be imported into the Russian Empire and Ukraine in the 19th century, mostly from

France. The modern industry emerged in Ukraine only in the early 20th century, when the first cosmetic factories were built in Kharkiv and Mykolaiv. Among the former Soviet republics Ukraine is second only to Russia in the manufacture of cosmetics. It accounted for 50 percent of the former USSR essence of rose output, 90 percent of its mint oil output, and 70 percent of its lavender oil output. The main plants are the Mykolaiv Perfume and Cosmetics Manufacturing Complex, the Kharkiv and Lviv perfume and cosmetics factories, and the Symferopil and Zolotonosha ethereal oil plants. Another 15 plants produce ethereal oils; the largest of them are in Bakhchesarai and Zuia, in the Crimea, and in Pryluka. Problems of the industry are studied at the former All-Union Scientific Research Institute of Ethereal Oil Cultures in Symferopil and at the Ukrainian Scientific Research Institute of the Oils and Fats Industry in Kharkiv.

Perilla (Ukrainian: *Peryla vasylkovydna*). An Asiatic mint plant of the family Labiatae. Perilla was introduced in Ukraine in the 1930s. It is cultivated for its oil in the Kuban and as an ornamental herbaceous plant in the forest-steppe region. Perilla seeds contain 35–52 percent of a light yellow oil that is used in the production of varnishes, paints, printing ink, and water-repellent fabrics. Perilla oil dries more quickly than linseed oil and forms harder films; it also has bactericidal properties.

Periodicals. See Press.

Periwinkle (*Vinca*; Ukrainian: *barvinok*). A trailing or woody evergreen herb of the dogbane family Apocynaceae, with shiny, dark green leaves and serrated lavender-blue or white flowers. Of its seven species, native to Europe and the Near and Far East, three grow in Ukraine – grassy periwinkle (*V. herbacea*; Ukrainian: *barvinok travianystyi*), in meadows and shrubbery of the forest-steppe and steppe zones and especially in Crimean forests, widely used as a cut flower; myrtle (*V. minor*) in Right-Bank regions, a long-standing favorite decorative creeper among Ukrainians that also plays an important role in folklore and Easter and *wedding rituals; and a cultivated garden species (*V. major*) that also grows wild in the Crimea. Periwinkle is a medicinal plant; in folk medicine it was believed to increase potency.

Perlo mnohotsinnoie (A Priceless Pearl). An important 17th-century literary monument by K. *Stavrovetsky-Tranquillon. It was published in Chernihiv in 1646 and again in Mohyliv in 1699. *Perlo ...* is a collection of edifying prose and 21 didactic religious poems written in the bookish language of the period but with many elements of folk poetics, particularly of the dumas. Much of it was reprinted in a 1978 anthology of late 16th- and early 17th-century Ukrainian poetry compiled by V. Kolosova and V. Krekoten.

Perlyk, Ivan, b 1880? d January 1919 in the Poltava region. Lieutenant colonel of the UNR Army. In March 1918 he organized the *Graycoats, which he commanded until August. During the anti-Hetman revolt he organized an insurgent unit that operated in the Poltava area. He was killed in battle with Bolshevik forces.

Permanent Representation of the Council of Ministers of the Ukrainian SSR at the Council of Ministers of the USSR (Postiine predstavnytstvo Rady Ministriv URSR pry Radi Ministriv SRSR). An institution created in 1924 to maintain direct contact between the governments of the Ukrainian SSR and the USSR. It was headed by a permanent representative appointed by the Council of Ministers of the Ukrainian SSR. Its legal status was defined in the decrees of the All-Ukrainian Central Executive Committee and Ukraine's Council of People's Commissars issued on 2 January 1924, 2 December 1925, and 11 January 1926 and in the special decrees of the USSR Council of People's Commissars issued on 4 February 1931 and 20 November 1940. By its decree of 29 December 1976 the Council of Ministers of the Ukrainian SSR empowered the Permanent Representation to establish direct contacts not only with the USSR Council of Ministers but also with individual ministries and committees and other federal institutions. The Permanent Representation participated in the sessions of the USSR Council of Ministers and advised it on all matters pertaining to the Ukrainian SSR, particularly when new laws, economic plans, and the budget were discussed. It also carried out special assignments of the Ukrainian government, delivered questions and interpellations from its government to the USSR government, and served as a channel of information. Prior to the dissolution of the USSR, proposals had been made to extend its role to international trade, interrepublic liaison, and cultural relations with the large Ukrainian colony in Moscow. The Permanent Representation had a staff of 50 in 1991. Its heads included M. Pidhirny, Yu. Dubin, and M. Pichuzhkin.

P. Potichnyj

Pernach (aka *pirnach, shestoper*). A mace used by Cossacks as a symbol of authority. Like the *bulava, the *pernach* was of Eastern origin. It consisted of a silver or gilded shaft and a pear-shaped gold-plated head divided into six or eight sharp-edged flanges (*pera*). Eventually the *pernach* became the special symbol of the colonel's office.

Perogies. See *Varenyky* and Foods, traditional.

Perohovsky, Vasyl [Perohovs'kyj, Vasyl'], b 1824, d 1881. Historian and ethnographer. A county court judge in Volhynia, he contributed articles on the local ethnography and history to *Volynskie gubernskie vedomosti* and *Kievskaia starina*.

Perovsky. An aristocratic family consisting of the illegitimate offspring (five sons and four daughters) of Oleksii, the son of Hetman K. *Rozumovsky, and their descendants. The surname was taken from Perovo village, in the Moscow region. The oldest son, Nikolai (d 1858), was governor of the Crimea and city governor of Teodosiia during the reign of Alexander I. Aleksei (1787–1836) was a botanist, member of the Imperial Academy if Sciences (from 1829), and successful author of novels (pseud: Antonii Pogorelsky). He was also a curator of Kharkiv University. Lev (1792–1856) was a senator and high official in St Petersburg. In 1841 he was appointed minister for internal affairs, and in 1852, minister of appanages and head of the cabinet. Vasilii (1794–1857) was a cavalry general. After being wounded in the Russo-Turkish War (1828) he became military governor in Orenburg (1833–42, 1851–6). Boris (1814–81) was a cavalry general. Aleksei's son, Lev (d 1890), was governor of St Petersburg in 1865–6 and then an official in the Ministry of Internal Affairs. His daughter, Sofiia (1853–81), renounced her family and joined the revolutionary movement in the 1870s. She married A. *Zheliabov and was involved in several attempts on the emperor's life. The first woman in Russia to be put to death for a political crime she, was executed for her role in the assassination of Alexander II.

Pavel Pershin

Pershin, Pavel [Peršin], b 4 January 1891 in Bubinskoe, Perm gubernia, Russia, d 11 November 1970 in Kiev. Economist and agronomist; full member of the AN URSR (now ANU) from 1948. A graduate of St Petersburg University (1916), in the interwar period he worked for several government institutions and taught economics and statistics at higher schools in Moscow, Voronezh, and Kharkiv. After the war he was director of the ANU Institute of Economics (1948–50) and head of its agrarian department (1951–7). He led the academy's expeditions for improving the performance of collective farms in the southern steppe (1950–4) and headed the Council for the Study of the Productive Resources of the Ukrainian SSR (1957–64). Pershin wrote or coauthored many articles and monographs on the history and the economics of agriculture in Russia, including *Narysy ahrarnoï revoliutsiï v Rosiï* (Outlines of the Agrarian Revolution in Russia, 1959), *Ahrarni peretvorennia Velykoï Zhovtnevoï sotsialistychnoï revoliutsiï* (Agrarian Transformations of the Great October Socialist Revolution, 1962), and *Narysy ahrarnykh problem budivnytstva sotsializmu* (Outlines of Agrarian Problems in the Construction of Socialism, 1973). A biography and bibliography of his works appeared in 1971 in Kiev.

Pershomaiske. See Pervomaiske (Mykolaiv oblast).

Pershotravenske [Peršotravens'ke]. V-17. A city (1989 pop 26,200) in Petropavlivka raion, Dnipropetrovske oblast, subordinated to the Pavlohrad city council. It was founded in 1954 as the coal-mining town of Shakhtarske and was renamed in 1960. In 1966 it received city status. Its economy depends on four coal mines and a metal-working plant.

Pershotravneve [Peršotravneve]. VI-18. A town smt (1986 pop 7,200) and raion center in Donetske oblast. The town developed out of a settlement called Manhush, founded by Greek settlers from the Crimea in 1779. It was renamed in 1946 and granted smt status in 1969. Its economy rests on agriculture.

Pershyi vinok (title page)

Pershyi vinok (The First Wreath). A pioneering miscellany by and about women. It was collected, subsidized, and published in Lviv in 1887 by N. Kobrynska and O. Pchilka with the editorial help of I. Franko. Its contents consisted of an introduction and feminist articles by N. Kobrynska; stories and poetry by H. Barvinok, O. Bazhanska-Ozarkevych, Dniprova Chaika, O. Pohoretska-Hrytsai, Kobrynska, U. Kravchenko, O. Huzar-Levytska, S. Navrotska-Paliiv, S. Okunevska-Moraczewska, A. Pavlyk, Pchilka, K. Popovych, M. Roshkevych, L. Starytska-Cherniakhivska, and Lesia Ukrainka; and ethnographic articles by K. Pavlyk-Dovbenchuk, Okunevska-Moraczewska, and O. Franko. The miscellany was reprinted in New York in 1984 with L. Onyshkevych's introduction and notes to commemorate the centenary of the Ukrainian women's movement.

Perun. One of the principal deities in eastern and northern Slavic mythology. In pre-Christian Kievan Rus' this was the chief god – the god of thunder, lightning, and rain, the ruler of the heavens, and, later, the god of war. According to the Primary Chronicle, when the pagans of Rus' entered into an agreement with Byzantium, they swore an oath to Perun. In 980 a wooden statue of Perun with a silver head and golden moustache stood on Perun Hill in Kiev. Perun's feast, celebrated with sacrifices, took place in July. On a clay calendar from the Cherniakhiv culture in the Kiev region Perun's Day (20 July OS) is marked with the sign of thunder – a six-spoked wheel. Human sacrifices to Perun (one boy and girl) were chosen by lot. After adopting Christianity Prince Volodymyr the Great ordered Perun's statue to be cast into the Dnieper and on its site built St Basil's Church. The cult of Perun, however, survived among the common people for many centuries. In Western Ukraine traces of the cult could be detected in the 20th century. The Lemkos still consider the expression 'May Perun strike you dead' as the most terrible curse. The Christian church replaced the cult of Perun with the cult of the prophet Elijah (feast day: 2 September, or 20 August OS), to whom all of Perun's qualities were transferred.

Pervisne hromadianstvo ta ioho perezhytky na Ukraïni (Primitive Society and Its Vestiges in Ukraine). A scholarly serial published in Kiev in 1926–9 (8 vols) by the VUAN Cultural-Historical Commission and again in 1928–9 by the Scientific Research Department of the History of Ukraine. It was edited by K. *Hrushevska, and contained anthropological and sociological studies on prehistoric society in Ukraine and on Ukrainian folk culture. The contributors included Hrushevska, M. Hrushevsky, F. Kolessa, K. Koperzhynsky, V. Kozlovska, K. Kvitka, F. Savchenko, L. Shevchenko, K. Shtepa, A. Stepovych, M. Vozniak, and D. Zelenin.

Pervomaiske [Pervomajs'ke]. VIII-14. A town smt (1986 pop 7,600) and raion center in Crimea oblast. The town, which is first mentioned in 1798, was called Dzhurchi until 1944. It has a food industry.

Pervomaiske or **Pervomaisk** [Pervomajs'ke or Pervomajs'k]. V-19, DB II-5. A city (1989 pop 49,800) on the Luhanka River in Luhanske oblast. From 1765 the settlement was known as Petromarivka; in 1920 it was renamed. A mine was opened there in 1872. The city is now a major coal-mining center, with eight coal mines and two enrichment plants. It also produces electric machines, building materials, reinforced-concrete goods, and footwear.

Pervomaiske or **Pervomaisk** [Pervomajs'ke or Pervomajs'k]. V-11. A city (1989 pop 82,000) at the confluence of the Syniukha and the Boh rivers and a raion center in Mykolaiv oblast. It was formed in 1919 through the amalgamation of three separate settlements, Olviopil, Bohopil, and Holta, each of which was founded by a different state. In 1420 the Lithuanian grand duke Vytautas constructed a bridge ~for merchants and traders near the present site of the city. Later a Zaporozhian fortress called Orlyka was built on the left bank of the Syniukha River, and by 1774 a village called Orlyk had arisen there. Eventually the settlement was renamed Yekaterynyshanets, and in 1782, Olviopil. Nearby, on the right bank of the Boh River, Cossacks and Ukrainian peasants founded Holta, which was under Turkish rule until 1791, when it was acquired by Russia. The third settlement, Bohopil, arose after the Poles built a fortress and a frontier post on the left bank of the Boh River. In the mid-18th century the frontiers of three states, the Russian (Zaporizhia), Ottoman, and Polish, met at that point. Today Pervomaiske is a major industrial center. Its plants produce sugar, beer, furniture, textiles, plastic goods, construction materials, and machines.

Pervomaiske Machine-Building Plant (Pervomaiskyi mashynobudivnyi zavod). A factory in Pervomaiske, Mykolaiv oblast, built in 1875 to produce agricultural and other machinery, including drive shafts, gears, pulleys, and equipment for mills and threshers. In 1927 it began to build diesel motors, and in 1934, gas motors. The factory was evacuated at the outset of the Second World War and rebuilt in 1945–6. Now the plant specializes in the production of diesel generators, diesel engines for ships, and spare parts.

Pervomaiske Milk-Canning Complex (Pervomaiskyi molochnokonservnyi kombinat). An enterprise of the canning industry, founded in 1952 in Pervomaiske,

Mykolaiv oblast. It consists of a canning factory in Pervomaiske and creameries in Kostiantynivka, Kryve Ozero, and Vradiivka. It produces 15 types of dairy products, including concentrated milk, kefir, and ice cream. In 1980 the enterprise had an annual capacity of 67.4 million standard cans.

Leonid Pervomaisky

Pervomaisky, Leonid [Pervomajs'kyj] (pseud of Illia Hurevych), b 17 May 1908 in Kostiantynohrad, now Krasnohrad in Kharkiv oblast, d 9 December 1973 in Kiev. Writer. He began his literary career with the short story 'A nad polem postril' (And There Was a Shot over the Field, 1924). He moved to Kharkiv in 1926 and worked there as an editor for newspapers, journals, and various publishing houses. He also worked for the All-Ukrainian Photo-Cinema Administration. His writing of the Kharkiv period is characterized by a romantic perception of the civil war and the postwar years, and the Komsomol is frequently chosen as a theme. Pervomaisky was one of the founders of the literary organization *Molodniak. From 1934 to 1941 he lived in Kiev. During that period he published *Komsomol's'ki povisti* (Komsomol Novelettes, 1935) and the poetry collections *Nova liryka* (New Lyric Poetry, 1937) and *Barvinkovyi svit* (A Periwinkle World, 1940). His prose of the period of the Second World War is collected in *Ataka na Vorskli* (The Attack on the Vorskla, 1946), and some poetry, in *Soldats'ki pisni* (Soldiers' Songs, 1946). Pervomaisky wrote his best poetry and prose in the post-Stalinist years. The collection of short stories *Materyn solodkyi khlib* (Mother's Sweet Bread, 1960) contains examples of masterful psychological prose that re-creates the 'unquiet poetry' of unfathomable incidents (eg, 'Chuzhe shchastia' [Other People's Happiness]). In places those short stories are of a completely modern style (eg 'Zamist' virshiv pro kokhannia' [Instead of Poems about Love]). The novel *Dykyi med* (Wild Honey, 1963), complex in its unexpected layering of events in the dimensions of time and space, is among the best novels of Soviet literature. The collection *Uroky poeziï* (Lessons of Poetry, 1966), which is characterized by maximum clarity of image and economy of expression, differentiates Pervomaisky from poets of his generation and places his writings closer in style to that of Western poets. Such characteristics also appear in his last collections, *Drevo piznannia* (The Tree of Knowledge, 1971) and the posthumous *Vchora i zavtra* (Yesterday and Tomorrow, 1974). The most complete edition of Pervomaisky's works is *Tvory v semy tomakh* (Works in Seven Volumes, 1968–70). Pervomaisky is the author of masterful translations of S. Petőfi, H. Heine, F. Viona, F.G. Lorca, and other writers.

I. Koshelivets

Pervomaiskyi [Pervomajs'kyj]. IV-17. A town smt (1986 pop 36,300) and raion center in Kharkiv oblast. It was founded in 1924 and was called Lykhacheve until 1952. It produces reinforced-concrete structures, knitwear, and food products.

Volodymyr Peshchansky

Peshchansky, Volodymyr [Peščans'kyj], b 10 November 1873 in Pereiaslav, Poltava gubernia, d 26 August 1926 in Lviv. Architect, art restorer, and art historian. A graduate of the St Petersburg Engineering and Architecture Institute, in 1913 he supervised the restoration of Kiev's St Nicholas's Military Cathedral and the Transfiguration Church in the Berestove district. An interwar émigré in Lviv from 1920, from 1922 he worked at the National Museum as the head restorer of its collection of medieval icons and supervisor of its folk-art collection. He wrote studies on Ukraine's ancient kilims (1925), Ukrainian and Russian icons (1926), and the Maniava Hermitage and Bohorodchany Iconostasis (1926, with M. Drahan and I. Svientsitsky).

Pestel, Pavel [Pestel'], b 5 July 1793 in Moscow, d 25 July 1826 in St Petersburg. Leader of the *Decembrist movement in Ukraine; son of a Russian senator and governor-general of Siberia (a Russified German). With other Russian officers who believed that Russia should become a democratic republic, he founded the clandestine *Union of Salvation (1816) and *Union of Welfare (1818) and headed the Tulchyn council of the latter group. In 1821 the council's members founded the revolutionary *Southern Society, and Pestel wrote its constitutional program, *Russkaia pravda* (Russian Justice), which was adopted at a secret meeting in Kiev in 1823. The society called for the overthrow of tsarism, the abolition of serfdom and oppressive *military settlements, and the establishment of a republic similar to that of the United States. Pestel did not, however, recognize the right to self-determination for the empire's non-Russians (except for the Poles), opposed the idea of a federal structure, and was consequently hostile to the separatist *Little Russian Secret Society. He was arrested on the way to Tulchyn on 25 December 1825 (the eve of the Decembrist revolt) and was tried and hanged

with four other Decembrist leaders in the Peter and Paul Fortress. L. Medvedska's book about him was published in Kiev in 1964.

Peter I (Russian: Petr), b 9 June 1672 in Moscow, d 8 February 1725 in Petersburg. Russian tsar from 1682 and first Russian emperor from 1721; son of Tsar Aleksei Mikhailovich. In 1696, after deposing the Muscovite regent, his half-sister *Sofiia Alekseevna, Peter conducted an aggressive, expansionist foreign policy that affected the *Hetman state, *Slobidksa Ukraine, and the *Zaporizhia throughout his reign. He exploited Ukraine economically and militarily as part of Russia's participation in the Holy League against the Ottoman Empire; the expansionist *Russo-Turkish wars of 1695–6 and 1710–13; the Northern War with *Sweden (1700–21), by which Russia gained a foothold on the Baltic coast; and the war with Persia (1722–3), which fortified Russia's hold in Transcaucasia and the Caspian littoral. Those wars exacted a heavy human and economic toll in Ukraine.

Peter's internal reforms had as their goal the modernization and Europeanization of Russia. His cultural revolution provided a sound basis for the further expansion of Russian absolutism and imperialism. In Russian-dominated Ukraine Peter's policies until 1708 continued the Muscovite tradition of the gradual erosion of Ukraine's sovereignty. In 1708, after Hetman I. *Mazepa and Otaman K. *Hordiienko sided with Charles XII of Sweden, and particularly after the Battle of Poltava (1709), he initiated a reign of terror in Ukraine. The Zaporozhian Sich and Mazepa's capital, Baturyn, were completely destroyed, and Baturyn's inhabitants were massacred; captured Cossacks were executed; and most of Mazepa's senior supporters were imprisoned in the *Solovets Islands. Thereafter the Russian military and civil authorities were brutally intrusive in all aspects of Ukrainian life. The powers of Mazepa's successor, I. *Skoropadsky, were strictly limited, and his actions were monitored by Peter's resident functionary, A. Izmailov. After Skoropadsky's death in 1722 Peter forbade the election of a successor, and the Hetmanate was controlled and virtually ruled by his *Little Russian Collegium. Opposition on the part of the Ukrainian government, led by the acting hetman P. *Po-

The Peter and Paul Fortress (engraving)

lubotok (1722–4), brought on further repressions. Polubotok and his General Officer Staff were imprisoned in St Petersburg's *Peter and Paul Fortress, where the hetman died. Peter's policies intensified serfdom, and the monetary taxes levied on the people increased from 45,500 rubles in 1722 to 241,300 in 1724. Peter forbade the publication of books in Ukrainian and ordered Ukrainian redactions of Old Church Slavonic texts to be made to correspond with Russian redactions. Thousands of Ukrainian conscripts died during the construction of Peter's new capital, *Saint Petersburg, and the Don-Volga and Ladoga canals.

(See also *Church, history of the Ukrainian, *History of Ukraine, *Holy Synod, *Little Russian Collegium, *Little Russian Office, *Poll tax, *Prokopovych, Teofan, *Ranks, Table of, *Russia, *Senate, and *Yavorsky, Stefan.)

BIBLIOGRAPHY
Herbil's'kyi, H. *Petro Pershyi v Zakhidnii Ukraïni, 1706–1707 rr.* (Lviv 1948)
Diadychenko, V. 'Petro i Ukraïna,' *UIZh*, 1972, no.6
Subtelny, O. 'Russia and the Ukraine: The Difference That Peter I Made,' *RR*, 39, no. 1 (January 1980)

O. Ohloblyn

Peter II (Russian: Petr Alekseevich), b 23 October 1715 in St Petersburg, d 29 January 1730 in Moscow. Russian emperor in 1727–30; grandson of Peter I and son of Tsarevich Aleksei, who was executed on his father's order. During the first year of his reign the de facto ruler was Prince A. *Menshikov.

Peter III (Karl-Peter Ulrich; Russian: Petr Fedorovich), b 21 February 1728 in Kiel, Holstein-Gottorp (now in Germany), d 17 July 1762 in Ropsha, near St Petersburg. Russian emperor in 1761–2; grandson of Peter I and husband of *Catherine II from 1745. Under the influence of his father, Duke Charles Frederick of Holstein-Gottorp, who had been a friend of the *Orlyk family and had defended Ukrainian causes at the imperial court, Peter III surrounded himself with Ukrainians, among them A. Hudovych (whom Peter appointed adjutant general and, it was rumored, planned to appoint hetman in place of K. Rozumovsky), V. Khanenko, and S. Karnovych. After he succeeded his aunt, Elizabeth I, as emperor, Peter abolished the Secret Chancery and compulsory military service for the gentry and ordered the secularization of monastic properties. Being pro-Prussian, he ended the *Seven Years' War and forged an alliance with Prussia in preparation for a new war with Denmark on behalf of Holstein. Peter's policies aroused opposition from his wife and other members of the imperial elite. In June 1762 Catherine staged a coup d'état, was recognized as empress by the imperial guard, senate, and Holy Synod, and had Peter arrested. After abdicating Peter was killed in a brawl by one of his captors.

Peter and Paul Fortress (Petropavlovskaia krepost). A stronghold on Zaiachii Island, near the mouth of the Neva River in St Petersburg. Its construction in 1703 marks the founding of the city. The fortress is infamous as a prison for political opponents of the tsarist regime, including many Ukrainians. In 1924 it was converted into a historical museum.

Peters, Ihor, b 21 September 1923 in Kremenchuk, Poltava gubernia. Soviet historian. A graduate of Kiev University (1949), he has worked since 1952 at the AN URSR (now ANU) Institute of History, where he received a candidate's degree in 1954 and a doctorate in 1968. He is the author of books on interwar Czechoslovak-Soviet relations, Czechoslovakia and European politics on the eve of the Munich Agreement (1971), and Czechoslovak foreign policy in 1945–60 (1976). He is also the coauthor of books on Soviet Ukraine and foreign socialist countries (1965), foreign internationalists who fought on the Bolshevik side in Ukraine in 1917–20 (1967), and Soviet Ukraine's economic co-operation with the socialist countries (1962).

Petipa, Tamara, b 18 September 1927 in Saratov, Russia. Hydrobiologist; corresponding member of the AN URSR (now ANU) since 1972. She completed study at Rostov University (1952) and worked at the Sevastopil Biological Station, from 1965 as laboratory director and from 1972 as departmental director. Her major research interest is the biology and nourishment of zooplankton.

Petiukh, Antin [Petjux] (real surname: Mytai), b 1884 in Medvyn, Kiev gubernia, d ca 1920 in the Zvenyhorod region. Bandurist. He studied the bandura in Kiev under I. Kucherenko-Kuchuhura. His repertoire consisted of dumas and historical and humorous songs. He died in a skirmish between partisans and Bolshevik troops.

Petliash-Barilotti, Olena [Petljaš-Barilotti], b 11 July 1890 in Kharkiv, d 4 October 1971 in Kiev. Opera singer (dramatic soprano); daughter of M. *Sadovsky. She studied singing under O. Muraviova in Kiev (1910–13) and A. Cotogni in Rome (1913–16). Her theatrical debut was with Sadovsky's Theater in 1907. She appeared on the opera stages of Odessa (1916–18, 1923–4), Kiev (1926–7), Saratov, Erevan, Tbilisi, and Kazan. She sang leading roles in M. Arkas's *Kateryna*, S. Hulak-Artemovsky's *Zaporozhian Cossack beyond the Danube* (Odarka), M. Lysenko's *Aeneid* (Didona), D. Sichynsky's *Roksoliana*, P. Tchaikovsky's *Mazepa* (Maria), G. Puccini's *Tosca*, and G. Verdi's *Aida*. In recital she often performed Ukrainian folk songs and romances.

Petlishenko, Marko [Petlišenko], b 30 December 1880 at Sochevaniv *khutir*, near Marianivka, Yelysavethrad county, Kherson gubernia, d 20 April 1938. Actor; brother of I. *Marianenko. He began his career as a chorister in the troupe of his uncle, M. Kropyvnytsky (1895–1900), and then worked in Saksahansky's Troupe (1900–7), Sadovsky's Theater (1907–14), the Society of Ukrainian Actors (1916), the Ukrainian National Theater (1917–18), the Poltava Rukh Theater (1919–22), the Kharkiv People's Theater (1924–8), the Kharkiv Chervonozavodskyi Ukrainian Drama Theater (1928–33), and the Kharkiv Theater of Working Youth (1934–7). His repertoire was extensive – from the ethnographically interesting Voznyi in I. Kotliarevsky's *Natalka Poltavka* (Natalka from Poltava) to the psychologically conceived Makar in V. Vynnychenko's *Moloda krov* (Young Blood). Petlishenko was arrested in 1937, and died in prison.

Petliura, Symon [Petljura] (pseuds: V. Marchenko, V. Salevsky, I. Rokytny, S. Prosvitianyn, O. Riast), b 10 May

Symon Petliura

1879 in Poltava, d 25 May 1926 in Paris. Statesman and publicist; supreme commander of the UNR Army and president of the Directory of the Ukrainian National Republic. He entered the Poltava Theological Seminary in 1895 but was expelled in 1901 for belonging to a clandestine Ukrainian hromada, which he had joined in 1898. From 1900 he was also active in a political cell in Poltava that became the nucleus of the Revolutionary Ukrainian party (RUP). To avoid arrest he moved in the autumn of 1902 to Katerynodar, in the Kuban, where he worked as a teacher and then, under the supervision of F. Shcherbyna, cataloged the archives of the Kuban Cossack Army. For his involvement in Katerynodar in the local RUP branch (the Black Sea Free Hromada) and in RUP periodicals (notably *Dobra novyna*) published in Austrian-ruled Lviv, he was arrested in December 1903. After being released on bail in March 1904, he went to Kiev and from there, in the autumn, to Lviv to do RUP work and to edit its organ *Selianyn*. In 1905, after the general amnesty, he returned to Kiev. In January 1906 he left for St Petersburg to edit, with P. Poniatenko and M. Porsh, the social democratic monthly *Vil'na Ukraïna*. After returning to Kiev in July 1906, he worked as secretary of the newspaper *Rada*, coedited (in 1907–8) *Slovo*, the organ of the Ukrainian Social Democratic Workers' party (USDRP), and contributed to the monthly *Ukraïna*. In 1909 he moved to Moscow and worked there as a bookkeeper until 1912, when he became coeditor, with O. Salikovsky, of the Russian-language monthly *Ukrainskaia zhizn'*

(1912–17). In 1916 and until the beginning of 1917 he was deputy plenipotentiary of the All-Russian Union of Zemstvos aid committee on the Russian western front.

After the February Revolution of 1917 Petliura was elected head of the Ukrainian Military Committee of the Western Front. He was sent as a delegate to the First *All-Ukrainian Military Congress (18–21 May 1917) in Kiev, where he was elected chairman of the Ukrainian General Military Committee. In June 1917 he was appointed general secretary of military affairs in the first *General Secretariat of the Central Rada, and directed all his energies to organizing and building up the Ukrainian armed forces, while facing opposition from certain members of the Central Rada as well as open and active hostility from Russian circles. In late 1917, disagreeing with the policies of V. Vynnychenko, the chairman of the General Secretariat, Petliura resigned and went to Left-Bank Ukraine. There he organized and commanded the *Haidamaka Battalion of Slobidska Ukraine, a military formation that played a decisive role in the January–February 1918 battles for Kiev and suppression of the Bolshevik Arsenal uprising there.

After Hetman P. Skoropadsky's coup in April 1918, Petliura headed the Kiev Gubernial Zemstvo and *All-Ukrainian Union of Zemstvos. He was arrested by the Hetman government in July 1918 but was released after four months, and went to Bila Tserkva. There he took part in the popular uprising against Skoropadsky's regime and was then elected a member of the UNR *Directory and supreme otaman of the UNR Army. On 11 February 1919, after the army's retreat from Kiev and Vynnychenko's flight abroad, Petliura succeeded him as president of the Directory and resigned from the USDRP. In the difficult conditions of the next 10 months he commanded the UNR and later joint UNR–Ukrainian Galician (UHA) armies against the Red and Russian Volunteer armies (see *Ukrainian-Soviet War). On 5 December 1919, surrounded by the enemy and faced with certain defeat after the UHA established a separate alliance with the Volunteer Army, Petliura and some members of his government fled Ukraine and made for Warsaw in the hope of finding support and allies there. In the meantime Petliura ordered the UNR Army to begin its first *winter campaign.

After the signing of the UNR-Polish Treaty of *Warsaw in April 1920, the UNR Army under Petliura's command and its Polish military ally mounted an offensive against the Bolshevik occupation in Ukraine. The joint forces took Kiev on 7 May 1920 but were forced to retreat in June. Thereafter Petliura continued the war against the Bolsheviks without Polish involvement. Poland and Soviet Russia concluded an armistice in October 1920, and in November the major UNR Army formations were forced to retreat across the Zbruch into Polish-held territory and to submit to internment. Petliura and his government resided temporarily in Tarnów. Later, under an assumed name, Petliura moved to Warsaw. In late 1923, faced with increased Soviet demands that Poland hand him over, he was forced to leave for Budapest. From there he went to Vienna and Geneva, and in late 1924 he settled in Paris. In Paris he founded the weekly *Tryzub*, and from there he oversaw the activities of the UNR *government-in-exile until his assassination by a Bessarabian Jew claiming vengeance for Petliura's purported responsibility for the pogroms in Ukraine (see *Schwartzbard Trial). He was buried in Montparnasse Cemetery.

Petliura debuted as a publicist in 1902 in *Literaturno-naukovyi vistnyk*. There and in the periodicals he edited he published many articles on political, civic, and cultural affairs, particularly on the question of Ukraine's national liberation. His articles had a discernible impact on the formation of Ukrainian national consciousness before the Revolution of 1917. As an émigré in Poland Petliura wrote a brochure on contemporary Ukrainian émigrés and their responsibility (1923). In *Tryzub* he wrote mainly about the 1917–21 attempts at Ukrainian nation building, the responsibility of émigrés, and Ukraine under Bolshevik rule.

The entire 1917–21 period of struggle for Ukrainian statehood is indissolubly linked with Petliura. As a publicist, politician, and military leader he was uncompromising on the issue of Ukrainian independence. Petliura's broad outlook was particularly evident in his definition of the tasks of Ukrainian émigrés and their role in the struggle for Ukrainian statehood. Despite the initially negative, if not openly hostile, attitudes of certain émigré (particularly Western Ukrainian) circles to Petliura because of his central role in the Treaty of *Warsaw and the Ukrainian-Polish alliance, since the mid-1920s he has personified, perhaps more than any other person, the struggle for Ukrainian independence. The personification seemingly also extends to the issue of the *pogroms that took place in Ukraine during the revolutionary period of 1918–20, and Petliura has frequently been invested with the responsibility for those acts. Petliura's own personal convictions render such responsibility highly unlikely, and all the documentary evidence indicates that he consistently made efforts to stem pogrom activity by UNR troops. The Russian and Soviet authorities also made Petliura a symbol of Ukrainian efforts at independence, although in their rendition he was a traitor to the Ukrainian people, and his followers (Petliurites) were unprincipled opportunists.

BIBLIOGRAPHY
Documents sur les pogromes en Ukraine et l'assassinat de Simon Petliura à Paris (Paris 1927)
Zbirnyk pam'iaty Symona Petliury (1879–1926) (Prague 1930)
Lotots'kyi, O. *Symon Petliura* (Warsaw 1936)
Zhuk, A. (ed). *Symon Petliura v molodosti: Zbirka spomyniv* (Lviv 1936)
Ivanys, V. *Symon Petliura – prezydent Ukraïny, 1879–1926* (Toronto 1952)
Symon Petliura: Statti, lysty, dokumenty, 2 vols (New York 1956, 1979)
Pidhainy, O. *Symon Petlura: A Bibliography* (Toronto and New York 1977)
Hunczak, T. *Symon Petliura and the Jews: A Reappraisal* (Toronto and Munich 1985)
Mark, R. 'Symon Petljura und die UNR: Vom Sturz des Hetmans Skoropadśkyj bis zum Exil in Polen,' *Forschungen zur Osteuropäischen Geschichte*, 40 (Berlin 1988)
T. Hunczak

Petliura Ukrainian Library (Ukrainska biblioteka im. Symona Petliury; French: Bibliothèque Ukrainienne Symon Petlura à Paris). Established in Paris in 1926 and officially opened in 1929. By 1940 it had approx 15,000 books, documents, and museum exhibits. In January 1941 the Germans confiscated its holdings and took them to the environs of Leipzig (which became a Soviet zone at the end of the Second World War), from which location they were never recovered. In 1946 the library reopened, and in 1958 it began an active campaign of renovation and acquisition. The number of books in its collection increased from 3,000 in the early 1950s to 10,000 in 1958, 12,000 in 1971, 18,000 in 1979 (not including 6,000 duplicates, 105 periodicals, and 30 newspapers), and over 30,000 in 1984. The library also contains documents on the struggle for independence in 1917–21 and some of the archives of the diplomatic missions of the UNR. It has published an informative bulletin, biannually from 1959 and annually from 1980 (53 issues by 1990). A museum of S. *Petliura's personal effects and of military insignia from 1917–20 is also housed on the premises of the library. The presidents of the library council have been V. Prokopovych (1926–42), I. Kosenko (1942–50), O. Udovychenko (1950–7), Ye. Prokopovych (1957–64), P. Plevako (1964–8), P. Shumovsky (1968–81), Yu. Yeremiiv (1981–3), and A. Zhukovsky (since 1983). The library's directors and the editors of its *Informatsiinyi biuleten'* have been I. Rudychiv, H. Dovzhenko, P. Yosypyshyn (1958–89), and V. Mykhalchuk (since 1989).

BIBLIOGRAPHY
Joukovsky, A. 'Petliura Library in Paris,' *HUS*, 14, no. 1/2 (June 1990)

Petlovany, Vitalii [Petl'ovanyj, Vitalij], b 16 December 1914 in Vinnytsia, d 4 January 1990. Writer. He began publishing in 1935 and was the author of 10 short-prose collections and of numerous novels, such as *Khotyntsi* (1949), *Divchyna z peredmistia* (The Girl from the Suburb, 1955), *Pleche druha* (A Friend's Shoulder, 1961), *Ta tse zh vesna!* (But This Is Spring!, 2 vols, 1962, 1965), *Antoniv vohon'* (Antin's Fire, 1963), *Bakeny na bystryni* (Buoys on the Current, 1967), *Kremlivs'kyi patrul'* (The Kremlin Patrol, 1969), *Syrena z mechem* (A Siren with a Sword, 2 vols, 1972, 1975), *Vohon' dlia Prometeia* (Fire for Prometheus, 1979), *Spomyn ratnoho polia* (Memoir of the Warring Field, 1981), and *Huliai-Hora* (1987).

Petlychny, Ivan [Petlyčnyj], b 1900 in Kobeliaky, Poltava gubernia, d ? Linguist. A graduate of the Kharkiv Institute of People's Education, he taught at the Kharkiv Linguistic and Pedagogical institutes (1930–41) and in the department of Ukrainian language at Lviv University (from 1945). He wrote over 40 articles on subjects such as the language of the *Samovydets Chronicle, the Hutsul dialect in M. Cheremshyna's works (candidate's diss, 1949), syntax and apposition in I. Franko's works, and the sentence in Ukrainian.

Petrakhnovych, Mykola [Petraxnovyč] (Morokhovsky), b ca 1600, d after 1666 in Lviv. Painter. He was a student and then successor of the Lviv painter F. *Senkovych and a leading member of the Lviv painters' guild. His works include the iconostasis in the Dormition Cathedral in Lviv (1637, now in Hrybovychi, near Lviv) and the *Theotokos* (1635) above the entrance to the cathedral, seven passion scenes, and six angels (1664, now lost). He is believed to have painted the portraits of K. Korniakt and his sons.

Petrakivska, Yuliia [Petrakivs'ka, Julija], b 29 November 1900 in Kiev, d 25 June 1969 in Kiev. Pedagogue. A graduate of the Kiev Institute of People's Education

(1929), she directed (1924–67) the renowned day-care facility of the Arsenal factory in Kiev and wrote extensively about early childhood education.

Petranovsky, Yarema [Petranovs'kyj, Jarema], b and d ? Cossack officer from Podilia. He was Uman regimental judge under Hetman B. Khmelnytsky, envoy to Turkey under I. Vyhovsky, and colonel of Lysianka (1648–9) and Chyhyryn (1671–6) regiments and general judge under D. Doroshenko (1669), as well as his ambassador to Poland.

Petranovych, Vasyl [Petranovyč, Vasyl'], b ca 1680 in Zhovkva, Galicia, d 12 August 1759 in Zhovkva. Painter. He painted icons for the Basilian monasteries in Krasnopushcha, Vitsyn, Krekhiv, Zhovkva, and Pidhirtsi; the iconostasis of the church in Vitsyn (fragments of the *Theotokos* and *John the Baptist* have been preserved); and the royal gate with a depiction of the Annunciation in the Good Friday Church in Krekhiv. A number of works now in the Lviv Art Gallery have been attributed to him, including the icons *Theotokos* and *Christ's Childhood*, portraits of W. and S. Rzewuski, *F. Rákóczi and I. Zriny before the Mother of God*, and *Crown Prince James with His Patron Saint, James*.

Halyna Petrashevych: *My Child* (marble, 1957)

Petrashevych, Halyna [Petraševyč], b 23 March 1903 in Dubova, Uman county, Kiev gubernia. Sculptor. She studied at the Uman Art and Decoration Studio (1920–3) and the Kiev State Art Institute (1925–9). She sculpted over 300 works in the socialist realist manner, mostly portraits such as *Oksana* (1932), *Self-Portrait* (1936), *Dream* (1946), *Woman*

Serf (1959); *Lesia Ukrainka* (1937), *T. Shevchenko* (1939, 1959), *O. Korniichuk* (1945, 1949, 1957), and Soviet war heroes and leaders; and the Victory monument in Chernivtsi (1946). I. Verba's book about her was published in Kiev in 1965.

Petrashiv, Petro [Petrašiv], b 1738 in Rybtsi, Poltava regiment, d 19 March 1772. Cossack painter. He painted icons, portraits, and landscapes at the Zaporozhian Sich. His known works include the iconostases of the Dormition Church in Kremenchuk (1767) and those in the military cathedral in Lokhvytsia commissioned by Otaman P. Kalnyshevsky (1770), icons and portraits in Dykanka commissioned by Col V. Kochubei (1768), an icon of the Holy Protectress depicting Cossacks and clergy (1772), and landscapes commissioned by Gen Isakov in Kremenchuk (1768). In composition his works are close to folk paintings.

Petrazhytsky-Kulaha, Ivan [Petražyc'kyj], b ?, d 1632 in Kaniv. Hetman of the *registered Cossacks in 1631–2. He petitioned the Polish Sejm to grant privileges to the Cossacks, demanded that it allow them to participate in the election of the Polish king after the death of Sigismund III Vasa, and defended the rights of the Orthodox church. Together with the Zaporozhian Host he petitioned Metropolitan P. Mohyla to fund a new school at the Kiev Epiphany Brotherhood. His attempts to prevent Zaporozhian sea campaigns against Turkey and his pro-Polish policies antagonized the Zaporozhians, and at the Cossack council in Maslovyi Stav in September 1632 he was deposed. Soon thereafter he was executed.

Andrii Petrenko

Petrenko, Andrii, b 1881 in the Poltava region, d July 1957 in Lviv. Civic leader. After the outbreak of the Revolution of 1917 he moved from Siberia, where he had worked as a bookkeeper for the Chief Railway Construction Administration, to Kiev, from which he was posted to Georgia as a member of a UNR diplomatic mission. In the early 1920s he settled in Lviv and worked at the head office of the Prosvita society. At the same time he was active in the Ukrainian Society of Aid to Emigrants from Eastern Ukraine and a director of the Khortytsia publishing house. During the Soviet and German occupations of Galicia (1939–44) he served as executive director of the Lviv Opera Theater. After the war he was seized by the Soviet secret police in Vienna. He was released from a labor camp shortly before his death.

Petrenko, Mykhailo, b 1817 in Slovianske, Izium county, Kharkiv gubernia, d ? Poet of the *Kharkiv Romantic School. After graduating from Kharkiv University in 1841, he worked as a civil servant. He wrote lyrical and elegiac poetry, genres uncommon at that time. Nineteen of his poems appeared in three literary miscellanies, O. Korsun's *Snip* (The Sheaf, 1841), I. Betsky's *Molodyk* (The New Moon, 1843), and A. Metlynsky's *Iuzhno-russkii sbornik* (South Russian Collection, 1848). Some of them became folk songs (eg, 'Dyvlius' ia na nebo' [I Gaze at the Sky]). Petrenko's poetry was published in an edition with V. Zabila's in 1960.

Petrenko, Nazar, b 1893, d ? Political activist. From 1918 he was a member of the CC of the centrist *Ukrainian Party of Socialist Revolutionaries (UPSR), and later he joined the Central Ukrainian Insurgent Committee in Kamianets-Podilskyi that was assisting the UNR in its struggle against A. Denikin. In 1921 Petrenko was convicted, together with V. Holubovych and other UPSR figures, in a Bolshevik show trial. His further fate is unknown.

Petrenko, Pavlo, b 15 November 1903, d 2 September 1982. Literary scholar. In the 1930s he was an associate of the Institute of Literature of the AN URSR (now ANU) and taught Ukrainian literature at various postsecondary schools in Kharkiv. He wrote books on the Marxist method in literary scholarship (1928), H. Kvitka-Osnovianenko (1931), I. Kotliarevsky (1931), and M. Vovchok (1932) and was one of the authors of a general course on the history of Ukrainian literature edited by O. Biletsky. After the Second World War he was a refugee in Germany and then emigrated to the United States. He contributed articles on Ukrainian literature to émigré periodicals and wrote a short biography of D. *Solovei (1968).

Petrenko, Serhii, b 8 December 1956 in Khmelnytskyi. Canoeist. He and A. Vinogradov won the 1976 Olympic gold medals in the 500-m and 1,000-m Canadian pairs. He was also a world and European champion in the 1974 and 1975 500-m Canadian singles and the 1977 10,000-m Canadian pairs, and a USSR champion in the 1975 4 × 500-m relay, the 1976 500-m Canadian pairs, and the 1979 10,000-m Canadian pairs.

Petrenko, Yevhen, b 1946 in Luhanske oblast. Painter. Petrenko studied in Kiev and at the Moscow Higher Art and Design School, from which he was expelled for attempting to organize a Ukrainian students' group. He creates fantastic, nonrepresentational compositions echoing abstract expressionism. His pictures are evocative of cataclysmic explosions and flights of fancy into unknown galaxies and black holes. Petrenko uses highly saturated colors in myriad tonalities of swirling pigment. His work was not exhibited in Ukraine until 1988.

Petrenko-Krytchenko, Pavlo [Krytčenko], b 9 July 1866 in Kherson, d 21 January 1944. Organic chemist; VUAN/AN URSR (now ANU) corresponding member from 1932. A graduate of the university in Odessa (1888), he taught there, and became a professor in 1903. In the 1920s he chaired the Scientific Council of the Odessa Chemical-Radiological Institute and the chemistry department at the Odessa Tekhnikum of Applied Chemistry. He studied

heterocyclic compounds, the substituent effect on the reactivity of organic compounds (esp ketones), and general structure-property relationships. He introduced the concept of steric hindrance on the basis of his esterification studies on aromatic carboxylic acids.

Ivanna Petriv   Gen Vsevolod Petriv

Petriv, Ivanna, b 20 January 1892 in Lviv, d 6 November 1971 in Toronto. A teacher at Ukrainian schools in Lviv (1918–44), she wrote handbooks and textbooks on teaching methodology and was active in the *Prosvita society and the *Ukrainian Teachers' Mutual Aid Society. In 1954, after spending several years in Germany and Belgium following the Second World War, she emigrated to Canada. She remained active in Ukrainian community affairs, particularly as a member of the *Ukrainian Catholic Women's League of Canada.

Petriv, Vsevolod, b 2 January 1883 in Kiev, d 10 July 1948 in Augsburg. Senior UNR Army officer; full member of the Shevchenko Scientific Society from 1948. A colonel of the general staff in the Russian army during the First World War, in early 1917 he was chief of staff in the Turkestan Division. He organized the Ukrainian troops of the division into the *Haidamaka Cavalry Regiment, and commanded it in battles for Kiev during January and March–April 1918 and then in the Crimean campaign. Under the Hetman government he served on the General Staff in the Department of Military Education, and during 1919 he organized and commanded the unified military youth school in Zhytomyr and then the Volhynian Group. Later, he served as defense minister in the government of I. Mazepa (1919), UNR Army inspector of infantry, and chief of general staff, and was promoted to brigadier general. In the interwar period he lived in Prague, where he lectured and wrote articles on military topics. His major work is *Spomyny z chasiv ukraïns'koï revoliutsiï (1917–1921)* (Memoirs from the Times of the Ukrainian Revolution [1917–21], 4 vols, 1927–9).

Petrivka. V-20, DB II-6. A town smt (1986 pop 6,500) near the confluence of the Yevsuh and the Kovsiuh rivers in Stanychno-Luhanske raion, Luhanske oblast. It was founded in the second half of the 17th century by Don Cossacks and runaway serfs. The settlement was called Karaiashnyk until 1771 and Petropavlivka until 1923. The town produces concrete and sand for the building industry.

Petrivske [Petrivs'ke] (Petrovs'ke). V-19, DB III-5. A city (1989 pop 17,800) in Luhanske oblast. It was founded in 1896 and called Shterivske until 1920. In 1963 it was granted city status and placed under the jurisdiction of the Krasnyi Luch municipal council. It has a building-materials and a food industry.

Petrivske fortified settlement. A Romen-Borsheve culture fortified settlement of the 9th to 12th century on the Vorsklo River near Petrivske, Velyka Pysarivka raion, Sumy oblast. Excavations in 1938 uncovered the remains of semi-pit dwellings and agricultural structures, work implements, and the bones of domesticated animals. Further occupation during the 11th and 12th century testified that Petrivske sheltered the inhabitants of surrounding settlements during onslaughts by steppe nomads.

Petrivske graphite region (Petrivskyi hrafitonosnyi raion). A number of graphite deposits in southeastern Kirovohrad and western Dnipropetrovske oblasts. The largest deposits are in Petrivske, Velyko Vodianske, and Babenkivske. Total reserves of graphite are estimated at 7.5 million t (1980). The graphite is found in seams that are 40–50 m in depth and extend to 2.5 km in width. The graphite concentration in the ore is 2–15 percent. Graphite was discovered in the area in 1872.

Petrivsky, Mykhailo [Petrivs'kyj, Myxajlo] (Petrowsky, Michael), b 15 November 1897 in Rozhubovychi, Peremyshl county, Galicia, d 7 April 1982 in Toronto. Writer and translator. After emigrating to Canada with his parents in 1912, he completed his education at the University of Ottawa and worked as a translator and investigator for the Royal Canadian Mounted Police. In this capacity he prepared a report in October 1939 on Ukrainians in Canada that strongly influenced government policy toward Ukrainian Canadians during the Second World War. He contributed articles to the Ukrainian and Canadian press and wrote plays, such as *Kanadiis'kyi zhenykh* (The Canadian Bridegroom, 1921) and *Katy biloho orla* (Executioners of the White Eagle, 1922), as well as the novelette *Magichne misto* (The Magical City, 1929). His short stories were published in the collections *Mrii sl'ozamy oblyti* (Dreams Drenched in Tears, 1973) and *Oi, Kanado Kanadon'ko* (Oh, Canada, Dear Canada, 1974). Some of his works have been translated into English.

Petro, b and d ? Metropolitan of Kiev. He was born in Volhynia, and entered a monastery at the age of 12. He founded his own monastery in Ratna, near Lviv. In 1305 Prince Yurii Lvovych of Galicia-Volhynia sent him to Constantinople to be consecrated metropolitan of Halych. Since Maximos, the metropolitan of Kiev, had recently died, Patriarch Athanasios named Petro metropolitan of Kiev and Halych (1308–26), on the condition that he transfer his see to Moscow to satisfy the demands of the Muscovite princes. The transfer led to the development of a separate Muscovite church jurisdiction and strengthened the authority of the Moscow princes. Petro was canonized in 1340.

Petrochemical industry. A branch of the *chemical industry that processes products of the *petroleum and *natural gas industries. The major products of the industry are polymers (synthetic rubber, plastics, synthetic fibers, etc), olefins, and various other organic and inorganic chemicals. Those products have important industrial and domestic uses. The petrochemical industry emerged in the USSR in the early 1930s, following the introduction of modern petroleum refining. In Ukraine, however, the industry began to develop only after the Second World War. In the 1960s its output increased by more than a factor of 3.5, yet overall production remained low. Recently, considerable emphasis has been placed on increasing the production of plastics, synthetic tar, and synthetic fibers. The main centers of the industry are the petroleum-producing regions of western Ukraine (near Drohobych and Boryslav) and the Donets Basin.

Petrograd. See Saint Petersburg.

Petrograd Ukrainian Drama Theater. See Zhovten Theater in Petrograd-Leningrad.

Petroleum deposits. There are three petroleum-bearing regions in Ukraine, the Carpathian, the Dnieper-Donets, and the Crimean-Caucasian. The Carpathian region, which has had the longest history of petroleum extraction, extends along the northeastern flank of the Carpathian Mountains. Petroleum deposits are located along the southwestern edge of the inner zone of the Subcarpathian Depression in Jurassic, Upper Cretaceous, Paleogene, and Neogene strata. Overlain in places by the Berehove Nappe, the deposits lie anywhere from 100 to 4,800 m, but mostly from 2,000 to 3,500 m, below the surface. Petroleum or crude oil from the Carpathian region is of the paraffin-petrogenic type. It contains up to 10 percent paraffin, has little sulfur, is rich in light fractions (35–60 percent, of benzene and gas), has a specific gravity ranging from 0.835 to 0.975, and can generate about 10,000 kcal/kg. Historically the most important petroleum deposit is the Boryslav field, which provided the longest period of exploitation and contributed up to 90 percent of petroleum production in the Carpathian region before the Second World War. Today the most important fields in the region are the Dolyna (discovered in 1949) and the Bytkiv (near Nadvirna; commercial extraction started in 1962). A number of small deposits, worked since the late 19th century, have been abandoned.

The Dnieper-Donets region contains (since 1965) the largest and most productive petroleum deposits in Ukraine. Exploration for petroleum began there in 1936 and commercial extraction started in 1952. By the time Ukrainian petroleum production peaked in 1972, the fields in the region accounted for about 85 percent of the republic's output. Petroleum deposits are located within a graben that extends from the northwest to the southeast through the central part of the Dnieper-Donets Trough. The graben, about 150–200 km wide and 800 km long, contains proven petroleum and gas-bearing strata of the mid-Jurassic, Permian-Triassic, and lower Permian-Carboniferous periods at depths of 940–2,600 m. There are prospects that petroleum might be discovered even deeper, in the Devonian deposits. The petroleum from the region is light to medium (specific gravity, 0.783–0.875), is low in paraffin (1–4 percent, seldom 4–7 percent), and contains less than 1 percent sulfur. The major commercial petroleum deposits of the region include Radchenky, Sahaidak, Rozbyshivka, Mykhailivka, and Zachepylivka, in Poltava oblast; Kachanivka and Rybalske, in Sumy oblast; and Pryluka, Hnidyntsi, and (the largest) Leliaky, in Chernihiv oblast.

The Crimean-Caucasian region extends along the northern flank of the western end of the Caucasus Mountains and crosses the Kerch Strait to the Kerch Peninsula, in the Crimea. Petroleum deposits are located in Tertiary sandstones at depths of 500–2,300 m and partially in the Cretaceous and Jurassic porous sedimentary rocks at even greater depths. The petroleum from the region is of high quality. It is both light and sulfur-free. In the Crimea oil fields were discovered in the Kerch Peninsula before the First World War, but most of them have been exhausted and only partly replaced. In the Kuban region the earliest oil fields were located near Maikop and to the southwest (at Apsheronske, Naftohorske, and Khadyzhenske). After the Second World War more oil fields were discovered southwest of Krasnodar (at Ilskyi, Akhtyrskyi, Krymske, and elsewhere) and in the Kuban Delta (centered on Anastasiivska). The last two areas are major producers at present.

Petroleum reserves for Ukraine have not been reported for nearly two decades. It is obvious that discoveries of new deposits have not kept up with the rates of extraction, and production since 1975 has fallen. There are prospects for new discoveries in the deeper strata of all three regions, especially in the lower Carboniferous and Devonian of the Dnieper-Donets region, and in the Cretaceous and Jurassic of the Crimean-Caucasian region, which have not yet been explored.

BIBLIOGRAPHY

Vitenko, V.; et al. *Naftovi ta hazovi rodovyshcha Ukraïny* (Kiev 1961)

Honta, Z.; Honta, T. *Naftovi bahatstva Ukraïny* (Kiev 1962)

Glushko, V.; et al. *Geologiia neftianykh i gazovykh mestorozhdenii Ukrainskoi SSR* (Moscow 1963)

Burshtar, M.; L'vov, M. *Geografiia i geologiia nefti i gaza SSSR i zarubezhnykh stran* (Moscow 1979)

Geologicheskie formatsii neftegazonosnykh provintsii Ukrainy (Kiev 1984)

I. Stebelsky

Petroleum industry. A branch of heavy industry that involves the extraction and refinement of petroleum resources. The petroleum industry in Ukraine is concentrated in three geographic regions: Galicia (in the foothills of the Carpathian Mountains), the Dnieper-Donets area, and the Black Sea coast. Petroleum output in Ukraine peaked in the mid-1970s.

In Galicia petroleum extracting began as early as 1617. Until the end of the 19th century petroleum was extracted manually with buckets and hand-pumps from oil springs (4–6 m below the surface) and, later, from wells (35–40 m deep). The petroleum was used in its natural state as lubricating material, lamp oil, and ointment. By 1836 Galicia's oil output had reached some 350 t per year. The discovery of a distillation process for naphtha and the invention of the naphtha lamp in 1851 spurred the development of the petroleum industry that was concentrated in the *Drohobych-Boryslav Industrial Region. By 1870 annual output had reached 20,000 t. The extracted oil was not refined locally, but shipped outside Galicia. The first significant oil refinery was established in Drohobych only in 1909. New technology had made it possible to drill deeper wells by the end of the 19th century. In 1908 the Oil City Company drilled a 1,015-m well that opened up the deeper, sandstone layers for exploitation. Small-scale entrepreneurs were displaced by large Austrian, British, German, and French companies. At the beginning of the 20th century British-Austrian interests controlled 78 percent of oil output and 73 percent of its processing. Ukrainian peasants who owned the oil-bearing land benefited little from the rapid development of the industry; many of them sold their land at very low prices. Petroleum production in Galicia peaked at 2.1 million t (5 percent of world output) in 1909 and then declined quickly to 877,000 t in 1914, as easily accessible resources were exhausted, and little was spent on exploration. Eighty percent of Galicia's oil and oil products were exported.

In the interwar period petroleum output in Galicia continued to decline. The industry was controlled by large foreign cartels (British, Belgian, French, and American), which accounted for 84 percent of its capital investment in 1933. The economic depression, competition from cheap Middle Eastern oil, and technological obsolescence contributed to the decline of Galicia's oil industry. Its output dropped from 700,000 t in 1928 to 370,000 t in 1938 (or 0.1 percent of world output). That quantity was enough to supply all of Poland's demand and even to export some surplus to other countries.

In central and eastern Ukraine petroleum was not extracted until the 1950s. Before then imported Caucasian oil was refined in Odessa, Kherson, and Berdianske. By the mid-1930s Ukraine was importing almost 2 million t of petroleum annually. In that period a pipeline was constructed from Armavir in the Caucasus to Trudove in the Donets Basin. In the 1930s, oil exploration was begun in the Dnieper-Donets Trough, and several productive wells were drilled. The Second World War, however, interrupted the development of that region's petroleum resources. In 1940 Ukraine's entire output of 400,000 t came from Galicia, which had been annexed by the Ukrainian SSR (see the table). During the war Galicia's oil industry was severely damaged. In 1946, therefore, Ukraine extracted only 213,000 t of petroleum.

Ukraine's oil production expanded after the war. By 1960 Ukraine was producing 2.2 million t of petroleum (including gas condensate), and by 1972, 14.5 million t (or about 4 percent of the USSR output). The increase was brought about partly by improvements in oil recovery technology. In the second half of the 1950s deep-drilling efforts were intensified, and secondary recovery methods were put to use. Furthermore, in 1950 a number of new oil fields were brought into production in Western Ukraine, including the Dolyna and Northern Dolyna oil fields in Ivano-Frankisvke oblast and the Olkhivske oil field in Transcarpathia. By 1960 the oil output in western Ukraine accounted for 70–80 percent of Ukraine's output. Since then production has declined: the reserves seem to be largely depleted, although drilling for small traps is continuing. In 1974 the estimated reserves of the Carpathian region were 426 million barrels of oil and condensate.

In the 1950s oil exploration of the large Dnieper-Donets

PETROLEUM INDUSTRY

graben system was intensified, and oil fields were developed in Poltava, Sumy, and Chernihiv oblasts. By 1965 over 60 percent of Ukraine's oil production came from that region. Predictions of large Devonian oil resources were confirmed partly in 1978 by deep drilling to 5,000 m. Such depths were inaccessible to Soviet technology. In 1974 the estimated reserves of the area, excluding the Devonian reserves, were 1,029 million barrels of oil and condensate.

The Black Sea region contains Ukraine's newest oil fields. The first oil field was discovered only in 1959. Exploration there has been fragmentary, because most of the potential is offshore. (See *Petroleum deposits.)

Ukraine's output of petroleum
(including gas condensate), 1940–87

Year	Output (in million t)
1940	0.4
1950	0.3
1960	2.2
1970	13.9
1980	7.5
1987	5.6

In the 1970s, Ukrainian petroleum production began a gradual decline as a result of the depletion of old reserves, and a lack of capital necessary for exploiting new sources – the Soviet government concentrated resources on the development of oil in Siberia and the north. Oil production (including gas condensate) declined from 14.5 million t in 1974 to 5.4 million t in 1988. The latter figure represented a mere 0.9 percent of total USSR production. Ukraine relies heavily on oil imported from Russia. In 1988 it paid almost 40 billion rubles for imported work oil and natural gas.

Historically the oil refining industry in Ukraine has lagged behind the extraction industry. In the 1950s and 1960s new refineries were built, and existing facilities were expanded. Today there are eight large refinery complexes in Ukraine: Boryslav, Drohobych, Lviv, Odessa, Kherson, Berdianske, Kremenchuk, and Lysychanske. Relatively outdated equipment and an irregular oil supply from Russia hindered the growth of Ukraine's refining industry in the second half of the 1980s.

BIBLIOGRAPHY
Jensen, R.; Shabad, T.; Wright, A. (eds). *Soviet Natural Resources in the World Economy* (Chicago 1983)
Kompleksnoe ispol'zovanie toplivo-energeticheskikh resursov (Kiev 1983)

B. Krawchenko, S. Protsiuk

Petropavlivka. V-17. A town smt (1986 pop 10,200) on the Byk River and a raion center in Dnipropetrovske oblast. A settlement of former members of the Luhanske Pike Regiment was established at the site in 1775. By 1846 it had become a volost center with a population of about 4,700. In 1923 it became a raion center. Today the town has a creamery and a hemp-processing plant.

Petrov, Aleksei, b 16 March 1859 in St Petersburg, d 5 January 1932 in Prague. Russian historian and Slavist; full member of the Shevchenko Scientific Society from 1925. A graduate of St Petersburg University (1880), he taught in St Petersburg secondary schools in 1880–7, the school of Higher Courses for Women from 1887, and the university from 1911. From 1922 he lived as an émigré in Prague. He wrote many studies on the history and ethnography of Transcarpathia. Among his works published separately were studies, in Russian, of the ethnographic border of the Ruthenian (ie, Ukrainian) people in Austria-Hungary (1915), Magyar hegemony in Hungary and Hungarian Rus' (ie, Transcarpathia, 1915), monuments of 16th- and 17th-century Transcarpathian Ruthenian church life (1921), the issue of the Slovak-Ruthenian ethnographic border (1923), and Carpatho-Ruthenian place-names from the mid-19th to the early 20th century (1927). Many of his studies appeared or were reprinted in *Materialy dlia istorii Ugorskoi Rusi* (Materials on the History of Hungarian Rus', 9 vols, 1905–14, 1923, 1932), which he edited. Petrov also contributed to the *Naukovyi zbirnyk* of the Uzhhorod Prosvita Society, *Karpatorusskii sbornik*, *Česká revue*, and other Czech scholarly publications.

Petrov, Aleksei, b 28 October 1910 in Koshki, Samara gubernia, Russia, d 9 May 1972 in Kiev. Theoretical physicist; AN URSR (now ANU) full member from 1969. He graduated from Kazan University in 1937 and worked there in 1943–69. He became head of a section of the ANU Institute of Theoretical Physics in 1970. His research dealt primarily with the theory of gravitational fields and gravitational radiation.

Petrov, Artem, b 31 October 1779 in Khomutets, Hadiache county, Poltava region, d 15 October 1849 in Moscow. Veterinarian. One of the founders of veterinary education in the Russian Empire, he graduated from the Kievan Mohyla Academy (1799) and the St Petersburg Medico-Surgical Academy (1807) and taught at the veterinary school of the Moscow Medico-Surgical Academy (1809–42). His work was mostly with horses.

Petrov, Mykola (Nikolai), b 6 May 1840 in Voznesenskoe, Makarev county, Kostroma gubernia, Russia, d 20 June 1921 in Kiev. Literary scholar, historian, ethnographer, archeologist, and pedagogue; full member of the Historical Society of Nestor the Chronicler, the Ukrainian Scientific Society from 1907, the Shevchenko Scientific Society from 1911, and the VUAN from 1918; corresponding member of the Russian Academy of Sciences from 1916. He graduated from the Kiev Theological Academy (1865) and taught at the Volhynian Theological Seminary in Kremianets (1865–70) and at the Kiev Theological Academy (1870–1911), where he organized and directed its Church History and Archeological Museum from 1872 and became a full professor in 1876. He received doctorates in

Mykola (Nikolai) Petrov (1840–1921)

theology (1875) and Russian language and literature (1907). Many of his articles appeared in *Trudy Kievskoi dukhovnoi akademii* and *Kievskaia starina*.

Petrov was one of the first scholars in the Russian Empire to write about Ukrainian literature. His studies, which he wrote using the comparative-historical method, are valuable for the facts they provide. Some of his earliest works were six articles on literary scholarship and activity at the Kievan Mohyla Academy (1866–8). In his studies of 17th- and 18th-century Ukrainian literature (1880, 1911) he described and analyzed Ukrainian *school drama. In his pioneering book on the history of 19th-century Ukrainian literature (1884) he examined Ukrainian literature as a 'self-sufficient branch,' but emphasized the influence of Russian literature; his eclectic approach, which did not take into account Western Ukrainian literature, was critiqued by M. *Dashkevych. He also wrote articles on H. Skovoroda, H. Konysky, M. Dovhalevsky, O. Lobysevych, I. Kotliarevsky, V. Hohol-Yanovsky and N. Gogol, and Ukrainian polemical literature.

As a church historian Petrov wrote books on the Kievan Mohyla Academy in the second half of the 17th century (1895) and its importance in the development of religious schools in Russia in the 18th century (1904), and nine articles on the history of the Basilian order in Poland (1870–2). He wrote authoritative descriptions of the manuscript collections at the Kiev Theological Academy's museum (1875, 1877, 1879) and elsewhere in Kiev (1891, 1897, 1904) and compiled the collection *Akty i dokumenty, otnosiashchiesia k istorii Kievskoi akademii* (Acts and Documents Pertaining to the History of the Kievan Academy, 5 vols, 1904–7). His works in archeology, museum studies, and art include a book of essays on the history and topography of ancient Kiev (1897), a study of building construction in Chernihiv in the 11th and 12th centuries (1919), and an album of Kiev's temples and monuments (1896). His contributions to ethnography include articles on Ukrainian folkloric elements in N. Gogol's early works, Ukrainian historical songs and legends, the influence of Russian *byliny* on Ukrainian oral literature, Ukrainian folk celebrations, old Ukrainian theater and the *vertep*, and intermedes. His historical monographs on the Kholm region (1887), Volhynia (1888), Belarus and Lithuania (1890), Podilia (1891), and Bessarabia (1892) form a distinct group of works within his scholarship.

R. Senkus

Petrov, Mykola, b 1875 in Elets, Orel gubernia, Russia, d 9 April 1940 in Kiev. Photographer and photography scholar. After graduating from the Riga Polytechnical Institute (1900) he founded (1901) and presided over (1906–12) the Daguerre Society, one of the earliest photographic societies in the world. Petrov taught photography at the Kiev Polytechnical Institute (1905–20), the Kiev State Art Institute (1924–30), and the Kiev Institute of Cinematography (1930–40), and also chaired the photography department of the Kiev Institute of Forensic Medicine. His photographs were published in various Soviet magazines and were shown at international exhibitions. He made technical improvements in the printing process and wrote numerous works on photography.

Viktor Petrov

Petrov, Viktor (pseud: V. Domontovych, V. Ber), b 22 October 1894 in Katerynoslav (now Dnipropetrovske), d 8 June 1969 in Kiev. Writer, literary scholar, archeologist, and ethnographer; member of the Shevchenko Scientific Society. A graduate of Kiev University (1918), from 1920 he worked for the VUAN Ethnographic Commission. He became coeditor (with A. Loboda) of its *Etnohrafichnyi visnyk* (1925–9) and head of the commission (1927–33). During that time he also worked as a literary scholar and writer and was close to the *Neoclassicists. In 1941 he was briefly director of the AN URSR (now ANU) Institute of Ukrainian Folklore. In 1942–3 he edited the literary journal *Ukraïns'kyi zasiv* in Kharkiv and Kirovohrad under German rule. In 1944 he fled to the West and became an associate of the Ukrainian Scientific Institute in Berlin (1944–5). As a refugee in postwar Munich he was a professor at the Ukrainian Free University and at the Theological Academy of the Ukrainian Autocephalous Orthodox Church and a member of the editorial boards of the literary and art monthly *Arka* and the MUR collections. In 1949 he 'reappeared' in the USSR and worked at the Institute of the History of Material Culture of the USSR Academy of Sciences in Moscow. From 1956 he was a senior associate of the ANU Institute of Archeology in Kiev and the custodian of its scientific archive.

Petrov wrote the biographical novel *Alina i Kostomarov* (Alina and [P.] Kostomarov, 1929) and, under the pen name V. Domontovych, the novels *Divchyna z vedmedykom* (Girl with a Teddy Bear, 1928), *Doktor Serafikus* (Doctor Seraficus, 1947), and *Bez gruntu* (Without Foundation, 1948). He also wrote stories, some of them under the pen name Viktor Ber. His literary works were republished in three volumes (1988–9). As a literary scholar he wrote books on

P. Kulish in the 1850s (1929) and Kulish's romances (1929), and articles on Kulish, T. Shevchenko, H. Skovoroda, and contemporary literature in VUAN serials and collections and the journal *Zhyttia i revoliutsiia*. As an émigré he published philosophical and critical articles in several periodicals and a brochure on the principal stages in the development of Shevchenko studies (1946). A pamphlet he wrote in the early 1940s on Ukrainian cultural figures destroyed by the Bolsheviks in 1920–40 was published in the West in 1959.

As an ethnographer Petrov wrote several dozen articles on such topics as the place of folklore in regional studies, the sun in Ukrainian folk beliefs, the legend of the origin of evil women, and the agrarian cult of fire, and entries on Slavic mythology in the Soviet Ukrainian encyclopedia. He also wrote a collection of articles on preclass society (1933). With Loboda he coedited a book of materials on the Dnieper boatmen (1929) and Ye. Markovsky's book on the Ukrainian *vertep* (1929). As an archeologist he was involved in excavations of late Trypilian and early Slavic settlements. He studied Scythian monuments and the Burial Fields culture of the Antes. He wrote books on the origin of the Ukrainian people (1947), the Scythians' language and ethnos (1968), slash-and-burn tillage (1968), and the ethnogenesis of the Slavs (1972). He also wrote articles on the Trypilian, Zarubyntsi, and Cherniakhiv cultures, on the ancient Slavs, and on Scythian and ancient East Slavic names, hydronyms, and toponyms, and published V. Khvoika's diary of excavations at Zarubyntsi.

R. Senkus

Petrov, Yosyp, b 15 November 1807 in Yelysavethrad (now Kirovohrad), d 11 March 1878 in St Petersburg. Opera singer (bass). In the years 1830–78 he appeared at the St Petersburg Theater. With a remarkable acting proficiency as well as a singing range of almost four octaves, Petrov is known as the founder of the vocal school in Russia. He premiered the leading parts (usually created for him) in notable Russian operas: M. Glinka's *Ruslan and Liudmila* and *Ivan Susanin*, A. Dargomyzhsky's *Rusalka* and *The Stone Guest*, A. Rubinstein's *The Demon*, P. Tchaikovsky's *Vakula the Smith* and *Mazepa*, N. Rimsky-Korsakov's *The Maid of Pskov*, and M. Mussorgsky's *Boris Godunov*. Mussorgsky was composing the comic opera *The Fair at Sorochyntsi* with the intention of casting Petrov in a leading part, but left the opera unfinished when Petrov died. A biography, by Ye. Lostochkina, appeared in 1950 and another, by V. Stasov, in 1952.

Petrova, Yevheniia, b 6 January 1903 in Kiev, d 12 January 1989 in Kiev. Stage actress; wife of M. Krushelnytsky. She began her theatrical career in an amateur theater of Kievan railway workers (1919) and in the Kameniar Theater under V. Vasylko (1922–3) and worked in Berezil (1923–33), the Kharkiv Ukrainian Drama Theater (from 1935), and the Kiev Ukrainian Drama Theater (1952–9).

Petrove. V-14. A town smt (1986 pop 8,700) on the Inhulets River and a raion center in Kirovohrad oblast. The town was founded as a Cossack settlement at the end of the 17th century. In 1923 it became a raion center of Kryvyi Rih okruha, and in 1963 it attained smt status. A water reservoir was built there in 1956. The town has a food industry and an iron-ore mine nearby.

Petrovske. See Petrivske.

Petrovsky, Heorhii [Petrovs'kyj, Heorhij], b 7 December 1901 in Velyki Sorochyntsi, Myrhorod county, Poltava gubernia, d 15 August 1957 in Lviv. Pharmacologist and internal medicine specialist. A graduate of the Kharkiv Medical Institute (1926), he was a professor at the Dnipropetrovske (1932–41) and the Lviv (1945–57) medical institutes. He proposed a classification system of choleretic drugs.

Hryhorii Petrovsky (portrait by Mykhailo Zhuk, 1928)   Mykola Petrovsky

Petrovsky, Hryhorii [Petrovs'kyi, Hryhorij], b 4 February 1878 in Kharkiv, d 9 January 1958 in Moscow. Soviet state official and Party leader. During the revolution he served as people's commissar of internal affairs of the RSFSR and then chaired the All-Ukrainian Central Executive Committee (1919–38) and the All-Ukrainian Committee of Poor Peasants (1920–33). He was a long-term member of the Politburo of the CP(B)U (1920–38). Petrovsky belonged to the Bolshevik majority that opposed the Ukrainian national-communist orientation represented by Yu. *Lapchynsky and O. *Shumsky, although in the 1920s he supported Ukrainization and defended Ukraine's economic, cultural, and political rights against growing centralization. After the purge of the Politburo of the CP(B)U he was removed from Ukraine (1938) and appointed deputy director of the USSR Museum of the Revolution in Moscow. In 1926 the city of Katerynoslav was renamed Dnipropetrovske in his honour.

Petrovsky, Mykola [Petrovs'kyj], b 26 November 1894 in Kudrivka, Sosnytsia county, Chernihiv gubernia, d 20 July 1951 in Kiev. Historian; AN URSR (now ANU) corresponding member from 1945. He studied at the Nizhen Historical-Philological Institute (1915–19). In 1924–33 he was a history professor at the Nizhen Institute of People's Education and edited its *Zapysky* (12 vols). From 1934 he chaired the department of Ukraine's history at Kiev University. He was also an associate of the ANU Institute of History from 1937, received a doctorate in 1939, and served as the institute's director in 1942–7. He was a member of the Ukrainian SSR delegations at the UN assemblies in San Francisco (1945) and London (1946) and at the Paris Peace Conference of 1946.

Petrovsky is the author of many works on 17th-century Ukrainian history. He wrote books about the Samovydets Chronicle (1930) and the Cossack-Polish War of 1648–57 (1939) and articles about Yu. Dunin-Borkovsky (1927), S. Zorka's pseudo-diary (1928), the Ruin (1929), the Hetmanate's regimental system (1929), T. Tsiutsiura (1929), the last years of Hetman P. Doroshenko (1930), I. Bohun (1930), R. Rakushka (1931), and the state structure of 17th-century Ukraine (1931). He is also a coauthor of two ANU histories of Ukraine (1942, 1943) and a collection of articles on the Cossack-Polish War (1940), and he compiled a collection of documents and materials pertaining to the history of Kievan Rus' (1939, 1946) and Ukraine in 1569–1654 (1941, with V. Putilov). His articles of the 1940s have propagandistic rather than scholarly value.

Petrovsky, Oleksander [Petrovs'kyj], b 12 September 1908 in Katerynoslav, d 21 October 1983 in Kiev. Conductor and educator. In 1941 he graduated from the Moscow Conservatory and in 1951 completed his graduate studies at the Kiev Conservatory. He served as artistic director and conductor of the All-Union Radio Committee choir (1938–4), artistic director of the DUMKA kapelle (1944–6), chief choirmaster and conductor of the opera studio of the Kiev Conservatory (1947–57), and chief conductor of the Kiev Theater of Opera and Ballet (1952–4). He lectured at the Kiev Pedagogical Institute from 1956. His works include a monograph on the Bilshovyk Plant kapelle (1956) and several collections, among them *Khrestomatiia z khorovoho dyryhuvannia* (The Choir Conducting Anthology, 1973).

Petrovych, Liudmyla [Petrovyč, Ljudmyla] (real name: Kravchukivna-Smaleva, Vanda), b 5 November 1882 in Chernivtsi, Bukovyna, d 27 December 1971 in Borshchiv, Ternopil oblast, Galicia. Singer (mezzo-soprano); sister of F. *Lopatynska and wife of V. *Petrovych. She studied voice under V. Vysotsky and M. Kossak in Lviv and sang as a soloist with the Chernivtsi City Choir (1897–9), the opera group of the Ruska Besida Theater (1899–1914), and V. Kossak's troupe (1920–1). Her main roles were Natalka in M. Lysenko's *Natalka from Poltava* and Kulyna in his *The Black Sea Cossacks*, Oksana and Odarka in S. Hulak-Artemovsky's *Zaporozhian Cossack beyond the Danube*, Hanna in M. Arkas's *Kateryna*, Olga in P. Tchaikovsky's *Eugene Onegin*, Siebel in C. Gounod's *Faust*, and Carmen in G. Bizet's *Carmen*. After the Second World War she directed the Borshchiv People's Theater.

Petrovych, Vasyl [Petrovyč, Vasyl'] (real surname: Senyk), b 1 January 1880 in Ivankivtsi, Zhydachiv county, Galicia, d 31 October 1914 in Lviv. Actor and singer (tenor). He joined the Ruska Besida Theater in 1897. He played roles in melodramas, operas, and operettas from the Ukrainian and non-Ukrainian repertoire. Petrovych died prematurely following a nervous breakdown.

Petrowska, Christina [Petrovs'ka, Khrystyna] (married name: Brégent), b 30 December 1948 in Ottawa. Ukrainian-Canadian concert pianist, teacher, poet, and graphic artist. She studied at the Toronto Conservatory, graduated in 1969 from the Juilliard School of Music, continued her studies with K. Stockhausen and G. Ligeti in Europe, and subsequently obtained a PH D in musicology from the

Sorbonne. At present she teaches music at York University in Toronto. She has appeared throughout North America and Europe, including Ukraine, in solo recitals, as a soloist with orchestra, and on radio and television. Her main interest and forte is contemporary music, including that of A. Schönberg, P. Boulez, M. Brégent, M. Kouzan, and V. Sylvestrov. She has several recordings. Her graphic art has been exhibited in Canada, the United States, and France, and her poetry has appeared in several journals.

Petrowsky, Michael. See Petrivsky, Mykhailo.

Petruk, Roman, b 17 October 1940 in Rudnyky, Sniatyn county, Galicia. Ceramist and printmaker. After graduating from the Lviv Institute of Applied and Decorative Arts (1964) he worked in the monument workshop of the Lviv Art Manufacturing Complex. He does ceramic sculptures and household ceramics. He has produced several series of relief dishes, such as 'Work,' 'Assemblers,' and 'The Tree of Peace' (1968), and large decorative panels, such as *Amateur Art* for the foyer of the culture building of the sugar refinery in Dubno (1969). He has also done ink drawings; monotypes such as *Icarus, The Muse, The Last Supper,* and *Dovbush's Death* (1968–70); and illustrations for an edition of V. Stefanyk's short stories (1971) and I. Kalynets's *Pidsumovuiuchy movchannia* (The Summing up of Silence, 1971), a proscribed collection of verses published in the West.

Roman Petruk: *The Kiss of Judas* (illustration to a poem by Ihor Kalynets)

Petrun, Fedir [Petrun'], b 1 March 1894 in Ustie, Kamianets-Podilskyi county, Podilia gubernia, d ? Historical geographer and bibliographer. In the 1920s he taught at the Odessa Institute of People's Education, headed a department at the Odessa Central Scientific Library, and was learned secretary of the Odessa branch of the All-Ukrainian Association of Oriental Studies. He is the author of articles in VUAN and other serials on the eastern boundary of the Grand Duchy of Lithuania in the 1630s (1928), Kachybei on old maps (1928), a map of roads in Ukraine in the first half of the 19th century (1928), ancient roads in the Odessa region (1929), and the pre-Odessa period of V. Hryhorovych's activity and its relation to Ukraine (1929). He was arrested during the Stalinist terror of the early 1930s, and most likely perished in a labor camp.

Petrunkevych [Petrunkevyč]. A family of Cossack *starshyna* and civic figures in the Chernihiv region. Stepan Petrunkevych was chancellor of Starodub regiment (1741–54) and acting general chancellor of the Hetman state (1750). Opanas (d 1766 in Sosnytsia) was acting captain of Sosnytsia company (1724) and a fellow of the banner (from 1740) in Chernihiv regiment. Opanas's descendant Illia was a lawyer and chairman of the Chernihiv Criminal Court from 1860. Illia's son Ivan (b 22 November 1843 in Plysky, Borzna county, Chernihiv gubernia, d 14 June 1928 in Prague) was a leading member of the zemstvo assembly in Chernihiv gubernia (1868–79) and a justice of the peace there. After administrative exile in Varnava, Smolensk, and Tver (1879–86) he was a zemstvo leader in Tver gubernia (1890–1905). He was a founding member of the Union of Liberation (1903) and its chairman (1905), a founding member of the *Constitutional Democratic (Kadet) party (1905) and chairman of its CC (1909–15), a member of the First Russian State Duma, and editor of the Kadet newspaper, *Rech'* (1908–17). From 1919 he lived as an émigré in Greece, France, the United States, Switzerland, and Czechoslovakia. His memoirs were published as vol 21 of *Arkhiv russkoi revoliutsii* (Berlin 1934). Ivan's brother, Mykhailo (Mikhail, b 1845 in Plysky, d 1912 in Yalta), was a doctor, a member of the First Duma, a civic activist, and an industrialist. Ivan's son, Alexander Petrunkevitch (b 22 December 1875 in Plysky, d 9 March 1964 in New Haven, Connecticut), was a zoology professor at Yale University (1910–44) and a renowned arachnologist who wrote numerous monographs.

Petrus Italus (Peter the Italian), b ? in Lugano, Switzerland, d ? Sixteenth-century builder. He built the Dormition Church (1547–59, destroyed in 1571) and a residential building (now on Virmenska St) in Lviv. His style is typical of the Italian Renaissance.

Petrusenko, Oksana (real surname: Borodavkina), b 18 February 1900 in Balakliia, Kupianske county, Kharkiv gubernia, d 15 July 1940 in Kiev. Opera and concert singer (lyric and dramatic soprano). A student of P. Saksahansky, from 1916 she appeared with traveling troupes of I. Sahatovsky, V. Krasenko, and Saksahansky, and subsequently (1927–33) sang in the opera theaters of Kazan, Samara, and Sverdlovsk. From 1934 she was a soloist of the Kiev Opera, with which she appeared as Gilda in G. Verdi's *Rigoletto*, Natasha in A. Dargomyzhsky's *Rusalka*, Koupava in N. Rimsky-Korsakov's *The Snow Maiden*,

Oksana Petrusenko   Rev Antin Petrushevych

Yaroslavna in A. Borodin's *Prince Igor*, Oksana and Odarka in S. Hulak-Artemovsky's *Zaporozhian Cossack beyond the Danube,* and Natalka in M. Lysenko's *Natalka from Poltava.* She was also noted for her performances of Ukrainian folk song arrangements. Biographies of Petrusenko were written by Yu. Martych (1961), H. Filipenko (1964), and M. Kaharlytsky (1973).

Petrushevych, Antin (Antonii) [Petruševyč] (pseuds: Antonii iz Dobrian, Halychanyn, A. Halytsky, Rusyn Halychanyn, A. Rusoliubovych, A. Totsamovych), b 18 January 1821 in Dobriany, Stryi circle, Galicia, d 23 September 1913 in Lviv. Galician church and cultural figure, politician, and scholar; son of S. *Petrushevych. He graduated from Lviv University and the Greek Catholic Theological Seminary in Lviv (1845). He was ordained in 1847 and was appointed chaplain and personal secretary to Cardinal M. Levytsky in Lviv. In 1848 he was a founding member of the *Supreme Ruthenian Council and the *Halytsko-Ruska Matytsia society, and he participated in the *Congress of Ruthenian Scholars. Under the tutelage of D. Zubrytsky Petrushevych became a Russophile sympathizer in the early 1850s. Thereafter he wrote in the artificial *yazychiie*, which he deemed to be the proto-Rus' language. In 1857 he was elevated to the position of honorary canon of the metropolitan's chapter in Lviv, and from 1861 he served as canon of St George's Cathedral in Lviv and administrator of the metropolitan's chancery. From 1873 he was also custodian and librarian of the metropolitan chapter. As an elected member of the Galician Diet (1861–77) and the Austrian parliament (1873–8) he was a spokesman for the introduction of Ukrainian as an official language in Galicia's schools, courts, and administration.

Petrushevych was a pioneer of the Galician national revival. In an 1848 polemical brochure defending the Ruthenians and the use of their language in the schools and government, he argued that they were historically, culturally, and linguistically distinct from the Poles and Russians. He was the first to collect unstudied and unpublished sources for the history of the Western Ukrainian lands from the archives of Galicia, Bukovyna, Rumania, Vienna, and Prague, which he excerpted in his valuable Galician-Ruthenian chronicles for the years 1600–1700 (2 vols, 1874, 1891), 1700–72 (3 vols, 1887, 1896–

7), and 1772–1800 (1889). He published many historical documents and charters, including the 17th-century Lviv Chronicle (1868), the medieval Galician-Volhynian Chronicle (1871–2), and collections of official documents pertaining to the history of southern and western Rus' (1869, 1877) and the Lviv Dormition Brotherhood (1879). He wrote books on the medieval Galician bishops (1854), the history of Kholm eparchy (1867), the medieval St Panteleimon's Church near Halych (1881), the introduction of Christianity in the Carpathian lands (1882), the first printer in Ukraine, I. Fedorovych (1883), and the origins of Lviv and its environs (1893); a collection of linguistic history studies (1887); and articles on medieval and early modern Galician church and secular history and ethnography and on Slavic literature (eg, on translations of the Bible). He was one of the first scholars of Galician archeology; he wrote a book (1888) and articles about medieval Halych and other archeological studies (eg, on the Zbruch idol). He also compiled materials for a million-word comparative Slavic–Indo-European etymological dictionary; they were donated to the Russian Academy of Sciences and never published.

For his scholarly contributions Petrushevych was appointed a consistorial councillor by Cardinal Levytsky (1851) and elected a member of the Cracow Academy of Sciences (1874), the Bohemian Academy of Sciences and Arts, and the Odessa Society of History and Antiquities (1888); he was also granted honorary memberships in the Historical Society of Nestor the Chronicler (1881) in Kiev, the Rumanian (1890) and Russian (1904) academies of sciences, and the Moscow Archeological Society (1894). His large collection (15,000 items) of books, manuscripts, maps, documents, portraits, artworks, and archeological objects was deposited in the People's Home in Lviv (Petrushevych was one of its councillors from 1863), where it later became the Petrushevych Museum.

R. Senkus

Ivan Petrushevych

Petrushevych, Ivan [Petruševyč], b 29 April 1875 in Yezupil, Stanyslaviv county, Galicia, d 28 July 1950 in San Mateo, California. Co-operative leader. After studying the co-operative movement in England in 1905, he returned to organize Rochdale consumer co-operatives in Yezupil and other Galician towns. As secretary of Narodna Torhovlia he prepared a plan to reorganize it into a union of consumer co-operatives. He wrote articles on the theory and practice of co-operation for the weekly *Ekonomist* and on Ukrainian issues for the London journal *East European Review*. His translations of French, English, and American literary works appeared in *Literaturno-naukovyi vistnyk* or were published separately by the Ukrainian-Ruthenian Publishing Association. After emigrating to Canada in 1913 he organized the Ruthenian Farmers' Elevator Company and edited the paper *Kanadiis'kyi rusyn*. He was sent by Ukrainian Canadians to the Paris Peace Conference in 1918 and became a member of L. Botha's commission in 1919. Then he served in London as secretary of the delegation from the Government-in-exile of the Western Ukrainian National Republic (1920–3). In the mid-1920s he moved to California, where using the pseudonym Pedro Savidge he wrote film scripts for Hollywood and the novel *Flying Submarine*. In 1945 he was invited to act as adviser to the delegation of Ukrainian Canadians and Americans to the United Nations Conference in San Francisco.

Petrushevych, Lev [Petruševyč], b ca 1880, d 1940. Lawyer and political activist in Galicia; son of S. *Petrushevych. In November 1918, while working as an attorney in Berezhany, he was delegated to the Ukrainian National Rada of the Western Ukrainian National Republic (ZUNR). He then served in Kamianets-Podilskyi as senior legal consultant to the UNR Ministry of Internal Affairs and in Vienna as chief of the presidium chancery of the ZUNR dictator. Upon returning to Galicia he practiced law and was legal adviser to the Dnister insurance company in Lviv.

Petrushevych, Mykhailo [Petruševyč, Myxajlo], b 1803 in Stryi circle, Galicia, d 1876. Greek Catholic priest and pomologist; son of S. and brother of A. *Petrushevych. He collected Galician vernacular plant names and worked on an etymological dictionary of the 'Ruthenian' language (Church Slavonic words with Greek, Latin, and German equivalents), of which only the first fascicle was published (80 pp, Kolomyia 1865).

Petrushevych, Stepan [Petruševyč], b 1772, d 1860. Priest, writer, and civic figure; father of A. and M. *Petrushevych. A school inspector in the Stryi district of Galicia, he collected fables, anecdotes, and folk sayings. Some of the sayings were published in a Polish newspaper (1857). He also wrote poetry and plays, such as *Muzh staryi, zhinka moloda* (Old Husband, Young Wife).

Petrushevych, Stepan [Petruševyč], b 1855, d 1920. Greek Catholic priest and political and economic organizer in Galicia; brother of Ye. *Petrushevych and father of L. *Petrushevych. A co-operative organizer in Radekhiv county, he was sent in 1918 as a delegate from the county to the Ukrainian National Rada of the Western Ukrainian National Republic. During the subsequent war for independence he served as field chaplain of the Ukrainian Galician Army. He died of typhus while in the field.

Petrushevych, Yevhen [Petruševyč, Jevhen], b 3 June 1863 in Buzke, Kaminka-Strumylova county, Galicia, d 29 August 1940 in Berlin. Lawyer, political leader, and president of the Western Ukrainian National Republic (ZUNR). As a law student at Lviv University he was president of the Academic Brotherhood. While practicing law in Sokal

Yevhen Petrushevych

(1896–1910) and then in Skole, he organized and led various local societies. An executive member of the National Democratic party, he was elected to the Austrian parliament (1907, 1911) and to the Galician Diet (1910, 1913) and served as vice-chairman of the Ukrainian Parliamentary Representation in Vienna (1910–16) and the Ukrainian caucus in the Diet (1910–14). He rejected political compromises with the Austrian government and led a determined struggle in both assemblies for the rights of the Ukrainian people; in particular he played a key role in the Galician Diet's electoral reforms of 1913, which gave Ukrainians a greater voice in the Diet. After becoming vice-president of the General Ukrainian Council (1915) Petrushevych resigned from that body because of what he regarded as its naive trust in the Austrian government. At the end of 1916 he was elected chairman of the Ukrainian Parliamentary Representation in the Austrian parliament and was recognized as the leading Ukrainian politician of his day. With a number of other Slavic leaders he proposed transforming Austria-Hungary into a federation of national states, including a Ukrainian one composed of eastern Galicia, northern Bukovyna, and Transcarpathia.

While the emperor vacillated, Petrushevych summoned a Ukrainian constituent assembly to Lviv to decide the future of those territories. At its first session on 18 October 1918, the assembly named itself the *Ukrainian National Rada, chose Petrushevych as its president, and proclaimed an independent Ukrainian state. Petrushevych was re-elected president of the Rada on 3 January 1919 in Stanyslaviv and proved himself a capable leader and mediator. With the merging of the ZUNR with the UNR in January 1919, Petrushevych became the sixth member of the UNR Directory. By mid-1919 the National Rada and the State Secretariat had recognized that military and political setbacks made it impossible for them to govern, and on 9 June they transferred their powers to Petrushevych, whom they nominated as dictator (see *Dictatorship of the Western Province of the UNR). Under his regime the Chortkiv offensive was conducted, the Ukrainian Galician Army (UHA) crossed the Zbruch River, and the combined forces of the UNR Army and the UHA liberated Kiev. The divergencies between S. Petliura's and Petrushevych's governments in domestic and foreign policy increased during their stay in Kamianets-Podilskyi and finally led to a break, in November 1919. Petrushevych left Ukraine to pursue the fight for independence abroad by diplomatic means.

On 25 July 1920 Petrushevych formed a government-in-exile in Vienna and lobbied for international recognition of Western Ukrainian statehood. Having gained a certain measure of support for his quest, he rejected Polish overtures for a degree of Ukrainian autonomy in exchange for recognition of their control over Galicia. His campaign collapsed after March 1923, however, when the Conference of Ambassadors recognized Galicia as part of the new Polish state. Petrushevych, then in Berlin, began to look for Soviet assistance in his aspirations. This tack also proved unfruitful, and support for him soon withered away.

I. Sokhotsky

Petryk, Petro (Ivanenko), b and d ? Cossack figure at the end of the 17th century, descended from a Cossack officer family in Poltava regiment. In 1691 he abandoned his post of senior scribe at Hetman I. Mazepa's General Military Chancellery and fled to the Zaporozhian Sich, where he was elected military chancellor. In 1692 he concluded a treaty with the Crimean Tatars against Muscovy and began a long struggle against the Cossack *starshyna* and Muscovite 'landlords.' With his 500 Zaporozhian followers and Tatar allies he tried to instigate popular revolts in Ukraine in 1692, 1693, 1694, and 1696. Having failed in those attempts he settled in Tatar territory between the Boh and the Dnieper rivers and served until 1712 as 'hetman' of so-called Khan Ukraine.

Petrykivka. V-15. A town smt (1986 pop 5,300) on the Chaplynka River in Tsarychanka raion, Dnipropetrovske oblast. In the mid-18th century a Cossack and peasant settlement sprang up around Petryk's homestead. It soon became known for its distinctive pattern of decorative *Petrykivka painting. In the late 1940s a painting school was set up. The town is also known for its embroidery, kilims, and fabrics.

Petrykivka painting. The name given to folk painting on the whitewashed walls of peasant houses. Petrykivka painting is now an independent decorative art form. Its name derives from the village of *Petrykivka, near Dnipropetrovske, which in the 19th century became the center of this type of painting and produced several of the better-known folk artists. The artists create stylized floral and plant motifs arranged in two basic types of compositions, *kvity* (flowers) of bouquets and *bihuntsi* (runners) of friezes. Originally these designs were used to decorate traditional stoves, the main wall of the house, and the frames of windows and doors. Chalk, local clays, soot, and paints produced from plants and bound with egg yolk, milk, or cherry glue were used to execute the decorations. As the demand for such decorations increased, village artists started producing *malovky*. Sold at local farm markets, these designs were painted on transparent or semitransparent paper that could be attached to walls. Eventually the decorations became independent pictures created on paper with tempera pigments. In 1936 a special art school was established in Petrykivka.

The four brush strokes traditional in the Petrykivka designs are: (1) *hrebinchyk* (comb), which begins with pressure and ends in a wisp and is used for flowers, leaves, and grasses with rounded shapes; (2) *zerniatko* (seed), which begins with a light touch and ends with full pressure of the brush and is used for leaves with jagged edges;

Petrykivka painting: *Bird of Happiness, Bird of Life* by Uliana Sklia

(3) *horishok* (nut), a variant of *hrebinchyk*, which is used to depict the flower pistils and buds; and (4) a transitional stroke in which the brush is dipped in several pigments, which is used for painting flower petals and leaves requiring tonal shading. Traditionally the painting is done with a cat's-hair brush directly on paper without any preliminary drawing.

Some of the better-known artists of the Petrykivka school of painting are T. *Pata, M. *Tymchenko, N. Bilokin, I. Pylypenko, H. Isaieva, V. Klymenko, V. and H. Pavlenko, V. Kucherenko, M. Shyshatska, F. Panko, P. Hlushchenko, N. Shulyk, and Z. Kudish.

D. Zelska-Darevych

Petryna, Dmytro, b 23 March 1934 in Torhanovychi, Sambir county, Galicia. Mathematician and theoretical physicist; corresponding member of the AN URSR (now ANU) since 1988. A graduate of Lviv University (1956), he has worked at the Institute of Theoretical Physics and the Institute of Mathematics of the ANU in Kiev, where he heads the section of mathematical methods in statistical mechanics. In 1979 he became a professor at Kiev University. Petryna is a specialist in contemporary mathematical physics, statistical mechanics, and quantum field theory. His scientific articles and three research monographs (some published jointly with other specialists) have made significant contributions to each of these areas.

Petrynenko, Diana, b 8 February 1930 in Bilousivka, Cherkasy okruha. Singer (lyric soprano). After graduating from (1955) and completing graduate studies at the Kiev Conservatory (1961), she began to lecture there (assistant professor in 1981). She also sang as soloist with the DUMKA kapelle (1955–8) and the Kiev Philharmonic Orchestra (from 1962). Her repertoire includes works by Ukrainian composers such as L. Revutsky, A. Kos-Anatolsky, H. and P. Maiboroda, and O. Bilash; Ukrainian folk songs; and opera arias by Soviet and Western composers.

Petryshyn, Arcadia. See Olenska-Petryshyn, Arcadia.

Petryshyn, Ivan [Petryšyn] (pseud: Liubomyr Seliansky), 1850–1913. Elementary school teacher in Galicia, journalist, and writer. He edited the journal *Prapor* (Kolomyia 1908–12) and worked on the satirical and political magazines *Komar*, *Zerkalo* (Lviv), *Khlops'ka pravda*, and *Zoria* (Kolomyia) and the almanac-calendar *Zaporozhets'*. He was the author of several works, among them *U 50-u richnytsiu znesennia panshchyny i vidrodzhennia Halyts'koï Rusy* (On the 50th Anniversary of the Repeal of Serfdom and the Rebirth of Galician Rus', 1898), *Hostynets' z Ameryky, abo nauka pro se, iak u sviti zhyty* (Gift from America, or a Lesson on How to Live in the World, 1906), and the historical stories 'Iasne sonychko Rusy-Ukraïny' (The Bright Sun of Rus'-Ukraine, 1911) and 'Orleans'ka divchyna' (The Maid of Orleans, 1912).

Petryshyn, Roman [Petryšyn], b 28 July 1946 in Neumarkt, Germany. Social activist and community figure. He was educated at Lakehead University in Thunder Bay, Ontario, the University of Birmingham, and the University of Bristol (PH D, 1981) and was active in the Ukrainian-Canadian students' movement of the late 1960s and early 1970s. He became a research associate of the Canadian Institute of Ukrainian Studies (1976–80) and then northern director of multicultural (cultural heritage) programming at Alberta Culture; he founded and since 1986 has directed the *Ukrainian Resource and Development Center at Grant MacEwan College in Edmonton. He has been a member and head of the *Ukrainian Community Development Committee, a strong supporter of Ukrainian Canadian Social Services, and editor of *Changing Realities: Social Trends among Ukrainian Canadians* (1980). He has made particularly valuable contributions in the development of the concept of multiculturalism in Canada and its incorporation into societal structures.

Petryshyn, Wolodymyr [Petryšyn, Volodymyr], b 22 January 1929 in Liashky Murovani, Lviv county, Galicia. Mathematician; full member of the Shevchenko Scientific Society since 1980 and foreign member of the Academy of Sciences of Ukraine since March 1992. A postwar displaced person, he emigrated from Germany to the United States in 1950, completed his education at Columbia University (PH D, 1961), and taught at the University of Chicago (1964–7) and Rutgers University (since 1967). He has lectured in Europe (including Ukraine), China, and Israel.

Petryshyn's main achievements are in nonlinear functional analysis. His major results include the development of the theory of iterative and projective methods for the constructive solution of linear and nonlinear abstract and differential equations with K-positive operators; new fixed-point theorems for $P(\gamma)$-compact and 1-set-contractive maps, and the development with (P. Fitzpatrick) of topological degree and index theories for multivalued condensing maps. Petryshyn is a founder and principal developer of the theory of approximation-proper (A-proper) maps, a new class of maps which attracted considerable attention in the mathematical community. He has shown that the theory of A-proper type maps not only extends and unifies the classical theory of compact maps with some recent theories of condensing and monotone-accretive maps, but also provides a new approach to the constructive solution of nonlinear abstract and differential equations. The topological degree for A-proper maps was constructed with F. Browder and the index theory with Fitzpatrick. The theory has been applied to ordinary and partial differential equations. Petryshyn was the mathematics subject editor for the *Encyclopedia of Ukraine*. In 1989 he was elected honorary member of the newly revived Kiev Mathematics Society.

R. Andrushkiv

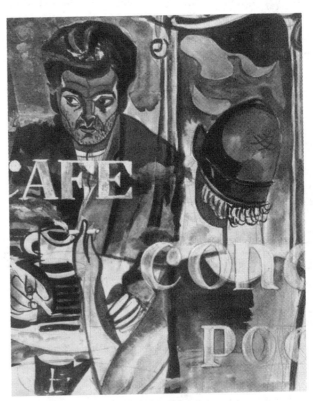

Anatol Petrytsky: *Portrait of Mykhailo Semenko* (watercolor, 1929)

Wolodymyr Petryshyn

Petrytsky, Anatol [Petryc'kyj, Anatol'], b 31 January 1895 in Kiev, d 6 March 1964 in Kiev. Ukrainian painter and stage designer. He studied at the Kiev Art School (1912–17) and the Advanced Artistic Theatrical Workshop in Moscow (1922–4) and worked as stage designer in the Molodyi Teatr (1916–19) and the Shevchenko First Theater of the Ukrainian Soviet Republic. In 1925–41 he continued to design in Ukrainian operatic and drama theaters in Kharkiv, Kiev, and Odessa. He also designed sets for performances in the Moscow Bolshoi and Malyi theaters, in 1942–3 in the Opera Theater in Alma-Ata, and in 1945–59 (with interruptions) in the Kiev Theater of Opera and Ballet.

Petrytsky's early work, particularly his painting, was influenced by cubism and futurism. As a stage designer he was an adherent of theatrical conventionality and readily employed Ukrainian popular print and ornamentation. In *Vertep* he created stylized costumes for actors who appeared in the puppet show; in O. Vyshnia's *Vii* he united screens with stylized costumes. From 1930 he specialized mostly in design for opera and ballet (M. Lysenko's *Taras Bulba*, K. Dankevych's *Lileia* [The Lily], and M. Mussorgsky's *Sorochyntsi Fair*). Even under pressure to adhere to norms of socialist realism he preserved a national coloring in his theater and dance (State Dance Ensemble of the Ukrainian SSR) work. Petrytsky was also a renowed portraitist, painter, and graphic artist. Albums of his art works were published in Kiev in 1968 and 1991.

V. Revutsky

Petrytsky, Mykhailo [Petryc'kyj, Myxajlo], b 1865 in Kopychyntsi, Husiatyn county, Galicia, d February 1921 in Kharkiv. Civic activist, publisher, and teacher; brother of P. Petrytsky. A former teacher who had gone into business selling silverware, he published and edited the Lviv nationalist weekly *Haidamaky* (1902–7) and published a number of Ukrainian literary works. He organized the 1902 agrarian strike in his home county and helped found local branches of the Ukrainian Pedagogical Society and Silskyi Hospodar. A candidate of the National Democratic party, he was elected to the Austrian parliament in 1907 and 1911. In 1918 he served as deputy to the Ukrainian National Rada and then as propaganda officer in the Ukrainian Galician Army. In 1920 he remained in Soviet-occupied Ukraine, where he was arrested and tortured to death by the Bolsheviks.

Petsukh, Hryhorii [Pecux, Hryhorij], b 23 January 1923 in Florynka, Nowy Sącz county, Galicia. Ukrainian-Polish sculptor. A graduate of the Zakopane Lyceum of Plastic Techniques (1950) and the Warsaw Academy of Arts (1955), he has taught sculpting in Zakopane. His animal and human figures, such as *Mother with Child*, *Banduryst*, *Lemko*, *I. Franko*, *Orchard*, *Tree of Life*, and *Girl*, are done mostly in wood and are closely associated with Lemko traditions. His work has beeen exhibited not only in Poland but also in New York, Washington, Prague, Vienna, Budapest, and Stockholm.

Petty gentry. Members of the nobility (mainly in Western Ukraine) who had the legal rights of that estate but did not own serfs, and worked their relatively small landholdings by themselves. They tended to live in compact groups, in whole villages or parts of villages. The greatest

Hryhorii Petsukh: *Mother and Child* (wood sculpture)

number of such villages were in Subcarpathia (particularly Sambir and Skole counties), Podilia (Bar county), and central and eastern Polisia (the Ovruch and Liubech areas). The petty gentry became a distinct social class in Galicia in the 14th century; it consisted mainly of impoverished boyars, the retainers of princes, and the free peasantry of the Galician-Volhynian principality. The families of petty nobility often adopted the name of the village they resided in as their own (Bereziv–Berezovsky, Chaikovychi–Chaikivsky, Terlo–Terletsky, Krushelnytsia–Krushelnytsky, Hordynia–Hordynsky, Kulchytsi–Kulchytsky). The Polish coats of arms most often used were the Sas (an arrow above a crescent moon with stars at each end) and Korczak (three horizontal rivers of unequal length). The petty nobility participated in anti-Polish uprisings, particularly those led by Mukha and B. Khmelnytsky. Hetman P. Sahaidachny and a number of Greek Catholic leaders and educators came from that class. After the abolition of serfdom they lost their social privileges but still differed from former serfs in their everyday habits and specific traditions. In the 1920s and 1930s, attempts made to Polonize them were largely unsuccessful.

Ya. Isaievych

Pevny, Bohdan [Pevnyj], b 4 June 1931 in Lutske, Volhynia. Artist and art critic; son of P. *Pevny; full member of the Ukrainian Academy of Arts and Sciences in the US. A postwar émigré, he studied art at the Art Students' League, the National Academy of Design, New York University, and Columbia University in New York. He became head of the Society of Young Painters of New York in 1955 and vice-president of the Ukrainian Artists' Association in the USA in 1963. He has taken part in many group exhibitions, illustrated books and journals, contributed articles on art to the émigré press, and edited a book about M. Nedilko (1983). He became art editor of the monthly *Suchasnist'* in 1984. Since 1989 he has published articles on art in journals in Ukraine, such as *Dzvin, Pam'iatky Ukraïny,* and *Ukraïna.*

Pevny, Petro [Pevnyj], b 18 August 1888 in Poltava, d 8 August 1957 in New York. Civic and political leader and journalist. He helped edit the daily *Vidrodzhennia* in Kiev (1918) and *Ukraïna* in Kamianets-Podilskyi (1919). With the collapse of the UNR he emigrated to Poland, and in 1929 he moved to Volhynia. He was president of the Volhynian Ukrainian Alliance (1928–35) and editor of its weekly *Ukraïns'ka nyva in Warsaw and Lutske (1926–35). He was also president of the Ridna Khata society in Lutske. He was elected to the Polish Sejm as an Alliance candidate (1930, 1935) and pursued a policy of accommodation with the Poles. After the Second World War he fled to Germany and then emigrated to the United States.

Hryhorii Pezhansky   Heorhii Pfeiffer

Pezhansky, Hryhorii [Pežans'kyj, Hryhorij], b 1860 in Pchany, Zhydachiv county, Galicia, d 16 January 1925 in Lviv. Architectural engineer and civic activist. A graduate of the Lviv and Vienna polytechnics, he worked as an engineer in the public service. He took part in the construction of many public buildings in Lviv, including the Trade School, pavilions for the 1894 Provincial Exhibition, the buildings of the university's physics and chemistry institutes and library, and the Women Teachers' Seminary. His works can also be seen in other Galician towns. A consultant on building projects for Ukrainian institutions, he was

a founder and president of the Ukrainian Technical Society as well as an executive member of the Dnister insurance company, the Shevchenko Scientific Society, the Ukrainian Pedagogical Society, the People's Home in Lviv, and the Stauropegion Institute.

Pezhansky, Mykhailo [Pežans'kyj, Myxajlo], b 29 September 1900 in Lviv, d 16 June 1987 in New York. Civil engineer and educator; son of H. Pezhansky; member of the Shevchenko Scientific Society (NTSh) from 1936. After graduating from the Vienna Technische Hochschule in 1927, he worked as a civil engineer in Lviv. After the Second World War he lectured in Munich at the United Nations Relief and Rehabilitation Administration University and then (1949) settled in the United States, where he worked as an engineer in a number of construction firms. He was a founder of the *Ukrainian Engineers' Society of America (TUIA) and the *Ukrainian Terminological Center of America and served on the terminological commissions of TUIA and NTSh. He was a member of the US executive and the chief executive of the *Plast Ukrainian Youth Association.

Pfeiffer, Heorhii [Pfejffer, Heorhij] (Georgii, Yurii), b 23 December 1872 in Sokyryntsi, Pryluka county, Poltava gubernia, d 10 October 1946 in Kiev. Mathematician; full member of the AN URSR (now ANU) from 1920. After graduating from Kiev University in 1896, he taught at the Kiev Polytechnical Institute (1899–1909) and at Kiev University (1900–46). He served as chairman of the VUAN Commission on Pure Mathematics (from 1920), research associate of the ANU Institute of Mathematics in Kiev (1934–41, 1944–6), and director of the (combined) Institute of Mathematics and Physics in Ufa (1941–4). Pfeiffer made significant contributions to the theory of partial differential equations (PDEs) and to the theory of Lie and Lagrange integrals. Among his many contributions is a general method for the formal integration of nonlinear equations and complete systems of nonlinear PDEs of the first order.

Pfister, Jan, b 1573 in Wrocław, Poland, d 1642 in Berezhany, Galicia. Polish sculptor of German origin. Ca 1611 he settled in Lviv and then in Berezhany. He took part in carving the decorative sculptures in the dome of the Boim Chapel in Lviv (1609–11) and engraved the side altar and the epitaphs of J. and J. Boim there. He also sculpted the burial monuments of Archbishop J. Zamoyski in the Roman Catholic cathedral (1610), J. Swoszowski in the old Dominican church (ca 1614) in Lviv, the Ostrozky family in the cathedral in Tarnów (1620), and A. Sieniawski in the castle chapel in Berezhany (after 1627).